February 2015

Audit and Assurance

Standards and Guidance

Ireland Edition

PREFACE

This edition of 'Standards and Guidance' contains all the FRC audit and assurance standards in issue at 1 February 2015 and selected guidance documents. A full list of extant standards and guidance at 1 February 2015 is provided in the Appendix. Individual pronouncements can be obtained from the Publications section of the FRC website.

References to legislation and regulations

Some standards and guidance include cross references to legislation and regulations that apply at the time of issuance of those pronouncements. Such references may have become out of date due to changes in the relevant legislation or regulations and users are advised to check the continuing relevance of them as necessary when applying the FRC's pronouncements.

International standards

The International Standards on Auditing (ISAs) (UK and Ireland), the International Standard on Quality Control (ISQC) (UK and Ireland) 1 and the International Standard on Review Engagements (ISRE) (UK and Ireland) 2410 are based on standards that have been issued by the International Auditing and Assurance Standards Board (IAASB), published by the International Federation of Accountants (IFAC), and are used with the permission of IFAC. Further explanation of this is given in the Statement in Section 2 that explains the scope and authority of the FRC's audit and assurance pronouncements.

CONTENTS

Section 1: SUMMARY OF 2014 ACTIVITIES

Auditing Standards

Revisions to auditing standards to implement the recommendations of the Sharman Inquiry and support changes to the UK Corporate Governance Code and guidance for directors on risk management

In September 2014 the FRC issued[1]:

- UK Corporate Governance Code September 2014

- Guidance on Risk Management, Internal Control and Related Financial and Business Reporting

- Guidance for Directors of Banks on Solvency and Liquidity Risk Management and the Going Concern Basis of Accounting

The FRC also issued extracts from ISAs (UK and Ireland) 260, *Communications With Those Charged With Governance*, 570, *Going Concern*, and 700, *The Independent Auditor's Report on Financial Statements*, to show the related revisions that had been finalised requiring auditors to consider and report on narrative disclosures, including risks. Accordingly auditors will need to consider the going concern basis of accounting (and material uncertainties relating thereto) and the longer term viability statement and the risk management disclosure. Those revisions are incorporated in the full versions of the standards included in this compendium.

The revised standards are effective for audits of financial statements for periods commencing on or after 1 October 2014. A high level summary of the main revisions to the requirements is set out below.

Revisions to ISA (UK and Ireland) 260

Revisions include requiring the auditor to communicate to the audit committee the auditor's views about:

- The robustness of the directors' assessment of the principal risks facing the entity, including the related disclosures in the annual report confirming that the directors have carried out such an assessment.

- The directors' explanation in the annual report as to how they have assessed the prospects of the entity, and their statements:

---

[1] The documents issued in September 2014 can be obtained from the FRC website: www.frc.org.uk/News-and-Events/FRC-Press/Press/2014/September/FRC-updates-UK-Corporate-Governance-Code.aspx

(i) in the financial statements, as to whether they considered it appropriate to adopt the going concern basis of accounting in preparing them, including any related disclosures identifying any material uncertainties; and

(ii) in the annual report as to whether they have a reasonable expectation that the entity will be able to continue in operation and meet its liabilities as they fall due over the period of their assessment, including any related disclosures drawing attention to any necessary qualifications or assumptions.

Revisions to ISA (UK and Ireland) 570

Revisions include:

- In the case of entities that are required, and those that choose voluntarily, to report on how they have applied the UK Corporate Governance Code, or to explain why they have not, the auditor is required to read and consider in light of the knowledge the auditor has acquired during the audit:

   (a) The directors' confirmation in the annual report that they have carried out a robust assessment of the principal risks facing the entity, including those that would threaten its business model, future performance, solvency or liquidity;

   (b) The disclosures in the annual report that describe those risks and explain how they are being managed or mitigated;

   (c) The directors' statement in the financial statements about whether they considered it appropriate to adopt the going concern basis of accounting in preparing them, and their identification of any material uncertainties; and

   (d) The directors' explanation in the annual report as to how they have assessed the prospects of the entity, and their statement as to whether they have a reasonable expectation that the entity will be able to continue in operation and meet its liabilities as they fall due over the period of their assessment.

The auditor is required to determine whether the auditor has anything material to add or to draw attention to in the auditor's report on the financial statements in relation to these disclosures.

- Matters the auditor considers when determining whether there is anything to add or to emphasize in the auditor's report on the financial statements include whether:

   ○ The auditor is aware of information that would indicate that the annual report and accounts taken as a whole are not fair balanced and understandable in relation to the principal risks facing the entity; and

   ○ Matters relating to the robustness of the directors' assessment of the principal risks facing the entity and its outcome, including the related disclosures in the annual report and accounts, that the auditor communicated to the audit

**FINANCIAL
REPORTING COUNCIL**

committee and that are not appropriately addressed in the section of the annual report that describes the work of the audit committee.

Revisions to ISA (UK and Ireland) 700

Revisions include:

- In the case of entities that are required, and those that choose voluntarily, to report on how they have applied the UK Corporate Governance Code or to explain why they have not, the auditor is required, having regard to the work performed in accordance with the requirements of ISA (UK and Ireland) 570, to give a statement as to whether the auditor has anything material to add or to draw attention to in relation to:

    (a) The directors' confirmation in the annual report that they have carried out a robust assessment of the principal risks facing the entity, including those that would threaten its business model, future performance, solvency or liquidity;

    (b) The disclosures in the annual report that describe those risks and explain how they are being managed or mitigated;

    (c) The directors' statement in the financial statements about whether they considered it appropriate to adopt the going concern basis of accounting in preparing them, and their identification of any material uncertainties; and

    (d) The directors' explanation in the annual report as to how they have assessed the prospects of the entity and their statement as to whether they have a reasonable expectation that the entity will be able to continue in operation and meet its liabilities as they fall due over the period of their assessment.

Auditing Guidance

Practice Note 14 – Auditing UK housing associations

In January 2014, following consultation in 2013, the FRC issued an update of Practice Note 14, *The audit of housing associations in the United Kingdom*. in the light of the landscape in which the social housing sector now operates. Reductions in grant funding, welfare reform and the impact on availability of funding following the financial crisis have led many associations to diversify their activities and funding models. Some associations augment their traditional housing activities with more commercial activities such as student accommodation or care homes. Some have moved away from long term bank financing to bond financing and an increased use of interest rate swaps. The new guidance is intended to assist auditors to understand the relevant business risks and to identify risks of material misstatement of Housing Associations financial statements in, among other things, the context of regulatory developments, pressures on public expenditure and changes in the ways in which some Housing Associations finance their activities.

The previous version of Practice Note 14 was issued in 2006. It was withdrawn in 2012 because almost all of its references to laws, regulations and ISAs (UK and Ireland) had become outdated. In deciding that a completely updated version of Practice Note 14 should be developed, the FRC agreed that it should be considerably shorter than the 2006 version but more comprehensive in that it would deal with each of the four regulatory regimes even-handedly rather than focusing primarily on the English regime.

Practice Note 14 is not included in this edition of the compendium of standards and guidance but may be obtained from the Publications section of the FRC website[2].

Bulletin 4 – Recent Developments in Company Law, The Listing Rules and Auditing Standards that affect United Kingdom Auditor's reports

In April 2014, the FRC issued Bulletin 4 which highlights matters giving rise to changes to auditors' responsibilities which have a significant impact commencing in 2014, affecting both the auditor's duties and the wording of auditor's reports on the financial statements of companies. These include the introduction of the Strategic Report and changes to the content of the Directors' Remuneration Report, including the requirement for companies to report a single total remuneration figure for each director.

The Bulletin notes that auditors have the same statutory reporting responsibility for the new Strategic Report as for the Directors' Report. The Bulletin also sets out the auditors' responsibilities in relation to the Directors' Remuneration Report. The auditor is required to audit some but not all elements of the Directors' Remuneration Report and it is particularly important, therefore, that the auditor describes clearly within its report the elements that it has audited.

The Bulletin is included in this compendium.

Other Activities

EU Audit Directive and Regulation

In May 2014 the European Commission published a Directive[3] amending the Statutory Audit Directive[4] and a new Audit Regulation[5]. The Audit Directive establishes specific requirements concerning the statutory audit of annual and consolidated financial statements. The Audit Regulation establishes further specific requirements regarding the statutory audit of 'public interest entities'. The new requirements come into effect on 17 June 2016 and will apply to financial years starting on or after that date.

The Audit Regulation has the direct effect of law and Member States are required to adopt appropriate provisions to ensure its effective application. The Audit Directive does not have a direct effect in law and Member States are required to adopt and publish the measures

---

[2] www.frc.org.uk/Our-Work/Codes-Standards/Audit-and-assurance/Standards-and-guidance/Standards-and-guidance-for-auditors/Practice-notes.aspx

[3] Directive 2014/56/EU.

[4] Directive 2006/43/EC.

[5] Regulation 537/2014.

necessary to comply with it. The Department for Business, Innovation and Skills (BIS) issued a Discussion Document[6] in December 2014 seeking views on the implementation of the Audit Directive and Audit Regulation in the UK.

Articles in both the Audit Directive and Audit Regulation establish provisions that relate to matters that are the subject of the FRC's auditing standards and ethical standards for auditors. In relation to a number of these provisions there are Member State options. BIS and the FRC consider that it would be most appropriate for the application of the provisions that clearly relate to matters currently covered by the FRC's standards to be allocated to the FRC to implement via development of the audit and ethical standards framework and revision of the relevant standards.

BIS, in their Discussion Document, are therefore seeking views on whether, in a revised statutory framework, the FRC should be given the specific responsibility to deal with the subject matter of these Articles, including the ability to exercise all the associated Member State options, in accordance with the FRC's usual processes for setting such standards.

Also in December 2014, the FRC issued a Consultation Document[7] that identifies and explains the range of positions the FRC is considering with respect to these Member State options, should it have a delegated power to exercise them and seeks stakeholder views. In some respects, the UK's current requirements go beyond those of the legislation. In those cases, and where the Member State options allow, the FRC seeks views on whether or not to retain current provisions, or to extend them further, or to align with the new legislation, including:

- **Entities not covered by the definition of Public Interest Entities** – The EU definition of a public interest entity (PIE) is different from the scope of the FRC's definition of a 'listed entity' for which incremental requirements are established in the FRC's auditing and ethical standards;

- **Non-audit services** – The Regulation prohibits the provision of certain non-audit services by auditors of PIEs through a 'black list' and places a cap on permitted services. The FRC is consulting on how to apply the cap and the list most effectively in the UK; and

- **The geographic extent of application** – Under the Regulation, the prohibitions on non-audit services to PIEs or their controlled entities within Europe, apply to auditors and their network firms. The consultation seeks views on whether these prohibitions should apply in relation to all audited group entities, irrespective of their location.

The FRC consultation period closes on 20 March 2015.

---

6   Auditor Regulation – Discussion document on the implications of the EU and wider reforms – December 2014.
7   The FRC Consultation Document can be obtained from the FRC website: www.frc.org.uk/News-and-Events/FRC-Press/Press/2014/December/FRC-consults-on-EU-Audit-Directive-and-Regulation.aspx

The Audit Directive and Audit Regulation also introduce some new requirements for which there are no options (the BIS Discussion Document gives more details of these). The FRC will consult later in 2015 on proposed specific revisions to the audit and ethical standards to implement those requirements. That consultation will also address the implementation of Member State options, taking into consideration the responses received to the December 2014 consultation, if it has been confirmed that the FRC will have the ability to exercise them.

The International Auditing and Assurance Standards Board (IAASB) has recently finalised revisions to some International Standards on Auditing (ISAs) relating to auditor reporting and conforming amendments to other ISAs. Where appropriate and practicable, the FRC will seek to ensure that revisions to the standards for the Audit Directive and Audit Regulation, the wider review of the ethical framework for auditors (see below) and the IAASB revisions are made at the same time to avoid multiple revisions to standards over a relatively short period of time.

Review of the ethical framework for auditors

In April 2014, the FRC set out its work to enhance justifiable confidence in the quality of audit[8]. A key element of that work is a review of the ethical framework for auditors, including the ethical standards. Further revisions to the ethical standards that may be proposed as a result of that review will be consulted on in 2015 at the same time as the proposed detailed revisions to implement the Audit Directive and Audit Regulation.

---

[8] www.frc.org.uk/News-and-Events/FRC-Press/Press/2014/April/FRCs-work-to-enhance-justifiable-confidence-in-au.aspx

Section 2: THE FINANCIAL REPORTING COUNCIL – SCOPE AND AUTHORITY OF AUDIT AND ASSURANCE PRONOUNCEMENTS

CONTENTS

Nature and Scope of FRC Audit and Assurance Pronouncements

1.   Audit and assurance pronouncements issued by the FRC include:

 *   Quality control standards for firms that perform audits of financial statements, reports in connection with investment circulars and other assurance engagements,

 *   A framework of fundamental principles, 'The Auditors' Code' which the FRC expects to guide the conduct of auditors (see Appendix 2),

 *   Ethical and engagement standards for audits of financial statements, reports in connection with investment circulars and other assurance engagements, and

 *   Guidance for auditors of financial statements, reporting accountants acting in connection with an investment circular and auditors involved in other assurance engagements.

 The structure of the audit and assurance pronouncements is shown in Appendix 1.

2.   Auditors and reporting accountants should not claim compliance with the FRC's audit and assurance standards unless they have complied fully with all of those standards relevant to an engagement.

3.   The Auditors' Code, which is set out in Appendix 2, provides a framework of fundamental principles which encapsulate the concepts that govern the conduct of audits and underlie the ethical and engagement standards for audits of financial statements.

4.   Quality control standards and engagement standards for audits of financial statements (the International Standards on Quality Control (ISQC) (UK and Ireland) and the International Standards on Auditing (ISAs) (UK and Ireland)) include objectives for the auditor, together with requirements[1] and related application and other explanatory material. It is necessary to have an understanding of the entire text of a standard, including its guidance, to understand its objectives and to apply its requirements properly. Further explanation of the scope, authority and structure of the engagement standards are set out in ISA (UK and Ireland) 200, *Overall Objectives of the Independent Auditor and the Conduct of an Audit in Accordance with International Standards on Auditing (UK and Ireland)*.

5.   Engagement standards for reporting accountants acting in connection with an investment circular (the Standards for Investment Reporting (SIRs)) and auditors involved in other assurance engagements contain basic principles and essential procedures (identified in bold type lettering[2]) together with related guidance. The basic

---

[1]   The level of authority of the text in requirements paragraphs is identified by use of the term "shall" (e.g. 'the auditor shall ...').

[2]   The level of authority of the text in these paragraphs is identified by use of the expression "the auditor should ...".

principles and essential procedures are to be understood and applied in the context of the explanatory and other material that provide guidance for their application. It is therefore necessary to consider the whole text of a standard to understand and apply the basic principles and essential procedures.

6. Ethical Standards for Auditors and Reporting Accountants contain requirements (identified in bold type lettering) together with related guidance.

7. The ISAs (UK and Ireland) and ISQC (UK and Ireland) 1 are based on the corresponding international standards issued by the International Auditing and Assurance Standards Board[3] (IAASB). Where necessary, the international standards have been augmented with additional requirements to address specific UK and Irish legal and regulatory requirements; and additional guidance that is appropriate in the UK and Irish national legislative, cultural and business context. This additional material is clearly differentiated from the original text of the international standards by the use of grey shading. For the audit of UK and Irish groups, the group auditor needs to be satisfied that the audit of the group financial statements, on which the group auditor gives an audit opinion, is in accordance with the ISAs (UK and Ireland). Auditors of overseas components are not required to have regard to the additional requirements and guidance material, although the group auditor may decide to refer to it in their instructions to component auditors[4].

8. The auditor reporting standard issued by the FRC, ISA (UK and Ireland) 700, *The Auditor's Report on Financial Statements,* has not been based on ISA 700, *Forming an Opinion and Reporting on Financial Statements*, as issued by the IAASB. The FRC standard addresses the requirements of company law and also provides for a more concise auditor's report, reflecting feedback to consultations. ISA (UK and Ireland) 700 has been designed to ensure that compliance with it will not preclude the auditor from being able to assert compliance with the ISAs issued by the IAASB[5]. However, the form of UK and Ireland auditor's reports may not be exactly aligned with that required in other circumstances by ISA 700 issued by the IAASB.

9. The ISAs and ISQC 1 as issued by the IAASB, require compliance with 'relevant ethical requirements' which are described, in the application material, as ordinarily comprising Parts A and B of the International Ethics Standards Board for Accountants (IESBA) *Code of Ethics for Professional Accountants* (the IESBA Code[6])

---

[3] IAASB is a committee of the International Federation of Accountants (IFAC). The IAASB's constitution and due process is described in its 'Preface to the International Quality Control, Auditing, Review, Other Assurance, and Related Services Pronouncements'.

[4] If the auditor of an overseas component is a part of the same firm as the group auditor (i.e. the same legal entity) consideration needs to be given to whether the auditor of the overseas component has the same legal obligations as the group auditor and, therefore, is required to comply with the legal or regulatory requirements of the ISAs (UK and Ireland). If such obligations exist, consideration needs to be given to the implications for communication between the group auditor and component auditor (for example where necessary to fulfil obligations for reporting money laundering offences or reporting matters to a regulator).

[5] See ISA (UK and Ireland) 700, paragraph 5.

[6] The IESBA Code is included in the IFAC "Handbook of the Code of Ethics for Professional Accountants" and can be downloaded free of charge from the publications section of the IAASB website (www.ifac.org/IAASB).

related to an audit of financial statements together with national requirements that are more restrictive. The ISAs (UK and Ireland) and ISQC (UK and Ireland) 1 have supplementary material that makes clear that auditors in the UK and Ireland are subject to ethical requirements from two sources: the Ethical Standards for Auditors concerning the integrity, objectivity and independence of the auditor, and the ethical pronouncements established by the auditor's relevant professional body. ISQC (UK and Ireland) 1 also has supplementary material that makes clear that the Ethical Standard for Reporting Accountants applies to all engagements that are subject to the Standards for Investment Reporting and involve investment circulars in which a report from the reporting accountant is to be published.

10. The Ethical Standards for Auditors and Reporting Accountants were developed with the intent that they should adhere to the principles of the IESBA Code. The FRC is not aware of any significant instances where the relevant parts of the IESBA Code are more restrictive than the Ethical Standards[7].

Standards and Guidance for Audits of Financial Statements

11. Ethical and engagement standards for audits of financial statements, which comprise the Ethical Standards for Auditors and International Standards on Auditing (ISAs) (UK and Ireland), apply to auditors carrying out:

* Statutory audits of companies in accordance with the Companies Acts[8];

* Audits of financial statements of entities in accordance with other UK or Irish legislation e.g. building societies, credit unions, friendly societies, pension funds, charities and registered social landlords;

* Public sector financial statement audits in the UK, including those carried out either on behalf of the national audit agencies or under contract to those agencies. (The standards governing the conduct and reporting of the audit of financial statements are a matter for the national audit agencies to determine. However, the heads of the national audit agencies[9] in the UK have chosen to adopt the ethical, engagement and quality control standards issued by the FRC for audits as the basis of their approach to the audit of financial statements);

* Other audits performed by audit firms registered with the members of the Consultative Committee of Accountancy Bodies (CCAB)[10] unless the nature of the engagement requires the use of other recognised auditing standards; and

---

[7] Should auditors wish to state that an audit has been conducted in compliance with ISAs as issued by IAASB they will need to ensure that they have complied with the relevant parts of the IESBA Code.
[8] Companies Act 2006 in the UK and the Companies Acts 1963–2003 in the Republic of Ireland.
[9] National audit agencies in the UK are the National Audit Office (for the Comptroller and Auditor General), the Wales Audit Office (for the Auditor General for Wales), the Audit Commission, Audit Scotland (for the Auditor General for Scotland and the Accounts Commission) and the Northern Ireland Audit Office (for the Comptroller and Auditor General for Northern Ireland).
[10] Members of CCAB are The Institute of Chartered Accountants in England & Wales, The Institute of Chartered Accountants of Scotland, Chartered Accountants Ireland, The Association of Chartered Certified Accountants and The Chartered Institute of Public Finance and Accountancy.

- Other audits where audit firms not registered with members of the CCAB elect, or are required by contract, to perform the work in accordance with UK or Irish auditing standards.

12. Guidance for auditors of financial statements is also issued in the form of Practice Notes and Bulletins. Practice Notes and Bulletins are persuasive rather than prescriptive and are indicative of good practice. Practice Notes assist auditors in applying engagement standards to particular circumstances and industries and Bulletins provide timely guidance on new or emerging issues. Auditors should be aware of and consider Practice Notes applicable to the engagement. Auditors who do not consider and apply the guidance included in a relevant Practice Note should be prepared to explain how the engagement standards have been complied with.

Standards and Guidance for Reporting Accountants Acting in Connection With an Investment Circular

13. The Ethical Standard for Reporting Accountants (ESRA) and Standards for Investment Reporting (SIRs) issued by the FRC apply to reporting accountants when carrying out engagements involving investment circulars intended to be issued in connection with a securities transaction governed wholly or in part by the laws and regulations of the United Kingdom or the Republic of Ireland.

Statements of Standards for Reporting Accountants

14. The FRC also issues standards and guidance for accountants on assurance engagements closely related to an audit of the financial statements. This includes the International Standard on Reporting Engagements (ISRE) (UK and Ireland) 2410, *Review of Interim Financial Information Performed by the Independent Auditor of the Entity*. ISRE (UK and Ireland) 2410 adopts the text of ISRE 2410 issued by the IAASB and, as with ISAs (UK and Ireland), a relatively small amount of additional material (highlighted with grey shading) has been added in order to clarify certain matters (for example in relation to the rules and regulations implementing the requirements of the European Transparency Directive applicable to UK and Irish listed companies) and to perpetuate previous guidance that remains pertinent. Other pronouncements on assurance engagements take the form of Bulletins (e.g. the auditor's statement on summary financial statements and guidance on providing assurance on client assets).

Authority of FRC Audit and Assurance Pronouncements

15. In order to be eligible for appointment in the UK as auditors of companies, or of any of the other entities which require their auditors to be eligible for appointment as auditors under section 1212 of the Companies Act 2006, persons must be registered with a Recognised Supervisory Body (RSB)[11] recognised under that Act and must be eligible

---

[11] The Institute of Chartered Accountants in England & Wales, The Institute of Chartered Accountants of Scotland, Chartered Accountants Ireland, the Association of Authorised Public Accountants and The Association of Chartered Certified Accountants are Recognised Supervisory Bodies for the purpose of regulating auditors in the UK.

for appointment under the rules of that RSB. The Companies Act 2006 requires RSBs to have rules and practices as to the technical standards to be applied in company audit work and the manner in which those standards are to be applied in practice. Each RSB is also required to have arrangements in place for the effective monitoring and enforcement of compliance with those standards.

16. In the Republic of Ireland legislative requirements concerning qualifications for appointment as auditor and recognition of bodies[12] of accountants are contained in the Companies Act 1990 as amended by the Companies (Auditing and Accounting) Act 2003 and in Statutory Instrument No. 220 of 2010, The European Communities (Statutory Audits) (Directive 2006/43/EC) Regulations. SI 220 implemented in Ireland Directive 2006/43/EC, the Statutory Audit Directive. The 2003 Act requires bodies of accountants to have satisfactory rules and practices as to technical and other standards. The Act also empowers the Irish Auditing and Accounting Supervisory Authority to revoke or suspend recognition or authorisation of a body of accountants or individual auditor.

17. The members of the CCAB have undertaken to adopt the ethical and engagement standards and guidance issued by the FRC. In the Republic of Ireland, accountancy bodies which are not members of the CCAB but which are also recognised bodies for the supervision of auditors may choose to require their members to comply with these standards.

18. Apparent failures by auditors to comply with applicable ethical or engagement standards are liable to be investigated by the relevant accountancy body. Auditors who do not comply with the applicable ethical or engagement standards when performing company or other audits make themselves liable to regulatory action which may include the withdrawal of registration and hence of eligibility to perform company audits.

19. All relevant FRC pronouncements are likely to be taken into account when the adequacy of the work of auditors is being considered in a court of law or in other contested situations.

20. The nature of the ethical and engagement standards and associated guidance requires professional accountants to exercise professional judgment in applying them. Where, in exceptional circumstances, auditors and reporting accountants judge it necessary to depart from a requirement, basic principle or essential procedure that is relevant in the circumstances of the engagement, the auditor or reporting accountant documents how the alternative procedures performed achieve the objective of the engagement and, unless otherwise clear, the reasons for the departure.

---

[12] Chartered Accountants Ireland, the Institute of Certified Public Accountants in Ireland, the Institute of Incorporated Public Accountants, The Association of Chartered Certified Accountants, The Institute of Chartered Accountants in England and Wales and The Institute of Chartered Accountants in Scotland are "Recognised Bodies" in the Republic of Ireland.

Appendix 1

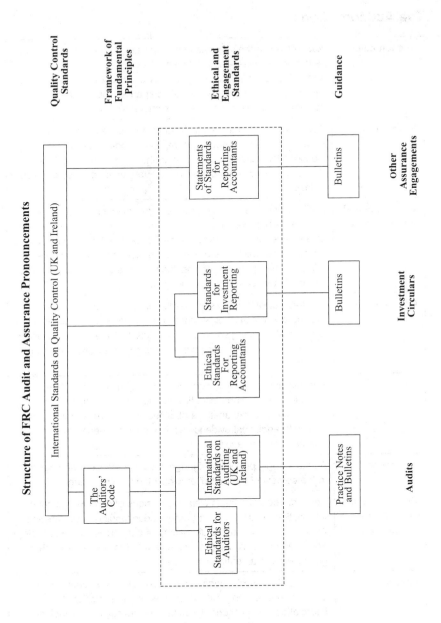

Structure of FRC Audit and Assurance Pronouncements

Quality Control Standards

Framework of Fundamental Principles

Ethical and Engagement Standards

Guidance

International Standards on Quality Control (UK and Ireland)

Statements of Standards for Reporting Accountants

Bulletins

Other Assurance Engagements

Standards for Investment Reporting

Ethical Standards For Reporting Accountants

Bulletins

Investment Circulars

The Auditors' Code

International Standards on Auditing (UK and Ireland)

Ethical Standards for Auditors

Practice Notes and Bulletins

Audits

Appendix 2

The Auditors' Code

Accountability	Auditors act in the interests of primary stakeholders, whilst having regard to the wider public interest. The identity of primary stakeholders is determined by reference to the statute or agreement requiring an audit: in the case of companies, the primary stakeholder is the general body of shareholders.
Integrity	Auditors act with integrity, fulfilling their responsibilities with honesty, fairness, candour, courage and confidentiality. Confidential information obtained in the course of the audit is disclosed only when required in the public interest, or by operation of law.
Objectivity and independence	Auditors are objective and provide impartial opinions unaffected by bias, prejudice, compromise and conflicts of interest. Auditors are also independent, this requires them to be free from situations and relationships which would make it probable that a reasonable and informed third party would conclude that the auditors' objectivity either is impaired or could be impaired.
Competence	Auditors act with professional skill, derived from their qualification, training and practical experience. This demands an understanding of financial reporting and business issues, together with expertise in accumulating and assessing the evidence necessary to form an opinion.
Rigour	Auditors approach their work with thoroughness and with an attitude of professional scepticism. They assess critically the information and explanations obtained in the course of their work and such additional evidence as they consider necessary for the purposes of their audit.
Judgment	Auditors apply professional judgment taking account of materiality in the context of the matter on which they are reporting.
Clear, complete and effective communication	Auditors' reports contain clear expressions of opinion and set out information necessary for a proper understanding of the opinion. Auditors communicate audit matters of governance interest arising from the audit of financial statements with those charged with governance of an entity.
Association	Auditors allow their reports to be included in documents containing other information only if they consider that the additional information is not in conflict with the matters covered by their report and they have no cause to believe it to be misleading.
Providing value	Auditors add to the reliability and quality of financial reporting; they provide to directors and officers constructive observations arising from the audit process; and thereby contribute to the effective operation of business, capital markets and the public sector.

FINANCIAL REPORTING COUNCIL

Section 3: ETHICAL STANDARDS

APB ETHICAL STANDARD 1 (REVISED)

INTEGRITY, OBJECTIVITY AND INDEPENDENCE

(Revised December 2010, updated December 2011)

CONTENTS

PREFACE

APB Ethical Standards apply in the audit of financial statements. They are read in the context of the Statement "The Financial Reporting Council – Scope and Authority of Audit and Assurance Pronouncements" which sets out the application and authority of APB Ethical Standards.

The terms used in APB Ethical Standards are explained in the Glossary.

APB Ethical Standards apply to audits of financial statements in both the private and the public sectors. However, auditors in the public sector are subject to more complex ethical requirements than their private sector counterparts. This includes, for example, compliance with legislation such as the Prevention of Corruption Act 1916, concerning gifts and hospitality, and with Cabinet Office guidance.

INTRODUCTION

1 The financial statements of an entity may have a number of different users. For example, they may be used by suppliers and customers, joint venture partners, bankers and other suppliers of finance, taxation and regulatory authorities, employees, trades unions and environmental groups. In the case of a listed company, the financial statements are an important source of information to the capital markets. But the primary purpose of the financial statements of an entity is to provide its owners – the shareholders (or those in an equivalent position) – with information on the state of affairs of the entity and its performance and to assist them in assessing the stewardship exercised by the directors (or those in an equivalent position) over the business that has been entrusted to them.

2 The financial statements of an entity are the responsibility of its board of directors and are prepared by them, or by others on their behalf, for the shareholders or, in some circumstances, for other third parties.

3 The primary objective of an audit of the financial statements is for the auditor to provide independent assurance to the shareholders that the directors have prepared the financial statements properly. The auditor issues a report that includes an opinion as to whether or not the financial statements give a true and fair view[1]. Thus the auditor assists the shareholders to exercise their proprietary powers as shareholders in the Annual General Meeting.

4 Public confidence in the operation of the capital markets and in the conduct of public interest entities depends, in part, upon the credibility of the opinions and reports issued by the auditor in connection with the audit of the financial statements. Such credibility depends on beliefs concerning the integrity, objectivity and independence of the auditor and the quality of audit work performed. APB establishes quality control, auditing and ethical standards to provide a framework for audit practice. The Auditors' Code underlies APB's standards and sets out the fundamental principles, which APB expects to guide the conduct of auditors.

5 APB Ethical Standards are concerned with the integrity, objectivity and independence of auditors. Ethical guidance on other matters, together with statements of fundamental ethical principles governing the work of all professional accountants, are issued by professional accountancy bodies.

6 **Auditors shall conduct the audit of the financial statements of an entity with integrity, objectivity and independence.**

---

[1] In the case of certain bodies in the public sector, the auditor expresses an opinion as to whether the financial statements 'present fairly' the financial position.

Integrity

7   Integrity is a prerequisite for all those who act in the public interest. It is essential that auditors act, and are seen to act, with integrity, which requires not only honesty but a broad range of related qualities such as fairness, candour, courage, intellectual honesty and confidentiality.

8   Integrity requires that the auditor is not affected, and is not seen to be affected, by conflicts of interest. Conflicts of interest may arise from personal, financial, business, employment, and other relationships which the audit engagement team, the audit firm or its partners or staff have with the audited entity and its connected parties.[2]

9   It is important that the directors and management of an audited entity can rely on the auditor to treat the information obtained during an audit as confidential[3], unless they have authorised its disclosure, unless it is already known to third parties or unless the auditor has a legal right or duty to disclose it. Without this, there is a danger that the directors and management will fail to disclose such information to the auditor and that the effectiveness of the audit will thereby be impaired.

Objectivity

10   Objectivity is a state of mind that excludes bias, prejudice and compromise and that gives fair and impartial consideration to all matters that are relevant to the task in hand, disregarding those that are not. Like integrity, objectivity is a fundamental ethical principle and requires that the auditor's judgment is not affected by conflicts of interest.

11   The need for auditors to be objective arises from the fact that many of the important issues involved in the preparation of financial statements do not relate to questions of fact but rather to questions of judgment. For example, there are choices to be made by the board of directors in deciding on the accounting policies to be adopted by the entity: the directors have to select the ones that they consider most appropriate and this decision can have a material impact on the financial statements. Furthermore, many items included in the financial statements cannot be measured with absolute precision and certainty. In many cases, estimates have to be made and the directors may have to choose one value from a range of possible outcomes. When exercising discretion in these areas, the directors have regard to the applicable financial reporting

---

[2]   For this purpose an audited entity's connected parties are:
a. its affiliates;
b. key members of management (including but not limited to directors and those charged with governance) of the audited entity and its significant affiliates; and
c. any person or entity with an ability to influence (other than in their capacity as professional advisor), whether directly or indirectly, key members of management and those charged with governance of the audited entity and its significant affiliates in relation to their responsibility for, or approach to, any matter or judgment that is material to the entity's financial statements.
[3]   The fundamental principle of confidentiality is addressed in the ethical guidance issued by the auditor's professional accountancy body. This principle does not constrain the proper communication between the auditor and shareholders (or equivalent) of the audited entity.

framework. If the directors, whether deliberately or inadvertently, make a biased judgment or an otherwise inappropriate decision, the financial statements may be misstated or misleading.

12   It is against this background that the auditor is required to express an opinion on the financial statements. The audit involves considering the process followed and the choices made by the directors in preparing the financial statements and concluding whether the result gives a true and fair view. The auditor's objectivity requires that an impartial opinion is expressed in the light of all the available audit evidence and the auditor's professional judgment. Objectivity also requires that the auditor adopts a rigorous and robust approach and is prepared to disagree, where necessary, with the directors' judgments.

Independence

13   Independence is freedom from situations and relationships which make it probable that a reasonable and informed third party would conclude that objectivity either is impaired or could be impaired. Independence is related to and underpins objectivity. However, whereas objectivity is a personal behavioural characteristic concerning the auditor's state of mind, independence relates to the circumstances surrounding the audit, including the financial, employment, business and personal relationships between the auditor and the audited entity and its connected parties. Relationships with parties whose interests may be contrary to the interests of the audited entity (for example, a hostile bidder) may also be relevant to the appearance of the auditor's independence.

14   The need for independence arises because, in most cases, users of the financial statements and other third parties do not have all the information necessary for judging whether the auditor is, in fact, objective. Although the auditor may be satisfied that the auditor's objectivity is not impaired by a particular situation, a third party may reach a different conclusion. For example, if a third party were aware that the auditor had certain financial, employment, business or personal relationships with the audited entity, that individual might reasonably conclude that the auditor could be subject to undue influence from the directors or would not be impartial or unbiased. Public confidence in the auditor's objectivity could therefore suffer as a result of this perception, irrespective of whether there is any actual impairment.

15   Accordingly, in evaluating the likely consequences of such situations and relationships, the test to be applied is not whether the auditor considers that the auditor's objectivity is impaired but whether it is probable that a reasonable and informed third party would conclude that the auditor's objectivity either is impaired or is likely to be impaired. As a result of the influence that the board of directors and management have over the appointment and remuneration of the auditor absolute independence cannot be achieved or maintained. The audit engagement partner considers the application of safeguards where there are threats to auditor independence (both actual and perceived).

COMPLIANCE WITH ETHICAL STANDARDS

16 **The audit firm shall establish policies and procedures, appropriately documented and communicated, designed to ensure that, in relation to each audit engagement, the audit firm, and all those who are in a position to influence the conduct and outcome of the audit, act with integrity, objectivity and independence.**

17 For the purposes of APB Ethical Standards, a person in a position to influence the conduct and outcome of the audit is:

  (a) any person who is directly involved in the audit ('the engagement team'), including:

    (i) the audit partners, audit managers and audit staff ('the audit team');

    (ii) professional personnel from other disciplines involved in the audit (for example, lawyers, actuaries, taxation specialists, IT specialists, treasury management specialists);[4]

    (iii) those who provide quality control or direct oversight of the audit;

  (b) any person who forms part of the chain of command for the audit within the audit firm;

  (c) any person within the audit firm who, due to any other circumstances, may be in a position to exert such influence.

18 Compliance with the requirements regarding the auditor's integrity, objectivity and independence is a responsibility of both the audit firm and of individual partners and professional staff. The audit firm establishes policies and procedures, appropriate to the size and nature of the audit firm, to promote and monitor compliance with those requirements by any person who is in a position to influence the conduct and outcome of the audit.[5, 6]

19 **The leadership of the audit firm shall take responsibility for establishing a control environment within the firm that places adherence to ethical principles and compliance with APB Ethical Standards above commercial considerations.**

---

[4] Where external consultants are involved in the audit, ISA (UK and Ireland) 620 *'Using the Work of an Auditor's Expert'* states that the auditor shall evaluate the objectivity of the expert.

[5] Monitoring of compliance with ethical requirements will often be performed as part of a broader quality control process. ISQC (UK & Ireland) 1 *'Quality Control for Firms that Perform Audits and Reviews of Financial Statements and other Assurance and Related Services Engagements'* establishes requirements in relation to a firm's responsibilities for its system of quality control for audits.

[6] In addition, UK legislation provides that each of the Recognised Supervisory Bodies must have adequate rules and practices to ensure that the audit firm has arrangements to prevent any person from being able to exert any influence over the way in which a statutory audit is conducted in circumstances in which that influence would be likely to affect the independence or integrity of the audit.

20   The leadership of the audit firm influences the internal culture of the firm by its actions and by its example ('the tone at the top'). Achieving a robust control environment requires that the leadership gives clear, consistent and frequent messages, backed up by appropriate actions, which emphasise the importance of compliance with APB Ethical Standards.

21   In order to promote a strong control environment, the audit firm establishes policies and procedures that include:

(a)   requirements for partners and staff to report where applicable:

- family and other personal relationships involving an entity audited by the firm;

- financial interests in an entity audited by the firm;

- decisions to join an audited entity.

(b)   monitoring of compliance with the firm's policies and procedures relating to integrity, objectivity and independence. Such monitoring procedures include, on a test basis, periodic review of the audit engagement partners' documentation of the consideration of the auditor's objectivity and independence, addressing, for example:

- financial interests in audited entities;

- economic dependence on audited entities;

- the performance of non-audit services;

- audit partner rotation;

(c)   identification of the audited entities which partners in the chain of command and their immediate family need to be independent from[7];

(d)   prompt communication of possible or actual breaches of the firm's policies and procedures to the relevant audit engagement partners;

(e)   evaluation by audit engagement partners of the implications of any identified possible or actual breaches of the firm's policies and procedures that are reported to them;

(f)   reporting by audit engagement partners of particular circumstances or relationships as required by APB Ethical Standards;

---

[7]   Such identification is necessary for those in the chain of command to understand how their firm responsibilities result in connections with different entities audited by the firm. It can be achieved by listing the individual audited entities or by a broader statement regarding categories of audited entity, for example, those of a certain business unit.

(g) operation of an enforcement mechanism to promote compliance with policies and procedures;

(h) empowerment of staff to communicate to senior levels within the firm any issue of objectivity or independence that concerns them; this includes establishing clear communication channels open to staff, encouraging staff to use these channels and ensuring that staff who use these channels are not subject to disciplinary proceedings as a result.

22 **Save where the circumstances contemplated in paragraph 26 apply, the audit firm shall designate a partner in the firm ('the Ethics Partner') as having responsibility for:**

(a) **the adequacy of the firm's policies and procedures relating to integrity, objectivity and independence, its compliance with APB Ethical Standards, and the effectiveness of its communication to partners and staff on these matters within the firm; and**

(b) **providing related guidance to individual partners with a view to achieving a consistent approach to the application of the APB Ethical Standards.**

23 In this role, the Ethics Partner has particular responsibility for engendering a culture in which the audit firm approaches ethical issues following the principles in the Ethical Standards. The Ethics Partner is an individual possessing seniority, relevant experience, and authority at leadership levels within the audit firm. Where the Ethics Partner undertakes this role together with a role such as Compliance or Risk Management he or she ensures that the responsibilities of the Ethics Partner set out in paragraph 22 above take precedence over the responsibilities of other functions.

24 In the case of audit firms that audit listed companies, the Ethics Partner has direct access to the independent non-executives[8] where such roles are introduced in an audit firm or, alternatively, to the firm's most senior governance body.

25 In assessing the effectiveness of the firm's communication of its policies and procedures relating to integrity, objectivity and independence, Ethics Partners consider whether the ethics are covered properly in induction programmes, professional training and continuing professional development for all partners and staff. Ethics Partners also provide guidance on matters referred to them and on matters which they otherwise become aware of, where a difficult and objective judgment needs to be made or a consistent position reached. Ethics Partners are proactive in considering the ethical implications of developments in the business of the audit firm and the environment in which it operates and in providing advice and guidance to partners and staff where appropriate.

---

[8] Independent non-executives appointed in accordance with the Audit Firm Governance Code are not regarded as part of the Chain of Command for the purposes of these Ethical Standards.

26   In audit firms with three or fewer partners who are 'responsible individuals'[9], it may not be practicable for an Ethics Partner to be designated. In these circumstances all partners will regularly discuss ethical issues amongst themselves, so ensuring that they act in a consistent manner and observe the principles set out in APB Ethical Standards. In the case of a sole practitioner, advice on matters where a difficult and objective judgment needs to be made is obtained through the ethics helpline of the auditor's professional body, or through discussion with a practitioner from another firm. In all cases, it is important that such discussions are documented.

27   To be able to discharge his or her responsibilities, the Ethics Partner is provided with sufficient staff support and other resources, commensurate with the size of the firm. Alternative arrangements are established to allow for:

- the provision of guidance on those audits where the Ethics Partner is the audit engagement partner; and

- situations where the Ethics Partner is unavailable, for example due to illness or holidays.

Where such support is shared with other functions such as Compliance or Risk Management, the Ethics Partner establishes policies and procedures to ensure that:

- matters delegated to support staff by the Ethics Partner, whether directly or indirectly through the operation of delegation policies established by the Ethics Partner, are clearly identified in internal documentation as relating to the Ethics Partner role and are addressed and supervised in a manner consistent with the Ethics Partner role, avoiding conflicts with other objectives; and

- all matters required to be communicated to, consulted upon with, or approved by the Ethics Partner are communicated to him or her or an authorised delegate personally, on a timely basis.

28   Whenever a possible or actual breach of an APB Ethical Standard, or of policies and procedures established pursuant to the requirements of an APB Ethical Standard, is identified, the audit engagement partner, in the first instance, and the Ethics Partner, where appropriate, assesses the implications of the breach, determines whether there are safeguards that can be put in place or other actions that can be taken to address any potential adverse consequences and considers whether there is a need to resign from the audit engagement.

29   An inadvertent violation of this Standard does not necessarily call into question the audit firm's ability to give an audit opinion, provided that:

---

9 A 'responsible individual' is a partner or employee of the audit firm who is responsible for audit work and designated as such under the audit regulations of a Recognised Supervisory Body.

(a) the audit firm has established policies and procedures that require all partners and staff to report any breach promptly to the audit engagement partner or to the Ethics Partner, as appropriate;

(b) the audit engagement partner or Ethics Partner promptly notifies the relevant partner or member of staff that any matter which has given rise to a breach is to be addressed as soon as possible and ensures that such action is taken;

(c) safeguards, where appropriate, are applied, (for example, having another partner review the work done by the relevant partner or member of staff or removing him or her from the engagement team); and

(d) the actions taken and the rationale for them are documented.

IDENTIFICATION AND ASSESSMENT OF THREATS

30 The auditor identifies and assesses the circumstances which could adversely affect the auditor's objectivity ('threats'), including any perceived loss of independence, and applies procedures ('safeguards'), which will either:

(a) eliminate the threat (for example, by eliminating the circumstances, such as removing an individual from the engagement team or disposing of a financial interest in the audited entity); or

(b) reduce the threat to an acceptable level, that is a level at which it is not probable that a reasonable and informed third party would conclude that the auditor's objectivity is impaired or is likely to be impaired (for example, by having the audit work reviewed by another partner or by another audit firm).

When considering safeguards, where the audit engagement partner chooses to reduce rather than to eliminate a threat to objectivity and independence, he or she recognises that this judgment may not be shared by users of the financial statements and that he or she may be required to justify the decision.

Threats to objectivity and independence

31 **The audit firm shall establish policies and procedures to require persons in a position to influence the conduct and outcome of the audit to be constantly alert to circumstances that might reasonably be considered threats to their objectivity or the perceived loss of independence and, where such circumstances are identified, to report them to the audit engagement partner or to the Ethics Partner, as appropriate.**

32 Such policies and procedures require that threats to the auditor's objectivity and independence are communicated to the appropriate person, having regard to the nature of the threats and to the part of the firm and the identity of any person involved.

The consideration of all threats on an individual and cumulative[10] basis and the action taken is documented. If the audit engagement partner is personally involved, or is unsure about the action to be taken, the matter is resolved through consultation with the Ethics Partner.

33 **The audit firm shall establish policies and procedures which require that partners and employees of the firm, including those providing non-audit services to an audited entity or its affiliates, do not take decisions that are the responsibility of management of the audited entity.**

34 It is not possible to specify all types of decision that are the responsibility of management, but they typically involve leading and directing the audited entity, including making significant judgments and taking decisions regarding the acquisition, deployment and control of human, financial, physical and intangible resources. Examples of judgments and decisions that are not made by the auditor include:

- Setting policies and strategic direction;

- Directing and taking responsibility for the actions of the entity's employees;

- Authorising transactions;

- Deciding which recommendations of the audit firm or other third parties should be implemented;

- Taking responsibility for the preparation and fair presentation of the financial statements in accordance with the applicable financial reporting framework; and

- Taking responsibility for designing, implementing and maintaining internal control.

35 The principal types of threats to the auditor's objectivity and independence are:

- *self-interest threat*
  A self-interest threat arises when the auditor has financial or other interests which might cause the auditor to be reluctant to take actions that would be adverse to the interests of the audit firm or any individual in a position to influence the conduct or outcome of the audit (for example, where the auditor has an investment in the audited entity, is seeking to provide additional services to the audited entity or needs to recover long-outstanding fees from the audited entity).

- *self-review threat*
  A self-review threat arises when the results of a non-audit service performed by the auditor or by others within the audit firm are reflected in the amounts included or disclosed in the financial statements (for example, where the audit firm has been involved in maintaining the accounting records, or undertaking valuations that are

---

[10] For this purpose, 'cumulative' means all current relationships and any past completed relationships that may be expected to have a continuing relevance to the auditor's independence and consideration of the threats that might exist.

incorporated in the financial statements). In the course of the audit, the auditor may need to re-evaluate the work performed in the non-audit service. As, by virtue of providing the non-audit service, the audit firm is associated with aspects of the preparation of the financial statements, the auditor may be (or may be perceived to be) unable to take an impartial view of relevant aspects of those financial statements.

- ***management threat***

  Paragraph 30 prohibits partners and employees of the audit firm from taking decisions on behalf of the management of the audited entity. A management threat can also arise when the audit firm undertakes an engagement to provide non-audit services in relation to which management are required to make judgments and take decisions based on that work (for example, the design, selection and implementation of a financial information technology system). In such work, the audit firm may become closely aligned with the views and interests of management and the auditor's objectivity and independence may be impaired, or may be perceived to be, impaired.

- ***advocacy threat***

  An advocacy threat arises when the audit firm undertakes work that involves acting as an advocate for an audited entity and supporting a position taken by management in an adversarial context (for example, by acting as a legal advocate for the audited entity in litigation or a regulatory investigation). In order to act in an advocacy role, the audit firm has to adopt a position closely aligned to that of management. This creates both actual and perceived threats to the auditor's objectivity and independence.

- ***familiarity (or trust) threat***

  A familiarity (or trust) threat arises when the auditor is predisposed to accept, or is insufficiently questioning of, the audited entity's point of view (for example, where close personal relationships are developed with the audited entity's personnel through long association with the audited entity).

- ***intimidation threat***

  An intimidation threat arises when the auditor's conduct is influenced by fear or threats (for example, where the auditor encounters an aggressive and dominating individual).

These categories may not be entirely distinct: certain circumstances may give rise to more than one type of threat. For example, where an audit firm wishes to retain the fee income from a large audited entity, but encounters an aggressive and dominating individual, there may be a self-interest threat as well as an intimidation threat. Furthermore, relationships with the audited entity's connected parties may give rise to similar threats.

36   Threats to the auditor's objectivity, including a perceived loss of independence, may arise where the audit firm is appointed to a non-audit service engagement for an entity not audited by the firm, but where an audited entity makes this decision. In such cases, even if the entity not audited by the firm pays the fee for the non-audit service

engagement, the auditor considers the implication of the threats (especially the self-interest threat) that arise from the appointment.

37　Similarly threats may arise where the auditor has a relationship with any connected party of the audited entity. Where any member of the engagement team is aware of such relationships, an assessment of the threats and available safeguards is made.

38　**The audit firm shall establish policies and procedures to require the audit engagement partner to identify and assess the significance of threats to the auditor's objectivity on an individual and cumulative[10] basis, including any perceived loss of independence:**

　　(a)　**when considering whether to accept or retain an audit engagement;[11]**

　　(b)　**when planning the audit;**

　　(c)　**when forming an opinion on the financial statements;[12]**

　　(d)　**when considering whether to accept or retain an engagement to provide non-audit services to an audited entity; and**

　　(e)　**when potential threats are reported to him or her.**

39　An initial assessment of the threats to objectivity and independence is required when the audit engagement partner is considering whether to accept or retain an audit engagement. That assessment is reviewed and updated at the planning stage of each audit. At the end of the audit process, when forming an opinion on the financial statements but before issuing the report, the audit engagement partner draws an overall conclusion as to whether all threats to objectivity and independence have been properly addressed on an individual and cumulative basis in accordance with APB Ethical Standards. If, at any time, the auditor is invited to accept an engagement to provide non-audit services, the audit engagement partner considers the impact this may have on the auditor's objectivity and independence.

40　When identifying and assessing threats to the auditor's objectivity and independence, the audit engagement partner takes into account current relationships with the audited entity (including non-audit service engagements and known relationships with connected parties of the audited entity) and with other parties in certain circumstances (see paragraph 41), those that existed prior to the current audit engagement and any known to be in prospect following the current audit engagement. This is because those prior and subsequent relationships may be perceived as likely to influence the auditor in the performance of the audit or as otherwise impairing the auditor's objectivity and independence.

---

[11]　Consideration of whether to accept or retain an audit engagement does not arise with those bodies in the public sector where responsibility for the audit is assigned by legislation.

[12]　In the case of listed companies, the auditor also assesses whether there is any threat to the auditor's objectivity and independence when discharging responsibilities in relation to preliminary announcements and when reporting on interim results.

41   Threats to the auditor's objectivity, including a perceived loss of independence, may arise where a non-audit service is provided by the audit firm to a third party which is connected (through a relationship) to an audited entity, and the outcome of that service has a material impact on the financial statements of the audited entity. For example, if the audit firm provides actuarial services to the pension scheme of an audited entity, which is in deficit, and the audit firm subsequently gives an opinion on financial statements that include judgments given in connection with that service.

42   Where the audited entity or a third party calls into question the objectivity and independence of the audit firm in relation to a particular audited entity, the Ethics Partner carries out such investigations as may be appropriate.

IDENTIFICATION AND ASSESSMENT OF SAFEGUARDS

43   **If the audit engagement partner identifies threats to the auditor's objectivity, including any perceived loss of independence, he or she shall identify and assess the effectiveness of the available safeguards and apply such safeguards as are sufficient to eliminate the threats or reduce them to an acceptable level.**

44   The nature and extent of safeguards to be applied depend on the significance of the threats. Where a threat is clearly insignificant, no safeguards are needed.

45   Other APB Ethical Standards address specific circumstances which can create threats to the auditor's objectivity or loss of independence. They give examples of safeguards that can, in some circumstances, eliminate the threat or reduce it to an acceptable level. In circumstances where this is not possible, the auditor either does not accept or withdraws from the audit engagement as appropriate.

46   APB Ethical Standards contain certain additional requirements or prohibitions that apply only in the case of listed company audited entities:

- ES 1, paragraphs 51 and 67;

- ES 3, paragraphs 12, 19 and 20;

- ES 4, paragraphs 22, 31 and 35;

- ES 5, paragraphs 28, 77, 84, 99, 110, 117, 153 and 160.

These additional requirements also apply where regulation or legislation requires that the audit of an entity is conducted in accordance with the auditing standards or ethical requirements that are applicable to the audit of listed companies.

47   **The audit firm shall establish policies and procedures which set out the circumstances in which those additional requirements listed in paragraph 46 that apply to listed companies are applied to other audit engagements.**

48   Such policies and procedures take into consideration any additional criteria set by the audit firm, such as the nature of the entity's business, its size, the number of its employees and the range of its stakeholders. For example, a firm may decide to extend the additional requirements to audit engagements of certain regulated financial institutions such as large non-listed banks and insurance companies.

49   **The audit engagement partner shall not accept or shall not continue an audit engagement if he or she concludes that any threats to the auditor's objectivity and independence cannot be reduced to an acceptable level.**

50   Where a reasonable and informed third party would regard ceasing to act as the auditor as detrimental to the shareholders (or equivalent) of the audited entity, then resignation may not be immediate. However, the audit firm discloses full details of the position to those charged with governance of the audited entity, and establishes appropriate safeguards.

ENGAGEMENT QUALITY CONTROL REVIEW

51   **In the case of listed companies the engagement quality control reviewer[13] shall:**

   (a)   **consider the audit firm's compliance with APB Ethical Standards in relation to the audit engagement;**

   (b)   **form an independent opinion as to the appropriateness and adequacy of the safeguards applied; and**

   (c)   **consider the adequacy of the documentation of the audit engagement partner's consideration of the auditor's objectivity and independence.**

52   The audit firm's policies and procedures set out whether there are circumstances in which an engagement quality control review is performed for other audit engagements as described in paragraph 47.

53   Where the involvement of an engagement quality control reviewer provides a safeguard to reduce to an acceptable level those threats to independence that have been identified as potentially arising from the provision of non-audit services, his or her review specifically addresses the related threat by ensuring that the work that was performed in the course of the non-audit service engagement has been properly and effectively assessed in the context of the audit of the financial statements.

---

[13] ISA (UK and Ireland) 220 *'Quality Control for an Audit of Financial Statements'*, requires the audit engagement partner to determine that an engagement quality control reviewer has been appointed for all audits of listed entities. The engagement quality control review involves consideration of the engagement team's evaluation of the firm's independence in relation to the audit engagement.

OVERALL CONCLUSION

54　**At the end of the audit process, when forming an opinion but before issuing the report on the financial statements, the audit engagement partner shall reach an overall conclusion that any threats to objectivity and independence on an individual and cumulative basis have been properly addressed in accordance with APB Ethical Standards. If the audit engagement partner cannot make such a conclusion, he or she shall not report and the audit firm shall resign as auditor.**

55　In addition to assessing individual threats to auditor objectivity and independence, the audit engagement partner assesses the cumulative impact of all the threats identified on the audit engagement so as to reach a conclusion that the threats identified, when viewed individually and cumulatively, have been reduced to an acceptable level through the application of safeguards.

56　If the audit engagement partner remains unable to conclude that any individual threats to objectivity and independence, or all threats to objectivity and independence viewed on a cumulative basis, have been properly addressed in accordance with APB Ethical Standards, or if there is a disagreement between the audit engagement partner and the engagement quality control reviewer, he or she consults the Ethics Partner.

57　In concluding on compliance with the requirements for objectivity and independence, the audit engagement partner is entitled to rely on the completeness and accuracy of the data developed by the audit firm's systems relating to independence (for example, in relation to the reporting of financial interests by staff), unless informed otherwise by the firm.

OTHER AUDITORS INVOLVED IN THE AUDIT OF GROUP FINANCIAL STATEMENTS

58　**The group audit engagement partner shall be satisfied that other auditors (whether a network firm or another audit firm) involved in the audit of the group financial statements, who are not subject to APB Ethical Standards, are objective and document the rationale for that conclusion.**

59　The group audit engagement partner obtains appropriate evidence[14] that the other auditors have a sufficient understanding of and have complied with the current Code of Ethics for Professional Accountants, including the independence requirements[15].

---

[14]　ISA (UK and Ireland) 600 *'Special Considerations – Audits of Group Financial Statements (Including the Work of Component Auditors)'* requires that the group engagement team shall obtain an understanding of whether the component auditor understands and will comply with the ethical requirements that are relevant to the group audit and, in particular, is independent.

[15]　The Code of Ethics for Professional Accountants (the IESBA Code) issued by the International Ethics Standards Board for Accountants establishes a conceptual framework for applying the fundamental principles of professional ethics for professional accountants. Section 290 of the IESBA Code illustrates the application of the conceptual framework to independence requirements for audit engagements and represents the international standard on which national standards should be based. No Member Body of the International Federation of Accountants (IFAC) is allowed to apply less stringent standards than those stated in that section. In addition, members of the IFAC Forum of Firms have agreed to apply ethical standards, which are at least as rigorous as those of the IESBA Code.

60   In the case of a listed company, the group audit engagement partner establishes that the company has communicated its policy[16] on the engagement of the external auditor to supply non-audit services to its affiliates and obtains confirmation that the other auditors will comply with this policy.

NETWORK FIRMS NOT INVOLVED IN THE AUDIT

61   **The audit firm shall establish that network firms which are not involved in the audit are required to comply with global policies and procedures that are designed to meet the requirements of the current IESBA Code[15].**

62   The IESBA Code requires all network firms to be independent of the entities audited by other network firms[17]. International audit networks commonly meet this requirement through global independence policies and procedures designed to comply with the current IESBA Code which are supported by appropriate monitoring and compliance processes within the network.

COMMUNICATION WITH THOSE CHARGED WITH GOVERNANCE

63   **The audit engagement partner shall ensure that those charged with governance of the audited entity are appropriately informed on a timely basis of all significant facts and matters that bear upon the auditor's objectivity and independence.**

64   The audit committee, where one exists, is usually responsible for oversight of the relationship between the auditor and the entity and of the conduct of the audit process. It therefore has a particular interest in being informed about the auditor's ability to express an objective opinion on the financial statements. Where there is no audit committee, this role is undertaken by the board of directors.[18, 19]

65   The aim of these communications is to ensure full and fair disclosure by the auditor to those charged with governance of the audited entity on matters in which they have an interest. These will generally include the key elements of the audit engagement partner's consideration of objectivity and independence, such as:

- the principal threats, if any, to objectivity and independence identified by the auditor, including consideration of all relationships between the audited entity, its affiliates and directors and the audit firm;

---

[16] The UK Corporate Governance Code requires audit committees to develop the company's policy on the engagement of the external auditor to supply non-audit services.

[17] Paragraph 290.13 of the IESBA Code, as updated in July 2009.

[18] Where there is no audit committee, references to communication with the audit committee are to be construed as including communication with the board of directors.

[19] Some bodies in the public sector have audit committees but others have different governance models.

- any safeguards adopted and the reasons why they are considered to be effective, including any independent partner review;

- the overall assessment of threats and safeguards;

- information about the general policies and processes within the audit firm for maintaining objectivity and independence.

66   Communications between the auditor and those charged with the governance of the audited entity will be needed at the planning stage and whenever significant judgments are made about threats to objectivity and independence and the appropriateness of safeguards put in place, for example, when accepting an engagement to provide non-audit services.

Additional provisions related to audits of listed companies

67   **In the case of listed companies, the audit engagement partner shall ensure that the audit committee is provided with:**

(a)   **a written disclosure of relationships (including the provision of non-audit services) that bear on the auditor's objectivity and independence, the threats to auditor independence that these create, any safeguards that have been put in place and why they address such threats, together with any other information necessary to enable the auditor's objectivity and independence to be assessed;**

(b)   **details of non-audit services provided and the fees charged in relation thereto;**

(c)   **written confirmation that the auditor is independent;**

(d)   **details of any inconsistencies between APB Ethical Standards and the company's policy for the supply of non-audit services by the audit firm and any apparent breach of that policy.**

(e)   **an opportunity to discuss auditor independence issues.**

68   The most appropriate time for these final written confirmations of independence is usually at the conclusion of the audit.

69   The auditor of a listed company discloses in writing details of all relationships between the auditor and the audited entity, and its directors and senior management and its affiliates, including all services provided by the audit firm and its network to the audited entity, its directors and senior management and its affiliates, and other services provided to other known connected parties that the auditor considers may reasonably be thought to bear on the auditor's objectivity and independence and the related safeguards that are in place.

70   The auditor ensures that the total amount of fees that the auditor and its network firms have charged to the audited entity and its affiliates for the provision of services during the reporting period, analysed into appropriate categories are disclosed. The Appendix contains an illustrative template for the provision of such information to an audit committee[20]. Separately, the auditor provides information on any contingent fee arrangements[21], the amounts of any future services which have been contracted, and details of any written proposal to provide non-audit services that has been submitted.

71   The written confirmation that the auditor is independent indicates that the auditor considers that the audit firm complies with APB Ethical Standards and that, in the auditor's professional judgment, the audit firm is independent and its objectivity is not compromised. If it is not possible to make such a confirmation, the communication will include any concerns that the auditor has that the audit firm's objectivity and independence may be compromised (including instances where the group audit engagement partner does not consider an other auditor to be objective) and an explanation of the actions which necessarily follow from this.

DOCUMENTATION

72   **The audit engagement partner shall ensure that his or her consideration of the auditor's objectivity and independence is appropriately documented on a timely basis.**

73   The requirement to document these issues contributes to the clarity and rigour of the audit engagement partner's thinking and the quality of his or her judgments. In addition, such documentation provides evidence that the audit engagement partner's consideration of the auditor's objectivity and independence was properly performed and, for listed companies, provides the basis for review by the engagement quality control reviewer.

74   Matters to be documented[22] include all key elements of the process and any significant judgments concerning:

- threats identified, other than those which are clearly insignificant, and the process used in identifying them;

- safeguards adopted and the reasons why they are considered to be effective;

---

[20] When considering how to present this analysis of fees, the auditor takes account of any applicable legislation.

[21] Paragraph 22 of ES 4 requires the audit engagement partner to disclose to the audit committee, in writing, any contingent fee arrangements for non-audit services provided by the auditor or its network firms.

[22] The necessary working papers can be combined with those prepared pursuant to paragraph 24 of ISA (UK and Ireland) 220 'Quality Control for an Audit of Financial Statements', which requires that: "The auditor shall include in the audit documentation conclusions on compliance with independence requirements that apply to the audit engagement, and any relevant discussions with the firm that support these conclusions."

- review by an engagement quality control reviewer or an independent partner;

- overall assessment of threats, on an individual and cumulative basis, and safeguards; and

- communication with those charged with governance.

EFFECTIVE DATE

75 This revised Ethical Standard becomes effective on 30 April 2011.

76 Firms may complete audit engagements relating to periods commencing on or before 31 December 2010 in accordance with existing ethical standards, putting in place any necessary changes in the subsequent engagement period.

APPENDIX: Illustrative template for communicating information on audit and non-audit services provided to the group

	Current year £m	Prior year £m
Audit of company	X	X
Audit of subsidiaries	X	X
Total audit	X	X
Audit related assurance services[23]	X	X
Other assurance services[24] [25]	X	X
Total assurance services	X	X
Tax compliance services (i.e. related to assistance with corporate tax returns)	X	X
Tax advisory services	X	X
Services relating to taxation	X	X
Internal audit services	X	X
Services related to corporate finance transactions not covered above	X	X
Other non-audit services not covered above	X	X
Total other non-audit services	X	X
Total non-audit services	X	X
Total fees	X	X
Occupational pension scheme audits	X	X
Non-audit services in respect of the audited entity provided to a third party[26].	X	X

---

[23] This will, and will only, include those services which are identified as audit related services in paragraph 55 of ES 5.

[24] This will not include any tax or internal audit services, all of which should be disclosed under those headings.

[25] The definition of an assurance engagement is provided in the Glossary of Terms included in APB's Compendium of Standards and Guidance which is published annually. Services provided under such engagements will include assurance engagements such as those which involve reporting on historical financial information which are included in an investment circular in accordance with the Standards for Investment Reporting 2000 (Revised): Investment reporting standards applicable to public reporting engagements on historical financial information.

[26] For the purposes of APB Ethical Standards non-audit services include services provided to another entity in respect of the audited entity, for example, where the audit firm provides transaction related services, in respect of an audited entity's financial information, to a prospective acquirer of the audited entity (see paragraph 12 of ES 5).

Disclosure of contingent fee arrangements under paragraph 22 of ES 4 can also be facilitated through the use of a footnote to this template.

Disclosures required under UK company legislation[27] are indicated by those categories in bold type above. Fuller information can be provided by companies if desired.

---

[27] Disclosure requirements in the Republic of Ireland are set out in European Communities (Statutory Audits) (Directive 2006/43/EC) Regulations 2010. An information sheet on this topic "Disclosure of auditors' remuneration" was developed by the Consultative Committee of Accountancy Bodies in Ireland and published by Chartered Accountants Ireland in January 2011: this is available at: http://www.charteredaccountants.ie/Members/Technical1/Financial-Reporting/Resources/Disclosure-of-Auditor-Remuneration/.

APB ETHICAL STANDARD 2 (REVISED)

FINANCIAL, BUSINESS, EMPLOYMENT AND PERSONAL RELATIONSHIPS

(Revised December 2010)

CONTENTS

PREFACE

APB Ethical Standards apply in the audit of financial statements. They are read in the context of the Statement "The Financial Reporting Council – Scope and Authority of Audit and Assurance Pronouncements" which sets out the application and authority of APB Ethical Standards.

The terms used in APB Ethical Standards are explained in the Glossary.

APB Ethical Standards apply to audits of financial statements in both the private and the public sectors. However, auditors in the public sector are subject to more complex ethical requirements than their private sector counterparts. This includes, for example, compliance with legislation such as the Prevention of Corruption Act 1916, concerning gifts and hospitality, and with Cabinet Office guidance.

INTRODUCTION

1   APB Ethical Standard 1 requires the audit engagement partner to identify and assess the circumstances which could adversely affect the auditor's objectivity ('threats'), including any perceived loss of independence, and to apply procedures ('safeguards') which will either:

(a)   eliminate the threat; or

(b)   reduce the threat to an acceptable level (that is, a level at which it is not probable that a reasonable and informed third party would conclude that the auditor's objectivity and independence is impaired or is likely to be impaired).

When considering safeguards, where the audit engagement partner chooses to reduce rather than to eliminate a threat to objectivity and independence, he or she recognises that this judgment may not be shared by users of the financial statements and that he or she may be required to justify the decision.

2   This Standard provides requirements and guidance on specific circumstances arising out of financial, business, employment and personal relationships with the audited entity, which may create threats to the auditor's objectivity or perceived loss of independence. It gives examples of safeguards that can, in some circumstances, eliminate the threat or reduce it to an acceptable level. In circumstances where this is not possible, either the relationship in question is not entered into or the auditor either does not accept or withdraws from the audit engagement, as appropriate.

3   Whenever a possible or actual breach of an APB Ethical Standard is identified, the audit engagement partner, in the first instance, and the Ethics Partner, where appropriate, assesses the implications of the breach, determines whether there are safeguards that can be put in place or other actions that can be taken to address any potential adverse consequences and considers whether there is a need to resign from the audit engagement.

4   An inadvertent violation of this Standard does not necessarily call into question the audit firm's ability to give an audit opinion provided that:

(a)   the audit firm has established policies and procedures that require all partners and staff to report any breach promptly to the audit engagement partner or to the Ethics Partner as appropriate;

(b)   the audit engagement partner or Ethics Partner promptly notifies the partner or member of staff that any matter which has given rise to a breach is to be addressed as soon as possible and ensures that such action is taken;

(c)   safeguards, if appropriate, are applied (for example, having another partner review the work done by the relevant partner or member of staff or by removing him or her from the engagement team); and

(d)   the actions taken and the rationale for them are documented.

FINANCIAL RELATIONSHIPS

General considerations

5   A financial interest is an equity or other security, debenture, loan or other debt instrument of an entity, including rights and obligations to acquire such an interest and derivatives directly related to such an interest.

6   Financial interests may be:

    (a)   owned directly, rather than through intermediaries (a 'direct financial interest'); or

    (b)   owned through intermediaries, for example, an open ended investment company or a pension scheme (an 'indirect financial interest').

7   **Save where the circumstances contemplated in paragraphs 9, 10, 12, 19 or 21 apply, the audit firm, any partner in the audit firm, a person in a position to influence the conduct and outcome of the audit or an immediate family member of such a person shall not hold:**

    (a)   any direct financial interest in an audited entity or an affiliate of an audited entity; or

    (b)   any indirect financial interest in an audited entity or an affiliate of an audited entity, where the investment is material to the audit firm or the individual, or to the intermediary; or

    (c)   any indirect financial interest in an audited entity or an affiliate of an audited entity, where the person holding it has both:

        (i)   the ability to influence the investment decisions of the intermediary; and

        (ii)   actual knowledge of the existence of the underlying investment in the audited entity.

8   The threats to the auditor's objectivity and independence, where a direct financial interest or a material indirect financial interest in the audited entity is held by the audit firm or by one of the individuals specified in paragraph 7, are such that no safeguards can eliminate them or reduce them to an acceptable level.

9   Where a person joins the audit firm as a partner, he or she or an immediate family member is not required to dispose of financial interests held where:

    (a)   the financial interests were acquired before the new partner joined the audit firm; and

    (b)   the individual is not able to influence the affairs of the audited entity; and

(c) either there is no market for such interests, or the individual does not have the power to sell or direct the sale of the interest; and

(d) the new partner:

- is not in a position to influence the conduct and outcome of the audit;

- does not work in the same part of the firm as the audit engagement partner; and

- is not involved in the provision of a non-audit service to the audit client.

Such a financial interest is disposed of as soon as possible after the individual becomes able to make a disposal. The audit firm ensures that:

- such financial interests are approved by the Ethics Partner;

- a record is maintained of such individuals, including a description of the circumstances; and

- this information is communicated to the relevant audit engagement partner.

10 Where an immediate family member of a partner who is not in a position to influence the conduct and outcome of the audit holds a financial interest in an audited entity or an affiliate of an audited entity as a consequence of:

- their compensation arrangements (for example, a share option scheme, where the shares have not vested); or

- a decision made, or a transaction undertaken, by an entity with whom that immediate family member has a contractual business or employment arrangement (for example, a partnership agreement);

such financial interests are not generally considered to threaten the auditor's objectivity and independence. However, where such interests are significant or the relevant partner has close working contacts with the engagement team, the Ethics Partner considers whether any safeguards need to be put in place.

11 For the purposes of paragraph 7, where holdings in an authorised unit or investment trust, an open ended investment company or an equivalent investment vehicle which is audited by the audit firm, are held by a partner in the audit firm, who is not in a position to influence the conduct and outcome of the audit, or an immediate family member of such a partner, these are to be treated as indirect financial interests. Such interests can therefore be held as long as:

(a) they are not material to the individual; and

(b) the individual has no influence over the investment decisions of the audited entity.

12 Where a person in a position to influence the conduct and outcome of the audit or a partner in the audit firm, or any of their immediate family members are members or shareholders of an audited entity, as a result of membership requirements, or equivalent, the audit firm ensures that no more than the minimum number of shares necessary to comply with the requirement are held and that this shareholding is not material to either the audited entity or the individual. Disclosure of such shareholdings will be made to those charged with governance of the audited entity, in accordance with APB Ethical Standard 1, paragraph 63.

13 Where one of the financial interests specified in paragraph 7 is held by:

(a) *the audit firm, a partner in the audit firm or an immediate family member of such a partner:* the entire financial interest is disposed of, a sufficient amount of an indirect financial interest is disposed of so that the remaining interest is no longer material, or the firm does not accept (or withdraws from) the audit engagement;

(b) *a person in a position to influence the conduct and outcome of the audit:* the entire financial interest is disposed of, a sufficient amount of an indirect financial interest is disposed of so that the remaining interest is no longer material, or that person does not retain a position in which they exert such influence on the audit engagement;

(c) *an immediate family member of a person in a position to influence the conduct and outcome of the audit:* the entire financial interest is disposed of, a sufficient amount of an indirect financial interest is disposed of so that the remaining interest is no longer material, or the person in a position to influence the conduct and outcome of the audit does not retain a position in which they exert such influence on the audit engagement.

14 Where one of the financial interests specified in paragraph 7 is acquired unintentionally, as a result of an external event (for example, inheritance, gift, or merger of firms or companies), the disposal of the financial interest is required immediately, or as soon as possible after the relevant person has actual knowledge of, and the right to dispose of, the interest.

15 Where the disposal of a financial interest does not take place immediately, the audit firm adopts safeguards to preserve its objectivity until the financial interest is disposed of. These may include the temporary exclusion of the person in a position to influence the conduct and outcome of the audit from such influence on the audit, or a review of the relevant person's audit work by an audit partner having sufficient experience and authority to fulfill the role who is not involved in the audit engagement.

16 Where the audit firm or one of the individuals specified in paragraph 7 holds an indirect financial interest but does not have both:

(a) the ability to influence the investment decisions of the intermediary; and

(b) actual knowledge of the existence of the underlying investment in the audited entity;

there may not be a threat to the auditor's objectivity and independence. For example, where the indirect financial interest takes the form of an investment in a pension fund, the composition of the funds and the size and nature of any underlying investment in the audited entity may be known but there is unlikely to be any influence on investment decisions, as the fund will generally be managed independently on a discretionary basis. In the case of an 'index tracker' fund, the investment in the audited entity is determined by the composition of the relevant index and there may be no threat to objectivity. As long as the person holding the indirect interest is not directly involved in the audit of the intermediary, nor able to influence the individual investment decisions of the intermediary, any threat to the auditor's objectivity and independence may be regarded as insignificant.

17 Where the audit firm or one of the individuals specified in paragraph 7 holds a beneficial interest in a properly operated 'blind' trust, they are (by definition) completely unaware of the identity of the underlying investments. If these include an investment in the audited entity, this means that they are unaware of the existence of an indirect financial interest. In these circumstances, there is no threat to the auditor's objectivity and independence.

18 **Where a person in a position to influence the conduct and outcome of the audit or a partner in the audit firm becomes aware that a close family member holds one of the financial interests specified in paragraph 7, that individual shall report the matter to the audit engagement partner to take appropriate action. If it is a close family member of the audit engagement partner, or if the audit engagement partner is in doubt as to the action to be taken, the audit engagement partner shall resolve the matter through consultation with the Ethics Partner.**

Financial interests held as trustee

19 Where a direct or an indirect financial interest in the audited entity or its affiliates is held in a trustee capacity by a person in a position to influence the conduct and outcome of the audit, or an immediate family member of such a person, a self-interest threat may be created because either the existence of the trustee interest may influence the conduct of the audit or the trust may influence the actions of the audited entity. Accordingly, such a trustee interest is only held when:

- the relevant person is not an identified potential beneficiary of the trust; and

- the financial interest held by the trust in the audited entity is not material to the trust; and

- the trust is not able to exercise significant influence over the audited entity or an affiliate of the audited entity; and

- the relevant person does not have significant influence over the investment decisions made by the trust, in so far as they relate to the financial interest in the audited entity.

20   Where it is not clear whether the financial interest held by the trust in the audited entity is material to the trust or whether the trust is able to exercise significant influence over the audited entity, the financial interest is reported to the Ethics Partner, so that a decision can be made as to the steps that need to be taken.

21   A direct or an indirect financial interest in the audited entity or its affiliates held in a trustee capacity by the audit firm or by a partner in the audit firm (other than a partner in a position to influence the conduct and outcome of the audit), or an immediate family member of such a person, can only be held when the relevant person is not an identified potential beneficiary of the trust.

Financial interests held by audit firm pension schemes

22   Where the pension scheme of an audit firm has a financial interest in an audited entity or its affiliates and the firm has any influence over the trustees' investment decisions (other than indirect strategic and policy decisions), the self-interest threat created is such that no safeguards can eliminate it or reduce it to an acceptable level. In other cases (for example, where the pension scheme invests through a collective investment scheme and the firm's influence is limited to investment policy decisions, such as the allocation between different categories of investment), the Ethics Partner considers the acceptability of the position, having regard to the materiality of the financial interest to the pension scheme.

Loans and guarantees

23   Where audit firms, persons in a position to influence the conduct and outcome of the audit or immediate family members of such persons:

(a)   accept a loan[1] or a guarantee of their borrowings from an audited entity; or

(b)   make a loan to or guarantee the borrowings of an audited entity,

a self-interest threat and an intimidation threat to the auditor's objectivity can be created or there may be a perceived loss of independence. In a number of situations, no safeguards can eliminate this threat or reduce it to an acceptable level.

24   **Audit firms, persons in a position to influence the conduct and outcome of the audit and immediate family members of such persons shall not make a loan to, or guarantee the borrowings of, an audited entity or its affiliates unless this represents a deposit made with a bank or similar deposit taking institution in the ordinary course of business and on normal business terms.**

---

[1]   For the purpose of this standard, the term 'loan' does not include ordinary trade credit arrangements or deposits placed for goods or services, unless they are material to either party (see paragraph 29).

25   **Audit firms shall not accept a loan from, or have their borrowings guaranteed by, the audited entity or its affiliates unless:**

   (a)   **the audited entity is a bank or similar deposit taking institution; and**

   (b)   **the loan or guarantee is made in the ordinary course of business on normal business terms; and**

   (c)   **the loan or guarantee is not material to both the audit firm and the audited entity.**

26   **Persons in a position to influence the conduct and outcome of the audit and immediate family members of such persons shall not accept a loan from, or have their borrowings guaranteed by, the audited entity or its affiliates unless:**

   (a)   **the audited entity is a bank or similar deposit taking institution; and**

   (b)   **the loan or guarantee is made in the ordinary course of business on normal business terms; and**

   (c)   **the loan or guarantee is not material to the audited entity.**

27   Loans by an audited entity that is a bank or similar institution to a person in a position to influence the conduct and outcome of the audit, or an immediate family member of such a person (for example, home mortgages, bank overdrafts or car loans), do not create an unacceptable threat to objectivity and independence, provided that normal business terms apply. However, where such loans are in arrears by a significant amount, this creates an intimidation threat that is unacceptable. Where such a situation arises, the person in a position to influence the conduct and outcome of the audit reports the matter to the audit engagement partner or to the Ethics Partner, as appropriate and ceases to have any involvement with the audit. The audit engagement partner or, where appropriate, the Ethics Partner considers whether any audit work is to be reperformed.

BUSINESS RELATIONSHIPS

28   A business relationship between:

   (a)   the audit firm or a person who is in a position to influence the conduct and outcome of the audit, or an immediate family member of such a person; and

   (b)   the audited entity or its affiliates, or its management;

   involves the two parties having a common commercial interest. Business relationships may create self-interest, advocacy or intimidation threats to the auditor's objectivity and perceived loss of independence. Examples include:

- joint ventures with the audited entity or with a director, officer or other individual who performs a management role for the audited entity;

- arrangements to combine one or more services or products of the audit firm with one or more services or products of the audited entity and to market the package with reference to both parties;

- distribution or marketing arrangements under which the audit firm acts as a distributor or marketer of any of the audited entity's products or services, or the audited entity acts as the distributor or marketer of any of the products or services of the audit firm;

- other commercial transactions, such as the audit firm leasing its office space from the audited entity.

29 **Audit firms, persons in a position to influence the conduct and outcome of the audit and immediate family members of such persons shall not enter into business relationships with an audited entity, its management or its affiliates except where they:**

- **involve the purchase of goods and services from the audit firm or the audited entity in the ordinary course of business and on an arm's length basis and which are not material to either party; or**

- **are clearly inconsequential to either party.**

30 Where a business relationship exists, that is not permitted under paragraph 29, and has been entered into by:

(a) *the audit firm:* either the relationship is terminated or the firm does not accept (or withdraws from) the audit engagement;

(b) *a person in a position to influence the conduct and outcome of the audit:* either the relationship is terminated or that person does not retain a position in which they exert such influence on the audit engagement;

(c) *an immediate family member of a person in a position to influence the conduct and outcome of the audit:* either the relationship is terminated or the person in a position to influence the conduct and outcome of the audit does not retain such a position.

Where there is an unavoidable delay in the termination of a business relationship, the audit firm adopts safeguards to preserve its objectivity until the relationship is terminated. These may include a review of the relevant person's audit work or a temporary exclusion of the relevant person from influence on conduct and outcome of the audit.

41   **Where a partner or employee returns to the firm on completion of a loan staff assignment, that individual shall not be given any role on the audit involving any function or activity that he or she performed or supervised during that assignment.**

42   In considering for how long this restriction is to be observed, the need to realise the potential value to the effectiveness of the audit of the increased knowledge of the audited entity's business gained through the assignment has to be weighed against the potential threats to objectivity and independence. Those threats increase with the length of the assignment and with the intended level of responsibility of the individual within the engagement team. As a minimum, this restriction will apply to at least the first audit of the financial statements following the completion of the loan staff assignment.

Partners and engagement team members joining an audited entity

43   **Where a former partner in the audit firm joins the audited entity, the audit firm shall take action as quickly as possible – and, in any event, before any further work is done by the audit firm in connection with the audit – to ensure that no significant connections remain between the firm and the individual.**

44   Ensuring that no significant connections remain between the firm and the individual requires that:

- all capital balances and similar financial interests be fully settled (including retirement benefits) unless these are made in accordance with pre-determined arrangements that cannot be influenced by any remaining connections between the individual and the firm; and

- the individual does not participate or appear to participate in the audit firm's business or professional activities.

45   **Audit firms shall establish policies and procedures that require:**

    (a)   all partners in the audit firm to notify the firm of any situation involving their potential employment with any entity audited by the firm; and

    (b)   senior members of any engagement team to notify the audit firm of any situation involving their potential employment with the relevant audited entity; and

    (c)   other members of any engagement team to notify the audit firm of any situation involving their probable employment with the relevant audited entity; and

    (d)   anyone who has given such notice to be removed from the engagement team; and

    (e)   a review of the audit work performed by the resigning or former engagement team member in the current and, where appropriate, the most recent audit.

46   Objectivity and independence may be threatened where a director, an officer or an employee of the audited entity who is in a position to exert direct and significant influence over the preparation of the financial statements, has recently been a partner in the audit firm or a member of the engagement team. Such circumstances may create self-interest, familiarity and intimidation threats, particularly when significant connections remain between the individual and the audit firm. Similarly, objectivity and independence may be threatened when an individual knows, or has reason to believe, that he or she will or may be joining the audited entity at some time in the future.

47   Where a partner in the audit firm or a member of the engagement team for a particular audited entity has left the audit firm and taken up employment with that entity, the significance of the self-interest, familiarity and intimidation threats is assessed and normally depends on such factors as:

- the position that individual had in the engagement team or firm;

- the position that individual has taken at the audited entity;

- the amount of involvement that individual will have with the engagement team (especially where it includes former colleagues with whom he or she worked);

- the length of time since that individual was a member of the engagement team or employed by the audit firm.

Following the assessment of any such threats, appropriate safeguards are applied where necessary.

48   Any review of audit work is performed by a more senior audit professional. If the individual joining the audited entity is an audit partner, the review is performed by an audit partner who is not involved in the audit engagement. Where, due to its size, the audit firm does not have a partner who was not involved in the audit engagement, it seeks either a review by another audit firm or advice from its professional body.

49   **Where a partner leaves the firm and is appointed as a director (including as a non-executive director) or to a key management position with an audited entity[4], having acted as audit engagement partner (or as an engagement quality control reviewer, key partner involved in the audit or a partner in the chain of command) at any time in the two years prior to this appointment, the firm shall resign as**

---

[4] UK legislation provides that each of the Recognised Supervisory Bodies must have adequate rules and practices to ensure that a key audit partner (the individual responsible for the statutory audit and individuals responsible for a parent undertaking or a material subsidiary undertaking) of a firm appointed by a public interest entity as auditor is prohibited from being appointed as a director or other officer of the entity during a period of two years commencing on the date on which his or her work as key audit partner ended.

auditor.[5] The firm shall not accept re-appointment as auditor until a two-year period, commencing when the former partner ceased to have an ability to influence the conduct and outcome of the audit, has elapsed or the former partner ceases employment with the former audited entity, whichever is the sooner.

50   Where a former member of the engagement team (other than an audit engagement partner, a key partner involved in the audit or a partner in the chain of command) leaves the audit firm and, within two years of ceasing to hold that position, joins the audited entity as a director (including as a non-executive director) or in a key management position, the audit firm shall consider whether the composition of the audit team is appropriate.

51   In such circumstances, the audit firm evaluates the appropriateness of the composition of the audit team by reference to the factors listed in paragraph 47 and alters or strengthens the audit team to address any threat to the auditor's objectivity and independence that may be identified.

Family members employed by an audited entity

52   Where a person in a position to influence the conduct and outcome of the audit, or a partner in the audit firm, becomes aware that an immediate or close family member is employed by an audited entity in a position to exercise influence on the accounting records or financial statements, that individual shall either:

(a)   in the case of an immediate family member of a person in a position to influence the conduct and outcome of the audit, cease to hold a position in which they exert such influence on the audit; or

(b)   in the case of a close family member of a person in a position to influence the conduct and outcome of the audit, or any family member of a partner in the audit firm, report the matter to the audit engagement partner to take appropriate action. If it is a close family member of the audit engagement partner or if the audit engagement partner is in doubt as to the action to be taken, the audit engagement partner shall resolve the matter in consultation with the Ethics Partner.

---

[5]   The timing of the audit firm's resignation as auditor is determined in accordance with paragraph 50 of APB Ethical Standard 1. In the case of those public sector bodies where the responsibility for the audit is assigned by legislation, the auditor cannot resign from the audit engagement and considers alternative safeguards that can be put in place.

GOVERNANCE ROLE WITH AN AUDITED ENTITY

53   Paragraphs 54 to 56 are supplementary to certain statutory or regulatory provisions that prohibit directors of entities from being appointed as their auditor.[6]

54   **The audit firm or a partner or employee of the audit firm shall not accept appointment or perform a role:**

(a)   **as an officer[7] or member of the board of directors of the audited entity;**

(b)   **as a member of any subcommittee of that board; or**

(c)   **in such a position in an entity which holds directly or indirectly more than 20% of the voting rights in the audited entity, or in an entity in which the audited entity holds directly or indirectly more than 20% of the voting rights.**

55   **Where a person in a position to influence the conduct and outcome of the audit becomes aware that an immediate or close family member holds a position described in paragraph 54, the audit firm shall take appropriate steps to ensure that the relevant person does not retain a position in which they exert influence on the conduct and outcome of the audit engagement.**

56   **Where a partner or employee of the audit firm, not being a member of the engagement team, becomes aware that an immediate or close family member holds a position described in paragraph 54, that individual shall report that fact to the audit engagement partner, who shall consider whether the relationship might be regarded by a reasonable and informed third party as impairing, or being thought to impair, the auditor's objectivity. If the audit engagement partner concludes that the auditor's objectivity may be impaired, that individual shall consult with the Ethics Partner to determine whether appropriate safeguards exist. If no such safeguards exist, the audit firm withdraws from the audit engagement.**

EMPLOYMENT WITH AUDIT FIRM

57   Objectivity and independence may be threatened where a former director or employee of the audited entity becomes a member of the engagement team. Self-interest, self-review and familiarity threats may be created where a member of the engagement team has to report on, for example, financial statements which he or she prepared, or elements of the financial statements for which he or she had responsibility, while with the audited entity.

---

[6]   For example, in the case of limited companies and certain other organisations, section 1214 of the Companies Act 2006 contains detailed provisions. Amongst other things, these state that:
'...A person may not act as statutory auditor of an audited person if [he] is (a) an officer or employee of the audited person, or (b) a partner or employee of such a person, or a partnership of which such a person is a partner.'

[7]   As defined in Section 1173 of the Companies Act 2006 as including a director, manager or secretary.

58   **Where a former director or a former employee of an audited entity, who was in a position to exert significant influence over the preparation of the financial statements, joins the audit firm, that individual shall not be assigned to a position in which he or she is able to influence the conduct and outcome of the audit for that entity or its affiliates for a period of two years following the date of leaving the audited entity.**

59   In certain circumstances, a longer period of exclusion from the engagement team may be appropriate. For example, threats to objectivity and independence may exist in relation to the audit of the financial statements of any period which are materially affected by the work of that person whilst occupying his or her former position of influence with the audited entity. The significance of these threats depends on factors such as:

  • the position the individual held with the audited entity;

  • the length of time since the individual left the audited entity;

  • the position the individual holds in the engagement team.

FAMILY AND OTHER PERSONAL RELATIONSHIPS

60   A relationship between a person who is in a position to influence the conduct and outcome of the audit and another party does not generally affect the consideration of the auditor's objectivity and independence. However, if it is a family relationship, and if the family member also has a financial, business or employment relationship with the audited entity, then self-interest, familiarity or intimidation threats to the auditor's objectivity and independence may be created. The significance of any such threats depends on such factors as:

  • the relevant person's involvement in the audit;

  • the nature of the relationship between the relevant person and his or her family member;

  • the family member's relationship with the audited entity.

61   A distinction is made between immediate family relationships and close family relationships. Immediate family members comprise an individual's spouse (or equivalent) and dependents, whereas close family members comprise parents, non-dependent children and siblings. While an individual can usually be presumed to be aware of matters concerning his or her immediate family members and to be able to influence their behaviour, it is generally recognised that the same levels of knowledge and influence do not exist in the case of close family members.

62   When considering family relationships, it needs to be acknowledged that, in an increasingly secular, open and inclusive society, the concept of what constitutes a family is evolving and relationships between individuals which have no status formally

recognised by law may nevertheless be considered as significant as those which do. It may therefore be appropriate to regard certain other personal relationships, particularly those that would be considered close personal relationships, as if they are family relationships.

63 **The audit firm shall establish policies and procedures that require:**

(a) **partners and professional staff to report to the audit firm any immediate family, close family and other personal relationships involving an entity audited by the firm, to which they are a party and which they consider might create a threat to the auditor's objectivity or a perceived loss of independence;**

(b) **the relevant audit engagement partners to be notified promptly of any immediate family, close family and other personal relationships reported by partners and other professional staff.**

64 **The audit engagement partner shall:**

(a) **assess the threats to the auditor's objectivity and independence arising from immediate family, close family and other personal relationships on the basis of the information reported to the firm by persons in a position to influence the conduct and outcome of the audit;**

(b) **apply appropriate safeguards to eliminate the threat or reduce it to an acceptable level; and**

(c) **where there are unresolved matters or the need for clarification, consult with the Ethics Partner.**

65 Where such matters are identified or reported, the audit engagement partner or the Ethics Partner assesses the information available and the potential for there to be a threat to the auditor's objectivity and independence, treating any personal relationship as if it were a family relationship.

EXTERNAL CONSULTANTS INVOLVED IN THE AUDIT

66 Audit firms may employ external consultants as experts in order to obtain sufficient appropriate audit evidence regarding certain financial statement assertions.[8] There is a risk that an expert's objectivity and independence will be impaired if the expert is related to the entity, for example by being financially dependent upon or having an investment in, the entity.

---

[8] ISA (UK and Ireland) 620 *'Using the Work of an Auditor's Expert'* requires that the auditor shall evaluate whether the expert has the necessary objectivity.

67 **The audit engagement partner shall be satisfied that any external consultant involved in the audit will be objective and document the rationale for that conclusion.**

68 The audit engagement partner obtains information from the external consultant as to the existence of any connections that they have with the audited entity including:

- financial interests;

- business relationships;

- employment (past, present and future);

- family and other personal relationships.

EFFECTIVE DATE

69 This revised Ethical Standard becomes effective on 30 April 2011.

70 Firms may complete audit engagements relating to periods commencing prior to 31 December 2010 in accordance with existing ethical standards, putting in place any necessary changes in the subsequent engagement period.

71 On appointment as auditor to an entity, an audit firm may continue in a business relationship or a loan staff arrangement which is already contracted at the date of appointment, until the earlier of either:

(i) the completion of the specific obligations under the contract or the end of the contract term, where this is set out in the contract; or

(ii) one year after the date of appointment, where obligations or a term are not defined,

provided that the need for additional safeguards is assessed and if considered necessary, those additional safeguards are applied.

APB ETHICAL STANDARD 3 (REVISED)

LONG ASSOCIATION WITH THE AUDIT ENGAGEMENT

(Revised October 2009)

CONTENTS

PREFACE

APB Ethical Standards apply in the audit of financial statements. They are read in the context of the Statement "The Financial Reporting Council – Scope and Authority of Audit and Assurance Pronouncements" which sets out the application and authority of APB Ethical Standards.

The terms used in APB Ethical Standards are explained in the Glossary.

APB Ethical Standards apply to audits of financial statements in both the private and the public sectors. However, auditors in the public sector are subject to more complex ethical requirements than their private sector counterparts. This includes, for example, compliance with legislation such as the Prevention of Corruption Act 1916, concerning gifts and hospitality, and with Cabinet Office guidance.

INTRODUCTION

1   APB Ethical Standard 1 requires the audit engagement partner to identify and assess the circumstances which could adversely affect the auditor's objectivity ('threats'), including any perceived loss of independence, and to apply procedures ('safeguards') which will either:

(a)   eliminate the threat; or

(b)   reduce the threat to an acceptable level (that is, a level at which it is not probable that a reasonable and informed third party would conclude that the auditor's objectivity and independence either is impaired or is likely to be impaired).

When considering safeguards, where the audit engagement partner chooses to reduce rather than to eliminate a threat to objectivity and independence, he or she recognises that this judgment may not be shared by users of the financial statements and that he or she may be required to justify the decision.

2   This Standard provides requirements and guidance on specific circumstances arising out of long association with the audit engagement, which may create threats to the auditor's objectivity or perceived loss of independence. It gives examples of safeguards that can, in some circumstances, eliminate the threat or reduce it to an acceptable level. In circumstances where this is not possible, the auditor either does not accept or withdraws from the audit engagement, as appropriate.

3   Whenever a possible or actual breach of an APB Ethical Standard is identified, the audit engagement partner, in the first instance, and the Ethics Partner, where appropriate, assesses the implications of the breach, determines whether there are safeguards that can be put in place or other actions that can be taken to address any potential adverse consequences and considers whether there is a need to resign from the audit engagement.

4   An inadvertent violation of this Standard does not necessarily call into question the audit firm's ability to give an audit opinion provided that:

(a)   the audit firm has established policies and procedures that require all partners and staff to report any breach promptly to the audit engagement partner or to the Ethics Partner, as appropriate;

(b)   the audit engagement partner or Ethics Partner ensures that any matter which has given rise to a breach is addressed as soon as possible;

(c)   safeguards, if appropriate, are applied (for example, by having another partner review the work done by the relevant partner or member of staff or by removing him or her from the engagement team): and

(d)   the actions taken and the rationale for them are documented.

GENERAL PROVISIONS

5   **The audit firm shall establish policies and procedures to monitor the length of time that audit engagement partners, key partners involved in the audit and partners and staff in senior positions, including those from other disciplines, serve as members of the engagement team for each audit.**

6   **Where audit engagement partners, key partners involved in the audit, and partners and staff in senior positions have a long association with the audit, the audit firm shall assess the threats to the auditor's objectivity and independence and shall apply safeguards to reduce the threats to an acceptable level. Where appropriate safeguards cannot be applied, the audit firm shall either resign as auditor or not stand for reappointment, as appropriate.[1]**

7   Where audit engagement partners, key partners involved in the audit, other partners and staff in senior positions have a long association with the audited entity, self-interest, self-review and familiarity threats to the auditor's objectivity may arise. Similarly, such circumstances may result in an actual or perceived loss of independence. The significance of such threats depends upon factors such as:

- the role of the individual in the engagement team;

- the proportion of time that the audited entity contributes to the individual's annual billable hours;

- the length of time that the individual has been associated with that audit engagement.

8   In order to address such threats, audit firms apply safeguards. Appropriate safeguards may include:

- removing ('rotating') the partners and the other senior members of the engagement team after a pre-determined number of years;

- involving an additional partner, who is not and has not recently been a member of the engagement team, to review the work done by the partners and the other senior members of the engagement team and to advise as necessary;

- applying independent internal quality reviews to the engagement in question.

9   Once an audit engagement partner has held this role for a continuous period of ten years, careful consideration is given as to whether a reasonable and informed third party would consider the audit firm's objectivity and independence to be impaired. Where the individual concerned is not rotated after ten years, it is important that:

---

[1] In the case of those public sector bodies where the responsibility for the audit is assigned by legislation, the auditor cannot resign from the audit engagement and considers alternative safeguards that can be put in place.

(a) safeguards other than rotation, such as those noted in paragraph 8, are applied; or

(b) (i) the reasoning as to why the individual continues to participate in the audit engagement without any safeguards is documented; and

(ii) the facts are communicated to those charged with governance of the audited entity in accordance with paragraphs 63 – 71 of APB Ethical Standard 1.

10 The audit firm's policies and procedures set out whether there are circumstances in which the audit engagement partners, engagement quality control reviewers and key partners involved in the audit of non-listed entities are subject to accelerated rotation requirements, such as those set out in paragraph 12, as described in paragraph 47 of APB Ethical Standard 1.

11 Any scheme of rotation of partners and other senior members of the engagement team needs to take into account the factors which affect the quality of the audit work, including the experience and continuity of members of the engagement team and the need to ensure appropriate succession planning.

ADDITIONAL PROVISIONS RELATED TO AUDITS OF LISTED COMPANIES

The audit engagement partner

12 **In the case of listed companies, save where the circumstances contemplated in paragraph 15 and 16 apply, the audit firm shall establish policies and procedures to ensure that:**

(a) **no one shall act as audit engagement partner for more than five years; and**

(b) **anyone who has acted as the audit engagement partner for a particular audited entity for a period of five years, shall not subsequently participate in the audit engagement until a further period of five years has elapsed.**

13 The roles that constitute participating in an audit engagement for the purposes of paragraph 12(b), include providing quality control for the engagement, advising or consulting with the engagement team or the client regarding technical or industry specific issues, transactions or events, or otherwise directly influencing the outcome of the audit engagement. This does not include responding to queries in relation to any completed audit engagement. This is not intended to preclude partners whose primary responsibility within a firm is to be consulted on technical or industry specific issues from providing such consultation to the engagement team or client after a period of two years has elapsed from their ceasing to act as audit engagement partner, provided that such consultation is in respect of new issues or new types of transactions or events that were not previously required to be considered by that individual in the course of acting as audit engagement partner.

14   Where an audit engagement partner continues in a non-audit role having been rotated off the engagement team, the new audit engagement partner and the individual concerned ensure that that person, while acting in this new role, does not exert any influence on the audit engagement. Positions in which an individual is responsible for the firm's client relationship with the particular audited entity would not be an acceptable non-audit role.

15   When an audited entity becomes a listed company, the length of time the audit engagement partner has served the audited entity in that capacity is taken into account in calculating the period before the audit engagement partner is rotated off the engagement team. However, where the audit engagement partner has already served for four or more years, that individual may continue to serve as the audit engagement partner for not more than two years after the audited entity becomes a listed company.

16   In circumstances where the audit committee (or equivalent) of the audited entity decide that a degree of flexibility over the timing of rotation is necessary to safeguard the quality of the audit and the audit firm agrees, the audit engagement partner may continue in this position for an additional period of up to two years, so that no longer than seven years in total is spent in the position of audit engagement partner. An audit committee and the audit firm may consider that such flexibility safeguards the quality of the audit, for example, where:

-    substantial change has recently been made or will soon be made to the nature or structure of the audited entity's business; or

-    there are unexpected changes in the senior management of the audited entity.

In these circumstances alternative safeguards are applied to reduce any threats to an acceptable level. Such safeguards may include ensuring that an expanded review of the audit work is undertaken by the engagement quality control reviewer or an audit partner, who is not involved in the audit engagement.

17   Where it has been determined that the audit engagement partner may act for a further period (not to exceed two years) in the interests of audit quality, this fact and the reasons for it, are to be disclosed to the audited entity's shareholders as early as practicable and in each of the additional years. If the audited entity is not prepared to make such a disclosure, the audit firm does not permit the audit engagement partner to continue in this role.

18   In the case of joint audit arrangements for listed companies, audit firms will make arrangements for changes of audit engagement partners over a five-year period so that the familiarity threat is avoided, whilst also taking into consideration factors that affect the quality of the audit work.

Engagement quality control reviewers and key partners involved in the audit

19   In the case of listed companies, the audit firm shall establish policies and procedures to ensure that:

(a)   no one shall act as the engagement quality control reviewer or a key partner involved in the audit for a period longer than seven years;

(b)   where an engagement quality control reviewer or a key partner involved in the audit becomes the audit engagement partner, the combined period of service in these positions shall not exceed seven years; and

(c)   anyone who has acted:

(i)   as an engagement quality control reviewer for a particular audited entity for a period of seven years, whether continuously or in aggregate, shall not participate in the audit engagement until a further period of five years has elapsed;

(ii)   as a key partner involved in the audit for a particular audited entity for a period of seven years, whether continuously or in aggregate, shall not participate in the audit engagement until a further period of two years has elapsed;

(iii)   in a combination of roles as:

•   the engagement quality control reviewer,

•   a key partner involved in the audit, or

•   the audit engagement partner

for a particular audited entity for a period of seven years, whether continuously or in aggregate, shall not participate in the audit engagement until a further period of five years has elapsed.

Other partners and staff in senior positions

20   In the case of listed companies, the audit engagement partner shall review the safeguards put in place to address the threats to the auditor's objectivity and independence arising where partners and staff have been involved in the audit in senior positions for a continuous period longer than seven years and shall discuss those situations with the engagement quality control reviewer. Any unresolved problems or issues shall be referred to the Ethics Partner.

21 The significance of the threats arising where partners and staff have been involved in the audit in senior positions for a continuous period longer than seven years will depend on:

- the total period of time that the individual has been involved in the audit;

- changes in the nature of the work and the role performed by the individual during that period; and

the portion of time the individual has spent on the audit and non-audit engagements with the audited entity during that period.

22 Following the assessment of any such threats, appropriate safeguards are applied where necessary. Safeguards that address these threats might include:

- changes in the roles within the engagement team;

- an additional review of the work done by the individual by the audit engagement partner or other partners in the engagement team;

- additional procedures carried out as part of the engagement quality control review.

If such safeguards do not reduce the threats to an acceptable level, the partner or member of staff is removed from the engagement team.

EFFECTIVE DATE

23 Revisions to this Ethical Standard become effective for audits of financial statements for periods commencing on or after 15 December 2009. Earlier adoption of the revisions is permitted.

24 Where a partner becomes a key partner involved in the audit as a result of the change in definition introduced with effect from 6 April 2008 the transitional arrangements in the previous version of ES 3 (Revised) continue to apply.

APB ETHICAL STANDARD 4 (REVISED)

FEES, REMUNERATION AND EVALUATION POLICIES, LITIGATION, GIFTS AND HOSPITALITY

(Revised December 2010)

CONTENTS

PREFACE

APB Ethical Standards apply in the audit of financial statements. They are read in the context of the Statement "The Financial Reporting Council – Scope and Authority of Audit and Assurance Pronouncements" which sets out the application and authority of APB Ethical Standards.

The terms used in APB Ethical Standards are explained in the Glossary.

APB Ethical Standards apply to audits of financial statements in both the private and the public sectors. However, auditors in the public sector are subject to more complex ethical requirements than their private sector counterparts. This includes, for example, compliance with legislation such as the Prevention of Corruption Act 1916, concerning gifts and hospitality, and with Cabinet Office guidance.

INTRODUCTION

1 APB Ethical Standard 1 requires the audit engagement partner to identify and assess the circumstances which could adversely affect the auditor's objectivity ('threats'), including any perceived loss of independence, and to apply procedures ('safeguards') which will either:

(a) eliminate the threat; or

(b) reduce the threat to an acceptable level (that is, a level at which it is not probable that a reasonable and informed third party would conclude that the auditor's objectivity and independence either is impaired or is likely to be impaired).

When considering safeguards, where the audit engagement partner chooses to reduce rather than to eliminate a threat to objectivity and independence, he or she recognises that this judgment may not be shared by users of the financial statements and that he or she may be required to justify the decision.

2 This Standard provides requirements and guidance on specific circumstances arising out of fees, economic dependence, litigation, remuneration and evaluation of partners and staff, and gifts and hospitality, which may create threats to the auditor's objectivity or perceived loss of independence. It gives examples of safeguards that can, in some situations, eliminate the threat or reduce it to an acceptable level. In circumstances where this is not possible, either the situation is avoided or the auditor either does not accept or withdraws from the audit engagement, as appropriate.

3 Whenever a possible or actual breach of an APB Ethical Standard is identified, the audit engagement partner, in the first instance, and the Ethics Partner, where appropriate, assesses the implications of the breach, determines whether there are safeguards that can be put in place or other actions that can be taken to address any potential adverse consequences and considers whether there is a need to resign from the audit engagement.

4 An inadvertent violation of this Standard does not necessarily call into question the audit firm's ability to give an audit opinion provided that:

(a) the audit firm has established policies and procedures that require all partners and staff to report any breach promptly to the audit engagement partner or to the Ethics Partner, as appropriate;

(b) the audit engagement partner or Ethics Partner ensures that any matter which has given rise to a breach is addressed as soon as possible;

(c) safeguards, if appropriate, are applied (for example, having another partner review the work done by the relevant partner or member of staff or by removing him or her from the engagement team); and

(d) the actions taken and the rationale for them are documented.

FEES

5   **The audit engagement partner shall be satisfied and able to demonstrate that the audit engagement has assigned to it sufficient partners and staff with appropriate time and skill to perform the audit in accordance with all applicable Auditing and Ethical Standards, irrespective of the audit fee to be charged.**

6   Paragraph 5 is not intended to prescribe the approach to be taken by audit firms to the setting of audit fees, but rather to emphasise that there are no circumstances where the amount of the audit fee can justify any lack of appropriate resource or time taken to perform a proper audit in accordance with applicable Auditing and Ethical Standards.

7   **The audit engagement partner shall ensure that audit fees are not influenced or determined by the provision of non-audit services to the audited entity.**

8   The audit fee ordinarily reflects the time spent, the skills and experience of the personnel performing the audit in accordance with all the relevant requirements, and the competitive situation in the audit market. Paragraph 7 is intended to prevent any relationship between the appropriate cost of the audit and the actual or potential provision of non-audit services.

9   Paragraph 7 is not intended to prohibit proper cost savings that can be achieved as a result of providing non-audit services in accordance with APB Ethical Standard 5 to the audited entity, for example, where information gained through undertaking a non-audit service is referred to by audit staff when carrying out the audit of the financial statements.

10   **An audit shall not be undertaken on a contingent fee basis.**

11   A contingent fee basis is any arrangement made under which a fee is calculated on a pre-determined basis relating to the outcome or result of a transaction, or other event, or the result of the work performed. A fee that is established by a court or other public authority is not a contingent fee.

12   Contingent fee arrangements in respect of audit engagements create self-interest threats to the auditor's objectivity and independence that are so significant that they cannot be eliminated or reduced to an acceptable level by the application of any safeguards.

13   The audit fee does not depend on whether the auditor's report on the financial statements is qualified or unqualified. The basis for the calculation of the audit fee is agreed with the audited entity each year before significant audit work is undertaken. Arrangements under which estimated audit fees are agreed with the audited entity on terms where the fees may be varied based on the level of audit work required do not constitute contingent fee arrangements.

14   Contingent fee arrangements in respect of non-audit services provided by the auditor in respect of an audited entity can create significant self-interest threats to the auditor's

objectivity and independence as the auditor may have, or may appear to have, an interest in the outcome of the non-audit service.

15 **The audit firm shall not undertake an engagement to provide non-audit services in respect of an audited entity on a contingent fee basis where:**

(a) **the contingent fee is material to the audit firm, or that part of the firm by reference to which the audit engagement partner's profit share is calculated; or**

(b) **the outcome of those non-audit services (and, therefore, the amount of the fee) is dependent on a future or contemporary audit judgment relating to a material matter in the financial statements of an audited entity.**

16 Where non-audit services are provided on a contingent fee basis, there may be a perception that the audit firm's interests are so closely aligned with the audited entity that the auditor's objectivity and independence is threatened. The significance of the self-interest threat is primarily determined by the materiality of the contingent fee to the audit firm or to the part of the firm by reference to which the audit engagement partner's profit share is calculated. Where the contingent fee and the outcome of the non-audit service is dependent on a future or contemporary audit judgment on a material matter included in the financial statements of an audited entity, the self interest threat cannot be eliminated or reduced to an acceptable level by the application of safeguards.

17 Paragraph 15 is not intended to prohibit an audit firm from charging a lower fee where the engagement relates to a transaction or engagement that was either aborted or prematurely terminated for whatever reason and where the rationale for the lower fee is to take account of either the reduced risk and responsibility involved or the fact that less work was undertaken than had been anticipated.

18 For non-audit services provided on a contingent fee basis, other than those prohibited under paragraph 15, the audit engagement partner assesses the significance of the self-interest threat and considers whether there are safeguards that could be applied which would be effective to eliminate the threat or reduce it to an acceptable level. The significance of the self-interest threat will depend on factors such as:

- the range of possible fee amounts;

- the nature of the non-audit service;

- the effect of the outcome of the non-audit service on the financial statements of the audited entity.

19 Examples of safeguards that might be applied to reduce to an acceptable level any self-interest threats arising from the provision of non-audit services on a contingent fee basis (other than those set out in paragraph 15 above) include:

- the provision of such non-audit services by partners and staff who have no involvement in the external audit of the financial statements;

- review of the audit of the financial statements by an audit partner who is not involved in the audit engagement to ensure that the subject matter of the non-audit service engagement has been properly and effectively addressed in the context of the audit of the financial statements.

20 **The audit firm shall establish policies and procedures to ensure that the audit engagement partner and the Ethics Partner are notified where others within the audit firm propose to adopt contingent fee arrangements in relation to the provision of non-audit services to the audited entity or its affiliates.**

21 Contingent fee arrangements in respect of non-audit services provided by the auditor may create a threat to the auditor's objectivity and independence. The circumstances in which such fee arrangements are not permitted for non-audit services are dealt with in paragraph 15 of this standard and paragraph 95 of APB Ethical Standard 5.

22 **In the case of listed companies the audit engagement partner shall disclose to the audit committee, in writing, any contingent fee arrangements for non-audit services provided by the auditor or its network firms.**

23 In the case of a group audit of a listed company, which involves other auditors, the letter of instruction sent by the group audit engagement partner to the other auditors requests disclosure of any contingent fees for non-audit services charged or proposed to be charged by the other auditors.

24 **The actual amount of the audit fee for the previous audit and the arrangements for its payment shall be agreed with the audited entity before the audit firm formally accepts appointment as auditor in respect of the following period.**

25 Ordinarily, any outstanding fees for the previous audit period are paid before the audit firm commences any new audit work. Where they are not, it is important for the audit engagement partner to understand the nature of any disagreement or other issue.

26 **Where fees for professional services from the audited entity are overdue and the amount cannot be regarded as trivial, the audit engagement partner, in consultation with the Ethics Partner, shall consider whether the audit firm can continue as auditor or whether it is necessary to resign.**

27 Where fees due from an audited entity, whether for audit or for non-audit services, remain unpaid for a long time – and, in particular, where a significant part is not paid before the auditor's report on the financial statements for the following year is due to be issued – a self-interest threat to the auditor's objectivity and independence is created because the issue of an unqualified audit report may enhance the audit firm's prospects of securing payment of such overdue fees.

28 Where the outstanding fees are in dispute and the amount involved is significant, the threats to the auditor's objectivity and independence may be such that no safeguards

can eliminate them or reduce them to an acceptable level. The audit engagement partner therefore considers whether the audit firm can continue with the audit engagement.

29   Where the outstanding fees are unpaid because of exceptional circumstances (including financial distress), the audit engagement partner considers whether the audited entity will be able to resolve its difficulties. In deciding what action to take, the audit engagement partner weighs the threats to the auditor's objectivity and independence, if the audit firm were to remain in office, against the difficulties the audited entity would be likely to face in finding a successor, and therefore the public interest considerations, if the audit firm were to resign.

30   In any case where the audit firm does not resign from the audit engagement, the audit engagement partner applies appropriate safeguards (such as a review by an audit partner who is not involved in the audit engagement) and notifies the Ethics Partner of the facts concerning the overdue fees.

31   **Where it is expected that the total fees for both audit and non-audit services receivable from a listed audited entity and its subsidiaries audited by the audit firm[1] will regularly exceed 10% of the annual fee income of the audit firm[2] or, where profits are not shared on a firm-wide basis, of the part of the firm by reference to which the audit engagement partner's profit share is calculated, the firm shall not act as the auditor of that entity and shall either resign as auditor or not stand for reappointment, as appropriate.[3]**

32   **Where it is expected that the total fees for both audit and non-audit services receivable from a non-listed audited entity and its subsidiaries audited by the audit firm will regularly exceed 15% of the annual fee income of the audit firm or, where profits are not shared on a firm-wide basis, of the part of the firm by reference to which the audit engagement partner's profit share is calculated, the firm shall not act as the auditor of that entity and shall either resign as auditor or not stand for reappointment, as appropriate.**

33   Where it is expected that the total fees for both audit and non-audit services receivable from an audited entity and its subsidiaries that are audited by the audit firm will regularly exceed 10% in the case of listed companies and 15% in the case of non-listed entities of the annual fee income of the part of the firm by reference to which the audit engagement partner's profit share is calculated, it may be possible to assign the engagement to another part of the firm.

---

[1]   Total fees will include those billed by others where the audit firm is entitled to the fees, but will not include fees billed by the audit firm where it is acting as agent for another party.

[2]   In the case of a sole practitioner, annual fee income of the audit firm includes all earned income received by the individual.

[3]   Paragraphs 31 to 40 do not apply to the audits of those public sector bodies where the responsibility for the audit is assigned by legislation. In such cases, the auditor cannot resign from the audit engagement, irrespective of considerations of economic dependence.

34   Paragraphs 31 and 32 are not intended to require the audit firm to resign as auditor or not stand for reappointment as a result of an individual event or engagement, the nature or size of which was unpredictable and where a reasonable and informed third party would regard ceasing to act as detrimental to the shareholders (or equivalent) of the audited entity. However, in such circumstances, the auditor discloses full details of the position to the Ethics Partner and to those charged with governance of the audited entity and discusses with both what, if any, safeguards may be appropriate.

35   **Where it is expected that the total fees for both audit and non-audit services receivable from a listed audited entity and its subsidiaries audited by the audit firm will regularly exceed 5% of the annual fee income of the audit firm or the part of the firm by reference to which the audit engagement partner's profit share is calculated, but will not regularly exceed 10%, the audit engagement partner shall disclose that expectation to the Ethics Partner and to those charged with governance of the audited entity and consider whether appropriate safeguards need to be applied to eliminate or reduce to an acceptable level the threat to the auditor's objectivity and independence.**

36   It is fundamental to the auditor's objectivity that the auditor be willing and able, if necessary, to disagree with the directors and management, regardless of the consequences to its own position. Where the auditor is, to any significant extent, economically dependent on the audited entity, this may inhibit the auditor's willingness or constrain the auditor's ability to express a qualified opinion on the financial statements, since this could be viewed as likely to lead to the auditor losing the audit engagement and the entity as a client.

37   An audit firm is deemed to be economically dependent on a listed audited entity if the total fees for audit and all other services from that entity and its subsidiaries which are audited by the audit firm represent 10% of the total fees of the audit firm or the part of the firm by reference to which the audit engagement partner's profit share is calculated. Where such fees are between 5% and 10%, the audit engagement partner and the Ethics Partner consider the significance of the threat and the need for appropriate safeguards.

38   Such safeguards might include:

   • taking steps to reduce the non-audit work to be undertaken and therefore the fees earned from the audited entity;

   • applying independent internal quality control reviews.

39   **Where it is expected that the total fees for both audit and non-audit services receivable from a non-listed audited entity and its subsidiaries audited by the audit firm will regularly exceed 10% of the annual fee income of the audit firm or the part of the firm by reference to which the audit engagement partner's profit share is calculated, but will not regularly exceed 15%, the audit engagement partner shall disclose that expectation to the Ethics Partner and to those charged with governance of the audited entity and the firm shall arrange an external**

independent quality control review of the audit engagement to be undertaken before the auditor's report is finalised.

40   A quality control review involves discussion with the audit engagement partner, a review of the financial statements and the auditor's report, and consideration of whether the report is appropriate. It also involves a review of selected working papers relating to the significant judgments the engagement team has made and the conclusions they have reached. The extent of the review depends on the complexity of the engagement and the risk that the report might not be appropriate in the circumstances. The review includes considering the following:

- Significant risks identified during the audit and the responses to those risks.

- Judgments made, particularly with respect to materiality and significant risks.

- Whether appropriate consultation has taken place on matters involving differences of opinion or other difficult or contentious matters, and the conclusions arising from those consultations.

- The significance and disposition of corrected and uncorrected misstatements identified during the audit.

- The appropriateness of the report to be issued.

Where the quality control reviewer makes recommendations that the audit engagement partner does not accept and the matter is not resolved to the reviewer's satisfaction, the report is not issued until the matter is resolved by following the audit firm's procedures for dealing with differences of opinion.

41   A new audit firm seeking to establish itself may find the requirements relating to economic dependence difficult to comply with in the short term. In these circumstances, such firms would:

(a)   not undertake any audits of listed companies, where fees from such an audited entity would represent 10% or more of the annual fee income of the firm; and

(b)   for a period not exceeding two years, require external independent quality control reviews of those audits of unlisted entities that represent more than 15% of the annual fee income before the audit opinion is issued.

The firm might also develop its practice by accepting work from entities not audited by the firm so as to bring the fees payable by each audited entity below 15%.

42   A self-interest threat may also be created where an audit partner in the engagement team:

- is employed exclusively or principally on that audit engagement; and

- is remunerated on the basis of the performance of part of the firm which is substantially dependent on fees from that audited entity.

43 Where the circumstances described in paragraph 42 arise, the audit firm assesses the significance of the threat and applies safeguards to reduce the threat to an acceptable level. Such safeguards might include:

- reducing the dependence of the office, partner or person in a position to influence the conduct and outcome of the audit by reallocating the work within the practice;

- a review by an audit partner who is not involved with the audit engagement to ensure that the auditor's objectivity and independence is not affected by the self-interest threat.

REMUNERATION AND EVALUATION POLICIES

44 **The audit firm shall establish policies and procedures to ensure that each of the following is true in relation to each audited entity:**

(a) **the objectives of the members of the engagement team do not include selling non-audit services to the entity they audit;**

(b) **the criteria for evaluating the performance or promotion of members of the engagement team do not include success in selling non-audit services to the entity they audit; and**

(c) **no specific element of the remuneration of a member of the engagement team is based on his or her success in selling non-audit services to the entity they audit.**

This requirement does not apply to those members of the engagement team from specialist practice areas where the nature and extent of their involvement in the audit is clearly insignificant.

45 Where the auditor identifies areas for possible improvement in an audited entity the auditor may provide general business advice, which might include suggested solutions to problems. Before discussing any non-audit service that might be provided by the audit firm or effecting any introductions to colleagues from outside the engagement team, the audit engagement partner considers the threats that such a service would have on the audit engagement, in line with the requirements of APB Ethical Standard 5.

46 The last sentence of paragraph 44 recognises the fact that an engagement team may include personnel from specialist practice areas and that it would be inappropriate to limit the business development activities of such persons where their involvement in the audit is clearly insignificant.

47 The policies and procedures required for compliance with paragraph 44 are not intended to inhibit normal profit-sharing arrangements. However, such policies and procedures are central to an audit firm's ability to demonstrate its objectivity and independence and to rebut any suggestion that an audit that it has undertaken and the opinion that it has given are influenced by the nature and extent of any non-audit services that it has provided to that audited entity. Because it is possible that, despite such policies and procedures, such factors may be taken into account in the evaluation and remuneration of members of an engagement team, the Ethics Partner pays particular attention to the actual implementation of those policies and procedures and is available for consultation when needed.

THREATENED AND ACTUAL LITIGATION

48 **Where litigation in relation to audit or non-audit services between the audited entity or its affiliates and the audit firm, which is other than insignificant, is already in progress, or where the audit engagement partner considers such litigation to be probable, the audit firm shall either not continue with or not accept the audit engagement.[4]**

49 Where litigation (in relation to audit or non-audit services) actually takes place between the audit firm (or any person in a position to influence the conduct and outcome of the audit) and the audited entity, or where litigation is threatened and there is a realistic prospect of such litigation being commenced, self-interest, advocacy and intimidation threats to the auditor's objectivity and independence are created because the audit firm's interest will be the achievement of an outcome to the dispute or litigation that is favourable to itself. In addition, an effective audit process requires complete candour and full disclosure between the audited entity's management and the engagement team: such disputes or litigation may place the two parties in opposing adversarial positions and may affect management's willingness to make complete disclosure of relevant information. Where the auditor can foresee that such a threat may arise, the auditor informs the audit committee of its intention to resign or, where there is no audit committee, the board of directors.

50 The auditor is not required to resign immediately in circumstances where a reasonable and informed third party would not regard it as being in the interests of the shareholders for it to do so. Such circumstances might arise, for example, where:

- the litigation was commenced as the audit was about to be completed and shareholder interests would be adversely affected by a delay in the audit of the financial statements;

- on appropriate legal advice, the audit firm deems that the threatened or actual litigation is vexatious or designed solely to bring pressure to bear on the opinion to be expressed by the auditor.

---

[4] Paragraphs 48 to 50 do not apply to the audits of those public sector bodies where the responsibility for the audit is assigned by legislation. In such cases, the auditor cannot resign from the audit engagement: the auditor reports significant litigation to the relevant legislative authority.

GIFTS AND HOSPITALITY

51   **The audit firm, those in a position to influence the conduct and outcome of the audit and immediate family members of such persons shall not accept gifts from the audited entity, unless the value is clearly insignificant.**

52   **Those in a position to influence the conduct and outcome of the audit and immediate family members of such persons shall not accept hospitality from the audited entity, unless it is reasonable in terms of its frequency, nature and cost.**

53   Where gifts or hospitality are accepted from an audited entity, self-interest and familiarity threats to the auditor's objectivity and independence are created. Familiarity threats also arise where gifts or hospitality are offered to an audited entity.

54   Gifts from the audited entity, unless their value is clearly insignificant, create threats to objectivity and independence which no safeguards can eliminate or reduce.

55   Hospitality is a component of many business relationships and can provide valuable opportunities for developing an understanding of the audited entity's business and for gaining the insight on which an effective and successful working relationship depends. Therefore, the auditor's objectivity and independence is not necessarily impaired as a result of accepting hospitality from the audited entity, provided it is reasonable in terms of its frequency, its nature and its cost.

56   **The audit firm shall establish policies on the nature and value of gifts and hospitality that may be accepted from and offered to audited entities, their directors, officers and employees, and shall issue guidance to assist partners and staff to comply with such policies.**

57   In assessing the acceptability of gifts and hospitality, the test to be applied is not whether the auditor considers that the auditor's objectivity is impaired but whether it is probable that a reasonable and informed third party would conclude that it is or is likely to be impaired.

58   Where there is any doubt as to the acceptability of gifts or hospitality offered by the audited entity, members of the engagement team discuss the position with the audit engagement partner. If there is any doubt as to the acceptability of gifts or hospitality offered to the audit engagement partner, or if the audit engagement partner has any residual doubt about the acceptability of gifts or hospitality to other individuals, the audit engagement partner reports the facts to the Ethics Partner, for further consideration regarding any action to be taken.

59   Where the cumulative amount of gifts or hospitality accepted from the audited entity appears abnormally high, the audit engagement partner reports the facts to both:

 • the Ethics Partner; and

 • the audit committee (or, where there is no audit committee, the board of directors), together with other significant facts and matters that bear upon the auditor's objectivity and independence.

EFFECTIVE DATE

60   This revised Ethical Standard becomes effective on 30 April 2011.

61   Firms may complete audit engagements relating to periods commencing on or before 31 December 2010 in accordance with existing ethical standards, putting in place any necessary changes in the subsequent engagement period.

62   An audit firm may continue to provide non-audit services that would be prohibited under paragraph 15, where these have already been contracted at 31 December 2010, until the earlier of either:

    a.   the completion of the specific task or the end of the contract term, where one is set out in the contract; or

    b.   31 December 2011.

APB ETHICAL STANDARD 5 (REVISED)

NON-AUDIT SERVICES PROVIDED TO AUDITED ENTITIES

(Revised December 2010, updated December 2011)

CONTENTS

PREFACE

APB Ethical Standards apply in the audit of financial statements. They are read in the context of the Statement "The Financial Reporting Council – Scope and Authority of Audit and Assurance Pronouncements" which sets out the application and authority of APB Ethical Standards.

The terms used in APB Ethical Standards are explained in the Glossary.

APB Ethical Standards apply to audits of financial statements in both the private and the public sectors. However, auditors in the public sector are subject to more complex ethical requirements than their private sector counterparts. This includes, for example, compliance with legislation such as the Prevention of Corruption Act 1916, concerning gifts and hospitality, and with Cabinet Office guidance.

INTRODUCTION

1   APB Ethical Standard 1 requires the audit engagement partner to identify and assess the circumstances which could adversely affect the auditor's objectivity ('threats'), including any perceived loss of independence, and to apply procedures ('safeguards') which will either:

   (a)   eliminate the threat; or

   (b)   reduce the threat to an acceptable level (that is, a level at which it is not probable that a reasonable and informed third party would conclude that the auditor's objectivity and independence either is impaired or is likely to be impaired).

   When considering safeguards, where the audit engagement partner chooses to reduce rather than to eliminate a threat to objectivity and independence, he or she recognises that this judgment may not be shared by users of the financial statements and that he or she may be required to justify the decision.

2   This Standard provides requirements and guidance on specific circumstances arising from the provision of non-audit services by audit firms to entities audited by them which may create threats to the auditor's objectivity or perceived loss of independence. It gives examples of safeguards that can, in some circumstances, eliminate the threat or reduce it to an acceptable level. In circumstances where this is not possible, either the non-audit service engagement in question is not undertaken or the auditor either does not accept or withdraws from the audit engagement, as appropriate.

3   Whenever a possible or actual breach of an APB Ethical Standard is identified, the audit engagement partner, in the first instance, and the Ethics Partner, where appropriate, assess the implications of the breach, determine whether there are safeguards that can be put in place or other actions that can be taken to address any potential adverse consequences and consider whether there is a need to resign from the audit engagement.

4   An inadvertent violation of this Standard does not necessarily call into question the audit firm's ability to give an audit opinion provided that:

   (a)   the audit firm has established policies and procedures that require all partners and staff to report any breach promptly to the audit engagement partner or to the Ethics Partner, as appropriate;

   (b)   the audit engagement partner promptly notifies the partner or member of staff that any matter which has given rise to a breach is to be addressed as soon as possible and ensures that such action is taken;

   (c)   safeguards, if appropriate, are applied (for example, by having another partner review the work done by the relevant partner or member of staff or by removing him or her from the engagement team); and

(d)   the actions taken and the rationale for them are documented.

GENERAL APPROACH TO NON-AUDIT SERVICES

5   Paragraphs 6 to 53 of this Standard set out the general approach to be adopted by audit firms and auditors in relation to the provision of non-audit services to entities audited by them. This approach is applicable irrespective of the nature of the non-audit services, which may be in question in a given case. (Paragraphs 54 to 168 of this Standard illustrate the application of the general approach to a number of common non-audit services.)

6   An audit is the term used to describe the work that is undertaken by the auditor to enable him or her to express an independent audit opinion on an entity's financial statements and, where the entity is a parent company, on the group financial statements and/or the separate financial statements of its components[1].

7   International Standards on Auditing (UK and Ireland) require that the auditor exercise professional judgment and maintain professional scepticism throughout the planning and performance of the audit and, among other things:

- Identify and assess risks of material misstatement, whether due to fraud or error, based on an understanding of the entity and its environment, including the entity's internal control.

- Obtain sufficient appropriate audit evidence about whether material misstatements exist, through designing and implementing appropriate responses to the assessed risks.

- Form an opinion on the financial statements based on conclusions drawn from the audit evidence obtained[2].

8   Judgments regarding the nature and extent of evidence necessary to support the audit opinion are a matter for the auditor but will include:

- Identifying, evaluating and testing, where appropriate, those internal control systems the effectiveness of which is necessary for the audit of the financial statements and where, if any control weaknesses are identified, extended testing will be required; and

- additional work undertaken to respond to risks identified by management or the audit committee that the auditor considers could impact the auditor's opinion on the financial statements.

---

[1]   In the public sector the statutory scope of an audit can extend beyond expressing an independent opinion on an entity's financial statements to include reporting on an entity's arrangements to ensure the proper conduct of its financial affairs, manage its performance or use of its resources.

[2]   ISA (UK and Ireland) 200 'Overall Objectives of the Independent Auditor and the Conduct of an Audit in Accordance with International Standards on Auditing (UK and Ireland)' paragraph 7.

9   Other work undertaken by the engagement team at the request of management or
     those charged with governance will not be categorised as part of the audit irrespective
     of whether it forms part of the audit proposal or engagement, unless it is clear that the
     predominant rationale for the performance of the work in question is to enable a
     soundly based audit opinion on the financial statements to be expressed. Therefore,
     an audit of financial statements does not include work where:

     - The objective of that work is not to gather evidence to support the auditor's opinion
       on the financial statements; or

     - The nature and extent of testing is not determined by the external auditor, or in the
       case of a group, the component auditors, in the context of expressing an opinion
       on the financial statements; or

     - The principal terms and conditions differ from that of the audit.

10   If additional work on financial information[3] and/or financial controls is authorised by
     those charged with governance, but the objective of that work is not to enable the
     auditor to provide an audit opinion on the entity's financial statements, it will be
     considered as an 'audit related service' for the purpose of this Standard provided that
     it:

     - is integrated with the work performed in the audit and performed largely by the
       existing audit team; and

     - is performed on the same principal terms and conditions as the audit.

     As a consequence of these factors, any threats to auditor independence arising from
     the performance of such additional work are considered to be clearly insignificant.

11   Other additional work that:

     - does not relate to financial information and/or financial controls; or

     - is not integrated with the work performed in the audit, or is not performed largely
       by the existing audit team, or

     - is not on the same principal terms and conditions as the audit;

     will be regarded as an 'other non-audit service' for the purpose of this Standard.

12   'Non-audit services' comprise any engagement in which an audit firm provides
     professional services to:

     −   an audited entity;

---

[3] This does not include accounting services.

    – an audited entity's affiliates; or

    – another entity in respect of the audited entity[4];

other than the audit of financial statements of the audited entity.

13   There may be circumstances where the audit firm is engaged to provide a non-audit service and where that engagement and its scope are determined by an entity which is not audited by the firm. However, it might be contemplated that an audited entity may gain some benefit from that engagement[5]. In these circumstances, whilst there may be no threat to the audit firm's objectivity and independence at the time of appointment, the audit firm considers how the engagement may be expected to develop, whether there are any threats that the audit firm may be subject to if additional relevant parties which are audited entities are identified, and whether any safeguards need to be put in place.

14   **The audit firm shall establish policies and procedures that require others within the firm, when considering whether to accept a proposed engagement to provide a non-audit service to an audited entity or any of its affiliates, to communicate details of the proposed engagement to the audit engagement partner.**

15   The audit firm establishes appropriate channels of internal communication to ensure that, in relation to an entity audited by the firm, the audit engagement partner (or their delegate) is informed about any proposed engagement to provide a non-audit service to the audited entity or any of its affiliates and that he or she considers the implications for the auditor's objectivity and independence before the engagement is accepted. Additionally, when addressing services provided to another entity in respect of the audited entity, the procedures address any requirement to preserve client confidentiality.

16   In the case of a listed company, the group audit engagement partner establishes that the company has communicated its policy on the engagement of the external auditor to supply non-audit services to its affiliates and obtains confirmation that the auditors of the affiliates will comply with this policy.[6] The group audit engagement partner also requires that relevant information on non-audit services provided by network firms is communicated on a timely basis.

---

[4]   For example, where an engagement is undertaken to assist in the preparation of listing particulars for a company acquiring the audited entity.

[5]   For example, in a vendor due diligence engagement, the engagement is initiated and scoped by the vendor before the purchaser is identified. If an entity audited by the firm undertaking the due diligence engagement is the purchaser, that audited entity may gain the benefit of the report issued by its auditor, it may be a party to the engagement letter and it may pay an element of the fee.

[6]   The UK Corporate Governance Code requires audit committees to develop the company's policy on the engagement of the external auditor to supply non-audit services.

IDENTIFICATION AND ASSESSMENT OF THREATS AND SAFEGUARDS

17   Before the audit firm accepts a proposed engagement to provide a non-audit service, the audit engagement partner shall:

(a)   consider whether it is probable that a reasonable and informed third party would regard the objectives of the proposed engagement as being inconsistent with the objectives of the audit of the financial statements; and

(b)   identify and assess the significance of any related threats to the auditor's objectivity, including any perceived loss of independence; and

(c)   identify and assess the effectiveness of the available safeguards to eliminate the threats or reduce them to an acceptable level.

18   When assessing the significance of threats to the auditor's objectivity and independence, the audit engagement partner considers the following factors:

- The likely relevance and impact of the subject matter on the financial statements;

- The extent to which performance of the proposed engagement will involve the exercise of professional judgment;

- The size of the engagement and the associated fee;

- The basis on which the fee is to be calculated;

- The staff who would be carrying out the non-audit service[7];

- The staff from the audited entity who would be involved in the non-audit service[8].

To ensure that this assessment is made with a proper understanding of the nature of the engagement, it may be necessary to refer to a draft engagement letter in respect of the proposed non-audit services or to discuss the engagement with the partner involved.

19   The assessment of the threats to the auditor's objectivity and independence arising from any particular non-audit engagement is a matter for the audit engagement partner. The audit engagement partner may decide to delegate some information gathering activities to senior personnel on the audit team and may allow such

---

[7]   For example, where those handling the non-audit service engagement are particularly expert so that the audit team (or persons advising it) may have difficulty in reviewing effectively the advice given or the work undertaken by the non-audit service team in the course of conducting a subsequent audit, with the result that the effectiveness of the audit might be compromised.

[8]   For example, the safeguards necessary to address any self-review threat will require careful consideration where those involved are particularly senior and can be expected to be actively involved in any audit discussion as this may also create an intimidation threat.

personnel to make decisions in relation to routine non-audit services. If this is the case, the audit engagement partner will:

- provide specific criteria for such decisions that reflect both the requirements of APB Ethical Standards and the audited entity's policy for the purchase of non-audit services; and

- monitor the decisions being made on a regular basis.

20 Where the audit engagement partner is not able to undertake the assessment of the significance of threats in relation to a proposed engagement to provide a non-audit service to an audited entity, for example due to illness or holidays, alternative arrangements are established (for example, by authorising the engagement quality control reviewer to consider the proposed engagement).

21 The objective of the audit of financial statements is to express an opinion on the preparation and presentation of those financial statements. For example, in the case of a limited company, legislation requires the auditor to make a report to the members on all annual accounts laid before the company in general meeting during its tenure of office. The report must include a statement as to whether, in the auditor's opinion, the accounts have been properly prepared in accordance with the requirements of the legislation, and, in particular, whether they give a true and fair view of the state of the affairs and profit or loss for the year.

22 **Where the audit engagement partner considers that it is probable that a reasonable and informed third party would regard the objectives of the proposed non-audit service engagement as being inconsistent with the objectives of the audit of the financial statements, the audit firm shall either:**

(a) **not undertake the non-audit service engagement; or**

(b) **not accept or withdraw from the audit engagement.**

23 The objectives of engagements to provide non-audit services vary and depend on the specific terms of the engagement. In some cases these objectives may be inconsistent with those of the audit, and, in such cases, this may give rise to a threat to the auditor's objectivity and to the appearance of its independence. Audit firms do not undertake non-audit service engagements where the objectives of such engagements are inconsistent with the objectives of the audit, or they do not accept or withdraw from the audit engagement as appropriate.

24 Similarly, in relation to a possible appointment as auditor to an entity that the audit firm has not audited before, consideration needs to be given to recent, current and potential engagements to provide non-audit services by the audit firm and whether the scope and objectives of those engagements are consistent with the proposed audit engagement. In the case of listed companies, when tendering for a new audit engagement, the audit firm ensures that relevant information on recent non-audit services is drawn to the attention of the audit committee, including:

- when recent non-audit services were provided;

- the materiality of those non-audit services to the proposed audit engagement;

- whether those non-audit services would have been prohibited if the entity had been an audited entity at the time when they were undertaken; and

- the extent to which the outcomes of non-audit services have been audited or reviewed by another audit firm.

Threats to objectivity and independence

25 The principal types of threats to the auditor's objectivity and independence are:

- self-interest threat;

- self-review threat;

- management threat;

- advocacy threat;

- familiarity (or trust) threat; and

- intimidation threat.

The auditor remains alert to the possibility that any of these threats may occur in connection with non-audit services. However, the threats most commonly associated with non-audit services are self-interest threat, self-review threat, management threat and advocacy threat.

26 A **self-interest threat** exists when the auditor has financial or other interests which might cause the auditor to be reluctant to take actions that would be adverse to the interests of the audit firm or any individual in a position to influence the conduct or outcome of the audit. In relation to non-audit services, the main self-interest threat concerns fees and economic dependence and these are addressed in APB Ethical Standard 4.

27 Where substantial fees are regularly generated from the provision of non-audit services and the fees for non-audit services are greater than the annual audit fees, the audit engagement partner has regard to the possibility that there may be perceived to be a loss of independence resulting from the expected or actual level of fees for non-audit services. The audit engagement partner determines whether there is any risk that there will be an actual loss of independence and objectivity by the engagement team. In making that assessment, the audit engagement partner considers matters such as whether the engagement or engagements giving rise to the fees for non-audit services were:

- audit related services;

- provided on a contingent fee basis;

- consistent with the engagements undertaken and fees received on a consistent basis in previous years;

- in the case of a group, disproportionate in relation to any individual group entity;

- unusual in size but unlikely to recur; and/or

- of such a size and nature that a reasonable and informed third party would be concerned at the effect that such engagements would have on the objectivity and independence of the engagement team.

Having made that assessment, the audit engagement partner determines whether the threats to independence from the level of fees for non-audit services are at an acceptable level (or can be reduced to an acceptable level by putting in place appropriate safeguards) and appropriately informs those charged with governance of the position on a timely basis in accordance with paragraphs 48 to 50 of this Standard.

28 **In the case of listed companies where the fees for non-audit services for a financial year are expected to be greater than the annual audit fees, the audit engagement partner shall provide details of the circumstances to the Ethics Partner and discuss them with him or her. Where the audit firm provides audit services to a group, the obligation to provide information to the Ethics Partner shall be on a group basis for all services provided by the audit firm and its network firms to all entities in the group.**

29 Discussing the level of fees for non-audit services with the Ethics Partner ensures that appropriate attention is paid to the issue by the audit firm. The audit firm's policies and procedures will set out whether there are circumstances in which the audit engagement partner discusses the level of non-audit fees with the Ethics Partner for non-listed audited entities as described in paragraph 47 of APB Ethical Standard 1.

30 Where fees for non-audit services are calculated on a contingent fee basis, there is a risk that a reasonable and informed third party may regard the audit firm's interests to be so closely aligned with the audited entity that it threatens the auditor's objectivity and independence. Consequently, the audit firm does not accept a non-audit services engagement on a contingent fee basis where:

(a) that contingent fee is material to the audit firm, or that part of the firm by reference to which the audit engagement partner's profit share is calculated; or

(b) the outcome of the service (and, therefore, the amount of the fee) is dependent on a future or contemporary audit judgment relating to a material matter in the financial statements of an audited entity.

31 A **self-review threat** exists when the results of a non-audit service performed by the engagement team or by others within the audit firm are reflected in the amounts included or disclosed in the financial statements.

32 A threat to objectivity and independence arises because, in the course of the audit, the auditor may need to re-evaluate the work performed in the non-audit service. As, by virtue of providing the non-audit service, the audit firm is associated with aspects of the preparation of the financial statements, it may be (or may appear to be) unable to take an impartial view of relevant aspects of those financial statements.

33 In assessing the significance of the self-review threat, the auditor considers the extent to which the non-audit service will:

- involve a significant degree of subjective judgment; and

- have a material effect on the preparation and presentation of the financial statements.

34 Where a significant degree of judgment relating to the financial statements is involved in a non-audit service engagement, the auditor may be inhibited from questioning that judgment in the course of the audit. Whether a significant degree of subjective judgment is involved will depend upon whether the non-audit service involves the application of well-established principles and procedures, and whether reliable information is available. If such circumstances do not exist because the non-audit service is based on concepts, methodologies or assumptions that require judgment and are not established by the audited entity or by authoritative guidance, the auditor's objectivity and the appearance of its independence may be adversely affected. Where the provision of a proposed non-audit service would also have a material effect on the financial statements, it is unlikely that any safeguard can eliminate or reduce to an acceptable level the self-review threat.

35 A **management threat** exists when the audit firm undertakes work that involves making judgments and taking decisions that are properly the responsibility of management.

36 Paragraph 33 of APB Ethical Standard 1 prohibits partners and employees of the audit firm from taking decisions on behalf of the management of the audited entity. A threat to objectivity and independence also arises where the audit firm undertakes an engagement to provide non-audit services in relation to which management are required to make judgments and take decisions based on that work. The auditor may become closely aligned with the views and interests of management and this may erode the distinction between the audited entity and the audit firm, in turn, impairing or calling into question the auditor's ability to apply a proper degree of professional scepticism in auditing the financial statements. The auditor's objectivity and the appearance of its independence therefore may be, or may be perceived to be, impaired.

37   In determining whether a non-audit service does or does not give rise to a management threat, the auditor considers whether there is informed management. Informed management exists when:

- the auditor is satisfied that a member of management (or senior employee of the audited entity) has been designated by the audited entity to receive the results of the non-audit service and has been given the authority to make any judgments and decisions of the type set out in paragraph 34 of APB Ethical Standard 1 that are needed;

- the auditor concludes that that member of management has the capability to make independent management judgments and decisions on the basis of the information provided; and

- the results of the non-audit service are communicated to the audited entity and, where judgments or decisions are to be made they are supported by an objective analysis of the issues to consider and the audited entity is given the opportunity to decide between reasonable alternatives.

38   In the absence of such informed management it is unlikely that any other safeguards can eliminate a management threat or reduce it to an acceptable level.

39   An **advocacy threat** exists when the audit firm undertakes work that involves acting as an advocate for an audited entity and supporting a position taken by management in an adversarial context.

40   A threat to objectivity and independence arises because, in order to act in an advocacy role, the audit firm has to adopt a position closely aligned to that of management. This creates both actual and perceived threats to the auditor's objectivity and independence. For example, where the audit firm, acting as advocate, has supported a particular contention of management, it may be difficult for the auditor to take an impartial view of this in the context of the audit of the financial statements.

41   Where the provision of a non-audit service would require the auditor to act as an advocate for the audited entity in relation to matters that are material to the financial statements, it is unlikely that any safeguards can eliminate or reduce to an acceptable level the advocacy threat that would exist.

42   Threats to the auditor's objectivity, including a perceived loss of independence, may arise where a non-audit service is provided by the audit firm to a third party which is connected (through a relationship) to an audited entity, and the outcome of that service has a material impact on the financial statements of the audited entity. For example, if the audit firm provides actuarial services to the pension scheme of an audited entity, which is in deficit and the audit firm subsequently gives an opinion on financial statements that include judgments given in connection with that service.

Safeguards

43   Where any threat to the auditor's objectivity and the appearance of its independence is identified, the audit engagement partner assesses the significance of that threat and considers whether there are safeguards that could be applied and which would be effective to eliminate the threat or reduce it to an acceptable level. If such safeguards can be identified and are applied, the non-audit service may be provided. However, where no such safeguards are applied, the only course is for the audit firm either not to undertake the engagement to provide the non-audit service in question or not to accept (or to withdraw from) the audit engagement.

44   When considering what safeguards, if any, would be effective in reducing the threats to independence and objectivity to an acceptable level, the audit engagement partner has regard to the following safeguards which, individually or in combination, may be effective, depending on the circumstances:

(a)   The non-audit services are provided by a separate team from the engagement team, and:

   •   if circumstances require, to address the threat identified, there is effective physical and electronic segregation of the individuals in each team, and of their documentation, at all times during the provision of the audit and non-audit services; and/or

   •   the team providing the non-audit services avoids taking any action or making any statement that compromises the independence or objectivity of the engagement team, for example, expressing any opinion about the approach that the engagement team might take or the conclusion it might reach when considering the appropriateness of accounting or other audit judgments.

   The Ethics Partner establishes policies and procedures to ensure that, where safeguards of this nature are considered appropriate, the arrangements put in place are effective at all times. This will involve the Ethics Partner being satisfied that there are effective arrangements in place for each member of the non-audit services team to acknowledge their responsibilities and for each member of the engagement team to notify him or her of any breach of this requirement that the team member becomes aware. Where notified of a breach, the Ethics Partner considers together with the audit engagement partner the significance of the breach and the implications for the independence and objectivity of the engagement team, including whether any further safeguards are necessary and whether the matter should be reported to those charged with governance of the audited entity;

(b)   The Engagement Quality Control Reviewer, or another audit partner of sufficient relevant experience and seniority who is, and is seen to be, an effective challenge to both the audit engagement partner and the partner leading the non-audit services engagement, reviews the work and conclusions of the engagement team in relation to their consideration of the audit judgments, if any, relating to the subject matter of the non-audit service, having regard to the self-review threat identified, and determines and documents his or her conclusions as to whether the work is sufficient and the conclusions of the engagement team are appropriate. Where the review partner has concerns, the audit engagement partner does not sign the audit opinion until those concerns have been subject to full consultation, including escalation through any processes required by the audit firm's policies. Where this safeguard is considered appropriate, the Ethics Partner is satisfied that the review partner undertaking this role is appropriate, that the review partner is aware of the circumstances leading to the conclusion that there is a significant self-review threat and that any concerns raised by the review partner have been satisfactorily resolved before signature of the audit opinion.

45 **Where the audit engagement partner concludes that no appropriate safeguards are available to eliminate or reduce to an acceptable level the threats to the auditor's objectivity, including any perceived loss of independence, related to a proposed engagement to provide a non-audit service to an audited entity, he or she shall inform the others concerned within the audit firm of that conclusion and the firm shall either:**

(a) **not undertake the non-audit service engagement; or**

(b) **not accept or withdraw from the audit engagement.**

If the audit engagement partner is in doubt as to the appropriate action to be taken, he or she shall resolve the matter through consultation with the Ethics Partner.

46 An initial assessment of the threats to objectivity and independence and the safeguards to be applied is required when the audit engagement partner is considering the acceptance of an engagement to provide a non-audit service. The assessment of the threats and the safeguards applied is reviewed whenever the scope and objectives of the non-audit service change significantly. If such a review suggests that safeguards cannot reduce the threat to an acceptable level, the audit firm withdraws from the non-audit service engagement, or does not accept or withdraws from the audit engagement as appropriate.

47 Where there is doubt as to the appropriate action to be taken, consultation with the Ethics Partner ensures that an objective judgment is made and the firm's position is consistent.

COMMUNICATION WITH THOSE CHARGED WITH GOVERNANCE

48 **The audit engagement partner shall ensure that those charged with governance of the audited entity are appropriately informed on a timely basis of:**

(a) **all significant facts and matters that bear upon the auditor's objectivity and independence, related to the provision of non-audit services, including the safeguards put in place; and**

(b) **for listed companies, any inconsistencies between APB Ethical Standards and the company's policy for the supply of non-audit services by the audit firm and any apparent breach of that policy.[6]**

49 Transparency is a key element in addressing the issues raised by the provision of non-audit services by audit firms to the entities audited by them. This can be facilitated by timely communication with those charged with governance of the audited entity (see APB Ethical Standard 1, paragraphs 63 to 71). Such communications are addressed to the audit committee, where there is one; in other circumstances, they are addressed to the board of directors (or those in an equivalent position). In the case of listed companies, ensuring that the audit committee is properly informed about the issues associated with the provision of non-audit services will assist them to comply with the provisions of the UK Corporate Governance Code relating to reviewing and monitoring the external auditor's independence and objectivity and to developing a policy on the engagement of the external auditor to supply non-audit services. This will include discussion of any inconsistencies between the company's policy and APB Ethical Standards and ensuring that the policy is communicated to affiliates.

50 Communications with those charged with governance regarding the impact on auditor objectivity of non-audit services are likely to be facilitated if disclosure of such non-audit services distinguishes between audit related services and other non-audit services (as defined in this Standard).

DOCUMENTATION

51 **The audit engagement partner shall ensure that the reasoning for a decision to undertake an engagement to provide non-audit services, and any safeguards adopted, is appropriately documented.**

52 Matters to be documented include any significant judgments concerning:

- threats identified;

- safeguards adopted and the reasons why they are considered to be effective; and

- communication with those charged with governance.

53 In situations where a management threat is identified in connection with the provision of non-audit services, this documentation will include the auditor's assessment of whether there is informed management. The documentation of communications with the audited entity where judgments and decisions are made by management may take a variety of forms, for example an informal meeting note covering the matters discussed.

APPLICATION OF GENERAL PRINCIPLES TO SPECIFIC NON-AUDIT SERVICES

AUDIT RELATED SERVICES

54   Audit related services are those non-audit services specified in this Standard that are largely carried out by members of the engagement team and where the work involved is closely related to the work performed in the audit and the threats to auditor independence are clearly insignificant and, as a consequence, safeguards need not be applied.

55   Audit related services are:

- Reporting required by law or regulation to be provided by the auditor;

- Reviews of interim financial information;

- Reporting on regulatory returns;

- Reporting to a regulator on client assets:

- Reporting on government grants;

- Reporting on internal financial controls when required by law or regulation;

- Extended audit work that is authorised by those charged with governance performed on financial information[9] and/or financial controls where this work is integrated with the audit work and is performed on the same principal terms and conditions.

56   **The audit engagement partner shall ensure that only those non-audit services listed in paragraph 55 are described as audit related services in communications with those charged with governance of the audited entity.**

57   There may be other services that the auditor considers are closely related to an audit. However the threats to auditor independence arising from such services are not necessarily clearly insignificant and the auditor considers whether such services give rise to threats to independence and, where appropriate, the need to apply safeguards.

INTERNAL AUDIT SERVICES

58   The range of 'internal audit services' is wide and they may not be termed as such by the audited entity. For example, the audit firm may be engaged:

- to outsource the audited entity's entire internal audit function; or

---

[9]   This does not include accounting services.

- to supplement the audited entity's internal audit function in specific areas (for example, by providing specialised technical services or resources in particular locations); or

- to provide occasional internal audit services to the audited entity on an *ad hoc* basis.

All such engagements would fall within the term 'internal audit services'.

59 The nature of possible internal audit services is also wide. While the internal audit remit will vary from company to company, it often involves assurance activities designed to assess the design and operating effectiveness of existing or proposed systems or controls and advisory activities where advice is given to an entity on the design and implementation of risk management, control and governance processes.

60 The nature and extent of the threats to the external auditor's independence when undertaking internal audit services vary depending on the nature of the services provided. The main threats to the auditor's objectivity and independence arising from the provision of internal audit services are the self-review threat and the management threat. Generally these will be lower for activities that are primarily designed to provide assurance to those charged with governance, for example that internal controls are operating effectively, than for advisory activities designed to assist the entity in improving the effectiveness of its risk management, control and governance processes.

61 Engagements to provide internal audit services – other than those prohibited in paragraph 63 – may be undertaken, provided that the auditor is satisfied that there is informed management and appropriate safeguards are applied to reduce the self-review threat to an acceptable level.

62 Examples of safeguards that may be appropriate when internal audit services are provided to an audited entity include ensuring that:

- internal audit projects undertaken by the audit firm are performed by partners and staff who have no involvement in the external audit of the financial statements;

- the audit of the financial statements is reviewed by an audit partner who is not involved in the audit engagement, to ensure that the internal audit work performed by the audit firm has been properly and effectively assessed in the context of the audit of the financial statements.

63 **The audit firm shall not undertake an engagement to provide internal audit services to an audited entity where it is reasonably foreseeable that:**

(a) **for the purposes of the audit of the financial statements, the auditor would place significant reliance on the internal audit work performed by the audit firm; or**

(b) for the purposes of the internal audit services, the audit firm would undertake part of the role of management.

64 The self-review threat is unacceptably high where substantially all of the internal audit activity is outsourced to the audit firm and this is significant to the audited entity or the auditor cannot perform the audit of the financial statements without placing significant reliance on the work performed for the purposes of the internal audit services engagement. In the case of listed companies the provision of internal audit services in relation to the following examples is likely to be unacceptable as the external audit team is likely to place significant reliance on the work performed by the internal audit team in relation to the audited entity's internal financial controls:

- a significant part of the internal controls over financial reporting;

- financial accounting systems which generate information that is significant to the client's accounting records;

- amounts or disclosures that are material to the financial statements of the audited entity.

65 The management threat is unacceptably high where the audit firm provides internal audit services that involve audit firm personnel taking decisions or making judgments, which are properly the responsibility of management. For example, such situations arise where the internal audit function is outsourced to the audit firm and this is significant to the audited entity or where the nature of the internal audit work involves:

- Taking decisions on the scope and nature of the internal audit services to be provided to the audited entity;

- Designing internal controls or implementing changes thereto;

- Taking responsibility for risk management decisions;

- Undertaking work to evaluate the cost effectiveness of activities, systems and controls;

- Undertaking pre-implementation work on non-financial systems.

66 During the course of the audit, the auditor generally evaluates the design and tests the operating effectiveness of some of the entity's internal financial controls, and the operation of any relevant internal audit function, and provides management with observations on matters that have come to the attention of the auditor, including comments on weaknesses in the internal control systems and/or the internal audit function together with suggestions for addressing them. This work is a by-product of the audit service rather than the result of a specific engagement to provide non-audit services and therefore does not constitute internal audit services for the purposes of this Standard.

67 In some circumstances, additional work is undertaken to respond to risks identified by management or those charged with governance. Where the auditor considers that such risks could impact their opinion on the financial statements, such work is considered to be audit work for the purposes of this Standard (see paragraphs 10 and 11).

68 If extended audit work on financial information and/or financial controls is authorised by those charged with governance, it will be considered as an 'audit related service' provided that it is integrated with the work performed in the audit and performed largely by the existing audit team, and is performed on the same principal terms and conditions as the audit.

69 Additional work will not be considered an audit related service if it:

- does not relate to financial information and/or financial controls; or

- is not authorised by those charged with governance; or

- is not integrated with the work performed in the audit, or is not performed largely by the existing audit team; or

- is not on the same principal terms and conditions as the audit.

In such circumstances the threats and the safeguards will be communicated to those charged with governance. The audit engagement partner reviews the scope and objectives of the proposed work and assesses the threats to which it gives rise and the safeguards available. Whether it is appropriate for this work to be undertaken by the audit firm will depend on the extent to which it gives rise to threats to the auditor's objectivity and independence.

INFORMATION TECHNOLOGY SERVICES

70 Design, provision and implementation of information technology (including financial information technology) systems by audit firms for entities audited by them creates threats to the auditor's objectivity and independence. The principal threats are the self-review threat and the management threat.

71 Engagements to design, provide or implement information technology systems that are not important to any significant part of the accounting system or to the production of the financial statements and do not have significant reliance placed on them by the auditor, may be undertaken, provided that there is informed management and appropriate safeguards are applied to reduce the self-review threat to an acceptable level.

72 Examples of safeguards that may be appropriate when information technology services are provided to an audited entity include ensuring that:

- information technology projects undertaken by the audit firm are performed by partners and staff who have no involvement in the external audit of the financial statements;

- the audit of the financial statements is reviewed by an audit partner who is not involved in the audit engagement to ensure that the information technology work performed has been properly and effectively assessed in the context of the audit of the financial statements.

73 **The audit firm shall not undertake an engagement to design, provide or implement information technology systems for an audited entity where:**

(a) **the systems concerned would be important to any significant part of the accounting system or to the production of the financial statements and the auditor would place significant reliance upon them as part of the audit of the financial statements; or**

(b) **for the purposes of the information technology services, the audit firm would undertake part of the role of management.**

74 Where it is reasonably apparent that, having regard to the activities and size of the audited entity and the range and complexity of the proposed system, management lacks the expertise required to take responsibility for the systems concerned, it is unlikely that any safeguards would be sufficient to eliminate these threats or to reduce them to an acceptable level. In particular, formal acceptance by management of the systems designed and installed by the audit firm is unlikely to be an effective safeguard when, in substance, the audit firm has been retained by management as experts and makes important decisions in relation to the design or implementation of systems of internal control and financial reporting.

75 The provision and installation of information technology services associated with a standard 'off the shelf accounting package' (including basic set-up procedures to make the package operate on the audited entity's existing platform and peripherals, setting up the chart of accounts and the entry of standard data such as the audited entity's product names and prices) is unlikely to create a level of threat to the auditor's objectivity and independence that cannot be addressed through applying appropriate safeguards.

VALUATION SERVICES

76 A valuation comprises the making of assumptions with regard to future developments, the application of appropriate methodologies and techniques, and the combination of both to compute a certain value, or range of values, for an asset, a liability or for a business as a whole.

77 **The audit firm shall not undertake an engagement to provide a valuation to:**

(a) an audited entity that is a listed company or a significant affiliate of such an entity, where the valuation would have a material effect on the listed company's financial statements, either separately or in aggregate with other valuations provided; or

(b) any other audited entity, where the valuation would both involve a significant degree of subjective judgment and have a material effect on the financial statements either separately or in aggregate with other valuations provided.

78 The main threats to the auditor's objectivity and independence arising from the provision of valuation services are the self-review threat and the management threat. In all cases, the self-review threat is considered too high to allow the provision of valuation services which involve the valuation of amounts with a significant degree of subjectivity and have a material effect on the financial statements.

79 For listed companies, or significant affiliates of such entities, the threats to the auditor's objectivity and independence that would be perceived to be created are too high to allow the audit firm to undertake any valuation that has a material effect on the listed company's financial statements.

80 The audit firm's policies and procedures will set out whether there are circumstances in which valuation services are not undertaken for non-listed audited entities as described in paragraph 47 of APB Ethical Standard 1.

81 In circumstances where the auditor is designated by legislation or regulation as being required to carry out a valuation the restrictions in paragraph 77 do not apply. In such circumstances, the audit engagement partner applies relevant safeguards.

82 It is usual for the auditor to provide management with accounting advice in relation to valuation matters that have come to the auditor's attention during the course of the audit. Such matters might typically include:

- comments on valuation assumptions and their appropriateness;

- errors identified in a valuation calculation and suggestions for correcting them;

- advice on accounting policies and any valuation methodologies used in their application.

Advice on such matters does not constitute valuation services for the purpose of this Standard.

83 Where the auditor is engaged to collect and verify the accuracy of data to be used in a valuation to be performed by others, such engagements do not constitute valuation services under this Standard.

ACTUARIAL VALUATION SERVICES

84　The audit firm shall not undertake an engagement to provide actuarial valuation services to:

(a)　an audited entity that is a listed company or a significant affiliate of such an entity, unless the firm is satisfied that the valuation has no material effect on the listed company's financial statements, either separately or in aggregate with other valuations provided; or

(b)　any other audited entity, unless the firm is satisfied that either all significant judgments, including the assumptions, are made by informed management or the valuation has no material effect on the financial statements, either separately or in aggregate with other valuations provided.

85　Actuarial valuation services are subject to the same general principles as other valuation services. In all cases, where they involve the audit firm in making a subjective judgment and have a material effect on the financial statements, actuarial valuations give rise to an unacceptable level of self-review threat and so may not be performed by audit firms for entities audited by them.

86　In the case of non-listed companies where all significant judgments concerning the assumptions, methodology and data for the actuarial valuation are made by informed management and the audit firm's role is limited to applying proven methodologies using the given data, for which the management takes responsibility, it may be possible to establish effective safeguards to protect the auditors' objectivity and the appearance of its independence.

87　For listed companies, or significant affiliates of such entities, the threats to the auditor's objectivity and independence that would be perceived to be created are too high to allow the audit firm to undertake any actuarial valuation unless the firm is satisfied that the valuation has no material effect on the listed company's financial statements.

88　The audit firm's policies and procedures will set out whether there are circumstances in which actuarial valuation services are not undertaken for non-listed audited entities as described in paragraph 47 of APB Ethical Standard 1.

TAX SERVICES

89　The range of activities encompassed by the term 'tax services' is wide. Three broad categories of tax service can be distinguished. They are where the audit firm:

(a)　provides advice to the audited entity on one or more specific matters at the request of the audited entity; or

(b)　undertakes a substantial proportion of the tax planning or compliance work for the audited entity; or

(c)   promotes tax structures or products to the audited entity, the effectiveness of which is likely to be influenced by the manner in which they are accounted for in the financial statements.

Whilst it is possible to consider tax services under broad headings, such as tax planning or compliance, in practice these services are often interrelated and it is impracticable to analyse services in this way for the purposes of attempting to identify generically the threats to which specific engagements give rise. As a result, audit firms need to identify and assess, on a case-by-case basis, the potential threats to the auditor's objectivity and independence before deciding whether to undertake a proposed engagement to provide tax services to an audited entity.

90   The provision of tax services by audit firms to entities audited by them may give rise to a number of threats to the auditor's objectivity and independence, including the self-interest threat, the management threat, the advocacy threat and, where the work involves a significant degree of subjective judgment and has a material effect on the financial statements, the self-review threat.

91   Where the audit firm provides advice to the audited entity on one or more specific matters at the request of the audited entity, a self-review threat may be created. This self-review threat is more significant where the audit firm undertakes a substantial proportion of the tax planning and compliance work for the audited entity. However, the auditor may be able to undertake such engagements, provided that there is informed management and appropriate safeguards are applied to reduce the self-review threat to an acceptable level.

92   Examples of such safeguards that may be appropriate when tax services are provided to an audited entity include ensuring that:

• the tax services are provided by partners and staff who have no involvement in the audit of the financial statements;

• the tax services are reviewed by an independent tax partner, or other senior tax employee;

• external independent advice is obtained on the tax work;

• tax computations prepared by the audit team are reviewed by a partner or senior staff member with appropriate expertise who is not a member of the audit team; or

• an audit partner not involved in the audit engagement reviews whether the tax work has been properly and effectively addressed in the context of the audit of the financial statements.

93   **The audit firm shall not promote tax structures or products or undertake an engagement to provide tax advice to an audited entity where the audit engagement partner has, or ought to have, reasonable doubt as to whether the related accounting treatment involved is based on well established interpretations or is appropriate, having regard to the requirement for the**

financial statements to give a true and fair view in accordance with the relevant financial reporting framework.

94   Where the audit firm promotes tax structures or products or undertakes an engagement to provide tax advice to the audited entity, it may be necessary to adopt an accounting treatment that is not based on well established interpretations or may not be appropriate, in order to achieve the desired result. A self-review threat arises in the course of an audit because the auditor may be unable to form an impartial view of the accounting treatment to be adopted for the purposes of the proposed arrangements. Accordingly, this Standard does not permit the promotion of tax structures or products by audit firms to entities audited by them where, in the view of the audit engagement partner, after such consultation as is appropriate, there is reasonable doubt as to whether the effectiveness of the tax structure or product depends on an accounting treatment that is well established and appropriate.

95   **The audit firm shall not undertake an engagement to provide tax services wholly or partly on a contingent fee basis where the outcome of those tax services (and, therefore, the amount of the fee) is dependent on the proposed application of tax law which is uncertain or has not been established.**

96   Where tax services, such as advising on corporate structures and structuring transactions to achieve a particular effect, are undertaken on a contingent fee basis, self-interest threats to the auditor's objectivity and independence may arise. The auditor may have, or may appear to have, an interest in the success of the tax services, causing the audit firm to make an audit judgment about which there is reasonable doubt as to its appropriateness. Where the contingent fee is determined by the outcome of the application of tax law which is uncertain or has not been established, the self-interest threat cannot be eliminated or reduced to an acceptable level by the application of any safeguards.

97   **The audit firm shall not undertake an engagement to provide tax services to an audited entity where the engagement would involve the audit firm undertaking a management role.**

98   When providing tax services to an audited entity, there is a risk that the audit firm undertakes a management role, unless the firm is working with informed management.

99   **Where an audited entity is a listed company or a significant affiliate of such an entity, the audit firm shall not undertake an engagement to prepare current or deferred tax calculations that are or may reasonably be expected to be used when preparing accounting entries that are material to the financial statements of the audited entity, save where the circumstances contemplated in paragraph 164 apply.**

100   For listed companies or significant affiliates of such entities, the threats to the auditor's objectivity and independence that would be created are too high to allow the audit firm to undertake an engagement to prepare calculations of current or deferred tax liabilities (or assets) for the purpose of preparing accounting entries that are material to

the relevant financial statements, together with associated disclosure notes, save where the circumstances contemplated in paragraph 164 apply.

101 Paragraph 99 is not intended to prevent an audit firm preparing tax calculations after the completion of the audit for the purpose of submitting tax returns.

102 For entities other than listed companies or significant affiliates of listed companies, the auditor may undertake an engagement to prepare current or deferred tax calculations for the purpose of preparing accounting entries, provided that:

(a) such services:

(i) do not involve initiating transactions or taking management decisions; and

(ii) are of a technical, mechanical or an informative nature; and

(b) appropriate safeguards are applied.

103 The audit firm's policies and procedures will set out whether there are circumstances in which current or deferred tax calculations for the purpose of preparing accounting entries are not prepared for non-listed audited entities as described in paragraph 47 of APB Ethical Standard 1.

104 **The audit firm shall not undertake an engagement to provide tax services to an audited entity where this would involve acting as an advocate for the audited entity, before an appeals tribunal or court[10] in the resolution of an issue:**

(a) **that is material to the financial statements; or**

(b) **where the outcome of the tax issue is dependent on a future or contemporary audit judgment.**

105 Where the tax services to be provided by the audit firm include representing the audited entity in any negotiations or proceedings involving the tax authorities, advocacy threats to the auditor's objectivity and independence may arise.

106 The audit firm is not acting as an advocate where the tax services involve the provision of information to the tax authorities (including an explanation of the approach being taken and the arguments being advanced by the audited entity). In such circumstances effective safeguards may exist and the tax authorities will undertake their own review of the issues.

107 Where the tax authorities indicate that they are minded to reject the audited entity's arguments on a particular issue and the matter is likely to be determined by an appeals tribunal or court, the audit firm may become so closely identified with management's

---

[10] The restriction applies to the first level of Tax Court that is independent of the tax authorities and to more authoritative bodies. In the UK this would be the General or Special Commissioners of HM Revenue & Customs or the VAT and Duties Tribunal.

arguments that the auditor is inhibited from forming an impartial view of the treatment of the issue in the financial statements. In such circumstances, if the issue is material to the financial statements or is dependent on a future or contemporary audit judgment, the audit firm discusses the matter with the audited entity and makes it clear that it will have to withdraw from that element of the engagement to provide tax services that requires it to act as advocate for the audited entity, or resign from the audit engagement from the time when the matter is formally listed for hearing before the appeals tribunal.

108 The audit firm is not, however, precluded from having a continuing role (for example, responding to specific requests for information) for the audited entity in relation to the appeal. The audit firm assesses the threat associated with any continuing role in accordance with the provisions of paragraphs 109 to 112 of this Standard.

LITIGATION SUPPORT SERVICES

109 Although management and advocacy threats may arise in litigation support services, such as acting as an expert witness, the primary issue is that a self-review threat will arise in all cases where such services involve a subjective estimation of the likely outcome of a matter that is material to the amounts to be included or the disclosures to be made in the financial statements.

110 **The audit firm shall not undertake an engagement to provide litigation support services to:**

(a) **an audited entity that is a listed company or a significant affiliate of such an entity, where this would involve the estimation by the audit firm of the likely outcome of a pending legal matter that could be material to the amounts to be included or the disclosures to be made in the listed company's financial statements, either separately or in aggregate with other estimates and valuations provided; or**

(b) **any other audited entity, where this would involve the estimation by the audit firm of the likely outcome of a pending legal matter that could be material to the amounts to be included or the disclosures to be made in the financial statements, either separately or in aggregate with other estimates and valuations provided and there is a significant degree of subjectivity involved.**

111 In the case of non-listed entities, litigation support services that do not involve such subjective estimations are not prohibited, provided that the audit firm has carefully considered the implications of any threats and established appropriate safeguards.

112 The audit firm's policies and procedures will set out whether there are circumstances in which litigation support services are not undertaken for non-listed audited entities as described in paragraph 47 of APB Ethical Standard 1.

LEGAL SERVICES

113 **The audit firm shall not undertake an engagement to provide legal services to an audited entity where this would involve acting as the solicitor formally nominated to represent the audited entity in the resolution of a dispute or litigation which is material to the amounts to be included or the disclosures to be made in the financial statements.**

114 Although the provision by the auditor of certain types of legal services to its audited entities may create advocacy, self-review and management threats, this Standard does not impose a general prohibition on the provision of legal services. However, in view of the degree of advocacy involved in litigation or other types of dispute resolution procedures and the potential importance of any assessment by the auditor of the merits of the audited entity's position when auditing its financial statements, this Standard prohibits an audit firm from acting as the formally nominated representative for an audited entity in the resolution of a dispute or litigation which is material to the financial statements (either in terms of the amounts recognised or disclosed in the financial statements).

RECRUITMENT AND REMUNERATION SERVICES

115 **The audit firm shall not undertake an engagement to provide recruitment services to an audited entity that would involve the firm taking responsibility for the appointment of any director or employee of the audited entity.**

116 A management threat arises where audit firm personnel take responsibility for any decision as to who is appointed by the audited entity.

117 **For an audited entity that is a listed company, the audit firm shall not undertake an engagement to provide recruitment services in relation to a key management position of the audited entity, or a significant affiliate of such an entity.**

118 A familiarity threat arises if the audit firm plays a significant role in relation to the identification and recruitment of senior members of management within the company, as the engagement team may be less likely to be critical of the information or explanations provided by such individuals than might otherwise be the case. Accordingly, for listed companies, and for significant affiliates of such entities, the audit firm does not undertake engagements that involve the recruitment of individuals for key management positions.

119 The audit firm's policies and procedures will set out whether there are circumstances in which recruitment services are not undertaken for non-listed audited entities as described in paragraph 47 of APB Ethical Standard 1.

120 Recruitment services involve a specifically identifiable, and separately remunerated, engagement. Audit firms and engagement teams may contribute to an entity's recruitment process in less formal ways. The prohibition set out in paragraph 117 does not extend to:

- senior members of an audit team interviewing prospective directors or employees of the audited entity and advising on the candidate's technical financial competence; or

- the audit entity using information gathered by the audit firm, including that relating to salary surveys.

121 **The audit firm shall not undertake an engagement to provide advice on the quantum of the remuneration package or the measurement criteria on which the quantum is calculated, for a director or key management position of an audited entity.**

122 The provision of advice on remuneration packages (including bonus arrangements, incentive plans and other benefits) to existing or prospective employees of the audited entity gives rise to familiarity threats. The significance of the familiarity threat is considered too high to allow advice on the overall amounts to be paid or on the quantitative measurement criteria included in remuneration packages for directors and key management positions.

123 For other employees, these threats can be adequately addressed by the application of safeguards, such as the advice being provided by partners and staff who have no involvement in the audit of the financial statements.

124 In cases where all significant judgments concerning the assumptions, methodology and data for the calculation of remuneration packages for directors and key management are made by informed management or a third party and the audit firm's role is limited to applying proven methodologies using the given data, for which the management takes responsibility, it may be possible to establish effective safeguards to protect the auditor's objectivity and independence.

125 Advice on tax, pensions and interpretation of accounting standards relating to remuneration packages for directors and key management can be provided by the audit firm, provided they are not prohibited by the requirements of this Standard relating to tax, actuarial valuations and accounting services. Disclosure of the provision of any such advice would be made to those charged with governance of the audited entity (see APB Ethical Standard 1, paragraphs 63 to 71).

CORPORATE FINANCE SERVICES

126 The range of services encompassed by the term 'corporate finance services' is wide. For example, the audit firm may be engaged:

- to identify possible purchasers for parts of the audited entity's business and provide advisory services in the course of such sales; or

- to identify possible 'targets' for the audited entity to acquire; or

- to advise the audited entity on how to fund its financing requirements; or

- to act as sponsor on admission to listing on the London Stock Exchange, or as Nominated Advisor on the admission of the audited entity on the Alternative Investments Market (AIM); or

- to act as financial adviser to audited entity offerors or offerees in connection with public takeovers.

127 The potential for the auditor's objectivity and independence to be impaired through the provision of corporate finance services varies considerably depending on the precise nature of the service provided. The main threats to auditor's objectivity and independence arising from the provision of corporate finance services are the self-review, management and advocacy threats. Self-interest threats may also arise, especially in situations where the audit firm is paid on a contingent fee basis.

128 When providing corporate finance services to an audited entity, there is a risk that the audit firm undertakes a management role, unless the firm is working with informed management. Appropriate safeguards are applied to reduce the self-review threat to an acceptable level.

129 Examples of safeguards that may be appropriate when corporate finance services are provided to an audited entity include ensuring that:

- the corporate finance advice is provided by partners and staff who have no involvement in the audit of the financial statements;

- any advice provided is reviewed by an independent corporate finance partner within the audit firm;

- external independent advice on the corporate finance work is obtained;

- an audit partner who is not involved in the audit engagement reviews the audit work performed in relation to the subject matter of the corporate finance services provided to ensure that such audit work has been properly and effectively reviewed and assessed in the context of the audit of the financial statements.

130 Where the audit firm undertakes an engagement to provide corporate finance services to an audited entity in connection with conducting the sale or purchase of a material part of the audited entity's business, the audit engagement partner informs the audit committee (or equivalent) about the engagement, as set out in paragraphs 63 to 71 of APB Ethical Standard 1.

131 **The audit firm shall not undertake an engagement to provide corporate finance services in respect of an audited entity where:**

(a) **the engagement would involve the audit firm taking responsibility for dealing in, underwriting, or promoting shares; or**

(b) **the audit engagement partner has, or ought to have, reasonable doubt as to whether an accounting treatment that is subject to a contemporary or future** audit judgment relating to a material matter in the financial statements of the audited entity, and upon which the success of the related transaction depends:

(i)   is based on well established interpretations; or

(ii) is appropriate,

having regard to the requirement for the financial statements to give a true and fair view in accordance with the relevant financial reporting framework; or

(c)   the engagement would involve the audit firm undertaking a management role in the audited entity.

132   An unacceptable advocacy threat arises where, in the course of providing a corporate finance service, the audit firm promotes the interests of the audited entity by taking responsibility for dealing in, underwriting, or promoting shares.

133   Where the audit firm acts as a sponsor under the Listing Rules[11], or as Nominated Adviser on the admission of the audited entity to the AIM, the audit firm is required to confirm that the audited entity has satisfied all applicable conditions for listing and other relevant requirements of the listing (or AIM) rules. Where there is, or there ought to be, reasonable doubt that the audit firm will be able to give that confirmation, it does not enter into such an engagement.

134   A self-review threat arises where the outcome or consequences of the corporate finance service provided by the audit firm may be material to the financial statements of the audited entity, which are, or will be, subject to audit by the same firm. Where the audit firm provides corporate finance services, for example advice to the audited entity on financing arrangements, it may be necessary to adopt an accounting treatment that is not based on well established interpretations or which may not be appropriate, in order to achieve the desired result. A self-review threat is created because the auditor may be unable to form an impartial view of the accounting treatment to be adopted for the purposes of the proposed arrangements. Accordingly, this Standard does not permit the provision of such services by audit firms in respect of entities audited by them where there is or ought to be reasonable doubt as to whether an accounting treatment that is subject to a contemporary or future audit judgment relating to a material matter in the financial statements of the audited entity and on which the success of a transaction depends is well established and appropriate.

135   Advice to audited entities on funding issues and banking arrangements, where there is no reasonable doubt as to the appropriateness of the accounting treatment, is not prohibited provided this does not involve the audit firm in taking decisions or making judgments which are properly the responsibility of management.

---

[11] In the United Kingdom, the UK Listing Authority's publication the 'Listing Rules'. In the Republic of Ireland, the United Kingdom 'Listing Rules' as modified by the 'Notes on the Listing Rules' published by the Irish Stock Exchange.

136 These restrictions do not apply in circumstances where the auditor is designated by legislation or regulation as being required to carry out a particular service. In such circumstances, the audit engagement partner establishes appropriate safeguards.

TRANSACTION RELATED SERVICES

137 In addition to corporate finance services, there are other non-audit services associated with transactions that an audit firm may undertake for an audited entity. For example:

- investigations into possible acquisitions or disposals ('due diligence' investigations); or

- investigations into the tax affairs of possible acquisitions or disposals; or

- the provision of information to management or sponsors in relation to prospectuses and other investment circulars (for example, long form reports, comfort letters on the adequacy of working capital); or

- agreed upon procedures or reports provided to management in relation to particular transactions (for example, securitisations).

138 When providing transaction related services to an audited entity, there is a risk that the audit firm may face a management threat, unless the firm is working with informed management. Appropriate safeguards are applied to reduce the self-review threat to an acceptable level.

139 Examples of safeguards that may be appropriate when transaction related services are provided to an audited entity include ensuring that:

- the transaction related advice is provided by partners and staff who have no involvement in the audit of the financial statements;

- any advice provided is reviewed by an independent transactions partner within the audit firm;

- external independent advice on the transaction related work is obtained;

- an audit partner who is not involved in the audit engagement reviews the audit work performed in relation to the subject matter of the transaction related service provided to ensure that such audit work has been properly and effectively reviewed and assessed in the context of the audit of the financial statements.

140 **The audit firm shall not undertake an engagement to provide transaction related services in respect of an audited entity where:**

(a) **the audit engagement partner has, or ought to have, reasonable doubt as to whether an accounting treatment that is subject to a contemporary or future audit judgment relating to a material matter in the financial statements of the** audited entity, and upon which the success of the related transaction depends;

       (i)   is based on well established interpretations; or

       (ii) is appropriate,

       having regard to the requirement for the financial statements to give a true and fair view in accordance with the relevant financial reporting framework; or

(b) the engagement would involve the audit firm undertaking a management role in the audited entity.

141 A self-review threat arises where the outcome of the transaction related services undertaken by the audit firm may be material to the financial statements of the audited entity which are, or will be, subject to audit by the same firm. Where the audited entity proposes to undertake a transaction, it may be necessary to adopt an accounting treatment that is not based on well established interpretations or may not be appropriate, in order to achieve the desired result of the transaction (for example, to take assets off the balance sheet). A self-review threat is created if the auditor undertakes transaction related services in connection with such a transaction. Accordingly, this Standard does not permit the provision of services by audit firms in respect of entities audited by them where there is or ought to be reasonable doubt as to whether an accounting treatment, that is subject to a contemporary or future audit judgment relating to a material matter in the financial statements of the audited entity and on which the success of a related transaction depends, is well established and appropriate.

142 These restrictions do not apply in circumstances where the auditor is designated by legislation or regulation as being required to carry out a particular service. In such circumstances, the audit engagement partner establishes appropriate safeguards.

RESTRUCTURING SERVICES

143 Restructuring services are any non-audit services provided to an audited entity in connection with the entity's development or implementation of a transaction or package of transactions (a 'restructuring plan') designed to change its equity or debt financing structure, its corporate structure, or its operating structure. There are a variety of possible purposes for developing a restructuring plan, for example to address financial or operating difficulties, to support tax planning, to improve operating efficiency, or to improve the cost of capital. The range of non-audit services that may be regarded as 'Restructuring Services' is extensive, and the nature of those services may encompass many of the other types of non-audit services discussed in this Ethical Standard. Where applicable, the related requirements and guidance covered elsewhere in this standard apply to Restructuring Services.

144 The services that an entity may engage an audit firm to provide may vary considerably and may range from the incidental and routine to advice that is fundamental to the efficacy of the restructuring plan. Consequently, where such services are provided by the entity's auditor, the audit engagement partner evaluates:

- the threats that the services may present to the audit firm's ability to conduct any contemporary or future audit with objectivity and independence; and

- the likelihood that a reasonable and informed third party would conclude that the auditor's objectivity and independence would be compromised.

145 **The audit firm shall not undertake an engagement to provide restructuring services in respect of an audited entity where:**

(a) **the engagement would involve the audit firm undertaking a management role in or on behalf of the audited entity; or**

(b) **the engagement would require the audit firm to act as an advocate for the audited entity in relation to matters that are material to the financial statements.**

146 The potential for the auditor's objectivity and independence to be impaired through the provision of restructuring services varies depending on the nature of the service provided. Two of the main threats to auditor objectivity and independence arising from the provision of restructuring services arise where the auditor undertakes a management or advocacy role:

- An audit firm undertakes a management role if the entity does not have informed management capable of taking responsibility for the decisions to be made.

- To avoid undertaking an advocacy role on behalf of the audited entity, the audit firm takes particular care not to assume (or seen to be assuming) responsibility for the entity's proposals or being regarded as negotiating on behalf of the entity or advocating the appropriateness of the proposals such that its independence is compromised. This is particularly important when the auditor attends meetings with the entity's bank or other interested parties.

If the audit firm undertakes a management role or acts as advocate for the audited entity, the threats to that auditor's objectivity and independence are such that no safeguards can reduce the threat to an acceptable level[12].

147 **The audit firm shall not undertake an engagement to provide restructuring services in respect of an audited entity where that engagement may give rise to a self review threat in the course of a contemporary or future audit unless it is**

---

[12] 'ES – Provisions Available for Small Entities (Revised)' provides exemptions relating to informed management and the advocacy threat for auditors of small entities.

satisfied that such threats can be reduced to an acceptable level by appropriate safeguards and that such safeguards have been put in place.

148 The provision of restructuring services gives rise to a self review threat where the restructuring services to be provided involve advice or judgments which are likely to be material to a contemporary or future audit judgment.

149 Examples of restructuring services that the audit firm may be requested to undertake and which may give rise to a self review threat include:

- Providing preliminary general advice on the options and choices available to management or stakeholders of an entity facing urgent financial or other difficulties.

- Undertaking a review of the business of the entity with a view to advising the audited entity on liquidity management or operational restructuring options.

- Advising on the development of forecasts or projections, for presentation to lenders and other stakeholders, including assumptions.

- Advising the audited entity on how to fund its financing requirements, including equity and debt restructuring programmes.

- Participating in the design or implementation of an overall restructuring plan including, for example, participating in the preparation of cash flow and other forecasts and financial models underpinning the overall restructuring plan.

150 The self review threat arising from the provision of such services is particularly significant where it has potential to impact the auditor's assessment of whether it is appropriate to prepare the entity's financial statements on a going concern basis. Where the audit firm has been involved in aspects of the preparation of a cash flow, a forecast or a financial model, it is probable that a reasonable and informed third party would conclude that the auditor would have a significant self-review threat in considering the going concern assumption.

151 The self review threat arising from the provision of such services is also particularly significant where the restructuring services are provided in respect of an audited entity and involve developing or implementing a restructuring plan to address the actual or anticipated financial or operational difficulties that threaten the survival of that entity as a going concern (an 'audited entity in distress').

152 The audit firm puts in place those safeguards that it regards as appropriate to reduce the threats to its objectivity and independence to an acceptable level. If the audit firm concludes that the threats arising from some or all of the restructuring services involved cannot be addressed by putting appropriate safeguards in place, it declines the engagement, or those parts of the engagement affected by those threats that cannot be addressed.

153 **Where an audited entity in distress is a listed company or a significant affiliate of a listed audited entity, the restructuring services provided by the audit firm shall be limited to providing:**

(a) **preliminary general advice to an entity in distress;**

(b) **assistance with the implementation of elements of an overall restructuring plan, such as the sale of a non-significant component business, provided those elements are not material to the overall restructuring plan;**

(c) **challenging, but in no circumstances developing, the projections and assumptions within a financial model that has been produced by the audited entity;**

(d) **reporting on a restructuring plan, or aspects of it, in connection with the proposed issue of an investment circular; and**

(e) **where specifically permitted by a regulatory body with oversight of the audited entity.**

154 Except to the extent identified in paragraph 153, the significance of the self-review threat is too high to permit the provision of other restructuring services to an audited entity in distress that is a listed company or a significant affiliate of a listed audited entity because there are no safeguards that would be sufficient to reduce the resultant threats to an acceptable level.

155 The audit firm's policies and procedures will set out whether there are circumstances in which restructuring services are not undertaken for non-listed audited entities in distress as described in paragraph 47 of APB Ethical Standard 1.

ACCOUNTING SERVICES

156 In this Standard, the term 'accounting services' is defined as the provision of services that involve the maintenance of accounting records or the preparation of financial statements that are then subject to audit. Advice on the implementation of current and proposed accounting standards is not included in the term 'accounting services'.

157 The range of activities encompassed by the term 'accounting services' is wide. In some cases, the audited entity may ask the audit firm to provide a complete service including maintaining all of the accounting records and the preparation of the financial statements. Other common situations are:

- the audit firm may take over the provision of a specific accounting function on an outsourced basis (for example, payroll);

- the audited entity maintains the accounting records, undertakes basic bookkeeping and prepares a year-end trial balance and asks the audit firm to assist with the preparation of the necessary adjustments and the financial statements.

158 The provision of accounting services by the audit firm to the audited entity creates threats to the auditor's objectivity and independence, principally self-review and management threats, the significance of which depends on the nature and extent of the accounting services in question and upon the level of public interest in the audited entity.

159 When providing accounting services to an audited entity, unless the firm is working with informed management, there is a risk that the audit firm undertakes a management role.

160 **The audit firm shall not undertake an engagement to provide accounting services to:**

    (a) **an audited entity that is a listed company or a significant affiliate of such an entity, save where the circumstances contemplated in paragraph 164 apply; or**

    (b) **any other audited entity, where those accounting services would involve the audit firm undertaking part of the role of management.**

161 Even where there is no engagement to provide any accounting services, it is usual for the auditor to provide the management with accounting advice on matters that have come to the auditor's attention during the course of the audit. Such matters might typically include:

- comments on weaknesses in the accounting records and suggestions for addressing them;

- errors identified in the accounting records and in the financial statements and suggestions for correcting them;

- advice on the accounting policies in use and on the application of current and proposed accounting standards.

This advice is a by-product of the audit service rather than the result of any engagement to provide non-audit services. Consequently, as it is part of the audit service, such advice is not regarded as giving rise to any threat to the auditor's objectivity and independence.

162 For listed companies or significant affiliates of such entities, the threats to the auditor's objectivity and independence that would be created are too high to allow the audit firm to undertake an engagement to provide any accounting services, save where the circumstances contemplated in paragraph 164 apply.

163 The audit firm's policies and procedures will set out whether there are circumstances in which accounting services are not undertaken for non-listed audited entities as described in paragraph 47 of APB Ethical Standard 1.

164 In emergency situations, the audit firm may provide a listed audited entity, or a significant affiliate of such a company, with accounting services to assist the company in the timely preparation of its financial statements. This might arise when, due to external and unforeseeable events, the audit firm personnel are the only people with the necessary knowledge of the audited entity's systems and procedures. A situation could be considered an emergency where the audit firm's refusal to provide these services would result in a severe burden for the audited entity (for example, withdrawal of credit lines), or would even threaten its going concern status. In such circumstances, the audit firm ensures that:

(a) any staff involved in the accounting services have no involvement in the audit of the financial statements; and

(b) the engagement would not lead to any audit firm staff or partners taking decisions or making judgments which are properly the responsibility of management.

165 For entities other than listed companies or significant affiliates of listed companies, the auditor may undertake an engagement to provide accounting services, provided that:

(a) such services:

(i) do not involve initiating transactions or taking management decisions; and

(ii) are of a technical, mechanical or an informative nature; and

(b) appropriate safeguards are applied to reduce the self-review threat to an acceptable level.

166 The maintenance of the accounting records and the preparation of the financial statements are the responsibility of the management of the audited entity. Accordingly, in any engagement to provide the audited entity with accounting services, the audit firm does not initiate any transactions or take any decisions or make any judgments, which are properly the responsibility of the management. These include:

• authorising or approving transactions;

• preparing originating data (including valuation assumptions);

• determining or changing journal entries, or the classifications for accounts or transactions, or other accounting records without management approval.

167 Examples of accounting services of a technical or mechanical nature or of an informative nature include:

- recording transactions for which management has determined the appropriate account classification, posting coded transactions to the general ledger, posting entries approved by management to the trial balance or providing certain data-processing services (for example, payroll);

- assistance with the preparation of the financial statements where management takes all decisions on issues requiring the exercise of judgment and has prepared the underlying accounting records.

168 Examples of safeguards that may be appropriate when accounting services are provided to an audited entity include:

- accounting services provided by the audit firm are performed by partners and staff who have no involvement in the external audit of the financial statements;

- the accounting services are reviewed by a partner or other senior staff member with appropriate expertise who is not a member of the audit team;

- the audit of the financial statements is reviewed by an audit partner who is not involved in the audit engagement to ensure that the accounting services performed have been properly and effectively assessed in the context of the audit of the financial statements.

EFFECTIVE DATE

169 This revised Ethical Standard becomes effective on 30 April 2011.

170 Firms may complete audit engagements relating to periods commencing on or before 31 December 2010 in accordance with existing ethical standards, putting in place any necessary changes in the subsequent engagement period.

171 Where compliance with the requirements of ES 5 would result in a service not being supplied, services contracted before 31 December 2010 may continue to be provided until the earlier of either:

(a) the completion of the specific task or the end of the contract term, where this is set out in the contract; or

(b) 31 December 2011 (or, in the case of services prohibited under paragraph 95, 31 December 2014) as long as the following apply:

- the engagement was permitted by existing ethical standards (including transitional provisions);

- any safeguards required by existing ethical standards continue to be applied; and

- the need for additional safeguards is assessed, including where possible any additional safeguards specified by ES 5, and if considered necessary, those additional safeguards are applied.

172 In the first year of appointment as auditor to an audited entity, an audit firm may continue to provide non-audit services which are already contracted at the date of appointment, until the earlier of either:

(i) the completion of the specific task or the end of the contract term, where this is set out in the contract; or

(ii) one year after the date of appointment, where a task or term is not defined,

provided that the need for additional safeguards is assessed and if considered necessary, those additional safeguards are applied.

APB ETHICAL STANDARD

PROVISIONS AVAILABLE FOR SMALL ENTITIES (REVISED)

(Revised December 2010)

CONTENTS

PREFACE

APB Ethical Standards apply in the audit of financial statements. They are read in the context of the Statement "The Financial Reporting Council – Scope and Authority of Audit and Assurance Pronouncements" which sets out the application and authority of APB Ethical Standards.

The terms used in APB Ethical Standards are explained in the Glossary.

INTRODUCTION

1   The APB issues Ethical Standards which set out the standards that auditors are required to comply with in order to discharge their responsibilities in respect of their integrity, objectivity and independence. The Ethical Standards 1 to 5 address such matters as:

- How audit firms set policies and procedures to ensure that, in relation to each audit, the audit firm and all those who are in a position to influence the conduct and outcome of an audit act with integrity, objectivity and independence;

- Financial, business, employment and personal relationships;

- Long association with the audit engagement;

- Fees, remuneration and evaluation policies, litigation, gifts and hospitality;

- Non-audit services provided to audited entities.

These Ethical Standards apply to all audit firms and to all audits and must be read in order to understand the alternative provisions and exemptions contained in this Standard.

2   The APB is aware that a limited number of the requirements in Ethical Standards 1 to 5 are difficult for certain audit firms to comply with, particularly when auditing a small entity. Whilst the APB is clear that those standards are appropriate in the interests of establishing the integrity, objectivity and independence of auditors, it accepts that certain dispensations, as set out in this Standard, are appropriate to facilitate the cost effective audit of the financial statements of Small Entities (as defined below).

3   This Standard provides alternative provisions for auditors of Small Entities to apply in respect of the threats arising from economic dependence and where tax or accounting services are provided and allows the option of taking advantage of exemptions from certain of the requirements in APB Ethical Standards 1 to 5 for a Small Entity audit engagement. Where an audit firm takes advantage of the exemptions within this Standard, it is required to:

(a)   take the steps described in this Standard; and

(b)   disclose in the audit report the fact that the firm has applied APB Ethical Standard – Provisions Available for Small Entities.

4   (i)   In this Standard, for the UK a 'Small Entity' is:

   (a)   any company, which is not a UK listed company or an affiliate thereof, that qualifies as a small company under Section 382 of the Companies Act 2006;

   (b)   where group accounts are produced, any group that qualifies as small under Section 383 of the Companies Act 2006;

(c) any charity with an income of less than the turnover threshold applicable to small companies as identified in Section 382 of the Companies Act 2006;

(d) any pension fund with less than 100 members (including active, deferred and pensioner members)[1];

(e) any firm regulated by the FSA, which is not required to appoint an auditor in accordance with chapter 3 of the FSA Supervision Manual which forms a part of the FSA Handbook[2];

(f) any credit union which is a mutually owned financial co-operative established under the Credit Unions Act 1979 and the Industrial and Provident Societies Act 1965 (or equivalent legislation), which meets the criteria set out in (a) above;

(g) any entity registered under the Industrial and Provident Societies Act 1965, incorporated under the Friendly Societies Act 1992 or registered under the Friendly Societies Act 1974 (or equivalent legislation), which meets the criteria set out in (a) above;

(h) any registered social landlord with less than 250 units; and

(i) any other entity, such as a club, which would be a Small Entity if it were a company.

(ii) In this Standard, for the Republic of Ireland a 'Small Entity' is:

(a) any company, which is not an Irish listed company or an affiliate thereof, that meets two or more of the following requirements in both the current financial year and the preceding financial year:

- not more than €7.3 million turnover;

- not more than €3.65 million balance sheet total;

- not more than 50 employees.

(b) any charity with an income of less than €7.3 million;

(c) any pension fund with less than 1,000 members (including active, deferred and pensioner members)[3]; and

---

[1] In cases where a scheme with more than 100 members has been in wind-up over a number of years, such a scheme does not qualify as a Small Entity, even where the remaining number of members falls below 100.

[2] This relates to those firms that are not required to appoint an auditor under rule SUP 3.3.2R of the FSA Supervision Manual.

[3] In cases where a scheme with more than 1,000 members has been in wind-up over a number of years, such a scheme does not qualify as a Small Entity, even where the remaining number of members falls below 1,000.

(d) any other entity, such as a club or credit union, which would be a Small Entity if it were a company.

Where an entity falls into more than one of the above categories, it is only regarded as a 'Small Entity' if it meets the criteria of all relevant categories.

ALTERNATIVE PROVISIONS

ECONOMIC DEPENDENCE

5   **When auditing the financial statements of a Small Entity an audit firm is not required to comply with the requirement in APB Ethical Standard 4, paragraph 39 that an external independent quality control review is performed.**

6   APB Ethical Standard 4, paragraph 39 provides that, where it is expected that the total fees for both audit and non-audit services receivable from a non-listed audited entity and its subsidiaries audited by the audit firm will regularly exceed 10% of the annual fee income of the audit firm or the part of the firm by reference to which the audit engagement partner's profit share is calculated, but will not regularly exceed 15% the firm shall arrange an external independent quality control review of the audit engagement to be undertaken before the auditors' report is finalised. Although an external independent quality control review is not required, nevertheless the audit engagement partner discloses the expectation that fees will amount to between 10% and 15% of the firm's annual fee income to the Ethics Partner and to those charged with governance of the audited entity.

SELF-REVIEW THREAT – NON-AUDIT SERVICES

7   **When undertaking non-audit services for a Small Entity audited entity, the audit firm is not required to apply safeguards to address a self-review threat provided:**

(a) **the audited entity has 'informed management'; and**

(b) **the audit firm extends the cyclical inspection of completed engagements that is performed for quality control purposes.**

8   APB Ethical Standard 5 requires that, when an audit firm provides non-audit services to an audited entity, appropriate safeguards are applied in order to reduce any self-review threat to an acceptable level. APB Ethical Standard 5 provides examples of safeguards that may be appropriate when non-audit services are provided to an audited entity (for example in paragraphs 92 for tax services and 168 for accounting services). In the case of an audit of a Small Entity, alternative procedures involve discussions with 'informed management', supplemented by an extension of the firm's cyclical inspection of completed engagements that is performed for quality control purposes.

9 The audit firm extends the number of engagements inspected under the requirements of ISQC (UK and Ireland) 1 *'Quality Control for Firms that Perform Audits and Reviews of Financial Statements, and other Assurance and Related Services Engagements'*[4] to include a random selection of audit engagements where non-audit services have been provided. Particular attention is given to ensuring that there is documentary evidence that 'informed management' has made such judgments and decisions that are needed in relation to the presentation and disclosure of information in the financial statements.

10 Those inspecting the engagements are not involved in performing the engagement. Small audit firms may wish to use a suitably qualified external person or another firm to carry out engagement inspections.

11 In addition to the documentation requirements of ISQC (UK and Ireland) 1, those inspecting the engagements document their evaluation of whether the documentary evidence that 'informed management' made such judgments and decisions that were needed in relation to the presentation and disclosure of information in the financial statements.

EXEMPTIONS

MANAGEMENT THREAT – NON-AUDIT SERVICES

12 **When undertaking non-audit services for Small Entity audited entities, the audit firm is not required to adhere to the prohibitions in APB Ethical Standard 5, relating to providing non-audit services that involve the audit firm undertaking part of the role of management, provided that:**

(a) **it discusses objectivity and independence issues related to the provision of non-audit services with those charged with governance, confirming that management accept responsibility for any decisions taken; and**

(b) **it discloses the fact that it has applied this Standard in accordance with paragraph 24.**

13 APB Ethical Standard 5, paragraph 38 provides that where an audit firm provides non-audit services to an audited entity where there is no 'informed management', it is unlikely that any other safeguards can eliminate a management threat or reduce it to an acceptable level with the consequence that such non-audit services may not be provided to that audited entity. This is because the absence of a member of management, who has the authority and capability to:

• receive the results of the non-audit services provided by the audit firm; and

---

[4] ISQC (UK and Ireland) 1 requires audit firms to establish policies and procedures which include a periodic inspection of a selection of completed engagements. Engagements selected for inspection include at least one engagement for each engagement partner over the inspection cycle, which ordinarily spans no more than three years.

- make any judgments and decisions that are needed, on the basis of the information provided,

means that there is an increased management threat since the audit firm will be closer to those decisions and judgments which are properly the responsibility of management and more aligned with the views and interests of management.

14 An audit firm auditing a Small Entity is exempted from the requirements of APB Ethical Standard 5, paragraphs 63(b) (internal audit services), 73(b) (information technology services), 97 (tax services), 131(c) (corporate finance services), 140(b) (transaction related services), 145(a) (restructuring services) and 160(b) (accounting services) in circumstances when there is no 'informed management' as envisioned by APB Ethical Standard 5, provided it discusses objectivity and independence issues related to the provision of non-audit services with those charged with governance, confirming that management accept responsibility for any decisions taken and discloses the fact that it has applied this Standard in accordance with paragraph 24.

ADVOCACY THREAT – NON-AUDIT SERVICES

15 **The audit firm of a Small Entity is not required to comply with APB Ethical Standard 5, paragraphs 104 and 145(b) provided that it discloses the fact that it has applied this Standard in accordance with paragraph 24.**

16 APB Ethical Standard 5, paragraph 104 provides that 'the audit firm shall not undertake an engagement to provide tax services to an audited entity where this would involve acting as an advocate for the audited entity, before an appeals tribunal or court in the resolution of an issue:

(a) that is material to the financial statements; or

(b) where the outcome of the tax issue is dependent on a future or contemporary audit judgment'.

Such circumstances may create an advocacy threat which it is unlikely any safeguards can eliminate or reduce to an acceptable level.

17 APB Ethical Standard 5, paragraph 145(b) provides that 'the audit firm shall not undertake an engagement to provide restructuring services in respect of an audited entity where the engagement would require the auditor to act as an advocate for the entity in relation to matters that are material to the financial statements'.

18 Such circumstances may create an advocacy threat which it is unlikely any safeguards can eliminate or reduce to an acceptable level.

19 Where an audit firm auditing a Small Entity takes advantage of the dispensation in paragraph 15, it discloses the fact that it has applied this Standard in accordance with paragraph 24.

PARTNERS JOINING AN AUDITED ENTITY

20 **The audit firm of a Small Entity is not required to comply with APB Ethical Standard 2, paragraph 49 provided that:**

    (a) **it takes appropriate steps to determine that there has been no significant threat to the audit team's integrity, objectivity and independence; and**

    (b) **it discloses the fact that it has applied this Standard in accordance with paragraph 24.**

21 APB Ethical Standard 2, paragraph 49 provides that where a former partner 'is appointed as a director (including as a non-executive director) or to a key management position with an audited entity, having acted as audit engagement partner (or as an engagement quality control reviewer, key partner involved in the audit or a partner in the chain of command) at any time in the two years prior to this appointment, the firm shall resign as auditors. The firm shall not accept re-appointment until a two-year period, commencing when the former partner ceased to have an ability to influence the conduct and outcome of the audit, has elapsed or the former partner ceases employment with the former audited entity, whichever is the sooner'. Such circumstances may create self-interest, familiarity and intimidation threats.

22 An audit firm takes appropriate steps to determine that there has been no significant threat to the audit team's integrity, objectivity and independence as a result of the former partner's employment by an audited entity that is a Small Entity by:

    (a) assessing the significance of the self-interest, familiarity or intimidation threats, having regard to the following factors:

        • the position the individual has taken at the audited entity;

        • the nature and amount of any involvement the individual will have with the audit team or the audit process;

        • the length of time that has passed since the individual was a member of the audit team or firm; and

        • the former position of the individual within the audit team or firm, and

    (b) if the threat is other than clearly insignificant, applying alternative procedures such as:

        • considering the appropriateness or necessity of modifying the audit plan for the audit engagement;

        • assigning an audit team to the subsequent audit engagement that is of sufficient experience in relation to the individual who has joined the audited entity;

- involving an audit partner or senior staff member with appropriate expertise, who was not a member of the audit team, to review the work done or otherwise advise as necessary; or

- undertaking an engagement quality control review of the audit engagement.

23 When an audit firm auditing a Small Entity takes advantage of paragraph 20 it discloses the fact that it has applied this Standard in accordance with paragraph 24 and documents the steps that it has taken to comply with this Standard.

DISCLOSURE REQUIREMENTS

24 **Where the audit firm has taken advantage of an exemption provided in paragraphs 12, 15 or 20 of this Standard, the audit engagement partner shall ensure that:**

(a) **the auditor's report discloses this fact, and**

(b) **either the financial statements, or the auditor's report, discloses the type of non-audit services provided to the audited entity or the fact that a former audit engagement partner has joined the audited entity.**

25 The fact that an audit firm has taken advantage of an exemption from APB Ethical Standard – Provisions Available for Small Entities is set out in the auditor's report as part of the auditor's responsibilities paragraph. It does not affect the Opinion paragraph. An illustrative example of such disclosure is set out in the Appendix.

26 The audit engagement partner ensures that within the financial statements reference is made to the type of non-audit services provided to the audited entity or the fact that a former partner has joined the audited entity. An illustration of possible disclosures is set out in the Appendix. Where such a disclosure is not made within the financial statements it is included in the auditor's report.

EFFECTIVE DATE

27 This revised Ethical Standard becomes effective on 30 April 2011.

APPENDIX: Illustrative disclosures

(a) Illustrative disclosure of the fact that the audit firm has taken advantage of an exemption within the auditor's report

Respective responsibilities of directors and auditor

As explained more fully in the Directors' Responsibilities Statement [set out [on page ...]], the directors are responsible for the preparation of the financial statements and for being satisfied that they give a true and fair view. Our responsibility is to audit and express an opinion on the financial statements in accordance with applicable law and International Standards on Auditing (UK and Ireland). Those standards require us to comply with the Auditing Practices Board's (APB's) Ethical Standards for Auditors, including "APB Ethical Standard – Provisions Available for Small Entities (Revised)", in the circumstances set out in note [x] to the financial statements.

Scope of the audit of the financial statements

Either:

> A description of the scope of an audit of financial statements is [provided on the APB's website at ...] / [set out [on page ...] of the Annual Report].

Or:

> An audit involves obtaining evidence about the amounts and disclosures in the financial statements ...

Opinion on financial statements

In our opinion the financial statements:

- give a true and fair view of the state of the company's affairs as at ...and of its profit [loss] for the year then ended; ...

[Date of the auditor's report, *auditor's signature and* address]

(b) Illustrative disclosure of relevant circumstances within the financial statements

Note [x]   In common with many other businesses of our size and nature we use our auditors to prepare and submit returns to the tax authorities and assist with the preparation of the financial statements[5].

---

[5]   Where exemption in paragraph 12 (Management threat in relation non-audit services) is applied.

Note [x]   In common with many other businesses of our size and nature we use our auditors to provide tax advice and to represent us, as necessary, at tax tribunals[6].

Note [x]   XYZ, a former partner of [audit firm] joined [audited entity] as [a director] on [date][7].

---

[6]   Where exemption in paragraph 15 (Advocacy threat – tax services) is applied.
[7]   Where exemption in paragraph 20 (Partners joining an audited entity) is applied.

ETHICAL STANDARD FOR REPORTING ACCOUNTANTS

(Issued October 2006)

CONTENTS

PREFACE

The APB Ethical Standard for Reporting Accountants applies to all engagements:

- that are subject to the requirements of the Standards for Investment Reporting (SIRs), and

- which are in connection with an investment circular in which a report from the reporting accountant is to be published.

It should be read in the context of the Statement "The Financial Reporting Council – Scope and Authority of Audit and Assurance Pronouncements" which sets out the application and authority of APB Ethical Standards.

The terms used in the APB Ethical Standard for Reporting Accountants are explained in the Glossary of terms at Appendix 1.

SECTION 1

INTRODUCTION

1.1   APB Ethical Standards for Auditors require an auditor to be independent from the entity that it is appointed to audit. There is a substantial degree of similarity between an audit opinion and the nature of assurance provided by accountants reporting for the purposes of an investment circular prepared in accordance with the statutory or regulatory requirements of a recognised stock exchange. Accordingly, the Auditing Practices Board (APB) believes that users of investment circulars will expect an equivalent standard of independence of reporting accountants to that required of auditors.

1.2   This standard is based on the APB Ethical Standards for Auditors and applies to all engagements:

- that are subject to the requirements of the Standards for Investment Reporting (SIRs) issued by the APB, and

- which are in connection with an investment circular in which a report from the reporting accountant is to be published.

This standard applies to all public reporting engagements undertaken in accordance with the SIRs. It also applies to all private reporting engagements that are directly linked to such public reporting engagements.

1.3   Where a private reporting engagement is undertaken, but it is not intended that the reporting accountant will issue a public report, the reporting accountant follows the ethical guidance issued by the professional accountancy body of which the reporting accountant is a member. The APB is not aware of any significant instances where the relevant parts of the ethical guidance issued by professional accountancy bodies in the UK and Ireland are more restrictive than this standard.

1.4   An investment circular is a document issued by an entity pursuant to statutory or regulatory requirements relating to securities on which it is intended that a third party should make an investment decision, including a prospectus, listing particulars, a circular to shareholders or similar document.

1.5   Public confidence in the operation of the capital markets and in the conduct of public interest entities depends, in part, upon the credibility of the opinions and reports issued by reporting accountants in connection with investment circulars. Such credibility depends on beliefs concerning the integrity, objectivity and independence of reporting accountants and the quality of work they perform. The APB establishes quality control, investment reporting[1] and ethical standards to provide a framework for the practice of reporting accountants.

---

[1]   SIR 1000 paragraph 18 states *'In the conduct of an engagement involving an investment circular, the reporting accountant should comply with the applicable ethical standards issued by the Auditing Practices Board'*.

1.6   **Reporting Accountants should conduct an investment circular reporting engagement with integrity, objectivity and independence.**

Integrity

1.7   Integrity is a prerequisite for all those who act in the public interest. It is essential that reporting accountants act, and are seen to act, with integrity, which requires not only honesty but a broad range of related qualities such as fairness, candour, courage, intellectual honesty and confidentiality.

1.8   It is important that the directors and management of an engagement client can rely on the reporting accountant to treat the information obtained during an engagement as confidential, unless they have authorised its disclosure, it is already known to third parties or the reporting accountant has a legal right or duty to disclose it. Without this, there is a danger that the directors and management will fail to disclose such information to the reporting accountant and that the outcome of the engagement will thereby be impaired.

Objectivity

1.9   Objectivity is a state of mind that excludes bias, prejudice and compromise and that gives fair and impartial consideration to all matters that are relevant to the task in hand, disregarding those that are not. Objectivity requires that the reporting accountant's judgment is not affected by conflicts of interests. Like integrity, objectivity is a fundamental ethical principle.

1.10   The need for reporting accountants to be objective arises from the fact that the important issues involved in an engagement are likely to relate to questions of judgment rather than to questions of fact. For example, in relation to historical financial information included in an investment circular directors have to form a view as to whether it is necessary to make adjustments to previously published financial statements. If the directors, whether deliberately or inadvertently, make a biased judgment or an otherwise inappropriate decision, the financial information may be misstated or misleading.

1.11   It is against this background that reporting accountants are engaged to undertake an investment circular reporting engagement. The reporting accountant's objectivity requires that it expresses an impartial opinion in the light of all the available information and its professional judgment. Objectivity also requires that the reporting accountant adopts a rigorous and robust approach and is prepared to disagree, where necessary, with the directors' judgments.

Independence

1.12   Independence is freedom from situations and relationships which make it probable that a reasonable and informed third party would conclude that objectivity either is impaired or could be impaired. Independence is related to and underpins objectivity. However, whereas objectivity is a personal behavioural characteristic concerning the reporting accountant's state of mind, independence relates to the circumstances surrounding the engagement, including the financial, employment, business and personal relationships between the reporting accountant and its engagement client and other parties who are connected with the investment circular.

1.13 The need for independence arises because, in most cases, users of the financial information and other third parties do not have all the information necessary to assess whether reporting accountants are, in fact, objective. Although reporting accountants themselves may be satisfied that their objectivity is not impaired by a particular situation, a third party may reach a different conclusion. For example, if a third party were aware that the reporting accountant had certain financial, employment, business or personal relationships with the engagement client, that individual might reasonably conclude that the reporting accountant could be subject to undue influence from the engagement client or would not be impartial or unbiased. Public confidence in the reporting accountant's objectivity could therefore suffer as a result of this perception, irrespective of whether there is any actual impairment.

1.14 Accordingly, in evaluating the likely consequences of such situations and relationships, the test to be applied is not whether the reporting accountant considers that its objectivity is impaired but whether it is probable that a reasonable and informed third party would conclude that the reporting accountant's objectivity either is impaired or is likely to be impaired. There are inherent threats to the level of independence (both actual and perceived) that the reporting accountant can achieve as a result of the influence that the board of directors and management have over its appointment and remuneration. The reporting accountant considers the application of safeguards where there are threats to their independence (both actual and perceived).

COMPLIANCE WITH ETHICAL STANDARDS

1.15 **The reporting accountant should establish policies and procedures, appropriately documented and communicated, designed to ensure that, in relation to each investment circular reporting engagement, the firm, and all those who are in a position directly to influence the conduct and outcome of the investment circular reporting engagement, act with integrity, objectivity and independence.**

1.16 For the purposes of the APB Ethical Standard for Reporting Accountants, a person in a position directly to influence the conduct and outcome of the investment circular reporting engagement is:

(a) any person within the firm who is directly involved in the investment circular reporting engagement ('the engagement team'), including:

      (i)   the partners, managers and staff from assurance and other disciplines involved in the engagement (for example, taxation specialists, IT specialists, treasury management specialists, lawyers, actuaries);[2]

      (ii)   those who provide quality control or direct oversight of the engagement;

    (b)   any person within the firm who can directly influence the conduct and outcome of the investment circular reporting engagement through the provision of direct supervisory, management or other oversight of the engagement team in the context of the investment circular reporting engagement.

1.17   Because investment circulars may relate to transactions that are price sensitive and therefore confidential, the fact that a firm has been engaged to undertake an investment circular reporting engagement is likely to be known by only a limited number of individuals within the firm. For this reason, the requirements of this standard apply only to:

    (a)   individuals within the engagement team and those with a direct supervisory, management or other oversight responsibility for the engagement team who have actual knowledge of the investment circular reporting engagement; and

    (b)   where required by this Standard, the firm.

1.18   Compliance with the requirements regarding the reporting accountant's integrity, objectivity and independence is a responsibility of both the firm and of individual partners and professional staff. The firm establishes policies and procedures, appropriate to the size and nature of the firm, to promote and monitor compliance with those requirements by any person who is in a position directly to influence the conduct and outcome of the investment circular reporting engagement.[3]

1.19   **The leadership of the firm should take responsibility for establishing a control environment within the firm that places adherence to ethical principles and compliance with the APB Ethical Standard for Reporting Accountants above commercial considerations.**

1.20   The leadership of the firm influences the internal culture of the organisation by its actions and by its example ('the tone at the top'). Achieving a robust control environment requires that the leadership gives clear, consistent and frequent messages, backed up by appropriate actions, which emphasise the importance of compliance with the APB Ethical Standard for Reporting Accountants.

---

[2] Where external consultants are engaged by the reporting accountant and involved in the engagement, the reporting accountant should evaluate the objectivity of the expert in accordance with paragraphs 2.53 to 2.55 of this Standard.

[3] Monitoring of compliance with ethical requirements will often be performed as part of a broader quality control process. ISQC (UK & Ireland) 1 *'Quality Control for firms that perform audits and reviews of historical financial information and other assurance and related services engagements'* establishes the basic principles and essential procedures in relation to a firm's responsibilities for its system of quality control for engagements in connection with an investment circular.

1.21 In order to promote a strong control environment, the firm establishes policies and procedures (including the maintenance of appropriate records) that include:

(a) reporting by partners and staff as required by the APB Ethical Standard for Reporting Accountants of particular circumstances including:

- family and other personal relationships involving an engagement client of the firm;

- financial interests in an engagement client of the firm; and

- decisions to join an engagement client;

(b) monitoring of compliance with the firm's policies and procedures relating to integrity, objectivity and independence. Such monitoring procedures include, on a test basis, periodic review of the engagement partners' documentation of their consideration of the reporting accountant's objectivity and independence, addressing, for example:

- financial interests in engagement clients;

- contingent fee arrangements;

- economic dependence on clients;

- the performance of other service engagements for the engagement client;

(c) a mechanism for prompt communication of possible or actual breaches of the firm's policies and procedures to the relevant engagement partners;

(d) evaluation by engagement partners of the implications of any identified possible or actual breaches of the firm's policies and procedures that are reported to them;

(e) prohibiting members of the engagement team from making, or assuming responsibility for, management decisions for the engagement client;

(f) operation of an enforcement mechanism to promote compliance with policies and procedures; and

(g) empowerment of staff to communicate to senior levels within the firm any issue of objectivity or independence that concerns them; this includes establishing clear communication channels open to staff, encouraging staff to use these channels and ensuring that staff who use these channels are not subject to disciplinary proceedings as a result.

1.22 **Save where the circumstances contemplated in paragraph 1.24 apply, the firm should designate a partner in the firm ('the ethics partner'[4]) as having responsibility for:**

(a) **the adequacy of the firm's policies and procedures relating to integrity, objectivity and independence, their compliance with the APB Ethical Standard for Reporting Accountants, and the effectiveness of their communication to partners and staff within the firm; and**

(b) **providing related guidance to individual partners.**

1.23 In assessing the effectiveness of the firm's communication of its policies and procedures relating to integrity, objectivity and independence, ethics partners consider whether these matters are properly covered in induction programmes, professional training and continuing professional development for all partners and staff with direct involvement in investment circular reporting engagements. Ethics partners also provide guidance on matters referred to them and on matters which they otherwise become aware of, where a difficult and objective judgment needs to be made or a consistent position reached.

1.24 In firms with three or less partners, it may not be practicable for an ethics partner to be designated. In these circumstances all partners will regularly discuss ethical issues amongst themselves, so ensuring that they act in a consistent manner and observe the principles set out in the APB Ethical Standard for Reporting Accountants. In the case of a sole practitioner, advice on matters where a difficult and objective judgment needs to be made is obtained through the ethics helpline of their professional body, or through discussion with a practitioner from another firm. In all cases, it is important that such discussions are documented.

1.25 To be able to discharge his or her responsibilities, the ethics partner is an individual possessing seniority, relevant experience and authority within the firm and is provided with sufficient staff support and other resources, commensurate with the size of the firm. Alternative arrangements are established to allow for:

- the provision of guidance on those engagements where the ethics partner is the engagement partner; and

- situations where the ethics partner is unavailable, for example due to illness or holidays.

1.26 Whenever a possible or actual breach of the APB Ethical Standard for Reporting Accountants, or of policies and procedures established pursuant to the requirements of the APB Ethical Standard for Reporting Accountants, is identified, the engagement partner, in the first instance, and the ethics partner, where appropriate, assesses the implications of the breach, determines whether there are safeguards that can be put

---

[4] This individual may be the same person who is designated as the ethics partner for the purposes of the APB Ethical Standards for Auditors.

in place or other actions that can be taken to address any potential adverse consequences and considers whether there is a need to withdraw from the investment circular reporting engagement.

1.27 An inadvertent violation of this Standard does not necessarily call into question the firm's ability to undertake an investment circular reporting engagement, provided that:

(a) the firm has established policies and procedures that require all partners and staff to report any breach promptly to the engagement partner or to the ethics partner, as appropriate;

(b) the engagement partner or ethics partner promptly notifies the relevant partner or member of staff that any matter which has given rise to a breach is to be addressed as soon as possible and ensures that such action is taken;

(c) safeguards, where appropriate, are applied, (for example, having another partner review the work done by the relevant partner or member of staff or removing him or her from the engagement team); and

(d) the actions taken and the rationale for them are documented.

IDENTIFICATION AND ASSESSMENT OF THREATS

1.28 Reporting accountants identify and assess the circumstances, which could adversely affect their objectivity ('threats'), including any perceived loss of independence, and apply procedures ('safeguards'), which will either:

(a) eliminate the threat (for example, by eliminating the circumstances, such as removing an individual from the engagement team or disposing of a financial interest in the engagement client); or

(b) reduce the threat to an acceptable level; that is a level at which it is not probable that a reasonable and informed third party would conclude that the reporting accountant's objectivity is impaired or is likely to be impaired (for example, by having the work reviewed by another partner or by another firm).

When considering safeguards, where the engagement partner chooses to reduce rather than to eliminate a threat to objectivity and independence, he or she recognises that this judgment may not be shared by third parties and that he or she may be required to justify the decision.

Threats to objectivity and independence

1.29 The principal types of threats to the reporting accountant's objectivity and independence are:

- self-interest threat;

- self-review threat;

- management threat;

- advocacy threat;

- familiarity (or trust) threat; and

- intimidation threat.

1.30 A **self-interest threat** arises when reporting accountants have financial or other interests which might cause them to be reluctant to take actions that would be adverse to the interests of the firm or any individual in a position directly to influence the conduct or outcome of the engagement (for example, when the engagement partner has a financial interest in the company issuing the investment circular).

1.31 A **self-review threat** arises when the results of a service performed by the engagement team or others within the firm are reflected in the amounts included or disclosed in the financial information that is the subject of the investment circular reporting engagement (for example, when reporting in relation to an initial public offering for a company where the firm has been involved in maintaining the accounting records of that company). A threat to objectivity arises because, in the course of the investment circular reporting engagement, the reporting accountant may need to re-evaluate the work performed in the course of the other service previously provided by the firm. As, by virtue of providing the other service, the firm is associated with aspects of the financial information being reported upon, the reporting accountant may be (or may be perceived to be) unable to take an impartial view of relevant aspects of that financial information.

1.32 There is a self-review threat where a firm prepares an accountant's report on historical financial information which has been included in, or formed part of, financial statements which have already been subject to audit by the same firm. In such situations, where the two engagement teams are not completely independent of each other, the engagement partner evaluates the significance of the self-review threat created. If this is other than clearly insignificant, safeguards are applied, such as the appointment of an engagement quality control reviewer who has not been involved in the audit.

1.33 In assessing the significance of the self-review threat in relation to an investment circular reporting engagement, the reporting accountant considers the extent to which the other service will:

- involve a significant degree of subjective judgment; and

- have a material effect on the preparation and presentation of the financial information that is the subject of the investment circular reporting engagement.

1.34 Where a significant degree of subjective judgment relating to the financial information is involved in an other service engagement, the reporting accountant may be inhibited from questioning that judgment in the course of the investment circular reporting engagement. Whether a significant degree of subjective judgment is involved will depend upon whether the other service involves the application of well-established principles and procedures, and whether reliable information is available. If such circumstances do not exist because the other service is based on concepts, methodologies or assumptions that require judgment and are not established by the engagement client or by authoritative guidance, the reporting accountant's objectivity and the appearance of its independence may be adversely affected. Where the provision of the other service during the relevant period also has a material effect on the financial information that is the subject of the investment circular reporting engagement, it is unlikely that any safeguard can eliminate or reduce to an acceptable level the self-review threat.

1.35   A **management threat** arises when the firm undertakes work that involves making judgments and taking decisions, which are the responsibility of the management of the party responsible for issuing the investment circular containing the financial information or the party on whose financial information the firm is reporting (the engagement client) in relation to:

- the transaction (for example, where it has been working closely with a company in developing a divestment strategy); or

- the financial information that is the subject of the investment circular reporting engagement (for example, deciding on the assumptions to be used in a profit forecast).

A threat to objectivity and independence arises because, by making judgments and taking decisions that are properly the responsibility of management, the firm erodes the distinction between the engagement client and the reporting accountant. The firm may become closely aligned with the views and interests of management and this may, in turn, impair or call into question the reporting accountant's ability to apply a proper degree of professional scepticism in performing the investment circular reporting engagement. The reporting accountant's objectivity and independence therefore may be impaired, or may be perceived to be, impaired.

1.36   Factors to be considered in determining whether an other service does or does not give rise to a management threat include whether:

- the other service results in recommendations by the firm justified by objective and transparent analyses or the engagement client being given the opportunity to decide between reasonable alternatives;

- the reporting accountant is satisfied that a member of management (or senior employee) has been designated by the engagement client to receive the results of the other service and make any judgments and decisions that are needed; and

- that member of management has the capability to make independent management judgments and decisions on the basis of the information provided ('informed management').

1.37   Where there is 'informed management', the reporting accountant assesses whether there are safeguards that can be introduced that would be effective to avoid a management threat or to reduce it to a level at which it can be disregarded. Such safeguards would include the investment circular reporting engagement being provided by partners and staff who have no involvement in those other services. In the absence of 'informed management', it is unlikely that any safeguards can eliminate the management threat or reduce it to an acceptable level.

1.38   An **advocacy threat** arises when the firm undertakes work that involves acting as an advocate for an engagement client and supporting a position taken by management in an adversarial context (for example, by undertaking an active responsibility for the marketing of an entity's shares). In order to act in an advocacy role, the firm has to adopt a position closely aligned to that of management. This creates both actual and perceived threats to the reporting accountant's objectivity and independence. For example, where the firm, acting as advocate, has supported a particular contention of management, it may be difficult for the reporting accountant to take an impartial view of this in the context of its review of the financial information.

1.39   Where the provision of an other service would require the reporting accountant to act as an advocate for the engagement client in relation to matters that are material to the financial information that is the subject of the investment circular reporting engagement, it is unlikely that any safeguards can eliminate or reduce to an acceptable level the advocacy threat that would exist.

1.40   A **familiarity threat** arises when reporting accountants are predisposed to accept or are insufficiently questioning of the engagement client's point of view (for example, where they develop close personal relationships with client personnel through long association with the engagement client).

1.41   An **intimidation threat** arises when the conduct of reporting accountants is influenced by fear or threats (for example, where they encounter an aggressive and dominating party).

1.42   These categories may not be entirely distinct: certain circumstances may give rise to more than one type of threat. For example, where a firm wishes to retain the fee income from a large client, but encounters an aggressive and dominating individual, there may be a self-interest threat as well as an intimidation threat.

1.43   When identifying threats to objectivity and independence, reporting accountants consider circumstances and relationships with a number of different parties. The engagement client may constitute one or more parties, dependent on the circumstances of the transaction which is the subject of the investment circular[5]. Where the party responsible for issuing the investment circular is different from the party whose financial information is included in the investment circular, the reporting

---

[5]   For example, where a report on a target company's financial statements is included in the acquiring company's investment circular.

accountant makes an assessment of independence with respect to both these parties, applying the alternative procedures set out in paragraph 1.44 as necessary.

1.44 Where either:

- an investment circular reporting engagement is undertaken to provide a report on the financial information relating to an audit client but the reporting accountant's report is to be published in an investment circular issued by another entity that is not an audit client; or

- the reporting accountant's report is to be published in an investment circular issued by an audit client but the reporting accountant's report is on financial information relating to another entity that is not an audit client,

it may not be practicable in the time available to identify all relationships and other service engagements recently undertaken by the firm for the non-audit client and its significant affiliates. In such instances the reporting accountant undertakes those enquiries[6] that are practical in the time available into the relationships and other service engagements that the firm has with the non-audit client and, having regard to its obligations to maintain confidentiality, addresses any identified threats. Having done so, the reporting accountant discloses to those charged with governance of the issuing engagement client that a consideration of all known threats has been undertaken and, where appropriate, safeguards applied, but this does not constitute a full evaluation of all relationships and other services provided to the non-audit client.

1.45 **The firm should establish policies and procedures to require persons in a position directly to influence the conduct and outcome of the investment circular reporting engagement to be constantly alert to circumstances and relationships with:**

(a) **the engagement client, and**

(b) **other parties who are connected with the investment circular,**

that might reasonably be considered threats to their objectivity or the perceived loss of their independence, and, where such circumstances or relationships are identified, to report them to the engagement partner or to the ethics partner, as appropriate.

1.46 Such policies and procedures require that threats to the reporting accountant's objectivity and independence are communicated to the appropriate person, having regard to the nature of the threats and the part of the firm and the identity of any person involved. The consideration of all threats and the action taken is documented.

---

[6] For example, these enquiries are likely to include reviewing the list of engagements recorded in the firm's accounting systems and an enquiry of individuals within the firm who are responsible for maintaining such systems as to whether any confidentially coded engagements could be relevant.

If the engagement partner is personally involved, or if he or she is unsure about the action to be taken, the matter is resolved through consultation with the ethics partner.

1.47 In addition to considering independence in the context of the engagement client, the reporting accountant also considers relationships with other parties who are connected with the investment circular. These parties will include the sponsor or nominated advisor, other parties from whom, in accordance with the engagement letter, the reporting accountant takes instructions and other entities directly involved in the transaction which is the subject of the investment circular.[7] The reporting accountant considers the circumstances involved and uses judgment to assess whether it is probable that a reasonable and informed third party would conclude that the reporting accountant's objectivity either is impaired or is likely to be impaired as a result of relationships held with any of these parties.

1.48 In the case of established financial institutions or advisers, the reporting accountant may have extensive relationships with these parties, including for the provision of other services or the purchase of goods and services in the ordinary course of business. These relationships will not generally give rise to a significant threat to the reporting accountant's objectivity.

1.49 Relationships with other parties who are connected with the investment circular which are outside the ordinary course of business or which are material to any party are more likely to give rise to a significant threat to the reporting accountant's objectivity. Consideration of the threats to the reporting accountant's objectivity in relation to other entities will primarily be concerned with matters that could give rise to self-interest and intimidation threats, for example:

- where there is financial dependence on the relationship with the other party arising from fees (including any contingent element) for investment circular reporting engagements undertaken by the firm as a result of connections with the other parties;

- joint ventures or similar relationships with the other party or with a senior member of their management;

- significant purchases of goods or services which are not in the ordinary course of business or are not on an arm's length basis;

- personal relationships between engagement team members and individuals in senior positions within the other party; or

- large direct financial interests in, or loans made by, the other party.

---

[7] Where such entities are part of a complex group or corporate structure, the reporting accountant considers issues relating to the wider group and not just the entity directly involved in the transaction.

1.50 **The firm should establish policies and procedures to require the engagement partner to identify and assess the significance of threats to the reporting accountant's objectivity, including any perceived loss of independence:**

    (a) **when considering whether to accept an investment circular reporting engagement and planning the work to be undertaken;**

    (b) **when signing the report;**

    (c) **when considering whether the firm can accept or retain an engagement to provide other services to an engagement client during the relevant period; and**

    (d) **when potential threats are reported to him or her.**

1.51 An initial assessment of the threats to objectivity and independence is required when the engagement partner is considering whether to accept an investment circular reporting engagement and planning the engagement. At the end of the engagement, when reporting on the work undertaken but before issuing the report, the engagement partner draws an overall conclusion as to whether any threats to objectivity and independence have been properly addressed in accordance with the APB Ethical Standard for Reporting Accountants. If, at any time, the reporting accountant is invited to accept an engagement to provide other services to an engagement client for which the firm is undertaking an investment circular reporting engagement, the engagement partner considers the impact this new engagement may have on the reporting accountant's objectivity and independence.

1.52 When identifying and assessing threats to their objectivity and independence, reporting accountants take into account their current relationships with the engagement client (including other service engagements) and those that existed prior to the current engagement in the relevant period. The relevant period covers the period during which the engagement is undertaken and any additional period before the engagement period but subsequent to the balance sheet date of the most recent audited financial statements[8]. This is because those prior relationships may be perceived as likely to influence the reporting accountant in the performance of the investment circular reporting engagement or as otherwise impairing the reporting accountant's objectivity and independence.

1.53 A firm's procedures will include reference to records of past and current engagements whenever a new investment circular reporting engagement is proposed.

1.54 Where the engagement client or a third party calls into question the objectivity and independence of the firm in relation to a particular client, the ethics partner carries out such investigations as may be appropriate.

---

[8] In the case of newly incorporated clients (not part of an established group of companies), where there has been no financial statement audit, this period is from the date of incorporation.

IDENTIFICATION AND ASSESSMENT OF SAFEGUARDS

1.55 **If the engagement partner identifies threats to the reporting accountant's objectivity, including any perceived loss of independence, he or she should identify and assess the effectiveness of the available safeguards and apply such safeguards as are sufficient to eliminate the threats or reduce them to an acceptable level.**

1.56 The nature and extent of safeguards to be applied depend on the significance of the threats. Where a threat is clearly insignificant, no safeguards are needed.

1.57 Sections 2 and 3 of this Standard address specific circumstances which can create threats to the reporting accountant's objectivity or loss of independence. They give examples of safeguards that can, in some circumstances, eliminate the threat or reduce it to an acceptable level. In circumstances where this is not possible, either the reporting accountant does not accept (or withdraws from) the investment circular reporting engagement or, in the case of threats arising from the current provision of other services, does not undertake the engagement to provide the other service.

1.58 **The engagement partner should not accept or should not continue an investment circular reporting engagement if he or she concludes that any threats to the reporting accountant's objectivity and independence cannot be reduced to an acceptable level.**

1.59 If during the conduct of the investment circular reporting engagement the engagement partner becomes aware of a threat and concludes that it cannot be reduced to an acceptable level, the firm withdraws immediately from the engagement, save in circumstances where a reasonable and informed third party would regard ceasing to act as the reporting accountant would be contrary to the public interest. In such cases withdrawal from the investment circular reporting engagement may not be appropriate. The firm discloses on a timely basis full details of the position to those charged with governance of the issuing engagement client and those the reporting accountant is instructed to advise, as set out in paragraphs 1.68 to 1.76, and establishes appropriate safeguards.

ENGAGEMENT QUALITY CONTROL REVIEW

1.60 Paragraph 22 of SIR 1000 requires the reporting accountant to comply with applicable standards and guidance set out in ISQC (UK and Ireland) 1 *'Quality control for firms that perform audits and reviews of historical financial information and other assurance and related services engagements'* and ISA (UK and Ireland) 220 *'Quality control for audits of historical financial information'*. This includes the appointment of an engagement quality control reviewer for all public reporting engagements.

1.61 **The engagement quality control reviewer should:**

   (a) consider the firm's compliance with the APB Ethical Standard for Reporting Accountants in relation to the investment circular reporting engagement;

(b) form an independent opinion as to the appropriateness and adequacy of the safeguards applied; and

(c) consider the adequacy of the documentation of the engagement partner's consideration of the reporting accountant's objectivity and independence.

1.62 The requirements of paragraph 1.61 supplement the requirements relating to the engagement quality control review established by ISA (UK and Ireland) 220. The engagement quality control reviewer will be a partner or other person performing the function of a partner who is not otherwise involved in the engagement. The experience required of the engagement quality control reviewer is determined by the nature of the engagement and the seniority and experience of the engagement partner.

OVERALL CONCLUSION

1.63 **At the end of the investment circular reporting engagement, when reporting on the work undertaken but before issuing the report, the engagement partner should reach an overall conclusion that any threats to objectivity and independence have been properly addressed in accordance with the APB Ethical Standard for Reporting Accountants. If the engagement partner cannot make such a conclusion, he or she should not report and the firm should withdraw from the investment circular reporting engagement.**

1.64 If the engagement partner remains unable to conclude that any threat to objectivity and independence has been properly addressed in accordance with the APB Ethical Standard for Reporting Accountants, or if there is a disagreement between the engagement partner and the engagement quality control reviewer, he or she consults the ethics partner.

1.65 In concluding on compliance with the requirements for objectivity and independence, the engagement partner is entitled to rely on the completeness and accuracy of the data developed by the firm's systems relating to independence (for example, in relation to the reporting of financial interests by staff), unless informed otherwise by the firm.

OTHER ACCOUNTANTS INVOLVED IN AN INVESTMENT CIRCULAR REPORTING ENGAGEMENT

1.66 **The engagement partner should be satisfied that other accountants (whether a network firm or another firm) involved in the investment circular reporting engagement, who are not subject to the APB Ethical Standard for Reporting Accountants, are objective and document the rationale for that conclusion.**

1.67 The engagement partner obtains written confirmation from the other accountants that they have a sufficient understanding of and have complied with the applicable provisions of the IESBA Code of Ethics for Professional Accountants, including the independence requirements.[9]

COMMUNICATION WITH THOSE CHARGED WITH GOVERNANCE

1.68 **The engagement partner should ensure that those charged with governance of the issuing engagement client, and any other persons or entities the reporting accountant is instructed to advise, are appropriately informed on a timely basis of all significant facts and matters that bear upon the reporting accountant's objectivity and independence.**

1.69 Those charged with governance of the issuing engagement client are responsible for oversight of the relationship between the reporting accountant and the entity and of the conduct of the investment circular reporting engagement. This group therefore has a particular interest in being informed about the reporting accountant's ability to report objectively on the engagement.

1.70 The aim of these communications by the reporting accountant is to ensure full and fair disclosure to those charged with governance of the issuing engagement client and to those from whom, in accordance with the engagement letter, the reporting accountant takes instructions of matters in which they have an interest.

1.71 It may be that all of the parties to the engagement letter wish to be informed about all significant facts and matters that bear upon the reporting accountant's objectivity and independence. In other cases, however, the parties to the engagement letter (other than the engagement client) may not wish to be directly involved and may appoint one or more of their number to review these matters on their behalf. At the time of appointment, the reporting accountant ensures that it is clear in the engagement letter to whom these communications are provided. If no such provision is included in the engagement letter, the reporting accountant will make disclosures to all those from whom, in accordance with the engagement letter, the reporting accountant takes instructions.

1.72 Matters communicated will generally include the key elements of the engagement partner's consideration of objectivity and independence, such as:

- the principal threats, if any, to objectivity and independence identified by the reporting accountant, including consideration of relationships between the firm and:

---

[9] The IESBA Code of Ethics for Professional Accountants (the IESBA Code) establishes a conceptual framework for ethical requirements for professional accountants and includes independence requirements for assurance engagements. No Member Body of IFAC is allowed to apply less stringent standards than those stated in the IESBA Code. In addition, members of the IFAC Forum of Firms have agreed to apply ethical standards, which are at least as rigorous as those of the IESBA Code.

      –   the engagement client, its affiliates and directors, and

      –   the sponsor and such other parties from whom the reporting accountant takes instructions, and

      –   other entities directly involved in the transaction which is the subject of the investment circular;

- any safeguards adopted and the reasons why they are considered to be effective;

- the considerations of the engagement quality control review;

- the overall assessment of threats and safeguards;

- information about the general policies and processes within the firm for maintaining objectivity and independence.

1.73   The reporting accountant, as a minimum:

    (a)   discloses in writing to those charged with governance of the issuing engagement client, and any other persons or entities the reporting accountant is instructed to advise:

        (i)   details of all relationships that the reporting accountant considers may reasonably be thought to bear on the objectivity and independence of the reporting accountant,[10] having regard to its relationships with the engagement client, its directors and senior management and its affiliates;

        (ii)   details of all relationships that the reporting accountant considers give rise to a threat to its objectivity between the reporting accountant and:

           - the sponsor and such other parties from whom the reporting accountant takes instructions[11];

           - other entities directly involved in the transaction which is the subject of the investment circular;

        (iii)   whether the total amount of fees that the reporting accountant is likely to charge to the engagement client and its significant affiliates for the provision of services relating to the transaction which is the subject of the

---

[10] Relationships include significant services previously provided by the firm and network firms involved in the investment circular reporting engagement to the engagement client and its significant affiliates. In considering the significance of such services the reporting accountant takes into account whether those services have been the subject of independent review after they were provided.

[11] Where a party to the engagement letter is an established financial institution or adviser, a generic disclosure that the firm has extensive relationships entered into in the ordinary course of business with these parties is sufficient with specific disclosure only being made in the case of relationships which are outside the ordinary course of business or which are material to any party.

investment circular during the relevant period is greater than 5% of the fee income of the firm in the relevant period or the part of the firm by reference to which the engagement partner's profit share is calculated during the relevant period; and

(iv) the related safeguards that are in place;

(b) confirms in writing that:

(i) it complies with the APB Ethical Standard for Reporting Accountants and that it is independent and its objectivity is not compromised, and

(ii) where relevant, the circumstances contemplated in paragraph 1.44 exist and a consideration of all known threats and safeguards has been undertaken, but this does not constitute a full evaluation of all business relationships and other services provided to the entity.

1.74 The reporting accountant seeks to discuss these matters with those charged with governance of the issuing engagement client and those others the reporting accountant is instructed to advise.

1.75 The most appropriate time for final confirmation of such matters is usually at the conclusion of the investment circular reporting engagement. However, communications between the reporting accountant and those charged with governance of the issuing engagement client and those others the reporting accountant is instructed to advise will also be needed at the planning stage and whenever significant judgments are made about threats to objectivity and independence and the appropriateness of safeguards put in place, for example, when accepting an engagement to provide other services.

1.76 Transparency is a key element in addressing the issues raised by the provision of other services by reporting accountants to their clients. This can be facilitated by timely communication with those charged with governance of the issuing engagement client. In the case of companies that are seeking a listing, ensuring that the audit committee is properly informed about the issues associated with the provision of other services will assist the audit committee to comply on an ongoing basis with the provisions of the Combined Code on Corporate Governance[12] relating to reviewing and monitoring the external auditors' independence and objectivity.

DOCUMENTATION

1.77 **The engagement partner should ensure that his or her consideration of the reporting accountant's objectivity and independence is appropriately documented on a timely basis.**

---

[12] Provision C.3.2 provides that 'the main role and responsibilities of the audit committee should be set out in written terms of reference and should include ... to develop and implement a policy on the engagement of the external auditor to supply non-audit services ...'

1.78 The requirement to document these issues contributes to the clarity and rigour of the engagement partner's thinking and the quality of his or her judgments. In addition, such documentation provides evidence that the engagement partner's consideration of the reporting accountant's objectivity and independence was properly performed and provides the basis for the engagement quality control review.

1.79 Matters to be documented include all key elements of the process and any significant judgments concerning:

- threats identified (in relation to the engagement client, those from whom, in accordance with the engagement letter, the reporting accountant takes instructions and other entities directly involved in the transaction which is the subject of the investment circular) and the process used in identifying them;

- safeguards adopted and the reasons why they are considered to be effective;

- the engagement quality control review;

- overall assessment of threats and safeguards; and

- communication with those charged with governance of the issuing engagement client and those others the reporting accountant is instructed to advise.

SECTION 2 – SPECIFIC CIRCUMSTANCES CREATING THREATS TO A REPORTING ACCOUNTANT'S OBJECTIVITY AND INDEPENDENCE

INTRODUCTION

2.1   Paragraphs 1.50 and 1.55 require the engagement partner to identify and assess the circumstances which could adversely affect the reporting accountant's objectivity ('threats'), including any perceived loss of independence, and to apply procedures ('safeguards') which will either:

(a)   eliminate the threat; or

(b)   reduce the threat to an acceptable level (that is, a level at which it is not probable that a reasonable and informed third party would conclude that the reporting accountant's objectivity and independence is impaired or is likely to be impaired).

When considering safeguards, where the engagement partner chooses to reduce rather than to eliminate a threat to objectivity and independence, he or she recognises that this judgment may not be shared by third parties and that he or she may be required to justify the decision.

2.2   This section of the APB Ethical Standard for Reporting Accountants provides requirements and guidance on specific circumstances arising out of relationships with the engagement client, which may create threats to the reporting accountant's objectivity or a perceived loss of independence. It gives examples of safeguards that can, in some circumstances, eliminate the threat or reduce it to an acceptable level. In circumstances where this is not possible, either the relationship in question is not entered into or the reporting accountant either does not accept or withdraws from the investment circular reporting engagement, as appropriate.

FINANCIAL RELATIONSHIPS

General considerations

2.3   A financial interest is an interest in an equity or other security, debenture, loan or other debt instrument of an entity, including rights and obligations to acquire such an interest and derivatives directly related to such an interest.

2.4   Financial interests may be:

•   owned directly, rather than through intermediaries (a 'direct financial interest'); or

•   owned through intermediaries, for example, an open ended investment company or a pension scheme (an 'indirect financial interest').

2.5 **Where a firm is engaged to undertake an investment circular reporting engagement for a client, the firm, a person in a position directly to influence the conduct and outcome of the investment circular reporting engagement or an immediate family member of such a person should not hold during the engagement period:**

    (a) **any direct financial interest in the engagement client or an affiliate of the engagement client; or**

    (b) **any indirect financial interest in the engagement client or an affiliate of the engagement client, where the investment is material to the firm or the individual and to the intermediary; or**

    (c) **any indirect financial interest in the engagement client or an affiliate of the engagement client, where the person holding it has both:**

        (i) **the ability to influence the investment decisions of the intermediary; and**

        (ii) **actual knowledge of the existence of the underlying investment in the engagement client.**

2.6 The threats to the reporting accountant's objectivity and independence, where a direct financial interest or a material indirect financial interest in the engagement client is held by the firm or by one of the individuals specified in paragraph 2.5 are such that no safeguards can eliminate them or reduce them to an acceptable level. If the existence of the transaction which is connected with the investment circular is price sensitive information then disposal of the financial interest may not be possible and the firm either does not accept the engagement or the relevant individuals are not included in the engagement team. Where a partner with one of the financial interests specified normally has direct supervisory or management responsibility over the engagement team, he or she is excluded from this responsibility for the purposes of the particular investment circular reporting engagement.

2.7 Where one of the financial interests specified in paragraph 2.5 is held by:

    (a) *the firm:* the entire financial interest is disposed of, a sufficient amount of an indirect financial interest is disposed of so that the remaining interest is no longer material, or the firm does not accept (or withdraws from) the investment circular reporting engagement;

    (b) *a person in a position directly to influence the conduct and outcome of the investment circular reporting engagement:* the entire financial interest is disposed of, a sufficient amount of an indirect financial interest is disposed of so that the remaining interest is no longer material, or that person does not retain a position in which they exert such direct influence on the investment circular reporting engagement;

(c) *an immediate family member of a person in a position directly to influence the conduct and outcome of the investment circular reporting engagement:* the entire financial interest is disposed of, a sufficient amount of an indirect financial interest is disposed of so that the remaining interest is no longer material, or the person in a position directly to influence the conduct and outcome of the investment circular reporting engagement does not retain a position in which they exert such direct influence on the investment circular reporting engagement.

2.8 Where the firm or one of the individuals specified in paragraph 2.5 holds an indirect financial interest but does not have both:

(a) the ability to influence the investment decisions of the intermediary; and

(b) actual knowledge of the existence of the underlying investment in the engagement client,

there may not be a threat to the reporting accountant's objectivity and independence. For example, where the indirect financial interest takes the form of an investment in a pension fund, the composition of the funds and the size and nature of any underlying investment in the engagement client may be known but there is unlikely to be any influence on investment decisions, as the fund will generally be managed independently on a discretionary basis. In the case of an 'index tracker' fund, the investment in the engagement client is determined by the composition of the relevant index and there may be no threat to objectivity. As long as the person holding the indirect interest is not directly involved in an investment circular reporting engagement involving the intermediary, nor able to influence the individual investment decisions of the intermediary, any threat to the reporting accountant's objectivity and independence may be regarded as insignificant.

2.9 Where the firm or one of the individuals specified in paragraph 2.5 holds a beneficial interest in a properly operated 'blind' trust, they are (by definition) completely unaware of the identity of the underlying investments. If these include an investment in the engagement client, this means that they are unaware of the existence of an indirect financial interest. In these circumstances, there is no threat to the reporting accountant's objectivity and independence.

2.10 **Where a person in a position directly to influence the conduct and outcome of the investment circular reporting engagement becomes aware that a close family member holds one of the financial interests specified in paragraph 2.5, that individual should report the matter to the engagement partner to take appropriate action. If it is a close family member of the engagement partner, or if the engagement partner is in doubt as to the action to be taken, the engagement partner should resolve the matter through consultation with the ethics partner.**

Financial interests held as trustee

2.11 Where a direct or an indirect financial interest in the engagement client or its affiliates is held in a trustee capacity by a person in a position directly to influence the conduct and outcome of the investment circular reporting engagement, or an immediate family member of such a person, a self-interest threat may be created because either the existence of the trustee interest may influence the conduct of the investment circular reporting engagement or the trust may influence the actions of the engagement client. Accordingly, such a trustee interest is only held when:

- the relevant person is not an identified potential beneficiary of the trust; and

- the financial interest held by the trust in the engagement client is not material to the trust; and

- the trust is not able to exercise significant influence over the engagement client or an affiliate of the engagement client; and

- the relevant person does not have significant influence over the investment decisions made by the trust, in so far as they relate to the financial interest in the engagement client.

2.12 Where it is not clear whether the financial interest held by the trust in the engagement client is material to the trust or whether the trust is able to exercise significant influence over the engagement client, the financial interest is reported to the ethics partner, so that a decision can be made as to the steps that need to be taken.

Financial interests held by firm pension schemes

2.13 Where the pension scheme of a firm has a financial interest in an engagement client or its affiliates and the firm has any influence over the trustees' investment decisions (other than indirect strategic and policy decisions), the self-interest threat created is such that no safeguards can eliminate it or reduce it to an acceptable level. In other cases (for example, where the pension scheme invests through a collective investment scheme and the firm's influence is limited to investment policy decisions, such as the allocation between different categories of investment), the ethics partner considers the acceptability of the position, having regard to the materiality of the financial interest to the pension scheme.

Loans and guarantees

2.14 Where reporting accountants, persons in a position directly to influence the conduct and outcome of the investment circular reporting engagement or immediate family members of such persons:

(a) accept a loan[13] or a guarantee of their borrowings from an engagement client; or

(b) make a loan to or guarantee the borrowings of an engagement client,

---

[13] For the purpose of this standard, the term 'loan' does not include ordinary trade credit arrangements or deposits placed for goods or services (see paragraph 2.20).

a self-interest threat and an intimidation threat to the reporting accountant's objectivity can be created or there may be a perceived loss of independence. No safeguards can eliminate this threat or reduce it to an acceptable level.

2.15 **The firm, persons in a position directly to influence the conduct and outcome of the investment circular reporting engagement and immediate family members of such persons should not during the engagement period have a loan outstanding to, or guarantee the borrowings of, an engagement client or its affiliates unless this represents a deposit made with a bank or similar deposit taking institution in the ordinary course of business and on normal business terms.**

2.16 **The firm should not during the engagement period have a loan from, or have its borrowings guaranteed by, the engagement client or its affiliates unless:**

(a) **the engagement client is a bank or similar deposit taking institution; and**

(b) **the loan or guarantee is made in the ordinary course of business on normal business terms; and**

(c) **the loan or guarantee is not material to both the firm and the engagement client.**

2.17 **Persons in a position directly to influence the conduct and outcome of the investment circular reporting engagement and immediate family members of such persons should not during the engagement period have a loan from, or have their borrowings guaranteed by, the engagement client or its affiliates unless:**

(a) **the engagement client is a bank or similar deposit taking institution; and**

(b) **the loan or guarantee is made in the ordinary course of business on normal business terms; and**

(c) **the loan or guarantee is not material to the engagement client.**

2.18 Loans by an engagement client that is a bank or similar institution to a person in a position directly to influence the conduct and outcome of the investment circular reporting engagement, or an immediate family member of such a person (for example, home mortgages, bank overdrafts or car loans), do not create an unacceptable threat to objectivity and independence, provided that normal business terms apply. However, where such loans are in arrears by a significant amount, this creates an intimidation threat that is unacceptable. Where such a situation arises, the person in a position directly to influence the conduct and outcome of the investment circular reporting engagement reports the matter to the engagement partner, or to the ethics partner, as appropriate and ceases to have any involvement with the investment circular reporting engagement. The engagement partner or, where appropriate, the ethics partner considers whether any work is to be reperformed.

BUSINESS RELATIONSHIPS

2.19 A business relationship between:

    (a) the firm or a person who is in a position directly to influence the conduct and outcome of the investment circular reporting engagement, or an immediate family member of such a person, and

    (b) the engagement client or its affiliates, or its management

involves the two parties having a common commercial interest. Business relationships may create self-interest, advocacy or intimidation threats to the reporting accountant's objectivity and perceived loss of independence. Examples include:

- joint ventures with the engagement client or with a director, officer or other individual who performs senior managerial functions for the client;

- arrangements to combine one or more services or products of the firm with one or more services or products of the engagement client and to market the package with reference to both parties;

- distribution or marketing arrangements under which the firm acts as a distributor or marketer of any of the engagement client's products or services, or the engagement client acts as the distributor or marketer of any of the products or services of the firm;

- other commercial transactions, such as the firm leasing its office space from the engagement client.

Subject to the alternative procedures outlined in paragraphs 1.44, a firm will identify all business relationships entered into by the firm, persons in a position directly to influence the conduct and outcome of the investment circular reporting engagement, or an immediate family member of such a person.

2.20 **Where a firm is engaged to undertake an investment circular reporting engagement for a client, the firm, persons in a position directly to influence the conduct and outcome of the investment circular reporting engagement and immediate family members of such persons should not have business relationships with the engagement client, its management or its affiliates during the relevant period except where they:**

- **are entered into in the ordinary course of business and are clearly trivial; or**

- **involve the purchase of goods and services from the firm or the engagement client in the ordinary course of business and on an arm's length basis.**

2.21 Where a business relationship exists, that is not permitted under paragraph 2.20, and has been entered into by:

(a) *the firm:* either the relationship is terminated before the start of the relevant period or the firm does not accept (or withdraws from) the investment circular reporting engagement;

(b) *a person in a position directly to influence the conduct and outcome of the investment circular reporting engagement:* either the relationship is terminated before the start of the relevant period or that person does not retain a position in which they exert such direct influence on the investment circular reporting engagement[14];

(c) *an immediate family member of a person in a position directly to influence the conduct and outcome of the investment circular reporting engagement:* either the relationship is terminated before the start of the relevant period or that person does not retain a position in which they exert such direct influence on the investment circular reporting engagement[14].

2.22 **Where a person in a position directly to influence the conduct and outcome of the investment circular reporting engagement becomes aware that a close family member has one of the business relationships specified in paragraph 2.20, that individual should report the matter to the engagement partner to take appropriate action. If it is a close family member of the engagement partner or if the engagement partner is in doubt as to the action to be taken, the engagement partner should resolve the matter through consultation with the ethics partner.**

2.23 Where there are doubts as to whether a transaction or series of transactions are either in the ordinary course of business or on an arm's length basis, the engagement partner reports the issue to the ethics partner, so that a decision can be made as to the appropriate action that needs to be taken to ensure that the matter is resolved.

2.24 **A firm should not act as reporting accountant to any entity or person able to influence the affairs of the firm or the performance of any investment circular reporting engagement undertaken by the firm.**

2.25 This prohibition applies to:

(a) any entity that owns any significant part of a firm, or is an affiliate of such an entity; or

(b) any shareholder, director or other person in a position to direct the affairs of such an entity or its affiliate.

---

[14] If the existence of the transaction which is connected with the investment circular is price sensitive information then termination of the business relationship may not be possible and the firm either does not accept the engagement or the relevant individuals are not included in the engagement team. Where a partner with one of the business relationships specified normally has direct supervisory or management responsibility over the engagement team, he or she is excluded from this responsibility for the purposes of the particular investment circular reporting engagement.

A significant ownership is one that carries the ability materially to influence the policy of an entity.[15]

EMPLOYMENT RELATIONSHIPS

MANAGEMENT ROLE WITH ENGAGEMENT CLIENT

2.26 **A firm undertaking an investment circular reporting engagement should not have as a partner or employ a person in a position directly to influence the conduct and outcome of the investment circular reporting engagement any person who is also employed by the engagement client or its affiliates ('dual employment').**

Loan staff assignments

2.27 **A reporting accountant should not enter into an agreement with an engagement client to provide a partner or employee to work for a temporary period as if that individual were an employee of the engagement client or its affiliates (a 'loan staff assignment') during the relevant period or for a period of one year before it, unless the client:**

   (a) **agrees that the individual concerned will not hold a management position in relation to the transaction or the financial information that is the subject of the investment circular reporting engagement, and**

   (b) **acknowledges its responsibility for directing and supervising the work to be performed, which will not include such matters as:**

   • **making management decisions; or**

   • **exercising discretionary authority to commit the engagement client to a particular position or accounting treatment.**

2.28 Where a firm agrees to assist an engagement client by providing loan staff, threats to objectivity and independence may be created. A management threat may arise if the employee undertakes work that involves making judgments and taking decisions that are properly the responsibility of management of the engagement client in relation to the transaction or the financial information that is the subject of the investment circular reporting engagement. Thus, for example, interim management arrangements involving participation in the financial reporting function involved in producing the financial information that is the subject of the investment circular reporting engagement are not acceptable.

---

[15] For companies, competition authorities have generally treated a 15% shareholding as sufficient to provide a material ability to influence policy.

2.29   A self-review threat may also arise if the individual, during the loan staff assignment, is in a position directly to influence the preparation of the engagement client's financial information and then, on completion of that assignment, is assigned to the engagement team for that client.

2.30   **Where a partner or employee returns to the firm on completion of a loan staff assignment, that individual should not be given any role on an investment circular reporting engagement for the engagement client which involves a review of, or any work in relation to, any function or activity that he or she performed or supervised during that assignment.**

2.31   In considering for how long this restriction is to be observed, the need to realise the potential value to the effectiveness of the investment circular reporting engagement of the increased knowledge of the client's business gained through the assignment has to be weighed against the potential threats to objectivity and independence. Those threats increase with the length of the assignment and with the intended level of responsibility of the individual within the engagement team. As a minimum, this restriction will apply to at least the period until an audit has been undertaken of the financial statements following the completion of the loan staff assignment.

Partners and engagement team members joining an engagement client

2.32   **Where a former partner in the firm joins the engagement client, the firm should take action before any further work is done by the firm in connection with the investment circular reporting engagement to ensure that no significant connections remain between the firm and the individual.**

2.33   Ensuring that no significant connections remain between the firm and the individual requires that:

- all capital balances and similar financial interests be fully settled (including retirement benefits) unless these are made in accordance with pre-determined arrangements that cannot be influenced by any remaining connections between the individual and the firm; and

- the individual does not participate or appear to participate in the firm's business or professional activities.

2.34   **Reporting accountants should establish policies and procedures that require:**

   (a)   **senior members of the engagement team to notify the firm of any situation involving their potential employment with the engagement client; and**

   (b)   **other members of the engagement team to notify the firm of any situation involving their probable employment with the engagement client; and**

   (c)   **anyone who has given such notice to be removed from the engagement team; and**

(d) **a review of the work performed by the resigning or former engagement team member in relation to the investment circular reporting engagement.**

2.35 Objectivity and independence may be threatened where a director, an officer or an employee of the engagement client who is in a position to exert direct and significant influence over the preparation of the financial information has recently been a partner in the firm or a member of an engagement team. Such circumstances may create self-interest, familiarity and intimidation threats, particularly when significant connections remain between the individual and the firm. Similarly, objectivity and independence may be threatened when an individual knows, or has reason to believe that he or she will or may be joining the engagement client at some time in the future.

2.36 Where a partner in the firm or a member of the engagement team for a particular client has left the firm and taken up employment with that client, the significance of the self-interest, familiarity and intimidation threats is assessed and normally depends on such factors as:

- the position that individual had in an engagement team or the firm;

- the position that individual has taken at the engagement client;

- the amount of involvement that individual will have with the engagement team (especially where it includes former colleagues with whom he or she worked);

- the length of time since that individual was a member of an engagement team or employed by the firm.

Following the assessment of any such threats, appropriate safeguards are applied where necessary.

2.37 Any review of work is performed by a more senior professional. If the individual joining the engagement client is a partner, the review is performed by a partner who is not involved in the engagement. Where, due to its size, the firm does not have a partner who was not involved in the engagement, it seeks either a review by another firm or advice from its professional body.

2.38 **Where a partner leaves the firm and is appointed as a director (including as a non-executive director) or to a key management position with an engagement client, having acted as an audit engagement partner, engagement quality control reviewer, key audit partner, reporting accountant or a partner in the chain of command at any time in the two years prior to such appointment, the firm should not accept an appointment as reporting accountant for a period of two years commencing when the former partner ceased to act for the engagement client or the former partner ceases employment with the engagement client, whichever is the sooner.**

2.39 **Where a partner (other than as specified in paragraph 2.38) or an employee joins the engagement client as a director (including as a non-executive director)** or in a key management position, the firm should consider whether the composition of the engagement team is appropriate.

2.40 In such circumstances, the firm evaluates the appropriateness of the composition of the engagement team by reference to the factors listed in paragraph 2.36 and alters or strengthens the team to address any threat to the reporting accountant's objectivity and independence that may be identified.

Family members employed by an engagement client

2.41 Where a person in a position directly to influence the conduct and outcome of the investment circular reporting engagement becomes aware that an immediate or close family member is employed by the engagement client in a position to exercise influence on the accounting records or financial information, that individual should either:

(a) in the case of an immediate family member, cease to hold a position in which they exert such direct influence on the investment circular reporting engagement; or

(b) in the case of a close family member, report the matter to the engagement partner to take appropriate action. If it is a close family member of the engagement partner or if the engagement partner is in doubt as to the action to be taken, the engagement partner should resolve the matter in consultation with the ethics partner.

GOVERNANCE ROLE WITH ENGAGEMENT CLIENT

2.42 A firm that undertakes an investment circular reporting engagement should not have as a partner or employ a person who during the engagement period is:

(a) on the board of directors of the engagement client;

(b) on any subcommittee of that board; or

(c) in such a position in an entity which holds directly or indirectly more than 20% of the voting rights in the engagement client, or in which the engagement client holds directly or indirectly more than 20% of the voting rights.

2.43 Where a person in a position directly to influence the conduct and outcome of the investment circular reporting engagement has an immediate or close family member who holds a position described in paragraph 2.42, the firm should take appropriate steps to ensure that the relevant person does not retain a position in which they exert direct influence on the conduct and outcome of the investment circular reporting engagement.

EMPLOYMENT WITH FIRM

2.44   Objectivity and independence may be threatened where a former director or employee of the engagement client becomes a member of the engagement team. Self-interest, self-review and familiarity threats may be created where a member of the engagement team has to report on, for example, financial information which he or she prepared, or elements of the financial information for which he or she had responsibility, while with the client.

2.45   **Where a former director or a former employee of an engagement client, who was in a position to exert significant influence over the preparation of the financial information, joins the firm, that individual should not be assigned to a position in which he or she is able directly to influence the conduct and outcome of an investment circular reporting engagement for that client or its affiliates for a period of two years following the date of leaving the client.**

2.46   In certain circumstances, a longer period of exclusion from the engagement team may be appropriate. For example, threats to objectivity and independence may exist in relation to an investment circular reporting engagement relating to the financial information of any period which was materially affected by the work of that person whilst occupying his or her former position of influence with the engagement client. The significance of these threats depends on factors such as:

- the position the individual held with the engagement client;

- the length of time since the individual left the engagement client;

- the position the individual holds in the engagement team.

FAMILY AND OTHER PERSONAL RELATIONSHIPS

2.47   A relationship between a person who is in a position directly to influence the conduct and outcome of the investment circular reporting engagement and another party does not generally affect the consideration of the reporting accountant's objectivity and independence. However, if it is a family relationship, and if the family member also has a financial, business or employment relationship with the engagement client, then self-interest, familiarity or intimidation threats to the reporting accountant's objectivity and independence may be created. The significance of any such threats depends on such factors as:

- the relevant person's involvement in the investment circular reporting engagement;

- the nature of the relationship between the relevant person and his or her family member;

- the family member's relationship with the engagement client.

2.48 A distinction is made between immediate family relationships and close family relationships. Immediate family members comprise an individual's spouse (or equivalent) and dependents, whereas close family members comprise parents, non-dependent children and siblings. While an individual can usually be presumed to be aware of matters concerning his or her immediate family members and to be able to influence their behaviour, it is generally recognised that the same levels of knowledge and influence do not exist in the case of close family members.

2.49 When considering family relationships, it needs to be acknowledged that, in an increasingly secular, open and inclusive society, the concept of what constitutes a family is evolving and relationships between individuals which have no status formally recognised by law may nevertheless be considered as significant as those which do. It may therefore be appropriate to regard certain other personal relationships, particularly those that would be considered close personal relationships, as if they are family relationships.

2.50 **The reporting accountant should establish policies and procedures that require:**

(a) **partners and professional staff to report to the firm where they become aware of any immediate family, close family and other relationships involving an engagement client of the firm and which they consider might create a threat to the reporting accountant's objectivity or a perceived loss of independence;**

(b) **the relevant engagement partners to be notified promptly of any immediate family, close family and other personal relationships reported by partners and other professional staff.**

2.51 **The engagement partner should:**

(a) **assess the threats to the reporting accountant's objectivity and independence arising from immediate family, close family and other personal relationships on the basis of the information reported to the firm;**

(b) **apply appropriate safeguards to eliminate the threat or reduce it to an acceptable level; and**

(c) **where there are unresolved matters or the need for clarification, consult with the ethics partner.**

2.52 Where such matters are identified or reported, the engagement partner or the ethics partner assesses the information available and the potential for there to be a threat to the reporting accountant's objectivity and independence, treating any personal relationship as if it were a family relationship.

EXTERNAL CONSULTANTS INVOLVED IN AN INVESTMENT CIRCULAR REPORTING ENGAGEMENT

2.53 Reporting accountants may employ external consultants as part of their investment circular reporting engagement. There is a risk that an expert's objectivity and independence will be impaired if the expert is related to the entity, for example by being financially dependent upon or having an investment in, the entity.

2.54 **The engagement partner should be satisfied that any external consultant engaged by the reporting accountant in the investment circular reporting engagement will be objective and document the rationale for that conclusion.**

2.55 The engagement partner obtains information from the external consultant as to the existence of any connections that they have with the engagement client including:

- financial interests;

- business relationships;

- employment (past, present and future);

- family and other personal relationships.

ASSOCIATION WITH AN ENGAGEMENT CLIENT

2.56 Where partners and staff in senior positions have been part of engagement teams acting for a client on a number of audit, corporate finance or other transaction related engagements they gain a deep knowledge of the client and its operations. This association may also create close personal relationships with client personnel, which may create threats to the reporting accountant's objectivity or perceived loss of independence.

2.57 **The firm should establish policies and procedures to monitor the extent of involvement of partners and staff in senior positions where the firm acts in connection with investment circulars on a regular basis for an engagement client.**

2.58 **Where partners and staff in senior positions in the engagement team have had extensive involvement with the engagement client, the firm should assess the threats to the reporting accountant's objectivity and independence and, where the threats are other than clearly insignificant, should:**

- **disclose the engagements previously undertaken by the reporting accountant for the engagement client to those charged with governance of the issuing engagement client and any other persons or entities the reporting accountant is instructed to advise, and**

- **apply safeguards to reduce the threats to an acceptable level.**

Where appropriate safeguards cannot be applied, the firm should either not accept or withdraw from the investment circular reporting engagement as appropriate.

2.59 Where partners and staff in senior positions in the engagement team have had extensive involvement with a particular engagement client, self-interest, self-review and familiarity threats to the reporting accountant's objectivity may arise. Similarly, such circumstances may result in an actual or perceived loss of independence.

2.60 To evaluate such threats, the reporting accountant gives careful consideration to which individual is appointed as the engagement partner on an investment circular reporting engagement. This consideration will reflect the need for relevant expertise[16] as well as factors such as:

- the nature of the investment circular reporting engagement and whether it will involve the reappraisal of previously audited financial information,

- the length of time that the audit engagement partner has been associated with the audit engagement,

- the length of time that other partners have acted for the client on corporate finance and other transaction related engagements,

- whether the objectivity of the engagement partner on a subsequent audit could be adversely affected by an opinion on a profit forecast included in the investment circular, and

- the scope of the engagement quality control review.

2.61 A self-interest threat may be created where a partner in the engagement team:

- is employed exclusively or principally on an investment circular reporting engagement that extends for a significant period of time; or

- is remunerated on the basis of the performance of a part of the firm which is substantially dependent on fees from that engagement client.

2.62 In order to address those threats that are identified, firms apply safeguards to reduce the threat to an acceptable level. Appropriate safeguards may include:

- appointing a partner who has no previous involvement with the engagement client as the engagement partner;

- arranging an engagement quality control review of the investment circular reporting engagement by a partner who is not involved with the client and, if

---

[16] Paragraph 25 of SIR 1000 requires that a partner with appropriate experience should be involved in the conduct of the work.

relevant, is not remunerated on the basis of the performance of part of the firm which is substantially dependent on fees from that client;

- arranging an external engagement quality control review of the investment circular reporting engagement.

FEES

2.63 **The engagement partner should be satisfied and able to demonstrate that the investment circular reporting engagement has assigned to it sufficient partners and staff with appropriate time and skill to perform the investment circular reporting engagement in accordance with all applicable Investment Reporting and Ethical Standards, irrespective of the fee to be charged.**

2.64 Paragraph 2.63 is not intended to prescribe the approach to be taken by reporting accountants to the setting of fees, but rather to emphasise that there are no circumstances where the amount of the fee can justify any lack of appropriate resource or time taken to perform an investment circular reporting engagement in accordance with applicable Investment Reporting and Ethical Standards.

2.65 **An investment circular reporting engagement should not be undertaken on a contingent fee basis.**

2.66 A contingent fee basis is any arrangement made at the outset of an engagement under which a pre-determined amount or a specified commission on or percentage of any consideration or saving is payable to the firm upon the happening of a specified event or the achievement of an outcome (or alternative outcomes). Differential hourly fee rates, or arrangements under which the fee payable will be negotiated after the completion of the engagement, do not constitute contingent fee arrangements.

2.67 Contingent fee arrangements in respect of investment circular reporting engagements create self-interest threats to the reporting accountant's objectivity and independence that are so significant that they cannot be eliminated or reduced to an acceptable level by the application of any safeguards.

2.68 The fee ordinarily reflects the time spent and the skills and experience of the personnel performing the engagement in accordance with all the relevant requirements.

2.69 The basis for the calculation of the fee is agreed with the engagement client prior to the commencement of the engagement. The engagement partner explains to the engagement client that the estimated fee is based on the expected level of work required and that, if unforeseen problems are encountered, the cost of any additional work found to be necessary will be reflected in the fee actually charged. This is not a contingent fee arrangement.

2.70   Investigations into possible acquisitions or disposals ('due diligence engagements'), particularly those performed in relation to a prospective transaction, typically involve a high level of risk and responsibility. A firm carrying out a due diligence engagement may charge a higher fee for work relating to a completed transaction than for the same transaction if it is not completed, for whatever reason, provided that the difference is related to such additional risk and responsibility and not the outcome of the due diligence engagement.

2.71   Where the reporting accountant is aware that the engagement client has a record of seeking substantial discounts to the fee payable where a transaction is unsuccessful or abortive, the engagement partner discusses the position with the ethics partner. An appropriate safeguard may involve arranging an engagement quality control review of the investment circular reporting engagement.

2.72   **The firm should establish policies and procedures to ensure that the engagement partner and the ethics partner are notified where others within the firm have agreed contingent fee arrangements in relation to the provision of other services to the engagement client or its affiliates.**

2.73   Contingent fee arrangements in respect of other services provided by the firm to an engagement client may create a threat to the reporting accountant's objectivity and independence. Where fees for other services are calculated on a contingent fee basis, the perception may be that the firm's interests are so closely aligned with the engagement client that it threatens the reporting accountant's objectivity and independence. Any contingent fee that is material to the firm, or that part of the firm by reference to which the engagement partner's profit share is calculated, will create an unacceptable self-interest threat and the firm does not undertake such an engagement at the same time as an investment circular reporting engagement.

2.74   **Where fees for professional services from the engagement client are overdue and the amount cannot be regarded as trivial, the engagement partner, in consultation with the ethics partner, should consider whether the firm should not accept or should withdraw from the investment circular reporting engagement.**

2.75   Where fees due from an engagement client, whether for audit, investment circular reporting engagements or for other professional services, remain unpaid for a long time a self-interest threat to the reporting accountant's objectivity and independence is created because the signing of a report may enhance the firm's prospects of securing payment of such overdue fees.

2.76   Where the outstanding fees are in dispute and the amount involved is significant, the threats to the reporting accountant's objectivity and independence may be such that no safeguards can eliminate them or reduce them to an acceptable level. The engagement partner therefore considers whether the firm can continue with the investment circular reporting engagement.

2.77   Where the outstanding fees are unpaid because of exceptional circumstances (including financial distress), the engagement partner considers whether the engagement client will be able to resolve its difficulties. In deciding what action to take, the engagement partner weighs the threats to the reporting accountant's objectivity and independence if the firm were to continue with the investment circular reporting engagement, against the difficulties the engagement client would be likely to face in finding a successor, and therefore the public interest considerations, if the firm were to withdraw from the investment circular reporting engagement.

2.78   In any case where the firm does not withdraw from the investment circular reporting engagement, the engagement partner applies appropriate safeguards (such as a review by a partner who is not involved in the engagement) and notifies the ethics partner of the facts concerning the overdue fees.

THREATENED AND ACTUAL LITIGATION

2.79   **Where litigation in relation to professional services between the engagement client or its affiliates and the firm, which is other than insignificant, is already in progress, or where the engagement partner considers such litigation to be probable, the reporting accountant should either not continue with or not accept the investment circular reporting engagement.**

2.80   Where litigation actually takes place between the firm (or any person in a position directly to influence the conduct and outcome of the investment circular reporting engagement) and the engagement client, or where litigation is threatened and there is a realistic prospect of such litigation being commenced, self-interest, advocacy and intimidation threats to the reporting accountant's objectivity and independence are created because the firm's interest will be the achievement of an outcome to the dispute or litigation that is favourable to itself. In addition, an effective investment circular reporting engagement requires complete candour and full disclosure between the engagement client management and the engagement team: such disputes or litigation may place the two parties in opposing adversarial positions and may affect management's willingness to make complete disclosure of relevant information. Where the reporting accountant can foresee that such a threat may arise, it informs those charged with governance of the issuing engagement client and any other persons or entities the reporting accountant is instructed to advise of its intention to withdraw from the investment circular reporting engagement.

2.81   The reporting accountant is not required to withdraw from the investment circular reporting engagement in circumstances where a reasonable and informed third party would not regard it as being in the public interest for it to do so. Such circumstances might arise, for example, where:

- the litigation was commenced as the investment circular reporting engagement was about to be completed and stakeholder interests would be adversely affected by a delay in the completion of the work (for example where the engagement relates to the restructuring of a company to avoid its imminent collapse);

- on appropriate legal advice, the firm deems that the threatened or actual litigation is vexatious or designed solely to bring pressure to bear on the opinion to be expressed by the reporting accountant.

GIFTS AND HOSPITALITY

2.82 **The reporting accountant, those in a position directly to influence the conduct and outcome of the investment circular reporting engagement and immediate family members of such persons should not accept gifts from the engagement client, unless the value is clearly insignificant.**

2.83 **Those in a position directly to influence the conduct and outcome of the investment circular reporting engagement and immediate family members of such persons should not accept hospitality from the engagement client, unless it is reasonable in terms of its frequency, nature and cost.**

2.84 Where gifts or hospitality are accepted from an engagement client, self-interest and familiarity threats to the reporting accountant's objectivity and independence are created. Familiarity threats also arise where gifts or hospitality are offered to an engagement client.

2.85 Gifts from the engagement client, unless their value is clearly insignificant, create threats to objectivity and independence which no safeguards can eliminate or reduce.

2.86 Hospitality is a component of many business relationships and can provide valuable opportunities for developing an understanding of the client's business and for gaining the insight on which an effective and successful working relationship depends. Therefore, the reporting accountant's objectivity and independence is not necessarily impaired as a result of accepting hospitality from the engagement client, provided it is reasonable in terms of its frequency, its nature and its cost.

2.87 **The firm should establish policies on the nature and value of gifts and hospitality that may be accepted from and offered to clients, their directors, officers and employees, and should issue guidance to assist partners and staff to comply with such policies.**

2.88 In assessing the acceptability of gifts and hospitality, the test to be applied is not whether the reporting accountant considers that its objectivity is impaired but whether it is probable that a reasonable and informed third party would conclude that it is or is likely to be impaired.

2.89 Where there is any doubt as to the acceptability of gifts or hospitality offered by the engagement client, members of the engagement team discuss the position with the engagement partner. If the cumulative amount of gifts or hospitality accepted from the engagement client appears abnormally high or there is any doubt as to the acceptability of gifts or hospitality offered to the engagement partner, or if the engagement partner has any residual doubt about the acceptability of gifts or hospitality to other individuals, the engagement partner reports the facts to the ethics partner, for further consideration regarding any action to be taken.

SECTION 3 – THE PROVISION OF OTHER SERVICES

INTRODUCTION

3.1 The provision of other services by reporting accountants to the engagement client may create threats to their objectivity or perceived loss of independence. The threats and safeguards approach set out in Section 1 sets out the general approach to be adopted by reporting accountants in relation to the provision of other services to their clients. This approach is applicable irrespective of the nature of the services, which may be in question in a given case. This Section illustrates the application of the general approach to a number of commonly provided services.

3.2 In this Standard, 'other services' comprise any engagement in which a reporting accountant provides professional services to an engagement client other than pursuant to:

(a) any investment circular reporting engagement;

(b) the audit of financial statements; and

(c) those other roles which legislation or regulation specify can be performed by the auditors of the entity (for example, considering the preliminary announcements of listed companies, complying with the procedural and reporting requirements of regulators, such as requirements relating to the audit of the client's internal controls and reports in accordance with Section 151 or 173 of the Companies Act 1985).

3.3 Where the engagement client is a member of a group, other services, for the purposes of this Standard, include:

- services provided by the firm, to the parent company or to any of its significant affiliates; and

- services provided by a network firm which is involved in the investment circular reporting engagement to the engagement client or any of its significant affiliates.

3.4 The provisions of this section apply only to those other services provided by the reporting accountant to the engagement client during the relevant period. The relevant period covers the period during which the engagement is undertaken and any additional period subsequent to the date of the most recent audited financial statements. Other services provided prior to that date are unlikely to create threats to the reporting accountant's objectivity because:

- where the reporting accountant undertook the last audit of the engagement client's financial statements and complied with the APB Ethical Standards for Auditors, the requirements applicable to the provision of other services will have been observed; or

- where the last audit of the engagement client's financial statements was undertaken by a different firm, the work done by the reporting accountant in providing other services will have been the subject of independent review in the course of the audit.

3.5 **The firm should establish policies and procedures, including the alternative procedures outlined in paragraphs 1.44, that enable it to identify circumstances where others within the firm and network firms involved in the investment circular reporting engagement have accepted an engagement to provide during the relevant period, an other service to an engagement client or any of that client's significant affiliates.**

3.6 The firm establishes appropriate policies and procedures to ensure that, in relation to an engagement client, any engagement to provide an other service to the client or any of its significant affiliates during the relevant period is identified so that the engagement partner can consider the implications for the reporting accountant's objectivity and independence before the investment circular reporting engagement is accepted. Such policies and procedures are likely to involve:

i) enquiries of the engagement client;

ii) reference to records of past and current other service engagements provided by the firm;

iii) enquiries of network firms involved in the investment circular reporting engagement as to whether they have provided any other service engagement to the client or any of its significant affiliates during the relevant period.

Such enquiries are undertaken in a manner which seeks to protect confidentiality.

3.7 **Where the engagement partner considers that it is probable that a reasonable and informed third party would regard the objectives of an other service engagement[17] undertaken during the relevant period as being inconsistent with the objectives of the investment circular reporting engagement, the firm should not accept or withdraw from the investment circular reporting engagement.**

3.8 The objectives of engagements to provide other services vary and depend on the specific terms of the engagement. In some cases these objectives may be inconsistent with those of the investment circular reporting engagement, and, in such cases, this may give rise to a threat to the reporting accountant's objectivity and to the appearance of its independence. Firms do not undertake other service engagements during the relevant period, where the objectives of such engagements are inconsistent with the objectives of the investment circular reporting engagement, or do not accept or withdraw from the investment circular reporting engagement.

---

[17] This includes consideration of any private reporting engagements associated with the transaction which is the subject of the investment circular that were undertaken before the investment circular was contemplated.

3.9   Similarly, in relation to a possible new investment circular reporting engagement, consideration needs to be given to recent and current engagements to provide other services by the firm to the client and whether the scope and objectives of those engagements are consistent with the proposed investment circular reporting engagement. In making this assessment, the engagement partner gives consideration to the provisions and guidance given on specific other services in paragraphs 3.13 to 3.89.

3.10   When tendering for a new investment circular reporting engagement, the firm ensures that relevant information on recent other services is drawn to the attention of those charged with governance of the issuing engagement client and any other persons or entities the reporting accountant is instructed to advise, including:

- when recent services were provided to the client;

- the materiality of those services to the proposed investment circular reporting engagement;

- whether those services would have been prohibited if the firm had been undertaking an investment circular reporting engagement at the time when they were undertaken; and

- the extent to which the outcomes of other services have been reviewed by another firm.

3.11   Where both an investment circular reporting engagement and an engagement to undertake other services are provided concurrently the initial assessment of the threats to objectivity and independence and the safeguards to be applied are reviewed whenever the scope and objectives of the other service or the investment circular reporting engagement change significantly. If such a review suggests that safeguards cannot reduce the threat to an acceptable level, the firm withdraws from the other service engagement, or withdraws from the investment circular reporting engagement.

3.12   The following paragraphs provide requirements and guidance on the provision of specific other services by the reporting accountant during the relevant period to the engagement client once the assessment of threats to independence and objectivity at the time of appointment has been made.

INTERNAL AUDIT SERVICES

3.13   The range of 'internal audit services' is wide and they may not be termed as such by the engagement client. For example, the firm may be engaged:

- to outsource the engagement client's entire internal audit function; or

- to supplement the engagement client's internal audit function in specific areas (for example, by providing specialised technical services or resources in particular locations); or

- to provide occasional internal audit services to the engagement client on an *ad hoc* basis.

All such engagements would fall within the term 'internal audit services'.

3.14 The main threats to the reporting accountant's objectivity and independence arising from the provision of internal audit services are the self-review threat and the management threat.

3.15 Engagements to provide internal audit services – other than those prohibited in paragraph 3.17 – may be undertaken, provided that the reporting accountant is satisfied that 'informed management'[18] has been designated by the client and provided that appropriate safeguards are applied.

3.16 Examples of safeguards that may be appropriate when internal audit services are provided to an engagement client include ensuring that:

- internal audit projects undertaken by the firm are performed by partners and staff who have no involvement in the investment circular reporting engagement;

- the work of the reporting accountant is reviewed by a partner who is not involved in the engagement, to ensure that the internal audit work performed by the firm has been properly and effectively assessed in the context of the investment circular reporting engagement.

3.17 **The firm should not undertake an engagement to provide internal audit services to an engagement client where it is reasonably foreseeable that:**

(a) **for the purposes of the investment circular reporting engagement, the reporting accountant would place significant reliance on the internal audit work performed by the firm; or**

(b) **for the purposes of the internal audit services, the firm would undertake part of the role of management of the engagement client in relation to the transaction or the financial information that is the subject of the investment circular reporting engagement.**

3.18 The self-review threat is unacceptably high where the reporting accountant cannot perform the investment circular reporting engagement without placing significant reliance on the work performed for the purposes of the internal audit services engagement. For example, the provision of internal audit services on the internal financial controls for an engagement client which is a large bank, is likely to be

---

[18] See paragraph 1.36.

unacceptable as the reporting accountant is likely to place significant reliance on the work performed by the internal audit team in relation to the bank's internal financial controls.

3.19 The management threat is unacceptably high where the firm provides internal audit services that involve firm personnel taking decisions or making judgments which are properly the responsibility of management. For example, such situations can arise where the nature of the internal audit work involves the firm in taking decisions in relation to the transaction or the financial information that is the subject of the investment circular reporting engagement, as to:

- the scope and nature of the internal audit services to be provided to the engagement client, or

- the design of internal controls or implementing changes thereto.

3.20 During the course of an investment circular reporting engagement the reporting accountant may evaluate the design and test the operating effectiveness of some of the entity's internal financial controls, including the operation of any internal audit function and provide management with observations on matters that have come to their attention, including comments on weaknesses in the internal control systems (including the internal audit function) and suggestions for addressing them. This work is a by-product of the investment circular reporting engagement rather than the result of a specific engagement to provide other services and therefore does not constitute internal audit services for the purposes of this Standard.

3.21 In some circumstances, additional internal financial controls work is performed during the course of the investment circular reporting engagement in response to a specific request. Whether it is appropriate for this work to be undertaken by the firm will depend on the extent to which it gives rise to a management threat to the reporting accountant's objectivity and independence. The engagement partner reviews the scope and objectives of the proposed work and assesses the threats to which it gives rise and the safeguards available.

INFORMATION TECHNOLOGY SERVICES

3.22 Design, provision and implementation of information technology (including financial information technology) systems by firms for their clients creates threats to the reporting accountant's objectivity and independence. The principal threats are the self-review threat and the management threat.

3.23 Engagements to design, provide or implement information technology systems that are not important to any significant part of the accounting system or to the production of the financial information that is the subject of the investment circular reporting engagement and do not have significant reliance placed on them by the reporting accountant, may be undertaken, provided that 'informed management'[18] has been designated by the engagement client and provided that appropriate safeguards are applied.

3.24 Examples of safeguards that may be appropriate when information technology services are provided to an engagement client include ensuring that:

- information technology projects undertaken by the firm are performed by partners and staff who have no involvement in the investment circular reporting engagement;

- the work undertaken in the course of the investment circular reporting engagement is reviewed by a partner who is not involved in the engagement to ensure that the information technology work performed has been properly and effectively assessed.

3.25 **The firm should not undertake an engagement to design, provide or implement information technology systems for an engagement client where:**

(a) **the systems concerned would be important to any significant part of the accounting system or to the production of the financial information that is the subject of an investment circular reporting engagement and the reporting accountant would place significant reliance upon them as part of the investment circular reporting engagement; or**

(b) **for the purposes of the information technology services, the firm would undertake part of the role of management of the engagement client in relation to the transaction or the financial information that is the subject of the investment circular reporting engagement.**

3.26 Where it is reasonably apparent that, having regard to the activities and size of the engagement client and the range and complexity of the system, the management lacks the expertise required to take responsibility for the systems concerned, it is unlikely that any safeguards would be sufficient to eliminate these threats or to reduce them to an acceptable level. In particular, formal acceptance by management of the systems designed and installed by the firm is unlikely to be an effective safeguard when, in substance, the firm has been retained by management for its expertise and has made important decisions in relation to the design or implementation of systems of internal control and financial reporting in relation to the transaction or the financial information that is the subject of the investment circular reporting engagement.

3.27 The provision and installation of information technology services associated with a standard 'off the shelf accounting package' (including basic set-up procedures to make the package operate on the client's existing platform and peripherals, setting up the chart of accounts and the entry of standard data such as the client's product names and prices) is unlikely to create a level of threat to the reporting accountant's objectivity and independence that cannot be addressed through applying appropriate safeguards.

VALUATION SERVICES

3.28 **The firm should not undertake an engagement to provide a valuation to an engagement client where the valuation would both:**

(a) **involve a significant degree of subjective judgment; and**

(b) **have a material effect on the financial information that is the subject of the investment circular reporting engagement.**

3.29 The main threats to the reporting accountant's objectivity and independence arising from the provision of valuation services are the self-review threat and the management threat. The self-review threat is considered too high to allow the provision of valuation services which involve the valuation of amounts with a significant degree of subjectivity that may have a material effect on the financial information that is the subject of the investment circular reporting engagement.

3.30 It is usual for the reporting accountant to provide the management with accounting advice in relation to valuation matters that have come to its attention during the course of the investment circular reporting engagement. Such matters might typically include:

- comments on valuation assumptions and their appropriateness;

- errors identified in a valuation calculation and suggestions for correcting them;

- advice on accounting policies and any valuation methodologies used in their application.

Advice on such matters does not constitute valuation services for the purpose of this Standard.

3.31 Where reporting accountants are engaged to collect and verify the accuracy of data to be used in a valuation to be performed by others, such engagements do not constitute valuation services under this Standard.

ACTUARIAL VALUATION SERVICES

3.32 **The firm should not undertake an engagement to provide actuarial valuation services to an engagement client, unless the firm is satisfied that either:**

(a) **all significant judgments, including the assumptions, are made by 'informed management'[18]; or**

(b) **the valuation has no material effect on the financial information that is the subject of the investment circular reporting engagement.**

3.33 Actuarial valuation services are subject to the same general principles as other valuation services. Where they involve the firm in making a subjective judgment and have a material effect on the financial information that is the subject of the investment circular reporting engagement, actuarial valuations give rise to an unacceptable level of self-review threat and so may not be performed by reporting accountants for their clients.

3.34 However, in cases where all significant judgments concerning the assumptions, methodology and data for the actuarial valuation are made by 'informed management' and the firm's role is limited to applying proven methodologies using the given data, for which the management takes responsibility, it may be possible to establish effective safeguards to protect the reporting accountant's objectivity and the appearance of its independence.

TAX SERVICES

3.35 The range of activities encompassed by the term 'tax services' is wide. Three broad categories of tax service can be distinguished. They are where the firm:

(a) provides advice to the engagement client on one or more specific matters at the request of the client; or

(b) undertakes a substantial proportion of the tax planning or compliance work for the engagement client; or

(c) promotes tax structures or products to the engagement client, the effectiveness of which is likely to be influenced by the manner in which they are accounted for in the financial information that is the subject of the investment circular reporting engagement.

Whilst it is possible to consider tax services under broad headings, such as tax planning or compliance, in practice these services are often interrelated and it is impracticable to analyse services in this way for the purposes of attempting to identify generically the threats to which specific engagements give rise. As a result, firms need to identify and assess, on a case-by-case basis, the potential threats to the reporting accountant's objectivity and independence before deciding whether to undertake an engagement to provide tax services to an engagement client.

3.36 The provision of tax services by firms to their engagement clients may give rise to a number of threats to the reporting accountant's objectivity and independence, including the self-interest threat, the management threat, the advocacy threat and, where the work involves a significant degree of subjective judgment and has a material effect on the financial information that is the subject of the investment circular reporting engagement, the self-review threat.

3.37 Where the firm provides advice to the engagement client on one or more specific matters at the request of the client, a self-review threat may be created. This self-review threat is more significant where the firm undertakes a substantial proportion of the tax planning and compliance work for the engagement client. However, the reporting accountant may be able to adopt appropriate safeguards.

3.38 Examples of such safeguards that may be appropriate when tax services are provided to an engagement client include ensuring that:

- the tax services are provided by partners and staff who have no involvement in the investment circular reporting engagement;

- the tax services are reviewed by an independent tax partner, or other senior tax employee;

- external independent advice is obtained on the tax work;

- tax computations prepared by the firm are reviewed by a partner or senior staff member with appropriate expertise who is not a member of the investment circular reporting engagement team; or

- a partner not involved in the engagement reviews whether the tax work has been properly and effectively addressed in the context of the investment circular reporting engagement.

3.39 **The firm should not promote tax structures or products or undertake an engagement to provide tax advice to an engagement client where the engagement partner has, or ought to have, reasonable doubt as to the appropriateness of the related accounting treatment involved, having regard to the requirement for the financial information to give a true and fair view, in the context of the relevant financial reporting framework.**

3.40 Where the firm promotes tax structures or products or undertakes an engagement to provide tax advice to the engagement client, it may be necessary to adopt an accounting treatment about which there is reasonable doubt as to its appropriateness, in order to achieve the desired result. A self-review threat arises in the course of an investment circular reporting engagement because the reporting accountant may be unable to form an impartial view of the accounting treatment to be adopted for the purposes of the proposed arrangements. Accordingly, this Standard does not permit the promotion of tax structures or products by firms to their engagement clients where, in the view of the engagement partner, after such consultation as is appropriate, the effectiveness of the tax structure or product depends on an accounting treatment about which there is reasonable doubt as to its appropriateness.

3.41 **The firm should not undertake an engagement to provide tax services to an engagement client wholly or partly on a contingent fee basis where:**

  (a) the engagement fees are material to the firm or the part of the firm by reference to which the engagement partner's profit share is calculated; or

(b) the outcome of those tax services (and, therefore, the entitlement to the fee) is dependent on:

(i) the application of tax law which is uncertain or has not been established; and

(ii) a judgment made by the reporting accountant in relation to a material aspect of the investment circular reporting engagement.

3.42 Where tax services, such as advising on corporate structures and structuring transactions to achieve a particular effect, are undertaken on a contingent fee basis, self-interest threats to the reporting accountant's objectivity and independence may arise. The reporting accountant may have, or may appear to have, an interest in the success of the tax services, causing it to make a judgment about which there is reasonable doubt as to its appropriateness. Where the contingent fee is determined by the outcome of the application of tax law, which is uncertain or has not been established, and a judgment made by the reporting accountant in relation to a material aspect of the investment circular reporting engagement, the self-interest threat cannot be eliminated or reduced to an acceptable level by the application of any safeguards.

3.43 **The firm should not undertake an engagement to provide tax services to an engagement client where the engagement would involve the firm undertaking a management role for the engagement client in relation to the transaction or the financial information that is the subject of the investment circular reporting engagement.**

3.44 When providing tax services to an engagement client, there is a risk that the reporting accountant undertakes a management role, unless the firm is working with 'informed management'[18] and appropriate safeguards are applied, such as the tax services being provided by partners and staff who have no involvement in the investment circular reporting engagement.

3.45 **The firm should not undertake an engagement to provide tax services to an engagement client where this would involve acting as an advocate for the client, before an appeals tribunal or court[19] in the resolution of an issue:**

(a) that is material to the financial information that is the subject of the investment circular reporting engagement; or

(b) where the outcome of the tax issue is dependent on a judgment made by the reporting accountant in relation to a material aspect of the investment circular reporting engagement.

---

[19] The restriction applies to the first level of Tax Court that is independent of the tax authorities and to more authoritative bodies. In the UK this would be the General or Special Commissioners of the Inland Revenue or the VAT and Duties Tribunal.

3.46   Where the tax services to be provided by the firm include representing the client in any negotiations or proceedings involving the tax authorities, advocacy threats to the reporting accountant's objectivity and independence may arise.

3.47   The firm is not acting as an advocate where the tax services involve the provision of information to the tax authorities (including an explanation of the approach being taken and the arguments being advanced by the client). In such circumstances effective safeguards may exist and the tax authorities will undertake their own review of the issues.

3.48   Where the tax authorities indicate that they are minded to reject the client's arguments on a particular issue and the matter is likely to be determined by an appeals tribunal or court, the firm may become so closely identified with management's arguments that the reporting accountant is inhibited from forming an impartial view of the treatment of the issue in the financial information that is the subject of the investment circular reporting engagement. In such circumstances, if the issue is material to the financial information or is dependent on a judgment made by the reporting accountant in relation to a material aspect of the investment circular reporting engagement, the firm discusses the matter with the engagement client and makes it clear to the engagement client that it will have to withdraw from that element of the engagement to provide tax services that requires it to act as advocate for the engagement client, or withdraw from the investment circular reporting engagement from the time when the matter is formally listed for hearing before the appeals tribunal.

3.49   The firm is not, however, precluded from having a continuing role (for example, responding to specific requests for information) for the engagement client in relation to the appeal. The firm assesses the threat associated with any continuing role in accordance with the provisions of paragraphs 3.50 to 3.52 of this Standard.

LITIGATION SUPPORT SERVICES

3.50   **The firm should not undertake an engagement to provide litigation support services to an engagement client where this would involve the estimation by the firm of the likely outcome of a pending legal matter that could be material to the amounts to be included or the disclosures to be made in the financial information that is the subject of the investment circular reporting engagement and there is a significant degree of subjectivity involved.**

3.51   Although management and advocacy threats may arise in litigation support services, such as acting as an expert witness, the primary issue is that a self-review threat will arise where such services involve a subjective estimation of the likely outcome of a matter that is material to the amounts to be included or the disclosures to be made in the financial information that is the subject of the investment circular reporting engagement.

3.52 Litigation support services that do not involve such subjective estimations are not prohibited, provided that the firm has carefully considered the implications of any threats and established appropriate safeguards.

LEGAL SERVICES

3.53 **The firm should not undertake an engagement to provide legal services to an engagement client where this would involve acting as the solicitor formally nominated to represent the client in the resolution of a dispute or litigation which is material to the amounts to be included or the disclosures to be made in the financial information that is the subject of the investment circular reporting engagement.**

3.54 Although the provision by reporting accountants of certain types of legal services to their clients may create advocacy, self-review and management threats, this Standard does not impose a general prohibition on the provision of legal services. However, in view of the degree of advocacy involved in litigation or other types of dispute resolution procedures and the potential importance of any assessment by the reporting accountant of the merits of the client's position when reviewing the financial information, this Standard prohibits a reporting accountant from acting as the formally nominated representative for an engagement client in the resolution of a dispute or litigation which is material to the financial information that is the subject of the investment circular reporting engagement (either in terms of the amounts recognised or disclosed in the financial information).

RECRUITMENT AND REMUNERATION SERVICES

3.55 **The firm should not undertake an engagement to provide recruitment services to an engagement client in relation to the appointment of:**

- **any director or**

- **any employee of the engagement client who will be involved in an area that is directly concerned with the transaction which is the subject of the investment circular.**

3.56 A management threat arises where firm personnel take responsibility for any decision as to who should be appointed by the engagement client. Furthermore, a familiarity threat arises if the firm plays a significant role in relation to the identification and recruitment of senior members of management within the company, as the engagement team may be less likely to be critical of the information or explanations provided by such individuals than might otherwise be the case. Accordingly, the firm does not undertake engagements that involve the recruitment of individuals for key management positions during the relevant period.

3.57 Where the firm has played a significant role in relation to the identification and recruitment of a senior member of management within the company, including all directors, prior to the relevant period, the engagement partner considers whether a familiarity threat exists, taking account of factors such as:

- the closeness of personal relationships between the firm's partners and staff and client personnel;

- the length of time since the recruitment of the individual in question;

- the position held by the individual at the engagement client;

- the extent of involvement that the individual will have with the transaction which is the subject of the investment circular;

- whether the individual is in a position to exercise influence on the accounting records or financial information.

Following the assessment of any such threats, appropriate safeguards are applied where necessary, such as ensuring that the engagement team does not include individuals with a close relationship to the senior member of management or who were involved in the recruitment exercise.

3.58   Recruitment services involve a specifically identifiable, and separately remunerated, engagement. Reporting accountants may contribute to an entity's recruitment process in less formal ways. The prohibition set out in paragraph 3.55 does not extend to senior members of an engagement team interviewing prospective employees of the engagement client or to the entity using information gathered by the firm, including that relating to salary surveys.

3.59   **The firm should not undertake an engagement to provide advice on the quantum of the remuneration package or the measurement criteria on which the quantum is calculated, for a director or key management position of an engagement client.**

3.60   The provision of advice on remuneration packages (including bonus arrangements, incentive plans and other benefits) to existing or prospective employees of the engagement client gives rise to familiarity threats. The significance of the familiarity threat is considered too high to allow advice on the overall amounts to be paid or on the quantitative measurement criteria included in remuneration packages for directors and key management positions.

3.61   For other employees, these threats can be adequately addressed by the application of safeguards, such as the advice being provided by partners and staff who have no involvement in the investment circular reporting engagement.

3.62   In cases where all significant judgments concerning the assumptions, methodology and data for the calculation of remuneration packages for directors and key management are made by 'informed management'[18] or a third party and the firm's role is limited to applying proven methodologies using the given data, for which the management takes responsibility, it may be possible to establish effective safeguards to protect the reporting accountant's objectivity and independence.

3.63   Advice on tax, pensions and interpretation of accounting standards relating to remuneration packages for directors and key management can be provided by the firm, provided they are not prohibited by the requirements of this Standard relating to tax, actuarial valuations and accounting services.

CORPORATE FINANCE SERVICES

3.64   The range of services encompassed by the term 'corporate finance services' is wide. For example, the firm may be engaged:

- to identify possible purchasers for parts of the client's business and provide advisory services in the course of such sales; or

- to identify possible 'targets' for the client to acquire; or

- to advise the client on how to fund its financing requirements, including advising on debt restructuring and securitisation programmes; or

- to act as sponsor on admission to listing on the London Stock Exchange or the Irish Stock Exchange, as Nominated Advisor on the admission of the client on the Alternative Investments Market (AIM); or as an IEX Adviser on the admission of the client to the Irish Enterprise Exchange (IEX) of the Irish Stock Exchange; or

- to act as financial adviser to client offerors or offerees in connection with public takeovers.

3.65   The potential for the reporting accountant's objectivity and independence to be impaired through the provision of corporate finance services varies considerably depending on the precise nature of the service provided. The main threats to reporting accountant's objectivity and independence arising from the provision of corporate finance services are the self-review, management and advocacy threats. Self-interest threats may also arise, especially in situations where the firm is paid on a contingent fee basis.

3.66   When providing corporate finance services to an engagement client, there is a risk that the firm undertakes a management role, unless the firm is working with 'informed management'[18] and appropriate safeguards are applied.

3.67   Examples of safeguards that may be appropriate when corporate finance services are provided to an engagement client include ensuring that:

- the corporate finance advice is provided by partners and staff who have no involvement in the investment circular reporting engagement,

- any advice provided is reviewed by an independent corporate finance partner within the firm,

- external independent advice on the corporate finance work is obtained,

- a partner who is not involved in the investment circular reporting engagement or the corporate finance services reviews the work performed in the investment circular reporting engagement.

3.68 Where the firm undertakes an engagement to provide corporate finance services to an engagement client in connection with conducting the sale or purchase of a material part of the client's business, the engagement partner should inform those charged with governance of the issuing engagement client and any other person or entity the reporting accountant is instructed to advise about the engagement, as set out in paragraphs 1.68 to 1.76.

3.69 **The firm should not undertake an engagement to provide corporate finance services to an engagement client where:**

(a) **the engagement would involve the firm taking responsibility for dealing in, underwriting or promoting shares; or**

(b) **the engagement partner has, or ought to have, reasonable doubt as to the appropriateness of an accounting treatment that is related to the advice provided, having regard to the requirement for the financial information to give a true and fair view in accordance with the relevant financial reporting framework; or**

(c) **such corporate finance services are to be provided on a contingent fee basis and:**

   (i) **the engagement fees are material to the firm or the part of the firm by reference to which the engagement partner's profit share is calculated; or**

   (ii) **the outcome of those corporate finance services (and, therefore, the entitlement to the fee) is dependent on a judgment made by the reporting accountant in relation to a material aspect of the investment circular reporting engagement[20]; or**

(d) **the engagement would involve the firm undertaking a management role for the engagement client in relation to the transaction or the financial**

---

[20] A reporting accountant judgment made in relation to a material aspect of the investment circular reporting engagement would be one which could adversely affect the successful completion of the transaction to which the investment circular relates, for example, where a reporting accountant is considering a qualification to an accountant's report as a result of a disagreement in relation to an accounting treatment which would affect revenue recognition and where a qualified opinion would be likely to render the company unsuitable for listing.

information that is the subject of the investment circular reporting engagement.

3.70   An unacceptable advocacy threat arises where, in the course of providing a corporate finance service, the firm promotes the interests of the engagement client by taking responsibility for dealing in, underwriting, or promoting shares.

3.71   Where the firm acts as a Sponsor under the Listing Rules[21], as Nominated Adviser on the admission of the engagement client to the AIM or as IEX Adviser on the admission of the engagement client to IEX, the firm is required to confirm that the client has satisfied all applicable conditions for listing and other relevant requirements of the Listing Rules, AIM Rules or IEX Rules, respectively. Where there is, or there ought to be, reasonable doubt that the firm will be able to give that confirmation, it does not enter into such an engagement.

3.72   A self-review threat arises where the outcome or consequences of the corporate finance service provided by the firm may be material to the financial information that is the subject of the investment circular reporting engagement. Where the firm provides corporate finance services, for example advice to the engagement client on financing arrangements, it may be necessary to adopt an accounting treatment about which there is reasonable doubt as to its appropriateness in order to achieve the desired result. A self-review threat is created because the reporting accountant may be unable to form an impartial view of the accounting treatment to be adopted for the purposes of the proposed arrangements. Accordingly, this Standard does not permit the provision of advice by firms to their engagement clients where there is reasonable doubt about the appropriateness of the related accounting treatments.

3.73   Advice to engagement clients on issues such as funding and banking arrangements, where there is no reasonable doubt as to the appropriateness of the accounting treatment, is not prohibited provided this does not involve the firm in taking decisions or making judgments which are properly the responsibility of management.

3.74   Where a corporate finance engagement is undertaken on a contingent fee basis, self-interest threats to the reporting accountant's objectivity and independence also arise as the reporting accountant may have, or may appear to have, an interest in the success of the corporate finance services. The significance of the self-interest threat is primarily determined by the materiality of the contingent fee to the firm, or to the part of the firm by reference to which the engagement partner's profit share is calculated. Where the contingent fee and the outcome of the corporate finance services is dependent on a judgment made by the reporting accountant in relation to a material aspect of the investment circular reporting engagement, the self-interest threat cannot be eliminated or reduced to an acceptable level by the application of any safeguards.

---

[21]   In the United Kingdom, the UK Listing Authority's publication the 'Listing Rules'. In the Republic of Ireland, the Irish Stock Exchange's publication the 'Listing Rules'.

3.75 In situations where a reporting accountant can see at the outset of the investment circular reporting engagement that there is likely to be a judgment that will be made in relation to a material aspect of the investment circular reporting engagement which could adversely affect the successful completion of the transaction to which the investment circular relates, the firm will not agree to undertake any corporate finance engagements in relation to the transaction on a contingent fee basis, or will not accept the investment circular reporting engagement. Where corporate finance engagements are entered into on a contingent fee basis and a judgment needs to be made in relation to a material aspect of the investment circular reporting engagement during the course of an investment circular reporting engagement, then the firm changes the terms of the corporate finance engagement so that it no longer involves a contingent fee or withdraws from either the relevant corporate finance engagement or the investment circular reporting engagement.

3.76 Where the firm provides a range of corporate finance services to the engagement client, including acting as a Sponsor, Nominated Advisor or IEX Adviser on terms that involve a contingent fee, and that firm also undertakes a public reporting engagement for the engagement client, the self-interest threat caused by contingent fee arrangements may be reduced to an acceptable level by the application of safeguards, such as the corporate finance services being provided by partners and staff who have no involvement in the investment circular reporting engagement. In such circumstances the reporting accountant ensures that the situation is fully disclosed to the Financial Services Authority, the Irish Stock Exchange or the London Stock Exchange and any related regulatory requirements have been complied with.[22]

TRANSACTION RELATED SERVICES

3.77 In addition to corporate finance services, there are other services associated with transactions that a firm may undertake for an engagement client. For example:

- investigations into possible acquisitions or disposals ('due diligence' engagements); or

- investigations into the tax implications of possible acquisitions or disposals.

---

[22] At the date of issue:

- FSA Listing Rule 8.7.12 states that a sponsor must provide written confirmation to the UKLA that it is independent of the issuer or new applicant by way of a 'Sponsor's Confirmation of Independence' form.
- Irish Stock Exchange Listing Rule 2.2.1(2) requires that for each transaction in respect of which a firm acts as sponsor in accordance with the listing rules, the sponsor must submit to the Exchange at an early stage a confirmation of independence in the form set out in 'Schedule 1'.
- Part Two of the *AIM Nominated Adviser eligibility criteria* states that a nominated adviser may not act as both reporting accountant and nominated adviser to an AIM company unless it has satisfied the London Stock Exchange that appropriate safeguards are in place.
- Part Two of the *IEX Adviser Eligibility Criteria* states that an IEX adviser may not act as both reporting accountant and IEX adviser to an IEX company unless it has satisfied the Irish Stock Exchange that appropriate safeguards are in place.

3.78   When providing transaction related services to an engagement client, unless the firm is working with 'informed management'[18] and appropriate safeguards are applied, there is a risk that the firm undertakes a management role.

3.79   Examples of safeguards that may be appropriate when transaction related services are provided to an engagement client include ensuring that:

- the transaction related advice is provided by partners and staff who have no involvement in the investment circular reporting engagement,

- any advice provided is reviewed by an independent transactions partner within the firm,

- external independent advice on the transaction related work is obtained,

- a partner who is not involved in the investment circular reporting engagement reviews the work performed in relation to the subject matter of the transaction related service provided to ensure that such work has been properly and effectively reviewed and assessed in the context of the investment circular reporting engagement.

3.80   **The reporting accountant should not undertake an engagement to provide transaction related services to an engagement client where:**

(a)   **the engagement partner has, or ought to have, reasonable doubt as to the appropriateness of an accounting treatment that is related to the advice provided, having regard to the requirement for the financial information to give a true and fair view in accordance with the relevant financial reporting framework; or**

(b)   **such transaction related services are to be provided on a contingent fee basis and:**

(i)   **the engagement fees are material to the firm or the part of the firm by reference to which the engagement partner's profit share is calculated; or**

(ii)   **the outcome of those transaction related services (and, therefore, the entitlement to the fee) is dependent on a judgment made by the reporting accountant in relation to a material aspect of the investment circular reporting engagement; or**

(c)   **the engagement would involve the firm undertaking a management role for the engagement client in relation to the transaction or the financial information that is the subject of the investment circular reporting engagement.**

3.81   A self-review threat arises where the outcome of the transaction related service undertaken by the firm may be material to the financial information that is the subject of the investment circular reporting engagement. Where the engagement client proposes to undertake a transaction, it may be necessary to adopt an inappropriate accounting treatment in order to achieve the desired result. A self-review threat is created if the reporting accountant undertakes transaction related services in connection with such a transaction. Accordingly, this Standard does not permit the provision of advice by firms to their engagement clients where there is reasonable doubt about the appropriateness of the accounting treatments related to the transaction advice given.

3.82   Where a transaction related services engagement is undertaken on a contingent fee basis, self-interest threats to the reporting accountant's objectivity and independence also arise as the reporting accountant may have, or may appear to have, an interest in the success of the transaction. The significance of the self-interest threat is primarily determined by the materiality of the contingent fee to the firm, or to the part of the firm by reference to which the engagement partner's profit share is calculated. Where the contingent fee and the outcome of the transaction related services is dependent on a judgment made by the reporting accountant in relation to a material aspect of the investment circular reporting engagement, the self-interest threat cannot be eliminated or reduced to an acceptable level by the application of any safeguards, other than where the transaction is subject to a pre-established dispute resolution procedure.

ACCOUNTING SERVICES

3.83   In this Standard, the term 'accounting services' is defined as the provision of services that involve the maintenance of accounting records or the preparation of financial statements or information that is then subject to review in an investment circular reporting engagement. Advice on the implementation of current and proposed accounting standards is not included in the term 'accounting services'.

3.84   The range of activities encompassed by the term 'accounting services' is wide. In some cases, the client may ask the firm to provide a complete service including maintaining all of the accounting records and the preparation of the financial information. Other common situations are:

- the firm may take over the provision of a specific accounting function on an outsourced basis (for example, payroll);

- the client maintains the accounting records, undertakes basic bookkeeping and prepares trial balance information and asks the firm to assist with the preparation of the necessary adjustments and financial information.

3.85   The provision of accounting services by the firm to the engagement client creates threats to the reporting accountant's objectivity and independence, principally self-review and management threats, the significance of which depends on the nature and extent of the accounting services in question and upon the level of public interest in the client.

3.86 **The firm should not undertake an engagement to provide accounting services in relation to the financial information that is the subject of the investment circular reporting engagement save where the circumstances contemplated in paragraph 3.89 apply.**

3.87 Even where there is no engagement to provide any accounting services, it is usual for the reporting accountant to provide the management with accounting advice on matters that have come to its attention during the course of an engagement. Such matters might typically include:

- comments on weaknesses in the accounting records and suggestions for addressing them;

- errors identified in the accounting records and in the financial information and suggestions for correcting them;

- advice on the accounting policies in use and on the application of current and proposed accounting standards.

This advice is a by-product of the investment circular reporting engagement rather than the result of any engagement to provide other services. Consequently, as it is part of the reporting accountant's engagement, such advice cannot be regarded as giving rise to any threat to the reporting accountant's objectivity and independence.

3.88 The threats to the reporting accountant's objectivity and independence that would be created are too high to allow the firm to undertake an engagement to provide any accounting services in relation to the financial information that is the subject of the investment circular reporting engagement, save where the circumstances contemplated in paragraph 3.89 apply.

3.89 In emergency situations, the firm may provide an engagement client, or a significant affiliate of such a company, with accounting services to assist the company in the timely preparation of its financial statements or information. This might arise when, due to external and unforeseeable events, the firm personnel are the only people with the necessary knowledge of the client's systems and procedures. A situation could be considered an emergency where the firm's refusal to provide these services would result in a severe burden for the client (for example, withdrawal of credit lines), or would even threaten its going concern status. In such circumstances, the firm ensures that:

(a) any staff involved in the accounting services have no involvement in the investment circular reporting engagement; and

(b) the engagement would not lead to any firm staff or partners taking decisions or making judgments which are properly the responsibility of management.

SECTION 4 – EFFECTIVE DATE

4.1 Effective for investment circular reporting engagements commencing on or after 1 April 2007.

4.2 Firms may complete investment circular reporting engagements commenced prior to 1 April 2007 in accordance with existing ethical guidance applicable to them at the time of their engagement from the relevant professional body.

4.3 Business relationships existing at 31 October 2006 that were permissible in accordance with existing ethical guidance from the relevant professional body, but are prohibited by the requirements of paragraph 2.20, may continue until 31 December 2007 provided that:

- no new contracts (or extensions of contracts) under the business relationship are entered into;

- the reporting accountant satisfies itself that there are adequate safeguards in place to reduce the threat to acceptable levels; and

- disclosure is made to those charged with governance of the issuing engagement client and those the reporting accountant is instructed to advise.

4.4 Loan staff assignments existing at 31 October 2006 that are prohibited by the requirements of paragraph 2.27, may continue until the earlier of:

(a) the completion of the specific task or the end of the contract term, where this is set out in the contract; or

(b) 31 December 2007, where a task or term is not defined,

as long as the following apply:

- the investment circular reporting engagement was permitted by existing ethical guidance from the relevant professional body;

- any safeguards required by existing ethical guidance continue to be applied;

- the need for additional safeguards is assessed, including where possible safeguards specified in section 3, and if considered necessary, those additional safeguards are applied; and

- disclosure is made to those charged with governance of the issuing engagement client and those the reporting accountant is instructed to advise.

4.5 The requirements of paragraph 2.38 in respect of employment with the engagement client do not apply if:

- the relevant person has notified an intention to join the client, or has entered into contractual arrangements, prior to 31 October 2006;

- undertaking the investment circular reporting engagement was permitted by existing ethical guidance from the relevant professional body; and

- disclosure is made to those charged with governance of the issuing engagement client and those the reporting accountant is instructed to advise.

4.6 Where compliance with the requirements of section 3 would result in an investment circular reporting engagement or other service not being supplied, other services contracted before 31 October 2006 may continue to be provided until the earlier of:

(a) the completion of the specific task or the end of the contract term, where this is set out in the contract; or

(b) 31 December 2007, where a task or term is not defined,

as long as the following apply:

- the investment circular reporting engagement was permitted by existing ethical guidance from the relevant professional body;

- any safeguards required by existing ethical guidance continue to be applied;

- the need for additional safeguards is assessed, including where possible safeguards specified in section 3, and if considered necessary, those additional safeguards are applied; and

- disclosure is made to those charged with governance of the issuing engagement client and those the reporting accountant is instructed to advise.

APPENDIX 1 – GLOSSARY OF TERMS

accounting services The provision of services that involve the maintenance of accounting records or the preparation of financial statements or information that is then subject to review in an investment circular reporting engagement

affiliate Any undertaking which is connected to another by means of common ownership, control or management.

audit engagement partner The partner or other person in the firm who is responsible for the audit engagement and its performance and for the report that is issued on behalf of the firm, and who, where required, has the appropriate authority from a professional, legal or regulatory body.

chain of command All persons who have a direct supervisory, management or other oversight responsibility for the engagement team who have actual knowledge of the investment circular reporting engagement. This includes all partners, principals and shareholders who prepare, review or directly influence the performance appraisal of any partner of the engagement team as a result of their involvement with the investment circular reporting engagement.

close family A non-dependent parent, child or sibling.

contingent fee basis Any arrangement made at the outset of an engagement under which a pre-determined amount or a specified commission on or percentage of any consideration or saving is payable to the firm upon the happening of a specified event or the achievement of an outcome (or alternative outcomes).
Differential hourly fee rates, or arrangements under which the fee payable will be negotiated after the completion of the engagement, do not constitute contingent fee arrangements.

engagement client The party responsible for issuing the investment circular containing the financial information[23] (the issuing engagement client) and, if different the party on whose financial information the firm is reporting.

engagement partner The partner or other person in the firm who is responsible for the investment circular reporting engagement and its performance and for the report that is issued on behalf of the firm, and who, where required, has the appropriate authority from a professional, legal or regulatory body.

engagement period The engagement period starts when the firm accepts the investment circular reporting engagement and ends on the date of the report.

---

[23] The financial information is described in SIR 1000 as being the 'outcome' of a reporting engagement.

engagement team   All professional personnel who are directly involved in the acceptance and performance of a particular investment circular reporting engagement. This includes those who provide quality control or direct oversight of the engagement.

ethics partner   The partner or other person in the firm having responsibility for the adequacy of the firm's policies and procedures relating to integrity, objectivity and independence, their compliance with APB Ethical Standards and the effectiveness of their communication to partners and staff within the firm and providing related guidance to individual partners.

financial interest   An interest in an equity or other security, debenture, loan or other debt instrument of an entity, including rights and obligations to acquire such an interest and derivatives directly related to such an interest.

firm   The sole practitioner, partnership, limited liability partnership or other corporate entity engaged as a reporting accountant. For the purpose of APB Ethical Standards, the firm includes network firms in the UK and Ireland, which are controlled by the firm or its partners.

immediate family   A spouse (or equivalent) or dependent.

issuing engagement client   The party responsible for issuing the investment circular containing the financial information being reported on.

investment circular   An investment circular is a document issued by an entity pursuant to statutory or regulatory requirements relating to securities on which it is intended that a third party should make an investment decision, including a prospectus, listing particulars, a circular to shareholders or similar document.

investment circular reporting engagement   Any public or private reporting engagement in connection with an investment circular where the engagement is undertaken in accordance with Standards for Investment Reporting (SIRs).

key audit partner   An audit partner, or other person performing the function of an audit partner, of the engagement team (other than the audit engagement partner) who is involved at the group level and is responsible for key decisions or judgments on significant matters, such as on significant subsidiaries or divisions of the audit client, or on significant risk factors that relate to the audit of that client.

key management position	Any position at the engagement client which involves the responsibility for fundamental management decisions at the client (e.g. as a CEO or CFO), including an ability to influence the accounting policies and the preparation of the financial statements of the client. A key management position also arises where there are contractual and factual arrangements which in substance allow an individual to participate in exercising such a management function in a different way (e.g. via a consulting contract).
network firm	Any entity:

(i)   controlled by the firm or

(ii)   under common control, ownership or management or

(iii) otherwise affiliated or associated with the firm through the use of a common name or through the sharing of significant common professional resources.

person in a position directly to influence the conduct and outcome of the investment circular reporting engagement

(a) Any person who is directly involved in the investment circular reporting engagement (the engagement team), including:

    (i)   professional personnel from all disciplines involved in the engagement, for example, lawyers, actuaries, taxation specialists, IT specialists, treasury management specialists;

    (ii)   those who provide quality control or direct oversight of the engagement;

(b) Any person within the firm who can directly influence the conduct and outcome of the investment circular reporting engagement through the provision of direct supervisory, management or other oversight of the engagement team in the context of the investment circular reporting engagement.

private reporting engagement

An engagement, in connection with an investment circular, in which a reporting accountant does not express a conclusion that is published in an investment circular

public reporting engagement

An engagement in which a reporting accountant expresses a conclusion that is published in an investment circular and which is designed to enhance the degree of confidence of the intended users of the report about the 'outcome' of the directors' evaluation or measurement of 'subject matter' (usually financial information) against 'suitable criteria'.

relevant period

The engagement period and any additional period before the engagement period but subsequent to the balance sheet date of the most recent audited financial statements of the engagement client.

reporting accountant An accountant engaged to prepare a report for inclusion in, or in connection with, an investment circular. The reporting accountant may or may not be the auditor of the entity issuing the investment circular. The term "reporting accountant" is used to describe either the engagement partner or the engagement partner's firm[24]. The reporting accountant could be a limited company or a principal employed by the company.

---

[24] Where the term applies to the engagement partner, it describes the responsibilities or obligations of the engagement partner. Such obligations or responsibilities may be fulfilled by either the engagement partner or another member of the engagement team.

Section 4: AUDITING STANDARDS

INTERNATIONAL STANDARD ON QUALITY CONTROL (UK AND IRELAND) 1

QUALITY CONTROL FOR FIRMS THAT PERFORM AUDITS AND REVIEWS OF FINANCIAL STATEMENTS, AND OTHER ASSURANCE AND RELATED SERVICES ENGAGEMENTS

(Effective for engagements relating to financial periods ending on or after 15 December 2010)[1a]

CONTENTS

[1a] Conforming amendments to this standard as a result of ISA (UK and Ireland) 610 (Revised June 2013), *Using the Work of Internal Auditors*, are included that are effective for audits of financial statements for periods ending on or after 15 June 2014. Details of the amendments are given in the Annexure to ISA (UK and Ireland) 610 (Revised June 2013).

Application and Other Explanatory Material

International Standard on Quality Control (UK and Ireland) (ISQC (UK and Ireland)) 1, "Quality Control for Firms that Perform Audits and Reviews of Financial Statements, and Other Assurance and Related Services Engagements" should be read in conjunction with ISA (UK and Ireland) 200, "Overall Objectives of the Independent Auditor and the Conduct of an Audit in Accordance with International Standards on Auditing (UK and Ireland)."

Introduction

Scope of this ISQC (UK and Ireland)

1.   This International Standard on Quality Control (UK and Ireland) (ISQC (UK and Ireland)) deals with a firm's responsibilities for its system of quality control for audits and reviews of financial statements, and other assurance and related services engagements. This ISQC (UK and Ireland) is to be read in conjunction with relevant ethical requirements.

1-1.   In the UK and Ireland, ISQC (UK and Ireland) 1 applies to firms that perform audits of financial statements, report in connection with investment circulars and provide other assurance services where they relate to activities that are reported in the public domain and are therefore in the public interest.

2.   Other pronouncements of the International Auditing and Assurance Standards Board (IAASB) set out additional standards and guidance on the responsibilities of firm personnel regarding quality control procedures for specific types of engagements. ISA (UK and Ireland) 220,[1] for example, deals with quality control procedures for audits of financial statements.

3.   A system of quality control consists of policies designed to achieve the objective set out in paragraph 11 and the procedures necessary to implement and monitor compliance with those policies.

Authority of this ISQC (UK and Ireland)

4.   This ISQC (UK and Ireland) applies to all firms of professional accountants in respect of audits and reviews of financial statements, and other assurance and related services engagements. The nature and extent of the policies and procedures developed by an individual firm to comply with this ISQC (UK and Ireland) will depend on various factors such as the size and operating characteristics of the firm, and whether it is part of a network.

5.   This ISQC (UK and Ireland) contains the objective of the firm in following the ISQC (UK and Ireland), and requirements designed to enable the firm to meet that stated objective. In addition, it contains related guidance in the form of application and other explanatory material, as discussed further in paragraph 8, and introductory material that provides context relevant to a proper understanding of the ISQC (UK and Ireland), and definitions.

6.   The objective provides the context in which the requirements of this ISQC (UK and Ireland) are set, and is intended to assist the firm in:

    • Understanding what needs to be accomplished; and

---

[1]   ISA (UK and Ireland) 220, "Quality Control for an Audit of Financial Statements."

- Deciding whether more needs to be done to achieve the objective.

7.   The requirements of this ISQC (UK and Ireland) are expressed using "shall."

8.   Where necessary, the application and other explanatory material provides further explanation of the requirements and guidance for carrying them out. In particular, it may:

- Explain more precisely what a requirement means or is intended to cover.

- Include examples of policies and procedures that may be appropriate in the circumstances.

While such guidance does not in itself impose a requirement, it is relevant to the proper application of the requirements. The application and other explanatory material may also provide background information on matters addressed in this ISQC (UK and Ireland). Where appropriate, additional considerations specific to public sector audit organizations or smaller firms are included within the application and other explanatory material. These additional considerations assist in the application of the requirements in this ISQC (UK and Ireland). They do not, however, limit or reduce the responsibility of the firm to apply and comply with the requirements in this ISQC (UK and Ireland).

9.   This ISQC (UK and Ireland) includes, under the heading "Definitions," a description of the meanings attributed to certain terms for purposes of this ISQC (UK and Ireland). These are provided to assist in the consistent application and interpretation of this ISQC (UK and Ireland), and are not intended to override definitions that may be established for other purposes, whether in law, regulation or otherwise. The Glossary of Terms[1b] relating to International Standards issued by the IAASB in the *Handbook of International Quality Control, Auditing, Review, Other Assurance, and Related Services Pronouncements* published by IFAC includes the terms defined in this ISQC (UK and Ireland). It also includes descriptions of other terms found in this ISQC (UK and Ireland) to assist in common and consistent interpretation and translation.

Effective Date

10. Systems of quality control in compliance with this ISQC (UK and Ireland) are required to be established for engagements relating to financial periods ending on or after 15 December 2010.[1a]

Objective

11. The objective of the firm is to establish and maintain a system of quality control to provide it with reasonable assurance that:

[1b] The APB's Glossary of Terms defines terms used in the ISAs (UK and Ireland). It comprises the Glossary of Terms issued by the IAASB supplemented by a small number of additional definitions.

(a) The firm and its personnel comply with professional standards and applicable legal and regulatory requirements; and

(b) Reports issued by the firm or engagement partners are appropriate in the circumstances.

Definitions

12. In this ISQC (UK and Ireland), the following terms have the meanings attributed below:

(a) Date of report – The date selected by the practitioner to date the report.

(b) Engagement documentation – The record of work performed, results obtained, and conclusions the practitioner reached (terms such as "working papers" or "workpapers" are sometimes used).

(c) Engagement partner[2] – The partner or other person in the firm who is responsible for the engagement and its performance, and for the report that is issued on behalf of the firm, and who, where required, has the appropriate authority from a professional, legal or regulatory body.

(d) Engagement quality control review – A process designed to provide an objective evaluation, on or before the date of the report, of the significant judgments the engagement team made and the conclusions it reached in formulating the report. The engagement quality control review process is for audits of financial statements of listed entities, and those other engagements, if any, for which the firm has determined an engagement quality control review is required.

(e) Engagement quality control reviewer – A partner, other person in the firm, suitably qualified external person, or a team made up of such individuals, none of whom is part of the engagement team, with sufficient and appropriate experience and authority to objectively evaluate the significant judgments the engagement team made and the conclusions it reached in formulating the report.

(f) Engagement team – All partners and staff performing the engagement, and any individuals engaged by the firm or a network firm who perform procedures on the engagement. This excludes an auditor's external expert engaged by the firm or by a network firm. The term "engagement team" also excludes individuals within the client's internal audit function who provide direct assistance on an audit engagement when the external auditor complies with the requirements of ISA (UK and Ireland) 610 (Revised June 2013)[3].

---

[2] "Engagement partner," "partner," and "firm" should be read as referring to their public sector equivalents where relevant.

[3] ISA 610 (Revised June 2013), "Using the Work of Internal Auditors", establishes limits on the use of direct assistance. It also acknowledges that the external auditor may be prohibited by law or regulation from obtaining direct assistance from internal auditors. Therefore, the use of direct assistance is restricted to situations where it is permitted.
The use of internal auditors to provide direct assistance is prohibited in an audit conducted in accordance with ISAs (UK and Ireland) – see ISA (UK and Ireland) 610 (Revised June 2013), paragraph 5-1.

(g) Firm – A sole practitioner, partnership or corporation or other entity of professional accountants.

(h) Inspection – In relation to completed engagements, procedures designed to provide evidence of compliance by engagement teams with the firm's quality control policies and procedures.

(i) Listed entity – An entity whose shares, stock or debt are quoted or listed on a recognized stock exchange, or are marketed under the regulations of a recognized stock exchange or other equivalent body.

(j) Monitoring – A process comprising an ongoing consideration and evaluation of the firm's system of quality control, including a periodic inspection of a selection of completed engagements, designed to provide the firm with reasonable assurance that its system of quality control is operating effectively.

(k) Network firm – A firm or entity that belongs to a network.

(l) Network – A larger structure:

(i) That is aimed at cooperation, and

(ii) That is clearly aimed at profit or cost-sharing or shares common ownership, control or management, common quality control policies and procedures, common business strategy, the use of a common brand name, or a significant part of professional resources.

(m) Partner – Any individual with authority to bind the firm with respect to the performance of a professional services engagement.

(n) Personnel – Partners and staff.

(o) Professional standards – IAASB Engagement Standards, as defined in the IAASB's *Preface to the International Quality Control, Auditing, Review, Other Assurance, and Related Services Pronouncements*, and relevant ethical requirements.

In the UK and Ireland, professional standards in the context of ISQC (UK and Ireland) 1 are the Ethical and Engagement Standards described in the Statement "The Financial Reporting Council – Scope and Authority of Audit and Assurance Pronouncements."

(p) Reasonable assurance – In the context of this ISQC (UK and Ireland), a high, but not absolute, level of assurance.

(q) Relevant ethical requirements – Ethical requirements to which the engagement team and engagement quality control reviewer are subject, which ordinarily comprise Parts A and B of the International Ethics Standards Board for Accountants' *Code of Ethics for Professional Accountants* (IESBA Code) together with national requirements that are more restrictive.

Auditors in the UK and Ireland are subject to ethical requirements from two sources: the APB Ethical Standards for Auditors concerning the integrity, objectivity and independence of the auditor, and the ethical pronouncements established by the auditor's relevant professional body. The APB is not aware of any significant instances where the relevant parts of the IESBA Code of Ethics are more restrictive than the Ethical Standards for Auditors.

The APB Ethical Standard for Reporting Accountants applies to all engagements:

- that are subject to the requirements of the Standards for Investment Reporting (SIRs), and

- which are in connection with an investment circular in which a report from the reporting accountant is to be published.

(r) Staff – Professionals, other than partners, including any experts the firm employs.

(s) Suitably qualified external person – An individual outside the firm with the competence and capabilities to act as an engagement partner, for example a partner of another firm, or an employee (with appropriate experience) of either a professional accountancy body whose members may perform audits and reviews of historical financial information, or other assurance or related services engagements, or of an organization that provides relevant quality control services.

Requirements

Applying, and Complying with, Relevant Requirements

13. Personnel within the firm responsible for establishing and maintaining the firm's system of quality control shall have an understanding of the entire text of this ISQC (UK and Ireland), including its application and other explanatory material, to understand its objective and to apply its requirements properly.

14. The firm shall comply with each requirement of this ISQC (UK and Ireland) unless, in the circumstances of the firm, the requirement is not relevant to the services provided in respect of audits and reviews of financial statements, and other assurance and related services engagements. (Ref: Para. A1)

15. The requirements are designed to enable the firm to achieve the objective stated in this ISQC (UK and Ireland). The proper application of the requirements is therefore expected to provide a sufficient basis for the achievement of the objective. However, because circumstances vary widely and all such circumstances cannot be anticipated, the firm shall consider whether there are particular matters or circumstances that require the firm to establish policies and procedures in addition to those required by this ISQC (UK and Ireland) to meet the stated objective.

Elements of a System of Quality Control

16. The firm shall establish and maintain a system of quality control that includes policies and procedures that address each of the following elements:

    (a) Leadership responsibilities for quality within the firm.

    (b) Relevant ethical requirements.

    (c) Acceptance and continuance of client relationships and specific engagements.

    (d) Human resources.

    (e) Engagement performance.

    (f) Monitoring.

17. The firm shall document its policies and procedures and communicate them to the firm's personnel. (Ref: Para. A2-A3)

Leadership Responsibilities for Quality within the Firm

18. The firm shall establish policies and procedures designed to promote an internal culture recognizing that quality is essential in performing engagements. Such policies and procedures shall require the firm's chief executive officer (or equivalent) or, if appropriate, the firm's managing board of partners (or equivalent) to assume ultimate responsibility for the firm's system of quality control. (Ref: Para. A4-A5)

19. The firm shall establish policies and procedures such that any person or persons assigned operational responsibility for the firm's system of quality control by the firm's chief executive officer or managing board of partners has sufficient and appropriate experience and ability, and the necessary authority, to assume that responsibility. (Ref: Para. A6)

Relevant Ethical Requirements

20. The firm shall establish policies and procedures designed to provide it with reasonable assurance that the firm and its personnel comply with relevant ethical requirements. (Ref: Para. A7-A10)

Independence

21. The firm shall establish policies and procedures designed to provide it with reasonable assurance that the firm, its personnel and, where applicable, others subject to independence requirements (including network firm personnel) maintain independence where required by relevant ethical requirements. Such policies and procedures shall enable the firm to:

(a) Communicate its independence requirements to its personnel and, where applicable, others subject to them; and

(b) Identify and evaluate circumstances and relationships that create threats to independence, and to take appropriate action to eliminate those threats or reduce them to an acceptable level by applying safeguards, or, if considered appropriate, to withdraw from the engagement, where withdrawal is permitted by law or regulation. (Ref: Para. A10)

22. Such policies and procedures shall require:

(a) Engagement partners to provide the firm with relevant information about client engagements, including the scope of services, to enable the firm to evaluate the overall impact, if any, on independence requirements;

(b) Personnel to promptly notify the firm of circumstances and relationships that create a threat to independence so that appropriate action can be taken; and

(c) The accumulation and communication of relevant information to appropriate personnel so that:

   (i) The firm and its personnel can readily determine whether they satisfy independence requirements;

   (ii) The firm can maintain and update its records relating to independence; and

   (iii) The firm can take appropriate action regarding identified threats to independence that are not at an acceptable level. (Ref: Para. A10)

23. The firm shall establish policies and procedures designed to provide it with reasonable assurance that it is notified of breaches of independence requirements, and to enable it to take appropriate actions to resolve such situations. The policies and procedures shall include requirements for:

(a) Personnel to promptly notify the firm of independence breaches of which they become aware;

(b) The firm to promptly communicate identified breaches of these policies and procedures to:

   (i) The engagement partner who, with the firm, needs to address the breach; and

   (ii) Other relevant personnel in the firm and, where appropriate, the network, and those subject to the independence requirements who need to take appropriate action; and

(c) Prompt communication to the firm, if necessary, by the engagement partner and the other individuals referred to in subparagragph (b)(ii) of the actions taken to resolve the matter, so that the firm can determine whether it should take further action. (Ref: Para. A10)

24. At least annually, the firm shall obtain written confirmation of compliance with its policies and procedures on independence from all firm personnel required to be independent by relevant ethical requirements. (Ref: Para. A10-A11)

25. The firm shall establish policies and procedures:

    (a) Setting out criteria for determining the need for safeguards to reduce the familiarity threat to an acceptable level when using the same senior personnel on an assurance engagement over a long period of time; and

    (b) Requiring, for audits of financial statements of listed entities, the rotation of the engagement partner and the individuals responsible for engagement quality control review, and where applicable, others subject to rotation requirements, after a specified period in compliance with relevant ethical requirements. (Ref: Para. A10, A12-A17)

Acceptance and Continuance of Client Relationships and Specific Engagements

26. The firm shall establish policies and procedures for the acceptance and continuance of client relationships and specific engagements, designed to provide the firm with reasonable assurance that it will only undertake or continue relationships and engagements where the firm:

    (a) Is competent to perform the engagement and has the capabilities, including time and resources, to do so; (Ref: Para. A18, A23)

    (b) Can comply with relevant ethical requirements; and

    (c) Has considered the integrity of the client, and does not have information that would lead it to conclude that the client lacks integrity. (Ref: Para. A19-A20, A23)

27. Such policies and procedures shall require:

    (a) The firm to obtain such information as it considers necessary in the circumstances before accepting an engagement with a new client, when deciding whether to continue an existing engagement, and when considering acceptance of a new engagement with an existing client. (Ref: Para. A21, A23)

    (b) If a potential conflict of interest is identified in accepting an engagement from a new or an existing client, the firm to determine whether it is appropriate to accept the engagement.

    (c) If issues have been identified, and the firm decides to accept or continue the client relationship or a specific engagement, the firm to document how the issues were resolved.

28. The firm shall establish policies and procedures on continuing an engagement and the client relationship, addressing the circumstances where the firm obtains information that would have caused it to decline the engagement had that information been available earlier. Such policies and procedures shall include consideration of:

   (a) The professional and legal responsibilities that apply to the circumstances, including whether there is a requirement for the firm to report to the person or persons who made the appointment or, in some cases, to regulatory authorities; and

   (b) The possibility of withdrawing from the engagement or from both the engagement and the client relationship. (Ref: Para. A22-A23)

Human Resources

29. The firm shall establish policies and procedures designed to provide it with reasonable assurance that it has sufficient personnel with the competence, capabilities, and commitment to ethical principles necessary to:

   (a) Perform engagements in accordance with professional standards and applicable legal and regulatory requirements; and

   (b) Enable the firm or engagement partners to issue reports that are appropriate in the circumstances. (Ref: Para. A24-A29)

Assignment of Engagement Teams

30. The firm shall assign responsibility for each engagement to an engagement partner and shall establish policies and procedures requiring that:

   (a) The identity and role of the engagement partner are communicated to key members of client management and those charged with governance;

   (b) The engagement partner has the appropriate competence, capabilities, and authority to perform the role; and

   (c) The responsibilities of the engagement partner are clearly defined and communicated to that partner. (Ref: Para. A30)

31. The firm shall also establish policies and procedures to assign appropriate personnel with the necessary competence, and capabilities to:

   (a) Perform engagements in accordance with professional standards and applicable legal and regulatory requirements; and

   (b) Enable the firm or engagement partners to issue reports that are appropriate in the circumstances. (Ref: Para. A31)

Engagement Performance

32. The firm shall establish policies and procedures designed to provide it with reasonable assurance that engagements are performed in accordance with professional standards and applicable legal and regulatory requirements, and that the firm or the engagement partner issue reports that are appropriate in the circumstances. Such policies and procedures shall include:

    (a) Matters relevant to promoting consistency in the quality of engagement performance; (Ref: Para. A32-A33)

    (b) Supervision responsibilities; and (Ref: Para. A34)

    (c) Review responsibilities. (Ref: Para. A35)

33. The firm's review responsibility policies and procedures shall be determined on the basis that work of less experienced team members is reviewed by more experienced engagement team members.

Consultation

34. The firm shall establish policies and procedures designed to provide it with reasonable assurance that:

    (a) Appropriate consultation takes place on difficult or contentious matters;

    (b) Sufficient resources are available to enable appropriate consultation to take place;

    (c) The nature and scope of, and conclusions resulting from, such consultations are documented and are agreed by both the individual seeking consultation and the individual consulted; and

    (d) Conclusions resulting from consultations are implemented. (Ref: Para. A36-A40)

Engagement Quality Control Review

35. The firm shall establish policies and procedures requiring, for appropriate engagements, an engagement quality control review that provides an objective evaluation of the significant judgments made by the engagement team and the conclusions reached in formulating the report. Such policies and procedures shall:

    (a) Require an engagement quality control review for all audits of financial statements of listed entities;

    (b) Set out criteria against which all other audits and reviews of historical financial information and other assurance and related services engagements shall be evaluated to determine whether an engagement quality control review should be performed; and (Ref: Para. A41)

(c)   Require an engagement quality control review for all engagements, if any, meeting the criteria established in compliance with subparagraph (b).

36.   The firm shall establish policies and procedures setting out the nature, timing and extent of an engagement quality control review. Such policies and procedures shall require that the engagement report not be dated until the completion of the engagement quality control review. (Ref: Para. A42-A43)

37.   The firm shall establish policies and procedures to require the engagement quality control review to include:

(a)   Discussion of significant matters with the engagement partner;

(b)   Review of the financial statements or other subject matter information and the proposed report;

(c)   Review of selected engagement documentation relating to significant judgments the engagement team made and the conclusions it reached; and

(d)   Evaluation of the conclusions reached in formulating the report and consideration of whether the proposed report is appropriate. (Ref: Para. A44)

38.   For audits of financial statements of listed entities, the firm shall establish policies and procedures to require the engagement quality control review to also include consideration of the following:

(a)   The engagement team's evaluation of the firm's independence in relation to the specific engagement;

(b)   Whether appropriate consultation has taken place on matters involving differences of opinion or other difficult or contentious matters, and the conclusions arising from those consultations; and

(c)   Whether documentation selected for review reflects the work performed in relation to the significant judgments and supports the conclusions reached. (Ref: Para. A45-A46)

Criteria for the Eligibility of Engagement Quality Control Reviewers

39.   The firm shall establish policies and procedures to address the appointment of engagement quality control reviewers and establish their eligibility through:

(a)   The technical qualifications required to perform the role, including the necessary experience and authority; and (Ref: Para. A47)

(b)   The degree to which an engagement quality control reviewer can be consulted on the engagement without compromising the reviewer's objectivity. (Ref: Para. A48)

40. The firm shall establish policies and procedures designed to maintain the objectivity of the engagement quality control reviewer. (Ref: Para. A49-A51)

41. The firm's policies and procedures shall provide for the replacement of the engagement quality control reviewer where the reviewer's ability to perform an objective review may be impaired.

Documentation of the Engagement Quality Control Review

42. The firm shall establish policies and procedures on documentation of the engagement quality control review which require documentation that:

    (a) The procedures required by the firm's policies on engagement quality control review have been performed;

    (b) The engagement quality control review has been completed on or before the date of the report; and

    (c) The reviewer is not aware of any unresolved matters that would cause the reviewer to believe that the significant judgments the engagement team made and the conclusions it reached were not appropriate.

Differences of Opinion

43. The firm shall establish policies and procedures for dealing with and resolving differences of opinion within the engagement team, with those consulted and, where applicable, between the engagement partner and the engagement quality control reviewer. (Ref: Para. A52-A53)

44. Such policies and procedures shall require that:

    (a) Conclusions reached be documented and implemented; and

    (b) The report not be dated until the matter is resolved.

Engagement Documentation

Completion of the Assembly of Final Engagement Files

45. The firm shall establish policies and procedures for engagement teams to complete the assembly of final engagement files on a timely basis after the engagement reports have been finalized. (Ref: Para. A54-A55)

Confidentiality, Safe Custody, Integrity, Accessibility and Retrievability of Engagement Documentation

46. The firm shall establish policies and procedures designed to maintain the confidentiality, safe custody, integrity, accessibility and retrievability of engagement documentation. (Ref: Para. A56-A59)

Retention of Engagement Documentation

47.   The firm shall establish policies and procedures for the retention of engagement documentation for a period sufficient to meet the needs of the firm or as required by law or regulation. (Ref: Para. A60-A63)

Monitoring

Monitoring the Firm's Quality Control Policies and Procedures

48.   The firm shall establish a monitoring process designed to provide it with reasonable assurance that the policies and procedures relating to the system of quality control are relevant, adequate, and operating effectively. This process shall:

   (a)   Include an ongoing consideration and evaluation of the firm's system of quality control including, on a cyclical basis, inspection of at least one completed engagement for each engagement partner;

   (b)   Require responsibility for the monitoring process to be assigned to a partner or partners or other persons with sufficient and appropriate experience and authority in the firm to assume that responsibility; and

   (c)   Require that those performing the engagement or the engagement quality control review are not involved in inspecting the engagement. (Ref: Para. A64-A68)

Evaluating, Communicating and Remedying Identified Deficiencies

49.   The firm shall evaluate the effect of deficiencies noted as a result of the monitoring process and determine whether they are either:

   (a)   Instances that do not necessarily indicate that the firm's system of quality control is insufficient to provide it with reasonable assurance that it complies with professional standards and applicable legal and regulatory requirements, and that the reports issued by the firm or engagement partners are appropriate in the circumstances; or

   (b)   Systemic, repetitive or other significant deficiencies that require prompt corrective action.

50.   The firm shall communicate to relevant engagement partners and other appropriate personnel deficiencies noted as a result of the monitoring process and recommendations for appropriate remedial action. (Ref: Para. A69)

51.   Recommendations for appropriate remedial actions for deficiencies noted shall include one or more of the following:

   (a)   Taking appropriate remedial action in relation to an individual engagement or member of personnel;

(b) The communication of the findings to those responsible for training and professional development;

(c) Changes to the quality control policies and procedures; and

(d) Disciplinary action against those who fail to comply with the policies and procedures of the firm, especially those who do so repeatedly.

52. The firm shall establish policies and procedures to address cases where the results of the monitoring procedures indicate that a report may be inappropriate or that procedures were omitted during the performance of the engagement. Such policies and procedures shall require the firm to determine what further action is appropriate to comply with relevant professional standards and legal and regulatory requirements and to consider whether to obtain legal advice.

53. The firm shall communicate at least annually the results of the monitoring of its system of quality control to engagement partners and other appropriate individuals within the firm, including the firm's chief executive officer or, if appropriate, its managing board of partners. This communication shall be sufficient to enable the firm and these individuals to take prompt and appropriate action where necessary in accordance with their defined roles and responsibilities. Information communicated shall include the following:

(a) A description of the monitoring procedures performed.

(b) The conclusions drawn from the monitoring procedures.

(c) Where relevant, a description of systemic, repetitive or other significant deficiencies and of the actions taken to resolve or amend those deficiencies.

54. Some firms operate as part of a network and, for consistency, may implement some of their monitoring procedures on a network basis. Where firms within a network operate under common monitoring policies and procedures designed to comply with this ISQC (UK and Ireland), and these firms place reliance on such a monitoring system, the firm's policies and procedures shall require that:

(a) At least annually, the network communicate the overall scope, extent and results of the monitoring process to appropriate individuals within the network firms; and

(b) The network communicate promptly any identified deficiencies in the system of quality control to appropriate individuals within the relevant network firm or firms so that the necessary action can be taken,

in order that engagement partners in the network firms can rely on the results of the monitoring process implemented within the network, unless the firms or the network advise otherwise.

Complaints and Allegations

55. The firm shall establish policies and procedures designed to provide it with reasonable assurance that it deals appropriately with:

    (a) Complaints and allegations that the work performed by the firm fails to comply with professional standards and applicable legal and regulatory requirements; and

    (b) Allegations of non-compliance with the firm's system of quality control.

    As part of this process, the firm shall establish clearly defined channels for firm personnel to raise any concerns in a manner that enables them to come forward without fear of reprisals. (Ref: Para. A70)

56. If during the investigations into complaints and allegations, deficiencies in the design or operation of the firm's quality control policies and procedures or non-compliance with the firm's system of quality control by an individual or individuals are identified, the firm shall take appropriate actions as set out in paragraph 51. (Ref: Para. A71-A72)

Documentation of the System of Quality Control

57. The firm shall establish policies and procedures requiring appropriate documentation to provide evidence of the operation of each element of its system of quality control. (Ref: Para. A73-A75)

58. The firm shall establish policies and procedures that require retention of documentation for a period of time sufficient to permit those performing monitoring procedures to evaluate the firm's compliance with its system of quality control, or for a longer period if required by law or regulation.

59. The firm shall establish policies and procedures requiring documentation of complaints and allegations and the responses to them.

***

Application and Other Explanatory Material

Applying, and Complying with, Relevant Requirements

Considerations Specific to Smaller Firms (Ref: Para. 14)

A1. This ISQC (UK and Ireland) does not call for compliance with requirements that are not relevant, for example, in the circumstances of a sole practitioner with no staff. Requirements in this ISQC (UK and Ireland) such as those for policies and procedures for the assignment of appropriate personnel to the engagement team (see paragraph 31), for review responsibilities (see paragraph 33), and for the annual communication of the results of monitoring to engagement partners within the firm (see paragraph 53) are not relevant in the absence of staff.

Elements of a System of Quality Control (Ref: Para. 17)

A2. In general, communication of quality control policies and procedures to firm personnel includes a description of the quality control policies and procedures and the objectives they are designed to achieve, and the message that each individual has a personal responsibility for quality and is expected to comply with these policies and procedures. Encouraging firm personnel to communicate their views or concerns on quality control matters recognizes the importance of obtaining feedback on the firm's system of quality control.

Considerations Specific to Smaller Firms

A3. Documentation and communication of policies and procedures for smaller firms may be less formal and extensive than for larger firms.

Leadership Responsibilities for Quality within the Firm

Promoting an Internal Culture of Quality (Ref: Para. 18)

A4. The firm's leadership and the examples it sets significantly influence the internal culture of the firm. The promotion of a quality-oriented internal culture depends on clear, consistent and frequent actions and messages from all levels of the firm's management that emphasize the firm's quality control policies and procedures, and the requirement to:

(a) Perform work that complies with professional standards and applicable legal and regulatory requirements; and

(b) Issue reports that are appropriate in the circumstances.

Such actions and messages encourage a culture that recognizes and rewards high quality work. These actions and messages may be communicated by, but are not limited to, training seminars, meetings, formal or informal dialogue, mission statements, newsletters, or briefing memoranda. They may be incorporated in the firm's internal documentation and training materials, and in partner and staff appraisal procedures such that they will support and reinforce the firm's view on the importance of quality and how, practically, it is to be achieved.

A5. Of particular importance in promoting an internal culture based on quality is the need for the firm's leadership to recognize that the firm's business strategy is subject to the overriding requirement for the firm to achieve quality in all the engagements that the firm performs. Promoting such an internal culture includes:

(a) Establishment of policies and procedures that address performance evaluation, compensation, and promotion (including incentive systems) with regard to its personnel, in order to demonstrate the firm's overriding commitment to quality;

(b) Assignment of management responsibilities so that commercial considerations do not override the quality of work performed; and

(c) Provision of sufficient resources for the development, documentation and support of its quality control policies and procedures.

Assigning Operational Responsibility for the Firm's System of Quality Control (Ref: Para. 19)

A6. Sufficient and appropriate experience and ability enables the person or persons responsible for the firm's system of quality control to identify and understand quality control issues and to develop appropriate policies and procedures. Necessary authority enables the person or persons to implement those policies and procedures.

Relevant Ethical Requirements

Compliance with Relevant Ethical Requirements (Ref: Para. 20)

A7. The IESBA Code[3a] establishes the fundamental principles of professional ethics, which include:

(a) Integrity;

(b) Objectivity;

(c) Professional competence and due care;

(d) Confidentiality; and

(e) Professional behavior.

A8. Part B of the IESBA Code[3a] illustrates how the conceptual framework is to be applied in specific situations. It provides examples of safeguards that may be appropriate to address threats to compliance with the fundamental principles and also provides examples of situations where safeguards are not available to address the threats.

A9. The fundamental principles are reinforced in particular by:

• The leadership of the firm;

• Education and training;

• Monitoring; and

[3a] See paragraph 12(q). Auditors and reporting accountants in the UK and Ireland are subject to ethical requirements from two sources: the APB Ethical Standards and the ethical pronouncements established by the auditor's relevant professional body. The APB is not aware of any significant instances where the relevant parts of the IESBA Code of Ethics are more restrictive than the APB Ethical Standards.

- A process for dealing with non-compliance.

Definition of "Firm," "Network" and "Network Firm" (Ref: Para. 20-25)

A10. The definitions of "firm," network" or "network firm" in relevant ethical requirements may differ from those set out in this ISQC (UK and Ireland). For example, the IESBA Code[4] defines the "firm" as:

    (i)   A sole practitioner, partnership or corporation of professional accountants;

    (ii) An entity that controls such parties through ownership, management or other means; and

    (iii) An entity controlled by such parties through ownership, management or other means.

The IESBA Code also provides guidance in relation to the terms "network" and "network firm."

In complying with the requirements in paragraphs 20-25, the definitions used in the relevant ethical requirements apply in so far as is necessary to interpret those ethical requirements.

Written Confirmation (Ref: Para. 24)

A11. Written confirmation may be in paper or electronic form. By obtaining confirmation and taking appropriate action on information indicating non-compliance, the firm demonstrates the importance that it attaches to independence and makes the issue current for, and visible to, its personnel.

Familiarity Threat (Ref: Para. 25)

A12. The IESBA Code[3a] discusses the familiarity threat that may be created by using the same senior personnel on an assurance engagement over a long period of time and the safeguards that might be appropriate to address such threats.

A13. Determining appropriate criteria to address familiarity threat may include matters such as:

- The nature of the engagement, including the extent to which it involves a matter of public interest; and

- The length of service of the senior personnel on the engagement.

Examples of safeguards include rotating the senior personnel or requiring an engagement quality control review.

---

[4] "*IESBA Code of Ethics for Professional Accountants.*" See footnote 3a.

A14. The IESBA Code[3a] recognizes that the familiarity threat is particularly relevant in the context of financial statement audits of listed entities. For these audits, the IESBA Code requires the rotation of the key audit partner[5] after a pre-defined period, normally no more than seven years[5a], and provides related standards and guidance. National requirements may establish shorter rotation periods.

Considerations specific to public sector audit organizations

A15. Statutory measures may provide safeguards for the independence of public sector auditors. However, threats to independence may still exist regardless of any statutory measures designed to protect it. Therefore, in establishing the policies and procedures required by paragraphs 20-25, the public sector auditor may have regard to the public sector mandate and address any threats to independence in that context.

A16. Listed entities as referred to in paragraphs 25 and A14 are not common in the public sector. However, there may be other public sector entities that are significant due to size, complexity or public interest aspects, and which consequently have a wide range of stakeholders. Therefore, there may be instances when a firm determines, based on its quality control policies and procedures, that a public sector entity is significant for the purposes of expanded quality control procedures.

A17. In the public sector, legislation may establish the appointments and terms of office of the auditor with engagement partner responsibility. As a result, it may not be possible to comply strictly with the engagement partner rotation requirements envisaged for listed entities. Nonetheless, for public sector entities considered significant, as noted in paragraph A16, it may be in the public interest for public sector audit organizations to establish policies and procedures to promote compliance with the spirit of rotation of engagement partner responsibility.

Acceptance and Continuance of Client Relationships and Specific Engagements

Competence, Capabilities, and Resources (Ref: Para. 26(a))

A18. Consideration of whether the firm has the competence, capabilities, and resources to undertake a new engagement from a new or an existing client involves reviewing the specific requirements of the engagement and the existing partner and staff profiles at all relevant levels, and including whether:

- Firm personnel have knowledge of relevant industries or subject matters;

- Firm personnel have experience with relevant regulatory or reporting requirements, or the ability to gain the necessary skills and knowledge effectively;

---

[5] IESBA Code, Definitions. See footnote 1b.
[5a] APB Ethical Standard 3 (Revised), "Long Association With The Audit Engagement," specifies for the audits of listed companies the rotation periods for the audit engagement partner, the engagement quality control reviewer, and key partners involved in the audit.

- The firm has sufficient personnel with the necessary competence and capabilities;

- Experts are available, if needed;

- Individuals meeting the criteria and eligibility requirements to perform engagement quality control review are available, where applicable; and

- The firm is able to complete the engagement within the reporting deadline.

Integrity of Client (Ref: Para. 26(c))

A19. With regard to the integrity of a client, matters to consider include, for example:

- The identity and business reputation of the client's principal owners, key management, and those charged with its governance.

- The nature of the client's operations, including its business practices.

- Information concerning the attitude of the client's principal owners, key management and those charged with its governance towards such matters as aggressive interpretation of accounting standards and the internal control environment.

- Whether the client is aggressively concerned with maintaining the firm's fees as low as possible.

- Indications of an inappropriate limitation in the scope of work.

- Indications that the client might be involved in money laundering or other criminal activities.

- The reasons for the proposed appointment of the firm and non-reappointment of the previous firm.

- The identity and business reputation of related parties.

The extent of knowledge a firm will have regarding the integrity of a client will generally grow within the context of an ongoing relationship with that client.

A20. Sources of information on such matters obtained by the firm may include the following:

- Communications with existing or previous providers of professional accountancy services to the client in accordance with relevant ethical requirements, and discussions with other third parties.

- Inquiry of other firm personnel or third parties such as bankers, legal counsel and industry peers.

- Background searches of relevant databases.

Continuance of Client Relationship (Ref: Para. 27(a))

A21. Deciding whether to continue a client relationship includes consideration of significant matters that have arisen during the current or previous engagements, and their implications for continuing the relationship. For example, a client may have started to expand its business operations into an area where the firm does not possess the necessary expertise.

Withdrawal (Ref: Para. 28)

A22. Policies and procedures on withdrawal from an engagement or from both the engagement and the client relationship address issues that include the following:

- Discussing with the appropriate level of the client's management and those charged with its governance the appropriate action that the firm might take based on the relevant facts and circumstances.

- If the firm determines that it is appropriate to withdraw, discussing with the appropriate level of the client's management and those charged with its governance withdrawal from the engagement or from both the engagement and the client relationship, and the reasons for the withdrawal.

- Considering whether there is a professional, legal or regulatory requirement for the firm to remain in place, or for the firm to report the withdrawal from the engagement, or from both the engagement and the client relationship, together with the reasons for the withdrawal, to regulatory authorities.

- Documenting significant matters, consultations, conclusions and the basis for the conclusions.

Considerations Specific to Public Sector Audit Organizations (Ref: Para. 26-28)

A23. In the public sector, auditors may be appointed in accordance with statutory procedures. Accordingly, certain of the requirements and considerations regarding the acceptance and continuance of client relationships and specific engagements as set out paragraphs 26-28 and A18-A22 may not be relevant. Nonetheless, establishing policies and procedures as described may provide valuable information to public sector auditors in performing risk assessments and in carrying out reporting responsibilities.

Human Resources (Ref: Para. 29)

A24. Personnel issues relevant to the firm's policies and procedures related to human resources include, for example:

- Recruitment.

- Performance evaluation.

- Capabilities, including time to perform assignments.

- Competence.

- Career development.

- Promotion.

- Compensation.

- The estimation of personnel needs.

Effective recruitment processes and procedures help the firm select individuals of integrity who have the capacity to develop the competence and capabilities necessary to perform the firm's work and possess the appropriate characteristics to enable them to perform competently.

A25. Competence can be developed through a variety of methods, including the following:

- Professional education.

- Continuing professional development, including training.

- Work experience.

- Coaching by more experienced staff, for example, other members of the engagement team.

- Independence education for personnel who are required to be independent.

A26. The continuing competence of the firm's personnel depends to a significant extent on an appropriate level of continuing professional development so that personnel maintain their knowledge and capabilities. Effective policies and procedures emphasize the need for continuing training for all levels of firm personnel, and provide the necessary training resources and assistance to enable personnel to develop and maintain the required competence and capabilities.

A27. The firm may use a suitably qualified external person, for example, when internal technical and training resources are unavailable.

A28. Performance evaluation, compensation and promotion procedures give due recognition and reward to the development and maintenance of competence and commitment to ethical principles. Steps a firm may take in developing and maintaining competence and commitment to ethical principles include:

- Making personnel aware of the firm's expectations regarding performance and ethical principles;

- Providing personnel with evaluation of, and counseling on, performance, progress and career development; and

- Helping personnel understand that advancement to positions of greater responsibility depends, among other things, upon performance quality and adherence to ethical principles, and that failure to comply with the firm's policies and procedures may result in disciplinary action.

Considerations Specific to Smaller Firms

A29. The size and circumstances of the firm will influence the structure of the firm's performance evaluation process. Smaller firms, in particular, may employ less formal methods of evaluating the performance of their personnel.

Assignment of Engagement Teams

Engagement Partners (Ref: Para. 30)

A30. Policies and procedures may include systems to monitor the workload and availability of engagement partners so as to enable these individuals to have sufficient time to adequately discharge their responsibilities.

Engagement Teams (Ref: Para. 31)

A31. The firm's assignment of engagement teams and the determination of the level of supervision required, include for example, consideration of the engagement team's:

- Understanding of, and practical experience with, engagements of a similar nature and complexity through appropriate training and participation;

- Understanding of professional standards and legal and regulatory requirements;

- Technical knowledge and expertise, including knowledge of relevant information technology;

- Knowledge of relevant industries in which the clients operate;

- Ability to apply professional judgment; and

- Understanding of the firm's quality control policies and procedures.

Engagement Performance

Consistency in the Quality of Engagement Performance (Ref: Para. 32(a))

A32. The firm promotes consistency in the quality of engagement performance through its policies and procedures. This is often accomplished through written or electronic manuals, software tools or other forms of standardized documentation, and industry or subject matter-specific guidance materials. Matters addressed may include:

- How engagement teams are briefed on the engagement to obtain an understanding of the objectives of their work.

- Processes for complying with applicable engagement standards.

- Processes of engagement supervision, staff training and coaching.

- Methods of reviewing the work performed, the significant judgments made and the form of report being issued.

- Appropriate documentation of the work performed and of the timing and extent of the review.

- Processes to keep all policies and procedures current.

A33. Appropriate teamwork and training assist less experienced members of the engagement team to clearly understand the objectives of the assigned work.

Supervision (Ref: Para. 32(b))

A34. Engagement supervision includes the following:

- Tracking the progress of the engagement;

- Considering the competence and capabilities of individual members of the engagement team, whether they have sufficient time to carry out their work, whether they understand their instructions and whether the work is being carried out in accordance with the planned approach to the engagement;

- Addressing significant matters arising during the engagement, considering their significance and modifying the planned approach appropriately; and

- Identifying matters for consultation or consideration by more experienced engagement team members during the engagement.

Review (Ref: Para. 32(c))

A35. A review consists of consideration of whether:

- The work has been performed in accordance with professional standards and applicable legal and regulatory requirements;

- Significant matters have been raised for further consideration;

- Appropriate consultations have taken place and the resulting conclusions have been documented and implemented;

- There is a need to revise the nature, timing and extent of work performed;

- The work performed supports the conclusions reached and is appropriately documented;

- The evidence obtained is sufficient and appropriate to support the report; and

- The objectives of the engagement procedures have been achieved.

Consultation (Ref: Para. 34)

A36. Consultation includes discussion at the appropriate professional level, with individuals within or outside the firm who have specialized expertise.

A37. Consultation uses appropriate research resources as well as the collective experience and technical expertise of the firm. Consultation helps to promote quality and improves the application of professional judgment. Appropriate recognition of consultation in the firm's policies and procedures helps to promote a culture in which consultation is recognized as a strength and encourages personnel to consult on difficult or contentious matters.

A38. Effective consultation on significant technical, ethical and other matters within the firm, or where applicable, outside the firm can be achieved when those consulted:

- are given all the relevant facts that will enable them to provide informed advice; and

- have appropriate knowledge, seniority and experience,

and when conclusions resulting from consultations are appropriately documented and implemented.

A39. Documentation of consultations with other professionals that involve difficult or contentious matters that is sufficiently complete and detailed contributes to an understanding of:

- The issue on which consultation was sought; and

- The results of the consultation, including any decisions taken, the basis for those decisions and how they were implemented.

Considerations Specific to Smaller Firms

A40. A firm needing to consult externally, for example, a firm without appropriate internal resources, may take advantage of advisory services provided by:

- Other firms;

- Professional and regulatory bodies; or

- Commercial organizations that provide relevant quality control services.

Before contracting for such services, consideration of the competence and capabilities of the external provider helps the firm to determine whether the external provider is suitably qualified for that purpose.

Engagement Quality Control Review

Criteria for an Engagement Quality Control Review (Ref: Para. 35(b))

A41. Criteria for determining which engagements other than audits of financial statements of listed entities are to be subject to an engagement quality control review may include, for example:

- The nature of the engagement, including the extent to which it involves a matter of public interest.

- The identification of unusual circumstances or risks in an engagement or class of engagements.

- Whether laws or regulations require an engagement quality control review.

Nature, Timing and Extent of the Engagement Quality Control Review (Ref: Para. 36-37)

A42. The engagement report is not dated until the completion of the engagement quality control review. However, documentation of the engagement quality control review may be completed after the date of the report.

A43. Conducting the engagement quality control review in a timely manner at appropriate stages during the engagement allows significant matters to be promptly resolved to the engagement quality control reviewer's satisfaction on or before the date of the report.

A44. The extent of the engagement quality control review may depend, among other things, on the complexity of the engagement, whether the entity is a listed entity, and the risk that the report might not be appropriate in the circumstances. The performance of an engagement quality control review does not reduce the responsibilities of the engagement partner.

Engagement Quality Control Review of a Listed Entity (Ref: Para. 38)

A45. Other matters relevant to evaluating the significant judgments made by the engagement team that may be considered in an engagement quality control review of an audit of financial statements of a listed entity include:

- Significant risks identified during the engagement and the responses to those risks.

- Judgments made, particularly with respect to materiality and significant risks.

- The significance and disposition of corrected and uncorrected misstatements identified during the engagement.

- The matters to be communicated to management and those charged with governance and, where applicable, other parties such as regulatory bodies.

These other matters, depending on the circumstances, may also be applicable for engagement quality control reviews for audits of the financial statements of other entities as well as reviews of financial statements and other assurance and related services engagements.

Considerations specific to public sector audit organizations

A46. Although not referred to as listed entities, as described in paragraph A16, certain public sector entities may be of sufficient significance to warrant performance of an engagement quality control review.

Criteria for the Eligibility of Engagement Quality Control Reviewers

Sufficient and Appropriate Technical Expertise, Experience and Authority (Ref: Para. 39(a))

A47. What constitutes sufficient and appropriate technical expertise, experience and authority depends on the circumstances of the engagement. For example, the engagement quality control reviewer for an audit of the financial statements of a listed entity is likely to be an individual with sufficient and appropriate experience and authority to act as an audit engagement partner on audits of financial statements of listed entities.

Consultation with the Engagement Quality Control Reviewer (Ref: Para. 39(b))

A48. The engagement partner may consult the engagement quality control reviewer during the engagement, for example, to establish that a judgment made by the engagement partner will be acceptable to the engagement quality control reviewer. Such consultation avoids identification of differences of opinion at a late stage of the engagement and need not compromise the engagement quality control reviewer's eligibility to perform the role. Where the nature and extent of the consultations become significant the reviewer's objectivity may be compromised unless care is taken by both the engagement team and the reviewer to maintain the reviewer's objectivity. Where this is not possible, another individual within the firm or a suitably qualified external person may be appointed to take on the role of either the engagement quality control reviewer or the person to be consulted on the engagement.

Objectivity of the Engagement Quality Control Reviewer (Ref: Para. 40)

A49. The firm is required to establish policies and procedures designed to maintain objectivity of the engagement quality control reviewer. Accordingly, such policies and procedures provide that the engagement quality control reviewer:

- Where practicable, is not selected by the engagement partner;

- Does not otherwise participate in the engagement during the period of review;

- Does not make decisions for the engagement team; and

- Is not subject to other considerations that would threaten the reviewer's objectivity.

Considerations specific to smaller firms

A50. It may not be practicable, in the case of firms with few partners, for the engagement partner not to be involved in selecting the engagement quality control reviewer. Suitably qualified external persons may be contracted where sole practitioners or small firms identify engagements requiring engagement quality control reviews. Alternatively, some sole practitioners or small firms may wish to use other firms to facilitate engagement quality control reviews. Where the firm contracts suitably qualified external persons, the requirements in paragraphs 39-41 and guidance in paragraphs A47-A48 apply.

Considerations specific to public sector audit organizations

A51. In the public sector, a statutorily appointed auditor (for example, an Auditor General, or other suitably qualified person appointed on behalf of the Auditor General) may act in a role equivalent to that of engagement partner with overall responsibility for public sector audits. In such circumstances, where applicable, the selection of the engagement quality control reviewer includes consideration of the need for independence from the audited entity and the ability of the engagement quality control reviewer to provide an objective evaluation.

Differences of Opinion (Ref: Para. 43)

A52. Effective procedures encourage identification of differences of opinion at an early stage, provide clear guidelines as to the successive steps to be taken thereafter, and require documentation regarding the resolution of the differences and the implementation of the conclusions reached.

A53. Procedures to resolve such differences may include consulting with another practitioner or firm, or a professional or regulatory body.

Engagement Documentation

Completion of the Assembly of Final Engagement Files (Ref: Para. 45)

A54. Law or regulation may prescribe the time limits by which the assembly of final engagement files for specific types of engagement is to be completed. Where no such time limits are prescribed in law or regulation, paragraph 45 requires the firm to establish time limits that reflect the need to complete the assembly of final engagement files on a timely basis. In the case of an audit, for example, such a time limit would ordinarily not be more than 60 days after the date of the auditor's report.

A55. Where two or more different reports are issued in respect of the same subject matter information of an entity, the firm's policies and procedures relating to time limits for the assembly of final engagement files address each report as if it were for a separate engagement. This may, for example, be the case when the firm issues an auditor's report on a component's financial information for group consolidation purposes and, at a subsequent date, an auditor's report on the same financial information for statutory purposes.

Confidentiality, Safe Custody, Integrity, Accessibility and Retrievability of Engagement Documentation (Ref: Para. 46)

A56. Relevant ethical requirements establish an obligation for the firm's personnel to observe at all times the confidentiality of information contained in engagement documentation, unless specific client authority has been given to disclose information, or there is a legal or professional duty to do so. Specific laws or regulations may impose additional obligations on the firm's personnel to maintain client confidentiality, particularly where data of a personal nature are concerned.

A57. Whether engagement documentation is in paper, electronic or other media, the integrity, accessibility or retrievability of the underlying data may be compromised if the documentation could be altered, added to or deleted without the firm's knowledge, or if it could be permanently lost or damaged. Accordingly, controls that the firm designs and implements to avoid unauthorized alteration or loss of engagement documentation may include those that:

- Enable the determination of when and by whom engagement documentation was created, changed or reviewed;

- Protect the integrity of the information at all stages of the engagement, especially when the information is shared within the engagement team or transmitted to other parties via the Internet;

- Prevent unauthorized changes to the engagement documentation; and

- Allow access to the engagement documentation by the engagement team and other authorized parties as necessary to properly discharge their responsibilities.

A58. Controls that the firm designs and implements to maintain the confidentiality, safe custody, integrity, accessibility and retrievability of engagement documentation may include the following:

- The use of a password among engagement team members to restrict access to electronic engagement documentation to authorized users.

- Appropriate back-up routines for electronic engagement documentation at appropriate stages during the engagement.

- Procedures for properly distributing engagement documentation to the team members at the start of the engagement, processing it during engagement, and collating it at the end of engagement.

- Procedures for restricting access to, and enabling proper distribution and confidential storage of, hardcopy engagement documentation.

A59. For practical reasons, original paper documentation may be electronically scanned for inclusion in engagement files. In such cases, the firm's procedures designed to maintain the integrity, accessibility, and retrievability of the documentation may include requiring the engagement teams to:

- Generate scanned copies that reflect the entire content of the original paper documentation, including manual signatures, cross-references and annotations;

- Integrate the scanned copies into the engagement files, including indexing and signing off on the scanned copies as necessary; and

- Enable the scanned copies to be retrieved and printed as necessary.

There may be legal, regulatory or other reasons for a firm to retain original paper documentation that has been scanned.

Retention of Engagement Documentation (Ref: Para. 47)

A60. The needs of the firm for retention of engagement documentation, and the period of such retention, will vary with the nature of the engagement and the firm's circumstances, for example, whether the engagement documentation is needed to provide a record of matters of continuing significance to future engagements. The retention period may also depend on other factors, such as whether local law or regulation prescribes specific retention periods for certain types of engagements, or whether there are generally accepted retention periods in the jurisdiction in the absence of specific legal or regulatory requirements.

A61. In the specific case of audit engagements, the retention period would ordinarily be no shorter than five years from the date of the auditor's report, or, if later, the date of the group auditor's report.[5b]

A62. Procedures that the firm adopts for retention of engagement documentation include those that enable the requirements of paragraph 47 to be met during the retention period, for example to:

- Enable the retrieval of, and access to, the engagement documentation during the retention period, particularly in the case of electronic documentation since the underlying technology may be upgraded or changed over time;

[5b] In the UK and Ireland this requirement is applied having regard to specific requirements of the auditor's relevant professional body.

- Provide, where necessary, a record of changes made to engagement documentation after the engagement files have been completed; and

- Enable authorized external parties to access and review specific engagement documentation for quality control or other purposes.

Ownership of engagement documentation

A63. Unless otherwise specified by law or regulation, engagement documentation is the property of the firm. The firm may, at its discretion, make portions of, or extracts from, engagement documentation available to clients, provided such disclosure does not undermine the validity of the work performed, or, in the case of assurance engagements, the independence of the firm or its personnel.

Monitoring

Monitoring the Firm's Quality Control Policies and Procedures (Ref: Para. 48)

A64. The purpose of monitoring compliance with quality control policies and procedures is to provide an evaluation of:

- Adherence to professional standards and legal and regulatory requirements;

- Whether the system of quality control has been appropriately designed and effectively implemented; and

- Whether the firm's quality control policies and procedures have been appropriately applied, so that reports that are issued by the firm or engagement partners are appropriate in the circumstances.

A65. Ongoing consideration and evaluation of the system of quality control include matters such as the following:

- Analysis of:

  - New developments in professional standards and legal and regulatory requirements, and how they are reflected in the firm's policies and procedures where appropriate;

  - Written confirmation of compliance with policies and procedures on independence;

  - Continuing professional development, including training; and

  - Decisions related to acceptance and continuance of client relationships and specific engagements.

- Determination of corrective actions to be taken and improvements to be made in the system, including the provision of feedback into the firm's policies and procedures relating to education and training.

- Communication to appropriate firm personnel of weaknesses identified in the system, in the level of understanding of the system, or compliance with it.

- Follow-up by appropriate firm personnel so that necessary modifications are promptly made to the quality control policies and procedures.

A66. Inspection cycle policies and procedures may, for example, specify a cycle that spans three years. The manner in which the inspection cycle is organized, including the timing of selection of individual engagements, depends on many factors, such as the following:

- The size of the firm.

- The number and geographical location of offices.

- The results of previous monitoring procedures.

- The degree of authority both personnel and offices have (for example, whether individual offices are authorized to conduct their own inspections or whether only the head office may conduct them).

- The nature and complexity of the firm's practice and organization.

- The risks associated with the firm's clients and specific engagements.

A67. The inspection process includes the selection of individual engagements, some of which may be selected without prior notification to the engagement team. In determining the scope of the inspections, the firm may take into account the scope or conclusions of an independent external inspection program. However, an independent external inspection program does not act as a substitute for the firm's own internal monitoring program.

Considerations Specific to Smaller Firms

A68. In the case of small firms, monitoring procedures may need to be performed by individuals who are responsible for design and implementation of the firm's quality control policies and procedures, or who may be involved in performing the engagement quality control review. A firm with a limited number of persons may choose to use a suitably qualified external person or another firm to carry out engagement inspections and other monitoring procedures. Alternatively, the firm may establish arrangements to share resources with other appropriate organizations to facilitate monitoring activities.

Communicating Deficiencies (Ref: Para. 50)

A69. The reporting of identified deficiencies to individuals other than the relevant engagement partners need not include an identification of the specific engagements concerned, although there may be cases where such identification may be necessary for the proper discharge of the responsibilities of the individuals other than the engagement partners.

Complaints and Allegations

Source of Complaints and Allegations (Ref: Para. 55)

A70. Complaints and allegations (which do not include those that are clearly frivolous) may originate from within or outside the firm. They may be made by firm personnel, clients or other third parties. They may be received by engagement team members or other firm personnel.

Investigation Policies and Procedures (Ref: Para. 56)

A71. Policies and procedures established for the investigation of complaints and allegations may include for example, that the partner supervising the investigation:

- Has sufficient and appropriate experience;

- Has authority within the firm; and

- Is otherwise not involved in the engagement.

The partner supervising the investigation may involve legal counsel as necessary.

Considerations specific to smaller firms

A72. It may not be practicable, in the case of firms with few partners, for the partner supervising the investigation not to be involved in the engagement. These small firms and sole practitioners may use the services of a suitably qualified external person or another firm to carry out the investigation into complaints and allegations.

Documentation of the System of Quality Control (Ref: Para. 57)

A73. The form and content of documentation evidencing the operation of each of the elements of the system of quality control is a matter of judgment and depends on a number of factors, including the following:

- The size of the firm and the number of offices.

- The nature and complexity of the firm's practice and organization.

For example, large firms may use electronic databases to document matters such as independence confirmations, performance evaluations and the results of monitoring inspections.

A74. Appropriate documentation relating to monitoring includes, for example:

- Monitoring procedures, including the procedure for selecting completed engagements to be inspected.

- A record of the evaluation of:

  ○ Adherence to professional standards and applicable legal and regulatory requirements;

  ○ Whether the system of quality control has been appropriately designed and effectively implemented; and

  ○ Whether the firm's quality control policies and procedures have been appropriately applied, so that reports that are issued by the firm or engagement partners are appropriate in the circumstances.

- Identification of the deficiencies noted, an evaluation of their effect, and the basis for determining whether and what further action is necessary.

Considerations Specific to Smaller Firms

A75. Smaller firms may use more informal methods in the documentation of their systems of quality control such as manual notes, checklists and forms.

INTERNATIONAL STANDARD ON AUDITING
(UK AND IRELAND) 200

OVERALL OBJECTIVES OF THE INDEPENDENT AUDITOR AND THE CONDUCT OF AN AUDIT IN ACCORDANCE WITH INTERNATIONAL STANDARDS ON AUDITING (UK AND IRELAND)

(Effective for audits of financial statements for periods ending on or after 15 December 2010)[1a]

CONTENTS

[1a] Conforming amendments to this standard as a result of ISA (UK and Ireland) 610 (Revised June 2013), *Using the Work of Internal Auditors*, are included that are effective for audits of financial statements for periods ending on or after 15 June 2014. Details of the amendments are given in the Annexure to ISA (UK and Ireland) 610 (Revised June 2013).

Introduction

Scope of this ISA (UK and Ireland)

1. This International Standard on Auditing (UK and Ireland) (ISA (UK and Ireland)) deals with the independent auditor's overall responsibilities when conducting an audit of financial statements in accordance with ISAs (UK and Ireland). Specifically, it sets out the overall objectives of the independent auditor, and explains the nature and scope of an audit designed to enable the independent auditor to meet those objectives. It also explains the scope, authority and structure of the ISAs (UK and Ireland), and includes requirements establishing the general responsibilities of the independent auditor applicable in all audits, including the obligation to comply with the ISAs (UK and Ireland). The independent auditor is referred to as "the auditor" hereafter.

2. ISAs (UK and Ireland) are written in the context of an audit of financial statements by an auditor. They are to be adapted as necessary in the circumstances when applied to audits of other historical financial information. ISAs (UK and Ireland) do not address the responsibilities of the auditor that may exist in legislation, regulation or otherwise in connection with, for example, the offering of securities to the public[1b]. Such responsibilities may differ from those established in the ISAs (UK and Ireland). Accordingly, while the auditor may find aspects of the ISAs (UK and Ireland) helpful in such circumstances, it is the responsibility of the auditor to ensure compliance with all relevant legal, regulatory or professional obligations.

An Audit of Financial Statements

3. The purpose of an audit is to enhance the degree of confidence of intended users in the financial statements. This is achieved by the expression of an opinion by the auditor on whether the financial statements are prepared, in all material respects, in accordance with an applicable financial reporting framework. In the case of most general purpose frameworks, that opinion is on whether the financial statements are presented fairly, in all material respects, or give a true and fair view in accordance with the framework. An audit conducted in accordance with ISAs (UK and Ireland) and relevant ethical requirements enables the auditor to form that opinion. (Ref: Para. A1)

4. The financial statements subject to audit are those of the entity, prepared by management of the entity with oversight from those charged with governance[1c]. ISAs (UK and Ireland) do not impose responsibilities on management or those charged with governance and do not override laws and regulations that govern their responsibilities. However, an audit in accordance with ISAs (UK and Ireland) is conducted on the premise that management and, where appropriate, those charged

---

[1b] In the UK and Ireland, standards and guidance for accountants undertaking engagements in connection with an investment circular are set out in APB's Standards for Investment Reporting (SIRS).
[1c] In the UK and Ireland, those charged with governance are responsible for the preparation of the financial statements. For corporate entities, directors have a collective responsibility; those charged with governance of other types of entity may also have a collective responsibility established in applicable law or regulation or under the terms of their appointment.

with governance have acknowledged certain responsibilities that are fundamental to the conduct of the audit. The audit of the financial statements does not relieve management or those charged with governance of their responsibilities. (Ref: Para. A2-A11)

5.   As the basis for the auditor's opinion, ISAs (UK and Ireland) require the auditor to obtain reasonable assurance about whether the financial statements as a whole are free from material misstatement, whether due to fraud or error. Reasonable assurance is a high level of assurance. It is obtained when the auditor has obtained sufficient appropriate audit evidence to reduce audit risk (that is, the risk that the auditor expresses an inappropriate opinion when the financial statements are materially misstated) to an acceptably low level. However, reasonable assurance is not an absolute level of assurance, because there are inherent limitations of an audit which result in most of the audit evidence on which the auditor draws conclusions and bases the auditor's opinion being persuasive rather than conclusive. (Ref: Para. A28-A52)

6.   The concept of materiality is applied by the auditor both in planning and performing the audit, and in evaluating the effect of identified misstatements on the audit and of uncorrected misstatements, if any, on the financial statements.[1] In general, misstatements, including omissions, are considered to be material if, individually or in the aggregate, they could reasonably be expected to influence the economic decisions of users taken on the basis of the financial statements. Judgments about materiality are made in the light of surrounding circumstances, and are affected by the auditor's perception of the financial information needs of users of the financial statements, and by the size or nature of a misstatement, or a combination of both. The auditor's opinion deals with the financial statements as a whole and therefore the auditor is not responsible for the detection of misstatements that are not material to the financial statements as a whole.

7.   The ISAs (UK and Ireland) contain objectives, requirements and application and other explanatory material that are designed to support the auditor in obtaining reasonable assurance. The ISAs (UK and Ireland) require that the auditor exercise professional judgment and maintain professional skepticism throughout the planning and performance of the audit and, among other things:

- Identify and assess risks of material misstatement, whether due to fraud or error, based on an understanding of the entity and its environment, including the entity's internal control.

- Obtain sufficient appropriate audit evidence about whether material misstatements exist, through designing and implementing appropriate responses to the assessed risks.

---

[1]   ISA (UK and Ireland) 320, "Materiality in Planning and Performing an Audit" and ISA (UK and Ireland) 450, "Evaluation of Misstatements Identified during the Audit."

- Form an opinion on the financial statements based on conclusions drawn from the audit evidence obtained.

8. The form of opinion expressed by the auditor will depend upon the applicable financial reporting framework and any applicable law or regulation. (Ref: Para. A12-A13)

9. The auditor may also have certain other communication and reporting responsibilities to users, management, those charged with governance, or parties outside the entity, in relation to matters arising from the audit. These may be established by the ISAs (UK and Ireland) or by applicable law or regulation.[2]

Effective Date

10. This ISA (UK and Ireland) is effective for audits of financial statements for periods ending on or after 15 December 2010.[1a]

Overall Objectives of the Auditor

11. In conducting an audit of financial statements, the overall objectives of the auditor are:

   (a) To obtain reasonable assurance about whether the financial statements as a whole are free from material misstatement, whether due to fraud or error, thereby enabling the auditor to express an opinion on whether the financial statements are prepared, in all material respects, in accordance with an applicable financial reporting framework; and

   (b) To report on the financial statements, and communicate as required by the ISAs (UK and Ireland), in accordance with the auditor's findings.

12. In all cases when reasonable assurance cannot be obtained and a qualified opinion in the auditor's report is insufficient in the circumstances for purposes of reporting to the intended users of the financial statements, the ISAs (UK and Ireland) require that the auditor disclaim an opinion or withdraw (or resign)[3] from the engagement, where withdrawal is possible under applicable law or regulation.

Definitions

13. For purposes of the ISAs (UK and Ireland), the following terms have the meanings attributed below:

---

[2] See, for example, ISA (UK and Ireland) 260, "Communication with Those Charged with Governance;" and paragraph 43 of ISA (UK and Ireland) 240, "The Auditor's Responsibilities Relating to Fraud in an Audit of Financial Statements."

[3] In the ISAs (UK and Ireland), only the term "withdrawal" is used.

(a) Applicable financial reporting framework – The financial reporting framework adopted by management and, where appropriate, those charged with governance in the preparation of the financial statements that is acceptable in view of the nature of the entity and the objective of the financial statements, or that is required by law or regulation.

The term "fair presentation framework" is used to refer to a financial reporting framework that requires compliance with the requirements of the framework and:

(i) Acknowledges explicitly or implicitly that, to achieve fair presentation of the financial statements, it may be necessary for management to provide disclosures beyond those specifically required by the framework; or

(ii) Acknowledges explicitly that it may be necessary for management to depart from a requirement of the framework to achieve fair presentation of the financial statements. Such departures are expected to be necessary only in extremely rare circumstances.

The term "compliance framework" is used to refer to a financial reporting framework that requires compliance with the requirements of the framework, but does not contain the acknowledgements in (i) or (ii) above.

(b) Audit evidence – Information used by the auditor in arriving at the conclusions on which the auditor's opinion is based. Audit evidence includes both information contained in the accounting records underlying the financial statements and other information. For purposes of the ISAs (UK and Ireland):

(i) Sufficiency of audit evidence is the measure of the quantity of audit evidence. The quantity of the audit evidence needed is affected by the auditor's assessment of the risks of material misstatement and also by the quality of such audit evidence.

(ii) Appropriateness of audit evidence is the measure of the quality of audit evidence; that is, its relevance and its reliability in providing support for the conclusions on which the auditor's opinion is based.

(c) Audit risk – The risk that the auditor expresses an inappropriate audit opinion when the financial statements are materially misstated. Audit risk is a function of the risks of material misstatement and detection risk.

(d) Auditor – "Auditor" is used to refer to the person or persons conducting the audit, usually the engagement partner or other members of the engagement team, or, as applicable, the firm. Where an ISA (UK and Ireland) expressly intends that a requirement or responsibility be fulfilled by the engagement partner, the term "engagement partner" rather than "auditor" is used. "Engagement partner" and "firm" are to be read as referring to their public sector equivalents where relevant.

(e) Detection risk – The risk that the procedures performed by the auditor to reduce audit risk to an acceptably low level will not detect a misstatement that exists and that could be material, either individually or when aggregated with other misstatements.

(f) Financial statements – A structured representation of historical financial information, including related notes, intended to communicate an entity's economic resources or obligations at a point in time or the changes therein for a period of time in accordance with a financial reporting framework. The related notes ordinarily comprise a summary of significant accounting policies and other explanatory information. The term "financial statements" ordinarily refers to a complete set of financial statements as determined by the requirements of the applicable financial reporting framework, but can also refer to a single financial statement.

(g) Historical financial information – Information expressed in financial terms in relation to a particular entity, derived primarily from that entity's accounting system, about economic events occurring in past time periods or about economic conditions or circumstances at points in time in the past.

(h) Management – The person(s) with executive responsibility for the conduct of the entity's operations. For some entities in some jurisdictions, management includes some or all of those charged with governance, for example, executive members of a governance board, or an owner-manager.

In the UK and Ireland, management will not normally include non-executive directors.

(i) Misstatement – A difference between the amount, classification, presentation, or disclosure of a reported financial statement item and the amount, classification, presentation, or disclosure that is required for the item to be in accordance with the applicable financial reporting framework. Misstatements can arise from error or fraud.

Where the auditor expresses an opinion on whether the financial statements are presented fairly, in all material respects, or give a true and fair view, misstatements also include those adjustments of amounts, classifications, presentation, or disclosures that, in the auditor's judgment, are necessary for the financial statements to be presented fairly, in all material respects, or to give a true and fair view.

(j) Premise, relating to the responsibilities of management and, where appropriate, those charged with governance, on which an audit is conducted – That management and, where appropriate, those charged with governance have acknowledged and understand that they have the following responsibilities that are fundamental to the conduct of an audit in accordance with ISAs (UK and Ireland). That is, responsibility:

(i)   For the preparation of the financial statements in accordance with the applicable financial reporting framework, including where relevant their fair presentation;

(ii)   For such internal control as management and, where appropriate, those charged with governance determine is necessary to enable the preparation of financial statements that are free from material misstatement, whether due to fraud or error; and

(iii)   To provide the auditor with:

    a.   Access to all information of which management and, where appropriate, those charged with governance are aware that is relevant to the preparation of the financial statements such as records, documentation and other matters;

    b.   Additional information that the auditor may request from management and, where appropriate, those charged with governance for the purpose of the audit; and

    c.   Unrestricted access to persons within the entity from whom the auditor determines it necessary to obtain audit evidence.

In the case of a fair presentation framework, (i) above may be restated as "for the preparation and *fair* presentation of the financial statements in accordance with the financial reporting framework," or "for the preparation of financial statements *that give a true and fair view* in accordance with the financial reporting framework."

The "premise, relating to the responsibilities of management and, where appropriate, those charged with governance, on which an audit is conducted" may also be referred to as the "premise."

(k)   Professional judgment – The application of relevant training, knowledge and experience, within the context provided by auditing, accounting and ethical standards, in making informed decisions about the courses of action that are appropriate in the circumstances of the audit engagement.

(l)   Professional skepticism – An attitude that includes a questioning mind, being alert to conditions which may indicate possible misstatement due to error or fraud, and a critical assessment of audit evidence.

(m)   Reasonable assurance – In the context of an audit of financial statements, a high, but not absolute, level of assurance.

(n)   Risk of material misstatement – The risk that the financial statements are materially misstated prior to audit. This consists of two components, described as follows at the assertion level:

(i)   Inherent risk – The susceptibility of an assertion about a class of transaction, account balance or disclosure to a misstatement that could be material, either individually or when aggregated with other misstatements, before consideration of any related controls.

(ii)   Control risk – The risk that a misstatement that could occur in an assertion about a class of transaction, account balance or disclosure and that could be material, either individually or when aggregated with other misstatements, will not be prevented, or detected and corrected, on a timely basis by the entity's internal control.

(o)   Those charged with governance – The person(s) or organization(s) (for example, a corporate trustee) with responsibility for overseeing the strategic direction of the entity and obligations related to the accountability of the entity. This includes overseeing the financial reporting process. For some entities in some jurisdictions, those charged with governance may include management personnel, for example, executive members of a governance board of a private or public sector entity, or an owner-manager.

In the UK and Ireland, those charged with governance include the directors (executive and non-executive) of a company and the members of an audit committee where one exists. For other types of entity it usually includes equivalent persons such as the partners, proprietors, committee of management or trustees.

Requirements

Ethical Requirements Relating to an Audit of Financial Statements

14.   The auditor shall comply with relevant ethical requirements, including those pertaining to independence, relating to financial statement audit engagements. (Ref: Para. A14-A17)

Professional Skepticism

15.   The auditor shall plan and perform an audit with professional skepticism recognizing that circumstances may exist that cause the financial statements to be materially misstated. (Ref: Para. A18-A22)

Professional Judgment

16.   The auditor shall exercise professional judgment in planning and performing an audit of financial statements. (Ref: Para. A23-A27)

Sufficient Appropriate Audit Evidence and Audit Risk

17.   To obtain reasonable assurance, the auditor shall obtain sufficient appropriate audit evidence to reduce audit risk to an acceptably low level and thereby enable the

auditor to draw reasonable conclusions on which to base the auditor's opinion. (Ref: Para. A28-A52)

Conduct of an Audit in Accordance with ISAs (UK and Ireland)

Complying with ISAs (UK and Ireland) Relevant to the Audit

18. The auditor shall comply with all ISAs (UK and Ireland) relevant to the audit. An ISA (UK and Ireland) is relevant to the audit when the ISA (UK and Ireland) is in effect and the circumstances addressed by the ISA (UK and Ireland) exist. (Ref: Para. A53-A57)

19. The auditor shall have an understanding of the entire text of an ISA (UK and Ireland), including its application and other explanatory material, to understand its objectives and to apply its requirements properly. (Ref: Para. A58-A66)

20. The auditor shall not represent compliance with ISAs (UK and Ireland) in the auditor's report unless the auditor has complied with the requirements of this ISA and all other ISAs (UK and Ireland) relevant to the audit.

Objectives Stated in Individual ISAs (UK and Ireland)

21. To achieve the overall objectives of the auditor, the auditor shall use the objectives stated in relevant ISAs (UK and Ireland) in planning and performing the audit, having regard to the interrelationships among the ISAs (UK and Ireland), to: (Ref: Para. A67-A69)

    (a) Determine whether any audit procedures in addition to those required by the ISAs (UK and Ireland) are necessary in pursuance of the objectives stated in the ISAs (UK and Ireland); and (Ref: Para. A70)

    (b) Evaluate whether sufficient appropriate audit evidence has been obtained. (Ref: Para. A71)

Complying with Relevant Requirements

22. Subject to paragraph 23, the auditor shall comply with each requirement of an ISA (UK and Ireland) unless, in the circumstances of the audit:

    (a) The entire ISA (UK and Ireland) is not relevant; or

    (b) The requirement is not relevant because it is conditional and the condition does not exist. (Ref: Para. A72-A73)

23. In exceptional circumstances, the auditor may judge it necessary to depart from a relevant requirement in an ISA (UK and Ireland). In such circumstances, the auditor shall perform alternative audit procedures to achieve the aim of that requirement. The need for the auditor to depart from a relevant requirement is expected to arise only where the requirement is for a specific procedure to be performed and, in the specific

circumstances of the audit, that procedure would be ineffective in achieving the aim of the requirement. (Ref: Para. A74)

Failure to Achieve an Objective

24.   If an objective in a relevant ISA (UK and Ireland) cannot be achieved, the auditor shall evaluate whether this prevents the auditor from achieving the overall objectives of the auditor and thereby requires the auditor, in accordance with the ISAs (UK and Ireland), to modify the auditor's opinion or withdraw from the engagement (where withdrawal is possible under applicable law or regulation). Failure to achieve an objective represents a significant matter requiring documentation in accordance with ISA (UK and Ireland) 230.[4] (Ref: Para. A75-A76)

***

Application and Other Explanatory Material

An Audit of Financial Statements

Scope of the Audit (Ref: Para. 3)

A1.   The auditor's opinion on the financial statements deals with whether the financial statements are prepared, in all material respects, in accordance with the applicable financial reporting framework. Such an opinion is common to all audits of financial statements. The auditor's opinion therefore does not assure, for example, the future viability of the entity nor the efficiency or effectiveness with which management has conducted the affairs of the entity. In some jurisdictions, however, applicable law or regulation may require auditors to provide opinions on other specific matters, such as the effectiveness of internal control, or the consistency of a separate management report with the financial statements. While the ISAs (UK and Ireland) include requirements and guidance in relation to such matters to the extent that they are relevant to forming an opinion on the financial statements, the auditor would be required to undertake further work if the auditor had additional responsibilities to provide such opinions.

Preparation of the Financial Statements (Ref: Para. 4)

A2.   Law or regulation may establish the responsibilities of management and, where appropriate, those charged with governance in relation to financial reporting. However, the extent of these responsibilities, or the way in which they are described, may differ across jurisdictions. Despite these differences, an audit in accordance with ISAs (UK and Ireland) is conducted on the premise that management and, where appropriate, those charged with governance have acknowledged and understand that they have responsibility:

---

[4]   ISA (UK and Ireland) 230, "Audit Documentation," paragraph 8(c).

(a) For the preparation of the financial statements in accordance with the applicable financial reporting framework, including where relevant their fair presentation;

(b) For such internal control as management and, where appropriate, those charged with governance determine is necessary to enable the preparation of financial statements that are free from material misstatement, whether due to fraud or error; and

(c) To provide the auditor with:

    (i) Access to all information of which management and, where appropriate, those charged with governance are aware that is relevant to the preparation of the financial statements such as records, documentation and other matters;

    (ii) Additional information that the auditor may request from management and, where appropriate, those charged with governance for the purpose of the audit; and

    (iii) Unrestricted access to persons within the entity from whom the auditor determines it necessary to obtain audit evidence.

A3. The preparation of the financial statements by management and, where appropriate, those charged with governance requires:

• The identification of the applicable financial reporting framework, in the context of any relevant laws or regulations.

• The preparation of the financial statements in accordance with that framework.

• The inclusion of an adequate description of that framework in the financial statements.

The preparation of the financial statements requires management to exercise judgment in making accounting estimates that are reasonable in the circumstances, as well as to select and apply appropriate accounting policies. These judgments are made in the context of the applicable financial reporting framework.

A4. The financial statements may be prepared in accordance with a financial reporting framework designed to meet:

• The common financial information needs of a wide range of users (that is, "general purpose financial statements"); or

• The financial information needs of specific users (that is, "special purpose financial statements").

A5.   The applicable financial reporting framework often encompasses financial reporting standards established by an authorized or recognized standards setting organization, or legislative or regulatory requirements. In some cases, the financial reporting framework may encompass both financial reporting standards established by an authorized or recognized standards setting organization and legislative or regulatory requirements. Other sources may provide direction on the application of the applicable financial reporting framework. In some cases, the applicable financial reporting framework may encompass such other sources, or may even consist only of such sources. Such other sources may include:

- The legal and ethical environment, including statutes, regulations, court decisions, and professional ethical obligations in relation to accounting matters;

- Published accounting interpretations of varying authority issued by standards setting, professional or regulatory organizations;

- Published views of varying authority on emerging accounting issues issued by standards setting, professional or regulatory organizations;

- General and industry practices widely recognized and prevalent; and

- Accounting literature.

Where conflicts exist between the financial reporting framework and the sources from which direction on its application may be obtained, or among the sources that encompass the financial reporting framework, the source with the highest authority prevails.

A6.   The requirements of the applicable financial reporting framework determine the form and content of the financial statements. Although the framework may not specify how to account for or disclose all transactions or events, it ordinarily embodies sufficient broad principles that can serve as a basis for developing and applying accounting policies that are consistent with the concepts underlying the requirements of the framework.

A7.   Some financial reporting frameworks are fair presentation frameworks, while others are compliance frameworks. Financial reporting frameworks that encompass primarily the financial reporting standards established by an organization that is authorized or recognized to promulgate standards to be used by entities for preparing general purpose financial statements are often designed to achieve fair presentation, for example, International Financial Reporting Standards (IFRSs) issued by the International Accounting Standards Board (IASB).

A8.   The requirements of the applicable financial reporting framework also determine what constitutes a complete set of financial statements. In the case of many frameworks, financial statements are intended to provide information about the financial position, financial performance and cash flows of an entity. For such frameworks, a complete set of financial statements would include a balance sheet; an income statement; a statement of changes in equity; a cash flow statement; and related notes. For some other financial reporting frameworks, a single financial statement and the related notes might constitute a complete set of financial statements:

- For example, the International Public Sector Accounting Standard (IPSAS), "Financial Reporting Under the Cash Basis of Accounting" issued by the International Public Sector Accounting Standards Board states that the primary financial statement is a statement of cash receipts and payments when a public sector entity prepares its financial statements in accordance with that IPSAS.

- Other examples of a single financial statement, each of which would include related notes, are:

  - Balance sheet.

  - Statement of income or statement of operations.

  - Statement of retained earnings.

  - Statement of cash flows.

  - Statement of assets and liabilities that does not include owner's equity.

  - Statement of changes in owners' equity.

  - Statement of revenue and expenses.

  - Statement of operations by product lines.

A9. ISA (UK and Ireland) 210 establishes requirements and provides guidance on determining the acceptability of the applicable financial reporting framework.[5] ISA 800 deals with special considerations when financial statements are prepared in accordance with a special purpose framework.[6]

A10. Because of the significance of the premise to the conduct of an audit, the auditor is required to obtain the agreement of management and, where appropriate, those charged with governance that they acknowledge and understand that they have the responsibilities set out in paragraph A2 as a precondition for accepting the audit engagement.[7]

Considerations Specific to Audits in the Public Sector

A11. The mandates for audits of the financial statements of public sector entities may be broader than those of other entities. As a result, the premise, relating to

---

[5] ISA (UK and Ireland) 210, "Agreeing the Terms of Audit Engagements," paragraph 6(a).
[6] ISA 800, "Special Considerations—Audits of Financial Statements Prepared in Accordance with Special Purpose Frameworks," paragraph 8.
ISA 800 has not been promulgated by the APB for application in the UK and Ireland.
[7] ISA (UK and Ireland) 210, paragraph 6(b).

management's responsibilities, on which an audit of the financial statements of a public sector entity is conducted may include additional responsibilities, such as the responsibility for the execution of transactions and events in accordance with law, regulation or other authority.[8]

Form of the Auditor's Opinion (Ref: Para. 8)

A12. The opinion expressed by the auditor is on whether the financial statements are prepared, in all material respects, in accordance with the applicable financial reporting framework. The form of the auditor's opinion, however, will depend upon the applicable financial reporting framework and any applicable law or regulation. Most financial reporting frameworks include requirements relating to the presentation of the financial statements; for such frameworks, *preparation* of the financial statements in accordance with the applicable financial reporting framework includes *presentation*.

A13. Where the financial reporting framework is a fair presentation framework, as is generally the case for general purpose financial statements, the opinion required by the ISAs (UK and Ireland) is on whether the financial statements are presented fairly, in all material respects, or give a true and fair view. Where the financial reporting framework is a compliance framework, the opinion required is on whether the financial statements are prepared, in all material respects, in accordance with the framework. Unless specifically stated otherwise, references in the ISAs (UK and Ireland) to the auditor's opinion cover both forms of opinion.

Ethical Requirements Relating to an Audit of Financial Statements (Ref: Para. 14)

A14. The auditor is subject to relevant ethical requirements, including those pertaining to independence, relating to financial statement audit engagements. Relevant ethical requirements ordinarily comprise Parts A and B of the International Ethics Standards Board for Accountants' *Code of Ethics for Professional Accountants* (IESBA Code) related to an audit of financial statements together with national requirements that are more restrictive.

A14-1. Auditors in the UK and Ireland are subject to ethical requirements from two sources: the APB Ethical Standards for Auditors concerning the integrity, objectivity and independence of the auditor, and the ethical pronouncements established by the auditor's relevant professional body. The APB is not aware of any significant instances where the relevant parts of the IESBA Code of Ethics are more restrictive than the APB Ethical Standards for Auditors.

A15. Part A of the IESBA Code establishes the fundamental principles of professional ethics relevant to the auditor when conducting an audit of financial statements and provides a conceptual framework for applying those principles. The fundamental principles with which the auditor is required to comply by the IESBA Code are:

---

[8] See paragraph A57.

(a) Integrity;

(b) Objectivity;

(c) Professional competence and due care;

(d) Confidentiality; and

(e) Professional behavior.

Part B of the IESBA Code illustrates how the conceptual framework is to be applied in specific situations.

A16. In the case of an audit engagement it is in the public interest and, therefore, required by the IESBA Code, that the auditor be independent of the entity subject to the audit. The IESBA Code describes independence as comprising both independence of mind and independence in appearance. The auditor's independence from the entity safeguards the auditor's ability to form an audit opinion without being affected by influences that might compromise that opinion. Independence enhances the auditor's ability to act with integrity, to be objective and to maintain an attitude of professional skepticism.

A17. International Standard on Quality Control (ISQC) 1[9], or national requirements that are at least as demanding,[10] deal with the firm's responsibilities to establish and maintain its system of quality control for audit engagements. ISQC 1 sets out the responsibilities of the firm for establishing policies and procedures designed to provide it with reasonable assurance that the firm and its personnel comply with relevant ethical requirements, including those pertaining to independence.[11] ISA (UK and Ireland) 220 sets out the engagement partner's responsibilities with respect to relevant ethical requirements. These include remaining alert, through observation and making inquiries as necessary, for evidence of non-compliance with relevant ethical requirements by members of the engagement team, determining the appropriate action if matters come to the engagement partner's attention that indicate that members of the engagement team have not complied with relevant ethical requirements, and forming a conclusion on compliance with independence requirements that apply to the audit engagement.[12] ISA (UK and Ireland) 220 recognizes that the engagement team is entitled to rely on a firm's system of quality control in meeting its responsibilities with respect to quality control procedures applicable to the individual audit engagement, unless information provided by the firm or other parties suggests otherwise.

---

[9] International Standard on Quality Control (ISQC) 1, "Quality Control for Firms that Perform Audits and Reviews of Financial Statements, and Other Assurance and Related Services Engagements."

[10] ISA (UK and Ireland) 220, "Quality Control for an Audit of Financial Statements," paragraph 2.

[11] ISQC (UK and Ireland) 1, paragraphs 20-25.

[12] ISA (UK and Ireland) 220, paragraphs 9-11.

Professional Skepticism (Ref: Para. 15)

A18. Professional skepticism includes being alert to, for example:

- Audit evidence that contradicts other audit evidence obtained.

- Information that brings into question the reliability of documents and responses to inquiries to be used as audit evidence.

- Conditions that may indicate possible fraud.

- Circumstances that suggest the need for audit procedures in addition to those required by the ISAs (UK and Ireland).

A19. Maintaining professional skepticism throughout the audit is necessary if the auditor is, for example, to reduce the risks of:

- Overlooking unusual circumstances.

- Over generalizing when drawing conclusions from audit observations.

- Using inappropriate assumptions in determining the nature, timing, and extent of the audit procedures and evaluating the results thereof.

A20. Professional skepticism is necessary to the critical assessment of audit evidence. This includes questioning contradictory audit evidence and the reliability of documents and responses to inquiries and other information obtained from management and those charged with governance. It also includes consideration of the sufficiency and appropriateness of audit evidence obtained in the light of the circumstances, for example in the case where fraud risk factors exist and a single document, of a nature that is susceptible to fraud, is the sole supporting evidence for a material financial statement amount.

A21. The auditor may accept records and documents as genuine unless the auditor has reason to believe the contrary. Nevertheless, the auditor is required to consider the reliability of information to be used as audit evidence.[13] In cases of doubt about the reliability of information or indications of possible fraud (for example, if conditions identified during the audit cause the auditor to believe that a document may not be authentic or that terms in a document may have been falsified), the ISAs (UK and Ireland) require that the auditor investigate further and determine what modifications or additions to audit procedures are necessary to resolve the matter.[14]

A22 The auditor cannot be expected to disregard past experience of the honesty and integrity of the entity's management and those charged with governance. Nevertheless, a belief that management and those charged with governance are

---

[13] ISA (UK and Ireland) 500, "Audit Evidence," paragraphs 7-9.

[14] ISA (UK and Ireland) 240, paragraph 13; ISA (UK and Ireland) 500, paragraph 11; ISA (UK and Ireland) 505, "External Confirmations," paragraphs 10-11, and 16.

honest and have integrity does not relieve the auditor of the need to maintain professional skepticism or allow the auditor to be satisfied with less-than-persuasive audit evidence when obtaining reasonable assurance.

Professional Judgment (Ref: Para. 16)

A23. Professional judgment is essential to the proper conduct of an audit. This is because interpretation of relevant ethical requirements and the ISAs (UK and Ireland) and the informed decisions required throughout the audit cannot be made without the application of relevant knowledge and experience to the facts and circumstances. Professional judgment is necessary in particular regarding decisions about:

- Materiality and audit risk.

- The nature, timing, and extent of audit procedures used to meet the requirements of the ISAs (UK and Ireland) and gather audit evidence.

- Evaluating whether sufficient appropriate audit evidence has been obtained, and whether more needs to be done to achieve the objectives of the ISAs (UK and Ireland) and thereby, the overall objectives of the auditor.

- The evaluation of management's judgments in applying the entity's applicable financial reporting framework.

- The drawing of conclusions based on the audit evidence obtained, for example, assessing the reasonableness of the estimates made by management in preparing the financial statements.

A24. The distinguishing feature of the professional judgment expected of an auditor is that it is exercised by an auditor whose training, knowledge and experience have assisted in developing the necessary competencies to achieve reasonable judgments.

A25. The exercise of professional judgment in any particular case is based on the facts and circumstances that are known by the auditor. Consultation on difficult or contentious matters during the course of the audit, both within the engagement team and between the engagement team and others at the appropriate level within or outside the firm, such as that required by ISA (UK and Ireland) 220,[15] assist the auditor in making informed and reasonable judgments.

A26. Professional judgment can be evaluated based on whether the judgment reached reflects a competent application of auditing and accounting principles and is appropriate in the light of, and consistent with, the facts and circumstances that were known to the auditor up to the date of the auditor's report.

A27. Professional judgment needs to be exercised throughout the audit. It also needs to be appropriately documented. In this regard, the auditor is required to prepare audit

---

[15] ISA (UK and Ireland) 220, paragraph 18.

documentation sufficient to enable an experienced auditor, having no previous connection with the audit, to understand the significant professional judgments made in reaching conclusions on significant matters arising during the audit.[16] Professional judgment is not to be used as the justification for decisions that are not otherwise supported by the facts and circumstances of the engagement or sufficient appropriate audit evidence.

Sufficient Appropriate Audit Evidence and Audit Risk (Ref: Para. 5 and 17)

Sufficiency and Appropriateness of Audit Evidence

A28. Audit evidence is necessary to support the auditor's opinion and report. It is cumulative in nature and is primarily obtained from audit procedures performed during the course of the audit. It may, however, also include information obtained from other sources such as previous audits (provided the auditor has determined whether changes have occurred since the previous audit that may affect its relevance to the current audit[17]) or a firm's quality control procedures for client acceptance and continuance. In addition to other sources inside and outside the entity, the entity's accounting records are an important source of audit evidence. Also, information that may be used as audit evidence may have been prepared by an expert employed or engaged by the entity. Audit evidence comprises both information that supports and corroborates management's assertions, and any information that contradicts such assertions. In addition, in some cases, the absence of information (for example, management's refusal to provide a requested representation) is used by the auditor, and therefore, also constitutes audit evidence. Most of the auditor's work in forming the auditor's opinion consists of obtaining and evaluating audit evidence.

A29. The sufficiency and appropriateness of audit evidence are interrelated. Sufficiency is the measure of the quantity of audit evidence. The quantity of audit evidence needed is affected by the auditor's assessment of the risks of misstatement (the higher the assessed risks, the more audit evidence is likely to be required) and also by the quality of such audit evidence (the higher the quality, the less may be required). Obtaining more audit evidence, however, may not compensate for its poor quality.

A30. Appropriateness is the measure of the quality of audit evidence; that is, its relevance and its reliability in providing support for the conclusions on which the auditor's opinion is based. The reliability of evidence is influenced by its source and by its nature, and is dependent on the individual circumstances under which it is obtained.

A31. Whether sufficient appropriate audit evidence has been obtained to reduce audit risk to an acceptably low level, and thereby enable the auditor to draw reasonable conclusions on which to base the auditor's opinion, is a matter of professional judgment. ISA (UK and Ireland) 500 and other relevant ISAs (UK and Ireland) establish additional requirements and provide further guidance applicable throughout

---

[16] ISA (UK and Ireland) 230, paragraph 8.

[17] ISA (UK and Ireland) 315, "Identifying and Assessing the Risks of Material Misstatement through Understanding the Entity and Its Environment," paragraph 9.

the audit regarding the auditor's considerations in obtaining sufficient appropriate audit evidence.

Audit Risk

A32. Audit risk is a function of the risks of material misstatement and detection risk. The assessment of risks is based on audit procedures to obtain information necessary for that purpose and evidence obtained throughout the audit. The assessment of risks is a matter of professional judgment, rather than a matter capable of precise measurement.

A33. For purposes of the ISAs (UK and Ireland), audit risk does not include the risk that the auditor might express an opinion that the financial statements are materially misstated when they are not. This risk is ordinarily insignificant. Further, audit risk is a technical term related to the process of auditing; it does not refer to the auditor's business risks such as loss from litigation, adverse publicity, or other events arising in connection with the audit of financial statements.

Risks of Material Misstatement

A34. The risks of material misstatement may exist at two levels:

- The overall financial statement level; and

- The assertion level for classes of transactions, account balances, and disclosures.

A35. Risks of material misstatement at the overall financial statement level refer to risks of material misstatement that relate pervasively to the financial statements as a whole and potentially affect many assertions.

A36. Risks of material misstatement at the assertion level are assessed in order to determine the nature, timing, and extent of further audit procedures necessary to obtain sufficient appropriate audit evidence. This evidence enables the auditor to express an opinion on the financial statements at an acceptably low level of audit risk. Auditors use various approaches to accomplish the objective of assessing the risks of material misstatement. For example, the auditor may make use of a model that expresses the general relationship of the components of audit risk in mathematical terms to arrive at an acceptable level of detection risk. Some auditors find such a model to be useful when planning audit procedures.

A37. The risks of material misstatement at the assertion level consist of two components: inherent risk and control risk. Inherent risk and control risk are the entity's risks; they exist independently of the audit of the financial statements.

A38. Inherent risk is higher for some assertions and related classes of transactions, account balances, and disclosures than for others. For example, it may be higher for complex calculations or for accounts consisting of amounts derived from accounting estimates that are subject to significant estimation uncertainty. External circumstances giving rise to business risks may also influence inherent risk. For example, technological developments might make a particular product obsolete, thereby causing inventory to be more susceptible to overstatement. Factors in the entity and its environment that relate to several or all of the classes of transactions, account balances, or disclosures may also influence the inherent risk related to a specific assertion. Such factors may include, for example, a lack of sufficient working capital to continue operations or a declining industry characterized by a large number of business failures.

A39. Control risk is a function of the effectiveness of the design, implementation and maintenance of internal control by management to address identified risks that threaten the achievement of the entity's objectives relevant to preparation of the entity's financial statements. However, internal control, no matter how well designed and operated, can only reduce, but not eliminate, risks of material misstatement in the financial statements, because of the inherent limitations of internal control. These include, for example, the possibility of human errors or mistakes, or of controls being circumvented by collusion or inappropriate management override. Accordingly, some control risk will always exist. The ISAs (UK and Ireland) provide the conditions under which the auditor is required to, or may choose to, test the operating effectiveness of controls in determining the nature, timing and extent of substantive procedures to be performed.[18]

A40. The ISAs (UK and Ireland) do not ordinarily refer to inherent risk and control risk separately, but rather to a combined assessment of the "risks of material misstatement." However, the auditor may make separate or combined assessments of inherent and control risk depending on preferred audit techniques or methodologies and practical considerations. The assessment of the risks of material misstatement may be expressed in quantitative terms, such as in percentages, or in non-quantitative terms. In any case, the need for the auditor to make appropriate risk assessments is more important than the different approaches by which they may be made.

A41. ISA (UK and Ireland) 315 establishes requirements and provides guidance on identifying and assessing the risks of material misstatement at the financial statement and assertion levels.

Detection Risk

A42. For a given level of audit risk, the acceptable level of detection risk bears an inverse relationship to the assessed risks of material misstatement at the assertion level. For example, the greater the risks of material misstatement the auditor believes exists, the less the detection risk that can be accepted and, accordingly, the more persuasive the audit evidence required by the auditor.

A43. Detection risk relates to the nature, timing, and extent of the auditor's procedures that are determined by the auditor to reduce audit risk to an acceptably low level. It is

---

[18] ISA (UK and Ireland) 330, "The Auditor's Reponses to Assessed Risks," paragraphs 7-17.

therefore a function of the effectiveness of an audit procedure and of its application by the auditor. Matters such as:

- adequate planning;

- proper assignment of personnel to the engagement team;

- the application of professional scepticism; and

- supervision and review of the audit work performed,

assist to enhance the effectiveness of an audit procedure and of its application and reduce the possibility that an auditor might select an inappropriate audit procedure, misapply an appropriate audit procedure, or misinterpret the audit results.

A44. ISA (UK and Ireland) 300 [19] and ISA (UK and Ireland) 330 establish requirements and provide guidance on planning an audit of financial statements and the auditor's responses to assessed risks. Detection risk, however, can only be reduced, not eliminated, because of the inherent limitations of an audit. Accordingly, some detection risk will always exist.

Inherent Limitations of an Audit

A45. The auditor is not expected to, and cannot, reduce audit risk to zero and cannot therefore obtain absolute assurance that the financial statements are free from material misstatement due to fraud or error. This is because there are inherent limitations of an audit, which result in most of the audit evidence on which the auditor draws conclusions and bases the auditor's opinion being persuasive rather than conclusive. The inherent limitations of an audit arise from:

- The nature of financial reporting;

- The nature of audit procedures; and

- The need for the audit to be conducted within a reasonable period of time and at a reasonable cost.

The Nature of Financial Reporting

A46. The preparation of financial statements involves judgment by management in applying the requirements of the entity's applicable financial reporting framework to the facts and circumstances of the entity. In addition, many financial statement items involve subjective decisions or assessments or a degree of uncertainty, and there may be a range of acceptable interpretations or judgments that may be made. Consequently, some financial statement items are subject to an inherent level of variability which cannot be eliminated by the application of additional auditing

---

[19] ISA (UK and Ireland) 300, "Planning an Audit of Financial Statements."

procedures. For example, this is often the case with respect to certain accounting estimates. Nevertheless, the ISAs (UK and Ireland) require the auditor to give specific consideration to whether accounting estimates are reasonable in the context of the applicable financial reporting framework and related disclosures, and to the qualitative aspects of the entity's accounting practices, including indicators of possible bias in management's judgments.[20]

The Nature of Audit Procedures

A47. There are practical and legal limitations on the auditor's ability to obtain audit evidence. For example:

- There is the possibility that management or others may not provide, intentionally or unintentionally, the complete information that is relevant to the preparation of the financial statements or that has been requested by the auditor. Accordingly, the auditor cannot be certain of the completeness of information, even though the auditor has performed audit procedures to obtain assurance that all relevant information has been obtained.

- Fraud may involve sophisticated and carefully organized schemes designed to conceal it. Therefore, audit procedures used to gather audit evidence may be ineffective for detecting an intentional misstatement that involves, for example, collusion to falsify documentation which may cause the auditor to believe that audit evidence is valid when it is not. The auditor is neither trained as nor expected to be an expert in the authentication of documents.

- An audit is not an official investigation into alleged wrongdoing. Accordingly, the auditor is not given specific legal powers, such as the power of search, which may be necessary for such an investigation.

Timeliness of Financial Reporting and the Balance between Benefit and Cost

A48. The matter of difficulty, time, or cost involved is not in itself a valid basis for the auditor to omit an audit procedure for which there is no alternative or to be satisfied with audit evidence that is less than persuasive. Appropriate planning assists in making sufficient time and resources available for the conduct of the audit. Notwithstanding this, the relevance of information, and thereby its value, tends to diminish over time, and there is a balance to be struck between the reliability of information and its cost. This is recognized in certain financial reporting frameworks (see, for example, the IASB's "Framework for the Preparation and Presentation of Financial Statements"). Therefore, there is an expectation by users of financial statements that the auditor will

---

[20] ISA (UK and Ireland) 540, "Auditing Accounting Estimates, Including Fair Value Accounting Estimates, and Related Disclosures," and ISA 700, "Forming an Opinion and Reporting on Financial Statements," paragraph 12.

The APB has not promulgated ISA 700 as issued by the IAASB for application in the UK and Ireland. In the UK and Ireland the applicable auditing standard is ISA (UK and Ireland) 700, "The Auditor's Report on Financial Statements." Paragraph 8 of ISA (UK and Ireland) 700 includes requirements equivalent to those in paragraph 12 of ISA 700.

form an opinion on the financial statements within a reasonable period of time and at a reasonable cost, recognizing that it is impracticable to address all information that may exist or to pursue every matter exhaustively on the assumption that information is in error or fraudulent until proved otherwise.

A49. Consequently, it is necessary for the auditor to:

- Plan the audit so that it will be performed in an effective manner;

- Direct audit effort to areas most expected to contain risks of material misstatement, whether due to fraud or error, with correspondingly less effort directed at other areas; and

- Use testing and other means of examining populations for misstatements.

A50. In light of the approaches described in paragraph A49, the ISAs (UK and Ireland) contain requirements for the planning and performance of the audit and require the auditor, among other things, to:

- Have a basis for the identification and assessment of risks of material misstatement at the financial statement and assertion levels by performing risk assessment procedures and related activities;[21] and

- Use testing and other means of examining populations in a manner that provides a reasonable basis for the auditor to draw conclusions about the population.[22]

Other Matters that Affect the Inherent Limitations of an Audit

A51. In the case of certain assertions or subject matters, the potential effects of the inherent limitations on the auditor's ability to detect material misstatements are particularly significant. Such assertions or subject matters include:

- Fraud, particularly fraud involving senior management or collusion. See ISA (UK and Ireland) 240 for further discussion.

- The existence and completeness of related party relationships and transactions. See ISA (UK and Ireland) 550[23] for further discussion.

- The occurrence of non-compliance with laws and regulations. See ISA (UK and Ireland) 250[24] for further discussion.

---

[21] ISA (UK and Ireland) 315, paragraphs 5-10.
[22] ISA (UK and Ireland) 330; ISA (UK and Ireland) 500; ISA 520, "Analytical Procedures;" ISA (UK and Ireland) 530, "Audit Sampling."
[23] ISA (UK and Ireland) 550, "Related Parties."
[24] ISA (UK and Ireland) 250, "Consideration of Laws and Regulations in an Audit of Financial Statements."

- Future events or conditions that may cause an entity to cease to continue as a going concern. See ISA (UK and Ireland) 570[25] for further discussion.

Relevant ISAs (UK and Ireland) identify specific audit procedures to assist in mitigating the effect of the inherent limitations.

A52. Because of the inherent limitations of an audit, there is an unavoidable risk that some material misstatements of the financial statements may not be detected, even though the audit is properly planned and performed in accordance with ISAs (UK and Ireland). Accordingly, the subsequent discovery of a material misstatement of the financial statements resulting from fraud or error does not by itself indicate a failure to conduct an audit in accordance with ISAs (UK and Ireland). However, the inherent limitations of an audit are not a justification for the auditor to be satisfied with less-than-persuasive audit evidence. Whether the auditor has performed an audit in accordance with ISAs is determined by the audit procedures performed in the circumstances, the sufficiency and appropriateness of the audit evidence obtained as a result thereof and the suitability of the auditor's report based on an evaluation of that evidence in light of the overall objectives of the auditor.

Conduct of an Audit in Accordance with ISAs (UK and Ireland)

Nature of the ISAs (UK and Ireland) (Ref: Para. 18)

A53. The ISAs (UK and Ireland), taken together, provide the standards for the auditor's work in fulfilling the overall objectives of the auditor. The ISAs (UK and Ireland) deal with the general responsibilities of the auditor, as well as the auditor's further considerations relevant to the application of those responsibilities to specific topics.

A54. The scope, effective date and any specific limitation of the applicability of a specific ISA (UK and Ireland) is made clear in the ISA (UK and Ireland). Unless otherwise stated in the ISA (UK and Ireland), the auditor is permitted to apply an ISA (UK and Ireland) before the effective date specified therein.

A55. In performing an audit, the auditor may be required to comply with legal or regulatory requirements in addition to the ISAs (UK and Ireland). The ISAs (UK and Ireland) do not override law or regulation that governs an audit of financial statements. In the event that such law or regulation differs from the ISAs (UK and Ireland), an audit conducted only in accordance with law or regulation will not automatically comply with ISAs (UK and Ireland).

A56. The auditor may also conduct the audit in accordance with both ISAs (UK and Ireland) and auditing standards of a specific jurisdiction or country. In such cases, in addition to complying with each of the ISAs (UK and Ireland) relevant to the audit, it may be necessary for the auditor to perform additional audit procedures in order to comply with the relevant standards of that jurisdiction or country.

---

[25] ISA (UK and Ireland) 570, "Going Concern."

Considerations Specific to Audits in the Public Sector

A57. The ISAs (UK and Ireland) are relevant to engagements in the public sector. The public sector auditor's responsibilities, however, may be affected by the audit mandate, or by obligations on public sector entities arising from law, regulation or other authority (such as ministerial directives, government policy requirements, or resolutions of the legislature), which may encompass a broader scope than an audit of financial statements in accordance with the ISAs (UK and Ireland). These additional responsibilities are not dealt with in the ISAs (UK and Ireland). They may be dealt with in the pronouncements of the International Organization of Supreme Audit Institutions or national standard setters, or in guidance developed by government audit agencies.

Contents of the ISAs (UK and Ireland) (Ref: Para. 19)

A58. In addition to objectives and requirements (requirements are expressed in the ISAs (UK and Ireland) using "shall"), an ISA (UK and Ireland) contains related guidance in the form of application and other explanatory material. It may also contain introductory material that provides context relevant to a proper understanding of the ISA (UK and Ireland), and definitions. The entire text of an ISA (UK and Ireland), therefore, is relevant to an understanding of the objectives stated in an ISA (UK and Ireland) and the proper application of the requirements of an ISA (UK and Ireland).

A59. Where necessary, the application and other explanatory material provides further explanation of the requirements of an ISA (UK and Ireland) and guidance for carrying them out. In particular, it may:

- Explain more precisely what a requirement means or is intended to cover.

- Include examples of procedures that may be appropriate in the circumstances.

While such guidance does not in itself impose a requirement, it is relevant to the proper application of the requirements of an ISA (UK and Ireland). The application and other explanatory material may also provide background information on matters addressed in an ISA (UK and Ireland).

A60. Appendices form part of the application and other explanatory material. The purpose and intended use of an appendix are explained in the body of the related ISA (UK and Ireland) or within the title and introduction of the appendix itself.

A61. Introductory material may include, as needed, such matters as explanation of:

- The purpose and scope of the ISA (UK and Ireland), including how the ISA (UK and Ireland) relates to other ISAs (UK and Ireland).

- The subject matter of the ISA (UK and Ireland).

- The respective responsibilities of the auditor and others in relation to the subject matter of the ISA (UK and Ireland).

- The context in which the ISA (UK and Ireland) is set.

A62. An ISA (UK and Ireland) may include, in a separate section under the heading "Definitions," a description of the meanings attributed to certain terms for purposes of the ISAs (UK and Ireland). These are provided to assist in the consistent application and interpretation of the ISAs (UK and Ireland), and are not intended to override definitions that may be established for other purposes, whether in law, regulation or otherwise. Unless otherwise indicated, those terms will carry the same meanings throughout the ISAs (UK and Ireland). The Glossary of Terms relating to International Standards issued by the International Auditing and Assurance Standards Board in the *Handbook of International Quality Control, Auditing, Review, Other Assurance, and Related Services Pronouncements* published by IFAC contains a complete listing of terms defined in the ISAs (UK and Ireland). It also includes descriptions of other terms found in ISAs (UK and Ireland) to assist in common and consistent interpretation and translation.

A63. When appropriate, additional considerations specific to audits of smaller entities and public sector entities are included within the application and other explanatory material of an ISA (UK and Ireland). These additional considerations assist in the application of the requirements of the ISA (UK and Ireland) in the audit of such entities. They do not, however, limit or reduce the responsibility of the auditor to apply and comply with the requirements of the ISAs (UK and Ireland).

Considerations Specific to Smaller Entities

A64. For purposes of specifying additional considerations to audits of smaller entities, a "smaller entity" refers to an entity which typically possesses qualitative characteristics such as:

(a) Concentration of ownership and management in a small number of individuals (often a single individual – either a natural person or another enterprise that owns the entity provided the owner exhibits the relevant qualitative characteristics); and

(b) One or more of the following:

(i) Straightforward or uncomplicated transactions;

(ii) Simple record-keeping;

(iii) Few lines of business and few products within business lines;

(iv) Few internal controls;

(v) Few levels of management with responsibility for a broad range of controls; or

(vi) Few personnel, many having a wide range of duties.

These qualitative characteristics are not exhaustive, they are not exclusive to smaller entities, and smaller entities do not necessarily display all of these characteristics.

A65. The considerations specific to smaller entities included in the ISAs (UK and Ireland) have been developed primarily with unlisted entities in mind. Some of the considerations, however, may be helpful in audits of smaller listed entities.

A66. The ISAs (UK and Ireland) refer to the proprietor of a smaller entity who is involved in running the entity on a day-to-day basis as the "owner-manager."

Objectives Stated in Individual ISAs (UK and Ireland) (Ref: Para. 21)

A67. Each ISA (UK and Ireland) contains one or more objectives which provide a link between the requirements and the overall objectives of the auditor. The objectives in individual ISAs (UK and Ireland) serve to focus the auditor on the desired outcome of the ISA (UK and Ireland), while being specific enough to assist the auditor in:

- Understanding what needs to be accomplished and, where necessary, the appropriate means of doing so; and

- Deciding whether more needs to be done to achieve them in the particular circumstances of the audit.

A68. Objectives are to be understood in the context of the overall objectives of the auditor stated in paragraph 11 of this ISA (UK and Ireland). As with the overall objectives of the auditor, the ability to achieve an individual objective is equally subject to the inherent limitations of an audit.

A69. In using the objectives, the auditor is required to have regard to the interrelationships among the ISAs (UK and Ireland). This is because, as indicated in paragraph A53, the ISAs (UK and Ireland) deal in some cases with general responsibilities and in others with the application of those responsibilities to specific topics. For example, this ISA (UK and Ireland) requires the auditor to adopt an attitude of professional skepticism; this is necessary in all aspects of planning and performing an audit but is not repeated as a requirement of each ISA (UK and Ireland). At a more detailed level, ISA (UK and Ireland) 315 and ISA (UK and Ireland) 330 contain, among other things, objectives and requirements that deal with the auditor's responsibilities to identify and assess the risks of material misstatement and to design and perform further audit procedures to respond to those assessed risks, respectively; these objectives and requirements apply throughout the audit. An ISA (UK and Ireland) dealing with specific aspects of the audit (for example, ISA (UK and Ireland) 540) may expand on how the objectives and requirements of such ISAs (UK and Ireland) as ISA (UK and Ireland) 315 and ISA (UK and Ireland) 330 are to be applied in relation to the subject of the ISA (UK and Ireland) but does not repeat them. Thus, in achieving the objective stated in ISA (UK and Ireland) 540, the auditor has regard to the objectives and requirements of other relevant ISAs (UK and Ireland).

Use of Objectives to Determine Need for Additional Audit Procedures (Ref: Para. 21(a))

A70. The requirements of the ISAs (UK and Ireland) are designed to enable the auditor to achieve the objectives specified in the ISAs (UK and Ireland), and thereby the overall objectives of the auditor. The proper application of the requirements of the ISAs (UK and Ireland) by the auditor is therefore expected to provide a sufficient basis for the auditor's achievement of the objectives. However, because the circumstances of audit engagements vary widely and all such circumstances cannot be anticipated in the ISAs (UK and Ireland), the auditor is responsible for determining the audit procedures necessary to fulfill the requirements of the ISAs (UK and Ireland) and to achieve the objectives. In the circumstances of an engagement, there may be particular matters that require the auditor to perform audit procedures in addition to those required by the ISAs (UK and Ireland) to meet the objectives specified in the ISAs (UK and Ireland).

Use of Objectives to Evaluate Whether Sufficient Appropriate Audit Evidence Has Been Obtained (Ref: Para. 21(b))

A71. The auditor is required to use the objectives to evaluate whether sufficient appropriate audit evidence has been obtained in the context of the overall objectives of the auditor. If as a result the auditor concludes that the audit evidence is not sufficient and appropriate, then the auditor may follow one or more of the following approaches to meeting the requirement of paragraph 21(b):

- Evaluate whether further relevant audit evidence has been, or will be, obtained as a result of complying with other ISAs (UK and Ireland);

- Extend the work performed in applying one or more requirements; or

- Perform other procedures judged by the auditor to be necessary in the circumstances.

Where none of the above is expected to be practical or possible in the circumstances, the auditor will not be able to obtain sufficient appropriate audit evidence and is required by the ISAs (UK and Ireland) to determine the effect on the auditor's report or on the auditor's ability to complete the engagement.

Complying with Relevant Requirements

Relevant Requirements (Ref: Para. 22)

A72. In some cases, an ISA (UK and Ireland) (and therefore all of its requirements) may not be relevant in the circumstances. For example, if an entity does not have an internal audit function, nothing in ISA (UK and Ireland) 610 (Revised June 2013)[26] is relevant.

---

[26] ISA (UK and Ireland) 610 (Revised June 2013), "Using the Work of Internal Auditors," paragraph 2.

A73. Within a relevant ISA (UK and Ireland), there may be conditional requirements. Such a requirement is relevant when the circumstances envisioned in the requirement apply and the condition exists. In general, the conditionality of a requirement will either be explicit or implicit, for example:

- The requirement to modify the auditor's opinion if there is a limitation of scope[27] represents an explicit conditional requirement.

- The requirement to communicate significant deficiencies in internal control identified during the audit to those charged with governance,[28] which depends on the existence of such identified significant deficiencies; and the requirement to obtain sufficient appropriate audit evidence regarding the presentation and disclosure of segment information in accordance with the applicable financial reporting framework,[29] which depends on that framework requiring or permitting such disclosure, represent implicit conditional requirements.

In some cases, a requirement may be expressed as being conditional on applicable law or regulation. For example, the auditor may be required to withdraw from the audit engagement, *where withdrawal is possible under applicable law or regulation*, or the auditor may be required to do something, *unless prohibited by law or regulation*. Depending on the jurisdiction, the legal or regulatory permission or prohibition may be explicit or implicit.

Departure from a Requirement (Ref: Para. 23)

A74. ISA (UK and Ireland) 230 establishes documentation requirements in those exceptional circumstances where the auditor departs from a relevant requirement.[30] The ISAs (UK and Ireland) do not call for compliance with a requirement that is not relevant in the circumstances of the audit.

Failure to Achieve an Objective (Ref: Para. 24)

A75. Whether an objective has been achieved is a matter for the auditor's professional judgment. That judgment takes account of the results of audit procedures performed in complying with the requirements of the ISAs (UK and Ireland), and the auditor's evaluation of whether sufficient appropriate audit evidence has been obtained and whether more needs to be done in the particular circumstances of the audit to achieve the objectives stated in the ISAs (UK and Ireland). Accordingly, circumstances that may give rise to a failure to achieve an objective include those that:

---

[27] ISA (UK and Ireland) 705, "Modifications to the Opinion in the Independent Auditor's Report," paragraph 13.

[28] ISA (UK and Ireland) 265, "Communicating Deficiencies in Internal Control to Those Charged with Governance and Management," paragraph 9.

[29] ISA (UK and Ireland) 501, "Audit Evidence—Specific Considerations for Selected Items," paragraph 13.

[30] ISA (UK and Ireland) 230, paragraph 12.

- Prevent the auditor from complying with the relevant requirements of an ISA (UK and Ireland).

- Result in its not being practicable or possible for the auditor to carry out the additional audit procedures or obtain further audit evidence as determined necessary from the use of the objectives in accordance with paragraph 21, for example due to a limitation in the available audit evidence.

A76. Audit documentation that meets the requirements of ISA (UK and Ireland) 230 and the specific documentation requirements of other relevant ISAs (UK and Ireland) provides evidence of the auditor's basis for a conclusion about the achievement of the overall objectives of the auditor. While it is unnecessary for the auditor to document separately (as in a checklist, for example) that individual objectives have been achieved, the documentation of a failure to achieve an objective assists the auditor's evaluation of whether such a failure has prevented the auditor from achieving the overall objectives of the auditor.

INTERNATIONAL STANDARD ON AUDITING (UK AND IRELAND) 210

AGREEING THE TERMS OF AUDIT ENGAGEMENTS

(Effective for audits of financial statements for periods ending on or after 15 December 2010)

CONTENTS

International Standard on Auditing (UK and Ireland) (ISA (UK and Ireland)) 210, "Agreeing the Terms of Audit Engagements" should be read in conjunction with ISA (UK and Ireland) 200, "Overall Objectives of the Independent Auditor and the Conduct of an Audit in Accordance with International Standards on Auditing (UK and Ireland)."

Introduction

Scope of this ISA (UK and Ireland)

1. This International Standard on Auditing (UK and Ireland) (ISA (UK and Ireland)) deals with the auditor's responsibilities in agreeing the terms of the audit engagement with management and, where appropriate, those charged with governance. This includes establishing that certain preconditions for an audit, responsibility for which rests with management and, where appropriate, those charged with governance, are present. ISA (UK and Ireland) 220[1] deals with those aspects of engagement acceptance that are within the control of the auditor. (Ref: Para. A1)

Effective Date

2. This ISA (UK and Ireland) is effective for audits of financial statements for periods ending on or after 15 December 2010.

Objective

3. The objective of the auditor is to accept or continue an audit engagement only when the basis upon which it is to be performed has been agreed, through:

    (a) Establishing whether the preconditions for an audit are present; and

    (b) Confirming that there is a common understanding between the auditor and management and, where appropriate, those charged with governance of the terms of the audit engagement.

Definitions

4. For purposes of the ISAs (UK and Ireland), the following term has the meaning attributed below:

    Preconditions for an audit – The use by management[1a] of an acceptable financial reporting framework in the preparation of the financial statements and the agreement of management and, where appropriate, those charged with governance to the premise[2] on which an audit is conducted.

5. For the purposes of this ISA (UK and Ireland), references to "management" should be read hereafter as "management and, where appropriate, those charged with governance."

---

[1] ISA (UK and Ireland) 220, "Quality Control for an Audit of Financial Statements."
[1a] In the UK and Ireland those charged with governance are responsible for the preparation of the financial statements.
[2] ISA (UK and Ireland) 200, "Overall Objectives of the Independent Auditor and the Conduct of an Audit in Accordance with International Standards on Auditing," paragraph 13.

Requirements

Preconditions for an Audit

6. In order to establish whether the preconditions for an audit are present, the auditor shall:

 (a) Determine whether the financial reporting framework to be applied in the preparation of the financial statements is acceptable; and (Ref: Para. A2-A10)

 (b) Obtain the agreement of management that it acknowledges and understands its responsibility: (Ref: Para. A11-A14, A20)

  (i) For the preparation of the financial statements in accordance with the applicable financial reporting framework, including where relevant their fair presentation; (Ref: Para. A15)

  (ii) For such internal control as management determines is necessary to enable the preparation of financial statements that are free from material misstatement, whether due to fraud or error; and (Ref: Para. A16-A19)

  (iii) To provide the auditor with[2a]:

   a. Access to all information of which management is aware that is relevant to the preparation of the financial statements such as records, documentation and other matters;

   b. Additional information that the auditor may request from management for the purpose of the audit; and

   c. Unrestricted access to persons within the entity from whom the auditor determines it necessary to obtain audit evidence.

Limitation on Scope Prior to Audit Engagement Acceptance

7. If management or those charged with governance impose a limitation on the scope of the auditor's work in the terms of a proposed audit engagement such that the auditor believes the limitation will result in the auditor disclaiming an opinion on the financial statements, the auditor shall not accept such a limited engagement as an audit engagement, unless required by law or regulation to do so.

[2a] Sections 499 and 500 of the Companies Act 2006 set legal requirements in relation to the auditor's right to obtain information. For the Republic of Ireland, relevant requirements are set out in Section 193(3), Companies Act 1990.

Other Factors Affecting Audit Engagement Acceptance

8.   If the preconditions for an audit are not present, the auditor shall discuss the matter with management. Unless required by law or regulation to do so, the auditor shall not accept the proposed audit engagement:

(a)   If the auditor has determined that the financial reporting framework to be applied in the preparation of the financial statements is unacceptable, except as provided in paragraph 19; or

(b)   If the agreement referred to in paragraph 6(b) has not been obtained.

Agreement on Audit Engagement Terms

9.   The auditor shall agree the terms of the audit engagement with management or those charged with governance, as appropriate. (Ref: Para. A21)

10.   Subject to paragraph 11, the agreed terms of the audit engagement shall be recorded in an audit engagement letter or other suitable form of written agreement and shall include: (Ref: Para. A22-A25)

(a)   The objective and scope of the audit of the financial statements;

(b)   The responsibilities of the auditor;

(c)   The responsibilities of management[2b];

(d)   Identification of the applicable financial reporting framework for the preparation of the financial statements; and

(e)   Reference to the expected form and content of any reports to be issued by the auditor and a statement that there may be circumstances in which a report may differ from its expected form and content.

11.   If law or regulation prescribes in sufficient detail the terms of the audit engagement referred to in paragraph 10, the auditor need not record them in a written agreement, except for the fact that such law or regulation applies and that management acknowledges and understands its responsibilities as set out in paragraph 6(b). (Ref: Para. A22, A26-A27)

12.   If law or regulation prescribes responsibilities of management similar to those described in paragraph 6(b), the auditor may determine that the law or regulation includes responsibilities that, in the auditor's judgment, are equivalent in effect to those set out in that paragraph. For such responsibilities that are equivalent, the auditor may use the wording of the law or regulation to describe them in the written

---

[2b] In the UK and Ireland, the engagement letter sets out the responsibilities of those charged with governance.

agreement. For those responsibilities that are not prescribed by law or regulation such that their effect is equivalent, the written agreement shall use the description in paragraph 6(b). (Ref: Para. A26)

Recurring Audits

13.   On recurring audits, the auditor shall assess whether circumstances require the terms of the audit engagement to be revised and whether there is a need to remind the entity of the existing terms of the audit engagement. (Ref: Para. A28)

Acceptance of a Change in the Terms of the Audit Engagement

14.   The auditor shall not agree to a change in the terms of the audit engagement where there is no reasonable justification for doing so. (Ref: Para. A29-A31)

15.   If, prior to completing the audit engagement, the auditor is requested to change the audit engagement to an engagement that conveys a lower level of assurance, the auditor shall determine whether there is reasonable justification for doing so. (Ref: Para. A32-A33)

16.   If the terms of the audit engagement are changed, the auditor and management shall agree on and record the new terms of the engagement in an engagement letter or other suitable form of written agreement.

17.   If the auditor is unable to agree to a change of the terms of the audit engagement and is not permitted by management to continue the original audit engagement, the auditor shall:

   (a)   Withdraw from the audit engagement where possible under applicable law or regulation; and

   (b)   Determine whether there is any obligation, either contractual or otherwise, to report the circumstances to other parties, such as those charged with governance, owners or regulators. (Ref: Para. A33-1)

Additional Considerations in Engagement Acceptance

Financial Reporting Standards Supplemented by Law or Regulation

18.   If financial reporting standards established by an authorized or recognized standards setting organization are supplemented by law or regulation, the auditor shall determine whether there are any conflicts between the financial reporting standards and the additional requirements. If such conflicts exist, the auditor shall discuss with management the nature of the additional requirements and shall agree whether:

   (a)   The additional requirements can be met through additional disclosures in the financial statements; or

**FINANCIAL
REPORTING COUNCIL**

(b)   The description of the applicable financial reporting framework in the financial statements can be amended accordingly.

If neither of the above actions is possible, the auditor shall determine whether it will be necessary to modify the auditor's opinion in accordance with ISA (UK and Ireland) 705.[3] (Ref: Para. A34)

Financial Reporting Framework Prescribed by Law or Regulation—Other Matters Affecting Acceptance

19.   If the auditor has determined that the financial reporting framework prescribed by law or regulation would be unacceptable but for the fact that it is prescribed by law or regulation, the auditor shall accept the audit engagement only if the following conditions are present: (Ref: Para. A35)

(a)   Management agrees to provide additional disclosures in the financial statements required to avoid the financial statements being misleading; and

(b)   It is recognized in the terms of the audit engagement that:

(i)   The auditor's report on the financial statements will incorporate an Emphasis of Matter paragraph, drawing users' attention to the additional disclosures, in accordance with ISA (UK and Ireland) 706;[4] and

(ii)   Unless the auditor is required by law or regulation to express the auditor's opinion on the financial statements by using the phrases "present fairly, in all material respects," or "give a true and fair view" in accordance with the applicable financial reporting framework, the auditor's opinion on the financial statements will not include such phrases.

20.   If the conditions outlined in paragraph 19 are not present and the auditor is required by law or regulation to undertake the audit engagement, the auditor shall:

(a)   Evaluate the effect of the misleading nature of the financial statements on the auditor's report; and

(b)   Include appropriate reference to this matter in the terms of the audit engagement.

Auditor's Report Prescribed by Law or Regulation

21.   In some cases, law or regulation of the relevant jurisdiction prescribes the layout or wording of the auditor's report in a form or in terms that are significantly different from the requirements of ISAs (UK and Ireland). In these circumstances, the auditor shall evaluate:

---

[3]   ISA (UK and Ireland) 705, "Modifications to the Opinion in the Independent Auditor's Report."
[4]   ISA (UK and Ireland) 706, "Emphasis of Matter Paragraphs and Other Matter Paragraphs in the Independent Auditor's Report."

(a) Whether users might misunderstand the assurance obtained from the audit of the financial statements and, if so,

(b) Whether additional explanation in the auditor's report can mitigate possible misunderstanding.[5]

If the auditor concludes that additional explanation in the auditor's report cannot mitigate possible misunderstanding, the auditor shall not accept the audit engagement, unless required by law or regulation to do so. An audit conducted in accordance with such law or regulation does not comply with ISAs (UK and Ireland). Accordingly, the auditor shall not include any reference within the auditor's report to the audit having been conducted in accordance with ISAs (UK and Ireland).[6] (Ref: Para. A36-A37)

***

Application and Other Explanatory Material

Scope of this ISA (UK and Ireland) (Ref: Para. 1)

A1. Assurance engagements, which include audit engagements, may only be accepted when the practitioner considers that relevant ethical requirements such as independence and professional competence will be satisfied, and when the engagement exhibits certain characteristics.[7] The auditor's responsibilities in respect of ethical requirements in the context of the acceptance of an audit engagement and in so far as they are within the control of the auditor are dealt with in ISA (UK and Ireland) 220.[8] This ISA (UK and Ireland) deals with those matters (or preconditions) that are within the control of the entity and upon which it is necessary for the auditor and the entity's management to agree.

---

[5] ISA (UK and Ireland) 706.

[6] See also ISA 700, "Forming an Opinion and Reporting on Financial Statements," paragraph 43.
The APB has not promulgated ISA 700 as issued by the IAASB for application in the UK and Ireland. In the UK and Ireland the applicable auditing standard is ISA (UK and Ireland) 700, "The Auditor's Report on Financial Statements." Paragraph 5 of ISA (UK and Ireland) 700 explains that compliance with that ISA (UK and Ireland) does not preclude the auditor from being able to assert compliance with ISAs.

[7] "International Framework for Assurance Engagements," paragraph 17.
The "International Framework for Assurance Engagements" has not been promulgated by the APB for application in the UK and Ireland.

[8] ISA (UK and Ireland) 220, paragraphs 9-11.

Preconditions for an Audit

The Financial Reporting Framework (Ref: Para. 6(a))

A2. A condition for acceptance of an assurance engagement is that the criteria referred to in the definition of an assurance engagement are suitable and available to intended users.[9] Criteria are the benchmarks used to evaluate or measure the subject matter including, where relevant, benchmarks for presentation and disclosure. Suitable criteria enable reasonably consistent evaluation or measurement of a subject matter within the context of professional judgment. For purposes of the ISAs (UK and Ireland), the applicable financial reporting framework provides the criteria the auditor uses to audit the financial statements, including where relevant their fair presentation.

A3. Without an acceptable financial reporting framework, management does not have an appropriate basis for the preparation of the financial statements and the auditor does not have suitable criteria for auditing the financial statements. In many cases the auditor may presume that the applicable financial reporting framework is acceptable, as described in paragraphs A8-A9.

Determining the Acceptability of the Financial Reporting Framework

A4. Factors that are relevant to the auditor's determination of the acceptability of the financial reporting framework to be applied in the preparation of the financial statements include:

- The nature of the entity (for example, whether it is a business enterprise, a public sector entity or a not for profit organization);

- The purpose of the financial statements (for example, whether they are prepared to meet the common financial information needs of a wide range of users or the financial information needs of specific users);

- The nature of the financial statements (for example, whether the financial statements are a complete set of financial statements or a single financial statement); and

- Whether law or regulation prescribes the applicable financial reporting framework.

A5. Many users of financial statements are not in a position to demand financial statements tailored to meet their specific information needs. While all the information needs of specific users cannot be met, there are financial information needs that are common to a wide range of users. Financial statements prepared in accordance with a financial reporting framework designed to meet the common financial information

---

[9] "International Framework for Assurance Engagements," paragraph 17(b)(ii).
The "International Framework for Assurance Engagements" has not been promulgated by the APB for application in the UK and Ireland.

needs of a wide range of users are referred to as general purpose financial statements.

A6. In some cases, the financial statements will be prepared in accordance with a financial reporting framework designed to meet the financial information needs of specific users. Such financial statements are referred to as special purpose financial statements. The financial information needs of the intended users will determine the applicable financial reporting framework in these circumstances. ISA 800 discusses the acceptability of financial reporting frameworks designed to meet the financial information needs of specific users.[10]

A7. Deficiencies in the applicable financial reporting framework that indicate that the framework is not acceptable may be encountered after the audit engagement has been accepted. When use of that framework is prescribed by law or regulation, the requirements of paragraphs 19-20 apply. When use of that framework is not prescribed by law or regulation, management may decide to adopt another framework that is acceptable. When management does so, as required by paragraph 16, new terms of the audit engagement are agreed to reflect the change in the framework as the previously agreed terms will no longer be accurate.

General purpose frameworks

A8. At present, there is no objective and authoritative basis that has been generally recognized globally for judging the acceptability of general purpose frameworks. In the absence of such a basis, financial reporting standards established by organizations that are authorized or recognized to promulgate standards to be used by certain types of entities are presumed to be acceptable for general purpose financial statements prepared by such entities, provided the organizations follow an established and transparent process involving deliberation and consideration of the views of a wide range of stakeholders. Examples of such financial reporting standards include:

- International Financial Reporting Standards (IFRSs) promulgated by the International Accounting Standards Board;

- International Public Sector Accounting Standards (IPSASs) promulgated by the International Public Sector Accounting Standards Board; and

- Accounting principles promulgated by an authorized or recognized standards setting organization in a particular jurisdiction, provided the organization follows an established and transparent process involving deliberation and consideration of the views of a wide range of stakeholders.

---

[10] ISA 800, "Special Considerations—Audits of Financial Statements Prepared in Accordance with Special Purpose Frameworks," paragraph 8.
ISA 800 has not been promulgated by the APB for application in the UK and Ireland.

These financial reporting standards are often identified as the applicable financial reporting framework in law or regulation governing the preparation of general purpose financial statements.

Financial reporting frameworks prescribed by law or regulation

A9. In accordance with paragraph 6(a), the auditor is required to determine whether the financial reporting framework, to be applied in the preparation of the financial statements, is acceptable. In some jurisdictions, law or regulation may prescribe the financial reporting framework to be used in the preparation of general purpose financial statements for certain types of entities. In the absence of indications to the contrary, such a financial reporting framework is presumed to be acceptable for general purpose financial statements prepared by such entities. In the event that the framework is not considered to be acceptable, paragraphs 19-20 apply.

Jurisdictions that do not have standards setting organizations or prescribed financial reporting frameworks

A10. When an entity is registered or operating in a jurisdiction that does not have an authorized or recognized standards setting organization, or where use of the financial reporting framework is not prescribed by law or regulation, management identifies a financial reporting framework to be applied in the preparation of the financial statements. Appendix 2 contains guidance on determining the acceptability of financial reporting frameworks in such circumstances.

Agreement of the Responsibilities of Management (Ref: Para. 6(b))

A11. An audit in accordance with ISAs is conducted on the premise that management has acknowledged and understands that it has the responsibilities set out in paragraph 6(b).[11] In certain jurisdictions, such responsibilities may be specified in law or regulation. In others, there may be little or no legal or regulatory definition of such responsibilities. ISAs (UK and Ireland) do not override law or regulation in such matters. However, the concept of an independent audit requires that the auditor's role does not involve taking responsibility for the preparation of the financial statements or for the entity's related internal control, and that the auditor has a reasonable expectation of obtaining the information necessary for the audit in so far as management is able to provide or procure it. Accordingly, the premise is fundamental to the conduct of an independent audit. To avoid misunderstanding, agreement is reached with management that it acknowledges and understands that it has such responsibilities as part of agreeing and recording the terms of the audit engagement in paragraphs 9-12.

A12. The way in which the responsibilities for financial reporting are divided between management and those charged with governance will vary according to the resources and structure of the entity and any relevant law or regulation, and the respective roles of management and those charged with governance within the entity.

---

[11] ISA (UK and Ireland) 200, paragraph A2.

In most cases, management is responsible for execution while those charged with governance have oversight of management. In some cases, those charged with governance will have, or will assume, responsibility for approving the financial statements or monitoring the entity's internal control related to financial reporting. In larger or public entities, a subgroup of those charged with governance, such as an audit committee, may be charged with certain oversight responsibilities.

A13. ISA (UK and Ireland) 580 requires the auditor to request management to provide written representations that it has fulfilled certain of its responsibilities.[12] It may therefore be appropriate to make management aware that receipt of such written representations will be expected, together with written representations required by other ISAs (UK and Ireland) and, where necessary, written representations to support other audit evidence relevant to the financial statements or one or more specific assertions in the financial statements.

A14. Where management will not acknowledge its responsibilities, or agree to provide the written representations, the auditor will be unable to obtain sufficient appropriate audit evidence.[13] In such circumstances, it would not be appropriate for the auditor to accept the audit engagement, unless law or regulation requires the auditor to do so. In cases where the auditor is required to accept the audit engagement, the auditor may need to explain to management the importance of these matters, and the implications for the auditor's report.

Preparation of the Financial Statements (Ref: Para. 6(b)(i))

A15. Most financial reporting frameworks include requirements relating to the presentation of the financial statements; for such frameworks, *preparation* of the financial statements in accordance with the financial reporting framework includes *presentation*. In the case of a fair presentation framework the importance of the reporting objective of fair presentation is such that the premise agreed with management includes specific reference to fair presentation, or to the responsibility to ensure that the financial statements will "give a true and fair view" in accordance with the financial reporting framework.

Internal Control (Ref: Para. 6(b)(ii))

A16. Management maintains such internal control as it determines is necessary to enable the preparation of financial statements that are free from material misstatement, whether due to fraud or error. Internal control, no matter how effective, can provide an entity with only reasonable assurance about achieving the entity's financial reporting objectives due to the inherent limitations of internal control.[14]

A17. An independent audit conducted in accordance with the ISAs (UK and Ireland) does not act as a substitute for the maintenance of internal control necessary for the

---

[12] ISA (UK and Ireland) 580, "Written Representations," paragraphs 10-11.
[13] ISA (UK and Ireland) 580, paragraph A26.
[14] ISA (UK and Ireland) 315, "Identifying and Assessing the Risks of Material Misstatement through Understanding the Entity and Its Environment," paragraph A46.

preparation of financial statements by management. Accordingly, the auditor is required to obtain the agreement of management that it acknowledges and understands its responsibility for internal control. However, the agreement required by paragraph 6(b)(ii) does not imply that the auditor will find that internal control maintained by management has achieved its purpose or will be free of deficiencies.

A18. It is for management to determine what internal control is necessary to enable the preparation of the financial statements. The term "internal control" encompasses a wide range of activities within components that may be described as the control environment; the entity's risk assessment process; the information system, including the related business processes relevant to financial reporting, and communication; control activities; and monitoring of controls. This division, however, does not necessarily reflect how a particular entity may design, implement and maintain its internal control, or how it may classify any particular component.[15] An entity's internal control (in particular, its accounting books and records, or accounting systems) will reflect the needs of management, the complexity of the business, the nature of the risks to which the entity is subject, and relevant laws or regulation.

A19. In some jurisdictions, law or regulation may refer to the responsibility of management for the adequacy of accounting books and records, or accounting systems. In some cases, general practice may assume a distinction between accounting books and records or accounting systems on the one hand, and internal control or controls on the other. As accounting books and records, or accounting systems, are an integral part of internal control as referred to in paragraph A18, no specific reference is made to them in paragraph 6(b)(ii) for the description of the responsibility of management. To avoid misunderstanding, it may be appropriate for the auditor to explain to management the scope of this responsibility.

Considerations Relevant to Smaller Entities (Ref: Para. 6(b))

A20. One of the purposes of agreeing the terms of the audit engagement is to avoid misunderstanding about the respective responsibilities of management and the auditor. For example, when a third party has assisted with the preparation of the financial statements, it may be useful to remind management that the preparation of the financial statements in accordance with the applicable financial reporting framework remains its responsibility.

Agreement on Audit Engagement Terms

Agreeing the Terms of the Audit Engagement (Ref: Para. 9)

A21. The roles of management and those charged with governance in agreeing the terms of the audit engagement for the entity depend on the governance structure of the entity and relevant law or regulation.

---

[15] ISA (UK and Ireland) 315, paragraph A51 and Appendix 1.

Audit Engagement Letter or Other Form of Written Agreement[16] (Ref: Para. 10-11)

A22. It is in the interests of both the entity and the auditor that the auditor sends an audit engagement letter before the commencement of the audit to help avoid misunderstandings with respect to the audit. In some countries, however, the objective and scope of an audit and the responsibilities of management and of the auditor may be sufficiently established by law, that is, they prescribe the matters described in paragraph 10. Although in these circumstances paragraph 11 permits the auditor to include in the engagement letter only reference to the fact that relevant law or regulation applies and that management acknowledges and understands its responsibilities as set out in paragraph 6(b), the auditor may nevertheless consider it appropriate to include the matters described in paragraph 10 in an engagement letter for the information of management.

Form and Content of the Audit Engagement Letter

A23. The form and content of the audit engagement letter may vary for each entity. Information included in the audit engagement letter on the auditor's responsibilities may be based on ISA (UK and Ireland) 200.[17] Paragraphs 6(b) and 12 of this ISA (UK and Ireland) deal with the description of the responsibilities of management. In addition to including the matters required by paragraph 10, an audit engagement letter may make reference to, for example:

- Elaboration of the scope of the audit, including reference to applicable legislation, regulations, ISAs (UK and Ireland), and ethical and other pronouncements of professional bodies to which the auditor adheres.

- The form of any other communication of results of the audit engagement.

- The fact that because of the inherent limitations of an audit, together with the inherent limitations of internal control, there is an unavoidable risk that some material misstatements may not be detected, even though the audit is properly planned and performed in accordance with ISAs (UK and Ireland).

- Arrangements regarding the planning and performance of the audit, including the composition of the engagement team.

- The expectation that management will provide written representations (see also paragraph A13).

- The agreement of management to make available to the auditor draft financial statements and any accompanying other information in time to allow the auditor to complete the audit in accordance with the proposed timetable.

---

[16] In the paragraphs that follow, any reference to an audit engagement letter is to be taken as a reference to an audit engagement letter or other suitable form of written agreement.

[17] ISA (UK and Ireland) 200, paragraphs 3-9.

- The agreement of management to inform the auditor of facts that may affect the financial statements, of which management may become aware during the period from the date of the auditor's report to the date the financial statements are issued.

- The basis on which fees are computed and any billing arrangements.

- A request for management to acknowledge receipt of the audit engagement letter and to agree to the terms of the engagement outlined therein.

A24. When relevant, the following points could also be made in the audit engagement letter:

- Arrangements concerning the involvement of other auditors and experts in some aspects of the audit.

- Arrangements concerning the involvement of internal auditors and other staff of the entity.

- Arrangements to be made with the predecessor auditor, if any, in the case of an initial audit.

- Any restriction of the auditor's liability when such possibility exists.

- A reference to any further agreements between the auditor and the entity.

- Any obligations to provide audit working papers to other parties.

An example of an audit engagement letter is set out in Appendix 1[17a].

Audits of Components

A25. When the auditor of a parent entity is also the auditor of a component, the factors that may influence the decision whether to send a separate audit engagement letter to the component include the following:

- Who appoints the component auditor;

- Whether a separate auditor's report is to be issued on the component;

- Legal requirements in relation to audit appointments;

- Degree of ownership by parent; and

- Degree of independence of the component management from the parent entity.

[17a] The example letter in the Appendix has not been tailored for the UK and Ireland.

Responsibilities of Management Prescribed by Law or Regulation (Ref: Para. 11-12)

A26.   If, in the circumstances described in paragraphs A22 and A27, the auditor concludes that it is not necessary to record certain terms of the audit engagement in an audit engagement letter, the auditor is still required by paragraph 11 to seek the written agreement from management that it acknowledges and understands that it has the responsibilities set out in paragraph 6(b). However, in accordance with paragraph 12, such written agreement may use the wording of the law or regulation if such law or regulation establishes responsibilities for management that are equivalent in effect to those described in paragraph 6(b). The accounting profession, audit standards setter, or audit regulator in a jurisdiction may have provided guidance as to whether the description in law or regulation is equivalent.

Considerations specific to public sector entities

A27.   Law or regulation governing the operations of public sector audits generally mandate the appointment of a public sector auditor and commonly set out the public sector auditor's responsibilities and powers, including the power to access an entity's records and other information. When law or regulation prescribes in sufficient detail the terms of the audit engagement, the public sector auditor may nonetheless consider that there are benefits in issuing a fuller audit engagement letter than permitted by paragraph 11.

Recurring Audits (Ref: Para. 13)

A28.   The auditor may decide not to send a new audit engagement letter or other written agreement each period. However, the following factors may make it appropriate to revise the terms of the audit engagement or to remind the entity of existing terms:

- Any indication that the entity misunderstands the objective and scope of the audit.

- Any revised or special terms of the audit engagement.

- A recent change of senior management.

- A significant change in ownership.

- A significant change in nature or size of the entity's business.

- A change in legal or regulatory requirements.

- A change in the financial reporting framework adopted in the preparation of the financial statements.

- A change in other reporting requirements.

Acceptance of a Change in the Terms of the Audit Engagement

Request to Change the Terms of the Audit Engagement (Ref: Para. 14)

A29. A request from the entity for the auditor to change the terms of the audit engagement may result from a change in circumstances affecting the need for the service, a misunderstanding as to the nature of an audit as originally requested or a restriction on the scope of the audit engagement, whether imposed by management or caused by other circumstances. The auditor, as required by paragraph 14, considers the justification given for the request, particularly the implications of a restriction on the scope of the audit engagement.

A30. A change in circumstances that affects the entity's requirements or a misunderstanding concerning the nature of the service originally requested may be considered a reasonable basis for requesting a change in the audit engagement.

A31. In contrast, a change may not be considered reasonable if it appears that the change relates to information that is incorrect, incomplete or otherwise unsatisfactory. An example might be where the auditor is unable to obtain sufficient appropriate audit evidence regarding receivables and the entity asks for the audit engagement to be changed to a review engagement to avoid a qualified opinion or a disclaimer of opinion.

Request to Change to a Review or a Related Service (Ref: Para. 15)

A32. Before agreeing to change an audit engagement to a review or a related service, an auditor who was engaged to perform an audit in accordance with ISAs (UK and Ireland) may need to assess, in addition to the matters referred to in paragraphs A29-A31 above, any legal or contractual implications of the change.

A33. If the auditor concludes that there is reasonable justification to change the audit engagement to a review or a related service, the audit work performed to the date of change may be relevant to the changed engagement; however, the work required to be performed and the report to be issued would be those appropriate to the revised engagement. In order to avoid confusing the reader, the report on the related service would not include reference to:

(a) The original audit engagement; or

(b) Any procedures that may have been performed in the original audit engagement, except where the audit engagement is changed to an engagement to undertake agreed-upon procedures and thus reference to the procedures performed is a normal part of the report.

Statement by Auditor on Ceasing to Hold Office (Ref: Para. 17)

A33-1. The auditor of a limited company in the UK who ceases to hold office as auditor is required to comply with the requirements of sections 519 and 521 of the Companies Act 2006 regarding the statement to be made by the auditor in relation to ceasing to hold office. For the Republic of Ireland, equivalent requirements are contained in section 185 of the Companies Act 1990. In addition, in the UK the auditor may need to notify the appropriate audit authority in accordance with section 522 of the Companies Act 2006.

Additional Considerations in Engagement Acceptance

Financial Reporting Standards Supplemented by Law or Regulation (Ref: Para. 18)

A34. In some jurisdictions, law or regulation may supplement the financial reporting standards established by an authorized or recognized standards setting organization with additional requirements relating to the preparation of financial statements. In those jurisdictions, the applicable financial reporting framework for the purposes of applying the ISAs (UK and Ireland) encompasses both the identified financial reporting framework and such additional requirements provided they do not conflict with the identified financial reporting framework. This may, for example, be the case when law or regulation prescribes disclosures in addition to those required by the financial reporting standards or when they narrow the range of acceptable choices that can be made within the financial reporting standards.[18]

Financial Reporting Framework Prescribed by Law or Regulation—Other Matters Affecting Acceptance (Ref: Para. 19)

A35. Law or regulation may prescribe that the wording of the auditor's opinion use the phrases "present fairly, in all material respects" or "give a true and fair view" in a case where the auditor concludes that the applicable financial reporting framework prescribed by law or regulation would otherwise have been unacceptable. In this case, the terms of the prescribed wording of the auditor's report are significantly different from the requirements of ISAs (UK and Ireland) (see paragraph 21).

Auditor's Report Prescribed by Law or Regulation (Ref: Para. 21)

A36. ISAs (UK and Ireland) require that the auditor shall not represent compliance with ISAs (UK and Ireland) unless the auditor has complied with all of the ISAs (UK and Ireland) relevant to the audit.[19] When law or regulation prescribes the layout or wording of the auditor's report in a form or in terms that are significantly different from the requirements of ISAs (UK and Ireland) and the auditor concludes that additional explanation in the auditor's report cannot mitigate possible misunderstanding, the auditor may consider including a statement in the auditor's report that the audit is not conducted in accordance with ISAs (UK and Ireland). The auditor is, however,

---

[18] ISA 700, paragraph 15, includes a requirement regarding the evaluation of whether the financial statements adequately refer to or describe the applicable financial reporting framework.

The APB has not promulgated ISA 700 as issued by the IAASB for application in the UK and Ireland. In the UK and Ireland the applicable auditing standard is ISA (UK and Ireland) 700, "The Auditor's Report on Financial Statements." Paragraph 9(a) of ISA (UK and Ireland) 700 includes a requirement regarding evaluation of whether the financial statements adequately refer to or describe the relevant financial reporting framework.

[19] ISA (UK and Ireland) 200, paragraph 20.

encouraged to apply ISAs (UK and Ireland), including the ISAs (UK and Ireland) that address the auditor's report, to the extent practicable, notwithstanding that the auditor is not permitted to refer to the audit being conducted in accordance with ISAs (UK and Ireland).

Considerations Specific to Public Sector Entities

A37. In the public sector, specific requirements may exist within the legislation governing the audit mandate; for example, the auditor may be required to report directly to a minister, the legislature or the public if the entity attempts to limit the scope of the audit.

Appendix 1

(Ref: Paras. A23-24)

The example letter in this Appendix has not been tailored for the UK and Ireland.

Example of an Audit Engagement Letter

The following is an example of an audit engagement letter for an audit of general purpose financial statements prepared in accordance with International Financial Reporting Standards. This letter is not authoritative but is intended only to be a guide that may be used in conjunction with the considerations outlined in this ISA. It will need to be varied according to individual requirements and circumstances. It is drafted to refer to the audit of financial statements for a single reporting period and would require adaptation if intended or expected to apply to recurring audits (see paragraph 13 of this ISA). It may be appropriate to seek legal advice that any proposed letter is suitable.

***

To the appropriate representative of management or those charged with governance of ABC Company:[20]

[*The objective and scope of the audit*]

You[21] have requested that we audit the financial statements of ABC Company, which comprise the balance sheet as at December 31, 20X1, and the income statement, statement of changes in equity and cash flow statement for the year then ended, and a summary of significant accounting policies and other explanatory information. We are pleased to confirm our acceptance and our understanding of this audit engagement by means of this letter. Our audit will be conducted with the objective of our expressing an opinion on the financial statements.

[*The responsibilities of the auditor*]

We will conduct our audit in accordance with International Standards on Auditing (ISAs). Those standards require that we comply with ethical requirements and plan and perform the audit to obtain reasonable assurance about whether the financial statements are free from material misstatement. An audit involves performing procedures to obtain audit evidence about the amounts and disclosures in the financial statements. The procedures selected depend on the auditor's judgment, including the assessment of the risks of material misstatement of the financial statements, whether due to fraud or error. An audit also includes evaluating the appropriateness of accounting policies used and the

---

[20] The addressees and references in the letter would be those that are appropriate in the circumstances of the engagement, including the relevant jurisdiction. It is important to refer to the appropriate persons – see paragraph A21.

[21] Throughout this letter, references to "you," "we," "us," "management," "those charged with governance" and "auditor" would be used or amended as appropriate in the circumstances.

reasonableness of accounting estimates made by management, as well as evaluating the overall presentation of the financial statements.

Because of the inherent limitations of an audit, together with the inherent limitations of internal control, there is an unavoidable risk that some material misstatements may not be detected, even though the audit is properly planned and performed in accordance with ISAs.

In making our risk assessments, we consider internal control relevant to the entity's preparation of the financial statements in order to design audit procedures that are appropriate in the circumstances, but not for the purpose of expressing an opinion on the effectiveness of the entity's internal control. However, we will communicate to you in writing concerning any significant deficiencies in internal control relevant to the audit of the financial statements that we have identified during the audit.

[*The responsibilities of management and identification of the applicable financial reporting framework (for purposes of this example it is assumed that the auditor has not determined that the law or regulation prescribes those responsibilities in appropriate terms; the descriptions in paragraph 6(b) of this ISA are therefore used).*]

Our audit will be conducted on the basis that [management and, where appropriate, those charged with governance][22] acknowledge and understand that they have responsibility:

(a)   For the preparation and fair presentation of the financial statements in accordance with International Financial Reporting Standards;[23]

(b)   For such internal control as [management] determines is necessary to enable the preparation of financial statements that are free from material misstatement, whether due to fraud or error; and

(c)   To provide us with:

(i)   Access to all information of which [management] is aware that is relevant to the preparation of the financial statements such as records, documentation and other matters;

(ii)   Additional information that we may request from [management] for the purpose of the audit; and

(iii)   Unrestricted access to persons within the entity from whom we determine it necessary to obtain audit evidence.

As part of our audit process, we will request from [management and, where appropriate, those charged with governance], written confirmation concerning representations made to us in connection with the audit.

---

[22] Use terminology as appropriate in the circumstances.

[23] Or, if appropriate, "For the preparation of financial statements that give a true and fair view in accordance with International Financial Reporting Standards."

We look forward to full cooperation from your staff during our audit.

[*Other relevant information*]

[*Insert other information, such as fee arrangements, billings and other specific terms, as appropriate.*]

[*Reporting*]

[*Insert appropriate reference to the expected form and content of the auditor's report.*]

The form and content of our report may need to be amended in the light of our audit findings.

Please sign and return the attached copy of this letter to indicate your acknowledgement of, and agreement with, the arrangements for our audit of the financial statements including our respective responsibilities.

XYZ & Co.

Acknowledged and agreed on behalf of ABC Company by

(signed)

....

Name and Title

Date

Appendix 2

(Ref: Para. A10)

Determining the Acceptability of General Purpose Frameworks

Jurisdictions that Do Not Have Authorized or Recognized Standards Setting Organizations or Financial Reporting Frameworks Prescribed by Law or Regulation

1. As explained in paragraph A10 of this ISA (UK and Ireland), when an entity is registered or operating in a jurisdiction that does not have an authorized or recognized standards setting organization, or where use of the financial reporting framework is not prescribed by law or regulation, management identifies an applicable financial reporting framework. Practice in such jurisdictions is often to use the financial reporting standards established by one of the organizations described in paragraph A8 of this ISA (UK and Ireland).

2. Alternatively, there may be established accounting conventions in a particular jurisdiction that are generally recognized as the financial reporting framework for general purpose financial statements prepared by certain specified entities operating in that jurisdiction. When such a financial reporting framework is adopted, the auditor is required by paragraph 6(a) of this ISA (UK and Ireland) to determine whether the accounting conventions collectively can be considered to constitute an acceptable financial reporting framework for general purpose financial statements. When the accounting conventions are widely used in a particular jurisdiction, the accounting profession in that jurisdiction may have considered the acceptability of the financial reporting framework on behalf of the auditors. Alternatively, the auditor may make this determination by considering whether the accounting conventions exhibit attributes normally exhibited by acceptable financial reporting frameworks (see paragraph 3 below), or by comparing the accounting conventions to the requirements of an existing financial reporting framework considered to be acceptable (see paragraph 4 below).

3. Acceptable financial reporting frameworks normally exhibit the following attributes that result in information provided in financial statements that is useful to the intended users:

    (a) Relevance, in that the information provided in the financial statements is relevant to the nature of the entity and the purpose of the financial statements. For example, in the case of a business enterprise that prepares general purpose financial statements, relevance is assessed in terms of the information necessary to meet the common financial information needs of a wide range of users in making economic decisions. These needs are ordinarily met by presenting the financial position, financial performance and cash flows of the business enterprise.

(b) Completeness, in that transactions and events, account balances and disclosures that could affect conclusions based on the financial statements are not omitted.

(c) Reliability, in that the information provided in the financial statements:

(i) Where applicable, reflects the economic substance of events and transactions and not merely their legal form; and

(ii) Results in reasonably consistent evaluation, measurement, presentation and disclosure, when used in similar circumstances.

(d) Neutrality, in that it contributes to information in the financial statements that is free from bias.

(e) Understandability, in that the information in the financial statements is clear and comprehensive and not subject to significantly different interpretation.

4. The auditor may decide to compare the accounting conventions to the requirements of an existing financial reporting framework considered to be acceptable. For example, the auditor may compare the accounting conventions to IFRSs. For an audit of a small entity, the auditor may decide to compare the accounting conventions to a financial reporting framework specifically developed for such entities by an authorized or recognized standards setting organization. When the auditor makes such a comparison and differences are identified, the decision as to whether the accounting conventions adopted in the preparation of the financial statements constitute an acceptable financial reporting framework includes considering the reasons for the differences and whether application of the accounting conventions, or the description of the financial reporting framework in the financial statements, could result in financial statements that are misleading.

5. A conglomeration of accounting conventions devised to suit individual preferences is not an acceptable financial reporting framework for general purpose financial statements. Similarly, a compliance framework will not be an acceptable financial reporting framework, unless it is generally accepted in the particular jurisdictions by preparers and users.

INTERNATIONAL STANDARD ON AUDITING (UK AND IRELAND) 220

QUALITY CONTROL FOR AN AUDIT OF FINANCIAL STATEMENTS

(Effective for audits of financial statements for periods ending on or after 15 December 2010)[1a]

CONTENTS

[1a] Conforming amendments to this standard as a result of ISA (UK and Ireland) 610 (Revised June 2013), *Using the Work of Internal Auditors*, are included that are effective for audits of financial statements for periods ending on or after 15 June 2014. Details of the amendments are given in the Annexure to ISA (UK and Ireland) 610 (Revised June 2013).

International Standard on Auditing (UK and Ireland) (ISA (UK and Ireland)) 220, "Quality Control for an Audit of Financial Statements" should be read in conjunction with ISA (UK and Ireland) 200, "Overall Objectives of the Independent Auditor and the Conduct of an Audit in Accordance with International Standards on Auditing (UK and Ireland)."

Introduction

Scope of this ISA (UK and Ireland)

1. This International Standard on Auditing (UK and Ireland) (ISA (UK and Ireland)) deals with the specific responsibilities of the auditor regarding quality control procedures for an audit of financial statements. It also addresses, where applicable, the responsibilities of the engagement quality control reviewer. This ISA (UK and Ireland) is to be read in conjunction with relevant ethical requirements.

System of Quality Control and Role of Engagement Teams

2. Quality control systems, policies and procedures are the responsibility of the audit firm. Under ISQC (UK and Ireland) 1, the firm has an obligation to establish and maintain a system of quality control to provide it with reasonable assurance that:

    (a) The firm and its personnel comply with professional standards and applicable legal and regulatory requirements; and

    (b) The reports issued by the firm or engagement partners are appropriate in the circumstances.[1]

    This ISA (UK and Ireland) is premised on the basis that the firm is subject to ISQC (UK and Ireland) 1 or to national requirements that are at least as demanding. (Ref: Para. A1)

3. Within the context of the firm's system of quality control, engagement teams have a responsibility to implement quality control procedures that are applicable to the audit engagement and provide the firm with relevant information to enable the functioning of that part of the firm's system of quality control relating to independence.

4. Engagement teams are entitled to rely on the firm's system of quality control, unless information provided by the firm or other parties suggests otherwise. (Ref: Para. A2)

Effective Date

5. This ISA (UK and Ireland) is effective for audits of financial statements for periods ending on or after 15 December 2010.[1a]

Objective

6. The objective of the auditor is to implement quality control procedures at the engagement level that provide the auditor with reasonable assurance that:

---

[1]   ISQC (UK and Ireland) 1, "Quality Control for Firms that Perform Audits and Reviews of Financial Statements, and Other Assurance and Related Services Engagements," paragraph 11.

(a) The audit complies with professional standards and applicable legal and regulatory requirements; and

(b) The auditor's report issued is appropriate in the circumstances.

Definitions

7. For purposes of the ISAs (UK and Ireland), the following terms have the meanings attributed below:

(a) Engagement partner[2] – The partner or other person in the firm who is responsible for the audit engagement and its performance, and for the auditor's report that is issued on behalf of the firm, and who, where required, has the appropriate authority from a professional, legal or regulatory body.

(b) Engagement quality control review – A process designed to provide an objective evaluation, on or before the date of the auditor's report, of the significant judgments the engagement team made and the conclusions it reached in formulating the auditor's report. The engagement quality control review process is only for audits of financial statements of listed entities and those other audit engagements, if any, for which the firm has determined an engagement quality control review is required.

(c) Engagement quality control reviewer – A partner, other person in the firm, suitably qualified external person, or a team made up of such individuals, none of whom is part of the engagement team, with sufficient and appropriate experience and authority to objectively evaluate the significant judgments the engagement team made and the conclusions it reached in formulating the auditor's report.

(d) Engagement team – All partners and staff performing the engagement, and any individuals engaged by the firm or a network firm who perform audit procedures on the engagement. This excludes an auditor's external expert engaged by the firm or by a network firm.[3] The term "engagement team" also excludes individuals within the client's internal audit function who provide direct assistance on an audit engagement when the external auditor complies with the requirements of ISA (UK and Ireland) 610 (Revised June 2013).[4]

---

[2] "Engagement partner," "partner," and "firm" should be read as referring to their public sector equivalents where relevant.

[3] ISA (UK and Ireland) 620, "Using the Work of an Auditor's Expert," paragraph 6(a), defines the term "auditor's expert."

[4] ISA 610 (Revised June 2013), "Using the Work of Internal Auditors", establishes limits on the use of direct assistance. It also acknowledges that the external auditor may be prohibited by law or regulation from obtaining direct assistance from internal auditors. Therefore, the use of direct assistance is restricted to situations where it is permitted.

The use of internal auditors to provide direct assistance is prohibited in an audit conducted in accordance with ISAs (UK and Ireland) – see ISA (UK and Ireland) 610 (Revised June 2013), paragraph 5-1.

(e) Firm – A sole practitioner, partnership or corporation or other entity of professional accountants.

(f) Inspection – In relation to completed audit engagements, procedures designed to provide evidence of compliance by engagement teams with the firm's quality control policies and procedures.

(g) Listed entity – An entity whose shares, stock or debt are quoted or listed on a recognized stock exchange, or are marketed under the regulations of a recognized stock exchange or other equivalent body.

(h) Monitoring – A process comprising an ongoing consideration and evaluation of the firm's system of quality control, including a periodic inspection of a selection of completed engagements, designed to provide the firm with reasonable assurance that its system of quality control is operating effectively.

(i) Network firm – A firm or entity that belongs to a network.

(j) Network – A larger structure:

    (i) That is aimed at cooperation, and

    (ii) That is clearly aimed at profit or cost-sharing or shares common ownership, control or management, common quality control policies and procedures, common business strategy, the use of a common brand name, or a significant part of professional resources.

(k) Partner – Any individual with authority to bind the firm with respect to the performance of a professional services engagement.

(l) Personnel – Partners and staff.

(m) Professional standards – International Standards on Auditing (UK and Ireland) (ISAs (UK and Ireland)) and relevant ethical requirements.

(n) Relevant ethical requirements – Ethical requirements to which the engagement team and engagement quality control reviewer are subject, which ordinarily comprise Parts A and B of the International Ethics Standards Board for Accountants' *Code of Ethics for Professional Accountants* (IESBA Code) related to an audit of financial statements together with national requirements that are more restrictive.

Auditors in the UK and Ireland are subject to ethical requirements from two sources: the APB Ethical Standards for Auditors concerning the integrity, objectivity and independence of the auditor, and the ethical pronouncements established by the auditor's relevant professional body. The APB is not aware of any significant instances where the relevant parts of the IESBA Code of Ethics are more restrictive than the APB Ethical Standards for Auditors.

(o) Staff – Professionals, other than partners, including any experts the firm employs.

(p) Suitably qualified external person – An individual outside the firm with the competence and capabilities to act as an engagement partner, for example a partner of another firm, or an employee (with appropriate experience) of either a professional accountancy body whose members may perform audits of historical financial information or of an organization that provides relevant quality control services.

Requirements

Leadership Responsibilities for Quality on Audits

8.   The engagement partner shall take responsibility for the overall quality on each audit engagement to which that partner is assigned. (Ref: Para. A3)

Relevant Ethical Requirements

9.   Throughout the audit engagement, the engagement partner shall remain alert, through observation and making inquiries as necessary, for evidence of non-compliance with relevant ethical requirements by members of the engagement team. (Ref: Para. A4-A5)

10. If matters come to the engagement partner's attention through the firm's system of quality control or otherwise that indicate that members of the engagement team have not complied with relevant ethical requirements, the engagement partner, in consultation with others in the firm, shall determine the appropriate action. (Ref: Para. A5)

Independence

11. The engagement partner shall form a conclusion on compliance with independence requirements that apply to the audit engagement. In doing so, the engagement partner shall: (Ref: Para. A5)

(a) Obtain relevant information from the firm and, where applicable, network firms, to identify and evaluate circumstances and relationships that create threats to independence;

(b) Evaluate information on identified breaches, if any, of the firm's independence policies and procedures to determine whether they create a threat to independence for the audit engagement; and

(c) Take appropriate action to eliminate such threats or reduce them to an acceptable level by applying safeguards, or, if considered appropriate, to withdraw from the audit engagement, where withdrawal is possible under applicable law or regulation. The engagement partner shall promptly report to the firm any inability to resolve the matter for appropriate action. (Ref: Para. A6-A7)

Acceptance and Continuance of Client Relationships and Audit Engagements

12. The engagement partner shall be satisfied that appropriate procedures regarding the acceptance and continuance of client relationships and audit engagements have been followed, and shall determine that conclusions reached in this regard are appropriate. (Ref: Para. A8-A9)

13. If the engagement partner obtains information that would have caused the firm to decline the audit engagement had that information been available earlier, the engagement partner shall communicate that information promptly to the firm, so that the firm and the engagement partner can take the necessary action. (Ref: Para. A9)

Assignment of Engagement Teams

14. The engagement partner shall be satisfied that the engagement team, and any auditor's experts who are not part of the engagement team, collectively have the appropriate competence and capabilities to:

(a) Perform the audit engagement in accordance with professional standards and applicable legal and regulatory requirements; and

(b) Enable an auditor's report that is appropriate in the circumstances to be issued. (Ref: Para. A10-A12)

Engagement Performance

Direction, Supervision and Performance

15. The engagement partner shall take responsibility for:

(a) The direction, supervision and performance of the audit engagement in compliance with professional standards and applicable legal and regulatory requirements; and (Ref: Para. A13-A15, A20)

(b) The auditor's report being appropriate in the circumstances.

Reviews

16. The engagement partner shall take responsibility for reviews being performed in accordance with the firm's review policies and procedures. (Ref: Para. A16-A17, A20)

17. On or before the date of the auditor's report, the engagement partner shall, through a review of the audit documentation and discussion with the engagement team, be satisfied that sufficient appropriate audit evidence has been obtained to support the conclusions reached and for the auditor's report to be issued. (Ref: Para. A18-A20)

Consultation

18.   The engagement partner shall:

   (a)   Take responsibility for the engagement team undertaking appropriate consultation on difficult or contentious matters;

   (b)   Be satisfied that members of the engagement team have undertaken appropriate consultation during the course of the engagement, both within the engagement team and between the engagement team and others at the appropriate level within or outside the firm;

   (c)   Be satisfied that the nature and scope of, and conclusions resulting from, such consultations are agreed with the party consulted; and

   (d)   Determine that conclusions resulting from such consultations have been implemented. (Ref: Para. A21-A22)

Engagement Quality Control Review

19.   For audits of financial statements of listed entities, and those other audit engagements, if any, for which the firm has determined that an engagement quality control review is required, the engagement partner shall:

   (a)   Determine that an engagement quality control reviewer has been appointed;

   (b)   Discuss significant matters arising during the audit engagement, including those identified during the engagement quality control review, with the engagement quality control reviewer; and

   (c)   Not date the auditor's report until the completion of the engagement quality control review. (Ref: Para. A23-A25)

20.   The engagement quality control reviewer shall perform an objective evaluation of the significant judgments made by the engagement team, and the conclusions reached in formulating the auditor's report. This evaluation shall involve:

   (a)   Discussion of significant matters with the engagement partner;

   (b)   Review of the financial statements and the proposed auditor's report;

   (c)   Review of selected audit documentation relating to the significant judgments the engagement team made and the conclusions it reached; and

   (d)   Evaluation of the conclusions reached in formulating the auditor's report and consideration of whether the proposed auditor's report is appropriate. (Ref: Para. A26-A27, A29-A31)

21. For audits of financial statements of listed entities, the engagement quality control reviewer, on performing an engagement quality control review, shall also consider the following:

    (a) The engagement team's evaluation of the firm's independence in relation to the audit engagement;

    (b) Whether appropriate consultation has taken place on matters involving differences of opinion or other difficult or contentious matters, and the conclusions arising from those consultations; and

    (c) Whether audit documentation selected for review reflects the work performed in relation to the significant judgments and supports the conclusions reached. (Ref: Para. A28-A31)

Differences of Opinion

22. If differences of opinion arise within the engagement team, with those consulted or, where applicable, between the engagement partner and the engagement quality control reviewer, the engagement team shall follow the firm's policies and procedures for dealing with and resolving differences of opinion.

Monitoring

23. An effective system of quality control includes a monitoring process designed to provide the firm with reasonable assurance that its policies and procedures relating to the system of quality control are relevant, adequate, and operating effectively. The engagement partner shall consider the results of the firm's monitoring process as evidenced in the latest information circulated by the firm and, if applicable, other network firms and whether deficiencies noted in that information may affect the audit engagement. (Ref: Para A32-A34)

Documentation

24. The auditor shall include in the audit documentation:[5]

    (a) Issues identified with respect to compliance with relevant ethical requirements and how they were resolved.

    (b) Conclusions on compliance with independence requirements that apply to the audit engagement, and any relevant discussions with the firm that support these conclusions.

    (c) Conclusions reached regarding the acceptance and continuance of client relationships and audit engagements.

---

[5] ISA (UK and Ireland) 230, "Audit Documentation," paragraphs 8-11, and paragraph A6.

      (d)   The nature and scope of, and conclusions resulting from, consultations undertaken during the course of the audit engagement. (Ref: Para. A35)

25.   The engagement quality control reviewer shall document, for the audit engagement reviewed, that:

      (a)   The procedures required by the firm's policies on engagement quality control review have been performed;

      (b)   The engagement quality control review has been completed on or before the date of the auditor's report; and

      (c)   The reviewer is not aware of any unresolved matters that would cause the reviewer to believe that the significant judgments the engagement team made and the conclusions it reached were not appropriate.

***

Application and Other Explanatory Material

System of Quality Control and Role of Engagement Teams (Ref: Para. 2)

A1.   ISQC (UK and Ireland) 1, or national requirements that are at least as demanding, deals with the firm's responsibilities to establish and maintain its system of quality control for audit engagements. The system of quality control includes policies and procedures that address each of the following elements:

- Leadership responsibilities for quality within the firm;

- Relevant ethical requirements;

- Acceptance and continuance of client relationships and specific engagements;

- Human resources;

- Engagement performance; and

- Monitoring.

   National requirements that deal with the firm's responsibilities to establish and maintain a system of quality control are at least as demanding as ISQC (UK and Ireland) 1 when they address all the elements referred to in this paragraph and impose obligations on the firm that achieve the aims of the requirements set out in ISQC (UK and Ireland) 1.

Reliance on the Firm's System of Quality Control (Ref: Para. 4)

A2.   Unless information provided by the firm or other parties suggest otherwise, the engagement team may rely on the firm's system of quality control in relation to, for example:

- Competence of personnel through their recruitment and formal training.

- Independence through the accumulation and communication of relevant independence information.

- Maintenance of client relationships through acceptance and continuance systems.

- Adherence to applicable legal and regulatory requirements through the monitoring process.

Leadership Responsibilities for Quality on Audits (Ref: Para. 8)

A3.   The actions of the engagement partner and appropriate messages to the other members of the engagement team, in taking responsibility for the overall quality on each audit engagement, emphasize:

(a)   The importance to audit quality of:

(i)   Performing work that complies with professional standards and applicable legal and regulatory requirements;

(ii)   Complying with the firm's quality control policies and procedures as applicable;

(iii)   Issuing auditor's reports that are appropriate in the circumstances; and

(iv)   The engagement team's ability to raise concerns without fear of reprisals; and

(b)   The fact that quality is essential in performing audit engagements.

Relevant Ethical Requirements

Compliance with Relevant Ethical Requirements (Ref: Para. 9)

A4.   The IESBA Code[5a] establishes the fundamental principles of professional ethics, which include:

(a)   Integrity;

(b)   Objectivity;

(c)   Professional competence and due care;

(d)   Confidentiality; and

(e)   Professional behavior.

Definition of "Firm," "Network" and "Network Firm" (Ref: Para. 9-11)

A5.   The definitions of "firm," "network" or "network firm" in relevant ethical requirements may differ from those set out in this ISA (UK and Ireland). For example, the IESBA Code[5a] defines the "firm" as:

(a)   A sole practitioner, partnership or corporation of professional accountants;

(b)   An entity that controls such parties through ownership, management or other means; and

(c)   An entity controlled by such parties through ownership, management or other means.

The IESBA Code also provides guidance in relation to the terms "network" and "network firm."

In complying with the requirements in paragraphs 9-11, the definitions used in the relevant ethical requirements apply in so far as is necessary to interpret those ethical requirements.

Threats to Independence (Ref: Para. 11(c))

A6.   The engagement partner may identify a threat to independence regarding the audit engagement that safeguards may not be able to eliminate or reduce to an acceptable level. In that case, as required by paragraph 11(c), the engagement partner reports to

---

[5a]   Auditors in the UK and Ireland are subject to ethical requirements from two sources: the APB Ethical Standards for Auditors concerning the integrity, objectivity and independence of the auditor, and the ethical pronouncements established by the auditor's relevant professional body. The APB is not aware of any significant instances where the relevant parts of the IESBA Code of Ethics are more restrictive than the APB Ethical Standards for Auditors.

the relevant person(s) within the firm to determine appropriate action, which may include eliminating the activity or interest that creates the threat, or withdrawing from the audit engagement, where withdrawal is possible under applicable law or regulation.

Considerations Specific to Public Sector Entities

A7.   Statutory measures may provide safeguards for the independence of public sector auditors. However, public sector auditors or audit firms carrying out public sector audits on behalf of the statutory auditor may, depending on the terms of the mandate in a particular jurisdiction, need to adapt their approach in order to promote compliance with the spirit of paragraph 11. This may include, where the public sector auditor's mandate does not permit withdrawal from the engagement, disclosure through a public report, of circumstances that have arisen that would, if they were in the private sector, lead the auditor to withdraw.

Acceptance and Continuance of Client Relationships and Audit Engagements (Ref: Para. 12)

A8.   ISQC (UK and Ireland) 1 requires the firm to obtain information considered necessary in the circumstances before accepting an engagement with a new client, when deciding whether to continue an existing engagement, and when considering acceptance of a new engagement with an existing client.[6] Information such as the following assists the engagement partner in determining whether the conclusions reached regarding the acceptance and continuance of client relationships and audit engagements are appropriate:

- The integrity of the principal owners, key management and those charged with governance of the entity;

- Whether the engagement team is competent to perform the audit engagement and has the necessary capabilities, including time and resources;

- Whether the firm and the engagement team can comply with relevant ethical requirements; and

- Significant matters that have arisen during the current or previous audit engagement, and their implications for continuing the relationship.

Considerations Specific to Public Sector Entities (Ref: Para. 12-13)

A9.   In the public sector, auditors may be appointed in accordance with statutory procedures. Accordingly, certain of the requirements and considerations regarding the acceptance and continuance of client relationships and audit engagements as set out in paragraphs 12, 13 and A8 may not be relevant. Nonetheless, information

---

[6]   ISQC (UK and Ireland) 1, paragraph 27(a).

gathered as a result of the process described may be valuable to public sector auditors in performing risk assessments and in carrying out reporting responsibilities.

Assignment of Engagement Teams (Ref: Para. 14)

A10. An engagement team includes a person using expertise in a specialized area of accounting or auditing, whether engaged or employed by the firm, if any, who performs audit procedures on the engagement. However, a person with such expertise is not a member of the engagement team if that person's involvement with the engagement is only consultation. Consultations are addressed in paragraph 18, and paragraph A21-A22.

A11. When considering the appropriate competence and capabilities expected of the engagement team as a whole, the engagement partner may take into consideration such matters as the team's:

- Understanding of, and practical experience with, audit engagements of a similar nature and complexity through appropriate training and participation.

- Understanding of professional standards and applicable legal and regulatory requirements.

- Technical expertise, including expertise with relevant information technology and specialized areas of accounting or auditing.

- Knowledge of relevant industries in which the client operates.

- Ability to apply professional judgment.

- Understanding of the firm's quality control policies and procedures.

Considerations Specific to Public Sector Entities

A12. In the public sector, additional appropriate competence may include skills that are necessary to discharge the terms of the audit mandate in a particular jurisdiction. Such competence may include an understanding of the applicable reporting arrangements, including reporting to the legislature or other governing body or in the public interest. The wider scope of a public sector audit may include, for example, some aspects of performance auditing or a comprehensive assessment of compliance with law, regulation or other authority and preventing and detecting fraud and corruption.

Engagement Performance

Direction, Supervision and Performance (Ref: Para. 15(a))

A13. Direction of the engagement team involves informing the members of the engagement team of matters such as:

- Their responsibilities, including the need to comply with relevant ethical requirements, and to plan and perform an audit with professional skepticism as required by ISA (UK and Ireland) 200.[7]

- Responsibilities of respective partners where more than one partner is involved in the conduct of an audit engagement.

- The objectives of the work to be performed.

- The nature of the entity's business.

- Risk-related issues.

- Problems that may arise.

- The detailed approach to the performance of the engagement.

Discussion among members of the engagement team allows less experienced team members to raise questions with more experienced team members so that appropriate communication can occur within the engagement team.

A14. Appropriate teamwork and training assist less experienced members of the engagement team to clearly understand the objectives of the assigned work.

A15. Supervision includes matters such as:

- Tracking the progress of the audit engagement.

- Considering the competence and capabilities of individual members of the engagement team, including whether they have sufficient time to carry out their work, whether they understand their instructions, and whether the work is being carried out in accordance with the planned approach to the audit engagement.

- Addressing significant matters arising during the audit engagement, considering their significance and modifying the planned approach appropriately.

- Identifying matters for consultation or consideration by more experienced engagement team members during the audit engagement.

---

[7] ISA (UK and Ireland) 200, "Overall Objectives of the Independent Auditor and the Conduct of an Audit in Accordance with International Standards on Auditing (UK and Ireland)," paragraph 15.

Reviews

Review Responsibilities (Ref: Para. 16)

A16. Under ISQC (UK and Ireland) 1, the firm's review responsibility policies and procedures are determined on the basis that work of less experienced team members is reviewed by more experienced team members.[8]

A17. A review consists of consideration whether, for example:

- The work has been performed in accordance with professional standards and applicable legal and regulatory requirements;

- Significant matters have been raised for further consideration;

- Appropriate consultations have taken place and the resulting conclusions have been documented and implemented;

- There is a need to revise the nature, timing and extent of work performed;

- The work performed supports the conclusions reached and is appropriately documented;

- The evidence obtained is sufficient and appropriate to support the auditor's report; and

- The objectives of the engagement procedures have been achieved.

The Engagement Partner's Review of Work Performed (Ref: Para. 17)

A18. Timely reviews of the following by the engagement partner at appropriate stages during the engagement allow significant matters to be resolved on a timely basis to the engagement partner's satisfaction on or before the date of the auditor's report:

- Critical areas of judgment, especially those relating to difficult or contentious matters identified during the course of the engagement;

- Significant risks; and

- Other areas the engagement partner considers important.

The engagement partner need not review all audit documentation, but may do so. However, as required by ISA (UK and Ireland) 230, the partner documents the extent and timing of the reviews.[9]

---

[8] ISQC (UK and Ireland) 1, paragraph 33.
[9] ISA (UK and Ireland) 230, paragraph 9(c).

A19. An engagement partner taking over an audit during the engagement may apply the review procedures as described in paragraphs A18 to review the work performed to the date of a change in order to assume the responsibilities of an engagement partner.

Considerations Relevant Where a Member of the Engagement Team with Expertise in a Specialized Area of Accounting or Auditing Is Used (Ref: Para. 15-17)

A20. Where a member of the engagement team with expertise in a specialized area of accounting or auditing is used, direction, supervision and review of that engagement team member's work may include matters such as:

- Agreeing with that member the nature, scope and objectives of that member's work; and the respective roles of, and the nature, timing and extent of communication between that member and other members of the engagement team.

- Evaluating the adequacy of that member's work including the relevance and reasonableness of that member's findings or conclusions and their consistency with other audit evidence.

Consultation (Ref: Para. 18)

A21. Effective consultation on significant technical, ethical, and other matters within the firm or, where applicable, outside the firm can be achieved when those consulted:

- Are given all the relevant facts that will enable them to provide informed advice; and

- Have appropriate knowledge, seniority and experience.

A22. It may be appropriate for the engagement team to consult outside the firm, for example, where the firm lacks appropriate internal resources. They may take advantage of advisory services provided by other firms, professional and regulatory bodies, or commercial organizations that provide relevant quality control services.

Engagement Quality Control Review

Completion of the Engagement Quality Control Review before Dating of the Auditor's Report (Ref: Para. 19(c))

A23. ISA (UK and Ireland) 700 requires the auditor's report to be dated no earlier than the date on which the auditor has obtained sufficient appropriate evidence on which to base the auditor's opinion on the financial statements.[10] In cases of an audit of

---

[10] ISA 700, "Forming an Opinion and Reporting on Financial Statements," paragraph 41.

The APB has not promulgated ISA 700 as issued by the IAASB for application in the UK and Ireland. In the UK and Ireland the applicable auditing standard is ISA (UK and Ireland) 700, "The Auditor's Report on Financial Statements." Paragraphs 23 and 24 of ISA (UK and Ireland) 700 establish requirements regarding dating of the auditor's report.

financial statements of listed entities or when an engagement meets the criteria for an engagement quality control review, such a review assists the auditor in determining whether sufficient appropriate evidence has been obtained.

A24. Conducting the engagement quality control review in a timely manner at appropriate stages during the engagement allows significant matters to be promptly resolved to the engagement quality control reviewer's satisfaction on or before the date of the auditor's report.

A25. Completion of the engagement quality control review means the completion by the engagement quality control reviewer of the requirements in paragraphs 20-21, and where applicable, compliance with paragraph 22. Documentation of the engagement quality control review may be completed after the date of the auditor's report as part of the assembly of the final audit file. ISA (UK and Ireland) 230 establishes requirements and provides guidance in this regard.[11]

Nature, Extent and Timing of Engagement Quality Control Review (Ref: Para. 20)

A26. Remaining alert for changes in circumstances allows the engagement partner to identify situations in which an engagement quality control review is necessary, even though at the start of the engagement, such a review was not required.

A27. The extent of the engagement quality control review may depend, among other things, on the complexity of the audit engagement, whether the entity is a listed entity, and the risk that the auditor's report might not be appropriate in the circumstances. The performance of an engagement quality control review does not reduce the responsibilities of the engagement partner for the audit engagement and its performance.

Engagement Quality Control Review of Listed Entities (Ref: Para. 21)

A28. Other matters relevant to evaluating the significant judgments made by the engagement team that may be considered in an engagement quality control review of a listed entity include:

- Significant risks identified during the engagement in accordance with ISA (UK and Ireland) 315,[12] and the responses to those risks in accordance with ISA (UK and Ireland) 330,[13] including the engagement team's assessment of, and response to, the risk of fraud in accordance with ISA (UK and Ireland) 240.[14]

- Judgments made, particularly with respect to materiality and significant risks

---

[11] ISA (UK and Ireland) 230, paragraphs 14-16.
[12] ISA (UK and Ireland) 315, "Identifying and Assessing the Risks of Material Misstatement through Understanding the Entity and Its Environment."
[13] ISA (UK and Ireland) 330, "The Auditor's Responses to Assessed Risks."
[14] ISA (UK and Ireland) 240, "The Auditor's Responsibilities Relating to Fraud in an Audit of Financial Statements."

- The significance and disposition of corrected and uncorrected misstatements identified during the audit.

- The matters to be communicated to management and those charged with governance and, where applicable, other parties such as regulatory bodies.

These other matters, depending on the circumstances, may also be applicable for engagement quality control reviews for audits of financial statements of other entities.

Considerations Specific to Smaller Entities (Ref: Para. 20-21)

A29. In addition to the audits of financial statements of listed entities, an engagement quality control review is required for audit engagements that meet the criteria established by the firm that subjects engagements to an engagement quality control review. In some cases, none of the firm's audit engagements may meet the criteria that would subject them to such a review.

Considerations Specific to Public Sector Entities (Ref: Para. 20-21)

A30. In the public sector, a statutorily appointed auditor (for example, an Auditor General, or other suitably qualified person appointed on behalf of the Auditor General), may act in a role equivalent to that of engagement partner with overall responsibility for public sector audits. In such circumstances, where applicable, the selection of the engagement quality control reviewer includes consideration of the need for independence from the audited entity and the ability of the engagement quality control reviewer to provide an objective evaluation.

A31. Listed entities as referred to in paragraphs 21 and A28 are not common in the public sector. However, there may be other public sector entities that are significant due to size, complexity or public interest aspects, and which consequently have a wide range of stakeholders. Examples include state owned corporations and public utilities. Ongoing transformations within the public sector may also give rise to new types of significant entities. There are no fixed objective criteria on which the determination of significance is based. Nonetheless, public sector auditors evaluate which entities may be of sufficient significance to warrant performance of an engagement quality control review.

Monitoring (Ref: Para. 23)

A32. ISQC (UK and Ireland) 1 requires the firm to establish a monitoring process designed to provide it with reasonable assurance that the policies and procedures relating to the system of quality control are relevant, adequate and operating effectively.[15]

A33. In considering deficiencies that may affect the audit engagement, the engagement partner may have regard to measures the firm took to rectify the situation that the engagement partner considers are sufficient in the context of that audit.

---

[15] ISQC (UK and Ireland) 1, paragraph 48.

A34. A deficiency in the firm's system of quality control does not necessarily indicate that a particular audit engagement was not performed in accordance with professional standards and applicable legal and regulatory requirements, or that the auditor's report was not appropriate.

Documentation

Documentation of Consultations (Ref: Para. 24(d))

A35. Documentation of consultations with other professionals that involve difficult or contentious matters that is sufficiently complete and detailed contributes to an understanding of:

- The issue on which consultation was sought; and

- The results of the consultation, including any decisions taken, the basis for those decisions and how they were implemented.

INTERNATIONAL STANDARD ON AUDITING
(UK AND IRELAND) 230

AUDIT DOCUMENTATION

(Effective for audits of financial statements for periods ending on or after 15 December 2010)[1a]

CONTENTS

International Standard on Auditing (UK and Ireland) (ISA (UK and Ireland)) 230, "Audit Documentation" should be read in conjunction with ISA (UK and Ireland) 200, "Overall Objectives of the Independent Auditor and the Conduct of an Audit in Accordance with International Standards on Auditing (UK and Ireland)."

[1a] Conforming amendments to this standard as a result of ISA (UK and Ireland) 610 (Revised June 2013), *Using the Work of Internal Auditors*, are included that are effective for audits of financial statements for periods ending on or after 15 June 2014. Details of the amendments are given in the Annexure to ISA (UK and Ireland) 610 (Revised June 2013).

Introduction

Scope of this ISA (UK and Ireland)

1.   This International Standard on Auditing (UK and Ireland) (ISA (UK and Ireland)) deals with the auditor's responsibility to prepare audit documentation for an audit of financial statements. The Appendix lists other ISAs (UK and Ireland) that contain specific documentation requirements and guidance. The specific documentation requirements of other ISAs (UK and Ireland) do not limit the application of this ISA (UK and Ireland). Law or regulation may establish additional documentation requirements.

Nature and Purposes of Audit Documentation

2.   Audit documentation that meets the requirements of this ISA (UK and Ireland) and the specific documentation requirements of other relevant ISAs (UK and Ireland) provides:

   (a)   Evidence of the auditor's basis for a conclusion about the achievement of the overall objectives of the auditor;[1] and

   (b)   Evidence that the audit was planned and performed in accordance with ISAs (UK and Ireland) and applicable legal and regulatory requirements.

3.   Audit documentation serves a number of additional purposes, including the following:

   •   Assisting the engagement team to plan and perform the audit.

   •   Assisting members of the engagement team responsible for supervision to direct and supervise the audit work, and to discharge their review responsibilities in accordance with ISA (UK and Ireland) 220.[2]

   •   Enabling the engagement team to be accountable for its work.

   •   Retaining a record of matters of continuing significance to future audits.

   •   Enabling the conduct of quality control reviews and inspections in accordance with ISQC (UK and Ireland) 1[3] or national requirements that are at least as demanding.[4]

---

[1]   ISA (UK and Ireland) 200, "Overall Objectives of the Independent Auditor and the Conduct of an Audit in Accordance with International Standards on Auditing (UK and Ireland)," paragraph 11.
[2]   ISA (UK and Ireland) 220, "Quality Control for an Audit of Financial Statements," paragraphs 15-17.
[3]   ISQC (UK and Ireland) 1, "Quality Control for Firms that Perform Audits and Reviews of Financial Statements, and Other Assurance and Related Services Engagements," paragraphs 32-33, 35-38, and 48].
[4]   ISA (UK and Ireland) 220, paragraph 2.

- Enabling the conduct of external inspections in accordance with applicable legal, regulatory or other requirements.

Effective Date

4. This ISA (UK and Ireland) is effective for audits of financial statements for periods ending on or after 15 December 2010.[1a]

Objective

5. The objective of the auditor is to prepare documentation that provides:

(a) A sufficient and appropriate record of the basis for the auditor's report; and

(b) Evidence that the audit was planned and performed in accordance with ISAs (UK and Ireland) and applicable legal and regulatory requirements.

Definitions

6. For purposes of the ISAs (UK and Ireland), the following terms have the meanings attributed below:

(a) Audit documentation – The record of audit procedures performed, relevant audit evidence obtained, and conclusions the auditor reached (terms such as "working papers" or "workpapers" are also sometimes used).

(b) Audit file – One or more folders or other storage media, in physical or electronic form, containing the records that comprise the audit documentation for a specific engagement.

(c) Experienced auditor – An individual (whether internal or external to the firm) who has practical audit experience, and a reasonable understanding of:

(i) Audit processes;

(ii) ISAs and applicable legal and regulatory requirements;

(iii) The business environment in which the entity operates; and

(iv) Auditing and financial reporting issues relevant to the entity's industry.

Requirements

Timely Preparation of Audit Documentation

7. The auditor shall prepare audit documentation on a timely basis. (Ref: Para. A1)

Documentation of the Audit Procedures Performed and Audit Evidence Obtained

Form, Content and Extent of Audit Documentation

8.   The auditor shall prepare audit documentation that is sufficient to enable an experienced auditor, having no previous connection with the audit, to understand: (Ref: Para. A2-A5, A16-A17)

    (a)   The nature, timing and extent of the audit procedures performed to comply with the ISAs (UK and Ireland) and applicable legal and regulatory requirements; (Ref: Para. A6-A7)

    (b)   The results of the audit procedures performed, and the audit evidence obtained; and

    (c)   Significant matters arising during the audit, the conclusions reached thereon, and significant professional judgments made in reaching those conclusions. (Ref: Para. A8-A11)

9.   In documenting the nature, timing and extent of audit procedures performed, the auditor shall record:

    (a)   The identifying characteristics of the specific items or matters tested; (Ref: Para. A12)

    (b)   Who performed the audit work and the date such work was completed; and

    (c)   Who reviewed the audit work performed and the date and extent of such review. (Ref: Para. A13)

10.   The auditor shall document discussions of significant matters with management, those charged with governance, and others, including the nature of the significant matters discussed and when and with whom the discussions took place. (Ref: Para. A14)

11.   If the auditor identified information that is inconsistent with the auditor's final conclusion regarding a significant matter, the auditor shall document how the auditor addressed the inconsistency. (Ref: Para. A15)

Departure from a Relevant Requirement

12.   If, in exceptional circumstances, the auditor judges it necessary to depart from a relevant requirement in an ISA (UK and Ireland), the auditor shall document how the alternative audit procedures performed achieve the aim of that requirement, and the reasons for the departure. (Ref: Para. A18-A19)

Matters Arising after the Date of the Auditor's Report

13. If, in exceptional circumstances, the auditor performs new or additional audit procedures or draws new conclusions after the date of the auditor's report, the auditor shall document: (Ref: Para. A20)

    (a) The circumstances encountered;

    (b) The new or additional audit procedures performed, audit evidence obtained, and conclusions reached, and their effect on the auditor's report; and

    (c) When and by whom the resulting changes to audit documentation were made and reviewed.

Assembly of the Final Audit File

14. The auditor shall assemble the audit documentation in an audit file and complete the administrative process of assembling the final audit file on a timely basis after the date of the auditor's report. (Ref: Para. A21-A22)

15. After the assembly of the final audit file has been completed, the auditor shall not delete or discard audit documentation of any nature before the end of its retention period. (Ref: Para. A23)

16. In circumstances other than those envisaged in paragraph 13 where the auditor finds it necessary to modify existing audit documentation or add new audit documentation after the assembly of the final audit file has been completed, the auditor shall, regardless of the nature of the modifications or additions, document: (Ref: Para. A24)

    (a) The specific reasons for making them; and

    (b) When and by whom they were made and reviewed.

***

Application and Other Explanatory Material

Timely Preparation of Audit Documentation (Ref: Para. 7)

A1. Preparing sufficient and appropriate audit documentation on a timely basis helps to enhance the quality of the audit and facilitates the effective review and evaluation of the audit evidence obtained and conclusions reached before the auditor's report is finalized. Documentation prepared after the audit work has been performed is likely to be less accurate than documentation prepared at the time such work is performed.

Documentation of the Audit Procedures Performed and Audit Evidence Obtained

Form, Content and Extent of Audit Documentation (Ref: Para. 8)

A2.   The form, content and extent of audit documentation depend on factors such as:

- The size and complexity of the entity.

- The nature of the audit procedures to be performed.

- The identified risks of material misstatement.

- The significance of the audit evidence obtained.

- The nature and extent of exceptions identified.

- The need to document a conclusion or the basis for a conclusion not readily determinable from the documentation of the work performed or audit evidence obtained.

- The audit methodology and tools used.

A3.   Audit documentation may be recorded on paper or on electronic or other media. Examples of audit documentation include:

- Audit programs.

- Analyses.

- Issues memoranda.

- Summaries of significant matters.

- Letters of confirmation and representation.

- Checklists.

- Correspondence (including e-mail) concerning significant matters.

The auditor may include abstracts or copies of the entity's records (for example, significant and specific contracts and agreements) as part of audit documentation. Audit documentation, however, is not a substitute for the entity's accounting records.

A4.   The auditor need not include in audit documentation superseded drafts of working papers and financial statements, notes that reflect incomplete or preliminary thinking, previous copies of documents corrected for typographical or other errors, and duplicates of documents.

A5.   Oral explanations by the auditor, on their own, do not represent adequate support for the work the auditor performed or conclusions the auditor reached, but may be used to explain or clarify information contained in the audit documentation.

Documentation of Compliance with ISAs (Ref: Para. 8(a))

A6.   In principle, compliance with the requirements of this ISA (UK and Ireland) will result in the audit documentation being sufficient and appropriate in the circumstances. Other ISAs (UK and Ireland) contain specific documentation requirements that are intended to clarify the application of this ISA (UK and Ireland) in the particular circumstances of those other ISAs (UK and Ireland). The specific documentation requirements of other ISAs do not limit the application of this ISA (UK and Ireland). Furthermore, the absence of a documentation requirement in any particular ISA (UK and Ireland) is not intended to suggest that there is no documentation that will be prepared as a result of complying with that ISA (UK and Ireland).

A7.   Audit documentation provides evidence that the audit complies with the ISAs (UK and Ireland). However, it is neither necessary nor practicable for the auditor to document every matter considered, or professional judgment made, in an audit. Further, it is unnecessary for the auditor to document separately (as in a checklist, for example) compliance with matters for which compliance is demonstrated by documents included within the audit file. For example:

- The existence of an adequately documented audit plan demonstrates that the auditor has planned the audit.

- The existence of a signed engagement letter in the audit file demonstrates that the auditor has agreed the terms of the audit engagement with management or, where appropriate, those charged with governance.

- An auditor's report containing an appropriately qualified opinion on the financial statements demonstrates that the auditor has complied with the requirement to express a qualified opinion under the circumstances specified in the ISAs (UK and Ireland).

- In relation to requirements that apply generally throughout the audit, there may be a number of ways in which compliance with them may be demonstrated within the audit file:

    o   For example, there may be no single way in which the auditor's professional skepticism is documented. But the audit documentation may nevertheless provide evidence of the auditor's exercise of professional skepticism in accordance with the ISAs (UK and Ireland). Such evidence may include specific procedures performed to corroborate management's responses to the auditor's inquiries.

    o   Similarly, that the engagement partner has taken responsibility for the direction, supervision and performance of the audit in compliance with the ISAs (UK and Ireland) may be evidenced in a number of ways within the audit documentation. This may include documentation of the engagement partner's timely involvement in aspects of the audit, such as participation in the team discussions required by ISA (UK and Ireland) 315.[5]

Documentation of Significant Matters and Related Significant Professional Judgments (Ref: Para. 8(c))

A8. Judging the significance of a matter requires an objective analysis of the facts and circumstances. Examples of significant matters include:

- Matters that give rise to significant risks (as defined in ISA (UK and Ireland) 315).[6]

- Results of audit procedures indicating (a) that the financial statements could be materially misstated, or (b) a need to revise the auditor's previous assessment of the risks of material misstatement and the auditor's responses to those risks.

- Circumstances that cause the auditor significant difficulty in applying necessary audit procedures.

- Findings that could result in a modification to the audit opinion or the inclusion of an Emphasis of Matter paragraph in the auditor's report.

- Concerns about the entity's ability to continue as a going concern.

A9. An important factor in determining the form, content and extent of audit documentation of significant matters is the extent of professional judgment exercised in performing the work and evaluating the results. Documentation of the professional judgments made, where significant, serves to explain the auditor's conclusions and to reinforce the quality of the judgment. Such matters are of particular interest to those responsible for reviewing audit documentation, including those carrying out subsequent audits when reviewing matters of continuing significance (for example, when performing a retrospective review of accounting estimates).

A10. Some examples of circumstances in which, in accordance with paragraph 8, it is appropriate to prepare audit documentation relating to the use of professional judgment include, where the matters and judgments are significant:

- The rationale for the auditor's conclusion when a requirement provides that the auditor "shall consider" certain information or factors, and that consideration is significant in the context of the particular engagement.

---

[5] ISA (UK and Ireland) 315, "Identifying and Assessing the Risks of Material Misstatement through Understanding the Entity and Its Environment," paragraph 10.

[6] ISA (UK and Ireland) 315, paragraph 4(e).

- The basis for the auditor's conclusion on the reasonableness of areas of subjective judgments (for example, the reasonableness of significant accounting estimates).

- The basis for the auditor's conclusions about the authenticity of a document when further investigation (such as making appropriate use of an expert or of confirmation procedures) is undertaken in response to conditions identified during the audit that caused the auditor to believe that the document may not be authentic.

A11. The auditor may consider it helpful to prepare and retain as part of the audit documentation a summary (sometimes known as a completion memorandum) that describes the significant matters identified during the audit and how they were addressed, or that includes cross-references to other relevant supporting audit documentation that provides such information. Such a summary may facilitate effective and efficient reviews and inspections of the audit documentation, particularly for large and complex audits. Further, the preparation of such a summary may assist the auditor's consideration of the significant matters. It may also help the auditor to consider whether, in light of the audit procedures performed and conclusions reached, there is any individual relevant ISA (UK and Ireland) objective that the auditor cannot achieve that would prevent the auditor from achieving the overall objectives of the auditor.

Identification of Specific Items or Matters Tested, and of the Preparer and Reviewer (Ref: Para. 9)

A12. Recording the identifying characteristics serves a number of purposes. For example, it enables the engagement team to be accountable for its work and facilitates the investigation of exceptions or inconsistencies. Identifying characteristics will vary with the nature of the audit procedure and the item or matter tested. For example:

- For a detailed test of entity-generated purchase orders, the auditor may identify the documents selected for testing by their dates and unique purchase order numbers.

- For a procedure requiring selection or review of all items over a specific amount from a given population, the auditor may record the scope of the procedure and identify the population (for example, all journal entries over a specified amount from the journal register).

- For a procedure requiring systematic sampling from a population of documents, the auditor may identify the documents selected by recording their source, the starting point and the sampling interval (for example, a systematic sample of shipping reports selected from the shipping log for the period from April 1 to September 30, starting with report number 12345 and selecting every 125th report).

- For a procedure requiring inquiries of specific entity personnel, the auditor may record the dates of the inquiries and the names and job designations of the entity personnel.

- For an observation procedure, the auditor may record the process or matter being observed, the relevant individuals, their respective responsibilities, and where and when the observation was carried out.

A13. ISA (UK and Ireland) 220 requires the auditor to review the audit work performed through review of the audit documentation.[7] The requirement to document who reviewed the audit work performed does not imply a need for each specific working paper to include evidence of review. The requirement, however, means documenting what audit work was reviewed, who reviewed such work, and when it was reviewed.

Documentation of Discussions of Significant Matters with Management, Those Charged with Governance, and Others (Ref: Para. 10)

A14. The documentation is not limited to records prepared by the auditor but may include other appropriate records such as minutes of meetings prepared by the entity's personnel and agreed by the auditor. Others with whom the auditor may discuss significant matters may include other personnel within the entity, and external parties, such as persons providing professional advice to the entity.

Documentation of How Inconsistencies have been Addressed (Ref: Para. 11)

A15. The requirement to document how the auditor addressed inconsistencies in information does not imply that the auditor needs to retain documentation that is incorrect or superseded.

Considerations Specific to Smaller Entities (Ref: Para. 8)

A16. The audit documentation for the audit of a smaller entity is generally less extensive than that for the audit of a larger entity. Further, in the case of an audit where the engagement partner performs all the audit work, the documentation will not include matters that might have to be documented solely to inform or instruct members of an engagement team, or to provide evidence of review by other members of the team (for example, there will be no matters to document relating to team discussions or supervision). Nevertheless, the engagement partner complies with the overriding requirement in paragraph 8 to prepare audit documentation that can be understood by an experienced auditor, as the audit documentation may be subject to review by external parties for regulatory or other purposes.

A17. When preparing audit documentation, the auditor of a smaller entity may also find it helpful and efficient to record various aspects of the audit together in a single document, with cross-references to supporting working papers as appropriate. Examples of matters that may be documented together in the audit of a smaller entity

---

[7] ISA (UK and Ireland) 220, paragraph 17.

include the understanding of the entity and its internal control, the overall audit strategy and audit plan, materiality determined in accordance with ISA (UK and Ireland) 320,[8] assessed risks, significant matters noted during the audit, and conclusions reached.

Departure from a Relevant Requirement (Ref: Para. 12)

A18. The requirements of the ISAs (UK and Ireland) are designed to enable the auditor to achieve the objectives specified in the ISAs (UK and Ireland), and thereby the overall objectives of the auditor. Accordingly, other than in exceptional circumstances, the ISAs (UK and Ireland) call for compliance with each requirement that is relevant in the circumstances of the audit.

A19. The documentation requirement applies only to requirements that are relevant in the circumstances. A requirement is not relevant[9] only in the cases where:

(a) The entire ISA (UK and Ireland) is not relevant (for example, if an entity does not have an internal audit function, nothing in ISA (UK and Ireland) 610 (Revised June 2013)[10] is relevant); or

(b) The requirement is conditional and the condition does not exist (for example, the requirement to modify the auditor's opinion where there is an inability to obtain sufficient appropriate audit evidence, and there is no such inability).

Matters Arising after the Date of the Auditor's Report (Ref: Para. 13)

A20. Examples of exceptional circumstances include facts which become known to the auditor after the date of the auditor's report but which existed at that date and which, if known at that date, might have caused the financial statements to be amended or the auditor to modify the opinion in the auditor's report.[11] The resulting changes to the audit documentation are reviewed in accordance with the review responsibilities set out in ISA (UK and Ireland) 220,[12] with the engagement partner taking final responsibility for the changes.

Assembly of the Final Audit File (Ref: Para. 14-16)

A21. ISQC (UK and Ireland) 1 (or national requirements that are at least as demanding) requires firms to establish policies and procedures for the timely completion of the assembly of audit files.[13] An appropriate time limit within which to complete the assembly of the final audit file is ordinarily not more than 60 days after the date of the auditor's report.[14]

---

[8] ISA (UK and Ireland) 320, "Materiality in Planning and Performing an Audit."
[9] ISA (UK and Ireland) 200, paragraph 22.
[10] ISA (UK and Ireland) 610 (Revised June 2013), "Using the Work of Internal Auditors," paragraph 2.
[11] ISA (UK and Ireland) 560, "Subsequent Events," paragraph 14.
[12] ISA (UK and Ireland) 220, paragraph 16.
[13] ISQC (UK and Ireland) 1, paragraph 45.
[14] ISQC (UK and Ireland) 1, paragraph A54.

A22. The completion of the assembly of the final audit file after the date of the auditor's report is an administrative process that does not involve the performance of new audit procedures or the drawing of new conclusions. Changes may, however, be made to the audit documentation during the final assembly process if they are administrative in nature. Examples of such changes include:

- Deleting or discarding superseded documentation.

- Sorting, collating and cross-referencing working papers.

- Signing off on completion checklists relating to the file assembly process.

- Documenting audit evidence that the auditor has obtained, discussed and agreed with the relevant members of the engagement team before the date of the auditor's report.

A23. ISQC (UK and Ireland) 1 (or national requirements that are at least as demanding) requires firms to establish policies and procedures for the retention of engagement documentation.[15] The retention period for audit engagements ordinarily is no shorter than five years from the date of the auditor's report, or, if later, the date of the group auditor's report.[16]

A24. An example of a circumstance in which the auditor may find it necessary to modify existing audit documentation or add new audit documentation after file assembly has been completed is the need to clarify existing audit documentation arising from comments received during monitoring inspections performed by internal or external parties.

---

[15] ISQC (UK and Ireland) 1, paragraph 47.
[16] ISQC (UK and Ireland) 1, paragraph A61.
In the UK and Ireland the auditor has regard to specific requirements of the auditor's relevant professional body.

Appendix

(Ref: Para. 1)

Specific Audit Documentation Requirements in Other ISAs

This appendix identifies paragraphs in other ISAs (UK and Ireland) in effect for audits of financial statements for periods ending on or after 15 December 2010 that contain specific documentation requirements. The list is not a substitute for considering the requirements and related application and other explanatory material in ISAs.

- ISA (UK and Ireland) 210, "Agreeing the Terms of Audit Engagements" – paragraphs 10-12

- ISA (UK and Ireland) 220, "Quality Control for an Audit of Financial Statements" – paragraphs 24-25

- ISA (UK and Ireland) 240, "The Auditor's Responsibilities Relating to Fraud in an Audit of Financial Statements" – paragraphs 44-47

- ISA (UK and Ireland) 250, Section A "Consideration of Laws and Regulations in an Audit of Financial Statements" – paragraph 29

- ISA (UK and Ireland) 260, "Communication with Those Charged with Governance" – paragraph 23

- ISA (UK and Ireland) 300, "Planning an Audit of Financial Statements" – paragraph 12

- ISA (UK and Ireland) 315, "Identifying and Assessing the Risks of Material Misstatement through Understanding the Entity and Its Environment" – paragraph 32

- ISA (UK and Ireland) 320, "Materiality in Planning and Performing an Audit" – paragraph 14

- ISA (UK and Ireland) 330, "The Auditor's Responses to Assessed Risks" – paragraphs 28-30

- ISA (UK and Ireland) 450, "Evaluation of Misstatements Identified During the Audit" – paragraph 15

- ISA (UK and Ireland) 540, "Auditing Accounting Estimates, Including Fair Value Accounting Estimates, and Related Disclosures" – paragraph 23

- ISA (UK and Ireland) 550, "Related Parties" – paragraph 28

- ISA (UK and Ireland) 600, "Special Considerations—Audits of Group Financial Statements (Including the Work of Component Auditors)" – paragraph 50

- ISA (UK and Ireland) 610, "Using the Work of Internal Auditors" – paragraph 13

- ISA (UK and Ireland) 720, Section B "The Auditor's Statutory Reporting Responsibility in Relation to Directors' reports" – paragraph 12

INTERNATIONAL STANDARD ON AUDITING
(UK AND IRELAND) 240

THE AUDITOR'S RESPONSIBILITIES RELATING TO
FRAUD IN AN AUDIT OF FINANCIAL STATEMENTS

(Effective for audits of financial statements for periods ending on or after 15 December 2010)[1a]

CONTENTS

[1a] Conforming amendments to this standard as a result of ISA (UK and Ireland) 610 (Revised June 2013), *Using the Work of Internal Auditors*, are included that are effective for audits of financial statements for periods ending on or after 15 June 2014. Details of the amendments are given in the Annexure to ISA (UK and Ireland) 610 (Revised June 2013).

International Standard on Auditing (UK and Ireland) (ISA (UK and Ireland)) 240, "The Auditor's Responsibilities Relating to Fraud in an Audit of Financial Statements" should be read in conjunction with ISA (UK and Ireland) 200, "Overall Objectives of the Independent Auditor and the Conduct of an Audit in Accordance with International Standards on Auditing (UK and Ireland)."

Introduction

Scope of this ISA (UK and Ireland)

1. This International Standard on Auditing (UK and Ireland) (ISA (UK and Ireland)) deals with the auditor's responsibilities relating to fraud in an audit of financial statements. Specifically, it expands on how ISA (UK and Ireland) 315[1] and ISA (UK and Ireland) 330[2] are to be applied in relation to risks of material misstatement due to fraud.

Characteristics of Fraud

2. Misstatements in the financial statements can arise from either fraud or error. The distinguishing factor between fraud and error is whether the underlying action that results in the misstatement of the financial statements is intentional or unintentional.

3. Although fraud is a broad legal concept, for the purposes of the ISAs (UK and Ireland), the auditor is concerned with fraud that causes a material misstatement in the financial statements. Two types of intentional misstatements are relevant to the auditor – misstatements resulting from fraudulent financial reporting and misstatements resulting from misappropriation of assets. Although the auditor may suspect or, in rare cases, identify the occurrence of fraud, the auditor does not make legal determinations of whether fraud has actually occurred. (Ref: Para. A1-A6)

Responsibility for the Prevention and Detection of Fraud

4. The primary responsibility for the prevention and detection of fraud rests with both those charged with governance of the entity and management. It is important that management, with the oversight of those charged with governance, place a strong emphasis on fraud prevention, which may reduce opportunities for fraud to take place, and fraud deterrence, which could persuade individuals not to commit fraud because of the likelihood of detection and punishment. This involves a commitment to creating a culture of honesty and ethical behavior which can be reinforced by an active oversight by those charged with governance. Oversight by those charged with governance includes considering the potential for override of controls or other inappropriate influence over the financial reporting process, such as efforts by management to manage earnings in order to influence the perceptions of analysts as to the entity's performance and profitability.

Responsibilities of the Auditor

5. An auditor conducting an audit in accordance with ISAs (UK and Ireland) is responsible for obtaining reasonable assurance that the financial statements taken as a whole are free from material misstatement, whether caused by fraud or error. Owing to the inherent limitations of an audit, there is an unavoidable risk that some material

---

[1] ISA (UK and Ireland) 315, "Identifying and Assessing the Risks of Material Misstatement through Understanding the Entity and Its Environment."

[2] ISA (UK and Ireland) 330, "The Auditor's Responses to Assessed Risks."

misstatements of the financial statements may not be detected, even though the audit is properly planned and performed in accordance with the ISAs (UK and Ireland).[3]

6. As described in ISA (UK and Ireland) 200,[4] the potential effects of inherent limitations are particularly significant in the case of misstatement resulting from fraud. The risk of not detecting a material misstatement resulting from fraud is higher than the risk of not detecting one resulting from error. This is because fraud may involve sophisticated and carefully organized schemes designed to conceal it, such as forgery, deliberate failure to record transactions, or intentional misrepresentations being made to the auditor. Such attempts at concealment may be even more difficult to detect when accompanied by collusion. Collusion may cause the auditor to believe that audit evidence is persuasive when it is, in fact, false. The auditor's ability to detect a fraud depends on factors such as the skillfulness of the perpetrator, the frequency and extent of manipulation, the degree of collusion involved, the relative size of individual amounts manipulated, and the seniority of those individuals involved. While the auditor may be able to identify potential opportunities for fraud to be perpetrated, it is difficult for the auditor to determine whether misstatements in judgment areas such as accounting estimates are caused by fraud or error.

7. Furthermore, the risk of the auditor not detecting a material misstatement resulting from management fraud is greater than for employee fraud, because management is frequently in a position to directly or indirectly manipulate accounting records, present fraudulent financial information or override control procedures designed to prevent similar frauds by other employees.

8. When obtaining reasonable assurance, the auditor is responsible for maintaining professional skepticism throughout the audit, considering the potential for management override of controls and recognizing the fact that audit procedures that are effective for detecting error may not be effective in detecting fraud. The requirements in this ISA (UK and Ireland) are designed to assist the auditor in identifying and assessing the risks of material misstatement due to fraud and in designing procedures to detect such misstatement.

Effective Date

9. This ISA (UK and Ireland) is effective for audits of financial statements for periods ending on or after 15 December 2010.[1a]

Objectives

10. The objectives of the auditor are:

(a) To identify and assess the risks of material misstatement of the financial statements due to fraud;

---

[3] ISA (UK and Ireland) 200, "Overall Objectives of the Independent Auditor and the Conduct of an Audit in Accordance with International Standards on Auditing (UK and Ireland)," paragraphs A51-A52.

[4] ISA (UK and Ireland) 200, paragraph A51.

(b)   To obtain sufficient appropriate audit evidence regarding the assessed risks of material misstatement due to fraud, through designing and implementing appropriate responses; and

(c)   To respond appropriately to fraud or suspected fraud identified during the audit.

Definitions

11.   For purposes of the ISAs (UK and Ireland), the following terms have the meanings attributed below:

(a)   Fraud – An intentional act by one or more individuals among management, those charged with governance, employees, or third parties, involving the use of deception to obtain an unjust or illegal advantage.

(b)   Fraud risk factors – Events or conditions that indicate an incentive or pressure to commit fraud or provide an opportunity to commit fraud.

Requirements

Professional Skepticism

12.   In accordance with ISA (UK and Ireland) 200, the auditor shall maintain professional skepticism throughout the audit, recognizing the possibility that a material misstatement due to fraud could exist, notwithstanding the auditor's past experience of the honesty and integrity of the entity's management and those charged with governance. (Ref: Para. A7- A8)

13.   Unless the auditor has reason to believe the contrary, the auditor may accept records and documents as genuine. If conditions identified during the audit cause the auditor to believe that a document may not be authentic or that terms in a document have been modified but not disclosed to the auditor, the auditor shall investigate further. (Ref: Para. A9)

14.   Where responses to inquiries of management or those charged with governance are inconsistent, the auditor shall investigate the inconsistencies.

Discussion among the Engagement Team

15.   ISA (UK and Ireland) 315 requires a discussion among the engagement team members and a determination by the engagement partner of which matters are to be communicated to those team members not involved in the discussion.[5] This discussion shall place particular emphasis on how and where the entity's financial statements may be susceptible to material misstatement due to fraud, including how

---

[5]   ISA (UK and Ireland) 315, paragraph 10.

fraud might occur. The discussion shall occur setting aside beliefs that the engagement team members may have that management and those charged with governance are honest and have integrity. (Ref: Para. A10-A11)

Risk Assessment Procedures and Related Activities

16.   When performing risk assessment procedures and related activities to obtain an understanding of the entity and its environment, including the entity's internal control, required by ISA (UK and Ireland) 315,[6] the auditor shall perform the procedures in paragraphs 17-24 to obtain information for use in identifying the risks of material misstatement due to fraud.

Management and Others within the Entity

17.   The auditor shall make inquiries of management regarding:

(a)   Management's assessment of the risk that the financial statements may be materially misstated due to fraud, including the nature, extent and frequency of such assessments; (Ref: Para. A12-A13)

(b)   Management's process for identifying and responding to the risks of fraud in the entity, including any specific risks of fraud that management has identified or that have been brought to its attention, or classes of transactions, account balances, or disclosures for which a risk of fraud is likely to exist; (Ref: Para. A14)

(c)   Management's communication, if any, to those charged with governance regarding its processes for identifying and responding to the risks of fraud in the entity; and

(d)   Management's communication, if any, to employees regarding its views on business practices and ethical behavior.

18.   The auditor shall make inquiries of management, and others within the entity as appropriate, to determine whether they have knowledge of any actual, suspected or alleged fraud affecting the entity. (Ref: Para. A15-A17)

19.   For those entities that have an internal audit function, the auditor shall make inquiries of appropriate individuals within the function to determine whether they have knowledge of any actual, suspected or alleged fraud affecting the entity, and to obtain its views about the risks of fraud. (Ref: Para. A18)

Those Charged with Governance

20.   Unless all of those charged with governance are involved in managing the entity,[7] the auditor shall obtain an understanding of how those charged with governance

---

[6]   ISA (UK and Ireland) 315, paragraphs 5-24.

[7]   ISA (UK and Ireland) 260, "Communication with Those Charged with Governance," paragraph 13.

exercise oversight of management's processes for identifying and responding to the risks of fraud in the entity and the internal control that management has established to mitigate these risks. (Ref: Para. A19-A21)

21. Unless all of those charged with governance are involved in managing the entity, the auditor shall make inquiries of those charged with governance to determine whether they have knowledge of any actual, suspected or alleged fraud affecting the entity. These inquiries are made in part to corroborate the responses to the inquiries of management.

Unusual or Unexpected Relationships Identified

22. The auditor shall evaluate whether unusual or unexpected relationships that have been identified in performing analytical procedures, including those related to revenue accounts, may indicate risks of material misstatement due to fraud.

Other Information

23. The auditor shall consider whether other information obtained by the auditor indicates risks of material misstatement due to fraud. (Ref: Para. A22)

Evaluation of Fraud Risk Factors

24. The auditor shall evaluate whether the information obtained from the other risk assessment procedures and related activities performed indicates that one or more fraud risk factors are present. While fraud risk factors may not necessarily indicate the existence of fraud, they have often been present in circumstances where frauds have occurred and therefore may indicate risks of material misstatement due to fraud. (Ref: Para. A23-A27)

Identification and Assessment of the Risks of Material Misstatement Due to Fraud

25. In accordance with ISA (UK and Ireland) 315, the auditor shall identify and assess the risks of material misstatement due to fraud at the financial statement level, and at the assertion level for classes of transactions, account balances and disclosures.[8]

26. When identifying and assessing the risks of material misstatement due to fraud, the auditor shall, based on a presumption that there are risks of fraud in revenue recognition, evaluate which types of revenue, revenue transactions or assertions give rise to such risks. Paragraph 47 specifies the documentation required where the auditor concludes that the presumption is not applicable in the circumstances of the engagement and, accordingly, has not identified revenue recognition as a risk of material misstatement due to fraud. (Ref: Para. A28-A30)

---

[8] ISA (UK and Ireland) 315, paragraph 25.

27. The auditor shall treat those assessed risks of material misstatement due to fraud as significant risks and accordingly, to the extent not already done so, the auditor shall obtain an understanding of the entity's related controls, including control activities, relevant to such risks. (Ref: Para. A31-A32)

Responses to the Assessed Risks of Material Misstatement Due to Fraud

Overall Responses

28. In accordance with ISA (UK and Ireland) 330, the auditor shall determine overall responses to address the assessed risks of material misstatement due to fraud at the financial statement level.[9] (Ref: Para. A33)

29. In determining overall responses to address the assessed risks of material misstatement due to fraud at the financial statement level, the auditor shall:

    (a) Assign and supervise personnel taking account of the knowledge, skill and ability of the individuals to be given significant engagement responsibilities and the auditor's assessment of the risks of material misstatement due to fraud for the engagement; (Ref: Para. A34-A35)

    (b) Evaluate whether the selection and application of accounting policies by the entity, particularly those related to subjective measurements and complex transactions, may be indicative of fraudulent financial reporting resulting from management's effort to manage earnings; and

    (c) Incorporate an element of unpredictability in the selection of the nature, timing and extent of audit procedures. (Ref: Para. A36)

Audit Procedures Responsive to Assessed Risks of Material Misstatement Due to Fraud at the Assertion Level

30. In accordance with ISA (UK and Ireland) 330, the auditor shall design and perform further audit procedures whose nature, timing and extent are responsive to the assessed risks of material misstatement due to fraud at the assertion level.[10] (Ref: Para. A37-A40)

Audit Procedures Responsive to Risks Related to Management Override of Controls

31. Management is in a unique position to perpetrate fraud because of management's ability to manipulate accounting records and prepare fraudulent financial statements by overriding controls that otherwise appear to be operating effectively. Although the level of risk of management override of controls will vary from entity to entity, the risk is nevertheless present in all entities. Due to the unpredictable way in which such

---

[9] ISA (UK and Ireland) 330, paragraph 5.
[10] ISA (UK and Ireland) 330, paragraph 6.

override could occur, it is a risk of material misstatement due to fraud and thus a significant risk.

32. Irrespective of the auditor's assessment of the risks of management override of controls, the auditor shall design and perform audit procedures to:

(a) Test the appropriateness of journal entries recorded in the general ledger and other adjustments made in the preparation of the financial statements. In designing and performing audit procedures for such tests, the auditor shall:

(i) Make inquiries of individuals involved in the financial reporting process about inappropriate or unusual activity relating to the processing of journal entries and other adjustments;

(ii) Select journal entries and other adjustments made at the end of a reporting period; and

(iii) Consider the need to test journal entries and other adjustments throughout the period. (Ref: Para. A41-A44)

(b) Review accounting estimates for biases and evaluate whether the circumstances producing the bias, if any, represent a risk of material misstatement due to fraud. In performing this review, the auditor shall:

(i) Evaluate whether the judgments and decisions made by management in making the accounting estimates included in the financial statements, even if they are individually reasonable, indicate a possible bias on the part of the entity's management that may represent a risk of material misstatement due to fraud. If so, the auditor shall reevaluate the accounting estimates taken as a whole; and

(ii) Perform a retrospective review of management judgments and assumptions related to significant accounting estimates reflected in the financial statements of the prior year. (Ref: Para. A45-A47)

(c) For significant transactions that are outside the normal course of business for the entity, or that otherwise appear to be unusual given the auditor's understanding of the entity and its environment and other information obtained during the audit, the auditor shall evaluate whether the business rationale (or the lack thereof) of the transactions suggests that they may have been entered into to engage in fraudulent financial reporting or to conceal misappropriation of assets. (Ref: Para. A48)

33. The auditor shall determine whether, in order to respond to the identified risks of management override of controls, the auditor needs to perform other audit procedures in addition to those specifically referred to above (that is, where there are specific additional risks of management override that are not covered as part of the procedures performed to address the requirements in paragraph 32).

Evaluation of Audit Evidence (Ref: Para. A49)

34. The auditor shall evaluate whether analytical procedures that are performed near the end of the audit, when forming an overall conclusion as to whether the financial statements are consistent with the auditor's understanding of the entity, indicate a previously unrecognized risk of material misstatement due to fraud. (Ref: Para. A50)

35. If the auditor identifies a misstatement, the auditor shall evaluate whether such a misstatement is indicative of fraud. If there is such an indication, the auditor shall evaluate the implications of the misstatement in relation to other aspects of the audit, particularly the reliability of management representations, recognizing that an instance of fraud is unlikely to be an isolated occurrence. (Ref: Para. A51)

36. If the auditor identifies a misstatement, whether material or not, and the auditor has reason to believe that it is or may be the result of fraud and that management (in particular, senior management) is involved, the auditor shall reevaluate the assessment of the risks of material misstatement due to fraud and its resulting impact on the nature, timing and extent of audit procedures to respond to the assessed risks. The auditor shall also consider whether circumstances or conditions indicate possible collusion involving employees, management or third parties when reconsidering the reliability of evidence previously obtained. (Ref: Para. A52)

37. If the auditor confirms that, or is unable to conclude whether, the financial statements are materially misstated as a result of fraud the auditor shall evaluate the implications for the audit. (Ref: Para. A53)

Auditor Unable to Continue the Engagement

38. If, as a result of a misstatement resulting from fraud or suspected fraud, the auditor encounters exceptional circumstances that bring into question the auditor's ability to continue performing the audit, the auditor shall:

    (a) Determine the professional and legal responsibilities applicable in the circumstances, including whether there is a requirement for the auditor to report to the person or persons who made the audit appointment or, in some cases, to regulatory authorities;

    (b) Consider whether it is appropriate to withdraw from the engagement, where withdrawal is possible under applicable law or regulation; and

    (c) If the auditor withdraws;

        (i) Discuss with the appropriate level of management and those charged with governance the auditor's withdrawal from the engagement and the reasons for the withdrawal; and

        (ii) Determine whether there is a professional or legal requirement to report to the person or persons who made the audit appointment or, in some cases, to regulatory authorities, the auditor's withdrawal from the engagement and the reasons for the withdrawal. (Ref: Para. A54-A57)

Written Representations

39. The auditor shall obtain written representations from management and, where appropriate, those charged with governance that:

    (a) They acknowledge their responsibility for the design, implementation and maintenance of internal control to prevent and detect fraud;

    (b) They have disclosed to the auditor the results of management's assessment of the risk that the financial statements may be materially misstated as a result of fraud;

    (c) They have disclosed to the auditor their knowledge of fraud or suspected fraud affecting the entity involving:

        (i) Management;

        (ii) Employees who have significant roles in internal control; or

        (iii) Others where the fraud could have a material effect on the financial statements; and

    (d) They have disclosed to the auditor their knowledge of any allegations of fraud, or suspected fraud, affecting the entity's financial statements communicated by employees, former employees, analysts, regulators or others. (Ref: Para. A58-A59)

Communications to Management and with Those Charged with Governance

40. If the auditor has identified a fraud or has obtained information that indicates that a fraud may exist, the auditor shall communicate these matters on a timely basis to the appropriate level of management in order to inform those with primary responsibility for the prevention and detection of fraud of matters relevant to their responsibilities. (Ref: Para. A60)

41. Unless all of those charged with governance are involved in managing the entity, if the auditor has identified or suspects fraud involving:

    (a) management;

    (b) employees who have significant roles in internal control; or

    (c) others where the fraud results in a material misstatement in the financial statements, the auditor shall communicate these matters to those charged with governance on a timely basis. If the auditor suspects fraud involving management, the auditor shall communicate these suspicions to those charged with governance and discuss with them the nature, timing and extent of audit procedures necessary to complete the audit. (Ref: Para. A61-A63)

42. The auditor shall communicate with those charged with governance any other matters related to fraud that are, in the auditor's judgment, relevant to their responsibilities. (Ref: Para. A64)

Communications to Regulatory and Enforcement Authorities

43. If the auditor has identified or suspects a fraud, the auditor shall determine whether there is a responsibility to report the occurrence or suspicion to a party outside the entity. Although the auditor's professional duty to maintain the confidentiality of client information may preclude such reporting, the auditor's legal responsibilities may override the duty of confidentiality in some circumstances. (Ref: Para. A65-A67)

Documentation

44. The auditor shall include the following in the audit documentation[11] of the auditor's understanding of the entity and its environment and the assessment of the risks of material misstatement required by ISA (UK and Ireland) 315:[12]

   (a) The significant decisions reached during the discussion among the engagement team regarding the susceptibility of the entity's financial statements to material misstatement due to fraud; and

   (b) The identified and assessed risks of material misstatement due to fraud at the financial statement level and at the assertion level.

45. The auditor shall include the following in the audit documentation of the auditor's responses to the assessed risks of material misstatement required by ISA (UK and Ireland) 330:[13]

   (a) The overall responses to the assessed risks of material misstatement due to fraud at the financial statement level and the nature, timing and extent of audit procedures, and the linkage of those procedures with the assessed risks of material misstatement due to fraud at the assertion level; and

   (b) The results of the audit procedures, including those designed to address the risk of management override of controls.

46. The auditor shall include in the audit documentation communications about fraud made to management, those charged with governance, regulators and others.

---

[11] ISA (UK and Ireland) 230, "Audit Documentation," paragraphs 8-11, and paragraph A6.
[12] ISA (UK and Ireland) 315, paragraph 32.
[13] ISA (UK and Ireland) 330, paragraph 28.

47. If the auditor has concluded that the presumption that there is a risk of material misstatement due to fraud related to revenue recognition is not applicable in the circumstances of the engagement, the auditor shall include in the audit documentation the reasons for that conclusion.

***

Application and Other Explanatory Material

Characteristics of Fraud (Ref: Para. 3)

A1. Fraud, whether fraudulent financial reporting or misappropriation of assets, involves incentive or pressure to commit fraud, a perceived opportunity to do so and some rationalization of the act. For example:

- Incentive or pressure to commit fraudulent financial reporting may exist when management is under pressure, from sources outside or inside the entity, to achieve an expected (and perhaps unrealistic) earnings target or financial outcome – particularly since the consequences to management for failing to meet financial goals can be significant. Similarly, individuals may have an incentive to misappropriate assets, for example, because the individuals are living beyond their means.

- A perceived opportunity to commit fraud may exist when an individual believes internal control can be overridden, for example, because the individual is in a position of trust or has knowledge of specific deficiencies in internal control.

- Individuals may be able to rationalize committing a fraudulent act. Some individuals possess an attitude, character or set of ethical values that allow them knowingly and intentionally to commit a dishonest act. However, even otherwise honest individuals can commit fraud in an environment that imposes sufficient pressure on them.

A2. Fraudulent financial reporting involves intentional misstatements including omissions of amounts or disclosures in financial statements to deceive financial statement users. It can be caused by the efforts of management to manage earnings in order to deceive financial statement users by influencing their perceptions as to the entity's performance and profitability. Such earnings management may start out with small actions or inappropriate adjustment of assumptions and changes in judgments by management. Pressures and incentives may lead these actions to increase to the extent that they result in fraudulent financial reporting. Such a situation could occur when, due to pressures to meet market expectations or a desire to maximize compensation based on performance, management intentionally takes positions that lead to fraudulent financial reporting by materially misstating the financial statements. In some entities, management may be motivated to reduce earnings by a material amount to minimize tax or to inflate earnings to secure bank financing.

A3. Fraudulent financial reporting may be accomplished by the following:

- Manipulation, falsification (including forgery), or alteration of accounting records or supporting documentation from which the financial statements are prepared.

- Misrepresentation in, or intentional omission from, the financial statements of events, transactions or other significant information.

- Intentional misapplication of accounting principles relating to amounts, classification, manner of presentation, or disclosure.

A4.   Fraudulent financial reporting often involves management override of controls that otherwise may appear to be operating effectively. Fraud can be committed by management overriding controls using such techniques as:

- Recording fictitious journal entries, particularly close to the end of an accounting period, to manipulate operating results or achieve other objectives.

- Inappropriately adjusting assumptions and changing judgments used to estimate account balances.

- Omitting, advancing or delaying recognition in the financial statements of events and transactions that have occurred during the reporting period.

- Concealing, or not disclosing, facts that could affect the amounts recorded in the financial statements.

- Engaging in complex transactions that are structured to misrepresent the financial position or financial performance of the entity.

- Altering records and terms related to significant and unusual transactions.

A5.   Misappropriation of assets involves the theft of an entity's assets and is often perpetrated by employees in relatively small and immaterial amounts. However, it can also involve management who are usually more able to disguise or conceal misappropriations in ways that are difficult to detect. Misappropriation of assets can be accomplished in a variety of ways including:

- Embezzling receipts (for example, misappropriating collections on accounts receivable or diverting receipts in respect of written-off accounts to personal bank accounts).

- Stealing physical assets or intellectual property (for example, stealing inventory for personal use or for sale, stealing scrap for resale, colluding with a competitor by disclosing technological data in return for payment).

- Causing an entity to pay for goods and services not received (for example, payments to fictitious vendors, kickbacks paid by vendors to the entity's purchasing agents in return for inflating prices, payments to fictitious employees).

- Using an entity's assets for personal use (for example, using the entity's assets as collateral for a personal loan or a loan to a related party).

Misappropriation of assets is often accompanied by false or misleading records or documents in order to conceal the fact that the assets are missing or have been pledged without proper authorization.

Considerations Specific to Public Sector Entities

A6. The public sector auditor's responsibilities relating to fraud may be a result of law, regulation or other authority applicable to public sector entities or separately covered by the auditor's mandate. Consequently, the public sector auditor's responsibilities may not be limited to consideration of risks of material misstatement of the financial statements, but may also include a broader responsibility to consider risks of fraud.

Professional Skepticism (Ref: Para. 12-14)

A7. Maintaining professional skepticism requires an ongoing questioning of whether the information and audit evidence obtained suggests that a material misstatement due to fraud may exist. It includes considering the reliability of the information to be used as audit evidence and the controls over its preparation and maintenance where relevant. Due to the characteristics of fraud, the auditor's professional skepticism is particularly important when considering the risks of material misstatement due to fraud.

A8. Although the auditor cannot be expected to disregard past experience of the honesty and integrity of the entity's management and those charged with governance, the auditor's professional skepticism is particularly important in considering the risks of material misstatement due to fraud because there may have been changes in circumstances.

A9. An audit performed in accordance with ISAs (UK and Ireland) rarely involves the authentication of documents, nor is the auditor trained as or expected to be an expert in such authentication.[14] However, when the auditor identifies conditions that cause the auditor to believe that a document may not be authentic or that terms in a document have been modified but not disclosed to the auditor, possible procedures to investigate further may include:

- Confirming directly with the third party.

- Using the work of an expert to assess the document's authenticity.

Discussion among the Engagement Team (Ref: Para. 15)

A10. Discussing the susceptibility of the entity's financial statements to material misstatement due to fraud with the engagement team:

---

[14] ISA (UK and Ireland) 200, paragraph A47.

- Provides an opportunity for more experienced engagement team members to share their insights about how and where the financial statements may be susceptible to material misstatement due to fraud.

- Enables the auditor to consider an appropriate response to such susceptibility and to determine which members of the engagement team will conduct certain audit procedures.

- Permits the auditor to determine how the results of audit procedures will be shared among the engagement team and how to deal with any allegations of fraud that may come to the auditor's attention.

A11. The discussion may include such matters as:

- An exchange of ideas among engagement team members about how and where they believe the entity's financial statements may be susceptible to material misstatement due to fraud, how management could perpetrate and conceal fraudulent financial reporting, and how assets of the entity could be misappropriated.

- A consideration of circumstances that might be indicative of earnings management and the practices that might be followed by management to manage earnings that could lead to fraudulent financial reporting.

- A consideration of the known external and internal factors affecting the entity that may create an incentive or pressure for management or others to commit fraud, provide the opportunity for fraud to be perpetrated, and indicate a culture or environment that enables management or others to rationalize committing fraud.

- A consideration of management's involvement in overseeing employees with access to cash or other assets susceptible to misappropriation.

- A consideration of any unusual or unexplained changes in behavior or lifestyle of management or employees which have come to the attention of the engagement team.

- An emphasis on the importance of maintaining a proper state of mind throughout the audit regarding the potential for material misstatement due to fraud.

- A consideration of the types of circumstances that, if encountered, might indicate the possibility of fraud.

- A consideration of how an element of unpredictability will be incorporated into the nature, timing and extent of the audit procedures to be performed.

- A consideration of the audit procedures that might be selected to respond to the susceptibility of the entity's financial statement to material misstatement due to fraud and whether certain types of audit procedures are more effective than others.

- A consideration of any allegations of fraud that have come to the auditor's attention.

- A consideration of the risk of management override of controls.

Risk Assessment Procedures and Related Activities

Inquiries of Management

Management's Assessment of the Risk of Material Misstatement Due to Fraud (Ref: Para. 17(a))

A12. Management[14a] accepts responsibility for the entity's internal control and for the preparation of the entity's financial statements. Accordingly, it is appropriate for the auditor to make inquiries of management regarding management's own assessment of the risk of fraud and the controls in place to prevent and detect it. The nature, extent and frequency of management's assessment of such risk and controls may vary from entity to entity. In some entities, management may make detailed assessments on an annual basis or as part of continuous monitoring. In other entities, management's assessment may be less structured and less frequent. The nature, extent and frequency of management's assessment are relevant to the auditor's understanding of the entity's control environment. For example, the fact that management has not made an assessment of the risk of fraud may in some circumstances be indicative of the lack of importance that management places on internal control.

Considerations specific to smaller entities

A13. In some entities, particularly smaller entities, the focus of management's assessment may be on the risks of employee fraud or misappropriation of assets.

Management's Process for Identifying and Responding to the Risks of Fraud (Ref: Para. 17(b))

A14. In the case of entities with multiple locations management's processes may include different levels of monitoring of operating locations, or business segments. Management may also have identified particular operating locations or business segments for which a risk of fraud may be more likely to exist.

Inquiry of Management and Others within the Entity (Ref: Para. 18)

A15. The auditor's inquiries of management may provide useful information concerning the risks of material misstatements in the financial statements resulting from employee fraud. However, such inquiries are unlikely to provide useful information regarding the risks of material misstatement in the financial statements resulting from

---

[14a] In the UK and Ireland those charged with governance are responsible for the preparation of the financial statements.

management fraud. Making inquiries of others within the entity may provide individuals with an opportunity to convey information to the auditor that may not otherwise be communicated.

A16. Examples of others within the entity to whom the auditor may direct inquiries about the existence or suspicion of fraud include:

- Operating personnel not directly involved in the financial reporting process.

- Employees with different levels of authority.

- Employees involved in initiating, processing or recording complex or unusual transactions and those who supervise or monitor such employees.

- In-house legal counsel.

- Chief ethics officer or equivalent person.

- The person or persons charged with dealing with allegations of fraud.

A17. Management is often in the best position to perpetrate fraud. Accordingly, when evaluating management's responses to inquiries with an attitude of professional skepticism, the auditor may judge it necessary to corroborate responses to inquiries with other information.

Inquiries of the Internal Audit Function (Ref: Para. 19)

A18. ISA (UK and Ireland) 315 (Revised June 2013) and ISA (UK and Ireland) 610 (Revised June 2013) establish requirements and provide guidance relevant to audits of those entities that have an internal audit function.[15] In carrying out the requirements of those ISAs (UK and Ireland) in the context of fraud, the auditor may inquire about specific activities of the function including, for example:

- The procedures performed, if any, by the internal audit function during the year to detect fraud.

- Whether management has satisfactorily responded to any findings resulting from those procedures.

Obtaining an Understanding of Oversight Exercised by Those Charged with Governance (Ref: Para. 20)

A19. Those charged with governance of an entity oversee the entity's systems for monitoring risk, financial control and compliance with the law. In many countries, corporate governance practices are well developed and those charged with

---

[15] ISA (UK and Ireland) 315 (Revised June 2013), paragraphs 6(a) and 23 and ISA 610 (Revised June 2013), "Using the Work of Internal Auditors."

governance play an active role in oversight of the entity's assessment of the risks of fraud and of the relevant internal control. Since the responsibilities of those charged with governance and management may vary by entity and by country, it is important that the auditor understands their respective responsibilities to enable the auditor to obtain an understanding of the oversight exercised by the appropriate individuals.[16]

A20. An understanding of the oversight exercised by those charged with governance may provide insights regarding the susceptibility of the entity to management fraud, the adequacy of internal control over risks of fraud, and the competency and integrity of management. The auditor may obtain this understanding in a number of ways, such as by attending meetings where such discussions take place, reading the minutes from such meetings or making inquiries of those charged with governance.

Considerations Specific to Smaller Entities

A21. In some cases, all of those charged with governance are involved in managing the entity. This may be the case in a small entity where a single owner manages the entity and no one else has a governance role. In these cases, there is ordinarily no action on the part of the auditor because there is no oversight separate from management.

Consideration of Other Information (Ref: Para. 23)

A22. In addition to information obtained from applying analytical procedures, other information obtained about the entity and its environment may be helpful in identifying the risks of material misstatement due to fraud. The discussion among team members may provide information that is helpful in identifying such risks. In addition, information obtained from the auditor's client acceptance and retention processes, and experience gained on other engagements performed for the entity, for example engagements to review interim financial information, may be relevant in the identification of the risks of material misstatement due to fraud.

Evaluation of Fraud Risk Factors (Ref: Para. 24)

A23. The fact that fraud is usually concealed can make it very difficult to detect. Nevertheless, the auditor may identify events or conditions that indicate an incentive or pressure to commit fraud or provide an opportunity to commit fraud (fraud risk factors). For example:

- The need to meet expectations of third parties to obtain additional equity financing may create pressure to commit fraud;

- The granting of significant bonuses if unrealistic profit targets are met may create an incentive to commit fraud; and

---

[16] ISA (UK and Ireland) 260, paragraphs A1-A8, discuss with whom the auditor communicates when the entity's governance structure is not well defined.

- A control environment that is not effective may create an opportunity to commit fraud.

A24. Fraud risk factors cannot easily be ranked in order of importance. The significance of fraud risk factors varies widely. Some of these factors will be present in entities where the specific conditions do not present risks of material misstatement. Accordingly, the determination of whether a fraud risk factor is present and whether it is to be considered in assessing the risks of material misstatement of the financial statements due to fraud requires the exercise of professional judgment.

A25. Examples of fraud risk factors related to fraudulent financial reporting and misappropriation of assets are presented in Appendix 1. These illustrative risk factors are classified based on the three conditions that are generally present when fraud exists:

- An incentive or pressure to commit fraud;

- A perceived opportunity to commit fraud; and

- An ability to rationalize the fraudulent action.

Risk factors reflective of an attitude that permits rationalization of the fraudulent action may not be susceptible to observation by the auditor. Nevertheless, the auditor may become aware of the existence of such information. Although the fraud risk factors described in Appendix 1 cover a broad range of situations that may be faced by auditors, they are only examples and other risk factors may exist.

A26. The size, complexity, and ownership characteristics of the entity have a significant influence on the consideration of relevant fraud risk factors. For example, in the case of a large entity, there may be factors that generally constrain improper conduct by management, such as:

- Effective oversight by those charged with governance.

- An effective internal audit function.

- The existence and enforcement of a written code of conduct.

Furthermore, fraud risk factors considered at a business segment operating level may provide different insights when compared with those obtained when considered at an entity-wide level.

Considerations Specific to Smaller Entities

A27. In the case of a small entity, some or all of these considerations may be inapplicable or less relevant. For example, a smaller entity may not have a written code of conduct but, instead, may have developed a culture that emphasizes the importance of integrity and ethical behavior through oral communication and by management example. Domination of management by a single individual in a small entity does not generally, in and of itself, indicate a failure by management to display and communicate an appropriate attitude regarding internal control and the financial reporting process. In some entities, the need for management authorization can compensate for otherwise deficient controls and reduce the risk of employee fraud. However, domination of management by a single individual can be a potential deficiency in internal control since there is an opportunity for management override of controls.

Identification and Assessment of the Risks of Material Misstatement Due to Fraud

Risks of Fraud in Revenue Recognition (Ref: Para. 26)

A28. Material misstatement due to fraudulent financial reporting relating to revenue recognition often results from an overstatement of revenues through, for example, premature revenue recognition or recording fictitious revenues. It may result also from an understatement of revenues through, for example, improperly shifting revenues to a later period.

A29. The risks of fraud in revenue recognition may be greater in some entities than others. For example, there may be pressures or incentives on management to commit fraudulent financial reporting through inappropriate revenue recognition in the case of listed entities when, for example, performance is measured in terms of year-over-year revenue growth or profit. Similarly, for example, there may be greater risks of fraud in revenue recognition in the case of entities that generate a substantial portion of revenues through cash sales.

A30. The presumption that there are risks of fraud in revenue recognition may be rebutted. For example, the auditor may conclude that there is no risk of material misstatement due to fraud relating to revenue recognition in the case where a there is a single type of simple revenue transaction, for example, leasehold revenue from a single unit rental property.

Identifying and Assessing the Risks of Material Misstatement Due to Fraud and Understanding the Entity's Related Controls (Ref: Para. 27)

A31. Management may make judgments on the nature and extent of the controls it chooses to implement, and the nature and extent of the risks it chooses to assume.[17] In determining which controls to implement to prevent and detect fraud, management considers the risks that the financial statements may be materially misstated as a result of fraud. As part of this consideration, management may conclude that it is not cost effective to implement and maintain a particular control in relation to the reduction in the risks of material misstatement due to fraud to be achieved.

A32. It is therefore important for the auditor to obtain an understanding of the controls that management has designed, implemented and maintained to prevent and detect

---

[17] ISA (UK and Ireland) 315, paragraph A48.

fraud. In doing so, the auditor may learn, for example, that management has consciously chosen to accept the risks associated with a lack of segregation of duties. Information from obtaining this understanding may also be useful in identifying fraud risks factors that may affect the auditor's assessment of the risks that the financial statements may contain material misstatement due to fraud.

Responses to the Assessed Risks of Material Misstatement Due to Fraud

Overall Responses (Ref: Para. 28)

A33. Determining overall responses to address the assessed risks of material misstatement due to fraud generally includes the consideration of how the overall conduct of the audit can reflect increased professional skepticism, for example, through:

- Increased sensitivity in the selection of the nature and extent of documentation to be examined in support of material transactions.

- Increased recognition of the need to corroborate management explanations or representations concerning material matters.

It also involves more general considerations apart from the specific procedures otherwise planned; these considerations include the matters listed in paragraph 29, which are discussed below.

Assignment and Supervision of Personnel (Ref: Para. 29(a))

A34. The auditor may respond to identified risks of material misstatement due to fraud by, for example, assigning additional individuals with specialized skill and knowledge, such as forensic and IT experts, or by assigning more experienced individuals to the engagement.

A35. The extent of supervision reflects the auditor's assessment of risks of material misstatement due to fraud and the competencies of the engagement team members performing the work.

Unpredictability in the Selection of Audit Procedures (Ref: Para. 29(c))

A36. Incorporating an element of unpredictability in the selection of the nature, timing and extent of audit procedures to be performed is important as individuals within the entity who are familiar with the audit procedures normally performed on engagements may be more able to conceal fraudulent financial reporting. This can be achieved by, for example:

- Performing substantive procedures on selected account balances and assertions not otherwise tested due to their materiality or risk.

- Adjusting the timing of audit procedures from that otherwise expected.

- Using different sampling methods.

- Performing audit procedures at different locations or at locations on an unannounced basis.

Audit Procedures Responsive to Assessed Risks of Material Misstatement Due to Fraud at the Assertion Level (Ref: Para. 30)

A37. The auditor's responses to address the assessed risks of material misstatement due to fraud at the assertion level may include changing the nature, timing and extent of audit procedures in the following ways:

- The nature of audit procedures to be performed may need to be changed to obtain audit evidence that is more reliable and relevant or to obtain additional corroborative information. This may affect both the type of audit procedures to be performed and their combination. For example:

  ○ Physical observation or inspection of certain assets may become more important or the auditor may choose to use computer-assisted audit techniques to gather more evidence about data contained in significant accounts or electronic transaction files.

  ○ The auditor may design procedures to obtain additional corroborative information. For example, if the auditor identifies that management is under pressure to meet earnings expectations, there may be a related risk that management is inflating sales by entering into sales agreements that include terms that preclude revenue recognition or by invoicing sales before delivery. In these circumstances, the auditor may, for example, design external confirmations not only to confirm outstanding amounts, but also to confirm the details of the sales agreements, including date, any rights of return and delivery terms. In addition, the auditor might find it effective to supplement such external confirmations with inquiries of non-financial personnel in the entity regarding any changes in sales agreements and delivery terms.

- The timing of substantive procedures may need to be modified. The auditor may conclude that performing substantive testing at or near the period end better addresses an assessed risk of material misstatement due to fraud. The auditor may conclude that, given the assessed risks of intentional misstatement or manipulation, audit procedures to extend audit conclusions from an interim date to the period end would not be effective. In contrast, because an intentional misstatement – for example, a misstatement involving improper revenue recognition – may have been initiated in an interim period, the auditor may elect to apply substantive procedures to transactions occurring earlier in or throughout the reporting period.

- The extent of the procedures applied reflects the assessment of the risks of material misstatement due to fraud. For example, increasing sample sizes or performing analytical procedures at a more detailed level may be appropriate. Also, computer-assisted audit techniques may enable more extensive testing of electronic transactions and account files. Such techniques can be used to select sample transactions from key electronic files, to sort transactions with specific characteristics, or to test an entire population instead of a sample.

A38. If the auditor identifies a risk of material misstatement due to fraud that affects inventory quantities, examining the entity's inventory records may help to identify locations or items that require specific attention during or after the physical inventory count. Such a review may lead to a decision to observe inventory counts at certain locations on an unannounced basis or to conduct inventory counts at all locations on the same date.

A39. The auditor may identify a risk of material misstatement due to fraud affecting a number of accounts and assertions. These may include asset valuation, estimates relating to specific transactions (such as acquisitions, restructurings, or disposals of a segment of the business), and other significant accrued liabilities (such as pension and other post-employment benefit obligations, or environmental remediation liabilities). The risk may also relate to significant changes in assumptions relating to recurring estimates. Information gathered through obtaining an understanding of the entity and its environment may assist the auditor in evaluating the reasonableness of such management estimates and underlying judgments and assumptions. A retrospective review of similar management judgments and assumptions applied in prior periods may also provide insight about the reasonableness of judgments and assumptions supporting management estimates.

A40. Examples of possible audit procedures to address the assessed risks of material misstatement due to fraud, including those that illustrate the incorporation of an element of unpredictability, are presented in Appendix 2. The appendix includes examples of responses to the auditor's assessment of the risks of material misstatement resulting from both fraudulent financial reporting, including fraudulent financial reporting resulting from revenue recognition, and misappropriation of assets.

Audit Procedures Responsive to Risks Related to Management Override of Controls

Journal Entries and Other Adjustments (Ref: Para. 32(a))

A41. Material misstatement of financial statements due to fraud often involve the manipulation of the financial reporting process by recording inappropriate or unauthorized journal entries. This may occur throughout the year or at period end, or by management making adjustments to amounts reported in the financial statements that are not reflected in journal entries, such as through consolidating adjustments and reclassifications.

A42. Further, the auditor's consideration of the risks of material misstatement associated with inappropriate override of controls over journal entries is important since automated processes and controls may reduce the risk of inadvertent error but do not overcome the risk that individuals may inappropriately override such automated processes, for example, by changing the amounts being automatically passed to the general ledger or to the financial reporting system. Furthermore, where IT is used to transfer information automatically, there may be little or no visible evidence of such intervention in the information systems.

A43. When identifying and selecting journal entries and other adjustments for testing and determining the appropriate method of examining the underlying support for the items selected, the following matters are of relevance:

- *The assessment of the risks of material misstatement due to fraud* – the presence of fraud risk factors and other information obtained during the auditor's assessment of the risks of material misstatement due to fraud may assist the auditor to identify specific classes of journal entries and other adjustments for testing.

- *Controls that have been implemented over journal entries and other adjustments* – effective controls over the preparation and posting of journal entries and other adjustments may reduce the extent of substantive testing necessary, provided that the auditor has tested the operating effectiveness of the controls.

- *The entity's financial reporting process and the nature of evidence that can be obtained* – for many entities routine processing of transactions involves a combination of manual and automated steps and procedures. Similarly, the processing of journal entries and other adjustments may involve both manual and automated procedures and controls. Where information technology is used in the financial reporting process, journal entries and other adjustments may exist only in electronic form.

- *The characteristics of fraudulent journal entries or other adjustments* – inappropriate journal entries or other adjustments often have unique identifying characteristics. Such characteristics may include entries (a) made to unrelated, unusual, or seldom-used accounts, (b) made by individuals who typically do not make journal entries, (c) recorded at the end of the period or as post-closing entries that have little or no explanation or description, (d) made either before or during the preparation of the financial statements that do not have account numbers, or (e) containing round numbers or consistent ending numbers.

- *The nature and complexity of the accounts* – inappropriate journal entries or adjustments may be applied to accounts that (a) contain transactions that are complex or unusual in nature, (b) contain significant estimates and period-end adjustments, (c) have been prone to misstatements in the past, (d) have not been reconciled on a timely basis or contain unreconciled differences, (e) contain inter-company transactions, or (f) are otherwise associated with an identified risk of material misstatement due to fraud. In audits of entities that have several locations or components, consideration is given to the need to select journal entries from multiple locations.

- *Journal entries or other adjustments processed outside the normal course of business* – non standard journal entries may not be subject to the same level of internal control as those journal entries used on a recurring basis to record transactions such as monthly sales, purchases and cash disbursements.

A44. The auditor uses professional judgment in determining the nature, timing and extent of testing of journal entries and other adjustments. However, because fraudulent journal entries and other adjustments are often made at the end of a reporting period, paragraph 32(a)(ii) requires the auditor to select the journal entries and other adjustments made at that time. Further, because material misstatements in financial statements due to fraud can occur throughout the period and may involve extensive efforts to conceal how the fraud is accomplished, paragraph 32(a)(iii) requires the auditor to consider whether there is also a need to test journal entries and other adjustments throughout the period.

Accounting Estimates (Ref: Para. 32(b))

A45. The preparation of the financial statements requires management[14a] to make a number of judgments or assumptions that affect significant accounting estimates and to monitor the reasonableness of such estimates on an ongoing basis. Fraudulent financial reporting is often accomplished through intentional misstatement of accounting estimates. This may be achieved by, for example, understating or overstating all provisions or reserves in the same fashion so as to be designed either to smooth earnings over two or more accounting periods, or to achieve a designated earnings level in order to deceive financial statement users by influencing their perceptions as to the entity's performance and profitability.

A46. The purpose of performing a retrospective review of management judgments and assumptions related to significant accounting estimates reflected in the financial statements of the prior year is to determine whether there is an indication of a possible bias on the part of management. It is not intended to call into question the auditor's professional judgments made in the prior year that were based on information available at the time.

A47. A retrospective review is also required by ISA (UK and Ireland) 540.[18] That review is conducted as a risk assessment procedure to obtain information regarding the effectiveness of management's prior period estimation process, audit evidence about the outcome, or where applicable, the subsequent re-estimation of prior period accounting estimates that is pertinent to making current period accounting estimates, and audit evidence of matters, such as estimation uncertainty, that may be required to be disclosed in the financial statements. As a practical matter, the auditor's review of management judgments and assumptions for biases that could represent a risk of material misstatement due to fraud in accordance with this ISA (UK and Ireland) may be carried out in conjunction with the review required by ISA (UK and Ireland) 540.

---

[18] ISA (UK and Ireland) 540, "Auditing Accounting Estimates, Including Fair Value Accounting Estimates, and Related Disclosures," paragraph 9.

Business Rationale for Significant Transactions (Ref: Para. 32(c))

A48. Indicators that may suggest that significant transactions that are outside the normal course of business for the entity, or that otherwise appear to be unusual, may have been entered into to engage in fraudulent financial reporting or to conceal misappropriation of assets include:

- The form of such transactions appears overly complex (for example, the transaction involves multiple entities within a consolidated group or multiple unrelated third parties).

- Management has not discussed the nature of and accounting for such transactions with those charged with governance of the entity, and there is inadequate documentation.

- Management is placing more emphasis on the need for a particular accounting treatment than on the underlying economics of the transaction.

- Transactions that involve non-consolidated related parties, including special purpose entities, have not been properly reviewed or approved by those charged with governance of the entity.

- The transactions involve previously unidentified related parties or parties that do not have the substance or the financial strength to support the transaction without assistance from the entity under audit.

Evaluation of Audit Evidence (Ref: Para. 34-37)

A49. ISA (UK and Ireland) 330 requires the auditor, based on the audit procedures performed and the audit evidence obtained, to evaluate whether the assessments of the risks of material misstatement at the assertion level remain appropriate.[19] This evaluation is primarily a qualitative matter based on the auditor's judgment. Such an evaluation may provide further insight about the risks of material misstatement due to fraud and whether there is a need to perform additional or different audit procedures. Appendix 3 contains examples of circumstances that may indicate the possibility of fraud.

Analytical Procedures Performed Near the End of the Audit in Forming an Overall Conclusion (Ref: Para. 34)

A50. Determining which particular trends and relationships may indicate a risk of material misstatement due to fraud requires professional judgment. Unusual relationships involving year-end revenue and income are particularly relevant. These might include, for example: uncharacteristically large amounts of income being reported in the last few weeks of the reporting period or unusual transactions; or income that is inconsistent with trends in cash flow from operations.

---

[19] ISA (UK and Ireland) 330, paragraph 25.

Consideration of Identified Misstatements (Ref: Para. 35-37)

A51. Since fraud involves incentive or pressure to commit fraud, a perceived opportunity to do so or some rationalization of the act, an instance of fraud is unlikely to be an isolated occurrence. Accordingly, misstatements, such as numerous misstatements at a specific location even though the cumulative effect is not material, may be indicative of a risk of material misstatement due to fraud.

A52. The implications of identified fraud depend on the circumstances. For example, an otherwise insignificant fraud may be significant if it involves senior management. In such circumstances, the reliability of evidence previously obtained may be called into question, since there may be doubts about the completeness and truthfulness of representations made and about the genuineness of accounting records and documentation. There may also be a possibility of collusion involving employees, management or third parties.

A53. ISA (UK and Ireland) 450[20] and ISA (UK and Ireland) 700[21] establish requirements and provide guidance on the evaluation and disposition of misstatements and the effect on the auditor's opinion in the auditor's report.

Auditor Unable to Continue the Engagement (Ref: Para. 38)

A54. Examples of exceptional circumstances that may arise and that may bring into question the auditor's ability to continue performing the audit include:

- The entity does not take the appropriate action regarding fraud that the auditor considers necessary in the circumstances, even where the fraud is not material to the financial statements;

- The auditor's consideration of the risks of material misstatement due to fraud and the results of audit tests indicate a significant risk of material and pervasive fraud; or

- The auditor has significant concern about the competence or integrity of management or those charged with governance.

A55. Because of the variety of the circumstances that may arise, it is not possible to describe definitively when withdrawal from an engagement is appropriate. Factors that affect the auditor's conclusion include the implications of the involvement of a member of management or of those charged with governance (which may affect the reliability of management representations) and the effects on the auditor of a continuing association with the entity.

---

[20] ISA (UK and Ireland) 450, "Evaluation of Misstatements Identified during the Audit."
[21] ISA 700, "Forming an Opinion and Reporting on Financial Statements."
   The APB has not promulgated ISA 700 as issued by the IAASB for application in the UK and Ireland. In the UK and Ireland the applicable auditing standard is ISA (UK and Ireland) 700, "The Auditor's Report on Financial Statements." Paragraph 8(b) of ISA (UK and Ireland) 700 requires evaluation of whether uncorrected misstatements are material, individually or in aggregate.

A56.   The auditor has professional and legal responsibilities in such circumstances and these responsibilities may vary by country. In some countries, for example, the auditor may be entitled to, or required to, make a statement or report to the person or persons who made the audit appointment or, in some cases, to regulatory authorities. Given the exceptional nature of the circumstances and the need to consider the legal requirements, the auditor may consider it appropriate to seek legal advice when deciding whether to withdraw from an engagement and in determining an appropriate course of action, including the possibility of reporting to shareholders, regulators or others.[22]

Considerations Specific to Public Sector Entities

A57.   In many cases in the public sector, the option of withdrawing from the engagement may not be available to the auditor due to the nature of the mandate or public interest considerations.

Written Representations (Ref: Para. 39)

A58.   ISA (UK and Ireland) 580[23] establishes requirements and provides guidance on obtaining appropriate representations from management and, where appropriate, those charged with governance in the audit. In addition to acknowledging that they have fulfilled their responsibility for the preparation of the financial statements, it is important that, irrespective of the size of the entity, management and, where appropriate, those charged with governance acknowledge their responsibility for internal control designed, implemented and maintained to prevent and detect fraud.

A59.   Because of the nature of fraud and the difficulties encountered by auditors in detecting material misstatements in the financial statements resulting from fraud, it is important that the auditor obtain a written representation from management and, where appropriate, those charged with governance confirming that they have disclosed to the auditor:

(a)   The results of management's assessment of the risk that the financial statements may be materially misstated as a result of fraud; and

(b)   Their knowledge of actual, suspected or alleged fraud affecting the entity.

---

[22]   The IESBA *Code of Ethics for Professional Accountants* provides guidance on communications with an auditor replacing the existing auditor

In the UK and Ireland the relevant ethical guidance on proposed communications with a successor auditor is provided by the ethical pronouncements relating to the work of auditors issued by the auditor's relevant professional body.

[23]   ISA (UK and Ireland) 580, "Written Representations."

Communications to Management and with Those Charged with Governance

Communication to Management (Ref: Para. 40)

A60. When the auditor has obtained evidence that fraud exists or may exist, it is important that the matter be brought to the attention of the appropriate level of management as soon as practicable. This is so even if the matter might be considered inconsequential (for example, a minor defalcation by an employee at a low level in the entity's organization). The determination of which level of management is the appropriate one is a matter of professional judgment and is affected by such factors as the likelihood of collusion and the nature and magnitude of the suspected fraud. Ordinarily, the appropriate level of management is at least one level above the persons who appear to be involved with the suspected fraud.

Communication with Those Charged with Governance (Ref: Para. 41)

A61. The auditor's communication with those charged with governance may be made orally or in writing. ISA (UK and Ireland) 260 identifies factors the auditor considers in determining whether to communicate orally or in writing.[24] Due to the nature and sensitivity of fraud involving senior management, or fraud that results in a material misstatement in the financial statements, the auditor reports such matters on a timely basis and may consider it necessary to also report such matters in writing.

A62. In some cases, the auditor may consider it appropriate to communicate with those charged with governance when the auditor becomes aware of fraud involving employees other than management that does not result in a material misstatement. Similarly, those charged with governance may wish to be informed of such circumstances. The communication process is assisted if the auditor and those charged with governance agree at an early stage in the audit about the nature and extent of the auditor's communications in this regard.

A63. In the exceptional circumstances where the auditor has doubts about the integrity or honesty of management or those charged with governance, the auditor may consider it appropriate to obtain legal advice to assist in determining the appropriate course of action.

Other Matters Related to Fraud (Ref: Para. 42)

A64. Other matters related to fraud to be discussed with those charged with governance of the entity may include, for example:

- Concerns about the nature, extent and frequency of management's assessments of the controls in place to prevent and detect fraud and of the risk that the financial statements may be misstated.

---

[24] ISA (UK and Ireland) 260, paragraph A38.

- A failure by management to appropriately address identified significant deficiencies in internal control, or to appropriately respond to an identified fraud.

- The auditor's evaluation of the entity's control environment, including questions regarding the competence and integrity of management.

- Actions by management that may be indicative of fraudulent financial reporting, such as management's selection and application of accounting policies that may be indicative of management's effort to manage earnings in order to deceive financial statement users by influencing their perceptions as to the entity's performance and profitability.

- Concerns about the adequacy and completeness of the authorization of transactions that appear to be outside the normal course of business.

Communications to Regulatory and Enforcement Authorities (Ref: Para. 43)

A65. The auditor's professional duty to maintain the confidentiality of client information may preclude reporting fraud to a party outside the client entity. However, the auditor's legal responsibilities vary by country[24a] and, in certain circumstances, the duty of confidentiality may be overridden by statute, the law or courts of law. In some countries, the auditor of a financial institution has a statutory duty to report the occurrence of fraud to supervisory authorities. Also, in some countries the auditor has a duty to report misstatements to authorities in those cases where management and those charged with governance fail to take corrective action.

A66. The auditor may consider it appropriate to obtain legal advice to determine the appropriate course of action in the circumstances, the purpose of which is to ascertain the steps necessary in considering the public interest aspects of identified fraud.

Considerations Specific to Public Sector Entities

A67. In the public sector, requirements for reporting fraud, whether or not discovered through the audit process, may be subject to specific provisions of the audit mandate or related law, regulation or other authority.

[24a] In the UK and Ireland, anti-money laundering legislation imposes a duty on auditors to report suspected money laundering activity. Suspicions relating to fraud are likely to be required to be reported under this legislation (see paragraph A11-1 in ISA (UK and Ireland) 250 Section A, "Consideration of laws and regulations").

Appendix 1

(Ref: Para. A25)

Examples of Fraud Risk Factors

The fraud risk factors identified in this Appendix are examples of such factors that may be faced by auditors in a broad range of situations. Separately presented are examples relating to the two types of fraud relevant to the auditor's consideration – that is, fraudulent financial reporting and misappropriation of assets. For each of these types of fraud, the risk factors are further classified based on the three conditions generally present when material misstatements due to fraud occur: (a) incentives/pressures, (b) opportunities, and (c) attitudes/rationalizations. Although the risk factors cover a broad range of situations, they are only examples and, accordingly, the auditor may identify additional or different risk factors. Not all of these examples are relevant in all circumstances, and some may be of greater or lesser significance in entities of different size or with different ownership characteristics or circumstances. Also, the order of the examples of risk factors provided is not intended to reflect their relative importance or frequency of occurrence.

Risk Factors Relating to Misstatements Arising from Fraudulent Financial Reporting

The following are examples of risk factors relating to misstatements arising from fraudulent financial reporting.

Incentives/Pressures

Financial stability or profitability is threatened by economic, industry, or entity operating conditions, such as (or as indicated by):

- High degree of competition or market saturation, accompanied by declining margins.

- High vulnerability to rapid changes, such as changes in technology, product obsolescence, or interest rates.

- Significant declines in customer demand and increasing business failures in either the industry or overall economy.

- Operating losses making the threat of bankruptcy, foreclosure, or hostile takeover imminent.

- Recurring negative cash flows from operations or an inability to generate cash flows from operations while reporting earnings and earnings growth.

- Rapid growth or unusual profitability especially compared to that of other companies in the same industry.

- New accounting, statutory, or regulatory requirements.

Excessive pressure exists for management to meet the requirements or expectations of third parties due to the following:

- Profitability or trend level expectations of investment analysts, institutional investors, significant creditors, or other external parties (particularly expectations that are unduly aggressive or unrealistic), including expectations created by management in, for example, overly optimistic press releases or annual report messages.

- Need to obtain additional debt or equity financing to stay competitive – including financing of major research and development or capital expenditures.

- Marginal ability to meet exchange listing requirements or debt repayment or other debt covenant requirements.

- Perceived or real adverse effects of reporting poor financial results on significant pending transactions, such as business combinations or contract awards.

Information available indicates that the personal financial situation of management or those charged with governance is threatened by the entity's financial performance arising from the following:

- Significant financial interests in the entity.

- Significant portions of their compensation (for example, bonuses, stock options, and earn-out arrangements) being contingent upon achieving aggressive targets for stock price, operating results, financial position, or cash flow.[25]

- Personal guarantees of debts of the entity.

There is excessive pressure on management or operating personnel to meet financial targets established by those charged with governance, including sales or profitability incentive goals.

Opportunities

The nature of the industry or the entity's operations provides opportunities to engage in fraudulent financial reporting that can arise from the following:

- Significant related-party transactions not in the ordinary course of business or with related entities not audited or audited by another firm.

- A strong financial presence or ability to dominate a certain industry sector that allows the entity to dictate terms or conditions to suppliers or customers that may result in inappropriate or non-arm's-length transactions.

---

[25] Management incentive plans may be contingent upon achieving targets relating only to certain accounts or selected activities of the entity, even though the related accounts or activities may not be material to the entity as a whole.

- Assets, liabilities, revenues, or expenses based on significant estimates that involve subjective judgments or uncertainties that are difficult to corroborate.

- Significant, unusual, or highly complex transactions, especially those close to period end that pose difficult "substance over form" questions.

- Significant operations located or conducted across international borders in jurisdictions where differing business environments and cultures exist.

- Use of business intermediaries for which there appears to be no clear business justification.

- Significant bank accounts or subsidiary or branch operations in tax-haven jurisdictions for which there appears to be no clear business justification.

The monitoring of management is not effective as a result of the following:

- Domination of management by a single person or small group (in a non owner-managed business) without compensating controls.

- Oversight by those charged with governance over the financial reporting process and internal control is not effective.

There is a complex or unstable organizational structure, as evidenced by the following:

- Difficulty in determining the organization or individuals that have controlling interest in the entity.

- Overly complex organizational structure involving unusual legal entities or managerial lines of authority.

- High turnover of senior management, legal counsel, or those charged with governance.

Internal control components are deficient as a result of the following:

- Inadequate monitoring of controls, including automated controls and controls over interim financial reporting (where external reporting is required).

- High turnover rates or employment of staff in accounting, information technology, or the internal audit function that are not effective.

- Accounting and information systems that are not effective, including situations involving significant deficiencies in internal control.

Attitudes/Rationalizations

- Communication, implementation, support, or enforcement of the entity's values or ethical standards by management, or the communication of inappropriate values or ethical standards, that are not effective.

- Nonfinancial management's excessive participation in or preoccupation with the selection of accounting policies or the determination of significant estimates.

- Known history of violations of securities laws or other laws and regulations, or claims against the entity, its senior management, or those charged with governance alleging fraud or violations of laws and regulations.

- Excessive interest by management in maintaining or increasing the entity's stock price or earnings trend.

- The practice by management of committing to analysts, creditors, and other third parties to achieve aggressive or unrealistic forecasts.

- Management failing to remedy known significant deficiencies in internal control on a timely basis.

- An interest by management in employing inappropriate means to minimize reported earnings for tax-motivated reasons.

- Low morale among senior management.

- The owner-manager makes no distinction between personal and business transactions.

- Dispute between shareholders in a closely held entity.

- Recurring attempts by management to justify marginal or inappropriate accounting on the basis of materiality.

- The relationship between management and the current or predecessor auditor is strained, as exhibited by the following:

  - Frequent disputes with the current or predecessor auditor on accounting, auditing, or reporting matters.

  - Unreasonable demands on the auditor, such as unrealistic time constraints regarding the completion of the audit or the issuance of the auditor's report.

  - Restrictions on the auditor that inappropriately limit access to people or information or the ability to communicate effectively with those charged with governance.

○ Domineering management behavior in dealing with the auditor, especially involving attempts to influence the scope of the auditor's work or the selection or continuance of personnel assigned to or consulted on the audit engagement.

Risk Factors Arising from Misstatements Arising from Misappropriation of Assets

Risk factors that relate to misstatements arising from misappropriation of assets are also classified according to the three conditions generally present when fraud exists: incentives/pressures, opportunities, and attitudes/rationalization. Some of the risk factors related to misstatements arising from fraudulent financial reporting also may be present when misstatements arising from misappropriation of assets occur. For example, ineffective monitoring of management and other deficiencies in internal control may be present when misstatements due to either fraudulent financial reporting or misappropriation of assets exist. The following are examples of risk factors related to misstatements arising from misappropriation of assets.

Incentives/Pressures

Personal financial obligations may create pressure on management or employees with access to cash or other assets susceptible to theft to misappropriate those assets.

Adverse relationships between the entity and employees with access to cash or other assets susceptible to theft may motivate those employees to misappropriate those assets. For example, adverse relationships may be created by the following:

• Known or anticipated future employee layoffs.

• Recent or anticipated changes to employee compensation or benefit plans.

• Promotions, compensation, or other rewards inconsistent with expectations.

Opportunities

Certain characteristics or circumstances may increase the susceptibility of assets to misappropriation. For example, opportunities to misappropriate assets increase when there are the following:

• Large amounts of cash on hand or processed.

• Inventory items that are small in size, of high value, or in high demand.

• Easily convertible assets, such as bearer bonds, diamonds, or computer chips.

• Fixed assets which are small in size, marketable, or lacking observable identification of ownership.

Inadequate internal control over assets may increase the susceptibility of misappropriation of those assets. For example, misappropriation of assets may occur because there is the following:

- Inadequate segregation of duties or independent checks.

- Inadequate oversight of senior management expenditures, such as travel and other re-imbursements.

- Inadequate management oversight of employees responsible for assets, for example, inadequate supervision or monitoring of remote locations.

- Inadequate job applicant screening of employees with access to assets.

- Inadequate record keeping with respect to assets.

- Inadequate system of authorization and approval of transactions (for example, in purchasing).

- Inadequate physical safeguards over cash, investments, inventory, or fixed assets.

- Lack of complete and timely reconciliations of assets.

- Lack of timely and appropriate documentation of transactions, for example, credits for merchandise returns.

- Lack of mandatory vacations for employees performing key control functions.

- Inadequate management understanding of information technology, which enables information technology employees to perpetrate a misappropriation.

- Inadequate access controls over automated records, including controls over and review of computer systems event logs.

Attitudes/Rationalizations

- Disregard for the need for monitoring or reducing risks related to misappropriations of assets.

- Disregard for internal control over misappropriation of assets by overriding existing controls or by failing to take appropriate remedial action on known deficiencies in internal control.

- Behavior indicating displeasure or dissatisfaction with the entity or its treatment of the employee.

- Changes in behavior or lifestyle that may indicate assets have been misappropriated.

- Tolerance of petty theft.

Appendix 2

(Ref: Para. A40)

Examples of Possible Audit Procedures to Address the Assessed Risks of Material Misstatement Due to Fraud

The following are examples of possible audit procedures to address the assessed risks of material misstatement due to fraud resulting from both fraudulent financial reporting and misappropriation of assets. Although these procedures cover a broad range of situations, they are only examples and, accordingly they may not be the most appropriate nor necessary in each circumstance. Also the order of the procedures provided is not intended to reflect their relative importance.

Consideration at the Assertion Level

Specific responses to the auditor's assessment of the risks of material misstatement due to fraud will vary depending upon the types or combinations of fraud risk factors or conditions identified, and the classes of transactions, account balances, disclosures and assertions they may affect.

The following are specific examples of responses:

- Visiting locations or performing certain tests on a surprise or unannounced basis. For example, observing inventory at locations where auditor attendance has not been previously announced or counting cash at a particular date on a surprise basis.

- Requesting that inventories be counted at the end of the reporting period or on a date closer to period end to minimize the risk of manipulation of balances in the period between the date of completion of the count and the end of the reporting period.

- Altering the audit approach in the current year. For example, contacting major customers and suppliers orally in addition to sending written confirmation, sending confirmation requests to a specific party within an organization, or seeking more or different information.

- Performing a detailed review of the entity's quarter-end or year-end adjusting entries and investigating any that appear unusual as to nature or amount.

- For significant and unusual transactions, particularly those occurring at or near year-end, investigating the possibility of related parties and the sources of financial resources supporting the transactions.

- Performing substantive analytical procedures using disaggregated data. For example, comparing sales and cost of sales by location, line of business or month to expectations developed by the auditor.

- Conducting interviews of personnel involved in areas where a risk of material misstatement due to fraud has been identified, to obtain their insights about the risk and whether, or how, controls address the risk.

- When other independent auditors are auditing the financial statements of one or more subsidiaries, divisions or branches, discussing with them the extent of work necessary to be performed to address the assessed risk of material misstatement due to fraud resulting from transactions and activities among these components.

- If the work of an expert becomes particularly significant with respect to a financial statement item for which the assessed risk of misstatement due to fraud is high, performing additional procedures relating to some or all of the expert's assumptions, methods or findings to determine that the findings are not unreasonable, or engaging another expert for that purpose.

- Performing audit procedures to analyze selected opening balance sheet accounts of previously audited financial statements to assess how certain issues involving accounting estimates and judgments, for example, an allowance for sales returns, were resolved with the benefit of hindsight.

- Performing procedures on account or other reconciliations prepared by the entity, including considering reconciliations performed at interim periods.

- Performing computer-assisted techniques, such as data mining to test for anomalies in a population.

- Testing the integrity of computer-produced records and transactions.

- Seeking additional audit evidence from sources outside of the entity being audited.

Specific Responses—Misstatement Resulting from Fraudulent Financial Reporting

Examples of responses to the auditor's assessment of the risks of material misstatement due to fraudulent financial reporting are as follows:

Revenue Recognition

- Performing substantive analytical procedures relating to revenue using disaggregated data, for example, comparing revenue reported by month and by product line or business segment during the current reporting period with comparable prior periods. Computer-assisted audit techniques may be useful in identifying unusual or unexpected revenue relationships or transactions.

- Confirming with customers certain relevant contract terms and the absence of side agreements, because the appropriate accounting often is influenced by such terms or agreements and basis for rebates or the period to which they relate are often poorly documented. For example, acceptance criteria, delivery and payment terms, the absence of future or continuing vendor obligations, the right to return the product, guaranteed resale amounts, and cancellation or refund provisions often are relevant in such circumstances.

- Inquiring of the entity's sales and marketing personnel or in-house legal counsel regarding sales or shipments near the end of the period and their knowledge of any unusual terms or conditions associated with these transactions.

- Being physically present at one or more locations at period end to observe goods being shipped or being readied for shipment (or returns awaiting processing) and performing other appropriate sales and inventory cutoff procedures.

- For those situations for which revenue transactions are electronically initiated, processed, and recorded, testing controls to determine whether they provide assurance that recorded revenue transactions occurred and are properly recorded.

Inventory Quantities

- Examining the entity's inventory records to identify locations or items that require specific attention during or after the physical inventory count.

- Observing inventory counts at certain locations on an unannounced basis or conducting inventory counts at all locations on the same date.

- Conducting inventory counts at or near the end of the reporting period to minimize the risk of inappropriate manipulation during the period between the count and the end of the reporting period.

- Performing additional procedures during the observation of the count, for example, more rigorously examining the contents of boxed items, the manner in which the goods are stacked (for example, hollow squares) or labeled, and the quality (that is, purity, grade, or concentration) of liquid substances such as perfumes or specialty chemicals. Using the work of an expert may be helpful in this regard.

- Comparing the quantities for the current period with prior periods by class or category of inventory, location or other criteria, or comparison of quantities counted with perpetual records.

- Using computer-assisted audit techniques to further test the compilation of the physical inventory counts – for example, sorting by tag number to test tag controls or by item serial number to test the possibility of item omission or duplication.

Management Estimates

- Using an expert to develop an independent estimate for comparison to management's estimate.

- Extending inquiries to individuals outside of management and the accounting department to corroborate management's ability and intent to carry out plans that are relevant to developing the estimate.

Specific Responses—Misstatements Due to Misappropriation of Assets

Differing circumstances would necessarily dictate different responses. Ordinarily, the audit response to an assessed risk of material misstatement due to fraud relating to misappropriation of assets will be directed toward certain account balances and classes of transactions. Although some of the audit responses noted in the two categories above may apply in such circumstances, the scope of the work is to be linked to the specific information about the misappropriation risk that has been identified.

Examples of responses to the auditor's assessment of the risk of material misstatements due to misappropriation of assets are as follows:

- Counting cash or securities at or near year-end.

- Confirming directly with customers the account activity (including credit memo and sales return activity as well as dates payments were made) for the period under audit.

- Analyzing recoveries of written-off accounts.

- Analyzing inventory shortages by location or product type.

- Comparing key inventory ratios to industry norm.

- Reviewing supporting documentation for reductions to the perpetual inventory records.

- Performing a computerized match of the vendor list with a list of employees to identify matches of addresses or phone numbers.

- Performing a computerized search of payroll records to identify duplicate addresses, employee identification or taxing authority numbers or bank accounts

- Reviewing personnel files for those that contain little or no evidence of activity, for example, lack of performance evaluations.

- Analyzing sales discounts and returns for unusual patterns or trends.

- Confirming specific terms of contracts with third parties.

- Obtaining evidence that contracts are being carried out in accordance with their terms.

- Reviewing the propriety of large and unusual expenses.

- Reviewing the authorization and carrying value of senior management and related party loans.

- Reviewing the level and propriety of expense reports submitted by senior management.

Examples of Circumstances that Indicate the Possibility of Fraud

The following are examples of circumstances that may indicate the possibility that the financial statements may contain a material misstatement resulting from fraud.

Discrepancies in the accounting records, including:

- Transactions that are not recorded in a complete or timely manner or are improperly recorded as to amount, accounting period, classification, or entity policy.

- Unsupported or unauthorized balances or transactions.

- Last-minute adjustments that significantly affect financial results.

- Evidence of employees' access to systems and records inconsistent with that necessary to perform their authorized duties.

- Tips or complaints to the auditor about alleged fraud.

Conflicting or missing evidence, including:

- Missing documents.

- Documents that appear to have been altered.

- Unavailability of other than photocopied or electronically transmitted documents when documents in original form are expected to exist.

- Significant unexplained items on reconciliations.

- Unusual balance sheet changes, or changes in trends or important financial statement ratios or relationships – for example, receivables growing faster than revenues.

- Inconsistent, vague, or implausible responses from management or employees arising from inquiries or analytical procedures.

- Unusual discrepancies between the entity's records and confirmation replies.

- Large numbers of credit entries and other adjustments made to accounts receivable records.

- Unexplained or inadequately explained differences between the accounts receivable sub-ledger and the control account, or between the customer statements and the accounts receivable sub-ledger.

- Missing or non-existent cancelled checks in circumstances where cancelled checks are ordinarily returned to the entity with the bank statement.

- Missing inventory or physical assets of significant magnitude.

- Unavailable or missing electronic evidence, inconsistent with the entity's record retention practices or policies.

- Fewer responses to confirmations than anticipated or a greater number of responses than anticipated.

- Inability to produce evidence of key systems development and program change testing and implementation activities for current-year system changes and deployments.

Problematic or unusual relationships between the auditor and management, including:

- Denial of access to records, facilities, certain employees, customers, vendors, or others from whom audit evidence might be sought.

- Undue time pressures imposed by management to resolve complex or contentious issues.

- Complaints by management about the conduct of the audit or management intimidation of engagement team members, particularly in connection with the auditor's critical assessment of audit evidence or in the resolution of potential disagreements with management.

- Unusual delays by the entity in providing requested information.

- Unwillingness to facilitate auditor access to key electronic files for testing through the use of computer-assisted audit techniques.

- Denial of access to key IT operations staff and facilities, including security, operations, and systems development personnel.

- An unwillingness to add or revise disclosures in the financial statements to make them more complete and understandable.

- An unwillingness to address identified deficiencies in internal control on a timely basis.

Other

- Unwillingness by management to permit the auditor to meet privately with those charged with governance.

- Accounting policies that appear to be at variance with industry norms.

- Frequent changes in accounting estimates that do not appear to result from changed circumstances.

- Tolerance of violations of the entity's code of conduct.

INTERNATIONAL STANDARD ON AUDITING (UK AND IRELAND) 250

SECTION A – CONSIDERATION OF LAWS AND REGULATIONS IN AN AUDIT OF FINANCIAL STATEMENTS

(Effective for audits of financial statements for periods ending on or after 15 December 2010)

CONTENTS

International Standard on Auditing (UK and Ireland) (ISA (UK and Ireland)) 250, "Consideration of Laws and Regulations in an Audit of Financial Statements" should be read in conjunction with ISA (UK and Ireland) 200, "Overall Objectives of the Independent Auditor and the Conduct of an Audit in Accordance with International Standards on Auditing (UK and Ireland)."

Introduction

Scope of this ISA (UK and Ireland)

1. This International Standard on Auditing (UK and Ireland) (ISA (UK and Ireland)) deals with the auditor's responsibility to consider laws and regulations in an audit of financial statements. This ISA (UK and Ireland) does not apply to other assurance engagements in which the auditor is specifically engaged to test and report separately on compliance with specific laws or regulations.

1-1. Guidance on the auditor's responsibility to report direct to regulators in the financial sector is provided in Section B of this ISA (UK and Ireland).

Effect of Laws and Regulations

2. The effect on financial statements of laws and regulations varies considerably. Those laws and regulations to which an entity is subject constitute the legal and regulatory framework. The provisions of some laws or regulations have a direct effect on the financial statements in that they determine the reported amounts and disclosures in an entity's financial statements. Other laws or regulations are to be complied with by management or set the provisions under which the entity is allowed to conduct its business but do not have a direct effect on an entity's financial statements. Some entities operate in heavily regulated industries (such as banks and chemical companies). Others are subject only to the many laws and regulations that relate generally to the operating aspects of the business (such as those related to occupational safety and health, and equal employment opportunity). Non-compliance with laws and regulations may result in fines, litigation or other consequences for the entity that may have a material effect on the financial statements.

Responsibility for Compliance with Laws and Regulations (Ref: Para. A1-A6)

3. It is the responsibility of management, with the oversight of those charged with governance, to ensure that the entity's operations are conducted in accordance with the provisions of laws and regulations, including compliance with the provisions of laws and regulations that determine the reported amounts and disclosures in an entity's financial statements.[1a]

Responsibility of the Auditor

4. The requirements in this ISA (UK and Ireland) are designed to assist the auditor in identifying material misstatement of the financial statements due to non-compliance with laws and regulations. However, the auditor is not responsible for preventing non-compliance and cannot be expected to detect non-compliance with all laws and regulations.

[1a] In the UK and Ireland those charged with governance are responsible for the preparation of the financial statements.

5.   The auditor is responsible for obtaining reasonable assurance that the financial statements, taken as a whole, are free from material misstatement, whether caused by fraud or error.[1] In conducting an audit of financial statements, the auditor takes into account the applicable legal and regulatory framework. Owing to the inherent limitations of an audit, there is an unavoidable risk that some material misstatements in the financial statements may not be detected, even though the audit is properly planned and performed in accordance with the ISAs (UK and Ireland).[2] In the context of laws and regulations, the potential effects of inherent limitations on the auditor's ability to detect material misstatements are greater for such reasons as the following:

•   There are many laws and regulations, relating principally to the operating aspects of an entity, that typically do not affect the financial statements and are not captured by the entity's information systems relevant to financial reporting.

•   Non-compliance may involve conduct designed to conceal it, such as collusion, forgery, deliberate failure to record transactions, management override of controls or intentional misrepresentations being made to the auditor.

•   Whether an act constitutes non-compliance is ultimately a matter for legal determination by a court of law.

Ordinarily, the further removed non-compliance is from the events and transactions reflected in the financial statements, the less likely the auditor is to become aware of it or to recognize the non-compliance.

6.   This ISA (UK and Ireland) distinguishes the auditor's responsibilities in relation to compliance with two different categories of laws and regulations as follows:

(a)   The provisions of those laws and regulations generally recognized to have a direct effect on the determination of material amounts and disclosures in the financial statements such as tax and pension laws and regulations (see paragraph 13); and

(b)   Other laws and regulations that do not have a direct effect on the determination of the amounts and disclosures in the financial statements, but compliance with which may be fundamental to the operating aspects of the business, to an entity's ability to continue its business, or to avoid material penalties (for example, compliance with the terms of an operating license, compliance with regulatory solvency requirements, or compliance with environmental regulations); non-compliance with such laws and regulations may therefore have a material effect on the financial statements (see paragraph 14).

7.   In this ISA (UK and Ireland), differing requirements are specified for each of the above categories of laws and regulations. For the category referred to in paragraph 6(a), the auditor's responsibility is to obtain sufficient appropriate audit evidence regarding

---

[1]   ISA (UK and Ireland) 200, "Overall Objectives of the Independent Auditor and the Conduct of an Audit in Accordance with International Standards on Auditing," paragraph 5.
[2]   ISA (UK and Ireland) 200, paragraph A51.

compliance with the provisions of those laws and regulations. For the category referred to in paragraph 6(b), the auditor's responsibility is limited to undertaking specified audit procedures to help identify non-compliance with those laws and regulations that may have a material effect on the financial statements.

8. The auditor is required by this ISA (UK and Ireland) to remain alert to the possibility that other audit procedures applied for the purpose of forming an opinion on financial statements may bring instances of identified or suspected non-compliance to the auditor's attention. Maintaining professional skepticism throughout the audit, as required by ISA (UK and Ireland) 200,[3] is important in this context, given the extent of laws and regulations that affect the entity.

Effective Date

9. This ISA (UK and Ireland) is effective for audits of financial statements for periods ending on or after 15 December 2010.

Objectives

10. The objectives of the auditor are:

    (a) To obtain sufficient appropriate audit evidence regarding compliance with the provisions of those laws and regulations generally recognized to have a direct effect on the determination of material amounts and disclosures in the financial statements;

    (b) To perform specified audit procedures to help identify instances of non-compliance with other laws and regulations that may have a material effect on the financial statements; and

    (c) To respond appropriately to non-compliance or suspected non-compliance with laws and regulations identified during the audit.

Definition

11. For the purposes of this ISA (UK and Ireland), the following term has the meaning attributed below:

    Non-compliance – Acts of omission or commission by the entity, either intentional or unintentional, which are contrary to the prevailing laws or regulations. Such acts

---

[3] ISA (UK and Ireland) 200, paragraph 15.

include transactions entered into by, or in the name of, the entity, or on its behalf, by those charged with governance, management or employees. Non-compliance does not include personal misconduct (unrelated to the business activities of the entity) by those charged with governance, management or employees of the entity.

11-1. This ISA (UK and Ireland) also refers to 'money laundering'. 'Money laundering' is defined in legislation[3a] and in general terms involves an act which conceals, disguises, converts, transfers, removes, uses, acquires or possesses property resulting from criminal conduct.

Requirements

The Auditor's Consideration of Compliance with Laws and Regulations

12.   As part of obtaining an understanding of the entity and its environment in accordance with ISA (UK and Ireland) 315,[4] the auditor shall obtain a general understanding of:

(a)   The legal and regulatory framework applicable to the entity and the industry or sector in which the entity operates; and

(b)   How the entity is complying with that framework. (Ref: Para. A7)

13.   The auditor shall obtain sufficient appropriate audit evidence regarding compliance with the provisions of those laws and regulations generally recognized to have a direct effect on the determination of material amounts and disclosures in the financial statements. (Ref: Para. A8 – A8-1)

14.   The auditor shall perform the following audit procedures to help identify instances of non-compliance with other laws and regulations that may have a material effect on the financial statements: (Ref: Para. A9 – A10-1)

(a)   Inquiring of management and, where appropriate, those charged with governance, as to whether the entity is in compliance with such laws and regulations; and

(b)   Inspecting correspondence, if any, with the relevant licensing or regulatory authorities.

[3a] In the UK, the Money Laundering Regulations 2007 and the requirements of the Proceeds of Crime Act 2002 (POCA) bring auditors within the regulated sector, requiring them to report suspected money laundering activity and adopt rigorous client identification procedures and appropriate anti-money laundering procedures.

In Ireland, the Criminal Justice Act 1994 (Section 32) Regulations 2003 designate accountants, auditors, and tax advisors and others for the purposes of the anti-money laundering provisions of the Criminal Justice Act, 1994, as amended.

[4]   ISA (UK and Ireland) 315, "Identifying and Assessing the Risks of Material Misstatement through Understanding the Entity and Its Environment," paragraph 11.

15.   During the audit, the auditor shall remain alert to the possibility that other audit procedures applied may bring instances of non-compliance or suspected non-compliance with laws and regulations to the auditor's attention. (Ref: Para. A11 – A11-2)

16.   The auditor shall request management and, where appropriate, those charged with governance to provide written representations that all known instances of non-compliance or suspected non-compliance with laws and regulations whose effects should be considered when preparing financial statements have been disclosed to the auditor. (Ref: Para. A12)

17.   In the absence of identified or suspected non-compliance, the auditor is not required to perform audit procedures regarding the entity's compliance with laws and regulations, other than those set out in paragraphs 12-16.

Audit Procedures When Non-Compliance Is Identified or Suspected

18.   If the auditor becomes aware of information concerning an instance of non-compliance or suspected non-compliance with laws and regulations, the auditor shall obtain: (Ref: Para. A13)

(a)   An understanding of the nature of the act and the circumstances in which it has occurred; and

(b)   Further information to evaluate the possible effect on the financial statements. (Ref: Para. A14)

19.   If the auditor suspects there may be non-compliance, the auditor shall[4a] discuss the matter with management and, where appropriate, those charged with governance. If management or, as appropriate, those charged with governance do not provide sufficient information that supports that the entity is in compliance with laws and

---

[4a]   Subject to compliance with legislation relating to 'tipping off' or "prejudicing an investigation".

In the UK, 'tipping off' is an offence under POCA section 333A. It arises when an individual discloses:

(a)   that a report (internal or external) has already been made where the disclosure by the individual is likely to prejudice an investigation which might be conducted following the internal or external report that has been made; or

(b)   that an investigation is being contemplated or is being carried out into allegations that a money laundering offence has been committed and the disclosure by the individual is likely to prejudice that investigation.

Whilst 'tipping off' requires a person to have knowledge or suspicion that a report has been or will be made, a further offence of prejudicing an investigation is included in POCA section 342. Under this provision, it is an offence to make any disclosure which may prejudice an investigation of which a person has knowledge or suspicion, or to falsify, conceal, destroy or otherwise dispose of, or cause or permit the falsification, concealment, destruction or disposal of, documents relevant to such an investigation.

The disclosure offences under sections 333A and 342 are not committed if the person disclosing does not know or suspect that it is likely to prejudice an investigation.

In Ireland Section 58 of the Criminal Justice Act, 1994, as amended, establishes the offence of "prejudicing an investigation". This relates both to when a person, knowing or suspecting that an investigation is taking place, makes any disclosure likely to prejudice the investigation or when a person, knowing that a report has been made, makes any disclosure likely to prejudice any investigation arising from the report.

regulations and, in the auditor's judgment, the effect of the suspected non-compliance may be material to the financial statements, the auditor shall consider the need to obtain legal advice. (Ref: Para. A15-A16)

20. If sufficient information about suspected non-compliance cannot be obtained, the auditor shall evaluate the effect of the lack of sufficient appropriate audit evidence on the auditor's opinion.

21. The auditor shall evaluate the implications of non-compliance in relation to other aspects of the audit, including the auditor's risk assessment and the reliability of written representations, and take appropriate action. (Ref: Para. A17- A18-1)

Reporting of Identified or Suspected Non-Compliance

Reporting Non-Compliance to Those Charged with Governance

22. Unless all of those charged with governance are involved in management of the entity, and therefore are aware of matters involving identified or suspected non-compliance already communicated by the auditor,[5] the auditor shall[4a] communicate with those charged with governance matters involving non-compliance with laws and regulations that come to the auditor's attention during the course of the audit, other than when the matters are clearly inconsequential.

23. If, in the auditor's judgment, the non-compliance referred to in paragraph 22 is believed to be intentional and material, the auditor shall[4a] communicate the matter to those charged with governance as soon as practicable. (Ref: Para. A18-2)

24. If the auditor suspects that management or those charged with governance are involved in non-compliance, the auditor shall[4a] communicate the matter to the next higher level of authority at the entity, if it exists, such as an audit committee or supervisory board. Where no higher authority exists, or if the auditor believes that the communication may not be acted upon or is unsure as to the person to whom to report, the auditor shall consider the need to obtain legal advice. (Ref: Para. A18-3)

Reporting Non-Compliance in the Auditor's Report on the Financial Statements

25. If the auditor concludes that the non-compliance has a material effect on the financial statements, and has not been adequately reflected in the financial statements, the auditor shall,[4a] in accordance with ISA (UK and Ireland) 705, express a qualified opinion or an adverse opinion on the financial statements.[6]

26. If the auditor is precluded by management or those charged with governance from obtaining sufficient appropriate audit evidence to evaluate whether non-compliance that may be material to the financial statements has, or is likely to have, occurred, the auditor shall[4a] express a qualified opinion or disclaim an opinion on the financial

---

[5] ISA (UK and Ireland) 260, "Communication with Those Charged with Governance," paragraph 13.
[6] ISA (UK and Ireland) 705, "Modifications to the Opinion in the Independent Auditor's Report," paragraphs 7-8.

statements on the basis of a limitation on the scope of the audit in accordance with ISA (UK and Ireland) 705.

27. If the auditor is unable to determine whether non-compliance has occurred because of limitations imposed by the circumstances rather than by management or those charged with governance, the auditor shall evaluate the effect on the auditor's opinion in accordance with ISA (UK and Ireland) 705. (Ref: Para. A18-4)

Reporting Non-Compliance to Regulatory and Enforcement Authorities

28. If the auditor has identified or suspects non-compliance with laws and regulations, the auditor shall determine whether the auditor has a responsibility to report the identified or suspected non-compliance to parties outside the entity. (Ref: Para. A19-A20)

Documentation

29. The auditor shall include in the audit documentation identified or suspected non-compliance with laws and regulations and the results of discussion with management and, where applicable, those charged with governance and other parties outside the entity.[7] (Ref: Para. A21)

***

Application and Other Explanatory Material

Responsibility for Compliance with Laws and Regulations (Ref: Para. 3-8)

A1. It is the responsibility of management, with the oversight of those charged with governance, to ensure that the entity's operations are conducted in accordance with laws and regulations. Laws and regulations may affect an entity's financial statements in different ways: for example, most directly, they may affect specific disclosures required of the entity in the financial statements or they may prescribe the applicable financial reporting framework. They may also establish certain legal rights and obligations of the entity, some of which will be recognized in the entity's financial statements. In addition, laws and regulations may impose penalties in cases of non-compliance.

A2. The following are examples of the types of policies and procedures an entity may implement to assist in the prevention and detection of non-compliance with laws and regulations:

- Monitoring legal requirements and ensuring that operating procedures are designed to meet these requirements.

---

[7] ISA (UK and Ireland) 230, "Audit Documentation," paragraphs 8-11, and paragraph A6.

- Instituting and operating appropriate systems of internal control.

- Developing, publicizing and following a code of conduct.

- Ensuring employees are properly trained and understand the code of conduct.

- Monitoring compliance with the code of conduct and acting appropriately to discipline employees who fail to comply with it.

- Engaging legal advisors to assist in monitoring legal requirements.

- Maintaining a register of significant laws and regulations with which the entity has to comply within its particular industry and a record of complaints.

In larger entities, these policies and procedures may be supplemented by assigning appropriate responsibilities to the following:

- An internal audit function.

- An audit committee.

- A compliance function.

A2-1. In the UK and Ireland, in certain sectors or activities (for example financial services), there are detailed laws and regulations that specifically require directors to have systems to ensure compliance. Breaches of these laws and regulations could have a material effect on the financial statements.

A2-2. In the UK and Ireland, it is the directors' responsibility to prepare financial statements that give a true and fair view of the state of affairs of a company or group and of its profit or loss for the financial year. Accordingly it is necessary, where possible non-compliance with law or regulations has occurred which may result in a material misstatement in the financial statements, for them to ensure that the matter is appropriately reflected and/or disclosed in the financial statements.

A2-3. In the UK and Ireland directors and officers of companies have responsibility to provide information required by the auditor, to which they have a legal right of access[7a]. Such legislation also provides that it is a criminal offence to give to the auditor information or explanations which are misleading, false or deceptive.

Responsibility of the Auditor

A3. Non-compliance by the entity with laws and regulations may result in a material misstatement of the financial statements. Detection of non-compliance, regardless of

---

[7a] In the UK under Section 499 of the Companies Act 2006 or Sections 193(3) and 197 of the Companies Act 1990 in Ireland.

materiality, may affect other aspects of the audit including, for example, the auditor's consideration of the integrity of management or employees.

A4.   Whether an act constitutes non-compliance with laws and regulations is a matter for legal determination, which is ordinarily beyond the auditor's professional competence to determine. Nevertheless, the auditor's training, experience and understanding of the entity and its industry or sector may provide a basis to recognize that some acts, coming to the auditor's attention, may constitute non-compliance with laws and regulations.

A5.   In accordance with specific statutory requirements, the auditor may be specifically required to report, as part of the audit of the financial statements, on whether the entity complies with certain provisions of laws or regulations. In these circumstances, ISA (UK and Ireland) 700[8] or ISA 800[9] deal with how these audit responsibilities are addressed in the auditor's report. Furthermore, where there are specific statutory reporting requirements, it may be necessary for the audit plan to include appropriate tests for compliance with these provisions of the laws and regulations.

Considerations Specific to Public Sector Entities

A6.   In the public sector, there may be additional audit responsibilities with respect to the consideration of laws and regulations which may relate to the audit of financial statements or may extend to other aspects of the entity's operations.

The Auditor's Consideration of Compliance with Laws and Regulations

Obtaining an Understanding of the Legal and Regulatory Framework (Ref: Para. 12)

A7.   To obtain a general understanding of the legal and regulatory framework, and how the entity complies with that framework, the auditor may, for example:

- Use the auditor's existing understanding of the entity's industry, regulatory and other external factors;

- Update the understanding of those laws and regulations that directly determine the reported amounts and disclosures in the financial statements;

- Inquire of management as to other laws or regulations that may be expected to have a fundamental effect on the operations of the entity;

---

[8]   ISA (UK and Ireland) 700, "Forming an Opinion and Reporting on Financial Statements," paragraph 38.
The APB has not promulgated ISA 700 as issued by the IAASB for application in the UK and Ireland. In the UK and Ireland the applicable auditing standard is ISA (UK and Ireland) 700, "The Auditor's Report on Financial Statements." Paragraph 21 of ISA (UK and Ireland) 700 is the equivalent to paragraph 38 of ISA 700.
[9]   ISA 800 "Special Considerations—Audits of Financial Statements Prepared in Accordance with Special Purpose Frameworks," paragraph 11.
ISA 800 has not been promulgated by the APB for application in the UK and Ireland.

- Inquire of management concerning the entity's policies and procedures regarding compliance with laws and regulations; and

- Inquire of management regarding the policies or procedures adopted for identifying, evaluating and accounting for litigation claims.

Laws and Regulations Generally Recognized to Have a Direct Effect on the Determination of Material Amounts and Disclosures in the Financial Statements (Ref: Para. 13)

A8. Certain laws and regulations are well-established, known to the entity and within the entity's industry or sector, and relevant to the entity's financial statements (as described in paragraph 6(a)). They could include those that relate to, for example:

- The form and content of financial statements[9a];

- Industry-specific financial reporting issues;

- Accounting for transactions under government contracts; or

- The accrual or recognition of expenses for income tax or pension costs.

In the UK and Ireland, these laws and regulations include:

- Those which determine the circumstances under which a company is prohibited from making a distribution except out of profits available for the purpose[9b].

- Those laws which require auditors expressly to report non-compliance, such as the requirements relating to the maintenance of adequate accounting records[9c] or the disclosure of particulars of directors' remuneration in a company's financial statements[9d].

Some provisions in those laws and regulations may be directly relevant to specific assertions in the financial statements (for example, the completeness of income tax provisions), while others may be directly relevant to the financial statements as a whole (for example, the required statements constituting a complete set of financial statements). The aim of the requirement in paragraph 13 is for the auditor to obtain sufficient appropriate audit evidence regarding the determination of amounts and disclosures in the financial statements in compliance with the relevant provisions of those laws and regulations.

[9a] In the UK under The Small Companies and Groups (Accounts and Directors' Report) Regulations 2008 (SI 2008-409) and The Large and Medium-sized Companies and Groups (Accounts and Reports) Regulations 2008 (SI 2008-410) or The Companies (Amendment) Act, 1986 in Ireland.

[9b] In the UK under Section 830 of the Companies Act 2006 or Section 45 of the Companies (Amendment) Act, 1983 in Ireland.

[9c] In the UK under Section 498 of the Companies Act 2006 and, in Ireland, under Section 193 and 194 of the Companies Act 1990.

[9d] In the UK under Section 497 of the Companies Act 2006. There is no equivalent in Ireland.

Non-compliance with other provisions of such laws and regulations and other laws and regulations may result in fines, litigation or other consequences for the entity, the costs of which may need to be provided for in the financial statements, but are not considered to have a direct effect on the financial statements as described in paragraph 6(a).

A8-1. In the UK and Ireland, the auditor's responsibility to express an opinion on an entity's financial statements does not extend to determining whether the entity has complied in every respect with applicable tax legislation. The auditor needs to obtain sufficient appropriate evidence to give reasonable assurance that the amounts included in the financial statements in respect of taxation are not materially misstated. This will usually include making appropriate enquiries of those advising the entity on taxation matters (whether within the audit firm or elsewhere). If the auditor becomes aware that the entity has failed to comply with the requirements of tax legislation, the auditor considers whether to report the matter to parties outside the entity.

Procedures to Identify Instances of Non-Compliance – Other Laws and Regulations (Ref: Para. 14)

A9. Certain other laws and regulations may need particular attention by the auditor because they have a fundamental effect on the operations of the entity (as described in paragraph 6(b)). Non-compliance with laws and regulations that have a fundamental effect on the operations of the entity may cause the entity to cease operations, or call into question the entity's continuance as a going concern. For example, non-compliance with the requirements of the entity's license or other entitlement to perform its operations could have such an impact (for example, for a bank, non-compliance with capital or investment requirements)[9e]. There are also many laws and regulations relating principally to the operating aspects of the entity that typically do not affect the financial statements and are not captured by the entity's information systems relevant to financial reporting.

A10. As the financial reporting consequences of other laws and regulations can vary depending on the entity's operations, the audit procedures required by paragraph 14 are directed to bringing to the auditor's attention instances of non-compliance with laws and regulations that may have a material effect on the financial statements.

A10-1. When determining the type of procedures necessary in a particular instance the auditor takes account of the particular entity concerned and the complexity of the regulations with which it is required to comply. In general, a small company which does not operate in a regulated area will require few specific procedures compared with a large multinational corporation carrying on complex, regulated business.

[9e] Such requirements exist in the UK under the Financial Services and Markets Act 2000 and in Ireland under the Investment Intermediaries Act 1995, the Central Bank Acts 1942 to 1989 and the Credit Union Act, 1997.

Non-Compliance Brought to the Auditor's Attention by Other Audit Procedures (Ref: Para. 15)

A11. Audit procedures applied to form an opinion on the financial statements may bring instances of non-compliance or suspected non-compliance with laws and regulations to the auditor's attention. For example, such audit procedures may include:

- Reading minutes;

- Inquiring of the entity's management and in-house legal counsel or external legal counsel concerning litigation, claims and assessments; and

- Performing substantive tests of details of classes of transactions, account balances or disclosures.

A11-1. In the UK and Ireland, the auditor is alert for instances of possible or actual non-compliance with laws and regulations including those that might incur obligations for partners and staff in audit firms to report to a regulatory or other enforcement authority. See paragraphs A11-2 and A19-1 – A19-12.

Money Laundering Offences

A11-2. Anti-money laundering legislation in the UK and Ireland imposes a duty on the auditor to report suspected money laundering activity. There are similar laws and regulations relating to financing terrorist offences[9f]. The detailed legislation in both countries differs but the impact on the auditor can broadly be summarised as follows:

- Partners and staff in audit firms are required to report suspicions of conduct which would constitute a criminal offence which gives rise to direct or indirect benefit.

- Partners and staff in audit firms need to be alert to the dangers of 'tipping-off' (in the UK) or 'prejudicing an investigation' (in Ireland), as this will constitute a criminal offence under the anti-money laundering legislation.[4a]

For the UK further detail is set out in Practice Note 12 (Revised): Money Laundering – Guidance for auditors on UK legislation.

Written Representations (Ref: Para. 16)

A12. Because the effect on financial statements of laws and regulations can vary considerably, written representations provide necessary audit evidence about

---

[9f] In the UK, the Terrorism Act 2000 contains reporting requirements for the laundering of terrorist funds which include any funds that are likely to be used for the financing of terrorism.
In Ireland, the Criminal Justice Act 1994 (as amended) requires reporting suspicions of terrorist financing to the appropriate authorities.

management's knowledge of identified or suspected non-compliance with laws and regulations, whose effects may have a material effect on the financial statements. However, written representations do not provide sufficient appropriate audit evidence on their own and, accordingly, do not affect the nature and extent of other audit evidence that is to be obtained by the auditor.[10]

Audit Procedures When Non-Compliance Is Identified or Suspected

Indications of Non-Compliance with Laws and Regulations (Ref: Para. 18)

A13. If the auditor becomes aware of the existence of, or information about, the following matters, it may be an indication of non-compliance with laws and regulations:

- Investigations by regulatory organizations and government departments or payment of fines or penalties.

- Payments for unspecified services or loans to consultants, related parties, employees or government employees.

- Sales commissions or agent's fees that appear excessive in relation to those ordinarily paid by the entity or in its industry or to the services actually received.

- Purchasing at prices significantly above or below market price.

- Unusual payments in cash, purchases in the form of cashiers' cheques payable to bearer or transfers to numbered bank accounts.

- Unusual transactions with companies registered in tax havens.

- Payments for goods or services made other than to the country from which the goods or services originated.

- Payments without proper exchange control documentation.

- Existence of an information system which fails, whether by design or by accident, to provide an adequate audit trail or sufficient evidence.

- Unauthorized transactions or improperly recorded transactions.

- Adverse media comment.

---

[10] ISA (UK and Ireland) 580, "Written Representations," paragraph 4.

Matters Relevant to the Auditor's Evaluation (Ref: Para. 18(b))

A14. Matters relevant to the auditor's evaluation[10a] of the possible effect on the financial statements include:

- The potential financial consequences of non-compliance with laws and regulations on the financial statements including, for example, the imposition of fines, penalties, damages, threat of expropriation of assets[10b], enforced discontinuation of operations, and litigation.

- Whether the potential financial consequences require disclosure.

- Whether the potential financial consequences are so serious as to call into question the fair presentation of the financial statements, or otherwise make the financial statements misleading.

Audit Procedures (Ref: Para. 19)

A15. The auditor may discuss the findings with those charged with governance where they may be able to provide additional audit evidence. For example, the auditor may confirm that those charged with governance have the same understanding of the facts and circumstances relevant to transactions or events that have led to the possibility of non-compliance with laws and regulations.

A16. If management or, as appropriate, those charged with governance do not provide sufficient information to the auditor that the entity is in fact in compliance with laws and regulations, the auditor may consider it appropriate to consult with the entity's in-house legal counsel or external legal counsel about the application of the laws and regulations to the circumstances, including the possibility of fraud, and the possible effects on the financial statements. If it is not considered appropriate to consult with the entity's legal counsel or if the auditor is not satisfied with the legal counsel's opinion, the auditor may consider it appropriate to consult the auditor's own legal counsel as to whether a contravention of a law or regulation is involved, the possible legal consequences, including the possibility of fraud, and what further action, if any, the auditor would take.

Evaluating the Implications of Non-Compliance (Ref: Para. 21)

A17. As required by paragraph 21, the auditor evaluates the implications of non-compliance in relation to other aspects of the audit, including the auditor's risk assessment and the reliability of written representations. The implications of particular

---

[10a] ISA (UK and Ireland) 620, "Using the Work of an Auditor's Expert" applies if the auditor judges it necessary to obtain appropriate expert advice in connection with the evaluation of the possible effect of legal matters on the financial statements.

[10b] The Proceeds of Crime Act 2002 ("POCA") provides procedures to enable the authorities to confiscate in criminal proceedings or bring an action for civil recovery of assets which represent the benefits of criminal conduct.

In Ireland, the Criminal Assets Bureau, an agency responsible for the confiscation of assets, was established by the Criminal Assets Bureau Act 1996.

instances of non-compliance identified by the auditor will depend on the relationship of the perpetration and concealment, if any, of the act to specific control activities and the level of management or employees involved, especially implications arising from the involvement of the highest authority within the entity.

A18. In exceptional cases, the auditor may consider whether withdrawal from the engagement, where withdrawal is possible under applicable law or regulation, is necessary when management or those charged with governance do not take the remedial action that the auditor considers appropriate in the circumstances, even when the non-compliance is not material to the financial statements. When deciding whether withdrawal from the engagement is necessary, the auditor may consider seeking legal advice. If withdrawal from the engagement is not possible, the auditor may consider alternative actions, including describing the non-compliance in an Other Matter(s) paragraph in the auditor's report.[11]

A18-1. Withdrawal from the engagement by the auditor is a step of last resort. It is normally preferable for the auditor to remain in office to fulfil the auditor's statutory duties, particularly where minority interests are involved. However, there are circumstances where there may be no alternative to withdrawal, for example where the directors of a company refuse to issue its financial statements or the auditor wishes to inform the shareholders or creditors of the company of the auditor's concerns and there is no immediate occasion to do so.

Reporting of Identified or Suspected Non-Compliance

Reporting Non-Compliance to Those Charged with Governance (Ref: Para. 23)

A18-2. If a non-compliance is intentional but not material the auditor considers whether the nature and circumstances make it appropriate to communicate to those charged with governance as soon as practicable.

Suspicion that Management or Those Charged with Governance are Involved in Non-Compliance (Ref: Para. 24)

A18-3. In the case of suspected Money Laundering it may be appropriate to report the matter direct to the appropriate authority.

---

[11] ISA (UK and Ireland) 706, "Emphasis of Matter Paragraphs and Other Matter Paragraphs in the Independent Auditor's Report," paragraph 8.

In the UK and Ireland, if the auditor concludes that the view given by the financial statements could be affected by a level of uncertainty concerning the consequences of a suspected or actual non-compliance which, in the auditor's opinion, is significant, the auditor, subject to a consideration of 'tipping off' or 'prejudicing an investigation' (see footnote 4a), includes an explanatory paragraph referring to the matter in the auditor's report.

Reporting Non-Compliance in the Auditor's Report on the Financial Statements (Ref: Para. 27)

A18-4. In the UK and Ireland, when considering whether the financial statements reflect the possible consequences of any suspected or actual non-compliance, the auditor has regard to the requirements of applicable accounting standards. Suspected or actual non-compliance with laws or regulations may require disclosure in the financial statements because, although the immediate financial effect on the entity may not be material[11a], there could be future material consequences such as fines or litigation. For example, an illegal payment may not itself be material but may result in criminal proceedings against the entity or loss of business which could have a material effect on the true and fair view given by the financial statements.

Reporting Non-Compliance to Regulatory and Enforcement Authorities (Ref: Para. 28)

A19. The auditor's professional duty to maintain the confidentiality of client information may preclude reporting identified or suspected non-compliance with laws and regulations to a party outside the entity. However, the auditor's legal responsibilities vary by jurisdiction and, in certain circumstances, the duty of confidentiality may be overridden by statute, the law or courts of law. In some jurisdictions, the auditor of a financial institution has a statutory duty to report the occurrence, or suspected occurrence, of non-compliance with laws and regulations to supervisory authorities. Also, in some jurisdictions, the auditor has a duty to report misstatements to authorities in those cases where management and, where applicable, those charged with governance fail to take corrective action. The auditor may consider it appropriate to obtain legal advice to determine the appropriate course of action.

A19-1. Legislation in the UK and Ireland establishes specific responsibilities for the auditor to report suspicions regarding certain criminal offences (for example, in relation to money laundering offences (see paragraph A11-2) and, in the Republic of Ireland, indictable offences under company law and the Criminal Justice (Theft and Fraud Offences) Act 2001). In addition, the auditor of entities subject to statutory regulation[11b], has separate responsibilities to report certain information direct to the relevant regulator. Standards and guidance on these responsibilities is given in Section B of this ISA (UK and Ireland) and relevant APB Practice Notes.

A19-2. The procedures and guidance in Section B of this ISA (UK and Ireland) can be adapted to circumstances in which the auditor of other types of entity becomes

---

[11a] As discussed in ISA (UK and Ireland) 320, "Materiality in Planning and Performing an Audit," judgments about materiality are made in light of surrounding circumstances and are affected by the size or nature of a matter or a combination of both.

[11b] Auditors of financial service entities, pension schemes and, in the UK, charities have a statutory responsibility, subject to compliance with legislation relating to 'tipping off' or 'prejudicing an investigation' (see footnote 4a), to report matters that are likely to be of material significance to the regulator.

aware of a suspected instance of non-compliance with laws or regulations which the auditor is under a statutory duty to report.

Timing of Reports

A19-3.   Some laws and regulations stipulate a period within which reports are to be made. If the auditor becomes aware of a suspected or actual non-compliance with law and regulations which gives rise to a statutory duty to report, the auditor complies with any such stipulated periods for reporting. Ordinarily the auditor makes a report to the appropriate authority as soon as practicable.

Reporting in the Public Interest

A19-4.   Where the auditor becomes aware of a suspected or actual instance of non-compliance with law or regulations which does not give rise to a statutory duty to report to an appropriate authority the auditor considers whether the matter may be one that ought to be reported to a proper authority in the public interest and, where this is the case, except in the circumstances covered in paragraph A19-6 below, discusses the matter with those charged with governance, including any audit committee[11c].

A19-5.   If, having considered any views expressed on behalf of the entity and in the light of any legal advice obtained, the auditor concludes that the matter ought to be reported to an appropriate authority in the public interest, the auditor notifies those charged with governance in writing of the view and, if the entity does not voluntarily do so itself or is unable to provide evidence that the matter has been reported, the auditor reports it.

A19-6.   The auditor reports a matter direct to a proper authority in the public interest and without discussing the matter with the entity if the auditor concludes that the suspected or actual instance of non-compliance has caused the auditor no longer to have confidence in the integrity of those charged with governance.

A19-7.   Examples of circumstances which may cause the auditor no longer to have confidence in the integrity of those charged with governance include situations:

- Where the auditor suspects or has evidence of the involvement or intended involvement of those charged with governance in possible non-compliance with law or regulations which could have a material effect on the financial statements; or

---

[11c] In rare circumstances, according to common law, disclosure might also be justified in the public interest where there is no instance of non-compliance with law or regulations, e.g. where the public is being misled or their financial interests are being damaged; where a miscarriage of justice has occurred; where the health and safety of members of the public or the environment is being endangered – although such events may well constitute breaches of law or regulation.

- Where the auditor is aware that those charged with governance are aware of such non-compliance and, contrary to regulatory requirements or the public interest, have not reported it to a proper authority within a reasonable period. In such a case, if the auditor determines that continued holding of office is untenable or the auditor is removed from office by the client, the auditor will be mindful of the auditor's reporting duties[11d].

A19-8. Determination of where the balance of public interest lies requires careful consideration. An auditor whose suspicions have been aroused uses professional judgment to determine whether the auditor's misgivings justify the auditor in carrying the matter further or are too insubstantial to deserve reporting. The auditor is protected from the risk of liability for breach of confidence or defamation provided that:

- In the case of breach of confidence, disclosure is made in the public interest, and such disclosure is made to an appropriate body or person[11e], and there is no malice motivating the disclosure; and

- In the case of defamation disclosure is made in the auditor's capacity as auditor of the entity concerned, and there is no malice motivating the disclosure.

In addition, the auditor is protected from such risks where the auditor is expressly permitted or required by legislation to disclose information[11f].

A19-9. 'Public interest' is a concept that is not capable of general definition. Each situation must be considered individually. In the UK, legal precedent indicates that matters to be taken into account when considering whether disclosure is justified in the public interest may include:

- The extent to which the suspected or actual non-compliance with law or regulations is likely to affect members of the public;

[11d] In the UK, under Part 16 of the Companies Act 2006.

[11e] In the UK, proper authorities could include the Serious Fraud Office, the Crown Prosecution Service, police forces, the Financial Services Authority the Panel on Takeovers and Mergers, the Society of Lloyd's, local authorities, the Charity Commissioners for England and Wales, the Scottish Office For Scottish Charities, HM Revenue and Customs, the Department of Business Innovation and Skills and the Health and Safety Executive.
In Ireland, comparable bodies could include the Garda Bureau of Fraud Investigation, the Revenue Commissioners, the Irish Stock Exchange, the Irish Financial Services Regulatory Authority, the Pensions Board, the Director of Corporate Enforcement, the Health and Safety Authority, The Charities Regulatory Authority and the Department of Enterprise Trade and Employment.

[11f] In the UK, the Employments Rights Act 1996 would give similar protection to an individual member of the audit engagement team who made an appropriate report in the public interest. However, ordinarily a member of the engagement team who believed there was a reportable matter would follow the audit firm's policies and procedures to address such matters. ISA (UK and Ireland) 220, "Quality Control for an Audit of Financial Statements," paragraph 18(a), requires that the engagement partner shall take responsibility for the engagement team undertaking appropriate consultation on difficult or contentious matters. If differences of opinion arise within the engagement team, ISA (UK and Ireland) 220, paragraph 22, requires that the engagement team shall follow the firm's policies and procedures for dealing with and resolving differences of opinion.

FINANCIAL REPORTING COUNCIL

- Whether those charged with governance have rectified the matter or are taking, or are likely to take, effective corrective action;

- The extent to which non-disclosure is likely to enable the suspected or actual non-compliance with law or regulations to recur with impunity;

- The gravity of the matter;

- Whether there is a general ethos within the entity of disregarding law or regulations; and

- The weight of evidence and the degree of the auditor's suspicion that there has been an instance of non-compliance with law or regulations.

A19-10. An auditor who can demonstrate having acted reasonably and in good faith in informing an authority of a breach of law or regulations which the auditor thinks has been committed would not be held by the court to be in breach of duty to the client even if, an investigation or prosecution having occurred, it were found that there had been no offence.

A19-11. The auditor needs to remember that the auditor's decision as to whether to report, and if so to whom, may be called into question at a future date, for example on the basis of:

- What the auditor knew at the time;

- What the auditor ought to have known in the course of the audit;

- What the auditor ought to have concluded; and

- What the auditor ought to have done.

The auditor may also wish to consider the possible consequences if financial loss is occasioned by non-compliance with law or regulations which the auditor suspects (or ought to suspect) has occurred but decided not to report.

A19-12. The auditor may need to take legal advice before making a decision on whether the matter needs to be reported to a proper authority in the public interest.

Considerations Specific to Public Sector Entities

A20. A public sector auditor may be obliged to report on instances of non-compliance to the legislature or other governing body or to report them in the auditor's report.

Documentation (Ref: Para. 29)

A21. The auditor's documentation of findings regarding identified or suspected non-compliance with laws and regulations may include, for example:

- Copies of records or documents.

- Minutes of discussions held with management, those charged with governance or parties outside the entity.

INTERNATIONAL STANDARD ON AUDITING (UK AND IRELAND) 250

SECTION B – THE AUDITOR'S RIGHT AND DUTY TO REPORT TO REGULATORS IN THE FINANCIAL SECTOR

(Effective for audits of financial statements for periods ending on or after 15 December 2010)

CONTENTS

International Standard on Auditing (UK and Ireland) (ISA (UK and Ireland)) 250, "Consideration of Laws and Regulations in an Audit of Financial Statements" should be read in conjunction with ISA (UK and Ireland) 200, "Overall Objectives of the Independent Auditor and the Conduct of an Audit in Accordance with International Standards on Auditing (UK and Ireland)."

Introduction

Scope of this Section

1.   This Section of ISA (UK and Ireland) 250 deals with the circumstances in which the auditor of a financial institution subject to statutory regulation (a 'regulated entity') is required to report direct to a regulator information which comes to the auditor's attention in the course of the work undertaken in the auditor's capacity as auditor of the regulated entity. This may include work undertaken to express an opinion on the entity's financial statements, other financial information or on other matters specified by legislation or by a regulator.

The Auditor's Responsibilities (Ref: Para. A1-A8)

2.   The auditor of a regulated entity generally has special reporting responsibilities in addition to the responsibility to report on financial statements. These special reporting responsibilities take two forms:

   (a)   *A responsibility to provide a report on matters specified in legislation or by a regulator.* This form of report is often made on an annual or other routine basis and does not derive from another set of reporting responsibilities. The auditor is required to carry out appropriate procedures sufficient to form an opinion on the matters concerned. These procedures may be in addition to those carried out to form an opinion on the financial statements; and

   (b)   *A statutory duty to report certain information, relevant to the regulators' functions, that come to the auditor's attention in the course of the audit work.* The auditor has no responsibility to carry out procedures to search out the information relevant to the regulator. This form of report is derivative in nature, arising only in the context of another set of reporting responsibilities, and is initiated by the auditor on discovery of a reportable matter.

3.   This section of this ISA (UK and Ireland) deals with both forms of direct reports. Guidance on the auditor's responsibility to provide special reports on a routine basis on other matters specified in legislation or by a regulator is given in the Practice Notes dealing with regulated business, for example banks, building societies, investment businesses and insurers.

4.   The statutory duty to report to a regulator applies to information which comes to the attention of the auditor in the auditor's capacity as auditor. In determining whether information is obtained in that capacity, two criteria in particular need to be considered: first, whether the person who obtained the information also undertook the audit work; and if so, whether it was obtained in the course of or as a result of undertaking the audit work. Appendix 2 to this Section of this ISA (UK and Ireland) sets out guidance on the application of these criteria.

5. The auditor may have a statutory right to bring information to the attention of the regulator in particular circumstances which lie outside those giving rise to a statutory duty to initiate a direct report. Where this is so, the auditor may use that right to make a direct report relevant to the regulator on a specific matter which comes to the auditor's attention when the auditor concludes that doing so is necessary to protect the interests of those for whose benefit the regulator is required to act.

6. The requirements and explanatory material in this section of this ISA (UK and Ireland) complement but do not replace the legal and regulatory requirements applicable to each regulated entity. Where the application of those legal and regulatory requirements, taking into account any published interpretations, is insufficiently clear for the auditor to determine whether a particular circumstance results in a legal duty to make a report to a regulator, or a right to make such a report, it may be appropriate to take legal advice.

Effective Date

7. This Section of ISA (UK and Ireland) 250 is effective for audits of financial statements for periods ending on or after 15 December 2010.

Objective

8. The objective of the auditor of a regulated entity is to bring information of which the auditor has become aware in the ordinary course of performing work undertaken to fulfil the auditor's audit responsibilities to the attention of the appropriate regulator as soon as practicable when:

    (a) The auditor concludes that it is relevant to the regulator's functions having regard to such matters as may be specified in statute or any related regulations; and

    (b) In the auditor's opinion there is reasonable cause to believe it is or may be of material significance to the regulator.

Definitions

9. For purposes of this Section of this ISA (UK and Ireland), the following terms have the meanings attributed below:

    (a) **The Act(s)**: means those Acts that give rise to a duty to report to a regulator. For example:

    In the United Kingdom, this includes the Financial Services and Markets Act 2000 and regulations made under that Act, and any future legislation including provisions relating to the duties of auditors similar to those contained in that statute.

In the Republic of Ireland, this includes the Central Bank Acts 1942 to 1989, the Building Societies Act 1989, The Central Bank and Financial Services Authority of Ireland Act, 2003, the Trustees Savings Bank Act 1989, the Insurance Act 1989, the European Communities (Undertakings for Collective Investment in Transferable Securities) Regulations 1989, the Unit Trusts Act 1990 and, in the case of investment companies, the Companies Act 1990 and any future legislation including provisions relating to the duties of auditors similar to those contained in those Acts, together with other regulations made under them.

(b) **Audit**: for the purpose of this Section of this ISA (UK and Ireland), the term *audit* refers both to an engagement to report on the financial statements of a regulated entity and to an engagement to provide a report on other matters specified by statute or by a regulator undertaken in the capacity of auditor.

(c) **Auditor**: the term 'auditor' should be interpreted in accordance with the requirements of the Acts. Guidance on its interpretation is contained in Practice Notes relating to each area of the financial sector to which the duty applies.

(d) **Material significance**: the term 'material significance' requires interpretation in the context of the specific legislation applicable to the regulated entity. A matter or group of matters is normally of material significance to a regulator's functions when, due either to its nature or its potential financial impact, it is likely of itself to require investigation by the regulator. Further guidance on the interpretation of the term in the context of specific legislation is contained in Practice Notes dealing with the rights and duties of auditors of regulated entities to report direct to regulators.

(e) **Regulated entity**: an individual, company or other type of entity authorised to carry on business in the financial sector which is subject to statutory regulation.

(f) **Regulator**: such persons as are empowered by the Act to regulate business in the financial sector. The term includes the Financial Services Authority (FSA), Irish Financial Services Regulatory Authority (IFSRA) and such other bodies as may be so empowered in future legislation.

(g) **'Tipping off'** involves a disclosure that is likely to prejudice any investigation into suspected money laundering which might arise from a report being made to a regulatory authority[1]. Money laundering involves an act which conceals, disguises, converts, transfers, removes, uses, acquires or possesses property which constitutes or represents a benefit from criminal conduct.

---

[1] More detail is provided in the definition contained in Section A of ISA (UK and Ireland) 250.

Requirements

Conduct of the Audit

Planning

10. When obtaining an understanding of the business for the purpose of the audit, the auditor of a regulated entity shall obtain an understanding of its current activities, the scope of its authorisation and the effectiveness of its control environment. (Ref: Para. A9-A16)

Supervision and Control

11. The auditor shall ensure that all staff involved in the audit of a regulated entity have an understanding of:

    (a) The provisions of applicable legislation;

    (b) The regulator's rules and any guidance issued by the regulator; and

    (c) Any specific requirements which apply to the particular regulated entity,

    appropriate to their role in the audit and sufficient (in the context of that role) to enable them to identify situations which may give reasonable cause to believe that a matter should be reported to the regulator. (Ref: Para. A17-A23)

Identifying Matters Requiring a Report Direct to Regulators

12. Where an apparent breach of statutory or regulatory requirements comes to the auditor's attention, the auditor shall:

    (a) Obtain such evidence as is available to assess its implications for the auditor's reporting responsibilities;

    (b) Determine whether, in the auditor's opinion, there is reasonable cause to believe that the breach is of material significance to the regulator; and

    (c) Consider whether the apparent breach is criminal conduct that gives rise to criminal property and, as such, should be reported to the specified authorities. (Ref: Para. A24-A30)

Reporting (Ref: Para. A31-A46)

The Auditor's Statutory Duty to Report Direct to Regulators

13. When the auditor concludes, after appropriate discussion and investigations, that a matter which has come to the auditor's attention gives rise to a statutory duty to make

a report the auditor shall[2] bring the matter to the attention of the regulator as soon as practicable in a form and manner which will facilitate appropriate action by the regulator. When the initial report is made orally, the auditor shall make a contemporaneous written record of the oral report and shall confirm the matter in writing to the regulator. (Ref: Para. A31-A35)

14. When the matter giving rise to a statutory duty to make a report direct to a regulator casts doubt on the integrity of those charged with governance or their competence to conduct the business of the regulated entity, the auditor shall[2] make the report to the regulator as soon as practicable and without informing those charged with governance in advance. (Ref: Para. A35)

The Auditor's Right to Report Direct to Regulators

15. When a matter comes to the auditor's attention which the auditor concludes does not give rise to a statutory duty to report but nevertheless may be relevant to the regulator's exercise of its functions, the auditor shall[2]:

    (a) Consider whether the matter should be brought to the attention of the regulator under the terms of the appropriate legal provisions enabling the auditor to report direct to the regulator; and, if so

    (b) Advise those charged with governance that in the auditor's opinion the matter should be drawn to the regulators' attention.

    Where the auditor is unable to obtain, within a reasonable period, adequate evidence that those charged with governance have properly informed the regulator of the matter, the auditor shall[2] make a report direct to the regulator as soon as practicable. (Ref: Para. A36-A37)

Contents of a Report Initiated by the Auditor

16. When making or confirming in writing a report direct to a regulator, the auditor shall:

    (a) State the name of the regulated entity concerned;

    (b) State the statutory power under which the report is made;

    (c) State that the report has been prepared in accordance with ISA (UK and Ireland) 250, Section B 'The Auditor's Right and Duty to Report to Regulators in the Financial Sector';

    (d) Describe the context in which the report is given;

    (e) Describe the matter giving rise to the report;

---

[2] In the UK, subject to compliance with legislation relating to 'tipping off'.

(f) Request the regulator to confirm that the report has been received; and

(g) State the name of the auditor, the date of the written report and, where appropriate, the date on which an oral report was made to the regulator and the name and title of the individual to whom the oral report was made. (Ref: Para. A38-A39)

Relationship With Other Reporting Responsibilities

17. When issuing a report expressing an opinion on a regulated entity's financial statements or on other matters specified by legislation or a regulator, the auditor:

(a) Shall consider whether there are consequential reporting issues affecting the auditor's opinion which arise from any report previously made direct to the regulator in the course of the auditor's appointment; and

(b) Shall assess whether any matters encountered in the course of the audit indicate a need for a further direct report. (Ref: Para. A40-A43)

***

Application and Other Explanatory Material

The Auditor's Responsibilities (Ref: Para. 2-6)

A1. Before accepting appointment, the auditor follows the procedures identified in the APB's Ethical Standards for Auditors and the ethical pronouncements and Audit Regulations issued by the auditor's relevant professional body.

A2. In the case of regulated entities, the auditor would in particular obtain an understanding of the appropriate statutory and regulatory requirements and a preliminary knowledge of the management and operations of the entity, so as to enable the auditor to determine whether a level of knowledge of the business adequate to perform the audit can be obtained. The procedures carried out by the auditor in seeking to obtain this preliminary understanding may include discussion with the previous auditor and, in some circumstances, with the regulator.

A3. On ceasing to hold office, the auditor may be required by statute or by regulation to make specific reports concerning the circumstances relating to that event, and would also follow the procedures identified in the ethical guidance issued by the relevant professional body.

A4. In addition, the auditor of a regulated entity would assess whether it is appropriate to bring any matters of which the auditor is then aware to the notice of the regulator. Under legislation in the UK, this may be done either before or after ceasing to hold office, as the auditor's statutory right to disclose to a regulator information obtained in the course of the auditor's appointment is not affected by the auditor's removal, resignation or otherwise ceasing to hold office.

A5.   The duty to make a report direct to a regulator does not impose upon the auditor a duty to carry out specific work: it arises solely in the context of work carried out to fulfil other reporting responsibilities. Accordingly, no auditing procedures in addition to those carried out in the normal course of auditing the financial statements, or for the purpose of making any other specified report, are necessary for the fulfilment of the auditor's responsibilities.

A6.   It will, however, be necessary for the auditor to take additional time in carrying out a financial statement audit or other engagement to assess whether matters which come to the auditor's attention should be included in a direct report and, where appropriate, to prepare and submit the report. These additional planning and follow-up procedures do not constitute an extension of the scope of the financial statement audit or of other work undertaken to provide a specified report relating to a regulated entity. They are necessary solely in order to understand and clarify the reporting responsibility and, where appropriate, to make a report.

A7.   The circumstances in which the auditor is required by statute to make a report direct to a regulator include matters which are not considered as part of the audit of financial statements or of work undertaken to discharge other routine responsibilities. For example, the duty to report would apply to information of which the auditor became aware in the course of the auditor's work which is relevant to the FSA's criteria for approved persons, although the auditor is not otherwise required to express an opinion on such matters. However, the legislation imposing a duty to make reports direct to regulators does not require the auditor to change the scope of the audit work, nor does it place on the auditor an obligation to conduct the audit work in such a way that there is reasonable certainty that the auditor will discover all matters which regulators might consider as being of material significance. Therefore, whilst the auditor of a regulated entity is required to be alert to matters which may require a report, the auditor is not expected to be aware of all circumstances which, had the auditor known of them, would have led the auditor to make such a report. It is only when the auditor becomes aware of such a matter during the conduct of the normal audit work that the auditor has an obligation to determine whether a report to the regulator is required by statute or appropriate for other reasons.

A8.   Similarly, the auditor is not responsible for reporting on a regulated entity's overall compliance with rules with which it is required to comply nor is the auditor required to conduct the audit work in such a way that there is reasonable certainty that the auditor will discover breaches. Nevertheless, breaches of rules with which a regulated entity is required to comply may have implications for the financial statements and, accordingly, the auditor of a regulated entity needs to consider whether any actual or contingent liabilities may have arisen from breaches of regulatory requirements. Breaches of a regulator's requirements may also have consequences for other matters on which the auditor of a regulated entity is required to express an opinion and, if such breaches represent criminal conduct, could give rise to the need to report to specified authorities.

Conduct of the Audit

Planning (Ref: Para. 10)

A9. ISAs (UK and Ireland) require the auditor to obtain an understanding of the entity and its environment[3].

A10. In the context of a regulated entity, the auditor's understanding of its business needs to extend to the applicable statutory provisions, the rules of the regulator concerned and any guidance issued by the regulator on the interpretation of those rules, together with other guidance issued by the APB.

A11. The auditor is also required to identify and assess the risks of material misstatements to provide a basis for designing and performing further audit procedures[4]. In making such an assessment the auditor takes into account the control environment, including the entity's higher level procedures for complying with the requirements of its regulator. Such a review gives an indication of the extent to which the general atmosphere and controls in the regulated entity are conducive to compliance, for example through consideration of *inter alia:*

- The adequacy of procedures and training to inform staff of the requirements of relevant legislation and the rules or other regulations of the regulator;

- The adequacy of procedures for authorisation of transactions;

- Procedures for internal review of the entity's compliance with regulatory or other requirements;

- The authority of, and any resources available to, the compliance officer/Money Laundering Reporting Officer ('MLRO'); and

- Procedures to ensure that possible breaches of requirements are investigated by an appropriate person and are brought to the attention of senior management.

A12. In some areas of the financial sector, conducting business outside the scope of the entity's authorisation is a serious regulatory breach, and therefore of material significance to the regulator. In addition, it may result in fines, suspension or loss of authorisation.

A13. Where the auditor's review of the reporting entity's activities indicates that published guidance by the regulator may not be sufficiently precise to enable the auditor to identify circumstances in which it is necessary to initiate a report, the auditor would consider whether it is necessary to discuss the matters specified in legislation with the appropriate regulator with a view to reaching agreement on its interpretation.

---

[3] ISA (UK and Ireland) 315, "Identifying and Assessing the Risks of Material Misstatement through Understanding the Entity and Its Environment," paragraph 11.

[4] ISA (UK and Ireland) 315, paragraph 25.

A14. Similarly, where a group includes two or more companies separately regulated by different regulators, there may be a need to clarify the regulators' requirements in any overlapping areas of activity. However, the statutory duty to make a report as presently defined arises only in respect of the legal entity subject to regulation. Therefore the auditor of an unregulated company in a group that includes one or more other companies which are authorised by regulators would not have a duty to report matters to the regulators of those companies.

A15. When a regulated entity is subject to provisions of two or more regulators, the auditor needs to take account of the separate reporting requirements in planning and conducting the audit work. Arrangements may exist for one regulatory body to rely on financial monitoring being carried out by another body (the 'lead regulator') and where this is the case, routine reports by the regulated entity's auditor may be made to the lead regulator alone.

A16. However, the auditor's statutory duty to report cannot be discharged by reliance on the lead regulator informing others. Therefore, where the auditor concludes that a matter is of material significance to one regulator, the auditor needs to assess the need for separate reports informing each regulator of matters which the auditor concludes are or may be of material significance to it.

Supervision and Control (Ref: Para. 11)

A17. ISAs (UK and Ireland) require the engagement partner to take responsibility for the direction, supervision and performance of the audit engagement in compliance with professional standards and applicable legal and regulatory requirements[5]. Consequently, in planning and conducting the audit of a regulated entity the auditor needs to ensure that staff are alert to the possibility that a report to its regulator may be required.

A18. Auditing firms also need to establish adequate procedures to ensure that any matters which are discovered in the course of or as a result of audit work and may give rise to a duty to report are brought to the attention of the partner responsible for the audit on a timely basis.

A19. The right and duty to report to a regulator applies to information of which the auditor becomes aware in the auditor's capacity as such. They do not extend automatically to any information obtained by an accounting firm regardless of its source. Consequently partners and staff undertaking work in another capacity are not required to have detailed knowledge of the regulator's requirements (unless necessary for that other work) nor to bring information to the attention of the partner responsible for the audit on a routine basis.

A20. However, as discussed further in Appendix 2, firms need to establish lines of communications, commensurate with their size and complexity, sufficient to ensure that non-audit work undertaken for a regulated entity which is likely to have an effect

---

[5] ISA (UK and Ireland) 220, "Quality Control for an Audit of Financial Statements," paragraph 15.

on the audit is brought to the attention of the partner responsible for the audit, who will need to determine whether the results of non-audit work undertaken for a regulated entity ought to be assessed as part of the audit process.

Reliance on Other Auditors

A21. An auditor with responsibilities for reporting on financial statements including financial information of one or more components audited by other auditors is required to obtain sufficient appropriate audit evidence that the work of the other auditors is adequate for the purposes of the audit. The same principle applies to reliance on another auditor in a different type of engagement. The auditor of a regulated entity who relies on work undertaken by other auditors needs to establish reporting arrangements such that the other auditors bring to the attention of the auditor of the regulated entity matters arising from their work which may give rise to a duty to report to a regulator.

A22. The nature of the reporting arrangements will depend on the nature of the work undertaken by the other auditors. For example, the statutory duty to make a report relates to the legal entity subject to regulation rather than to the entire group to which that entity may belong. Consequently, the auditor of a holding company authorised by one regulator would not be expected to have knowledge of all matters which come to the attention of a subsidiary's auditor. The auditor of the regulated entity would, however, have a duty to report, where appropriate, matters which arise from the audit of the regulated entity's own financial statements and of the consolidated group figures.

A23. Where the audit of a regulated entity is undertaken by joint auditors, knowledge obtained by one auditing firm is likely to be deemed to be known by the other. Care will therefore be needed in agreeing and implementing arrangements to exchange information relating to matters which may give rise to a duty to report to a regulator.

Identifying Matters Requiring a Report Direct to Regulators (Ref: Para. 12)

A24. The precise matters which give rise to a statutory duty on auditors to make a report to a regulator derive from the relevant Acts. Broadly, such matters fall into three general categories:

(a) The financial position of the regulated entity;

(b) Its compliance with requirements for the management of its business; and

(c) The status of those charged with governance as fit and proper persons.

Further detailed guidance on the interpretation of these matters in the context of specific legislation applicable to each type of regulated entity is contained in Practice Notes dealing with the rights and duties of auditors of regulated entities to report direct to regulators.

A25. In assessing the effect of an apparent breach, the auditor takes into account the quantity and type of evidence concerning such a matter which may reasonably be expected to be available. If the auditor concludes that the auditor has been prevented from obtaining all such evidence concerning a matter which may give rise to a duty to report, the auditor would normally make a report direct to the regulator as soon as practicable.

A26. An apparent breach of statutory or regulatory requirements may not of itself give rise to a statutory duty to make a report to a regulator. There will normally be a need for some further investigation and discussion of the circumstances surrounding the apparent breach with the directors in order to obtain sufficient information to determine whether it points to a matter which is or may be of material significance to the regulator. For example, a minor breach which has been corrected by the regulated entity and reported (if appropriate) to the regulator, and which from the evidence available to the auditor appears to be an isolated occurrence, would not normally give the auditor reasonable cause to believe that it is or may be of material significance to the regulator. However a minor breach that results in a criminal offence that gave rise to the criminal property would be reportable to the specified authorities under the anti-money laundering legislation.

A27. When determining whether a breach of statutory or regulatory requirements gives rise to a statutory duty to make a report direct to a regulator, the auditor considers factors such as:

- Whether the breach, though minor, is indicative of a general lack of compliance with the regulator's requirements or otherwise casts doubt on the status of those charged with governance as fit and proper persons;

- Whether a breach which occurred before the auditor's visit to the regulated entity was reported by the entity itself and has since been corrected, such that, at the date of the auditor's discovery, no breach exists;

- Whether the circumstances giving rise to a breach which occurred before the auditors visit to the regulated entity continue to exist, or those charged with governance have not taken corrective action, or the breach has re-occurred; and

- Whether the circumstances suggest that an immediate report to the regulator is necessary in order to protect the interests of depositors, investors, policyholders, clients of the entity or others in whose interests the regulator is required to act.

A28. The auditor would normally seek evidence to assess the implications of a suspected breach before reporting a matter to the regulator. However, the auditor's responsibility to make a report does not require the auditor to determine the full implications of a matter before reporting: the auditor is required to exercise professional judgment as to whether or not there is reasonable cause to believe that a matter is or may be of material significance to the regulator. In forming that judgment, the auditor undertakes appropriate investigations to determine the circumstances but does not require the degree of evidence which would be a normal part of forming an opinion on financial statements. Such investigations would normally include:

- Enquiry of appropriate level of staff;

- Review of correspondence and documents relating to the transaction or event concerned; and

- Discussion with those charged with governance, or other senior management where appropriate.

In the case of a life company, it would also be appropriate to consult with the appointed actuary, who also has various statutory duties under insurance companies legislation.

A29. The potential gravity of some apparent breaches may be such that an immediate report to the regulator is essential in order to enable the regulator to take appropriate action: in particular, prompt reporting of a loss of client assets may be necessary to avoid further loss to investors or others in whose interests the regulator is required to act. The auditor is therefore required to balance the need for further investigation of the matter with the need for prompt reporting.

A30. On completion of the auditor's investigations, the auditor needs to ensure that the facts and the basis for the auditor's decision (whether to report or not) is adequately documented such that the reasons for that decision may be clearly demonstrated should the need to do so arise in future.

Reporting

The Auditor's Statutory Duty to Report Direct to Regulators (Ref: Para. 13-14)

A31. Except in the circumstances referred to in paragraph 14 the auditor seeks to reach agreement with those charged with governance on the circumstances giving rise to a report direct to the regulator. However, where a statutory duty to report arises, the auditor is required to make such a report regardless of:

(a) Whether the matter has been referred to the regulator by other parties (including the company, whether by those charged with governance or otherwise); and

(b) Any duty owed to other parties, including those charged with governance of the regulated entity and its shareholders (or equivalent persons).

A32. Except in the circumstances set out in paragraph 14, the auditor sends a copy of the auditor's written report to those charged with governance and (where appropriate) audit committee of the regulated entity.

A33. In normal circumstances, the auditor would wish to communicate with the regulator with the knowledge and agreement of those charged with governance of the regulated entity. However, in some circumstances immediate notification of the discovery of a matter giving reasonable grounds to believe that a reportable matter exists will be necessary - for example, a phone call to alert the regulator followed by a meeting to discuss the circumstances.

A34. Speed of reporting is essential where the circumstances cause the auditor no longer to have confidence in the integrity of those charged with governance. In such circumstances, there may be a serious and immediate threat to the interests of depositors or other persons for whose protection the regulator is required to act; for example where the auditor believes that a fraud or other irregularity may have been committed by, or with the knowledge of, those charged with governance, or have evidence of the intention of those charged with governance to commit or condone a suspected fraud or other irregularity.

A35. In circumstances where the auditor no longer has confidence in the integrity of those charged with governance, it is not appropriate to provide those charged with governance with copies of the auditor's report. Since such circumstances will be exceptional and extreme, the auditor may wish to seek legal advice as to the auditor's responsibilities and the appropriate course of action.

The Auditor's Right to Report Direct to Regulators (Ref: Para. 15)

A36. The auditor may become aware of matters which the auditor concludes are relevant to the exercise of the regulator's functions even though they fall outside the statutory definition of matters which must be reported to a regulator. In such circumstances, the Acts in the UK provide the auditor with protection for making disclosure of the matter to the appropriate regulator[6].

A37. Where the auditor considers that a matter which does not give rise to a statutory duty to report is nevertheless, in the auditor's professional judgment, such that it should be brought to the attention of the regulator, it is normally appropriate for the auditor to request those charged with governance of the regulated entity in writing to draw it to the attention of the regulator.

Contents of a Report Initiated by the Auditor (Ref: Para. 16)

A38. Such a report is a by-product of other work undertaken by the auditor. As a result it is not possible for the auditor or the regulator to conclude that all matters relevant to the regulator were encountered in the course of the auditor's work. The auditor's report therefore sets out the context in which the information reported was identified and indicates the extent to which the matter has been investigated and discussed with those charged with governance.

A39. Matters to which the auditor may wish to refer when describing the context in which a report is made direct to a regulator include:

---

[6] There is no statutory provision of protection for a voluntary report under the Acts in the Republic of Ireland.

- The nature of the appointment from which the report derives. For example, it may be appropriate to distinguish between a report made in the course of an audit of financial statements and one which arises in the course of a more limited engagement, such as an appointment to report on specified matters by the FSA or IFSRA;

- The applicable legislative requirements and interpretations of those requirements which have informed the auditor's judgment;

- The extent to which the auditor has investigated the circumstances giving rise to the matter reported;

- Whether the matter reported has been discussed with those charged with governance;

- Whether steps to rectify the matter have been taken.

Relationship With Other Reporting Responsibilities (Ref: Para. 17)

A40. The circumstances which give rise to a report direct to a regulator may involve an uncertainty or other matter which requires disclosure in the financial statements. The auditor will therefore need to consider whether the disclosures made in the financial statements are adequate for the purposes of giving a true and fair view of the regulated entity's state of affairs and profit or loss. Where the auditor considers it necessary to draw users' attention to a matter presented or disclosed in the financial statements that, in the auditor's judgment, is of such importance that it is fundamental to users' understanding of the financial statements, the auditor is required to include an emphasis of matter paragraph in the auditor's report[7].

A41. Similarly, circumstances giving rise to a report direct to a regulator may also require reflection in the auditor's reports on other matters required by legislation or another regulator.

A42. In fulfilling the responsibility to report direct to a regulator, it is important that the auditor not only assess the significance of individual transactions or events but also consider whether a combination of such items over the course of the work undertaken for the auditor's primary reporting responsibilities may give the auditor reasonable grounds to believe that they constitute a matter of material significance to the regulator, and so give rise to a statutory duty to make a report.

A43. As there is no requirement for the auditor to extend the scope of the audit work to search for matters which may give rise to a statutory duty to report, such an assessment of the cumulative effect of evidence obtained in the course of an audit would be made when reviewing the evidence in support of the opinions to be expressed in the reports the auditor has been appointed to make. Where such a

---

[7] ISA (UK and Ireland) 706 "Emphasis of Matter Paragraphs and Other Matter Paragraphs in the Independent Auditor's Report," paragraph 6.

review leads to the conclusion that the cumulative effect of matters noted in the course of the audit is of material significance to the regulator, it will be appropriate for a report to be made as set out in paragraph 16 above. However, reports indicating a 'nil return' are not appropriate.

Communication of Information by the Regulator

A44. The Acts provide that, in certain exceptional circumstances, regulators may pass confidential information to another party. The precise circumstances in which regulators may disclose information varies, but in general they may do so if considered necessary to fulfil their own obligations under the appropriate Act, or, in some cases, to enable the auditor to fulfil the auditor's duties either to the regulated entity or, in other cases, to the regulator. Confidential information remains confidential in the hands of the recipient.

A45. In so far as the law permits, regulators have confirmed that they will consider taking the initiative in bringing a matter to the attention of the auditor of a regulated entity in circumstances where:

(a) They believe the matter is of such importance that the auditor's knowledge of it could significantly affect the form of the auditor's report on the entity's financial statements or other matters on which the auditor is required to report, or the way in which the auditor discharges the auditor's reporting responsibilities; and

(b) The disclosure is for the purpose of enabling or assisting the regulator to discharge its functions under the Acts.

A46. The auditor needs to be aware that there may be circumstances in which the regulators are unable to disclose such information. Where the auditor of a regulated entity is not informed by the regulator of any matter, therefore, the auditor cannot assume that there are no matters known to the regulator which could affect the auditor's judgment as to whether information is of material significance. However, in the absence of disclosure by the regulator, the auditor can only form a judgment in the light of evidence to which the auditor has access.

Appendix 1

The Regulatory Framework

1. In both the UK and Ireland, legislation exists in the principal areas of financial services to protect the interests of investors, depositors in banks and other users of financial services. Regulated entities operating in the financial sector are required to comply with legal and regulatory requirements concerning the way their business is conducted. Compliance with those rules is monitored in four principal ways:

    *   Internal monitoring by those charged with governance of the regulated entity;

    *   Submission of regular returns by the regulated entity to the regulator;

    *   Monitoring and, in some cases, inspection of the entity by the regulator;

    *   Reports[2] by the reporting entity's auditor on its financial statements and other specified matters required by legislation or by the regulator.

Responsibility for Ensuring Compliance

2. Ensuring compliance with the requirements with which a regulated entity is required to comply in carrying out its business is the responsibility of those charged with governance of a regulated entity. It requires adequate organisation and systems of controls. The regulatory framework provides that adequate procedures for compliance must be established and maintained. Those charged with governance of a regulated entity are also normally required to undertake regular reviews of compliance and to inform the regulator of any breach of the rules and regulations applicable to its regulated business. In addition, regulators may undertake compliance visits.

3. The auditor of a regulated entity normally has responsibilities for reporting[2] on particular aspects of its compliance with the regulator's requirements. However, the auditor has no direct responsibility for expressing an opinion on an entity's overall compliance with the requirements for the conduct of its business, nor does an audit provide any assurance that breaches of requirements which are not the subject of regular auditors' reports will be detected.

The Role of Auditors

4. Those charged with governance of regulated entities have primary responsibility for ensuring that all appropriate information is made available to regulators. Normal reporting procedures (including auditor's reports on records, systems and returns, and regular meetings with those charged with governance and/or management and auditors) supplemented by any inspection visits considered necessary by the regulators should provide the regulators with all the information they need to carry out their responsibilities under the relevant Act.

Routine Reporting by Auditors

5. Regulators' requirements for reports by auditors vary. In general terms, however, such reports may include opinions on:

    - The regulated entity's annual financial statements;

    - The regulated entity's compliance with requirements for financial resources; and

    - The adequacy of the regulated entity's system of controls over its transactions and in particular over its clients' money and other property.

6. As a result of performing the work necessary to discharge their routine reporting responsibilities, or those arising from an appointment to provide a special report required by the regulator, the auditor of a regulated entity may become aware of matters which the auditor considers need to be brought to the regulator's attention sooner than would be achieved by routine reports by the entity or its auditor.

7. The auditor of a regulated entity normally has a right to communicate in good faith[2] information the auditor considers is relevant to the regulators' functions.

The Auditor's Statutory Duty to Report to the Regulator

8. In addition, the auditor is required by law to report[2] direct to a regulator when the auditor concludes that there is reasonable cause to believe that a matter is or may be of material significance to the regulator. The precise matters which result in a statutory duty to make such a report vary, depending upon the specific requirements of relevant legislation and the regulator's rules. In general, however, a duty to report to a regulator arises when the auditor becomes aware that:

    - The regulated entity is in serious breach of:

        ○ Requirements to maintain adequate financial resources; or

        ○ Requirements for those charged with governance to conduct its business in a sound and prudent manner (including the maintenance of systems of control over transactions and over any clients' assets held by the business); or

    - There are circumstances which give reason to doubt the status of those charged with governance or senior management as fit and proper persons.

Confidentiality

9. Confidentiality is an implied term of the auditor's contracts with client entities. However[2] in the circumstances leading to a right or duty to report, the auditor is entitled to communicate to regulators in good faith information or opinions relating to the business or affairs of the entity or any associated body without contravening the duty of confidence owed to the entity and, in the case of a bank, building society and friendly society, its associated bodies.

10. The statutory provisions permitting the auditor to communicate information to regulators relate to information obtained in the auditor's capacity as auditor of the regulated entity concerned. Auditors and regulators therefore should be aware that confidential information obtained in other capacities may not normally be disclosed to another party.

Appendix 2

The Application of the Statutory Duty to Report to Regulators

Introduction

1. The statutory duty to report to a regulator[2] applies to information which comes to the attention of the auditor in the auditor's capacity as auditor. However, neither the term 'auditor' nor the phrase "in the capacity of auditor" are defined in the legislation, nor has the court determined how these expressions should be construed.

2. As a result, it is not always clearly apparent when an accounting firm should regard itself as having a duty to report to a regulator. For example, information about a regulated entity may be obtained when partners or staff of the firm which is appointed as its auditor carry out work for another client entity; or when the firm undertakes other work for the regulated entity. Auditors, regulated entities and regulators need to be clear as to when the normal duty of confidentiality will be overridden by the auditor's statutory duty to report to the regulator.

3. In order to clarify whether or not an accounting firm should regard itself as bound by the duty, the APB has developed, in conjunction with HM Treasury, the IFSRA and the regulators, guidance on the interpretation of the key conditions for the existence of that duty, namely that the firm is to be regarded as auditor of a regulated entity and that information is obtained in the capacity of auditor.

4. Guidance on the interpretation of the term 'auditor' in the context of each Act is contained in the separate Practice Notes dealing with each area affected by the legislation.

5. This appendix sets out guidance on the interpretation of the phrase "in the capacity of auditor". The Board nevertheless continues to hold the view that the meaning of the phrase should be clarified in legislation in the longer term.

In the Capacity of Auditor

6. In determining whether information is obtained in the capacity of auditor, two criteria in particular should be considered:

   (a) Whether the person who obtained the information also undertook the audit work; and if so

   (b) Whether it was obtained in the course of or as a result of undertaking the audit work,

7. It is then necessary to apply these criteria to information about a regulated entity which may become known from a number of sources, and by a number of different individuals within an accounting firm. Within a large firm, for example, information may come to the attention of the partner responsible for the audit of a regulated entity, a partner in another office who undertakes a different type of work, or members of the

firm's staff at any level. In the case of a sole practitioner who is the auditor of a regulated entity, information about a regulated entity may also be obtained by the practitioner in the course of work other than its audit.

Non-Audit Work Carried out in Relation to a Regulated Entity

8. Where partners or staff involved in the audit of a regulated entity carry out work other than its audit (non-audit work) information about the regulated entity will be known to them as individuals. In circumstances which suggest that a matter would otherwise give rise to a statutory duty to report[2] if obtained in the capacity of auditor, it will be prudent for them to make enquiries in the course of their audit work in order to establish whether this is the case from information obtained in that capacity.

9. However where non-audit work is carried out by other partners or staff, neither of the criteria set out in paragraph 6 is met in respect of information which becomes known to them. Nevertheless the firm should take proper account of such information when it could affect the audit so that it is treated in a responsible manner, particularly since in partnership law the knowledge obtained by one partner in the course of the partnership business may be imputed to the entire partnership. In doing so, two types of work may be distinguished: first, work which could affect the firm's work as auditor and, secondly, work which is undertaken purely in an advisory capacity.

10. A firm appointed as auditor of a regulated entity needs to have in place appropriate procedures to ensure that the partner responsible for the audit function is made aware of any other relationship which exists between any department of the firm and the regulated entity when that relationship could affect the firm's work as auditor. Common examples of such work include accounting work, particularly for smaller entities, and provision of tax services to the regulated entity.

11. *Prima facie*, information obtained in the course of non-audit work is not covered by either the right or the duty to report to a regulator. However, the firm appointed as auditor needs to consider whether the results of other work undertaken for a regulated entity need to be assessed as part of the audit process. In principle, this is no different to seeking to review a report prepared by outside consultants on, say, the entity's accounting systems so as to ensure that the auditor makes a proper assessment of the risks of misstatement in the financial statements and of the work needed to form an opinion. Consequently, the partner responsible for the audit needs to make appropriate enquiries in the process of planning and completing the audit (see paragraph 17 above). Such enquiries would be directed to those aspects of the non-audit work which might reasonably be expected to be relevant to the audit. When, as a result of such enquiries, those involved in the audit become aware of issues which may be of material significance to a regulator such issues should be considered, and if appropriate reported[2] following the requirements set out in this Section of this ISA (UK and Ireland).

12. Work which is undertaken in an advisory capacity, for example to assist the directors of a regulated entity to determine effective and efficient methods of discharging their duties, would not normally affect the work undertaken for the audit. Nevertheless, in rare instances, the partner responsible for such advisory work may conclude that

steps considered necessary in order to comply with the regulator's requirements have not been taken by the directors or that the directors intend in some respect not to comply with the regulator's requirements. Such circumstances would require consideration in the course of work undertaken for the audit, both to consider the effect on the auditor's routine reports and to determine whether the possible non-compliance is or is likely to be of material significance to the regulator.

Work Relating to a Separate Entity

13. Information obtained in the course of work relating to another entity audited by the same firm (or the same practitioner) is confidential to that other entity. The auditor is not required, and has no right, to report to a regulator confidential information which arises from work undertaken by the same auditing firm for another client. However, as a matter of sound practice, individuals involved in the audit of a regulated entity who become aware (in a capacity other than that of auditor of a regulated entity) of a matter which could otherwise give rise to a statutory duty to report would normally make enquiries in the course of their audit of the regulated entity to establish whether the information concerned is substantiated.

14. In carrying out the audit work, the auditor is required to have due regard to whether disclosure of non-compliance with laws and regulations to a proper authority is appropriate in the public interest. standards and guidance on this general professional obligation is set out in Section A of this ISA (UK and Ireland).

Conclusion

15. The phrase "in his capacity as auditor" limits information subject to the duty to report to matters of which the auditor becomes aware in the auditor's capacity as such. Consequently, it is unlikely that a partnership can be said to be acting in its capacity as auditor of a particular regulated entity whenever any apparently unrelated material comes to the attention of a partner or member of staff not engaged in that audit, particularly if that material is confidential to another client.

16. The statutory duty to report to a regulator[2] therefore does not extend automatically to any information obtained by an accounting firm regardless of its source. Accounting firms undertaking audits of regulated entities need, however, to establish lines of communication, commensurate with their size and organisational structure, sufficient to ensure that non-audit work undertaken for a regulated entity which is likely to have an effect on the audit is brought to the attention of the partner responsible for the audit and to establish procedures for the partner responsible for the audit to make appropriate enquiries of those conducting such other work as part of the process of planning and completing the audit.

Appendix 3

Action by the Auditor on Discovery of a Breach of a Regulator's Requirements

1.   This appendix sets out in the form of a flowchart the steps involved in assessing whether a report to a regulator is required when a breach of the regulator's requirements comes to the attention of the auditor.

2.   The flowchart is intended to provide guidance to readers in understanding this Section of this ISA (UK and Ireland). It does not form part of the auditing standards contained in the ISA (UK and Ireland).

Action by the Auditor on Discovery of a Breach of a Regulator's Requirement

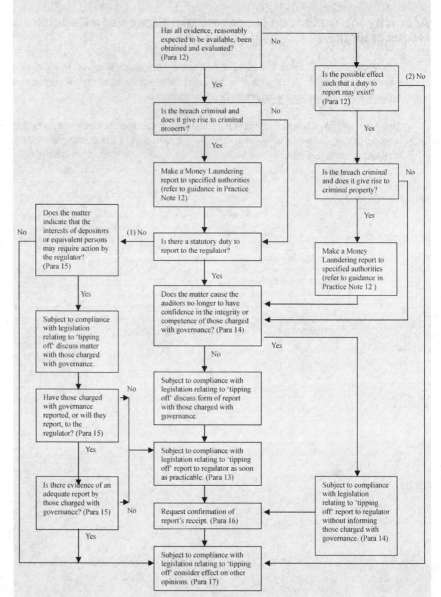

(1) This route would be only followed when a distinct right to report to the regulator exists. Otherwise, where no duty to report exists, the auditor would next consider the effect on other opinions.

(2) Where the auditor considers that a distinct right to report to the regulator exists, the auditor would next consider the question marked (1).

INTERNATIONAL STANDARD ON AUDITING (UK AND IRELAND) 260 (REVISED SEPTEMBER 2014)

COMMUNICATION WITH THOSE CHARGED WITH GOVERNANCE

(Effective for audits of financial statements for periods commencing on or after 1 October 2014)

CONTENTS

International Standard on Auditing (UK and Ireland) (ISA (UK and Ireland)) 260, "Communication with Those Charged with Governance" should be read in conjunction with ISA (UK and Ireland) 200, "Overall Objectives of the Independent Auditor and the Conduct of an Audit in Accordance with International Standards on Auditing (UK and Ireland)."

Introduction

Scope of this ISA (UK and Ireland)

1. This International Standard on Auditing (UK and Ireland) (ISA (UK and Ireland)) deals with the auditor's responsibility to communicate with those charged with governance in an audit of financial statements. Although this ISA (UK and Ireland) applies irrespective of an entity's governance structure or size, particular considerations apply where all of those charged with governance are involved in managing an entity, and for listed entities. This ISA (UK and Ireland) does not establish requirements regarding the auditor's communication with an entity's management or owners unless they are also charged with a governance role.

2. This ISA (UK and Ireland) is written in the context of an audit of financial statements, but may also be applicable, adapted as necessary in the circumstances, to audits of other historical financial information when those charged with governance have a responsibility to oversee the preparation of the other historical financial information.

3. Recognizing the importance of effective two-way communication in an audit of financial statements, this ISA (UK and Ireland) provides an overarching framework for the auditor's communication with those charged with governance, and identifies some specific matters to be communicated with them. Additional matters to be communicated, which complement the requirements of this ISA (UK and Ireland), are identified in other ISAs (UK and Ireland) (see Appendix 1). In addition, ISA (UK and Ireland) 265[1] establishes specific requirements regarding the communication of significant deficiencies in internal control the auditor has identified during the audit to those charged with governance. Further matters, not required by this or other ISAs (UK and Ireland), may be required to be communicated by law or regulation, by agreement with the entity, or by additional requirements applicable to the engagement, for example, the standards of a national professional accountancy body. Nothing in this ISA (UK and Ireland) precludes the auditor from communicating any other matters to those charged with governance. (Ref: Para. A24-A27)

The Role of Communication

4. This ISA (UK and Ireland) focuses primarily on communications from the auditor to those charged with governance. Nevertheless, effective two-way communication is important in assisting:

    (a) The auditor and those charged with governance in understanding matters related to the audit in context, and in developing a constructive working relationship. This relationship is developed while maintaining the auditor's independence and objectivity;

---

[1] ISA (UK and Ireland) 265, "Communicating Deficiencies in Internal Control to Those Charged with Governance and Management."

(b)   The auditor in obtaining from those charged with governance information relevant to the audit[1a]. For example, those charged with governance may assist the auditor in understanding the entity and its environment, in identifying appropriate sources of audit evidence, and in providing information about specific transactions or events; and

(c)   Those charged with governance in fulfilling their responsibility to oversee the financial reporting process, thereby reducing the risks of material misstatement of the financial statements.

5.   Although the auditor is responsible for communicating matters required by this ISA (UK and Ireland), management also has a responsibility to communicate matters of governance interest to those charged with governance. Communication by the auditor does not relieve management of this responsibility. Similarly, communication by management with those charged with governance of matters that the auditor is required to communicate does not relieve the auditor of the responsibility to also communicate them. Communication of these matters by management may, however, affect the form or timing of the auditor's communication with those charged with governance.

6.   Clear communication of specific matters required to be communicated by ISAs (UK and Ireland) is an integral part of every audit. ISAs (UK and Ireland) do not, however, require the auditor to perform procedures specifically to identify any other matters to communicate with those charged with governance.

7.   Law or regulation may restrict the auditor's communication of certain matters with those charged with governance. For example, laws or regulations may specifically prohibit a communication, or other action, that might prejudice an investigation by an appropriate authority into an actual, or suspected, illegal act. In some circumstances, potential conflicts between the auditor's obligations of confidentiality and obligations to communicate may be complex. In such cases, the auditor may consider obtaining legal advice.

Effective Date

8.   This ISA (UK and Ireland) is effective for audits of financial statements for periods commencing on or after 1 October 2014.

Objectives

9.   The objectives of the auditor are:

[1a] Sections 499 and 500 of the Companies Act 2006 set legal requirements in relation to the auditor's right to obtain information. For the Republic of Ireland, relevant requirements are set out in Sections 193(3) and 196, Companies Act 1990.

(a)   To communicate clearly with those charged with governance the responsibilities of the auditor in relation to the financial statement audit, and an overview of the planned scope and timing of the audit;

(b)   To obtain from those charged with governance information relevant to the audit;

(c)   To provide those charged with governance with timely observations arising from the audit that are significant and relevant to their responsibility to oversee the financial reporting process; and

(d)   To promote effective two-way communication between the auditor and those charged with governance.

Definitions

10.   For purposes of the ISAs (UK and Ireland), the following terms have the meanings attributed below:

(a)   Those charged with governance – The person(s) or organization(s) (for example, a corporate trustee) with responsibility for overseeing the strategic direction of the entity and obligations related to the accountability of the entity. This includes overseeing the financial reporting process. For some entities in some jurisdictions, those charged with governance may include management personnel, for example, executive members of a governance board of a private or public sector entity, or an owner-manager.For discussion of the diversity of governance structures, see paragraphs A1-A8.

In the UK and Ireland, those charged with governance include the directors (executive and non-executive) of a company and the members of an audit committee where one exists. For other types of entity it usually includes equivalent persons such as the partners, proprietors, committee of management or trustees.

(b)   Management – The person(s) with executive responsibility for the conduct of the entity's operations. For some entities in some jurisdictions, management includes some or all of those charged with governance, for example, executive members of a governance board, or an owner-manager.

In the UK and Ireland, management will not normally include non-executive directors.

Requirements

Those Charged with Governance

11.   The auditor shall determine the appropriate person(s) within the entity's governance structure with whom to communicate. (Ref: Para. A1-A4)

Communication with a Subgroup of Those Charged with Governance

12. If the auditor communicates with a subgroup of those charged with governance, for example, an audit committee, or an individual, the auditor shall determine whether the auditor also needs to communicate with the governing body. (Ref: Para. A5-A7)

When All of Those Charged with Governance Are Involved in Managing the Entity

13. In some cases, all of those charged with governance are involved in managing the entity, for example, a small business where a single owner manages the entity and no one else has a governance role. In these cases, if matters required by this ISA (UK and Ireland) are communicated with person(s) with management responsibilities, and those person(s) also have governance responsibilities, the matters need not be communicated again with those same person(s) in their governance role. These matters are noted in paragraph 16(c). The auditor shall nonetheless be satisfied that communication with person(s) with management responsibilities adequately informs all of those with whom the auditor would otherwise communicate in their governance capacity. (Ref: Para. A8)

Matters to Be Communicated

The Auditor's Responsibilities in Relation to the Financial Statement Audit

14. The auditor shall communicate with those charged with governance the responsibilities of the auditor in relation to the financial statement audit, including that:

(a) The auditor is responsible for forming and expressing an opinion on the financial statements that have been prepared by management[1b] with the oversight of those charged with governance; and

(b) The audit of the financial statements does not relieve management or those charged with governance of their responsibilities. (Ref: Para. A9-A10)

Planned Scope and Timing of the Audit

15. The auditor shall communicate with those charged with governance an overview of the planned scope and timing of the audit. (Ref: Para. A11-A15)

Significant Findings from the Audit

16. The auditor shall communicate with those charged with governance: (Ref: Para. A16)

(a) The auditor's views about significant qualitative aspects of the entity's accounting practices, including accounting policies, accounting estimates and

---

[1b] In the UK and Ireland those charged with governance are responsible for the preparation of the financial statements.

financial statement disclosures. When applicable, the auditor shall explain to those charged with governance why the auditor considers a significant accounting practice, that is acceptable under the applicable financial reporting framework, not to be most appropriate to the particular circumstances of the entity; (Ref: Para. A17)

(b) Significant difficulties, if any, encountered during the audit; (Ref: Para. A18)

(c) Unless all of those charged with governance are involved in managing the entity:

    (i) Significant matters, if any, arising from the audit that were discussed, or subject to correspondence with management; and (Ref: Para. A19)

    (ii) Written representations the auditor is requesting; and

(d) Other matters, if any, arising from the audit that, in the auditor's professional judgment, are significant to the oversight of the financial reporting process. (Ref: Para. A20)

Entities that Report on Application of the UK Corporate Governance Code

16-1. In the case of entities that are required[1c], and those that choose voluntarily, to report on how they have applied the UK Corporate Governance Code, or to explain why they have not, the auditor shall communicate to the audit committee the information that the auditor believes will be relevant to: (Ref: Para. A20-1)

- The board (in the context of fulfilling its responsibilities under Code provisions C.1.1, C.1.3, C.2.1, C.2.2 and C.2.3) and, where applicable, the audit committee (in the context of fulfilling its responsibilities under Code provision C.3.4); and

- The audit committee (in the context of fulfilling its responsibilities under Code provision C.3.2) in order to understand the rationale and the supporting evidence the auditor has relied on when making significant professional judgments in the course of the audit and in reaching an opinion on the financial statements.

If not already covered by communications under paragraphs 15 and 16 above and paragraph 23 of ISA (UK and Ireland) 570, "Going Concern", this information shall include the auditor's views: (Ref: Para. A20-2 – A20-5)

(a) About business risks relevant to financial reporting objectives, the application of materiality and the implications of their judgments in relation to these for the overall audit strategy, the audit plan and the evaluation of misstatements identified;

(b) On the significant accounting policies (both individually and in aggregate);

[1c] In the UK, these include companies with a Premium listing of equity shares regardless of whether they are incorporated in the UK or elsewhere. In Ireland, these include Irish incorporated companies with a primary or secondary listing of equity shares on the Irish Stock Exchange.

(c) On management's valuations of the entity's material assets and liabilities and the related disclosures provided by management;

(d) Without expressing an opinion on the effectiveness of the entity's system of internal control as a whole, and based solely on the audit procedures performed in the audit of the financial statements, about:

(i) The effectiveness of the entity's system of internal control relevant to risks that may affect financial reporting; and

(ii) Other risks arising from the entity's business model and the effectiveness of related internal controls to the extent, if any, the auditor has obtained an understanding of these matters;

(e) About the robustness of the directors' assessment of the principal risks facing the entity, including those that would threaten its business model, future performance, solvency or liquidity and its outcome, including the related disclosures in the annual report confirming that they have carried out such an assessment and describing those risks and explaining how they are being managed or mitigated (in accordance with Code provision C.2.1);

(f) About the directors' explanation in the annual report as to how they have assessed the prospects of the entity, over what period they have done so and why they consider that period to be appropriate (in accordance with Code provision C.2.2), and their statements:

(i) in the financial statements, as to whether they considered it appropriate to adopt the going concern basis of accounting in preparing them, including any related disclosures identifying any material uncertainties to the entity's ability to continue to do so over a period of at least twelve months from the date of approval of the financial statements (in accordance with Code provision C.1.3); and

(ii) in the annual report as to whether they have a reasonable expectation that the entity will be able to continue in operation and meet its liabilities as they fall due over the period of their assessment, including any related disclosures drawing attention to any necessary qualifications or assumptions (in accordance with Code provision C.2.2); and

(g) On any other matters identified in the course of the audit that the auditor believes will be relevant to the board or the audit committee in the context of fulfilling their responsibilities referred to above.

The auditor shall include with this communication sufficient explanation to enable the audit committee to understand the context within which the auditor's views relating to the matters in paragraph (d) above are expressed, including the extent to which the auditor has developed an understanding of these matters in the course of the audit and, if not already communicated to the audit committee, that the audit included consideration of internal control relevant to the preparation of the financial statements only in order to design audit procedures that are appropriate in the circumstances, and not for the purpose of expressing an opinion on the effectiveness of internal control.

Auditor Independence

17. In the case of listed entities, the auditor shall communicate with those charged with governance:

   (a) A statement that the engagement team and others in the firm as appropriate, the firm and, when applicable, network firms have complied with relevant ethical requirements regarding independence[1d]; and

   (b) (i) All relationships and other matters between the firm, network firms, and the entity that, in the auditor's professional judgment, may reasonably be thought to bear on independence. This shall include total fees charged during the period covered by the financial statements for audit and non-audit services provided by the firm and network firms to the entity and components controlled by the entity. These fees shall be allocated to categories that are appropriate to assist those charged with governance in assessing the effect of services on the independence of the auditor; and

   (ii) The related safeguards that have been applied to eliminate identified threats to independence or reduce them to an acceptable level. (Ref: Para. A21-A23)

The Communication Process

Establishing the Communication Process

18. The auditor shall communicate with those charged with governance the form, timing and expected general content of communications. (Ref: Para. A28-A36)

Forms of Communication

19. The auditor shall communicate in writing with those charged with governance regarding significant findings from the audit if, in the auditor's professional judgment, oral communication would not be adequate. Written communications need not include all matters that arose during the course of the audit. (Ref: Para. A37-A39)

20. The auditor shall communicate in writing with those charged with governance regarding auditor independence when required by paragraph 17.

[1d] In the UK and Ireland, auditors are subject to ethical requirements from two sources: the APB's Ethical Standards for Auditors (ESs), including ES 1 (Revised), "Integrity, Objectivity and Independence," and the ethical pronouncements established by the auditor's relevant professional body. In the case of listed companies, ES 1 (Revised) specifies information to be communicated to those charged with governance (see Para A21-1 in this ISA (UK and Ireland)).

Timing of Communications

21.   The auditor shall communicate with those charged with governance on a timely basis. (Ref: Para. A40 - A41-1)

Adequacy of the Communication Process

22.   The auditor shall evaluate whether the two-way communication between the auditor and those charged with governance has been adequate for the purpose of the audit. If it has not, the auditor shall evaluate the effect, if any, on the auditor's assessment of the risks of material misstatement and ability to obtain sufficient appropriate audit evidence, and shall take appropriate action. (Ref: Para. A42-A44)

Documentation

23.   Where matters required by this ISA (UK and Ireland) to be communicated are communicated orally, the auditor shall include them in the audit documentation, and when and to whom they were communicated. Where matters have been communicated in writing, the auditor shall retain a copy of the communication as part of the audit documentation.[2] (Ref: Para. A45)

***

Application and Other Explanatory Material

Those Charged with Governance (Ref: Para. 11)

A1.   Governance structures vary by jurisdiction and by entity, reflecting influences such as different cultural and legal backgrounds, and size and ownership characteristics. For example:

- In some jurisdictions a supervisory (wholly or mainly non-executive) board exists that is legally separate from an executive (management) board (a "two-tier board" structure). In other jurisdictions, both the supervisory and executive functions are the legal responsibility of a single, or unitary, board (a "one-tier board" structure).

- In some entities, those charged with governance hold positions that are an integral part of the entity's legal structure, for example, company directors. In others, for example, some government entities, a body that is not part of the entity is charged with governance.

- In some cases, some or all of those charged with governance are involved in managing the entity. In others, those charged with governance and management comprise different persons.

---

[2]   ISA (UK and Ireland) 230, "Audit Documentation," paragraphs 8-11, and paragraph A6.

- In some cases, those charged with governance are responsible for approving[3] the entity's financial statements (in other cases management has this responsibility).

A2. In most entities, governance is the collective responsibility of a governing body, such as a board of directors, a supervisory board, partners, proprietors, a committee of management, a council of governors, trustees, or equivalent persons. In some smaller entities, however, one person may be charged with governance, for example, the owner-manager where there are no other owners, or a sole trustee. When governance is a collective responsibility, a subgroup such as an audit committee or even an individual, may be charged with specific tasks to assist the governing body in meeting its responsibilities. Alternatively, a subgroup or individual may have specific, legally identified responsibilities that differ from those of the governing body.

A3. Such diversity means that it is not possible for this ISA (UK and Ireland) to specify for all audits the person(s) with whom the auditor is to communicate particular matters. Also, in some cases the appropriate person(s) with whom to communicate may not be clearly identifiable from the applicable legal framework or other engagement circumstances, for example, entities where the governance structure is not formally defined, such as some family-owned entities, some not-for-profit organizations, and some government entities. In such cases, the auditor may need to discuss and agree with the engaging party the relevant person(s) with whom to communicate. In deciding with whom to communicate, the auditor's understanding of an entity's governance structure and processes obtained in accordance with ISA (UK and Ireland) 315 (Revised June 2013)[4] is relevant. The appropriate person(s) with whom to communicate may vary depending on the matter to be communicated.

A4. ISA (UK and Ireland) 600 includes specific matters to be communicated by group auditors with those charged with governance.[5] When the entity is a component of a group, the appropriate person(s) with whom the component auditor communicates depends on the engagement circumstances and the matter to be communicated. In some cases, a number of components may be conducting the same businesses within the same system of internal control and using the same accounting practices. Where those charged with governance of those components are the same (for example, common board of directors), duplication may be avoided by dealing with these components concurrently for the purpose of communication.

---

[3] As described at paragraph A40 of ISA 700, "Forming an Opinion and Reporting on Financial Statements," having responsibility for approving in this context means having the authority to conclude that all the statements that comprise the financial statements, including the related notes, have been prepared.

In the UK and Ireland, those charged with governance are responsible for the approval of the financial statements.

The FRC has not promulgated ISA 700 as issued by the IAASB for application in the UK and Ireland. In the UK and Ireland the applicable auditing standard is ISA (UK and Ireland) 700, "The Independent Auditor's Report on Financial Statements."

[4] ISA (UK and Ireland) 315 (Revised June 2013), "Identifying and Assessing the Risks of Material Misstatement through Understanding the Entity and Its Environment."

[5] ISA (UK and Ireland) 600, "Special Considerations—Audits of Group Financial Statements (Including the Work of Component Auditors)," paragraphs 46-49.

A4-1. In the UK and Ireland there are statutory obligations on corporate subsidiary undertakings, and their auditors and other parties, to provide the auditor of a corporate parent undertaking with such information and explanations as that auditor may reasonably require for the purposes of the audit[5a]. Where there is no such statutory obligation (e.g. for non corporate entities), permission may be needed by the auditors of the subsidiary undertakings, from those charged with governance of the subsidiary undertakings, to disclose the contents of any communication to them to the auditor of the parent undertaking and also for the auditor of the parent undertaking to pass those disclosures onto those charged with governance of the parent undertaking. The auditor of the parent undertaking seeks to ensure that appropriate arrangements are made at the planning stage for these disclosures. Normally, such arrangements for groups are recorded in the instructions to the auditors of subsidiary undertakings and relevant engagement letters.

Communication with a Subgroup of Those Charged with Governance (Ref: Para. 12)

A5. When considering communicating with a subgroup of those charged with governance, the auditor may take into account such matters as:

- The respective responsibilities of the subgroup and the governing body.

- The nature of the matter to be communicated.

- Relevant legal or regulatory requirements.

- Whether the subgroup has the authority to take action in relation to the information communicated, and can provide further information and explanations the auditor may need.

A6. When deciding whether there is also a need to communicate information, in full or in summary form, with the governing body, the auditor may be influenced by the auditor's assessment of how effectively and appropriately the subgroup communicates relevant information with the governing body. The auditor may make explicit in agreeing the terms of engagement that, unless prohibited by law or

---

[5a] In the UK, Section 499 of the Companies Act 2006 specifies that the auditor of a company may require any subsidiary undertaking of the company which is a body corporate incorporated in the UK, and any officer, employee or auditor of any such subsidiary undertaking or any person holding or accountable for any books, accounts or vouchers of any such subsidiary undertaking, to provide him with such information or explanations as he thinks necessary for the performance of his duties as auditor. If a parent company has a subsidiary undertaking that is not a body corporate incorporated in the UK, Section 500 of the Companies Act 2006 specifies that the auditor of the parent company may require it to take all such steps as are reasonably open to it to obtain from the subsidiary undertaking, any officer, employee or auditor of the undertaking, or any person holding or accountable for any of the undertaking's books, accounts or vouchers, such information and explanations as he may reasonably require for the purposes of his duties as auditor. Similar obligations regarding companies incorporated in the Republic of Ireland are set out in Section 196, Companies Act 1990.

regulation, the auditor retains the right to communicate directly with the governing body.

A6-1. Audit committees report to the board on various matters related to the discharge of their responsibilities, including those related to the financial statements, the annual report and the audit process (see paragraph A20-1 below). The auditor, when assessing whether there is a need to communicate with the full board regarding matters communicated by the auditor to the audit committee, takes into consideration the adequacy of the communications between the audit committee and the board, including whether they appropriately address relevant matters communicated to the audit committee by the auditor. This may be achieved in one or more ways including: where judged appropriate attending the relevant part of a board meeting where the audit committee reports to the board, holding discussions with individual board members, or reviewing any written reports from the audit committee to the board.

A7. Audit committees (or similar subgroups with different names) exist in many jurisdictions. Although their specific authority and functions may differ, communication with the audit committee, where one exists, has become a key element in the auditor's communication with those charged with governance. Good governance principles suggest that:

- The auditor will be invited to regularly attend meetings of the audit committee.

- The chair of the audit committee and, when relevant, the other members of the audit committee, will liaise with the auditor periodically.

- The audit committee will meet the auditor without management present at least annually.

When All of Those Charged with Governance Are Involved in Managing the Entity (Ref: Para.13)

A8. In some cases, all of those charged with governance are involved in managing the entity, and the application of communication requirements is modified to recognize this position. In such cases, communication with person(s) with management responsibilities may not adequately inform all of those with whom the auditor would otherwise communicate in their governance capacity. For example, in a company where all directors are involved in managing the entity, some of those directors (for example, one responsible for marketing) may be unaware of significant matters discussed with another director (for example, one responsible for the preparation of the financial statements).

Matters to Be Communicated

The Auditor's Responsibilities in Relation to the Financial Statement Audit (Ref: Para. 14)

A9. The auditor's responsibilities in relation to the financial statement audit are often included in the engagement letter or other suitable form of written agreement that records the agreed terms of the engagement. Providing those charged with governance with a copy of that engagement letter or other suitable form of written agreement may be an appropriate way to communicate with them regarding such matters as:

- The auditor's responsibility for performing the audit in accordance with ISAs (UK and Ireland), which is directed towards the expression of an opinion on the financial statements. The matters that ISAs (UK and Ireland) require to be communicated, therefore, include significant matters arising from the audit of the financial statements that are relevant to those charged with governance in overseeing the financial reporting process.

- The fact that ISAs (UK and Ireland) do not require the auditor to design procedures for the purpose of identifying supplementary matters to communicate with those charged with governance.

- When applicable, the auditor's responsibility for communicating particular matters required by law or regulation, by agreement with the entity or by additional requirements applicable to the engagement, for example, the standards of a national professional accountancy body.

A9-1. The provision of copies of the audit engagement letter to the audit committees of listed companies facilitates their review and agreement of the audit engagement letter as recommended by the FRC Guidance on Audit Committees. As part of their review, the guidance further recommends the audit committee to consider whether the audit engagement letter has been updated to reflect changes in circumstances since the previous year.

A10. Law or regulation, an agreement with the entity or additional requirements applicable to the engagement may provide for broader communication with those charged with governance. For example, (a) an agreement with the entity may provide for particular matters to be communicated when they arise from services provided by a firm or network firm other than the financial statement audit; or (b) the mandate of a public sector auditor may provide for matters to be communicated that come to the auditor's attention as a result of other work, such as performance audits.

Planned Scope and Timing of the Audit (Ref: Para. 15)

A11. Communication regarding the planned scope and timing of the audit may:

(a) Assist those charged with governance to understand better the consequences of the auditor's work, to discuss issues of risk and the concept of materiality with the auditor, and to identify any areas in which they may request the auditor to undertake additional procedures[5b]; and

(b) Assist the auditor to understand better the entity and its environment.

[5b] The UK Corporate Governance Code and the FRC Guidance on Audit Committees contain, inter alia, recommendations about the audit committee's relationship with the auditor

A11-1. The communication of the planned scope of the audit includes, where relevant, any limitations on the work the auditor proposes to undertake (e.g. if limitations are imposed by management)[5c].

A12. Care is required when communicating with those charged with governance about the planned scope and timing of the audit so as not to compromise the effectiveness of the audit, particularly where some or all of those charged with governance are involved in managing the entity. For example, communicating the nature and timing of detailed audit procedures may reduce the effectiveness of those procedures by making them too predictable.

A13. Matters communicated may include:

- How the auditor proposes to address the significant risks of material misstatement, whether due to fraud or error.

- The auditor's approach to internal control relevant to the audit.

- The application of the concept of materiality in the context of an audit.[6]

A13-1. The nature and detail of the planning information communicated will reflect the size and nature of the entity and the manner in which those charged with governance operate.

A13-2 In any particular year, the auditor may decide that there are no significant changes in the planned scope and timing of the audit that have been communicated previously and judge that it is unnecessary to remind those charged with governance of all or part of that information. In these circumstances, the auditor need only make those charged with governance aware that the auditor has no new matters to communicate concerning the planned scope and timing of the audit. Matters that are included in the audit engagement letter need not be repeated.

A14. Other planning matters that it may be appropriate to discuss with those charged with governance include:

- Where the entity has an internal audit function, how the external auditor and internal auditors can work in a constructive and complementary manner, including any planned use of the work of the internal audit function, and the nature and extent of any planned use of internal auditors to provide direct assistance.[7]

[5c] ISA (UK and Ireland) 210, "Agreeing the Terms of Audit Engagements," paragraph 7 requires that if management or those charged with governance impose a limitation on the scope of the auditor's work in the terms of a proposed audit engagement such that the auditor believes the limitation will result in the auditor disclaiming an opinion on the financial statements, the auditor shall not accept such a limited engagement as an audit engagement, unless required by law or regulation to do so.

[6] ISA (UK and Ireland) 320, "Materiality in Planning and Performing an Audit."

[7] ISA (UK and Ireland) 610 (Revised June 2013), "Using the Work of Internal Auditors", paragraphs 20 and 31.

The use of internal auditors to provide direct assistance is prohibited in an audit conducted in accordance with ISAs (UK and Ireland) – see ISA (UK and Ireland) 610 (Revised June 2013), paragraph 5-1.

- The views of those charged with governance of:

  ○ The appropriate person(s) in the entity's governance structure with whom to communicate.

  ○ The allocation of responsibilities between those charged with governance and management.

  ○ The entity's objectives and strategies, and the related business risks that may result in material misstatements.

  ○ Matters those charged with governance consider warrant particular attention during the audit, and any areas where they request additional procedures to be undertaken.

  ○ Significant communications with regulators.

  ○ Other matters those charged with governance consider may influence the audit of the financial statements.

- The attitudes, awareness, and actions of those charged with governance concerning (a) the entity's internal control and its importance in the entity, including how those charged with governance oversee the effectiveness of internal control, and (b) the detection or possibility of fraud.

- The actions of those charged with governance in response to developments in accounting standards, corporate governance practices, exchange listing rules, and related matters.

- The responses of those charged with governance to previous communications with the auditor.

A15. While communication with those charged with governance may assist the auditor to plan the scope and timing of the audit, it does not change the auditor's sole responsibility to establish the overall audit strategy and the audit plan, including the nature, timing and extent of procedures necessary to obtain sufficient appropriate audit evidence.

Significant Findings from the Audit (Ref: Para. 16)

A16. The communication of findings from the audit may include requesting further information from those charged with governance in order to complete the audit evidence obtained. For example, the auditor may confirm that those charged with governance have the same understanding of the facts and circumstances relevant to specific transactions or events.

Significant Qualitative Aspects of Accounting Practices (Ref: Para. 16(a))

A17. Financial reporting frameworks ordinarily allow for the entity to make accounting estimates, and judgments about accounting policies and financial statement disclosures. Open and constructive communication about significant qualitative aspects of the entity's accounting practices may include comment on the acceptability of significant accounting practices. Appendix 2 identifies matters that may be included in this communication.

Significant Difficulties Encountered during the Audit (Ref: Para. 16(b))

A18. Significant difficulties encountered during the audit may include such matters as:

- Significant delays in management providing required information.

- An unnecessarily brief time within which to complete the audit.

- Extensive unexpected effort required to obtain sufficient appropriate audit evidence.

- The unavailability of expected information.

- Restrictions imposed on the auditor by management.

- Management's unwillingness to make or extend its assessment of the entity's ability to continue as a going concern when requested.

In some circumstances, such difficulties may constitute a scope limitation that leads to a modification of the auditor's opinion.[8]

Significant Matters Discussed, or Subject to Correspondence with Management (Ref: Para. 16(c)(i))

A19. Significant matters discussed, or subject to correspondence with management may include such matters as:

- Business conditions affecting the entity, and business plans and strategies that may affect the risks of material misstatement.

- Concerns about management's consultations with other accountants on accounting or auditing matters.

- Discussions or correspondence in connection with the initial or recurring appointment of the auditor regarding accounting practices, the application of auditing standards, or fees for audit or other services.

---

[8] ISA (UK and Ireland) 705, "Modifications to the Opinion in the Independent Auditor's Report."

Other Significant Matters Relevant to the Financial Reporting Process (Ref: Para. 16(d))

A20. Other significant matters arising from the audit that are directly relevant to those charged with governance in overseeing the financial reporting process may include such matters as material misstatements of fact or material inconsistencies in information accompanying the audited financial statements that have been corrected.

Entities that Report on Application of the UK Corporate Governance Code (Ref: Para. 16-1)

A20-1. Under the UK Corporate Governance Code, the responsibilities of the directors under Code provision C.1.1 include making a statement that they consider the annual report and accounts taken as a whole is fair, balanced and understandable and provides the information necessary for shareholders to assess the entity's position and performance, business model and strategy. The responsibilities of the audit committee under Code provision C.3.4 include, where requested by the board, providing advice in relation to that statement[8a]. The responsibilities of the board under Code provision C.2.3 include monitoring the entity's risk management and internal control systems and, at least annually, carrying out a review of their effectiveness and reporting on that review in the annual report[8b]. The responsibilities of the board under Code provisions C.1.3, C.2.1 and C.2.2 are described in paragraphs 16-1 (e) and (f). The responsibilities of the audit committee under Code provision C.3.2 include: monitoring the integrity of the financial statements of the entity and any formal announcements relating to the entity's financial performance, reviewing significant financial reporting judgments contained in them; reviewing the entity's internal financial controls and, unless expressly addressed by a separate board risk committee composed of independent directors or by the board itself, the entity's internal control and risk management systems[8c]; review and monitor the effectiveness of the audit process; and reporting to the board on how it has discharged its responsibilities. The supporting Guidance on Audit Committees indicates that the report to the board should include, inter alia[8d]:

- The significant issues that the audit committee considered in relation to the financial statements and how these issues were addressed; and

---

[8a] Responsibility for ensuring the annual report is fair, balanced and understandable rests with the board as a whole. The board may ask the audit committee to provide advice on this.

[8b] In addition, FCA Rule DTR 7.2.5 R requires companies to describe the main features of the internal control and risk management systems in relation to the financial reporting process.

[8c] The FRC issues 'Guidance on Risk Management and Internal Control and Related Financial and Business Reporting' for directors on their responsibilities under the UK Corporate Governance Code. The guidance indicates that it is for the board to decide what arrangements to put in place to enable it to exercise its responsibilities. The guidance also indicates the nature of the information the board may include in its narrative statement about these matters. Supplementary considerations for the banking sector are provided in 'Guidance for Directors of Banks on Solvency and Liquidity Risk Management and the Going Concern Basis of Accounting'.

[8d] The Guidance on Audit Committees also sets out other matters the audit committee should consider in relation to the annual audit cycle, including in relation to the audit plan and the auditor's findings.

- The basis for its advice, where requested by the board, that the annual report and accounts taken as a whole is fair, balanced and understandable and provides the information necessary for shareholders to assess the entity's performance, business model and strategy.

A20-2. In fulfilling these responsibilities, the audit committee and the board will be assisted by an understanding of:

(a) Issues that involve significant judgment; and

(b) Other matters communicated to them by the auditor relevant to those responsibilities.

This will include an understanding of the rationale and supporting evidence for the auditor's significant professional judgments made in the course of the audit and in reaching the opinion on the financial statements, and of other matters communicated to the audit committee by the auditor in accordance with the requirements of paragraph 16-1, including relevant information communicated in accordance with the requirements of paragraphs 15 and 16. The auditor's communications include information regarding separate components of a group where relevant. In fulfilling its responsibilities set out above, the board will be assisted by the report from the audit committee on how the audit committee has discharged its responsibilities.

A20-3. The audit procedures that the auditor designs as part of the audit of the financial statements are not designed for the purpose of expressing an opinion on the effectiveness of the entity's system of internal control as a whole and accordingly the auditor does not express such an opinion on the basis of those procedures. However, communication of the auditor's views about the effectiveness of elements of the entity's system of internal control, based on the audit procedures performed in the audit of the financial statements, may help the audit committee and the board fulfil their respective responsibilities with respect to the entity's internal control and risk management systems.

A20-4. The auditor's understanding of the entity includes the entity's objectives and strategies and those related business risks that may result in risks of material misstatement, obtained in compliance with ISA (UK and Ireland) 315 (Revised June 2013)[8e], and may also include other risks arising from the entity's business model that are relevant to an understanding of that model and the entity's strategy. To the extent that the auditor has obtained an understanding of such risks and the effectiveness of the entity's system of internal control in addressing them, communicating its views on those matters may be helpful to the audit committee and the board in their evaluation of whether the annual report is fair, balanced and understandable and provides the information necessary for users to assess the entity's position and performance, business model and strategy. However, the auditor is not required to design and perform audit procedures expressly for the

---

[8e] ISA (UK and Ireland) 315 (Revised June 2013), paragraph 11(d).

purpose of forming views about the effectiveness of the entity's internal control in addressing such risks. Accordingly, to the extent applicable, the auditor may communicate that they have not obtained an understanding of, and therefore are not able to express views about, such risks and related aspects of the entity's internal control.

A20-5. The auditor's communication of views about the effectiveness of the entity's internal control may include, or refer to, the communication of significant deficiencies in internal control, if any, that is required by ISA (UK and Ireland) 265. However, views about effectiveness can go beyond just identifying such deficiencies. For example they may include views about such matters as the entity's strategies for identifying and responding quickly to significant new financial or operational risks; the quality of the reports that the board receives to provide them with information about risks and the operation of internal control; or how the entity's systems compare in general terms with those of other relevant entities of which the auditor has knowledge, such as the impact on internal control effectiveness that may result from different approaches to maintaining an appropriate control environment. The auditor's communications include its views relating to separate components of a group where relevant.

Auditor Independence (Ref: Para. 17)

A21. The auditor is required to comply with relevant ethical requirements, including those pertaining to independence, relating to financial statement audit engagements.[9]

A21-1 In the UK and Ireland, auditors are subject to ethical requirements from two sources: the APB's Ethical Standards for Auditors (ESs), including ES 1 (Revised), "Integrity, Objectivity and Independence," and the ethical pronouncements established by the auditor's relevant professional body. In the case of listed companies ES 1 (Revised) requires that:

"The audit engagement partner shall ensure that those charged with the governance of the audited entity are appropriately informed on a timely basis of all significant facts and matters that bear upon the auditor's objectivity and independence." and

"In the case of listed companies, the audit engagement partner shall ensure that the audit committee is provided with:

(a) a written disclosure of relationships (including the provision of non-audit services) that bear on the auditor's objectivity and independence, the threats to auditor independence that these create, any safeguards that have been put in place and why they address such threats, together with any other information necessary to enable the auditor's objectivity and independence to be assessed;

---

[9] ISA (UK and Ireland) 200, "Overall Objectives of the Independent Auditor and the Conduct of an Audit in Accordance with International Standards on Auditing," paragraph 14.

(b) details of non-audit services provided to the audited entity and the fees charged in relation thereto;

(c) written confirmation that the auditor is independent;

(d) details of any inconsistencies between APB Ethical Standards and the company's policy for the supply of non-audit services by the audit firm and any apparent breach of that policy.

(e) an opportunity to discuss auditor independence issues."

A22. The relationships and other matters, and safeguards to be communicated, vary with the circumstances of the engagement, but generally address:

(a) Threats to independence, which may be categorized as: self-interest threats, self-review threats, advocacy threats, familiarity threats, and intimidation threats; and

(b) Safeguards created by the profession, legislation or regulation, safeguards within the entity, and safeguards within the firm's own systems and procedures.

The communication required by paragraph 17(a) may include an inadvertent violation of relevant ethical requirements as they relate to auditor independence, and any remedial action taken or proposed.

A23. The communication requirements relating to auditor independence that apply in the case of listed entities may also be relevant in the case of some other entities, particularly those that may be of significant public interest because, as a result of their business, their size or their corporate status, they have a wide range of stakeholders. Examples of entities that are not listed entities, but where communication of auditor independence may be appropriate, include public sector entities, credit institutions, insurance companies, and retirement benefit funds. On the other hand, there may be situations where communications regarding independence may not be relevant, for example, where all of those charged with governance have been informed of relevant facts through their management activities. This is particularly likely where the entity is owner-managed, and the auditor's firm and network firms have little involvement with the entity beyond a financial statement audit.

Supplementary Matters (Ref: Para. 3)

A24. The oversight of management by those charged with governance includes ensuring that the entity designs, implements and maintains appropriate internal control with regard to reliability of financial reporting, effectiveness and efficiency of operations and compliance with applicable laws and regulations.

A25. The auditor may become aware of supplementary matters that do not necessarily relate to the oversight of the financial reporting process but which are, nevertheless, likely to be significant to the responsibilities of those charged with governance in overseeing the strategic direction of the entity or the entity's obligations related to accountability. Such matters may include, for example, significant issues regarding governance structures or processes, and significant decisions or actions by senior management that lack appropriate authorization.

A26. In determining whether to communicate supplementary matters with those charged with governance, the auditor may discuss matters of this kind of which the auditor has become aware with the appropriate level of management, unless it is inappropriate to do so in the circumstances.

A27. If a supplementary matter is communicated, it may be appropriate for the auditor to make those charged with governance aware that:

(a) Identification and communication of such matters is incidental to the purpose of the audit, which is to form an opinion on the financial statements;

(b) No procedures were carried out with respect to the matter other than any that were necessary to form an opinion on the financial statements; and

(c) No procedures were carried out to determine whether other such matters exist.

The Communication Process

Establishing the Communication Process (Ref: Para. 18)

A28. Clear communication of the auditor's responsibilities, the planned scope and timing of the audit, and the expected general content of communications helps establish the basis for effective two-way communication.

A29. Matters that may also contribute to effective two-way communication include discussion of:

- The purpose of communications. When the purpose is clear, the auditor and those charged with governance are better placed to have a mutual understanding of relevant issues and the expected actions arising from the communication process.

- The form in which communications will be made.

- The person(s) in the engagement team and amongst those charged with governance who will communicate regarding particular matters.

- The auditor's expectation that communication will be two-way, and that those charged with governance will communicate with the auditor matters they consider relevant to the audit, for example, strategic decisions that may significantly affect the nature, timing and extent of audit procedures, the suspicion or the detection of fraud, and concerns with the integrity or competence of senior management.

- The process for taking action and reporting back on matters communicated by the auditor.

- The process for taking action and reporting back on matters communicated by those charged with governance.

A30. The communication process will vary with the circumstances, including the size and governance structure of the entity, how those charged with governance operate, and the auditor's view of the significance of matters to be communicated. Difficulty in establishing effective two-way communication may indicate that the communication between the auditor and those charged with governance is not adequate for the purpose of the audit (see paragraph A44).

Considerations Specific to Smaller Entities

A31. In the case of audits of smaller entities, the auditor may communicate in a less structured manner with those charged with governance than in the case of listed or larger entities.

Communication with Management

A32. Many matters may be discussed with management in the ordinary course of an audit, including matters required by this ISA (UK and Ireland) to be communicated with those charged with governance. Such discussions recognize management's executive responsibility for the conduct of the entity's operations and, in particular, management's responsibility for the preparation of the financial statements.

A33. Before communicating matters with those charged with governance, the auditor may discuss them with management, unless that is inappropriate. For example, it may not be appropriate to discuss questions of management's competence or integrity with management. In addition to recognizing management's executive responsibility, these initial discussions may clarify facts and issues, and give management an opportunity to provide further information and explanations. Similarly, when the entity has an internal audit function, the auditor may discuss matters with appropriate individuals within the function before communicating with those charged with governance.

Communication with Third Parties

A34. Those charged with governance may wish to provide third parties, for example, bankers or certain regulatory authorities, with copies of a written communication from the auditor. In some cases, disclosure to third parties may be illegal or otherwise inappropriate. When a written communication prepared for those charged with governance is provided to third parties, it may be important in the circumstances that the third parties be informed that the communication was not prepared with them in mind, for example, by stating in written communications with those charged with governance:

(a) That the communication has been prepared for the sole use of those charged with governance and, where applicable, the group management and the group auditor, and should not be relied upon by third parties;

    (b) That no responsibility is assumed by the auditor to third parties; and

    (c) Any restrictions on disclosure or distribution to third parties.

A35. In some jurisdictions the auditor may be required by law or regulation to, for example:

- Notify a regulatory or enforcement body of certain matters communicated with those charged with governance. For example, in some countries the auditor has a duty to report misstatements to authorities where management and those charged with governance fail to take corrective action;

- Submit copies of certain reports prepared for those charged with governance to relevant regulatory or funding bodies, or other bodies such as a central authority in the case of some public sector entities; or

- Make reports prepared for those charged with governance publicly available.

A36. Unless required by law or regulation to provide a third party with a copy of the auditor's written communications with those charged with governance, the auditor may need the prior consent of those charged with governance before doing so.

Forms of Communication (Ref: Para. 19-20)

A37. Effective communication may involve structured presentations and written reports as well as less structured communications, including discussions. The auditor may communicate matters other than those identified in paragraphs 19 and 20 either orally or in writing. Written communications may include an engagement letter that is provided to those charged with governance.

A37-1. The auditor discusses issues clearly and unequivocally with those charged with governance so that the implications of those issues are likely to be fully comprehended by them.

A38. In addition to the significance of a particular matter, the form of communication (for example, whether to communicate orally or in writing, the extent of detail or summarization in the communication, and whether to communicate in a structured or unstructured manner) may be affected by such factors as:

- Whether the matter has been satisfactorily resolved.

- Whether management has previously communicated the matter.

- The size, operating structure, control environment, and legal structure of the entity.

- In the case of an audit of special purpose financial statements, whether the auditor also audits the entity's general purpose financial statements.

- Legal requirements. In some jurisdictions, a written communication with those charged with governance is required in a prescribed form by local law.

- The expectations of those charged with governance, including arrangements made for periodic meetings or communications with the auditor.

- The amount of ongoing contact and dialogue the auditor has with those charged with governance.

- Whether there have been significant changes in the membership of a governing body.

A38-1. The judgment of whether to communicate significant matters orally or in writing may also be affected by the evaluation, required by paragraph 22, of whether the two-way communication between the auditor and those charged with governance has been adequate for the purpose of the audit. The auditor may judge also that for effective communication a written communication is issued even if its content is limited to explaining that there is nothing the auditor wishes to draw to the attention of those charged with governance. To avoid doubt where there are no matters the auditor wishes to communicate in writing, the auditor may communicate that fact in writing to those charged with governance.

A39. When a significant matter is discussed with an individual member of those charged with governance, for example, the chair of an audit committee, it may be appropriate for the auditor to summarize the matter in later communications so that all of those charged with governance have full and balanced information.

Timing of Communications (Ref: Para. 21)

A40. The appropriate timing for communications will vary with the circumstances of the engagement. Relevant circumstances include the significance and nature of the matter, and the action expected to be taken by those charged with governance. For example:

- Communications regarding planning matters may often be made early in the audit engagement and, for an initial engagement, may be made as part of agreeing the terms of the engagement.

- It may be appropriate to communicate a significant difficulty encountered during the audit as soon as practicable if those charged with governance are able to assist the auditor to overcome the difficulty, or if it is likely to lead to a modified opinion. Similarly, the auditor may communicate orally to those charged with governance as soon as practicable significant deficiencies in internal control that the auditor has identified, prior to communicating these in writing as required by ISA (UK and Ireland) 265.[10] Communications regarding independence may be appropriate whenever significant judgments are made about threats to

---

[10] ISA (UK and Ireland) 265, paragraphs 9 and A14.

independence and related safeguards, for example, when accepting an engagement to provide non-audit services, and at a concluding discussion. A concluding discussion may also be an appropriate time to communicate findings from the audit, including the auditor's views about the qualitative aspects of the entity's accounting practices.

- When auditing both general purpose and special purpose financial statements, it may be appropriate to coordinate the timing of communications.

A41.   Other factors that may be relevant to the timing of communications include:

- The size, operating structure, control environment, and legal structure of the entity being audited.

- Any legal obligation to communicate certain matters within a specified timeframe.

- The expectations of those charged with governance, including arrangements made for periodic meetings or communications with the auditor.

- The time at which the auditor identifies certain matters, for example, the auditor may not identify a particular matter (for example, noncompliance with a law) in time for preventive action to be taken, but communication of the matter may enable remedial action to be taken.

A41-1. Findings from the audit that are relevant to the financial statements, including the auditor's views about the qualitative aspects of the entity's accounting and financial reporting, are ordinarily communicated to those charged with governance before they approve the financial statements.

Adequacy of the Communication Process (Ref: Para. 22)

A42.   The auditor need not design specific procedures to support the evaluation of the two-way communication between the auditor and those charged with governance; rather, that evaluation may be based on observations resulting from audit procedures performed for other purposes. Such observations may include:

- The appropriateness and timeliness of actions taken by those charged with governance in response to matters raised by the auditor. Where significant matters raised in previous communications have not been dealt with effectively, it may be appropriate for the auditor to inquire as to why appropriate action has not been taken, and to consider raising the point again. This avoids the risk of giving an impression that the auditor is satisfied that the matter has been adequately addressed or is no longer significant.

- The apparent openness of those charged with governance in their communications with the auditor.

- The willingness and capacity of those charged with governance to meet with the auditor without management present.

- The apparent ability of those charged with governance to fully comprehend matters raised by the auditor, for example, the extent to which those charged with governance probe issues, and question recommendations made to them.

- Difficulty in establishing with those charged with governance a mutual understanding of the form, timing and expected general content of communications.

- Where all or some of those charged with governance are involved in managing the entity, their apparent awareness of how matters discussed with the auditor affect their broader governance responsibilities, as well as their management responsibilities.

- Whether the two-way communication between the auditor and those charged with governance meets applicable legal and regulatory requirements.

A43. As noted in paragraph 4, effective two-way communication assists both the auditor and those charged with governance. Further, ISA (UK and Ireland) 315 (Revised June 2013) identifies participation by those charged with governance, including their interaction with the internal audit function, if any, and external auditors, as an element of the entity's control environment.[11] Inadequate two-way communication may indicate an unsatisfactory control environment and influence the auditor's assessment of the risks of material misstatements. There is also a risk that the auditor may not have obtained sufficient appropriate audit evidence to form an opinion on the financial statements.

A44. If the two-way communication between the auditor and those charged with governance is not adequate and the situation cannot be resolved, the auditor may take such actions as:

- Modifying the auditor's opinion on the basis of a scope limitation.

- Obtaining legal advice about the consequences of different courses of action.

- Communicating with third parties (for example, a regulator), or a higher authority in the governance structure that is outside the entity, such as the owners of a business (for example, shareholders in a general meeting), or the responsible government minister or parliament in the public sector.

- Withdrawing from the engagement, where withdrawal is possible under applicable law or regulation.

Documentation (Ref: Para. 23)

A45. Documentation of oral communication may include a copy of minutes prepared by the entity retained as part of the audit documentation where those minutes are an appropriate record of the communication.

---

[11] ISA (UK and Ireland) 315 (Revised June 2013), paragraph A77.

Appendix 1

(Ref: Para. 3)

Specific Requirements in ISQC (UK and Ireland) 1 and Other ISAs (UK and Ireland) that Refer to Communications with Those Charged With Governance

This appendix identifies paragraphs in ISQC (UK and Ireland) 1[12] and other ISAs (UK and Ireland) in effect for audits of financial statements for periods ending on or after 15 December 2010 that require communication of specific matters with those charged with governance. The list is not a substitute for considering the requirements and related application and other explanatory material in ISAs (UK and Ireland).

- ISQC (UK and Ireland) 1, "Quality Control for Firms that Perform Audits and Reviews of Financial Statements, and Other Assurance and Related Services Engagements" – paragraph 30(a)

- ISA (UK and Ireland) 240, "The Auditor's Responsibilities Relating to Fraud in an Audit of Financial Statements" – paragraphs 21, 38(c)(i) and 40-42

- ISA (UK and Ireland) 250, "Consideration of Laws and Regulations in an Audit of Financial Statements" – paragraphs 14, 19 and 22-24

- ISA (UK and Ireland) 265, "Communicating Deficiencies in Internal Control to Those Charged with Governance and Management" – paragraph 9

- ISA (UK and Ireland) 450, "Evaluation of Misstatements Identified during the Audit" – paragraphs 12-13

- ISA (UK and Ireland) 505, "External Confirmations" – paragraph 9

- ISA (UK and Ireland) 510, "Initial Audit Engagements—Opening Balances" – paragraph 7

- ISA (UK and Ireland) 550, "Related Parties" – paragraph 27

- ISA (UK and Ireland) 560, "Subsequent Events" – paragraphs 7(b)-(c), 10(a), 13(b), 14(a) and 17

- ISA (UK and Ireland) 570, "Going Concern" – paragraph 23

- ISA (UK and Ireland) 600, "Special Considerations – Audits of Group Financial Statements (Including the Work of Component Auditors)" – paragraph 49

---

[12] ISQC (UK and Ireland) 1, "Quality Control for Firms that Perform Audits and Reviews of Financial Statements, and Other Assurance and Related Services Engagements."

- ISA (UK and Ireland) 610 (Revised June 2013), "Using the Work of Internal Auditors" – paragraphs 20 and 31

- ISA (UK and Ireland) 705, "Modifications to the Opinion in the Independent Auditor's Report" – paragraphs 12, 14, 19(a) and 28

- ISA (UK and Ireland) 706, "Emphasis of Matter Paragraphs and Other Matter Paragraphs in the Independent Auditor's Report" – paragraph 9

- ISA (UK and Ireland) 710, "Comparative Information—Corresponding Figures and Comparative Financial Statements" – paragraph 18

- ISA (UK and Ireland) 720, "The Auditor's Responsibilities Relating to Other Information in Documents Containing Audited Financial Statements" – paragraphs 10, 13 and 16

Appendix 2

(Ref: Para. 16(a), A17)

Qualitative Aspects of Accounting Practices

The communication required by paragraph 16(a), and discussed in paragraph A17, may include such matters as:

Accounting Policies

- The appropriateness of the accounting policies to the particular circumstances of the entity, having regard to the need to balance the cost of providing information with the likely benefit to users of the entity's financial statements. Where acceptable alternative accounting policies exist, the communication may include identification of the financial statement items that are affected by the choice of significant accounting policies as well as information on accounting policies used by similar entities.

- The initial selection of, and changes in significant accounting policies, including the application of new accounting pronouncements. The communication may include: the effect of the timing and method of adoption of a change in accounting policy on the current and future earnings of the entity; and the timing of a change in accounting policies in relation to expected new accounting pronouncements.

- The effect of significant accounting policies in controversial or emerging areas (or those unique to an industry, particularly when there is a lack of authoritative guidance or consensus).

- The effect of the timing of transactions in relation to the period in which they are recorded.

Accounting Estimates

- For items for which estimates are significant, issues discussed in ISA (UK and Ireland) 540,[13] including, for example:

  - Management's identification of accounting estimates.

  - Management's process for making accounting estimates.

  - Risks of material misstatement.

  - Indicators of possible management bias.

  - Disclosure of estimation uncertainty in the financial statements.

---

[13] ISA (UK and Ireland) 540, "Auditing Accounting Estimates, Including Fair Value Accounting Estimates, and Related Disclosures."

Financial Statement Disclosures

- The issues involved, and related judgments made, in formulating particularly sensitive financial statement disclosures (for example, disclosures related to revenue recognition, remuneration, going concern, subsequent events, and contingency issues).

- The overall neutrality, consistency and clarity of the disclosures in the financial statements.

Related Matters

- The potential effect on the financial statements of significant risks, exposures and uncertainties, such as pending litigation, that are disclosed in the financial statements.

- The extent to which the financial statements are affected by unusual transactions, including non-recurring amounts recognized during the period, and the extent to which such transactions are separately disclosed in the financial statements.

- The factors affecting asset and liability carrying values, including the entity's bases for determining useful lives assigned to tangible and intangible assets. The communication may explain how factors affecting carrying values were selected and how alternative selections would have affected the financial statements.

- The selective correction of misstatements, for example, correcting misstatements with the effect of increasing reported earnings, but not those that have the effect of decreasing reported earnings.

INTERNATIONAL STANDARD ON AUDITING (UK AND IRELAND) 265

COMMUNICATING DEFICIENCIES IN INTERNAL CONTROL TO THOSE CHARGED WITH GOVERNANCE AND MANAGEMENT

(Effective for audits of financial statements for periods ending on or after 15 December 2010)[1a]

CONTENTS

International Standard on Auditing (UK and Ireland) (ISA (UK and Ireland)) 265, "Communicating Deficiencies in Internal Control to Those Charged with Governance and Management" should be read in conjunction with ISA (UK and Ireland) 200, "Overall Objectives of the Independent Auditor and the Conduct of an Audit in Accordance with International Standards on Auditing (UK and Ireland)."

[1a] Conforming amendments to this standard as a result of ISA (UK and Ireland) 610 (Revised June 2013), *Using the Work of Internal Auditors*, are included that are effective for audits of financial statements for periods ending on or after 15 June 2014. Details of the amendments are given in the Annexure to ISA (UK and Ireland) 610 (Revised June 2013).

Introduction

Scope of this ISA (UK and Ireland)

1. This International Standard on Auditing (UK and Ireland) (ISA (UK and Ireland)) deals with the auditor's responsibility to communicate appropriately to those charged with governance and management deficiencies in internal control[1] that the auditor has identified in an audit of financial statements. This ISA (UK and Ireland) does not impose additional responsibilities on the auditor regarding obtaining an understanding of internal control and designing and performing tests of controls over and above the requirements of ISA (UK and Ireland) 315 and ISA (UK and Ireland) 330.[2] ISA (UK and Ireland) 260[3] establishes further requirements and provides guidance regarding the auditor's responsibility to communicate with those charged with governance in relation to the audit.

2. The auditor is required to obtain an understanding of internal control relevant to the audit when identifying and assessing the risks of material misstatement.[4] In making those risk assessments, the auditor considers internal control in order to design audit procedures that are appropriate in the circumstances, but not for the purpose of expressing an opinion on the effectiveness of internal control. The auditor may identify deficiencies in internal control not only during this risk assessment process but also at any other stage of the audit. This ISA (UK and Ireland) specifies which identified deficiencies the auditor is required to communicate to those charged with governance and management.

3. Nothing in this ISA (UK and Ireland) precludes the auditor from communicating to those charged with governance and management other internal control matters that the auditor has identified during the audit.

Effective Date

4. This ISA (UK and Ireland) is effective for audits of financial statements for periods ending on or after 15 December 2010.[1a]

Objective

5. The objective of the auditor is to communicate appropriately to those charged with governance and management deficiencies in internal control that the auditor has identified during the audit and that, in the auditor's professional judgment, are of sufficient importance to merit their respective attentions.

---

[1] ISA (UK and Ireland) 315, "Identifying and Assessing the Risks of Material Misstatement through Understanding the Entity and Its Environment," paragraphs 4 and 12.
[2] ISA (UK and Ireland) 330, "The Auditor's Responses to Assessed Risks."
[3] ISA (UK and Ireland) 260, "Communication with Those Charged with Governance."
[4] ISA (UK and Ireland) 315, paragraph 12. Paragraphs A60-A65 provide guidance on controls relevant to the audit.

Definitions

6. For purposes of the ISAs (UK and Ireland), the following terms have the meanings attributed below:

    (a) Deficiency in internal control – This exists when:

        (i) A control is designed, implemented or operated in such a way that it is unable to prevent, or detect and correct, misstatements in the financial statements on a timely basis; or

        (ii) A control necessary to prevent, or detect and correct, misstatements in the financial statements on a timely basis is missing.

    (b) Significant deficiency in internal control – A deficiency or combination of deficiencies in internal control that, in the auditor's professional judgment, is of sufficient importance to merit the attention of those charged with governance. (Ref: Para. A5)

Requirements

7. The auditor shall determine whether, on the basis of the audit work performed, the auditor has identified one or more deficiencies in internal control. (Ref: Para. A1-A4)

8. If the auditor has identified one or more deficiencies in internal control, the auditor shall determine, on the basis of the audit work performed, whether, individually or in combination, they constitute significant deficiencies. (Ref: Para. A5-A11)

9. The auditor shall communicate in writing significant deficiencies in internal control identified during the audit to those charged with governance on a timely basis. (Ref: Para. A12-A18, A27)

10. The auditor shall also communicate to management at an appropriate level of responsibility on a timely basis: (Ref: Para. A19, A27)

    (a) In writing, significant deficiencies in internal control that the auditor has communicated or intends to communicate to those charged with governance, unless it would be inappropriate to communicate directly to management in the circumstances; and (Ref: Para. A14, A20-A21)

    (b) Other deficiencies in internal control identified during the audit that have not been communicated to management by other parties and that, in the auditor's professional judgment, are of sufficient importance to merit management's attention. (Ref: Para. A22-A26)

11. The auditor shall include in the written communication of significant deficiencies in internal control:

(a) A description of the deficiencies and an explanation of their potential effects; and (Ref: Para. A28)

(b) Sufficient information to enable those charged with governance and management to understand the context of the communication. In particular, the auditor shall explain that: (Ref: Para. A29-A30)

(i) The purpose of the audit was for the auditor to express an opinion on the financial statements;

(ii) The audit included consideration of internal control relevant to the preparation of the financial statements in order to design audit procedures that are appropriate in the circumstances, but not for the purpose of expressing an opinion on the effectiveness of internal control; and

(iii) The matters being reported are limited to those deficiencies that the auditor has identified during the audit and that the auditor has concluded are of sufficient importance to merit being reported to those charged with governance.

***

Application and Other Explanatory Material

Determination of Whether Deficiencies in Internal Control Have Been Identified (Ref: Para. 7)

A1. In determining whether the auditor has identified one or more deficiencies in internal control, the auditor may discuss the relevant facts and circumstances of the auditor's findings with the appropriate level of management. This discussion provides an opportunity for the auditor to alert management on a timely basis to the existence of deficiencies of which management may not have been previously aware. The level of management with whom it is appropriate to discuss the findings is one that is familiar with the internal control area concerned and that has the authority to take remedial action on any identified deficiencies in internal control. In some circumstances, it may not be appropriate for the auditor to discuss the auditor's findings directly with management, for example, if the findings appear to call management's integrity or competence into question (see paragraph A20).

A2. In discussing the facts and circumstances of the auditor's findings with management, the auditor may obtain other relevant information for further consideration, such as:

• Management's understanding of the actual or suspected causes of the deficiencies.

• Exceptions arising from the deficiencies that management may have noted, for example, misstatements that were not prevented by the relevant information technology (IT) controls.

- A preliminary indication from management of its response to the findings.

Considerations Specific to Smaller Entities

A3. While the concepts underlying control activities in smaller entities are likely to be similar to those in larger entities, the formality with which they operate will vary. Further, smaller entities may find that certain types of control activities are not necessary because of controls applied by management. For example, management's sole authority for granting credit to customers and approving significant purchases can provide effective control over important account balances and transactions, lessening or removing the need for more detailed control activities.

A4. Also, smaller entities often have fewer employees which may limit the extent to which segregation of duties is practicable. However, in a small owner-managed entity, the owner-manager may be able to exercise more effective oversight than in a larger entity. This higher level of management oversight needs to be balanced against the greater potential for management override of controls.

Significant Deficiencies in Internal Control (Ref: Para. 6(b), 8)

A5. The significance of a deficiency or a combination of deficiencies in internal control depends not only on whether a misstatement has actually occurred, but also on the likelihood that a misstatement could occur and the potential magnitude of the misstatement. Significant deficiencies may therefore exist even though the auditor has not identified misstatements during the audit.

A6. Examples of matters that the auditor may consider in determining whether a deficiency or combination of deficiencies in internal control constitutes a significant deficiency include:

- The likelihood of the deficiencies leading to material misstatements in the financial statements in the future.

- The susceptibility to loss or fraud of the related asset or liability.

- The subjectivity and complexity of determining estimated amounts, such as fair value accounting estimates.

- The financial statement amounts exposed to the deficiencies.

- The volume of activity that has occurred or could occur in the account balance or class of transactions exposed to the deficiency or deficiencies.

- The importance of the controls to the financial reporting process; for example:

  o General monitoring controls (such as oversight of management).

  o Controls over the prevention and detection of fraud.

- ○ Controls over the selection and application of significant accounting policies.

- ○ Controls over significant transactions with related parties.

- ○ Controls over significant transactions outside the entity's normal course of business.

- ○ Controls over the period-end financial reporting process (such as controls over non-recurring journal entries).

- The cause and frequency of the exceptions detected as a result of the deficiencies in the controls.

- The interaction of the deficiency with other deficiencies in internal control.

A7. Indicators of significant deficiencies in internal control include, for example:

- Evidence of ineffective aspects of the control environment, such as:

  - ○ Indications that significant transactions in which management is financially interested are not being appropriately scrutinized by those charged with governance.

  - ○ Identification of management fraud, whether or not material, that was not prevented by the entity's internal control.

  - ○ Management's failure to implement appropriate remedial action on significant deficiencies previously communicated.

- Absence of a risk assessment process within the entity where such a process would ordinarily be expected to have been established.

- Evidence of an ineffective entity risk assessment process, such as management's failure to identify a risk of material misstatement that the auditor would expect the entity's risk assessment process to have identified.

- Evidence of an ineffective response to identified significant risks (for example, absence of controls over such a risk).

- Misstatements detected by the auditor's procedures that were not prevented, or detected and corrected, by the entity's internal control.

- Restatement of previously issued financial statements to reflect the correction of a material misstatement due to error or fraud.

- Evidence of management's inability to oversee the preparation of the financial statements.

A8.   Controls may be designed to operate individually or in combination to effectively prevent, or detect and correct, misstatements.[5] For example, controls over accounts receivable may consist of both automated and manual controls designed to operate together to prevent, or detect and correct, misstatements in the account balance. A deficiency in internal control on its own may not be sufficiently important to constitute a significant deficiency. However, a combination of deficiencies affecting the same account balance or disclosure, relevant assertion, or component of internal control may increase the risks of misstatement to such an extent as to give rise to a significant deficiency.

A9.   Law or regulation in some jurisdictions may establish a requirement (particularly for audits of listed entities) for the auditor to communicate to those charged with governance or to other relevant parties (such as regulators) one or more specific types of deficiency in internal control that the auditor has identified during the audit. Where law or regulation has established specific terms and definitions for these types of deficiency and requires the auditor to use these terms and definitions for the purpose of the communication, the auditor uses such terms and definitions when communicating in accordance with the legal or regulatory requirement.

A10.   Where the jurisdiction has established specific terms for the types of deficiency in internal control to be communicated but has not defined such terms, it may be necessary for the auditor to use judgment to determine the matters to be communicated further to the legal or regulatory requirement. In doing so, the auditor may consider it appropriate to have regard to the requirements and guidance in this ISA (UK and Ireland). For example, if the purpose of the legal or regulatory requirement is to bring to the attention of those charged with governance certain internal control matters of which they should be aware, it may be appropriate to regard such matters as being generally equivalent to the significant deficiencies required by this ISA (UK and Ireland) to be communicated to those charged with governance.

A11.   The requirements of this ISA (UK and Ireland) remain applicable notwithstanding that law or regulation may require the auditor to use specific terms or definitions.

Communication of Deficiencies in Internal Control

Communication of Significant Deficiencies in Internal Control to Those Charged with Governance (Ref: Para. 9)

A12.   Communicating significant deficiencies in writing to those charged with governance reflects the importance of these matters, and assists those charged with governance in fulfilling their oversight responsibilities. ISA (UK and Ireland) 260 establishes relevant considerations regarding communication with those charged with governance when all of them are involved in managing the entity.[6]

---

5   ISA (UK and Ireland) 315, paragraph A66.
6   ISA (UK and Ireland) 260, paragraph 13.

A12-1. In the UK and Ireland, where applicable, timely communication of significant deficiencies in writing to directors of listed entities can assist them apply the revised "Turnbull Guidance"[6a] on the requirements of the Combined Code relating to internal control and reporting to shareholders thereon.

A13. In determining when to issue the written communication, the auditor may consider whether receipt of such communication would be an important factor in enabling those charged with governance to discharge their oversight responsibilities. In addition, for listed entities in certain jurisdictions, those charged with governance may need to receive the auditor's written communication before the date of approval of the financial statements in order to discharge specific responsibilities in relation to internal control for regulatory or other purposes. For other entities, the auditor may issue the written communication at a later date. Nevertheless, in the latter case, as the auditor's written communication of significant deficiencies forms part of the final audit file, the written communication is subject to the overriding requirement[7] for the auditor to complete the assembly of the final audit file on a timely basis. ISA (UK and Ireland) 230 states that an appropriate time limit within which to complete the assembly of the final audit file is ordinarily not more than 60 days after the date of the auditor's report.[8]

A14. Regardless of the timing of the written communication of significant deficiencies, the auditor may communicate these orally in the first instance to management and, when appropriate, to those charged with governance to assist them in taking timely remedial action to minimize the risks of material misstatement. Doing so, however, does not relieve the auditor of the responsibility to communicate the significant deficiencies in writing, as this ISA (UK and Ireland) requires.

A15. The level of detail at which to communicate significant deficiencies is a matter of the auditor's professional judgment in the circumstances. Factors that the auditor may consider in determining an appropriate level of detail for the communication include, for example:

- The nature of the entity. For instance, the communication required for a public interest entity may be different from that for a non-public interest entity.

- The size and complexity of the entity. For instance, the communication required for a complex entity may be different from that for an entity operating a simple business.

- The nature of significant deficiencies that the auditor has identified.

[6a] "Internal Control – Revised Guidance for Directors on the Combined Code" issued by the Financial Reporting Council, October 2005.
[7] ISA (UK and Ireland) 230, "Audit Documentation," paragraph 14.
[8] ISA (UK and Ireland) 230, paragraph A21.

- The entity's governance composition. For instance, more detail may be needed if those charged with governance include members who do not have significant experience in the entity's industry or in the affected areas.

- Legal or regulatory requirements regarding the communication of specific types of deficiency in internal control.

A16. Management and those charged with governance may already be aware of significant deficiencies that the auditor has identified during the audit and may have chosen not to remedy them because of cost or other considerations. The responsibility for evaluating the costs and benefits of implementing remedial action rests with management and those charged with governance. Accordingly, the requirement in paragraph 9 applies regardless of cost or other considerations that management and those charged with governance may consider relevant in determining whether to remedy such deficiencies.

A17. The fact that the auditor communicated a significant deficiency to those charged with governance and management in a previous audit does not eliminate the need for the auditor to repeat the communication if remedial action has not yet been taken. If a previously communicated significant deficiency remains, the current year's communication may repeat the description from the previous communication, or simply reference the previous communication. The auditor may ask management or, where appropriate, those charged with governance, why the significant deficiency has not yet been remedied. A failure to act, in the absence of a rational explanation, may in itself represent a significant deficiency.

Considerations Specific to Smaller Entities

A18. In the case of audits of smaller entities, the auditor may communicate in a less structured manner with those charged with governance than in the case of larger entities.

Communication of Deficiencies in Internal Control to Management (Ref: Para. 10)

A19. Ordinarily, the appropriate level of management is the one that has responsibility and authority to evaluate the deficiencies in internal control and to take the necessary remedial action. For significant deficiencies, the appropriate level is likely to be the chief executive officer or chief financial officer (or equivalent) as these matters are also required to be communicated to those charged with governance. For other deficiencies in internal control, the appropriate level may be operational management with more direct involvement in the control areas affected and with the authority to take appropriate remedial action.

Communication of Significant Deficiencies in Internal Control to Management (Ref: Para. 10(a))

A20. Certain identified significant deficiencies in internal control may call into question the integrity or competence of management. For example, there may be evidence of fraud or intentional non-compliance with laws and regulations by management, or management may exhibit an inability to oversee the preparation of adequate financial statements that may raise doubt about management's competence. Accordingly, it may not be appropriate to communicate such deficiencies directly to management.

A21. ISA (UK and Ireland) 250 establishes requirements and provides guidance on the reporting of identified or suspected non-compliance with laws and regulations, including when those charged with governance are themselves involved in such non-compliance.[9] ISA (UK and Ireland) 240 establishes requirements and provides guidance regarding communication to those charged with governance when the auditor has identified fraud or suspected fraud involving management.[10]

Communication of Other Deficiencies in Internal Control to Management (Ref: Para. 10(b))

A22. During the audit, the auditor may identify other deficiencies in internal control that are not significant deficiencies but that may be of sufficient importance to merit management's attention. The determination as to which other deficiencies in internal control merit management's attention is a matter of professional judgment in the circumstances, taking into account the likelihood and potential magnitude of misstatements that may arise in the financial statements as a result of those deficiencies.

A23. The communication of other deficiencies in internal control that merit management's attention need not be in writing but may be oral. Where the auditor has discussed the facts and circumstances of the auditor's findings with management, the auditor may consider an oral communication of the other deficiencies to have been made to management at the time of these discussions. Accordingly, a formal communication need not be made subsequently.

A24. If the auditor has communicated deficiencies in internal control other than significant deficiencies to management in a prior period and management has chosen not to remedy them for cost or other reasons, the auditor need not repeat the communication in the current period. The auditor is also not required to repeat information about such deficiencies if it has been previously communicated to management by other parties, such as the internal audit function or regulators. It may, however, be appropriate for the auditor to re-communicate these other deficiencies if there has been a change of management, or if new information has come to the auditor's attention that alters the prior understanding of the auditor and management regarding the deficiencies. Nevertheless, the failure of management to remedy other deficiencies in internal control that were previously communicated may become a significant deficiency requiring communication with those charged with governance. Whether this is the case depends on the auditor's judgment in the circumstances.

---

[9] ISA (UK and Ireland) 250, "Consideration of Laws and Regulations in an Audit of Financial Statements," paragraphs 22-28.

[10] ISA (UK and Ireland) 240, "The Auditor's Responsibilities Relating to Fraud in an Audit of Financial Statements," paragraph 41.

A25. In some circumstances, those charged with governance may wish to be made aware of the details of other deficiencies in internal control the auditor has communicated to management, or be briefly informed of the nature of the other deficiencies. Alternatively, the auditor may consider it appropriate to inform those charged with governance of the communication of the other deficiencies to management. In either case, the auditor may report orally or in writing to those charged with governance as appropriate.

A26. ISA (UK and Ireland) 260 establishes relevant considerations regarding communication with those charged with governance when all of them are involved in managing the entity.[11]

Considerations Specific to Public Sector Entities (Ref: Para. 9-10)

A27. Public sector auditors may have additional responsibilities to communicate deficiencies in internal control that the auditor has identified during the audit, in ways, at a level of detail and to parties not envisaged in this ISA (UK and Ireland). For example, significant deficiencies may have to be communicated to the legislature or other governing body. Law, regulation or other authority may also mandate that public sector auditors report deficiencies in internal control, irrespective of the significance of the potential effects of those deficiencies. Further, legislation may require public sector auditors to report on broader internal control-related matters than the deficiencies in internal control required to be communicated by this ISA (UK and Ireland), for example, controls related to compliance with legislative authorities, regulations, or provisions of contracts or grant agreements.

Content of Written Communication of Significant Deficiencies in Internal Control (Ref: Para. 11)

A28. In explaining the potential effects of the significant deficiencies, the auditor need not quantify those effects. The significant deficiencies may be grouped together for reporting purposes where it is appropriate to do so. The auditor may also include in the written communication suggestions for remedial action on the deficiencies, management's actual or proposed responses, and a statement as to whether or not the auditor has undertaken any steps to verify whether management's responses have been implemented.

A29. The auditor may consider it appropriate to include the following information as additional context for the communication:

- An indication that if the auditor had performed more extensive procedures on internal control, the auditor might have identified more deficiencies to be reported, or concluded that some of the reported deficiencies need not, in fact, have been reported.

---

[11] ISA (UK and Ireland) 260, paragraph 13.

- An indication that such communication has been provided for the purposes of those charged with governance, and that it may not be suitable for other purposes.

A30. Law or regulation may require the auditor or management to furnish a copy of the auditor's written communication on significant deficiencies to appropriate regulatory authorities. Where this is the case, the auditor's written communication may identify such regulatory authorities.

INTERNATIONAL STANDARD ON AUDITING
(UK AND IRELAND) 300

PLANNING AN AUDIT OF FINANCIAL STATEMENTS

(Effective for audits of financial statements for periods ending on or after 15 December 2010)[1a]

CONTENTS

Paragraphs

[1a] Conforming amendments to this standard as a result of ISA (UK and Ireland) 610 (Revised June 2013), *Using the Work of Internal Auditors*, are included that are effective for audits of financial statements for periods ending on or after 15 June 2014. Details of the amendments are given in the Annexure to ISA (UK and Ireland) 610 (Revised June 2013).

International Standard on Auditing (UK and Ireland) (ISA (UK and Ireland)) 300, "Planning an Audit of Financial Statements" should be read in conjunction with ISA (UK and Ireland) 200, "Overall Objectives of the Independent Auditor and the Conduct of an Audit in Accordance with International Standards on Auditing (UK and Ireland)."

Introduction

Scope of this ISA (UK and Ireland)

1. This International Standard on Auditing (UK and Ireland) (ISA (UK and Ireland)) deals with the auditor's responsibility to plan an audit of financial statements. This ISA (UK and Ireland) is written in the context of recurring audits. Additional considerations in an initial audit engagement are separately identified.

The Role and Timing of Planning

2. Planning an audit involves establishing the overall audit strategy for the engagement and developing an audit plan. Adequate planning benefits the audit of financial statements in several ways, including the following: (Ref: Para. A1-A3)

    *   Helping the auditor to devote appropriate attention to important areas of the audit.

    *   Helping the auditor identify and resolve potential problems on a timely basis.

    *   Helping the auditor properly organize and manage the audit engagement so that it is performed in an effective and efficient manner.

    *   Assisting in the selection of engagement team members with appropriate levels of capabilities and competence to respond to anticipated risks, and the proper assignment of work to them.

    *   Facilitating the direction and supervision of engagement team members and the review of their work.

    *   Assisting, where applicable, in coordination of work done by auditors of components and experts.

Effective Date

3. This ISA (UK and Ireland) is effective for audits of financial statements for periods ending on or after 15 December 2010.[1a]

Objective

4. The objective of the auditor is to plan the audit so that it will be performed in an effective manner.

Requirements

Involvement of Key Engagement Team Members

5.   The engagement partner and other key members of the engagement team shall be involved in planning the audit, including planning and participating in the discussion among engagement team members. (Ref: Para. A4)

Preliminary Engagement Activities

6.   The auditor shall undertake the following activities at the beginning of the current audit engagement:

(a)   Performing procedures required by ISA (UK and Ireland) 220 regarding the continuance of the client relationship and the specific audit engagement;[1]

(b)   Evaluating compliance with relevant ethical requirements, including independence, in accordance with ISA (UK and Ireland) 220;[2] and

(c)   Establishing an understanding of the terms of the engagement, as required by ISA (UK and Ireland) 210.[3] (Ref: Para. A5-A7)

Planning Activities

7.   The auditor shall establish an overall audit strategy that sets the scope, timing and direction of the audit, and that guides the development of the audit plan.

8.   In establishing the overall audit strategy, the auditor shall:

(a)   Identify the characteristics of the engagement that define its scope;

(b)   Ascertain the reporting objectives of the engagement to plan the timing of the audit and the nature of the communications required;

(c)   Consider the factors that, in the auditor's professional judgment, are significant in directing the engagement team's efforts;

(d)   Consider the results of preliminary engagement activities and, where applicable, whether knowledge gained on other engagements performed by the engagement partner for the entity is relevant; and

(e)   Ascertain the nature, timing and extent of resources necessary to perform the engagement. (Ref: Para. A8-A11)

9.   The auditor shall develop an audit plan that shall include a description of:

---

[1]   ISA (UK and Ireland) 220, "Quality Control for an Audit of Financial Statements," paragraphs 12-13.
[2]   ISA (UK and Ireland) 220, paragraphs 9-11.
[3]   ISA (UK and Ireland) 210, "Agreeing the Terms of Audit Engagements," paragraphs 9-13.

**FINANCIAL
REPORTING COUNCIL**

(a) The nature, timing and extent of planned risk assessment procedures, as determined under ISA (UK and Ireland) 315.[4]

(b) The nature, timing and extent of planned further audit procedures at the assertion level, as determined under ISA (UK and Ireland) 330.[5]

(c) Other planned audit procedures that are required to be carried out so that the engagement complies with ISAs (UK and Ireland). (Ref: Para. A12)

10. The auditor shall update and change the overall audit strategy and the audit plan as necessary during the course of the audit. (Ref: Para. A13)

11. The auditor shall plan the nature, timing and extent of direction and supervision of engagement team members and the review of their work. (Ref: Para. A14-A15)

Documentation

12. The auditor shall include in the audit documentation:[6]

(a) The overall audit strategy;

(b) The audit plan; and

(c) Any significant changes made during the audit engagement to the overall audit strategy or the audit plan, and the reasons for such changes. (Ref: Para. A16-A19)

Additional Considerations in Initial Audit Engagements

13. The auditor shall undertake the following activities prior to starting an initial audit:

(a) Performing procedures required by ISA (UK and Ireland) 220 regarding the acceptance of the client relationship and the specific audit engagement;[7] and

(b) Communicating with the predecessor auditor, where there has been a change of auditors, in compliance with relevant ethical requirements. (Ref: Para. A20)

***

---

[4] ISA (UK and Ireland) 315, "Identifying and Assessing the Risks of Material Misstatement through Understanding the Entity and Its Environment."
[5] ISA (UK and Ireland) 330, "The Auditor's Responses to Assessed Risks."
[6] ISA (UK and Ireland) 230, "Audit Documentation," paragraphs 8-11, and paragraph A6.
[7] ISA (UK and Ireland) 220, paragraphs 12-13.

Application and Other Explanatory Material

The Role and Timing of Planning (Ref: Para. 2)

A1. The nature and extent of planning activities will vary according to the size and complexity of the entity, the key engagement team members' previous experience with the entity, and changes in circumstances that occur during the audit engagement.

A2. Planning is not a discrete phase of an audit, but rather a continual and iterative process that often begins shortly after (or in connection with) the completion of the previous audit and continues until the completion of the current audit engagement. Planning, however, includes consideration of the timing of certain activities and audit procedures that need to be completed prior to the performance of further audit procedures. For example, planning includes the need to consider, prior to the auditor's identification and assessment of the risks of material misstatement, such matters as:

  * The analytical procedures to be applied as risk assessment procedures.

  * Obtaining a general understanding of the legal and regulatory framework applicable to the entity and how the entity is complying with that framework.

  * The determination of materiality.

  * The involvement of experts.

  * The performance of other risk assessment procedures.

A3. The auditor may decide to discuss elements of planning with the entity's management to facilitate the conduct and management of the audit engagement (for example, to coordinate some of the planned audit procedures with the work of the entity's personnel). Although these discussions often occur, the overall audit strategy and the audit plan remain the auditor's responsibility. When discussing matters included in the overall audit strategy or audit plan, care is required in order not to compromise the effectiveness of the audit. For example, discussing the nature and timing of detailed audit procedures with management may compromise the effectiveness of the audit by making the audit procedures too predictable.

Involvement of Key Engagement Team Members (Ref: Para. 5)

A4.   The involvement of the engagement partner and other key members of the engagement team in planning the audit draws on their experience and insight, thereby enhancing the effectiveness and efficiency of the planning process.[8]

Preliminary Engagement Activities (Ref: Para. 6)

A5.   Performing the preliminary engagement activities specified in paragraph 6 at the beginning of the current audit engagement assists the auditor in identifying and evaluating events or circumstances that may adversely affect the auditor's ability to plan and perform the audit engagement.

A6.   Performing these preliminary engagement activities enables the auditor to plan an audit engagement for which, for example:

- The auditor maintains the necessary independence and ability to perform the engagement.

- There are no issues with management[8a] integrity that may affect the auditor's willingness to continue the engagement.

- There is no misunderstanding with the client as to the terms of the engagement.

A7.   The auditor's consideration of client continuance and relevant ethical requirements, including independence, occurs throughout the audit engagement as conditions and changes in circumstances occur. Performing initial procedures on both client continuance and evaluation of relevant ethical requirements (including independence) at the beginning of the current audit engagement means that they are completed prior to the performance of other significant activities for the current audit engagement. For continuing audit engagements, such initial procedures often occur shortly after (or in connection with) the completion of the previous audit.

Planning Activities

The Overall Audit Strategy (Ref: Para. 7-8)

A8.   The process of establishing the overall audit strategy assists the auditor to determine, subject to the completion of the auditor's risk assessment procedures, such matters as:

---

[8]   ISA (UK and Ireland) 315, paragraph 10, establishes requirements and provides guidance on the engagement team's discussion of the susceptibility of the entity to material misstatements of the financial statements. ISA (UK and Ireland) 240, "The Auditor's Responsibilities Relating to Fraud in an Audit of Financial Statements," paragraph 15, provides guidance on the emphasis given during this discussion to the susceptibility of the entity's financial statements to material misstatement due to fraud.

[8a] In the UK and Ireland, the auditor is also concerned to establish that there are no issues with the integrity of those charged with governance that may affect the auditor's willingness to continue the engagement.

- The resources to deploy for specific audit areas, such as the use of appropriately experienced team members for high risk areas or the involvement of experts on complex matters;

- The amount of resources to allocate to specific audit areas, such as the number of team members assigned to observe the inventory count at material locations, the extent of review of other auditors' work in the case of group audits, or the audit budget in hours to allocate to high risk areas;

- When these resources are to be deployed, such as whether at an interim audit stage or at key cut-off dates; and

- How such resources are managed, directed and supervised, such as when team briefing and debriefing meetings are expected to be held, how engagement partner and manager reviews are expected to take place (for example, on-site or off-site), and whether to complete engagement quality control reviews.

A9. The Appendix lists examples of considerations in establishing the overall audit strategy.

A10. Once the overall audit strategy has been established, an audit plan can be developed to address the various matters identified in the overall audit strategy, taking into account the need to achieve the audit objectives through the efficient use of the auditor's resources. The establishment of the overall audit strategy and the detailed audit plan are not necessarily discrete or sequential processes, but are closely inter-related since changes in one may result in consequential changes to the other.

Considerations Specific to Smaller Entities

A11. In audits of small entities, the entire audit may be conducted by a very small engagement team. Many audits of small entities involve the engagement partner (who may be a sole practitioner) working with one engagement team member (or without any engagement team members). With a smaller team, co-ordination of, and communication between, team members are easier. Establishing the overall audit strategy for the audit of a small entity need not be a complex or time-consuming exercise; it varies according to the size of the entity, the complexity of the audit, and the size of the engagement team. For example, a brief memorandum prepared at the completion of the previous audit, based on a review of the working papers and highlighting issues identified in the audit just completed, updated in the current period based on discussions with the owner-manager, can serve as the documented audit strategy for the current audit engagement if it covers the matters noted in paragraph 8.

The Audit Plan (Ref: Para. 9)

A12. The audit plan is more detailed than the overall audit strategy in that it includes the nature, timing and extent of audit procedures to be performed by engagement team members. Planning for these audit procedures takes place over the course of the audit as the audit plan for the engagement develops. For example, planning of the auditor's risk assessment procedures occurs early in the audit process. However, planning the nature, timing and extent of specific further audit procedures depends on the outcome of those risk assessment procedures. In addition, the auditor may begin the execution of further audit procedures for some classes of transactions, account balances and disclosures before planning all remaining further audit procedures.

Changes to Planning Decisions during the Course of the Audit (Ref: Para. 10)

A13. As a result of unexpected events, changes in conditions, or the audit evidence obtained from the results of audit procedures, the auditor may need to modify the overall audit strategy and audit plan and thereby the resulting planned nature, timing and extent of further audit procedures, based on the revised consideration of assessed risks. This may be the case when information comes to the auditor's attention that differs significantly from the information available when the auditor planned the audit procedures. For example, audit evidence obtained through the performance of substantive procedures may contradict the audit evidence obtained through tests of controls.

Direction, Supervision and Review (Ref: Para. 11)

A14. The nature, timing and extent of the direction and supervision of engagement team members and review of their work vary depending on many factors, including:

- The size and complexity of the entity.

- The area of the audit.

- The assessed risks of material misstatement (for example, an increase in the assessed risk of material misstatement for a given area of the audit ordinarily requires a corresponding increase in the extent and timeliness of direction and supervision of engagement team members, and a more detailed review of their work).

- The capabilities and competence of the individual team members performing the audit work.

   ISA (UK and Ireland) 220 contains further guidance on the direction, supervision and review of audit work.[9]

Considerations Specific to Smaller Entities

A15. If an audit is carried out entirely by the engagement partner, questions of direction and supervision of engagement team members and review of their work do not arise. In such cases, the engagement partner, having personally conducted all aspects of the work, will be aware of all material issues. Forming an objective view on the

---

[9]   ISA (UK and Ireland) 220, paragraphs 15-17.

appropriateness of the judgments made in the course of the audit can present practical problems when the same individual also performs the entire audit. If particularly complex or unusual issues are involved, and the audit is performed by a sole practitioner, it may be desirable to consult with other suitably-experienced auditors or the auditor's professional body.

Documentation (Ref: Para. 12)

A16. The documentation of the overall audit strategy is a record of the key decisions considered necessary to properly plan the audit and to communicate significant matters to the engagement team. For example, the auditor may summarize the overall audit strategy in the form of a memorandum that contains key decisions regarding the overall scope, timing and conduct of the audit.

A17. The documentation of the audit plan is a record of the planned nature, timing and extent of risk assessment procedures and further audit procedures at the assertion level in response to the assessed risks. It also serves as a record of the proper planning of the audit procedures that can be reviewed and approved prior to their performance. The auditor may use standard audit programs or audit completion checklists, tailored as needed to reflect the particular engagement circumstances.

A18. A record of the significant changes to the overall audit strategy and the audit plan, and resulting changes to the planned nature, timing and extent of audit procedures, explains why the significant changes were made, and the overall strategy and audit plan finally adopted for the audit. It also reflects the appropriate response to the significant changes occurring during the audit.

Considerations Specific to Smaller Entities

A19. As discussed in paragraph A11, a suitable, brief memorandum may serve as the documented strategy for the audit of a smaller entity. For the audit plan, standard audit programs or checklists (see paragraph A17) drawn up on the assumption of few relevant control activities, as is likely to be the case in a smaller entity, may be used provided that they are tailored to the circumstances of the engagement, including the auditor's risk assessments.

Additional Considerations in Initial Audit Engagements (Ref: Para. 13)

A20. The purpose and objective of planning the audit are the same whether the audit is an initial or recurring engagement. However, for an initial audit, the auditor may need to expand the planning activities because the auditor does not ordinarily have the previous experience with the entity that is considered when planning recurring engagements. For an initial audit engagement, additional matters the auditor may consider in establishing the overall audit strategy and audit plan include the following:

- Unless prohibited by law or regulation, arrangements to be made with the predecessor auditor, for example, to review the predecessor auditor's working papers.

- Any major issues (including the application of accounting principles or of auditing and reporting standards) discussed with management in connection with the initial selection as auditor, the communication of these matters to those charged with governance and how these matters affect the overall audit strategy and audit plan.

- The audit procedures necessary to obtain sufficient appropriate audit evidence regarding opening balances.[10]

- Other procedures required by the firm's system of quality control for initial audit engagements (for example, the firm's system of quality control may require the involvement of another partner or senior individual to review the overall audit strategy prior to commencing significant audit procedures or to review reports prior to their issuance).

---

[10] ISA (UK and Ireland) 510, "Initial Audit Engagements—Opening Balances."

Appendix

(Ref: Para. 7-8, A8-A11)

Considerations in Establishing the Overall Audit Strategy

This appendix provides examples of matters the auditor may consider in establishing the overall audit strategy. Many of these matters will also influence the auditor's detailed audit plan. The examples provided cover a broad range of matters applicable to many engagements. While some of the matters referred to below may be required by other ISAs (UK and Ireland), not all matters are relevant to every audit engagement and the list is not necessarily complete.

Characteristics of the Engagement

- The financial reporting framework on which the financial information to be audited has been prepared, including any need for reconciliations to another financial reporting framework.

- Industry-specific reporting requirements such as reports mandated by industry regulators.

- The expected audit coverage, including the number and locations of components to be included.

- The nature of the control relationships between a parent and its components that determine how the group is to be consolidated.

- The extent to which components are audited by other auditors.

- The nature of the business segments to be audited, including the need for specialized knowledge.

- The reporting currency to be used, including any need for currency translation for the financial information audited.

- The need for a statutory audit of standalone financial statements in addition to an audit for consolidation purposes.

- Whether the entity has an internal audit function and if so, whether, in which areas and to what extent, the work of the function can be used, or internal auditors can be used to provide direct assistance[10a], for purposes of the audit.

[10a] The use of internal auditors to provide direct assistance is prohibited in an audit conducted in accordance with ISAs (UK and Ireland) – see ISA (UK and Ireland) 610 (Revised June 2013), "Using the Work of Internal Auditors", paragraph 5-1.

- The entity's use of service organizations and how the auditor may obtain evidence concerning the design or operation of controls performed by them.

- The expected use of audit evidence obtained in previous audits, for example, audit evidence related to risk assessment procedures and tests of controls.

- The effect of information technology on the audit procedures, including the availability of data and the expected use of computer-assisted audit techniques.

- The coordination of the expected coverage and timing of the audit work with any reviews of interim financial information and the effect on the audit of the information obtained during such reviews.

- The availability of client personnel and data.

Reporting Objectives, Timing of the Audit, and Nature of Communications

- The entity's timetable for reporting, such as at interim and final stages.

- The organization of meetings with management and those charged with governance to discuss the nature, timing and extent of the audit work.

- The discussion with management and those charged with governance regarding the expected type and timing of reports to be issued and other communications, both written and oral, including the auditor's report, management letters and communications to those charged with governance.

- The discussion with management regarding the expected communications on the status of audit work throughout the engagement.

- Communication with auditors of components regarding the expected types and timing of reports to be issued and other communications in connection with the audit of components.

- The expected nature and timing of communications among engagement team members, including the nature and timing of team meetings and timing of the review of work performed.

- Whether there are any other expected communications with third parties, including any statutory or contractual reporting responsibilities arising from the audit.

Significant Factors, Preliminary Engagement Activities, and Knowledge Gained on Other Engagements

- The determination of materiality in accordance with ISA (UK and Ireland) 320[11] and, where applicable:

---

[11] ISA (UK and Ireland) 320, "Materiality in Planning and Performing an Audit."

- ○ The determination of materiality for components and communication thereof to component auditors in accordance with ISA (UK and Ireland) 600.[12]

- ○ The preliminary identification of significant components and material classes of transactions, account balances and disclosures.

- Preliminary identification of areas where there may be a higher risk of material misstatement.

- The impact of the assessed risk of material misstatement at the overall financial statement level on direction, supervision and review.

- The manner in which the auditor emphasizes to engagement team members the need to maintain a questioning mind and to exercise professional skepticism in gathering and evaluating audit evidence.

- Results of previous audits that involved evaluating the operating effectiveness of internal control, including the nature of identified deficiencies and action taken to address them.

- The discussion of matters that may affect the audit with firm personnel responsible for performing other services to the entity.

- Evidence of management's[12a] commitment to the design, implementation and maintenance of sound internal control, including evidence of appropriate documentation of such internal control.

- Volume of transactions, which may determine whether it is more efficient for the auditor to rely on internal control.

- Importance attached to internal control throughout the entity to the successful operation of the business.

- Significant business developments affecting the entity, including changes in information technology and business processes, changes in key management, and acquisitions, mergers and divestments.

- Significant industry developments such as changes in industry regulations and new reporting requirements.

- Significant changes in the financial reporting framework, such as changes in accounting standards.

---

[12] ISA (UK and Ireland) 600, "Special Considerations—Audits of Group Financial Statements (Including the Work of Component Auditors), paragraphs 21-23 and 40(c).

[12a] In the UK and Ireland, the auditor also considers evidence of the commitment of those charged with governance to the design and operation of sound internal control.

- Other significant relevant developments, such as changes in the legal environment affecting the entity.

Nature, Timing and Extent of Resources

- The selection of the engagement team (including, where necessary, the engagement quality control reviewer) and the assignment of audit work to the team members, including the assignment of appropriately experienced team members to areas where there may be higher risks of material misstatement.

- Engagement budgeting, including considering the appropriate amount of time to set aside for areas where there may be higher risks of material misstatement.

INTERNATIONAL STANDARD ON AUDITING (UK AND IRELAND) 315 (REVISED JUNE 2013)

IDENTIFYING AND ASSESSING THE RISKS OF MATERIAL MISSTATEMENT THROUGH UNDERSTANDING THE ENTITY AND ITS ENVIRONMENT

(Effective for audits of financial statements for periods ending on or after 15 June 2014)

CONTENTS

International Standard on Auditing (UK and Ireland) (ISA (UK and Ireland)) 315 (Revised June 2013), "Identifying and Assessing the Risks of Material Misstatement through Understanding the Entity and Its Environment" should be read in conjunction with ISA (UK and Ireland) 200, "Overall Objectives of the Independent Auditor and the Conduct of an Audit in Accordance with International Standards on Auditing (UK and Ireland)."

Introduction

Scope of this ISA (UK and Ireland)

1. This International Standard on Auditing (UK and Ireland) (ISA (UK and Ireland)) deals with the auditor's responsibility to identify and assess the risks of material misstatement in the financial statements, through understanding the entity and its environment, including the entity's internal control.

Effective Date

2. This ISA (UK and Ireland) is effective for audits of financial statements for periods ending on or after 15 June 2014.

Objective

3. The objective of the auditor is to identify and assess the risks of material misstatement, whether due to fraud or error, at the financial statement and assertion levels, through understanding the entity and its environment, including the entity's internal control, thereby providing a basis for designing and implementing responses to the assessed risks of material misstatement.

Definitions

4. For purposes of the ISAs (UK and Ireland), the following terms have the meanings attributed below:

    (a) Assertions – Representations by management[1a], explicit or otherwise, that are embodied in the financial statements, as used by the auditor to consider the different types of potential misstatements that may occur.

    (b) Business risk – A risk resulting from significant conditions, events, circumstances, actions or inactions that could adversely affect an entity's ability to achieve its objectives and execute its strategies, or from the setting of inappropriate objectives and strategies.

    (c) Internal control – The process designed, implemented and maintained by those charged with governance, management and other personnel to provide reasonable assurance about the achievement of an entity's objectives with regard to reliability of financial reporting, effectiveness and efficiency of operations, and compliance with applicable laws and regulations. The term "controls" refers to any aspects of one or more of the components of internal control.

[1a] In the UK and Ireland, those charged with governance are responsible for preparing the financial statements.

(d) Risk assessment procedures – The audit procedures performed to obtain an understanding of the entity and its environment, including the entity's internal control, to identify and assess the risks of material misstatement, whether due to fraud or error, at the financial statement and assertion levels.

(e) Significant risk – An identified and assessed risk of material misstatement that, in the auditor's judgment, requires special audit consideration.

Requirements

Risk Assessment Procedures and Related Activities

5. The auditor shall perform risk assessment procedures to provide a basis for the identification and assessment of risks of material misstatement at the financial statement and assertion levels. Risk assessment procedures by themselves, however, do not provide sufficient appropriate audit evidence on which to base the audit opinion. (Ref: Para. A1-A5)

6. The risk assessment procedures shall include the following:

(a) Inquiries of management, of appropriate individuals within the internal audit function (if the function exists), and of others within the entity who in the auditor's judgment may have information that is likely to assist in identifying risks of material misstatement due to fraud or error. (Ref: Para. A6-A13)

(b) Analytical procedures. (Ref: Para. A14-A17)

(c) Observation and inspection. (Ref: Para. A18)

7. The auditor shall consider whether information obtained from the auditor's client acceptance or continuance process is relevant to identifying risks of material misstatement.

8. If the engagement partner has performed other engagements for the entity, the engagement partner shall consider whether information obtained is relevant to identifying risks of material misstatement.

9. Where the auditor intends to use information obtained from the auditor's previous experience with the entity and from audit procedures performed in previous audits, the auditor shall determine whether changes have occurred since the previous audit that may affect its relevance to the current audit. (Ref: Para. A19-A20)

10. The engagement partner and other key engagement team members shall discuss the susceptibility of the entity's financial statements to material misstatement, and the application of the applicable financial reporting framework to the entity's facts and circumstances. The engagement partner shall determine which matters are to be communicated to engagement team members not involved in the discussion. (Ref: Para. A21-A23)

The Required Understanding of the Entity and Its Environment, Including the Entity's Internal Control

The Entity and Its Environment

11.   The auditor shall obtain an understanding of the following:

   (a)   Relevant industry, regulatory, and other external factors including the applicable financial reporting framework. (Ref: Para. A24-A29)

   (b)   The nature of the entity, including:

   (i)   its operations;

   (ii)   its ownership and governance structures;

   (iii) the types of investments that the entity is making and plans to make, including investments in special-purpose entities; and

   (iv)   the way that the entity is structured and how it is financed

   to enable the auditor to understand the classes of transactions, account balances, and disclosures to be expected in the financial statements. (Ref: Para. A30-A34)

   (c)   The entity's selection and application of accounting policies, including the reasons for changes thereto. The auditor shall evaluate whether the entity's accounting policies are appropriate for its business and consistent with the applicable financial reporting framework and accounting policies used in the relevant industry. (Ref: Para. A35)

   (d)   The entity's objectives and strategies, and those related business risks that may result in risks of material misstatement. (Ref: Para. A36-A42)

   (e)   The measurement and review of the entity's financial performance. (Ref: Para. A43-A48)

The Entity's Internal Control

12.   The auditor shall obtain an understanding of internal control relevant to the audit. Although most controls relevant to the audit are likely to relate to financial reporting, not all controls that relate to financial reporting are relevant to the audit. It is a matter of the auditor's professional judgment whether a control, individually or in combination with others, is relevant to the audit. (Ref: Para. A49-A72)

Nature and Extent of the Understanding of Relevant Controls

13.   When obtaining an understanding of controls that are relevant to the audit, the auditor shall evaluate the design of those controls and determine whether they have been

implemented, by performing procedures in addition to inquiry of the entity's personnel. (Ref: Para. A73-A75)

Components of Internal Control

Control environment

14. The auditor shall obtain an understanding of the control environment. As part of obtaining this understanding, the auditor shall evaluate whether:

   (a) Management, with the oversight of those charged with governance, has created and maintained a culture of honesty and ethical behavior; and

   (b) The strengths in the control environment elements collectively provide an appropriate foundation for the other components of internal control, and whether those other components are not undermined by deficiencies in the control environment. (Ref: Para. A76-A86)

The entity's risk assessment process

15. The auditor shall obtain an understanding of whether the entity has a process for:

   (a) Identifying business risks relevant to financial reporting objectives;

   (b) Estimating the significance of the risks;

   (c) Assessing the likelihood of their occurrence; and

   (d) Deciding about actions to address those risks. (Ref: Para. A87)

16. If the entity has established such a process (referred to hereafter as the "entity's risk assessment process"), the auditor shall obtain an understanding of it, and the results thereof. If the auditor identifies risks of material misstatement that management failed to identify, the auditor shall evaluate whether there was an underlying risk of a kind that the auditor expects would have been identified by the entity's risk assessment process. If there is such a risk, the auditor shall obtain an understanding of why that process failed to identify it, and evaluate whether the process is appropriate to its circumstances or determine if there is a significant deficiency in internal control with regard to the entity's risk assessment process.

17. If the entity has not established such a process or has an ad hoc process, the auditor shall discuss with management whether business risks relevant to financial reporting objectives have been identified and how they have been addressed. The auditor shall evaluate whether the absence of a documented risk assessment process is appropriate in the circumstances, or determine whether it represents a significant deficiency in internal control. (Ref: Para. A88)

The information system, including the related business processes, relevant to financial reporting, and communication

18.   The auditor shall obtain an understanding of the information system, including the related business processes, relevant to financial reporting, including the following areas:

   (a)   The classes of transactions in the entity's operations that are significant to the financial statements;

   (b)   The procedures, within both information technology (IT) and manual systems, by which those transactions are initiated, recorded, processed, corrected as necessary, transferred to the general ledger and reported in the financial statements;

   (c)   The related accounting records, supporting information and specific accounts in the financial statements that are used to initiate, record, process and report transactions; this includes the correction of incorrect information and how information is transferred to the general ledger. The records may be in either manual or electronic form;

   (d)   How the information system captures events and conditions, other than transactions, that are significant to the financial statements;

   (e)   The financial reporting process used to prepare the entity's financial statements, including significant accounting estimates and disclosures; and

   (f)   Controls surrounding journal entries, including non-standard journal entries used to record non-recurring, unusual transactions or adjustments. (Ref: Para. A89-A93)

19.   The auditor shall obtain an understanding of how the entity communicates financial reporting roles and responsibilities and significant matters relating to financial reporting, including: (Ref: Para. A94-A95)

   (a)   Communications between management and those charged with governance; and

   (b)   External communications, such as those with regulatory authorities.

Control activities relevant to the audit

20.   The auditor shall obtain an understanding of control activities relevant to the audit, being those the auditor judges it necessary to understand in order to assess the risks of material misstatement at the assertion level and design further audit procedures responsive to assessed risks. An audit does not require an understanding of all the control activities related to each significant class of transactions, account balance, and disclosure in the financial statements or to every assertion relevant to them. (Ref: Para. A96-A102)

21.   In understanding the entity's control activities, the auditor shall obtain an understanding of how the entity has responded to risks arising from IT. (Ref: Para. A103-A105)

Monitoring of controls

22.   The auditor shall obtain an understanding of the major activities that the entity uses to monitor internal control relevant to financial reporting, including those related to those control activities relevant to the audit, and how the entity initiates remedial actions to deficiencies in its controls. (Ref: Para. A106-A108)

23.   If the entity has an internal audit function,[1] the auditor shall obtain an understanding of the nature of the internal audit function's responsibilities, its organizational status, and the activities performed, or to be performed. (Ref: Para A109-A116)

24.   The auditor shall obtain an understanding of the sources of the information used in the entity's monitoring activities, and the basis upon which management considers the information to be sufficiently reliable for the purpose. (Ref: Para. A117)

Identifying and Assessing the Risks of Material Misstatement

25.   The auditor shall identify and assess the risks of material misstatement at:

(a)   the financial statement level; and (Ref: Para. A118-A121)

(b)   the assertion level for classes of transactions, account balances, and disclosures (Ref: Para. A122-A126)

to provide a basis for designing and performing further audit procedures.

26.   For this purpose, the auditor shall:

(a)   Identify risks throughout the process of obtaining an understanding of the entity and its environment, including relevant controls that relate to the risks, and by considering the classes of transactions, account balances, and disclosures in the financial statements; (Ref: Para. A127-A128)

(b)   Assess the identified risks, and evaluate whether they relate more pervasively to the financial statements as a whole and potentially affect many assertions;

(c)   Relate the identified risks to what can go wrong at the assertion level, taking account of relevant controls that the auditor intends to test; and (Ref: Para. A129-A131)

---

[1]   ISA (UK and Ireland) 610 (Revised June 2013), *Using the Work of Internal Auditors,* paragraph 14, defines the term "internal audit function" for purposes of the ISAs (UK and Ireland).

(d) Consider the likelihood of misstatement, including the possibility of multiple misstatements, and whether the potential misstatement is of a magnitude that could result in a material misstatement.

Risks That Require Special Audit Consideration

27. As part of the risk assessment as described in paragraph 25, the auditor shall determine whether any of the risks identified are, in the auditor's judgment, a significant risk. In exercising this judgment, the auditor shall exclude the effects of identified controls related to the risk.

28. In exercising judgment as to which risks are significant risks, the auditor shall consider at least the following:

(a) Whether the risk is a risk of fraud;

(b) Whether the risk is related to recent significant economic, accounting or other developments and, therefore, requires specific attention;

(c) The complexity of transactions;

(d) Whether the risk involves significant transactions with related parties;

(e) The degree of subjectivity in the measurement of financial information related to the risk, especially those measurements involving a wide range of measurement uncertainty; and

(f) Whether the risk involves significant transactions that are outside the normal course of business for the entity, or that otherwise appear to be unusual. (Ref: Para. A132-A136)

29. If the auditor has determined that a significant risk exists, the auditor shall obtain an understanding of the entity's controls, including control activities, relevant to that risk. (Ref: Para. A137-A139)

Risks for Which Substantive Procedures Alone Do Not Provide Sufficient Appropriate Audit Evidence

30. In respect of some risks, the auditor may judge that it is not possible or practicable to obtain sufficient appropriate audit evidence only from substantive procedures. Such risks may relate to the inaccurate or incomplete recording of routine and significant classes of transactions or account balances, the characteristics of which often permit highly automated processing with little or no manual intervention. In such cases, the entity's controls over such risks are relevant to the audit and the auditor shall obtain an understanding of them. (Ref: Para. A140-A142)

Revision of Risk Assessment

31.   The auditor's assessment of the risks of material misstatement at the assertion level may change during the course of the audit as additional audit evidence is obtained. In circumstances where the auditor obtains audit evidence from performing further audit procedures, or if new information is obtained, either of which is inconsistent with the audit evidence on which the auditor originally based the assessment, the auditor shall revise the assessment and modify the further planned audit procedures accordingly. (Ref: Para. A143)

Documentation

32.   The auditor shall include in the audit documentation:[2]

   (a)   The discussion among the engagement team where required by paragraph 10, and the significant decisions reached;

   (b)   Key elements of the understanding obtained regarding each of the aspects of the entity and its environment specified in paragraph 11 and of each of the internal control components specified in paragraphs 14-24; the sources of information from which the understanding was obtained; and the risk assessment procedures performed;

   (c)   The identified and assessed risks of material misstatement at the financial statement level and at the assertion level as required by paragraph 25; and

   (d)   The risks identified, and related controls about which the auditor has obtained an understanding, as a result of the requirements in paragraphs 27-30. (Ref: Para. A144-A147)

***

Application and Other Explanatory Material

Risk Assessment Procedures and Related Activities (Ref: Para. 5)

A1.   Obtaining an understanding of the entity and its environment, including the entity's internal control (referred to hereafter as an "understanding of the entity"), is a continuous, dynamic process of gathering, updating and analyzing information throughout the audit. The understanding establishes a frame of reference within which the auditor plans the audit and exercises professional judgment throughout the audit, for example, when:

   •   Assessing risks of material misstatement of the financial statements;

---

[2]   ISA (UK and Ireland) 230, *Audit Documentation*, paragraphs 8-11, and A6.

- Determining materiality in accordance with ISA (UK and Ireland) 320;[3]

- Considering the appropriateness of the selection and application of accounting policies, and the adequacy of financial statement disclosures;

- Identifying areas where special audit consideration may be necessary, for example, related party transactions, the appropriateness of management's use of the going concern assumption, or considering the business purpose of transactions;

- Developing expectations for use when performing analytical procedures;

- Responding to the assessed risks of material misstatement, including designing and performing further audit procedures to obtain sufficient appropriate audit evidence; and

- Evaluating the sufficiency and appropriateness of audit evidence obtained, such as the appropriateness of assumptions and of management's[3a] oral and written representations.

A2.   Information obtained by performing risk assessment procedures and related activities may be used by the auditor as audit evidence to support assessments of the risks of material misstatement. In addition, the auditor may obtain audit evidence about classes of transactions, account balances, or disclosures and related assertions and about the operating effectiveness of controls, even though such procedures were not specifically planned as substantive procedures or as tests of controls. The auditor also may choose to perform substantive procedures or tests of controls concurrently with risk assessment procedures because it is efficient to do so.

A3.   The auditor uses professional judgment to determine the extent of the understanding required. The auditor's primary consideration is whether the understanding that has been obtained is sufficient to meet the objective stated in this ISA (UK and Ireland). The depth of the overall understanding that is required by the auditor is less than that possessed by management in managing the entity.

A4.   The risks to be assessed include both those due to error and those due to fraud, and both are covered by this ISA (UK and Ireland). However, the significance of fraud is such that further requirements and guidance are included in ISA (UK and Ireland) 240 in relation to risk assessment procedures and related activities to obtain information that is used to identify the risks of material misstatement due to fraud.[4]

---

[3]   ISA (UK and Ireland) 320, *Materiality in Planning and Performing an Audit.*
[3a]   In the UK and Ireland, as explained in paragraph A2-1 of ISA (UK and Ireland) 580, *Written Representations*, it is appropriate for written representations that are critical to obtaining sufficient appropriate audit evidence to be provided by those charged with governance, rather than other levels of the entity's management.
[4]   ISA (UK and Ireland) 240, *The Auditor's Responsibilities Relating to Fraud in an Audit of Financial Statements*, paragraphs 12-24.

A5. Although the auditor is required to perform all the risk assessment procedures described in paragraph 6 in the course of obtaining the required understanding of the entity (see paragraphs 11-24), the auditor is not required to perform all of them for each aspect of that understanding. Other procedures may be performed where the information to be obtained therefrom may be helpful in identifying risks of material misstatement. Examples of such procedures include:

- Reviewing information obtained from external sources such as trade and economic journals; reports by analysts, banks, or rating agencies; or regulatory or financial publications.

- Making inquiries of the entity's external legal counsel or of valuation experts that the entity has used.

Inquiries of Management, the Internal Audit Function and Others within the Entity (Ref: Para. 6(a))

A6. Much of the information obtained by the auditor's inquiries is obtained from management and those responsible for financial reporting. Information may also be obtained by the auditor through inquiries with the internal audit function, if the entity has such a function, and others within the entity.

A7. The auditor may also obtain information, or a different perspective in identifying risks of material misstatement, through inquiries of others within the entity and other employees with different levels of authority. For example:

- Inquiries directed towards those charged with governance may help the auditor understand the environment in which the financial statements are prepared. ISA (UK and Ireland) 260[5] identifies the importance of effective two-way communication in assisting the auditor to obtain information from those charged with governance in this regard.

- Inquiries of employees involved in initiating, processing or recording complex or unusual transactions may help the auditor to evaluate the appropriateness of the selection and application of certain accounting policies.

- Inquiries directed toward in-house legal counsel may provide information about such matters as litigation, compliance with laws and regulations, knowledge of fraud or suspected fraud affecting the entity, warranties, post-sales obligations, arrangements (such as joint ventures) with business partners and the meaning of contract terms.

- Inquiries directed towards marketing or sales personnel may provide information about changes in the entity's marketing strategies, sales trends, or contractual arrangements with its customers.

---

[5] ISA (UK and Ireland) 260, *Communication with Those Charged with Governance*, paragraph 4(b).

- Inquiries directed to the risk management function (or those performing such roles) may provide information about operational and regulatory risks that may affect financial reporting.

- Inquiries directed to information systems personnel may provide information about system changes, system or control failures, or other information system-related risks.

A8. As obtaining an understanding of the entity and its environment is a continual, dynamic process, the auditor's inquiries may occur throughout the audit engagement.

Inquiries of the Internal Audit Function

A9. If an entity has an internal audit function, inquiries of the appropriate individuals within the function may provide information that is useful to the auditor in obtaining an understanding of the entity and its environment, and in identifying and assessing risks of material misstatement at the financial statement and assertion levels. In performing its work, the internal audit function is likely to have obtained insight into the entity's operations and business risks, and may have findings based on its work, such as identified control deficiencies or risks, that may provide valuable input into the auditor's understanding of the entity, the auditor's risk assessments or other aspects of the audit. The auditor's inquiries are therefore made whether or not the auditor expects to use the work of the internal audit function to modify the nature or timing, or reduce the extent, of audit procedures to be performed.[6] Inquiries of particular relevance may be about matters the internal audit function has raised with those charged with governance and the outcomes of the function's own risk assessment process.

A10. If, based on responses to the auditor's inquiries, it appears that there are findings that may be relevant to the entity's financial reporting and the audit, the auditor may consider it appropriate to read related reports of the internal audit function. Examples of reports of the internal audit function that may be relevant include the function's strategy and planning documents and reports that have been prepared for management or those charged with governance describing the findings of the internal audit function's examinations.

A11. In addition, in accordance with ISA (UK and Ireland) 240,[7] if the internal audit function provides information to the auditor regarding any actual, suspected or alleged fraud, the auditor takes this into account in the auditor's identification of risk of material misstatement due to fraud.

A12. Appropriate individuals within the internal audit function with whom inquiries are made are those who, in the auditor's judgment, have the appropriate knowledge, experience and authority, such as the chief internal audit executive or, depending on

---

[6] The relevant requirements are contained in ISA (UK and Ireland) 610 (Revised June 2013).

[7] ISA (UK and Ireland) 240, paragraph 19.

the circumstances, other personnel within the function. The auditor may also consider it appropriate to have periodic meetings with these individuals.

Considerations specific to public sector entities (Ref: Para 6(a))

A13. Auditors of public sector entities often have additional responsibilities with regard to internal control and compliance with applicable laws and regulations. Inquiries of appropriate individuals in the internal audit function can assist the auditors in identifying the risk of material noncompliance with applicable laws and regulations and the risk of deficiencies in internal control over financial reporting.

Analytical Procedures (Ref: Para. 6(b))

A14. Analytical procedures performed as risk assessment procedures may identify aspects of the entity of which the auditor was unaware and may assist in assessing the risks of material misstatement in order to provide a basis for designing and implementing responses to the assessed risks. Analytical procedures performed as risk assessment procedures may include both financial and non-financial information, for example, the relationship between sales and square footage of selling space or volume of goods sold.

A15. Analytical procedures may help identify the existence of unusual transactions or events, and amounts, ratios, and trends that might indicate matters that have audit implications. Unusual or unexpected relationships that are identified may assist the auditor in identifying risks of material misstatement, especially risks of material misstatement due to fraud.

A16. However, when such analytical procedures use data aggregated at a high level (which may be the situation with analytical procedures performed as risk assessment procedures), the results of those analytical procedures only provide a broad initial indication about whether a material misstatement may exist. Accordingly, in such cases, consideration of other information that has been gathered when identifying the risks of material misstatement together with the results of such analytical procedures may assist the auditor in understanding and evaluating the results of the analytical procedures.

Considerations Specific to Smaller Entities

A17. Some smaller entities may not have interim or monthly financial information that can be used for purposes of analytical procedures. In these circumstances, although the auditor may be able to perform limited analytical procedures for purposes of planning the audit or obtain some information through inquiry, the auditor may need to plan to perform analytical procedures to identify and assess the risks of material misstatement when an early draft of the entity's financial statements is available.

Observation and Inspection (Ref: Para. 6(c))

A18. Observation and inspection may support inquiries of management and others, and may also provide information about the entity and its environment. Examples of such audit procedures include observation or inspection of the following:

- The entity's operations.

- Documents (such as business plans and strategies), records, and internal control manuals.

- Reports prepared by management (such as quarterly management reports and interim financial statements) and those charged with governance (such as minutes of board of directors' meetings).

- The entity's premises and plant facilities.

Information Obtained in Prior Periods (Ref: Para. 9)

A19. The auditor's previous experience with the entity and audit procedures performed in previous audits may provide the auditor with information about such matters as:

- Past misstatements and whether they were corrected on a timely basis.

- The nature of the entity and its environment, and the entity's internal control (including deficiencies in internal control).

- Significant changes that the entity or its operations may have undergone since the prior financial period, which may assist the auditor in gaining a sufficient understanding of the entity to identify and assess risks of material misstatement.

A20. The auditor is required to determine whether information obtained in prior periods remains relevant, if the auditor intends to use that information for the purposes of the current audit. This is because changes in the control environment, for example, may affect the relevance of information obtained in the prior year. To determine whether changes have occurred that may affect the relevance of such information, the auditor may make inquiries and perform other appropriate audit procedures, such as walk-throughs of relevant systems.

Discussion among the Engagement Team (Ref: Para. 10)

A21. The discussion among the engagement team about the susceptibility of the entity's financial statements to material misstatement:

- Provides an opportunity for more experienced engagement team members, including the engagement partner, to share their insights based on their knowledge of the entity.

- Allows the engagement team members to exchange information about the business risks to which the entity is subject and about how and where the financial statements might be susceptible to material misstatement due to fraud or error.

- Assists the engagement team members to gain a better understanding of the potential for material misstatement of the financial statements in the specific areas assigned to them, and to understand how the results of the audit procedures that they perform may affect other aspects of the audit including the decisions about the nature, timing, and extent of further audit procedures.

- Provides a basis upon which engagement team members communicate and share new information obtained throughout the audit that may affect the assessment of risks of material misstatement or the audit procedures performed to address these risks.

ISA (UK and Ireland) 240 provides further requirements and guidance in relation to the discussion among the engagement team about the risks of fraud.[8]

A22. It is not always necessary or practical for the discussion to include all members in a single discussion (as, for example, in a multi-location audit), nor is it necessary for all of the members of the engagement team to be informed of all of the decisions reached in the discussion. The engagement partner may discuss matters with key members of the engagement team including, if considered appropriate, those with specific skills or knowledge, and those responsible for the audits of components, while delegating discussion with others, taking account of the extent of communication considered necessary throughout the engagement team. A communications plan, agreed by the engagement partner, may be useful.

Considerations Specific to Smaller Entities

A23. Many small audits are carried out entirely by the engagement partner (who may be a sole practitioner). In such situations, it is the engagement partner who, having personally conducted the planning of the audit, would be responsible for considering the susceptibility of the entity's financial statements to material misstatement due to fraud or error.

---

[8]   ISA (UK and Ireland) 240, paragraph 15.

The Required Understanding of the Entity and Its Environment, Including the Entity's Internal Control

The Entity and Its Environment

Industry, Regulatory and Other External Factors (Ref: Para. 11(a))

Industry Factors

A24. Relevant industry factors include industry conditions such as the competitive environment, supplier and customer relationships, and technological developments. Examples of matters the auditor may consider include:

- The market and competition, including demand, capacity, and price competition.

- Cyclical or seasonal activity.

- Product technology relating to the entity's products.

- Energy supply and cost.

A25. The industry in which the entity operates may give rise to specific risks of material misstatement arising from the nature of the business or the degree of regulation. For example, long-term contracts may involve significant estimates of revenues and expenses that give rise to risks of material misstatement. In such cases, it is important that the engagement team include members with sufficient relevant knowledge and experience.[9]

Regulatory Factors

A26. Relevant regulatory factors include the regulatory environment. The regulatory environment encompasses, among other matters, the applicable financial reporting framework and the legal and political environment. Examples of matters the auditor may consider include:

- Accounting principles and industry specific practices.

- Regulatory framework for a regulated industry.

- Legislation and regulation that significantly affect the entity's operations, including direct supervisory activities.

- Taxation (corporate and other).

---

[9] ISA (UK and Ireland) 220, *Quality Control for an Audit of Financial Statements*, paragraph 14.

- Government policies currently affecting the conduct of the entity's business, such as monetary, including foreign exchange controls, fiscal, financial incentives (for example, government aid programs), and tariffs or trade restrictions policies.

- Environmental requirements affecting the industry and the entity's business.

A27. ISA (UK and Ireland) 250 includes some specific requirements related to the legal and regulatory framework applicable to the entity and the industry or sector in which the entity operates.[10]

Considerations specific to public sector entities

A28. For the audits of public sector entities, law, regulation or other authority may affect the entity's operations. Such elements are essential to consider when obtaining an understanding of the entity and its environment.

Other External Factors

A29. Examples of other external factors affecting the entity that the auditor may consider include the general economic conditions, interest rates and availability of financing, and inflation or currency revaluation.

Nature of the Entity (Ref: Para. 11(b))

A30. An understanding of the nature of an entity enables the auditor to understand such matters as:

- Whether the entity has a complex structure, for example with subsidiaries or other components in multiple locations. Complex structures often introduce issues that may give rise to risks of material misstatement. Such issues may include whether goodwill, joint ventures, investments, or special-purpose entities are accounted for appropriately.

- The ownership, and relations between owners and other people or entities. This understanding assists in determining whether related party transactions have been identified and accounted for appropriately. ISA (UK and Ireland) 550[11] establishes requirements and provides guidance on the auditor's considerations relevant to related parties.

A31. Examples of matters that the auditor may consider when obtaining an understanding of the nature of the entity include:

- Business operations such as:

---

[10] ISA (UK and Ireland) 250, *Consideration of Laws and Regulations in an Audit of Financial Statements*, paragraph 12.
[11] ISA (UK and Ireland) 550, *Related Parties*.

- Nature of revenue sources, products or services, and markets, including involvement in electronic commerce such as Internet sales and marketing activities.

- Conduct of operations (for example, stages and methods of production, or activities exposed to environmental risks).

- Alliances, joint ventures, and outsourcing activities.

- Geographic dispersion and industry segmentation.

- Location of production facilities, warehouses, and offices, and location and quantities of inventories.

- Key customers and important suppliers of goods and services, employment arrangements (including the existence of union contracts, pension and other post employment benefits, stock option or incentive bonus arrangements, and government regulation related to employment matters).

- Research and development activities and expenditures.

- Transactions with related parties.

• Investments and investment activities such as:

- Planned or recently executed acquisitions or divestitures.

- Investments and dispositions of securities and loans.

- Capital investment activities.

- Investments in non-consolidated entities, including partnerships, joint ventures and special-purpose entities.

• Financing and financing activities such as:

- Major subsidiaries and associated entities, including consolidated and non-consolidated structures.

- Debt structure and related terms, including off-balance-sheet financing arrangements and leasing arrangements.

- Beneficial owners (local, foreign, business reputation and experience) and related parties.

- Use of derivative financial instruments.

- Financial reporting such as:

  - Accounting principles and industry specific practices, including industry-specific significant categories (for example, loans and investments for banks, or research and development for pharmaceuticals).

  - Revenue recognition practices.

  - Accounting for fair values.

  - Foreign currency assets, liabilities and transactions.

  - Accounting for unusual or complex transactions including those in controversial or emerging areas (for example, accounting for stock-based compensation).

A32. Significant changes in the entity from prior periods may give rise to, or change, risks of material misstatement.

Nature of Special-Purpose Entities

A33. A special-purpose entity (sometimes referred to as a special-purpose vehicle) is an entity that is generally established for a narrow and well-defined purpose, such as to effect a lease or a securitization of financial assets, or to carry out research and development activities. It may take the form of a corporation, trust, partnership or unincorporated entity. The entity on behalf of which the special-purpose entity has been created may often transfer assets to the latter (for example, as part of a derecognition transaction involving financial assets), obtain the right to use the latter's assets, or perform services for the latter, while other parties may provide the funding to the latter. As ISA (UK and Ireland) 550 indicates, in some circumstances, a special-purpose entity may be a related party of the entity.[12]

A34. Financial reporting frameworks often specify detailed conditions that are deemed to amount to control, or circumstances under which the special-purpose entity should be considered for consolidation. The interpretation of the requirements of such frameworks often demands a detailed knowledge of the relevant agreements involving the special-purpose entity.

The Entity's Selection and Application of Accounting Policies (Ref: Para. 11(c))

A35. An understanding of the entity's selection and application of accounting policies may encompass such matters as:

- The methods the entity uses to account for significant and unusual transactions.

- The effect of significant accounting policies in controversial or emerging areas for which there is a lack of authoritative guidance or consensus.

---

[12] ISA (UK and Ireland) 550, paragraph A7.

- Changes in the entity's accounting policies.

- Financial reporting standards and laws and regulations that are new to the entity and when and how the entity will adopt such requirements.

Objectives and Strategies and Related Business Risks (Ref: Para. 11(d))

A36. The entity conducts its business in the context of industry, regulatory and other internal and external factors. To respond to these factors, the entity's management or those charged with governance define objectives, which are the overall plans for the entity. Strategies are the approaches by which management intends to achieve its objectives. The entity's objectives and strategies may change over time.

A37. Business risk is broader than the risk of material misstatement of the financial statements, though it includes the latter. Business risk may arise from change or complexity. A failure to recognize the need for change may also give rise to business risk. Business risk may arise, for example, from:

- The development of new products or services that may fail;

- A market which, even if successfully developed, is inadequate to support a product or service; or

- Flaws in a product or service that may result in liabilities and reputational risk.

A38. An understanding of the business risks facing the entity increases the likelihood of identifying risks of material misstatement, since most business risks will eventually have financial consequences and, therefore, an effect on the financial statements. However, the auditor does not have a responsibility to identify or assess all business risks because not all business risks give rise to risks of material misstatement.

A39. Examples of matters that the auditor may consider when obtaining an understanding of the entity's objectives, strategies and related business risks that may result in a risk of material misstatement of the financial statements include:

- Industry developments (a potential related business risk might be, for example, that the entity does not have the personnel or expertise to deal with the changes in the industry).

- New products and services (a potential related business risk might be, for example, that there is increased product liability).

- Expansion of the business (a potential related business risk might be, for example, that the demand has not been accurately estimated).

- New accounting requirements (a potential related business risk might be, for example, incomplete or improper implementation, or increased costs).

- Regulatory requirements (a potential related business risk might be, for example, that there is increased legal exposure).

- Current and prospective financing requirements (a potential related business risk might be, for example, the loss of financing due to the entity's inability to meet requirements).

- Use of IT (a potential related business risk might be, for example, that systems and processes are incompatible).

- The effects of implementing a strategy, particularly any effects that will lead to new accounting requirements (a potential related business risk might be, for example, incomplete or improper implementation).

A40. A business risk may have an immediate consequence for the risk of material misstatement for classes of transactions, account balances, and disclosures at the assertion level or the financial statement level. For example, the business risk arising from a contracting customer base may increase the risk of material misstatement associated with the valuation of receivables. However, the same risk, particularly in combination with a contracting economy, may also have a longer-term consequence, which the auditor considers when assessing the appropriateness of the going concern assumption. Whether a business risk may result in a risk of material misstatement is, therefore, considered in light of the entity's circumstances. Examples of conditions and events that may indicate risks of material misstatement are indicated in Appendix 2.

A41. Usually, management identifies business risks and develops approaches to address them. Such a risk assessment process is part of internal control and is discussed in paragraph 15 and paragraphs A87-A88.

Considerations Specific to Public Sector Entities

A42. For the audits of public sector entities, "management objectives" may be influenced by concerns regarding public accountability and may include objectives which have their source in law, regulation or other authority.

Measurement and Review of the Entity's Financial Performance (Ref: Para.11(e))

A43. Management and others will measure and review those things they regard as important. Performance measures, whether external or internal, create pressures on the entity. These pressures, in turn, may motivate management to take action to improve the business performance or to misstate the financial statements. Accordingly, an understanding of the entity's performance measures assists the auditor in considering whether pressures to achieve performance targets may result in management actions that increase the risks of material misstatement, including those due to fraud. See ISA (UK and Ireland) 240 for requirements and guidance in relation to the risks of fraud.

A44. The measurement and review of financial performance is not the same as the monitoring of controls (discussed as a component of internal control in paragraphs A106-A117), though their purposes may overlap:

- The measurement and review of performance is directed at whether business performance is meeting the objectives set by management (or third parties).

- Monitoring of controls is specifically concerned with the effective operation of internal control.

In some cases, however, performance indicators also provide information that enables management to identify deficiencies in internal control.

A45. Examples of internally-generated information used by management for measuring and reviewing financial performance, and which the auditor may consider, include:

- Key performance indicators (financial and non-financial) and key ratios, trends and operating statistics.

- Period-on-period financial performance analyses.

- Budgets, forecasts, variance analyses, segment information and divisional, departmental or other level performance reports.

- Employee performance measures and incentive compensation policies.

- Comparisons of an entity's performance with that of competitors.

A46. External parties may also measure and review the entity's financial performance. For example, external information such as analysts' reports and credit rating agency reports may represent useful information for the auditor. Such reports can often be obtained from the entity being audited.

A47. Internal measures may highlight unexpected results or trends requiring management to determine their cause and take corrective action (including, in some cases, the detection and correction of misstatements on a timely basis). Performance measures may also indicate to the auditor that risks of misstatement of related financial statement information do exist. For example, performance measures may indicate that the entity has unusually rapid growth or profitability when compared to that of other entities in the same industry. Such information, particularly if combined with other factors such as performance-based bonus or incentive remuneration, may indicate the potential risk of management bias in the preparation of the financial statements.

Considerations Specific to Smaller Entities

A48. Smaller entities often do not have processes to measure and review financial performance. Inquiry of management may reveal that it relies on certain key indicators for evaluating financial performance and taking appropriate action. If such inquiry indicates an absence of performance measurement or review, there may be an increased risk of misstatements not being detected and corrected.

The Entity's Internal Control (Ref: Para. 12)

A49. An understanding of internal control assists the auditor in identifying types of potential misstatements and factors that affect the risks of material misstatement, and in designing the nature, timing, and extent of further audit procedures.

A50. The following application material on internal control is presented in four sections, as follows:

- General Nature and Characteristics of Internal Control.

- Controls Relevant to the Audit.

- Nature and Extent of the Understanding of Relevant Controls.

- Components of Internal Control.

General Nature and Characteristics of Internal Control

Purpose of Internal Control

A51. Internal control is designed, implemented and maintained to address identified business risks that threaten the achievement of any of the entity's objectives that concern:

- The reliability of the entity's financial reporting;

- The effectiveness and efficiency of its operations; and

- Its compliance with applicable laws and regulations.

The way in which internal control is designed, implemented and maintained varies with an entity's size and complexity.

Considerations specific to smaller entities

A52. Smaller entities may use less structured means and simpler processes and procedures to achieve their objectives.

Limitations of Internal Control

A53. Internal control, no matter how effective, can provide an entity with only reasonable assurance about achieving the entity's financial reporting objectives. The likelihood of their achievement is affected by the inherent limitations of internal control. These include the realities that human judgment in decision-making can be faulty and that breakdowns in internal control can occur because of human error. For example, there may be an error in the design of, or in the change to, a control. Equally, the operation of a control may not be effective, such as where information produced for the purposes of internal control (for example, an exception report) is not effectively used because the individual responsible for reviewing the information does not understand its purpose or fails to take appropriate action.

A54. Additionally, controls can be circumvented by the collusion of two or more people or inappropriate management override of internal control. For example, management may enter into side agreements with customers that alter the terms and conditions of the entity's standard sales contracts, which may result in improper revenue recognition. Also, edit checks in a software program that are designed to identify and report transactions that exceed specified credit limits may be overridden or disabled.

A55. Further, in designing and implementing controls, management may make judgments on the nature and extent of the controls it chooses to implement, and the nature and extent of the risks it chooses to assume.

Considerations specific to smaller entities

A56. Smaller entities often have fewer employees which may limit the extent to which segregation of duties is practicable. However, in a small owner-managed entity, the owner-manager may be able to exercise more effective oversight than in a larger entity. This oversight may compensate for the generally more limited opportunities for segregation of duties.

A57. On the other hand, the owner-manager may be more able to override controls because the system of internal control is less structured. This is taken into account by the auditor when identifying the risks of material misstatement due to fraud.

Division of Internal Control into Components

A58. The division of internal control into the following five components, for purposes of the ISAs (UK and Ireland), provides a useful framework for auditors to consider how different aspects of an entity's internal control may affect the audit:

(a) The control environment;

(b) The entity's risk assessment process;

(c) The information system, including the related business processes, relevant to financial reporting, and communication;

(d) Control activities; and

(e) Monitoring of controls.

The division does not necessarily reflect how an entity designs, implements and maintains internal control, or how it may classify any particular component. Auditors may use different terminology or frameworks to describe the various aspects of internal control, and their effect on the audit than those used in this ISA (UK and Ireland), provided all the components described in this ISA (UK and Ireland) are addressed.

A59. Application material relating to the five components of internal control as they relate to a financial statement audit is set out in paragraphs A76-A117 below. Appendix 1 provides further explanation of these components of internal control.

Characteristics of Manual and Automated Elements of Internal Control Relevant to the Auditor's Risk Assessment

A60. An entity's system of internal control contains manual elements and often contains automated elements. The characteristics of manual or automated elements are relevant to the auditor's risk assessment and further audit procedures based thereon.

A61. The use of manual or automated elements in internal control also affects the manner in which transactions are initiated, recorded, processed, and reported:

- Controls in a manual system may include such procedures as approvals and reviews of transactions, and reconciliations and follow-up of reconciling items. Alternatively, an entity may use automated procedures to initiate, record, process, and report transactions, in which case records in electronic format replace paper documents.

- Controls in IT systems consist of a combination of automated controls (for example, controls embedded in computer programs) and manual controls. Further, manual controls may be independent of IT, may use information produced by IT, or may be limited to monitoring the effective functioning of IT and of automated controls, and to handling exceptions. When IT is used to initiate, record, process or report transactions, or other financial data for inclusion in financial statements, the systems and programs may include controls related to the corresponding assertions for material accounts or may be critical to the effective functioning of manual controls that depend on IT.

An entity's mix of manual and automated elements in internal control varies with the nature and complexity of the entity's use of IT.

A62. Generally, IT benefits an entity's internal control by enabling an entity to:

- Consistently apply predefined business rules and perform complex calculations in processing large volumes of transactions or data;

- Enhance the timeliness, availability, and accuracy of information;

- Facilitate the additional analysis of information;

- Enhance the ability to monitor the performance of the entity's activities and its policies and procedures;

- Reduce the risk that controls will be circumvented; and

- Enhance the ability to achieve effective segregation of duties by implementing security controls in applications, databases, and operating systems.

A63. IT also poses specific risks to an entity's internal control, including, for example:

- Reliance on systems or programs that are inaccurately processing data, processing inaccurate data, or both.

- Unauthorized access to data that may result in destruction of data or improper changes to data, including the recording of unauthorized or non-existent transactions, or inaccurate recording of transactions. Particular risks may arise where multiple users access a common database.

- The possibility of IT personnel gaining access privileges beyond those necessary to perform their assigned duties thereby breaking down segregation of duties.

- Unauthorized changes to data in master files.

- Unauthorized changes to systems or programs.

- Failure to make necessary changes to systems or programs.

- Inappropriate manual intervention.

- Potential loss of data or inability to access data as required.

A64. Manual elements in internal control may be more suitable where judgment and discretion are required such as for the following circumstances:

- Large, unusual or non-recurring transactions.

- Circumstances where errors are difficult to define, anticipate or predict.

- In changing circumstances that require a control response outside the scope of an existing automated control.

- In monitoring the effectiveness of automated controls.

A65. Manual elements in internal control may be less reliable than automated elements because they can be more easily bypassed, ignored, or overridden and they are also more prone to simple errors and mistakes. Consistency of application of a manual control element cannot therefore be assumed. Manual control elements may be less suitable for the following circumstances:

- High volume or recurring transactions, or in situations where errors that can be anticipated or predicted can be prevented, or detected and corrected, by control parameters that are automated.

> - Control activities where the specific ways to perform the control can be adequately designed and automated.

A66. The extent and nature of the risks to internal control vary depending on the nature and characteristics of the entity's information system. The entity responds to the risks arising from the use of IT or from use of manual elements in internal control by establishing effective controls in light of the characteristics of the entity's information system.

Controls Relevant to the Audit

A67. There is a direct relationship between an entity's objectives and the controls it implements to provide reasonable assurance about their achievement. The entity's objectives, and therefore controls, relate to financial reporting, operations and compliance; however, not all of these objectives and controls are relevant to the auditor's risk assessment.

A68. Factors relevant to the auditor's judgment about whether a control, individually or in combination with others, is relevant to the audit may include such matters as the following:

- Materiality.

- The significance of the related risk.

- The size of the entity.

- The nature of the entity's business, including its organization and ownership characteristics.

- The diversity and complexity of the entity's operations.

- Applicable legal and regulatory requirements.

- The circumstances and the applicable component of internal control.

- The nature and complexity of the systems that are part of the entity's internal control, including the use of service organizations.

- Whether, and how, a specific control, individually or in combination with others, prevents, or detects and corrects, material misstatement.

A69. Controls over the completeness and accuracy of information produced by the entity may be relevant to the audit if the auditor intends to make use of the information in designing and performing further procedures. Controls relating to operations and compliance objectives may also be relevant to an audit if they relate to data the auditor evaluates or uses in applying audit procedures.

A70. Internal control over safeguarding of assets against unauthorized acquisition, use, or disposition may include controls relating to both financial reporting and operations objectives. The auditor's consideration of such controls is generally limited to those relevant to the reliability of financial reporting.

A71. An entity generally has controls relating to objectives that are not relevant to an audit and therefore need not be considered. For example, an entity may rely on a sophisticated system of automated controls to provide efficient and effective operations (such as an airline's system of automated controls to maintain flight schedules), but these controls ordinarily would not be relevant to the audit. Further, although internal control applies to the entire entity or to any of its operating units or business processes, an understanding of internal control relating to each of the entity's operating units and business processes may not be relevant to the audit.

Considerations Specific to Public Sector Entities

A72. Public sector auditors often have additional responsibilities with respect to internal control, for example to report on compliance with an established code of practice. Public sector auditors can also have responsibilities to report on compliance with law, regulation or other authority. As a result, their review of internal control may be broader and more detailed.

Nature and Extent of the Understanding of Relevant Controls (Ref: Para. 13)

A73. Evaluating the design of a control involves considering whether the control, individually or in combination with other controls, is capable of effectively preventing, or detecting and correcting, material misstatements. Implementation of a control means that the control exists and that the entity is using it. There is little point in assessing the implementation of a control that is not effective, and so the design of a control is considered first. An improperly designed control may represent a significant deficiency in internal control.

A74. Risk assessment procedures to obtain audit evidence about the design and implementation of relevant controls may include:

- Inquiring of entity personnel.

- Observing the application of specific controls.

- Inspecting documents and reports.

- Tracing transactions through the information system relevant to financial reporting.

Inquiry alone, however, is not sufficient for such purposes.

A75. Obtaining an understanding of an entity's controls is not sufficient to test their operating effectiveness, unless there is some automation that provides for the consistent operation of the controls. For example, obtaining audit evidence about the implementation of a manual control at a point in time does not provide audit evidence about the operating effectiveness of the control at other times during the period under audit. However, because of the inherent consistency of IT processing (see paragraph A62), performing audit procedures to determine whether an automated control has been implemented may serve as a test of that control's operating effectiveness, depending on the auditor's assessment and testing of controls such as those over program changes. Tests of the operating effectiveness of controls are further described in ISA (UK and Ireland) 330.[13]

Components of Internal Control—Control Environment (Ref: Para. 14)

A76. The control environment includes the governance and management functions and the attitudes, awareness, and actions of those charged with governance and management concerning the entity's internal control and its importance in the entity. The control environment sets the tone of an organization, influencing the control consciousness of its people.

A77. Elements of the control environment that may be relevant when obtaining an understanding of the control environment include the following:

(a) *Communication and enforcement of integrity and ethical values* – These are essential elements that influence the effectiveness of the design, administration and monitoring of controls.

(b) *Commitment to competence* – Matters such as management's consideration of the competence levels for particular jobs and how those levels translate into requisite skills and knowledge.

(c) *Participation by those charged with governance* – Attributes of those charged with governance such as:

- Their independence from management.

- Their experience and stature.

- The extent of their involvement and the information they receive, and the scrutiny of activities.

- The appropriateness of their actions, including the degree to which difficult questions are raised and pursued with management, and their interaction with internal and external auditors.

(d) *Management's philosophy and operating style* – Characteristics such as management's:

- Approach to taking and managing business risks.

---

[13] ISA (UK and Ireland) 330, *The Auditor's Responses to Assessed Risks.*

- Attitudes and actions toward financial reporting.

- Attitudes toward information processing and accounting functions and personnel.

(e) *Organizational structure* – The framework within which an entity's activities for achieving its objectives are planned, executed, controlled, and reviewed.

(f) *Assignment of authority and responsibility* – Matters such as how authority and responsibility for operating activities are assigned and how reporting relationships and authorization hierarchies are established.

(g) *Human resource policies and practices* – Policies and practices that relate to, for example, recruitment, orientation, training, evaluation, counselling, promotion, compensation, and remedial actions.

Audit Evidence for Elements of the Control Environment

A78. Relevant audit evidence may be obtained through a combination of inquiries and other risk assessment procedures such as corroborating inquiries through observation or inspection of documents. For example, through inquiries of management and employees, the auditor may obtain an understanding of how management communicates to employees its views on business practices and ethical behavior. The auditor may then determine whether relevant controls have been implemented by considering, for example, whether management has a written code of conduct and whether it acts in a manner that supports the code.

A79. The auditor may also consider how management has responded to the findings and recommendations of the internal audit function regarding identified deficiencies in internal control relevant to the audit, including whether and how such responses have been implemented, and whether they have been subsequently evaluated by the internal audit function.

Effect of the Control Environment on the Assessment of the Risks of Material Misstatement

A80. Some elements of an entity's control environment have a pervasive effect on assessing the risks of material misstatement. For example, an entity's control consciousness is influenced significantly by those charged with governance, because one of their roles is to counterbalance pressures on management in relation to financial reporting that may arise from market demands or remuneration schemes. The effectiveness of the design of the control environment in relation to participation by those charged with governance is therefore influenced by such matters as:

- Their independence from management and their ability to evaluate the actions of management.

- Whether they understand the entity's business transactions.

- The extent to which they evaluate whether the financial statements are prepared in accordance with the applicable financial reporting framework.

A81. An active and independent board of directors may influence the philosophy and operating style of senior management. However, other elements may be more limited in their effect. For example, although human resource policies and practices directed toward hiring competent financial, accounting, and IT personnel may reduce the risk of errors in processing financial information, they may not mitigate a strong bias by top management to overstate earnings.

A82. The existence of a satisfactory control environment can be a positive factor when the auditor assesses the risks of material misstatement. However, although it may help reduce the risk of fraud, a satisfactory control environment is not an absolute deterrent to fraud. Conversely, deficiencies in the control environment may undermine the effectiveness of controls, in particular in relation to fraud. For example, management's failure to commit sufficient resources to address IT security risks may adversely affect internal control by allowing improper changes to be made to computer programs or to data, or unauthorized transactions to be processed. As explained in ISA (UK and Ireland) 330, the control environment also influences the nature, timing, and extent of the auditor's further procedures.[14]

A83. The control environment in itself does not prevent, or detect and correct, a material misstatement. It may, however, influence the auditor's evaluation of the effectiveness of other controls (for example, the monitoring of controls and the operation of specific control activities) and thereby, the auditor's assessment of the risks of material misstatement.

Considerations Specific to Smaller Entities

A84. The control environment within small entities is likely to differ from larger entities. For example, those charged with governance in small entities may not include an independent or outside member, and the role of governance may be undertaken directly by the owner-manager where there are no other owners. The nature of the control environment may also influence the significance of other controls, or their absence. For example, the active involvement of an owner-manager may mitigate certain of the risks arising from a lack of segregation of duties in a small entity; it may, however, increase other risks, for example, the risk of override of controls.

A85. In addition, audit evidence for elements of the control environment in smaller entities may not be available in documentary form, in particular where communication between management and other personnel may be informal, yet effective. For example, small entities might not have a written code of conduct but, instead, develop a culture that emphasizes the importance of integrity and ethical behavior through oral communication and by management example.

---

[14] ISA (UK and Ireland) 330, paragraphs A2-A3.

A86. Consequently, the attitudes, awareness and actions of management or the owner-manager are of particular importance to the auditor's understanding of a smaller entity's control environment.

Components of Internal Control—The Entity's Risk Assessment Process (Ref: Para. 15)

A87. The entity's risk assessment process forms the basis for how management determines the risks to be managed. If that process is appropriate to the circumstances, including the nature, size and complexity of the entity, it assists the auditor in identifying risks of material misstatement. Whether the entity's risk assessment process is appropriate to the circumstances is a matter of judgment.

Considerations Specific to Smaller Entities (Ref: Para. 17)

A88. There is unlikely to be an established risk assessment process in a small entity. In such cases, it is likely that management will identify risks through direct personal involvement in the business. Irrespective of the circumstances, however, inquiry about identified risks and how they are addressed by management is still necessary.

Components of Internal Control—The Information System, Including Related Business Processes, Relevant to Financial Reporting, and Communication

The Information System, Including Related Business Processes, Relevant to Financial Reporting (Ref: Para. 18)

A89. The information system relevant to financial reporting objectives, which includes the accounting system, consists of the procedures and records designed and established to:

- Initiate, record, process, and report entity transactions (as well as events and conditions) and to maintain accountability for the related assets, liabilities, and equity;

- Resolve incorrect processing of transactions, for example, automated suspense files and procedures followed to clear suspense items out on a timely basis;

- Process and account for system overrides or bypasses to controls;

- Transfer information from transaction processing systems to the general ledger;

- Capture information relevant to financial reporting for events and conditions other than transactions, such as the depreciation and amortization of assets and changes in the recoverability of accounts receivables; and

- Ensure information required to be disclosed by the applicable financial reporting framework is accumulated, recorded, processed, summarized and appropriately reported in the financial statements.

Journal entries

A90. An entity's information system typically includes the use of standard journal entries that are required on a recurring basis to record transactions. Examples might be journal entries to record sales, purchases, and cash disbursements in the general ledger, or to record accounting estimates that are periodically made by management, such as changes in the estimate of uncollectible accounts receivable.

A91. An entity's financial reporting process also includes the use of non-standard journal entries to record non-recurring, unusual transactions or adjustments. Examples of such entries include consolidating adjustments and entries for a business combination or disposal or non-recurring estimates such as the impairment of an asset. In manual general ledger systems, non-standard journal entries may be identified through inspection of ledgers, journals, and supporting documentation. When automated procedures are used to maintain the general ledger and prepare financial statements, such entries may exist only in electronic form and may therefore be more easily identified through the use of computer-assisted audit techniques.

Related business processes

A92. An entity's business processes are the activities designed to:

- Develop, purchase, produce, sell and distribute an entity's products and services;

- Ensure compliance with laws and regulations; and

- Record information, including accounting and financial reporting information.

Business processes result in the transactions that are recorded, processed and reported by the information system. Obtaining an understanding of the entity's business processes, which include how transactions are originated, assists the auditor obtain an understanding of the entity's information system relevant to financial reporting in a manner that is appropriate to the entity's circumstances.

Considerations specific to smaller entities

A93. Information systems and related business processes relevant to financial reporting in small entities are likely to be less sophisticated than in larger entities, but their role is just as significant. Small entities with active management involvement may not need extensive descriptions of accounting procedures, sophisticated accounting records, or written policies. Understanding the entity's systems and processes may therefore be easier in an audit of smaller entities, and may be more dependent on inquiry than on review of documentation. The need to obtain an understanding, however, remains important.

Communication (Ref: Para. 19)

A94. Communication by the entity of the financial reporting roles and responsibilities and of significant matters relating to financial reporting involves providing an understanding of individual roles and responsibilities pertaining to internal control over financial reporting. It includes such matters as the extent to which personnel understand how their activities in the financial reporting information system relate to the work of others and the means of reporting exceptions to an appropriate higher level within the entity. Communication may take such forms as policy manuals and financial reporting manuals. Open communication channels help ensure that exceptions are reported and acted on.

Considerations specific to smaller entities

A95. Communication may be less structured and easier to achieve in a small entity than in a larger entity due to fewer levels of responsibility and management's greater visibility and availability.

Components of Internal Control—Control Activities Relevant to the Audit (Ref: Para. 20)

A96. Control activities are the policies and procedures that help ensure that management directives are carried out. Control activities, whether within IT or manual systems, have various objectives and are applied at various organizational and functional levels. Examples of specific control activities include those relating to the following:

- Authorization.

- Performance reviews.

- Information processing.

- Physical controls.

- Segregation of duties.

A97. Control activities that are relevant to the audit are:

- Those that are required to be treated as such, being control activities that relate to significant risks and those that relate to risks for which substantive procedures alone do not provide sufficient appropriate audit evidence, as required by paragraphs 29 and 30, respectively; or

- Those that are considered to be relevant in the judgment of the auditor.

A98. The auditor's judgment about whether a control activity is relevant to the audit is influenced by the risk that the auditor has identified that may give rise to a material misstatement and whether the auditor thinks it is likely to be appropriate to test the operating effectiveness of the control in determining the extent of substantive testing.

A99. The auditor's emphasis may be on identifying and obtaining an understanding of control activities that address the areas where the auditor considers that risks of material misstatement are likely to be higher. When multiple control activities each achieve the same objective, it is unnecessary to obtain an understanding of each of the control activities related to such objective.

A100. The auditor's knowledge about the presence or absence of control activities obtained from the understanding of the other components of internal control assists the auditor in determining whether it is necessary to devote additional attention to obtaining an understanding of control activities.

Considerations Specific to Smaller Entities

A101. The concepts underlying control activities in small entities are likely to be similar to those in larger entities, but the formality with which they operate may vary. Further, small entities may find that certain types of control activities are not relevant because of controls applied by management. For example, management's sole authority for granting credit to customers and approving significant purchases can provide strong control over important account balances and transactions, lessening or removing the need for more detailed control activities.

A102. Control activities relevant to the audit of a smaller entity are likely to relate to the main transaction cycles such as revenues, purchases and employment expenses.

Risks Arising from IT(Ref: Para. 21)

A103. The use of IT affects the way that control activities are implemented. From the auditor's perspective, controls over IT systems are effective when they maintain the integrity of information and the security of the data such systems process, and include effective general IT controls and application controls.

A104. General IT controls are policies and procedures that relate to many applications and support the effective functioning of application controls. They apply to mainframe, miniframe, and end-user environments. General IT controls that maintain the integrity of information and security of data commonly include controls over the following:

- Data center and network operations.

- System software acquisition, change and maintenance.

- Program change.

- Access security.

- Application system acquisition, development, and maintenance.

They are generally implemented to deal with the risks referred to in paragraph A63 above.

A105. Application controls are manual or automated procedures that typically operate at a business process level and apply to the processing of transactions by individual applications. Application controls can be preventive or detective in nature and are designed to ensure the integrity of the accounting records. Accordingly, application controls relate to procedures used to initiate, record, process and report transactions or other financial data. These controls help ensure that transactions occurred, are authorized, and are completely and accurately recorded and processed. Examples include edit checks of input data, and numerical sequence checks with manual follow-up of exception reports or correction at the point of data entry.

Components of Internal Control—Monitoring of Controls (Ref: Para. 22)

A106. Monitoring of controls is a process to assess the effectiveness of internal control performance over time. It involves assessing the effectiveness of controls on a timely basis and taking necessary remedial actions. Management accomplishes monitoring of controls through ongoing activities, separate evaluations, or a combination of the two. Ongoing monitoring activities are often built into the normal recurring activities of an entity and include regular management and supervisory activities.

A107. Management's monitoring activities may include using information from communications from external parties such as customer complaints and regulator comments that may indicate problems or highlight areas in need of improvement.

Considerations Specific to Smaller Entities

A108. Management's monitoring of control is often accomplished by management's or the owner-manager's close involvement in operations. This involvement often will identify significant variances from expectations and inaccuracies in financial data leading to remedial action to the control.

The Entity's Internal Audit Function (Ref: Para. 23)

A109. If the entity has an internal audit function, obtaining an understanding of that function contributes to the auditor's understanding of the entity and its environment, including internal control, in particular the role that the function plays in the entity's monitoring of internal control over financial reporting. This understanding, together with the information obtained from the auditor's inquiries in paragraph 6(a) of this ISA (UK and Ireland), may also provide information that is directly relevant to the auditor's identification and assessment of the risks of material misstatement.

A110. The objectives and scope of an internal audit function, the nature of its responsibilities and its status within the organization, including the function's authority and accountability, vary widely and depend on the size and structure of the entity and the requirements of management and, where applicable, those charged with governance. These matters may be set out in an internal audit charter or terms of reference.

A111. The responsibilities of an internal audit function may include performing procedures and evaluating the results to provide assurance to management and those charged with governance regarding the design and effectiveness of risk management, internal control and governance processes. If so, the internal audit function may play an important role in the entity's monitoring of internal control over financial reporting.

However, the responsibilities of the internal audit function may be focused on evaluating the economy, efficiency and effectiveness of operations and, if so, the work of the function may not directly relate to the entity's financial reporting.

A112. The auditor's inquiries of appropriate individuals within the internal audit function in accordance with paragraph 6(a) of this ISA (UK and Ireland) help the auditor obtain an understanding of the nature of the internal audit function's responsibilities. If the auditor determines that the function's responsibilities are related to the entity's financial reporting, the auditor may obtain further understanding of the activities performed, or to be performed, by the internal audit function by reviewing the internal audit function's audit plan for the period, if any, and discussing that plan with the appropriate individuals within the function.

A113. If the nature of the internal audit function's responsibilities and assurance activities are related to the entity's financial reporting, the auditor may also be able to use the work of the internal audit function to modify the nature or timing, or reduce the extent, of audit procedures to be performed directly by the auditor in obtaining audit evidence. Auditors may be more likely to be able to use the work of an entity's internal audit function when it appears, for example, based on experience in previous audits or the auditor's risk assessment procedures, that the entity has an internal audit function that is adequately and appropriately resourced relative to the size of the entity and the nature of its operations, and has a direct reporting relationship to those charged with governance.

A114. If, based on the auditor's preliminary understanding of the internal audit function, the auditor expects to use the work of the internal audit function to modify the nature or timing, or reduce the extent, of audit procedures to be performed, ISA (UK and Ireland) 610 (Revised June 2013) applies.

A115. As is further discussed in ISA (UK and Ireland) 610 (Revised June 2013), the activities of an internal audit function are distinct from other monitoring controls that may be relevant to financial reporting, such as reviews of management accounting information that are designed to contribute to how the entity prevents or detects misstatements.

A116. Establishing communications with the appropriate individuals within an entity's internal audit function early in the engagement, and maintaining such communications throughout the engagement, can facilitate effective sharing of information. It creates an environment in which the auditor can be informed of significant matters that may come to the attention of the internal audit function when such matters may affect the work of the auditor. ISA (UK and Ireland) 200 discusses the importance of the auditor planning and performing the audit with professional skepticism, including being alert to information that brings into question the reliability of documents and responses to inquiries to be used as audit evidence. Accordingly, communication with the internal audit function throughout the engagement may provide opportunities for internal auditors to bring such information to the auditor's attention. The auditor is then able to take such information into account in the auditor's identification and assessment of risks of material misstatement.

Sources of Information (Ref: Para. 24)

A117. Much of the information used in monitoring may be produced by the entity's information system. If management assumes that data used for monitoring are accurate without having a basis for that assumption, errors that may exist in the information could potentially lead management to incorrect conclusions from its monitoring activities. Accordingly, an understanding of:

- the sources of the information related to the entity's monitoring activities; and

- the basis upon which management considers the information to be sufficiently reliable for the purpose,

is required as part of the auditor's understanding of the entity's monitoring activities as a component of internal control.

Identifying and Assessing the Risks of Material Misstatement

Assessment of Risks of Material Misstatement at the Financial Statement Level
(Ref: Para. 25 (a))

A118. Risks of material misstatement at the financial statement level refer to risks that relate pervasively to the financial statements as a whole and potentially affect many assertions. Risks of this nature are not necessarily risks identifiable with specific assertions at the class of transactions, account balance, or disclosure level. Rather, they represent circumstances that may increase the risks of material misstatement at the assertion level, for example, through management override of internal control. Financial statement level risks may be especially relevant to the auditor's consideration of the risks of material misstatement arising from fraud.

A119. Risks at the financial statement level may derive in particular from a deficient control environment (although these risks may also relate to other factors, such as declining economic conditions). For example, deficiencies such as management's lack of competence may have a more pervasive effect on the financial statements and may require an overall response by the auditor.

A120. The auditor's understanding of internal control may raise doubts about the auditability of an entity's financial statements. For example:

- Concerns about the integrity of the entity's management may be so serious as to cause the auditor to conclude that the risk of management misrepresentation in the financial statements is such that an audit cannot be conducted.

- Concerns about the condition and reliability of an entity's records may cause the auditor to conclude that it is unlikely that sufficient appropriate audit evidence will be available to support an unmodified opinion on the financial statements.

A121. ISA (UK and Ireland) 705[15] establishes requirements and provides guidance in determining whether there is a need for the auditor to express a qualified opinion or disclaim an opinion or, as may be required in some cases, to withdraw from the engagement where withdrawal is possible under applicable law or regulation.

Assessment of Risks of Material Misstatement at the Assertion Level (Ref: Para. 25(b))

A122. Risks of material misstatement at the assertion level for classes of transactions, account balances, and disclosures need to be considered because such consideration directly assists in determining the nature, timing, and extent of further audit procedures at the assertion level necessary to obtain sufficient appropriate audit evidence. In identifying and assessing risks of material misstatement at the assertion level, the auditor may conclude that the identified risks relate more pervasively to the financial statements as a whole and potentially affect many assertions.

The Use of Assertions

A123. In representing that the financial statements are in accordance with the applicable financial reporting framework, management[1a] implicitly or explicitly makes assertions regarding the recognition, measurement, presentation and disclosure of the various elements of financial statements and related disclosures.

A124. Assertions used by the auditor to consider the different types of potential misstatements that may occur fall into the following three categories and may take the following forms:

  (a) Assertions about classes of transactions and events for the period under audit:

      (i)   Occurrence—transactions and events that have been recorded have occurred and pertain to the entity.

      (ii)   Completeness—all transactions and events that should have been recorded have been recorded.

      (iii) Accuracy—amounts and other data relating to recorded transactions and events have been recorded appropriately.

      (iv) Cutoff—transactions and events have been recorded in the correct accounting period.

      (v)   Classification—transactions and events have been recorded in the proper accounts.

  (b) Assertions about account balances at the period end:

---

[15] ISA (UK and Ireland) 705, *Modifications to the Opinion in the Independent Auditor's Report.*

     (i)   Existence—assets, liabilities, and equity interests exist.

     (ii)   Rights and obligations—the entity holds or controls the rights to assets, and liabilities are the obligations of the entity.

     (iii)   Completeness—all assets, liabilities and equity interests that should have been recorded have been recorded.

     (iv)   Valuation and allocation—assets, liabilities, and equity interests are included in the financial statements at appropriate amounts and any resulting valuation or allocation adjustments are appropriately recorded.

(c)   Assertions about presentation and disclosure:

     (i)   Occurrence and rights and obligations—disclosed events, transactions, and other matters have occurred and pertain to the entity.

     (ii)   Completeness—all disclosures that should have been included in the financial statements have been included.

     (iii)   Classification and understandability—financial information is appropriately presented and described, and disclosures are clearly expressed.

     (iv)   Accuracy and valuation—financial and other information are disclosed fairly and at appropriate amounts.

A125. The auditor may use the assertions as described above or may express them differently provided all aspects described above have been covered. For example, the auditor may choose to combine the assertions about transactions and events with the assertions about account balances.

Considerations specific to public sector entities

A126. When making assertions about the financial statements of public sector entities, in addition to those assertions set out in paragraph A124, management[1a] may often assert that transactions and events have been carried out in accordance with law, regulation or other authority. Such assertions may fall within the scope of the financial statement audit.

Process of Identifying Risks of Material Misstatement (Ref: Para. 26(a))

A127. Information gathered by performing risk assessment procedures, including the audit evidence obtained in evaluating the design of controls and determining whether they have been implemented, is used as audit evidence to support the risk assessment. The risk assessment determines the nature, timing, and extent of further audit procedures to be performed.

A128. Appendix 2 provides examples of conditions and events that may indicate the existence of risks of material misstatement.

Relating Controls to Assertions (Ref: Para. 26(c))

A129. In making risk assessments, the auditor may identify the controls that are likely to prevent, or detect and correct, material misstatement in specific assertions. Generally, it is useful to obtain an understanding of controls and relate them to assertions in the context of processes and systems in which they exist because individual control activities often do not in themselves address a risk. Often, only multiple control activities, together with other components of internal control, will be sufficient to address a risk.

A130. Conversely, some control activities may have a specific effect on an individual assertion embodied in a particular class of transactions or account balance. For example, the control activities that an entity established to ensure that its personnel are properly counting and recording the annual physical inventory relate directly to the existence and completeness assertions for the inventory account balance.

A131. Controls can be either directly or indirectly related to an assertion. The more indirect the relationship, the less effective that control may be in preventing, or detecting and correcting, misstatements in that assertion. For example, a sales manager's review of a summary of sales activity for specific stores by region ordinarily is only indirectly related to the completeness assertion for sales revenue. Accordingly, it may be less effective in reducing risk for that assertion than controls more directly related to that assertion, such as matching shipping documents with billing documents.

Significant Risks

Identifying Significant Risks (Ref: Para. 28)

A132. Significant risks often relate to significant non-routine transactions or judgmental matters. Non-routine transactions are transactions that are unusual, due to either size or nature, and that therefore occur infrequently. Judgmental matters may include the development of accounting estimates for which there is significant measurement uncertainty. Routine, non-complex transactions that are subject to systematic processing are less likely to give rise to significant risks.

A133. Risks of material misstatement may be greater for significant non-routine transactions arising from matters such as the following:

- Greater management intervention to specify the accounting treatment.

- Greater manual intervention for data collection and processing.

- Complex calculations or accounting principles.

- The nature of non-routine transactions, which may make it difficult for the entity to implement effective controls over the risks.

A134. Risks of material misstatement may be greater for significant judgmental matters that require the development of accounting estimates, arising from matters such as the following:

- Accounting principles for accounting estimates or revenue recognition may be subject to differing interpretation.

- Required judgment may be subjective or complex, or require assumptions about the effects of future events, for example, judgment about fair value.

A135. ISA (UK and Ireland) 330 describes the consequences for further audit procedures of identifying a risk as significant.[16]

Significant risks relating to the risks of material misstatement due to fraud

A136. ISA (UK and Ireland) 240 provides further requirements and guidance in relation to the identification and assessment of the risks of material misstatement due to fraud.[17]

Understanding Controls Related to Significant Risks (Ref: Para. 29)

A137. Although risks relating to significant non-routine or judgmental matters are often less likely to be subject to routine controls, management may have other responses intended to deal with such risks. Accordingly, the auditor's understanding of whether the entity has designed and implemented controls for significant risks arising from non-routine or judgmental matters includes whether and how management responds to the risks. Such responses might include:

- Control activities such as a review of assumptions by senior management or experts.

- Documented processes for estimations.

- Approval by those charged with governance.

A138. For example, where there are one-off events such as the receipt of notice of a significant lawsuit, consideration of the entity's response may include such matters as whether it has been referred to appropriate experts (such as internal or external legal counsel), whether an assessment has been made of the potential effect, and how it is proposed that the circumstances are to be disclosed in the financial statements.

A139. In some cases, management may not have appropriately responded to significant risks of material misstatement by implementing controls over these significant risks. Failure by management to implement such controls is an indicator of a significant deficiency in internal control.[18]

---

[16] ISA (UK and Ireland) 330, paragraphs 15 and 21.

[17] ISA (UK and Ireland) 240, paragraphs 25-27.

[18] ISA (UK and Ireland) 265, *Communicating Deficiencies in Internal Control to Those Charged with Governance and Management*, paragraph A7.

Risks for Which Substantive Procedures Alone Do Not Provide Sufficient Appropriate Audit Evidence (Ref: Para. 30)

A140. Risks of material misstatement may relate directly to the recording of routine classes of transactions or account balances, and the preparation of reliable financial statements. Such risks may include risks of inaccurate or incomplete processing for routine and significant classes of transactions such as an entity's revenue, purchases, and cash receipts or cash payments.

A141. Where such routine business transactions are subject to highly automated processing with little or no manual intervention, it may not be possible to perform only substantive procedures in relation to the risk. For example, the auditor may consider this to be the case in circumstances where a significant amount of an entity's information is initiated, recorded, processed, or reported only in electronic form such as in an integrated system. In such cases:

- Audit evidence may be available only in electronic form, and its sufficiency and appropriateness usually depend on the effectiveness of controls over its accuracy and completeness.

- The potential for improper initiation or alteration of information to occur and not be detected may be greater if appropriate controls are not operating effectively.

A142. The consequences for further audit procedures of identifying such risks are described in ISA (UK and Ireland) 330.[19]

Revision of Risk Assessment (Ref: Para. 31)

A143. During the audit, information may come to the auditor's attention that differs significantly from the information on which the risk assessment was based. For example, the risk assessment may be based on an expectation that certain controls are operating effectively. In performing tests of those controls, the auditor may obtain audit evidence that they were not operating effectively at relevant times during the audit. Similarly, in performing substantive procedures the auditor may detect misstatements in amounts or frequency greater than is consistent with the auditor's risk assessments. In such circumstances, the risk assessment may not appropriately reflect the true circumstances of the entity and the further planned audit procedures may not be effective in detecting material misstatements. See ISA (UK and Ireland) 330 for further guidance.

Documentation (Ref: Para. 32)

A144. The manner in which the requirements of paragraph 32 are documented is for the auditor to determine using professional judgment. For example, in audits of small entities the documentation may be incorporated in the auditor's documentation of the

---

[19] ISA (UK and Ireland) 330, paragraph 8.

overall strategy and audit plan.[20] Similarly, for example, the results of the risk assessment may be documented separately, or may be documented as part of the auditor's documentation of further procedures.[21] The form and extent of the documentation is influenced by the nature, size and complexity of the entity and its internal control, availability of information from the entity and the audit methodology and technology used in the course of the audit.

A145. For entities that have uncomplicated businesses and processes relevant to financial reporting, the documentation may be simple in form and relatively brief. It is not necessary to document the entirety of the auditor's understanding of the entity and matters related to it. Key elements of understanding documented by the auditor include those on which the auditor based the assessment of the risks of material misstatement.

A146. The extent of documentation may also reflect the experience and capabilities of the members of the audit engagement team. Provided the requirements of ISA (UK and Ireland) 230 are always met, an audit undertaken by an engagement team comprising less experienced individuals may require more detailed documentation to assist them to obtain an appropriate understanding of the entity than one that includes experienced individuals.

A147. For recurring audits, certain documentation may be carried forward, updated as necessary to reflect changes in the entity's business or processes.

---

[20] ISA (UK and Ireland) 300, *Planning an Audit of Financial Statements*, paragraphs 7 and 9.
[21] ISA (UK and Ireland) 330, paragraph 28.

Appendix 1

(Ref: Paras. 4(c), 14-24, A76-A117)

Internal Control Components

1.   This appendix further explains the components of internal control, as set out in paragraphs 4(c), 14-24 and A76-A117, as they relate to a financial statement audit.

Control Environment

2.   The control environment encompasses the following elements:

(a)   *Communication and enforcement of integrity and ethical values*. The effectiveness of controls cannot rise above the integrity and ethical values of the people who create, administer, and monitor them. Integrity and ethical behavior are the product of the entity's ethical and behavioral standards, how they are communicated, and how they are reinforced in practice. The enforcement of integrity and ethical values includes, for example, management actions to eliminate or mitigate incentives or temptations that might prompt personnel to engage in dishonest, illegal, or unethical acts. The communication of entity policies on integrity and ethical values may include the communication of behavioral standards to personnel through policy statements and codes of conduct and by example.

(b)   *Commitment to competence*. Competence is the knowledge and skills necessary to accomplish tasks that define the individual's job.

(c)   *Participation by those charged with governance*. An entity's control consciousness is influenced significantly by those charged with governance. The importance of the responsibilities of those charged with governance is recognized in codes of practice and other laws and regulations or guidance produced for the benefit of those charged with governance. Other responsibilities of those charged with governance include oversight of the design and effective operation of whistle blower procedures and the process for reviewing the effectiveness of the entity's internal control.

(d)   *Management's philosophy and operating style*. Management's philosophy and operating style encompass a broad range of characteristics. For example, management's attitudes and actions toward financial reporting may manifest themselves through conservative or aggressive selection from available alternative accounting principles, or conscientiousness and conservatism with which accounting estimates are developed.

(e)   *Organizational structure*. Establishing a relevant organizational structure includes considering key areas of authority and responsibility and appropriate lines of reporting. The appropriateness of an entity's organizational structure depends, in part, on its size and the nature of its activities.

(f) *Assignment of authority and responsibility.* The assignment of authority and responsibility may include policies relating to appropriate business practices, knowledge and experience of key personnel, and resources provided for carrying out duties. In addition, it may include policies and communications directed at ensuring that all personnel understand the entity's objectives, know how their individual actions interrelate and contribute to those objectives, and recognize how and for what they will be held accountable.

(g) *Human resource policies and practices.* Human resource policies and practices often demonstrate important matters in relation to the control consciousness of an entity. For example, standards for recruiting the most qualified individuals – with emphasis on educational background, prior work experience, past accomplishments, and evidence of integrity and ethical behavior – demonstrate an entity's commitment to competent and trustworthy people. Training policies that communicate prospective roles and responsibilities and include practices such as training schools and seminars illustrate expected levels of performance and behavior. Promotions driven by periodic performance appraisals demonstrate the entity's commitment to the advancement of qualified personnel to higher levels of responsibility.

Entity's Risk Assessment Process

3. For financial reporting purposes, the entity's risk assessment process includes how management identifies business risks relevant to the preparation of financial statements in accordance with the entity's applicable financial reporting framework, estimates their significance, assesses the likelihood of their occurrence, and decides upon actions to respond to and manage them and the results thereof. For example, the entity's risk assessment process may address how the entity considers the possibility of unrecorded transactions or identifies and analyzes significant estimates recorded in the financial statements.

4. Risks relevant to reliable financial reporting include external and internal events, transactions or circumstances that may occur and adversely affect an entity's ability to initiate, record, process, and report financial data consistent with the assertions of management[1a] in the financial statements. Management may initiate plans, programs, or actions to address specific risks or it may decide to accept a risk because of cost or other considerations. Risks can arise or change due to circumstances such as the following:

- *Changes in operating environment.* Changes in the regulatory or operating environment can result in changes in competitive pressures and significantly different risks.

- *New personnel.* New personnel may have a different focus on or understanding of internal control.

- *New or revamped information systems.* Significant and rapid changes in information systems can change the risk relating to internal control.

- *Rapid growth*. Significant and rapid expansion of operations can strain controls and increase the risk of a breakdown in controls.

- *New technology*. Incorporating new technologies into production processes or information systems may change the risk associated with internal control.

- *New business models, products, or activities*. Entering into business areas or transactions with which an entity has little experience may introduce new risks associated with internal control.

- *Corporate restructurings*. Restructurings may be accompanied by staff reductions and changes in supervision and segregation of duties that may change the risk associated with internal control.

- *Expanded foreign operations*. The expansion or acquisition of foreign operations carries new and often unique risks that may affect internal control, for example, additional or changed risks from foreign currency transactions.

- *New accounting pronouncements*. Adoption of new accounting principles or changing accounting principles may affect risks in preparing financial statements.

Information System, Including the Related Business Processes, Relevant to Financial Reporting, and Communication

5. An information system consists of infrastructure (physical and hardware components), software, people, procedures, and data. Many information systems make extensive use of information technology (IT).

6. The information system relevant to financial reporting objectives, which includes the financial reporting system, encompasses methods and records that:

- Identify and record all valid transactions.

- Describe on a timely basis the transactions in sufficient detail to permit proper classification of transactions for financial reporting.

- Measure the value of transactions in a manner that permits recording their proper monetary value in the financial statements.

- Determine the time period in which transactions occurred to permit recording of transactions in the proper accounting period.

- Present properly the transactions and related disclosures in the financial statements.

7. The quality of system-generated information affects management's ability to make appropriate decisions in managing and controlling the entity's activities and to prepare reliable financial reports.

8. Communication, which involves providing an understanding of individual roles and responsibilities pertaining to internal control over financial reporting, may take such forms as policy manuals, accounting and financial reporting manuals, and memoranda. Communication also can be made electronically, orally, and through the actions of management.

Control Activities

9. Generally, control activities that may be relevant to an audit may be categorized as policies and procedures that pertain to the following:

    *   *Performance reviews.* These control activities include reviews and analyses of actual performance versus budgets, forecasts, and prior period performance; relating different sets of data – operating or financial – to one another, together with analyses of the relationships and investigative and corrective actions; comparing internal data with external sources of information; and review of functional or activity performance.

    *   *Information processing.* The two broad groupings of information systems control activities are application controls, which apply to the processing of individual applications, and general IT controls, which are policies and procedures that relate to many applications and support the effective functioning of application controls by helping to ensure the continued proper operation of information systems. Examples of application controls include checking the arithmetical accuracy of records, maintaining and reviewing accounts and trial balances, automated controls such as edit checks of input data and numerical sequence checks, and manual follow-up of exception reports. Examples of general IT controls are program change controls, controls that restrict access to programs or data, controls over the implementation of new releases of packaged software applications, and controls over system software that restrict access to or monitor the use of system utilities that could change financial data or records without leaving an audit trail.

    *   *Physical controls.* Controls that encompass:

        ○   The physical security of assets, including adequate safeguards such as secured facilities over access to assets and records.

        ○   The authorization for access to computer programs and data files.

        ○   The periodic counting and comparison with amounts shown on control records (for example, comparing the results of cash, security and inventory counts with accounting records).

        The extent to which physical controls intended to prevent theft of assets are relevant to the reliability of financial statement preparation, and therefore the audit, depends on circumstances such as when assets are highly susceptible to misappropriation.

- *Segregation of duties.* Assigning different people the responsibilities of authorizing transactions, recording transactions, and maintaining custody of assets. Segregation of duties is intended to reduce the opportunities to allow any person to be in a position to both perpetrate and conceal errors or fraud in the normal course of the person's duties.

10. Certain control activities may depend on the existence of appropriate higher level policies established by management or those charged with governance. For example, authorization controls may be delegated under established guidelines, such as investment criteria set by those charged with governance; alternatively, non-routine transactions such as major acquisitions or divestments may require specific high level approval, including in some cases that of shareholders.

Monitoring of Controls

11. An important management responsibility is to establish and maintain internal control on an ongoing basis. Management's monitoring of controls includes considering whether they are operating as intended and that they are modified as appropriate for changes in conditions. Monitoring of controls may include activities such as management's review of whether bank reconciliations are being prepared on a timely basis, internal auditors' evaluation of sales personnel's compliance with the entity's policies on terms of sales contracts, and a legal department's oversight of compliance with the entity's ethical or business practice policies. Monitoring is done also to ensure that controls continue to operate effectively over time. For example, if the timeliness and accuracy of bank reconciliations are not monitored, personnel are likely to stop preparing them.

12. Internal auditors or personnel performing similar functions may contribute to the monitoring of an entity's controls through separate evaluations. Ordinarily, they regularly provide information about the functioning of internal control, focusing considerable attention on evaluating the effectiveness of internal control, and communicate information about strengths and deficiencies in internal control and recommendations for improving internal control.

13. Monitoring activities may include using information from communications from external parties that may indicate problems or highlight areas in need of improvement. Customers implicitly corroborate billing data by paying their invoices or complaining about their charges. In addition, regulators may communicate with the entity concerning matters that affect the functioning of internal control, for example, communications concerning examinations by bank regulatory agencies. Also, management may consider communications relating to internal control from external auditors in performing monitoring activities.

Appendix 2

(Ref: Para. A40, A128)

Conditions and Events That May Indicate Risks of Material Misstatement

The following are examples of conditions and events that may indicate the existence of risks of material misstatement. The examples provided cover a broad range of conditions and events; however, not all conditions and events are relevant to every audit engagement and the list of examples is not necessarily complete.

• Operations in regions that are economically unstable, for example, countries with significant currency devaluation or highly inflationary economies.

• Operations exposed to volatile markets, for example, futures trading.

• Operations that are subject to a high degree of complex regulation.

• Going concern and liquidity issues including loss of significant customers.

• Constraints on the availability of capital and credit.

• Changes in the industry in which the entity operates.

• Changes in the supply chain.

• Developing or offering new products or services, or moving into new lines of business.

• Expanding into new locations.

• Changes in the entity such as large acquisitions or reorganizations or other unusual events.

• Entities or business segments likely to be sold.

• The existence of complex alliances and joint ventures.

• Use of off balance sheet finance, special-purpose entities, and other complex financing arrangements.

• Significant transactions with related parties.

• Lack of personnel with appropriate accounting and financial reporting skills.

• Changes in key personnel including departure of key executives.

• Deficiencies in internal control, especially those not addressed by management.

- Inconsistencies between the entity's IT strategy and its business strategies.

- Changes in the IT environment.

- Installation of significant new IT systems related to financial reporting.

- Inquiries into the entity's operations or financial results by regulatory or government bodies.

- Past misstatements, history of errors or a significant amount of adjustments at period end.

- Significant amount of non-routine or non-systematic transactions including intercompany transactions and large revenue transactions at period end.

- Transactions that are recorded based on management's intent, for example, debt refinancing, assets to be sold and classification of marketable securities.

- Application of new accounting pronouncements.

- Accounting measurements that involve complex processes.

- Events or transactions that involve significant measurement uncertainty, including accounting estimates.

- Pending litigation and contingent liabilities, for example, sales warranties, financial guarantees and environmental remediation.

INTERNATIONAL STANDARD ON AUDITING (UK AND IRELAND) 320

MATERIALITY IN PLANNING AND PERFORMING AN AUDIT

(Effective for audits of financial statements for periods ending on or after 15 December 2010)

CONTENTS

International Standard on Auditing (UK and Ireland) (ISA (UK and Ireland)) 320, "Materiality in Planning and Performing an Audit" should be read in the context of ISA (UK and Ireland) 200, "Overall Objectives of the Independent Auditor and the Conduct of an Audit in Accordance with International Standards on Auditing (UK and Ireland)."

Introduction

Scope of this ISA (UK and Ireland)

1. This International Standard on Auditing (UK and Ireland) (ISA (UK and Ireland)) deals with the auditor's responsibility to apply the concept of materiality in planning and performing an audit of financial statements. ISA (UK and Ireland) 450[1] explains how materiality is applied in evaluating the effect of identified misstatements on the audit and of uncorrected misstatements, if any, on the financial statements.

Materiality in the Context of an Audit

2. Financial reporting frameworks often discuss the concept of materiality in the context of the preparation and presentation of financial statements. Although financial reporting frameworks may discuss materiality in different terms, they generally explain that:

    *   Misstatements, including omissions, are considered to be material if they, individually or in the aggregate, could reasonably be expected to influence the economic decisions of users taken on the basis of the financial statements;

    *   Judgments about materiality are made in light of surrounding circumstances, and are affected by the size or nature of a misstatement, or a combination of both; and

    *   Judgments about matters that are material to users of the financial statements are based on a consideration of the common financial information needs of users as a group.[2] The possible effect of misstatements on specific individual users, whose needs may vary widely, is not considered.

3. Such a discussion, if present in the applicable financial reporting framework, provides a frame of reference to the auditor in determining materiality for the audit. If the applicable financial reporting framework does not include a discussion of the concept of materiality, the characteristics referred to in paragraph 2 provide the auditor with such a frame of reference.

4. The auditor's determination of materiality is a matter of professional judgment, and is affected by the auditor's perception of the financial information needs of users of the financial statements. In this context, it is reasonable for the auditor to assume that users:

---

[1] ISA (UK and Ireland) 450, "Evaluation of Misstatements Identified during the Audit."

[2] For example, the "Framework for the Preparation and Presentation of Financial Statements," adopted by the International Accounting Standards Board in April 2001, indicates that, for a profit-oriented entity, as investors are providers of risk capital to the enterprise, the provision of financial statements that meet their needs will also meet most of the needs of other users that financial statements can satisfy.

The "Framework for the Preparation and Presentation of Financial Statements," has not been promulgated by the APB for application in the UK and Ireland.

(a) Have a reasonable knowledge of business and economic activities and accounting and a willingness to study the information in the financial statements with reasonable diligence;

(b) Understand that financial statements are prepared, presented and audited to levels of materiality;

(c) Recognize the uncertainties inherent in the measurement of amounts based on the use of estimates, judgment and the consideration of future events; and

(d) Make reasonable economic decisions on the basis of the information in the financial statements.

5. The concept of materiality is applied by the auditor both in planning and performing the audit, and in evaluating the effect of identified misstatements on the audit and of uncorrected misstatements, if any, on the financial statements and in forming the opinion in the auditor's report. (Ref: Para. A1)

6. In planning the audit, the auditor makes judgments about the size of misstatements that will be considered material. These judgments provide a basis for:

(a) Determining the nature, timing and extent of risk assessment procedures;

(b) Identifying and assessing the risks of material misstatement; and

(c) Determining the nature, timing and extent of further audit procedures.

The materiality determined when planning the audit does not necessarily establish an amount below which uncorrected misstatements, individually or in the aggregate, will always be evaluated as immaterial. The circumstances related to some misstatements may cause the auditor to evaluate them as material even if they are below materiality. Although it is not practicable to design audit procedures to detect misstatements that could be material solely because of their nature, the auditor considers not only the size but also the nature of uncorrected misstatements, and the particular circumstances of their occurrence, when evaluating their effect on the financial statements.[3]

Effective Date

7. This ISA (UK and Ireland) is effective for audits of financial statements for periods ending on or after 15 December 2010.

---

[3] ISA (UK and Ireland) 450, paragraph A16.

Objective

8.   The objective of the auditor is to apply the concept of materiality appropriately in planning and performing the audit.

Definition

9.   For purposes of the ISAs (UK and Ireland), performance materiality means the amount or amounts set by the auditor at less than materiality for the financial statements as a whole to reduce to an appropriately low level the probability that the aggregate of uncorrected and undetected misstatements exceeds materiality for the financial statements as a whole. If applicable, performance materiality also refers to the amount or amounts set by the auditor at less than the materiality level or levels for particular classes of transactions, account balances or disclosures.

Requirements

Determining Materiality and Performance Materiality When Planning the Audit

10.   When establishing the overall audit strategy, the auditor shall determine materiality for the financial statements as a whole. If, in the specific circumstances of the entity, there is one or more particular classes of transactions, account balances or disclosures for which misstatements of lesser amounts than materiality for the financial statements as a whole could reasonably be expected to influence the economic decisions of users taken on the basis of the financial statements, the auditor shall also determine the materiality level or levels to be applied to those particular classes of transactions, account balances or disclosures. (Ref: Para. A2-A11)

11.   The auditor shall determine performance materiality for purposes of assessing the risks of material misstatement and determining the nature, timing and extent of further audit procedures. (Ref: Para. A12)

Revision as the Audit Progresses

12.   The auditor shall revise materiality for the financial statements as a whole (and, if applicable, the materiality level or levels for particular classes of transactions, account balances or disclosures) in the event of becoming aware of information during the audit that would have caused the auditor to have determined a different amount (or amounts) initially. (Ref: Para. A13)

13.   If the auditor concludes that a lower materiality for the financial statements as a whole (and, if applicable, materiality level or levels for particular classes of transactions, account balances or disclosures) than that initially determined is appropriate, the auditor shall determine whether it is necessary to revise performance materiality, and

whether the nature, timing and extent of the further audit procedures remain appropriate.

Documentation

14. The auditor shall include in the audit documentation the following amounts and the factors considered in their determination:[4]

    (a) Materiality for the financial statements as a whole (see paragraph 10);

    (b) If applicable, the materiality level or levels for particular classes of transactions, account balances or disclosures (see paragraph 10);

    (c) Performance materiality (see paragraph 11); and

    (d) Any revision of (a)-(c) as the audit progressed (see paragraphs 12-13).

***

Application and Other Explanatory Material

Materiality and Audit Risk (Ref: Para. 5)

A1. In conducting an audit of financial statements, the overall objectives of the auditor are to obtain reasonable assurance about whether the financial statements as a whole are free from material misstatement, whether due to fraud or error, thereby enabling the auditor to express an opinion on whether the financial statements are prepared, in all material respects, in accordance with an applicable financial reporting framework; and to report on the financial statements, and communicate as required by the ISAs (UK and Ireland), in accordance with the auditor's findings.[5] The auditor obtains reasonable assurance by obtaining sufficient appropriate audit evidence to reduce audit risk to an acceptably low level.[6] Audit risk is the risk that the auditor expresses an inappropriate audit opinion when the financial statements are materially misstated. Audit risk is a function of the risks of material misstatement and detection risk.[7] Materiality and audit risk are considered throughout the audit, in particular, when:

    (a) Identifying and assessing the risks of material misstatement;[8]

    (b) Determining the nature, timing and extent of further audit procedures;[9] and

---

[4] ISA (UK and Ireland) 230, "Audit Documentation," paragraphs 8-11, and paragraph A6.

[5] ISA (UK and Ireland) 200, "Overall Objectives of the Independent Auditor and the Conduct of an Audit in Accordance with International Standards on Auditing (UK and Ireland)," paragraph 11.

[6] ISA (UK and Ireland) 200, paragraph 17.

[7] ISA (UK and Ireland) 200, paragraph 13(c).

[8] ISA (UK and Ireland) 315, "Identifying and Assessing the Risks of Material Misstatements through Understanding the Entity and Its Environment."

[9] ISA (UK and Ireland) 330, "The Auditor's Responses to Assessed Risks."

(c) Evaluating the effect of uncorrected misstatements, if any, on the financial statements[10] and in forming the opinion in the auditor's report.[11]

Determining Materiality and Performance Materiality When Planning the Audit

Considerations Specific to Public Sector Entities (Ref: Para. 10)

A2. In the case of a public sector entity, legislators and regulators are often the primary users of its financial statements. Furthermore, the financial statements may be used to make decisions other than economic decisions. The determination of materiality for the financial statements as a whole (and, if applicable, materiality level or levels for particular classes of transactions, account balances or disclosures) in an audit of the financial statements of a public sector entity is therefore influenced by law, regulation or other authority, and by the financial information needs of legislators and the public in relation to public sector programs.

Use of Benchmarks in Determining Materiality for the Financial Statements as a Whole (Ref: Para. 10)

A3. Determining materiality involves the exercise of professional judgment. A percentage is often applied to a chosen benchmark as a starting point in determining materiality for the financial statements as a whole. Factors that may affect the identification of an appropriate benchmark include the following:

- The elements of the financial statements (for example, assets, liabilities, equity, revenue, expenses);

- Whether there are items on which the attention of the users of the particular entity's financial statements tends to be focused (for example, for the purpose of evaluating financial performance users may tend to focus on profit, revenue or net assets);

- The nature of the entity, where the entity is in its life cycle, and the industry and economic environment in which the entity operates;

- The entity's ownership structure and the way it is financed (for example, if an entity is financed solely by debt rather than equity, users may put more emphasis on assets, and claims on them, than on the entity's earnings); and

- The relative volatility of the benchmark.

---

[10] ISA (UK and Ireland) 450.
[11] ISA 700, "Forming an Opinion and Reporting on Financial Statements."
The APB has not promulgated ISA 700 as issued by the IAASB for application in the UK and Ireland. In the UK and Ireland the applicable auditing standard is ISA (UK and Ireland) 700, "The Auditor's Report on Financial Statements." Paragraph 8(b) of ISA (UK and Ireland) 700 requires evaluation of whether uncorrected misstatements are material, individually or in aggregate.

A4.   Examples of benchmarks that may be appropriate, depending on the circumstances of the entity, include categories of reported income such as profit before tax, total revenue, gross profit and total expenses, total equity or net asset value. Profit before tax from continuing operations is often used for profit-oriented entities. When profit before tax from continuing operations is volatile, other benchmarks may be more appropriate, such as gross profit or total revenues.

A5.   In relation to the chosen benchmark, relevant financial data ordinarily includes prior periods' financial results and financial positions, the period-to-date financial results and financial position, and budgets or forecasts for the current period, adjusted for significant changes in the circumstances of the entity (for example, a significant business acquisition) and relevant changes of conditions in the industry or economic environment in which the entity operates. For example, when, as a starting point, materiality for the financial statements as a whole is determined for a particular entity based on a percentage of profit before tax from continuing operations, circumstances that give rise to an exceptional decrease or increase in such profit may lead the auditor to conclude that materiality for the financial statements as a whole is more appropriately determined using a normalized profit before tax from continuing operations figure based on past results.

A6.   Materiality relates to the financial statements on which the auditor is reporting. Where the financial statements are prepared for a financial reporting period of more or less than twelve months, such as may be the case for a new entity or a change in the financial reporting period, materiality relates to the financial statements prepared for that financial reporting period.

A7.   Determining a percentage to be applied to a chosen benchmark involves the exercise of professional judgment. There is a relationship between the percentage and the chosen benchmark, such that a percentage applied to profit before tax from continuing operations will normally be higher than a percentage applied to total revenue. For example, the auditor may consider five percent of profit before tax from continuing operations to be appropriate for a profit-oriented entity in a manufacturing industry, while the auditor may consider one percent of total revenue or total expenses to be appropriate for a not-for-profit entity. Higher or lower percentages, however, may be deemed appropriate in the circumstances.

Considerations Specific to Small Entities

A8.   When an entity's profit before tax from continuing operations is consistently nominal, as might be the case for an owner-managed business where the owner takes much of the profit before tax in the form of remuneration, a benchmark such as profit before remuneration and tax may be more relevant.

Considerations Specific to Public Sector Entities

A9.   In an audit of a public sector entity, total cost or net cost (expenses less revenues or expenditure less receipts) may be appropriate benchmarks for program activities. Where a public sector entity has custody of public assets, assets may be an appropriate benchmark.

Materiality Level or Levels for Particular Classes of Transactions, Account Balances or Disclosures (Ref: Para. 10)

A10. Factors that may indicate the existence of one or more particular classes of transactions, account balances or disclosures for which misstatements of lesser amounts than materiality for the financial statements as a whole could reasonably be expected to influence the economic decisions of users taken on the basis of the financial statements include the following:

- Whether law, regulation or the applicable financial reporting framework affect users' expectations regarding the measurement or disclosure of certain items (for example, related party transactions, and the remuneration of management and those charged with governance).

- The key disclosures in relation to the industry in which the entity operates (for example, research and development costs for a pharmaceutical company).

- Whether attention is focused on a particular aspect of the entity's business that is separately disclosed in the financial statements (for example, a newly acquired business).

A11. In considering whether, in the specific circumstances of the entity, such classes of transactions, account balances or disclosures exist, the auditor may find it useful to obtain an understanding of the views and expectations of those charged with governance and management.

Performance Materiality (Ref: Para. 11)

A12. Planning the audit solely to detect individually material misstatements overlooks the fact that the aggregate of individually immaterial misstatements may cause the financial statements to be materially misstated, and leaves no margin for possible undetected misstatements. Performance materiality (which, as defined, is one or more amounts) is set to reduce to an appropriately low level the probability that the aggregate of uncorrected and undetected misstatements in the financial statements exceeds materiality for the financial statements as a whole. Similarly, performance materiality relating to a materiality level determined for a particular class of transactions, account balance or disclosure is set to reduce to an appropriately low level the probability that the aggregate of uncorrected and undetected misstatements in that particular class of transactions, account balance or disclosure exceeds the materiality level for that particular class of transactions, account balance or disclosure. The determination of performance materiality is not a simple mechanical calculation and involves the exercise of professional judgment. It is affected by the auditor's understanding of the entity, updated during the performance of the risk assessment procedures; and the nature and extent of misstatements identified in previous audits and thereby the auditor's expectations in relation to misstatements in the current period.

Revision as the Audit Progresses (Ref: Para. 12)

A13. Materiality for the financial statements as a whole (and, if applicable, the materiality level or levels for particular classes of transactions, account balances or disclosures) may need to be revised as a result of a change in circumstances that occurred during the audit (for example, a decision to dispose of a major part of the entity's business), new information, or a change in the auditor's understanding of the entity and its operations as a result of performing further audit procedures. For example, if during the audit it appears as though actual financial results are likely to be substantially different from the anticipated period end financial results that were used initially to determine materiality for the financial statements as a whole, the auditor revises that materiality.

INTERNATIONAL STANDARD ON AUDITING (UK AND IRELAND) 330

THE AUDITOR'S RESPONSES TO ASSESSED RISKS

(Effective for audits of financial statements for periods ending on or after 15 December 2010)

CONTENTS

International Standard on Auditing (UK and Ireland) (ISA (UK and Ireland)) 330, "The Auditor's Responses to Assessed Risks" should be read in conjunction with ISA (UK and Ireland) 200, "Overall Objectives of the Independent Auditor and the Conduct of an Audit in Accordance with International Standards on Auditing (UK and Ireland)."

Introduction

Scope of this ISA (UK and Ireland)

1.   This International Standard on Auditing (UK and Ireland) (ISA (UK and Ireland)) deals with the auditor's responsibility to design and implement responses to the risks of material misstatement identified and assessed by the auditor in accordance with ISA (UK and Ireland) 315[1] in an audit of financial statements.

Effective Date

2.   This ISA (UK and Ireland) is effective for audits of financial statements for periods ending on or after 15 December 2010.

Objective

3.   The objective of the auditor is to obtain sufficient appropriate audit evidence regarding the assessed risks of material misstatement, through designing and implementing appropriate responses to those risks.

Definitions

4.   For purposes of the ISAs (UK and Ireland), the following terms have the meanings attributed below:

    (a)   Substantive procedure – An audit procedure designed to detect material misstatements at the assertion level. Substantive procedures comprise:

        (i)   Tests of details (of classes of transactions, account balances, and disclosures); and

        (ii)   Substantive analytical procedures.

    (b)   Test of controls – An audit procedure designed to evaluate the operating effectiveness of controls in preventing, or detecting and correcting, material misstatements at the assertion level.

---

[1]   ISA (UK and Ireland) 315, "Identifying and Assessing the Risks of Material Misstatement through Understanding the Entity and Its Environment."

Requirements

Overall Responses

5. The auditor shall design and implement overall responses to address the assessed risks of material misstatement at the financial statement level. (Ref: Para. A1-A3)

Audit Procedures Responsive to the Assessed Risks of Material Misstatement at the Assertion Level

6. The auditor shall design and perform further audit procedures whose nature, timing, and extent are based on and are responsive to the assessed risks of material misstatement at the assertion level. (Ref: Para. A4-A8)

7. In designing the further audit procedures to be performed, the auditor shall:

    (a) Consider the reasons for the assessment given to the risk of material misstatement at the assertion level for each class of transactions, account balance, and disclosure, including:

        (i) The likelihood of material misstatement due to the particular characteristics of the relevant class of transactions, account balance, or disclosure (that is, the inherent risk); and

        (ii) Whether the risk assessment takes account of relevant controls (that is, the control risk), thereby requiring the auditor to obtain audit evidence to determine whether the controls are operating effectively (that is, the auditor intends to rely on the operating effectiveness of controls in determining the nature, timing and extent of substantive procedures); and (Ref: Para. A9-A18)

    (b) Obtain more persuasive audit evidence the higher the auditor's assessment of risk. (Ref: Para. A19)

Tests of Controls

8. The auditor shall design and perform tests of controls to obtain sufficient appropriate audit evidence as to the operating effectiveness of relevant controls if:

    (a) The auditor's assessment of risks of material misstatement at the assertion level includes an expectation that the controls are operating effectively (that is, the auditor intends to rely on the operating effectiveness of controls in determining the nature, timing and extent of substantive procedures); or

    (b) Substantive procedures alone cannot provide sufficient appropriate audit evidence at the assertion level. (Ref: Para. A20-A24)

9.   In designing and performing tests of controls, the auditor shall obtain more persuasive audit evidence the greater the reliance the auditor places on the effectiveness of a control. (Ref: Para. A25)

Nature and Extent of Tests of Controls

10.   In designing and performing tests of controls, the auditor shall:

(a)   Perform other audit procedures in combination with inquiry to obtain audit evidence about the operating effectiveness of the controls, including:

(i)   How the controls were applied at relevant times during the period under audit;

(ii)   The consistency with which they were applied; and

(iii) By whom or by what means they were applied. (Ref: Para. A26-29)

(b)   Determine whether the controls to be tested depend upon other controls (indirect controls) and, if so, whether it is necessary to obtain audit evidence supporting the effective operation of those indirect controls. (Ref: Para. A30-A31)

Timing of Tests of Controls

11.   The auditor shall test controls for the particular time, or throughout the period, for which the auditor intends to rely on those controls, subject to paragraphs 12 and 15 below, in order to provide an appropriate basis for the auditor's intended reliance. (Ref: Para. A32)

Using audit evidence obtained during an interim period

12.   If the auditor obtains audit evidence about the operating effectiveness of controls during an interim period, the auditor shall:

(a)   Obtain audit evidence about significant changes to those controls subsequent to the interim period; and

(b)   Determine the additional audit evidence to be obtained for the remaining period. (Ref: Para. A33-A34)

Using audit evidence obtained in previous audits

13.   In determining whether it is appropriate to use audit evidence about the operating effectiveness of controls obtained in previous audits, and, if so, the length of the time period that may elapse before retesting a control, the auditor shall consider the following:

(a) The effectiveness of other elements of internal control, including the control environment, the entity's monitoring of controls, and the entity's risk assessment process;

(b) The risks arising from the characteristics of the control, including whether it is manual or automated;

(c) The effectiveness of general IT-controls;

(d) The effectiveness of the control and its application by the entity, including the nature and extent of deviations in the application of the control noted in previous audits, and whether there have been personnel changes that significantly affect the application of the control;

(e) Whether the lack of a change in a particular control poses a risk due to changing circumstances; and

(f) The risks of material misstatement and the extent of reliance on the control. (Ref: Para. A35)

14. If the auditor plans to use audit evidence from a previous audit about the operating effectiveness of specific controls, the auditor shall establish the continuing relevance of that evidence by obtaining audit evidence about whether significant changes in those controls have occurred subsequent to the previous audit. The auditor shall obtain this evidence by performing inquiry combined with observation or inspection, to confirm the understanding of those specific controls, and:

(a) If there have been changes that affect the continuing relevance of the audit evidence from the previous audit, the auditor shall test the controls in the current audit. (Ref: Para. A36)

(b) If there have not been such changes, the auditor shall test the controls at least once in every third audit, and shall test some controls each audit to avoid the possibility of testing all the controls on which the auditor intends to rely in a single audit period with no testing of controls in the subsequent two audit periods. (Ref: Para. A37-A39)

Controls over significant risks

15. If the auditor plans to rely on controls over a risk the auditor has determined to be a significant risk, the auditor shall test those controls in the current period.

Evaluating the Operating Effectiveness of Controls

16. When evaluating the operating effectiveness of relevant controls, the auditor shall evaluate whether misstatements that have been detected by substantive procedures indicate that controls are not operating effectively. The absence of misstatements detected by substantive procedures, however, does not provide audit evidence that controls related to the assertion being tested are effective. (Ref: Para. A40)

17. If deviations from controls upon which the auditor intends to rely are detected, the auditor shall make specific inquiries to understand these matters and their potential consequences, and shall determine whether: (Ref: Para. A41)

(a) The tests of controls that have been performed provide an appropriate basis for reliance on the controls;

(b) Additional tests of controls are necessary; or

(c) The potential risks of misstatement need to be addressed using substantive procedures.

Substantive Procedures

18. Irrespective of the assessed risks of material misstatement, the auditor shall design and perform substantive procedures for each material class of transactions, account balance, and disclosure. (Ref: Para. A42-A47)

19. The auditor shall consider whether external confirmation procedures are to be performed as substantive audit procedures. (Ref: Para. A48-A51)

Substantive Procedures Related to the Financial Statement Closing Process

20. The auditor's substantive procedures shall include the following audit procedures related to the financial statement closing process:

(a) Agreeing or reconciling the financial statements with the underlying accounting records; and

(b) Examining material journal entries and other adjustments made during the course of preparing the financial statements. (Ref: Para. A52)

Substantive Procedures Responsive to Significant Risks

21. If the auditor has determined that an assessed risk of material misstatement at the assertion level is a significant risk, the auditor shall perform substantive procedures that are specifically responsive to that risk. When the approach to a significant risk consists only of substantive procedures, those procedures shall include tests of details. (Ref: Para. A53)

Timing of Substantive Procedures

22. If substantive procedures are performed at an interim date, the auditor shall cover the remaining period by performing:

(a) substantive procedures, combined with tests of controls for the intervening period; or

(b) if the auditor determines that it is sufficient, further substantive procedures only that provide a reasonable basis for extending the audit conclusions from the interim date to the period end. (Ref: Para. A54-A57)

23. If misstatements that the auditor did not expect when assessing the risks of material misstatement are detected at an interim date, the auditor shall evaluate whether the related assessment of risk and the planned nature, timing, or extent of substantive procedures covering the remaining period need to be modified. (Ref: Para. A58)

Adequacy of Presentation and Disclosure

24. The auditor shall perform audit procedures to evaluate whether the overall presentation of the financial statements, including the related disclosures, is in accordance with the applicable financial reporting framework. (Ref: Para. A59)

Evaluating the Sufficiency and Appropriateness of Audit Evidence

25. Based on the audit procedures performed and the audit evidence obtained, the auditor shall evaluate before the conclusion of the audit whether the assessments of the risks of material misstatement at the assertion level remain appropriate. (Ref: Para. A60-A61)

26. The auditor shall conclude whether sufficient appropriate audit evidence has been obtained. In forming an opinion, the auditor shall consider all relevant audit evidence, regardless of whether it appears to corroborate or to contradict the assertions in the financial statements. (Ref: Para. A62)

27. If the auditor has not obtained sufficient appropriate audit evidence as to a material financial statement assertion, the auditor shall attempt to obtain further audit evidence. If the auditor is unable to obtain sufficient appropriate audit evidence, the auditor shall express a qualified opinion or disclaim an opinion on the financial statements.

Documentation

28. The auditor shall include in the audit documentation:[2]

   (a) The overall responses to address the assessed risks of material misstatement at the financial statement level, and the nature, timing, and extent of the further audit procedures performed;

   (b) The linkage of those procedures with the assessed risks at the assertion level; and

   (c) The results of the audit procedures, including the conclusions where these are not otherwise clear. (Ref: Para. A63)

---

[2] ISA (UK and Ireland) 230, "Audit Documentation," paragraphs 8-11, and paragraph A6.

29. If the auditor plans to use audit evidence about the operating effectiveness of controls obtained in previous audits, the auditor shall include in the audit documentation the conclusions reached about relying on such controls that were tested in a previous audit.

30. The auditor's documentation shall demonstrate that the financial statements agree or reconcile with the underlying accounting records.

***

Application and Other Explanatory Material

Overall Responses (Ref: Para. 5)

A1. Overall responses to address the assessed risks of material misstatement at the financial statement level may include:

- Emphasizing to the engagement team the need to maintain professional skepticism.

- Assigning more experienced staff or those with special skills or using experts.

- Providing more supervision.

- Incorporating additional elements of unpredictability in the selection of further audit procedures to be performed.

- Making general changes to the nature, timing, or extent of audit procedures, for example: performing substantive procedures at the period end instead of at an interim date; or modifying the nature of audit procedures to obtain more persuasive audit evidence.

A2. The assessment of the risks of material misstatement at the financial statement level, and thereby the auditor's overall responses, is affected by the auditor's understanding of the control environment. An effective control environment may allow the auditor to have more confidence in internal control and the reliability of audit evidence generated internally within the entity and thus, for example, allow the auditor to conduct some audit procedures at an interim date rather than at the period end. Deficiencies in the control environment, however, have the opposite effect; for example, the auditor may respond to an ineffective control environment by:

- Conducting more audit procedures as of the period end rather than at an interim date.

- Obtaining more extensive audit evidence from substantive procedures.

- Increasing the number of locations to be included in the audit scope.

A3. Such considerations, therefore, have a significant bearing on the auditor's general approach, for example, an emphasis on substantive procedures (substantive approach), or an approach that uses tests of controls as well as substantive procedures (combined approach).

Audit Procedures Responsive to the Assessed Risks of Material Misstatement at the Assertion Level

The Nature, Timing, and Extent of Further Audit Procedures (Ref: Para. 6)

A4. The auditor's assessment of the identified risks at the assertion level provides a basis for considering the appropriate audit approach for designing and performing further audit procedures. For example, the auditor may determine that:

(a) Only by performing tests of controls may the auditor achieve an effective response to the assessed risk of material misstatement for a particular assertion;

(b) Performing only substantive procedures is appropriate for particular assertions and, therefore, the auditor excludes the effect of controls from the relevant risk assessment. This may be because the auditor's risk assessment procedures have not identified any effective controls relevant to the assertion, or because testing controls would be inefficient and therefore the auditor does not intend to rely on the operating effectiveness of controls in determining the nature, timing and extent of substantive procedures; or

(c) A combined approach using both tests of controls and substantive procedures is an effective approach.

However, as required by paragraph 18, irrespective of the approach selected, the auditor designs and performs substantive procedures for each material class of transactions, account balance, and disclosure.

A5. The nature of an audit procedure refers to its purpose (i.e., test of controls or substantive procedure) and its type (that is, inspection, observation, inquiry, confirmation, recalculation, reperformance, or analytical procedure). The nature of the audit procedures is of most importance in responding to the assessed risks.

A6. Timing of an audit procedure refers to when it is performed, or the period or date to which the audit evidence applies.

A7. Extent of an audit procedure refers to the quantity to be performed, for example, a sample size or the number of observations of a control activity.

A8. Designing and performing further audit procedures whose nature, timing, and extent are based on and are responsive to the assessed risks of material misstatement at the assertion level provides a clear linkage between the auditor's further audit procedures and the risk assessment.

Responding to the Assessed Risks at the Assertion Level (Ref: Para. 7(a))

Nature

A9.   The auditor's assessed risks may affect both the types of audit procedures to be performed and their combination. For example, when an assessed risk is high, the auditor may confirm the completeness of the terms of a contract with the counterparty, in addition to inspecting the document. Further, certain audit procedures may be more appropriate for some assertions than others. For example, in relation to revenue, tests of controls may be most responsive to the assessed risk of misstatement of the completeness assertion, whereas substantive procedures may be most responsive to the assessed risk of misstatement of the occurrence assertion.

A10. The reasons for the assessment given to a risk are relevant in determining the nature of audit procedures. For example, if an assessed risk is lower because of the particular characteristics of a class of transactions without consideration of the related controls, then the auditor may determine that substantive analytical procedures alone provide sufficient appropriate audit evidence. On the other hand, if the assessed risk is lower because of internal controls, and the auditor intends to base the substantive procedures on that low assessment, then the auditor performs tests of those controls, as required by paragraph 8(a). This may be the case, for example, for a class of transactions of reasonably uniform, non-complex characteristics that are routinely processed and controlled by the entity's information system.

Timing

A11. The auditor may perform tests of controls or substantive procedures at an interim date or at the period end. The higher the risk of material misstatement, the more likely it is that the auditor may decide it is more effective to perform substantive procedures nearer to, or at, the period end rather than at an earlier date, or to perform audit procedures unannounced or at unpredictable times (for example, performing audit procedures at selected locations on an unannounced basis). This is particularly relevant when considering the response to the risks of fraud. For example, the auditor may conclude that, when the risks of intentional misstatement or manipulation have been identified, audit procedures to extend audit conclusions from interim date to the period end would not be effective.

A12. On the other hand, performing audit procedures before the period end may assist the auditor in identifying significant matters at an early stage of the audit, and consequently resolving them with the assistance of management or developing an effective audit approach to address such matters.

A13. In addition, certain audit procedures can be performed only at or after the period end, for example:

- Agreeing the financial statements to the accounting records;

- Examining adjustments made during the course of preparing the financial statements; and

- Procedures to respond to a risk that, at the period end, the entity may have entered into improper sales contracts, or transactions may not have been finalized.

A14. Further relevant factors that influence the auditor's consideration of when to perform audit procedures include the following:

- The control environment.

- When relevant information is available (for example, electronic files may subsequently be overwritten, or procedures to be observed may occur only at certain times).

- The nature of the risk (for example, if there is a risk of inflated revenues to meet earnings expectations by subsequent creation of false sales agreements, the auditor may wish to examine contracts available on the date of the period end).

- The period or date to which the audit evidence relates.

Extent

A15. The extent of an audit procedure judged necessary is determined after considering the materiality, the assessed risk, and the degree of assurance the auditor plans to obtain. When a single purpose is met by a combination of procedures, the extent of each procedure is considered separately. In general, the extent of audit procedures increases as the risk of material misstatement increases. For example, in response to the assessed risk of material misstatement due to fraud, increasing sample sizes or performing substantive analytical procedures at a more detailed level may be appropriate. However, increasing the extent of an audit procedure is effective only if the audit procedure itself is relevant to the specific risk.

A16. The use of computer-assisted audit techniques (CAATs) may enable more extensive testing of electronic transactions and account files, which may be useful when the auditor decides to modify the extent of testing, for example, in responding to the risks of material misstatement due to fraud. Such techniques can be used to select sample transactions from key electronic files, to sort transactions with specific characteristics, or to test an entire population instead of a sample.

Considerations specific to public sector entities

A17. For the audits of public sector entities, the audit mandate and any other special auditing requirements may affect the auditor's consideration of the nature, timing and extent of further audit procedures.

Considerations specific to smaller entities

A18. In the case of very small entities, there may not be many control activities that could be identified by the auditor, or the extent to which their existence or operation have been documented by the entity may be limited. In such cases, it may be more efficient for the auditor to perform further audit procedures that are primarily substantive procedures. In some rare cases, however, the absence of control activities or of other components of control may make it impossible to obtain sufficient appropriate audit evidence.

Higher Assessments of Risk (Ref: Para 7(b))

A19. When obtaining more persuasive audit evidence because of a higher assessment of risk, the auditor may increase the quantity of the evidence, or obtain evidence that is more relevant or reliable, for example, by placing more emphasis on obtaining third party evidence or by obtaining corroborating evidence from a number of independent sources.

Tests of Controls

Designing and Performing Tests of Controls (Ref: Para. 8)

A20. Tests of controls are performed only on those controls that the auditor has determined are suitably designed to prevent, or detect and correct, a material misstatement in an assertion. If substantially different controls were used at different times during the period under audit, each is considered separately.

A21. Testing the operating effectiveness of controls is different from obtaining an understanding of and evaluating the design and implementation of controls. However, the same types of audit procedures are used. The auditor may, therefore, decide it is efficient to test the operating effectiveness of controls at the same time as evaluating their design and determining that they have been implemented.

A22. Further, although some risk assessment procedures may not have been specifically designed as tests of controls, they may nevertheless provide audit evidence about the operating effectiveness of the controls and, consequently, serve as tests of controls. For example, the auditor's risk assessment procedures may have included:

- Inquiring about management's use of budgets.

- Observing management's comparison of monthly budgeted and actual expenses.

- Inspecting reports pertaining to the investigation of variances between budgeted and actual amounts.

These audit procedures provide knowledge about the design of the entity's budgeting policies and whether they have been implemented, but may also provide audit evidence about the effectiveness of the operation of budgeting policies in preventing or detecting material misstatements in the classification of expenses.

A23. In addition, the auditor may design a test of controls to be performed concurrently with a test of details on the same transaction. Although the purpose of a test of controls is different from the purpose of a test of details, both may be accomplished concurrently by performing a test of controls and a test of details on the same transaction, also known as a dual-purpose test. For example, the auditor may design, and evaluate the results of, a test to examine an invoice to determine whether it has been approved and to provide substantive audit evidence of a transaction. A dual-purpose test is designed and evaluated by considering each purpose of the test separately.

A24. In some cases, the auditor may find it impossible to design effective substantive procedures that by themselves provide sufficient appropriate audit evidence at the assertion level.[3] This may occur when an entity conducts its business using IT and no documentation of transactions is produced or maintained, other than through the IT system. In such cases, paragraph 8(b) requires the auditor to perform tests of relevant controls.

Audit Evidence and Intended Reliance (Ref: Para. 9)

A25. A higher level of assurance may be sought about the operating effectiveness of controls when the approach adopted consists primarily of tests of controls, in particular where it is not possible or practicable to obtain sufficient appropriate audit evidence only from substantive procedures.

Nature and Extent of Tests of Controls

Other audit procedures in combination with inquiry (Ref: Para. 10(a))

A26. Inquiry alone is not sufficient to test the operating effectiveness of controls. Accordingly, other audit procedures are performed in combination with inquiry. In this regard, inquiry combined with inspection or reperformance may provide more assurance than inquiry and observation, since an observation is pertinent only at the point in time at which it is made.

A27. The nature of the particular control influences the type of procedure required to obtain audit evidence about whether the control was operating effectively. For example, if operating effectiveness is evidenced by documentation, the auditor may decide to inspect it to obtain audit evidence about operating effectiveness. For other controls, however, documentation may not be available or relevant. For example, documentation of operation may not exist for some factors in the control environment, such as assignment of authority and responsibility, or for some types of control activities, such as control activities performed by a computer. In such circumstances,

---

[3] ISA (UK and Ireland) 315, paragraph 30.

audit evidence about operating effectiveness may be obtained through inquiry in combination with other audit procedures such as observation or the use of CAATs.

Extent of tests of controls

A28. When more persuasive audit evidence is needed regarding the effectiveness of a control, it may be appropriate to increase the extent of testing of the control. As well as the degree of reliance on controls, matters the auditor may consider in determining the extent of tests of controls include the following:

- The frequency of the performance of the control by the entity during the period.

- The length of time during the audit period that the auditor is relying on the operating effectiveness of the control.

- The expected rate of deviation from a control.

- The relevance and reliability of the audit evidence to be obtained regarding the operating effectiveness of the control at the assertion level.

- The extent to which audit evidence is obtained from tests of other controls related to the assertion.

ISA (UK and Ireland) 530[4] contains further guidance on the extent of testing.

A29. Because of the inherent consistency of IT processing, it may not be necessary to increase the extent of testing of an automated control. An automated control can be expected to function consistently unless the program (including the tables, files, or other permanent data used by the program) is changed. Once the auditor determines that an automated control is functioning as intended (which could be done at the time the control is initially implemented or at some other date), the auditor may consider performing tests to determine that the control continues to function effectively. Such tests might include determining that:

- Changes to the program are not made without being subject to the appropriate program change controls;

- The authorized version of the program is used for processing transactions; and

- Other relevant general controls are effective.

Such tests also might include determining that changes to the programs have not been made, as may be the case when the entity uses packaged software applications without modifying or maintaining them. For example, the auditor may inspect the record of the administration of IT security to obtain audit evidence that unauthorized access has not occurred during the period.

---

[4] ISA (UK and Ireland) 530, "Audit Sampling."

Testing of indirect controls (Ref: Para. 10(b))

A30. In some circumstances, it may be necessary to obtain audit evidence supporting the effective operation of indirect controls. For example, when the auditor decides to test the effectiveness of a user review of exception reports detailing sales in excess of authorized credit limits, the user review and related follow up is the control that is directly of relevance to the auditor. Controls over the accuracy of the information in the reports (for example, the general IT-controls) are described as "indirect" controls.

A31. Because of the inherent consistency of IT processing, audit evidence about the implementation of an automated application control, when considered in combination with audit evidence about the operating effectiveness of the entity's general controls (in particular, change controls), may also provide substantial audit evidence about its operating effectiveness.

Timing of Tests of Controls

Intended period of reliance (Ref: Para. 11)

A32. Audit evidence pertaining only to a point in time may be sufficient for the auditor's purpose, for example, when testing controls over the entity's physical inventory counting at the period end. If, on the other hand, the auditor intends to rely on a control over a period, tests that are capable of providing audit evidence that the control operated effectively at relevant times during that period are appropriate. Such tests may include tests of the entity's monitoring of controls.

Using audit evidence obtained during an interim period (Ref: Para. 12b)

A33. Relevant factors in determining what additional audit evidence to obtain about controls that were operating during the period remaining after an interim period, include:

- The significance of the assessed risks of material misstatement at the assertion level.

- The specific controls that were tested during the interim period, and significant changes to them since they were tested, including changes in the information system, processes, and personnel.

- The degree to which audit evidence about the operating effectiveness of those controls was obtained.

- The length of the remaining period.

- The extent to which the auditor intends to reduce further substantive procedures based on the reliance of controls.

- The control environment.

A34. Additional audit evidence may be obtained, for example, by extending tests of controls over the remaining period or testing the entity's monitoring of controls.

Using audit evidence obtained in previous audits (Ref: Para. 13)

A35. In certain circumstances, audit evidence obtained from previous audits may provide audit evidence where the auditor performs audit procedures to establish its continuing relevance. For example, in performing a previous audit, the auditor may have determined that an automated control was functioning as intended. The auditor may obtain audit evidence to determine whether changes to the automated control have been made that affect its continued effective functioning through, for example, inquiries of management and the inspection of logs to indicate what controls have been changed. Consideration of audit evidence about these changes may support either increasing or decreasing the expected audit evidence to be obtained in the current period about the operating effectiveness of the controls.

Controls that have changed from previous audits (Ref: Para. 14(a))

A36. Changes may affect the relevance of the audit evidence obtained in previous audits such that there may no longer be a basis for continued reliance. For example, changes in a system that enable an entity to receive a new report from the system probably do not affect the relevance of audit evidence from a previous audit; however, a change that causes data to be accumulated or calculated differently does affect it.

Controls that have not changed from previous audits (Ref: Para. 14(b))

A37. The auditor's decision on whether to rely on audit evidence obtained in previous audits for controls that:

(a)   have not changed since they were last tested; and

(b)   are not controls that mitigate a significant risk,

is a matter of professional judgment. In addition, the length of time between retesting such controls is also a matter of professional judgment, but is required by paragraph 14 (b) to be at least once in every third year.

A38. In general, the higher the risk of material misstatement, or the greater the reliance on controls, the shorter the time period elapsed, if any, is likely to be. Factors that may decrease the period for retesting a control, or result in not relying on audit evidence obtained in previous audits at all, include the following:

*   A deficient control environment.

*   Deficient monitoring of controls.

*   A significant manual element to the relevant controls.

- Personnel changes that significantly affect the application of the control.

- Changing circumstances that indicate the need for changes in the control.

- Deficient general IT-controls.

A39. When there are a number of controls for which the auditor intends to rely on audit evidence obtained in previous audits, testing some of those controls in each audit provides corroborating information about the continuing effectiveness of the control environment. This contributes to the auditor's decision about whether it is appropriate to rely on audit evidence obtained in previous audits.

Evaluating the Operating Effectiveness of Controls (Ref: Para. 16-17)

A40. A material misstatement detected by the auditor's procedures is a strong indicator of the existence of a significant deficiency in internal control.

A41. The concept of effectiveness of the operation of controls recognizes that some deviations in the way controls are applied by the entity may occur. Deviations from prescribed controls may be caused by such factors as changes in key personnel, significant seasonal fluctuations in volume of transactions and human error. The detected rate of deviation, in particular in comparison with the expected rate, may indicate that the control cannot be relied on to reduce risk at the assertion level to that assessed by the auditor.

Substantive Procedures (Ref: Para. 18)

A42. Paragraph 18 requires the auditor to design and perform substantive procedures for each material class of transactions, account balance, and disclosure, irrespective of the assessed risks of material misstatement. This requirement reflects the facts that: (a) the auditor's assessment of risk is judgmental and so may not identify all risks of material misstatement; and (b) there are inherent limitations to internal control, including management override.

Nature and Extent of Substantive Procedures

A43. Depending on the circumstances, the auditor may determine that:

- Performing only substantive analytical procedures will be sufficient to reduce audit risk to an acceptably low level. For example, where the auditor's assessment of risk is supported by audit evidence from tests of controls.

- Only tests of details are appropriate.

- A combination of substantive analytical procedures and tests of details are most responsive to the assessed risks.

A44. Substantive analytical procedures are generally more applicable to large volumes of transactions that tend to be predictable over time. ISA (UK and Ireland) 520[5] establishes requirements and provides guidance on the application of analytical procedures during an audit.

A45. The nature of the risk and assertion is relevant to the design of tests of details. For example, tests of details related to the existence or occurrence assertion may involve selecting from items contained in a financial statement amount and obtaining the relevant audit evidence. On the other hand, tests of details related to the completeness assertion may involve selecting from items that are expected to be included in the relevant financial statement amount and investigating whether they are included.

A46. Because the assessment of the risk of material misstatement takes account of internal control, the extent of substantive procedures may need to be increased when the results from tests of controls are unsatisfactory. However, increasing the extent of an audit procedure is appropriate only if the audit procedure itself is relevant to the specific risk.

A47. In designing tests of details, the extent of testing is ordinarily thought of in terms of the sample size. However, other matters are also relevant, including whether it is more effective to use other selective means of testing. See ISA (UK and Ireland) 500.[6]

Considering Whether External Confirmation Procedures Are to Be Performed (Ref: Para. 19)

A48. External confirmation procedures frequently are relevant when addressing assertions associated with account balances and their elements, but need not be restricted to these items. For example, the auditor may request external confirmation of the terms of agreements, contracts, or transactions between an entity and other parties. External confirmation procedures also may be performed to obtain audit evidence about the absence of certain conditions. For example, a request may specifically seek confirmation that no "side agreement" exists that may be relevant to an entity's revenue cut-off assertion. Other situations where external confirmation procedures may provide relevant audit evidence in responding to assessed risks of material misstatement include:

- Bank balances and other information relevant to banking relationships.

- Accounts receivable balances and terms.

- Inventories held by third parties at bonded warehouses for processing or on consignment.

- Property title deeds held by lawyers or financiers for safe custody or as security.

---

[5] ISA (UK and Ireland) 520, "Analytical Procedures."
[6] ISA (UK and Ireland) 500, "Audit Evidence," paragraph 10.

- Investments held for safekeeping by third parties, or purchased from stockbrokers but not delivered at the balance sheet date.

- Amounts due to lenders, including relevant terms of repayment and restrictive covenants.

- Accounts payable balances and terms.

A49. Although external confirmations may provide relevant audit evidence relating to certain assertions, there are some assertions for which external confirmations provide less relevant audit evidence. For example, external confirmations provide less relevant audit evidence relating to the recoverability of accounts receivable balances, than they do of their existence.

A50. The auditor may determine that external confirmation procedures performed for one purpose provide an opportunity to obtain audit evidence about other matters. For example, confirmation requests for bank balances often include requests for information relevant to other financial statement assertions. Such considerations may influence the auditor's decision about whether to perform external confirmation procedures.

A51. Factors that may assist the auditor in determining whether external confirmation procedures are to be performed as substantive audit procedures include:

- The confirming party's knowledge of the subject matter – responses may be more reliable if provided by a person at the confirming party who has the requisite knowledge about the information being confirmed.

- The ability or willingness of the intended confirming party to respond – for example, the confirming party:

  ○ May not accept responsibility for responding to a confirmation request;

  ○ May consider responding too costly or time consuming;

  ○ May have concerns about the potential legal liability resulting from responding;

  ○ May account for transactions in different currencies; or

  ○ May operate in an environment where responding to confirmation requests is not a significant aspect of day-to-day operations.

  In such situations, confirming parties may not respond, may respond in a casual manner or may attempt to restrict the reliance placed on the response.

- The objectivity of the intended confirming party – if the confirming party is a related party of the entity, responses to confirmation requests may be less reliable.

Substantive Procedures Related to the Financial Statement Closing Process (Ref: Para. 20(b))

A52. The nature, and also the extent, of the auditor's examination of journal entries and other adjustments depends on the nature and complexity of the entity's financial reporting process and the related risks of material misstatement.

Substantive Procedures Responsive to Significant Risks (Ref: Para. 21)

A53. Paragraph 21 of this ISA (UK and Ireland) requires the auditor to perform substantive procedures that are specifically responsive to risks the auditor has determined to be significant risks. Audit evidence in the form of external confirmations received directly by the auditor from appropriate confirming parties may assist the auditor in obtaining audit evidence with the high level of reliability that the auditor requires to respond to significant risks of material misstatement, whether due to fraud or error. For example, if the auditor identifies that management is under pressure to meet earnings expectations, there may be a risk that management is inflating sales by improperly recognizing revenue related to sales agreements with terms that preclude revenue recognition or by invoicing sales before shipment. In these circumstances, the auditor may, for example, design external confirmation procedures not only to confirm outstanding amounts, but also to confirm the details of the sales agreements, including date, any rights of return and delivery terms. In addition, the auditor may find it effective to supplement such external confirmation procedures with inquiries of non-financial personnel in the entity regarding any changes in sales agreements and delivery terms.

Timing of Substantive Procedures (Ref: Para. 22-23)

A54. In most cases, audit evidence from a previous audit's substantive procedures provides little or no audit evidence for the current period. There are, however, exceptions, for example, a legal opinion obtained in a previous audit related to the structure of a securitization to which no changes have occurred, may be relevant in the current period. In such cases, it may be appropriate to use audit evidence from a previous audit's substantive procedures if that evidence and the related subject matter have not fundamentally changed, and audit procedures have been performed during the current period to establish its continuing relevance.

Using audit evidence obtained during an interim period (Ref: Para. 22)

A55. In some circumstances, the auditor may determine that it is effective to perform substantive procedures at an interim date, and to compare and reconcile information concerning the balance at the period end with the comparable information at the interim date to:

(a)   Identify amounts that appear unusual;

(b)   Investigate any such amounts; and

(c) Perform substantive analytical procedures or tests of details to test the intervening period.

A56. Performing substantive procedures at an interim date without undertaking additional procedures at a later date increases the risk that the auditor will not detect misstatements that may exist at the period end. This risk increases as the remaining period is lengthened. Factors such as the following may influence whether to perform substantive procedures at an interim date:

- The control environment and other relevant controls.

- The availability at a later date of information necessary for the auditor's procedures.

- The purpose of the substantive procedure.

- The assessed risk of material misstatement.

- The nature of the class of transactions or account balance and related assertions.

- The ability of the auditor to perform appropriate substantive procedures or substantive procedures combined with tests of controls to cover the remaining period in order to reduce the risk that misstatements that may exist at the period end will not be detected.

A57. Factors such as the following may influence whether to perform substantive analytical procedures with respect to the period between the interim date and the period end:

- Whether the period end balances of the particular classes of transactions or account balances are reasonably predictable with respect to amount, relative significance, and composition.

- Whether the entity's procedures for analyzing and adjusting such classes of transactions or account balances at interim dates and for establishing proper accounting cutoffs are appropriate.

- Whether the information system relevant to financial reporting will provide information concerning the balances at the period end and the transactions in the remaining period that is sufficient to permit investigation of:

    (a) Significant unusual transactions or entries (including those at or near the period end);

    (b) Other causes of significant fluctuations, or expected fluctuations that did not occur; and

    (c) Changes in the composition of the classes of transactions or account balances.

Misstatements detected at an interim date (Ref: Para. 23)

A58. When the auditor concludes that the planned nature, timing, or extent of substantive procedures covering the remaining period need to be modified as a result of unexpected misstatements detected at an interim date, such modification may include extending or repeating the procedures performed at the interim date at the period end.

Adequacy of Presentation and Disclosure (Ref: Para. 24)

A59. Evaluating the overall presentation of the financial statements, including the related disclosures, relates to whether the individual financial statements are presented in a manner that reflects the appropriate classification and description of financial information, and the form, arrangement, and content of the financial statements and their appended notes. This includes, for example, the terminology used, the amount of detail given, the classification of items in the statements, and the bases of amounts set forth.

Evaluating the Sufficiency and Appropriateness of Audit Evidence (Ref: Para. 25-27)

A60. An audit of financial statements is a cumulative and iterative process. As the auditor performs planned audit procedures, the audit evidence obtained may cause the auditor to modify the nature, timing or extent of other planned audit procedures. Information may come to the auditor's attention that differs significantly from the information on which the risk assessment was based. For example:

- The extent of misstatements that the auditor detects by performing substantive procedures may alter the auditor's judgment about the risk assessments and may indicate a significant deficiency in internal control.

- The auditor may become aware of discrepancies in accounting records, or conflicting or missing evidence.

- Analytical procedures performed at the overall review stage of the audit may indicate a previously unrecognized risk of material misstatement.

In such circumstances, the auditor may need to reevaluate the planned audit procedures, based on the revised consideration of assessed risks for all or some of the classes of transactions, account balances, or disclosures and related assertions. ISA (UK and Ireland) 315 contains further guidance on revising the auditor's risk assessment.[7]

A61. The auditor cannot assume that an instance of fraud or error is an isolated occurrence. Therefore, the consideration of how the detection of a misstatement

---

[7] ISA (UK and Ireland) 315, paragraph 31.

affects the assessed risks of material misstatement is important in determining whether the assessment remains appropriate.

A62. The auditor's judgment as to what constitutes sufficient appropriate audit evidence is influenced by such factors as the following:

- Significance of the potential misstatement in the assertion and the likelihood of its having a material effect, individually or aggregated with other potential misstatements, on the financial statements.

- Effectiveness of management's responses and controls to address the risks.

- Experience gained during previous audits with respect to similar potential misstatements.

- Results of audit procedures performed, including whether such audit procedures identified specific instances of fraud or error.

- Source and reliability of the available information.

- Persuasiveness of the audit evidence.

- Understanding of the entity and its environment, including the entity's internal control.

Documentation (Ref: Para. 28)

A63. The form and extent of audit documentation is a matter of professional judgment, and is influenced by the nature, size and complexity of the entity and its internal control, availability of information from the entity and the audit methodology and technology used in the audit.

INTERNATIONAL STANDARD ON AUDITING (UK AND IRELAND) 402

AUDIT CONSIDERATIONS RELATING TO AN ENTITY USING A SERVICE ORGANIZATION

(Effective for audits of financial statements for periods ending on or after 15 December 2010)[1a]

CONTENTS

[1a] Conforming amendments to this standard as a result of ISA (UK and Ireland) 610 (Revised June 2013), *Using the Work of Internal Auditors*, are included that are effective for audits of financial statements for periods ending on or after 15 June 2014. Details of the amendments are given in the Annexure to ISA (UK and Ireland) 610 (Revised June 2013).

International Standard on Auditing (UK and Ireland) (ISA (UK and Ireland)) 402, "Audit Considerations Relating to an Entity Using a Service Organization" should be read in conjunction with ISA (UK and Ireland) 200, "Overall Objectives of the Independent Auditor and the Conduct of an Audit in Accordance with International Standards on Auditing (UK and Ireland)."

Introduction

Scope of this ISA (UK and Ireland)

1.   This International Standard on Auditing (UK and Ireland) (ISA (UK and Ireland)) deals with the user auditor's responsibility to obtain sufficient appropriate audit evidence when a user entity uses the services of one or more service organizations. Specifically, it expands on how the user auditor applies ISA (UK and Ireland) 315[1] and ISA (UK and Ireland) 330[2] in obtaining an understanding of the user entity, including internal control relevant to the audit, sufficient to identify and assess the risks of material misstatement and in designing and performing further audit procedures responsive to those risks.

2.   Many entities outsource aspects of their business to organizations that provide services ranging from performing a specific task under the direction of an entity to replacing an entity's entire business units or functions, such as the tax compliance function. Many of the services provided by such organizations are integral to the entity's business operations; however, not all those services are relevant to the audit.

3.   Services provided by a service organization are relevant to the audit of a user entity's financial statements when those services, and the controls over them, are part of the user entity's information system, including related business processes, relevant to financial reporting. Although most controls at the service organization are likely to relate to financial reporting, there may be other controls that may also be relevant to the audit, such as controls over the safeguarding of assets. A service organization's services are part of a user entity's information system, including related business processes, relevant to financial reporting if these services affect any of the following:

   (a)   The classes of transactions in the user entity's operations that are significant to the user entity's financial statements;

   (b)   The procedures, within both information technology (IT) and manual systems, by which the user entity's transactions are initiated, recorded, processed, corrected as necessary, transferred to the general ledger and reported in the financial statements;

   (c)   The related accounting records, either in electronic or manual form, supporting information and specific accounts in the user entity's financial statements that are used to initiate, record, process and report the user entity's transactions; this includes the correction of incorrect information and how information is transferred to the general ledger;

   (d)   How the user entity's information system captures events and conditions, other than transactions, that are significant to the financial statements;

---

[1]   ISA (UK and Ireland) 315, "Identifying and Assessing the Risks of Material Misstatement through Understanding the Entity and Its Environment."
[2]   ISA (UK and Ireland) 330, "The Auditor's Responses to Assessed Risks."

(e) The financial reporting process used to prepare the user entity's financial statements, including significant accounting estimates and disclosures; and

(f) Controls surrounding journal entries, including non-standard journal entries used to record non-recurring, unusual transactions or adjustments.

4. The nature and extent of work to be performed by the user auditor regarding the services provided by a service organization depend on the nature and significance of those services to the user entity and the relevance of those services to the audit.

5. This ISA (UK and Ireland) does not apply to services provided by financial institutions that are limited to processing, for an entity's account held at the financial institution, transactions that are specifically authorized by the entity, such as the processing of checking account transactions by a bank or the processing of securities transactions by a broker. In addition, this ISA (UK and Ireland) does not apply to the audit of transactions arising from proprietary financial interests in other entities, such as partnerships, corporations and joint ventures, when proprietary interests are accounted for and reported to interest holders.

Effective Date

6. This ISA (UK and Ireland) is effective for audits of financial statements for periods ending on or after 15 December 2010.[1a]

Objectives

7. The objectives of the user auditor, when the user entity uses the services of a service organization, are:

(a) To obtain an understanding of the nature and significance of the services provided by the service organization and their effect on the user entity's internal control relevant to the audit, sufficient to identify and assess the risks of material misstatement; and

(b) To design and perform audit procedures responsive to those risks.

Definitions

8. For purposes of the ISAs (UK and Ireland), the following terms have the meanings attributed below:

(a) Complementary user entity controls – Controls that the service organization assumes, in the design of its service, will be implemented by user entities, and which, if necessary to achieve control objectives, are identified in the description of its system.

(b) Report on the description and design of controls at a service organization (referred to in this ISA (UK and Ireland) as a type 1 report) – A report that comprises:

   (i)   A description, prepared by management of the service organization, of the service organization's system, control objectives and related controls that have been designed and implemented as at a specified date; and

   (ii) A report by the service auditor with the objective of conveying reasonable assurance that includes the service auditor's opinion on the description of the service organization's system, control objectives and related controls and the suitability of the design of the controls to achieve the specified control objectives.

(c) Report on the description, design, and operating effectiveness of controls at a service organization (referred to in this ISA (UK and Ireland) as a type 2 report) – A report that comprises:

   (i)   A description, prepared by management of the service organization, of the service organization's system, control objectives and related controls, their design and implementation as at a specified date or throughout a specified period and, in some cases, their operating effectiveness throughout a specified period; and

   (ii) A report by the service auditor with the objective of conveying reasonable assurance that includes:

      a.   The service auditor's opinion on the description of the service organization's system, control objectives and related controls, the suitability of the design of the controls to achieve the specified control objectives, and the operating effectiveness of the controls; and

      b.   A description of the service auditor's tests of the controls and the results thereof.

(d) Service auditor – An auditor who, at the request of the service organization, provides an assurance report on the controls of a service organization.

(e) Service organization – A third-party organization (or segment of a third-party organization) that provides services to user entities that are part of those entities' information systems relevant to financial reporting.

(f) Service organization's system – The policies and procedures designed, implemented and maintained by the service organization to provide user entities with the services covered by the service auditor's report.

(g) Subservice organization – A service organization used by another service organization to perform some of the services provided to user entities that are part of those user entities' information systems relevant to financial reporting.

(h)   User auditor – An auditor who audits and reports on the financial statements of a user entity.

(i)   User entity – An entity that uses a service organization and whose financial statements are being audited.

Requirements

Obtaining an Understanding of the Services Provided by a Service Organization, Including Internal Control

9.   When obtaining an understanding of the user entity in accordance with ISA (UK and Ireland) 315,[3] the user auditor shall obtain an understanding of how a user entity uses the services of a service organization in the user entity's operations, including: (Ref: Para. A1-A2)

(a)   The nature of the services provided by the service organization and the significance of those services to the user entity, including the effect thereof on the user entity's internal control; (Ref: Para. A3-A5)

(b)   The nature and materiality of the transactions processed or accounts or financial reporting processes affected by the service organization; (Ref: Para. A6)

(c)   The degree of interaction between the activities of the service organization and those of the user entity; and (Ref: Para. A7)

(d)   The nature of the relationship between the user entity and the service organization, including the relevant contractual terms for the activities undertaken by the service organization. (Ref: Para. A8-A11)

(e)   If the service organisation maintains all or part of a user entity's accounting records, whether those arrangements impact the work the auditor performs to fulfil reporting responsibilities in relation to accounting records that are established in law or regulation. (Ref: Para. A11-1 – A11-3)

10.   When obtaining an understanding of internal control relevant to the audit in accordance with ISA (UK and Ireland) 315,[4] the user auditor shall evaluate the design and implementation of relevant controls at the user entity that relate to the services provided by the service organization, including those that are applied to the transactions processed by the service organization. (Ref: Para. A12-A14)

11.   The user auditor shall determine whether a sufficient understanding of the nature and significance of the services provided by the service organization and their effect on

---

[3]   ISA (UK and Ireland) 315, paragraph 11.
[4]   ISA (UK and Ireland) 315, paragraph 12.

the user entity's internal control relevant to the audit has been obtained to provide a basis for the identification and assessment of risks of material misstatement.

12.   If the user auditor is unable to obtain a sufficient understanding from the user entity, the user auditor shall obtain that understanding from one or more of the following procedures:

   (a)   Obtaining a type 1 or type 2 report, if available;

   (b)   Contacting the service organization, through the user entity, to obtain specific information;

   (c)   Visiting the service organization and performing procedures that will provide the necessary information about the relevant controls at the service organization; or

   (d)   Using another auditor to perform procedures that will provide the necessary information about the relevant controls at the service organization. (Ref: Para. A15-A20)

Using a Type 1 or Type 2 Report to Support the User Auditor's Understanding of the Service Organization

13.   In determining the sufficiency and appropriateness of the audit evidence provided by a type 1 or type 2 report, the user auditor shall be satisfied as to:

   (a)   The service auditor's professional competence and independence from the service organization; and

   (b)   The adequacy of the standards under which the type 1 or type 2 report was issued. (Ref: Para. A21)

14.   If the user auditor plans to use a type 1 or type 2 report as audit evidence to support the user auditor's understanding about the design and implementation of controls at the service organization, the user auditor shall:

   (a)   Evaluate whether the description and design of controls at the service organization is at a date or for a period that is appropriate for the user auditor's purposes;

   (b)   Evaluate the sufficiency and appropriateness of the evidence provided by the report for the understanding of the user entity's internal control relevant to the audit; and

   (c)   Determine whether complementary user entity controls identified by the service organization are relevant to the user entity and, if so, obtain an understanding of whether the user entity has designed and implemented such controls. (Ref: Para. A22-A23)

Responding to the Assessed Risks of Material Misstatement

15. In responding to assessed risks in accordance with ISA (UK and Ireland) 330, the user auditor shall:

    (a) Determine whether sufficient appropriate audit evidence concerning the relevant financial statement assertions is available from records held at the user entity; and, if not,

    (b) Perform further audit procedures to obtain sufficient appropriate audit evidence or use another auditor to perform those procedures at the service organization on the user auditor's behalf. (Ref: Para. A24-A28)

Tests of Controls

16. When the user auditor's risk assessment includes an expectation that controls at the service organization are operating effectively, the user auditor shall obtain audit evidence about the operating effectiveness of those controls from one or more of the following procedures:

    (a) Obtaining a type 2 report, if available;

    (b) Performing appropriate tests of controls at the service organization; or

    (c) Using another auditor to perform tests of controls at the service organization on behalf of the user auditor. (Ref: Para. A29-A30)

Using a Type 2 Report as Audit Evidence that Controls at the Service Organization Are Operating Effectively

17. If, in accordance with paragraph 16(a), the user auditor plans to use a type 2 report as audit evidence that controls at the service organization are operating effectively, the user auditor shall determine whether the service auditor's report provides sufficient appropriate audit evidence about the effectiveness of the controls to support the user auditor's risk assessment by:

    (a) Evaluating whether the description, design and operating effectiveness of controls at the service organization is at a date or for a period that is appropriate for the user auditor's purposes;

    (b) Determining whether complementary user entity controls identified by the service organization are relevant to the user entity and, if so, obtaining an understanding of whether the user entity has designed and implemented such controls and, if so, testing their operating effectiveness;

    (c) Evaluating the adequacy of the time period covered by the tests of controls and the time elapsed since the performance of the tests of controls; and

(d)   Evaluating whether the tests of controls performed by the service auditor and the results thereof, as described in the service auditor's report, are relevant to the assertions in the user entity's financial statements and provide sufficient appropriate audit evidence to support the user auditor's risk assessment. (Ref: Para. A31-A39)

Type 1 and Type 2 Reports that Exclude the Services of a Subservice Organization

18.   If the user auditor plans to use a type 1 or a type 2 report that excludes the services provided by a subservice organization and those services are relevant to the audit of the user entity's financial statements, the user auditor shall apply the requirements of this ISA (UK and Ireland) with respect to the services provided by the subservice organization. (Ref: Para. A40)

Fraud, Non-Compliance with Laws and Regulations and Uncorrected Misstatements in Relation to Activities at the Service Organization

19.   The user auditor shall inquire of management of the user entity whether the service organization has reported to the user entity, or whether the user entity is otherwise aware of, any fraud, non-compliance with laws and regulations or uncorrected misstatements affecting the financial statements of the user entity. The user auditor shall evaluate how such matters affect the nature, timing and extent of the user auditor's further audit procedures, including the effect on the user auditor's conclusions and user auditor's report. (Ref: Para. A41)

Reporting by the User Auditor

20.   The user auditor shall modify the opinion in the user auditor's report in accordance with ISA (UK and Ireland) 705[5] if the user auditor is unable to obtain sufficient appropriate audit evidence regarding the services provided by the service organization relevant to the audit of the user entity's financial statements. (Ref: Para. A42)

21.   The user auditor shall not refer to the work of a service auditor in the user auditor's report containing an unmodified opinion unless required by law or regulation to do so. If such reference is required by law or regulation, the user auditor's report shall indicate that the reference does not diminish the user auditor's responsibility for the audit opinion. (Ref: Para. A43)

22.   If reference to the work of a service auditor is relevant to an understanding of a modification to the user auditor's opinion, the user auditor's report shall indicate that such reference does not diminish the user auditor's responsibility for that opinion. (Ref: Para. A44)

---

[5]   ISA (UK and Ireland) 705, "Modifications to the Opinion in the Independent Auditor's Report," paragraph 6.

***

Application and Other Explanatory Material

Obtaining an Understanding of the Services Provided by a Service Organization, Including Internal Control

Sources of Information (Ref: Para. 9)

A1. Information on the nature of the services provided by a service organization may be available from a wide variety of sources, such as:

- User manuals.

- System overviews.

- Technical manuals.

- The contract or service level agreement between the user entity and the service organization.

- Reports by service organizations, the internal audit function or regulatory authorities on controls at the service organization.

- Reports by the service auditor, including management letters, if available.

A2. Knowledge obtained through the user auditor's experience with the service organization, for example through experience with other audit engagements, may also be helpful in obtaining an understanding of the nature of the services provided by the service organization. This may be particularly helpful if the services and controls at the service organization over those services are highly standardized.

Nature of the Services Provided by the Service Organization (Ref: Para. 9(a))

A3. A user entity may use a service organization such as one that processes transactions and maintains related accountability, or records transactions and processes related data. Service organizations that provide such services include, for example, bank trust departments that invest and service assets for employee benefit plans or for others; mortgage bankers that service mortgages for others; and application service providers that provide packaged software applications and a technology environment that enables customers to process financial and operational transactions.

A4. Examples of service organization services that are relevant to the audit include:

- Maintenance of the user entity's accounting records.

- Management of assets.

- Initiating, recording or processing transactions as agent of the user entity.

Compliance with Law and Regulations

A4-1. The user auditor considers whether the activities undertaken by the service organisation are in an area in which the user entity is required to comply with requirements of law and regulations (for example, there are legal requirements relating to the maintenance of accounting records by companies – see paragraphs A11-1 – A11-3). In such circumstances, non-compliance may have a significant effect on the financial statements. The user auditor therefore determines whether the law and regulations concerned are to be regarded as relevant to the audit[5a] in order to meet the requirements of ISA (UK and Ireland) 250 Section A "Consideration of Laws and Regulations in an Audit of Financial Statements" and undertake procedures to assess the risk of a misstatement arising from non-compliance as set out in that ISA (UK and Ireland).

Considerations Specific to Smaller Entities

A5. Smaller entities may use external bookkeeping services ranging from the processing of certain transactions (for example, payment of payroll taxes) and maintenance of their accounting records to the preparation of their financial statements. The use of such a service organization for the preparation of its financial statements does not relieve management of the smaller entity and, where appropriate, those charged with governance of their responsibilities for the financial statements.[6]

Nature and Materiality of Transactions Processed by the Service Organization (Ref: Para. 9(b))

A6. A service organization may establish policies and procedures that affect the user entity's internal control. These policies and procedures are at least in part physically and operationally separate from the user entity. The significance of the controls of the service organization to those of the user entity depends on the nature of the services provided by the service organization, including the nature and materiality of the transactions it processes for the user entity. In certain situations, the transactions processed and the accounts affected by the service organization may not appear to be material to the user entity's financial statements, but the nature of the transactions processed may be significant and the user auditor may determine that an understanding of those controls is necessary in the circumstances.

The Degree of Interaction between the Activities of the Service Organization and the User Entity (Ref: Para. 9(c))

A7. The significance of the controls of the service organization to those of the user entity also depends on the degree of interaction between its activities and those of the user

---

[5a] Laws and regulations are relevant to the audit when they either relate directly to the preparation of the financial statements of the entity, or are fundamental to the operating aspects of its business (ISA (UK and Ireland) 250 Section A, "Consideration of Laws and Regulations in an Audit of Financial Statements," paragraph 6).

[6] ISA (UK and Ireland) 200, "Overall Objectives of the Independent Auditor and the Conduct of an Audit in Accordance with International Standards on Auditing," paragraphs 4 and A2-A3.

entity. The degree of interaction refers to the extent to which a user entity is able to and elects to implement effective controls over the processing performed by the service organization. For example, a high degree of interaction exists between the activities of the user entity and those at the service organization when the user entity authorizes transactions and the service organization processes and does the accounting for those transactions. In these circumstances, it may be practicable for the user entity to implement effective controls over those transactions. On the other hand, when the service organization initiates or initially records, processes, and does the accounting for the user entity's transactions, there is a lower degree of interaction between the two organizations. In these circumstances, the user entity may be unable to, or may elect not to, implement effective controls over these transactions at the user entity and may rely on controls at the service organization.

Nature of the Relationship between the User Entity and the Service Organization (Ref: Para. 9(d))

A8. The contract or service level agreement between the user entity and the service organization may provide for matters such as:

- The information to be provided to the user entity and responsibilities for initiating transactions relating to the activities undertaken by the service organization;

- The application of requirements of regulatory bodies concerning the form of records to be maintained, or access to them;

- The indemnification, if any, to be provided to the user entity in the event of a performance failure;

- Whether the service organization will provide a report on its controls and, if so, whether such report would be a type 1 or type 2 report;

- Whether the user auditor has rights of access to the accounting records of the user entity maintained by the service organization and other information necessary for the conduct of the audit; and

- Whether the agreement allows for direct communication between the user auditor and the service auditor.

A8-1. Other matters which the auditor may consider include:

- The way that accounting records relating to relevant activities are maintained.

- Whether the entity has rights of access to accounting records prepared by the service organisation concerning the activities undertaken, and relevant underlying information held by it, and the conditions in which such access may be sought.

- The nature of relevant performance standards.

- The way in which the entity monitors performance of relevant activities and the extent to which its monitoring process relies on controls operated by the service organization.

A8-2. Agreement by a service organisation to provide an indemnity does not provide information directly relevant to the user auditor's assessment of the risk of material misstatements relating to financial statement assertions. However, such agreements may help to inform the user auditor's judgment concerning the effect of performance failure on the user entity's financial statements: this may be relevant in instances of performance failure, when the existence of an indemnity may help to ensure that the user entity's status as a going concern is not threatened. Where the user auditor wishes to rely on the operation of the indemnity for this purpose, the resources available to the service organisation also need to be considered.

A8-3. The financial standing of a service organisation is relevant to the audit insofar as the user auditor considers it necessary to rely on the operation of an indemnity from the service organisation in assessing the entity's status as a going concern (see paragraph A8-2). However, a service organisation whose cash and/or capital resources are low in relation to the nature of services provided or the volume of its customers may be susceptible to pressures resulting in errors or deliberate misstatements in reporting to the entity, or fraud. If the user auditor considers that this factor may be relevant to the assessment of risk, the user auditor also takes into account the existence of binding arrangements to provide resources to the service organisations from a holding company or other group company, and the financial strength of the group as a whole.

A9. There is a direct relationship between the service organization and the user entity and between the service organization and the service auditor. These relationships do not necessarily create a direct relationship between the user auditor and the service auditor. When there is no direct relationship between the user auditor and the service auditor, communications between the user auditor and the service auditor are usually conducted through the user entity and the service organization. A direct relationship may also be created between a user auditor and a service auditor, taking into account the relevant ethical and confidentiality considerations. A user auditor, for example, may use a service auditor to perform procedures on the user auditor's behalf, such as:

(a) Tests of controls at the service organization; or

(b) Substantive procedures on the user entity's financial statement transactions and balances maintained by a service organization.

Considerations Specific to Public Sector Entities

A10. Public sector auditors generally have broad rights of access established by legislation. However, there may be situations where such rights of access are not available, for example when the service organization is located in a different jurisdiction. In such cases, a public sector auditor may need to obtain an understanding of the legislation applicable in the different jurisdiction to determine whether appropriate access rights can be obtained. A public sector auditor may also obtain or ask the user entity to incorporate rights of access in any contractual arrangements between the user entity and the service organization.

A11. Public sector auditors may also use another auditor to perform tests of controls or substantive procedures in relation to compliance with law, regulation or other authority.

Accounting Records (Ref: Para. 9(e))

A11-1. Use of a service organisation does not diminish the ultimate responsibility of those charged with governance of a user entity for conducting its business in a manner which meets their legal responsibilities, including those of safeguarding the user entity's assets, maintaining adequate accounting records and preparing financial statements which provide information about its economic activities and financial position. Practical issues, including the way in which accounting records will be kept and the manner in which those charged with governance assess the quality of the service, need to be addressed.

A11-2. An auditor of an entity incorporated under company law has statutory reporting obligations relating to compliance with requirements for companies to maintain adequate accounting records. Where such an entity outsources the preparation of its accounting records to a service organisation, issues relating to whether the arrangements with the service organisation are such as to permit the user entity to meet its statutory obligations may require careful consideration, by both those charged with governance and the user auditor. Where there is doubt, the user auditor may wish to encourage those charged with governance to take legal advice before issuing the auditor's report on its financial statements.

A11-3. A particular issue arises in relation to companies incorporated in the United Kingdom. The wording of UK company law appears to be prescriptive and to require the company itself to keep accounting records. Consequently, whether a company 'keeps' records (as opposed to 'causes records to be kept') will depend upon the particular terms of the outsourcing arrangements and, in particular, the extent to which the company retains ownership of, has access to, or holds copies of, those records[6b].

Understanding the Controls Relating to Services Provided by the Service Organization (Ref: Para. 10)

A12. The user entity may establish controls over the service organization's services that may be tested by the user auditor and that may enable the user auditor to conclude that the user entity's controls are operating effectively for some or all of the related assertions, regardless of the controls in place at the service organization. If a user entity, for example, uses a service organization to process its payroll transactions, the

---

[6b] In Ireland, company law requires that companies shall cause records to be kept in accordance with its requirements.

user entity may establish controls over the submission and receipt of payroll information that could prevent or detect material misstatements. These controls may include:

- Comparing the data submitted to the service organization with reports of information received from the service organization after the data has been processed.

- Recomputing a sample of the payroll amounts for clerical accuracy and reviewing the total amount of the payroll for reasonableness.

A13. In this situation, the user auditor may perform tests of the user entity's controls over payroll processing that would provide a basis for the user auditor to conclude that the user entity's controls are operating effectively for the assertions related to payroll transactions.

A14. As noted in ISA (UK and Ireland) 315,[7] in respect of some risks, the user auditor may judge that it is not possible or practicable to obtain sufficient appropriate audit evidence only from substantive procedures. Such risks may relate to the inaccurate or incomplete recording of routine and significant classes of transactions and account balances, the characteristics of which often permit highly automated processing with little or no manual intervention. Such automated processing characteristics may be particularly present when the user entity uses service organizations. In such cases, the user entity's controls over such risks are relevant to the audit and the user auditor is required to obtain an understanding of, and to evaluate, such controls in accordance with paragraphs 9 and 10 of this ISA (UK and Ireland).

Further Procedures When a Sufficient Understanding Cannot Be Obtained from the User Entity (Ref: Para. 12)

A15. The user auditor's decision as to which procedure, individually or in combination, in paragraph 12 to undertake, in order to obtain the information necessary to provide a basis for the identification and assessment of the risks of material misstatement in relation to the user entity's use of the service organization, may be influenced by such matters as:

- The size of both the user entity and the service organization;

- The complexity of the transactions at the user entity and the complexity of the services provided by the service organization;

- The location of the service organization (for example, the user auditor may decide to use another auditor to perform procedures at the service organization on the user auditor's behalf if the service organization is in a remote location);

---

[7] ISA (UK and Ireland) 315, paragraph 30.

- Whether the procedure(s) is expected to effectively provide the user auditor with sufficient appropriate audit evidence; and

- The nature of the relationship between the user entity and the service organization.

A16. A service organization may engage a service auditor to report on the description and design of its controls (type 1 report) or on the description and design of its controls and their operating effectiveness (type 2 report). Type 1 or type 2 reports may be issued under [proposed] International Standard on Assurance Engagements (ISAE) 3402[8] or under standards established by an authorized or recognized standards setting organization (which may identify them by different names, such as Type A or Type B reports).

A17. The availability of a type 1 or type 2 report will generally depend on whether the contract between a service organization and a user entity includes the provision of such a report by the service organization. A service organization may also elect, for practical reasons, to make a type 1 or type 2 report available to the user entities. However, in some cases, a type 1 or type 2 report may not be available to user entities.

A18. In some circumstances, a user entity may outsource one or more significant business units or functions, such as its entire tax planning and compliance functions, or finance and accounting or the controllership function to one or more service organizations. As a report on controls at the service organization may not be available in these circumstances, visiting the service organization may be the most effective procedure for the user auditor to gain an understanding of controls at the service organization, as there is likely to be direct interaction of management of the user entity with management at the service organization.

A19. Another auditor may be used to perform procedures that will provide the necessary information about the relevant controls at the service organization. If a type 1 or type 2 report has been issued, the user auditor may use the service auditor to perform these procedures as the service auditor has an existing relationship with the service organization. The user auditor using the work of another auditor may find the guidance in ISA (UK and Ireland) 600[9] useful as it relates to understanding another auditor (including that auditor's independence and professional competence), involvement in the work of another auditor in planning the nature, extent and timing of such work, and in evaluating the sufficiency and appropriateness of the audit evidence obtained.

---

[8] [Proposed] ISAE 3402, "Assurance Reports on Controls at a Third Party Service Organization."

[9] ISA (UK and Ireland) 600, "Special Considerations-Audits of Group Financial Statements (Including the Work of Component Auditors)," paragraph 2, states: "An auditor may find this ISA (UK and Ireland), adapted as necessary in the circumstances, useful when that auditor involves other auditors in the audit of financial statements that are not group financial statements ..." See also paragraph 19 of ISA (UK and Ireland) 600.

A20. A user entity may use a service organization that in turn uses a subservice organization to provide some of the services provided to a user entity that are part of the user entity's information system relevant to financial reporting. The subservice organization may be a separate entity from the service organization or may be related to the service organization. A user auditor may need to consider controls at the subservice organization. In situations where one or more subservice organizations are used, the interaction between the activities of the user entity and those of the service organization is expanded to include the interaction between the user entity, the service organization and the subservice organizations. The degree of this interaction, as well as the nature and materiality of the transactions processed by the service organization and the subservice organizations are the most important factors for the user auditor to consider in determining the significance of the service organization's and subservice organization's controls to the user entity's controls.

Using a Type 1 or Type 2 Report to Support the User Auditor's Understanding of the Service Organization (Ref: Para. 13-14)

A21. The user auditor may make inquiries about the service auditor to the service auditor's professional organization or other practitioners and inquire whether the service auditor is subject to regulatory oversight. The service auditor may be practicing in a jurisdiction where different standards are followed in respect of reports on controls at a service organization, and the user auditor may obtain information about the standards used by the service auditor from the standard setting organization.

A22. A type 1 or type 2 report, along with information about the user entity, may assist the user auditor in obtaining an understanding of:

(a) The aspects of controls at the service organization that may affect the processing of the user entity's transactions, including the use of subservice organizations;

(b) The flow of significant transactions through the service organization to determine the points in the transaction flow where material misstatements in the user entity's financial statements could occur;

(c) The control objectives at the service organization that are relevant to the user entity's financial statement assertions; and

(d) Whether controls at the service organization are suitably designed and implemented to prevent or detect processing errors that could result in material misstatements in the user entity's financial statements.

A type 1 or type 2 report may assist the user auditor in obtaining a sufficient understanding to identify and assess the risks of material misstatement. A type 1 report, however, does not provide any evidence of the operating effectiveness of the relevant controls.

A23. A type 1 or type 2 report that is as of a date or for a period that is outside of the reporting period of a user entity may assist the user auditor in obtaining a preliminary understanding of the controls implemented at the service organization if the report is supplemented by additional current information from other sources. If the service organization's description of controls is as of a date or for a period that precedes the beginning of the period under audit, the user auditor may perform procedures to update the information in a type 1 or type 2 report, such as:

- Discussing the changes at the service organization with user entity personnel who would be in a position to know of such changes;

- Reviewing current documentation and correspondence issued by the service organization; or

- Discussing the changes with service organization personnel.

Responding to the Assessed Risks of Material Misstatement (Ref: Para. 15)

A24. Whether the use of a service organization increases a user entity's risk of material misstatement depends on the nature of the services provided and the controls over these services; in some cases, the use of a service organization may decrease a user entity's risk of material misstatement, particularly if the user entity itself does not possess the expertise necessary to undertake particular activities, such as initiating, processing, and recording transactions, or does not have adequate resources (for example, an IT system).

A25. When the service organization maintains material elements of the accounting records of the user entity, direct access to those records may be necessary in order for the user auditor to obtain sufficient appropriate audit evidence relating to the operations of controls over those records or to substantiate transactions and balances recorded in them, or both. Such access may involve either physical inspection of records at the service organization's premises or interrogation of records maintained electronically from the user entity or another location, or both. Where direct access is achieved electronically, the user auditor may thereby obtain evidence as to the adequacy of controls operated by the service organization over the completeness and integrity of the user entity's data for which the service organization is responsible.

A26. In determining the nature and extent of audit evidence to be obtained in relation to balances representing assets held or transactions undertaken by a service organization on behalf of the user entity, the following procedures may be considered by the user auditor:

(a) Inspecting records and documents held by the user entity: the reliability of this source of evidence is determined by the nature and extent of the accounting records and supporting documentation retained by the user entity. In some cases, the user entity may not maintain independent detailed records or documentation of specific transactions undertaken on its behalf.

(b) Inspecting records and documents held by the service organization: the user auditor's access to the records of the service organization may be established as part of the contractual arrangements between the user entity and the service organization. The user auditor may also use another auditor, on its behalf, to gain access to the user entity's records maintained by the service organization.

(c)   Obtaining confirmations of balances and transactions from the service organization: where the user entity maintains independent records of balances and transactions, confirmation from the service organization corroborating the user entity's records may constitute reliable audit evidence concerning the existence of the transactions and assets concerned. For example, when multiple service organizations are used, such as an investment manager and a custodian, and these service organizations maintain independent records, the user auditor may confirm balances with these organizations in order to compare this information with the independent records of the user entity.

If the user entity does not maintain independent records, information obtained in confirmations from the service organization is merely a statement of what is reflected in the records maintained by the service organization. Therefore, such confirmations do not, taken alone, constitute reliable audit evidence. In these circumstances, the user auditor may consider whether an alternative source of independent evidence can be identified.

(d)   Performing analytical procedures on the records maintained by the user entity or on the reports received from the service organization: the effectiveness of analytical procedures is likely to vary by assertion and will be affected by the extent and detail of information available.

A27.   Another auditor may perform procedures that are substantive in nature for the benefit of user auditors. Such an engagement may involve the performance, by another auditor, of procedures agreed upon by the user entity and its user auditor and by the service organization and its service auditor. The findings resulting from the procedures performed by another auditor are reviewed by the user auditor to determine whether they constitute sufficient appropriate audit evidence. In addition, there may be requirements imposed by governmental authorities or through contractual arrangements whereby a service auditor performs designated procedures that are substantive in nature. The results of the application of the required procedures to balances and transactions processed by the service organization may be used by user auditors as part of the evidence necessary to support their audit opinions. In these circumstances, it may be useful for the user auditor and the service auditor to agree, prior to the performance of the procedures, to the audit documentation or access to audit documentation that will be provided to the user auditor.

A28.   In certain circumstances, in particular when a user entity outsources some or all of its finance function to a service organization, the user auditor may face a situation where a significant portion of the audit evidence resides at the service organization. Substantive procedures may need to be performed at the service organization by the user auditor or another auditor on its behalf. A service auditor may provide a type 2 report and, in addition, may perform substantive procedures on behalf of the user auditor. The involvement of another auditor does not alter the user auditor's responsibility to obtain sufficient appropriate audit evidence to afford a reasonable basis to support the user auditor's opinion. Accordingly, the user auditor's consideration of whether sufficient appropriate audit evidence has been obtained and whether the user auditor needs to perform further substantive procedures includes the user auditor's involvement with, or evidence of, the direction, supervision and performance of the substantive procedures performed by another auditor.

Tests of Controls (Ref: Para. 16)

A29. The user auditor is required by ISA (UK and Ireland) 330[10] to design and perform tests of controls to obtain sufficient appropriate audit evidence as to the operating effectiveness of relevant controls in certain circumstances. In the context of a service organization, this requirement applies when:

(a) The user auditor's assessment of risks of material misstatement includes an expectation that the controls at the service organization are operating effectively (that is, the user auditor intends to rely on the operating effectiveness of controls at the service organization in determining the nature, timing and extent of substantive procedures); or

(b) Substantive procedures alone, or in combination with tests of the operating effectiveness of controls at the user entity, cannot provide sufficient appropriate audit evidence at the assertion level.

A30. If a type 2 report is not available, a user auditor may contact the service organization, through the user entity, to request that a service auditor be engaged to provide a type 2 report that includes tests of the operating effectiveness of the relevant controls or the user auditor may use another auditor to perform procedures at the service organization that test the operating effectiveness of those controls. A user auditor may also visit the service organization and perform tests of relevant controls if the service organization agrees to it. The user auditor's risk assessments are based on the combined evidence provided by the work of another auditor and the user auditor's own procedures.

Using a Type 2 Report as Audit Evidence that Controls at the Service Organization Are Operating Effectively (Ref: Para. 17)

A31. A type 2 report may be intended to satisfy the needs of several different user auditors; therefore tests of controls and results described in the service auditor's report may not be relevant to assertions that are significant in the user entity's financial statements. The relevant tests of controls and results are evaluated to determine that the service auditor's report provides sufficient appropriate audit evidence about the effectiveness of the controls to support the user auditor's risk assessment. In doing so, the user auditor may consider the following factors:

---

[10] ISA (UK and Ireland) 330, paragraph 8.

(a)   The time period covered by the tests of controls and the time elapsed since the performance of the tests of controls;

(b)   The scope of the service auditor's work and the services and processes covered, the controls tested and tests that were performed, and the way in which tested controls relate to the user entity's controls; and

(c)   The results of those tests of controls and the service auditor's opinion on the operating effectiveness of the controls.

A32.   For certain assertions, the shorter the period covered by a specific test and the longer the time elapsed since the performance of the test, the less audit evidence the test may provide. In comparing the period covered by the type 2 report to the user entity's financial reporting period, the user auditor may conclude that the type 2 report offers less audit evidence if there is little overlap between the period covered by the type 2 report and the period for which the user auditor intends to rely on the report. When this is the case, a type 2 report covering a preceding or subsequent period may provide additional audit evidence. In other cases, the user auditor may determine it is necessary to perform, or use another auditor to perform, tests of controls at the service organization in order to obtain sufficient appropriate audit evidence about the operating effectiveness of those controls.

A33.   It may also be necessary for the user auditor to obtain additional evidence about significant changes to the relevant controls at the service organization outside of the period covered by the type 2 report or determine additional audit procedures to be performed. Relevant factors in determining what additional audit evidence to obtain about controls at the service organization that were operating outside of the period covered by the service auditor's report may include:

- The significance of the assessed risks of material misstatement at the assertion level;

- The specific controls that were tested during the interim period, and significant changes to them since they were tested, including changes in the information system, processes, and personnel;

- The degree to which audit evidence about the operating effectiveness of those controls was obtained;

- The length of the remaining period;

- The extent to which the user auditor intends to reduce further substantive procedures based on the reliance on controls; and

- The effectiveness of the control environment and monitoring of controls at the user entity.

A34.   Additional audit evidence may be obtained, for example, by extending tests of controls over the remaining period or testing the user entity's monitoring of controls.

A35. If the service auditor's testing period is completely outside the user entity's financial reporting period, the user auditor will be unable to rely on such tests for the user auditor to conclude that the user entity's controls are operating effectively because they do not provide current audit period evidence of the effectiveness of the controls, unless other procedures are performed.

A36. In certain circumstances, a service provided by the service organization may be designed with the assumption that certain controls will be implemented by the user entity. For example, the service may be designed with the assumption that the user entity will have controls in place for authorizing transactions before they are sent to the service organization for processing. In such a situation, the service organization's description of controls may include a description of those complementary user entity controls. The user auditor considers whether those complementary user entity controls are relevant to the service provided to the user entity.

A37. If the user auditor believes that the service auditor's report may not provide sufficient appropriate audit evidence, for example, if a service auditor's report does not contain a description of the service auditor's tests of controls and results thereon, the user auditor may supplement the understanding of the service auditor's procedures and conclusions by contacting the service organization, through the user entity, to request a discussion with the service auditor about the scope and results of the service auditor's work. Also, if the user auditor believes it is necessary, the user auditor may contact the service organization, through the user entity, to request that the service auditor perform procedures at the service organization. Alternatively, the user auditor, or another auditor at the request of the user auditor, may perform such procedures.

A38. The service auditor's type 2 report identifies results of tests, including exceptions and other information that could affect the user auditor's conclusions. Exceptions noted by the service auditor or a modified opinion in the service auditor's type 2 report do not automatically mean that the service auditor's type 2 report will not be useful for the audit of the user entity's financial statements in assessing the risks of material misstatement. Rather, the exceptions and the matter giving rise to a modified opinion in the service auditor's type 2 report are considered in the user auditor's assessment of the testing of controls performed by the service auditor. In considering the exceptions and matters giving rise to a modified opinion, the user auditor may discuss such matters with the service auditor. Such communication is dependent upon the user entity contacting the service organization, and obtaining the service organization's approval for the communication to take place.

Communication of deficiencies in internal control identified during the audit

A39. The user auditor is required to communicate in writing significant deficiencies identified during the audit to both management and those charged with governance on a timely basis.[11] The user auditor is also required to communicate to management

---

[11] ISA (UK and Ireland) 265, "Communicating Deficiencies in Internal Control to Those Charged with Governance and Management," paragraphs 9-10.

at an appropriate level of responsibility on a timely basis other deficiencies in internal control identified during the audit that, in the user auditor's professional judgment, are of sufficient importance to merit management's attention.[12] Matters that the user auditor may identify during the audit and may communicate to management and those charged with governance of the user entity include:

- Any monitoring of controls that could be implemented by the user entity, including those identified as a result of obtaining a type 1 or type 2 report;

- Instances where complementary user entity controls are noted in the type 1 or type 2 report and are not implemented at the user entity; and

- Controls that may be needed at the service organization that do not appear to have been implemented or that are not specifically covered by a type 2 report.

Type 1 and Type 2 Reports that Exclude the Services of a Subservice Organization (Ref: Para. 18)

A40. If a service organization uses a subservice organization, the service auditor's report may either include or exclude the subservice organization's relevant control objectives and related controls in the service organization's description of its system and in the scope of the service auditor's engagement. These two methods of reporting are known as the inclusive method and the carve-out method, respectively. If the type 1 or type 2 report excludes the controls at a subservice organization, and the services provided by the subservice organization are relevant to the audit of the user entity's financial statements, the user auditor is required to apply the requirements of this ISA (UK and Ireland) in respect of the subservice organization. The nature and extent of work to be performed by the user auditor regarding the services provided by a subservice organization depend on the nature and significance of those services to the user entity and the relevance of those services to the audit. The application of the requirement in paragraph 9 assists the user auditor in determining the effect of the subservice organization and the nature and extent of work to be performed.

Fraud, Non-Compliance with Laws and Regulations and Uncorrected Misstatements in Relation to Activities at the Service Organization (Ref: Para. 19)

A41. A service organization may be required under the terms of the contract with user entities to disclose to affected user entities any fraud, non-compliance with laws and regulations or uncorrected misstatements attributable to the service organization's management or employees. As required by paragraph 19, the user auditor makes inquiries of the user entity management regarding whether the service organization has reported any such matters and evaluates whether any matters reported by the service organization affect the nature, timing and extent of the user auditor's further audit procedures. In certain circumstances, the user auditor may require additional

---

[12] ISA (UK and Ireland) 265, paragraph 10.

information to perform this evaluation, and may request the user entity to contact the service organization to obtain the necessary information.

Reporting by the User Auditor (Ref: Para. 20)

A42. When a user auditor is unable to obtain sufficient appropriate audit evidence regarding the services provided by the service organization relevant to the audit of the user entity's financial statements, a limitation on the scope of the audit exists. This may be the case when:

- The user auditor is unable to obtain a sufficient understanding of the services provided by the service organization and does not have a basis for the identification and assessment of the risks of material misstatement;

- A user auditor's risk assessment includes an expectation that controls at the service organization are operating effectively and the user auditor is unable to obtain sufficient appropriate audit evidence about the operating effectiveness of these controls; or

- Sufficient appropriate audit evidence is only available from records held at the service organization, and the user auditor is unable to obtain direct access to these records.

Whether the user auditor expresses a qualified opinion or disclaims an opinion depends on the user auditor's conclusion as to whether the possible effects on the financial statements are material or pervasive.

Reference to the Work of a Service Auditor (Ref: Para. 21-22)

A43. In some cases, law or regulation may require a reference to the work of a service auditor in the user auditor's report, for example, for the purposes of transparency in the public sector. In such circumstances, the user auditor may need the consent of the service auditor before making such a reference.

A44. The fact that a user entity uses a service organization does not alter the user auditor's responsibility under ISAs (UK and Ireland) to obtain sufficient appropriate audit evidence to afford a reasonable basis to support the user auditor's opinion. Therefore, the user auditor does not make reference to the service auditor's report as a basis, in part, for the user auditor's opinion on the user entity's financial statements. However, when the user auditor expresses a modified opinion because of a modified opinion in a service auditor's report, the user auditor is not precluded from referring to the service auditor's report if such reference assists in explaining the reason for the user auditor's modified opinion. In such circumstances, the user auditor may need the consent of the service auditor before making such a reference.

INTERNATIONAL STANDARD ON AUDITING (UK AND IRELAND) 450

EVALUATION OF MISSTATEMENTS IDENTIFIED DURING THE AUDIT

(Effective for audits of financial statements for periods ending on or after 15 December 2010)

CONTENTS

International Standard on Auditing (UK and Ireland) (ISA (UK and Ireland)) 450, "Evaluation of Misstatements Identified during the Audit" should be read in the context of ISA (UK and Ireland) 200, "Overall Objectives of the Independent Auditor and the Conduct of an Audit in Accordance with International Standards on Auditing (UK and Ireland)."

Introduction

Scope of this ISA (UK and Ireland)

1. This International Standard on Auditing (UK and Ireland) (ISA (UK and Ireland)) deals with the auditor's responsibility to evaluate the effect of identified misstatements on the audit and of uncorrected misstatements, if any, on the financial statements. ISA (UK and Ireland) 700 deals with the auditor's responsibility, in forming an opinion on the financial statements, to conclude whether reasonable assurance has been obtained about whether the financial statements as a whole are free from material misstatement. The auditor's conclusion required by ISA (UK and Ireland) 700 takes into account the auditor's evaluation of uncorrected misstatements, if any, on the financial statements, in accordance with this ISA (UK and Ireland).[1] ISA (UK and Ireland) 320[2] deals with the auditor's responsibility to apply the concept of materiality appropriately in planning and performing an audit of financial statements.

Effective Date

2. This ISA (UK and Ireland) is effective for audits of financial statements for periods ending on or after 15 December 2010.

Objective

3. The objective of the auditor is to evaluate:

    (a) The effect of identified misstatements on the audit; and

    (b) The effect of uncorrected misstatements, if any, on the financial statements.

Definitions

4. For purposes of the ISAs (UK and Ireland), the following terms have the meanings attributed below:

    (a) Misstatement – A difference between the amount, classification, presentation, or disclosure of a reported financial statement item and the amount, classification, presentation, or disclosure that is required for the item to be in accordance with the applicable financial reporting framework. Misstatements can arise from error or fraud. (Ref: Para. A1)

---

[1] ISA 700, "Forming an Opinion and Reporting on Financial Statements," paragraphs 10-11.
The APB has not promulgated ISA 700 as issued by the IAASB for application in the UK and Ireland. In the UK and Ireland the applicable auditing standard is ISA (UK and Ireland) 700, "The Auditor's Report on Financial Statements." Paragraph 8(b) of ISA (UK and Ireland) 700 requires evaluation of whether uncorrected misstatements are material, individually or in aggregate.
[2] ISA (UK and Ireland) 320, "Materiality in Planning and Performing an Audit."

When the auditor expresses an opinion on whether the financial statements are presented fairly, in all material respects, or give a true and fair view, misstatements also include those adjustments of amounts, classifications, presentation, or disclosures that, in the auditor's judgment, are necessary for the financial statements to be presented fairly, in all material respects, or to give a true and fair view.

(b)   Uncorrected misstatements – Misstatements that the auditor has accumulated during the audit and that have not been corrected.

Requirements

Accumulation of Identified Misstatements

5.   The auditor shall accumulate misstatements identified during the audit, other than those that are clearly trivial. (Ref: Para. A2-A3)

Consideration of Identified Misstatements as the Audit Progresses

6.   The auditor shall determine whether the overall audit strategy and audit plan need to be revised if:

(a)   The nature of identified misstatements and the circumstances of their occurrence indicate that other misstatements may exist that, when aggregated with misstatements accumulated during the audit, could be material; or (Ref: Para. A4)

(b)   The aggregate of misstatements accumulated during the audit approaches materiality determined in accordance with ISA (UK and Ireland) 320. (Ref: Para. A5)

7.   If, at the auditor's request, management has examined a class of transactions, account balance or disclosure and corrected misstatements that were detected, the auditor shall perform additional audit procedures to determine whether misstatements remain. (Ref: Para. A6)

Communication and Correction of Misstatements

8.   The auditor shall communicate on a timely basis all misstatements accumulated during the audit with the appropriate level of management, unless prohibited by law or regulation.[3] The auditor shall request management to correct those misstatements. (Ref: Para. A7-A9)

9.   If management refuses to correct some or all of the misstatements communicated by the auditor, the auditor shall obtain an understanding of management's reasons for

---

[3]   ISA (UK and Ireland) 260, "Communication with Those Charged with Governance," paragraph 7.

not making the corrections and shall take that understanding into account when evaluating whether the financial statements as a whole are free from material misstatement. (Ref: Para. A10)

Evaluating the Effect of Uncorrected Misstatements

10. Prior to evaluating the effect of uncorrected misstatements, the auditor shall reassess materiality determined in accordance with ISA (UK and Ireland) 320 to confirm whether it remains appropriate in the context of the entity's actual financial results. (Ref: Para. A11-A12)

11. The auditor shall determine whether uncorrected misstatements are material, individually or in aggregate. In making this determination, the auditor shall consider:

    (a) The size and nature of the misstatements, both in relation to particular classes of transactions, account balances or disclosures and the financial statements as a whole, and the particular circumstances of their occurrence; and (Ref: Para. A13-A17, A19-A20)

    (b) The effect of uncorrected misstatements related to prior periods on the relevant classes of transactions, account balances or disclosures, and the financial statements as a whole. (Ref: Para. A18)

Communication with Those Charged with Governance

12. The auditor shall communicate with those charged with governance uncorrected misstatements and the effect that they, individually or in aggregate, may have on the opinion in the auditor's report, unless prohibited by law or regulation.[4] The auditor's communication shall identify material uncorrected misstatements individually. The auditor shall request that uncorrected misstatements be corrected. (Ref: Para. A21-A23)

13. The auditor shall also communicate with those charged with governance the effect of uncorrected misstatements related to prior periods on the relevant classes of transactions, account balances or disclosures, and the financial statements as a whole.

Written Representation

14. The auditor shall request a written representation from management and, where appropriate, those charged with governance whether they believe the effects of uncorrected misstatements are immaterial, individually and in aggregate, to the financial statements as a whole. A summary of such items shall be included in or attached to the written representation. (Ref: Para. A24 – A24-1)

---

[4] See footnote 3.

Documentation

15. The auditor shall include in the audit documentation:[5] (Ref: Para. A25)

   (a) The amount below which misstatements would be regarded as clearly trivial (paragraph 5);

   (b) All misstatements accumulated during the audit and whether they have been corrected (paragraphs 5, 8 and 12); and

   (c) The auditor's conclusion as to whether uncorrected misstatements are material, individually or in aggregate, and the basis for that conclusion (paragraph 11).

***

Application and Other Explanatory Material

Definition of Misstatement (Ref: Para. 4(a))

A1. Misstatements may result from:

   (a) An inaccuracy in gathering or processing data from which the financial statements are prepared;

   (b) An omission of an amount or disclosure;

   (c) An incorrect accounting estimate arising from overlooking, or clear misinterpretation of, facts; and

   (d) Judgments of management concerning accounting estimates that the auditor considers unreasonable or the selection and application of accounting policies that the auditor considers inappropriate.

   Examples of misstatements arising from fraud are provided in ISA (UK and Ireland) 240.[6]

Accumulation of Identified Misstatements (Ref: Para. 5)

A2. The auditor may designate an amount below which misstatements would be clearly trivial and would not need to be accumulated because the auditor expects that the accumulation of such amounts clearly would not have a material effect on the financial statements. "Clearly trivial" is not another expression for "not material." Matters that are clearly trivial will be of a wholly different (smaller) order of magnitude than materiality determined in accordance with ISA (UK and Ireland) 320, and will be

---

[5] ISA (UK and Ireland) 230, "Audit Documentation," paragraphs 8-11, and paragraph A6.
[6] ISA (UK and Ireland) 240, "The Auditor's Responsibilities Relating to Fraud in an Audit of Financial Statements," paragraphs A1-A6.

matters that are clearly inconsequential, whether taken individually or in aggregate and whether judged by any criteria of size, nature or circumstances. When there is any uncertainty about whether one or more items are clearly trivial, the matter is considered not to be clearly trivial.

A3.   To assist the auditor in evaluating the effect of misstatements accumulated during the audit and in communicating misstatements to management and those charged with governance, it may be useful to distinguish between factual misstatements, judgmental misstatements and projected misstatements.

- Factual misstatements are misstatements about which there is no doubt.

- Judgmental misstatements are differences arising from the judgments of management concerning accounting estimates that the auditor considers unreasonable, or the selection or application of accounting policies that the auditor considers inappropriate.

- Projected misstatements are the auditor's best estimate of misstatements in populations, involving the projection of misstatements identified in audit samples to the entire populations from which the samples were drawn. Guidance on the determination of projected misstatements and evaluation of the results is set out in ISA (UK and Ireland) 530.[7]

Consideration of Identified Misstatements as the Audit Progresses (Ref: Para. 6-7)

A4.   A misstatement may not be an isolated occurrence. Evidence that other misstatements may exist include, for example, where the auditor identifies that a misstatement arose from a breakdown in internal control or from inappropriate assumptions or valuation methods that have been widely applied by the entity.

A5.   If the aggregate of misstatements accumulated during the audit approaches materiality determined in accordance with ISA (UK and Ireland) 320, there may be a greater than acceptably low level of risk that possible undetected misstatements, when taken with the aggregate of misstatements accumulated during the audit, could exceed materiality. Undetected misstatements could exist because of the presence of sampling risk and non-sampling risk.[8]

A6.   The auditor may request management to examine a class of transactions, account balance or disclosure in order for management to understand the cause of a misstatement identified by the auditor, perform procedures to determine the amount of the actual misstatement in the class of transactions, account balance or disclosure, and to make appropriate adjustments to the financial statements. Such a request may be made, for example, based on the auditor's projection of misstatements identified in an audit sample to the entire population from which it was drawn.

---

[7]   ISA (UK and Ireland) 530, "Audit Sampling," paragraphs 14-15.
[8]   ISA (UK and Ireland) 530, paragraph 5(c)-(d).

Communication and Correction of Misstatements (Ref: Para. 8-9)

A7. Timely communication of misstatements to the appropriate level of management is important as it enables management to evaluate whether the items are misstatements, inform the auditor if it disagrees, and take action as necessary. Ordinarily, the appropriate level of management is the one that has responsibility and authority to evaluate the misstatements and to take the necessary action.

A8. Law or regulation may restrict the auditor's communication of certain misstatements to management, or others, within the entity. For example, laws or regulations may specifically prohibit a communication, or other action, that might prejudice an investigation by an appropriate authority into an actual, or suspected, illegal act. In some circumstances, potential conflicts between the auditor's obligations of confidentiality and obligations to communicate may be complex. In such cases, the auditor may consider seeking legal advice.

A9. The correction by management of all misstatements, including those communicated by the auditor, enables management to maintain accurate accounting books and records and reduces the risks of material misstatement of future financial statements because of the cumulative effect of immaterial uncorrected misstatements related to prior periods.

A10. ISA (UK and Ireland) 700 requires the auditor to evaluate whether the financial statements are prepared and presented, in all material respects, in accordance with the requirements of the applicable financial reporting framework. This evaluation includes consideration of the qualitative aspects of the entity's accounting practices, including indicators of possible bias in management's judgments,[9] which may be affected by the auditor's understanding of management's reasons for not making the corrections.

Evaluating the Effect of Uncorrected Misstatements (Ref: Para. 10-11)

A11. The auditor's determination of materiality in accordance with ISA (UK and Ireland) 320 is often based on estimates of the entity's financial results, because the actual financial results may not yet be known. Therefore, prior to the auditor's evaluation of the effect of uncorrected misstatements, it may be necessary to revise materiality determined in accordance with ISA (UK and Ireland) 320 based on the actual financial results.

A12. ISA (UK and Ireland) 320 explains that, as the audit progresses, materiality for the financial statements as a whole (and, if applicable, the materiality level or levels for particular classes of transactions, account balances or disclosures) is revised in the event of the auditor becoming aware of information during the audit that would have

---

[9] ISA 700, paragraph 12.

The APB has not promulgated ISA 700 as issued by the IAASB for application in the UK and Ireland. In the UK and Ireland the applicable auditing standard is ISA (UK and Ireland) 700, "The Auditor's Report on Financial Statements." Paragraph 8 of ISA (UK and Ireland) 700 includes requirements equivalent to those in paragraph 12 of ISA 700.

caused the auditor to have determined a different amount (or amounts) initially.[10] Thus, any significant revision is likely to have been made before the auditor evaluates the effect of uncorrected misstatements. However, if the auditor's reassessment of materiality determined in accordance with ISA (UK and Ireland) 320 (see paragraph 10 of this ISA (UK and Ireland)) gives rise to a lower amount (or amounts), then performance materiality and the appropriateness of the nature, timing and extent of the further audit procedures are reconsidered so as to obtain sufficient appropriate audit evidence on which to base the audit opinion.

A13. Each individual misstatement is considered to evaluate its effect on the relevant classes of transactions, account balances or disclosures, including whether the materiality level for that particular class of transactions, account balance or disclosure, if any, has been exceeded.

A14. If an individual misstatement is judged to be material, it is unlikely that it can be offset by other misstatements. For example, if revenue has been materially overstated, the financial statements as a whole will be materially misstated, even if the effect of the misstatement on earnings is completely offset by an equivalent overstatement of expenses. It may be appropriate to offset misstatements within the same account balance or class of transactions; however, the risk that further undetected misstatements may exist is considered before concluding that offsetting even immaterial misstatements is appropriate.[11]

A15. Determining whether a classification misstatement is material involves the evaluation of qualitative considerations, such as the effect of the classification misstatement on debt or other contractual covenants, the effect on individual line items or sub-totals, or the effect on key ratios. There may be circumstances where the auditor concludes that a classification misstatement is not material in the context of the financial statements as a whole, even though it may exceed the materiality level or levels applied in evaluating other misstatements. For example, a misclassification between balance sheet line items may not be considered material in the context of the financial statements as a whole when the amount of the misclassification is small in relation to the size of the related balance sheet line items and the misclassification does not affect the income statement or any key ratios.

A16. The circumstances related to some misstatements may cause the auditor to evaluate them as material, individually or when considered together with other misstatements accumulated during the audit, even if they are lower than materiality for the financial statements as a whole. Circumstances that may affect the evaluation include the extent to which the misstatement:

- Affects compliance with regulatory requirements;

- Affects compliance with debt covenants or other contractual requirements;

---

[10] ISA (UK and Ireland) 320, paragraph 12.
[11] The identification of a number of immaterial misstatements within the same account balance or class of transactions may require the auditor to reassess the risk of material misstatement for that account balance or class of transactions.

- Relates to the incorrect selection or application of an accounting policy that has an immaterial effect on the current period's financial statements but is likely to have a material effect on future periods' financial statements;

- Masks a change in earnings or other trends, especially in the context of general economic and industry conditions;

- Affects ratios used to evaluate the entity's financial position, results of operations or cash flows;

- Affects segment information presented in the financial statements (for example, the significance of the matter to a segment or other portion of the entity's business that has been identified as playing a significant role in the entity's operations or profitability);

- Has the effect of increasing management compensation, for example, by ensuring that the requirements for the award of bonuses or other incentives are satisfied;

- Is significant having regard to the auditor's understanding of known previous communications to users, for example, in relation to forecast earnings;

- Relates to items involving particular parties (for example, whether external parties to the transaction are related to members of the entity's management);

- Is an omission of information not specifically required by the applicable financial reporting framework but which, in the judgment of the auditor, is important to the users' understanding of the financial position, financial performance or cash flows of the entity; or

- Affects other information that will be communicated in documents containing the audited financial statements (for example, information to be included in a "Management Discussion and Analysis" or an "Operating and Financial Review") that may reasonably be expected to influence the economic decisions of the users of the financial statements. ISA (UK and Ireland) 720[12] deals with the auditor's consideration of other information, on which the auditor has no obligation to report, in documents containing audited financial statements.

These circumstances are only examples; not all are likely to be present in all audits nor is the list necessarily complete. The existence of any circumstances such as these does not necessarily lead to a conclusion that the misstatement is material.

A17. ISA (UK and Ireland) 240[13] explains how the implications of a misstatement that is, or may be, the result of fraud ought to be considered in relation to other aspects of the

---

[12] ISA (UK and Ireland) 720, "The Auditor's Responsibilities Relating to Other Information in Documents Containing Audited Financial Statements."
[13] ISA (UK and Ireland) 240, paragraph 35.

FINANCIAL REPORTING COUNCIL

audit, even if the size of the misstatement is not material in relation to the financial statements.

A18. The cumulative effect of immaterial uncorrected misstatements related to prior periods may have a material effect on the current period's financial statements. There are different acceptable approaches to the auditor's evaluation of such uncorrected misstatements on the current period's financial statements. Using the same evaluation approach provides consistency from period to period.

Considerations Specific to Public Sector Entities

A19. In the case of an audit of a public sector entity, the evaluation whether a misstatement is material may also be affected by the auditor's responsibilities established by law, regulation or other authority to report specific matters, including, for example, fraud.

A20. Furthermore, issues such as public interest, accountability, probity and ensuring effective legislative oversight, in particular, may affect the assessment whether an item is material by virtue of its nature. This is particularly so for items that relate to compliance with law, regulation or other authority.

Communication with Those Charged with Governance (Ref: Para. 12)

A21. If uncorrected misstatements have been communicated with person(s) with management responsibilities, and those person(s) also have governance responsibilities, they need not be communicated again with those same person(s) in their governance role. The auditor nonetheless has to be satisfied that communication with person(s) with management responsibilities adequately informs all of those with whom the auditor would otherwise communicate in their governance capacity.[14]

A22. Where there is a large number of individual immaterial uncorrected misstatements, the auditor may communicate the number and overall monetary effect of the uncorrected misstatements, rather than the details of each individual uncorrected misstatement.

A23. ISA (UK and Ireland) 260 requires the auditor to communicate with those charged with governance the written representations the auditor is requesting (see paragraph 14 of this ISA (UK and Ireland)).[15] The auditor may discuss with those charged with governance the reasons for, and the implications of, a failure to correct misstatements, having regard to the size and nature of the misstatement judged in the surrounding circumstances, and possible implications in relation to future financial statements.

A23-1. If management have corrected material misstatements, communicating those corrections of which the auditor is aware to those charged with governance may

---

[14] ISA (UK and Ireland) 260, paragraph 13.
[15] ISA (UK and Ireland) 260, paragraph 16(c)(ii).

assist them to fulfill their governance responsibilities, including reviewing the effectiveness of the system of internal control.

Written Representation (Ref: Para. 14)

A24. Because the preparation of the financial statements requires management and, where appropriate, those charged with governance to adjust the financial statements to correct material misstatements, the auditor is required to request them to provide a written representation about uncorrected misstatements. In some circumstances, management and, where appropriate, those charged with governance may not believe that certain uncorrected misstatements are misstatements. For that reason, they may want to add to their written representation words such as: "We do not agree that items ... and ... constitute misstatements because [description of reasons]." Obtaining this representation does not, however, relieve the auditor of the need to form a conclusion on the effect of uncorrected misstatements.

A24-1 Requesting those charged with governance to provide written representations that set out their reasons for not correcting misstatements brought to their attention by the auditor may help focus the attention of those charged with governance on those misstatements and the circumstances giving rise to them.

Documentation (Ref: Para. 15)

A25. The auditor's documentation of uncorrected misstatements may take into account:

(a) The consideration of the aggregate effect of uncorrected misstatements;

(b) The evaluation of whether the materiality level or levels for particular classes of transactions, account balances or disclosures, if any, have been exceeded; and

(c) The evaluation of the effect of uncorrected misstatements on key ratios or trends, and compliance with legal, regulatory and contractual requirements (for example, debt covenants).

INTERNATIONAL STANDARD ON AUDITING
(UK AND IRELAND) 500

AUDIT EVIDENCE

(Effective for audits of financial statements for periods ending on or after 15 December 2010)[1a]

CONTENTS

International Standard on Auditing (UK and Ireland) (ISA (UK and Ireland)) 500, "Audit Evidence" should be read in conjunction with ISA (UK and Ireland) 200, "Overall Objectives of the Independent Auditor and the Conduct of an Audit in Accordance with International Standards on Auditing (UK and Ireland)."

[1a] Conforming amendments to this standard as a result of ISA (UK and Ireland) 610 (Revised June 2013), *Using the Work of Internal Auditors*, are included that are effective for audits of financial statements for periods ending on or after 15 June 2014. Details of the amendments are given in the Annexure to ISA (UK and Ireland) 610 (Revised June 2013).

Introduction

Scope of this ISA (UK and Ireland)

1. This International Standard on Auditing (UK and Ireland) (ISA (UK and Ireland)) explains what constitutes audit evidence in an audit of financial statements, and deals with the auditor's responsibility to design and perform audit procedures to obtain sufficient appropriate audit evidence to be able to draw reasonable conclusions on which to base the auditor's opinion.

2. This ISA (UK and Ireland) is applicable to all the audit evidence obtained during the course of the audit. Other ISAs (UK and Ireland) deal with specific aspects of the audit (for example, ISA (UK and Ireland) 315[1]), the audit evidence to be obtained in relation to a particular topic (for example, ISA (UK and Ireland) 570[2]), specific procedures to obtain audit evidence (for example, ISA (UK and Ireland) 520[3]), and the evaluation of whether sufficient appropriate audit evidence has been obtained (ISA (UK and Ireland) 200[4] and ISA (UK and Ireland) 330[5]).

Effective Date

3. This ISA (UK and Ireland) is effective for audits of financial statements for periods ending on or after 15 December 2010.[1a]

Objective

4. The objective of the auditor is to design and perform audit procedures in such a way as to enable the auditor to obtain sufficient appropriate audit evidence to be able to draw reasonable conclusions on which to base the auditor's opinion.

Definitions

5. For purposes of the ISAs (UK and Ireland), the following terms have the meanings attributed below:

    (a) Accounting records – The records of initial accounting entries and supporting records, such as checks and records of electronic fund transfers; invoices; contracts; the general and subsidiary ledgers, journal entries and other adjustments to the financial statements that are not reflected in journal

---

[1] ISA (UK and Ireland) 315, "Identifying and Assessing the Risks of Material Misstatement through Understanding the Entity and Its Environment."

[2] ISA (UK and Ireland) 570, "Going Concern."

[3] ISA (UK and Ireland) 520, "Analytical Procedures."

[4] ISA (UK and Ireland) 200, "Overall Objectives of the Independent Auditor and the Conduct of an Audit in Accordance with International Standards on Auditing (UK and Ireland)."

[5] ISA (UK and Ireland) 330, "The Auditor's Responses to Assessed Risks."

entries; and records such as work sheets and spreadsheets supporting cost allocations, computations, reconciliations and disclosures.

(b) Appropriateness (of audit evidence) – The measure of the quality of audit evidence; that is, its relevance and its reliability in providing support for the conclusions on which the auditor's opinion is based.

(c) Audit evidence – Information used by the auditor in arriving at the conclusions on which the auditor's opinion is based. Audit evidence includes both information contained in the accounting records underlying the financial statements and other information.

(d) Management's expert – An individual or organization possessing expertise in a field other than accounting or auditing, whose work in that field is used by the entity to assist the entity in preparing the financial statements.

(e) Sufficiency (of audit evidence) – The measure of the quantity of audit evidence. The quantity of the audit evidence needed is affected by the auditor's assessment of the risks of material misstatement and also by the quality of such audit evidence.

Requirements

Sufficient Appropriate Audit Evidence

6. The auditor shall design and perform audit procedures that are appropriate in the circumstances for the purpose of obtaining sufficient appropriate audit evidence. (Ref: Para. A1-A25)

Information to Be Used as Audit Evidence

7. When designing and performing audit procedures, the auditor shall consider the relevance and reliability of the information to be used as audit evidence. (Ref: Para. A26-A33)

8. If information to be used as audit evidence has been prepared using the work of a management's expert, the auditor shall, to the extent necessary, having regard to the significance of that expert's work for the auditor's purposes,: (Ref: Para. A34-A36)

(a) Evaluate the competence, capabilities and objectivity of that expert; (Ref: Para. A37-A43)

(b) Obtain an understanding of the work of that expert; and (Ref: Para. A44-A47)

(c) Evaluate the appropriateness of that expert's work as audit evidence for the relevant assertion. (Ref: Para. A48)

9. When using information produced by the entity, the auditor shall evaluate whether the information is sufficiently reliable for the auditor's purposes, including as necessary in the circumstances:

   (a) Obtaining audit evidence about the accuracy and completeness of the information; and (Ref: Para. A49-A50)

   (b) Evaluating whether the information is sufficiently precise and detailed for the auditor's purposes. (Ref: Para. A51)

Selecting Items for Testing to Obtain Audit Evidence

10. When designing tests of controls and tests of details, the auditor shall determine means of selecting items for testing that are effective in meeting the purpose of the audit procedure. (Ref: Para. A52-A56)

Inconsistency in, or Doubts over Reliability of, Audit Evidence

11. If:

   (a) audit evidence obtained from one source is inconsistent with that obtained from another; or

   (b) the auditor has doubts over the reliability of information to be used as audit evidence,

   the auditor shall determine what modifications or additions to audit procedures are necessary to resolve the matter, and shall consider the effect of the matter, if any, on other aspects of the audit. (Ref: Para. A57)

***

Application and Other Explanatory Material

Sufficient Appropriate Audit Evidence (Ref: Para. 6)

A1. Audit evidence is necessary to support the auditor's opinion and report. It is cumulative in nature and is primarily obtained from audit procedures performed during the course of the audit. It may, however, also include information obtained from other sources such as previous audits (provided the auditor has determined whether changes have occurred since the previous audit that may affect its relevance to the current audit[6]) or a firm's quality control procedures for client acceptance and continuance. In addition to other sources inside and outside the entity, the entity's accounting records are an important source of audit evidence. Also, information that may be used as audit evidence may have been prepared using the work of a

---

[6] ISA (UK and Ireland) 315, paragraph 9.

management's expert. Audit evidence comprises both information that supports and corroborates management's assertions, and any information that contradicts such assertions. In addition, in some cases the absence of information (for example, management's refusal to provide a requested representation) is used by the auditor, and therefore, also constitutes audit evidence.

A2. Most of the auditor's work in forming the auditor's opinion consists of obtaining and evaluating audit evidence. Audit procedures to obtain audit evidence can include inspection, observation, confirmation, recalculation, reperformance and analytical procedures, often in some combination, in addition to inquiry. Although inquiry may provide important audit evidence, and may even produce evidence of a misstatement, inquiry alone ordinarily does not provide sufficient audit evidence of the absence of a material misstatement at the assertion level, nor of the operating effectiveness of controls.

A3. As explained in ISA (UK and Ireland) 200,[7] reasonable assurance is obtained when the auditor has obtained sufficient appropriate audit evidence to reduce audit risk (that is, the risk that the auditor expresses an inappropriate opinion when the financial statements are materially misstated) to an acceptably low level.

A4. The sufficiency and appropriateness of audit evidence are interrelated. Sufficiency is the measure of the quantity of audit evidence. The quantity of audit evidence needed is affected by the auditor's assessment of the risks of misstatement (the higher the assessed risks, the more audit evidence is likely to be required) and also by the quality of such audit evidence (the higher the quality, the less may be required). Obtaining more audit evidence, however, may not compensate for its poor quality.

A5. Appropriateness is the measure of the quality of audit evidence; that is, its relevance and its reliability in providing support for the conclusions on which the auditor's opinion is based. The reliability of evidence is influenced by its source and by its nature, and is dependent on the individual circumstances under which it is obtained.

A6. ISA (UK and Ireland) 330 requires the auditor to conclude whether sufficient appropriate audit evidence has been obtained.[8] Whether sufficient appropriate audit evidence has been obtained to reduce audit risk to an acceptably low level, and thereby enable the auditor to draw reasonable conclusions on which to base the auditor's opinion, is a matter of professional judgment. ISA (UK and Ireland) 200 contains discussion of such matters as the nature of audit procedures, the timeliness of financial reporting, and the balance between benefit and cost, which are relevant factors when the auditor exercises professional judgment regarding whether sufficient appropriate audit evidence has been obtained.

---

[7] ISA (UK and Ireland) 200, paragraph 5.
[8] ISA (UK and Ireland) 330, paragraph 26.

Sources of Audit Evidence

A7. Some audit evidence is obtained by performing audit procedures to test the accounting records, for example, through analysis and review, reperforming procedures followed in the financial reporting process, and reconciling related types and applications of the same information. Through the performance of such audit procedures, the auditor may determine that the accounting records are internally consistent and agree to the financial statements.

A8. More assurance is ordinarily obtained from consistent audit evidence obtained from different sources or of a different nature than from items of audit evidence considered individually. For example, corroborating information obtained from a source independent of the entity may increase the assurance the auditor obtains from audit evidence that is generated internally, such as evidence existing within the accounting records, minutes of meetings, or a management representation.

A9. Information from sources independent of the entity that the auditor may use as audit evidence may include confirmations from third parties, analysts' reports, and comparable data about competitors (benchmarking data).

Audit Procedures for Obtaining Audit Evidence

A10. As required by, and explained further in, ISA (UK and Ireland) 315 and ISA (UK and Ireland) 330, audit evidence to draw reasonable conclusions on which to base the auditor's opinion is obtained by performing:

(a) Risk assessment procedures; and

(b) Further audit procedures, which comprise:

(i) Tests of controls, when required by the ISAs (UK and Ireland) or when the auditor has chosen to do so; and

(ii) Substantive procedures, including tests of details and substantive analytical procedures.

A11. The audit procedures described in paragraphs A14-A25 below may be used as risk assessment procedures, tests of controls or substantive procedures, depending on the context in which they are applied by the auditor. As explained in ISA (UK and Ireland) 330, audit evidence obtained from previous audits may, in certain circumstances, provide appropriate audit evidence where the auditor performs audit procedures to establish its continuing relevance.[9]

A12. The nature and timing of the audit procedures to be used may be affected by the fact that some of the accounting data and other information may be available only in electronic form or only at certain points or periods in time. For example, source

---

[9] ISA (UK and Ireland) 330, paragraph A35.

documents, such as purchase orders and invoices, may exist only in electronic form when an entity uses electronic commerce, or may be discarded after scanning when an entity uses image processing systems to facilitate storage and reference.

A13. Certain electronic information may not be retrievable after a specified period of time, for example, if files are changed and if backup files do not exist. Accordingly, the auditor may find it necessary as a result of an entity's data retention policies to request retention of some information for the auditor's review or to perform audit procedures at a time when the information is available.

Inspection

A14. Inspection involves examining records or documents, whether internal or external, in paper form, electronic form, or other media, or a physical examination of an asset. Inspection of records and documents provides audit evidence of varying degrees of reliability, depending on their nature and source and, in the case of internal records and documents, on the effectiveness of the controls over their production. An example of inspection used as a test of controls is inspection of records for evidence of authorization.

A15. Some documents represent direct audit evidence of the existence of an asset, for example, a document constituting a financial instrument such as a stock or bond. Inspection of such documents may not necessarily provide audit evidence about ownership or value. In addition, inspecting an executed contract may provide audit evidence relevant to the entity's application of accounting policies, such as revenue recognition.

A16. Inspection of tangible assets may provide reliable audit evidence with respect to their existence, but not necessarily about the entity's rights and obligations or the valuation of the assets. Inspection of individual inventory items may accompany the observation of inventory counting.

Observation

A17. Observation consists of looking at a process or procedure being performed by others, for example, the auditor's observation of inventory counting by the entity's personnel, or of the performance of control activities. Observation provides audit evidence about the performance of a process or procedure, but is limited to the point in time at which the observation takes place, and by the fact that the act of being observed may affect how the process or procedure is performed. See ISA (UK and Ireland) 501 for further guidance on observation of the counting of inventory.[10]

External Confirmation

A18. An external confirmation represents audit evidence obtained by the auditor as a direct written response to the auditor from a third party (the confirming party), in paper form,

---

[10] ISA (UK and Ireland) 501, "Audit Evidence—Specific Considerations for Selected Items."

or by electronic or other medium. External confirmation procedures frequently are relevant when addressing assertions associated with certain account balances and their elements. However, external confirmations need not be restricted to account balances only. For example, the auditor may request confirmation of the terms of agreements or transactions an entity has with third parties; the confirmation request may be designed to ask if any modifications have been made to the agreement and, if so, what the relevant details are. External confirmation procedures also are used to obtain audit evidence about the absence of certain conditions, for example, the absence of a "side agreement" that may influence revenue recognition. See ISA (UK and Ireland) 505 for further guidance.[11]

Recalculation

A19. Recalculation consists of checking the mathematical accuracy of documents or records. Recalculation may be performed manually or electronically.

Reperformance

A20. Reperformance involves the auditor's independent execution of procedures or controls that were originally performed as part of the entity's internal control.

Analytical Procedures

A21. Analytical procedures consist of evaluations of financial information through analysis of plausible relationships among both financial and non-financial data. Analytical procedures also encompass such investigation as is necessary of identified fluctuations or relationships that are inconsistent with other relevant information or that differ from expected values by a significant amount. See ISA (UK and Ireland) 520 for further guidance.

Inquiry

A22. Inquiry consists of seeking information of knowledgeable persons, both financial and non-financial, within the entity or outside the entity. Inquiry is used extensively throughout the audit in addition to other audit procedures. Inquiries may range from formal written inquiries to informal oral inquiries. Evaluating responses to inquiries is an integral part of the inquiry process.

A23. Responses to inquiries may provide the auditor with information not previously possessed or with corroborative audit evidence. Alternatively, responses might provide information that differs significantly from other information that the auditor has obtained, for example, information regarding the possibility of management override of controls. In some cases, responses to inquiries provide a basis for the auditor to modify or perform additional audit procedures.

---

[11] ISA (UK and Ireland) 505, "External Confirmations."

A24. Although corroboration of evidence obtained through inquiry is often of particular importance, in the case of inquiries about management intent, the information available to support management's intent may be limited. In these cases, understanding management's past history of carrying out its stated intentions, management's stated reasons for choosing a particular course of action, and management's ability to pursue a specific course of action may provide relevant information to corroborate the evidence obtained through inquiry.

A25. In respect of some matters, the auditor may consider it necessary to obtain written representations from management and, where appropriate, those charged with governance to confirm responses to oral inquiries. See ISA (UK and Ireland) 580 for further guidance.[12]

Information to Be Used as Audit Evidence

Relevance and Reliability (Ref: Para. 7)

A26. As noted in paragraph A1, while audit evidence is primarily obtained from audit procedures performed during the course of the audit, it may also include information obtained from other sources such as, for example, previous audits, in certain circumstances, and a firm's quality control procedures for client acceptance and continuance. The quality of all audit evidence is affected by the relevance and reliability of the information upon which it is based.

Relevance

A27. Relevance deals with the logical connection with, or bearing upon, the purpose of the audit procedure and, where appropriate, the assertion under consideration. The relevance of information to be used as audit evidence may be affected by the direction of testing. For example, if the purpose of an audit procedure is to test for overstatement in the existence or valuation of accounts payable, testing the recorded accounts payable may be a relevant audit procedure. On the other hand, when testing for understatement in the existence or valuation of accounts payable, testing the recorded accounts payable would not be relevant, but testing such information as subsequent disbursements, unpaid invoices, suppliers' statements, and unmatched receiving reports may be relevant.

A28. A given set of audit procedures may provide audit evidence that is relevant to certain assertions, but not others. For example, inspection of documents related to the collection of receivables after the period end may provide audit evidence regarding existence and valuation, but not necessarily cutoff. Similarly, obtaining audit evidence regarding a particular assertion, for example, the existence of inventory, is not a substitute for obtaining audit evidence regarding another assertion, for example, the valuation of that inventory. On the other hand, audit evidence from different sources or of a different nature may often be relevant to the same assertion.

---

[12] ISA (UK and Ireland) 580, "Written Representations."

A29. Tests of controls are designed to evaluate the operating effectiveness of controls in preventing, or detecting and correcting, material misstatements at the assertion level. Designing tests of controls to obtain relevant audit evidence includes identifying conditions (characteristics or attributes) that indicate performance of a control, and deviation conditions which indicate departures from adequate performance. The presence or absence of those conditions can then be tested by the auditor.

A30. Substantive procedures are designed to detect material misstatements at the assertion level. They comprise tests of details and substantive analytical procedures. Designing substantive procedures includes identifying conditions relevant to the purpose of the test that constitute a misstatement in the relevant assertion.

Reliability

A31. The reliability of information to be used as audit evidence, and therefore of the audit evidence itself, is influenced by its source and its nature, and the circumstances under which it is obtained, including the controls over its preparation and maintenance where relevant. Therefore, generalizations about the reliability of various kinds of audit evidence are subject to important exceptions. Even when information to be used as audit evidence is obtained from sources external to the entity, circumstances may exist that could affect its reliability. For example, information obtained from an independent external source may not be reliable if the source is not knowledgeable, or a management's expert may lack objectivity. While recognizing that exceptions may exist, the following generalizations about the reliability of audit evidence may be useful:

- The reliability of audit evidence is increased when it is obtained from independent sources outside the entity.

- The reliability of audit evidence that is generated internally is increased when the related controls, including those over its preparation and maintenance, imposed by the entity are effective.

- Audit evidence obtained directly by the auditor (for example, observation of the application of a control) is more reliable than audit evidence obtained indirectly or by inference (for example, inquiry about the application of a control).

- Audit evidence in documentary form, whether paper, electronic, or other medium, is more reliable than evidence obtained orally (for example, a contemporaneously written record of a meeting is more reliable than a subsequent oral representation of the matters discussed).

- Audit evidence provided by original documents is more reliable than audit evidence provided by photocopies or facsimiles, or documents that have been filmed, digitized or otherwise transformed into electronic form, the reliability of which may depend on the controls over their preparation and maintenance.

A32. ISA (UK and Ireland) 520 provides further guidance regarding the reliability of data used for purposes of designing analytical procedures as substantive procedures.[13]

A33. ISA (UK and Ireland) 240 deals with circumstances where the auditor has reason to believe that a document may not be authentic, or may have been modified without that modification having been disclosed to the auditor.[14]

Reliability of Information Produced by a Management's Expert (Ref: Para. 8)

A34. The preparation of an entity's financial statements may require expertise in a field other than accounting or auditing, such as actuarial calculations, valuations, or engineering data. The entity may employ or engage experts in these fields to obtain the needed expertise to prepare the financial statements. Failure to do so when such expertise is necessary increases the risks of material misstatement.

A35. When information to be used as audit evidence has been prepared using the work of a management's expert, the requirement in paragraph 8 of this ISA (UK and Ireland) applies. For example, an individual or organization may possess expertise in the application of models to estimate the fair value of securities for which there is no observable market. If the individual or organization applies that expertise in making an estimate which the entity uses in preparing its financial statements, the individual or organization is a management's expert and paragraph 8 applies. If, on the other hand, that individual or organization merely provides price data regarding private transactions not otherwise available to the entity which the entity uses in its own estimation methods, such information, if used as audit evidence, is subject to paragraph 7 of this ISA (UK and Ireland), but is not the use of a management's expert by the entity.

A36. The nature, timing and extent of audit procedures in relation to the requirement in paragraph 8 of this ISA (UK and Ireland), may be affected by such matters as:

- The nature and complexity of the matter to which the management's expert relates.

- The risks of material misstatement in the matter.

- The availability of alternative sources of audit evidence.

- The nature, scope and objectives of the management's expert's work.

- Whether the management's expert is employed by the entity, or is a party engaged by it to provide relevant services.

- The extent to which management can exercise control or influence over the work of the management's expert.

---

[13] ISA (UK and Ireland) 520, paragraph 5(a).
[14] ISA (UK and Ireland) 240, "The Auditor's Responsibilities Relating to Fraud in an Audit of Financial Statements," paragraph 13.

- Whether the management's expert is subject to technical performance standards or other professional or industry requirements.

- The nature and extent of any controls within the entity over the management's expert's work.

- The auditor's knowledge and experience of the management's expert's field of expertise.

- The auditor's previous experience of the work of that expert.

The Competence, Capabilities and Objectivity of a Management's Expert (Ref: Para. 8(a))

A37. Competence relates to the nature and level of expertise of the management's expert. Capability relates the ability of the management's expert to exercise that competence in the circumstances. Factors that influence capability may include, for example, geographic location, and the availability of time and resources. Objectivity relates to the possible effects that bias, conflict of interest or the influence of others may have on the professional or business judgment of the management's expert. The competence, capabilities and objectivity of a management's expert, and any controls within the entity over that expert's work, are important factors in relation to the reliability of any information produced by a management's expert.

A38. Information regarding the competence, capabilities and objectivity of a management's expert may come from a variety of sources, such as:

- Personal experience with previous work of that expert.

- Discussions with that expert.

- Discussions with others who are familiar with that expert's work.

- Knowledge of that expert's qualifications, membership of a professional body or industry association, license to practice, or other forms of external recognition.

- Published papers or books written by that expert.

- An auditor's expert, if any, who assists the auditor in obtaining sufficient appropriate audit evidence with respect to information produced by the management's expert.

A39. Matters relevant to evaluating the competence, capabilities and objectivity of a management's expert include whether that expert's work is subject to technical performance standards or other professional or industry requirements, for example, ethical standards and other membership requirements of a professional body or industry association, accreditation standards of a licensing body, or requirements imposed by law or regulation.

A40. Other matters that may be relevant include:

- The relevance of the management's expert's competence to the matter for which that expert's work will be used, including any areas of specialty within that expert's field. For example, a particular actuary may specialize in property and casualty insurance, but have limited expertise regarding pension calculations.

- The management's expert's competence with respect to relevant accounting requirements, for example, knowledge of assumptions and methods, including models where applicable, that are consistent with the applicable financial reporting framework.

- Whether unexpected events, changes in conditions, or the audit evidence obtained from the results of audit procedures indicate that it may be necessary to reconsider the initial evaluation of the competence, capabilities and objectivity of the management's expert as the audit progresses.

A41. A broad range of circumstances may threaten objectivity, for example, self-interest threats, advocacy threats, familiarity threats, self-review threats and intimidation threats. Safeguards may reduce such threats, and may be created either by external structures (for example, the management's expert's profession, legislation or regulation), or by the management's expert's work environment (for example, quality control policies and procedures).

A42. Although safeguards cannot eliminate all threats to a management's expert's objectivity, threats such as intimidation threats may be of less significance to an expert engaged by the entity than to an expert employed by the entity, and the effectiveness of safeguards such as quality control policies and procedures may be greater. Because the threat to objectivity created by being an employee of the entity will always be present, an expert employed by the entity cannot ordinarily be regarded as being more likely to be objective than other employees of the entity.

A43. When evaluating the objectivity of an expert engaged by the entity, it may be relevant to discuss with management and that expert any interests and relationships that may create threats to the expert's objectivity, and any applicable safeguards, including any professional requirements that apply to the expert; and to evaluate whether the safeguards are adequate. Interests and relationships creating threats may include:

- Financial interests.

- Business and personal relationships.

- Provision of other services.

Obtaining an Understanding of the Work of the Management's Expert (Ref: Para. 8(b))

A44. An understanding of the work of the management's expert includes an understanding of the relevant field of expertise. An understanding of the relevant field of expertise may be obtained in conjunction with the auditor's determination of whether the auditor has the expertise to evaluate the work of the management's expert, or whether the auditor needs an auditor's expert for this purpose.[15]

A45. Aspects of the management's expert's field relevant to the auditor's understanding may include:

- Whether that expert's field has areas of specialty within it that are relevant to the audit.

- Whether any professional or other standards, and regulatory or legal requirements apply.

- What assumptions and methods are used by the management's expert, and whether they are generally accepted within that expert's field and appropriate for financial reporting purposes.

- The nature of internal and external data or information the auditor's expert uses.

A46. In the case of a management's expert engaged by the entity, there will ordinarily be an engagement letter or other written form of agreement between the entity and that expert. Evaluating that agreement when obtaining an understanding of the work of the management's expert may assist the auditor in determining the appropriateness of the following for the auditor's purposes:

- The nature, scope and objectives of that expert's work;

- The respective roles and responsibilities of management and that expert; and

- The nature, timing and extent of communication between management and that expert, including the form of any report to be provided by that expert.

A47. In the case of a management's expert employed by the entity, it is less likely there will be a written agreement of this kind. Inquiry of the expert and other members of management may be the most appropriate way for the auditor to obtain the necessary understanding.

Evaluating the Appropriateness of the Management's Expert's Work (Ref: Para. 8(c))

A48. Considerations when evaluating the appropriateness of the management's expert's work as audit evidence for the relevant assertion may include:

- The relevance and reasonableness of that expert's findings or conclusions, their consistency with other audit evidence, and whether they have been appropriately reflected in the financial statements;

---

[15] ISA (UK and Ireland) 620, "Using the Work of an Auditor's Expert," paragraph 7.

- If that expert's work involves use of significant assumptions and methods, the relevance and reasonableness of those assumptions and methods; and

- If that expert's work involves significant use of source data the relevance, completeness, and accuracy of that source data.

Information Produced by the Entity and Used for the Auditor's Purposes (Ref: Para. 9(a)-(b))

A49. In order for the auditor to obtain reliable audit evidence, information produced by the entity that is used for performing audit procedures needs to be sufficiently complete and accurate. For example, the effectiveness of auditing revenue by applying standard prices to records of sales volume is affected by the accuracy of the price information and the completeness and accuracy of the sales volume data. Similarly, if the auditor intends to test a population (for example, payments) for a certain characteristic (for example, authorization), the results of the test will be less reliable if the population from which items are selected for testing is not complete.

A50. Obtaining audit evidence about the accuracy and completeness of such information may be performed concurrently with the actual audit procedure applied to the information when obtaining such audit evidence is an integral part of the audit procedure itself. In other situations, the auditor may have obtained audit evidence of the accuracy and completeness of such information by testing controls over the preparation and maintenance of the information. In some situations, however, the auditor may determine that additional audit procedures are needed.

A51. In some cases, the auditor may intend to use information produced by the entity for other audit purposes. For example, the auditor may intend to make use of the entity's performance measures for the purpose of analytical procedures, or to make use of the entity's information produced for monitoring activities, such as reports of the internal audit function. In such cases, the appropriateness of the audit evidence obtained is affected by whether the information is sufficiently precise or detailed for the auditor's purposes. For example, performance measures used by management may not be precise enough to detect material misstatements.

Selecting Items for Testing to Obtain Audit Evidence (Ref: Para. 10)

A52. An effective test provides appropriate audit evidence to an extent that, taken with other audit evidence obtained or to be obtained, will be sufficient for the auditor's purposes. In selecting items for testing, the auditor is required by paragraph 7 to determine the relevance and reliability of information to be used as audit evidence; the other aspect of effectiveness (sufficiency) is an important consideration in selecting items to test. The means available to the auditor for selecting items for testing are:

(a)   Selecting all items (100% examination);

(b)   Selecting specific items; and

(c)   Audit sampling.

The application of any one or combination of these means may be appropriate depending on the particular circumstances, for example, the risks of material misstatement related to the assertion being tested, and the practicality and efficiency of the different means.

Selecting All Items

A53. The auditor may decide that it will be most appropriate to examine the entire population of items that make up a class of transactions or account balance (or a stratum within that population). 100% examination is unlikely in the case of tests of controls; however, it is more common for tests of details. 100% examination may be appropriate when, for example:

- The population constitutes a small number of large value items;

- There is a significant risk and other means do not provide sufficient appropriate audit evidence; or

- The repetitive nature of a calculation or other process performed automatically by an information system makes a 100% examination cost effective.

Selecting Specific Items

A54. The auditor may decide to select specific items from a population. In making this decision, factors that may be relevant include the auditor's understanding of the entity, the assessed risks of material misstatement, and the characteristics of the population being tested. The judgmental selection of specific items is subject to non-sampling risk. Specific items selected may include:

- *High value or key items*. The auditor may decide to select specific items within a population because they are of high value, or exhibit some other characteristic, for example, items that are suspicious, unusual, particularly risk-prone or that have a history of error.

- *All items over a certain amount*. The auditor may decide to examine items whose recorded values exceed a certain amount so as to verify a large proportion of the total amount of a class of transactions or account balance.

- *Items to obtain information*. The auditor may examine items to obtain information about matters such as the nature of the entity or the nature of transactions.

A55. While selective examination of specific items from a class of transactions or account balance will often be an efficient means of obtaining audit evidence, it does not constitute audit sampling. The results of audit procedures applied to items selected in this way cannot be projected to the entire population; accordingly, selective examination of specific items does not provide audit evidence concerning the remainder of the population.

Audit Sampling

A56. Audit sampling is designed to enable conclusions to be drawn about an entire population on the basis of testing a sample drawn from it. Audit sampling is discussed in ISA (UK and Ireland) 530.[16]

Inconsistency in, or Doubts over Reliability of, Audit Evidence (Ref: Para. 11)

A57. Obtaining audit evidence from different sources or of a different nature may indicate that an individual item of audit evidence is not reliable, such as when audit evidence obtained from one source is inconsistent with that obtained from another. This may be the case when, for example, responses to inquiries of management, internal auditors, and others are inconsistent, or when responses to inquiries of those charged with governance made to corroborate the responses to inquiries of management are inconsistent with the response by management. ISA (UK and Ireland) 230 includes a specific documentation requirement if the auditor identified information that is inconsistent with the auditor's final conclusion regarding a significant matter.[17]

---

[16] ISA (UK and Ireland) 530, "Audit Sampling."
[17] ISA (UK and Ireland) 230, "Audit Documentation," paragraph 11.

INTERNATIONAL STANDARD ON AUDITING (UK AND IRELAND) 501

AUDIT EVIDENCE—SPECIFIC CONSIDERATIONS FOR SELECTED ITEMS

(Effective for audits of financial statements for periods ending on or after 15 December 2010)

CONTENTS

International Standard on Auditing (UK and Ireland) (ISA (UK and Ireland)) 501, "Audit Evidence—Specific Considerations for Selected Items" should be read in conjunction with ISA (UK and Ireland) 200, "Overall Objectives of the Independent Auditor and the Conduct of an Audit in Accordance with International Standards on Auditing (UK and Ireland)."

Introduction

Scope of this ISA (UK and Ireland)

1.   This International Standard on Auditing (UK and Ireland) (ISA (UK and Ireland)) deals with specific considerations by the auditor in obtaining sufficient appropriate audit evidence in accordance with ISA (UK and Ireland) 330,[1] ISA (UK and Ireland) 500[2] and other relevant ISAs (UK and Ireland), with respect to certain aspects of inventory, litigation and claims involving the entity, and segment information in an audit of financial statements.

Effective Date

2.   This ISA (UK and Ireland) is effective for audits of financial statements for periods ending on or after 15 December 2010.

Objective

3.   The objective of the auditor is to obtain sufficient appropriate audit evidence regarding the:

    (a)   Existence and condition of inventory;

    (b)   Completeness of litigation and claims involving the entity; and

    (c)   Presentation and disclosure of segment information in accordance with the applicable financial reporting framework.

Requirements

Inventory

4.   If inventory is material to the financial statements, the auditor shall obtain sufficient appropriate audit evidence regarding the existence and condition of inventory by:

    (a)   Attendance at physical inventory counting, unless impracticable, to: (Ref: Para. A1-A3)

        (i)   Evaluate management's instructions and procedures for recording and controlling the results of the entity's physical inventory counting; (Ref: Para. A4)

---

[1]   ISA (UK and Ireland) 330, "The Auditor's Responses to Assessed Risks."
[2]   ISA (UK and Ireland) 500, "Audit Evidence."

> (ii)   Observe the performance of management's count procedures; (Ref: Para. A5)
>
> (iii)   Inspect the inventory; and (Ref: Para. A6)
>
> (iv)   Perform test counts; and (Ref: Para. A7-A8)

(b)   Performing audit procedures over the entity's final inventory records to determine whether they accurately reflect actual inventory count results.

5.   If physical inventory counting is conducted at a date other than the date of the financial statements, the auditor shall, in addition to the procedures required by paragraph 4, perform audit procedures to obtain audit evidence about whether changes in inventory between the count date and the date of the financial statements are properly recorded. (Ref: Para. A9-A11)

6.   If the auditor is unable to attend physical inventory counting due to unforeseen circumstances, the auditor shall make or observe some physical counts on an alternative date, and perform audit procedures on intervening transactions.

7.   If attendance at physical inventory counting is impracticable, the auditor shall perform alternative audit procedures to obtain sufficient appropriate audit evidence regarding the existence and condition of inventory. If it is not possible to do so, the auditor shall modify the opinion in the auditor's report in accordance with ISA (UK and Ireland) 705.[3] (Ref: Para. A12-A14)

8.   If inventory under the custody and control of a third party is material to the financial statements, the auditor shall obtain sufficient appropriate audit evidence regarding the existence and condition of that inventory by performing one or both of the following:

(a)   Request confirmation from the third party as to the quantities and condition of inventory held on behalf of the entity. (Ref: Para. A15)

(b)   Perform inspection or other audit procedures appropriate in the circumstances. (Ref: Para. A16)

Litigation and Claims

9.   The auditor shall design and perform audit procedures in order to identify litigation and claims involving the entity which may give rise to a risk of material misstatement, including: (Ref: Para. A17-A19)

(a)   Inquiry of management[3a] and, where applicable, others within the entity, including in-house legal counsel;

---

[3]   ISA (UK and Ireland) 705, "Modifications to the Opinion in the Independent Auditor's Report."
[3a]   In the UK and Ireland the auditor also makes appropriate inquiry of those charged with governance.

      (b)   Reviewing minutes of meetings of those charged with governance and correspondence between the entity and its external legal counsel; and

      (c)   Reviewing legal expense accounts. (Ref: Para. A20)

10.   If the auditor assesses a risk of material misstatement regarding litigation or claims that have been identified, or when audit procedures performed indicate that other material litigation or claims may exist, the auditor shall, in addition to the procedures required by other ISAs (UK and Ireland), seek direct communication with the entity's external legal counsel. The auditor shall do so through a letter of inquiry, prepared by management[3b] and sent by the auditor, requesting the entity's external legal counsel to communicate directly with the auditor. If law, regulation or the respective legal professional body prohibits the entity's external legal counsel from communicating directly with the auditor, the auditor shall perform alternative audit procedures. (Ref: Para. A21-A25)

11.   If:

      (a)   management[3c] refuses to give the auditor permission to communicate or meet with the entity's external legal counsel, or the entity's external legal counsel refuses to respond appropriately to the letter of inquiry, or is prohibited from responding; and

      (b)   the auditor is unable to obtain sufficient appropriate audit evidence by performing alternative audit procedures,

the auditor shall modify the opinion in the auditor's report in accordance with ISA (UK and Ireland) 705.

Written Representations

12.   The auditor shall request management and, where appropriate, those charged with governance to provide written representations that all known actual or possible litigation and claims whose effects should be considered when preparing the financial statements have been disclosed to the auditor and accounted for and disclosed in accordance with the applicable financial reporting framework.

Segment Information

13.   The auditor shall obtain sufficient appropriate audit evidence regarding the presentation and disclosure of segment information in accordance with the applicable financial reporting framework by: (Ref: Para. A26)

      (a)   Obtaining an understanding of the methods used by management in determining segment information, and: (Ref: Para. A27)

[3b] In the UK and Ireland the letter may need to be prepared by those charged with governance.
[3c] In the UK and Ireland permission may be denied by those charged with governance.

     (i)   Evaluating whether such methods are likely to result in disclosure in accordance with the applicable financial reporting framework; and

     (ii)   Where appropriate, testing the application of such methods; and

  (b) Performing analytical procedures or other audit procedures appropriate in the circumstances.

***

Application and Other Explanatory Material

Inventory[3d]

Attendance at Physical Inventory Counting (Ref: Para. 4(a))

A1.   Management ordinarily establishes procedures under which inventory is physically counted at least once a year to serve as a basis for the preparation of the financial statements and, if applicable, to ascertain the reliability of the entity's perpetual inventory system.

A2.   Attendance at physical inventory counting involves:

- Inspecting the inventory to ascertain its existence and evaluate its condition, and performing test counts;

- Observing compliance with management's instructions and the performance of procedures for recording and controlling the results of the physical inventory count; and

- Obtaining audit evidence as to the reliability of management's count procedures.

These procedures may serve as test of controls or substantive procedures depending on the auditor's risk assessment, planned approach and the specific procedures carried out.

A3.   Matters relevant in planning attendance at physical inventory counting (or in designing and performing audit procedures pursuant to paragraphs 4-8 of this ISA (UK and Ireland)) include, for example:

- The risks of material misstatement related to inventory.

- The nature of the internal control related to inventory.

[3d] For auditors in the UK and Ireland further guidance has been promulgated by the APB in Practice Note 25, "Attendance at Stocktaking."

- Whether adequate procedures are expected to be established and proper instructions issued for physical inventory counting.

- The timing of physical inventory counting.

- Whether the entity maintains a perpetual inventory system.

- The locations at which inventory is held, including the materiality of the inventory and the risks of material misstatement at different locations, in deciding at which locations attendance is appropriate. ISA (UK and Ireland) 600[4] deals with the involvement of other auditors and accordingly may be relevant if such involvement is with regards to attendance of physical inventory counting at a remote location.

- Whether the assistance of an auditor's expert is needed. ISA (UK and Ireland) 620[5] deals with the use of an auditor's expert to assist the auditor to obtain sufficient appropriate audit evidence.

Evaluate Management's Instructions and Procedures (Ref: Para. 4(a)(i))

A4. Matters relevant in evaluating management's instructions and procedures for recording and controlling the physical inventory counting include whether they address, for example:

- The application of appropriate control activities, for example, collection of used physical inventory count records, accounting for unused physical inventory count records, and count and re-count procedures.

- The accurate identification of the stage of completion of work in progress, of slow moving, obsolete or damaged items and of inventory owned by a third party, for example, on consignment.

- The procedures used to estimate physical quantities, where applicable, such as may be needed in estimating the physical quantity of a coal pile.

- Control over the movement of inventory between areas and the shipping and receipt of inventory before and after the cutoff date.

Observe the Performance of Management's Count Procedures (Ref: Para. 4(a)(ii))

A5. Observing the performance of management's count procedures, for example those relating to control over the movement of inventory before, during and after the count, assists the auditor in obtaining audit evidence that management's instructions and count procedures are adequately designed and implemented. In addition, the auditor

---

[4] ISA (UK and Ireland) 600, "Special Considerations—Audits of Group Financial Statements (Including the Work of Component Auditors)."

[5] ISA (UK and Ireland) 620, "Using the Work of an Auditor's Expert."

may obtain copies of cutoff information, such as details of the movement of inventory, to assist the auditor in performing audit procedures over the accounting for such movements at a later date.

Inspect the Inventory (Ref: Para. 4(a)(iii))

A6.   Inspecting inventory when attending physical inventory counting assists the auditor in ascertaining the existence of the inventory (though not necessarily its ownership), and in identifying, for example, obsolete, damaged or ageing inventory.

Perform Test Counts (Ref: Para. 4(a)(iv))

A7.   Performing test counts, for example by tracing items selected from management's count records to the physical inventory and tracing items selected from the physical inventory to management's count records, provides audit evidence about the completeness and the accuracy of those records.

A8.   In addition to recording the auditor's test counts, obtaining copies of management's completed physical inventory count records assists the auditor in performing subsequent audit procedures to determine whether the entity's final inventory records accurately reflect actual inventory count results.

Physical Inventory Counting Conducted Other than At the Date of the Financial Statements (Ref: Para. 5)

A9.   For practical reasons, the physical inventory counting may be conducted at a date, or dates, other than the date of the financial statements. This may be done irrespective of whether management determines inventory quantities by an annual physical inventory counting or maintains a perpetual inventory system. In either case, the effectiveness of the design, implementation and maintenance of controls over changes in inventory determines whether the conduct of physical inventory counting at a date, or dates, other than the date of the financial statements is appropriate for audit purposes. ISA (UK and Ireland) 330 establishes requirements and provides guidance on substantive procedures performed at an interim date.[6]

A10.   Where a perpetual inventory system is maintained, management may perform physical counts or other tests to ascertain the reliability of inventory quantity information included in the entity's perpetual inventory records. In some cases, management or the auditor may identify differences between the perpetual inventory records and actual physical inventory quantities on hand; this may indicate that the controls over changes in inventory are not operating effectively.

A11.   Relevant matters for consideration when designing audit procedures to obtain audit evidence about whether changes in inventory amounts between the count date, or dates, and the final inventory records are properly recorded include:

---

[6]   ISA (UK and Ireland) 330, paragraphs 22-23.

- Whether the perpetual inventory records are properly adjusted.

- Reliability of the entity's perpetual inventory records.

- Reasons for significant differences between the information obtained during the physical count and the perpetual inventory records.

Attendance at Physical Inventory Counting Is Impracticable (Ref: Para. 7)

A12. In some cases, attendance at physical inventory counting may be impracticable. This may be due to factors such as the nature and location of the inventory, for example, where inventory is held in a location that may pose threats to the safety of the auditor. The matter of general inconvenience to the auditor, however, is not sufficient to support a decision by the auditor that attendance is impracticable. Further, as explained in ISA (UK and Ireland) 200,[7] the matter of difficulty, time, or cost involved is not in itself a valid basis for the auditor to omit an audit procedure for which there is no alternative or to be satisfied with audit evidence that is less than persuasive.

A13. In some cases where attendance is impracticable, alternative audit procedures, for example inspection of documentation of the subsequent sale of specific inventory items acquired or purchased prior to the physical inventory counting, may provide sufficient appropriate audit evidence about the existence and condition of inventory.

A14. In other cases, however, it may not be possible to obtain sufficient appropriate audit evidence regarding the existence and condition of inventory by performing alternative audit procedures. In such cases, ISA (UK and Ireland) 705 requires the auditor to modify the opinion in the auditor's report as a result of the scope limitation.[8]

Inventory under the Custody and Control of a Third Party

Confirmation (Ref: Para. 8(a))

A15. ISA (UK and Ireland) 505[9] establishes requirements and provides guidance for performing external confirmation procedures.

Other Audit Procedures (Ref: Para. 8(b))

A16. Depending on the circumstances, for example where information is obtained that raises doubt about the integrity and objectivity of the third party, the auditor may consider it appropriate to perform other audit procedures instead of, or in addition to, confirmation with the third party. Examples of other audit procedures include:

- Attending, or arranging for another auditor to attend, the third party's physical counting of inventory, if practicable.

---

[7] ISA (UK and Ireland) 200, "Overall Objectives of the Independent Auditor and the Conduct of an Audit in Accordance with International Standards on Auditing (UK and Ireland)," paragraph A48.

[8] ISA (UK and Ireland) 705, paragraph 13.

[9] ISA (UK and Ireland) 505, "External Confirmations."

- Obtaining another auditor's report, or a service auditor's report, on the adequacy of the third party's internal control for ensuring that inventory is properly counted and adequately safeguarded.

- Inspecting documentation regarding inventory held by third parties, for example, warehouse receipts.

- Requesting confirmation from other parties when inventory has been pledged as collateral.

Litigation and Claims

Completeness of Litigations and Claims (Ref: Para. 9)

A17. Litigation and claims involving the entity may have a material effect on the financial statements and thus may be required to be disclosed or accounted for in the financial statements.

A18. In addition to the procedures identified in paragraph 9, other relevant procedures include, for example, using information obtained through risk assessment procedures carried out as part of obtaining an understanding of the entity and its environment to assist the auditor to become aware of litigation and claims involving the entity.

A19. Audit evidence obtained for purposes of identifying litigation and claims that may give rise to a risk of material misstatement also may provide audit evidence regarding other relevant considerations, such as valuation or measurement, regarding litigation and claims. ISA (UK and Ireland) 540[10] establishes requirements and provides guidance relevant to the auditor's consideration of litigation and claims requiring accounting estimates or related disclosures in the financial statements.

Reviewing Legal Expense Accounts (Ref: Para. 9(c))

A20. Depending on the circumstances, the auditor may judge it appropriate to examine related source documents, such as invoices for legal expenses, as part of the auditor's review of legal expense accounts.

Communication with the Entity's External Legal Counsel (Ref: Para. 10-11)

A21. Direct communication with the entity's external legal counsel assists the auditor in obtaining sufficient appropriate audit evidence as to whether potentially material litigation and claims are known and management's estimates of the financial implications, including costs, are reasonable.

---

[10] ISA (UK and Ireland) 540, "Auditing Accounting Estimates, Including Fair Value Accounting Estimates, and Related Disclosures."

A22. In some cases, the auditor may seek direct communication with the entity's external legal counsel through a letter of general inquiry. For this purpose, a letter of general inquiry requests the entity's external legal counsel to inform the auditor of any litigation and claims that the counsel is aware of, together with an assessment of the outcome of the litigation and claims, and an estimate of the financial implications, including costs involved.

A23. If it is considered unlikely that the entity's external legal counsel will respond appropriately to a letter of general inquiry, for example if the professional body to which the external legal counsel belongs prohibits response to such a letter[10a], the auditor may seek direct communication through a letter of specific inquiry. For this purpose, a letter of specific inquiry includes:

(a) A list of litigation and claims;

(b) Where available, management's assessment of the outcome of each of the identified litigation and claims and its estimate of the financial implications, including costs involved; and

(c) A request that the entity's external legal counsel confirm the reasonableness of management's assessments and provide the auditor with further information if the list is considered by the entity's external legal counsel to be incomplete or incorrect.

A24. In certain circumstances, the auditor also may judge it necessary to meet with the entity's external legal counsel to discuss the likely outcome of the litigation or claims. This may be the case, for example, where:

• The auditor determines that the matter is a significant risk.

• The matter is complex.

• There is disagreement between management and the entity's external legal counsel.

Ordinarily, such meetings require management's permission[3c] and are held with a representative of management in attendance.

A25. In accordance with ISA (UK and Ireland) 700,[11] the auditor is required to date the auditor's report no earlier than the date on which the auditor has obtained sufficient appropriate audit evidence on which to base the auditor's opinion on the financial

---

[10a] In the UK, the Council of the Law Society has advised solicitors that it is unable to recommend them to comply with non-specific requests for information.

[11] ISA 700, "Forming an Opinion and Reporting on Financial Statements," paragraph 41.

The APB has not promulgated ISA 700 as issued by the IAASB for application in the UK and Ireland. In the UK and Ireland the applicable auditing standard is ISA (UK and Ireland) 700, "The Auditor's Report on Financial Statements." Paragraphs 23 and 24 of ISA (UK and Ireland) 700 establish requirements regarding dating of the auditor's report.

statements. Audit evidence about the status of litigation and claims up to the date of the auditor's report may be obtained by inquiry of management[3a], including in-house legal counsel, responsible for dealing with the relevant matters. In some instances, the auditor may need to obtain updated information from the entity's external legal counsel.

Segment Information (Ref: Para. 13)

A26. Depending on the applicable financial reporting framework, the entity may be required or permitted to disclose segment information in the financial statements. The auditor's responsibility regarding the presentation and disclosure of segment information is in relation to the financial statements taken as a whole. Accordingly, the auditor is not required to perform audit procedures that would be necessary to express an opinion on the segment information presented on a stand alone basis.

Understanding of the Methods Used by Management (Ref: Para. 13(a))

A27. Depending on the circumstances, example of matters that may be relevant when obtaining an understanding of the methods used by management in determining segment information and whether such methods are likely to result in disclosure in accordance with the applicable financial reporting framework include:

- Sales, transfers and charges between segments, and elimination of inter-segment amounts.

- Comparisons with budgets and other expected results, for example, operating profits as a percentage of sales.

- The allocation of assets and costs among segments.

- Consistency with prior periods, and the adequacy of the disclosures with respect to inconsistencies.

INTERNATIONAL STANDARD ON AUDITING
(UK AND IRELAND) 505

EXTERNAL CONFIRMATIONS

(Effective for audits of financial statements for periods ending on or after 15 December 2010)

CONTENTS

International Standard on Auditing (UK and Ireland) (ISA (UK and Ireland)) 505, "External Confirmations" should be read in conjunction with ISA (UK and Ireland) 200, "Overall Objectives of the Independent Auditor and the Conduct of an Audit in Accordance with International Standards on Auditing (UK and Ireland)."

Introduction

Scope of this ISA (UK and Ireland)

1. This International Standard on Auditing (UK and Ireland) (ISA (UK and Ireland)) deals with the auditor's use of external confirmation procedures to obtain audit evidence in accordance with the requirements of ISA (UK and Ireland) 330[1] and ISA (UK and Ireland) 500.[2] It does not address inquiries regarding litigation and claims, which are dealt with in ISA (UK and Ireland) 501.[3]

External Confirmation Procedures to Obtain Audit Evidence

2. ISA (UK and Ireland) 500 indicates that the reliability of audit evidence is influenced by its source and by its nature, and is dependent on the individual circumstances under which it is obtained.[4] That ISA (UK and Ireland) also includes the following generalizations applicable to audit evidence:[5]

   - Audit evidence is more reliable when it is obtained from independent sources outside the entity.

   - Audit evidence obtained directly by the auditor is more reliable than audit evidence obtained indirectly or by inference.

   - Audit evidence is more reliable when it exists in documentary form, whether paper, electronic or other medium.

   Accordingly, depending on the circumstances of the audit, audit evidence in the form of external confirmations received directly by the auditor from confirming parties may be more reliable than evidence generated internally by the entity. This ISA (UK and Ireland) is intended to assist the auditor in designing and performing external confirmation procedures to obtain relevant and reliable audit evidence.

3. Other ISAs (UK and Ireland) recognize the importance of external confirmations as audit evidence, for example:

   - ISA (UK and Ireland) 330 discusses the auditor's responsibility to design and implement overall responses to address the assessed risks of material misstatement at the financial statement level, and to design and perform further audit procedures whose nature, timing and extent are based on, and are responsive to, the assessed risks of material misstatement at the assertion level.[6] In addition, ISA (UK and Ireland) 330 requires that, irrespective of the assessed risks of material misstatement, the auditor designs and performs substantive

---

[1] ISA (UK and Ireland) 330, "The Auditor's Responses to Assessed Risks."
[2] ISA (UK and Ireland) 500, "Audit Evidence."
[3] ISA (UK and Ireland) 501, "Audit Evidence—Specific Considerations for Selected Items."
[4] ISA (UK and Ireland) 500, paragraph A5.
[5] ISA (UK and Ireland) 500, paragraph A31.
[6] ISA (UK and Ireland) 330, paragraphs 5-6.

procedures for each material class of transactions, account balance, and disclosure. The auditor is also required to consider whether external confirmation procedures are to be performed as substantive audit procedures.[7]

- ISA (UK and Ireland) 330 requires that the auditor obtain more persuasive audit evidence the higher the auditor's assessment of risk.[8] To do this, the auditor may increase the quantity of the evidence or obtain evidence that is more relevant or reliable, or both. For example, the auditor may place more emphasis on obtaining evidence directly from third parties or obtaining corroborating evidence from a number of independent sources. ISA (UK and Ireland) 330 also indicates that external confirmation procedures may assist the auditor in obtaining audit evidence with the high level of reliability that the auditor requires to respond to significant risks of material misstatement, whether due to fraud or error.[9]

- ISA (UK and Ireland) 240 indicates that the auditor may design confirmation requests to obtain additional corroborative information as a response to address the assessed risks of material misstatement due to fraud at the assertion level.[10]

- ISA (UK and Ireland) 500 indicates that corroborating information obtained from a source independent of the entity, such as external confirmations, may increase the assurance the auditor obtains from evidence existing within the accounting records or from representations made by management.[11]

Effective Date

4.   This ISA (UK and Ireland) is effective for audits of financial statements for periods ending on or after 15 December 2010.

Objective

5.   The objective of the auditor, when using external confirmation procedures, is to design and perform such procedures to obtain relevant and reliable audit evidence.

Definitions

6.   For purposes of the ISAs (UK and Ireland), the following terms have the meanings attributed below:

(a)   External confirmation – Audit evidence obtained as a direct written response to the auditor from a third party (the confirming party), in paper form, or by electronic or other medium.

---

[7]   ISA (UK and Ireland) 330, paragraphs 18-19.
[8]   ISA (UK and Ireland) 330, paragraph 7(b).
[9]   ISA (UK and Ireland) 330, paragraph A53.
[10] ISA (UK and Ireland) 240, "The Auditor's Responsibilities Relating to Fraud in an Audit of Financial Statements," paragraph A37.
[11] ISA (UK and Ireland) 500, paragraph A8-A9.

(b) Positive confirmation request – A request that the confirming party respond directly to the auditor indicating whether the confirming party agrees or disagrees with the information in the request, or providing the requested information.

(c) Negative confirmation request – A request that the confirming party respond directly to the auditor only if the confirming party disagrees with the information provided in the request.

(d) Non-response – A failure of the confirming party to respond, or fully respond, to a positive confirmation request, or a confirmation request returned undelivered.

(e) Exception – A response that indicates a difference between information requested to be confirmed, or contained in the entity's records, and information provided by the confirming party.

Requirements

External Confirmation Procedures

7. When using external confirmation procedures, the auditor shall maintain control over external confirmation requests, including:

(a) Determining the information to be confirmed or requested; (Ref: Para. A1)

(b) Selecting the appropriate confirming party; (Ref: Para. A2)

(c) Designing the confirmation requests, including determining that requests are properly addressed and contain return information for responses to be sent directly to the auditor; and (Ref: Para. A3-A6)

(d) Sending the requests, including follow-up requests when applicable, to the confirming party. (Ref: Para. A7)

Management's Refusal to Allow the Auditor to Send a Confirmation Request

8. If management refuses to allow the auditor to send a confirmation request, the auditor shall:

(a) Inquire as to management's reasons for the refusal, and seek audit evidence as to their validity and reasonableness; (Ref: Para. A8)

(b) Evaluate the implications of management's refusal on the auditor's assessment of the relevant risks of material misstatement, including the risk of fraud, and on the nature, timing and extent of other audit procedures; and (Ref: Para. A9)

(c) Perform alternative audit procedures designed to obtain relevant and reliable audit evidence. (Ref: Para. A10)

9.   If the auditor concludes that management's refusal to allow the auditor to send a confirmation request is unreasonable, or the auditor is unable to obtain relevant and reliable audit evidence from alternative audit procedures, the auditor shall communicate with those charged with governance in accordance with ISA (UK and Ireland) 260.[12] The auditor also shall determine the implications for the audit and the auditor's opinion in accordance with ISA (UK and Ireland) 705.[13]

Results of the External Confirmation Procedures

Reliability of Responses to Confirmation Requests

10.   If the auditor identifies factors that give rise to doubts about the reliability of the response to a confirmation request, the auditor shall obtain further audit evidence to resolve those doubts. (Ref: Para. A11-A16)

11.   If the auditor determines that a response to a confirmation request is not reliable, the auditor shall evaluate the implications on the assessment of the relevant risks of material misstatement, including the risk of fraud, and on the related nature, timing and extent of other audit procedures. (Ref: Para. A17)

Non-Responses

12.   In the case of each non-response, the auditor shall perform alternative audit procedures to obtain relevant and reliable audit evidence. (Ref: Para A18-A19)

When a Response to a Positive Confirmation Request Is Necessary to Obtain Sufficient Appropriate Audit Evidence

13.   If the auditor has determined that a response to a positive confirmation request is necessary to obtain sufficient appropriate audit evidence, alternative audit procedures will not provide the audit evidence the auditor requires. If the auditor does not obtain such confirmation, the auditor shall determine the implications for the audit and the auditor's opinion in accordance with ISA (UK and Ireland) 705. (Ref: Para A20)

Exceptions

14.   The auditor shall investigate exceptions to determine whether or not they are indicative of misstatements. (Ref: Para. A21-A22)

Negative Confirmations

15.   Negative confirmations provide less persuasive audit evidence than positive confirmations. Accordingly, the auditor shall not use negative confirmation requests as the sole substantive audit procedure to address an assessed risk of material

---

[12]   ISA (UK and Ireland) 260, "Communication with Those Charged with Governance," paragraph 16.

[13]   ISA (UK and Ireland) 705, "Modifications to the Opinion in the Independent Auditor's Report."

misstatement at the assertion level unless all of the following are present: (Ref: Para. A23)

(a) The auditor has assessed the risk of material misstatement as low and has obtained sufficient appropriate audit evidence regarding the operating effectiveness of controls relevant to the assertion;

(b) The population of items subject to negative confirmation procedures comprises a large number of small, homogeneous, account balances, transactions or conditions;

(c) A very low exception rate is expected; and

(d) The auditor is not aware of circumstances or conditions that would cause recipients of negative confirmation requests to disregard such requests.

Evaluating the Evidence Obtained

16. The auditor shall evaluate whether the results of the external confirmation procedures provide relevant and reliable audit evidence, or whether further audit evidence is necessary. (Ref: Para A24-A25)

***

Application and Other Explanatory Material

External Confirmation Procedures

Determining the Information to Be Confirmed or Requested (Ref: Para. 7(a))

A1. External confirmation procedures frequently are performed to confirm or request information regarding account balances and their elements. They may also be used to confirm terms of agreements, contracts, or transactions between an entity and other parties, or to confirm the absence of certain conditions, such as a "side agreement."

Selecting the Appropriate Confirming Party (Ref: Para. 7(b))

A2. Responses to confirmation requests provide more relevant and reliable audit evidence when confirmation requests are sent to a confirming party the auditor believes is knowledgeable about the information to be confirmed. For example, a financial institution official who is knowledgeable about the transactions or arrangements for which confirmation is requested may be the most appropriate person at the financial institution from whom to request confirmation.

Designing Confirmation Requests (Ref: Para. 7(c))

A3. The design of a confirmation request may directly affect the confirmation response rate, and the reliability and the nature of the audit evidence obtained from responses.

A4. Factors to consider when designing confirmation requests include:

- The assertions being addressed.

- Specific identified risks of material misstatement, including fraud risks.

- The layout and presentation of the confirmation request.

- Prior experience on the audit or similar engagements.

- The method of communication (for example, in paper form, or by electronic or other medium).

- Management's authorization or encouragement to the confirming parties to respond to the auditor. Confirming parties may only be willing to respond to a confirmation request containing management's authorization.

- The ability of the intended confirming party to confirm or provide the requested information (for example, individual invoice amount versus total balance).

A5. A positive external confirmation request asks the confirming party to reply to the auditor in all cases, either by indicating the confirming party's agreement with the given information, or by asking the confirming party to provide information. A response to a positive confirmation request ordinarily is expected to provide reliable audit evidence. There is a risk, however, that a confirming party may reply to the confirmation request without verifying that the information is correct. The auditor may reduce this risk by using positive confirmation requests that do not state the amount (or other information) on the confirmation request, and ask the confirming party to fill in the amount or furnish other information. On the other hand, use of this type of "blank" confirmation request may result in lower response rates because additional effort is required of the confirming parties.

A6. Determining that requests are properly addressed includes testing the validity of some or all of the addresses on confirmation requests before they are sent out.

Follow-Up on Confirmation Requests (Ref: Para. 7(d))

A7. The auditor may send an additional confirmation request when a reply to a previous request has not been received within a reasonable time. For example, the auditor may, having re-verified the accuracy of the original address, send an additional or follow-up request.

Management's Refusal to Allow the Auditor to Send a Confirmation Request

Reasonableness of Management's Refusal (Ref: Para. 8(a))

A8.   A refusal by management to allow the auditor to send a confirmation request is a limitation on the audit evidence the auditor may wish to obtain. The auditor is therefore required to inquire as to the reasons for the limitation. A common reason advanced is the existence of a legal dispute or ongoing negotiation with the intended confirming party, the resolution of which may be affected by an untimely confirmation request. The auditor is required to seek audit evidence as to the validity and reasonableness of the reasons because of the risk that management may be attempting to deny the auditor access to audit evidence that may reveal fraud or error.

Implications for the Assessment of Risks of Material Misstatement (Ref: Para. 8(b))

A9.   The auditor may conclude from the evaluation in paragraph 8(b) that it would be appropriate to revise the assessment of the risks of material misstatement at the assertion level and modify planned audit procedures in accordance with ISA (UK and Ireland) 315.[14] For example, if management's request to not confirm is unreasonable, this may indicate a fraud risk factor that requires evaluation in accordance with ISA (UK and Ireland) 240.[15]

Alternative Audit Procedures (Ref: Para. 8(c))

A10.   The alternative audit procedures performed may be similar to those appropriate for a non-response as set out in paragraphs A18-A19 of this ISA (UK and Ireland). Such procedures also would take account of the results of the auditor's evaluation in paragraph 8(b) of this ISA (UK and Ireland).

Results of the External Confirmation Procedures

Reliability of Responses to Confirmation Requests (Ref: Para. 10)

A11.   ISA (UK and Ireland) 500 indicates that even when audit evidence is obtained from sources external to the entity, circumstances may exist that affect its reliability.[16] All responses carry some risk of interception, alteration or fraud. Such risk exists regardless of whether a response is obtained in paper form, or by electronic or other medium. Factors that may indicate doubts about the reliability of a response include that it:

- Was received by the auditor indirectly; or

- Appeared not to come from the originally intended confirming party.

---

[14]   ISA (UK and Ireland) 315, "Identifying and Assessing the Risks of Material Misstatement through Understanding the Entity and Its Environment," paragraph 31.

[15]   ISA (UK and Ireland) 240, paragraph 24.

[16]   ISA (UK and Ireland) 500, paragraph A31.

A12. Responses received electronically, for example by facsimile or electronic mail, involve risks as to reliability because proof of origin and authority of the respondent may be difficult to establish, and alterations may be difficult to detect. A process used by the auditor and the respondent that creates a secure environment for responses received electronically may mitigate these risks. If the auditor is satisfied that such a process is secure and properly controlled, the reliability of the related responses is enhanced. An electronic confirmation process might incorporate various techniques for validating the identity of a sender of information in electronic form, for example, through the use of encryption, electronic digital signatures, and procedures to verify web site authenticity.

A13. If a confirming party uses a third party to coordinate and provide responses to confirmation requests, the auditor may perform procedures to address the risks that:

(a) The response may not be from the proper source;

(b) A respondent may not be authorized to respond; and

(c) The integrity of the transmission may have been compromised.

A14. The auditor is required by ISA (UK and Ireland) 500 to determine whether to modify or add procedures to resolve doubts over the reliability of information to be used as audit evidence.[17] The auditor may choose to verify the source and contents of a response to a confirmation request by contacting the confirming party. For example, when a confirming party responds by electronic mail, the auditor may telephone the confirming party to determine whether the confirming party did, in fact, send the response. When a response has been returned to the auditor indirectly (for example, because the confirming party incorrectly addressed it to the entity rather than to the auditor), the auditor may request the confirming party to respond in writing directly to the auditor.

A15. On its own, an oral response to a confirmation request does not meet the definition of an external confirmation because it is not a direct written response to the auditor. However, upon obtaining an oral response to a confirmation request, the auditor may, depending on the circumstances, request the confirming party to respond in writing directly to the auditor. If no such response is received, in accordance with paragraph 12, the auditor seeks other audit evidence to support the information in the oral response.

A16. A response to a confirmation request may contain restrictive language regarding its use. Such restrictions do not necessarily invalidate the reliability of the response as audit evidence.

---

[17] ISA (UK and Ireland) 500, paragraph 11.

Unreliable Responses (Ref: Para. 11)

A17. When the auditor concludes that a response is unreliable, the auditor may need to revise the assessment of the risks of material misstatement at the assertion level and modify planned audit procedures accordingly, in accordance with ISA (UK and Ireland) 315.[18] For example, an unreliable response may indicate a fraud risk factor that requires evaluation in accordance with ISA (UK and Ireland) 240.[19]

Non-Responses (Ref: Para. 12)

A18. Examples of alternative audit procedures the auditor may perform include:

- For accounts receivable balances – examining specific subsequent cash receipts, shipping documentation, and sales near the period-end.

- For accounts payable balances – examining subsequent cash disbursements or correspondence from third parties, and other records, such as goods received notes.

A19. The nature and extent of alternative audit procedures are affected by the account and assertion in question. A non-response to a confirmation request may indicate a previously unidentified risk of material misstatement. In such situations, the auditor may need to revise the assessed risk of material misstatement at the assertion level, and modify planned audit procedures, in accordance with ISA (UK and Ireland) 315.[20] For example, fewer responses to confirmation requests than anticipated, or a greater number of responses than anticipated, may indicate a previously unidentified fraud risk factor that requires evaluation in accordance with ISA (UK and Ireland) 240.[21]

When a Response to a Positive Confirmation Request Is Necessary to Obtain Sufficient Appropriate Audit Evidence (Ref. Para. 13)

A20. In certain circumstances, the auditor may identify an assessed risk of material misstatement at the assertion level for which a response to a positive confirmation request is necessary to obtain sufficient appropriate audit evidence. Such circumstances may include where:

- The information available to corroborate management's assertion(s) is only available outside the entity.

- Specific fraud risk factors, such as the risk of management override of controls, or the risk of collusion which can involve employee(s) and/or management, prevent the auditor from relying on evidence from the entity.

---

[18] ISA (UK and Ireland) 315, paragraph 31.
[19] ISA (UK and Ireland) 240, paragraph 24.
[20] ISA (UK and Ireland) 315, paragraph 31.
[21] ISA (UK and Ireland) 240, paragraph 24.

Exceptions (Ref: Para. 14)

A21. Exceptions noted in responses to confirmation requests may indicate misstatements or potential misstatements in the financial statements. When a misstatement is identified, the auditor is required by ISA (UK and Ireland) 240 to evaluate whether such misstatement is indicative of fraud.[22] Exceptions may provide a guide to the quality of responses from similar confirming parties or for similar accounts. Exceptions also may indicate a deficiency, or deficiencies, in the entity's internal control over financial reporting.

A22. Some exceptions do not represent misstatements. For example, the auditor may conclude that differences in responses to confirmation requests are due to timing, measurement, or clerical errors in the external confirmation procedures.

Negative Confirmations (Ref: Para. 15)

A23. The failure to receive a response to a negative confirmation request does not explicitly indicate receipt by the intended confirming party of the confirmation request or verification of the accuracy of the information contained in the request. Accordingly, a failure of a confirming party to respond to a negative confirmation request provides significantly less persuasive audit evidence than does a response to a positive confirmation request. Confirming parties also may be more likely to respond indicating their disagreement with a confirmation request when the information in the request is not in their favor, and less likely to respond otherwise. For example, holders of bank deposit accounts may be more likely to respond if they believe that the balance in their account is understated in the confirmation request, but may be less likely to respond when they believe the balance is overstated. Therefore, sending negative confirmation requests to holders of bank deposit accounts may be a useful procedure in considering whether such balances may be understated, but is unlikely to be effective if the auditor is seeking evidence regarding overstatement.

Evaluating the Evidence Obtained (Ref: Para. 16)

A24. When evaluating the results of individual external confirmation requests, the auditor may categorize such results as follows:

(a) A response by the appropriate confirming party indicating agreement with the information provided in the confirmation request, or providing requested information without exception;

(b) A response deemed unreliable;

(c) A non-response; or

(d) A response indicating an exception.

---

[22] ISA (UK and Ireland) 240, paragraph 35.

A25. The auditor's evaluation, when taken into account with other audit procedures the auditor may have performed, may assist the auditor in concluding whether sufficient appropriate audit evidence has been obtained or whether further audit evidence is necessary, as required by ISA (UK and Ireland) 330.[23]

---

[23] ISA (UK and Ireland) 330, paragraphs 26-27.

INTERNATIONAL STANDARD ON AUDITING (UK AND IRELAND) 510

INITIAL AUDIT ENGAGEMENTS—OPENING BALANCES

(Effective for audits of financial statements for periods ending on or after 15 December 2010)

CONTENTS

International Standard on Auditing (UK and Ireland) (ISA (UK and Ireland)) 510, "Initial Audit Engagements—Opening Balances" should be read in conjunction with ISA (UK and Ireland) 200, "Overall Objectives of the Independent Auditor and the Conduct of an Audit in Accordance with International Standards on Auditing (UK and Ireland)."

Introduction

Scope of this ISA (UK and Ireland)

1. This International Standard on Auditing (UK and Ireland) (ISA (UK and Ireland)) deals with the auditor's responsibilities relating to opening balances in an initial audit engagement. In addition to financial statement amounts, opening balances include matters requiring disclosure that existed at the beginning of the period, such as contingencies and commitments. When the financial statements include comparative financial information, the requirements and guidance in ISA (UK and Ireland) 710[1] also apply. ISA (UK and Ireland) 300[2] includes additional requirements and guidance regarding activities prior to starting an initial audit.

Effective Date

2. This ISA (UK and Ireland) is effective for audits of financial statements for periods ending on or after 15 December 2010.

Objective

3. In conducting an initial audit engagement, the objective of the auditor with respect to opening balances is to obtain sufficient appropriate audit evidence about whether:

    (a) Opening balances contain misstatements that materially affect the current period's financial statements; and

    (b) Appropriate accounting policies reflected in the opening balances have been consistently applied in the current period's financial statements, or changes thereto are appropriately accounted for and adequately presented and disclosed in accordance with the applicable financial reporting framework.

Definitions

4. For the purposes of the ISAs (UK and Ireland), the following terms have the meanings attributed below:

    (a) Initial audit engagement – An engagement in which either:

        (i) The financial statements for the prior period were not audited; or

        (ii) The financial statements for the prior period were audited by a predecessor auditor.

---

[1] ISA (UK and Ireland) 710, "Comparative Information—Corresponding Figures and Comparative Financial Statements."

[2] ISA 300 (UK and Ireland), "Planning an Audit of Financial Statements."

(b)　Opening balances – Those account balances that exist at the beginning of the period. Opening balances are based upon the closing balances of the prior period and reflect the effects of transactions and events of prior periods and accounting policies applied in the prior period. Opening balances also include matters requiring disclosure that existed at the beginning of the period, such as contingencies and commitments.

(c)　Predecessor auditor – The auditor from a different audit firm, who audited the financial statements of an entity in the prior period and who has been replaced by the current auditor.

Requirements

Audit Procedures

Opening Balances

5.　The auditor shall read the most recent financial statements, if any, and the predecessor auditor's report thereon, if any, for information relevant to opening balances, including disclosures.

6.　The auditor shall obtain sufficient appropriate audit evidence about whether the opening balances contain misstatements that materially affect the current period's financial statements by: (Ref: Para. A1–A2)

(a)　Determining whether the prior period's closing balances have been correctly brought forward to the current period or, when appropriate, have been restated;

(b)　Determining whether the opening balances reflect the application of appropriate accounting policies; and

(c)　Performing one or more of the following: (Ref: Para. A3–A7)

(i)　Where the prior year financial statements were audited, reviewing the predecessor auditor's working papers to obtain evidence regarding the opening balances;

(ii)　Evaluating whether audit procedures performed in the current period provide evidence relevant to the opening balances; or

(iii)　Performing specific audit procedures to obtain evidence regarding the opening balances.

7.　If the auditor obtains audit evidence that the opening balances contain misstatements that could materially affect the current period's financial statements, the auditor shall perform such additional audit procedures as are appropriate in the circumstances to determine the effect on the current period's financial statements. If the auditor concludes that such misstatements exist in the current period's financial statements, the auditor shall communicate the misstatements with the appropriate level of management and those charged with governance in accordance with ISA (UK and Ireland) 450.[3]

Consistency of Accounting Policies

8. The auditor shall obtain sufficient appropriate audit evidence about whether the accounting policies reflected in the opening balances have been consistently applied in the current period's financial statements, and whether changes in the accounting policies have been appropriately accounted for and adequately presented and disclosed in accordance with the applicable financial reporting framework.

Relevant Information in the Predecessor Auditor's Report

9. If the prior period's financial statements were audited by a predecessor auditor and there was a modification to the opinion, the auditor shall evaluate the effect of the matter giving rise to the modification in assessing the risks of material misstatement in the current period's financial statements in accordance with ISA (UK and Ireland) 315.[4]

Audit Conclusions and Reporting

Opening Balances

10. If the auditor is unable to obtain sufficient appropriate audit evidence regarding the opening balances, the auditor shall express a qualified opinion or disclaim an opinion on the financial statements, as appropriate, in accordance with ISA (UK and Ireland) 705.[5] (Ref: Para. A8)

11. If the auditor concludes that the opening balances contain a misstatement that materially affects the current period's financial statements, and the effect of the misstatement is not appropriately accounted for or not adequately presented or disclosed, the auditor shall express a qualified opinion or an adverse opinion, as appropriate, in accordance with ISA (UK and Ireland) 705.

Consistency of Accounting Policies

12. If the auditor concludes that:

    (a) the current period's accounting policies are not consistently applied in relation to opening balances in accordance with the applicable financial reporting framework; or

---

[3] ISA (UK and Ireland) 450, "Evaluation of Misstatements Identified during the Audit," paragraphs 8 and 12.

[4] ISA (UK and Ireland) 315, "Identifying and Assessing the Risks of Material Misstatement through Understanding the Entity and Its Environment."

[5] ISA (UK and Ireland) 705, "Modifications to the Opinion in the Independent Auditor's Report."

(b) a change in accounting policies is not appropriately accounted for or not adequately presented or disclosed in accordance with the applicable financial reporting framework,

the auditor shall express a qualified opinion or an adverse opinion as appropriate in accordance with ISA (UK and Ireland) 705.

Modification to the Opinion in the Predecessor Auditor's Report

13. If the predecessor auditor's opinion regarding the prior period's financial statements included a modification to the auditor's opinion that remains relevant and material to the current period's financial statements, the auditor shall modify the auditor's opinion on the current period's financial statements in accordance with ISA (UK and Ireland) 705 and ISA (UK and Ireland) 710. (Ref: Para. A9)

***

Application and Other Explanatory Material

Audit Procedures

Considerations Specific to Public Sector Entities (Ref: Para. 6)

A1. In the public sector, there may be legal or regulatory limitations on the information that the current auditor can obtain from a predecessor auditor. For example, if a public sector entity that has previously been audited by a statutorily appointed auditor (for example, an Auditor General, or other suitably qualified person appointed on behalf of the Auditor General) is privatized, the amount of access to working papers or other information that the statutorily appointed auditor can provide a newly-appointed auditor that is in the private sector may be constrained by privacy or secrecy laws or regulations. In situations where such communications are constrained, audit evidence may need to be obtained through other means and, if sufficient appropriate audit evidence cannot be obtained, consideration given to the effect on the auditor's opinion.

A2. If the statutorily appointed auditor outsources an audit of a public sector entity to a private sector audit firm, and the statutorily appointed auditor appoints an audit firm other than the firm that audited the financial statements of the public sector entity in the prior period, this is not usually regarded as a change in auditors for the statutorily appointed auditor. Depending on the nature of the outsourcing arrangement, however, the audit engagement may be considered an initial audit engagement from the perspective of the private sector auditor in fulfilling their responsibilities, and therefore this ISA (UK and Ireland) applies.

Opening Balances (Ref: Para. 6(c))

A3. The nature and extent of audit procedures necessary to obtain sufficient appropriate audit evidence regarding opening balances depend on such matters as:

- The accounting policies followed by the entity.

- The nature of the account balances, classes of transactions and disclosures and the risks of material misstatement in the current period's financial statements.

- The significance of the opening balances relative to the current period's financial statements.

- Whether the prior period's financial statements were audited and, if so, whether the predecessor auditor's opinion was modified.

A4. If the prior period's financial statements were audited by a predecessor auditor, the auditor may be able to obtain sufficient appropriate audit evidence regarding the opening balances by reviewing the predecessor auditor's working papers. Whether such a review provides sufficient appropriate audit evidence is influenced by the professional competence and independence of the predecessor auditor.

A5. Relevant ethical and professional requirements guide the current auditor's communications with the predecessor auditor.

A5-1. In the UK and Ireland the relevant ethical guidance on proposed communications with a predecessor auditor is provided by the ethical pronouncements relating to the work of auditors issued by the auditor's relevant professional body.

A6. For current assets and liabilities, some audit evidence about opening balances may be obtained as part of the current period's audit procedures. For example, the collection (payment) of opening accounts receivable (accounts payable) during the current period will provide some audit evidence of their existence, rights and obligations, completeness and valuation at the beginning of the period. In the case of inventories, however, the current period's audit procedures on the closing inventory balance provide little audit evidence regarding inventory on hand at the beginning of the period. Therefore, additional audit procedures may be necessary, and one or more of the following may provide sufficient appropriate audit evidence:

- Observing a current physical inventory count and reconciling it to the opening inventory quantities.

- Performing audit procedures on the valuation of the opening inventory items.

- Performing audit procedures on gross profit and cutoff.

A7. For non-current assets and liabilities, such as property plant and equipment, investments and long-term debt, some audit evidence may be obtained by examining the accounting records and other information underlying the opening balances. In certain cases, the auditor may be able to obtain some audit evidence regarding opening balances through confirmation with third parties, for example, for long-term debt and investments. In other cases, the auditor may need to carry out additional audit procedures.

Audit Conclusions and Reporting

Opening Balances (Ref: Para. 10)

A8. ISA (UK and Ireland) 705 establishes requirements and provides guidance on circumstances that may result in a modification to the auditor's opinion on the financial statements, the type of opinion appropriate in the circumstances, and the content of the auditor's report when the auditor's opinion is modified. The inability of the auditor to obtain sufficient appropriate audit evidence regarding opening balances may result in one of the following modifications to the opinion in the auditor's report:

(a) A qualified opinion or a disclaimer of opinion, as is appropriate in the circumstances; or

(b) Unless prohibited by law or regulation, an opinion which is qualified or disclaimed, as appropriate, regarding the results of operations, and cash flows, where relevant, and unmodified regarding financial position.

The Appendix includes illustrative auditors' reports.[5a]

Modification to the Opinion in the Predecessor Auditor's Report (Ref: Para. 13)

A9. In some situations, a modification to the predecessor auditor's opinion may not be relevant and material to the opinion on the current period's financial statements. This may be the case where, for example, there was a scope limitation in the prior period, but the matter giving rise to the scope limitation has been resolved in the current period.

[5a] The examples in the Appendix have not been tailored for the UK and Ireland. Illustrative auditor's reports tailored for use with audits conducted in accordance with ISAs (UK and Ireland) are given in the current versions of the APB Compendia Auditor's Report Bulletins.

Appendix

(Ref: Para. A8)

Illustrations of Auditors' Reports with Modified Opinions

The examples in the Appendix have not been tailored for the UK and Ireland. Illustrative auditor's reports tailored for use with audits conducted in accordance with ISAs (UK and Ireland) are given in the current versions of the APB Compendia Auditor's Report Bulletins.

Illustration 1:

Circumstances described in paragraph A8(a) include the following:

- **The auditor did not observe the counting of the physical inventory at the beginning of the current period and was unable to obtain sufficient appropriate audit evidence regarding the opening balances of inventory.**

- **The possible effects of the inability to obtain sufficient appropriate audit evidence regarding opening balances of inventory are deemed to be material but not pervasive to the entity's financial performance and cash flows.[6]**

- **The financial position at year end is fairly presented.**

- **In this particular jurisdiction, law and regulation prohibit the auditor from giving an opinion which is qualified regarding the financial performance and cash flows and unmodified regarding financial position.**

INDEPENDENT AUDITOR'S REPORT

[Appropriate Addressee]

Report on the Financial Statements[7]

We have audited the accompanying financial statements of ABC Company, which comprise the balance sheet as at December 31, 20X1, and the income statement, statement of changes in equity and cash flow statement for the year then ended, and a summary of significant accounting policies and other explanatory information.

---

[6] If the possible effects, in the auditor's judgment, are considered to be material and pervasive to the entity's financial performance and cash flows, the auditor would disclaim an opinion on the financial performance and cash flows.

[7] The sub-title "Report on the Financial Statements" is unnecessary in circumstances when the second sub-title "Report on Other Legal and Regulatory Requirements" is not applicable.

Management's[8] Responsibility for the Financial Statements

Management is responsible for the preparation and fair presentation of these financial statements in accordance with International Financial Reporting Standards,[9] and for such internal control as management determines is necessary to enable the preparation of financial statements that are free from material misstatement, whether due to fraud or error.

Auditor's Responsibility

Our responsibility is to express an opinion on these financial statements based on our audit. We conducted our audit in accordance with International Standards on Auditing. Those standards require that we comply with ethical requirements and plan and perform the audit to obtain reasonable assurance about whether the financial statements are free from material misstatement.

An audit involves performing procedures to obtain audit evidence about the amounts and disclosures in the financial statements. The procedures selected depend on the auditor's judgment, including the assessment of the risks of material misstatement of the financial statements, whether due to fraud or error. In making those risk assessments, the auditor considers internal control relevant to the entity's preparation and fair presentation[10] of the financial statements in order to design audit procedures that are appropriate in the circumstances, but not for the purpose of expressing an opinion on the effectiveness of the entity's internal control.[11] An audit also includes evaluating the appropriateness of accounting policies used and the reasonableness of accounting estimates made by management, as well as evaluating the overall presentation of the financial statements.

We believe that the audit evidence we have obtained is sufficient and appropriate to provide a basis for our qualified audit opinion.

Basis for Qualified Opinion

We were appointed as auditors of the company on June 30, 20X1 and thus did not observe the counting of the physical inventories at the beginning of the year. We were unable to satisfy ourselves by alternative means concerning inventory quantities held at December

---

[8] Or other term that is appropriate in the context of the legal framework in the particular jurisdiction.

[9] Where management's responsibility is to prepare financial statements that give a true and fair view, this may read: "Management is responsible for the preparation of financial statements that give a true and fair view in accordance with International Financial Reporting Standards, and for such ..."

[10] In the case of footnote 9, this may read: "In making those risk assessments, the auditor considers internal control relevant to the entity's preparation of financial statements that give a true and fair view in order to design audit procedures that are appropriate in the circumstances, but not for the purpose of expressing an opinion on the effectiveness of the entity's internal control."

[11] In circumstances when the auditor also has responsibility to express an opinion on the effectiveness of internal control in conjunction with the audit of the financial statements, this sentence would be worded as follows: "In making those risk assessments, the auditor considers internal control relevant to the entity's preparation and fair presentation of the financial statements in order to design audit procedures that are appropriate in the circumstances." In the case of footnote 9, this may read: "In making those risk assessments, the auditor considers internal control relevant to the entity's preparation of financial statements that give a true and fair view in order to design audit procedures that are appropriate in the circumstances."

31, 20X0. Since opening inventories enter into the determination of the financial performance and cash flows, we were unable to determine whether adjustments might have been necessary in respect of the profit for the year reported in the income statement and the net cash flows from operating activities reported in the cash flow statement.

Qualified Opinion

In our opinion, except for the possible effects of the matter described in the Basis for Qualified Opinion paragraph, the financial statements present fairly, in all material respects, (or *give a true and fair view of*) the financial position of ABC Company as at December 31, 20X1, and (*of*) its financial performance and its cash flows for the year then ended in accordance with International Financial Reporting Standards.

Other Matter

The financial statements of ABC Company for the year ended December 31, 20X0 were audited by another auditor who expressed an unmodified opinion on those statements on March 31, 20X1.

Report on Other Legal and Regulatory Requirements

[Form and content of this section of the auditor's report will vary depending on the nature of the auditor's other reporting responsibilities.]

[Auditor's signature]

[Date of the auditor's report]

[Auditor's address]

Illustration 2:

Circumstances described in paragraph A8(b) include the following:

- **The auditor did not observe the counting of the physical inventory at the beginning of the current period and was unable to obtain sufficient appropriate audit evidence regarding the opening balances of inventory.**

- **The possible effects of the inability to obtain sufficient appropriate audit evidence regarding opening balances of inventory are deemed to be material but not pervasive to the entity's financial performance and cash flows.[12]**

- **The financial position at year end is fairly presented.**

- **An opinion that is qualified regarding the financial performance and cash flows and unmodified regarding financial position is considered appropriate in the circumstances.**

INDEPENDENT AUDITOR'S REPORT

[Appropriate Addressee]

Report on the Financial Statements[13]

We have audited the accompanying financial statements of ABC Company, which comprise the balance sheet as at December 31, 20X1, and the income statement, statement of changes in equity and cash flow statement for the year then ended, and a summary of significant accounting policies and other explanatory information.

Management's[14] Responsibility for the Financial Statements

Management is responsible for the preparation and fair presentation of these financial statements in accordance with International Financial Reporting Standards,[15] and for such internal control as management determines is necessary to enable the preparation of financial statements that are free from material misstatement, whether due to fraud or error.

---

[12] If the possible effects, in the auditor's judgment, are considered to be material and pervasive to the entity's financial performance and cash flows, the auditor would disclaim the opinion on the financial performance and cash flows.

[13] The sub-title "Report on the Financial Statements" is unnecessary in circumstances when the second sub-title "Report on Other Legal and Regulatory Requirements" is not applicable.

[14] Or other term that is appropriate in the context of the legal framework in the particular jurisdiction.

[15] Where management's responsibility is to prepare financial statements that give a true and fair view, this may read: "Management is responsible for the preparation of financial statements that give a true and fair view in accordance with International Financial Reporting Standards, and for such ...."

Auditor's Responsibility

Our responsibility is to express an opinion on these financial statements based on our audit. We conducted our audit in accordance with International Standards on Auditing. Those standards require that we comply with ethical requirements and plan and perform the audit to obtain reasonable assurance about whether the financial statements are free from material misstatement.

An audit involves performing procedures to obtain audit evidence about the amounts and disclosures in the financial statements. The procedures selected depend on the auditor's judgment, including the assessment of the risks of material misstatement of the financial statements, whether due to fraud or error. In making those risk assessments, the auditor considers internal control relevant to the entity's preparation and fair presentation[16] of the financial statements in order to design audit procedures that are appropriate in the circumstances, but not for the purpose of expressing an opinion on the effectiveness of the entity's internal control.[17] An audit also includes evaluating the appropriateness of accounting policies used and the reasonableness of accounting estimates made by management, as well as evaluating the overall presentation of the financial statements.

We believe that the audit evidence we have obtained is sufficient and appropriate to provide a basis for our unmodified opinion on the financial position and our qualified audit opinion on the financial performance and cash flows.

Basis for Qualified Opinion on the Financial Performance and Cash Flows

We were appointed as auditors of the company on June 30, 20X1 and thus did not observe the counting of the physical inventories at the beginning of the year. We were unable to satisfy ourselves by alternative means concerning inventory quantities held at December 31, 20X0. Since opening inventories enter into the determination of the financial performance and cash flows, we were unable to determine whether adjustments might have been necessary in respect of the profit for the year reported in the income statement and the net cash flows from operating activities reported in the cash flow statement.

Qualified Opinion on the Financial Performance and Cash Flows

In our opinion, except for the possible effects of the matter described in the Basis for Qualified Opinion paragraph, the Income Statement and Cash Flow Statement present

---

[16] In the case of footnote 15, this may read: "In making those risk assessments, the auditor considers internal control relevant to the entity's preparation of financial statements that give a true and fair view in order to design audit procedures that are appropriate in the circumstances, but not for the purpose of expressing an opinion on the effectiveness of the entity's internal control."

[17] In circumstances when the auditor also has responsibility to express an opinion on the effectiveness of internal control in conjunction with the audit of the financial statements, this sentence would be worded as follows: "In making those risk assessments, the auditor considers internal control relevant to the entity's preparation and fair presentation of the financial statements in order to design audit procedures that are appropriate in the circumstances." In the case of footnote 15, this may read: "In making those risk assessments, the auditor considers internal control relevant to the entity's preparation of financial statements that give a true and fair view in order to design audit procedures that are appropriate in the circumstances."

fairly, in all material respects (or *give a true and fair view of*) the financial performance and cash flows of ABC Company for the year ended December 31, 20X1 in accordance with International Financial Reporting Standards.

Opinion on the financial position

In our opinion, the balance sheet presents fairly, in all material respects (or *gives a true and fair view of*) the financial position of ABC Company as at December 31, 20X1 in accordance with International Financial Reporting Standards.

Other Matter

The financial statements of ABC Company for the year ended December 31, 20X0 were audited by another auditor who expressed an unmodified opinion on those statements on March 31, 20X1.

Report on Other Legal and Regulatory Requirements

[Form and content of this section of the auditor's report will vary depending on the nature of the auditor's other reporting responsibilities.]

[Auditor's signature]

[Date of the auditor's report]

[Auditor's address]

INTERNATIONAL STANDARD ON AUDITING
(UK AND IRELAND) 520

ANALYTICAL PROCEDURES

(Effective for audits of financial statements for periods ending on or after 15 December 2010)

CONTENTS

International Standard on Auditing (UK and Ireland) (ISA (UK and Ireland)) 520, "Analytical Procedures" should be read in conjunction with ISA (UK and Ireland) 200, "Overall Objectives of the Independent Auditor and the Conduct of an Audit in Accordance with International Standards on Auditing (UK and Ireland)."

Introduction

Scope of this ISA (UK and Ireland)

1. This International Standard on Auditing (UK and Ireland) (ISA (UK and Ireland)) deals with the auditor's use of analytical procedures as substantive procedures ("substantive analytical procedures"). It also deals with the auditor's responsibility to perform analytical procedures near the end of the audit that assist the auditor when forming an overall conclusion on the financial statements. ISA (UK and Ireland) 315[1] deals with the use of analytical procedures as risk assessment procedures. ISA (UK and Ireland) 330 includes requirements and guidance regarding the nature, timing and extent of audit procedures in response to assessed risks; these audit procedures may include substantive analytical procedures.[2]

Effective Date

2. This ISA (UK and Ireland) is effective for audits of financial statements for periods ending on or after 15 December 2010.

Objectives

3. The objectives of the auditor are:

    (a) To obtain relevant and reliable audit evidence when using substantive analytical procedures; and

    (b) To design and perform analytical procedures near the end of the audit that assist the auditor when forming an overall conclusion as to whether the financial statements are consistent with the auditor's understanding of the entity.

Definition

4. For the purposes of the ISAs (UK and Ireland), the term "analytical procedures" means evaluations of financial information through analysis of plausible relationships among both financial and non-financial data. Analytical procedures also encompass such investigation as is necessary of identified fluctuations or relationships that are inconsistent with other relevant information or that differ from expected values by a significant amount. (Ref: Para. A1-A3)

---

[1] ISA (UK and Ireland) 315, "Identifying and Assessing the Risks of Material Misstatement through Understanding the Entity and Its Environment," paragraph 6(b).

[2] ISA (UK and Ireland) 330, "The Auditor's Reponses to Assessed Risks," paragraphs 6 and 18.

Requirements

Substantive Analytical Procedures

5. When designing and performing substantive analytical procedures, either alone or in combination with tests of details, as substantive procedures in accordance with ISA (UK and Ireland) 330,[3] the auditor shall: (Ref: Para. A4-A5)

   (a) Determine the suitability of particular substantive analytical procedures for given assertions, taking account of the assessed risks of material misstatement and tests of details, if any, for these assertions; (Ref: Para. A6-A11)

   (b) Evaluate the reliability of data from which the auditor's expectation of recorded amounts or ratios is developed, taking account of source, comparability, and nature and relevance of information available, and controls over preparation; (Ref: Para. A12-A14)

   (c) Develop an expectation of recorded amounts or ratios and evaluate whether the expectation is sufficiently precise to identify a misstatement that, individually or when aggregated with other misstatements, may cause the financial statements to be materially misstated; and (Ref: Para. A15)

   (d) Determine the amount of any difference of recorded amounts from expected values that is acceptable without further investigation as required by paragraph 7. (Ref: Para. A16)

Analytical Procedures that Assist When Forming an Overall Conclusion

6. The auditor shall design and perform analytical procedures near the end of the audit that assist the auditor when forming an overall conclusion as to whether the financial statements are consistent with the auditor's understanding of the entity. (Ref: Para. A17-A19)

Investigating Results of Analytical Procedures

7. If analytical procedures performed in accordance with this ISA (UK and Ireland) identify fluctuations or relationships that are inconsistent with other relevant information or that differ from expected values by a significant amount, the auditor shall investigate such differences by:

   (a) Inquiring of management and obtaining appropriate audit evidence relevant to management's responses; and

   (b) Performing other audit procedures as necessary in the circumstances. (Ref: Para. A20-A21)

---

[3] ISA (UK and Ireland) 330, paragraph 18.

***

Application and Other Explanatory Material

Definition of Analytical Procedures (Ref: Para. 4)

A1.   Analytical procedures include the consideration of comparisons of the entity's financial information with, for example:

- Comparable information for prior periods.

- Anticipated results of the entity, such as budgets or forecasts, or expectations of the auditor, such as an estimation of depreciation.

- Similar industry information, such as a comparison of the entity's ratio of sales to accounts receivable with industry averages or with other entities of comparable size in the same industry.

A2.   Analytical procedures also include consideration of relationships, for example:

- Among elements of financial information that would be expected to conform to a predictable pattern based on the entity's experience, such as gross margin percentages.

- Between financial information and relevant non-financial information, such as payroll costs to number of employees.

A3.   Various methods may be used to perform analytical procedures. These methods range from performing simple comparisons to performing complex analyses using advanced statistical techniques. Analytical procedures may be applied to consolidated financial statements, components and individual elements of information.

Substantive Analytical Procedures (Ref: Para. 5)

A4.   The auditor's substantive procedures at the assertion level may be tests of details, substantive analytical procedures, or a combination of both. The decision about which audit procedures to perform, including whether to use substantive analytical procedures, is based on the auditor's judgment about the expected effectiveness and efficiency of the available audit procedures to reduce audit risk at the assertion level to an acceptably low level.

A5.   The auditor may inquire of management as to the availability and reliability of information needed to apply substantive analytical procedures, and the results of any such analytical procedures performed by the entity. It may be effective to use analytical data prepared by management, provided the auditor is satisfied that such data is properly prepared.

Suitability of Particular Analytical Procedures for Given Assertions (Ref: Para. 5(a))

A6. Substantive analytical procedures are generally more applicable to large volumes of transactions that tend to be predictable over time. The application of planned analytical procedures is based on the expectation that relationships among data exist and continue in the absence of known conditions to the contrary. However, the suitability of a particular analytical procedure will depend upon the auditor's assessment of how effective it will be in detecting a misstatement that, individually or when aggregated with other misstatements, may cause the financial statements to be materially misstated.

A7. In some cases, even an unsophisticated predictive model may be effective as an analytical procedure. For example, where an entity has a known number of employees at fixed rates of pay throughout the period, it may be possible for the auditor to use this data to estimate the total payroll costs for the period with a high degree of accuracy, thereby providing audit evidence for a significant item in the financial statements and reducing the need to perform tests of details on the payroll. The use of widely recognized trade ratios (such as profit margins for different types of retail entities) can often be used effectively in substantive analytical procedures to provide evidence to support the reasonableness of recorded amounts.

A8. Different types of analytical procedures provide different levels of assurance. Analytical procedures involving, for example, the prediction of total rental income on a building divided into apartments, taking the rental rates, the number of apartments and vacancy rates into consideration, can provide persuasive evidence and may eliminate the need for further verification by means of tests of details, provided the elements are appropriately verified. In contrast, calculation and comparison of gross margin percentages as a means of confirming a revenue figure may provide less persuasive evidence, but may provide useful corroboration if used in combination with other audit procedures.

A9. The determination of the suitability of particular substantive analytical procedures is influenced by the nature of the assertion and the auditor's assessment of the risk of material misstatement. For example, if controls over sales order processing are deficient, the auditor may place more reliance on tests of details rather than on substantive analytical procedures for assertions related to receivables.

A10. Particular substantive analytical procedures may also be considered suitable when tests of details are performed on the same assertion. For example, when obtaining audit evidence regarding the valuation assertion for accounts receivable balances, the auditor may apply analytical procedures to an aging of customers' accounts in addition to performing tests of details on subsequent cash receipts to determine the collectability of the receivables.

Considerations Specific to Public Sector Entities

A11. The relationships between individual financial statement items traditionally considered in the audit of business entities may not always be relevant in the audit of governments or other non-business public sector entities; for example, in many public sector entities there may be little direct relationship between revenue and expenditure. In addition, because expenditure on the acquisition of assets may not be capitalized, there may be no relationship between expenditures on, for example, inventories and fixed assets and the amount of those assets reported in the financial statements. Also, industry data or statistics for comparative purposes may not be available in the public sector. However, other relationships may be relevant, for example, variations in the cost per kilometer of road construction or the number of vehicles acquired compared with vehicles retired.

The Reliability of the Data (Ref: Para. 5(b))

A12. The reliability of data is influenced by its source and nature and is dependent on the circumstances under which it is obtained. Accordingly, the following are relevant when determining whether data is reliable for purposes of designing substantive analytical procedures:

(a) Source of the information available. For example, information may be more reliable when it is obtained from independent sources outside the entity;[4]

(b) Comparability of the information available. For example, broad industry data may need to be supplemented to be comparable to that of an entity that produces and sells specialized products;

(c) Nature and relevance of the information available. For example, whether budgets have been established as results to be expected rather than as goals to be achieved; and

(d) Controls over the preparation of the information that are designed to ensure its completeness, accuracy and validity. For example, controls over the preparation, review and maintenance of budgets.

(e) Prior year knowledge and understanding. For example, the knowledge gained during previous audits, together with the auditor's understanding of the effectiveness of the accounting and internal control systems and the types of problems that in prior periods have given rise to accounting adjustments.

A13. The auditor may consider testing the operating effectiveness of controls, if any, over the entity's preparation of information used by the auditor in performing substantive analytical procedures in response to assessed risks. When such controls are effective, the auditor generally has greater confidence in the reliability of the information and, therefore, in the results of analytical procedures. The operating effectiveness of controls over non-financial information may often be tested in conjunction with other tests of controls. For example, in establishing controls over the processing of sales invoices, an entity may include controls over the recording of unit sales. In these circumstances, the auditor may test the operating effectiveness of controls over the recording of unit sales in conjunction with tests of the operating

---

[4] ISA (UK and Ireland) 500, "Audit Evidence," paragraph A31.

effectiveness of controls over the processing of sales invoices. Alternatively, the auditor may consider whether the information was subjected to audit testing. ISA (UK and Ireland) 500 establishes requirements and provides guidance in determining the audit procedures to be performed on the information to be used for substantive analytical procedures.[5]

A14. The matters discussed in paragraphs A12(a)-A12(d) are relevant irrespective of whether the auditor performs substantive analytical procedures on the entity's period end financial statements, or at an interim date and plans to perform substantive analytical procedures for the remaining period. ISA (UK and Ireland) 330 establishes requirements and provides guidance on substantive procedures performed at an interim date. [6]

Evaluation Whether the Expectation Is Sufficiently Precise (Ref: Para. 5(c))

A15. Matters relevant to the auditor's evaluation of whether the expectation can be developed sufficiently precisely to identify a misstatement that, when aggregated with other misstatements, may cause the financial statements to be materially misstated, include:

- The accuracy with which the expected results of substantive analytical procedures can be predicted. For example, the auditor may expect greater consistency in comparing gross profit margins from one period to another than in comparing discretionary expenses, such as research or advertising.

- The degree to which information can be disaggregated. For example, substantive analytical procedures may be more effective when applied to financial information on individual sections of an operation or to financial statements of components of a diversified entity, than when applied to the financial statements of the entity as a whole.

- The availability of the information, both financial and non-financial. For example, the auditor may consider whether financial information, such as budgets or forecasts, and non-financial information, such as the number of units produced or sold, is available to design substantive analytical procedures. If the information is available, the auditor may also consider the reliability of the information as discussed in paragraphs A12-A13 above.

Amount of Difference of Recorded Amounts from Expected Values that Is Acceptable (Ref: Para. 5(d))

A16. The auditor's determination of the amount of difference from the expectation that can be accepted without further investigation is influenced by materiality[7] and the consistency with the desired level of assurance, taking account of the possibility that a misstatement, individually or when aggregated with other misstatements, may

---

[5] ISA (UK and Ireland) 500, paragraph 10.
[6] ISA (UK and Ireland) 330, paragraphs 22-23.
[7] ISA (UK and Ireland) 320, "Materiality in Planning and Performing an Audit," paragraph A13.

cause the financial statements to be materially misstated. ISA (UK and Ireland) 330 requires the auditor to obtain more persuasive audit evidence the higher the auditor's assessment of risk.[8] Accordingly, as the assessed risk increases, the amount of difference considered acceptable without investigation decreases in order to achieve the desired level of persuasive evidence.[9]

Analytical Procedures that Assist When Forming an Overall Conclusion (Ref: Para. 6)

A17. The conclusions drawn from the results of analytical procedures designed and performed in accordance with paragraph 6 are intended to corroborate conclusions formed during the audit of individual components or elements of the financial statements. This assists the auditor to draw reasonable conclusions on which to base the auditor's opinion.

A17-1. Considerations when carrying out such procedures may include:

(a) Whether the financial statements adequately reflect the information and explanations previously obtained and conclusions previously reached during the course of the audit;

(b) Whether the procedures reveal any new factors which may affect the presentation of, or disclosures in, the financial statements;

(c) Whether analytical procedures applied when completing the audit, such as comparing the information in the financial statements with other pertinent data, produce results which assist in arriving at the overall conclusion as to whether the financial statements as a whole are consistent with the auditor's knowledge of the entity's business;

(d) Whether the presentation adopted in the financial statements may have been unduly influenced by the desire of those charged with governance to present matters in a favourable or unfavourable light; and

(e) The potential impact on the financial statements of the aggregate of uncorrected misstatements (including those arising from bias in making accounting estimates) identified during the course of the audit and the preceding period's audit, if any.

A18. The results of such analytical procedures may identify a previously unrecognized risk of material misstatement. In such circumstances, ISA (UK and Ireland) 315 requires the auditor to revise the auditor's assessment of the risks of material misstatement and modify the further planned audit procedures accordingly.[10]

---

[8] ISA (UK and Ireland) 330, paragraph 7(b).
[9] ISA (UK and Ireland) 330, paragraph A19.
[10] ISA (UK and Ireland) 315, paragraph 31.

A19. The analytical procedures performed in accordance with paragraph 6 may be similar to those that would be used as risk assessment procedures.

Investigating Results of Analytical Procedures (Ref: Para. 7)

A20. Audit evidence relevant to management's responses may be obtained by evaluating those responses taking into account the auditor's understanding of the entity and its environment, and with other audit evidence obtained during the course of the audit.

A21. The need to perform other audit procedures may arise when, for example, management is unable to provide an explanation, or the explanation, together with the audit evidence obtained relevant to management's response, is not considered adequate.

INTERNATIONAL STANDARD ON AUDITING (UK AND IRELAND) 530

AUDIT SAMPLING

(Effective for audits of financial statements for periods ending on or after 15 December 2010)

CONTENTS

International Standard on Auditing (UK and Ireland) (ISA (UK and Ireland)) 530, "Audit Sampling" should be read in conjunction with ISA 200 (UK and Ireland), "Overall Objectives of the Independent Auditor and the Conduct of an Audit in Accordance with International Standards on Auditing (UK and Ireland)."

Introduction

Scope of this ISA (UK and Ireland)

1. This International Standard on Auditing (UK and Ireland) (ISA (UK and Ireland)) applies when the auditor has decided to use audit sampling in performing audit procedures. It deals with the auditor's use of statistical and non-statistical sampling when designing and selecting the audit sample, performing tests of controls and tests of details, and evaluating the results from the sample.

2. This ISA (UK and Ireland) complements ISA (UK and Ireland) 500,[1] which deals with the auditor's responsibility to design and perform audit procedures to obtain sufficient appropriate audit evidence to be able to draw reasonable conclusions on which to base the auditor's opinion. ISA (UK and Ireland) 500 provides guidance on the means available to the auditor for selecting items for testing, of which audit sampling is one means.

Effective Date

3. This ISA (UK and Ireland) is effective for audits of financial statements for periods ending on or after 15 December 2010.

Objective

4. The objective of the auditor, when using audit sampling, is to provide a reasonable basis for the auditor to draw conclusions about the population from which the sample is selected.

Definitions

5. For purposes of the ISAs (UK and Ireland), the following terms have the meanings attributed below:

   (a) Audit sampling (sampling) – The application of audit procedures to less than 100% of items within a population of audit relevance such that all sampling units have a chance of selection in order to provide the auditor with a reasonable basis on which to draw conclusions about the entire population.

   (b) Population – The entire set of data from which a sample is selected and about which the auditor wishes to draw conclusions.

   (c) Sampling risk – The risk that the auditor's conclusion based on a sample may be different from the conclusion if the entire population were subjected to the same audit procedure. Sampling risk can lead to two types of erroneous conclusions:

---

[1] ISA (UK and Ireland) 500, "Audit Evidence."

(i) In the case of a test of controls, that controls are more effective than they actually are, or in the case of a test of details, that a material misstatement does not exist when in fact it does. The auditor is primarily concerned with this type of erroneous conclusion because it affects audit effectiveness and is more likely to lead to an inappropriate audit opinion.

(ii) In the case of a test of controls, that controls are less effective than they actually are, or in the case of a test of details, that a material misstatement exists when in fact it does not. This type of erroneous conclusion affects audit efficiency as it would usually lead to additional work to establish that initial conclusions were incorrect.

(d) Non-sampling risk – The risk that the auditor reaches an erroneous conclusion for any reason not related to sampling risk. (Ref: Para A1)

(e) Anomaly – A misstatement or deviation that is demonstrably not representative of misstatements or deviations in a population.

(f) Sampling unit – The individual items constituting a population. (Ref: Para A2)

(g) Statistical sampling – An approach to sampling that has the following characteristics:

(i) Random selection of the sample items; and

(ii) The use of probability theory to evaluate sample results, including measurement of sampling risk.

A sampling approach that does not have characteristics (i) and (ii) is considered non-statistical sampling.

(h) Stratification – The process of dividing a population into sub-populations, each of which is a group of sampling units which have similar characteristics (often monetary value).

(i) Tolerable misstatement – A monetary amount set by the auditor in respect of which the auditor seeks to obtain an appropriate level of assurance that the monetary amount set by the auditor is not exceeded by the actual misstatement in the population. (Ref: Para A3)

(j) Tolerable rate of deviation – A rate of deviation from prescribed internal control procedures set by the auditor in respect of which the auditor seeks to obtain an appropriate level of assurance that the rate of deviation set by the auditor is not exceeded by the actual rate of deviation in the population.

Requirements

Sample Design, Size and Selection of Items for Testing

6. When designing an audit sample, the auditor shall consider the purpose of the audit procedure and the characteristics of the population from which the sample will be drawn. (Ref: Para. A4-A9)

7. The auditor shall determine a sample size sufficient to reduce sampling risk to an acceptably low level. (Ref: Para. A10-A11)

8. The auditor shall select items for the sample in such a way that each sampling unit in the population has a chance of selection. (Ref: Para. A12-A13)

Performing Audit Procedures

9. The auditor shall perform audit procedures, appropriate to the purpose, on each item selected.

10. If the audit procedure is not applicable to the selected item, the auditor shall perform the procedure on a replacement item. (Ref: Para. A14)

11. If the auditor is unable to apply the designed audit procedures, or suitable alternative procedures, to a selected item, the auditor shall treat that item as a deviation from the prescribed control, in the case of tests of controls, or a misstatement, in the case of tests of details. (Ref: Para. A15-A16)

Nature and Cause of Deviations and Misstatements

12. The auditor shall investigate the nature and cause of any deviations or misstatements identified, and evaluate their possible effect on the purpose of the audit procedure and on other areas of the audit. (Ref: Para. A17)

13. In the extremely rare circumstances when the auditor considers a misstatement or deviation discovered in a sample to be an anomaly, the auditor shall obtain a high degree of certainty that such misstatement or deviation is not representative of the population. The auditor shall obtain this degree of certainty by performing additional audit procedures to obtain sufficient appropriate audit evidence that the misstatement or deviation does not affect the remainder of the population.

Projecting Misstatements

14. For tests of details, the auditor shall project misstatements found in the sample to the population. (Ref: Para. A18-A20)

Evaluating Results of Audit Sampling

15. The auditor shall evaluate:

(a) The results of the sample; and (Ref: Para. A21-A22)

(b) Whether the use of audit sampling has provided a reasonable basis for conclusions about the population that has been tested. (Ref: Para. A23)

***

Application and Other Explanatory Material

Definitions

Non-Sampling Risk (Ref: Para. 5(d))

A1. Examples of non-sampling risk include use of inappropriate audit procedures, or misinterpretation of audit evidence and failure to recognize a misstatement or deviation.

Sampling Unit (Ref: Para. 5(f))

A2. The sampling units might be physical items (for example, checks listed on deposit slips, credit entries on bank statements, sales invoices or debtors' balances) or monetary units.

Tolerable Misstatement (Ref: Para. 5(i))

A3. When designing a sample, the auditor determines tolerable misstatement in order to address the risk that the aggregate of individually immaterial misstatements may cause the financial statements to be materially misstated and provide a margin for possible undetected misstatements. Tolerable misstatement is the application of performance materiality, as defined in ISA (UK and Ireland) 320,[2] to a particular sampling procedure. Tolerable misstatement may be the same amount or an amount lower than performance materiality.

Sample Design, Size and Selection of Items for Testing

Sample Design (Ref: Para. 6)

A4. Audit sampling enables the auditor to obtain and evaluate audit evidence about some characteristic of the items selected in order to form or assist in forming a conclusion concerning the population from which the sample is drawn. Audit sampling can be applied using either non-statistical or statistical sampling approaches.

A5. When designing an audit sample, the auditor's consideration includes the specific purpose to be achieved and the combination of audit procedures that is likely to best achieve that purpose. Consideration of the nature of the audit evidence sought and

---

[2] ISA (UK and Ireland) 320, "Materiality in Planning and Performing an Audit," paragraph 9.

possible deviation or misstatement conditions or other characteristics relating to that audit evidence will assist the auditor in defining what constitutes a deviation or misstatement and what population to use for sampling. In fulfilling the requirement of paragraph 10 of ISA (UK and Ireland) 500, when performing audit sampling, the auditor performs audit procedures to obtain evidence that the population from which the audit sample is drawn is complete.

A6. The auditor's consideration of the purpose of the audit procedure, as required by paragraph 6, includes a clear understanding of what constitutes a deviation or misstatement so that all, and only, those conditions that are relevant to the purpose of the audit procedure are included in the evaluation of deviations or projection of misstatements. For example, in a test of details relating to the existence of accounts receivable, such as confirmation, payments made by the customer before the confirmation date but received shortly after that date by the client, are not considered a misstatement. Also, a misposting between customer accounts does not affect the total accounts receivable balance. Therefore, it may not be appropriate to consider this a misstatement in evaluating the sample results of this particular audit procedure, even though it may have an important effect on other areas of the audit, such as the assessment of the risk of fraud or the adequacy of the allowance for doubtful accounts.

A7. In considering the characteristics of a population, for tests of controls, the auditor makes an assessment of the expected rate of deviation based on the auditor's understanding of the relevant controls or on the examination of a small number of items from the population. This assessment is made in order to design an audit sample and to determine sample size. For example, if the expected rate of deviation is unacceptably high, the auditor will normally decide not to perform tests of controls. Similarly, for tests of details, the auditor makes an assessment of the expected misstatement in the population. If the expected misstatement is high, 100% examination or use of a large sample size may be appropriate when performing tests of details.

A8. In considering the characteristics of the population from which the sample will be drawn, the auditor may determine that stratification or value-weighted selection is appropriate. Appendix 1 provides further discussion on stratification and value-weighted selection.

A9. The decision whether to use a statistical or non-statistical sampling approach is a matter for the auditor's judgment; however, sample size is not a valid criterion to distinguish between statistical and non-statistical approaches.

Sample Size (Ref: Para. 7)

A10. The level of sampling risk that the auditor is willing to accept affects the sample size required. The lower the risk the auditor is willing to accept, the greater the sample size will need to be.

A11. The sample size can be determined by the application of a statistically-based formula or through the exercise of professional judgment. Appendices 2 and 3 indicate the influences that various factors typically have on the determination of sample size. When circumstances are similar, the effect on sample size of factors such as those identified in Appendices 2 and 3 will be similar regardless of whether a statistical or non-statistical approach is chosen.

Selection of Items for Testing (Ref: Para. 8)

A12. With statistical sampling, sample items are selected in a way that each sampling unit has a known probability of being selected. With non-statistical sampling, judgment is used to select sample items. Because the purpose of sampling is to provide a reasonable basis for the auditor to draw conclusions about the population from which the sample is selected, it is important that the auditor selects a representative sample, so that bias is avoided, by choosing sample items which have characteristics typical of the population.

A13. The principal methods of selecting samples are the use of random selection, systematic selection and haphazard selection. Each of these methods is discussed in Appendix 4.

Performing Audit Procedures (Ref: Para. 10-11)

A14. An example of when it is necessary to perform the procedure on a replacement item is when a voided check is selected while testing for evidence of payment authorization. If the auditor is satisfied that the check has been properly voided such that it does not constitute a deviation, an appropriately chosen replacement is examined.

A15. An example of when the auditor is unable to apply the designed audit procedures to a selected item is when documentation relating to that item has been lost.

A16. An example of a suitable alternative procedure might be the examination of subsequent cash receipts together with evidence of their source and the items they are intended to settle when no reply has been received in response to a positive confirmation request.

Nature and Cause of Deviations and Misstatements (Ref: Para. 12)

A17. In analyzing the deviations and misstatements identified, the auditor may observe that many have a common feature, for example, type of transaction, location, product line or period of time. In such circumstances, the auditor may decide to identify all items in the population that possess the common feature, and extend audit procedures to those items. In addition, such deviations or misstatements may be intentional, and may indicate the possibility of fraud.

Projecting Misstatements (Ref: Para. 14)

A18. The auditor is required to project misstatements for the population to obtain a broad view of the scale of misstatement but this projection may not be sufficient to determine an amount to be recorded.

A19. When a misstatement has been established as an anomaly, it may be excluded when projecting misstatements to the population. However, the effect of any such misstatement, if uncorrected, still needs to be considered in addition to the projection of the non-anomalous misstatements.

A20. For tests of controls, no explicit projection of deviations is necessary since the sample deviation rate is also the projected deviation rate for the population as a whole. ISA (UK and Ireland) 330[3] provides guidance when deviations from controls upon which the auditor intends to rely are detected.

Evaluating Results of Audit Sampling (Ref: Para. 15)

A21. For tests of controls, an unexpectedly high sample deviation rate may lead to an increase in the assessed risk of material misstatement, unless further audit evidence substantiating the initial assessment is obtained. For tests of details, an unexpectedly high misstatement amount in a sample may cause the auditor to believe that a class of transactions or account balance is materially misstated, in the absence of further audit evidence that no material misstatement exists.

A22. In the case of tests of details, the projected misstatement plus anomalous misstatement, if any, is the auditor's best estimate of misstatement in the population. When the projected misstatement plus anomalous misstatement, if any, exceeds tolerable misstatement, the sample does not provide a reasonable basis for conclusions about the population that has been tested. The closer the projected misstatement plus anomalous misstatement is to tolerable misstatement, the more likely that actual misstatement in the population may exceed tolerable misstatement. Also if the projected misstatement is greater than the auditor's expectations of misstatement used to determine the sample size, the auditor may conclude that there is an unacceptable sampling risk that the actual misstatement in the population exceeds the tolerable misstatement. Considering the results of other audit procedures helps the auditor to assess the risk that actual misstatement in the population exceeds tolerable misstatement, and the risk may be reduced if additional audit evidence is obtained.

A23. If the auditor concludes that audit sampling has not provided a reasonable basis for conclusions about the population that has been tested, the auditor may:

- Request management to investigate misstatements that have been identified and the potential for further misstatements and to make any necessary adjustments; or

- Tailor the nature, timing and extent of those further audit procedures to best achieve the required assurance. For example, in the case of tests of controls, the auditor might extend the sample size, test an alternative control or modify related substantive procedures.

---

[3] ISA (UK and Ireland) 330, "The Auditor's Responses to Assessed Risks," paragraph 17.

Appendix 1

(Ref: Para. A8)

Stratification and Value-Weighted Selection

In considering the characteristics of the population from which the sample will be drawn, the auditor may determine that stratification or value-weighted selection is appropriate. This Appendix provides guidance to the auditor on the use of stratification and value-weighted sampling techniques.

Stratification

1. Audit efficiency may be improved if the auditor stratifies a population by dividing it into discrete sub-populations which have an identifying characteristic. The objective of stratification is to reduce the variability of items within each stratum and therefore allow sample size to be reduced without increasing sampling risk.

2. When performing tests of details, the population is often stratified by monetary value. This allows greater audit effort to be directed to the larger value items, as these items may contain the greatest potential misstatement in terms of overstatement. Similarly, a population may be stratified according to a particular characteristic that indicates a higher risk of misstatement, for example, when testing the allowance for doubtful accounts in the valuation of accounts receivable, balances may be stratified by age.

3. The results of audit procedures applied to a sample of items within a stratum can only be projected to the items that make up that stratum. To draw a conclusion on the entire population, the auditor will need to consider the risk of material misstatement in relation to whatever other strata make up the entire population. For example, 20% of the items in a population may make up 90% of the value of an account balance. The auditor may decide to examine a sample of these items. The auditor evaluates the results of this sample and reaches a conclusion on the 90% of value separately from the remaining 10% (on which a further sample or other means of gathering audit evidence will be used, or which may be considered immaterial).

4. If a class of transactions or account balance has been divided into strata, the misstatement is projected for each stratum separately. Projected misstatements for each stratum are then combined when considering the possible effect of misstatements on the total class of transactions or account balance.

Value-Weighted Selection

5. When performing tests of details it may be efficient to identify the sampling unit as the individual monetary units that make up the population. Having selected specific monetary units from within the population, for example, the accounts receivable balance, the auditor may then examine the particular items, for example, individual balances, that contain those monetary units. One benefit of this approach to defining the sampling unit is that audit effort is directed to the larger value items because they

have a greater chance of selection, and can result in smaller sample sizes. This approach may be used in conjunction with the systematic method of sample selection (described in Appendix 4) and is most efficient when selecting items using random selection.

Examples of Factors Influencing Sample Size for Tests of Controls

The following are factors that the auditor may consider when determining the sample size for tests of controls. These factors, which need to be considered together, assume the auditor does not modify the nature or timing of tests of controls or otherwise modify the approach to substantive procedures in response to assessed risks.

FACTOR	EFFECT ON SAMPLE SIZE	
1. An increase in the extent to which the auditor's risk assessment takes into account relevant controls	Increase	The more assurance the auditor intends to obtain from the operating effectiveness of controls, the lower the auditor's assessment of the risk of material misstatement will be, and the larger the sample size will need to be. When the auditor's assessment of the risk of material misstatement at the assertion level includes an expectation of the operating effectiveness of controls, the auditor is required to perform tests of controls. Other things being equal, the greater the reliance the auditor places on the operating effectiveness of controls in the risk assessment, the greater is the extent of the auditor's tests of controls (and therefore, the sample size is increased).
2. An increase in the tolerable rate of deviation	Decrease	The lower the tolerable rate of deviation, the larger the sample size needs to be.

FACTOR	EFFECT ON SAMPLE SIZE	
3. An increase in the expected rate of deviation of the population to be tested	Increase	The higher the expected rate of deviation, the larger the sample size needs to be so that the auditor is in a position to make a reasonable estimate of the actual rate of deviation. Factors relevant to the auditor's consideration of the expected rate of deviation include the auditor's understanding of the business (in particular, risk assessment procedures undertaken to obtain an understanding of internal control), changes in personnel or in internal control, the results of audit procedures applied in prior periods and the results of other audit procedures. High expected control deviation rates ordinarily warrant little, if any, reduction of the assessed risk of material misstatement.
4. An increase in the auditor's desired level of assurance that the tolerable rate of deviation is not exceeded by the actual rate of deviation in the population	Increase	The greater the level of assurance that the auditor desires that the results of the sample are in fact indicative of the actual incidence of deviation in the population, the larger the sample size needs to be.
5. An increase in the number of sampling units in the population	Negligible effect	For large populations, the actual size of the population has little, if any, effect on sample size. For small populations however, audit sampling may not be as efficient as alternative means of obtaining sufficient appropriate audit evidence.

Appendix 3

(Ref: Para. A11)

Examples of Factors Influencing Sample Size for Tests of Details

The following are factors that the auditor may consider when determining the sample size for tests of details. These factors, which need to be considered together, assume the auditor does not modify the approach to tests of controls or otherwise modify the nature or timing of substantive procedures in response to the assessed risks.

FACTOR	EFFECT ON SAMPLE SIZE	
1. An increase in the auditor's assessment of the risk of material misstatement	Increase	The higher the auditor's assessment of the risk of material misstatement, the larger the sample size needs to be. The auditor's assessment of the risk of material misstatement is affected by inherent risk and control risk. For example, if the auditor does not perform tests of controls, the auditor's risk assessment cannot be reduced for the effective operation of internal controls with respect to the particular assertion. Therefore, in order to reduce audit risk to an acceptably low level, the auditor needs a low detection risk and will rely more on substantive procedures. The more audit evidence that is obtained from tests of details (that is, the lower the detection risk), the larger the sample size will need to be.
2. An increase in the use of other substantive procedures directed at the same assertion	Decrease	The more the auditor is relying on other substantive procedures (tests of details or substantive analytical procedures) to reduce to an acceptable level the detection risk regarding a particular population, the less assurance the auditor will require from sampling and, therefore, the smaller the sample size can be.

FACTOR	EFFECT ON SAMPLE SIZE	
3. An increase in the auditor's desired level of assurance that tolerable misstatement is not exceeded by actual misstatement in the population	Increase	The greater the level of assurance that the auditor requires that the results of the sample are in fact indicative of the actual amount of misstatement in the population, the larger the sample size needs to be.
4. An increase in tolerable misstatement	Decrease	The lower the tolerable misstatement, the larger the sample size needs to be.
5. An increase in the amount of misstatement the auditor expects to find in the population	Increase	The greater the amount of misstatement the auditor expects to find in the population, the larger the sample size needs to be in order to make a reasonable estimate of the actual amount of misstatement in the population. Factors relevant to the auditor's consideration of the expected misstatement amount include the extent to which item values are determined subjectively, the results of risk assessment procedures, the results of tests of control, the results of audit procedures applied in prior periods, and the results of other substantive procedures.
6. Stratification of the population when appropriate	Decrease	When there is a wide range (variability) in the monetary size of items in the population, it may be useful to stratify the population. When a population can be appropriately stratified, the aggregate of the sample sizes from the strata generally will be less than the sample size that would have been required to attain a given level of sampling risk, had one sample been drawn from the whole population.

FACTOR	EFFECT ON SAMPLE SIZE	
7. The number of sampling units in the population	Negligible effect	For large populations, the actual size of the population has little, if any, effect on sample size. Thus, for small populations, audit sampling is often not as efficient as alternative means of obtaining sufficient appropriate audit evidence. (However, when using monetary unit sampling, an increase in the monetary value of the population increases sample size, unless this is offset by a proportional increase in materiality for the financial statements as a whole [and, if applicable, materiality level or levels for particular classes of transactions, account balances or disclosures].)

Appendix 4

(Ref: Para. A13)

Sample Selection Methods

There are many methods of selecting samples. The principal methods are as follows:

(a) Random selection (applied through random number generators, for example, random number tables).

(b) Systematic selection, in which the number of sampling units in the population is divided by the sample size to give a sampling interval, for example 50, and having determined a starting point within the first 50, each 50th sampling unit thereafter is selected. Although the starting point may be determined haphazardly, the sample is more likely to be truly random if it is determined by use of a computerized random number generator or random number tables. When using systematic selection, the auditor would need to determine that sampling units within the population are not structured in such a way that the sampling interval corresponds with a particular pattern in the population.

(c) Monetary Unit Sampling is a type of value-weighted selection (as described in Appendix 1) in which sample size, selection and evaluation results in a conclusion in monetary amounts.

(d) Haphazard selection, in which the auditor selects the sample without following a structured technique. Although no structured technique is used, the auditor would nonetheless avoid any conscious bias or predictability (for example, avoiding difficult to locate items, or always choosing or avoiding the first or last entries on a page) and thus attempt to ensure that all items in the population have a chance of selection. Haphazard selection is not appropriate when using statistical sampling.

(e) Block selection involves selection of a block(s) of contiguous items from within the population. Block selection cannot ordinarily be used in audit sampling because most populations are structured such that items in a sequence can be expected to have similar characteristics to each other, but different characteristics from items elsewhere in the population. Although in some circumstances it may be an appropriate audit procedure to examine a block of items, it would rarely be an appropriate sample selection technique when the auditor intends to draw valid inferences about the entire population based on the sample.

INTERNATIONAL STANDARD ON AUDITING (UK AND IRELAND) 540

AUDITING ACCOUNTING ESTIMATES, INCLUDING FAIR VALUE ACCOUNTING ESTIMATES, AND RELATED DISCLOSURES

(Effective for audits of financial statements for periods ending on or after 15 December 2010)

CONTENTS

International Standard on Auditing (UK and Ireland) (ISA (UK and Ireland)) 540, "Auditing Accounting Estimates, Including Fair Value Accounting Estimates, and Related Disclosures" should be read in conjunction with ISA (UK and Ireland) 200, "Overall Objectives of the Independent Auditor and the Conduct of an Audit in Accordance with International Standards on Auditing (UK and Ireland)."

Introduction

Scope of this ISA (UK and Ireland)

1. This International Standard on Auditing (UK and Ireland) (ISA (UK and Ireland)) deals with the auditor's responsibilities relating to accounting estimates, including fair value accounting estimates, and related disclosures in an audit of financial statements. Specifically, it expands on how ISA (UK and Ireland) 315[1] and ISA (UK and Ireland) 330[2] and other relevant ISAs (UK and Ireland) are to be applied in relation to accounting estimates. It also includes requirements and guidance on misstatements of individual accounting estimates, and indicators of possible management bias.

Nature of Accounting Estimates

2. Some financial statement items cannot be measured precisely, but can only be estimated. For purposes of this ISA (UK and Ireland), such financial statement items are referred to as accounting estimates. The nature and reliability of information available to management to support the making of an accounting estimate varies widely, which thereby affects the degree of estimation uncertainty associated with accounting estimates. The degree of estimation uncertainty affects, in turn, the risks of material misstatement of accounting estimates, including their susceptibility to unintentional or intentional management bias. (Ref: Para. A1-A11)

3. The measurement objective of accounting estimates can vary depending on the applicable financial reporting framework and the financial item being reported. The measurement objective for some accounting estimates is to forecast the outcome of one or more transactions, events or conditions giving rise to the need for the accounting estimate. For other accounting estimates, including many fair value accounting estimates, the measurement objective is different, and is expressed in terms of the value of a current transaction or financial statement item based on conditions prevalent at the measurement date, such as estimated market price for a particular type of asset or liability. For example, the applicable financial reporting framework may require fair value measurement based on an assumed hypothetical current transaction between knowledgeable, willing parties (sometimes referred to as "marketplace participants" or equivalent) in an arm's length transaction, rather than the settlement of a transaction at some past or future date.[3]

4. A difference between the outcome of an accounting estimate and the amount originally recognized or disclosed in the financial statements does not necessarily represent a misstatement of the financial statements. This is particularly the case for fair value accounting estimates, as any observed outcome is invariably affected by events or conditions subsequent to the date at which the measurement is estimated for purposes of the financial statements.

---

[1] ISA (UK and Ireland) 315, "Identifying and Assessing the Risks of Material Misstatement through Understanding the Entity and Its Environment."
[2] ISA (UK and Ireland) 330, "The Auditor's Responses to Assessed Risks."
[3] Different definitions of fair value may exist among financial reporting frameworks.

Effective Date

5. This ISA (UK and Ireland) is effective for audits of financial statements for periods ending on or after 15 December 2010.

Objective

6. The objective of the auditor is to obtain sufficient appropriate audit evidence about whether:

(a) accounting estimates, including fair value accounting estimates, in the financial statements, whether recognized or disclosed, are reasonable; and

(b) related disclosures in the financial statements are adequate,

in the context of the applicable financial reporting framework.

Definitions

7. For purposes of the ISAs (UK and Ireland), the following terms have the meanings attributed below:

(a) Accounting estimate – An approximation of a monetary amount in the absence of a precise means of measurement. This term is used for an amount measured at fair value where there is estimation uncertainty, as well as for other amounts that require estimation. Where this ISA (UK and Ireland) addresses only accounting estimates involving measurement at fair value, the term "fair value accounting estimates" is used.

(b) Auditor's point estimate or auditor's range – The amount, or range of amounts, respectively, derived from audit evidence for use in evaluating management's point estimate.

(c) Estimation uncertainty – The susceptibility of an accounting estimate and related disclosures to an inherent lack of precision in its measurement.

(d) Management bias – A lack of neutrality by management in the preparation of information.

(e) Management's point estimate – The amount selected by management for recognition or disclosure in the financial statements as an accounting estimate.

(f) Outcome of an accounting estimate – The actual monetary amount which results from the resolution of the underlying transaction(s), event(s) or condition(s) addressed by the accounting estimate.

Requirements

Risk Assessment Procedures and Related Activities

8. When performing risk assessment procedures and related activities to obtain an understanding of the entity and its environment, including the entity's internal control, as required by ISA (UK and Ireland) 315,[4] the auditor shall obtain an understanding of the following in order to provide a basis for the identification and assessment of the risks of material misstatement for accounting estimates: (Ref: Para. A12)

   (a) The requirements of the applicable financial reporting framework relevant to accounting estimates, including related disclosures. (Ref: Para. A13-A15)

   (b) How management identifies those transactions, events and conditions that may give rise to the need for accounting estimates to be recognized or disclosed in the financial statements. In obtaining this understanding, the auditor shall make inquiries of management about changes in circumstances that may give rise to new, or the need to revise existing, accounting estimates. (Ref: Para. A16-A21)

   (c) How management makes the accounting estimates, and an understanding of the data on which they are based, including: (Ref: Para. A22-A23)

      (i) The method, including where applicable the model, used in making the accounting estimate; (Ref: Para. A24-A26)

      (ii) Relevant controls; (Ref: Para. A27-A28)

      (iii) Whether management has used an expert; (Ref: Para. A29-A30)

      (iv) The assumptions underlying the accounting estimates; (Ref: Para. A31-A36)

      (v) Whether there has been or ought to have been a change from the prior period in the methods for making the accounting estimates, and if so, why; and (Ref: Para. A37)

      (vi) Whether and, if so, how management has assessed the effect of estimation uncertainty. (Ref: Para. A38)

9. The auditor shall review the outcome of accounting estimates included in the prior period financial statements, or, where applicable, their subsequent re-estimation for the purpose of the current period. The nature and extent of the auditor's review takes account of the nature of the accounting estimates, and whether the information obtained from the review would be relevant to identifying and assessing risks of material misstatement of accounting estimates made in the current period financial statements. However, the review is not intended to call into question the judgments

---

[4] ISA (UK and Ireland) 315, paragraphs 5-6 and 11-12.

made in the prior periods that were based on information available at the time. (Ref: Para. A39-A44)

Identifying and Assessing the Risks of Material Misstatement

10.   In identifying and assessing the risks of material misstatement, as required by ISA (UK and Ireland) 315,[5] the auditor shall evaluate the degree of estimation uncertainty associated with an accounting estimate. (Ref: Para. A45-A46)

11.   The auditor shall determine whether, in the auditor's judgment, any of those accounting estimates that have been identified as having high estimation uncertainty give rise to significant risks. (Ref: Para. A47-A51)

Responses to the Assessed Risks of Material Misstatement

12.   Based on the assessed risks of material misstatement, the auditor shall determine: (Ref: Para. A52)

    (a)   Whether management has appropriately applied the requirements of the applicable financial reporting framework relevant to the accounting estimate; and (Ref: Para. A53-A56)

    (b)   Whether the methods for making the accounting estimates are appropriate and have been applied consistently, and whether changes, if any, in accounting estimates or in the method for making them from the prior period are appropriate in the circumstances. (Ref: Para. A57-A58)

13.   In responding to the assessed risks of material misstatement, as required by ISA (UK and Ireland) 330,[6] the auditor shall undertake one or more of the following, taking account of the nature of the accounting estimate: (Ref: Para. A59-A61)

    (a)   Determine whether events occurring up to the date of the auditor's report provide audit evidence regarding the accounting estimate. (Ref: Para. A62-A67)

    (b)   Test how management made the accounting estimate and the data on which it is based. In doing so, the auditor shall evaluate whether: (Ref: Para. A68-A70)

        (i)   The method of measurement used is appropriate in the circumstances; and (Ref: Para. A71-A76)

        (ii)   The assumptions used by management are reasonable in light of the measurement objectives of the applicable financial reporting framework. (Ref: Para. A77-A83)

---

[5]   ISA (UK and Ireland) 315, paragraph 25.
[6]   ISA (UK and Ireland) 330, paragraph 5.

(c)   Test the operating effectiveness of the controls over how management made the accounting estimate, together with appropriate substantive procedures. (Ref: Para. A84-A86)

(d)   Develop a point estimate or a range to evaluate management's point estimate. For this purpose: (Ref: Para. A87-A91)

      (i)   If the auditor uses assumptions or methods that differ from management's, the auditor shall obtain an understanding of management's assumptions or methods sufficient to establish that the auditor's point estimate or range takes into account relevant variables and to evaluate any significant differences from management's point estimate. (Ref: Para. A92)

      (ii)   If the auditor concludes that it is appropriate to use a range, the auditor shall narrow the range, based on audit evidence available, until all outcomes within the range are considered reasonable. (Ref: Para. A93-A95)

14.   In determining the matters identified in paragraph 12 or in responding to the assessed risks of material misstatement in accordance with paragraph 13, the auditor shall consider whether specialized skills or knowledge in relation to one or more aspects of the accounting estimates are required in order to obtain sufficient appropriate audit evidence. (Ref: Para. A96-A101)

Further Substantive Procedures to Respond to Significant Risks

Estimation Uncertainty

15.   For accounting estimates that give rise to significant risks, in addition to other substantive procedures performed to meet the requirements of ISA (UK and Ireland) 330,[7] the auditor shall evaluate the following: (Ref: Para. A102)

(a)   How management has considered alternative assumptions or outcomes, and why it has rejected them, or how management has otherwise addressed estimation uncertainty in making the accounting estimate. (Ref: Para. A103-A106)

(b)   Whether the significant assumptions used by management are reasonable. (Ref: Para. A107-A109)

(c)   Where relevant to the reasonableness of the significant assumptions used by management or the appropriate application of the applicable financial reporting framework, management's intent to carry out specific courses of action and its ability to do so. (Ref: Para. A110)

---

[7]   ISA (UK and Ireland) 330, paragraph 18.

16.   If, in the auditor's judgment, management has not adequately addressed the effects of estimation uncertainty on the accounting estimates that give rise to significant risks, the auditor shall, if considered necessary, develop a range with which to evaluate the reasonableness of the accounting estimate. (Ref: Para. A111-A112)

Recognition and Measurement Criteria

17.   For accounting estimates that give rise to significant risks, the auditor shall obtain sufficient appropriate audit evidence about whether:

(a)   management's decision to recognize, or to not recognize, the accounting estimates in the financial statements; and (Ref: Para. A113-A114)

(b)   the selected measurement basis for the accounting estimates, (Ref: Para. A115)

are in accordance with the requirements of the applicable financial reporting framework.

Evaluating the Reasonableness of the Accounting Estimates, and Determining Misstatements

18.   The auditor shall evaluate, based on the audit evidence, whether the accounting estimates in the financial statements are either reasonable in the context of the applicable financial reporting framework, or are misstated. (Ref: Para. A116-A119)

Disclosures Related to Accounting Estimates

19.   The auditor shall obtain sufficient appropriate audit evidence about whether the disclosures in the financial statements related to accounting estimates are in accordance with the requirements of the applicable financial reporting framework. (Ref: Para. A120-A121)

20.   For accounting estimates that give rise to significant risks, the auditor shall also evaluate the adequacy of the disclosure of their estimation uncertainty in the financial statements in the context of the applicable financial reporting framework. (Ref: Para. A122-A123)

Indicators of Possible Management Bias

21.   The auditor shall review the judgments and decisions made by management in the making of accounting estimates to identify whether there are indicators of possible management bias. Indicators of possible management bias do not themselves constitute misstatements for the purposes of drawing conclusions on the reasonableness of individual accounting estimates. (Ref: Para. A124-A125)

Written Representations

22.   The auditor shall obtain written representations from management and, where appropriate, those charged with governance whether they believe significant

assumptions used in making accounting estimates are reasonable. (Ref: Para. A126-A127)

Documentation

23.   The auditor shall include in the audit documentation:[8]

   (a)   The basis for the auditor's conclusions about the reasonableness of accounting estimates and their disclosure that give rise to significant risks; and

   (b)   Indicators of possible management bias, if any. (Ref: Para. A128)

***

Application and Other Explanatory Material

Nature of Accounting Estimates (Ref: Para. 2)

A1.   Because of the uncertainties inherent in business activities, some financial statement items can only be estimated. Further, the specific characteristics of an asset, liability or component of equity, or the basis of or method of measurement prescribed by the financial reporting framework, may give rise to the need to estimate a financial statement item. Some financial reporting frameworks prescribe specific methods of measurement and the disclosures that are required to be made in the financial statements, while other financial reporting frameworks are less specific. The Appendix to this ISA (UK and Ireland) discusses fair value measurements and disclosures under different financial reporting frameworks.

A2.   Some accounting estimates involve relatively low estimation uncertainty and may give rise to lower risks of material misstatements, for example:

   •   Accounting estimates arising in entities that engage in business activities that are not complex.

   •   Accounting estimates that are frequently made and updated because they relate to routine transactions.

   •   Accounting estimates derived from data that is readily available, such as published interest rate data or exchange-traded prices of securities. Such data may be referred to as "observable" in the context of a fair value accounting estimate.

   •   Fair value accounting estimates where the method of measurement prescribed by the applicable financial reporting framework is simple and applied easily to the asset or liability requiring measurement at fair value.

---

[8]   ISA (UK and Ireland) 230, "Audit Documentation," paragraphs 8-11, and paragraph A6.

- Fair value accounting estimates where the model used to measure the accounting estimate is well-known or generally accepted, provided that the assumptions or inputs to the model are observable.

A3. For some accounting estimates, however, there may be relatively high estimation uncertainty, particularly where they are based on significant assumptions, for example:

- Accounting estimates relating to the outcome of litigation.

- Fair value accounting estimates for derivative financial instruments not publicly traded.

- Fair value accounting estimates for which a highly specialized entity-developed model is used or for which there are assumptions or inputs that cannot be observed in the marketplace.

A4. The degree of estimation uncertainty varies based on the nature of the accounting estimate, the extent to which there is a generally accepted method or model used to make the accounting estimate, and the subjectivity of the assumptions used to make the accounting estimate. In some cases, estimation uncertainty associated with an accounting estimate may be so great that the recognition criteria in the applicable financial reporting framework are not met and the accounting estimate cannot be made.

A5. Not all financial statement items requiring measurement at fair value, involve estimation uncertainty. For example, this may be the case for some financial statement items where there is an active and open market that provides readily available and reliable information on the prices at which actual exchanges occur, in which case the existence of published price quotations ordinarily is the best audit evidence of fair value. However, estimation uncertainty may exist even when the valuation method and data are well defined. For example, valuation of securities quoted on an active and open market at the listed market price may require adjustment if the holding is significant in relation to the market or is subject to restrictions in marketability. In addition, general economic circumstances prevailing at the time, for example, illiquidity in a particular market, may impact estimation uncertainty.

A6. Additional examples of situations where accounting estimates, other than fair value accounting estimates, may be required include:

- Allowance for doubtful accounts.

- Inventory obsolescence.

- Warranty obligations.

- Depreciation method or asset useful life.

- Provision against the carrying amount of an investment where there is uncertainty regarding its recoverability.

- Outcome of long term contracts.

- Costs arising from litigation settlements and judgments.

A7. Additional examples of situations where fair value accounting estimates may be required include:

- Complex financial instruments, which are not traded in an active and open market.

- Share-based payments.

- Property or equipment held for disposal.

- Certain assets or liabilities acquired in a business combination, including goodwill and intangible assets.

- Transactions involving the exchange of assets or liabilities between independent parties without monetary consideration, for example, a non-monetary exchange of plant facilities in different lines of business.

A8. Estimation involves judgments based on information available when the financial statements are prepared. For many accounting estimates, these include making assumptions about matters that are uncertain at the time of estimation. The auditor is not responsible for predicting future conditions, transactions or events that, if known at the time of the audit, might have significantly affected management's actions or the assumptions used by management.

Management Bias

A9. Financial reporting frameworks often call for neutrality, that is, freedom from bias. Accounting estimates are imprecise, however, and can be influenced by management judgment. Such judgment may involve unintentional or intentional management bias (for example, as a result of motivation to achieve a desired result). The susceptibility of an accounting estimate to management bias increases with the subjectivity involved in making it. Unintentional management bias and the potential for intentional management bias are inherent in subjective decisions that are often required in making an accounting estimate. For continuing audits, indicators of possible management bias identified during the audit of the preceding periods influence the planning and risk identification and assessment activities of the auditor in the current period.

A10. Management bias can be difficult to detect at an account level. It may only be identified when considered in the aggregate of groups of accounting estimates or all accounting estimates, or when observed over a number of accounting periods. Although some form of management bias is inherent in subjective decisions, in making such judgments there may be no intention by management to mislead the users of financial statements. Where, however, there is intention to mislead, management bias is fraudulent in nature.

Considerations Specific to Public Sector Entities

A11. Public sector entities may have significant holdings of specialized assets for which there are no readily available and reliable sources of information for purposes of measurement at fair value or other current value bases, or a combination of both. Often specialized assets held do not generate cash flows and do not have an active market. Measurement at fair value therefore ordinarily requires estimation and may be complex, and in some rare cases may not be possible at all.

Risk Assessment Procedures and Related Activities (Ref: Para. 8)

A12. The risk assessment procedures and related activities required by paragraph 8 of this ISA (UK and Ireland) assist the auditor in developing an expectation of the nature and type of accounting estimates that an entity may have. The auditor's primary consideration is whether the understanding that has been obtained is sufficient to identify and assess the risks of material misstatement in relation to accounting estimates, and to plan the nature, timing and extent of further audit procedures.

Obtaining an Understanding of the Requirements of the Applicable Financial Reporting Framework (Ref: Para. 8(a))

A13. Obtaining an understanding of the requirements of the applicable financial reporting framework assists the auditor in determining whether it, for example:

- Prescribes certain conditions for the recognition,[9] or methods for the measurement, of accounting estimates.

- Specifies certain conditions that permit or require measurement at a fair value, for example, by referring to management's intentions to carry out certain courses of action with respect to an asset or liability.

- Specifies required or permitted disclosures.

Obtaining this understanding also provides the auditor with a basis for discussion with management about how management has applied those requirements relevant to the accounting estimate, and the auditor's determination of whether they have been applied appropriately.

A14. Financial reporting frameworks may provide guidance for management on determining point estimates where alternatives exist. Some financial reporting

---

[9] Most financial reporting frameworks require incorporation in the balance sheet or income statement of items that satisfy their criteria for recognition. Disclosure of accounting policies or adding notes to the financial statements does not rectify a failure to recognize such items, including accounting estimates.

frameworks, for example, require that the point estimate selected be the alternative that reflects management's judgment of the most likely outcome.[10] Others may require, for example, use of a discounted probability-weighted expected value. In some cases, management may be able to make a point estimate directly. In other cases, management may be able to make a reliable point estimate only after considering alternative assumptions or outcomes from which it is able to determine a point estimate.

A15. Financial reporting frameworks may require the disclosure of information concerning the significant assumptions to which the accounting estimate is particularly sensitive. Furthermore, where there is a high degree of estimation uncertainty, some financial reporting frameworks do not permit an accounting estimate to be recognized in the financial statements, but certain disclosures may be required in the notes to the financial statements.

Obtaining an Understanding of How Management Identifies the Need for Accounting Estimates (Ref: Para. 8(b))

A16. The preparation of the financial statements requires management to determine whether a transaction, event or condition gives rise to the need to make an accounting estimate, and that all necessary accounting estimates have been recognized, measured and disclosed in the financial statements in accordance with the applicable financial reporting framework.

A17. Management's identification of transactions, events and conditions that give rise to the need for accounting estimates is likely to be based on:

- Management's knowledge of the entity's business and the industry in which it operates.

- Management's knowledge of the implementation of business strategies in the current period.

- Where applicable, management's cumulative experience of preparing the entity's financial statements in prior periods.

In such cases, the auditor may obtain an understanding of how management identifies the need for accounting estimates primarily through inquiry of management. In other cases, where management's process is more structured, for example, when management has a formal risk management function, the auditor may perform risk assessment procedures directed at the methods and practices followed by management for periodically reviewing the circumstances that give rise to the accounting estimates and re-estimating the accounting estimates as necessary. The completeness of accounting estimates is often an important consideration of the auditor, particularly accounting estimates relating to liabilities.

---

[10] Different financial reporting frameworks may use different terminology to describe point estimates determined in this way.

A18. The auditor's understanding of the entity and its environment obtained during the performance of risk assessment procedures, together with other audit evidence obtained during the course of the audit, assist the auditor in identifying circumstances, or changes in circumstances, that may give rise to the need for an accounting estimate.

A19. Inquiries of management about changes in circumstances may include, for example, inquiries about whether:

- The entity has engaged in new types of transactions that may give rise to accounting estimates.

- Terms of transactions that gave rise to accounting estimates have changed.

- Accounting policies relating to accounting estimates have changed, as a result of changes to the requirements of the applicable financial reporting framework or otherwise.

- Regulatory or other changes outside the control of management have occurred that may require management to revise, or make new, accounting estimates.

- New conditions or events have occurred that may give rise to the need for new or revised accounting estimates.

A20. During the audit, the auditor may identify transactions, events and conditions that give rise to the need for accounting estimates that management failed to identify. ISA (UK and Ireland) 315 deals with circumstances where the auditor identifies risks of material misstatement that management failed to identify, including determining whether there is a significant deficiency in internal control with regard to the entity's risk assessment processes.[11]

Considerations Specific to Smaller Entities

A21. Obtaining this understanding for smaller entities is often less complex as their business activities are often limited and transactions are less complex. Further, often a single person, for example the owner-manager, identifies the need to make an accounting estimate and the auditor may focus inquiries accordingly.

Obtaining an Understanding of How Management Makes the Accounting Estimates (Ref: Para. 8(c))

A22. The preparation of the financial statements also requires management to establish financial reporting processes for making accounting estimates, including adequate internal control. Such processes include the following:

---

[11] ISA (UK and Ireland) 315, paragraph 16.

- Selecting appropriate accounting policies and prescribing estimation processes, including appropriate estimation or valuation methods, including, where applicable, models.

- Developing or identifying relevant data and assumptions that affect accounting estimates.

- Periodically reviewing the circumstances that give rise to the accounting estimates and re-estimating the accounting estimates as necessary.

A23. Matters that the auditor may consider in obtaining an understanding of how management makes the accounting estimates include, for example:

- The types of accounts or transactions to which the accounting estimates relate (for example, whether the accounting estimates arise from the recording of routine and recurring transactions or whether they arise from non-recurring or unusual transactions).

- Whether and, if so, how management has used recognized measurement techniques for making particular accounting estimates.

- Whether the accounting estimates were made based on data available at an interim date and, if so, whether and how management has taken into account the effect of events, transactions and changes in circumstances occurring between that date and the period end.

Method of Measurement, Including the Use of Models (Ref: Para. 8(c)(i))

A24. In some cases, the applicable financial reporting framework may prescribe the method of measurement for an accounting estimate, for example, a particular model that is to be used in measuring a fair value estimate. In many cases, however, the applicable financial reporting framework does not prescribe the method of measurement, or may specify alternative methods for measurement.

A25. When the applicable financial reporting framework does not prescribe a particular method to be used in the circumstances, matters that the auditor may consider in obtaining an understanding of the method or, where applicable the model, used to make accounting estimates include, for example:

- How management considered the nature of the asset or liability being estimated when selecting a particular method.

- Whether the entity operates in a particular business, industry or environment in which there are methods commonly used to make the particular type of accounting estimate.

A26. There may be greater risks of material misstatement, for example, in cases when management has internally developed a model to be used to make the accounting estimate or is departing from a method commonly used in a particular industry or environment.

Relevant Controls (Ref: Para. 8(c)(ii))

A27. Matters that the auditor may consider in obtaining an understanding of relevant controls include, for example, the experience and competence of those who make the accounting estimates, and controls related to:

- How management determines the completeness, relevance and accuracy of the data used to develop accounting estimates.

- The review and approval of accounting estimates, including the assumptions or inputs used in their development, by appropriate levels of management and, where appropriate, those charged with governance.

- The segregation of duties between those committing the entity to the underlying transactions and those responsible for making the accounting estimates, including whether the assignment of responsibilities appropriately takes account of the nature of the entity and its products or services (for example, in the case of a large financial institution, relevant segregation of duties may include an independent function responsible for estimation and validation of fair value pricing of the entity's proprietary financial products staffed by individuals whose remuneration is not tied to such products).

A28. Other controls may be relevant to making the accounting estimates depending on the circumstances. For example, if the entity uses specific models for making accounting estimates, management may put into place specific policies and procedures around such models. Relevant controls may include, for example, those established over:

- The design and development, or selection, of a particular model for a particular purpose.

- The use of the model.

- The maintenance and periodic validation of the integrity of the model.

Management's Use of Experts (Ref: Para. 8(c)(iii))

A29. Management may have, or the entity may employ individuals with, the experience and competence necessary to make the required point estimates. In some cases, however, management may need to engage an expert to make, or assist in making, them. This need may arise because of, for example:

- The specialized nature of the matter requiring estimation, for example, the measurement of mineral or hydrocarbon reserves in extractive industries.

- The technical nature of the models required to meet the relevant requirements of the applicable financial reporting framework, as may be the case in certain measurements at fair value.

- The unusual or infrequent nature of the condition, transaction or event requiring an accounting estimate.

Considerations specific to smaller entities

A30. In smaller entities, the circumstances requiring an accounting estimate often are such that the owner-manager is capable of making the required point estimate. In some cases, however, an expert will be needed. Discussion with the owner-manager early in the audit process about the nature of any accounting estimates, the completeness of the required accounting estimates, and the adequacy of the estimating process may assist the owner-manager in determining the need to use an expert.

Assumptions (Ref: Para. 8(c)(iv))

A31. Assumptions are integral components of accounting estimates. Matters that the auditor may consider in obtaining an understanding of the assumptions underlying the accounting estimates include, for example:

- The nature of the assumptions, including which of the assumptions are likely to be significant assumptions.

- How management assesses whether the assumptions are relevant and complete (that is, that all relevant variables have been taken into account).

- Where applicable, how management determines that the assumptions used are internally consistent.

- Whether the assumptions relate to matters within the control of management (for example, assumptions about the maintenance programs that may affect the estimation of an asset's useful life), and how they conform to the entity's business plans and the external environment, or to matters that are outside its control (for example, assumptions about interest rates, mortality rates, potential judicial or regulatory actions, or the variability and the timing of future cash flows).

- The nature and extent of documentation, if any, supporting the assumptions.

Assumptions may be made or identified by an expert to assist management in making the accounting estimates. Such assumptions, when used by management, become management's assumptions.

A32. In some cases, assumptions may be referred to as inputs, for example, where management uses a model to make an accounting estimate, though the term inputs may also be used to refer to the underlying data to which specific assumptions are applied.

A33. Management may support assumptions with different types of information drawn from internal and external sources, the relevance and reliability of which will vary. In some cases, an assumption may be reliably based on applicable information from either external sources (for example, published interest rate or other statistical data) or internal sources (for example, historical information or previous conditions experienced by the entity). In other cases, an assumption may be more subjective, for example, where the entity has no experience or external sources from which to draw.

A34. In the case of fair value accounting estimates, assumptions reflect, or are consistent with, what knowledgeable, willing arm's length parties (sometimes referred to as "marketplace participants" or equivalent) would use in determining fair value when exchanging an asset or settling a liability. Specific assumptions will also vary with the characteristics of the asset or liability being valued, the valuation method used (for example, a market approach, or an income approach) and the requirements of the applicable financial reporting framework.

A35. With respect to fair value accounting estimates, assumptions or inputs vary in terms of their source and bases, as follows:

(a) Those that reflect what marketplace participants would use in pricing an asset or liability developed based on market data obtained from sources independent of the reporting entity (sometimes referred to as "observable inputs" or equivalent).

(b) Those that reflect the entity's own judgments about what assumptions marketplace participants would use in pricing the asset or liability developed based on the best information available in the circumstances (sometimes referred to as "unobservable inputs" or equivalent).

In practice, however, the distinction between (a) and (b) is not always apparent. Further, it may be necessary for management to select from a number of different assumptions used by different marketplace participants.

A36. The extent of subjectivity, such as whether an assumption or input is observable, influences the degree of estimation uncertainty and thereby the auditor's assessment of the risks of material misstatement for a particular accounting estimate.

Changes in Methods for Making Accounting Estimates (Ref: Para. 8(c)(v))

A37. In evaluating how management makes the accounting estimates, the auditor is required to understand whether there has been or ought to have been a change from the prior period in the methods for making the accounting estimates. A specific estimation method may need to be changed in response to changes in the environment or circumstances affecting the entity or in the requirements of the applicable financial reporting framework. If management has changed the method for making an accounting estimate, it is important that management can demonstrate that the new method is more appropriate, or is itself a response to such changes. For example, if management changes the basis of making an accounting estimate from a mark-to-market approach to using a model, the auditor challenges whether management's assumptions about the marketplace are reasonable in light of economic circumstances.

Estimation Uncertainty (Ref: Para. 8(c)(vi))

A38. Matters that the auditor may consider in obtaining an understanding of whether and, if so, how management has assessed the effect of estimation uncertainty include, for example:

- Whether and, if so, how management has considered alternative assumptions or outcomes by, for example, performing a sensitivity analysis to determine the effect of changes in the assumptions on an accounting estimate.

- How management determines the accounting estimate when analysis indicates a number of outcome scenarios.

- Whether management monitors the outcome of accounting estimates made in the prior period, and whether management has appropriately responded to the outcome of that monitoring procedure.

Reviewing Prior Period Accounting Estimates (Ref: Para. 9)

A39. The outcome of an accounting estimate will often differ from the accounting estimate recognized in the prior period financial statements. By performing risk assessment procedures to identify and understand the reasons for such differences, the auditor may obtain:

- Information regarding the effectiveness of management's prior period estimation process, from which the auditor can judge the likely effectiveness of management's current process.

- Audit evidence that is pertinent to the re-estimation, in the current period, of prior period accounting estimates.

- Audit evidence of matters, such as estimation uncertainty, that may be required to be disclosed in the financial statements.

A40. The review of prior period accounting estimates may also assist the auditor, in the current period, in identifying circumstances or conditions that increase the susceptibility of accounting estimates to, or indicate the presence of, possible management bias. The auditor's professional skepticism assists in identifying such circumstances or conditions and in determining the nature, timing and extent of further audit procedures.

A41. A retrospective review of management judgments and assumptions related to significant accounting estimates is also required by ISA (UK and Ireland) 240.[12] That review is conducted as part of the requirement for the auditor to design and perform procedures to review accounting estimates for biases that could represent a risk of material misstatement due to fraud, in response to the risks of management override of controls. As a practical matter, the auditor's review of prior period accounting estimates as a risk assessment procedure in accordance with this ISA (UK and Ireland) may be carried out in conjunction with the review required by ISA (UK and Ireland) 240.

A42. The auditor may judge that a more detailed review is required for those accounting estimates that were identified during the prior period audit as having high estimation uncertainty, or for those accounting estimates that have changed significantly from the prior period. On the other hand, for example, for accounting estimates that arise from the recording of routine and recurring transactions, the auditor may judge that the application of analytical procedures as risk assessment procedures is sufficient for purposes of the review.

A43. For fair value accounting estimates and other accounting estimates based on current conditions at the measurement date, more variation may exist between the fair value amount recognized in the prior period financial statements and the outcome or the amount re-estimated for the purpose of the current period. This is because the measurement objective for such accounting estimates deals with perceptions about value at a point in time, which may change significantly and rapidly as the environment in which the entity operates changes. The auditor may therefore focus the review on obtaining information that would be relevant to identifying and assessing risks of material misstatement. For example, in some cases obtaining an understanding of changes in marketplace participant assumptions which affected the outcome of a prior period fair value accounting estimate may be unlikely to provide relevant information for audit purposes. If so, then the auditor's consideration of the outcome of prior period fair value accounting estimates may be directed more towards understanding the effectiveness of management's prior estimation process, that is, management's track record, from which the auditor can judge the likely effectiveness of management's current process.

A44. A difference between the outcome of an accounting estimate and the amount recognized in the prior period financial statements does not necessarily represent a misstatement of the prior period financial statements. However, it may do so if, for example, the difference arises from information that was available to management when the prior period's financial statements were finalized, or that could reasonably be expected to have been obtained and taken into account in the preparation of those financial statements. Many financial reporting frameworks contain guidance on distinguishing between changes in accounting estimates that constitute misstatements and changes that do not, and the accounting treatment required to be followed.

---

[12] ISA (UK and Ireland) 240, "The Auditor's Responsibilities Relating to Fraud in an Audit of Financial Statements," paragraph 32(b)(ii).

Identifying and Assessing the Risks of Material Misstatement

Estimation Uncertainty (Ref: Para. 10)

A45. The degree of estimation uncertainty associated with an accounting estimate may be influenced by factors such as:

- The extent to which the accounting estimate depends on judgment.

- The sensitivity of the accounting estimate to changes in assumptions.

- The existence of recognized measurement techniques that may mitigate the estimation uncertainty (though the subjectivity of the assumptions used as inputs may nevertheless give rise to estimation uncertainty).

- The length of the forecast period, and the relevance of data drawn from past events to forecast future events.

- The availability of reliable data from external sources.

- The extent to which the accounting estimate is based on observable or unobservable inputs.

The degree of estimation uncertainty associated with an accounting estimate may influence the estimate's susceptibility to bias.

A46. Matters that the auditor considers in assessing the risks of material misstatement may also include:

- The actual or expected magnitude of an accounting estimate.

- The recorded amount of the accounting estimate (that is, management's point estimate) in relation to the amount expected by the auditor to be recorded.

- Whether management has used an expert in making the accounting estimate.

- The outcome of the review of prior period accounting estimates.

High Estimation Uncertainty and Significant Risks (Ref: Para. 11)

A47. Examples of accounting estimates that may have high estimation uncertainty include the following:

- Accounting estimates that are highly dependent upon judgment, for example, judgments about the outcome of pending litigation or the amount and timing of future cash flows dependent on uncertain events many years in the future.

- Accounting estimates that are not calculated using recognized measurement techniques.

- Accounting estimates where the results of the auditor's review of similar accounting estimates made in the prior period financial statements indicate a substantial difference between the original accounting estimate and the actual outcome.

- Fair value accounting estimates for which a highly specialized entity-developed model is used or for which there are no observable inputs.

A48. A seemingly immaterial accounting estimate may have the potential to result in a material misstatement due to the estimation uncertainty associated with the estimation; that is, the size of the amount recognized or disclosed in the financial statements for an accounting estimate may not be an indicator of its estimation uncertainty.

A49. In some circumstances, the estimation uncertainty is so high that a reasonable accounting estimate cannot be made. The applicable financial reporting framework may, therefore, preclude recognition of the item in the financial statements, or its measurement at fair value. In such cases, the significant risks relate not only to whether an accounting estimate should be recognized, or whether it should be measured at fair value, but also to the adequacy of the disclosures. With respect to such accounting estimates, the applicable financial reporting framework may require disclosure of the accounting estimates and the high estimation uncertainty associated with them (see paragraphs A120-A123).

A50. If the auditor determines that an accounting estimate gives rise to a significant risk, the auditor is required to obtain an understanding of the entity's controls, including control activities.[13]

A51. In some cases, the estimation uncertainty of an accounting estimate may cast significant doubt about the entity's ability to continue as a going concern. ISA (UK and Ireland) 570[14] establishes requirements and provides guidance in such circumstances.

Responses to the Assessed Risks of Material Misstatement (Ref: Para. 12)

A52. ISA (UK and Ireland) 330 requires the auditor to design and perform audit procedures whose nature, timing and extent are responsive to the assessed risks of material misstatement in relation to accounting estimates at both the financial statement and assertion levels.[15] Paragraphs A53-A115 focus on specific responses at the assertion level only.

---

[13] ISA (UK and Ireland) 315, paragraph 29.
[14] ISA (UK and Ireland) 570, "Going Concern."
[15] ISA (UK and Ireland) 330, paragraphs 5-6.

Application of the Requirements of the Applicable Financial Reporting Framework (Ref: Para. 12(a))

A53. Many financial reporting frameworks prescribe certain conditions for the recognition of accounting estimates and specify the methods for making them and required disclosures. Such requirements may be complex and require the application of judgment. Based on the understanding obtained in performing risk assessment procedures, the requirements of the applicable financial reporting framework that may be susceptible to misapplication or differing interpretations become the focus of the auditor's attention.

A54. Determining whether management has appropriately applied the requirements of the applicable financial reporting framework is based, in part, on the auditor's understanding of the entity and its environment. For example, the measurement of the fair value of some items, such as intangible assets acquired in a business combination, may involve special considerations that are affected by the nature of the entity and its operations.

A55. In some situations, additional audit procedures, such as the inspection by the auditor of the current physical condition of an asset, may be necessary to determine whether management has appropriately applied the requirements of the applicable financial reporting framework.

A56. The application of the requirements of the applicable financial reporting framework requires management to consider changes in the environment or circumstances that affect the entity. For example, the introduction of an active market for a particular class of asset or liability may indicate that the use of discounted cash flows to estimate the fair value of such asset or liability is no longer appropriate.

Consistency in Methods and Basis for Changes (Ref: Para. 12(b))

A57. The auditor's consideration of a change in an accounting estimate, or in the method for making it from the prior period, is important because a change that is not based on a change in circumstances or new information is considered arbitrary. Arbitrary changes in an accounting estimate result in inconsistent financial statements over time and may give rise to a financial statement misstatement or be an indicator of possible management bias.

A58. Management often is able to demonstrate good reason for a change in an accounting estimate or the method for making an accounting estimate from one period to another based on a change in circumstances. What constitutes a good reason, and the adequacy of support for management's contention that there has been a change in circumstances that warrants a change in an accounting estimate or the method for making an accounting estimate, are matters of judgment.

Responses to the Assessed Risks of Material Misstatements (Ref: Para. 13)

A59. The auditor's decision as to which response, individually or in combination, in paragraph 13 to undertake to respond to the risks of material misstatement may be influenced by such matters as:

- The nature of the accounting estimate, including whether it arises from routine or non routine transactions.

- Whether the procedure(s) is expected to effectively provide the auditor with sufficient appropriate audit evidence.

- The assessed risk of material misstatement, including whether the assessed risk is a significant risk.

A60. For example, when evaluating the reasonableness of the allowance for doubtful accounts, an effective procedure for the auditor may be to review subsequent cash collections in combination with other procedures. Where the estimation uncertainty associated with an accounting estimate is high, for example, an accounting estimate based on a proprietary model for which there are unobservable inputs, it may be that a combination of the responses to assessed risks in paragraph 13 is necessary in order to obtain sufficient appropriate audit evidence.

A61. Additional guidance explaining the circumstances in which each of the responses may be appropriate is provided in paragraphs A62-A95.

Events Occurring Up to the Date of the Auditor's Report (Ref: Para. 13(a))

A62. Determining whether events occurring up to the date of the auditor's report provide audit evidence regarding the accounting estimate may be an appropriate response when such events are expected to:

- Occur; and

- Provide audit evidence that confirms or contradicts the accounting estimate.

A63. Events occurring up to the date of the auditor's report may sometimes provide sufficient appropriate audit evidence about an accounting estimate. For example, sale of the complete inventory of a superseded product shortly after the period end may provide audit evidence relating to the estimate of its net realizable value. In such cases, there may be no need to perform additional audit procedures on the accounting estimate, provided that sufficient appropriate evidence about the events is obtained.

A64. For some accounting estimates, events occurring up to the date of the auditor's report are unlikely to provide audit evidence regarding the accounting estimate. For example, the conditions or events relating to some accounting estimates develop only over an extended period. Also, because of the measurement objective of fair value accounting estimates, information after the period-end may not reflect the events or conditions existing at the balance sheet date and therefore may not be relevant to the measurement of the fair value accounting estimate. Paragraph 13 identifies other responses to the risks of material misstatement that the auditor may undertake.

A65. In some cases, events that contradict the accounting estimate may indicate that management has ineffective processes for making accounting estimates, or that there is management bias in the making of accounting estimates.

A66. Even though the auditor may decide not to undertake this approach in respect of specific accounting estimates, the auditor is required to comply with ISA (UK and Ireland) 560.[16] The auditor is required to perform audit procedures designed to obtain sufficient appropriate audit evidence that all events occurring between the date of the financial statements and the date of the auditor's report that require adjustment of, or disclosure in, the financial statements have been identified[17] and appropriately reflected in the financial statements.[18] Because the measurement of many accounting estimates, other than fair value accounting estimates, usually depends on the outcome of future conditions, transactions or events, the auditor's work under ISA (UK and Ireland) 560 is particularly relevant.

Considerations specific to smaller entities

A67. When there is a longer period between the balance sheet date and the date of the auditor's report, the auditor's review of events in this period may be an effective response for accounting estimates other than fair value accounting estimates. This may particularly be the case in some smaller owner-managed entities, especially when management does not have formalized control procedures over accounting estimates.

Testing How Management Made the Accounting Estimate (Ref: Para. 13(b))

A68. Testing how management made the accounting estimate and the data on which it is based may be an appropriate response when the accounting estimate is a fair value accounting estimate developed on a model that uses observable and unobservable inputs. It may also be appropriate when, for example:

- The accounting estimate is derived from the routine processing of data by the entity's accounting system.

- The auditor's review of similar accounting estimates made in the prior period financial statements suggests that management's current period process is likely to be effective.

- The accounting estimate is based on a large population of items of a similar nature that individually are not significant.

---

[16] ISA (UK and Ireland) 560, "Subsequent Events."
[17] ISA (UK and Ireland) 560, paragraph 6.
[18] ISA (UK and Ireland) 560, paragraph 8.

A69. Testing how management made the accounting estimate may involve, for example:

- Testing the extent to which data on which the accounting estimate is based is accurate, complete and relevant, and whether the accounting estimate has been properly determined using such data and management assumptions.

- Considering the source, relevance and reliability of external data or information, including that received from external experts engaged by management to assist in making an accounting estimate.

- Recalculating the accounting estimate, and reviewing information about an accounting estimate for internal consistency.

- Considering management's review and approval processes.

Considerations specific to smaller entities

A70. In smaller entities, the process for making accounting estimates is likely to be less structured than in larger entities. Smaller entities with active management involvement may not have extensive descriptions of accounting procedures, sophisticated accounting records, or written policies. Even if the entity has no formal established process, it does not mean that management is not able to provide a basis upon which the auditor can test the accounting estimate.

Evaluating the method of measurement (Ref: Para. 13(b)(i))

A71. When the applicable financial reporting framework does not prescribe the method of measurement, evaluating whether the method used, including any applicable model, is appropriate in the circumstances is a matter of professional judgment.

A72. For this purpose, matters that the auditor may consider include, for example, whether:

- Management's rationale for the method selected is reasonable.

- Management has sufficiently evaluated and appropriately applied the criteria, if any, provided in the applicable financial reporting framework to support the selected method.

- The method is appropriate in the circumstances given the nature of the asset or liability being estimated and the requirements of the applicable financial reporting framework relevant to accounting estimates.

- The method is appropriate in relation to the business, industry and environment in which the entity operates.

A73. In some cases, management may have determined that different methods result in a range of significantly different estimates. In such cases, obtaining an understanding of how the entity has investigated the reasons for these differences may assist the auditor in evaluating the appropriateness of the method selected.

Evaluating the use of models

A74. In some cases, particularly when making fair value accounting estimates, management may use a model. Whether the model used is appropriate in the circumstances may depend on a number of factors, such as the nature of the entity and its environment, including the industry in which it operates, and the specific asset or liability being measured.

A75. The extent to which the following considerations are relevant depends on the circumstances, including whether the model is one that is commercially available for use in a particular sector or industry, or a proprietary model. In some cases, an entity may use an expert to develop and test a model.

A76. Depending on the circumstances, matters that the auditor may also consider in testing the model include, for example, whether:

- The model is validated prior to usage, with periodic reviews to ensure it is still suitable for its intended use. The entity's validation process may include evaluation of:

    o The model's theoretical soundness and mathematical integrity, including the appropriateness of model parameters.

    o The consistency and completeness of the model's inputs with market practices.

    o The model's output as compared to actual transactions.

- Appropriate change control policies and procedures exist.

- The model is periodically calibrated and tested for validity, particularly when inputs are subjective.

- Adjustments are made to the output of the model, including in the case of fair value accounting estimates, whether such adjustments reflect the assumptions marketplace participants would use in similar circumstances.

- The model is adequately documented, including the model's intended applications and limitations and its key parameters, required inputs, and results of any validation analysis performed.

Assumptions used by management (Ref: Para. 13(b)(ii))

A77. The auditor's evaluation of the assumptions used by management is based only on information available to the auditor at the time of the audit. Audit procedures dealing with management assumptions are performed in the context of the audit of the entity's financial statements, and not for the purpose of providing an opinion on assumptions themselves.

A78. Matters that the auditor may consider in evaluating the reasonableness of the assumptions used by management include, for example:

- Whether individual assumptions appear reasonable.

- Whether the assumptions are interdependent and internally consistent.

- Whether the assumptions appear reasonable when considered collectively or in conjunction with other assumptions, either for that accounting estimate or for other accounting estimates.

- In the case of fair value accounting estimates, whether the assumptions appropriately reflect observable marketplace assumptions.

A79. The assumptions on which accounting estimates are based may reflect what management expects will be the outcome of specific objectives and strategies. In such cases, the auditor may perform audit procedures to evaluate the reasonableness of such assumptions by considering, for example, whether the assumptions are consistent with:

- The general economic environment and the entity's economic circumstances.

- The plans of the entity.

- Assumptions made in prior periods, if relevant.

- Experience of, or previous conditions experienced by, the entity, to the extent this historical information may be considered representative of future conditions or events.

- Other assumptions used by management relating to the financial statements.

A80. The reasonableness of the assumptions used may depend on management's intent and ability to carry out certain courses of action. Management often documents plans and intentions relevant to specific assets or liabilities and the financial reporting framework may require it to do so. Although the extent of audit evidence to be obtained about management's intent and ability is a matter of professional judgment, the auditor's procedures may include the following:

- Review of management's history of carrying out its stated intentions.

- Review of written plans and other documentation, including, where applicable, formally approved budgets, authorizations or minutes.

- Inquiry of management about its reasons for a particular course of action.

- Review of events occurring subsequent to the date of the financial statements and up to the date of the auditor's report.

- Evaluation of the entity's ability to carry out a particular course of action given the entity's economic circumstances, including the implications of its existing commitments.

Certain financial reporting frameworks, however, may not permit management's intentions or plans to be taken into account when making an accounting estimate. This is often the case for fair value accounting estimates because their measurement objective requires that assumptions reflect those used by marketplace participants.

A81. Matters that the auditor may consider in evaluating the reasonableness of assumptions used by management underlying fair value accounting estimates, in addition to those discussed above where applicable, may include, for example:

- Where relevant, whether and, if so, how management has incorporated market-specific inputs into the development of assumptions.

- Whether the assumptions are consistent with observable market conditions, and the characteristics of the asset or liability being measured at fair value.

- Whether the sources of market-participant assumptions are relevant and reliable, and how management has selected the assumptions to use when a number of different market participant assumptions exist.

- Where appropriate, whether and, if so, how management considered assumptions used in, or information about, comparable transactions, assets or liabilities.

A82. Further, fair value accounting estimates may comprise observable inputs as well as unobservable inputs. Where fair value accounting estimates are based on unobservable inputs, matters that the auditor may consider include, for example, how management supports the following:

- The identification of the characteristics of marketplace participants relevant to the accounting estimate.

- Modifications it has made to its own assumptions to reflect its view of assumptions marketplace participants would use.

- Whether it has incorporated the best information available in the circumstances.

- Where applicable, how its assumptions take account of comparable transactions, assets or liabilities.

If there are unobservable inputs, it is more likely that the auditor's evaluation of the assumptions will need to be combined with other responses to assessed risks in paragraph 13 in order to obtain sufficient appropriate audit evidence. In such cases, it may be necessary for the auditor to perform other audit procedures, for example, examining documentation supporting the review and approval of the accounting estimate by appropriate levels of management and, where appropriate, by those charged with governance.

A83. In evaluating the reasonableness of the assumptions supporting an accounting estimate, the auditor may identify one or more significant assumptions. If so, it may indicate that the accounting estimate has high estimation uncertainty and may, therefore, give rise to a significant risk. Additional responses to significant risks are described in paragraphs A102-A115.

Testing the Operating Effectiveness of Controls (Ref: Para. 13(c))

A84. Testing the operating effectiveness of the controls over how management made the accounting estimate may be an appropriate response when management's process has been well-designed, implemented and maintained, for example:

- Controls exist for the review and approval of the accounting estimates by appropriate levels of management and, where appropriate, by those charged with governance.

- The accounting estimate is derived from the routine processing of data by the entity's accounting system.

A85. Testing the operating effectiveness of the controls is required when:

(a) The auditor's assessment of risks of material misstatement at the assertion level includes an expectation that controls over the process are operating effectively; or

(b) Substantive procedures alone do not provide sufficient appropriate audit evidence at the assertion level.[19]

Considerations specific to smaller entities

A86. Controls over the process to make an accounting estimate may exist in smaller entities, but the formality with which they operate varies. Further, smaller entities may determine that certain types of controls are not necessary because of active management involvement in the financial reporting process. In the case of very small entities, however, there may not be many controls that the auditor can identify. For this reason, the auditor's response to the assessed risks is likely to be substantive in nature, with the auditor performing one or more of the other responses in paragraph 13.

---

[19]   ISA (UK and Ireland) 330, paragraph 8.

Developing a Point Estimate or Range (Ref: Para. 13(d))

A87. Developing a point estimate or a range to evaluate management's point estimate may be an appropriate response where, for example:

- An accounting estimate is not derived from the routine processing of data by the accounting system.

- The auditor's review of similar accounting estimates made in the prior period financial statements suggests that management's current period process is unlikely to be effective.

- The entity's controls within and over management's processes for determining accounting estimates are not well designed or properly implemented.

- Events or transactions between the period end and the date of the auditor's report contradict management's point estimate.

- There are alternative sources of relevant data available to the auditor which can be used in making a point estimate or a range.

A88. Even where the entity's controls are well designed and properly implemented, developing a point estimate or a range may be an effective or efficient response to the assessed risks. In other situations, the auditor may consider this approach as part of determining whether further procedures are necessary and, if so, their nature and extent.

A89. The approach taken by the auditor in developing either a point estimate or a range may vary based on what is considered most effective in the circumstances. For example, the auditor may initially develop a preliminary point estimate, and then assess its sensitivity to changes in assumptions to ascertain a range with which to evaluate management's point estimate. Alternatively, the auditor may begin by developing a range for purposes of determining, where possible, a point estimate.

A90. The ability of the auditor to make a point estimate, as opposed to a range, depends on several factors, including the model used, the nature and extent of data available and the estimation uncertainty involved with the accounting estimate. Further, the decision to develop a point estimate or range may be influenced by the applicable financial reporting framework, which may prescribe the point estimate that is to be used after consideration of the alternative outcomes and assumptions, or prescribe a specific measurement method (for example, the use of a discounted probability-weighted expected value).

A91. The auditor may develop a point estimate or a range in a number of ways, for example, by:

- Using a model, for example, one that is commercially available for use in a particular sector or industry, or a proprietary or auditor-developed model.

- Further developing management's consideration of alternative assumptions or outcomes, for example, by introducing a different set of assumptions.

- Employing or engaging a person with specialized expertise to develop or execute the model, or to provide relevant assumptions.

- Making reference to other comparable conditions, transactions or events, or, where relevant, markets for comparable assets or liabilities.

Understanding Management's Assumptions or Method (Ref: Para. 13(d)(i))

A92. When the auditor makes a point estimate or a range and uses assumptions or a method different from those used by management, paragraph 13(d)(i) requires the auditor to obtain a sufficient understanding of the assumptions or method used by management in making the accounting estimate. This understanding provides the auditor with information that may be relevant to the auditor's development of an appropriate point estimate or range. Further, it assists the auditor to understand and evaluate any significant differences from management's point estimate. For example, a difference may arise because the auditor used different, but equally valid, assumptions as compared with those used by management. This may reveal that the accounting estimate is highly sensitive to certain assumptions and therefore subject to high estimation uncertainty, indicating that the accounting estimate may be a significant risk. Alternatively, a difference may arise as a result of a factual error made by management. Depending on the circumstances, the auditor may find it helpful in drawing conclusions to discuss with management the basis for the assumptions used and their validity, and the difference, if any, in the approach taken to making the accounting estimate.

Narrowing a Range (Ref: Para. 13(d)(ii))

A93. When the auditor concludes that it is appropriate to use a range to evaluate the reasonableness of management's point estimate (the auditor's range), paragraph 13(d)(ii) requires that range to encompass all "reasonable outcomes" rather than all possible outcomes. The range cannot be one that comprises all possible outcomes if it is to be useful, as such a range would be too wide to be effective for purposes of the audit. The auditor's range is useful and effective when it is sufficiently narrow to enable the auditor to conclude whether the accounting estimate is misstated.

A94. Ordinarily, a range that has been narrowed to be equal to or less than performance materiality is adequate for the purposes of evaluating the reasonableness of management's point estimate. However, particularly in certain industries, it may not be possible to narrow the range to below such an amount. This does not necessarily preclude recognition of the accounting estimate. It may indicate, however, that the estimation uncertainty associated with the accounting estimate is such that it gives rise to a significant risk. Additional responses to significant risks are described in paragraphs A102-A115.

A95. Narrowing the range to a position where all outcomes within the range are considered reasonable may be achieved by:

(a)   Eliminating from the range those outcomes at the extremities of the range judged by the auditor to be unlikely to occur; and

(b)   Continuing to narrow the range, based on audit evidence available, until the auditor concludes that all outcomes within the range are considered reasonable. In some rare cases, the auditor may be able to narrow the range until the audit evidence indicates a point estimate.

Considering whether Specialized Skills or Knowledge Are Required (Ref: Para. 14)

A96.   In planning the audit, the auditor is required to ascertain the nature, timing and extent of resources necessary to perform the audit engagement.[20] This may include, as necessary, the involvement of those with specialized skills or knowledge. In addition, ISA (UK and Ireland) 220 requires the engagement partner to be satisfied that the engagement team, and any auditor's external experts who are not part of the engagement team, collectively have the appropriate competence and capabilities to perform the audit engagement.[21] During the course of the audit of accounting estimates the auditor may identify, in light of the experience of the auditor and the circumstances of the engagement, the need for specialized skills or knowledge to be applied in relation to one or more aspects of the accounting estimates.

A97.   Matters that may affect the auditor's consideration of whether specialized skills or knowledge is required include, for example:

*   The nature of the underlying asset, liability or component of equity in a particular business or industry (for example, mineral deposits, agricultural assets, complex financial instruments).

*   A high degree of estimation uncertainty.

*   Complex calculations or specialized models are involved, for example, when estimating fair values when there is no observable market.

*   The complexity of the requirements of the applicable financial reporting framework relevant to accounting estimates, including whether there are areas known to be subject to differing interpretation or practice is inconsistent or developing.

*   The procedures the auditor intends to undertake in responding to assessed risks.

A98.   For the majority of accounting estimates, even when there is estimation uncertainty, it is unlikely that specialized skills or knowledge will be required. For example, it is unlikely that specialized skills or knowledge would be necessary for an auditor to evaluate an allowance for doubtful accounts.

---

[20]   ISA (UK and Ireland) 300, "Planning an Audit of Financial Statements," paragraph 8(e).
[21]   ISA (UK and Ireland) 220, "Quality Control for an Audit of Financial Statements," paragraph 14.

A99. However, the auditor may not possess the specialized skills or knowledge required when the matter involved is in a field other than accounting or auditing and may need to obtain it from an auditor's expert. ISA (UK and Ireland) 620[22] establishes requirements and provides guidance in determining the need to employ or engage an auditor's expert and the auditor's responsibilities when using the work of an auditor's expert.

A100. Further, in some cases, the auditor may conclude that it is necessary to obtain specialized skills or knowledge related to specific areas of accounting or auditing. Individuals with such skills or knowledge may be employed by the auditor's firm or engaged from an external organization outside of the auditor's firm. Where such individuals perform audit procedures on the engagement, they are part of the engagement team and accordingly, they are subject to the requirements in ISA (UK and Ireland) 220.

A101. Depending on the auditor's understanding and experience of working with the auditor's expert or those other individuals with specialized skills or knowledge, the auditor may consider it appropriate to discuss matters such as the requirements of the applicable financial reporting framework with the individuals involved to establish that their work is relevant for audit purposes.

Further Substantive Procedures to Respond to Significant Risks
(Ref: Para. 15)

A102. In auditing accounting estimates that give rise to significant risks, the auditor's further substantive procedures are focused on the evaluation of:

(a) How management has assessed the effect of estimation uncertainty on the accounting estimate, and the effect such uncertainty may have on the appropriateness of the recognition of the accounting estimate in the financial statements; and

(b) The adequacy of related disclosures.

Estimation Uncertainty

Management's Consideration of Estimation Uncertainty (Ref: Para. 15(a))

A103. Management may evaluate alternative assumptions or outcomes of the accounting estimates through a number of methods, depending on the circumstances. One possible method used by management is to undertake a sensitivity analysis. This might involve determining how the monetary amount of an accounting estimate varies with different assumptions. Even for accounting estimates measured at fair value there can be variation because different market participants will use different assumptions. A sensitivity analysis could lead to the development of a number of

---

[22] ISA (UK and Ireland) 620, "Using the Work of an Auditor's Expert."

outcome scenarios, sometimes characterized as a range of outcomes by management, such as "pessimistic" and "optimistic" scenarios.

A104. A sensitivity analysis may demonstrate that an accounting estimate is not sensitive to changes in particular assumptions. Alternatively, it may demonstrate that the accounting estimate is sensitive to one or more assumptions that then become the focus of the auditor's attention.

A105. This is not intended to suggest that one particular method of addressing estimation uncertainty (such as sensitivity analysis) is more suitable than another, or that management's consideration of alternative assumptions or outcomes needs to be conducted through a detailed process supported by extensive documentation. Rather, it is whether management has assessed how estimation uncertainty may affect the accounting estimate that is important, not the specific manner in which it is done. Accordingly, where management has not considered alternative assumptions or outcomes, it may be necessary for the auditor to discuss with management, and request support for, how it has addressed the effects of estimation uncertainty on the accounting estimate.

Considerations specific to smaller entities

A106. Smaller entities may use simple means to assess the estimation uncertainty. In addition to the auditor's review of available documentation, the auditor may obtain other audit evidence of management consideration of alternative assumptions or outcomes by inquiry of management. In addition, management may not have the expertise to consider alternative outcomes or otherwise address the estimation uncertainty of the accounting estimate. In such cases, the auditor may explain to management the process or the different methods available for doing so, and the documentation thereof. This would not, however, change the responsibilities of management[a] for the preparation of the financial statements.

Significant Assumptions (Ref: Para. 15(b))

A107. An assumption used in making an accounting estimate may be deemed to be significant if a reasonable variation in the assumption would materially affect the measurement of the accounting estimate.

A108. Support for significant assumptions derived from management's knowledge may be obtained from management's continuing processes of strategic analysis and risk management. Even without formal established processes, such as may be the case in smaller entities, the auditor may be able to evaluate the assumptions through inquiries of and discussions with management, along with other audit procedures in order to obtain sufficient appropriate audit evidence.

A109. The auditor's considerations in evaluating assumptions made by management are described in paragraphs A77-A83.

Management Intent and Ability (Ref: Para. 15(c))

A110. The auditor's considerations in relation to assumptions made by management and management's intent and ability are described in paragraphs A13 and A80.

Development of a Range (Ref: Para. 16)

A111. In preparing the financial statements, management may be satisfied that it has adequately addressed the effects of estimation uncertainty on the accounting estimates that give rise to significant risks. In some circumstances, however, the auditor may view the efforts of management as inadequate. This may be the case, for example, where, in the auditor's judgment:

- Sufficient appropriate audit evidence could not be obtained through the auditor's evaluation of how management has addressed the effects of estimation uncertainty.

- It is necessary to explore further the degree of estimation uncertainty associated with an accounting estimate, for example, where the auditor is aware of wide variation in outcomes for similar accounting estimates in similar circumstances.

- It is unlikely that other audit evidence can be obtained, for example, through the review of events occurring up to the date of the auditor's report.

- Indicators of management bias in the making of accounting estimates may exist.

A112. The auditor's considerations in determining a range for this purpose are described in paragraphs A87-A95.

Recognition and Measurement Criteria

Recognition of the Accounting Estimates in the Financial Statements (Ref: Para. 17(a))

A113. Where management has recognized an accounting estimate in the financial statements, the focus of the auditor's evaluation is on whether the measurement of the accounting estimate is sufficiently reliable to meet the recognition criteria of the applicable financial reporting framework.

A114. With respect to accounting estimates that have not been recognized, the focus of the auditor's evaluation is on whether the recognition criteria of the applicable financial reporting framework have in fact been met. Even where an accounting estimate has not been recognized, and the auditor concludes that this treatment is appropriate, there may be a need for disclosure of the circumstances in the notes to the financial statements. The auditor may also determine that there is a need to draw the reader's attention to a significant uncertainty by adding an Emphasis of Matter paragraph to the auditor's report. ISA (UK and Ireland) 706[23] establishes requirements and provides guidance concerning such paragraphs.

Measurement Basis for the Accounting Estimates (Ref: Para. 17(b))

A115. With respect to fair value accounting estimates, some financial reporting frameworks presume that fair value can be measured reliably as a prerequisite to either requiring or permitting fair value measurements and disclosures. In some cases, this presumption may be overcome when, for example, there is no appropriate method or basis for measurement. In such cases, the focus of the auditor's evaluation is on whether management's basis for overcoming the presumption relating to the use of fair value set forth under the applicable financial reporting framework is appropriate.

Evaluating the Reasonableness of the Accounting Estimates, and Determining Misstatements (Ref: Para. 18)

A116. Based on the audit evidence obtained, the auditor may conclude that the evidence points to an accounting estimate that differs from management's point estimate. Where the audit evidence supports a point estimate, the difference between the auditor's point estimate and management's point estimate constitutes a misstatement. Where the auditor has concluded that using the auditor's range provides sufficient appropriate audit evidence, a management point estimate that lies outside the auditor's range would not be supported by audit evidence. In such cases, the misstatement is no less than the difference between management's point estimate and the nearest point of the auditor's range.

A117. Where management has changed an accounting estimate, or the method in making it, from the prior period based on a subjective assessment that there has been a change in circumstances, the auditor may conclude based on the audit evidence that the accounting estimate is misstated as a result of an arbitrary change by management, or may regard it as an indicator of possible management bias (see paragraphs A124-A125).

A118. ISA (UK and Ireland) 450[24] provides guidance on distinguishing misstatements for purposes of the auditor's evaluation of the effect of uncorrected misstatements on the financial statements. In relation to accounting estimates, a misstatement, whether caused by fraud or error, may arise as a result of:

• Misstatements about which there is no doubt (factual misstatements).

• Differences arising from management's judgments concerning accounting estimates that the auditor considers unreasonable, or the selection or application of accounting policies that the auditor considers inappropriate (judgmental misstatements).

---

[23] ISA (UK and Ireland) 706, "Emphasis of Matter Paragraphs and Other Matter Paragraphs in the Independent Auditor's Report."
[24] ISA (UK and Ireland) 450, "Evaluation of Misstatements Identified during the Audit."

• The auditor's best estimate of misstatements in populations, involving the projection of misstatements identified in audit samples to the entire populations from which the samples were drawn (projected misstatements).

In some cases involving accounting estimates, a misstatement could arise as a result of a combination of these circumstances, making separate identification difficult or impossible.

A119. Evaluating the reasonableness of accounting estimates and related disclosures included in the notes to the financial statements, whether required by the applicable financial reporting framework or disclosed voluntarily, involves essentially the same types of considerations applied when auditing an accounting estimate recognized in the financial statements.

Disclosures Related to Accounting Estimates

Disclosures in Accordance with the Applicable Financial Reporting Framework (Ref: Para. 19)

A120. The presentation of financial statements in accordance with the applicable financial reporting framework includes adequate disclosure of material matters. The applicable financial reporting framework may permit, or prescribe, disclosures related to accounting estimates, and some entities may disclose voluntarily additional information in the notes to the financial statements. These disclosures may include, for example:

• The assumptions used.

• The method of estimation used, including any applicable model.

• The basis for the selection of the method of estimation.

• The effect of any changes to the method of estimation from the prior period.

• The sources and implications of estimation uncertainty.

Such disclosures are relevant to users in understanding the accounting estimates recognized or disclosed in the financial statements, and sufficient appropriate audit evidence needs to be obtained about whether the disclosures are in accordance with the requirements of the applicable financial reporting framework.

A121. In some cases, the applicable financial reporting framework may require specific disclosures regarding uncertainties. For example, some financial reporting frameworks prescribe:

• The disclosure of key assumptions and other sources of estimation uncertainty that have a significant risk of causing a material adjustment to the carrying amounts of assets and liabilities. Such requirements may be described using terms such as "Key Sources of Estimation Uncertainty" or "Critical Accounting Estimates."

- The disclosure of the range of possible outcomes, and the assumptions used in determining the range.

- The disclosure of information regarding the significance of fair value accounting estimates to the entity's financial position and performance.

- Qualitative disclosures such as the exposures to risk and how they arise, the entity's objectives, policies and procedures for managing the risk and the methods used to measure the risk and any changes from the previous period of these qualitative concepts.

- Quantitative disclosures such as the extent to which the entity is exposed to risk, based on information provided internally to the entity's key management personnel, including credit risk, liquidity risk and market risk.

Disclosures of Estimation Uncertainty for Accounting Estimates that Give Rise to Significant Risks (Ref: Para. 20)

A122. In relation to accounting estimates having significant risk, even where the disclosures are in accordance with the applicable financial reporting framework, the auditor may conclude that the disclosure of estimation uncertainty is inadequate in light of the circumstances and facts involved. The auditor's evaluation of the adequacy of disclosure of estimation uncertainty increases in importance the greater the range of possible outcomes of the accounting estimate is in relation to materiality (see related discussion in paragraph A94).

A123. In some cases, the auditor may consider it appropriate to encourage management to describe, in the notes to the financial statements, the circumstances relating to the estimation uncertainty. ISA (UK and Ireland) 705[25] provides guidance on the implications for the auditor's opinion when the auditor believes that management's disclosure of estimation uncertainty in the financial statements is inadequate or misleading.

Indicators of Possible Management Bias (Ref: Para. 21)

A124. During the audit, the auditor may become aware of judgments and decisions made by management which give rise to indicators of possible management bias. Such indicators may affect the auditor's conclusion as to whether the auditor's risk assessment and related responses remain appropriate, and the auditor may need to consider the implications for the rest of the audit. Further, they may affect the

---

[25] ISA (UK and Ireland) 705, "Modifications to the Opinion in the Independent Auditor's Report."

auditor's evaluation of whether the financial statements as a whole are free from material misstatement, as discussed in ISA (UK and Ireland) 700.[26]

A125. Examples of indicators of possible management bias with respect to accounting estimates include:

- Changes in an accounting estimate, or the method for making it, where management has made a subjective assessment that there has been a change in circumstances.

- Use of an entity's own assumptions for fair value accounting estimates when they are inconsistent with observable marketplace assumptions.

- Selection or construction of significant assumptions that yield a point estimate favorable for management objectives.

- Selection of a point estimate that may indicate a pattern of optimism or pessimism.

Written Representations (Ref: Para. 22)

A126. ISA (UK and Ireland) 580[27] discusses the use of written representations. Depending on the nature, materiality and extent of estimation uncertainty, written representations about accounting estimates recognized or disclosed in the financial statements may include representations:

- About the appropriateness of the measurement processes, including related assumptions and models, used by management in determining accounting estimates in the context of the applicable financial reporting framework, and the consistency in application of the processes.

- That the assumptions appropriately reflect management's intent and ability to carry out specific courses of action on behalf of the entity, where relevant to the accounting estimates and disclosures.

- That disclosures related to accounting estimates are complete and appropriate under the applicable financial reporting framework.

- That no subsequent event requires adjustment to the accounting estimates and disclosures included in the financial statements.

---

[26] ISA 700, "Forming an Opinion and Reporting on Financial Statements."
The APB has not promulgated ISA 700 as issued by the IAASB for application in the UK and Ireland. In the UK and Ireland the applicable auditing standard is ISA (UK and Ireland) 700, "The Auditor's Report on Financial Statements." Paragraph 8(b) of ISA (UK and Ireland) requires the auditor's evaluation of whether uncorrected misstatements are material. This evaluation is required to include consideration of possible indicators of management bias.
[27] ISA (UK and Ireland) 580, "Written Representations."

A127. For those accounting estimates not recognized or disclosed in the financial statements, written representations may also include representations about:

- The appropriateness of the basis used by management for determining that the recognition or disclosure criteria of the applicable financial reporting framework have not been met (see paragraph A114).

- The appropriateness of the basis used by management to overcome the presumption relating to the use of fair value set forth under the entity's applicable financial reporting framework, for those accounting estimates not measured or disclosed at fair value (see paragraph A115).

Documentation (Ref: Para. 23)

A128. Documentation of indicators of possible management bias identified during the audit assists the auditor in concluding whether the auditor's risk assessment and related responses remain appropriate, and in evaluating whether the financial statements as a whole are free from material misstatement. See paragraph A125 for examples of indicators of possible management bias.

Appendix

(Ref: Para. A1)

Fair Value Measurements and Disclosures under Different Financial Reporting Frameworks

The purpose of this appendix is only to provide a general discussion of fair value measurements and disclosures under different financial reporting frameworks, for background and context.

1.   Different financial reporting frameworks require or permit a variety of fair value measurements and disclosures in financial statements. They also vary in the level of guidance that they provide on the basis for measuring assets and liabilities or the related disclosures. Some financial reporting frameworks give prescriptive guidance, others give general guidance, and some give no guidance at all. In addition, certain industry-specific measurement and disclosure practices for fair values also exist.

2.   Definitions of fair value may differ among financial reporting frameworks, or for different assets, liabilities or disclosures within a particular framework. For example, International Accounting Standard (IAS) 39[28] defines fair value as "the amount for which an asset could be exchanged, or a liability settled, between knowledgeable, willing parties in an arm's length transaction." The concept of fair value ordinarily assumes a current transaction, rather than settlement at some past or future date. Accordingly, the process of measuring fair value would be a search for the estimated price at which that transaction would occur. Additionally, different financial reporting frameworks may use such terms as "entity-specific value," "value in use," or similar terms, but may still fall within the concept of fair value in this ISA (UK and Ireland).

3.   Financial reporting frameworks may treat changes in fair value measurements that occur over time in different ways. For example, a particular financial reporting framework may require that changes in fair value measurements of certain assets or liabilities be reflected directly in equity, while such changes might be reflected in income under another framework. In some frameworks, the determination of whether to use fair value accounting or how it is applied is influenced by management's intent to carry out certain courses of action with respect to the specific asset or liability.

4.   Different financial reporting frameworks may require certain specific fair value measurements and disclosures in financial statements and prescribe or permit them in varying degrees. The financial reporting frameworks may:

   •   Prescribe measurement, presentation and disclosure requirements for certain information included in the financial statements or for information disclosed in notes to financial statements or presented as supplementary information;

---

[28] IAS 39, "Financial Instruments: Recognition and Measurement."

- Permit certain measurements using fair values at the option of an entity or only when certain criteria have been met;

- Prescribe a specific method for determining fair value, for example, through the use of an independent appraisal or specified ways of using discounted cash flows;

- Permit a choice of method for determining fair value from among several alternative methods (the criteria for selection may or may not be provided by the financial reporting framework); or

- Provide no guidance on the fair value measurements or disclosures of fair value other than their use being evident through custom or practice, for example, an industry practice.

5.   Some financial reporting frameworks presume that fair value can be measured reliably for assets or liabilities as a prerequisite to either requiring or permitting fair value measurements or disclosures. In some cases, this presumption may be overcome when an asset or liability does not have a quoted market price in an active market and for which other methods of reasonably estimating fair value are clearly inappropriate or unworkable. Some financial reporting frameworks may specify a fair value hierarchy that distinguishes inputs for use in arriving at fair values ranging from those that involve clearly "observable inputs" based on quoted prices and active markets and those "unobservable inputs" that involve an entity's own judgments about assumptions that marketplace participants would use.

6.   Some financial reporting frameworks require certain specified adjustments or modifications to valuation information, or other considerations unique to a particular asset or liability. For example, accounting for investment properties may require adjustments to be made to an appraised market value, such as adjustments for estimated closing costs on sale, adjustments related to the property's condition and location, and other matters. Similarly, if the market for a particular asset is not an active market, published price quotations may have to be adjusted or modified to arrive at a more suitable measure of fair value. For example, quoted market prices may not be indicative of fair value if there is infrequent activity in the market, the market is not well established, or small volumes of units are traded relative to the aggregate number of trading units in existence. Accordingly, such market prices may have to be adjusted or modified. Alternative sources of market information may be needed to make such adjustments or modifications. Further, in some cases, collateral assigned (for example, when collateral is assigned for certain types of investment in debt) may need to be considered in determining the fair value or possible impairment of an asset or liability.

7.   In most financial reporting frameworks, underlying the concept of fair value measurements is a presumption that the entity is a going concern without any intention or need to liquidate, curtail materially the scale of its operations, or undertake a transaction on adverse terms. Therefore, in this case, fair value would not be the amount that an entity would receive or pay in a forced transaction, involuntary liquidation, or distress sale. On the other hand, general economic conditions or

economic conditions specific to certain industries may cause illiquidity in the marketplace and require fair values to be predicated upon depressed prices, potentially significantly depressed prices. An entity, however, may need to take its current economic or operating situation into account in determining the fair values of its assets and liabilities if prescribed or permitted to do so by its financial reporting framework and such framework may or may not specify how that is done. For example, management's plan to dispose of an asset on an accelerated basis to meet specific business objectives may be relevant to the determination of the fair value of that asset.

Prevalence of Fair Value Measurements

8. Measurements and disclosures based on fair value are becoming increasingly prevalent in financial reporting frameworks. Fair values may occur in, and affect the determination of, financial statements in a number of ways, including the measurement at fair value of the following:

    *   Specific assets or liabilities, such as marketable securities or liabilities to settle an obligation under a financial instrument, routinely or periodically "marked-to-market."

    *   Specific components of equity, for example when accounting for the recognition, measurement and presentation of certain financial instruments with equity features, such as a bond convertible by the holder into common shares of the issuer.

    *   Specific assets or liabilities acquired in a business combination. For example, the initial determination of goodwill arising on the purchase of an entity in a business combination usually is based on the fair value measurement of the identifiable assets and liabilities acquired and the fair value of the consideration given.

    *   Specific assets or liabilities adjusted to fair value on a one-time basis. Some financial reporting frameworks may require the use of a fair value measurement to quantify an adjustment to an asset or a group of assets as part of an asset impairment determination, for example, a test of impairment of goodwill acquired in a business combination based on the fair value of a defined operating entity or reporting unit, the value of which is then allocated among the entity's or unit's group of assets and liabilities in order to derive an implied goodwill for comparison to the recorded goodwill.

    *   Aggregations of assets and liabilities. In some circumstances, the measurement of a class or group of assets or liabilities calls for an aggregation of fair values of some of the individual assets or liabilities in such class or group. For example, under an entity's applicable financial reporting framework, the measurement of a diversified loan portfolio might be determined based on the fair value of some categories of loans comprising the portfolio.

    *   Information disclosed in notes to financial statements or presented as supplementary information, but not recognized in the financial statements.

INTERNATIONAL STANDARD ON AUDITING (UK AND IRELAND) 550

RELATED PARTIES

(Effective for audits of financial statements for periods ending on or after 15 December 2010)[1a]

CONTENTS

[1a] Conforming amendments to this standard as a result of ISA (UK and Ireland) 610 (Revised June 2013), *Using the Work of Internal Auditors*, are included that are effective for audits of financial statements for periods ending on or after 15 June 2014. Details of the amendments are given in the Annexure to ISA (UK and Ireland) 610 (Revised June 2013).

International Standard on Auditing (UK and Ireland) (ISA (UK and Ireland)) 550, "Related Parties" should be read in conjunction with ISA (UK and Ireland) 200, "Overall Objectives of the Independent Auditor and the Conduct of an Audit in Accordance with International Standards on Auditing (UK and Ireland)."

Introduction

Scope of this ISA (UK and Ireland)

1. This International Standard on Auditing (UK and Ireland) (ISA (UK and Ireland)) deals with the auditor's responsibilities relating to related party relationships and transactions in an audit of financial statements. Specifically, it expands on how ISA (UK and Ireland) 315,[1] ISA (UK and Ireland) 330,[2] and ISA (UK and Ireland) 240[3] are to be applied in relation to risks of material misstatement associated with related party relationships and transactions.

Nature of Related Party Relationships and Transactions

2. Many related party transactions are in the normal course of business. In such circumstances, they may carry no higher risk of material misstatement of the financial statements than similar transactions with unrelated parties. However, the nature of related party relationships and transactions may, in some circumstances, give rise to higher risks of material misstatement of the financial statements than transactions with unrelated parties. For example:

    *   Related parties may operate through an extensive and complex range of relationships and structures, with a corresponding increase in the complexity of related party transactions.

    *   Information systems may be ineffective at identifying or summarizing transactions and outstanding balances between an entity and its related parties.

    *   Related party transactions may not be conducted under normal market terms and conditions; for example, some related party transactions may be conducted with no exchange of consideration.

Responsibilities of the Auditor

3. Because related parties are not independent of each other, many financial reporting frameworks establish specific accounting and disclosure requirements for related party relationships, transactions and balances to enable users of the financial statements to understand their nature and actual or potential effects on the financial statements. Where the applicable financial reporting framework establishes such requirements[3a], the auditor has a responsibility to perform audit procedures to identify, assess and respond to the risks of material misstatement arising from the

---

[1] ISA (UK and Ireland) 315, "Identifying and Assessing the Risks of Material Misstatement through Understanding the Entity and Its Environment."

[2] ISA (UK and Ireland) 330, "The Auditor's Responses to Assessed Risks."

[3] ISA (UK and Ireland) 240, "The Auditor's Responsibilities Relating to Fraud in an Audit of Financial Statements."

[3a] In the UK and Ireland, specific accounting and disclosure requirements for related party relationships, transactions and balances are established in accounting standards and in law and regulations.

entity's failure to appropriately account for or disclose related party relationships, transactions or balances in accordance with the requirements of the framework.

4. Even if the applicable financial reporting framework establishes minimal or no related party requirements, the auditor nevertheless needs to obtain an understanding of the entity's related party relationships and transactions sufficient to be able to conclude whether the financial statements, insofar as they are affected by those relationships and transactions: (Ref: Para. A1)

 (a) Achieve fair presentation (for fair presentation frameworks); or (Ref: Para. A2)

 (b) Are not misleading (for compliance frameworks). (Ref: Para. A3)

5. In addition, an understanding of the entity's related party relationships and transactions is relevant to the auditor's evaluation of whether one or more fraud risk factors are present as required by ISA (UK and Ireland) 240,[4] because fraud may be more easily committed through related parties.

6. Owing to the inherent limitations of an audit, there is an unavoidable risk that some material misstatements of the financial statements may not be detected, even though the audit is properly planned and performed in accordance with the ISAs (UK and Ireland).[5] In the context of related parties, the potential effects of inherent limitations on the auditor's ability to detect material misstatements are greater for such reasons as the following:

- Management may be unaware of the existence of all related party relationships and transactions, particularly if the applicable financial reporting framework does not establish related party requirements.

- Related party relationships may present a greater opportunity for collusion, concealment or manipulation by management.

7. Planning and performing the audit with professional skepticism as required by ISA (UK and Ireland) 200[6] is therefore particularly important in this context, given the potential for undisclosed related party relationships and transactions. The requirements in this ISA (UK and Ireland) are designed to assist the auditor in identifying and assessing the risks of material misstatement associated with related party relationships and transactions, and in designing audit procedures to respond to the assessed risks.

Effective Date

8. This ISA (UK and Ireland) is effective for audits of financial statements for periods ending on or after 15 December 2010.[1a]

---

[4] ISA (UK and Ireland) 240, paragraph 24.
[5] ISA (UK and Ireland) 200, "Overall Objectives of the Independent Auditor and the Conduct of an Audit in Accordance with International Standards on Auditing," paragraphs A51-A52.
[6] ISA (UK and Ireland) 200, paragraph 15.

Objectives

9.   The objectives of the auditor are:

(a)   Irrespective of whether the applicable financial reporting framework establishes related party requirements, to obtain an understanding of related party relationships and transactions sufficient to be able:

(i)   To recognize fraud risk factors, if any, arising from related party relationships and transactions that are relevant to the identification and assessment of the risks of material misstatement due to fraud; and

(ii)   To conclude, based on the audit evidence obtained, whether the financial statements, insofar as they are affected by those relationships and transactions:

a.   Achieve fair presentation (for fair presentation frameworks); or

b.   Are not misleading (for compliance frameworks); and

(b)   In addition, where the applicable financial reporting framework establishes related party requirements, to obtain sufficient appropriate audit evidence about whether related party relationships and transactions have been appropriately identified, accounted for and disclosed in the financial statements in accordance with the framework.

Definitions

10.   For purposes of the ISAs (UK and Ireland), the following terms have the meanings attributed below:

(a)   Arm's length transaction – A transaction conducted on such terms and conditions as between a willing buyer and a willing seller who are unrelated and are acting independently of each other and pursuing their own best interests.

(b)   Related party – A party that is either: (Ref: Para. A4-A7)

(i)   A related party as defined in the applicable financial reporting framework; or

(ii)   Where the applicable financial reporting framework establishes minimal or no related party requirements:

a.   A person or other entity that has control or significant influence, directly or indirectly through one or more intermediaries, over the reporting entity;

b. Another entity over which the reporting entity has control or significant influence, directly or indirectly through one or more intermediaries; or

c. Another entity that is under common control with the reporting entity through having:

  i. Common controlling ownership;

  ii. Owners who are close family members; or

  iii. Common key management.

  However, entities that are under common control by a state (that is, a national, regional or local government) are not considered related unless they engage in significant transactions or share resources to a significant extent with one another.

Requirements

Risk Assessment Procedures and Related Activities

11. As part of the risk assessment procedures and related activities that ISA (UK and Ireland) 315 and ISA (UK and Ireland) 240 require the auditor to perform during the audit,[7] the auditor shall perform the audit procedures and related activities set out in paragraphs 12-17 to obtain information relevant to identifying the risks of material misstatement associated with related party relationships and transactions. (Ref: Para. A8)

Understanding the Entity's Related Party Relationships and Transactions

12. The engagement team discussion that ISA (UK and Ireland) 315 and ISA (UK and Ireland) 240 require[8] shall include specific consideration of the susceptibility of the financial statements to material misstatement due to fraud or error that could result from the entity's related party relationships and transactions. (Ref: Para. A9-A10)

13. The auditor shall inquire of management regarding:

  (a) The identity of the entity's related parties, including changes from the prior period; (Ref: Para. A11-A14)

  (b) The nature of the relationships between the entity and these related parties; and

  (c) Whether the entity entered into any transactions with these related parties during the period and, if so, the type and purpose of the transactions.

---

[7] ISA (UK and Ireland) 315, paragraph 5; ISA 240, paragraph 16.
[8] ISA (UK and Ireland) 315, paragraph 10; ISA 240, paragraph 15.

14. The auditor shall inquire of management and others within the entity, and perform other risk assessment procedures considered appropriate, to obtain an understanding of the controls, if any, that management has established to: (Ref: Para. A15-A20)

   (a) Identify, account for, and disclose related party relationships and transactions in accordance with the applicable financial reporting framework;

   (b) Authorize and approve significant transactions and arrangements with related parties; and (Ref: Para. A21)

   (c) Authorize and approve significant transactions and arrangements outside the normal course of business.

Maintaining Alertness for Related Party Information When Reviewing Records or Documents

15. During the audit, the auditor shall remain alert, when inspecting records or documents, for arrangements or other information that may indicate the existence of related party relationships or transactions that management has not previously identified or disclosed to the auditor. (Ref: Para. A22-A23)

   In particular, the auditor shall inspect the following for indications of the existence of related party relationships or transactions that management has not previously identified or disclosed to the auditor:

   (a) Bank and legal confirmations obtained as part of the auditor's procedures;

   (b) Minutes of meetings of shareholders and of those charged with governance; and

   (c) Such other records or documents as the auditor considers necessary in the circumstances of the entity.

16. If the auditor identifies significant transactions outside the entity's normal course of business when performing the audit procedures required by paragraph 15 or through other audit procedures, the auditor shall inquire of management about: (Ref: Para. A24-A25)

   (a) The nature of these transactions; and (Ref: Para. A26)

   (b) Whether related parties could be involved. (Ref: Para. A27)

Sharing Related Party Information with the Engagement Team

17. The auditor shall share relevant information obtained about the entity's related parties with the other members of the engagement team. (Ref: Para. A28)

Identification and Assessment of the Risks of Material Misstatement Associated with Related Party Relationships and Transactions

18.　In meeting the ISA (UK and Ireland) 315 requirement to identify and assess the risks of material misstatement,[9] the auditor shall identify and assess the risks of material misstatement associated with related party relationships and transactions and determine whether any of those risks are significant risks. In making this determination, the auditor shall treat identified significant related party transactions outside the entity's normal course of business as giving rise to significant risks.

19.　If the auditor identifies fraud risk factors (including circumstances relating to the existence of a related party with dominant influence) when performing the risk assessment procedures and related activities in connection with related parties, the auditor shall consider such information when identifying and assessing the risks of material misstatement due to fraud in accordance with ISA (UK and Ireland) 240. (Ref: Para. A6 and A29-A30)

Responses to the Risks of Material Misstatement Associated with Related Party Relationships and Transactions

20.　As part of the ISA (UK and Ireland) 330 requirement that the auditor respond to assessed risks,[10] the auditor designs and performs further audit procedures to obtain sufficient appropriate audit evidence about the assessed risks of material misstatement associated with related party relationships and transactions. These audit procedures shall include those required by paragraphs 21-24. (Ref: Para. A31-A34)

Identification of Previously Unidentified or Undisclosed Related Parties or Significant Related Party Transactions

21.　If the auditor identifies arrangements or information that suggests the existence of related party relationships or transactions that management has not previously identified or disclosed to the auditor, the auditor shall determine whether the underlying circumstances confirm the existence of those relationships or transactions.

22.　If the auditor identifies related parties or significant related party transactions that management has not previously identified or disclosed to the auditor, the auditor shall:

(a)　Promptly communicate the relevant information to the other members of the engagement team; (Ref: Para. A35)

(b)　Where the applicable financial reporting framework establishes related party requirements:

---

[9]　ISA (UK and Ireland) 315, paragraph 25.
[10]　ISA (UK and Ireland) 330, paragraphs 5-6.

(i)   Request management to identify all transactions with the newly identified related parties for the auditor's further evaluation; and

(ii)   Inquire as to why the entity's controls over related party relationships and transactions failed to enable the identification or disclosure of the related party relationships or transactions;

(c)   Perform appropriate substantive audit procedures relating to such newly identified related parties or significant related party transactions; (Ref: Para. A36)

(d)   Reconsider the risk that other related parties or significant related party transactions may exist that management has not previously identified or disclosed to the auditor, and perform additional audit procedures as necessary; and

(e)   If the non-disclosure by management appears intentional (and therefore indicative of a risk of material misstatement due to fraud), evaluate the implications for the audit. (Ref: Para. A37)

Identified Significant Related Party Transactions outside the Entity's Normal Course of Business

23.   For identified significant related party transactions outside the entity's normal course of business, the auditor shall:

(a)   Inspect the underlying contracts or agreements, if any, and evaluate whether:

(i)   The business rationale (or lack thereof) of the transactions suggests that they may have been entered into to engage in fraudulent financial reporting or to conceal misappropriation of assets;[11] (Ref: Para. A38-A39)

(ii)   The terms of the transactions are consistent with management's explanations; and

(iii)   The transactions have been appropriately accounted for and disclosed in accordance with the applicable financial reporting framework; and

(b)   Obtain audit evidence that the transactions have been appropriately authorized and approved. (Ref: Para. A40-A41)

Assertions That Related Party Transactions Were Conducted on Terms Equivalent to Those Prevailing in an Arm's Length Transaction

24.   If management has made an assertion in the financial statements to the effect that a related party transaction was conducted on terms equivalent to those prevailing in an

---

[11]   ISA (UK and Ireland) 240, paragraph 32(c).

arm's length transaction, the auditor shall obtain sufficient appropriate audit evidence about the assertion. (Ref: Para. A42-A45)

Evaluation of the Accounting for and Disclosure of Identified Related Party Relationships and Transactions

25. In forming an opinion on the financial statements in accordance with ISA (UK and Ireland) 700,[12] the auditor shall evaluate: (Ref: Para. A46)

    (a) Whether the identified related party relationships and transactions have been appropriately accounted for and disclosed in accordance with the applicable financial reporting framework; and (Ref: Para. A47 – A47-1)

    (b) Whether the effects of the related party relationships and transactions:

        (i) Prevent the financial statements from achieving fair presentation (for fair presentation frameworks); or

        (ii) Cause the financial statements to be misleading (for compliance frameworks).

Written Representations

26. Where the applicable financial reporting framework establishes related party requirements, the auditor shall obtain written representations from management and, where appropriate, those charged with governance that: (Ref: Para. A48 - A49-1)

    (a) They have disclosed to the auditor the identity of the entity's related parties and all the related party relationships and transactions of which they are aware; and

    (b) They have appropriately accounted for and disclosed such relationships and transactions in accordance with the requirements of the framework.

Communication with Those Charged with Governance

27. Unless all of those charged with governance are involved in managing the entity,[13] the auditor shall communicate with those charged with governance significant matters arising during the audit in connection with the entity's related parties. (Ref: Para. A50)

---

[12] ISA 700, "Forming an Opinion and Reporting on Financial Statements," paragraphs 10-15.
The APB has not promulgated ISA 700 as issued by the IAASB for application in the UK and Ireland. In the UK and Ireland the applicable auditing standard is ISA (UK and Ireland) 700, "The Auditor's Report on Financial Statements." Paragraphs 8 - 11 of ISA (UK and Ireland) 700 establish requirements regarding forming an opinion on the financial statements.

[13] ISA (UK and Ireland) 260, "Communication with Those Charged with Governance," paragraph 13.

Documentation

28. The auditor shall include in the audit documentation the names of the identified related parties and the nature of the related party relationships.[14]

***

Application and Other Explanatory Material

Responsibilities of the Auditor

Financial Reporting Frameworks That Establish Minimal Related Party Requirements (Ref: Para. 4)

A1. An applicable financial reporting framework that establishes minimal related party requirements is one that defines the meaning of a related party but that definition has a substantially narrower scope than the definition set out in paragraph 10(b)(ii) of this ISA (UK and Ireland), so that a requirement in the framework to disclose related party relationships and transactions would apply to substantially fewer related party relationships and transactions.

Fair Presentation Frameworks (Ref: Para. 4(a))

A2. In the context of a fair presentation framework,[15] related party relationships and transactions may cause the financial statements to fail to achieve fair presentation if, for example, the economic reality of such relationships and transactions is not appropriately reflected in the financial statements. For instance, fair presentation may not be achieved if the sale of a property by the entity to a controlling shareholder at a price above or below fair market value has been accounted for as a transaction involving a profit or loss for the entity when it may constitute a contribution or return of capital or the payment of a dividend.

Compliance Frameworks (Ref: Para. 4(b))

A3. In the context of a compliance framework, whether related party relationships and transactions cause the financial statements to be misleading as discussed in ISA (UK and Ireland) 700 depends upon the particular circumstances of the engagement. For example, even if non-disclosure of related party transactions in the financial statements is in compliance with the framework and applicable law or regulation, the financial statements could be misleading if the entity derives a very substantial portion of its revenue from transactions with related parties, and that fact is not disclosed. However, it will be extremely rare for the auditor to consider financial statements that are prepared and presented in accordance with a compliance

---

[14] ISA (UK and Ireland) 230, "Audit Documentation," paragraphs 8-11, and paragraph A6.
[15] ISA 200, paragraph 13(a), defines the meaning of fair presentation and compliance frameworks.

framework to be misleading if in accordance with ISA (UK and Ireland) 210[16] the auditor determined that the framework is acceptable.[17]

Definition of a Related Party (Ref: Para. 10(b))

A4. Many financial reporting frameworks discuss the concepts of control and significant influence. Although they may discuss these concepts using different terms, they generally explain that:

(a) Control is the power to govern the financial and operating policies of an entity so as to obtain benefits from its activities; and

(b) Significant influence (which may be gained by share ownership, statute or agreement) is the power to participate in the financial and operating policy decisions of an entity, but is not control over those policies.

A5. The existence of the following relationships may indicate the presence of control or significant influence:

(a) Direct or indirect equity holdings or other financial interests in the entity.

(b) The entity's holdings of direct or indirect equity or other financial interests in other entities.

(c) Being part of those charged with governance or key management (that is, those members of management who have the authority and responsibility for planning, directing and controlling the activities of the entity).

(d) Being a close family member of any person referred to in subparagraph (c).

(e) Having a significant business relationship with any person referred to in subparagraph (c).

Related Parties with Dominant Influence

A6. Related parties, by virtue of their ability to exert control or significant influence, may be in a position to exert dominant influence over the entity or its management. Consideration of such behavior is relevant when identifying and assessing the risks of material misstatement due to fraud, as further explained in paragraphs A29-A30.

---

[16] ISA (UK and Ireland) 210, "Agreeing the Terms of Audit Engagements," paragraph 6(a).
[17] ISA 700, paragraph A12.
The APB has not promulgated ISA 700 as issued by the IAASB for application in the UK and Ireland. In the UK and Ireland the applicable auditing standard is ISA (UK and Ireland) 700, "The Auditor's Report on Financial Statements." Paragraph A12 of ISA 700 states "It will be extremely rare for the auditor to consider financial statements that are prepared in accordance with a compliance framework to be misleading if, in accordance with ISA 210, the auditor determined that the framework is acceptable."

Special-Purpose Entities as Related Parties

A7.   In some circumstances, a special-purpose entity[18] may be a related party of the entity because the entity may in substance control it, even if the entity owns little or none of the special-purpose entity's equity.

Risk Assessment Procedures and Related Activities

Risks of Material Misstatement Associated with Related Party Relationships and Transactions (Ref: Para. 11)

Considerations Specific to Public Sector Entities

A8.   The public sector auditor's responsibilities regarding related party relationships and transactions may be affected by the audit mandate, or by obligations on public sector entities arising from law, regulation or other authority. Consequently, the public sector auditor's responsibilities may not be limited to addressing the risks of material misstatement associated with related party relationships and transactions, but may also include a broader responsibility to address the risks of non-compliance with law, regulation and other authority governing public sector bodies that lay down specific requirements in the conduct of business with related parties. Further, the public sector auditor may need to have regard to public sector financial reporting requirements for related party relationships and transactions that may differ from those in the private sector.

Understanding the Entity's Related Party Relationships and Transactions

Discussion among the Engagement Team (Ref: Para. 12)

A9.   Matters that may be addressed in the discussion among the engagement team include:

- The nature and extent of the entity's relationships and transactions with related parties (using, for example, the auditor's record of identified related parties updated after each audit).

- An emphasis on the importance of maintaining professional skepticism throughout the audit regarding the potential for material misstatement associated with related party relationships and transactions.

- The circumstances or conditions of the entity that may indicate the existence of related party relationships or transactions that management has not identified or disclosed to the auditor for example, a complex organizational structure, use of special-purpose entities for off-balance sheet transactions, or an inadequate information system).

---

[18] ISA (UK and Ireland) 315, paragraphs A26-A27, provides guidance regarding the nature of a special-purpose entity.

- The records or documents that may indicate the existence of related party relationships or transactions.

- The importance that management and those charged with governance attach to the identification, appropriate accounting for, and disclosure of related party relationships and transactions (if the applicable financial reporting framework establishes related party requirements), and the related risk of management override of relevant controls.

A10. In addition, the discussion in the context of fraud may include specific consideration of how related parties may be involved in fraud. For example:

- How special-purpose entities controlled by management might be used to facilitate earnings management.

- How transactions between the entity and a known business partner of a key member of management could be arranged to facilitate misappropriation of the entity's assets.

The Identity of the Entity's Related Parties (Ref: Para. 13(a))

A11. Where the applicable financial reporting framework establishes related party requirements, information regarding the identity of the entity's related parties is likely to be readily available to management because the entity's information systems will need to record, process and summarize related party relationships and transactions to enable the entity to meet the accounting and disclosure requirements of the framework. Management is therefore likely to have a comprehensive list of related parties and changes from the prior period. For recurring engagements, making the inquiries provides a basis for comparing the information supplied by management with the auditor's record of related parties noted in previous audits.

A12. However, where the framework does not establish related party requirements, the entity may not have such information systems in place. Under such circumstances, it is possible that management may not be aware of the existence of all related parties. Nevertheless, the requirement to make the inquiries specified by paragraph 13 still applies because management may be aware of parties that meet the related party definition set out in this ISA (UK and Ireland). In such a case, however, the auditor's inquiries regarding the identity of the entity's related parties are likely to form part of the auditor's risk assessment procedures and related activities performed in accordance with ISA (UK and Ireland) 315 to obtain information regarding:

- The entity's ownership and governance structures;

- The types of investments that the entity is making and plans to make; and

- The way the entity is structured and how it is financed.

In the particular case of common control relationships, as management is more likely to be aware of such relationships if they have economic significance to the entity, the auditor's inquiries are likely to be more effective if they are focused on whether parties with which the entity engages in significant transactions, or shares resources to a significant degree, are related parties.

A13. In the context of a group audit, ISA (UK and Ireland) 600 requires the group engagement team to provide each component auditor with a list of related parties prepared by group management and any other related parties of which the group engagement team is aware.[19] Where the entity is a component within a group, this information provides a useful basis for the auditor's inquiries of management regarding the identity of the entity's related parties.

A14. The auditor may also obtain some information regarding the identity of the entity's related parties through inquiries of management during the engagement acceptance or continuance process.

The Entity's Controls over Related Party Relationships and Transactions (Ref: Para. 14)

A15. Others within the entity are those considered likely to have knowledge of the entity's related party relationships and transactions, and the entity's controls over such relationships and transactions. These may include, to the extent that they do not form part of management:

- Those charged with governance;

- Personnel in a position to initiate, process, or record transactions that are both significant and outside the entity's normal course of business, and those who supervise or monitor such personnel;

- The internal audit function;

- In-house legal counsel; and

- The chief ethics officer or equivalent person.

A16. The audit is conducted on the premise that management and, where appropriate, those charged with governance have acknowledged and understand that they have responsibility for the preparation of the financial statements in accordance with the applicable financial reporting framework, including where relevant their fair presentation, and for such internal control as management and, where appropriate, those charged with governance determine is necessary to enable the preparation of financial statements that are free from material misstatement, whether due to fraud or error.[20] Accordingly, where the framework establishes related party requirements, the

---

[19] ISA (UK and Ireland) 600, "Special Considerations—Audits of Group Financial Statements (Including the Work of Component Auditors)," paragraph 40(e).
[20] ISA (UK and Ireland) 200, paragraph A2.

preparation of the financial statements requires management, with oversight from those charged with governance, to design, implement and maintain adequate controls over related party relationships and transactions so that these are identified and appropriately accounted for and disclosed in accordance with the framework. In their oversight role, those charged with governance monitor how management is discharging its responsibility for such controls. Regardless of any related party requirements the framework may establish, those charged with governance may, in their oversight role, obtain information from management to enable them to understand the nature and business rationale of the entity's related party relationships and transactions.

A17. In meeting the ISA (UK and Ireland) 315 (Revised June 2013) requirement to obtain an understanding of the control environment,[21] the auditor may consider features of the control environment relevant to mitigating the risks of material misstatement associated with related party relationships and transactions, such as:

- Internal ethical codes, appropriately communicated to the entity's personnel and enforced, governing the circumstances in which the entity may enter into specific types of related party transactions.

- Policies and procedures for open and timely disclosure of the interests that management and those charged with governance have in related party transactions.

- The assignment of responsibilities within the entity for identifying, recording, summarizing, and disclosing related party transactions.

- Timely disclosure and discussion between management and those charged with governance of significant related party transactions outside the entity's normal course of business, including whether those charged with governance have appropriately challenged the business rationale of such transactions (for example, by seeking advice from external professional advisors).

- Clear guidelines for the approval of related party transactions involving actual or perceived conflicts of interest, such as approval by a subcommittee of those charged with governance comprising individuals independent of management.

- Periodic reviews by the internal audit function, where applicable.

- Proactive action taken by management to resolve related party disclosure issues, such as by seeking advice from the auditor or external legal counsel.

- The existence of whistle-blowing policies and procedures, where applicable.

A18. Controls over related party relationships and transactions within some entities may be deficient or non-existent for a number of reasons, such as:

---

[21] ISA (UK and Ireland) 315 (Revised June 2013), paragraph 14.

- The low importance attached by management to identifying and disclosing related party relationships and transactions.

- The lack of appropriate oversight by those charged with governance.

- An intentional disregard for such controls because related party disclosures may reveal information that management considers sensitive, for example, the existence of transactions involving family members of management.

- An insufficient understanding by management of the related party requirements of the applicable financial reporting framework.

- The absence of disclosure requirements under the applicable financial reporting framework.

Where such controls are ineffective or non-existent, the auditor may be unable to obtain sufficient appropriate audit evidence about related party relationships and transactions. If this were the case, the auditor would, in accordance with ISA (UK and Ireland) 705,[22] consider the implications for the audit, including the opinion in the auditor's report.

A19. Fraudulent financial reporting often involves management override of controls that otherwise may appear to be operating effectively.[23] The risk of management override of controls is higher if management has relationships that involve control or significant influence with parties with which the entity does business because these relationships may present management with greater incentives and opportunities to perpetrate fraud. For example, management's financial interests in certain related parties may provide incentives for management to override controls by (a) directing the entity, against its interests, to conclude transactions for the benefit of these parties, or (b) colluding with such parties or controlling their actions. Examples of possible fraud include:

- Creating fictitious terms of transactions with related parties designed to misrepresent the business rationale of these transactions.

- Fraudulently organizing the transfer of assets from or to management or others at amounts significantly above or below market value.

- Engaging in complex transactions with related parties, such as special-purpose entities, that are structured to misrepresent the financial position or financial performance of the entity.

---

[22] ISA (UK and Ireland) 705, "Modifications to the Opinion in the Independent Auditor's Report."
[23] ISA (UK and Ireland) 240, paragraphs 31 and A4.

Considerations specific to smaller entities

A20. Control activities in smaller entities are likely to be less formal and smaller entities may have no documented processes for dealing with related party relationships and transactions. An owner-manager may mitigate some of the risks arising from related party transactions, or potentially increase those risks, through active involvement in all the main aspects of the transactions. For such entities, the auditor may obtain an understanding of the related party relationships and transactions, and any controls that may exist over these, through inquiry of management combined with other procedures, such as observation of management's oversight and review activities, and inspection of available relevant documentation.

Authorization and approval of significant transactions and arrangements (Ref: Para. 14(b))

A21. Authorization involves the granting of permission by a party or parties with the appropriate authority (whether management, those charged with governance or the entity's shareholders) for the entity to enter into specific transactions in accordance with pre-determined criteria, whether judgmental or not. Approval involves those parties' acceptance of the transactions the entity has entered into as having satisfied the criteria on which authorization was granted. Examples of controls the entity may have established to authorize and approve significant transactions and arrangements with related parties or significant transactions and arrangements outside the normal course of business include:

- Monitoring controls to identify such transactions and arrangements for authorization and approval.

- Approval of the terms and conditions of the transactions and arrangements by management, those charged with governance or, where applicable, shareholders.

Maintaining Alertness for Related Party Information When Reviewing Records or Documents

Records or Documents That the Auditor May Inspect (Ref: Para. 15)

A22. During the audit, the auditor may inspect records or documents that may provide information about related party relationships and transactions, for example:

- Third-party confirmations obtained by the auditor (in addition to bank and legal confirmations).

- Entity income tax returns.

- Information supplied by the entity to regulatory authorities.

- Shareholder registers to identify the entity's principal shareholders.

- Statements of conflicts of interest from management and those charged with governance.

- Records of the entity's investments and those of its pension plans.

- Contracts and agreements with key management or those charged with governance.

- Significant contracts and agreements not in the entity's ordinary course of business.

- Specific invoices and correspondence from the entity's professional advisors.

- Life insurance policies acquired by the entity.

- Significant contracts re-negotiated by the entity during the period.

- Reports of the internal audit function.

- Documents associated with the entity's filings with a securities regulator (for example, prospectuses).

Arrangements that may indicate the existence of previously unidentified or undisclosed related party relationships or transactions

A23. An arrangement involves a formal or informal agreement between the entity and one or more other parties for such purposes as:

- The establishment of a business relationship through appropriate vehicles or structures.

- The conduct of certain types of transactions under specific terms and conditions.

- The provision of designated services or financial support.

Examples of arrangements that may indicate the existence of related party relationships or transactions that management has not previously identified or disclosed to the auditor include:

- Participation in unincorporated partnerships with other parties.

- Agreements for the provision of services to certain parties under terms and conditions that are outside the entity's normal course of business.

- Guarantees and guarantor relationships.

Identification of Significant Transactions outside the Normal Course of Business (Ref: Para. 16)

A24. Obtaining further information on significant transactions outside the entity's normal course of business enables the auditor to evaluate whether fraud risk factors, if any, are present and, where the applicable financial reporting framework establishes related party requirements, to identify the risks of material misstatement.

A25. Examples of transactions outside the entity's normal course of business may include:

- Complex equity transactions, such as corporate restructurings or acquisitions.

- Transactions with offshore entities in jurisdictions with weak corporate laws.

- The leasing of premises or the rendering of management services by the entity to another party if no consideration is exchanged.

- Sales transactions with unusually large discounts or returns.

- Transactions with circular arrangements, for example, sales with a commitment to repurchase.

- Transactions under contracts whose terms are changed before expiry.

Understanding the nature of significant transactions outside the normal course of business (Ref: Para. 16(a))

A26. Inquiring into the nature of the significant transactions outside the entity's normal course of business involves obtaining an understanding of the business rationale of the transactions, and the terms and conditions under which these have been entered into.

Inquiring into whether related parties could be involved (Ref: Para. 16(b))

A27. A related party could be involved in a significant transaction outside the entity's normal course of business not only by directly influencing the transaction through being a party to the transaction, but also by indirectly influencing it through an intermediary. Such influence may indicate the presence of a fraud risk factor.

Sharing Related Party Information with the Engagement Team (Ref: Para. 17)

A28. Relevant related party information that may be shared among the engagement team members includes, for example:

- The identity of the entity's related parties.

- The nature of the related party relationships and transactions.

- Significant or complex related party relationships or transactions that may require special audit consideration, in particular transactions in which management or those charged with governance are financially involved.

Identification and Assessment of the Risks of Material Misstatement Associated with Related Party Relationships and Transactions

Fraud Risk Factors Associated with a Related Party with Dominant Influence (Ref: Para. 19)

A29. Domination of management by a single person or small group of persons without compensating controls is a fraud risk factor.[24] Indicators of dominant influence exerted by a related party include:

- The related party has vetoed significant business decisions taken by management or those charged with governance.

- Significant transactions are referred to the related party for final approval.

- There is little or no debate among management and those charged with governance regarding business proposals initiated by the related party.

- Transactions involving the related party (or a close family member of the related party) are rarely independently reviewed and approved.

Dominant influence may also exist in some cases if the related party has played a leading role in founding the entity and continues to play a leading role in managing the entity.

A30. In the presence of other risk factors, the existence of a related party with dominant influence may indicate significant risks of material misstatement due to fraud. For example:

- An unusually high turnover of senior management or professional advisors may suggest unethical or fraudulent business practices that serve the related party's purposes.

- The use of business intermediaries for significant transactions for which there appears to be no clear business justification may suggest that the related party could have an interest in such transactions through control of such intermediaries for fraudulent purposes.

- Evidence of the related party's excessive participation in or preoccupation with the selection of accounting policies or the determination of significant estimates may suggest the possibility of fraudulent financial reporting.

---

[24] ISA (UK and Ireland) 240, Appendix 1.

Responses to the Risks of Material Misstatement Associated with Related Party Relationships and Transactions (Ref: Para. 20)

A31. The nature, timing and extent of the further audit procedures that the auditor may select to respond to the assessed risks of material misstatement associated with related party relationships and transactions depend upon the nature of those risks and the circumstances of the entity.[25]

A32. Examples of substantive audit procedures that the auditor may perform when the auditor has assessed a significant risk that management has not appropriately accounted for or disclosed specific related party transactions in accordance with the applicable financial reporting framework (whether due to fraud or error) include:

- Confirming or discussing specific aspects of the transactions with intermediaries such as banks, law firms, guarantors, or agents, where practicable and not prohibited by law, regulation or ethical rules.

- Confirming the purposes, specific terms or amounts of the transactions with the related parties (this audit procedure may be less effective where the auditor judges that the entity is likely to influence the related parties in their responses to the auditor).

- Where applicable, reading the financial statements or other relevant financial information, if available, of the related parties for evidence of the accounting of the transactions in the related parties' accounting records.

A33. If the auditor has assessed a significant risk of material misstatement due to fraud as a result of the presence of a related party with dominant influence, the auditor may, in addition to the general requirements of ISA (UK and Ireland) 240, perform audit procedures such as the following to obtain an understanding of the business relationships that such a related party may have established directly or indirectly with the entity and to determine the need for further appropriate substantive audit procedures:

- Inquiries of, and discussion with, management and those charged with governance.

- Inquiries of the related party.

- Inspection of significant contracts with the related party.

- Appropriate background research, such as through the Internet or specific external business information databases.

- Review of employee whistle-blowing reports where these are retained.

---

[25] ISA (UK and Ireland) 330 provides further guidance on considering the nature, timing and extent of further audit procedures. ISA 240 establishes requirements and provides guidance on appropriate responses to assessed risks of material misstatement due to fraud.

A34. Depending upon the results of the auditor's risk assessment procedures, the auditor may consider it appropriate to obtain audit evidence without testing the entity's controls over related party relationships and transactions. In some circumstances, however, it may not be possible to obtain sufficient appropriate audit evidence from substantive audit procedures alone in relation to the risks of material misstatement associated with related party relationships and transactions. For example, where intra-group transactions between the entity and its components are numerous and a significant amount of information regarding these transactions is initiated, recorded, processed or reported electronically in an integrated system, the auditor may determine that it is not possible to design effective substantive audit procedures that by themselves would reduce the risks of material misstatement associated with these transactions to an acceptably low level. In such a case, in meeting the ISA (UK and Ireland) 330 requirement to obtain sufficient appropriate audit evidence as to the operating effectiveness of relevant controls,[26] the auditor is required to test the entity's controls over the completeness and accuracy of the recording of the related party relationships and transactions.

Identification of Previously Unidentified or Undisclosed Related Parties or Significant Related Party Transactions

Communicating Newly Identified Related Party Information to the Engagement Team (Ref: Para. 22(a))

A35. Communicating promptly any newly identified related parties to the other members of the engagement team assists them in determining whether this information affects the results of, and conclusions drawn from, risk assessment procedures already performed, including whether the risks of material misstatement need to be reassessed.

Substantive Procedures Relating to Newly Identified Related Parties or Significant Related Party Transactions (Ref: Para. 22(c))

A36. Examples of substantive audit procedures that the auditor may perform relating to newly identified related parties or significant related party transactions include:

- Making inquiries regarding the nature of the entity's relationships with the newly identified related parties, including (where appropriate and not prohibited by law, regulation or ethical rules) inquiring of parties outside the entity who are presumed to have significant knowledge of the entity and its business, such as legal counsel, principal agents, major representatives, consultants, guarantors, or other close business partners.

- Conducting an analysis of accounting records for transactions with the newly identified related parties. Such an analysis may be facilitated using computer-assisted audit techniques.

---

[26] ISA (UK and Ireland) 330, paragraph 8(b).

- Verifying the terms and conditions of the newly identified related party transactions, and evaluating whether the transactions have been appropriately accounted for and disclosed in accordance with the applicable financial reporting framework.

Intentional Non-Disclosure by Management (Ref: Para. 22(e))

A37. The requirements and guidance in ISA (UK and Ireland) 240 regarding the auditor's responsibilities relating to fraud in an audit of financial statements are relevant where management appears to have intentionally failed to disclose related parties or significant related party transactions to the auditor. The auditor may also consider whether it is necessary to re-evaluate the reliability of management's responses to the auditor's inquiries and management's representations to the auditor.

Identified Significant Related Party Transactions outside the Entity's Normal Course of Business

Evaluating the Business Rationale of Significant Related Party Transactions (Ref: Para. 23)

A38. In evaluating the business rationale of a significant related party transaction outside the entity's normal course of business, the auditor may consider the following:

- Whether the transaction:

  ○ Is overly complex (for example, it may involve multiple related parties within a consolidated group).

  ○ Has unusual terms of trade, such as unusual prices, interest rates, guarantees and repayment terms.

  ○ Lacks an apparent logical business reason for its occurrence.

  ○ Involves previously unidentified related parties.

  ○ Is processed in an unusual manner.

- Whether management has discussed the nature of, and accounting for, such a transaction with those charged with governance.

- Whether management is placing more emphasis on a particular accounting treatment rather than giving due regard to the underlying economics of the transaction.

  If management's explanations are materially inconsistent with the terms of the related party transaction, the auditor is required, in accordance with ISA (UK and Ireland)

500,[27] to consider the reliability of management's explanations and representations on other significant matters.

A39. The auditor may also seek to understand the business rationale of such a transaction from the related party's perspective, as this may help the auditor to better understand the economic reality of the transaction and why it was carried out. A business rationale from the related party's perspective that appears inconsistent with the nature of its business may represent a fraud risk factor.

Authorization and Approval of Significant Related Party Transactions (Ref: Para. 23(b))

A40. Authorization and approval by management, those charged with governance, or, where applicable, the shareholders of significant related party transactions outside the entity's normal course of business may provide audit evidence that these have been duly considered at the appropriate levels within the entity and that their terms and conditions have been appropriately reflected in the financial statements. The existence of transactions of this nature that were not subject to such authorization and approval, in the absence of rational explanations based on discussion with management or those charged with governance, may indicate risks of material misstatement due to error or fraud. In these circumstances, the auditor may need to be alert for other transactions of a similar nature. Authorization and approval alone, however, may not be sufficient in concluding whether risks of material misstatement due to fraud are absent because authorization and approval may be ineffective if there has been collusion between the related parties or if the entity is subject to the dominant influence of a related party.

Considerations specific to smaller entities

A41. A smaller entity may not have the same controls provided by different levels of authority and approval that may exist in a larger entity. Accordingly, when auditing a smaller entity, the auditor may rely to a lesser degree on authorization and approval for audit evidence regarding the validity of significant related party transactions outside the entity's normal course of business. Instead, the auditor may consider performing other audit procedures such as inspecting relevant documents, confirming specific aspects of the transactions with relevant parties, or observing the owner-manager's involvement with the transactions.

Assertions That Related Party Transactions Were Conducted on Terms Equivalent to Those Prevailing in an Arm's Length Transaction (Ref: Para. 24)

A42. Although audit evidence may be readily available regarding how the price of a related party transaction compares to that of a similar arm's length transaction, there are ordinarily practical difficulties that limit the auditor's ability to obtain audit evidence that all other aspects of the transaction are equivalent to those of the arm's length transaction. For example, although the auditor may be able to confirm that a related

---

[27] ISA (UK and Ireland) 500, "Audit Evidence," paragraph 11.

party transaction has been conducted at a market price, it may be impracticable to confirm whether other terms and conditions of the transaction (such as credit terms, contingencies and specific charges) are equivalent to those that would ordinarily be agreed between independent parties. Accordingly, there may be a risk that management's assertion that a related party transaction was conducted on terms equivalent to those prevailing in an arm's length transaction may be materially misstated.

A43. The preparation of the financial statements requires management to substantiate an assertion that a related party transaction was conducted on terms equivalent to those prevailing in an arm's length transaction. Management's support for the assertion may include:

- Comparing the terms of the related party transaction to those of an identical or similar transaction with one or more unrelated parties.

- Engaging an external expert to determine a market value and to confirm market terms and conditions for the transaction.

- Comparing the terms of the transaction to known market terms for broadly similar transactions on an open market.

A44. Evaluating management's support for this assertion may involve one or more of the following:

- Considering the appropriateness of management's process for supporting the assertion.

- Verifying the source of the internal or external data supporting the assertion, and testing the data to determine their accuracy, completeness and relevance.

- Evaluating the reasonableness of any significant assumptions on which the assertion is based.

A45. Some financial reporting frameworks require the disclosure of related party transactions not conducted on terms equivalent to those prevailing in arm's length transactions. In these circumstances, if management has not disclosed a related party transaction in the financial statements, there may be an implicit assertion that the transaction was conducted on terms equivalent to those prevailing in an arm's length transaction.

Evaluation of the Accounting for and Disclosure of Identified Related Party Relationships and Transactions

Materiality Considerations in Evaluating Misstatements (Ref: Para. 25)

A46. ISA (UK and Ireland) 450 requires the auditor to consider both the size and the nature of a misstatement, and the particular circumstances of its occurrence, when evaluating whether the misstatement is material.[28] The significance of the transaction to the financial statement users may not depend solely on the recorded amount of the transaction but also on other specific relevant factors, such as the nature of the related party relationship.

Evaluation of Related Party Disclosures (Ref: Para. 25(a))

A47. Evaluating the related party disclosures in the context of the disclosure requirements of the applicable financial reporting framework means considering whether the facts and circumstances of the entity's related party relationships and transactions have been appropriately summarized and presented so that the disclosures are understandable. Disclosures of related party transactions may not be understandable if:

(a) The business rationale and the effects of the transactions on the financial statements are unclear or misstated; or

(b) Key terms, conditions, or other important elements of the transactions necessary for understanding them are not appropriately disclosed.

A47-1. Accounting standards and corporate law applicable in the UK and Ireland include requirements for many entities for disclosures relating to control of the entity. The auditor may only be able to determine the name of the entity's ultimate controlling party through specific inquiry of management or those charged with governance. When the auditor considers it necessary, the auditor obtains corroboration from the ultimate controlling party confirming representations received in this regard.

Written Representations (Ref: Para. 26)

A48. Circumstances in which it may be appropriate to obtain written representations from those charged with governance include:

- When they have approved specific related party transactions that (a) materially affect the financial statements, or (b) involve management.

- When they have made specific oral representations to the auditor on details of certain related party transactions.

---

[28] ISA (UK and Ireland) 450, "Evaluation of Misstatements Identified during the Audit," paragraph 11(a). Paragraph A16 of ISA 450 provides guidance on the circumstances that may affect the evaluation of a misstatement.

- When they have financial or other interests in the related parties or the related party transactions.

A49. The auditor may also decide to obtain written representations regarding specific assertions that management may have made, such as a representation that specific related party transactions do not involve undisclosed side agreements.

A49-1. An entity may require its management and those charged with governance to sign individual declarations in relation to related party matters. It may be helpful if any such declarations are addressed jointly to a designated official of the entity and also to the auditor. In other cases, the auditor may wish to obtain written representations directly from each of those charged with governance and from members of management.

Communication with Those Charged with Governance (Ref: Para. 27)

A50. Communicating significant matters arising during the audit[29] in connection with the entity's related parties helps the auditor to establish a common understanding with those charged with governance of the nature and resolution of these matters. Examples of significant related party matters include:

- Non-disclosure (whether intentional or not) by management to the auditor of related parties or significant related party transactions, which may alert those charged with governance to significant related party relationships and transactions of which they may not have been previously aware.

- The identification of significant related party transactions that have not been appropriately authorized and approved, which may give rise to suspected fraud.

- Disagreement with management regarding the accounting for and disclosure of significant related party transactions in accordance with the applicable financial reporting framework.

- Non-compliance with applicable law or regulations prohibiting or restricting specific types of related party transactions.

- Difficulties in identifying the party that ultimately controls the entity.

---

[29] ISA (UK and Ireland) 230, paragraph A8, provides further guidance on the nature of significant matters arising during the audit.

INTERNATIONAL STANDARD ON AUDITING
(UK AND IRELAND) 560

SUBSEQUENT EVENTS

(Effective for audits of financial statements for periods ending on or after 15 December 2010)

CONTENTS

International Standard on Auditing (UK and Ireland) (ISA (UK and Ireland)) 560, "Subsequent Events" should be read in conjunction with ISA (UK and Ireland) 200, "Overall Objectives of the Independent Auditor and the Conduct of an Audit in Accordance with International Standards on Auditing (UK and Ireland)."

Introduction

Scope of this ISA (UK and Ireland)

1. This International Standard on Auditing (UK and Ireland) (ISA (UK and Ireland)) deals with the auditor's responsibilities relating to subsequent events in an audit of financial statements. (Ref: Para. A1)

Subsequent Events

2. Financial statements may be affected by certain events that occur after the date of the financial statements. Many financial reporting frameworks specifically refer to such events.[1] Such financial reporting frameworks ordinarily identify two types of events:

    (a) Those that provide evidence of conditions that existed at the date of the financial statements; and

    (b) Those that provide evidence of conditions that arose after the date of the financial statements.

    ISA (UK and Ireland) 700 explains that the date of the auditor's report informs the reader that the auditor has considered the effect of events and transactions of which the auditor becomes aware and that occurred up to that date.[2]

Effective Date

3. This ISA (UK and Ireland) is effective for audits of financial statements for periods ending on or after 15 December 2010.

Objectives

4. The objectives of the auditor are:

    (a) To obtain sufficient appropriate audit evidence about whether events occurring between the date of the financial statements and the date of the auditor's report that require adjustment of, or disclosure in, the financial statements are

---

[1] For example, International Accounting Standard (IAS) 10, "Events After the Reporting Period" deals with the treatment in financial statements of events, both favorable and unfavorable, that occur between the date of the financial statements (referred to as the "end of the reporting period" in the IAS) and the date when the financial statements are authorized for issue.

[2] ISA (UK and Ireland) 700, "Forming an Opinion and Reporting on Financial Statements," paragraph A38.
The APB has not promulgated ISA 700 as issued by the IAASB for application in the UK and Ireland. In the UK and Ireland the applicable auditing standard is ISA (UK and Ireland) 700, "The Auditor's Report on Financial Statements." Paragraph A19 of ISA (UK and Ireland) 700 explains that the date of the auditor's report informs the reader that the auditor has considered the effect of events and transactions of which the auditor becomes aware and that occurred up to that date.

appropriately reflected in those financial statements in accordance with the applicable financial reporting framework; and

(b) To respond appropriately to facts that become known to the auditor after the date of the auditor's report, that, had they been known to the auditor at that date, may have caused the auditor to amend the auditor's report.

Definitions

5. For purposes of the ISAs (UK and Ireland), the following terms have the meanings attributed below:

(a) Date of the financial statements – The date of the end of the latest period covered by the financial statements.

(b) Date of approval of the financial statements – The date on which all the statements that comprise the financial statements, including the related notes, have been prepared and those with the recognized authority have asserted that they have taken responsibility for those financial statements. (Ref: Para. A2)

(c) Date of the auditor's report – The date the auditor dates the report on the financial statements in accordance with ISA (UK and Ireland) 700. (Ref: Para. A3)

(d) Date the financial statements are issued – The date that the auditor's report and audited financial statements are made available to third parties. (Ref: Para. A4-A5)

(e) Subsequent events – Events occurring between the date of the financial statements and the date of the auditor's report, and facts that become known to the auditor after the date of the auditor's report.

Requirements

Events Occurring between the Date of the Financial Statements and the Date of the Auditor's Report

6. The auditor shall perform audit procedures designed to obtain sufficient appropriate audit evidence that all events occurring between the date of the financial statements and the date of the auditor's report that require adjustment of, or disclosure in, the financial statements have been identified. The auditor is not, however, expected to perform additional audit procedures on matters to which previously applied audit procedures have provided satisfactory conclusions. (Ref: Para. A6)

7. The auditor shall perform the procedures required by paragraph 6 so that they cover the period from the date of the financial statements to the date of the auditor's report, or as near as practicable thereto. The auditor shall take into account the auditor's risk

assessment in determining the nature and extent of such audit procedures, which shall include the following: (Ref: Para. A7-A8)

(a) Obtaining an understanding of any procedures management has established to ensure that subsequent events are identified.

(b) Inquiring of management and, where appropriate, those charged with governance as to whether any subsequent events have occurred which might affect the financial statements. (Ref: Para. A9)

(c) Reading minutes, if any, of the meetings, of the entity's owners, management and those charged with governance, that have been held after the date of the financial statements and inquiring about matters discussed at any such meetings for which minutes are not yet available. (Ref: Para. A10)

(d) Reading the entity's latest subsequent interim financial statements, if any.

8. If, as a result of the procedures performed as required by paragraphs 6 and 7, the auditor identifies events that require adjustment of, or disclosure in, the financial statements, the auditor shall determine whether each such event is appropriately reflected in those financial statements in accordance with the applicable financial reporting framework.

Written Representations

9. The auditor shall request management and, where appropriate, those charged with governance, to provide a written representation in accordance with ISA (UK and Ireland) 580[3] that all events occurring subsequent to the date of the financial statements and for which the applicable financial reporting framework requires adjustment or disclosure have been adjusted or disclosed.

Facts Which Become Known to the Auditor after the Date of the Auditor's Report but before the Date the Financial Statements Are Issued

10. The auditor has no obligation to perform any audit procedures regarding the financial statements after the date of the auditor's report. However, if, after the date of the auditor's report but before the date the financial statements are issued, a fact becomes known to the auditor that, had it been known to the auditor at the date of the auditor's report, may have caused the auditor to amend the auditor's report, the auditor shall: (Ref: Para. A11)

(a) Discuss the matter with management and, where appropriate, those charged with governance.

(b) Determine whether the financial statements need amendment and, if so,

---

[3] ISA (UK and Ireland) 580, "Written Representations."

(c) Inquire how management intends to address the matter in the financial statements.

11. If management[3a] amends the financial statements, the auditor shall:

    (a) Carry out the audit procedures necessary in the circumstances on the amendment.

    (b) Unless the circumstances in paragraph 12 apply:

        (i) Extend the audit procedures referred to in paragraphs 6 and 7 to the date of the new auditor's report; and

        (ii) Provide a new auditor's report on the amended financial statements. The new auditor's report shall not be dated earlier than the date of approval of the amended financial statements.

12. Where law, regulation or the financial reporting framework does not prohibit management[3a] from restricting the amendment of the financial statements to the effects of the subsequent event or events causing that amendment and those responsible for approving the financial statements are not prohibited from restricting their approval to that amendment, the auditor is permitted to restrict the audit procedures on subsequent events required in paragraph 11(b)(i) to that amendment. In such cases, the auditor shall either:

    (a) Amend the auditor's report to include an additional date restricted to that amendment that thereby indicates that the auditor's procedures on subsequent events are restricted solely to the amendment of the financial statements described in the relevant note to the financial statements; or (Ref: Para. A12)

    (b) Provide a new or amended auditor's report that includes a statement in an Emphasis of Matter paragraph[4] or Other Matter paragraph that conveys that the auditor's procedures on subsequent events are restricted solely to the amendment of the financial statements as described in the relevant note to the financial statements.

13. In some jurisdictions, management[3a] may not be required by law, regulation or the financial reporting framework to issue amended financial statements and, accordingly, the auditor need not provide an amended or new auditor's report. However, if management does not amend the financial statements in circumstances where the auditor believes they need to be amended, then: (Ref: Para. A13-A14)

[3a] In the UK and Ireland the responsibility for amending the financial statements rests with those charged with governance.

[4] See ISA (UK and Ireland) 706, "Emphasis of Matter Paragraphs and Other Matter Paragraphs in the Independent Auditor's Report."

(a)   If the auditor's report has not yet been provided to the entity, the auditor shall modify the opinion as required by ISA (UK and Ireland) 705[5] and then provide the auditor's report; or

(b)   If the auditor's report has already been provided to the entity, the auditor shall notify management and, unless all of those charged with governance are involved in managing the entity, those charged with governance, not to issue the financial statements to third parties before the necessary amendments have been made. If the financial statements are nevertheless subsequently issued without the necessary amendments, the auditor shall take appropriate action, to seek to prevent reliance on the auditor's report. (Ref. Para: A15-A16)

Facts Which Become Known to the Auditor after the Financial Statements Have Been Issued

14.   After the financial statements have been issued, the auditor has no obligation to perform any audit procedures regarding such financial statements. However, if, after the financial statements have been issued, a fact becomes known to the auditor that, had it been known to the auditor at the date of the auditor's report, may have caused the auditor to amend the auditor's report, the auditor shall:

(a)   Discuss the matter with management and, where appropriate, those charged with governance;

(b)   Determine whether the financial statements need amendment; and, if so,

(c)   Inquire how management intends to address the matter in the financial statements. (Ref: Para. A16-1 – A16-3)

15.   If management[3a] amends the financial statements[5a], the auditor shall: (Ref: Para. A17)

(a)   Carry out the audit procedures necessary in the circumstances on the amendment.

(b)   Review the steps taken by management to ensure that anyone in receipt of the previously issued financial statements together with the auditor's report thereon is informed of the situation.

(c)   Unless the circumstances in paragraph 12 apply:

     (i)   Extend the audit procedures referred to in paragraphs 6 and 7 to the date of the new auditor's report, and date the new auditor's report no earlier than the date of approval of the amended financial statements; and

---

[5]   ISA (UK and Ireland) 705, "Modifications to the Opinion in the Independent Auditor's Report."

[5a]   In the UK the detailed regulations governing revised financial statements and directors' reports, where the revision is voluntary, are set out in section 454 of the Companies Act 2006. There are no provisions in the Companies Acts of the Republic of Ireland for revising financial statements.

(ii)   Provide a new auditor's report on the amended financial statements.

(d)   When the circumstances in paragraph 12 apply, amend the auditor's report, or provide a new auditor's report as required by paragraph 12.

16.   The auditor shall include in the new or amended auditor's report an Emphasis of Matter paragraph or Other Matter(s) paragraph referring to a note to the financial statements that more extensively discusses the reason for the amendment of the previously issued financial statements and to the earlier report provided by the auditor.

17.   If management[5b] does not take the necessary steps to ensure that anyone in receipt of the previously issued financial statements is informed of the situation and does not amend the financial statements in circumstances where the auditor believes they need to be amended, the auditor shall notify management and, unless all of those charged with governance are involved in managing the entity[6], those charged with governance, that the auditor will seek to prevent future reliance on the auditor's report. If, despite such notification, management or those charged with governance do not take these necessary steps, the auditor shall take appropriate action to seek to prevent reliance on the auditor's report. (Ref: Para. A18 – A18-1)

***

Application and Other Explanatory Material

Scope of this ISA (UK and Ireland) (Ref: Para. 1)

A1.   When the audited financial statements are included in other documents subsequent to the issuance of the financial statements, the auditor may have additional responsibilities relating to subsequent events that the auditor may need to consider, such as legal or regulatory requirements involving the offering of securities to the public in jurisdictions in which the securities are being offered. For example, the auditor may be required to perform additional audit procedures to the date of the final offering document. These procedures may include those referred to in paragraphs 6 and 7 performed up to a date at or near the effective date of the final offering document, and reading the offering document to assess whether the other information in the offering document is consistent with the financial information with which the auditor is associated.[7]

[5b]   In the UK and Ireland, those charged with governance have responsibility for taking the steps referred to in paragraph 17.

[6]   ISA (UK and Ireland) 260, "Communication with Those Charged with Governance," paragraph 13.

[7]   See ISA (UK and Ireland) 200, "Overall Objectives of the Independent Auditor and the Conduct of an Audit in Accordance with International Standards on Auditing," paragraph 2.

In the UK and Ireland, standards and guidance for accountants engaged to prepare a report and/or letter for inclusion in, or in connection with, an investment circular are set out in APB's Statements of Investment Circular Reporting Standards (SIRS).

Definitions

Date of Approval of the Financial Statements (Ref: Para. 5(b))

A2.   In some jurisdictions, law or regulation identifies the individuals or bodies (for example, management or those charged with governance) that are responsible for concluding that all the statements that comprise the financial statements, including the related notes, have been prepared, and specifies the necessary approval process. In other jurisdictions, the approval process is not prescribed in law or regulation and the entity follows its own procedures in preparing and finalizing its financial statements in view of its management and governance structures. In some jurisdictions, final approval of the financial statements by shareholders is required. In these jurisdictions, final approval by shareholders is not necessary for the auditor to conclude that sufficient appropriate audit evidence on which to base the auditor's opinion on the financial statements has been obtained. The date of approval of the financial statements for purposes of the ISAs (UK and Ireland) is the earlier date on which those with the recognized authority determine that all the statements that comprise the financial statements, including the related notes, have been prepared and that those with the recognized authority have asserted that they have taken responsibility for those financial statements.

Date of the Auditor's Report (Ref: Para. 5(c))

A3.   The auditor's report cannot be dated earlier than the date on which the auditor has obtained sufficient appropriate audit evidence on which to base the opinion on the financial statements including evidence that all the statements that comprise the financial statements, including the related notes, have been prepared and that those with the recognized authority have asserted that they have taken responsibility for those financial statements.[8] Consequently, the date of the auditor's report cannot be earlier than the date of approval of the financial statements as defined in paragraph 5(b). A time period may elapse due to administrative issues between the date of the auditor's report as defined in paragraph 5(c) and the date the auditor's report is provided to the entity.

Date the Financial Statements Are Issued (Ref: Para. 5(d))

A4.   The date the financial statements are issued generally depends on the regulatory environment of the entity. In some circumstances, the date the financial statements are issued may be the date that they are filed with a regulatory authority. Since audited financial statements cannot be issued without an auditor's report, the date that the audited financial statements are issued must not only be at or later than the

---

[8]   ISA 700, paragraph 41. In some cases, law or regulation also identifies the point in the financial statement reporting process at which the audit is expected to be complete.

The APB has not promulgated ISA 700 as issued by the IAASB for application in the UK and Ireland. In the UK and Ireland the applicable auditing standard is ISA (UK and Ireland) 700, "The Auditor's Report on Financial Statements." Paragraph 24 of ISA (UK and Ireland) 700 establishes requirements regarding dating of the auditor's report, including that this shall not be earlier than the date the auditor has considered all necessary available evidence.

date of the auditor's report, but must also be at or later than the date the auditor's report is provided to the entity.

Considerations Specific to Public Sector Entities

A5. In the case of the public sector, the date the financial statements are issued may be the date the audited financial statements and the auditor's report thereon are presented to the legislature or otherwise made public.

Events Occurring between the Date of the Financial Statements and the Date of the Auditor's Report (Ref: Para. 6-9)

A6. Depending on the auditor's risk assessment, the audit procedures required by paragraph 6 may include procedures, necessary to obtain sufficient appropriate audit evidence, involving the review or testing of accounting records or transactions occurring between the date of the financial statements and the date of the auditor's report. The audit procedures required by paragraphs 6 and 7 are in addition to procedures that the auditor may perform for other purposes that, nevertheless, may provide evidence about subsequent events (for example, to obtain audit evidence for account balances as at the date of the financial statements, such as cut-off procedures or procedures in relation to subsequent receipts of accounts receivable).

A7. Paragraph 7 stipulates certain audit procedures in this context that the auditor is required to perform pursuant to paragraph 6. The subsequent events procedures that the auditor performs may, however, depend on the information that is available and, in particular, the extent to which the accounting records have been prepared since the date of the financial statements. Where the accounting records are not up-to-date, and accordingly no interim financial statements (whether for internal or external purposes) have been prepared, or minutes of meetings of management or those charged with governance have not been prepared, relevant audit procedures may take the form of inspection of available books and records, including bank statements. Paragraph A8 gives examples of some of the additional matters that the auditor may consider in the course of these inquiries.

A8. In addition to the audit procedures required by paragraph 7, the auditor may consider it necessary and appropriate to:

- Read the entity's latest available budgets, cash flow forecasts and other related management reports for periods after the date of the financial statements;

- Inquire, or extend previous oral or written inquiries, of the entity's legal counsel concerning litigation and claims; or

- Consider whether written representations covering particular subsequent events may be necessary to support other audit evidence and thereby obtain sufficient appropriate audit evidence.

Inquiry (Ref. Para. 7(b))

A9.   In inquiring of management and, where appropriate, those charged with governance, as to whether any subsequent events have occurred that might affect the financial statements, the auditor may inquire as to the current status of items that were accounted for on the basis of preliminary or inconclusive data and may make specific inquiries about the following matters:

- Whether new commitments, borrowings or guarantees have been entered into.

- Whether sales or acquisitions of assets have occurred or are planned.

- Whether there have been increases in capital or issuance of debt instruments, such as the issue of new shares or debentures, or an agreement to merge or liquidate has been made or is planned.

- Whether any assets have been appropriated by government or destroyed, for example, by fire or flood.

- Whether there have been any developments regarding contingencies.

- Whether any unusual accounting adjustments have been made or are contemplated.

- Whether any events have occurred or are likely to occur that will bring into question the appropriateness of accounting policies used in the financial statements, as would be the case, for example, if such events call into question the validity of the going concern assumption.

- Whether any events have occurred that are relevant to the measurement of estimates or provisions made in the financial statements.

- Whether any events have occurred that are relevant to the recoverability of assets.

Reading Minutes (Ref. Para. 7(c))

Considerations Specific to Public Sector Entities

A10. In the public sector, the auditor may read the official records of relevant proceedings of the legislature and inquire about matters addressed in proceedings for which official records are not yet available.

Facts Which Become Known to the Auditor after the Date of the Auditor's Report but before the Date the Financial Statements Are Issued

Management Responsibility towards Auditor (Ref: Para. 10)

A11. As explained in ISA (UK and Ireland) 210, the terms of the audit engagement include the agreement of management[8a] to inform the auditor of facts that may affect the financial statements, of which management may become aware during the period from the date of the auditor's report to the date the financial statements are issued.[9]

Dual Dating (Ref: Para. 12(a))

A12. When, in the circumstances described in paragraph 12(a), the auditor amends the auditor's report to include an additional date restricted to that amendment, the date of the auditor's report on the financial statements prior to their subsequent amendment by management[3a] remains unchanged because this date informs the reader as to when the audit work on those financial statements was completed. However, an additional date is included in the auditor's report to inform users that the auditor's procedures subsequent to that date were restricted to the subsequent amendment of the financial statements. The following is an illustration of such an additional date:

> "(Date of auditor's report), except as to Note Y, which is as of (date of completion of audit procedures restricted to amendment described in Note Y)."

No Amendment of Financial Statements by Management (Ref: Para. 13)

A13. In some jurisdictions, management[3a] may not be required by law, regulation or the financial reporting framework to issue amended financial statements. This is often the case when issuance of the financial statements for the following period is imminent, provided appropriate disclosures are made in such statements.

Considerations Specific to Public Sector Entities

A14. In the public sector, the actions taken in accordance with paragraph 13 when management does not amend the financial statements may also include reporting separately to the legislature, or other relevant body in the reporting hierarchy, on the implications of the subsequent event for the financial statements and the auditor's report.

Auditor Action to Seek to Prevent Reliance on Auditor's Report (Ref: Para. 13(b))

A15. The auditor may need to fulfill additional legal obligations even when the auditor has notified management not to issue the financial statements and management has agreed to this request.

[8a] In the UK and Ireland the responsibility to inform the auditor of facts which may affect the financial statements usually rests with those charged with governance.

[9] ISA (UK and Ireland) 210, "Agreeing the Terms of Audit Engagements," paragraph A23.

A16. Where management has issued the financial statements despite the auditor's notification not to issue the financial statements to third parties, the auditor's course of action to prevent reliance on the auditor's report on the financial statements depends upon the auditor's legal rights and obligations. Consequently, the auditor may consider it appropriate to seek legal advice.

Facts Which Become Known to the Auditor after the Financial Statements Have Been Issued

A16-1. When issuing a new report the auditor has regard to the regulations relating to reports on revised annual financial statements and directors' reports[5a].

A16-2. Where the auditor becomes aware of a fact relevant to the audited financial statements which did not exist at the date of the auditor's report there are no statutory provisions for revising financial statements. The auditor discusses with those charged with governance whether they should withdraw the financial statements and where those charged with governance decide not to do so the auditor may wish to take advice on whether it might be possible to withdraw their report. In both cases, other possible courses of action include the making of a statement by those charged with governance or the auditor at the annual general meeting. In any event legal advice may be helpful.

A16-3. In the UK or the Republic of Ireland the auditor of a company has a statutory right to attend the Annual General Meeting and be heard on any part of the business of the meeting which concerns them as auditor. This right could include making a statement about facts discovered after the date of the auditor's report and where subsequent events come to the attention of the auditor, the auditor needs to consider what to do in relation to them.

No Amendment of Financial Statements by Management (Ref: Para. 15)

Considerations Specific to Public Sector Entities

A17. In some jurisdictions, entities in the public sector may be prohibited from issuing amended financial statements by law or regulation. In such circumstances, the appropriate course of action for the auditor may be to report to the appropriate statutory body.

Auditor Action to Seek to Prevent Reliance on Auditor's Report (Ref: Para. 17)

A18. Where the auditor believes that management, or those charged with governance, have failed to take the necessary steps to prevent reliance on the auditor's report on financial statements previously issued by the entity despite the auditor's prior notification that the auditor will take action to seek to prevent such reliance, the auditor's course of action depends upon the auditor's legal rights and obligations. Consequently, the auditor may consider it appropriate to seek legal advice.

A18-1. Where the financial statements of companies are issued but have not yet been laid before the members or equivalent, or if those charged with governance do not intend to make an appropriate statement at the annual general meeting, then the auditor may consider making an appropriate statement at the annual general meeting. The auditor does not have a statutory right to communicate directly in writing with the members although, if the auditor resigns or is removed or is not reappointed, the auditor has, for example, various duties under company law[9a].

[9a] The auditor of a limited company in Great Britain who ceases to hold office as auditor is required to comply with the requirements of section 519 of the Companies Act 2006 regarding the statement to be made by the auditor in relation to ceasing to hold office. Equivalent requirements for the Republic of Ireland, are contained in section 185 of the Companies Act 1990.

INTERNATIONAL STANDARD ON AUDITING (UK AND IRELAND) 570 (REVISED SEPTEMBER 2014)

GOING CONCERN

(Effective for audits of financial statements for periods commencing on or after 1 October 2014)

CONTENTS

International Standard on Auditing (UK and Ireland) (ISA (UK and Ireland)) 570, "Going Concern" should be read in conjunction with ISA (UK and Ireland) 200, "Overall Objectives of the Independent Auditor and the Conduct of an Audit in Accordance with International Standards on Auditing (UK and Ireland)."

Interpreting the term 'going concern' in this ISA (UK and Ireland)

The financial reporting frameworks applicable in the UK and Ireland generally require the adoption of the **going concern basis of accounting** in financial statements, except in circumstances where management intends to liquidate the entity or to cease trading, or has no realistic alternative to liquidation or cessation of operations. In effect, an entity that does not meet the threshold for that exception is described as a **going concern**. This requirement applies even when there are uncertainties about events or conditions that may cast significant doubt upon the entity's ability to continue as a going concern in the future. Such uncertainties are required to be disclosed in the financial statements when they are material.

The term **going concern assumption** is the defining assumption about the condition of an entity for which adoption of the going concern basis of accounting is appropriate: that the entity is, and will be able to continue as, a going concern.

Accordingly, as used in this ISA (UK and Ireland):

A. The term 'going concern' applies to any entity unless its management intends to liquidate the entity or to cease trading, or has no realistic alternative to liquidation or cessation of operations; and

B. The term 'ability to continue as a going concern' is equivalent to the term 'ability to continue to adopt the going concern basis of accounting' in the future.

Introduction

Scope of this ISA (UK and Ireland)

1. This International Standard on Auditing (UK and Ireland) (ISA (UK and Ireland)) deals with the auditor's responsibilities in the audit of financial statements relating to management's use of the going concern assumption in the preparation of the financial statements.

Going Concern Assumption

2. Under the going concern assumption, an entity is viewed as continuing in business for the foreseeable future. General purpose financial statements are prepared on a going concern basis, unless management either intends to liquidate the entity or to cease operations, or has no realistic alternative but to do so. Special purpose financial statements may or may not be prepared in accordance with a financial reporting framework for which the going concern basis is relevant for example, the going concern basis is not relevant for some financial statements prepared on a tax basis in particular jurisdictions). When the use of the going concern assumption is appropriate, assets and liabilities are recorded on the basis that the entity will be able to realize its assets and discharge its liabilities in the normal course of business. (Ref: Para. A1)

Responsibility for Assessment of the Entity's Ability to Continue as a Going Concern

3. Some financial reporting frameworks contain an explicit requirement for management[1a] to make a specific assessment of the entity's ability to continue as a going concern, and standards regarding matters to be considered and disclosures to be made in connection with going concern. For example, International Accounting Standard (IAS) 1 requires management to make an assessment of an entity's ability to continue as a going concern.[1] The detailed requirements regarding management's responsibility to assess the entity's ability to continue as a going concern and related financial statement disclosures may also be set out in law or regulation.

4. In other financial reporting frameworks, there may be no explicit requirement for management to make a specific assessment of the entity's ability to continue as a going concern. Nevertheless, since the going concern assumption is a fundamental principle in the preparation of financial statements as discussed in paragraph 2, the preparation of the financial statements requires management to assess the entity's ability to continue as a going concern even if the financial reporting framework does not include an explicit requirement to do so.

5. Management's[1a] assessment of the entity's ability to continue as a going concern involves making a judgment, at a particular point in time, about inherently uncertain

---

[1a] In the UK and Ireland those charged with governance are responsible for the preparation of the financial statements and the assessment of the entity's ability to continue as a going concern.

[1] IAS 1, "Presentation of Financial Statements" as at 1 January 2009, paragraphs 25-26.

future outcomes of events or conditions. The following factors are relevant to that judgment:

- The degree of uncertainty associated with the outcome of an event or condition increases significantly the further into the future an event or condition or the outcome occurs. For that reason, most financial reporting frameworks that require an explicit management assessment specify the period for which management is required to take into account all available information.

- The size and complexity of the entity, the nature and condition of its business and the degree to which it is affected by external factors affect the judgment regarding the outcome of events or conditions.

- Any judgment about the future is based on information available at the time at which the judgment is made. Subsequent events may result in outcomes that are inconsistent with judgments that were reasonable at the time they were made.

Responsibilities of the Auditor

6.   The auditor's responsibility is to obtain sufficient appropriate audit evidence about the appropriateness of management's[1a] use of the going concern assumption in the preparation and presentation of the financial statements and to conclude whether there is a material uncertainty about the entity's ability to continue as a going concern. This responsibility exists even if the financial reporting framework used in the preparation of the financial statements does not include an explicit requirement for management to make a specific assessment of the entity's ability to continue as a going concern.

7.   However, as described in ISA (UK and Ireland) 200,[2] the potential effects of inherent limitations on the auditor's ability to detect material misstatements are greater for future events or conditions that may cause an entity to cease to continue as a going concern. The auditor cannot predict such future events or conditions. Accordingly, the absence of any reference to going concern uncertainty in an auditor's report cannot be viewed as a guarantee as to the entity's ability to continue as a going concern.

Effective Date

8.   This ISA (UK and Ireland) is effective for audits of financial statements for periods commencing on or after 1 October 2014.

Objectives

9.   The objectives of the auditor are:

---

[2]   ISA (UK and Ireland) 200, "Overall Objectives of the Independent Auditor and the Conduct of an Audit in Accordance with International Standards on Auditing."

(a) To obtain sufficient appropriate audit evidence regarding the appropriateness of management's[1a] use of the going concern assumption in the preparation of the financial statements;

(b) To conclude, based on the audit evidence obtained, whether a material uncertainty exists related to events or conditions that may cast significant doubt on the entity's ability to continue as a going concern; and

(c) To determine the implications for the auditor's report.

Requirements

Risk Assessment Procedures and Related Activities

10. When performing risk assessment procedures as required by ISA (UK and Ireland) 315 (Revised June 2013),[3] the auditor shall consider whether there are events or conditions that may cast significant doubt on the entity's ability to continue as a going concern. In so doing, the auditor shall determine whether management[1a] has already performed a preliminary assessment of the entity's ability to continue as a going concern, and: (Ref: Para. A2-A5)

(a) If such an assessment has been performed, the auditor shall discuss the assessment with management and determine whether management has identified events or conditions that, individually or collectively, may cast significant doubt on the entity's ability to continue as a going concern and, if so, management's plans to address them; or

(b) If such an assessment has not yet been performed, the auditor shall discuss with management the basis for the intended use of the going concern assumption, and inquire of management whether events or conditions exist that, individually or collectively, may cast significant doubt on the entity's ability to continue as a going concern.

11. The auditor shall remain alert throughout the audit for audit evidence of events or conditions that may cast significant doubt on the entity's ability to continue as a going concern. (Ref: Para. A6)

Evaluating Management's Assessment

12. The auditor shall evaluate management's[1a] assessment of the entity's ability to continue as a going concern. (Ref: Para. A7-A9; A11-A12)

13. In evaluating management's[1a] assessment of the entity's ability to continue as a going concern, the auditor shall cover the same period as that used by management to make

---

[3] ISA (UK and Ireland) 315 (Revised June 2013), "Identifying and Assessing the Risks of Material Misstatement through Understanding the Entity and Its Environment," paragraph 5.

its assessment as required by the applicable financial reporting framework, or by law or regulation if it specifies a longer period. If management's assessment of the entity's ability to continue as a going concern covers less than twelve months from the date of the financial statements as defined in ISA 560,[4] the auditor shall request management to extend its assessment period to at least twelve months from that date[4a]. (Ref: Para. A10-A12)

14. In evaluating management's[1a] assessment, the auditor shall consider whether management's assessment includes all relevant information of which the auditor is aware as a result of the audit.

Period beyond Management's[1a] Assessment

15. The auditor shall inquire of management as to its knowledge of events or conditions beyond the period of management's[1a] assessment that may cast significant doubt on the entity's ability to continue as a going concern. (Ref: Para. A13-A14)

Additional Audit Procedures When Events or Conditions Are Identified

16. If events or conditions have been identified that may cast significant doubt on the entity's ability to continue as a going concern, the auditor shall obtain sufficient appropriate audit evidence to determine whether or not a material uncertainty exists through performing additional audit procedures, including consideration of mitigating factors. These procedures shall include: (Ref: Para. A15)

(a) Where management[1a] has not yet performed an assessment of the entity's ability to continue as a going concern, requesting management to make its assessment.

(b) Evaluating management's[1a] plans for future actions in relation to its going concern assessment, whether the outcome of these plans is likely to improve the situation and whether management's plans are feasible in the circumstances. (Ref: Para. A16)

(c) Where the entity has prepared a cash flow forecast, and analysis of the forecast is a significant factor in considering the future outcome of events or conditions in the evaluation of management's[1a] plans for future action: (Ref: Para. A17-A18)

(i) Evaluating the reliability of the underlying data generated to prepare the forecast; and

(ii) Determining whether there is adequate support for the assumptions underlying the forecast.

---

[4] ISA (UK and Ireland) 560, "Subsequent Events," paragraph 5(a).
[4a] In the UK and Ireland the period used by those charged with governance in making their assessment is usually at least one year from the date of approval of the financial statements.

(d) Considering whether any additional facts or information have become available since the date on which management made its assessment.

(e) Requesting written representations from management and, where appropriate, those charged with governance, regarding their plans for future action and the feasibility of these plans[1a].

Audit Conclusions and Reporting

17. Based on the audit evidence obtained, the auditor shall conclude whether, in the auditor's judgment, a material uncertainty exists related to events or conditions that, individually or collectively, may cast significant doubt on the entity's ability to continue as a going concern. A material uncertainty exists when the magnitude of its potential impact and likelihood of occurrence is such that, in the auditor's judgment, appropriate disclosure of the nature and implications of the uncertainty is necessary for: (Ref: Para. A19 – A19-2)

(a) In the case of a fair presentation financial reporting framework, the fair presentation of the financial statements, or

(b) In the case of a compliance framework, the financial statements not to be misleading.

17-1 If the period to which those charged with governance have paid particular attention in assessing going concern is less than one year from the date of approval of the financial statements, and those charged with governance have not disclosed that fact, the auditor shall do so within the auditor's report[4b]. (Ref: Para A19-1)

17-2. In the case of entities that are required[4c], and those that choose voluntarily, to report on how they have applied the UK Corporate Governance Code, or to explain why they have not, the auditor shall read and consider in light of the knowledge the auditor has acquired during the audit, including that acquired in the evaluation of management's[1a] assessment of the entity's ability to continue as a going concern:

(a) The directors' confirmation in the annual report that they have carried out a robust assessment of the principal risks facing the entity, including those that would threaten its business model, future performance, solvency or liquidity;

(b) The disclosures in the annual report that describe those risks and explain how they are being managed or mitigated;

[4b] If the non-disclosure of the fact in the financial statements is a departure from the requirements of the applicable financial reporting framework, the auditor would give a qualified opinion ("except for").

[4c] In the UK, these include companies with a Premium listing of equity shares regardless of whether they are incorporated in the UK or elsewhere. In Ireland, these include Irish incorporated companies with a primary or secondary listing of equity shares on the Irish Stock Exchange.

(c) The directors' statement in the financial statements about whether they considered it appropriate to adopt the going concern basis of accounting in preparing them, and their identification of any material uncertainties to the entity's ability to continue to do so over a period of at least twelve months from the date of approval of the financial statements; and

(d) The director's explanation in the annual report as to how they have assessed the prospects of the entity, over what period they have done so and why they consider that period to be appropriate, and their statement as to whether they have a reasonable expectation that the entity will be able to continue in operation and meet its liabilities as they fall due over the period of their assessment, including any related disclosures drawing attention to any necessary qualifications or assumptions.

The auditor shall determine whether the auditor has anything material to add or to draw attention to in the auditor's report on the financial statements in relation to these disclosures, and shall report in accordance with the requirements of ISA (UK and Ireland) 700[4d].

17-3. Matters the auditor considers when determining whether there is anything to add or to emphasise in the auditor's report on the financial statements shall include, based on the knowledge the auditor has acquired during the audit, including that acquired in the evaluation of management's[1a] assessment of the entity's ability to continue as a going concern:

- Whether the auditor is aware of information that would indicate that the annual report and accounts taken as a whole are not fair, balanced and understandable in relation to the principal risks facing the entity including those that would threaten its business model, future performance, solvency or liquidity; and

- Matters relating to the robustness of the directors' assessment of the principal risks facing the entity and its outcome, including the related disclosures in the annual report and accounts, that the auditor communicated to the audit committee[4e] and that are not appropriately addressed in the section of the annual report that describes the work of the audit committee.

Use of Going Concern Assumption Appropriate but a Material Uncertainty Exists

18. If the auditor concludes that the use of the going concern assumption is appropriate in the circumstances but a material uncertainty exists, the auditor shall determine whether the financial statements:

[4d] ISA (UK and Ireland) 700, "The Independent Auditor's Report on Financial Statements", paragraph 22C.

[4e] ISA (UK and Ireland) 260, "Communication with Those Charged with Governance", paragraph 16-1(e).

(a) Adequately describe the principal events or conditions that may cast significant doubt on the entity's ability to continue as a going concern and management's[1a] plans to deal with these events or conditions; and

(b) Disclose clearly that there is a material uncertainty related to events or conditions that may cast significant doubt on the entity's ability to continue as a going concern and, therefore, that it may be unable to realize its assets and discharge its liabilities in the normal course of business. (Ref: Para. A20)

19. If adequate disclosure is made in the financial statements, the auditor shall express an unmodified opinion and include an Emphasis of Matter paragraph in the auditor's report to:

(a) Highlight the existence of a material uncertainty relating to the event or condition that may cast significant doubt on the entity's ability to continue as a going concern; and to

(b) Draw attention to the note in the financial statements that discloses the matters set out in paragraph 18. (See ISA (UK and Ireland) 706.[5]) (Ref: Para. A21-A22)

20. If adequate disclosure is not made in the financial statements, the auditor shall express a qualified opinion or adverse opinion, as appropriate, in accordance with ISA (UK and Ireland) 705.[6] The auditor shall state in the auditor's report that there is a material uncertainty that may cast significant doubt about the entity's ability to continue as a going concern. (Ref: Para. A23-A24)

Use of Going Concern Assumption Inappropriate

21. If the financial statements have been prepared on a going concern basis but, in the auditor's judgment, management's[1a] use of the going concern assumption in the financial statements is inappropriate, the auditor shall express an adverse opinion. (Ref: Para. A25-A26)

Management Unwilling to Make or Extend Its Assessment

22. If management[1a] is unwilling to make or extend its assessment when requested to do so by the auditor, the auditor shall consider the implications for the auditor's report. (Ref: Para. A27)

Communication with Those Charged with Governance

23. Unless all those charged with governance are involved in managing the entity,[7] the auditor shall communicate with those charged with governance events or conditions identified that may cast significant doubt on the entity's ability to continue as a going

---

[5] ISA (UK and Ireland) 706, "Emphasis of Matter Paragraphs and Other Matter Paragraphs in the Independent Auditor's Report."

[6] ISA (UK and Ireland) 705, "Modifications to the Opinion in the Independent Auditor's Report."

[7] ISA (UK and Ireland) 260, "Communication with Those Charged with Governance," paragraph 13.

concern. Such communication with those charged with governance shall include the following:

(a) Whether the events or conditions constitute a material uncertainty;

(b) Whether the use of the going concern assumption is appropriate in the preparation and presentation of the financial statements; and

(c) The adequacy of related disclosures in the financial statements.

Significant Delay in the Approval of Financial Statements

24. If there is significant delay in the approval of the financial statements by management or those charged with governance after the date of the financial statements, the auditor shall inquire as to the reasons for the delay. If the auditor believes that the delay could be related to events or conditions relating to the going concern assessment, the auditor shall perform those additional audit procedures necessary, as described in paragraph 16, as well as consider the effect on the auditor's conclusion regarding the existence of a material uncertainty, as described in paragraph 17.

***

Application and Other Explanatory Material

Going Concern Assumption (Ref: Para. 2)

Considerations Specific to Public Sector Entities

A1. Management's[1a] use of the going concern assumption is also relevant to public sector entities. For example, International Public Sector Accounting Standard (IPSAS) 1 addresses the issue of the ability of public sector entities to continue as going concerns.[8] Going concern risks may arise, but are not limited to, situations where public sector entities operate on a for-profit basis, where government support may be reduced or withdrawn, or in the case of privatization. Events or conditions that may cast significant doubt on an entity's ability to continue as a going concern in the public sector may include situations where the public sector entity lacks funding for its continued existence or when policy decisions are made that affect the services provided by the public sector entity.

Risk Assessment Procedures and Related Activities

Events or Conditions That May Cast Doubt about Going Concern Assumption (Ref: Para. 10)

A2. The following are examples of events or conditions that, individually or collectively, may cast significant doubt about the going concern assumption. This listing is not all-

---

[8] IPSAS 1, "Presentation of Financial Statements" as at 1 January 2009, paragraphs 38-41.

inclusive nor does the existence of one or more of the items always signify that a material uncertainty exists.

Financial

- Net liability or net current liability position.

- Fixed-term borrowings approaching maturity without realistic prospects of renewal or repayment; or excessive reliance on short-term borrowings to finance long-term assets.

- Indications of withdrawal of financial support by creditors.

- Negative operating cash flows indicated by historical or prospective financial statements.

- Adverse key financial ratios.

- Substantial operating losses or significant deterioration in the value of assets used to generate cash flows.

- Arrears or discontinuance of dividends.

- Inability to pay creditors on due dates.

- Inability to comply with the terms of loan agreements.

- Change from credit to cash-on-delivery transactions with suppliers.

- Inability to obtain financing for essential new product development or other essential investments.

Operating

- Management intentions to liquidate the entity or to cease operations.

- Loss of key management without replacement.

- Loss of a major market, key customer(s), franchise, license, or principal supplier(s).

- Labor difficulties.

- Shortages of important supplies.

- Emergence of a highly successful competitor.

Other

- Non-compliance with capital or other statutory requirements.

- Pending legal or regulatory proceedings against the entity that may, if successful, result in claims that the entity is unlikely to be able to satisfy.

- Changes in law or regulation or government policy expected to adversely affect the entity.

- Uninsured or underinsured catastrophes when they occur.

The significance of such events or conditions often can be mitigated by other factors. For example, the effect of an entity being unable to make its normal debt repayments may be counter-balanced by management's plans to maintain adequate cash flows by alternative means, such as by disposing of assets, rescheduling loan repayments, or obtaining additional capital. Similarly, the loss of a principal supplier may be mitigated by the availability of a suitable alternative source of supply.

A3.   The risk assessment procedures required by paragraph 10 help the auditor to determine whether management's use of the going concern assumption is likely to be an important issue and its impact on planning the audit. These procedures also allow for more timely discussions with management, including a discussion of management's[1a] plans and resolution of any identified going concern issues.

Considerations Specific to Smaller Entities

A4.   The size of an entity may affect its ability to withstand adverse conditions. Small entities may be able to respond quickly to exploit opportunities, but may lack reserves to sustain operations.

A5.   Conditions of particular relevance to small entities include the risk that banks and other lenders may cease to support the entity, as well as the possible loss of a principal supplier, major customer, key employee, or the right to operate under a license, franchise or other legal agreement.

Remaining Alert throughout the Audit for Audit Evidence about Events or Conditions (Ref: Para. 11)

A6.   ISA (UK and Ireland) 315 (Revised June 2013) requires the auditor to revise the auditor's risk assessment and modify the further planned audit procedures accordingly when additional audit evidence is obtained during the course of the audit that affects the auditor's assessment of risk.[9] If events or conditions that may cast significant doubt on the entity's ability to continue as a going concern are identified after the auditor's risk assessments are made, in addition to performing the procedures in paragraph 16, the auditor's assessment of the risks of material misstatement may need to be revised. The existence of such events or conditions may also affect the nature, timing and extent of the auditor's further procedures in

---

[9]   ISA (UK and Ireland) 315 (Revised June 2013), paragraph 31.

response to the assessed risks. ISA (UK and Ireland) 330[10] establishes requirements and provides guidance on this issue.

Evaluating Management's[1a] Assessment

Management's[1a] Assessment and Supporting Analysis and the Auditor's Evaluation (Ref: Para. 12)

A7. Management's[1a] assessment of the entity's ability to continue as a going concern is a key part of the auditor's consideration of management's use of the going concern assumption.

A8. It is not the auditor's responsibility to rectify the lack of analysis by management[1a]. In some circumstances, however, the lack of detailed analysis by management to support its assessment may not prevent the auditor from concluding whether management's use of the going concern assumption is appropriate in the circumstances. For example, when there is a history of profitable operations and a ready access to financial resources, management may make its assessment without detailed analysis. In this case, the auditor's evaluation of the appropriateness of management's assessment may be made without performing detailed evaluation procedures if the auditor's other audit procedures are sufficient to enable the auditor to conclude whether management's use of the going concern assumption in the preparation of the financial statements is appropriate in the circumstances.

A9. In other circumstances, evaluating management's[1a] assessment of the entity's ability to continue as a going concern, as required by paragraph 12, may include an evaluation of the process management followed to make its assessment, the assumptions on which the assessment is based and management's plans for future action and whether management's plans are feasible in the circumstances.

The Period of Management's[1a] Assessment (Ref: Para. 13)

A10. Most financial reporting frameworks requiring an explicit management[1a] assessment specify the period for which management is required to take into account all available information.[11]

---

[10] ISA (UK and Ireland) 330, "The Auditor's Responses to Assessed Risks."

[11] Accounting frameworks do not normally specify a maximum period that should be reviewed as part of the assessment of going concern. However, IAS 1 and FRS 18 both provide that management takes into account all available information about the future.

For example, IAS 1 defines this as a period that should be at least, but is not limited to, twelve months from the end of the reporting period.

FRS 18 does not specify a period but does require that where the foreseeable future considered by the directors has been limited to a period of less than one year from the date of approval of the financial statements, that fact should be disclosed in the financial statements.

Guidance issued by the FRC for directors of listed companies in "An Update for Directors of Listed Companies: Going Concern and Liquidity Risk" (November 2008) states that "Where the period considered by the directors has been limited, for example to a period of less than twelve months from the date of the approval of the annual report and accounts, the directors need to consider whether additional disclosures are necessary to explain adequately the assumptions that underlie the adoption of the going concern basis."

A10-1. If the future period to which those charged with governance have paid particular attention has been limited, for example, to a period of less than one year from the date of approval of the financial statements, those charged with governance will have determined whether, in their opinion, the financial statements require any additional disclosures to explain adequately the assumptions that underlie the adoption of the going concern basis.

A10-2. The auditor assesses whether to concur with the judgments of those charged with governance regarding the need for additional disclosures and their adequacy. Disclosure, however, does not eliminate the need to make appropriate judgments about the suitability of the future period as an adequate basis for assessing the going concern position. Paragraph 17-1 requires the auditor to disclose in the auditor's report if the period to which those charged with governance have paid particular attention in assessing going concern is less than one year from the date of approval of the financial statements, and those charged with governance have not disclosed that fact. The auditor through discussion with those charged with governance of their plans and expectations may be able to obtain satisfaction that those charged with governance have in fact paid particular attention to a period of one year from the date of approval of the financial statements.

Procedures to Identify Material Matters Indicating Concern

A10-3. Having regard to the future period to which those charged with governance have paid particular attention in assessing going concern, the auditor plans and performs procedures specifically designed to identify any material matters which could indicate concern about the entity's ability to continue as a going concern.

A10-4. The extent of the auditor's procedures is influenced primarily by the excess of the financial resources available to the entity over the financial resources that it requires. The entity's procedures (and the auditor's procedures) need not always be elaborate in order to provide sufficient appropriate audit evidence. A determination of the sufficiency of the evidence supplied to the auditor by those charged with governance will depend on the particular circumstances. For example, to be sufficient the evidence may not require formal cash flow forecasts and budgets to have been prepared for the period ending one year from the date of approval of the financial statements. Although such forecasts and budgets are likely to provide the most persuasive evidence, alternative sources of evidence may also be acceptable. This is particularly likely to be the case in respect of entities with uncomplicated circumstances. Many smaller companies fall into this category.

Considerations Specific to Smaller Entities (Ref: Para. 12-13)

A11. In many cases, the management[1a] of smaller entities may not have prepared a detailed assessment of the entity's ability to continue as a going concern, but instead may rely on in-depth knowledge of the business and anticipated future prospects. Nevertheless, in accordance with the requirements of this ISA (UK and Ireland), the auditor needs to evaluate management's assessment of the entity's ability to continue as a going concern. For smaller entities, it may be appropriate to discuss the medium and long-term financing of the entity with management, provided that management's contentions can be corroborated by sufficient documentary evidence and are not inconsistent with the auditor's understanding of the entity. Therefore, the requirement in paragraph 13 for the auditor to request management to extend its assessment may, for example, be satisfied by discussion, inquiry and inspection of supporting documentation, for example, orders received for future supply, evaluated as to their feasibility or otherwise substantiated.

A12. Continued support by owner-managers is often important to smaller entities' ability to continue as a going concern. Where a small entity is largely financed by a loan from the owner-manager, it may be important that these funds are not withdrawn. For example, the continuance of a small entity in financial difficulty may be dependent on the owner-manager subordinating a loan to the entity in favor of banks or other creditors, or the owner manager supporting a loan for the entity by providing a guarantee with his or her personal assets as collateral. In such circumstances the auditor may obtain appropriate documentary evidence of the subordination of the owner-manager's loan or of the guarantee. Where an entity is dependent on additional support from the owner-manager, the auditor may evaluate the owner-manager's ability to meet the obligation under the support arrangement. In addition, the auditor may request written confirmation of the terms and conditions attaching to such support and the owner-manager's intention or understanding.

Period beyond Management's[1a] Assessment (Ref: Para. 15)

A13. As required by paragraph 11, the auditor remains alert to the possibility that there may be known events, scheduled or otherwise, or conditions that will occur beyond the period of assessment used by management[1a] that may bring into question the appropriateness of management's use of the going concern assumption in preparing the financial statements. Since the degree of uncertainty associated with the outcome of an event or condition increases as the event or condition is further into the future, in considering events or conditions further in the future, the indications of going concern issues need to be significant before the auditor needs to consider taking further action. If such events or conditions are identified, the auditor may need to request management to evaluate the potential significance of the event or condition on its assessment of the entity's ability to continue as a going concern. In these circumstances the procedures in paragraph 16 apply.

A14. Other than inquiry of management, the auditor does not have a responsibility to perform any other audit procedures to identify events or conditions that may cast significant doubt on the entity's ability to continue as a going concern beyond the period assessed by management[1a], which, as discussed in paragraph 13, would be at least twelve months from the date of the financial statements.

Additional Audit Procedures When Events or Conditions Are Identified (Ref: Para. 16)

A15. Audit procedures that are relevant to the requirement in paragraph 16 may include the following:

- Analyzing and discussing cash flow, profit and other relevant forecasts with management.

- Analyzing and discussing the entity's latest available interim financial statements.

- Reading the terms of debentures and loan agreements and determining whether any have been breached.

- Reading minutes of the meetings of shareholders, those charged with governance and relevant committees for reference to financing difficulties.

- Inquiring of the entity's legal counsel regarding the existence of litigation and claims and the reasonableness of management's[1a] assessments of their outcome and the estimate of their financial implications.

- Confirming the existence, legality and enforceability of arrangements to provide or maintain financial support with related and third parties and assessing the financial ability of such parties to provide additional funds.

- Evaluating the entity's plans to deal with unfilled customer orders.

- Performing audit procedures regarding subsequent events to identify those that either mitigate or otherwise affect the entity's ability to continue as a going concern.

- Confirming the existence, terms and adequacy of borrowing facilities.

- Obtaining and reviewing reports of regulatory actions.

- Determining the adequacy of support for any planned disposals of assets.

Evaluating Management's Plans for Future Actions (Ref: Para. 16(b))

A16. Evaluating management's[1a] plans for future actions may include inquiries of management as to its plans for future action, including, for example, its plans to liquidate assets, borrow money or restructure debt, reduce or delay expenditures, or increase capital.

The Period of Management's[1a] Assessment (Ref: Para. 16(c))

A17. In addition to the procedures required in paragraph 16(c), the auditor may compare:

- The prospective financial information for recent prior periods with historical results; and

- The prospective financial information for the current period with results achieved to date.

A18. Where management's[1a] assumptions include continued support by third parties, whether through the subordination of loans, commitments to maintain or provide additional funding, or guarantees, and such support is important to an entity's ability to continue as a going concern, the auditor may need to consider requesting written confirmation (including of terms and conditions) from those third parties and to obtain evidence of their ability to provide such support.

Audit Conclusions and Reporting (Ref: Para. 17 – 17-1)

A19. The phrase "material uncertainty" is used in IAS 1 in discussing the uncertainties related to events or conditions which may cast significant doubt on the entity's ability to continue as a going concern that should be disclosed in the financial statements. In some other financial reporting frameworks the phrase "significant uncertainty" is used in similar circumstances.

A19-1 Where, in forming their opinion, the auditor's assessment of going concern is based on a period to which those charged with governance have paid particular attention which is less than one year from the date of approval of the financial statements, it is appropriate for the auditor to disclose that fact within the basis of the audit opinion, unless it is disclosed in the financial statements or accompanying information (for example, a Corporate Governance Statement). In deciding whether to disclose the fact, the auditor assesses whether the evidence supplied by those charged with governance is sufficient to demonstrate that those charged with governance have, in assessing going concern, paid particular attention to a period of one year from the date of approval of the financial statements (see paragraph A10-3).

A19-2 In complying with the requirements of ISA (UK and Ireland) 230 to document significant matters arising during the audit,[11a] the auditor documents concerns (if any) about the entity's ability to continue as a going concern.

Use of Going Concern Assumption Appropriate but a Material Uncertainty Exists

Adequacy of Disclosure of Material Uncertainty (Ref: Para. 18)

A20. The determination of the adequacy of the financial statement disclosure may involve determining whether the information explicitly draws the reader's attention to the possibility that the entity may be unable to continue realizing its assets and discharging its liabilities in the normal course of business.

[11a] ISA (UK and Ireland) 230, "Audit Documentation," paragraph 8(c).

Audit Reporting When Disclosure of Material Uncertainty Is Adequate (Ref: Para. 19)

A21. The following is an illustration of an Emphasis of Matter paragraph when the auditor is satisfied as to the adequacy of the note disclosure:[11b]

> Emphasis of Matter
>
> Without qualifying our opinion, we draw attention to Note X in the financial statements which indicates that the Company incurred a net loss of ZZZ during the year ended December 31, 20X1 and, as of that date, the Company's current liabilities exceeded its total assets by YYY. These conditions, along with other matters as set forth in Note X, indicate the existence of a material uncertainty that may cast significant doubt about the Company's ability to continue as a going concern.

A22. In situations involving multiple material uncertainties that are significant to the financial statements as a whole, the auditor may consider it appropriate in extremely rare cases to express a disclaimer of opinion instead of adding an Emphasis of Matter paragraph. ISA (UK and Ireland) 705 provides guidance on this issue.

Audit Reporting When Disclosure of Material Uncertainty Is Inadequate (Ref: Para. 20)

A23. The following is an illustration of the relevant paragraphs when a qualified opinion is to be expressed:[11b]

> Basis for Qualified Opinion
>
> The Company's financing arrangements expire and amounts outstanding are payable on March 19, 20X1. The Company has been unable to re-negotiate or obtain replacement financing. This situation indicates the existence of a material uncertainty that may cast significant doubt on the Company's ability to continue as a going concern and therefore the Company may be unable to realize its assets and discharge its liabilities in the normal course of business. The financial statements (and notes thereto) do not fully disclose this fact.
>
> Qualified Opinion
>
> In our opinion, except for the incomplete disclosure of the information referred to in the Basis for Qualified Opinion paragraph, the financial statements present fairly, in all material respects (or "give a true and fair view of") the financial position of the Company at December 31, 20X0 and of its financial performance and its cash flows for the year then ended in accordance with ...

[11b] Illustrative auditor's reports tailored for use with audits conducted in accordance with ISAs (UK and Ireland) are given in the current versions of the APB Compendia Auditor's Report Bulletins.

A24. The following is an illustration of the relevant paragraphs when an adverse opinion is to be expressed:[11b]

Basis for Adverse Opinion

The Company's financing arrangements expired and the amount outstanding was payable on December 31, 20X0. The Company has been unable to re-negotiate or obtain replacement financing and is considering filing for bankruptcy. These events indicate a material uncertainty that may cast significant doubt on the Company's ability to continue as a going concern and therefore it may be unable to realize its assets and discharge its liabilities in the normal course of business. The financial statements (and notes thereto) do not disclose this fact.

Adverse Opinion

In our opinion, because of the omission of the information mentioned in the Basis for Adverse Opinion paragraph, the financial statements do not present fairly (or "give a true and fair view of") the financial position of the Company as at December 31, 20X0, and of its financial performance and its cash flows for the year then ended in accordance with...

Use of Going Concern Assumption Inappropriate (Ref: Para. 21)

A25. If the financial statements have been prepared on a going concern basis but, in the auditor's judgment, management's use of the going concern assumption in the financial statements is inappropriate, the requirement of paragraph 21 for the auditor to express an adverse opinion applies regardless of whether or not the financial statements include disclosure of the inappropriateness of management's[1a] use of the going concern assumption.

A26. If the entity's management[1a] is required, or elects, to prepare financial statements when the use of the going concern assumption is not appropriate in the circumstances, the financial statements are prepared on an alternative basis (for example, liquidation basis). The auditor may be able to perform an audit of those financial statements provided that the auditor determines that the alternative basis is an acceptable financial reporting framework in the circumstances. The auditor may be able to express an unmodified opinion on those financial statements, provided there is adequate disclosure therein but may consider it appropriate or necessary to include an Emphasis of Matter paragraph in the auditor's report to draw the user's attention to that alternative basis and the reasons for its use.

Management[1a] Unwilling to Make or Extend Its Assessment (Ref: Para. 22)

A27. In certain circumstances, the auditor may believe it necessary to request management[1a] to make or extend its assessment. If management is unwilling to do so, a qualified opinion or a disclaimer of opinion in the auditor's report may be appropriate, because it may not be possible for the auditor to obtain sufficient appropriate audit evidence regarding the use of the going concern assumption in the preparation of the financial statements, such as audit evidence regarding the existence of plans management has put in place or the existence of other mitigating factors.

Regulated Entities

A27-1. When the auditor of a regulated financial entity considers that it might be necessary to either qualify the audit opinion or add an explanatory paragraph to the audit report, the auditor may have a duty to inform the appropriate regulator at an early stage in the audit. In such cases the regulator might, if it has not already done so, specify corrective action to be taken by the entity. At the time at which the auditor formulates the audit report, the auditor takes account of matters such as:

- Any views expressed by the regulator.

- Any legal advice obtained by those charged with governance.

- The actual and planned corrective action.

INTERNATIONAL STANDARD ON AUDITING (UK AND IRELAND) 580

WRITTEN REPRESENTATIONS

(Effective for audits of financial statements for periods ending on or after 15 December 2010)

CONTENTS

Appendix 1: List of ISAs (UK and Ireland) Containing Requirements for Written
        Representations

Appendix 2: Illustrative Representation Letter

International Standard on Auditing (UK and Ireland) (ISA (UK and Ireland)) 580, "Written Representations" should be read in conjunction with ISA (UK and Ireland) 200, "Overall Objectives of the Independent Auditor and the Conduct of an Audit in Accordance with International Standards on Auditing (UK and Ireland)."

Introduction

Scope of this ISA (UK and Ireland)

1. This International Standard on Auditing (UK and Ireland) (ISA (UK and Ireland)) deals with the auditor's responsibility to obtain written representations from management and, where appropriate, those charged with governance in an audit of financial statements.

2. Appendix 1 lists other ISAs (UK and Ireland) containing subject-matter specific requirements for written representations. The specific requirements for written representations of other ISAs (UK and Ireland) do not limit the application of this ISA (UK and Ireland).

Written Representations as Audit Evidence

3. Audit evidence is the information used by the auditor in arriving at the conclusions on which the auditor's opinion is based.[1] Written representations are necessary information that the auditor requires in connection with the audit of the entity's financial statements. Accordingly, similar to responses to inquiries, written representations are audit evidence. (Ref: Para. A1)

4. Although written representations provide necessary audit evidence, they do not provide sufficient appropriate audit evidence on their own about any of the matters with which they deal. Furthermore, the fact that management has provided reliable written representations does not affect the nature or extent of other audit evidence that the auditor obtains about the fulfillment of management's responsibilities, or about specific assertions.

Effective Date

5. This ISA (UK and Ireland) is effective for audits of financial statements for periods ending on or after 15 December 2010.

Objectives

6. The objectives of the auditor are:

    (a) To obtain written representations from management and, where appropriate, those charged with governance that they believe that they have fulfilled their responsibility for the preparation of the financial statements and for the completeness of the information provided to the auditor;

    (b) To support other audit evidence relevant to the financial statements or specific assertions in the financial statements by means of written representations if

---

[1] ISA (UK and Ireland) 500, "Audit Evidence," paragraph 5(c).

determined necessary by the auditor or required by other ISAs (UK and Ireland); and

(c) To respond appropriately to written representations provided by management and, where appropriate, those charged with governance, or if management or, where appropriate, those charged with governance do not provide the written representations requested by the auditor.

Definitions

7. For purposes of the ISAs (UK and Ireland), the following term has the meaning attributed below:

Written representation – A written statement by management provided to the auditor to confirm certain matters or to support other audit evidence. Written representations in this context do not include financial statements, the assertions therein, or supporting books and records.

8. For purposes of this ISA (UK and Ireland), references to "management" should be read as "management and, where appropriate, those charged with governance." Furthermore, in the case of a fair presentation framework, management is responsible for the preparation and *fair* presentation of the financial statements in accordance with the applicable financial reporting framework; or the preparation of financial statements *that give a true and fair view* in accordance with the applicable financial reporting framework.

Requirements

Management from whom Written Representations Requested

9. The auditor shall request written representations from management with appropriate responsibilities for the financial statements and knowledge of the matters concerned. (Ref: Para. A2-A6)

Written Representations about Management's Responsibilities

Preparation of the Financial Statements

10. The auditor shall request management to provide a written representation that it has fulfilled its responsibility for the preparation of the financial statements in accordance with the applicable financial reporting framework, including where relevant their fair presentation, as set out in the terms of the audit engagement.[2] (Ref: Para. A7-A9, A14, A22)

---

[2] ISA (UK and Ireland) 210, "Agreeing the Terms of Audit Engagements," paragraph 6(b)(i).

Information Provided and Completeness of Transactions

11. The auditor shall request management to provide a written representation that:

    (a) It has provided the auditor with all relevant information and access as agreed in the terms of the audit engagement,[3] and

    (b) All transactions have been recorded and are reflected in the financial statements. (Ref: Para. A7-A9, A14, A22 – A22-1)

11-1 Management may include in the written representations required by paragraphs 10 and 11 qualifying language to the effect that the representations are made to the best of its knowledge and belief. Such qualifying language does not cause paragraph 20 to apply if, during the audit, the auditor found no evidence that the representations are incorrect. (Ref; Para A5, A8-1)

Description of Management's Responsibilities in the Written Representations

12. Management's responsibilities shall be described in the written representations required by paragraphs 10 and 11 in the manner in which these responsibilities are described in the terms of the audit engagement.

Other Written Representations

13. Other ISAs (UK and Ireland) require the auditor to request written representations. If, in addition to such required representations, the auditor determines that it is necessary to obtain one or more written representations to support other audit evidence relevant to the financial statements or one or more specific assertions in the financial statements, the auditor shall request such other written representations. (Ref: Para. A10-A13, A14, A22 – A22-1)

Date of and Period(s) Covered by Written Representations

14. The date of the written representations shall be as near as practicable to, but not after, the date of the auditor's report on the financial statements. The written representations shall be for all financial statements and period(s) referred to in the auditor's report. (Ref: Para. A15-A18)

Form of Written Representations

15. The written representations shall be in the form of a representation letter addressed to the auditor. If law or regulation requires management to make written public statements about its responsibilities, and the auditor determines that such statements provide some or all of the representations required by paragraphs 10 or 11, the relevant matters covered by such statements need not be included in the representation letter. (Ref: Para. A19-A21)

---

[3] ISA (UK and Ireland) 210, paragraph 6(b)(iii).

Doubt as to the Reliability of Written Representations and Requested Written Representations Not Provided

Doubt as to the Reliability of Written Representations

16. If the auditor has concerns about the competence, integrity, ethical values or diligence of management, or about its commitment to or enforcement of these, the auditor shall determine the effect that such concerns may have on the reliability of representations (oral or written) and audit evidence in general. (Ref: Para. A24-A25)

17. In particular, if written representations are inconsistent with other audit evidence, the auditor shall perform audit procedures to attempt to resolve the matter. If the matter remains unresolved, the auditor shall reconsider the assessment of the competence, integrity, ethical values or diligence of management, or of its commitment to or enforcement of these, and shall determine the effect that this may have on the reliability of representations (oral or written) and audit evidence in general. (Ref: Para. A23)

18. If the auditor concludes that the written representations are not reliable, the auditor shall take appropriate actions, including determining the possible effect on the opinion in the auditor's report in accordance with ISA (UK and Ireland) 705,[4] having regard to the requirement in paragraph 20 of this ISA (UK and Ireland).

Requested Written Representations Not Provided

19. If management does not provide one or more of the requested written representations, the auditor shall:

    (a) Discuss the matter with management;

    (b) Reevaluate the integrity of management and evaluate the effect that this may have on the reliability of representations (oral or written) and audit evidence in general; and

    (c) Take appropriate actions, including determining the possible effect on the opinion in the auditor's report in accordance with ISA (UK and Ireland) 705, having regard to the requirement in paragraph 20 of this ISA (UK and Ireland).

Written Representations about Management's Responsibilities

20. The auditor shall disclaim an opinion on the financial statements in accordance with ISA (UK and Ireland) 705 if:

    (a) The auditor concludes that there is sufficient doubt about the integrity of management such that the written representations required by paragraphs 10 and 11 are not reliable; or

---

[4] ISA (UK and Ireland) 705, "Modifications to the Opinion in the Independent Auditor's Report."

(b) Management does not provide the written representations required by paragraphs 10 and 11. (Ref: Para. A26-A27)

***

Application and Other Explanatory Material

Written Representations as Audit Evidence (Ref: Para. 3)

A1. Written representations are an important source of audit evidence. If management modifies or does not provide the requested written representations, it may alert the auditor to the possibility that one or more significant issues may exist. Further, a request for written, rather than oral, representations in many cases may prompt management to consider such matters more rigorously, thereby enhancing the quality of the representations.

Management from whom Written Representations Requested (Ref: Para. 9)

A2. Written representations are requested from those responsible for the preparation of the financial statements. Those individuals may vary depending on the governance structure of the entity, and relevant law or regulation; however, management (rather than those charged with governance) is often the responsible party. Written representations may therefore be requested from the entity's chief executive officer and chief financial officer, or other equivalent persons in entities that do not use such titles. In some circumstances, however, other parties, such as those charged with governance, are also responsible for the preparation and presentation of the financial statements[4a].

A2-1 In view of their importance, it is appropriate for written representations that are critical to obtaining sufficient appropriate audit evidence to be provided by those charged with governance rather than the entity's management.

A3. Due to its responsibility for the preparation of the financial statements, and its responsibilities for the conduct of the entity's business, management would be expected to have sufficient knowledge of the process followed by the entity in preparing and presenting the financial statements and the assertions therein on which to base the written representations.

A4. In some cases, however, management may decide to make inquiries of others who participate in preparing and presenting the financial statements and assertions therein, including individuals who have specialized knowledge relating to the matters about which written representations are requested. Such individuals may include:

*   An actuary responsible for actuarially determined accounting measurements.

[4a] In the UK and Ireland, those charged with governance are responsible for the preparation of the financial statements.

- Staff engineers who may have responsibility for and specialized knowledge about environmental liability measurements.

- Internal counsel who may provide information essential to provisions for legal claims.

A5. In some cases, management may include in the written representations qualifying language to the effect that representations are made to the best of its knowledge and belief. It is reasonable for the auditor to accept such wording if the auditor is satisfied that the representations are being made by those with appropriate responsibilities and knowledge of the matters included in the representations.

A6. To reinforce the need for management to make informed representations, the auditor may request that management include in the written representations confirmation that it has made such inquiries as it considered appropriate to place it in the position to be able to make the requested written representations. It is not expected that such inquiries would usually require a formal internal process beyond those already established by the entity.

Written Representations about Management's Responsibilities (Ref: Para. 10-11)

A7. Audit evidence obtained during the audit that management has fulfilled the responsibilities referred to in paragraphs 10 and 11 is not sufficient without obtaining confirmation from management that it believes that it has fulfilled those responsibilities. This is because the auditor is not able to judge solely on other audit evidence whether management has prepared and presented the financial statements and provided information to the auditor on the basis of the agreed acknowledgement and understanding of its responsibilities. For example, the auditor could not conclude that management has provided the auditor with all relevant information agreed in the terms of the audit engagement without asking it whether, and receiving confirmation that, such information has been provided.

A7-1. A signed copy of the financial statements for a company may be sufficient evidence of the directors' acknowledgement of their collective responsibility for the preparation of the financial statements where it incorporates a statement to that effect. A signed copy of the financial statements, however, is not, by itself, sufficient appropriate evidence to confirm other representations given to the auditor as it does not, ordinarily, clearly identify and explain the specific separate representations.

A8. The written representations required by paragraphs 10 and 11 draw on the agreed acknowledgement and understanding of management of its responsibilities in the terms of the audit engagement by requesting confirmation that it has fulfilled them. The auditor may also ask management to reconfirm its acknowledgement and understanding of those responsibilities in written representations. This is common in certain jurisdictions, but in any event may be particularly appropriate when:

- Those who signed the terms of the audit engagement on behalf of the entity no longer have the relevant responsibilities;

- The terms of the audit engagement were prepared in a previous year;

- There is any indication that management misunderstands those responsibilities; or

- Changes in circumstances make it appropriate to do so.

Consistent with the requirement of ISA (UK and Ireland) 210,[5] such reconfirmation of management's acknowledgement and understanding of its responsibilities is not made subject to the best of management's knowledge and belief (as discussed in paragraph A5 of this ISA (UK and Ireland)).

A8-1 Although reconfirmation of management's acknowledgement and understanding of its responsibilities is not made subject to the best of management's knowledge and belief, as discussed in paragraph A8, this does not prevent management from stating that the written representations required by paragraphs 10 and 11 relating to the fulfillment of its responsibilities are given to the best of its knowledge and belief.

Considerations Specific to Public Sector Entities

A9. The mandates for audits of the financial statements of public sector entities may be broader than those of other entities. As a result, the premise, relating to management's responsibilities, on which an audit of the financial statements of a public sector entity is conducted may give rise to additional written representations. These may include written representations confirming that transactions and events have been carried out in accordance with law, regulation or other authority.

Other Written Representations (Ref: Para. 13)

Additional Written Representations about the Financial Statements

A10. In addition to the written representation required by paragraph 10, the auditor may consider it necessary to request other written representations about the financial statements. Such written representations may supplement, but do not form part of, the written representation required by paragraph 10. They may include representations about the following:

- Whether the selection and application of accounting policies are appropriate; and

- Whether matters such as the following, where relevant under the applicable financial reporting framework, have been recognized, measured, presented or disclosed in accordance with that framework:

  o Plans or intentions that may affect the carrying value or classification of assets and liabilities;

---

[5] ISA (UK and Ireland) 210, paragraph 6(b).

- Liabilities, both actual and contingent;

- Title to, or control over, assets, the liens or encumbrances on assets, and assets pledged as collateral; and

- Aspects of laws, regulations and contractual agreements that may affect the financial statements, including non-compliance.

Additional Written Representations about Information Provided to the Auditor

A11. In addition to the written representation required by paragraph 11, the auditor may consider it necessary to request management to provide a written representation that it has communicated to the auditor all deficiencies in internal control of which management is aware.

Written Representations about Specific Assertions

A12. When obtaining evidence about, or evaluating, judgments and intentions, the auditor may consider one or more of the following:

- The entity's past history in carrying out its stated intentions.

- The entity's reasons for choosing a particular course of action.

- The entity's ability to pursue a specific course of action.

- The existence or lack of any other information that might have been obtained during the course of the audit that may be inconsistent with management's judgment or intent.

A13. In addition, the auditor may consider it necessary to request management to provide written representations about specific assertions in the financial statements; in particular, to support an understanding that the auditor has obtained from other audit evidence of management's judgment or intent in relation to, or the completeness of, a specific assertion. For example, if the intent of management is important to the valuation basis for investments, it may not be possible to obtain sufficient appropriate audit evidence without a written representation from management about its intentions. Although such written representations provide necessary audit evidence, they do not provide sufficient appropriate audit evidence on their own for that assertion.

Communicating a Threshold Amount (Ref: Para. 10-11, 13)

A14. ISA (UK and Ireland) 450 requires the auditor to accumulate misstatements identified during the audit, other than those that are clearly trivial.[6] The auditor may determine a threshold above which misstatements cannot be regarded as clearly trivial. In the

---

[6] ISA (UK and Ireland) 450, "Evaluation of Misstatements Identified during the Audit," paragraph 5.

same way, the auditor may consider communicating to management a threshold for purposes of the requested written representations.

Date of and Period(s) Covered by Written Representations (Ref: Para. 14)

A15. Because written representations are necessary audit evidence, the auditor's opinion cannot be expressed, and the auditor's report cannot be dated, before the date of the written representations. Furthermore, because the auditor is concerned with events occurring up to the date of the auditor's report that may require adjustment to or disclosure in the financial statements, the written representations are dated as near as practicable to, but not after, the date of the auditor's report on the financial statements.

A16. In some circumstances it may be appropriate for the auditor to obtain a written representation about a specific assertion in the financial statements during the course of the audit. Where this is the case, it may be necessary to request an updated written representation.

A17. The written representations are for all periods referred to in the auditor's report because management needs to reaffirm that the written representations it previously made with respect to the prior periods remain appropriate. The auditor and management may agree to a form of written representation that updates written representations relating to the prior periods by addressing whether there are any changes to such written representations and, if so, what they are.

A18. Situations may arise where current management were not present during all periods referred to in the auditor's report. Such persons may assert that they are not in a position to provide some or all of the written representations because they were not in place during the period. This fact, however, does not diminish such persons' responsibilities for the financial statements as a whole. Accordingly, the requirement for the auditor to request from them written representations that cover the whole of the relevant period(s) still applies.

Form of Written Representations (Ref: Para. 15)

A19. Written representations are required to be included in a representation letter addressed to the auditor. In some jurisdictions, however, management may be required by law or regulation to make a written public statement about its responsibilities. Although such statement is a representation to the users of the financial statements, or to relevant authorities, the auditor may determine that it is an appropriate form of written representation in respect of some or all of the representations required by paragraph 10 or 11. Consequently, the relevant matters covered by such statement need not be included in the representation letter. Factors that may affect the auditor's determination include:

- Whether the statement includes confirmation of the fulfillment of the responsibilities referred to in paragraphs 10 and 11.

- Whether the statement has been given or approved by those from whom the auditor requests the relevant written representations.

- Whether a copy of the statement is provided to the auditor as near as practicable to, but not after, the date of the auditor's report on the financial statements (see paragraph 14).

A20. A formal statement of compliance with law or regulation, or of approval of the financial statements, would not contain sufficient information for the auditor to be satisfied that all necessary representations have been consciously made. The expression of management's responsibilities in law or regulation is also not a substitute for the requested written representations.

A21. Appendix 2 provides an illustrative example of a representation letter.

Communication with Those Charged with Governance (Ref: Para. 10-11, 13)

A22. ISA (UK and Ireland) 260 requires the auditor to communicate with those charged with governance the written representations which the auditor has requested from management.[7]

A22-1. In the UK and Ireland these communications are made before those charged with governance approve the financial statements, to ensure that they are aware of the representations on which the auditor intends to rely in expressing the auditor's opinion on those financial statements.

Doubt as to the Reliability of Written Representations and Requested Written Representations Not Provided

Doubt as to the Reliability of Written Representations (Ref: Para. 16-17)

A23. In the case of identified inconsistencies between one or more written representations and audit evidence obtained from another source, the auditor may consider whether the risk assessment remains appropriate and, if not, revise the risk assessment and determine the nature, timing and extent of further audit procedures to respond to the assessed risks.

A24. Concerns about the competence, integrity, ethical values or diligence of management, or about its commitment to or enforcement of these, may cause the auditor to conclude that the risk of management misrepresentation in the financial statements is such that an audit cannot be conducted. In such a case, the auditor may consider withdrawing from the engagement, where withdrawal is possible under applicable law or regulation, unless those charged with governance put in place appropriate corrective measures. Such measures, however, may not be sufficient to enable the auditor to issue an unmodified audit opinion.

---

[7] ISA (UK and Ireland) 260, "Communication with Those Charged with Governance," paragraph 16(c)(ii).

A25. ISA (UK and Ireland) 230 requires the auditor to document significant matters arising during the audit, the conclusions reached thereon, and significant professional judgments made in reaching those conclusions.[8] The auditor may have identified significant issues relating to the competence, integrity, ethical values or diligence of management, or about its commitment to or enforcement of these, but concluded that the written representations are nevertheless reliable. In such a case, this significant matter is documented in accordance with ISA (UK and Ireland) 230.

Written Representations about Management's Responsibilities (Ref: Para. 20)

A26. As explained in paragraph A7, the auditor is not able to judge solely on other audit evidence whether management has fulfilled the responsibilities referred to in paragraphs 10 and 11. Therefore, if, as described in paragraph 20(a), the auditor concludes that the written representations about these matters are unreliable, or if management does not provide those written representations, the auditor is unable to obtain sufficient appropriate audit evidence. The possible effects on the financial statements of such inability are not confined to specific elements, accounts or items of the financial statements and are hence pervasive. ISA (UK and Ireland) 705 requires the auditor to disclaim an opinion on the financial statements in such circumstances.[9]

A27. A written representation that has been modified from that requested by the auditor does not necessarily mean that management did not provide the written representation. However, the underlying reason for such modification may affect the opinion in the auditor's report. For example:

- The written representation about management's fulfillment of its responsibility for the preparation of the financial statements may state that management believes that, except for material non-compliance with a particular requirement of the applicable financial reporting framework, the financial statements are prepared in accordance with that framework. The requirement in paragraph 20 does not apply because the auditor concluded that management has provided reliable written representations. However, the auditor is required to consider the effect of the non-compliance on the opinion in the auditor's report in accordance with ISA (UK and Ireland) 705.

- The written representation about the responsibility of management to provide the auditor with all relevant information agreed in the terms of the audit engagement may state that management believes that, except for information destroyed in a fire, it has provided the auditor with such information. The requirement in paragraph 20 does not apply because the auditor concluded that management has provided reliable written representations. However, the auditor is required to consider the effects of the pervasiveness of the information destroyed in the fire on the financial statements and the effect thereof on the opinion in the auditor's report in accordance with ISA (UK and Ireland) 705.

---

[8] ISA (UK and Ireland) 230, "Audit Documentation," paragraphs 8(c) and 10.
[9] ISA (UK and Ireland) 705, paragraph 9.

- The written representation that all transactions have been recorded and are reflected in the financial statements may be modified, for example to refer a threshold amount agreed with the auditor (see paragraph A14) or to state that all transactions that may have a material effect on the financial statements have been recorded.

Appendix 1

(Ref: Para. 2)

List of ISAs (UK and Ireland) Containing Requirements for Written Representations

This appendix identifies paragraphs in other ISAs (UK and Ireland) in effect for audits of financial statements for periods ending on or after 15 December 2010 that require subject-matter specific written representations. The list is not a substitute for considering the requirements and related application and other explanatory material in ISAs (UK and Ireland).

- ISA 240 (UK and Ireland), "The Auditor's Responsibilities Relating to Fraud in an Audit of Financial Statements" – paragraph 39

- ISA 250 (UK and Ireland), "Consideration of Laws and Regulations in an Audit of Financial Statements" – paragraph 16

- ISA 450 (UK and Ireland), "Evaluation of Misstatements Identified during the Audit" – paragraph 14

- ISA 501 (UK and Ireland), "Audit Evidence—Specific Considerations for Selected Items" – paragraph 12

- ISA 540 (UK and Ireland), "Auditing Accounting Estimates, Including Fair Value Accounting Estimates, and Related Disclosures" – paragraph 22

- ISA 550 (UK and Ireland), "Related Parties" – paragraph 26

- ISA 560 (UK and Ireland), "Subsequent Events" – paragraph 9

- ISA 570 (UK and Ireland), "Going Concern" – paragraph 16(e)

- ISA 710 (UK and Ireland), "Comparative Information—Corresponding Figures and Comparative Financial Statements" – paragraph 9

Appendix 2

This illustrative representation letter has not been tailored for the UK and Ireland. For example, when describing the responsibilities of management and those charged with governance for the financial statements and providing information to the auditor, the auditor has regard to the manner in which those responsibilities are described in the terms of the audit engagement (see ISA (UK and Ireland) 210).

Illustrative Representation Letter

The following illustrative letter includes written representations that are required by this and other ISAs in effect for audits of financial statements for periods ending on or after 15 December 2010. It is assumed in this illustration that the applicable financial reporting framework is International Financial Reporting Standards; the requirement of ISA 570[10] to obtain a written representation is not relevant; and that there are no exceptions to the requested written representations. If there were exceptions, the representations would need to be modified to reflect the exceptions.

(Entity Letterhead)

(To Auditor) (Date)

This representation letter is provided in connection with your audit of the financial statements of ABC Company for the year ended December 31, 20XX[11] for the purpose of expressing an opinion as to whether the financial statements are presented fairly, in all material respects, (or *give a true and fair view*) in accordance with International Financial Reporting Standards.

We confirm that (*, to the best of our knowledge and belief, having made such inquiries as we considered necessary for the purpose of appropriately informing ourselves*):

Financial Statements

- We have fulfilled our responsibilities, as set out in the terms of the audit engagement dated [insert date], for the preparation of the financial statements in accordance with International Financial Reporting Standards; in particular the financial statements are fairly presented (or *give a true and fair view*) in accordance therewith.

- Significant assumptions used by us in making accounting estimates, including those measured at fair value, are reasonable. (ISA 540)

---

[10] ISA 570, "Going Concern."

[11] Where the auditor reports on more than one period, the auditor adjusts the date so that the letter pertains to all periods covered by the auditor's report.

- Related party relationships and transactions have been appropriately accounted for and disclosed in accordance with the requirements of International Financial Reporting Standards. (ISA 550)

- All events subsequent to the date of the financial statements and for which International Financial Reporting Standards require adjustment or disclosure have been adjusted or disclosed. (ISA 560)

- The effects of uncorrected misstatements are immaterial, both individually and in the aggregate, to the financial statements as a whole. A list of the uncorrected misstatements is attached to the representation letter. (ISA 450)

- [Any other matters that the auditor may consider appropriate (see paragraph A10 of this ISA).]

Information Provided

- We have provided you with:

  - Access to all information of which we are aware that is relevant to the preparation of the financial statements such as records, documentation and other matters;

  - Additional information that you have requested from us for the purpose of the audit; and

  - Unrestricted access to persons within the entity from whom you determined it necessary to obtain audit evidence.

- All transactions have been recorded in the accounting records and are reflected in the financial statements.

- We have disclosed to you the results of our assessment of the risk that the financial statements may be materially misstated as a result of fraud. (ISA 240)

- We have disclosed to you all information in relation to fraud or suspected fraud that we are aware of and that affects the entity and involves:

  - Management;

  - Employees who have significant roles in internal control; or

  - Others where the fraud could have a material effect on the financial statements. (ISA 240)

- We have disclosed to you all information in relation to allegations of fraud, or suspected fraud, affecting the entity's financial statements communicated by employees, former employees, analysts, regulators or others. (ISA 240)

- We have disclosed to you all known instances of non-compliance or suspected non-compliance with laws and regulations whose effects should be considered when preparing financial statements. (ISA 250)

- We have disclosed to you the identity of the entity's related parties and all the related party relationships and transactions of which we are aware. 550)

- [Any other matters that the auditor may consider necessary (see paragraph A11 of this ISA).]

Management   Management

INTERNATIONAL STANDARD ON AUDITING
(UK AND IRELAND) 600

SPECIAL CONSIDERATIONS—AUDITS OF GROUP
FINANCIAL STATEMENTS (INCLUDING THE WORK OF
COMPONENT AUDITORS)

(Effective for audits of group financial statements for periods ending on or after 15 December 2010)[1a]

CONTENTS

Paragraphs

[1a] Conforming amendments to this standard as a result of ISA (UK and Ireland) 610 (Revised June 2013), *Using the Work of Internal Auditors*, are included that are effective for audits of financial statements for periods ending on or after 15 June 2014. Details of the amendments are given in the Annexure to ISA (UK and Ireland) 610 (Revised June 2013).

Appendix 1: Example of a Qualified Opinion Where the Group Engagement Team Is Not Able to Obtain Sufficient Appropriate Audit Evidence on Which to Base the Group Audit Opinion

Appendix 2: Examples of Matters about Which the Group Engagement Team Obtains an Understanding

Appendix 3: Examples of Conditions or Events that May Indicate Risks of Material Misstatement of the Group Financial Statements

Appendix 4: Examples of a Component Auditor's Confirmations

Appendix 5: Required and Additional Matters Included in the Group Engagement Team's Letter of Instruction

---

International Standard on Auditing (UK and Ireland) (ISA (UK and Ireland)) 600, "Special Considerations—Audits of Group Financial Statements (Including the Work of Component Auditors)" should be read in conjunction with ISA (UK and Ireland) 200, "Overall Objectives of the Independent Auditor and the Conduct of an Audit in Accordance with International Standards on Auditing (UK and Ireland)."

Introduction

Scope of this ISA (UK and Ireland)

1.   The International Standards on Auditing (UK and Ireland) (ISAs (UK and Ireland)) apply to group audits. This ISA (UK and Ireland) deals with special considerations that apply to group audits, in particular those that involve component auditors.

2.   An auditor may find this ISA (UK and Ireland), adapted as necessary in the circumstances, useful when that auditor involves other auditors in the audit of financial statements that are not group financial statements. For example, an auditor may involve another auditor to observe the inventory count or inspect physical fixed assets at a remote location.

3.   A component auditor may be required by statute, regulation or for another reason, to express an audit opinion on the financial statements of a component. The group engagement team may decide to use the audit evidence on which the audit opinion on the financial statements of the component is based to provide audit evidence for the group audit, but the requirements of this ISA (UK and Ireland) nevertheless apply. (Ref: Para. A1)

4.   In accordance with ISA (UK and Ireland) 220,[1] the group engagement partner is required to be satisfied that those performing the group audit engagement, including component auditors, collectively have the appropriate competence and capabilities. The group engagement partner is also responsible for the direction, supervision and performance of the group audit engagement.

5.   The group engagement partner applies the requirements of ISA (UK and Ireland) 220 regardless of whether the group engagement team or a component auditor performs the work on the financial information of a component. This ISA (UK and Ireland) assists the group engagement partner to meet the requirements of ISA (UK and Ireland) 220 where component auditors perform work on the financial information of components.

6.   Audit risk is a function of the risk of material misstatement of the financial statements and the risk that the auditor will not detect such misstatements.[2] In a group audit, this includes the risk that the component auditor may not detect a misstatement in the financial information of the component that could cause a material misstatement of the group financial statements, and the risk that the group engagement team may not detect this misstatement. This ISA (UK and Ireland) explains the matters that the group engagement team considers when determining the nature, timing and extent of its involvement in the risk assessment procedures and further audit procedures performed by the component auditors on the financial information of the

---

[1]   ISA (UK and Ireland) 220, "Quality Control for an Audit of Financial Statements," paragraphs 14 and 15.

[2]   ISA (UK and Ireland) 200, "Overall Objectives of the Independent Auditor and the Conduct of an Audit in Accordance with International Standards on Auditing (UK and Ireland)," paragraph A32.

components. The purpose of this involvement is to obtain sufficient appropriate audit evidence on which to base the audit opinion on the group financial statements.

Effective Date

7.   This ISA (UK and Ireland) is effective for audits of group financial statements for periods ending on or after 15 December 2010.[1a]

Objectives

8.   The objectives of the auditor are:

    (a)   To determine whether to act as the auditor of the group financial statements; and

    (b)   If acting as the auditor of the group financial statements:

        (i)   To communicate clearly with component auditors about the scope and timing of their work on financial information related to components and their findings; and

        (ii)   To obtain sufficient appropriate audit evidence regarding the financial information of the components and the consolidation process to express an opinion on whether the group financial statements are prepared, in all material respects, in accordance with the applicable financial reporting framework.

Definitions

9.   For purposes of the ISAs (UK and Ireland), the following terms have the meanings attributed below:

    (a)   Component – An entity or business activity for which group or component management prepares financial information that should be included in the group financial statements. (Ref: Para. A2-A4)

    (b)   Component auditor – An auditor who, at the request of the group engagement team, performs work on financial information related to a component for the group audit. (Ref: Para. A7)

    (c)   Component management – Management responsible for the preparation of the financial information of a component.

    (d)   Component materiality – The materiality for a component determined by the group engagement team.

(e)　Group – All the components whose financial information is included in the group financial statements. A group always has more than one component.

(f)　Group audit – The audit of group financial statements.

(g)　Group audit opinion – The audit opinion on the group financial statements.

(h)　Group engagement partner – The partner or other person in the firm who is responsible for the group audit engagement and its performance, and for the auditor's report on the group financial statements that is issued on behalf of the firm. Where joint auditors conduct the group audit, the joint engagement partners and their engagement teams collectively constitute the group engagement partner and the group engagement team. This ISA (UK and Ireland) does not, however, deal with the relationship between joint auditors or the work that one joint auditor performs in relation to the work of the other joint auditor.

(i)　Group engagement team – Partners, including the group engagement partner, and staff who establish the overall group audit strategy, communicate with component auditors, perform work on the consolidation process, and evaluate the conclusions drawn from the audit evidence as the basis for forming an opinion on the group financial statements.

(j)　Group financial statements – Financial statements that include the financial information of more than one component. The term "group financial statements" also refers to combined financial statements aggregating the financial information prepared by components that have no parent but are under common control.

(k)　Group management – Management responsible for the preparation of the group financial statements.

(l)　Group-wide controls – Controls designed, implemented and maintained by group management over group financial reporting.

(m)　Significant component – A component identified by the group engagement team (i) that is of individual financial significance to the group, or (ii) that, due to its specific nature or circumstances, is likely to include significant risks of material misstatement of the group financial statements. (Ref: Para. A5-A6)

10.　Reference to "the applicable financial reporting framework" means the financial reporting framework that applies to the group financial statements. Reference to "the consolidation process" includes:

(a)　The recognition, measurement, presentation, and disclosure of the financial information of the components in the group financial statements by way of consolidation, proportionate consolidation, or the equity or cost methods of accounting; and

(b) The aggregation in combined financial statements of the financial information of components that have no parent but are under common control.

Requirements

Responsibility

11. The group engagement partner is responsible for the direction, supervision and performance of the group audit engagement in compliance with professional standards and applicable legal and regulatory requirements, and whether the auditor's report that is issued is appropriate in the circumstances.[3]; As a result, the auditor's report on the group financial statements shall not refer to a component auditor, unless required by law or regulation to include such reference. If such reference is required by law or regulation, the auditor's report shall indicate that the reference does not diminish the group engagement partner's or the group engagement partner's firm's responsibility for the group audit opinion. (Ref: Para. A8-A9)

Acceptance and Continuance

12. In applying ISA (UK and Ireland) 220, the group engagement partner shall determine whether sufficient appropriate audit evidence can reasonably be expected to be obtained in relation to the consolidation process and the financial information of the components on which to base the group audit opinion. For this purpose, the group engagement team shall obtain an understanding of the group, its components, and their environments that is sufficient to identify components that are likely to be significant components. Where component auditors will perform work on the financial information of such components, the group engagement partner shall evaluate whether the group engagement team will be able to be involved in the work of those component auditors to the extent necessary to obtain sufficient appropriate audit evidence. (Ref: Para. A10-A12)

13. If the group engagement partner concludes that:

(a) it will not be possible for the group engagement team to obtain sufficient appropriate audit evidence due to restrictions imposed by group management; and

(b) the possible effect of this inability will result in a disclaimer of opinion on the group financial statements),[4]

the group engagement partner shall either:

---

[3] ISA (UK and Ireland) 220, paragraph 15.
[4] ISA (UK and Ireland) 705, "Modifications to the Opinion in the Independent Auditor's Report."

- in the case of a new engagement, not accept the engagement, or, in the case of a continuing engagement, withdraw from the engagement, where withdrawal is possible under applicable law or regulation; or

- where law or regulation prohibits an auditor from declining an engagement or where withdrawal from an engagement is not otherwise possible, having performed the audit of the group financial statements to the extent possible, disclaim an opinion on the group financial statements. (Ref: Para. A13-A19)

Terms of Engagement

14. The group engagement partner shall agree on the terms of the group audit engagement in accordance with ISA (UK and Ireland) 210.[5] (Ref: Para. A20-A21)

Overall Audit Strategy and Audit Plan

15. The group engagement team shall establish an overall group audit strategy and shall develop a group audit plan in accordance with ISA (UK and Ireland) 300.[6]

16. The group engagement partner shall review the overall group audit strategy and group audit plan. (Ref: Para. A22)

Understanding the Group, Its Components and Their Environments

17. The auditor is required to identify and assess the risks of material misstatement through obtaining an understanding of the entity and its environment.[7] The group engagement team shall:

    (a) Enhance its understanding of the group, its components, and their environments, including group-wide controls, obtained during the acceptance or continuance stage; and

    (b) Obtain an understanding of the consolidation process, including the instructions issued by group management to components. (Ref: Para. A23-A29)

18. The group engagement team shall obtain an understanding that is sufficient to:

    (a) Confirm or revise its initial identification of components that are likely to be significant; and

    (b) Assess the risks of material misstatement of the group financial statements, whether due to fraud or error.[8] (Ref: Para. A30-A31)

---

[5] ISA (UK and Ireland) 210, "Agreeing the Terms of Audit Engagements."
[6] ISA (UK and Ireland) 300, "Planning an Audit of Financial Statements," paragraphs 7-12.
[7] ISA (UK and Ireland) 315, "Identifying and Assessing the Risks of Material Misstatement through Understanding the Entity and Its Environment."
[8] ISA (UK and Ireland) 315.

Understanding the Component Auditor

19. If the group engagement team plans to request a component auditor to perform work on the financial information of a component, the group engagement team shall obtain an understanding of the following: (Ref: Para. A32-A35)

 (a) Whether the component auditor understands and will comply with the ethical requirements that are relevant to the group audit and, in particular, is independent. (Ref: Para. A37)

 (b) The component auditor's professional competence. (Ref: Para. A38)

 (c) Whether the group engagement team will be able to be involved in the work of the component auditor to the extent necessary to obtain sufficient appropriate audit evidence.

 (d) Whether the component auditor operates in a regulatory environment that actively oversees auditors. (Ref: Para. A36)

20. If a component auditor does not meet the independence requirements that are relevant to the group audit, or the group engagement team has serious concerns about the other matters listed in paragraph 19(a)-(c), the group engagement team shall obtain sufficient appropriate audit evidence relating to the financial information of the component without requesting that component auditor to perform work on the financial information of that component. (Ref: Para. A39-A41)

Materiality

21. The group engagement team shall determine the following: (Ref: Para. A42)

 (a) Materiality for the group financial statements as a whole when establishing the overall group audit strategy.

 (b) If, in the specific circumstances of the group, there are particular classes of transactions, account balances or disclosures in the group financial statements for which misstatements of lesser amounts than materiality for the group financial statements as a whole could reasonably be expected to influence the economic decisions of users taken on the basis of the group financial statements, the materiality level or levels to be applied to those particular classes of transactions, account balances or disclosures.

 (c) Component materiality for those components where component auditors will perform an audit or a review for purposes of the group audit. To reduce to an appropriately low level the probability that the aggregate of uncorrected and undetected misstatements in the group financial statements exceeds materiality for the group financial statements as a whole, component materiality shall be lower than materiality for the group financial statements as a whole. (Ref: Para. A43-A44)

(d) The threshold above which misstatements cannot be regarded as clearly trivial to the group financial statements. (Ref: Para. A45)

22. Where component auditors will perform an audit for purposes of the group audit, the group engagement team shall evaluate the appropriateness of performance materiality determined at the component level. (Ref: Para. A46)

23. If a component is subject to audit by statute, regulation or other reason, and the group engagement team decides to use that audit to provide audit evidence for the group audit, the group engagement team shall determine whether:

(a) materiality for the component financial statements as a whole; and

(b) performance materiality at the component level

meet the requirements of this ISA (UK and Ireland).

Responding to Assessed Risks

24. The auditor is required to design and implement appropriate responses to address the assessed risks of material misstatement of the financial statements.[9] The group engagement team shall determine the type of work to be performed by the group engagement team, or the component auditors on its behalf, on the financial information of the components (see paragraphs 26-29). The group engagement team shall also determine the nature, timing and extent of its involvement in the work of the component auditors (see paragraphs 30-31).

25. If the nature, timing and extent of the work to be performed on the consolidation process or the financial information of the components are based on an expectation that group-wide controls are operating effectively, or if substantive procedures alone cannot provide sufficient appropriate audit evidence at the assertion level, the group engagement team shall test, or request a component auditor to test, the operating effectiveness of those controls.

Determining the Type of Work to Be Performed on the Financial Information of Components (Ref: Para. A47)

Significant Components

26. For a component that is significant due to its individual financial significance to the group, the group engagement team, or a component auditor on its behalf, shall perform an audit of the financial information of the component using component materiality.

27. For a component that is significant because it is likely to include significant risks of material misstatement of the group financial statements due to its specific nature or

---

[9] ISA (UK and Ireland) 330, "The Auditor's Responses to Assessed Risks."

circumstances, the group engagement team, or a component auditor on its behalf, shall perform one or more of the following:

(a) An audit of the financial information of the component using component materiality.

(b) An audit of one or more account balances, classes of transactions or disclosures relating to the likely significant risks of material misstatement of the group financial statements. (Ref: Para. A48)

(c) Specified audit procedures relating to the likely significant risks of material misstatement of the group financial statements. (Ref: Para. A49)

Components that Are Not Significant Components

28. For components that are not significant components, the group engagement team shall perform analytical procedures at group level. (Ref: Para. A50)

29. If the group engagement team does not consider that sufficient appropriate audit evidence on which to base the group audit opinion will be obtained from:

(a) the work performed on the financial information of significant components;

(b) the work performed on group-wide controls and the consolidation process; and

(c) the analytical procedures performed at group level,

the group engagement team shall select components that are not significant components and shall perform, or request a component auditor to perform, one or more of the following on the financial information of the individual components selected: (Ref: Para. A51-A53)

- An audit of the financial information of the component using component materiality.

- An audit of one or more account balances, classes of transactions or disclosures.

- A review of the financial information of the component using component materiality.

- Specified procedures.

The group engagement team shall vary the selection of components over a period of time.

Involvement in the Work Performed by Component Auditors (Ref: Para. A54-A55)

Significant Components—Risk Assessment

30.   If a component auditor performs an audit of the financial information of a significant component, the group engagement team shall be involved in the component auditor's risk assessment to identify significant risks of material misstatement of the group financial statements. The nature, timing and extent of this involvement are affected by the group engagement team's understanding of the component auditor, but at a minimum shall include:

(a)   Discussing with the component auditor or component management those of the component's business activities that are significant to the group;

(b)   Discussing with the component auditor the susceptibility of the component to material misstatement of the financial information due to fraud or error; and

(c)   Reviewing the component auditor's documentation of identified significant risks of material misstatement of the group financial statements. Such documentation may take the form of a memorandum that reflects the component auditor's conclusion with regard to the identified significant risks.

Identified Significant Risks of Material Misstatement of the Group Financial Statements—Further Audit Procedures

31.   If significant risks of material misstatement of the group financial statements have been identified in a component on which a component auditor performs the work, the group engagement team shall evaluate the appropriateness of the further audit procedures to be performed to respond to the identified significant risks of material misstatement of the group financial statements. Based on its understanding of the component auditor, the group engagement team shall determine whether it is necessary to be involved in the further audit procedures.

Consolidation Process

32.   In accordance with paragraph 17, the group engagement team obtains an understanding of group-wide controls and the consolidation process, including the instructions issued by group management to components. In accordance with paragraph 25, the group engagement team, or component auditor at the request of the group engagement team, tests the operating effectiveness of group-wide controls if the nature, timing and extent of the work to be performed on the consolidation process are based on an expectation that group-wide controls are operating effectively, or if substantive procedures alone cannot provide sufficient appropriate audit evidence at the assertion level.

33.   The group engagement team shall design and perform further audit procedures on the consolidation process to respond to the assessed risks of material misstatement of the group financial statements arising from the consolidation process. This shall

include evaluating whether all components have been included in the group financial statements.

34.   The group engagement team shall evaluate the appropriateness, completeness and accuracy of consolidation adjustments and reclassifications, and shall evaluate whether any fraud risk factors or indicators of possible management bias exist. (Ref: Para. A56)

35.   If the financial information of a component has not been prepared in accordance with the same accounting policies applied to the group financial statements, the group engagement team shall evaluate whether the financial information of that component has been appropriately adjusted for purposes of preparing and presenting the group financial statements.

36.   The group engagement team shall determine whether the financial information identified in the component auditor's communication (see paragraph 41(c)) is the financial information that is incorporated in the group financial statements.

37.   If the group financial statements include the financial statements of a component with a financial reporting period-end that differs from that of the group, the group engagement team shall evaluate whether appropriate adjustments have been made to those financial statements in accordance with the applicable financial reporting framework.

Subsequent Events

38.   Where the group engagement team or component auditors perform audits on the financial information of components, the group engagement team or the component auditors shall perform procedures designed to identify events at those components that occur between the dates of the financial information of the components and the date of the auditor's report on the group financial statements, and that may require adjustment to or disclosure in the group financial statements.

39.   Where component auditors perform work other than audits of the financial information of components, the group engagement team shall request the component auditors to notify the group engagement team if they become aware of subsequent events that may require an adjustment to or disclosure in the group financial statements.

Communication with the Component Auditor

40.   The group engagement team shall communicate its requirements to the component auditor on a timely basis. This communication shall set out the work to be performed, the use to be made of that work, and the form and content of the component auditor's communication with the group engagement team. It shall also include the following: (Ref: Para. A57, A58, A60)

    (a)   A request that the component auditor, knowing the context in which the group engagement team will use the work of the component auditor, confirms that the component auditor will cooperate with the group engagement team. (Ref: Para. A59)

(b) The ethical requirements that are relevant to the group audit and, in particular, the independence requirements.

(c) In the case of an audit or review of the financial information of the component, component materiality (and, if applicable, the materiality level or levels for particular classes of transactions, account balances or disclosures) and the threshold above which misstatements cannot be regarded as clearly trivial to the group financial statements.

(d) Identified significant risks of material misstatement of the group financial statements, due to fraud or error, that are relevant to the work of the component auditor. The group engagement team shall request the component auditor to communicate on a timely basis any other identified significant risks of material misstatement of the group financial statements, due to fraud or error, in the component, and the component auditor's responses to such risks.

(e) A list of related parties prepared by group management, and any other related parties of which the group engagement team is aware. The group engagement team shall request the component auditor to communicate on a timely basis related parties not previously identified by group management or the group engagement team. The group engagement team shall determine whether to identify such additional related parties to other component auditors.

41. The group engagement team shall request the component auditor to communicate matters relevant to the group engagement team's conclusion with regard to the group audit. Such communication shall include: (Ref: Para. A60)

(a) Whether the component auditor has complied with ethical requirements that are relevant to the group audit, including independence and professional competence;

(b) Whether the component auditor has complied with the group engagement team's requirements;

(c) Identification of the financial information of the component on which the component auditor is reporting;

(d) Information on instances of non-compliance with laws or regulations that could give rise to a material misstatement of the group financial statements;

(e) A list of uncorrected misstatements of the financial information of the component (the list need not include misstatements that are below the threshold for clearly trivial misstatements communicated by the group engagement team (see paragraph 40(c));

(f) Indicators of possible management bias;

(g) Description of any identified significant deficiencies in internal control at the component level;

(h) Other significant matters that the component auditor communicated or expects to communicate to those charged with governance of the component, including fraud or suspected fraud involving component management, employees who have significant roles in internal control at the component level or others where the fraud resulted in a material misstatement of the financial information of the component;

(i) Any other matters that may be relevant to the group audit, or that the component auditor wishes to draw to the attention of the group engagement team, including exceptions noted in the written representations that the component auditor requested from component management; and

(j) The component auditor's overall findings, conclusions or opinion.

Evaluating the Sufficiency and Appropriateness of Audit Evidence Obtained

Evaluating the Component Auditor's Communication and Adequacy of their Work

42. The group engagement team shall evaluate the component auditor's communication (see paragraph 41). The group engagement team shall:

(a) Discuss significant matters arising from that evaluation with the component auditor, component management or group management, as appropriate; and

(b) Determine whether it is necessary to review other relevant parts of the component auditor's audit documentation. (Ref: Para. A61)

43. If the group engagement team concludes that the work of the component auditor is insufficient, the group engagement team shall determine what additional procedures are to be performed, and whether they are to be performed by the component auditor or by the group engagement team.

Sufficiency and Appropriateness of Audit Evidence

44. The auditor is required to obtain sufficient appropriate audit evidence to reduce audit risk to an acceptably low level and thereby enable the auditor to draw reasonable conclusions on which to base the auditor's opinion.[10] The group engagement team shall evaluate whether sufficient appropriate audit evidence has been obtained from the audit procedures performed on the consolidation process and the work performed by the group engagement team and the component auditors on the financial information of the components, on which to base the group audit opinion. (Ref: Para. A62)

---

[10] ISA (UK and Ireland) 200, paragraph 17.

45. The group engagement partner shall evaluate the effect on the group audit opinion of any uncorrected misstatements (either identified by the group engagement team or communicated by component auditors) and any instances where there has been an inability to obtain sufficient appropriate audit evidence. (Ref: Para. A63)

Communication with Group Management and Those Charged with Governance of the Group

Communication with Group Management

46. The group engagement team shall determine which identified deficiencies in internal control to communicate to those charged with governance and group management in accordance with ISA (UK and Ireland) 265.[11] In making this determination, the group engagement team shall consider:

    (a) Deficiencies in group-wide internal control that the group engagement team has identified;

    (b) Deficiencies in internal control that the group engagement team has identified in internal controls at components; and

    (c) Deficiencies in internal control that component auditors have brought to the attention of the group engagement team.

47. If fraud has been identified by the group engagement team or brought to its attention by a component auditor (see paragraph 41(h)), or information indicates that a fraud may exist, the group engagement team shall communicate this on a timely basis to the appropriate level of group management in order to inform those with primary responsibility for the prevention and detection of fraud of matters relevant to their responsibilities. (Ref. Para. A64)

48. A component auditor may be required by statute, regulation or for another reason, to express an audit opinion on the financial statements of a component. In that case, the group engagement team shall request group management to inform component management of any matter of which the group engagement team becomes aware that may be significant to the financial statements of the component, but of which component management may be unaware. If group management refuses to communicate the matter to component management, the group engagement team shall discuss the matter with those charged with governance of the group. If the matter remains unresolved, the group engagement team, subject to legal and professional confidentiality considerations, shall consider whether to advise the component auditor not to issue the auditor's report on the financial statements of the component until the matter is resolved. (Ref: Para. A65)

---

[11] ISA (UK and Ireland) 265, "Communicating Deficiencies in Internal Control to Those Charged with Governance and Management."

Communication with Those Charged with Governance of the Group

49. The group engagement team shall communicate the following matters with those charged with governance of the group, in addition to those required by ISA (UK and Ireland) 260[12] and other ISAs (UK and Ireland): (Ref: Para. A66)

    (a) An overview of the type of work to be performed on the financial information of the components.

    (b) An overview of the nature of the group engagement team's planned involvement in the work to be performed by the component auditors on the financial information of significant components.

    (c) Instances where the group engagement team's evaluation of the work of a component auditor gave rise to a concern about the quality of that auditor's work.

    (d) Any limitations on the group audit, for example, where the group engagement team's access to information may have been restricted.

    (e) Fraud or suspected fraud involving group management, component management, employees who have significant roles in group-wide controls or others where the fraud resulted in a material misstatement of the group financial statements.

Documentation

50. The group engagement team shall include in the audit documentation the following matters:[13]

    (a) An analysis of components, indicating those that are significant, and the type of work performed on the financial information of the components.

    (b) The nature, timing and extent of the group engagement team's involvement in the work performed by the component auditors on significant components including, where applicable, the group engagement team's review of relevant parts of the component auditors' audit documentation and conclusions thereon. (Ref: Para. A66-1)

    (c) Written communications between the group engagement team and the component auditors about the group engagement team's requirements.

***

---

[12] ISA (UK and Ireland) 260, "Communication with Those Charged with Governance."
[13] ISA (UK and Ireland) 230, "Audit Documentation," paragraphs 8-11, and paragraph A6.

Application and Other Explanatory Material

Components Subject to Audit by Statute, Regulation or Other Reason (Ref: Para. 3)

A1. Factors that may affect the group engagement team's decision whether to use an audit required by statute, regulation or for another reason to provide audit evidence for the group audit include the following:

- Differences in the financial reporting framework applied in preparing the financial statements of the component and that applied in preparing the group financial statements.

- Differences in the auditing and other standards applied by the component auditor and those applied in the audit of the group financial statements.

- Whether the audit of the financial statements of the component will be completed in time to meet the group reporting timetable.

Considerations Specific to Public Sector Entities

A1-1 In certain parts of the public sector where the responsibilities of principal and other auditors are governed by statutory provisions, these override the provisions of this ISA (UK and Ireland).

Definitions

Component (Ref: Para. 9(a))

A2. The structure of a group affects how components are identified. For example, the group financial reporting system may be based on an organizational structure that provides for financial information to be prepared by a parent and one or more subsidiaries, joint ventures, or investees accounted for by the equity or cost methods of accounting; by a head office and one or more divisions or branches; or by a combination of both. Some groups, however, may organize their financial reporting system by function, process, product or service (or by groups of products or services), or geographical locations. In these cases, the entity or business activity for which group or component management prepares financial information that is included in the group financial statements may be a function, process, product or service (or group of products or services), or geographical location.

A3. Various levels of components may exist within the group financial reporting system, in which case it may be more appropriate to identify components at certain levels of aggregation rather than individually.

A4. Components aggregated at a certain level may constitute a component for purposes of the group audit; however, such a component may also prepare group financial statements that incorporate the financial information of the components it encompasses (that is, a subgroup). This ISA (UK and Ireland) may therefore be applied by different group engagement partners and teams for different subgroups within a larger group.

Significant Component (Ref: Para. 9(m))

A5. As the individual financial significance of a component increases, the risks of material misstatement of the group financial statements ordinarily increase. The group engagement team may apply a percentage to a chosen benchmark as an aid to identify components that are of individual financial significance. Identifying a benchmark and determining a percentage to be applied to it involve the exercise of professional judgment. Depending on the nature and circumstances of the group, appropriate benchmarks might include group assets, liabilities, cash flows, profit or turnover. For example, the group engagement team may consider that components exceeding 15% of the chosen benchmark are significant components. A higher or lower percentage may, however, be deemed appropriate in the circumstances.

A6. The group engagement team may also identify a component as likely to include significant risks of material misstatement of the group financial statements due to its specific nature or circumstances (that is, risks that require special audit consideration[14]). For example, a component could be responsible for foreign exchange trading and thus expose the group to a significant risk of material misstatement, even though the component is not otherwise of individual financial significance to the group.

Component Auditor (Ref: Para. 9(b))

A7. A member of the group engagement team may perform work on the financial information of a component for the group audit at the request of the group engagement team. Where this is the case, such a member of the engagement team is also a component auditor.

Responsibility (Ref: Para. 11)

A8. Although component auditors may perform work on the financial information of the components for the group audit and as such are responsible for their overall findings, conclusions or opinions, the group engagement partner or the group engagement partner's firm is responsible for the group audit opinion.

A9. When the group audit opinion is modified because the group engagement team was unable to obtain sufficient appropriate audit evidence in relation to the financial information of one or more components, the Basis for Modification paragraph in the auditor's report on the group financial statements describes the reasons for that inability without referring to the component auditor, unless such a reference is necessary for an adequate explanation of the circumstances.[15]

---

[14] ISA (UK and Ireland) 315, paragraphs 27-29.
[15] ISA (UK and Ireland) 705, paragraph 20.

Acceptance and Continuance

Obtaining an Understanding at the Acceptance or Continuance Stage (Ref: Para. 12)

A10. In the case of a new engagement, the group engagement team's understanding of the group, its components, and their environments may be obtained from:

- Information provided by group management;

- Communication with group management; and

- Where applicable, communication with the previous group engagement team, component management, or component auditors.

A11. The group engagement team's understanding may include matters such as the following:

- The group structure, including both the legal and organizational structure (that is, how the group financial reporting system is organized).

- Components' business activities that are significant to the group, including the industry and regulatory, economic and political environments in which those activities take place.

- The use of service organizations, including shared service centers.

- A description of group-wide controls.

- The complexity of the consolidation process.

- Whether component auditors that are not from the group engagement partner's firm or network will perform work on the financial information of any of the components, and group management's rationale for appointing more than one auditor.

- Whether the group engagement team:

  ○ Will have unrestricted access to those charged with governance of the group, group management, those charged with governance of the component, component management, component information, and the component auditors (including relevant audit documentation sought by the group engagement team); and

  ○ Will be able to perform necessary work on the financial information of the components.

A12. In the case of a continuing engagement, the group engagement team's ability to obtain sufficient appropriate audit evidence may be affected by significant changes, for example:

- Changes in the group structure (for example, acquisitions, disposals, reorganizations, or changes in how the group financial reporting system is organized).

- Changes in components' business activities that are significant to the group.

- Changes in the composition of those charged with governance of the group, group management, or key management of significant components.

- Concerns the group engagement team has with regard to the integrity and competence of group or component management.

- Changes in group-wide controls.

- Changes in the applicable financial reporting framework.

Expectation to Obtain Sufficient Appropriate Audit Evidence (Ref: Para. 13)

A13. A group may consist only of components not considered significant components. In these circumstances, the group engagement partner can reasonably expect to obtain sufficient appropriate audit evidence on which to base the group audit opinion if the group engagement team will be able to:

(a) Perform the work on the financial information of some of these components; and

(b) Be involved in the work performed by component auditors on the financial information of other components to the extent necessary to obtain sufficient appropriate audit evidence.

Access to Information (Ref: Para. 13)

A14. The group engagement team's access to information may be restricted by circumstances that cannot be overcome by group management, for example, laws relating to confidentiality and data privacy, or denial by the component auditor of access to relevant audit documentation sought by the group engagement team. It may also be restricted by group management.

A14-1. In the UK and Ireland there are statutory obligations on corporate subsidiary undertakings, and their auditors and other parties, in the UK and Ireland to provide the auditor of a corporate parent undertaking with such information and explanations as that auditor may reasonably require for the purposes of the audit[15a]. Where there is no such statutory obligation (e.g. for non corporate entities and overseas subsidiary undertakings), permission may be needed by the auditors of the subsidiary undertakings, from those charged with governance of the subsidiary undertakings, to disclose information to the auditor of the parent undertaking. Permission may also be needed from those charged with governance of the subsidiary undertakings for the auditor of the parent undertaking to pass those disclosures on to those charged with governance of the parent undertaking. The auditor of the parent undertaking seeks to ensure that appropriate arrangements are made at the planning stage for these disclosures. Normally, such arrangements for groups are recorded in the instructions to the auditors of subsidiary undertakings and relevant engagement letters.

A15. Where access to information is restricted by circumstances, the group engagement team may still be able to obtain sufficient appropriate audit evidence; however, this is less likely as the significance of the component increases. For example, the group engagement team may not have access to those charged with governance, management, or the auditor (including relevant audit documentation sought by the group engagement team) of a component that is accounted for by the equity method of accounting. If the component is not a significant component, and the group engagement team has a complete set of financial statements of the component, including the auditor's report thereon, and has access to information kept by group management in relation to that component, the group engagement team may conclude that this information constitutes sufficient appropriate audit evidence in relation to that component. If the component is a significant component, however, the group engagement team will not be able to comply with the requirements of this ISA (UK and Ireland) relevant in the circumstances of the group audit. For example, the group engagement team will not be able to comply with the requirement in paragraphs 30-31 to be involved in the work of the component auditor. The group engagement team will not, therefore, be able to obtain sufficient appropriate audit evidence in relation to that component. The effect of the group engagement team's

---

[15a] In the UK, Section 499 of the Companies Act 2006 specifies that the auditor of a company may require any subsidiary undertaking of the company which is a body corporate incorporated in the UK, and any officer, employee or auditor of any such subsidiary undertaking or any person holding or accountable for any books, accounts or vouchers of any such subsidiary undertaking, to provide him with such information or explanations as he thinks necessary for the performance of his duties as auditor. (Similar obligations regarding companies incorporated in the Republic of Ireland are set out in Section 196, Companies Act 1990.) If a parent company has a subsidiary undertaking that is not a body corporate incorporated in the UK, Section 500 of the Companies Act 2006 specifies that the auditor of the parent company may require it to take all such steps as are reasonably open to it to obtain from the subsidiary undertaking, any officer, employee or auditor of the undertaking, or any person holding or accountable for any of the undertaking's books, accounts or vouchers, such information and explanations as he may reasonably require for the purposes of his duties as auditor. Schedule 10, paragraph 10A, to the Companies Act 2006 includes provisions relating to arrangements to enable Recognised Supervisory Bodies and other bodies involved in monitoring audits to have access to the audit documentation of certain other auditors involved in the group audit. These provisions are addressed in audit regulations not in ISAs (UK and Ireland).

inability to obtain sufficient appropriate audit evidence is considered in terms of ISA (UK and Ireland) 705.

A16. The group engagement team will not be able to obtain sufficient appropriate audit evidence if group management restricts the access of the group engagement team or a component auditor to the information of a significant component.

A17. Although the group engagement team may be able to obtain sufficient appropriate audit evidence if such restriction relates to a component considered not a significant component, the reason for the restriction may affect the group audit opinion. For example, it may affect the reliability of group management's responses to the group engagement team's inquiries and group management's representations to the group engagement team.

A18. Law or regulation may prohibit the group engagement partner from declining or withdrawing from an engagement. For example, in some jurisdictions the auditor is appointed for a specified period of time and is prohibited from withdrawing before the end of that period. Also, in the public sector, the option of declining or withdrawing from an engagement may not be available to the auditor due to the nature of the mandate or public interest considerations. In these circumstances, this ISA (UK and Ireland) still applies to the group audit, and the effect of the group engagement team's inability to obtain sufficient appropriate audit evidence is considered in terms of ISA (UK and Ireland) 705.

A19. Appendix 1 contains an example of an auditor's report containing a qualified opinion based on the group engagement team's inability to obtain sufficient appropriate audit evidence in relation to a significant component accounted for by the equity method of accounting, but where, in the group engagement team's judgment, the effect is material but not pervasive[15b].

Terms of Engagement (Ref: Para. 14)

A20. The terms of engagement identify the applicable financial reporting framework.[16] Additional matters may be included in the terms of a group audit engagement, such as the fact that:

- The communication between the group engagement team and the component auditors should be unrestricted to the extent possible under law or regulation;

- Important communications between the component auditors, those charged with governance of the component, and component management, including communications on significant deficiencies in internal control, should be communicated as well to the group engagement team;

[15b] The example in the Appendix has not been tailored for the UK and Ireland. Illustrative auditor's reports tailored for use with audits conducted in accordance with ISAs (UK and Ireland) are given in the current versions of the APB Compendia Auditor's Report Bulletins.

[16] ISA (UK and Ireland) 210, paragraph 8.

- Important communications between regulatory authorities and components related to financial reporting matters should be communicated to the group engagement team; and

- To the extent the group engagement team considers necessary, it should be permitted:

  - Access to component information, those charged with governance of components, component management, and the component auditors (including relevant audit documentation sought by the group engagement team); and

  - To perform work or request a component auditor to perform work on the financial information of the components.

A21. Restrictions imposed on:

- the group engagement team's access to component information, those charged with governance of components, component management, or the component auditors (including relevant audit documentation sought by the group engagement team); or

- the work to be performed on the financial information of the components

after the group engagement partner's acceptance of the group audit engagement, constitute an inability to obtain sufficient appropriate audit evidence that may affect the group audit opinion. In exceptional circumstances it may even lead to withdrawal from the engagement where withdrawal is possible under applicable law or regulation.

Overall Audit Strategy and Audit Plan (Ref: Para. 16)

A22. The group engagement partner's review of the overall group audit strategy and group audit plan is an important part of fulfilling the group engagement partner's responsibility for the direction of the group audit engagement.

Understanding the Group, Its Components and Their Environments

Matters about Which the Group Engagement Team Obtains an Understanding (Ref: Para. 17)

A23. ISA (UK and Ireland) 315 contains guidance on matters the auditor may consider when obtaining an understanding of the industry, regulatory, and other external factors that affect the entity, including the applicable financial reporting framework; the nature of the entity; objectives and strategies and related business risks; and measurement and review of the entity's financial performance.[17] Appendix 2 of this

---

[17] ISA (UK and Ireland) 315, paragraphs A17-A41.

ISA (UK and Ireland) contains guidance on matters specific to a group, including the consolidation process.

Instructions Issued by Group Management to Components (Ref: Para. 17)

A24. To achieve uniformity and comparability of financial information, group management ordinarily issues instructions to components. Such instructions specify the requirements for financial information of the components to be included in the group financial statements and often include financial reporting procedures manuals and a reporting package. A reporting package ordinarily consists of standard formats for providing financial information for incorporation in the group financial statements. Reporting packages generally do not, however, take the form of complete financial statements prepared and presented in accordance with the applicable financial reporting framework.

A25. The instructions ordinarily cover:

- The accounting policies to be applied;

- Statutory and other disclosure requirements applicable to the group financial statements, including:

  ○ The identification and reporting of segments;

  ○ Related party relationships and transactions;

  ○ Intra-group transactions and unrealized profits;

  ○ Intra-group account balances; and

- A reporting timetable.

A26. The group engagement team's understanding of the instructions may include the following:

- The clarity and practicality of the instructions for completing the reporting package.

- Whether the instructions:

  ○ Adequately describe the characteristics of the applicable financial reporting framework;

  ○ Provide for disclosures that are sufficient to comply with the requirements of the applicable financial reporting framework, for example, disclosure of related party relationships and transactions, and segment information;

○ Provide for the identification of consolidation adjustments, for example, intra-group transactions and unrealized profits, and intra-group account balances; and

○ Provide for the approval of the financial information by component management.

Fraud (Ref: Para. 17)

A27. The auditor is required to identify and assess the risks of material misstatement of the financial statements due to fraud, and to design and implement appropriate responses to the assessed risks.[18] Information used to identify the risks of material misstatement of the group financial statements due to fraud may include the following:

- Group management's assessment of the risks that the group financial statements may be materially misstated as a result of fraud.

- Group management's process for identifying and responding to the risks of fraud in the group, including any specific fraud risks identified by group management, or account balances, classes of transactions, or disclosures for which a risk of fraud is likely.

- Whether there are particular components for which a risk of fraud is likely.

- How those charged with governance of the group monitor group management's processes for identifying and responding to the risks of fraud in the group, and the controls group management has established to mitigate these risks.

- Responses of those charged with governance of the group, group management, appropriate individuals within the internal audit function (and if considered appropriate, component management, the component auditors, and others) to the group engagement team's inquiry whether they have knowledge of any actual, suspected, or alleged fraud affecting a component or the group.

Discussion among Group Engagement Team Members and Component Auditors Regarding the Risks of Material Misstatement of the Group Financial Statements, Including Risks of Fraud (Ref: Para. 17)

A28. The key members of the engagement team are required to discuss the susceptibility of an entity to material misstatement of the financial statements due to fraud or error, specifically emphasizing the risks due to fraud. In a group audit, these discussions may also include the component auditors.[19] The group engagement partner's determination of who to include in the discussions, how and when they occur, and their extent, is affected by factors such as prior experience with the group.

---

[18] ISA (UK and Ireland) 240, "The Auditor's Responsibilities Relating to Fraud in an Audit of Financial Statements."

[19] ISA (UK and Ireland) 240, paragraph 15, and ISA 315, paragraph 10.

A29. The discussions provide an opportunity to:

- Share knowledge of the components and their environments, including group-wide controls.

- Exchange information about the business risks of the components or the group.

- Exchange ideas about how and where the group financial statements may be susceptible to material misstatement due to fraud or error, how group management and component management could perpetrate and conceal fraudulent financial reporting, and how assets of the components could be misappropriated.

- Identify practices followed by group or component management that may be biased or designed to manage earnings that could lead to fraudulent financial reporting, for example, revenue recognition practices that do not comply with the applicable financial reporting framework.

- Consider known external and internal factors affecting the group that may create an incentive or pressure for group management, component management, or others to commit fraud, provide the opportunity for fraud to be perpetrated, or indicate a culture or environment that enables group management, component management, or others to rationalize committing fraud.

- Consider the risk that group or component management may override controls.

- Consider whether uniform accounting policies are used to prepare the financial information of the components for the group financial statements and, where not, how differences in accounting policies are identified and adjusted (where required by the applicable financial reporting framework).

- Discuss fraud that has been identified in components, or information that indicates existence of a fraud in a component.

- Share information that may indicate non-compliance with national laws or regulations, for example, payments of bribes and improper transfer pricing practices.

Risk Factors (Ref: Para. 18)

A30. Appendix 3 sets out examples of conditions or events that, individually or together, may indicate risks of material misstatement of the group financial statements, including risks due to fraud.

Risk Assessment (Ref: Para. 18)

A31. The group engagement team's assessment at group level of the risks of material misstatement of the group financial statements is based on information such as the following:

- Information obtained from the understanding of the group, its components, and their environments, and of the consolidation process, including audit evidence obtained in evaluating the design and implementation of group-wide controls and controls that are relevant to the consolidation.

- Information obtained from the component auditors.

Understanding the Component Auditor (Ref: Para. 19)

A32. The group engagement team obtains an understanding of a component auditor only when it plans to request the component auditor to perform work on the financial information of a component for the group audit. For example, it will not be necessary to obtain an understanding of the auditors of those components for which the group engagement team plans to perform analytical procedures at group level only.

Group Engagement Team's Procedures to Obtain an Understanding of the Component Auditor and Sources of Audit Evidence (Ref: Para. 19)

A33. The nature, timing and extent of the group engagement team's procedures to obtain an understanding of the component auditor are affected by factors such as previous experience with or knowledge of the component auditor, and the degree to which the group engagement team and the component auditor are subject to common policies and procedures, for example:

- Whether the group engagement team and a component auditor share:

  ○ Common policies and procedures for performing the work (for example, audit methodologies);

  ○ Common quality control policies and procedures; or

  ○ Common monitoring policies and procedures.

- The consistency or similarity of:

  ○ Laws and regulations or legal system;

  ○ Professional oversight, discipline, and external quality assurance;

  ○ Education and training;

  ○ Professional organizations and standards; or

  ○ Language and culture.

A34. These factors interact and are not mutually exclusive. For example, the extent of the group engagement team's procedures to obtain an understanding of Component Auditor A, who consistently applies common quality control and monitoring policies and procedures and a common audit methodology or operates in the same jurisdiction as the group engagement partner, may be less than the extent of the group engagement team's procedures to obtain an understanding of Component Auditor B, who is not consistently applying common quality control and monitoring policies and procedures and a common audit methodology or operates in a foreign jurisdiction. The nature of the procedures performed in relation to Component Auditors A and B may also be different.

A35. The group engagement team may obtain an understanding of the component auditor in a number of ways. In the first year of involving a component auditor, the group engagement team may, for example:

- Evaluate the results of the quality control monitoring system where the group engagement team and component auditor are from a firm or network that operates under and complies with common monitoring policies and procedures;[20]

- Visit the component auditor to discuss the matters in paragraph 19(a)-(c);

- Request the component auditor to confirm the matters referred to in paragraph 19(a)-(c) in writing. Appendix 4 contains an example of written confirmations by a component auditor;

- Request the component auditor to complete questionnaires about the matters in paragraph 19(a)-(c);

- Discuss the component auditor with colleagues in the group engagement partner's firm, or with a reputable third party that has knowledge of the component auditor; or

- Obtain confirmations from the professional body or bodies to which the component auditor belongs, the authorities by which the component auditor is licensed, or other third parties.

In subsequent years, the understanding of the component auditor may be based on the group engagement team's previous experience with the component auditor. The group engagement team may request the component auditor to confirm whether anything in relation to the matters listed in paragraph 19(a)-(c) has changed since the previous year.

A36. Where independent oversight bodies have been established to oversee the auditing profession and monitor the quality of audits, awareness of the regulatory environment may assist the group engagement team in evaluating the independence and competence of the component auditor. Information about the regulatory environment may be obtained from the component auditor or information provided by the independent oversight bodies.

---

[20] As required by ISQC (UK and Ireland) 1, "Quality Control for Firms that Perform Audits and Reviews of Financial Statements, and Other Assurance and Related Services Engagements," paragraph 54, or national requirements that are at least as demanding.

Ethical Requirements that Are Relevant to the Group Audit (Ref: Para. 19(a))

A37. When performing work on the financial information of a component for a group audit, the component auditor is subject to ethical requirements that are relevant to the group audit. Such requirements may be different or in addition to those applying to the component auditor when performing a statutory audit in the component auditor's jurisdiction. The group engagement team therefore obtains an understanding whether the component auditor understands and will comply with the ethical requirements that are relevant to the group audit, sufficient to fulfill the component auditor's responsibilities in the group audit.

The Component Auditor's Professional Competence (Ref: Para. 19(b))

A38. The group engagement team's understanding of the component auditor's professional competence may include whether the component auditor:

- Possesses an understanding of auditing and other standards applicable to the group audit that is sufficient to fulfill the component auditor's responsibilities in the group audit;

- Has sufficient resources (e.g. personnel with the necessary capabilities) to perform the work on the financial information of the particular component;

- Possesses the special skills (for example, industry specific knowledge) necessary to perform the work on the financial information of the particular component; and

- Where relevant, possesses an understanding of the applicable financial reporting framework that is sufficient to fulfill the component auditor's responsibilities in the group audit (instructions issued by group management to components often describe the characteristics of the applicable financial reporting framework).

Application of the Group Engagement Team's Understanding of a Component Auditor (Ref: Para. 20)

A39. The group engagement team cannot overcome the fact that a component auditor is not independent by being involved in the work of the component auditor or by performing additional risk assessment or further audit procedures on the financial information of the component.

A40. However, the group engagement team may be able to overcome less than serious concerns about the component auditor's professional competency (for example, lack of industry specific knowledge), or the fact that the component auditor does not operate in an environment that actively oversees auditors, by being involved in the work of the component auditor or by performing additional risk assessment or further audit procedures on the financial information of the component.

A41. Where law or regulation prohibits access to relevant parts of the audit documentation of the component auditor, the group engagement team may request the component auditor to overcome this by preparing a memorandum that covers the relevant information.

Materiality (Ref: Para. 21-23)

A42. The auditor is required:[21]

(a) When establishing the overall audit strategy, to determine:

(i) Materiality for the financial statements as a whole; and

(ii) If, in the specific circumstances of the entity, there are particular classes of transactions, account balances or disclosures for which misstatements of lesser amounts than materiality for the financial statements as a whole could reasonably be expected to influence the economic decisions of users taken on the basis of the financial statements, the materiality level or levels to be applied to those particular classes of transactions, account balances or disclosures; and

(b) To determine performance materiality.

In the context of a group audit, materiality is established for both the group financial statements as a whole, and for the financial information of the components. Materiality for the group financial statements as a whole is used when establishing the overall group audit strategy.

A43. To reduce to an appropriately low level the probability that the aggregate of uncorrected and undetected misstatements in the group financial statements exceeds materiality for the group financial statements as a whole, component materiality is set lower than materiality for the group financial statements as a whole. Different component materiality may be established for different components. Component materiality need not be an arithmetical portion of the materiality for the group financial statements as a whole and, consequently, the aggregate of component materiality for the different components may exceed the materiality for the group financial statements as a whole. Component materiality is used when establishing the overall audit strategy for a component.

A44. Component materiality is determined for those components whose financial information will be audited or reviewed as part of the group audit in accordance with paragraphs 26, 27(a) and 29. Component materiality is used by the component auditor to evaluate whether uncorrected detected misstatements are material, individually or in the aggregate.

A45. A threshold for misstatements is determined in addition to component materiality. Misstatements identified in the financial information of the component that are above the threshold for misstatements are communicated to the group engagement team.

---

[21] ISA (UK and Ireland) 320, "Materiality in Planning and Performing an Audit," paragraphs 10-11.

A46. In the case of an audit of the financial information of a component, the component auditor (or group engagement team) determines performance materiality at the component level. This is necessary to reduce to an appropriately low level the probability that the aggregate of uncorrected and undetected misstatements in the financial information of the component exceeds component materiality. In practice, the group engagement team may set component materiality at this lower level. Where this is the case, the component auditor uses component materiality for purposes of assessing the risks of material misstatement of the financial information of the component and to design further audit procedures in response to assessed risks as well as for evaluating whether detected misstatements are material individually or in the aggregate.

Responding to Assessed Risks

Determining the Type of Work to Be Performed on the Financial Information of Components (Ref: Para. 26-27)

A47. The group engagement team's determination of the type of work to be performed on the financial information of a component and its involvement in the work of the component auditor is affected by:

(a)   The significance of the component;

(b)   The identified significant risks of material misstatement of the group financial statements;

(c)   The group engagement team's evaluation of the design of group-wide controls and determination whether they have been implemented; and

(d)   The group engagement team's understanding of the component auditor.

The diagram shows how the significance of the component affects the group engagement team's determination of the type of work to be performed on the financial information of the component.

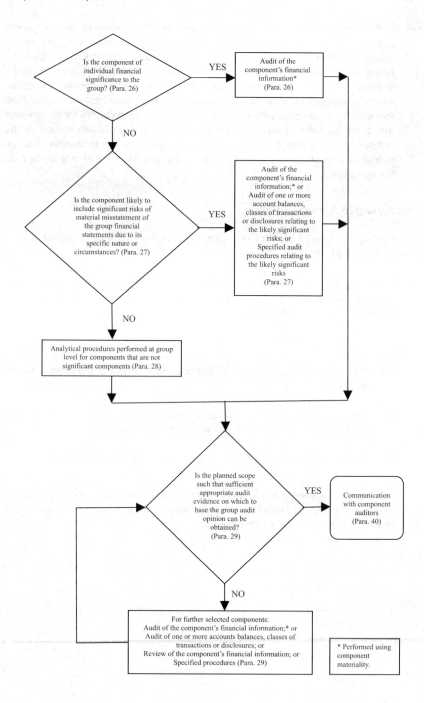

Significant Components (Ref: Para. 27(b)-(c))

A48.   The group engagement team may identify a component as a significant component because that component is likely to include significant risks of material misstatement of the group financial statements due to its specific nature or circumstances. In that case, the group engagement team may be able to identify the account balances, classes of transactions or disclosures affected by the likely significant risks. Where this is the case, the group engagement team may decide to perform, or request a component auditor to perform, an audit of only those account balances, classes of transactions or disclosures. For example, in the situation described in paragraph A6, the work on the financial information of the component may be limited to an audit of the account balances, classes of transactions and disclosures affected by the foreign exchange trading of that component. Where the group engagement team requests a component auditor to perform an audit of one or more specific account balances, classes of transactions or disclosures, the communication of the group engagement team (see paragraph 40) takes account of the fact that many financial statement items are interrelated.

A49.   The group engagement team may design audit procedures that respond to a likely significant risk of material misstatement of the group financial statements. For example, in the case of a likely significant risk of inventory obsolescence, the group engagement team may perform, or request a component auditor to perform, specified audit procedures on the valuation of inventory at a component that holds a large volume of potentially obsolete inventory, but that is not otherwise significant.

Components that Are Not Significant Components (Ref: Para. 28-29)

A50.   Depending on the circumstances of the engagement, the financial information of the components may be aggregated at various levels for purposes of the analytical procedures. The results of the analytical procedures corroborate the group engagement team's conclusions that there are no significant risks of material misstatement of the aggregated financial information of components that are not significant components.

A51.   The group engagement team's decision as to how many components to select in accordance with paragraph 29, which components to select, and the type of work to be performed on the financial information of the individual components selected may be affected by factors such as the following:

- The extent of audit evidence expected to be obtained on the financial information of the significant components.

- Whether the component has been newly formed or acquired.

- Whether significant changes have taken place in the component.

- Whether the internal audit function has performed work at the component and any effect of that work on the group audit.

- Whether the components apply common systems and processes.

- The operating effectiveness of group-wide controls.

- Abnormal fluctuations identified by analytical procedures performed at group level.

- The individual financial significance of, or the risk posed by, the component in comparison with other components within this category.

- Whether the component is subject to audit required by statute, regulation or for another reason.

Including an element of unpredictability in selecting components in this category may increase the likelihood of identifying material misstatement of the components' financial information. The selection of components is often varied on a cyclical basis.

A52. A review of the financial information of a component may be performed in accordance with International Standard on Review Engagements (ISRE) 2400[22] or ISRE (UK and Ireland) 2410,[23] adapted as necessary in the circumstances. The group engagement team may also specify additional procedures to supplement this work.

A53. As explained in paragraph A13, a group may consist only of components that are not significant components. In these circumstances, the group engagement team can obtain sufficient appropriate audit evidence on which to base the group audit opinion by determining the type of work to be performed on the financial information of the components in accordance with paragraph 29. It is unlikely that the group engagement team will obtain sufficient appropriate audit evidence on which to base the group audit opinion if the group engagement team, or a component auditor, only tests group-wide controls and performs analytical procedures on the financial information of the components.

Involvement in the Work Performed by Component Auditors (Ref: Para. 30-31)

A54. Factors that may affect the group engagement team's involvement in the work of the component auditor include:

(a) The significance of the component;

(b) The identified significant risks of material misstatement of the group financial statements; and

(c) The group engagement team's understanding of the component auditor.

---

[22] ISRE 2400, "Engagements to Review Financial Statements."
ISRE 2400 has not been promulgated by APB for application in the UK and Ireland.
[23] ISRE (UK and Ireland) 2410, "Review of Interim Financial Information Performed by the Independent Auditor of the Entity."

In the case of a significant component or identified significant risks, the group engagement team performs the procedures described in paragraphs 30-31. In the case of a component that is not a significant component, the nature, timing and extent of the group engagement team's involvement in the work of the component auditor will vary based on the group engagement team's understanding of that component auditor. The fact that the component is not a significant component becomes secondary. For example, even though a component is not considered a significant component, the group engagement team nevertheless may decide to be involved in the component auditor's risk assessment, because it has less than serious concerns about the component auditor's professional competency (for example, lack of industry specific knowledge), or the component auditor does not operate in an environment that actively oversees auditors.

A55. Forms of involvement in the work of a component auditor other than those described in paragraphs 30-31 and 42 may, based on the group engagement team's understanding of the component auditor, include one or more of the following:

(a) Meeting with component management or the component auditors to obtain an understanding of the component and its environment.

(b) Reviewing the component auditors' overall audit strategy and audit plan.

(c) Performing risk assessment procedures to identify and assess the risks of material misstatement at the component level. These may be performed with the component auditors, or by the group engagement team.

(d) Designing and performing further audit procedures. These may be designed and performed with the component auditors, or by the group engagement team.

(e) Participating in the closing and other key meetings between the component auditors and component management.

(f) Reviewing other relevant parts of the component auditors' audit documentation.

Consolidation Process

Consolidation Adjustments and Reclassifications (Ref: Para. 34)

A56. The consolidation process may require adjustments to amounts reported in the group financial statements that do not pass through the usual transaction processing systems, and may not be subject to the same internal controls to which other financial information is subject. The group engagement team's evaluation of the appropriateness, completeness and accuracy of the adjustments may include:

• Evaluating whether significant adjustments appropriately reflect the events and transactions underlying them;

- Determining whether significant adjustments have been correctly calculated, processed and authorized by group management and, where applicable, by component management;

- Determining whether significant adjustments are properly supported and sufficiently documented; and

- Checking the reconciliation and elimination of intra-group transactions and unrealized profits, and intra-group account balances.

Communication with the Component Auditor (Ref: Para. 40-41)

A57. If effective two-way communication between the group engagement team and the component auditors does not exist, there is a risk that the group engagement team may not obtain sufficient appropriate audit evidence on which to base the group audit opinion. Clear and timely communication of the group engagement team's requirements forms the basis of effective two-way communication between the group engagement team and the component auditor.

A58. The group engagement team's requirements are often communicated in a letter of instruction. Appendix 5 contains guidance on required and additional matters that may be included in such a letter of instruction. The component auditor's communication with the group engagement team often takes the form of a memorandum or report of work performed. Communication between the group engagement team and the component auditor, however, may not necessarily be in writing. For example, the group engagement team may visit the component auditor to discuss identified significant risks or review relevant parts of the component auditor's audit documentation. Nevertheless, the documentation requirements of this and other ISAs (UK and Ireland) apply.

A59. In cooperating with the group engagement team, the component auditor, for example, would provide the group engagement team with access to relevant audit documentation if not prohibited by law or regulation.

A60. Where a member of the group engagement team is also a component auditor, the objective for the group engagement team to communicate clearly with the component auditor can often be achieved by means other than specific written communication. For example:

- Access by the component auditor to the overall audit strategy and audit plan may be sufficient to communicate the group engagement team's requirements set out in paragraph 40; and

- A review of the component auditor's audit documentation by the group engagement team may be sufficient to communicate matters relevant to the group engagement team's conclusion set out in paragraph 41.

Evaluating the Sufficiency and Appropriateness of Audit Evidence Obtained

Reviewing the Component Auditor's Audit Documentation (Ref: Para. 42(b))

A61. What parts of the audit documentation of the component auditor will be relevant to the group audit may vary depending on the circumstances. Often the focus is on audit documentation that is relevant to the significant risks of material misstatement of the group financial statements. The extent of the review may be affected by the fact that the component auditor's audit documentation has been subjected to the component auditor's firm's review procedures.

Sufficiency and Appropriateness of Audit Evidence (Ref: Para. 44-45)

A62. If the group engagement team concludes that sufficient appropriate audit evidence on which to base the group audit opinion has not been obtained, the group engagement team may request the component auditor to perform additional procedures. If this is not feasible, the group engagement team may perform its own procedures on the financial information of the component.

A63. The group engagement partner's evaluation of the aggregate effect of any misstatements (either identified by the group engagement team or communicated by component auditors) allows the group engagement partner to determine whether the group financial statements as a whole are materially misstated.

Communication with Group Management and Those Charged with Governance of the Group

Communication with Group Management (Ref: Para. 46-48)

A64. ISA (UK and Ireland) 240 contains requirements and guidance on communication of fraud to management and, where management may be involved in the fraud, to those charged with governance.[24]

A65. Group management may need to keep certain material sensitive information confidential. Examples of matters that may be significant to the financial statements of the component of which component management may be unaware include the following:

- Potential litigation.

- Plans for abandonment of material operating assets.

- Subsequent events.

- Significant legal agreements.

---

[24] ISA (UK and Ireland) 240, paragraphs 40-42.

A65-1. Information that group management has determined needs to be kept confidential would ordinarily be known to those charged with governance of the group[24a].

Communication with Those Charged with Governance of the Group (Ref: Para. 49)

A66. The matters the group engagement team communicates to those charged with governance of the group may include those brought to the attention of the group engagement team by component auditors that the group engagement team judges to be significant to the responsibilities of those charged with governance of the group. Communication with those charged with governance of the group takes place at various times during the group audit. For example, the matters referred to in paragraph 49(a)-(b) may be communicated after the group engagement team has determined the work to be performed on the financial information of the components. On the other hand, the matter referred to in paragraph 49(c) may be communicated at the end of the audit, and the matters referred to in paragraph 49(d)-(e) may be communicated when they occur.

Documentation (Ref: Para. 50(b))

A66-1. In the UK legislation[24b] has been enacted to implement Article 27(b) of the Statutory Audit Directive which requires that group auditors:

(a) review for the purposes of a group audit the audit work conducted by other persons, and

(b) record that review.

Accordingly, the documentation of the group engagement team's involvement in the work performed by the component auditors includes any review that the group engagement team undertook, for the purpose of the group audit, of the audit work conducted by component auditors.

[24a] ISA (UK and Ireland) 260, paragraph 16(c), requires that, unless all of those charged with governance are involved in managing the entity, the auditor shall communicate with those charged with governance significant matters, if any, arising from the audit that were discussed, or subject to correspondence with management.

[24b] UK Companies Act 2006, Schedule 10, paragraph 10A(1).

Appendix 1

(Ref: Para. A19)

The example in this Appendix has not been tailored for the UK and Ireland. Illustrative auditor's reports tailored for use with audits conducted in accordance with ISAs (UK and Ireland) are given in the current versions of the APB Compendia Auditor's Report Bulletins.

Example of a Qualified Opinion Where the Group Engagement Team Is Not Able to Obtain Sufficient Appropriate Audit Evidence on Which to Base the Group Audit Opinion

In this example, the group engagement team is unable to obtain sufficient appropriate audit evidence relating to a significant component accounted for by the equity method (recognized at $15 million in the balance sheet, which reflects total assets of $60 million) because the group engagement team did not have access to the accounting records, management, or auditor of the component.

The group engagement team has read the audited financial statements of the component as of December 31, 20X1, including the auditor's report thereon, and considered related financial information kept by group management in relation to the component.

In the group engagement partner's judgment, the effect on the group financial statements of this inability to obtain sufficient appropriate audit evidence is material but not pervasive.

INDEPENDENT AUDITOR'S REPORT

[Appropriate Addressee]

Report on the Consolidated Financial Statements[25]

We have audited the accompanying consolidated financial statements of ABC Company and its subsidiaries, which comprise the consolidated balance sheet as at December 31, 20X1, and the consolidated income statement, statement of changes in equity and cash flow statement for the year then ended, and a summary of significant accounting policies and other explanatory information.

Management's[26] Responsibility for the Consolidated Financial Statements

Management is responsible for the preparation and fair presentation of these consolidated financial statements in accordance with International Financial

---

[25] The sub-title, "Report on the Consolidated Financial Statements" is unnecessary in circumstances when the second sub-title, "Report on Other Legal and Regulatory Requirements" is not applicable.

[26] Or other term that is appropriate in the context of the legal framework in the particular jurisdiction.

Reporting Standards,[27] and for such internal control as management determines is necessary to enable the preparation of consolidated financial statements that are free from material misstatement, whether due to fraud or error.

Auditor's Responsibility

Our responsibility is to express an opinion on these consolidated financial statements based on our audit. We conducted our audit in accordance with International Standards on Auditing. Those standards require that we comply with ethical requirements and plan and perform the audit to obtain reasonable assurance about whether the consolidated financial statements are free from material misstatement.

An audit involves performing procedures to obtain audit evidence about the amounts and disclosures in the consolidated financial statements. The procedures selected depend on the auditor's judgment, including the assessment of the risks of material misstatement of the consolidated financial statements, whether due to fraud or error. In making those risk assessments, the auditor considers internal control relevant to the entity's preparation and fair presentation[28] of the consolidated financial statements in order to design audit procedures that are appropriate in the circumstances, but not for the purpose of expressing an opinion on the effectiveness of the entity's internal control.[29] An audit also includes evaluating the appropriateness of accounting policies used and the reasonableness of accounting estimates made by management, as well as evaluating the overall presentation of the consolidated financial statements.

We believe that the audit evidence we have obtained is sufficient and appropriate to provide a basis for our qualified audit opinion.

Basis for Qualified Opinion

ABC Company's investment in XYZ Company, a foreign associate acquired during the year and accounted for by the equity method, is carried at $15 million on the consolidated balance sheet as at December 31, 20X1, and ABC's share of XYZ's

---

[27] Where management's responsibility is to prepare consolidated financial statements that give a true and fair view, this may read: "Management is responsible for the preparation of consolidated financial statements that give a true and fair view in accordance with International Financial Reporting Standards, and for such ..."

[28] In the case of footnote 27, this may read: "In making those risk assessments, the auditor considers internal control relevant to the entity's preparation of consolidated financial statements that give a true and fair view in order to design audit procedures that are appropriate in the circumstances, but not for the purpose of expressing an opinion on the effectiveness of the entity's internal control."

[29] In circumstances when the auditor also has responsibility to express an opinion on the effectiveness of internal control in conjunction with the audit of the consolidated financial statements, this sentence would be worded as follows: "In making those risk assessments, the auditor considers internal control relevant to the entity's preparation and fair presentation of the consolidated financial statements in order to design audit procedures that are appropriate in the circumstances." In the case of footnote 27, this may read: "In making those risk assessments, the auditor considers internal control relevant to the entity's preparation of consolidated financial statements that give a true and fair view in order to design audit procedures that are appropriate in the circumstances."

net income of $1 million is included in the consolidated income statement for the year then ended. We were unable to obtain sufficient appropriate audit evidence about the carrying amount of ABC's investment in XYZ as at December 31, 20X1 and ABC's share of XYZ's net income for the year because we were denied access to the financial information, management, and the auditors of XYZ. Consequently, we were unable to determine whether any adjustments to these amounts were necessary.

Qualified Opinion

In our opinion, except for the possible effects of the matter described in the Basis for Qualified Opinion paragraph, the consolidated financial statements present fairly, in all material respects, *(or give a true and fair view of)* the financial position of ABC Company and its subsidiaries as at December 31, 20X1, and *(of)* their financial performance and cash flows for the year then ended in accordance with International Financial Reporting Standards.

Report on Other Legal and Regulatory Requirements

[Form and content of this section of the auditor's report will vary depending on the nature of the auditor's other reporting responsibilities.]

[Auditor's signature]

[Date of the auditor's report]

[Auditor's address]

If, in the group engagement partner's judgment, the effect on the group financial statements of the inability to obtain sufficient appropriate audit evidence is material and pervasive, the group engagement partner would disclaim an opinion in accordance with ISA (UK and Ireland) 705.

Appendix 2

(Ref: Para. A23)

Examples of Matters about Which the Group Engagement Team Obtains an Understanding

The examples provided cover a broad range of matters; however, not all matters are relevant to every group audit engagement and the list of examples is not necessarily complete.

Group-Wide Controls

1.   Group-wide controls may include a combination of the following:

-    Regular meetings between group and component management to discuss business developments and to review performance.

-    Monitoring of components' operations and their financial results, including regular reporting routines, which enables group management to monitor components' performance against budgets, and to take appropriate action.

-    Group management's risk assessment process, that is, the process for identifying, analyzing and managing business risks, including the risk of fraud, that may result in material misstatement of the group financial statements.

-    Monitoring, controlling, reconciling, and eliminating intra-group transactions and unrealized profits, and intra-group account balances at group level.

-    A process for monitoring the timeliness and assessing the accuracy and completeness of financial information received from components.

-    A central IT system controlled by the same general IT controls for all or part of the group.

-    Control activities within an IT system that is common for all or some components.

-    Monitoring of controls, including activities of the internal audit function and self-assessment programs.

-    Consistent policies and procedures, including a group financial reporting procedures manual.

-    Group-wide programs, such as codes of conduct and fraud prevention programs.

-    Arrangements for assigning authority and responsibility to component management.

2. The internal audit function may be regarded as part of group-wide controls, for example, when the function is centralized. ISA (UK and Ireland) 610 (Revised June 2013)[30] deals with the group engagement team's evaluation of whether the internal audit function's organizational status and relevant policies and procedures adequately supports the objectivity of internal auditors, the level of competence of the internal audit function, and whether the function applies a systematic and disciplined approach where the group engagement team expects to use the function's work.

Consolidation Process

3. The group engagement team's understanding of the consolidation process may include matters such as the following:

Matters relating to the applicable financial reporting framework:

*   The extent to which component management has an understanding of the applicable financial reporting framework.

*   The process for identifying and accounting for components in accordance with the applicable financial reporting framework.

*   The process for identifying reportable segments for segment reporting in accordance with the applicable financial reporting framework.

*   The process for identifying related party relationships and related party transactions for reporting in accordance with the applicable financial reporting framework.

*   The accounting policies applied to the group financial statements, changes from those of the previous financial year, and changes resulting from new or revised standards under the applicable financial reporting framework.

*   The procedures for dealing with components with financial year-ends different from the group's year-end.

Matters relating to the consolidation process:

*   Group management's process for obtaining an understanding of the accounting policies used by components, and, where applicable, ensuring that uniform accounting policies are used to prepare the financial information of the components for the group financial statements, and that differences in accounting policies are identified, and adjusted where required in terms of the applicable financial reporting framework. Uniform accounting policies are the specific principles, bases, conventions, rules, and practices adopted by the group, based on the applicable financial reporting framework, that the

---

[30] ISA (UK and Ireland) 610 (Revised June 2013), "Using the Work of Internal Auditors," paragraphs 15-16.

components use to report similar transactions consistently. These policies are ordinarily described in the financial reporting procedures manual and reporting package issued by group management.

- Group management's process for ensuring complete, accurate and timely financial reporting by the components for the consolidation.

- The process for translating the financial information of foreign components into the currency of the group financial statements.

- How IT is organized for the consolidation, including the manual and automated stages of the process, and the manual and programmed controls in place at various stages of the consolidation process.

- Group management's process for obtaining information on subsequent events.

Matters relating to consolidation adjustments:

- The process for recording consolidation adjustments, including the preparation, authorization and processing of related journal entries, and the experience of personnel responsible for the consolidation.

- The consolidation adjustments required by the applicable financial reporting framework.

- Business rationale for the events and transactions that gave rise to the consolidation adjustments.

- Frequency, nature and size of transactions between components.

- Procedures for monitoring, controlling, reconciling and eliminating intra-group transactions and unrealized profits, and intra-group account balances.

- Steps taken to arrive at the fair value of acquired assets and liabilities, procedures for amortizing goodwill (where applicable), and impairment testing of goodwill, in accordance with the applicable financial reporting framework.

- Arrangements with a majority owner or minority interests regarding losses incurred by a component (for example, an obligation of the minority interest to make good such losses).

Appendix 3

(Ref: Para. A30)

Examples of Conditions or Events that May Indicate Risks of Material Misstatement of the Group Financial Statements

The examples provided cover a broad range of conditions or events; however, not all conditions or events are relevant to every group audit engagement and the list of examples is not necessarily complete.

- A complex group structure, especially where there are frequent acquisitions, disposals or reorganizations.

- Poor corporate governance structures, including decision-making processes, that are not transparent.

- Non-existent or ineffective group-wide controls, including inadequate group management information on monitoring of components' operations and their results.

- Components operating in foreign jurisdictions that may be exposed to factors such as unusual government intervention in areas such as trade and fiscal policy, and restrictions on currency and dividend movements; and fluctuations in exchange rates.

- Business activities of components that involve high risk, such as long-term contracts or trading in innovative or complex financial instruments.

- Uncertainties regarding which components' financial information require incorporation in the group financial statements in accordance with the applicable financial reporting framework, for example, whether any special-purpose entities or non-trading entities exist and require incorporation.

- Unusual related party relationships and transactions.

- Prior occurrences of intra-group account balances that did not balance or reconcile on consolidation.

- The existence of complex transactions that are accounted for in more than one component.

- Components' application of accounting policies that differ from those applied to the group financial statements.

- Components with different financial year-ends, which may be utilized to manipulate the timing of transactions.

- Prior occurrences of unauthorized or incomplete consolidation adjustments.

- Aggressive tax planning within the group, or large cash transactions with entities in tax havens.

- Frequent changes of auditors engaged to audit the financial statements of components.

Examples of a Component Auditor's Confirmations

The following is not intended to be a standard letter. Confirmations may vary from one component auditor to another and from one period to the next.

Confirmations often are obtained before work on the financial information of the component commences.

[Component Auditor Letterhead]

[Date]

[To Group Engagement Partner]

This letter is provided in connection with your audit of the group financial statements of [name of parent] for the year ended [date] for the purpose of expressing an opinion on whether the group financial statements present fairly, in all material respects (give a true and fair view of) the financial position of the group as of [date] and of its financial performance and cash flows for the year then ended in accordance with [indicate applicable financial reporting framework].

We acknowledge receipt of your instructions dated [date], requesting us to perform the specified work on the financial information of [name of component] for the year ended [date].

We confirm that:

1.   We will be able to comply with the instructions. / We advise you that we will not be able to comply with the following instructions [specify instructions] for the following reasons [specify reasons].

2.   The instructions are clear and we understand them. / We would appreciate it if you could clarify the following instructions [specify instructions].

3.   We will cooperate with you and provide you with access to relevant audit documentation.

We acknowledge that:

1.   The financial information of [name of component] will be included in the group financial statements of [name of parent].

2.   You may consider it necessary to be involved in the work you have requested us to perform on the financial information of [name of component] for the year ended [date].

3.   You intend to evaluate and, if considered appropriate, use our work for the audit of the group financial statements of [name of parent].

In connection with the work that we will perform on the financial information of [name of component], a [describe component, for example, wholly-owned subsidiary, subsidiary, joint venture, investee accounted for by the equity or cost methods of accounting] of [name of parent], we confirm the following:

1.   We have an understanding of [indicate relevant ethical requirements] that is sufficient to fulfill our responsibilities in the audit of the group financial statements, and will comply therewith. In particular, and with respect to [name of parent] and the other components in the group, we are independent within the meaning of [indicate relevant ethical requirements] and comply with the applicable requirements of [refer to rules] promulgated by [name of regulatory agency].

2.   We have an understanding of International Standards on Auditing and [indicate other national standards applicable to the audit of the group financial statements] that is sufficient to fulfill our responsibilities in the audit of the group financial statements and will conduct our work on the financial information of [name of component] for the year ended [date] in accordance with those standards.

3.   We possess the special skills (for example, industry specific knowledge) necessary to perform the work on the financial information of the particular component.

4.   We have an understanding of [indicate applicable financial reporting framework or group financial reporting procedures manual] that is sufficient to fulfill our responsibilities in the audit of the group financial statements.

We will inform you of any changes in the above representations during the course of our work on the financial information of [name of component].

[Auditor's signature]

[Date]

[Auditor's address]

Appendix 5

(Ref: Para. A58)

Required and Additional Matters Included in the Group Engagement Team's Letter of Instruction

Matters required by this ISA (UK and Ireland) to be communicated to the component auditor are shown in italicized text.

Matters that are relevant to the planning of the work of the component auditor:

• *A request for the component auditor, knowing the context in which the group engagement team will use the work of the component auditor, to confirm that the component auditor will cooperate with the group engagement team.*

• The timetable for completing the audit.

• Dates of planned visits by group management and the group engagement team, and dates of planned meetings with component management and the component auditor.

• A list of key contacts.

• *The work to be performed by the component auditor, the use to be made of that work*, and arrangements for coordinating efforts at the initial stage of and during the audit, including the group engagement team's planned involvement in the work of the component auditor.

• *The ethical requirements that are relevant to the group audit and, in particular, the independence requirements*, for example, where the group auditor is prohibited by law or regulation from using internal auditors to provide direct assistance, it is relevant for the group auditor to consider whether the prohibition also extends to component auditors and, if so, to address this in the communication to the component auditors.[31]

• *In the case of an audit or review of the financial information of the component, component materiality (and, if applicable, the materiality level or levels for particular classes of transactions, account balances or disclosures), and the threshold above which misstatements cannot be regarded as clearly trivial to the group financial statements.*

• *A list of related parties prepared by group management, and any other related parties that the group engagement team is aware of, and a request that the component auditor*

---

[31] ISA 610 (Revised June 2013), "Using the Work of Internal Auditors", paragraph A31.
The use of internal auditors to provide direct assistance is prohibited in an audit conducted in accordance with ISAs (UK and Ireland). For a group audit this prohibition extends to the work of any component auditor which is relied upon by the group auditor, including for overseas components – see ISA (UK and Ireland) 610 (Revised June 2013), paragraph 5-1.

communicates on a timely basis to the group engagement team related parties not previously identified by group management or the group engagement team.

- Work to be performed on intra-group transactions and unrealized profits and intra-group account balances.

- Guidance on other statutory reporting responsibilities, for example, reporting on group management's assertion on the effectiveness of internal control.

- Where time lag between completion of the work on the financial information of the components and the group engagement team's conclusion on the group financial statements is likely, specific instructions for a subsequent events review.

Matters that are relevant to the conduct of the work of the component auditor

- The findings of the group engagement team's tests of control activities of a processing system that is common for all or some components, and tests of controls to be performed by the component auditor.

- *Identified significant risks of material misstatement of the group financial statements, due to fraud or error, that are relevant to the work of the component auditor, and a request that the component auditor communicates on a timely basis any other significant risks of material misstatement of the group financial statements, due to fraud or error, identified in the component and the component auditor's response to such risks.*

- The findings of the internal audit function, based on work performed on controls at or relevant to components.

- A request for timely communication of audit evidence obtained from performing work on the financial information of the components that contradicts the audit evidence on which the group engagement team originally based the risk assessment performed at group level.

- A request for a written representation on component management's compliance with the applicable financial reporting framework, or a statement that differences between the accounting policies applied to the financial information of the component and those applied to the group financial statements have been disclosed.

- Matters to be documented by the component auditor.

Other information

- A request that the following be reported to the group engagement team on a timely basis:

  - Significant accounting, financial reporting and auditing matters, including accounting estimates and related judgments.

- ○ Matters relating to the going concern status of the component.

- ○ Matters relating to litigation and claims.

- ○ Significant deficiencies in internal control that the component auditor has identified during the performance of the work on the financial information of the component, and information that indicates the existence of fraud.

- A request that the group engagement team be notified of any significant or unusual events as early as possible.

- *A request that the matters listed in paragraph 41 be communicated to the group engagement team when the work on the financial information of the component is completed.*

INTERNATIONAL STANDARD ON AUDITING (UK AND IRELAND) 610 (REVISED JUNE 2013)

USING THE WORK OF INTERNAL AUDITORS

(Effective for audits of financial statements for periods ending on or after 15 June 2014)

CONTENTS

Annexure: Conforming Amendments to Other ISAs (UK and Ireland)

International Standard on Auditing (ISA) (UK and Ireland) 610 (Revised June 2013), *Using the Work of Internal Auditors,* should be read in conjunction with ISA (UK and Ireland) 200, *Overall Objectives of the Independent Auditor and the Conduct of an Audit in Accordance with International Standards on Auditing.*

Introduction

Scope of this ISA (UK and Ireland)

1. This International Standard on Auditing (ISA) (UK and Ireland) deals with the external auditor's responsibilities if using the work of internal auditors. This includes (a) using the work of the internal audit function in obtaining audit evidence and (b) using internal auditors to provide direct assistance under the direction, supervision and review of the external auditor.

2. This ISA (UK and Ireland) does not apply if the entity does not have an internal audit function. (Ref: Para. A2)

3. If the entity has an internal audit function, the requirements in this ISA (UK and Ireland) relating to using the work of that function do not apply if:

    (a) The responsibilities and activities of the function are not relevant to the audit; or

    (b) Based on the auditor's preliminary understanding of the function obtained as a result of procedures performed under ISA (UK and Ireland) 315 (Revised June 2013),[1] the external auditor does not expect to use the work of the function in obtaining audit evidence.

    Nothing in this ISA (UK and Ireland) requires the external auditor to use the work of the internal audit function to modify the nature or timing, or reduce the extent, of audit procedures to be performed directly by the external auditor; it remains a decision of the external auditor in establishing the overall audit strategy.

4. Furthermore, the requirements in this ISA (UK and Ireland) relating to direct assistance do not apply if the external auditor does not plan to use internal auditors to provide direct assistance.

5. In some jurisdictions, the external auditor may be prohibited, or restricted to some extent, by law or regulation from using the work of the internal audit function or using internal auditors to provide direct assistance. The ISAs (UK and Ireland) do not override laws or regulations that govern an audit of financial statements.[2] Such prohibitions or restrictions will therefore not prevent the external auditor from complying with the ISAs (UK and Ireland). (Ref: Para. A31)

5-1. The use of internal auditors to provide direct assistance is prohibited in an audit conducted in accordance with ISAs (UK and Ireland). For a group audit this prohibition extends to the work of any component auditor which is relied upon by the

---

[1] ISA (UK and Ireland) 315 (Revised June 2013), *Identifying and Assessing the Risks of Material Misstatement through Understanding the Entity and Its Environment.*
[2] ISA (UK and Ireland) 200, *Overall Objectives of the Independent Auditor and the Conduct of an Audit in Accordance with International Standards on Auditing*, paragraph A55.

group auditor, including for overseas components. Accordingly, the requirements and related application material in this ISA (UK and Ireland) relating to direct assistance are not applicable[2a].

Relationship between ISA (UK and Ireland) 315 (Revised June 2013) and ISA (UK and Ireland) 610 (Revised June 2013)

6.   Many entities establish internal audit functions as part of their internal control and governance structures. The objectives and scope of an internal audit function, the nature of its responsibilities and its organizational status, including the function's authority and accountability, vary widely and depend on the size and structure of the entity and the requirements of management and, where applicable, those charged with governance.

7.   ISA (UK and Ireland) 315 (Revised June 2013) addresses how the knowledge and experience of the internal audit function can inform the external auditor's understanding of the entity and its environment and identification and assessment of risks of material misstatement. ISA (UK and Ireland) 315 (Revised 2013)[3] also explains how effective communication between the internal and external auditors also creates an environment in which the external auditor can be informed of significant matters that may affect the external auditor's work.

8.   Depending on whether the internal audit function's organizational status and relevant policies and procedures adequately support the objectivity of the internal auditors, the level of competency of the internal audit function, and whether the function applies a systematic and disciplined approach, the external auditor may also be able to use the work of the internal audit function in a constructive and complementary manner. This ISA (UK and Ireland) addresses the external auditor's responsibilities when, based on the external auditor's preliminary understanding of the internal audit function obtained as a result of procedures performed under ISA (UK and Ireland) 315 (Revised 2013), the external auditor expects to use the work of the internal audit function as part of the audit evidence obtained.[4] Such use of that work modifies the nature or timing, or reduces the extent, of audit procedures to be performed directly by the external auditor.

9.   In addition, this ISA (UK and Ireland) also addresses the external auditor's responsibilities if considering using internal auditors to provide direct assistance under the direction, supervision and review of the external auditor.

10.   There may be individuals in an entity that perform procedures similar to those performed by an internal audit function. However, unless performed by an objective and competent function that applies a systematic and disciplined approach, including quality control, such procedures would be considered internal controls and obtaining

---

[2a] The non-applicable requirements are those set out in paragraphs 27-35 and 37. The non-applicable application material is that set out in paragraphs A32-A41.
[3]   ISA UK and Ireland) 315 (Revised June 2013), paragraph A116.
[4]   See paragraphs 15–25.

evidence regarding the effectiveness of such controls would be part of the auditor's responses to assessed risks in accordance with ISA (UK and Ireland) 330.[5]

The External Auditor's Responsibility for the Audit

11. The external auditor has sole responsibility for the audit opinion expressed, and that responsibility is not reduced by the external auditor's use of the work of the internal audit function or internal auditors to provide direct assistance on the engagement. Although they may perform audit procedures similar to those performed by the external auditor, neither the internal audit function nor the internal auditors are independent of the entity as is required of the external auditor in an audit of financial statements in accordance with ISA (UK and Ireland) 200.[6] This ISA (UK and Ireland), therefore, defines the conditions that are necessary for the external auditor to be able to use the work of internal auditors. It also defines the necessary work effort to obtain sufficient appropriate evidence that the work of the internal audit function, or internal auditors providing direct assistance, is adequate for the purposes of the audit. The requirements are designed to provide a framework for the external auditor's judgments regarding the use of the work of internal auditors to prevent over or undue use of such work.

Effective Date

12. This ISA (UK and Ireland) is effective for audits of financial statements for periods ending on or after 15 June 2014[6a].

Objectives

13. The objectives of the external auditor, where the entity has an internal audit function and the external auditor expects to use the work of the function to modify the nature or timing, or reduce the extent, of audit procedures to be performed directly by the external auditor, or to use internal auditors to provide direct assistance, are:

    (a) To determine whether the work of the internal audit function or direct assistance from internal auditors can be used, and if so, in which areas and to what extent;

    and having made that determination:

    (b) If using the work of the internal audit function, to determine whether that work is adequate for purposes of the audit; and

---

[5] ISA (UK and Ireland) 330, *The Auditor's Responses to Assessed Risks.*

[6] ISA (UK and Ireland) 200, paragraph 14.

[6a] For the purpose of audits under ISAs as issued by the IAASB, the material pertaining to the use of direct assistance has an effective date of audits of financial statements for periods ending on or after 15 December 2014. However, as stated in paragraph 5-1, the use of internal auditors to provide direct assistance is prohibited in an audit conducted in accordance with ISAs (UK and Ireland) – such prohibition being effective from the effective date of this ISA (UK and Ireland), audits of financial statements for periods ending on or after 15 June 2014.

    (c)   If using internal auditors to provide direct assistance, to appropriately direct, supervise and review their work.

Definitions

14.   For purposes of the ISAs (UK and Ireland), the following terms have the meanings attributed below:

    (a)   Internal audit function – A function of an entity that performs assurance and consulting activities designed to evaluate and improve the effectiveness of the entity's governance, risk management and internal control processes. (Ref: Para. A1–A4)

    (b)   Direct assistance – The use of internal auditors to perform audit procedures under the direction, supervision and review of the external auditor.

Requirements

Determining Whether, in Which Areas, and to What Extent the Work of the Internal Audit Function Can Be Used

Evaluating the Internal Audit Function

15.   The external auditor shall determine whether the work of the internal audit function can be used for purposes of the audit by evaluating the following:

    (a)   The extent to which the internal audit function's organizational status and relevant policies and procedures support the objectivity of the internal auditors; (Ref: Para. A5–A9)

    (b)   The level of competence of the internal audit function; and (Ref: Para. A5–A9)

    (c)   Whether the internal audit function applies a systematic and disciplined approach, including quality control. (Ref: Para. A10–A11)

16.   The external auditor shall not use the work of the internal audit function if the external auditor determines that:

    (a)   The function's organizational status and relevant policies and procedures do not adequately support the objectivity of internal auditors;

    (b)   The function lacks sufficient competence; or

    (c)   The function does not apply a systematic and disciplined approach, including quality control. (Ref: Para. A12–A14)

Determining the Nature and Extent of Work of the Internal Audit Function that Can Be Used

17.   As a basis for determining the areas and the extent to which the work of the internal audit function can be used, the external auditor shall consider the nature and scope of the work that has been performed, or is planned to be performed, by the internal audit function and its relevance to the external auditor's overall audit strategy and audit plan. (Ref: Para. A15–A17)

18.   The external auditor shall make all significant judgments in the audit engagement and, to prevent undue use of the work of the internal audit function, shall plan to use less of the work of the function and perform more of the work directly: (Ref: Para. A15–A17)

   (a)   The more judgment is involved in:

      (i)   Planning and performing relevant audit procedures; and

      (ii)   Evaluating the audit evidence gathered; (Ref: Para. A18–A19)

   (b)   The higher the assessed risk of material misstatement at the assertion level, with special consideration given to risks identified as significant; (Ref: Para. A20–A22)

   (c)   The less the internal audit function's organizational status and relevant policies and procedures adequately support the objectivity of the internal auditors; and

   (d)   The lower the level of competence of the internal audit function.

19.   The external auditor shall also evaluate whether, in aggregate, using the work of the internal audit function to the extent planned would still result in the external auditor being sufficiently involved in the audit, given the external auditor's sole responsibility for the audit opinion expressed. (Ref: Para. A15–A22)

20.   The external auditor shall, in communicating with those charged with governance an overview of the planned scope and timing of the audit in accordance with ISA (UK and Ireland) 260,[7] communicate how the external auditor has planned to use the work of the internal audit function. (Ref: Para. A23)

Using the Work of the Internal Audit Function

21.   If the external auditor plans to use the work of the internal audit function, the external auditor shall discuss the planned use of its work with the function as a basis for coordinating their respective activities. (Ref: Para. A24–A26)

---

[7]   ISA (UK and Ireland) 260, *Communication with Those Charged with Governance*, paragraph 15.

22.   The external auditor shall read the reports of the internal audit function relating to the work of the function that the external auditor plans to use to obtain an understanding of the nature and extent of audit procedures it performed and the related findings.

23.   The external auditor shall perform sufficient audit procedures on the body of work of the internal audit function as a whole that the external auditor plans to use to determine its adequacy for purposes of the audit, including evaluating whether:

(a)   The work of the function had been properly planned, performed, supervised, reviewed and documented;

(b)   Sufficient appropriate evidence had been obtained to enable the function to draw reasonable conclusions; and

(c)   Conclusions reached are appropriate in the circumstances and the reports prepared by the function are consistent with the results of the work performed. (Ref: Para. A27–A30)

24.   The nature and extent of the external auditor's audit procedures shall be responsive to the external auditor's evaluation of:

(a)   The amount of judgment involved;

(b)   The assessed risk of material misstatement;

(c)   The extent to which the internal audit function's organizational status and relevant policies and procedures support the objectivity of the internal auditors; and

(d)   The level of competence of the function;[8] (Ref: Para. A27–A29)

and shall include reperformance of some of the work. (Ref: Para. A30)

25.   The external auditor shall also evaluate whether the external auditor's conclusions regarding the internal audit function in paragraph 15 of this ISA (UK and Ireland) and the determination of the nature and extent of use of the work of the function for purposes of the audit in paragraphs 18–19 of this ISA (UK and Ireland) remain appropriate.

---

[8]   See paragraph 18.

Determining Whether, in Which Areas, and to What Extent Internal Auditors Can Be Used to Provide Direct Assistance

Determining Whether Internal Auditors Can Be Used to Provide Direct Assistance for Purposes of the Audit

26. The external auditor may be prohibited by law or regulation from obtaining direct assistance from internal auditors. If so, paragraphs 27–35 and 37 do not apply[8a]. (Ref: Para. A31)

27. If using internal auditors to provide direct assistance is not prohibited by law or regulation, and the external auditor plans to use internal auditors to provide direct assistance on the audit, the external auditor shall evaluate the existence and significance of threats to objectivity and the level of competence of the internal auditors who will be providing such assistance. The external auditor's evaluation of the existence and significance of threats to the internal auditors' objectivity shall include inquiry of the internal auditors regarding interests and relationships that may create a threat to their objectivity. (Ref: Para. A32–A34)

28. The external auditor shall not use an internal auditor to provide direct assistance if:

    (a) There are significant threats to the objectivity of the internal auditor; or

    (b) The internal auditor lacks sufficient competence to perform the proposed work. (Ref: Para. A32–A34)

Determining the Nature and Extent of Work that Can Be Assigned to Internal Auditors Providing Direct Assistance

29. In determining the nature and extent of work that may be assigned to internal auditors and the nature, timing and extent of direction, supervision and review that is appropriate in the circumstances, the external auditor shall consider:

    (a) The amount of judgment involved in:

        (i) Planning and performing relevant audit procedures; and

        (ii) Evaluating the audit evidence gathered;

    (b) The assessed risk of material misstatement; and

    (c) The external auditor's evaluation of the existence and significance of threats to the objectivity and level of competence of the internal auditors who will be providing such assistance. (Ref: Para. A35–A39)

[8a] The use of internal auditors to provide direct assistance is prohibited in an audit conducted in accordance with ISAs (UK and Ireland). See paragraph 5-1 above of this ISA (UK and Ireland).

30.   The external auditor shall not use internal auditors to provide direct assistance to perform procedures that:

(a)   Involve making significant judgments in the audit; (Ref: Para. A19)

(b)   Relate to higher assessed risks of material misstatement where the judgment required in performing the relevant audit procedures or evaluating the audit evidence gathered is more than limited; (Ref: Para. A38)

(c)   Relate to work with which the internal auditors have been involved and which has already been, or will be, reported to management or those charged with governance by the internal audit function; or

(d)   Relate to decisions the external auditor makes in accordance with this ISA (UK and Ireland) regarding the internal audit function and the use of its work or direct assistance. (Ref: Para. A35–A39)

31.   Having appropriately evaluated whether and, if so, to what extent internal auditors can be used to provide direct assistance on the audit, the external auditor shall, in communicating with those charged with governance an overview of the planned scope and timing of the audit in accordance with ISA (UK and Ireland) 260,[9] communicate the nature and extent of the planned use of internal auditors to provide direct assistance so as to reach a mutual understanding that such use is not excessive in the circumstances of the engagement. (Ref: Para. A39)

32.   The external auditor shall evaluate whether, in aggregate, using internal auditors to provide direct assistance to the extent planned, together with the planned use of the work of the internal audit function, would still result in the external auditor being sufficiently involved in the audit, given the external auditor's sole responsibility for the audit opinion expressed.

Using Internal Auditors to Provide Direct Assistance

33.   Prior to using internal auditors to provide direct assistance for purposes of the audit, the external auditor shall:

(a)   Obtain written agreement from an authorized representative of the entity that the internal auditors will be allowed to follow the external auditor's instructions, and that the entity will not intervene in the work the internal auditor performs for the external auditor; and

(b)   Obtain written agreement from the internal auditors that they will keep confidential specific matters as instructed by the external auditor and inform the external auditor of any threat to their objectivity.

---

[9]   ISA (UK and Ireland) 260, paragraph 15.

34. The external auditor shall direct, supervise and review the work performed by internal auditors on the engagement in accordance with ISA (UK and Ireland) 220.[10] In so doing:

   (a) The nature, timing and extent of direction, supervision, and review shall recognize that the internal auditors are not independent of the entity and be responsive to the outcome of the evaluation of the factors in paragraph 29 of this ISA (UK and Ireland); and

   (b) The review procedures shall include the external auditor checking back to the underlying audit evidence for some of the work performed by the internal auditors.

   The direction, supervision and review by the external auditor of the work performed by the internal auditors shall be sufficient in order for the external auditor to be satisfied that the internal auditors have obtained sufficient appropriate audit evidence to support the conclusions based on that work. (Ref: Para. A40–A41)

35. In directing, supervising and reviewing the work performed by internal auditors, the external auditor shall remain alert for indications that the external auditor's evaluations in paragraph 27 are no longer appropriate.

Documentation

36. If the external auditor uses the work of the internal audit function, the external auditor shall include in the audit documentation:

   (a) The evaluation of:

      (i) Whether the function's organizational status and relevant policies and procedures adequately support the objectivity of the internal auditors;

      (ii) The level of competence of the function; and

      (iii) Whether the function applies a systematic and disciplined approach, including quality control;

   (b) The nature and extent of the work used and the basis for that decision; and

   (c) The audit procedures performed by the external auditor to evaluate the adequacy of the work used.

37. If the external auditor uses internal auditors to provide direct assistance on the audit, the external auditor shall include in the audit documentation:

---

[10] ISA (UK and Ireland) 220, *Quality Control for an Audit of Financial Statements*.

(a) The evaluation of the existence and significance of threats to the objectivity of the internal auditors, and the level of competence of the internal auditors used to provide direct assistance;

(b) The basis for the decision regarding the nature and extent of the work performed by the internal auditors;

(c) Who reviewed the work performed and the date and extent of that review in accordance with ISA (UK and Ireland) 230;[11]

(d) The written agreements obtained from an authorized representative of the entity and the internal auditors under paragraph 33 of this ISA (UK and Ireland); and

(e) The working papers prepared by the internal auditors who provided direct assistance on the audit engagement.

***

Application and Other Explanatory Material

Definition of Internal Audit Function (Ref: Para. 2, 14(a))

A1. The objectives and scope of internal audit functions typically include assurance and consulting activities designed to evaluate and improve the effectiveness of the entity's governance processes, risk management and internal control such as the following:

Activities Relating to Governance

* The internal audit function may assess the governance process in its accomplishment of objectives on ethics and values, performance management and accountability, communicating risk and control information to appropriate areas of the organization and effectiveness of communication among those charged with governance, external and internal auditors, and management.

Activities Relating to Risk Management

* The internal audit function may assist the entity by identifying and evaluating significant exposures to risk and contributing to the improvement of risk management and internal control (including effectiveness of the financial reporting process).

* The internal audit function may perform procedures to assist the entity in the detection of fraud.

---

[11] ISA (UK and Ireland) 230, *Audit Documentation*.

Activities Relating to Internal Control

- Evaluation of internal control. The internal audit function may be assigned specific responsibility for reviewing controls, evaluating their operation and recommending improvements thereto. In doing so, the internal audit function provides assurance on the control. For example, the internal audit function might plan and perform tests or other procedures to provide assurance to management and those charged with governance regarding the design, implementation and operating effectiveness of internal control, including those controls that are relevant to the audit.

- Examination of financial and operating information. The internal audit function may be assigned to review the means used to identify, recognize, measure, classify and report financial and operating information, and to make specific inquiry into individual items, including detailed testing of transactions, balances and procedures.

- Review of operating activities. The internal audit function may be assigned to review the economy, efficiency and effectiveness of operating activities, including non-financial activities of an entity.

- Review of compliance with laws and regulations. The internal audit function may be assigned to review compliance with laws, regulations and other external requirements, and with management policies and directives and other internal requirements.

A2. Activities similar to those performed by an internal audit function may be conducted by functions with other titles within an entity. Some or all of the activities of an internal audit function may also be outsourced to a third-party service provider. Neither the title of the function, nor whether it is performed by the entity or a third-party service provider, are sole determinants of whether or not the external auditor can use the work of the function. Rather, it is the nature of the activities; the extent to which the internal audit function's organizational status and relevant policies and procedures support the objectivity of the internal auditors; competence; and systematic and disciplined approach of the function that are relevant. References in this ISA (UK and Ireland) to the work of the internal audit function include relevant activities of other functions or third-party providers that have these characteristics.

A3. In addition, those in the entity with operational and managerial duties and responsibilities outside of the internal audit function would ordinarily face threats to their objectivity that would preclude them from being treated as part of an internal audit function for the purpose of this ISA (UK and Ireland), although they may perform control activities that can be tested in accordance with ISA (UK and Ireland) 330.[12] For this reason, monitoring controls performed by an owner-manager would not be considered equivalent to an internal audit function.

---

[12] See paragraph 10.

A4. While the objectives of an entity's internal audit function and the external auditor differ, the function may perform audit procedures similar to those performed by the external auditor in an audit of financial statements. If so, the external auditor may make use of the function for purposes of the audit in one or more of the following ways:

- To obtain information that is relevant to the external auditor's assessments of the risks of material misstatement due to error or fraud. In this regard, ISA (UK and Ireland) 315 (Revised June 2013)[13] requires the external auditor to obtain an understanding of the nature of the internal audit function's responsibilities, its status within the organization, and the activities performed, or to be performed, and make inquiries of appropriate individuals within the internal audit function (if the entity has such a function); or

- Unless prohibited, or restricted to some extent, by law or regulation, the external auditor, after appropriate evaluation, may decide to use work that has been performed by the internal audit function during the period in partial substitution for audit evidence to be obtained directly by the external auditor.[14]

In addition, unless prohibited, or restricted to some extent, by law or regulation, the external auditor may use internal auditors to perform audit procedures under the direction, supervision and review of the external auditor (referred to as "direct assistance" in this ISA (UK and Ireland)).[15]

Determining Whether, in Which Areas, and to What Extent the Work of the Internal Audit Function Can Be Used

Evaluating the Internal Audit Function

Objectivity and Competence (Ref: Para. 15(a)–(b))

A5. The external auditor exercises professional judgment in determining whether the work of the internal audit function can be used for purposes of the audit, and the nature and extent to which the work of the internal audit function can be used in the circumstances.

A6. The extent to which the internal audit function's organizational status and relevant policies and procedures support the objectivity of the internal auditors and the level of competence of the function are particularly important in determining whether to use and, if so, the nature and extent of the use of the work of the function that is appropriate in the circumstances.

---

[13] ISA (UK and Ireland) 315 (Revised June 2013), paragraph 6(a).

[14] See paragraphs 15–25.

[15] See paragraphs 26–35. The use of internal auditors to provide direct assistance is prohibited in an audit conducted in accordance with ISAs (UK and Ireland) – see paragraph 5-1.

A7.   Objectivity refers to the ability to perform those tasks without allowing bias, conflict of interest or undue influence of others to override professional judgments. Factors that may affect the external auditor's evaluation include the following:

- Whether the organizational status of the internal audit function, including the function's authority and accountability, supports the ability of the function to be free from bias, conflict of interest or undue influence of others to override professional judgments. For example, whether the internal audit function reports to those charged with governance or an officer with appropriate authority, or if the function reports to management, whether it has direct access to those charged with governance.

- Whether the internal audit function is free of any conflicting responsibilities, for example, having managerial or operational duties or responsibilities that are outside of the internal audit function.

- Whether those charged with governance oversee employment decisions related to the internal audit function, for example, determining the appropriate remuneration policy.

- Whether there are any constraints or restrictions placed on the internal audit function by management or those charged with governance, for example, in communicating the internal audit function's findings to the external auditor.

- Whether the internal auditors are members of relevant professional bodies and their memberships obligate their compliance with relevant professional standards relating to objectivity, or whether their internal policies achieve the same objectives.

A8.   Competence of the internal audit function refers to the attainment and maintenance of knowledge and skills of the function as a whole at the level required to enable assigned tasks to be performed diligently and in accordance with applicable professional standards. Factors that may affect the external auditor's determination include the following:

- Whether the internal audit function is adequately and appropriately resourced relative to the size of the entity and the nature of its operations.

- Whether there are established policies for hiring, training and assigning internal auditors to internal audit engagements.

- Whether the internal auditors have adequate technical training and proficiency in auditing. Relevant criteria that may be considered by the external auditor in making the assessment may include, for example, the internal auditors' possession of a relevant professional designation and experience.

- Whether the internal auditors possess the required knowledge relating to the entity's financial reporting and the applicable financial reporting framework and whether the internal audit function possesses the necessary skills (for example, industry-specific knowledge) to perform work related to the entity's financial statements.

- Whether the internal auditors are members of relevant professional bodies that oblige them to comply with the relevant professional standards including continuing professional development requirements.

A9. Objectivity and competence may be viewed as a continuum. The more the internal audit function's organizational status and relevant policies and procedures adequately support the objectivity of the internal auditors and the higher the level of competence of the function, the more likely the external auditor may make use of the work of the function and in more areas. However, an organizational status and relevant policies and procedures that provide strong support for the objectivity of the internal auditors cannot compensate for the lack of sufficient competence of the internal audit function. Equally, a high level of competence of the internal audit function cannot compensate for an organizational status and policies and procedures that do not adequately support the objectivity of the internal auditors.

Application of a Systematic and Disciplined Approach (Ref: Para. 15(c))

A10. The application of a systematic and disciplined approach to planning, performing, supervising, reviewing and documenting its activities distinguishes the activities of the internal audit function from other monitoring control activities that may be performed within the entity.

A11. Factors that may affect the external auditor's determination of whether the internal audit function applies a systematic and disciplined approach include the following:

- The existence, adequacy and use of documented internal audit procedures or guidance covering such areas as risk assessments, work programs, documentation and reporting, the nature and extent of which is commensurate with the size and circumstances of an entity.

- Whether the internal audit function has appropriate quality control policies and procedures, for example, such as those policies and procedures in ISQC (UK and Ireland) 1[16] that would be applicable to an internal audit function (such as those relating to leadership, human resources and engagement performance) or quality control requirements in standards set by the relevant professional bodies for internal auditors. Such bodies may also establish other appropriate requirements such as conducting periodic external quality assessments.

---

[16] International Standard on Quality Control (ISQC) (UK and Ireland) 1, *Quality Control for Firms that Perform Audits and Reviews of Financial Statements, and Other Assurance and Related Services Engagements.*

Circumstances When Work of the Internal Audit Function Cannot Be Used (Ref: Para. 16)

A12. The external auditor's evaluation of whether the internal audit function's organizational status and relevant policies and procedures adequately support the objectivity of the internal auditors, the level of competence of the internal audit function, and whether it applies a systematic and disciplined approach may indicate that the risks to the quality of the work of the function are too significant and therefore it is not appropriate to use any of the work of the function as audit evidence.

A13. Consideration of the factors in paragraphs A7, A8 and A11 of this ISA (UK and Ireland) individually and in aggregate is important because an individual factor is often not sufficient to conclude that the work of the internal audit function cannot be used for purposes of the audit. For example, the internal audit function's organizational status is particularly important in evaluating threats to the objectivity of the internal auditors. If the internal audit function reports to management, this would be considered a significant threat to the function's objectivity unless other factors such as those described in paragraph A7 of this ISA (UK and Ireland) collectively provide sufficient safeguards to reduce the threat to an acceptable level.

A14. In addition, the IESBA Code[17] states that a self-review threat is created when the external auditor accepts an engagement to provide internal audit services to an audit client, and the results of those services will be used in conducting the audit. This is because of the possibility that the engagement team will use the results of the internal audit service without properly evaluating those results or without exercising the same level of professional skepticism as would be exercised when the internal audit work is performed by individuals who are not members of the firm. The IESBA Code[18] discusses the prohibitions that apply in certain circumstances and the threats and the safeguards that can be applied to reduce the threats to an acceptable level in other circumstances.

A14-1. Auditors in the UK and Ireland are subject to ethical requirements from two sources: the APB Ethical Standards for Auditors (ESs) concerning the integrity, objectivity and independence of the auditor, and the ethical pronouncements established by the auditor's relevant professional body. Requirements and guidance concerning the provision of internal audit services, including to address the self-review threat, are set out in ES 5[18a].

---

[17] The International Ethics Standards Board for Accountants' (IESBA) *Code of Ethics for Professional Accountants* (IESBA Code), Section 290.199.

[18] IESBA Code, Section 290.195–290.200.

[18a] ES 5, *Non-audit services provided to audited entities*, paragraphs 58-69.

Determining the Nature and Extent of Work of the Internal Audit Function that Can Be Used

Factors Affecting the Determination of the Nature and Extent of the Work of the Internal Audit Function that Can Be Used (Ref: Para. 17–19)

A15. Once the external auditor has determined that the work of the internal audit function can be used for purposes of the audit, a first consideration is whether the planned nature and scope of the work of the internal audit function that has been performed, or is planned to be performed, is relevant to the overall audit strategy and audit plan that the external auditor has established in accordance with ISA (UK and Ireland) 300.[19]

A16. Examples of work of the internal audit function that can be used by the external auditor include the following:

- Testing of the operating effectiveness of controls.

- Substantive procedures involving limited judgment.

- Observations of inventory counts.

- Tracing transactions through the information system relevant to financial reporting.

- Testing of compliance with regulatory requirements.

- In some circumstances, audits or reviews of the financial information of subsidiaries that are not significant components to the group (where this does not conflict with the requirements of ISA (UK and Ireland) 600).[20]

A17. The external auditor's determination of the planned nature and extent of use of the work of the internal audit function will be influenced by the external auditor's evaluation of the extent to which the internal audit function's organizational status and relevant policies and procedures adequately support the objectivity of the internal auditors and the level of competence of the internal audit function in paragraph 18 of this ISA (UK and Ireland). In addition, the amount of judgment needed in planning, performing and evaluating such work and the assessed risk of material misstatement at the assertion level are inputs to the external auditor's determination. Further, there are circumstances in which the external auditor cannot use the work of the internal audit function for purpose of the audit as described in paragraph 16 of this ISA (UK and Ireland).

---

[19] ISA (UK and Ireland) 300, *Planning an Audit of Financial Statements.*
[20] ISA (UK and Ireland) 600, *Special Considerations—Audits of Group Financial Statements (Including the Work of Component Auditors).*

Judgments in planning and performing audit procedures and evaluating results (Ref: Para. 18(a), 30(a))

A18. The greater the judgment needed to be exercised in planning and performing the audit procedures and evaluating the audit evidence, the external auditor will need to perform more procedures directly in accordance with paragraph 18 of this ISA (UK and Ireland), because using the work of the internal audit function alone will not provide the external auditor with sufficient appropriate audit evidence.

A19. Since the external auditor has sole responsibility for the audit opinion expressed, the external auditor needs to make the significant judgments in the audit engagement in accordance with paragraph 18. Significant judgments include the following:

- Assessing the risks of material misstatement;

- Evaluating the sufficiency of tests performed;

- Evaluating the appropriateness of management's use of the going concern assumption;

- Evaluating significant accounting estimates; and

- Evaluating the adequacy of disclosures in the financial statements, and other matters affecting the auditor's report.

Assessed risk of material misstatement (Ref: Para. 18(b))

A20. For a particular account balance, class of transaction or disclosure, the higher an assessed risk of material misstatement at the assertion level, the more judgment is often involved in planning and performing the audit procedures and evaluating the results thereof. In such circumstances, the external auditor will need to perform more procedures directly in accordance with paragraph 18 of this ISA (UK and Ireland), and accordingly, make less use of the work of the internal audit function in obtaining sufficient appropriate audit evidence. Furthermore, as explained in ISA (UK and Ireland) 200,[21] the higher the assessed risks of material misstatement, the more persuasive the audit evidence required by the external auditor will need to be, and, therefore, the external auditor will need to perform more of the work directly.

A21. As explained in ISA (UK and Ireland) 315 (Revised June 2013),[22] significant risks require special audit consideration and therefore the external auditor's ability to use the work of the internal audit function in relation to significant risks will be restricted to procedures that involve limited judgment. In addition, where the risk of material misstatement is other than low, the use of the work of the internal audit function alone is unlikely to reduce audit risk to an acceptably low level and eliminate the need for the external auditor to perform some tests directly.

---

[21] ISA (UK and Ireland) 200, paragraph A29.
[22] ISA (UK and Ireland) 315 (Revised June 2013), paragraph 4(e).

A22. Carrying out procedures in accordance with this ISA (UK and Ireland) may cause the external auditor to reevaluate the external auditor's assessment of the risks of material misstatement. Consequently, this may affect the external auditor's determination of whether to use the work of the internal audit function and whether further application of this ISA (UK and Ireland) is necessary.

Communication with Those Charged with Governance (Ref: Para. 20)

A23. In accordance with ISA (UK and Ireland) 260,[23] the external auditor is required to communicate with those charged with governance an overview of the planned scope and timing of the audit. The planned use of the work of the internal audit function is an integral part of the external auditor's overall audit strategy and is therefore relevant to those charged with governance for their understanding of the proposed audit approach.

Using the Work of the Internal Audit Function

Discussion and Coordination with the Internal Audit Function (Ref: Para. 21)

A24. In discussing the planned use of their work with the internal audit function as a basis for coordinating the respective activities, it may be useful to address the following:

- The timing of such work.

- The nature of the work performed.

- The extent of audit coverage.

- Materiality for the financial statements as a whole (and, if applicable, materiality level or levels for particular classes of transactions, account balances or disclosures), and performance materiality.

- Proposed methods of item selection and sample sizes.

- Documentation of the work performed.

- Review and reporting procedures.

A25. Coordination between the external auditor and the internal audit function is effective when, for example:

- Discussions take place at appropriate intervals throughout the period.

- The external auditor informs the internal audit function of significant matters that may affect the function.

---

[23] ISA (UK and Ireland) 260, paragraph 15.

- The external auditor is advised of and has access to relevant reports of the internal audit function and is informed of any significant matters that come to the attention of the function when such matters may affect the work of the external auditor so that the external auditor is able to consider the implications of such matters for the audit engagement.

A26. ISA (UK and Ireland) 200[24] discusses the importance of the auditor planning and performing the audit with professional skepticism, including being alert to information that brings into question the reliability of documents and responses to inquiries to be used as audit evidence. Accordingly, communication with the internal audit function throughout the engagement may provide opportunities for internal auditors to bring matters that may affect the work of the external auditor to the external auditor's attention.[25] The external auditor is then able to take such information into account in the external auditor's identification and assessment of risks of material misstatement. In addition, if such information may be indicative of a heightened risk of a material misstatement of the financial statements or may be regarding any actual, suspected or alleged fraud, the external auditor can take this into account in the external auditor's identification of risk of material misstatement due to fraud in accordance with ISA (UK and Ireland) 240.[26]

Procedures to Determine the Adequacy of Work of the Internal Audit Function (Ref: Para. 23–24)

A27. The external auditor's audit procedures on the body of work of the internal audit function as a whole that the external auditor plans to use provide a basis for evaluating the overall quality of the function's work and the objectivity with which it has been performed.

A28. The procedures the external auditor may perform to evaluate the quality of the work performed and the conclusions reached by the internal audit function, in addition to reperformance in accordance with paragraph 24, include the following:

- Making inquiries of appropriate individuals within the internal audit function.

- Observing procedures performed by the internal audit function.

- Reviewing the internal audit function's work program and working papers.

A29. The more judgment involved, the higher the assessed risk of material misstatement, the less the internal audit function's organizational status and relevant policies and procedures adequately support the objectivity of the internal auditors, or the lower the level of competence of the internal audit function, the more audit procedures are needed to be performed by the external auditor on the overall body of work of the

---

[24] ISA (UK and Ireland) 200, paragraphs 15 and A18.
[25] ISA (UK and Ireland) 315 (Revised June 2013), paragraph A116.
[26] ISA (UK and Ireland) 315 (Revised June 2013), paragraph A11 in relation to ISA (UK and Ireland) 240, *The Auditor's Responsibilities Relating to Fraud in an Audit of Financial Statements.*

function to support the decision to use the work of the function in obtaining sufficient appropriate audit evidence on which to base the audit opinion.

Reperformance (Ref: Para. 24)

A30. For purposes of this ISA (UK and Ireland), reperformance involves the external auditor's independent execution of procedures to validate the conclusions reached by the internal audit function. This objective may be accomplished by examining items already examined by the internal audit function, or where it is not possible to do so, the same objective may also be accomplished by examining sufficient other similar items not actually examined by the internal audit function. Reperformance provides more persuasive evidence regarding the adequacy of the work of the internal audit function compared to other procedures the external auditor may perform in paragraph A28. While it is not necessary for the external auditor to do reperformance in each area of work of the internal audit function that is being used, some reperformance is required on the body of work of the internal audit function as a whole that the external auditor plans to use in accordance with paragraph 24. The external auditor is more likely to focus reperformance in those areas where more judgment was exercised by the internal audit function in planning, performing and evaluating the results of the audit procedures and in areas of higher risk of material misstatement.

Determining Whether, in Which Areas and to What Extent Internal Auditors Can Be Used to Provide Direct Assistance

Determining Whether Internal Auditors Can Be Used to Provide Direct Assistance for Purposes of the Audit (Ref: Para. 5, 26–28)

A31. In jurisdictions where the external auditor is prohibited by law or regulation from using internal auditors to provide direct assistance, it is relevant for the group auditors to consider whether the prohibition also extends to component auditors and, if so, to address this in the communication to the component auditors.[27]

A32. As stated in paragraph A7 of this ISA (UK and Ireland), objectivity refers to the ability to perform the proposed work without allowing bias, conflict of interest or undue influence of others to override professional judgments. In evaluating the existence and significance of threats to the objectivity of an internal auditor, the following factors may be relevant:

- The extent to which the internal audit function's organizational status and relevant policies and procedures support the objectivity of the internal auditors.[28]

---

[27] ISA 600, paragraph 40(b). The use of internal auditors to provide direct assistance is prohibited in an audit conducted in accordance with ISAs (UK and Ireland). For a group audit this prohibition extends to the work of any component auditor which is relied upon by the group auditor, including for overseas components – see paragraph 5-1 above of this ISA (UK and Ireland).

[28] See paragraph A7.

- Family and personal relationships with an individual working in, or responsible for, the aspect of the entity to which the work relates.

- Association with the division or department in the entity to which the work relates.

- Significant financial interests in the entity other than remuneration on terms consistent with those applicable to other employees at a similar level of seniority.

Material issued by relevant professional bodies for internal auditors may provide additional useful guidance.

A33. There may also be some circumstances in which the significance of the threats to the objectivity of an internal auditor is such that there are no safeguards that could reduce them to an acceptable level. For example, because the adequacy of safeguards is influenced by the significance of the work in the context of the audit, paragraph 30 (a) and (b) prohibits the use of internal auditors to provide direct assistance in relation to performing procedures that involve making significant judgments in the audit or that relate to higher assessed risks of material misstatement where the judgment required in performing the relevant audit procedures or evaluating the audit evidence gathered is more than limited. This would also be the case where the work involved creates a self-review threat, which is why internal auditors are prohibited from performing procedures in the circumstances described in paragraph 30 (c) and (d).

A34. In evaluating the level of competence of an internal auditor, many of the factors in paragraph A8 of this ISA (UK and Ireland) may also be relevant applied in the context of individual internal auditors and the work to which they may be assigned.

Determining the Nature and Extent of Work that Can Be Assigned to Internal Auditors Providing Direct Assistance (Ref: Para. 29–31)

A35. Paragraphs A15-A22 of this ISA (UK and Ireland) provide relevant guidance in determining the nature and extent of work that may be assigned to internal auditors.

A36. In determining the nature of work that may be assigned to internal auditors, the external auditor is careful to limit such work to those areas that would be appropriate to be assigned. Examples of activities and tasks that would not be appropriate to use internal auditors to provide direct assistance include the following:

- Discussion of fraud risks. However, the external auditors may make inquiries of internal auditors about fraud risks in the organization in accordance with ISA (UK and Ireland) 315 (Revised June 2013).[29]

- Determination of unannounced audit procedures as addressed in ISA (UK and Ireland) 240.

---

[29] ISA 315 (Revised), paragraph 6(a).

A37. Similarly, since in accordance with ISA (UK and Ireland) 505[30] the external auditor is required to maintain control over external confirmation requests and evaluate the results of external confirmation procedures, it would not be appropriate to assign these responsibilities to internal auditors. However, internal auditors may assist in assembling information necessary for the external auditor to resolve exceptions in confirmation responses.

A38. The amount of judgment involved and the risk of material misstatement are also relevant in determining the work that may be assigned to internal auditors providing direct assistance. For example, in circumstances where the valuation of accounts receivable is assessed as an area of higher risk, the external auditor could assign the checking of the accuracy of the aging to an internal auditor providing direct assistance. However, because the evaluation of the adequacy of the provision based on the aging would involve more than limited judgment, it would not be appropriate to assign that latter procedure to an internal auditor providing direct assistance.

A39. Notwithstanding the direction, supervision and review by the external auditor, excessive use of internal auditors to provide direct assistance may affect perceptions regarding the independence of the external audit engagement.

Using Internal Auditors to Provide Direct Assistance (Ref: Para. 34)

A40. As individuals in the internal audit function are not independent of the entity as is required of the external auditor when expressing an opinion on financial statements, the external auditor's direction, supervision and review of the work performed by internal auditors providing direct assistance will generally be of a different nature and more extensive than if members of the engagement team perform the work.

A41. In directing the internal auditors, the external auditor may for example, remind the internal auditors to bring accounting and auditing issues identified during the audit to the attention of the external auditor. In reviewing the work performed by the internal auditors, the external auditor's considerations include whether the evidence obtained is sufficient and appropriate in the circumstances, and that it supports the conclusions reached.

---

[30] ISA 505, *External Confirmations*, paragraphs 7 and 16.

Annexure

CONFORMING AMENDMENTS TO OTHER ISAs (UK AND IRELAND)

> This annexure shows the conforming amendments to ISQC (UK and Ireland) 1 and other ISAs (UK and Ireland) as a result of ISA (UK and Ireland) 610 (Revised June 2013), *Using the Work of Internal Auditors*. These amendments are effective for audits of financial statements for periods ending on or after 15 June 2014[1]. The footnote numbers within these amendments do not align with the ISAs (UK and Ireland) that will be amended, and reference should be made to those ISAs (UK and Ireland).

ISQC (UK and Ireland) 1, *Quality Control for Firms that Perform Audits and Reviews of Financial Statements, and Other Assurance and Related Services Engagements*

Definitions

12. In this ISQC (UK and Ireland), the following terms have the meanings attributed below:

(f) Engagement team – All partners and staff performing the engagement, and any individuals engaged by the firm or a network firm who perform procedures on the engagement. This excludes an auditor's external experts engaged by the firm or by a network firm. The term "engagement team" also excludes individuals within the client's internal audit function who provide direct assistance on an audit engagement when the external auditor complies with the requirements of ISA (UK and Ireland) 610 (Revised June 2013)[2].

***

---

[1] For the purpose of audits under ISAs as issued by the IAASB, the material pertaining to the use of direct assistance has an effective date of audits of financial statements for periods ending on or after 15 December 2014. However, as stated in paragraph 5-1 of ISA (UK and Ireland) 610 (Revised June 2013), the use of internal auditors to provide direct assistance is prohibited in an audit conducted in accordance with ISAs (UK and Ireland) – such prohibition being effective from the effective date of ISA (UK and Ireland) 610 (Revised June 2013), audits of financial statements for periods ending on or after 15 June 2014.

[2] ISA 610 (Revised June 2013), *Using the Work of Internal Auditors*, establishes limits on the use of direct assistance. It also acknowledges that the external auditor may be prohibited by law or regulation from obtaining direct assistance from internal auditors. Therefore, the use of direct assistance is restricted to situations where it is permitted. The use of internal auditors to provide direct assistance is prohibited in an audit conducted in accordance with ISAs (UK and Ireland) – see ISA (UK and Ireland) 610 (Revised June 2013), paragraph 5-1.

ISA (UK and Ireland) 200, *Overall Objectives of the Independent Auditor and the Conduct of an Audit in Accordance with International Standards on Auditing*

A72. In some cases, an ISA (UK and Ireland) (and therefore all of its requirements) may not be relevant in the circumstances. For example, if an entity does not have an internal audit function, nothing in ISA (UK and Ireland) 610 (Revised June 2013)[3] is relevant.

***

ISA (UK and Ireland) 220, *Quality Control for an Audit of Financial Statements*

Definitions

7. For purposes of the ISAs (UK and Ireland), the following terms have the meanings attributed below:

   (d) Engagement team – All partners and staff performing the engagement, and any individuals engaged by the firm or a network firm who perform audit procedures on the engagement. This excludes an auditor's external expert engaged by the firm or by a network firm.[4] The term "engagement team" also excludes individuals within the client's internal audit function who provide direct assistance on an audit engagement when the external auditor complies with the requirements of ISA (UK and Ireland) 610 (Revised June 2013).[5]

***

ISA (UK and Ireland) 230, *Audit Documentation*

A19. The documentation requirement applies only to requirements that are relevant in the circumstances. A requirement is not relevant[6] only in the cases where:

   (a) The entire ISA (UK and Ireland) is not relevant (for example, if an entity does not have an internal audit function, nothing in ISA (UK and Ireland) 610 (Revised June 2013)[7] is relevant); or

---

[3] ISA (UK and Ireland) 610 (Revised June 2013), *Using the Work of Internal Auditors*, paragraph 2.
[4] ISA (UK and Ireland) 620, *Using the Work of an Auditor's Expert*, paragraph 6(a), defines the term "auditor's expert."
[5] ISA 610 (Revised June 2013), *Using the Work of Internal Auditors*, establishes limits on the use of direct assistance. It also acknowledges that the external auditor may be prohibited by law or regulation from obtaining direct assistance from internal auditors. Therefore, the use of direct assistance is restricted to situations where it is permitted. The use of internal auditors to provide direct assistance is prohibited in an audit conducted in accordance with ISAs (UK and Ireland) – see ISA (UK and Ireland) 610 (Revised June 2013), paragraph 5-1.
[6] ISA (UK and Ireland) 200, paragraph 22.
[7] ISA (UK and Ireland) 610 (Revised June 2013), *Using the Work of Internal Auditors*, paragraph 2.

(b)   The requirement is conditional and the condition does not exist (for example, the requirement to modify the auditor's opinion where there is an inability to obtain sufficient appropriate audit evidence, and there is no such inability).

***

ISA (UK and Ireland) 240, *The Auditor's Responsibilities Relating to Fraud in an Audit of Financial Statements*

19.   For those entities that have an internal audit function, the auditor shall make inquiries of appropriate individuals within the function ~~internal audit~~ to determine whether ~~it~~ they ~~has~~ve knowledge of any actual, suspected or alleged fraud affecting the entity, and to obtain its views about the risks of fraud. (Ref: Para. A18)

Inquiries~~y~~ of the Internal Audit Function (Ref: Para. 19)

A18.   ISA (UK and Ireland) 315 (Revised June 2013) and ISA (UK and Ireland) 610 (Revised June 2013) establish requirements and provide guidance relevant to ~~in~~ audits of those entities that have an internal audit function.[8] In carrying out the requirements of those ISAs (UK and Ireland) in the context of fraud, the auditor may inquire about specific activities of the function ~~internal audit activities~~ including, for example:

*   The procedures performed, if any, by the internal ~~auditors~~ function during the year to detect fraud.

*   Whether management has satisfactorily responded to any findings resulting from those procedures.

Appendix 1

Examples of Fraud Risk Factors

Internal control components are deficient as a result of the following:

*   Inadequate monitoring of controls, including automated controls and controls over interim financial reporting (where external reporting is required).

*   High turnover rates or employment of staff in accounting, ~~internal audit, or~~ information technology, or the internal audit function ~~staff~~ that are not effective.

***

---

[8]   ISA (UK and Ireland) 315 (Revised June 2013), paragraphs 6(a) and 23, and ISA (UK and Ireland) 610 (Revised June 2013), *Using the Work of Internal Auditors*.

ISA (UK and Ireland) 260, *Communication with Those Charged with Governance*

A14. Other planning matters that it may be appropriate to discuss with those charged with governance include:

- Where the entity has an internal audit function, ~~the extent to which~~ how the external auditor ~~will use the work of internal audit, and how the external~~ and internal auditors can ~~best~~ work ~~together~~ in a constructive and complementary manner, including any planned use of the work of the internal audit function, and the nature and extent of any planned use of internal auditors to provide direct assistance.[9]

- ...

A33. Before communicating matters with those charged with governance, the auditor may discuss them with management, unless that is inappropriate. For example, it may not be appropriate to discuss questions of management's competence or integrity with management. In addition to recognizing management's executive responsibility, these initial discussions may clarify facts and issues, and give management an opportunity to provide further information and explanations. Similarly, when the entity has an internal audit function, the auditor may discuss matters with ~~the~~ appropriate individuals within the function ~~internal auditor~~ before communicating with those charged with governance.

A43. As noted in paragraph 4, effective two-way communication assists both the auditor and those charged with governance. Further, ISA (UK and Ireland) 315 (Revised June 2013) identifies participation by those charged with governance, including their interaction with the internal audit function, if any, and external auditors, as an element of the entity's control environment.[10] Inadequate two-way communication may indicate an unsatisfactory control environment and influence the auditor's assessment of the risks of material misstatements. There is also a risk that the auditor may not have obtained sufficient appropriate audit evidence to form an opinion on the financial statements.

***

---

[9] ISA (UK and Ireland) 610 (Revised June 2013), *Using the Work of Internal Auditors*, paragraphs 20 and 31. The use of internal auditors to provide direct assistance is prohibited in an audit conducted in accordance with ISAs (UK and Ireland) – see ISA (UK and Ireland) 610 (Revised June 2013), paragraph 5-1.

[10] ISA (UK and Ireland) 315 (Revised June 2013), paragraph A77~~70~~.

ISA (UK and Ireland) 265, *Communicating Deficiencies in Internal Control to Those Charged with Governance and Management*

A24. If the auditor has communicated deficiencies in internal control other than significant deficiencies to management in a prior period and management has chosen not to remedy them for cost or other reasons, the auditor need not repeat the communication in the current period. The auditor is also not required to repeat information about such deficiencies if it has been previously communicated to management by other parties, such as the internal ~~auditors~~ function or regulators. It may, however, be appropriate for the auditor to re-communicate these other deficiencies if there has been a change of management, or if new information has come to the auditor's attention that alters the prior understanding of the auditor and management regarding the deficiencies. ...

***

ISA (UK and Ireland) 300, *Planning an Audit of Financial Statements*

Appendix

Characteristics of the Engagement

...

- The need for a statutory audit of standalone financial statements in addition to an audit for consolidation purposes.

- ~~The availability of the work of internal auditors and the extent of the auditor's potential reliance on such work~~ Whether the entity has an internal audit function and if so, whether, in which areas and to what extent, the work of the function can be used, or internal auditors can be used to provide direct assistance[11], for purposes of the audit.

    ...

***

---

[11] The use of internal auditors to provide direct assistance is prohibited in an audit conducted in accordance with ISAs (UK and Ireland) – see ISA (UK and Ireland) 610 (Revised June 2013), *Using the Work of Internal Auditors,* paragraph 5-1.

ISA (UK and Ireland) 402, *Audit Considerations Relating to an Entity Using a Service Organization*

A1. Information on the nature of the services provided by a service organization may be available from a wide variety of sources, such as:

- User manuals.

- System overviews.

- Technical manuals.

- The contract or service level agreement between the user entity and the service organization.

- Reports by service organizations, the internal auditors function or regulatory authorities on controls at the service organization.

- Reports by the service auditor, including management letters, if available.

***

ISA (UK and Ireland) 500, *Audit Evidence*

A51. In some cases, the auditor may intend to use information produced by the entity for other audit purposes. For example, the auditor may intend to make use of the entity's performance measures for the purpose of analytical procedures, or to make use of the entity's information produced for monitoring activities, such as internal auditor's reports of the internal audit function. In such cases, the appropriateness of the audit evidence obtained is affected by whether the information is sufficiently precise or detailed for the auditor's purposes. For example, performance measures used by management may not be precise enough to detect material misstatements.

Inconsistency in, or Doubts over Reliability of, Audit Evidence (Ref: Para. 11)

A57. Obtaining audit evidence from different sources or of a different nature may indicate that an individual item of audit evidence is not reliable, such as when audit evidence obtained from one source is inconsistent with that obtained from another. This may be the case when, for example, responses to inquiries of management, internal auditors, and others are inconsistent, or when responses to inquiries of those charged with governance made to corroborate the responses to inquiries of management are inconsistent with the response by management. ISA (UK and Ireland) 230 includes a specific documentation requirement if the auditor identified information that is inconsistent with the auditor's final conclusion regarding a significant matter.[12]

***

---

[12] ISA (UK and Ireland) 230, *Audit Documentation*, paragraph 11.

ISA (UK and Ireland) 550, *Related Parties*

A15. Others within the entity are those considered likely to have knowledge of the entity's related party relationships and transactions, and the entity's controls over such relationships and transactions. These may include, to the extent that they do not form part of management:

- Those charged with governance;

- Personnel in a position to initiate, process, or record transactions that are both significant and outside the entity's normal course of business, and those who supervise or monitor such personnel;

- The ~~I~~internal audit~~ors~~ function;

- In-house legal counsel; and

- The chief ethics officer or equivalent person.

A17. In meeting the ISA (UK and Ireland) 315 (Revised June 2013) requirement to obtain an understanding of the control environment,[13] the auditor may consider features of the control environment relevant to mitigating the risks of material misstatement associated with related party relationships and transactions, such as:

- Internal ethical codes, appropriately communicated to the entity's personnel and enforced, governing the circumstances in which the entity may enter into specific types of related party transactions.

  ...

- Periodic reviews by the internal audit~~ors~~ function, where applicable.

  ...

A22. During the audit, the auditor may inspect records or documents that may provide information about related party relationships and transactions, for example:

- Third-party confirmations obtained by the auditor (in addition to bank and legal confirmations).

  ...

- ~~Internal auditors' r~~Reports of the internal audit function.

  ...

---

[13] ISA (UK and Ireland) 315 (Revised June 2013), paragraph 14.

***

ISA (UK and Ireland) 600, *Special Considerations—Audits of Group Financial Statements (Including the Work of Component Auditors)*

A27. The auditor is required to identify and assess the risks of material misstatement of the financial statements due to fraud, and to design and implement appropriate responses to the assessed risks.[14] Information used to identify the risks of material misstatement of the group financial statements due to fraud may include the following:

...

- Responses of those charged with governance of the group, group management, appropriate individuals within the internal audit function (and if considered appropriate, component management, the component auditors, and others) to the group engagement team's *inquiry* whether they have knowledge of any actual, suspected, or alleged fraud affecting a component or the group.

A51. The group engagement team's decision as to how many components to select in accordance with paragraph 29, which components to select, and the type of work to be performed on the financial information of the individual components selected may be affected by factors such as the following:

- ...

- Whether the internal audit function has performed work at the component and any effect of that work on the group audit.

- ...

Appendix 2

Examples of Matters about Which the Group Engagement Team Obtains an Understanding

The examples provided cover a broad range of matters; however, not all matters are relevant to every group audit engagement and the list of examples is not necessarily complete.

---

[14] ISA (UK and Ireland) 240, *The Auditor's Responsibilities Relating to Fraud in an Audit of Financial Statements*.

Group-Wide Controls

1.　Group-wide controls may include a combination of the following:

- ...

- Monitoring of controls, including activities of the internal audit function and self-assessment programs.

- ...

2.　The ~~l~~internal audit function may be regarded as part of group-wide controls, for example, when the ~~internal audit~~ function is centralized. ISA (UK and Ireland) 610 (Revised June 2013)[15] deals with the group engagement team's evaluation of ~~the~~ whether the internal audit function's organizational status and relevant policies and procedures adequately supports the ~~competence and~~ objectivity of ~~the~~ internal auditors, the level of competence of the internal audit function, and whether the function applies a systematic and disciplined approach where the group engagement team expects ~~it plans~~ to use ~~their~~ the function's work.

Appendix 5

Required and Additional Matters Included in the Group Engagement Team's Letter of Instruction

Matters required by this ISA (UK and Ireland) to be communicated to the component auditor are shown in italicized text.

Matters that are relevant to the planning of the work of the component auditor:

- *The ethical requirements that are relevant to the group audit and, in particular, the independence requirements, for example, where the group auditor is prohibited by law or regulation from using internal auditors to provide direct assistance, it is relevant for the group auditor to consider whether the prohibition also extends to component auditors and, if so, to address this in the communication to the component auditors.*[16]

...

---

[15]　ISA (UK and Ireland) 610 (Revised June 2013), *Using the Work of Internal Auditors*, paragraphs 15-16 ~~9~~.

[16]　ISA 610 (Revised June 2013), *Using the Work of Internal Auditors*, paragraph A31. The use of internal auditors to provide direct assistance is prohibited in an audit conducted in accordance with ISAs (UK and Ireland). For a group audit this prohibition extends to the work of any component auditor which is relied upon by the group auditor, including for overseas components – see ISA (UK and Ireland) 610 (Revised June 2013), paragraph 5-1.

Matters that are relevant to the conduct of the work of the component auditor:

- ...

- The findings of the internal audit function, based on work performed on controls at or relevant to components...

INTERNATIONAL STANDARD ON AUDITING (UK AND IRELAND) 620

USING THE WORK OF AN AUDITOR'S EXPERT

(Effective for audits of financial statements for periods ending on or after 15 December 2010)

CONTENTS

International Standard on Auditing (UK and Ireland) (ISA (UK and Ireland)) 620, "Using the Work of an Auditor's Expert" should be read in conjunction with ISA (UK and Ireland) 200, "Overall Objectives of the Independent Auditor and the Conduct of an Audit in Accordance with International Standards on Auditing (UK and Ireland)."

Introduction

Scope of this ISA (UK and Ireland)

1. This International Standard on Auditing (UK and Ireland) (ISA (UK and Ireland)) deals with the auditor's responsibilities relating to the work of an individual or organization in a field of expertise other than accounting or auditing, when that work is used to assist the auditor in obtaining sufficient appropriate audit evidence.

2. This ISA (UK and Ireland) does not deal with:

    (a) Situations where the engagement team includes a member, or consults an individual or organization, with expertise in a specialized area of accounting or auditing, which are dealt with in ISA (UK and Ireland) 220;[1] or

    (b) The auditor's use of the work of an individual or organization possessing expertise in a field other than accounting or auditing, whose work in that field is used by the entity to assist the entity in preparing the financial statements (a management's expert), which is dealt with in ISA (UK and Ireland) 500.[2]

The Auditor's Responsibility for the Audit Opinion

3. The auditor has sole responsibility for the audit opinion expressed, and that responsibility is not reduced by the auditor's use of the work of an auditor's expert. Nonetheless, if the auditor using the work of an auditor's expert, having followed this ISA (UK and Ireland), concludes that the work of that expert is adequate for the auditor's purposes, the auditor may accept that expert's findings or conclusions in the expert's field as appropriate audit evidence.

Effective Date

4. This ISA (UK and Ireland) is effective for audits of financial statements for periods ending on or after 15 December 2010.

Objectives

5. The objectives of the auditor are:

    (a) To determine whether to use the work of an auditor's expert; and

    (b) If using the work of an auditor's expert, to determine whether that work is adequate for the auditor's purposes.

---

[1] ISA (UK and Ireland) 220, "Quality Control for an Audit of Financial Statements," paragraphs A10, A20-A22.

[2] ISA (UK and Ireland) 500, "Audit Evidence," paragraphs A34-A48.

Definitions

6. For purposes of the ISAs (UK and Ireland), the following terms have the meanings attributed below:

    (a) Auditor's expert – An individual or organization possessing expertise in a field other than accounting or auditing, whose work in that field is used by the auditor to assist the auditor in obtaining sufficient appropriate audit evidence. An auditor's expert may be either an auditor's internal expert (who is a partner[3] or staff, including temporary staff, of the auditor's firm or a network firm), or an auditor's external expert. (Ref: Para. A1-A3)

    (b) Expertise – Skills, knowledge and experience in a particular field.

    (c) Management's expert – An individual or organization possessing expertise in a field other than accounting or auditing, whose work in that field is used by the entity to assist the entity in preparing the financial statements.

Requirements

Determining the Need for an Auditor's Expert

7. If expertise in a field other than accounting or auditing is necessary to obtain sufficient appropriate audit evidence, the auditor shall determine whether to use the work of an auditor's expert. (Ref: Para. A4-A9)

Nature, Timing and Extent of Audit Procedures

8. The nature, timing and extent of the auditor's procedures with respect to the requirements in paragraphs 9-13 of this ISA (UK and Ireland) will vary depending on the circumstances. In determining the nature, timing and extent of those procedures, the auditor shall consider matters including: (Ref: Para. A10)

    (a) The nature of the matter to which that expert's work relates;

    (b) The risks of material misstatement in the matter to which that expert's work relates;

    (c) The significance of that expert's work in the context of the audit;

    (d) The auditor's knowledge of and experience with previous work performed by that expert; and

    (e) Whether that expert is subject to the auditor's firm's quality control policies and procedures. (Ref: Para. A11-A13)

---

[3] "Partner" and "firm" should be read as referring to their public sector equivalents where relevant.

The Competence, Capabilities and Objectivity of the Auditor's Expert

9. The auditor shall evaluate whether the auditor's expert has the necessary competence, capabilities and objectivity for the auditor's purposes. In the case of an auditor's external expert, the evaluation of objectivity shall include inquiry regarding interests and relationships that may create a threat to that expert's objectivity. (Ref: Para. A14-A20)

Obtaining an Understanding of the Field of Expertise of the Auditor's Expert

10. The auditor shall obtain a sufficient understanding of the field of expertise of the auditor's expert to enable the auditor to: (Ref: Para. A21-A22)

    (a) Determine the nature, scope and objectives of that expert's work for the auditor's purposes; and

    (b) Evaluate the adequacy of that work for the auditor's purposes.

Agreement with the Auditor's Expert

11. The auditor shall agree, in writing when appropriate, on the following matters with the auditor's expert: (Ref: Para. A23-A26)

    (a) The nature, scope and objectives of that expert's work; (Ref: Para. A27)

    (b) The respective roles and responsibilities of the auditor and that expert; (Ref: Para. A28-A29)

    (c) The nature, timing and extent of communication between the auditor and that expert, including the form of any report to be provided by that expert; and (Ref: Para. A30)

    (d) The need for the auditor's expert to observe confidentiality requirements. (Ref: Para. A31)

Evaluating the Adequacy of the Auditor's Expert's Work

12. The auditor shall evaluate the adequacy of the auditor's expert's work for the auditor's purposes, including: (Ref: Para. A32)

    (a) The relevance and reasonableness of that expert's findings or conclusions, and their consistency with other audit evidence; (Ref: Para. A33-A34)

    (b) If that expert's work involves use of significant assumptions and methods, the relevance and reasonableness of those assumptions and methods in the circumstances; and (Ref: Para. A35-A37)

(c)   If that expert's work involves the use of source data that is significant to that expert's work, the relevance, completeness, and accuracy of that source data. (Ref: Para. A38-A39)

13.   If the auditor determines that the work of the auditor's expert is not adequate for the auditor's purposes, the auditor shall: (Ref: Para. A40)

(a)   Agree with that expert on the nature and extent of further work to be performed by that expert; or

(b)   Perform additional audit procedures appropriate to the circumstances.

Reference to the Auditor's Expert in the Auditor's Report

14.   The auditor shall not refer to the work of an auditor's expert in an auditor's report containing an unmodified opinion unless required by law or regulation to do so. If such reference is required by law or regulation, the auditor shall indicate in the auditor's report that the reference does not reduce the auditor's responsibility for the auditor's opinion. (Ref: Para. A41)

15.   If the auditor makes reference to the work of an auditor's expert in the auditor's report because such reference is relevant to an understanding of a modification to the auditor's opinion, the auditor shall indicate in the auditor's report that such reference does not reduce the auditor's responsibility for that opinion. (Ref: Para. A42)

***

Application and Other Explanatory Material

Definition of an Auditor's Expert (Ref: Para. 6(a))

A1.   Expertise in a field other than accounting or auditing may include expertise in relation to such matters as:

- The valuation of complex financial instruments, land and buildings, plant and machinery, jewelry, works of art, antiques, intangible assets, assets acquired and liabilities assumed in business combinations and assets that may have been impaired.

- The actuarial calculation of liabilities associated with insurance contracts or employee benefit plans.

- The estimation of oil and gas reserves.

- The valuation of environmental liabilities, and site clean-up costs.

- The interpretation of contracts, laws and regulations.

- The analysis of complex or unusual tax compliance issues.

A2. In many cases, distinguishing between expertise in accounting or auditing, and expertise in another field, will be straightforward, even where this involves a specialized area of accounting or auditing. For example, an individual with expertise in applying methods of accounting for deferred income tax can often be easily distinguished from an expert in taxation law. The former is not an expert for the purposes of this ISA (UK and Ireland) as this constitutes accounting expertise; the latter is an expert for the purposes of this ISA (UK and Ireland) as this constitutes legal expertise. Similar distinctions may also be able to be made in other areas, for example, between expertise in methods of accounting for financial instruments, and expertise in complex modeling for the purpose of valuing financial instruments. In some cases, however, particularly those involving an emerging area of accounting or auditing expertise, distinguishing between specialized areas of accounting or auditing, and expertise in another field, will be a matter of professional judgment. Applicable professional rules and standards regarding education and competency requirements for accountants and auditors may assist the auditor in exercising that judgment.[4]

A3. It is necessary to apply judgment when considering how the requirements of this ISA (UK and Ireland) are affected by the fact that an auditor's expert may be either an individual or an organization. For example, when evaluating the competence, capabilities and objectivity of an auditor's expert, it may be that the expert is an organization the auditor has previously used, but the auditor has no prior experience of the individual expert assigned by the organization for the particular engagement; or it may be the reverse, that is, the auditor may be familiar with the work of an individual expert but not with the organization that expert has joined. In either case, both the personal attributes of the individual and the managerial attributes of the organization (such as systems of quality control the organization implements) may be relevant to the auditor's evaluation.

Determining the Need for an Auditor's Expert (Ref: Para. 7)

A4. An auditor's expert may be needed to assist the auditor in one or more of the following:

- Obtaining an understanding of the entity and its environment, including its internal control.

- Identifying and assessing the risks of material misstatement.

- Determining and implementing overall responses to assessed risks at the financial statement level.

---

[4] For example, International Education Standard 8, "Competence Requirements for Audit Professionals" may be of assistance.

- Designing and performing further audit procedures to respond to assessed risks at the assertion level, comprising tests of controls or substantive procedures.

- Evaluating the sufficiency and appropriateness of audit evidence obtained in forming an opinion on the financial statements.

A5.   The risks of material misstatement may increase when expertise in a field other than accounting is needed for management[4a] to prepare the financial statements, for example, because this may indicate some complexity, or because management may not possess knowledge of the field of expertise. If in preparing the financial statements management does not possess the necessary expertise, a management's expert may be used in addressing those risks. Relevant controls, including controls that relate to the work of a management's expert, if any, may also reduce the risks of material misstatement.

A6.   If the preparation of the financial statements involves the use of expertise in a field other than accounting, the auditor, who is skilled in accounting and auditing, may not possess the necessary expertise to audit those financial statements. The engagement partner is required to be satisfied that the engagement team, and any auditor's experts who are not part of the engagement team, collectively have the appropriate competence and capabilities to perform the audit engagement.[5] Further, the auditor is required to ascertain the nature, timing and extent of resources necessary to perform the engagement.[6] The auditor's determination of whether to use the work of an auditor's expert, and if so when and to what extent, assists the auditor in meeting these requirements. As the audit progresses, or as circumstances change, the auditor may need to revise earlier decisions about using the work of an auditor's expert.

A7.   An auditor who is not an expert in a relevant field other than accounting or auditing may nevertheless be able to obtain a sufficient understanding of that field to perform the audit without an auditor's expert. This understanding may be obtained through, for example:

- Experience in auditing entities that require such expertise in the preparation of their financial statements.

- Education or professional development in the particular field. This may include formal courses, or discussion with individuals possessing expertise in the relevant field for the purpose of enhancing the auditor's own capacity to deal with matters in that field. Such discussion differs from consultation with an auditor's expert regarding a specific set of circumstances encountered on the engagement where that expert is given all the relevant facts that will enable the expert to provide informed advice about the particular matter.[7]

[4a] In the UK and Ireland those charged with governance are responsible for the preparation of the financial statements.
[5] ISA (UK and Ireland) 220, paragraph 14.
[6] ISA (UK and Ireland) 300, "Planning an Audit of Financial Statements," paragraph 8(e).
[7] ISA (UK and Ireland) 220, paragraph A21.

- Discussion with auditors who have performed similar engagements.

A8. In other cases, however, the auditor may determine that it is necessary, or may choose, to use an auditor's expert to assist in obtaining sufficient appropriate audit evidence. Considerations when deciding whether to use an auditor's expert may include:

- Whether management[4a] has used a management's expert in preparing the financial statements (see paragraph A9).

- The nature and significance of the matter, including its complexity.

- The risks of material misstatement in the matter.

- The expected nature of procedures to respond to identified risks, including: the auditor's knowledge of and experience with the work of experts in relation to such matters; and the availability of alternative sources of audit evidence.

A9. When management has used a management's expert in preparing the financial statements, the auditor's decision on whether to use an auditor's expert may also be influenced by such factors as:

- The nature, scope and objectives of the management's expert's work.

- Whether the management's expert is employed by the entity, or is a party engaged by it to provide relevant services.

- The extent to which management can exercise control or influence over the work of the management's expert.

- The management's expert's competence and capabilities.

- Whether the management's expert is subject to technical performance standards or other professional or industry requirements

- Any controls within the entity over the management's expert's work.

ISA (UK and Ireland) 500[8] includes requirements and guidance regarding the effect of the competence, capabilities and objectivity of management's experts on the reliability of audit evidence.

Nature, Timing and Extent of Audit Procedures (Ref: Para. 8)

A10. The nature, timing and extent of audit procedures with respect to the requirements in paragraphs 9-13 of this ISA (UK and Ireland) will vary depending on the

---

[8] ISA (UK and Ireland) 500, paragraph 8.

circumstances. For example, the following factors may suggest the need for different or more extensive procedures than would otherwise be the case:

- The work of the auditor's expert relates to a significant matter that involves subjective and complex judgments.

- The auditor has not previously used the work of the auditor's expert, and has no prior knowledge of that expert's competence, capabilities and objectivity.

- The auditor's expert is performing procedures that are integral to the audit, rather than being consulted to provide advice on an individual matter.

- The expert is an auditor's external expert and is not, therefore, subject to the firm's quality control policies and procedures.

The Auditor's Firm's Quality Control Policies and Procedures (Ref: Para. 8(e))

A11. An auditor's internal expert may be a partner or staff, including temporary staff, of the auditor's firm, and therefore subject to the quality control policies and procedures of that firm in accordance with ISQC (UK and Ireland) 1[9] or national requirements that are at least as demanding.[10] Alternatively, an auditor's internal expert may be a partner or staff, including temporary staff, of a network firm, which may share common quality control policies and procedures with the auditor's firm.

A12. An auditor's external expert is not a member of the engagement team and is not subject to quality control policies and procedures in accordance with ISQC (UK and Ireland) 1.[11] In some jurisdictions, however, law or regulation may require that an auditor's external expert be treated as a member of the engagement team, and may therefore be subject to relevant ethical requirements, including those pertaining to independence, and other professional requirements, as determined by that law or regulation.

A13. Engagement teams are entitled to rely on the firm's system of quality control, unless information provided by the firm or other parties suggests otherwise.[12] The extent of that reliance will vary with the circumstances, and may affect the nature, timing and extent of the auditor's procedures with respect to such matters as:

- Competence and capabilities, through recruitment and training programs.

- Objectivity. Auditor's internal experts are subject to relevant ethical requirements, including those pertaining to independence.

---

[9] ISQC (UK and Ireland) 1, "Quality Control for Firms that Perform Audits and Reviews of Financial Statements, and Other Assurance and Related Services Engagements," paragraph 12(f).
[10] ISA (UK and Ireland) 220, paragraph 2.
[11] ISQC (UK and Ireland) 1, paragraph 12(f).
[12] ISA (UK and Ireland) 220, paragraph 4.

FINANCIAL REPORTING COUNCIL

- The auditor's evaluation of the adequacy of the auditor's expert's work. For example, the firm's training programs may provide auditor's internal experts with an appropriate understanding of the interrelationship of their expertise with the audit process. Reliance on such training and other firm processes, such as protocols for scoping the work of auditor's internal experts, may affect the nature, timing and extent of the auditor's procedures to evaluate the adequacy of the auditor's expert's work.

- Adherence to regulatory and legal requirements, through monitoring processes.

- Agreement with the auditor's expert.

Such reliance does not reduce the auditor's responsibility to meet the requirements of this ISA (UK and Ireland).

The Competence, Capabilities and Objectivity of the Auditor's Expert (Ref: Para. 9)

A14. The competence, capabilities and objectivity of an auditor's expert are factors that significantly affect whether the work of the auditor's expert will be adequate for the auditor's purposes. Competence relates to the nature and level of expertise of the auditor's expert. Capability relates to the ability of the auditor's expert to exercise that competence in the circumstances of the engagement. Factors that influence capability may include, for example, geographic location, and the availability of time and resources. Objectivity relates to the possible effects that bias, conflict of interest, or the influence of others may have on the professional or business judgment of the auditor's expert.

A15. Information regarding the competence, capabilities and objectivity of an auditor's expert may come from a variety of sources, such as:

- Personal experience with previous work of that expert.

- Discussions with that expert.

- Discussions with other auditors or others who are familiar with that expert's work.

- Knowledge of that expert's qualifications, membership of a professional body or industry association, license to practice, or other forms of external recognition.

- Published papers or books written by that expert.

- The auditor's firm's quality control policies and procedures (see paragraphs A11-A13).

A16. Matters relevant to evaluating the competence, capabilities and objectivity of the auditor's expert include whether that expert's work is subject to technical performance standards or other professional or industry requirements, for example, ethical standards and other membership requirements of a professional body or industry association, accreditation standards of a licensing body, or requirements imposed by law or regulation.

A17. Other matters that may be relevant include:

- The relevance of the auditor's expert's competence to the matter for which that expert's work will be used, including any areas of specialty within that expert's field. For example, a particular actuary may specialize in property and casualty insurance, but have limited expertise regarding pension calculations.

- The auditor's expert's competence with respect to relevant accounting and auditing requirements, for example, knowledge of assumptions and methods, including models where applicable, that are consistent with the applicable financial reporting framework.

- Whether unexpected events, changes in conditions, or the audit evidence obtained from the results of audit procedures indicate that it may be necessary to reconsider the initial evaluation of the competence, capabilities and objectivity of the auditor's expert as the audit progresses.

A18. A broad range of circumstances may threaten objectivity, for example, self-interest threats, advocacy threats, familiarity threats, self-review threats, and intimidation threats. Safeguards may eliminate or reduce such threats, and may be created by external structures (for example, the auditor's expert's profession, legislation or regulation), or by the auditor's expert's work environment (for example, quality control policies and procedures). There may also be safeguards specific to the audit engagement.

A19. The evaluation of the significance of threats to objectivity and of whether there is a need for safeguards may depend upon the role of the auditor's expert and the significance of the expert's work in the context of the audit. There may be some circumstances in which safeguards cannot reduce threats to an acceptable level, for example, if a proposed auditor's expert is an individual who has played a significant role in preparing the information that is being audited, that is, if the auditor's expert is a management's expert.

A20. When evaluating the objectivity of an auditor's external expert, it may be relevant to:

   (a) Inquire of the entity about any known interests or relationships that the entity has with the auditor's external expert that may affect that expert's objectivity.

   (b) Discuss with that expert any applicable safeguards, including any professional requirements that apply to that expert; and evaluate whether the safeguards are adequate to reduce threats to an acceptable level. Interests and relationships that it may be relevant to discuss with the auditor's expert include:

      - Financial interests.

      - Business and personal relationships.

- Provision of other services by the expert, including by the organization in the case of an external expert that is an organization.

In some cases, it may also be appropriate for the auditor to obtain a written representation from the auditor's external expert about any interests or relationships with the entity of which that expert is aware.

Obtaining an Understanding of the Field of Expertise of the Auditor's Expert (Ref: Para. 10)

A21. The auditor may obtain an understanding of the auditor's expert's field of expertise through the means described in paragraph A7, or through discussion with that expert.

A22. Aspects of the auditor's expert's field relevant to the auditor's understanding may include:

- Whether that expert's field has areas of specialty within it that are relevant to the audit (see paragraph A17).

- Whether any professional or other standards, and regulatory or legal requirements apply.

- What assumptions and methods, including models where applicable, are used by the auditor's expert, and whether they are generally accepted within that expert's field and appropriate for financial reporting purposes.

- The nature of internal and external data or information the auditor's expert uses.

Agreement with the Auditor's Expert (Ref: Para. 11)

A23. The nature, scope and objectives of the auditor's expert's work may vary considerably with the circumstances, as may the respective roles and responsibilities of the auditor and the auditor's expert, and the nature, timing and extent of communication between the auditor and the auditor's expert. It is therefore required that these matters are agreed between the auditor and the auditor's expert regardless of whether the expert is an auditor's external expert or an auditor's internal expert.

A24. The matters noted in paragraph 8 may affect the level of detail and formality of the agreement between the auditor and the auditor's expert, including whether it is appropriate that the agreement be in writing. For example, the following factors may suggest the need for more a detailed agreement than would otherwise be the case, or for the agreement to be set out in writing:

- The auditor's expert will have access to sensitive or confidential entity information.

- The respective roles or responsibilities of the auditor and the auditor's expert are different from those normally expected.

- Multi-jurisdictional legal or regulatory requirements apply.

- The matter to which the auditor's expert's work relates is highly complex.

- The auditor has not previously used work performed by that expert.

- The greater the extent of the auditor's expert's work, and its significance in the context of the audit.

A25. The agreement between the auditor and an auditor's external expert is often in the form of an engagement letter. The Appendix lists matters that the auditor may consider for inclusion in such an engagement letter, or in any other form of agreement with an auditor's external expert.

A26. When there is no written agreement between the auditor and the auditor's expert, evidence of the agreement may be included in, for example:

- Planning memoranda, or related working papers such as the audit program.

- The policies and procedures of the auditor's firm. In the case of an auditor's internal expert, the established policies and procedures to which that expert is subject may include particular policies and procedures in relation to that expert's work. The extent of documentation in the auditor's working papers depends on the nature of such policies and procedures. For example, no documentation may be required in the auditor's working papers if the auditor's firm has detailed protocols covering the circumstances in which the work of such an expert is used.

Nature, Scope and Objectives of Work (Ref: Para. 11(a))

A27. It may often be relevant when agreeing on the nature, scope and objectives of the auditor's expert's work to include discussion of any relevant technical performance standards or other professional or industry requirements that the expert will follow.

Respective Roles and Responsibilities (Ref: Para. 11(b))

A28. Agreement on the respective roles and responsibilities of the auditor and the auditor's expert may include:

- Whether the auditor or the auditor's expert will perform detailed testing of source data.

- Consent for the auditor to discuss the auditor's expert's findings or conclusions with the entity and others, and to include details of that expert's findings or conclusions in the basis for a modified opinion in the auditor's report, if necessary (see paragraph A42).

- Any agreement to inform the auditor's expert of the auditor's conclusions concerning that expert's work.

Working Papers

A29. Agreement on the respective roles and responsibilities of the auditor and the auditor's expert may also include agreement about access to, and retention of, each other's working papers. When the auditor's expert is a member of the engagement team, that expert's working papers form part of the audit documentation. Subject to any agreement to the contrary, auditor's external experts' working papers are their own and do not form part of the audit documentation.

Communication (Ref: Para. 11(c))

A30. Effective two-way communication facilitates the proper integration of the nature, timing and extent of the auditor's expert's procedures with other work on the audit, and appropriate modification of the auditor's expert's objectives during the course of the audit. For example, when the work of the auditor's expert relates to the auditor's conclusions regarding a significant risk, both a formal written report at the conclusion of that expert's work, and oral reports as the work progresses, may be appropriate. Identification of specific partners or staff who will liaise with the auditor's expert, and procedures for communication between that expert and the entity, assists timely and effective communication, particularly on larger engagements.

Confidentiality (Ref: Para. 11(d))

A31. It is necessary for the confidentiality provisions of relevant ethical requirements that apply to the auditor also to apply to the auditor's expert. Additional requirements may be imposed by law or regulation. The entity may also have requested that specific confidentiality provisions be agreed with auditor's external experts.

Evaluating the Adequacy of the Auditor's Expert's Work (Ref: Para. 12)

A32. The auditor's evaluation of the auditor's expert's competence, capabilities and objectivity, the auditor's familiarity with the auditor's expert's field of expertise, and the nature of the work performed by the auditor's expert affect the nature, timing and extent of audit procedures to evaluate the adequacy of that expert's work for the auditor's purposes.

The Findings and Conclusions of the Auditor's Expert (Ref: Para. 12(a))

A33. Specific procedures to evaluate the adequacy of the auditor's expert's work for the auditor's purposes may include:

- Inquiries of the auditor's expert.

- Reviewing the auditor's expert's working papers and reports.

- Corroborative procedures, such as:

  - Observing the auditor's expert's work;

- ○ Examining published data, such as statistical reports from reputable, authoritative sources;

- ○ Confirming relevant matters with third parties;

- ○ Performing detailed analytical procedures; and

- ○ Reperforming calculations.

- Discussion with another expert with relevant expertise when, for example, the findings or conclusions of the auditor's expert are not consistent with other audit evidence.

- Discussing the auditor's expert's report with management.

A34. Relevant factors when evaluating the relevance and reasonableness of the findings or conclusions of the auditor's expert, whether in a report or other form, may include whether they are:

- Presented in a manner that is consistent with any standards of the auditor's expert's profession or industry;

- Clearly expressed, including reference to the objectives agreed with the auditor, the scope of the work performed and standards applied;

- Based on an appropriate period and take into account subsequent events, where relevant;

- Subject to any reservation, limitation or restriction on use, and if so, whether this has implications for the auditor; and

- Based on appropriate consideration of errors or deviations encountered by the auditor's expert.

Assumptions, Methods and Source Data

Assumptions and Methods (Ref: Para. 12(b))

A35. When the auditor's expert's work is to evaluate underlying assumptions and methods, including models where applicable, used by management in developing an accounting estimate, the auditor's procedures are likely to be primarily directed to evaluating whether the auditor's expert has adequately reviewed those assumptions and methods. When the auditor's expert's work is to develop an auditor's point estimate or an auditor's range for comparison with management's point estimate, the auditor's procedures may be primarily directed to evaluating the assumptions and methods, including models where appropriate, used by the auditor's expert.

A36. ISA (UK and Ireland) 540[13] discusses the assumptions and methods used by management in making accounting estimates, including the use in some cases of highly specialized, entity-developed models. Although that discussion is written in the context of the auditor obtaining sufficient appropriate audit evidence regarding management's assumptions and methods, it may also assist the auditor when evaluating an auditor's expert's assumptions and methods.

A37. When an auditor's expert's work involves the use of significant assumptions and methods, factors relevant to the auditor's evaluation of those assumptions and methods include whether they are:

- Generally accepted within the auditor's expert's field;

- Consistent with the requirements of the applicable financial reporting framework;

- Dependent on the use of specialized models; and

- Consistent with those of management, and if not, the reason for, and effects of, the differences.

Source Data Used by the Auditor's Expert (Ref: Para. 12(c))

A38. When an auditor's expert's work involves the use of source data that is significant to that expert's work, procedures such as the following may be used to test that data:

- Verifying the origin of the data, including obtaining an understanding of, and where applicable testing, the internal controls over the data and, where relevant, its transmission to the expert.

- Reviewing the data for completeness and internal consistency.

A39. In many cases, the auditor may test source data. However, in other cases, when the nature of the source data used by an auditor's expert is highly technical in relation to the expert's field, that expert may test the source data. If the auditor's expert has tested the source data, inquiry of that expert by the auditor, or supervision or review of that expert's tests may be an appropriate way for the auditor to evaluate that data's relevance, completeness, and accuracy.

Inadequate Work (Ref: Para. 13)

A40. If the auditor concludes that the work of the auditor's expert is not adequate for the auditor's purposes and the auditor cannot resolve the matter through the additional audit procedures required by paragraph 13, which may involve further work being performed by both the expert and the auditor, or include employing or engaging another expert, it may be necessary to express a modified opinion in the auditor's

---

[13] ISA (UK and Ireland) 540, "Auditing Accounting Estimates, Including Fair Value Accounting Estimates, and Related Disclosures," paragraphs 8, 13 and 15.

report in accordance with ISA (UK and Ireland) 705 because the auditor has not obtained sufficient appropriate audit evidence.[14]

Reference to the Auditor's Expert in the Auditor's Report (Ref: Para. 14-15)

A41. In some cases, law or regulation may require a reference to the work of an auditor's expert, for example, for the purposes of transparency in the public sector.

A42. It may be appropriate in some circumstances to refer to the auditor's expert in an auditor's report containing a modified opinion, to explain the nature of the modification. In such circumstances, the auditor may need the permission of the auditor's expert before making such a reference.

---

[14] ISA (UK and Ireland) 705, "Modifications to the Opinion in the Independent Auditor's Report," paragraph 6(b).

Appendix

(Ref: Para. A25)

Considerations for Agreement between the Auditor and an Auditor's External Expert

This Appendix lists matters that the auditor may consider for inclusion in any agreement with an auditor's external expert. The following list is illustrative and is not exhaustive; it is intended only to be a guide that may be used in conjunction with the considerations outlined in this ISA (UK and Ireland). Whether to include particular matters in the agreement depends on the circumstances of the engagement. The list may also be of assistance in considering the matters to be included in an agreement with an auditor's internal expert.

Nature, Scope and Objectives of the Auditor's External Expert's Work

- The nature and scope of the procedures to be performed by the auditor's external expert.

- The objectives of the auditor's external expert's work in the context of materiality and risk considerations concerning the matter to which the auditor's external expert's work relates, and, when relevant, the applicable financial reporting framework.

- Any relevant technical performance standards or other professional or industry requirements the auditor's external expert will follow.

- The assumptions and methods, including models where applicable, the auditor's external expert will use, and their authority.

- The effective date of, or when applicable the testing period for, the subject matter of the auditor's external expert's work, and requirements regarding subsequent events.

The Respective Roles and Responsibilities of the Auditor and the Auditor's External Expert

- Relevant auditing and accounting standards, and relevant regulatory or legal requirements.

- The auditor's external expert's consent to the auditor's intended use of that expert's report, including any reference to it, or disclosure of it, to others, for example reference to it in the basis for a modified opinion in the auditor's report, if necessary, or disclosure of it to management or an audit committee.

- The nature and extent of the auditor's review of the auditor's external expert's work.

- Whether the auditor or the auditor's external expert will test source data.

- The auditor's external expert's access to the entity's records, files, personnel and to experts engaged by the entity.

- Procedures for communication between the auditor's external expert and the entity.

- The auditor's and the auditor's external expert's access to each other's working papers.

- Ownership and control of working papers during and after the engagement, including any file retention requirements.

- The auditor's external expert's responsibility to perform work with due skill and care.

- The auditor's external expert's competence and capability to perform the work.

- The expectation that the auditor's external expert will use all knowledge that expert has that is relevant to the audit or, if not, will inform the auditor.

- Any restriction on the auditor's external expert's association with the auditor's report.

- Any agreement to inform the auditor's external expert of the auditor's conclusions concerning that expert's work

Communications and Reporting

- Methods and frequency of communications, including:

  - How the auditor's external expert's findings or conclusions will be reported (written report, oral report, ongoing input to the engagement team, for example.).

  - Identification of specific persons within the engagement team who will liaise with the auditor's external expert.

- When the auditor's external expert will complete the work and report findings or conclusions to the auditor.

- The auditor's external expert's responsibility to communicate promptly any potential delay in completing the work, and any potential reservation or limitation on that expert's findings or conclusions.

- The auditor's external expert's responsibility to communicate promptly instances in which the entity restricts that expert's access to records, files, personnel or experts engaged by the entity.

- The auditor's external expert's responsibility to communicate to the auditor all information that expert believes may be relevant to the audit, including any changes in circumstances previously communicated.

- The auditor's external expert's responsibility to communicate circumstances that may create threats to that expert's objectivity, and any relevant safeguards that may eliminate or reduce such threats to an acceptable level.

Confidentiality

- The need for the auditor's expert to observe confidentiality requirements, including:

  ○ The confidentiality provisions of relevant ethical requirements that apply to the auditor.

  ○ Additional requirements that may be imposed by law or regulation, if any.

  ○ Specific confidentiality provisions requested by the entity, if any.

ISA (UK and Ireland) 700 – Clarification Statement

This document sets out a clarification statement issued by the FRC in relation to paragraph 19A of ISA (UK and Ireland) 700 *The Independent Auditor's Report on Financial Statements.*

Background

Paragraph 19A of ISA (UK and Ireland) 700 establishes requirements with respect to the content of auditor's reports of entities that are required, and those that choose voluntarily, to report on how they have applied the UK Corporate Governance Code, or to explain why they have not.

An auditor's report for a group may include the auditor's report with respect to both the group and the parent company financial statements. This is typically the case where both sets of financial statements are presented in accordance with IFRS as adopted in the EU. However, the FRC's compendium of auditor's reports (Bulletin 2010/2) notes that, where the financial statements of the group and the parent company are presented in accordance with different financial reporting frameworks, the financial statements might be presented separately within the Annual Report and in such circumstances separate auditor's reports in respect of the group and the parent company financial statements might be provided within the Annual Report.

Issue

With respect to groups, some stakeholders have sought clarification as to whether the requirements of paragraph 19A are intended to apply with respect to the auditor's report(s) on both the group and the parent company financial statements of entities that are within the scope of Paragraph 19A, both when the auditor's reports thereon are combined in a single report and when they are provided separately.

The FRC's intention

The focus of the FRC's intention was that the requirements of paragraph 19A should apply primarily to the auditor's report on the group financial statements. The standard was not, however, written to exclude the application of the requirements to the separate audit of the individual parent company financial statements.

Further analysis

Most of the risks of material misstatement addressed in the audit of the parent company would likely also be risks of material misstatement in the audit of the group financial statements, subject to any differences in quantitative materiality considerations that may apply in those audits. However, the FRC recognises that there may be important risks of material misstatement that only arise in relation to the audit of the parent company financial statements (such as risks relating to investments in subsidiaries that could, for example, have implications for distributable reserves).

An understanding of such risks may be of interest to readers of auditor's reports where such risks have had the greatest effect on the overall audit strategy for the parent company audit.

Readers may find such risks to be of particular interest when their implications are relevant in the context of the parent company's reported distributable reserves. However, readers of the auditor's report(s) on the group and parent company financial statements will be assisted by avoiding unnecessary duplication or disaggregation of matters arising from these audits in such report(s).

Application where there is a single auditor's report

Where the auditor's reports on both the group and parent company financial statements are combined within a single report, it may be appropriate for any relevant risks and other information required by paragraph 19A that are unique to the parent company audit to be separately identified but integrated within the disclosures in that report of corresponding matters arising from the audit of the group financial statements.

Application where the auditor reports separately on the group and parent company financial statements

Where the auditor provides separate auditor's reports on the group and parent company financial statements, it may also be appropriate for any relevant risks and other information required by paragraph 19A that are unique to the parent company audit to be separately identified but integrated within the disclosures within the group auditor's report of corresponding matters arising from the group audit. Where this is so, the parent company auditor's report could make reference to this fact in the other matter paragraph that refers to the separate auditor's report on the group financial statements rather than repeating the information.

INTERNATIONAL STANDARD ON AUDITING (UK AND IRELAND) 700 (REVISED SEPTEMBER 2014)

THE INDEPENDENT AUDITOR'S REPORT ON FINANCIAL STATEMENTS

(Effective for audits of financial statements for periods commencing on or after 1 October 2014)

CONTENTS

International Standard on Auditing (UK and Ireland) (ISA (UK and Ireland) 700, "The Independent Auditor's Report on Financial Statements (Revised September 2014)" should be read in conjunction with ISA (UK and Ireland) 200, "Overall Objectives of the Independent Auditor and the Conduct of an Audit in Accordance with International Standards on Auditing (UK and Ireland)."

NOTE: The FRC has not at this time adopted ISA 700 "Forming an Opinion and Reporting on Financial Statements". The FRC has instead issued ISA (UK and Ireland) 700 "The Independent Auditor's Report on Financial Statements (Revised September 2014)". The main effect of this is that the form of auditor's reports may not be exactly aligned with the precise format required by ISA 700 issued by the IAASB. However, ISA (UK and Ireland) 700 (Revised September 2014) has been drafted such that compliance with it will not preclude the auditor from being able to assert compliance with the ISAs issued by the IAASB.

Introduction

Scope of this ISA (UK and Ireland)

1.   This International Standard on Auditing (UK and Ireland) (ISA (UK and Ireland)) establishes standards and provides guidance on the form and content of the auditor's report issued as a result of an audit performed by an independent auditor of the financial statements.

2.   This ISA (UK and Ireland) is written to address both "true and fair frameworks[1]" and "compliance frameworks". A "true and fair framework" is one that requires compliance with the framework but which acknowledges that to achieve a true and fair view:

(a)   It may be necessary to provide disclosures additional to those specifically required by the framework[2]; and

(b)   It may be necessary to depart from a requirement of the framework[3].

A "compliance framework" is one that requires compliance with the framework and does not contain the acknowledgements in (a) or (b) above.

3.   Illustrative examples of auditor's reports tailored for use with audits conducted in accordance with ISAs (UK and Ireland) are provided in compendia Bulletins issued by the FRC[4]. Illustrative examples of auditor's reports on regulatory returns are provided in various Practice Notes issued by the FRC.

4.   ISA (UK and Ireland) 705 and ISA (UK and Ireland) 706 deal with how the form and content of the auditor's report are affected when the auditor expresses a modified opinion or includes an Emphasis of Matter paragraph or an Other Matter paragraph in the auditor's report.

---

[1]   True and fair frameworks are sometimes referred to as "fair presentation frameworks".

[2]   In the IFRS Framework this is acknowledged in paragraph 17(c) of IAS 1. In UK GAAP this is acknowledged in Sections 396(4) and 404(4) of the Companies Act 2006. Under Generally Accepted Accounting Practice in Ireland this is acknowledged, for example, in Section 3(c) of the Companies (Amendment) Act 1986 and Regulation 14 of the European Communities (Companies: Group Accounts) Regulations 1992.

[3]   This is sometimes referred to as the "true and fair override". In the IFRS Framework this is acknowledged in paragraph 19 of IAS 1. In UK GAAP this is acknowledged in Sections 396(5) and 404(5) of the Companies Act 2006. Under Generally Accepted Accounting Practice in Ireland this is acknowledged, for example, in Section 3(d) of the Companies (Amendment) Act 1986 and Regulation 14(3) of the European Communities (Companies: Group Accounts) Regulations 1992.

[4]   At the date of publication of this ISA (UK and Ireland), Bulletins 2010/2 (Revised) "Compendium of Illustrative Auditor's Reports on United Kingdom Private Sector Financial Statements for periods ended on or after 15 December 2010" and 1(I) "Compendium of Illustrative Auditor's Reports on Irish Financial Statements" were the current compendia Bulletins.

Status of this ISA (UK and Ireland)

5.   Paragraph 43 of ISA 700, "Forming an opinion and reporting on financial statements," as issued by the IAASB specifies the minimum elements of auditor's reports where the regulation of a specific jurisdiction specify wording of the auditor's report. Reports prepared in accordance with ISA (UK and Ireland) 700 contain those minimum elements and consequently compliance with this ISA (UK and Ireland) does not preclude the auditor from being able to assert compliance with International Standards on Auditing issued by the IAASB.

Effective Date

6.   This ISA (UK and Ireland) is effective for audits of financial statements for periods commencing on or after 1 October 2014.

Objectives

7.   The objectives of the auditor are to:

(a)   Form an opinion on the financial statements based on an evaluation of the conclusions drawn from the audit evidence obtained; and

(b)   Express clearly that opinion through a written report that also describes the basis for the opinion.

Requirements

Forming an Opinion on the Financial Statements

8.   The auditor's report on the financial statements shall contain a clear written expression of opinion on the financial statements taken as a whole, based on the auditor evaluating the conclusions drawn from the audit evidence obtained, including evaluating whether:

(a)   Sufficient appropriate audit evidence as to whether the financial statements as a whole are free from material misstatement, whether due to fraud or error has been obtained;

(b)   Uncorrected misstatements are material, individually or in aggregate. This evaluation shall include consideration of the qualitative aspects of the entity's accounting practices, including indicators of possible bias in management's judgments; (Ref: Para. A1-A3)

(c)   In respect of a true and fair framework, the financial statements, including the related notes, give a true and fair view; and

(d) In respect of all frameworks the financial statements have been prepared in all material respects in accordance with the framework, including the requirements of applicable law.

9.   In particular, the auditor shall evaluate whether:

(a) The financial statements adequately refer to or describe the relevant financial reporting framework;

(b) The financial statements adequately disclose the significant accounting policies selected and applied;

(c) The accounting policies selected and applied are consistent with the applicable financial reporting framework, and are appropriate in the circumstances;

(d) Accounting estimates are reasonable;

(e) The information presented in the financial statements is relevant, reliable, comparable and understandable;

(f) The financial statements provide adequate disclosures to enable the intended users to understand the effect of material transactions and events on the information conveyed in the financial statements; and

(g) The terminology used in the financial statements, including the title of each financial statement, is appropriate.

10. With respect to compliance frameworks an unqualified opinion on the financial statements shall be expressed only when the auditor concludes that they have been prepared in accordance with the identified financial reporting framework, including the requirements of applicable law.

11. With respect to true and fair frameworks an unqualified opinion on the financial statements shall be expressed only when the auditor concludes that they have been prepared in accordance with the identified financial reporting framework, including the requirements of applicable law, and the financial statements give a true and fair view.

Auditor's Report

Title

12. The auditor's report shall have an appropriate title. (Ref: Para A4)

Addressee

13. The auditor's report shall be appropriately addressed as required by the circumstances of the engagement. (Ref: Para A5)

Introductory Paragraph

14. The auditor's report shall identify the financial statements of the entity that have been audited, including the date of, and period covered by, the financial statements.

Respective Responsibilities of Those Charged with Governance and Auditors

15. The auditor's report shall include a statement that those charged with governance are responsible for the preparation of the financial statements and a statement that the responsibility of the auditor is to audit and express an opinion on the financial statements in accordance with applicable legal requirements and International Standards on Auditing (UK and Ireland). The report shall also state that those standards require the auditor to comply with the APB's Ethical Standards for Auditors. (Ref: Para A6 - A7)

Description of the Generic Scope of an Audit

16. The auditor's report shall include a description of the generic scope of an audit by either:

    (a) Cross referring to the applicable version of a "Statement of the Scope of an Audit" that is maintained on the FRC's web-site; or

    (b) Cross referring to a "Statement of the Scope of an Audit" that is included elsewhere within the Annual Report; or

    (c) Including verbatim within the report the following:

        "An audit involves obtaining evidence about the amounts and disclosures in the financial statements sufficient to give reasonable assurance that the financial statements are free from material misstatement, whether caused by fraud or error. This includes an assessment of: whether the accounting policies are appropriate to the *[describe nature of entity]* circumstances and have been consistently applied and adequately disclosed; the reasonableness of significant accounting estimates made by *[describe those charged with governance]*; and the overall presentation of the financial statements. In addition, we read all the financial and non-financial information in the *[describe the annual report]* to identify material inconsistencies with the audited financial statements and to identify any information that is apparently materially incorrect based on, or materially inconsistent with, the knowledge acquired by us in the course of performing the audit. If we become aware of any apparent material misstatements or inconsistencies we consider the implications for our report." (Ref: Para A8 – A9)

Opinion on the Financial Statements

17. The opinion paragraph of the auditor's report shall clearly state the auditor's opinion as required by the relevant financial reporting framework used to prepare the financial statements, including applicable law.

18. When expressing an unqualified opinion on financial statements prepared in accordance with a true and fair framework the opinion paragraph shall clearly state that the financial statements give a true and fair view[5]. It is not sufficient for the auditor to conclude that the financial statements give a true and fair view solely on the basis that the financial statements were prepared in accordance with accounting standards and any other applicable legal requirements. (Ref: Para A10 – A12)

Opinion in Respect of an Additional Financial Reporting Framework

19. When an auditor is engaged to issue an opinion on the compliance of the financial statements with an additional financial reporting framework the second opinion shall be clearly separated from the first opinion on the financial statements, by use of an appropriate heading. (Ref: Para A13)

Entities that Report on Application of the UK Corporate Governance Code

19A. In the case of entities[6] that are required, and those that choose voluntarily, to report on how they have applied the UK Corporate Governance Code, or to explain why they have not, the auditor's report shall:

   (a) Describe those assessed risks of material misstatement that were identified by the auditor and which had the greatest effect on: the overall audit strategy; the allocation of resources in the audit; and directing the efforts of the engagement team;

   (b) Provide an explanation of how the auditor applied the concept of materiality in planning and performing the audit. Such explanation shall specify the threshold used by the auditor as being materiality for the financial statements as a whole[7]; and

   (c) Provide an overview of the scope of the audit[8], including an explanation of how such scope addressed the assessed risks of material misstatement disclosed in accordance with (a) and was influenced by the auditor's application of materiality disclosed in accordance with (b). (Ref. Para A13A – A13C)

---

[5] United Kingdom auditor's reports prepared in accordance with section 495(3) of the UK Companies Act 2006 will meet this requirement. Irish auditor's reports prepared in accordance with Section 193(4C) of the Irish Companies Act 1990 and, therefore, expressing an opinion in terms of "true and fair view, in accordance with the relevant financial reporting framework" also meets this requirement. This is supported by recital 10 of EU Directive 2003/51/EC which states "The fundamental requirement that an audit opinion states whether the annual or consolidated accounts give a true and fair view in accordance with the relevant financial reporting framework does not represent a restriction of the scope of that opinion but clarifies the context in which it is expressed".

[6] In the UK, these include companies with a Premium listing of equity shares regardless of whether they are incorporated in the UK or elsewhere. In Ireland, these include Irish incorporated companies with a primary or secondary listing of equity shares on the Irish Stock Exchange.

[7] As required by paragraph 10 of ISA (UK and Ireland) 320 "Materiality in Planning and Performing an Audit".

[8] See also paragraphs 15 and A11 to A15 of ISA (UK and Ireland) 260 "Communication with Those Charged with Governance" and paragraph 49 of ISA (UK and Ireland) 600 "Special considerations – Audits of Group Financial Statements (Including the Work of Component Auditors).

FINANCIAL REPORTING COUNCIL

19B. In order to be useful to users of the financial statements, the explanations of the matters required to be set out in the auditor's report by paragraph 19A shall be described:

- So as to enable a user to understand their significance in the context of the audit of the financial statements as a whole and not as discrete opinions on separate elements of the financial statements.

- In a way that enables them to be related directly to the specific circumstances of the audited entity and are not, therefore, generic or abstract matters expressed in standardised language.

- In a manner that complements the description of significant issues relating to the financial statements, required to be set out in the separate section of the annual report describing the work of the audit committee in discharging its responsibilities[9]. The auditor seeks to coordinate descriptions of overlapping topics addressed in these communications, to avoid duplication of reporting about them, whilst having appropriate regard to the separate responsibilities of the auditor and the board for directly communicating information primarily in their respective domains.

Requirement Specific to Public Sector Entities where an Opinion on Regularity is Given.

20. The auditor shall address other reporting responsibilities in [a] separate section[s] of the auditor's report following the opinion[s] on the financial statements and, where there is one, the opinion on regularity. (Ref: Para A14)

Opinions on Other Matters

21. When the auditor addresses other reporting responsibilities within the auditor's report on the financial statements, the opinion arising from such other responsibilities shall be set out in a separate section of the auditor's report following the opinion[s] on the financial statements or, where there is one, the opinion on regularity. (Ref: Para A15 – A16)

22. If the auditor is required to report on certain matters by exception the auditor shall describe its responsibilities under the heading "Matters on which we are required to report by exception" and incorporate a suitable conclusion in respect of such matters. (Ref: Para A17 - A18)

22A. In the case of entities that are required[6], and those that choose voluntarily, to report on how they have applied the UK Corporate Governance Code or to explain why they have not, the auditor shall report by exception if, when reading the other financial and non-financial information included in the annual report, the auditor has identified information that is materially inconsistent with the information in the audited financial

---

[9] In accordance with provision C.3.8 of the UK Corporate Governance Code.

statements or is apparently materially incorrect based on, or materially inconsistent with, the knowledge acquired by the auditor in the course of performing the audit or that is otherwise misleading. (Ref: Para A18A)

22B. Matters that the auditor shall report on by exception in accordance with paragraph 22A include circumstances where the annual report includes:

(a) A statement given by the directors that they consider the annual report and accounts taken as a whole is fair, balanced and understandable and provides the information necessary for shareholders to assess the entity's performance, business model and strategy, that is inconsistent with the knowledge acquired by the auditor in the course of performing the audit; or

(b) A section describing the work of the audit committee that does not appropriately address matters communicated by the auditor to the audit committee; or

(c) An explanation, as to why the annual report does not include such a statement or section, that is materially inconsistent with the knowledge acquired by the auditor in the course of performing the audit; or

(d) Other information that, in the auditor's judgment, contains a material inconsistency or a material misstatement of fact.

The auditor shall include a suitable conclusion on these matters in the auditor's report in accordance with paragraph 22 and, if applicable, shall describe why the auditor believes that any such statement, section, explanation or other information is materially inconsistent with the knowledge acquired by the auditor in the course of performing the audit or otherwise contains a material inconsistency or a material misstatement of fact. If a section of the annual report describing the work of the audit committee does not appropriately disclose any matters communicated by the auditor to the audit committee that in the auditor's judgment should have been disclosed, or if the annual report does not contain such a section, the auditor's report shall also include any such information.

Statement on the Directors' Assessment of the Principal Risks that Would Threaten the Solvency or Liquidity of the Entity

22C. In the case of entities that are required[6], and those that choose voluntarily, to report on how they have applied the UK Corporate Governance Code or to explain why they have not, the auditor shall, having regard to the work performed in accordance with the requirement of paragraph 17-2 of ISA (UK and Ireland) 570, give a statement as to whether the auditor has anything material to add or to draw attention to in relation to:

(a) The directors' confirmation in the annual report that they have carried out a robust assessment of the principal risks facing the entity, including those that would threaten its business model, future performance, solvency or liquidity,

(b) The disclosures in the annual report that describe those risks and explain how they are being managed or mitigated,

(c) The directors' statement in the financial statements about whether they considered it appropriate to adopt the going concern basis of accounting in preparing them, and their identification of any material uncertainties to the entity's ability to continue to do so over a period of at least twelve months from the date of approval of the financial statements, and

(d) The director's explanation in the annual report as to how they have assessed the prospects of the entity, over what period they have done so and why they consider that period to be appropriate, and their statement as to whether they have a reasonable expectation that the entity will be able to continue in operation and meet its liabilities as they fall due over the period of their assessment, including any related disclosures drawing attention to any necessary qualifications or assumptions.

Date of Report

23. The date of an auditor's report on a reporting entity's financial statements shall be the date on which the auditor signed the report expressing an opinion on those financial statements. (Ref. Para A19)

24. The auditor shall not sign, and hence date, the report earlier than the date on which all other information contained in a report of which the audited financial statements form a part have been approved by those charged with governance and the auditor has considered all necessary available evidence. (Ref. Para A20 – A23)

Location of Auditor's Office

25. The report shall name the location of the office where the auditor is based.

Auditor's Signature

26. The auditor's report shall state the name of the auditor and be signed and dated. (Ref. Para A24)

***

Application and Other Explanatory Material

Qualitative Aspects of the Entity's Accounting Practices (Ref: Para 8)

A1. Management makes a number of judgments about the amounts and disclosures in the financial statements.

A2. ISA (UK and Ireland) 260 contains a discussion of the qualitative aspects of accounting practices.[10] In considering the qualitative aspects of the entity's accounting practices, the auditor may become aware of possible bias in

---

[10] ISA (UK and Ireland) 260, "Communication with Those Charged with Governance," Appendix 2.

management's judgments. The auditor may conclude that the cumulative effect of a lack of neutrality, together with the effect of uncorrected misstatements, causes the financial statements as a whole to be materially misstated. Indicators of a lack of neutrality that may affect the auditor's evaluation of whether the financial statements as a whole are materially misstated include the following:

- The selective correction of misstatements brought to management's attention during the audit (e.g., correcting misstatements with the effect of increasing reported earnings, but not correcting misstatements that have the effect of decreasing reported earnings).

- Possible management bias in the making of accounting estimates.

A3. ISA (UK and Ireland) 540 addresses possible management bias in making accounting estimates.[11] Indicators of possible management bias do not constitute misstatements for purposes of drawing conclusions on the reasonableness of individual accounting estimates. They may, however, affect the auditor's evaluation of whether the financial statements as a whole are free from material misstatement.

Auditor's Report

Title (Ref: Para 12)

A4. The term "Independent Auditor" is usually used in the title in order to distinguish the auditor's report from reports that might be issued by others, such as by those charged with governance, or from the reports of other auditors who may not have to comply with the APB's Ethical Standards for Auditors.

Addressee (Ref: Para 13)

A5. The Companies Acts[12] require the auditor to report to the company's members because the audit is undertaken on their behalf. Such auditor's reports are, therefore, typically addressed to either the members or the shareholders of the company. The auditor's report on financial statements of other types of reporting entity is addressed to the appropriate person or persons, as defined by statute or by the terms of the individual engagement.

Respective Responsibilities of Those Charged with Governance and Auditors (Ref: Para 15)

A6. An appreciation of the interrelationship between the responsibilities of those who prepare financial statements and those who audit them facilitates an understanding of the nature and context of the opinion expressed by the auditor.

---

[11] ISA (UK and Ireland) 540, "Auditing Accounting Estimates, Including Fair Value Accounting Estimates, and Related Disclosures," paragraph 21.

[12] In the United Kingdom the Companies Act 2006 establishes this requirement. In Ireland the Companies Acts 1963 to 2006 establish this requirement.

A7.   The preparation of financial statements requires those charged with governance to make significant accounting estimates and judgments, as well as to determine the appropriate accounting principles and methods used in preparation of the financial statements. This determination will be made in the context of the financial reporting framework that those charged with governance choose, or are required, to use. In contrast, the auditor's responsibility is to audit the financial statements in order to express an opinion on them.

Description of the Generic Scope of an Audit (Ref: Para 16)

A8.   The FRC maintains on its web-site generic descriptions of the scope of an audit of the financial statements of private sector entities[13]. These descriptions address the auditor's responsibilities under ISAs (UK and Ireland).

A9.   Where the generic scope of the audit is described within the Annual Report but not in the auditor's report, such description includes the prescribed text set out in paragraph 16 (c). The content of the description of the generic scope of the audit is determined by the auditor regardless of whether it is incorporated into the auditor's report or published as a separate statement elsewhere in the annual report.

Opinion on the Financial Statements (Ref: Para 18)

A10. Although the "true and fair" concept has been central to accounting and auditing practice in the UK and Ireland for many years it is not defined in legislation. In 2008, the Financial Reporting Council published a legal opinion, that it had commissioned, entitled "The true and fair requirement revisited" (The Opinion)[14]. The Opinion confirms the overarching nature of the true and fair requirement to the preparation of financial statements in the United Kingdom, whether they are prepared in accordance with international or national accounting standards[15].

A11. The Opinion states that "The preparation of financial statements is not a mechanical process where compliance with relevant accounting standards will automatically ensure that those financial statements show a true and fair view, or a fair presentation. Such compliance may be highly likely to produce such an outcome; but it does not guarantee it".

A12. To advise the reader of the context in which the auditor's opinion is expressed, the auditor's opinion indicates the financial reporting framework upon which the financial statements are based. The financial reporting framework is normally one of:

   • "International Financial Reporting Standards (IFRSs) as adopted by the European Union", and the national law that is applicable when using IFRSs

---

[13] The web-site reference relevant to the UK is www.frc.org.uk/auditscopeukprivate and the web-site reference relevant to Ireland is www.frc.org.uk/audit-scope-ireland.

[14] The opinion can be downloaded from the FRC web-site at http://www.frc.org.uk/about/trueandfair.cfm

[15] UK and Irish law differ but follow similar principles.

and, in the case of consolidated financial statements of publicly traded companies[16], Article 4 of the IAS Regulation (1606/2002/EC); or

- "Generally Accepted Accounting Practice in Ireland", which comprises applicable Irish law and accounting standards issued by the Financial Reporting Council (FRC) and promulgated by the Institute of Chartered Accountants in Ireland; or

- "UK Generally Accepted Accounting Practice", which comprises applicable UK law and UK Accounting Standards as issued by the FRC.

Opinion in Respect of an Additional Financial Reporting Framework (Ref: Para 19)

A13. The financial statements of some entities may comply with two financial reporting frameworks (for example "IFRSs as issued by the IASB" and "IFRSs as adopted by the European Union" and those charged with governance may engage the auditor to express an opinion in respect of both frameworks. Once the auditor is satisfied that there are no differences between the two financial reporting frameworks that affect the financial statements being reported on, the auditor states a second separate opinion with regard to the other financial reporting framework.

Entities that Report on Application of the UK Corporate Governance Code

A13A. Such assessed risks of material misstatement are likely to have been identified by the auditor in meeting the requirements of ISA (UK and Ireland) 315 "Identifying and assessing the risks of material misstatement through understanding the entity and its environment"[17], including those relating to significant risks. However, the auditor uses its judgment to determine which, if any, of the significant risks and which, if any, of the other identified risks meet the criteria set out in paragraph 19A(a) and are to be described in the auditor's report. If the auditor significantly revises its risk assessment during the audit the auditor considers whether to disclose that fact and the circumstances giving rise to the changed assessment.

A13B. The explanation, of how the auditor applied the concept of materiality in planning and performing the audit, is tailored to the particular circumstances and complexity of the audit and, in addition to specifying the threshold used by the auditor as being materiality for the financial statements as a whole, might include, for example:

- Materiality level or levels for those classes of transactions, account balances or disclosures where such materiality levels are lower than materiality for the financial statements as a whole (as described in paragraph 10 of ISA (UK and Ireland) 320).

---

[16] A publicly traded company is one whose securities are admitted to trading on a regulated market in any Member State in the European Union.

[17] The relevant section of the ISA (UK and Ireland) is "Identifying and Assessing the Risks of Material Misstatement" (paragraphs 25 to 31).

- Performance materiality (as described in paragraph 11 of ISA (UK and Ireland) 320).

- Any significant revisions of materiality thresholds that were made as the audit progressed.

- The threshold used for reporting unadjusted differences to the audit committee.

- Significant qualitative considerations relating to the auditor's evaluation of materiality.

A13C.The content of the overview of the scope of the audit is tailored to the particular circumstances of the audit and how the scope was influenced by the auditor's application of materiality and addressed the assessed risks of material misstatement described in the auditor's report. Such a summary might also include, for example:

- The coverage of revenue, total assets and profit before tax achieved.

- The coverage of revenue, total assets and profit before tax of reportable segments achieved.

- The number of locations visited by the auditor as a proportion of the total number of locations, and the rationale underlying any programme of visits.

- The effect of the group structure on the scope. The audit approach to a group consisting of autonomous subsidiary companies may differ from that applied to one which consists of a number of non-autonomous divisions.

- The nature and extent of the group auditor's involvement in the work of component auditors.

Requirement Specific to Public Sector Entities where an Opinion on Regularity is Given. (Ref: Para 20)

A14. For the audit of certain public sector entities the audit mandate may require the auditor to express an opinion on regularity[18]. Regularity is the requirement that financial transactions are in accordance with the legislation authorising them.

Opinion on Other Matters (Ref: Para 21 – 22B)

A15. The auditor sets out its opinion[s] on these other reporting responsibilities in [a] separate section[s] of the report in order to clearly distinguish it from the auditor's opinion[s] on the financial statements.

---

[18] Guidance for auditors of public sector bodies in the UK and Ireland is given in Practice Note 10 "Audit of Financial Statements of Public Sector Bodies in the United Kingdom (Revised)" and Practice Note 10 (I) "Audit of Central Government Financial Statements in the Republic of Ireland".

A16. Other reporting responsibilities may be determined by specific statutory requirements applicable to the reporting entity, or, in some circumstances, by the terms of the auditor's engagement[19]. Such matters may be required to be dealt with by either:

(a)   a positive statement in the auditor's report; or

(b)   by exception.

An example of (a) arises where the auditor of a company is required to state whether, in the auditor's opinion, the information given in the directors' report for the financial year for which the accounts are prepared is consistent with those accounts[20]. An example of (b) arises in the United Kingdom where company legislation requires the auditor of a company to report when a company has not maintained adequate accounting records[21]. An example of (b) arises in Ireland where company legislation requires the auditor to report when the disclosures of directors' remuneration and transactions specified by law are not made[22].

A17. Where the auditor has discharged such responsibilities and has nothing to report in respect of them, the conclusion could be expressed in the form of the following phrase: "We have nothing to report in respect of the following".

A18. Where the auditor expresses a modified conclusion in respect of other reporting responsibilities (including those on which they are required to report by exception) this may give rise to a modification of the auditor's opinion on the financial statements. For example, if adequate accounting records have not been maintained and as a result it proves impracticable for the auditor to obtain sufficient appropriate evidence concerning material matters in the financial statements, the auditor's report on the financial statements includes a qualified opinion or disclaimer of opinion arising from that limitation.[23]

A18A. For entities that apply the UK Corporate Governance Code, the directors are required to give a statement in the annual report that they consider the annual report and accounts taken as a whole is fair, balanced and understandable and provides the information necessary for shareholders to assess the entity's performance, business model and strategy. Such entities are also required to include a separate section of the annual report that describes the work of the audit committee in discharging its responsibilities. This should include, inter alia, the significant issues that the audit committee considered in relation to the financial statements, including appropriate matters considered that were communicated to it by the auditor, and how these issues were addressed.

---

[19] An example of a reporting responsibility determined by the terms of the auditor's engagement is where the directors of a listed company are required by the rules of a Listing Authority to ensure that the auditor reviews certain statements made by the directors before the annual report is published.

[20] In the UK section 496 of the Companies Act 2006 and in Ireland section 15 of Companies (Amendment Act) 1986.

[21] Section 498(2) of the Companies Act 2006

[22] Section 191(8) of the Companies Act 1963 and section 46 of the Companies Act 1990.

[23] International Standard on Auditing (UK and Ireland) 705 "Modifications to the opinion in the independent auditor's report" sets out the requirements relating to qualified opinions and disclaimer of opinions on financial statements.

Date of Report (Ref: Para 23 – 24)

A19. This informs the reader that the auditor has considered the effect on the financial statements and on the auditor's report of events and transactions of which the auditor became aware and that occurred up to that date.

A20. The auditor is not in a position to form the opinion until the financial statements (and any other information contained in a report of which the audited financial statements form a part) have been approved by those charged with governance and the auditor has completed the assessment of all the evidence the auditor considers necessary for the opinion or opinions to be given in the auditor's report. This assessment includes events occurring up to the date the opinion is expressed. The auditor, therefore, plans the conduct of the audit to take account of the need to ensure, before expressing an opinion on financial statements, that those charged with governance have approved the financial statements and any accompanying other information and that the auditor has completed a sufficient review of post balance sheet events.

A21. The date of the auditor's report is, therefore, the date on which the auditor signs the auditor's report expressing an opinion on the financial statements for distribution with those financial statements, following:

    (a) Receipt of the financial statements and accompanying documents in the form approved by those charged with governance for release;

    (b) Review of all documents which the auditor is required to consider in addition to the financial statements (for example the directors' report, chairman's statement or other review of an entity's affairs which will accompany the financial statements): and

    (c) Completion of all procedures necessary to form an opinion on the financial statements (and any other opinions required by law or regulation) including a review of post balance sheet events,

A22. The form of the financial statements and other information approved by those charged with governance, and considered by the auditor when signing a report expressing the auditor's opinion, may be in the form of final drafts from which printed documents will be prepared. Subsequent production of printed copies of the financial statements and the auditor's report does not constitute the creation of a new document. Copies of the report produced for circulation to shareholders or others may, therefore, reproduce a printed version of the auditor's signature showing the date of actual signature.

A23. If the date on which the auditor signs the report is later than that on which those charged with governance approved the financial statements, the auditor takes such steps as are appropriate:

    (a) To obtain assurance that those charged with governance would have approved the financial statements on that later date (for example, by obtaining confirmation from specified individual members of the Board to whom authority has been delegated for this purpose); and

(b)   To ensure that its procedures for reviewing subsequent events cover the period up to that date.

Auditor's Signature (Ref: Para 26)

A24. The report is signed in the name of the audit firm, the personal name of the auditor or both, as required by law. In the case of a UK company and certain other entities UK law requires:

(a)   where the auditor is an individual that the report is signed by the individual; or

(b)   where the auditor is a firm that the report is signed by the senior statutory auditor[24] in his or her own name, for and on behalf of the auditor.

In the case of an Irish company and certain other entities Irish law requires:

- where the auditor is a statutory auditor (a natural person) that the report is signed by that person; or

- where the auditor is a statutory audit firm:

  o   that the report is signed by the statutory auditor designated by the statutory audit firm as being primarily responsible for carrying out the statutory audit on behalf of the audit firm; or

  o   in the case of a group audit at least the statutory auditor designated by the statutory audit firm as being primarily responsible for carrying out the statutory audit at the level of the group;

in his or her own name, for and on behalf of, the audit firm[25].

---

[24] See Bulletin 2008/6 "The "Senior Statutory Auditor" under the United Kingdom Companies Act 2006". That Bulletin at paragraphs 8-10 also explains the meaning of "signing the auditor's report" in a UK context.

[25] See Statutory Instrument 220 of 2010.

INTERNATIONAL STANDARD ON AUDITING (UK AND IRELAND) 705 (REVISED OCTOBER 2012)

MODIFICATIONS TO THE OPINION IN THE INDEPENDENT AUDITOR'S REPORT

(Effective for audits of financial statements for periods commencing on or after 1 October 2012)

CONTENTS

International Standard on Auditing (UK and Ireland) (ISA (UK and Ireland)) 705, "Modifications to the Opinion in the Independent Auditor's Report" should be read in conjunction with ISA (UK and Ireland) 200, "Overall Objectives of the Independent Auditor and the Conduct of an Audit in Accordance with International Standards on Auditing (UK and Ireland)."

Introduction

Scope of this ISA (UK and Ireland)

1. This International Standard on Auditing (UK and Ireland) (ISA (UK and Ireland)) deals with the auditor's responsibility to issue an appropriate report in circumstances when, in forming an opinion in accordance with ISA (UK and Ireland) 700,[1] the auditor concludes that a modification to the auditor's opinion on the financial statements is necessary.

Types of Modified Opinions

2. This ISA (UK and Ireland) establishes three types of modified opinions, namely, a qualified opinion, an adverse opinion, and a disclaimer of opinion. The decision regarding which type of modified opinion is appropriate depends upon:

    (a) The nature of the matter giving rise to the modification, that is, whether the financial statements are materially misstated or, in the case of an inability to obtain sufficient appropriate audit evidence, may be materially misstated; and

    (b) The auditor's judgment about the pervasiveness of the effects or possible effects of the matter on the financial statements. (Ref: Para. A1)

Effective Date

3. This ISA (UK and Ireland) is effective for audits of financial statements for periods commencing on or after 1 October 2012. Earlier adoption is permitted.

Objective

4. The objective of the auditor is to express clearly an appropriately modified opinion on the financial statements that is necessary when:

    (a) The auditor concludes, based on the audit evidence obtained, that the financial statements as a whole are not free from material misstatement; or

    (b) The auditor is unable to obtain sufficient appropriate audit evidence to conclude that the financial statements as a whole are free from material misstatement.

Definitions

5. For purposes of the ISAs (UK and Ireland), the following terms have the meanings attributed below:

---

[1] ISA (UK and Ireland) 700, "The Auditor's Report on Financial Statements."

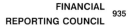

(a) Pervasive – A term used, in the context of misstatements, to describe the effects on the financial statements of misstatements or the possible effects on the financial statements of misstatements, if any, that are undetected due to an inability to obtain sufficient appropriate audit evidence. Pervasive effects on the financial statements are those that, in the auditor's judgment:

    (i) Are not confined to specific elements, accounts or items of the financial statements;

    (ii) If so confined, represent or could represent a substantial proportion of the financial statements; or

    (iii) In relation to disclosures, are fundamental to users' understanding of the financial statements.

(b) Modified opinion – A qualified opinion, an adverse opinion or a disclaimer of opinion.

Requirements

Circumstances When a Modification to the Auditor's Opinion Is Required

6. The auditor shall modify the opinion in the auditor's report when:

(a) The auditor concludes that, based on the audit evidence obtained, the financial statements as a whole are not free from material misstatement; or (Ref: Para. A2-A7)

(b) The auditor is unable to obtain sufficient appropriate audit evidence to conclude that the financial statements as a whole are free from material misstatement. (Ref: Para. A8-A12)

Determining the Type of Modification to the Auditor's Opinion

Qualified Opinion

7. The auditor shall express a qualified opinion when:

(a) The auditor, having obtained sufficient appropriate audit evidence, concludes that misstatements, individually or in the aggregate, are material, but not pervasive, to the financial statements; or

(b) The auditor is unable to obtain sufficient appropriate audit evidence on which to base the opinion, but the auditor concludes that the possible effects on the financial statements of undetected misstatements, if any, could be material but not pervasive.

Adverse Opinion

8.   The auditor shall express an adverse opinion when the auditor, having obtained sufficient appropriate audit evidence, concludes that misstatements, individually or in the aggregate, are both material and pervasive to the financial statements.

Disclaimer of Opinion

9.   The auditor shall disclaim an opinion when the auditor is unable to obtain sufficient appropriate audit evidence on which to base the opinion, and the auditor concludes that the possible effects on the financial statements of undetected misstatements, if any, could be both material and pervasive.

10.   The auditor shall disclaim an opinion when, in extremely rare circumstances involving multiple uncertainties, the auditor concludes that, notwithstanding having obtained sufficient appropriate audit evidence regarding each of the individual uncertainties, it is not possible to form an opinion on the financial statements due to the potential interaction of the uncertainties and their possible cumulative effect on the financial statements.

Consequence of an Inability to Obtain Sufficient Appropriate Audit Evidence Due to a Management-Imposed Limitation after the Auditor Has Accepted the Engagement

11.   If, after accepting the engagement, the auditor becomes aware that management has imposed a limitation on the scope of the audit that the auditor considers likely to result in the need to express a qualified opinion or to disclaim an opinion on the financial statements, the auditor shall request that management remove the limitation.

12.   If management refuses to remove the limitation referred to in paragraph 11, the auditor shall communicate the matter to those charged with governance, unless all of those charged with governance are involved in managing the entity,[2] and determine whether it is possible to perform alternative procedures to obtain sufficient appropriate audit evidence.

13.   If the auditor is unable to obtain sufficient appropriate audit evidence, the auditor shall determine the implications as follows:

(a)   If the auditor concludes that the possible effects on the financial statements of undetected misstatements, if any, could be material but not pervasive, the auditor shall qualify the opinion; or

(b)   If the auditor concludes that the possible effects on the financial statements of undetected misstatements, if any, could be both material and pervasive so that a qualification of the opinion would be inadequate to communicate the gravity of the situation, the auditor shall:

---

[2]   ISA (UK and Ireland) 260, "Communication with Those Charged with Governance," paragraph 13.

(i)   Withdraw from the audit, where practicable and possible under applicable law or regulation; or (Ref: Para. A13-A14)

(ii)   If withdrawal from the audit before issuing the auditor's report is not practicable or possible, disclaim an opinion on the financial statements.

14.   If the auditor withdraws as contemplated by paragraph 13(b)(i), before withdrawing, the auditor shall communicate to those charged with governance any matters regarding misstatements identified during the audit that would have given rise to a modification of the opinion. (Ref: Para. A15 – A15-1)

Other Considerations Relating to an Adverse Opinion or Disclaimer of Opinion

15.   When the auditor considers it necessary to express an adverse opinion or disclaim an opinion on the financial statements as a whole, the auditor's report shall not also include an unmodified opinion with respect to the same financial reporting framework on a single financial statement or one or more specific elements, accounts or items of a financial statement. To include such an unmodified opinion in the same report[3] in these circumstances would contradict the auditor's adverse opinion or disclaimer of opinion on the financial statements as a whole. (Ref: Para. A16)

Form and Content of the Auditor's Report When the Opinion Is Modified

Basis for Modification Paragraph

16.   When the auditor modifies the opinion on the financial statements, the auditor shall, in addition to the specific elements required by ISA (UK and Ireland) 700, include a paragraph in the auditor's report that provides a description of the matter giving rise to the modification. The auditor shall place this paragraph immediately before the opinion paragraph in the auditor's report and use the heading "Basis for Qualified Opinion on Financial Statements," "Basis for Adverse Opinion on Financial Statements," or "Basis for Disclaimer of Opinion on Financial Statements," as appropriate. (Ref: Para. A17)

17.   If there is a material misstatement of the financial statements that relates to specific amounts in the financial statements (including quantitative disclosures), the auditor shall include in the basis for modification paragraph a description and quantification of the financial effects of the misstatement, unless impracticable. If it is not practicable to quantify the financial effects, the auditor shall so state in the basis for modification paragraph. (Ref: Para. A18)

---

[3] ISA 805, "Special Considerations—Audits of Single Financial Statements and Specific Elements, Accounts or Items of a Financial Statement," deals with circumstances where the auditor is engaged to express a separate opinion on one or more specific elements, accounts or items of a financial statement.
ISA 805 has not been promulgated by the FRC for application in the UK and Ireland.

18.   If there is a material misstatement of the financial statements that relates to narrative disclosures, the auditor shall include in the basis for modification paragraph an explanation of how the disclosures are misstated.

19.   If there is a material misstatement of the financial statements that relates to the non-disclosure of information required to be disclosed, the auditor shall:

   (a)   Discuss the non-disclosure with those charged with governance;

   (b)   Describe in the basis for modification paragraph the nature of the omitted information; and

   (c)   Unless prohibited by law or regulation, include the omitted disclosures, provided it is practicable to do so and the auditor has obtained sufficient appropriate audit evidence about the omitted information. (Ref: Para. A19)

20.   If the modification results from an inability to obtain sufficient appropriate audit evidence, the auditor shall include in the basis for modification paragraph the reasons for that inability.

21.   Even If the auditor has expressed an adverse opinion or disclaimed an opinion on the financial statements, the auditor shall describe in the basis for modification paragraph the reasons for any other matters of which the auditor is aware that would have required a modification to the opinion, and the effects thereof. (Ref: Para. A20)

Opinion on the Financial Statements Paragraph

22.   When the auditor modifies the audit opinion, the auditor shall use the heading "Qualified Opinion on Financial Statements," "Adverse Opinion on Financial Statements," or "Disclaimer of Opinion on Financial Statements," as appropriate, for the opinion paragraph. (Ref: Para. A21, A23-A24)

23.   When the auditor expresses a qualified opinion due to a material misstatement in the financial statements, the auditor shall state in the Qualified Opinion on Financial Statements paragraph that, in the auditor's opinion, except for the effects of the matter(s) described in the Basis for Qualified Opinion paragraph:

   (a)   The financial statements present fairly, in all material respects (or give a true and fair view when reporting in accordance with a fair presentation framework[3a]; or

   (b)   The financial statements have been prepared, in all material respects, in accordance with the applicable financial reporting framework when reporting in accordance with a compliance framework.

[3a] Auditor's reports prepared in accordance with Section 193 (4C) of the Irish Companies Act 1990 will express the opinion in terms of "true and fair view in accordance with the relevant financial reporting framework".

When the modification arises from an inability to obtain sufficient appropriate audit evidence, the auditor shall use the corresponding phrase "except for the possible effects of the matter(s) ..." for the modified opinion. (Ref: Para. A22)

24. When the auditor expresses an adverse opinion, the auditor shall state in the Qualified Opinion on Financial Statements paragraph that, in the auditor's opinion, because of the significance of the matter(s) described in the Basis for Adverse Opinion paragraph:

    (a) The financial statements do not present fairly (or give a true and fair view) when reporting in accordance with a fair presentation framework[4]; or

    (b) The financial statements have not been prepared, in all material respects, in accordance with the applicable financial reporting framework when reporting in accordance with a compliance framework.

25. When the auditor disclaims an opinion due to an inability to obtain sufficient appropriate audit evidence, the auditor shall state in the Qualified Opinion on Financial Statements paragraph that:

    (a) Because of the significance of the matter(s) described in the Basis for Disclaimer of Opinion paragraph, the auditor has not been able to obtain sufficient appropriate audit evidence to provide a basis for an audit opinion; and, accordingly,

    (b) The auditor does not express an opinion on the financial statements.

26. *[Deliberately left blank]*

Description of Auditor's Responsibility When the Auditor Disclaims an Opinion

27. When the auditor disclaims an opinion due to an inability to obtain sufficient appropriate audit evidence, the auditor shall amend the introductory paragraph of the auditor's report to state that the auditor was engaged to audit the financial statements.

Communication with Those Charged with Governance

28. When the auditor expects to modify the opinion in the auditor's report, the auditor shall communicate with those charged with governance the circumstances that led to the expected modification and the proposed wording of the modification. (Ref: Para. A25)

***

Application and Other Explanatory Material

Types of Modified Opinions (Ref: Para. 2)

A1. The table below illustrates how the auditor's judgment about the nature of the matter giving rise to the modification, and the pervasiveness of its effects or possible effects on the financial statements, affects the type of opinion to be expressed.

Nature of Matter Giving Rise to the Modification	Auditor's Judgment about the Pervasiveness of the Effects or Possible Effects on the Financial Statements	
	Material but Not Pervasive	Material and Pervasive
Financial statements are materially misstated	Qualified opinion	Adverse opinion
Inability to obtain sufficient appropriate audit evidence	Qualified opinion	Disclaimer of opinion

Nature of Material Misstatements (Ref: Para. 6(a))

A2. ISA (UK and Ireland) 700 requires the auditor, in order to form an opinion on the financial statements, to conclude as to whether reasonable assurance has been obtained about whether the financial statements as a whole are free from material misstatement.[4] This conclusion takes into account the auditor's evaluation of uncorrected misstatements, if any, on the financial statements in accordance with ISA (UK and Ireland) 450.[5]

A3. ISA (UK and Ireland) 450 defines a misstatement as a difference between the amount, classification, presentation, or disclosure of a reported financial statement item and the amount, classification, presentation, or disclosure that is required for the item to be in accordance with the applicable financial reporting framework. Accordingly, a material misstatement of the financial statements may arise in relation to:

(a) The appropriateness of the selected accounting policies;

(b) The application of the selected accounting policies; or

(c) The appropriateness or adequacy of disclosures in the financial statements.

Appropriateness of the Selected Accounting Policies

A4. In relation to the appropriateness of the accounting policies management has selected, material misstatements of the financial statements may arise when:

---

[4] ISA 700, paragraph 11.

The FRC has not promulgated ISA 700 as issued by the IAASB for application in the UK and Ireland. In the UK and Ireland the applicable auditing standard is ISA (UK and Ireland) 700, "The Auditor's Report on Financial Statements." Paragraph 8 of ISA (UK and Ireland) 700 requires evaluation of whether sufficient appropriate audit evidence has been obtained.

[5] ISA (UK and Ireland) 450, "Evaluation of Misstatements Identified during the Audit," paragraph 11.

(a) The selected accounting policies are not consistent with the applicable financial reporting framework; or

(b) The financial statements, including the related notes, do not represent the underlying transactions and events in a manner that achieves fair presentation.

A5. Financial reporting frameworks often contain requirements for the accounting for, and disclosure of, changes in accounting policies. Where the entity has changed its selection of significant accounting policies, a material misstatement of the financial statements may arise when the entity has not complied with these requirements.

Application of the Selected Accounting Policies

A6. In relation to the application of the selected accounting policies, material misstatements of the financial statements may arise:

(a) When management has not applied the selected accounting policies consistently with the financial reporting framework, including when management has not applied the selected accounting policies consistently between periods or to similar transactions and events (consistency in application); or

(b) Due to the method of application of the selected accounting policies (such as an unintentional error in application).

Appropriateness or Adequacy of Disclosures in the Financial Statements

A7. In relation to the appropriateness or adequacy of disclosures in the financial statements, material misstatements of the financial statements may arise when:

(a) The financial statements do not include all of the disclosures required by the applicable financial reporting framework;

(b) The disclosures in the financial statements are not presented in accordance with the applicable financial reporting framework; or

(c) The financial statements do not provide the disclosures necessary to achieve fair presentation.

Nature of an Inability to Obtain Sufficient Appropriate Audit Evidence
(Ref: Para. 6(b))

A8. The auditor's inability to obtain sufficient appropriate audit evidence (also referred to as a limitation on the scope of the audit) may arise from:

(a) Circumstances beyond the control of the entity;

(b) Circumstances relating to the nature or timing of the auditor's work; or

(c) Limitations imposed by management.

A9. An inability to perform a specific procedure does not constitute a limitation on the scope of the audit if the auditor is able to obtain sufficient appropriate audit evidence by performing alternative procedures. If this is not possible, the requirements of paragraphs 7(b) and 10 apply as appropriate. Limitations imposed by management may have other implications for the audit, such as for the auditor's assessment of fraud risks and consideration of engagement continuance.

A10. Examples of circumstances beyond the control of the entity include when:

- The entity's accounting records have been destroyed.

- The accounting records of a significant component have been seized indefinitely by governmental authorities.

A11. Examples of circumstances relating to the nature or timing of the auditor's work include when:

- The entity is required to use the equity method of accounting for an associated entity, and the auditor is unable to obtain sufficient appropriate audit evidence about the latter's financial information to evaluate whether the equity method has been appropriately applied.

- The timing of the auditor's appointment is such that the auditor is unable to observe the counting of the physical inventories.

- The auditor determines that performing substantive procedures alone is not sufficient, but the entity's controls are not effective.

A12. Examples of an inability to obtain sufficient appropriate audit evidence arising from a limitation on the scope of the audit imposed by management include when:

- Management prevents the auditor from observing the counting of the physical inventory.

- Management prevents the auditor from requesting external confirmation of specific account balances.

Consequence of an Inability to Obtain Sufficient Appropriate Audit Evidence Due to a Management-Imposed Limitation after the Auditor Has Accepted the Engagement
(Ref: Para. 13(b)-14)

A13. The practicality of withdrawing from the audit may depend on the stage of completion of the engagement at the time that management imposes the scope limitation. If the auditor has substantially completed the audit, the auditor may decide to complete the audit to the extent possible, disclaim an opinion and explain the scope limitation in the Basis for Disclaimer of Opinion paragraph prior to withdrawing.

A14. In certain circumstances, withdrawal from the audit may not be possible if the auditor is required by law or regulation to continue the audit engagement. This may be the case for an auditor that is appointed to audit the financial statements of public sector entities. It may also be the case in jurisdictions where the auditor is appointed to audit the financial statements covering a specific period, or appointed for a specific period and is prohibited from withdrawing before the completion of the audit of those financial statements or before the end of that period, respectively. The auditor may also consider it necessary to include an Other Matter paragraph in the auditor's report.[6]

A15. When the auditor concludes that withdrawal from the audit is necessary because of a scope limitation, there may be a professional, legal or regulatory requirement for the auditor to communicate matters relating to the withdrawal from the engagement to regulators or the entity's owners.

Statement by Auditor on Ceasing to Hold Office

A15-1. The auditor of a company in the UK who ceases to hold office as auditor is required to comply with the requirements of sections 519 and 521 of the Companies Act 2006 regarding the statement to be made by the auditor in relation to ceasing to hold office. In addition, the auditor may need to notify the appropriate audit authority in accordance with section 522 of the Companies Act 2006.

A15-2 Auditors of Irish Companies, generally, are obliged to notify the Irish Auditing and Accounting Supervisory Authority (IAASA) within one month of ceasing to hold office on the appropriate form which includes stating the reason for resignation notwithstanding that the auditor may have nothing to report to the members or creditors regarding their ceasing to hold office[6a].

Other Considerations Relating to an Adverse Opinion or Disclaimer of Opinion
(Ref: Para. 15)

A16. The following are examples of reporting circumstances that would not contradict the auditor's adverse opinion or disclaimer of opinion:

- The expression of an unmodified opinion on financial statements prepared under a given financial reporting framework and, within the same report, the expression of an adverse opinion on the same financial statements under a different financial reporting framework.[7]

---

[6] ISA (UK and Ireland) 706, "Emphasis of Matter Paragraphs and Other Matter Paragraphs in the Independent Auditor's Report," paragraph A5.

[6a] See section 161A. (1) of the Companies Act of 1990.

[7] See paragraph A32 of ISA 700 for a description of this circumstance.

The FRC has not promulgated ISA 700 as issued by the IAASB for application in the UK and Ireland. In the UK and Ireland the applicable auditing standard is ISA (UK and Ireland) 700, "The Auditor's Report on Financial Statements." Paragraph A13 of ISA (UK and Ireland) 700 provides guidance on expressing an opinion in respect of an additional financial reporting framework.

- The expression of a disclaimer of opinion regarding the results of operations, and cash flows, where relevant, and an unmodified opinion regarding the financial position (see ISA (UK and Ireland) 510[8]). In this case, the auditor has not expressed a disclaimer of opinion on the financial statements as a whole.

Form and Content of the Auditor's Report When the Opinion Is Modified

Basis for Modification Paragraph (Ref: Para. 16-17, 19, 21)

A17. Consistency in the auditor's report helps to promote users' understanding and to identify unusual circumstances when they occur. Accordingly, although uniformity in the wording of a modified opinion and in the description of the basis for the modification may not be possible, consistency in both the form and content of the auditor's report is desirable.

A18. An example of the financial effects of material misstatements that the auditor may describe in the basis for modification paragraph in the auditor's report is the quantification of the effects on income tax, income before taxes, net income and equity if inventory is overstated.

A19. Disclosing the omitted information in the basis for modification paragraph would not be practicable if:

(a) The disclosures have not been prepared by management or the disclosures are otherwise not readily available to the auditor; or

(b) In the auditor's judgment, the disclosures would be unduly voluminous in relation to the auditor's report.

A20. An adverse opinion or a disclaimer of opinion relating to a specific matter described in the basis for qualification paragraph does not justify the omission of a description of other identified matters that would have otherwise required a modification of the auditor's opinion. In such cases, the disclosure of such other matters of which the auditor is aware may be relevant to users of the financial statements.

Opinion on the Financial Statements Paragraph (Ref: Para. 22-23)

A21. Inclusion of this paragraph heading makes it clear to the user that the auditor's opinion is modified and indicates the type of modification.

A22. When the auditor expresses a qualified opinion, it would not be appropriate to use phrases such as "with the foregoing explanation" or "subject to" in the opinion paragraph as these are not sufficiently clear or forceful.

---

[8] ISA (UK and Ireland) 510, "Initial Audit Engagements – Opening Balances," paragraph 10.

Illustrative Auditors' Reports[8a]

A23. *Illustrative auditor's reports tailored for use with audits conducted in accordance with ISAs (UK and Ireland) are given in the current versions of the FRC's compendia Auditor's Report Bulletins[8a].*

A24. *[Deliberately left blank]*

Communication with Those Charged with Governance (Ref: Para. 28)

A25. Communicating with those charged with governance the circumstances that lead to an expected modification to the auditor's opinion and the proposed wording of the modification enables:

(a) The auditor to give notice to those charged with governance of the intended modification(s) and the reasons (or circumstances) for the modification(s);

(b) The auditor to seek the concurrence of those charged with governance regarding the facts of the matter(s) giving rise to the expected modification(s), or to confirm matters of disagreement with management as such; and

(c) Those charged with governance to have an opportunity, where appropriate, to provide the auditor with further information and explanations in respect of the matter(s) giving rise to the expected modification(s).

[8a] At the date of publication of this ISA (UK and Ireland), Bulletins 2010/2 (Revised) "Compendium of Illustrative Auditor's Reports on United Kingdom Private Sector Financial Statements for periods ended on or after 15 December 2010" and 1(I) "Compendium of Illustrative Auditor's Reports on Irish Financial Statements" were the current compendia Bulletins.

INTERNATIONAL STANDARD ON AUDITING (UK AND IRELAND) 706 (REVISED OCTOBER 2012)

EMPHASIS OF MATTER PARAGRAPHS AND OTHER MATTER PARAGRAPHS IN THE INDEPENDENT AUDITOR'S REPORT

(Effective for audits of financial statements for periods commencing on or after 1 October 2012)

CONTENTS

International Standard on Auditing (UK and Ireland) (ISA (UK and Ireland)) 706, "Emphasis of Matter Paragraphs and Other Matter Paragraphs in the Independent Auditor's Report" should be read in conjunction with ISA (UK and Ireland) 200, "Overall Objectives of the Independent Auditor and the Conduct of an Audit in Accordance with International Standards on Auditing (UK and Ireland)."

Introduction

Scope of this ISA (UK and Ireland)

1.   This International Standard on Auditing (UK and Ireland) (ISA (UK and Ireland)) deals with additional communication in the auditor's report when the auditor considers it necessary to:

(a)   Draw users' attention to a matter or matters presented or disclosed in the financial statements that are of such importance that they are fundamental to users' understanding of the financial statements; or

(b)   Draw users' attention to any matter or matters other than those presented or disclosed in the financial statements that are relevant to users' understanding of the audit, the auditor's responsibilities or the auditor's report.

2.   Appendices 1 and 2 identify ISAs (UK and Ireland) that contain specific requirements for the auditor to include Emphasis of Matter paragraphs or Other Matter paragraphs in the auditor's report. In those circumstances, the requirements in this ISA regarding the form and placement of such paragraphs apply.

2-1   At the date of publication of this ISA (UK and Ireland) illustrative examples of emphasis of matter paragraphs for UK and Irish financial statements are contained in the compendia Bulletins 2010/2 "Compendium of Illustrative Auditor's Reports on United Kingdom Private Sector Financial Statements for periods ended on or after 15 December 2010" (Revised) and 1(I) "Compendium of Illustrative Auditor's Reports on Irish Financial Statements".

Effective Date

3.   This ISA (UK and Ireland) is effective for audits of financial statements for periods commencing on or after 1 October 2012. Earlier adoption is permitted.

Objective

4.   The objective of the auditor, having formed an opinion on the financial statements, is to draw users' attention, when in the auditor's judgment it is necessary to do so, by way of clear additional communication in the auditor's report, to:

(a)   A matter, although appropriately presented or disclosed in the financial statements, that is of such importance that it is fundamental to users' understanding of the financial statements; or

(b)   As appropriate, any other matter that is relevant to users' understanding of the audit, the auditor's responsibilities or the auditor's report.

Definitions

5.   For the purposes of the ISAs (UK and Ireland), the following terms have the meanings
       attributed below:

   (a) Emphasis of Matter paragraph – A paragraph included in the auditor's report that
        refers to a matter appropriately presented or disclosed in the financial
        statements that, in the auditor's judgment, is of such importance that it is
        fundamental to users' understanding of the financial statements.

   (b) Other Matter paragraph – A paragraph included in the auditor's report that refers
        to a matter other than those presented or disclosed in the financial statements
        that, in the auditor's judgment, is relevant to users' understanding of the audit,
        the auditor's responsibilities or the auditor's report.

Requirements

Emphasis of Matter Paragraphs in the Auditor's Report

6.   If the auditor considers it necessary to draw users' attention to a matter presented or
       disclosed in the financial statements that, in the auditor's judgment, is of such
       importance that it is fundamental to users' understanding of the financial statements,
       the auditor shall include an Emphasis of Matter paragraph in the auditor's report
       provided the auditor has obtained sufficient appropriate audit evidence that the
       matter is not materially misstated in the financial statements[1a]. Such a paragraph
       shall refer only to information presented or disclosed in the financial statements. (Ref:
       Para. A1-A2)

7.   When the auditor includes an Emphasis of Matter paragraph in the auditor's report,
       the auditor shall:

   (a) Include it immediately after the Opinion on Financial Statements paragraph in
        the auditor's report;

   (b) Use the heading "Emphasis of Matter," or other appropriate heading;

   (c) Include in the paragraph a clear reference to the matter being emphasized and
        to where relevant disclosures that fully describe the matter can be found in the
        financial statements; and

   (d) Indicate that the auditor's opinion is not modified in respect of the matter
        emphasized. (Ref: Para. A3-A4)

[1a] Paragraph 19 of ISA (UK and Ireland) 570, "Going Concern," requires, where adequate disclosure is
     made in the financial statements, the auditor always include an Emphasis of Matter paragraph in the
     auditor's report to highlight the existence of a material uncertainty relating to an event or condition
     that may cast significant doubt on the entity's ability to continue as a going concern.

Other Matter Paragraphs in the Auditor's Report

8.   If the auditor considers it necessary to communicate a matter other than those that are presented or disclosed in the financial statements that, in the auditor's judgment, is relevant to users' understanding of the audit, the auditor's responsibilities or the auditor's report and this is not prohibited by law or regulation, the auditor shall do so in a paragraph in the auditor's report, with the heading "Other Matter," or other appropriate heading. The auditor shall include this paragraph immediately after the Opinion on Financial Statements paragraph and any Emphasis of Matter paragraph, or elsewhere in the auditor's report if the content of the Other Matter paragraph is relevant to the Other Reporting Responsibilities section. (Ref: Para. A5-A11)

Communication with Those Charged with Governance

9.   If the auditor expects to include an Emphasis of Matter or an Other Matter paragraph in the auditor's report, the auditor shall communicate with those charged with governance regarding this expectation and the proposed wording of this paragraph. (Ref: Para. A12)

***

Application and Other Explanatory Material

Emphasis of Matter Paragraphs in the Auditor's Report

Circumstances in Which an Emphasis of Matter Paragraph May Be Necessary (Ref: Para. 6)

A1.   Examples of circumstances where the auditor may consider it necessary to include an Emphasis of Matter paragraph are:

*   An uncertainty relating to the future outcome of exceptional litigation or regulatory action.

*   Early application (where permitted) of a new accounting standard (for example, a new International Financial Reporting Standard) that has a pervasive effect on the financial statements in advance of its effective date.

*   A major catastrophe that has had, or continues to have, a significant effect on the entity's financial position.

A2.   A widespread use of Emphasis of Matter paragraphs diminishes the effectiveness of the auditor's communication of such matters. Additionally, to include more information in an Emphasis of Matter paragraph than is presented or disclosed in the financial statements may imply that the matter has not been appropriately presented or disclosed; accordingly, paragraph 6 limits the use of an Emphasis of Matter paragraph to matters presented or disclosed in the financial statements.

Including an Emphasis of Matter Paragraph in the Auditor's Report (Ref: Para. 7)

A3. The inclusion of an Emphasis of Matter paragraph in the auditor's report does not affect the auditor's opinion. An Emphasis of Matter paragraph is not a substitute for either:

(a) The auditor expressing a qualified opinion or an adverse opinion, or disclaiming an opinion, when required by the circumstances of a specific audit engagement (see ISA (UK and Ireland) 705[1]); or

(b) Disclosures in the financial statements that the applicable financial reporting framework requires management to make.

A4. *[Deliberately left blank].*

Other Matter Paragraphs in the Auditor's Report (Ref: Para. 8)

Circumstances in Which an Other Matter Paragraph May Be Necessary

Relevant to Users' Understanding of the Audit

A5. In the rare circumstance where the auditor is unable to withdraw from an engagement even though the possible effect of an inability to obtain sufficient appropriate audit evidence due to a limitation on the scope of the audit imposed by management is pervasive,[2] the auditor may consider it necessary to include an Other Matter paragraph in the auditor's report to explain why it is not possible for the auditor to withdraw from the engagement.

Relevant to Users' Understanding of the Auditor's Responsibilities or the Auditor's Report

A6. Law, regulation or generally accepted practice in a jurisdiction may require or permit the auditor to elaborate on matters that provide further explanation of the auditor's responsibilities in the audit of the financial statements or of the auditor's report thereon. Where relevant, one or more sub-headings may be used that describe the content of the Other Matter paragraph.

A7. An Other Matter paragraph does not deal with circumstances where the auditor has other reporting responsibilities that are in addition to the auditor's responsibility under the ISAs (UK and Ireland) to report on the financial statements (see "Other Reporting Responsibilities" section in ISA (UK and Ireland) 700[3]), or where the auditor has been

---

[1] ISA (UK and Ireland) 705, "Modifications to the Opinion in the Independent Auditor's Report."

[2] See paragraph 13(b)(ii) of ISA (UK and Ireland) 705 for a discussion of this circumstance.

[3] ISA 700, "Forming an Opinion and Reporting on Financial Statements," paragraphs 38-39.
The FRC has not promulgated ISA 700 as issued by the IAASB for application in the UK and Ireland. In the UK and Ireland the applicable auditing standard is ISA (UK and Ireland) 700, "The Auditor's Report on Financial Statements." Paragraphs 21 and 22 of ISA (UK and Ireland) 700 are the equivalent paragraphs to 38 -39 of ISA 700.

asked to perform and report on additional specified procedures, or to express an opinion on specific matters.

Reporting on more than one set of financial statements

A8. An entity may prepare one set of financial statements in accordance with a general purpose framework (for example, the national framework) and another set of financial statements in accordance with another general purpose framework (for example, International Financial Reporting Standards), and engage the auditor to report on both sets of financial statements. If the auditor has determined that the frameworks are acceptable in the respective circumstances, the auditor may include an Other Matter paragraph in the auditor's report, referring to the fact that another set of financial statements has been prepared by the same entity in accordance with another general purpose framework and that the auditor has issued a report on those financial statements.

A8-1 The situation described in paragraph A8 is differentiated from the requirement in paragraph 19 of ISA (UK and Ireland) 700 in that, in the latter case, the auditor is engaged to express in the same auditor's report an opinion on the compliance of the financial statements with an additional financial reporting framework. This is only permissible if the auditor is satisfied that there are no differences between the two financial reporting frameworks that affect the financial statements being reported on.

Restriction on distribution or use of the auditor's report

A9. Financial statements prepared for a specific purpose may be prepared in accordance with a general purpose framework because the intended users have determined that such general purpose financial statements meet their financial information needs. Since the auditor's report is intended for specific users, the auditor may consider it necessary in the circumstances to include an Other Matter paragraph, stating that the auditor's report is intended solely for the intended users, and should not be distributed to or used by other parties.

Including an Other Matter Paragraph in the Auditor's Report

A10. The content of an Other Matter paragraph reflects clearly that such other matter is not required to be presented and disclosed in the financial statements. An Other Matter paragraph does not include information that the auditor is prohibited from providing by law, regulation or other professional standards, for example, ethical standards relating to confidentiality of information. An Other Matter paragraph also does not include information that is required to be provided by management.

A11. The placement of an Other Matter paragraph depends on the nature of the information to be communicated. When an Other Matter paragraph is included to draw users' attention to a matter relevant to their understanding of the audit of the financial statements, the paragraph is included immediately after the Opinion on Financial Statements paragraph and any Emphasis of Matter paragraph. When an Other Matter paragraph is included to draw users' attention to a matter relating to Other Reporting Responsibilities addressed in the auditor's report, the paragraph may be included in the Opinion on Other Matters (prescribed by applicable legislation under the terms of our engagement) paragraph. Alternatively, when relevant to all the auditor's responsibilities or users' understanding of the auditor's report, the Other Matter paragraph may be included as a separate section at the end of the auditor's report[3a].

Communication with Those Charged with Governance (Ref. Para. 9)

A12. Such communication enables those charged with governance to be made aware of the nature of any specific matters that the auditor intends to highlight in the auditor's report, and provides them with an opportunity to obtain further clarification from the auditor where necessary. Where the inclusion of an Other Matter paragraph on a particular matter in the auditor's report recurs on each successive engagement, the auditor may determine that it is unnecessary to repeat the communication on each engagement.

[3a] In the UK and Ireland separate auditor's reports may be provided where the consolidated financial statements of a group of companies and the financial statements of the parent company are presented separately. In such cases, an "Other Matter" paragraph explaining that separate auditor's reports have been provided is usually included as the final paragraph of both of the auditor's reports.

Appendix 1

(Ref: Para. 2)

List of ISAs (UK and Ireland) Containing Requirements for Emphasis of Matter Paragraphs

This appendix identifies paragraphs in other ISAs (UK and Ireland) in effect for audits of financial statements for periods ending on or after 15 December 2010 that require the auditor to include an Emphasis of Matter paragraph in the auditor's report in certain circumstances. The list is not a substitute for considering the requirements and related application and other explanatory material in ISAs.

- ISA (UK and Ireland) 210, "Agreeing the Terms of Audit Engagements" – paragraph 19(b)

- ISA (UK and Ireland) 560, "Subsequent Events" – paragraphs 12(b) and 16

- ISA (UK and Ireland) 570, "Going Concern" – paragraph 19

- ISA 800[3b], "Special Considerations—Audits of Financial Statements Prepared in Accordance with Special Purpose Frameworks" – paragraph 14

[3b] ISA 800 has not been promulgated by the FRC for application in the UK and Ireland.

Appendix 2

(Ref: Para. 2)

List of ISAs (UK and Ireland) Containing Requirements for Other Matter Paragraphs

This appendix identifies paragraphs in other ISAs (UK and Ireland) in effect for audits of financial statements for periods ending on or after 15 December 2010 that require the auditor to include an Other Matter paragraph in the auditor's report in certain circumstances. The list is not a substitute for considering the requirements and related application and other explanatory material in ISAs.

- ISA (UK and Ireland) 560, "Subsequent Events" – paragraphs 12(b) and 16

- ISA (UK and Ireland) 710, "Comparative Information—Corresponding Figures and Comparative Financial Statements" – paragraphs 13-14, 16-17 and 19

- ISA (UK and Ireland) 720 Section A, "The Auditor's Responsibilities Relating to Other Information in Documents Containing Audited Financial Statements" – paragraph 10(a)

INTERNATIONAL STANDARD ON AUDITING (UK AND IRELAND) 710

COMPARATIVE INFORMATION— CORRESPONDING FIGURES AND COMPARATIVE FINANCIAL STATEMENTS

(Effective for audits of financial statements for periods ending on or after 15 December 2010)

CONTENTS

International Standard on Auditing (UK and Ireland) (ISA (UK and Ireland)) 710, "Comparative Information—Corresponding Figures and Comparative Financial Statements" should be read in conjunction with ISA (UK and Ireland) 200, "Overall Objectives of the Independent Auditor and the Conduct of an Audit in Accordance with International Standards on Auditing (UK and Ireland)."

Introduction

Scope of this ISA (UK and Ireland)

1. This International Standard on Auditing (UK and Ireland) (ISA (UK and Ireland)) deals with the auditor's responsibilities relating to comparative information in an audit of financial statements. When the financial statements of the prior period have been audited by a predecessor auditor or were not audited, the requirements and guidance in ISA (UK and Ireland) 510[1] regarding opening balances also apply.

The Nature of Comparative Information

2. The nature of the comparative information that is presented in an entity's financial statements depends on the requirements of the applicable financial reporting framework. There are two different broad approaches to the auditor's reporting responsibilities in respect of such comparative information: corresponding figures and comparative financial statements. The approach to be adopted is often specified by law or regulation but may also be specified in the terms of engagement.

2-1. In the UK and Ireland the corresponding figures method of presentation is usually required.

3. The essential audit reporting differences between the approaches are:

   (a) For corresponding figures, the auditor's opinion on the financial statements refers to the current period only; whereas

   (b) For comparative financial statements, the auditor's opinion refers to each period for which financial statements are presented.

   This ISA (UK and Ireland) addresses separately the auditor's reporting requirements for each approach.

Effective Date

4. This ISA (UK and Ireland) is effective for audits of financial statements for periods ending on or after 15 December 2010.

Objectives

5. The objectives of the auditor are:

   (a) To obtain sufficient appropriate audit evidence about whether the comparative information included in the financial statements has been presented, in all

---

[1] ISA (UK and Ireland) 510, "Initial Audit Engagements—Opening Balances."

material respects, in accordance with the requirements for comparative information in the applicable financial reporting framework; and

(b) To report in accordance with the auditor's reporting responsibilities.

Definitions

6. For purposes of the ISAs (UK and Ireland), the following terms have the meanings attributed below:

(a) Comparative information – The amounts and disclosures included in the financial statements in respect of one or more prior periods in accordance with the applicable financial reporting framework.

(b) Corresponding figures – Comparative information where amounts and other disclosures for the prior period are included as an integral part of the current period financial statements, and are intended to be read only in relation to the amounts and other disclosures relating to the current period (referred to as "current period figures"). The level of detail presented in the corresponding amounts and disclosures is dictated primarily by its relevance to the current period figures.

(c) Comparative financial statements – Comparative information where amounts and other disclosures for the prior period are included for comparison with the financial statements of the current period but, if audited, are referred to in the auditor's opinion. The level of information included in those comparative financial statements is comparable with that of the financial statements of the current period.

For purposes of this ISA (UK and Ireland), references to "prior period" should be read as "prior periods" when the comparative information includes amounts and disclosures for more than one period.

Requirements

Audit Procedures

7. The auditor shall determine whether the financial statements include the comparative information required by the applicable financial reporting framework and whether such information is appropriately classified. For this purpose, the auditor shall evaluate whether:

(a) The comparative information agrees with the amounts and other disclosures presented in the prior period or, when appropriate, have been restated; (Ref: Para. A1-1) and

(b)   The accounting policies reflected in the comparative information are consistent with those applied in the current period or, if there have been changes in accounting policies, whether those changes have been properly accounted for and adequately presented and disclosed.

8.   If the auditor becomes aware of a possible material misstatement in the comparative information while performing the current period audit, the auditor shall perform such additional audit procedures as are necessary in the circumstances to obtain sufficient appropriate audit evidence to determine whether a material misstatement exists. If the auditor had audited the prior period's financial statements, the auditor shall also follow the relevant requirements of ISA (UK and Ireland) 560.[2] If the prior period financial statements are amended, the auditor shall determine that the comparative information agrees with the amended financial statements.

9.   As required by ISA (UK and Ireland) 580,[3] the auditor shall request written representations for all periods referred to in the auditor's opinion. The auditor shall also obtain a specific written representation regarding any restatement made to correct a material misstatement in prior period financial statements that affect the comparative information. (Ref: Para. A1)

Audit Reporting

Corresponding Figures

10.   When corresponding figures are presented, the auditor's opinion shall not refer to the corresponding figures except in the circumstances described in paragraphs 11, 12, and 14. (Ref: Para. A2)

11.   If the auditor's report on the prior period, as previously issued, included a qualified opinion, a disclaimer of opinion, or an adverse opinion and the matter which gave rise to the modification is unresolved, the auditor shall modify the auditor's opinion on the current period's financial statements. In the Basis for Modification paragraph in the auditor's report, the auditor shall either:

(a)   Refer to both the current period's figures and the corresponding figures in the description of the matter giving rise to the modification when the effects or possible effects of the matter on the current period's figures are material; or

(b)   In other cases, explain that the audit opinion has been modified because of the effects or possible effects of the unresolved matter on the comparability of the current period's figures and the corresponding figures. (Ref: Para. A3-A5)

12.   If the auditor obtains audit evidence that a material misstatement exists in the prior period financial statements on which an unmodified opinion has been previously issued, and the corresponding figures have not been properly restated or appropriate

---

[2]   ISA (UK and Ireland) 560, "Subsequent Events," paragraphs 14-17.
[3]   ISA (UK and Ireland) 580, "Written Representations," paragraph 14.

disclosures have not been made, the auditor shall express a qualified opinion or an adverse opinion in the auditor's report on the current period financial statements, modified with respect to the corresponding figures included therein. (Ref: Para. A6)

Prior Period Financial Statements Audited by a Predecessor Auditor

13. If the financial statements of the prior period were audited by a predecessor auditor and the auditor is not prohibited by law or regulation from referring to the predecessor auditor's report on the corresponding figures and decides to do so, the auditor shall state in an Other Matter paragraph in the auditor's report:

    (a) That the financial statements of the prior period were audited by the predecessor auditor;

    (b) The type of opinion expressed by the predecessor auditor and, if the opinion was modified, the reasons therefore; and

    (c) The date of that report. (Ref: Para. A7 – A7-2)

Prior Period Financial Statements Not Audited

14. If the prior period financial statements were not audited, the auditor shall state in an Other Matter paragraph in the auditor's report that the corresponding figures are unaudited. Such a statement does not, however, relieve the auditor of the requirement to obtain sufficient appropriate audit evidence that the opening balances do not contain misstatements that materially affect the current period's financial statements.[4]

Comparative Financial Statements

15. When comparative financial statements are presented, the auditor's opinion shall refer to each period for which financial statements are presented and on which an audit opinion is expressed. (Ref: Para. A8-A9)

16. When reporting on prior period financial statements in connection with the current period's audit, if the auditor's opinion on such prior period financial statements differs from the opinion the auditor previously expressed, the auditor shall disclose the substantive reasons for the different opinion in an Other Matter paragraph in accordance with ISA (UK and Ireland) 706.[5] (Ref: Para. A10)

Prior Period Financial Statements Audited by a Predecessor Auditor

17. If the financial statements of the prior period were audited by a predecessor auditor, in addition to expressing an opinion on the current period's financial statements, the auditor shall state in an Other Matter paragraph:

---

[4] ISA (UK and Ireland) 510, paragraph 6.
[5] ISA (UK and Ireland) 706, "Emphasis of Matter Paragraphs and Other Matter Paragraphs in the Independent Auditor's Report," paragraph 8.

(a)   that the financial statements of the prior period were audited by a predecessor auditor;

(b)   the type of opinion expressed by the predecessor auditor and, if the opinion was modified, the reasons therefore; and

(c)   the date of that report,

unless the predecessor auditor's report on the prior period's financial statements is reissued with the financial statements.

18.   If the auditor concludes that a material misstatement exists that affects the prior period financial statements on which the predecessor auditor had previously reported without modification, the auditor shall communicate the misstatement with the appropriate level of management and, unless all of those charged with governance are involved in managing the entity,[6] those charged with governance and request that the predecessor auditor be informed. If the prior period financial statements are amended, and the predecessor auditor agrees to issue a new auditor's report on the amended financial statements of the prior period, the auditor shall report only on the current period. (Ref: Para. A11)

Prior Period Financial Statements Not Audited

19.   If the prior period financial statements were not audited, the auditor shall state in an Other Matter paragraph that the comparative financial statements are unaudited. Such a statement does not, however, relieve the auditor of the requirement to obtain sufficient appropriate audit evidence that the opening balances do not contain misstatements that materially affect the current period's financial statements.[7]

***

Application and Other Explanatory Material

Audit Procedures (Ref: Para. 7(a))

A1-1. When evaluating whether the comparative information agrees with the amounts and other disclosures presented in the prior period or, where appropriate, have been restated, the auditor's procedures include checking whether the related opening balances in the accounting records were appropriately brought forward.

Written Representations (Ref: Para. 9)

A1.   In the case of comparative financial statements, the written representations are requested for all periods referred to in the auditor's opinion because management

---

[6]   ISA (UK and Ireland) 260, "Communication with Those Charged with Governance," paragraph 13.
[7]   ISA (UK and Ireland) 510, paragraph 6.

needs to reaffirm that the written representations it previously made with respect to the prior period remain appropriate. In the case of corresponding figures, the written representations are requested for the financial statements of the current period only because the auditor's opinion is on those financial statements, which include the corresponding figures. However, the auditor requests a specific written representation regarding any restatement made to correct a material misstatement in the prior period financial statements that affect the comparative information.

Audit Reporting

Corresponding Figures

No Reference in Auditor's Opinion (Ref: Para. 10)

A2. The auditor's opinion does not refer to the corresponding figures because the auditor's opinion is on the current period financial statements as a whole, including the corresponding figures.

Modification in Auditor's Report on the Prior Period Unresolved (Ref: Para. 11)

A3. When the auditor's report on the prior period, as previously issued, included a qualified opinion, a disclaimer of opinion, or an adverse opinion and the matter which gave rise to the modified opinion is resolved and properly accounted for or disclosed in the financial statements in accordance with the applicable financial reporting framework, the auditor's opinion on the current period need not refer to the previous modification.

A3-1. In some circumstances the auditor may consider it appropriate to qualify the audit opinion on the current period's financial statements. For example, if a provision which the auditor considered should have been made in the previous period is made in the current period.

A4. When the auditor's opinion on the prior period, as previously expressed, was modified, the unresolved matter that gave rise to the modification may not be relevant to the current period figures. Nevertheless, a qualified opinion, a disclaimer of opinion, or an adverse opinion (as applicable) may be required on the current period's financial statements because of the effects or possible effects of the unresolved matter on the comparability of the current and corresponding figures.

A5. Illustrative examples of the auditor's report if the auditor's report on the prior period included a modified opinion and the matter giving rise to the modification is unresolved are contained in Illustrations 1 and 2 of the Appendix.[7a]

[7a] The examples in the Appendix have not been tailored for the UK and Ireland. Illustrative auditor's reports tailored for use with audits conducted in accordance with ISAs (UK and Ireland) are given in the current versions of the APB Compendia Auditor's Report Bulletins.

Misstatement in Prior Period Financial Statements (Ref: Para. 12)

A6. When the prior period financial statements that are misstated have not been amended and an auditor's report has not been reissued, but the corresponding figures have been properly restated or appropriate disclosures have been made in the current period financial statements, the auditor's report may include an Emphasis of Matter paragraph describing the circumstances and referring to where relevant disclosures that fully describe the matter can be found in the financial statements (see ISA (UK and Ireland) 706).

Prior Period Financial Statements Audited by a Predecessor Auditor (Ref: Para. 13)

A7. An illustrative example of the auditor's report if the prior period financial statements were audited by a predecessor auditor and the auditor is not prohibited by law or regulation from referring to the predecessor auditor's report on the corresponding figures is contained in Illustration 3 of the Appendix.[7a]

A7-1. In the UK and Ireland the incoming auditor does not refer to the predecessor auditor's report on the corresponding figures in the incoming auditor's report for the current period. The incoming auditor assumes audit responsibility for the corresponding figures only in the context of the financial statements as a whole. The incoming auditor reads the preceding period's financial statements and, using the knowledge gained during the current audit, considers whether they have been properly reflected as corresponding figures in the current period's financial statements.

A7-2. Although the incoming auditor is not required to re-audit the financial statements of the preceding period, if the incoming auditor becomes aware of a possible material misstatement of corresponding figures, the requirement and guidance in paragraphs 12 and A6 apply.

Comparative Financial Statements

Reference in Auditor's Opinion (Ref: Para. 15)

A8. Because the auditor's report on comparative financial statements applies to the financial statements for each of the periods presented, the auditor may express a qualified opinion or an adverse opinion, disclaim an opinion, or include an Emphasis of Matter paragraph with respect to one or more periods, while expressing a different auditor's opinion on the financial statements of the other period.

A9. An illustrative example of the auditor's report if the auditor is required to report on both the current and the prior period financial statements in connection with the current year's audit and the prior period included a modified opinion and the matter giving rise to the modification is unresolved, is contained in Illustration 4 of the Appendix.[7a]

Opinion on Prior Period Financial Statements Different from Previous Opinion (Ref: Para. 16)

A10. When reporting on the prior period financial statements in connection with the current period's audit, the opinion expressed on the prior period financial statements may be different from the opinion previously expressed if the auditor becomes aware of circumstances or events that materially affect the financial statements of a prior period during the course of the audit of the current period. In some jurisdictions, the auditor may have additional reporting responsibilities designed to prevent future reliance on the auditor's previously issued report on the prior period financial statements.

Prior Period Financial Statements Audited by a Predecessor Auditor (Ref: Para. 18)

A11. The predecessor auditor may be unable or unwilling to reissue the auditor's report on the prior period financial statements. An Other Matter paragraph of the auditor's report may indicate that the predecessor auditor reported on the financial statements of the prior period before amendment. In addition, if the auditor is engaged to audit and obtains sufficient appropriate audit evidence to be satisfied as to the appropriateness of the amendment, the auditor's report may also include the following paragraph:

As part of our audit of the 20X2 financial statements, we also audited the adjustments described in Note X that were applied to amend the 20X1 financial statements. In our opinion, such adjustments are appropriate and have been properly applied. We were not engaged to audit, review, or apply any procedures to the 20X1 financial statements of the company other than with respect to the adjustments and, accordingly, we do not express an opinion or any other form of assurance on the 20X1 financial statements taken as a whole.

Appendix

Example Auditors' Reports

The examples in the Appendix have not been tailored for the UK and Ireland. Illustrative auditor's reports tailored for use with audits conducted in accordance with ISAs (UK and Ireland) are given in the current versions of the APB Compendia Auditor's Report Bulletins.

Example A – Corresponding Figures (Ref: Para. A5)

> **Report illustrative of the circumstances described in paragraph 11(a), as follows:**
>
> • **The auditor's report on the prior period, as previously issued, included a qualified opinion.**
>
> • **The matter giving rise to the modification is unresolved.**
>
> • **The effects or possible effects of the matter on the current period's figures are material and require a modification to the auditor's opinion regarding the current period figures.**

INDEPENDENT AUDITOR'S REPORT

[Appropriate Addressee]

Report on the Financial Statements[8]

We have audited the accompanying financial statements of ABC Company, which comprise the balance sheet as at December 31, 20X1, and the income statement, statement of changes in equity and cash flow statement for the year then ended, and a summary of significant accounting policies and other explanatory information.

Management's[9] Responsibility for the Financial Statements

Management is responsible for the preparation and fair presentation of these financial statements in accordance with International Financial Reporting Standards,[10] and for such internal control as management determines is necessary to enable the preparation of financial statements that are free from material misstatement, whether due to fraud or error.

---

[8] The sub-title "Report on the Financial Statements" is unnecessary in circumstances when the second sub-title "Report on Other Legal and Regulatory Requirements" is not applicable.

[9] Or other term that is appropriate in the context of the legal framework in the particular jurisdiction.

[10] Where management's responsibility is to prepare financial statements that give a true and fair view, this may read: "Management is responsible for the preparation of financial statements that give a true and fair view in accordance with International Financial Reporting Standards, and for such ..."

Auditor's Responsibility

Our responsibility is to express an opinion on these financial statements based on our audit. We conducted our audit in accordance with International Standards on Auditing. Those standards require that we comply with ethical requirements and plan and perform the audit to obtain reasonable assurance about whether the financial statements are free from material misstatement.

An audit involves performing procedures to obtain audit evidence about the amounts and disclosures in the financial statements. The procedures selected depend on the auditor's judgment, including the assessment of the risks of material misstatement of the financial statements, whether due to fraud or error. In making those risk assessments, the auditor considers internal control relevant to the entity's preparation and fair presentation[11] of the financial statements in order to design audit procedures that are appropriate in the circumstances, but not for the purpose of expressing an opinion on the effectiveness of the entity's internal control.[12] An audit also includes evaluating the appropriateness of accounting policies used and the reasonableness of accounting estimates made by management, as well as evaluating the overall presentation of the financial statements.

We believe that the audit evidence we have obtained is sufficient and appropriate to provide a basis for our qualified audit opinion.

Basis for Qualified Opinion

As discussed in Note X to the financial statements, no depreciation has been provided in the financial statements, which constitutes a departure from International Financial Reporting Standards. This is the result of a decision taken by management at the start of the preceding financial year and caused us to qualify our audit opinion on the financial statements relating to that year. Based on the straight-line method of depreciation and annual rates of 5% for the building and 20% for the equipment, the loss for the year should be increased by xxx in 20X1 and xxx in 20X0, property, plant and equipment should be reduced by accumulated depreciation of xxx in 20X1 and xxx in 20X0, and the accumulated loss should be increased by xxx in 20X1 and xxx in 20X0.

---

[11] In the case of footnote 10, this may read: "In making those risk assessments, the auditor considers internal control relevant to the entity's preparation of financial statements that give a true and fair view in order to design audit procedures that are appropriate in the circumstances, but not for the purpose of expressing an opinion on the effectiveness of the entity's internal control."

[12] In circumstances when the auditor also has responsibility to express an opinion on the effectiveness of internal control in conjunction with the audit of the financial statements, this sentence would be worded as follows: "In making those risk assessments, the auditor considers internal control relevant to the entity's preparation and fair presentation of the financial statements in order to design audit procedures that are appropriate in the circumstances." In the case of footnote 10, this may read: "In making those risk assessments, the auditor considers internal control relevant to the entity's preparation of financial statements that give a true and fair view in order to design audit procedures that are appropriate in the circumstances."

Qualified Opinion

In our opinion, except for the effects of the matter described in the Basis for Qualified Opinion paragraph, the financial statements present fairly, in all material respects, (or *give a true and fair view of*) the financial position of ABC Company as at December 31, 20X1, and (*of*) its financial performance and its cash flows for the year then ended in accordance with International Financial Reporting Standards.

Report on Other Legal and Regulatory Requirements

[Form and content of this section of the auditor's report will vary depending on the nature of the auditor's other reporting responsibilities.]

[Auditor's signature]

[Date of the auditor's report]

[Auditor's address]

Example B – Corresponding Figures (Ref: Para. A5)

> **Report illustrative of the circumstances described in paragraph 11(b), as follows:**
>
> - **The auditor's report on the prior period, as previously issued, included a qualified opinion.**
>
> - **The matter giving rise to the modification is unresolved.**
>
> - **The effects or possible effects of the matter on the current period's figures are immaterial but require a modification to the auditor's opinion because of the effects or possible effects of the unresolved matter on the comparability of the current period's figures and the corresponding figures.**

INDEPENDENT AUDITOR'S REPORT

[Appropriate Addressee]

Report on the Financial Statements[13]

We have audited the accompanying financial statements of ABC Company, which comprise the balance sheet as at December 31, 20X1, and the income statement, statement of changes in equity and cash flow statement for the year then ended, and a summary of significant accounting policies and other explanatory information.

Management's[14] Responsibility for the Financial Statements

Management is responsible for the preparation and fair presentation of these financial statements in accordance with International Financial Reporting Standards,[15] and for such internal control as management determines is necessary to enable the preparation of financial statements that are free from material misstatement, whether due to fraud or error.

Auditor's Responsibility

Our responsibility is to express an opinion on these financial statements based on our audit. We conducted our audit in accordance with International Standards on Auditing. Those standards require that we comply with ethical requirements and plan and perform the audit to obtain reasonable assurance about whether the financial statements are free from material misstatement.

---

[13] The sub-title "Report on the Financial Statements" is unnecessary in circumstances when the second sub-title "Report on Other Legal and Regulatory Requirements" is not applicable.

[14] Or other term that is appropriate in the context of the legal framework in the particular jurisdiction.

[15] Where management's responsibility is to prepare financial statements that give a true and fair view, this may read: "Management is responsible for the preparation of financial statements that give a true and fair view in accordance with International Financial Reporting Standards, and for such ..."

An audit involves performing procedures to obtain audit evidence about the amounts and disclosures in the financial statements. The procedures selected depend on the auditor's judgment, including the assessment of the risks of material misstatement of the financial statements, whether due to fraud or error. In making those risk assessments, the auditor considers internal control relevant to the entity's preparation and fair presentation[16] of the financial statements in order to design audit procedures that are appropriate in the circumstances, but not for the purpose of expressing an opinion on the effectiveness of the entity's internal control.[17] An audit also includes evaluating the appropriateness of accounting policies used and the reasonableness of accounting estimates made by management, as well as evaluating the overall presentation of the financial statements.

We believe that the audit evidence we have obtained is sufficient and appropriate to provide a basis for our qualified audit opinion.

Basis for Qualified Opinion

Because we were appointed auditors of ABC Company during 20X0, we were not able to observe the counting of the physical inventories at the beginning of that period or satisfy ourselves concerning those inventory quantities by alternative means. Since opening inventories affect the determination of the results of operations, we were unable to determine whether adjustments to the results of operations and opening retained earnings might be necessary for 20X0. Our audit opinion on the financial statements for the period ended December 31, 20X0 was modified accordingly. Our opinion on the current period's financial statements is also modified because of the possible effect of this matter on the comparability of the current period's figures and the corresponding figures.

Qualified Opinion

In our opinion, except for the possible effects on the corresponding figures of the matter described in the Basis for Qualified Opinion paragraph, the financial statements present fairly, in all material respects, (or *give a true and fair view of*) the financial position of ABC Company as at December 31, 20X1, and (*of*) its financial performance and its cash flows for the year then ended in accordance with International Financial Reporting Standards.

---

[16] In the case of footnote 15, this may read: "In making those risk assessments, the auditor considers internal control relevant to the entity's preparation of financial statements that give a true and fair view in order to design audit procedures that are appropriate in the circumstances, but not for the purpose of expressing an opinion on the effectiveness of the entity's internal control."

[17] In circumstances when the auditor also has responsibility to express an opinion on the effectiveness of internal control in conjunction with the audit of the financial statements, this sentence would be worded as follows: "In making those risk assessments, the auditor considers internal control relevant to the entity's preparation and fair presentation of the financial statements in order to design audit procedures that are appropriate in the circumstances." In the case of footnote 15, this may read: "In making those risk assessments, the auditor considers internal control relevant to the entity's preparation of financial statements that give a true and fair view in order to design audit procedures that are appropriate in the circumstances."

Report on Other Legal and Regulatory Requirements

[Form and content of this section of the auditor's report will vary depending on the nature of the auditor's other reporting responsibilities.]

[Auditor's signature]

[Date of the auditor's report]

[Auditor's address]

Example C – Corresponding Figures: (Ref: Para. A7)

> **Report illustrative of the circumstances described in paragraph 13, as follows:**
>
> • **The prior period's financial statements were audited by a predecessor auditor.**
>
> • **The auditor is not prohibited by law or regulation from referring to the predecessor auditor's report on the corresponding figures and decides to do so.**

INDEPENDENT AUDITOR'S REPORT

[Appropriate Addressee]

Report on the Financial Statements[18]

We have audited the accompanying financial statements of ABC Company, which comprise the balance sheet as at December 31, 20X1, and the income statement, statement of changes in equity and cash flow statement for the year then ended, and a summary of significant accounting policies and other explanatory information.

Management's[19] Responsibility for the Financial Statements

Management is responsible for the preparation and fair presentation of these financial statements in accordance with International Financial Reporting Standards,[20] and for such internal control as management determines is necessary to enable the preparation of financial statements that are free from material misstatement, whether due to fraud or error.

Auditor's Responsibility

Our responsibility is to express an opinion on these financial statements based on our audit. We conducted our audit in accordance with International Standards on Auditing. Those standards require that we comply with ethical requirements and plan and perform the audit to obtain reasonable assurance about whether the financial statements are free from material misstatement.

An audit involves performing procedures to obtain audit evidence about the amounts and disclosures in the financial statements. The procedures selected depend on the auditor's

---

[18] The sub-title "Report on the Financial Statements" is unnecessary in circumstances when the second sub-title "Report on Other Legal and Regulatory Requirements" is not applicable.

[19] Or other term that is appropriate in the context of the legal framework in the particular jurisdiction.

[20] Where management's responsibility is to prepare financial statements that give a true and fair view, this may read: "Management is responsible for the preparation of financial statements that give a true and fair view in accordance with International Financial Reporting Standards, and for such ..."

judgment, including the assessment of the risks of material misstatement of the financial statements, whether due to fraud or error. In making those risk assessments, the auditor considers internal control relevant to the entity's preparation and fair presentation[21] of the financial statements in order to design audit procedures that are appropriate in the circumstances, but not for the purpose of expressing an opinion on the effectiveness of the entity's internal control.[22] An audit also includes evaluating the appropriateness of accounting policies used and the reasonableness of accounting estimates made by management, as well as evaluating the overall presentation of the financial statements.

We believe that the audit evidence we have obtained is sufficient and appropriate to provide a basis for our audit opinion.

Opinion

In our opinion, the financial statements present fairly, in all material respects, (or *give a true and fair view of*) the financial position of ABC Company as at December 31, 20X1, and (*of*) its financial performance and its cash flows for the year then ended in accordance with International Financial Reporting Standards.

Other Matter

The financial statements of ABC Company for the year ended December 31, 20X0, were audited by another auditor who expressed an unmodified opinion on those statements on March 31, 20X1.

Report on Other Legal and Regulatory Requirements

[Form and content of this section of the auditor's report will vary depending on the nature of the auditor's other reporting responsibilities.]

[Auditor's signature]

[Date of the auditor's report]

[Auditor's address]

---

[21] In the case of footnote 20, this may read: "In making those risk assessments, the auditor considers internal control relevant to the entity's preparation of financial statements that give a true and fair view in order to design audit procedures that are appropriate in the circumstances, but not for the purpose of expressing an opinion on the effectiveness of the entity's internal control."

[22] In circumstances when the auditor also has responsibility to express an opinion on the effectiveness of internal control in conjunction with the audit of the financial statements, this sentence would be worded as follows: "In making those risk assessments, the auditor considers internal control relevant to the entity's preparation and fair presentation of the financial statements in order to design audit procedures that are appropriate in the circumstances." In the case of footnote 20, this may read: "In making those risk assessments, the auditor considers internal control relevant to the entity's preparation of financial statements that give a true and fair view in order to design audit procedures that are appropriate in the circumstances."

Example D – Comparative Financial Statements: (Ref: Para. A9)

> Report illustrative of the circumstances described in paragraph 15, as follows:
>
> • Auditor is required to report on both the current period financial statements and the prior period financial statements in connection with the current year's audit.
>
> • The auditor's report on the prior period, as previously issued, included a qualified opinion.
>
> • The matter giving rise to the modification is unresolved.
>
> • The effects or possible effects of the matter on the current period's figures are material to both the current period financial statements and prior period financial statements and require a modification to the auditor's opinion.

INDEPENDENT AUDITOR'S REPORT

[Appropriate Addressee]

Report on the Financial Statements[23]

We have audited the accompanying financial statements of ABC Company, which comprise the balance sheets as at December 31, 20X1 and 20X0, and the income statements, statements of changes in equity and cash flow statements for the years then ended, and a summary of significant accounting policies and other explanatory information.

Management's[24] Responsibility for the Financial Statements

Management is responsible for the preparation and fair presentation of these financial statements in accordance with International Financial Reporting Standards,[25] and for such internal control as management determines is necessary to enable the preparation of financial statements that are free from material misstatement, whether due to fraud or error.

Auditor's Responsibility

Our responsibility is to express an opinion on these financial statements based on our audits. We conducted our audits in accordance with International Standards on Auditing. Those standards require that we comply with ethical requirements and plan and perform the

---

[23] The sub-title "Report on the Financial Statements" is unnecessary in circumstances when the second sub-title "Report on Other Legal and Regulatory Requirements" is not applicable.

[24] Or other term that is appropriate in the context of the legal framework in the particular jurisdiction.

[25] Where management's responsibility is to prepare financial statements that give a true and fair view, this may read: "Management is responsible for the preparation of financial statements that give a true and fair view in accordance with International Financial Reporting Standards, and for such ..."

audit to obtain reasonable assurance about whether the financial statements are free from material misstatement.

An audit involves performing procedures to obtain audit evidence about the amounts and disclosures in the financial statements. The procedures selected depend on the auditor's judgment, including the assessment of the risks of material misstatement of the financial statements, whether due to fraud or error. In making those risk assessments, the auditor considers internal control relevant to the entity's preparation and fair presentation[26] of the financial statements in order to design audit procedures that are appropriate in the circumstances, but not for the purpose of expressing an opinion on the effectiveness of the entity's internal control.[27] An audit also includes evaluating the appropriateness of accounting policies used and the reasonableness of accounting estimates made by management, as well as evaluating the overall presentation of the financial statements.

We believe that the audit evidence we have obtained in our audits is sufficient and appropriate to provide a basis for our qualified audit opinion.

Basis for Qualified Opinion

As discussed in Note X to the financial statements, no depreciation has been provided in the financial statements, which constitutes a departure from International Financial Reporting Standards. Based on the straight-line method of depreciation and annual rates of 5% for the building and 20% for the equipment, the loss for the year should be increased by xxx in 20X1 and xxx in 20X0, property, plant and equipment should be reduced by accumulated depreciation of xxx in 20X1 and xxx in 20X0, and the accumulated loss should be increased by xxx in 20X1 and xxx in 20X0.

Qualified Opinion

In our opinion, except for the effects of the matter described in the Basis for Qualified Opinion paragraph, the financial statements present fairly, in all material respects, (or *give a true and fair view of*) the financial position of ABC Company as at December 31, 20X1 and 20X0 and (*of*) its financial performance and its cash flows for the years then ended in accordance with International Financial Reporting Standards.

---

[26] In the case of footnote 25, this may read: "In making those risk assessments, the auditor considers internal control relevant to the entity's preparation of financial statements that give a true and fair view in order to design audit procedures that are appropriate in the circumstances, but not for the purpose of expressing an opinion on the effectiveness of the entity's internal control."

[27] In circumstances when the auditor also has responsibility to express an opinion on the effectiveness of internal control in conjunction with the audit of the financial statements, this sentence would be worded as follows: "In making those risk assessments, the auditor considers internal control relevant to the entity's preparation and fair presentation of the financial statements in order to design audit procedures that are appropriate in the circumstances." In the case of footnote 25, this may read: "In making those risk assessments, the auditor considers internal control relevant to the entity's preparation of financial statements that give a true and fair view in order to design audit procedures that are appropriate in the circumstances."

Report on Other Legal and Regulatory Requirements

[Form and content of this section of the auditor's report will vary depending on the nature of the auditor's other reporting responsibilities.]

[Auditor's signature]

[Date of the auditor's report]

[Auditor's address]

INTERNATIONAL STANDARD ON AUDITING (UK AND IRELAND) 720 (REVISED OCTOBER 2012)

SECTION A – THE AUDITOR'S RESPONSIBILITIES RELATING TO OTHER INFORMATION IN DOCUMENTS CONTAINING AUDITED FINANCIAL STATEMENTS

(Effective for audits of financial statements for periods commencing on or after 1 October 2012)

CONTENTS

International Standard on Auditing (UK and Ireland) (ISA (UK and Ireland)) 720 Section A, "The Auditor's Responsibilities Relating to Other Information in Documents Containing Audited Financial Statements" should be read in conjunction with ISA (UK and Ireland) 200, "Overall Objectives of the Independent Auditor and the Conduct of an Audit in Accordance with International Standards on Auditing (UK and Ireland)."

Introduction

Scope of this ISA (UK and Ireland)

1. This International Standard on Auditing (UK and Ireland) (ISA (UK and Ireland)) deals with the auditor's responsibilities relating to other information in documents containing audited financial statements and the auditor's report thereon. In the absence of any separate requirement in the particular circumstances of the engagement, the auditor's opinion does not cover other information and the auditor has no specific responsibility for determining whether or not other information is properly stated. However, the auditor reads the other information because the credibility of the audited financial statements may be undermined by material inconsistencies between the audited financial statements and other information. (Ref: Para. A1)

1-1. The standards and guidance in this Section apply to all other information included in documents containing audited financial statements, including the directors' report. Further standards and guidance on the auditor's statutory reporting obligations in relation to directors' reports are set out in Section B.

2. In this ISA (UK and Ireland) "documents containing audited financial statements" refers to annual reports (or similar documents), that are issued to owners (or similar stakeholders), containing audited financial statements and the auditor's report thereon. This ISA (UK and Ireland) may also be applied, adapted as necessary in the circumstances, to other documents containing audited financial statements, such as those used in securities offerings.[1] (Ref: Para. A2)

Effective Date

3. This ISA (UK and Ireland) is effective for audits of financial statements for periods commencing on or after 1 October 2012.

Objective

4. The objective of the auditor is to respond appropriately when documents containing audited financial statements and the auditor's report thereon include other

---

[1] See ISA (UK and Ireland) 200, "Overall Objectives of the Independent Auditor and the Conduct of an Audit in Accordance with International Standards on Auditing," paragraph 2.

Paragraph 2 of ISA (UK and Ireland) 200 includes the statement that "ISAs (UK and Ireland) do not address the responsibilities of the auditor that may exist in legislation, regulation or otherwise in connection with, for example, the offering of securities to the public. Such responsibilities may differ from those established in the ISAs (UK and Ireland). Accordingly, while the auditor may find aspects of the ISAs (UK and Ireland) helpful in such circumstances, it is the responsibility of the auditor to ensure compliance with all relevant legal, regulatory or professional obligations." Guidance on other information issued with investment circulars is covered in the FRC's Statement of Investment Reporting Standard (SIR) 1000. Accordingly, the guidance in this ISA (UK and Ireland) is limited to Annual Reports and statutory audits.

information that could undermine the credibility of those financial statements and the auditor's report.

Definitions

5. For purposes of the ISAs (UK and Ireland) the following terms have the meanings attributed below:

    (a) Other information – Financial and non-financial information (other than the financial statements and the auditor's report thereon) which is included, either by law, regulation or custom, in a document containing audited financial statements and the auditor's report thereon. (Ref: Para. A3-A4)

    (b) Inconsistency – Other information that contradicts information contained in the audited financial statements. A material inconsistency may raise doubt about the audit conclusions drawn from audit evidence previously obtained and, possibly, about the basis for the auditor's opinion on the financial statements.

    (c) Misstatement of fact – Other information that is unrelated to matters appearing in the audited financial statements that is incorrectly stated or presented. A material misstatement of fact may undermine the credibility of the document containing audited financial statements.

    In the context of an audit conducted in accordance with ISAs (UK and Ireland), other information that is incorrectly stated or presented includes other information that is apparently incorrect based on, or inconsistent with, the knowledge acquired by the auditor in the course of performing the audit or that is otherwise misleading.

Requirements

Reading Other Information

6. The auditor shall read the other information to identify material inconsistencies, if any, with the audited financial statements. (Ref: Para. A4-1 – A4-2)

6-1. The auditor shall also read the other information to identify any information that is apparently materially incorrect based on, or materially inconsistent with, the knowledge acquired by the auditor in the course of performing the audit. (Ref: Para. A4-1 – A4-2)

**FINANCIAL
REPORTING COUNCIL**

7. The auditor shall make appropriate arrangements with management or those charged with governance to obtain the other information prior to the date of the auditor's report. If it is not possible to obtain all the other information prior to the date of the auditor's report, the auditor shall read such other information as soon as practicable[1a]. (Ref: Para. A5)

Material Inconsistencies

8. If, on reading the other information, the auditor identifies a material inconsistency, the auditor shall determine whether the audited financial statements or the other information needs to be revised.

Material Inconsistencies Identified in Other Information Obtained Prior to the Date of the Auditor's Report

9. If revision of the audited financial statements is necessary and management[1b] refuses to make the revision, the auditor shall modify the opinion in the auditor's report in accordance with ISA (UK and Ireland) 705.[2]

10. If revision of the other information is necessary and management refuses to make the revision, the auditor shall communicate this matter to those charged with governance, unless all of those charged with governance are involved in managing the entity;[3] and

    (a) Include in the auditor's report an Other Matter(s) paragraph describing the material inconsistency in accordance with ISA (UK and Ireland) 706;[4] or

    (b) Withhold the auditor's report; or

    (c) Withdraw from the engagements, where withdrawal is possible under applicable law or regulation. (Ref: Para. A6-A7, A11-2 – A11-3)

Material Inconsistencies Identified in Other Information Obtained Subsequent to the Date of the Auditor's Report

Paragraphs 11 to 13 deal with other information obtained subsequent to the date of the auditor's report. These are not applicable in an audit conducted in accordance with ISAs (UK and Ireland) because ISA (UK and Ireland) 700, "The Auditor's Report on Financial Statements" requires that "The auditor shall not sign, and hence date, the report earlier than the date on which all other information contained in a report of

---

[1a] ISA (UK and Ireland) 700 requires that "The auditor shall not sign, and hence date, the report earlier than the date on which all other information contained in a report of which the audited financial statements form a part have been approved by those charged with governance and the auditor has considered all necessary available evidence."

[1b] In the UK and Ireland those charged with governance are responsible for the preparation of the financial statements.

[2] ISA (UK and Ireland) 705, "Modifications to the Opinion in the Independent Auditor's Report."

[3] ISA (UK and Ireland) 260, "Communication with Those Charged with Governance," paragraph 13.

[4] ISA (UK and Ireland) 706, "Emphasis of Matter Paragraphs and Other Matter Paragraphs in the Independent Auditor's Report," paragraph 8.

which the audited financial statements forma part have been approved by those charged with governance and the auditor has considered all necessary available evidence."

11. If revision of the audited financial statements is necessary, the auditor shall follow the relevant requirements in ISA (UK and Ireland) 560.[5]

12. If revision of the other information is necessary and management agrees to make the revision, the auditor shall carry out the procedures necessary under the circumstances. (Ref: Para. A8)

13. If revision of the other information is necessary, but management refuses to make the revision, the auditor shall notify those charged with governance, unless all of those charged with governance are involved in managing the entity, of the auditor's concern regarding the other information and take any further appropriate action. (Ref: Para. A9)

Material Misstatements of Fact

14. If, on reading the other information for the purpose of identifying material inconsistencies, the auditor becomes aware of an apparent material misstatement of fact, the auditor shall discuss the matter with management. (Ref: Para. A10)

14-1. If, on reading the other information for the purpose of identifying any information that is apparently materially incorrect based on, or materially inconsistent with, the knowledge acquired by the auditor in the course of performing the audit, the auditor becomes aware of an apparent misstatement of fact, the auditor shall discuss the matter with management. (Ref: Para. A10 – A10-2)

15. If, following such discussions, the auditor still considers that there is an apparent material misstatement of fact, the auditor shall request management to consult with a qualified third party, such as the entity's legal counsel, and the auditor shall consider the advice received.

16. If the auditor concludes that there is a material misstatement of fact in the other information which management refuses to correct, the auditor shall notify those charged with governance, unless all of those charged with governance are involved in managing the entity, of the auditor's concern regarding the other information and take any further appropriate action. (Ref: Para. A11 – A11-3)

***

---

[5] ISA (UK and Ireland) 560, "Subsequent Events," paragraphs 10-17.

Application and Other Explanatory Material

Scope of this ISA (UK and Ireland)

Additional Responsibilities, through Statutory or Other Regulatory Requirements, in Relation to Other Information (Ref: Para. 1)

A1. The auditor may have additional responsibilities, through statutory or other regulatory requirements, in relation to other information that are beyond the scope of this ISA (UK and Ireland). For example, some jurisdictions may require the auditor to apply specific procedures to certain of the other information such as required supplementary data or to express an opinion on the reliability of performance indicators described in the other information. Where there are such obligations, the auditor's additional responsibilities are determined by the nature of the engagement and by law, regulation and professional standards. If such other information is omitted or contains deficiencies, the auditor may be required by law or regulation to refer to the matter in the auditor's report.

A1-1. In the UK and Ireland an example of an auditor's additional responsibilities for a listed company would include the auditor's review of whether the Corporate Governance Statement reflects the company's compliance with the provisions of the UK Corporate Governance Code specified by the Listing Rules for review by the auditor.

Documents Containing Audited Financial Statements (Ref: Para. 2)

Considerations Specific to Smaller Entities

A2. Unless required by law or regulation, smaller entities are less likely to issue documents containing audited financial statements. However, an example of such a document would be where a legal requirement exists for an accompanying report by those charged with governance. Examples of other information that may be included in a document containing the audited financial statements of a smaller entity are a detailed income statement and a management report.

Definition of Other Information (Ref: Para. 5(a))

A3. Other information may comprise, for example:

- A report by management or those charged with governance on operations.

- Financial summaries or highlights.

- Employment data.

- Planned capital expenditures.

- Financial ratios.

- Names of officers and directors.

• Selected quarterly data.

A3-1. Further examples relevant in the UK and Ireland are a directors' report required by statute (see Section B), statements relating to corporate governance, as required by the Listing Rules, a chairman's statement, a voluntary Operating and Financial Review and non-statutory financial information included within the annual report[5a].

A4. For purposes of the ISAs (UK and Ireland), other information does not encompass, for example:

• A press release or a transmittal memorandum, such as a covering letter, accompanying the document containing audited financial statements and the auditor's report thereon.

• Information contained in analyst briefings.

• Information contained on the entity's website.

Reading Other Information (Ref: Para. 6-7)

A4-1. When the auditor reads the other information, the auditor does so in the light of the knowledge the auditor has acquired during the audit. The auditor is not expected to verify any of the other information. The audit engagement partner (and, where appropriate, other senior members of the engagement team who can reasonably be expected to be aware of the more important matters arising during the audit and to have a general understanding of the entity's affairs), reads the other information with a view to identifying significant misstatements therein or matters which are inconsistent with the financial statements or the knowledge acquired by the auditor in the course of performing the audit.

A4-2 If the auditor believes that the other information contains a material misstatement of fact, is materially inconsistent with the financial statements, or is otherwise misleading, and the auditor is unable to resolve the matter with management and those charged with governance, the auditor considers the implications for the auditor's report and what further actions may be appropriate. The auditor has regard to the guidance in paragraphs A11-1 and A11-2 below and, for entities that are required, and those that choose voluntarily, to report on how they have applied the UK Corporate Governance Code, the requirements in paragraphs 22A and 22B, and

---

[5a] The FRC recognises that in some circumstances the presentation of non-statutory financial information and associated narrative explanations with the statutory results may help shareholders understand better the financial performance of a company. However, the FRC is concerned that in other circumstances such non-statutory information in annual reports has the potential to be misleading and shareholders may sometimes be misinformed by the manner in which non-statutory information is presented. The FRC believes that the potential for non-statutory information to be misleading is considerable when undue and inappropriate prominence is given to the non-statutory information, when there is no description of the non-statutory information and, where appropriate, the adjusted numbers are not reconciled to the statutory financial information.

related guidance in paragraph A18A, of ISA (UK and Ireland) 700 (Revised) to report on matters by exception.

A5.   Obtaining the other information prior to the date of the auditor's report enables the auditor to resolve possible material inconsistencies and apparent material misstatements of fact with management on a timely basis. An agreement with management as to when the other information will be available may be helpful.

A5-1. Guidance to auditors in the UK and Ireland on the consideration of other information where the annual financial statements accompanied by the auditor's report are published on an entity's website, or in the UK where companies can meet their statutory reporting obligations to shareholders by distributing annual financial statements and certain other reports electronically, is given in the Appendix to this Section[5b].

Material Inconsistencies

Material Inconsistencies Identified in Other Information Obtained Prior to the Date of the Auditor's Report (Ref: Para. 10)

A6.   When management refuses to revise the other information, the auditor may base any decision on what further action to take on advice from the auditor's legal counsel.

A6-1. If the auditor concludes that the other information contains inconsistencies with the financial statements, and the auditor is unable to resolve them through discussion with those charged with governance, the auditor considers requesting those charged with governance to consult with a qualified third party, such as the entity's legal counsel and considers the advice received.

Considerations Specific to Public Sector Entities

A7.   In the public sector, withdrawal from the engagement or withholding the auditor's report may not be options. In such cases, the auditor may issue a report to the appropriate statutory body giving details of the inconsistency.

Material Inconsistencies Identified in Other Information Obtained Subsequent to the Date of the Auditor's Report (Ref: Para. 12-13)

A8.   *When management agrees to revise the other information, the auditor's procedures may include reviewing the steps taken by management to ensure that individuals in receipt of the previously issued financial statements, the auditor's report thereon, and the other information are informed of the revision.*

[5b] In the UK, the Companies Act 2006 enables companies, subject to certain conditions set out in Schedule 5 thereto, to make communications in electronic form, including by means of a website. Further, section 430 of the Companies Act 2006 requires that a quoted company must ensure that its annual accounts and reports are made available on a website.

A9. *When management refuses to make the revision of such other information that the auditor concludes is necessary, appropriate further actions by the auditor may include obtaining advice from the auditor's legal counsel.*

Material Misstatements of Fact (Ref: Para. 14-16)

A10. When discussing an apparent material misstatement of fact with management, the auditor may not be able to evaluate the validity of some disclosures included within the other information and management's responses to the auditor's inquiries, and may conclude that valid differences of judgment or opinion exist.

A10-1 A material misstatement of fact in other information would potentially include an inconsistency between information obtained by the auditor during the audit (such as information obtained as part of the planning process or analytical procedures, or as written representations) and information which is included in the other information.

A10-2. The auditor has regard to the nature of the inconsistency or misstatement that in the auditor's opinion exists. A distinction may be drawn between a matter of fact and one of judgment. It is generally more difficult for the auditor to take issue with a matter of judgment (such as the view of those charged with governance of the likely out-turn for the following year) than a factual error. Although an auditor does not substitute the auditor's judgment for that of management and those charged with governance in such matters, there may be circumstances in which the auditor is aware that the expressed view of management and those charged with governance is significantly at variance with the entity's internal assessment or is so unreasonable as not to be credible to someone with the auditor's knowledge.

A11. When the auditor concludes that there is a material misstatement of fact that management refuses to correct, appropriate further actions by the auditor may include obtaining advice from the auditor's legal counsel.

A11-1. When the auditor concludes that there is a material misstatement of fact that management refuses to correct, appropriate further actions may also include including in the auditor's report an Other Matter(s) paragraph describing the material misstatement of fact.

Further Actions Available to the Auditor when a Material Inconsistency or Material Misstatement of Fact in Other Information is not Corrected

A11-2. The auditor of a limited company in the United Kingdom or the Republic of Ireland may use the auditor's right to be heard at any general meeting of the members on any part of the business of the meeting which concerns the auditor as auditor[5c].

[5c] The relevant reference for the UK is section 502 of the Companies Act 2006, and for the Republic of Ireland is section 193(5) of the Companies Act 1990.

A11-3. The auditor may also consider resigning from the audit engagement. In the case of auditors of limited companies in the United Kingdom or the Republic of Ireland, the requirements for the auditor to make a statement on ceasing to hold office as auditor apply[5d]. When making a statement in these circumstances, the considerations set out in paragraph A10-2 above would normally be applicable. In addition, in the UK the auditor may need to notify the relevant audit authority.

[5d] The relevant reference for the UK is section 519 of the Companies Act 2006, and for the Republic of Ireland is section 185 of the Companies Act 1990.

Appendix

Electronic Publication of the Auditor's Report

Introduction

1. In the UK, section 430 of the Companies Act 2006 requires that a quoted company must ensure that its annual accounts and reports are made available on a website. The Companies Act 2006 also enables all companies, subject to certain conditions set out in Schedule 5 thereto, to make communications in electronic form, including by means of a website.

2. Various types of financial information can be found on websites including information that has been audited (for example the annual financial statements), information which the auditor may have reviewed (for example interim financial information) and information with which the auditor has had no direct involvement, such as financial highlights from a company's Annual Report or may never have seen, such as presentations for analysts. In addition, websites typically contain a considerable amount of non-financial information.

3. The purpose of this Appendix is to provide guidance to auditors on the consideration of other information in situations where the annual financial statements accompanied by the auditor's report are published on an entity's website[5e].

The Auditor's Consideration of Other Information Issued with the Annual Report

Checking Information Presented Electronically

4. When companies include the annual financial statements and the auditor's report on their website or, in the UK, decide to distribute annual financial statements to their shareholders electronically, the auditor:

    (a) Reviews the process by which the financial statements to be published electronically are derived from the financial information contained in the manually signed accounts;

    (b) Checks that the proposed electronic version is identical in content with the manually signed accounts; and

    (c) Checks that the conversion of the manually signed accounts into an electronic format has not distorted the overall presentation of the financial information, for example, by highlighting certain information so as to give it greater prominence.

[5e] This guidance is generally applicable both to auditors in the UK (where the provisions of the Companies Act 2006 apply) and the Republic of Ireland (where they do not).

5.   It is recommended that the auditor retains a printout or disk of the final electronic version for future reference if necessary.

Auditor's Report Wording

6.   The auditor considers whether the wording of the auditor's report is suitable for electronic distribution. Issues include:

- Identifying the financial statements that have been audited and the information that has been reviewed, or read, by the auditor.

- Limiting the auditor's association with any other information distributed with the Annual Report.

Identification of the Financial Statements That Have Been Audited

7.   In Annual Reports produced in a hard copy format, the auditor's report usually identifies the financial statements which have been audited by reference to page numbers. The use of page numbers is often not a suitable method of identifying particular financial information presented on a website[5f]. The auditor's report therefore needs to specify in another way the location and description of the information that has been audited.

8.   The FRC recommends that the auditor's report describes, by name, the primary statements that comprise the financial statements. The same technique can also be used to specify the information that has been reviewed or, because it is included in the Annual Report, read by the auditor.

9.   The auditor ensures that the auditor's statutory report on the full financial statements is not associated with extracts from, or summaries of, those audited financial statements.

Identification of the Nationality of the Accounting and Auditing Standards Applied

10.   Auditor's reports on websites will be accessible internationally, and it is therefore important that the auditor's report indicates clearly the nationality of the accounting standards used in the preparation of the financial statements and the nationality of the auditing standards applied. For the same reason, the auditor ensures that the auditor's report discloses sufficient of the auditor's address to enable readers to understand in which country the auditor is located.

[5f]   The audited financial statements can be presented on the website using a variety of webfile formats. As at the date of this Bulletin, examples of these are the Portable Document Format (PDF) or Hypertext Mark-up Language (HTML). Page numbers generally continue to be an effective referencing mechanism for PDF files but this is not always the case when data is represented 'in HTML.

Limitation of the Auditor's Association With any Other Information Distributed With the Annual Report

11.   In addition to the Annual Report many companies publish on their websites a considerable volume of financial and non-financial information. This information could take the form of additional analyses or alternative presentations of audited financial information. Users of the website are likely to find it difficult to distinguish financial information which the auditor has audited, or read, from other data. This issue is exacerbated when there are hyperlinks which allow users to move easily from one area of the website to another.

12.   The auditor gives careful consideration to the use of hyperlinks between the audited financial statements and information contained on the website that has not been subject to audit or 'reading' by the auditor ('other information'). To avoid possible misunderstandings concerning the scope of the audit, the auditor requests those charged with governance to ensure that hyperlinks contain warnings that the linkage is from audited to unaudited information.

13.   Sometimes audited information is not included in the financial statements themselves (e.g. certain information relating to directors' remuneration may be set out as part of a company's corporate governance disclosures). The FRC is of the view that companies should be encouraged to make disclosures that are required to be audited, as part of the financial statements or included in the Annual Report in such a way that it is clear which elements of it have been audited. In other circumstances the auditor assesses whether the scope of the audit will be capable of being clearly described. If this cannot be achieved to the satisfaction of the auditor it may be necessary to describe the particulars that have been audited within the auditor's report.

14.   The auditor is concerned to establish that the auditor's report on the financial statements is not inappropriately associated with other information. The auditor takes steps to satisfy themselves that information that they have audited or, because it is included in the Annual Report, read, is distinguished from other information in a manner appropriate to the electronic format used by the entity. Techniques that can be used to differentiate material within a website include

   •   Icons or watermarks.

   •   Colour borders.

   •   Labels/banners such as 'annual report' or 'audited financial statements'.

   The appropriate mode of differentiation between audited and unaudited information will be dependent on the electronic format selected, and the nature and extent of other information presented on the website. The method of differentiation would normally also be clearly stated in an introduction page within the website.

15.   During the course of the audit, the auditor discusses with those charged with governance or, where appropriate, the audit committee how the financial statements

and auditor's report will be presented on the entity's website with a view to minimizing the possibility that the auditor's report is inappropriately associated with other information. If the auditor is not satisfied with the proposed electronic presentation of the audited financial statements and auditor's report, the auditor requests that the presentation be amended. If the presentation is not amended the auditor will, in accordance with the terms of the engagement, not give consent for the electronic release of the audit opinion.

16.   If the auditor's report is used without the auditor's consent, and the auditor has concerns about the electronic presentation of the audited financial statements or the auditor's report and appropriate action is not taken by those charged with governance, the auditor seeks legal advice as necessary. The auditor also considers whether it would be appropriate to resign.

INTERNATIONAL STANDARD ON AUDITING (UK AND IRELAND) 720

SECTION B – THE AUDITOR'S STATUTORY REPORTING RESPONSIBILITY IN RELATION TO DIRECTORS' REPORTS

(Effective for audits of financial statements for periods ending on or after 15 December 2010)

CONTENTS

International Standard on Auditing (UK and Ireland) (ISA (UK and Ireland)) 720 Section B, "The Auditor's Statutory Reporting Responsibility in Relation to Directors' Reports" should be read in conjunction with ISA (UK and Ireland) 200, "Overall Objectives of the Independent Auditor and the Conduct of an Audit in Accordance with International Standards on Auditing (UK and Ireland)."

Introduction

Scope of this Section

1.   This Section of International Standard on Auditing (UK and Ireland) (ISA (UK and Ireland)) 720 deals with the auditor's statutory reporting responsibility in relation to directors' reports.

2.   In the United Kingdom and the Republic of Ireland, legislation[1] requires the auditor of a company to state in the auditor's report whether, in the auditor's opinion, the information given in the directors' report is consistent with the financial statements.

3.   "Information given in the directors' report" includes information that is included by way of cross reference to other information presented separately from the directors' report. For example, a UK company may decide to present a voluntary Operating and Financial Review (OFR) which includes some or all of the matters required for the Business Review section of the directors' report. Rather than duplicate the information, the company may cross refer from the Business Review section in the directors' report to the relevant information provided in the OFR.

4.   The auditor is not required to verify, or report on, the completeness of the information in the directors' report. If, however, the auditor becomes aware that information that is required by law or regulations to be in the directors' report has been omitted the auditor communicates the matter to those charged with governance. This communication includes situations where the required information is presented separately from the directors' report without appropriate cross references.

5.   Illustrative auditor's reports tailored for use with audits conducted in accordance with ISAs (UK and Ireland) are given in the current versions of the APB Compendia Auditor's Report Bulletins.

Effective Date

6.   This Section of ISA (UK and Ireland) 720 is effective for audits of financial statements for periods ending on or after 15 December 2010.

Objective

7.   The objective of the auditor is to form an opinion on whether the information given in the directors' report is consistent with the financial statements and to respond appropriately if it is not consistent.

---

[1]   Relevant legislation includes:
*   In the UK, Section 496 of the Companies Act 2006
*   In the Republic of Ireland, Section 15 of the Companies (Amendment) Act 1986.

FINANCIAL
REPORTING COUNCIL

Requirements

Reading the Directors' Report

8.   The auditor shall read the information in the directors' report and assess whether it is consistent with the financial statements. (Ref: Para. A1)

Inconsistencies

9.   If the auditor identifies any inconsistencies between the information in the directors' report and the financial statements the auditor shall seek to resolve them. (Ref: Para. A2)

10.   If the auditor is of the opinion that the information in the directors' report is materially inconsistent[2] with the financial statements, and has been unable to resolve the inconsistency, the auditor shall state that opinion and describe the inconsistency in the auditor's report.

11.   If an amendment is necessary to the financial statements and management and those charged with governance refuse to make the amendment, the auditor shall express a qualified or adverse opinion on the financial statements.

Documentation

12.   The auditor shall document:

       (a)   The results of those procedures performed to assess whether the information in the directors' report is consistent with the financial statements, including details of any material inconsistencies identified and how they were resolved; and

       (b)   The conclusion reached as to whether the information in the directors' report is consistent with the financial statements.

***

Application and Other Explanatory Material

Reading the Directors' Report (Ref: Para. 8)

A1.   Much of the information in the directors' report is likely to be extracted or directly derived from the financial statements and will therefore be directly comparable with them. Some financial information may, however, be more detailed or prepared on a different basis from that in the financial statements. Where the financial information is more detailed, the auditor agrees the information to the auditor's working papers or

---

[2]   Materiality is addressed in ISA (UK and Ireland) 320 "Audit Materiality". An inconsistency is "material" if it could influence the economic decisions of users.

the entity's accounting records. Where the financial information has been prepared on a different basis, the auditor considers whether there is adequate disclosure of the differences in the bases of preparation to enable an understanding of the differences in the information, and checks the reconciliation of the information to the financial statements.

Inconsistencies (Ref: Para. 9)

A2.   Inconsistencies include:

- Differences between amounts or narrative appearing in the financial statements and the directors' report.

- Differences between the bases of preparation of related items appearing in the financial statements and the directors' report, where the figures themselves are not directly comparable and the different bases are not disclosed.

- Contradictions between figures contained in the financial statements and narrative explanations of those figures in the directors' report.

The auditor ordinarily seeks to resolve inconsistencies through discussion with management and those charged with governance.

Section 5: STATEMENTS OF STANDARDS FOR REPORTING ACCOUNTANTS

INTERNATIONAL STANDARD ON REVIEW ENGAGEMENTS (UK AND IRELAND) 2410

REVIEW OF INTERIM FINANCIAL INFORMATION PERFORMED BY THE INDEPENDENT AUDITOR OF THE ENTITY

(Effective for reviews of interim financial information for periods ending on or after 20 September 2007. Early adoption is permitted.)

CONTENTS

Appendix 7: Examples of Review Reports with an Adverse Conclusion for a Departure from the Applicable Financial Reporting Framework

Appendix 8: Example Review Report for a UK or Irish Company Listed in the UK or Ireland Preparing a Half-Yearly Financial Report in Compliance with IAS 34 as Adopted by the European Union

Appendix 9: Summary of Particular Requirements of Half-Yearly Financial Reports Prepared by Listed Companies in the UK and Ireland

International Standard on Review Engagements (UK and Ireland) (ISRE (UK and Ireland)) 2410, "Review of Interim Financial Information Performed by the Independent Auditor of the Entity" should be read in the context of the Statement "The Financial Reporting Council – Scope and Authority of Audit and Assurance Pronouncements" which sets out the application and authority of FRC pronouncements.

ISRE (UK and Ireland) 2410 adopts the text of ISRE 2410 as issued by the International Auditing and Assurance Standards Board (IAASB) in July 2005. Supplementary material added by the FRC is differentiated by the use of grey shading.

Introduction

1. The purpose of this International Standard on Review Engagements (UK and Ireland) (ISRE (UK and Ireland)) is to establish standards and provide guidance on the auditor's professional responsibilities when the auditor undertakes an engagement to review interim financial information of an audit client, and on the form and content of the report. The term "auditor" is used throughout this ISRE (UK and Ireland), not because the auditor is performing an audit function but because the scope of this ISRE (UK and Ireland) is limited to a review of interim financial information performed by the independent auditor of the financial statements of the entity.

1-1. This ISRE (UK and Ireland) uses the terms 'those charged with governance' and 'management'. The term 'governance' describes the role of persons entrusted with the supervision, control and direction of an entity. Ordinarily, those charged with governance are accountable for ensuring that the entity achieves its objectives, and for the quality of its financial reporting and reporting to interested parties. Those charged with governance include management only when they perform such functions.

1-2. In the UK and Ireland, those charged with governance include the directors (executive and non-executive) of a company or other body, the members of an audit committee where one exists, the partners, proprietors, committee of management or trustees of other forms of entity, or equivalent persons responsible for directing the entity's affairs and preparing its financial statements.

1-3. 'Management' comprises those persons who perform senior managerial functions.

1-4. In the UK and Ireland, depending on the nature and circumstances of the entity, management may include some or all of those charged with governance (e.g. executive directors). Management will not normally include non-executive directors.

2. For purposes of this ISRE (UK and Ireland), interim financial information is financial information that is prepared and presented in accordance with an applicable financial reporting frameworkFor example, International Financial Reporting Standards as issued by the International Accounting Standards Board. and comprises either a complete or a condensed set of financial statements for a period that is shorter than the entity's financial year.

2-1. In the UK and Ireland, interim financial information usually comprises condensed financial information prepared for the first six months of the financial year. For entities listed on the London Stock Exchange the applicable financial reporting framework is established by the Disclosure and Transparency Rules of the Financial Services Authority (FSA)[1a]. For entities listed on the Irish Stock Exchange the applicable

---

[1a] Disclosure and Transparency Rule (DTR) 4.2 "Half-yearly financial reports" applies to all issuers whose shares or debt securities are admitted to trading and whose home state is the UK, subject to the exemptions set out in DTR 4.4.

financial reporting framework is established by the Transparency (Directive 2004/109/EC) Regulations 2007 and the Transparency Rules of the Financial Regulator[1b].

2-2.   For entities listed on the London or Irish Stock Exchanges, issuers that are required to prepare consolidated annual accounts using International Financial Reporting Standards (IFRS) are required to prepare half-yearly financial reports that include a condensed set of financial statements that comply with International Accounting Standard (IAS) 34, "Interim Financial Reporting," as adopted by the European Union. The relatively few issuers that do not prepare consolidated accounts are required to comply with the minimum disclosure requirements set out in the relevant rules of the UK FSA and the Irish Transparency Regulations and rules of the Irish Financial Regulator as applicable. These rules and regulations also make clear that the persons making the required responsibility statements can satisfy the requirement to confirm that the condensed set of financial statements give a true and fair view by giving a statement that they have been prepared in accordance with IAS 34 as adopted by the European Union or, for UK or Irish issuers not using IFRS, pronouncements on interim reporting issued by the Accounting Standards Board[1c], provided always that such persons have reasonable grounds to be satisfied that the condensed set of financial statements is not misleading. Further information on the rules and regulations applicable to issuers is given in Appendix 9.

2-3.   In the context of a review of consolidated interim financial information "the entity," as referred to in this ISRE (UK and Ireland), is the group.

3.   **The auditor who is engaged to perform a review of interim financial information should perform the review in accordance with this ISRE (UK and Ireland).** Through performing the audit of the annual financial statements, the auditor obtains an understanding of the entity and its environment, including its internal control. When the auditor is engaged to review the interim financial information, this understanding is updated through inquiries made in the course of the review, and assists the auditor in focusing the inquiries to be made and the analytical and other review procedures to be applied. A practitioner who is engaged to perform a review of interim financial information, and who is not the auditor of the entity, performs the review in accordance with ISRE 2400, "Engagements to Review Financial Statements."[1d] As the practitioner does not ordinarily have the same understanding of the entity and its environment, including its internal control, as the auditor of the entity, the practitioner needs to carry out different inquiries and procedures to meet the objective of the review.

3-1.   In some cases the auditor may be asked to carry out specific agreed-upon procedures as an alternative to a review, or the auditor may be approached for advice and guidance on specific accounting and financial reporting issues such as the

---

[1b] Requirements for half yearly financial reports are set out in regulations 6 to 8 of Part 2 of the Transparency (Directive 2004/109/EC) Regulations 2007, subject to the exemptions set out in Part 3. Further requirements applicable to half-yearly financial reports are set out in the Transparency Rules issued by The Financial Regulator in Ireland.

[1c] For half-yearly periods ending on or after 20 September 2007, the relevant ASB pronouncement is the Statement "Half-Yearly Financial Reports".

[1d] ISRE 2400 has not been promulgated by the APB for application in the UK and Ireland.

policies relating to asset impairment or the useful life of an intangible asset. In such circumstances the auditor first agrees the procedures to be carried out, and then reports within that context. Such engagements are outside the scope of this ISRE (UK and Ireland) and, in such circumstances, the auditor requests the entity to describe interim financial information as 'neither audited nor reviewed'[1e].

General Principles of a Review of Interim Financial Information

4. **The auditor should comply with the ethical requirements relevant to the audit of the annual financial statements of the entity[1f].** These ethical requirements govern the auditor's professional responsibilities in the following areas: independence, integrity, objectivity, professional competence and due care, confidentiality, professional behavior, and technical standards.

5. **The auditor should implement quality control procedures that are applicable to the individual engagement.** The elements of quality control that are relevant to an individual engagement include leadership responsibilities for quality on the engagement, ethical requirements, acceptance and continuance of client relationships and specific engagements, assignment of engagement teams, engagement performance, and monitoring.

6. **The auditor should plan and perform the review with an attitude of professional skepticism, recognizing that circumstances may exist that cause the interim financial information to require a material adjustment for it to be prepared, in all material respects, in accordance with the applicable financial reporting framework.** An attitude of professional skepticism means that the auditor makes a critical assessment, with a questioning mind, of the validity of evidence obtained and is alert to evidence that contradicts or brings into question the reliability of documents or representations by management of the entity.

Objective of an Engagement to Review Interim Financial Information

7. The objective of an engagement to review interim financial information is to enable the auditor to express a conclusion whether, on the basis of the review, anything has come to the auditor's attention that causes the auditor to believe that the interim financial information is not prepared, in all material respects, in accordance with an applicable

---

[1e] The FSA's Disclosure and Transparency Rule 4.2.9(1), and the Irish Regulation 8(4)(a), requires that if the half-yearly financial report has been audited or reviewed by auditors pursuant to the Auditing Practices Board guidance on Review of Interim Financial Information, the audit report or review report must be reproduced in full.
The FSA's Disclosure and Transparency Rule 4.2.9(2), and the Irish Regulation 8(4)(b), requires that if the half-yearly financial report has not been audited or reviewed by auditors pursuant to the Auditing Practices Board guidance on Review of Interim Financial Information, an issuer must make a statement to this effect in its report.
[1f] In the UK and Ireland the relevant ethical pronouncements with which the auditor complies are the APB's Ethical Standards for Auditors and the ethical pronouncements relating to the work of auditors issued by the auditor's relevant professional body.

financial reporting framework. The auditor makes inquiries, and performs analytical and other review procedures in order to reduce to a moderate level the risk of expressing an inappropriate conclusion when the interim financial information is materially misstated.

8. The objective of a review of interim financial information differs significantly from that of an audit conducted in accordance with International Standards on Auditing (UK and Ireland) (ISAs (UK and Ireland)). A review of interim financial information does not provide a basis for expressing an opinion whether the financial information gives a true and fair view, or is presented fairly, in all material respects, in accordance with an applicable financial reporting framework.

9. A review, in contrast to an audit, is not designed to obtain reasonable assurance that the interim financial information is free from material misstatement. A review consists of making inquiries, primarily of persons responsible for financial and accounting matters, and applying analytical and other review procedures. A review may bring significant matters affecting the interim financial information to the auditor's attention, but it does not provide all of the evidence that would be required in an audit.

Agreeing the Terms of the Engagement

10. **The auditor and the client should agree on the terms of the engagement.**

11. The agreed terms of the engagement are ordinarily recorded in an engagement letter. Such a communication helps to avoid misunderstandings regarding the nature of the engagement and, in particular, the objective and scope of the review, management's responsibilities, the extent of the auditor's responsibilities, the assurance obtained, and the nature and form of the report. The communication ordinarily covers the following matters:

- The objective of a review of interim financial information.

- The scope of the review.

- Management's responsibility for the interim financial information.

- The applicable financial reporting framework (e.g. IAS 34 as adopted by the European Union and/or, where applicable, rules and regulations of a listing/ regulatory authority relating to the form and content of interim financial information)

- Management's responsibility for establishing and maintaining effective internal control relevant to the preparation of interim financial information.

- Management's responsibility for making all financial records and related information available to the auditor.

- Management's agreement to provide written representations to the auditor to confirm representations made orally during the review, as well as representations that are implicit in the entity's records.

- The anticipated form and content of the report to be issued, including the identity of the addressee of the report.

- Management's agreement that where any document containing interim financial information indicates that the interim financial information has been reviewed by the entity's auditor, the review report will also be included in the document.

An illustrative engagement letter is set out in Appendix 1 to this ISRE (UK and Ireland). The terms of engagement to review interim financial information can also be combined with the terms of engagement to audit the annual financial statements.

Procedures for a Review of Interim Financial Information

Understanding the Entity and its Environment, Including its Internal Control

12. **The auditor should have an understanding of the entity and its environment, including its internal control, as it relates to the preparation of both annual and interim financial information, sufficient to plan and conduct the engagement so as to be able to:**

    (a) **Identify the types of potential material misstatement and consider the likelihood of their occurrence; and**

    (b) **Select the inquiries, analytical and other review procedures that will provide the auditor with a basis for reporting whether anything has come to the auditor's attention that causes the auditor to believe that the interim financial information is not prepared, in all material respects, in accordance with the applicable financial reporting framework.**

13. As required by ISA (UK and Ireland) 315, "Understanding the Entity and its Environment and Assessing the Risks of Material Misstatement," the auditor who has audited the entity's financial statements for one or more annual periods has obtained an understanding of the entity and its environment, including its internal control, as it relates to the preparation of annual financial information that was sufficient to conduct the audit. In planning a review of interim financial information, the auditor updates this understanding. The auditor also obtains a sufficient understanding of internal control as it relates to the preparation of interim financial information as it may differ from internal control as it relates to annual financial information.

14. The auditor uses the understanding of the entity and its environment, including its internal control, to determine the inquiries to be made and the analytical and other review procedures to be applied, and to identify the particular events, transactions or assertions to which inquiries may be directed or analytical or other review procedures applied.

15. The procedures performed by the auditor to update the understanding of the entity and its environment, including its internal control, ordinarily include the following:

- Reading the documentation, to the extent necessary, of the preceding year's audit and reviews of prior interim period(s) of the current year and corresponding interim period(s) of the prior year, to enable the auditor to identify matters that may affect the current-period interim financial information.

- Considering any significant risks, including the risk of management override of controls, that were identified in the audit of the prior year's financial statements.

- Reading the most recent annual and comparable prior period interim financial information.

- Considering materiality with reference to the applicable financial reporting framework as it relates to interim financial information to assist in determining the nature and extent of the procedures to be performed and evaluating the effect of misstatements.

- Considering the nature of any corrected material misstatements and any identified uncorrected immaterial misstatements in the prior year's financial statements.

- Considering significant financial accounting and reporting matters that may be of continuing significance such as material weaknesses in internal control.

- Considering the results of any audit procedures performed with respect to the current year's financial statements.

- Considering the results of any internal audit performed and the subsequent actions taken by management.

- Reading management accounts and commentaries for the period.

- Considering any findings from prior periods relating to the quality and reliability of management accounts.

- Inquiring of management about the results of management's assessment of the risk that the interim financial information may be materially misstated as a result of fraud.

- Inquiring of management about the effect of changes in the entity's business activities.

- Inquiring of management about any significant changes in internal control and the potential effect of any such changes on the preparation of interim financial information.

- Inquiring of management of the process by which the interim financial information has been prepared and the reliability of the underlying accounting records to which the interim financial information is agreed or reconciled.

16. The auditor determines the nature of the review procedures, if any, to be performed for components and, where applicable, communicates these matters to other auditors involved in the review. Factors to be considered include the materiality of, and risk of misstatement in, the interim financial information of components, and the auditor's understanding of the extent to which internal control over the preparation of such information is centralized or decentralized.

17. **In order to plan and conduct a review of interim financial information, a recently appointed auditor, who has not yet performed an audit of the annual financial statements in accordance with ISAs (UK and Ireland), should obtain an understanding of the entity and its environment, including its internal control, as it relates to the preparation of both annual and interim financial information.**

18. This understanding enables the auditor to focus the inquiries made, and the analytical and other review procedures applied in performing a review of interim financial information in accordance with this ISRE (UK and Ireland). As part of obtaining this understanding, the auditor ordinarily makes inquiries of the predecessor auditor and, where practicable, reviews the predecessor auditor's documentation for the preceding annual audit, and for any prior interim periods in the current year that have been reviewed by the predecessor auditor. In doing so, the auditor considers the nature of any corrected misstatements, and any uncorrected misstatements aggregated by the predecessor auditor, any significant risks, including the risk of management override of controls, and significant accounting and any reporting matters that may be of continuing significance, such as material weaknesses in internal control.

Inquiries, Analytical and Other Review Procedures

19. **The auditor should make inquiries, primarily of persons responsible for financial and accounting matters, and perform analytical and other review procedures to enable the auditor to conclude whether, on the basis of the procedures performed, anything has come to the auditor's attention that causes the auditor to believe that the interim financial information is not prepared, in all material respects, in accordance with the applicable financial reporting framework.**

20. A review ordinarily does not require tests of the accounting records through inspection, observation or confirmation. Procedures for performing a review of interim financial information are ordinarily limited to making inquiries, primarily of persons responsible for financial and accounting matters, and applying analytical and other review procedures, rather than corroborating information obtained concerning significant accounting matters relating to the interim financial information. The auditor's understanding of the entity and its environment, including its internal control, the results of the risk assessments relating to the preceding audit and the auditor's consideration of materiality as it relates to the interim financial information, affects the nature and extent of the inquiries made, and analytical and other review procedures applied.

21. The auditor ordinarily performs the following procedures:

- Reading the minutes of the meetings of shareholders, those charged with governance, and other appropriate committees to identify matters that may affect the interim financial information, and inquiring about matters dealt with at meetings for which minutes are not available that may affect the interim financial information.

- Considering the effect, if any, of matters giving rise to a modification of the audit or review report, accounting adjustments or unadjusted misstatements, at the time of the previous audit or reviews.

- Communicating, where appropriate, with other auditors who are performing a review of the interim financial information of the reporting entity's significant components.

- Inquiring of members of management responsible for financial and accounting matters, and others as appropriate about the following:

  ○ Whether the interim financial information has been prepared and presented in accordance with the applicable financial reporting framework.

  ○ Whether there have been any changes in accounting principles or in the methods of applying them.

  ○ Whether any new transactions have necessitated the application of a new accounting principle.

  ○ Whether the interim financial information contains any known uncorrected misstatements.

  ○ Unusual or complex situations that may have affected the interim financial information, such as a business combination or disposal of a segment of the business.

  ○ Significant assumptions that are relevant to the fair value measurement or disclosures and management's intention and ability to carry out specific courses of action on behalf of the entity.

  ○ Whether related party transactions have been appropriately accounted for and disclosed in the interim financial information.

  ○ Significant changes in commitments and contractual obligations.

  ○ Significant changes in contingent liabilities including litigation or claims.

  ○ Compliance with debt covenants.

  ○ Matters about which questions have arisen in the course of applying the review procedures.

- ○ Significant transactions occurring in the last several days of the interim period or the first several days of the next interim period.

- ○ Knowledge of any fraud or suspected fraud affecting the entity involving:

  - – Management;

  - – Employees who have significant roles in internal control; or

  - – Others where the fraud could have a material effect on the interim financial information.

- ○ Knowledge of any allegations of fraud, or suspected fraud, affecting the entity's interim financial information communicated by employees, former employees, analysts, regulators, or others.

- ○ Knowledge of any actual or possible noncompliance with laws and regulations that could have a material effect on the interim financial information.

- • For group interim financial information, reviewing consolidation adjustments for consistency with the preceding annual financial statements and enquiring into large or unusual adjustments, and into adjustments made in the preceding annual financial statements but not made in the financial information in the interim report.

- • Reviewing correspondence with regulators where applicable.

- • Applying analytical procedures to the interim financial information designed to identify relationships and individual items that appear to be unusual and that may reflect a material misstatement in the interim financial information. Analytical procedures may include ratio analysis and statistical techniques such as trend analysis or regression analysis and may be performed manually or with the use of computer-assisted techniques. Appendix 2 to this ISRE (UK and Ireland) contains examples of analytical procedures the auditor may consider when performing a review of interim financial information.

- • Reading the interim financial information, and considering whether anything has come to the auditor's attention that causes the auditor to believe that the interim financial information is not prepared, in all material respects, in accordance with the applicable financial reporting framework.

22. The auditor may perform many of the review procedures before or simultaneously with the entity's preparation of the interim financial information. For example, it may be practicable to update the understanding of the entity and its environment, including its internal control, and begin reading applicable minutes before the end of the interim period. Performing some of the review procedures earlier in the interim period also permits early identification and consideration of significant accounting matters affecting the interim financial information.

23. The auditor performing the review of interim financial information is also engaged to perform an audit of the annual financial statements of the entity. For convenience and efficiency, the auditor may decide to perform certain audit procedures concurrently with the review of interim financial information. For example, information gained from reading the minutes of meetings of the board of directors in connection with the review of the interim financial information also may be used for the annual audit. The auditor may also decide to perform, at the time of the interim review, auditing procedures that would need to be performed for the purpose of the audit of the annual financial statements, for example, performing audit procedures on significant or unusual transactions that occurred during the period, such as business combinations, restructurings, or significant revenue transactions.

24. A review of interim financial information ordinarily does not require corroborating the inquiries about litigation or claims. It is, therefore, ordinarily not necessary to send an inquiry letter to the entity's lawyer. Direct communication with the entity's lawyer with respect to litigation or claims may, however, be appropriate if a matter comes to the auditor's attention that causes the auditor to question whether the interim financial information is not prepared, in all material respects, in accordance with the applicable financial reporting framework, and the auditor believes the entity's lawyer may have pertinent information.

25. **The auditor should obtain evidence that the interim financial information agrees or reconciles with the underlying accounting records**. The auditor may obtain evidence that the interim financial information agrees or reconciles with the underlying accounting records by tracing the interim financial information to:

    (a) The accounting records, such as the general ledger, or a consolidating schedule that agrees or reconciles with the accounting records; and

    (b) Other supporting data in the entity's records as necessary.

25-1. For a review of consolidated group interim financial information, the auditor traces the financial information of group components to the consolidation schedules and records of significant consolidation journals and adjustments. The auditor is not required to check the financial information back to the accounting records of individual group components.

26. **The auditor should inquire whether management has identified all events up to the date of the review report that may require adjustment to or disclosure in the interim financial information.** It is not necessary for the auditor to perform other procedures to identify events occurring after the date of the review report.

27. **The auditor should inquire whether management has changed its assessment of the entity's ability to continue as a going concern. When, as a result of this inquiry or other review procedures, the auditor becomes aware of events or conditions that may cast significant doubt on the entity's ability to continue as a going concern, the auditor should:**

(a) Inquire of management as to its plans for future actions based on its going concern assessment, the feasibility of these plans, and whether management believes that the outcome of these plans will improve the situation; and

(b) Consider the adequacy of the disclosure about such matters in the interim financial information.

27-1. The guidance in "Going concern and financial reporting - guidance for directors of listed companies registered in the UK" issued in 1994 states "Directors cannot be expected to consider going concern as fully at the interim, but they should undertake a review of their previous work." Paragraph 57 of that guidance also states: "They should look at the position at the previous year-end to see whether any of the significant factors which they had identified at that time have changed in the interim to such an extent as to affect the appropriateness of the going concern assumption."

28. Events or conditions which may cast significant doubt on the entity's ability to continue as a going concern may have existed at the date of the annual financial statements or may be identified as a result of inquiries of management or in the course of performing other review procedures. When such events or conditions come to the auditor's attention, the auditor inquires of management as to its plans for future action, such as its plans to liquidate assets, borrow money or restructure debt, reduce or delay expenditures, or increase capital. The auditor also inquires as to the feasibility of management's plans and whether management believes that the outcome of these plans will improve the situation. However, it is not ordinarily necessary for the auditor to corroborate the feasibility of management's plans and whether the outcome of these plans will improve the situation.

29. When a matter comes to the auditor's attention that leads the auditor to question whether a material adjustment should be made for the interim financial information to be prepared, in all material respects, in accordance with the applicable financial reporting framework, the auditor should make additional inquiries or perform other procedures to enable the auditor to express a conclusion in the review report. For example, if the auditor's review procedures lead the auditor to question whether a significant sales transaction is recorded in accordance with the applicable financial reporting framework, the auditor performs additional procedures sufficient to resolve the auditor's questions, such as discussing the terms of the transaction with senior marketing and accounting personnel, or reading the sales contract.

Comparative Interim Financial Information

29-1. When comparative interim financial information is presented, the auditor should consider whether:

(a) The accounting policies used for the comparative financial information are consistent with those of the current period and appropriate adjustments and disclosures have been made where this is not the case; and

(b) **The comparative amounts agree with the amounts and other disclosures presented in the preceding interim financial report for the corresponding period or whether appropriate disclosures and adjustments have been made where this is not the case.**

Evaluation of Misstatements

30. **The auditor should evaluate, individually and in the aggregate, whether uncorrected misstatements that have come to the auditor's attention are material to the interim financial information.**

31. A review of interim financial information, in contrast to an audit engagement, is not designed to obtain reasonable assurance that the interim financial information is free from material misstatement. However, misstatements which come to the auditor's attention, including inadequate disclosures, are evaluated individually and in the aggregate to determine whether a material adjustment is required to be made to the interim financial information for it to be prepared, in all material respects, in accordance with the applicable financial reporting framework.

32. The auditor exercises professional judgment in evaluating the materiality of any misstatements that the entity has not corrected. The auditor considers matters such as the nature, cause and amount of the misstatements, whether the misstatements originated in the preceding year or interim period of the current year, and the potential effect of the misstatements on future interim or annual periods.

33. The auditor may designate an amount below which misstatements need not be aggregated, because the auditor expects that the aggregation of such amounts clearly would not have a material effect on the interim financial information. In so doing, the auditor considers the fact that the determination of materiality involves quantitative as well as qualitative considerations, and that misstatements of a relatively small amount could nevertheless have a material effect on the interim financial information.

33-1. The amount designated by the auditor, below which misstatements that have come to the auditors attention need not be aggregated, is the amount below which the auditor believes misstatements are clearly trivial[19].

---

[19] This is not another expression for 'immaterial'. Matters which are 'clearly trivial' will be of an wholly different (smaller) order of magnitude than the materiality thresholds used in the review, and will be matters that are clearly inconsequential, whether taken individually or in aggregate and whether judged by any quantitative and/or qualitative criteria. Further, whenever there is any uncertainty about whether one or more items are 'clearly trivial' (in accordance with this definition), the presumption should be that the matter is not 'clearly trivial'.

Management Representations

34. **The auditor should obtain written representation from management that:**

   (a) **It acknowledges its responsibility for the design and implementation of internal control to prevent and detect fraud and error;**

   (b) **The interim financial information is prepared and presented in accordance with the applicable financial reporting framework;**

   (c) **It believes the effect of those uncorrected misstatements aggregated by the auditor during the review are immaterial, both individually and in the aggregate, to the interim financial information taken as a whole. A summary of such items is included in or attached to the written representations;**

   (d) **It has disclosed to the auditor all significant facts relating to any frauds or suspected frauds known to management that may have affected the entity;**

   (e) **It has disclosed to the auditor the results of its assessment of the risks that the interim financial information may be materially misstated as a result of fraud;[2]**

   (f) **It has disclosed to the auditor all known actual or possible noncompliance with laws and regulations whose effects are to be considered when preparing the interim financial information; and**

   (g) **It has disclosed to the auditor all significant events that have occurred subsequent to the balance sheet date and through to the date of the review report that may require adjustment to or disclosure in the interim financial information.**

35. The auditor obtains additional representations as are appropriate related to matters specific to the entity's business or industry. An illustrative management representation letter is set out in Appendix 3 to this ISRE (UK and Ireland).

Auditor's Responsibility for Accompanying Information[2a]

36. **The auditor should read the other information that accompanies the interim financial information to consider whether any such information is materially**

---

[2] Paragraph 35 of ISA (UK and Ireland) 240, "The Auditor's Responsibility to Consider Fraud in an Audit of Financial Statements" explains that the nature, extent and frequency of such an assessment vary from entity to entity and that management may make a detailed assessment on an annual basis or as part of continuous monitoring. Accordingly, this representation, insofar as it relates to the interim financial information, is tailored to the entity's specific circumstances.

[2a] Other information in the half-yearly financial report of a listed entity includes the interim management report and the responsibility statements required by the rules and regulations of the listing/regulatory authorities. It may also include, for example, performance summaries, prospective information and a chairman's statement.

inconsistent with the interim financial information. If the auditor identifies a material inconsistency, the auditor considers whether the interim financial information or the other information needs to be amended. If an amendment is necessary in the interim financial information and management refuses to make the amendment, the auditor considers the implications for the review report. If an amendment is necessary in the other information and management refuses to make the amendment, the auditor considers including in the review report an additional paragraph describing the material inconsistency, or taking other actions, such as withholding the issuance of the review report or withdrawing from the engagement. For example, management may present alternative measures of earnings that more positively portray financial performance than the interim financial information, and such alternative measures are given excessive prominence, are not clearly defined, or not clearly reconciled to the interim financial information such that they are confusing and potentially misleading[2b].

37. **If a matter comes to the auditor's attention that causes the auditor to believe that the other information appears to include a material misstatement of fact, the auditor should discuss the matter with the entity's management.** While reading the other information for the purpose of identifying material inconsistencies, an apparent material misstatement of fact may come to the auditor's attention (i.e., information, not related to matters appearing in the interim financial information, that is incorrectly stated or presented). When discussing the matter with the entity's management, the auditor considers the validity of the other information and management's responses to the auditor's inquiries, whether valid differences of judgment or opinion exist and whether to request management to consult with a qualified third party to resolve the apparent misstatement of fact. If an amendment is necessary to correct a material misstatement of fact and management refuses to make the amendment, the auditor considers taking further action as appropriate, such as notifying those charged with governance and obtaining legal advice.

[2b] The APB recognises that in some circumstances the presentation of alternative performance measures and associated narrative explanations may help shareholders understand better the financial performance of a company. However, the APB is concerned that in other circumstances such alternative performance measures have the potential to be misleading and shareholders may sometimes be misinformed by the manner in which alternative performance measures are presented. The APB believes that the potential for alternative performance measures to be misleading is considerable when they are given undue and inappropriate prominence, when there is no description of the basis on which the information was produced and, where appropriate, the adjusted numbers are not reconciled to the financial information that is presented in accordance with the applicable financial reporting framework.

The APB's concerns are shared by the UK Listing Authority (UKLA). In its September 2005 newsletter, List!, the UKLA reminded issuers that they were free to disclose additional non-GAAP numbers in their interim accounts but, where they did, the UKLA said they should make clear the basis on which the numbers are calculated in order to avoid misleading investors. The UKLA also explained that it would not expect non-GAAP figures to be given greater prominence in interim announcements than any GAAP numbers. On 3 November 2005, the Committee of European Securities Regulators (CESR) published a recommendation on the use of alternative performance measures. In the February 2006 edition of List! the UKLA indicated that in its view the CESR recommendation represents best practice for the disclosure of alternative performance measures and encouraged issuers to follow the recommendation.

Communication

38. **When, as a result of performing the review of interim financial information, a matter comes to the auditor's attention that causes the auditor to believe that it is necessary to make a material adjustment to the interim financial information for it to be prepared, in all material respects, in accordance with the applicable financial reporting framework, the auditor should communicate this matter as soon as practicable to the appropriate level of management.**

39. **When, in the auditor's judgment, management does not respond appropriately within a reasonable period of time, the auditor should inform those charged with governance.** The communication is made as soon as practicable, either orally or in writing. The auditor's decision whether to communicate orally or in writing is affected by factors such as the nature, sensitivity and significance of the matter to be communicated and the timing of such communications. If the information is communicated orally, the auditor documents the communication.

40. **When, in the auditor's judgment, those charged with governance do not respond appropriately within a reasonable period of time, the auditor should consider:**

    (a) **Whether to modify the report; or**

    (b) **The possibility of withdrawing from the engagement; and**

    (c) **The possibility of resigning from the appointment to audit the annual financial statements.**

41. **When, as a result of performing the review of interim financial information, a matter comes to the auditor's attention that causes the auditor to believe in the existence of fraud or noncompliance by the entity with laws and regulations the auditor should communicate the matter as soon as practicable to the appropriate level of management.** The determination of which level of management is the appropriate one is affected by the likelihood of collusion or the involvement of a member of management. The auditor also considers the need to report such matters to those charged with governance and considers the implication for the review.

42. **The auditor should communicate relevant matters of governance interest arising from the review of interim financial information to those charged with governance.** As a result of performing the review of the interim financial information, the auditor may become aware of matters that in the opinion of the auditor are both important and relevant to those charged with governance in overseeing the financial reporting and disclosure process. The auditor communicates such matters to those charged with governance.

Reporting the Nature, Extent and Results of the Review of Interim Financial Information

43. **The auditor should issue a written report that contains the following:**

(a) **An appropriate title.**

(b) **An addressee, as required by the circumstances of the engagement.**

(c) **Identification of the interim financial information reviewed, including identification of the title of each of the statements contained in the complete or condensed set of financial statements and the date and period covered by the interim financial information.**

(d) **If the interim financial information comprises a complete set of general purpose financial statements prepared in accordance with a financial reporting framework designed to achieve fair presentation, a statement that management is responsible for the preparation and fair presentation of the interim financial information in accordance with the applicable financial reporting framework.**

(e) **In other circumstances, a statement that management is responsible for the preparation and presentation of the interim financial information in accordance with the applicable financial reporting framework.**

(f) **A statement that the auditor is responsible for expressing a conclusion on the interim financial information based on the review.**

(g) **A statement that the review of the interim financial information was conducted in accordance with International Standard on Review Engagements (UK and Ireland) (ISRE (UK and Ireland)) 2410, "Review of Interim Financial Information Performed by the Independent Auditor of the Entity," and a statement that that such a review consists of making inquiries, primarily of persons responsible for financial and accounting matters, and applying analytical and other review procedures.**

(h) **A statement that a review is substantially less in scope than an audit conducted in accordance with International Standards on Auditing (UK and Ireland) and consequently does not enable the auditor to obtain assurance that the auditor would become aware of all significant matters that might be identified in an audit and that accordingly no audit opinion is expressed.**

(i) **If the interim financial information comprises a complete set of general purpose financial statements prepared in accordance with a financial reporting framework designed to achieve fair presentation, a conclusion as to whether anything has come to the auditor's attention that causes the auditor to believe that the interim financial information does not give a true and fair view, or does not present fairly, in all material respects, in accordance with the applicable financial reporting framework (including a reference to the jurisdiction or country of origin of the financial reporting framework when the financial reporting framework used is not International Financial Reporting Standards); or**

(j)   In other circumstances, a conclusion as to whether anything has come to the auditor's attention that causes the auditor to believe that the interim financial information is not prepared, in all material respects, in accordance with the applicable financial reporting framework (including a reference to the jurisdiction or country of origin of the financial reporting framework when the financial reporting framework used is not International Financial Reporting Standards).

(k)   The date of the report.

(l)   The location in the country or jurisdiction where the auditor practices.

(m)   The auditor's signature.

Illustrative review reports are set out in Appendix 4 to this ISRE (UK and Ireland).

43-1.   An illustrative review report for a UK or Irish Company listed in the UK or Ireland and complying with IAS 34 as adopted by the European Union is set out in Appendix 8 to this ISRE (UK and Ireland).

44.   In some jurisdictions, law or regulation governing the review of interim financial information may prescribe wording for the auditor's conclusion that is different from the wording described in paragraph 43(i) or (j). Although the auditor may be obliged to use the prescribed wording, the auditor's responsibilities as described in this ISRE (UK and Ireland) for coming to the conclusion remain the same.

Date of the Review Report

44-1.   The date of the review report on an entity's financial information is the date on which the auditor signs the review report. The auditor should not date the review report earlier than the date on which the financial information is approved by management and those charged with governance.

Departure from the Applicable Financial Reporting Framework

45.   The auditor should express a qualified or adverse conclusion when a matter has come to the auditor's attention that causes the auditor to believe that a material adjustment should be made to the interim financial information for it to be prepared, in all material respects, in accordance with the applicable financial reporting framework.

46.   If matters have come to the auditor's attention that cause the auditor to believe that the interim financial information is or may be materially affected by a departure from the applicable financial reporting framework, and management does not correct the interim financial information, the auditor modifies the review report. The modification describes the nature of the departure and, if practicable, states the effects on the interim financial information. If the information that the auditor believes is necessary for adequate disclosure is not included in the interim financial information, the auditor

modifies the review report and, if practicable, includes the necessary information in the review report. The modification to the review report is ordinarily accomplished by adding an explanatory paragraph to the review report, and qualifying the conclusion. Illustrative review reports with a qualified conclusion are set out in Appendix 5 to this ISRE (UK and Ireland).

47. When the effect of the departure is so material and pervasive to the interim financial information that the auditor concludes a qualified conclusion is not adequate to disclose the misleading or incomplete nature of the interim financial information, the auditor expresses an adverse conclusion. Illustrative review reports with an adverse conclusion are set out in Appendix 7 to this ISRE (UK and Ireland).

Limitation on Scope

48. A limitation on scope ordinarily prevents the auditor from completing the review.

49. **When the auditor is unable to complete the review, the auditor should communicate, in writing, to the appropriate level of management and to those charged with governance the reason why the review cannot be completed, and consider whether it is appropriate to issue a report.**

Limitation on Scope Imposed by Management

50. The auditor does not accept an engagement to review the interim financial information if the auditor's preliminary knowledge of the engagement circumstances indicates that the auditor would be unable to complete the review because there will be a limitation on the scope of the auditor's review imposed by management of the entity.

51. If, after accepting the engagement, management imposes a limitation on the scope of the review, the auditor requests the removal of that limitation. If management refuses to do so, the auditor is unable to complete the review and express a conclusion. In such cases, the auditor communicates, in writing, to the appropriate level of management and those charged with governance the reason why the review cannot be completed. Nevertheless, if a matter comes to the auditor's attention that causes the auditor to believe that a material adjustment to the interim financial information is necessary for it to be prepared, in all material respects, in accordance with the applicable financial reporting framework, the auditor communicates such matters in accordance with the guidance in paragraphs 38-40.

52. The auditor also considers the legal and regulatory responsibilities, including whether there is a requirement for the auditor to issue a report. If there is such a requirement, the auditor disclaims a conclusion, and provides in the review report the reason why the review cannot be completed. However, if a matter comes to the auditor's attention that causes the auditor to believe that a material adjustment to the interim financial information is necessary for it to be prepared, in all material respects, in accordance with the applicable financial reporting framework, the auditor also communicates such a matter in the report.

Other Limitations on Scope

53. A limitation on scope may occur due to circumstances other than a limitation on scope imposed by management. In such circumstances, the auditor is ordinarily unable to complete the review and express a conclusion and is guided by paragraphs 51-52. There may be, however, some rare circumstances where the limitation on the scope of the auditor's work is clearly confined to one or more specific matters that, while material, are not in the auditor's judgment pervasive to the interim financial information. In such circumstances, the auditor modifies the review report by indicating that, except for the matter which is described in an explanatory paragraph to the review report, the review was conducted in accordance with this ISRE (UK and Ireland), and by qualifying the conclusion. Illustrative review reports with a qualified conclusion are set out in Appendix 6 to this ISRE (UK and Ireland).

54. The auditor may have expressed a qualified opinion on the audit of the latest annual financial statements because of a limitation on the scope of that audit. The auditor considers whether that limitation on scope still exists and, if so, the implications for the review report.

Going Concern and Significant Uncertainties

55. In certain circumstances, an emphasis of matter paragraph may be added to a review report, without affecting the auditor's conclusion, to highlight a matter that is included in a note to the interim financial information that more extensively discusses the matter. The paragraph would preferably be included after the conclusion paragraph and ordinarily refers to the fact that the conclusion is not qualified in this respect.

56. **If adequate disclosure is made in the interim financial information, the auditor should add an emphasis of matter paragraph to the review report to highlight a material uncertainty relating to an event or condition that may cast significant doubt on the entity's ability to continue as a going concern.**

57. The auditor may have modified a prior audit or review report by adding an emphasis of matter paragraph to highlight a material uncertainty relating to an event or condition that may cast significant doubt on the entity's ability to continue as a going concern. If the material uncertainty still exists and adequate disclosure is made in the interim financial information, the auditor modifies the review report on the current interim financial information by adding a paragraph to highlight the continued material uncertainty.

58. If, as a result of inquiries or other review procedures, a material uncertainty relating to an event or condition comes to the auditor's attention that may cast significant doubt on the entity's ability to continue as a going concern, and adequate disclosure is made in the interim financial information the auditor modifies the review report by adding an emphasis of matter paragraph.

59. **If a material uncertainty that casts significant doubt about the entity's ability to continue as a going concern is not adequately disclosed in the interim financial information, the auditor should express a qualified or adverse conclusion, as**

appropriate. **The report should include specific reference to the fact that there is such a material uncertainty.**

60. **The auditor should consider modifying the review report by adding a paragraph to highlight a significant uncertainty (other than a going concern problem) that came to the auditor's attention, the resolution of which is dependent upon future events and which may affect the interim financial information.**

Requests to Discontinue an Interim Review Engagement

60-1. There may be rare circumstances in which the auditor indicates in advance to management and those charged with governance that the review report may be modified for one or more of the reasons set out in paragraphs 45 to 60 above. In these cases the auditor may be requested to discontinue the review engagement rather than include a modified review report with the interim financial information.

60-2. The auditor informs the audit committee, where one exists, of this situation as soon as practicable. If information is communicated orally, the auditor subsequently documents the communication as appropriate. For a listed entity, if, in the auditor's judgment, the entity does not take appropriate action to address the auditor's concerns regarding the financial information to be published, the auditor considers requesting those charged with governance to discuss the matter with the entity's brokers, including whether the matter should be reported to the relevant regulatory authority. The auditor also evaluates whether to resign as the entity's auditor and include the auditor's reasons for resigning in a statement of circumstances as required by the Companies Act. The auditor may wish to take legal advice when considering resignation.

Other Considerations

61. The terms of the engagement include management's agreement that where any document containing interim financial information indicates that such information has been reviewed by the entity's auditor, the review report will also be included in the document. If management has not included the review report in the document, the auditor considers seeking legal advice to assist in determining the appropriate course of action in the circumstances.

62. If the auditor has issued a modified review report and management issues the interim financial information without including the modified review report in the document containing the interim financial information, the auditor considers seeking legal advice to assist in determining the appropriate course of action in the circumstances, and the possibility of resigning from the appointment to audit the annual financial statements.

63. Interim financial information consisting of a condensed set of financial statements does not necessarily include all the information that would be included in a complete set of financial statements, but may rather present an explanation of the events and changes that are significant to an understanding of the changes in the financial position and performance of the entity since the annual reporting date. This is because it is presumed that the users of the interim financial information will have access to the

latest audited financial statements, such as is the case with listed entities. In other circumstances, the auditor discusses with management the need for such interim financial information to include a statement that it is to be read in conjunction with the latest audited financial statements. In the absence of such a statement, the auditor considers whether, without a reference to the latest audited financial statements, the interim financial information is misleading in the circumstances, and the implications for the review report.

Documentation

64. **The auditor should prepare review documentation that is sufficient and appropriate to provide a basis for the auditor's conclusion and to provide evidence that the review was performed in accordance with this ISRE (UK and Ireland) and applicable legal and regulatory requirements.** The documentation enables an experienced auditor having no previous connection with the engagement to understand the nature, timing and extent of the inquiries made, and analytical and other review procedures applied, information obtained, and any significant matters considered during the performance of the review, including the disposition of such matters.

Effective Date

65. This ISRE (UK and Ireland) is effective for reviews of interim financial information for periods ending on or after 20 September 2007. Early adoption is permitted.

Public Sector Perspective

66. *Paragraph 10 requires that the auditor and the client agree on the terms of engagement. Paragraph 11 explains that an engagement letter helps to avoid misunderstandings regarding the nature of the engagement and, in particular, the objective and scope of the review, management's responsibilities, the extent of the auditor's responsibilities, the assurance obtained, and the nature and form of the report. Law or regulation governing review engagements in the public sector ordinarily mandates the appointment of the auditor. Consequently, engagement letters may not be a widespread practice in the public sector. Nevertheless, an engagement letter setting out the matters referred to in paragraph 11 may be useful to both the public sector auditor and the client. Public sector auditors, therefore, consider agreeing with the client the terms of a review engagement by way of an engagement letter.*

67. *In the public sector, the auditor's statutory audit obligation may extend to other work, such as a review of interim financial information. Where this is the case, the public sector auditor cannot avoid such an obligation and, consequently, may not be in a position not to accept (see paragraph 50) or to withdraw from a review engagement (see paragraphs 36 and 40(b)). The public sector auditor also may not be in the position to resign from the appointment to audit the annual financial statements (see paragraphs 40(c)) and 62).*

68. *Paragraph 41 discusses the auditor's responsibility when a matter comes to the auditor's attention that causes the auditor to believe in the existence of fraud or noncompliance by the entity with laws and regulations. In the public sector, the auditor may be subject to statutory or other regulatory requirements to report such a matter to regulatory or other public authorities.*

Appendix 1

Example of an Engagement Letter for a Review of Interim Financial Information

The following letter is to be used as a guide in conjunction with the consideration outlined in paragraph 10 of this ISRE (UK and Ireland) and will need to be adapted according to individual requirements and circumstances.

For an engagement to review interim financial information prepared by a listed company in the UK or Ireland, the letter would ordinarily include paragraphs such as:

> "As directors of XYZ PLC you are responsible under the [Companies Act 1985] [Companies Act 1990] for keeping proper accounting records. You are also responsible for presenting the half-yearly financial report in accordance with [International Accounting Standard 34, "Interim Financial Reporting," as adopted by the European Union] [the Accounting Standards Board Statement "Half-Yearly Financial Reports"] and the requirements of the [Disclosure and Transparency Rules of the Financial Services Authority] [Transparency (Directive 2004/109/EC) Regulations 2007 and the Transparency Rules of the Financial Regulator]." [*The second sentence identifies the applicable financial reporting framework for the entity and should be amended as necessary.*]

> "For the purpose of our review you will make available to us all of the company's accounting records and all other related information, including minutes of directors' shareholders', and audit committee meetings and of all relevant management meetings, that we consider necessary."

To the Board of Directors (or the appropriate representative of senior management)

We are providing this letter to confirm our understanding of the terms and objectives of our engagement to review the entity's interim balance sheet as at June 30, 20X1 and the related statements of income, changes in equity and cash flows for the six-month period then ended.

Our review will be conducted in accordance with International Standard on Review Engagements (UK and Ireland) 2410, "Review of Interim Financial Information Performed by the Independent Auditor of the Entity" issued by the Auditing Practices Board with the objective of providing us with a basis for reporting whether anything has come to our attention that causes us to believe that the interim financial information is not prepared, in all material respects, in accordance with the [indicate applicable financial reporting framework, including a reference to the jurisdiction or country of origin of the financial reporting when the financial reporting framework used is not International Financial Reporting Standards]. Such a review consists of making inquiries, primarily of persons responsible for financial and accounting matters, and applying analytical and other review procedures and does not, ordinarily, require corroboration of the information obtained. The scope of a review of interim financial information is substantially less than the scope of an audit conducted in accordance with International Standards on Auditing (UK and Ireland) whose objective is the expression of an opinion regarding the financial statements and, accordingly, we shall express no such opinion.

We expect to report on the interim financial information as follows:

[Include text of sample report]

Responsibility for the interim financial information, including adequate disclosure, is that of management of the entity. This includes designing, implementing and maintaining internal control relevant to the preparation and presentation of interim financial information that is free from material misstatement, whether due to fraud or error; selecting and applying appropriate accounting policies; and making accounting estimates that are reasonable in the circumstances. As part of our review, we will request written representations from management concerning assertions made in connection with the review. We will also request that where any document containing interim financial information indicates that the interim financial information has been reviewed, our report will also be included in the document.

A review of interim financial information does not provide assurance that we will become aware of all significant matters that might be identified in an audit. Further, our engagement cannot be relied upon to disclose whether fraud or errors, or illegal acts exist. However, we will inform you of any material matters that come to our attention.

We look forward to full cooperation with your staff ~~and we trust that they will make available to us whatever records, documentation and other information are requested in connection with our review.~~[2c]

[Insert additional information here regarding fee arrangements and billings, as appropriate.]

This letter will be effective for future years unless it is terminated, amended or superseded (if applicable).

Please sign and return the attached copy of this letter to indicate that it is in accordance with your understanding of the arrangements for our review of the financial statements.

Acknowledged on behalf of ABC Entity by

(signed)

Name and Title

Date

[2c] Rendered unnecessary by the alternative text presented in the shaded note immediately before this example letter.

Appendix 2

Analytical Procedures the Auditor May Consider When Performing a Review of Interim Financial Information

Examples of analytical procedures the auditor may consider when performing a review of interim financial information include the following:

- Comparing the interim financial information with the interim financial information of the immediately preceding interim period, with the interim financial information of the corresponding interim period of the preceding financial year, with the interim financial information that was expected by management for the current period, and with the most recent audited annual financial statements.

- Comparing current interim financial information with anticipated results, such as budgets or forecasts (for example, comparing tax balances and the relationship between the provision for income taxes to pretax income in the current interim financial information with corresponding information in (a) budgets, using expected rates, and (b) financial information for prior periods).

- Comparing current interim financial information with relevant non-financial information.

- Comparing the recorded amounts, or ratios developed from recorded amounts, to expectations developed by the auditor. The auditor develops such expectations by identifying and applying relationships that are reasonably expected to exist based on the auditor's understanding of the entity and of the industry in which the entity operates.

- Comparing ratios and indicators for the current interim period with those of entities in the same industry.

- Comparing relationships among elements in the current interim financial information with corresponding relationships in the interim financial information of prior periods, for example, expense by type as a percentage of sales, assets by type as a percentage of total assets, and percentage of change in sales to percentage of change in receivables.

- Comparing disaggregated data. The following are examples of how data may be disaggregated:

  ○ By period, for example, revenue or expense items disaggregated into quarterly, monthly, or weekly amounts.

  ○ By product line or source of revenue.

  ○ By location, for example, by component.

○ By attributes of the transaction, for example, revenue generated by designers, architects, or craftsmen.

○ By several attributes of the transaction, for example, sales by product and month.

Appendix 3

Example of a Management Representation Letter

The following letter is not intended to be a standard letter. Representations by management will vary from entity to entity and from one interim period to the next.

(Entity Letterhead)

(To Auditor)   (Date)

Opening paragraphs if interim financial information comprises condensed financial statements:

This representation letter is provided in connection with your review of the condensed balance sheet of ABC Entity as of March 31, 20X1 and the related condensed statements of income, changes in equity and cash flows for the three-month period then ended for the purposes of expressing a conclusion whether anything has come to your attention that causes you to believe that the interim financial information is not prepared, in all material respects, in accordance with [indicate applicable financial reporting framework, including a reference to the jurisdiction or country of origin of the financial reporting framework when the financial reporting framework used is not International Financial Reporting Standards].

We acknowledge our responsibility for the preparation and presentation of the interim financial information in accordance with [indicate applicable financial reporting framework].

Opening paragraphs if interim financial information comprises a complete set of general purpose financial statements prepared in accordance with a financial reporting framework designed to achieve fair presentation:

This representation letter is provided in connection with your review of the balance sheet of ABC Entity as of March 31, 20X1 and the related statements of income, changes in equity and cash flows for the three-month period then ended and a summary of the significant accounting policies and other explanatory notes for the purposes of expressing a conclusion whether anything has come to your attention that causes you to believe that the interim financial information does not give a true and fair view of *(or "does not present fairly, in all material respects,")* the financial position of ABC Entity as at March 31, 20X1, and of its financial performance and its cash flows in accordance with [indicate applicable financial reporting framework, including a reference to the jurisdiction or country of origin of the financial reporting framework when the financial reporting framework used is not International Financial Reporting Standards].

We acknowledge our responsibility for the fair presentation of the interim financial information in accordance with [indicate applicable financial reporting framework].

We confirm, to the best of our knowledge and belief, the following representations:

- The interim financial information referred to above has been prepared and presented in accordance with [indicate applicable financial reporting framework].

- We have made available to you all books of account and supporting documentation, and all minutes of meetings of shareholders and the board of directors (namely those held on [insert applicable dates]).

- There are no material transactions that have not been properly recorded in the accounting records underlying the interim financial information.

- There has been no known actual or possible noncompliance with laws and regulations that could have a material effect on the interim financial information in the event of noncompliance.

- We acknowledge responsibility for the design and implementation of internal control to prevent and detect fraud and error.

- We have disclosed to you all significant facts relating to any known frauds or suspected frauds that may have affected the entity.

- We have disclosed to you the results of our assessment of the risk that the interim financial information may be materially misstated as the result of fraud.

- We believe the effects of uncorrected misstatements summarized in the accompanying schedule are immaterial, both individually and in the aggregate, to the interim financial information taken as a whole.

- We confirm the completeness of the information provided to you regarding the identification of related parties.

- The following have been properly recorded and, when appropriate, adequately disclosed in the interim financial information:

  - Related party transactions, including sales, purchases, loans, transfers, leasing arrangements and guarantees, and amounts receivable from or payable to related parties;

  - Guarantees, whether written or oral, under which the entity is contingently liable; and

  - Agreements and options to buy back assets previously sold.

- The presentation and disclosure of the fair value measurements of assets and liabilities are in accordance with [indicate applicable financial reporting framework]. The assumptions used reflect our intent and ability to carry specific courses of action on behalf of the entity, where relevant to the fair value measurements or disclosure.

- We have no plans or intentions that may materially affect the carrying value or classification of assets and liabilities reflected in the interim financial information.

- We have no plans to abandon lines of product or other plans or intentions that will result in any excess or obsolete inventory, and no inventory is stated at an amount in excess of realizable value.

- The entity has satisfactory title to all assets and there are no liens or encumbrances on the entity's assets.

- We have recorded or disclosed, as appropriate, all liabilities, both actual and contingent.

- [Add any additional representations related to new accounting standards that are being implemented for the first time and consider any additional representations required by a new International Standard on Auditing (UK and Ireland) that are relevant to interim financial information.]

To the best of our knowledge and belief, no events have occurred subsequent to the balance sheet date and through the date of this letter that may require adjustment to or disclosure in the aforementioned interim financial information.

_____

(Senior Executive Officer)

_____

(Senior Financial Officer)

Appendix 4

Examples of Review Reports on Interim Financial Information

An example review report for a UK or Irish company listed in the UK or Ireland is set out in Appendix 8.

Complete Set of General Purpose Financial Statements Prepared in Accordance with a Financial Reporting Framework Designed to Achieve Fair Presentation (see paragraph 43(i))

Report on Review of Interim Financial Information

(Appropriate addressee)

Introduction

We have reviewed the accompanying balance sheet of ABC Entity as of March 31, 20X1 and the related statements of income, changes in equity and cash flows for the three-month period then ended, and a summary of significant accounting policies and other explanatory notes.The auditor may wish to specify the regulatory authority or equivalent with whom the interim financial information is filed. Management is responsible for the preparation and fair presentation of this interim financial information in accordance with [indicate applicable financial reporting framework]. Our responsibility is to express a conclusion on this interim financial information based on our review.

Scope of Review

We conducted our review in accordance with International Standard on Review Engagements 2410, "Review of Interim Financial Information Performed by the Independent Auditor of the Entity." A review of interim financial information consists of making inquiries, primarily of persons responsible for financial and accounting matters, and applying analytical and other review procedures. A review is substantially less in scope than an audit conducted in accordance with International Standards on Auditing and consequently does not enable us to obtain assurance that we would become aware of all significant matters that might be identified in an audit. Accordingly, we do not express an audit opinion.

Conclusion

Based on our review, nothing has come to our attention that causes us to believe that the accompanying interim financial information does not give a true and fair view of (or "does not present fairly, in all material respects,") the financial position of the entity as at March 31, 20X1, and of its financial performance and its cash flows for the three-month period then ended in accordance with [applicable financial reporting framework, including a reference to the jurisdiction or country of origin of the financial reporting framework when the financial reporting framework used is not International Financial Reporting Standards].

AUDITOR

Date

Address

Other Interim Financial Information (see paragraph 43(j))

Report on Review of Interim Financial Information

(Appropriate addressee)

Introduction

We have reviewed the accompanying [condensed] balance sheet of ABC Entity as of March 31, 20X1 and the related [condensed] statements of income, changes in equity and cash flows for the three-month period then ended. The auditor may wish to specify the regulatory authority or equivalent with whom the interim financial information is filed. Management is responsible for the preparation and presentation of this interim financial information in accordance with [indicate applicable financial reporting framework]. Our responsibility is to express a conclusion on this interim financial information based on our review.

Scope of Review

We conducted our review in accordance with International Standard on Review Engagements 2410, "Review of Interim Financial Information Performed by the Independent Auditor of the Entity." A review of interim financial information consists of making inquiries, primarily of persons responsible for financial and accounting matters, and applying analytical and other review procedures. A review is substantially less in scope than an audit conducted in accordance with International Standards on Auditing and consequently does not enable us to obtain assurance that we would become aware of all significant matters that might be identified in an audit. Accordingly, we do not express an audit opinion.

Conclusion

Based on our review, nothing has come to our attention that causes us to believe that the accompanying interim financial information is not prepared, in all material respects, in accordance with [applicable financial reporting framework, including a reference to the jurisdiction or country of origin of the financial reporting framework when the financial reporting framework used is not International Financial Reporting Standards].

AUDITOR

Date

Address

Appendix 5

Examples of Review Reports with a Qualified Conclusion for a Departure from the Applicable Financial Reporting Framework

An example unqualified review report for a UK or Irish company listed in the UK or Ireland is set out in Appendix 8 and can be tailored to give a report with a qualified conclusion when appropriate.

Complete Set of General Purpose Financial Statements Prepared in Accordance with a Financial Reporting Framework Designed to Achieve Fair Presentation (see paragraph 43(i))

Report on Review of Interim Financial Information

(Appropriate addressee)

Introduction

We have reviewed the accompanying balance sheet of ABC Entity as of March 31, 20X1 and the related statements of income, changes in equity and cash flows for the three-month period then ended, and a summary of significant accounting policies and other explanatory notes.The auditor may wish to specify the regulatory authority or equivalent with whom the interim financial information is filed. Management is responsible for the preparation and fair presentation of this interim financial information in accordance with [indicate applicable financial reporting framework]. Our responsibility is to express a conclusion on this interim financial information based on our review.

Scope of Review

We conducted our review in accordance with International Standard on Review Engagements 2410, "Review of Interim Financial Information Performed by the Independent Auditor of the Entity." A review of interim financial information consists of making inquiries, primarily of persons responsible for financial and accounting matters, and applying analytical and other review procedures. A review is substantially less in scope than an audit conducted in accordance with International Standards on Auditing and consequently does not enable us to obtain assurance that we would become aware of all significant matters that might be identified in an audit. Accordingly, we do not express an audit opinion.

Basis for Qualified Conclusion

Based on information provided to us by management, ABC Entity has excluded from property and long-term debt certain lease obligations that we believe should be capitalized to conform with [indicate applicable financial reporting framework]. This information indicates that if these lease obligations were capitalized at March 31, 20X1, property would be increased by $_____, long-term debt by $_____, and net income and earnings per share would be increased (decreased) by $_____, $_____, $_____, and $_____, respectively for the three-month period then ended.

Qualified Conclusion

Based on our review, with the exception of the matter described in the preceding paragraph, nothing has come to our attention that causes us to believe that the accompanying interim financial information does not give a true and fair view of (or "does not present fairly, in all material respects,") the financial position of the entity as at March 31, 20X1, and of its financial performance and its cash flows for the three-month period then ended in accordance with [indicate applicable financial reporting framework, including the reference to the jurisdiction or country of origin of the financial reporting framework when the financial reporting framework used is not International Financial Reporting Standards].

AUDITOR

Date

Address

Other Interim Financial Information (see paragraph 43(j))

Report on Review of Interim Financial Information

(Appropriate addressee)

Introduction

We have reviewed the accompanying [condensed] balance sheet of ABC Entity as of March 31, 20X1 and the related [condensed] statements of income, changes in equity and cash flows for the three-month period then ended. The auditor may wish to specify the regulatory authority or equivalent with whom the interim financial information is filed. Management is responsible for the preparation and presentation of this interim financial information in accordance with [indicate applicable financial reporting framework]. Our responsibility is to express a conclusion on this interim financial information based on our review.

Scope of Review

We conducted our review in accordance with International Standard on Review Engagements 2410, "Review of Interim Financial Information Performed by the Independent Auditor of the Entity." A review of interim financial information consists of making inquiries, primarily of persons responsible for financial and accounting matters, and applying analytical and other review procedures. A review is substantially less in scope than an audit conducted in accordance with International Standards on Auditing and consequently does not enable us to obtain assurance that we would become aware of all significant matters that might be identified in an audit. Accordingly, we do not express an audit opinion.

Basis for Qualified Conclusion

Based on information provided to us by management, ABC Entity has excluded from property and long-term debt certain lease obligations that we believe should be capitalized to conform with [indicate applicable financial reporting framework]. This information indicates that if these lease obligations were capitalized at March 31, 20X1, property would be increased by $\_\_\_\_\_$, long-term debt by $\_\_\_\_\_$, and net income and earnings per share would be increased (decreased) by $_____$, $_____$, $_____$, and $_____$, respectively for the three-month period then ended.

Qualified Conclusion

Based on our review, with the exception of the matter described in the preceding paragraph, nothing has come to our attention that causes us to believe that the accompanying interim financial information is not prepared, in all material respects, in accordance with [indicate applicable financial reporting framework, including a reference to the jurisdiction or country of origin of the financial reporting framework when the financial reporting framework used is not International Financial Reporting Standards].

AUDITOR

Date

Address

FINANCIAL REPORTING COUNCIL

Appendix 6

Examples of Review Reports with a Qualified Conclusion for a Limitation on Scope Not Imposed By Management

An example unqualified review report for a UK or Irish company listed in the UK or Ireland is set out in Appendix 8 and can be tailored to give a report with a qualified conclusion when appropriate.

Complete Set of General Purpose Financial Statements Prepared in Accordance with a Financial Reporting Framework Designed to Achieve Fair Presentation (see paragraph 43(i))

Report on Review of Interim Financial Information

(Appropriate addressee)

Introduction

We have reviewed the accompanying balance sheet of ABC Entity as of March 31, 20X1 and the related statements of income, changes in equity and cash flows for the three-month period then ended, and a summary of significant accounting policies and other explanatory notes.The auditor may wish to specify the regulatory authority or equivalent with whom the interim financial information is filed. Management is responsible for the preparation and fair presentation of this interim financial information in accordance with [indicate applicable financial reporting framework]. Our responsibility is to express a conclusion on this interim financial information based on our review.

Scope of Review

Except as explained in the following paragraph, we conducted our review in accordance with International Standard on Review Engagements 2410, "Review of Interim Financial Information Performed by the Independent Auditor of the Entity." A review of interim financial information consists of making inquiries, primarily of persons responsible for financial and accounting matters, and applying analytical and other review procedures. A review is substantially less in scope than an audit conducted in accordance with International Standards on Auditing and consequently does not enable us to obtain assurance that we would become aware of all significant matters that might be identified in an audit. Accordingly, we do not express an audit opinion.

Basis for Qualified Conclusion

As a result of a fire in a branch office on (date) that destroyed its accounts receivable records, we were unable to complete our review of accounts receivable totaling $_____ included in the interim financial information. The entity is in the process of reconstructing these records and is uncertain as to whether these records will support the amount shown above and the related allowance for uncollectible accounts. Had we been able to complete our review of accounts receivable, matters might have come to our attention indicating that adjustments might be necessary to the interim financial information.

Qualified Conclusion

Except for the adjustments to the interim financial information that we might have become aware of had it not been for the situation described above, based on our review, nothing has come to our attention that causes us to believe that the accompanying interim financial information does not give a true and fair view of (or "does not present fairly, in all material respects,") the financial position of the entity as at March 31, 20X1, and of its financial performance and its cash flows for the three-month period then ended in accordance with [indicate applicable financial reporting framework, including a reference to the jurisdiction or country of origin of the financial reporting framework when the financial reporting framework used is not International Financial Reporting Standards].

AUDITOR

Date

Address

Other Interim Financial Information (see paragraph 43(j))

Report on Review of Interim Financial Information

(Appropriate addressee)

Introduction

We have reviewed the accompanying [condensed] balance sheet of ABC Entity as of March 31, 20X1 and the related [condensed] statements of income, changes in equity and cash flows for the three-month period then ended.The auditor may wish to specify the regulatory authority or equivalent with whom the interim financial information is filed. Management is responsible for the preparation and presentation of this interim financial information in accordance with [indicate applicable financial reporting framework]. Our responsibility is to express a conclusion on this interim financial information based on our review.

Scope of Review

Except as explained in the following paragraph, we conducted our review in accordance with International Standards on Review Engagements 2410, "Review of Interim Financial Information Performed by the Auditor of the Entity." A review of interim financial information consists of making inquiries, primarily of persons responsible for financial and accounting matters, and applying analytical and other review procedures. A review is substantially less in scope than an audit conducted in accordance with International Standards on Auditing and consequently does not enable us to obtain assurance that we would become aware of all significant matters that might be identified in an audit. Accordingly, we do not express an audit opinion.

Basis for Qualified Conclusion

As a result of a fire in a branch office on (date) that destroyed its accounts receivable records, we were unable to complete our review of accounts receivable totaling $_____ included in the interim financial information. The entity is in the process of reconstructing these records and is uncertain as to whether these records will support the amount shown above and the related allowance for uncollectible accounts. Had we been able to complete our review of accounts receivable, matters might have come to our attention indicating that adjustments might be necessary to the interim financial information.

Qualified Conclusion

Except for the adjustments to the interim financial information that we might have become aware of had it not been for the situation described above, based on our review, nothing has come to our attention that causes us to believe that the accompanying interim financial information is not prepared, in all material respects, in accordance with [indicate applicable financial reporting framework, including a reference to the jurisdiction or country of origin of the financial reporting framework when the financial reporting framework used is not International Financial Reporting Standards].

AUDITOR

Date

Address

Appendix 7

Examples of Review Reports with an Adverse Conclusion for a Departure from the Applicable Financial Reporting Framework

An example unqualified review report for a UK or Irish company listed in the UK or Ireland is set out in Appendix 8 and can be tailored to give a report with an adverse conclusion when appropriate.

Complete Set of General Purpose Financial Statements Prepared in Accordance with a Financial Reporting Framework Designed to Achieve Fair Presentation (see paragraph 43(i))

Report on Review of Interim Financial Information

(Appropriate addressee)

Introduction

We have reviewed the accompanying balance sheet of ABC Entity as of March 31, 20X1 and the related statements of income, changes in equity and cash flows for the three-month period then ended, and a summary of significant accounting policies and other explanatory notes. The auditor may wish to specify the regulatory authority or equivalent with whom the interim financial information is filed. Management is responsible for the preparation and fair presentation of this interim financial information in accordance with [indicate applicable financial reporting framework]. Our responsibility is to express a conclusion on this interim financial information based on our review.

Scope of Review

We conducted our review in accordance with International Standard on Review Engagements 2410, "Review of Interim Financial Information Performed by the Auditor of the Entity." A review of interim financial information consists of making inquiries, primarily of persons responsible for financial and accounting matters, and applying analytical and other review procedures. A review is substantially less in scope than an audit conducted in accordance with International Standards on Auditing and consequently does not enable us to obtain assurance that we would become aware of all significant matters that might be identified in an audit. Accordingly, we do not express an audit opinion.

Basis for Adverse Conclusion

Commencing this period, management of the entity ceased to consolidate the financial statements of its subsidiary companies since management considers consolidation to be inappropriate because of the existence of new substantial non-controlling interests. This is not in accordance with [indicate applicable financial reporting framework, including a reference to the jurisdiction or country of origin of the financial reporting framework when the financial reporting framework used is not International Financial Reporting Standards]. Had consolidated financial statements been prepared, virtually every account in the interim financial information would have been materially different.

Adverse Conclusion

Our review indicates that, because the entity's investment in subsidiary companies is not accounted for on a consolidated basis, as described in the preceding paragraph, this interim financial information does not give a true and fair view of (or "does not present fairly, in all material respects,") the financial position of the entity as at March 31, 20X1, and of its financial performance and its cash flows for the three-month period then ended in accordance with [indicate applicable financial reporting framework, including a reference to the jurisdiction or country of origin of the financial reporting framework when the financial reporting framework used is not International Financial Reporting Standards].

AUDITOR

Date

Address

Other Interim Financial Information (see paragraph 43(j))

Report on Review of Interim Financial Information

(Appropriate addressee)

Introduction

We have reviewed the accompanying [condensed] balance sheet of ABC Entity as of March 31, 20X1 and the related [condensed] statements of income, changes in equity and cash flows for the three-month period then ended. The auditor may wish to specify the regulatory authority or equivalent with whom the interim financial information is filed. Management is responsible for the preparation and presentation of this interim financial information in accordance with [indicate applicable financial reporting framework]. Our responsibility is to express a conclusion on this interim financial information based on our review.

Scope of Review

We conducted our review in accordance with International Standard on Review Engagements 2410, "Review of Interim Financial Information Performed by the Independence Auditor of the Entity." A review of interim financial information consists of making inquiries, primarily of persons responsible for financial and accounting matters, and applying analytical and other review procedures. A review is substantially less in scope than an audit conducted in accordance with International Standards on Auditing and consequently does not enable us to obtain assurance that we would become aware of all significant matters that might be identified in an audit. Accordingly, we do not express an audit opinion.

Basis for Adverse Conclusion

Commencing this period, management of the entity ceased to consolidate the financial statements of its subsidiary companies since management considers consolidation to be inappropriate because of the existence of new substantial non-controlling interests. This is not in accordance with [indicate applicable financial reporting framework, including the reference to the jurisdiction or country of origin of the financial reporting framework when the financial reporting framework used is not International Financial Reporting Standards]. Had consolidated financial statements been prepared, virtually every account in the interim financial information would have been materially different.

Adverse Conclusion

Our review indicates that, because the entity's investment in subsidiary companies is not accounted for on a consolidated basis, as described in the preceding paragraph, this interim financial information is not prepared, in all material respects, in accordance with [indicate applicable financial reporting framework, including a reference to the jurisdiction or country of origin of the financial reporting framework when the financial reporting framework used is not International Financial Reporting Standards].

AUDITOR

Date

Address

Appendix 8

Example Review Report for a UK or Irish Company Listed in the UK or Ireland Preparing a Half-Yearly Financial Report in Compliance with IAS 34 as Adopted by the European Union

INDEPENDENT REVIEW REPORT TO XYZ PLC

Introduction

We have been engaged by the company to review the condensed set of financial statements in the half-yearly financial report for the six months ended ... which comprises [specify the primary financial statements and the related explanatory notes that have been reviewed].[10a] We have read the other information contained in the half-yearly financial report and considered whether it contains any apparent misstatements or material inconsistencies with the information in the condensed set of financial statements.

Directors' Responsibilities

The half-yearly financial report is the responsibility of, and has been approved by, the directors. The directors are responsible for preparing the half-yearly financial report in accordance with the [Disclosure and Transparency Rules of the United Kingdom's Financial Services Authority] [Transparency (Directive 2004/109/EC) Regulations 2007 and the Transparency Rules of the Republic of Ireland's Financial Regulator].

As disclosed in note X, the annual financial statements of the [group/company] are prepared in accordance with IFRSs as adopted by the European Union. The condensed set of financial statements included in this half-yearly financial report has been prepared in accordance with International Accounting Standard 34, "Interim Financial Reporting," as adopted by the European Union.

Our Responsibility

Our responsibility is to express to the Company a conclusion on the condensed set of financial statements in the half-yearly financial report based on our review.

Scope of Review

We conducted our review in accordance with International Standard on Review Engagements (UK and Ireland) 2410, "Review of Interim Financial Information Performed by the Independent Auditor of the Entity" issued by the Auditing Practices Board for use in [the United Kingdom] [Ireland]. A review of interim financial information consists of making enquiries, primarily of persons responsible for financial and accounting matters, and applying analytical and other review procedures. A review is substantially less in scope than an audit conducted in accordance with International Standards on Auditing (UK and Ireland)

[10a] Review reports of entities that do not publish their half-yearly reports on a web site or publish them using 'PDF' format may continue to refer to the pages of the half-yearly report.

and consequently does not enable us to obtain assurance that we would become aware of all significant matters that might be identified in an audit. Accordingly, we do not express an audit opinion.

Conclusion

Based on our review, nothing has come to our attention that causes us to believe that the condensed set of financial statements in the half-yearly financial report for the six months ended .... is not prepared, in all material respects, in accordance with International Accounting Standard 34 as adopted by the European Union and [the Disclosure and Transparency Rules of the United Kingdom's Financial Services Authority] [the Transparency (Directive 2004/109/EC) Regulations 2007 and the Transparency Rules of the Republic of Ireland's Financial Regulator].

AUDITOR

Date

Address

Appendix 9

Summary of Particular Requirements of Half-Yearly Reports Prepared by Listed Companies in the UK and Ireland

This Appendix sets out a summary of particular requirements of the FSA's Disclosure and Transparency Rules (DTRs) applicable to half-yearly financial reports prepared by an 'issuer' whose shares or debt securities are admitted to trading and whose home state is the United Kingdom, subject to the exemptions in DTR 4.4. Equivalent requirements are included in the Irish Transparency (Directive 2004/109/EC) Regulations 2007 (specifically Regulations 6 – 8 in Part 2, subject to the exemptions in Part 3) and Transparency Rules of the Financial Regulator in the Republic of Ireland (specifically Rule 6.2). It also gives a summary of Companies Act requirements relevant to the publication of non-statutory accounts. It does not set out in full all the applicable requirements and, therefore, is not intended to provide a substitute for the auditor reading the applicable Rules, Regulations and legislation to obtain an understanding of them.

FSA Disclosure and Transparency Rules

Rule 4.2.3 requires that an issuer publish a half-yearly financial report, containing:

(1)   a condensed set of financial statements;

(2)   an interim management report; and

(3)   responsibility statements.

Rule 4.2.4 requires that if an issuer is required to prepare consolidated accounts, the condensed set of financial statements must be prepared in accordance with International Accounting Standard 34 "Interim Financial Reporting". (Under the FSA's definitions of "International Accounting Standards" this will be IAS 34 as adopted by the European Union.)

If an issuer is not required to prepare consolidated accounts, the condensed set of financial information must contain, as a minimum, the following:

(a)   a condensed balance sheet;

(b)   a condensed profit and loss account; and

(c)   explanatory notes on these accounts.

Rule 4.2.5 requires that the condensed balance sheet and condensed profit and loss account referred to in (a) and (b) above must:

•   follow the same principles for recognising and measuring as when preparing annual financial reports,

- show each of the headings and subtotals included in the most recent annual financial statements of the issuer. Additional line items must be included if, as a result of their omission, the half-yearly financial statements would give a misleading view of the assets, liabilities, financial position and profit or loss of the issuer.

For issuers not required to prepare consolidated accounts the Rules also set out further specific requirements in relation to comparative information and the content of the explanatory notes.

Rule 4.2.6 requires that the accounting policies and presentation applied to the half-yearly figures must be consistent with those applied in the latest published annual accounts except where:

(1) the accounting policies and presentation are to be changed in the subsequent annual financial statements, in which case the new accounting policies and presentation should be followed, and the changes and the reasons for the changes should be disclosed in the half-yearly report; or

(2) the FSA otherwise agrees.

Companies may choose to have the half-yearly financial report reviewed or audited by an auditor. Rule 4.2.9 requires that "if the half-yearly financial report has been audited or reviewed by auditors pursuant to the Auditing Practices Board guidance on Review of Interim Financial Information, the audit report or review report must be reproduced in full."

Responsibility Statements

Rule 4.2.10 requires that for each person making a responsibility statement, the statement must confirm that to the best of his or her knowledge, inter alia:

"the condensed set of financial statements, which has been prepared in accordance with the applicable set of accounting standards, gives a true and fair view of the assets, liabilities, financial position and profit or loss of the issuer, or the undertakings included in the consolidation as a whole ..."

However, Rule 4.2.10 also provides that:

"A person making a responsibility statement will satisfy the requirement ... to confirm that the condensed set of financial statements gives a true and fair view ... by including a statement that the condensed set of financial statements have been prepared in accordance with:

(a) IAS 34; or

(b) for UK issuers not using IFRS, pronouncements on interim reporting issued by the Accounting Standards Board[10b]; or

---

[10b] For half-yearly periods ending on or after 20 September 2007, the relevant ASB pronouncement is the Statement "Half-Yearly Financial Reports".

(c)   for all other issuers not using IFRS, a national accounting standard relating to interim reporting,

provided always that a person making such a statement has reasonable grounds to be satisfied that the condensed set of financial statements prepared in accordance with such a standard is not misleading."

Companies Act Requirements

United Kingdom

Financial statements included in half-yearly financial reports constitute non-statutory accounts under the provisions of the Companies Act[10c] and therefore must include a statement indicating:

(a)   that they are not the statutory accounts;

(b)   whether statutory accounts for any relevant financial year have been delivered to the registrar of companies;

(c)   whether the auditors reported on the statutory accounts for any such year; and

(d)   if so, whether it was qualified or unqualified, or included an emphasis of matter, or contained a statement by the auditor required under the Companies Act[10d] (accounting records or returns inadequate or accounts or directors' remuneration report not agreeing with records and returns, or failure to obtain necessary information and explanations).

Republic of Ireland

In the Republic of Ireland, financial statements included in a half-yearly report made by a single entity constitute abbreviated accounts under section 19 of the Companies (Amendment) Act, 1986. Financial statements included in a half-yearly report made by a group constitute abbreviated group accounts under regulation 40 of the European Communities (Companies: Group Accounts) Regulations, 1992. This states that where a parent undertaking publishes abbreviated group accounts relating to any financial year, it shall also publish a statement indicating:

(a)   that the abbreviated group accounts are not the group accounts, copies of which are required by law to be annexed to the annual return,

(b)   whether the copies of the group accounts so required to be annexed have in fact been so annexed,

---

[10c] Relevant references are: for the Companies Act 1985 – section 240 (the equivalent legislation in Northern Ireland is Article 243(3) of the Companies (Northern Ireland) Order, 1986); for the Companies Act 2006 –section 435 (this also applies in Northern Ireland).

[10d] Relevant references are: for the Companies Act 1985 – section 237(2) and (3); for the Companies Act 2006 – section 498(2) and (3).

(c) whether the auditors have made a report under section 193 of the Companies Act, 1990 in respect of the group accounts which relate to any financial year with which the abbreviated group accounts purport to deal, and

(d) whether the report of the auditors contained any qualifications.

The statement required for a single entity is similar.

Section 6: STANDARDS FOR INVESTMENT REPORTING

STANDARDS FOR INVESTMENT REPORTING

1000 – INVESTMENT REPORTING STANDARDS APPLICABLE TO ALL ENGAGEMENTS IN CONNECTION WITH AN INVESTMENT CIRCULAR

CONTENTS

SIR 1000 contains basic principles and essential procedures ("Investment Reporting Standards"), indicated by paragraphs in bold type, with which a reporting accountant is required to comply in the conduct of all engagements in connection with an investment circular prepared for issue in connection with a securities transaction governed wholly or in part by the laws and regulations of the United Kingdom.

SIR 1000 also includes explanatory and other material, including appendices, in the context of which the basic principles and essential procedures are to be understood and applied. It is necessary to consider the whole text of the SIR to understand and apply the basic principles and essential procedures.

The definitions in the glossary of terms set out in Appendix 4 are to be applied in the interpretation of this and all other SIRs. Terms defined in the glossary are underlined the first time that they occur in the text.

This SIR replaces SIR 100 "Investment circulars and reporting accountants" issued in December 1997.

To assist readers, SIRs contain references to, and extracts from, certain legislation and chapters of the Rules of the UK Listing Authority. Readers are cautioned that these references may change subsequent to publication.

Introduction

1.　The application of Standards for Investment Reporting (SIRs) is best understood by reference to the following four defined terms used throughout the SIRs:

(a)　**investment circular** is a generic term defined as *"Any document issued by an entity pursuant to statutory or regulatory requirements relating to securities on which it is intended that a third party should make an investment decision, including a prospectus, listing particulars, a circular to shareholders or similar document"*;

(b)　**reporting accountant** is defined as *"An accountant engaged to prepare a report for inclusion in, or in connection with, an investment circular. The reporting accountant may or may not be the auditor of the entity issuing the investment circular. The term "reporting accountant" is used to describe either the engagement partner or the engagement partner's firm[1]. The reporting accountant could be a limited company or an engagement principal employed by the company;*

(c)　**public reporting engagement** is defined as *"An engagement in which a reporting accountant expresses a conclusion that is published in an investment circular, and which is designed to enhance the degree of confidence of the intended users of*

---

[1]　Where the term applies to the engagement partner, it describes the responsibilities or obligations of the engagement partner. Such obligations or responsibilities may be fulfilled by either the engagement partner or a member of the engagement partner's team.

the report about the '_outcome_[2]' of the directors' evaluation or measurement of '_subject matter_' against '_suitable criteria_'"; and

(d) **private reporting engagement** is defined as "_An engagement, in connection with an investment circular, in which a reporting accountant does not express a conclusion that is published in an investment circular_". Private reporting engagements are likely to involve the reporting accountant reporting privately to one or more of an issuer, sponsor or regulator.

2. In order to provide flexibility to develop SIRs for a wide range of possible public reporting engagements, the description of public reporting engagement includes three generic terms. Their meanings are as follows:

(a) the "**subject matter**" of the engagement is that which is being evaluated or measured against suitable criteria. Examples of subject matter are the entity's financial position and the directors' expectation of the issuer's profit for the period covered by a profit forecast;

(b) criteria are the benchmarks used to evaluate or measure the subject matter. "**Suitable criteria**" are usually derived from laws and regulations and are required by directors to enable them to make reasonably consistent evaluations or measurements of the subject matter. With respect to public reporting engagements the suitable criteria for specific types of engagement are described in the individual SIR dealing with such engagements. Where the reporting accountant's engagement requires it to consider only certain criteria, such criteria are described as "reporting accountant's criteria". Reporting accountant's criteria are set out in the SIRs. Where a SIR has not been issued with respect to a particular type of reporting engagement, the reporting accountant uses those criteria that are specified by legislation or regulation. The evaluation or measurement of a subject matter solely on the basis of the reporting accountant's own expectations, judgments and individual experience would not constitute suitable criteria; and

(c) the "**outcome**" of the evaluation or measurement of a subject matter is the information that results from the directors applying the suitable criteria to the subject matter. Examples of outcomes are historical financial information and a directors' profit forecast and related disclosures that are included in an investment circular.

3. Not all engagements performed by a reporting accountant are public reporting engagements. Examples of engagements that are not public reporting engagements include:

- Engagements involving the preparation of a comfort letter.

- Engagements involving the preparation of a long form report.

---

[2] The "outcome" is sometimes described as "subject matter information."

Such engagements are private reporting engagements.

4. This SIR establishes basic principles and essential procedures for the work of reporting accountants that are common to all reporting engagements (both public and private) relating to investment circulars. Other SIRs set out basic principles and essential procedures to address the particular issues and requirements arising on specific public reporting engagements. These comprise:

   (a) SIR 2000 "Investment reporting standards applicable to public reporting engagements on historical financial information";

   (b) SIR 3000 "Investment reporting standards applicable to public reporting engagements on profit forecasts"; and

   (c) SIR 4000 "Investment reporting standards applicable to public reporting engagements on pro forma financial information.

5. Appendix 1 summarises public reporting engagements that reporting accountants may be required to undertake under the Prospectus Rules.

Engagement acceptance and continuance

6. **The reporting accountant should accept (or continue where applicable) a reporting engagement only if, on the basis of a preliminary knowledge of the engagement circumstances, nothing comes to the attention of the reporting accountant to indicate that the requirements of relevant ethical standards and guidance, issued by the Auditing Practices Board and the professional bodies of which the reporting accountant is a member, will not be satisfied. (SIR 1000.1)**

7. **The reporting accountant should accept (or continue where applicable) a reporting engagement only if:**

   (a) **the scope of the engagement is expected to be sufficient to support the required report;**

   (b) **the reporting accountant expects to be able to carry out the procedures required by the SIRs; and**

   (c) **those persons who are to perform the engagement collectively possess the necessary professional competencies. (SIR 1000.2)**

8. In determining whether the scope of the engagement is expected to be sufficient to support the required report, the reporting accountant considers whether there appear to be any significant limitations on the scope of the reporting accountant's work.

9. A reporting accountant may be requested to perform reporting engagements on a wide range of matters. Some engagements may require specialised skills and

knowledge. In these circumstances the reporting accountant considers using internal or external specialists having the appropriate skills.

Agreeing the terms of the engagement

10. **The reporting accountant should agree the terms of the engagement with those from whom they accept instructions. All the terms of the engagement should be recorded in writing. (SIR 1000.3)**

11. Generally, a letter is prepared by the reporting accountant, covering all aspects of the engagement, and accepted in writing by the directors of the issuer and, where relevant, the sponsor. With respect to a public reporting engagement the letter will record the reporting accountant's understanding of what constitutes the subject matter of the engagement, the suitable criteria, and the information that constitutes the outcome of the evaluation or measurement of the subject matter against the suitable criteria.

12. As an alternative to a letter drafted by the reporting accountant, an instruction letter may be issued by the directors and, where relevant, the sponsor. In these circumstances, its terms are formally acknowledged by the reporting accountant in writing, clarifying particular aspects of the instructions and covering any matters that may not have been addressed.

13. This letter, or exchange of letters (together referred to as "the engagement letter"), provides evidence of the contractual relationship between the reporting accountant, the entity and, where relevant, the sponsor. It sets out clearly the scope and limitations of the work to be performed by the reporting accountant. It also confirms the reporting accountant's acceptance of the engagement and includes a summary of the reporting accountant's responsibilities and those of the directors and, where relevant, the sponsor as they relate to the reporting accountant's role.

14. The engagement letter establishes a direct responsibility to the other parties from the reporting accountant. It is also the mechanism by which the scope of the reporting accountant's contribution is defined and agreed. If in the course of the engagement the terms of the engagement are changed, such changes are similarly agreed, and recorded in writing.

15. The engagement letter will usually set out the form of any reports (public or private) required (including, in each case, the nature of any opinion to be expressed by the reporting accountant). Accordingly, it is important to clarify those from whom the reporting accountant has agreed to accept instructions including, where relevant, sponsors, and determine their requirements and the scope of such reports, at an early stage.

16. **The engagement letter should specify those reports that are intended for publication in the investment circular and any other reports that are required. The engagement letter should specify, in respect of each report, to whom it is to be addressed. (SIR 1000.4)**

17. The engagement letter sets out the express terms governing the reporting accountant's contractual responsibilities in connection with the transaction to those instructing them. Reporting accountants do not accept responsibility beyond the matters or entities in respect of which they are specifically instructed. Nor are they expected to comment or report on matters which more properly fall within the skill and experience of other experts or advisers. They understand, however, the need to apply their own professional skill and experience in interpreting and carrying out their instructions. The reporting accountant may find information outside the defined scope of the engagement that it believes should be disclosed, because, in its view such information is material to the purpose of the investment circular or to the proposed transaction. The reporting accountant discusses such matters with the directors of the issuer and the sponsor, where relevant, and agrees a course of action.

Ethical requirements

18. **In the conduct of an engagement involving an investment circular, the reporting accountant should comply with the applicable ethical standards issued by the Auditing Practices Board. The reporting accountant should also adhere to the relevant ethical guidance of the professional bodies of which the reporting accountant is a member. (SIR 1000.5)**

19. While it is not the responsibility of the reporting accountant to judge the appropriateness, or otherwise, of a proposed transaction, in respect of which they have been engaged, there may be rare circumstances where a reporting accountant considers the proposed transaction, or their proposed association with the transaction, to be so inappropriate that the reporting accountant cannot properly commence work or continue to act.

Legal and regulatory requirements

20. **The reporting accountant should be familiar with the applicable laws and regulations governing the report which is to be given. (SIR 1000.6)**

21. The principal legal and regulatory requirements applicable to reporting accountants in the United Kingdom are summarised in Appendix 2. Readers are cautioned that these references may change subsequent to publication of this SIR.

Quality control

22. **The reporting accountant should comply with the applicable standards and guidance set out in International Standard on Quality Control (UK and Ireland) 1 and ISA (UK and Ireland) 220. (SIR 1000.7)**

23. International Standard on Quality Control (UK and Ireland) 1 "Quality control for firms that perform audits and reviews of historical financial information, and other assurance

and related services engagements" provides standards and guidance on the system of quality control that a firm establishes.

24. The quality control procedures that an engagement partner applies are those set out in ISA (UK and Ireland) 220 "Quality control for audits of historical financial information". In applying ISA (UK and Ireland) 220, the terms "audit" and "audit engagement" are read as "reporting accountant's engagement" and the term "auditor's report" is read as "reporting accountant's report".

25. **When undertaking any engagement involving an investment circular a partner with appropriate experience should be involved in the conduct of the work. (SIR 1000.8)**

26. Reporting accountants are frequently from a firm that is also the auditor of the entity. The audit partner, although having knowledge of the entity, may not have the necessary experience to take responsibility for all aspects of an engagement involving an investment circular. The extent of involvement of a partner with the requisite experience of dealing with investment circulars is determined, for example, by the expertise required to make the reports that the reporting accountant has agreed to provide and the experience of the audit partner.

27. In some cases it may be appropriate for the partner with the requisite experience of dealing with investment circulars to act as a second partner. In other cases it may be appropriate for such a partner to be the lead engagement partner.

Planning and performing the engagement

28. **The reporting accountant should develop and document a plan for the work so as to perform the engagement in an effective manner. (SIR 1000.9)**

29. Planning is an essential component of all reporting accountant's engagements. Examples of the main matters to be considered include:

- The terms of the engagement.

- Ethical considerations.

- Whether the timetable is realistic.

- The reporting accountant's understanding of the entity and its environment.

- Identifying potential problems that could impact the performance of the engagement.

- The need for the involvement of specialists.

30. Planning is not a discrete phase, but rather an iterative process throughout the engagement. As a result of unexpected events, changes in conditions or the evidence

obtained from the results of evidence-gathering procedures, the reporting accountant may need to revise the overall strategy and engagement plan, and thereby the resulting planned nature, timing and extent of further procedures.

31. A preliminary review of the available information may provide an indication of potential issues that might need to be addressed in carrying out the engagement. If the preliminary review indicates that there are factors which may give rise to a qualification or other modification of any report, then such factors are reported immediately to the directors and, where relevant, the sponsor.

32. Changes in circumstances, or unexpected results of work carried out, may require the plan to be amended as work progresses. Any such amendments are documented. Where the changes affect the work set out in the engagement letter, the engagement letter is also amended as necessary following agreement with the directors, and where relevant, the sponsor.

33. **The reporting accountant should consider materiality in planning its work in accordance with its instructions and in determining the effect of its findings on the report to be issued. (SIR 1000.10)**

34. Matters are material if their omission or misstatement could, individually or collectively, influence the economic decisions of users of the outcome. Materiality depends on the size and nature of the omission or misstatement judged in light of the surrounding circumstances. The size or nature of the matter, or a combination of both, could be the determining factor.

35. In certain circumstances, such as private reporting engagements to report the results of agreed-upon procedures, materiality may have been determined for the reporting accountant within the scope of the engagement.

36. **The reporting accountant should obtain sufficient appropriate evidence on which to base the report provided. (SIR 1000.11)**

37. The reporting accountant, either directly or indirectly, will seek to obtain evidence derived from one or more of the following procedures: inspection, observation, enquiry, confirmation, computation and analytical procedures. The choice of which of these, or which combination, is appropriate will depend on the circumstances of each engagement and on the form of opinion (if any) to be given. Guidance on considerations applicable in particular circumstances is given in other SIRs which address the particular issues and requirements arising on specific engagements.

38. The evidence gathered in support of an individual report takes account of the information gathered and conclusions drawn in support of other reporting engagements in connection with the transaction.

39. **If the reporting accountant becomes aware of any withholding, concealment or misrepresentation of information, it should take steps, as soon as practicable, to consider its obligation to report such findings and, if necessary, take legal advice to determine the appropriate response. (SIR 1000.12)**

40. In preparing any report the reporting accountant relies on information supplied to it by the directors, employees or agents of the entity that is the subject of the reporting accountant's enquiries. The engagement letter may limit the extent of the reporting accountant's responsibility where information which is material to the report has been withheld from, concealed from or misrepresented to the reporting accountant. Notwithstanding any such limitation, the reporting accountant does not accept such information without further inquiry where, applying its professional skill and experience to the engagement, the information provided, prima facie, gives rise to doubts about its validity.

41. The reporting accountant normally informs the directors of the issuer and the sponsor, where relevant, as soon as practicable, of any withholding, concealment or misrepresentation of information. The reporting accountant's duty of confidentiality would ordinarily preclude reporting to a third party. However, in certain circumstances, that duty of confidentiality is overridden by law, for example, in the case of suspected money laundering it may be appropriate to report the matter direct to the appropriate authority. The reporting accountant may need to seek legal advice in such circumstances, giving due consideration to any public interest considerations.

42. **The reporting accountant should obtain appropriate written confirmation of representations from the directors of the entity. (SIR 1000.13)**

43. Written confirmation of representations made by the directors on matters material to the reporting accountant's report is ordinarily obtained. These representations also encompass statements or opinions attributed to directors, management, employees or agents of an entity, which are relied upon by the reporting accountant.

44. This may be achieved by the directors confirming that they have read a final draft of the report and that to the best of their knowledge and belief:

    (a) they have made available to the reporting accountant all significant information, relevant to the report, of which they have knowledge;

    (b) the report is factually accurate, no material facts have been omitted and the report is not otherwise misleading; and

    (c) the report accurately reflects any opinion or statements attributed therein to the directors, management, employees or agents of the entity.

45. Representations by the directors of the entity cannot replace the evidence that the reporting accountant could reasonably expect to be available to support any opinion given, if any. An inability to obtain sufficient appropriate evidence regarding a matter could represent a limitation of scope even if a representation has been received on the matter.

Documentation

46. **The reporting accountant should document matters that are significant in providing evidence that supports the report provided and in providing evidence that the engagement was performed in accordance with SIRs. (SIR 1000.14)**

47. **The reporting accountant should record in the working papers (or, if applicable, the report) the reporting accountant's reasoning on all significant matters that require the exercise of judgment, and related conclusions. (SIR 1000.15)**

48. The information to be recorded in working papers is a matter of professional judgment since it is neither necessary nor practical to document every matter considered by the reporting accountant. When applying professional judgment in assessing the extent of documentation to be prepared and retained, the reporting accountant may consider what is necessary to provide an understanding of the work performed and the basis of the principal decisions taken to another person, such as a reporting accountant, who has no previous experience with the engagement. That other person may, however, only be able to obtain an understanding of detailed aspects of the engagement by discussing them with the reporting accountant who prepared the documentation.

49. The form and content of working papers are affected by matters such as:

- The nature and scope of the engagement.

- The form of the report and the opinion, if any, to be given.

- The nature and complexity of the entity's business.

- The nature and condition of the entity's accounting and internal control systems.

- The needs in the particular circumstances for direction, supervision and review of the work of members of the reporting accountant's team.

- The specific methodology and technology that the reporting accountant uses.

Professional scepticism

50. **The reporting accountant should plan and perform an engagement with an attitude of professional scepticism. (SIR 1000.16)**

51. An attitude of professional scepticism is essential to ensure that the reporting accountant makes a critical assessment, with a questioning mind, of the validity of evidence obtained and is alert to evidence that contradicts or brings into question the reliability of documents or representations.

52. Whilst the reporting accountant may proceed on the basis that information and explanations provided by the directors and management of the issuer are reliable, it assesses them critically and considers them in the context of its knowledge and

findings derived from other areas of its work. The reporting accountant is alert for, and, where appropriate reports, on a timely basis, to the directors and sponsors, where relevant, any inconsistencies it considers to be significant. The extent to which the reporting accountant is required to perform further procedures on the information and explanations received will depend upon the reporting accountant's specific instructions, and the level of assurance, if any, it is to provide and the requirements of relevant SIRs.

Reporting

53. **In all reports the reporting accountant should:**

    (a) **address reports only to those parties who are party to the engagement letter (and on the basis agreed in the engagement letter) or to a relevant regulatory body;**

    (b) **identify the matters to which the report relates;**

    (c) **address all matters that are required by the engagement letter;**

    (d) **explain the basis of the reporting accountant's work;**

    (e) **give, where applicable, a clear expression of opinion;**

    (f) **include the reporting accountant's manuscript or printed signature;**

    (g) **include the reporting accountant's address; and**

    (h) **date the report. (SIR 1000.17)**

54. **In all public reporting engagements the reporting accountant should explain the basis of the reporting accountant's opinion by including in its report:**

    (a) **a statement as to the reporting accountant's compliance, or otherwise, with applicable Standards for Investment Reporting; and**

    (b) **a summary description of the work performed by the reporting accountant. (SIR 1000.18)**

55. Certain of the reports prepared in connection with investment circulars are public reporting engagements and, therefore, intended for publication in the investment circular. Examples of such reports are accountant's reports, reports on profit forecasts and reports on pro forma financial information. Additional basic principles and essential procedures on the expression of opinions or conclusions relating to these example public reporting engagements are provided as follows:

    (a) accountant's reports on historical financial information, in SIR 2000;

(b)   reports on profit forecasts, in SIR 3000; and

(c)   reports on pro forma financial information, in SIR 4000.

56.   In private reporting engagements the reporting accountant would ordinarily include in its report:

(a)   a statement of compliance with this SIR; and

(b)   either a summary description of the work performed or a cross reference to the description of work to be performed in the engagement letter.

In some private reporting engagements those engaging the reporting accountant agree with the reporting accountant the procedures to be performed[3]. In such cases it may be unnecessary for the report of the reporting accountant to repeat the description of the procedures that is set out in the engagement letter.

57.   **Before signing the report, the reporting accountant should consider whether it is appropriate to make the required report, having regard to the scope of the work performed and the evidence obtained. (SIR 1000.19)**

58.   The date of a report is the date on which the reporting accountant signs the report as being suitable for release. However, the reporting accountant should not sign the report (whether modified or not) unless sufficient appropriate evidence has been obtained and all relevant procedures have been finalised. Such procedures include the review procedures of both the engagement partner and the engagement quality control reviewer.

59.   As noted in paragraph 15 above, the engagement letter usually sets out the form of the report to be issued, including, where applicable, the form of opinion to be expressed. The reporting accountant ensures that the form of report or opinion is consistent with the terms of the engagement letter.

60.   The level of assurance, if any, provided by the reporting accountant may vary from engagement to engagement. This reflects the wide range of characteristics of the matters to which the engagements undertaken by reporting accountants relate. To avoid any misunderstanding by the user of the report as to the scope of the opinion or the level of assurance provided, it is important that the matters to which the engagements undertaken by reporting accountants relate are clearly identified and that the reporting accountant's opinion or other assurance is expressed in terms that are appropriate to the particular engagement. Standards and guidance on the form and scope of reports appropriate in particular circumstances is given in other SIRs which address particular issues and requirements relevant to individual reports.

61.   In certain circumstances the Prospectus Rules require, "a declaration by those responsible for certain parts of the registration document that, having taken all

---

[3]   These are often referred to as "agreed-upon procedures engagements"

reasonable care to ensure that such is the case, the information contained in the part of the registration document for which they are responsible is, to the best of their knowledge, in accordance with the facts and contains no omission likely to affect its import". The reporting accountant is responsible for its reports included in investment circulars and ordinarily includes this declaration (when satisfied it is able to do so) at the end of each public report included in an investment circular to which the Prospectus Rules apply.

Modified opinions

62. **The reporting accountant should not express an unmodified opinion when the following circumstances exist and, in the reporting accountant's judgment, the effect of the matter is or may be material:**

    (a) **there is a limitation on the scope of the reporting accountant's work, that is, circumstances prevent, or there are restrictions imposed that prevent, the reporting accountant from obtaining evidence required to reduce engagement risk to the appropriate level; or**

    (b) **the outcome is materially misstated. (SIR 1000.20)**

63. Where not precluded by regulation, the reporting accountant expresses a qualified opinion when the effect of a matter described in paragraph 62 is not so material or pervasive as to require an adverse opinion or a disclaimer of opinion. When giving a qualified opinion, the opinion is expressed "except for" the matter to which the qualification relates.

64. Some regulations require a positive and unmodified opinion. Consequently, in the event that the reporting accountant is unable to report in the manner prescribed it considers, with the parties to whom it is to report, whether the outcome can be amended to alleviate its concerns, or whether the outcome should be omitted from the investment circular.

Pre-existing financial information

65. With respect to historical financial information, where the issuer already has available:

    (a) audited annual financial statements; or

    (b) audited or reviewed financial information, which meet the requirements of the applicable rules in respect of the preparation and presentation of historical financial information to be included in the investment circular,

    it may choose to include these financial statements, or financial information, in the investment circular together with the pre-existing reports of the auditor. In these circumstances the audit firm is not required by the Prospectus Rules to consent to the inclusion of its reports in the investment circular.

Consent

66. Where the reporting accountant is required to give consent to the inclusion of its public report, or references to its name, in an investment circular the reporting accountant should, before doing so, consider its public report in the form and context in which it appears, or is referred to, in the investment circular as a whole by:

    (a) comparing its public report together with the information being reported on to the other information in the rest of the investment circular and assessing whether the reporting accountant has any cause to believe that such other information is inconsistent with the information being reported on; and

    (b) assessing whether the reporting accountant has any cause to believe that any information in the investment circular is misleading.

    When the reporting accountant believes information in the investment circular is either inconsistent with its public report, together with the information being reported on, or misleading, the reporting accountant should withhold its consent until the reporting accountant is satisfied that its concerns are unwarranted or until the investment circular has been appropriately amended. (SIR 1000.21)

67. The reporting accountant should give consent to the inclusion of any report in an investment circular only when all relevant reports that it has agreed to make, in that investment circular, have been finalised. (SIR 1000.22)

68. In order to comply with the relevant legislation or regulations, the issuer of an investment circular may ask a reporting accountant to provide a consent letter, consenting to the inclusion of public reports in investment circulars in a number of different circumstances. An example consent letter is set out in Appendix 3. The various circumstances include:

    (a) under the Prospectus Rules. These relate to a prospectus issued by an issuer (other than under the Listing Rules). No consent is required to the inclusion of previously issued reports. Where a reporting accountant prepares an accountant's report on a financial information table for the purposes of the prospectus, the reporting accountant's consent must be obtained. A statement referring to the reporting accountant's consent to the inclusion of such report in the prospectus is required, by item 23.1 of Annex I of the Prospectus Rules, to be included in the Prospectus;

    (b) under the Listing Rules. Where these relate to listing particulars prepared in connection with an application for admission of securities to listing, the same consent requirements, that is item 23.1 of Annex I of the Prospectus Rules, apply;

    (c) under the Listing Rules. Where these relate to a Class 1 circular, paragraph 13.4.1 (6) of the Listing Rules sets out similar consent requirements;

(d) under the City Code. In connection with a takeover, Rule 28.4 requires a similar consent requirement in respect of a public report on a profit forecast. Rule 28.5 requires a similar consent in connection with a subsequent document issued in connection with the offer; and

(e) under the AIM Rules. The consent requirements of item 23.1 of Annex I of the Prospectus Rules apply.

69. Whilst the reporting accountant's reporting responsibilities do not extend beyond its report, the process of giving consent involves an awareness of the overall process whereby the investment circular is prepared, and may entail discussions with those responsible for the document as a whole in relation to its contents.

70. In deciding whether to give its consent, a reporting accountant reads the final version of the investment circular with a view to assessing the overall impression given by the document, having regard to the purposes for which it has been prepared, as well as considering whether there are any inconsistencies between its report and the information in the rest of the document. As part of this process the reporting accountant considers whether it has any cause to believe that any information in the investment circular may be misleading such that the reporting accountant would not wish to be associated with it.

71. For this purpose the engagement partner uses the knowledge of the partners and professional staff working on the engagement. If particular issues are identified the engagement partner may make enquiries of partners and professional staff previously engaged on the audit of financial statements that are the basis of financial information in the investment circular, and any other partners and professional staff who may have been previously consulted regarding such issues, including the engagement quality review partner who is independent of the engagement. The engagement partner is not expected to make enquiries more widely within the reporting accountant's firm.

72. Because of the degree of knowledge required and the increased responsibility that may be assumed, it is inappropriate for a reporting accountant to provide consent unless the reporting accountant has been commissioned to undertake work specifically in connection with the relevant document in relation to the matter for which consent is sought. Hence, if an investment circular includes a reference to a report or opinion, previously provided by the reporting accountant, which is already in the public domain, the reporting accountant is not expected to provide consent to the inclusion of that information and does not generally do so. As discussed in paragraph 65, an example would be the inclusion or incorporation by reference in a prospectus of a previously published audit report or interim review report.

73. An exception to this general rule would be where the reporting accountant has previously consented to the inclusion in an investment circular of that earlier report or opinion and it is being repeated or referred to in connection with the same transaction in respect of which it was originally issued. For example, as noted in paragraph 68 above, Rule 28.5 of the City Code requires a profit forecast made and reported on in one document to be confirmed in any subsequent document in connection with the same offer, and for the reporting accountant to indicate that it has no objection to its

report continuing to apply. In such a case, before issuing its consent the reporting accountant makes enquiries as to whether there have been any material events subsequent to the date of its original report which might require modification of or disclosure in that report.

74. Letters of consent are dated the same date as the relevant document. The City Code requires the letter of consent to be available for public inspection. The letter of consent may be made available for public inspection in other cases.

Events occurring between the date of the reporting accountant's report and the completion date of the transaction

75. **If, in the period between the date of the reporting accountant's report and the completion date of the transaction, the reporting accountant becomes aware of events and other matters which, had they occurred and been known at the date of the report, might have caused it to issue a different report or withhold consent, the reporting accountant should discuss the implications of them with those responsible for the investment circular and take additional action as appropriate. (SIR 1000.23)**

76. If, as a result of discussion with those responsible for the investment circular concerning an event that occurred prior to the completion date of the transaction, the reporting accountant is either uncertain about or disagrees with the course of action proposed, it may consider it necessary to take legal advice with respect to its responsibilities in the particular circumstances.

77. After the date of its report, the reporting accountant has no obligation to perform procedures or make enquiries regarding the investment circular.

Effective date

78. A reporting accountant is required to comply with the Investment Reporting Standards contained in this SIR for reports signed after 31 August 2005. Earlier adoption is encouraged.

Appendix 1

SUMMARY OF POSSIBLE REPORTING ACCOUNTANT'S PUBLIC REPORTING ENGAGEMENTS UNDER THE PROSPECTUS RULES

In the following table possible reporting accountant's responsibilities, as set out in the Prospectus Rules, are shaded.

	Shares	Debt, units < €50k	Debt, units =/> €50k	Derivatives, units < €50k	Derivatives, units =/> €50K	Asset backed securities, units < €50k	Asset backed securities, units =/> €50k	Depository receipts, units < €50k	Depository receipts, units =/> €50k	Banks issuing anything other than equity securities
Applicable annex:										
Registration document	I, II	IV	IX	IV	IX	VII	VII	X	X	XI
Securities note	III	V	XIII	XII	XII	VIII	VIII	X	X	As relevant instrument type
Historical financial information	I, 20.1	IV, 13.1	IX, 11.1	IV, 13.1	IX, 11.1	VII, 8.2	VII, 8.2 bis	X, 20.1	X, 20.1 bis	XI, 11.1
Number of years	3 years with latest 2 years on new GAAP	2 years with latest year on new GAAP	2 years with latest year on new GAAP	2 years with latest year on new GAAP	2 years with latest year on new GAAP	2 years with latest year on new GAAP	2 years with latest year on new GAAP	3 years with latest 2 years on new GAAP	3 years with latest 2 years on new GAAP	2 years with latest year on new GAAP

	Shares	Debt, units < €50k	Debt, units =/> €50k	Derivatives, units < €50K	Derivatives, units =/> €50K	Asset backed securities, units < €50k	Asset backed securities, units =/> €50k	Depository receipts, units < €50k	Depository receipts, units =/> €50k	Banks issuing anything other than equity securities
GAAP	National GAAP or IFRS[1] as applicable to EU issuer. IFRS or GAAP equivalent to IFRS for non-EU issuers	National GAAP or IFRS[1] as applicable to EU issuer. IFRS or GAAP equivalent to IFRS for non-EU issuers	National GAAP or IFRS[1] as applicable to EU issuer. Non-EU issuers may use local GAAP with a narrative description of differences	National GAAP or IFRS[1] as applicable to EU issuer. IFRS or GAAP equivalent to IFRS for non-EU issuers	National GAAP or IFRS[1] as applicable to EU issuer. Non-EU issuers may use local GAAP with a narrative description of differences	National GAAP or IFRS[1] as applicable to EU issuer. IFRS or GAAP equivalent to IFRS for non-EU issuers	National GAAP or IFRS[1] as applicable to EU issuer. Non-EU issuers may use local GAAP with a narrative description of differences	National GAAP or IFRS[1] as applicable to EU issuer. IFRS or GAAP equivalent to IFRS for non-EU issuers	National GAAP or IFRS[1] as applicable to EU issuer. Non-EU issuers may use local GAAP with a narrative description of differences	National GAAP or IFRS[1] as applicable to EU issuer. IFRS or GAAP equivalent to IFRS for non-EU issuers
Issuers operating less than one year	Special purpose financial information must be included	Special purpose financial information must be included	No additional requirements	Special purpose financial information must be included	No additional requirements	Special purpose financial information must be included	No additional requirements	Special purpose financial information must be included	No additional requirements	Special purpose financial information must be included
Report on financial information	Auditor's report or accountant's report as applicable	Auditor's report or accountant's report as applicable	Auditor's report or accountant's report as applicable	Auditor's report or accountant's report as applicable	Auditor's report or accountant's report as applicable	Auditor's report or accountant's report as applicable	Auditor's report or accountant's report as applicable	Auditor's report or accountant's report as applicable	Auditor's report or accountant's report as applicable	Auditor's report or accountant's report as applicable

1   In this table the expression IFRS is intended to refer to "those IFRSs as adopted for use in the European Union".

	Shares	Debt, units < €50k	Debt, units =/> €50k	Derivatives, units < €50k	Derivatives, units =/> €50K	Asset backed securities, units < €50k	Asset backed securities, units =/> €50k	Depository receipts, units < €50k	Depository receipts, units =/> €50k	Banks issuing anything other than equity securities
Age of latest financial information	I, 20.5	IV, 13.4	IX, 11.4	IV, 13.4	IX, 11.4	-	-	X, 20.4	X, 20.4	XI, 11.4
Age of audited information	No more than 15 months if unaudited interims or 18 months if audited interims	No more than 18 months	No more than 18 months	No more than 18 months	No more than 18 months	No requirements	No requirements	No more than 15 months if unaudited interims or 18 months if audited interims	No more than 15 months if unaudited interims or 18 months if audited interims	No more than 18 months
Pro forma financial information	I, 20.2 & II	-	-	-	-	-	-	-	-	-
Information	Required to show effect of significant gross changes	No requirements	No requirements	No requirements	No requirements	No requirements	No requirements	No requirements	No requirements	No requirements
Report on proper compilation	Required, where pro forma included	No requirements	No requirements	No requirements	No requirements	No requirements	No requirements	No requirements	No requirements	No requirements

Profit forecasts and estimates	Shares	Debt, units < €50k	Debt, units =/> €50k	Derivatives, units < €50k	Derivatives, units =/> €50K	Asset backed securities, units < €50k	Asset backed securities, units =/> €50k	Depository receipts, units < €50k	Depository receipts, units =/> €50k	Banks issuing anything other than equity securities
	I, 13	IV, 9	IX, 8	IV, 9	IX, 8	-	-	X, 13	X, 13	XI, 8
Disclosure of assumptions	Required	Required	Required	Required	Required	No requirements	No requirements	Required	Required	Required
Report on proper compilation	Required	Required	No requirements	Required	No requirements	No requirements	No requirements	Required	Required	Required
Outstanding forecasts	Update statement required	No requirements	No requirements	No requirements	No requirements	No requirements	No requirements	Update statement required	Update statement required	No requirements

Appendix 2

PRINCIPAL LEGAL AND REGULATORY REQUIREMENTS

The description of legal and regulatory requirements provided in this appendix is intended to be a guide and not intended to be a definitive interpretation of such requirements.

The FSA Handbook

1   In July 2005 the then existing listing rules were modified to take account of the implementation of the Prospectus Directive in the United Kingdom. At the same time the opportunity was taken to revise the rules applying to the continuing obligations of listed companies.

2   The FSA Handbook now includes three parts relevant to securities and their issuers, namely: the "Prospectus Rules", the "Listing Rules" and the "Disclosure Rules".

3   The Prospectus Rules effect the practical implementation of the Prospectus Directive. They apply to all prospectuses required to be issued by UK companies either offering securities to the public or seeking admission of securities to a regulated market. The annexes to the PD Regulation provide detailed rules on prospectuses and, in particular, the content requirements of prospectuses. In respect of prospectus content requirements, the Prospectus Rules reproduce the Annexes to the PD Regulation. Accordingly, references to the contents requirements in Annexes to the Prospectus Rules are also references to the Annexes to the PD Regulation.

4   The Prospectus Rules also make it clear that the FSA expect "CESR's recommendations for the consistent implementation of the European Commission's Regulation on Prospectuses no. 809/2004"[1] to be followed by issuers when preparing a prospectus.

5   The Listing Rules provide the rules and guidance applicable to issuers of securities both seeking admission to, and once admitted to, the Official List. They include the conditions for admission to listing, the requirements concerning Sponsors under the Listing Rules, Class 1 and related party transactions and the requirements for listing particulars when a prospectus is not required to be prepared.

6   The Disclosure Rules contain rules and guidance in relation to the publication and control of "inside information" and the disclosure of transactions by persons discharging managerial responsibilities and their connected persons.

7   The annexes to the Prospectus Rules provide that historical financial information for the last three completed financial years, where it exists, is to be included in a prospectus. This information can either be extracted or incorporated by reference from the issuer's annual financial statements or presented in the prospectus specifically for

---

[1]   "CESR" is the Committee of European Securities Regulators. Its recommendations were issued in February 2005 and are sometimes referred to as the "Level 3 Guidance of the Lamfalussy Process". This guidance can be accessed on the CESR website www.cesr-eu.org.

that purpose. The Prospectus Rules provide that where the accounting framework to be applied in an issuer's next annual financial statements is different from that previously applied, at least some of the historical financial information must be represented on the basis of those new policies. The historical financial information must either be accompanied by the auditor's report on the statutory financial statements or by a new opinion by reporting accountants where the information has been presented for the purpose of the prospectus.

8   Where an issuer with listed equity securities proposes to undertake a Class 1 acquisition, Listing Rule 13.5 requires that certain historical financial information is presented in relation to the target and, where relevant, the target's subsidiary undertakings. The last three years historical financial information must be presented in a financial information table on a basis consistent with accounting policies of the issuer. Unless the target is itself admitted to trading on an EU regulated market or on an overseas regulated market or listed on an overseas investment exchange, the financial information table must be reported on by a reporting accountant. However, if there is no report by reporting accountants on the financial information table itself, it is necessary for the issuer to consider whether any material adjustment is required to achieve consistency between the target's historical financial information and the accounting policies of the issuer, in which event a reconciliation of key financial statement components must be presented and the reconciliation reported on by reporting accountants.

9   If an issuer chooses to include a profit forecast or profit estimate in a prospectus the registration document may be required to contain the following information:

(a)   a statement setting out the principal assumptions upon which the issuer has based its forecast or estimate. See item 13.1 of Annex I to the Prospectus Rules for more detailed requirements regarding assumptions; and

(b)   a report prepared by independent accountants or auditors stating that in the opinion of the independent accountants or auditors the forecast or estimate has been properly compiled on the basis stated and that the basis of accounting used for the profit forecast or estimate is consistent with the accounting policies of the issuer.

The profit forecast or estimate must be prepared on a basis comparable with the historical financial information.

10   If a profit forecast in a prospectus has been published which is still outstanding, the issuer must provide a statement setting out whether or not that forecast is still correct as at the time of the registration document, and an explanation of why such forecast is no longer valid if that is the case.

11   Where an issuer includes pro forma financial information in a prospectus, (relating to shares, transferable securities equivalent to shares and certain other securities convertible into shares), Annex I item 20.2 and Annex II of the Prospectus Rules require any such information to be reported on by the reporting accountants. The

Listing Rules also require a reporting accountant's report on any pro forma financial information that an issuer chooses to include in a Class 1 circular.

12   Where a statement or report attributed to an expert (including reporting accountants) is included in a prospectus at the issuer's request, the Prospectus Rules require a statement of consent from the expert. This is discussed in more detail in paragraphs 66 to 74 in the body of this SIR. The consent of the auditor is not required where reports (audit or review) previously issued by the auditor are included in a prospectus.

13   Other rules apply in particular circumstances. By replication of the Prospectus Rules requirements an expert is required, by the Listing Rules, to consent to the inclusion of any report in any listing particulars. However, the consent of the auditor is not required where reports (audit or review) previously issued by the auditor are included in the listing particulars.

14   The Listing Rules also require pro forma financial information in a Class 1 circular to be reported on by an issuer's reporting accountants and to contain provisions requiring an expert's consent to any report included in a Class 1 circular.

Admission to the Main Market of the London Stock Exchange

15   A two-stage admission process applies to companies who want to have their securities admitted to the Main Market for listed securities of the London Stock Exchange. The securities need to be admitted to the Official List by the UK Listing Authority (UKLA), a division of the Financial Services Authority, and also admitted to trading by the London Stock Exchange. To be admitted to trading the Admission and Disclosure Standards need to be met. Once both processes are complete the securities are officially listed on the Exchange.

AIM requirements

16   Under the AIM Rules of the London Stock Exchange, companies seeking admission to AIM must publish an AIM admission document. This is the case whether or not they are required by the Prospectus Rules to prepare a prospectus (because they are also making an offer of securities to the public which is not exempt from the requirement to produce a prospectus).

17   The AIM Rules provide that the content of an admission document should be based on the share disclosure requirements in the Prospectus Rules, modified to allow issuers to elect not to include certain financial information where no prospectus is required, notably profit forecasts and pro forma financial information. However, if such information is included the Prospectus Rules requirements must be followed.

The Professional Securities Market

18   From 1 July 2005, issuers listing debt, convertibles or depository receipts in London will have a choice of being admitted to a regulated market or the Professional Securities Market, which is a market operated and regulated by the London Stock Exchange. Issuers listing on the Professional Securities Market will not be required to

report historical financial information under IFRSs or an EU approved equivalent standard either in listing documents or as a continuing obligation requirement.

The City Code

19   Where a document sent to shareholders in connection with an offer falling within the scope of the City Code contains a profit forecast or estimate, with certain exceptions, Rule 28.3 of the City Code requires that forecast or estimate to be reported on by reporting accountants and by the financial advisers. The City Code's requirements for such reports are similar to those under the Prospectus Rules. In certain circumstances, the City Code also provides for a reporting accountant to report on merger benefit statements (Rule 19.1) and interim financial information (Rule 28.6 (c)).

Companies legislation

20   In the United Kingdom, financial information presented in an investment circular may constitute "non statutory accounts" within the meaning of section 240 of the Companies Act 1985. The document in which the financial information is presented will usually, therefore, contain a statement complying with section 240(3) of the Companies Act 1985. However, this statement is only appropriate where the financial information comprises non-statutory accounts of the company issuing the document. No statement is needed in respect of financial information on a target company in an acquisition circular, for example, unless the directors of the target company explicitly accept responsibility for that part of the document. The statement is also the responsibility of the directors of the company publishing the document, not the reporting accountants.

Financial Services and Markets Act 2000

21   Upon implementation of the Prospectus Directive into UK law with effect from 1 July 2005, the existing regime regarding the issue of prospectuses in the UK whether in connection with an official listing of securities or a public offer was repealed.

22   Under Part VI, the FSA's function is a statutory one. Part VI covers not only the whole process by which securities are admitted to official listing but also the obligations to which companies are subject once they have obtained listing. The Listing Rules represent listing rules for the purposes of Part VI.

23   Prospectus Rule 5.5 (in relation to prospectuses), and regulation 6 of The Financial Services and Markets Act 2000 (Official Listing of Securities) Regulations 2001 (in relation to listing particulars, i.e. not prospectuses within the meaning of the Prospectus Directive) provide that each person:

(a)   who accepts, and is stated in the particulars as accepting, responsibility for the particulars or for any part of the particulars; or

(b)   who has authorised the contents of, or any part of, the particulars;

is deemed to accept responsibility for the particulars (or that part of them).

24 This raises potential issues for reporting accountants, for example:

- If they are involved in advising on an investment circular but are not named in it.

- If they issue a report or letter which is included in the investment circular.

25 In the first example the Prospectus Rules and The Financial Services and Markets Act 2000 (Official Listing of Securities) Regulations 2001 relieve professional advisers from responsibility for the circular where they are solely giving advice as to the contents of the listing particulars in a professional capacity.

26 In the second example the Prospectus Rules and The Financial Services and Markets Act 2000 (Official Listing of Securities) Regulations 2001 limit the responsibility of experts, including reporting accountants, to the part for which they accept responsibility and only if the part for which they accept responsibility is included in (or substantially in) the form and context to which they have agreed.

Appendix 3

EXAMPLE OF A CONSENT LETTER

The Directors
ABC plc

Dear Sirs

We hereby give our consent to the inclusion in the [describe Investment Circular] dated [ ] issued by ABC plc of [our accountant's report]/[our report relating to the profit estimate for the year ended 20 ,]/[our report relating to the profit forecast for the year ending 20 ,]/[our report relating to the pro forma financial information for the year ended 20] dated [ ] [[and] the references to our name[2]] in the form and context in which [it]/[they] are included, as shown in the enclosed proof of the [describe Investment Circular] which we have signed for identification.

[We also hereby authorise the contents of the [report[s]] referred to above which [is/are] included in the Prospectus for the purposes of Prospectus Rule [5.5.3R (2)(f)] [5.5.4R (2)(f)] **OR** [We also hereby authorise the contents of the [report[s]] referred to above which [is/are] included in the Listing Particulars for the purposes of Regulation 6(1)(e) of The Financial Services and Markets Act 2000 (Official Listing of Securities) Regulations 2001.] **OR** [We also hereby authorise the contents of the report[s] referred to above which [is/are] included in the Admission Document for the purposes of the Schedule Two to the AIM Rules][3]

Yours faithfully

Reporting accountant

---

[2] This is required only when a statement is attributed to a reporting accountant as an expert outside the context of a report from the reporting accountant included in the investment circular.

[3] This paragraph is not required in respect of a Class 1 Circular.

Appendix 4

GLOSSARY OF TERMS

Accountant's report - A report by a reporting accountant included in an investment circular, in which the reporting accountant normally expresses a "true and fair, for the purposes of the investment circular" opinion on historical financial information relating to the issuer and its subsidiaries in accordance with SIR 2000 "Investment Reporting Standards applicable to public reporting engagements on historical financial information ".

Admission and Disclosure Standards - The Admission and Disclosure Standards published by the London Stock Exchange, for companies admitted or seeking to be admitted to trading by the Exchange.

Agreed-upon procedures [engagements] - An engagement where the reporting accountant is engaged to carry out procedures of an audit or assurance nature, that the reporting accountant, the entity and any appropriate third parties have agreed, and to report on factual findings. The recipients of the report must form their own conclusions from the report by the reporting accountant. The report is restricted to those parties that have agreed to the procedures to be performed, since others, unaware of the reasons for the procedures, may misinterpret the results.

AIM - The Alternative Investment Market operated by the London Stock Exchange plc. The market is for smaller growing companies. Securities admitted to AIM are unlisted.

AIM Admission Document - The document prepared in connection with an application for admission of an issuer's securities to trading on AIM. If upon admission a prospectus is required in accordance with the Prospectus Rules, such prospectus may serve as the AIM Admission Document.

AIM Rules - The Rules of the Alternative Investment Market.

CESR - The Committee of European Securities Regulators.

Circular - A circular issued by any company to its shareholders and/or holders of its debt securities in connection with a transaction, which does not constitute a prospectus, listing particulars or AIM admission document.

City Code - The City Code on Takeovers and Mergers, published by the Panel on Takeovers and Mergers.

Class 1 circular - A circular relating to a Class 1 transaction.

Class 1 transaction - A transaction where one or more of a number of specified percentage ratios exceed a predetermined level as specified in Chapter 10 of the Listing Rules.

Comfort letter - A private letter from the reporting accountant, usually prepared at the request of the issuer and/or the sponsor, where relevant. It is intended to provide the addressees with comfort (in the form of an opinion or a report on the results of specific procedures carried out by the reporting accountants) regarding matters relevant to the addressees' responsibilities.

Completion date of the transaction - The date by which any offer contained in the circular must have been accepted or application made for shares or other securities to be issued, or the date on which shareholders vote to approve the transaction.

Consent letter - A letter whereby the reporting accountant consents to the inclusion in an investment circular of references to its name or the inclusion of any of its reports or letters which are to be published therein.

Due diligence - The process whereby the directors of the issuer and other parties, whether as principal or in an advisory capacity, satisfy themselves that the transaction is entered into after due and careful enquiry and that all relevant regulatory and/or legal requirements have been properly complied with. There is no generally accepted definition of required procedures for this purpose and where others (such as reporting accountants) are engaged to carry out work that will form part of the process, it is for the instructing parties to make clear what is required of those others in the particular circumstances.

Engagement partner - The partner or other person in the firm who is responsible for the engagement and its performance, and for reports that are issued on behalf of the firm, and who, where required, has the appropriate authority from a professional, legal or regulatory body.

Financial information - The term is used to signify the specific information presented in the form of a table upon which a reporting accountant reports. Typically, this information encompasses a number of accounting periods.

Financial statements - A balance sheet, profit and loss account (or other form of income statement), statement of cash flow, and statement of total recognised gains and losses (or statement of changes in equity), notes and other statements and explanatory material. In order to avoid confusion the term financial information is used throughout the SIRs to refer to the information upon which the reporting accountant reports. When the term financial statements is used within the SIRs this refers to financial statements from which the financial information has been derived by the issuer.

FSA - Financial Services Authority.

FSMA - Financial Services and Markets Act 2000.

IFRSs - International Financial Reporting Standards issued by the International Accounting Standards Board. This term incorporates all International Financial Reporting Standards, International Accounting Standards (IASs) and Interpretations originated by the International Financial Reporting Interpretations Committee (IFRIC) or the former Standards Interpretation Committee of the IASC.

Investment circular - A generic term describing any document issued by an entity pursuant to statutory or regulatory requirements relating to securities on which it is intended that a third party should make an investment decision, including a prospectus, listing particulars, circular to shareholders or similar document.

ISAs (UK and Ireland) - International Standards on Auditing (UK and Ireland) issued by the Auditing Practices Board.

Issuer - For the purposes of the Prospectus Rules "A legal person who issues or proposes to issue securities". For the purposes of the Listing Rules "Any company or other legal person or undertaking (including a public sector issuer), any class of whose securities has been admitted to listing, or is the subject of an application for admission to listing".

Listing particulars - A document not being a Prospectus prepared in connection with an admission of securities to the Official List.

Listing Rules - The part of the FSA's Handbook entitled "Listing Rules" governing the conduct of companies whose securities are admitted to the Official List.

London Stock Exchange - The London Stock Exchange plc.

Long form report - A private report with a restricted circulation, normally prepared by the reporting accountants on the instructions of, and addressed to, the sponsor, where relevant, and the directors of the issuer as part of their due diligence, dealing with agreed matters including commentary on financial and other information in an orderly and relevant form for a specific purpose.

Main Market - The London Stock Exchange's market for larger and established companies. Securities admitted to the Main Market are listed.

Nominated adviser - A corporate broker, investment banker or other professional adviser approved by the London Stock Exchange to act as a nominated adviser to an AIM company under the AIM Rules.

Ofex - An independent, self regulated, UK market for smaller companies.

Official List - The Official List maintained by the FSA.

Outcome - The outcome of the evaluation or measurement of a subject matter is the information that results from the directors applying the suitable criteria to the subject matter. Examples of outcomes are historical financial information and a directors' profit forecast and related disclosures that are included in an investment circular.

Partner - Any individual with authority to bind a firm of reporting accountants with respect to the performance of any engagement in connection with an investment circular.

PD Regulation - The implementing EU Regulation 809/2004 that provides the detailed rules concerning Prospectuses and their contents. Much of the text of this regulation is included within the Prospectus Rules.

Private reporting engagement - An engagement in which a reporting accountant does not express a conclusion that is published in an investment circular.

Professional Securities Market - A market for debt, convertibles and depository receipts, which is operated and regulated by the London Stock Exchange. This is not a regulated market as defined by the Prospectus and Transparency Directives.

Profit estimate - Historical financial information for a financial period which has expired but for which the results have not yet been published.

Profit forecast - The PD Regulation defines a profit forecast as "a form of words which expressly states or by implication indicates a figure or a minimum or maximum figure for the likely level of profits or losses for the current financial period and/or financial periods subsequent to that period, or contains data from which calculation of such a figure for future profits or losses may be made, even if no particular figure is mentioned and the word "profit" is not used. Where a profit forecast relates to an extended period and/or is subject to significant uncertainty it is sometimes referred to as a projection.

Pro forma financial information - Financial information such as net assets, profit or cash flow statements that demonstrate the impact of a transaction on previously published financial information together with the explanatory notes thereto.

Projection - See "Profit forecast".

Prospectus - The document issued in accordance with the Prospectus Rules in connection with either a public offer or an admission of securities to trading on a regulated market.

Prospectus Regulations - The UK statutory instrument which makes amendments to Part VI of FSMA and to certain secondary legislation.

Prospectus Rules - The FSA's Handbook part "Prospectus Rules" which together with the PD Regulation and the changes to FSMA Part VI made by the Prospectus Regulations, implement the Prospectus Directive into UK law. In respect of Prospectus content requirements, the Prospectus Rules reproduce the Annexes to the PD Regulation. Accordingly, references to the contents requirements in Annexes to the Prospectus Rules are also references to the Annexes to the PD Regulation.

Public offer - An offer to the public in any form to subscribe for securities in an issuer.

Public reporting engagement - An engagement in which a reporting accountant expresses a conclusion that is published in an investment circular and which is designed to enhance the degree of confidence of the intended users of the report about the "outcome" of the directors' evaluation or measurement of "subject matter" (usually financial information) against "suitable criteria".

Report - This term encompasses letters that the reporting accountant may be required to send by regulation or arising from the terms of the engagement.

Reporting accountant - An accountant engaged to prepare a report for inclusion in, or in connection with, an investment circular. The reporting accountant may or may not be the auditor of the entity issuing the investment circular. The term "reporting accountant" is used to describe either the engagement partner or the engagement partner's firm. The reporting accountant could be a limited company or an engagement principal employed by the company.

Reporting accountant's criteria - A subset of suitable criteria which the reporting accountant's engagement requires the reporting accountant to consider. Reporting accountant's criteria are set out in appendices to the SIRs.

Securities - Are as defined by Article 4 of the EU's Markets in Financial Instruments Directive with the exception of money-market instruments having a maturity of less than twelve months.

Sponsor - For the purposes of SIRs, "sponsor" is a generic term which includes any one or more of the following to whom the reporting accountant has agreed, in its engagement letter, to address a relevant report:

(a) a person approved, under section 88 of FSMA, by the FSA as a sponsor. The FSA's sponsor regime applies to applications for admission to listing and major transactions. The sponsor regime is designed to ensure that effective due diligence is undertaken on issuers and transactions to ensure that issuers are eligible for listing, that major transactions are properly evaluated and that all relevant information has been included in the investment circular. Listing Rule 8.2.1 sets out the circumstances when an issuer must appoint a sponsor;

(b) a nominated adviser approved by the London Stock Exchange in connection with an application for admission to AIM and subsequent transactions by a company with securities traded on AIM; and

(c) in connection with any transaction, any party, other than the issuer, who may have specific responsibility for the preparation and/or contents of an investment circular.

Subject matter - The subject matter of an engagement is that which is being evaluated or measured against "suitable criteria". Examples of subject matter are the entity's financial position and the directors' expectation of the issuer's profit for the period covered by a profit forecast.

Suitable criteria - Criteria are the benchmarks used to evaluate or measure the subject matter. Suitable criteria are usually derived from laws and regulations and are required by directors to enable them to make reasonably consistent evaluations or measurements of the subject matter. With respect to public reporting engagements the suitable criteria for specific types of engagement are described in the individual SIR dealing with such engagements.

STANDARDS FOR INVESTMENT REPORTING

2000 – INVESTMENT REPORTING STANDARDS APPLICABLE TO PUBLIC REPORTING ENGAGEMENTS ON HISTORICAL FINANCIAL INFORMATION (REVISED)

CONTENTS

Appendices

ANNEXURE

Accounting conventions commonly used in the preparation of historical financial information in investment circulars[1]

---

[1] The Annexure has been compiled by the APB from a number of sources. It does not include basic principles, essential procedures or guidance promulgated by the APB.

SIR 1000 "Investment reporting standards applicable to all engagements in connection with an investment circular" contains basic principles and essential procedures ("Investment Reporting Standards") that are applicable to all engagements involving an investment circular. The definitions in the glossary of terms set out in Appendix 4 of SIR 1000 are to be applied in the interpretation of this and all other SIRs. Terms defined in the glossary are underlined the first time that they occur in the text.

SIR 2000 contains additional Investment Reporting Standards, indicated by paragraphs in bold type, with which a reporting accountant is required to comply in the conduct of an engagement involving the examination of historical financial information which is intended to give a true and fair view, for the purposes of the relevant investment circular, included within an investment circular prepared for issue in connection with a securities transaction governed wholly or in part by the laws and regulations of the United Kingdom or the Republic of Ireland.

SIR 2000 also includes explanatory and other material, including appendices, in the context of which the Investment Reporting Standards are to be understood and applied. It is necessary to consider the whole text of the SIR to understand and apply the basic principles and essential procedures.

To assist readers, SIRs contain references to, and extracts from, certain legislation and chapters of the Rules of the UK Listing Authority (UKLA) and the Listing Rules of the Irish Stock Exchange Limited (ISE) (together "the Listing Rules"). Readers are cautioned that these references may change subsequent to publication.

This version of SIR 2000 replaces the version issued in July 2005.

Introduction

1. The purpose of this Standard for Investment Reporting (SIR) is to establish standards and provide guidance on the reporting accountant's responsibilities and procedures when preparing an "accountant's report" on historical financial information. The work required to prepare an "accountant's report" is referred to in this SIR as the "reporting accountant's exercise". The objective of the reporting accountant's exercise is to enable the reporting accountant to express an opinion as to whether, for the purposes of the relevant investment circular, the financial information gives a true and fair view of the state of affairs and profits, cash flows and statements of changes in equity of the issuer, or where applicable the target.

2. **When the reporting accountant is engaged to prepare an accountant's report, the reporting accountant should obtain sufficient appropriate evidence to express an opinion as to whether the financial information presents a true and fair view, for the purposes of the investment circular. (SIR 2000.1)**

3. An engagement to prepare an accountant's report is a public reporting engagement as described in SIR 1000. The description of a public reporting engagement includes three generic terms having the following meanings in the context of an engagement to report on historical financial information:

(a) With respect to historical financial information the "**subject matter**" is the entity's financial position for the periods being reported on;

(b) The "**suitable criteria**" are the requirements of the applicable financial reporting framework, the PD Regulation, and Listing Rules together with any "accepted conventions", as set out in the Annexure, that are applicable; and

(c) With respect to historical financial information the "**outcome**" is the directors' historical financial information that is included in the investment circular and which has resulted from the directors applying the suitable criteria to the subject matter. The reporting accountant expresses an opinion (in the "**accountant's report**") as to whether the historical financial information gives, for the purposes of the investment circular, a true and fair view.

4. The Prospectus Rules set out certain requirements, derived from the PD Regulation, relating to the presentation of historical financial information in a prospectus. Annex I of the PD Regulation (and there are equivalent requirements in a number of the other annexes) requires that historical financial information is either audited or "reported on as to whether or not, for the purposes of the registration document, it gives a true and fair view, in accordance with auditing standards applicable in a Member State or an equivalent standard."[2].

5. With respect to Class 1 acquisitions, Chapter 13 of the Listing Rules sets out requirements for a financial information table relating to a target company and the accountant's opinion on that table. The accountant's opinion is required to state whether, for the purposes of the Class 1 circular, the financial information table gives a true and fair view of the financial matters set out in it, and whether the financial information table has been prepared in a form that is consistent with the accounting policies adopted in the listed company's latest annual accounts.

6. In this SIR, accountant's opinions on such financial information tables are described as "accountant's reports".

7. An accountant's report is likely to be used where the issuer's audited annual financial statements do not meet the standards of preparation and presentation prescribed in the applicable rules and need, therefore, to be adjusted in order that historical financial information which complies with the applicable rules can be presented. For example, where the entity is seeking a listing, the financial information for the last two years is required to be prepared and presented in a form consistent with that which will be adopted in the issuer's next published annual financial statements, having regard to accounting standards and policies and legislation applicable to such annual financial statements. In the context of Class 1 circulars, the objective may be to present the financial information of the target for all periods in a form which is consistent and comparable with the accounting policies adopted by the listed company in its latest annual accounts.

---

[2] In respect of prospectus content requirements, the Prospectus Rules reproduce the Annexes to the PD Regulation. Accordingly, references to the contents requirements in the Annexes to the Prospectus Rules are also references to the Annexes to the PD Regulation.

8. In addition, an accountant's report is used where the issuer has a complex financial history and there are no underlying financial statements that have been audited. Conventions for accounting where there are complex financial histories are described in the Annexure to this SIR.

9. The nature of the accountant's report is such that the objective of the reporting accountant's exercise does not differ in essence from that of an auditor. The underlying requirement of this SIR is that the reporting accountant will, in conducting the work necessary to provide the accountant's report, perform its own procedures, and/or use the work of the auditor(s), that meet those requirements of ISAs (UK and Ireland) that are relevant to the reporting accountant's exercise. The reporting accountant applies ISAs (UK and Ireland) on the basis set out in this SIR in the context of the following:

    (a) The reporting accountant is often reporting on financial information that has been included in, or formed part of, financial statements which have themselves already been subject to audit by an independent auditor. In consequence, there may be available to the reporting accountant a body of independent evidence relating to the historical financial information which would not be available to an auditor examining the financial information for the first time;

    (b) The financial information being examined may relate to accounting periods in circumstances where financial statements for one, and possibly two, subsequent periods have been prepared and audited. These circumstances mean that in assessing risks that may affect the historical financial information in relation to earlier periods the reporting accountant has the benefit of information relating to uncertainties affecting the financial information which would not have been available to an auditor auditing the information for the first time; and

    (c) The reporting accountant does not have the statutory reporting responsibilities of an auditor.

10. This SIR provides standards that address those aspects of the reporting accountant's exercise that require the reporting accountant to perform procedures directly, for example risk assessment procedures. It also provides guidance on the application of ISAs (UK and Ireland) to the reporting accountant's exercise.

11. This SIR recognises that the reporting accountant may wish to use evidence previously obtained by the auditor who audited the historical financial statements for the relevant period covered by the reporting accountant's exercise. Guidance is provided on the steps that the reporting accountant undertakes, including initial planning considerations, in order to assess the suitability of the audit evidence for this purpose.

12. Subject to the considerations set out in this SIR, references in the ISAs (UK and Ireland) to the auditor performing audit procedures or obtaining audit evidence may be read as references to the reporting accountant being satisfied that the procedures have been performed, or the evidence has been obtained, either by the reporting accountant or an auditor.

13. Certain requirements of ISAs (UK and Ireland) will not be relevant to the reporting accountant's exercise, for example, when a requirement of an ISA (UK and Ireland) is predicated on a continuing relationship between an auditor and the entity being audited, or because of the specific nature of the reporting accountant's responsibilities, under applicable regulations, as discussed in this SIR.

14. This SIR also provides guidance to the reporting accountant in the context of assessing whether the financial information shows a true and fair view, for the purposes of the investment circular. In situations where the issuer has a historical record of audited financial statements, the true and fair view for the purposes of the investment circular may be a financial reporting framework such as International Financial Reporting Standards as adopted by the European Union. In situations where the issuer has a complex financial history the conventions to support the true and fair view for the purposes of the investment circular are set out in the Annexure to this SIR.

Pre-existing financial information

15. With respect to historical financial information, where the issuer already has available:

(a) Audited annual financial statements; or

(b) Audited or reviewed interim financial information,

which meet the requirements of the applicable rules in respect of the preparation and presentation of historical financial information to be included in the investment circular, it may choose to include these financial statements, or financial information, in the investment circular together with the pre-existing reports of the auditor. In these circumstances an accountant's report is not prepared and this SIR does not apply to such circumstances. Furthermore, in these circumstances the audit firm is not required by the Prospectus Rules to consent to the inclusion of its reports in the investment circular.

16. Notwithstanding that the audit firm is not required to give consent, a reporting accountant that is also the auditor of the company may become aware that the financial statements are defective. For example, a material error may have been detected in the original financial statements. If the reporting accountant does become aware that the financial statements are defective and that the directors have not revised them as permitted by section 454 of the Companies Act 2006, it discusses the matter with those charged with governance. If the directors do not decide to revise the financial statements the reporting accountant considers the need to take legal advice[3].

---

[3] See also Bulletin 2008/5 "Auditor's Reports on Revised Accounts and Reports, in the United Kingdom".

True and fair view, for the purposes of the investment circular

17. **The reporting accountant should:**

    (a) **Obtain an understanding of the purpose of the investment circular;**

    (b) **Ascertain which financial reporting framework is required to be used by the applicable regulations and which, if any, accepted conventions as to the preparation and presentation of historical financial information for inclusion in investment circulars are to be applied[4]; and**

    (c) **Review the appropriateness of the accounting policies**

    in order to determine whether the proposed historical financial information prepared by the issuer is capable of giving a true and fair view, for the purposes of the investment circular. (SIR 2000.2)

18. Where historical financial information is presented in a prospectus the Prospectus Rules generally determine the applicable financial reporting framework. The Prospectus Rules require the most recent year's financial information to be presented in a form consistent with that which will be adopted in the issuer's next published annual financial statements, having regard to the accounting standards, policies and legislation applicable to such annual financial statements.

19. The reporting accountant satisfies itself that the directors have performed a thorough review of the accounting policies used in preparing the historical financial information in determining the accounting policies appropriate for the business following the transaction that is the subject of the prospectus. The reporting accountant also considers whether the policies are consistent with the applicable financial reporting framework, and accounting policies used in the relevant industry. Where the reporting accountant does not agree with the directors' final proposed accounting policies they refer to the guidance on reporting set out in paragraphs 70 to 76 of this SIR.

20. Where information is presented in a Class 1 circular, the suitable criteria regarding its presentation are those set out in the Listing Rules. These rules require financial information to be presented in a form consistent with the accounting policies adopted in the issuer's latest annual consolidated accounts.

21. The directors have regard to, and make appropriate disclosure of, accepted conventions which have been developed for the preparation and presentation of historical financial information in investment circulars (including those relating to additional disclosures). These conventions have been developed to assist the directors, to the extent consistent with established accounting principles, to fulfil the criteria set out in the relevant regulations, present the information in an easily analysable form, and give a true and fair view for the purposes of the applicable investment circular.

---

[4] See Annexure.

22. The Annexure provides a summary of these conventions including, among others, conventions that address:

- Making adjustments to previously published financial statements and dealing with entities which have not previously prepared consolidated accounts.

- Carve outs.

- Acquisitions.

- Newly-formed issuers.

In certain circumstances applying the conventions may result in combined or aggregated, rather than consolidated, financial information being presented in order to meet the requirement to present financial information that gives a true and fair view, for the purposes of the investment circular.

General professional considerations

23. SIR 1000.3 and SIR 1000.4 set out basic principles and essential procedures applicable to agreeing the terms of the engagement. Paragraphs 11 to 15 and paragraph 17 of SIR 1000 provide guidance with respect to these basic principles and essential procedures. Illustrative examples of engagement letter clauses are set out in Appendix 1. SIR 1000.5 sets out the basic principles and essential procedures with respect to the ethical requirements that apply to a reporting accountant.

24. Where the evidence used by the reporting accountant includes that contained within the audit documentation of an auditor, the reporting accountant's documentation identifies the working papers reviewed and the nature of the work performed. Whilst it is not necessary for the reporting accountant's documentation to replicate all of the detailed findings contained in the audit documentation reporting accountants do document the basis on which the auditor addressed the particular risks identified in the reporting accountant's risk assessment procedures.

25. In considering the requirements of ISA (UK and Ireland) 240 "The auditor's responsibilities relating to fraud in an audit of financial statements", ISA (UK and Ireland) 250 "Section A - Consideration of laws and regulations in an audit of financial statements and Section B - The auditor's right and duty to report to regulators in the financial sector" for the auditor to report any matters arising to certain authorities, the reporting accountant will need to assess the effect of these requirements when reporting in terms of the true and fair view, for the purposes of the investment circular. Where matters arise which may potentially require disclosure by the reporting accountant and the reporting accountant is unsure how to proceed, the reporting accountant takes legal advice.

26. In applying ISAs (UK and Ireland) 240, 250, 260 "Communication with those charged with governance", 265 "Communicating deficiencies in internal control to those charged with governance and management" and 450 "Evaluation of misstatements

identified during the audit", the reporting accountant considers who, in relation to the investment circular, should be regarded as a person charged with governance. Where the issuer has already formed an audit committee, the reporting accountant communicates with the audit committee in accordance with the guidance set out in this SIR. In the absence of an audit committee those responsible for governance will usually be the directors of the issuer.

Planning

27. **The reporting accountant should perform and document risk assessment procedures to support the reporting accountant's exercise. (SIR 2000.3)**

28. In addition to those matters that a reporting accountant considers when applying SIR 1000, a reporting accountant may consider:

- Any previous modifications to the opinion in the auditor's report on underlying financial statements or emphasis of matter or other matters paragraphs and their potential impact on the approach to the reporting accountant's exercise.

- The nature of adjustments to previously published historical financial information which may be proposed by the preparer of the historical financial information (for example as a result of changing the applicable accounting framework) and the sources of evidence to support an examination of the adjustments.

- The interaction with other roles undertaken by the reporting accountant in connection with the transaction, for example preparing a long form report.

- Staffing, including relevant experience and skills linked to investment circular reporting, and sources of consultation.

- Liaison with the auditor and arrangements for terms of access to the audit documentation, or equivalent evidence if maintained in machine readable form.

- The nature and timing of procedures to support any decision to rely on audit evidence obtained by the auditor.

- Whether the financial reporting framework applicable to the audited financial statements is the same as that applicable to the financial information contained in the investment circular.

- Whether there are any special circumstances concerning the appointment, resignation or reporting responsibilities of the auditor.

- Whether there is evidence of any limitation having been placed on the work of the auditor.

- Whether corrections or adjustments to subsequent financial statements indicate possible inadequacies in the audits of earlier periods.

29. **Where the reporting accountant is considering using audit evidence obtained by an auditor as part of the evidence for the reporting accountant's exercise, the reporting accountant should consider the professional qualification, independence and professional competence of the auditor and the quality control systems applied by the audit firm to that engagement. (SIR 2000.4)**

30. Matters that the reporting accountant considers include:

    • The integrity and experience of the auditor.

    • Whether the auditor was required to comply with the APB's Ethical Standards for Auditors, International Standard on Quality Control (UK and Ireland) 1, ISAs (UK and Ireland) or equivalent standards.

Understanding of the entity, its environment and risk assessment

31. **The reporting accountant should obtain an understanding of the entity and its environment, including its internal control, sufficient to identify and assess the risks of material misstatement of the historical financial information covered by the accountant's report whether due to fraud or error, and sufficient to design and perform further procedures. As part of this risk assessment the reporting accountant should determine whether any of the risks identified are, in the reporting accountant's judgment, significant risks. (SIR 2000.5)**

32. Such an understanding is ordinarily obtained by:

    (a) Meeting the directors and management of the entity;

    (b) Visiting the entity's premises;

    (c) Discussing the financial information and recent results with management;

    (d) Applying analytical procedures to the financial information; and

    (e) Obtaining from management an understanding of the principal transaction flows, internal controls and reporting arrangements of the business.

33. If this process indicates that there are factors which may give rise to a modification of the accountant's opinion or an emphasis of matter and other matter paragraphs then such factors are reported immediately to those responsible for the investment circular, usually the directors, and any other responsible parties.

34. In considering areas of risk in relation to the periods for which historical financial information is presented, the reporting accountant has regard to the probability that misstatements in earlier periods, if they exist, are likely to have been detected in subsequent periods. Account is also taken of the fact that other uncertainties,

particularly those affecting subjective matters in the historical financial information, may have been resolved with the passage of time.

35. **When performing the risk assessment, the reporting accountant should take into account the evidence obtained from all other relevant work performed in connection with the investment circular. (SIR 2000.6)**

36. The reporting accountant may be undertaking other relevant work related to the transaction giving rise to the accountant's report. For example, the reporting accountant may have been commissioned to prepare a long form report, or a comfort letter on a statement of sufficiency of working capital.

37. If other relevant work has been performed by another firm the reporting accountant requests the issuer to provide access to the documentation of such work. If the reporting accountant is not allowed access to such documentation it considers the implications for its report.

Materiality

38. The reporting accountant determines both materiality and performance materiality for the purposes of the reporting accountant's work independently from the auditor, if any, who audited the underlying financial statements, and accordingly the reporting accountant's determination of materiality and performance materiality may differ from that of the auditor. In determining materiality and performance materiality for the purposes of reporting on historical financial information, regard is had to the context in which the opinion is to be given (which includes the fact that the information may relate to a trend of results over a three year period).

The reporting accountant's procedures

39. **The reporting accountant should perform procedures to obtain sufficient appropriate evidence as to whether the work of an auditor, which the reporting accountant plans to use, is adequate for the reporting accountant's purposes. Where the reporting accountant, concludes that the auditor's work is not adequate, does not have access to the auditor's audit documentation, or an audit has not previously been performed, the reporting accountant should perform procedures that compensate for this. The procedures of the auditor and the reporting accountant, taken together, should comply with the requirements of ISAs (UK and Ireland) unless:**

   (a) **An entire ISA (UK and Ireland) is not relevant to the reporting accountant's engagement; or**

   (b) **A particular requirement is:**

      (i) **Conditional and the condition does not exist; or**

(ii) **Less relevant than an equivalent requirement of a SIR; or**

(iii) **Predicated on the concept of a recurring engagement or an ongoing relationship with a client which is usually not relevant to engagements to report on an investment circular; or**

(c) **It is not practicable for the reporting accountant to undertake such procedures.**

If the reporting accountant decides not to comply with a requirement of ISAs (UK and Ireland) because it is not practicable for it to undertake such procedures, it should document the reason for not complying with the requirement and why its omission does not have an impact on its opinion. (SIR 2000.7)

40. In approaching the procedures to be performed in response to the assessed risk of material misstatement at the assertion level, the reporting accountant considers the extent to which the procedures that the reporting accountant wishes to perform have previously been performed by an auditor. Where such procedures have been performed by an auditor, the reporting accountant may, subject to the considerations discussed in this SIR, use the evidence obtained by the auditor from those procedures as part of the reporting accountant's own evidence.

41. In exceptional circumstances a reporting accountant may judge it necessary to depart from a relevant requirement in an ISA (UK and Ireland) to achieve the aim of that requirement. In such circumstances the reporting accountant performs alternative procedures to achieve the aim of that requirement. When such a situation arises the reporting accountant documents the reason for the departure.

42. Where applicable auditing standards have changed during the period covered by the historical financial information, or it is not practicable for the reporting accountant to undertake procedures that meet the requirements of ISAs (UK and Ireland), the reporting accountant considers the implications for the reporting accountant's exercise, having regard to its risk assessment. The reporting accountant may be able to conclude that it is unnecessary to apply certain requirements of the ISAs (UK and Ireland) throughout the three year period covered by the accountant's report because:

(a) It is sufficient to apply them with respect to the latest period only, because sufficient appropriate evidence relating to earlier periods can be obtained from the latest period; or

(b) The auditing standards that were applicable at the time met the same objectives as the requirements of ISAs (UK and Ireland).

In such cases the reporting accountant documents the reason or justification for not meeting the requirement and why omitting it does not have an impact on its opinion.

43. **When the reporting accountant intends to use audit evidence obtained by the auditor, it should evaluate whether the audit procedures performed by the auditor**

adequately respond to the reporting accountant's assessment of the risks (including significant risks) of material misstatement of the financial information to be included in the investment circular. (SIR 2000.8)

44. **The reporting accountant's procedures should include:**

    (a) Examining material adjustments from previously published historical financial statements made during the course of preparing the historical financial information and considering the responsible party's basis for satisfying itself that the adjustments are necessary and whether they have been correctly determined;

    (b) Evaluating whether all necessary adjustments to previously published historical financial statements have been made; and

    (c) Where the information is based on previously published financial statements, comparing the historical financial information to those financial statements and assessing whether the information has been accurately extracted therefrom. (SIR 2000.9)

45. In certain areas, use of the work of the auditor may be the only practicable means of obtaining the evidence necessary to support the reporting accountant's opinion[5]. The timing of the reporting accountant's own work will inevitably be dictated by the timing of the preparation of the historical financial information and the related investment circular and this may be some time after the end of the periods to which the report relates.

Evidence

46. The reporting accountant reconsiders the matters considered at the planning stage as described in paragraphs 28 and 30.

47. Where the financial information to be reported on has previously been subject to audit, the audit documentation will be a useful source for the evidence which the reporting accountant may need to support its opinion on the financial information.

48. If planning to use the work of the auditor, the reporting accountant considers whether:

    (a) The work of the auditor was conducted to an appropriate materiality level; and

    (b) The auditor appears to have complied with the auditing standards that were applicable to the auditor's work.

---

[5] Procedures which require the reporting accountant to be physically present at a relevant date (for example attendance at physical inventory counting) will clearly be impossible to perform.

49. The reporting accountant accepts evidence in audit documentation as being prima facie truthful and genuine, but in considering that evidence adopts an attitude of professional scepticism, whether the documentation was produced by an auditor from the reporting accountant's own firm or by another auditor. However, with respect to audit documentation from the reporting accountant's own firm, the reporting accountant is more familiar with the detailed quality control procedures that will have been applied in the conduct of the audit. The application of professional scepticism will include considering the evidence contained in the audit documentation in the light of the understanding of the entity and its environment, including its internal control and such other evidence as the reporting accountant obtains directly.

50. The extent to which independent testing of the evidence obtained by the auditor (for example, reperformance of tests performed by the auditor) will be necessary is a matter for the reporting accountant's judgment on the basis of the information available at the time, including the reporting accountant's evaluation of the auditor's work.

51. **The reporting accountant should evaluate the quality of the audit evidence obtained by the auditor that the reporting accountant intends to rely on. Where the reporting accountant concludes that such audit evidence is either not sufficient or is inappropriate for the purposes of the reporting accountant's exercise the reporting accountant should obtain evidence directly. Where the evidence is not available, the reporting accountant should consider the implications for its report. (SIR 2000.10)**

52. Where the reporting accountant intends to rely on internal controls the reporting accountant performs tests of control when unable to rely on the auditor's tests of such internal controls. This is likely to arise when the auditor:

    (a) Has not performed tests of those internal controls; or

    (b) Has performed tests of internal controls but the internal controls have subsequently changed.

53. Where relevant information is not available from the audit documentation, the reporting accountant will need to obtain the relevant evidence directly. The audit documentation is unlikely, for example, to contain information concerning post balance sheet events up to the date of signing the accountant's report or to contain evidence relating to any adjustments made to the financial statements in preparing the historical financial information.

Obtaining access to information in audit documentation

54. When the company's auditor, or former auditor, is not appointed as the reporting accountant, the auditor will be aware that the reporting accountant may need access to information contained in the audit documentation. The auditor or former auditor is normally prepared, in accordance with relevant professional guidance, to make the

audit documentation available to reporting accountants for the purpose of work under this SIR.

55. Access may be granted only on the basis that the auditor accepts no responsibility or liability to the reporting accountant in connection with the use of the audit documentation by the reporting accountant. This has no effect on the reporting accountant's judgment regarding the extent to which reliance is placed on such audit documentation.

56. In cases where the reporting accountant is not able to obtain access to information in audit documentation, the reporting accountant will have no option other than to obtain the relevant evidence directly.

57. Irrespective of whether the reporting accountant has access to the auditor's documentation, the reporting accountant seeks to obtain, either from the directors or from the auditor, copies of all relevant communications sent by the auditor to those charged with governance of the entity, including those required to be sent by auditing standards applicable at the time, and copies of any responses to such communications made by management. A relevant communication would, for example, be one that discussed internal control and other weaknesses.

Events occurring up to the date of the accountant's report

58. Unless a post balance sheet event indicates that there has been an error in the preparation of the historical financial information in an earlier period, the reporting accountant will, having regard to the convention for treating post balance sheet events for the purposes of historical financial information in an investment circular (as referred to in the Annexure), only consider the impact of post balance sheet events occurring up to the date of the accountant's report on the final period presented.

Events occurring between the date of the accountant's report and the completion date of the transaction

59. **If, in the period between the date of the accountant's report and the <u>completion date of the transaction</u>, the reporting accountant becomes aware of events and other matters which, had they occurred and been known at the date of the report, might have caused it to issue a different report or to withhold consent, the reporting accountant should discuss the implications of them with those responsible for the investment circular and take additional action as appropriate. (SIR 2000.11)**

60. After the date of the accountant's report, the reporting accountant has no obligation to perform procedures or make enquiries regarding the investment circular.

61. Under Chapter 3 of the Prospectus Rules, a supplementary prospectus must be prepared if, after the date the prospectus has been formally approved by the FSA and before the final closing of the offer of securities to the public or the commencement of

trading in the relevant securities, there is a significant change affecting any matter contained in the document or a significant new matter has arisen (or a material mistake or inaccuracy is noted).

62. If, as a result of discussions with those responsible for the investment circular concerning a subsequent event that occurred prior to the completion date of the transaction, the reporting accountant is either uncertain about or disagrees with the course of action proposed, the reporting accountant may consider it necessary to take legal advice with respect to an appropriate course of action.

Going concern

63. References to an emphasis of matter of a material uncertainty related to events or conditions that may cast significant doubt about the ability of the entity to continue as a going concern that is relevant at the time the accountant's report is signed, and which will not be resolved by a satisfactory outcome to the transaction to which the investment circular relates, will be included in the reporting accountants' report immediately after the reporting accountant's opinion on the financial information.

64. Where the material uncertainty, related to events or conditions that may cast significant doubt about the ability of the entity to continue as a going concern, will be resolved if the outcome of transactions to which the investment circular containing the report relates is satisfactory (for example the successful raising of money through a share issue or shareholder approval of a transaction), the reporting accountant will consider whether adequate disclosure of that matter or uncertainty is made in a basis of preparation note to the historical financial information. If adequate disclosure is made in the historical financial information it is unlikely to be necessary for the reporting accountant to include an emphasis of matter paragraph in its report.

Representations

65. SIR 1000.13 sets out the basic principles and essential procedures with respect to obtaining written confirmation of representations from the directors of the entity.

66. A number of specific representations are required by ISAs (UK and Ireland). Where representations have been obtained by the auditor, subject to the considerations set out in this SIR, it may not be necessary for the reporting accountant to seek further representations covering the same matters, other than in relation to the period since the audit opinion relating to the final period included in the historical financial information was given.

67. Representations additional to those pursuant to ISAs (UK and Ireland) that a reporting accountant may consider for incorporation in the letter of representation or board minute include:

- Confirmation from the directors or management of the entity that they are responsible for the preparation of the historical financial information.

- Confirmation that any adjustments made to historical financial statements for the purposes of preparing the historical financial information are necessary, have been correctly determined and that there are no other adjustments that are necessary.

68. In relation to a Class 1 acquisition, the acquirer may not be in a position to make representations in relation to the historical financial information of the target entity on matters such as fraud, non-compliance with laws and regulation and related parties. In such circumstances representations may be sought from the management of the target entity.

Joint reporting accountants

69. When joint reporting accountants are appointed, the division of work as between them is a matter for agreement. The arrangements between the joint reporting accountants may form part of the engagement letter. Irrespective of any such arrangement, the joint reporting accountants are jointly and severally responsible for the report to be given. Each of the joint reporting accountants participates in the planning of the engagement and they agree upon the scope of work and any changes subsequently found to be necessary thereto. Each of the joint reporting accountants has regard to the considerations set out in this SIR in respect of using the work of an auditor in determining the extent to which it is appropriate to rely on the evidence obtained by the other reporting accountants or the extent to which they consider it necessary to carry out their own work. Each of the joint reporting accountants reviews the work of the other to the extent considered necessary and records the results of that review. A common record of documentation, in accordance with paragraphs 46-48 of SIR 1000, is normally maintained.

Reporting

70. SIRs 1000.17, 1000.18, 1000.19 and 1000.20 set out the basic principles and essential procedures with respect to reporting. Appendices 2 and 3 set out illustrative examples of accountant's reports on historical financial information.

71. The reporting accountant's opinion is usually expressed in terms of whether, for the purpose of the relevant investment circular, the financial information gives a true and fair view of the state of affairs and profits, cash flows and statement of changes in equity.

72. When there is a limitation on the scope of the reporting accountant's work, the reporting accountant considers whether the limitation results in a lack of sufficient appropriate evidence necessary to form an opinion. When the possible effect is, in the opinion of the reporting accountant, material to the financial information, there will be insufficient evidence to support an unqualified opinion. The nature of the work of reporting accountants is such that in the absence of reliable contemporary evidence relating to significant accounts and balances it may not be possible to form an opinion on the financial information. This might be the case where there has been no audit of

the underlying financial information in the past or where the auditor has given a qualified opinion because of a limitation in the scope of work.

73. As a consequence of the purpose for which financial information is presented and the importance which may be attached to it by readers of the document, a reporting accountant does not normally agree to be associated with financial information where a disclaimer of opinion needs to be given on the information for the entire period.

74. The reporting accountant needs to be satisfied that the financial information adequately describes both the applicable financial reporting framework used in the preparation of the financial information and any of the accounting conventions from the Annexure that have been used. Usually these are referred to within the financial information in a basis of preparation note.

75. Where the financial information has been prepared fully in accordance with a recognised financial reporting framework such as "International Financial Reporting Standards as adopted by the European Union" the accountant's opinion is expressed in terms of the financial information giving a true and fair view in accordance with that framework (see Appendix 2 for an illustration).

76. Where the financial information has not been prepared fully in accordance with a recognised financial reporting framework but, for example, in accordance with a financial reporting framework modified by applying a convention described in the Annexure to this SIR, the accountant's opinion is expressed in terms of the financial information being prepared in accordance with the basis of preparation described in note x to the financial information, rather than in accordance with the financial reporting framework. The basis of preparation note states which accounting convention has been applied and how it departs from the requirements of the recognised financial reporting framework. A statement is made in the note that in all other respects the recognised financial reporting framework has been applied (see Appendix 3 for an illustration of the accountant's report).

Other information – references to previous audit opinions

77. The reporting accountant's opinion is arrived at independently of any audit opinion previously given on the financial statements which form the basis for the financial information to be reported on. It is not part of the reporting accountant's role to explain (where this is the case) why the reporting accountant's opinion differs from the opinion of the auditor. In some cases, however, there may be an obligation on an issuer to disclose details of modified opinions contained in auditor's reports prepared by the statutory auditor. In such cases, the reporting accountant considers the disclosures made by the issuer relating to such modified opinions and whether any matters disclosed might give rise to questions as to how the reporting accountant has dealt with matters giving rise to the modified opinions. If the reporting accountant is not satisfied with the disclosures, the reporting accountant discusses the matter with those responsible for the investment circular and ensures that the appropriate information is included by the issuer or is included in the accountant's report. Where the audit has

been undertaken by another firm, the reporting accountant does not normally refer to the name of the auditor in the accountant's report.

Comparatives

78. The reporting accountant is required to provide a report on each period included in the historical financial information to which the reporting requirement relates. In consequence the financial information does not constitute either "comparative information", "corresponding figures" or "comparative financial statements" as contemplated by ISA (UK and Ireland) 710 "Comparative information – corresponding figures and comparative financial statements". Accordingly ISA (UK and Ireland) 710 is not relevant to the work of the reporting accountant.

Consent in the context of investment circulars containing a report by a reporting accountant

79. Paragraphs 66 to 74 of SIR 1000 deal with consent in relation to the inclusion of an accountant's report in an investment circular.

Effective date

80. A reporting accountant is required to comply with the Investment Reporting Standards contained in this SIR for reports on financial information for periods ending on or after 15 December 2010.

Appendix 1

EXAMPLES OF ENGAGEMENT LETTER CLAUSES

These examples of engagement letter clauses are intended for consideration in the context of an accountant's report. They should be tailored to the specific circumstances and supplemented by such other clauses as are relevant and appropriate. Suitably adapted, this example may be used for reporting accountant's engagements with respect to AIM admission documents.

For a prospectus

Financial information upon which the report is to be given

We understand that the directors of ABC plc will include in the Prospectus historical financial information for the [three] years ended [ ] in relation to ABC plc, the last [two years] of which will be presented and prepared in a form consistent with that which will be adopted in ABC plc's next published annual financial statements, having regard to accounting standards and policies and legislation applicable to such annual financial statements in accordance with the requirements of Annex I item 20.1 of the Prospectus Rules.

Responsibilities

The directors of ABC plc are responsible for the historical financial information.

It is our responsibility to form an opinion as to whether the financial information gives a true and fair view for the purposes of the Prospectus and to report our opinion to the directors of ABC plc.

Scope of work

We shall expect to obtain such evidence as we consider sufficient and appropriate to enable us to draw reasonable conclusions therefrom. The nature and extent of our procedures will vary according to our assessment of the appropriate sources of evidence. Our work will be directed to those matters which in our view materially affect the overall financial information upon which our opinion is to be given, and will not be directed to the discovery of errors or misstatements which we consider to be immaterial.

It is expected that a substantial part of the evidence which we may require will be contained in the audit files of LMN Accountants. ABC plc has agreed that it will use its best endeavours to ensure that the relevant files are made available to us.

Our work may also depend upon receiving without undue delay full co-operation from all relevant officials of ABC plc and their disclosure to us of all the accounting records of ABC plc and all other records and related information (including certain representations) as we may need for the purposes of our examination.

For a Class 1 circular

Financial information upon which the report is to be given

We understand that the directors of ABC plc will include in the Class 1 Circular a historical financial information table for the [three] years ended [ ] in relation to XYZ Limited which will be presented and prepared in a form consistent with the accounting policies adopted in ABC plc's latest annual consolidated accounts in accordance with the requirements of chapter 13 of the Listing Rules.

Responsibilities

The directors of ABC plc are responsible for the historical financial information table.

It is our responsibility to form an opinion as to whether the financial information gives a true and fair view for the purposes of the Class 1 circular and whether the financial information table has been prepared in a form that is consistent with the accounting policies adopted in ABC plc's latest annual accounts and to report our opinion to the directors of ABC plc.

Scope of work

We shall expect to obtain such evidence as we consider sufficient and appropriate to enable us to draw reasonable conclusions therefrom. The nature and extent of our procedures will vary according to our assessment of the appropriate sources of evidence. Our work will be directed to those matters which in our view materially affect the overall financial information upon which our opinion is to be given, and will not be directed to the discovery of errors or misstatements which we consider to be immaterial.

It is expected that a substantial part of the evidence which we may require will be contained in the audit files of LMN Accountants. ABC plc has agreed that it will use its best endeavours to ensure that the relevant files are made available to us.

Our work may also depend upon receiving without undue delay full co-operation from all relevant officials of ABC plc and XYZ Limited and their disclosure to us of all the accounting records of XYZ Limited and all other records and related information (including certain representations) as we may need for the purposes of our examination.

Appendix 2

EXAMPLE OF AN ACCOUNTANT'S REPORT ON HISTORICAL FINANCIAL INFORMATION PREPARED IN ACCORDANCE WITH INTERNATIONAL FINANCIAL REPORTING STANDARDS AS ADOPTED BY THE EUROPEAN UNION

Date

Reporting accountant's address

Addressees, as agreed between the parties in the engagement letter

Dear Sirs

[ABC plc]/[XYZ Limited]

We report on the financial information [set out in paragraphs .... to ....] [which comprises[1]], for the *[specify periods]*. This financial information has been prepared for inclusion in the [*describe Document*[2]] dated..........of ABC plc on the basis of the accounting policies set out in paragraph [ ]. This report is required by [*Relevant Regulation*] and is given for the purpose of complying with that [paragraph] and for no other purpose. [We have not audited or reviewed the financial information for the [*26 weeks ended* ...] [which has been included for comparative purposes only,] and accordingly do not express an opinion thereon.[3]]

Responsibilities
The Directors of ABC plc are responsible for preparing the financial information in accordance with International Financial Reporting Standards as adopted by the European Union.

It is our responsibility to form an opinion on the financial information and to report our opinion to you.

Basis of opinion
We conducted our work in accordance with Standards for Investment Reporting issued by the Auditing Practices Board in the United Kingdom. Our work included an assessment of evidence relevant to the amounts and disclosures in the financial information. It also included an assessment of significant estimates and judgments made by those responsible for the preparation of the financial information and whether the accounting policies are appropriate to the entity's circumstances, consistently applied and adequately disclosed.

---

[1]   Where paragraph numbers are not referred to specify the titles of the primary statements on which the opinion is being expressed and refer to the notes to those primary statements.

[2]   For example, "prospectus", "listing particulars", "Class 1 circular" and "AIM admission document."

[3]   This wording is relevant where financial information for an interim period is required to be reported on in circumstances where comparative information for the same interim period in the prior financial period is also to be presented, but not reported on.

We planned and performed our work so as to obtain all the information and explanations which we considered necessary in order to provide us with sufficient evidence to give reasonable assurance that the financial information is free from material misstatement whether caused by fraud or other irregularity or error.

Opinion on financial information

In our opinion, the financial information gives, for the purposes of the [*describe Document*] dated ....., a true and fair view of the state of affairs of [ABC plc]/[XYZ Limited] as at [*specify dates*] and of its profits, cash flows and [recognised gains and losses] [changes in equity] for the [*specify periods*] in accordance with International Financial Reporting Standards as adopted by the European Union [and has been prepared in a form that is consistent with the accounting policies adopted in [ABC plc's] latest annual accounts[4]].

Declaration[5]

For the purposes of [Prospectus Rule [5.5.3R(2)(f)] [5.5.4R(2)(f)]] [Paragraph a of Schedule Two of the AIM Rules] we are responsible for [this report as part] [the following part(s)] of the [prospectus] [registration document] [AIM admission document] and declare that we have taken all reasonable care to ensure that the information contained in [this report] [those parts] is, to the best of our knowledge, in accordance with the facts and contains no omission likely to affect its import. This declaration is included in the [prospectus] [registration document] [AIM admission document] in compliance with [item 1.2 of annex 1 of the Prospectus Regulation] [item 1.2 of annex 3 of the Prospectus Regulation] [Schedule Two of the AIM Rules].

Yours faithfully

Reporting accountant

---

[4] The wording in these square brackets is appropriate for inclusion where the report relates to historical financial information included in a Class 1 circular.
[5] This declaration is a requirement of the Prospectus Rules and is appropriate for inclusion when the report is included in a Prospectus, see Appendix 2 of SIR 1000. It is also appropriate for inclusion in an AIM admission document under Schedule Two of the AIM Rules.

Appendix 3

EXAMPLE OF AN ACCOUNTANT'S REPORT ON HISTORICAL FINANCIAL INFORMATION PREPARED IN ACCORDANCE WITH THE BASIS DESCRIBED IN A BASIS OF PREPARATION NOTE

Date

Reporting accountant's address

Addressees, as agreed between the parties in the engagement letter

Dear Sirs

[ABC plc]/[XYZ Limited]

We report on the financial information [set out in paragraphs .... to ....] [which comprises[1]], for the *[specify periods]*. This financial information has been prepared for inclusion in the [*describe Document*[2]] dated..........of ABC plc on the basis of the accounting policies set out in paragraph [ ]. This report is required by [*Relevant Regulation*] and is given for the purpose of complying with that [paragraph] and for no other purpose. We have not audited or reviewed the financial information for the [*26 weeks ended* ...] [which has been included for comparative purposes only,] and accordingly do not express an opinion thereon.[3]

Responsibilities

As described in paragraph [ ] the Directors of ABC plc are responsible for preparing the financial information on the basis of preparation set out in note x to the financial information.

It is our responsibility to form an opinion on the financial information and to report our opinion to you.

Basis of opinion

We conducted our work in accordance with Standards for Investment Reporting issued by the Auditing Practices Board in the United Kingdom. Our work included an assessment of evidence relevant to the amounts and disclosures in the financial information. It also included an assessment of significant estimates and judgments made by those responsible for the preparation of the financial information and whether the accounting policies are appropriate to the entity's circumstances, consistently applied and adequately disclosed.

We planned and performed our work so as to obtain all the information and explanations which we considered necessary in order to provide us with sufficient evidence to give

---

[1] Where paragraph numbers are not referred to specify the titles of the primary statements on which the opinion is being expressed and refer to the notes to those primary statements.

[2] For example, "prospectus", "listing particulars", "Class 1 circular" and "AIM admission document."

[3] This wording is relevant where financial information for an interim period is required to be reported on in circumstances where comparative information for the same interim period in the prior financial period is also to be presented, but not reported on.

reasonable assurance that the financial information is free from material misstatement whether caused by fraud or other irregularity or error.

Opinion on financial information

In our opinion, the financial information gives, for the purposes of the [*describe Document*] dated ....., a true and fair view of the state of affairs of [ABC plc]/[XYZ Limited] as at [*specify dates*] and of its profits, cash flows and [recognised gains and losses] [changes in equity] for the [*specify periods*] in accordance with the basis of preparation set out in note x[4] [and has been prepared in a form that is consistent with the accounting policies adopted in [ABC plc's] latest annual accounts[5]].

Declaration[6]

For the purposes of [Prospectus Rule [5.5.3R(2)(f)] [5.5.4R(2)(f)]] [Paragraph a of Schedule Two of the AIM Rules] we are responsible for [this report as part] [the following part(s)] of the [prospectus] [registration document] [AIM admission document] and declare that we have taken all reasonable care to ensure that the information contained in [this report] [those parts] is, to the best of our knowledge, in accordance with the facts and contains no omission likely to affect its import. This declaration is included in the [prospectus] [registration document] [AIM admission document] in compliance with [item 1.2 of annex 1 of the Prospectus Regulation] [item 1.2 of annex 3 of the Prospectus Regulation] [Schedule Two of the AIM Rules].

Yours faithfully

Reporting accountant

---

[4] Where the financial information has not been prepared fully in accordance with a recognised financial reporting framework but, for example, in accordance with a financial reporting framework modified by applying a convention described in the Annexure to this SIR, the accountant's opinion is expressed in terms of the financial information being prepared in accordance with the basis of preparation described in note x to the financial information, rather than in accordance with the financial reporting framework. The basis of preparation note states which accounting convention has been applied and how it departs from the requirements of the recognised financial reporting framework. A statement is made in the note that in all other respects the recognised financial reporting framework has been applied.

[5] The wording in these square brackets is appropriate for inclusion where the report relates to historical financial information included in a Class 1 circular.

[6] This declaration is a requirement of the Prospectus Rules and is appropriate for inclusion when the report is included in a Prospectus, see Appendix 2 of SIR 1000. It is also appropriate for inclusion in an AIM admission document under Schedule Two of the AIM Rules.

ACCOUNTING CONVENTIONS COMMONLY USED IN THE PREPARATION OF HISTORICAL FINANCIAL INFORMATION IN INVESTMENT CIRCULARS

This Annexure has been compiled by the APB from a number of sources to describe conventions commonly used for the preparation of historical financial information intended to show a true and fair view for the purposes of an investment circular. It does not include basic principles, essential procedures, or guidance promulgated by the APB.

Introduction

1   Preparers[1] have regard to accepted conventions which have been developed for the preparation and presentation of historical financial information in investment circulars. They seek to assist preparers, to the extent consistent with established accounting principles, to meet the obligation that the historical financial information should give a true and fair view for the purposes of the relevant investment circular. These conventions also take into account the requirement contained in the Prospectus Directive that the information should be presented in an easily analysable and comprehensible form. The conventions are described in the material presented below.

Disclosure of the financial reporting framework adopted

2   Preparers summarise the applicable financial reporting framework within the notes to the financial information. Where one of the conventions described in this Annexure is applied and its application has a material effect on the financial information or is necessary for an understanding of the basis of preparation of the financial information, it is appropriate to describe the treatment adopted in the basis of preparation note in the historical financial information.

Adjustments to the financial information

3   Preparers make adjustments, only in respect of material items, in order to:

(a)   Present the financial information for all relevant years on the basis of consistent, acceptable and appropriately applied accounting policies, in accordance with the applicable requirements;

(b)   Correct errors; and

(c)   Record adjusting post balance sheet events where appropriate (see paragraph 13 below).

---

[1]   The directors and management of an entity are responsible for the preparation and presentation of the financial statements of an entity. In this Annexure they are collectively referred to as "the preparers".

4   The historical financial information presented will be based on the records of the entity whose historical financial information is presented in the investment circular (referred to as "the entity" throughout this Annexure), for the periods reported on. These records reflect the representations and intentions of the entity's management at the time the underlying financial information was drawn up. Matters such as the selection of accounting policies, accounting estimates and valuation judgments form part of the responsibilities of management in compiling a record of their stewardship.

5   In presenting historical financial information in an investment circular, except insofar as necessary to achieve the objectives set out above, preparers do not seek to replace accounting policies, accounting estimates or valuation judgments with alternatives subsequently selected by themselves. They consider whether the specific application of the basis of accounting originally adopted by management falls within an acceptable range of alternatives (if not, the conclusion will usually be that an error has occurred, which may need to be adjusted). Furthermore, it is not normally appropriate for adjustments to be made to eliminate items of earned income or expenses incurred, nor, in any circumstances, to recognise notional items of income or expense. The historical financial information presented in the investment circular is thus a version of the historical record as presented by the entity's management and adjustments are introduced only to achieve those specific objectives set out in paragraph 3 of this Annexure.

Trend of results

6   The historical financial information included in an investment circular presents a trend of results for the relevant period. In this respect the financial information may be distinguished from the financial information contained in statutory accounts.

7   Notional, or other, adjustments that impact net profits or net assets are not introduced in order to make the "track record" more consistent with the entity's expected operations or structure following the transaction. Such adjustments would anticipate future events and are not consistent with the principle that the historical financial information should record the events which actually occurred during the period of the historical financial information.

Adjustments for change in basis of accounting

8   Adjustments are made to ensure that, wherever practicable, the financial information is stated on the basis of consistent accounting policies. Under the PD Regulation (subject to certain transitional provisions in Article 35 of the PD Regulation), the financial information for the most recent year (where audited historical financial information is required for the latest 2 financial years) or most recent 2 years (where audited historical financial information is required for the latest 3 financial years) is required to be prepared and presented in a form consistent with that which will be adopted in the issuer's next published annual financial statements (having regard to accounting standards and policies and legislation applicable to such annual financial statements). The requirements do not prevent entities from presenting the financial

information for all periods in a form which is consistent with that which will be adopted in the next published financial statements if they so choose. In other contexts such as in a Class 1 transaction, the objective may be for the financial information for all periods to be presented in a form consistent with the accounting policies adopted by the acquirer in its latest annual consolidated accounts.

9   When considering the adjustments that may be necessary where a new International Financial Reporting Standard or other relevant accounting standard has been introduced during, or (where applicable under the regulations) subsequent to, the period to which the regulations apply, a relevant factor will be whether the requirements for implementing the new accounting standard provide that it should be applied retroactively once adopted. Where adoption of a new accounting standard leads to the inclusion of a prior year adjustment in the accounts, adjustments are made, to the extent practicable, to reflect the effect of the policy in any relevant earlier period. Where the adoption of a new accounting standard does not lead to the inclusion of a prior year adjustment, for example where the accounting standard is stated to apply to transactions first accounted for after a certain date; no such adjustment is made to the financial information. Where an entity chooses to adopt a new accounting standard early and this is permitted or encouraged, although not required, by that standard, the financial information reflects the same treatment as adopted by the entity.

10 Although adjustments may be made for changes in accounting policies, adjustments are not normally made for changes in the methods of applying an accounting policy (whether a one-off change or a series of gradual refinements) or otherwise to correct the entity's accounting estimates, provided that there were no errors. The effect of correcting an estimate in a later period is normally reflected in the result of that period. Consideration may be given to whether an understanding of the trend of results would be assisted by separate or additional disclosure in relation to changes in the methods of applying accounting policies or the impact of a correction of an accounting estimate.

11 Occasionally, an accounting policy may have been applied on the basis of considerations other than relevant economic ones (for example where financial statements measure the carrying amount of depreciable fixed assets in accordance with depreciation policies which are influenced by taxation considerations – as is the case in certain jurisdictions). Those presenting historical financial information in an investment circular may determine that an adjustment is necessary in order for the financial information to present a true and fair view, for the purposes of the relevant investment circular.

Audit qualifications relating to non-compliance with accounting standards

12 Where the auditor's report(s) on the underlying financial statements was qualified on grounds for example of failure to comply with an applicable accounting standard or disagreement over an accounting treatment, it may be possible to make adjustments so as to remove the need for a similar qualification in a report on the adjusted historical financial information.

Post balance sheet events

13 In determining whether adjustment is to be made for post balance sheet events, subject to the guidance set out above, it is normal practice to consider events only up to the date on which the audit report on the relevant underlying financial statements was originally signed by the auditors except in relation to the final period presented. In respect of this final period, it will be necessary for post balance sheet events to be reflected up to the date on which the historical financial information to be presented in the investment circular is approved by the responsible party. Where the financial information is based upon financial records which were not audited, the relevant date for post balance sheet event considerations in the earlier periods is normally taken to be the date at which the underlying balance sheet was finalised.

Presentation of the financial information

14 Subject to the requirements of any applicable regulation, the financial information is presented on a consistent and comparable basis from period to period and includes such presentational changes to the financial information as are necessary in order to achieve this.

15 Presentational changes might be made to:

(a) Present the financial information in a comparable way; and

(b) Give due prominence to matters of particular importance in the context of the document in which the financial information is included.

16 The financial information contained in the entity's records may not have been presented on a comparable basis from period to period because the convention for presenting financial information adopted in earlier periods may have been different from that adopted in later periods.

17 Whenever practicable, financial information is presented in such a way that information which a user of the investment circular might wish to compare, is in fact comparable. Presentational changes of this nature may be categorised as follows:

(a) Reclassifications (for example, cost of sales reclassified as distribution costs);

(b) Re-analyses (for example, restatements of analyses between continuing and discontinued activities);

(c) Grossing up of items netted off in earlier periods (for example, matched assets and liabilities previously left off balance sheet);

(d) Derivation or computation of information undisclosed in earlier periods (for example, profit and loss account subtotals or cash flow statements); and

(e) Harmonisation of note disclosures (for example the editing of notes for earlier periods to integrate them with notes for later periods).

18 For example, a business classed as a continuing operation in one year may have been designated a discontinued activity in financial statements drawn up for a later period. It will be desirable for the relevant information within continuing operations in the earlier periods to be reclassified as discontinued. Where separate disclosure of information relating to entities acquired during the period has been presented in the financial statements, it is customary to reclassify such information for the purposes of the historical financial information as continuing activities, other than in respect of acquisitions made in the final period of the track record.

19 Changes are not, however, made to the presentation adopted in the financial statements on which the financial information is based, unless such changes are consistent with the requirement to give a true and fair view for the purposes of the investment circular.

20 Where it is considered that the significance of certain items to an understanding of the financial information may be obscured by the presentation adopted in the financial statements, it is usually appropriate for that presentation to be changed, relevant disclosures to be made or relevant explanations to be introduced to highlight their significance. This approach may be adopted for example to highlight certain categories of expense, such as proprietors' remuneration, in the trading record of a company seeking flotation. It may also be adopted to highlight the results of different classes of business, particularly in cases where there are proposals that a class of business is to be discontinued.

21 However, in all cases, changes in presentation would be inappropriate if they are in conflict with applicable accounting standards.

22 As noted above, in certain cases regulatory requirements stipulate that information for the most recent two of the three years is to be presented on a basis comparable with that which would be adopted in an issuer's next annual financial statements. In such cases, in order that the reader is able to relate the first year's information to the final two years, preparers may present financial information for the second year on the basis originally reported (and thus comparable with the first year) as well as on the adjusted basis required by the regulation.

Issues connected with underlying financial statements

23 Where the entity has prepared accounts consolidating all its subsidiaries during the period, the financial information will, subject to any adjustments made, be the information set out in the consolidated accounts.

24 There may be cases where historical financial information is to be prepared for an entity in circumstances where consolidated financial statements do not exist. This may arise for example where the business is a sub-group, the parent company of which was exempt from the requirement to prepare consolidated accounts, or where the

business comprises companies under common ownership but which were not constituted as a legal sub-group.

Unconsolidated accounts

25 Where there has been a legal sub-group it will usually be appropriate, for ease of analysis and comprehension, for the accounts of the subsidiaries to be consolidated into the accounts of the parent company. For this purpose, specially prepared consolidated accounts may be compiled by the relevant entity, applying the normal conventions for consolidation.

Entities under common management and control

26 Where the entities have been under common management and control but do not form a legal group, the historical financial information will normally be presented on a combined or aggregated basis. Under this method, the results and net assets of the relevant entities are aggregated (with eliminations for intercompany transactions and balances), as are the related share capital balances and reserves. If the information is not presented on a combined or aggregated basis then separate historical financial information for entities accounting for substantially the whole of the historical revenue earning record is likely to be required.

Carve outs

27 Where a business has formed part of a larger group ("overall group") during the three year period, but has not been accounted for separately, it may be desirable to present a separate track record (a "carve out") for that business ("carve out business"), derived from the records of the overall group. This approach may be preferable to the alternative approach of presenting the track record of the overall group, with appropriate disclosures of operations discontinuing or not acquired. Circumstances where a carve out approach might be followed include flotations of businesses in a demerger and Class 1 acquisitions of divisions of a selling group.

28 When considering whether it is appropriate to present carve out financial information, the following factors will be relevant:

(a) The extent to which the carve out business has been separately managed and financially controlled within the overall group; and

(b) The extent to which it is practicable to identify the historical financial information attributable to the carve out business.

29 Where the omission of the results and assets of those operations not the subject of the transaction concerned would be misleading in the context of the circumstances in which the historical financial information is to be presented, it will generally be appropriate to adopt the approach of presenting financial information on the overall group. Disclosures are made to assist the user to understand the contribution made by the operations not the subject of the transaction concerned. However, each case will need to be assessed on its own facts and circumstances.

30   In preparing the track record for the carve out business, the guidance in paragraph 5 of this Annexure will be relevant. The objective will be, so far as possible, to present a historical record reflecting the events which actually occurred in the reporting period. Whilst it may be possible to identify certain transactions and balances which clearly relate to the carve out business, there will often be cases where the accounting records do not differentiate between items which relate to the carve out business and items which relate to the remainder of the overall group's business. Examples include management overheads, funding arrangements and shared assets. The guidance below discusses some of the elements typically encountered in preparing a carve out track record.

31   Clear and comprehensive disclosure in the notes to the historical financial information will normally be needed in the basis of preparation in order for the nature of the historical financial information to be clearly understood. The description would be expected to give a general indication of the process adopted for the preparation of the historical financial information, and describe any factors which are particularly important to an understanding of the manner in which the information has been prepared.

32   The accounting policies to be adopted in the carve out accounts will need to reflect the requirements relating to the presentation of historical financial information and may differ from those previously adopted. The question of functional currency should also be considered having regard to the economic environment of the carve out business, which may lead to the adoption of a different functional currency from that of the overall group.

Allocations

33   Where transactions or balances are not accounted for within the overall group in a manner which clearly attributes them to the carve out business, it will generally be desirable for a method for allocating the relevant amounts to the carve out business to be identified with a view to providing the fairest approximation to the amounts actually attributable to the carve out business. Any method should be adopted and applied on a rational and consistent basis. It will not, however, be appropriate to make allocations where there is no rational or consistent basis for doing so.

Bases for allocating transactions and balances

34   The appropriate basis for allocating group income and expenditure to a carve out business will vary according to the circumstances. It may, for example, be appropriate to allocate centrally accounted-for human resources costs on the basis of headcount (but account might be taken also of relative levels of staff turnover or other factors which indicate greater or less than average use in deciding whether the approach was in fact appropriate). The costs of a head office accounts department might be allocated by reference to the relevant sizes of the carve out business and remaining group. Again if other factors suggest that size is not a good indicator – if for example a disproportionate number of the accounting team is engaged in work for one part of the business and not the other – refinements to the approach might be considered appropriate.

35 It is important to recognise that the purpose of the allocation is to attribute an appropriate element of the overall group record to the carve out business. As a consequence, the position shown will frequently not be that which might have existed if the carve out business had been a stand-alone business. The position will be affected by the arrangements which apply to the group as a whole, which are a matter of historical fact and which it is not the purpose of the carve out financial information to alter. Frequently, disclosure will be made accompanying the financial information highlighting that the information presented may not be representative of the position which may prevail after the transaction.

36 Where an element of overall group third party debt is to be assumed by the carve out business, it may be appropriate to allocate an appropriate element of such debt to the carve out business during the historical track record period. The basis for such an allocation may be by reference to the terms of the separation agreement. In other cases, the debt may be treated as part of the carve out business' balance with the overall group. Finance lease borrowings would be expected to be allocated in line with the allocation of the related asset. The allocation of interest income/costs would follow the way in which the related debt and debt instruments have been apportioned.

Relationship with the remaining group

37 In addition to transactions with 'third parties', the results of the business will also include transactions with the part of the overall group which is not part of the carve out business (the "remaining group"). Hence, for example, sales which were previously regarded as 'intra group' will need to be re-examined to determine whether they relate to entities within the carve out business or outside it.

38 The remaining group will normally also be regarded as a related party for the purposes of disclosing related party transactions, and it will normally be necessary to identify the extent of the relationships between the carve out business and the remaining group. Balances with the remaining group may have comprised elements of trading balances and short term or long term funding balances, which may or may not have been interest bearing. Balances of a trading nature will normally be presented as an element of debtors or creditors. Balances which are considered to be funding in nature (having regard inter alia to the use made of the balances, the period for which they remain outstanding and the level of other capital) will normally be classified according to their general nature. Where the balance is interest bearing and has other characteristics of debt, it will be presented in the manner of debt financing. Where the balance does not have the characteristics of debt, it will be re-classified from creditors into capital and be presented in the manner of equity, typically aggregated with the share capital and reserves of companies comprising carve out business, as 'parent company net investment' in the carve out business.

39 Balances with the remaining group may also contain elements of third party debtors or creditors which have been accounted for on behalf of the carve out business by the remaining group. Examples might be VAT costs, payroll taxes, certain customers or suppliers common to the carve out business and the remaining group, and external funding balances. Such elements of the balance with the remaining group would be expected to be reallocated to the appropriate third party captions.

40   Consolidation journals within the overall group accounting records will need to be analysed and, if appropriate, allocated to the carve out business.

Pension costs

41   Where employees of the carve out business participate in a pension scheme relating to the overall group, the track record of the carve out business would reflect the apportioned costs applicable to the carve out business. The accounting implications of any pension surplus/deficit attributable to the carve out business would also normally be expected to be reflected in the track record.

Acquisitions

42   Acquisitions will be treated in accordance with the guidance in paragraphs 50 to 52 of this Annexure. It should be noted that acquisitions previously regarded as too small for separate disclosure in the overall group accounts may become sufficiently material to require separate disclosure in the context of the carve out business.

Disposals, non recurring and exceptional items

43   Non recurring and exceptional items are generally allocated to the carve out business and accounted for in accordance with the applicable accounting standard. The treatment of disposals follows that described in paragraph 53 of this Annexure.

Taxation

44   Tax charges are generally allocated to the carve out business to reflect the proportion of the overall group charge attributable to the carve out business. The approach will typically involve the aggregation of the tax charges actually incurred by the companies within the carve out business (and will therefore reflect the benefits, reliefs and charges arising as a result of membership of the overall group), after taking account of the tax effects of any adjustments. Where the information relating to the tax charges actually incurred is not available, the tax charge may be recomputed on the basis of the results of the carve out business. The tax rate applied is selected having regard to the tax position of the overall group and might thus include the impact of benefits, reliefs and charges arising as a result of membership of the overall group, to the extent that they would have been available to or imposed upon the carve out business.

Cash flow statements

45   A cash flow statement is prepared for the carve out business based on the carve out information. Where the overall group operates a central cash account, cash flows relating to centrally settled costs are allocated to the carve out business to the extent that the related balances are allocated to the carve out business.

Investments in subsidiaries, joint ventures and associates

46   The status of an entity in the overall group's accounts (that is, whether it is recorded as a subsidiary, joint venture or associate) may be the result of investments in the relevant

entity by more than one group company. If not all the investing companies are to be part of the carve out business, this may mean that the status of the entity in the track record of the carve out business is different from that within the overall group. Additional or new disclosures may therefore be required.

Treatment of other items

47 Dividends are expected to be reflected in the track record of the carve out business where companies within the carve out business have paid dividends to members of the remaining group.

48 In relation to the disclosure of directors' remuneration, it is normal to present information for those individuals who are to be directors of the carve out business or who were employed by the overall group in a capacity equivalent to that of a director of the carve out business. The information disclosed will reflect the salaries and benefits paid in respect of services to the carve out business by any member of the overall group to those individuals (irrespective of whether the individuals were directors or not) during the period covered by the track record. No information is presented for proposed directors of the carve out business who were not employed by the overall group, or for individuals who served as directors of companies within the carve out group but who are not to be directors of the carve out group's holding company following the transaction.

49 A segmental analysis is prepared for the carve out business to reflect the segments which the carve out business has decided to adopt.

Acquisitions

50 Entities acquired during the period covered by the historical financial information will typically be accounted for, in the records of the acquiring entity, in accordance with the accounting treatment applicable, having regard to the set of accounting standards adopted. Hence, for example, if the accounting standards require acquisition accounting, the acquired subsidiary will be accounted for from the date of acquisition by the acquiring entity.

51 Chapter 13 of the Listing Rules states that, in the case of a Class 1 acquisition when, during the three year period to be covered by the historical financial information (or in the lesser period up to the date of the acquisition if the target's business has been in operation for less than 3 years), the target has acquired or has agreed to acquire an undertaking which would have been classified, at the date of the acquisition, as a Class 1 acquisition, financial information on that undertaking must be given, which covers as a minimum the period from the beginning of the three year period to the date of acquisition.

52 Generally (and typically where the acquisition has been or will be accounted for under the acquisition method), the requirement outlined in paragraph 50 of this Annexure leads to a separate table of historical financial information covering the results of the acquired subsidiary undertaking during the period prior to acquisition. The Listing Rules contain no express contents requirements for acquisitions which would have

been classified as smaller than Class 1 (ie a Class 2 or Class 3 transaction), although Listing Rule 13.3 contains contents requirements applicable to all circulars. Additional financial information may be required where the financial information presented in the entity's own track record does not account for substantially all of the track record of the business during the three year period.

Disposals

53   Disposals of subsidiaries or a discontinuation of a material section of the business are reflected by separate analysis between the continuing business and the disposed or discontinued business, either under the relevant headings in the profit and loss table or in the notes to the historical financial information. It is not normally appropriate to make adjustments to eliminate the results of subsidiaries that have been disposed of or discontinued operations from the trading record. However, it may not be necessary to introduce the results of a subsidiary that has been disposed of or a discontinued operation into specially prepared consolidated accounts or combined accounts prepared having regard to the considerations set out in paragraphs 25 to 49 of this Annexure, unless the inclusion of such information is relevant to an understanding of the business to which the historical financial information relates.

Financial information on newly formed issuers

54   In many cases, investment circulars are prepared in relation to newly formed companies (for example start up businesses, investment trusts, newly formed holding companies etc). Generally such companies will not have prepared accounts for a financial year at the time the investment circular is to be issued and consequently financial statements will need to be prepared for the purposes of the investment circular.

Unincorporated entities and entities producing limited accounting information

55   Acquisitions may involve entities which do not prepare financial information which meets the standards required for statutory accounts in the UK (and additionally may not have been subject to the disciplines of an external audit). The accounting conventions adopted may be devised for internal management accounting purposes rather than to meet more generally applicable accounting standards. In such cases, it may not be possible to present financial information meeting the requirements of the relevant regulations. The decision as to what information to present will depend upon the degree to which the information can be regarded as sufficiently relevant and reliable having regard to the purpose for which it is presented. Frequently the purpose will be to assist shareholders in a decision; it is for those responsible for the investment circular to weigh up the balance between depriving shareholders of information which may be relevant to a decision and being satisfied that the information presented is of sufficient quality to be properly used as the basis for a decision. Where there is significant doubt about the quality of the financial information available, those responsible for the investment circular would be advised not to present it in the investment circular. This may lead to very limited financial information appearing in the relevant investment circular. In the case of an investment circular regulated by the UK

Listing Authority, the position should be discussed in advance with the UK Listing Authority.

Changes in the legal form of entities

56   There may be circumstances where businesses have been carried on during the period covered by the report by different legal entities with the consequence that the relevant financial information may be found in the accounts of different legal entities. A typical example is a management buy-out, where prior to the buy-out, the business might have been accounted for in the financial statements of a subsidiary undertaking of the vendor, but, following the buy-out, the financial information may be that of the entity formed to effect the acquisition.

57   In cases where the legal entity accounting for the business has changed (for example where a business has been transferred from one entity to another – typically a newly formed company) but where there is no essential change in the underlying business, it is normal for the financial information to be presented as part of a single table, with the results of the predecessor entity shown next to those of the successor entity (generally on a combined basis in the period during which the transaction took place).

58   A consequence of the change in legal entity may be a change in the capital structure. Frequently, where there is a management buy-out, debt becomes a significant part of the capitalisation of the business. In order to highlight for the reader the potential lack of comparability between periods, a statement is often included within the introduction or beneath the profit and loss account (and in the relevant notes) referring to the change in capital structure and alerting the reader to the fact that the information relating to financing costs may not be comparable throughout the period. In certain cases, where the effect is material to an appreciation of the figures, it may also be necessary to draw attention to a discontinuity in values attributed to balance sheet items. In circumstances where, as in the case of a management buy-out, fair value adjustments have been made during the period covered by the historical financial information, it is inappropriate to attempt to show the impact of such adjustments on the results prior to the acquisition. However, the impact of the fair value adjustments is, where practicable, highlighted in respect of the post-acquisition results.

Earnings per share

59   In cases where there has been a capital reorganisation since the date at which the last balance sheet was drawn up, it will usually be appropriate for the earnings per share figures disclosed to be adjusted to reflect the reorganisation (to the extent that it involves issues of shares for no consideration, issues containing a bonus element, share splits etc). In such cases, the number of shares used in the earnings per share calculation is adjusted so that the shares originally in issue are replaced by the number of new shares, representing the shares originally in issue, following the reorganisation. Where shares have been issued during the period, this is taken into account in calculating the equivalent weighted average number of post-reorganisation shares. Where the reconstruction involves conversions, for example of preference shares or loan stock, the earnings figures used in the calculation of earnings per share may also

need to be adjusted to eliminate the effect of any related preference dividends or interest.

60   Difficulties may also arise over the relevance of the earnings per share figure in certain cases, for example where prior to flotation a new holding company has been created. In such cases an earnings per share figure based on the share capital of the subsidiary may be of limited significance to investors. Accordingly, it is usually appropriate to include a supplementary earnings per share figure, in addition to the historical earnings per share figure, based on the relevant number of shares in the new parent company (before the issue of shares to raise new funds). This approach is also generally adopted in the case of a carve out business which did not have share capital during the reporting period. Where the effect is material and where practicable, the number of shares used for the purposes of the calculation is adjusted to reflect variations in the levels of capital funding the operations arising, for example, from issues of equity for cash during the period under review. In some circumstances, such as where there has been a management buy out during the period reported on, the differences in the capital structure may be such that a comparison of the earnings per share figures is not meaningful. Where this is the case, the statement to be included beneath the profit and loss table mentioned above generally refers also to the lack of comparability of the earnings per share information.

Reporting currency

61   Where historical financial information is to be presented on a target entity, and that target has reported historically in a currency other than that of the acquiring entity, it is normal to present the financial information in the target's original reporting currency.

Extraction without material adjustment

62   In a Class 1 circular, the listed company must (in addition to citing the source of the information) state whether the financial information that has been extracted from audited accounts was extracted without material adjustment. It is not possible to prescribe conditions for determining whether an adjustment will be a material adjustment in any given case, although presentational changes which do not have the effect of altering net assets, are normally permitted to be made. The UK Listing Authority will need to agree the approach in individual cases.

STANDARDS FOR INVESTMENT REPORTING

3000 – INVESTMENT REPORTING STANDARDS APPLICABLE TO PUBLIC REPORTING ENGAGEMENTS ON PROFIT FORECASTS

CONTENTS

SIR 3000 contains basic principles and essential procedures ("Investment Reporting Standards"), indicated by paragraphs in bold type, with which a reporting accountant is required to comply in the conduct of an engagement to report on a profit forecast which is included within an investment circular prepared for issue in connection with a securities *transaction governed wholly or in part by the law and regulations of the United Kingdom.*

SIR 3000 also includes explanatory and other material, including appendices, in the context of which the basic principles and essential procedures are to be understood and applied. It is necessary to consider the whole text of the SIR to understand and apply the basic principles and essential procedures.

For the purposes of SIRs, an investment circular is defined as: "any document issued by an entity pursuant to statutory or regulatory requirements relating to listed or unlisted securities on which it is intended that a third party should make an investment decision, including a prospectus, listing particulars, circular *to shareholders or similar document".*

SIR 1000 "Investment reporting standards applicable to all engagements involving an investment circular" contains basic principles and essential procedures that are applicable to all engagements involving an investment circular. The definitions in the Glossary of terms set out in Appendix 4 of SIR 1000 are to be applied in the interpretation of this and all other SIRs. Terms defined in the glossary are underlined the first time that they occur in the text.

To assist readers, SIRs contain references to, and extracts from, certain legislation and chapters of the Rules of the UK Listing Authority. Readers are cautioned that these references may change subsequent to publication.

Introduction

1. Standard for Investment Reporting (SIR) 1000 "Investment Reporting Standards applicable to all engagements in connection with an investment circular" establishes the Investment Reporting Standards applicable to all engagements involving investment circulars. The purpose of this SIR is to establish specific additional Investment Reporting Standards and provide guidance for a reporting accountant engaged to report publicly on profit forecasts to be included in an investment circular under the PD Regulation, other regulations with similar requirements[1], the City Code, or if required by the London Stock Exchange in respect of an AIM Admission Document.

2. An engagement to report publicly on the proper compilation of a profit forecast is a public reporting engagement as described in SIR 1000. The description of a public reporting engagement includes three generic terms having the following meanings in the context of an engagement to report on the proper compilation of a profit forecast:

---

[1] In the UK the Prospectus Directive is implemented into law through amendments to Part VI of FSMA and to certain secondary legislation. The Annexes to the PD Regulation have been incorporated into the Prospectus Rules issued by the FSA.

(a) with respect to a profit forecast the "**subject matter**" is the directors' expectation of the issuer's profit for the period of the forecast;

(b) "**suitable criteria**" to be used by directors in the preparation of the profit forecast are provided by the requirements of the PD Regulation and the guidance[2] issued by CESR (CESR Recommendations). In forming its opinion as to whether the profit forecast has been properly compiled the reporting accountant considers whether certain of those criteria ("**reporting accountant's criteria**") have been properly applied. Reporting accountant's criteria are set out in Appendix 2 of this SIR; and

(c) with respect to a profit forecast the "**outcome**"[3] is the directors' profit forecast and related disclosures, that is included in the investment circular, and on which the reporting accountant expresses an opinion (in the "**reporting accountant's report**") as to whether that forecast is properly compiled on the basis stated and the basis of accounting used is consistent with the accounting policies of the issuer.

3. The PD Regulation defines a profit forecast as "a form of words which expressly states or by implication indicates a figure or a minimum or maximum figure for the likely level of profits or losses for the current financial period and/or financial periods subsequent to that period, or contains data from which a calculation of such a figure for future profits or losses may be made, even if no particular figure is mentioned and the word "profit" is not used"[4]. Where a profit forecast relates to an extended period and/or is subject to significant uncertainty it is sometimes referred to as a projection.

4. A profit forecast may include historical financial information relating to a past period. For example, a forecast made on 15 October 20xx for the profit for the year ended 31 December 20xx may include the profit for the six months ended 30 June 20xx included in the issuer's half yearly report and amounts extracted from management accounts for July and August. A profit estimate is historical financial information for a financial period which has expired but for which the results have not yet been published.

5. In this SIR requirements relating to "profit forecasts" also apply to statements typically referred to as "profit estimates" or "projections". The Investment Circular Reporting Standards in this SIR are applied to the whole period of the profit forecast including historical financial information included therein.

The nature of profit forecasts

6. A profit forecast is, by definition, uncertain because events and circumstances may not occur as expected or may not be predicted at all, or because the directors may take actions different to those previously intended. A profit forecast will usually include

---

[2] CESR issued "CESR's Recommendations for the Consistent Implementation of the European Commission's Regulation on Prospectuses No. 809/2004" in February 2005.

[3] The "outcome" is sometimes described as "subject matter information".

[4] The definition of a profit forecast in the City Code is similar to that used by the PD Regulation.

disclosures which provide information to assist the intended users understand the uncertainties involved.

7.   A profit forecast is usually based on assumptions, relating to the expected outcome of future events and possible actions by the entity. As assumptions on which any forward-looking element of a profit forecast is based are a critical element of the profit forecast, the various regulations require, among other things, the disclosure of the principal assumptions which could have a material effect on the achievement of the profit forecast including those within the influence and control of the directors.

8.   The extent to which a profit forecast will differ materially from the actual out-turn will depend on a profit forecast's particular circumstances. The length of the period into the future to which the profit forecast relates is only one, and not necessarily the most significant, factor. For example, an established business may be able to predict with greater certainty its results for the following year, particularly if it operates in a very stable environment, than a start-up business or an established business entering a new field.

9.   Profit forecasts are inherently uncertain and the probability that a profit forecast will correctly predict the actual out-turn is dependent upon the many factors which determine that uncertainty. The fact that a profit forecast does not correctly predict the actual out-turn does not mean that the profit forecast was not properly compiled.

10.   The Institute of Chartered Accountants in England and Wales issued guidance entitled "Prospective Financial Information – Guidance for UK directors" in September 2003 ("ICAEW Guidance") to assist directors in meeting the needs of the intended users of such information and of regulators and to promote the production of high quality prospective financial information, including profit forecasts.

11.   As explained in Appendix 1 of this SIR the CESR Recommendations state that profit forecasts should be:

(a)   reliable;

(b)   understandable;

(c)   comparable; and

(d)   relevant.

Directors are required to form a judgment as to whether the profit forecast is relevant to the purpose of the investment circular[5] and, therefore, whether or not it is appropriate for the profit forecast to be included in the investment circular. The directors' judgment

---

[5]   The ICAEW Guidance considers that a profit forecast will only be "relevant" if it:
(a)   has the ability to influence economic decisions of investors;
(b)   is provided in time to influence the economic decisions of investors; and
(c)   has predictive value or, by helping to confirm or correct past evaluations or assessments, it has confirmatory value.

in this regard will be influenced by the applicable regulatory requirements. The role of the reporting accountant is to report on whether a profit forecast, that the directors have decided to include in an investment circular, has been properly compiled. The role of the reporting accountant does not include questioning the directors' decision to include a profit forecast in an investment circular.

12. In order to provide an opinion on the proper compilation of a profit forecast the reporting accountant carries out the procedures required by this SIR and SIR 1000, and any others it considers necessary, to satisfy itself that the profit forecast is:

   (a) reliable[6];

   (b) understandable[7]; and

   (c) comparable[8].

   Consequently, these three principles are considered to be suitable criteria for the evaluation of profit forecasts by the reporting accountant (see Appendix 2 of this SIR).

Reliability

13. The ICAEW Guidance explains that to be *reliable* a profit forecast will possess the following attributes:

   (a) it can be depended upon by the intended users as a faithful representation of what it either purports to represent or could reasonably be expected to represent;

   (b) it is neutral because it is free from deliberate or systematic bias intended to influence a decision or judgment to achieve a predetermined result;

   (c) it is free from material error;

   (d) it is complete within the bounds of what is material; and

   (e) it is prudent in that a degree of caution is applied in making judgments under conditions of uncertainty.

   The ICAEW Guidance explains that a profit forecast will be a faithful representation where it reflects an entity's strategies, plans and risk analysis in a way that is appropriate for the purpose for which the profit forecast is being prepared. The fact that a profit forecast does not correctly predict the actual out-turn once reported, does not necessarily mean that it was not reliable when made.

14. A profit forecast, including the assumptions used, is more likely to possess the above attributes when the issuer has undertaken an analysis of the underlying business and

---

[6] The business analysis principle in the ICAEW Guidance.
[7] The reasonable disclosure principle in the ICAEW Guidance.
[8] The subsequent validation principle in the ICAEW Guidance.

its strategies, plans and risks (the directors' business analysis) and when the forecast is prepared as a faithful representation of that business analysis, taking prudent account of the risk analysis. The reliability of a profit forecast is, therefore, a function of:

(a)   the quality of the analysis undertaken; and

(b)   the degree to which that analysis is reflected in the profit forecast.

Understandability

15.   To be **understandable** a profit forecast contains the information necessary for intended users to appreciate the degree of uncertainty attaching to the information and how that uncertainty might impact it. This requires the disclosure of assumptions and other matters relevant to the basis of preparation of the profit forecast which are of importance in assisting the intended users' understanding of the profit forecast. The omission of important information may prevent a profit forecast from being understandable and equally, if the disclosure is too complex or too extensive the understandability of the profit forecast may be also impaired. What constitutes reasonable disclosure will therefore depend upon the particular circumstances of each profit forecast but will need to take into consideration:

(a)   sources of uncertainty and the related assumptions made relating to uncertainties;

(b)   the factors that will affect whether assumptions will be borne out in practice; and

(c)   alternative outcomes, being the consequences of assumptions not being borne out.

Comparability

16.   The usefulness of a profit forecast is derived partly from its **comparability**, namely the expectation that it will be possible to compare it to the actual results and that it can be compared to equivalent information for other reporting periods. For this to be the case profit forecasts need to be prepared and presented on a basis comparable with the actual financial information for that period and will involve the application of the accounting policies used by the entity in preparing the historical financial information included in the investment circular.

Compilation process

17.   The compilation of a profit forecast is the gathering, classification and summarisation of relevant financial information. The process followed by the preparer would be expected to include:

(a)   an appropriate analysis of the business (what is appropriate will depend on a number of factors including the complexity and predictability of the business and the length of the period being forecast and accordingly the content, degree of detail and presentation of such analyses may vary significantly);

(b)   identification of material uncertainties;

(c)   selection of appropriate assumptions;

(d)   where relevant, identification of and reference to, appropriate third party information (eg. market research reports);

(e)   arithmetic computation of the profit forecast;

(f)   appropriate sensitivity analysis;

(g)   appropriate disclosures to enable the intended users to understand the profit forecast; and

(h)   appropriate consideration of the profit forecast and approval of it by the directors of the entity.

Engagement acceptance and continuance

18.   SIR 1000.1 and SIR 1000.2 set out the basic principles and essential procedures, with respect to engagement acceptance and continuance, which are applicable to all engagements involving an investment circular.

19.   When accepting or continuing an engagement to report publicly on a profit forecast, the reporting accountant ascertains whether the directors intend to comply with all relevant regulatory requirements, in particular those that are the basis of the reporting accountant's criteria set out in Appendix 2 of this SIR.

Agreeing the terms of the engagement

20.   SIR 1000.3 and SIR 1000.4 set out the basic principles and essential procedures with respect to agreeing the terms of the engagement. Examples of engagement letter clauses are set out in Appendix 4 of this SIR.

Ethical requirements

21.   SIR 1000.5 sets out the basic principles and essential procedures with respect to the ethical requirements that apply to a reporting accountant[9].

---

[9]   In January 2006 the APB issued an Exposure Draft of an Ethical Standard for Reporting Accountants (ESRA).

Legal and regulatory requirements

22. The PD Regulation requires any profit forecast or estimate included in a prospectus to be reported on by independent accountants or auditors (referred to in this SIR as "a reporting accountant") and specifies the form of opinion to be given[10]. The City Code contains provisions in relation to profit forecasts included in offer documents and requires reports from the auditors or reporting accountants in certain circumstances.

23. SIR 1000.6 sets out the basic principles with respect to the legal and regulatory requirements applicable to a reporting accountant.

24. Appendices 1, 2 and 3 to this SIR set out those provisions of the PD Regulation, the CESR Recommendations relating to the implementation of the PD Regulation, and the City Code, that provide the suitable criteria for directors. Those provisions that are the basis of criteria for a reporting accountant expressing an opinion on whether the profit forecast has been properly compiled are set out in Appendix 2 of this SIR.

Quality control

25. SIR 1000.7 and SIR 1000.8 set out the basic principles and essential procedures with respect to the quality control of engagements to report on profit forecasts.

Planning and performing the engagement

26. SIR 1000.9 and SIR 1000.10 set out the basic principles and essential procedures with respect to the planning of all reporting engagements. Additional essential procedures and guidance are set out below.

27. **The reporting accountant should obtain an understanding of the key factors affecting the subject matter sufficient to identify and assess the risk of the profit forecast not being properly compiled and sufficient to design and perform evidence gathering procedures including:**

    (a) **the background to and nature of the circumstances in which the profit forecast, which is included in the investment circular, was made;**

    (b) **the entity's business; and**

    (c) **the procedures adopted, or planned to be adopted, by the directors for the preparation of the profit forecast. (SIR 3000.1)**

28. The reporting accountant gains an understanding of the background to and nature of the circumstances in which the profit forecast is being prepared, by discussion with the

---

[10] The PD Regulation requirements are reproduced verbatim in the Prospectus Rules issued by the FSA.

directors or management of the issuer and by reading relevant supporting documentation. In particular, the reporting accountant ascertains whether the profit forecast is being made for the first time or whether it is a forecast that has previously been made by the issuer that may be required to be updated by the directors.

29. The reporting accountant uses professional judgment to determine the extent of the understanding required of the entity's business. In a start-up situation or where an established business is entering a new field the reporting accountant's understanding of the prospective business is necessarily limited to general knowledge of the field being entered and an understanding of the business analysis undertaken by the entity.

30. Reporting on the proper compilation of a profit forecast generally requires an understanding of the entity's management accounting, budgeting and forecasting systems and procedures beyond that normally considered necessary for an audit of historical financial statements.

31. Discussion with the preparers of a profit forecast will identify the process by which the profit forecast has been, or will be prepared, the extent to which the ICAEW guidance has been followed, the sources of information used, areas of significant uncertainty where assumptions have been made and the basis for those assumptions and how those assumptions have been documented. Specific matters for consideration include:

- The organisational structure of the entity and the extent to which subsidiaries or local operating units have been involved in the preparation of the profit forecast.

- Whether the profit forecast is prepared on a basis comparable with the most recent historical financial information in the investment circular.

- The extent to which the period of the forecast includes historical financial information.

- Whether the profit forecast will be capable of comparison to subsequently published historical financial information.

32. Where profit forecasts are regularly prepared by the entity either for internal management purposes or for publication, the reporting accountant considers the closeness to actual out-turns achieved in previous forecasts and the analysis of any variances. As well as helping to provide an understanding of the entity's business this may be helpful in identifying those aspects of the business which are subject to significant uncertainty.

33. **The reporting accountant should consider materiality and public reporting engagement risk in planning its work in accordance with its instructions and in determining the effect of its findings on the report to be issued. (SIR 3000.2)**

Materiality

34. The ICAEW Guidance states that in order for a profit forecast to be **reliable** it will, amongst other things, be free of material error. An error in the context of the proper compilation of a profit forecast includes:

- Assumptions that are not consistent with the analysis of the business.

- Mathematical or clerical mistakes in the compilation of the profit forecast.

- Misapplication of accounting policies.

- Misapplication of a stated assumption.

- Known misstatements in historical financial information embodied in the forecast without adjustment.

35. Additionally, there may be deficiencies in the presentation of a profit forecast which may impair the understandability or comparability of the forecast in a way that is material. An error could, therefore, also include:

(a) failure to disclose an assumption or other explanation which is necessary for an understanding of the forecast; or

(b) presenting the forecast in a way that it is not capable of being compared with subsequent published results.

36. Matters are material if their omission or misstatement could, individually or collectively, influence the economic decisions of the intended users of the profit forecast. Materiality depends on the size and nature of the omission or misstatement judged in light of the surrounding circumstances. The size or nature of the matter, or a combination of both, could be the determining factor.

37. Evaluating whether an omission or misstatement could influence economic decisions of the intended users of the profit forecast, and so be material, requires consideration of the characteristics of those intended users. The intended users are assumed to:

(a) have a reasonable knowledge of business and economic activities and accounting and a willingness to study the profit forecast with reasonable diligence; and

(b) make reasonable economic decisions on the basis of the profit forecast.

The determination of materiality, therefore, takes into account how intended users with such characteristics could reasonably be expected to be influenced in making economic decisions.

38. The fact that the out-turn differs from the forecast does not necessarily mean that the forecast was not properly compiled as, for example, actual economic conditions may have differed from those reasonably assumed in the preparation of the profit forecast.

Public reporting engagement risk

39. "Public reporting engagement risk" is the risk that the reporting accountant expresses the positive and unmodified opinion required by the PD Regulation or the City Code when the profit forecast has not been properly compiled on the basis stated or the basis of accounting used for the profit forecast is not consistent with the accounting policies of the issuer.

40. SIR 1000.11 and SIR 1000.12 set out the basic principles and essential procedures, with respect to obtaining evidence, that are applicable to all engagements involving an investment circular. Additional basic principles, essential procedures and guidance relating to engagements to report on profit forecasts are set out below.

41. **To form an opinion that the profit forecast has been properly compiled, the reporting accountant should obtain sufficient appropriate evidence that the forecast is free from material error in its compilation by:**

    (a) **obtaining evidence that the directors have applied the criteria set out in Appendix 2 of this SIR;**

    (b) **checking that the profit forecast has been accurately computed based upon the disclosed assumptions and the preparer's accounting policies;**

    (c) **considering whether the assumptions used are consistent with the directors' business analysis and the reporting accountant's own knowledge of the business; and**

    (d) **where applicable, evaluating the basis on which any historical financial information included in the profit forecast has been prepared. (SIR 3000.3)**

42. The reporting accountant considers the business analysis carried out by the preparer of the profit forecast and whether there is prima facie evidence that it has been used by the directors in compiling the profit forecast. The extent and nature of the analysis that is necessary to support a forecast, and therefore the extent of the reporting accountant's consideration of such analysis, will be dependent upon the specific circumstances in which the forecast is being prepared. The reporting accountant discusses the preparer's plans, strategies and risk analysis with the preparer of the profit forecast, considers documentary support for them and assesses whether they are consistent with the analysis of the business. Where the outcome is dependent upon the intent of the directors and management the reporting accountant will ordinarily obtain representations from the directors concerning such matters.

43. The preparer can be expected to document the assumptions that have been made relating to matters significant to the profit forecast. The reporting accountant will, therefore, obtain from preparers of the profit forecast details of those assumptions

identified as being relevant to the compilation of the profit forecast. It will usually be the case that not all of the assumptions made in support of the profit forecast will be published. This is because only those that are material to an understanding of the profit forecast are required to be disclosed.

44. There may be a range of appropriate assumptions which can be used as the basis for a profit forecast and the resulting forecast may differ significantly depending on which assumptions are adopted. The reporting accountant is not required to express an opinion on the appropriateness of the assumptions used or the achievability of the results reflected in a profit forecast. The reporting accountant does however:

   (a) consider if any of the assumptions adopted by the directors which, in the opinion of the reporting accountant are necessary for a proper understanding of the profit forecast, have not been adequately disclosed; and

   (b) consider whether any material assumption made by the directors appears to be unrealistic.

45. When checking whether the profit forecast has been accurately computed the reporting accountant considers whether cash flow statements and balance sheets have been prepared to act as checks against omissions and inconsistencies. If cash flow statements and balance sheets have not been prepared, in circumstances where the reporting accountant considers this to be necessary, the reporting accountant discusses with the directors whether their preparation is necessary in order to properly compile the profit forecast.

Historical financial information

46. **When evaluating the basis on which any historical financial information included in the profit forecast has been prepared the reporting accountant should:**

   (a) **consider whether any element of that historical financial information has been audited or reviewed by the auditors and, if so, the results of that audit or review;**

   (b) **evaluate the suitability of unaudited historical financial information included in the profit forecast;**

   (c) **evaluate how the historical financial information has been embodied into the profit forecast; and**

   (d) **if adjustments have been made to previously published historical financial information evaluate whether the adjustments appear appropriate in the circumstances. (SIR 3000.4)**

47. If historical financial information has been audited or reviewed the reporting accountant evaluates the scope of the audit or review procedures performed. In performing such an evaluation the reporting accountant ordinarily seeks access to the working papers of the auditor or reviewer and considers whether the results of those

procedures indicate that the historical financial information may be unreliable or reveal uncertainties that ought to require the directors to make and disclose assumptions in the forecast.

48. In order to evaluate the suitability of unaudited historical financial information included in the profit forecast the reporting accountant[11]:

   (a) understands the internal control environment of the entity relevant to the historical financial information;

   (b) discusses with the management of the issuer the accounting policies applied and any differences from the method of preparing the entity's published financial statements;

   (c) enquires of management, including internal audit, whether there have been any changes in the financial reporting systems or internal controls, or any breakdowns in systems and controls, which might affect the reliability of the financial information;

   (d) enquires about changes in the entity's procedures for recording, classifying and summarising transactions, accumulating information for disclosure, and preparing the financial information;

   (e) considers the accuracy of unaudited historical financial information by comparing it to audited financial statements for the same period;

   (f) compares the historical financial information to previous budgets or forecasts prepared by the entity in respect of the period covered by the historical financial information and gains an understanding of the reasons for any significant differences; and

   (g) checks the historical financial information used in the profit forecast agrees to, or reconciles with, the underlying accounting records of the entity.

49. Where the reporting accountant determines that it is not able to obtain sufficient appropriate evidence from the above procedures to indicate that the financial information for the expired part of the forecast period forms a suitable basis for inclusion in the profit forecast the reporting accountant discusses the matter with the directors of the issuer and, if appropriate, the issuer's advisers.

50. In considering historical financial information included in a profit forecast, it is important that the reporting accountant understands the manner in which such information has been included in the profit forecast. Where different systems or processes have been used to produce prospective financial information and the historical information, there is a risk that there may be inconsistencies in the cut-off

---

[11] Some of these procedures may already have been performed as part of a review.

between these two sources of information which could lead to a material error in the compilation of the profit forecast.

Consistent accounting policies

51. **The reporting accountant should compare the accounting policies used in connection with the profit forecast with those used by the entity in preparing the most recent historical financial information in the investment circular, and evaluate whether they are consistent with each other and continue to be appropriate so far as concerns the profit forecast. (SIR 3000.5)**

52. Where the profit forecast relates to the expansion of an existing business the reporting accountant's primary consideration is the consistency of the accounting policies used. However, the reporting accountant also considers the ongoing appropriateness of the accounting policies in the light of the business plans underlying the profit forecast.

53. Where the profit forecast relates to a start-up situation the reporting accountant considers the appropriateness of the accounting policies chosen.

Presentation of the profit forecast

54. **The reporting accountant should consider whether it has become aware of anything to cause it to believe that:**

    (a) **the profit forecast is presented in a way that is not understandable;**

    (b) **a material assumption is unrealistic;**

    (c) **an assumption or other information which appears to it to be material to a proper understanding of the profit forecast has not been disclosed; or**

    (d) **the profit forecast is not capable of subsequently being compared with historical financial information.**

    If the reporting accountant is aware of such matters it should discuss them with the parties responsible for the profit forecast and with those persons to whom its report is to be addressed and consider whether it is able to issue its opinion. (SIR 3000.6)

55. The ICAEW Guidance provides guidance to directors with regard to the matters that should be disclosed in connection with a profit forecast. This covers both the manner in which the profit forecast is presented and the use of disclosure to deal with uncertainty. It is important that useful information is not obscured through the inclusion of immaterial items or the use of headings or financial measures which are not meaningful to, or may be misunderstood by, the intended users.

56. When evaluating the presentation of a profit forecast the reporting accountant considers whether the components of the profit forecast are clearly described and whether the descriptions are adequate to allow an intended user to understand the

profit forecast. For example, if a profit forecast is presented as a single figure for profit before tax, and this was to be achieved by the inclusion of a significant non-recurring profit from the sale of a fixed asset, consideration is given as to whether additional disclosure is necessary to make the profit forecast understandable.

57. When evaluating whether the disclosures made in respect of a profit forecast are sufficient to make it understandable, the reporting accountant considers whether the degree of uncertainty inherent in the information is clearly disclosed. Disclosure of an assumption may not make the profit forecast understandable if the significance of that assumption is not apparent from the disclosure made.

58. Where a profit forecast is subject to significant uncertainty it is common practice for the preparers to perform a sensitivity analysis in respect of those assumptions which are either believed to be subject to the greatest uncertainty and/or where the profit forecast is most sensitive to variations in such assumptions. The reporting accountant considers such sensitivity analysis, as it may assist in the identification of material assumptions or other aspects of the profit forecast where the uncertainty requires additional disclosure to enable it to be understood.

59. The manner in which the profit forecast is presented in the investment circular will also be considered in respect of whether the profit forecast is capable of being compared with subsequent historical financial information. The choice of captions and disclosure or emphasis of particular numbers or attributes may determine how the profit forecast will be interpreted and consideration is given as to whether this is consistent with the purpose for which the profit forecast has been prepared.

Representation letter

60. SIR 1000.13 sets out the basic principles and essential procedures, with respect to representation letters, that are applicable to all engagements involving an investment circular. Examples of representation letter clauses are set out in Appendix 5 of this SIR.

61. Some of the assumptions used in the compilation of a profit forecast will be dependent on the intent of the directors and management. Consequently the representations of directors and management as to their intent are a particularly important source of evidence for the reporting accountant.

Documentation

62. SIR 1000.14 and SIR 1000.15 set out the basic principles and essential procedures with respect to the reporting accountant's working papers.

Professional scepticism

63. SIR 1000.16 sets out the basic principle with respect to the attitude of professional scepticism adopted by the reporting accountant in planning and performing an engagement.

Reporting

64. SIR 1000.17, SIR 1000.18 and SIR 1000.19 set out the basic principles and essential procedures, with respect to reporting, that are applicable to all engagements involving an investment circular. Additional basic principles and essential procedures relating to engagements to report on profit forecasts are set out below.

Responsibilities

65. **In all reports on profit forecasts in investment circulars the reporting accountant should explain the extent of its responsibility in respect of the profit forecast by including in its report:**

   (a) **a statement that the reporting accountant's responsibility is to form an opinion (as required by the relevant regulatory requirement) on the compilation of the profit forecast and to report its opinion to the addressees of the report; and**

   (b) **a statement that the profit forecast and the assumptions on which it is based are the responsibility of the directors. (SIR 3000.7)**

Basis of preparation of the profit forecast

66. **The reporting accountant should include a basis of preparation section of its report that cross refers to disclosures that explain the basis of preparation of the profit forecast including:**

   (a) **assumptions made;**

   (b) **the accounting policies applied; and**

   (c) **where appropriate, the source of historical financial information embodied in the profit forecast. (SIR 3000.8)**

67. Where the entity is reporting on the expansion of an established business it is usual for it to report that the basis of accounting is consistent with the existing accounting policies. Where the accounting policies used in the profit forecast differ from those previously published a more detailed explanation of the accounting policies used in the preparation of the profit forecast will be appropriate.

Basis of opinion

68. SIR 1000.18 sets out the basic principles and essential procedures, with respect to the basis of the reporting accountant's opinion, that are applicable to all engagements involving an investment circular. Additional basic principles and essential procedures relating to engagements to report on profit forecasts are set out below.

69. **The reporting accountant should explain the basis of its opinion by including in its report a statement that where the profit forecast and any assumptions on which it**

is based relate to the future and may, therefore, be affected by unforeseen events, the reporting accountant does not express any opinion as to whether the actual results achieved will correspond to those shown in the profit forecast. (SIR 3000.9)

70. By its nature financial information relating to the future is inherently uncertain. For a profit forecast to be understandable sufficient information must be disclosed to allow an intended user to understand this uncertainty. As the reporting accountant is not required to form or express an opinion on the achievability of the result shown in the profit forecast, it is inappropriate for the reporting accountant to include in the basis of preparation section of its report cautionary language relating to uncertainty beyond that referred to above.

Expression of opinion

71. **The report should contain a clear expression of opinion that complies with applicable regulatory requirements. (SIR 3000.10)**

72. In forming its opinion the reporting accountant takes account of those events or information which the reporting accountant becomes aware of occurring up to the date on which the reporting accountant signs the report, that affect the opinion expressed in the report.

73. The investment circular in which the reporting accountant's report is included may be made available in other countries, such as the United States of America, which have their own standards for accountants when reporting on profit forecasts. In such circumstances, the reporting accountant considers whether to include a reference to the fact that a report issued in accordance with the SIRs should not be relied upon as if it had been issued in accordance with the standards applicable in that other country. An example of such a reference is included in the example reports set out in Appendices 6 and 7 of this SIR.

Modified opinions

74. SIR 1000.20 sets out the basic principles and essential procedures, with respect to modified opinions, that are applicable to all engagements involving an investment circular. Additional basic principles and essential procedures relating to engagements to report on profit forecasts are set out below.

75. **The reporting accountant should not express an unmodified opinion when the directors have not applied the criteria set out in Appendix 2 of this SIR and in the reporting accountant's judgment the effect of not doing so is, or may be, material. (SIR 3000.11)**

76. The PD and other regulations, such as the City Code, usually require a positive and unmodified opinion. Consequently, in the event that the reporting accountant concludes that it is unable to report in the manner prescribed it invites those responsible for the profit forecast to consider whether the profit forecast can be

amended to alleviate its concerns or whether the profit forecast should be omitted from the investment circular.

77. Examples of reports on a profit forecast and a profit estimate expressing such positive and unmodified opinions are set out in Appendices 6 and 7 of this SIR.

Consent

78. SIR 1000.21 and SIR 1000.22 set out the basic principles and essential procedures with respect to the giving of consent by the reporting accountant.

79. The reporting accountant considers whether disclosures in the investment circular, such as those in the "Risk Factors" section, are consistent with the assumptions and other disclosures made in connection with the profit forecast before consent is given by the reporting accountant to its report on the profit forecast being included in the investment circular.

Events occurring between the date of the reporting accountant's report and the completion date of the transaction

80. SIR 1000.23 sets out the basic principles and essential procedures with respect to events occurring between the date of the reporting accountant's report and the completion date of the transaction.

81. Under Sections 81 and 87G of the FSMA, Prospectus Rule 3.4, and Listing Rule 4.4.1, a supplementary investment circular must be prepared if, after the date the investment circular has been formally approved by a regulator and before dealings in the relevant securities commence, the issuer becomes aware that there has been a significant change affecting any matter contained in the document or a significant new matter has arisen, the inclusion of information in respect of which would have been required if it had arisen at the time of its preparation. A similar obligation arises under Article 16 of the Prospectus Directive in respect of the period following registration of the investment circular during which an agreement in respect of the securities can be entered into in pursuance of the offer contained in the investment circular.

82. If, as a result of discussion with those responsible for the investment circular concerning an event that occurred prior to the completion date of the transaction, the reporting accountant is either uncertain about or disagrees with the course of action proposed the reporting accountant may consider it necessary to take legal advice with respect to its responsibilities in the particular circumstances.

83. After the date of its report, the reporting accountant has no obligation to perform procedures or make enquiries regarding the investment circular.

Effective date

84. A reporting accountant is required to comply with the Investment Reporting Standards contained in this SIR for reports signed after 31 March 2006. Earlier adoption is encouraged.

Appendix 1

THE REGULATORY BACKGROUND

Prospectus Directive Requirements

The **Prospectus Directive** and **PD Regulation** determine the requirements for the content of a prospectus. In determining whether the PD Regulation has been complied with, the FSA will take into account whether a person has complied with the CESR Recommendations.

The PD Regulation requires that where an issuer chooses to include a profit forecast (including a profit estimate) in a prospectus it must:

(a) be prepared on a basis comparable with the historical financial information in the prospectus;

(b) include a statement setting out the principal assumptions upon which the issuer has based its forecast or estimate. There must be a clear distinction between assumptions about factors which the members of the administrative, management or supervisory bodies can influence and assumptions about factors which are exclusively outside the influence of the members of the administrative, management or supervisory bodies; the assumptions must be readily understandable by investors, be specific and precise and not relate to the general accuracy of the estimates underlying the forecast; and

(c) other than for issuers of high denomination debt and derivative securities, include a report prepared by independent accountants or auditors stating that in their opinion the forecast or estimate has been properly compiled on the basis stated and that the basis of accounting used for the profit forecast or estimate is consistent with the accounting policies of the issuer.

The CESR Recommendations provide further guidance concerning the principles that should be applied in preparing a profit forecast in a prospectus. In addition to due care and diligence being taken to ensure that profit forecasts or estimates are not misleading to investors, the following principles should be taken into consideration when profit forecasts are being compiled. Profit forecasts and estimates should be:

(a) *reliable* - they should be supported by a thorough analysis of the issuer's business and should represent factual and not hypothetical strategies, plans and risk analysis; (a criterion for a reporting accountant see Appendix 2 of this SIR)

(b) *understandable* - they should contain disclosure that is not too complex or extensive for investors to understand; (a criterion for a reporting accountant see Appendix 2 of this SIR)

(c) *comparable* - they should be capable of justification by comparison with outcomes in the form of historical financial information (a criterion for a reporting accountant see Appendix 2 of this SIR); and

(d) **relevant** - they must have an ability to influence economic decisions of investors and provided on a timely basis so as to influence such decisions and assist in confirming or correcting past evaluations or assessments. (Not a criterion for a reporting accountant see paragraph 11 of this SIR).

The City Code

The City Code requires that:

(a) all communications to shareholders in an offer, including forecasts, must maintain the highest standard of accuracy and fair presentation;

(b) assumptions should be drafted in a way that allows shareholders to understand their implications; and

(c) the forecast is compiled with due care and consideration by the directors and the disclosure of assumptions should provide useful information to assist shareholders to help them to form a view as to the reasonableness and reliability of the forecast.

Notes 1(c) and (d) to Rule 28.2 of the City Code state:

"The forecast and the assumptions on which it is based are the sole responsibility of the directors. However, a duty is placed on the financial advisers to discuss the assumptions with their client and to satisfy themselves that the forecast has been made with due care and consideration. Auditors or consultant accountants must satisfy themselves that the forecast, so far as the accounting policies and calculations are concerned, has been properly compiled on the basis of the assumptions made.

Although the accountants have no responsibility for the assumptions, they will as a result of their review be in a position to advise the company on what assumptions should be listed in the circular and the way in which they should be described. The financial advisers and accountants obviously have substantial influence on the information about assumptions to be given in the circular; neither should allow an assumption to be published which appears to be unrealistic, or one to be omitted which appears to be important, without commenting appropriately in its report".

Whilst the City Code does not explicitly identify the principles contained in the CESR Recommendations those principles are consistent with the requirement of the Code.

REPORTING ACCOUNTANT'S CRITERIA

	PD Regulation	Annex I[1] of PD Regulation	CESR Recommendations
A statement setting out the principal assumptions upon which the issuer has based its forecast or estimate.		13.1	
There must be a clear distinction between assumptions about factors which the members of the administrative, management or supervisory bodies can influence and assumptions about factors which are exclusively outside the influence of the members of the administrative, management or supervisory bodies; the assumptions must be readily understandable by investors, be specific and precise and not relate to the general accuracy of the estimates underlying the forecast.		13.1	
The profit forecast or estimate must be prepared on a basis comparable with the historical financial information.		13.3	
The following principles should be taken into consideration when profit forecasts or estimates are being compiled. Profit forecasts or estimates should be • **Understandable,** ie Profit forecasts or estimates should contain disclosure that is not too complex or extensive for investors to understand; • **Reliable,** ie Profit forecasts should be supported by a thorough analysis of the issuer's business and should represent factual and not hypothetical strategies, plans and risk analysis; • **Comparable,** ie Profit forecasts or estimates should be capable of justification by comparison with outcomes in the form of historical financial information;			para 41

[1] The column illustrates Annex I as an example. Other annexes to the PD Regulation contain identical requirements with respect to profit forecasts. See Appendix 1 of SIR 1000.

Appendix 3

OTHER REGULATORY PROVISIONS RELEVANT TO THE PREPARERS OF PROFIT FORECASTS

	PD Regulation	Annex I of PD Regulation	CESR Recommendations
(8) Voluntary disclosure of profit forecasts in a share registration document should be presented in a consistent and comparable manner and accompanied by a statement prepared by independent accountants or auditors. This information should not be confused with the disclosure of known trends or other factual data with material impact on the issuer's prospects. Moreover, they should provide an explanation of any changes in disclosure policy relating to profit forecasts when supplementing a prospectus or drafting a new prospectus.	Recital 8		
Profit forecast means a form of words which expressly states or by implication indicates a figure or a minimum or maximum figure for the likely level of profits or losses for the current financial period and/or financial periods subsequent to that period, or contains data from which a calculation of such a figure for future profits or losses may be made, even if no particular figure is mentioned and the word "profit" is not used.	Article 2		
Profit estimate means a profit forecast for a financial period which has expired and for which results have not yet been published.	Article 2		
If an issuer chooses to include a profit forecast or profit estimate the registration document must contain the information set out in items 13.1 and 13.2.		13	
A report prepared by independent accountants or auditors stating that in the opinion of the independent accountants or auditors the forecast or estimate has been properly compiled on the basis stated and that the basis of accounting used for the profit forecast or estimate is consistent with the accounting policies of the issuer.		13.2	

	PD Regulation	Annex I of PD Regulation	CESR Recommendations
If a profit forecast in a prospectus has been published which is still outstanding, then provide a statement setting out whether or not that forecast is still correct as at the time of the registration document, and an explanation of why such forecast is no longer valid if that is the case.		13.4	
The inclusion of a profit forecast or estimate in a prospectus is the responsibility of the issuer and persons responsible for the prospectus and due care and diligence must be taken to ensure that profit forecasts or estimates are not misleading to investors.			para 40
The following principles should be taken into consideration when profit forecasts or estimates are being compiled. Profit forecasts or estimates should be • **Relevant,** ie profit forecasts and estimates must have an ability to influence economic decisions of investors and provided on a timely basis so as to influence such decisions and assist in confirming or correcting past evaluations or assessments.			para 41
Where an issuer provides a profit forecast or estimate in a registration document, if the related schedules so requires, it must be reported on by independent accountants or auditors in the registration document (as described in item 13.2 of Annex I of the Regulation). Where the issuer does not produce a single prospectus, upon the issuance of the securities note and summary at a later time, the issuer should either: • Confirm the profit forecasts or estimates; or • State that the profit forecasts or estimates are no longer valid or correct; or • Make appropriate alteration of profit forecasts or estimates. In this case they must be reported upon as described in item 13.2 of Annex I of the Regulation.			para 42
If an issuer has made a statement other than in a previous prospectus that would constitute a profit forecast or estimate if made in a prospectus, for instance, in a regulatory announcement, and that statement is still outstanding at the time of publication of the prospectus, the issuer should consider whether the forecasts or estimates are still material and valid and choose whether or not to include them in the prospectus. CESR considers that there is a presumption that an outstanding forecast made other than in a previous prospectus will be material in the case of share issues (especially in the context of an IPO). This is not necessarily the presumption in case of non-equity securities.			paras 43 & 44

	PD Regulation	Annex I of PD Regulation	CESR Recommendations
When there is an outstanding profit forecast or estimate in relation to a material undertaking which the issuer has acquired, the issuer should consider whether it is appropriate to make a statement as to whether or not the profit forecast or estimate is still valid or correct. The issuer should also evaluate the effects of the acquisition and the profit forecast made by that undertaking on its own financial position and report on it as it would have done if the profit forecast or estimate had been made by the issuer.			paras 45 & 46
The forecast or estimate should normally be of profit before tax (disclosing separately any non-recurrent items and tax charges if they are expected to be abnormally high or low). If the forecast or estimate is not of profit before tax, the reasons for presenting another figure from the profit and loss account must be disclosed and clearly explained. Furthermore the tax effect should be clearly explained. When the results are published relating to a period covered by a forecast or estimate, the published financial statements must disclose the relevant figure so as to enable the forecast and actual results to be directly compared.			paras 47 & 48
CESR recognises that often in practice, there is a fine line between what constitutes a profit forecast and what constitutes trend information as detailed in item 12 of Annex I of the Regulation. A general discussion about the future or prospects of the issuer under trend information will not normally constitute a profit forecast or estimate as defined in Articles 2.10 and 2.11 of the Regulation. Whether or not a statement constitutes profit forecasts or estimates is a question of fact and will depend upon the circumstances of the particular issuer.			para 49
This is a non-exhaustive list of factors that an issuer is expected to take into consideration when preparing forecasts: • Past results, market analysis, strategic evolutions, market share and position of the issuer • Financial position and possible changes therein • Description of the impact of an acquisition or disposal, change in strategy or any major change in environmental matters and technology • Changes in legal and tax environment • Commitments towards third parties.			para 50

Appendix 4

EXAMPLES OF ENGAGEMENT LETTER CLAUSES

The examples of engagement letter clauses are intended for consideration in the context of a public reporting engagement on a profit forecast. They should be tailored to the specific circumstances and supplemented by such other clauses as are relevant and appropriate.

Financial information upon which the report is to be given

The [investment circular] will contain a profit [forecast] [estimate] for the company for the period [ending] [ended] [date] (the "PFI") prepared and presented in accordance with [item 13 of Annex I of the PD Regulation] [the requirements of the City Code] [other applicable regulation]. We will prepare a report on the profit [forecast] [estimate] addressed to [...] expressing our opinion on the profit [forecast] [estimate], in the form described below, to be included in the [investment circular].

We will ask the Directors to make certain representations to us regarding the PFI. If the PFI is intended only to be a hypothetical illustration, or the Directors are unable to make such representations to us, we will not wish to be associated with the PFI and accordingly, will be unable to report publicly on it.

Responsibilities

The preparation and presentation of the profit forecast will be the responsibility solely of the Directors. [This responsibility includes the identification and disclosure of the assumptions underlying the profit forecast. (omit if no assumptions)] The Directors are also responsible for ensuring that the PFI is prepared and presented in accordance with [item 13 of Annex I of the PD Regulation] [the requirements of the City Code] [other applicable regulation].

We will require the Directors to formally adopt the PFI before we report on it. We understand that the Directors will have regard to the guidance issued by The Institute of Chartered Accountants in England & Wales entitled "Prospective Financial Information – Guidance for UK directors" in preparing the PFI.

It is our responsibility to form an opinion as to whether the profit [forecast] [estimate] has been properly compiled on the basis stated and whether such basis is consistent with the accounting policies normally adopted by ABC plc.

If the results of our work are satisfactory, and having regard to the requirements of [item 13.2 of Annex I of the PD Regulation] [the City Code] [other applicable regulation], we shall prepare a report on the profit [forecast] [estimate] for inclusion in the [investment circular]. An illustration of the form of our report is attached.

Scope of work

Our work will be undertaken in accordance with Standard for Investment Reporting (SIR) 3000 "Investment Reporting Standards Applicable to Public Reporting Engagements on Profit Forecasts" issued by the Auditing Practices Board and will be subject to the limitations described therein.

We draw your attention in particular to paragraph 75 of SIR 3000 which would preclude us from expressing any opinion if the Directors have not complied with the regulatory requirements set out in Appendix 2 of that SIR.

As the purpose of our engagement is restricted as described above and since the PFI and the assumptions on which it is based relate to the future and may be affected by unforeseen events, we will not provide any opinion as to how closely the actual result achieved will correspond to the profit [forecast] [estimate]. Accordingly we neither confirm nor otherwise accept responsibility for the ultimate accuracy and achievability of the PFI.

Assumptions

We will discuss the assumptions with the persons responsible for preparing the PFI together with the evidence they have to support the assumptions, but we will not seek to independently verify or audit those assumptions. We are not responsible for identifying the assumptions.

In the event that anything comes to our attention to indicate that any of the assumptions adopted by the Directors which, in our opinion, are necessary for a proper understanding of the PFI have not been disclosed or if any material assumption made by the Directors appears to us to be unrealistic we will inform the directors so that steps can be taken to resolve the matter. However, we are required to comment in our report if an assumption is published which appears to us to be unrealistic or an assumption is omitted which appears to us to be important to an understanding of the PFI.

Appendix 5

EXAMPLES OF MANAGEMENT REPRESENTATION LETTER CLAUSES

Similar clauses to those below could be amended to be used in connection with a report on a profit estimate.

Introduction

We refer to the forecast of *[insert description of items forecast]*, profit for the financial year and earnings per share of ABC plc ("the Company") and its subsidiaries together ("the ABC Group") for the year ending *[date]* ("the profit forecast") set out on page [•] of the [Prospectus]/[Circular]/[Offer Document] to be issued on *[date]*. We acknowledge that we are solely responsible for the profit forecast and the assumptions on which it is based as set out on page [•] and confirm on behalf of the Directors [and Proposed Directors] of the Company to the best of our knowledge and belief, having made appropriate enquiries of officials of the Company, the following representations made to you in the course of your work:

Specific representations

* The profit forecast is based on our assessment of the financial position and results of operations and cash flow for the period and is presented on a basis consistent with the accounting policies [normally] [to be] adopted by the ABC Group and has been prepared in accordance with relevant legislative requirements.[1]

* We believe the forecast results are likely to be achieved although achievement of the forecast may be favourably or unfavourably affected by unforeseeable and uncontrollable events.

* We have made available to you all significant information relevant to the profit forecast of which we have knowledge.

* All significant assumptions have been disclosed and the assumptions underlying the profit forecast are reasonable and appropriate.

* The results shown in the [audited/unaudited] financial results for the six months ended *[date]* and the unaudited management accounts for the [•] months ended *[date]* which are included in the profit forecast have been prepared in accordance with the accounting policies [normally] [to be] adopted by the ABC Group and are free from material misstatement.

---

[1] The reporting accountant may also wish to obtain a representation that the profit forecast has been prepared in accordance with 'Prospective Financial Information - Guidance for UK directors' published by the Institute of Chartered Accountants in England and Wales.

- There are no contingencies, (other than those which have been taken into account in making the forecast), that are material in the context of the profit forecast which should be disclosed or taken into account in the profit forecast.

- The profit forecast is presented in a manner which is balanced and fair and not misleading and contains all information necessary for a proper understanding of the profit forecast.

- The profit forecast together with the assumptions and the representations in this letter have been approved by the board of directors.

Representations in respect of specific assumptions such as;

- The assumed like for like increase in sales of 5% in the last quarter of 200X incorporates expected price increases of 2% based on preliminary discussions with three of our major customers.

- The assumed increase in gross margin of 2 percentage points from 1 July 200X is based on manufacturing cost savings as a result of the realisation of efficiencies resulting from the factory reorganisation which we expect to be completed by the end of May 200X.

- The assumed increase in sales prices by 2% more than the general level of inflation in 200Y is based upon the expectation that our major competitor will announce a price increase of at least that amount in November 200X. Our expectation takes account of similar timing of increases in previous years and information derived from conversations with mutual customers.

- The opening of two new sales outlets in the current financial year assumes that negotiations to agree a lease on one out of the three potential units in Guildford will be completed and that refitting and pre-opening will be completed within 10 weeks which is 25% longer than the historical average due to additional building works being required in one of the potential sites.

- The profit forecast assumes that a forward sale of $x million will be designated as a hedge against expected US$ income.

Appendix 6

EXAMPLE OF A REPORT ON A PROFIT FORECAST

Date

Reporting accountant's address

Addressees, as agreed between the parties in the engagement letter

Dear Sirs

[ABC plc]

We report on the profit forecast comprising [*insert description of items comprising the prospective financial information, e.g.* [forecast of turnover, operating profit, profit before tax and earnings per share]/[projected profit and loss account]] of ABC plc ("the Company") and its subsidiaries (together "the ABC Group") for the [*specify period*] ending [*date*] (the "Profit Forecast"). The Profit Forecast, and the material assumptions upon which it is based, are set out on pages [•] to [•] of the [*describe document*] ("the [Document]") issued by the Company dated [*date*]. This report is required by [Relevant Regulation] [guidance issued by the London Stock Exchange with respect to the AIM market] and is given for the purpose of complying with that [Relevant Regulation] [guidance issued by the London Stock Exchange] and for no other purpose.

[*Substitute the following text for the last sentence of the immediately preceding paragraph, where a profit forecast is made by an offeree in the context of a takeover.* This report is required by Rule 28.3(b) of the City Code and is given for the purpose of complying with that rule and for no other purpose. Accordingly, we assume no responsibility in respect of this report to the Offeror or any person connected to, or acting in concert with, the Offeror or to any other person who is seeking or may in future seek to acquire control of the Company (an "Alternative Offeror") or to any other person connected to, or acting in concert with, an Alternative Offeror.]

Responsibilities

It is the responsibility of the Directors of ABC plc to prepare the Profit Forecast in accordance with the requirements of the [PD Regulation]/[Listing Rules]/[City Code] [guidance issued by the London Stock Exchange].

It is our responsibility to form an opinion as required by the [PD Regulation]/[Listing Rules]/ [City Code] [guidance issued by the London Stock Exchange] as to the proper compilation of the Profit Forecast and to report that opinion to you.

Basis of preparation of the Profit Forecast

The Profit Forecast has been prepared on the basis stated on page [ ] of the [Document][1] and is based on the [audited/unaudited] interim financial results for the [six] months ended [date], the unaudited management accounts for the [x] months ended [date] and a forecast to [date]. The Profit Forecast is required to be presented on a basis consistent with the accounting policies of the ABC Group.

Basis of opinion

We conducted our work in accordance with the Standards for Investment Reporting issued by the Auditing Practices Board in the United Kingdom. Our work included [evaluating the basis on which the historical financial information included in the Profit Forecast has been prepared and] considering whether the Profit Forecast has been accurately computed based upon the disclosed assumptions and the accounting policies of the ABC Group. Whilst the assumptions upon which the Profit Forecast are based are solely the responsibility of the Directors, we considered whether anything came to our attention to indicate that any of the assumptions adopted by the Directors which, in our opinion, are necessary for a proper understanding of the Profit Forecast have not been disclosed and whether any material assumption made by the Directors appears to us to be unrealistic.

We planned and performed our work so as to obtain the information and explanations we considered necessary in order to provide us with reasonable assurance that the Profit Forecast has been properly compiled on the basis stated.

Since the Profit Forecast and the assumptions on which it is based relate to the future and may therefore be affected by unforeseen events, we can express no opinion as to whether the actual results reported will correspond to those shown in the Profit Forecast and differences may be material.

[*This paragraph may be omitted if the document is not to be distributed outside the UK* - Our work has not been carried out in accordance with auditing or other standards and practices generally accepted in the United States of America [or other jurisdictions] and accordingly should not be relied upon as if it had been carried out in accordance with those standards and practices.]

---

[1] The disclosures presented with the profit forecast should explain the basis on which the forecast has been prepared. This will include identification of the accounting policies used and the financial information used in compiling the forecast. Typically this may include reference to audited/unaudited financial statements of the entity for an interim period, unaudited management accounts and management's forecast for the period for which no management accounts are available.

Opinion

In our opinion, the Profit Forecast has been properly compiled on the basis [stated] [of the assumptions made by the Directors/][2] and the basis of accounting used is consistent with the accounting policies of the ABC Group[3].

Declaration[4]

For the purposes of [Prospectus Rule [5.5.3R(2)(f)] [5.5.4R(2)(f)] [guidance issued by the London Stock Exchange] we are responsible for [this report as part] [the following part(s) of the [prospectus] [registration document] [AIM admission document] and declare that we have taken all reasonable care to ensure that the information contained [in this report] [those parts] is, to the best of our knowledge, in accordance with the facts and contains no omission likely to affect its import. This declaration is included in the [prospectus] [registration document] [AIM admission document] in compliance with [item 1.2 of annex I of the PD Regulation] [item 1.2 of annex III of the PD Regulation] [guidance issued by the London Stock Exchange].

Yours faithfully

Reporting Accountant

---

[2] The City Code requires 'on the basis of the assumptions made by the Directors' but the PD Regulation requires 'on the basis stated'.

[3] Where the accounting policies used in the profit forecast either differ from those used by the company in its latest published financial statements or where the company has never published financial statements reference should be made to the accounting policies which have been used.

[4] This declaration is a requirement of the PD Regulation and is appropriate for inclusion when the report is included in a Prospectus, see Appendix 2 of SIR 1000.

Appendix 7

EXAMPLE OF A REPORT ON A PROFIT ESTIMATE THAT IS NOT SUBJECT TO ASSUMPTIONS

Date

Reporting accountant's address

Addressees, as agreed between the parties in the engagement letter

Dear Sirs

[ABC plc]

We report on the profit estimate comprising [*insert description of items comprising the prospective financial information, e.g. [*estimate of turnover, operating profit, profit before tax and earnings per share*]//[estimated profit and loss account*]] of ABC plc ("the Company") and its subsidiaries (together "the ABC Group") for the [*specify period*] ended [*date*] (the "Profit Estimate"). The Profit Estimate and the basis on which it is prepared is set out on pages [•] to [•] of the [*describe document*] ("the [Document]") issued by the Company dated [*date*]. This report is required by [Relevant Regulation] [guidance issued by the London Stock Exchange with respect to the AIM market] and is given for the purpose of complying with that [Relevant Regulation] [guidance issued by the London Stock Exchange] and for no other purpose.

[*Substitute the following text for the last sentence of the immediately preceding paragraph, where a profit estimate is made by an offeree in the context of a takeover.* This report is required by Rule 28.3(b) of the City Code and is given for the purpose of complying with that rule and for no other purpose. Accordingly, we assume no responsibility in respect of this report to the Offeror or any person connected to, or acting in concert with, the Offeror or to any other person who is seeking or may in future seek to acquire control of the Company (an "Alternative Offeror") or to any other person connected to, or acting in concert with, an Alternative Offeror.]

Responsibilities

It is the responsibility of the directors of ABC plc to prepare the Profit Estimate in accordance with the requirements of the [PD Regulation]/[Listing Rules]/[City Code]. In preparing the Profit Estimate the directors of ABC plc are responsible for correcting errors that they have identified which may have arisen in unaudited financial results and unaudited management accounts used as the basis of preparation for the Profit Estimate.

It is our responsibility to form an opinion as required by the [PD Regulation]/[Listing Rules]/[City Code] as to the proper compilation of the Profit Estimate and to report that opinion to you.

Basis of preparation of the Profit Estimate

The Profit Estimate has been prepared on the basis stated on page [ ] of the [Document][1] and is based on the [audited/unaudited] interim financial results for the [six] months ended [date], the unaudited management accounts for the [x] months ended [date] and an estimate for the [month] to [date]. The Profit Estimate is required to be presented on a basis consistent with the accounting policies of the ABC Group.

Basis of opinion

We conducted our work in accordance with the Standards for Investment Reporting issued by the Auditing Practices Board in the United Kingdom. Our work included evaluating the basis on which the historical financial information for the [x] months to [date] included in the Profit Estimate has been prepared and considering whether the Profit Estimate has been accurately computed using that information and whether the basis of accounting used is consistent with the accounting policies of the ABC Group.

We planned and performed our work so as to obtain the information and explanations we considered necessary in order to provide us with reasonable assurance that the Profit Estimate has been properly compiled on the basis stated.

However, the Profit Estimate has not been audited. The actual results reported, therefore, may be affected by revisions required to accounting estimates due to changes in circumstances, the impact of unforeseen events and the correction of errors in the [interim financial results] [management accounts]. Consequently we can express no opinion as to whether the actual results achieved will correspond to those shown in the Profit Estimate and the difference may be material.

[*This paragraph may be omitted if the document is not to be distributed outside the UK* Our work has not been carried out in accordance with auditing or other standards and practices generally accepted in the United States of America [or other jurisdictions] and accordingly should not be relied upon as if it had been carried out in accordance with those standards and practices.]

Opinion

In our opinion, the Profit Estimate has been properly compiled on the basis stated and the basis of accounting used is consistent with the accounting policies of the ABC Group[2].

---

[1]   The disclosures presented with the profit estimate should explain the basis on which the estimate has been prepared. This will include identification of the accounting policies used and the financial information used in compiling the estimate. Typically this may include reference to audited/unaudited financial statements of the entity for an interim period, unaudited management accounts and management's estimate (which may itself be based on other forms of management information for the period for which no management accounts are available.

[2]   Where the accounting policies used in the profit estimate either differ from those used by the company in its latest published financial statements or where the company has never published financial statements reference should be made to the accounting policies which have been used.

Declaration[3]

For the purposes of [Prospectus Rule [5.5.3R(2)(f)] [5.5.4R(2)(f)] [guidance issued by the London Stock Exchange] we are responsible for [this report as part] [the following part(s) of the [prospectus] [registration document] [AIM admission document] and declare that we have taken all reasonable care to ensure that the information contained [in this report] [those parts] is, to the best of our knowledge, in accordance with the facts and contains no omission likely to affect its import. This declaration is included in the [prospectus] [registration document] [AIM admission document] in compliance with [item 1.2 of annex I of the PD Regulation] [item 1.2 of annex III of the PD Regulation] [guidance issued by the London Stock Exchange].

Yours faithfully

Reporting Accountant

---

[3] This declaration is a requirement of the PD Regulation and is appropriate for inclusion when the report is included in a Prospectus, see Appendix 2 of SIR 1000.

STANDARDS FOR INVESTMENT REPORTING

4000 – INVESTMENT REPORTING STANDARDS APPLICABLE TO PUBLIC REPORTING ENGAGEMENTS ON PRO FORMA FINANCIAL INFORMATION

CONTENTS

Appendices
1 *Reporting accountant's criteria*
2 *Other regulatory provisions relevant to the preparers of pro forma financial information*
3 *Examples of engagement letter clauses*
4 *Examples of management representation letter clauses*
5 *Example report on pro forma financial information in accordance with the PD Regulation
   or the Listing Rules*

ANNEXURE

Sections of TECH 18/98 "Pro forma financial information – Guidance for preparers
under the Listing Rules" (published by the Institute of Chartered Accountants in
England & Wales) that remain relevant

SIR 4000 contains basic principles and essential procedures ("Investment Reporting Standards"), indicated by paragraphs in bold type, with which a reporting accountant is required to comply in the conduct of an engagement to report on pro forma financial information, which is included within an investment circular prepared for issue in connection with a securities transaction governed wholly or in part by the laws and regulations of the United Kingdom.

SIR 4000 also includes explanatory and other material, including appendices, in the context of which the basic principles and essential procedures are to be understood and applied. It is necessary to consider the whole text of the SIR to understand and apply the basic principles and essential procedures.

For the purposes of the SIRs, an investment circular is defined as: "any document issued by an entity pursuant to statutory or regulatory requirements relating to listed or unlisted securities on which it is intended that a third party should make an investment decision, including a prospectus, listing particulars, circular to shareholders or similar document".

SIR 1000 "Investment reporting standards applicable to all engagements involving an investment circular" contains basic principles and essential procedures that are applicable to all engagements involving an investment circular. The definitions in the glossary of terms set out in Appendix 4 of SIR 1000 are to be applied in the interpretation of this and all other SIRs. Terms defined in the glossary are underlined the first time that they occur in the text.

To assist readers, SIRs contain references to, and extracts from, certain legislation and chapters of the Rules of the UK Listing Authority. Readers are cautioned that these references may change subsequent to publication.

Introduction

1. Standard for Investment Reporting (SIR) 1000 "Investment Reporting Standards applicable to all engagements in connection with an investment circular" establishes the Investment Reporting Standards applicable to all engagements involving investment circulars. The purpose of this SIR is to establish specific additional Investment Reporting Standards and provide guidance for a reporting accountant engaged to report publicly on pro forma financial information to be included in an investment circular under the PD Regulation, the Listing Rules[1], or if required by the London Stock Exchange in respect of an AIM Admission Document.

2. An engagement to report publicly on the proper compilation of pro forma financial information is a public reporting engagement as described in SIR 1000. The description of a public reporting engagement includes three generic terms having the following meanings in the context of an engagement to report on the proper compilation of pro forma financial information:

---

[1] In the UK the Prospectus Directive is implemented into law through amendments to Part VI of FSMA and to certain secondary legislation. The Annexes to the PD Regulation have been incorporated into the Prospectus Rules issued by the FSA.

(a) with respect to pro forma financial information the "**subject matter**" is the impact that the transaction, that is the subject of the investment circular, would have had on the earnings of the issuer (assuming that the transaction had been undertaken at the commencement of the financial period used for the illustration) or on the assets and liabilities of the issuer (assuming that the transaction had been undertaken at the end of the financial period used for the illustration);

(b) "**suitable criteria**" to be used by directors in the preparation of the pro forma financial information are provided by the requirements of the PD Regulation and the guidance issued by CESR[2] (CESR Recommendations). In forming its opinion as to whether the pro forma financial information has been properly compiled the reporting accountant considers whether certain of those criteria ("**reporting accountant's criteria**") have been properly applied. Reporting accountant's criteria are set out in Appendix 1 of this SIR; and

(c) with respect to pro forma financial information the "**outcome**"[3] is the pro forma financial information and related disclosures that are included in the investment circular and on which the reporting accountant expresses an opinion (in the "**reporting accountant's report**") as to whether that information is properly compiled on the basis stated and whether such basis is consistent with the accounting policies of the issuer.

The nature of pro forma financial information

3. For the purpose of this SIR "pro forma financial information" is defined to include financial information such as net assets, profit or cash flow statements that demonstrate the impact of a transaction on previously published financial information together with the explanatory notes thereto. Under item 1 of Annex II of the PD Regulation the pro forma financial information must be accompanied by introductory text describing the transaction, the businesses or entities involved, the period to which it refers and its purpose and limitations.

4. The Institute of Chartered Accountants in England and Wales (ICAEW) issued guidance entitled "Pro forma financial information - Guidance for preparers under the Listing Rules"[4] in September 1998 (the "ICAEW Guidance") to assist directors when preparing pro forma financial information for inclusion in documents subject to approval by the FSA prior to their issue. While aspects of this guidance remain of assistance to directors there are differences between the requirements of the PD Regulation, the CESR Recommendations and the requirements on which the ICAEW guidance was based. The Annexure has been prepared to assist in determining which parts of the ICAEW guidance continue to be relevant.

---

[2] CESR issued "CESR's Recommendations for the Consistent Implementation of the European Commission's Regulation on Prospectuses No. 809/2004" in February 2005.
[3] The "outcome" is sometimes described as "subject matter information".
[4] TECH 18/98

Compilation process

5. The compilation of pro forma information is the gathering, classification and summarisation of relevant financial information. The process followed by the preparer would be expected to include the following:

   (a) the accurate extraction of information from sources permitted under the PD Regulation;

   (b) the making of adjustments to the source information that are arithmetically correct, appropriate and complete for the purpose for which the pro forma financial information is presented;

   (c) arithmetic computation of the pro forma information;

   (d) consideration of accounting policies;

   (e) appropriate disclosure to enable the intended users to understand the pro forma financial information; and

   (f) appropriate consideration of the pro forma financial information and approval by the directors of the entity.

Engagement acceptance and continuance

6. SIR 1000.1 and SIR 1000.2 set out the basic principles and essential procedures, with respect to engagement acceptance and continuance, that are applicable to all engagements involving an investment circular.

7. When accepting or continuing an engagement to report publicly on pro forma information, the reporting accountant ascertains whether the directors intend to comply with all relevant regulatory requirements, in particular those that constitute the reporting accountant's criteria set out in Appendix 1 of this SIR.

Agreeing the terms of the engagement

8. SIR 1000.3 and SIR 1000.4 set out the basic principles and essential procedures with respect to agreeing the terms of the engagement. Examples of engagement letter clauses are set out in Appendix 3 of this SIR.

Ethical requirements

9. SIR 1000.5 sets out the basic principles and essential procedures with respect to the ethical requirements that apply to a reporting accountant[5].

Legal and regulatory requirements

10. The PD Regulation requires any pro forma financial information included in a prospectus to be reported on by independent accountants or auditors (referred to in this SIR as the "reporting accountant") and specifies the form of opinion to be given. The Listing Rules require any pro forma financial information included in a Class 1 circular to be reported on in the same way. References in the SIR to the PD Regulation apply equally to the Listing Rules where those Rules apply.

11. SIR 1000.6 sets out the basic principles with respect to the legal and regulatory requirements applicable to a reporting accountant.

12. Appendices 1 and 2 to this SIR set out those provisions of the PD Regulation and the CESR Recommendations, relating to the implementation of the Regulation, that provide the suitable criteria for directors. Those provisions that constitute criteria for a reporting accountant expressing an opinion on whether the pro forma information has been properly compiled are set out in Appendix 1 of this SIR.

Quality control

13. SIR 1000.7 and SIR 1000.8 set out the basic principles and essential procedures with respect to the quality control of engagements to report on pro forma financial information.

Planning and performing the engagement

14. SIR 1000.9 and SIR 1000.10 set out the basic principles and essential procedures with respect to the planning of all reporting engagements. Additional basic principles, essential procedures and guidance are set out below.

15. **The reporting accountant should obtain an understanding of the key factors affecting the subject matter sufficient to identify and assess the risk of the pro forma financial information not being properly compiled and sufficient to design and perform evidence gathering procedures including:**

    (a) the nature of the transaction being undertaken by the issuer;

---

[5] In January 2006 the APB issued an Exposure Draft of an Ethical Standard for Reporting Accountants (ESRA).

(b) the entity's business; and

(c) the procedures adopted, or planned to be adopted, by the directors for the preparation of the pro forma financial information. (SIR 4000.1)

16. The reporting accountant gains an understanding of the transaction, in respect of which the pro forma financial information is being prepared, by discussion with the directors or management of the issuer and by reading relevant supporting documentation.

17. The reporting accountant uses professional judgment to determine the extent of the understanding required of the entity's business.

18. Other matters for consideration by the reporting accountant include the availability of evidence to provide factual support for the proposed adjustments and the accounting policies that will form the basis of the adjustments to the pro forma financial information.

19. **The reporting accountant should consider materiality and public reporting engagement risk in planning its work in accordance with its instructions and in determining the effect of its findings on the report to be issued. (SIR 4000.2)**

Materiality

20. Matters are material if their omission or misstatement could, individually or collectively, influence the economic decisions of the intended users of the pro forma financial information. Materiality depends on the size and nature of the omission or misstatement judged in light of the surrounding circumstances. The size or nature of the matter, or a combination of both, could be the determining factor.

21. A misstatement in the context of the compilation of pro forma financial information includes, for example:

- Use of an inappropriate source for the unadjusted financial information.

- Incorrect extraction of the unadjusted financial information from an appropriate source.

- In relation to adjustments, the misapplication of accounting policies or failure to use the accounting policies adopted in the last, or to be adopted in the next, financial statements.

- Failure to make an adjustment required by the PD regulation.

- Making an adjustment that does not comply with the PD regulation.

- A mathematical or clerical mistake.

- Inadequate, or incorrect, disclosures.

22. Evaluating whether an omission or misstatement could influence economic decisions of the intended users of the pro forma financial information, and so be material, requires consideration of the characteristics of those intended users. The intended users are assumed to:

   (a) have a reasonable knowledge of business and economic activities and accounting and a willingness to study the pro forma financial information with reasonable diligence; and

   (b) make reasonable economic decisions on the basis of the pro forma financial information.

   The determination of materiality, therefore, takes into account how intended users with such characteristics could reasonably be expected to be influenced in making economic decisions.

Public reporting engagement risk

23. "Public reporting engagement risk" is the risk that the reporting accountant expresses an inappropriate opinion when the pro forma financial information has not been properly compiled on the basis stated or that basis is not consistent with the accounting policies of the issuer[6].

24. SIR 1000.11 and SIR 1000.12 set out the basic principles and essential procedures, with respect to obtaining evidence, that are applicable to all engagements involving an investment circular. Additional basic principles, essential procedures and guidance relating to engagements to report on pro forma financial information are set out below.

25. **The reporting accountant should obtain sufficient appropriate evidence that the pro forma financial information is free from material error in its compilation by:**

   (a) **checking that the unadjusted financial information of the issuer has been accurately extracted from a source that is both appropriate and in accordance with the relevant regulation;**

   (b) **obtaining evidence that the directors have applied the criteria set out in Appendix 1 of this SIR and, therefore, that the adjustments are appropriate and complete for the purpose for which the pro forma financial information is presented; and**

   (c) **checking that the calculations within the pro forma financial information are arithmetically correct. (SIR 4000.3)**

26. Item 5 of Annex II of the PD Regulation permits pro forma financial information to be published only in respect of:

---

[6] The PD Regulation requires a positive and unmodified opinion – for this reason there is no risk that the reporting accountant will inappropriately modify its opinion.

(a)   the current financial period;

(b)   the most recently completed financial period; and

(c)   the most recent interim period for which relevant unadjusted information has been or will be published or is being published in the same investment circular.

Unadjusted financial information of the issuer

27.   The reporting accountant considers whether the period in respect of which the pro forma financial information is proposed to be published is permitted under the PD Regulation. The reporting accountant also considers whether the source of the unadjusted financial information for the issuer is appropriate and whether the source of the unadjusted financial information is clearly stated.

28.   The reporting accountant is not required to perform specific procedures on the unadjusted financial information of the issuer other than as described in paragraph 27. However, if the reporting accountant has reason to believe that the unadjusted financial information is, or may be, unreliable, or if a report thereon has identified any uncertainties or disagreements, the reporting accountant considers the effect on the pro forma financial information.

29.   The reporting accountant checks the extraction of the unadjusted financial information from the source concerned.

Adjustments

30.   Item 6 of Annex II to the PD Regulation requires pro forma adjustments to be:

(a)   clearly shown and explained;

(b)   directly attributable to the transaction; and

(c)   factually supportable.

31.   In addition, in respect of a pro forma profit and loss or cash flow statement, they must be clearly identified as to those adjustments which are expected to have a continuing impact on the issuer and those which are not.

32.   More detailed guidance for directors concerning the implementation of these requirements is provided by the CESR Recommendations and those parts of the ICAEW Guidance that remain relevant (see Annexure).

33.   The reporting accountant considers the way in which the directors have fulfilled their responsibilities. With its understanding of the transaction and the entity's business as background the reporting accountant discusses with the directors the steps the directors have taken to identify relevant adjustments and whether such adjustments are permitted to be made.

34. If, as a result of these enquiries, the reporting accountant becomes aware of a significant adjustment which, in its opinion, ought to be made for the purposes of the pro forma financial information it discusses the position with the directors of the issuer and, if necessary, the issuer's advisers. If the reporting accountant is not able to agree with the directors and the issuer's advisers as to how the matter is to be resolved it considers the consequences for its report.

35. The reporting accountant considers the adjustments to assess whether they are "directly attributable" to the transaction whose impact is being illustrated by the pro forma financial information, that is, they are an integral part of the transaction concerned. If a potential adjustment is not directly attributable to the transaction or transactions described in the investment circular, it cannot be made (although it may be appropriate to disclose by way of note to the pro forma financial information the nature of a prohibited potential adjustment and the effect it would have had if it had been permissible to include it).

36. In assessing whether adjustments are directly attributable to the transaction the reporting accountant considers whether the adjustments relate to future events and/or decisions. This is because adjustments that are related to the transaction being illustrated but which are dependent on actions to be taken once the transaction has been completed, cannot be said to be "directly attributable".

37. The reporting accountant considers whether the adjustments have been clearly shown and explained and, in respect of a pro forma profit and loss or cash flow statement, whether they have been clearly identified as to those which are expected to have a continuing impact on the issuer (that is, relate to events or circumstances that are expected to recur) and to those which are not.

38. The reporting accountant obtains appropriate evidence that the directors of the issuer have factual support for each adjustment. Sources of such evidence would include published financial statements, other financial information or valuations disclosed elsewhere in the investment circular, purchase and sale agreements and other agreements relating to the transaction.

Omitted adjustments

39. In view of the specific restrictions on the nature of the adjustments permitted to be made under item 6 of Annex II of the PD Regulation, the directors may not be permitted to make all the adjustments that they would otherwise wish to. For example, an adjustment which is directly attributable but which is not factually supportable could not be included in pro forma financial information.

40. If any adjustments are excluded because of the requirement in item 6 of Annex II of the PD Regulation for adjustments to be factually supportable, the reporting accountant considers the effect on the pro forma financial information and in particular whether the exclusion renders the pro forma financial information misleading. In such circumstances, the reporting accountant may consider that disclosure in the notes to the pro forma financial information of the fact that such an adjustment has not been

made is sufficient in the context of the overall purpose of the pro forma financial information.

41. However, if the reporting accountant concludes that an omitted adjustment is so fundamental as to render the pro forma statement misleading in the context of the investment circular, it discusses the matter with the directors and, if necessary, the issuer's advisers and in the event that acceptable changes to the disclosures are not made, considers whether it is able to issue its report.

Checking the calculations

42. The reporting accountant ascertains whether the adjustments made in the pro forma financial information are included under the appropriate financial statement caption as well as the arithmetical accuracy of the calculations within the pro forma financial information itself.

Consistent accounting policies

43. **The reporting accountant should evaluate whether the adjustments made to the unadjusted financial information are consistent with the accounting policies adopted in the last, or to be adopted in the next, financial statements of the entity presenting the pro forma financial information. (SIR 4000.4)**

44. It is the responsibility of the directors of the issuer to ensure that in accordance with item 4 of Annex II of the PD Regulation the pro forma financial information is prepared in a manner consistent with either the accounting policies adopted in the last, or to be adopted in the next, financial statements of the issuer.

45. Where the reporting accountant is not the auditor of the issuer or has not otherwise reported on the financial information relating to the subject of the transaction, it evaluates the steps taken to ensure that the pro forma financial information has been prepared in a manner consistent with the accounting policies of the issuer. Guidance for directors with respect to the consistency of accounting policies is provided by the ICAEW Guidance.

Presentation of pro forma financial information

46. **The reporting accountant should consider whether it has become aware of anything to cause it to believe that the pro forma financial information is presented in a way that is not understandable or is misleading in the context in which it is provided. If the reporting accountant is aware of such matters it should discuss them with the parties responsible for the pro forma financial information and with those persons to whom its report is to be addressed, and consider whether it is able to issue its report. (SIR 4000.5)**

47. The reporting accountant reads the pro forma financial information to assess whether:

    (a) as required by item 1 of Annex II of the PD Regulation, the pro forma financial information includes a description of the transaction, the businesses or entities involved and the period to which it refers and clearly states the purpose for which it has been prepared, that it has been prepared for illustrative purposes only and that, because of its nature, it addresses a hypothetical situation and, therefore, does not represent the company's actual financial position or results;

(b) in accordance with the normal form of presentation under item 3 of Annex II of the PD Regulation, the pro forma financial information is presented in columnar format composed of (a) the historical unadjusted information, (b) the pro forma adjustments and (c) the resulting pro forma financial information in the final column; and

(c) disclosures, in the notes to the pro forma financial information, concerning omitted adjustments are satisfactory (see paragraphs 40 and 41 above).

Representation letter

48. SIR 1000.13 sets out the basic principles and essential procedures, with respect to representation letters, that are applicable to all engagements involving an investment circular. Examples of management representation letter clauses are set out in Appendix 4 of this SIR.

Documentation

49. SIR 1000.14 and SIR 1000.15 set out the basic principles and essential procedures with respect to the reporting accountant's working papers.

Professional scepticism

50. SIR 1000.16 sets out the basic principle with respect to the attitude of professional scepticism adopted by the reporting accountant in planning and performing an engagement.

Reporting

51. SIRs 1000.17, SIR 1000.18 and SIR 1000.19 set out the basic principles and essential procedures, with respect to reporting, that are applicable to all engagements involving an investment circular. Additional basic principles and essential procedures relating to engagements to report on pro forma financial information are set out below.

Responsibilities

52. **In all reports on pro forma financial information in investment circulars the reporting accountant should explain the extent of its responsibility in respect of the pro forma financial information by including in its report:**

(a) **a statement that the reporting accountant's responsibility is to form an opinion (as required by the applicable regulatory requirements) on the proper compilation of the pro forma financial information and to report its opinion to the addressees of the report; and**

(b) a statement that the pro forma financial information is the responsibility of the directors. (SIR 4000.6)

53. The reporting accountant's responsibility in relation to the opinion required by the PD Regulation is limited to the provision of the report and the opinion expressed.

Basis of preparation of the pro forma financial information

54. **The reporting accountant should include a basis of preparation section of its report that cross refers to disclosures that explain the basis of preparation of the pro forma financial information. (SIR 4000.7)**

55. The basis of preparation section of the report will make clear whether the accounting policies applied in the preparation of the pro forma information are those adopted by the entity in preparing the last published financial statements or those that it plans to adopt in the next published financial statements.

Expression of opinion

56. **The report on the pro forma financial information should contain a clear expression of opinion that complies with applicable regulatory requirements. (SIR 4000.8)**

57. In forming its opinion the reporting accountant takes account of those events which the reporting accountant becomes aware of occurring up to the date on which the reporting accountant signs the report, that affect the opinion expressed in the report.

58. In providing the opinion required by the PD Regulation the reporting accountant is not providing any assurance in relation to any source financial information on which the pro forma financial information is based beyond that opinion. In particular, the reporting accountant is not refreshing or updating any opinion that it may have given in any other capacity on that source financial information.

59. The investment circular in which the reporting accountant's report is included may be made available in other countries, such as the United States of America, which have their own standards for accountants when reporting on pro forma financial information. In such circumstances, the reporting accountant considers whether to include a reference to the fact that a report issued in accordance with the SIRs should not be relied upon as if it had been issued in accordance with the standards applicable in that other country. An example of such a reference is included in the example report set out in Appendix 5 of this SIR.

Modified opinions

60. SIR 1000.20 sets out the basic principles and essential procedures, with respect to modified opinions, that are applicable to all engagements involving an investment circular. Additional basic principles and essential procedures relating to engagements to report on pro forma financial information are set out below.

61. In the event that the reporting accountant concludes that it is unable to report in the manner prescribed it considers, with the parties to whom it is to report, whether the pro forma financial information can be amended to alleviate its concerns or whether the pro forma information should be omitted from the investment circular and the requirement for information to be given on the effect of the transaction satisfied in some other way.

62. **As the PD Regulation requires a positive and unmodified opinion, the reporting accountant should not express an opinion when the directors have not applied the criteria set out in Appendix 1 of this SIR and, in the reporting accountant's judgment the effect of not doing so is, or may be, material. (SIR 4000.9)**

63. An example of a report on pro forma financial information expressing a positive and unmodified opinion, pursuant to the PD Regulation, is set out in Appendix 5 of this SIR.

Consent

64. SIR 1000.21 and SIR 1000.22 set out the basic principles and essential procedures with respect to the giving of consent by the reporting accountant.

Events occurring between the date of the reporting accountant's report and the completion date of the transaction

65. SIR 1000.23 sets out the basic principles and essential procedures with respect to events occurring between the date of the reporting accountant's report and the completion date of the transaction.

66. Under Section 81 and 87G of the FSMA, Prospectus Rule 3.4 and Listing Rule 4.4.1, a supplementary investment circular must be prepared if, after the date the investment circular has been formally approved by a regulator and before dealings in the relevant securities commence, the issuer becomes aware that there has been a significant change affecting any matter contained in the document or a significant new matter has arisen, the inclusion of information in respect of which would have been required if it had arisen at the time of its preparation. A similar obligation arises, under Article 16 of the Prospectus Directive, in respect of the period following registration of the investment circular during which an agreement in respect of the securities can be entered into in pursuance of the offer contained in the investment circular.

67. If, as a result of discussions with those responsible for the Investment circular concerning an event that occurred prior to the completion date of the transaction, the reporting accountant is either uncertain about or disagrees with the course of action proposed it may consider it necessary to take legal advice with respect to its responsibilities in the particular circumstances.

68. After the date of its report, the reporting accountant has no obligation to perform procedures or make enquiries regarding the investment circular.

Effective date

69. A reporting accountant is required to comply with the Investment Reporting Standards contained in this SIR for reports signed after 31 March 2006. Earlier adoption is encouraged.

Appendix 1

REPORTING ACCOUNTANT'S CRITERIA

	Annex I of PD Regulation	Annex II of PD Regulation	CESR Recommendations
In the case of a significant gross change, a description of how the transaction might have affected the assets and liabilities and earnings of the issuer, had the transaction been undertaken at the commencement of the period being reported on or at the date reported. This requirement will normally be satisfied by the inclusion of pro forma financial information.	20.2		
The pro forma information must normally be presented in columnar format composed of: a) the historical unadjusted information; b) the pro forma adjustments; and c) the resulting pro forma financial information in the final column		3	
The sources of the pro forma financial information have to be stated.		3	
The pro forma information must be prepared in a manner consistent with the accounting policies adopted by the issuer in its last or next financial statements and shall identify the following: a) the basis upon which it is prepared; b) the source of each item of information and adjustment.		4	
Pro forma adjustments related to the pro forma financial information must be: a) clearly shown and explained.		6	
Pro forma adjustments related to the pro forma financial information must be: b) directly attributable to the transaction.		6	

	Annex I of PD Regulation	Annex II of PD Regulation	CESR Recommendations
"Directly attributable to transactions". Pro forma information should only reflect matters that are an integral part of the transactions which are described in the prospectus. In particular, pro forma financial information should not include adjustments which are dependent on actions to be taken once the current transactions have been completed, even where such actions are central to the issuer's purpose in entering into the transactions.			Para 88
Pro forma adjustments related to the pro forma financial information must be: c) factually supportable.		6	
"Factually supportable". The nature of the facts supporting an adjustment will vary according to the circumstances. Nevertheless, facts are expected to be capable of some reasonable degree of objective determination. Support might typically be provided by published accounts, management accounts, other financial information and valuations contained in the document, purchase and sale agreements and other agreements to the transaction covered by the prospectus. For instance in relation to management accounts, the interim figures for an undertaking being acquired may be derived from the consolidation schedules underlying that undertaking's interim statements.			Para 87
In respect of a pro forma profit and loss or cash flow statement, the adjustments must be clearly identified as to those expected to have a continuing impact on the issuer and those which are not.		6	
The accounting treatment applied to adjustments should be presented and prepared in a form consistent with the policy the issuer would adopt in its last or next published financial statements.			Para 89[1]

[1]Paragraph 89 of the CESR guidance also makes recommendations that do not constitute criteria but provide useful guidance with respect to this criterion.

Appendix 2

OTHER REGULATORY PROVISIONS RELEVANT TO THE PREPARERS OF PRO FORMA FINANCIAL INFORMATION

	PD Regulation	Annex I of PD Regulation	Annex II of PD Regulation	CESR Recommendations
(9) Pro forma financial information is needed in case of significant gross change i.e. a variation of more than 25% relative to one or more indicators of the size of the issuer's business, in the situation of an issuer due to a particular transaction, with the exception of those situations where merger accounting is required.	Recital 9			
For these purposes, "Significant gross change" is described in recital 9 of the PD Regulation. Thus, in order to assess whether the variation to an issuer's business as a result of a transaction is more than 25%, the size of the transaction should be assessed relative to the size of the issuer by using appropriate indicators of size prior to the relevant transaction. A transaction will constitute a significant gross change where at least one of the indicators of size is more than 25%. A non-exhaustive list of indicators of size is provided below: - Total assets - Revenue - Profit or loss Other indicators of size can be applied by the issuer especially where the stated indicators of size produce an anomalous result or are inappropriate to the specific industry of the issuer, in these cases the issuers should address these anomalies by agreement of the competent authority. The appropriate indicators of size should refer to figures from the issuer's last or next published annual financial statements.				Paras 90 to 94

	PD Regulation	Annex I of PD Regulation	Annex II of PD Regulation	CESR Recommendations
Pro forma financial information should be preceded by an introductory explanatory paragraph that states in clear terms the purpose of including this information in the prospectus	Article 5			
This pro forma financial information is to be presented as set out in Annex II and must include the information indicated therein. Pro forma financial information must be accompanied by a report prepared by independent accountants or auditors.		20.2		
The pro forma information must include a description of the transaction, the businesses or entities involved and the period to which it refers.			1	
The pro forma information must clearly state the purpose to which it has been prepared			1	
The pro forma information must clearly state that it has been prepared for illustrative purposes only			1	
The pro forma information must clearly state that, because of its nature, it addresses a hypothetical situation and, therefore, does not represent the company's actual financial position or results.			1	
In order to present pro forma financial information, a balance sheet and profit and loss account, and accompanying explanatory notes, depending on the circumstances may be included			2	

	PD Regulation	Annex I of PD Regulation	Annex II of PD Regulation	CESR Recommendations
Where applicable the financial statements of the acquired businesses or entities must be included in the prospectus.			3	
Pro forma information may only be published in respect of: a) the current financial period; b) the most recently completed financial period; and/or c) the most recent interim period for which relevant unadjusted information has been or will be published or is being published in the same document			5	

Appendix 3

EXAMPLES OF ENGAGEMENT LETTER CLAUSES

The examples of engagement letter clauses are intended for consideration in the context of a public reporting engagement on pro forma financial information. They should be tailored to the specific circumstances and supplemented by such other clauses as are relevant and appropriate.

Financial information upon which the report is to be given

The [investment circular] will include a pro forma [balance sheet/profit and loss account] together with a description of the basis of presentation (including the accounting policies used) and supporting notes to illustrate how the transaction might have affected the financial information of the company had the transaction been undertaken at the beginning of the period[s] concerned or as at the date[s] stated (the "pro forma financial information").

Responsibilities

The pro forma financial information, which will be the responsibility solely of the directors, will be prepared for illustrative purposes only. This is required to be prepared in accordance with items 1 to 6 of Annex II of the PD Regulation.

It is our responsibility to form an opinion as to whether the pro forma financial information has been properly compiled on the basis stated and that such basis is consistent with the accounting policies of ABC plc.

If the results of our work are satisfactory, and having regard to the requirements of item 7 of Annex II of the PD Regulation, we shall prepare a report on the pro forma financial information for inclusion in the [*describe document*]. An illustration of the form of our report is attached.

Scope of work

Our work will be undertaken in accordance with Standard for Investment Reporting (SIR) 4000 "Investment Reporting Standards Applicable to Public Reporting Engagements on Pro Forma Financial Information" issued by the Auditing Practices Board and will be subject to the limitations described therein.

We draw your attention in particular to paragraph 62 of SIR 4000 which would preclude us from expressing any opinion if the directors have not complied with the regulatory requirements set out in Appendix 1 of that SIR.

Appendix 4

EXAMPLES OF MANAGEMENT REPRESENTATION LETTER CLAUSES

The following are examples of management representation letter clauses relating to a report on pro forma financial information, issued pursuant to the PD Regulation or Listing Rules, which may be obtained from the issuer. Alternatively they may form the basis for a board minute.

Introduction

We refer to the pro forma financial information set out in Part [...] of the [investment circular] dated...to be issued in connection with [...] dated. We acknowledge that we are solely responsible for the pro forma financial information and confirm on behalf of the Directors of the Company to the best of our knowledge and belief, having made appropriate enquiries of officials of the Company [and the directors and officials of the target company], the following representations made to you in the course of your work.

Specific representations

- We acknowledge as duly appointed officials of the Company our responsibility for the pro forma financial information (which has been prepared in accordance with [CESR's Recommendations for the Consistent Implementation of the European Commission's Regulation on Prospectuses No. 809/2004"] [and, to the extent applicable, with Technical Release TECH 18/98 published by the Institute of Chartered Accountants in England and Wales].

- We have considered the pro forma financial information and we confirm that, in our opinion, as required by item 20.2 of Annex I of the PD Regulation, the pro forma financial information provides investors with information about the impact of the transaction by illustrating how that transaction might have affected the [assets and liabilities] [and] [earnings] of the issuer, had the transaction been undertaken at the commencement of the period being reported on or at the date reported. Furthermore, we confirm that, in our opinion, the pro forma financial information is not misleading.

- We have considered the adjustments included in the pro forma financial information. We confirm that, in our opinion, the pro forma financial information includes all appropriate adjustments permitted by item 6 of Annex II of the PD Regulation, of which we are aware, necessary to give effect to the transaction as if the transaction had been undertaken [at the date reported on} [at the commencement of the period being reported on].

- [We have considered those adjustments which have been omitted by virtue of not being permitted to be included by item 6 of Annex II of the PD Regulation and the disclosures made in respect thereof. In our opinion the omission of these adjustments does not render the pro forma financial information misleading.]

- [*Where the accounting policies in the issuer's next financial statements are used.* The accounting policies used in compiling the pro forma financial information are those to be adopted in the Company's next financial statements, and all changes necessary to reflect those policies have been made.]

- [*Any specific representations relating to information included in the pro forma financial information.*]

Appendix 5

EXAMPLE REPORT ON PRO FORMA FINANCIAL INFORMATION IN ACCORDANCE WITH THE PD REGULATION OR THE LISTING RULES

Date

Reporting accountant's address

Addressees, as agreed between the parties in the engagement letter

Dear Sirs,

[ABC plc]

We report on the pro forma [financial information] (the "Pro forma financial information") set out in Part [...] of the [investment circular] dated......., which has been prepared on the basis described [in note x], for illustrative purposes only, to provide information about how the [transaction] might have affected the financial information presented on the basis of the accounting policies [adopted/to be adopted[1]] by ABC plc in preparing the financial statements for the period [ended/ending] [*date*]. This report is required by [Relevant Regulation] [guidance issued by the London Stock Exchange with respect to the AIM market] and is given for the purpose of complying with that [Relevant Regulation] [guidance issued by the London Stock Exchange] and for no other purpose.

Responsibilities

It is the responsibility of the directors of ABC plc to prepare the Pro forma financial information in accordance with [item 20.2 of Annex I of the PD Regulation] [guidance issued by the London Stock Exchange].

It is our responsibility to form an opinion, as required by [item 7 of Annex II of the PD Regulation] [guidance issued by the London Stock Exchange], as to the proper compilation of the Pro forma financial information and to report that opinion to you.

In providing this opinion we are not updating or refreshing any reports or opinions previously made by us on any financial information used in the compilation of the Pro forma financial information, nor do we accept responsibility for such reports or opinions beyond that owed to those to whom those reports or opinions were addressed by us at the dates of their issue.

Basis of Opinion

We conducted our work in accordance with the Standards for Investment Reporting issued by the Auditing Practices Board in the United Kingdom. The work that we performed for the

---

[1]   See paragraph 44 of SIR 4000

purpose of making this report, which involved no independent examination of any of the underlying financial information, consisted primarily of comparing the unadjusted financial information with the source documents, considering the evidence supporting the adjustments and discussing the Pro forma financial information with the directors of ABC plc.

We planned and performed our work so as to obtain the information and explanations we considered necessary in order to provide us with reasonable assurance that the Pro forma financial information has been properly compiled on the basis stated and that such basis is consistent with the accounting policies of ABC plc.

[*This paragraph may be omitted if the document is not to be distributed outside the UK* - Our work has not been carried out in accordance with auditing or other standards and practices generally accepted in the United States of America [or other jurisdictions] and accordingly should not be relied upon as if it had been carried out in accordance with those standards and practices.]

Opinion

In our opinion:

(a) the Pro forma financial information has been properly compiled on the basis stated; and

(b) such basis is consistent with the accounting policies of ABC plc.

Declaration[2]

For the purposes of [Prospectus Rule [5.5.3R(2)(f)] [5.5.4R(2)(f)]] [guidance issued by the London Stock Exchange] we are responsible for [this report as part] [the following part(s)] of the [prospectus] [registration document] [AIM Admission Document] and declare that we have taken all reasonable care to ensure that the information contained [in this report] [those parts] is, to the best of our knowledge, in accordance with the facts and contains no omission likely to affect its import. This declaration is included in the [prospectus] [registration document] [AIM Admission Document] in compliance with [item 1.2 of Annex I of the PD Regulation] [item 1.2 of Annex III of the Prospectus Regulation] [guidance issued by the London Stock Exchange].

Yours faithfully

Reporting accountant

---

[2] This declaration is a requirement of the Prospectus Rules and is appropriate for inclusion when the report is included in a Prospectus, see Appendix 2 of SIR 1000. It is also appropriate for inclusion in an AIM admission document under Schedule Two of the AIM Rules.

SECTIONS OF TECH 18/98 "PRO FORMA FINANCIAL INFORMATION – GUIDANCE FOR PREPARERS UNDER THE LISTING RULES"[1] (PUBLISHED BY THE INSTITUTE OF CHARTERED ACCOUNTANTS IN ENGLAND & WALES) THAT REMAIN RELEVANT

This Annexure has been compiled by the APB to indicate those paragraphs of TECH 18/98 that continue to be relevant. (There are differences between the requirements of the PD Regulation and the CESR Recommendations compared to the requirements on which TECH 18/98 was based.) The Annexure does not include either basic principles, essential procedures, or guidance promulgated by the APB.

Paragraphs in TECH 18/98	Application under the PD Regulation
1 to 5	*Not applicable*
6	Principles still applicable, save that under Item 20.2 of Annex I of the PD Regulation inclusion of pro forma information is now normally included where there has been a "significant gross change" (as defined in Recital (9))
7 and 8	Principles still applicable
9	*Not applicable – replaced by the following:* *Item 20.2 of Annex 1 of the PD Regulation. In the case of a significant gross change, a description of how the transaction might have affected the assets and liabilities and earnings of the issuer, had the transaction been undertaken at the commencement of the period being reported on or at the date reported.* *This requirement will normally be satisfied by the inclusion of pro forma financial information.* *This pro forma financial information is to be presented as set out in Annex II and must include the information indicated therein.* *Pro forma financial information must be accompanied by a report prepared by independent accountants or auditors.*
10 and 11	Principles still applicable
12 to 19	Principles still applicable save that there is no express requirement under the PD Regulation for all appropriate adjustments to be included, nor for the pro forma financial information not to be misleading
20	*Not applicable – replaced by the following (the words **emphasised** are additional to the original Listing Rule and certain other words have been deleted):* *Item 1 of Annex II of the PD Regulation. The pro forma information **must include a description of the transaction, the businesses or entities involved and the period to which it refers**, and must clearly state the following:* *a) the purpose **to** which it has been prepared;* *b) the fact that it has been prepared for illustrative purposes only;* *c) the fact that because of its nature, **the pro forma financial information addresses a hypothetical situation and, therefore, does not represent the company's actual financial position or results.***

---

[1] This Annexure applies to TECH 18/98 which was published by the ICAEW in 1998 and is available for download from its website. The ICAEW has indicated that it intends to update and reissue TECH 18/98. When it is reissued this Annexure will no longer be applicable and should not be used.

	Item 2 of Annex II of the PD Regulation **In order to present pro forma financial information, a balance sheet and profit and loss account, and accompanying explanatory notes, depending on the circumstances may be included.**
21 to 24	Principles still applicable
25	*Not applicable – replaced by the following:* *Item 3 of Annex II of the PD Regulation. Pro forma financial information must* **normally** *be presented in columnar format,* **composed of:** *a) the* **historical** *unadjusted information;* *b) the pro forma adjustments; and* *c) the* **resulting** *pro forma financial information* **in the final column**. **The sources of the pro forma financial information have to be stated and, if applicable, the financial statements of the acquired businesses or entities must be included in the prospectus** *Item 4 of Annex II of the PD Regulation. The pro forma information must be prepared in a manner consistent with the accounting policies adopted by the issuer in its* **last or next** *financial statements and shall identify the following:* *a) the basis upon which it is prepared;* *b) the source of each item of information and adjustment.*
26	Principles still applicable
27	Principles still applicable, save that the accounting policies to be used in the next financial statements may also be applied
28 to 29	Principles still applicable
30	*Not applicable*
31 and 32	Principles still applicable
33	*Not applicable*
34	Applicable, save that the words *"and, in the case of a pro forma balance sheet or net asset statement, as at the date on which such periods end or ended"* are omitted
35 to 43	Principles still applicable
44 and 45	*Not applicable*
46 to 71	Principles still applicable
72 to 74	*Not applicable*

STANDARDS FOR INVESTMENT REPORTING

5000 – INVESTMENT REPORTING STANDARDS APPLICABLE TO PUBLIC REPORTING ENGAGEMENTS ON FINANCIAL INFORMATION RECONCILIATIONS UNDER THE LISTING RULES

CONTENTS

Appendices

ANNEXURE

*Accounting conventions and processes used in preparing financial information
reconciliations for inclusion in Class 1 circulars.*

SIR 1000 "Investment reporting standards applicable to all engagements in connection with an investment circular" contains basic principles and essential procedures ("Investment Reporting Standards") that are applicable to all engagements involving an investment circular. The definitions in the glossary of terms set out in Appendix 4 of SIR 1000 are to be applied in the interpretation of this and all other SIRs. Terms defined in the glossary are underlined the first time that they occur in the text.

SIR 5000 contains additional Investment Reporting Standards, indicated by paragraphs in bold type, with which a reporting accountant is required to comply in the conduct of an engagement to report on financial information reconciliations which are included within a Class 1 circular prepared for issue in connection with a securities transaction governed wholly or in part by the laws and regulations of the United Kingdom or the Republic of Ireland.

SIR 5000 also includes explanatory and other material, including appendices, in the context of which the Investment Reporting Standards are to be understood and applied. It is necessary to consider the whole text of the SIR to understand and apply the basic principles and essential procedures.

To assist readers, SIRs contain references to, and extracts from, certain legislation and chapters of the Rules of the UK Listing Authority (UKLA) and the Listing Rules of the Irish Stock Exchange Limited (ISE) (together "the Listing Rules"). Readers are cautioned that these references may change subsequent to publication.

Introduction

1. Standard for Investment Reporting (SIR) 1000 "Investment Reporting Standards applicable to all engagements in connection with an Investment Circular" establishes the Investment Reporting Standards applicable to all engagements involving investment circulars. The purpose of SIR 5000 is to establish specific additional Investment Reporting Standards and provide guidance for a reporting accountant engaged to report publicly on reconciliations of the financial information of a target[1] to the accounting policies of an issuer (financial information reconciliations) to be included in a Class 1 circular under the Listing Rules.

2. Financial information reconciliations (sometimes referred to as GAAP reconciliations) may be included in investment circulars other than Class 1 circulars. If the reporting accountant is requested to report in similar terms to those for a Class 1 circular in such a context, and agrees to do so, the guidance in this SIR may be helpful. However, this SIR is not intended to be used in connection with GAAP reconciliations that are included within a note to financial statements included in an investment circular.

3. An engagement to report on the proper compilation of financial information reconciliations is a public reporting engagement as described in SIR 1000. The description of a public reporting engagement includes three generic terms having the

---

[1] Under UKLA LR 13.5.1R(1): ISE LR 10.5.1(1) where a listed company is seeking to acquire an interest in another company, that company is described as a "target".

following meanings in the context of an engagement to report on the proper compilation of financial information reconciliations:

(a) the "**subject matter**" is the target's financial information for the periods being reported on, presented in accordance with the target's accounting policies (ie the target's unadjusted financial information);

(b) the "**suitable criteria**" are the requirements of the financial reporting framework adopted by the issuer, the accounting policies of the issuer and any "accepted conventions", as set out in the Annexure, that have been applied; and

(c) the "**outcome[2]**" is the financial information of the target, as adjusted, together with the adjustments, that is included in the Class 1 circular and which has resulted from the directors applying the suitable criteria to the subject matter. The reporting accountant expresses an opinion as to whether that financial information (as adjusted) is properly compiled on the basis stated and whether the adjustments are appropriate for presenting the financial information (as adjusted) on a basis consistent in all material respects with the issuer's accounting policies.

4. In order to express an opinion on the reconciliation the reporting accountant is not required to re-assess any judgments or estimates underlying the subject matter or provide an opinion on the subject matter.

The nature of financial information reconciliations

5. Paragraph 5 of SIR 2000 "Investment Reporting Standards Applicable to Public Reporting Engagements on Historical Financial Information" describes, with respect to Class 1 acquisitions, the requirements of the Listing Rules for a Class 1 circular to include a financial information table relating to the target and an accountant's opinion on that table.

6. However, under the Listing Rules, when an issuer seeks to acquire a publicly traded company (a target) a financial information table is not required to be presented on the basis of the issuer's accounting policies but is presented on the basis of the target's accounting policies. Consequently the accountant's opinion described in SIR 2000 is not required and there are additional Listing Rules that apply[3].

7. Under these additional rules (see Appendix 1), where a material adjustment needs to be made to the financial information presented in respect of the target in the Class 1

---

[2] The "outcome" is sometimes described as "subject matter information".
[3] These rules are UKLA LR 13.5.27R and 13.5.28R: ISE LR 10.5.27 and 10.5.28.

circular to achieve consistency with the issuer's accounting policies, the issuer is required to include the following in the Class 1 circular[4]:

(a) a reconciliation of financial information on the target, for all periods covered by the financial information table, normally on the basis of the accounting policies used in the issuer's last published accounts[5];

(b) an accountant's opinion that sets out:

    (i) whether the reconciliation of financial information in the financial information table has been properly compiled on the basis stated; and

    (ii) whether the adjustments are appropriate for the purpose of presenting the financial information (as adjusted) on a basis consistent in all material respects with the issuer's accounting policies.

If no material adjustment needs to be made to the target's financial information, in order to achieve consistency with the issuer's accounting policies, then the Class 1 circular is not required to include a financial information reconciliation.

8. The need for a financial information reconciliation usually arises because the target and the issuer prepare their respective financial statements in accordance with different financial reporting frameworks (for example, the issuer may prepare its financial statements in accordance with International Financial Reporting Standards as adopted by the European Union and the target may prepare its financial statements in accordance with United States Generally Accepted Accounting Principles) but may also arise through different choices made within the same financial reporting framework.

9. Other than the need for the financial information to be presented on a basis consistent in all material respects with the listed company's accounting policies, the Listing Rules contain no further requirements regarding the proper compilation of the financial information reconciliation, or the appropriateness of adjustments. In particular, the Listing Rules do not specify the individual financial statements or financial statement components that should comprise "financial information" for this purpose. Consequently the directors have regard to accepted conventions which have developed for the preparation and presentation of financial information reconciliations in Class 1 circulars. The Annexure provides a summary of these accepted conventions.

---

[4] Under UKLA LR 13.5.30R(2) and ISE LR 10.5.30(2) similar requirements apply where the target has published half yearly or quarterly financial information subsequent to the end of its last financial year and a material adjustment needs to be made to the financial information presented in respect of the relevant interim period of the target in the Class 1 circular to achieve consistency with the issuer's accounting policies.

[5] The UKLA's publication "List!" 16 at paragraph 2.5 discusses certain circumstances where accounting policies other than those used in the issuer's last published accounts are used.

Engagement acceptance and continuance

10. SIR 1000.1 and SIR 1000.2 set out the Investment Reporting Standards with respect to engagement acceptance and continuance that are applicable to all engagements involving an investment circular. Additional Investment Reporting Standards and guidance are set out below.

11. When accepting or continuing an engagement to report publicly on financial information reconciliations, the reporting accountant ascertains whether the directors intend to comply with the relevant regulatory requirements.

12. **In determining whether the persons who are to perform the engagement collectively possess the necessary professional competence the reporting accountant should:**

    (a) **assess whether the engagement team[6], or those with whom the engagement team intend to consult, have sufficient knowledge and experience of the issuer's financial reporting framework; and**

    (b) **consider the extent to which the engagement team requires knowledge of the target's financial reporting framework or are able to consult with those having such knowledge having regard to management's processes. (SIR 5000.1)**

13. Where the target's or the issuer's financial information has been prepared in accordance with a financial reporting framework other than that of the country in which the reporting accountant practises[7], the reporting accountant determines whether it has, or can obtain, the necessary professional competence to evaluate whether the financial information reconciliation has been prepared in accordance with the requirements of the Listing Rules.

14. The successful completion of the reporting accountant's engagement will depend on receiving, on a timely basis, the co-operation of the management and directors both of the issuer and of the target including their disclosure to the reporting accountant of all the pertinent accounting records and any other relevant records and related information. In a hostile bid, or other limited access situation, the reporting accountant is unlikely to obtain the necessary access to the officials and records of the target and, therefore, is unlikely to be in a position to report on a financial

---

[6] The "engagement team" is any person within the reporting accountant's firm who is directly involved in the engagement including:
  (a) the partners, managers and staff from assurance and other disciplines involved in the engagement (for example, taxation specialists, IT specialists, treasury management specialists, lawyers, actuaries), and
  (b) those who provide quality control or direct oversight of the engagement

[7] UKLA LR 13.5.23R and ISE LR 10.5.23 require that the accountant's opinion must be given by an independent accountant who is qualified to act as an auditor. With the exception of paragraph 56, this SIR is drafted on the presumption that the opinion is provided by the issuer's reporting accountant or auditor. However, this need not be the case.

information reconciliation. In such situations the circumstances are discussed with the UK Listing Authority[8] (UKLA) or the Irish Stock Exchange (ISE).

Agreeing the terms of the engagement

15. SIR 1000.3 and SIR 1000.4 set out the Investment Reporting Standards with respect to agreeing the terms of the engagement. Examples of engagement letter clauses are set out in Appendix 2 of this SIR.

Ethical requirements

16. SIR 1000.5 sets out the Investment Reporting Standard with respect to the ethical requirements that apply to a reporting accountant[9].

Legal and regulatory requirements

17. The legal and regulatory requirements relating to financial information reconciliations in Class 1 circulars are set out in Chapter 13 of the UKLA Listing Rules and Chapter 10 of the ISE Listing Rules. These chapters also set out the requirements for the inclusion of financial information tables in Class 1 circulars.

18. SIR 1000.6 sets out the Investment Reporting Standards with respect to the legal and regulatory requirements applicable to a reporting accountant.

19. Appendix 1 summarises the relevant requirements of the Listing Rules and illustrates those requirements that are dealt with by SIR 2000 and those dealt with by SIR 5000.

Quality control

20. SIR 1000.7 and SIR 1000.8 set out the Investment Reporting Standards with respect to the quality control of engagements to report on financial information reconciliations.

Planning and performing the engagement

21. SIR 1000.9 and SIR 1000.10 set out the Investment Reporting Standards with respect to the planning of all reporting engagements. Additional Investment Reporting Standards and guidance are set out below.

---

[8] The UKLA generally encourages advisers or issuers preparing an investment circular in a limited access situation to contact them as soon as possible to discuss the exact disclosure requirements. In certain circumstances it may be appropriate for a financial information reconciliation to be published in a supplementary circular within 28 days of a contested offer becoming unconditional.

[9] In October 2006 the APB issued the Ethical Standard for Reporting Accountants (ESRA).

22. **The reporting accountant should obtain an understanding of those factors affecting the subject matter sufficient to identify and assess the risk of the financial information reconciliation not being properly compiled and the adjustments being inappropriate for the purpose of presenting the financial information (as adjusted) on a basis consistent in all material respects with the issuer's accounting policies. The reporting accountant's understanding should be sufficient to design and perform evidence gathering procedures and in particular should include:**

   (a) **the nature of the target's and the issuer's businesses;**

   (b) **the accounting policies of the target and of the issuer and the application of those policies;**

   (c) **the requirements of the issuer's financial reporting framework;**

   (d) **the extent to which the issuer has employees with the requisite knowledge of the financial reporting framework used by the target, or the ability to consult with those having such knowledge; and**

   (e) **the procedures and controls adopted, or planned to be adopted, by the directors for the preparation of the financial information reconciliation. (SIR 5000.2)**

23. The reporting accountant may gain an understanding of the nature of the target's business in a number of ways, for example:

   • Reviewing publicly available information on the target.

   • Through discussion with the issuer's directors or management.

   • Through discussion with the target's directors or management.

   • Through discussion with the target's auditor, where that auditor is prepared to assist the reporting accountant to gain a wider understanding of the target, its financial reporting procedures and the way in which its accounting policies are applied.

24. In obtaining an understanding of the target's and the issuer's businesses the reporting accountant may consider the following, for example:

   • Business operations:

     ○ Conduct of operations and nature of revenue sources.

     ○ Products or services and markets.

   • Financing and Investments:

- ○ Group structure.

- ○ Finance structure.

- ○ Investments in non-consolidated entities, including partnerships, joint ventures and special purpose entities.

- • Financial reporting:

- ○ Industry specific practices.

- ○ Revenue recognition practices.

- ○ Accounting for unusual or complex transactions including those in emerging areas.

25. Under the Listing Rules the financial information reconciliation on the target is required to be prepared on the basis of the accounting policies of the issuer[10]. Guidance in the Listing Rules indicates that "accounting policies" includes accounting standards and accounting disclosures[11]. A financial information reconciliation, therefore, is not confined to a reconciliation to the published accounting policies of an issuer but also to those accounting standards comprising the issuer's financial reporting framework, regardless of whether they are articulated within the issuer's statement of accounting policies, even if they have not previously been relevant to the issuer. Accordingly, both the issuer and the reporting accountant consider the extent to which they will need access to expertise in the target's financial reporting framework. However financial information reconciliations do not normally extend to reconciling note disclosures.

26. Other matters for consideration by the reporting accountant include the availability of evidence to support the proposed adjustments and the accounting policies that will form the basis of the adjustments to the target's financial information.

27. **The reporting accountant should consider materiality and public reporting engagement risk in planning its work in accordance with its instructions and in determining the effect of its findings on the report to be issued. (SIR 5000.3)**

Materiality

28. The Listing Rules require a financial information reconciliation to be included in a Class 1 circular only when a material adjustment needs to be made to the target's financial information to achieve consistency with the listed company's accounting policies[12]. The judgment concerning materiality to comply with the Listing Rules is the responsibility of the issuer. The reporting accountant is not required to evaluate this determination of materiality made by the issuer. However, if the reporting accountant becomes aware that a material adjustment may need to be made to the target's

---

[10] UKLA LR 13.5.4R and ISE LR10.5.4

[11] UKLA LR 13.5.5G and ISE LR 10.5.5.

[12] UKLA LRs 13.5.27R and 13.5.28R and ISE LRs 10.5.27 and 10.5.28.

financial statements to achieve consistency with the listed company's accounting policies, and the issuer has not prepared a financial information reconciliation, it discusses the matter with the directors of the issuer.

29. The following guidance on materiality addresses the reporting accountant's responsibilities with respect to a financial information reconciliation once the issuer is satisfied that the preparation of a financial information reconciliation is required under the Listing Rules.

30. Matters are material if their omission or misstatement could, individually or collectively, influence the economic decisions of the intended users of the financial information reconciliation. Materiality depends on the size and nature of the omission or misstatement judged in the light of the surrounding circumstances. Materiality is determined by reference to the financial information of the target, as adjusted in the financial information reconciliation.

31. A misstatement in the context of the compilation of a financial information reconciliation includes, for example:

- Use of an inappropriate source for the target's financial information.

- Incorrect extraction of the target's financial information from an appropriate source.

- In relation to adjustments, the misapplication of accounting policies or failure to use the issuer's accounting policies.

- Failure to make an adjustment necessary for the purpose of presenting the financial information (as adjusted) on a basis consistent in all material respects with the issuer's accounting policies.

- Disclosing as an adjustment the rectification of an error in the underlying financial information of the target[13].

- A mathematical or clerical mistake.

32. If the reporting accountant becomes aware of a material misstatement in the financial information reconciliation it discusses the matter with the directors of the issuer. If the reporting accountant is not able to agree with the directors as to how the matter is to be resolved it considers the consequences for its opinion.

Public reporting engagement risk

33. "Public reporting engagement risk" is the risk that the reporting accountant expresses an inappropriate opinion when the financial information reconciliation has not been properly compiled on the basis stated or when the adjustments are not appropriate for

---

[13] See discussion in paragraph 12 of Annexure concerning the manner in which a rectification of a misstatement in the underlying financial information may be disclosed.

the purpose of presenting the financial information (as adjusted) on a basis consistent, in all material respects, with the accounting policies of the issuer.

34. SIR 1000.11 and SIR 1000.12 set out the Investment Reporting Standards with respect to obtaining evidence that are applicable to all engagements involving an investment circular. Additional Investment Reporting Standards and guidance relating to engagements to report on financial information reconciliations are set out below.

35. **The reporting accountant should assess whether the reconciliation of financial information in the financial information table has been properly compiled on the basis stated and whether the adjustments are appropriate for the purpose of presenting the financial information (as adjusted) on a basis consistent in all material respects with the issuer's accounting policies. In making these assessments the reporting accountant should, having regard to the procedures and controls adopted by the directors:**

   (a) **check whether the financial information of the target has been accurately extracted from an appropriate source;**

   (b) **assess whether all adjustments necessary for the purpose of presenting the financial information (as adjusted) on a basis consistent in all material respects with the issuer's accounting policies have been made; and**

   (c) **check the arithmetical accuracy of the calculations within the financial information reconciliation. (SIR 5000.4)**

Consideration of directors' procedures and controls

36. In assessing whether the financial information reconciliation has been properly compiled on the basis stated and whether the adjustments are appropriate the reporting accountant has regard to the procedures and controls adopted by the issuer. Such procedures and controls may encompass both high-level internal controls over the reconciliation process and lower level accounting control activities.

37. High-level internal controls over the reconciliation process that the reporting accountant may wish to assess include, whether:

   • Employees (or outside experts utilised by the issuer), have the requisite knowledge and experience to prepare and monitor the preparation of the reconciliation.

   • The directors of the issuer have been involved to an appropriate extent in the preparation of the financial information reconciliation.

   • Where applicable, management has compared the reconciliation to any that may have been made before.

38. Examples of accounting control activities that the reporting accountant may wish to assess include, whether:

- When making adjustments management sought to ensure that the principles of double-entry bookkeeping were followed such that "one-sided" entries were not made.

- Management considered the tax effects of the adjustments and assessed whether the resultant effective tax rate is understandable and meaningful.

- Management analysed the differences between the opening and closing equity account balances, as adjusted. (This is sometimes referred to as an equity roll forward reconciliation.) Such an analysis would have assisted management in seeking to ensure that the principles of double-entry bookkeeping have been followed where the other side of an adjustment is to an equity account.

- Management considered whether the cash and cash equivalent position, as adjusted, is (and should be) the same as that shown by the unadjusted financial statements. If there is a difference between the cash position reported on the two bases management should be able to explain how the difference arises and, in particular, to have considered whether the difference may reflect an error in the double-entry bookkeeping applied to the reconciliation process.

Unadjusted financial information of the target

39. The reporting accountant assesses whether the unadjusted financial information has been extracted from an appropriate source: namely the financial information table of the target included in the Class 1 circular or such published half yearly or quarterly financial information that is required, by the Listing Rules[14], to be reproduced in the Class 1 circular.

40. The reporting accountant is not required to perform specific procedures on the unadjusted financial information of the target other than as described in paragraph 39, and in particular is not required to audit the unadjusted financial information. However, if the reporting accountant has reason to believe that the unadjusted financial information is, or may be, unreliable, or if a report thereon has identified any uncertainties or disagreements, the reporting accountant considers the effect on the financial information reconciliation.

41. When the directors have identified an error in the underlying financial information that does not reflect a genuine difference between the accounting policies of the target and the issuer it is not rectified by being presented as an adjustment. The issuer would discuss the proposed presentation of the rectification of the error with the UKLA or the ISE. The reporting accountant would wish to see evidence, based on such discussions, of the agreement of the UKLA or the ISE to the proposed presentation of the rectification of the error.

---

[14] UKLA LR13.5.30R(1) and ISE LR10.5.30(1)

Completeness of adjustments and consistency of accounting policies

42. In assessing the completeness of the adjustments and whether the adjustments are appropriate for the purpose of presenting the financial information (as adjusted) on a basis consistent, in all material respects, with the issuer's accounting policies, the reporting accountant utilises its expertise, and the expertise of those with whom they have consulted, in the issuer's financial reporting framework.

43. The reporting accountant assesses the thoroughness with which the directors have fulfilled their responsibility for ensuring the completeness of adjustments. In view of the importance of the accuracy of a financial reconciliation to potential investors the directors will be expected to have carefully analysed the target's accounting policies and prepared an "impact analysis" of the effect of applying the issuer's accounting policies to the target's financial information. With its understanding of the target and the issuer's business as background (see paragraph 24) the reporting accountant discusses with the directors the steps the directors have taken to identify relevant adjustments.

44. As described in paragraph 25 the definition of accounting policies in the Listing Rules encompasses the accounting standards of the applicable financial reporting framework. The reporting accountant's assessment of the completeness of adjustments is likely to include gaining an understanding of the differences between the financial reporting frameworks of the target and the issuer and, in particular:

    (a) identifying those accounting standards in the issuer's or the target's financial reporting framework that may have a particular impact on the target's or issuer's industries;

    (b) assessing the adequacy of the directors' impact analysis;

    (c) considering the adequacy of the process followed by the issuer in ensuring the completeness of the adjustments, in particular the depth of involvement of senior management in the preparation of the reconciliation. Paragraphs 23 to 33 of the Annexure describe in more detail the processes that management may use when preparing a financial information reconciliation; and

    (d) assessing whether the reconciliation, taken as a whole, appears to have any material omissions.

45. **The reporting accountant should obtain sufficient appropriate evidence that the issuer can support each adjustment (including the detailed calculation of the adjustment) and that, where appropriate, such support has been obtained from the appropriate level of management of the target. (SIR 5000.5)**

46. If the reporting accountant becomes aware of an adjustment which:

    (a) in its opinion, ought to be made for the purposes of the financial information reconciliation; or

(b) in its opinion, ought not to have been made for the purposes of the financial information reconciliation; or

(c) the directors of the issuer cannot support (either in principle or in matters of detail and computation),

it discusses the position with the directors of the issuer and, if necessary, the issuer's advisers. If the reporting accountant is not able to agree with the directors of the issuer and the issuer's advisers as to how the matter is to be resolved it considers the consequences for its report.

Checking the calculations

47. The reporting accountant ascertains whether the adjustments made in the financial information reconciliation are included under the appropriate financial statement captions as well as the arithmetical accuracy of the calculations within the financial information reconciliation itself.

48. In respect of the adjustments the reporting accountant checks the calculation of the effect on the target's financial information of applying the accounting policy of the issuer rather than the accounting policies of the target.

Presentation of the financial information reconciliation

49. **The reporting accountant should consider whether it has become aware of anything to cause it to believe that the financial information reconciliation is presented in a way that is not understandable or is misleading in the context in which it is provided. If the reporting accountant is aware of such matters it should discuss them with the directors of the issuer and any other persons to whom its report is to be addressed, and consider whether it is able to issue its opinion. (SIR 5000.6)**

50. The underlying principle is that a reader of the Class 1 circular will be able to understand how the adjustments that have been made affect the underlying financial information. The reporting accountant may wish to assess whether, for example, there is adequate disclosure of the specific line items of the income statement or balance sheet that give rise to an adjustment.

Representation letter

51. SIR 1000.13 sets out the Investment Reporting Standard with respect to representation letters that is applicable to all engagements involving an investment circular. Examples of representation letter clauses applicable to financial information reconciliations are set out in Appendix 3.

Documentation

52. SIR 1000.14 and SIR 1000.15 set out the Investment Reporting Standards with respect to the reporting accountant's working papers.

Professional scepticism

53. SIR 1000.16 sets out the Investment Reporting Standard with respect to the attitude of professional scepticism adopted by the reporting accountant in planning and performing an engagement.

Reporting

54. SIR 1000.17, SIR 1000.18 and SIR 1000.19 set out the Investment Reporting Standards with respect to reporting that are applicable to all engagements involving an investment circular. Additional Investment Reporting Standards relating to engagements to report on financial information reconciliations are set out below. An example report on a financial information reconciliation prepared in accordance with the Listing Rules is set out in Appendix 4.

Responsibilities

55. **In all reports on financial information reconciliations in Class 1 circulars the reporting accountant should explain the extent of its responsibility in respect of the reconciliations by including in its report:**

    (a) **a statement that the reporting accountant's responsibility is to form an opinion as to whether the reconciliations have been properly compiled on the basis stated and the adjustments are appropriate for the purpose of presenting the financial information (as adjusted) on a basis consistent in all material respects with the accounting policies of the issuer and to report its opinion to the addressees of the report; and**

    (b) **a statement that the financial information reconciliation is the responsibility of the directors. (SIR 5000.7)**

56. The reporting accountant's responsibility in relation to the opinion required by the Listing Rules is limited to the provision of the report and the opinion expressed. Where an audit or other opinion has been expressed on the financial information of the target by a firm other than the reporting accountant, the reporting accountant may state in the responsibilities section that it does not accept any responsibility for any of the historical financial statements of the target and that it expresses no opinion on those financial statements. An example of such a reference is included in the example report in Appendix 4.

57. Where the reporting accountant has provided an audit or other opinion on the financial information of the target the reporting accountant may state in the responsibilities section that:

    (a) it is not updating or refreshing any reports or opinions previously made by it on any financial information used in the compilation of the reconciliations; and

    (b) it accepts no responsibility for such reports or opinions beyond that owed to those to whom those reports or opinions were addressed at the date of their issue.

    An example of such a reference is included in the example report in Appendix 4.

Basis of preparation of the financial information reconciliation

58. **The reporting accountant should, in its report, cross refer to disclosures that explain the basis of preparation of the financial information reconciliation (SIR 5000.8).**

Expression of opinion

59. **The report on the financial information reconciliation should contain a clear expression of opinion that complies with the requirements of the Listing Rules. (SIR 5000.9)**

60. The Class 1 circular in which the reporting accountant's report is included may be made available in other countries, such as the United States of America, which have their own standards for accountants when reporting on financial information reconciliations. In such circumstances, the reporting accountant considers whether to include a reference to the fact that a report issued in accordance with the SIRs should not be relied upon as if it had been issued in accordance with the standards applicable in that other country. An example of such a reference is included in the example report in Appendix 4.

Modified opinions

61. SIR 1000.20 sets out the Investment Reporting Standard, with respect to modified opinions, that is applicable to all engagements involving an investment circular.

62. With respect to the compilation of a financial information reconciliation, the reporting accountant may conclude that the outcome is materially misstated, (for example, in the circumstances described in paragraph 31 above), and in such circumstances considers the impact of such misstatements on its opinion.

63. In the event that the reporting accountant concludes that it is necessary to express a modified opinion it explains the circumstances to the directors of the issuer and any other parties to whom it is to report so that the issuer has an opportunity to amend the financial information reconciliation to alleviate the reporting accountant's concerns.

Consent

64. SIR 1000.21 and SIR 1000.22 set out the Investment Reporting Standards with respect to the giving of consent by the reporting accountant.

Events occurring between the date of the reporting accountant's report and the completion date of the transaction

65. After the date of its report, the reporting accountant has no obligation to perform procedures or make enquiries regarding the Class 1 circular. However, the reporting accountant may become aware of events and other matters which, had they occurred and been known at the date of the report, might have caused it to issue a different report or to withhold consent. SIR 1000.23 sets out the Investment Reporting Standards with respect to such events occurring between the date of the reporting accountant's report and the completion date of the transaction.

Effective date

66. A reporting accountant is required to comply with the Investment Reporting Standards contained in this SIR for reports signed after 31 May 2008. Earlier adoption is encouraged.

REGULATORY PROVISIONS APPLICABLE TO CLASS 1 CIRCULARS

Appendix 1

Type of Class 1 Transaction	Requirement for a financial information table	← SIR 2000 → Requirement for an accountant's opinion in true and fair terms	Possibility of a modified opinion	← SIR 5000 → Requirement for a financial information reconciliation	Requirement for an accountant's opinion in properly compiled terms	Possibility of a modified opinion
Class 1 Acquisition of a target that is neither admitted to trading, listed on an overseas investment exchange, nor admitted to trading on an overseas regulated market.	✓ UKLA 13.5.12R UKLA 13.5.14R ISE 10.5.12 ISE 10.5.14	✓ UKLA 13.5.21R UKLA 13.5.22R ISE 10.5.21 ISE 10.5.22	✓ UKLA 13.5.25R ISE 10.5.25	✗	✗	n/a
Class 1 Acquisition of a target that is admitted to trading ...and a material adjustment needs to be made.	✓ UKLA 13.5.12R UKLA 13.5.14R ISE 10.5.12 ISE 10.5.14	✗ UKLA 13.5.21R ISE 10.5.21	n/a	✓ UKLA 13.5.27R(2)(a) UKLA 13.5.30R(2) ISE 10.5.27(2)(a) ISE 10.5.30(2)	✓ UKLA 13.5.27R(2)(b) UKLA 13.5.30R(2) ISE 10.5.27(2)(b) ISE 10.5.30(2)	✓ UKLA 13.5.27R(2)(b) UKLA 13.5.30R ISE 10.5.27(2)(b) ISE 10.5.30
Class 1 Acquisition of a target that is admitted to trading ... and NO material adjustment needs to be made	✓ UKLA 13.5.12R UKLA 13.5.14R ISE 10.5.12 ISE 10.5.14	✗ UKLA 13.5.21R ISE 10.5.21	n/a	✗ If no material adjustment required then not in scope of UKLA 13.5.27R: ISE 10.5.27	✗ UKLA 13.5.28R ISE 10.5.28	n/a
Class 1 disposal	✓ UKLA 13.5.12R UKLA 13.5.19R ISE 10.5.12 ISE 10.5.19	✗ UKLA 13.5.21R UKLA 13.5.29G ISE 10.5.21 ISE 10.5.29	n/a	✗	✗	n/a

Note 1: With in Chapter 13 of the UKLA Listing Rules and Chapter 10 of the ISE Listing Rules the terms "financial information" and "financial information table" are used. The terms have different meanings in that the requirements for a financial information table are set out in UKLA LR 13.5.18R and ISE 10.5.18 whereas the term financial information is not defined.

Note 2: Within Chapter 13 of the UKLA Listing Rules and Chapter 10 of the ISE Listing Rules two different types of accountant's opinion are discussed. The opinion relevant to financial information reconciliations is set out in UKLA 13.5.27R (2)(b) and ISE 10.5.27(2)(b) and is dealt with in this SIR. The other opinion which is relevant to opinions on financial information 'ables is set out in UKLA LR 13.5.22R and ISE 10.5.22 and dealt with in SIR 2000.

Note 3: UKLA LR13.5.30R(2) and ISE 10.5.30(2) require a financial information reconciliation of a target to be produced with respect to subsequent half yearly or quarterly financial information

Appendix 2

EXAMPLES OF ENGAGEMENT LETTER CLAUSES

The examples of engagement letter clauses are intended for consideration in the context of a public reporting engagement on a financial information reconciliation in a Class 1 circular. They should be tailored to the specific circumstances and supplemented by such other clauses as are relevant and appropriate.

Financial information upon which the report is to be given

The Class 1 circular will include a financial information table relating to ABC Inc. prepared in accordance with the requirements of Listing Rule [13.5.18R] [10.5.18] [and interim financial information relating to ABC Inc. reproduced in accordance with Listing Rule [13.5.30R(2)] [10.5.30(2)]].

We understand that the Class 1 circular will also include a financial information reconciliation of ABC Inc. for the three years ended [31 December 200X] [and the interim period ended [*date*]] (the "Reconciliation"). The Reconciliation will comprise [the income statements] and [balance sheets] of ABC Inc. showing the adjustments necessary to restate them to conform to XYZ plc's stated accounting policies. The Reconciliation will include supporting notes to explain the adjustments made.

Responsibilities

The preparation of the Reconciliation in accordance with the requirements of the Listing Rules will be the responsibility solely of the directors.

It is our responsibility to form an opinion as to whether the Reconciliation has been properly compiled on the basis stated and the adjustments are appropriate for the purpose of presenting the financial information (as adjusted) on a basis consistent in all material respects with the accounting policies of XYZ plc.

If the results of our work are satisfactory, and having regard to the requirements of Listing Rule [13.5.27R (2)(b)] [10.5.27(2)(b)] [and Listing Rule [13.5.30(2)] [10.5.30(2)]], we shall prepare a report on the Reconciliation for inclusion in the Class 1 circular. An illustration of the form of our report if the results of our work are satisfactory is attached.

Scope of work

Our work will be undertaken in accordance with the Standards for Investment Reporting issued by the Auditing Practices Board and will be subject to the limitations described therein.

In performing this engagement we will expect to receive, without undue delay, such;

(a) co-operation from all relevant officials of XYZ plc and ABC Inc. [including its auditors];

(b) access to all the pertinent accounting records of XYZ plc and ABC Inc. and any other relevant records and related information; [and]

(c) representations from XYZ plc[; and]

(d) [access to the files of the auditors of ABC Inc.],

as we may need for the purposes of our examination.

Appendix 3

EXAMPLES OF MANAGEMENT REPRESENTATION LETTER CLAUSES

The following are examples of management representation letter clauses relating to reports on financial information reconciliations, issued pursuant to the Listing Rules, which may be obtained from the issuer. Alternatively they may form the basis for a board minute.

Introduction

We refer to the financial information reconciliation set out in Part [...] of the [Class 1 circular] dated...(the "Reconciliation"). We acknowledge that we are solely responsible for the Reconciliation and confirm on behalf of the directors of the company to the best of our knowledge and belief, having made appropriate enquiries of officials of the company [and the directors and officials of the [target]], the following representations made to you in the course of your work.

Specific representations

- We acknowledge as duly appointed officials of the company our responsibility for the Reconciliation which has been prepared in accordance with the requirements of the Listing Rules of [the United Kingdom Listing Authority] [the Irish Stock Exchange Limited].

- We have considered the adjustments included in the Reconciliation. We confirm that, in our opinion, the Reconciliation includes all adjustments that are appropriate for the purpose of presenting the financial information (as adjusted) on a basis consistent in all material respects with the accounting policies of XYZ plc.

- We have made available to you all significant information relevant to the Reconciliation of which we have knowledge.

- [...*Any specific representations relating to information included in the Reconciliations (for example representations concerning accounting policies in greater detail than that included in the published financial statements).*]

EXAMPLE REPORT ON A FINANCIAL INFORMATION RECONCILIATION IN ACCORDANCE WITH THE LISTING RULES

Date

Reporting accountant's address

Addressees, as agreed between the parties in the engagement letter

Dear Sirs,

XYZ plc (the "Company"): proposed acquisition of ABC Inc (the "Target")

We report on the reconciliation of [*describe items reconciled* the consolidated income statement for each of the years in the three-year period ended [*date*] [and the interim period ended [*date*]], and of *describe items reconciled* the consolidated balance sheet as at[*dates*]], together the "financial information", as previously reported in the financial statements of the Target prepared under [United States Generally Accepted Accounting Principles], showing the adjustments necessary to restate it on the basis of the Company's accounting policies [specify the accounting policies e.g. those used in preparing the Company's last set of annual financial statements] (the "Reconciliation"), set out in Part [ ] of the Class 1 circular of the Company dated [*date*]. This report is required by Listing Rule[s] [13.5.27R(2)(b) [and 13.5.30R(2)] of the United Kingdom Listing Authority] [10.5.27(2)(b) [and 10.5.30(2) of the Irish Stock Exchange Limited]] and is given for the purpose of complying with [that] [those] Listing Rule[s] and for no other purpose.

Responsibilities

It is the responsibility of the directors of the Company (the "Directors") to prepare the Reconciliation in accordance with Listing Rule[s] [13.5.27R(2)(a) [and 13.5.30R(2)]] [10.5.27(2)(a) [and 10.5.30(2)]].

It is our responsibility to form an opinion, as required by Listing Rule[s] [13.5.27R(2(b)] [and 13.5.30R(2)]] [10.5.27(2)(a) and 10.5.30(2)]], as to whether:

(a) the Reconciliation has been properly compiled on the basis stated; and

(b) the adjustments are appropriate for the purpose of presenting the financial information (as adjusted) on a basis consistent in all material respects with the Company's accounting policies,

and to report that opinion to you.

[Insert where an audit or other opinion has been expressed on the financial statements of the Target upon which the Reconciliation is based by a firm other than the reporting accountant, or where such information is unaudited: The Reconciliation is based on the [un]audited balance sheet[s] as at *[dates]* and income statement[s] for [each of] the [year[s]]/ [period[s]] then ended of [the Target] which were the responsibility of the directors of [the Target] [and were audited by another firm of accountants]. We do not accept any responsibility for any of the historical financial statements of [the Target], nor do we express any opinion on those financial statements.]

[Insert where the reporting accountant has provided an audit or other opinion on the financial statements of the Target upon which the Reconciliation is based: In providing this opinion we are not updating or refreshing any reports or opinions previously made by us on any financial information used in the compilation of the Reconciliation, nor do we accept responsibility for such reports or opinions beyond that owed to those to whom those reports or opinions were addressed at the date of their issue.]

Basis of Opinion

We conducted our work in accordance with the Standards for Investment Reporting issued by the Auditing Practices Board in [the United Kingdom] [Ireland]. The work that we performed for the purpose of making this report, which involved no independent examination of any of the underlying financial information, consisted primarily of checking whether the unadjusted financial information of [the Target] has been accurately extracted from an appropriate source, assessing whether all adjustments necessary for the purpose of presenting the financial information on a basis consistent in all material respects with [the Company's] accounting policies have been made, examination of evidence supporting the adjustments in the Reconciliation and checking the arithmetical accuracy of the calculations within the Reconciliation.

We planned and performed our work so as to obtain the information and explanations we considered necessary in order to provide us with reasonable assurance that the Reconciliation has been properly compiled on the basis stated and that the adjustments are appropriate for the purpose of presenting the financial information (as adjusted) on a basis consistent in all material respects with the Company's accounting policies.

[This paragraph may be omitted if the document is not to be distributed outside [the UK] [Ireland] – Our work has not been carried out in accordance with auditing or other standards and practices generally accepted in the United States of America [or other jurisdictions] and accordingly should not be relied upon as if it had been carried out in accordance with those standards and practices.]

Opinion

In our opinion:

(a)   the Reconciliation has been properly compiled on the basis stated; and

(b) the adjustments are appropriate for the purpose of presenting the financial information (as adjusted) on a basis consistent in all material respects with the Company's accounting policies.

Declaration

[*This paragraph is only included if the investment circular is also a prospectus*. For the purposes of [Prospectus Rule [5.5.3R(2)(f)] [5.5.4R(2)(f)]] /[Paragraph 2(2)(f) of Schedule 1 to "The Prospectus (Directive 2003/71/EC) Regulations 2005"] [Paragraph 3(2)(f) of Schedule 1 to "the Prospectus (Directive 2003/71/EC) Regulations 2005"] we are responsible for this report as part of the [prospectus] [registration document] and declare that we have taken all reasonable care to ensure that the information contained [in this report] [those parts] is, to the best of our knowledge, in accordance with the facts and contains no omission likely to affect its import. This declaration is included in the [prospectus] [registration document] in compliance with [item 1.2 of Annex I of the PD Regulation] [item 1.2 of Annex III of the PD Regulation].]

Yours faithfully

Reporting accountant

ACCOUNTING CONVENTIONS AND PROCESSES USED IN PREPARING FINANCIAL INFORMATION RECONCILIATIONS FOR INCLUSION IN CLASS 1 CIRCULARS

This Annexure has been compiled by the APB from a number of sources to describe conventions and processes commonly used for the proper compilation of financial information reconciliations. It does not constitute basic principles, essential procedures, or guidance promulgated by the APB.

Introduction

Financial information tables

1   With respect to Class 1 acquisitions, Chapter 13 of the Listing Rules of the UK Listing Authority (UKLA) and Chapter 10 of the Listing Rules of the Irish Stock Exchange Limited (ISE) set out requirements for a financial information table relating to targets[1].

2   A financial information table is required to include, for each of the periods covered by the table:

(a)   a balance sheet and its explanatory notes;

(b)   an income statement and its explanatory notes;

(c)   a cash flow statement and its explanatory notes;

(d)   a statement showing either all changes in equity or changes in equity other than those arising from capital transactions with owners and distributions to owners;

(e)   the accounting policies; and

(f)   any additional explanatory notes.

3   When an issuer seeks to acquire a target that is not publicly traded[2], the financial information table is presented on the basis of the issuer's accounting policies. However, when an issuer seeks to acquire a publicly traded target the financial information table is presented on the basis of the target's accounting policies.

4   With respect to a target that is not publicly traded a reporting accountant's opinion is required as to whether, for the purposes of the Class 1 circular, the financial

---

[1]   Where a listed company is seeking to acquire an interest in another company, that company is described as a target.

[2]   A target that is not publicly traded is one that is neither admitted to the Official List nor admitted to trading, listed on an overseas investment exchange nor admitted to trading on an overseas regulated market.

information table gives a true and fair view of the financial matters set out in it, and whether the financial information table has been prepared in a form that is consistent with the accounting policies adopted in the listed company's latest annual consolidated accounts.

Financial information of publicly traded targets

5   With respect to targets that are publicly traded a reporting accountant's opinion on the financial information table is not required. However, with respect to a publicly traded target, if a material adjustment needs to be made to the target's financial statements to achieve consistency with the issuer's accounting policies there are additional requirements.

6   Therefore, with respect to a publicly traded target, the issuer is required to make a determination as to whether material adjustments need to be made to the target's financial statements in order to achieve consistency with the issuer's accounting policies. Such a determination will need to be made by a staff member or outside expert having appropriate qualifications (see paragraph 23) and involve the identification of material differences (if any) between the accounting policies of the issuer and the accounting policies of the target (see paragraph 24).

7   Where such a material adjustment does need to be made the issuer is required to include the following in the Class 1 circular in addition to the financial information table referred to above[3]:

(a)   a reconciliation of "financial information" on the target, for all periods covered by the financial information table, normally on the basis of the accounting policies used in the issuer's last published accounts[4];

(b)   a reporting accountant's opinion on that reconciliation that sets out:

(i)   whether the reconciliation of financial information in the financial information table has been properly compiled on the basis stated; and

(ii)   whether the adjustments are appropriate for the purpose of presenting the financial information (as adjusted) on a basis consistent in all material respects with the issuer's accounting policies.

---

[3]   Under UKLA LR 13.5.30R(2) and ISE LR 10.5.30(2) similar requirements apply where the target has published half yearly or quarterly financial information subsequent to the end of its last financial year and a material adjustment needs to be made to the financial information presented in respect of the relevant interim period of the target in the Class 1 circular to achieve consistency with the issuer's accounting policies.

[4]   The UKLA's publication "List!" 16 at paragraph 2.5 discusses certain circumstances where accounting policies other than those used in the issuer's last published accounts are used.

The need for accounting conventions

8   The term "financial information" is not defined by the Listing Rules nor are there any detailed rules regarding the "proper compilation" of a financial information reconciliation. The directors, therefore, have regard to accepted conventions which have developed for the preparation and presentation of financial information reconciliation tables in Class 1 circulars. These conventions are summarised in paragraphs 9 to 22 that follow. In paragraphs 23 to 33 there is a discussion of processes that the issuer may adopt when preparing financial information reconciliations.

Conventions

Format of financial information reconciliations

9   The overriding principle regarding the format of the presentation of a financial information reconciliation is that the presentation discloses all the material adjustments that are required to be made in order to present the financial information (as adjusted) on a basis consistent with the issuer's accounting policies. The relevant accounting policies of the issuer are normally those adopted by the issuer in its last published accounts.

10   Financial information reconciliations typically address the balance sheet and income statement or extracts of the balance sheet and income statement. However, if there is a material adjustment required, for example, to the cash flow statement or the Statement of Changes in Equity then relevant financial information from the relevant statement may also be presented. A material adjustment may arise to the cash flow statement where the target and the issuer use different definitions of the composition of cash and cash equivalents.

11   There is no prescribed format for the presentation of the reconciliation. Sometimes they are presented in columnar form using as a basis the descriptions of financial statement items in the target's financial information. However, alternative presentations are commonly used and the underlying principle is that the reader of the Class 1 circular should be able to understand how the adjustments affect the underlying financial information.

Errors in the underlying financial information

12   Where an error in the underlying financial information is identified that does not reflect a genuine difference between the accounting policies of the target and the issuer it is not rectified by being presented as an adjustment. The issuer discusses the proposed presentation of the rectification of the error with the UKLA or the ISE.

13   What constitutes an error will be defined by the financial reporting framework used by the issuer. In the case of International Financial Reporting Standards (IFRSs) as adopted by the EU, for example, an error is defined as: "omissions from, and

misstatements in, the target's financial statements, for one or more prior periods arising from a failure to use, or misuse of, reliable information that:

(a) was available when financial statements for those periods were authorised for issue; and

(b) could reasonably be expected to have been obtained and taken into account in the preparation and presentation of those financial statements.

Such errors include the effects of mathematical mistakes, mistakes in applying accounting policies, oversights or misinterpretations of fact and fraud".

Accounting policies

14 Guidance in UKLA Listing Rule 13.5.5G and ISE Listing Rule 10.5.5 indicates that "accounting policies include accounting standards and accounting disclosures". A financial information reconciliation, therefore, is not confined to a reconciliation to the stated accounting policies of an issuer but to those policies and the accounting standards comprising the financial reporting framework of the issuer regardless of whether they are articulated within the issuer's statement of accounting policies. However, reconciliations do not normally extend to reconciling note disclosures.

15 Under many financial reporting frameworks, such as IFRSs as adopted by the EU, the application of different measurement bases to financial statement items is evidence that different accounting policies have been applied. IAS 8 states "A change in the measurement basis applied is a change in an accounting policy and is not a change in an accounting estimate"[5]. Examples of measurement bases, described in IFRSs as adopted by the EU are: historical cost, current cost, net realisable value, fair value or recoverable amount[6].

16 In the process of applying the entity's accounting policies, management makes various judgments, apart from those involving estimations (see paragraph 19) that can have a significant effect on the amounts recognised in the financial statements. Under IFRSs as adopted by the EU the entity is required to disclose those judgments that have the most significant effect on the amounts recognised in the financial statements[7].

17 Examples of such judgments are:

- Whether financial assets are held-to-maturity investments.

- When substantially all the significant risks and rewards of ownership of financial assets and lease assets are transferred to other entities.

---

[5] IAS 8 "Accounting Policies, Changes in Accounting Estimates and Errors" paragraph 35
[6] IAS 1 "Presentation of financial statements" paragraph 109
[7] IAS 1 paragraphs 113 and 114

- Whether, in substance, particular sales of goods are financing arrangements and therefore do not give rise to revenue.

- Whether the substance of the relationship between the entity and a special purpose entity indicates that the special purpose entity is controlled by the entity.

Where the target and the issuer have made, or would make, different judgments in similar circumstances this gives rise to the need for an adjustment.

Accounting estimates

18 Although adjustments are made for differences in accounting policies (as defined), adjustments are not made to replace the target's accounting estimates with new estimates made by the issuer. However, in rare circumstances the effect of a difference from applying an accounting estimate may be material to the adjusted financial information and the issuer may consider that it is necessary to explain this through supplemental disclosure to allow the financial information reconciliation to be considered in context. An example of such a circumstance is where the issuer and the target both have a policy of depreciating a particular class of property, plant and equipment on a straight line basis over its expected useful life. However, the target's estimate of the expected useful life differs significantly from the issuer's estimated useful life and the effect of the difference in estimate is material to the financial information reconciliation.

Distinguishing between accounting policies and accounting estimates

19 Many financial reporting frameworks recognise that it can be difficult to distinguish changes in accounting policies from changes in accounting estimates and that in such instances of uncertainty the change is treated as a change in accounting estimate[8]. A similar principle applies when determining whether a target uses different accounting policies to those used by the issuer.

Explanation of adjustments

20 The overriding principle that the issuer follows is to ensure that the adjustments are clearly shown and explained.

21 The convention is that material adjustments are presented on a disaggregated basis (that is offsetting adjustments are not netted off) as such presentation enhances the understanding of the users of the reconciliation.

Material adjustments

22 The requirement for a reconciliation arises where a material adjustment needs to be made to the target's financial statements to achieve consistency with the listed company's accounting policies. It is not possible to prescribe conditions for

---

[8] IAS 8 paragraph 35

determining whether an adjustment will be a material adjustment in any given case, although presentational accounting policy differences, which do not have the effect of altering net assets, net income or cash flows are not normally treated as material. The UKLA or the ISE will usually wish to agree the approach in individual cases.

Processes for preparing a financial information reconciliation

Identification of all material differences

23 In order to identify all material differences between the accounting policies of the issuer and the accounting policies of the target the issuer's staff responsible for preparation of the reconciliation will need to have (or acquire) a requisite degree of expertise with respect to both financial reporting frameworks. Such expertise may be augmented by the use of appropriate reference material and technical guides. In complex cases the issuer may have to employ an outside expert having appropriate qualifications.

Preparing a financial information reconciliation

24 There are four basic steps involved in preparing a financial information reconciliation. These are:

(a) identification of all material differences between the accounting policies of the issuer and the accounting policies of the target (See paragraph 6);

(b) performing an "impact analysis" by performing a detailed analysis of the application of those policies and gathering the relevant data to enable either:

(i) the adjustments to be calculated; or

(ii) a determination to be made that no adjustments are required.

(c) in respect of each material difference calculating the effect on the target's financial information of applying the accounting policies of the issuer rather than the accounting policies of the target; and

(d) ensuring that the bookkeeping underpinning the financial information reconciliation is complete and accurate.

25 In practice these steps will need to be undertaken by the issuer's staff responsible for preparation of the reconciliation in consultation with, and with the cooperation of, the relevant finance staff of the target. It is unlikely that the issuer's staff will be able to achieve the necessary understanding of the target's financial information without a high degree of involvement of the target's finance staff in the process. In a hostile bid, or other limited access situation, the issuer is unlikely to be in a position to prepare a financial information reconciliation. In such situations the circumstances are discussed with the UKLA or the ISE.

26   The UKLA generally encourages issuers preparing an investment circular in a limited access situation to contact them as soon as possible to discuss the exact disclosure requirements. In certain circumstances it may be appropriate for a financial information reconciliation to be published in a supplementary circular within 28 days of a contested offer becoming unconditional.

Identification of all material differences between the accounting policies of the issuer and the target

27   As explained in paragraph 14 the identification is not confined to the stated accounting policies of the issuer or the target but also encompasses differences between those accounting standards that affect the financial statements of the issuer or the target regardless of whether the application of the accounting standards has been articulated in the statement of accounting policies.

Impact analysis

28   The issuer, therefore, gains an understanding of the differences between the financial reporting frameworks of the target and the issuer and may prepare an "impact analysis". Such an impact analysis may be prepared in conjunction with, or as a development of, the initial determination prepared by the issuer referred to in paragraph 6.

29   The impact analysis should in particular identify those accounting standards in the issuer's or target's financial reporting frameworks that may have a particular impact on the target's or issuer's industries.

30   Using proprietary checklists or synopses of the requirements of accounting standards may assist issuers in preparing an impact analysis.

Calculating the effect on the target's financial information of applying the issuer's accounting policies

31   In order to calculate the adjustments required to be made in respect of each identified difference, between the accounting policies of the target and the issuer, the issuer is likely to require access to the accounting records and related information of the target. To provide support for the calculation of each adjustment the issuer retains appropriate documented evidence.

Ensuring that the bookkeeping is complete and accurate

32   When preparing a financial information reconciliation there are a number of accounting controls that an issuer may apply, for example:

- Ensuring, when making adjustments, that the principles of double-entry bookkeeping are followed. The risk of making one-sided adjustments is mitigated to a great extent if working papers are prepared covering an adjusted income statement, an adjusted balance sheet and an adjusted statement of equity, even if not all of these are to be published.

- Considering the income, and other, tax effects of the adjustments and assessing whether the resultant effective tax rate is understandable and meaningful.

- Analysing the differences between the (adjusted) opening and closing equity account balances. (This is sometimes referred to as an equity roll forward reconciliation.) Such an analysis will be of assistance in checking that the principles of double-entry bookkeeping have been followed where the other side of an adjustment is to an equity account.

- Proving that the cash and cash equivalent position, as adjusted, is the same as that shown by the unadjusted financial statements (unless there is a reason for there being a difference). If there is a difference between the cash position reported on the two bases the issuer should understand how this difference arises and consider whether it may reflect an error in the double-entry bookkeeping applied to the reconciliation process[9].

Internal controls over the reconciliation

33   The following high level internal controls should typically be in place:

- The issuer should have employees (or access to outside experts), and other technical resources, with requisite knowledge and experience to prepare and monitor the preparation of the financial information reconciliation.

- The directors of the issuer should be committed to the proper preparation of financial information reconciliations as evidenced by a careful review of the financial information reconciliations being performed.

- Where applicable, comparing the reconciliation to those made in earlier periods. This may be applicable where the listed company has made an unsuccessful bid for the target in a previous period or a bid for other targets that use the same financial reporting framework.

---

[9]   Cash flow statements are usually not published as part of a financial information reconciliation. Nevertheless, comparing the resultant cash position from moving from the target's financial reporting framework to that of the issuer may be a useful accounting control.

Section 7: GUIDANCE

BULLETIN 2006/4

REGULATORY AND LEGISLATIVE BACKGROUND TO THE APPLICATION OF STANDARDS FOR INVESTMENT REPORTING IN THE REPUBLIC OF IRELAND

CONTENTS

Introduction

1. The Auditing Practices Board (APB) has recently issued four Standards for Investment Reporting (SIRs):

   (a) SIR 1000 "Investment Reporting Standards Applicable To All Engagements In Connection With An Investment Circular" ("SIR 1000");

   (b) SIR 2000 "Investment Reporting Standards Applicable To Public Reporting Engagements on Historical Financial Information" ("SIR 2000");

   (c) SIR 3000 "Investment Reporting Standards Applicable to Public Reporting Engagements on Profit Forecasts" ("SIR 3000"); and

   (d) SIR 4000 "Investment Reporting Standards Applicable to Public Reporting Engagements on Pro Forma Financial Information" (SIR 4000).

2. The SIRs reflect the requirements of the EU Prospectus Directive, the implementing EU Regulation 809/2004 that provides the detailed rules concerning Prospectuses and their contents (Referred to in the SIRs as the PD Regulation and in "Irish Prospectus Law[1]" as the Prospectus Regulation[2]), and other related regulations that came into force on 1 July 2005.

3. The SIRs contain basic principles and essential procedures (Investment Reporting Standards), indicated by paragraphs in bold type, with which a reporting accountant is required to comply in the conduct of all engagements in connection with an investment circular.

SIRs 1000 and 2000

4. Under the new regulations issuers, rather than reporting accountants, are responsible for preparing and presenting historical financial information in an investment circular and the reporting accountant's role is to express an opinion as to whether that financial information gives a true and fair view.

5. SIR 1000 provides Investment Reporting Standards applicable to all engagements involving investment circulars. SIR 2000 establishes additional Investment Reporting Standards for reporting accountants when examining historical financial information which is intended to give a true and fair view.

6. SIRs 1000 and 2000 apply to reports signed by reporting accountants after 31 August 2005. SIRs 100 and 200 (which were issued in 1997) were withdrawn with effect from the same date.

---

[1] See Appendix 1 for definition of this term.
[2] In this Bulletin the term "the Prospectus Regulation" refers to EU Regulation 809/2004. The equivalent term used in the published SIRs is "PD Regulation".

SIRs 3000 and 4000

7. Under the Prospectus Regulation a reporting accountant has to express an opinion as to whether or not a profit forecast and pro forma financial information has been "properly compiled" on the basis stated by the issuer.

8. SIRs 3000 and 4000 establish Investment Reporting Standards for reporting accountants when reporting on profit forecasts and pro forma financial information respectively. These are additional to the requirements of SIR 1000. Among other things the SIRs require the reporting accountant to obtain sufficient appropriate evidence that the directors have applied the criteria provided by the Prospectus Regulation and the CESR recommendations that affect the "proper compilation" of the profit forecast or pro forma financial information.

9. SIRs 3000 and 4000 apply to reports signed after 31 March 2006. With effect from the same date Bulletin 1998/08 "Reporting on Pro forma Financial Information Pursuant to the Listing Rules" was withdrawn.

Application of the SIRs in the Republic of Ireland

10. The SIRs have been drafted with reference to legislation and regulations implementing the Prospectus Directive in the United Kingdom. The provisions and the principles contained within the SIRs are applicable to the Irish legislative and regulatory environment. The purpose of this Bulletin, therefore, is to provide an explanation of the background to the legislative and regulatory environment in Ireland and to provide a mapping of legislative and technical references within the SIRs, as published, to the Irish equivalent.

Ethical Standard for Reporting Accountants (ESRA)

11. Bulletin 2005/7 "Integrity, Objectivity and Independence – Guidance for reporting Accountants Undertaking Engagements in Connection with an Investment Circular" provides interim guidance to reporting accountants as to how to apply Ethical Standards ES1 to 5 to assist them in complying with the requirement of SIR 1000 to "comply with the applicable ethical standards issued by the Auditing Practices Board".

12. In January 2006 the APB issued an Exposure Draft of an Ethical Standard for Reporting Accountants (ESRA) which in due course will supersede Bulletin 2005/7.

Principal Legislation and the Prospectus Directive

(1) Principal Legislation

13. The principal legislation governing the regulation of companies and the publication of financial information in Ireland are the Companies Acts, 1963 – 2005 (the "Companies Acts").

14. The Companies Acts 1963 -2005 include the "Investment Funds, Companies and Miscellaneous Provisions Act, 2005" enacted on 29 June 2005 as Act Number 12 of 2005.

(2) Prospectus (Directive 2003/71/EC) Regulations, 2005 ("the Regulation[3]")

15. The Regulation made by the Minister for Enterprise, Trade and Employment, came into operation on 1 July 2005. This Regulation transposed the EU Prospectus Directive into Irish law by statutory instrument.

16. Upon implementation of the Prospectus Directive, the existing regime regarding the issue of listing particulars in connection with an application for listing or prospectuses in connection with a public offer of securities in Ireland, pursuant to Council Directive 80/390/EEC or Council Directive 89/298EEC, respectively, was repealed.

17. The Regulation along with Part 5 of the Investment Funds, Companies and Miscellaneous Provisions Act 2005 (the Act of 2005) give effect to the Prospectus Directive in Ireland on prospectuses to be published when securities are offered to the public or admitted to trading on a regulated market. The annexes to the Prospectus Regulation provide detailed rules on prospectuses and, in particular, the content requirements of prospectuses.

(3) Market Abuse (Directive2003/6/EC) Regulations, 2005 (the "Market Abuse Directive")

18. The Market Abuse Regulations made by the Minister for Enterprise, Trade and Employment, came substantially into operation on 6 July 2005, these regulations transposed the EU Market Abuse Directive into Irish law by statutory instrument, remaining provisions of the Market Abuse Directive (insider lists, manager transactions) came into effect on 1 October 2005.

19. The Market Abuse (Directive 2003/6/EC) Regulations 2005 along with Part 4 of the Investment Funds, Companies and Miscellaneous Provisions Act 2005 give effect to the Market Abuse Directive in Ireland, as well as implementing Directives 2003/124/EC, 2003/125/EC and 2004/72/EC on insider dealing and market manipulation.

(4) Role of the Financial Regulator, Prospectus Rules, Market Abuse Rules and CESR

Role of the Financial Regulator

20. Under the Prospectus Directive and the Market Abuse Directive, the Financial Regulator (previously titled the Irish Financial Services Regulatory Authority) ("the Financial Regulator") is the competent authority.

---

[3] These regulations are referred to as "The Regulation" in the definition of Irish Prospectus Law. See Appendix 1 and also item 1.2 of the "Prospectus Rules"

Prospectus Rules

21. The Financial Regulator, in exercising its functions as competent authority under the Prospectus Directive, has published finalised "Prospectus Rules Issued Under Section 51 of the Investment Funds, Companies and Miscellaneous Provisions Act, 2005" (the "Prospectus Rules"). The Prospectus Rules will replace the Interim Rules and Guidance Note that have been in place since the Prospectus Regulations came into operation in July 2005. The Prospectus Rules set out procedural and administrative requirements and guidance in respect of the Directives.

22. The Prospectus Rules indicate that in determining whether Commission Regulation (EC) No 809/2004 has been complied with, the Financial Regulator will take into account whether an issuer has complied with "CESR's[4] recommendations for the consistent implementation of the European Commission's Regulation on Prospectuses no. 809/2004 (CESR/05-054b)" to be followed when preparing a prospectus.

Market Abuse Rules

23. The Financial Regulator, in exercising its functions as competent authority under the Market Abuse Directive, has issued "Rules Issued Under Section 34 of the Investment Funds, Companies and Miscellaneous Provisions Act 2005" (the "Market Abuse Rules"). The Rules set out procedural and administrative requirements and guidance in respect of the Directives.

24. The Market Abuse Rules make it clear that in determining whether Commission Regulation (EC) No 809/2004 has been complied with, the Financial Regulator will take into account whether an issuer has complied with "CESR's Guidance and Information on the Common Operation of the Market Abuse Directive (CESR/04-505b)" to be followed when preparing a prospectus.

25. Copies of the Prospectus Rules and the Market Abuse Rules are available from www.financialregulator.ie.

Rules of the Irish Stock Exchange

(1) Irish Stock Exchange Listing Rules

26. In relation to the Listing Rules, the Irish Stock Exchange is performing its functions as the competent authority under Regulation 7 of the European Communities (Stock Exchange) Regulations, 1984.

---

[4] The Committee of European Securities Regulators ("CESR") is an independent committee of European Securities Regulators, the Financial Regulator is a member of CESR.
The role of CESR is to:
(i) Improve co-ordination among securities regulators;
(ii) Act as an advisory group to assist the EU Commission; and
(iii) Work to ensure more consistent and timely day-today implementation of community legislation in Member States.
Further information about CESR can be found on its web-site: www.cesr-eu.org

27. Given the new regulatory environment following implementation of the Prospectus Directive and Market Abuse Directive, the Irish Stock Exchange no longer adopts the Listing Rules of the Financial Services Authority (FSA) in the UK, and instead has developed its own stand alone listing rule book. To facilitate the dual listing of securities on the Irish and London stock exchanges, the Irish Stock Exchange has retained its policy of maintaining parity of listing standards with the FSA.

28. From 1 July 2005 the Exchange's Listing Rules cover *inter alia*:

   • conditions for listing.

   • listing applications procedures.

   • listing principles.

   • continuing obligation requirements, including super-equivalent requirements.

   • requirements for sponsors.

29. The Listing Rules are available on the Exchange's website at the following address: www.ise.ie

(2) Alternative Securities Market ("ASM") Rules

30. From 1 July 2005, issuers seeking a listing of asset backed, debt or derivative securities on the Irish Stock Exchange may choose to have those securities admitted to trading on the Alternative Securities Market (ASM), rather than the "regulated market" (as defined by Article 1(13) of Directive 93/22/EEC). Issuers seeking a listing on the ASM must prepare a listing particulars document which is reviewed, and subject to approval, by the Exchange. Certain third country issuers are not required to report historical financial information under IFRSs or an EU approved equivalent standard either in listing particulars or as a continuing obligation requirement.

(3) Irish Enterprise Exchange ("IEX") Rules

31. Under the Irish Enterprise Exchange ("IEX") Rules of the Irish Stock Exchange, companies seeking admission to IEX must publish an IEX admission document. This is the case whether or not they are required by Prospectus Law to prepare a prospectus (because they are also making an offer of securities to the public which is not exempt from the requirement to produce a prospectus).

32. The IEX Rules provide that the content of an admission document should be based on the disclosure requirements that apply to issuers of shares in the Prospectus Regulation, modified as set out in the IEX Rules, as well as certain additional IEX disclosure requirements.

Appendix 1

Glossary of terms

Alternative Securities Market – A market for debt and derivative securities which is operated and regulated by the Irish Stock Exchange. This is not a "regulated market" as defined by Article 1(13) of Directive 93/22/EEC.

ASM – The Alternative Securities Market

CESR – The Committee of European Securities Regulators

CESR Recommendations – "CESR's recommendations for the consistent implementation of the European Commission's Regulation on Prospectuses no. 809/2004 (CESR/05-054b)"

Circular – A circular issued by any company to its shareholders and/or holders of its debt securities in connection with a transaction, which does not constitute a prospectus, listing particulars or IEX admission document.

City Code – Takeover Rules and Substantial Acquisition Rules. The application of these rules is monitored by the Irish Takeover Panel.

Class 1 transaction – A transaction where one or more of a number of specified percentage ratios exceed a predetermined level as specified in Chapter 7 of the Listing Rules.

Financial Regulator – Irish Financial Services Authority of Ireland (IFSRA).

IEX - The Irish Enterprise Exchange.

IEX Admission Document – The document prepared in connection with an application for admission of an issuer's securities to IEX.

IEX adviser – An adviser whose name appears on the Irish Stock Exchange's most recently published register of IEX advisers.

IEX Rules – The Rules of the Irish Enterprise Exchange.

IFSRA – The Irish Financial Services Regulatory Authority (Financial Regulator)

Irish Enterprise Exchange – A market for small to mid-sized companies which is operated and regulated by the Irish Stock Exchange.

Irish Stock Exchange – The Irish Stock Exchange Limited.

Issuer – For the purposes of Prospectus Law "A body corporate or other legal entity which issues or proposes to issue securities". For the purposes of the Listing Rules "Any company or other legal person or undertaking (including a public sector issuer), any class of whose securities has been admitted to listing or is the subject of an application for admission to listing".

Listing Rules – The Listing Rules of the Irish Stock Exchange.

Official List – Official List of the Irish Stock Exchange.

Prospectus Law – Any or all of the following as the context so requires:

(1) Part 5 of the Investment Funds, Companies and Miscellaneous Provisions Act 2005 (the Act of 2005);
(2) The Regulation;
(3) The Prospectus Regulation;
(4) CESR Recommendations; and
(5) Prospectus Rules.

Prospectus Rules – Rules issued under Section 51 of the Investment Funds, Companies and Miscellaneous Provisions Act, 2005.[5]

(The) Prospectus Regulation Commission Regulation (EC) No 809/2004 of 29 April 2004[6]. (The equivalent term used in the published SIRs is PD Regulation).

(The) Regulation – Prospectus (Directive 2003/71/EC) Regulations 2005.

Sponsor – A person approved by the Irish Stock Exchange as a registered sponsor.

---

[5] Readers are cautioned that in the UK, and in the SIRs as published, the expression "Prospectus Rules" has a different meaning. For the purposes of this Bulletin the equivalent Irish term to the UK "Prospectus Rules" is "Prospectus Law".

[6] Readers are cautioned that in the UK, and in the SIRs as published, the expression "Prospectus Regulations" has a different meaning. For the purposes of this Bulletin the equivalent Irish term to the UK "Prospectus Regulations" is "Prospectus Law".

Appendix 2

Mapping from SIRS to Equivalent Irish References

(1) SIR 1000 "Investment Reporting Standards Applicable To All Engagements In Connection With An Investment Circular"

SIR 1000 – Paragraph Reference	UK Reference	Irish Equivalent
Main Document		
5, 61, 65, 68(a), Appendix 1	Prospectus Rules	Prospectus Law
68(a), 68(b), 68(c)	Listing Rules	Listing Rules of the Irish Stock Exchange
68(a), 68(b)	Item 23.1 of Annex I of the Prospectus Rules	Item 23.1 of Annex I of the Prospectus Regulation
68(c)	Paragraph 13.4.1(6) of the Listing Rules	Paragraph 10.4.1(6) of the Listing Rules of the Irish Stock Exchange
68(d), 74	City Code	Takeover Rules and Substantial Acquisition Rules.
68(d)	Rule 28.4 City Code	Rule 28.4 – Takeover Rules
68(d),73	Rule 28.5 City Code	Rule 28.5 – Takeover Rules
68(e), Appendix 2	Alternative Investment Market (AIM) Rules	IEX Rules
68(e)	Item 23.1 of Annex I of the Prospectus Rules	Item 23.1 of Annex I of The Prospectus Regulation
Appendix 2	**Principal Legal and Regulatory Requirements**	
Paragraphs 1 to 6	FSA Handbook	Listing Rules of the Irish Stock Exchange and the Prospectus Regulation.
7	Annexes to the Prospectus Rules	Annexes to the Prospectus Regulation
8	Listing Rule 13.5	Section 10.5 of the Listing Rules of the Irish Stock Exchange
9(a)	Item 13.1 of Annex I to the Prospectus Directive	Item 13.1 of Annex I of the Prospectus Regulation
11	Annex I item 20.2 and Annex II of the Prospectus Rules	Annex I item 20.2 and Annex II of the Prospectus Regulation
15	Admission to Main Market of the London Stock Exchange	Admission to a regulated market of the Irish Stock Exchange
18	Professional Securities Market	Alternative Securities Market

SIR 1000 – Paragraph Reference	UK Reference	Irish Equivalent
19	City Code Rule 28.3	Rule 28.3 – Takeover Rules
19	City Code Rule 19.1	Rule 19.1 – Takeover Rules
19	City Code Rule 28.6(c)	Rule 28.6 (d)- Takeover Rules
20	S. 240 Companies Act 1985, ("non-statutory accounts")	S. 19 Companies Amendment Act 1986 ("abbreviated accounts")
20	S. 240 (3) Companies Act 1985	S. 19 (2) Companies Amendment Act 1986 ("abbreviated accounts")
Paragraphs 21 to 26	Financial Services and Markets Act 2000	"the Regulation"
Appendix 3	**Example of Consent Letter**	
Paragraph 2	Prospectus Rule 5.5.3R(2)(f)	Paragraph 2(2)(f) of Schedule 1 to "the Regulation"
Paragraph 2	Prospectus Rule 5.5.4R(2)(f)	Paragraph 3(2)(f) of Schedule 1 to "the Regulation"
Paragraph 2	Regulation 6(1)(e) of The Financial Services and Markets Act 2000 (Official Listing of Securities) Regulations 2001	Chapter 16 of the Listing Rules of the Irish Stock Exchange
Paragraph 2	Schedule Two to the AIM Rules	Schedule Two to the IEX Rules

(2) SIR 2000 "Investment Reporting Standards Applicable To Public Reporting Engagements on Historical Financial Information"

SIR 2000 – Paragraph Reference	UK Reference	Irish Equivalent
Main Document		
3(b), 4	PD Regulation	The Prospectus Regulation
3(b), 21, Annex I	Listing Rules	Listing Rules of the Irish Stock Exchange
4, 19, Appendix 3	Prospectus Rules	Prospectus Law
4	Annex I of the PD Regulation	Annex I of the Prospectus Regulation
5, Appendix 2	Chapter 13 of the Listing Rules	Chapter 10 of the Listing Rules of the Irish Stock Exchange
17	Companies Act 1985	Companies Acts 1963 to 2005
63	Chapter 3 of the Prospectus Rules	Regulations 51 and 52 of "the Regulation"
63	FSA	The Financial Regulator
Appendix 2	**Examples of Engagement Letter Clauses**	
For a Prospectus Paragraph 1	Annex I item 20.1 of the Prospectus Rules	Annex I item 20.1 of the Prospectus Regulation
For a Class 1 circular Paragraph 1	Chapter 13 of the Listing Rules	Chapter 10 of the Listing Rules of the Irish Stock Exchange
Appendix 3	**Example of an Accountant's Report on Historical Financial Information**	
Footnote 1	AIM admission document	IEX admission document
Declaration	Prospectus Rule 5.5.3R(2)(f)	Paragraph 2(2)(f) of Schedule 1 to "the Regulation"
Declaration	Prospectus Rule 5.5.4R(2)(f)	Paragraph 3(2)(f) of Schedule 1 to "the Regulation"
Declaration	Item 1.2 of Annex I of the PD Regulation	Item 1.2 of Annex I of Prospectus Regulation
Declaration	Item 1.2 of Annex III of the PD Regulation	Item 1.2 of Annex III of Prospectus Regulation
Declaration	Schedule 2 of the AIM Rules	Schedule 2 of the IEX Rules
Footnote 3	AIM admission document under Schedule Two of the AIM Rules	IEX admission document under Schedule Two of the IEX Rules

SIR 2000 – Paragraph Reference	UK Reference	Irish Equivalent
Annexure		
8	PD Regulation (subject to certain transitional provisions in Article 35 of the PD Regulation)	The Prospectus Regulation (subject to certain transitional provisions in Article 35 of the Prospectus Regulation)
51	Chapter 13 of the Listing Rules	Chapter 10 of the Listing Rules of the Irish Stock Exchange
52	Listing Rule 13.3	Listing Rule 10.3 of the Irish Stock Exchange
55, 62	UK Listing Authority	Irish Stock Exchange

(3) SIR 3000 "Investment Reporting Standards Applicable To Public Reporting Engagements On Profit Forecasts"

(i) Main Body of Document

SIR 3000 – Paragraph Reference	UK Reference	Irish Equivalent
1, 2(b), 3, 22, 24, 39	PD Regulation	The Prospectus Regulation
1	Listing Rules	Listing Rules of the Irish Stock Exchange
1, 22, 39, 76	City Code	Takeover Rules and Substantial Acquisition Rules
1	AIM Admission Document	Irish Enterprise Exchange ("IEX") Admission Document
10	Prospective Financial Information – Guidance for UK directors – ICAEW[7] Guidance	Prospective Financial Information – Guidance for UK directors – ICAEW Guidance (for information)
81	Sections 81 and 87G of the FSMA, Prospectus Rule 3.4, and Listing Rule 4.4.1, preparation.	Regulation 51 of "the Regulation" and Irish Stock Exchange Listing Rule 16.4.
Appendix 1	Notes 1(c) and (d) to Rule 28.2 of the City Code	Notes 1(c) and (d) to Rule 28.2 of the Takeover Rules

---

[7] Institute of Chartered Accountants in England & Wales

(ii) Appendix 2 – Reporting Accountant's Criteria

	Prospectus Regulation	Annex I[8] Prospectus Regulation	CESR Recommendations
A statement setting out the principal assumptions upon which the issuer has based its forecast or estimate.		13.1	
There must be a clear distinction between assumptions about factors which the members of the administrative, management or supervisory bodies can influence and assumptions about factors which are exclusively outside the influence of the members of the administrative, management or supervisory bodies; the assumptions must be readily understandable by investors, be specific and precise and not relate to the general accuracy of the estimates underlying the forecast.		13.1	
The profit forecast or estimate must be prepared on a basis comparable with the historical financial information.		13.3	
The following principles should be taken into consideration when profit forecasts or estimates are being compiled. Profit forecasts or estimates should be • **Understandable,** ie Profit forecasts or estimates should contain disclosure that is not too complex or extensive for investors to understand; • **Reliable,** ie Profit forecasts should be supported by a thorough analysis of the issuer's business and should represent factual and not hypothetical strategies, plans and risk analysis; • **Comparable,** ie Profit forecasts or estimates should be capable of justification by comparison with outcomes in the form of historical financial information;			para 41

8   The column illustrates Annex I as an example. Other annexes to the Prospectus Regulation contain identical requirements with respect to profit forecasts. See Appendix 1 of SIR 1000.

(iii) Appendix 3 – Other Regulatory Provisions Relevant to the Preparers of Profit Forecasts

	Prospectus Regulation	Annex I of Prospectus Regulation	CESR Recommendations
(8) Voluntary disclosure of profit forecasts in a share registration document should be presented in a consistent and comparable manner and accompanied by a statement prepared by independent accountants or auditors. This information should not be confused with the disclosure of known trends or other factual data with material impact on the issuer's prospects. Moreover, they should provide an explanation of any changes in disclosure policy relating to profit forecasts when supplementing a prospectus or drafting a new prospectus.	Recital 8		
Profit forecast means a form of words which expressly states or by implication indicates a figure or a minimum or maximum figure for the likely level of profits or losses for the current financial period and/or financial periods subsequent to that period, or contains data from which a calculation of such a figure for future profits or losses may be made, even if no particular figure is mentioned and the word "profit" is not used.	Article 2		
Profit estimate means a profit forecast or profit estimate for a financial period which has expired and for which results have not yet been published	Article 2		
If an issuer chooses to include a profit forecast or profit estimate the registration document must contain the information set out in items 13.1 and 13.2		13	
A report prepared by independent accountants or auditors stating that in the opinion of the independent accountants or auditors the forecast or estimate has been properly compiled on the basis stated and that the basis of accounting used for the profit forecast or estimate is consistent with the accounting policies of the issuer		13.2	

	Prospectus Regulation	Annex I of Prospectus Regulation	CESR Recommendations
If a profit forecast in a prospectus has been published which is still outstanding, then provide a statement setting out whether or not that forecast is still correct as at the time of the registration document, and an explanation of why such forecast is no longer valid if that is the case.		13.4	
The inclusion of a profit forecast or estimate in a prospectus is the responsibility of the issuer and persons responsible for the prospectus and due care and diligence must be taken to ensure that profit forecasts or estimates are not misleading to investors			para 40
The following principles should be taken into consideration when profit forecasts or estimates are being compiled. Profit forecasts or estimates should be • **Relevant,** ie profit forecasts and estimates must have an ability to influence economic decisions of investors and provided on a timely basis so as to influence such decisions and assist in confirming or correcting past evaluations or assessments			para 41
Where an issuer provides a profit forecast or estimate in a registration document, if the related schedules so requires, it must be reported on by independent accountants or auditors in the registration document (as described in item 13.2 of Annex I of the Regulation) Where the issuer does not produce a single prospectus, upon the issuance of the securities note and summary at a later time, the issuer should either: • Confirm the profit estimates or forecasts; or • State that the profit forecasts or estimates are no longer valid or correct; or Make appropriate alteration of profit forecasts or estimates. In this case they must be reported upon as described in item 13.2 of Annex I of the Regulation.			para 42

	Prospectus Regulation	Annex I of Prospectus Regulation	CESR Recommendations
If an issuer has made a statement other than in a previous prospectus that would constitute a profit forecast or estimate if made in a prospectus, for instance, in a regulatory announcement, and that statement is still outstanding at the time of publication of the prospectus, the issuer should consider whether the forecasts or estimates are still material and valid and choose whether or not to include them in the prospectus. CESR considers that there is a presumption that an outstanding forecast made other than in a previous prospectus will be material in the case of share issues (especially in the context of an IPO). This is not necessarily the presumption in case of non-equity securities.			paras 43 & 44
When there is an outstanding profit forecast or estimate in relation to a material undertaking which the issuer has acquired, the issuer should consider whether it is appropriate to make a statement as to whether or not the profit forecast or estimate is still valid or correct. The issuer should also evaluate the effects of the acquisition and the profit forecast made by that undertaking on its own financial position and report on it as it would have done if the profit forecast or estimate had been made by the issuer.			paras 45 & 46
The forecast or estimate should normally be of profit before tax (disclosing separately any non-recurrent items and tax charges if they are expected to be abnormally high or low). If the forecast or estimate is not of profit before tax, the reasons for presenting another figure from the profit and loss account must be disclosed and clearly explained. Furthermore the tax effect should be clearly explained. When the results are published relating to a period covered by a forecast or estimate, the published financial statements must disclose the relevant figure so as to enable the forecast and actual results to be directly compared.			paras 47 & 48

	Prospectus Regulation	Annex I of Prospectus Regulation	CESR Recommendations
CESR recognises that often in practice, there is a fine line between what constitutes a profit forecast and what constitutes trend information as detailed in item 12 of Annex I of the Regulation. A general discussion about the future or prospects of the issuer under trend information will not normally constitute a profit forecast or estimate as defined in Articles 2.10 and 2.1¹ of the Regulation. Whether or not a statement constitutes a profit forecast is a question of fact and will depend upon the circumstances of the particular issuer.			para 49
This is a non-exhaustive list of factors that an issuer is expected to take into consideration when preparing forecasts: • Past results, market analysis, strategic evolutions, market share and position of the issuer • Financial position and possible changes therein • Description of the impact of an acquisition or disposal, change in strategy or any major change in environmental matters and technology • Changes in legal and tax environment • Commitments towards third parties			para 50

(4) SIR 4000 "Investment Reporting Standards Applicable To Public Reporting Engagements on Pro Forma Financial Information"

(i) Main Body of Document

SIR 4000 – Paragraph Reference	UK Reference	Irish Equivalent
1, 4, 5(a), 10, 12, 27, 58, 62, 63,	PD Regulation	The Prospectus Regulation
1, 10	Listing Rules of the FSA	Listing Rules of the Irish Stock Exchange
1	City Code	Takeover Rules and Substantial Acquisition Rules
1	AIM Admission Document	Irish Enterprise Exchange ("IEX") Admission Document
3	Item 1 of Annex II of the PD Regulation	Item 1 of Annex II of the Prospectus Regulation
4	Prospective Financial Information – Guidance for UK directors – ICAEW Guidance	Prospective Financial Information – Guidance for UK directors – ICAEW Guidance (for information)
26	Item 5 of Annex II of the PD Regulation	Item 5 of Annex II of the Prospectus Regulation
30, 39, 40	Item 6 of Annex II to the PD Regulation	Item 6 of Annex II to the Prospectus Regulation
44	Item 4 of Annex II of the PD Regulation	Item 4 of Annex II of the Prospectus Regulation
47 (a)	Item 1 of Annex II of the PD Regulation	Item 1 of Annex II of the Prospectus Regulation
47 (b)	Item 3 of Annex II of the PD Regulation	Item 3 of Annex II of the Prospectus Regulation
66	Section 81 and 87G of the FSMA, Prospectus Rule 3.4 and Listing Rule 4.4.1	Regulation 51 of "the Regulation" and Irish Stock Exchange Listing Rule 16.4.

(ii) Appendix 1 – Reporting Accountant's Criteria

	Annex I of Prospectus Regulation	Annex II of Prospectus Regulation	CESR Recommendations
In the case of a significant gross change, a description of how the transaction might have affected the assets and liabilities and earnings of the issuer, had the transaction been undertaken at the commencement of the period being reported on or at the date reported. This requirement will normally be satisfied by the inclusion of pro forma financial information.	20.2		
The pro forma information must normally be presented in columnar format composed of: a) the historical unadjusted information; b) the pro forma adjustments; and c) the resulting pro forma financial information in the final column		3	
The sources of the pro forma financial information have to be stated.		3	
The pro forma information must be prepared in a manner consistent with the accounting policies adopted by the issuer in its last or next financial statements and shall identify the following: a) the basis upon which it is prepared; b) the source of each item of information and adjustment.		4	
Pro forma adjustments related to the pro forma financial information must be: a) clearly shown and explained.		6	
Pro forma adjustments related to the pro forma financial information must be: b) directly attributable to the transaction.		6	

	Annex I of Prospectus Regulation	Annex II of Prospectus Regulation	CESR Recommendations
"Directly attributable to transactions". Pro forma information should only reflect matters that are an integral part of the transactions which are described in the prospectus. In particular, pro forma financial information should not include adjustments which are dependent on actions to be taken once the current transaction has been completed, even where such actions are central to the issuer's purpose in entering into the transactions			Para 88
Pro forma adjustments related to the pro forma financial information must be: c) factually supportable.		6	
"Factually supportable". The nature of the facts supporting an adjustment will vary according to the circumstances. Nevertheless, facts are expected to be capable of some reasonable degree of objective determination. Support might typically be provided by published accounts, management accounts, other financial information and valuations contained in the document, purchase and sale agreements and other agreements to the transaction covered by the prospectus. For instance in relation to management accounts, the interim figures for an undertaking being acquired may be derived from the consolidation schedules underlying that undertaking's interim statements			Para 87
In respect of a pro forma profit and loss or cash flow statement, the adjustments must be clearly identified as to those expected to have a continuing impact on the issuer and those which are not.		6	
The accounting treatment applied to adjustments should be presented and prepared in a form consistent with the policy the issuer would adopt in its last or next published financial statements.			Para 89[9]

9 Paragraph 89 of the CESR guidance also provides guidance that although not constituting a criterion is useful guidance to this criterion.

(iii) Appendix 2– Other Regulatory Provisions Relevant to the Preparers of Pro Forma Financial Information

	Prospectus Regulation	Annex I & II of Prospectus Regulation	CESR Recommendations
(9) Pro forma financial information is needed in case of significant gross change, i.e. a variation of more than 25% relative to one or more indicators of the size of the issuers business, in the situation of an issuer due to a particular transaction, with the exception of those situations where merger accounting is required.	Recital 9		
For these purposes, "Significant gross change" is described in recital 9 of the PD Regulation. Thus, in order to assess whether the variation to an issuer's business as a result of a transaction is more than 25%, the size of the transaction should be assessed relative to the size of the issuer by using appropriate indicators of size prior to the relevant transaction. A transaction will constitute a significant gross change where at least one of the indicators of size is more than 25%. A non-exhaustive list of indicators is provided below: – Total assets – Revenue – Profit or loss Other indicators of size can be applied by the issuer especially where the stated indicators of size produce an anomalous result or are inappropriate to the specific industry of the issuer, in these cases the issuers should address these anomalies by agreement of the competent authority. The appropriate indicators of size should refer to figures from the issuer's last or next published annual financial statements.			Paras 90 to 94
Pro forma financial information should be preceded by an introductory explanatory paragraph that states in clear terms the purpose of including this information in the prospectus	Article 5		

	Prospectus Regulation	Annex I & II of Prospectus Regulation	CESR Recommendations
This pro forma financial information is to be presented as set out in Annex II and must include the information indicated therein. Pro forma financial information must be accompanied by a report prepared by independent accountants or auditors.		20.2 (I)	
The pro forma information must include a description of the transaction, the business involved and the period to which it refers.		1 (II)	
The pro forma information must clearly state the purpose to which it has been prepared		1 (II)	
The pro forma information must clearly state that it has been prepared for illustrative purposes only		1 (II)	
The pro forma information must clearly state that it addresses a hypothetical situation and, therefore, does not represent the company's actual financial position or results.		1 (II)	
In order to present pro forma financial information, a balance sheet and profit and loss account, and accompanying explanatory notes, depending on the circumstances may be included		2 (II)	
Where applicable the financial statements of the acquired businesses or entities must be included in the prospectus.		3 (II)	

	Prospectus Regulation	Annex I & II of Prospectus Regulation	CESR Recommendations
Pro forma information may only be published in respect of: a) the current financial period; b) the most recently completed financial period; c) the most recent interim period for which relevant unadjusted information has been or will be published or is being published in the same document		5 (II)	

BULLETIN 2006/5

THE COMBINED CODE ON CORPORATE GOVERNANCE: REQUIREMENTS OF AUDITORS UNDER THE LISTING RULES OF THE FINANCIAL SERVICES AUTHORITY AND THE IRISH STOCK EXCHANGE

CONTENTS

Introduction

1. This Bulletin provides guidance for auditors when reviewing a company's statement made in relation to "The Combined Code on Corporate Governance" ("Combined Code") in accordance with Listing Rule ("LR") 9.8.10R of the Financial Services Authority ("FSA") or LR 6.8.9 of the Irish Stock Exchange ("ISE"). It replaces the guidance in:

    *   APB Bulletin 2004/3, "The Combined Code on Corporate Governance: Requirements of Auditors under the Listing Rules of the Financial Services Authority" published in November 2004; and

    *   APB Bulletin 2004/4 "The Combined Code on Corporate Governance: Requirements of Auditors under the Listing Rules of the Irish Stock Exchange" published in December 2004.

2. This Bulletin reflects the following:

    (a) The issuance of "Internal Control: Revised Guidance for Directors on the Combined Code" ("Turnbull Guidance") by the Financial Reporting Council in October 2005. The Turnbull Review Group made only a small number of changes to the Turnbull Guidance as first issued in 1999. One of these changes is that the board's statement on internal control should confirm that necessary actions have been, or are being, taken to remedy any significant failings or weaknesses identified from its review of the effectiveness of the system of internal control. This development is set out in paragraph 36 of the revised Turnbull Guidance and is discussed in paragraphs 40 to 44 in this Bulletin.

    (b) The issuance of revised Listing Rules in July 2005. Although there has been no change to the substance of the requirements of the Listing Rules in this regard the text of the rules differs from the previous rules.

3. This Bulletin provides guidance for auditors of both:

    (a) companies listed on the Official List maintained by the FSA that are incorporated in the United Kingdom; and

    (b) companies listed on the Official List maintained by the ISE that are incorporated in Ireland.

    The text of the applicable revised Listing Rules issued by the FSA is set out in Appendix 1. Appendix 2 sets out the references to the equivalent Listing Rules of the ISE. In the remainder of this Bulletin reference is made to the "Listing Rules" and footnotes provide the specific references to the Listing Rules issued by the FSA and the ISE.

4.   This Bulletin does not address the report to shareholders on executive directors' remuneration that is required by the Listing Rules[1].

Requirements of the Listing Rules relating to corporate governance matters

Requirement for companies to "comply or explain"

5.   The FSA Listing Rules require listed companies[2] that are incorporated in the United Kingdom to include in their annual report and accounts a two-part disclosure statement in relation to the Combined Code. The Listing Rules of the ISE have a similar requirement with respect to listed companies that are incorporated in the Republic of Ireland. The first part of the disclosure statement is to explain how the company has applied the principles set out in Section 1 of the Combined Code, in a manner that would enable shareholders to evaluate how the principles have been applied[3].

6.   The second part of the disclosure statement requires the company to either[4]:

(a)   Comply - include "*a statement as to whether the listed company has complied throughout the accounting period with all relevant provisions set out in Section 1 of the Combined Code*"; or

(b)   Explain – include "*a statement as to whether the listed company has not complied throughout the accounting period with all relevant provisions set out in Section 1 of the Combined Code and if so, setting out:*

(i)   *those provisions, if any, it has not complied with;*

(ii)   *in the case of provisions whose requirements are of a continuing nature, the period within which, if any, it did not comply with some or all of those provisions; and*

(iii) *the company's reasons for non-compliance*".

7.   It is expected that listed companies will comply with the provisions of the Combined Code most of the time. However, it is recognised that departures from the provisions of the Code may be justified in particular circumstances. The auditor has no responsibility to review or otherwise assess and comment upon a company's decision to depart from the provisions of the Code. It is for shareholders and others to evaluate any such departure and the company's explanation for it.

---

[1]   FSA LR 9.8.6R(7) and LR 9.8.8R; ISE LR 6.8.6(8) and LR 6.8.8.
[2]   A listed company is defined by the FSA and the Irish Stock Exchange as "a company that has any class of its securities listed".
[3]   FSA LR 9.8.6R(5); ISE LR 6.8.6(6)
[4]   FSA LR 9.8.6R(6); ISE LR 6.8.6(7)

8.   The Listing Rules[5] requires an overseas company with a primary listing to disclose in its annual report and accounts certain matters relating to its corporate governance. There are no requirements relating to auditors in respect of these Listing Rules.

Review of the company's disclosure statement by the auditor

9.   The Listing Rules[6] require that *"A listed company must ensure that the auditors review the parts of the statement that relate to the following provisions of the Combined Code C1.1, C2.1, and C3.1 to C3.7."* They require the auditor to review nine of the ten objectively verifiable Combined Code provisions relating to accountability and audit.

10. The tenth accountability and audit Combined Code provision (C.1.2 on going concern) is addressed by different Listing Rules[7]. These Listing Rules require the directors to make a statement that the business is a going concern, together with supporting assumptions or qualifications as necessary. This statement is required to be included in the annual report and accounts and to be reviewed by the auditor before publication.

The auditor's review of the statement of compliance

11. The scope of the auditor's review required by the Listing Rules[8], in comparison to the totality of the Combined Code, is narrow. The auditor is not required to review the directors' narrative statement of how they have applied the Code principles and is required only to review the directors' compliance statement in relation to nine of the forty-eight Code provisions applicable to companies. Nevertheless, because the directors' narrative statement comprises other information included in a document containing audited financial statements there is a broader requirement under Auditing Standards[9] for the auditor to read such "other information" and if the auditor becomes aware of any apparent misstatements therein, or identifies any material inconsistencies with the audited financial statements, to seek to resolve them.

12. The Listing Rules are silent as to whether the auditor should report on the auditor's review of the directors' compliance statement and whether any such report should be published or referred to in the annual report. The APB is of the view that if the auditor's report itself contains a description of the auditor's responsibilities (including the auditor's responsibilities under the Listing Rules), as discussed in paragraphs 24 to 29, there is no necessity for a separate auditor's report dealing with the auditor's review of corporate governance matters.

13. Because of the limited nature of the auditor's review and in order to avoid the possibility of misunderstandings arising the APB recommends that:

---

[5]   FSA LR 9.8.7R; ISE LR 6.8.7
[6]   FSA LR 9.8.10R(2); ISE LR 6.8.9(2)
[7]   FSA LR 9.8.6R(3) and LR 9.8.10R(1); ISE LR 6.8.6(3) and LR 6.8.9(1)
[8]   FSA LR 9.8.10R; ISE LR 6.8.9
[9]   ISA (UK and Ireland) 720 (Revised) Section A, "Other information in documents containing audited financial statements".

(a) the auditor's engagement letter explains the scope of the auditor's review. Example paragraphs are set out in Appendix 3; and

(b) prior to the release of the annual report and accounts the auditor communicates, and discusses, with those charged with governance the factual findings of the auditor's review.

Combined Code provisions that the auditor is required to review

14. The provisions of the Combined Code that the auditor is required to review are set out below, together with a reference to the specific procedures recommended by the APB:

Provision	Detailed recommendation	Specific procedures
C.1.1	The directors should explain in the annual report their responsibility for preparing the accounts and there should be a statement by the auditors about their reporting responsibilities.	23-29
C.2.1	The board should, at least annually, conduct a review of the effectiveness of the group's system of internal controls and should report to shareholders that they have done so. The review should cover all material controls, including financial, operational and compliance controls and risk management systems.	30-55
C.3.1	The board should establish an audit committee of at least three, or in the case of smaller companies[10] two, members, who should all be independent non-executive directors. The board should satisfy itself that at least one member of the audit committee has recent and relevant financial experience.	56-59
C.3.2	The main role and responsibilities of the audit committee should be set out in written terms of reference and should include: • to monitor the integrity of the financial statements of the company, and any formal announcements relating to the company's financial performance, reviewing significant financial reporting judgements contained in them; • to review the company's internal financial controls and, unless expressly addressed by a separate board risk committee composed of independent directors,	60

---

[10] In the UK, a smaller company is one that is below the FTSE 350 throughout the year immediately prior to the reporting year. The Irish Stock Exchange considers a smaller company to be one that is included in the ISEQ Small Cap Index throughout the year immediately prior to the reporting year.

	or by the board itself, to review the company's internal control and risk management systems; • to monitor and review the effectiveness of the company's internal audit function; • to make recommendations to the board, for it to put to the shareholders for their approval in general meeting, in relation to the appointment, re-appointment and removal of the external auditor and to approve the remuneration and terms of engagement of the external auditor; • to review and monitor the external auditor's independence and objectivity and the effectiveness of the audit process, taking into consideration relevant UK professional and regulatory requirements; • to develop and implement policy on the engagement of the external auditor to supply non-audit services, taking into account relevant ethical guidance regarding the provision of non-audit services by the external audit firm; and to report to the board, identifying any matters in respect of which it considers that action or improvement is needed and making recommendations as to the steps to be taken.	
C.3.3	The terms of reference of the audit committee, including its role and the authority delegated to it by the board, should be made available. A separate section of the annual report should describe the work of the committee in discharging those responsibilities.	61
C.3.4	The audit committee should review arrangements by which staff of the company may, in confidence, raise concerns about possible improprieties in matters of financial reporting or other matters. The audit committee's objective should be to ensure that arrangements are in place for the proportionate and independent investigation of such matters and for appropriate follow-up action.	62
C.3.5	The audit committee should monitor and review the effectiveness of the internal audit activities. Where there is no internal audit function, the audit committee should consider annually whether there is a need for an internal audit function and make a recommendation to the board, and the reasons for the absence of such a function should be explained in the relevant section of the annual report.	63
C.3.6	The audit committee should have primary responsibility for making a recommendation on the appointment,	64

	reappointment and removal of the external auditors. If the board does not accept the audit committee's recommendation, it should include in the annual report, and in any papers recommending appointment or re- appointment, a statement from the audit committee explaining the recommendation and should set out reasons why the board has taken a different position.	
C.3.7	The annual report should explain to shareholders how, if the auditor provides non-audit services, auditor objectivity and independence is safeguarded.	65-67

General procedures

15. Paragraphs 16 to 22 set out general procedures relating to the auditor's review of the statement of compliance. These general procedures are applicable to all of the nine provisions of the Combined Code that the auditor is required to review.

16. In relation to all elements of the corporate governance disclosures relating to the provisions of the Combined Code that are within the scope of the auditor's review, the auditor obtains appropriate evidence to support the compliance statement made by the company. The type of procedures usually performed include:

   (a) reviewing the minutes of the meetings of the board of directors, and of relevant board committees;

   (b) reviewing supporting documents prepared for the board of directors or board committees that are relevant to those matters specified for review by the auditor;

   (c) making enquiries of certain directors (such as the chairman of the board of directors and the chairmen of relevant board committees) and the company secretary to satisfy themselves on matters relevant to those provisions of the Combined Code specified for review by the auditor; and

   (d) attending meetings of the audit committee (or the full board if there is no audit committee) at which the annual report and accounts, including the statement of compliance, are considered and approved for submission to the board of directors.

17. The auditor may request the directors to provide written confirmation of oral representations made during the course of the review.

Non-compliance with provisions of the Combined Code

18. Where the auditor becomes aware of any provision of the Combined Code that is within the scope of the auditor's review and with which the company has not complied, the auditor establishes that the departure is described in the directors' statement of compliance. However, the auditor is not required to, and does not, perform additional

procedures to investigate the appropriateness of reasons given for non-compliance with the provision.

19. Where there is a departure from a provision specified for the auditor's review but there is proper disclosure of this fact and of the reasons for the departure, as envisaged by the Listing Rules[11], the auditor does not refer to this in its report on the financial statements.

20. However, where the auditor considers that there is not proper disclosure of a departure from a provision of the Combined Code specified for the auditor's review the auditor reports this in the auditor's report on the financial statements. Paragraph 55 describes the way in which such a matter (which does not give rise to a qualified opinion on the financial statements) is reported and provides an example of such an opinion.

Auditor's association with company's corporate governance disclosures

21. The auditor would not wish to be associated with either the statement of compliance or the company's narrative statement of how it has applied the Code principles if the auditor has reason to believe that they may be misleading. The auditor, therefore, reads both of these statements and considers whether any information in either of them is apparently misstated or materially inconsistent with other information of which the auditor has become aware in the course of either the review of the company's compliance statement (insofar as it relates to the nine provisions of the Combined Code that the auditor is required to review under the Listing Rules) or the audit of the financial statements.

22. The auditor is not expected actively to search for misstatements or inconsistencies. However, if the auditor becomes aware of such a matter the auditor discusses it with the directors in order to establish the significance of the lack of proper disclosure. If such lack of proper disclosure is considered significant by the auditor and the directors cannot be persuaded to amend the disclosure to the auditor's satisfaction, the auditor considers the implications for the auditor's reporting responsibilities and the auditor may need to take legal advice.

Specific procedures

Responsibilities of the directors and the auditor

> C.1.1 The directors should explain in the annual report their responsibility for preparing the accounts and there should be a statement by the auditors about their reporting responsibilities.

---

[11] FSA LR 9.8.10R; ISE LR 6.8.9

Directors' responsibilities

23. While the content of the statement of the directors' responsibilities is determined by the directors, the auditor establishes that the directors' responsibility for preparing the accounts is explained in the annual report.

Auditor's responsibilities

24. The auditor has different responsibilities with respect to the various component parts of the annual report. For example, the auditor is required to "audit" the financial statements, "review" the company's compliance with certain aspects of the Combined Code and "read" all information in the annual report that is not subject to any other requirement. The auditor reads such "other information" because the credibility of the financial statements and the related auditor's report may be undermined by material inconsistencies between the financial statements and the "other information", or by apparent misstatements within the other information.

25. In some instances the auditor has to report positively the results of the work whereas in other instances the auditor only has to report by exception. The APB is of the view that users of annual reports will find it difficult to understand the scope of the auditor's involvement in the absence of a clear statement of the auditor's responsibilities towards the whole annual report.

26. The key elements of a statement of the auditor's responsibilities relate to the requirements of:

    (a) statute and Auditing Standards with respect to the audit of the financial statements;

    (b) statute with respect to the auditor's opinion as to whether the information given in the directors report for the financial year for which the financial statements are prepared is consistent with those financial statements;

    (c) statute and the Listing Rules where the auditor is only required to report by exception;

    (d) the Listing Rules for the auditor to review the statement concerning the company's compliance with certain provisions of the Combined Code; and

    (e) Auditing Standards to read the "other information" in the annual report.

27. A description of the auditor's responsibilities may either be included as a separate section of the auditor's report on the financial statements or set out as a separate statement within the annual report. The APB encourages auditors to include a description of the auditor's responsibilities within the auditor's report on the financial statements. Illustrative examples of auditor's reports containing descriptions of the

auditor's responsibilities are given in the most recent version of the APB Bulletin "Auditor's Reports on Financial Statements"[12].

28. The content of the statement of the auditor's responsibilities ought to be determined by the auditor regardless of whether it is published as a separate statement, or incorporated into the auditor's report on the financial statements.

29. Appendix 3 to this Bulletin includes illustrative paragraphs that may be included in the auditor's engagement letter to describe the auditor's responsibilities with respect to the company's compliance with the Listing Rules[13]. In practice the auditor tailors the engagement letter to the specific circumstances of the engagement.

Internal control

> **C.2.1 The board should, at least annually, conduct a review of the effectiveness of the group's system of internal controls and should report to shareholders that they have done so. The review should cover all material controls, including financial, operational and compliance controls and risk management systems.**

The auditor's responsibilities with respect to the directors' narrative statement

30. The annual report will contain a narrative statement of how the company has applied Code principle C.2. The Turnbull Guidance recommends that, "In its narrative statement of how the company has applied Code Principle C.2, the board should, as a minimum, disclose that there is an ongoing process for identifying, evaluating and managing the significant risks faced by the company, that it has been in place for the year under review and up to the date of approval of the annual report and accounts, that is regularly reviewed by the board...".[14] The Turnbull Guidance also states that "The annual report and accounts should include such meaningful, high-level information as the board considers necessary to assist shareholders' understanding of the main features of the company's risk management processes and system of internal control, and should not give a misleading impression"[15]. The content of such narrative statements is likely, therefore, to vary widely from company to company.

31. Although the Listing Rules do not require the auditor to review the narrative statement, there are requirements under Auditing Standards for the auditor to read the other information (of which the company's narrative statement forms a part) issued with the audited financial statements and to seek to resolve any apparent misstatements or material inconsistencies with the audited financial statements.

---

[12] At the date of publication of this Bulletin the most recent version was Bulletin 2005/4
[13] FSA LR 9.8.10R; ISE LR 6.8.9
[14] Paragraph 34 of the Turnbull Guidance.
[15] Paragraph 33 of the Turnbull Guidance

Auditor's review of compliance

32. The Turnbull Guidance[16], recommends that the company discloses a summary of the process the board (and where applicable, its committees) has adopted in reviewing the effectiveness of the system of internal control. The Turnbull Guidance[17] describes the directors' process for reviewing effectiveness and in particular states[18]: *"The board should define the process to be adopted for its review of the effectiveness of internal control. This should encompass both the scope and frequency of the reports it receives and reviews during the year, and also the process for its annual assessment, such that it will be provided with sound, appropriately documented, support for its statement on internal control in the company's annual report and accounts".*

33. The objective of the auditor's review of compliance is to assess whether the company's summary of the process the board (and where applicable its committees) has adopted in reviewing the effectiveness of the system of internal control, is both supported by the documentation prepared by or for the directors and appropriately reflects that process.

34. To achieve this objective the auditor, in addition to the procedures outlined in paragraph 16;

   (a) obtains an understanding, through enquiry of the directors, of the process defined by the board for its review of the effectiveness of all material internal controls and compares that understanding to the statement made by the board in the annual report and accounts;

   (b) reviews the documentation prepared by or for the directors to support their statement made in connection with Code provision C.2.1 and assesses whether or not it provides sound support for that statement; and

   (c) relates the statement made by the directors to the auditor's knowledge of the company obtained during the audit of the financial statements. As explained in paragraph 36, the scope of the directors' review will be considerably broader in its scope than the knowledge the auditor can be expected to have based on their audit.

35. The auditor considers whether the directors' statement covers the year under review and the period to the date of approval of the annual report and accounts, as recommended by the Turnbull Guidance[19].

36. In carrying out the review, the auditor will have regard to the knowledge of the company the auditor has obtained from the audit work. To enable the auditor to

---

[16] Paragraphs 26-32 and 36 of the Turnbull Guidance.
[17] Paragraphs 26-32 of the Turnbull Guidance.
[18] Paragraph 27 of the Turnbull Guidance.
[19] Paragraph 26 of the Turnbull Guidance.

perform the audit and express an opinion on the financial statements, the auditor is required by Auditing Standards[20] to obtain an understanding of the entity and its environment, including its internal control, sufficient to identify and assess the risks of material misstatement of the financial statements. Consequently, the auditor's assessment required by Auditing Standards will be considerably narrower in scope than the review performed by the directors for the purpose of reporting on compliance with Code provision C.2.1.

37. The auditor, therefore, is not expected to assess whether all risks and controls have been addressed by the directors or that risks are satisfactorily addressed by internal controls. In order to communicate this fact to users of the annual report, the following sentence is included in the auditor's report on the financial statements.

> "We are not required to consider whether the board's statements on internal control cover all risks and controls, or form an opinion on the effectiveness of the company's corporate governance procedures or its risk and control procedures."

38. However, ISA (UK and Ireland) 260 "Communication of audit matters with those charged with governance" requires, among other things, that the auditor communicates, on a timely basis, to those charged with governance material weaknesses in internal control identified during the audit. A material weakness in internal control is a deficiency in design or operation which could adversely affect the entity's ability to record, process, summarize and report financial and other relevant data so as to result in a material misstatement in the financial statements. A material weakness in control identified by the auditor will be considered by the directors, in the context of the reports they receive and review during the year as part of their overall process for undertaking an annual assessment of the effectiveness of the company's internal control procedures, and it may be considered by them to be a significant failing or weakness as described in the Turnbull Guidance.

39. In view of the obligations placed on directors by the Turnbull Guidance the APB recommends that any material weaknesses in internal control identified by the auditor be reported to those charged with governance as soon as is practicable. The auditor does not wait until the financial statement audit has been completed before reporting such weaknesses. In this way, the directors will be aware of the weaknesses that the auditor has identified and be able to take account of them in making their statements on internal control[21].

---

[20] ISA (UK and Ireland) 315, "Obtaining an understanding of the entity and its environment and assessing the risks of material misstatement".

[21] The auditor has a responsibility under ISA (UK and Ireland) 260 to consider whether there is adequate two-way communication between the auditor and those charged with governance, such that an effective audit can take place. As part of this responsibility, amongst other things, the auditor will need to consider the appropriateness and timeliness of actions taken by those charged with governance in response to the recommendations made by the auditor including those regarding material weaknesses in internal control.

Actions taken by the directors to remedy significant failings or weaknesses

40. A revision made to the Turnbull Guidance in October 2005 was to expand the existing recommendation regarding the board's statement on internal control in the annual report in relation to Code provision C2.1. The recommendation was expanded to say that the board should in its statement on internal control, *"confirm that necessary actions have been or are being taken to remedy any significant failings or weaknesses identified from that review"*[22] (The reference to "that review" relates to the board's annual review of the effectiveness of the system of internal control).

41. The auditor's review responsibility with respect to this recommendation includes:

   (a) reviewing the documentation prepared by or for the directors supporting their statement made in connection with Code provision C2.1 that discusses those failings or weaknesses, if any, in internal control that they have assessed as "significant" and assessing whether or not it provides sound support for that statement;

   (b) discussing with the directors the actions they have already taken, or consider necessary to take, with respect to the identified significant failings or weaknesses; and

   (c) relating the statement made by the directors to the auditor's knowledge of the company obtained during the audit of the financial statements.

42. With respect to 41(c) above, the auditor assesses whether the directors, in making their statement, have taken into consideration the material weaknesses in internal control reported to those charged with governance by the auditor in accordance with ISA (UK and Ireland) 260 (See paragraph 38 above).

43. However, the auditor is not required to assess either the directors' decision as to what constitutes a significant failing or weakness, or whether the actions, taken or to be taken by the directors, will in fact remedy the significant failings or weaknesses identified by the directors. The APB recommends that a statement to this effect be included in the engagement letter (see Appendix 3).

44. If the auditor:

   (a) considers that the documentation and discussions do not support the directors' confirmation that necessary actions have been, or are being, taken or

   (b) based on its audit findings is aware of material weaknesses in internal control that have not been considered by the directors

---

[22] Paragraph 36 of the Turnbull Guidance

it discusses the position with the directors. If the auditor is not satisfied with the directors' explanations it considers the consequences for its opinion (see paragraph 54).

Internal control aspects of problems disclosed in the annual report

45. The Turnbull Guidance[23] also recommends that the board discloses *"the process it has applied to deal with material internal control aspects of any significant problems disclosed in the annual report and accounts"*.

46. This may be a difficult recommendation for directors to satisfy, and for the auditor to review, because what is meant by "significant problems" is not defined and the word "problem" encompasses more than financial matters. A directors' description, for example, of difficulties obtaining raw materials at a remote overseas location may be seen as a significant problem by directors of some companies but not the directors of others. Even when the directors have identified a problem it may not always be clear whether the problem has material internal control aspects. A significant loss-making contract, for example, will necessitate an assessment of whether the problem is attributable to changes in circumstances that could not reasonably have been foreseen as opposed to weaknesses in internal control.

47. The auditor's review responsibility with respect to this recommendation includes:

(a) discussing with the directors the steps the directors have taken to determine what "significant problems" are disclosed in the annual report and accounts; and

(b) assessing whether disclosures made by the board of the processes it has applied to deal with material internal control aspects of any significant problems disclosed in the annual report and accounts appropriately reflect those processes.

48. The auditor is not required to assess whether the processes described by the directors will, in fact, remedy the problem described in the annual report and accounts.

49. If the auditor is aware of a significant problem that is disclosed in the annual report and accounts for which the board has not disclosed the material internal control aspects it discusses the position with the directors of the company.

50. If the auditor is not able to agree with the directors as to how the matter should be resolved it considers the consequences for its opinion (see paragraph 54).

Failure to conduct a review

51. The Listing Rules[24] require the company to disclose if the board has failed to conduct a review of the effectiveness of internal control. The Turnbull Guidance[25] recommends

---

[23] Paragraph 36 of the Turnbull Guidance.
[24] FSA LR 9.8.6R(6)(b); ISE LR 6.8.6(7)(b)
[25] Paragraph 37 of the Turnbull Guidance

that where it has not made the required disclosures the board should state that fact and provide an explanation. The auditor considers whether this recommendation is met and whether the explanation is consistent with the auditor's understanding.

Groups of companies

52. The Turnbull Guidance establishes that, for groups of companies, the review of effectiveness should be from the perspective of the group as a whole[26]. Accordingly, the auditor's consideration of the board's description of its process for reviewing the effectiveness of internal control encompasses the group as a whole.

53. Where material joint ventures and associated companies have not been dealt with as part of the group for the purposes of applying the Turnbull Guidance, this fact should be disclosed by the board[27]. The auditor assesses, based on the auditor's knowledge of the group obtained during the audit of the financial statements, whether any material joint ventures or associated companies have not been dealt with and, therefore, if such a disclosure is necessary.

Reporting by exception

54. If the auditor concludes:

(a) that the board's summary of the process it has applied in reviewing the effectiveness of internal control is either not supported by or does not appropriately reflect the auditor's understanding of the process undertaken (paragraphs 32 to 39);

(b) that the documentation and discussions do not support the directors' confirmation that necessary actions have been, or are being taken; (paragraphs 40 to 44);

(c) that the processes disclosed to deal with material internal control aspects of significant problems disclosed in the annual report and accounts do not appropriately reflect the auditor's understanding of the process undertaken (paragraphs 45 to 50);

(d) that no disclosure has been made by the board that it has failed to conduct a review of the effectiveness of internal control (paragraph 51);

(e) where the board discloses that it has not reviewed the effectiveness of internal control, that its explanation is not consistent with the auditor's understanding (paragraph 51); or

---

[26] Paragraph 13 of the Turnbull Guidance
[27] Paragraph 38 of the Turnbull Guidance

(f)　that no disclosure has been made by the board that a material joint venture or associated company has not been dealt with as part of the group (paragraphs 52 to 53),

they report this in their report on the financial statements.

55.　However, as this does not give rise to a qualified audit opinion on the financial statements the APB recommends that the auditor's comments be included under the heading "Other matter" which would be included in the auditor's report below the auditor's opinion and any emphasis of matter related to the auditor's report on the financial statements as illustrated below:

Opinion

[Standard opinion wording for an auditor's report on group (not including parent company) financial statements of a publicly traded company incorporated in Great Britain[28]]

Emphasis of matter

Where applicable any emphasis of matter paragraph relating to the auditor's report on the financial statements.

Other matter

We have reviewed the board's description of its process for reviewing the effectiveness of internal control set out on page x of the annual report. In our opinion the board's comments concerning ... do not appropriately reflect our understanding of the process undertaken by the board because.....

An audit committee of independent non-executive directors

C.3.1　**The board should establish an audit committee of at least three, or in the case of smaller companies[29] two, members, who should all be independent non-executive directors. The board should satisfy itself that at least one member of the audit committee has recent and relevant financial experience.**

Auditor's review of compliance

56.　When reviewing the company's compliance with this provision of the Combined Code the APB recommends that the auditor performs the following procedures:

(a)　Checking that the audit committee comprises at least three, or in the case of smaller companies two, members.

---

[28]　See Example 7 in Bulletin 2005/4

[29]　In the UK a smaller company is one that is below the FTSE 350 throughout the year immediately prior to the reporting year. The Irish Stock Exchange considers a smaller company to be one that is included in the ISEQ Small Cap Index throughout the year immediately prior to the reporting year.

(b) Obtaining an understanding of the process adopted by the board for determining whether:

    (i) the members of the audit committee are all independent non-executive directors (see paragraphs 57 to 58); and

    (ii) at least one member of the audit committee has recent and relevant financial experience (see paragraph 59).

(c) Reviewing evidence such as minutes and other documentation supporting the board's view that the non-executive directors on the audit committee are independent and, where appropriate, have recent and relevant financial experience.

57. Provision A.3.1 of the Combined Code, requires the board to identify in the annual report each non-executive director it considers to be independent. This provision includes guidance on how independence might be interpreted by listing a number of relationships or circumstances that may indicate that a director is not independent[30]. The Code makes clear, however, that notwithstanding such relationships or circumstances the company is entitled to explain why a director is considered independent.

58. It is not the auditor's responsibility to satisfy itself whether directors are properly described as being "independent" non-executives. Nor does the auditor lay down more precise criteria with respect to the meaning of the term "independent" than those set out in the Combined Code. When reviewing the company's compliance with this provision of the Combined Code the APB recommends that the review procedures be limited to establishing that the audit committee is comprised of non-executive directors who are identified in the annual report as being, in the opinion of the board, independent. However, if the auditor doubts whether the directors are properly described as being "independent" non-executives the auditor communicates those concerns to the audit committee and the board of directors.

59. Similarly, it is not the auditor's responsibility to satisfy itself whether the company is correct in concluding that a particular audit committee member has "recent and relevant financial experience". Nor should the auditor lay down more precise criteria with respect to the meaning of the term "recent and relevant financial experience". When reviewing the company's compliance with this provision of the Combined Code the APB recommends that the review procedures be limited to considering the process adopted by the board for determining that at least one member of the audit committee has "recent and relevant financial experience". However, if the auditor doubts whether

---

[30] A footnote to A.3.1 explains 'A.2.2 states that the chairman should on appointment meet the independence criteria set out in this provision, but thereafter the test of independence is not appropriate in relation to the chairman'.

the company is correct in concluding that a particular audit committee member has "recent and relevant financial experience" the auditor communicates those concerns to the audit committee and the board of directors.[31]

Role and responsibilities of the audit committee[32]

> **C.3.2** **The main role and responsibilities of the audit committee should be set out in written terms of reference and should include:**
> * **to monitor the integrity of the financial statements of the company, and any formal announcements relating to the company's financial performance, reviewing significant financial reporting judgements contained in them;**
> * **to review the company's internal financial controls and, unless expressly addressed by a separate board risk committee composed of independent directors, or by the board itself, to review the company's internal control and risk management systems;**
> * **to monitor and review the effectiveness of the company's internal audit function;**
> * **to make recommendations to the board, for it to put to the shareholders for their approval in general meeting, in relation to the appointment, re-appointment and removal of the external auditor and to approve the remuneration and terms of engagement of the external auditor;**
> * **to review and monitor the external auditor's independence and objectivity and the effectiveness of the audit process, taking into consideration relevant UK professional and regulatory requirements;**
> * **to develop and implement policy on the engagement of the external auditor to supply non-audit services, taking into account relevant ethical guidance regarding the provision of non-audit services by the external audit firm; and to report to the board, identifying any matters in respect of which it considers that action or improvement is needed and making recommendations as to the steps to be taken.**

Auditor's review of compliance

60. When reviewing the company's compliance with this provision of the Combined Code the APB recommends that the auditor obtains a copy of the terms of reference of the audit committee and reviews whether the roles and responsibilities of the audit committee described in the terms of reference reflect the recommendations of Code provision C.3.2. It is not the auditor's responsibility to consider whether the audit committee has fulfilled its roles and responsibilities.

---

[31] The Combined Code recommends that the board should satisfy itself that at least one member of the audit committee has recent and relevant financial experience. Where this is not the case there is a need for an explanation such as the board has concluded that the audit committee "collectively" has recent and relevant financial experience.

[32] In Ireland Section 42(2) of the Companies (Auditing and Accounting) Act 2003 requires the board of directors to establish an audit committee and sets out its responsibilities.

Terms of reference of the audit committee

> **C.3.3** **The terms of reference of the audit committee, including its role and the authority delegated to it by the board, should be made available[23]. A separate section of the annual report should describe the work of the committee in discharging those responsibilities.**

Auditor's review of compliance

61. When reviewing the company's compliance with this provision of the Combined Code the APB recommends that the auditor performs the following procedures:

    (a) Reviewing whether the terms of reference of the audit committee are included on the company's website or that the terms of reference have been reasonably made available or communicated by another method.

    (b) Reviewing whether a description of the work performed by the audit committee in discharging its responsibilities, is included in a separate section of the annual report, and is not materially inconsistent with the information that the auditor has obtained in the course of the audit work on the financial statements.

Arrangements by which company's staff may raise concerns

> **C.3.4** **The audit committee should review arrangements by which staff of the company may, in confidence, raise concerns about possible improprieties in matters of financial reporting or other matters. The audit committee's objective should be to ensure that arrangements are in place for the proportionate and independent investigation of such matters and for appropriate follow-up action.**

Auditor's review of compliance

62. When reviewing the company's compliance with this provision of the Combined Code the APB recommends that the auditor performs the following procedures:

    (a) Reviewing supporting documentation to determine whether there is evidence that the audit committee has reviewed the arrangements and, if necessary, discussing with members of the audit committee what review procedures they performed.

    (b) Reviewing documentation supporting the company's arrangements for the proportionate and independent investigation of concerns raised in confidence by staff relating to possible improprieties in matters of financial reporting or other matters and for appropriate follow-up action. It is not the responsibility of the auditor to consider whether such arrangements will facilitate "proportionate and independent" investigation or "appropriate" follow-up action but the auditor reviews the process by which the audit committee satisfies itself that the recommendation of the Combined Code has been satisfied.

Monitoring and review of the effectiveness of the internal audit activities

> **C.3.5** The audit committee should monitor and review the effectiveness of the internal audit activities. Where there is no internal audit function, the audit committee should consider annually whether there is a need for an internal audit function and make a recommendation to the board, and the reasons for the absence of such a function should be explained in the relevant section of the annual report.

Auditor's review of compliance

63. When reviewing the company's compliance with this provision of the Combined Code the APB recommends that the auditor performs the following procedures:

   (a) Where there is an internal audit function discussing with the audit committee chairman and reviewing the supporting documentation to establish that the audit committee has monitored and reviewed the effectiveness of the internal audit activities. It is not the auditor's responsibility to consider whether the internal audit activities are effective.

   (b) Where there is no internal audit function, reviewing whether:

   (i) the audit committee has considered whether there is a need for an internal audit function;

   (ii) there is documentation that evidences the audit committee's recommendation to the board;

   (iii) the reasons for the absence of such a function are explained in the relevant section of the annual report. It is not the auditor's responsibility to consider whether the reasons given are appropriate.

Appointment, reappointment and removal of the external auditor

> **C.3.6** The audit committee should have primary responsibility for making a recommendation on the appointment, reappointment and removal of the external auditors. If the board does not accept the audit committee's recommendation, it should include in the annual report, and in any papers recommending appointment or re-appointment, a statement from the audit committee explaining the recommendation and should set out reasons why the board has taken a different position.

Auditor's review of compliance

64. When reviewing the company's compliance with this provision of the Combined Code the APB recommends that the auditor performs the following procedures:

(a) Reviewing documentation, for example inclusion in the terms of reference of the audit committee, which explains that the audit committee has primary responsibility for making a recommendation on the appointment, reappointment and removal of the external auditors.

(b) Reviewing documentation that evidences the audit committee's recommendation to the board.

(c) Where the board has not accepted the audit committee's recommendation, reviewing whether there is included in the annual report and in any papers recommending appointment or re-appointment of the auditors:

    (i) a statement from the audit committee explaining its recommendation; and

    (ii) a statement from the board setting out reasons why the board has taken a different position from that recommended by the audit committee.

Non-audit activities

> **C.3.7** **The annual report should explain to shareholders how, if the auditor provides non-audit services, auditor objectivity and independence is safeguarded.**

Auditor's review of compliance

65. When reviewing the company's compliance with this provision of the Combined Code the APB recommends that the auditor establishes whether the annual report includes a statement explaining to shareholders how, if the auditor provides non-audit services, auditor objectivity and independence is safeguarded.

66. The auditor considers the explanation of how auditor objectivity and independence is safeguarded in the context of the information of which they are aware. While it is not the auditor's responsibility to establish that the audit committee has fulfilled its responsibilities as set out in the terms of reference recommended by the Combined Code (to review and monitor the independence and objectivity of the external auditor and to develop and implement policy on the engagement of the external auditor to supply non- audit services taking into account relevant ethical guidance regarding the provision of non-audit services by the external auditor[24]) the auditor will be aware of whether the audit committee has undertaken these responsibilities and:

(a) notifies the audit committee and the board of directors if they believe these responsibilities have not been undertaken; and

(b) considers the requirements of Auditing Standards in relation to other information issued with audited financial statements if they believe the explanation is misleading.

67. APB Ethical Standards ("ESs") 1 to 5 set out the integrity, objectivity and independence requirements for auditors in the audit of financial statements. ES1[33] requires the audit engagement partner to ensure that those charged with governance of the audit client are appropriately informed on a timely basis of all significant facts and matters that bear upon the auditors "objectivity and independence". In relation to non-audit services, ES5[34] requires the audit engagement partner to ensure that those charged with governance are informed of any inconsistencies between APB Ethical Standards and the company's policy for the supply of non-audit services by the audit firm and any apparent breach of that policy.

Directors' statement on going concern

> **C.1.2** **The directors should report that the business is a going concern, with supporting assumptions or qualifications as necessary.**

Auditor's review of compliance

68. The Listing Rules[35] require the directors of certain listed companies[36] to include in the annual report and accounts a statement that:

> *"the business is a going concern, together with supporting assumptions or qualification as necessary, that has been prepared in accordance with "Going Concern and Financial Reporting: Guidance for directors of listed companies registered in the United Kingdom, published in November 1994[37]".*

69. The Listing Rules[38] require a listed company to ensure that the auditor reviews the directors' going concern statement. In order for the auditor to meet the review requirements of this rule the auditor:

   (a) assesses the consistency of the directors' going concern statement with the knowledge obtained in the course of the audit of the financial statements. This knowledge will primarily have been obtained in meeting Auditing Standards[39] relating to going concern; and

   (b) assesses whether the directors' statement meets the disclosure requirements of the guidance for directors referred to in the Listing Rules[40]. Illustrative suggested disclosures for directors are set out in paragraphs 47 to 54 of that guidance.

---

[33] Paragraph 49
[34] Paragraph 35
[35] FSA LR 9.8.6R(3); ISE LR 6.8.6R(3)
[36] In the case of the FSA the Listing Rule applies to companies incorporated in the United Kingdom and in the case of the ISE the Listing Rule applies to companies incorporated in the Republic of Ireland.
[37] Going Concern and Financial Reporting: Guidance for directors of listed companies registered in the UK, ICAEW, November 1994. This guidance can be downloaded from the ICAEW web-site.
[38] FSA LR 9.8.10R(1); ISE LR 6.8.9(1)
[39] ISA (UK and Ireland) 570, 'The going concern basis in financial statements".
[40] FSA 9.8.6R(3); ISE LR 6.8.6(3)

70. The auditor does not assess or report on whether the directors have complied with any other detailed requirements of the guidance for directors. In particular, as the auditor does not express an opinion on the ability of the company to continue in operational existence they do not undertake additional procedures that would support such an opinion.

71. Paragraph 49 of the guidance for directors (dealing with going concern) provides the following illustrative example of the basic disclosure that directors make when the going concern presumption is appropriate:

> "After making enquiries, the directors have a reasonable expectation that the company has adequate resources to continue in operational existence for the foreseeable future. For this reason, they continue to adopt the going concern basis in preparing the accounts".

72. It is particularly important that the directors' statement on going concern is not inconsistent with any disclosures regarding going concern in either the financial statements or the auditor's report thereon. Where going concern matters are discussed in the financial statements one method of achieving consistency is for the directors' statement to include a cross reference to the relevant note to the financial statements.

Reporting requirements derived from other Auditing Standards

73. Auditing Standards set out the auditor's responsibilities in relation to other information in documents containing audited financial statements. These responsibilities extend to the Combined Code disclosures where there is either a material misstatement of fact or a material inconsistency with the audited financial statements. Application of these Standards requires that:

(a) Where the auditor identifies a material inconsistency between the audited financial statements and the Combined Code disclosures the auditor determines whether the audited financial statements or the Combined Code disclosures need to be amended and seeks to resolve the matter through discussion with those charged with governance:

(i) If an amendment is necessary in the audited financial statements and the entity refuses to make the amendment, the auditor expresses a qualified or adverse opinion on the financial statements.

(ii) If an amendment is necessary in the Combined Code disclosures and the entity refuses to make the amendment, the auditor considers including in the auditor's report an emphasis of matter paragraph describing the material inconsistency[41] or taking other actions.

---

[41] As explained in paragraph 55, the APB recommends that the auditor's comments be included under the heading 'other matter' which would be included in the auditor's report below the auditor's opinion.

(b) Where the auditor identifies a material misstatement of fact in the Combined Code disclosures the auditor discusses the matter with those charged with governance. Where, after discussion, the auditor still considers that there is an apparent misstatement of fact, the auditor requests those charged with governance to consult with a qualified third party, such as the entity's legal counsel, and considers the advice received.

If the auditor concludes that an amendment is necessary in the Combined Code disclosures, which the entity refuses to correct, the auditor considers taking further appropriate action and considers including in the auditor's report an emphasis of matter paragraph describing the material misstatement.

Appendix 1

Extracts from the FSA Listing Rules[42]

Additional information

LR 9.8.6R
In the case of a *listed company* incorporated in the *United Kingdom*, the following additional items must be included in its annual report and accounts:

(3) a statement made by the *directors* that the business is a going concern, together with supporting assumptions or qualifications as necessary, that has been prepared in accordance with "Going Concern and Financial Reporting: Guidance for Directors of listed companies registered in the United Kingdom", published in November 1994;

(5) a statement of how the *listed company* has applied the principles set out in Section 1 of the *Combined Code*, in a manner that would enable shareholders to evaluate how the principles have been applied;

(6) a statement as to whether the *listed company* has;

    (a) complied throughout the accounting period with all relevant provisions set out in Section 1 of the *Combined Code*; or

    (b) not complied throughout the accounting period with all relevant provisions set out in Section 1 of the *Combined Code* and if so, setting out:

        i. those provisions, if any, it has not complied with;

        ii. in the case of provisions whose requirements are of a continuing nature, the period within which, if any, it did not comply with some or all of those provisions; and

        iii. the *company's* reasons for non-compliance; ...

LR 9.8.7R
An *overseas company* with a *primary listing* must disclose in its annual report and accounts:

(1) whether or not it complies with the corporate governance regime of its country of incorporation;

(2) the significant ways in which its actual corporate governance practices differ from those set out in the *Combined Code*; and

---

[42] See Appendix 2 for references to equivalent Irish Stock Exchange Listing Rules

(3) the unexpired term of the service contract of any *director* proposed for election or re-election at the forthcoming annual general meeting and, if any *director* for election or re-election does not have a service contract, a statement to that effect.

Auditors report

LR 9.8.10R   A *listed company* must ensure that the auditors review each of the following before the annual report is published:

(1) LR 9.8.6R (3) (statement by the directors that the business is a going concern); and

(2) the parts of the statement required by LR9.8.6R (6) (corporate governance) that relate to the following provisions of the *Combined Code:*

a.   C1.1;

b.   C.2.1; and

c.   C3.1 to C3.7

Appendix 2

Equivalent Irish Stock Exchange Listing Rules

FSA Listing Rule	Equivalent Listing Rule of the Irish Stock Exchange
LR 9.8.6R	LR 6.8.6
LR 9.8.6R (3)	LR 6.8.6 (3)
LR 9.8.6R (5)	LR 6.8.6 (6)
LR 9.8.6R (6)	LR 6.8.6 (7)
LR 9.8.6R (7)	LR 6.8.6 (8)
LR 9.8.7R	LR 6.8.7
LR 9.8.8R	LR 6.8.8
LR 9.8.10R	LR 6.8.9
LR 9.8.10R(1)	LR 6.8.9(1)
LR 9.8.10R(2)	LR 6.8.9(2)

Appendix 3

Example Terms of Engagement Paragraphs

The following is an illustrative example of paragraphs that may be included in the auditor's engagement letter dealing with the auditor's responsibilities with respect to the company's compliance with FSA LR 9.8.10R or ISE LR 6.8.9. In practice the auditor tailors the engagement letter to the specific circumstances of the engagement.

The auditor may wish to include a statement in its engagement letter limiting the auditor's liability in respect of the engagement to review the directors' corporate governance disclosures. The auditor is recommended to take legal advice concerning the wording of such a statement and how it is communicated.

Review of the company's disclosures relating to corporate governance and going concern.

Responsibilities of directors

As directors of the company you are responsible for ensuring that the company complies with the Listing Rules of the [Financial Services Authority including rules LR 9.8.6R (3), (5) and (6) "Additional information" and LR 9.8.10R "Auditors report"] [Irish Stock Exchange including rules LR 6.8.6 (3), (6) and(7) "Additional information" and LR 6.8.9 "Auditors Report"].

Responsibilities of the auditor

Listing Rule [9.8.10R] [6.8.9] states that "A listed company must ensure that the auditors review each of the following before the annual report is published:

(1) [LR9.8.6R (3)] [LR 6.8.6 (3)] (statement by the directors that the business is a going concern); and

(2) the parts of the statement required by [LR 9.8.6R (6)] [LR 6.8.6(7)] (corporate governance) that relate to the following provisions of the Combined Code:

   (a) C1.1;

   (b) C2.1; and

   (c) C3.1 to C3.7.

As we have agreed, we will carry out the review required of us by the Listing Rules having regard to the guidance published in APB Bulletin 2006/5. We are not required to form an opinion on the company's corporate governance procedures.

Having finalised our review we expect to communicate and discuss with you the factual findings of our review.

Scope of review

You will provide us with such information and explanations as we consider necessary. We may request you to provide written confirmation of oral representations which you make to us during the course of our review. We shall request sight of all documents or statements which are due to be issued with either the statement of compliance or the going concern statement and all documentation prepared by or for the board in support of the company's statements.

As we have agreed we will attend the meeting of the audit committee [full board] at which the annual report and accounts, including the going concern statement and the statement of compliance, are considered and approved for submission to the board of directors.

Internal control

With respect to Code Provision C.2.1, our work will be restricted to:

(a) assessing, based on enquiry of the directors, the supporting documentation prepared by or for the directors and our knowledge obtained during the audit of the financial statements, whether the company's summary of the process the board (and where applicable its committees) has adopted in reviewing the effectiveness of internal control appropriately reflects that process; and

(b) assessing whether the company's disclosures of the processes it has applied to deal with material internal control aspects of any significant problems disclosed in the annual report and accounts appropriately reflects those processes.

As our work is not designed to:

(a) consider whether the board's statements on internal control cover all risks and controls; or

(b) form an opinion on the effectiveness of the company's risk and control procedures; or

(c) assess either the directors' decision as to what constitutes a significant failing or weakness, or whether the actions, taken or to be taken, will in fact remedy the significant failings or weaknesses identified by the directors,

our work on internal control will not be sufficient to enable us to express any assurance as to whether or not your internal controls are effective. In addition our financial statement audit should not be relied upon to draw to your attention matters that may be relevant to your consideration as to whether or not your system of internal control is effective.

Going concern

With respect to the company's going concern statement our work will be restricted to a consideration of whether the statement provides the disclosures required by [LR 9.8.6R (3)] [LR 6.8.6 (3)] and is not inconsistent with the information of which we are aware from our audit work on the financial statements. We will not carry out the additional work necessary to give an opinion that the company has adequate resources to continue in operational existence.

Statement of auditor's responsibilities

Code provision C.1.1 recommends, among other things, that there should be a statement in the annual report about the auditor's reporting responsibilities. As we have agreed we will incorporate a description of our reporting responsibilities in our audit report on the financial statements.

BULLETIN 2007/2

THE DUTY OF AUDITORS IN THE REPUBLIC OF IRELAND TO REPORT TO THE DIRECTOR OF CORPORATE ENFORCEMENT

CONTENTS

1.0 Introduction

1.1 Under the Companies Acts and other legislation, the primary responsibility for a company's compliance with legal and regulatory requirements rests with its directors. This responsibility includes reporting to the company's shareholders, keeping proper books of account, safeguarding the assets of the company and taking appropriate steps to prevent fraud and other irregularities.

1.2 The corporate governance structure established in the Companies Acts also provides that, subject to the exemption introduced by Part III of the Companies (Amendment) (No. 2) Act 1999 (as amended), shareholders are entitled to receive a report from an independent auditor as to whether, in that auditor's opinion, the financial statements presented by the directors give a true and fair view of the state of affairs of the company and of its profits (or losses) for the period under review and have been properly prepared in accordance with the accounting provisions of the Companies Acts and on certain other aspects of the directors' responsibilities for financial reporting.

1.3 While auditors perform these duties in the interests of a company's primary stakeholders, namely its shareholders, they also have to have regard to the public interest. Accordingly, in addition to requiring an auditor to report to shareholders, the Companies Acts and other legislation also impose certain duties on auditors to make disclosures to regulatory authorities in the public interest.

1.4 In 2001, the Oireachtas decided that auditors should be required to report to the Director of Corporate Enforcement ("the Director") instances of the suspected commission of indictable offences under the Companies Acts by a company, its officers or agents. Section 74 of the Company Law Enforcement Act 2001 ("the 2001 Act") accordingly introduced this new duty by amending the existing duties of auditors in section 194 of the Companies Act 1990 ("the 1990 Act"). Section 74 was brought into effect on 28 November 2001[1].

1.5 In 2003, section 37 of the Companies (Auditing and Accounting) Act 2003 ("the 2003 Act") made a number of further changes to section 194 of the 1990 Act. These changes sought to provide inter alia that the failure to comply with certain obligations to file annual returns would be exempted from the obligation to report to the Director and that auditors would be required to give additional assistance to the Director in his investigation of reported suspected indictable offences under the Companies Acts.

1.6 Sections 73(2)(d) and (3) of the Investment Funds, Companies and Miscellaneous Provisions Act 2005 ("the 2005 Act") made a further amendment to section 194 which clarified the provision in the 2003 Act relating to the exemption of auditors from the requirement to report filing defaults to the Director. This exemption provision was commenced with effect from 1 September 2005[2].

---

[1] Commencement was achieved in the Investment Funds, Companies and Miscellaneous Provisions Act 2005 (Commencement) Order 2005 (S.I. No. 323 of 2005).

[2] Commencement was achieved in the Investment Funds, Companies and Miscellaneous Provisions Act 2005 (Commencement) Order 2005 (S.I. No.323 of 2005).

1.7 The guidance set out in this Bulletin cannot be construed as a definitive legal interpretation of the relevant provisions. However, this guidance discusses the scope of section 194(5), (5A) and (5B) of the 1990 Act (as amended) and takes into account and applies the terms of relevant auditing standards to that provision. It has been developed in conjunction with the Office of the Director of Corporate Enforcement and the Consultative Committee of Accountancy Bodies – Ireland.

2.0 Section 194 (as amended) of the Companies Act, 1990

2.1 The original section 194 of the 1990 Act sets out the duties of auditors where they form the opinion that proper books of account are not being kept by a company and its directors. The amendments to section 194 made by the 2001, 2003 and the 2005 Acts prescribe new or amended reporting requirements for auditors. A copy of section 194 of the 1990 Act, following amendment by section 74 of the 2001 Act, section 37 of the 2003 Act and section 73 of the 2005 Act, is attached at Appendix 1 to this Bulletin.

2.2 The purpose of this Bulletin is to outline the scope of the duties which arise for auditors in this context and to address certain issues arising within each part of section 194(5), (5A) and 5(B) of the 1990 Act as amended. The requirement under section 194(5) provides as follows:

"Where, in the course of, and by virtue of, their carrying out an audit of the accounts of the company, information comes into the possession of the auditors of a company that leads them to form the opinion that there are reasonable grounds for believing that the company or an officer or an agent of it has committed an indictable offence under the Companies Acts (other than an indictable offence under section 125(2) or 127(12) of the Principal Act), the auditors shall, forthwith after having formed it, notify that opinion to the Director and provide the Director with details of the grounds on which they have formed that opinion."[3].

2.3 Section 37(e) of the 2003 Act introduced sections 194(5A) and (5B) as follows:

"(5A) Where the auditors of a company notify the Director of any matter pursuant to subsection (5), they shall, in addition to performing their obligations under that subsection, if requested by the Director—

(a) *furnish the Director with such further information in their possession or control relating to the matter as the Director may require, including further information relating to the details of the grounds on which they formed the opinion referred to in that subsection,*

(b) *give the Director such access to books and documents in their possession or control relating to the matter as the Director may require, and*

---

[3] As amended by Section 73(2)(d) of the Investment Funds, Companies and Miscellaneous Provisions Act 2005.

(c) give the Director such access to facilities for the taking of copies of or extracts from those books and documents as the Director may require.

(5B) Nothing in this section compels the disclosure by any person of any information that the person would be entitled to refuse to produce on the grounds of legal professional privilege or authorises the inspection or copying of any document containing such information that is in the person's possession."

2.4 The reporting obligation applies to all persons practising as Responsible Individuals / Registered Auditors[4] of companies to which the provision applies. This includes auditors resident outside the State who are legally permitted under the Companies Acts to audit the accounts of such companies.

2.5 Auditing standards[5] also require auditors to exercise adequate control and supervision over their staff conducting audit work. Consequently, as indicated in ISA (UK and Ireland) 250(B), "The Auditor's Right and Duty to Report to Regulators in the Financial Sector", (paragraph 35), in planning and conducting the audit of a company, auditors need to ensure that staff are alert to the possibility that a report may be required. Auditors should also refer to ISA (UK and Ireland) 220 "Quality Control for Audits of Historical Financial Information" for further guidance on this matter. ISA (UK and Ireland) 250(B) also states that auditing firms need to establish adequate procedures to ensure that any matters which are discovered in the course of, or as a result of, audit work which may give rise to a report are brought to the attention of the engagement partner on a timely basis (ISA (UK and Ireland) 250(B) paragraph 36).

3.0 Auditing Standards

3.1 A number of standards are of relevance to this subject. These include, primarily, ISA (UK and Ireland) 250(A) "Consideration of Law and Regulations in an Audit of Financial Statements" and ISA (UK and Ireland) 250(B) "The Auditor's Right and Duty to Report to Regulators in the Financial Sector". Paragraph 38-3 of ISA (UK and Ireland) 250(A) indicates that the procedures and guidance set out in ISA (UK and Ireland) 250(B) can be adapted to other circumstances in which the auditor becomes aware of a suspected instance of non-compliance with laws or regulations which the auditor is under a statutory duty to report. Where applicable, reference is made to these Standards in the text of this guidance.

---

[4] The Institutes of Chartered Accountants in Ireland (ICAI), England & Wales (ICAEW) and Scotland (ICAS) register firms for audit. The Institute of Certified Public Accountants in Ireland (ICPAI) also registers firms. Persons within those firms who are entitled to sign audit reports are known as Responsible Individuals. The Association of Chartered Certified Accountants (ACCA) registers both firms and individuals for audit while the Institute of Incorporated Public Accountants Ltd. (IIPA) registers individuals for audit. Individuals registered by these bodies are known as Registered Auditors.

[5] International Standards on Auditing (UK and Ireland) may be accessed through the APB website at www.frc.org.uk/apb.

4.0 Non-Audit Assignments

"Where in the course of, and by virtue of, their carrying out an audit of the accounts of a company..."

4.1   The subsection indicates that the obligation on auditors to report a suspected indictable offence under the Companies Acts to the Director of Corporate Enforcement arises where auditors are undertaking an audit of the financial statements of a company. Therefore, the reporting obligation does not apply to persons providing non-audit services to a company. Similarly, the subsection does not impose a legal obligation on persons undertaking non-audit services to inform the auditors within their firm of the information which has come into their possession.

4.2   However, where a person performs, or has performed, non-audit work for a company for whom s/he also acts, or subsequently accepts appointment, as auditor, that auditor, acting as such, has certain responsibilities in relation to any information suggesting the commission of an indictable offence which came to attention during the course of the non-audit work.

4.3   The statutory duty to report to a regulator applies to information which comes to the attention of auditors in their capacity as such. In determining whether information is obtained in that capacity, ISA (UK and Ireland) 250(B) identifies two criteria in particular which need to be considered, namely:

   (i)   whether the person who obtained the information also undertook the audit work and, if so,

   (ii)   whether it was obtained in the course of, or as a result of, undertaking the audit work (ISA (UK and Ireland) 250(B) Appendix 2 - paragraph 6).

4.4   Where partners or staff, involved in the audit of an entity, carry out work other than the audit (i.e. non-audit work), information about the entity will be known to them as individuals. In circumstances which suggest that a matter would otherwise give rise to a statutory duty to report if obtained in the capacity of auditor, it will be prudent for them to make enquiries in the course of their audit work in order to establish whether this is the case from information obtained in that capacity (ISA (UK and Ireland) 250(B) Appendix 2 - paragraph 8).

4.5   Where non-audit work is carried out by other partners or staff, neither of the aforementioned criteria (at (i) and (ii) above) are satisfied in respect of the information that becomes known to them. Nevertheless, in such circumstances, ISA (UK and Ireland) 250(B) states that the firm in question should take proper account of such information when it could affect the audit so that it is treated in a responsible manner, particularly since in partnership law the knowledge obtained by one partner in the course of partnership business may be imputed to the entire partnership (ISA (UK and Ireland) 250(B) Appendix 2 - paragraph 9).

4.6 A firm appointed as auditor of an entity needs to have in place appropriate procedures to ensure that the partner responsible for the audit function is made aware of any relationship which exists between any department of the firm and the regulated entity when that relationship could affect the firm's work as auditor (ISA (UK and Ireland) 250(B) Appendix 2 - paragraph 10).

4.7 The ISA goes on to state that, *prima facie*, information obtained in the course of non-audit work is not covered by the duty to report. However, the firm appointed as auditor needs to consider whether the results of other work undertaken for the entity in question needs to be assessed as part of the audit process. In principle this is no different to seeking to review a report prepared by outside consultants on the entity's accounting systems so as to ensure that the auditor makes a proper assessment of the risks of misstatement in the financial statements and of the work needed to form an opinion. Consequently, the partner responsible for the audit needs to make appropriate enquiries in the process of planning (see below) and completing the audit. Such enquiries would be directed to those aspects of the non-audit work which might reasonably be expected to be relevant to the audit (ISA (UK and Ireland) 250(B) Appendix 2 - paragraph 11).

4.8 In the context of the foregoing, the provisions of ISA (UK and Ireland) 300 "Planning an Audit of Financial Statements", ISA (UK and Ireland) 210 "Terms of Audit Engagements", and ISA (UK and Ireland) 315 "Understanding the Entity and its Environment and Assessing the Risks of Material Misstatement" are also of particular relevance. Auditors are required by these standards to:

- plan the audit (ISA (UK and Ireland) 300),

- agree the terms of engagement with the client (ISA (UK and Ireland) 210), and

- obtain an understanding of the entity and its environment (ISA (UK and Ireland) 315).

4.9 In planning the audit, agreeing the terms of engagement, and obtaining a knowledge of the business, the auditor is expected to consider all material relevant to the audit including:

- internal control relevant to the audit (ISA (UK and Ireland) 315 paragraph 41),

- relevant industry, regulatory and other external factors (ISA (UK and Ireland) 315 paragraph 22),

- scope of the audit, including reference to applicable legislation (ISA (UK and Ireland) 210 paragraph 6), and

- where relevant, information about the entity and its environment obtained in prior periods (ISA (UK and Ireland) 315 paragraph 12).

4.10 ISA (UK and Ireland) 300 is framed in the context of recurring audits. However, it draws auditors' attention (in paragraph 29) to the fact that "*for an initial audit, the auditor may need to expand the planning activities because the auditor does not ordinarily have the previous experience with the entity that is considered when planning recurring engagements".*

4.11 Compliance with the provisions of ISAs (UK and Ireland) 250, 300 and 315 respectively may result in auditors successfully identifying any matters arising from non-audit work that may require them to make a report to the Director pursuant to their obligations under section 194(5) of the 1990 Act.

4.12 With regard to the point in time at which auditors' reporting obligations arise in respect of matters first identified in the course of providing non-audit services:

- where a person providing non-audit services to a company becomes aware of an indictable offence and s/he also acts as the auditor of that company, the obligation to report the suspected indictable offence will arise when the auditor comes into possession of the information in question as part of the undertaking of the audit, and

- where a person providing non-audit services to a company becomes aware of an indictable offence and s/he is subsequently appointed to act as the auditor of that company, the obligation to report the suspected indictable offence will arise when the auditor comes into possession of the information in question as part of the undertaking of the audit.

5.0 Reportable Information

"...information comes into the possession of the auditors of a company..."

5.1 The provision indicates that the obligation on auditors to report to the Director of Corporate Enforcement arises when information comes into their possession as part of the undertaking of the audit. Without prejudice to the above guidance on the need for proper audit planning and associated requirements, the Director does not regard the obligation as requiring auditors to seek out possible indictable offences as part of the audit process. However, auditors react to information coming into their possession which suggests that a possible indictable offence has occurred and to make the necessary enquiries to enable them to form a considered opinion on the question.

5.2 ISA (UK and Ireland) 250(A) sets out standards and guidance for auditors on the consideration of law and regulations. It requires that *"the auditor should plan and perform the audit with an attitude of professional scepticism, recognising that the audit may reveal conditions or events that could lead to questioning whether an entity is complying with law and regulations."* (ISA (UK and Ireland) 250(A) paragraph 13).

5.3 ISA (UK and Ireland) 250(A) requires that *"in order to plan the audit, the auditor should obtain a general understanding of the legal and regulatory framework applicable to the entity and the industry and how the entity is complying with that framework."* (ISA (UK and Ireland) 250(A) paragraph 15).

5.4 The ISA also indicates that in obtaining a general understanding of the legal and regulatory framework applicable to an entity and procedures followed to ensure compliance with this framework, auditors would particularly recognise that non-compliance with some laws and regulations may give rise to business risks that have a fundamental effect on the operations of the entity. That is, non-compliance with certain laws and regulations may cause the entity to cease operations, or call into question the entity's continuance as a going concern. For example, non-compliance with the requirements of the entity's license or other title to perform its operations could have such an impact (for example, for a bank, non-compliance with capital or investment requirements) (ISA (UK and Ireland) 250(A) paragraph 16).

5.5 The ISA goes on to state that *"To obtain the general understanding of laws and regulations, the auditor would ordinarily:*

- *Use the existing understanding of the entity's industry, regulatory and other external factors;*

- *Inquire of management concerning the entity's policies and procedures regarding compliance with laws and regulations;*

- *Inquire of management as to the laws or regulations that may be expected to have a fundamental effect on the operations of the entity;*

- *Discuss with management the policies or procedures adopted for identifying, evaluating and accounting for litigation claims and assessments; and*

- *Discuss the legal and regulatory framework with auditors of subsidiaries in other countries (for example, if the subsidiary is required to adhere to the securities regulations of the parent company)."* (ISA (UK and Ireland) 250(A) paragraph 17).

5.6 The auditor should then perform further audit procedures to help identify instances of non-compliance with those laws and regulations where non-compliance should be considered when preparing financial statements, specifically:

- Inquiring of management as to whether the entity is in compliance with such laws and regulations;

- Inspecting correspondence with the relevant licensing or regulatory authorities; and

- Enquiring of those charged with governance as to whether they are on notice of any such possible instances of non-compliance with law or regulations. (ISA (UK and Ireland) 250(A) paragraph 18).

5.7 The auditor's procedures should be designed to help identify possible or actual instances of non-compliance with those laws and regulations which provide a legal framework within which the entity conducts its business and which are central to the entity's ability to conduct its business and hence to its financial statements (ISA (UK and Ireland) 250(A) paragraph 18-1).

5.8 On discovery of a possible instance of non-compliance, the ISA provides the following direction to auditors: *"when the auditor becomes aware of information concerning a possible instance of non-compliance, the auditor should obtain an understanding of the nature of the act and the circumstances in which it has occurred and sufficient other information to evaluate the possible effect on the financial statements"* (ISA (UK and Ireland) 250(A) paragraph 26).

5.9 The ISA goes on to state that when evaluating the possible effect on the financial statements, the auditor considers, *inter alia*, *"the potential financial consequences, such as fines, penalties, damages, threat of expropriation of assets, enforced discontinuation of operations and litigation"* (ISA (UK and Ireland) 250(A) paragraph 27).

5.10 It is clear, therefore, that where auditors detect the suspected commission of an indictable offence under the Companies Acts, they are required by professional standards to carry out such further investigations into the matter as to provide them with an understanding of the nature of the act and to allow them to properly evaluate the possible effects on the financial statements, including the potential consequences of any fines or other sanctions (imposed on the company, its directors or officers) which might result from that non-compliance.

5.11 In general the maximum penalty on conviction on indictment (see [section 10.0] – Indictable Offences) of an indictable offence under the Companies Acts is €12,700 and/or 5 years' imprisonment. However, the Companies Acts also provide for considerably higher sanctions in respect of certain offences, e.g. fraudulent trading (€63,000 and/or 7 years imprisonment) and insider dealing/market abuse (€10,000,000 and/or 10 years' imprisonment). Moreover, persons convicted on indictment of an indictable offence involving fraud or dishonesty are automatically disqualified from acting as company directors/officers. The Director of Corporate Enforcement can also apply to the Courts seeking the disqualification of any person:

• guilty of two or more offences of failing to maintain proper books and records, or,

• guilty of three or more defaults under the Companies Acts.

5.12 Accordingly, the conviction on indictment of a company or any of its officers under the Companies Acts and any consequential claims arising can have potentially very serious consequences for the company and its continuing operations, and by extension on its financial statements.

5.13 In the context of their investigations, section 193(3) of the Companies Act 1990 entitles auditors, *inter alia*, to require from the officers of the company such information as they think necessary for the performance of their duties. If an auditor is unable, as part of the audit, to obtain information regarding a potential breach due to the non co-operation of one of the company's officers or agents, this in itself constitutes a suspected indictable offence under section 197[6] of the 1990 Act. Naturally, any such non co-operation will also have to be taken into account by an auditor when:

- forming his or her audit opinion,

- drafting the audit report under section 193(4) of the Companies Act 1990,

- deciding whether to continue in office or to decline re-appointment.

5.14 In the event that an auditor was to resign or to decline re-appointment in such circumstances, s/he would be obliged under section 185 of the 1990 Act to:

- serve a notice of resignation on the company (subsection (1)),

- provide in the notice a statement of the circumstances which should be brought to the attention of the members or creditors of the company (subsection (2)), and

- copy the notice to the Registrar of Companies within 14 days (subsection (3)).

6.0 Legal or Other Professional Advice

> "...that leads them to form the opinion that there are reasonable grounds for believing..."

6.1 Section 194(5) requires auditors to exercise their professional judgement in determining if the information and evidence in their possession leads to the formation of the opinion that the matter is reportable to the Director of Corporate Enforcement by virtue of providing reasonable grounds for a belief that an indictable offence has been committed. A collective judgement may be made in the case of an auditing firm. While there is no obligation on auditors to obtain legal or other professional advice before forming that opinion, the Director recognises that auditors may wish to seek such independent advice as part of the process of forming their opinion.

6.2 Where legal or other professional advice is obtained by the company in relation to the matter(s) about which the auditor has concerns, the auditor is similarly required to exercise professional judgement in determining if the information is reportable to the Director of Corporate Enforcement. While in many cases, auditors could expect to be

---

[6] Section 197(3) Companies Act, 1990 states: "An officer of a company who fails to provide to the auditors of the company or of the holding company of the company, within two days of the making of the relevant request, any information or explanations that the auditors require as auditors of the company or of the holding company of the company and that is within the knowledge of or can be procured by the officer shall be guilty of an offence".

satisfied with legal advice emanating from a reputable source, auditors would not be entitled to rely on such advice if, having taken it into account, they formed the opinion that the advice was in error, incomplete or otherwise inadequate by reference to the information in their possession.

7.0 Reportable Persons

"...that the company or an officer or an agent of it..."

7.1 In the subsection, *"the company"* is the company which is being audited by the auditor ("Company A"). Subject to what follows, the reporting obligation does not therefore extend to another company ("Company B"), which the auditor of Company A may believe has committed a reportable offence.

7.2 In addition, the term *"company"* must comply with the general definition of company in the Companies Act 1963 which is *"a company formed and registered under this Act, or an existing company"*.

7.3 The term *"existing company"* is separately defined as *"a company formed and registered in a register kept in the State under the Joint Stock Companies Acts, the Companies Act, 1862 or the Companies (Consolidation) Act, 1908"*.

7.4 The reporting obligation on auditors imposed by the subsection does not extend to companies formed outside the State, even where they may be registered as having an established place of business within the State under the Companies Acts or where they operate through a branch (under the European Communities (Branch Disclosure) Regulations, 1993).

7.5 The term *"officer"* is defined in section 2(1) of the Companies Act, 1963. It states that *"'officer' in relation to a body corporate includes a director or secretary"*. The term officer also includes the company's auditor in certain specified circumstances.

7.6 In relation to certain offences under the Companies Acts, the term officer is extended to include shadow directors. The term *'shadow director'* is specifically defined in section 27 of the 1990 Act as *"a person in accordance with whose directions or instructions the directors of a company are accustomed to act"*. Accordingly, where the suspected offence is one which applies to shadow directors, the term officer includes shadow directors.

7.7 Where the audit is of the consolidated financial statements of a group of companies, the obligation to report applies to each group company individually.

7.8 The reporting obligation extends to either of the following circumstances:

- where the reportable offence by the officer of Company A relates to that company, or,

- where the reportable offence by the officer of Company A relates to a matter outside of that company. In other words, a suspected indictable offence by an officer of Company A relating to his or her involvement in Company B is eligible to be reported by the auditor of Company A.

7.9 In the subsection, the term *"agent"* must comply with the general definition of agent in section 2(1) of the Companies Act, 1963, which states *"'agent' does not include a person's counsel acting as such"*. The term "agent" is commonly understood to refer to any person authorised to bind the company. Therefore, a company's solicitor, acting in a capacity that binds the company, may be an agent of the company in certain circumstances.

7.10 Again, the reporting obligation extends to either of the following circumstances:

- where the reportable offence by the agent of Company A relates to that company, or

- where the reportable offence by the agent of Company A relates to a matter outside of that company. In other words, a suspected indictable offence by an agent of Company A relating to his or her involvement in Company B is eligible to be reported by the auditor of Company A.

7.11 While the preceding paragraphs set out the general guidance to auditors on this matter, it is recognised that in many circumstances, auditors will not be in a position to obtain sufficient information to allow the formation of an opinion as to whether an officer or an agent of Company A has committed an indictable offence in relation to Company B.

8.0 Standard of Certainty

"...has committed..."

8.1 The term *"has committed"* is obviously of a higher standard of certainty than *"might have committed"* or even *"may have committed"*. Where auditors detect a suspected reportable breach of the Companies Acts, they should obtain sufficient information to enable the formation of the opinion as to whether there are reasonable grounds to conclude that an indictable offence has been committed.

8.2 ISA (UK and Ireland) 250(B) provides the following guidance to auditors in this regard: *"In assessing the effect of an apparent breach, the auditor takes into account the quantity and type of evidence concerning such a matter which may reasonably be expected to be available. If the auditor concludes that the auditor has been prevented from obtaining all such evidence concerning a matter which may give rise to a duty to report, the auditor would normally make a report direct to the regulator without delay."* (ISA (UK and Ireland) 250(B) paragraph 41).

8.3 ISA (UK and Ireland) 250(B) requires auditors to exercise their professional judgement. In forming that judgement, auditors undertake appropriate investigations to determine the circumstances but do not require the degree of evidence which would be a normal part of forming an opinion on financial statements. ISA (UK and Ireland) 250(B) goes on to state that the appropriate investigations performed by auditors in these circumstances would normally include:

- enquiry of staff at an appropriate level,

- review of correspondence and documents relating to the transaction or event concerned, and

- discussion with those charged with governance or other senior management where appropriate (ISA (UK and Ireland) 250(B) paragraph 44).

9.0 Indictable Offences

"...an indictable offence under the Companies Acts (other than an indictable offence under section 125(2) or 127(12) of the Principal Act)..."

9.1 Under the Companies Acts, provision is made for two types of criminal offence, namely summary and indictable offences. A summary offence is generally of a less serious nature and is tried before a judge only in the District Court. Indictable offences are generally of a more serious nature. Indictable offences can, in the same way as summary offences, be tried in the District Court before a judge only. However, the distinction between a summary offence and an indictable offence is that, due to their more serious nature, indictable offences can also be tried in the Circuit Court, i.e. before a judge and jury. Where this course is taken, the indictable offence is said to be prosecuted on indictment. Where an offence is prosecuted on indictment, the penalties provided for by the law on conviction are generally considerably higher than had the offence been prosecuted summarily.

9.2 The sole prosecuting authority for indictable offences is the Director of Public Prosecutions (DPP). It is a matter for the Director of Corporate Enforcement to determine in any particular case if the suspected indictable offence reported to him by an auditor should be prosecuted summarily or referred to the DPP. Where a case is referred to the DPP by the Director of Corporate Enforcement, the DPP will subsequently make an independent decision as to whether or not it should actually be prosecuted on indictment. In practice, the DPP may decide to refer a matter to the Garda Síochána for further investigation before making a final decision.

9.3 With regard to the Company Law Enforcement Act 2001, the Oireachtas has decided that the obligation on auditors to report applies only to indictable offences and not to all offences under the Companies Acts[7]. The only exceptions to this are sections 125(2) and 127(12) of the Companies Act, 1963 (as amended) which relate to the filing of annual returns.

9.4 In considering whether or not to report a suspected offence, auditors are required to determine if in fact the offence in question is an indictable offence. It is not the duty of auditors under section 194(5) to make any other evaluation as to the seriousness or otherwise of an actual or potential offence. For example, it is of no relevance to the formation of an auditor's opinion under section 194(5) as to:

- whether the suspected offence has any impact on the company's financial statements or on the auditor's opinion as to whether or not the financial statements give a true and fair view of the state of affairs of the company. It is quite possible that an auditor may be in a position to give an unqualified audit report and yet be required to report a suspected indictable offence to the Director;

- what the policy of the Director of Corporate Enforcement or the Director of Public Prosecutions is with respect to the prosecution of indictable offences of a particular type. In other words even if it is their policy to prosecute certain offences summarily, this is not a matter which should affect the formation of the auditor's opinion in respect of the reporting of any suspected indictable offence;

- the extent to which the suspected indictable offence might involve a financial or other loss to any person. While this may be taken into account by the prosecuting authority in deciding whether or not to prosecute a case, the auditor has no role in making that adjudication on behalf of the prosecutor;

- whether the suspected offence may or may not have already been brought to the attention of the Director of Corporate Enforcement by the company, one of its officers or agents or another party. It is possible that any such report may not have included all relevant facts and details of the circumstances giving rise to the auditor's concerns. Accordingly, it is necessary that the auditor provide his or her independent opinion of the suspected indictable offence which has been committed;

- whether or not circumstances giving rise to the offence have been rectified or otherwise settled. Again, this is a matter which may be taken into account by the prosecuting authority in deciding whether or not to prosecute a case, but it is likely that circumstances will arise from time to time where rectification of the circumstances is not in itself a sufficient response to the indicated offence.

9.5 In addition to considering whether a suspected offence falls to be reported to the Director of Corporate Enforcement, the auditor assesses whether the particular

---

[7] A current list of indictable offences under the Companies Acts is available on the ODCE website (http://www.odce.ie) for the convenience of auditors. It is the Director of Corporate Enforcement's intention to update this list as required.

circumstances indicate reportable offences under the Criminal Justice Act 1994 (in respect of money laundering) and the Criminal Justice (Theft and Fraud Offences) Act, 2001 and, where appropriate, report these to the Garda Síochána and the Revenue Commissioners.

10.0 Timing of Formation and Notification of Opinion

"...the auditors shall, forthwith after having formed it, notify that opinion to the Director..."

10.1 The provision indicates that auditors are required to notify the Director of their opinion immediately after forming an opinion that there are reasonable grounds to conclude that an indictable offence has been committed. ISA (UK and Ireland) 250(B) is broadly consistent with this provision in requiring that *"when the auditor concludes, after appropriate discussion and investigations, that a matter which has come to the auditor's attention gives rise to a statutory duty to make a report, the auditor should bring the matter to the attention of the regulator without undue delay..."* (ISA (UK and Ireland) 250(B) paragraph 50).

10.2 While there will be circumstances where it is readily apparent that an indictable offence has been committed and that a report is required, there will be other circumstances where the immediate formation of an opinion may not be possible by virtue of auditors having to obtain and assess additional information from the company, its officers and employees.

10.3 Notwithstanding the foregoing, auditors will have to consider carefully the nature of the circumstances which have come to light in determining whether the formation of an opinion is urgent and, having formed that opinion, whether to report immediately to the Director. Such circumstances might for example include those where the effectiveness of any enforcement or other remedial action by the Director would be compromised by any delay in the formation and notification of the auditor's opinion. Such instances might typically include (but are not restricted to) those involving:

- breaches of requirements concerning the issue of shares;

- failure to observe the requirements of section 60 of the Companies Act 1963 while providing financial assistance for the purchase by a company of its own shares;

- falsification of records and/or documents;

- fraudulent trading;

- acquisition of own shares in contravention of a prohibition on their acquisition;

- illegal transactions involving directors;

- insider dealing/market abuse;

- disqualified person acting in contravention of a disqualification order;

- restricted director acting in contravention of the terms of a restriction order;

- failure to keep proper books of account;

- furnishing false information in purported compliance with any provision of the Companies Acts;

- knowingly or recklessly making a statement to an auditor, which is materially misleading, false or deceptive.

11.0 Details of the Grounds

"...and provide the Director with details of the grounds on which they have formed that opinion."

11.1 Auditors provide sufficient information in support of their opinion to enable the Director to evaluate properly the circumstances suggesting the commission of an indictable offence. This guidance is supported by ISA (UK and Ireland) 250(B) which requires, *inter alia, "the auditor should bring the matter to the attention of the regulator...in a form and manner which will facilitate appropriate action by the regulator"* (ISA (UK and Ireland) 250(B) paragraph 50).

11.2 The information provided by auditors as part of their reports to the Director of Corporate Enforcement should include:

- auditor details;

- statutory authority under which the report is being made;

- details of the company/person(s) who are the subject of the report;

- whether the matter has been discussed with the directors and/or relevant officer(s) and/or agent(s) of the company;

- details of the suspected indictable offence(s);

- details of the grounds on which the auditor has formed the opinion that an indictable offence has been committed. Auditors should ensure that this description is of sufficient detail to facilitate appropriate action by the Director;

- the context in which the report is being made. ISA (UK and Ireland) 250(B) offers guidance to auditors as to the type of information that might be included in this regard e.g.

  - the extent to which the auditor has investigated the circumstances giving rise to the matter reported, and

  - whether steps to rectify the matter have been taken (ISA (UK and Ireland) 250(B) paragraph 63).

- any other information considered relevant by the auditor;

- auditor's signature;

- date of report.

11.3 The ODCE publication 'A Guide to Transactions Involving Directors' sets out information that, if known to the auditor as a result of audit work, the Director considers useful to include as part of the report to his Office where the subject matter of the report is a suspected offence under section 40 of the Companies Act 1990 indicating a loan to a director(s) exceeding 10% of the company's relevant assets. Such information includes, if possible:

- the date(s) on which the loan(s) was/were advanced;

- the identity of each individual to whom the loan(s) was/were given;

- the value of the loan(s);

- whether the company's relevant assets were calculated by reference to the company's net assets as shown in the last preceding financial statements laid before an AGM or by reference to the company's called up share capital; and

- the extent to which 10% of the company's relevant assets were exceeded by the loan(s)[8].

Where such information is not readily available to the auditor (ie from information contained in the audit working papers), the auditor refers the Director to the company and its directors.

11.4 Auditors may afford the company's officer(s) or agent(s), as appropriate, the opportunity to compile a statement for submission to the Director of Corporate Enforcement together with the auditor's report. Issues that the officer(s) or agent(s) may wish to address if they choose to prepare such a statement might include, for

---

[8] Section 8.2, Contents of Auditors' Reports, excerpt from 'A Guide to Transactions Involving Directors', published by the ODCE in November 2003.

example, their views on the report's subject matter and details of any corrective or remedial action taken or proposed.

11.5 However, where the officer(s) or agent(s) elect to submit a statement to the Director, auditors should ensure that their reports are not delayed. Accordingly, it is recommended that in such circumstances, auditors should allow a period of two days for the furnishing of statements by the officer(s) or agent(s), after which time auditors should submit their report. Naturally, the officer(s) or agent(s) can, if they so wish, subsequently furnish a statement to the Director.

12.0 Provision of Further Information by Auditors to the Director

12.1 Section 37(e) of the Companies (Auditing and Accounting) Act 2003 extends the responsibilities of auditors in situations where they make a report to the Director under Section 194(5) of the Companies Act 1990. In particular, it provides in a new subsection (5A) that if requested by the Director, auditors shall:

"(a) furnish the Director with such further information in their possession or control relating to the matter as the Director may require, including further information relating to the details of the grounds on which they formed the opinion referred to in that subsection,

(b) give the Director such access to books and documents in their possession or control relating to the matter as the Director may require, and

(c) give the Director such access to facilities for the taking of copies of or extracts from those books and documents as the Director may require."

12.2 The purpose of this additional provision is to enable the Director to acquire on an efficient and effective basis the quality of information and evidence which initially led the auditor to report the suspected offence and thereby to facilitate the Director in reaching an informed decision as to what enforcement action (if any) is warranted by him as a result of the indicated circumstances.

12.3 The decision of the Director as to whether he will close the case without further action, recommend administrative resolution of the case perhaps by way of letter, or commence the preparation of a case for legal proceedings, depends on him having access to the fullest possible information concerning the incident or incidents that gave rise to the auditor's report. Every report made to the Office is dealt with in this manner so it is to the benefit of all parties that this information be gathered as efficiently as possible.

12.4 The information or books and documents to be made available is limited only to that which is actually in the possession of the auditor or under his control. The term "books and documents" is defined in section 3(1) of the 1990 Act as including "accounts, deeds, writings and records made in any other manner". Accordingly, the information, books and documents to be made available comprise both electronic and physical material. It should be noted that the auditor is not required to provide original documentation and there is no requirement to seek out additional information beyond that which is in the auditor's possession or control as a result of a request under this section.

12.5 Section 194(5B) of the 1990 Act makes clear that the Director's right to the information, books and documents referred to in section 194(5A) does not extend to material which is covered by legal professional privilege. An auditor can accordingly properly refuse to provide such material. Appendix 2 provides commentary on legal professional privilege.

12.6 The meaning of the phrase "relating to the matter" will depend on the particular circumstances of each report and the nature and amount of information in the possession of the auditor. It would be impossible to produce a definitive list of all information that could relate to the matter and could be in the possession or control of the auditor, as this will vary with each offence and with the amount and quality of information that the auditor has in his/her possession or control.

12.7 Books and documents may include records of meetings or discussions considering the issue directly, documentation on how the opinion that there are reasonable grounds for believing that an indictable offence has been committed was reached, working papers that highlight the matter as part of the audit fieldwork, as well as any other documents in the possession or control of the auditors that relate to the matter. Other documents may include client records and files or other documents relating to non-audit services provided to the company and that relate to the matter reported and are in the possession or control of the auditor.

12.8 In response to the receipt of an indictable offence report, an officer or officers of the Director may, pursuant to section 194(5A) of the 1990 Act, seek to acquire the further information and documents relating to the matter by way of correspondence and/or meeting and/or discussion. Where an officer or officers attends at the office of an auditor, the auditor may be required to make available facilities for the copying of relevant books or documents in the auditor's possession.

13.0 Protection Against Liability

13.1 Section 194(6) of the 1990 Act, which was inserted by section 74(e) of the 2001 Act, protects auditors from liability in discharging their legal duties under section 194. This protection covers the following circumstances:

- the reporting to the Registrar of Companies by auditors of any failure to keep proper books of account (section 194(1)(b) of the 1990 Act);

- the requirement on auditors to give the Director of Corporate Enforcement access to documentation and provide such information and explanations as the Director may require to investigate the circumstances giving rise to the auditor's notice to the Registrar above (section 194(3A) of the 1990 Act);

- the requirement on auditors to report to the Director their opinion that a suspected indictable offence has been committed under the Companies Acts and to provide the Director with details of the grounds for that opinion (section 194(5) of the 1990 Act);

- the new requirement on auditors to give the Director information, and access to books and documents relating to the suspected indictable offence report (new section 194(5A) of the 1990 Act).

13.2 In addition to the statutory protection afforded to auditors under the section, professional standards also offer auditors guidance on this matter. ISA (UK and Ireland) 250(B) (Appendix 1 paragraph 9) states *"Confidentiality is an implied term of the auditor's contracts with client entities. However, in the circumstances leading to a right or duty to report, the auditor is entitled to communicate with regulators in good faith information or opinions relating to the business or affairs of the entity or any associated body without contravening the duty of confidence owed to the entity."*

14 Reporting of Suspected Offences Beyond the Scope of Section 194(5) in the Public Interest

14.1 ISA (UK and Ireland) 250(A) indicates, *inter alia*, that where the auditor becomes aware of a suspected or actual instance of non-compliance with law or regulations which does not give rise to a statutory duty to report to an appropriate authority, the auditor considers whether the matter is one that ought to be reported to a proper authority in the public interest, and where this is the case, they discuss the matter with those charged with governance. (ISA (UK and Ireland) 250(A) paragraph 38-4).

14.2 ISA (UK and Ireland) 250(A) (paragraph 38-9) states that 'Public Interest' is a concept that is not capable of general definition. Each situation must be considered individually. Matters to be taken into account when considering whether disclosure is justified in the public interest may include:

- the extent to which the suspected or actual non-compliance is likely to affect members of the public;

- whether those charged with governance have rectified the matter or are taking, or likely to take, effective corrective action;

- the extent to which non-disclosure is likely to enable the suspected or actual non-compliance to recur with impunity;

- the gravity of the matter;

- whether there is a general ethos within the entity of disregarding law or regulations;

- the weight of evidence and the degree of the auditors' suspicion that there has been an instance of non-compliance with law or regulations.

14.3 The protection afforded to auditors under section 194(6) of the 1990 Act does not extend to public interest reporting. ISA (UK and Ireland) 250(A) provides guidance to auditors under these circumstances. While ISA (UK and Ireland) 250(A) provides the following guidance, auditors may need to take legal advice before making a decision on whether the matter should be reported to a proper authority in the public interest.

14.4 ISA (UK and Ireland) 250(A) states that *"determination of where the balance of public interest lies requires careful consideration. An auditor whose suspicions have been aroused uses professional judgment to determine whether the auditor's misgivings justify the auditor in carrying the matter further or are too insubstantial to deserve reporting.* (ISA (UK and Ireland) 250(A) paragraph 38-8).

14.5 Auditors are protected from the risk of liability for breach of confidence or defamation provided that:

- in the case of breach of confidence:

  ○ the disclosure has been made in the public interest, and,

  ○ such disclosure has been made to an appropriate body or person, and,

  ○ there has been no malice motivating the disclosure (ISA (UK and Ireland) 250(A) paragraph 38-8).

- in the case of defamation:

  ○ disclosure has been made in their capacity as auditors of the entity concerned, and,

  ○ there has been no malice motivating the disclosure (ISA (UK and Ireland) 250(A) paragraph 38-8).

14.6 It is important, in order for auditors to retain the protection of qualified privilege that they report to the proper authorities. A footnote to paragraph 38-8 of ISA (UK and Ireland) 250(A) identifies the Department of Enterprise, Trade & Employment and the Director of Corporate Enforcement as being among those authorities to whom it is proper to make a report in the public interest. Auditors receive the same protection even if they have only a reasonable suspicion that non-compliance with law or regulations has occurred. Paragraph 38-10 of ISA (UK and Ireland) 250(A) indicates that auditors who can demonstrate that they have acted reasonably and in good faith in informing an authority of a breach of law or regulations which they think has been committed would not be held by the court to have been in breach of duty to the client even if, an investigation or prosecution having occurred, it were to be found that there had been no offence.

14.7 The ISA goes on to state that:

- the auditor needs to remember that the auditor's decision as to whether to report, and if so to whom, may be called into question at a future date, for example on the basis of:

  ○ what the auditor knew at the time;

  ○ what the auditor ought to have known in the course of the audit;

  ○ what the auditor ought to have concluded, and;

  ○ what the auditor ought to have done (ISA (UK and Ireland) 250(A) paragraph 38-11).

- the auditor may also wish to consider the possible consequences if financial loss is occasioned by non-compliance with law or regulations which they suspect (or ought to suspect) has occurred but decide not to report (ISA (UK and Ireland) 250(A) paragraph 38-11).

14.8 Where, having considered any views expressed on behalf of the entity and in the light of any legal advice obtained, the auditor concludes that the matter ought to be reported to an appropriate authority in the public interest, the auditor notifies those charged with governance in writing of their view and, if the entity does not voluntarily do so itself or is unable to provide evidence that the matter has been reported, the auditor reports it (ISA (UK and Ireland) 250(A) paragraph 38-5). The auditor reports a matter to the proper authority in the public interest and without discussing the matter with the entity if the auditor concludes that the suspected or actual instance of non-compliance has caused the auditor no longer to have confidence in the integrity of those charged with governance (ISA (UK and Ireland) 250(A) paragraph 38-6).

15. The Director's Response to Auditors' Reports

15.1 Every auditor's report received will be examined by the Office of the Director of Corporate Enforcement and an acknowledgement issued. Where considered necessary, clarification or further information will be sought from the directors, auditor or other persons as required for example under the provisions of Section 194(5A) and (5B). Assuming that a *prima facie* breach of the Companies Acts is disclosed, the Director and his officers will consider various matters before determining the next step. These include:

- whether the offence is proper to the Director's Office. It may be, for instance, that the offence is better handled by another authority,

- what additional evidence may be required by way of documentation or oral statements from the company, its officers, agents or third parties to address the indicated breach and the manner in which such evidence should be obtained,

- the seriousness of the suspected offence,

- whether the offence has been remedied and the extent to which the remedy in itself is a sufficient outcome,

- the urgency of the case, and

- the extent to which viable options are available to the Director to remedy or sanction the suspected offence.

15.2 Where action is appropriate by his Office, the Director will endeavour to respond in a manner which is likely to be both effective and proportionate in relation to the indicated offence.

Appendix 1

Section 194 of the Companies Act 1990 as amended by Section 74 of the 2001 Act, Section 37 of the 2003 Act and Section 73 of the 2005 Act

(Please note that the text as amended by the 2003 and 2005 Acts is underlined)

Duty of auditors if proper books of account are not being kept

194.—(1) If, at any time, the auditors of a company form the opinion that the company is contravening, or has contravened, *section 202* by failing to cause to be kept proper books of account (within the meaning of that section) in relation to the matters specified in *subsections (1)* and *(2)* of that section, the auditors shall—

   (a)   as soon as may be, by recorded delivery, serve a notice in writing on the company stating their opinion, and

   (b)   not later than 7 days after the service of such notice on the company, notify the registrar of companies in the prescribed form of the notice and the registrar shall forthwith forward a copy of the notice to the Director.

(2) Where the auditors form the opinion that the company has contravened *section 202* but that, following such contravention, the directors of the company have taken the necessary steps to ensure that proper books of account are kept as required by that section, *subsection (1)(b)* shall not apply.

(3) This section shall not require the auditors to make the notifications referred to in *subsection (1)* if they are of opinion that the contraventions concerned are minor or otherwise immaterial in nature.

(3A) Where the auditors of a company file a notice pursuant to *subsection (1)(b)*, they shall, if requested by the Director-

   (a)   furnish to the Director such information, including an explanation of the reasons for their opinion that the company has contravened section 202, and

   (b)   give to the Director such access to books and documents, including facilities for inspecting and taking copies, being information, books or documents in their possession or control and relating to the matter the subject of the notice, as the Director may require.

(3B) Any written information given in response to a request of the Director under *subsection (3A)* shall in all legal proceedings be admissible without further proof, until the contrary is shown, as evidence of the facts stated therein.

(4) A person who contravenes *subsection (1), (3A), (5)* or *(5A)* shall be guilty of an offence.

(5) Where, in the course of, and by virtue of, their carrying out an audit of the accounts of the company, information comes into the possession of the auditors of a company that leads them to form the opinion that there are reasonable grounds for believing that the company or an officer or an agent of it has committed an indictable offence under the Companies Acts (other than an indictable offence under section 125(2) or 127(12) of the Principal Act), the auditors shall, forthwith after having formed it, notify that opinion to the Director and provide the Director with details of the grounds on which they have formed that opinion.

(5A) Where the auditors of a company notify the Director of any matter pursuant to subsection (5), they shall, in addition to performing their obligations under that subsection, if requested by the Director—

(a) furnish the Director with such further information in their possession or control relating to the matter as the Director may require, including further information relating to the details of the grounds on which they formed the opinion referred to in that subsection,

(b) give the Director such access to books and documents in their possession or control relating to the matter as the Director may require, and

(c) give the Director such access to facilities for the taking of copies of or extracts from those books and documents as the Director may require.

(5B) Nothing in this section compels the disclosure by any person of any information that the person would be entitled to refuse to produce on the grounds of legal professional privilege or authorises the inspection or copying of any document containing such information that is in the person's possession.

(6) No professional or legal duty to which an auditor is subject by virtue of his appointment as an auditor of a company shall be regarded as contravened by, and no liability to the company, its shareholders, creditors or other interested parties shall attach to, an auditor, by reason of his compliance with an obligation imposed on him by or under this section.

Appendix 2

Legal Professional Privilege
(The commentary below relates to the Republic of Ireland only)

Section 194(5B) of the 1990 Act states:

> *'Nothing in this section compels the disclosure by any person of any information that the person would be entitled to refuse to produce on the grounds of legal professional privilege or authorises the inspection or copying of any document containing such information that is in the person's possession.'*

The issue of whether information or documents attract legal professional privilege will need to be considered carefully. The question is one of law which, in appropriate circumstances, may fall to be determined by the Courts. ***Accordingly, auditors seeking to limit disclosure on the basis of legal professional privilege are advised to consider taking legal advice.***

A brief explanation of legal privilege and the circumstances in which it may apply are set out below. Such situations are likely to be rare. For example, it is unlikely that the audit work carried out and documented by the auditor which resulted in the identification of a reportable matter will be privileged. This is because such audit work would not have been in contemplation of litigation; identification of a reportable matter is incidental to the audit. Nor will it apply to other non-audit documentation prepared by the audit firm in advance of the formation of an opinion that a report should be made to the Director and which relates to the subject matter of that report.

Legal professional privilege exists in two forms – legal advice privilege and litigation privilege.

Legal advice privilege

Legal advice privilege prevents the disclosure of communications between a lawyer and a client where such communications are made for the purpose of obtaining legal advice. It is not necessary for litigation to be pending or contemplated for this to apply. However, for legal advice privilege to apply, the advice must come from a professionally-qualified lawyer (solicitor or barrister). Advice from an auditor or tax advisor to a client is not subject to privilege.

The subject matter of the document must be legal advice rather than legal assistance (eg company secretarial services).

As noted above, the circumstances in which this form of legal professional privilege will apply to an auditor are likely to be rare.

Litigation privilege

Litigation privilege prevents the disclosure of communications between the client and his lawyer or either the client or his lawyer and a third party, such as, in this case, the auditor.

For litigation privilege to apply, the Courts have set out certain criteria;

- litigation must be pending, contemplated, or reasonably apprehended[9];

- the dominant purpose for the creation of the document must have been that of pending/contemplated or reasonably apprehended litigation; there may be more than one purpose behind the preparation of the document;

- documents in existence prior to litigation being contemplated will not be privileged.

It is important to note that legal professional privilege "belongs" to the client who has sought the legal advice, or is party to the relevant litigation. It is for that client to decide whether to assert the privilege or, alternatively, whether he/she wishes to waive it.

Where the auditor or his/her firm has sought legal advice (including from the audit firm's professionally-qualified in-house lawyers) such advice clearly attracts legal professional privilege and it is for the auditor to decide whether or not to assert the privilege. The same situation applies where the auditor or his/her firm is a party to pending or contemplated litigation and documents have been created for the dominant purpose of that litigation.

Where an auditor or his/her firm is in possession of information or documents over which the audit client enjoys legal professional privilege the situation is somewhat more complicated. Legal professional privilege is concerned with protecting confidential communications and, accordingly, if a client has opted to substantially publicise those communications the privilege may be lost or may be taken to have been waived. However it is thought that confidential disclosure by a company to its statutory auditors of material over which it (the company) enjoys legal professional privilege will not ordinarily give rise to a loss or waiver of the company's privilege – certainly in cases where the auditor, as such, shares a common interest in the communications with the company.

---

[9] These terms have received judicial consideration and should be read in light of the relevant case law.

BULLETIN 2008/2

THE AUDITOR'S ASSOCIATION WITH PRELIMINARY ANNOUNCEMENTS MADE IN ACCORDANCE WITH THE REQUIREMENTS OF THE UK AND IRISH LISTING RULES

CONTENTS

Introduction

1. This Bulletin provides updated guidance for the auditor concerning its responsibilities with regard to preliminary announcements[1]. The updated Bulletin:

    (a) reflects the change in the Listing Rules to move from a mandatory to a permissive regime for the publication of preliminary announcements;

    (b) reflects the change in the Listing Rules to require preliminary announcements to give details of any likely modification (rather than qualification) of the auditor's report required to be included with the annual financial report;

    (c) reflects the introduction of International Standards on Auditing (ISAs) (UK and Ireland); and

    (d) continues to emphasise the need for the auditor to consider the way in which alternative performance measures and management commentary are presented in preliminary announcements before agreeing to their release.

2. In this Bulletin the term "Preliminary Announcement" encompasses:

    (a) the disclosures required to be made by United Kingdom Listing Authority (UKLA) Listing Rule 9.7A.1R and Irish Stock Exchange (ISE) Listing Rule 6.7.1; and

    (b) other additional information (highlights, Chairman's Statement, narrative disclosures, management commentary, press release etc) that is released to a Regulatory Information Service[2] as part of a preliminary announcement.

    Any presentation to analysts, trading statement, interim management statement or half-yearly financial report is not included within the definition of preliminary announcement.

3. If a company decides to make a preliminary announcement it will be the first public communication of that company's full year results and year-end financial position. Preliminary announcements form one of the focal points for investor interest, primarily because they confirm or update market expectations. Because of this the auditor of a listed company has an important role to play in the process leading to the orderly release of preliminary announcements.

4. Both the content and the preparation of any preliminary announcement are the responsibility of the company's directors. The directors of companies having equities on the Official List are required by the Listing Rules to have agreed the preliminary

---

[1] In the Listing Rules preliminary announcements are described as "preliminary statements of annual results".

[2] Regulatory Information Service is the term used for any organisation through which the Listing Rules require listed companies to disseminate price sensitive information. In the Republic of Ireland all price sensitive information must be sent to the Company Announcements Office of the ISE.

announcement with the auditor prior to publication (UKLA Listing Rule 9.7A.1R (2): ISE Listing Rule 6.7.1 (2)).

5. The Listing Rules do not indicate what form the agreement with the auditor should take, or the extent of work expected of the auditor before the auditor gives its agreement. This Bulletin provides guidance on the procedures that would normally be carried out by the auditor and on communicating the outcome of such procedures to the directors.

6. Many companies provide more information in their preliminary announcement than the minimum requirements of the Listing Rules. In the opinion of the APB it is neither practical nor desirable for the auditor to agree to anything less than the entire content of the preliminary announcement.

7. There is an expectation that the information in a preliminary announcement will be consistent with that in the audited financial statements. The risk of later changes to the figures in the preliminary announcement is not completely extinguished unless the preliminary announcement is issued at the same time that the full financial statements are approved by the directors and the auditor has signed the auditor's report on them. However, it has also been the accepted practice of some companies to issue the preliminary announcement, with their auditor's agreement, when the audit is at an "advanced stage" but before the auditor's report on the financial statements has been signed. This Bulletin provides guidance on interpreting the expression "advanced stage".

8. Although the APB would not wish to prevent the auditor from agreeing to the release of preliminary announcements before the auditor's report has been signed there is, in such circumstances, an unavoidable risk that the company may wish to revise its preliminary announcement in the light of audit findings or other developments arising between the preliminary announcement being issued and the completion of the audit.

9. There is no requirement for a preliminary announcement to include an auditor's report. In the view of the APB this is appropriate, as it is unlikely that a communication, that contains both a clear expression of opinion and sets out the information necessary for a proper understanding of that opinion, can be developed without producing a report of excessive length and complexity; which would be out of place in the context of the preliminary announcement as a whole. However, to avoid possible misunderstanding and to make explicit their agreement to the preliminary announcement the auditor issues a letter to the company signifying its agreement (see Appendix 1).

Listing Rule requirements

10. Under UKLA Listing Rule 9.7A.1R (1): ISE Listing Rule 6.7.1 (1) a company that prepares a preliminary announcement must publish it as soon as possible after it has been approved by the Board. The preliminary announcement must:

(a) be agreed with the company's auditor prior to publication;

(b) show the figures in the form of a table, including the items required for a half-yearly report, consistent with the presentation to be adopted in the annual accounts for that financial year;

(c) give details of the nature of any likely modification that may be contained in the auditor's report required to be included with the annual financial report; and

(d) include any significant additional information necessary for the purpose of assessing the results being announced.

11. In accordance with UKLA Listing Rule 9.7A.3 G: ISE Listing Rule 6.7.2 the Listing Authority[3] may authorise the omission from any preliminary announcement of information required by UKLA Listing Rule 9.7A.1 R: ISE Listing Rule 6.7.1 if it considers that disclosure of such information would be contrary to the public interest or seriously detrimental to the listed company, provided that such omission would not be likely to mislead the public with regard to facts and circumstances, knowledge of which is essential for the assessment of the shares.

Companies Act requirements

12. In the United Kingdom, preliminary announcements[4] constitute non-statutory accounts under section 435 of the Companies Act 2006[5] (CA 2006) and must include a statement indicating:

(a) that they are not the company's statutory accounts;

---

[3] In the UK the term "Listing Authority" refers to the United Kingdom Listing Authority of the Financial Services Authority ("FSA") acting in its capacity as the competent authority for the purposes of Part VI of the Financial Services and Markets Act 2000. In the Republic of Ireland, the ISE is the competent authority for the purposes of the European Communities (Admission to Listing and Miscellaneous Provisions) Regulations 2007 (S.I. No.286 of 2007).

[4] In the Republic of Ireland, a preliminary announcement made by a single entity constitutes abbreviated accounts under section 19 of the Companies (Amendment) Act, 1986. A preliminary announcement made by a group constitutes abbreviated group accounts under Regulation 40 of the European Communities (Companies: Group Accounts) Regulations, 1992. This states that where a parent undertaking publishes abbreviated group accounts relating to any financial year, it shall also publish a statement indicating:

    (a) that the abbreviated group accounts are not the group accounts, copies of which are required by law to be annexed to the annual return;

    (b) whether the copies of the group accounts so required to be annexed have in fact been so annexed;

    (c) whether the auditors have made a report under section 193 of the Companies Act, 1990 in respect of the group accounts which relate to any financial year with which the abbreviated group accounts purport to deal; and

    (d) whether the report of the auditors contained any qualifications.

Where a company publishes abbreviated accounts, it shall not publish with those accounts any such report of the auditors as is mentioned in (c) above. The statement required for a single entity is similar.

[5] The equivalent section in the Companies Act 1985 is section 240.

(b) whether statutory accounts dealing with any financial year with which the non-statutory accounts purport to deal have been delivered to the registrar of companies;

(c) whether the auditor has reported on the statutory accounts for any such year; and

(d) if so whether the auditor's report:

(i) was qualified or unqualified or included a reference to any matters to which the auditor drew attention by way of emphasis without qualifying its report; or

(ii) contained a statement under section 498(2) (accounting records or returns inadequate or accounts or directors' remuneration report not agreeing with records and returns), or section 498(3) (failure to obtain necessary information and explanations)[6].

Terms of engagement

13. It is in the interests of both the auditor and the company that the auditor's role in respect of the preliminary announcement is set out in writing; typically by including relevant paragraphs in the audit engagement letter. To avoid misunderstandings the engagement letter describes the auditor's understanding of the process of "agreeing" the preliminary announcement.

14. In circumstances where the auditor is to agree to a preliminary announcement based on financial statements on which its audit is not complete the engagement letter includes cautionary language to the effect that there is an unavoidable risk that the company may wish to revise its preliminary announcement in the light of audit findings or other developments occurring before the completion of the audit.

15. Matters that may be dealt with in the engagement letter include:

(a) the responsibility of the directors for the preparation of any preliminary announcement;

(b) the fact that the auditor will conduct its work in accordance with this Bulletin;

(c) a statement as to whether the auditor believes it is management's intention that the preliminary announcement will be based on audited financial statements or on draft financial statements upon which the auditor has not issued a report;

(d) a statement that the auditor will issue a letter confirming its agreement to the preliminary announcement; and

(e) a statement explaining the inherent limitations of the auditor's work.

---

[6] The equivalent sections in the Companies Act 1985 are sections 237(2) and 237(3).

16. Examples of suitable paragraphs for inclusion in a letter of engagement are given in Appendix 2 for circumstances where the preliminary announcement is to be based on audited financial statements and in Appendix 3 for circumstances where the preliminary announcement is to be based on draft financial statements.

Procedures

Planning

17. Where the preliminary announcement is to be based on draft financial statements the company's timetable should allow the auditor to have completed the audit other than for those matters set out in paragraph 21 below.

Preliminary announcements based on audited financial statements

18. There is an expectation on the part of users that the information in a preliminary announcement will be consistent with that in the audited financial statements. The only way of achieving absolute certainty of this is for the audit of the financial statements to have been completed and the contents of the preliminary announcement to have been extracted from audited financial statements that had been approved and signed by the directors and upon which the auditor has signed the auditor's report.

Preliminary announcements based on draft financial statements

19. Companies may wish to issue their preliminary announcement before the audit is complete. There are additional risks for directors in these circumstances if further information comes to light as a result of the auditor's procedures that the directors decide should be reflected in the financial statements and gives rise to the need for a revised announcement by the company. Before agreeing to the release of the preliminary announcement, therefore, the directors will need to ensure they are satisfied that the information it contains will be consistent with the information that will be contained in the audited financial statements.

20. The auditor will need to be satisfied that any matters outstanding with respect to the audit will be unlikely to result in changes to the information contained in the preliminary announcement. This means that the audit of the financial statements must be at an advanced stage and that, subject only to unforeseen events, the auditor expects to be in a position to issue the auditor's report on the financial statements incorporating the amounts upon which the preliminary announcement is based, and know what that auditor's report will state.

21. This means completing the audit, including the engagement quality control review as described in paragraphs 38 to 40 of ISA (UK and Ireland) 220 "Quality control for audits of historical financial information", subject only to the following:

    (a) clearing outstanding audit matters which the auditor is satisfied are unlikely to have a material impact on the financial statements or disclosures insofar as they affect the preliminary announcement;

(b) completing audit procedures on the detail of note disclosures to the financial statements that will not have a material impact on the primary financial statements and completing the auditor's reading of "other information" in the annual report, in accordance with ISA (UK and Ireland) 720 "Other information in documents containing audited financial statements";

(c) updating the subsequent events review to cover the period between the issue of the preliminary announcement and the date of the auditor's report on the financial statements; and

(d) obtaining final signed written representations from management and establishing that the financial statements have been reviewed and approved by the directors.

22. In advance of the preliminary announcement the auditor discusses with management the representations that the auditor will be likely to require in order to issue its report on the financial statements. If management expresses reservations about its ability or willingness to make such representations the auditor does not agree to the preliminary announcement.

All preliminary announcements

23. The following procedures will normally be carried out by the auditor in relation to the preliminary announcement itself regardless of whether it is based on draft financial statements or extracted from audited financial statements:

(a) checking that the figures in the preliminary announcement covering the full year have been accurately extracted from the audited or draft financial statements; and reflect the presentation to be adopted in the audited financial statements. For example, any summarisation should not change the order in which items are presented where this is specified by law or accounting standards;

(b) considering whether the information (including the management commentary) is consistent with other expected contents of the annual report of which the auditor is aware; and

(c) considering whether the financial information in the preliminary announcement is misstated. A misstatement exists when the information is stated incorrectly or presented in a misleading manner. A misstatement may arise, for example, as a result of an omission of a significant change of accounting policy disclosed, or due to be disclosed, in the audited financial statements.

24. The auditor considers whether the preliminary announcement includes a statement by directors as required by section 435[7] of CA 2006[8] (see paragraph 12) and whether the preliminary announcement includes the minimum information required by UKLA Listing Rule 9.7A.1: ISE Listing Rule 6.7.1 (see paragraph 10).

---

[7] The equivalent section in the Companies Act 1985 is section 240.

[8] See footnote 4 for the equivalent legislation in the Republic of Ireland.

Alternative performance measures

25. Regulators recognise that in some circumstances the presentation of alternative performance measures (APMs)[9] and associated narrative explanations with the statutory results may help shareholders understand better the financial performance of a company. However, regulators are concerned that in other instances such APMs have the potential to be misleading[10] and shareholders may sometimes be misinformed by the manner in which APMs are included in preliminary announcements with which the auditor is associated. In those circumstances the APB believes that the potential for APMs to be misleading is considerable when:

    (a) inappropriate prominence is given to the APMs;

    (b) there is no description of the APMs;

    (c) APMs resemble defined performance measures but do not actually have the characteristics of the defined measures; and

    (d) where relevant, the APMs are not reconciled to the statutory financial information.

    Appendix 4 is the UKLA's summary of a recommendation published by the Committee of European Securities Regulators (CESR) on the use of APMs.

26. In this context where the preliminary announcement includes APMs, before agreeing to its release, the auditor considers whether:

    (a) appropriate prominence is given to statutory financial information and related narrative explanations compared to the prominence given to APMs and their related narrative explanations;

    (b) APMs are reconciled, where appropriate, to the statutory financial information and sufficient prominence is given to that reconciliation;

    (c) APMs are clearly and accurately described; and

    (d) APMs are not otherwise misleading in the form and context in which they appear.

    If the auditor does not believe that the preliminary announcement satisfies these conditions, it seeks to resolve the issues arising with the directors. If it is unable to

---

[9] Alternative performance measures include the adjustment of statutory financial information to, for example:
  - Exclude certain items to give alternative earnings numbers eg earnings before interest, tax, depreciation and amortisation (EBITDA).
  - Exclude certain business segments or activities.
  - Reflect significant non-adjusting post balance sheet events eg disposals or acquisitions.

[10] UKLA Listing Rule 1.3.3R and ISE Listing Rule 1.3.3 require that "An issuer must take all reasonable care to ensure that any information it notifies to a Regulatory Information Service or makes available through the FSA/ISE is not misleading, false or deceptive and does not omit anything likely to affect the import of the information."

resolve the issues the auditor considers whether to withhold its consent to the release of the announcement.

Management commentary

27. An important feature of preliminary announcements is a management commentary on the company's performance during the year and its position at the year-end. Such management commentary may include comments on the final interim period in the preliminary announcement and separate presentation of the final interim period figures to the extent this is necessary to support the management commentary. The extent of information on the final interim period will vary from company to company and in some cases this may only consist of a reference to the key figures in the management commentary.

28. The auditor reads the management commentary, any other narrative disclosures and any final interim period figures and considers whether they are in conflict with the information that it has obtained in the course of the audit. If the auditor becomes aware of any apparent inconsistencies with information obtained during the audit or with the draft financial statements, it seeks to resolve them with the directors. If it is unable to resolve the matters the auditor withholds its consent to the publication of the preliminary announcement.

29. In the case of a preliminary announcement based on audited financial statements, the auditor will read the text of any Chairman's Statement, business review or similar document to be included in the annual report from which the management commentary in the preliminary announcement will usually be derived. For a preliminary announcement based on draft financial statements, this will be done on the latest draft of such documents that are available.

Directors' approval of the preliminary announcement

30. The auditor does not agree to the preliminary announcement until its entire content has been formally approved by the board or by a duly authorised committee[11] of the board.

Modification of the auditor's report

31. The Listing Rules require that, if the auditor's report (on the financial statements) is likely to be modified, the preliminary announcement should give details of the nature of the modification. In doing this, care should be taken to ensure compliance with section 435[12] of CA 2006[13] which states that an auditor's report on the statutory accounts may not be published with non-statutory accounts.

---

[11] The Combined Code states that one of the main roles and responsibilities of the audit committee is "to monitor the integrity of the financial statements of the company, and any formal announcements relating to the company's financial performance, reviewing significant financial reporting judgements contained in them"(Combined Code provision C.3.2).

[12] The equivalent section in the Companies Act 1985 is section 240.

[13] See footnote 4 for the equivalent legislation in the Republic of Ireland.

32. Where reference is made in a preliminary announcement to an actual or possible qualified opinion or emphasis of matter, the directors should give adequate prominence to that information in the announcement and the auditor should be satisfied in this regard. If the auditor has concerns about the appropriateness of the wording of a statement referring to a modified report it is encouraged to seek legal advice.

Communication of agreement

33. The APB encourages the auditor to make explicit its agreement to the issue of the preliminary announcement by sending a letter to the directors. An example of such a letter is given in Appendix 1. Similarly, if the auditor is not in agreement with the content of the preliminary announcement, it communicates this to the directors by sending them a letter setting out the reasons for its disagreement, advising the directors that the preliminary announcement should not be published.

34. The auditor may become aware that a company has released a preliminary announcement without first obtaining its agreement. There may be a number of reasons for this ranging from innocent oversight on the part of the directors to the directors knowingly releasing a preliminary announcement with which the auditor disagrees. The action that the auditor takes depends on the particular circumstances. In circumstances where a preliminary announcement is inadvertently released without the auditor's knowledge, but with which the auditor does in fact agree, the auditor may wish to remind the directors of their obligation under the Listing Rules to have obtained the auditor's agreement.

35. However, at the other end of the spectrum, where the auditor becomes aware that the directors have released an announcement with which it disagrees, it takes legal advice with a view to notifying the Listing Authority of the fact that it had not agreed to the announcement.

Appendix 1

ILLUSTRATIVE EXAMPLE LETTER TO DIRECTORS INDICATING AUDITOR'S AGREEMENT WITH PRELIMINARY ANNOUNCEMENT

Dear Sirs

XYZ plc: preliminary announcement of results for year ended [...]

In accordance with the terms of our engagement letter dated [ ], we have reviewed the attached proposed preliminary announcement of XYZ plc for the year ended [ ]. Our work was conducted having regard to Bulletin 2008/2 "The auditor's association with preliminary announcements made in accordance with the requirements of the UK and Irish listing rules" issued by the Auditing Practices Board. As directors you have accepted responsibility for preparing and issuing the preliminary announcement.

Our responsibility is solely to give our agreement to the preliminary announcement having carried out the procedures specified in the Bulletin as providing a basis for such agreement. In this regard we agree to the preliminary announcement being notified to [a Regulatory Information Service] [and/or the Company Announcements Office of the Irish Stock Exchange, as appropriate].

[As you are aware we are not in a position to sign our auditor's report on the annual financial statements as they have not yet been approved by the directors and we have not yet ... [insert significant procedures that are yet to be completed, for example completing the subsequent events review and obtaining final signed written representations from directors ...]. Consequently there can be no absolute certainty that we will be in a position to issue an unmodified audit report on financial statements consistent with the results and financial position reported in the preliminary announcement. However, at the present time, we are not aware of any matters that may give rise to a modification to our report. In the event that such matters do come to our attention we will inform you immediately.]

Yours faithfully

Appendix 2

ILLUSTRATIVE EXAMPLE TERMS OF ENGAGEMENT; AUDIT COMPLETED

Extract from Letter of Engagement

The Listing Rules require that "a preliminary statement[1] of annual results .... must be agreed with the company's auditor prior to publication". As directors of the company, you are responsible for preparing and issuing any preliminary announcement and ensuring that we agree to its release.

We undertake to review the preliminary announcement having regard to Bulletin 2008/2 "The auditor's association with preliminary announcements made in accordance with the requirements of the UK and Irish listing rules" issued by the Auditing Practices Board. Accordingly, our review will be limited to checking the accuracy of extraction of the financial information in the preliminary announcement from the audited financial statements of the company for that year, considering whether any "alternative performance measures" and associated narrative explanations may be misleading and reading the management commentary, including any comments on, or separate presentation of, the final interim period figures, and considering whether it is in conflict with the information that we obtained in the course of our audit.

You will provide us with such information and explanations as we consider necessary for the purposes of our work. We shall request sight of the preliminary announcement in sufficient time to enable us to complete our work. The Board/committee of the Board will formally approve the preliminary announcement before we agree to it.

Appendix 3

ILLUSTRATIVE EXAMPLE TERMS OF ENGAGEMENT; AUDIT NOT COMPLETED

Extract from Letter of Engagement

The Listing Rules require that "a preliminary statement[1] of annual results ...... must be agreed with the company's auditor prior to publication". As directors of the company, you are responsible for preparing and issuing any preliminary announcement and ensuring that we agree to its release.

We undertake to review the preliminary announcement having regard to Bulletin 2008/2 "The auditor's association with preliminary announcements made in accordance with the requirements of the UK and Irish listing rules" issued by the Auditing Practices Board. Accordingly, our review will be limited to checking the accuracy of extraction of the financial information in the preliminary announcement from the latest available draft financial statements of the company for that year, considering whether any "alternative performance measures" and associated narrative explanations may be misleading and reading the management commentary, including any comments on, or separate presentation of, the final interim period figures, and considering whether it is in conflict with the information that we have obtained in the course of our audit.

You will provide us with such information and explanations as we consider necessary for the purposes of our work. We shall request sight of the preliminary announcement in sufficient time to enable us to complete our work. The Board/committee of the Board will formally approve the preliminary announcement before we agree to it. You will also make available to us the proposed text of the company's annual report.

We will not agree to the release of the preliminary announcement until the audit is complete subject only to the following:

(a) clearing outstanding audit matters which we are satisfied are unlikely to have a material impact on the financial statements or disclosures insofar as they affect the preliminary announcement;

(b) completing audit procedures on the detail of note disclosures to the financial statements that will not have a material impact on the primary financial statements and completing our reading of other information in the annual report, in accordance with ISA (UK and Ireland) 720 "Other information in documents containing audited financial statements";

(c) updating the subsequent events review to cover the period between the date of the preliminary announcement and the date of our auditor's report on the financial statements; and

(d) obtaining final signed written representations from management and establishing that the financial statements have been reviewed and approved by the directors.

The scope of our work will be necessarily limited in that, we will only be able to check the consistency of the preliminary announcement with draft financial statements on which our audit is incomplete. Accordingly, we shall not, at that stage, know whether further adjustments may be required to those draft financial statements. Consequently, there is an unavoidable risk that the company may wish to revise its preliminary announcement in the light of audit findings or other developments occurring between the preliminary announcement being notified to [a Regulatory Information Service] [and/or the Company Announcements Office of the Irish Stock Exchange, as appropriate] and the completion of the audit.

In the event that we disagree with the release of the preliminary announcement we will send you a letter setting out the reasons why.

Appendix 4

UNITED KINGDOM LISTING AUTHORITY'S SUMMARY OF THE CESR "RECOMMENDATION ON THE USE OF ALTERNATIVE PERFORMANCE MEASURES"

In List! 12 of February 2006 the UKLA summarised the key points of a recommendation on the use of APMs issued by CESR as follows:

1. Under the IAS Framework, there are four qualitative characteristics that make the information provided in financial statements useful to users: understandability, relevance, reliability and comparability. CESR believes that issuers should follow these principles when preparing APMs.

2. Issuers should define the terminology used and the basis of calculation adopted (ie defining the components included in an APM). Clear disclosure is key to the understandability.

3. Where possible issuers should present APMs only in combination with defined measures (ie GAAP measures). Furthermore, issuers should explain the differences between both measures.

4. Comparatives should be provided for any APM presented.

5. APMs should be presented consistently over time.

6. To ensure that investors are not misled, CESR recommends that APMs should not be presented with greater prominence than defined GAAP measures. Where APMs are derived from audited financial statements and resemble defined performance measures but do not actually have the characteristics of the defined measures, CESR recommends that defined measures should have greater prominence than the APMs.

In our (ie the UKLA) view the CESR recommendation represents best practice for the disclosure of APMs and we would encourage issuers to follow the recommendation.

BULLETIN 2008/4

THE SPECIAL AUDITOR'S REPORT ON ABBREVIATED ACCOUNTS IN THE UNITED KINGDOM

CONTENTS

Appendices
1. *Filing options available to small companies*
2. *The two filing options available to medium-sized companies*
3. *Illustrative example of a special report on the abbreviated accounts of a small company*
4. *Illustrative example of a special report on the abbreviated accounts of a medium-sized company*

Introduction

1. This Bulletin provides guidance for auditors regarding the filing obligations of small and medium-sized companies, under the United Kingdom Companies Act 2006 (CA 2006). In particular, it provides guidance concerning the "Special Auditor's Report on Abbreviated Accounts".

Companies subject to the small companies regime

2. Section 381 of CA 2006 states that the small companies regime for accounts and reports applies to a company for a financial year in relation to which the company:

    (a) qualifies as small (see sections 382 and 383 of CA 2006); and

    (b) is not excluded from the regime (see section 384 of CA 2006).

3. With respect to companies preparing accounts under UK GAAP[1] (described in CA 2006 as Companies Act accounts), section 396 (3) of CA 2006 provides for the Secretary of State to make regulations as to:

    (a) the form and content of the balance sheet and profit and loss account; and

    (b) additional information to be provided by way of notes to the accounts.

    The Small Companies and Groups (Accounts and Directors' Report) Regulations 2008[2] (the SI 409 Regulations) provide the regulations that are applicable to companies subject to the small companies regime.

Accounts sent to members

4. A small company that prepares accounts under UK GAAP is required to prepare and send to its members its "full" annual accounts and a directors' report prepared in accordance with the relevant requirements of CA 2006, the SI 409 Regulations and either:

    (a) the Financial Reporting Standard for Smaller Entities (FRSSE)[3]; or

    (b) UK Financial Reporting Standards.

5. A small company that prepares IAS accounts is required to prepare and send to its members its "full" annual accounts and a directors' report prepared in accordance

---

[1] Generally accepted accounting practice.

[2] Statutory Instrument, SI 2008 No. 409.

[3] Example 1 of Appendix 1 of Bulletin 2006/6 "Auditor's Reports on Financial Statements in the United Kingdom" provides an illustrative example of an auditor's report of a non-publicly traded company preparing financial statements under the FRSSE.

with the relevant requirements of CA 2006, the SI 409 Regulations and International Financial Reporting Standards as adopted by the European Union.

6.   All small companies are required to send to their members an auditor's report prepared in accordance with sections 495 and 496 of CA 2006, except where the company is exempt from audit and the directors have taken advantage of that exemption[4].

Accounts placed on the public record

7.   With respect to the accounts that a small company is required to place on the public record, by delivering them to the Registrar of Companies[5], it has the following three choices. These are, delivering to the Registrar:

(a)   a copy of the balance sheet as sent to its members; or

(b)   a copy of the balance sheet and the profit and loss account as sent to its members; or

(c)   where its accounts are prepared using UK GAAP, abbreviated accounts prepared in accordance with Regulation 6 and Schedule 4 of the SI 409 Regulations.

In the case of (a) and (b) the company is required to deliver to the Registrar a copy of the auditor's report prepared in accordance with section 495 of CA 2006. In the case of (c) the company is required to deliver the "special auditor's report" prepared in accordance with section 449 of CA 2006.

8.   A small company is not required to deliver to the Registrar a copy of the directors' report. However, where it chooses to deliver a copy of the directors' report, the auditor's report prepared in connection with section 496 of CA 2006 on the directors' report must also be delivered to the Registrar[6].

9.   These requirements are discussed further in the following paragraphs and are summarised in the table in Appendix 1.

Delivering accounts subject to the small companies regime other than abbreviated accounts

10.   Where a small company delivers to the Registrar IAS accounts or UK GAAP accounts that are not abbreviated accounts and does not deliver a copy of the company's profit and loss account or a copy of the directors' report, the copy of the balance sheet delivered to the Registrar is required to contain in a prominent position a statement

---

[4]   This Bulletin provides guidance with respect to small companies that are either not exempt from audit; or, where exempt have not taken advantage of that exemption.

[5]   In CA 2006 the expressions "the registrar of companies" and "the registrar" mean the registrar of companies for England & Wales, Scotland or Northern Ireland, as the case may require (section 1060(3) CA 2006).

[6]   Section 444(2) CA 2006.

that the company's accounts and reports have been delivered in accordance with the provisions applicable to companies subject to the small companies regime[7].

11. The company is also required to deliver to the Registrar a copy of the auditor's report prepared in accordance with section 495 [and section 496 if a Directors' Report is filed] of CA 2006 notwithstanding that the auditor's opinion is expressed on the full accounts and report rather than being restricted in scope to the balance sheet [and directors' report] that has been filed. As the auditor's report that is filed has to be a copy of the report prepared in accordance with section 495 [and, if applicable, 496] of CA 2006 the auditor is not permitted to amend the report to refer to only those items that are delivered.

12. However, the auditor is not precluded from adding a preface to the copy report explaining that the auditor's report had been prepared in connection with the audit of the full annual accounts and directors' report and that certain primary statements and the directors' report originally reported on are not included within the filing. Illustrative wording for such a preface is as follows:

> Although the company is only required to file a balance sheet, the Companies Act 2006 requires the accompanying auditor's report to be a copy of our report to the members on the company's full annual accounts and directors' report. Readers are cautioned that the profit and loss account and certain other primary statements and the directors' report, referred to in the copy of our auditor's report, are not required to be filed with the Registrar of Companies.

Delivering abbreviated accounts

13. Abbreviated accounts for small companies:

   (a) comprise a balance sheet and prescribed notes (including the disclosure of accounting policies) drawn up in accordance with Schedule 4 of the SI 409 Regulations, and

   (b) if a profit and loss account is filed it may omit those items specified by the SI 409 Regulations[8].

14. If abbreviated accounts are delivered to the Registrar and an audit has been undertaken the obligation to deliver a copy of the auditor's report is to deliver a copy of the special auditor's report required by section 449 of CA 2006[9].

---

[7] Section 444(5) CA 2006.
[8] Section 444(3) CA 2006.
[9] Section 444(4) CA 2006.

Medium-sized companies

15. The criteria for a company to qualify as medium-sized are set out in sections 465 to 467 of CA 2006. The Large and Medium-sized Companies and Groups (Accounts and Reports) Regulations 2008[10] (the SI 410 Regulations) provide the regulations that are applicable to medium sized companies that prepare accounts under UK GAAP.

Accounts sent to members

16. A medium-sized company that prepares accounts under UK GAAP is required to prepare and send to its members its "full" annual accounts prepared in accordance with the relevant requirements of CA 2006, the SI 410 Regulations and UK Financial Reporting Standards.

17. A medium-sized company that prepares IAS accounts is required to prepare and send to its members its "full" annual accounts prepared in accordance with the relevant requirements of CA 2006 and International Financial Reporting Standards as adopted by the European Union.

Accounts placed on the public record

18. The directors of a company that qualifies as a medium-sized company in relation to a financial year must deliver to the Registrar a copy of:

    (a) the company's annual accounts; and

    (b) the directors' report[11].

    The directors are also required to deliver to the Registrar a copy of the auditor's report on the accounts and on the directors' report prepared in accordance with sections 495 and 496 of CA 2006[12] respectively.

19. However, where the company prepares UK GAAP accounts the directors may deliver to the Registrar abbreviated accounts rather than the company's full annual accounts and directors' report as described in paragraph 18[13].

20. The filing obligations of medium-sized companies, described above, are discussed further in the following paragraphs and summarised in tabular form in Appendix 2.

Delivering abbreviated accounts

21. Abbreviated accounts for medium-sized companies comprise:

    (a) a balance sheet; and

---

[10] Statutory Instrument, SI 2008 No. 410.
[11] Section 445(1) CA 2006.
[12] Section 445(2) CA 2006.
[13] Section 445(3) CA 2006.

(b)   a profit and loss account in which items are combined in accordance with the SI 410 Regulations[14] and that does not contain items whose omission is authorised by those Regulations[15] (See paragraphs 4, 5 and 6 of the SI 410 Regulations).

22.   If abbreviated accounts are delivered to the Registrar and an audit has been undertaken[16] the obligation to deliver a copy of the auditor's report is to deliver a copy of the special auditor's report required by section 449 of CA 2006.

Abbreviated accounts of small and medium-sized companies

23.   As described above, companies which are small companies or medium-sized companies in relation to a financial year and that are preparing "full" UK GAAP individual accounts are entitled to deliver "abbreviated accounts" to the Registrar. These provisions are only available to companies preparing UK GAAP accounts, as the format of accounts on which abbreviated accounts are based does not apply to companies preparing IAS accounts.

24.   Section 384 (for small companies) and 467 (for medium-sized companies) of CA 2006 specify cases in which the provisions permitting the delivery of abbreviated accounts do not apply.

25.   Section 450(3) of CA 2006 requires, with respect to abbreviated accounts that the balance sheet include a statement, in a prominent position above the director's signature, that the accounts are prepared in accordance with the special provisions of CA 2006 relating (as the case may be) to companies subject to the small companies regime or to medium-sized companies.

26.   CA 2006 provides for abbreviated accounts to be prepared in respect of an individual company only. CA 2006 does not provide for "abbreviated group accounts".

Auditor's procedures when reporting on abbreviated accounts

27.   Before issuing the special auditor's report on abbreviated accounts the auditor:

(a)   assesses by reference to section 444 (small companies) or section 445 (medium-sized companies) of CA 2006 whether the company is entitled to deliver abbreviated accounts;

---

[14] For companies that are not banking or insurance companies these regulations are set out in Schedule 1 of the SI 410 Regulations. (Schedules 2 and 3 of the SI 410 Regulations set out the requirements for banking and insurance companies).

[15] Section 445 (3) CA 2006.

[16] An audit exemption may arise with respect to non-profit making companies subject to public sector audit.

(b) compares the abbreviated accounts to the underlying audited annual accounts from which they have been derived and assesses whether the abbreviated accounts are consistent with the audited annual accounts;

(c) checks whether the content of the abbreviated accounts complies with the requirements of the SI 409 Regulations with respect to small companies and the SI 410 Regulations with respect to medium-sized companies; and

(d) considers whether the omission of information, other than through compliance with the relevant regulations, results in the abbreviated accounts being misleading.

Special report of the auditor on abbreviated accounts

28. If abbreviated accounts prepared in accordance with the relevant provision are delivered to the Registrar, sections 444(4), 445(4) and 449(2) of CA 2006 require that they be accompanied by a copy of a special report of the auditor.

29. By virtue of section 449(4) of CA 2006, the provisions of sections 503 to 506 (signature of auditor's report) and sections 507 to 509 (offences in connection with auditor's report) apply to the special report of the auditor as they apply to an auditor's report on the company's annual accounts prepared under Part 16 of CA 2006.

30. The elements of the special report of the auditor are set out in the following paragraphs and illustrated in appendices 3 to 6 of this Bulletin.

Title and addressee

31. CA 2006 does not state to whom the special report of the auditor should be addressed. In the absence of any requirement the auditor addresses the report to the company. It is appropriate to use the term "Independent Auditor" in the title.

Introductory paragraph

32. The auditor identifies the abbreviated accounts examined.

Respective responsibilities

33. The auditor includes a description of its responsibilities and also states that the directors are responsible for preparing the abbreviated accounts in accordance with the relevant section of CA 2006.

34. The auditor indicates that its work was conducted in accordance with this Bulletin and was limited to determining whether the company is entitled to deliver abbreviated accounts to the Registrar and whether the abbreviated accounts to be delivered are properly prepared in accordance with the relevant provisions.

Opinion

35. Although abbreviated accounts must be properly prepared in accordance with the relevant provisions, they are not required to give a true and fair view (in practice, they will not do so).

36. Section 449(2) of CA 2006 requires the auditor to state that in its opinion:

    (a) the company is entitled to deliver abbreviated accounts prepared in accordance with the section in question[17]; and

    (b) the abbreviated accounts to be delivered are properly prepared in accordance with regulations under that section.

37. The fact that the auditor's report under section 495 of CA 2006 on the "full" accounts was modified (e.g. qualified or contained an emphasis of matter paragraph), does not prevent the abbreviated accounts from being prepared in accordance with the relevant section of CA 2006.

38. The matter in question may, however, affect the company's eligibility as "small" or "medium-sized". The auditor therefore considers whether the maximum effect of the matter giving rise to the modification would cause two or more of the criteria for determining eligibility (that is, the turnover, employee or balance sheet totals) to exceed the relevant limits. An auditor may be unable to assess properly the criteria for small or medium sized eligibility where an adverse opinion or disclaimer of opinion has been given under section 495 of CA 2006.

39. Where either:

    (a) the criteria exceed the relevant limits; or

    (b) the auditor is unable to assess the criteria,

    the auditor will be unable to express an opinion that the company is entitled to deliver abbreviated accounts.

40. CA 2006 does not envisage a qualified opinion being expressed on the abbreviated accounts. An auditor unable to make the positive statements required, reports this fact to the directors. In such circumstances, the directors cannot deliver the abbreviated accounts to the Registrar.

Other information required in the Auditor's Special Report

41. Under section 449(3) of CA 2006, if the auditor's report under section 495 of CA 2006 on the "full" annual accounts:

---

[17] Section 444(3) of CA 2006 for a small company and section 445(3) of CA 2006 for a medium-sized company.

(a) was qualified, the special report must set out that report in full (together with any further material necessary to understand the qualification); or

(b) contained a statement under section 498(2)(a) or (b) (accounts, records or returns inadequate or accounts not agreeing with records or returns), or section 498(3) (failure to obtain necessary information and explanations) of CA 2006, the special report is required to set out the statement in full.

42. These are, however, minimum requirements and do not preclude the inclusion in the special auditor's report of other information which the auditor considers important to a proper understanding of that report. In particular, when the auditor's report under section 495 of CA 2006 is unqualified but contains an emphasis of matter paragraph, the APB considers that it is necessary for the auditor to include such a paragraph (together with any further material necessary to understand it) in the special auditor's report (see Appendix 5).

43. When a qualified report or an emphasis of matter paragraph includes a reference to a note to the "full" annual accounts, without stating explicitly all the relevant information contained in that note, the auditor includes the necessary information in their report on the abbreviated accounts, immediately following the reproduction of the text of its report on the "full" annual accounts. Alternatively the auditor could request the company to include such information in the notes to the abbreviated accounts.

44. For a medium-sized company, where the auditor's report under sections 495 and 496 of CA 2006 draws attention to an inconsistency between the directors' report and the "full" financial statements (as described in Example B to Section B of ISA (UK and Ireland) 720 (Revised)) the paragraph describing the inconsistency is likely to be included in the special report of the auditor as illustrated in Appendix 6[18].

Signature

45. Where the auditor is an individual the special report is signed by the individual. Where the auditor is a firm, the report must be signed by the senior statutory auditor in his own name for and on behalf of the auditor (See Bulletin 2008/6 "The 'Senior Statutory Auditor' under the United Kingdom Companies Act 2006".

Date

46. The auditor dates the special report with the date on which it is signed. The auditor does not sign the special report until the directors have approved and signed the abbreviated accounts. It is desirable that the auditor complete and sign its special report on the date that they complete and sign their report on the "full" annual accounts to avoid the impression that the special report in any way 'updates' the auditor's report on the "full" annual accounts. Where the auditor dates its special report after the date of their report on the "full" annual accounts, the special report

---

[18] For a small company the abbreviated accounts may exclude the directors' report and therefore the paragraph describing the inconsistency is unlikely to be included in the special report of the auditor as it does not affect the reader's understanding of the information in the abbreviated accounts.

states that the auditor has not considered the effects of any events between the two dates.

Change of auditor

47. Where there is to be a change of auditor, it is preferable for the auditor who reported on the "full" annual accounts to report on the abbreviated accounts for that financial year. Where this is not possible, the new auditor performing the latter function may decide to accept the "full" annual accounts audited by its predecessor as a basis for its work, unless it has grounds to doubt the company's eligibility to deliver abbreviated accounts (for example, because a qualified opinion affects the criteria for determining eligibility). If there is a need to refer in the special report to the predecessor auditor's report on the "full" annual accounts, the new auditor indicates in its report by whom the audit of the "full" annual accounts was carried out.

Appendix 1

Filing options available to small companies

Option	1 Full Accounts	2 Full Balance Sheet only	3 Full Abbreviated Accounts	4 Abbreviated Balance Sheet only
Applicability	UK GAAP and IAS companies	UK GAAP and IAS companies	UK GAAP companies only	UK GAAP companies only
Copy full Balance Sheet	✓	✓		
Balance sheet to include statement that the company's annual accounts and reports have been delivered in accordance with the provisions applicable to companies subject to the small companies regime	✗	✓		
Copy full Profit and Loss Account	✓	✗		
Copy Directors' Report	✓	✗		
Auditor's report required by section 495 of CA 2006	✓	✓		
Auditor's report required by section 496 of CA 2006	✓	✗		
Abbreviated balance sheet drawn up in accordance with the SI 409 Regulations			✓	✓
Abbreviated profit and loss account drawn up in accordance with the SI 409 Regulations			✓	✗
Copy Directors' Report			✓	✗
Special auditor's report required by section 449 of CA 2006			✓	✓

NOTE: It is a small company's choice as to whether it files its profit and loss account or director's report. Options 1 and 3 illustrate the filing of both. Options 2 and 4 illustrate the filing of neither. Small companies may also file one but not the other. For simplicity these other alternatives are not illustrated.

Appendix 2

The two filing options available to medium-sized companies

Option	1: Full Accounts	2: Abbreviated Accounts
Applicability	**UK GAAP and IAS companies**	**UK GAAP companies only**
Copy Annual Accounts	✓	
Copy Abbreviated Accounts drawn up in accordance with the SI 410 Regulations		✓
Copy Directors' Report	✓	✓
Auditors' report required by sections 495 and 496 of CA 2006	✓	
Special auditor's report required by section 449 of CA 2006		✓

Appendix 3

Illustrative example of a special report on the abbreviated accounts of a small company

INDEPENDENT AUDITOR'S REPORT TO XYZ LIMITED UNDER SECTION 449 OF THE COMPANIES ACT 2006

We have examined the abbreviated accounts set out on pages ... to ...[19], together with the financial statements of XYZ Limited for the year ended ... prepared under section 396 of the Companies Act 2006.

Respective responsibilities of directors and auditors

The directors are responsible for preparing the abbreviated accounts in accordance with section 444 of the Companies Act 2006. It is our responsibility to form an independent opinion as to whether the company is entitled to deliver abbreviated accounts to the Registrar of Companies and whether the abbreviated accounts have been properly prepared in accordance with the regulations made under that section and to report our opinion to you.

We conducted our work in accordance with Bulletin 2008/4 issued by the Auditing Practices Board. In accordance with that Bulletin we have carried out the procedures we consider necessary to confirm, by reference to the financial statements, that the company is entitled to deliver abbreviated accounts and that the abbreviated accounts are properly prepared[20].

Opinion

In our opinion the company is entitled to deliver abbreviated accounts prepared in accordance with section 444(3) of the Companies Act 2006, and the abbreviated accounts have been properly prepared in accordance with the regulations made under that section.

[Other information[21]]

[Signature]   *Address*
John Smith (senior statutory auditor)   *Date*
for and on behalf of ABC LLP, Statutory Auditors

---

[19]   If the profit and loss account and/or directors' report are included (as is permitted but not required) they are included within these page numbers.

[20]   Add appropriate wording such as "The scope of our work for the purposes of this report does not include examining events occurring after the date of our auditor's report on the full financial statements" where special report is dated after the signing of the auditor's report on the full annual accounts (see paragraph 46).

[21]   This section is included only in the circumstances described in paragraphs 41 to 44 (see Appendices 5 and 6).

Appendix 4

Illustrative example of a special report on the abbreviated accounts of a medium-sized company

INDEPENDENT AUDITOR'S REPORT TO XYZ LIMITED UNDER SECTION 449 OF THE COMPANIES ACT 2006

We have examined the abbreviated accounts set out on pages ... to ...,[22] together with the financial statements of XYZ Limited for the year ended ... prepared under section 396 of the Companies Act 2006.

Respective responsibilities of directors and auditors

The directors are responsible for preparing the abbreviated accounts in accordance with section 445 of the Companies Act 2006. It is our responsibility to form an independent opinion as to whether the company is entitled to deliver abbreviated accounts to the Registrar of Companies and whether the abbreviated accounts have been properly prepared in accordance with the regulations made under that section and to report our opinion to you.

We conducted our work in accordance with Bulletin 2008/4 issued by the Auditing Practices Board. In accordance with that Bulletin we have carried out the procedures we consider necessary to confirm, by reference to the financial statements, that the company is entitled to deliver abbreviated accounts and that the abbreviated accounts are properly prepared[23].

Opinion

In our opinion the company is entitled to deliver abbreviated accounts prepared in accordance with section 445(3) of the Companies Act 2006, and the abbreviated accounts have been properly prepared in accordance with the regulations made under that section.

[Other information[24]]

[Signature]   *Address*
John Smith (senior statutory auditor)   *Date*
for and on behalf of ABC LLP, Statutory Auditors

---

[22] The directors' report is included within these page numbers.

[23] Add appropriate wording such as "The scope of our work for the purposes of this report does not include examining events occurring after the date of our auditor's report on the full financial statements" where special report is dated after the signing of the auditor's report on the full annual accounts (see paragraph 46).

[24] This section is included only in the circumstances described in paragraphs 41 to 44 (see Appendices 5 and 6).

Appendix 5

Illustrative example of a special report on the abbreviated accounts of a small company including other information – emphasis of matter paragraph regarding a material uncertainty (going concern)

INDEPENDENT AUDITOR'S REPORT TO XYZ LIMITED UNDER SECTION 449 OF THE COMPANIES ACT 2006

We have examined the abbreviated accounts set out on pages ... to ...,[25] together with the financial statements of XYZ Limited for the year ended ... prepared under section 396 of the Companies Act 2006.

Respective responsibilities of directors and auditors

The directors are responsible for preparing the abbreviated accounts in accordance with section 444 of the Companies Act 2006. It is our responsibility to form an independent opinion as to whether the company is entitled to deliver abbreviated accounts to the Registrar of Companies and whether the abbreviated accounts have been properly prepared in accordance with the regulations made under that section and to report our opinion to you.

Basis of opinion

We conducted our work in accordance with Bulletin 2008/4 issued by the Auditing Practices Board. In accordance with that Bulletin we have carried out the procedures we consider necessary to confirm, by reference to the financial statements, that the company is entitled to deliver abbreviated accounts and that the abbreviated accounts are properly prepared[26].

Opinion

In our opinion the company is entitled to deliver abbreviated accounts prepared in accordance with section 444 of the Companies Act 2006, and the abbreviated accounts have been properly prepared in accordance with the regulations made under that section.

---

[25] If the profit and loss account and/or directors' report are included (as is permitted but not required) they are included within these page numbers.

[26] Add appropriate wording such as "The scope of our work for the purposes of this report does not include examining events occurring after the date of our auditor's report on the full annual accounts" where special report is dated after the signing of the auditor's report on the full annual accounts (see paragraph 46).

Other information

On ...[27] we reported as auditor to the members of the company on the financial statements prepared under section 396 of the Companies Act 2006 and our report [included the following paragraph][28] *[was as follows]*[29]

Emphasis of matter - Going concern

In forming our opinion on the financial statements, which is not qualified, we have considered the adequacy of the disclosure made in note x to the financial statements concerning the company's ability to continue as a going concern. The company incurred a net loss of £X during the year ended 31 December 20X1 and, at that date, the company's current liabilities exceeded its total assets by £Y. These conditions, along with the other matters explained in note x to the financial statements, indicate the existence of a material uncertainty which may cast significant doubt about the company's ability to continue as a going concern. The financial statements do not include the adjustments that would result if the company was unable to continue as a going concern.'[30]

[Signature]	*Address*
John Smith (senior statutory auditor)	*Date*
for and on behalf of ABC LLP, Statutory Auditors	

---

[27] The date of the auditor's report on the annual accounts.

[28] In this example, the "other information" section of the report on the abbreviated accounts reproduces an emphasis of matter paragraph from the auditors' report on the annual accounts and consequently the words "included the following paragraph" are used (see paragraph 42).

[29] Where the auditor's opinion is qualified the words "was as follows" are used.

[30] Further material necessary to understand the explanatory paragraph may be added (see paragraph 43).

Appendix 6

Illustrative example of a special report on the abbreviated accounts of a medium-sized company including a paragraph regarding a material inconsistency between the full annual accounts and the directors' report

INDEPENDENT AUDITOR'S REPORT TO XYZ LIMITED UNDER SECTION 449 OF THE COMPANIES ACT 2006

We have examined the abbreviated accounts set out on pages ... to ...,[31] together with the financial statements of XYZ Limited for the year ended ... prepared under section 396 of the Companies Act 2006.

Respective responsibilities of directors and auditors

The directors are responsible for preparing the abbreviated accounts in accordance with section 445 of the Companies Act 2006. It is our responsibility to form an independent opinion as to whether the company is entitled to deliver abbreviated accounts to the Registrar of Companies and whether the abbreviated accounts have been properly prepared in accordance with the regulations made under that section and to report our opinion to you.

We conducted our work in accordance with Bulletin 2008/4 issued by the Auditing Practices Board. In accordance with that Bulletin we have carried out the procedures we consider necessary to confirm, by reference to the financial statements, that the company is entitled to deliver abbreviated accounts and that the abbreviated accounts are properly prepared[32].

Opinion

In our opinion the company is entitled to deliver abbreviated accounts prepared in accordance with section 445(3) of the Companies Act 2006, and the abbreviated accounts have been properly prepared in accordance with the regulations made under that section.

Other information

On ...[33] we reported as auditor to the members of the company on the full financial statements prepared under section 396 of the Companies Act 2006 and our report included the following paragraph:[34]

---

[31] The directors' report is included within these page numbers.

[32] Add appropriate wording such as "The scope of our work for the purposes of this report does not include examining events occurring after the date of our auditor's report on the full annual accounts" where special report is dated after the signing of the auditor's report on the full financial statements (see paragraph 46).

[33] The date of the auditor's report on the financial statements.

[34] In this example, the "other information" section of the report on the abbreviated accounts reproduces a paragraph from the auditor's report on the financial statements drawing attention to an inconsistency between the directors' report and the full financial statements (see paragraph 44).

Material inconsistency between the full financial statements and the directors' report

In our opinion, the information given in the seventh paragraph of the Business Review in the directors' report is not consistent with the full financial statements. That paragraph states without amplification that "the company's trading for the period resulted in a 10% increase in profit over the previous period's profit. The income statement, however, shows that the company's profit for the period includes a profit of £Z which did not arise from trading but from the disposal of assets of a discontinued operation. Without this profit on the disposal of assets the company would have reported a profit for the year of £Y, representing a reduction in profit of 25% over the previous period's profit on a like for like basis. Except for this matter, in our opinion the information given in the directors' report is consistent with the full financial statements on which we separately reported on [insert date][35].

[Signature]   *Address*

John Smith (senior statutory auditor)   *Date*

for and on behalf of ABC LLP, Statutory Auditors

---

[35] Further material necessary to understand the explanatory paragraph may be added (see paragraph 43).

BULLETIN 2008/6

THE "SENIOR STATUTORY AUDITOR" UNDER THE UNITED KINGDOM COMPANIES ACT 2006

CONTENTS

Introduction

1. Section 503(3) of the Companies Act 2006 (CA 2006) requires, where the auditor is a firm, that the auditor's report must be signed by the "senior statutory auditor in his own name for and on behalf of the auditor". This is a new requirement and the Secretary of State has appointed the Auditing Practices Board[1] (APB) to issue guidance with respect to the meaning of the term "senior statutory auditor". This Bulletin constitutes that guidance.

2. Sections 503 and 504 of CA 2006 address the signature of the auditor's report and are reproduced in Appendix 1. The requirement for the senior statutory auditor to sign in his own name applies to auditor's reports:

    (a) prepared in accordance with the requirements of sections 495, 496 and 497 of CA 2006;

    (b) in respect of voluntary revisions of annual accounts and reports made in accordance with section 454 of CA 2006; and

    (c) on the special auditor's report where abbreviated accounts are delivered to the Registrar[2] (section 449 CA 2006),

    for financial years beginning on or after 6 April 2008.

3. CA 2006 sets out a number of requirements regarding the appointment of auditors. However, other than as described in paragraph 4, there are no legal requirements concerning eligibility for appointment as the senior statutory auditor. This is an internal matter for the audit firm as under section 504(1) of CA 2006 it is the firm which is required to identify which individual is the senior statutory auditor.

Eligibility for appointment as "Senior Statutory Auditor"

4. Section 504(2) of CA 2006 requires that the person identified as senior statutory auditor of a company must be eligible for appointment as auditor of the company in question. Eligibility for appointment is dealt with in sections 1212 to 1225 of CA 2006.

Meaning of "Senior Statutory Auditor"

5. Subject to meeting the CA 2006 requirement described in paragraph 4, the term "senior statutory auditor" has the same meaning as the term "engagement partner" when used in International Standards on Auditing (ISAs) (UK and Ireland).

---

[1] The Auditing Practices Board is appointed by virtue of Article 11 of the "Statutory Auditors (Delegation of Functions etc) Order 2008. SI 2008 No. 496

[2] In CA 2006 the expressions "the Registrar of Companies" and "the Registrar" mean the registrar of companies for England & Wales, Scotland or Northern Ireland, as the case may require. (section 1060 (3) CA 2006)

6. ISA (UK and Ireland) 220 "Quality Control for Audits of Historical Financial Information" contains the following definition of "engagement partner":

> The partner or other person in the firm who is responsible for the audit engagement and its performance, and for the auditor's report that is issued on behalf of the firm, and who, where required, has the appropriate authority from a professional, legal or regulatory body.

Involvement of more than one partner in an audit engagement

7. Where more than one partner is involved in the conduct of an audit engagement, it is important that the responsibilities of the respective partners are clearly defined and understood by the engagement team[3]. In particular, it is necessary for it to be clearly understood which partner is designated as the engagement partner and is, therefore, the senior statutory auditor identified by the firm in accordance with section 504(1) of CA 2006.

Meaning of "signing" the auditor's report

8. Section 503 of CA 2006 requires that where the auditor is a firm, the auditor's report must be signed by the senior statutory auditor in his own name, for and on behalf of the auditor (i.e. the firm). The signature of the senior statutory auditor is also required to be dated. An illustration of the presentation of these requirements in an auditor's report is shown in Appendix 2. Section 505(1) further requires that the name of the senior statutory auditor must be stated in copies of the auditor's report published by, or on behalf of, the company.

9. In paragraph 8 references to the auditor's report is to the auditor's report provided to the company by the auditor upon completion of the audit. Such references do not refer to the authentication of the copy auditor's reports required to be delivered to the Registrar.

10. Paragraphs 6 to 10 of Schedule 1 of "The Companies Act 2006 (Commencement No.5, Transitional Provisions and Savings) Order 2007"[4] address the authentication of accounts and reports filed with the Registrar. With effect from 6 April 2008 this order requires the copies of auditor's reports delivered to the Registrar to:

   (a) state the name of the auditor and (where the auditor is a firm) the name of the person who signed it as senior statutory auditor; and

   (b) be signed by the auditor or (where the auditor is a firm) in the name of the firm by a person authorised to sign on its behalf.

---

[3] ISA (UK and Ireland) 220 "Quality control for audits of historical financial information" paragraph 29
[4] SI 2007 No. 3495.

The senior statutory auditor, therefore, does not necessarily need to sign copy auditor's reports that are required to be delivered to the Registrar.[5]

Changing the senior statutory auditor during the reporting period

11. Where the audit firm changes the senior statutory auditor (i.e. the engagement partner) during the engagement the new senior statutory auditor reviews the audit work performed to the date of the change. The review procedures are sufficient to satisfy the new senior statutory auditor that the audit work performed to the date of the review had been planned and performed in accordance with professional standards and regulatory and legal requirements[6].

Senior statutory auditor unable to be present to sign the auditor's report

12. Under section 503(3) of CA 2006, the senior statutory auditor must sign the auditor's report. Another partner, or responsible individual, is not able to sign for and on behalf of the senior statutory auditor.

13. In circumstances where the senior statutory auditor is unable to continue to take responsibility for the direction, supervision and performance of the audit the audit firm appoints a replacement senior statutory auditor and the circumstances are treated in the same way as a change of senior statutory auditor described in paragraph 11.

14. In circumstances where the senior statutory auditor is absent but is still able to, and does, take responsibility for the direction, supervision and performance of the audit the senior statutory auditor may sign the auditor's report using electronic means (e.g. e-mail or fax).

15. In circumstances where the auditor's report needs to be signed by a certain date (e.g. listed entities and other public interest entities) it would be pragmatic for the audit firm to have a contingency plan as to who would succeed as senior statutory auditor in the

---

[5] Paragraph 10 describes transitional arrangements that came into force on 6 April 2008. Readers are cautioned that these arrangements are subject to change subsequent to the publication of this Bulletin.

[6] ISA (UK and Ireland) 220 paragraph 28.

event that the audit is at an advanced stage[7] but the senior statutory auditor is unable to sign the auditor's report. If another audit partner is actively involved in the audit engagement, a suitable contingency plan may be for that other partner to work in parallel with the senior statutory auditor and be able to take over as senior statutory auditor if the need arises. An efficient contingency plan would be one that was developed in conjunction with the firm's plans for partner rotation in accordance with the requirements of Ethical Standard 3 "Long association with the audit engagement".

16. The APB recognises that circumstances may arise where another partner has not worked in parallel with the senior statutory auditor. The APB is of the view that in such exceptional circumstances it is permissible for the engagement quality control reviewer[8] to be appointed as the replacement senior statutory auditor[9] where:

(a) the engagement quality control reviewer has completed his or her review; and

(b) the audit is at an "advanced stage".

17. However, once an engagement quality reviewer has been appointed as a replacement senior statutory auditor he or she can no longer act as the engagement quality control reviewer because his or her objectivity may have been impaired through assuming the role of senior statutory auditor.

Joint Audits

18. The Companies Act 2006 permits companies to appoint an auditor or auditors. Where a company appoints joint auditors each of the auditing firms appoints a senior statutory auditor both of which are required to sign the auditors' report in accordance with the requirements of section 503 of CA 2006.

---

[7] Bulletin 2008/2 "The auditor's association with preliminary announcements made in accordance with the requirements of the UK and Irish Listing Rules" describes an audit as being at an "advanced stage" when it is complete subject only to the following:
  (a) clearing outstanding matters which are unlikely to have a material impact on the financial statements;
  (b) completing audit procedures on the detail of note disclosures on the financial statements that will not have a material impact on the primary financial statements and completing the auditor's reading of "other information" in the annual report, in accordance with ISA (UK and Ireland) 720 "Other information in documents containing audited financial statements";
  (c) updating the subsequent events review covering the period to the date of the auditor's report on the financial statements; and
  (d) obtaining final written representations from management and establishing that the financial statements have been reviewed and approved by the directors.

[8] This is on the assumption that the engagement quality control reviewer is eligible to be appointed as the senior statutory auditor (see paragraph 4 for eligibility criterion).

[9] ISA (UK and Ireland) 220 "Quality control for audits of historical financial information" requires an engagement quality control reviewer to be appointed in respect of all listed entities.

Appendix 1

Sections 503 and 504 of the Companies Act 2006

503 Signature of auditor's report

(1) The auditor's report must state the name of the auditor and be signed and dated.

(2) Where the auditor is an individual, the report must be signed by him.

(3) Where the auditor is a firm, the report must be signed by the senior statutory auditor in his own name, for and on behalf of the auditor.

504 Senior statutory auditor

(1) The senior statutory auditor means the individual identified by the firm as senior statutory auditor in relation to the audit in accordance with –

    (a) standards issued by the European Commission, or

    (b) if there is no applicable standard so issued, any relevant guidance issued by –

        (i) the Secretary of State, or

        (ii) a body appointed by order of the Secretary of State.

(2) The person identified as senior statutory auditor must be eligible for appointment as auditor of the company in question (see Chapter 2 of Part 42 of this Act).

(3) The senior statutory auditor is not, by reason of being named or identified as senior statutory auditor or by reason of his having signed the auditor's report, subject to any civil liability to which he would not otherwise be subject.

(4) An order appointing a body for the purpose of subsection (1)(b)(ii) is subject to negative resolution procedure.

Appendix 2

Illustrative example of presentation of signature of senior statutory auditor on the auditor's report where the auditor is a firm

...

Opinion

In our opinion:

- the financial statements give a true and fair view of the state of the company's affairs as at ... and of its profit[loss] for the year then ended;

- the financial statements have been properly prepared in accordance with United Kingdom Generally Accepted Accounting Practice;

- the financial statements have been prepared in accordance with the Companies Act 2006; and

- the information given in the Directors' Report is consistent with the financial statements.

[Signature]   *Address*
John Smith (Senior Statutory Auditor)   *Date*
for and on behalf of ABC LLP, Statutory Auditor

BULLETIN 2008/10

GOING CONCERN ISSUES DURING THE CURRENT ECONOMIC CONDITIONS

CONTENTS

Introduction

1. Current economic conditions provide particular challenges to all involved with annual reports and accounts. One consequence is expected to be an increase in the disclosures in annual reports and accounts about going concern and liquidity risk. As a result, the current conditions will present challenges for:

   (a) directors – who will need to ensure that they prepare thoroughly for their assessment of going concern and make appropriate disclosures; and

   (b) auditors – who will need to ensure that they fully consider going concern assessments and only refer to going concern in their auditor's reports when appropriate.

2. In January 2008 the Auditing Practices Board (APB) issued Bulletin 2008/1[1] to provide guidance on matters that auditors needed to consider when conducting audits in the economic environment that was, at that time, characterised as the "credit crunch".

3. Since then the economic environment has worsened and the UK and Irish economies are entering a period of recession. This economic environment leads to added uncertainty regarding:

   (a) bank lending intentions and the availability of finance more generally;

   (b) the impact of the recession on a company's own business; and

   (c) the impact of the recession on counterparties, including customers and suppliers.

   These conditions will create a number of challenges for the preparers of financial statements and their auditors.

4. The effect of the current market conditions on any particular entity requires careful evaluation. However, the general economic situation at the present time does not, of itself, necessarily mean that a material uncertainty exists about an entity's ability to continue as a going concern or justify auditors modifying their auditor's reports to draw attention to going concern. The auditor makes a judgment on the need, or otherwise, to draw attention to going concern on the basis of the facts and circumstances of the entity at the time of signing the auditor's report. This Bulletin gives guidance on relevant factors to be considered and highlights certain requirements and guidance in the ISAs (UK and Ireland).

---

[1] Bulletin 2008/1 "Audit Issues when Financial Market Conditions are Difficult and Credit Facilities may be Restricted".

**FINANCIAL
REPORTING COUNCIL**

5.   This Bulletin supplements Bulletin 2008/1 and in particular:

    (a)   updates the list of risk factors included in that Bulletin (see appendices 2 and 3); and

    (b)   provides guidance on a number of going concern issues that auditors are likely to encounter during the forthcoming reporting cycle.

This guidance draws on ISA (UK and Ireland) 570 "Going concern" and does not establish any new requirements.

6.   To assist directors, the Financial Reporting Council (FRC), has published guidance entitled "An update for directors of listed companies: going concern and liquidity risk" (Update for Directors). Its purpose is to bring together existing guidance in the context of recent developments relating to going concern and liquidity risk disclosures to assist directors, audit committees and finance teams of listed companies during the forthcoming reporting season. It is expected that this Update for Directors will also be useful to directors of unlisted companies and other entities who have similar responsibilities to assess going concern and make appropriate disclosures. This Update for Directors is attached as Appendix 1 to this Bulletin.

7.   As with Bulletin 2008/1, this Bulletin has been written by reference to the challenges arising in relation to audits of all entities. The challenges arising in relation to audits of financial institutions such as banks, insurance companies and investment businesses give rise to additional specialist considerations that are not addressed in this Bulletin.

The potential impact of the economic outlook on the directors' approach to assessing going concern

8.   Accounting standards (both IFRS and UK GAAP) require directors to:

    (a)   make an assessment of a company's ability to continue as a going concern when preparing financial statements, and

    (b)   disclose the uncertainties that the directors are aware of in making their assessment of going concern where those uncertainties may cast significant doubt on the company's ability to continue as a going concern.

9.   The APB believes that the FRC's publication of the Update for Directors will assist auditors as it emphasises the need for directors to apply an appropriate degree of rigour and formality when making their judgments and suggests that directors will need to plan their assessment of going concern as early as practicable, including deciding on the information that will need to be produced (such as board papers) and the processes and procedures that will be undertaken. The Update for Directors further suggests that the directors should address the evidence to be obtained to support their conclusion and develop, where necessary, any remedial action plan.

10. To help minimise the risk of last minute surprises, the Update for Directors recommends companies have early discussions with their auditor about their plans. It also suggests that it may be useful for a draft of the relevant disclosures about going concern and liquidity risk to be prepared and discussed with the auditor before the end of the financial year. Such discussions may help the auditor plan its audit procedures and minimise the risk of the auditor qualifying its opinion on the grounds of a scope limitation or of a disagreement due to inadequate disclosure. It may also encourage the directors to develop a realistic remedial action plan where one is needed.

11. Notwithstanding early discussions between the company and its auditors both directors and auditors need to take account of subsequent developments as final assessments of going concern need to be made at the date that the directors approve the annual report and accounts taking into account the relevant facts and circumstances at that date.

Developments in corporate reporting

12. The Update for Directors describes recent developments in corporate reporting relating to:

   (a) the disclosure of the principal risks and uncertainties facing the company in the Business Review to be included in Director's Reports; and

   (b) additional disclosures relating to going concern and liquidity risk arising from changes to IFRS and UK GAAP.

13. The current squeeze on corporate cash-flows means that liquidity risk is likely to be a material risk this year for many more entities. As a consequence a greater number of companies are likely to need to present relevant disclosures concerning liquidity risk[2]. Examining the directors' processes underlying the preparation of these disclosures is likely to provide useful audit evidence for auditors with respect to the validity of the going concern assumption.

Planning

14. Risks arising from current economic circumstances are likely to impact a number of different aspects of the financial statements, for example the economic conditions may impact matters such as inventory obsolescence, goodwill impairments and cash flows, which may in turn affect whether the company is a going concern. It is important that auditor judgments on such matters are based on consistent underlying information and views.

---

[2] For IFRS, disclosures concerning liquidity risk are required by IFRS 7, IAS 1 and IAS 7. For UK GAAP, disclosures are required by FRS 18 and, where applicable, FRS 13 and FRS 29.

15. Because of the significance and pervasive nature of the current economic circumstances auditors need to take account of them at all stages of forthcoming audits and in particular when:

    (a) making risk assessments during the planning process and re-assessing those risks as the audit progresses;

    (b) performing audit procedures to respond to assessed risks;

    (c) evaluating the results of audit procedures (including as part of any engagement quality control review); and

    (d) forming an opinion on the financial statements.

Considering the directors' assessment of going concern

16. ISA (UK and Ireland) 570 requires the auditor to consider the appropriateness of the directors' use of the going concern assumption in the preparation of the financial statements, and consider whether there are material uncertainties about the entity's ability to continue as a going concern that need to be disclosed in the financial statements[3]. In order to meet this requirement the auditor's procedures will comprise:

    (a) evaluating the means by which the directors have satisfied themselves it is appropriate for them to adopt the going concern basis in preparing the financial statements, (see paragraphs 17 to 22);

    (b) concluding whether or not they concur with the directors' view, (see paragraphs 23 to 25);

    (c) assessing whether the financial statements contain adequate disclosures relating to going concern, (see paragraphs 26 to 28);

    (d) determining the implications for the auditor's report on the financial statements (see paragraphs 29 to 40); and

    (e) preparing appropriate documentation (see paragraph 41).

Evaluating how the directors have satisfied themselves that it is appropriate to adopt the going concern basis

17. Audit procedures that are likely to be relevant when evaluating the adequacy of the means by which the directors have satisfied themselves whether it is appropriate for them to adopt the going concern basis in preparing the financial statements include:

---

[3] Paragraphs 2 and 9 of ISA (UK and Ireland) 570.

- Analysing and discussing cash flow, profit and other relevant forecasts with management.

- Reviewing the terms of loan agreements and determining whether any may have been breached.

- Reading minutes of the meetings of shareholders, those charged with governance and relevant committees for references to financing difficulties.

- Reviewing events after period end to identify those that may mitigate or otherwise affect the entity's ability to continue as a going concern[4].

18. When analysis of cash flow is a significant factor in considering the future outcome of future events or conditions the auditor considers:

   (a) the reliability of the entity's information system for generating such information; and

   (b) whether there is adequate support for the assumptions underlying the forecast[5].

19. The Update for Directors notes that one impact of current conditions may be to limit finance available from trading counterparties (including suppliers and customers) and providers of finance. Furthermore, lenders may be more risk averse when considering whether to provide or renew finance facilities and may establish new conditions and these conditions may affect the company and its trading counterparties.

20. The Update for Directors indicates that directors will need to consider carefully the position in the light of the information available to them and the assumptions as to the future availability of finance. It:

   (a) notes that in the present economic environment, bankers may be reluctant to provide positive confirmations to the directors that facilities will continue to be available;

   (b) provides a number of examples of understandable reasons for this (see paragraph 37); and

   (c) concludes that the absence of bank confirmation of bank facilities does not, of itself, necessarily cast significant doubt upon the ability of an entity to continue as a going concern.

21. ISA (UK and Ireland) 570 requires that when events or conditions have been identified which may cast significant doubt on the entity's ability to continue as a going concern, the auditor should:

---

[4] Additional procedures are described in paragraph 28 of ISA (UK and Ireland) 570.
[5] Paragraph 29 of ISA (UK and Ireland) 570.

(a) review the directors' plans for future action based on their going concern assessment;

(b) gather sufficient appropriate audit evidence to confirm or dispel whether or not a material uncertainty exists through carrying out audit procedures considered necessary, including considering the effect of any plans of the directors and other mitigating factors; and

(c) seek written representations from the directors regarding their plans for future action[6].

In general terms, the greater the risks arising from current economic circumstances the more audit evidence will be required.

22. The auditor's procedures necessarily involve a consideration of the entity's ability to continue in operational existence for the foreseeable future. In turn, that necessitates consideration both of the current and the likely future circumstances of the business and the environment in which it operates[7]. The auditor may conclude that it will be appropriate to request from the directors written representations on specific matters relating to their assumptions and plans. Such representations may usefully include confirmation as to the completeness of the information provided to the auditor regarding events and conditions relating to going concern at the date of approval of the financial statements.

Concluding whether or not to concur with the directors' view

23. Assessing the going concern assumption involves making a judgment, at a particular point in time, about the future outcome of events or conditions which are inherently uncertain. Generally, the degree of uncertainty associated with the outcome of an event or condition increases the further into the future a judgment is being made about the outcome of an event or condition. Any judgment about the future is based on available evidence and reasonable assumptions about the outcome of the future events made at the time at which the judgment is made.

24. The basis for the auditor's conclusion is the information upon which the directors have based their assessment and their reasoning[8], including, where applicable, advice obtained from external advisers including lawyers. In evaluating the assessment of the directors, the auditor considers the process they followed to make their assessment, the assumptions on which the assessment is based and their plans for future action. The auditor considers whether the assessment has taken into account all relevant information of which the auditor is aware as a result of the audit[9].

---

[6] Paragraph 26 of ISA (UK and Ireland) 570.
[7] Paragraph 9-2 of ISA (UK and Ireland) 570.
[8] Paragraph 18-3 of ISA (UK and Ireland) 570.
[9] Paragraph 20 of ISA (UK and Ireland) 570.

25. Where there are events or conditions that cast significant doubt on the ability of the entity to continue as a going concern, the auditor assesses the directors' plans for future action, including plans to liquidate assets, borrow money or restructure debt, reduce or delay expenditures, or increase capital.

Adequacy of disclosures

26. Developments in accounting standards, including those relating to liquidity risk, together with the current economic conditions can be expected to give rise to a greater number of company annual reports and accounts containing liquidity and going-concern related disclosures.

27. The Update for Directors emphasises the importance, in the current economic conditions, of appropriate disclosures regarding liquidity risk and uncertainties. In its Appendix[10] it provides three illustrative examples of how directors might explain their going concern conclusion in a manner that would facilitate an understanding by readers of annual reports and accounts.

28. The IASB Framework notes that an essential quality of the information provided in financial statements is that it is readily understandable by users[11]. In reviewing the presentation of the disclosures the auditor considers whether the notes to the financial statements taken together with the primary financial statements present a true and fair view. The understandability of the disclosures is an important factor in determining whether the financial statements give a true and fair view.

Determining the implications for the auditor's report

29. ISAs (UK and Ireland) provide for a number of different auditor reports depending upon the specific facts and circumstances[12]. For example, if auditors conclude that the disclosures regarding going concern are not adequate to meet the requirements of accounting standards, including the need for financial statements to give a true and fair view, they are required either to express a qualified or adverse opinion, as appropriate. The report is also required to include specific reference to the fact that there is a material uncertainty that may cast significant doubt about the entity's ability to continue as a going concern[13].

30. If the auditor concludes that a material uncertainty exists that leads to significant doubt about the ability of the entity to continue as a going concern, and those uncertainties

---

[10] See page 1374 of this Bulletin.
[11] In UK GAAP, Chapter 1 of the Statement of Principles for financial reporting states that "the objective of financial statements is to provide information about the reporting entity's financial performance and position that is useful to a wide range of users for assessing the stewardship of the entity's management and for making economic decisions".
[12] See Appendix 4.
[13] Paragraph 34 of ISA (UK and Ireland) 570.

have been adequately disclosed in the financial statements, it is required to modify its report by including an emphasis of matter paragraph[14].

31. The current economic circumstances are likely to increase the level of uncertainty existing when the directors make their judgment about the outcome of future events or conditions. However, whilst the effect of current market conditions on individual entities requires careful evaluation, it should not be assumed that the general economic situation at the present time in itself means that a material uncertainty, which casts significant doubt on the ability of the entity to continue as a going concern, exists. Nor are extensive disclosures necessarily indicative of the existence of a significant doubt on the entity's ability to continue as a going concern. Indeed an objective of the disclosures may be to explain why the going concern issues that affect the company do not give rise to a significant doubt.

32. What constitutes a material uncertainty that may cast significant doubt on the entity's ability to continue as a going concern is a judgment involving not only

(a) the nature and materiality of the events or conditions giving rise to uncertainty; but also:

(b) the ability of the entity to adopt strategies that mitigate the uncertainty.

Nature and materiality of the events or conditions

33. Accounting standards do not define what constitutes a "material uncertainty". However, determining whether a "material uncertainty" exists involves assessing:

(a) the likelihood of events or conditions occurring; and

(b) their impact.

Assessment of these elements may require a high degree of judgment both by the directors and subsequently by the auditors depending upon the individual circumstances of the company and/or group.

34. Examples of possible events or conditions which may give rise to business risks, that individually or collectively may cast significant doubt about the going concern assumption are set out in ISA (UK and Ireland) 570 paragraph 8[15], these include:

• A net liability or current liability position.

---

[14] Paragraph 31 of ISA (UK and Ireland) 700 requires *"The auditor should modify the auditor's report by adding a paragraph to highlight a material matter regarding a going concern problem"*. Whereas, ISA (UK and Ireland) 570 uses the term *"material uncertainty relating to the event or condition that may cast significant doubt on the entity's ability to continue as a going concern"*. The term used in ISA (UK and Ireland) 570 is equivalent to the term "material matter regarding a going concern problem" used in ISA (UK and Ireland) 700.

[15] That paragraph also notes that the existence of one or more of the factors does not always signify that a material uncertainty that casts significant doubt on the entity's ability to continue as a going concern exists.

- Negative operating cash flows.

- Fixed-term borrowings approaching maturity without realistic prospects of renewal or repayment, or excessive reliance on short-term borrowings to finance long-term assets.

- Major debt repayment falling due where refinancing is necessary to the entity's continued existence.

- Inability to comply with the terms of loan agreements or to pay creditors on due dates.

- Loss of a major market, franchise, license or principal supplier.

A list of other possible events and conditions that may affect the auditor's assessment of going concern are set out in Appendix 2.

35. A factor listed in ISA (UK and Ireland) 570 is that necessary borrowing facilities have not been agreed. In examining borrowing facilities the auditor could decide, for example, that it is necessary:

    (a) to obtain confirmations of the existence and terms of bank facilities; and

    (b) to make its own assessment of the intentions of the bankers relating thereto.

    This latter assessment could involve the auditor examining written evidence or making notes of meetings which it would hold with the directors and, where appropriate, with the directors and the entity's bankers.

36. As discussed in paragraph 20(a), in the present economic environment bankers may be reluctant to confirm to entities or their auditors that facilities will be renewed. This reluctance may extend to companies with a profitable business and relatively small borrowing requirements. The lack of a positive confirmation from a bank does not of itself provide evidence of a material uncertainty that casts significant doubt on the entity's ability to continue as a going concern. Auditors seek to differentiate between circumstances where the lack of a confirmation reflects the existence of a material matter regarding going concern (which, therefore, falls to be emphasised in the auditor's report) and increased caution on the part of bankers that is not indicative of a material matter regarding going concern (and which, therefore, does not fall to be emphasised in the auditor's report).

37. There may be a number of reasons why a bank may be reluctant to confirm that a facility will be available in the future, which would not be a material matter regarding going concern, including:

- The bank responding that in the current economic environment, as a matter of policy, it is not providing such confirmations to its customers or their auditors.

- The entity and its bankers are engaged in negotiations about the terms of a facility (e.g. the interest rate), and where there is no evidence that the bank is reluctant to lend to the company.

- The bank renewed a rolling facility immediately prior to the date of the issuance of the annual report and accounts and is reluctant to go through the administrative burden to confirm that the facility will be renewed on expiry.

38. However, if the auditor concludes that an entity's bankers may be refusing to confirm facilities for reasons that are specific to the entity the auditor considers the significance of this and, where appropriate, discusses with the directors whether there are alternative strategies or sources of financing that would enable the financial statements to be prepared on the going concern basis.

Ability to adopt alternative strategies that mitigate an uncertainty

39. The adverse factors described in paragraph 34 may be mitigated by other favourable factors. For example, the effect of an entity being unable to make its debt repayments from operating cash flows may be counterbalanced by management's plans to maintain adequate cash flows by alternative means, such as by disposal of assets, rescheduling of loan repayments, or obtaining additional capital. Similarly the loss of a principal supplier may be mitigated by the availability of another suitable source of supply. Where an entity contends that it has alternative strategies to overcome any adverse factors the auditor assesses the effectiveness of such strategies and the ability of management to execute them.

40. If the auditor, in assessing the alternative strategies, considers that they:

(a) are realistic;

(b) have a reasonable expectation of resolving any problems foreseen; and

(c) that the directors are likely to put the strategies into place effectively[16],

the auditor may decide that it is unnecessary to include an emphasis of matter paragraph in the auditor's report[17].

Documentation

41. ISA (UK and Ireland) 230 (Revised) "Audit Documentation" requires the auditor to prepare audit documentation so as to enable an experienced auditor, having no previous connection with the audit, to understand significant matters arising during the

---

[16] Paragraph 20-1 of ISA (UK and Ireland) 570.
[17] Paragraph 26(b) of ISA (UK and Ireland) 570.

audit and the conclusions reached thereon. Significant matters include, amongst other things, findings that could result in a modification to the auditor's report. With respect to going concern, it is important, therefore, that the auditor documents its knowledge of conditions and events at the date of the auditor's report, and its reasoning with respect to the conclusions it has drawn.

Preliminary announcements

42. While preliminary announcements are no longer mandatory for listed companies, where a preliminary announcement is issued the directors are required by the Listing Rules to have agreed it with the auditor prior to publication.

43. The Listing Rules require that preliminary announcements "include any significant additional information necessary for the purposes of assessing the results being announced". An example of such information may be the disclosures that the directors propose to make in the annual report and accounts explaining their rationale for adopting the going concern basis in the annual accounts and setting out the uncertainties that they have considered in making their assessment.

44. Under both the UK and Irish Listing Rules a preliminary announcement is required to give details of the nature of any likely modification that may be contained in the auditor's report on the full financial statements. Under the Listing Rules modified auditor's reports encompass auditor's reports that contain an emphasis of matter paragraph. This would include a paragraph highlighting a material uncertainty relating to an event or condition that may cast significant doubt on the entity's ability to continue as a going concern.

45. Before agreeing to a preliminary announcement, therefore, the auditor assesses

    (a) whether the directors have given adequate prominence to significant additional information concerning going concern[18]; and

    (b) the adequacy of the directors' disclosure, within the announcement, of any likely modification relating to going concern that may be contained in the auditor's report.

Reviewing interim financial information

46. International Standard on Review Engagements (ISRE) (UK and Ireland) 2410 "Review of Interim Financial Information Performed by the Independent Auditor of the Entity", establishes standards and provides guidance on the auditor's professional responsibilities when the auditor undertakes an engagement to review interim financial information of an audit client and on the form and content of the report.

---

[18] Guidance for auditors on preliminary announcements is set out in Bulletin 2008/2 "The auditor's association with preliminary announcements made in accordance with the requirements of the UK and Irish Listing Rules".

47. If, as a result of enquiries or other review procedures, a material uncertainty relating to an event or condition comes to the auditor's attention that may cast significant doubt on the entity's ability to continue as a going concern, and adequate disclosure is made in the interim financial information the auditor modifies its review report by adding an emphasis of matter paragraph.

48. However, if a material uncertainty that casts significant doubt about the entity's ability to continue as a going concern is not adequately disclosed in the interim financial information, the auditor is required by ISRE 2410 to express a qualified or adverse conclusion as appropriate. In such circumstances the report is required to include specific reference to the fact that there is such a material uncertainty.

Ethical issues

49. The APB's Ethical Standards (ESs) are based on a "threats and safeguards approach" whereby auditors identify and assess the circumstances which could adversely affect the auditor's objectivity ("threats"), including any perceived loss of independence, and apply procedures ("safeguards"), which will either eliminate the threat or reduce it to an acceptable level, that is a level at which it is not probable that a reasonable and informed third party would conclude that the auditor's objectivity is impaired or is likely to be impaired.

50. In the current circumstances, where financial market conditions are difficult and credit facilities may be restricted, auditors need to be particularly alert to the possibility of self-review, management or advocacy threats arising from the provision of non-audit services in relation to a refinancing or restructuring that might jeopardise their objectivity and independence.

51. Examples of engagements that the audit firm may be requested to undertake in the current economic environment and which may give rise to threats to the auditor's independence and objectivity include:

    - Undertaking a review of the business with a view to advising the audited entity on restructuring options.

    - Advising on forecasts or projections, for presentation to lenders and other stakeholders, including assumptions.

    - Advising the audited entity on how to fund its financing requirements, including debt restructuring programmes.

52. When such work is undertaken a threat arises from the risk that the audit team may not review objectively the work undertaken in relation to going concern for audit purposes. Accordingly, where audit firms (and, in particular, members of the audit team) do undertake such engagements, consideration should be given to safeguards such as:

- A review of the going concern assessment and the conclusion reached by a partner or other senior staff member with appropriate expertise who is not a member of the audit team.

- Additional procedures undertaken as part of an Engagement Quality Control Review.

53. ES 5 (Revised) states that it is unlikely that safeguards can eliminate a threat or reduce it to an acceptable level:

    (a) in the absence of 'informed management' (paragraph 27 of ES 5 (Revised)) and

    (b) when the non-audit service would require the auditors to act as advocates for the entity in relation to matters that are material to the Financial Statements (paragraph 30 of ES 5 (Revised)).

54. Consequently, where an audit firm is engaged to provide advice to assist an entity it audits to demonstrate that it is a going concern, the audit firm ensures that the entity has "informed management"[19] capable of taking responsibility for the decisions to be made, thereby reducing the risk that the audit firm may be regarded as taking management decisions for the entity concerned. If the audit firm attends meetings with the entity's bank or other interested parties it takes particular care to avoid assuming responsibility for the entity's proposals or being regarded as negotiating on behalf of the entity or advocating the appropriateness of the proposals such that its independence is compromised.

---

[19] 'ES – Provisions Available for Small Entities' provides exemptions relating to informed management for auditors of small entities.

Financial Reporting Council

An Update for Directors of Listed Companies: Going Concern and Liquidity Risk

November 2008

Contents

		Page

One – Introduction

1. Current economic conditions provide particular challenges to all involved with annual reports and accounts. One consequence is expected to be an increase in the disclosures in annual reports and accounts about going concern and liquidity risk. As a result the current conditions will present challenges for all of the parties involved:

   - directors will need to ensure that they prepare thoroughly for their assessment of going concern and make appropriate disclosures;

   - auditors will need to ensure that they fully consider going concern assessments and only refer to going concern in their audit reports when appropriate; and

   - investors and lenders will need to be prepared to read all of the relevant information in annual reports and accounts before making decisions.

2. The purpose of this document is to bring together existing guidance in the context of recent developments relating to going concern and liquidity risk disclosures to assist directors, audit committees and finance teams of listed companies during the forthcoming reporting season. It does not establish any new requirements but it does highlight the importance of clear disclosure about going concern and liquidity risk in current economic conditions. This update may also be useful for directors of unlisted companies who have similar responsibilities to assess going concern and make appropriate disclosures.

3. Going concern is a fundamental accounting concept that underlies the preparation of the annual report and accounts of all UK companies. Under both International Financial Reporting Standards (IFRS) and UK Generally Accepted Accounting Principles (UK GAAP) directors are required to satisfy themselves that it is reasonable for them to conclude that it is appropriate to prepare financial statements on a going concern basis. These requirements are not intended to, and do not, guarantee that a company will remain a going concern until the next annual report and accounts is issued.

4. Both IFRS and UK GAAP require disclosure of the uncertainties that the directors are aware of in making their assessment of going concern where those uncertainties may cast significant doubt on the group's and company's ability to continue as a going concern.

5. The economic conditions being faced by many companies will necessitate careful consideration by directors when assessing whether it is reasonable for them to use the going concern basis of accounting, and whether adequate disclosure has been given of going concern risks and other uncertainties. Addressing these challenges well before the preparation of annual reports and accounts may help avoid a last minute problem that might unsettle investors and lenders unnecessarily.

6.   Directors will need to plan their assessment of going concern as early as practicable including deciding on the information and analysis that will need to be produced (such as board papers) and the processes and procedures that will be undertaken. These plans should also address the evidence to be obtained to support their conclusion and develop, where necessary, any remedial action plan.

7.   Early discussions with company auditors about these plans may help minimise the risk of last minute surprises, and it may be helpful for a draft of the relevant disclosures about going concern and liquidity risk to be prepared and discussed with the auditors before the end of the financial year.

8.   The Financial Reporting Council (FRC) published a consultation document on "Going concern and financial reporting: proposals to revise the guidance for directors of listed companies" (the 2008 Consultation) at the beginning of September 2008. Responses to the 2008 Consultation were due on 24 November 2008. The FRC anticipates that an exposure draft will be issued towards the end of the first quarter next year and will not become effective before mid 2009.

9.   The FRC would welcome further feedback on the practical challenges of applying the existing guidance "Going concern and financial reporting: guidance for directors of listed companies registered in the United Kingdom" (the 1994 Guidance), before the end of February 2009.

10. In the meantime the FRC believes that the existing guidance contained in the 1994 Guidance is fit for purpose even in these times of significant economic stress. This guidance can be found on the FRC website at: *http:// www.frc.org.uk/corporate/goingconcern.cfm*.

11. The 1994 Guidance indicates that directors may seek confirmation from their bankers regarding the existence and status of their finance arrangements. In the present economic environment bankers may be reluctant to provide positive confirmation that facilities will continue to be available. The absence of confirmations of bank facilities does not of itself necessarily cast significant doubt upon the ability of an entity to continue as a going concern nor necessarily require auditors to refer to going concern in their reports.

12. The effect of current market conditions on individual entities requires careful evaluation. The general economic situation at the present time does not of itself necessarily mean that a material uncertainty exists about a company's ability to continue as a going concern. However, it is important that annual accounts contain appropriate disclosure of liquidity risk and uncertainties such as are necessary in order to give a true and fair view.

13. Examples illustrating how directors might explain their going concern conclusion taking account of current economic conditions which would

facilitate an understanding by readers of annual reports and accounts are included in the appendix to this update.

14. The FRC has recently conducted a study of going concern and liquidity risk disclosures made by companies applying IFRS 7 (Financial instruments: Disclosures) in December 2007 and March 2008 year end annual reports and accounts. The study concluded that there are significant opportunities for improvement by way of better, rather than more, disclosure. In particular, it noted that there was often a significant lack of clarity about how liquidity risk is managed in practice and that much of the relevant information was distributed amongst different parts of annual reports, making it difficult for users to appreciate the full picture.

Two – Accounting requirements with respect to going concern

15. Going concern is a fundamental accounting concept that underlies the preparation of financial statements of all UK companies.

16. Preparing financial statements on a going concern basis is not compatible with the intention or the necessity of a company:

- entering into a scheme of arrangement with the company's creditors;
- making an application for an administration order; or
- being placed into administrative receivership or liquidation.

Assessment of going concern

17. International Accounting Standard (IAS) 1 (Presentation of financial statements) and UK Financial Reporting Standard (FRS) 18 (Accounting policies) require management/directors to make an assessment of an entity's ability to continue as a going concern when preparing financial statements. IAS 1.25 states:

> "When preparing financial statements, management shall make an assessment of an entity's ability to continue as a going concern. An entity shall prepare financial statements on a going concern basis unless management either intends to liquidate the entity or to cease trading, or has no realistic alternative but to do so. When management is aware, in making its assessment, of material uncertainties related to events or conditions that may cast significant doubt upon the entity's ability to continue as a going concern, the entity shall disclose those uncertainties."[1]

18. For financial reporting purposes, the assessment of going concern is made at the date that the directors approve the annual report and accounts and takes into account the relevant facts and circumstances at that date. IAS 1.26 also notes that the degree of consideration that may need to be given to the going concern assessment will depend upon the facts of each case.

19. The Listing Rules of the Financial Services Authority also require that the annual reports of listed companies include a statement by the directors that the business is a going concern, together with supporting assumptions or qualifications as necessary, that has been prepared in accordance with the 1994 Guidance.

20. The Directors statement on going concern is required to be prepared in accordance with the 1994 Guidance which outlines procedures that the directors may wish to adopt in making their assessment. The 1994 Guidance

---

1   Similar provision is made by FRS 18 paragraphs 21-25.

addresses both annual and interim accounts. In relation to the latter directors of listed companies will also need to consider the requirements of IAS 34 (Interim financial reporting).

21. The procedures that are necessary for the directors to comply with the requirements of IAS 1 or FRS 18 are likely to be similar to those adopted to meet their obligations under the Listing Rules. The 1994 Guidance places particular emphasis on the importance of the processes and procedures that directors carry out and highlights some major areas in which procedures are likely to be appropriate, including:

   - forecasts and budgets;
   - borrowing requirements;
   - liability management;
   - contingent liabilities;
   - products and markets;
   - financial risk management;
   - other factors; and
   - financial adaptability.

22. The 1994 Guidance notes that this list is not exhaustive and the significance of factors will vary from company to company. In the current economic climate many of these factors will have increased in significance which will require directors to consider them with more rigour and formality.

23. In forming their conclusion on going concern directors will need to evaluate which of three potential outcomes is appropriate to the specific circumstances of the group and company. The directors may conclude:

   - there are no material uncertainties that lead to significant doubt upon the entity's ability to continue as a going concern;
   - there are material uncertainties that lead to significant doubt upon the entity's ability to continue as a going concern; or
   - the use of the going concern basis is not appropriate.

24. In addition to the assessment that must be made by directors, auditors are required by auditing standards to determine if, in the auditors' judgment, a material uncertainty exists that may cast significant doubt on the entity's ability to continue as a going concern.

25. Auditing standards provide for a number of different audit reports depending upon the specific facts and circumstances. Auditors may conclude that it is necessary to qualify their opinion, disclaim an opinion, issue an adverse opinion or modify their report by including an emphasis of matter paragraph.

26. Auditors are required to consider the disclosures about going concern and liquidity risk made in the financial statements. If auditors conclude that the disclosures are not adequate to meet the requirements of accounting standards, including the need for financial statements to give a true and fair view, they are required to qualify their opinion and to provide their reasons for doing so. If auditors conclude that a material uncertainty exists that leads to significant doubt about the ability of the entity to continue as a going concern, and those uncertainties have been adequately disclosed in the financial statements, they are required to modify their report by including an emphasis of matter paragraph.

27. The combination of these requirements will generally result in one of the following three outcomes:

Outcome	Consequence for the directors' statement on going concern	Consequence for the auditors' report
No material uncertainties leading to significant doubt about going concern have been identified by the directors.	Disclosure explaining the conclusion on going concern and how that has been reached. *Examples 1 and 2 in the attached appendix illustrate this outcome.*	Unmodified report (clean) – provided the auditors concur with the directors' assessment and supporting disclosures.
Material uncertainties leading to significant doubt about going concern have been identified by the directors.	Disclosures explaining the specific nature of the material uncertainties and explaining why the going concern basis has still been adopted. *Example 3 in the attached appendix illustrates this outcome.*	Modified report including an emphasis of matter paragraph highlighting the existence of material uncertainties – provided auditors concur with the directors' assessment and supporting disclosures.
The directors conclude that the going concern basis is not appropriate.	Disclosures explaining the basis of the conclusion and the accounting policies applied in drawing up financial statements on a non-going concern basis.	Unmodified report (clean) – provided that the accounts contain the necessary disclosures and the auditors consider the basis to be appropriate to the specific facts and circumstances.

28. The 1994 Guidance also provides for disclosure when directors conclude that the going concern basis should be used despite having identified factors which cast doubt on the ability of the company to continue in existence for the foreseeable future. Significant changes to disclosure requirements about risks and uncertainties in IFRS, UK GAAP and the Companies Act 2006 (the Act) since 1994 may mean that sufficient disclosure of the factors giving rise

to the problem will have been provided through these disclosures (see paragraphs 40 to 49).

29. One impact of current conditions may be to limit finance available from trading counterparties including suppliers, customers and providers of finance. Furthermore, lenders may be more risk averse when considering whether to provide or renew finance facilities and may establish new conditions and these conditions may affect the company and the group and their trading counterparties.

30. In relation to bank and other facilities, paragraphs 30 to 32 of the 1994 Guidance may assist:

---

30. *The facilities available to the company should be reviewed and compared to the detailed cash flow forecasts for the period to the next balance sheet date, as a minimum. Sensitivity analyses on the critical assumptions should also be used in the comparison. The directors should seek to ensure that there are no anticipated:*

- *shortfalls in facilities against requirements;*

- *arrears of interest; or*

- *breaches of covenants.*

31. *The directors have responsibility to manage borrowing requirements actively. Any potential deficits, arrears or breaches should be discussed with the company's bankers in order to determine whether any action is appropriate. This may prevent potential problems crystallising. The onus is on the directors to be satisfied that there are likely to be appropriate and committed financing arrangements in place.*

32. *The directors may seek confirmation from their bankers regarding the existence and status of any finance arrangements which the company has entered into.*

---

31. Directors will need to consider carefully the position in the light of the information available to them and the assumptions as to the future availability of finance. Accounting standards do not define what constitutes a 'material uncertainty that may cast significant doubt upon the entity's ability to continue as a going concern'. This involves assessing both the probability of an event occurring and the impact it will have if it does occur. Assessment of these elements may require a high degree of judgment both by the directors, and subsequently by the auditors depending upon individual company and group circumstances.

32. In the present economic environment bankers may be reluctant to provide positive confirmations to the directors that facilities will continue to be

available. This reluctance may extend to companies with a profitable business and relatively small borrowing requirements. There may be a number of understandable reasons why a bank may be reluctant to confirm that a facility will be available in the future including:

- the bank responding that in the current economic environment, as a matter of policy, it is not providing such confirmations to its customers;

- the entity and its bankers are engaged in negotiations about the terms of a facility (e.g. the interest rate), however there is no evidence that the bank is reluctant to lend to the company; and

- the bank renewed a rolling facility immediately prior to the date of the issuance of the annual report and accounts and is reluctant to go through the administrative burden to confirm that the facility will be renewed again in a year's time.

33. The absence of confirmations of bank facilities does not of itself necessarily cast significant doubt upon the ability of an entity to continue as a going concern nor require necessarily auditors to refer to going concern in their reports.

Three – Going concern review period

34. IFRS contains specific requirements about the period which directors are required to review when assessing going concern. IAS 1.26 provides that management should take into account all available information about the future, which is at least, but not limited to, twelve months from the end of the reporting period.

35. FRS 18 requires disclosure if the period considered by the directors is less than twelve months from the date of approval of the financial statements.

36. Directors should consider the 1994 Guidance which provides that budgets and forecasts should be prepared to cover the period to the next balance sheet date as a minimum and notes that further periods are generally covered by medium or long-term plans which give an indication in general terms of how the directors expect the company to fare. The guidance also notes that the assessment is based on what is known to the directors at the date on which they approve the annual report and accounts which includes events or circumstances of which they are aware that arise after the end of the review period.

37. Where the period considered by the directors has been limited, for example, to a period of less than twelve months from the date of the approval of the annual report and accounts, the directors need to consider whether additional disclosures are necessary to explain adequately the assumptions that underlie the adoption of the going concern basis.

38. Auditing standards also address going concern and the period of the review by the directors. Auditors have an explicit obligation to include an extra paragraph in their audit report if the period covered by the directors' review is less than twelve months from the date of approval of the annual report and accounts and this fact is not disclosed by the directors.

Four – Insolvency

39. Doubts upon the ability of a company to remain a going concern do not necessarily mean that the company is, or is likely to become, insolvent. The solvency of a company is determined by reference to a comparison of its assets and liabilities and by its ability to meet liabilities as they fall due. Where the directors are unable to state that the going concern basis is appropriate, they should consider taking professional advice.

Five – Disclosures relevant to going concern and liquidity risk

Disclosure requirements of the Listing Rules about going concern

40. The Listing Rules require that the annual reports of listed companies include a statement by the directors that the business is a going concern, together with supporting assumptions or qualifications as necessary.

41. The 1994 Guidance notes that if there are doubts as to the appropriateness of the going concern presumption then the annual accounts may need to reflect any relevant factors in greater detail if they are to show a true and fair view. The guidance also notes that when there are factors which, in the event of an unfavourable outcome, cast doubt on the appropriateness of the going concern presumption, the directors should explain the circumstances so as to identify the factors which give rise to the problems (including any external factors outside their control which may affect the outcome) and an explanation of how they intend to deal with the problem so as to resolve it.

Disclosure requirements of IFRS and UK GAAP about going concern and liquidity risk

42. IAS 1 and FRS 18 have explicit disclosure requirements in the event that the directors conclude that there are material uncertainties that may cast significant doubt upon the entity's ability to continue as a going concern. In addition, in recent years there have also been significant changes to specific accounting standards that are relevant to disclosures about liquidity risk and other risks and uncertainties including:

Requirement	IFRS Reference (2008)	UK GAAP (2007/8)
Disclosures relating to risks arising from financial instruments, including liquidity risk where it is material.	IFRS 7 paragraphs 31 to 42	FRS 29 paragraphs 31 to 42
Estimating future cash flows (in connection with impairment of intangible assets).	IAS 36 paragraphs 33 to 54	FRS 11 paragraphs 36 to 40
Disclosure of undrawn borrowing facilities and any restrictions such as covenant requirements, where relevant.	IAS 7 paragraph 50 (a)	No explicit requirement
Disclosure of defaults and covenant breaches and potential reclassification of loans in default as current liabilities.	IAS 1 paragraphs 74 to 76	No explicit requirement
Disclosure of key sources of estimation uncertainty about the carrying amounts of assets and liabilities.	IAS 1 paragraphs 125 to 133	FRS 18 paragraphs 50 to 55

IFRS liquidity risk disclosures

43. Liquidity risk is the risk that an entity will encounter difficulty in meeting its obligations associated with financial liabilities. IFRS 7 (FRS 29) requires an entity to make both qualitative and quantitative disclosures concerning liquidity risk, where it is a material financial risk.

44. Where liquidity risk is material, IFRS 7 (FRS 29) requires:

   • disclosure of information that enables users to evaluate the nature and extent of the entity's exposure to liquidity risk;

   • narrative disclosures explaining how liquidity risk arises in the business and how it is managed in practice;

   • summary numerical data about liquidity risk based on the information that is provided to key management personnel, often the Board of Directors; and

   • certain mandatory disclosures such as a maturity analysis of financial liabilities.

45. The disclosures required by IFRS 7 are supplemented by disclosures required by other IFRS standards. For example, IAS 7 (Statement of cash flows) requires disclosure of undrawn borrowing facilities where relevant to users understanding of the financial position and liquidity of the entity, whilst IAS 1 requires disclosure of defaults and breaches of loan terms and conditions.

46. The current squeeze on corporate cash flows means that liquidity risk is likely to be a material risk this year for many more entities. As a consequence, a greater number of companies are likely to need to present relevant disclosures as required by IFRS 7 (FRS 29), IAS 1, IAS 7 and FRS 18.

Disclosure requirements of the Companies Act 2006 related to Directors' Reports

47. The Act requires the Directors' Report of all companies (except companies subject to the small companies' regime) to include a Business Review.

48. The Business Review is required to be a balanced and comprehensive analysis of the development and performance of the business of the company during the financial year and the position of the company at the end of that year, consistent with the size and complexity of the business. In particular it should include a description of the principal risks and uncertainties facing the company.

49. In the case of a quoted company, the Business Review is also required to provide information on a number of other matters including:

   • the main trends and factors likely to affect the future development, performance or position of the company's business; and

- information about persons with whom the company has contractual or other arrangements which are essential to the business of the company.

50. Directors will need to explain in the Business Review the principal risks and uncertainties facing the company arising from the current difficult economic conditions. One of the purposes of the Business Review is to help the members assess how the directors have performed their duties so it is reasonable to expect that it will also contain an account of how the directors intend to respond to these risks and uncertainties. Issues which may require disclosure depend upon individual facts and circumstances and may include:

   - uncertainties about current financing arrangements (whether committed or uncommitted);

   - potential changes in financing arrangements such as critical covenants and any need to increase borrowing levels ;

   - risks arising from current credit arrangements (including the availability of insurance where relevant) with either customers or suppliers;

   - a dependency on key suppliers and customers ; and

   - uncertainties posed by the potential impact of the economic outlook on business activities.

51. The Act also requires auditors to review the Directors' Report and to state in their report whether the information given in the Directors' Report is consistent with the financial statements. Auditing standards provide guidance for auditors on how they should carry out this work.

FRC review of going concern and liquidity risk disclosures

52. The FRC has published a study into going concern and liquidity risk disclosures in the financial statements of listed companies that have adopted IFRS 7. The study can be obtained from the FRC *http://www.frc.org.uk/ corporate/goingconcern.cfm*. The study notes that information about going concern and liquidity risk was distributed amongst a number of different parts of the annual report and accounts reviewed, thus making it difficult for users to determine and evaluate the extent to which liquidity concerns were relevant to the business and how liquidity risk was being managed in practice.

53. The study concluded that it would be particularly helpful if all of these disclosures could be brought together into a single section of a company's annual reports and accounts.

54. If it is not practical to provide the information in a single section, the study recommends that the key disclosures be brought together by way of a note including cross references to help readers of annual reports and accounts to find all of the relevant pieces of information.

55. It would be useful if such a note included the following components:

- Paragraph 1 explaining cash and borrowing positions and how liquidity risk is managed in practice.

- Paragraph 2 explaining whether confirmation of the renewal of banking and other facilities has been sought and if so whether those confirmations have been obtained[2].

- Paragraph 3 stating that the use of the going concern basis of accounting is appropriate and explaining the basis of that conclusion.

56. Examples illustrating these disclosures are included in the appendix to this update.

57. The FRC study also concluded that, while in general information about cash balances, borrowings and facilities was provided on a comprehensive basis, the level of detail about how liquidity risk was managed in practice and the information used by key management to monitor liquidity risk varied greatly. In particular:

- For many companies, the disclosures were generic rather than specific in nature. Only a minority of companies provided information that shed light on how the business managed its day to day cash flow and borrowing levels.

- A conclusion could not be reached on whether appropriate disclosure had been made of summarised data about liquidity risk as provided to key management personnel (generally the directors). Reaching such a conclusion would have required access to internal company documentation.

---

2   See paragraphs 29 to 33.

Six – Preliminary announcements

58. Preliminary announcements of annual results form one of the focal points for investor interest, primarily because they confirm or update market expectations. Under the Listing Rules such announcements are voluntary, although if made their contents are subject to minimum requirements. Where a company chooses to publish a preliminary announcement the directors are required by the Listing Rules to have agreed the preliminary announcement with their auditor prior to publication.

59. The Listing Rules provide that, if a preliminary announcement is made, it should give details of the nature of any likely modification that may be contained in the auditor's report required to be included with the annual report and accounts. Modified audit reports encompass audit reports that:

- are qualified;
- express an adverse opinion;
- express a disclaimer of opinion; or
- contain an emphasis of matter paragraph (including a paragraph highlighting a material matter regarding a going concern problem).

Appendix – examples of going concern disclosures

The purpose of this appendix is merely to illustrate the principles in paragraph 55 in bringing together going concern and liquidity risk disclosures. In practice such disclosures should be specific to the individual circumstances of each company.

Example 1 – A group with significant positive bank balances, uncomplicated circumstances and little or no exposure to uncertainties in the current economic environment which may impact the going concern assumption.

The group's business activities, together with the factors likely to affect its future development, performance and position are set out in the Business Review on pages X to Y. The financial position of the group, its cash flows, liquidity position and borrowing facilities are described in the Chief Financial Officer's Review on pages P to Q. In addition note A to the financial statements includes the group's objectives, policies and processes for managing its capital; its financial risk management objectives; details of its financial instruments and hedging activities; and its exposures to credit risk and liquidity risk.

The group has considerable financial resources together with long-term contracts with a number of customers and suppliers across different geographic areas and industries. As a consequence, the directors believe that the group is well placed to manage its business risks successfully despite the current uncertain economic outlook.

After making enquiries, the directors have a reasonable expectation that the company and the group have adequate resources to continue in operational existence for the foreseeable future. Accordingly, they continue to adopt the going concern basis in preparing the annual report and accounts.

Example 2 – A group with uncomplicated circumstances, some exposure to the current economic uncertainties and either a current material bank overdraft or loan and a need to renew this facility in the foreseeable future albeit not imminently.

Paragraph similar to example 1, paragraph 1.

As highlighted in note B to the financial statements, the group meets its day to day working capital requirements through an overdraft facility which is due for renewal on [date]. The current economic conditions create uncertainty particularly over (a) the level of demand for the group's products; (b) the exchange rate between sterling and currency X and thus the consequence for the cost of the group's raw materials; and (c) the availability of bank finance in the foreseeable future.

The group's forecasts and projections, taking account of reasonably possible changes in trading performance, show that the group should be able to operate within the level of its current facility. The group will open renewal negotiations with the bank in due course and has at this stage not sought any written commitment that the facility will be renewed. However, the group has held discussion with its bankers about its future borrowing needs and no matters have been drawn to its attention to suggest that renewal may not be forthcoming on acceptable terms.

Paragraph as per example 1, paragraph 3.

Example 3 – A group with complicated circumstances, considerable exposure to the current economic uncertainties and either a current material bank overdraft or loan which requires renewal and perhaps an increase in the year ahead.

Paragraph as example 1, paragraph 1.

As described in the directors' report on page X the current economic environment is challenging and the group has reported an operating loss for the year. The directors' consider that the outlook presents significant challenges in terms of sales volume and pricing as well as input costs. Whilst the directors have instituted measures to preserve cash and secure additional finance, these circumstances create material uncertainties over future trading results and cash flows.

As explained on page X, the directors are seeking to sell a property to provide additional working capital. The group is in negotiations with a potential purchaser but there can be no certainty that a sale will proceed. Based on negotiations conducted to date the directors have a reasonable expectation that it will proceed successfully, but if not the group will need to secure additional finance facilities.

As explained in the Business Review on Page Y, the group's has commenced discussions with its bankers about an additional facility that may prove to be necessary should the sale of the property not proceed or should material adverse changes in sales volumes or margins occur. It is likely that these discussions will not be completed for some time. The directors are also pursuing alternative sources of funding in case an additional facility is not forthcoming, but have not yet secured a commitment.

The directors have concluded that the combination of these circumstances represent a material uncertainty that casts significant doubt upon the group's and the company's ability to continue as a going concern. Nevertheless after making enquiries, and considering the uncertainties described above, the directors have a reasonable expectation that the group and the company have adequate resources to continue in operational existence for the foreseeable future. For these reasons, they continue to adopt the going concern basis in preparing the annual report and accounts.

Appendix 2

Events or Conditions That May Affect Going Concern

Possible events and conditions that may affect the auditor's assessment of going concern are listed below:

- Obtaining external finance:

  - Entity has experienced difficulties in the past in obtaining external finance facilities and/or complying with the related terms and covenants.

  - Borrowing agreements or executory contracts include clauses relating to debt covenants or subjective clauses (e.g. a "material adverse change clause") that trigger repayment.

  - Entity has breached some of the terms or covenants giving rise to the risk that the facilities may be withdrawn or not renewed.

  - Finance facilities are due for renewal in the next year.

  - Management have no plans for alternative arrangements should current facilities not be extended.

  - Finance facility is secured on assets (e.g. properties) that have decreased in value below the amount of the facility.

  - There are significant doubts about the financial strength of the entity's bankers.

  - Financing is provided by a syndicate of banks and other financial institutions and there are concerns about the viability of one or more of the members of the syndicate.

- Management plans to overcome financing difficulties include disposal of assets or possible rights issues:

  - Plans developed prior to current market conditions have not been updated or stress tested.

  - Lack of evidence that management can realise the assets at the values arising from planned disposals or obtain the support of shareholders in relation to a rights issue.

- Entity provides significant loans or guarantees:

  - Guarantees that may be called in.

  - Borrowers who may be unable to make payments.

- Entity dependent on guarantees provided by another party:

- Guarantor no longer able/prepared to provide the guarantee.

- Future cash flows:

    - Reduction in cash flows resulting from unfavourable economic conditions.

    - Customers taking longer/unable to pay.

    - Terms or covenants of renewed financing are changed and become more difficult to comply with (e.g. increased interest rates or charges).

    - Entity is subject to margin calls as a result of a decrease in fair market value of financial instruments that it holds.

    - Entities have issued loans (or received borrowings) having an introductory period during which favourable terms are in force which revert to normal market rates in the forthcoming year.

- Entity heavily dependent on counterparties such as suppliers and customers:

    - Suppliers facing financial difficulties provide essential goods/services.

    - Entity unable to find alternative suppliers.

Appendix 3

Risk Factors Arising From Current Economic Conditions

This Appendix identifies some factors that may increase the risk of material misstatement in financial statements during the current economic conditions, other than in relation to going concern.

Fair Values:

- Entity needs to change valuation model and/or management's assumptions to reflect current market conditions.

- Active market no longer exists, requiring use of a model for valuation purposes.

- Inputs to a model are not based on observable market inputs but rather are based on the entity's own data.

- Impairment of non-financial assets held at fair value (e.g. properties).

- Suspension of external valuation indices triggering a need for alternative valuation approaches.

- Entity uses an external pricing service for fair value measurements that needs to change its valuation model and/or assumptions to reflect current market conditions.

- Entity does not have necessary expertise to undertake valuations.

- Recent amendments to GAAP (IAS 39, IFRS 7, FRS 26 and FRS 29) may require or permit the reclassification of certain financial assets.

Impairments:

- Impairments of assets other than those held at fair value (e.g. need for increased doubtful debt provisions because previously reliable customers may not be able to pay their debts when due).

- Stock obsolescence resulting from significant decreases in demand for certain types of product.

- Impairment of the carrying amount of purchased goodwill.

- Increasing discount rates used in impairment calculations because capital has become more expensive.

- Effect on impairment calculations of subsequent events, in particular those relating to counterparties.

- Current credit market conditions may lead to the triggering of acceleration clauses which may lead to the impairment of financial assets.

Current versus non-current classification:

- Current market conditions may bring into question the classification of assets and liabilities as current or non-current. (For example the re-classification of liabilities as a result of a breach of loan covenants).

Revenue Recognition:

- Current credit market conditions may make it more difficult to demonstrate that the revenue recognition criteria, in (IAS 18/FRS 5) have been met.

Pensions:

- Pension obligations of an entity increased by reduction in value of assets in a related defined benefits pension scheme.

- Effect of illiquid investments and decreases in expected rates of return on investments.

Hedging:

- Hedging arrangements no longer effective when a derivative counterparty is experiencing financial difficulty or, more generally due to widening credit spreads on the derivative counterparty.

- In current market conditions, hedge effectiveness may have failed for the current period either because it is no longer probable that a derivative counterparty will meet its obligations, or because counterparty credit spreads have increased substantially, or because of the effect of changes in inter-bank lending rates on fair value interest rate hedges.

Insurance:

- The ability of an insurance company providing credit insurance to meet claims.

Deferred income taxes:

- If a company is reporting losses or is exposed to future losses there may be a need for a valuation allowance for deferred tax assets.

Appendix 4

Examples of conclusions the auditor might draw

Auditor's report	Circumstances	Example modified audit reports[1]
	Auditor agrees with the directors' assessment	
Clean	Preparing the financial statements on the going concern basis is appropriate, the going concern and liquidity disclosures are adequate and there are no material uncertainties that cast significant doubt on the entity's ability to continue as a going concern. (See examples 1 and 2 in the appendix to the Update for Directors)	n/a
Modified by inclusion of emphasis of matter paragraph[2]	Preparing the financial statements on the going concern basis is appropriate but there are material uncertainties described in the financial statements that cast significant doubt on the entity's ability to continue as a going concern. (See example 3 in the appendix to the Update for Directors)	Example 1
	Auditor disagrees with the directors' assessment	
Qualified opinion	Preparing the financial statements on the going concern basis is appropriate but there are material uncertainties that cast significant doubt on the entity's ability to continue as a going concern that are not adequately described in the financial statements	Example 5
Adverse opinion	The financial statements have been prepared on the going concern basis but the auditor has concluded that using the going concern basis is inappropriate.	–
Auditor's report	Circumstances	Example modified audit reports
	The directors refuse to undertake, or extend, an assessment of going concern	

---

[1] References are to the examples in Appendix 3 to Bulletin 2006/6 'Auditor's Reports on Financial Statements in the United Kingdom'

[2] ISA (UK and Ireland) 700 Paragraph 34 notes that in extreme cases, such as situations involving multiple uncertainties that are significant to the financial statements, the auditor may consider it appropriate to express a disclaimer of opinion.

Disclaimer of opinion	Where the directors' refusal either to undertake or to extend an assessment of going concern results in the auditor being unable to form an opinion on whether the financial statements give a true and fair view as the scope of the audit has been limited because the directors' consideration of going concern is completely inadequate.	Example 7

In all cases, if the period used by the directors in making their assessment of going concern is less than one year from the date of approval of the financial statements, and they have not disclosed that fact in the financial statements, the auditor is required by paragraph 31-4 of ISA (UK and Ireland) 570 to do so within the auditor's report.

BULLETIN 2009/4

DEVELOPMENTS IN CORPORATE GOVERNANCE AFFECTING THE RESPONSIBILITIES OF AUDITORS OF UK COMPANIES

CONTENTS

Introduction

1.   This Bulletin:

    (a)   updates and supersedes the guidance in paragraphs 68 to 72 of Bulletin 2006/5[1] issued by the Auditing Practices Board (APB) relating to the requirement in the Listing Rules for the auditor to review the directors' going concern statement. The need for the update arises from the issuance by the Financial Reporting Council of "Going Concern and Liquidity Risk: Guidance for Directors of UK Companies 2009" (FRC Guidance) which supersedes the guidance for directors to which the relevant guidance for auditors in Bulletin 2006/5 relates. The updated guidance for auditors is set out in paragraphs 2 to 12 of this Bulletin;

    (b)   provides guidance for the auditor with respect to its responsibilities under the Companies Act 2006 (CA 2006) regarding Corporate Governance Statements that the Disclosure Rules and Transparency Rules of the Financial Services Authority (FSA) require certain companies to make. This guidance is set out in paragraphs 13 to 34 and Appendix 1 of this Bulletin; and

    (c)   provides an illustration of how the example auditor's reports in Bulletin 2009/2 are amended to apply to "standard listed companies"[2] that are incorporated in the UK. The Listing Regime was changed with effect from 6 October 2009 to permit UK companies a choice of being either a "standard listed company" or a "premium listed company". Previously, all UK listed companies were subject to the regime that will apply to "premium listed companies". Guidance is set out in paragraphs 35 to 40 and Appendix 2 of this Bulletin.

Directors' statement on going concern required by the Listing Rules

Auditor's review of compliance

2.   The Listing Rules require the directors of certain listed companies[3] to include in the annual financial report a statement that:

---

[1]   APB Bulletin 2006/5, "The Combined Code on Corporate Governance: Requirements of Auditors under the Listing Rules of the Financial Services Authority and the Irish Stock Exchange" published in September 2006.

[2]   From 6 October 2009 to 6 April 2010, such companies will be described as "secondary listed companies". The change of name to "standard listed company" will be effective from 6 April 2010.

[3]   FSA LR 9.8.6R (3); ISE LR 6.8.3 (3). These Listing Rules apply to companies that have a primary listing of equity shares, preference shares or securities convertible into equity shares. The FSA's Listing Rule applies to such companies incorporated in the United Kingdom and the ISE's Listing Rule applies to such companies incorporated in the Republic of Ireland. From 6 April 2010, a primary listing will be described as a premium listing.

> "the business is a going concern, together with supporting assumptions or qualification as necessary, that has been prepared in accordance with Going Concern and Liquidity Risk: Guidance for directors of UK companies 2009, published by the Financial Reporting Council in October 2009".

3. The FRC Guidance provides a framework to assist directors in determining whether it is appropriate to adopt the going concern basis for preparing financial statements and in making balanced, proportionate and understandable disclosures. It encourages directors to focus on the three principles set out in the FRC Guidance and to apply them in a manner proportionate to the nature of their businesses.

4. The Listing Rules[4] also require a listed company to ensure that the auditor reviews the directors' going concern statement prior to the publication of the annual financial report. The auditor's review responsibility with respect to the directors' going concern statement includes:

    (a) reviewing the documentation prepared by or for the directors which explains the basis of the directors' conclusion with respect to going concern. If the going concern assessment has been prepared for the directors, the FRC Guidance recommends that the directors review and approve the documented assessment at the Board meeting at which the Board approves the financial statements;

Principle 1 of the FRC Guidance

Assessing Going Concern
Directors should make and document a rigorous assessment of whether the company is a going concern when preparing annual and half-yearly financial statements. The process carried out by the directors should be proportionate in nature and depth depending upon the size, level of financial risk and complexity of the company and its operations.

    (b) evaluating the consistency of the directors' going concern statement with the auditor's knowledge obtained in the course of the audit of the financial statements. This knowledge will primarily have been obtained in meeting the requirements of International Standard on Auditing (ISA) (UK and Ireland) 570 "Going Concern"; and

---

Principle 2 of the FRC Guidance

The Review Period
Directors should consider all available information about the future when concluding whether the company is a going concern at the date they approve the financial statements. Their review should usually cover a period of at least twelve months from the date of approval of annual and half-yearly financial statements.

---

[4] FSA LR 9.8.10R(1); ISE LR 6.8.6(1).

(c) whether the directors' statement meets the disclosure requirements of the FRC Guidance.

Principle 3 of the FRC Guidance

Disclosures

Directors should make balanced, proportionate and clear disclosures about going concern for the financial statements to give a true and fair view. Directors should disclose if the period that they have reviewed is less than twelve months from the date of approval of annual and half-yearly financial statements and explain their justification for limiting their review period.

Consistency with auditor's knowledge obtained in the course of the audit

5. ISA (UK and Ireland) 570 requires the auditor, based on the audit evidence obtained, to determine if, in its judgment, a material uncertainty exists related to events or conditions that alone or in aggregate may cast significant doubt on the company's ability to continue as a going concern[5]. The FRC Guidance requires the directors to make the same assessment.

No material uncertainties

6. If the directors conclude that there are no material uncertainties related to events or conditions that may cast significant doubt about the ability of the company to continue as a going concern, the Listing Rules require that a statement be made by the directors that the business is a going concern together with their supporting assumptions as necessary.

7. If the auditor also determines that there are no material uncertainties related to events or conditions that may cast doubt about the ability of the company to continue as a going concern, the auditor will be able to issue an unmodified opinion on the financial statements (i.e. there is no need for a going concern emphasis of matter paragraph).

8. However if, in the auditor's opinion, the directors' disclosures in their going concern statement are not balanced, proportionate or clear, the auditor considers whether it is necessary to communicate this fact in the auditor's report. If the auditor considers this to be necessary, paragraph 55 of ISA (UK and Ireland) 700 (Revised) requires the auditor to communicate this matter in an "other matter" paragraph in the auditor's report.

Material uncertainties but going concern basis appropriate

9. If the directors conclude that there is a material uncertainty related to events or conditions that may cast significant doubt about the ability of the company to continue as a going concern but that the going concern basis remains appropriate, the Listing

---

[5] ISA (UK and Ireland) 570 "Going concern" paragraph 30.

Rules require that a statement be made by the directors that the business is a going concern together with supporting assumptions or qualifications as necessary.

10. If the auditor also determines that there is a material uncertainty related to events or conditions that may cast significant doubt about the ability of the company to continue as a going concern, but that the going concern basis remains appropriate, the auditor assesses whether adequate disclosure has been made both in the financial statements and in the directors' going concern statement.

11. If adequate disclosure is made in the financial statements, the auditor should express an unqualified opinion on the financial statements but modify the auditor's report by adding an emphasis of matter paragraph. That paragraph highlights the existence of the material uncertainty, relating to the event or condition that may cast significant doubt on the company's ability to continue as a going concern, and draws attention to the note in the financial statements describing the uncertainty.

12. If adequate disclosure is made in the financial statements but in the auditor's opinion the directors' disclosures in their going concern statement are not balanced, proportionate or clear, the auditor considers whether it is necessary to communicate this fact in the auditor's report as described in paragraph 8 above.

The Corporate Governance Statement required by the "Disclosure Rules and Transparency Rules"

13. Directive 2006/46 (the Directive), of the European Parliament and the Council, on Company Reporting requires, among other things, that publicly traded companies[6] include a Corporate Governance Statement in their annual (directors') report. The requirements of the Directive and the responsibilities of the auditor with respect to Corporate Governance Statements have been implemented in the United Kingdom through:

(a) section 7.2 of the Disclosure Rules and Transparency Rules (DTR) of the FSA[7];

(b) section 496 of CA 2006; and

(c) Statutory Instrument 2009, No. 1581, "The Companies Act 2006 (Accounts, Reports and Audit) Regulations 2009" (the Regulations).

14. The FSA requirements for the preparation of a Corporate Governance Statement came into force on 29 June 2008 for financial years beginning on or after that date. The amendments to CA 2006 made by the Regulations came into force on 27 June 2009

---

[6] Companies whose securities are admitted to trading on a regulated market within the meaning of Article 4(1), point (14) of Directive 2004/39/EC. This definition includes both standard and premium listed companies (see paragraph 37 of this Bulletin).

[7] Section 7.2 was inserted by the Disclosure Rules and Transparency Rules Sourcebook (Corporate Governance Rules) Instrument 2008 (FSA 2008/32).

and are effective for financial years beginning on or after 29 June 2008 which had not ended by 27 June 2009.

Section 7.2 of the Disclosure Rules and Transparency Rules

15. Section 7.2 of the DTR requires disclosure of certain matters in the Corporate Governance Statement[8] many of which have, for some time, been required (by either company law or the Listing Rules) to be disclosed by UK listed companies in their annual reports (typically in the directors' report).

16. The requirements regarding the content of the Corporate Governance Statement are set out in the following DTRs.

DTR	Synopsis of requirement and comments
7.2.2R and 7.2.3R	**The Corporate Governance Code to which the issuer is subject** Requirements satisfied by compliance with LR 9.8.6R (3) (the "comply or explain" rule in the Combined Code) (see DTR 7.2.4G).
7.2.5R	**Description of the main features of the issuer's internal control and risk management systems in relation to the financial reporting process** A new requirement (see paragraph 17 below).
7.2.6R	**Takeover Directive disclosures about share capital** Required by paragraph 13(2)(c), (d), (f), (h) and (i) of Schedule 7 to the Large and Medium-sized Companies and Groups (Accounts and Reports) Regulations 2008.[9] These requirements are not new, having been in force for financial years beginning on or after 20 May 2006.
7.2.7R	**Description of the composition and operation of the issuer's administrative, management and supervisory bodies and their committees** In the FSA's view, the information specified in provisions A.1.1, A.1.2, A.4.6, B.2.1 and C.3.3 of the Combined Code satisfy this requirement (see DTR 7.2.8G).

17. Although the requirement in 7.2.5R is new, the Government has stated: "We do not believe that these regulations should add to the costs of audit because the test for consistency should not be onerous, and in a number of companies, the audited financial statements may not contain information on internal control and risk management systems".

18. Section 7.2 of the DTR requires those companies to which it applies to include a Corporate Governance Statement, either:

(a) as a specific section of the directors' report (DTR 7.2.1R); or

---

[8] The detailed requirements regarding the content of the Corporate Governance Statement are set out in DTRs 7.2.2R to 7.2.8G and 7.2.10R.

[9] Statutory Instrument (SI) 2008/410.

(b) in a separate report which is either;

    (i) published together with, and in the same manner as, its annual report (DTR 7.2.9 (1)R); or

    (ii) by means of a cross reference in its directors' report to where such document is publicly available on the company's website (DTR 7.2.9. (2) R).

Consistency of the Corporate Governance Statement with the financial statements

19. The auditor's responsibility with respect to assessing the consistency of the Corporate Governance Statement with the financial statements will differ dependent on whether the Statement:

(a) is included in the directors' report or is a separate Statement; and

(b) is included in a document containing audited financial statements (if it does so the requirements of ISA (UK and Ireland) 720 Section A are applicable).

20. The following table sets out, with respect to the various possible locations of the Corporate Governance Statement, what the appropriate requirements are and the relevant paragraphs of this Bulletin that provide guidance.

Location of Corporate Governance Statement	CA 2006			ISA (UK & I) 720	Paragraphs in Bulletin
	S 496	S 497A	S 498A		
In directors' report[10]	✓	n/a	n/a	✓ Sections A and B	21 – 28
Separate: in a document containing audited financial statements	n/a	✓	✓	✓ Section A	21 – 25 29 – 34
Separate: not in a document containing audited financial statements	n/a	✓	✓	n/a	21 – 24 29 – 32
No statement made by directors	n/a	n/a	✓	n/a	31 – 32

21. Regardless of whether the Corporate Governance Statement is included in the directors' report or is a separate Statement, the auditor is required to form an opinion as to whether the information given in the Statement for the financial year in relation to

---

[10] Directors may need to take legal advice to determine whether including a reference in a Directors' Report to "incorporating the Corporate Governance Statement by cross reference" is effective in determining that a Corporate Governance Statement is included in the Directors' Report.

the requirements of DTR 7.2.5R and 7.2.6R is consistent with the financial statements for that year.

22. An inconsistency arises when information in the Corporate Governance Statement contradicts information contained in the financial statements. If the auditor identifies an inconsistency, the auditor needs to determine whether the audited financial statements or the Corporate Governance Statement need to be revised.

23. Where there are no inconsistencies and the Corporate Governance Statement forms part of the directors' report, no additional words are required to be included in the auditor's report (see paragraphs 26 to 28 below). However, with respect to a Separate Corporate Governance Statement, the auditor is required to report (in the auditor's report on the financial statements) on the consistency of the information relating to DTRs 7.2.5R and 7.2.6R in the Statement with the financial statements (see paragraphs 29 to 30 below and Appendix 1).

24. In either case, if the auditor considers that revision of the audited financial statements is necessary, and the directors refuse to make the revision, the auditor is required to modify its opinion on the financial statements in accordance with the requirements of ISA (UK and Ireland) 700 (Revised) "The auditor's report on financial statements".

Apparent material misstatement of fact

25. If the Corporate Governance Statement is included in a document containing audited financial statements, the auditor, in meeting the requirements of ISA (UK and Ireland) 720 (Revised) Section A "Other information in documents containing audited financial statements", may become aware of apparent material misstatements of fact. A material misstatement of fact in the Statement exists when information in the Statement, which is not related to matters appearing in the audited financial statements, is incorrectly stated or presented. A material misstatement of fact would potentially include an inconsistency between information obtained by the auditor during the audit and information included in the Statement.

Corporate Governance Statement included in the directors' report

26. Where the Corporate Governance Statement is included in the directors' report, section 496 of CA 2006 requires:

> **Section 496 of CA 2006**
> The auditor must state in his report on the company's annual accounts whether in his opinion the information given in the directors' report for the financial year for which the accounts are prepared is consistent with those accounts.

27. Sections A and B of ISA (UK and Ireland) 720 (Revised) set out standards and guidance with respect to the auditor's statutory reporting responsibility with respect to a Corporate Governance Statement included in a directors' report.

28. Where the Corporate Governance Statement is included in the directors' report and the auditor has not identified any inconsistencies, the illustrative unmodified auditor's reports set out in Appendices 1 to 4 of Bulletin 2009/2 "Auditor's Reports on Financial Statements in the United Kingdom" do not need amendment. If the auditor does identify an inconsistency, Appendix 10 of Bulletin 2009/2 illustrates the way in which this would be done.

Separate Corporate Governance Statement

29. Where a Separate Corporate Governance Statement is issued, the Regulations insert a new section 497A into CA 2006 which requires:

Section 497A of CA 2006

(1) Where the company prepares a separate corporate governance statement in respect of a financial year the auditor must state in his report on the company's annual accounts for that year whether in his opinion the information given in the statement in compliance with rules 7.2.5 and 7.2.6 in the Disclosure Rules and Transparency Rules sourcebook issued by the Financial Service Authority (information about internal control and risk management systems in relation to financial reporting processes and about share capital structures) is consistent with those accounts.

---

30. Where there is a Separate Corporate Governance Statement, the auditor is required, therefore, to consider whether the information included in that statement in respect of DTR Rules 7.2.5 and 7.2.6 is consistent with the financial statements and report as required by section 497A of CA 2006.

31. The Regulations also insert into CA 2006 new section 498A which requires:

Section 498A of CA 2006

Where the company is required to prepare a corporate governance statement in respect of a financial year and no such statement is included in the directors' report:

(a) the company's auditor, in preparing his report on the company's annual accounts for that year, must ascertain whether a corporate governance statement has been prepared; and

(b) if it appears to the auditor that no such statement has been prepared, he must state that fact in his report.

---

32. Section 498A of CA 2006 merely requires the auditor to ascertain whether or not a Corporate Governance Statement has been prepared by the directors. It does not require the auditor to take steps additional to the requirements of sections 496 and 497A of CA 2006. In particular, section 498A of CA 2006 does not require the auditor to evaluate whether a Separate Corporate Governance Statement has been properly prepared by the directors in accordance with the Disclosure Rules and Transparency Rules.

33. However, if the Corporate Governance Statement forms part of a document that includes the audited financial statements, the requirements of ISA (UK and Ireland) 720 (Revised) Section A apply.

Amending the APB's illustrative auditor's reports when a Separate Corporate Governance Statement is issued

34. Where a company issues a Separate Corporate Governance Statement, the illustrative examples of auditor's reports of publicly traded companies and groups in Bulletin 2009/2 will need to be amended. In Appendix 1 to this Bulletin, example 4 from Bulletin 2009/2 is reproduced and marked up to illustrate the necessary changes. The other example auditor's reports in Bulletin 2009/2 relating to publicly traded companies and groups should be similarly amended where a separate corporate governance statement is issued.

Changes to the structure of the Listing Regime effective October 2009

35. In its Consultation Paper CP 09/24 "Listing Regime Review", the Financial Services Authority announced changes to the Listing Regime (and the detailed Listing Rules) which have the objective of providing more clarity about the Regime for market participants.

36. Most of the changes to the regime are effective from 6 April 2010. However, the Listing Rules have been changed with effect from 6 October 2009 to enable UK companies to join the Standard Listing Segment[11]. Prior to that date, this segment was only available to overseas companies.

37. The principal changes which are effective from 6 April 2010 are:

    • re-structuring the regime into two segments, Premium and Standard – the former denoting the more stringent super-equivalent standards (such as those relating to going concern and Corporate Governance Statements) and the latter, European Union minimum standards;

    • requiring overseas premium listed companies to "comply or explain" against the UK Combined Code;

    • requiring overseas standard listed companies to provide a Corporate Governance Statement which, among other things, describes the main features of their internal control and risk management systems;

38. If a UK company joins the Standard Listing Segment, or migrates to it from the Premium Listing Segment, there are implications for the content of its auditor's report.

---

[11] The Listing Rules have been changed with effect from 6 October 2009 to enable UK companies to be secondary listed companies. With effect from 6 April 2010, the category "secondary listed company" will be known as "standard listed company".

From 6 October 2009, secondary listed companies[11] incorporated in the UK are no longer required to make either the going concern statement required by Listing Rule 9.8.6(R) (3) or the corporate governance statement required by Listing Rule 9.8.6(R) (6) and, therefore, the auditors of such companies are no longer required to review such statements.

39. Appendix 2 of this Bulletin sets out how the section of the auditor's report relating to "Matters on which we are required to report by exception", as illustrated in the example illustrative auditor's reports in Bulletin 2009/2, is amended.

40. As the APB does not provide guidance for auditors of overseas listed companies, this Bulletin does not address the wording of auditor's reports for such companies.

Appendix 1

Illustrative auditor's report from Bulletin 2009/2 showing the additional wording that is required when a separate corporate governance statement is issued by the company either in its annual report or in a separate document[12]

- *Illustration based on Example 4 of Appendix 1 of Bulletin 2009/2*

INDEPENDENT AUDITOR'S REPORT TO THE MEMBERS OF XYZ PLC

We have audited the financial statements of (name of entity) for the year ended ... which comprise [specify the titles of the primary statements such as the Statement of Financial Position, the Statement of Comprehensive Income, the Statement of Cash Flow, the Statement of Changes in Equity] and the related notes. The financial reporting framework that has been applied in their preparation is applicable law and International Financial Reporting Standards (IFRSs) as adopted by the European Union.

Respective responsibilities of directors and auditors

As explained more fully in the Directors' Responsibilities Statement [set out [on page ...]], the directors are responsible for the preparation of the financial statements and for being satisfied that they give a true and fair view. Our responsibility is to audit the financial statements in accordance with applicable law and International Standards on Auditing (UK and Ireland). Those standards require us to comply with the Auditing Practices Board's [(APB's)] Ethical Standards for Auditors.

Scope of the audit of the financial statements

Either:

> A description of the scope of an audit of financial statements is [provided on the APB's website at www.frc.org.uk/apb/scope/UKP] / [set out [on page ...] of the Annual Report].

---

[12] The additional wording shown in this illustration is not required in an unmodified auditor's report where the Corporate Governance Statement is included in the Directors' Report.

Or:

> An audit involves obtaining evidence about the amounts and disclosures in the financial statements sufficient to give reasonable assurance that the financial statements are free from material misstatement, whether caused by fraud or error. This includes an assessment of: whether the accounting policies are appropriate to the company's circumstances and have been consistently applied and adequately disclosed; the reasonableness of significant accounting estimates made by the directors; and the overall presentation of the financial statements.

Opinion on financial statements

In our opinion, the financial statements:

- give a true and fair view of the state of the company's affairs as at ... and of its profit [loss] for the year then ended;

- have been properly prepared in accordance with IFRSs as adopted by the European Union; and

- have been prepared in accordance with the requirements of the Companies Act 2006.

[Separate opinion in relation to IFRSs as issued by the IASB

As explained in note [x] to the financial statements, the company in addition to applying IFRSs as adopted by the European Union, has also applied IFRSs as issued by the International Accounting Standards Board (IASB).

In our opinion, the financial statements comply with IFRSs as issued by the IASB.]

Opinion on other matters prescribed by the Companies Act 2006

In our opinion:

- the part of the Directors' Remuneration Report to be audited has been properly prepared in accordance with the Companies Act 2006; and

- the information given in the Directors' Report for the financial year for which the financial statements are prepared is consistent with the financial statements; and

- the information given in the Corporate Governance Statement set out [on pages] [in describe document] [at include web-address[13]] with respect to internal control

---

[13] Care should be taken to ensure that the web address is to the page on the website where the Corporate Governance Statement is located. As a website may be difficult to navigate it would be unhelpful if the web address is one, (for example that of the home page of the website), that does not lead directly to the Corporate Governance Statement.

and risk management systems in relation to financial reporting processes and about share capital structures is consistent with the financial statements[12].

Matters on which we are required to report by exception

We have nothing to report in respect of the following:

Under the Companies Act 2006, we are required to report to you if, in our opinion:

- adequate accounting records have not been kept, or returns adequate for our audit have not been received from branches not visited by us; or

- the financial statements and the part of the Directors' Remuneration Report to be audited are not in agreement with the accounting records and returns; or

- certain disclosures of directors' remuneration specified by law are not made; or

- we have not received all the information and explanations we require for our audit; or

- a Corporate Governance Statement has not been prepared by the company[12].

Under the Listing Rules, we are required to review:

- the directors' statement, [set out [on page...]], in relation to going concern; and

- the part of the Corporate Governance Statement [on pages] [in *describe* document] [at *include web* address] relating to the company's compliance with the nine provisions of the [2006] [June 2008] Combined Code specified for our review.

[Signature]   *Address*
John Smith (Senior Statutory Auditor)   *Date*
for and on behalf of ABC LLP, Statutory Auditor

Appendix 2

Illustrative auditor's report from Bulletin 2009/2 showing the changes necessary for it to apply to a standard listed company[14]

- *Illustration based on Example 4 of Appendix 1 of Bulletin 2009/2*

...

Opinion on other matters prescribed by the Companies Act 2006

In our opinion:

- the part of the Directors' Remuneration Report to be audited has been properly prepared in accordance with the Companies Act 2006; and

- the information given in the Directors' Report for the financial year for which the financial statements are prepared is consistent with the financial statements; and

- [the information given in the Corporate Governance Statement set out [on pages] [in *describe document*] [at *include web-address*[13]] with respect to internal control and risk management systems in relation to financial reporting processes and about share capital structures is consistent with the financial statements[12]].

Matters on which we are required to report by exception

We have nothing to report in respect of the following:

Under the Companies Act 2006, we are required to report to you if, in our opinion:

- adequate accounting records have not been kept, or returns adequate for our audit have not been received from branches not visited by us; or

- the financial statements and the part of the Directors' Remuneration Report to be audited are not in agreement with the accounting records and returns; or

- certain disclosures of directors' remuneration specified by law are not made; or

- we have not received all the information and explanations we require for our audit [; or

- a Corporate Governance Statement has not been prepared by the company[12]].

---

[14] The UK Listing Regime changed with effect from 6 October 2009 to permit UK companies to be "secondary listed companies". With effect from 6 April 2010 such companies will be described under the Listing Rules as "standard listed companies".

~~Under the Listing Rules we are required to review:~~

- ~~the directors' statement, [set out [on page...]], in relation to going concern; and~~

- ~~the part of the Corporate Governance Statement relating to the company's compliance with the nine provisions of the [2006] [June 2008] Combined Code specified for our review.~~[15]

[Signature]   *Address*
John Smith (Senior Statutory Auditor)   *Date*
for and on behalf of ABC LLP, Statutory Auditor

---

[15] The struck out words will continue to be included in the auditor's reports of UK "premium listed companies" (such companies are described as "primary listed companies" until 6 April 2010).

BULLETIN 2010/1

XBRL TAGGING OF INFORMATION IN AUDITED FINANCIAL STATEMENTS – GUIDANCE FOR AUDITORS

CONTENTS

Introduction

1. XBRL tagging of UK statutory financial statements is required for tax purposes in 2011. This Bulletin :

    *   Provides background information on the HM Revenue & Customs (HMRC) requirement and XBRL tagging,

    *   Explains that currently XBRL tagging is not within the scope of an audit performed under ISAs (UK and Ireland), and

    *   Provides guidance on the application of the APB's Ethical Standards for Auditors to non-audit services relating to XBRL tagging that auditors may be asked to perform. Particular threats to be considered include the 'management threat' and the 'self-review threat' as discussed below.

2. The use of XBRL is a developing area. Over time it is possible that XBRL will become integrated into accounting systems and will be used to generate the financial statements. The APB intends to keep its use by preparers of financial information, and the role of auditors in relation to it, under review and will issue updated guidance in the future as necessary to reflect changing circumstances.

HMRC requirement

3. In 2006 Lord Carter in his "Review of HMRC Online Services" recommended that all companies should be required to file their company tax returns online, using XBRL.

4. In September 2009, in a joint statement[1] issued with Companies House, HMRC announced that the Company Tax Return, including the supporting statutory accounts and tax computations showing the derivation from those accounts of the entries in the Company Tax Return, must be delivered electronically using the Inline XBRL (iXBRL) format. This will be mandatory when filing a Company Tax Return for accounting periods ending after 31 March 2010 and submitted to HMRC after 31 March 2011[2].

5. The HMRC requirement does not include a requirement for the auditor to provide assurance on the XBRL tagging of the information submitted. Indeed many of the companies that will be required to submit iXBRL financial statements will be below the audit exemption threshold and will not be subject to an audit.

6. In order to reduce potential administrative burdens on business, Companies House has announced that it will accept company accounts in the iXBRL format[3]. In the short

---

[1] Copies of the statement dated 1 September 2009 are available on the HMRC website at www.hmrc.gov.uk and the Companies House website at www.companieshouse.gov.uk.

[2] The legal requirement for delivering company tax returns electronically in a means approved by HMRC is established in SI 2009/3218, "The Income and Corporation Taxes (Electronic Communications) (Amendment) Regulations 2009."

[3] Companies House stated they will add iXBRL software filing for unaudited full accounts to their service by the summer of 2010, and then continue to develop their iXBRL capability for all the main types of accounts they receive by summer 2011.

term it is not expected that Companies House will make available the data in XBRL form (although the financial statements themselves will be viewable). However, in the longer term Companies House will be disseminating XBRL data to facilitate its use by users of company information.

XBRL

7.   XBRL, which stands for eXtensible Business Reporting Language, is a computer based language for the electronic communication of business data.

8.   XBRL works through tagging individual items of information with machine-readable codes (e.g. for the individual numbers in a set of financial statements). The codes are drawn from a library of codes referred to as a 'taxonomy'; taxonomies are pre-prepared by various organisations and are freely available[4].

9.   The value of XBRL tagging is that it allows data to become more easily accessible, manipulable and reviewable. XBRL allows users to customise their analysis and presentation of tagged information using computer software tools.

10.   Aspects of the tagging process may be automated but, in the case of financial statements, it is likely to be necessary for people to exercise judgement over the tag to be applied to a particular piece of information. Judgement will also be needed if the taxonomy does not cover all items of information that are disclosed in a set of financial statements. In such circumstances XBRL permits users to extend the taxonomy by creating new bespoke tags for data. This is why the word 'extensible' features in the name.

11.   'Inline XBRL' embeds XBRL tags within documents that can still be read by the human eye. When looked at on a computer screen the document looks like a normal document but the data will have underlying tags that can be revealed, for example by positioning the mouse cursor over the data.

12.   There are a number of ways for entities to create financial statements using XBRL:

   •   After they have been finalised, financial statements can be mapped into XBRL either manually or using "bolt-on" applications which consist of software that compiles XBRL data from the traditional financial statements into XBRL format.

   •   XBRL-aware accounting software products are becoming available which will support the export of data in XBRL form. These tools allow users to map charts of accounts and other structures to XBRL tags.

---

[4]   The taxonomy for International Financial Reporting Standards (IFRS) is the responsibility of the International Accounting Standards Committee Foundation (IASCF), the oversight body of the International Accounting Standards Board (IASB). In the UK, XBRL UK has issued a 'UK IFRS' taxonomy, which takes the IASCF taxonomy and adds the extra tags needed by UK listed companies (e.g. to cover data that is required by company law in addition to the accounting standards) and a 'UK GAAP' taxonomy.

13. The route which an individual entity may take will depend on its requirements and the accounting software and systems it currently uses.

14. To help with the introduction of mandatory online filing for tax returns, HMRC will initially accept accounts with only some of the data needing to be tagged[5]. HMRC has already published 'minimum tagging lists' for the UK GAAP taxonomies and will be doing so for UK IFRS. These lists specify the items that must be tagged if they are present in any given set of accounts. Companies may choose to adopt full tagging immediately.

Audit

15. As described above, HMRC is requiring the financial statements supporting a company's tax return to be transmitted to it using the iXBRL format. There is no requirement for an audit of the data or indeed the XBRL tagging.

16. With respect to the audit of financial statements, the current position is that ISAs (UK and Ireland) do not impose a general requirement on the auditor to check XBRL tagging of the financial statements as part of the audit. Furthermore, because the XBRL tagging is simply a machine-readable rendering of the data within the financial statements, rather than a discrete document, it does not constitute 'other information' as defined in ISA (UK and Ireland) 720 Section A. Accordingly the requirement of ISA (UK and Ireland) 720 Section A for the auditor to "read" the other information for the purpose of identifying material inconsistencies or material misstatements of fact is not applicable to XBRL tags.[6]

17. Whether management seeks to increase its confidence concerning the accuracy of its iXBRL tagging for HMRC through a service provided by the company's auditors, or another accountancy firm, is a matter for management to determine. If management does seek such a service, the extent and nature of the engagement to provide it is a matter for agreement between management and the auditor or other accountancy firm.

18. As usage of XBRL evolves in the UK and Ireland the APB will consider the needs of users and the extent to which an audit of financial statements should be expected to provide assurance on the accuracy of the tagging process. It is also possible that regulators may require auditors to provide assurance on XBRL-tagged data at some stage in the future.

---

[5] Guidance on online filing is provided on the HMRC website (www.hmrc.gov.uk/ct/ct-online/file-return). This includes a guidance document "XBRL- when to tag, how to tag, what to tag" (http://www.hmrc.gov.uk/ct/ct-online/file-return/online-xbrltag.pdf).

[6] This position is consistent with that set out in the Questions and Answers publication "XBRL: The Emerging Landscape," issued by the staff of the International Auditing and Assurance Standards Board (IAASB) in January 2010, clarifying that the IAASB's auditing pronouncements currently do not impose requirements on auditors with respect to XBRL-tagged data or the representation of this data.

Non-audit services and possible threats to auditor independence

19. While auditors do not provide assurance as to the accuracy of the tagging in the context of an audit of financial statements, there may be a demand for non-audit services to be performed by audit/accountancy firms. These may include:

    • Performing the tagging exercise;

    • Providing a service to the directors of the company as to accuracy of the tagging performed by management (e.g. by undertaking an agreed upon procedures engagement);

    • Providing advice on the selection of individual tags;

    • Supplying accounts preparation software that automates the tagging;

    • Training management in XBRL tagging.

20. Where non-audit services are provided by the company's auditor, the auditor considers possible threats to independence and objectivity and whether it is appropriate to accept the engagement and, if so, whether to apply appropriate safeguards. The differing nature of possible non-audit services means that the associated requirements and guidance fall under different headings in APB's Ethical Standard (ES) 5 including:

    • accounting services;

    • taxation services; and

    • information technology services.

21. The main threats addressed in these sections of ES5 relate to the management threat and the self-review threat.

Management threat

22. Unless they apply the provisions of ES – Provisions Available for Small Entities (ES-PASE)[7] the APB Ethical Standards[8] require audit firms to establish policies and procedures which require partners and employees of the firm, including those providing non-audit services to an audited entity, not to take decisions that are the responsibility of the management of the audited entity.

---

[7] ES – Provisions Available for Small Entities allows auditors of Small Entities to take advantage of exemptions from certain of the requirements in APB Ethical Standards 1 to 5 and provides alternative provisions.

[8] ES1 paragraph 30.

23. Some non-audit services related to XBRL may give rise to a management threat. In particular performing the XBRL tagging can involve judgements, especially when a transaction or balance is not covered by the taxonomy, or when more than one item within a taxonomy initially appears to be suitable for application to a particular disclosure. In such circumstances the audit firm will need to ensure that management in the audited entity takes responsibility for making the management decisions and that the entity has informed management in place to help it do so.

24. Under ES – PASE an audit firm can provide non-audit services that involve the firm undertaking part of the role of management to small entities, provided that it discusses these services with those charged with governance, confirms that management accepts responsibility for any decisions taken and discloses the fact that ES – PASE has been applied in the auditor's report.

Self-review threat

25. Some non-audit services related to XBRL may give rise to a self-review threat. A self-review threat exists when the results of a non-audit service are reflected in the amounts included or disclosed in the financial statements that are subject to audit. If the audit engagement partner identifies threats to the auditor's independence the APB Ethical Standards[9] require him to identify the effectiveness of the available safeguards and apply such safeguards as are sufficient to eliminate the threats or reduce them to an acceptable level[10].

26. Whether a self-review threat exists in an XBRL tagging engagement depends on whether XBRL tagging is used to generate the financial statements and whether the tagging is covered in the scope of the audit.

27. In the short term, it is likely that the tagging will take place after the financial statements have been generated and the audit has been completed. Accordingly a self-review threat will not arise in relation to the audit of those financial statements. However tagging performed in 'year one' may provide the basis for the tagging in future years. If an audit requirement is established at some stage in the future a self-review threat may exist in relation to this initial work. Because of this audit firms may wish to design an XBRL related non-audit service in a way that would avoid a potential future self-review threat.

28. In the longer term, if XBRL becomes integrated into accounting systems it may be difficult to separate XBRL tagging from accounting services. In such circumstances the provisions of ES 5 in relation to accounting services are likely to apply, including the prohibition in paragraph 127 that accounting services are not provided by audit firms to audited entities that are listed companies or significant affiliates of listed companies.

---

[9] ES1 paragraph 38.

[10] Where a small company is audited under ES – PASE the audit firm is not required to apply safeguards to address the self-review threat associated with non-audit services, as long as the audited entity has informed management and the audit firm extends the cyclical inspection of completed engagements that is performed for quality control purposes (ES – PASE, paragraph 7). In the absence of informed management, the firm needs to apply safeguards to address any self-review threat.

BULLETIN 2011/1

DEVELOPMENTS IN CORPORATE GOVERNANCE AFFECTING THE RESPONSIBILITIES OF AUDITORS OF COMPANIES INCORPORATED IN IRELAND

CONTENTS

Introduction

1. This Bulletin provides:

    (a) guidance with respect to the auditor's responsibilities under Statutory Instrument No. 450 of 2009 "European Communities (Directive 2006/46/EC) Regulations 2009" as amended by Statutory Instrument No. 83 of 2010 "European Communities (Directive 2006/46/EC) (Amendment) Regulations 2010", regarding the Corporate Governance Statement required for inclusion in Annual Reports, for accounting periods commencing on or after 18 November 2009, of certain companies whose securities are admitted to trading on a regulated market[1];

    (b) illustrations of how the example Auditor's Reports in Bulletin 2006/1 are amended when a Corporate Governance Statement is issued; and

    (c) a summary of the Irish legislative requirements in respect of the Corporate Governance Statement.

The Corporate Governance Statement required by Legislation in Ireland

2. Directive 2006/46/EC of the European Parliament and the Council, on Company Reporting ("the Directive") requires, among other things, that certain companies whose securities are admitted to trading on a regulated market include a Corporate Governance Statement in their Annual Report. The requirements of the Directive and the responsibilities of the auditor with respect to the Corporate Governance Statement have been implemented in Ireland through Statutory Instrument No. 450 of 2009 "European Communities (Directive 2009/46/EC) Regulations 2009" as amended by Statutory Instrument No. 83 of 2010 "European Communities (Directive 2006/46/EC) (Amendment) Regulations 2010" (the Regulations)

3. A summary of the Irish legislative requirements in respect of the Corporate Governance Statement for certain companies whose securities are admitted to trading on a regulated market is set out in Appendix 4 to this Bulletin.

4. The requirements regarding the content of the Corporate Governance Statement have been incorporated into section 158 of the Companies Act, 1963 by the Regulations with additional requirements for groups set out in Regulation 8 of the Regulations. The following table sets out a synopsis of the requirements of section 158 of the Companies Act, 1963 and how they relate to extant rules and guidance such as those provided by the Irish Stock Exchange Listing Rules or by other legislation or guidance.

---

[1] Within the meaning of Article 4(1), point (14) of Directive 2004/39/EC. The main securities market (MSM) of the Irish Stock Exchange (ISE) is a regulated market for this purpose.

S.158 CA 1963	Synopsis of requirements and comments
6D(a)	**The Corporate Governance Code**
	Requirements satisfied by compliance with Listing Rule (L.R.). 6.8.3(7) (the "comply or explain" rule in the 2008 Combined Code) together with disclosure of where the relevant text is publicly available. For periods beginning on or after 30 September 2010 the ISE's Listing Rules require compliance with the UK Corporate Governance Code (L.R. 6.8.3(6) and (7)) and for periods beginning on or after 18 December 2010 the Listing Rules also require compliance with the Irish Corporate Governance Annex to the ISE Listing Rules (L.R. 6.8.3(9)).
6D(b)	**Departure from a Corporate Governance Code**
	Requirement similar to L.R.6.8.3(7)(b) and for periods beginning on or after 18 December 2010 L.R. 6.8.3(9)(b) also refers.
6D(c)	**Description of the main features of the issuer's[1] internal control and risk management systems in relation to the financial reports process**
	Regulation 8(1) of Statutory Instrument No. 450 of 2009 also requires similar information in relation to Consolidated Financial Statements.
	There is overlap here with paragraph 33 of the Financial Reporting Council's (FRC) "Internal Control - Revised Guidance For Directors On The Combined Code" issued in October 2005: "The Annual Report and Accounts should include such meaningful, high-level information as the board considers necessary to assist shareholders' understanding of the main features of the company's risk management processes and system of internal control, and should not give a misleading impression."
6D(d)	**Takeover Bids Directive disclosures about share capital**
	Disclosures required by paragraph 2(c), (d), (f), (h) and (i) of Regulation 21 of the European Communities (Takeover Bids (Directive 2004/25/EC)) Regulations 2006 (S.I. No. 255 of 2006). These requirements are not new, having been in force since 2006[2] but are now required to be located in the Corporate Governance Statement.
6D(e)	**Description of the operation of the issuer's shareholder meeting, the key powers of the shareholder meeting, shareholders' rights and the exercise of such rights**
	A new requirement.

---

[2] Refer S.I. No. 255 of 2006 European Communities (Takeover Bids (Directive 2004/25/EC)) Regulations 2006.

S.158 CA 1963	Synopsis of requirements and comments
6D(f)	**Description of the composition of and operation of the issuer's board of directors and the committees of the board of directors with administrative, management and supervisory functions** The information specified in provisions A.1.1, A.1.2, A.4.6, B.2.1 and C.3.3 of the 2008 Combined Code[3] refer. The relevant provisions in the UK Corporate Governance Code are A1.1, A1.2, B2.4, C3.3 and D2.1.

5.   The legislation requires those issuers to which it applies to include a Corporate Governance Statement, either:

(a)   as a specific section of the Directors' Report[4]; or

(b)   in a separate report which is either;

(i)   published together with, and in conjunction with the Annual Report[5]; or

(ii)   incorporated by means of a cross reference in the Directors' Report to where such document is publicly available on the issuers' website.

The legislation also distinguishes between the Corporate Governance Statement for entities and for groups.

Consistency of the Corporate Governance Statement with the Financial Statements

6.   The auditor's responsibility with respect to assessing and reporting on the consistency of the Corporate Governance Statement with the financial statements will differ dependent on whether the statement addresses an entity or a group and whether it is included in:

(a)   the Directors' Report;

(b)   a document containing the audited financial statements (if it does so the requirements of the ISA (UK and Ireland) 720 Section A are applicable); or

(c)   a separate document not containing the audited financial statements.

---

[3]   For periods commencing prior to 30 September 2010 the ISE's listing rules require compliance with the 2008 Combined Code. For periods beginning on or after 30 September 2010 the ISE's listing rules require compliance with the UK Corporate Governance Code and for periods beginning on or after 18 December 2010 also the Irish Corporate Governance Annex to the ISE Listing Rules.

[4]   Paragraph 6(D) of S.158 of Companies Act, 1963 (as amended) and Regulation 8(2) of S.I. No. 450 (as amended).

[5]   Paragraph 6E and 6G(a) of S.158 of Companies Act, 1963 (as amended) and Regulation 8(3) of S.I. No. 450 (as amended).

7. The following table sets out, with respect to the various possible locations of the Corporate Governance Statement, the relevant legislative references and paragraphs of this Bulletin that provide guidance.

Summary of auditor's obligations – reporting on consistency of the Corporate Governance Statement.

Location of the Corporate Governance Statement:	Auditor's obligation to provide separate consistency opinion in the audit report	
	Entity financial statements	Consolidated financial statements
Included in the directors' report[6]	No additional reporting requirements other than the existing requirement under Section 15 of the Companies (Amendment) Act, 1986[7] ISA (UK & Ireland) 720 Bulletin paragraphs 8 & 16 to 19	Yes in respect solely of relevant aspects of internal control and risk management systems Regulation 9 of S.I. No. 450 of 2009 (as amended by S.I. No. 83 of 2010) Regulation 38 of S.I. No. 201 of 1992: European Communities (Companies: Group Accounts) Regulations, 1992[7] ISA (UK & Ireland) 720 Bulletin paragraphs 9 to 11 & 16 to 19 Example Auditor's Report: Appendix – 1
Separate: outside directors' report but included in a document containing the audited financial statements	Yes Section 158 (6H) of the Companies Act, 1963 Section 15 of the Companies (Amendment) Act, 1986[7]	Yes Regulation 9 of S.I. No. 450 of 2009 (as amended by S.I. No. 83 of 2010) Regulation 38 of S.I. No. 201 of 1992: European Communities (Companies:

---

[6] Directors may need to take legal advice to determine whether including a reference in a directors' report to "incorporating the Corporate Governance Statement by cross reference" is effective in determining that a Corporate Governance Statement is included in the directors' report.

[7] Similar consistency opinion requirements apply for credit institutions and insurance undertakings – refer: regulation 13 of S.I. No. 294 of 1992: European Communities (Credit Institutions: Accounts) Regulations, 1992 as amended by regulation 16 of S.I. No. 450 of 2009 (as amended by S.I. No. 83 of 2010) and regulation 16 of S.I. No. 23 of 1996: European Communities (Insurance Undertakings: Accounts) Regulations, 1996 as amended by regulation 23 of S.I. No. 450 of 2009 (as amended by S.I. No. 83 of 2010).

Location of the Corporate Governance Statement:	Auditor's obligation to provide separate consistency opinion in the audit report	
	Entity financial statements	**Consolidated financial statements**
	ISA (UK & Ireland) 720 Bulletin paragraphs 12, 13 & 16 to 19 Example Auditor's Report: Appendix – 3	Group Accounts) Regulations, 1992[7] ISA (UK & Ireland) 720 Bulletin paragraphs 14 & 16 to 19 Example Auditor's Report: Appendix – 2
Separate: not included in a document containing the audited financial statements	Yes Section 158 (6H) of the Companies Act, 1963 Bulletin paragraphs 15 to 19 Example Auditor's Report: Appendix – 3	Yes Regulation 9 of S.I. No. 450 of 2009 (as amended by S.I. No. 83 of 2010) Regulation 13 of S.I. No. 294 of 1992: European Communities (Credit Institutions: Accounts) Regulations, 1992 as amended by regulation 16 of S.I. No. 450 of 2009 (as amended by S.I. No. 83 of 2010) Regulation 16 of S.I. No. 23 of 1996: European Communities (Insurance Undertakings: Accounts) Regulations, 1996 as amended by regulation 23 of S.I. No. 450 of 2009 (as amended by S.I. No. 83 of 2010) Bulletin paragraphs 15 to 19 Example Auditor's Report: Appendix – 2

Corporate Governance Statement included in the Directors' Report

Entity financial statements

8. The auditor is not specifically obliged to report on the consistency of an Entity Corporate Governance Statement where such Statement is included in the Directors' Report. Therefore, no modification is required to the standard auditor's report on the entity's financial statements. However, section 15 of the Companies (Amendment) Act, 1986 requires the auditor to consider whether the information in the Directors' Report is consistent with the financial statements prepared by the company.

> **Section 15 of the Companies (Amendment) Act, 1986**
>
> It shall be the duty of the auditors of a company, in preparing the report in relation to the company required by section 193 of the Principal Act, to consider whether the information given in the report of the directors of the company relating to the financial year concerned is consistent with the accounts prepared by the company for that year and they shall state in the report whether, in their opinion, such information is consistent with those accounts.

Consolidated financial statements

9. Regulation 9 of S.I. No. 450 of 2009 (as amended) requires the auditor to state in its report on consolidated financial statements whether, in its opinion, the description, in the Corporate Governance Statement, of the main features of the internal control and risk management systems of the parent and its subsidiary undertakings in relation to the process for preparing the Consolidated Financial Statements, is consistent with the Consolidated Financial Statements for the year. This reporting obligation is the same whether the Group Corporate Governance Statement is included within the Directors' Report, included within a document containing the audited Financial Statements or included within a separate document i.e. not within a document containing the audited Financial Statements.

10. Whilst the specific requirements of the Regulations concerning descriptions of both internal control and risk management systems in relation to the issuer's financial reporting process and those relating to the consolidated financial statements are new, they are unlikely to give rise to a significant increase in the extent of audit work required. The auditor's procedures in relation to the descriptions of internal controls and risk management systems, and other information contained in the Corporate Governance statement, will be determined by reference to ISA (UK & Ireland) 720 Section B "The auditor's statutory reporting responsibility in relation to directors' reports". The auditor, therefore, assesses the information provided by comparison with the financial statements and should inconsistencies be identified, seeks to resolve them by discussion with management.

11. Existing guidance, which is set out in APB Bulletin 2006/5 "The Combined Code on Corporate Governance: Requirements of Auditors under the Listing Rules of the

Financial Services Authority and the Irish Stock Exchange", to consider application of the Combined Code provisions identified for review by the auditor remain unchanged.

Regulation 9 of S.I. No. 450 of 2009 (as amended)

Where a parent undertaking referred to in Regulation 8 produces a corporate governance statement in respect of a financial year –

(a) in the report by the directors in accordance with Regulation 8(1), or;

(b) in a separate report in accordance with Regulation 8(3),

the auditors of the parent undertaking, when preparing their report under section 193 of the Act of 1990 for that financial year, shall state in their report whether, in their opinion, the description, in the corporate governance statement, of the main features of the internal control and risk management systems referred to in Regulation 8(1) is consistent with the consolidated accounts for that financial year.

Corporate Governance Statement included in a document containing the Audited Financial Statements but outside the Directors' Report

Entity financial statements

12. The regulations insert a new section 158 (6H) into the Companies Act, 1963 which requires:

Section 158 (6H) of the Companies Act, 1963

6(H) Where a company, in accordance with subsection (6E) produces a corporate governance statement in a separate report in respect of a financial year-

(a) the auditors of the company, in their report under section 193 of the Act of 1990, shall state whether, in their opinion, the information in the corporate governance statement, required by paragraph (c) of subsection (6D) is consistent with the annual accounts for that financial year,

(b) the auditors of the company, in their report under section 193 of the Act of 1990, shall state whether, in their opinion, the information in the corporate governance statement, required by paragraph (d) of subsection (6D) is consistent with the annual accounts for that financial year, and

(c) the auditors of the company, when preparing their report under section 193 of the Act of 1990 in respect of the annual accounts for that year, shall ascertain that a separate corporate governance statement has, in accordance with subsection (6E), been produced and contains the information required by paragraphs (a), (b), (e) and (f) of subsection (6D).

---

13. Accordingly, the auditor's report for the entity financial statements of a company will reflect the obligations of the auditor in the respective responsibility section and in addition the opinion section of the report will contain specific references to the matters set out in Section 158(6D) (c) and (d).

Consolidated financial statements

14. Where a parent undertaking, preparing consolidated financial statements, includes the Corporate Governance Statement outside the Directors' Report but within a document containing the audited financial statements, the auditor's reporting obligations are as discussed in paragraphs 9 and 10 above.

Separate Corporate Governance Statement not included in a document containing the Audited Financial Statements

15. The reporting obligations of the auditor in the case of a separate Corporate Governance Statement for an entity or group preparing a Corporate Governance Statement which is not included in a document containing the audited financial statements are the same as those set out in paragraph 12 to 14 above. However, the obligations under ISA (UK and Ireland) 720 do not apply.

Inconsistency of the information

Entity and consolidated financial statements

16. An inconsistency arises when information in the Corporate Governance Statement contradicts information contained in the financial statements. If the auditor identifies an inconsistency, the auditor needs to determine whether the financial statements or the Corporate Governance Statement need to be revised.

17. If the auditor considers that revision of the financial statements is necessary, and the directors refuse to make the revision the auditor considers the need to modify the opinion on the financial statements in accordance with the requirements of ISA (UK and Ireland) 700 "The auditor's report on financial statements"[8].

Apparent material misstatement of fact

Entity and consolidated financial statements

18. If the Corporate Governance Statement is included in a document containing audited financial statements, the auditor, in meeting the requirements of ISA (UK and Ireland) 720 Section A "Other information in documents containing audited financial

---

[8] The version of ISA (UK and Ireland) 700 that was effective for periods commencing on or after 15 December 2004 remains in effect with respect to audits of Irish entities.

statements", may become aware of apparent material misstatements of fact. A material misstatement of fact in the Corporate Governance Statement exists when information in the statement, which is not related to matters appearing in the audited financial statements, is incorrectly stated or presented. A material misstatement of fact would potentially include an inconsistency between information obtained by the auditor during the audit and information included in the Statement.

19. Sections B of ISA (UK and Ireland) 720 set out standards and guidance with respect to the auditor's statutory reporting responsibility with respect to a Corporate Governance Statement included in a Directors' Report.

The Auditor's Report when a corporate governance statement is issued

Entity and consolidated financial statements

20. Where a Corporate Governance Statement is required, the illustrative examples of auditor's reports of publicly traded companies and groups in Bulletin 2006/1 need to be amended:

    (a) in all cases involving Group Corporate Governance Statements; and

    (b) for Entity Corporate Governance Statements presented separately to the Directors' Report.

    In Appendices 1 to 3 of this Bulletin, example 12 and example 5 from Bulletin 2006/1 are reproduced and marked up to illustrate the necessary changes. The other example auditor's reports in Bulletin 2006/1 relating to publicly traded companies and groups should be similarly amended whenever a Corporate Governance Statement is required.

21. A number of minor changes have been made to the wording used in the Bulletin 2006/1 examples:

    • The Companies Acts citation is updated from the Companies Acts 1963 to 2005 to the Companies Acts 1963 to 2009.

    • The phrase "as adopted for use in the European Union" has been replaced with "as adopted by the European Union".

    • In the group report examples, parent company rather than just company has been used to aid clarity.

    • Where there is reference to article 4 of the IAS regulations, wording has been added to make clear that this is just as regards the group accounts.

No, or non compliant, statement made by directors

Entity and consolidated financial statements

22. Regulation 26 specifies that, among other things, the contravention of regulation 8 (report of the directors to contain information required by Section 158 of the Companies Act, 1963 including a description of the main features of the internal control and risk management system of the parent and subsidiaries in relation to the process of preparing the consolidated financial statements) is an indictable offence. The auditor has regard to Bulletin 2007/2 ' The duty of auditors in the Republic of Ireland to report to the Director of Corporate Enforcement' in cases:

> Where, in the course of, and by the virtue of, their carrying out an audit of the accounts of the company, information comes into the possession of the auditors of a company that leads them to form the opinion that there are reasonable grounds for believing that the company or an officer or agent of it has committed an indictable offence under the Companies Acts (other than an indictable offence under section 125 (2) or 127(2) of the Principal Act), the auditor shall, forthwith after having formed it, notify that opinion to the Directors and provide the Directors with details of the grounds on which they have formed that opinion[9].

Effective date of the Corporate Government Statement requirement

23. The Corporate Governance Statement requirements reflected in this bulletin are effective for periods beginning on or after 18 November 2009.

---

[9] Section 194(5) of the Companies Act, 1990.

Appendix 1

Illustrative Auditor's Report from Bulletin 2006/1 incorporating the additional wording that is required when a Corporate Governance Statement issued by a group is included in the Directors' Report.

- Illustration based on Example 12 of Appendix 1 of Bulletin 2006/1

- Parent with securities admitted to trading on a regulated market[1] producing consolidated financial statements

- Corporate Governance Statement presented within the directors' report and covers parent and subsidiary undertakings

INDEPENDENT AUDITOR'S REPORT TO THE SHAREHOLDERS OF XYZ LIMITED

We have audited the group and parent company financial statements (the "financial statements") of (name of entity) for the year ended ... which comprise [state the primary statements such as the Group Income Statement, the Group and Parent Company Balance Sheets[10], the Group and Parent Company Cash Flow Statements, the Group Statement of Comprehensive Income, the Group and Parent Company Statements of Changes in Equity] and the related notes[11]. These financial statements have been prepared under the accounting policies set out therein.

Respective responsibilities of directors and auditors

The directors' responsibilities for preparing the Annual Report and the financial statements in accordance with applicable law and International Financial Reporting Standards (IFRSs) as adopted for use in by the European Union are set out in the Statement of Directors' Responsibilities.

Our responsibility is to audit the financial statements in accordance with relevant legal and regulatory requirements and International Standards on Auditing (UK and Ireland).

We report to you our opinion as to whether the consolidated financial statements give a true and fair view, in accordance with IFRSs as adopted for use in by the European Union. We report to you our opinion as to whether the parent company financial statements give a true

---

[10] With exception of the use of the term "balance sheet", the names of the primary statements given in the IFRS audit report example are those terms used in IAS 1 (2007) which applies for accounting periods beginning on or after 1 January 2009. IAS 1 (2007) refers to the balance sheet as the 'statement of financial position'. However, as this or any of the new titles are not mandatory, the example retains the better-known title of 'balance sheet'.

[11] Auditor's reports of entities that do not publish their financial statements on a web site or publish them using 'PDF' format may continue to refer to the financial statements by reference to page numbers.

and fair view, in accordance with IFRSs as adopted for use in by the European Union as applied in accordance with the provisions of the Companies Acts, 1963 to 20052009. We also report to you whether the financial statements have been properly prepared in accordance with the Companies Acts, 1963 to 20052009 and, as regards the group financial statements, Article 4 of the IAS Regulation. We also report to you whether, in our opinion: proper books of account have been kept by the parent company; whether at the balance sheet date, there exists a financial situation requiring the convening of an extraordinary general meeting of the parent company; and whether the information given in the directors' report is consistent with the financial statements. In addition, we state whether we have obtained all the information and explanations necessary for the purposes of our audit, and whether the financial statements are parent company balance sheet is in agreement with the books of account.

We also report to you if, in our opinion, any information specified by law or the Listing Rules of the Irish Stock Exchange regarding directors' remuneration and directors' transactions is not disclosed and, where practicable, include such information in our report.

We are required by law to report to you our opinion as to whether the description in the Corporate Governance Statement set out in the directors' report of the main features of the internal control and risk management systems in relation to the process for preparing the consolidated financial statements is consistent with the consolidated financial statements. In addition, we review whether the Corporate Governance Statement reflects the parent company's compliance with the nine provisions of the [20082003 FRC Combined Code[3]]/[UK Corporate Governance Code and the two provisions of the Irish Corporate Governance Annex] specified for our review by the Listing Rules of the Irish Stock Exchange, and we report if it does not. We are not required to consider whether the board's statements on internal control cover all risks and controls, or form an opinion on the effectiveness of the group's corporate governance procedures or its risk and control procedures.

We read the other information contained in the Annual Report and consider whether it is consistent with the audited financial statements. The other information comprises only [the Directors' Report, the Chairman's Statement, the Operating and Financial Review and the Corporate Governance Statement][12]. We consider the implications for our report if we become aware of any apparent misstatements or material inconsistencies with the financial statements. Our responsibilities do not extend to any other information.

Basis of audit opinion

We conducted our audit in accordance with International Standards on Auditing (UK and Ireland) issued by the Auditing Practices Board. An audit includes examination, on a test basis, of evidence relevant to the amounts and disclosures in the financial statements. It also includes an assessment of the significant estimates and judgments made by the directors in the preparation of the financial statements, and of whether the accounting policies are appropriate to the group's and parent company's circumstances, consistently applied and adequately disclosed.

---

[12] The other information that is 'read' is the content of the printed Annual Report other than the financial statements. The description of the information that has been read is tailored to reflect the terms used in the Annual Report.

We planned and performed our audit so as to obtain all the information and explanations which we considered necessary in order to provide us with sufficient evidence to give reasonable assurance that the financial statements are free from material misstatement, whether caused by fraud or other irregularity or error. In forming our opinion we also evaluated the overall adequacy of the presentation of information in the financial statements.

Opinion

In our opinion:

- the consolidated financial statements give a true and fair view, in accordance with IFRSs as adopted for use in by the European Union, of the state of the group's affairs as at ....and of its profit [loss] for the year then ended;

- the parent company financial statements give a true and fair view, in accordance with IFRSs as adopted for use in by the European Union as applied in accordance with the provisions of the Companies Acts, 1963 to 20052009, of the state of the parent company's affairs as at .... ; and

- the financial statements have been properly prepared in accordance with the Companies Acts, 1963 to 20052009 and, as regards the group financial statements, Article 4 of the IAS Regulation.

We have obtained all the information and explanations which we consider necessary for the purposes of our audit. In our opinion proper books of account have been kept by the parent company. The parent company balance sheet is in agreement with the books of account.

In our opinion the information given in the directors' report is consistent with the financial statements and the description in the Corporate Governance Statement of the main features of the internal control and risk management systems in relation to the process for preparing the consolidated financial statements is consistent with the consolidated financial statements.

The net assets of the parent company, as stated in the parent company balance sheet are more than half the amount of its called-up share capital and, in our opinion, on that basis there did not exist at ... a financial situation which under Section 40(1) of the Companies (Amendment) Act, 1983 would require the convening of an extraordinary general meeting of the parent company.

[Separate opinion in relation to IFRSs

As explained in Note X to the consolidated financial statements, the parent company and the group in addition to complying with its legal obligation to comply with IFRSs as adopted by the European Union, have also complied with the IFRSs as issued by the International Accounting Standards Board (IASB).

In our opinion the consolidated financial statements give a true and fair view, in accordance with IFRSs, of the state of the group's affairs as at........ and of the profit [loss] of the group for the year then ended.]

Registered auditors[13]   Address

Date

---

[13] For accounting periods commencing on or after 20 May 2010, the audit report should state the name of the statutory auditor and be signed by the statutory auditor in their own name for and on behalf of the statutory audit firm (section 193(4G) of the Companies Act, 1990 as amended by regulation 57 of S.I. No. 220 of 2010).

Appendix 2

Illustrative Auditor's Report from Bulletin 2006/1 incorporating the additional wording that is required when a Corporate Governance Statement is issued by a group outside the Directors' Report

- Illustration based on Example 12 of Appendix 1 of Bulletin 2006/1

- Parent with securities admitted to trading on a regulated market[1] producing consolidated financial statements

- Separate Corporate Governance Statement covering parent and subsidiaries presented outside the directors' report regardless where published

INDEPENDENT AUDITOR'S REPORT TO THE SHAREHOLDERS OF XYZ LIMITED

We have audited the group and parent company financial statements (the "financial statements") of (name of entity) for the year ended ... which comprise [specify the titles of the primary statements such as the Group Statement of Income, the Group and Parent Company Balance Sheets[10], the Group Statement of Comprehensive Income, the Group and Parent Company Cash Flow Statements, the Group and Parent Company Statements of Changes in Equity] and the related notes[11]. These financial statements have been prepared under the accounting policies set out therein.

Respective responsibilities of directors and auditors

The directors' responsibilities for preparing the Annual Report and the financial statements in accordance with applicable law and International Financial Reporting Standards (IFRSs) as adopted for use in by the European Union are set out in the Statement of Directors' Responsibilities.

Our responsibility is to audit the financial statements in accordance with relevant legal and regulatory requirements and International Standards on Auditing (UK and Ireland).

We report to you our opinion as to whether the consolidated financial statements give a true and fair view, in accordance with IFRSs as adopted for use in by the European Union. We report to you our opinion as to whether the parent company financial statements give a true and fair view, in accordance with IFRSs as adopted for use in by the European Union as applied in accordance with the provisions of the Companies Acts, 1963 to 20052009. We also report to you whether the financial statements have been properly prepared in accordance with the Companies Acts, 1963 to 20052009 and, as regards the group financial statements, Article 4 of the IAS Regulation. We also report to you whether, in our opinion: proper books of account have been kept by the parent company; whether at the balance sheet date, there exists a financial situation requiring the convening of an extraordinary general meeting of the parent company; and whether the information given in the directors' report is consistent with the financial statements. In addition, we state whether we have obtained all the information and explanations necessary for the purposes of our audit, and whether the ~~financial statements are~~ parent company balance sheet is in agreement with the books of account.

We also report to you if, in our opinion, any information specified by law or the Listing Rules of the Irish Stock Exchange regarding directors' remuneration and directors' transactions is not disclosed and, where practicable, include such information in our report.

We are required by law to ascertain whether the separate Corporate Governance Statement set out [on pages] [in describe document] [at include web address][14] contains the information required by law and report to you our opinion as to whether the information required by section 158(6D)(d) of the Companies Act, 1963 is consistent with the parent company financial statements. We are also required to report to you our opinion as to whether the information given in the Corporate Governance Statement of the main features of the internal control and risk management systems in relation to the process for preparing the group and parent company financial statements is consistent with the group and parent company financial statements. In addition, we review whether the Corporate Governance Statement reflects the parent company's compliance with the nine provisions of the [~~20082003 FRC~~ Combined Code[3]]/[UK Corporate Governance Code and the two provisions of the Irish Corporate Governance Annex] specified for our review by the Listing Rules of the Irish Stock Exchange, and we report if it does not. We are not required to consider whether the board's statements on internal control cover all risks and controls, or form an opinion on the effectiveness of the group's corporate governance procedures or its risk and control procedures.

We read the other information contained in the Annual Report and consider whether it is consistent with the audited financial statements. The other information comprises only [the Directors' Report, the Chairman's Statement, the Operating and Financial Review and the Corporate Governance Statement[15]].[12] We consider the implications for our report if we become aware of any apparent misstatements or material inconsistencies with the financial statements. Our responsibilities do not extend to any other information.

Basis of audit opinion

We conducted our audit in accordance with International Standards on Auditing (UK and Ireland) issued by the Auditing Practices Board. An audit includes examination, on a test basis, of evidence relevant to the amounts and disclosures in the financial statements. It also includes an assessment of the significant estimates and judgments made by the directors in the preparation of the financial statements, and of whether the accounting policies are appropriate to the group's and parent company's circumstances, consistently applied and adequately disclosed.

---

[14] Care should be taken to ensure that the web address is to the page on the website where the Corporate Governance Statement is located. As a website may be difficult to navigate it would be unhelpful if the web address is one, (for example that of the home page of the website), that does not lead directly to the Corporate Governance Statement.

[15] Include a reference to a Corporate Governance Statement only when the Corporate Governance Statement is included in a document containing audited financial statements.

We planned and performed our audit so as to obtain all the information and explanations which we considered necessary in order to provide us with sufficient evidence to give reasonable assurance that the financial statements are free from material misstatement, whether caused by fraud or other irregularity or error. In forming our opinion we also evaluated the overall adequacy of the presentation of information in the financial statements.

Opinion

In our opinion:

- the consolidated financial statements give a true and fair view, in accordance with IFRSs as adopted for use in by the European Union, of the state of the group's affairs as at .... and of its profit [loss] for the year then ended;

- the parent company financial statements give a true and fair view, in accordance with IFRSs as adopted for use in by the European Union as applied in accordance with the provisions of the Companies Acts, 1963 to 20052009, of the state of the parent company's affairs as at ....; and

- the financial statements have been properly prepared in accordance with the Companies Acts, 1963 to 20052009 and, as regards the group financial statements, Article 4 of the IAS Regulation.

We have obtained all the information and explanations which we consider necessary for the purposes of our audit. In our opinion proper books of account have been kept by the parent company. The parent company balance sheet is in agreement with the books of account.

In our opinion the information given in the directors' report is consistent with the financial statements. In our opinion the information required by section 158(6D)(d) of the Companies Act, 1963 [on pages] [in describe document] [at include web address][14] in the Corporate Governance Statement is consistent with the parent company financial statements and the description of the main features of the internal control and risk management systems in relation to the process for preparing the group and parent company financial statements in that statement is consistent with the group and parent company financial statements.

The net assets of the parent company, as stated in the parent company balance sheet are more than half the amount of its called-up share capital and, in our opinion, on that basis there did not exist at ... a financial situation which, under Section 40(1) of the Companies (Amendment) Act, 1983, would require the convening of an extraordinary general meeting of the parent company,

[Separate opinion in relation to IFRSs

As explained in Note X to the consolidated financial statements, the parent company and the group in addition to complying with its legal obligation to comply with IFRSs as adopted by the European Union, have also complied with the IFRSs as issued by the International Accounting Standards Board (IASB).

In our opinion the consolidated financial statements give a true and fair view, in accordance with IFRSs, of the state of the group's affairs as at........ and of the profit [loss] of the group for the year then ended.]

Registered auditors[13]   Address

Date

Appendix 3

Illustrative Auditor's Report from Bulletin 2006/1 incorporating the additional wording that is required when a Corporate Governance Statement is issued by a company outside the Directors' Report.

- Illustration based on Example 5 of Appendix 1 of Bulletin 2006/1

- Company (not being a parent) with securities admitted to trading on a regulated market[1] producing entity financial statements

- Separate Corporate Governance Statement outside the directors' report regardless where published

INDEPENDENT AUDITOR'S REPORT TO THE SHAREHOLDERS OF XYZ LIMITED

We have audited the ~~parent company~~ financial statements of (name of entity) for the year ended ... which comprise [state the primary financial statements such as the Income Statement, the Balance Sheet[10], the Cash flow Statement, the Statement of Changes in Shareholders' Equity] and the related notes[11]. These ~~parent company~~ financial statements have been prepared under the accounting policies set out therein.

~~We have reported separately on the consolidated financial statements of (name of entity) for the year ended....~~

Respective responsibilities of directors and auditors

The directors' responsibilities for preparing the Annual Report and the ~~parent company~~ financial statements in accordance with applicable law and International Financial Reporting Standards (IFRSs) as adopted ~~for use in~~ by the European Union are set out in the Statement of Directors' Responsibilities.

Our responsibility is to audit the financial statements in accordance with relevant legal and regulatory requirements and International Standards on Auditing (UK and Ireland).

We report to you our opinion as to whether the ~~parent company~~ financial statements give a true and fair view, in accordance with IFRSs as adopted ~~for use in~~ by the European Union, and have been properly prepared ~~in accordance~~ with the Companies Acts, 1963 to ~~2005~~2009. We also report to you whether, in our opinion: proper books of account have been kept by the ~~parent~~ company; whether at the balance sheet date, there exists a financial situation requiring the convening of an extraordinary general meeting of the company; and whether the information given in the directors' report is consistent with the financial statements. In addition, we state whether we have obtained all the information and explanations necessary for the purposes of our audit, and whether the ~~parent company~~ financial statements are in agreement with the books of account.

We also report to you if, in our opinion, any information specified by law or the Listing Rules of the Irish Stock Exchange regarding directors' remuneration and directors' transactions is not disclosed and, where practicable, include such information in our report.

We are required by law to ascertain whether the separate Corporate Governance Statement contains the information required by law and report to you our opinion as to whether the information given in the Corporate Governance Statement set out [on pages] [in describe document] [at include web address][14] with respect to a description of main features of the internal control and risk management systems in relation to the financial reporting process and the information required by section 158(6D)(d) of the Companies Act, 1963 is consistent with the financial statements. In addition, we review whether the Corporate Governance Statement reflects the company's compliance with the nine provisions of the [2008 Combined Code[3]]/[UK Corporate Governance Code and the two provisions of the Irish Corporate Governance Annex] specified for our review by the Listing Rules of the Irish Stock Exchange, and we report if it does not. We are not required to consider whether the board's statements on internal control cover all risks and controls, or form an opinion on the effectiveness of the company's corporate governance procedures or its risk and control procedures.

We read the other information contained in the Annual Report and consider whether it is consistent with the audited ~~parent company~~ financial statements. The other information comprises only [the Directors' Report, the Chairman's Statement, the Operating and Financial Review and the Corporate Governance Statement[15]][12].We consider the implications for our report if we become aware of any apparent misstatements or material inconsistencies with the ~~parent company~~ financial statements. Our responsibilities do not extend to any other information.

Basis of audit opinion

We conducted our audit in accordance with International Standards on Auditing (UK and Ireland) issued by the Auditing Practices Board. An audit includes examination, on a test basis, of evidence relevant to the amounts and disclosures in the ~~parent company~~ financial statements. It also includes an assessment of the significant estimates and judgments made by the directors in the preparation of the ~~parent company~~ financial statements, and of whether the accounting policies are appropriate to the company's circumstances, consistently applied and adequately disclosed.

We planned and performed our audit so as to obtain all the information and explanations which we considered necessary in order to provide us with sufficient evidence to give reasonable assurance that the ~~parent company~~ financial statements are free from material misstatement, whether caused by fraud or other irregularity or error. In forming our opinion we also evaluated the overall adequacy of the presentation of information in the ~~parent company~~ financial statements.

Opinion

In our opinion the ~~parent company~~ financial statements:

- give a true and fair view, in accordance with IFRSs as adopted ~~for use in~~ by the European Union, of the state of the company's affairs as at .... and of its profit [loss] for the year then ended; and

- the financial statements have been properly prepared in accordance with the Companies Acts, 1963 to ~~2005~~2009.

We have obtained all the information and explanations which we consider necessary for the purposes of our audit. In our opinion proper books of account have been kept by the company. The financial statements are in agreement with the books of account.

In our opinion the information given in the directors' report is consistent with the financial statements. In our opinion the description of the main features of the internal control and risk management systems in relation to the financial reporting process and the information required by section 158 (6D) (d) of the Companies Act, 1963 given in the separate Corporate Governance Statement [on pages] [in describe document] [at include web address][14] is consistent with the financial statements.

The net assets of the company, as stated in the balance sheet are more than half of the amount of its called-up share capital and, in our opinion, on that basis there did not exist at ... a financial situation which under Section 40 (1) of the Companies (Amendment) Act, 1983 would require the convening of an extraordinary general meeting of the company.

Registered auditors[13]   Address

Date

Appendix 4

Summary of the Corporate Governance Statement requirements for certain companies

The table below summarises the impact of Statutory Instrument No. 450 of 2009 (EUROPEAN COMMUNITIES (DIRECTIVE 2006/46/EC) REGULATIONS 2009) as amended by Statutory Instrument No. 83 of 2010 on annual reports for years beginning on or after 18 November 2009. Further details regarding the requirements may be found in the notes under the table below:

Issuer	Years beginning on or after 18 November 2009
Irish issuers with **equity listed** on a regulated market within the EU[1]. Irish issuers that are **closed ended funds listed** on a regulated market within the EU[1].	A Corporate Governance Statement is required **including** a description of the main features of the internal control and risk management systems in relation to the financial reporting process – for both the company and the group. No impact on the company audit report once the company Corporate Governance Statement is included directly or by cross reference in the directors' report. In the case of an issuer preparing consolidated financial statements, regulation 9 of S.I. No. 450 of 2009 requires the auditor to state in its report whether, in its opinion, the description in the Corporate Governance Statement, of the main features of the internal control and risk management systems of the parent and subsidiary undertaking in relation to the process for preparing the company and consolidated financial statements, is consistent with the consolidated financial statements for the year. This reporting obligation is the same whether the group Corporate Governance Statement is included within the directors' report, included within a document containing the audited financial statements or included within a separate document i.e. not within a document containing the audited financial statements.
Irish issuers that are **funds other than closed ended type listed** on a regulated market within the EU[1].	A Corporate Governance Statement is required including a description of the main features of the internal control and risk management systems in relation to the financial reporting process – for both the company and the group, but Section 158 6(D)(d) of Companies Act, 1963 does not apply. The audit report requirements are the same as referred to above for equity listed entities and closed ended funds.

Issuer	Years beginning on or after 18 November 2009
Irish issuers with **debt listed** on a regulated market within the EU[1] unless such companies have issued shares which are traded in a multilateral trading facility (MTF)[16] (in which case see equity listed above)	A Company Corporate Governance Statement is required to include only a description of the main features of the internal control and risk management systems in relation to the company financial reporting process and where debt securities carry voting rights the information under Section 158 6(D)(d) of the Companies Act, 1963. No impact on the company audit report once the Company Corporate Governance Statement is included directly or by cross reference in the directors' report.

Legally required contents of the Corporate Governance Statement

The following outlines the legally required disclosures for an Irish parent company with equity listed on a European Union regulated market[1] in respect of accounting periods beginning on or after 18 November 2009 by virtue of S.I. No. 450 of 2009 as amended by S.I. No. 83 of 2010, as an aide memoire for auditors:

Corporate Governance Statement for year ended [——————]

Code [Where a company is not subject to a corporate governance code and does not voluntarily apply one then this section is omitted].

(*a*) a reference to—

(i) the corporate governance code—

(I) to which the company is subject and where the relevant text is publicly available, or

(II) which the company has voluntarily decided to apply and where the relevant text is publicly available, and

(ii) all relevant information concerning corporate governance practices applied in respect of the company which are additional to any statutory requirement, and where the information on such corporate governance practices is available for inspection by the public;

(*b*) where the company departs, in accordance with any statutory provision, from a corporate governance code referred to in clause (I) or (II) of paragraph (*a*)(i)—

(i) an explanation by the company as to which parts of the corporate governance code it departs from in accordance with the statutory provision and the extent to which it departs from such code and

---

[16] The ISE has indicated that the Enterprise Securities Market (ESM) and the Global Exchange Market (GEM) are regarded as multilateral trading facilities.

(ii)   the reasons for such departure, and where the company has decided not to apply any provisions of a corporate governance code referred to in clause (I) or (II) of paragraph (a)(i), the company shall explain its reasons for doing so;

Internal control (c) a description of the main features of the internal control and risk management systems of the company [and group] in relation to the financial reporting process;

> [Such a description might include a description of the main features of internal control as well as the risk management systems for both the company and consolidated financial reporting processes over the headings of: the Control Environment; Risk Assessment; Information and Communication; Control Activities; and Monitoring]

Secretarial matters (d) where the company is subject to the European Communities (Takeover Bids (Directive 2004/25/EC)) Regulations 2006 (S.I. No. 255 of 2006);

(i)   to the extent not already required to be disclosed pursuant to section 67 or 91 of the Companies Act 1990, in the case of each person with a significant direct or indirect holding of securities in the company, such details as are known to the company of –

   (i)   the identity of the person,

   (ii) the size of the holding, and

   (iii) the nature of the holding

(ii) in the case of each person who holds securities carrying special rights with regard to control of the company –

   (i)   the identity of the person, and

   (ii) the nature of the rights

(iii) rights, including in particular –

   (i)   limitations on voting rights of holders of a given percentage or number of votes,

   (ii) deadlines for exercising voting rights, and

   (iii) arrangements by which, with the company's cooperation, financial rights carried by securities are held by a person other than the holder of the securities

(iv) any rules which the company has in force concerning –

   (i)   appointment and replacement of directors of the company, or

   (ii) amendment of the company's articles of association,

(v)   the powers of the company's directors, including in particular any powers in relation to the issuing or buying back by the company of its shares

(e) a description of the operation of the shareholder meeting, the key powers of the shareholder meeting, shareholders' rights and the exercise of such rights;

(f) the composition and operation of the board of directors and the committees of the board of directors with administrative, management and supervisory functions.

BULLETIN 1(I)

COMPENDIUM OF ILLUSTRATIVE AUDITOR'S REPORTS ON IRISH FINANCIAL STATEMENTS

For Audits of Irish Financial Statements for Periods Commencing On or After 1 October 2012

CONTENTS

**FINANCIAL
REPORTING COUNCIL**

Introduction

1. This Bulletin contains a compendium of illustrative auditor's reports applicable to Irish financial statements for periods commencing on or after 1 October 2012. The auditor's reports support and illustrate the requirements of ISAs (UK and Ireland) 700 *"The auditor's report on financial statements"*, 705 *"Modifications to the opinion in the independent auditor's report"* and 706 *"Emphasis of matter paragraphs and other matter paragraphs in the independent auditor's report"*[1]. They also support the requirements of the law and regulations applicable to the particular type of entity to which the illustration applies.

2. Whilst the majority of this Bulletin deals with companies, there are other entities for which a statutory audit obligation exists and, accordingly, Appendix 3 contains a number of examples of auditor's reports pertaining to such entities.

3. This Bulletin also states the legal requirements involved in preparing an auditor's report pursuant to Section 193 of the Companies Act 1990 ('1990 Act') to accompany the statutory financial statements to be laid in front of the members at the annual general meeting of a company incorporated under the Irish Companies Acts 1963 to 2012 ('Companies Acts').

Legislation governing the statutory auditor's report

4. In preparing an auditor's report pursuant to Section 193 of the 1990 Act to accompany the statutory financial statements to be laid in front of the members of an Irish company at the annual general meeting the auditor, among other things, will have regard to:

    *   Section 193 of the 1990 Act: Auditors' report and right of access to books and of attendance and audience at general meetings;

    *   Various pieces of legislation in relation to the consideration by auditors of consistency of directors' report with company's financial statements (see paragraph 45);

    *   Section 191(8) of the Companies Act 1963 ('1963 Act'): Particulars of directors' salaries and payments to be given in financial statements;

    *   Section 46 of the1990 Act: Duty of auditors of company in breach of Section 41 or 43;

    *   If publicly traded, Regulation 9 of S.I. No. 450 of 2009 as amended by S.I. No. 83 of 2010 ('S.I. No. 450 as amended');

---

[1] The relevant versions of ISAs (UK and Ireland) 700, 705 and 706 are those that are effective for audits of financial statements for periods commencing on or after 1 October 2012

- Other relevant legislation, FRC Practice Notes and Bulletins especially in the case of regulated entities.

The Requirements of Section 193 of the 1990 Act: Auditors' report and right of access to books and of attendance and audience at general meetings

5. Section 193(1) of the 1990 Act requires that :

> The auditors of a company shall make a report to the members on the individual accounts examined by them, and on every balance sheet and profit and loss account or income statement, and all group accounts, laid before the company in general meeting during their tenure of office.

6. Accordingly, auditors of a company have a duty under the Companies Acts to make a report to the members of the company on the financial statements examined by them. Specifically, they are required to report on every balance sheet and profit and loss account and on all group financial statements laid before the company in general meeting during their tenure of office. The expression 'financial statements' is used in this document to denote the annual accounts, prepared by directors to meet their obligations under Section 148 (company accounts) and/or Section 150 (group accounts) of the 1963 Act.

Requirement for auditor's report to be read out at AGM

7. Section 193(2) of the 1990 Act requires that :

> The auditors' report shall be read at the annual general meeting of the company and shall be open to inspection by any member.

8. It is noteworthy that while law requires the auditor's report to be read at the AGM it does not specifically impose this obligation on the auditor – it would appear that any person present at the meeting, e.g. the chairman, may read the report at the meeting.

Access to books and records and provision of information and explanations

9. Section 193(3) of the 1990 Act requires that :

> Every auditor of a company shall have a right of access at all reasonable times to the books, accounts and vouchers of the company and shall be entitled to require from the officers (within the meaning of section 197 (5)) of the company such information and explanations that are within their knowledge or can be procured by them as he thinks necessary for the performance of the duties of the auditors.

10. The above refers to the obligation on the auditor to report whether or not they consider that they have received all the information and explanations they consider necessary for the audit. Section 197 of the 1990 Act provides as follows:

Penalty for false statements to auditors.

(1) An officer of a company who knowingly or recklessly makes a statement to which this section applies that is misleading, false or deceptive in a material particular shall be guilty of an offence.

(2) This section applies to any statement made to the auditors of a company (whether orally or in writing) which conveys, or purports to convey, any information or explanation which they require under the Companies Acts, or are entitled so to require, as auditors of the company.

(3) An officer of a company who fails to provide to the auditors of the company or of the holding company of the company, within two days of the making of the relevant requirement, any information or explanations that the auditors require as auditors of the company or of the holding company of the company and that is within the knowledge of or can be procured by the officer shall be guilty of an offence.

(4) In a prosecution for an offence under this section, it shall be a defence for the defendant to show that it was not reasonably possible for him to comply with the requirement under subsection (3) to which the offence relates within the time specified in that subsection but that he complied therewith as soon as was reasonably possible after the expiration of such time.

(5) In this section "officer", in relation to a company, includes any employee of the company.

---

11. As breaches of Section 197 of the 1990 Act are an indictable offence, auditors have regard to Bulletin 2007/2 issued by the Auditing Practices Board (APB) concerning the auditors' duty to report to the Office of the Director of Corporate Enforcement (ODCE) in circumstances where a reporting obligation may arise.

Identification of accounting and auditing standards

12. Section 193(4) of the 1990 Act requires that :

The auditors' report shall include –

(a) an introduction identifying the individual accounts, and where appropriate, the group accounts, that are the subject of the audit and the financial reporting framework that has been applied in their preparation, and

---

> (b)   a description of the scope of the audit identifying the auditing standards in accordance with which the audit was conducted.

The "introduction" to the auditor's report

13.   For clarity the auditor will use language in the introduction that is consistent with the description of the financial statements used by the directors in preparing the financial statements subject to audit. There are a number of possible financial reporting frameworks that may be used in the preparation of financial statements. Where the "Companies Acts" framework has been adopted the auditor identifies the precise standards being used. Generally, the Companies Acts framework will be Irish law and accounting standards issued by the Financial Reporting Council and promulgated by the Institute of Chartered Accountants in Ireland (Generally Accepted Accounting Practice in Ireland). For companies permitted to adopt an alternative body of accounting standards the reference will be to Irish law and the body of accounting standards applied.

Description of the "scope of the audit"

14.   Paragraph 16 of ISA (UK and Ireland) 700 requires:

The auditor's report shall either

a)   Cross refer to the applicable version of a "Statement of the Scope of an Audit" that is maintained on the FRC's website; or

b)   Cross refer to a "Statement of the Scope of an Audit" that is included elsewhere within the Annual Report; or

c)   Include the following description of the scope of an audit:

"An audit involves obtaining evidence about the amounts and disclosures in the financial statements sufficient to give reasonable assurance that the financial statements are free from material misstatement, whether caused by fraud or error. This includes an assessment of: whether the accounting policies are appropriate to the [describe nature of entity] circumstances and have been consistently applied and adequately disclosed; the reasonableness of significant accounting estimates made by [describe those charged with governance]; and the overall presentation of the financial statements. In addition, we read all the financial and non-financial information in the [describe the annual report] to identify material inconsistencies with the audited financial statements. If we become aware of any apparent material misstatements or inconsistencies we consider the implications for our report."

15.   In the illustrative auditor's reports in this Bulletin these alternatives are shown by means of two text boxes. The alternative shown by the first text box is the wording that is used when the auditor's report cross refers to a Statement of the Scope of an Audit maintained on the FRC's website, or included elsewhere within the Annual Report. The

alternative shown by the second text box is the wording that must be used if the description of the Scope of an Audit is included within the auditor's report.

16. Effective for audits of financial statements for periods commencing on or after 1 October 2012 the Statement of the Scope of an Audit can be found on the FRC website at www.frc.org/audit-scope-ireland . A single statement can be used with respect to the auditor's reports of all Irish entities. The text of this statement is included in Appendix 10.

Reference to proper preparation of financial statements

17. Section 193(4A) of the 1990 Act provides as follows:

(4A)

(a) Except in the case of a company that has taken advantage of any of the provisions of Part III of the Sixth Schedule to the Principal Act, the auditors' report shall state clearly whether in the auditors' opinion the annual accounts have been properly prepared in accordance with the requirements of the Companies Acts (and, where applicable, Article 4 of the IAS Regulation).

(b) In the case of a company that has taken advantage of any of the provisions of Part III of the Sixth Schedule to the Principal Act, the auditors' report shall state whether, in their opinion, the annual accounts and, where it is a holding company submitting group accounts, the group accounts have been properly prepared in accordance with the Companies Acts (and, where applicable, Article 4 of the IAS Regulation) and give a true and fair view of the matters referred to in subsection (4B)(e)(i) and (ii) and, where appropriate, subsection (4B)(e)(iii) subject to the non-disclosure of any matters (to be indicated in the report) which by virtue of the said Part III are not required to be disclosed.

---

18. Accordingly, the opinion section of the auditor's report refers to whether the financial statements subject to audit have been properly prepared in accordance with the Companies Acts. In this context, the expression 'properly prepared' includes compliance with the requirements of the Companies Acts with respect to the form and content of the balance sheet and profit and loss account and any additional information to be provided by way of notes to the financial statements, subject to an overriding requirement that the financial statements should give a true and fair view.

19. Article 4 of the IAS Regulation provides as follows:

Regulation (EC) 1606/2002 The IAS Regulation

Article 4 Consolidated accounts of publicly traded companies
For each financial year starting on or after 1 January 2005, companies governed by the law of a Member State shall prepare their consolidated accounts in

---

> conformity with the international accounting standards adopted in accordance
> with the procedure laid down in Article 6(2) if, at their balance sheet date, their
> securities are admitted to trading on a regulated market of any Member State
> within the meaning of Article 1(13) of Council Directive 93/22/EEC of 10 May 1993
> on investment services in the securities field [1].
>
> (1) OJ L 141, 11.6.1993, p. 27. Directive as last amended by European Parliament
> and Council Directive 2000/64/EC (OJ L 290, 17.11.2000, p. 27).

20. In relation to Irish companies with a listing on a regulated market in any Member State
the auditor therefore makes reference to properly prepared in accordance with IAS 4 of
the IAS Regulation in relation to the consolidated financial statements only. For a
parent company with an Irish Stock Exchange listing this will only apply where
consolidated financial statements are prepared and either its debt or equity is listed on
the Main Securities Market of the Irish Stock Exchange.

Additional statements and opinions

21. Section 193(4B) of the 1990 Act imposes the following reporting obligations on the
auditor:

> (4B) The auditors' report shall also state –
>
> (a) whether they have obtained all the information and explanations which, to
> the best of their knowledge and belief, are necessary for the purposes of
> their audit,
>
> (b) whether, in their opinion, proper books of account have been kept by the
> company,
>
> (c) whether, in their opinion, proper returns adequate for their audit have been
> received from branches of the company not visited by them, and
>
> (d) whether the company's balance sheet and (unless it is framed as a
> consolidated profit and loss account) profit and loss account are in
> agreement with the books of account and returns.

Obtaining all necessary information and explanations

22. The auditor must state whether they have obtained all the information and
explanations necessary for the purpose of their audit. In particular circumstances,
for example where there has been a limitation of the scope of the audit giving rise to a
modification of the auditor's report, the auditor should consider whether they can
make that statement.

Proper books of account

23. The auditor must also opine whether proper books of account have been kept by the company. The auditor forms this opinion having regard to the definition of proper books set out in Section 202 of the 1990 Act. Where the auditor is of the opinion that, other than for matters that are minor or otherwise immaterial in nature, proper books have not been kept, in addition to modifying the proper books opinion the auditor will also consider their other consequential reporting duties:

- duty under ISA (UK and Ireland) 250A *Consideration of laws and regulations in an audit of financial statements* to report to those charged with governance;

- as breaches of Section 202 are an indictable offence, the auditor has regard to Bulletin 2007/2 issued by the APB concerning the auditors' duty to report to the ODCE in circumstances where a reporting obligation may arise;

- as required by Section 194 of the 1990 Act:

  ○ serve the written notice on the company as soon as may be; and

  ○ within seven days notify the CRO on form H4 unless the directors have taken the necessary steps to ensure that proper book are kept as required by Section 202 of the 1990 Act.

24. Where the failure to keep proper books reflects non-compliance with the Taxes Consolidation Act 1997 and/or the Criminal Justice Act 2011 and/or the Criminal Justice (Theft and Fraud Offences) Act 2001 and/or anti money laundering legislation the auditor also considers their reporting duties to the Gardaí and/or Revenue Commissioners.

The true and fair reporting requirement

25. Section 193(4C)(i) of the 1990 Act sets out the auditors obligation in relation to true and fair:

(4C) The auditor's report shall state, in particular –

(i) whether the annual accounts give a true and fair view in accordance with the relevant financial reporting framework–

(I) in the case of an individual balance sheet, of the state of affairs of the company as at the end of the financial year,

(II) in the case of an individual profit and loss account, of the profit or loss of the company for the financial year,

(III) in the case of group accounts, of the state of affairs as at the end of the financial year and of the profit or loss for the financial year of the undertakings included in the consolidation as a whole, so far as concerns members of the company...

26. Accounting standards set out in Financial Reporting Standards ('FRSs') and in International Financial Reporting Standards ('IFRSs') as adopted by the European Union require, in certain circumstances, further 'primary statements' in addition to the balance sheet and profit and loss account. These further primary statements are normally necessary in order that the annual financial statements give a true and fair view. The Companies Acts do not require the auditors to refer to those 'primary statements' in their report.

Reporting on a "financial situation"

27. Section 193(4C)(ii) of the 1990 Act sets out the auditor's obligation in relation to reporting on a financial situation:

> whether, in their opinion, there existed at the balance sheet date a financial situation which under section 40(1) of the Companies (Amendment) Act 1983 would require the convening of an extraordinary general meeting of the company.

28. Section 40 of the Companies (Amendment) Act 1983 ('1983 Act') refers to the financial situation where net assets are 'half or less of the company's called-up share capital' which in certain circumstances requires the convening of an extraordinary general meeting ('EGM'). In the case of a group, the Section 40 opinion is formed by reference to the parent company balance sheet. Matters to be considered by the auditor include:

a) the auditor bases the opinion, as to whether a financial situation exists, solely on the amounts of the assets (whether at cost or valuation) and liabilities included in the balance sheet (or statement of financial position) on which the auditor is reporting. Reporting on the financial situation shown in the balance sheet means that the auditor ignores disclosure of the market values of property and investments that is made merely by way of note to the balance sheet. Furthermore, non-adjusting post-balance sheet events as defined by FRS 21 or IAS 10 *Events after the balance sheet date* are not taken into account;

b) Section 40 of the 1983 Act does not apply to situations which existed and were known by the directors to exist before 13 October 1983, the day on which the 1983 Act came into force. In such situations, there is no obligation on the auditor to report as to whether or not a financial situation existed;

c) even though the balance sheet shows that a financial situation exists, there may be additional circumstances which avoid the need to convene an EGM. The auditor's responsibility is confined to reporting on the existence of the financial situation regardless of whether an EGM has been or will be held. The auditor may but need not comment in the auditor's report on such additional circumstances.

29. Where the auditor has added an "emphasis of matter" paragraph or an "other matter" paragraph (as defined in ISA (UK and Ireland) 706) to an unqualified auditor's report there is no change to the approach to the separate 'financial situation' opinion and it remains based on the financial information as shown by the balance sheet.

30. Where the auditor cannot report without modification to the effect that in their opinion the financial statements give a true and fair view, this may have an impact on the 'financial situation' opinion since that further opinion is based on the amounts shown by the balance sheet. The impact of auditor's report modifications in this context may be summarised as follows:

a) Where the auditor has modified their opinion because of the effect of a limitation on the scope of their work, the auditor considers whether the adjustments which might be required, had there been no limitation of scope, could result in the net assets of the company altering from more than half of the called-up share capital to half or less (or vice versa). Where the adjustments which might be required could result in the financial situation being affected in this way, the auditor appropriately modifies the separate 'financial situation' opinion.

b) Where the auditor has disclaimed an opinion because the possible effect of a limitation on the scope of their work is so material or pervasive that the auditor has not been able to obtain sufficient evidence to support, and accordingly is unable to express an opinion on the financial statements, it will be necessary for the auditor to give a disclaimer of opinion in relation to the separate 'financial situation'.

c) Finally, where the auditor has qualified their audit opinion due to disagreement affecting balance sheet amounts, the auditor expresses the 'financial situation' opinion based on the assumption that the balance sheet is adjusted for the amounts in disagreement.

31. Example 3 in Appendix 1 sets out the text of an auditor's report of a company limited by guarantee not having a share capital and not trading for gain. Readers will note that no reference is made to Section 40 of the 1983 Act.

Auditor's report modifications

32. Sections 193(4D) and (4E) of the 1990 Act state:

(4D) The auditors' report –

(a) [deleted]

(b) shall, in relation to each matter referred to in subsections (4A), (4B) and (4C) contain a statement or opinion, as the case may be, which shall be either –

(i) unqualified, or

(ii) qualified,

and

> (c) shall include a reference to any matters to which the auditors wish to draw attention by way of emphasis without qualifying the report.
>
> (4E) For the purposes of subsection (4D)(b)(ii), a statement or opinion may be qualified, including to the extent of an adverse opinion or a disclaimer of opinion, where there is a disagreement or limitation in scope of work.

33. Detailed guidance on the modification of the auditor's report and the use of emphasis of matter and other matter paragraphs may be found in International Standard on Auditing (UK and Ireland) 705 *Modifications to the opinion in the independent auditor's report* and International Standard on Auditing (UK and Ireland) 706 *Emphasis of matter paragraphs and other matter paragraphs in the independent auditor's report*.

34. The appendices to this Bulletin include example auditor's reports illustrating modified opinions (Appendices 5-8) and emphasis of matter paragraphs (Appendix 4).

35. Section 193(4F) of the 1990 Act states:

> (4F) Where the individual accounts of a parent undertaking are attached to the group accounts, the auditors' report on the group accounts may be combined with the report on the individual accounts.

36. Various example reports in this compendium illustrate the wording of the auditor's report where the annual report presents both the group and company financial statements (see Appendix 2). Please refer to paragraph 63 for a discussion of auditor's reports where the group and parent company financial statements are presented separately.

37. Section 193(4G) of the 1990 Act states:

> (4G) (a) The auditors' report shall state the name of the auditor and be signed, as provided for in paragraph (b), and dated.
>
> (b) Where the auditor is—
>
> (i) a statutory auditor (within the meaning of the European Communities (Statutory Audits) (Directive 2006/43/EC) Regulations 2010, the report shall be signed by that person, or
>
> (ii) a statutory audit firm (within the meaning of the foregoing Regulations),
> the report shall be signed by—
>
> (I) the statutory auditor (or, where more than one, each statutory auditor) designated by the statutory audit firm for the particular

> audit engagement as being primarily responsible for carrying out the statutory audit on behalf of the audit firm, or
>
> (II) in the case of a group audit, at least the statutory auditor (or, where more than one, each statutory auditor) designated by the statutory audit firm as being primarily responsible for carrying out the statutory audit at the level of the group, in his or her own name, for and on behalf of, the audit firm.

Dating of the auditor's report

38. The Companies Acts require that both the balance sheet and the profit and loss account are signed by two of the directors of the company on behalf of the board[2]. Paragraph 24 of ISA (UK and Ireland) 700 (Revised October 2012) *The auditor's report on financial statements* states that the auditor "shall not sign, and hence date, the report earlier than the date on which all other information contained in a report of which the audited financial statements form a part have been approved by those charged with governance and the auditor has considered all necessary available evidence." Please refer also to ISA (UK and Ireland) 560 *Subsequent events* for detailed requirements and guidance in this area.

39. Section 193(5) of the 1990 Act states:

> (5) The auditors of a company shall be entitled to attend any general meeting of the company and to receive all notices of, and other communications relating to, any general meeting which any member of the company is entitled to receive and to be heard at any general meeting which they attend on any part of the business of the meeting which concerns them as auditors.

40. This section gives the auditor a right to receive timely notice of general meetings. The auditor is also given the right but not an obligation to attend these meetings.

41. Section 193(6) of the 1990 Act states:

> (6) A person who is appointed as auditor of a company or as a public auditor shall be under a general duty to carry out such audit with professional integrity.

42. Compliance with the APB's Ethical Standards for Auditors, International Standard on Quality Control (UK and Ireland), International Standards on Auditing (UK and Ireland)

---

[2] Where the company is a bank, section 156 of the Companies Act 1963 provides that the balance sheet and profit and loss account (or income statement) must be signed by the company secretary and where there are more than three directors by at least three of the directors.

and the rules of the recognised professional body of which the auditor is a member, is required to carry out an audit with professional integrity.

43. Section 193(7) of the 1990 Act states:

> (7) Any reference in the Principal Act to section 163 of or the Seventh Schedule to that Act shall be construed as references to this section.

44. This section updates the references in the 1963 Act to point to Section 193 of the 1990 Act as far as concerns the statutory auditor's report.

Other Information required by the Companies Acts

Consistency of directors' report with financial statements

45. As indicated in the table below company law requires the auditor to state whether, in the auditor's opinion, the information given in the report of the directors relating to the financial year concerned is consistent with the financial statements prepared by the company for that year. A similar obligation for group financial statements is imposed. The auditor is not required to form an opinion on the directors' report itself.

Type	Individual Accounts	Group Accounts
Companies other than insurance undertakings and credit institutions	Section 15 Companies (Amendment) Act 1986	Regulation 38 European Communities (Companies: Group Accounts) Regulations, 1992
Insurance Undertakings	Section 15 Companies (Amendment) Act 1986	Regulation 16 European Communities (Insurance Undertakings: Accounts) Regulations 1996
Credit Institutions	Regulation 13(2) European Communities (Credit Institutions: Accounts) Regulations 1992	Regulation 13(2) European Communities (Credit Institutions: Accounts) Regulations 1992

46. The auditor has no statutory responsibilities in respect of items in the directors' report which, in the auditor's opinion, are misleading but not inconsistent with the financial statements. However, if the auditor considers that the other information is misleading and the auditor is unable to resolve the matter with management and those charged with governance, the auditor considers the implication for the auditor's report and what further actions may be appropriate. ISA (UK and Ireland) 720B *The auditor's statutory reporting responsibility in relation to directors' reports* also addresses this area.

Other requirements of the Companies Acts

47. The content of the auditor's report may also be affected by other requirements of the Companies Acts giving the auditor additional reporting responsibilities. In the circumstances specified in (i) and (ii) below the auditor must set out the required particulars in their report, so far as they are reasonably able to do so.

(i) Section 191(8) of the 1963 Act

If the financial statements do not comply with the requirements of Section 191 which deals with 'Particulars of directors' salaries and payments to be given in accounts'.

(ii) Section 46 of the 1990 Act

If the financial statements do not comply with the requirements of Section 41 or 43 which deal with particulars of substantial contracts, loans and other transactions with directors, together with particulars of related amounts outstanding at the balance sheet date. As breaches of Sections 41 or 43 are indictable offences, the auditor has regard to Bulletin 2007/2 issued by the APB concerning the auditors' duty to report to the ODCE in circumstances where a reporting obligation may arise.

(iii) Regulation 9 of S.I. No. 450 as amended

Bulletin 2011/01 *"Developments in Corporate Governance affecting the responsibilities of auditors of companies incorporated in Ireland"* issued by the APB gives guidance to auditors of companies listed on an EU regulated market with respect to this reporting duty. Examples 6-8 and 14-18 in this compendium set out example auditor's reports meeting this reporting requirement in the most commonly encountered circumstances.

Classifications of companies

Publicly traded and non-publicly traded

48. This Bulletin distinguishes between:

    a) "publicly traded companies" – defined as "those whose securities are admitted to trading on a regulated market in any Member State in the European Economic Area" (EEA); and

    b) "non-publicly traded companies" – defined as "those who do not have any securities that are admitted to trading on a regulated market in any Member State in the European Economic Area" (EEA).

49. Under Article 4 of the IAS Regulation[3], publicly traded companies governed by the law of a Member State are required to prepare their consolidated financial statements on the basis of accounting standards issued by the International Accounting Standards

---

[3] Regulation (EC) No. 1606/2002 of the European Parliament and of the Council of 19 July 2002 on the application of international accounting standards.

Board (IASB) that are adopted by the EU[4]. Such financial statements are referred to as "IFRS Group accounts" in the Companies Acts whereas in the auditor's reports in this Bulletin this framework is referred to as "IFRSs as adopted by the European Union"[5]

50. Article 4 does not apply to a publicly traded company that is not required to prepare consolidated financial statements.

51. In Ireland (as permitted under Article 5 of the IAS Regulation) the use of 'IFRS accounts' has been extended so that:

a) Publicly traded companies are permitted to use IFRSs as adopted by the European Union in their individual financial statements; and

b) Non publicly traded companies are permitted to use IFRSs as adopted by the European Union in both their individual and consolidated financial statements.

52. Charities are not permitted to use IFRSs[6]. In addition charities do not fall within the ambit of Article 4 of the IAS Regulation as non-profit making bodies are specifically excluded.

53. For the purposes of the auditor's report a further implication of being a publicly traded company is that such companies are required to include a Corporate Governance Statement in their annual report. The requirements relating to the content of the Corporate Governance Statement are set out in S.I. No. 450 as amended.

54. If the Corporate Governance Statement is not included in the directors' report there are specific reporting responsibilities imposed on the auditor. Guidance on the auditor's responsibilities with respect to the Corporate Governance Statement is set out more fully in Bulletin 2011/1 issued by the APB. Appendices 1 and 2 to the Bulletin contain illustrative examples of how the auditor is required to report in this circumstance.

Listed companies

55. Chapter 6 of the Listing Rules of the Irish Stock Exchange applies to a company that has a listing of equity shares on the Main Securities Market (MSM). There are implications for the auditor's report of having a listing on the MSM. They arise from the requirements in Listing Rule 6.8.6 for a MSM listed company to ensure that its auditor reviews:

- The directors' going concern statement (required by LR 6.8.3 (3)); and

---

[4] Refer to Section 150 of the 1963 Act.
[5] For companies that apply the requirements of Irish company law and the FRC's accounting standards the financial reporting framework is described as Irish Generally Accepted Accounting Practice (Irish GAAP).
[6] Refer to Section 148(3) of the 1963 Act.

- The parts of the directors' statement relating to the company's compliance with the UK Corporate Governance Code (required by LR 6.8.3 (7))[7]; and the Irish Annex (LR 6.8.3 (9))[6].

56. Listing Rule 6.8.7 requires a listed company to ensure that the auditor also reviews the following disclosures:

- amount of each element in the remuneration package & information on share options (required by LR 6.8.5 (2));

- details of long term incentive schemes for directors (required by LR 6.8.5 (3), (4) and (5));

- defined contribution schemes (required by LR 6.8.5 (11)); and

- defined benefit schemes (required by LR 6.8.5 (12)).

57. Listing Rule 6.8.8 requires that if, in the opinion of the auditors the listed company has not complied with any of the requirements set out in LR 6.8.7, the listed company must ensure that the auditor's report includes, to the extent possible, a statement giving details of the non-compliance.

58. The Listing Rules are silent as to whether the auditor should report on the auditor's review of the above matters. However, the FRC is of the view that the auditor should describe its responsibilities within the auditor's report and incorporate a suitable conclusion in respect of their review. Paragraph 22 of ISA (UK and Ireland) 700 (Revised October 2012) sets out this requirement and examples 6, 7, 14, 15 and 16 illustrate it.

Companies admitted to trading on other markets

59. The definition of publicly traded company exclude those with a listing on an exchange-regulated market such as both the Irish Stock Exchange's Enterprise Security Market (ESM) and the London Stock Exchange's international market for smaller growing companies (AIM). However, under both the rules of the ESM and the AIM, a company that is admitted to trading on the ESM or on the AIM market is required to prepare its financial statements in accordance with IFRSs as adopted by the European Union. Examples 5 and 13 are applicable to companies admitted to trading on ESM and/or AIM.

Treatment of the classifications in the illustrative examples

60. If not otherwise apparent from the title of a particular illustration in the appendices, the rubric to an example makes clear which of the above classifications apply to the illustration.

---

[7] These statements are different from the requirement for a corporate governance statement in S.I. No. 450 as amended described in paragraph 47(iii).

Alternative presentation options of the financial statements of a group

61. As explained in paragraph 51 above, group and parent company financial statements may be prepared in accordance with different financial reporting frameworks (for example IFRSs as adopted by the EU used for the group financial statements and Irish GAAP used for the parent company financial statements).

62. Where the financial statements of the group and the parent company are presented in accordance with different financial reporting frameworks the financial statements might be presented separately within the Annual Report and in such circumstances separate auditor's reports might be provided.

63. The examples in Appendix 2 of this Bulletin illustrate auditor's reports where the report on the group financial statements and the report on the parent company financial statements are presented as a single auditor's report. Where the group and parent company financial statements are presented separately, the auditor might provide separate auditor's reports on the group financial statements and on the parent company financial statements. Where this is the case:

   - The auditor refers explicitly to the *'parent company'* or *'group'* as appropriate in naming the primary financial statements, or generally referring to those financial statements, throughout the respective reports.

   - In the opinion section of the reports, the auditor refers to the *"true and fair view of the **company's** affairs as at ..."* regarding the parent company financial statements and the *"true and fair view of the **group's** affairs as at ..."* regarding the group financial statements.

   - The legal requirement to give an opinion on whether the company balance sheet agrees with the books of account, and on whether a 'financial situation' in accordance with Section 40 of the Companies Act 1983 exists, applies to the parent company alone and, accordingly, these opinions are not included in the separate auditor's report on the group financial statements.

   - Under 'other matters' (see also paragraph 71), the auditor includes the following text in the auditor's report on the parent company financial statements and the group financial statements respectively:

Other matter *(for inclusion in the auditor's report on the parent company financial statements)*

We have reported separately on the group financial statements of (name of company) for the year ended ... [That report includes an emphasis of matter] [The opinion in that report is (qualified)/(an adverse opinion)/(a disclaimer of opinion)].

> **Other matter** *(for inclusion in the auditor's report on the group financial statements)*
>
> We have reported separately on the parent company financial statements of (name of company) for the year ended ... [That report includes an emphasis of matter] [The opinion in that report is (qualified)/(an adverse opinion)/(a disclaimer of opinion)].

Omitting the parent company profit and loss account

64. Section 148(8) of the 1963 Act allows a company that prepares group financial statements to omit the parent company's profit and loss account from the company's annual financial statements provided that:

    a) the notes to the parent company's balance sheet show the company's profit or loss for the financial year determined in accordance with Section 149 or Section 149A of the 1963 Act as appropriate; and

    b) it is disclosed in the company's annual financial statements that the exemption applies.

65. Section 7(1A) of the Companies (Amendment) Act 1986 ('1986 Act') extends a similar exemption in respect of filing the parent company profit and loss account. Where advantage has been taken of the exemptions under Section 148(8) of the 1963 Act and Section 7(1A) of the 1986 Act and the parent company financial statements have been prepared in accordance with "IFRSs as adopted by the European Union" the financial reporting framework is described in the auditor's report as

> have been properly prepared in accordance with IFRSs as adopted by the European Union as applied in accordance with the provisions of the Companies Acts 1963 to 2012.

66. Example 11 illustrates an auditor's report where the exemptions have been taken in respect of the parent company's own profit and loss account. Example 12 illustrates an auditor's report where the exemptions have not been taken.

Opinion in respect of an additional financial reporting framework

67. The financial statements of some companies may comply with two financial reporting frameworks (for example IFRSs as adopted by the European Union and IFRSs as issued by the IASB) and those charged with governance may engage the auditor to express an opinion in respect of both frameworks.

68. ISA (UK and Ireland) 700 (Revised) requires that the second opinion should be clearly separated from the first opinion on the financial statements by use of an appropriate heading. This is illustrated in examples 7 and 14-18.[8]

Emphasis of matter paragraphs

69. An emphasis of matter paragraph refers to a matter that is appropriately presented or disclosed in the financial statements that, in the auditor's judgment, is of such importance that it is fundamental to a user's understanding of the financial statements. When the auditor includes an emphasis of matter paragraph ISA (UK and Ireland) 706 requires the auditor to indicate in its report that the auditor's opinion is not modified in respect of the matter emphasised.

70. Example of emphasis of matter paragraphs are set out in Appendix 4. These examples have been drafted in the context of auditor's reports on the financial statements of a company. However, the examples can be tailored for use in the auditor's reports of all entities.

Other matter paragraphs

71. A matter other than those presented or disclosed in the financial statements that, in the auditor's judgment, is relevant to a user's understanding of the audit, the auditor's responsibilities or the auditor's report, is referred to in the other matter paragraph.

Regulated entities

72. Examples 12 to 16 in Appendix 2, which provide examples of auditor's reports for publicly traded and non-publicly traded parent companies preparing financial statements in accordance with both Irish GAAP and IFRSs as adopted by the European Union, are appropriate for use in relation to the financial statements of banking and insurance parent companies. They should, therefore, be used rather than the example auditor's reports in Practice Notes – PN 19(I) (revised) and PN 20(I) (revised) issued by the APB. Similarly, example 20 in Appendix 3 supersedes the example auditor's report in Practice Note 27(I) on the audit of credit unions in Ireland and example 23 updates the example auditor's report in Practice Note 15(I) on the audit of occupational pension schemes in Ireland.

73. The abovementioned Practice Notes contain, however, illustrative examples of reports by auditors on other matters that arise from the requirements of regulations not subject to the reporting requirements of ISAs (UK and Ireland).

---

[8] The wording used in these examples is illustrative to reflect the requirement of the Securities and Exchange Commission of the USA whose Final Rule "Acceptance From Foreign Private Issuers of Financial Statements Prepared in Accordance With International Financial Reporting Standards Without Reconciliation to US GAAP" (4 January 2008) states "...the independent auditor must opine in its report on whether those financial statements comply with IFRS as issued by the IASB. ...the auditor's report can include this language in addition to any opinion relating to compliance with standards required by the home country".

Modifying the auditor's opinion on the financial statements

74. An auditor's opinion on financial statements is considered to be modified in the following situations.

   a) Qualified opinion arising from either a disagreement or a scope limitation (Illustrative examples set out in Appendix 5);

   b) Adverse opinion (Illustrative examples set out in Appendix 6); and

   c) Disclaimer of opinion (Illustrative examples set out in Appendix 7).

Modifying the auditor's opinion on the directors' report

75. Section 13 of the 1986 Act requires the auditor to state in its report on the company's annual financial statements whether in its opinion the information given in the directors' report for the financial year for which the financial statements are prepared is consistent with those financial statements. The example report in Appendix 8 illustrates a modified opinion on the consistency of the directors' report with the annual financial statements.

Illustrative directors' responsibilities statement

76. Appendix 9 contains an illustrative example of a Directors' Responsibilities Statement for a non-publicly traded company preparing its parent company financial statements under Irish GAAP. Illustrative examples of Directors' Responsibilities Statements for publicly traded companies are not provided as the directors' responsibilities will vary dependent on the rules of the market on which a company's securities are admitted to trading.

Appendix 1

Company does not prepare group financial statements

1. Non-publicly traded company incorporated in Ireland preparing financial statements under the FRSSE

2. Non-publicly traded company incorporated in Ireland preparing financial statements under Irish GAAP

3. Non-publicly traded company limited by guarantee incorporated in Ireland preparing financial statements under Irish GAAP

4. Company incorporated in Ireland with a listing on the Global Exchange Market preparing financial statements under Irish GAAP

5. Company incorporated in Ireland preparing financial statements under IFRSs as adopted by the European Union

6. Publicly traded company incorporated in Ireland preparing financial statements under Irish GAAP

7. Publicly traded company incorporated in Ireland preparing financial statements under IFRSs as adopted by the European Union

8. Publicly traded company with listed debt incorporated in Ireland preparing financial statements under Irish GAAP

9. Non-publicly traded collective investment fund incorporated in of Ireland preparing financial statements under Irish GAAP

10. Publicly traded company with collective investment funds incorporated in Ireland preparing financial statements under Irish GAAP

Example 1 – Non-publicly traded company incorporated in Ireland preparing financial statements under the FRSSE

- *Company is not a listed company.*

- *Company qualifies as a small company and chooses to prepare its financial statements in accordance with the FRSSE.*

- *Company does not prepare group financial statements.*

INDEPENDENT AUDITOR'S REPORT TO THE MEMBERS OF XYZ LIMITED

We have audited the financial statements of (name of company) for the year ended ... which comprise [specify the titles of the primary statements such as the Profit and Loss Account, the Balance Sheet, the Cash Flow Statement, the Statement of Total Recognised Gains and Losses] and the related notes[9]. The financial reporting framework that has been applied in their preparation is Irish law and the Financial Reporting Standard for Smaller Entities [(effective April 2008)][10] issued by the Financial Reporting Council and promulgated by the Institute of Chartered Accountants in Ireland (Generally Accepted Accounting Practice in Ireland applicable to Smaller Entities).

Respective responsibilities of directors and auditors

As explained more fully in the Directors' Responsibilities Statement [set out [on page ...]], the directors are responsible for the preparation of the financial statements giving a true and fair view. Our responsibility is to audit and express an opinion on the financial statements in accordance with Irish law and International Standards on Auditing (UK and Ireland). Those standards require us to comply with the Auditing Practices Board's [(APB's)] Ethical Standards for Auditors[, including "APB Ethical Standard – Provisions Available for Small Entities (Revised)", in the circumstances set out in note [x] to the financial statements][11].

Scope of the audit of the financial statements

Either:

A description of the scope of an audit of financial statements is [provided on the FRC's website at www.frc.org.uk/audit-scope-ireland] / [set out [on page ...] of the Annual Report].

---

[9] Auditor's reports of entities that do not publish their financial statements on a website or publish them using 'PDF' format may refer to the financial statements by reference to page numbers.

[10] Specify the version of the Financial Reporting Standard for Smaller Entities.

[11] Delete the words in square brackets if the relief and exemptions provided by "APB Ethical Standard – Provisions Available for Small Entities (revised)" (ES PASE) are not utilised. Paragraph 24 of ES PASE requires disclosure in the auditor's report where the audit firm has taken advantage of an exemption provided by ES PASE. The Appendix to ES PASE provides illustrative disclosures of relevant circumstances where the audit firm has taken advantage of an exemption provided by ES PASE.

Or:

An audit involves obtaining evidence about the amounts and disclosures in the financial statements sufficient to give reasonable assurance that the financial statements are free from material misstatement, whether caused by fraud or error. This includes an assessment of: whether the accounting policies are appropriate to the company's circumstances and have been consistently applied and adequately disclosed; the reasonableness of significant accounting estimates made by the directors; and the overall presentation of the financial statements. In addition, we read all the financial and non-financial information in the [describe the annual report] to identify material inconsistencies with the audited financial statements. If we become aware of any apparent material misstatements or inconsistencies we consider the implications for our report.

Opinion on financial statements

In our opinion the financial statements:

- give a true and fair view, in accordance with Generally Accepted Accounting Practice in Ireland applicable to Smaller Entities, of the state of the company's affairs as at .... and of its profit [loss] for the year then ended; and

- have been properly prepared in accordance with the requirements of the Companies Acts 1963 to 2012.

Matters on which we are required to report by the Companies Acts 1963 to 2012

- We have obtained all the information and explanations which we consider necessary for the purposes of our audit.

- In our opinion proper books of account have been kept by the company.

- The financial statements are in agreement with the books of account.

- In our opinion, the information given in the directors' report is consistent with the financial statements.

- The net assets of the company, as stated in the balance sheet are more than half of the amount of its called-up share capital and, in our opinion, on that basis there did not exist at ... a financial situation which under Section 40 (1) of the Companies (Amendment) Act, 1983 would require the convening of an extraordinary general meeting of the company.

Matters on which we are required to report by exception

We have nothing to report in respect of the provisions in the Companies Acts 1963 to 2012 which require us to report to you if, in our opinion, the disclosures of directors' remuneration and transactions specified by law are not made.

[Signature]   *Address*

Seán MacGabhan   *Date*

for and on behalf of ABC & Co

Example 2 – Non-publicly traded company incorporated in Ireland preparing financial statements under Irish GAAP

- *Company is not a listed company.*

- *Company either does not qualify as a small company or qualifies as a small company but chooses not to prepare financial statements in accordance with the FRSSE.*

- *Company does not prepare group financial statements.*

INDEPENDENT AUDITOR'S REPORT TO THE MEMBERS OF XYZ LIMITED

We have audited the financial statements of (name of company) for the year ended ... which comprise [specify the titles of the primary statements such as the Profit and Loss Account, the Balance Sheet, the Cash Flow Statement, the Statement of Total Recognised Gains and Losses, the Reconciliation of Movements in Shareholders' Funds] and the related notes[12]. The financial reporting framework that has been applied in their preparation is Irish law and accounting standards issued by the Financial Reporting Council and promulgated by the Institute of Chartered Accountants in Ireland (Generally Accepted Accounting Practice in Ireland).

Respective responsibilities of directors and auditors

As explained more fully in the Directors' Responsibilities Statement [set out [on page ....]] the directors are responsible for the preparation of the financial statements giving a true and fair view. Our responsibility is to audit and express an opinion on the financial statements in accordance with Irish law and International Standards on Auditing (UK and Ireland). Those standards require us to comply with the Auditing Practices Board's [APB's] Ethical Standards for Auditors[13].

---

[12] Auditor's reports of entities that do not publish their financial statements on a web site or publish them using 'PDF' format may continue to refer to the financial statements by reference to page numbers.

[13] If the company is a small entity as defined in paragraph 4(ii) of the APB Ethical Standard – Provisions Available for Small Entities (ES PASE), add 'including "APB Ethical Standard – Provisions Available for Small Entities (Revised)", in the circumstances set out in note [x] to the financial statements if the auditor has availed itself of the exemption set out in paragraph 24 of ES PASE. The Appendix to ES PASE provides illustrative disclosures of relevant circumstances where the auditor has taken advantage of such an exemption.

Scope of the audit of the financial statements

Either:

> A description of the scope of an audit of financial statements is [provided on the FRC's website at www.frc.org.uk/audit-scope-ireland] / [set out [on page...] of the Annual Report].

Or:

> An audit involves obtaining evidence about the amounts and disclosures in the financial statements sufficient to give reasonable assurance that the financial statements are free from material misstatement, whether caused by fraud or error. This includes an assessment of: whether the accounting policies are appropriate to the company's circumstances and have been consistently applied and adequately disclosed; the reasonableness of significant accounting estimates made by the directors; and the overall presentation of the financial statements. In addition, we read all the financial and non-financial information in the [describe the annual report] to identify material inconsistencies with the audited financial statements. If we become aware of any apparent material misstatements or inconsistencies we consider the implications for our report.

Opinion on financial statements

In our opinion the financial statements:

- give a true and fair view in accordance with Generally Accepted Accounting Practice in Ireland of the state of the company's affairs as at .... and of its profit [loss] for the year then ended; and

- have been properly prepared in accordance with the requirements of the Companies Acts 1963 to 2012.

Matters on which we are required to report by the Companies Acts 1963 to 2012

- We have obtained all the information and explanations which we consider necessary for the purposes of our audit.

- In our opinion proper books of account have been kept by the company.

- The financial statements are in agreement with the books of account.

- In our opinion the information given in the directors' report is consistent with the financial statements.

- The net assets of the company, as stated in the balance sheet are more than half of the amount of its called-up share capital and, in our opinion, on that basis there did not exist at .... a financial situation which under Section 40 (1) of the Companies (Amendment) Act, 1983 would require the convening of an extraordinary general meeting of the company.

Matters on which we are required to report by exception

We have nothing to report in respect of the provisions in the Companies Acts 1963 to 2012 which require us to report to you if, in our opinion the disclosures of directors' remuneration and transactions specified by law are not made.

[Signature]   Address
Seán MacGabhan   Date
for and on behalf of ABC & Co.

Example 3 – Non-publicly traded company limited by guarantee incorporated in Ireland preparing financial statements under Irish GAAP

- *Company is not a listed company.*

- *Company is limited by guarantee, does not have a share capital and is not subject to the Companies (Amendment) Act, 1986 as it is not trading for the acquisition of gain by the members.*

- *Company does not prepare group financial statements.*

INDEPENDENT AUDITOR'S REPORT TO THE MEMBERS OF XYZ LIMITED

We have audited the financial statements of (name of company) for the year ended ... which comprise [specify the titles of the primary statements such as the Profit and Loss Account, the Balance Sheet, the Cash Flow Statement, the Statement of Total Recognised Gains and Losses] and the related notes[14]. The financial reporting framework that has been applied in their preparation is Irish law and accounting standards issued by the Financial Reporting Council and promulgated by the Institute of Chartered Accountants in Ireland (Generally Accepted Accounting Practice in Ireland).

Respective responsibilities of directors and auditors

As explained more fully in the Directors' Responsibilities Statement [set out [on page ....]] the directors are responsible for the preparation of the financial statements giving a true and fair view. Our responsibility is to audit and express an opinion on the financial statements in accordance with Irish law and International Standards on Auditing (UK and Ireland). Those standards require us to comply with the Auditing Practices Board's [APB's] Ethical Standards for Auditors.

Scope of the audit of the financial statements

Either:

> A description of the scope of an audit of financial statements is [provided on the FRC's website at www.frc.org.uk/audit-scope-ireland] / [set out [on page...] of the Annual Report].

---

[14] Auditor's reports of entities that do not publish their financial statements on a web site or publish them using 'PDF' format may continue to refer to the financial statements by reference to page numbers.

Or:

An audit involves obtaining evidence about the amounts and disclosures in the financial statements sufficient to give reasonable assurance that the financial statements are free from material misstatement, whether caused by fraud or error. This includes an assessment of: whether the accounting policies are appropriate to the company's circumstances and have been consistently applied and adequately disclosed; the reasonableness of significant accounting estimates made by the directors; and the overall presentation of the financial statements. In addition, we read all the financial and non-financial information in the [describe the annual report] to identify material inconsistencies with the audited financial statements. If we become aware of any apparent material misstatements or inconsistencies we consider the implications for our report.

Opinion on financial statements

In our opinion the financial statements:

- give a true and fair view in accordance with Generally Accepted Accounting Practice in Ireland of the state of the company's affairs as at .... and of its profit [loss] for the year then ended; and

- have been properly prepared in accordance with the requirements of the Companies Acts 1963 to 2012.

Matters on which we are required to report by the Companies Acts 1963 to 2012

- We have obtained all the information and explanations which we consider necessary for the purposes of our audit.

- In our opinion proper books of account have been kept by the company.

- The financial statements are in agreement with the books of account.

Matters on which we are required to report by exception

We have nothing to report in respect of the provisions in the Companies Acts 1963 to 2012 which require us to report to you if, in our opinion the disclosures of directors' remuneration and transactions specified by law are not made.

[Signature]   Address
Seán MacGabhan   Date
for and on behalf of ABC & Co.

Example 4 – Company incorporated in Ireland with a listing on the Global Exchange Market preparing financial statements under Irish GAAP

- *Company is listed on the Global Exchange Market ("GEM") of the Irish Stock Exchange and subject to the continuing obligations in respect of Annual Financial Statements as set out in Chapter 5 of the Listing Rules of the GEM.*

- *Company does not prepare group financial statements.*

INDEPENDENT AUDITOR'S REPORT TO THE MEMBERS OF XYZ LIMITED

We have audited the financial statements of (name of company) for the year ended ... which comprise [specify the titles of the primary statements such as the Profit and Loss Account, the Balance Sheet, the Cash Flow Statement, the Statement of Total Recognised Gains and Losses, the Reconciliation of Movements in Shareholders' Funds] and the related notes[15]. The financial reporting framework that has been applied in their preparation is Irish law and accounting standards issued by the Financial Reporting Council and promulgated by the Institute of Chartered Accountants in Ireland (Generally Accepted Accounting Practice in Ireland).

Respective responsibilities of directors and auditors

As explained more fully in the Directors' Responsibilities Statement [set out [on page ....]] the directors are responsible for the preparation of the financial statements giving a true and fair view. Our responsibility is to audit and express an opinion on the financial statements in accordance with Irish law and International Standards on Auditing (UK and Ireland). Those standards require us to comply with the Auditing Practices Board's [APB's] Ethical Standards for Auditors[16] .

Scope of the audit of the financial statements

Either:

A description of the scope of an audit of financial statements is [provided on the FRC's website at www.frc.org.uk/audit-scope-ireland] / [set out [on page...] of the Annual Report].

---

[15] Auditor's reports of entities that do not publish their financial statements on a web site or publish them using 'PDF' format may continue to refer to the financial statements by reference to page numbers.

[16] If the company is a small entity as defined in paragraph 4(ii) of the APB Ethical Standard – Provisions Available for Small Entities (ES PASE), add 'including "APB Ethical Standard – Provisions Available for Small Entities (Revised)", in the circumstances set out in note [x] to the financial statements' if the auditor has availed itself of the exemption set out in paragraph 24 of ES PASE. The Appendix to ES PASE provides illustrative disclosures of relevant circumstances where the auditor has taken advantage of such an exemption.

Or:

An audit involves obtaining evidence about the amounts and disclosures in the financial statements sufficient to give reasonable assurance that the financial statements are free from material misstatement, whether caused by fraud or error. This includes an assessment of: whether the accounting policies are appropriate to the company's circumstances and have been consistently applied and adequately disclosed; the reasonableness of significant accounting estimates made by the directors; and the overall presentation of the financial statements. In addition, we read all the financial and non-financial information in the [describe the annual report] to identify material inconsistencies with the audited financial statements. If we become aware of any apparent material misstatements or inconsistencies we consider the implications for our report.

Opinion on financial statements

In our opinion the financial statements:

- give a true and fair view in accordance with Generally Accepted Accounting Practice in Ireland of the state of the company's affairs as at .... and of its profit [loss] for the year then ended; and

- have been properly prepared in accordance with the requirements of the Companies Acts 1963 to 2012.

Matters on which we are required to report by the Companies Acts 1963 to 2012

- We have obtained all the information and explanations which we consider necessary for the purposes of our audit.

- In our opinion proper books of account have been kept by the company.

- The financial statements are in agreement with the books of account.

- In our opinion the information given in the directors' report is consistent with the financial statements.

- The net assets of the company, as stated in the balance sheet are more than half of the amount of its called-up share capital and, in our opinion, on that basis there did not exist at .... a financial situation which under Section 40 (1) of the Companies (Amendment) Act, 1983 would require the convening of an extraordinary general meeting of the company.

Matters on which we are required to report by exception

We have nothing to report in respect of the provisions in the Companies Acts 1963 to 2012 which require us to report to you if, in our opinion the disclosures of directors' remuneration and transactions specified by law are not made.

[Signature]   *Address*
Seán MacGabhan   *Date*
for and on behalf of ABC & Co.

Example 5 – Company incorporated in Ireland preparing financial statements under IFRSs as adopted by the European Union

- *Company has a primary listing on the Enterprise Securities Market ("ESM") of the Irish Stock Exchange and is subject to the obligations in respect of Annual Financial Statements as set out in Part 1 of the Listing Rules of the ESM.*
  or

- *Company has a primary listing on "AIM", the London Stock Exchange's international market for smaller growing companies and is subject to the obligations in respect of Annual Financial Statements as set out in Rule 19 of the AIM Rules.*
  or

- *Company has opted to prepare 'IFRS individual accounts' in accordance with Section 148 of the Companies Act 1963.*
  and

- *Company does not prepare group financial statements.*

INDEPENDENT AUDITOR'S REPORT TO THE MEMBERS OF XYZ LIMITED/PLC

We have audited the financial statements of (name of company) for the year ended ... which comprise [specify the titles of the primary statements such as the Statement of Financial Position, the Statement of Comprehensive Income[17], the Statement of Cash Flow and the Statement of Changes in Equity] and the related notes[18]. The financial reporting framework that has been applied in their preparation is Irish law and International Financial Reporting Standards (IFRSs) as adopted by the European Union.

Respective responsibilities of directors and auditors

As explained more fully in the Directors' Responsibilities Statement [set out [on page ...]], the directors are responsible for the preparation of the financial statements giving a true and fair view. Our responsibility is to audit and express an opinion on the financial statements in accordance with Irish law and International Standards on Auditing (UK and Ireland). Those standards require us to comply with the Auditing Practices Board's [(APB's)] Ethical Standards for Auditors[19]].

---

[17] The names used for the primary statements in the auditor's report should reflect the precise titles used by the company for them.

[18] Auditor's reports of entities that do not publish their financial statements on a website or publish them using 'PDF' format may refer to the financial statements by reference to page numbers.

[19] Add the words "including 'APB Ethical Standard – Provisions Available for Small Entities (Revised)'" if the relief and exemptions provided by "APB Ethical Standard – Provisions Available for Small Entities (Revised)" (ES PASE) are utilised. Paragraph 24 of ES PASE requires disclosure in the auditor's report where the audit firm has taken advantage of an exemption provided by ES PASE. The Appendix to ES PASE provides illustrative disclosures of relevant circumstances where the audit firm has taken advantage of an exemption provided by the ES PASE.

Scope of the audit of the financial statements

Either:

> A description of the scope of an audit of financial statements is [provided on the FRC's website at www.frc.org.uk/audit-scope-ireland] / [set out [on page ...] of the Annual Report].

Or:

> An audit involves obtaining evidence about the amounts and disclosures in the financial statements sufficient to give reasonable assurance that the financial statements are free from material misstatement, whether caused by fraud or error. This includes an assessment of: whether the accounting policies are appropriate to the company's circumstances and have been consistently applied and adequately disclosed; the reasonableness of significant accounting estimates made by the directors; and the overall presentation of the financial statements. In addition, we read all the financial and non-financial information in the [describe the annual report] to identify material inconsistencies with the audited financial statements. If we become aware of any apparent material misstatements or inconsistencies we consider the implications for our report.

Opinion on financial statements

In our opinion the financial statements:

- give a true and fair view, in accordance with IFRSs as adopted by the European Union, of the state of the company's affairs as at .... and of its profit [loss] for the year then ended; and

- have been properly prepared in accordance with the requirements of the Companies Acts 1963 to 2012.

Matters on which we are required to report by the Companies Acts 1963 to 2012

- We have obtained all the information and explanations which we consider necessary for the purposes of our audit.

- In our opinion proper books of account have been kept by the company.

- The financial statements are in agreement with the books of account.

- In our opinion, the information given in the directors' report is consistent with the financial statements.

- The net assets of the company, as stated in the balance sheet are more than half of the amount of its called-up share capital and, in our opinion, on that basis there did not exist at ... a financial situation which under Section 40 (1) of the Companies (Amendment) Act, 1983 would require the convening of an extraordinary general meeting of the company.

Matters on which we are required to report by exception

We have nothing to report in respect of the provisions in the Companies Acts 1963 to 2012 which require us to report to you if, in our opinion, the disclosures of directors' remuneration and transactions specified by law are not made.

[Signature]   *Address*
Seán MacGabhan   *Date*
for and on behalf of ABC & Co

Example 6 – Publicly traded company incorporated in Ireland preparing financial statements under Irish GAAP

- *Company has equity shares with a primary listing on the Main Securities Market ("MSM") of the Irish Stock Exchange and is subject to the continuing obligations in relation to the annual report as set out in Chapter 6 of the Listing Rules of the MSM.*

- *Company does not prepare group financial statements.*

- *Corporate governance statement incorporated into the directors' report, either directly or by incorporation by reference as explained in Bulletin 2011/1 issued by the APB[20].*

INDEPENDENT AUDITOR'S REPORT TO THE MEMBERS OF XYZ PLC

We have audited the financial statements of (name of company) for the year ended ... which comprise [specify the titles of the primary statements such as the Profit and Loss Account, the Balance Sheet, the Cash Flow Statement, the Statement of Total Recognised Gains and Losses] and the related notes[21]. The financial reporting framework that has been applied in their preparation is Irish law and accounting standards issued by the Financial Reporting Council and promulgated by the Institute of Chartered Accountants in Ireland (Generally Accepted Accounting Practice in Ireland).

Respective responsibilities of directors and auditors

As explained more fully in the Directors' Responsibilities Statement [set out [on page ....]] the directors are responsible for the preparation of the financial statements giving a true and fair view. Our responsibility is to audit and express an opinion on the financial statements in accordance with Irish law and International Standards on Auditing (UK and Ireland). Those standards require us to comply with the Auditing Practices Board's [APB's] Ethical Standards for Auditors.

Scope of the audit of the financial statements

Either:

> A description of the scope of an audit of financial statements is [provided on the FRC's website at www.frc.org.uk/audit-scope-ireland] / [set out [on page...] of the Annual Report].

---

[20] See example 16 for an illustration of an auditor's report where the corporate governance statement is not incorporated into the director's report.

[21] Auditor's reports of entities that do not publish their financial statements on a web site or publish them using 'PDF' format may continue to refer to the financial statements by reference to page numbers.

Or:

> An audit involves obtaining evidence about the amounts and disclosures in the financial statements sufficient to give reasonable assurance that the financial statements are free from material misstatement, whether caused by fraud or error. This includes an assessment of: whether the accounting policies are appropriate to the company's circumstances and have been consistently applied and adequately disclosed; the reasonableness of significant accounting estimates made by the directors; and the overall presentation of the financial statements. In addition, we read all the financial and non-financial information in the [describe the annual report] to identify material inconsistencies with the audited financial statements. If we become aware of any apparent material misstatements or inconsistencies we consider the implications for our report.

Opinion on financial statements

In our opinion the financial statements:

- give a true and fair view in accordance with Generally Accepted Accounting Practice in Ireland of the state of the company's affairs as at .... and of its profit [loss] for the year then ended; and

- have been properly prepared in accordance with the requirements of the Companies Acts 1963 to 2012.

Matters on which we are required to report by the Companies Acts 1963 to 2012

- We have obtained all the information and explanations which we consider necessary for the purposes of our audit.

- In our opinion proper books of account have been kept by the company.

- The financial statements are in agreement with the books of account.

- In our opinion the information given in the directors' report is consistent with the financial statements.

- The net assets of the company, as stated in the balance sheet are more than half of the amount of its called-up share capital and, in our opinion, on that basis there did not exist at .... a financial situation which under Section 40 (1) of the Companies (Amendment) Act, 1983 would require the convening of an extraordinary general meeting of the company.

Matters on which we are required to report by exception

We have nothing to report in respect of the following:

Under the Companies Acts 1963 to 2012 we are required to report to you if, in our opinion the disclosures of directors' remuneration and transactions specified by law are not made.

Under the Listing Rules of the Irish Stock Exchange we are required to review:

- the directors' statement, [set out [on page...]], in relation to going concern;

- the part of the Corporate Governance Statement relating to the company's compliance with the nine provisions of the UK Corporate Governance Code and the two provisions of the Irish Corporate Governance Annex specified for our review;

- the six specified elements of the disclosures in the report to shareholders by the Board on directors' remuneration.

[Signature]   Address
Seán MacGabhan   Date
for and on behalf of ABC & Co

Example 7 – Publicly traded company incorporated in Ireland preparing financial statements under IFRSs as adopted by the European Union

- *Company has equity shares with a primary listing on the Main Securities Market ("MSM") of the Irish Stock Exchange and is subject to the continuing obligations in relation to the annual report as set out in Chapter 6 of the Listing Rules of the MSM.*

- *Company does not prepare group financial statements.*

- *Corporate governance statement incorporated into the directors' report, either directly or by incorporation by reference as explained in Bulletin 2011/1 issued by the APB[22].*

INDEPENDENT AUDITOR'S REPORT TO THE MEMBERS OF XYZ PLC

We have audited the financial statements of (name of company) for the year ended ... which comprise [specify the titles of the primary statements such as the Statement of Financial Position, the Statement of Comprehensive Income, the Statement of Cash Flows, the Statement of Changes in Equity[23]] and the related notes[24]. The financial reporting framework that has been applied in their preparation is Irish law and International Financial Reporting Standards (IFRSs) as adopted by the European Union.

Respective responsibilities of directors and auditors

As explained more fully in the Directors' Responsibilities Statement [set out [on page ....]] the directors are responsible for the preparation of the financial statements giving a true and fair view. Our responsibility is to audit and express an opinion on the financial statements in accordance with Irish law and International Standards on Auditing (UK and Ireland). Those standards require us to comply with the Auditing Practices Board's [APB's] Ethical Standards for Auditors.

Scope of the audit of the financial statements

Either:

> A description of the scope of an audit of financial statements is [provided on the FRC's website at www.frc.org.uk/audit-scope-ireland] / [set out [on page...] of the Annual Report].

---

[22] See example 16 for an illustration of an auditor's report where the corporate governance statement is not incorporated into the director's report.

[23] The names used for the primary statements in the auditor's report should reflect the precise titles used by the company for them.

[24] Auditor's reports of entities that do not publish their financial statements on a web site or publish them using 'PDF' format may continue to refer to the financial statements by reference to page numbers.

Or:

An audit involves obtaining evidence about the amounts and disclosures in the financial statements sufficient to give reasonable assurance that the financial statements are free from material misstatement, whether caused by fraud or error. This includes an assessment of: whether the accounting policies are appropriate to the company's circumstances and have been consistently applied and adequately disclosed; the reasonableness of significant accounting estimates made by the directors; and the overall presentation of the financial statements. In addition, we read all the financial and non-financial information in the [describe the annual report] to identify material inconsistencies with the audited financial statements. If we become aware of any apparent material misstatements or inconsistencies we consider the implications for our report.

Opinion on financial statements

In our opinion the financial statements:

- give a true and fair view in accordance with International Financial Reporting Standards (IFRSs) as adopted by the European Union of the state of the company's affairs as at .... and of its profit [loss] for the year then ended; and

- have been properly prepared in accordance with the requirements of the Companies Acts 1963 to 2012.

[Separate opinion in relation to IFRSs as issued by the IASB

As explained in note [x] to the financial statements, the company in addition to complying with its legal obligation to comply with IFRSs as adopted by the European Union, have also complied with the IFRSs as issued by the International Accounting Standards Board (IASB).

In our opinion the financial statements comply with IFRSs as issued by the IASB.]

Matters on which we are required to report by the Companies Acts 1963 to 2012

- We have obtained all the information and explanations which we consider necessary for the purposes of our audit

- In our opinion proper books of account have been kept by the company.

- The financial statements are in agreement with the books of account.

- In our opinion the information given in the directors' report is consistent with the financial statements.

- The net assets of the company, as stated in the statement of financial position are more than half of the amount of its called-up share capital and, in our opinion, on that basis there did not exist at .... a financial situation which under Section 40 (1) of the Companies (Amendment) Act, 1983 would require the convening of an extraordinary general meeting of the company.

Matters on which we are required to report by exception

We have nothing to report in respect of the following:

Under the Companies Acts 1963 to 2012 we are required to report to you if, in our opinion the disclosures of directors' remuneration and transactions specified by law are not made.

Under the Listing Rules of the Irish Stock Exchange we are required to review:

- the directors' statement, [set out [on page...]], in relation to going concern;

- the part of the Corporate Governance Statement relating to the company's compliance with the nine provisions of the UK Corporate Governance Code and the two provisions of the Irish Corporate Governance Annex specified for our review; and

- the six specified elements of the disclosures in the report to shareholders by the Board on directors' remuneration.

[Signature]   Address
Seán MacGabhan   Date
for and on behalf of ABC & Co

Example 8 – Publicly traded company with listed debt incorporated in Ireland preparing financial statements under Irish GAAP

- Company has debt securities only with a primary listing on the Main Securities Market ("MSM") of the Irish Stock Exchange ("ISE") and is subject to the continuing obligations in relation to the annual report as set out in Chapter 15 of the Listing Rules of the MSM.

- ISE debt listed only companies are not required to make the ISE corporate governance disclosures.

- Company does not prepare group financial statements.

- Corporate governance statement (pursuant to S.I. No. 450 of 2010) incorporated into the directors' report, either directly or by incorporation by reference as explained in Bulletin 2011/1 issued by the APB[25].

INDEPENDENT AUDITOR'S REPORT TO THE MEMBERS OF XYZ PLC

We have audited the financial statements of (name of company) for the year ended ... which comprise [specify the titles of the primary statements such as the Profit and Loss Account, the Balance Sheet, the Cash Flow Statement, the Statement of Total Recognised Gains and Losses] and the related notes[26]. The financial reporting framework that has been applied in their preparation is Irish law and accounting standards issued by the Financial Reporting Council and promulgated by the Institute of Chartered Accountants in Ireland (Generally Accepted Accounting Practice in Ireland).

Respective responsibilities of directors and auditors

As explained more fully in the Directors' Responsibilities Statement [set out [on page ....]] the directors are responsible for the preparation of the financial statements giving a true and fair view. Our responsibility is to audit and express an opinion on the financial statements in accordance with Irish law and International Standards on Auditing (UK and Ireland). Those standards require us to comply with the Auditing Practices Board's [APB's] Ethical Standards for Auditors.

---

[25] See example 16 for an illustration of an auditor's report where the corporate governance statement is not incorporated into the director's report.

[26] Auditor's reports of entities that do not publish their financial statements on a web site or publish them using 'PDF' format may continue to refer to the financial statements by reference to page numbers.

Scope of the audit of the financial statements

Either:

A description of the scope of an audit of financial statements is [provided on the FRC's website at www.frc.org.uk/audit-scope-ireland] / [set out [on page...] of the Annual Report].

Or:

An audit involves obtaining evidence about the amounts and disclosures in the financial statements sufficient to give reasonable assurance that the financial statements are free from material misstatement, whether caused by fraud or error. This includes an assessment of: whether the accounting policies are appropriate to the company's circumstances and have been consistently applied and adequately disclosed; the reasonableness of significant accounting estimates made by the directors; and the overall presentation of the financial statements. In addition, we read all the financial and non-financial information in the [describe the annual report] to identify material inconsistencies with the audited financial statements. If we become aware of any apparent material misstatements or inconsistencies we consider the implications for our report.

Opinion on financial statements

In our opinion the financial statements:

- give a true and fair view in accordance with Generally Accepted Accounting Practice in Ireland of the state of the company's affairs as at .... and of its profit [loss] for the year then ended; and

- have been properly prepared in accordance with the requirements of the Companies Acts 1963 to 2012.

Matters on which we are required to report by the Companies Acts 1963 to 2012

- We have obtained all the information and explanations which we consider necessary for the purposes of our audit.

- In our opinion proper books of account have been kept by the company.

- The financial statements are in agreement with the books of account.

- In our opinion the information given in the directors' report is consistent with the financial statements.

- The net assets of the company, as stated in the balance sheet are more than half of the amount of its called-up share capital and, in our opinion, on that basis there did not exist at .... a financial situation which under Section 40 (1) of the Companies (Amendment) Act, 1983 would require the convening of an extraordinary general meeting of the company.

Matters on which we are required to report by exception

We have nothing to report in respect of the provisions in the Companies Acts 1963 to 2012 which require us to report to you if, in our opinion the disclosures of directors' remuneration and transactions specified by law are not made.

[Signature]   *Address*
Seán MacGabhan   *Date*
for and on behalf of ABC & Co

Example 9 – Non-publicly traded collective investment fund incorporated in Ireland preparing financial statements under Irish GAAP

- Company is not a listed company.

- Company is a collective investment fund.

- Company does not prepare group financial statements.

INDEPENDENT AUDITOR'S REPORT TO THE MEMBERS OF XYZ LIMITED

We have audited the financial statements of (name of company) for the year ended ... which comprise [specify the titles of the primary statements such as the Profit and Loss Account, the Balance Sheet, the Cash Flow Statement, the Statement of Total Recognised Gains and Losses] and the related notes[27]. The financial reporting framework that has been applied in their preparation is Irish law and accounting standards issued by the Financial Reporting Council and promulgated by the Institute of Chartered Accountants in Ireland (Generally Accepted Accounting Practice in Ireland)[28].

Respective responsibilities of directors and auditors

As explained more fully in the Directors' Responsibilities Statement [set out [on page ....]] the directors are responsible for the preparation of the financial statements giving a true and fair view. Our responsibility is to audit and express an opinion on the financial statements in accordance with Irish law and International Standards on Auditing (UK and Ireland). Those standards require us to comply with the Auditing Practices Board's [APB's] Ethical Standards for Auditors.

Scope of the audit of the financial statements

Either:

> A description of the scope of an audit of financial statements is [provided on the FRC's website at www.frc.org.uk/audit-scope-ireland] / [set out [on page...] of the Annual Report].

---

[27] Auditor's reports of entities that do not publish their financial statements on a web site or publish them using 'PDF' format may continue to refer to the financial statements by reference to page numbers.

[28] Investment companies subject to Part XIII of the Companies Act 1990 or the European Communities (Undertakings for Collective Investment in Transferable Securities) Regulations 2011 may alternatively adopt an alternative body of accounting standards which apply in the United States of America, Canada or Japan.

Or:

> An audit involves obtaining evidence about the amounts and disclosures in the financial statements sufficient to give reasonable assurance that the financial statements are free from material misstatement, whether caused by fraud or error. This includes an assessment of: whether the accounting policies are appropriate to the company's circumstances and have been consistently applied and adequately disclosed; the reasonableness of significant accounting estimates made by the directors; and the overall presentation of the financial statements. In addition, we read all the financial and non-financial information in the [describe the annual report] to identify material inconsistencies with the audited financial statements. If we become aware of any apparent material misstatements or inconsistencies we consider the implications for our report.

Opinion on financial statements

In our opinion the financial statements:

- give a true and fair view in accordance with Generally Accepted Accounting Practice in Ireland[27] of the state of the company's affairs as at .... and of its profit [loss] for the year then ended; and

- have been properly prepared in accordance with the requirements of the Companies Acts 1963 to 2012 [and the European Communities (Undertakings for Collective Investment in Transferable Securities) Regulations, 2011][29].

Matters on which we are required to report by the Companies Acts 1963 to 2012

- We have obtained all the information and explanations which we consider necessary for the purposes of our audit.

- In our opinion proper books of account have been kept by the company.

- The financial statements are in agreement with the books of account.

- In our opinion the information given in the directors' report is consistent with the financial statements.

---

[29] Include if the fund is a UCITS fund.

Matters on which we are required to report by exception

We have nothing to report in respect of the provisions in the Companies Acts 1963 to 2012 which require us to report to you if, in our opinion the disclosures of directors' remuneration and transactions specified by law are not made.

[Signature]	*Address*
Seán MacGabhan	*Date*
for and on behalf of ABC & Co	

Example 10 – Publicly traded company with collective investment funds incorporated in Ireland preparing financial statements under Irish GAAP

- Company has collective investment funds with a primary listing on the Main Securities Market ("MSM") of the Irish Stock Exchange and is subject to the Annual Report and Financial Statements requirements as set out in the Code of Listing Requirements and Procedures for Investment Funds and/or Chapter 14 of the Listing Rules of the MSM.

- Company does not prepare group financial statements.

- Corporate governance statement incorporated into the directors' report, either directly or by incorporation by reference as explained in Bulletin 2011/1 issued by the APB[30].

INDEPENDENT AUDITOR'S REPORT TO THE MEMBERS OF XYZ LIMITED

We have audited the financial statements of (name of company) for the year ended ... which comprise [specify the titles of the primary statements such as the Profit and Loss Account, the Balance Sheet, the Statement of Changes in Net Assets Attributable to Participating Shareholders] and the related notes[31]. The financial reporting framework that has been applied in their preparation is Irish law and accounting standards issued by the Financial Reporting Council and promulgated by the Institute of Chartered Accountants in Ireland (Generally Accepted Accounting Practice in Ireland)[32].

Respective responsibilities of directors and auditors

As explained more fully in the Directors' Responsibilities Statement [set out [on page ....]] the directors are responsible for the preparation of the financial statements giving a true and fair view. Our responsibility is to audit and express an opinion on the financial statements in accordance with Irish law and International Standards on Auditing (UK and Ireland). Those standards require us to comply with the Auditing Practices Board's [APB's] Ethical Standards for Auditors.

---

[30] See example 16 for an illustration of an auditor's report where the corporate governance statement is not incorporated into the directors' report.

[31] Auditor's reports of entities that do not publish their financial statements on a web site or publish them using 'PDF' format may continue to refer to the financial statements by reference to page numbers.

[32] Investment companies subject to Part XIII of the Companies Act 1990 or the European Communities (Undertakings for Collective Investment in Transferable Securities) Regulations 2011 may alternatively adopt an alternative body of accounting standards which apply in the United States of America, Canada or Japan.

Scope of the audit of the financial statements

Either:

> A description of the scope of an audit of financial statements is [provided on the FRC's website at www.frc.org.uk/audit-scope-ireland] / [set out [on page...] of the Annual Report].

Or:

> An audit involves obtaining evidence about the amounts and disclosures in the financial statements sufficient to give reasonable assurance that the financial statements are free from material misstatement, whether caused by fraud or error. This includes an assessment of: whether the accounting policies are appropriate to the company's circumstances and have been consistently applied and adequately disclosed; the reasonableness of significant accounting estimates made by the directors; and the overall presentation of the financial statements. In addition, we read all the financial and non-financial information in the [describe the annual report] to identify material inconsistencies with the audited financial statements. If we become aware of any apparent material misstatements or inconsistencies we consider the implications for our report.

Opinion on financial statements

In our opinion the financial statements:

- give a true and fair view in accordance with Generally Accepted Accounting Practice in Ireland[31] of the state of the company's affairs as at .... and of its profit [loss] for the year then ended; and

- have been properly prepared in accordance with the requirements of the Companies Acts 1963 to 2012 [and the European Communities (Undertakings for Collective Investment in Transferable Securities) Regulations, 2011][33].

Matters on which we are required to report by the Companies Acts 1963 to 2012

- We have obtained all the information and explanations which we consider necessary for the purposes of our audit.

- In our opinion proper books of account have been kept by the company.

- The financial statements are in agreement with the books of account.

---

[33] Include if the fund is a UCITS fund.

- In our opinion the information given in the directors' report is consistent with the financial statements.

Matters on which we are required to report by exception

We have nothing to report in respect of the provisions in the Companies Acts 1963 to 2012 which require us to report to you if, in our opinion the disclosures of directors' remuneration and transactions specified by law are not made.

[Signature]   *Address*
Seán MacGabhan   *Date*
for and on behalf of ABC & Co

Appendix 2

Group and parent company financial statements reported on in a single auditor's report

11. Non-publicly traded group – Parent company incorporated in Ireland preparing financial statements under Irish GAAP (Section 148(8) exemption taken)

12. Non-publicly traded group – Parent company incorporated in Ireland preparing financial statements under Irish GAAP (Section 148(8) exemption not taken)

13. Non-publicly traded group – Parent company incorporated in Ireland prepares financial statement under IFRSs as adopted by the European Union

14. Publicly traded group – Parent company incorporated in Ireland prepares financial statements under IFRSs as adopted by the European Union

15. Publicly traded group – Parent company incorporated in Ireland prepares financial statements under Irish GAAP

16. Publicly traded group – Parent company incorporated in Ireland prepares financial statements under Irish GAAP and corporate governance statement not incorporated in the directors' report

17. Private company with publicly traded listed debt – Parent company incorporated in Ireland preparing financial statements under IFRSs as adopted by the European Union

18. Publicly traded collective investment fund – Parent company incorporated in Ireland prepares financial statements under IFRSs as adopted by the European Union

19. State Body incorporated in Ireland preparing group financial statements under Irish GAAP

Example 11 – Non-publicly traded group – Parent company incorporated in Ireland preparing financial statements under Irish GAAP (Section 148(8) exemption taken)

- *Company is not a listed company.*

- *Company prepares group financial statements under Irish GAAP and Section 148(8) Companies Act 1963 exemption taken for the parent company's own profit and loss account.*

- *This example report may also be used for the report on the group financial statements prepared under Irish GAAP of a company incorporated in Ireland and listed on the Global Exchange Market ("GEM") of the Irish Stock Exchange and subject to the continuing obligations in respect of Annual Financial Statements as set out in Chapter 5 of the Listing Rules of the GEM.*

INDEPENDENT AUDITOR'S REPORT TO THE MEMBERS OF XYZ LIMITED

We have audited the financial statements of (name of company) for the year ended ... which comprise [specify the titles of the primary statements such as the Group Profit and Loss Account, the Group and Parent Company Balance Sheets, the Group Cash Flow Statement, the Group Statement of Total Recognised Gains and Losses] and the related notes[34]. The financial reporting framework that has been applied in their preparation is Irish law and accounting standards issued by the Financial Reporting Council and promulgated by the Institute of Chartered Accountants in Ireland (Generally Accepted Accounting Practice in Ireland).

Respective responsibilities of directors and auditors

As explained more fully in the Directors' Responsibilities Statement [set out [on page ....]] the directors are responsible for the preparation of the financial statements giving a true and fair view. Our responsibility is to audit and express an opinion on the financial statements in accordance with Irish law and International Standards on Auditing (UK and Ireland). Those standards require us to comply with the Auditing Practices Board's [APB's] Ethical Standards for Auditors.

---

[34] Auditor's reports of entities that do not publish their financial statements on a web site or publish them using 'PDF' format may continue to refer to the financial statements by reference to page numbers.

Scope of the audit of the financial statements

Either:

A description of the scope of an audit of financial statements is [provided on the FRC's website at www.frc.org.uk/audit-scope-ireland] / [set out [on page...] of the Annual Report].

Or:

An audit involves obtaining evidence about the amounts and disclosures in the financial statements sufficient to give reasonable assurance that the financial statements are free from material misstatement, whether caused by fraud or error. This includes an assessment of: whether the accounting policies are appropriate to the group's and parent company's circumstances and have been consistently applied and adequately disclosed; the reasonableness of significant accounting estimates made by the directors; and the overall presentation of the financial statements. In addition, we read all the financial and non-financial information in the [describe the annual report] to identify material inconsistencies with the audited financial statements. If we become aware of any apparent material misstatements or inconsistencies we consider the implications for our report.

Opinion on financial statements

In our opinion the financial statements:

- give a true and fair view in accordance with Generally Accepted Accounting Practice in Ireland of the state of the group's and of the parent company's affairs as at .... and of the group's profit [loss] for the year then ended; and

- have been properly prepared in accordance with the requirements of the Companies Acts 1963 to 2012.

Matters on which we are required to report by the Companies Acts 1963 to 2012

- We have obtained all the information and explanations which we consider necessary for the purposes of our audit.

- In our opinion proper books of account have been kept by the parent company.

- The parent company balance sheet is in agreement with the books of account.

- In our opinion the information given in the directors' report is consistent with the financial statements.

* The net assets of the parent company, as stated in the parent company balance sheet are more than half of the amount of its called-up share capital and, in our opinion, on that basis there did not exist at .... a financial situation which under Section 40 (1) of the Companies (Amendment) Act, 1983 would require the convening of an extraordinary general meeting of the parent company.

Matters on which we are required to report by exception

We have nothing to report in respect of the provisions in the Companies Acts 1963 to 2012 which require us to report to you if, in our opinion the disclosures of directors' remuneration and transactions specified by law are not made.

[Signature]   *Address*
Seán MacGabhan   *Date*
for and on behalf of ABC & Co

Example 12 – Non-publicly traded group – Parent company incorporated in Ireland preparing financial statements under Irish GAAP (Section 148(8) exemption not taken)

- *Company is not a listed company.*

- *Company prepares group financial statements and Section 148(8) Companies Act 1963 exemption not taken for parent company's own profit and loss account.*

- *This example report may also be used for the report on the group financial statements prepared under Irish GAAP of a company listed on the Global Exchange Market ("GEM") of the Irish Stock Exchange and subject to the continuing obligations in respect of Annual Financial Statements as set out in Chapter 5 of the Listing Rules of the GEM.*

INDEPENDENT AUDITOR'S REPORT TO THE MEMBERS OF XYZ LIMITED

We have audited the financial statements of (name of company) for the year ended ... which comprise [specify the titles of the primary statements such as the Group and Parent Company Profit and Loss Account, the Group and Parent Company Balance Sheets, the Group Cash Flow Statement, the Group Statement of Total Recognised Gains and Losses,] and the related notes[35]. The financial reporting framework that has been applied in their preparation is Irish law and accounting standards issued by the Financial Reporting Council and promulgated by the Institute of Chartered Accountants in Ireland (Generally Accepted Accounting Practice in Ireland).

Respective responsibilities of directors and auditors

As explained more fully in the Directors' Responsibilities Statement [set out [on page ....]] the directors are responsible for the preparation of the financial statements giving a true and fair view. Our responsibility is to audit and express an opinion on the financial statements in accordance with Irish law and International Standards on Auditing (UK and Ireland). Those standards require us to comply with the Auditing Practices Board's [APB's] Ethical Standards for Auditors.

Scope of the audit of the financial statements

Either:

> A description of the scope of an audit of financial statements is [provided on the FRC's website at www.frc.org.uk/audit-scope-ireland] / [set out [on page...] of the Annual Report].

---

[35] Auditor's reports of entities that do not publish their financial statements on a web site or publish them using 'PDF' format may continue to refer to the financial statements by reference to page numbers.

Or:

> An audit involves obtaining evidence about the amounts and disclosures in the financial statements sufficient to give reasonable assurance that the financial statements are free from material misstatement, whether caused by fraud or error. This includes an assessment of: whether the accounting policies are appropriate to the group's and parent company's circumstances and have been consistently applied and adequately disclosed; the reasonableness of significant accounting estimates made by the directors; and the overall presentation of the financial statements. In addition, we read all the financial and non-financial information in the [describe the annual report] to identify material inconsistencies with the audited financial statements. If we become aware of any apparent material misstatements or inconsistencies we consider the implications for our report.

Opinion on financial statements

In our opinion the financial statements:

- give a true and fair view in accordance with Generally Accepted Accounting Practice in Ireland of the state of the group's and of the parent company's affairs as at .... and of the group's and parent company's profit [loss] for the year then ended; and

- have been properly prepared in accordance with the requirements of the Companies Acts 1963 to 2012.

Matters on which we are required to report by the Companies Acts 1963 to 2012

- We have obtained all the information and explanations which we consider necessary for the purposes of our audit.

- In our opinion proper books of account have been kept by the parent company.

- The parent company's financial statements are in agreement with the books of account.

- In our opinion the information given in the directors' report is consistent with the financial statements.

- The net assets of the parent company, as stated in the parent company balance sheet are more than half of the amount of its called-up share capital and, in our opinion, on that basis there did not exist at .... a financial situation which under Section 40 (1) of the Companies (Amendment) Act, 1983 would require the convening of an extraordinary general meeting of the parent company.

Matters on which we are required to report by exception

We have nothing to report in respect of the provisions in the Companies Acts 1963 to 2012 which require us to report to you if, in our opinion the disclosures of directors' remuneration and transactions specified by law are not made.

[Signature]   *Address*
Seán MacGabhan   *Date*
for and on behalf of ABC & Co

Example 13 – Non-publicly traded group – Parent company incorporated in Ireland prepares financial statements under IFRSs as adopted by the European Union

- *Company is not a company listed on the Main Securities Market of the Irish Stock Exchange.*

- *Company prepares group financial statements under IFRSs as adopted by the European Union and Section 148(8) Companies Act 1963 exemption taken in respect of the parent company's own statement of comprehensive income.*

- *This example report may also be used for the report on the group financial statements prepared under IFRSs as adopted by the EU of a parent company incorporated in Ireland and listed either on (a) the Enterprise Securities Market ("ESM") of the Irish Stock Exchange and is subject to the obligations in respect of Annual Financial Statements as set out in Part 1 of the Listing Rules of the ESM; or (b) "AIM", the London Stock Exchange's market for smaller and growing companies and is subject to the obligations in respect of Annual Financial Statements as set out Rule 19 of the AIM Rules.*

INDEPENDENT AUDITOR'S REPORT TO THE MEMBERS OF XYZ LIMITED

We have audited the financial statements of (name of company) for the year ended ... which comprise [specify the titles of the primary statements such as the Group and Parent Company Statements of Financial Position, the Group Statement of Comprehensive Income, the Group and Parent Company Cash Flow Statements, the Group and Parent Company Statements of Changes in Equity][36] and the related notes[37]. The financial reporting framework that has been applied in their preparation is Irish law and International Financial Reporting Standards (IFRSs) as adopted by the European Union and, as regards the parent company financial statements, as applied in accordance with the provisions of the Companies Acts 1963 to 2012.

Respective responsibilities of directors and auditors

As explained more fully in the Directors' Responsibilities Statement [set out [on page ....]] the directors are responsible for the preparation of the financial statements giving a true and fair view. Our responsibility is to audit and express an opinion on the financial statements in accordance with Irish law and International Standards on Auditing (UK and Ireland). Those standards require us to comply with the Auditing Practices Board's [APB's] Ethical Standards for Auditors.

---

[36] The names used for the primary statements in the auditor's report should reflect the precise titles used by the company for them.

[37] Auditor's reports of entities that do not publish their financial statements on a web site or publish them using 'PDF' format may continue to refer to the financial statements by reference to page numbers.

Scope of the audit of the financial statements

Either:

A description of the scope of an audit of financial statements is [provided on the FRC's website at www.frc.org.uk/audit-scope-ireland] / [set out [on page...] of the Annual Report].

Or:

An audit involves obtaining evidence about the amounts and disclosures in the financial statements sufficient to give reasonable assurance that the financial statements are free from material misstatement, whether caused by fraud or error. This includes an assessment of: whether the accounting policies are appropriate to the group's and the parent company's circumstances and have been consistently applied and adequately disclosed; the reasonableness of significant accounting estimates made by the directors; and the overall presentation of the financial statements. In addition, we read all the financial and non-financial information in the [describe the annual report] to identify material inconsistencies with the audited financial statements. If we become aware of any apparent material misstatements or inconsistencies we consider the implications for our report.

Opinion on financial statements

In our opinion:

- the group financial statements give a true and fair view, in accordance with IFRSs as adopted by the European Union, of the state of the group's affairs as at ...... and of its [profit/loss] for the year then ended;

- the parent company statement of financial position gives a true and fair view, in accordance with IFRSs as adopted by the European Union as applied in accordance with the provisions of the Companies Acts 1963 to 2012, of the state of the parent company's affairs as at ...... ; and

- the financial statements have been properly prepared in accordance with the requirements of the Companies Acts 1963 to 2012.

Matters on which we are required to report by the Companies Acts 1963 to 2012

- We have obtained all the information and explanations which we consider necessary for the purposes of our audit.

- In our opinion proper books of account have been kept by the parent company.

- The parent company statement of financial position is in agreement with the books of account.

- In our opinion the information given in the directors' report is consistent with the financial statements.

- The net assets of the parent company, as stated in the parent company statement of financial position are more than half of the amount of its called-up share capital and, in our opinion, on that basis there did not exist at .... a financial situation which under Section 40 (1) of the Companies (Amendment) Act, 1983 would require the convening of an extraordinary general meeting of the parent company.

Matters on which we are required to report by exception

We have nothing to report in respect of the provisions in the Companies Acts 1963 to 2012 which require us to report to you if, in our opinion the disclosures of directors' remuneration and transactions specified by law are not made.

[Signature]   *Address*
Seán MacGabhan   *Date*
for and on behalf of ABC & Co

Example 14 – Publicly traded group – Parent company incorporated in Ireland prepares financial statements under IFRSs as adopted by the European Union

- *Company has equity shares with a primary listing on the Main Securities Market ("MSM") of the Irish Stock Exchange and is subject to the continuing obligations in relation to the annual report as set out in Chapter 6 of the Listing Rules of the MSM.*

- *Company prepares group financial statements under IFRSs as adopted by the European Union and Section 148(8) exemption taken in respect of parent company's own statement of comprehensive income.*

- *Corporate governance statement incorporated into the directors' report, either directly or by incorporation by reference as explained in Bulletin 2011/1 issued by the APB[38].*

INDEPENDENT AUDITOR'S REPORT TO THE MEMBERS OF XYZ PLC

We have audited the financial statements of (name of company) for the year ended ... which comprise [specify the titles of the primary statements such as the Group and Parent Company Statements of Financial Position, the Group Statement of Comprehensive Income, the Group and Parent Company Cash Flow Statements, the Group and Parent Company Statements of Changes in Equity][39] and the related notes[40]. The financial reporting framework that has been applied in their preparation is Irish law and International Financial Reporting Standards (IFRSs) as adopted by the European Union and, as regards the parent company financial statements, as applied in accordance with the provisions of the Companies Acts 1963 to 2012.

Respective responsibilities of directors and auditors

As explained more fully in the Directors' Responsibilities Statement [set out [on page ....]] the directors are responsible for the preparation of the financial statements giving a true and fair view. Our responsibility is to audit and express an opinion on the financial statements in accordance with Irish law and International Standards on Auditing (UK and Ireland). Those standards require us to comply with the Auditing Practices Board's [APB's] Ethical Standards for Auditors.

---

[38] See example 16 for an illustration of an auditor's report where the corporate governance statement is not incorporated into the director's report.

[39] The names used for the primary statements in the auditor's report should reflect the precise titles used by the company for them.

[40] Auditor's reports of entities that do not publish their financial statements on a web site or publish them using 'PDF' format may continue to refer to the financial statements by reference to page numbers.

Scope of the audit of the financial statements

Either:

> A description of the scope of an audit of financial statements is [provided on the FRC's website at www.frc.org.uk/audit-scope-ireland] / [set out [on page...] of the Annual Report].

Or:

> An audit involves obtaining evidence about the amounts and disclosures in the financial statements sufficient to give reasonable assurance that the financial statements are free from material misstatement, whether caused by fraud or error. This includes an assessment of: whether the accounting policies are appropriate to the group's and parent company's circumstances and have been consistently applied and adequately disclosed; the reasonableness of significant accounting estimates made by the directors; and the overall presentation of the financial statements. In addition, we read all the financial and non-financial information in the [describe the annual report] to identify material inconsistencies with the audited financial statements. If we become aware of any apparent material misstatements or inconsistencies we consider the implications for our report.

Opinion on financial statements

In our opinion:

- the group financial statements give a true and fair view, in accordance with IFRSs as adopted by the European Union, of the state of the group's affairs as at ...... and of its [profit/loss] for the year then ended;

- the parent company statement of financial position gives a true and fair view, in accordance with IFRSs as adopted by the European Union as applied in accordance with the provisions of the Companies Acts 1963 to 2012, of the state of the parent company's affairs as at ...... ; and

- the financial statements have been properly prepared in accordance with the requirements of the Companies Acts 1963 to 2012 and, as regards the group financial statements, Article 4 of the IAS Regulation.

[Separate opinion in relation to IFRSs as issued by the IASB

As explained in note [x] to the financial statements, the group in addition to complying with its legal obligation to comply with IFRSs as adopted by the European Union, have also complied with the IFRSs as issued by the International Accounting Standards Board (IASB).

In our opinion the group financial statements comply with IFRSs as issued by the IASB.]

Matters on which we are required to report by the Companies Acts 1963 to 2012

- We have obtained all the information and explanations which we consider necessary for the purposes of our audit.

- In our opinion proper books of account have been kept by the parent company

- The parent company statement of financial position is in agreement with the books of account.

- In our opinion the information given in the directors' report is consistent with the financial statements and the description in the Corporate Governance Statement of the main features of the internal control and risk management systems in relation to the process for preparing the group financial statements is consistent with the group financial statements.

- The net assets of the parent company, as stated in the parent company statement of financial position are more than half of the amount of its called-up share capital and, in our opinion, on that basis there did not exist at .... a financial situation which under Section 40 (1) of the Companies (Amendment) Act, 1983 would require the convening of an extraordinary general meeting of the parent company.

Matters on which we are required to report by exception

We have nothing to report in respect of the following:

Under the Companies Acts 1963 to 2012 we are required to report to you if, in our opinion the disclosures of directors' remuneration and transactions specified by law are not made.

Under the Listing Rules of the Irish Stock Exchange we are required to review:

- the directors' statement, [set out [on page...]], in relation to going concern;

- the part of the Corporate Governance Statement relating to the company's compliance with the nine provisions of the UK Corporate Governance Code and the two provisions of the Irish Corporate Governance Annex specified for our review; and

- the six specified elements of disclosures in the report to shareholders by the Board on directors' remuneration.

[Signature]	Address
Seán MacGabhan	Date
for and on behalf of ABC & Co	

Example 15 – Publicly traded group – Parent company incorporated in Ireland prepares financial statements under Irish GAAP

- *Company has equity shares with a primary listing on the Main Securities Market ("MSM") of the Irish Stock Exchange and is subject to the continuing obligations in relation to the annual report as set out in Chapter 6 of the Listing Rules of the MSM.*

- *Company prepares group financial statements under IFRSs as adopted by the European Union and Section 148(8) exemption taken in respect of the parent company's own profit and loss account.*

- *Corporate governance statement incorporated into the directors' report, either directly or by incorporation by reference as explained in Bulletin 2011/1 issued by the APB[41].*

INDEPENDENT AUDITOR'S REPORT TO THE MEMBERS OF XYZ PLC

We have audited the financial statements of (name of company) for the year ended ... which comprise [specify the titles of the primary statements such as the Group Statement of Financial Position and Parent Company Balance Sheet, the Group Statement of Comprehensive Income, the Group Statement of Cash Flows, the Group Statement of Changes in Equity][42] and the related notes[43]. The financial reporting framework that has been applied in the preparation of the group financial statements is Irish law and International Financial Reporting Standards (IFRSs) as adopted by the European Union. The financial reporting framework that has been applied in the preparation of the parent company financial statements is Irish law and accounting standards issued by the Financial Reporting Council and promulgated by the Institute of Chartered Accountants in Ireland (Generally Accepted Accounting Practice in Ireland).

Respective responsibilities of directors and auditors

As explained more fully in the Directors' Responsibilities Statement [set out [on page ....]] the directors are responsible for the preparation of the financial statements giving a true and fair view. Our responsibility is to audit and express an opinion on the financial statements in accordance with Irish law and International Standards on Auditing (UK and Ireland). Those standards require us to comply with the Auditing Practices Board's [APB's] Ethical Standards for Auditors.

---

[41] See example 16 for an illustration of an auditor's report where the corporate governance statement is not incorporated into the directors' report.

[42] The names used for the primary statements in the auditor's report should reflect the precise titles used by the company for them.

[43] Auditor's reports of entities that do not publish their financial statements on a web site or publish them using 'PDF' format may continue to refer to the financial statements by reference to page numbers.

Scope of the audit of the financial statements

Either:

> A description of the scope of an audit of financial statements is [provided on the FRC's website at www.frc.org.uk/audit-scope-ireland] / [set out [on page...] of the Annual Report].

Or:

> An audit involves obtaining evidence about the amounts and disclosures in the financial statements sufficient to give reasonable assurance that the financial statements are free from material misstatement, whether caused by fraud or error. This includes an assessment of: whether the accounting policies are appropriate to the group and the parent company's circumstances and have been consistently applied and adequately disclosed; the reasonableness of significant accounting estimates made by the directors; and the overall presentation of the financial statements. In addition, we read all the financial and non-financial information in the [describe the annual report] to identify material inconsistencies with the audited financial statements. If we become aware of any apparent material misstatements or inconsistencies we consider the implications for our report.

Opinion on financial statements

In our opinion:

- the group financial statements give a true and fair view, in accordance with IFRSs as adopted by the European Union, of the state of the group's affairs as at ...... and of its [profit/loss] for the year then ended;

- the parent company balance sheet gives a true and fair view in accordance with Generally Accepted Accounting Practice in Ireland of the state of the parent company's affairs as at ....; and

- the financial statements have been properly prepared in accordance with the requirements of the Companies Acts 1963 to 2012 and, as regards the group financial statements, Article 4 of the IAS Regulation.

[Separate opinion in relation to IFRSs as issued by the IASB

As explained in note [x] to the financial statements, the group in addition to complying with its legal obligation to comply with IFRSs as adopted by the European Union, have also complied with the IFRSs as issued by the International Accounting Standards Board (IASB).

In our opinion the group financial statements comply with IFRSs as issued by the IASB.]

Matters on which we are required to report by the Companies Acts 1963 to 2012

- We have obtained all the information and explanations which we consider necessary for the purposes of our audit.

- In our opinion proper books of account have been kept by the parent company.

- The parent company balance sheet is in agreement with the books of account.

- In our opinion the information given in the directors' report is consistent with the financial statements.

- The net assets of the parent company, as stated in the parent company balance sheet are more than half of the amount of its called-up share capital and, in our opinion, on that basis there did not exist at .... a financial situation which under Section 40 (1) of the Companies (Amendment) Act, 1983 would require the convening of an extraordinary general meeting of the parent company.

- In our opinion the information given in the directors' report is consistent with the financial statements and the description in the Corporate Governance Statement of the main features of the internal control and risk management systems in relation to the process for preparing the group financial statements is consistent with the group financial statements.

Matters on which we are required to report by exception

We have nothing to report in respect of the following:

Under the Companies Acts 1963 to 2012 we are required to report to you if, in our opinion the disclosures of directors' remuneration and transactions specified by law are not made.

Under the Listing Rules of the Irish Stock Exchange we are required to review:

- the directors' statement, [set out [on page...]], in relation to going concern;

- the part of the Corporate Governance Statement relating to the company's compliance with the nine provisions of the UK Corporate Governance Code and the two provisions of the Irish Corporate Governance Annex specified for our review; and

- the six specified elements of the disclosures in the report to shareholders by the Board on directors' remuneration.

[Signature]   *Address*
Seán MacGabhan   *Date*
for and on behalf of ABC & Co

Example 16 – Publicly traded group – Parent company incorporated in Ireland prepares financial statements under Irish GAAP and corporate governance statement not incorporated in the directors' report

- *Company has equity shares with a primary listing on the Main Securities Market ("MSM") of the Irish Stock Exchange and is subject to the continuing obligations in relation to the annual report as set out in Chapter 6 of the Listing Rules of the MSM.*

- *Company does prepare group financial statements and Section 148(8) exemption taken in respect of parent company's own profit and loss account.*

- *Corporate governance statement not incorporated into the directors' report, either directly or by incorporation by reference as explained in Bulletin 2011/1 issued by the APB (the underlined text has been revised or included in the auditor's report as a consequence of the statement not being incorporated in the director's report).*

INDEPENDENT AUDITOR'S REPORT TO THE MEMBERS OF XYZ PLC

We have audited the financial statements of (name of company) for the year ended ... which comprise [specify the titles of the primary statements such as the Group Statement of Financial Position and Parent Company Balance Sheet, the Group Statement of Comprehensive Income, the Group Statement of Cash Flows, the Group Statement of Changes in Equity][44] and the related notes[45]. The financial reporting framework that has been applied in the preparation of the group financial statements is Irish law and International Financial Reporting Standards (IFRSs) as adopted by the European Union. The financial reporting framework that has been applied in the preparation of the parent company financial statements is Irish law and accounting standards issued by the Financial Reporting Council and promulgated by the Institute of Chartered Accountants in Ireland (Generally Accepted Accounting Practice in Ireland).

Respective responsibilities of directors and auditors

As explained more fully in the Directors' Responsibilities Statement [set out [on page ....]] the directors are responsible for the preparation of the financial statements giving a true and fair view. Our responsibility is to audit and express an opinion on the financial statements in accordance with Irish law and International Standards on Auditing (UK and Ireland). Those standards require us to comply with the Auditing Practices Board's [APB's] Ethical Standards for Auditors.

---

[44] The names used for the primary statements in the auditor's report should reflect the precise titles used by the company for them.

[45] Auditor's reports of entities that do not publish their financial statements on a web site or publish them using 'PDF' format may continue to refer to the financial statements by reference to page numbers.

Scope of the audit of the financial statements

Either:

A description of the scope of an audit of financial statements is [provided on the FRC's website at www.frc.org.uk/audit-scope-ireland] / [set out [on page...] of the Annual Report].

Or:

An audit involves obtaining evidence about the amounts and disclosures in the financial statements sufficient to give reasonable assurance that the financial statements are free from material misstatement, whether caused by fraud or error. This includes an assessment of: whether the accounting policies are appropriate to the group and the parent company's circumstances and have been consistently applied and adequately disclosed; the reasonableness of significant accounting estimates made by the directors; and the overall presentation of the financial statements. In addition, we read all the financial and non-financial information in the [describe the annual report] to identify material inconsistencies with the audited financial statements. If we become aware of any apparent material misstatements or inconsistencies we consider the implications for our report.

Opinion on financial statements

In our opinion:

- the group financial statements give a true and fair view, in accordance with IFRSs as adopted by the European Union, of the state of the group's affairs as at ...... and of its [profit/loss] for the year then ended;

- the parent company balance sheet gives a true and fair view in accordance with Generally Accepted Accounting Practice in Ireland of the state of the company's affairs as at ....; and

- the financial statements have been properly prepared in accordance with the requirements of the Companies Acts 1963 to 2012 and, as regards the group financial statements, Article 4 of the IAS Regulation.

[Separate opinion in relation to IFRSs as issued by the IASB

As explained in note [x] to the financial statements, the group in addition to complying with its legal obligation to comply with IFRSs as adopted by the European Union, have also complied with the IFRSs as issued by the International Accounting Standards Board (IASB).

In our opinion the group financial statements comply with IFRSs as issued by the IASB.]

Matters on which we are required to report by the Companies Acts 1963 to 2012

- We have obtained all the information and explanations which we consider necessary for the purposes of our audit.

- In our opinion proper books of account have been kept by the parent company.

- The parent company balance sheet is in agreement with the books of account.

- In our opinion the information given in the directors' report is consistent with the financial statements.

- The net assets of the parent company, as stated in the parent company balance sheet are more than half of the amount of its called-up share capital and, in our opinion, on that basis there did not exist at .... a financial situation which under Section 40 (1) of the Companies (Amendment) Act, 1983 would require the convening of an extraordinary general meeting of the parent company.

- In our opinion the information required by Section 158(6D)(d) of the Companies Act 1963 [on pages] [in describe document] [at include web address] in the Corporate Governance Statement is consistent with the parent company financial statements and the description of the main features of the internal control and risk management systems in relation to the process for preparing the group and parent company financial statements in that statement is consistent with the group and parent company financial statements.

Matters on which we are required to report by exception

We have nothing to report in respect of the following:

Under the Companies Acts 1963 to 2012 we are required to report to you if, in our opinion:

- the disclosures of directors' remuneration and transactions specified by law are not made; or

- a Corporate Governance Statement has not been prepared by the company; or

- the Corporate Governance Statement does not contain the information required by Section 158(6D) (a), (b), (e) and (f) of the Companies Act 1963.

Under the Listing Rules of the Irish Stock Exchange we are required to review:

- the directors' statement, [set out [on page...]], in relation to going concern;

- the part of the Corporate Governance Statement relating to the company's compliance with the nine provisions of the UK Corporate Governance Code and the two provisions of the Irish Corporate Governance Annex specified for our review; and

- the six specified elements of the disclosures in the report to shareholders by the Board on directors' remuneration.

[Signature]   *Address*
Seán MacGabhan   *Date*
for and on behalf of ABC & Co

Example 17 – Private company with publicly traded listed debt – Parent company incorporated in Ireland preparing financial statements under IFRSs as adopted by the European Union

- *Company has debt securities only with a primary listing on the Main Securities Market of the Irish Stock Exchange and is subject to the continuing obligations in relation to the annual report as set out in Chapter 15 of the Listing Rules of the MSM.*

- *Company prepares group financial statements under IFRSs as adopted by the European Union and Section 148(8) exemption taken in respect of the parent company's own statement of comprehensive income.*

- *Corporate governance statement incorporated into the directors' report, either directly or by incorporation by reference as explained in Bulletin 2011/1 issued by the APB[46].*

INDEPENDENT AUDITOR'S REPORT TO THE MEMBERS OF XYZ LIMITED

We have audited the financial statements of (name of company) for the year ended ... which comprise [specify the titles of the primary statements such as the Group and Parent Company Statements of Financial Position, the Group Statement of Comprehensive Income, the Group and Parent Company Cash Flow Statements, the Group and Parent Company Statements of Changes in Equity][47] and the related notes[48]. The financial reporting framework that has been applied in their preparation is Irish law and International Financial Reporting Standards (IFRSs) as adopted by the European Union and, as regards the parent company financial statements, as applied in accordance with the provisions of the Companies Acts 1963 to 2012.

Respective responsibilities of directors and auditors

As explained more fully in the Directors' Responsibilities Statement [set out [on page ....]] the directors are responsible for the preparation of the financial statements giving a true and fair view. Our responsibility is to audit and express an opinion on the financial statements in accordance with Irish law and International Standards on Auditing (UK and Ireland). Those standards require us to comply with the Auditing Practices Board's [APB's] Ethical Standards for Auditors.

---

[46] See example 16 for an illustration of an auditor's report where the corporate governance statement is not incorporated into the directors' report.

[47] The names used for the primary statements in the auditor's report should reflect the precise titles used by the company for them.

[48] Auditor's reports of entities that do not publish their financial statements on a web site or publish them using 'PDF' format may continue to refer to the financial statements by reference to page numbers.

Scope of the audit of the financial statements

Either:

A description of the scope of an audit of financial statements is [provided on the FRC's website at www.frc.org.uk/audit-scope-ireland] / [set out [on page...] of the Annual Report].

Or:

An audit involves obtaining evidence about the amounts and disclosures in the financial statements sufficient to give reasonable assurance that the financial statements are free from material misstatement, whether caused by fraud or error. This includes an assessment of: whether the accounting policies are appropriate to the group and the parent company's circumstances and have been consistently applied and adequately disclosed; the reasonableness of significant accounting estimates made by the directors; and the overall presentation of the financial statements. In addition, we read all the financial and non-financial information in the [describe the annual report] to identify material inconsistencies with the audited financial statements. If we become aware of any apparent material misstatements or inconsistencies we consider the implications for our report.

Opinion on financial statements

In our opinion:

- the group financial statements give a true and fair view, in accordance with IFRSs as adopted by the European Union, of the state of the group's affairs as at ...... and of its [profit/loss] for the year then ended;

- the parent company statement of financial position gives a true and fair view, in accordance with IFRSs as adopted by the European Union as applied in accordance with the provisions of the Companies Acts 1963 to 2012, of the state of the parent company's affairs as at ...... ; and

- the financial statements have been properly prepared in accordance with the requirements of the Companies Acts 1963 to 2012 and, as regards the group financial statements, Article 4 of the IAS Regulation.

[Separate opinion in relation to IFRSs as issued by the IASB

As explained in note [x] to the financial statements, the group in addition to complying with its legal obligation to comply with IFRSs as adopted by the European Union, have also complied with the IFRSs as issued by the International Accounting Standards Board (IASB).

In our opinion the group financial statements comply with IFRSs as issued by the IASB.]

Matters on which we are required to report by the Companies Acts 1963 to 2012

- We have obtained all the information and explanations which we consider necessary for the purposes of our audit.

- In our opinion proper books of account have been kept by the parent company.

- The parent company statement of financial position is in agreement with the books of account.

- In our opinion the information given in the directors' report is consistent with the financial statements and the description in the Corporate Governance Statement of the main features of the internal control and risk management systems in relation to the process for preparing the group financial statements is consistent with the group financial statements.

- The net assets of the parent company, as stated in the parent company statement of financial position is more than half of the amount of its called-up share capital and, in our opinion, on that basis there did not exist at .... a financial situation which under Section 40 (1) of the Companies (Amendment) Act, 1983 would require the convening of an extraordinary general meeting of the parent company.

Matters on which we are required to report by exception

We have nothing to report in respect of the provisions in the Companies Acts 1963 to 2012 which require us to report to you if, in our opinion the disclosures of directors' remuneration and transactions specified by law are not made.

[Signature]	*Address*
Seán MacGabhan	*Date*
for and on behalf of ABC & Co	

Example 18 – Publicly traded collective investment fund – Parent company incorporated in Ireland prepares financial statements under IFRSs as adopted by the European Union

- *Company is a collective investment fund with a primary listing on the Main Securities Market of the Irish Stock Exchange and is subject to the requirements for Annual Report and Financial Statements as set out in the Code of Listing Requirements and Procedures for Investment Funds and/or Chapter 14 of the Listing Rules of the MSM.*

- *Company prepares group financial statements under IFRSs as adopted by the European Union and Section 148(8) exemption taken in respect of the parent company's own statement of comprehensive income.*

- *Corporate governance statement incorporated into the directors' report, either directly or by incorporation by reference as explained in Bulletin 2011/1 issued by the APB[49].*

INDEPENDENT AUDITOR'S REPORT TO THE MEMBERS OF XYZ PLC

We have audited the financial statements of (name of company) for the year ended ... which comprise [specify the titles of the primary statements such as the Group and Parent Company Statements of Financial Position, the Group Statement of Comprehensive Income, the Group and Parent Company Statements of Changes in Net Assets attributable to holders of redeemable shares][50] and the related notes[51]. The financial reporting framework that has been applied in their preparation is Irish law and International Financial Reporting Standards (IFRSs) as adopted by the European Union and, as regards the parent company financial statements, as applied in accordance with the provisions of the Companies Acts 1963 to 2012 [and the European Communities (Undertakings for Collective Investment in Transferable Securities) Regulations, 2011][52].

Respective responsibilities of directors and auditors

As explained more fully in the Directors' Responsibilities Statement [set out [on page ....]] the directors are responsible for the preparation of the financial statements giving a true and fair view. Our responsibility is to audit and express an opinion on the financial statements in accordance with Irish law and International Standards on Auditing (UK and Ireland). Those

---

[49] See example 16 for an illustration of an auditor's report where the corporate governance statement is not incorporated into the directors' report.

[50] The names used for the primary statements in the auditor's report should reflect the precise titles used by the company for them.

[51] Auditor's reports of entities that do not publish their financial statements on a web site or publish them using 'PDF' format may continue to refer to the financial statements by reference to page numbers.

[52] Include if the fund is a UCITS fund.

standards require us to comply with the Auditing Practices Board's [APB's] Ethical Standards for Auditors.

Scope of the audit of the financial statements

Either:

> A description of the scope of an audit of financial statements is [provided on the FRC's website at www.frc.org.uk/audit-scope-ireland] / [set out [on page...] of the Annual Report].

Or:

> An audit involves obtaining evidence about the amounts and disclosures in the financial statements sufficient to give reasonable assurance that the financial statements are free from material misstatement, whether caused by fraud or error. This includes an assessment of: whether the accounting policies are appropriate to the group and the parent company's circumstances and have been consistently applied and adequately disclosed; the reasonableness of significant accounting estimates made by the directors; and the overall presentation of the financial statements. In addition, we read all the financial and non-financial information in the [describe the annual report] to identify material inconsistencies with the audited financial statements. If we become aware of any apparent material misstatements or inconsistencies we consider the implications for our report.

Opinion on financial statements

In our opinion:

- the group financial statements give a true and fair view, in accordance with IFRSs as adopted by the European Union, of the state of the group's affairs as at ...... and of its [profit/loss] for the year then ended;

- the parent company statement of financial position gives a true and fair view, in accordance with IFRSs as adopted by the European Union as applied in accordance with the provisions of the Companies Acts 1963 to 2012, of the state of the parent company's affairs as at ...... ; and

- the financial statements have been properly prepared in accordance with the requirements of the Companies Acts 1963 to 2012 [, the European Communities (Undertakings for Collective Investment in Transferable Securities) Regulations, 2011][53] and, as regards the group financial statements, Article 4 of the IAS Regulation.

---

[53] Include if the fund is a UCITS fund.

[Separate opinion in relation to IFRSs as issued by the IASB

As explained in note [x] to the financial statements, the group in addition to complying with its legal obligation to comply with IFRSs as adopted by the European Union, have also complied with the IFRSs as issued by the International Accounting Standards Board (IASB).

In our opinion the group financial statements comply with IFRSs as issued by the IASB.]

Matters on which we are required to report by the Companies Acts 1963 to 2012

- We have obtained all the information and explanations which we consider necessary for the purposes of our audit.

- In our opinion proper books of account have been kept by the parent company.

- The parent company statement of financial position is in agreement with the books of account.

- In our opinion the information given in the directors' report is consistent with the financial statements and the description in the Corporate Governance Statement of the main features of the internal control and risk management systems in relation to the process for preparing the group financial statements is consistent with the group financial statements.

Matters on which we are required to report by exception

We have nothing to report in respect of the provisions in the Companies Acts 1963 to 2012 which require us to report to you if, in our opinion the disclosures of directors' remuneration and transactions specified by law are not made.

[Signature]
Seán MacGabhan
for and on behalf of ABC & Co

Address
Date

Example 19 – State Body incorporated in Ireland preparing group financial statements under Irish GAAP

- *Company is a State Body subject to the Code of Practice for the Governance of State Bodies.*

- *Company is not a listed company.*

- *Company prepares group financial statements under Irish GAAP and Section 148(8) exemption taken in respect of the parent company's own profit and loss account.*

INDEPENDENT AUDITOR'S REPORT TO THE MEMBERS OF XYZ LIMITED

We have audited the financial statements of (name of company) for the year ended ... which comprise [specify the titles of the primary statements such as the Profit and Loss Account, the Group and Parent Company Balance Sheets, the Group Cash Flow Statement, the Group Statement of Total Recognised Gains and Losses] and the related notes[54]. The financial reporting framework that has been applied in their preparation is Irish law and accounting standards issued by the Financial Reporting Council and promulgated by the Institute of Chartered Accountants in Ireland (Generally Accepted Accounting Practice in Ireland).

Respective responsibilities of directors and auditors

As explained more fully in the Directors' Responsibilities Statement [set out [on page ....]] the directors are responsible for the preparation of the financial statements giving a true and fair view. Our responsibility is to audit and express an opinion on the financial statements in accordance with Irish law and International Standards on Auditing (UK and Ireland). Those standards require us to comply with the Auditing Practices Board's [APB's] Ethical Standards for Auditors.

Scope of the audit of the financial statements

Either:

> A description of the scope of an audit of financial statements is [provided on the FRC's website at www.frc.org.uk/audit-scope-ireland] / [set out [on page...] of the Annual Report].

---

[54] Auditor's reports of entities that do not publish their financial statements on a web site or publish them using 'PDF' format may continue to refer to the financial statements by reference to page numbers.

Or:

An audit involves obtaining evidence about the amounts and disclosures in the financial statements sufficient to give reasonable assurance that the financial statements are free from material misstatement, whether caused by fraud or error. This includes an assessment of: whether the accounting policies are appropriate to the group's and the parent company's circumstances and have been consistently applied and adequately disclosed; the reasonableness of significant accounting estimates made by the directors; and the overall presentation of the financial statements. In addition, we read all the financial and non-financial information in the [describe the annual report] to identify material inconsistencies with the audited financial statements. If we become aware of any apparent material misstatements or inconsistencies we consider the implications for our report.

Opinion on financial statements

In our opinion the financial statements:

- give a true and fair view in accordance with Generally Accepted Accounting Practice in Ireland of the state of the group's and parent company's affairs as at .... and of the group's [profit/loss] for the year then ended; and

- have been properly prepared in accordance with the requirements of the Companies Acts 1963 to 2012.

Matters on which we are required to report by the Companies Acts 1963 to 2012

- We have obtained all the information and explanations which we consider necessary for the purposes of our audit.

- In our opinion proper books of account have been kept by the parent company.

- The parent company balance sheet is in agreement with the books of account.

- In our opinion the information given in the directors' report is consistent with the financial statements.

- The net assets of the parent company, as stated in the parent company balance sheet are more than half of the amount of its called-up share capital and, in our opinion, on that basis there did not exist at .... a financial situation which under Section 40 (1) of the Companies (Amendment) Act, 1983 would require the convening of an extraordinary general meeting of the parent company.

Matters on which we are required to report by exception

We have nothing to report in respect of the following:

Under the Companies Acts 1963 to 2012 we are required to report to you if, in our opinion the disclosures of directors' remuneration and transactions specified by law are not made.

Under the Code of Practice for the Governance of State Bodies ("the Code") we are required to report to you if the statement regarding the system of internal financial control required under the Code [as included in the Corporate Governance Statement] on page(s) [to] does not reflect the group's compliance with paragraph 13.1 (iii) of the Code or if it is not consistent with the information of which we are aware from our audit work on the financial statements and we report if it does not.

[Signature]   *Address*
Seán MacGabhan   *Date*
for and on behalf of ABC & Co

Appendix 3

Other auditor's reports

20. Credit Union preparing financial statements under Irish GAAP

21. Industrial and Provident Society preparing financial statements under Irish GAAP

22. Friendly Society preparing financial statements under Irish GAAP

23. Defined Benefit/Defined Contribution Scheme/ Plan preparing financial statements under Irish GAAP

Example 20 – Credit Union preparing financial statements under Irish GAAP

- *Replacing Illustrative Auditor's Report on financial statements for a Credit Union – Appendix 1 PN 27(I).*

- *Group financial statements not prepared.*

INDEPENDENT AUDITOR'S REPORT TO THE MEMBERS OF XYZ CREDIT UNION LIMITED

We have audited the financial statements of (name of credit union) for the year ended ... which comprise [specify the titles of the primary statements such as the Income and Expenditure Account, the Balance Sheet, the Cash Flow Statement, the Statement of Total Recognised Gains and Losses][55] and the related notes[56]. The financial reporting framework that has been applied in their preparation is Irish law and accounting standards issued by the Financial Reporting Council and promulgated by the Institute of Chartered Accountants in Ireland (Generally Accepted Accounting Practice in Ireland).

Respective responsibilities of directors and auditor

As explained more fully in the Directors' Responsibilities Statement [set out [on page ...]], the directors are responsible for the preparation of the financial statements giving a true and fair view. Our responsibility is to audit and express an opinion on the financial statements in accordance with Irish law and International Standards on Auditing (UK and Ireland). Those standards require us to comply with the Auditing Practices Board's [(APB's)] Ethical Standards for Auditors.

Scope of the audit of the financial statements

Either:

> A description of the scope of an audit of financial statements is [provided on the FRC's website at www.frc.org.uk/audit-scope-ireland] / [set out [on page ...] of the Annual Report].

---

[55] The names used for the primary statements in the auditor's report should reflect the precise titles used by the company for them.

[56] Auditor's reports of entities that do not publish their financial statements on a website or publish them using 'PDF' format may refer to the financial statements by reference to page numbers.

Or:

> An audit involves obtaining evidence about the amounts and disclosures in the financial statements sufficient to give reasonable assurance that the financial statements are free from material misstatement, whether caused by fraud or error. This includes an assessment of: whether the accounting policies are appropriate to the credit union's circumstances and have been consistently applied and adequately disclosed; the reasonableness of significant accounting estimates made by the directors; and the overall presentation of the financial statements. In addition, we read all the financial and non-financial information in the [describe the annual report] to identify material inconsistencies with the audited financial statements. If we become aware of any apparent material misstatements or inconsistencies we consider the implications for our report.

Opinion on financial statements

In our opinion the financial statements:

- give a true and fair view of the state of the credit union's affairs as at .... and of its income and expenditure for the year then ended;

- have been prepared in accordance with Generally Accepted Accounting Practice in Ireland; and

- have been properly prepared so as to conform with the requirements of the Credit Union Act 1997.

Other matters prescribed by the Credit Union Act 1997

- We have obtained all the information and explanations which we considered were necessary for the purposes of our audit.

- In our opinion proper accounting records have been kept by the credit union.

- The financial statements are in agreement with the accounting records.

[Firm Signature]   *Address*
ABC & Co.   *Date*

Example 21 – Industrial and Provident Society preparing financial statements under Irish GAAP

- *Society does not prepare group financial statements.*

- *This auditor's report pertains to the annual financial statements of the Society and not to the annual return required by the Industrial and Provident Societies Acts 1893 to 1978.*

INDEPENDENT AUDITOR'S REPORT TO THE MEMBERS OF XYZ CO-OPERATIVE SOCIETY LIMITED

We have audited the financial statements of (name of company) for the year ended ... which comprise [specify the titles of the primary statements such as the Profit and Loss Account, the Balance Sheet, the Cash Flow Statement, the Statement of Total Recognised Gains and Losses, the Reconciliation of Movements in Shareholders' Funds] and the related notes[57]. The financial reporting framework that has been applied in their preparation is Irish law and accounting standards issued by the Financial Reporting Council and promulgated by the Institute of Chartered Accountants in Ireland (Generally Accepted Accounting Practice in Ireland).

Respective responsibilities of [committee of management][trustees] and auditors

As explained more fully in the [Committee of Management][Trustees'] Responsibilities Statement [set out [on page ....]] the [committee of management][trustees] are responsible for the preparation of the financial statements giving a true and fair view. Our responsibility is to audit and express an opinion on the financial statements in accordance with Irish law and International Standards on Auditing (UK and Ireland). Those standards require us to comply with the Auditing Practices Board's [APB's] Ethical Standards for Auditors[58].

Scope of the audit of the financial statements

Either:

A description of the scope of an audit of financial statements is [provided on the FRC's website at www.frc.org.uk/audit-scope-ireland] / [set out [on page...] of the Annual Report].

---

[57] Auditor's reports of entities that do not publish their financial statements on a web site or publish them using 'PDF' format may continue to refer to the financial statements by reference to page numbers.

[58] If the company is a small entity as defined in paragraph 4(ii) of the APB Ethical Standard – Provisions Available for Small Entities, add 'including "APB Ethical Standard – Provisions Available for Small Entities (revised)", in the circumstances set out in note [x] to the financial statements' if the auditor has availed of the exemption set out in paragraph 24 the Ethical Standard ("ES"). The Appendix to the ES provides illustrative disclosures of relevant circumstances where the auditor has taken advantage of such an exemption.

Or:

> An audit involves obtaining evidence about the amounts and disclosures in the financial statements sufficient to give reasonable assurance that the financial statements are free from material misstatement, whether caused by fraud or error. This includes an assessment of: whether the accounting policies are appropriate to the company's circumstances and have been consistently applied and adequately disclosed; the reasonableness of significant accounting estimates made by the [committee of management][trustees]; and the overall presentation of the financial statements. In addition, we read all the financial and non-financial information in the [describe the annual report] to identify material inconsistencies with the audited financial statements. If we become aware of any apparent material misstatements or inconsistencies we consider the implications for our report.

Opinion on financial statements

In our opinion the financial statements

- give a true and fair view of the state of the society's affairs as at .... and of its [profit [loss]] [surplus/[deficit]] for the year then ended; and

- have been prepared in accordance with Generally Accepted Accounting Practice in Ireland.

As required by Section 13(2) of the Industrial and Provident Societies Act 1893 we examined the balance sheets showing the receipts and expenditure, funds and effects of the society, and verified the same with the books, deeds, documents, accounts and vouchers relating thereto, and found them to be correct, duly vouched, and in accordance with law.

[Firm Signature]   *Address*
ABC & Co.   *Date*

Example 22 – Friendly Society preparing financial statements under Irish GAAP

- *Society does not prepare group financial statements.*

- *This auditor's report pertains to the annual financial statements of the Society and not to the annual return required by the Friendly Societies Acts 1896 to 1977.*

INDEPENDENT AUDITOR'S REPORT TO THE MEMBERS OF XYZ FRIENDLY SOCIETY LIMITED

We have audited the financial statements of (name of company) for the year ended ... which comprise [specify the titles of the primary statements such as the Profit and Loss Account, the Balance Sheet, the Cash Flow Statement, the Statement of Total Recognised Gains and Losses, the Reconciliation of Movements in Shareholders' Funds] and the related notes[59]. The financial reporting framework that has been applied in their preparation is Irish law and accounting standards issued by the Financial Reporting Council and promulgated by the Institute of Chartered Accountants in Ireland (Generally Accepted Accounting Practice in Ireland).

Respective responsibilities of [committee of management][trustees] and auditors

As explained more fully in the [Committee of Management][Trustees'] Responsibilities Statement [set out [on page ....]] the [committee of management][trustees] are responsible for the preparation of the financial statements giving a true and fair view. Our responsibility is to audit and express an opinion on the financial statements in accordance with Irish law and International Standards on Auditing (UK and Ireland). Those standards require us to comply with the Auditing Practices Board's [APB's] Ethical Standards for Auditors[60].

Scope of the audit of the financial statements

Either:

> A description of the scope of an audit of financial statements is [provided on the FRC's website at www.frc.org.uk/audit-scope-ireland] / [set out [on page...] of the Annual Report].

---

[59] Auditor's reports of entities that do not publish their financial statements on a web site or publish them using 'PDF' format may continue to refer to the financial statements by reference to page numbers.

[60] If the company is a small entity as defined in paragraph 4(ii) of the APB Ethical Standard – Provisions Available for Small Entities, add 'including "APB Ethical Standard – Provisions Available for Small Entities (revised)", in the circumstances set out in note [x] to the financial statements' if the auditor has availed of the exemption set out in paragraph 24 the Ethical Standard ("ES"). The Appendix to the ES provides illustrative disclosures of relevant circumstances where the auditor has taken advantage of such an exemption.

Or:

An audit involves obtaining evidence about the amounts and disclosures in the financial statements sufficient to give reasonable assurance that the financial statements are free from material misstatement, whether caused by fraud or error. This includes an assessment of: whether the accounting policies are appropriate to the company's circumstances and have been consistently applied and adequately disclosed; the reasonableness of significant accounting estimates made by the [committee of management] [trustees]; and the overall presentation of the financial statements. In addition, we read all the financial and non-financial information in the [describe the annual report] to identify material inconsistencies with the audited financial statements. If we become aware of any apparent material misstatements or inconsistencies we consider the implications for our report.

Opinion on financial statements

In our opinion the financial statements

- give a true and fair view of the state of the society's affairs as at .... and of its [profit [loss]] [surplus/[deficit]] for the year then ended; and

- have been prepared in accordance with Generally Accepted Accounting Practice in Ireland.

[Firm Signature]   *Address*
ABC & Co.   *Date*

Example 23 – Defined Benefit/Defined Contribution Scheme/ Plan preparing financial statements under Irish GAAP

INDEPENDENT AUDITOR'S REPORT TO THE TRUSTEE[S] OF XYZ PENSION SCHEME/PLAN

We have audited the financial statements of (name of scheme/plan) for the year ended ... which comprise [specify the titles of the primary statements such as the Fund Account, the Net Assets Statement] and the related notes[61]. The financial reporting framework that has been applied in their preparation is Irish pension law and accounting standards issued by the Financial Reporting Council and promulgated by the Institute of Chartered Accountants in Ireland (Generally Accepted Accounting Practice in Ireland).

Respective responsibilities of trustee[s] and auditors

As explained more fully in the Trustees' Responsibilities Statement [set out [on page ...]], the trustees are responsible for the preparation of the financial statements giving a true and fair view, and for ensuring that contributions are made to the [scheme/plan] in accordance with the [scheme's/plan's] rules [and the recommendation of the actuary][62]. Our responsibility is to audit and express an opinion on the financial statements in accordance with Irish pension law and International Standards on Auditing (UK and Ireland). Those standards require us to comply with the Auditing Practices Board's [(APB's)] Ethical Standards for Auditors.

Scope of the audit of the financial statements

Either:

> A description of the scope of an audit of financial statements is [provided on the FRC's website at www.frc.org.uk/audit-scope-ireland] / [set out [on page ...] of the Annual Report].

---

[61] Auditor's reports of entities that do not publish their financial statements on a web site or publish them using 'PDF' format may continue to refer to the financial statements by reference to page numbers.

[62] Only include text if the scheme/Plan is Defined Benefit.

Or:

> An audit involves obtaining evidence about the amounts and disclosures in the financial statements sufficient to give reasonable assurance that the financial statements are free from material misstatement, whether caused by fraud or error. This includes an assessment of: whether the accounting policies are appropriate to the [scheme's/plan's] circumstances and have been consistently applied and adequately disclosed; the reasonableness of significant accounting estimates made by the trustees; and the overall presentation of the financial statements. In addition, we read all the financial and non-financial information in the [describe the annual report] to identify material inconsistencies with the audited financial statements. If we become aware of any apparent material misstatements or inconsistencies we consider the implications for our report.

Opinion on financial statements

In our opinion the financial statements:

- give a true and fair view of the financial transactions of the [scheme/plan] during the year ended .... and of the amount and disposition of the assets and liabilities (other than liabilities to pay pensions and other benefits in the future) at that date; and

- are prepared in accordance with Generally Accepted Accounting Practice in Ireland.

Opinions on other matters prescribed by the Occupational Pension Scheme (Disclosure of Information) Regulations 2006

In our opinion:

- the financial statements include the information specified in Schedule A to the Occupational Pension Schemes (Disclosure of Information) Regulations 2006 which is applicable and material to the [scheme/plan];

- the contributions payable to the [scheme / plan] during the year ended.......... have been received by the trustees within thirty days of the end of the [scheme / plan] year; and

- the contributions have been paid in accordance with the rules of the [scheme / plan] [and the recommendation of the actuary][62].

[Firm Signature]   *Address*
ABC & Co.   *Date*

Appendix 4

Emphasis of matter paragraphs

24. Emphasis of matter: Material uncertainty that may cast significant doubt about the company's ability to continue as a going concern

25. Emphasis of matter: Uncertain outcome of a lawsuit

Example 24 – Emphasis of matter: Material uncertainty that may cast significant doubt about the company's ability to continue as a going concern

- *Irish non-publicly traded company prepares Irish GAAP financial statements (Example 2).*

- *The company incurred a net loss of €X during the year ended 31 December 20X1 and, as at that date, the company's current liabilities exceeded its total assets by €Y and it had net current liabilities of €Z.*

- *These conditions, along with other matters set forth in the notes to the financial statements, indicate the existence of a material uncertainty, which may cast significant doubt about the company's ability to continue as a going concern.*

- *The company makes relevant disclosures in the financial statements including those referred to in paragraphs 18 and 19 of ISA (UK and Ireland) 570 "Going Concern".*

- *The auditor issues an unmodified opinion with an emphasis of matter paragraph describing the situation giving rise to the emphasis of matter and its possible effects on the financial statements, including (where practicable) quantification.*

Extract from auditor's report

...

Opinion on financial statements

In our opinion the financial statements:

- give a true and fair view, in accordance with Generally Accepted Accounting Practice in Ireland, of the state of the company's affairs as at 31 December 20X1 and of its loss for the year then ended; and

- have been properly prepared in accordance with the requirements of the Companies Acts 1963 to 2012.

Emphasis of matter – Going concern

In forming our opinion on the financial statements, which is not modified, we have considered the adequacy of the disclosure made in note [x] to the financial statements concerning the company's ability to continue as a going concern. The company incurred a net loss of €X during the year ended 31 December 201X and, at that date, the company's current liabilities exceeded its total assets by €Y and it had net current liabilities of €Z. These conditions, along with the other matters explained in note [x] to the financial statements, indicate the existence of a material uncertainty which may cast significant doubt about the company's ability to continue as a going concern. The financial statements do not include the adjustments that would result if the company was unable to continue as a going concern.

Matters on which we are required to report by the Companies Acts 1963 to 2012

...

Example 25 – Emphasis of matter: Uncertain outcome of a lawsuit

- *Irish non-publicly traded company prepares Irish GAAP financial statements (Example 2).*

- *A lawsuit alleges that the company has infringed certain patent rights and claims royalties and damages. The company has filed a counter action, and preliminary hearings and discovery proceedings on both actions are in progress.*

- *The ultimate outcome of the matter cannot presently be determined, and no provision for any liability that may result has been made in the financial statements.*

- *The company makes relevant disclosures in the financial statements.*

- *The auditor issues an unmodified opinion with an emphasis of matter paragraph describing the situation giving rise to the emphasis of matter and its possible effects on the financial statements, including that the effect on the financial statements of the resolution of the uncertainty cannot be quantified.*

Extract from auditor's report

...

Opinion on financial statements

In our opinion the financial statements:

- give a true and fair view, in accordance with Generally Accepted Accounting Practice in Ireland, of the state of the company's affairs as at ... and of its profit [loss] for the year then ended; and

- have been properly prepared in accordance with the requirements of the Companies Acts 1963 to 2012.

Emphasis of matter – uncertain outcome of a lawsuit

In forming our opinion on the financial statements, which is not modified, we have considered the adequacy of the disclosures made in note [x] to the financial statements concerning the uncertain outcome of a lawsuit, alleging infringement of certain patent rights and claiming royalties and punitive damages, where the company is the defendant. The company has filed a counter action, and preliminary hearings and discovery proceedings on both actions are in progress. The ultimate outcome of the matter cannot presently be determined, and no provision for any liability that may result has been made in the financial statements.

Matters on which we are required to report by the Companies Acts 1963 to 2012

...

Appendix 5

Modified opinions – Qualified opinion on financial statements

26. Disagreement – Inappropriate accounting treatment of debtors

27. Disagreement – Non-disclosure of a going concern problem

28. Disagreement – Non-disclosure of information required to be disclosed

29. Limitation of Scope – Auditor not appointed at the time of the stocktaking

30. Limitation of Scope – Directors did not prepare cash flow forecasts sufficiently far into the future to be able to assess the going concern status of the company

Example 26 – Qualified opinion: Disagreement – Inappropriate accounting treatment of debtors

- *Irish non-publicly traded company prepares Irish GAAP financial statements (Example 2).*

- *The debtors shown on the balance sheet include an amount of €Y due from a company which has ceased trading. XYZ Limited has no security for this debt.*

- *The auditor's opinion is that the company is unlikely to receive any payment and full allowance of €Y should have been made.*

- *The auditor believes that the effect of the disagreement is material but not pervasive to the financial statements and accordingly issues a qualified opinion – except for disagreement about the accounting treatment of debtors.*

- *The auditor concludes that it is still possible to express the 'financial situation' opinion.*

Extract from auditor's report

...

Basis for qualified opinion on financial statements

Included in the debtors shown on the balance sheet is an amount of €Y due from a company which has ceased trading. XYZ Limited has no security for this debt. In our opinion the company is unlikely to receive any payment and full allowance of €Y should have been made. Accordingly, debtors should be reduced by €Y, the deferred tax liability should be reduced by €X and profit for the year and retained earnings should be reduced by €Z.

Qualified opinion on financial statements

In our opinion, except for the effects of the matter described in the Basis for qualified opinion paragraph, the financial statements:

- give a true and fair view, in accordance with Generally Accepted Accounting Practice in Ireland, of the state of the company's affairs as at ... and of its profit [loss] for the year then ended; and

- have been properly prepared in accordance with the requirements of the Companies Acts 1963 to 2012.

Matters on which we are required to report by the Companies Acts 1963 to 2012

- We have obtained all the information and explanations which we consider necessary for the purposes of our audit.

- In our opinion proper books of account have been kept by the company.

- The financial statements are in agreement with the books of account.

- In our opinion the information given in the directors' report is consistent with the financial statements.

- The net assets of the company, as stated in the balance sheet are more than half of the amount of its called-up share capital and, in our opinion, on that basis there did not exist at .... a financial situation which under Section 40 (1) of the Companies (Amendment) Act, 1983 would require the convening of an extraordinary general meeting of the company.

Matters on which we are required to report by exception

We have nothing to report in respect of the provisions in the Companies Acts 1963 to 2012 which require us to report to you if, in our opinion, the disclosures of directors' remuneration and transactions specified by law are not made.

Example 27 – Qualified opinion: Disagreement – Non-disclosure of a going concern problem

- *Irish non-publicly traded company prepares Irish GAAP financial statements (Example 2).*

- *The company's year-end is 31 December 20X1 and neither the financial statements nor the directors' report disclose that the company's financing arrangements expire and amounts outstanding are payable on 19 July 20X2 and that the company has been unable to re-negotiate or obtain replacement financing. The directors continue to talk to potential alternative providers of finance.*

- *This situation indicates the existence of a material uncertainty which may cast significant doubt on the company's ability to continue as a going concern and therefore it may be unable to realise its assets and discharge its liabilities in the normal course of business.*

- *The auditor concludes that there is a significant level of concern about going concern and disagrees with the failure to disclose this information in the financial statements. The auditor believes that the lack of disclosure although material is not pervasive to the financial statements and accordingly issues a qualified opinion describing the disagreement.*

Extract from auditor's report

...

Basis for qualified opinion on financial statements

The company's financing arrangements expire and amounts outstanding are payable on 19 July 20X2. While the directors continue to investigate alternative sources of finance, the company has so far been unable to re-negotiate or obtain replacement financing. This situation indicates the existence of a material uncertainty which may cast significant doubt on the company's ability to continue as a going concern and therefore it may be unable to realise its assets and discharge its liabilities in the normal course of business. The financial statements (and notes thereto) do not disclose this fact.

Qualified opinion on financial statements

In our opinion, except for the effects of the matter described in the Basis for qualified opinion paragraph, the financial statements:

- give a true and fair view, in accordance with Generally Accepted Accounting Practice in Ireland, of the state of the company's affairs as at 31 December 20X1 and of its profit [loss] for the year then ended; and

- have been properly prepared in accordance with the requirements of the Companies Acts 1963 to 2012.

Matters on which we are required to report by the Companies Acts 1963 to 2012

...

Example 28 – Qualified opinion: Disagreement – Non-disclosure of information required to be disclosed

- *Irish non-publicly traded company prepares Irish GAAP financial statements (Example 2).*

- *The company has not disclosed that one of its bankers has a fixed and floating charge over all of the company's assets as security for a long term loan. Such disclosure is required by paragraph 34 of Part IV to the Schedule of the Companies (Amendment) Act 1986.*

Extract from auditor's report

...

Basis for qualified opinion on financial statements

The notes to the financial statements do not disclose that one of the company's bankers has a fixed and floating charge over all of the company's assets as security for a bank loan of €5 million which is included in creditors: amounts falling due after more than one year. Such disclosure is required by the Companies (Amendment) Act 1986.

Qualified opinion on financial statements

In our opinion, except for the effects of the matter described in the Basis for qualified opinion paragraph, the financial statements:

- give a true and fair view, in accordance with Generally Accepted Accounting Practice in Ireland, of the state of the company's affairs as at 31 December 20X1 and of its profit [loss] for the year then ended; and

- have been properly prepared in accordance with the requirements of the Companies Acts 1963 to 2012.

Matters on which are required to report by the Companies Acts 1963 to 2012

...

Example 29 – Qualified opinion: Limitation on scope – Auditor not appointed at the time of the stocktaking

- *Irish non-publicly traded company prepares Irish GAAP financial statements (Example 2).*

- *The evidence available to the auditor was limited because the auditor did not observe the counting of the physical stock as at 31 December 20X1, since that date was prior to the time the auditor was initially engaged as auditor for the company. Owing to the nature of the company's records, the auditor was unable to satisfy itself as to stock quantities using other audit procedures.*

- *The limitation in audit scope causes the auditor to issue a qualified opinion "except for" any adjustments that might have been found to be necessary had it been able to obtain sufficient evidence concerning stock.*

- *The limitation of scope was determined by the auditor to be material but not pervasive to the financial statements.*

- *The auditor concludes that it is still possible to express the 'financial situation' opinion.*

Extract from auditor's report

...

Basis for qualified opinion on financial statements

With respect to stock having a carrying amount of €X the audit evidence available to us was limited because we did not observe the counting of the physical stock as at 31 December 20X1, since that date was prior to our appointment as auditor of the company. Owing to the nature of the company's records, we were unable to obtain sufficient appropriate audit evidence regarding the stock quantities by using other audit procedures.

Qualified opinion on financial statements

In our opinion, except for the possible effects of the matters described in the Basis for qualified opinion paragraph, the financial statements:

- give a true and fair view, in accordance with Generally Accepted Accounting Practice in Ireland, of the state of the company's affairs as at 31 December 20X1 and of its profit [loss] for the year then ended; and

- have been properly prepared in accordance with the requirements of the Companies Acts 1963 to 2012.

Matters on which we are required to report by the Companies Acts 1963 to 2012

- In respect solely of the limitation on our work relating to stock, described above:

  - we have not obtained all the information and explanations that we consider necessary for the purpose of our audit; and

  - we were unable to determine whether proper books of account have been kept.

- The financial statements are in agreement with the books of account.

- In our opinion the information given in the directors' report is consistent with the financial statements.

- The net assets of the company, as stated in the balance sheet are more than half of the amount of its called-up share capital and, in our opinion, on that basis there did not exist at .... a financial situation which under Section 40 (1) of the Companies (Amendment) Act, 1983 would require the convening of an extraordinary general meeting of the company.

Matters on which we are required to report by exception

We have nothing to report in respect of the provisions in the Companies Acts 1963 to 2012 which require us to report to you if, in our opinion, the disclosures of directors' remuneration and transactions specified by law are not made.

[Signature]   Address
Seán MacGabhan   Date
for and on behalf of ABC & Co

Example 30 – Qualified opinion: Limitation of scope – Directors did not prepare cash flow forecasts sufficiently far into the future to be able to assess the going concern status of the company

- Irish non-publicly traded company prepares Irish GAAP financial statements (Example 2).

- The evidence available to the auditor was limited because the company had prepared cash flow forecasts and other information needed for the assessment of the appropriateness of the going concern basis of preparation of the financial statements only for a period of nine months from the date of approval of the financial statements and there were no sufficient alternative procedures that the auditor could perform.

- Although this fact is disclosed in the financial statements had the information been available the auditor might have formed a different opinion. The auditor considers that the directors have not taken adequate steps to satisfy themselves that it is appropriate for them to adopt the going concern basis.

- The auditor does not consider that the future period to which the directors have paid particular attention in assessing going concern is reasonable in the company's circumstances. The auditor considers that the particular circumstances of the company and the nature of the company's business require that such information be prepared, and reviewed by the directors and auditor for a period of at least twelve months from the date of approval of the financial statements.

- The auditor considers that the possible effect of the limitation of scope is material but not pervasive.

- The auditor issues a qualified opinion referring to the adjustments that might have been found to be necessary had they obtained sufficient evidence concerning the appropriateness of the going concern basis of preparation of the financial statements.

Extract from auditor's report

...

Basis for qualified opinion on financial statements

The audit evidence available to us was limited because the directors of the company have prepared cash flow forecasts and other information needed for the assessment of the appropriateness of the going concern basis of preparation of the financial statements for a period of only nine months from the date of approval of these financial statements. We consider that the directors have not taken adequate steps to satisfy themselves that it is appropriate for them to adopt the going concern basis because the circumstances of the company and the nature of the business require that such information be prepared, and reviewed by the directors and ourselves, for a period of at least twelve months from the date of approval of the financial statements. Had this information been available to us we might have formed a different opinion on the financial statements.

Qualified opinion on financial statements

In our opinion, except for the possible effects of the matter described in the Basis for qualified opinion paragraph, the financial statements:

- give a true and fair view, in accordance with Generally Accepted Accounting Practice in Ireland, of the state of the company's affairs as at ... and of its profit [loss] for the year then ended; and

- have been properly prepared in accordance with the requirements of the Companies Acts 1963 to 2012.

Matters on which we are required to report by the Companies Acts 1963 to 2012

- In respect solely of the limitation on our work relating to the assessment of the appropriateness of the going concern basis of preparation of the financial statements, described above, we have not obtained all the information and explanations that we consider necessary for the purpose of our audit.

- In our opinion proper books of account have been kept by the company.

- The financial statements are in agreement with the books of account.

- In our opinion the information given in the directors' report is consistent with the financial statements.

- The net assets of the company, as stated in the balance sheet are more than half of the amount of its called-up share capital and, in our opinion, on that basis there did not exist at .... a financial situation which under Section 40 (1) of the Companies (Amendment) Act, 1983 would require the convening of an extraordinary general meeting of the company.

Matters on which we are required to report by exception

We have nothing to report in respect of the provisions in the Companies Acts 1963 to 2012 which require us to report to you if, in our opinion, the disclosures of directors' remuneration and transactions specified by law are not made.

[Signature]   *Address*
Seán MacGabhan   *Date*
for and on behalf of ABC & Co

Appendix 6

Modified opinions – Adverse opinion on financial statements

31. Adverse opinion: No provision made for losses expected to arise on long term contracts

32. Adverse opinion: Significant level of concern about going concern status that is not disclosed in the financial statements

Example 31 – Adverse opinion: No provision made for losses expected to arise on long-term contracts

- *Irish non-publicly traded company prepares Irish GAAP financial statements (Example 2).*

- *No provision has been made for losses expected to arise on certain long-term contracts currently in progress, as the directors consider that such losses should be off-set against amounts recoverable on other long-term contracts.*

- *In the auditor's opinion, provision should be made for foreseeable losses on individual contracts as required by SSAP 9.*

- *In the auditor's view, the financial effect of this disagreement in accounting treatment is both material and pervasive to the financial statements such that an "except for" qualification of the auditor's opinion would not be sufficient to disclose the misleading nature of the financial statements.*

- *The auditor issues an adverse opinion due to the failure to provide for the losses and quantifies the impact on the profit for the year, the contract work in progress and the deferred tax liability at the year end.*

- *The auditor considers that notwithstanding its adverse opinion on the financial statements that proper books of account have been kept by the company and that it had received all the information and explanations it required for the audit.*

- *The auditor concludes that it is still possible to express the 'financial situation' opinion.*

Extract from auditor's report

...

Basis for adverse opinion on financial statements

As more fully explained in note [x] to the financial statements no provision has been made for losses expected to arise on certain long-term contracts currently in progress, as the directors consider that such losses should be off-set against amounts recoverable on other long-term contracts. In our opinion, provision should be made for foreseeable losses on individual contracts as required by Statement of Standard Accounting Practice 9: *Stocks and long-term contracts*. If losses had been so recognised the effect would have been to reduce the carrying amount of contract work in progress by €X, the deferred tax liability by €Y and the profit for the year and retained earnings at 31 December 20X1 by €Z.

Adverse opinion on financial statements

In our opinion, because of the significance of the matter described in the Basis for adverse opinion paragraph, the financial statements do not give a true and fair view, in accordance with Generally Accepted Accounting Practice in Ireland, of the state of the company's affairs as at 31 December 20X1 and of its profit [loss] for the year then ended.

In all other respects, in our opinion the financial statements have been properly prepared in accordance with the requirements of the Companies Acts 1963 to 2012.

Matters on which we are required to report by the Companies Acts 1963 to 2012

Notwithstanding our adverse opinion on the financial statements:

- we have obtained all the information and explanations which we consider necessary for the purposes of our audit;

- in our opinion proper books of account have been kept by the company;

- the financial statements are in agreement with the books of account;

- in our opinion the information given in the directors' report is consistent with the financial statements; and

- the net assets of the company, as stated in the balance sheet are more than half of the amount of its called-up share capital and, in our opinion, on that basis there did not exist at .... a financial situation which under Section 40 (1) of the Companies (Amendment) Act, 1983 would require the convening of an extraordinary general meeting of the company.

Matters on which we are required to report by exception

We have nothing to report in respect of the provisions in the Companies Acts 1963 to 2012 which require us to report to you if, in our opinion, the disclosures of directors' remuneration and transactions specified by law are not made.

[Signature]   *Address*
Seán MacGabhan   *Date*
for and on behalf of ABC & Co

Example 32 – Adverse opinion: Significant level of concern about going concern status that is not disclosed in the financial statements

- *Irish non-publicly traded company prepares Irish GAAP financial statements (Example 2).*

- *Although there is a significant level of concern about the company's ability to continue as a going concern the financial statements and notes do not disclose this fact and the directors have prepared the financial statements on the going concern basis.*

- *The auditor considers that the financial statements should disclose that there is a material uncertainty, which may cast significant doubt on the company's ability to continue as a going concern.*

- *As the effect of this disagreement is both material and pervasive to the amounts included within the financial statements the auditor concludes that a qualification of the opinion is not adequate to disclose the misleading and incomplete nature of the financial statements.*

- *The auditor issues an adverse audit opinion stating that, because the material uncertainty regarding going concern is not disclosed, the financial statements do not give a true and fair view.*

Extract from auditor's report

...

Basis for adverse opinion on financial statements

As explained in note [x] to the financial statements the company's financing arrangements expired and the amount outstanding was payable on [a past date]. The company has been unable to re-negotiate or obtain replacement financing and the directors are continuing to investigate alternative sources of finance. If they are not successful, they will have no alternative but to cease trading. These events indicate a material uncertainty which may cast significant doubt on the company's ability to continue as a going concern and, therefore, it may be unable to realise its assets and discharge its liabilities in the normal course of business. The financial statements (and notes thereto) do not disclose this fact and have been prepared on the going concern basis.

Adverse opinion on financial statements

In our opinion, because of the significance of the matter described in the Basis for adverse opinion paragraph the financial statements do not give a true and fair view, in accordance with Generally Accepted Accounting Practice in Ireland, of the state of the company's affairs as at ... and of its profit [loss] for the year then ended

In all other respects, in our opinion the financial statements have been properly prepared in accordance with the requirements of the Companies Acts 1963 to 2012.

Matters on which we are required to report by the Companies Acts 1963 to 2012

Notwithstanding our adverse opinion on the financial statements:

- we have obtained all the information and explanations which we consider necessary for the purposes of our audit;

- in our opinion proper books of account have been kept by the company;

- the financial statements are in agreement with the books of account;

- in our opinion the information given in the directors' report is consistent with the financial statements; and

- the net assets of the company, as stated in the balance sheet are more than half of the amount of its called-up share capital and, in our opinion, on that basis there did not exist at .... a financial situation which under Section 40 (1) of the Companies (Amendment) Act, 1983 would require the convening of an extraordinary general meeting of the company.

Matters on which we are required to report by exception

We have nothing to report in respect of the provisions in the Companies Acts 1963 to 2012 which require us to report to you if, in our opinion, the disclosures of directors' remuneration and transactions specified by law are not made.

[Signature]   *Address*
Seán MacGabhan   *Date*
for and on behalf of ABC & Co

Modified opinions – Disclaimer of opinion on financial statements

33. Disclaimer of opinion: Auditor unable to attend stocktaking and confirm trade debtors

34. Disclaimer of opinion: Multiple uncertainties

Example 33 – Disclaimer of opinion: Auditor unable to attend stocktaking and confirm trade debtors

- Irish non-publicly traded company prepares Irish GAAP financial statements (Example 2).

- The evidence available to the auditor was limited because the auditor was not able to observe all physical stock and confirm trade debtors due to limitations placed on the scope of the auditor's work by the directors of the company.

- The limitation in scope is considered by the auditor to be both material and pervasive so that it is unable to form an opinion on the financial statements.

- As a result, the auditor issues a modified opinion disclaiming an opinion on the financial statements.

INDEPENDENT AUDITOR'S REPORT TO THE MEMBERS OF XYZ LIMITED

We were engaged to audit the financial statements of (name of entity) for the year ended ... which comprise [specify the titles of the primary statements such as the Profit and Loss Account, the Balance Sheet, the Cash Flow Statement, the Statement of Total Recognised Gains and Losses] and the related notes[63]. The financial reporting framework that has been applied in their preparation is Irish law and accounting standards issued by the Financial Reporting Council and promulgated by the Institute of Chartered Accountants in Ireland (Generally Accepted Accounting Practice in Ireland).

Respective responsibilities of directors and auditor

As explained more fully in the Directors' Responsibilities Statement [set out [on page ...]], the directors are responsible for the preparation of the financial statements giving a true and fair view. Our responsibility is to audit and express an opinion on the financial statements in accordance with law and International Standards on Auditing (UK and Ireland). Those standards require us to comply with the Auditing Practices Board's [(APB's)] Ethical Standards for Auditors. Because of the matter described in the Basis for disclaimer of opinion paragraph, however, we were not able to obtain sufficient appropriate audit evidence to provide a basis for an audit opinion.

Scope of the audit of the financial statements

Either:

> A description of the scope of an audit of financial statements is [provided on the FRC's website at www.frc.org.uk/audit-scope-ireland] / [set out [on page ...] of the Annual Report].

---

[63] Auditor's reports of entities that do not publish their financial statements on a website or publish them using 'PDF' format may refer to the financial statements by reference to page numbers.

Or:

An audit involves obtaining evidence about the amounts and disclosures in the financial statements sufficient to give reasonable assurance that the financial statements are free from material misstatement, whether caused by fraud or error. This includes an assessment of: whether the accounting policies are appropriate to the company's circumstances and have been consistently applied and adequately disclosed; the reasonableness of significant accounting estimates made by the directors; and the overall presentation of the financial statements. In addition, we read all the financial and non-financial information in the [describe the annual report] to identify material inconsistencies with the audited financial statements. If we become aware of any apparent material misstatements or inconsistencies we consider the implications for our report.

Basis for disclaimer of opinion on financial statements

The audit evidence available to us was limited because we were unable to observe the counting of physical stock having a carrying amount of €X and send confirmation letters to trade debtors having a carrying amount of €Y due to limitations placed on the scope of our work by the directors of the company. As a result of this we have been unable to obtain sufficient appropriate audit evidence concerning both stock and trade debtors.

Disclaimer of opinion on financial statements

Because of the significance of the matter described in the Basis for disclaimer of opinion paragraph, we have not been able to obtain sufficient appropriate audit evidence to provide a basis for an audit opinion. Accordingly we do not express an opinion on the financial statements.

Matters on which we are required to report by the Companies Acts 1963 to 2012

Arising from the limitation of our work referred to above:

- we have not obtained all the information and explanations that we consider necessary for the purpose of our audit;

- we were unable to determine whether proper books of account have been kept;

- we have been unable to form an opinion as to whether there did or did not exist at .... a financial situation which under Section 40 (1) of the Companies (Amendment) Act, 1983 would require the convening of an extraordinary general meeting of the company.

Notwithstanding our disclaimer of an opinion on the financial statements:

- the financial statements are in agreement with the books of account; and

- in our opinion the information given in the directors' report is consistent with the financial statements.

Matters on which we are required to report by exception

We have nothing to report in respect of the provisions in the Companies Acts 1963 to 2012 which require us to report to you if, in our opinion, the disclosures of directors' remuneration and transactions specified by law are not made.

[Signature]   *Address*
Seán MacGabhan   *Date*
for and on behalf of ABC & Co

Example 34 – Disclaimer of opinion: Multiple uncertainties

- *Irish non-publicly traded company prepares Irish GAAP financial statements (Example 2).*

- *As discussed in ISA (UK and Ireland) 705 paragraph 10 the auditor disclaims an opinion when, in extremely rare circumstances involving multiple uncertainties, the auditor concludes that, notwithstanding having obtained sufficient appropriate audit evidence regarding each of the individual uncertainties, it is not possible to form an opinion on the financial statements due to the potential interaction of the uncertainties and their possible cumulative effect on the financial statements.*

- *This example does not include a description of the multiple uncertainties that might lead to a disclaimer of opinion because circumstances will vary and auditors will have to use their judgment when deciding whether it is an extreme case involving multiple uncertainties that are significant to the financial statements. Often, if the matters constituting the multiple uncertainties were considered individually the auditor may be able to issue an unqualified auditor's opinion with an emphasis of matter paragraph describing the situation giving rise to the emphasis of matter and its possible effects on the financial statements, including (where practicable) quantification but the audit opinion would be unmodified.*

INDEPENDENT AUDITOR'S REPORT TO THE MEMBERS OF XYZ LIMITED

We were engaged to audit the financial statements of (name of entity) for the year ended ... which comprise [specify the titles of the primary statements such as the Profit and Loss Account, the Balance Sheet, the Cash Flow Statement, the Statement of Total Recognised Gains and Losses, the Reconciliation of Movements in Shareholders' Funds] and the related notes[64]. The financial reporting framework that has been applied in their preparation is Irish law and accounting standards issued by the Financial Reporting Council and promulgated by the Institute of Chartered Accountants in Ireland (Generally Accepted Accounting Practice in Ireland).

Respective responsibilities of directors and auditor

As explained more fully in the Directors' Responsibilities Statement [set out [on page ...]], the directors are responsible for the preparation of the financial statements and for being satisfied that they give a true and fair view. Our responsibility is to audit and express an opinion on the financial statements in accordance with Irish law and International Standards on Auditing (UK and Ireland). Those standards require us to comply with the Auditing Practices Board's [(APB's)] Ethical Standards for Auditors. Because of the matters described in the Basis for disclaimer of opinion paragraph, however, we were not able to obtain sufficient appropriate audit evidence to provide a basis for an audit opinion.

---

[64] Auditor's reports of entities that do not publish their financial statements on a website or publish them using 'PDF' format may refer to the financial statements by reference to page numbers.

Scope of the audit of the financial statements

Either:

A description of the scope of an audit of financial statements is [provided on the FRC's website at www.frc.org.uk/audit-scope-ireland] / [set out [on page ...] of the Annual Report].

Or:

An audit involves obtaining evidence about the amounts and disclosures in the financial statements sufficient to give reasonable assurance that the financial statements are free from material misstatement, whether caused by fraud or error. This includes an assessment of: whether the accounting policies are appropriate to the company's circumstances and have been consistently applied and adequately disclosed; the reasonableness of significant accounting estimates made by the directors; and the overall presentation of the financial statements. In addition, we read all the financial and non-financial information in the [describe the annual report] to identify material inconsistencies with the audited financial statements. If we become aware of any apparent material misstatements or inconsistencies we consider the implications for our report.

Basis for disclaimer of opinion on financial statements

In seeking to form an opinion on the financial statements we considered the implications of the significant uncertainties disclosed in the financial statements concerning the following matters:

- [Describe uncertainty 1]

- [Describe uncertainty 2]

There is potential for the uncertainties to interact with one another such that we have been unable to obtain sufficient appropriate audit evidence regarding the possible effect of the uncertainties taken together.

Disclaimer of opinion on financial statements

Because of the significance of the possible impact of the uncertainties, described in the Basis for disclaimer of opinion on financial statements paragraph, to the financial statements, we have not been able to obtain sufficient appropriate audit evidence to provide a basis for an audit opinion. Accordingly we do not express an opinion on the financial statements.

Matters on which we are required to report by the Companies Acts 1963 to 2012

We have been unable to form an opinion as to whether there did or did not exist at .... a financial situation which under Section 40 (1) of the Companies (Amendment) Act, 1983 would require the convening of an extraordinary general meeting of the company.

Notwithstanding our disclaimer of an opinion on the financial statements:

- we have obtained all the information and explanations which we consider necessary for the purposes of our audit;

- in our opinion proper books of account have been kept by the company;

- the financial statements are in agreement with the books of account;

- in our opinion the information given in the directors' report is consistent with the financial statements; and

Matters on which we are required to report by exception

We have nothing to report in respect of the provisions in the Companies Acts 1963 to 2012 which require us to report to you if, in our opinion, the disclosures of directors' remuneration and transactions specified by law are not made.

[Signature]   *Address*
Seán MacGabhan   *Date*
for and on behalf of ABC & Co

Appendix 8

Modified opinions – Other requirements of the Companies Acts

35. Modified opinion on the consistency of the financial statements with the directors' report

Example 35 – Modified opinion on the consistency of the financial statements with the directors' report

- *Irish non-publicly traded company prepares Irish GAAP financial statements (Example 2).*

- *Auditor gives an unqualified opinion on the financial statements.*

- *There is an unresolved inconsistency between the directors' report and the financial statements.*

Extract from auditor's report

...

Opinion on financial statements

In our opinion the financial statements:

- give a true and fair view, in accordance with Generally Accepted Accounting Practice in Ireland, of the state of the company's affairs as at .... and of its profit [loss] for the year then ended; and

- have been properly prepared in accordance with the requirements of the Companies Acts 1963 to 2012.

Matters on which we are required to report by the Companies Acts 1963 to 2012

In our opinion:

- the information given in the seventh paragraph of the Business Review in the Directors' Report is not consistent with the financial statements. That paragraph states without amplification that "the company's trading for the period resulted in a 10% increase in profit over the previous period's profit". The profit and loss account, however, shows that the company's profit for the period includes a profit of €Z which did not arise from trading but arose from the disposal of assets of a discontinued operation. Without this profit on the disposal of assets the company would have reported a profit for the year of €Y, representing a reduction in profit of 25% over the previous period's profit on a like for like basis. Except for this matter, in our opinion the information given in the Directors' Report is consistent with the financial statements;

- we have obtained all the information and explanations which we consider necessary for the purposes of our audit;

- in our opinion proper books of account have been kept by the company;

- the financial statements are in agreement with the books of account; and

- the net assets of the company, as stated in the balance sheet are more than half of the amount of its called-up share capital and, in our opinion, on that basis there did not exist at .... a financial situation which under Section 40 (1) of the Companies (Amendment) Act, 1983 would require the convening of an extraordinary general meeting of the company.

Matters on which we are required to report by exception

We have nothing to report in respect of the provisions in the Companies Acts 1963 to 2012 which require us to report to you if, in our opinion, the disclosures of directors' remuneration and transactions specified by law are not made.

[Signature]   *Address*
Seán MacGabhan   *Date*
for and on behalf of ABC & Co

Appendix 9

Illustrative *Directors' responsibilities statement* for a non-publicly traded company

> The FRC has not prepared an illustrative example of a Directors' responsibilities statement for a publicly traded company as the directors' responsibilities, which are in part dependant on the particular regulatory environment, will vary depending on the rules of the market on which its securities are admitted to trading.

A. Company prepares financial statements under Irish GAAP

Directors' responsibilities statement

The directors are responsible for preparing the Directors' Report and the financial statements in accordance with Irish law and regulations.

Irish company law requires the directors to prepare financial statements giving a true and fair view of the state of affairs of the company and the profit or loss of the company for each financial year. Under that law the directors have elected to prepare the financial statements in accordance with Irish Generally Accepted Accounting Practice (accounting standards issued by the Financial Reporting Council and promulgated by the Institute of Chartered Accountants in Ireland and Irish law).

In preparing these financial statements, the directors are required to:

- select suitable accounting policies and then apply them consistently;

- make judgments and accounting estimates that are reasonable and prudent;

- prepare the financial statements on the going concern basis unless it is inappropriate to presume that the company will continue in business[65].

The directors are responsible for keeping proper books of account that disclose with reasonable accuracy at any time the financial position of the company and enable them to ensure that the financial statements comply with the Companies Acts 1963 to 2012. They are also responsible for safeguarding the assets of the company and hence for taking reasonable steps for the prevention and detection of fraud and other irregularities.

---

[65] Included where no separate statement on going concern is made by the directors

Appendix 10

Description of the "Scope of an Audit" that may be cross referenced from auditor's reports

Scope of an Audit of Financial Statements arising from the requirements of ISAs (UK and Ireland)

Overview

An audit involves obtaining evidence about the amounts and disclosures in the financial statements sufficient to give reasonable assurance that the financial statements are free from material misstatement, whether caused by fraud or error. This includes an assessment of: whether the accounting policies are appropriate to the [entity's] circumstances and have been consistently applied and adequately disclosed; the reasonableness of significant accounting estimates made by the directors; and the overall presentation of the financial statements.

Overall objective

The overall objectives of the auditor are to:

a.   obtain reasonable assurance about whether the financial statements as a whole are free from material misstatement, whether due to fraud or error; and

b.   report on the financial statements and communicate, as required by ISAs (UK and Ireland), the auditor's findings.

Compliance with ISAs (UK and Ireland) and APB's Ethical Standards for Auditors

The auditor is required to comply with:

a.   all ISAs (UK and Ireland) that are relevant to the audit; and

b.   APB's Ethical Standards for Auditors.

ISAs (UK and Ireland):

•   Require the auditor to plan and perform an audit with professional scepticism recognising that circumstances may exist that cause the financial statements to be materially misstated.

•   Require the auditor to exercise professional judgment in planning and performing an audit.

•   Contain requirements which the auditor must comply with unless a particular ISA (UK and Ireland) or a requirement of an ISA (UK and Ireland) is not relevant.

Some ISAs (UK and Ireland) address the core aspects of the audit process such as:

- Planning the audit.

- Understanding the entity and its environment (including its internal controls).

- Identifying and assessing the risks of material misstatement.

- Responding to assessed risks.

Other ISAs (UK and Ireland) establish requirements in relation to those areas of the auditor's work where it is particularly important that the views of the auditor and users of financial statements regarding the nature and extent of work to be performed are aligned. Such areas include:

- Going concern.

- The auditor's responsibility to consider fraud.

- Consideration of laws and regulations.

Other information in documents containing audited financial statements

The auditor is required to read all financial and non-financial information, (other information), included in the document containing the audited financial statements and to consider whether such other information is consistent with the audited financial statements. The auditor considers the implications for its report if it becomes aware of any material inconsistencies with the financial statements or any apparent material misstatements in the other information.

Communicating with those charged with governance

The auditor is required to communicate its significant findings arising from the audit with those charged with governance. Those charged with governance are the persons with responsibility for overseeing the strategic direction of the entity and obligations relating to the accountability of the entity. This includes overseeing the financial reporting process.

Significant findings from the audit include:

a.   the auditor's view about significant qualitative aspects of the entity's accounting practices, including accounting policies, accounting estimates and financial statement disclosures;

b.   significant difficulties encountered during the audit; and

c.   material weaknesses in internal control identified during the audit.

Reporting on the financial statements

The auditor's report is required to contain a clear expression of opinion on the financial statements taken as a whole.

To form an opinion on the financial statements the auditor concludes as to whether:

a. sufficient appropriate audit evidence has been obtained;

b. uncorrected misstatements are material, individually or in aggregate;

c. the financial statements, including the related notes, give a true and fair view , in accordance with the requirements of the relevant financial reporting framework[69]; and

d. the financial statements are properly prepared in accordance with the requirements of applicable law.

In particular an audit involves evaluating whether:

a. the financial statements adequately refer to or describe the relevant financial reporting framework;

b. the financial statements adequately disclose the significant accounting policies selected and applied;

c. the accounting policies selected and applied are consistent with the applicable financial reporting framework, and are appropriate in the circumstances;

d. accounting estimates are reasonable;

e. the information presented in the financial statements is relevant, reliable, comparable and understandable;

f. the financial statements provide adequate disclosures to enable the intended users to understand the effect of material transactions and events on the information conveyed in the financial statements; and

g. the terminology used in the financial statements, including the title of each financial statement is appropriate.

Unqualified opinions

An unqualified opinion is expressed when the auditor is able to conclude that the financial statements [give a true and fair view in accordance with the relevant financial reporting

---

[69] This conclusion is required only with respect to financial statements which have been prepared in accordance with a true and fair framework (examples are, International Financial Reporting Standards as adopted by the European Union and Irish GAAP).

framework and][70] have been properly prepared in accordance with the requirements of applicable law.

Modified opinions

The auditor modifies the opinion when either:

    a.   the auditor concludes that, based on the audit evidence obtained, the financial statements as a whole are not free from material misstatement; or

    b.   the auditor is unable to obtain sufficient appropriate audit evidence to conclude that the financial statements as a whole are free from material misstatement.

The auditor expresses a qualified opinion when either:

    a.   misstatements, individually or in the aggregate, are material but not pervasive to the financial statements; or

    b.   the possible effect of undetected misstatements, arising from an ability to obtain sufficient appropriate audit evidence, could be material but not pervasive.

The auditor expresses an adverse opinion when the auditor, having obtained sufficient appropriate audit evidence, concludes that misstatements, individually or in the aggregate, are both material and pervasive to the financial statements.

The auditor disclaims an opinion when:

    a.   the possible effect of undetected misstatements, arising from an inability to obtain sufficient appropriate audit evidence, could be both material and pervasive to the financial statements; and

    b.   in extremely rare circumstances involving multiple uncertainties, the auditor concludes that notwithstanding having obtained sufficient appropriate audit evidence regarding each of the individual uncertainties, it is not possible to form an opinion on the financial statements due to the potential interaction of the uncertainties and their possible cumulative effect on the financial statements.

Emphasising certain matters without qualifying the opinion

In certain circumstances an auditor's report includes an emphasis of matter paragraph to highlight a matter fundamental to the user's understanding of the financial statements. An emphasis of matter paragraph does not affect the auditor's opinion. The auditor is required to consider adding an emphasis of matter paragraph where there is a significant uncertainty the resolution of which is dependent upon future events and which may affect the financial statements. The auditor is required to add an emphasis of matter paragraph to highlight a

---

[70] Only applicable with respect to "true and fair" frameworks.

material uncertainty relating to an event or condition that may cast significant doubt on the entity's ability to continue as a going concern.

Communicating "other matters"

If the auditor considers it necessary to communicate a matter other than those that are presented or disclosed in the financial statements that, in the auditor's judgment is relevant to the user's understanding of the audit, the auditor's responsibility or the auditor's report, the auditor does so in a paragraph in the auditor's report with the heading "Other Matter" or other appropriate heading.

Other Legal and Regulatory Requirements

The auditor is required to address other legal and regulatory requirements relating to the auditor's report in a separate section of the auditor's report following the opinion on the financial statements.

Illustrative Example of an Irish Auditor's Report Reflecting the Requirements of ISA (UK and Ireland) 700 (Revised June 2013)

The attached illustrative auditor's report updates Example 14 in Bulletin 1 (I) "Compendium of Illustrative Auditor's Reports on Irish Financial Statements" to reflect the changes to ISA (UK and Ireland) 700 made in October 2012 and June 2013. The changes shown in sections 1 and 2 reflect these changes. The change shown in section 3 reflects a recent change in Irish law.

The changes shown in section 1 and 2 apply to audits of financial statements for periods commencing on or after 1 October 2012.

1. Changes shown under the heading 'Scope of the audit of the financial statements'

The changes shown in bold should be made in respect of all auditor's reports.

2. Changes shown under the headings 'Our assessment of risk of material misstatement', 'Our application of materiality', 'An overview of the scope of our audit' and 'Matters on which we are required to report by exception'

The changes shown in italics also apply in respect of examples 6, 7, 15 and 16 in Bulletin 1 (I). These changes also apply in respect of auditor's reports of any entity that has voluntarily chosen to report on how it has applied the UK Corporate Governance Code.

3. Changes shown with strikethrough

The changes shown with strikethrough should be made in respect of all auditor's reports on companies which are signed on or after 24 December 2013.

Example 14 — Publicly traded group – Parent company incorporated in Ireland prepares financial statements under IFRSs as adopted by the European Union

- Company has equity shares with a primary listing on the Main Securities Market ("MSM") of the Irish Stock Exchange and is subject to the continuing obligations in relation to the annual report as set out in Chapter 6 of the Listing Rules of the MSM.

- Company prepares group financial statements under IFRSs as adopted by the European Union and Section 148(8) exemption taken in respect of parent company's own statement of comprehensive income.

- Corporate governance statement incorporated into the directors' report, either directly or by incorporation by reference as explained in Bulletin 2011/1 issued by the APB[1].

INDEPENDENT AUDITOR'S REPORT TO THE MEMBERS OF XYZ PLC

We have audited the financial statements of (name of company) for the year ended ... which comprise [specify the titles of the primary statements such as the Group and Parent Company Statements of Financial Position, the Group Statement of Comprehensive Income, the Group and Parent Company Cash Flow Statements, the Group and Parent Company Statements of Changes in Equity[2]] and the related notes[3]. The financial reporting framework that has been applied in their preparation is Irish law and International Financial Reporting Standards (IFRSs) as adopted by the European Union and, as regards the parent company financial statements, as applied in accordance with the provisions of the Companies Act 1963 to 2012 3.

Respective responsibilities of directors and auditors

As explained more fully in the Directors' Responsibilities Statement [set out [on page ....]] the directors are responsible for the preparation of the financial statements giving a true and fair view. Our responsibility is to audit and express an opinion on the financial statements in accordance with Irish law and International Standards on Auditing (ISAs) (UK and Ireland).

Those standards require us to comply with the Auditing Practices Board's [APB's] Ethical Standards for Auditors.

---

[1] See example 16 for an illustration of an auditor's report where the corporate governance statement is not incorporated into the directors' report.

[2] The names used for the primary statements in the auditor's report should reflect the precise titles used by the company for them.

[3] Auditor's reports of entities that do not publish their financial statements on a web site or publish them using 'PDF' format may continue to refer to the financial statements by reference to page numbers.

Scope of the audit of the financial statements

Either:

> A description of the scope of an audit of financial statements is [provided on the FRC's website at www.frc.org.uk/audit-scope-ireland] / [set out [on page...] of the Annual Report].

Or:

> An audit involves obtaining evidence about the amounts and disclosures in the financial statements sufficient to give reasonable assurance that the financial statements are free from material misstatement, whether caused by fraud or error. This includes an assessment of: whether the accounting policies are appropriate to the company's circumstances and have been consistently applied and adequately disclosed; the reasonableness of significant accounting estimates made by the directors; and the overall presentation of the financial statements. In addition, we read all the financial and non-financial information in the [describe the annual report] to identify material inconsistencies with the audited financial statements **and to identify any information that is apparently materially incorrect based on, or materially inconsistent with, the knowledge acquired by us in the course of performing the audit**. If we become aware of any apparent material misstatements or inconsistencies we consider the implications for our report.

Opinion on financial statements

In our opinion:

- the group financial statements give a true and fair view, in accordance with IFRSs as adopted by the European Union, of the state of the group's affairs as at ... and of its [profit/loss] for the year then ended;

- the parent company statement of financial position gives a true and fair view, in accordance with International Financial Reporting Standards (IFRSs) as applied in accordance with the provisions of the Companies Acts 1963 to 2012З, of the state of the parent company's affairs as at; and

- the financial statements have been properly prepared in accordance with the requirements of the Companies Acts 1963 to 2012З and, as regards the group financial statements, Article 4 of the IAS Regulation.

Our assessment of risks of material misstatement

[Insert a description of those specific assessed risks of material misstatement that were identified by the auditor and which had the greatest effect on the audit strategy; the allocation of resources in the audit; and directing the efforts of the engagement team.]

Our application of materiality

[Insert an explanation of how the auditor applied the concept of materiality in planning and performing the audit. Such explanation shall specify the threshold used by the auditor as being materiality for the financial statements as a whole.]

An overview of the scope of our audit

[Insert an overview of the scope of the audit, including an explanation of how the scope addressed the assessed risks of material misstatement and was influenced by the auditor's application of materiality.]

[The disclosures about the above three matters are made in a manner that complements the description of significant issues relating to the financial statements required to be set out in the separate section of the annual report describing the work of the audit committee in discharging its responsibilities (see paragraphs 19B and A13D)].

[Separate opinion in relation to IFRSs as issued by the IASB

As explained in note [x] to the financial statements, the group in addition to complying with its legal obligation to comply with IFRSs as adopted by the European Union, have also complied with the IFRSs as issued by the International Accounting Standards Board (IASB).

In our opinion the financial statements comply with IFRSs as issued by the IASB.]

Matters on which we are required to report by the Companies Acts 1963 to 20123

- We have obtained all the information and explanations which we consider necessary for the purposes of our audit

- In our opinion proper books of account have been kept by the parent company.

- The parent company statement of financial position is in agreement with the books of account.

- In our opinion the information given in the directors' report is consistent with the financial statements and the description in the Corporate Governance Statement of the main features of the internal control and risk management systems in relation to the process for preparing the group financial statements is consistent with the group financial statements.

- The net assets of the parent company, as stated in the parent company statement of financial position are more than half of the amount of its called-up share capital and, in our opinion, on that basis there did not exist at .... a financial situation which under Section 40 (1) of the Companies (Amendment) Act, 1983 would require the convening of an extraordinary general meeting of the parent company.

Matters on which we are required to report by exception

We have nothing to report in respect of the following:

Under the ISAs (UK and Ireland), we are required to report to you if, in our opinion, information in the annual report is:

- *materially inconsistent with the information in the audited financial statements; or*

- *apparently materially incorrect based on, or materially inconsistent with, our knowledge of the group acquired in the course of performing our audit; or*

- *is otherwise misleading.*

In particular, we are required to consider whether we have identified any inconsistencies between our knowledge acquired during the audit and the directors' statement that they consider the annual report is fair, balanced and understandable and whether the annual report appropriately discloses those matters that we communicated to the audit committee which we consider should have been disclosed.

Under the Companies Acts 1963 to 2013² we are required to report to you if, in our opinion the disclosures of directors' remuneration and transactions specified by law are not made.

Under the Listing Rules of the Irish Stock Exchange we are required to review:

- the directors' statement, [set out [on page...]], in relation to going concern;

- the part of the Corporate Governance Statement relating to the company's compliance with the nine provisions of the UK Corporate Governance Code and the two provisions of the Irish Corporate Governance Annex specified for our review; and

- the six specified elements of the disclosures in the report to shareholders by the Board on directors' remuneration.

[Signature]	Address
Seán MacGabhan	Date
for and on behalf of ABC & Co	

BULLETIN 2 (FEBRUARY 2013)

GUIDANCE FOR REPORTING ACCOUNTANTS OF STAKEHOLDER PENSION SCHEMES IN THE UNITED KINGDOM

CONTENTS

Introduction

1. Stakeholder pension schemes can be set up by trustees (trust schemes) or can be established by managers (contract schemes). The Pensions Regulator has responsibility for maintaining the register of stakeholder pension schemes, and for the governance of schemes. Under the regulations The Pensions Regulator cannot register, and must de-register, stakeholder schemes if they fail to meet the conditions for being a stakeholder scheme set out in legislation. The Financial Services Authority (FSA) has responsibility for regulating the sales and marketing of stakeholder pensions, and is also responsible for authorising and supervising the firms acting as stakeholder managers as well as firms involved in managing the funds invested in stakeholder schemes.

2. This Bulletin has been issued by the FRC to provide guidance for reporting accountants in relation to the requirements placed upon them in connection with stakeholder pension schemes. It does not constitute guidance from The Pensions Regulator or the FSA.

3. The principal legislation regulating Stakeholder pensions is The Welfare Reform and Pensions Act 1999 ('the Act') and The Stakeholder Pension Schemes Regulations 2000[1] ('the Regulations'). The relevant parts of the Regulations came into force on 1 October 2000 but have been subject to subsequent amending regulations. This Bulletin reflects the version of the Regulations in force as at 5 April 2012.

4. Regulation 12(2)(a) requires the trustees or manager to make an annual declaration[2] containing various statements in accordance with Regulation 12(5). Regulation 12(5)(a) requires a statement that in the opinion of the trustees or manager there are systems and controls in place which provide reasonable assurance that:

    (i)   Regulations 13, 14 and 14B[3] of the regulations have been complied with in relation to the scheme;

    (ii) transactions for the purposes of the scheme in securities, property or other assets have occurred at a fair market value;

    (iii) the value of members' rights has been determined in accordance with the provisions in the instruments establishing the scheme; and

    (iv) adequate records have been maintained for the purposes of providing to members the statement required by Regulation 18A(1)[4] of the regulations.

---

[1] SI 2000 no.1403.

[2] Regulation 12 of The Stakeholder Pension Schemes Regulations 2000, as amended, is reproduced in full in Appendix 2 of this Bulletin.

[3] These regulations impose limits on the amount of charges and deductions which may be made by a stakeholder pension scheme and on the manner in which charges may be made by such a scheme.

[4] This regulation requires a stakeholder pension scheme to provide an annual benefit statement to each member.

5. Regulation 12(5)(b) requires a statement describing the process that has been undertaken in order to arrive at the opinion expressed in the statement required by Regulation 12(5)(a).

6. Regulations 12(5)(c) and (d) require statements concerning compliance with the conditions in section 1(1) of the Act, and explaining the requirements of Regulations 13, 14, 14B and 18A(1).

7. Regulation 12(6) requires the trustees or manager to provide the reporting accountant with documentation to demonstrate that the process described in the statement in accordance with Regulation 12(5)(b) has taken place.

8. Regulation 12(2)(b) requires that the trustees or manager shall obtain from a reporting accountant[5] statements made in accordance with Regulation 12(7) that

   (i) the reporting accountant has been provided with documentation as required by Regulation 12(6); and

   (ii) nothing has come to the attention of the reporting accountant that is inconsistent with the statement made in accordance with Regulation 12(5)(b), or

   so far as the reporting accountant is unable to provide such statements, an explanation as to why he or she is unable to do so. The reporting accountant is not required to report on the statements made by the trustees or manager in accordance with Regulations 12(5)(c) or (d).

9. The trustees or managers are required by the Regulations to annex the reporting accountant's report to their declaration, and shall make the whole document available to members and beneficiaries of the scheme on request.

10. It is a condition of a scheme being a stakeholder pension scheme that the requirements of the Regulations are complied with.

11. The declarations by the trustees or managers and the reporting accountant's reports are due 6 months after the end of the scheme accounting period.

Trustees' or managers' declarations

12. As described above, the trustees or managers are required to make statements to the effect that systems and controls provide reasonable assurance that specified aspects of the Regulations have been complied with and to describe the process that has been undertaken to make such statements. Guidance for trustees and managers to assist

---

[5] Regulation 11 defines a reporting accountant as follows:
"A person is eligible for appointment as the reporting accountant if the person is eligible under section 1212 of the Companies Act 2006 for appointment as a company auditor

them in fulfilling these responsibilities has been issued by the Pensions Research Accountants Group (PRAG)[6].

Reporting Accountant's procedures

13. Regulation 11 sets out the processes to be followed for the appointment and resignation of the reporting accountant. The Regulation requires, in particular, that the reporting accountant acknowledge in writing within one month its receipt of the notice of appointment, and confirm that it will notify the trustees or managers of any conflict of interest to which the reporting accountant is subject in relation to the scheme immediately the reporting accountant becomes aware of its existence. The reporting accountant is also required, on resignation, to serve on the trustees or managers a written notice containing a statement specifying any circumstances connected with the resignation which in its opinion significantly affects the interests of the members or beneficiaries of the scheme, or a declaration that it knows of no such circumstances.

14. The objective of the reporting accountant's review in accordance with Regulation 12(2)(b) is to obtain evidence to support an assessment of whether the trustees' or managers' description of the process that has been undertaken in order to arrive at the opinion expressed in the statement required by Regulation 12(5)(a) is supported by the documentation provided to the reporting accountant in accordance with Regulation 12 (6) and demonstrates that the process described has taken place. Before commencing its review procedures, the reporting accountant:

    (a) plans the work to be undertaken in relation to the declaration by the trustees or managers so as to perform that work in an effective manner;

    (b) familiarises itself with the Stakeholder Pensions Regulations, particularly those sections governing the preparation of the trustees' or managers' declaration;

    (c) obtains an understanding of the structure and management of the scheme and its processing arrangements, including those that are outsourced;

    (d) ensures that it complies with the independence guidance issued by its professional body and discusses, where appropriate, with the trustees or managers any relationships which may affect the reporting accountant's independence or its objectivity and any related safeguards that are in place; and

    (e) agrees the terms of the engagement with the trustees or managers and records them in writing.

15. Appropriate evidence to support the reporting accountant's assessment will usually be obtained by performing the following procedures:

---

[6] "Making the Annual Declaration – A Guide for Trustees and Managers of Stakeholder Pension Schemes". Copies of this guidance may be obtained from PRAG's website: www.prag.org.uk.

(a) obtaining through enquiry of appropriate individuals an understanding both of the framework of controls relevant to the legislation referred to in Regulation 12(5)(a), and the process established by the trustees or managers for the review of the effectiveness of those controls, to enable the reporting accountant to arrive at its opinion and sign the declaration;

(b) enquiring of the trustees or managers whether they are familiar with, and have considered the applicability to their scheme of, relevant guidance issued to trustees and managers by PRAG[7] and The Pensions Regulator and, if necessary, recommending that they should so consider it;

(c) reviewing relevant minutes of the meetings of the trustees or managers, and of other committees (for example audit and risk management committees) together with supporting papers presented at those meetings;

(d) enquiring of the trustees or managers whether they are aware of any instances of non-compliance with the legislation referred to in Regulation 12(5)(a);

(e) reviewing any relevant correspondence with regulators, particularly The Pensions Regulator and the FSA;

(f) reviewing the documentation provided to the reporting accountant by the trustees or managers in accordance with Regulation 12(6), including any documentation relating to functions outsourced to a third party, to ascertain that it demonstrates that the process described in the statement made in accordance with Regulation 12(5)(b) has taken place;

(g) enquiring of the audit engagement partner whether any relevant matters have come to his or her attention during the audit work (see paragraph 18 below); and

(h) attending meetings at which the declaration made in accordance with Regulation 12(5)(a), including the statement concerning the review process made in accordance with Regulation 12(5)(b), is considered and approved for signature.

16. The reporting accountant also:

(a) records in its working papers

– details of the engagement planning,

– the nature, timing and extent of the procedures performed in relation to its report, and the conclusions drawn; and

– its reasoning and conclusions on all significant matters which require the exercise of judgment;

---

[7] In addition to the PRAG guidance referred to in paragraph 12, PRAG has also issued guidance on possible control procedures entitled "Stakeholder pension schemes – a controls checklist". This can also be downloaded from PRAG's website www.prag.org.uk.

(b) considers the matters which have come to its attention while performing the procedures on the declaration and whether they should result in a modification to the reporting accountant's statement or be included in a letter of comment to the trustees or managers; and

(c) takes steps to ensure that any delegated work is directed, supervised and reviewed in a manner which provides reasonable assurance that such work is performed competently.

17. The reporting accountant may request the trustees or managers to provide written confirmation of oral representations made during the course of the review.

18. The reporting accountant of a stakeholder pension scheme may also be the statutory auditor of the managing entity (in the case of contract schemes), or of the schemes managed by the trustees (in the case of trust schemes). Whilst the reporting accountant's assignment is entirely separate from the audit engagement, the partner in charge of the reporting accountant's work nevertheless requests the audit engagement partner to advise him of any breaches of the requirements specified in Regulation 12(5)(a) of which the audit engagement partner has become aware as a result of the audit.

19. The reporting accountant is not required to consider whether the trustees' or managers' description of the process made in accordance with Regulation 12(5)(b) covers all relevant risks and controls, or to reach a conclusion on the adequacy of the process or on the effectiveness of the controls. However the reporting accountant does consider:

- whether it has been provided with documentation which supports the trustees' or managers' description of the process, and

- whether it has become aware of matters which are inconsistent with the description of the process,

and, if necessary, the reporting accountant modifies its statement.

20. The reporting accountant is not required to obtain evidence concerning the specific requirements underlying Regulation 12(5)(a) – for example that the value of members' rights has been determined in accordance with the provisions establishing the scheme. However, if during its review of the trustees' or managers' documentation the reporting accountant identifies facts or circumstances which suggest that:

- the trustees or managers may not be justified in their belief that their systems and controls provide reasonable assurance to enable them to make the statement required by Regulation 12(5)(a), or

- because of apparent breaches of the legislation or other matters, the proposed statement required by Regulation 12(5)(a) is not supportable, the reporting accountant discusses its concerns with the trustees or managers as soon as is practicable.

21. If as a result of the discussion the reporting accountant remains of the view that significant internal control weaknesses or other matters exist which, in its opinion, call into question the credibility of the statement made by the trustees or managers in accordance with Regulation 12(5)(a), they consider modifying the statement in their report in respect of these matters.

22. Under normal circumstances the reporting accountant modifies its report in respect of apparent undisclosed breaches of the legislation, referred to in Regulation 12(5)(a), of which the reporting accountant becomes aware. In deciding whether to modify its report in respect of such breaches, the reporting accountant considers their significance. The materiality of the breach in monetary terms may not be relevant to a consideration of its significance. However, where breaches have occurred which were identified by the scheme's own control systems, which were not indicative of a systemic problem, and which were corrected subsequently such that there was no monetary impact on any member or beneficiary of the scheme, they are unlikely to be significant.

Reporting Accountant's reports

23. The reporting accountant's report on a declaration normally includes the following matters:

- a title identifying the persons to whom the report is addressed (which will normally be the trustees or managers of the scheme);

- an introductory paragraph identifying the Regulations which are covered by the report;

- separate sections, appropriately headed, dealing with

    - respective responsibilities of the trustees or managers and the reporting accountants, and

    - the basis of the reporting accountant's statement, including (where appropriate) a reference to compliance with the guidance in this Bulletin;

- the reporting accountant's statement on the matters required by the Regulations;

- the signature of the reporting accountant; and

- the date of the reporting accountant's report.

Appendix 1 of this Bulletin sets out an illustrative example of a reporting accountant's report on the declaration. This example wording may need to be tailored to reflect particular circumstances.

24. As indicated in paragraphs 19-22 above, the reporting accountant modifies the statement in its report if the reporting accountant:

   – has not been provided with documentation to demonstrate that the trustees' or managers' description of the process made in accordance with Regulation 12(5)(a) has taken place, or

   – is aware of matters that are inconsistent with the trustees' or managers' description of the process, made in accordance with Regulation 12(5)(b), or

   – is aware of matters which call into question the credibility of the statement made by the trustees or managers in accordance with Regulation 12(5)(a). These matters are likely to be connected with significant internal control weaknesses, or with breaches of the legislation referred to in Regulation 12(5)(a).

Reporting to the regulators

25. Section 70(1) of The Pensions Act 2004 imposes on "a person who is otherwise involved in advising trustees or managers of an occupational or personal pension scheme in relation to the scheme" a requirement to report to The Pensions Regulator. The Pensions Regulator's Regulatory Code of Practice 01 "Reporting breaches of the law" clarifies that a reporting accountant appointed to a stakeholder scheme is subject to this requirement.

26. The reporting requirement referred to in paragraph 25 will exist where the reporting accountant has reasonable cause to believe that:

   • a duty which is relevant to the administration of the scheme in question, and is imposed by or by virtue of an enactment or rule of law, has not been or is not being complied with; and

   • the failure to comply is likely to be of material significance to The Pensions Regulator in the exercise of any of its functions[8].

27. A reporting accountant of a contract scheme who is also the auditor of the managing entity considers whether it has a duty to report matters of material significance, of which it becomes aware in its capacity as auditor of the managing entity, to the FSA[9] under the FSMA[10] 2000 (Communications by Auditors) Regulations 2001. This is because there may be situations where it is not clear whether information coming to the attention of the reporting accountant is received in that capacity or in its role as auditor. Appendix 2 to ISA (UK and Ireland) 250 Section B provides guidance as to how information obtained in non-audit work may be relevant to the auditor in the

---

[8] Further guidance on reporting to The Pensions Regulator is set out in Practice Note 15 (Revised) – The audit of occupational schemes in the United Kingdom.

[9] Further guidance on reporting to the FSA is set out in Practice Note 20 (Revised) – The audit of insurers in the United Kingdom.

[10] The Financial Services and Markets Act.

planning and conduct of the audit and the steps that need to be taken to ensure the communication of information that is relevant to the audit.

28. In general, if a reporting accountant is in any doubt as to whether a report should be made to the regulator or not, it considers taking legal advice.

Letters of comment

29. As indicated in paragraph 24 above, if the reporting accountant considers that significant weaknesses in internal control or other matters exist which call into question whether the trustees' or managers' statements made in accordance with Regulations 12(5)(a) and (b) are justified, it modifies the statement in its report.

30. If, however, the reporting accountant is of the opinion that control weaknesses or other matters exist, but these do not affect the credibility of the statement made by the trustees or managers in accordance with Regulation 12(5)(a), it reports them in a letter of comment to the trustees or managers.

31. Where no significant weaknesses in the scheme's internal control systems come to the reporting accountant's attention during its review, the reporting accountant advises the trustees or managers in writing that no letter of comment is to be issued.

32. Trustees or managers will normally wish to have the opportunity of responding in writing to the comments made in letters of comment. The reporting accountant agrees with the trustees or managers the way in which their responses are to be presented. These discussions should not, however, be allowed to cause an unreasonable delay in issuing the letter of comment.

Appendix 1

Example report of the Reporting Accountant to the Trustees or Managers of a stakeholder pension scheme

The Trustees/Managers of the XYZ pension scheme,

Address.

XYZ STAKEHOLDER PENSION SCHEME

We report in accordance with the requirements of Regulation 12(7) of the Stakeholder Pension Schemes Regulations 2000 (as amended) (the Regulations), concerning the annual declaration by the trustees/managers of the XYZ pension scheme. The declaration is made in respect of the period of 12 months ended on xxxx.

Respective responsibilities of the trustees/managers and the reporting accountant

In accordance with Regulation 12(2)(a) the trustees/managers are responsible for the preparation of a declaration, which contains a statement describing the process that the trustees/ managers have undertaken, in order to arrive at their opinion as to whether systems and controls are in place which provide reasonable assurance that specified regulations in relation to stakeholder pensions have been complied with.

It is our responsibility to consider whether documentation has been provided to us to demonstrate that the process described by the trustees'/managers' has taken place, and to report if this is not the case and to consider whether anything has come to our attention that is inconsistent with the description of the process and to report if this is the case.

We are not required to consider whether the trustees'/managers' description of the process made in accordance with Regulation 12(5)(b) covers all relevant risks and controls, or to reach a conclusion on the adequacy of the process or on the effectiveness of the controls or to undertake any work in this regard.

Basis of reporting accountant's statement

We conducted our work in accordance with Bulletin 2 'Guidance for reporting accountants of stakeholder pension schemes in the United Kingdom' issued by the Financial Reporting Council. The work performed involved making enquiries of management and staff and examination of the documentary evidence supporting the existence of the process.

Statement

(Other than the Exception set out below)[11] In accordance with Regulation 12(7) we report that in our opinion:

- we have been provided by the trustees/managers with documentation, which is required by Regulation 12(6) to demonstrate that the process described in the trustees'/managers' statement has taken place; and

- nothing has come to our attention that is inconsistent with the trustees'/ managers' description of the process.

(Exception

The trustees'/managers' description concerning ... does not appropriately reflect our understanding of the process undertaken by you because.....")

Reporting accountants   Address
Date

---

[11] In cases where there are no exceptions, the wording in italics would be omitted.

Appendix 2

Regulation 12 of The Stakeholder Pension Schemes Regulations 2000

Requirement for declaration by trustees or manager

12.—(1) For the purposes of section 1(1)(b), it shall be a condition of a scheme being a stakeholder pension scheme that the requirements of this regulation are complied with.

(2) Subject to paragraph (11), the trustees or manager of the scheme shall, no later than the end of 6 months beginning with each reporting date—

   (a) make a declaration in writing signed by the trustees or manager containing the statements set out in paragraph (5) in relation to the reporting period or, in so far as they are unable to make those statements containing a statement explaining why they are unable to do so; and

   (b) obtain from the reporting accountant appointed by virtue of regulation 11 the statement specified in paragraph (7) or, in so far as the reporting accountant is unable to make that statement, a statement from the reporting accountant explaining why he is unable to do so.

(3) Subject to paragraph (10), in this regulation reporting date means—

   (a) in the case of the first reporting date, a date chosen by the trustees or manager that is no later than the last day of the period of 12 months beginning with the date on which the scheme is registered under section 2 of the Act; and

   (b) in the case of each subsequent reporting date, a date chosen by the trustees or manager that is no later than the last day of the period of 12 months beginning with the date immediately following the previous reporting date.

(4) Subject to paragraph (10), in this regulation reporting period means—

   (a) in the case of the first reporting period, the period beginning with the date of registration of the scheme under section 2 of the Act and ending on and including the first reporting date;

   (b) in the case of subsequent reporting periods, the period beginning on the date immediately following the previous reporting date and ending on and including the reporting date.

(5) The statements specified in paragraph (2)(a) shall be—

   (a) a statement that in the opinion of the trustees or manager there are systems and controls in place which provide reasonable assurance that —

     (i) regulations 13, 14 and 14B have been complied with in relation to the scheme;

     (ii) transactions for the purposes of the scheme in securities, property or other assets have occurred at a fair market value;

     (iii) the value of members' rights has been determined in accordance with the provisions in the instruments establishing the scheme; and

     (iv) adequate records have been maintained for the purposes of providing to members the statement required by regulation 18A(1);

   (b) a statement describing the process that the trustees or manager have or has undertaken in order to arrive at the opinion expressed in the statement described in paragraph (5)(a);

   (c) a statement that in the opinion of the trustees or manager there are systems and controls in place which provide reasonable assurance that the scheme has complied with the conditions in section 1(1) of the Act, apart from those conditions that are covered by the statement in paragraph (5)(a); and

(d)   a statement which explains that—

   (i)   regulations 13, 14 and 14B impose limits on the amount of charges and deductions which may be made by a stakeholder pension scheme and on the manner in which charges may be made by such a scheme; and

   (ii)   regulation 18A(1) requires a stakeholder pension scheme to provide an annual benefit statement to each member.

(6) The trustees or manager shall provide the reporting accountant with documentation to demonstrate that the process described in the statement in paragraph (5)(b) has taken place.

(7) The statement specified in paragraph (2)(b) shall be a statement that—

(a)   the reporting accountant has been provided with documentation as required by paragraph (6); and

(b)   nothing has come to the attention of the reporting accountant that is inconsistent with the statement made in paragraph (5)(b).

(8) The trustees or manager shall make available to members and beneficiaries of the scheme on request the declaration made by the trustees or manager and the statement obtained from the reporting accountant in accordance with paragraph (2).

(9) If the statement to be obtained by the trustees or manager under paragraph (2)(b) is obtained from the reporting accountant acting as such while ineligible in contravention of regulation 11(7A)(a)—

(a)   the trustees or manager shall not be regarded as having complied with paragraph (2)(b); and

(b)   for the purposes of paragraph (8), the statement from the reporting accountant shall not be regarded as obtained in accordance with paragraph (2)(b).

(10) Where a scheme is registered under section 2 of the Act on or before 6th April 2001—

(a)   the first reporting date shall be 5th April 2002; and

(b)   the first reporting period shall be the period commencing on and including 6th April 2001 and ending on and including 5th April 2002.

(11) Where the reporting date is on or before 30th September 2002 the trustees or manager of the scheme shall make the declaration specified in paragraph (2)(a) and obtain the statement specified in paragraph (2)(b) from the reporting accountant—

(a)   on or before 31st December 2002; or

(b)   by the end of 6 months beginning with the reporting date,

whichever is later.

BULLETIN 4 (APRIL 2014)

RECENT DEVELOPMENTS IN COMPANY LAW, THE LISTING RULES AND AUDITING STANDARDS THAT AFFECT UNITED KINGDOM AUDITOR'S REPORTS

CONTENTS

Introduction

1. There have been a number of recent developments in UK Company Law, the UK Listing Rules and ISAs (UK and Ireland) that affect both the auditor's duties and the wording of auditor's reports on the financial statements of companies.

2. These developments are:

    (a) The introduction of the Strategic Report;

    (b) The option for companies to provide its members with a stand-alone "Strategic Report with Supplementary Material" in place of the company's full accounts and reports. "The Strategic Report with Supplementary Material" replaces the previous option of providing a Summary Financial Statement;

    (c) Amendment of the Regulations that specify the information to be included in a quoted company's Directors' Remuneration Report;

    (d) Changes in the requirements of the Listing Rules with respect to directors' remuneration disclosures; and

    (e) Changes to ISA (UK and Ireland) 700 "The Independent Auditor's Report on Financial Statements" made in October 2012 and June 2013 and the issuance, in November 2013, of a Clarification Statement in respect thereof.

3. The effects of these developments on the auditor's report are illustrated in:

    • Appendix 1: Example 1 from Bulletin 2010/2 (Revised March 2012). Non-publicly traded company preparing financial statements under the FRSSE.

    • Appendix 2: Example 9 from Bulletin 2010/2 (Revised March 2012). Publicly traded premium listed group – Auditor's report on group financial statements prepared under IFRSs as adopted by the European Union.

    New text to be inserted is shown as underlined and text to be removed is shown as struck-out.

The strategic report

Background

4. The Companies Act 2006 (Strategic Report and Directors' Report) Regulations 2013[1] (SI 2013/1970) has amended the Companies Act 2006 (CA 2006) to insert new sections providing for the preparation, by certain companies, of a Strategic Report. The purpose of the Strategic Report is to inform members of the company and help

---

[1] The Regulations are set out in Statutory Instrument 2013 No. 1970.

them assess how the directors have performed their duty under section 172 (duty to promote the success of the company) of CA 2006.

Duty to prepare strategic report

5. The directors of all companies, other than those entitled to the small companies' exemption, must prepare a strategic report for each financial year of the company. A company is entitled to the small companies' exemption in relation to the strategic report for a financial year if:

    (a) It is entitled to prepare accounts for the year in accordance with the small companies' regime, or

    (b) It would be so entitled but for being or having been a member of an ineligible group.

6. If the company is a parent company and the directors prepare group accounts the strategic report must be a consolidated report (a "group strategic report") relating to the undertakings included in the consolidation. A group strategic report may, where appropriate, give greater emphasis to the matters that are significant to the undertaking included in the consolidation, taken as a whole.

Content of strategic report

7. Sections 414C (2) and (3) of CA 2006 require the strategic report to contain:

    (a) A fair review of the company's business, and

    (b) A description of the principal risks and uncertainties facing the company.

The review required is a balanced and comprehensive analysis of:

    (a) The development and performance of the company's business during the financial year, and

    (b) The position of the company's business at the end of that year.

The detailed requirements regarding the content of the strategic report are set out in Sections 414C (4) to (14) of CA 2006.

Approval and signing of strategic report

8. The strategic report is required to be approved by the board of directors and signed on behalf of the board by a director or the secretary of the company.

Effective date

9. The Regulations set out in SI 2013/1970 are effective for financial years ending on or after 30 September 2013.

Consequential changes to the content of the Directors' Report

10. There are a number of consequential changes to the content of the Directors' Report. The principal changes are as follows:

    (a) It is no longer a requirement for a Business Review to be prepared as part of the Directors' Report.

    (b) The Directors' Report no longer requires a statement by the company of its principal activities in the course of the year.

    (c) A number of detailed changes have been made to the requirements regarding the content of the Directors' Report set out in the Large and Medium-sized Companies and Groups (Accounts and Reports) Regulations 2008 (SI 2008/ 410) and the Small Companies and Groups (Accounts and Directors' Report) Regulations 2008 (SI 2008/409).

What the auditor needs to do

11. Section 496 of CA 2006 requires the auditor to state in his report on the company's annual accounts whether the information given in the strategic report (if any) for the financial year for which the accounts are prepared is consistent with those accounts. This is the same statutory reporting responsibility as that which applies to the Directors' Report.

12. ISA (UK and Ireland) 720, Section B – "The Auditor's Statutory Reporting Responsibility In Relation To Directors' Reports", deals with the auditor's statutory reporting responsibility in relation to the directors' report. When reporting on the strategic report the auditor applies the requirements and application and other explanatory material in ISA (UK and Ireland) 720, Section B to the extent that they are applicable to the Strategic Report.

13. Under subsection (5)(b) of section 498 of CA 2006 if the directors of a company have taken advantage of the small companies exemption from the requirement to prepare a strategic report and in the auditor's opinion they were not entitled to do so, the auditor is required to state that fact in the auditor's report.

Implications for the illustrative auditor's reports in Bulletin 2010/2 (Revised March 2012)

14. Where the directors of a company prepare a strategic report the bullet point relating to the Directors' Report in the section headed "Opinion on other matters prescribed by the Companies Act 2006" should now read (new text shown as underlined):

> • The information given in the <u>Strategic Report and the</u> Directors' Report for the financial year for which the financial statements are prepared is consistent with the financial statements.

15. This change applies to examples 2 to 11 in Bulletin 2010/2 (Revised March 2012).

16. Where the directors of a company have taken advantage of the small companies' exemption from the requirement to prepare a strategic report and in the auditor's opinion they were entitled to do so the final bullet point of example 1 in Bulletin 2010/2 (Revised March 2012) is amended as follows:

> "We have nothing to report in respect of the following matters where the Companies Act 2006 requires us to report to you if, in our opinion:
>
> * ...
>
> * the directors were not entitled to [prepare the financial statements in accordance with the small companies regime] [and] [take advantage of the small companies' exemption in preparing the directors' report] [and] [take advantage of the small companies exemption from the requirement to prepare a strategic report]".

The stand-alone "strategic report with supplementary material"

Background

17. The Companies (Receipt of Accounts and Reports) Regulations 2013[2] (SI 2013/1973) establish the circumstances under which a company may send to its members, in place of the company's full accounts and reports, a copy of the company's "Strategic Report with supplementary material" in accordance with section 426 of CA 2006.

18. Section 426 of CA 2006 (as originally enacted) provided that a company could send a summary financial statement to persons who were entitled to receive full copies of the company's accounts and reports. That section was amended by SI 2013/1970 to substitute for a "summary financial statement" a copy of the "strategic report and supplementary material".

19. The requirement for a company to prepare a strategic report is set out in section 414A of CA 2006 and what constitutes "supplementary material" is described in section 426A of CA 2006 as inserted into the Act by SI 2013/1970.

20. The supplementary material is required to:

    (a) Contain a statement that the strategic report is only part of the company's annual accounts and reports;

    (b) State how a person entitled to them can obtain a full copy of the company's annual accounts and reports;

---

[2] The Regulations are set out in Statutory Instrument 2013 No. 1973.

(c) State whether the auditor's report on the annual accounts was unqualified or qualified and, if it was qualified, set out the report in full together with any further material needed to understand the qualification;

(d) State whether, in that report, the auditor's statement under section 496 (whether strategic report and directors' report consistent with the accounts) was unqualified or qualified and, if it was qualified, set out the qualified statement in full together with any further material needed to understand the qualification; and

(e) In the case of a quoted company, contain a copy of that part of the directors' remuneration report which sets out the single total figure table in respect of the company's directors' remuneration in accordance with Schedule 8 to the Large and Medium-sized Companies (Accounts and Reports) Regulations 2008 (SI 2008/410).

21. The expression "qualified" in (c) and (d) above has the following meaning as set out in section 539 of CA 2006:

> " 'qualified', in relation to an auditor's report (or a statement contained in an auditor's report) means that the report or statement does not state the auditor's unqualified opinion that the accounts have been properly prepared in accordance with this Act or, in the case of an undertaking not required to prepare accounts in accordance with this Act, under any corresponding legislation under which it is required to prepare accounts."

22. Regulation 2 of SI 2013/1973 revoked the Companies (Summary Financial Statement) Regulations 2008 (SI 2008/374). Regulations 4 to 8 provide for the conditions under which a company may provide a copy of the strategic report with supplementary material and the procedures by which it can be ascertained whether a person wishes to receive full accounts and reports. These regulations are in substantially the same form as regulations 4 to 8 of SI 2008/374.

Effective date

23. The Regulations set out in SI 2013/1973 are effective for financial years ending on or after 30 September 2013.

What the auditor needs to do

Repeal of requirement for an auditor's statement

24. Sections 427(4)(d) and 428(4)(d) of CA 2006 as originally enacted required summary financial statements to contain a statement by the company's auditor of its opinion as to whether the summary financial statement is consistent with the full annual financial statements and the Directors' Report and complies with the applicable requirements of the Companies Act 2006 and the regulations made thereunder.

25. These requirements have been repealed and the newly inserted requirements relating to a stand-alone "Strategic Report and Supplementary Material" (i.e. one that is not included in the Annual Report) do not require a statement by the company's auditor to be included.

The auditor's procedures

26. When planning the audit of a company the auditor ascertains whether a stand-alone "Strategic Report and Supplementary Material" will be prepared for distribution to those members who elect to receive it instead of the full annual reports and accounts. If so, the audit engagement letter, or a separate engagement letter, records the respective responsibilities of the directors and the auditor with respect to the stand-alone Strategic Report.

27. In order for the auditor to carry out its work on the stand-alone "Strategic Report and Supplementary Material" at the same time as it completes the audit, the auditor encourages the directors to plan the year end timetable accordingly.

28. The auditor's procedures in relation to the stand-alone "Strategic Report and Supplementary Material" are:

   (a) Ensuring that the stand-alone strategic report is the same as the strategic report published in the annual report and accounts. Once the auditor has established that the stand-alone strategic report is the same as that included in the annual report no further work is required if the procedures outlined in paragraphs 11 to 13 have been satisfactorily completed; and

   (b) Assessing whether the requirements of CA 2006 with respect to the Supplementary Material have been complied with.

Implications for the illustrative auditor's reports in Bulletin 2010/2 (Revised March 2012)

29. There are no implications for the illustrative auditor's reports in Bulletin 2010/2 (Revised March 2012).

Auditing the directors' remuneration report

Background

The responsibility of directors

30. Section 420 of CA 2006 sets out the duty of directors of quoted companies (as defined below) to prepare a directors' remuneration report for each financial year of a company. Section 421 of CA 2006 addresses the content of the directors' remuneration report and provides that the Secretary of State may make provision by regulations as to:

(a)   The information that must be contained in a directors' remuneration report,

(b)   How information is to be set out in the report, and

(c)   What is to be the auditable part of the report.

31.   Section 421 of CA 2006 further provides that it is the duty of:

(a)   Any director of a company, and

(b)   Any person who is or has at any time in the preceding five years been a director of the company

to give notice to the company of such matters relating to himself as may be necessary for the purposes of regulations under this section.

32.   Section 422 of CA 2006 requires the directors' remuneration report to be approved by the board of directors and signed on behalf of the board by a director or the secretary of the company.

Definition of quoted company

33.   For this purpose a quoted company is defined in section 385 of CA 2006 as follows:

(a)   ...a company is a quoted company in relation to a financial year if it is a quoted company immediately before the end of the accounting reference period by reference to which that financial year was determined.

(b)   A "quoted company" means a company whose equity share capital:

a.   has been included in the official list[3] in accordance with the provisions of Part 6 of the Financial Services and Markets Act 2000 (c 8), or

b.   is officially listed in an EEA State, or

c.   is admitted to dealing on either the New York Stock Exchange or the exchange known as Nasdaq.

2013 Regulations

34.   Effective for year ends ending on or after 30 September 2013 "The Large and Medium-sized Companies and Groups (Accounts and Reports) (Amendment) Regulations 2013"[4] (SI 2013/1981) came into force. These Regulations amend Schedule 8 "Quoted Companies: Directors' Remuneration Report" of "The Large and Medium-

---

[3]   The "official list" has the meaning given by section 103(1) of the Financial Services and Markets Act 2000.

[4]   Statutory Instrument 2013 No. 1981.

sized Companies and Groups (Accounts and Reports) Regulations 2008". Schedule 8 specifies the information to be included in the Directors' Remuneration Report.

35. A significant change to Part 3 of Schedule 8 is that it now requires the Directors' Remuneration Report to include a single total figure table of remuneration in respect of each person who was a director during the relevant financial year.

What the auditor needs to do

The auditor's responsibility and duties

36. Section 497 of CA 2006 requires in respect of quoted companies that the auditor in its report on the company's annual accounts for the financial year, must:

    (a) Report to the company's members on the auditable part of the directors' remuneration report, and

    (b) State whether in its opinion that part of the directors' remuneration report has been properly prepared in accordance with this Act.

37. Section 498 (2) of CA 2006 also requires the auditor of a quoted company to form an opinion as to whether the auditable part of the company's directors' remuneration report is in agreement with the accounting records and returns. If the auditor is of the opinion that the auditable part of the report is not in agreement with the accounting records and returns he is required to state that fact in his report.

38. Section 498 (4) of CA 2006 further requires that if the requirements of regulations under section 421 CA 2006 as to information forming the auditable part of the directors' remuneration report are not complied with in that report the auditor is required to include in the auditor's report, so far as he is reasonably able to do so, a statement giving the required particulars.

39. Section 498 (4) has an identical requirement with respect to the disclosures made under section 412 of CA 2006 (disclosure of directors' benefits: remuneration, pensions and compensation for loss of office in the notes to the accounts). These latter requirements are separate from the requirements relating to the directors' remuneration report (see below).

Provisions of the Directors' Remuneration Report which are subject to audit

40. The information contained in the directors' remuneration report which is subject to audit is the information required by paragraphs 4 to 17 (inclusive) of Part 3 of Schedule 8. This information includes the single total figure table of remuneration described above.

Reporting on the Directors' Remuneration Report

41. As the auditor is not required to audit all of the information contained in the Directors' Remuneration Report the auditor will need, in its report, to describe accurately which

elements of the Directors' Remuneration Report it has audited. The auditor, therefore, makes arrangements with the directors, well in advance of the year end, to ensure that the audited disclosures will be clearly distinguished from those that have not been audited.

42. It would be unsatisfactory for an auditor, in its report, to describe what it has audited in an uninformative manner such as "the disclosures required by Part 3 of Schedule 8 to The Large and Medium-sized Companies and Groups (Accounts and Reports) Regulations" as this would require readers of the auditor's report to have a detailed knowledge of the requirements.

43. The auditor assesses whether the scope of its audit will be capable of being clearly described. If this cannot be achieved to its satisfaction by cross-reference, it sets out the particulars that have been audited within the auditor's report.

Difference between the disclosures required by Schedule 5 and Schedule 8 of The Large and Medium-sized Companies and Groups (Accounts and Reports) Regulations 2008

44. Schedule 5 of the Regulations requires a company to provide certain information concerning directors' remuneration by way of the notes to the company's financial statements. The majority of the provisions of Schedule 5 apply only to unquoted companies (as the information required to be disclosed would be duplicated by disclosures in the Directors' Remuneration Report). However, the provisions described as "Total amount of directors' remuneration etc." apply to both quoted and unquoted companies.

45. A consequence of this may be that the financial statements of a quoted company disclose aggregate directors' remuneration that may differ from the aggregate directors' remuneration disclosed in the Directors' Remuneration Report. This may arise because the definition of aggregate remuneration differs between the two Schedules.

46. Both of these disclosures are reported on by the auditor. Where both disclosures have been prepared in accordance with the requirements of the Act and the various Regulations any difference between the disclosures is, prima facie, an inconsistency. However, the difference is not an inconsistency as defined by ISA (UK and Ireland) 720 (Revised October 2012) Section A – "The Auditor's Responsibilities Relating to Other Information in Documents Containing Audited Financial Statements". This is because the inconsistency arises from complying with the law and it would, therefore, be inappropriate to "correct" the inconsistency. However, as users may think the inconsistency is a mistake the auditor encourages the directors to provide an explanation of any difference within the Annual Report.

Issuing the Directors' Remuneration Report as a separate document

47. If a quoted company issues its Directors' Remuneration Report as a separate document the scope of the auditor's report included in the Annual Report will, nevertheless, encompass the auditable part of the Directors' Remuneration Report.

For this reason the requirements of ISA (UK and Ireland) 720 (Revised October 2012) Section A apply to the content of a separate Directors' Remuneration Report, notwithstanding the fact that the Report is not included in a document containing audited financial statements.

48. When the Directors' Remuneration Report is issued as a separate document, although not required by the Act, the auditor:

    (a) When its report is unqualified, encourages the directors to indicate within the Directors' Remuneration Report where the auditor's report, prepared in accordance with section 495 of CA 2006, may be found; or

    (b) When its report expresses either a qualified or adverse opinion or disclaims an opinion, which is relevant to the Directors' Remuneration Report, require the directors to reproduce the relevant parts of the auditor's report as part of the Directors' Remuneration Report. In the event that the directors do not agree to do so, the auditor considers whether to resign.

Implications for the illustrative auditor's reports in Bulletin 2010/2 (Revised March 2012)

49. These changes have no implications for the illustrative auditor's reports in Bulletin 2010/2 (Revised March 2012).

Changes in listing rule requirements with respect to directors' remuneration disclosures

Background

50. On 12 December 2013 the Financial Conduct Authority (FCA) amended the Listing Rules to delete Listing Rules 9.8.11R and 9.8.12R. These Listing Rules had required premium listed companies to ensure that their auditors review certain disclosures of directors' remuneration and to provide in the auditor's report details of any non-compliance.

51. These Listing Rules were deleted in response to the new Directors Remuneration Reporting Regulations (SI 2013/1981) and Strategic Report Regulations (SI 2013/1970), outlined above, with the intention of reducing unnecessary administrative burdens for a premium listed company incorporated in the UK. The FCA commented "We consider that only having to comply with one set of requirements in relation to most remuneration related disclosures should ensure a simpler and more effective regime for firms".

Effective date

52. The changes apply to premium listed companies with a financial year ending on or after 30 September 2013 that had not published their annual financial report on or before 13 December 2013.

Implications for the illustrative auditor's reports in Bulletin 2010/2 (Revised March 2012)

53. In illustrative examples 4, 8 and 9 the following amendments should be made in the section headed "Under the Listing Rules we are required to review:"

> Under the Listing Rules we are required to review:
>
> - the directors statement [set out [on page...]], in relation to going concern; and
>
> - the part of the Corporate Governance Statement relating to the company's compliance with the nine provisions of the [June 2008 Combined Code] [UK Corporate Governance Code[26, 37, 42]]-specified for our review.; and
>
> - certain elements of the report to the shareholders by the Board on directors' remuneration[26, 38, 43].

Recent changes to ISA (UK and IRELAND) 700

Background

Changes applicable to all auditor's reports

54. Following changes made to ISA (UK and Ireland) 720A "The Auditor's Responsibilities Relating to Other Information in Documents Containing Audited Financial Statements" a consequential change was made to the required description of the scope of an audit prescribed by paragraph 16 (c) of ISA (UK and Ireland) 700. The change required the following wording to be added to the penultimate sentence of the description.

> In addition, we read all the financial and non-financial information in the *[describe the annual report]* to identify material inconsistencies with the audited financial statements and to identify any information that is apparently materially incorrect based on, or materially inconsistent with, the knowledge acquired by us in the course of performing the audit.

This change is required to be made to all of the example auditor's reports set out in Bulletin 2010/2 (Revised March 2012).

Changes applicable in respect only of entities that apply the UK Corporate Governance Code

55. Other recent changes to ISA (UK and Ireland) 700 apply only to entities that apply the UK Corporate Governance Code. The following paragraphs provide an overview of these developments.

56. In September 2012 the FRC revised a number of ISAs (UK and Ireland) in order to give effect to the proposals in *Effective Company Stewardship: Next Steps* published by the

FRC in September 2011, and to support changes to the UK Corporate Governance Code and Guidance for Audit Committees that were also issued in September 2012.

57.   The changes in the ISAs (UK and Ireland) were mainly directed at:

(a)   Enhancing auditor communications by requiring the auditor to communicate to the audit committee information that the auditor believes the audit committee will need to understand the significant professional judgments made in the audit; and

(b)   Extending auditor reporting by requiring the auditor to report, by exception, if the board's statement that the annual report is fair, balanced and understandable is inconsistent with the knowledge acquired by the auditor in the course of performing the audit, or if the matters disclosed in the report from the audit committee do not appropriately address matters communicated by the auditor to the committee.

58.   In order to reflect these changes in the auditor's report the following text is included under the heading "Matters on which we are required to report by exception".

Matters on which we are required to report by exception

We have nothing to report in respect of the following:

Under the ISAs (UK and Ireland), we are required to report to you if, in our opinion, information in the annual report is:

- materially inconsistent with the information in the audited financial statements; or

- apparently materially incorrect based on, or materially inconsistent with, our knowledge of the Group acquired in the course of performing our audit; or

- is otherwise misleading.

In particular, we are required to consider whether we have identified any inconsistencies between our knowledge acquired during the audit and the directors' statement that they consider the annual report is fair, balanced and understandable and whether the annual report appropriately discloses those matters that we communicated to the audit committee which we consider should have been disclosed.

---

59.   In June 2013 the FRC, following consultation, made further changes to ISA (UK and Ireland) 700 requiring auditors reporting on entities which apply the UK Corporate Governance Code to explain more about their work. In overview the auditor's report is required to:

(a)   Describe those assessed risks of material misstatement identified by the auditor that had the greatest effect on:

a.   The overall audit strategy;

  b. The allocation of resources in the audit;

  c. Directing the efforts of the engagement team.

 (b) Provide an explanation of how the auditor applied the concept of materiality in planning and performing the audit; and

 (c) Provide an overview of the scope of the audit, showing how this addressed the risk and materiality considerations.

60. This explanation follows the opinion on the financial statements and is reflected in the example auditor's reports as follows:

> **Our assessment of risks of material misstatement**
> *[Insert a description of those specific assessed risks of material misstatement that were identified by the auditor and which had the greatest effect on the audit strategy, the allocation of resources in the audit; and directing the efforts of the engagement team.]*
>
> **Our application of materiality**
> *[Insert an explanation of how the auditor applied the concept of materiality in planning and performing the audit. Such explanation shall specify the threshold used by the auditor as being materiality for the financial statements as a whole.]*
>
> **An overview of the scope of our audit**
> *[Insert an overview of the scope of the audit, including an explanation of how the scope addressed the assessed risks of material misstatement and was influenced by the auditor's application of materiality.]*
>
> *[The disclosures about the above three matters are made in a manner that complements the description of significant issues relating to the financial statements required to be set out in the separate section of the annual report describing the work of the audit committee in discharging its responsibilities (see paragraphs [19B] and A13D] of ISA (UK and Ireland) 700).*

Effective date

61. All of the above changes to ISA (UK and Ireland) 700 are effective for audits of financial statements for periods commencing on or after 1 October 2012. Although expressed differently this is the same effective date as applies to the legal and regulatory requirements described in paragraphs 4 to 53.

Clarification Statement

62. In November 2013 the FRC issued a clarification statement in respect of paragraph 19A of ISA (UK and Ireland) 700. The clarification statement addresses an issue raised by a number of stakeholders who sought clarification as to whether the requirements

of paragraph 19A of ISA (UK and Ireland) 700 are intended to apply with respect to the auditor's report of both the group and the parent company financial statements.

63. The text of the clarification statement can be found on the following page of the FRC's web-site.
https://frc.org.uk/Our-Work/Publications/Audit-and-Assurance-Team/ISA-700-Clarification-Statement.pdf

Appendix 1

Example 1 – Non-publicly traded company preparing financial statements under the FRSSE

- *Company qualifies as a small company.*

- *Company does not prepare group financial statements.*

Independent auditor's report to the members of XYZ Limited

We have audited the financial statements of (name of company) for the year ended ... which comprise [specify the titles of the primary statements such as the Profit and Loss Account, the Balance Sheet, [the Cash Flow Statement], the Statement of Total Recognised Gains and Losses, [the Reconciliation of Movements in Shareholders' Funds]] and the related notes[5]. The financial reporting framework that has been applied in their preparation is applicable law and the Financial Reporting Standard for Smaller Entities [(Effective April 2008)][6] (United Kingdom Generally Accepted Accounting Practice applicable to Smaller Entities).

Respective responsibilities of directors and auditor

As explained more fully in the Directors' Responsibilities Statement [set out [on page ...]], the directors are responsible for the preparation of the financial statements and for being satisfied that they give a true and fair view. Our responsibility is to audit and express an opinion on the financial statements in accordance with applicable law and International Standards on Auditing (UK and Ireland). Those standards require us to comply with the Auditing Practices Board's [(APB's)] Ethical Standards for Auditors[, including "APB Ethical Standard – Provisions Available for Small Entities (Revised)", in the circumstances set out in note [x] to the financial statements][7].

Scope of the audit of the financial statements

Either:

> A description of the scope of an audit of financial statements is [provided on the APB's website at www.frc.org.uk/auditscopeukprivate] / [set out [on page ...] of the Annual Report].

---

[5] Auditor's reports of entities that do not publish their financial statements on a website or publish them using 'PDF' format may refer to the financial statements by reference to page numbers.

[6] Specify the version of The Financial Reporting Standard for Smaller Entities.

[7] Delete the words in square brackets if the relief and exemptions provided by ES PASE are not utilised. Paragraph 22 of ES PASE requires disclosure in the auditor's report where the audit firm has taken advantage of an exemption provided by ES PASE. The Appendix to ES PASE provides illustrative disclosures of relevant circumstances where the audit firm has taken advantage of an exemption provided by ES PASE.

Or:

> An audit involves obtaining evidence about the amounts and disclosures in the financial statements sufficient to give reasonable assurance that the financial statements are free from material misstatement, whether caused by fraud or error. This includes an assessment of: whether the accounting policies are appropriate to the company's circumstances and have been consistently applied and adequately disclosed; the reasonableness of significant accounting estimates made by the directors; and the overall presentation of the financial statements. In addition, we read all the financial and non-financial information in the *[describe the annual report]* to identify material inconsistencies with the audited financial statements <u>and to identify any information that is apparently materially incorrect based on, or materially inconsistent with, the knowledge acquired by us in the course of performing the audit</u>[8]. If we become aware of any apparent material misstatements or inconsistencies we consider the implications for our report.

Opinion on financial statements

In our opinion the financial statements:

- give a true and fair view of the state of the company's affairs as at .... and of its profit [loss] for the year then ended[9];

- have been properly prepared in accordance with United Kingdom Generally Accepted Accounting Practice applicable to Smaller Entities; and

- have been prepared in accordance with the requirements of the Companies Act 2006.

Opinion on other matter prescribed by the Companies Act 2006

In our opinion the information given in the Directors' Report for the financial year for which the financial statements are prepared is consistent with the financial statements.[16]

Matters on which we are required to report by exception

We have nothing to report in respect of the following matters where the Companies Act 2006 requires us to report to you if, in our opinion:

- adequate accounting records have not been kept, or returns adequate for our audit have not been received from branches not visited by us; or

---

[8] See paragraph 54 for explanation of change.
[9] Guidance for auditors when a company takes advantage of the option in section 444(1) of CA 2006 not to file the profit and loss account or the directors' report is set out in paragraph 12 of APB Bulletin 2008/4 "The Special Auditor's Report on Abbreviated Accounts in the United Kingdom".

- the financial statements are not in agreement with the accounting records and returns; or

- certain disclosures of directors' remuneration specified by law are not made; or

- we have not received all the information and explanations we require for our audit; or

- the directors were not entitled to [prepare the financial statements in accordance with the small companies regime] [and] [take advantage of the small companies' exemption in preparing the directors' report] [and] [take advantage of the small companies exemption from the requirement to prepare a strategic report][10].

[Signature]   *Address*
John Smith (Senior statutory auditor)   *Date*
for and on behalf of ABC LLP, Statutory Auditor

---

[10] See paragraph 16 for explanation of change.

Appendix 2

Example 9 – Publicly traded premium listed group – Auditor's report on group financial statements prepared under IFRSs as adopted by the European Union

- *Company is a quoted company and has a premium listing.*

- *Corporate governance statement reported on in the auditor's report on the group financial statements and incorporated into the directors' report, either directly or by incorporation by reference as explained in APB Bulletin 2009/4 (see example 7 for an illustration of an auditor's report where the corporate governance statement is not incorporated into the directors' report).*

- *Directors' Remuneration Report reported on in the auditor's report on the parent company financial statements.*

- *Company does prepare group financial statements.*

Independent auditor's report to the members of XYZ Plc

We have audited the group financial statements of (name of company) for the year ended ... which comprise [specify the titles of the primary statements such as the Group Statement of Financial Position, the Group Statement of Comprehensive Income, the Group Statement of Cash Flows, the Group Statement of Changes in Equity][11] and the related notes[12]. The financial reporting framework that has been applied in their preparation is applicable law and International Financial Reporting Standards (IFRSs) as adopted by the European Union.

Respective responsibilities of directors and auditor

As explained more fully in the Directors' Responsibilities Statement [set out [on page ...]], the directors are responsible for the preparation of the group financial statements and for being satisfied that they give a true and fair view. Our responsibility is to audit and express an opinion on the group financial statements in accordance with applicable law and International Standards on Auditing (UK and Ireland). Those standards require us to comply with the Auditing Practices Board's [(APB's)] Ethical Standards for Auditors.

---

[11] The names used for the primary statements in the auditor's report should reflect the precise titles used by the company for them.

[12] Auditor's reports of entities that do not publish their financial statements on a website or publish them using 'PDF' format may refer to the financial statements by reference to page numbers.

Scope of the audit of the financial statements

Either:

A description of the scope of an audit of financial statements is [provided on the FRC's website at www.frc.org.uk/auditscopeukprivate] / [set out [on page ...] of the Annual Report].

Or:

An audit involves obtaining evidence about the amounts and disclosures in the financial statements sufficient to give reasonable assurance that the financial statements are free from material misstatement, whether caused by fraud or error. This includes an assessment of: whether the accounting policies are appropriate to the group's circumstances and have been consistently applied and adequately disclosed; the reasonableness of significant accounting estimates made by the directors; and the overall presentation of the financial statements. In addition, we read all the financial and non-financial information in the [describe the annual report] to identify material inconsistencies with the audited financial statements and to identify any information that is apparently materially incorrect based on, or materially inconsistent with, the knowledge acquired by us in the course of performing the audit[13]. If we become aware of any apparent material misstatements or inconsistencies we consider the implications for our report.

Opinion on financial statements

In our opinion the group financial statements:

- give a true and fair view of the state of the group's affairs as at .... and of its profit [loss] for the year then ended;

- have been properly prepared in accordance with IFRSs as adopted by the European Union; and

- have been prepared in accordance with the requirements of the Companies Act 2006 and Article 4 of the IAS Regulation.

Our assessment of risks of material misstatement

[Insert a description of those specific assessed risks of material misstatement that were identified by the auditor and which had the greatest effect on the audit strategy; the allocation of resources in the audit; and directing the efforts of the engagement team.]

---

[13] See paragraph 54 for explanation of change.

Our application of materiality

[Insert an explanation of how the auditor applied the concept of materiality in planning and performing the audit. Such explanation shall specify the threshold used by the auditor as being materiality for the financial statements as a whole.]

An overview of the scope of our audit

[Insert an overview of the scope of the audit, including an explanation of how the scope addressed the assessed risks of material misstatement and was influenced by the auditor's application of materiality.]

[The disclosures about the above three matters are made in a manner that complements the description of significant issues relating to the financial statements required to be set out in the separate section of the annual report describing the work of the audit committee in discharging its responsibilities (see paragraphs [19B] and A13D] of ISA (UK and Ireland) 700)[14].

Opinion on other matter prescribed by the Companies Act 2006

In our opinion the information given in the Strategic Report and the[15] Directors' Report for the financial year for which the group financial statements are prepared is consistent with the group financial statements.

Matters on which we are required to report by exception

We have nothing to report in respect of the following:

Under the ISAs (UK and Ireland), we are required to report to you if, in our opinion, information in the annual report is:

- materially inconsistent with the information in the audited financial statements; or

- apparently materially incorrect based on, or materially inconsistent with, our knowledge of the Group acquired in the course of performing our audit; or

- is otherwise misleading.

In particular, we are required to consider whether we have identified any inconsistencies between our knowledge acquired during the audit and the directors' statement that they consider the annual report is fair, balanced and understandable and whether the annual report appropriately discloses those matters that we communicated to the audit committee which we consider should have been disclosed[16].

---

[14] See paragraphs 59 to 60 for explanation of change.
[15] See paragraph 14 for explanation of change
[16] See paragraph 57 to 58 for explanation of change.

Under the Companies Act 2006 we are required to report to you if, in our opinion:

- certain disclosures of directors' remuneration specified by law are not made; or

- we have not received all the information and explanations we require for our audit.

Under the Listing Rules we are required to review:

- the directors' statement, [set out [on page...]], in relation to going concern; and

- the part of the Corporate Governance Statement relating to the company's compliance with the nine provisions of the [June 2008 Combined Code] [UK Corporate Governance Code[17]] specified for our review.; and

- certain elements of the report to shareholders by the Board on directors' remuneration[18].[19]

Other matter

We have reported separately on the parent company financial statements of (name of company) for the year ended ... and on the information in the Directors' Remuneration Report that is described as having been audited. [That report includes an emphasis of matter] [The opinion in that report is (qualified)/(an adverse opinion)/(a disclaimer of opinion)].

[Signature]   Address
John Smith (Senior statutory auditor)   Date
for and on behalf of ABC LLP, Statutory Auditor

---

[17] The UK Corporate Governance Code was issued in May 2010 and applies to financial years beginning on or after 29 June 2010.

[18] The report on directors' remuneration should clearly identify those elements that have been audited.

[19] See paragraph 53 for explanation of change.

**FINANCIAL
REPORTING COUNCIL**

PRACTICE NOTE 10(I) (REVISED)

AUDIT OF CENTRAL GOVERNMENT FINANCIAL STATEMENTS IN THE REPUBLIC OF IRELAND

CONTENTS

Preface

This Practice Note contains guidance on the application of auditing standards issued by the Auditing Practices Board (APB) to the audit of central government sector bodies in the Republic of Ireland.

This Practice Note is intended to assist auditors in applying the requirements of, and should be read in conjunction with, International Standards on Auditing (ISAs) (UK and Ireland), which apply to all audits undertaken in Ireland. The Practice Note sets out the special considerations relating to the audit of central government sector bodies which arise from individual ISAs (UK and Ireland) listed in the contents. The Practice Note does not provide commentary on all of the requirements in the ISAs (UK and Ireland) – it is not the intention of the Practice Note to provide step-by-step guidance on the audit of central government sector bodies, so where no special considerations arise from a particular ISA (UK and Ireland) no material is included. Extracts from the ISAs (UK and Ireland) are indicated by grey shading.

Foreword – Public Accountability and Audit

1. Central government entities are responsible for the conduct of public business and for spending public money and are accountable to Dáil Éireann and through Dáil Éireann to the public for ensuring that this business is conducted in accordance with the law and proper standards of accounting and governance and that public money is used economically, efficiently and effectively. Their principal source of funding is money voted by Dáil Éireann or by means of statutory levies and their powers to raise revenue in other ways are governed by legislation.

2. Financial statements produced in the central government sector normally have the following characteristics – they are:

    *   prepared on an annual basis;

    *   laid before Dáil Éireann; and

    *   available to the public in published form.

3. For the purpose of this Practice Note, central government sector entities include funds administered through the Exchequer, voted funds, departmental funds, the financial statements of non-commercial state sponsored bodies, health agencies, third level educational institutions, vocational educational committees and some regional and local bodies. In Ireland all financial statements of central government departments and non-commercial entities are audited by the Comptroller and Auditor General (C&AG).

4. The C&AG gives an independent opinion on the financial statements of central government entities and may review and, where appropriate, report on aspects of the arrangements set in place by those bodies to ensure the proper conduct of their financial affairs and to manage their performance and use of resources. As such, his audit is an essential element in the process of accountability and makes an important

contribution to the stewardship of public money and the corporate governance of public services.

5.   The standards governing the conduct and reporting of the audit of financial statements in the central government sector is a matter for the C&AG and he has chosen to adopt the Auditing Practices Board's engagement standards and quality control standards as the basis of his approach to the audit of financial statements. ISAs (UK and Ireland) apply to all audits of financial statements for periods ending on or after 15 December 2010.

The role of Accounting Officers

6.   A particular provision has been made for accountability in the case of government departments. An Accounting Officer is designated by the Minister for Finance[1] to be responsible for the preparation of Appropriation Account(s).

7.   An Accounting Officer is also responsible for:

- the regularity and propriety of transactions in the Appropriation Account(s);

- the economy and efficiency of the department in the use of its resources; and

- the systems procedures and practices employed by the department for the purpose of evaluating the effectiveness of the operations[2].

8.   The Comptroller and Auditor General (Amendment) Act 1993 (the 1993 Act) provides that an Accounting Officer may be required to give evidence to the Committee of Public Accounts on these matters.

9.   The Civil Service head of the department or office administering a Vote is normally appointed Accounting Officer on the premise that he/she alone is in a position to account for all monies entrusted to his/her department.

10. In a limited number of other entities an Accounting Officer has been provided for by way of primary legislation.

Responsibilities of the Comptroller and Auditor General

11. Article 33 of the Constitution of Ireland provides for a Comptroller and Auditor General and legislation provides the authority for the audit of each central government sector entity. The scope of audit is determined by:

- the legislation governing the accountability of, and audit provisions relating to, the audited entity; and

---

[1]   Section 22 of the Exchequer and Audit Departments Act 1866.
[2]   Section 19 of the 1993 Act.

- auditing standards and related guidance promulgated by the Auditing Practices Board.

12. In the case of all central government sector entities it extends in particular to:

- the financial audit of the accounts;

- the regularity of transactions included in such accounts; and

- the proper conduct of public business (propriety).

Committee of Public Accounts

13. The body in Dáil Éireann mainly concerned with the work of the C&AG is the Committee of Public Accounts (PAC). It examines and reports to Dáil Éireann on:

- all financial statements audited by the C&AG together with his reports thereon;

- the C&AG reports on Value for Money examinations; and

- other reports made by the C&AG under the 1993 Act.

14. The Committee consists of thirteen Deputies none of whom may be a member of the Government or Minister of State. By long tradition, the Chairman is a member of the Opposition.

15. The PAC possesses no executive powers and its power is one of recommendation only. The Committee is entitled to send for persons, papers and records and takes evidence primarily from the Accounting Officer of the entity under examination or in the case of other entities an accountable person designated for that purpose.

The Audit of Regularity

16. An audit of financial statements in the central government sector is similar in scope and nature to an audit of limited companies and other entities in the private sector. There is, however, a greater emphasis on compliance with authority, commonly known as regularity.

17. The general concern is with the administration of public monies in accordance with the legal authority governing them and therefore extends to the substance of transactions and the entitlement of recipients of public funds.

18. The concept of regularity reflects a concern that public money raised through taxation on the public should be used only for those purposes approved by Dáil Éireann. The preparation of financial statements by central government sector bodies is an important means by which they are accountable for the use of public funds made available to them. The financial statements of central government sector bodies include an implied assertion regarding the regularity of financial transactions, in

addition to the financial statement assertions identified in ISA (UK and Ireland) 500, 'Audit Evidence'.

19. Regularity, as applied in the audit of the Appropriation Accounts and the financial statements of Vocational Education Committees, is defined in the 1993 Act. In these cases, the C&AG must satisfy himself as to:

- whether amounts expended have been applied by the entity concerned for the purposes intended;

- whether transactions recorded in the account conform with the authority under which they purport to have been carried out.

20. Upon completion of the audit, the C&AG must refer to any material case in which the entity has failed to apply expenditure recorded in the financial statements for the purpose intended or transactions recorded in the financial statements do not conform to the authority under which they purport to have been carried out. As a matter of principle, the concept of regularity is also applied in the audit of all other central government sector entities which are within the audit remit of the C&AG.

21. By comparison, the auditors of private sector bodies are also concerned with applicable law and regulations. Nevertheless, the environment within which they work is different, as the operations of private sector bodies are generally subject to less detailed regulation than those in the central government sector. Indeed, ISA (UK and Ireland) 250 Section A, 'Consideration of Law and Regulations in an Audit of Financial Statements', draws attention to the fact that the auditor of bodies in the central government sector may have duties that go beyond those of auditors of private sector entities.

22. Part B to this Practice Note amplifies this guidance on the audit of regularity.

The Concept of Propriety

23. Propriety is concerned with the way in which public business is conducted including any conventions agreed with Dáil Éireann (and in particular the PAC), and any guidance issued on governance and ethics.

24. Whereas regularity is concerned with the compliance with appropriate authorities, propriety goes wider than this and extends to standards of conduct, behaviour and corporate governance. It is concerned with fairness and integrity including avoidance of personal profit from public business, even-handedness in the appointment of staff, open competition in the award of contracts and the avoidance of waste and extravagance.

25. Although of no less importance than regularity, propriety is less readily susceptible to objective verification and is not expressly covered in the opinion on financial statements. Nevertheless, the auditor of a central government account is expected to have regard to matters of propriety in conducting his audit.

26. When considering the measures taken by management to promote propriety the C&AG has regard to what is considered generally accepted practice in the central government sector. To ascertain what is acceptable practice, the auditor of central government accounts draws as necessary on recommendations or expression of opinion made by the PAC as accepted by the Executive following consideration of specific cases, guidance issued by Department of Finance or, in the case of other central government sector bodies, guidance issued by the supervising government departments.

Reporting the Results of Audit Activity

27. The results of audit activity are reported to Dáil Éireann in two main ways:

    • through certificates or reports which give an audit opinion on each account; and

    • through reports on matters relating to the management of individual entities and other matters likely to be of concern to Dáil Éireann.

28. Audit reports give two types of assurance:

    • an opinion giving explicit assurance on the financial statements usually in a form prescribed by law; and

    • assurance in relation to matters required to be reported on by exception, including the Statement on Internal Financial Control, regularity and propriety.

29. Other reports to Dáil Éireann cover matters of value for money, financial administration or outline any material issues that have arisen concerning the regularity of transactions or the propriety of public business.

30. This Practice Note does not apply to local authorities or the commercial state sponsored sector[3]. The guidance in this Practice Note relates only to audit work designed to support the issue of audit opinions on financial statements audited by the C&AG. Consequently the guidance does not cover other reports issued under section 11(2) of the 1993 Act such as value for money reports.

---

[3] Bodies in the commercial state sector are largely specified in the Second Schedule to the 1993 Act.

Part A – ISQC (UK and Ireland) 1 and ISAs (UK and Ireland)

International Standard on Quality Control (UK and Ireland) 1

Objective

The objective of the firm is to establish and maintain a system of quality control to provide it with reasonable assurance that:

(a) The firm and its personnel comply with professional standards and applicable legal and regulatory requirements; and

(b) Reports issued by the firm or engagement partners are appropriate in the circumstances. (Paragraph 11)

Definitions

31. In the context of the audit of public sector entities the following clarification of terms used in ISQC (UK and Ireland) 1 is relevant:

    - "firm" is taken as a general reference to the Office of the Comptroller and Auditor General or other auditors where the audit has been contracted-out; and

    - "engagement partner" is the nominated senior individual responsible for that engagement and its performance including the delivery of the engagement to the C&AG, in accordance with the ISAs (UK and Ireland).

32. In addition, for the purposes of this standard, the following definition applies:

    - Contracted-out engagement[4] is where responsibility for issuing the audit report remains with the C&AG, but all or some of the audit assignment is undertaken by another firm or auditor under contract or agreement.

Leadership

33. Overall responsibility for the system of quality control in the central government sector remains with the head of the organisation (the Accounting Officer). The organisation establishes policies and procedures such that any person or persons assigned operational responsibility for the organisation's system of quality control by the C&AG has the appropriate experience and ability, and the necessary authority, to assume that responsibility

34. For contracted-out engagements, responsibility for quality across all engagements remains with the C&AG. However, this does not absolve the contractor of responsibility

---

[4] In accordance with the 1993 Act the C&AG may arrange with an audit firm to undertake work on his behalf.

for systems of quality control within that firm in accordance with ISQC (UK and Ireland) 1. In practice, this may involve the C&AG obtaining assurances over quality from the contractor, and may involve the C&AG undertaking procedures to confirm that the systems of quality control are working effectively.

Ethics

35. The C&AG has chosen to adopt the Auditing Practices Board's Ethical Standards. Additional ethical and propriety standards may apply such as the Civil Service Code of Standards and Behaviour, Ethics legislation[5] and Official Secrets legislation. Compliance with these additional requirements does not compromise the ability of the auditor of a central government account to comply with relevant professional ethical requirements required by ISQC (UK and Ireland) 1.

36. For contracted out audits the C&AG confirms that the other firm meets the relevant ethical standards, including independence, on appointment and periodically thereafter, and that there are policies and procedures in place to identify and resolve potential conflicts.

Acceptance and Continuance of Client Relationships and Specific Engagements

37. In the central government sector, where the audit appointment is by or under statute, it is not possible to decline or withdraw from the engagement. However, in most cases the auditor of a central government account has the statutory authority to report publicly matters that may otherwise have caused withdrawal from the engagement. For example, in the central government sector such matters can be reported to the Dáil Éireann.

38. The auditor of a central government account therefore establishes policies and procedures equivalent to those envisaged within ISQC (UK and Ireland) 1 for acceptance and continuance of both client relationships and specific engagements in accordance with ISA (UK and Ireland) 220.

Human Resources

39. Where an engagement is contracted out steps are taken to ensure that the other auditor has sufficient personnel with the competencies, capabilities and commitment to ethical principles necessary for compliance with ISQC (UK and Ireland) 1.

Engagement Performance

40. For contracted-out audits, the auditor of a central government account remains responsible for engagement performance. This does not affect the contractor's responsibility for its engagement performance. Both undertake their own consideration of whether internal consultation and the appointment of an

---

[5]   Ethics in Public Office Acts 1995 and 2001

engagement quality control reviewer are necessary. The fact that either has undertaken, or chosen not to implement, this process does not absolve the other from considering the need for such procedures in accordance with ISQC (UK and Ireland) 1. Equally, a review by the engagement partner of the auditor of a central government account does not constitute an independent engagement quality control review for the purposes of ISQC (UK and Ireland) 1.

41. ISQC (UK and Ireland) 1 requires the appointment of an engagement quality control reviewer for listed companies, but acknowledges that certain public sector entities may be of sufficient significance to warrant performance of such a review. Each firm establishes a policy for determining which assignments are subject to an engagement quality control review, taking into account the complexity of the organisation, public interest issues, and other relevant factors determined corporately, for example whether a modification to the audit report is expected.

Monitoring

42. Each firm implements quality control monitoring policies and procedures. Where contractors perform assignments on a contracted-out basis, the auditor of a central government account ensures that the quality control monitoring system includes those assignments.

43. A firm undertaking an assignment on a contracted-out basis ensures that their quality control monitoring system includes such assignments.

44. Where deficiencies are identified as a result of monitoring an assignment undertaken on a contracted-out basis, these deficiencies are reported to the firm undertaking the assignment. Equally, if the contractor identifies deficiencies in any of its assignments that fall within the remit of the auditor of a central government account, these are communicated to that auditor, along with the action undertaken.

45. Each firm establishes policies and procedures designed to provide it with reasonable assurance that it deals appropriately with complaints and allegations relating to quality. These policies and procedures allow for escalation of such issues to the auditor of a central government account, where relevant.

Confidentiality, Safe Custody, Integrity, Accessibility and Retrievability of Engagement Documentation

The firm shall establish policies and procedures designed to maintain the confidentiality, safe custody, integrity, accessibility and retrievability of engagement documentation. (Paragraph 46)

46. Although the auditor of a central government account applies the provisions of ISQC (UK and Ireland) 1 in full, there may be additional statutory obligations relating to confidentiality. For example, when carrying out central government assignments the auditor of a central government account is aware of, and complies with, any applicable provisions of the Official Secrets Act 1963.

47. Where the C&AG has arranged for a firm or person to perform any audit work in accordance with the 1993 Act, it is normal practice to include a condition that audit documentation remains the property of the C&AG. The firm or person is equally bound by the legislation on confidentiality, retention of working papers and freedom of information.

48. The Freedom of Information Act 1997 does not apply to records created after the commencement of an audit[6]. However, records created before the commencement of an audit and other administrative documents are covered by the Act.

---

[6] Section 46(c) of the Act.

ISA (UK and Ireland) 200: Overall Objectives of the Independent Auditor and the Conduct of an Audit in Accordance with International Standards on Auditing (UK and Ireland)

Overall Objectives of the Auditor

In conducting an audit of financial statements, the overall objectives of the auditor are:

(a) To obtain reasonable assurance about whether the financial statements as a whole are free from material misstatement, whether due to fraud or error, thereby enabling the auditor to express an opinion on whether the financial statements are prepared, in all material respects, in accordance with an applicable financial reporting framework; and

(b) To report on the financial statements, and communicate as required by the ISAs (UK and Ireland), in accordance with the auditor's findings. (Paragraph 11)

In all cases when reasonable assurance cannot be obtained and a qualified opinion in the auditor's report is insufficient in the circumstances for purposes of reporting to the intended users of the financial statements, the ISAs (UK and Ireland) require that the auditor disclaim an opinion or withdraw (or resign) from the engagement, where withdrawal is possible under applicable law or regulation. (Paragraph 12)

49. Although the principles of auditing are the same in the public and private sectors, the auditor of a central government entity often has wider objectives and additional statutory responsibilities, laid down in legislation or otherwise.

The Audit of Regularity

50. In observing the requirements of ISA (UK and Ireland) 200, the auditor of a central government account is aware that:

• for central government sector entities, there is a requirement, laid out in statute or by convention, to obtain evidence on compliance with authorities (regularity); and

• in recognition of the importance of regularity to the audit of these entities, the matters addressed in the section of the auditor's report that deals with matters required to be reported on by exception includes the regularity of transactions.

The auditor of a central government account also considers propriety, internal control and corporate governance.

51. The audit opinion issued by the C&AG only refers to instances of departure from the norms of regularity, internal control or corporate governance. Issues of probity are generally reported separately from the audit opinion.

ISA (UK and Ireland) 210: Agreeing the Terms of Audit Engagements

Objective:

The objective of the auditor is to accept or continue an audit engagement only when the basis upon which it is to be performed has been agreed, through:

(a) Establishing whether the preconditions for an audit are present; and

(b) Confirming that there is a common understanding between the auditor and management and, where appropriate, those charged with governance of the terms of the audit engagement. (Paragraph 3)

52. In this section of the Practice Note, the client is considered to be the audited body.

Preconditions for an Audit

In order to establish whether the preconditions for an audit are present, the auditor shall:

(a) Determine whether the financial reporting framework to be applied in the preparation of the financial statements is acceptable; and

(b) Obtain the agreement of management that it acknowledges and understands its responsibility:

    (i) For the preparation of the financial statements in accordance with the applicable financial reporting framework, including where relevant their fair presentation;

    (ii) For such internal control as management determines is necessary to enable the preparation of financial statements that are free from material misstatement, whether due to fraud or error; and

    (iii) To provide the auditor with:

        a. Access to all information of which management is aware that is relevant to the preparation of the financial statements such as records, documentation and other matters;

        b. Additional information that the auditor may request from management for the purpose of the audit; and

        c. Unrestricted access to persons within the entity from whom the auditor determines it necessary to obtain audit evidence. (Paragraph 6)

53. In the central government sector, the preconditions for audit may derive from a number of sources, including legislation or 'by agreement' with the Minister for Finance.

Agreement on Audit Engagement Terms

The auditor shall agree the terms of the audit engagement with management or those charged with governance, as appropriate. (Paragraph 9)

Subject to paragraph 11 [of the standard], the agreed terms of the audit engagement shall be recorded in an audit engagement letter or other suitable form of written agreement and shall include:

(a) The objective and scope of the audit of the financial statements;

(b) The responsibilities of the auditor;

(c) The responsibilities of management;

(d) Identification of the applicable financial reporting framework for the preparation of the financial statements; and

(e) Reference to the expected form and content of any reports to be issued by the auditor and a statement that there may be circumstances in which a report may differ from its expected form and content. (Paragraph 10)

If law or regulation prescribes in sufficient detail the terms of the audit engagement referred to in paragraph 10 [of the standard], the auditor need not record them in a written agreement, except for the fact that such law or regulation applies and that management acknowledges and understands its responsibilities as set out in paragraph 6(b) [of the standard]. (Paragraph 11)

54. Statutory engagements in the central government sector normally differ substantially from those addressed in the private sector. In the central government sector there are often a number of parties with an interest in the terms of an engagement. In most other instances, the statutory framework allows a substantial part of the scope and objectives of the audit to be mandated by the auditor of a central government account.

55. For this reason, formal engagement letters for statutory engagements may not be necessary. However, it remains important that the client and the auditor formally recognise their respective responsibilities. It may also be necessary, where legislation does not provide sufficient detail on the scope of the audit, to ensure that is appropriately understood by those charged with governance. A letter of understanding may therefore be necessary. The annex to this chapter provides examples of areas such a letter may cover.

56. The auditor may find it appropriate to conclude letters of understanding with the audited entity to confirm the auditor's understanding of the roles of the parties with an interest in the engagement, the requirements of the audit, the responsibilities of each party, how the responsibilities will be met, and the expectations that each party can have of the other.

57. For audit engagements undertaken 'by agreement', an engagement letter is required, covering the matters set out in ISA (UK and Ireland) 210. The issuance of an engagement letter for such assignments makes clear the rights, responsibilities and duties of all parties.

Acceptance of a Change in Engagement

If, prior to completing the audit engagement, the auditor is requested to change the audit engagement to an engagement that conveys a lower level of assurance, the auditor shall determine whether there is reasonable justification for doing so. (Paragraph 15)

58. Where the responsibilities of the auditor of a central government account are set out in statute, the terms of the engagement cannot be changed to provide a lower level of assurance.

If the auditor is unable to agree to a change of the audit engagement and is not permitted to continue the original engagement, the auditor shall:

(a) Withdraw from the audit engagement where possible under applicable law or regulation; and

(b) Determine whether there is any obligation, either contractual or otherwise, to report to other parties, such as those charged with governance, owners or regulators. (Paragraph 17)

59. In the central government sector, where the appointment is under statute, it is not possible to decline or withdraw from the engagement. However, in most cases a central government auditor has the statutory authority to report publicly matters that may otherwise have caused withdrawal from the engagement. For example, in the central government sector such matters can be reported to Dáil Éireann.

60. Where appointment is not by statute, the requirements of ISA 210 (UK and Ireland) will apply in full with respect to considerations for acceptance of an engagement, or changes and restrictions to the terms of an engagement.

Annex

Areas that may be Covered in a Letter of Engagement or Understanding

The auditor of a central government account considers the areas that may be covered by the letter of engagement or understanding. These areas may change over time and the auditor of a central government account will need to consider developments that may be relevant to the client.

In preparing the letter of engagement or understanding the auditor of a central government account may consider the following:

- Individual responsibilities of the Accounting Officer or accountable person, as well as the general responsibilities of those charged with governance, where relevant;

- Responsibilities of the auditor of a central government account, with reference to the relevant legislative framework;

- Wider auditor responsibilities, such as obligations to report certain matters involving fraud and other offences in accordance with law[7];

- Reviewing the Accounting Officer or a Board's Statement on Internal Financial Control;

- Electronic Publication of Financial Statements;

- Value for Money Examinations;

- Audit Fees.

---

[7] Section 74 of the Company Law Enforcement Act 2001 requires that an auditor report to the Office of the Director of Corporate Enforcement instances of the suspected commission of indictable offences under the Companies Acts by a company, its officers or agents.
Section 59 Criminal Justice (Theft and Fraud Offences) Act 2001 requires that an auditor report to a member of the Garda Síochána in circumstances where information or documents indicate that certain offences under the Act may have been committed by a client entity, or by its management or employees.
Anti-money laundering legislation requires that an auditor report suspicions of money laundering to the Garda Síochána and the Revenue Commissioners.

ISA (UK and Ireland) 220: Quality Control for an Audit of Financial Statements

Objective

The objective of the auditor is to implement quality control procedures at the engagement level that provide the auditor with reasonable assurance that:

(a) The audit complies with professional standards and applicable legal and regulatory requirements; and

(b) The auditor's report issued is appropriate in the circumstances. (Paragraph 6)

61. In the context of the audit of public sector entities the following clarification of terms used in ISA (UK and Ireland) 220 is relevant:

- "firm" is taken as a general reference to the Office of the Comptroller and Auditor General or other auditors where the audit has been contracted-out; and

- "engagement partner" is taken as the nominated senior individual within the firm responsible for that engagement and its performance including the delivery of the engagement to the C&AG, in accordance with the ISAs (UK and Ireland).

Acceptance and Continuance of Client Relationships and Specific Audit Engagements

The engagement partner shall be satisfied that appropriate procedures regarding the acceptance and continuance of client relationships and specific audit engagements have been followed, and shall determine that conclusions reached in this regard are appropriate. (Paragraph 12)

62. A central government sector auditor may be specifically appointed under legislation to audit the financial statements of a central government entity, in which case it will not be open to the auditor to decline the appointment. For example, the Comptroller and Auditor General can be named as the auditor in the legislation that creates a new public sector entity. However, an assessment is carried out on initial appointment and annually thereafter of the matters outlined in the ISA (UK and Ireland) and put in place sufficient safeguards to mitigate the risks identified.

63. In all other respects the auditor of a central government account will follow the guidance set out in ISA (UK and Ireland) 220, and if necessary include in the auditor's report, for example, any constraints to undertaking sufficient work to be able to perform the audit in accordance with Auditing Standards or an imposed limitation in audit scope.

> If the engagement partner obtains information that would have caused the firm to decline the audit engagement had that information been available earlier, the engagement partner shall communicate that information promptly to the firm, so that the firm and the engagement partner can take the necessary action. (Paragraph 13)

64. Further guidance on declining or withdrawing from engagements in the public sector is provided in paragraph 88 of this Practice Note and in paragraph A7 to ISA 220 (UK and Ireland).

Engagement Quality Control Review

> For audits of financial statements of listed entities, and those other audit engagements, if any, for which the firm has determined that an engagement quality control review is required, the engagement partner shall:
>
> (a) Determine that an engagement quality control reviewer has been appointed;
>
> (b) Discuss significant matters arising during the audit engagement, including those identified during the engagement quality control review, with the engagement quality control reviewer; and
>
> (c) Not date the auditor's report until the completion of the engagement quality control review. (Paragraph 19)

65. The ISA (UK and Ireland) requires that an engagement quality control review is undertaken for all audit engagements where the entity is a listed company, and that firms establish policies setting out the circumstances in which an engagement quality control review is performed for other audit engagements, whether on the grounds of the public interest or risk.

66. In the central government sector, the auditor of a central government account considers the circumstances in which an engagement quality control review of the audit is necessary. In doing so consideration will need to be given to the size and characteristics of the entity. Generally engagement quality control reviews are more likely to be appropriate to larger, more complex, entities than smaller ones, and to higher profile entities than lower profile entities. An engagement quality control review may be appropriate for smaller entities with a high profile, for example if there is a particularly high level of Oireachtas, public or media interest in the entity or where the entity itself is not high profile, although the activities of the entity are. It is the decision of each firm to determine what constitutes a high profile entity taking into account both the size and profile of the entity.

ISA (UK and Ireland) 230: Audit Documentation

Objective:

The objective of the auditor is to prepare documentation that provides:

(a) A sufficient and appropriate record of the basis for the auditor's report; and

(b) Evidence that the audit was planned and performed in accordance with ISAs (UK and Ireland) and applicable legal and regulatory requirements. (Paragraph 5)

Assembly of the Final Audit File

67. Guidance on the confidentiality, safe custody, integrity, accessibility and retrievability of engagement documentation is provided in the ISQC (UK and Ireland) 1 section of this Practice Note.

After the assembly of the final audit file has been completed, the auditor shall not delete or discard audit documentation of any nature before the end of its retention period. (Paragraph 15)

68. The auditor of a central government account also considers whether there are specific statutory requirements for the retention of working papers. In certain circumstances the National Archives Act 1986 could apply to documentation relating to the audit of a central government sector entity. Where the auditor is uncertain as to his statutory duties, he considers seeking legal advice.

ISA (UK and Ireland) 240: The Auditor's Responsibilities Relating to Fraud in an Audit of Financial Statements

Objectives

The objectives of the auditor are:

(a) To identify and assess the risks of material misstatement of the financial statements due to fraud;

(b) To obtain sufficient appropriate audit evidence regarding the assessed risks of material misstatement due to fraud, through designing and implementing appropriate responses; and

(c) To respond appropriately to fraud or suspected fraud identified during the audit. (Paragraph 10)

69. An auditor conducting an audit in accordance with ISAs (UK and Ireland) is responsible for obtaining reasonable assurance that the financial statements taken as a whole are free from material misstatement, whether caused by fraud or error.

70. The central government sector auditor's responsibilities under ISA (UK and Ireland) 240 are not any different from those of private sector auditors as regards the audit of the financial statements (although in some instances they are different with respect to the other responsibilities relating to fraud as set out in paragraphs 74 and 82).

71. Further details regarding the requirements of central government audit with regard to loss and mismanagement (including the possibility of fraud) are set out in the Department of Finance's *Public Financial Procedures* and other appropriate guidance on corporate governance.

72. These other responsibilities are different from and wider than those to which ISA (UK and Ireland) 240 is directly relevant. The auditor of a central government account is concerned, to a greater or lesser extent, with reviewing and reporting upon the entity's arrangements for the prevention and detection of fraud. ISA (UK and Ireland) 240 is concerned with ensuring that the auditor considers the risks of material misstatement in the financial statements due to fraud and designs and performs further audit procedures whose nature, timing and extent are responsive to assessed risks.

Fraud in the Context of the Regularity Opinion

73. Only a court of law can determine whether a particular transaction is fraudulent. However, the auditor often encounters situations where there is suspicion of fraud, identified by management, internal audit, third parties or the auditor. Although the auditor does not have the authority to determine whether or not a fraud has actually occurred, the auditor does have a responsibility to determine whether, in the auditor's

opinion, the transactions concerned are in compliance with the authorities that govern them.

74. Fraudulent transactions cannot, by definition, be regular since they are without proper authority. Where there is a duty to give a regularity opinion (including 'by exception'), fraud that is material always results in a qualification of the regularity part of the opinion, regardless of the manner or extent of disclosure in the financial statements.

75. The definition of fraud in ISA (UK and Ireland) 240 includes acts committed by individuals both inside and outside the audited entity. Guidance in the ISA (UK and Ireland) is, however, primarily concerned with internal fraud as it is this type of fraud which is considered most likely to lead to material misstatements in the financial statements. The responsibility that the auditor of a central government account has to reach an opinion on regularity means that the auditor is also concerned with the extent of fraud perpetrated from outside the entity.

76. The guidance in appendix 1 of ISA (UK and Ireland) 240 provides examples of fraud risk factors. These are all relevant to central government, but in addition, the auditor considers those conditions and events which increase the risk of external fraud.

77. Paragraphs 28 and 30 of ISA (UK and Ireland) 240 require that the overall audit response to address the assessed risks of material misstatement due to fraud at the financial statement level be determined and further audit procedures whose nature, timing and extent are responsive to the assessed risks at the assertion level be designed and performed. However, as explained in paragraph 6 of ISA (UK and Ireland) 240, owing to the inherent limitations of an audit, there is an unavoidable risk that some material misstatements of the financial statements will not be detected, even though the audit is properly planned and performed in accordance with ISAs (UK and Ireland). In addition, the likelihood of the audit detecting material fraud, and in particular external fraud, is always lower than a reasonable expectation of detecting error, since fraud is usually accompanied by acts specifically designed to conceal its existence, or involving collusion between employees, or employees and third parties, or falsification of records. The auditor cannot be expected to identify forged documentation in support of claims for grants or other benefits, other than the most obvious forgeries, and generally does not have investigative powers or rights of access to individuals or organisations making claims.

78. Both for practical reasons and in recognition of the responsibilities of those charged with governance in this area, the audit is likely to focus on the adequacy of the entity's internal controls for preventing and detecting fraud.

79. Whilst ISA (UK and Ireland) 240 is not written to address, and should not be considered to address the audit of regularity, in some instances compliance with the requirements of ISA (UK and Ireland) 240 may be effectively extended to also gain assurance over regularity. For example, the requirements to:

- evaluate whether unusual or unexpected relationships that have been identified through analytical procedures are indicative of material misstatement due to fraud (ISA (UK and Ireland) 240 paragraph 22);

- test the appropriateness of journal entries made in the general ledger (ISA (UK and Ireland) 240 paragraph 32(a)); and

- consider the rationale for significant transactions undertaken outside the normal course of business (ISA (UK and Ireland) 240 paragraph 32(c)), may also be completed as part of the audit of the regularity assertion.

80. ISA (UK and Ireland) 240 explains that although fraud is a broad legal concept, for the purposes of the ISAs (UK and Ireland), the audit is concerned with fraud that causes a material misstatement in the financial statements. Two types of intentional misstatements are relevant to the auditor – misstatements resulting from fraudulent financial reporting and misstatements resulting from misappropriation of assets. Although the auditor of a central government account may suspect or, in rare cases, identify the occurrence of fraud, the auditor does not make legal determinations of whether fraud has actually occurred.

81. ISA (UK and Ireland) 240 is focussed upon the risks of fraudulent financial reporting and also considers the risks of misappropriation of assets. For the purposes of auditing regularity, fraudulent financial reporting, although it may disguise underlying irregular transactions, is not, itself, irregular. Therefore, it is considered by the central government sector auditor in accordance with ISA (UK and Ireland) 240. However, misappropriation of assets is irregular and risk of material misappropriation of assets due to fraud is considered in accordance with both ISA (UK and Ireland) 240, which places an emphasis on misappropriation by management or employees, and this section of the Practice Note.

Unless all of those charged with governance are involved in managing the entity[8], the auditor shall obtain an understanding of how those charged with governance exercise oversight of management's processes for identifying and responding to the risks of fraud in the entity and the internal control that management has established to mitigate these risks. (Paragraph 20)

82. The responsibilities of central government sector entities in relation to the prevention and detection of fraud and error are set out in statute, standards and other guidance. The Department of Finance's *Public Financial Procedures* set out the Accounting Officer's responsibility in relation to the proper presentation of financial statements for which he or she is answerable and for ensuring that:

- the transactions of the Department/Office are proper and regular;

- proper financial procedures are followed;

- public funds are properly controlled, well managed and safeguarded; and

- assets are safeguarded and controlled.

---

[8]   ISA (UK and Ireland) 260, "Communication with Those Charged with Governance," paragraph 13.

83. Similar responsibilities attach to the accountable persons or organs of non-commercial state sponsored bodies such as boards. These are expressly acknowledged in Statements of Responsibilities accompanying the financial statements.

84. Management in all central government entities has the general responsibility of developing and maintaining effective controls to prevent fraud and to ensure that, when it does occur, it is detected promptly.

Risk Assessment Procedures and Related Activities

When performing risk assessment procedures and related activities to obtain an understanding of the entity and its environment, including the entity's internal control, required by ISA (UK and Ireland) 315, the auditor shall perform procedures [specified in paragraphs 17-24 of the standard] to obtain information for use in identifying the risks of material misstatement due to fraud. (Paragraph 16)

85. The auditor of a central government account considers whether internal and external fraud risk factors are present when obtaining an understanding of audited entities. The risk of external fraud may be particularly high where a body is involved in issuing grants or benefits to the public or collecting tax revenues as there is an increased risk of fraudulent activity by individuals or groups outside of the immediate control of the audited entity, for example fraudulent benefit or prescription claims.

86. ISA (UK and Ireland) 240 describes two types of fraud that are relevant to the auditor:

- misstatements resulting from the misappropriation of assets; and

- misstatements resulting from fraudulent financial reporting.

In the central government sector consideration is also given to the risk of external fraud as explained above.

87. A central government sector auditor needs to consider misstatements that may arise from fraudulent financial reporting where the audited body may manipulate its results to meet externally set targets, for example, the achievement of a break-even responsibility.

Auditor Unable to Continue the Engagement

If, as a result of a misstatement resulting from fraud or suspected fraud, the auditor encounters exceptional circumstances that bring into question the auditor's ability to continue performing the audit the auditor shall:

(a) Determine the professional and legal responsibilities applicable in the circumstances, including whether there is a requirement for the auditor to report to the person or persons who made the audit appointment or, in some cases, to regulatory authorities;

(b) Consider whether it is appropriate to withdraw from the engagement, where withdrawal from the engagement is legally permitted and

(c) If the auditor withdraws:

   (i) Discuss with the appropriate level of management and those charged with governance the auditor's withdrawal from the engagement and the reasons for the withdrawal; and

   (ii) Determine whether there is a professional or legal requirement to report to the person or persons who made the audit appointment or, in some cases, to regulatory authorities, the auditor's withdrawal from the engagement and the reasons for the withdrawal. (Paragraph 38)

88. In the central government sector, where the appointment is under statute the auditor cannot decline or withdraw from the engagement. Where the auditor of a central government account is not appointed by statute there are still a number of avenues open to the auditor other than withdrawing from the engagement. In most cases a central government sector auditor has the statutory authority to report publicly matters that may otherwise have caused withdrawal from the engagement. For example, in the central government sector such matters can be reported to Dáil Éireann.

Documentation

The auditor shall include in the audit documentation communications about fraud made to management, those charged with governance, regulators and others. (Paragraph 46)

89. In considering whether to report a suspected or actual instance of fraud to a proper authority, the auditor of a central government sector entity has regard to paragraph 43 of ISA (UK and Ireland) 240 and to:

• the provisions relevant to the entity that set out the responsibilities of those charged with governance for the reporting of misconduct, fraud or other irregularity; and

• the duties under specific legislation[9] requiring the reporting to a third party such as An Garda Síochána or the Office of the Director of Corporate Enforcement.

---

[9] Section 59 Criminal Justice (Theft and Fraud Offences) Act 2001 requires that an auditor report to a member of the Garda Síochána in circumstances where information or documents indicate that certain offences under the Act may have been committed by a client entity, or by its management or employees. Section 74 of the Company Law Enforcement Act 2001 requires instances of the suspected commission of indictable offences under the Companies Acts by a company, its officers or agents to be reported by an auditor to the Office of the Director of Corporate Enforcement.

90. Where, in accordance with ISA (UK and Ireland) 240, a duty to report to an outside authority is considered to apply (e.g. because of the implication of those charged with governance in the matter or their refusal to report), the proper authorities to whom instances of suspected or actual fraud are expected to be made may differ. In the central government sector, and depending on the circumstances of the suspected or actual fraud, the supervising department would constitute the proper authority to whom a suspected or actual instance of fraud in a non-commercial state sponsored body is reported. For a central government department, the Department of Finance is the proper destination for reports of instances of suspected or actual fraud.

91. Because the public sector is covered by separate legislation on corruption[10], the auditor of a central government account considers to whom he may report suspected or actual acts of corruption, irrespective of whether, in his opinion, the consequences of the corruption could have a material effect on the financial statements. In the first instance, the matter is normally brought to the attention of those charged with governance. It is then the responsibility of those charged with governance to report the matter to the proper authorities. If the auditor of a central government entity identifies a suspected or actual instance of corruption, and if, having reported the matter to those charged with governance he is unable to establish whether those charged with governance have reported the matter to the relevant third party, the auditor takes the steps set out in paragraph 43 of ISA (UK and Ireland) 240.

92. The auditor of a central government account is also aware of the responsibilities in relation to reporting money laundering offences (see guidance in paragraphs 98 and 99 of this Practice Note), including those relating to 'tipping-off'. Auditors ensure that they liaise with their Money Laundering Reporting Officer in making any report.

> When identifying and assessing the risks of material misstatement due to fraud, the auditor shall, based on a presumption that there are risks of fraud in revenue recognition, evaluate which types of revenue, revenue transactions or assertions give rise to such risks. Paragraph 47 [of the standard] specifies the documentation required when the auditor concludes that the presumption is not applicable in the circumstances of the engagement and, accordingly, has not identified revenue recognition as a risk of material misstatement due to fraud. (Paragraph 26)

---

[10] Specific legislation on corruption applies to Irish public bodies of all descriptions and their agents, where an agent is a person serving under a public body. The generally applicable legislation comprises:
- the Prevention of Corruption Acts 1889 to 2010; and
- the Ethics in Public Office Act 1995 and 2001.

Section 2 of the Prevention of Corruption Act 1916 (as amended) states that:

'Where in any proceedings.... it is proved that any money, gift or other consideration has been paid or given to or received by an office holder or special adviser or a director of, or occupier of a position of employment in, a public body by or from a person or agent of a person holding or seeking to obtain a contract from a Minister of the Government or a public body, the money, gift or consideration shall be deemed to have been paid or given and received corruptly ... unless the contrary is proved.'

The importance of this particular provision is that, where a person employed by a public body has received any money, gift or consideration from a contractor or tenderer, the burden of proof is on that person to establish that such consideration was not paid or received corruptly.

93. ISA (UK and Ireland) 240 indicates, in paragraphs 26 and A28, that material misstatements due to fraudulent financial reporting often result from an overstatement of revenues (for example, through premature revenue recognition or recording fictitious revenues) or an understatement of revenues (for example, through improperly shifting revenues to a later period). Therefore, the auditor ordinarily presumes that there are risks of fraud in revenue recognition and considers which types of revenue, revenue transactions or assertions may give rise to such risks. Those assessed risks of material misstatement due to fraud related to revenue recognition are significant risks. For some central government sector entities this presumption regarding the risk of fraud relating to revenue recognition may not apply due to the immateriality of revenue streams. However, even in these cases, the central government sector auditor still needs to consider whether there is a risk of material misstatement due to fraud related to revenue recognition where the audited body is required to meet externally set targets. For example, within central government departments, income may be an immaterial transaction stream but could be manipulated in order to ensure that net expenditure is within the budget limits.

94. In the central government sector, the risk that material misstatements due to fraudulent financial reporting may arise from the manipulation of expenditure recognition (for instance by deferring expenditure to a later period) also needs to be considered. This may arise due to the audited body manipulating expenditure to meet externally set targets. As most central government bodies are net spending bodies, then the risk of material misstatement due to fraud related to expenditure recognition may in some cases be greater than the risk of material misstatements due to fraud related to revenue recognition and so the auditor of a central government account has regard to this when planning and performing audit procedures.

ISA (UK and Ireland) 250: Section A – Consideration of Laws and Regulations in an Audit of Financial Statements

Objectives

The objectives of the auditor are:

(a) To obtain sufficient appropriate audit evidence regarding compliance with the provisions of those laws and regulations generally recognised to have a direct effect on the determination of material amounts and disclosures in the financial statements;

(b) To perform specified audit procedures to help identify instances of non-compliance with other laws and regulations that may have a material effect on the financial statements; and

(c) To respond appropriately to non-compliance or suspected non-compliance with laws and regulations identified during the audit. (Paragraph 10)

Consideration of Laws and Regulations

95. An audit of financial statements in the public sector is similar in scope and nature to an entity in the private sector. The auditor has regard to the risk that financial statements might be materially affected by the entity's non-compliance with laws and regulation. For auditors of central government bodies, there is a specific reporting requirement commonly known as regularity.

96. ISA (UK and Ireland) 250 is concerned with laws and regulations that, if not complied with, may materially affect the financial statements of any entity. Such laws and regulations fall into two categories:

(a) The provisions of those laws and regulations generally recognised to have a direct effect on the determination of material amounts and disclosures in the financial statements such as tax and pension laws and regulations; and

(b) Other laws and regulations that do not have a direct effect on the determination of the amounts and disclosures in the financial statements, but compliance with which may be fundamental to the operating aspects of the business, to an entity's ability to continue its business, or to avoid material penalties (for example, compliance with environmental regulations); non-compliance with such laws and regulations may therefore have a material effect on the financial statements.

> As part of obtaining an understanding of the entity and its environment in accordance with ISA 315[11], the auditor shall obtain a general understanding of:
>
> (a) The legal and regulatory framework applicable to the entity and the industry or sector in which the entity operates; and
>
> (b) How the entity is complying with that framework. (Paragraph 12)

97. The audit of central government entities carries a specific reporting requirement commonly known as regularity which is discussed in Part B of this Practice Note.

Reporting of Identified or Suspected Non-Compliance

> If the auditor has identified or suspects non-compliance with laws and regulations, the auditor shall determine whether the auditor has a responsibility to report the identified or suspected non-compliance to parties outside the entity. (Paragraph 28)

98. Guidance on the auditor's responsibilities in relation to the anti-money laundering legislation when auditing and reporting on financial statements is provided in *Anti-Money Laundering Procedures Republic of Ireland* issued by the Consultative Committee of Accountancy Bodies – Ireland.

99. The auditor of a central government account considers the offence of tipping off under section 58(1) of the Criminal Justice Act 1994.

---

[11] ISA (UK and Ireland) 315 "Identifying and Assessing the Risks of Material Misstatement through Understanding the Entity and its Environment," paragraph 11.

ISA (UK and Ireland) 260: Communication with Those Charged With Governance

Objectives

The objectives of the auditor are:

(a) To communicate clearly with those charged with governance the responsibilities of the auditor in relation to the financial statement audit, and an overview of the planned scope and timing of the audit;

(b) To obtain from those charged with governance information relevant to the audit;

(c) To provide those charged with governance with timely observations arising from the audit that are significant and relevant to their responsibility to oversee the financial reporting process; and

(d) To promote effective two-way communication between the auditor and those charged with governance. (Paragraph 9)

100. In the central government sector the Accounting Officers or Chief Executive Officer (as accountable person) or equivalent head of the audited organisation is responsible not only for maintaining adequate internal controls, but also for the regularity of the public funds for which they are accountable. The audit of central government entities carries a specific reporting requirement commonly known as regularity which is discussed in Part B of this Practice Note

Those Charged with Governance

The auditor shall determine the appropriate person(s) within the entity's governance structure with whom to communicate. (Paragraph 11)

101. The auditor of a central government account determines who is charged with governance at the outset of the audit. This may be one or more of the Accounting Officer and a group or groups of individuals charged with that role. It may include a Board, council, governing body or another group.

102. The Accounting Officer has personal responsibilities for:

• ensuring that effective management systems appropriate for the achievement of the organisation's objectives including financial monitoring and control systems have been put in place;

• keeping proper accounts;

- ensuring internal audit is established and organised in accordance with appropriate standards; and

- ensuring the regularity and propriety of public finances.

103. When submitting a report on matters arising out of an audit to management, consideration is given to which members of senior management have the power to act on their findings. The Accounting Officer has both the power and responsibility to act on communications of audit matters. The auditor of a central government account is normally expected to address his communications to the Accounting Officer.

104. In other bodies, communication is to the Chief Executive Officer or equivalent who is the person accountable for the transactions of the entity even where:

- the entity is managed by a Board; or

- the entity has an audit committee.

105. In each of these instances the auditor of a central government account ensures that these other parties are made aware of the existence and content of the communication. While the governance of a body is primarily a matter for the Chief Executive Officer and board, or equivalent organ, as a matter of practice the C&AG will communicate matters arising from the audit in appropriate cases to sponsoring departments or in his report on the financial statements.

ISA (UK and Ireland) 265: Communicating Deficiencies in Internal Control to Those Charged with Governance and Management

Objective

The objective of the auditor is to communicate appropriately to those charged with governance and management deficiencies in internal control that the auditor has identified during the audit and that, in the auditor's professional judgment, are of sufficient importance to merit their respective attentions. (Paragraph 5)

The auditor shall communicate in writing significant deficiencies in internal control identified during the audit to those charged with governance on a timely basis. (Paragraph 9)

106. The C&AG often has a responsibility to report publicly, including in relation to deficiencies or failings in internal control, whether resulting in financial loss, irregular transactions, issues of propriety or breach of a statutory requirement. For example, under the 1993 Act the C&AG may report significant deficiencies identified from his audit of central government departments and the accounts of vocational education committees to Dáil Éireann.

107. Where legislation requires the auditor of a central government account to consider broader internal control-related matters than would be required under ISAs (UK and Ireland), deficiencies in these controls are reported to Those Charged with Governance and Management in accordance with ISA (UK and Ireland) 265. For example, controls related to compliance with legislative authorities, regulations, or provisions of contracts or grant agreements.

ISA (UK and Ireland) 300: Planning an Audit of Financial Statements

Objective

The objective of the auditor is to plan the audit so that it will be performed in an effective manner. (Paragraph 4)

108. Effective working by the central government sector auditor requires that the evidence needed to satisfy each responsibility and meet each duty (whether laid down in statute or by agreement with the Minister for Finance) is collected and considered in a structured way that contributes with greatest effect to the objectives of the audit considered as a whole. Where the auditor of a central government account has completed work in relation to other responsibilities and duties, he considers whether the work meets the requirements of ISAs (UK and Ireland) before seeking to place reliance on it for the purposes of the audit of the financial statements.

Preliminary Engagement Activities

The auditor shall undertake the following activities at the beginning of the current audit engagement:

a)   Performing procedures required by ISA (UK and Ireland) 220 regarding the continuance of the client relationship and the specific audit engagement.

b)   Evaluating compliance with ethical requirements, including independence, in accordance with ISA (UK and Ireland) 220; and.

c)   Establishing an understanding of the terms of the engagement, as required by ISA (UK and Ireland) 210. (Paragraph 6)

109. Further guidance on declining or withdrawing from engagements in the public sector is provided in paragraph 88 of this Practice Note.

110. When establishing an understanding of the terms of the engagement, the auditor of a central government account will need to consider the requirement to provide an opinion on the regularity of transactions. For further guidance on the audit of regularity, see Part B of this Practice Note on regularity.

Planning Activities

The auditor shall establish an overall audit strategy that sets the scope, timing and direction of the audit, and that guides the development of the audit plan. (Paragraph 7)

111. Where the auditor of a central government account is required to give a regularity opinion, in developing the overall audit strategy a sufficient understanding is obtained of the framework of authorities governing the audited entity and its activities that is sufficient to enable the auditor to identify events, transactions and practices that may have a significant effect on the regularity of transactions in the financial statements. Guidance on planning the audit of regularity is set out in Part B of this Practice Note on regularity.

112. In the central government sector, financial statements may include specific notation, for instance details of expenditure outturn variances or losses, which are required under the applicable reporting framework. In these circumstances, in developing the audit strategy the auditor of a central government account obtains an understanding of the reporting requirements and of the audited entity and its activities sufficient to design audit procedures to obtain assurance in respect of these additional requirements.

ISA (UK and Ireland) 315: Identifying and Assessing the Risks of Material Misstatement through Understanding the Entity and its Environment

Objective

The objective of the auditor is to identify and assess the risks of material misstatement, whether due to fraud or error, at the financial statement and assertion levels, through understanding the entity and its environment, including the entity's internal control, thereby providing a basis for designing and implementing responses to the assessed risks of material misstatement. (Paragraph 3)

The auditor shall perform risk assessment procedures to provide a basis for the identification and assessment of risks of material misstatement at the financial statement and assertion levels. Risk assessment procedures by themselves, however, do not provide sufficient appropriate audit evidence on which to base the audit opinion. (Paragraph 5)

113. This ISA (UK and Ireland) requires the auditor to make risk assessments at the financial statement and assertion levels based on an appropriate understanding of the entity and its environment. In the central government sector, consideration has to be given to the additional assertion of regularity. At the planning stage, the central government sector auditor therefore needs to obtain an understanding of the framework of authorities specific to the entity. For further guidance on obtaining an understanding of the framework of authorities refer to Part B of this Practice Note on regularity.

The Required Understanding of the Entity and Its Environment, Including the Entity's Internal Control

The auditor shall obtain an understanding of relevant industry, regulatory, and other external factors including the applicable financial reporting framework. (Paragraph 11(a))

114. The auditor of a central government account obtains an understanding of the financial reporting framework and regulatory factors under which the financial statements are prepared and their impact on the audit. The financial reporting framework and other regulations for the public sector include those set out in:

- the specific legislation that has established the audited entity and determines its activities;

- *Public Financial Procedures* for government departments published by the Department of Finance;

- standards that constitute International Financial Reporting Standards and/or Irish GAAP.

115. When considering compliance with the applicable financial reporting framework, the central government sector auditor's procedures are performed in the knowledge that entities have their own legislative framework and accounting provisions that prescribe the form and content of financial statements.

116. Where a report is given on statements made by those charged with governance relating to corporate governance, this is outside the scope of the audit of the financial statements, even though it may be based on work carried out for that audit. Whether an opinion is always given by the auditor or by exception, it is based on any specific guidance issued in laws, regulations or codes of practice applicable in Ireland.

Nature of the Entity

The auditor shall obtain an understanding of the following: ...

The nature of the entity, including:

(i)   its operations;

(ii)   its ownership and governance structures;

(iii)   the types of investments that the entity is making and plans to make; and

(iv)   the way that the entity is structured and how it is being financed

to enable the auditor to understand the classes of transactions, account balances, and disclosures to be expected in the financial statements. (Paragraph 11(b))

117. In the central government sector this will include obtaining an understanding of the legislative background of the body and the way in which it is funded.

Objectives and Strategies and Related Business Risks

The auditor shall obtain an understanding of ...

The entity's objectives and strategies, and related business risks that may result in risks of material misstatement. (Paragraph 11 (d))

118. There are a number of additional factors that may be considered when assessing business risks for central government sector entities. These arise from the particular coincidence in the public sector of a closely regulated regime, a large volume of transactions processed and a public reporting process. These additional factors may arise where:

- major new legislation or expenditure programmes have been introduced;

- there is the possibility of manipulation by management to achieve performance or other targets;

- an entity is likely to be wound up, reorganised, merged, sold or privatised;

- there is political pressure on an entity to complete transactions quickly; and

- the final form of account does not reflect the underlying management and accounting processes.

119. Where entities are required to work to annual limits on resources, the risk of transactions being recorded in the wrong accounting period is increased, since there is a temptation for an entity in surplus to bring forward payments and for an entity in deficit to delay them.

Assessing the Risks of Material Misstatement

The auditor shall identify and assess the risks of material misstatement at:

(a) The financial statement level; and

(b) The assertion level for classes of transactions, account balances, and disclosures. (Paragraph 25)

120. To assess the inherent risk of a material misstatement occurring, the auditor of a central government account uses judgement to evaluate a range of factors. In the context of the regularity opinion specific factors include those set out in the annex to this section of the Practice Note. Further guidance on the audit of regularity is set out Part B of this Practice Note.

As part of the risk assessment as described in paragraph 25 [of the standard], the auditor shall determine whether any of the risks identified are, in the auditor's judgment, a significant risk. In exercising this judgment, the auditor shall exclude the effects of identified controls related to the risk. (Paragraph 27)

121. Possible significant risks in the public sector include the risks that:

- organisations issuing grants may have been subject to fraudulent grant claims;

- financial reporting and disclosure requirements arising through the issuing of financial and/or statutory guarantees may not be met;

- the financial statements may have been manipulated to meet externally set targets, such as deliberate understatement of expenditure to meet a net expenditure limit;

- fixed asset valuations are incorrect;

- guarantees or other contingent liabilities which are subject to significant change in value; and

- financial transactions entered into by the entity in the period do not conform to the authorities that govern them (known as "regularity").

If the auditor has determined that a significant risk exists, the auditor shall obtain an understanding of the entity's controls, including control activities, relevant to that risk. (Paragraph 29)

122. For further guidance on possible control procedures relating to the identified risks to regularity refer to the annex to this section of the Practice Note.

Annex

Risks to regularity and possible control procedures

Risk	Description	Mitigating Controls
Complexity of Regulations	The more complex the regulations the greater the risk of error. This may occur either through a misunderstanding or misinterpretation of the regulation or through an error in application.	• Formal procedures for the translation of statutory requirements into operating instructions. • Formal control plans prepared and monitored by scheme managers. • Review of scheme control plans and operating manuals by internal audit or some other independent audit.
New Legislation	New legislation may require the introduction of new administrative and control procedures. This may result in errors in either the design or operation of controls required to ensure regularity.	The controls identified above involving formal procedures for the translation of statutory requirements into scheme rules. Formal control plans and the independent review of operating instructions and control plans will also apply where schemes are introduced following new legislation.
European Union Schemes	Where legislation is developed by the European Commission there is a risk that regulations and guidance may be misinterpreted or omitted from internal instructions.	The mitigating controls identified in connection with the complexity of regulations apply equally to EU funded schemes.

Risk	Description	Mitigating Controls
Services and programmes delivered through third parties	Where programmes are administered by agents, departments lose a degree of direct control and may have to rely on agents to ensure compliance with authorities.	• Formal agreements between the entity and the agent defining control procedures to be applied in the administration of services. • Management control and monitoring of third party activities. • Inspection visits by internal audit to third parties to review systems and procedures, including those relevant to regularity. • Independent certification of payments and receipts by the third parties' auditor.
Payments and receipts made on the basis of claims or declarations	An entity's ability to confirm compliance with authorities may be restricted where, for example, criteria specified for receipt of grant are not subject to direct verification.	• Established criteria for making claims, clearly set out in departmental instructions and guidance to claimants. • Standard requirements for documentation evidencing entitlement to be submitted in support of claims. (This may be a condition of payment of grant or a requirement once the activity supported by the grant has been completed). • Physical inspection of claimants' records etc., to confirm eligibility. • Procedures for assessing the financial standing of claimants before awarding a grant and for monitoring continuing solvency. • Independent certification of the application of grant by external auditor.

ISA (UK and Ireland) 320: Materiality in Planning and Performing an Audit

Objective

The objective of the auditor is to apply the concept of materiality appropriately in planning and performing the audit. (Paragraph 8)

123. The concept of materiality is applied by the auditor of a central government account both in planning and performing the audit, and in evaluating the effect of identified misstatements on the audit and uncorrected misstatements, if any, on the financial statements and in forming the opinion in the auditor's report.

124. The auditor of a central government account makes an assessment of materiality with reference to the auditor's understanding of the expectations of the users of the financial statements. However, in the consideration of materiality, the assessment remains the auditor's own and is not dictated directly by any explicit or implicit interest expressed by any individual with an interest in the financial statements.

125. A central government sector auditor may have other specific responsibilities and duties under statute or be required under the terms of engagement to make reports on matters that do not affect the opinion on the financial statements. Where this is the case, the auditor may adopt a level of significance appropriate to these other responsibilities and duties which differs from the materiality level applied to the audit of the financial statements. There is no necessary connection between the materiality of an item to the financial statements and its significance to one of the auditor's other responsibilities or duties.

126. For example, in the course of carrying out work relating to other responsibilities and duties, the auditor of a central government account may detect errors, omissions or weaknesses in accounting arrangements. In these instances the auditor considers the materiality of the findings for the audit of the financial statements and reviews the risk assessments on which the audit was based to ensure that they remain valid.

When establishing the overall audit strategy, the auditor shall determine materiality for the financial statements as a whole. If, in the specific circumstances of the entity, there is one or more particular classes of transactions, account balances or disclosures for which misstatements of lesser amounts than materiality for the financial statements as a whole could reasonably be expected to influence the economic decisions of users taken on the basis of the financial statements, the auditor shall also determine the materiality level or levels to be applied to those particular classes of transactions, account balances or disclosures. (Paragraph 10)

127. Where the auditor of a central government account has a duty to give a regularity opinion, the qualitative considerations applying to the assessment of materiality may reflect the interests expressed by principal users in the regularity of transactions. The

determination of materiality in the central government sector is therefore influenced by legislative and regulatory requirements, and by the financial information needs of legislators and the public in relation to public sector programmes. The list of matters will vary from audited body to audited body, however considerations may include:

- The need for openness and transparency, for example if there are particular disclosure requirements for senior staff or board members' remuneration;

- Public expectations and public interest which might deem separate disclosure of special payments, write offs and losses necessary; and

- The context in which a matter appears, for example if the matter is also subject to compliance with authorities, legislation or regulations. For example situations where a loss is turned into a deficit or in central government where expenditure limits are exceeded (Excess Vote).

128. Further guidance on the interaction between the regularity aspects and the audit of the financial statements is given in Part B of this Practice Note on regularity.

ISA (UK and Ireland) 330: The Auditor's Responses to Assessed Risks

Objective

The objective of the auditor is to obtain sufficient appropriate audit evidence regarding the assessed risks of material misstatement, through designing and implementing appropriate responses to those risks. (Paragraph 3)

Audit Procedures to Address Risks of Material Misstatement at the Assertion Level

If the auditor has determined that an assessed risk of material misstatement at the assertion level is a significant risk, the auditor shall perform substantive procedures that are specifically responsive to that risk. When the approach to a significant risk consists only of substantive procedures, those procedures shall include tests of details. (Paragraph 21)

129. Paragraph 121 in this Practice Note outlines the issues the central government sector auditor considers when assessing significant risks. The annex to the guidance in this Practice Note on ISA 315 (UK and Ireland) provides further guidance on possible control responses by management to risks to regularity. Where the auditor has identified a risk that expenditure may have been misstated to meet externally set targets, the auditor performs audit procedures to address this risk such as analytical procedures to identify anomalies in results, reviewing unusual transactions and reviewing significant judgments made by those charged with governance when preparing the financial statements.

ISA (UK and Ireland) 402: Audit Considerations Relating to an Entity Using a Service Organisation

Objective

The objectives of the user auditor, when the user entity uses the services of a service organisation, are:

(a) To obtain an understanding of the nature and significance of the services provided by the service organisation and their effect on the user entity's internal control relevant to the audit, sufficient to identify and assess the risks of material misstatement; and

(b) To design and perform audit procedures responsive to those risks. (Paragraph 7)

130. Central government sector entities may use shared service providers, often in a pooled arrangement, across a sector or departmental group. For example, transaction processing or payroll services may be outsourced to another entity, which could be private sector, another public sector organisation, or a joint venture between the two sectors.

Obtaining an Understanding of the Services Provided by a Service Organisation, Including Internal Control

When obtaining an understanding of the user entity in accordance with ISA (UK and Ireland) 315, the user auditor shall obtain an understanding of how a user entity uses the services of a service organisation in the user entity's operations, ... (Paragraph 9)

131. The responsibilities of an auditor of a central government account go beyond those in the private sector by virtue of statutory or other prescribed duties and obligations. This includes the need to give an opinion on the regularity of expenditure. This may require the central government sector auditor to inspect records maintained by service organisations in relation to activities undertaken on behalf of public sector entities. Guidance on the audit of regularity is set out in Part B of this Practice Note on regularity.

When obtaining an understanding of internal control relevant to the audit in accordance with ISA (UK and Ireland) 315, the user auditor shall evaluate the design and implementation of relevant controls at the user entity that relate to the services provided by the service organisation, including those that are applied to the transactions provided by the service organisation. (Paragraph 10)

132. Consideration is given in particular to how the user organisations oversee the performance by the provider, and consider whether this, itself raises the risk of

misstatement. Also, where the auditor of a central government account is the auditor of more than one user organisation for a service provider, an understanding is obtained of how each user entity is affected by the service organisation, and individual assessments are made of risk and impact on the audit approach for each user entity.

133. ISA (UK and Ireland) 402 in itself is not sufficient to secure access rights for the central government sector auditor, and it is important that such access rights and the purpose of such rights are recognised and provided for in the contract between the service organisation and the central government sector entity.

134. The Comptroller and Auditor General has the right of access under section 10 of the 1993 Act to every document relating to an entity subject to audit by him as he may reasonably require. The C&AG also has inspection rights under section 8 of the 1993 Act to the books of individuals or organisations who receive 50% or more of their funding from the Exchequer, either directly or indirectly. The Department of Finance *Compendium of Clauses for a DBFOM*[12] *Contract* specifies that an access clause for the Comptroller and Auditor General be included in all Public-Private Partnerships.

---

[12] Design, build, finance, operate and manage.

**FINANCIAL
REPORTING COUNCIL**

ISA (UK and Ireland) 500: Audit Evidence

Objective

The objective of the auditor is to design and perform audit procedures in such a way as to enable the auditor to obtain sufficient appropriate audit evidence to be able to draw reasonable conclusions on which to base the auditor's opinion. (Paragraph 4)

135. In the central government sector, sufficient audit evidence is obtained to support the regularity assertion. Entities will usually have established internal controls designed to secure the regularity of transactions. However, where the audited entity is responsible for giving grants or other financial assistance to other parties, it is often the case that the regularity of the transaction will depend on the other parties satisfying the criteria and meeting the terms for receiving assistance. Evidence might then be required on the entity's exercise of its responsibilities to satisfy itself about the transactions of these other parties. Guidance on audit evidence for regularity work is set out in Part B of this Practice Note on regularity.

136. In the central government sector financial statements may also include specific notation which are required under the relevant applicable reporting framework. Where the entity makes non-GAAP disclosures in accordance with the applicable framework then this is subject to audit testing.

ISA (UK and Ireland) 510: Initial Audit Engagements – Opening Balances

Objective

In conducting an initial audit engagement, the objective of the auditor with respect to opening balances is to obtain sufficient appropriate audit evidence about whether:

(a) Opening balances contain misstatements that materially affect the current period's financial statements; and

(b) Appropriate accounting policies reflected in the opening balances have been consistently applied in the current period's financial statements, or changes thereto are appropriately accounted for and adequately presented and disclosed in accordance with the applicable financial reporting framework. (Paragraph 3)

137. All of the requirements of ISA (UK and Ireland) 510 are relevant to the central government sector auditor. However, the variety of circumstances in which ISA (UK and Ireland) 510 will apply will be different from that in the private sector. New legislation and changes in Government policies mean that new audit appointments will arise from the imposed breaking-up or bringing-together of existing public sector entities or changes in public sector audit arrangements.

138. ISA (UK and Ireland) 510 is concerned with the opening balances for initial engagements. This can occur when the financial statements for the prior period were audited by another auditor, but is also relevant for "machinery of government changes" that transfer functions from one part of the public sector to another as a going concern.

139. For machinery of government changes, the following additional considerations may be relevant:

Nature of Opening Balances	Additional Guidance
Opening balance amounts are clearly identifiable from the preceding period's audited financial statements for the transferring entity	The auditor of a central government account adopts the requirements in paragraphs 6 and 7 of ISA (UK and Ireland) 510.

Nature of Opening Balances	Additional Guidance
Opening balance amounts are not identifiable from the preceding period's audited financial statements for another entity, but have been derived from balances contained in those statements.	If relevant, the auditor of a central government account discusses with the auditor of the predecessor organisation whether information is available that would provide substantive evidence for the opening balances. In the absence of such evidence, the auditor of a central government account carries out substantive testing of opening balances to confirm they have been brought-forward appropriately in accordance with the terms of the transfer, at an appropriate valuation in line with the accounting policies of the receiving body.
Opening balances have been calculated as part of a separate disaggregation/ merger exercise, subject to a separate specific review and report by an auditor	The auditor of a central government account considers the scope and outcomes of that separate review, and considers whether the conclusions can be relied on in accordance with ISA (UK and Ireland) 500. Where the work from the separate specific review cannot be used, the auditor of a central government account considers carrying out substantive testing of opening balances, in line with the box above.
Opening balances have been calculated as part of a separate disaggregation/ merger exercise, but not subject to separate specific review and report	The auditor of a central government account considers carrying out substantive testing of opening balances. Completeness of assets and liabilities, together with appropriate valuation can be risks in a disaggregation exercise, and engagement with the audited body is made at an early stage.

140. Where, after performing the procedures described in paragraph 6 of ISA (UK and Ireland) 510 and the table above, the auditor of a central government account is unable to obtain sufficient appropriate audit evidence concerning the opening balances of the entity, the auditor considers the implications for the auditor's report.

The Audit of Opening Balances by the Incoming Auditor

141. In the audit of central government sector entities, the incoming auditor to a new audit assignment is normally able to obtain audit evidence about the opening balances from the procedures outlined in the guidance supporting ISA (UK and Ireland) 510.

142. Paragraph 6 of ISA (UK and Ireland) 510 indicates that when the prior period's financial statements were audited by another auditor, the current auditor may be able to obtain sufficient audit evidence regarding opening balances by inter alia, reviewing the predecessor auditor's working papers. In the central government sector, in the interests of efficiency and reducing the audit burden, the predecessor auditor is expected by the auditor of a central government account to adopt a co-operative approach in dealing with enquiries and requests for information from the incoming auditor.

ISA (UK and Ireland) 520: Analytical Procedures

Objectives

The objectives of the auditor are:

(a) To obtain relevant and reliable audit evidence when using substantive analytical procedures; and

(b) To design and perform analytical procedures near the end of the audit that assist the auditor when forming an overall conclusion as to whether the financial statements are consistent with the auditor's understanding of the entity. (Paragraph 3)

143. All central government sector entities produce a comprehensive range of information and data. Much of the information is consolidated and published by Government entities and other bodies, particularly performance indicators. The auditor of a central government account can use this information both in performing analytical procedures that compare the activities of a single entity from one year to another and in making comparisons between similar entities. Auditors, however, validate the reliability and independence of data to form expectations in analytical procedures as outlined in ISA (UK and Ireland) 520 paragraphs 5 and A12. Data validation procedures could potentially be linked to data quality work carried out by auditors at specified entities.

Data Relationships

144. Relationships between individual financial statement items traditionally considered in the audit of business entities may not always be relevant in the audit of government or other non-business public sector entities. The central government sector auditor however, also considers relationships:

- between elements of financial information that would be expected to conform to a predictable pattern based on the entity's experience, such as staff costs; and

- where expenditure and income are expected to conform to a demand pattern that can be deduced from other related data, such as the number of people within a certain age range.

145. The central government sector auditor may also divide the financial information considered into two classes:

- programme expenditure and income; and

- administrative expenditure and income.

146. Each has a number of essential features that influence the nature of the analytical procedures that may be undertaken.

147. Programme expenditure and income relate to the actual function of the audited entity, and are disclosed in the financial statements as, for example, appropriations in aid, grant payments and healthcare treatments. Features of such transactions are that:

- they may be closely related to non-financial information such as the number of bodies in receipt of grant or persons receiving hospital treatment;

- they may not always be directly comparable to prior periods because of changes in eligibility rules and Government policy; and

- they are comparable to published departmental/entity strategy and expenditure plans.

148. Administrative costs relate to the running of the audited entity and can be distinguished from programme expenditure because they are:

- usually closely related to comparable information for prior periods and are less likely to experience significant fluctuation owing to changes in Government policy and the entity's strategy;

- closely related to information such as number of locations, number of employees and size of buildings; and

- usually directly comparable to other entities with similar establishment sizes.

149. Analytical procedures are unlikely, on their own, to provide the auditor of a central government account with sufficient appropriate evidence in support of a regularity opinion. They may nevertheless, in certain circumstances, assist the auditor in assessing whether amounts recorded in financial statements are consistent with expectations. For example, where allowances under a scheme are subject to a maximum value and the number of recipients is known the auditor may use analytical procedures to identify whether the permitted maximum may have been breached.

ISA (UK and Ireland) 540: Auditing Accounting Estimates, Including Fair Value Accounting Estimates, and Related Disclosures

Objective

The objective of the auditor is to obtain sufficient appropriate audit evidence about whether:

(a) accounting estimates, including fair value accounting estimates, in the financial statements, whether recognised or disclosed, are reasonable; and

(b) related disclosures in the financial statements are adequate,

in the context of the applicable financial reporting framework. (Paragraph 6)

Management Bias

The auditor shall review the judgments and decisions made by management in the making of accounting estimates to identify whether there are any indicators of possible management bias. Indicators of possible management bias do not themselves constitute misstatements for the purposes of drawing conclusions on the reasonableness of individual accounting estimates. (Paragraph 21)

150. In the central government sector, management decisions on accounting estimates can be influenced by financial factors that fall outside the scope of the financial reporting framework. For example, central government departments must adhere to Department of Finance budgetary controls, and so valuation of estimates within the financial statements can be influenced by the impact they have on departmental expenditure limits or the administration budget. In other sectors, statutory limits or targets can influence management decisions.

151. The auditor of a central government account therefore needs to understand these influences, some of which come from elsewhere within a departmental or sector group, when considering the appropriateness of accounting estimates and the assumptions applied by management.

Third Party Estimates

152. Some central government sector entities may be reliant on accounting estimates provided by other entities within the public sector. The auditor of a central government account understands how these estimates have been derived, and may need to communicate with the auditors of the entities compiling the accounting estimates relied on.

ISA (UK and Ireland) 550: Related Parties

Objectives

The objectives of the auditor are:

(a) Irrespective of whether the applicable financial reporting framework establishes related party requirements, to obtain an understanding of related party relationships and transactions sufficient to be able:

    (i) To recognise fraud risk factors, if any, arising from related party relationships and transactions that are relevant to the identification and assessment of the risks of material misstatement due to fraud; and

    (ii) To conclude, based on the audit evidence obtained, whether the financial statements, insofar as they are affected by those relationships and transactions:

        a. Achieve fair presentation (for fair presentation frameworks); or

        b. Are not misleading (for compliance frameworks); and

(b) In addition, where the applicable financial reporting framework establishes related party requirements, to obtain sufficient appropriate audit evidence about whether related party relationships and transactions have been appropriately identified, accounted for and disclosed in the financial statements in accordance with the framework. (Paragraph 9)

153. Because related parties are not independent of each other, many financial reporting frameworks establish specific accounting and disclosure requirements for related party relationships, transactions and balances to enable users of the financial statements to understand their nature and actual or potential effects on the financial statements. Where the applicable financial reporting framework establishes such requirements[13], the auditor of a central government account has a responsibility to perform audit procedures to identify, assess and respond to the risks of material misstatement arising from the entity's failure to appropriately account for or disclose related party relationships, transactions or balances in accordance with the requirements of the framework.

154. The related parties of central government sector entities are subject to either a statutory or non-statutory framework[14] which regulates their conduct and the relationships that they can enter into with the entity. The framework restricts practices that might be permissible in relationships outside the public sector.

---

[13] Specific accounting and disclosure requirements for related party relationships, transactions and balances are established in accounting standards and in law and regulations.

[14] The statutory framework covers public and civil servants as set out in Ethics legislation. Additional procedures and practices are set out in corporate governance guidance issued by the Minister for Finance.

ISA (UK and Ireland) 560: Subsequent Events

Objectives

The objectives of the auditor are:

(a) To obtain sufficient appropriate audit evidence about whether events occurring between the date of the financial statements and the date of the auditor's report that require adjustment of, or disclosure in, the financial statements are appropriately reflected in those financial statements in accordance with the applicable financial reporting framework; and

(b) To respond appropriately to facts that become known to the auditor after the date of the auditor's report, that, had they been known to the auditor at that date, may have caused the auditor to amend the auditor's report. (Paragraph 4)

Events Occurring between the Date of the Financial Statements and the Date of the Auditor's Report

The auditor shall perform audit procedures designed to obtain sufficient appropriate audit evidence that all events occurring between the date of the financial statements and the date of the auditor's report that require adjustment of, or disclosure in, the financial statements have been identified. The auditor is not, however, expected to perform additional audit procedures on matters to which previously applied audit procedures have provided satisfactory conclusions. (Paragraph 6)

155. In addition to the further procedures described in paragraph 7 of ISA (UK and Ireland) 560, the auditor of a central government account considers matters arising from relevant proceedings of the Oireachtas which the auditor may have become aware of during the course of the audit as being scheduled to take place at or after the period end, the outcome of which may have an impact on the audited entity.

Facts Which Become Known to the Auditor after the Date of the Auditor's Report but before the Financial Statements are Issued

156. In interpreting the requirements of ISA (UK and Ireland) 560, the financial statements of central government entities are considered to be "issued" where one of the following circumstances applies:

- for financial statements where the statutory responsibility of laying the financial statements before the Oireachtas rests with the C&AG, the financial statements are deemed to be issued when they are dispatched to the Houses of the Oireachtas;

- for financial statements where the statutory responsibility for laying them before the Oireachtas rests with a Minister of the Government, then the financial statements are deemed to be issued when the audited entity dispatch them to the Minister;

- where there is no statute or requirement to lay the financial statements before the Oireachtas the statements are deemed issued when they are published by the audited entity or other relevant authority.

157. In all cases, the date on which the financial statements of central government entities are laid before the Houses of the Oireachtas is the date on which they are received in the library of the Houses of the Oireachtas following their dispatch by the C&AG or Minister of the supervising department.

158. The impact of subsequent events which come to audit attention and occur between the date of the audit report and the date on which the financial statements are issued, is considered.

The auditor has no obligation to perform any audit procedures regarding the financial statements after the date of the auditor's report. However, when, after the date of the auditor's report but before the date the financial statements are issued, a fact becomes known to the auditor that, had it been known to the auditor at the date of the auditor's report, may have caused the auditor to amend the auditor's report, the auditor shall:

(a) Discuss the matter with management and, where appropriate, those charged with governance;

(b) Determine whether the financial statements need amendment and, if so,

(c) Inquire how management intends to address the matter in the financial statements. (Paragraph 10)

159. If the Accounting Officer or Chief Executive decides not to amend the financial statements, where the auditor of a central government account believes that they need to be revised, the auditor considers taking appropriate steps on a timely basis to prevent reliance on the auditor's report. Such steps could take the form of a statement reporting the specific public accountability concerns to the relevant supervising Department or body in the light of any legal advice taken. In certain instances the C&AG has the power under legislation to report the matter to the Houses of the Oireachtas.

160. Where the subsequent event occurred after the date of the auditor's report, the auditor may, in addition to seeking legal advice, discuss the matter with the entity's Chief Executive and with the sponsor department to establish whether it might be possible to withdraw the auditor's report before the financial statements are laid before the Houses of the Oireachtas.

Facts Which Become Known to the Auditor after the Financial Statements Have Been Issued

> The auditor shall include in the new or amended auditor's report an Emphasis of Matter paragraph or Other Matter(s) paragraph referring to a note to the financial statements that more extensively discusses the reason for the amendment of the previously issued financial statements and to the earlier report provided by the auditor. (Paragraph 16)

161. In the central government sector, the issue of the auditor's statutory audit opinion marks the end of the audit and once the financial statements have been issued they cannot be revised and the auditor's report cannot be re-issued.

162. If a matter that needs to be drawn to the attention of stakeholders arises once the financial statements have been issued, the auditor has other mechanisms available for making a public statement. For example, in the central government sector the Comptroller and Auditor General can issue a report and have it laid before the Houses of the Oireachtas.

ISA (UK and Ireland) 570: Going Concern

Objectives

The objectives of the auditor are:

(a) To obtain sufficient appropriate audit evidence regarding the appropriateness of management's use of the going concern assumption in the preparation of the financial statements;

(b) To conclude, based on the audit evidence obtained, whether a material uncertainty exists related to events or conditions that may cast significant doubt on the entity's ability to continue as a going concern; and

(c) To determine the implications for the auditor's report. (Paragraph 9)

163. Some financial reporting frameworks contain an explicit requirement for management to make a specific assessment of the entity's ability to continue as a going concern, and standards regarding matters to be considered and disclosures to be made in connection with going concern. For example, International Accounting Standard (IAS) 1 requires management to make an assessment of an entity's ability to continue as a going concern. The detailed requirements regarding management's responsibility to assess the entity's ability to continue as a going concern and related financial statement disclosures may also be set out in law or regulation.

164. Under some circumstances, the management of an audited body may not have made a formal assessment of the body's ability to continue as a going concern. Under these circumstances the auditor of a central government account discusses the going concern assumption with management and documents the considerations around the going concern assumption arising from that discussion.

165. The central government sector auditor may have other responsibilities relating to going concern different from those to which ISA (UK and Ireland) 570 is directly relevant. As a matter of practice the Comptroller and Auditor General reviews the entity's arrangements for maintaining its general financial health and in appropriate cases reports to those charged with governance, the sponsor department or in his report on the financial statements.

166. Where central government entities prepare financial statements on a cash basis, ISA (UK and Ireland) 570 does not apply to the audit as the going concern basis is not used in the preparation of the statements. However, the audit still considers whether there are any matters affecting the audited entity's ability to continue as a going concern. Where such matters are identified, the need to report separately to the Oireachtas on those matters and the inclusion of an emphasis of matter paragraph in the audit report is considered. The audit opinion is not, however, qualified on the proper presentation of the financial statements.

Risk Assessment Procedures and Related Activities

> When performing risk assessment procedures as required by ISA (UK and Ireland) 315, the auditor shall consider whether there are events or conditions that may cast significant doubt on the entity's ability to continue as a going concern. In so doing, the auditor shall determine whether management has already performed a preliminary assessment of the entity's ability to continue as a going concern ... (Paragraph 10)

167. To apply ISA (UK and Ireland) 570 in the central government sector, the auditor considers the circumstances in which a central government sector entity may cease to continue in its operational existence.

168. It is not uncommon in the central government sector for entities to spend more in one year than they have resources to cover or to become overstretched in their commitments, such that they might have a deficit of income over expenditure or an excess of liabilities over assets. However, it is less common that the operational existence of a central government sector entity will cease or its scale of operations be subject to a forced reduction as a result of an inability to finance its operations or of net liabilities (although this is possible where a central government entity operates at arm's length from Government, particularly in a trading capacity). The reasons for this are:

- entities which carry out essential functions may be revenue-raising bodies (without a specified limit on revenue-raising powers), and have the possibility, on application, of recovering losses over a period;

- there is a general assumption that no part of the central government sector will be allowed to cease operations other than by deliberate closure by government, announced in advance; and

- ultimately government departments can act to avoid financial failures by individual entities in central government and other parts of the public sector and thus secure continuation of the delivery of public services (although this may require Oireachtas authority).

169. In the central government sector it is not uncommon for statutory bodies to give guarantees which, if called upon, can not be met by the resources currently available to the organisation. In such circumstances, the auditor of a central government account considers if the matter needs to be referred to in an emphasis of matter paragraph within the audit report.

170. Cessation is most likely to result from a Government policy decision. A policy decision may be taken to:

- wind up and dissolve an entity in its entirety where the Government determines that its functions are no longer required;

- wind up and dissolve all or part of an entity, but transfer some or all of its functions to another entity in the same sector or another sector;

- merge the entity, or some part of it, with another in the same sector; or

- privatise an entity, or some part of it, where the Government decides that certain functions would be better delivered by the private sector.

171. In each of these cases the operational existence of all or part of the entity ceases, but only in the case of dissolution without any continuation of operations would the going concern basis cease clearly to be appropriate. In the other cases the auditor of a central government account considers the basis on which the activities are transferred, from the viewpoint of the entity that is relinquishing the assets and liabilities at the accounting date.

Consideration of the foreseeable future

172. ISA (UK and Ireland) 570 specifies that, in assessing whether the going concern assumption is appropriate, those charged with governance take into account all available information for the foreseeable future, which is at least twelve months from the balance sheet date. If the period to which those charged with governance have paid particular attention in assessing going concern is less than one year from the date of approval of the financial statements, and those charged with governance have not disclosed the fact, the auditor of a central government account complies with the requirements of paragraph 17-1 of ISA (UK and Ireland) 570.

Auditor's responsibilities for the consideration of the appropriateness of the going concern basis

173. In forming a view on the entity's ability to continue its operations, the audit consideration of going concern embraces two separate, but sometimes overlapping, factors:

- the risk associated with changes in policy direction; and

- the less common operational, or business, risk (for example, where an entity has insufficient working capital to continue its operations at its existing level).

174. To minimise the risk of it not coming to the auditor's attention that the Government has made, or is likely to make, a decision on policy direction which could impact on the going concern assumption, the auditor ascertains whether:

- the Government has a known intention to review an area of policy affecting the audited entity, for example as a result of a manifesto commitment;

- a review has been announced and is in progress;

- a review has indicated that the audited entity could be rationalised or that an entity's future may be re-examined; or

- there is a known intention to privatise the activities of the audited entity.

175. When the auditor of a central government account becomes aware of information which indicates that the Government has made, or plans to make, a policy decision which is likely to impact on the entity's continued operational existence, the auditor first establishes whether the entity's operational activities are likely to be transferred elsewhere in the public sector. If they are, irrespective of whether the entity will continue to operate, the going concern basis of preparation of the financial statements is likely to remain appropriate. If not, then in considering the going concern assumption, the auditor may decide to request that the audited entity secures from the relevant department or executive body a letter of financial support, confirming that the entity continues to have financial backing to utilise its assets and meet liabilities as they fall due.

176. Some central government sector bodies may have a duty to break even. The existence of such a requirement may influence the scope and nature of audit procedures, for instance it may be appropriate to consider the financial performance of the entity, including the effectiveness of financial recovery plans.

Additional Audit Procedures When Events or Conditions are Identified

If events or conditions have been identified that may cast significant doubt on the entity's ability to continue as a going concern, the auditor shall obtain sufficient appropriate audit evidence to determine whether or not a material uncertainty exists through performing additional audit procedures, including consideration of mitigating factors. These procedures shall include:

(a) Where management has not yet performed an assessment of the entity's ability to continue as a going concern, requesting management to make its assessment.

(b) Evaluating management's plans for future actions in relation to its going concern assessment, whether the outcome of these plans is likely to improve the situation and whether management's plans are feasible in the circumstances.

(c) Where the entity has prepared a cash flow forecast, and analysis of the forecast is a significant factor in considering the future outcome of events or conditions in the evaluation of management's plans for future action:

  (i) Evaluating the reliability of the underlying data generated to prepare the forecast; and

  (ii) Determining whether there is adequate support for the assumptions underlying the forecast.

(d) Considering whether any additional facts or information have become available since the date on which management made its assessment.

(e) Requesting written representations from management or, where appropriate, those charged with governance, regarding their plans for future action and feasibility of these plans. (Paragraph 16)

177. In certain circumstances, the evidence of the likelihood of continued financial support may be available from other sources including records relating to the estimates process and proceedings of Oireachtas committees.

178. Where the auditor of a central government account judges that the going concern basis is appropriate for the preparation of the entity's financial statements substantially on the basis of third party confirmations received from the department or body responsible for providing financial backing, the auditor considers whether this is a matter of such significance that the confirmations are referred to in the financial statements and in the audit report as being relevant to a proper understanding of the basis of the audit opinion.

179. If no appropriate representations or confirmations can be obtained, the auditor of a central government account considers whether there is a limitation on the scope of the audit work that requires a qualified opinion or a fundamental uncertainty that requires an emphasis of matter paragraph in the audit report.

Annex

Illustrative Examples of Audit Procedures and Auditor's Reports

Example – A Non-Commercial State Sponsored Body where the Minister of the parent department has announced a review of its operations

Situation 1

- *The auditor considers that the probability of any change in the nature of operations is remote.*

- *An unqualified auditor's report without an added emphasis of matter paragraph.*

180. When planning the audit, the auditor of a central government account becomes aware of the following matters:

- the Minister of the parent department has recently announced a review of the entity's operations. The review will examine the services provided by the entity and consider whether, together with the services provided by two other entities, they could be better provided by one entity; and

- the Chief Executive believes that the entity's services would be more expensive to provide under the new proposed arrangements and that the review is unlikely to recommend any significant change in operations.

181. The auditor's initial assessment might be that there is some uncertainty about the ability of the entity to continue as a going concern. The auditor plans to monitor the progress of the review by liaising with the Chief Executive and reconsider the position when the auditor has completed the audit.

182. Having completed all other aspects of the audit, the auditor of a central government account considers the progress of the review:

- the Chief Executive knows that the review is almost completed and the department has begun to consider its findings. The Chief Executive has been told that it is unlikely that the Minister will recommend the closure of the entity;

- the auditor informs the Chief Executive that the auditor intends to contact the department to confirm this understanding;

- on behalf of the Accounting Officer, the Finance Officer of the parent department gives a written representation to the auditor that, while the recommendations arising from the review have not been finalised, it is now unlikely that the entity would be significantly affected by them; and

- the auditor therefore considers that the probability of the entity not being a going concern is remote.

183. The Chief Executive considers that no special disclosures are required in the financial statements. The auditor of a central government account agrees and accordingly does not consider it necessary to qualify the audit opinion or to add an emphasis of matter paragraph to the auditor's report.

Situation 2

- *The auditor considers that there is significant uncertainty as to the future of the entity, but as yet the Minister has made no decision on the entity's future.*

- *An unqualified auditor's report with an added emphasis of matter paragraph.*

184. The circumstances and audit work are as in Situation 1 except as follows.

185. Having completed all other aspects of the audit, the auditor of a central government account considers the progress of the review:

- the Chief Executive knows that the review is almost completed and the department has begun to consider its findings. He does not know what the Minister's recommendation might be on the future of the entity;

- the Chief Executive arranges a meeting between himself, the auditor and officials of the parent department to discuss the situation;

- the departmental officials indicate that preliminary studies showed a merger might result in efficiencies and that a further cost benefit study is ongoing. Its results will not be known for some months; and

- in view of this uncertainty, the parent department's Finance Officer, acting for the Accounting Officer, is not willing to provide any written representation about the future of the entity.

186. The auditor believes there is significant uncertainty as to the future of the entity and discusses the concerns with the Chief Executive. The Chief Executive has already decided to make appropriate disclosures in the financial statements as follows.

Extract from the notes to the financial statements

Note 1 Basis of preparing financial statements

On 1 September 20XX the Minister for XXXX announced a review of the operations of the entity which would examine the different ways in which its current services can be provided in the future. The review is considering several options, including the possible merger of the entity with other entities. The Minister has not yet announced the outcome of the review and therefore the Chief Executive considers that it is appropriate to prepare financial statements on the going concern basis. The financial statements do not include any adjustments that would result from a decision to alter the operations of the entity, or to transfer its activities to another entity.

187. In these circumstances, the auditor of a central government account considers an audit opinion can be formed but has a significant level of concern about the ability of the entity to continue as a going concern. Hence, while the auditor does not qualify the audit opinion, the auditor includes a suitable emphasis of matter paragraph when setting out the basis of the opinion, as set out below.

188. Paragraph 19 of ISA (UK and Ireland) 570 requires that:

> "the auditor shall express an unmodified opinion and include an Emphasis of Matter paragraph in the auditor's report to: a) highlight the existence of a material uncertainty relating to the event or condition that may cast significant doubt on the entity's ability to continue as a going concern; and to b) draw attention to the note in the financial statements that discloses the matters set out in paragraph 18."

In this example, the auditor of a central government account does not disagree with the preparation of the financial statements on the going concern basis.

Extract from the auditor's report

Going concern

In forming my opinion, I have considered the adequacy of the disclosures made in Note 1 of the financial statements concerning the uncertainty as to the continuation of the entity in its present form. In view of the significance of this uncertainty to the financial statements, I consider that it should be drawn to your attention, but my opinion is not qualified in this respect.

Situation 3

- *The Minister has announced that the entity will cease operations at the end of the next financial year and its activities will be transferred to a new entity.*

- *The auditor is satisfied that the agency has made appropriate adjustments to, and disclosures in, its financial statements.*

- *An unqualified auditor's report without an added emphasis of matter paragraph.*

189. The circumstances and audit work are as in Situation 2 except as follows.

190. During the audit the Minister announces that the review has been completed and that the entity will cease operations and be wound up at the end of the next financial year. Its activities will be transferred to a new entity, together with the activities of two other entities.

191. The auditor of a central government account obtains further details of the restructuring plans through the Chief Executive. The auditor ascertains that all assets and liabilities will be transferred for nil consideration to the new entity. The majority of staff will be transferred to the new entity, but a number will be made redundant. The costs of redundancy will be borne by the entity in the next financial year. All operating leases

will be transferred to the new entity for nil consideration and there are no other contingent liabilities.

192. The Chief Executive considers that the entity cannot prepare financial statements on the going concern basis. The financial statements therefore show:

- full provision for the redundancy and early retirement costs expected to be incurred over the next year and the fact that the decision has been communicated to employees before the year-end; and

- all fixed assets written down to the fair value at which they will be taken into the new entity's books. The Chief Executive's budget for the next financial year shows the entity will break even and so no provision for future losses need be considered.

193. The auditor of a central government account reviews these treatments and audits the values attributed to fixed assets and the provision for redundancy costs. The auditor concludes that appropriate adjustments have been made.

194. The financial statements contain the following note.

Extract from the notes to the financial statements

Note 1 Basis of preparing financial statements

On 1 July 20XX the Minister for XXXX announced that the entity would be wound up on 31 December 20XX and its activities transferred to a new entity, the JKL Centre. The operations of the entity will not transfer to the JKL Centre as a going concern and the Chief Executive considers it inappropriate for the financial statements to be prepared on a going concern basis. Appropriate adjustments have been made to the values of fixed assets to bring them into line with the bases of measurement applicable to the new entity (see Note Z) and full provision has been made for the cost of redundancy and early retirement for staff who will not transfer to the JKL Centre.

195. The auditor of a central government account concludes that the entity has made appropriate disclosures in the financial statements. The auditor issues an unqualified opinion in the auditor's report.

Situation 4

- *As for situation 3, except that the auditor is not satisfied as to the appropriateness of adjustments and disclosures made and considers that the financial statements are materially misstated.*

- *A qualified auditor's report – disagreement with accounting treatment.*

196. The circumstances and audit work are as in Situation 3 except as follows.

197. The Chief Executive believes it is inappropriate to adjust the values of fixed assets, as they are being transferred with all other assets and liabilities for nil consideration. The

Chief Executive does not believe it appropriate to provide for redundancy costs on the grounds that the entity will receive specific additional funding in the following financial year.

198. The auditor of a central government account disagrees, as the audit determines:

- some fixed assets will be surplus to the requirements of the new entity and will have no value to it; and

- the decision on making some staff redundant was taken and communicated before the year-end and therefore full provision is made.

199. If the auditor of a central government account cannot persuade the Chief Executive to make appropriate adjustments to the financial statements, the auditor will qualify the audit opinion on the grounds of disagreement. As the opinion has been qualified, there is no need to include an emphasis of matter paragraph.

ISA (UK and Ireland) 580: Written Representations

Objectives

The objectives of the auditor are:

(a) To obtain written representations from management and, where appropriate, those charged with governance that they believe that they have fulfilled their responsibility for the preparation of the financial statements and for the completeness of the information provided to the auditor;

(b) To support other audit evidence relevant to the financial statements or specific assertions in the financial statements by means of written representations if determined necessary by the auditor or required by other ISAs (UK and Ireland); and

(c) To respond appropriately to written representations provided by management and, where appropriate, those charged with governance, or if management or, where appropriate, those charged with governance do not provide the written representations requested by the auditor. (Paragraph 6)

Written Representations about Management's Responsibilities

The auditor shall request management to provide a written representation that it has fulfilled its responsibility for the preparation of the financial statements in accordance with the applicable financial reporting framework, including where relevant their fair presentation, as set out in the terms of the audit engagement. (Paragraph 10)

200. In addition to the representations made relating to the financial statements in accordance with ISA (UK and Ireland) 580 the auditor of a central government sector entity may be required to meet other responsibilities additional to giving a true and fair opinion on the financial statements. For example, the auditor may be required to report by exception on the regularity of transactions entered into by the entity. The auditor may wish to obtain representations relevant to these additional responsibilities in the same letter or statement from the entity.

The auditor shall request written representations from management with appropriate responsibilities for the financial statements and knowledge of the matters concerned. (Paragraph 9)

201. The auditor of a central government account takes care to ensure that representations are only accepted from those competent to give them, such that:

• acknowledgement of the responsibilities of "directors" for the financial statements is made by those in whom the responsibilities are vested; and

- management representations on matters material to the financial statements are made by persons who have knowledge of the facts or who are authorised to make the judgment or express the opinion (for instance, a legal officer may be best placed to make representations about contingent liabilities) – this may be particularly relevant where the financial statements comprise a consolidation of information from lower tier accounts.

202. In government departments and offices, representations will usually be obtained from the Accounting Officer who has the role and responsibilities which are similar to that of the directors and, because the Accounting Officer has a personal responsibility for preparation and signing of the financial statements, the auditor of a central government account expects representations to be signed by the Accounting Officer. For non-commercial state sponsored bodies, boards, committees and funds the senior full-time official (Chief Executive Officer or equivalent) is responsible for the financial statements and as such is normally the accountable person for purposes of accountability to Dáil Éireann. However, the financial statements of such entities are formally adopted by their boards and the letter of representation is then signed on the board's behalf by the Chairman and Secretary.

203. Where the auditor of a central government account has a responsibility to give a regularity opinion (by exception), it may be necessary to obtain representations about knowledge and opinions relevant to the duty, such as the application of any grants or other financial assistance given by the audited entity to other parties and confirmation that all facts have been disclosed to the auditor, such as losses, write-offs and known or suspected frauds.

ISA (UK and Ireland) 600: Special Considerations – Audits of Group Financial Statements (Including the work of Component Auditors)

Objectives

The objectives of the auditor are:

(a) To determine whether to act as the auditor of the group financial statements; and

(b) If acting as the auditor of the group financial statements:

   (i)   To communicate clearly with component auditors about the scope and timing of their work on financial information related to components and their findings; and

   (ii) To obtain sufficient appropriate audit evidence regarding the financial information of the components and the consolidation process to express an opinion on whether the group financial statements are prepared, in all material respects, in accordance with the applicable financial reporting framework. (Paragraph 8)

204. Generally, the situations in which the central government sector auditor may encounter another auditor and become group auditor, such that the requirements of ISA (UK and Ireland) 600 need to be considered will be limited to where he audits an entity that consolidates or summarises the financial statements of lower tier or other bodies. This situation may occur where a State entity has established a subsidiary company under the Companies Acts audited by separate auditors and the subsidiary company results are consolidated in group financial statements of the entity.

205. Where the auditor of a central government account audits an entity that has contracted out services to another party outside of the entity or group, the requirements of ISA (UK and Ireland) 402 apply. In this situation, whether the auditor of a central government account needs access to the contractor and/or to the contractor's auditor depends on the particular nature of the service provided, the information available at the principal entity and the terms of engagement of the other auditor. The guidance on ISA (UK and Ireland) 402 discusses the requirements of an auditor in this position.

206. Where the auditor of a central government account has a duty to give a regularity opinion (by exception), it will be necessary to obtain assurance about the application of any material grants or other financial assistance given by the audited entity to other parties for example by using the work of the grantee's auditor and reducing the extent of his own audit procedures

Understanding the Component Auditor

If the group engagement team plans to request a component auditor perform work on the financial information of a component, the group engagement team shall obtain an understanding of the following:

(a) Whether the component auditor understands and will comply with the ethical requirements that are relevant to the group audit and, in particular, is independent.

(b) The component auditor's professional competence.

(c) Whether the group engagement team will be able to be involved in the work of the component auditor to the extent necessary to obtain sufficient appropriate audit evidence.

(d) Whether the component auditor operates in a regulatory environment that actively oversees auditors. (Paragraph 19)

207. Where the C&AG arranges with a person or firm for the performance of audit work on his behalf in accordance with the 1993 Act, the appointed person or firm will have had to demonstrate professional qualifications, experience and resources. Whilst this does not mean that the principal auditor can then assume the competence of this auditor, it provides a clear framework within which the assessment required by paragraph 19 can be made.

ISA (UK and Ireland) 610: Using the Work of Internal Auditors

Objectives

The objectives of the external auditor, where the entity has an internal audit function that the external auditor has determined is likely to be relevant to the audit, are:

(a) To determine whether, and to what extent, to use specific work of the internal auditors; and

(b) If using the specific work of the internal auditors, to determine whether that work is adequate for the purposes of the audit. (Paragraph 6)

208. A distinctive feature of internal audit in the central government sector is that it is normally a mandatory element of any entity's framework of internal control. Details of the role and responsibilities of internal audit, and applicable internal auditing standards and practices are set out in paragraph 211.

Determining Whether and to What Extent to Use the Work of the Internal Auditors

The external auditor shall determine:

(a) Whether the work of the internal auditors is likely to be adequate for purposes of the audit; and

(b) If so, the planned effect of the work of the internal auditors on the nature, timing or extent of the external auditor's procedures. (Paragraph 8)

209. Where the auditor of a central government account has other responsibilities in relation to systems of internal control, the work of internal audit may be considered as a part of that framework. An assessment of the internal audit function may be carried out for such purposes, even if the auditor considers that it may not be possible or desirable to rely on its work in specific areas for the purpose of the external audit of the financial statements. For example, where the auditor has a responsibility to report by exception on the Statement on Internal Financial Control and has assessed internal audit's work in this area, the auditor may rely on the Head of Internal Audit's annual assurance report.

210. The work of internal audit may also be considered in relation to the other responsibilities of the auditor of a central government account. The auditor of a central government account takes care to ensure that, where matters come to his attention relating to the work of internal audit in relation to his other responsibilities, these findings are properly reviewed in accordance with ISA (UK and Ireland) 610 for their potential impact on the audit of the financial statements.

In order for the external auditor to use specific work of the internal auditors, the external auditor shall evaluate and perform audit procedures on that work to determine its adequacy for the external auditor's purposes. (Paragraph 11)

211. Roles and responsibilities of internal audit, and applicable internal auditing standards and practices:

	Roles and responsibilities of internal audit	Internal auditing standards and practices
Central government entities	The precise responsibilities of an internal audit unit are determined by the head of a department as Accounting Officer. These include, the provision of assurance on risk management, internal control and governance established by management to: • achieve the entity's objectives; • ensure the economical, effective and efficient use of resources; • ensure compliance with established policies, procedures, laws and regulations; • safeguard the entity's assets and interests from losses of all kinds, including those arising from fraud, irregularity or corruption; and • ensure the integrity and reliability of information and data.	An Accounting Officer is charged with making arrangements for internal audit to accord with the objectives, standards and practices set out in the Internal Audit Standards. The guidelines relating to the standards to be followed are outlined in the Department of Finance's publication *Internal Audit Standards*. Internal audit is also covered in Sections 3.6–3.14 of the December 2003 Department of Finance Memorandum for Accounting Officers – The Role and Responsibilities of Accounting Officers. Departments may also refer as appropriate to the standards and guidelines issued by the Institute of Internal Auditors (IIA) – UK and Ireland and other appropriate professional bodies.

	Roles and responsibilities of internal audit	Internal auditing standards and practices
Non-Commercial State Bodies, Universities and Third Level Educational Institutions and Health Sector Bodies.	Applicable Codes of Practice set out the principles under which the internal audit function should operate within bodies including the responsibility for the Board (or equivalent) in ensuring that there is a properly constituted internal audit function which reports directly to the Board Audit Committee. Internal audit functions are agreed by the Board and set out in a written charter. The role of internal audit would be broadly similar to those set out above.	The internal audit function should serve the best interests of the body as a whole and carry out its work in a manner that is consistent with the Standards for the Professional Practice of Internal Auditors, published by the Institute of Internal Auditors (IIA) – UK and Ireland and other appropriate professional bodies.

ISA (UK and Ireland) 700 (Revised): The Auditor's Report on Financial Statements

Objectives

The objectives of the auditor are to:

(a) Form an opinion on the financial statements based on an evaluation of the conclusions drawn from the audit evidence obtained; and

(b) Express clearly that opinion through a written report that also describes the basis for the opinion. (Paragraph 7)

212. The APB has not mandated the application of the clarified ISAs (UK and Ireland) 700, 705 and 706 (the auditor's reporting standards) in the Republic of Ireland. This is because there are expected to be changes to Irish Company law that will affect the auditor's report. However, the C&AG considers the application of the clarified auditor's reporting standards to be appropriate for audits of central government financial statements in the Republic of Ireland and accordingly has adopted them.

Basic Elements of the Auditor's Report

The auditor's report shall be appropriately addressed as required by the circumstances of the engagement. (Paragraph 13)

213. ISA (UK and Ireland) 700 requires the title of an auditor's report to identify the person or persons to whom it is addressed. This is normally the person or persons on whose behalf the audit is undertaken.

214. The accounts of each entity together with the Report of the Comptroller and Auditor General are transmitted to the relevant House or Houses of the Oireachtas either directly by the C&AG or by a designated Minister of the Government. The audit reports of the C&AG are addressed to the Oireachtas. Accordingly reports are entitled 'Report of the Comptroller and Auditor General for presentation to the Houses of the Oireachtas'.

The auditor's report shall include a statement that those charged with governance are responsible for the preparation of the financial statements and a statement that the responsibility of the auditor is to audit and express an opinion on the financial statements in accordance with applicable legal requirements and International Standards on Auditing (UK and Ireland). The report shall also state that those standards require the auditor to comply with the APB's Ethical Standards for Auditors. (Paragraph 15)

215. For central government sector entities, the responsibilities equivalent to those of directors may lie with different individuals or groups.

- in the case of government departments and offices, responsibility for the financial statements rests with the Accounting Officer; and

- in the case of other central government entities, the responsibility for the financial statements rests with the board members or other organ, as designated by law, of the entity.

216. The financial statements are required to include a statement of those responsibilities. Where such accounting responsibilities are not set out in the financial statements or other statutory report, a separate statement of responsibilities is prepared.

217. In all cases the statement sets out

- the accounting provisions laid down by law in respect of the entity;

- the person or body upon whom responsibilities for preparing financial statements, maintaining accounting records and ensuring the regularity and propriety of public finances, rests.

218. Example disclosures in a central government sector entity's Statement of Responsibilities are set out in Annex I to this section of the Practice Note.

219. Where the requirement to audit an entity's financial statements is provided for under statute, the audit report refers to the relevant legislation in the introductory paragraph.

The opinion paragraph of the auditor's report shall clearly state the auditor's opinion as required by the relevant financial reporting framework used to prepare the financial statements, including applicable law. (Paragraph 17)

When expressing an unqualified opinion on financial statements prepared in accordance with a true and fair framework the opinion paragraph shall clearly state that the financial statements give a true and fair view. It is not sufficient for the auditor to conclude that the financial statements give a true and fair view solely on the basis that the financial statements were prepared in accordance with accounting standards and any other applicable legal requirements. (Paragraph 18)

220. For government departments and offices these requirements are set down in statute[15] and the Department of Finance's *Public Financial Procedures*. For other central government entities these requirements may be set out in specific standards approved

---

[15] Comptroller and Auditor General Acts, 1866 to 1998
Ministers and Secretaries Act 1924.

by a sponsoring government department or accounting standards promulgated by the accountancy bodies in Ireland.

221. Across the central government sector, most financial statements include an opinion as to whether the financial statements give a true and fair view. However, there are instances where the auditing framework requires an opinion as to whether the financial statements present fairly or properly present the entity's transactions or balances. Whichever wording is used for the opinion on the financial statements, this will not have an impact on the extent to which the auditor observes the requirements of Auditing Standards.

Illustrative report

222. Audit reports are issued on a wide variety of central government sector accounts. Annex II sets out an illustrative report for statutory corporate entities. While variations occur due to the regulatory provisions applying to different entities this report provides a basis for the audit reports on other central government sector accounts. These variations can arise out of the terms of establishing legislation in the case of statutory corporate bodies or in instances where the provisions of company law have been modified by legislation for bodies initially incorporated by a process of registration under the Companies Acts.

Special considerations which apply to audit by the CA&G

223. The audit of central government sector bodies is planned and performed to take into account the special considerations which apply to these bodies by virtue of the fact that they are established by legislation or are in receipt of substantial funding from the Exchequer. Special considerations refer to the matters of regularity and propriety.

Published reports other than audit opinions

224. The C&AG considers the need for reporting other than through the audit opinion where the audit opinion is qualified as a consequence of a material irregularity. The purpose of a separate report is to provide the Oireachtas with a detailed explanation beyond that given in the audit opinion and which could form the basis of a hearing by the Committee of Public Accounts.

225. In central government departments and offices a separate report will always be required where there is an Excess Vote on an Appropriation Account. An excess constitutes a breach of parliamentary control and, regardless of the amounts involved, the Committee of Public Accounts has to be informed of the background and reasons. In such circumstances the Oireachtas must be requested to give retrospective approval to the additional expenditure.

226. The C&AG has the statutory authority to report on value for money issues and general matters arising from his audits and where matters come to his attention in the course of the audit which he believes merit a public report, he considers the implications for his report and opinion on the statutory accounts. For example, he may wish to refer in the opinion section of his audit report to the fact that he intends to publish a separate report on a particular matter.

Annex I

Contents of statement of responsibilities

The examples in this Annex are based on particular assumptions about the adequacy of the disclosures made in the financial statements about the responsibilities of the entity, directors and officers for keeping accounting records and preparing the financial statements. Where these disclosures are not adequate, then the sections for respective responsibilities in the example auditor's reports might need to be extended.

Statements of responsibilities include disclosures with regard to the following matters:

Responsibility for:

1   Proper accounting records that disclose with reasonable accuracy at any time the financial position of the entity and enable the entity to ensure that financial statements are prepared to comply with statutory requirements

2   Safeguarding the assets of the entity and for taking reasonable steps for the prevention and detection of fraud and other irregularities

3   Preparation of financial statements for each financial year that give a true and fair view of/present fairly the state of affairs of the entity and its performance for that period

4   In preparing financial statements:

   •   selecting suitable accounting policies and then applying them consistently;

   •   making judgments and estimates that are reasonable and prudent;

   •   stating whether applicable accounting standards have been followed, subject to any material departures disclosed and explained in the financial statements; and

   •   preparing the financial statements on the going concern basis, unless it is inappropriate to presume that the entity will continue in business.

5   Where a regularity opinion is given, responsibility for the regularity of the public finances for which the Accounting/Accountable Officer is answerable.

Annex II

Illustrative audit report

Example – Audit Report on a State Sponsored Agency

Report of the Comptroller and Auditor General for presentation to the Houses of the Oireachtas

Name of Entity

I have audited the financial statements of the [name of entity] for the year ended [year-end date] under the [specify legislation/basis for audit]. The financial statements, which have been prepared under the accounting policies set out therein, comprise [list primary financial statements] and the related notes. The financial reporting framework that has been applied in their preparation is applicable law and the accounting standards issued by the Accounting Standards Board (generally accepted accounting practice in Ireland).

Responsibilities of the [Board or equivalent of the Entity]

The Board [or equivalent] is responsible for the preparation of the financial statements, for ensuring that they give a true and fair view of the state of the [entity]'s affairs and of its income and expenditure, and for ensuring the regularity of transactions.

Responsibilities of the Comptroller and Auditor General

My responsibility is to audit the financial statements and report on them in accordance with applicable law.

My audit is conducted by reference to the special considerations which attach to [State bodies **or** bodies in receipt of substantial funding from the State] in relation to their management and operation.

My audit is carried out in accordance with the International Standards on Auditing (UK and Ireland). These standards require me to comply with the Auditing Practices Board's Ethical Standards for Auditors.

Scope of Audit of the Financial Statements

An audit involves obtaining evidence about the amounts and disclosures in the financial statements, sufficient to give reasonable assurance that the financial statements are free from material misstatement, whether caused by fraud or error. This includes an assessment of:

- whether the accounting policies are appropriate to the [name of entity]'s circumstances, and have been consistently applied and adequately disclosed,

- the reasonableness of significant accounting estimates made in the preparation of the financial statements, and

- the overall presentation of the financial statements.

- I also seek to obtain evidence about the regularity of financial transactions in the course of audit.

[In addition, I read all the financial and non-financial information in the [describe the annual report] to identify material inconsistencies with the audited financial statements. If I become aware of any apparent material misstatements or inconsistencies I consider the implications for my report.]

Opinion on the Financial Statements

In my opinion, the financial statements, which have been properly prepared in accordance with generally accepted accounting practice in Ireland, give a true and fair view of the state of the [entity]'s affairs at [year end date] and of its income and expenditure for the year then ended.

In my opinion, proper books of account have been kept by [name of entity]. The financial statements are in agreement with the books of account.

Matters on Which I am Required to Report by Exception

I report by exception if:

- there was any material instance where moneys have not been applied for the purposes intended or where the transactions did not conform to the authorities governing them, or

- I have not received all the information and explanations I required for my audit, or

- [the information given in [the entity]'s Annual Report for the year for which the financial statements are prepared is not consistent with the financial statements, or]

- the Statement on Internal Financial Control does not reflect the [entity]'s compliance with the Code of Practice for the Governance of State Bodies, or

- I find there are other material matters relating to the manner in which public business has been conducted.

I have nothing to report in regard to those matters upon which reporting is by exception.

[Otherwise insert detail if reporting is warranted]

Comptroller and Auditor General
[Date]

ISA (UK and Ireland) 720: Section A – The Auditor's Responsibilities Relating to Other Information in Documents Containing Audited Financial Statements

Objective

The objective of the auditor is to respond appropriately when documents containing audited financial statements and the auditor's report thereon include other information that could undermine the credibility of those financial statements and the auditor's report. (Paragraph 4)

The auditor shall read the other information to identify material inconsistencies, if any, with the audited financial statements. (Paragraph 6)

The Annual Report

227. In the case of non-commercial state sponsored bodies, boards, committees or funds an annual report often accompanies the financial statements and where the body is also a company a Director's Report is published. Where there is a requirement to produce an Annual Report an additional paragraph is inserted into the report outlined in the example in Annex II to the section on ISA (UK and Ireland) 700 of this Practice Note.

Other Information

228. Part C of this Practice Note deals with Statements on Internal Financial Control and outlines the guidance applicable for entities in different central government sectors when preparing these statements. The auditor of a central government account reviews these statements and reports the results of his review 'by exception' i.e. he only reports where there is a material departure from the applicable guidance. This review is not to provide assurance on the statement, but to:

- consider the completeness of the disclosures in meeting the requirements of the applicable corporate governance guidance;

- identify whether the disclosures are misleading; and

- identify any inconsistencies between the disclosures and the information that the auditor is aware of from audit work.

In addition, as part of his review he is not required to consider whether the entity's statement covers all risk and controls, or to form an opinion on the effectiveness of the entity's corporate governance procedures or its risk and control procedures

If, on reading the other information for the purpose of identifying material inconsistencies, the auditor becomes aware of an apparent material misstatement of fact, the auditor shall discuss the matter with management. (Paragraph 14)

If, following such discussions, the auditor still considers that there is an apparent material misstatement of fact, the auditor shall request management to consult with a qualified third party, such as the entity's legal counsel, and the auditor shall consider the advice received. (Paragraph 15)

If the auditor concludes that there is a material misstatement of fact in the other information which management refuses to correct, the auditor shall notify those charged with governance, unless all of those charged with governance are involved in managing the entity, of the auditor's concern regarding the other information and take any further appropriate action. (Paragraph 16)

229. Where the auditor of a central government account:

- identifies an inconsistency between the other information and corresponding or related amounts or disclosures in the audited financial statements; and

- concludes that, under the circumstances, the other information needs to be amended,

the auditor considers whether to take action as recommended by ISA (UK and Ireland) 720.

230. In taking action, the auditor of a central government account is concerned to ensure that the credibility of the financial statements and the related auditor's report is not undermined. Possible steps that might be taken to protect the auditor's report include:

- no further action – subject to management agreeing to amend the other information, either after communicating concerns to the responsible officer or, where appropriate, to the sponsoring government department or other entity to which the entity might be accountable – requests might also be made that the responsible officer consults an appropriate third party if disagreement persists;

- consider the implications for the auditor's report – the impact on the opinion itself will only be considered where doubt remains that an amendment might be required to the financial statements themselves; or

- resigning from the appointment.

231. Where audits are conducted under statute the resignation option is not available and the auditor's reports may include an explanatory paragraph if the information is not corrected.

Part B – The Audit of Regularity

232. The Foreword notes the importance of regularity to the financial framework of the central government sector and the responsibility of the auditor of a central government account to provide assurance regarding regularity on accounts subject to audit by him.

233. The concept of regularity relates to the substance of transactions. It is concerned with the legal authority of central government entities to effect the transactions in question and the legal entitlement of recipients to the funds disbursed. The overall objective of the audit of the regularity of transactions included in a central government account is to gain assurance that moneys have been applied for the purposes intended and in accordance with the governing legal authority. There are analogous objectives in the area of receipts.

234. This section provides the auditor of a central government account with practical guidance on the audit of regularity and expands the guidance contained in this Practice Note on the areas of:

- *obtaining a sufficient understanding of the framework of authorities*. The auditor of a central government account needs to identify laws and regulations and the financial framework that are specific to the entity and obtain a broad understanding sufficient to enable identification of transactions or events that may have a significant effect on the regularity of transactions in the financial statements.

- *testing for regularity*. Tests on regularity are usually integrated with those relating to the audit of the financial statements and involve tests to detect transactions or classes of transaction where the regularity assertion cannot be sustained and when necessary tests on the operating effectiveness of controls in preventing, or detecting and correcting material misstatements of the regularity assertion.

- *reporting on regularity*. The auditor of a central government account reports in any material case where the entity has failed to comply with regularity requirements. This reporting by exception is done through his opinion on the financial statements.

Obtaining a Sufficient Understanding of the Framework of Authorities

235. The governing authorities which the auditor of a central government account considers when obtaining a knowledge of the entity's activities and identifying the framework of authorities will be drawn from a variety of sources including:

- the founding legislation establishing the functions, powers and limits of the transactions and fee levying authority of the central government entity;

- legislation governing entitlement to funding from a scheme, programme or project administered by the central government entity;

- general legislation governing specific central government entities including the Ministers and Secretaries Acts and, in particular, the statutory requirements to get

Department of Finance approval whether in specific form or on foot of global delegation for expenditure;

- legislation governing the appropriation of funds including the annual Appropriation Act and the Central Fund (Permanent Provisions) Act 1965;

- Statutory Instruments relevant to the entity.

236. Apart from direct reference to the above, other sources of guidance in identifying the framework of authorities include:

- the Department of Finance's Public Financial Procedures;

- directions issued under legal authority by the sponsoring department for other entities in the central government sector;

- documentation produced by the entity, for example, in a complex environment documents which outline the translation of authorities into relevant rules and procedures;

- discussions with personnel in the entity; and

- previous experience with the entity or similar entities.

Testing for Regularity

237. The principles and procedures applied to obtain sufficient appropriate evidence to support an opinion on the regularity of transactions recorded in the financial statements of an entity in the central government sector are the same as those applied to the audit of any other financial statement assertion.

238. In general, audit assurance is sought by a combination of 'top down' reviews of the framework of authorities governing classes of payments and 'bottom up' reviews of transactions. In this respect regularity is a key assertion in the course of all central government sector audits. The extent of the audit work on regularity will depend on the nature and complexity of the relevant legislation and other authorities.

239. Central government sector entities will usually have installed internal controls to ensure regularity in the course of transaction processing. These controls often operate alongside procedures which from the audit perspective provide evidence regarding other assertions. In testing controls embedded in the entity's systems, the auditor of a central government account considers how the entity's management ensures compliance with the framework of authorities and seeks to mitigate the risk of material irregularity through those controls. The consideration of controls to prevent or detect irregular transactions involves assessing the general control environment at the entity level and control procedures relating to individual transaction streams. The annex to the guidance in this Practice Note on ISA (UK and Ireland) 315 provides further guidance on possible control responses by management to risks to regularity.

240. Particular considerations may arise in the design of audit procedures in relation to the regularity assertion. For example:

- Testing controls over regularity may involve:

  - examining the design of the system, the process for translating statutory requirements into rules and operational procedures, and the control activities established within the system;

  - transaction authorisation mechanisms within the entity.

- Testing the regularity of individual transactions may involve:

  - examining the payment scheme to determine whether the purpose and rules are consistent with legislative and other authorities;

  - examining transaction streams or account categories in order to identify transactions that may be outside the intention of Dáil Éireann;

  - determining that expenditure has remained within specified limits;

  - examining vires and entitlement.

241. To audit the regularity assertion where the audit is of an account of a central government entity which has paid a grant to another entity, the auditor of a central government account may use the work of the grantee's auditor and reduce the extent of his own audit procedures. In some cases he does not have a right of access and will use the work of the Local Government Audit Service or other auditors. Examples of this situation include the grants paid by departments to fund State-sponsored bodies which are not audited by the C&AG and the grants paid by the Department of the Environment, Heritage and Local Government to local authorities.

242. The auditor of a central government account approaches the audit of regularity of receipts, including revenues from taxation and other sources, in the same way the auditor would approach the audit of the regularity of expenditure. There may, nevertheless, be particular considerations when auditing the regularity of fees and charges levied by central government sector entities for example:

- reviewing the relevant primary legislation to confirm that it provides appropriate authority to levy fees and charges;

- confirming that fee orders and other types of Statutory Instrument issued under the governing legislation are in accordance with those authorities;

- for vote funded activities, confirming that the Appropriation Act provides the appropriate authority for the receipts to be applied in aid of expenditure.

Regularity and Reporting

243. In Ireland, while regularity is a key assertion tested in the course of every audit and a specific statutory obligation in government departments and certain other bodies the form of reporting adopted is by 'exception' in each case. This is based on the existing statutory provisions which require the C&AG to report in his certificate of opinion any material instance where the entity has failed to apply expenditure recorded in the financial statements for the purposes intended or where the transactions do not conform to the authority under which they purport to have been carried out.

244. Cases of irregular transactions will usually be reported to the management of the entity to allow corrective action to be taken, for example, by recovering overpayments of grant. In addition, in appropriate cases separate reports are made to supervising departments on the regularity of the activities and the transactions of those entities under their aegis. In the audit of a central government department the 1993 Act outlines the process to be undertaken including the reporting thereof where the C&AG believe that the department has incurred expenditure not properly chargeable or incurred material expenditure which was not authorised.

245. For other central government sector entities where it is not possible for the entity to take corrective action the auditor of a central government account may encourage it to disclose the non-compliance in its financial statements by outlining the circumstances and the possible extent of irregular transactions. Even where a breach of regularity is disclosed, the auditor of a central government account will still consider the implications for the audit opinion on regularity and the need to present a separate report on the matter. In doing so, the auditor of a central government account considers the materiality of the matter at issue.

Part C – Statement on Internal Financial Control

Introduction

246. This part of the Practice Note provides additional guidance on the auditor's responsibilities in relation to statements on internal financial control in the central government sector.

247. Applicable guidance for Accounting Officers and other accountable persons in the central government sector is derived from:

- The Code of Practice for the Governance of State Bodies (the Code of Practice) which introduced corporate governance guidance for central government entities excluding government departments;

- The Report of the Working Group on the Accountability of Secretaries General and Accounting Officers which made recommendations regarding enhanced governance arrangements in government departments. These have been implemented under the general direction of the Department of Finance.

248. Among the corporate governance requirements introduced by this guidance were:

- the establishment of audit committees;

- ensuring that an internal audit function operates in the entity;

- the introduction of an annual Statement on Internal Financial Control (SIFC).

249. In addition, the Chairperson of each State body must report annually to the relevant Minister on compliance with the Code of Practice.

Audit Responsibility

250. By agreement with the Minister for Finance the auditor of a central government account is required to:

- review the SIFC to confirm that it reflects the entity's compliance with the applicable guidance on corporate governance; and

- consider if that statement is misleading or inconsistent with other information of which he is aware from his audit of the financial statements.

251. The auditor of a central government account reports 'by exception' in instances where the entity has not complied with these requirements.

252. The auditor of a central government account has no other additional responsibilities arising out of these governance arrangements. In particular, while it is open to him to do so, he is not required to consider whether the entity's statement covers all risks and controls, or form an opinion on the effectiveness of the entity's corporate governance

procedures or its risk and control procedures. In this regard it is a matter of practice for the C&AG to report, in appropriate cases, to Dáil Éireann or sponsoring departments on matters arising from his financial audit including any material concerns relating to governance arrangements.

Statements on Internal Financial Control

253. The Accounting Officer of a government department and the Chairperson or equivalent of any other body in the central government sector is required to submit along with the financial statements a Statement on Internal Financial Control. For government departments the format of the SIFC has been promulgated by the Department of Finance. In the case of other central government sector entities the format of the SIFC is set out in Appendix V of the Code of Practice.

254. Each SIFC is required to outline the key procedures put in place by entities designed to provide effective internal financial control, including:

- steps taken to ensure an appropriate control environment;

- processes used to identify risks (including business risks as appropriate) and to evaluate their financial implications;

- details of major information systems in place;

- the procedures for addressing the financial implications of major business risks;

- the procedures for monitoring the effectiveness of the system of internal financial control.

255. The entity also confirms that a review of the effectiveness of the system of internal financial control has taken place. Where a deficiency in controls has led to a material loss, contingency or uncertainty being disclosed in the financial statements the matter and any remedial action taken may be reported in the SIFC or in the audit report on the financial statements, or in both.

Responsibilities of the Auditor of a Central Government Account

Scope and limitations of audit work

256. The extent of the responsibility of the auditor of a central government account is limited to a *review* of whether the SIFC *reflects* the entity's compliance with applicable guidance on corporate governance. The auditor of a central government account considers whether the SIFC presents the information:

- specified by the Department of Finance for government departments, or

- required at Appendix V of the Code of Practice.

257. The auditor of a central government account also considers whether the SIFC reflects the process undertaken by the entity in reviewing the internal control system, and also whether there is appropriate evidence for the disclosures made in that statement.

258. The auditor of a central government account obtains *appropriate evidence* to support the statement made by the entity. Appropriate evidence is usually obtained from the following sources:

- reviewing relevant documentation (minutes and other supporting documents prepared for management/board/audit committee meetings);

- making enquiries of senior officials or directors;

- meetings of the audit committee;

- requesting the directors or in government departments, the responsible officials to provide written confirmation of oral representations made during the course of the review.

259. A key assertion attaching to the SIFC is that the entity has reviewed its controls. While the scope of this review may extend to operational and compliance control systems, the current requirement is to report only on its assessment of internal financial controls. The examination by the auditor of a central government account of the consistency of information contained in the statement with his own understanding from the audit is, therefore, limited to the internal financial controls.

260. Where the auditor of a central government account becomes aware of material misstatements or inconsistencies in the SIFC he takes the appropriate steps outlined in the guidance contained in this Practice Note on ISA (UK and Ireland) 720. However, the auditor of a central government account is not expected to assess whether the entity has addressed all risks and controls or that risks are satisfactorily addressed by internal controls.

261. Neither is the auditor of a central government account expected to actively search for misstatements or inconsistencies in the statement. The auditor of a central government account is not giving an opinion on the effectiveness of the entity's system of internal financial controls.

262. The SIFC covers the year under review and the period up to the date of approval of the financial statements (and annual report if applicable) and therefore the review by the auditor of a central government account must be consistent with this timeframe.

263. Because of the limited nature of the auditor's review and in order to avoid the possibility of misunderstandings arising, it is considered good practice:

- where a letter of understanding is issued to the client, that such letter explain the scope of the review by the auditor of a central government account;

- prior to the release of the annual report and financial statements, the auditor of a central government account communicates and discusses with the entity the factual findings of his review.

Programme of work

264. In addition to gathering evidence from the sources of evidence referred to above the following procedures are undertaken:

- enquiries of the directors or senior officials in order to obtain an understanding of the process defined by the management or board for its review of the effectiveness of internal control;

- examination of relevant documentation, including management or board minutes and any other material prepared by or for the managers or directors and which evidences this process;

- review of the SIFC in order to determine that it is in the required format;

- evaluation of whether or not the evidence examined provides sound support for that statement;

- considering whether the information contained in the SIFC is consistent with auditor's knowledge obtained during the audit of the financial statements.

265. In carrying out the review of the SIFC, the auditor of a central government account has regard to the knowledge of the entity obtained from the audit of the financial statements. To enable him to perform the audit and express an opinion on the financial statements, the auditor of a central government account is required by auditing standards to understand the entity's control environment and to assess the components of audit risk. Such an assessment may extend to the auditor's review of control risk to the extent that he has relied on such an assessment in order to reduce the extent of substantive audit procedures.

266. In the unlikely event that the SIFC describes procedures of which the auditor of a central government account is unaware, he satisfies himself through enquiry sufficient to allow him to conclude that the SIFC is not misleading. The auditor of a central government account does not necessarily review the operation of such procedures.

267. The audit report discloses the scope of the audit work in terms such as those set out in the example in Annex II to ISA (UK and Ireland) 700 of this Practice Note.

Communication of significant deficiencies discovered during audit

268. ISA (UK and Ireland) 265 requires the auditor to communicate significant deficiencies in internal control identified during the audit to those charged with governance on a timely basis. Significant deficiencies include those which in the opinion of the auditor of a central government account could lead to a material loss. Consequently, the auditor of a central government account does not wait until the financial statement

audit has been completed before reporting such deficiencies. In this way, the management or directors are made aware of the deficiencies that the auditor has identified and are able to take account of them when preparing the SIFC.

Significant internal financial control issues

269. Where appropriate, the entity is requested to disclose relevant information about deficiencies or weaknesses in internal financial control which have resulted in material losses, contingencies or uncertainties which require disclosure in the financial statements (or auditor's report) and also a description of the action taken or intended to be taken to correct the deficiencies. Where no action is proposed an explanation is given.

270. The responsibility of the auditor of a central government account in situations where deficiencies in internal controls have resulted in material losses, contingencies or uncertainties which require disclosure in the financial statements (or auditor's report), consists of:

- discussing with the entity the steps that have been taken to determine the significant deficiencies resulting in material loss, contingency or uncertainty being disclosed; and

- assessing whether disclosures made in the SIFC of the processes applied to deal with such deficiencies appropriately reflect those processes.

271. The auditor of a central government account is not required to assess whether the action proposed by the entity will, in fact, remedy the deficiency described.

272. If the auditor of a central government account is aware of a material loss, contingency or uncertainty being disclosed in the financial statements (and annual report) but the entity has not disclosed any related internal control deficiency, the auditor of a central government account discusses the position with the entity. If the auditor of a central government account is not able to agree with the directors or other relevant persons as to how the matter should be resolved he considers the consequences for the audit report.

Failure to conduct a review

273. Where the entity has not conducted an annual assessment as required by the Code of Practice, the chairperson should state that fact and provide an explanation in the SIFC. In these circumstances, the auditor of a central government account determines appropriate wording for the audit report.

Groups of entities

274. The SIFC covers the parent undertaking and all subsidiary undertakings. Accordingly the assessment of the system of internal financial control is made from the perspective of the group as a whole. Thus the auditor of a central government account considers materiality as it applies to the group and not to individual undertakings.

275. Where material joint ventures and associated companies have not been dealt with as part of the group when applying the Code of Practice, the board should disclose this fact. The auditor of a central government account assesses, based on his knowledge of the group, obtained during the audit of the financial statements, whether any material joint ventures or associated companies have not been dealt with and, therefore, if such a disclosure is necessary.

Reporting the Results

276. Based on his work the auditor of a central government account reports on any material instance where the SIFC does not comply with the applicable guidance or where it is misleading or inconsistent with other information which he is aware of from the audit of the financial statements. Where he is satisfied that there is material compliance he does not refer to the matter in his report.

Reporting by exception

277. If the auditor of a central government account concludes:

- that the description of the key procedures designed to provide effective internal financial control is either not supported by or does not appropriately reflect the auditor's understanding of the process undertaken;

- that the information disclosed about those deficiencies in internal financial control that have resulted in material losses, contingencies or other uncertainties being disclosed either in the financial statements or the audit report, is not consistent with his understanding;

- that no disclosure has been made by the entity of its failure to conduct an assessment of the system of internal financial control;

- that the explanation by the entity of the circumstances where it has not assessed the system of internal control is not consistent with the auditors' understanding; or

- that no disclosure has been made by the entity that a material joint venture or associated company has not been dealt with as part of the group,

the audit report states this in the opinion section.

278. However, as this does not give rise to a qualified audit opinion on the financial statements, such comments are included under the sub heading 'Other Matter' in the audit report.

Appendix

Glossary of terms

Accountable person – is the Chief Executive Officer or other appropriate person in central government entities other than government departments and offices who is given responsibilities similar to an Accounting Officer, although not formally designated as such.

Accounting Officer – the Civil Service head of a department or office administering a Vote is normally appointed Accounting Officer on the premise that he/she alone is in a position to account for all the moneys entrusted to his/her department. An Accounting Officer is personally responsible for the regularity and propriety of transactions, the economy and efficiency of the Department in the use of its resources and the systems procedures and practices employed by the Department for the purpose of evaluating the effectiveness of the operations. The appointment of an Accounting Officer is in accordance with the Exchequer and Audit Departments Act 1866 and his/her responsibilities are set out in the C&AG (Amendment) Act 1993. The detailed responsibilities of an Accounting Officer are further elaborated in the Department of Finance publication "Public Financial Procedures" and PAC guidelines for Accounting Officers appearing before that Committee.

Legislation establishing a public entity such as a non-commercial State sponsored body may also designate the chief officer of that body as the Accounting Officer.

Appropriation Account – is the account prepared for each voted service. It shows the outturn for the financial year against the amount provided by Dáil Éireann and also provides an outline of the services financed from the Vote. In addition to providing the statutory financial information on a cash basis of accounting the Appropriation Account also sets out some accrual-based information.

Audit report – is a report expressing an auditor's opinion on the truth and fairness, fair presentation or proper presentation of financial statements and on the regularity of the financial transactions included in them. In the central government sector, the audit report may also be referred to as a Certificate.

Cash account – is any set of financial statements which records receipts and payments on a cash basis. It would not normally disclose assets and liabilities, although, the Appropriation Accounts do so by way of memorandum information.

Central Bank of Ireland – amongst its responsibilities, the Central Bank of Ireland manages government bank accounts, maintains the register of government bonds and acts as custodian of the official external reserves. As banker to the government, the Central Bank holds the Exchequer Account together with the accounts of the Paymaster General and the main accounts of the Revenue Commissioners.

Central Fund – is the amount standing to the credit of the Exchequer Account which is kept at the Central Bank of Ireland. It is the destination of all State revenues and the source of all government spending except where otherwise provided by law.

Central government account – includes the financial statements of the Exchequer, government departments, activities administered through departmental funds, non-commercial state sponsored bodies, third level educational institutions, and non-elected regional and local authorities. It does not include the financial statements of local authorities or commercial state sponsored bodies. See also voted funds, departmental funds and non-commercial state sponsored bodies.

Certificate – is the term reserved for the formal mandatory audit report of the C&AG on financial statements audited under statute where there is a statutory requirement for his examination to be certified.

Dáil Éireann – lower house of parliament.

Departmental funds – refer to funds, the majority of which have been established by statute to enable the State to administer moneys, whether public or private, entrusted to it.

Entities – is the generic term used in the Practice Note for any central government sector body or legal persons.

Estimates – for the Supply Services must be presented to Dáil Éireann and circulated to members not less than seven days before the annual budget and not later than the 30th day of the financial year. The Estimates are published in the Book of Estimates. This publication contains a separate Estimate of the cost of each Departmental function for which Dáil Éireann will be asked to appropriate money by way of a separate Vote. When an Estimate is passed by Dáil Éireann it is technically known as a Vote.

Finance Accounts – are detailed annual accounts presented by the Minister for Finance to the Houses of the Oireachtas, containing analysis and classification of receipts and issues of the Central Fund as well as details relating to the National Debt.

National Treasury Management Agency (NTMA) – was established in 1990 to borrow moneys for the Exchequer and to manage the National Debt on behalf of the Minister for Finance.

Non-commercial state sponsored bodies – are non-trading entities which in the main are charged with promotional, developmental, training or regulatory functions.

Oireachtas (Houses of the) – Seanad Éireann and Dáil Éireann, the upper and lower houses of parliament.

Propriety – is concerned with the way in which public business is conducted including any conventions agreed with Dáil Éireann, and any guidance issued on governance and ethics.

Public Financial Procedures – the principles of Government accounting are mainly derived from the Constitution and from the institutional and financial relationships between parliament and the executive which have been developed over the years. The Public Financial Procedures is a guide which sets out these principles, as well as the more important ways they are applied in the day-to-day operations of government departments and offices.

Regularity – is concerned with the application of money under governing authority for the purpose intended. While the statutory requirement refers only to expenditure it is equally applicable to income.

Third level educational institutions – include universities and Institutes of Technology.

Voted funds – refer to money for the general service of departments or offices which is voted by Dáil Éireann on an annual basis.

PRACTICE NOTE 12 (REVISED)

MONEY LAUNDERING LEGISLATION – GUIDANCE FOR AUDITORS IN THE UNITED KINGDOM

CONTENTS

Introduction

1.   Practice Note 12 (Revised), "Money Laundering – Guidance for auditors on UK legislation", was last issued as interim guidance in March 2008. Practice Note 12 (Revised) has now been approved by HM Treasury in accordance with sections 330 and 331 of the Proceeds of Crime Act 2002 ("POCA"), section 21A of the Terrorism Act 2000 ("TA 2000") and Regulations 42 and 45 of the Money Laundering Regulations 2007 (the "ML Regulations"). This version reflects the legislation effective at 31 August 2010 and also the ISAs (UK and Ireland) that apply to audits relating to accounting periods ending on, or after, 15 December 2010[1]. Auditors need to be alert to subsequent changes in legislative requirements.

2.   Practice Note 12 (Revised) focuses on the impact of the UK anti-money laundering legislation on auditors' responsibilities when auditing and reporting on financial statements. It does not provide general guidance on the legislation. The Consultative Committee of Accountancy Bodies has issued "Anti-Money Laundering Guidance for the Accountancy Sector" ("CCAB Guidance") which provides general guidance on the legislation for all entities providing audit, accountancy, tax advisory or insolvency related services[2].

3.   The anti-money laundering legislation is complex and some uncertainty still exists as to how the courts will interpret it in practice. To obtain a full understanding of the legal requirements auditors will need to refer to the relevant provisions of the legislation and, if necessary, obtain legal advice.

4.   The use of the term 'auditor' in this Practice Note means anyone who is part of the engagement team (not necessarily only those employed by an audit firm). The engagement team comprises all persons who are directly involved in the acceptance and performance of a particular audit. This includes the audit team (including audit professionals contracted by the firm), professional personnel from other disciplines involved in the audit engagement and those who provide quality control or direct oversight of the audit engagement, but it does not include experts contracted by the firm. Appendix 2 sets out further guidance as to whom the anti-money laundering legislation applies.

---

[1]   Audits relating to accounting periods ending before 15 December 2010 will be undertaken with reference to Practice Note 12 (Revised), "Money Laundering – Interim guidance for auditors in the United Kingdom", published in March 2008.

[2]   Cross references in the Practice Note to "CCAB Guidance" are to the guidance issued by the CCAB in August 2008. This is available on the CCAB website at http://www.ccab.org.uk/documents.php.

Key legal requirements

5. The key legal requirements introduced by POCA (as subsequently amended by the Serious and Organised Crime and Police Act 2005 (SOCPA)), TA 2000 and the ML Regulations are as follows:

- Part 7 of POCA consolidated, updated and reformed criminal law in the UK with regard to money laundering. The definition of money laundering[3] comprises three principal money laundering offences[4] (behaviour that directly constitutes money laundering). These include possessing, or in any way dealing with, or concealing, the proceeds of any crime and includes crime committed by an entity or an individual.

- TA 2000 contains similar offences for the laundering of terrorist funds, although in such cases, the funds involved include any funds that are likely to be used for the financing of terrorism. There is no need for funds to have been obtained from a previous criminal offence for them to be terrorist funds.

- POCA and the ML Regulations do not extend the scope of the audit, but auditors are within the regulated sector and are required to report where:

  - they know or suspect, or have reasonable grounds to know or suspect, that another person is engaged in money laundering;

  - they can identify the other person or the whereabouts of any of the laundered property or that they believe, or it is reasonable to expect them to believe, that information that they have obtained will or may assist in identifying that other person or the whereabouts of the laundered property; and

  - the information has come to the auditor in the course of its regulated business.

---

[3] Section 340(11) of POCA states that "Money laundering is an act which:
   (a) constitutes an offence under section 327, 328 or 329,
   (b) constitutes an attempt, conspiracy or incitement to commit an offence specified in paragraph (a),
   (c) constitutes aiding, abetting, counselling or procuring the commission of an offence specified in paragraph (a), or
   (d) would constitute an offence specified in paragraph (a), (b) or (c) if done in the UK."
[4] The principal money laundering offences defined under POCA are:
   - s327 "Concealing" criminal property (including concealing or disguising its nature, source, location, disposition, movement, ownership or rights attaching; converting, transferring or removing from any part of the UK).
   - s328 "Arranging" (entering into or becoming concerned in an arrangement which the business or an individual knows or suspects facilitates the acquisition, retention, use or control of criminal property by or on behalf of another person).
   - s329 "Acquiring, using or possessing criminal property".

- Failure by an auditor to report knowledge or suspicion of, or reasonable grounds to know or suspect, money laundering in relation to the proceeds of any crime is a criminal offence[5]. Auditors (partners and staff) will face criminal penalties[6] if they breach the requirements.

- The requirement to report is not just related to matters that might be considered material to the financial statements; auditors have to report knowledge or suspicion, or reasonable grounds for knowledge or suspicion, of crimes that potentially have no material financial statement impact. POCA does not contain de minimis concessions.

- Where an auditor knows or suspects that they themselves are involved in money laundering, the auditor is required to report this in order that appropriate consent can be obtained.

- Firms must take appropriate measures so that partners and staff are made aware of the provisions of POCA, the ML Regulations and the TA 2000 and are given training in how to recognise and deal with actual or suspected money laundering activities.

- Auditors are required to adopt rigorous client identification procedures and appropriate anti-money laundering procedures.

The Proceeds of Crime Act 2002

6. POCA defines both the money laundering offences and the auditor's reporting responsibilities. The anti-money laundering legislation imposes a duty to report money laundering in respect of all criminal property. Property is criminal property if:

    (a) It constitutes a person's benefit from criminal conduct or it represents such a benefit (in whole or in part and whether directly or indirectly); and

    (b) The alleged offender knows or suspects that it constitutes or represents such a benefit.

---

[5] Subject to the provisions of POCA section 330(6) relating to information coming to a legal adviser or relevant professional adviser in "privileged circumstances" and section 330(7A) relating to offences committed overseas.

[6] Criminal penalties are covered under sections 334 and 336(6) of POCA. The maximum penalty for the three principal money laundering offences on conviction on indictment is fourteen years imprisonment. The maximum penalty on conviction on indictment is five years imprisonment for the following offences:
- a person in the regulated sector other than a nominated officer failing to disclose (section 330),
- the nominated officer failure to disclose offences (section 331 for the regulated sector, section 332 for those outside this sector),
- the giving of consent by a nominated officer inappropriately to prohibited acts (section 336(5)), and
- the 'tipping off' offence (sections 333A to 333E).
Furthermore in all cases, an unlimited fine can be imposed.
On summary conviction, the maximum penalty for all the above offences is six months' imprisonment and/or a fine not exceeding the statutory maximum. A person guilty of an offence under section 339(1A) of making a disclosure under section 330, 331, 332 or 338 otherwise than in the form prescribed by the Secretary of State or otherwise than in the manner so prescribed is liable on summary conviction to a fine not exceeding level 5 on the standard scale.

A very wide range of offences (including, for example, bribery and corruption outside the UK) may give rise to a responsibility to report money laundering suspicions. Examples of situations that may give rise to money laundering offences are set out in Appendix 1.

7. There are three principal money laundering offences[4] which define money laundering to encompass offences relating to the possession, acquisition, use, concealment or conversion of criminal property and involvement in arrangements relating to criminal property. These principal offences apply to all persons and businesses whether or not they are within the regulated sector.

8. Under section 330 of POCA persons working in the regulated sector are required to report knowledge or suspicion, or reasonable grounds for knowledge or suspicion, that another person is engaged in money laundering to a nominated officer where that knowledge or suspicion, or reasonable grounds for knowledge or suspicion, came to those persons in the course of their business or employment in the regulated sector. In audit firms the nominated officer is usually known as a Money Laundering Reporting Officer ("MLRO") and is referred to as such in this Practice Note.[7] If as a result of that report the MLRO has knowledge or suspicion of, or reasonable grounds to know or suspect money laundering, the MLRO then has a responsibility to report to the Serious Organised Crime Agency (SOCA). POCA does not contain de minimis concessions that affect the reporting requirements with the result that reports need to be made irrespective of the quantum of the benefits derived from, or the seriousness of, the offence. When a report has been made to SOCA partners and staff in audit firms need to be alert to the dangers of disseminating information that is likely to 'tip off' a money launderer or prejudice an investigation[8] as this may constitute a criminal offence under the anti-money laundering legislation.

9. Auditors who consider that the actions they plan to take, or may be asked to take, will result in themselves committing a principal money laundering offence are required to obtain prior consent to those actions from their MLRO and the MLRO is required to seek appropriate prior consent from SOCA (see paragraphs 48 to 50).

The Terrorism Act 2000

10. For the purposes of this guidance, money laundering includes activities relating to terrorist financing. This extends the money laundering reporting requirements for partners and staff in audit firms to terrorist fund-raising, the use of money or other property for the purposes of terrorism, or the possession of money or other property and arrangements where money or other property is to be made available to another, where a person intends, knows or has reasonable cause to suspect that it may be

---

[7] Section 20(3) of the ML Regulations recognises that the requirements relating to internal reporting procedures do not apply to sole practitioners, but the external reporting obligations under POCA remain. There is no obligation on a sole practitioner to appoint an MLRO where the sole practitioner does not employ any staff, or act in association with any other person. Where no MLRO is appointed and a sole practitioner has knowledge or suspicion of, or reasonable grounds to know or suspect, money laundering the sole practitioner has a responsibility to report to SOCA.

[8] See guidance on 'tipping off' and prejudicing an investigation in paragraphs 44 to 47.

used for the purposes of terrorism irrespective of whether those funds come from a legitimate source or not.

The Money Laundering Regulations 2007

11. The ML Regulations apply to persons, acting in the course of business as a statutory auditor within the meaning of Part 42 of the Companies Act 2006, when carrying out statutory audit work within the meaning of section 1210 of the Companies Act 2006[9]. For the purposes of this Practice Note "person" is interpreted as referring to a UK audit firm that is designated as a "Registered Auditor" to which the ML Regulations apply.

12. Where a Registered Auditor is not carrying out statutory audit work the ML Regulations will nevertheless often apply as they also cover a firm or sole practitioner who by way of business provides accountancy services to, or advice about the tax affairs of, other persons, when providing such services[10].

13. The ML Regulations impose requirements on businesses in the regulated sector relating to systems and training to prevent money laundering, identification procedures for clients, record keeping procedures and internal reporting procedures.

Firm-wide practices

14. The ML Regulations requires businesses in the regulated sector to establish risk-sensitive policies and procedures relating to:

- Customer identification and on-going monitoring of business relationships;

- Reporting internally and to SOCA[11];

- Record keeping;

- Internal control, risk assessment and management;

- Training for all relevant employees; and

- Monitoring and management of compliance with and the internal communication of such policies and procedures.

In addition, audit firms need to ensure sufficient senior management oversight of the systems used for monitoring compliance with these procedures. It may be helpful for this to be co-ordinated with the responsibility for the firm's quality control systems under ISQC (UK and Ireland) I. Detailed guidance on developing and applying a risk based approach is given in section 4 of the CCAB Guidance.

---

[9] Regulation 3(4) of the Money Laundering Regulations 2007.

[10] Regulations 3(7) and 3(8) of the Money Laundering Regulations 2007.

[11] Whilst a risk based approach is appropriate when devising policies and procedures, the auditor will not adopt a risk based approach to making reports either internally or to SOCA.

Client identification and on-going monitoring of business relationships

15. Appropriate identification procedures, as required by the ML Regulations, are mandatory when accepting appointment as auditor. The extent of information collected about the client and verification of identity undertaken will depend on the client risk assessment. Guidance on identification procedures, including references to financial restrictions regimes (i.e. sanctions), is given in section 5 of the CCAB Guidance.

16. Auditing standards on quality control require the audit firm to consider the integrity of the client. This involves the auditor making appropriate enquiries and may involve discussions with third parties, the obtaining of written references and searches of relevant databases. These procedures may provide some of the relevant client identification information but may need to be extended to comply with the ML Regulations.

17. It may be helpful for the auditor to explain to the client the reason for requiring evidence of identity and this can be achieved by including this matter in pre-engagement letter communications with the potential client. The following is an illustrative paragraph that could be included for this purpose:

> "Client identification
> As with other professional services firms, we are required to identify our clients for the purposes of the UK anti-money laundering legislation. We are likely to request from you, and retain, some information and documentation for these purposes and/ or to make searches of appropriate databases. If we are not able to obtain satisfactory evidence of your identity within a reasonable time, there may be circumstances in which we are not able to proceed with the audit appointment."

18. It may also be helpful to inform clients of the auditor's responsibilities under POCA to report knowledge or suspicion, or reasonable grounds to know or suspect, that a money laundering offence has been committed and the restrictions created by the 'tipping off' rules on the auditor's ability to discuss such matters with their clients. The following is an illustrative paragraph that could be included in the audit engagement letter for this purpose:

> "Money laundering disclosures
> The provision of audit services is a business in the regulated sector under the Proceeds of Crime Act 2002 and, as such, partners and staff in audit firms have to comply with this legislation which includes provisions that may require us to make a money laundering disclosure in relation to information we obtain as part of our normal audit work. It is not our practice to inform you when such a disclosure is made or the reasons for it because of the restrictions imposed by the 'tipping off' provisions of the legislation."

19. Whether or not to include these illustrative paragraphs in the audit engagement letter is a policy decision to be taken by individual firms.

20. The activities of and the relationship with the audit client will be monitored on an on-going basis. For example, if there has been a change in the client's circumstances, such as changes in beneficial ownership, control or directors, and this information was relied upon originally as part of the client identification procedures then, depending on the auditor's assessment of risk, the procedures may need to be re-performed and documented. However, annual reappointment as auditor does not, in itself, require the client identification procedures to be re-performed.

Money Laundering Reporting Officer

21. The ML Regulations require relevant businesses to appoint a nominated officer (usually known as the MLRO). A sole practitioner who does not employ any staff, or act in association with any other person, is by default an MLRO. Auditors are required to report where they know or suspect, or have reasonable grounds to know or suspect, that another person is engaged in money laundering or, for the purposes of obtaining consent, where they know or suspect that they themselves are involved in money laundering. Partners and staff in audit firms discharge their responsibilities by reporting to their MLRO or, in the case of sole practitioners, to SOCA and, where appropriate, by obtaining consent from the MLRO or SOCA to continue with any prohibited activities. The MLRO is responsible for deciding, on the basis of the information provided by the partners and staff, whether further enquiry is required, whether the matter should be reported to SOCA and for making the report to SOCA. Partners and staff may seek advice from the MLRO who will often act as the main source of guidance and if necessary act as the liaison point for communication with lawyers, SOCA and the relevant law enforcement agency. More detailed guidance on the role of the MLRO is given in section 7 of the CCAB Guidance.

Training

22. Firms are required to take appropriate measures so that partners and staff are made aware of the relevant provisions of POCA, the ML Regulations and the TA 2000 and are given training in how to recognise and deal with activities which may be related to money laundering. Guidance on training is given in section 3 of the CCAB Guidance. The level of training provided to individuals needs to be appropriate to both the level of exposure of the individual to money laundering risk and their role and seniority within the firm. Senior members of the firm whatever their role need to understand the requirements of POCA and the ML Regulations.

23. Apart from the training referred to in paragraph 22 above, additional training or expertise in criminal law is not required under POCA. However, paragraph 12 of ISA (UK and Ireland) 250 Section A 'Consideration of Laws and Regulations in an Audit of Financial Statements' requires an auditor to obtain a general understanding of the legal and regulatory framework applicable to the entity and the industry or sector in which the entity operates and how the entity is complying with that framework

Impact of legislation on audit procedures

Identification of knowledge or suspicions

24. ISA (UK and Ireland) 250 Section A establishes standards and provides guidance on the auditor's responsibility to consider law and regulations in an audit of financial

statements. The anti-money laundering legislation does not require the auditor to extend the scope of the audit, save as referred to in paragraph 32 below, but the normal audit work could give rise to knowledge or suspicion, or reasonable grounds for knowledge or suspicion, that will need to be reported.

25. Auditing standards on law and regulations require the auditor to obtain:

  • a general understanding of the legal and regulatory framework applicable to the entity and the industry or sector in which the entity operates and how the entity is complying with that framework (paragraph 12 of ISA (UK and Ireland) 250 Section A); and

  • sufficient appropriate audit evidence regarding compliance with the provisions of those laws and regulations generally recognised to have a direct effect on the determination of material amounts and disclosures in the financial statements (paragraph 13 of ISA (UK and Ireland) 250 Section A). This may cause the auditor to be suspicious that, for example, breaches of the Companies Act or tax offences have taken place, which may be criminal offences resulting in criminal property.

26. Paragraph 14 of ISA (UK and Ireland) 250 Section A also requires the auditor to perform procedures to help identify instances of non-compliance with other laws and regulations which may have a material effect on the financial statements. These procedures consist of:

  • enquiring of those charged with governance as to whether the entity is in compliance with such laws and regulations; and

  • inspecting correspondence with the relevant licensing or regulatory authorities;

This work may give the auditor grounds to suspect that criminal offences have been committed.

27. For businesses within the regulated sector[12], other laws and regulations that may have a material effect on the financial statements will include POCA and the ML Regulations.

---

[12] For the purposes of this Practice Note this includes (but is not restricted to) the following persons acting in the course of business in the United Kingdom:
  • credit institutions;
  • financial institutions (including money service operators);
  • auditors, insolvency practitioners, external accountants and tax advisers;
  • independent legal professionals;
  • trust or company service providers;
  • estate agents;
  • high value dealers when dealing in goods of any description which involves accepting a total cash payment of 15,000 euro or more
  • casinos.
The legislation from which this list is derived is complicated and comprises two sources. If in doubt, an auditor refers to the definitions of:
  • the regulated sector, defined in the Proceeds of Crime Act 2002 Schedule 9 Part 1 (as amended by Statutory Instrument 2003/3074 "The Proceeds of Crime Act 2002 (Business in the Regulated Sector and Supervisory Authorities) Order 2003" and Statutory Instrument 2007/3287 "The Proceeds of Crime Act 2002 (Business in the Regulated Sector and Supervisory Authorities) Order 2007); and
  • relevant businesses as defined in paragraph 3(1) of the ML Regulations.

When auditing the financial statements of businesses within the regulated sector the auditor reviews the steps taken by the entity to comply with the ML Regulations, assesses their effectiveness and obtains management representations concerning compliance with the ML Regulations. If the client's systems are thought to be ineffective the auditor considers whether there is a responsibility to report 'a matter of material significance' to the regulator in accordance with ISA (UK and Ireland) 250 Section B 'The Auditor's Right and Duty to Report to Regulators in the Financial Sector', and considers the possible impact of fines (which might be imposed if non-compliance with the ML Regulations or POCA is proven). Where the entity's business is outside the regulated sector, although the auditor's reporting responsibilities under the money laundering legislation are unchanged, the entity's management is not required to implement the ML Regulations. Whilst the principal money laundering offences apply to these entities, the laws relating to money laundering are unlikely to be considered by the auditor to be other laws and regulations that may have a material effect on the financial statements for the purposes of ISA (UK and Ireland) 250 Section A.

28. Auditing standards on laws and regulations require the auditor to be alert to the possibility that audit procedures applied for the purpose of forming an opinion on the financial statements may bring instances of possible non-compliance with other laws and regulations to the auditor's attention. This includes of non-compliance that might incur obligations for partners and staff in audit firms to report to a regulatory or other enforcement authority.

29. The auditor also gives consideration to whether any contingent liabilities might arise in this area. For example, there may be regulatory or criminal fines for offences under POCA or the ML Regulations. Even where no offence under POCA has been committed, civil recovery actions under POCA (Part 5) or other civil claims may give rise to contingent liabilities. The auditor will remain alert to the fact that discussions with the client on such matters may give rise to a risk of 'tipping off' (see paragraphs 44 to 47).

30. In some situations the audit client may have obtained legal advice to the effect that certain actions or circumstances do not give rise to criminal conduct and therefore cannot give rise to criminal property. Whether an act constitutes non-compliance with law or regulations may involve consideration of matters which do not lie within the competence and experience of individuals trained in the audit of financial information. Provided that the auditor considers that the advice has been obtained from a suitably qualified and independent lawyer and that the lawyer was made aware of all relevant circumstances known to the auditor, the auditor may rely on such advice, provided the auditor has complied with auditing standards on audit evidence and using the work of an expert.

31. The anti-money laundering legislation requires UK auditors to report the laundering of the proceeds of conduct which takes place overseas if that conduct would constitute an offence in any part of the UK, subject to certain exceptions. The anti-money laundering legislation does not change the scope of the audit and does not therefore impose any requirement for the UK parent company auditor to change or add to the normal instructions to auditors of overseas subsidiaries. However, when considering

non-UK parts of the group audit the UK parent company auditor will need to consider whether information obtained as part of the group audit procedures (for example reports made by non-UK subsidiary auditors, discussions with non-UK subsidiary auditors or discussions with UK and non-UK directors) gives rise to knowledge or suspicion, or reasonable grounds for knowledge or suspicion, such that there is a requirement for the UK parent company auditor to report to SOCA.

Further enquiry

32. Once the auditor suspects a possible breach of law or regulations, the auditor will need to make further enquiries to assess the implications of this for the audit of the financial statements. Auditing standards on laws and regulations require that when the auditor becomes aware of information concerning a possible instance of non-compliance, the auditor should obtain an understanding of the nature of the act and the circumstances in which it has occurred, and sufficient other information to evaluate the possible effect on the financial statements. Where the auditor knows or suspects, or has reasonable grounds to know or suspect, that another person is engaged in money laundering, a disclosure must be made to the firm's MLRO or, for sole practitioners, to SOCA. The anti-money laundering legislation does not require the auditor to undertake any additional enquiries to determine further details of the predicate criminal offence. If the auditor is genuinely uncertain as to whether or not there are grounds to make a disclosure, the auditor will bring the matter to the attention of the audit engagement partner who may wish to seek advice from the MLRO.

33. In performing any further enquiries in the context of the audit of the financial statements the auditor takes care not to alert a money launderer to the possibility that a report will be or has been made, especially if management and/or the directors are themselves involved in the suspected criminal activity.

Reporting to the MLRO and to SOCA

34. In the UK, auditors report to their MLRO or, in the case of sole practitioners, to SOCA where they know or suspect, or have reasonable grounds to know or suspect, that another person is engaged in money laundering. Money laundering reports need to be made irrespective of the quantum of the benefits derived from, or the seriousness of, the offence. There are no de minimis concessions applicable to the auditor contained in POCA, the ML Regulations or the TA 2000. There is no provision for the auditor not to make a report even where the auditor considers that the matter has already been reported (although in such cases the 'limited intelligence value' report may be appropriate).

35. However, the auditor is not required to report where:

   • the auditor does not have the information to identify the money launderer and the whereabouts of any of the laundered property, or

- the auditor does not believe, and it is unreasonable to expect the auditor to believe, that any information held by the auditor will or may assist in identifying the money launderer or the whereabouts of any of the laundered property.

For example, a company involved in the retail business is likely to have been the victim of shoplifting offences, but information that the auditor has is unlikely to be able to identify the money launderer or the whereabouts of any of the laundered property, and the auditor is therefore not normally required to report knowledge or suspicion of money laundering arising from such a crime.

36. Where suspected money laundering occurs wholly or partially overseas in relation to conduct that is lawful in the country where it occurred, the position is more complicated, and the auditor needs to be careful to ensure that the strict requirements of POCA have been satisfied if no report is to be made to the MLRO or to SOCA. In these circumstances, the auditor considers two questions:

- where the client or third party's money laundering is occurring wholly overseas: is the money laundering lawful there? If it is, a report is not required. However, auditors need to be careful to ensure that no consequences of the criminal conduct are, in fact, occurring in the UK;

- where the client or third party's money laundering is occurring in the UK in relation to underlying conduct which occurred overseas and was lawful there: would the conduct amount to a 'serious offence' under English law[13] if it had occurred here? If it would have amounted to such an offence, a report is required.

The duties to report on overseas money laundering activity are complex as they rely on knowledge of both overseas and UK law. In practice auditors may choose to report all overseas money laundering activity to their MLRO.

37. During the course of the audit work the auditor might obtain knowledge or form a suspicion about a prohibited act that would be a criminal offence under POCA sections 327, 328 or 329 but has yet to occur. Because attempting or conspiring to commit a money laundering offence is in itself a money laundering offence, it is possible that in some circumstances a report might need to be made.

38. Where the auditor has made a report to the MLRO and the MLRO has decided that further enquiry is necessary, the auditor will need to be made aware of the outcome of the enquiry to determine whether there are any implications for the audit report or the decision to accept reappointment as auditor.

39. The format of the internal report made to the MLRO is not specified by the ML Regulations. MLROs determine the form in which partners and staff in audit firms

---

[13] A 'serious offence' is conduct that would constitute an offence punishable by imprisonment for a maximum term in excess of 12 months if it occurred in any part of the UK, with the exception of:
   (a) an offence under the Gaming Act 1968;
   (b) an offence under the Lotteries and Amusements Act 1976; or
   (c) an offence under section 23 or 25 of the Financial Services and Markets Act 2000.

report knowledge or suspicion of, or reasonable grounds to know or suspect, money laundering offences internally to their MLRO, although this will need to provide the MLRO with sufficient information to enable a report to be made to SOCA if necessary. Reporting as soon as is practicable to the MLRO is the individual responsibility of the partner or audit staff member and although suspicions would normally be discussed within the engagement team before deciding whether or not to make an internal report to the MLRO this should not delay the report to the MLRO and, even where the rest of the engagement team disagrees, an individual should not be dissuaded from reporting to the MLRO if the individual still considers that it is necessary. In the case of a sole practitioner, who is not required to appoint an MLRO, the sole practitioner reports directly to SOCA.

40. The MLRO makes the decision as to whether a report is made by the audit firm to SOCA. Suspicious Activity Reports may be made using one of SOCA's forms and methods of submission (http://www.soca.gov.uk/financialIntel/suspectActivity.html). The SOCA reporting guidance permits aggregated reporting of suspicious activity that meets the SOCA criteria for 'limited intelligence value' reporting. These criteria are defined in SOCA guidance notes for completing the 'limited intelligence value' report form available on the SOCA website.

41. The timing of reporting by the MLRO to SOCA, or in the case of a sole practitioner their report to SOCA, is governed by section 331(4) of POCA which requires the disclosure to be made "as soon as is practicable" after the information or other matter comes to the attention of the MLRO. In practice this does not always mean "immediately". The timing of reports will be influenced by whether:

- the information includes time sensitive information (that may, for example, allow the recovery of proceeds of crime if communicated immediately) in which case the report will be made quickly;

- further information is required before a report can be made to SOCA, in which case, a report will be made as soon as all the required information has been obtained;

- the information indicates a minor irregularity but there is nothing to suggest dishonest behaviour, in which case a 'limited intelligence value' report can be made as soon as possible after the completion of the audit[14].

Guidance on the reporting of knowledge and suspicions by the MLRO to SOCA is given in section 7 of the CCAB Guidance.

42. Partners and staff in audit firms follow their firm's internal documentation procedures when considering whether to include documentation relating to money laundering reporting in the audit working papers. However, in order to prevent 'tipping off' where

---

[14] For the purposes of this Practice Note 'completion of the audit' is interpreted as being no later than the date the auditor's report is signed, although if there is likely to be a significant period between the date the audit work is completed and the date the auditor's report is signed the auditor considers submitting relevant reports earlier.

another auditor or professional advisor has access to the audit file, the auditor may wish to have all details of internal reports held by the MLRO and exclude these from client files.

Legal privilege

43. Legal privilege can provide a defence for a professional legal adviser to a charge of failing to report knowledge or suspicion of money laundering and is generally available to the legal profession when giving legal advice to a client or acting in relation to litigation.[15] If the auditor is given access to client information over which legal professional privilege may be asserted (for example, correspondence between clients and solicitors in relation to legal advice or litigation) and that information gives grounds to suspect money laundering, the auditor considers whether the auditor is nevertheless obliged to report to the MLRO. There is some ambiguity about how the issue of legal privilege is interpreted and a prudent approach is to assume that legal privilege does not extend to the auditor. Where the auditor is in possession of client information which is clearly privileged (for example, a solicitor's advice to an audit client), the auditor seeks legal advice to determine whether that privilege can be extended to the auditor.

'Tipping off' and prejudicing an investigation

44. In the UK, 'tipping off' is an offence for individuals in the regulated sector under section 333A of POCA. This offence arises:

   (a) When an individual discloses that a report (internal or external) has already been made where the report is based on information that came to that individual in the course of a business in the regulated sector and the disclosure by the individual is likely to prejudice an investigation which might be conducted following the internal or external report that has been made; or

   (b) When an individual discloses that an investigation is being contemplated or is being carried out into allegations that a money laundering offence has been committed and the disclosure by the individual is likely to prejudice that investigation and the information on which the report is based came to a person in the course of a business in the regulated sector.

45. There are a number of exceptions to this offence under sections 333B, 333C and 333D of POCA, including where disclosures are made:

---

[15] Statutory Instrument 2006/308 "The Proceeds of Crime Act 2002 and Money Laundering Regulations 2003 (Amendment) Order 2006" extended this defence to accountants, auditors or tax advisers who satisfy certain conditions where the information on which their suspicion of money laundering is based comes to their attention in privileged circumstances (as defined in POCA section 330(10)). Examples may be where a client provides information in connection with the provision by the auditor of advice on legal issues such as tax or company law. The giving of such advice would not normally arise as a result of an audit engagement, but may arise where the auditor has an additional contract with the client, to provide advisory services. In such circumstances, the auditor may discuss their money laundering suspicions with the MLRO without requiring the MLRO to make a disclosure to SOCA. Guidance on privilege reporting exemption is given in section 7 of the CCAB Guidance.

- to a fellow auditor employed by a firm that shares common ownership, management or control with the audit firm (some network firms may not meet this test);

- to an auditor in another firm in the EEA (or an equivalent jurisdiction for money laundering purposes, where both are subject to equivalent confidentiality and data protection obligations), in relation to the same client and a transaction or service involving them both, for the purpose of preventing a money laundering offence;

- to a supervisory authority for the person making the disclosure;

- for the purpose of the detection, investigation or prosecution of a criminal offence (whether in the UK or elsewhere);

- where the auditor is acting as a relevant professional adviser, to the client, for the purpose of dissuading the client from engaging in an offence; or

- in circumstances where the person making the disclosure does not know or suspect that the disclosure is likely to prejudice an investigation.

46. A further offence of prejudicing an investigation is included in section 342 of POCA. Under this provision, it is an offence to make any disclosure which is likely to prejudice an investigation of which a person has knowledge or suspicion, or to falsify, conceal, destroy or otherwise dispose of, or cause or permit the falsification, concealment, destruction or disposal of, documents relevant to such an investigation.

47. ISA (UK and Ireland) 260 requires the auditor to communicate significant findings from the audit with those charged with governance of an entity. The auditor will consider whether there is a need to communicate suspicions of money laundering to those charged with governance of an entity. As set out above, under section 333D of POCA a tipping off offence is not committed by an auditor (when he or she is acting as a relevant professional adviser) where a disclosure is made to the client in order to dissuade the client from engaging in a money laundering offence (for example, where an employee is engaged in money laundering using the client's financial systems, the auditor may inform the client of the situation in order to prevent the client from committing a money laundering offence). However, care will be taken as to whom the disclosure is made where senior management of the client or those charged with governance are or are suspected to be involved in the money laundering activity or complicit with it. For example, where a client develops a policy approved by the directors that duplicate payments on its invoices will not be returned to customers and that no credit is given against further invoices, the company may be committing a criminal offence (see Example 2 in Appendix 1 of this Practice Note).

Reporting to obtain appropriate consent

48. In addition to the auditor's duty to report knowledge or suspicion of, or reasonable grounds to know or suspect, money laundering under POCA sections 330 and 331, the auditor may need to obtain appropriate consent to perform an act which could otherwise constitute a principal money laundering offence (subject to the SOCPA

amendments to sections 327, 328 and 329 for overseas activities[16]). For example, if the auditor suspected that the audit report was necessary in order for financial statements to be issued in connection with a transaction involving the proceeds of crime, or if the auditor was to sign off an auditor's report on financial statements for a company that was a front for illegal activity, the auditor might be involved in an arrangement which facilitated the acquisition, retention, use or control of criminal property under section 328 of POCA. In these circumstances, in addition to the normal procedures, the auditor would generally need to obtain appropriate consent from SOCA via the MLRO as soon as is practicable. Consent may be given expressly or may be deemed to have been given following the expiry of certain time limits specified in section 336 of POCA. Where applicable the auditor understands the applicable time limits. Further guidance on seeking appropriate consent is given in section 8 of the CCAB Guidance.

49. The auditor will also need to consider whether continuing to act for the company could itself constitute money laundering, for example if it amounted to aiding or abetting the commission of one of the principal money laundering offences in sections 327, 328 or 329 of POCA, or if it amounted to one of the principal money laundering offences itself, in particular the offence of becoming involved in an arrangement under section 328 of POCA. In those circumstances the auditor may want to consider whether to resign, but should firstly contact the MLRO, both to report the suspicions and to seek guidance in respect of 'tipping off'. If the auditor wishes to continue to conduct the audit the auditor, through the MLRO, may need to seek appropriate consent from SOCA for such an action to be taken.

50. Appropriate consent from SOCA will protect the auditor from committing a principal money laundering offence but will not relieve the auditor from any civil liability or other professional, legal or ethical obligations. As an alternative to seeking appropriate consent, the auditor may wish to consider resignation from the audit but, in such circumstances, is still required to disclose suspicions to the MLRO. Further guidance on resignation is given in paragraphs 56 to 60 below.

Reporting to regulators

51. Reporting to SOCA does not relieve the auditor from other statutory duties. Examples of statutory reporting responsibilities include:

- *audits of entities in the financial sector*: the auditor has a statutory duty to report matters of 'material significance' to the FSA which come to the auditor's attention in the course of the audit work;

- *audits of entities in the public sector*: auditors of some public sector entities may be required to report on the entity's compliance with requirements to ensure the

---

[16] It is not a money laundering offence for a person to deal with the proceeds of conduct which that person knows, or believes on reasonable grounds, occurred in a particular country or territory outside the UK, and which was known to be lawful, at the time it occurred, under the criminal law then applying in that country or territory, and does not constitute a 'serious offence' under English law (see footnote 13).

regularity and propriety of financial transactions. Activity connected with money laundering may be a breach of those requirements; and

- *audits of other types of entity:* auditors of some other entities are also required to report matters of 'material significance' to regulators (for example, charities and occupational pension schemes).

52. Knowledge or suspicion, or reasonable grounds for knowledge or suspicion, of involvement of the entity's directors in money laundering, or of a failure of a regulated business to comply with the ML Regulations would normally be regarded as being of material significance to a regulator and so give rise to a statutory duty to report to the regulator in addition to the requirement to report to SOCA. In determining whether such a duty arises, the auditor follows the requirements of auditing standards on reporting to regulators in the financial sector and considers the specific guidance dealing with each area set out in related Practice Notes. A tipping off offence is not committed when a report is made to that person's supervisory authority or in any other circumstances where a disclosure is not likely to prejudice an investigation.

The auditor's report on financial statements

53. Where it is suspected that money laundering has occurred the auditor will need to apply the concept of materiality when considering whether the auditor's report on the financial statements needs to be qualified or modified, taking into account whether:

- the crime itself has a material effect on the financial statements;

- the consequences of the crime have a material effect on the financial statements; or

- the outcome of any subsequent investigation by the police or other investigatory body may have a material effect on the financial statements.

54. If it is known that money laundering has occurred and that directors or senior staff of the company were knowingly involved, the auditor will need to consider whether the auditor's report is likely to include a qualified opinion on the financial statements. In such circumstances the auditor considers whether disclosure in the report on the financial statements, either through qualifying the opinion or referring to fundamental uncertainty, could alert a money launderer.

55. Timing may be the crucial factor. Any delay in issuing the audit report pending the outcome of an investigation is likely to be impracticable and could in itself alert a money launderer. The auditor seeks advice from the MLRO who acts as the main source of guidance and if necessary is the liaison point for communication with lawyers, SOCA and the relevant law enforcement agency.

Resignation and communication with successor auditors

56. The auditor may wish to resign from the position as auditor if the auditor believes that the client or an employee is engaged in money laundering or any other illegal act,

particularly where a normal relationship of trust can no longer be maintained. Where the auditor intends to cease to hold office there may be a conflict between the requirements under section 519 of the Companies Act 2006 for the auditor to deposit a statement at a company's registered office of any circumstances that the auditor believes need to be brought to the attention of members or creditors and the risk of 'tipping off'. This may arise if, for example, the circumstances connected with the resignation of the auditor include knowledge or suspicion of money laundering and an internal or external disclosure being made. See section 9 of CCAB Guidance for guidance on cessation of work and resignation.

57. Where such disclosure of circumstances may amount to 'tipping off', the auditor seeks to agree the wording of the section 519 disclosure with the relevant law enforcement agency and, failing that, seeks legal advice. The auditor seeks advice from the MLRO who acts as the main source of guidance and if necessary is the liaison point for communication with lawyers, SOCA and the relevant law enforcement agency. The auditor may as a last resort need to apply to the court for direction as to what is included in the section 519 statement.

58. The offence of 'tipping off' may also cause a conflict with the need to communicate with the prospective successor auditor in accordance with legal and ethical requirements relating to changes in professional appointment. For example, the existing auditor might feel obliged to mention knowledge or suspicion regarding suspected money laundering and any external disclosure made to SOCA. Under section 333C of POCA this would not constitute 'tipping off' if it was done to prevent the incoming auditor from committing a money laundering offence. However, as an audit opinion is rarely used for money laundering purposes, this is unlikely to apply in an audit situation.

59. If information about internal and external reports made by the auditor is considered relevant information for the purposes of paragraph 9 of Schedule 10 of the Companies Act 2006[17], the auditor considers whether the disclosure of that information would constitute a 'tipping off' offence under section 333A, because it may prejudice an investigation. If the auditor considers a 'tipping off' offence might be committed, the auditor speaks to SOCA to see if they are content that disclosure in those circumstances would not prejudice any investigation. The auditor may, as a last resort, need to apply to the Court for directions as to what is disclosed to the incoming auditor.

60. Where the only information which needs to be disclosed is the underlying circumstances which gave rise to the disclosure, there are two scenarios to consider:

- Where the auditor only wishes to disclose the suspicions about the underlying criminal conduct and the basis for those suspicions, the auditor will not commit an

---

[17] Statutory Instrument 2007/3494 "The Statutory Auditors and Third Country Auditors Regulations 2007" came into force on 6th April 2008 and introduced a new Schedule 10 to the Companies Act 2006 which requires Recognised Supervisory Bodies to have rules obliging auditors to make available all relevant information held in relation to holding the office as auditor to a successor auditor.

offence under POCA if that information only is disclosed. For example, if audit files are made available to the incoming auditor containing working papers that detail circumstances which have lead the audit team to suspect the management of a fraud and this suspicion is noted on the file, this will not constitute a 'tipping off' offence[18].

- If the auditor wishes to disclose any suspicions specifically about money laundering (for example, if the working papers in the example above indicated that the suspected fraud also constituted a suspicion of money laundering), then as a matter of prudence, the approach adopted follows that described in paragraphs 56 and 57 in relation to the section 519 statement.

---

[18] Where the auditor knows or suspects that a confiscation, civil recovery, detained cash or money laundering investigation is being or is about to be conducted, the auditor also considers section 342 of POCA, which creates an offence of prejudicing an investigation. If the auditor suspects that the disclosure of the working papers would be likely to prejudice that investigation, the auditor takes the approach described in paragraphs 56 and 57 above in relation to the section 519 statement.

Appendix 1

Examples of situations that may give rise to money laundering offences that auditors may encounter during the course of the audit

These are examples of some of the situations that auditors may encounter during the course of the audit and some of the factors that auditors may wish to bear in mind when considering reporting suspicions of money laundering. They are intended to demonstrate the breadth of the money laundering legislation. This is not an exhaustive list of offences, nor a guide as to how such offences must be dealt with. The best way to deal with suspected money laundering will vary according to the particular facts of each case and should be dealt with in accordance with the firm's procedures.

The examples are based on the legislation and SOCA guidance current at the time the Practice Note was finalised. Auditors will wish to consider whether SOCA guidance has been updated as well as the extent to which they are prepared to follow any SOCA guidance, particularly if SOCA states in its guidance that in a particular type of case no report at all is required.

1. Offences where the client is the victim (for example, shoplifting)

The auditor acts for a large retail client. The auditor discovers there has been significant stock shrinkage in a number of stores. The client attributes at least some of this to shoplifting. In addition, the auditor is aware that some of the stores hold files detailing instances when the police have been called to deal with shoplifters caught by the security guards.

POCA does not require the auditor to undertake further enquiry outside the auditor's normal audit work to determine whether an offence has occurred or to find out further details of the offence. Accordingly, the auditor does not need to review the files containing the details of the police being called, unless the auditor would otherwise have done so for the purposes of the audit.

Where the auditor does not believe that the client's information will or may assist in identifying the shoplifter or the whereabouts of any of the goods stolen by the shoplifter, for example where the identity of the shoplifters cannot be deduced from the information and the proceeds have disappeared without trace, the auditor decides not to make a report to the MLRO.

In the circumstances where the information possessed by the client will assist in identifying the shoplifter or the whereabouts of any of the goods stolen by the shoplifter, the auditor must make a report to the MLRO briefly describing the situation and stating where the information on the identity of shoplifters may be found.

2. Offences that indicate dishonest behaviour (for example, overpayments not returned)

Some customers of the audit client have overpaid their invoices and some have paid twice. The auditor discovers that the audit client has a policy of retaining all overpayments by customers and crediting them to the profit and loss account if they are not claimed within a year.

The auditor considers whether the retention of the overpayments might amount to theft by the audit client from its customer. If so, the client will be in possession of the proceeds of its crime, a money laundering offence.

In the case of minor irregularities where there is nothing to suggest dishonest behaviour, (for example where the client attempted to return the overpayments to its customers, or if the overpayments were mistakenly overlooked), the person making the report may be satisfied that no criminal property is involved and therefore a report is not required.

If there are no such indications that the company has acted honestly, the auditor concludes that the client may have acted dishonestly. Following the firm's procedures, which take into account the SOCA guidance about minor irregularities where dishonest behaviour is suspected, and about multiple suspicions of limited intelligence value which arise during the course of one audit, the auditor must make a report to the MLRO but may do so at the end of the audit, briefly describing the situation and any other matters of limited intelligence value.

3. Companies Act offences that are civil offences (for example, illegal dividend payments)

During the course of the audit, the auditor discovers that the audit client has paid a dividend based on draft accounts. Audit adjustments subsequently reduce distributable reserves to the extent that the dividend is now illegal under the Companies Act.

The auditor recognises that the payment of an illegal dividend is not per se a criminal offence because the Companies Act imposes only civil sanctions on companies making illegal distributions and decides not to report the matter to the MLRO.

4. Offences that involve saved costs (for example, environmental offences)

The client has a factory which manufactures some of the goods sold in its retail business. In the course of reviewing board minutes, the auditor discovers that the client has been disposing of waste from the factory without a proper licence. There are concerns that pollutants from the waste have been leaking into a nearby river. The client is currently in discussion with the relevant licensing authorities to try to get proper authorisation.

The auditor has reasonable grounds to suspect that the client may have committed offences of disposing of waste without the relevant licence and of polluting the nearby river. The client has saved the costs of applying for a licence. It is also apparent that its methods of disposing of the waste are cheaper than processing it properly. These saved costs may represent the benefit of the client's crime. The client is in possession of the benefit of a crime and the auditor therefore suspects that it has committed a money laundering offence.

The firm's procedures take into account the SOCA guidance which states that in the case of regulatory matters, where the relevant government agency is already aware of an offence which also happens to be an instance of suspected money laundering, a limited intelligence value report can be made. A limited intelligence value report can also be made where the only benefit from criminal conduct is in the form of cost savings.

The authorities are aware of the licensing issue and the pollution of the nearby river. As the only benefit to the company is in the form of cost savings, the auditor decides to include this matter in the limited intelligence value report to the MLRO at the end of the audit.

Alternatively, if the client has accrued for back licence fees, fines and/or restitution costs, there may be no remaining proceeds to the original offence and therefore no need to report.

5.   **Conduct committed overseas that is a criminal offence under English law (for example, bribery, because English Law on bribery applies to overseas conduct)**

The client plans to expand its retail operations into a country where it has not operated before. Construction of its first outlets is underway and it is in consultation with the overseas Government about obtaining the necessary permits to sell its goods (although these negotiations are proving difficult). The client has engaged a consultancy firm to oversee the implementation of its plans and liaise 'on the ground', although it is not clear to the auditor exactly what the firm's role is. The auditor notices that the payments made to the firm are very large, particularly in comparison to the services provided. The auditor reviews the expenses claimed by the consultant and notes that some of these are for significant sums to meet government officials' expenses.

The auditor considers whether the payments may be for the consultant to use in paying bribes, for example to obtain the necessary permits. The country is one where corruption and facilitation payments are known to be widespread. The auditor makes some enquiries about the consultancy firm but cannot establish that it is a reputable business.

Taking into account compliance with legislation relating to 'tipping off' the auditor questions the client's Finance Director about the matter and the FD admits that the consultant has told him that some 'facilitation payments' will be necessary to move the project along and the FD agreed that some payments should be made to get the local officials to do the jobs that they should be doing anyway; for example, to get the traffic police to let the construction vehicles through nearby road blocks. The FD thought that such payments were acceptable in the country in question.

The auditor suspects that bribes have been paid and the auditor is aware that currently bribery of government officials is a criminal offence under UK law, even where it occurs wholly outside the UK, under Part 12 of the Anti-terrorism Crime and Security Act 2001. Although the relevant sections of the Anti-terrorism Crime and Security Act will be repealed when relevant provisions of the Bribery Act 2010 come into force, bribery of a foreign public official will remain a criminal offence under Section 6. In addition, under the Bribery Act 2010, when the provisions of Section 7 come into force, a commercial organisation is guilty of a bribery office if it cannot show that it has adequate procedures to prevent bribery. Accordingly, the auditor decides to make a full report to the MLRO.

6. Lawful Conduct Overseas which would amount to a serious offence if it occurred in England and Wales (for example, a cartel operation)

The client's overseas subsidiary is one of three key suppliers of goods to a particular market in Europe. The subsidiary has recently significantly increased its prices and margins and its principal competitors have done the same. There has been press speculation that the suppliers acted in concert, but publicly they have cited increased costs of production as driving the increase. Whilst this explains part of the reason for the increase, it is not the only reason because of the increase in margins.

On reviewing the accounting records, the auditor sees significant payments for consultancy services. He seeks an explanation for these costs and is informed that these relate to the recent price increase. Apparently, this related to an assessment of the impact of the price increase on the market as well as some compensation for any losses the competitors suffered on their business outside of Europe. Some of the increased profits have flowed back to the client parent company. The client informs the auditor that there is not a criminal cartel offence under local law.

The auditor has a number of concerns:

- the subsidiary may be engaged in conduct amounting to money laundering overseas. However, because the conduct is not criminal there it also does not constitute money laundering under local law. No report is therefore required about the subsidiary.

- the parent company has received profits from the subsidiary and may therefore be engaged in money laundering in England. The auditor suspects that the subsidiary's conduct, whilst lawful where it occurred, would be unlawful under English law if it was committed here, since the auditor suspects that the agreement to fix prices would have been dishonest. The auditor therefore makes a full disclosure to the MLRO.

In rare circumstances where the auditor is also concerned about being involved in a prohibited arrangement, the auditor also needs to consider whether the overseas conduct would amount to a serious criminal offence if it was committed in England and Wales. As a cartel offence is serious a report would be made to the MLRO and the auditor would await consent from the MLRO before proceeding further.

7. Offences committed overseas that are not criminal offences under UK law (for example, breach of exchange controls and importing religious material)

During the course of the audit, the auditor forms a suspicion that one of the overseas subsidiaries has been in breach of a number of local laws. In particular:

- Dividends have been paid to the parent company in breach of local exchange control requirements.

- The subsidiary has imported religious materials intended for the preaching of a particular faith, which is contrary to the laws of that jurisdiction.

Money laundering offences include conduct occurring overseas which would constitute an offence if it had occurred in the UK. Because the UK has no exchange control legislation and the preaching of any faith is allowed it is possible that neither of the offences committed by the overseas subsidiary constitute offences under UK law. The auditor considers whether any other offence might have been committed if this conduct took place in the UK, but the auditor decides not to make a report to the MLRO in these circumstances.

Appendix 2

Guidance as to whom the anti-money laundering legislation applies

The requirement to make a report under section 330 and 331 of POCA applies to information which comes to a person in the course of a business, or an MLRO, in the regulated sector. That information may relate to money laundering by persons or businesses inside or outside the regulated sector.

The offence of failing to report that another person is engaged in money laundering applies to all money laundering, including conduct taking place overseas that would be an offence if it took place in the UK (see paragraph 36 of this Practice Note). For that reason there may be an obligation to report information arising from the audit of non-UK companies or their subsidiaries.

When is an auditor in the UK regulated sector?

The regulated sector includes any firm or individual who acts in the course of a business carried on in the UK as an auditor.

A person is eligible for appointment as an auditor if the person is a member of a recognised supervisory body, (which is a body established in the UK which maintains and enforces rules as to the eligibility of persons to seek appointment as an auditor and the conduct of audit work, and which is recognised by the Secretary of State by Order) and is eligible for appointment under the rules of that body. A person will fall within the regulated sector in their capacity as an auditor when carrying out statutory audit work within the meaning of section 1210 of the Companies Act 2006. In summary, this comprises the audit of UK private or public companies, building societies, friendly societies, Lloyds syndicate aggregate accounts, insurance undertakings, limited liability partnerships, qualifying partnerships[19], and any other such bodies as the Secretary of State may prescribe by Order.

For the purposes of this Practice Note the anti-money laundering reporting requirements apply to all partners and staff within a UK audit firm who are involved in providing audit services in relation to statutory audit work (see above) in the UK. Where they become involved in audit work in the UK, such persons may include:

- Experts from other disciplines within the UK audit firm.

- Employees (both audit partners and staff and experts from other disciplines) of non-UK audit firms.

Where they are not involved in audit work in the UK such persons may fall within other parts of the regulated sector. For example, the provision of accountancy services to other persons by way of business is within the regulated sector regardless of whether the person

---

[19] These are defined by the "Partnerships (Accounts) Regulations" 2008/569.

providing the services is or is not a member of a UK professional auditing/accountancy body.

It is unlikely that it will be practicable or desirable for a UK audit firm which is within the regulated sector to distinguish for reporting purposes between partners and staff who are providing services in the regulated sector and those who are not. Accordingly, UK audit firms may choose to impose procedures across the firm requiring all partners and staff to report to the firm's MLRO[20].

The following table illustrates how the reporting requirements might apply to a number of different audit/client scenarios.[21] This table is intended as a guide and it is recognised that there may be factual scenarios which do not fall within the categories above. In case of any doubt, auditors should refer to the provisions of POCA and the ML Regulations, which take precedence over any guidance in this Appendix.

Persons	Offence discovered as part of audit of:	
	UK companies (including UK subsidiaries of UK or non-UK companies)	Non-UK companies (including non-UK subsidiaries of UK or non-UK companies)
• working in UK for UK audit firm	Yes	Yes. The auditor is unlikely to be carrying out statutory audit work within the meaning of s.1210 of the Companies Act 2006, however, the auditor or firm would likely be providing accountancy services and therefore fall within the UK regulated sector.
• working in UK for non-UK audit firm[22]	Possibly. Where the auditor or audit firm is not eligible for appointment as a UK auditor, in practice, it is likely that the auditor or firm would be providing accountancy services and therefore fall within the UK regulated sector.	
• seconded to UK audit firm	Yes	Yes – as above, the auditor or firm is likely to be providing accountancy services.

---

[20] Persons outside the regulated sector are not obliged to report to their MLRO under POCA section 330 and section 331 (the 'failure to report' offence), but can make voluntary reports under POCA section 337 of information they obtain in the course of their trade, profession, business or employment which causes them to know or suspect, or gives reasonable grounds for knowing or suspecting, that another person is engaged in money laundering. Such reports are protected from breach of client confidentiality in the same way as reports made under POCA section 330 and section 331.

[21] The audit/client reporting scenarios do not take into account the exemptions for activities occurring outside the UK.

[22] It is recognised that it would not be possible for a non-UK audit firm or auditor to be appointed as the auditor of a UK company. However, this category has been included for completeness.

Persons	Offence discovered as part of audit of:	
	UK companies (including UK subsidiaries of UK or non-UK companies)	**Non-UK companies (including non-UK subsidiaries of UK or non-UK companies)**
• working temporarily outside UK or on foreign secondments, or working permanently outside UK but employed by a UK audit firm	The position of an auditor working temporarily outside the UK or on foreign secondments, or working permanently outside the UK but still within a UK audit firm (but not necessarily employed by the UK firm), is more difficult. For example the duty to report may be influenced by the terms of the secondment. The following is a non-exhaustive list of issues to consider and firms may wish to take legal advice in relation to the need for their employees to comply with the UK's money laundering reporting regime as well as any local legal requirements. Issues to consider include: • If the auditor's work outside the UK is part of a UK audit then in some circumstances that information may have come to the auditor's attention in the course of engaging in UK regulated activities and therefore be reportable. • In the case of an auditor working permanently outside the UK for a UK firm, it may be appropriate to consider whether the auditor is working at a separate firm or at a branch office of a UK firm. • An auditor should be particularly cautious about any decision not to make a report on their return to the UK if the information relates to work that the auditor is undertaking in the UK. • Regardless of the strict legal position, firms may wish to consider putting in place a business-wide anti-money laundering strategy to protect their global reputation and UK regulated business. • An auditor working permanently or temporarily outside the UK considers the anti-money laundering legislation in their host country.	
• working permanently outside UK for non-UK audit firm	No	No

PRACTICE NOTE 15(I)

THE AUDIT OF OCCUPATIONAL PENSION SCHEMES IN IRELAND

CONTENTS

Preface

This Practice Note contains guidance on the application of auditing standards issued by the Auditing Practices Board (APB) to the audit of occupational pension schemes (pension schemes) in Ireland. Audits of pension schemes, where required by applicable legislation in Ireland, may only be carried out by registered auditors.

The Practice Note is supplementary to, and should be read in conjunction with, applicable International Standards on Auditing (UK and Ireland). In October 2009, APB issued an updated series of ISAs (UK and Ireland) that apply to audits of accounting periods ending on, or after, 15 December 2010. This Practice Note will be updated for these new standards during the course of 2010.

This Practice Note sets out the special considerations relating to the audit of pension schemes which arise from the individual ISAs (UK and Ireland). The Practice Note does not and is not intended to provide detailed guidance on the audits of pension schemes, so where no special considerations arise from a particular ISA (UK and Ireland), no material is included.

The trustees of occupational pension schemes are required to meet the general provisions of trust law (taking into account the particular circumstances of pension schemes) and to comply with the provisions of the Pensions Acts, 1990 to 2009 and associated regulations (the PA 1990). In addition, the activities of pension schemes are subject to taxation legislation. Scheme auditors need to be aware of the accounting and auditing implications of these requirements. Auditors of public sector schemes (and other statutory schemes established under separate statute) will need to be aware of the particular legislative requirements relating to the scheme concerned.

This Practice Note has been prepared with advice and assistance from staff of the Pensions Board (PB) and is based on the legislation and regulations in effect at 30 June 2009.

Introduction

1. The purpose of this Practice Note is to give guidance on the application of ISAs (UK and Ireland) to the audit of pension schemes in Ireland. They contain the basic principles and essential procedures, referred to as Auditing Standards, which are indicated in the text of the ISAs (UK and Ireland) in bold type, and with which auditors are required to comply in the conduct of any audit of financial statements.

2. Registered auditors are required to comply with Auditing Standards when conducting audits. This principle applies in the context of pension schemes in the same way as to entities in any sector, irrespective of their size, but the way in which Auditing Standards are applied needs to be adapted to suit the particular characteristics of the entity audited.

3. There is a variety of ways of providing pensions in Ireland. Most pension schemes in Ireland are required to produce annual financial statements and to appoint scheme auditors to report on those financial statements and on the payment of contributions to the scheme. There are some exemptions from the statutory audit requirement, including certain small schemes. Where statutory provisions do not require an audit, a scheme's trust deed and rules may still require its financial statements to be audited: however, a trust deed may not derogate from the statutory provisions in this regard.

4. The guidance in this Practice Note is written primarily for audits of financial statements of pension schemes carried out to meet the requirements of the PA 1990. However the guidance is also applicable to audits undertaken solely under the terms of a scheme's trust deed or other agreement requiring auditors to provide a similar report, including requests from trustees where the scheme is otherwise exempt from audit or for financial statements prepared other than at the normal scheme year end.

Legislative and regulatory requirements

5. Pension schemes operate within a framework of law and regulation which is complex and differs in a number of respects from that applicable to commercial enterprises. This framework involves both trust law and specific statutory provisions, set out primarily in the PA 1990. For a scheme, other than a public sector scheme, to obtain exempt approval for tax purposes it is essential that it is established under an 'irrevocable trust'. To the extent necessary to carry out their audit, it is essential for auditors of pension schemes to have a good understanding of current pensions legislation and associated regulations, including accounting and taxation aspects. In the case of public sector schemes, this extends to the specific requirements applicable to each scheme, which may differ in a number of respects from the requirements of the PA 1990.

Occupational pension schemes – key characteristics

6. The general duties and powers of pension scheme trustees are essentially the same as those of other trustees. The principal elements of their responsibilities under trust law and statute are the proper management of funds provided by sponsoring employers and, where applicable, employees during the course of their employment

so as to provide pension benefits and, subsequently, the payment of these benefits to those entitled to them.

7. Benefits at retirement may be provided by an employer on a funded basis or on an unfunded 'pay-as-you-go' basis. The latter involves payment by the employer of pension commitments out of the employer's available resources when the employee has retired: the provision of pensions in this way involves no advance funding.

8. Broadly, funded pension schemes fall into two principal types, differentiated by the way in which pensions payable are determined. In defined benefit schemes, the pension to be paid is determined in advance, for example by reference to average or final salary levels and accrual of periods of service as a member. By contrast, in defined contribution schemes (also called money purchase schemes) the benefits payable are determined by the extent of funds available when an individual pension commences. Hybrid or mixed benefit schemes may also be established, combining both forms of benefit structure.

9. In the case of schemes providing defined benefits, determining the extent of future obligations to pay pensions and of the funding necessary to meet those obligations requires actuarial assessment. Trustees of such schemes are therefore required to ensure that a scheme actuary is appointed to report on the funding required and the security of accrued and prospective rights of scheme members.

10. Trustees of defined contribution schemes are not normally required to appoint a scheme actuary, although they may take actuarial advice to assess the potential level of benefits available. Some, but not all, defined contribution schemes buy annuities from third parties to avoid uncertainty and the ongoing obligation to pay pensions.

11. Trustees of nearly all funded schemes (other than those schemes frozen prior to 1 January 1997), irrespective of the method of funding, are required by the PA 1990 to prepare and make available to members an annual report. The content of the annual report varies with the type of scheme. The specific information required in the annual report is set out in Schedule B to the Occupational Pension Schemes (Disclosure of Information) Regulations, 2006 (S.I. 301 of 2006) (the 2006 Regulations) and generally comprises the following:

    (a) a trustees' report, giving names of trustees and others acting for them, a review of the management of the scheme, membership statistics and developments during the period;

    (b) an investment report, reviewing the investment policy and performance of the scheme;

    (c) a statement of investment policy principles and a statement of risk where not already included in the trustees' report;

    (d) an actuarial funding certificate from the appointed scheme actuary (generally when the scheme provides defined benefits) and unless the effective date of the certificate is at, or later than, the scheme year end a further statement of the actuarial position at the year end;

(e) a report on the liabilities of the scheme, where it is a defined contribution scheme;

(f) financial statements showing a true and fair view of the financial transactions of the scheme during the period and of the disposition of its assets and liabilities at the end of the period other than liabilities to pay benefits after the scheme year end;

(g) an independent auditors' report on the financial statements; and

(h) auditors' opinions about contributions into the scheme.

The annual report may also include a compliance statement, containing administrative disclosures required by law or made voluntarily.

The PA 1990 requires scheme auditors to be qualified for appointment as an auditor of a company under the Companies Acts, 1963 to 1990 and to be independent of the scheme, and their function is to provide an objective opinion on the scheme's financial statements and statements of opinion in respect of contributions.

12. As indicated above, the statutory regime applying to schemes is complex and forms of scheme are diverse. In addition, because the activities of a scheme are governed by trust law, the scheme auditors need to be aware of the principal terms of the deed or other instrument establishing the scheme. The statutory regime and trust law have a significant effect on the scheme auditors' work, as do other factors concerning the way in which scheme trustees fulfil their responsibilities.

Financial statements

13. The form and content of a pension scheme's financial statements are specified in the 2006 Regulations. These require scheme trustees to make available financial statements which:

- contain specified information, set out in Schedule A to the 2006 Regulations; and

- show a true and fair view of the financial transactions of the scheme during the scheme year and of the amount and disposition as at the end of the scheme year of its assets and of its liabilities, other than liabilities to pay benefits after the end of the scheme year.

14. The 2006 Regulations (Schedule A, Paragraph 5) require the financial statements to state whether the financial statements have been prepared in accordance with the most recent applicable version of the Statement of Recommended Practice 'Financial Reports of Pension Schemes' ('the Pensions SORP')[1] and to indicate any material

---

[1] Issued by the Pensions Research Accountants Group (PRAG) in accordance with the Accounting Standards Board's code of practice for the development and issue of SORPs.

departures from its guidance. The Pensions SORP supplements general accounting principles set out in Financial Reporting Standards and Statements of Standard Accounting Practice, indicating best practice in accounting and financial reporting by pension schemes. Consequently it is normally necessary to follow the guidance in the Pensions SORP in order for pension scheme financial statements to show a true and fair view.

15. The nature of applicable accounting requirements and their effect on auditors' reports are considered in more detail in the Practice Note's section on ISA (UK and Ireland) 700 'The auditors' report on financial statements'.

Contents of the auditors' report on pension scheme financial statements

16. The responsibilities of pension scheme auditors reflect the nature of schemes' financial statements.

17. Occupational pension scheme financial statements exclude estimates of future pension benefits payable. In the case of defined benefit schemes, information about the extent of liabilities for future benefits and the adequacy of the scheme's funding are included in the section of the annual report dealing with the actuary's report. Trustees of defined contribution schemes are required to prepare a report on the liabilities of the scheme at each year end, split between those designated to members and those not designated to members. Because of the nature of defined contribution schemes, the liabilities are generally limited to their assets and the report is therefore usually relatively short and is not subject to audit. Thus, the 2006 Regulations do not require scheme auditors to express an opinion as to whether the financial statements of a pension scheme prepared by or on behalf of its trustees show a true and fair view of its state of affairs but whether the financial statements made available by or on behalf of the trustees:

   (i)   show a true and fair view of the scheme's financial transactions during the scheme year and assets, and liabilities as at the scheme year end, other than liabilities to pay benefits after the end of the scheme year; and

   (ii) contain the information specified in Schedule A to the 2006 Regulations.

18. Scheme auditors are also required to make a statement as to whether in their opinion:

   • the contributions payable to the scheme during the scheme year have been received by the trustees within 30 days of the end of the scheme year; and

   • that such contributions have been paid in accordance with the rules of the scheme and, if appropriate, the recommendation of the actuary.

   Contributions payable include:

   • all contributions deducted from employees

- contributions payable in accordance with the rules of the scheme and, if appropriate, the actuary's recommendations; and

- any additional or special contributions which the employer has committed to pay.

The rules of the scheme will generally include, inter alia, the basis of calculation for contributions, definition of pensionable pay, reference dates for determining pensionable pay and contribution rates.

19. Thus the focus of the scheme auditors' work differs, in certain respects, from that involved in the audit of a commercial entity's financial statements.

20. Scheme auditors' statutory responsibilities under the PA 1990 do not require them to undertake work to determine whether the trustees' report or other sections of the scheme's annual report are properly prepared. The scheme auditors' professional obligations under Auditing Standards are discussed in the section of the Practice Note dealing with ISA (UK and Ireland) 720 'Other information in documents containing audited financial statements'.

Reporting on contributions

21. The 2006 Regulations require the scheme auditors to provide a statement as to whether in their opinion the contributions payable to the scheme during the scheme year have been received by the trustees within 30 days of the end of the scheme year and, in their opinion, have been paid in accordance with the rules of the scheme and, if appropriate, the recommendation of the actuary. The work undertaken by scheme auditors in respect of contributions takes into account both their obligation to report their opinion on the financial statements and, separately, to report whether in their opinion contributions have been received within 30 days of the scheme year end and have been made in accordance with the rules of the scheme and, if appropriate, the recommendation of the actuary. This affects the determination of planning materiality, requiring the scheme auditors to consider more detailed aspects of the receipt of income from contributions than would be the case if reporting on the financial statements alone.

Reporting to the Pensions Board

22. In addition to reporting on a scheme's financial statements, scheme auditors appointed under the PA 1990 are required by section 83 of the Pensions Act 1990 to report directly to the Pensions Board (PB) in certain circumstances. The obligation to report under the section does not require scheme auditors to undertake additional work directed at identifying matters to report over and above that which is necessary to fulfil their obligations under the 2006 Regulations to report on a scheme's financial statements and on the contributions it has received. Scheme auditors are therefore not required to put into place arrangements to detect matters to be reported under section 83; their obligation is limited to reporting those which come to their attention.

23. Guidance on the interpretation of the matters to be reported is set out in the section dealing with Section B of ISA (UK and Ireland) 250. The statutory duty to report certain

matters to the PB applies to both scheme auditors and others, including scheme actuaries. Consequently, scheme auditors who become aware of a matter which may be reportable consider whether to discuss the circumstances with the scheme actuary where this may assist them in forming their opinion as to whether to report to the PB and the content of the report. Section 84 of the Pensions Act 1990 offers protection to scheme auditors making a report in good faith. A report made in good faith to the PB of any matter concerning the state or conduct of a scheme will not breach any duty (such as a duty of confidentiality) to which the person making the report is subject and no liability or action shall lie against that person in any court for so doing.

Going concern

24. The nature of the scheme auditors' statutory opinion and the extent of involvement of the scheme actuary mean that the nature of the scheme auditors' work in relation to going concern differs from that normally undertaken in relation to a commercial entity.

25. The principal liabilities of a defined benefit scheme consist of obligations to pay future pensions, the extent of which are assessed by the scheme actuary rather than the scheme auditors. Such liabilities do not arise in defined contribution schemes, as the benefits payable are determined, broadly speaking, by the extent of funds available and prevailing annuity rates. Nevertheless, the going concern basis is assumed in the preparation of the financial statements of pension schemes. Consequently, scheme auditors need to make enquiries of the trustees in order to determine whether they are aware of factors which may make it necessary to wind up the scheme.

26. This aspect of the scheme auditors' work is discussed further in the section dealing with ISA (UK and Ireland) 570 'Going concern'.

Reliance on third parties

27. Trustees of pension schemes – who do not necessarily have first hand actuarial, accounting or other relevant experience – frequently rely on advice or services from experts in order to fulfil their responsibilities to safeguard the interests of scheme members. The PA 1990 also requires trustees to ensure that actuaries and scheme auditors are appointed and are appropriately qualified.

Reliance on third parties – actuaries

28. To provide the actuarial skills needed to determine the funding requirements of a defined benefit scheme, trustees of such schemes are, in all but a few cases, specifically required by statute to ensure that a scheme actuary is appointed to provide them with necessary valuations and advice. Consideration of the action taken by trustees in response to advice from the scheme actuary consequently forms an important element of the work undertaken by the scheme auditors in order to form an opinion on contributions to a defined benefit scheme. Pension scheme trustees are also required to appoint a Registered Administrator one of whose responsibilities is to prepare an annual report for the scheme.

29. When forming an opinion on the view shown by a scheme's financial statements, scheme auditors are not required to express an opinion as to the completeness or accuracy of the long term liabilities determined by a scheme's actuary; the actuary's certificate and statement are the responsibility of the scheme actuary. However, as set out in the Auditors' Code[2], scheme auditors do not permit their names to be associated with information inconsistent with their report or which they consider to be misleading. Scheme auditors therefore normally seek to discuss with the scheme actuary any matters of mutual interest.

30. To facilitate effective liaison, scheme auditors and scheme actuaries seek agreement from the trustees of a scheme to communication between them as part of their terms of engagement when accepting appointment. Further commentary concerning liaison with the scheme actuary is set out in a separate section of this Practice Note.

Reliance on third parties – investment managers and custodians

31. Investments form the principal asset of a pension scheme, and income from investments is an important element in ensuring that the scheme can meet future pension obligations. The level of funds available and the expected future yield are also important elements of the scheme actuary's valuation of a defined benefit scheme.

32. Generally trustees appoint investment managers to undertake the management of the funds available for investment. The trustees nevertheless retain ultimate responsibility for the proper use of the scheme's funds, and generally are required to determine the investment policy appropriate to a particular scheme's circumstances. A statement of investment policy principles is included in the trustees report or attached to the annual report to scheme members.

33. Scheme auditors take steps to determine that all investments and income from investments due to the scheme are properly reflected in its financial statements. When trustees have appointed an investment manager or custodian to undertake work on the scheme's behalf, scheme auditors consider the controls operated by the trustees over the service provider.

34. Issues relating to obtaining sufficient appropriate evidence when the trustees have delegated some of their functions to investment managers or custodians are discussed in the sections dealing with ISA (UK and Ireland) 402 'Audit Considerations Relating to Entities Using Service Organisations'.

Reliance on third parties – administrators

35. As stated above, the trustees of pension schemes are required under the PA 1990 to appoint a Registered Administrator for the purposes of compliance with certain requirements under the PA 1990, including preparation of the annual report and annual benefit statements for members. Trustees of pension schemes may, if empowered to do so under the rules of the scheme, also delegate aspects of

---

[2] The Auditors' Code is appended to the APB's "Scope and Authority of Pronouncements" (Revised).

administration (although not ultimate responsibility), to a third party (including the sponsoring employer – see below). In such cases, the scheme auditors normally obtain direct access to the relevant records of the third party in order to obtain relevant audit evidence, as discussed in the section dealing with ISA (UK and Ireland) 402.

Reliance on third parties – sponsoring employers

36. In many cases, the relationship between the scheme and the sponsoring employer may consist only of trust or other contractual arrangements relating to the establishment of the scheme. However, in the case of on-going schemes, the sponsoring employer may also provide administrative services. Such services may be the subject of a separate contract between the employer and the trustees.

37. Where trustees delegate administrative functions to the sponsoring employer (or to another service provider), or, where the sponsoring employer has been appointed as Registered Administrator for the purposes of the PA 1990, scheme auditors assess the controls established by the trustees over the work being carried out to ensure inter alia the completeness and accuracy of records maintained by the sponsoring employer (or other service provider) on behalf of the scheme.

Ethical Standards

38. APB Ethical Standards for Auditors apply in the audit of financial statements, including those of pension schemes. Particular issues that the audit engagement partner of a pension scheme has regard to when assessing possible threats to the independence and objectivity and the nature and extent of the safeguards to be applied include:

- any professional relationships that he or his firm have with organisations that contribute to the scheme (e.g. whether the firm also audits the sponsoring employer);

- non-audit services provided to the trustees of the scheme by the firm (e.g. accounting, actuarial, administrative and risk management services), and

- non-audit services provided to the sponsoring employer by the firm.

The APB Ethical Standards include a small number of additional requirements that apply to the audits of listed companies[3]. They provide that an audit firm's policies and procedures will set out the circumstances in which these additional requirements apply to the audits of non-listed clients, taking into consideration the nature of the entity's business, its size, the number of its employees and the range of its stakeholders. These may include some pension schemes.

---

[3] ES1 paragraphs 41 and 42.

The audit of financial statements

ISAs (UK and Ireland) apply to the conduct of all audits in respect of accounting periods commencing on or after 15 December 2004. This includes audits of the financial statements of occupational pension schemes. The purpose of the following paragraphs is to identify the special considerations arising from the application of certain 'bold letter' requirements to the audits of occupational pension schemes, and to suggest ways in which these can be addressed (extracts from ISAs (UK and Ireland) are indicated by grey-shaded boxes below). This Practice Note does not contain commentary on all of the bold letter requirements included in the ISAs (UK and Ireland) and reading it should not be seen as an alternative to reading the relevant ISAs (UK and Ireland) in their entirety. In addition, where no special considerations arise from a particular ISA (UK and Ireland), no material is included.

ISA (UK and Ireland) 200: Objective and General Principles Governing an Audit of Financial Statements

Background note

The purpose of this ISA (UK and Ireland) is to establish standards and provide guidance on the objective and general principles governing an audit of financial statements.

The auditor should plan and perform an audit with an attitude of professional scepticism, recognising that circumstances may exist that cause the financial statements to be materially misstated (paragraph 6).

39. Auditing Standards include a requirement for auditors to comply with the APB's Ethical Standards and relevant ethical guidance issued by the auditors' professional body in the conduct of any audit of financial statements, which apply equally to audits of pension schemes. A fundamental principle is that practitioners should not accept or perform work which they are not competent to undertake. The importance of technical competence is also underlined in the Auditors' Code[2] and states that the necessary degree of professional skill demands an understanding of financial reporting and business. Practitioners should not undertake the audit of pension schemes unless they are satisfied that they have or can attain the necessary level of competence.

40. Before commencing the audit of a pension scheme, a firm ensures that it has enough staff that has adequate knowledge and experience of such audits. Staff involved in an audit of a pension scheme will have a broad understanding, commensurate with the individual's role and responsibilities in the audit process, of:

- the status (e.g. open, closed to new members, closed to future accrual) and nature of the scheme;

- the scheme's trust deed and rules and the benefit structure of the scheme;

- the most significant parts of the relevant regulator's guidance; and

- the relevant general principles of the Pensions SORP.

ISA (UK and Ireland) 210: Terms of Audit Engagements

Background note

The purpose of this ISA (UK and Ireland) is to establish standards and provide guidance on agreeing the terms of the engagement with the client.

The auditor and the client should agree on the terms of the engagement. (paragraph 2)

The auditor should confirm that the engagement letter documents and confirms the auditor's acceptance of the appointment, and includes a summary of the responsibilities of those charged with governance and of the auditor, the scope of the engagement and the form of any reports. (paragraph 5-1)

41. ISA (UK and Ireland) 210 requires that an engagement letter be obtained for all audit appointments.

42. Auditors should not accept the engagement until they have completed pre-acceptance procedures including, for example:

    (i) considering their competence to undertake the engagement (including their ability to identify potential conflicts of interest, and knowledge of the laws and regulations to which the scheme is subject);

    (ii) establishing requisite knowledge of the client, including the nature of the scheme and the benefits payable, the names of the trustees and previous scheme auditors, any investment managers or administrators or other professional advisors, the scheme year-end, and obtaining a copy of the trust deed and rules and the last set of audited financial statements;

    (iii) obtaining from the trustees a written confirmation of resignation of the previous scheme auditors, if any, and permission to correspond with them; and

    (iv) corresponding with the previous scheme auditors.

The letter of engagement

43. The same basic principles used in drafting engagement letters apply in relation to the audit of pension schemes as to the audit of any entity. Practical considerations arising from the particular characteristics of pension schemes are considered below.

44. Paragraph 1-5 of ISA (UK and Ireland) 210 indicates that the term 'client' used in paragraph 1 means the addressee of the scheme auditors' report (the client is the trustee(s)). Consequently, the scheme auditors agree the terms of their engagement with the trustees of the scheme and address their letter of engagement to the trustees.

45. The scheme auditors may consider ensuring that all the trustees receive a copy of the letter, and establishing that the trustees agree to the terms of the engagement by asking for a signed copy of the letter to be returned as confirmation of this. If the trustees are not engaged in the day-to-day running of the scheme, the scheme auditors may wish to request the trustees to send a copy of the engagement letter to the administrators, together with a more detailed description of the audit work to be undertaken and any client assistance to be given.

46. Scheme auditors set out the nature and scope of their audit obligations under the PA 1990 so as to ensure trustees are aware of the extent of those responsibilities. In particular, they include reference to their responsibility to report on the contributions payable to the scheme and to the statutory duty to report to the PB in certain circumstances, making it clear that the duty is to report matters if found, and does not involve undertaking additional work to identify reportable matters.

47. Scheme auditors do not have a right of access under the PA 1990 to information held by third parties. Consequently, it is necessary for scheme auditors to request such information, when necessary for their audit, through the trustees. Scheme auditors therefore include in the engagement letter a paragraph relating to access to third parties to whom the trustees delegate particular functions, and to their records relating to the scheme. Scheme auditors may require information from the:

- administrator;

- investment manager;

- custodian;

- sponsoring employer – or employers where there is a multi-employer scheme – and the sponsoring employer's auditors;

- scheme actuary.

48. In view of the importance of the scheme actuary's work to the information contained in a scheme's annual report, it is normally appropriate for scheme auditors to obtain the trustees' agreement to direct dealings with the scheme actuary, both in terms of ongoing liaison regarding the affairs of the scheme and also in respect of the scheme actuary's and scheme auditors' duty to report certain matters directly to the PB, and to document this agreement in their engagement letter.

49. Scheme auditors may wish to include a term in their engagement letter requiring the trustees to undertake to inform the scheme auditors of any matters which come to their attention which may be relevant to the audit.

50. Trustees may issue other reports to scheme members in addition to the annual report required by statute. For example, they may provide summary reports and financial statements, and periodic newsletters. Where this is the case, the engagement letter also sets out the scheme auditors' responsibilities, if any, in respect of such other

reports. Appendix 4 gives specimen paragraphs for engagement letters for the audit of a pension scheme.

> On recurring audits, the auditor should consider whether circumstances require the terms of engagement to be revised and whether there is a need to remind the client of the existing terms of the engagement. (paragraph 10)

51. The auditor considers annually whether changes to the legal and regulatory requirements may require the terms of the engagement letter to be revised.

**FINANCIAL
REPORTING COUNCIL**

ISA (UK and Ireland) 240: The Auditor's Responsibility to Consider Fraud in an Audit of Financial Statements

Background note

The purpose of this ISA (UK and Ireland) is to establish basic principles and essential procedures and to provide guidance on the auditor's responsibility to consider fraud in an audit of financial statements and expand on how the standards and guidance in ISA (UK and Ireland) 315 and ISA (UK and Ireland) 330 are to be applied in relation to the risks of material misstatement due to fraud. The standards and guidance in this ISA (UK and Ireland) are intended to be integrated into the overall audit process.

In planning and performing the audit to reduce audit risk to an acceptably low level, the auditor should consider the risks of material misstatements in the financial statements due to fraud. (paragraph 3)

The auditor should maintain an attitude of professional scepticism throughout the audit, recognising the possibility that a material misstatement due to fraud could exist, notwithstanding the auditor's past experience with the entity about the honesty and integrity of management and those charged with governance. (paragraph 24)

The auditor should make inquiries of management, internal audit, and others within the entity as appropriate, to determine whether they have knowledge of any actual, suspected or alleged fraud affecting the entity. (paragraph 38)

52. Auditors of pension schemes should be aware that the potential for fraud exists in all schemes. Although due to the nature of pension schemes (not profit-making and not trading) the risk of fraudulent financial reporting can generally be considered to be low, the risk of misappropriation of assets remains. Professional scepticism therefore remains key.

The auditor should make inquiries of those charged with governance to determine whether they have knowledge of any actual, suspected or alleged fraud affecting the entity (paragraph 46).

When obtaining an understanding of the entity and its environment, including its internal control, the auditor should consider whether the information obtained indicates that one or more fraud risk factors are present. (paragraph 48)

53. The trustees of a pension scheme are responsible for ensuring that the assets and revenues of the scheme are adequately safeguarded against the effects of fraud and error through the implementation of appropriate controls. This responsibility remains with trustees even if they have delegated some or all of their executive functions to third parties.

54. Examples of types of fraud which may occur in the context of a pension scheme include:

- misappropriation of assets;

- non-payment of contributions (employee/employer) to the scheme by the employer;

- using assets of the scheme directly or as collateral for borrowing by the employer or an associate of the employer;

- misapplying the assets of a scheme to meet the obligations and expenses of another scheme or of the sponsoring employer;

- buying/selling of scheme assets by the investment manager without the required mandate or authorisation;

- lending of scheme assets by the custodian without authorisation;

- exchange of assets without sufficient valuable consideration (for example, selling assets such as property at below market value);

- assets of the scheme used for the personal preferment of the trustees or used for the personal preferment of an individual scheme member;

- benefit claims by members or their beneficiaries to which they are not entitled – for example, failure to notify a scheme of the death of a true beneficiary;

- creation of fictitious scheme records by the administrator – for example, dummy beneficiary records.

55. These examples are only illustrative and do not cover all situations which may arise. Guidance on the internal control procedures which can be put in place by trustees, and are designed to minimise the risk of fraud or error occurring, is included in the section on ISA (UK and Ireland) 315 'Obtaining an Understanding of the Entity and Its Environment and Assessing the Risks of Material Misstatement'. Instances of actual or suspected fraud are also likely to involve breaches of specific statutory or trust law requirements relating to pension schemes.

56. Examples of conditions or events which may increase the risk of fraud are:

- trustees or scheme management displaying a significant disregard for the various regulatory authorities;

- trustees or scheme management having little or no involvement in the day-to-day administration of the scheme;

- trustees or scheme management having ready access to the scheme's assets and an ability to override any internal controls;

- trustees or scheme management failing to put in place arrangements to monitor activities undertaken by third parties, including the employer;

- trustees or scheme management displaying a lack of candour in dealings with members, the scheme actuary or the scheme auditors on significant matters affecting scheme assets;

- the sponsoring employer operating in an industry with increasing business failures, or itself having financial difficulties;

- significant levels, or unusual types, of related party transactions (including employer-related investments) involving unaudited entities or entities audited by other firms.

57. The audit planning process includes an assessment of the risk of material misstatements, whether arising from fraud or error. Conditions or events which increase the risk of fraud and error include previous experience or incidents which call into question the competence or integrity of persons involved in the operation of the scheme, which include:

- the trustees;

- the sponsoring employer, its directors or staff (and in the case of groups, those of the holding company or subsidiary undertakings);

- third parties to whom the trustees have delegated the conduct of scheme activities, for example:

  – the investment manager (including the insurance company) or investment adviser,

  – the property manager,

  – the scheme administrator,

  – the investment custodian, and

  – payroll administrator (both employee and pensioner payroll);

- professional advisers, principally

  – the actuary, and

  – the lawyer.

58. In assessing the risk of misstatement arising from fraud, scheme auditors also consider the extent of the trustees' involvement in the day-to-day administration of the scheme, their access to its resources and their ability, collectively or individually, to override any internal controls. Additionally, they consider the arrangements the

trustees have put in place to monitor work undertaken by third parties, for example custodianship of investments or the day-to-day administration of the scheme, including those circumstances where the services are provided by the sponsoring employer.

> When performing analytical procedures to obtain an understanding of the entity and its environment, including its internal control, the auditor should consider unusual or unexpected relationships that may indicate risks of material misstatement due to fraud. (paragraph 53)

> The auditor should consider whether analytical procedures that are performed at or near the end of the audit when forming an overall conclusion as to whether the financial statements as a whole are consistent with the auditor's knowledge of the business indicate a previously unrecognised risk of material misstatement due to fraud. (paragraph 85)

59. Detailed guidance on the analytical techniques that may be applied either to obtain an understanding of a scheme or at or near the end of the audit is set out in the section of this Practice Note dealing with ISA (UK and Ireland) 520.

60. Determining which particular trends and relationships may indicate risks of material misstatement due to fraud requires professional judgement. Unusual fluctuations in benefits and other payments, particularly when not matched by matching changes in the number and status of members, may indicate fraudulent activity.

> If the auditor has identified a fraud or has obtained information that indicates that a fraud may exist, the auditor should communicate these matters as soon as practicable to the appropriate level of management. (paragraph 93)

> The auditor should document communications about fraud made to management, those charged with governance, regulators and others. (paragraph 109)

Reporting to management

61. Scheme auditors communicate their findings to the appropriate level of management, unless it is concluded that the suspected or actual instance of fraud ought to be reported to the PB and / or An Garda Síochána and that the auditors no longer have confidence in the integrity of the directors or equivalents (in the case of a pension scheme, the trustees or managers). In this case, the scheme auditors make a report direct to the PB and / or An Garda Síochána in the public interest, without delay and without informing the trustees in advance.

62. In the case of pension schemes where the trustees are not involved in the day-to-day management of the scheme, having delegated this function to staff or a third party, and

it is the latter who are suspected of involvement in fraud, the scheme auditors may consider that it is appropriate to communicate with the trustees in the first instance.

Reporting to addressees of the scheme auditors' report on the financial statements

63. The scheme auditors' report on financial statements is addressed to the trustees of the scheme concerned, and to other parties if required by the trust deed or other applicable rules. Even where an actual or suspected fraud has already been communicated fully to the trustees, the scheme auditors' report on the financial statements includes details of any fundamental uncertainty, or disagreement over disclosure of a suspected or actual instance of fraud having a material effect on the financial statements.

Reporting to third parties

64. Any suspected or actual fraud found at a pension scheme will normally give rise to a statutory duty to report to the regulatory authority (the PB) and An Garda Síochána. Guidance on this area is contained in the section of this Practice Note dealing with Section B of ISA (UK and Ireland) 250.

> When the auditor has concluded that the presumption that there is a risk of material misstatement due to fraud related to revenue recognition is not applicable to the circumstances of the engagement, the auditor should document the reasons for that conclusion. (paragraph 110)

65. Auditors of pension schemes usually rebut the presumption that revenue recognition gives rise to a risk of material misstatement due to fraud. Revenue in a pension scheme is generally comprised of contributions and investment income. Pension schemes are not profit making entities and pension scheme financial statements are not publicly available. Unlike sales revenue of a commercial entity, there is little scope to manipulate revenue of a pension scheme, for example through false invoicing or misuse of credit notes. Given these facts, there is therefore likely to be little incentive for revenue to be fraudulently misstated.

ISA (UK and Ireland) 250: Section A – Consideration of Laws and Regulations in an Audit of Financial Statements

Background note

The purpose of this ISA (UK and Ireland) is to establish standards and provide guidance on the auditor's responsibility to consider laws and regulations in the audit of financial statements.

When designing and performing audit procedures and in evaluating and reporting the results thereof, the auditor should recognise that non-compliance by the entity with laws and regulations may materially affect the financial statements. (paragraph 2)

In accordance with ISA (UK and Ireland) 200, "Objective and General principles Governing an Audit of Financial Statements" the auditor should plan and perform the audit with an attitude of professional scepticism recognising that the audit may reveal conditions or events that would lead to questioning whether an entity is complying with laws and regulations. (paragraph 13)

In order to plan the audit, the auditor should obtain a general understanding of the legal and regulatory framework applicable to the entity and the industry and how the entity is complying with that framework. (paragraph 15)

66. Paragraph 2 of ISA (UK and Ireland) 250 states that auditors should recognise that non-compliance by the entity with laws and regulations may materially affect the financial statements. In the case of a pension scheme, relevant laws and regulations include trust law, and hence the specific requirements of the scheme's governing document (usually a trust deed).

The regulatory framework

67. The regulatory framework within which a pension scheme operates does not alter the nature of the scheme auditors' responsibility to consider laws and regulations in an audit of financial statements, as described by ISA (UK and Ireland 250).

68. The trustees of a pension scheme are responsible for ensuring that the necessary controls are in place to ensure compliance with applicable laws and regulations, and to detect and correct any breaches that have occurred, even if they have delegated some of their executive functions to professional staff or advisers.

After obtaining the general understanding, the auditor should perform further audit procedures to help identify instances of non-compliance with those laws and regulations where non-compliance should be considered when preparing financial statements, specifically:

(a) Inquiring of management as to whether the entity is in compliance with such laws and regulations;

(b) Inspecting correspondence with the relevant licensing or regulatory authorities; and.

(c) Enquiring of those charged with governance as to whether they are on notice of any such possible instances of non-compliance with law or regulations. (paragraph 18)

In the UK and Ireland, the auditor's procedures should be designed to help identify possible or actual instances of non-compliance with those laws and regulations which provide a legal framework within which the entity conducts its business and which are central to the entity's ability to conduct its business and hence to its financial statements. (paragraph 18-1)

Classification of laws and regulations

69. Laws and regulations relevant to the audit of a pension scheme can be regarded as falling into three main categories:

(a) those which relate directly to the preparation of the entity's financial statements, or the inclusion or disclosure of specific items in the financial statements,

(b) those which relate to the payment of contributions to the scheme; and

(c) those which provide a legal framework[4] within which the entity conducts its business and which are central to the entity's ability to conduct its business and hence to its financial statements.

70. Examples of items falling into each of these categories are discussed in the following paragraphs. Laws and regulations which do not fall into any of the above categories need not be taken into account in planning audit work to be undertaken: however, scheme auditors are required to remain alert to the possibility of breaches of other requirements, including trust law, and to investigate any which come to their attention.

---

[4] The PB has issued a series of Codes of Practice, which set out the regulator's expectations of how relevant laws and regulations should be complied with in practice.

Laws relating directly to the preparation of the financial statements

71. ISA (UK and Ireland) 250 requires auditors to obtain sufficient appropriate audit evidence about compliance with those laws and regulations which relate directly to the preparation of, or the inclusion or disclosure of specific items in, the financial statements. The ISA (UK and Ireland) also requires auditors to obtain evidence relating to compliance with laws and regulations where there is a statutory requirement for auditors to report, as part of the audit of financial statements, on whether the entity complies with those provisions.

72. The laws and regulations which relate directly to the preparation of financial statements of pension schemes, or where there is a statutory duty for scheme auditors to report on compliance as part of the audit, are included in the list of relevant legislation set out in Appendix 1. All staff involved in a scheme's audit need a broad understanding of the requirements of the PA 1990, in particular of the principal requirements of the 2006 Regulations and of the general principles of the Pensions SORP. All audit staff should also be aware of the requirement to report certain matters to the PB in accordance with section 83 of the Pensions Act 1990.

73. Further knowledge is required, commensurate with the individual's role and responsibilities in the audit process, of:

    • the trust deed and rules of a particular scheme;

    • the legal and regulatory framework applicable to pension schemes sufficient to meet the requirements of ISAs (UK and Ireland), including:

        – the responsibilities of pension scheme trustees under general trust law and the PA 1990; and

        – responsibilities of registered administrators, the sponsoring employer, any professional adviser or any prescribed person acting in connection with the scheme;

    • the detailed requirements concerning the preparation of the financial statements and other matters on which scheme auditors are required routinely to report.

74. Scheme auditors also gain an understanding of the pension scheme's trust deed and plan and conduct their audit so as to ensure that their audit procedures cover compliance with any special provisions as to the disclosure of information in the financial statements or reporting requirements. Users of the financial statements of a scheme reasonably expect that the transactions recorded within them are authorised by the governing document: hence, in order to show a true and fair view, due regard needs to be given to disclosure of any material non-compliance with the governing document.

Requirements to report on other legal requirements

75. ISA (UK and Ireland) 250 indicates that where statutory requirements exist which require the auditors to report, as part of the audit of the financial statements, whether the entity complies with certain provisions of laws or regulations, the auditors need to have a sufficient understanding of such laws and regulations and to test for compliance with such provisions.

Laws relating to the payment of contributions to the scheme

76. Scheme auditors are required, as part of their audit report on the financial statements, to give a statement as to whether in their opinion the trustees of the scheme have received contributions within 30 days of the scheme year end. The scheme auditors are also required to report on whether in their opinion contributions have been paid to the scheme in accordance with the rules of the scheme and with the recommendation of the actuary, if appropriate.

77. Issues that may require consideration include:

   - the date on which any change in the recommended contribution rate commences and its effect on employer contributions (and, where relevant, on employee contributions);

   - the correct basis of deduction (i.e. definition of pensionable earnings);

   - the arrangements made by the trustees to implement the actuary's recommendation (where appropriate); and

   - where annual benefit statements are issued to members showing the contributions made by them and on their behalf what queries, if any, have been raised by members on these statements.

Laws which are central to the pension scheme's conduct of its activities and to its financial statements

78. ISA (UK and Ireland) 250 requires auditors to carry out specified steps to help identify possible or actual instances of non-compliance with those laws and regulations which fall into the category of those that are central to the entity's ability to conduct its business.

79. 'Central' is described in the ISA (UK and Ireland) as relating to those laws and regulations where:

   (a) compliance is a pre-requisite of obtaining a license to operate; or

   (b) non-compliance may reasonably be expected to result in the entity ceasing operations, or call into question the entity's status as a going concern.

80. In the context of pension schemes, these two criteria indicate that laws and regulations are central to a particular scheme when breaches would have any of the following consequences:

   (a) action by the Revenue Commissioners to rescind tax exempt approved status (for example, as a result of a change to the constitution or the nature and value of benefits provided which do not comply with the legislation); or

   (b) action by the PB under sections 63-64 of the Pensions Act 1990 to remove or replace the scheme's trustees. Action to remove trustees can be taken, through an application to the High Court, where in the opinion of the PB the trustees have failed to carry out their duties or the rights and the interests of the members are jeopardised.

   The PB has the power to appoint trustees where there are no trustees or the trustees cannot be found.

81. The Pensions Ombudsman may also make recommendations concerning remedial action necessary in particular cases, which may lead to investigation and action by the PB. Scheme auditors therefore include a review of correspondence with that body, as well as correspondence with the PB and the Revenue Commissioners, as part of their procedures to assess the risk of non-compliance with laws and regulations which are central to a pension scheme.

82. In addition, each scheme is bound to comply with the terms of its governing document. Failure to comply will constitute a breach of trust, which may form grounds for intervention by the PB. Determination of laws and regulations which are central to a particular scheme therefore requires consideration of its governing document, as well as applicable laws and regulations and the requirements of trust law and statute.

Money laundering

> In the UK and Ireland, when carrying out procedures for the purpose of forming an opinion on the financial statements, the auditor should be alert for those instances of possible or actual non-compliance with laws and regulations that might incur obligations for partners and staff in audit firms to report money laundering offences. (paragraph 22-1)

83. Auditors in Ireland have reporting obligations under anti-money laundering legislation to report knowledge or suspicion of money laundering or terrorist financing offences to An Garda Siochána. The impact of the detailed legislation on auditors can broadly be summarised as follows:

   • money laundering includes concealing, disguising, converting, transferring, removing, using, acquiring or possessing property resulting from criminal conduct; the anti-money laundering legislation contains no de minimis concessions;

- partners and staff in audit firms are required to report suspicions that a criminal offence, giving rise to direct or indirect benefit from criminal conduct has been committed, regardless of whether that offence has been committed by a client or by a third party; and

- partners and staff in audit firms need to be alert to the dangers of making disclosures that are likely to prejudice an investigation as this will constitute a criminal offence under the anti-money laundering legislation.

Failure by an auditor to report knowledge or suspicion of money laundering is a criminal offence.

84. Trustees of pension schemes have no specific statutory responsibilities in connection with money laundering over and above those which apply generally to individuals and organisations.

The Criminal Justice (Theft and Fraud Offences) Act, 2001

85. Section 59 of the Criminal Justice (Theft and Fraud Offences) Act, 2001 (the "Theft and Fraud Act") requires a relevant person, including an auditor, to report to a member of An Garda Síochána in circumstances where information or documents indicate that certain offences under the Theft and Fraud Act may have been committed by a client or by its management or employees.

86. Section 59(2) of the Theft and Fraud Act states:

> "Where the accounts of a firm, or as the case may be any information or document mentioned in subsection (1) (b), indicates that – an offence under this Act (....) may have been committed by the firm concerned, or such an offence may have been committed in relation to its affairs by a partner in the firm or, in the case of a corporate or unincorporated body, by a director, manager, secretary or other employee thereof, or by the self-employed individual person concerned, the relevant person shall, notwithstanding any professional obligations of privilege or confidentiality, report that fact to a member of the Garda Síochána."

87. A "firm" above includes a pension scheme.

88. There are many reportable offences in the Act.

89. The Consultative Committee of Accountancy Bodies, Ireland has obtained legal advice to the effect that, within an accountancy practice, the term "relevant person" applies to the engagement partner, as the individual responsible for the audit or advice as the case may be.

Reporting to the Pensions Board

90. If the same circumstances that give rise to a report under the anti-money laundering legislation or a report under the Theft and Fraud Act also give rise to a belief that there was, is or may be a material misappropriation or a fraudulent conversion of the

resources of the pension scheme then there is an obligation to report that belief to the PB under section 83 of the Pensions Act 1990.

91. Even if the circumstances that gave rise to a report under anti-money laundering legislation or a report under the Theft and Fraud Act do not give rise to a belief that there was, is or may be a material misappropriation or a fraudulent conversion of the resources of the pension scheme, a scheme auditor may nonetheless wish to make voluntary report to the PB. Section 84 of the Pensions Act 1990 offers protection to scheme auditors making a voluntary report in good faith. A report made in good faith to the PB of any matter concerning the state or conduct of a scheme will not breach any duty (such as a duty of confidentiality) to which the person making the report is subject and no liability or action shall lie against that person in any court for so doing.

92. When reporting to the PB, partners and staff in audit firms need to be alert to the dangers of prejudicing an investigation under the anti-money laundering legislation.

Reporting non-compliance with law or regulations

The auditor should, as soon as practicable, either communicate with those charged with governance, or obtain audit evidence that they are appropriately informed, regarding non-compliance that comes to the auditor's attention. (paragraph 32)

Reporting to management

93. ISA (UK and Ireland) 250 requires auditors to communicate their findings to the appropriate level of management, unless they conclude that the suspected or actual instance of non-compliance ought to be reported to a 'proper authority' in the public interest and that they no longer have confidence in the integrity of the directors or equivalents (in the case of a pension scheme, the trustees or managers).

94. In this case, the scheme auditors make a report direct to a proper authority in the public interest, without delay and without informing the trustees in advance. In those cases where the trustees are not involved in the day-to-day management, having delegated this function to others, and it is the latter who are suspected of involvement in the breach of law or regulations, the scheme auditors may consider that it is appropriate to discuss the matter with the trustees in order to form an opinion as to whether to report to the PB.

Reporting to the addressees of the auditors' report on the financial statements

95. The scheme auditors' report on financial statements is addressed to the scheme's trustees. Although an actual or suspected breach of law or regulations may already have been reported to the trustees, the scheme auditors' report on the financial statements is nevertheless required to include details of any fundamental uncertainty, or disagreement over disclosure of a suspected or actual instance of non-compliance having a material effect on the financial statements.

Reporting to third parties

96. ISA (UK and Ireland) 250 deals with the reporting of actual or suspected non-compliance with law and regulations to third parties, in particular reporting to a 'proper authority' in the public interest. The ISA (UK and Ireland) states that the auditors only report to an authority 'with a proper interest to receive the information'. In the case of pension schemes, the proper authority is normally the PB and in the event of fraud includes An Garda Síochána.

ISA (UK and Ireland) 250: Section B – The Auditor's Right and Duty to Report to Regulators in the Financial Sector

The auditor of a regulated entity should bring information of which the auditor has become aware in the ordinary course of performing work undertaken to fulfil the auditor's audit responsibilities to the attention of the appropriate regulator without delay when:

(a) The auditor concludes that it is relevant to the regulator's functions having regard to such matters as may be specified in statute or any related regulations; and

(b) In the auditor's opinion there is reasonable cause to believe it is or may be of material significance to the regulator. (paragraph 2)

Where an apparent breach of statutory or regulatory requirements comes to the auditor's attention, the auditor should:

(a) Obtain such evidence as is available to assess its implications for the auditor's reporting responsibilities;

(b) Determine whether, in the auditor's opinion, there is reasonable cause to believe that the breach is of material significance to the regulator; and

(c) Consider whether the apparent breach is criminal conduct that gives rise to criminal property and, as such, should be reported to the specified authorities. (paragraph 39)

The regulatory framework

97. Pension schemes operate within a complex legal framework determined by general trust law and specific statutory provisions. The PA 1990 introduced specific statutory requirements concerning key areas of trustees' responsibilities and scheme administration which supplement, but do not replace, the requirements of trust law.

98. The PA 1990 established the PB to monitor and supervise the operations of the PA 1990 and pensions' development generally, and to issue guidelines and guidance notes in furtherance thereof. The PA 1990 provides the PB with a variety of powers (set out in Appendix 2 of this Practice Note) that it can use on application to the High Court to ensure that trustees and others comply with the legal requirements for the proper administration of pension schemes.

99. Appendix 2 contains a short description of the legal and regulatory framework for pension schemes.

100. Section 83 of the Pensions Act 1990 placed a duty on relevant persons (including scheme trustees, scheme auditors and actuaries) to report to the PB in writing where they have

> *'reasonable cause to believe that a material misappropriation or a fraudulent conversion of the resources of a scheme........... has occurred is occurring or is to be attempted.* ("a Reasonable Cause to Believe")'

101. The purpose of the statutory duty to report introduced by section 83 of the Pensions Act 1990 is to strengthen the protection of scheme assets and the system of regulation of pension schemes in Ireland by requiring scheme auditors and others (relevant persons) to communicate in particular circumstances with the PB, so assisting it in the exercise of its functions.

102. Although the title of ISA (UK and Ireland) 250: Section B refers to reports to regulators in the financial sector, the principles and essential procedures included in ISA (UK and Ireland) 250: Section B are equally applicable in respect of this statutory duty of scheme auditors under section 83 of the Pensions Act 1990 to report to the PB.

103. Even where there is no duty to report under section 83 of the Pensions Act 1990 there may be circumstances in which scheme auditors wish to make a voluntary report to the PB. Issues to be considered in relation to voluntary reporting to the PB are discussed below in paragraphs 119 to 123 below.

104. The obligation to report under section 83 of the Pensions Act 1990 does not require scheme auditors to undertake additional work directed at identifying matters to report over and above that which is necessary to fulfil their obligations under the 2006 Regulations and under Auditing Standards. Scheme auditors are therefore not required to put into place arrangements to detect matters to be reported under section 83 of the Pensions Act 1990; their obligation is limited to reporting those where a Reasonable Cause to Believe comes to their attention.

Duty to report to the PB

105. The following paragraphs should be read in conjunction with ISA (UK and Ireland) 240: 'The Auditor's Responsibility to Consider Fraud in an Audit of Financial Statements'.

106. Scheme auditors conducting activities under the PA 1990 need to assess information of which they become aware in the course of their work which indicates that a "material misappropriation" or a "fraudulent conversion" of scheme resources has occurred, is occurring or is to be attempted. The PA 1990 does not require scheme auditors to perform any additional audit work as a result of the statutory duty nor are scheme auditors required specifically to seek out breaches of the requirements applicable to a particular scheme. However, in circumstances where scheme auditors identify that a reportable matter may exist, they carry out such extra work, as considered necessary, to determine whether the facts and circumstances give them Reasonable Cause to Believe. This may require the scheme auditors to seek information from the sponsoring

employer, or any participating employer, its auditors or other third parties[5]. It should be noted that the scheme auditors' work does not need to prove that the reportable matter exists.

107. It should be noted the word 'material' in the phrase 'material misappropriation' does not have the same meaning as 'materiality', in the context of the materiality limits set, for the audit of the financial statements and the scheme auditors should consider the guidance set out in paragraphs 113 to 118.

108. Guidance notes provided by the PB refer to misappropriation as occurring when any of the scheme assets are appropriated by any person who is not entitled to them under the provisions of the scheme or under relevant laws or are appropriated for the use or benefit of any person otherwise than in accordance with the provisions of the scheme and any relevant laws. They note that a misappropriation need not necessarily be fraudulent but if it is, as it is likely to be fraudulent conversion, it must be automatically reported. If the misappropriation is not fraudulent, it should still be reported if it is material.

109. Guidance notes from the PB state that there is a fraudulent conversion of the resources of a scheme when any of the scheme assets are, with intent to defraud, converted to the use or benefit of any person other than the persons for whose benefit they are required to be applied under the provisions of the scheme or under relevant law. Fraudulent conversion must always be reported, whether the amounts involved are material or not.

110. The determination of whether a matter is, or is likely to be, a material misappropriation or a fraudulent conversion inevitably requires scheme auditors to exercise their judgment. In forming such judgments, scheme auditors need to consider not simply the facts of the matter but also their implications. In addition, it is possible that a matter, which is not a material misappropriation in isolation, may become so when other possible matters are considered.

111. In forming an opinion as to whether a matter is likely to constitute a material misappropriation, scheme auditors may wish to liaise with other relevant persons. This procedure helps to ensure that the cumulative effect of all breaches is considered and not only those identified by one professional adviser. It is important to ensure that the audit terms of engagement allow discussions with the scheme actuary and other advisers in this context. It may also be helpful to enquire of trustees whether they are aware of any statutory or voluntary reports to the PB by others within the scheme year under review.

112. In the context of ISA (UK and Ireland) 250: Section B, where an apparent breach of statutory or regulatory requirements comes to the auditors' attention, they should:

---

[5] In circumstances where the scheme auditors are uncertain whether an action or inaction constitutes a breach of law, they clarify the legal requirements to the extent necessary to decide whether they have a Reasonable Cause to Believe, as defined in section 83 of the Pensions Act 1990, that the law has been broken.

- obtain such evidence as is available to assess its implications for their reporting responsibilities;

- determine whether, in their opinion, there is a Reasonable Cause to Believe; and

- consider whether the apparent breach gives rise to a potential money laundering offence and, as such, should be reported to the specified authorities.

113. In assessing the effect of an apparent breach of duty which has come to their attention, scheme auditors take into account the quantity and type of evidence concerning such a matter which may reasonably be expected to be available. If the scheme auditors conclude that they have been prevented from obtaining all such evidence concerning a matter which may give rise to a duty to report, this may in itself provide foundation for a Reasonable Cause to Believe.

114. Matters are likely of themselves to give rise to a duty to report to the PB only if there is a Reasonable Cause to Believe. In these circumstances surrounding facts must be taken into account in determining the impact of the breach of law or legal duty.

115. The existence of incomplete accounting records is not a reportable matter of itself but may cause auditors to consider whether there may also be a matter giving rise to a Reasonable Cause to Believe.

Voluntary reports to the PB

116. Where a matter has come to light which does not trigger a duty to report under section 83 but is nonetheless a matter that is likely to be of concern to the PB scheme auditors should consider making a voluntary report to the PB. For example, voluntary reporting should be considered for significant breaches of law.

117. Matters which may cause the scheme auditors to consider making a voluntary report to the PB require careful consideration in the light of both:

- the gravity of the matter taken alone; and

- its implications when considered with other information known to the scheme auditors.

118. The potential gravity of some matters may be such that an individual matter is likely of itself to warrant the consideration by the PB of the use of its powers of application to the High Court to have any individual removed from acting as trustee, to have a new trustee appointed or otherwise to intervene in the running of a scheme.

119. All matters which are likely to be of interest to the PB therefore require careful assessment irrespective of their apparent individual significance. Matters which, of themselves, may not be of the gravity described in paragraphs 120 or 121 may be indicative of a general lack of compliance with legal requirements or of a more significant breach of duty, which is likely to be of interest to the PB.

120. Section 84 of the Pensions Act 1990 provides legal protection to any person making a voluntary report to the PB of any matter concerning the state and conduct of the scheme. The purpose is to enable persons to make voluntary reports in good faith without incurring liability. The types of matters which might be covered in such a voluntary report might include:

- fraudulent conversions or material misappropriation, reported by a person who is not obliged to make a compulsory report under section 83 of the Pensions Act 1990, e.g. a member of the scheme who becomes aware of material misappropriation or fraudulent conversion;

- any breach of the PA 1990, especially if any breaches were persistent and raised serious concerns about the running of the scheme;

- maladministration which the person making the report believes to be sufficiently serious to warrant a report to the PB;

- any matter which the person making the report believes would be of interest to the PB.

Prior to making a report it may be useful to discuss the issue of concern with the PB in order to establish if a report is warranted.

121. Insofar as the law permits, the PB will consider bringing a matter to the attention of the scheme auditors if it believes that the matter is of such importance that it could significantly affect the form of the scheme auditors' report on the scheme's financial statements or the way in which they discharge their other reporting responsibilities.

122. However, scheme auditors need to be aware that there will be circumstances in which the PB is unable to disclose information concerning a pension scheme which could affect their judgment as to the view given by its financial statements or whether a breach of law is likely to be of interest to the PB. Therefore scheme auditors proceed on the basis of the information available to them and do not make assumptions as to its interaction with information which may be held by the PB.

123. On completion of their enquiries, scheme auditors ensure that the facts and circumstances and the basis for their conclusion as to whether to report to the PB are adequately documented such that the reasons for their decision may be clearly demonstrated should the need to do so arise in future.

Conduct of the audit

124. Paragraph 34 of ISA (UK and Ireland) 250: Section B states that: 'The auditor should ensure that all staff involved in the audit of a regulated entity have an understanding of the following:

(a) the provisions of applicable legislation;

(b) the regulator's rules and any guidance issued by the regulator; and

(c)   any specific requirements which apply to the particular regulated entity.

appropriate to their role in the audit and sufficient (in the context of that role) to enable them to identify situations which may give reasonable cause to believe that a matter should be reported to the regulator.'

125. As stated above, the PA 1990 does not require scheme auditors to perform any additional work as a result of the statutory duty to report to the PB under Section 83 of the Pensions Act 1990 or as a result of any voluntary report made under that section, nor are they required specifically to seek out instances of material misappropriation or fraudulent conversion applicable to a particular pension scheme. However, scheme auditors should include procedures within their planning process to ensure that members of the audit team have sufficient understanding (in the context of their role) to enable them to recognise material misappropriation and fraudulent conversion and that such matters are reported to the audit engagement partner without delay so that a decision may be made as to the impact on the audit and potential reporting responsibilities.

126. The numbers of staff involved in the audit of a pension scheme will vary, depending on its size and complexity. While specific expertise will also vary, all staff will be aware of the main features of a pension scheme audit. In addition, at least the staff who are involved in a scheme's audit team in a supervisory or review role should have an understanding of the following :

- the general principles of the Pensions SORP;

- the principal requirements of Pensions Regulations;

- the PB Guidance, in particular Reporting to the PB;

- the trust deed and rules of the particular scheme; and

- the standards and guidance in Section B of ISA (UK and Ireland) 250.

127. Further knowledge is required, commensurate with the individual's role and responsibilities in the audit process, of:

- the legal and regulatory framework applicable to pension schemes sufficient to meet the requirements of ISAs (UK and Ireland), including:

  - the responsibilities of pension scheme trustees under general trust law and the PA 1990;

  - the responsibilities of registered administrators, the sponsoring employer and any relevant person acting in connection with the scheme; and

- the detailed requirements concerning the preparation of the financial statements and other matters on which scheme auditors are required routinely to report.

An overview of the major features of the legal and regulatory framework is set out in Appendix 2.

Protection for a scheme auditor making a report to the PB

128. Scheme auditors owe a duty of confidentiality to the trustees of a pension scheme in the same way as they do to any other audit client. However section 84 of the PA1990 makes it clear that scheme auditors will not incur any liability for breach of this duty or any other duty if they make a report in good faith to the PB. Section 84 of the Pensions Act 1990 states:

> 'Where a person makes a report, whether in writing or otherwise, in good faith to the Board of any matter concerning the state and conduct of a scheme,............ whether or not that person is a relevant person and whether or not the report is required to be made under section 83, no duty to which the person may be subject shall be regarded as contravened and no liability or action shall lie against the person in any court for so doing.'

129. Hence reporting to the PB under section 83 of the Pensions Act 1990 does not contravene the duty of confidentiality, provided that scheme auditors communicate in good faith, reporting matters in relation to which they have a Reasonable Cause to Believe.

130. Section 84 of the Pensions Act 1990 provides protection not only to a person who makes a compulsory report under section 83 of that Act but also to any person making a voluntary report of any matter concerning the state and conduct of a scheme. Hence a voluntary report made by scheme auditors to the PB, in circumstances where the scheme auditors do not have a duty to report under section 83, does not contravene the duty of confidentiality or any other duty, provided that the report is made in good faith.

131. Section 83 of the Pensions Act 1990 imposes a duty for reports to be made 'as soon as practicable'. However, the duty to report only arises once scheme auditors have concluded that there is a Reasonable Cause to Believe that a material misappropriation or a fraudulent conversion has occurred. In reaching this belief, scheme auditors may wish to take appropriate advice and consult with colleagues or lawyers. The obligation to report as soon as reasonably practicable does not prevent such consultation taking place as part of the process of forming an opinion that a duty to report arises. However, the more serious the nature of the breach, e.g. dishonesty, the more urgently consultation needs to take place.

132. The trustees are the persons principally responsible for the management of the scheme. In forming their opinion, scheme auditors will therefore normally seek to reach agreement with the trustees on the circumstances giving rise to a report to the PB and to understand whether they intend to make a report. However, paragraph 53 of ISA (UK and Ireland) 250: Section B stresses that in some circumstances, immediate notification of a matter giving reasonable grounds to believe that a reportable matter exists will be necessary. Paragraph 54 of ISA (UK and Ireland) 250: Section B also states that:

'When the matter giving rise to a statutory duty to make a report direct to a regulator casts doubt on the integrity of those charged with governance or their competence to conduct the business of the regulated entity, the auditors should, subject to compliance with legislation relating to "tipping off", make the report to the regulator without delay and without informing those charged with governance in advance.'

Therefore scheme auditors cannot undertake to inform trustees in advance of every matter which they bring to the PB's attention.

133. In certain circumstances joint reporting (i.e. a shared report between the trustees and auditors) of breaches to the regulator may be appropriate. A number of difficulties, however, may arise in practice, including:

- delays occurring due to the time taken to agree wording with all the signatories of the joint report, and

- scheme auditors finding it difficult to associate themselves with trustees' descriptions of action plans to avoid further breaches.

In the light of these practical difficulties, the APB recommends that scheme auditors do not delay reporting to the PB in order to participate in a joint report; rather they report to the PB directly once they have concluded that they have a Reasonable Cause to Believe.

Contents of a Report to the PB

134. When making a report concerning a material misappropriation or fraudulent conversion direct to a regulator, in accordance with Section B of ISA (UK and Ireland) 250, auditors are required to:

(a) state the name of the regulated entity concerned;

(b) state the statutory power under which the report is made;

(c) state that the report has been prepared in accordance with ISA (UK and Ireland) 250, Section B 'The Auditor's Right and Duty to Report to Regulators in the Financial Sector' and section 83 of the Pensions Act 1990;

(d) describe the context in which the report is given;

(e) describe the matter giving rise to the report;

(f) request the regulator to confirm that the report has been received; and

(g) state the name of the auditors, the date of the written report and, where appropriate, the date on which an oral report was made to the regulator and the name and title of the individual to whom the oral report was made (paragraph 61 of Section B).

135. Auditors should also refer to the PB's current guidance in relation to the contents of a report available from the PB directly or www.pensionsboard.ie.

Describing the context of a report

136. The description of the context in which the report is given sets out information relevant to a proper understanding of its subject matter, primarily concerning the way in which the matter was identified, and the extent to which it has been investigated and discussed with those responsible for stewardship of the scheme. Matters to which pension scheme auditors may wish to refer include:

- The nature of the engagement from which the report derives. For example, it may be appropriate to distinguish between a report made by the auditors of a defined benefit scheme or defined contribution scheme, who are required to express an opinion on the scheme's financial statements as well as to report on its contributions, and one which arises from a more limited engagement;

- the applicable provisions of the PA 1990 and any interpretations of those provisions which have informed the scheme auditors' judgment;

- The extent (if any) to which the scheme auditors have investigated the circumstances giving rise to the matter reported, including (in the case of defined benefit schemes) whether the matter has been discussed with the scheme actuary or other third parties; and

- whether or not the trustees have taken steps to rectify the matter.

137. Where trustees wish to make a submission to the PB as to the circumstances and steps being taken to address a reportable matter, the scheme auditors may attach such a memorandum or report prepared by the trustees to their report. Where such additional information is provided scheme auditors refer to the additional information in their report, and indicate whether or not they have undertaken additional procedures to determine whether any remedial actions described have been taken.

138. Section 83 of the Pensions Act 1990 refers to a Reasonable Cause to Believe arising in respect of schemes to which they are auditors. It does not specify that the information be obtained in the course of the audit. Accounting firms appointed as scheme auditors of pension schemes may undertake other non-audit work for such schemes, or may undertake work for other individuals (e.g. trustees) or organisations (e.g. administrators). Matters that are potentially reportable to the PB, and which arise in this context should be considered by the accounting firm and if appropriate reported, in accordance with ISA (UK and Ireland) 250: Section B, section 83 of the Pensions Act 1990 and applicable guidance from the PB.

139. Under section 83 (3) of the Pensions Act 1990 a relevant person is guilty of an offence if he fails to make a report in writing as soon as practicable. A relevant person (including a scheme auditor) is also guilty of an offence if he knowingly or wilfully makes a report which is incorrect. The PA 1990 provides for fines and penalties for relevant persons who fail to comply with their obligations and offers a defence for

those who can show that the contravention was attributable to another person failing to comply with Section 83 and that reasonable steps were taken to secure that person's compliance.

140. Section 59 of the Criminal Justice (Theft and Fraud Offences) Act, 2001 requires a relevant person, which would include auditors and would generally include an accountant providing professional services, to report to a member of the Garda Síochána in circumstances where information or documents indicate that certain offences under the Act such as theft, false accounting and forgery, may have been committed by an entity, or by its management or employees.

ISA (UK and Ireland) 260: Communication of Audit Matters with Those Charged with Governance

Background note

The purpose of this ISA (UK and Ireland) is to establish standards and provide guidance on communication of audit matters arising from the audit of financial statements between the auditor and those charged with governance of an entity. These communications relate to audit matters of governance interest as defined in this ISA (UK and Ireland). This ISA (UK and Ireland) does not provide guidance on communications by the auditor to parties outside the entity, for example, external regulatory or supervisory agencies.

The auditor should communicate audit matters of governance interest arising from the audit of financial statements with those charged with governance of an entity. (paragraph 2)

In the UK and Ireland, the auditor should communicate in writing to those charged with governance regarding the significant findings from the audit. (paragraph 16-1)

141. Auditors always issue written communication even if its content is limited to explaining there is nothing the auditors wish to draw to the attention of those charged with governance. However, ISA (UK and Ireland) 260 also stresses that communication should be active, two-way communication between the auditor and those charged with governance. This is unlikely to be achieved if communication is only by way of written reports. It encourages dialogue.

142. Scheme auditors notify trustees of all breaches discovered in the course of their work of duties relevant to the administration of the scheme imposed by any enactment or rule of law on the trustees or managers, the sponsoring employer (or any participating employer), any professional adviser or any prescribed person acting in connection with the scheme, regardless of whether the matter gave rise to a statutory duty to report to the PB. Such notification normally takes place in the course of assessing the consequences of each particular breach: however, scheme auditors may also summarise such breaches in their report of audit matters to those charged with governance.

ISA (UK and Ireland) 300: Planning an Audit of Financial Statements

Background note

The purpose of this ISA (UK and Ireland) is to establish standards and provide guidance on the considerations and activities applicable to planning an audit of financial statements. This ISA (UK and Ireland) is framed in the context of recurring audits. In addition, matters the auditor considers in initial audit engagements are included in paragraphs 28 and 29.

The auditor should plan the audit so that the engagement will be performed in an effective manner. (paragraph 2)

143. In developing the audit plan, the auditors consider the responsibilities as set out in statute or other regulation and the letter of engagement to ensure that the scope of the audit plan is sufficient and includes, where appropriate, reports required by statute.

144. Auditors obtain an understanding of the accounting principles under which the financial statements are prepared and their impact on the audit. Accounting principles for pension schemes include those set out in:

- specific legislation;

- accounting and other recommendations issued by the regulator;

- accounting standards; and

- the Pensions SORP.

The auditor should develop an audit plan for the audit in order to reduce audit risk to an acceptably low level. (paragraph 13)

145. In designing the audit procedures auditors seek, as far as practicable, to make use of the internal controls, work of internal audit (if any) and financial reporting arrangements which are in place at the pension scheme.

The auditor should document the overall audit strategy and the audit plan, including any significant changes made during the audit engagement. (paragraph 22)

146. When planning the work to be undertaken in respect of a pension scheme audit it is important to identify those areas which are key to its operations as reflected in its financial statements. The key areas of most schemes' financial statements include the following:

- contributions receivable;

- self-investment;

- investment income;

- benefits payable; and

- investment assets.

147. In addition to assessing the work to be undertaken to form an opinion on the financial statements, the scheme auditors' plan also takes account of the steps necessary to obtain sufficient appropriate evidence in order to discharge their statutory obligation to report on the payment of contributions.

148. Other areas which may have significant impact depending upon the circumstances of the scheme are transfer values paid and received, administration expenses and debtors and creditors.

149. When planning the work to be undertaken the scheme auditors consider the other information available to the scheme auditors, including:

- minutes of trustee meetings;

- information in the public domain regarding relevant developments at the sponsoring employer;

- membership records; and

- the actuarial valuation report (depending on the type of scheme being audited).

150. When planning the audit of a pension scheme's financial statements, scheme auditors also take into account the importance of the work of third parties in the administration and accounting on behalf of the trustees. Such third parties include the:

- administrator (including the Registered Administrator);

- investment manager;

- investment custodian;

- property manager; and

- sponsoring and participating employer(s).

151. At an early stage in planning the audit, scheme auditors seek agreement with the trustees for necessary access to third parties, when appropriate, and the timing and extent of the information required from them. The principal requirements are normally set out in the scheme auditors' engagement letter. More detailed arrangements for

obtaining access and information are likely to be one of the main subjects of discussion with the trustees, whether at a planning meeting or more informally, before the scheme auditors complete their audit plan.

152. In delegating particular matters to third parties, such as investment managers, trustees are legally obliged to do so in a manner which is consistent with their duty to act prudently. Hence, in addition to exercising care in the selection of advisers and other third parties to whom scheme activities are delegated, trustees need to lay down adequate guidelines for the way the third parties undertake those activities and for monitoring their performance. This is frequently achieved by using service agreements. Where significant functions have been delegated to third parties, scheme auditors review any such agreements with third parties as part of the planning process.

153. How such delegation actually works in practice also has an impact on the control environment and the audit plan. Effective segregation of duties between third parties and regular supervision and direction by the trustees can greatly strengthen the control environment while, in contrast, the blurring of responsibilities and poor communication and co-ordination can weaken the control environment.

154. The sections on ISA (UK and Ireland) 315 'Obtaining an Understanding of the Entity and Its Environment and Assessing the Risks of Material Misstatement', and ISA (UK and Ireland) 402 'Audit Considerations Relating to Entities Using Service Organisations' give guidance on the factors to be considered by scheme auditors when determining the evidence about outsourced functions which is necessary to support their report on the scheme's financial statements.

155. Scheme auditors may wish to discuss their audit plan with the trustees so as to enable the trustees to consider whether they require any specific additional procedures to be performed beyond those necessary to support the audit opinion. For example, the trustees may request the scheme auditors to carry out additional tests on the detailed membership records, or on the calculation of individual benefits, to provide the trustees with added assurance that reliable records are being maintained and that the individual payments being made are in accordance with the rules of the scheme.

ISA (UK and Ireland) 315: Obtaining an Understanding of the Entity and its Environment and Assessing the Risks of Material Misstatement

Background note

The purpose of this ISA (UK and Ireland) is to establish standards and to provide guidance on obtaining an understanding of the entity and its environment, including its internal control, and on assessing the risks of material misstatement in a financial statement audit.

156. The principles of obtaining and using knowledge of the scheme to be audited are the same as those applying to the audit of any entity.

157. However, ISA (UK and Ireland) 315 takes little account of the possible use of service organisations by a reporting entity. When planning an audit of a pension scheme, this ISA (UK and Ireland) should be read in conjunction with ISA (UK and Ireland) 402 'Audit Considerations Relating to Entities Using Service Organisations', which is discussed later in this Practice Note. The discussion in this section focuses on the control environment and controls of the entity (i.e. the pension scheme) itself, rather than those service organisations which may be relevant to the audit.

A. Understanding the Entity and Its Environment, Including Its Internal Controls

The auditor should obtain an understanding of relevant industry, regulatory, and other external factors including the applicable financial reporting framework. (paragraph 22)

Legislative and Regulatory Requirements

158. Pension schemes operate within a framework of law and regulation which is complex and differs in a number of respects from that applicable to commercial enterprises. This framework involves both trust law and specific statutory provisions, set out primarily in the PA 1990. It is essential for auditors of pension schemes to have a good understanding of relevant pensions legislation and associated regulations. In the case of public sector schemes, this extends to the specific requirements applicable to each scheme, which may differ in a number of respects from the requirements of the PA 1990.

Financial Reporting: Legal Requirements and Accounting Standards

159. The form and content of a pension scheme's financial statements are specified in the PA 1990. These require scheme trustees to obtain financial statements which:

(a) contain specified information, set out in Schedule A of the 2006 Regulations; and

(b) show a true and fair view of the financial transactions of the scheme during the scheme year and of the amount and disposition as at the end of the scheme year of its assets and of its liabilities, other than liabilities to pay pensions and benefits after the end of the scheme year.

160. The 2006 Regulations require the trustees to state whether the financial statements have been prepared in accordance with the Statement of Recommended Practice 'Financial Reports of Pension Schemes' (the Pensions SORP) and to indicate any material departures from its guidance. The Pensions SORP supplements general accounting principles set out in Financial Reporting Standards and Statements of Standard Accounting Practice, indicating best practice in accounting and financial reporting by pension schemes. Consequently it is normally necessary to follow the guidance in the Pensions SORP in order for pension scheme financial statements to show the true and fair view required by legislation.

> The auditor should obtain an understanding of the nature of the entity. (paragraph 25)

161. The scheme auditors understanding of the nature of the entity usually includes:

(a) scheme nature and documentation

– trust deed and rules

– the definition of pensionable earnings/pay, where not covered by the above

– membership numbers

– nature of the scheme and type of benefits provided

– scheme booklet

– documentation of the schemes "registered pension scheme" status

– correspondence with the Revenue Commissioners

– Revenue approval

– statement of risks

– internal dispute resolution procedures

(b) scheme governance

– membership of the trustee body and division of responsibilities

- outsourcing arrangements and principal terms of contractual agreements with third party service providers

- correspondence with PB/Pensions Ombudsman

- minutes of meetings of the trustee body and key sub-committees

- internal dispute resolution procedure and any disputes in progress

- arrangements for agreeing contribution rates with the sponsoring employer and taking actuarial advice where necessary

(c) sponsoring and participating employers

- identity of the sponsoring and other participating employer(s)

- agreements with employer(s) and related parties, including any relevant covenants or guarantees supporting the scheme

- details of employer auditors

- arrangements for payments of contributions in accordance with the rules of the scheme and the recommendation of the actuary where appropriate;

- arrangements for ensuring that contributions are paid to the trustees within the time limits specified in the PA 1990.

(d) scheme actuary (where appropriate)

- letter of appointment

- areas of responsibility

- valuation reports

- latest statements and certificates

(e) scheme administration

- responsibilities of pension scheme registered administrator, the sponsoring and participating employer, and any professional advisors or agents acting on behalf of the scheme or trustees;

- service agreements

- division of administrative responsibilities

- documentation of accounting systems and controls

–   accounting and membership records

–   stewardship reports

–   systems and controls documentation

(f)   investments

–   statement of investment policy principles

–   custody arrangements

–   service agreements with investment managers and custodians

–   investment managers' reports

–   nature of investments and extent of employer-related investment, use of complex financial instruments, stock lending, unquoted investments

–   borrowings

–   common investment fund arrangements

–   subsidiaries

–   AVC arrangements

(g)   other advisers

–   relationship/contracts with other advisers

> The auditor should obtain an understanding of the entity's selection and application of accounting policies and consider whether they are appropriate for its business and consistent with the applicable financial reporting framework and accounting policies used in the relevant industry. (paragraph 28)

162. The Pensions SORP provides detailed guidance on appropriate accounting policies. Material departures from the Pensions SORP must be disclosed in the financial statements.

163. In the case of most pension schemes, the following will be the key areas of the financial statements and therefore the choice of accounting policies in these areas will be of most significance to the financial statements:

•   contributions;

•   investments;

- investment return; and

- benefits and transfers.

164. As noted in paragraph 165 above, pension scheme financial statements are required to include a statement as to whether the financial statements have been prepared in accordance with the Pensions SORP and if they have not 'an indication of where there are any material departures from those guidelines'.

165. The principles underlying the Pensions SORP are as follows:

- investment assets are included at their market value, and

- income and expenditure items are included on the accruals basis.

166. As a result, trustees are left with little discretion as to the choice of accounting policies. Therefore the auditors primary concern will be to understand the manner in which these policies have been applied in the particular context of the individual scheme and to ensure that where the trustees have adopted a policy that is not in accordance with the Pensions SORP, such as where some income and expenditure items have been dealt with on the cash basis rather than the accruals basis, either the impact is not material to the financial statements or, where the impact is material, the alternative policy can be justified by the circumstances and is disclosed as a deviation from the Pensions SORP.

> The auditor should obtain an understanding of the entity's objectives and strategies, and the related business risks that may result in material misstatement of the financial statements (ISA (UK and Ireland) 315. (paragraph 30)

167. Scheme auditors need to be aware of the principal terms of the trust instrument governing the particular scheme. This is usually contained in the trust deed and rules which set out the objectives of the scheme and determine the powers of the trustees, along with the more detailed rules in respect of how the scheme affairs should be conducted. Failure to comply with the trust deed and rules would constitute a breach of trust, and may result in the auditor being required to make a report or consider a voluntary report to the PB.

Defined contribution schemes

168. The benefits payable by defined contribution schemes will be directly related to and determined by the assets attributable to an individual member at the date that their pension benefits become payable. The risk that the pension that can be secured with the assets available is inadequate is borne by the member, not the scheme. Therefore in the absence of a loss of the assets due to theft or mismanagement, such a scheme does not face "business risks" that threaten the achievement of the scheme's objective.

Defined benefit schemes

169. Due to the nature of the commitment of defined benefit schemes to pay benefits related to members' salaries and service at or close to retirement, such schemes face a risk of being under-funded, and therefore being unable to meet all benefits in full as they fall due for payment. This situation may arise from a number of factors, including:

    - inadequate contributions;

    - inadequate investment returns; and

    - adverse changes in experience affecting the amount and/or duration of benefit payments (e.g. improvements in pensioner survival).

170. Financial statements of pension schemes record the historical levels of contributions, investment return and benefit payments but are not designed to provide measures of the current or future levels of funding: these measures are provided by the outcomes of the work of the actuary, whose statements sit alongside the audited financial statements within the annual report.

> The auditor should obtain an understanding of the measurement and review of the entity's financial performance. (paragraph 35)

171. Conventional measures of financial performance, such as profit, return on capital or cash flow are typically not relevant to pension scheme financial statements. However the trustees should have procedures in place to monitor investment strategy and performance, and the auditor considers these as part of their audit work.

> The auditor should obtain an understanding of internal control relevant to the audit. (paragraph 41)

172. There is a wide variation between different schemes in terms of size, activity and organisation. Smaller schemes may be administered by the staff of the sponsoring employer or by third party administrators or a combination of both. Larger schemes may employ directly professionally qualified, full-time staff. However, the responsibilities of trustees for ensuring that the scheme is properly administered and its assets properly safeguarded apply irrespective of a scheme's size or administrative arrangements, and the attitude, role and involvement of each scheme's trustees are likely to be fundamental in determining the effectiveness of its control environment.

173. In addition to reviewing accounting systems and the control environment in order to assess the risk of material misstatement in a pension scheme's financial statements, scheme auditors also undertake a review of the arrangements made by the trustees to implement the contribution rates and timing of payments set out in the trust deed and rules (for defined contribution schemes) and as recommended by the actuary (for

defined benefit, hybrid and mixed benefit schemes). The scheme auditor may also undertake work to test the adequacy of internal controls instituted for this purpose.

174. Paragraph 48 of ISA (UK and Ireland) 315 makes it clear that a scheme's use of service organisations is relevant to the auditor's consideration of the controls that are relevant to the audit. For the purpose of compliance with this ISA (UK and Ireland), it is not necessary for the auditor to document and assess the control environment or controls of service organisations so long as his work at entity level has provided him with a sufficient understanding of risk on which to base his planning of audit procedures (see later discussion of ISA (UK and Ireland 402).

> The auditor should obtain an understanding of the control environment. (paragraph 67)

175. Trustees of a pension scheme are responsible for determining and implementing systems of control appropriate to a particular scheme and sufficient to allow them properly to discharge their legal and fiduciary duties.

176. Where trustees delegate the operation of the detailed controls, the trustees focus on the selection, appointment and monitoring of appropriate third party delegates. In the case of outsourced activities, the ultimate responsibility for these functions remains that of the trustees, who should have appropriate controls in place over these arrangements. These may include:

- risk assessment prior to contracting with the service provider, which includes a proper due diligence and periodic review of the appropriateness of the arrangement;

- appropriate contractual agreements or service level agreements;

- contingency plans should the provider fail in delivery of services;

- appropriate management information and reporting from the outsourced provider; and

- appropriate controls over scheme members' information.

177. The maintenance of an effective control environment is as important for pension schemes as it is for other entities, since it is a fundamental duty of pension scheme trustees to protect the assets of the scheme. Failure to do so can render the trustees personally liable for any loss occasioned to the scheme. The scheme auditor's statutory responsibilities do not include any requirement to report to the trustees on the design or operation of a scheme's systems of controls. However, auditing standards require auditors to report any material weaknesses in the accounting and internal control systems identified during the audit to directors (or equivalents) on a timely basis. For pension schemes this would therefore require any such report to be made to the trustees.

178. An effective control environment is likely to include the following features:

   (a) appropriate trustee competence, commitment and involvement;

   (b) properly trained and qualified staff, in relation to the tasks they have to perform;

   (c) adequate segregation of duties. Where the size of the pension scheme does not allow for segregation of duties between administrative staff, supervision by the trustees is especially important;

   (d) the trustees have adequate arrangements to obtain independent professional advice; and

   (e) in the case of larger schemes, budgetary controls in the form of estimates for each financial year of income, expenditure and (where expenses and benefit payments are significant) cash flows, including regular comparisons of actual figures to the estimates. For smaller schemes and in areas where future income and expenditure are difficult to predict (for example special contributions, death benefits, lump sum withdrawals which arise incidentally) trustees or managers may rely on specific procedures to approve items of expenditure and monitor the nature and levels of income and expenditure.

179. Factors taken into account when considering the attitude, role and involvement of a scheme's trustees include:

   • the skills and qualifications of individual trustees;

   • the regularity and effectiveness of trustee meetings;

   • arrangements to monitor adherence to the scheme's statement of investment principles;

   • training undertaken by trustees;

   • compliance with industry guidelines (for example PB Guidance for Trustees);

   • the independence of trustees from each other;

   • the policy on dealing with trustee conflicts;

   • adequacy of minutes of trustee meetings;

   • the division of duties between trustees;

   • the involvement of trustees in supervision and control procedures, including matters such as cheque-signing arrangements;

   • the trustees' attitude towards third parties to whom they delegate the conduct of scheme activities;

- arrangements for trustees to monitor scheme income and expenditure; and

- the attitude of trustees to previously identified breaches or control weaknesses.

> The auditor should obtain an understanding of the entity's process for identifying business risks relevant to financial reporting objectives and deciding about actions to address those risks, and the results thereof. (paragraph 76)

180. Where a scheme has a formal process for identifying business risks, (such as maintaining a risk register) the auditors review the process and consider its outcomes. For schemes without such a process, which is usually the case with smaller schemes, the auditors refer to paragraph 79 of ISA (UK and Ireland) 315.

181. The key operational risk of a defined benefit pension scheme is that it will become under-funded and, as a result, be unable to meet its obligations to pay pensions as they fall due for payment in the future. Pension scheme annual financial statements are not designed to provide a view of the adequacy of a scheme's state of funding and, as a result, this risk is not relevant to annual financial reporting by pension schemes.

> The auditor should obtain a sufficient understanding of control activities to assess the risks of material misstatement at the assertion level and to design further audit procedures responsive to assessed risks. (paragraph 90)

182. Aspects of the control activities which are pensions-related are described below. Control activities which are not specific to pension schemes (such as segregation of duties) are not included in the examples, but are relevant to the auditors' assessment of the components of audit risk.

Control activities

183. In any scheme, key activities consist of receiving contributions, and investing scheme funds to generate capital growth and income. Where members have retired, the scheme will also be involved in securing or paying pension benefits. Examples of controls which trustees may implement in each of these areas where they are material to the financial affairs of the scheme, both to reduce the risk of material misstatements and to minimise the risk of loss of the scheme's assets through fraud, are set out in the table below.

Contributions receivable	controls to monitor and check the accurate and timely receipt of contributions from the employer in accordance with the PA 1990, the scheme rules and/or recommendation of the actuary, such as monitoring date received, comparing contributions received to the prior month or carrying out full reconciliations of contributions received to expected amounts using source data
	procedures to identify special contributions, augmentations, AVCs or life premiums to actuarial advice and employer communications
	agreement of receipts to current membership records
	agreement of receipts to the trust deed and rules and the actuary's recommendation (where appropriate)
	reviewing reports from administrators on the results of checks that membership records are up to date
Benefits payable	agreement of benefits payable to list of current pensioners or beneficiaries
	agreement of benefits payable to scheme rules, actuarial advice, relevant legislation and trust law
	reconciling DC and AVC benefits to provider statements and member records
	scrutiny of claims made on the scheme to determine bona fide
	monitoring of queries arising from benefit statements and monitoring of disputes resolution procedures
Protection of scheme assets and investment return	physical security, where appropriate, over cash, cheques, share certificates, title deeds etc.
	monitoring of investment manager's performance against agreed investment objectives and service levels (including property management where significant)
	use of independent benchmarking services to monitor investment return
	obtaining indemnities from third parties providing services
Monitoring of custody arrangements	monitoring of investment cash flows (including use of budgets and forecasts)
	obtaining service auditor reports on internal controls

184. Trustees may seek to obtain (where available) copies of auditor reports on internal controls from investment and/or property managers, custodians, providers of scheme administration and/or fund accounting where these activities are carried out by third parties on behalf of the trustees.

185. Where trustees obtain copies of such reports, these are likely to provide useful information for scheme auditors in obtaining an understanding of risk and the impact of outsourced activities.

Accounting records

186. Section 59 of the Pensions Act 1990 requires the trustees to ensure that proper membership and financial records in respect of the scheme are kept.

187. The reporting responsibilities of pension scheme auditors do not include a requirement to report a breach of these requirements in their report on financial statements, as is the case for companies and various other entities. However, the auditors consider whether failure by the trustees to ensure that adequate accounting records are kept has implications for their ability to provide an opinion as to whether the financial statements give a true and fair view of the financial transactions of the scheme.

> The auditor should obtain an understanding of how the entity has responded to risks arising from IT. (paragraph 93)

188. Auditors consider whether adequate IT controls exist over financial systems and other systems relevant to the audit, including the administration and membership records.

B. Assessing the Risks of Material Misstatement

> The auditor should identify and assess the risks of material misstatement at the financial statement level, and at the assertion level for classes of transactions, account balances, and disclosures. (paragraph 100)

189. There is a wide variation between different schemes in terms of size, activity and organisation, so that there can be no standard approach to internal controls and risk. Scheme auditors assess risk and the adequacy of controls in relation to the circumstances of each scheme.

190. Factors considered by the auditor in assessing whether there may be an increased level of risk of material misstatement at the financial statement level include:

- complex scheme structure;

- major changes in the operation of the scheme or participating/sponsoring employers;

- outdated trust deed and rules, or a deed and rules with numerous amendments;

- inadequacy of administrative resources;

- informal arrangements for delegation of discretionary decisions;

- employer is the sole trustee;

- cash flow difficulties of the sponsoring or participating employer(s);

- the involvement of the sponsoring employer(s) in corporate acquisitions or disposals;

- previous enquiries by regulatory bodies; and

- experience from previous years' audits.

191. Factors considered by the auditor in assessing whether there may be an increased level of risk of material misstatement at the assertion level include:

- complex contribution arrangements, for example:

  - age-related rates;

  - a complex definition of pensionable earnings;

  - rates which are related to benefit accrual rates (DB arrangements) or which are subject to member choice, possibly with employer matching;

  - rates which are different for different participating employers;

- complex benefit structure, for example:

  - continuous service granted in respect of membership of previous pension arrangements;

  - elements of benefits that are subject to trustees' discretion;

  - "added years" purchased with AVCs;

- membership profile:

  - difficulties in establishing pensioner existence;

  - numbers of members leaving the scheme, giving rise to transfer payments;

  - the death rate among scheme members, and extent of consequential adjustments to benefits payable to surviving spouses;

- non compliance with contributions requirements as to rates and timing as set out in the trust deed and rules or recommended by the actuary;

- investment arrangements:

    –   investment in volatile markets or in assets that are difficult to value;

    –   use of complex financial instruments;

    –   insurance policies, including those linked with life-styling arrangements;

    –   remote location of assets and unregulated custodial arrangements;

    –   non-standard investment classes – works of art, loans;

    –   significant levels of employer-related investment.

> As part of the risk assessment, the auditor should determine which of the risks identified are, in the auditor's judgment, risks that require special audit consideration (such risks are defined as "significant risks"). (paragraph 108)
>
> For significant risks, to the extent the auditor has not already done so, the auditor should evaluate the design of the entity's related controls, including relevant control activities, and determine whether they have been implemented. (paragraph 113)

192. Significant risks may arise from significant changes to the scheme. For example:

- changes in third party service providers (such as a change in the scheme administrator or investment manager) including inadequate transitional procedures;

- a scheme reconstruction;

- changes in sponsoring or participating employers; or

- changes in funding arrangements by the employer.

193. Significant risks may also be presented by the following:

- investment types that are illiquid and/or difficult to value;

- benefits whose calculation are particularly complex and/or involve significant exercise of discretion in individual cases;

- contributions whose rates depend on the specific participating employer within a group, member age and/or members' management status or are variable at the discretion of the member and/or the employer.

194. Where the use of service organisations is relevant to material aspects of the scheme's financial statements, scheme auditors need to have a sufficient understanding of the possible impact of the involvement of the service organisation(s) on financial

information in order to assess the risks of material misstatement in the financial statements that might be controlled by the entity i.e. the trustees.

ISA (UK and Ireland) 320: Audit Materiality

> **Background note**
>
> The purpose of this ISA (UK and Ireland) is to establish standards and provide guidance on the concept of materiality and its relationship with audit risk.

> Materiality should be considered by the auditor when:
>
> (a) Determining the nature, timing and extent of audit procedures; and
>
> (b) Evaluating the effect of misstatements. (paragraph 8)

195. The principles of assessing materiality of a pension scheme to be audited are the same as those applying to the audit of any entity. However, the focus of attention in a set of financial statements of a pension scheme does not correspond to that of a commercial trading entity: net earnings or level of working capital are not among the prime indicators for a pension scheme and therefore when considering materiality the focus is directed at contributions receivable, benefits payable, returns on investment, the levels of other items of income and expenditure and the disposition of the scheme assets.

196. ISA (UK and Ireland) 320 indicates that materiality is considered at both the overall financial statement level and in relation to individual account balances, classes of transactions and disclosures. In the context of pension schemes, materiality is usually based on:

- a percentage of the total value of the assets in the scheme, or

- a percentage of the inflows or outflows from dealings with members.

197. Materiality for pension schemes may vary with the nature of the scheme – defined benefit/defined contribution – and needs to be assessed for each individual scheme rather than applying any general guidelines. It is also important to distinguish, especially for the benefit of the trustees, that materiality in relation to the audit of the pension scheme's financial statements will not necessarily coincide with the expectations of materiality of an individual member of the scheme in relation to his or her expected benefits. Even in the case of defined contribution arrangements, the scheme auditors' judgments about materiality are made in the context of the financial statements as a whole and the account balances and classes of transactions reported in those statements, rather than in the context of an individual member's designated assets, contributions or benefits.

198. The scheme auditors' statement of opinions on contributions require assessment of whether specific conditions have been met. A different level of materiality may be used in relation to the auditors' statement of opinions on contributions than that used in

If the auditor concludes that the activities of the service organisation are significant to the entity and relevant to the audit, the auditor should obtain a sufficient understanding of the entity and its environment, including its internal control to identify and assess the risks of material misstatement and design further audit procedures in response to the assessed risk. (paragraph 7)

209. If the auditors are able to obtain a sufficient understanding of risk on which to base their planning of audit procedures by considering the pension fund's controls and information available to the pension fund, for example by reviewing an auditor report on internal controls, the auditors will not need to supplement that understanding and assessment by making further enquiries about the control arrangements of relevant service providers.

210. If the auditors are unable to obtain a sufficient understanding of risk by considering information and controls at the entity level, the auditors take steps to obtain a more detailed understanding of the control arrangements of relevant service providers by such means as visiting the service organisation or requesting the service organisation's auditors or the entity's internal audit function to perform specified procedures. The feasibility of this approach will depend on whether the contractual arrangements between the trustees and the service provider entitle the trustees to obtain supplementary information when considered necessary.

Based on the auditor's understanding of the aspects of the entity's accounting system and control environment relating to relevant activities, the auditor should:

(a) Assess whether sufficient appropriate audit evidence concerning the relevant financial statement assertions is available from records held at the entity; and if not,

(b) Determine effective procedures to obtain evidence necessary for the audit, either by direct access to records kept by service organisations or through information obtained from the service organisations or their auditor. (paragraph 9-18)

211. Information prepared on behalf of the trustees of a pension scheme by outsourced service providers (e.g. registered administrators) should be considered as being "produced by the entity" and therefore the auditor is required to obtain audit evidence about the accuracy and completeness of that information (see also ISA (UK and Ireland) 500.

Administration of contributions and benefits

212. When a pension scheme uses another organisation or the sponsoring employer to deal with the administration of contributions and benefits and to maintain membership and financial records, the trustees arrange for the scheme auditors to have direct

access to the records and personnel of the relevant organisation acting as scheme administrator.

213. Where particular administrative functions such as the collection of contributions and the payment of benefits are delegated to sponsoring employers, the scheme auditors may, with the agreement of the trustees and the employers, request the employers' auditors or internal auditors to carry out specified procedures and to report their findings to the scheme auditors. Where such auditors are used, the requirements set out in ISA (UK and Ireland) 610 'Considering the work of internal audit' or ISA (UK and Ireland) 600 'Considering the work of another auditor', as applicable, should be followed. If the foregoing methods of obtaining audit evidence are not available to the scheme auditors, they may need to consider whether this will result in a limitation to the scope of their audit which affects their opinions on the financial statements and on the payment of contributions.

Investment management and custody

214. The relationship between the pension scheme and third party investment managers and custodians will often have a significant impact on the source, nature and timing of financial information available to the pension scheme and the accounting records maintained by it.

215. The scheme auditors will wish to consider how the contract(s) between the pension scheme and service organisations, and the manner in which the trustees of the pension scheme ensure compliance with the contract terms, affect audit evidence requirements in relation to the following assertions:

- existence: the investments exist at a given date;

- rights and obligations: the investments pertain to the scheme at the relevant date and any lien or other charge is properly identified;

- occurrence: investment income and purchases and sales of investments pertain to the scheme during the relevant period;

- completeness: there are no unrecorded investments or related assets and liabilities, investment income, transactions or events, or undisclosed items;

- valuation: investments are recorded at an appropriate carrying value;

- measurement: investment transactions are recorded at the proper amount and revenue or expense is allocated to the proper period; and

- presentation and disclosure: investment related items are disclosed, classified and described in accordance with the applicable accounting framework. In the case of pension schemes, the applicable accounting framework is established by the PA 1990, accounting standards issued by the ASB and the Pensions SORP.

216. The principal factors affecting the scheme auditors' judgment as to the extent and nature of audit evidence required in relation to investments managed by a third party are:

(a) the nature and extent of the investment services provided by the third party;

(b) the materiality and inherent risk of the financial statement assertions relating to activities delegated to the service organisations;

(c) the nature and extent of records maintained by the trustees or scheme administrators, and the level of supervision that the trustees exercise over any third parties;

(d) the reputation of the third party for providing accurate and timely information. The reputation of the entity may be enhanced in circumstances where the service provided is subject to regulatory oversight (as is the case in relation to investment management) and there is no evidence of regulatory action against the service organisation having been initiated by the regulator concerned; and

(e) the contract terms between the pension scheme and the various service organisations concerned, and the ways in which the trustees of the pension scheme monitor compliance with the contract terms, including any arrangements for independent check on the actions of one service organisation by another (for example, where duties are segregated between a custodian and investment manager who operate independently of each other).

217. A contract clause whereby the investment manager or custodian indemnifies the scheme in the event of loss caused by maladministration is unlikely to provide information directly relevant to the scheme auditors' judgment concerning the extent of evidence to be obtained in relation to investments and investment income. However, such a clause may, together with information concerning the financial resources available to the service organisation, be relevant to the auditors' understanding of the effect on the scheme's financial statements of performance failure by the investment manager or custodian.

Sources of evidence

218. The trustees or scheme administrator may maintain accounting records which are initiated independently from the investment manager and/or custodian, and are sufficient to monitor the transactions undertaken on behalf of the scheme. When such records are kept, and the scheme auditors' assessment of control risk is low, sufficient appropriate audit evidence may ordinarily be obtained by performing procedures on the records maintained by the scheme administrator, and agreeing them to the extent deemed appropriate with independent confirmations from third parties, including the investment manager and/or custodian.

219. Where trustees or administrators do not maintain accounting records in relation to investments and related transactions which are initiated independently from the investment manager and/ or custodian (for example, where the trustees have given the

investment manager discretionary powers) the scheme auditors consider whether sufficient appropriate audit evidence is available from other sources. Alternative sources of audit evidence are:

(a) Returns and/or confirmations from service organisations: reconciliation of representations from independent service organisations may provide valuable audit evidence especially in relation to the ownership and existence assertions. The quality of such evidence is determined by the degree to which there is segregation of responsibility between the custodian and investment manager. Hence such reconciliations form reliable audit evidence only if the scheme auditors can also obtain evidence that the two entities are operated and managed independently of each other and maintain separate records and databases;

(b) Funds reconciliations: analytical review of reconciliations between cash movements and investment transactions, possibly accompanied by more detailed substantive procedures, can provide useful evidence concerning the existence and ownership assertions but provides relatively little evidence in relation to other assertions including completeness of investment income;

(c) Controls reports provided by service organisations: as part of their approach to monitoring the activities of a service organisation, trustees may decide to obtain a 'controls report' from the service organisation covering the design and operating effectiveness of the organisation's accounting and internal control systems relevant to the scheme. Scheme auditors may find such a report on internal controls obtained by the trustees useful audit evidence, especially where:

　　(i) the scope of the work performed by the reporting accountants adequately addresses controls relevant to the financial statement assertions concerning the scheme's investments;

　　(ii) it contains an unqualified assurance report by the reporting accountant;

　　(iii) the scheme auditor has confidence, in the context of the specific assignment undertaken, regarding the professional competence of the reporting accountant;

　　(iv) the assurance report covers the full reporting period of the pension scheme or, where this is not the case, the scheme auditors conclude, after taking into account the reputation of the investment manager and/or custodian as a provider of reliable information, that they are able to carry out appropriate additional procedures in order to rely on returns from the investment manager and/or custodian in relation to the remainder of the reporting period;

(d) Agreed-upon procedures performed by service entity auditors: the effectiveness of this method of obtaining audit evidence will depend upon the ways in which the service organisation operates. For example, if investments are held on a pooled basis, confirmation of the specific investments owned by one scheme may be impracticable. In addition, such procedures may involve considerable cost;

(e) Direct inspection of the service provider's records by user auditors: some service contracts provide pension scheme trustees with access to the records of the service organisation. Unless such a contractual agreement exists, there is no right of auditor access to records maintained outside the scheme. If access is obtained, direct inspection, particularly in relation to a comparatively small fund operated by a large investment manager, is likely to give considerable practical difficulties and to involve considerable cost.

220. The above guidance relates to situations where the pension scheme has a portfolio of investments and these investments are disclosed in the financial statements. The guidance is not intended to address the situation where the scheme invests wholly in unitised products such as a managed fund. It is the units in the fund that are shown in the net assets statement as scheme assets rather than the underlying investments of the managed fund, and consequently the scheme auditors normally obtain evidence as to the existence and value of the units themselves rather than the underlying investments.

221. Similarly, where a scheme invests in a common investment fund constituted under a trust deed requiring the preparation of audited financial statements, the net assets statement of the scheme reflects the participation in the net assets and investment portfolio of the common investment fund, as reflected in its financial statements, rather than the individual underlying investments. In such cases, the scheme auditors normally agree the amount at which the investment is included in the net assets statement with the common investment funds' audited financial statements, and place reliance on the work of the fund's auditors following the requirements of ISA (UK and Ireland) 600.

222. Some outsourced activities are the subject of regulation, notably investment management. However, regulation does not by itself eliminate the need for pension scheme auditors to obtain independent evidence because controls required by regulators, and inspection work undertaken by them in service organisations, may not be relevant to or sufficiently focussed on aspects of importance to pension schemes. Furthermore, reports from the service organisation's auditors required by its regulator are not ordinarily available to a pension scheme or its auditors.

223. Many pension schemes outsource the maintenance of their accounting records to third parties. Scheme auditors obtain and document an understanding as to the way the accounting records are maintained, including the way in which trustees ensure that their records meet the PA 1990 and trust deed requirements for such records.

224. Scheme auditors may need to obtain audit evidence in relation to information provided by the relevant employer and in this may seek the assistance of the employer's auditors. It is the statutory duty of the employer and the employer's auditors to disclose on request to the trustees such information as is reasonably required for the performance of the duties of the trustees or scheme auditors. The trustees and employers in turn have a statutory duty to disclose such information to the scheme auditors as they reasonably require to perform their duties. If scheme auditors require the assistance of the employer's auditors in providing information or in carrying out

certain audit procedures, it is appropriate for the initial request to be made through the trustees and the employer.

225. The Pensions Research Accountants Group (PRAG) has issued guidance for scheme trustees entitled "Outsourcing for trustees"[6], which provides practical guidance on the management of the risks that can arise when functions are carried out by a service provider. As one of the risks concerns access to accounting records, it may be beneficial for scheme auditors to enquire whether trustees have obtained the PRAG guidance and considered its implications.

226. If the scheme auditors conclude that evidence from records held by a service provider is necessary in order to form an opinion on the financial statements of the pension scheme and they are unable to obtain such evidence, they consider how this will affect their audit opinion and whether or not the matter should be reported to the PB on a voluntary basis.

---

[6] Available from the PRAG Administrator, whose contact details may be obtained from PRAG's website – www.prag.org.uk.

ISA (UK and Ireland) 520: Analytical Procedures

Background note

The purpose of this ISA (UK and Ireland) is to establish standards and provide guidance on the application of analytical procedures during an audit.

The auditor should apply analytical procedures as risk assessment procedures to obtain an understanding of the entity and its environment and in the overall review at the end of the audit. (paragraph 2)

227. Analytical review techniques are likely to be particularly useful in the audit of pension schemes, not only at the planning and overall review stages of the audit but also as substantive procedures to supplement other evidence concerning the operation of controls or accuracy of individual balances and transactions.

228. Although pension schemes' income, resources and expenditure may fluctuate from year to year, for most transactions there are still ways in which the scheme auditor can establish whether the figures are internally consistent and reflect the pension scheme's operations during the year. Key techniques include comparison of information shown in the financial statements, for example:

- investment income is usually a substantial proportion of total income and analytical procedures can be used in this context;

- monthly and annual patterns of contribution income can be compared to expected amounts using rates set out in the trust deed and rules or actuary's recommendation (where appropriate). However, difficulties may be encountered when differing rates of contribution are used for different categories of members;

- monthly and annual patterns of pensions payments can be compared to movements in membership statistics and increases to benefits in payment;

- membership statistics and bench-marking reports on investment performance, which ought to correlate to financial information shown in the financial statements;

- non-financial information contained in documents issued by the scheme, such as summary reports, pensions newsletters, or in management information reports concerning scheme membership;

- minutes of trustees' meetings, including committees and sub-committees of the trustees, which can be expected to reflect major issues and events arising during the period under review;

- comparison of actual income and expenditure to prior years' figures and trends;

- comparison of actual expenditure to the scheme auditor's own expectation of expenditure that would be reasonable for the particular transaction under review, for example average pension payment per pensioner;

- comparison with published information, for example in respect of investment income, equity yields and rental income per square foot.

ISA (UK and Ireland) 550: Related Parties

Background note

The purpose of this ISA (UK and Ireland) is to establish standards and provide guidance on the auditor's responsibilities and audit procedures regarding related parties and transactions with such parties regardless of whether International Accounting Standard (IAS) 24, "Related Party Disclosures," or similar requirement, is part of the applicable financial reporting framework.

When planning the audit the auditor should assess the risk that material undisclosed related party transactions, or undisclosed outstanding balances between an entity and its related parties may exist. (paragraph 106-3)

229. The related parties of pension schemes fall into three broad categories:

- employer-related;

- trustee-related, or

- officers and managers.

230. The Pensions SORP recommends that for financial reporting purposes related parties should be deemed also to include other pension schemes for the benefit of employees of companies and businesses related to the employers, or for the benefit of the employees of any entity that is itself a related party of the reporting pension scheme.

231. The same principles and procedures set out in ISA (UK and Ireland) 550 apply to the audit of pension schemes as for other entities. The scheme auditors consider the possibility of related party transactions, for example where a pension scheme contracts with the employer or related third parties for the use of a property or for the supply of goods or services to the scheme, even if these result in more favourable terms for the pension scheme than would otherwise be available.

232. Scheme auditors enquire as to the procedures that the trustees have introduced to identify related parties and to authorise and record any related party transactions, including transactions with or loans to the sponsoring employer. Paragraphs 2.126 to 2.131 of the Pensions SORP provide guidance on the types of transaction that fall into the categories shown above and the form of disclosure recommended. Scheme auditors consider whether the trustees have made appropriate arrangements for identifying, authorising and recording such transactions in the circumstances of the particular scheme. Scheme auditors also obtain written representations from the trustees concerning the completeness of information provided regarding the related party disclosures in the financial statements.

233. It is a fundamental principle of trust law that trustees do not benefit from their trust. In addition, certain forms of employer-related investments are also prohibited or restricted by the legislation. The pension scheme trustee who is also a scheme member may, however, benefit as a scheme member from decisions taken as a trustee. Fees may be paid to trustees if specifically allowed by the trust deed.

ISA (UK and Ireland) 570: Going Concern

Background note

The purpose of this ISA (UK and Ireland) is to establish standards and provide guidance on the auditor's responsibility on the audit of financial statements with respect to the going concern assumption used in the preparation of the financial statements, including management's assessment of the entity's ability to continue as a going concern.

When planning and performing audit procedures and in evaluating the results thereof, the auditor should consider the appropriateness of management's use of the going concern assumption in the preparation of the financial statements. (paragraph 2)

The auditor should consider any relevant disclosures in the financial statements. (paragraph 2-1)

In obtaining an understanding of the entity, the auditor should consider whether there are events or conditions and related business risks which may cast significant doubt on the entity's ability to continue as a going concern. (paragraph 11)

The auditor should evaluate management's assessment of the entity's ability to continue as a going concern (paragraph 17).

234. The scheme auditors' assessment of a scheme's status as a going concern differs from that undertaken in the audit of the financial statements of a commercial entity.

235. As explained in the Pensions SORP, the going concern concept does not play the same fundamental role in the measurement and classification of assets and liabilities in pension scheme financial statements as it does in the financial statements of commercial entities. The basis of preparation of financial statements does not change unless the trustees have taken the decision to wind up the scheme (the Pensions SORP, paragraphs 2.33 to 2.34).

236. The scheme auditors' legal obligation in reporting on financial statements of a pension scheme is to express an opinion as to whether those statements show a true and fair view of the scheme's financial transactions and its assets and liabilities (excluding liabilities to pay pensions and benefits falling due after the scheme year end) rather than a true and fair view of the broader concept of an entity's state of affairs. This form of opinion reflects the nature of pension schemes' financial statements, which exclude long term obligations to meet pension commitments.

237. Information about the continued ability of a defined benefit scheme to meet future benefits is provided in the actuarial statement and actuarial funding certificate, neither of which form a basis of the audited financial statements but are included or referred to

in the annual report alongside the financial statements. Scheme auditors have no statutory responsibility to report on information contained in the annual report: however, they are required by ISA (UK and Ireland) 720 to read other information included in documents containing audited financial statements and, if they become aware of apparent misstatements or inconsistencies with the audited financial statements, to seek to resolve them. In addition, the Auditors' Code indicates that auditors do not allow their reports to be included in documents containing other information which they consider to be misleading.

238. Pension scheme auditors make enquiries of the trustees as to whether there are circumstances indicating that it may be appropriate to wind up the scheme.

239. In all cases where the scheme auditors conclude that there are circumstances which may lead to the scheme being wound up, they consider whether the trustees have provided relevant information in the trustees' report as recommended by the Pensions SORP. If the scheme auditors become aware that the trustees have taken a decision to wind up the scheme, they consider whether appropriate changes have been made in the bases of valuation of assets in the financial statements, as recommended by the Pensions SORP.

240. The trustees' consideration of the appropriateness of the going concern basis when preparing the financial statements does not involve their consideration of prospective financial information. Therefore, the ISA (UK and Ireland) 570 paragraph 17-1 b(ii) requirement for the auditors to identify any material matters which could indicate concern about a scheme's ability to continue as a going concern is not relevant to the audit of a pension scheme. Further, the auditors do not search for circumstances that might, as a result of a future uncertain event, lead to the scheme needing to be wound up.

241. Pension schemes will not be wound up solely due to the failure to meet minimum funding standards. Where minimum funding standards are not met trustees need to put in place a funding plan, which may plan to address the scheme's funding over a period of ten years or potentially longer. Failure to agree a funding plan does not necessarily result in trustees winding up the scheme as section 50 and section 50A of the Pensions Act 1990 provide alternatives to winding up the scheme. Those sections permit, in certain circumstances, the reduction of benefits provided by a scheme to facilitate a scheme not meeting the funding standard to be brought into alignment with the funding standard.

ISA (UK and Ireland) 580: Management Representations

Background note

The purpose of this ISA (UK and Ireland) is to establish standards and provide guidance on the use of management representations as audit evidence, the procedures to be applied in evaluating and documenting management representations and the action to be taken if management refuses to provide appropriate representations.

The auditor should obtain appropriate representations from management. (paragraph 2)

242. An important principle is that scheme auditors do not accept the unsupported representations of trustees or senior management of the pension scheme where these relate to matters which are material to the financial statements. Moreover, representations cannot substitute for evidence that the scheme auditors reasonably expect to be available.

Written confirmation of appropriate representations from management, as required by paragraph 4 below, should be obtained before the audit report is issued. (paragraph 2-1)

In the UK and Ireland, the auditor should obtain evidence that those charged with governance acknowledge their collective responsibility for the preparation of the financial statements and have approved the financial statements. (paragraph 3-1)

The auditor should obtain written representations from management on matters material to the financial statements when other sufficient appropriate audit evidence cannot reasonably be expected to exist. (paragraph 4)

243. ISA (UK and Ireland) 580 requires auditors to obtain written confirmation of appropriate representations from management. These commonly take the form of a representation letter and normally include a representation concerning the completeness of information made available to the scheme auditors, including minutes of trustee meetings and correspondence with the Pensions Ombudsman and the PB. In addition, ISA (UK and Ireland) 250 and ISA (UK and Ireland) 550 require auditors to obtain written confirmation in respect of the completeness of disclosure to the auditors of:

* known events which involve possible non-compliance with laws and regulations, together with the actual or contingent consequences which may arise therefrom; and

- information provided regarding the identification of related parties and the adequacy of related party disclosures.

244. The trustees as a body are responsible for the contents and presentation of the financial statements. Consequently, discussion of the content of any written representation by the trustee body as a whole may be appropriate before it is signed on behalf of the trustees, often by two of their members. The body of trustees as a whole is responsible for the contents and presentation of the financial statements.

245. For larger pension schemes where there is a non-trustee chief executive or pensions manager, it is also likely that in practice there are some representations that necessitate discussion with that person. Scheme auditors often find it useful to attend the meeting at which trustees consider the financial statements and representation letter, to encourage discussion of significant items or matters, including unadjusted errors, arising in the course of the audit.

246. An example of a representation letter is included in Appendix 5.

247. In many pension schemes day to day management may be delegated to a scheme management team, possibly provided by a service organisation. In these circumstances, the trustees may wish scheme management or the third party service organisation to provide a representation to them in relation to some or all aspects of the preparation of the financial statements. This is a relationship matter for the trustees and should not impact on the nature or strength of the representations made by the trustees to the auditors.

248. If there is a delay between the approval of the financial statements by the trustees and their receipt by the auditors for the approval of the audit report, the auditors consider whether to obtain an update of the trustees' representations, either by enquiry of the secretary to the trustees about any changes to the scheme's circumstances or by requesting the trustees to provide an updated representation letter.

ISA (UK and Ireland) 600: Using the Work of Another Auditor

Background note

The purpose of this ISA (UK and Ireland) is to establish standards and provide guidance when an auditor reporting on the financial statements of an entity ('the principal auditor') uses the work of another auditor ('the other auditor') on the financial information of one or more components included in the financial statements of the entity.

When the principal auditor uses the work of another auditor, the principal auditor should determine how the work of the other auditor will affect the audit. (paragraph 2)

When planning to use the work of another auditor, the principal auditor should consider the professional competence of the other auditor in the context of the specific assignment. (paragraph 7)

249. Where scheme auditors use the services of other auditors in the audit of statutory financial statements, then the scheme auditors advise the other auditors of the use that is to be made of their work and make the necessary arrangements for the co-ordination of their efforts at the initial planning stage of the audit.

250. Scheme auditors may request scheme trustees to ask the employer to request their auditors to carry out certain work on contributions paid to the scheme by the employer, rather than undertaking such work themselves. Typically this arises in multi-employer schemes, such as industry-wide arrangements. In such circumstances, scheme auditors specify the procedures to be undertaken and provide these to the trustees.

The principal auditor should perform procedures to obtain sufficient appropriate audit evidence that the work of the other auditor is adequate for the principal auditor's purposes in the context of the specific assignment. (paragraph 8)

251. Scheme auditors specify the procedures to be undertaken and provide these to the trustees. The trustees then pass these to the employer and the employer's auditor, who is engaged by the employer to undertake the work on the understanding that the results will be passed to the scheme trustees purely for the purposes of the scheme audit. If the trustees wish to contract directly with the employer's auditors to undertake work on their behalf, the employer's auditors will need to be appointed as a professional adviser to the scheme.

ISA (UK and Ireland) 620: Using the Work of an Expert

Background note

The purpose of this ISA (UK and Ireland) is to establish standards and provide guidance on using the work of an expert as audit evidence.

When using the work performed by an expert, the auditor should obtain sufficient appropriate audit evidence that such work is adequate for the purposes of the audit. (paragraph 2)

252. Areas in which the scheme auditors may, in conjunction with the trustees, use the work of an expert to provide audit evidence include:

  - valuations of certain investments, for example unquoted investments, insurance policies, properties and works of art and certain derivatives and alternative investment categories; and

  - legal opinions concerning the interpretation of the trust deed and rules.

253. The nature of the scheme auditors' statutory opinion excludes consideration of liabilities to pay pension and benefits after the end of the scheme year. As a result, scheme auditors do not ordinarily rely on the work of the scheme actuary to provide audit evidence to support their report on a scheme's financial statements.

254. Nevertheless, for a defined benefit scheme, the actuary's certificate and/or statement is an important element in the information accompanying the audited financial statements as part of the trustees' annual report. ISA (UK and Ireland) 720 requires scheme auditors to read such accompanying information and, if they become aware of any apparent misstatements or inconsistencies with the audited financial statements, to seek to resolve them. Steps to be taken to facilitate necessary liaison with the scheme actuary are discussed in this Practice Note under ISA (UK and Ireland) 720 (revised), Section A – Other Information in Documents Containing Audited Financial Statements in a section headed "Liaison with the scheme actuary".

ISA (UK and Ireland) 700: The Auditor's Report on Financial Statements

Background note

The purpose of this ISA (UK and Ireland) is to establish standards and provide guidance on the form and content of the auditor's report issued as a result of an audit performed by an independent auditor of the financial statements of an entity. Much of the guidance provided can be adapted to auditors' reports on financial information other than financial statements.

The auditor's report should contain a clear written expression of opinion on the financial statements taken as a whole. (paragraph 4)

The auditor's report should be appropriately addressed as required by the circumstances of the engagement and local regulations. (paragraph 7)

In the UK and Ireland:

(a) The auditor should distinguish between the auditor's responsibilities and the responsibilities of those charged with governance by including in their report a reference to a description of the relevant responsibilities of those charged with governance when that description is set out elsewhere in the financial statements or accompanying information; or

(b) Where the financial statements or accompanying information do not include an adequate description of relevant responsibilities of those charged with governance, the auditor's report should include a description of those responsibilities. (paragraph 9-1)

The auditor's report should describe the scope of the audit by stating that the audit was conducted in accordance with ISAs (UK and Ireland) or in accordance with relevant national standards or practices as appropriate. (paragraph 12)

The opinion paragraph of the auditor's report should clearly indicate the financial reporting framework used to prepare the financial statements (including identifying the country of origin of the financial reporting framework when the framework used is not International Accounting Standards) and state the auditor's opinion as to whether the financial statements give a true and fair view (or are presented fairly, in all material respects) in accordance with that financial reporting framework and, where appropriate, whether the financial statements comply with statutory requirements. (paragraph 17)

255. The form and content of auditors' reports on the financial statements of pension schemes follow the basic principles and procedures established by ISA (UK and Ireland) 700, which are explained in the following paragraphs.

Addressee of the report

256. Section 56 of the Pensions Act 1990 requires that the trustees cause the financial statements of the scheme to be audited: hence the scheme auditors, in accordance with the 2006 Regulations, address their report on a scheme's financial statements to the trustees of the scheme and to other parties if required by the trust deed or other applicable rules.

Statement of trustees' responsibilities

257. ISA (UK and Ireland) 700 requires auditors to include a statement distinguishing between their responsibilities and those of the entity's directors (in the case of a pension scheme, its trustees) and to refer to a description of the latter's responsibilities set out in the financial statements or accompanying information. If no adequate description is given, the ISA requires the auditors to provide details in their report.

258. The responsibilities of the trustees may vary according to the constitution of the particular pension scheme. Example Trustees' Responsibilities Statements are set out in Appendix 7, which may be adapted to the circumstances of individual schemes.

Compliance with relevant accounting requirements

259. The scheme auditors' opinion on a pension scheme's financial statements is expressed in the context of the particular accounting requirements applicable to the pension scheme concerned. ISA (UK and Ireland) 700 includes commentary on compliance with the requirements of law and accounting standards (see paragraphs 22-1 and 22-2). In general terms, unless exceptional circumstances apply, compliance with accounting standards is necessary to show a true and fair view.

260. Trustees are required to ensure the preparation of financial statements which contain the information specified in Schedule A to the 2006 Regulations and show a true and fair view of the financial transactions of the scheme during the scheme year, the amount and disposition of the assets at the end of the scheme year and the liabilities of the scheme, other than the liabilities to pay benefits after the end of the scheme year. The 2006 Regulations require the scheme auditors to state whether or not in their opinion the financial statements contain the information specified in Schedule A to the 2006 Regulations and show a true and fair view as required by the 2006 Regulations. If there is a qualified opinion the scheme auditors are required to state the reasons.

261. The Pensions SORP has been developed and issued by PRAG in accordance with the Accounting Standards Board's code of practice for the production and issue of SORPs. The Pensions SORP was last revised in May 2007 and sets out guidance intended to represent best practice on the form and content of the financial statements of pension schemes prepared in accordance with accounting standards current at the time of its issue.

262. The 2006 Regulations require trustees of a scheme to disclose in its financial statements whether those statements have been prepared following the Pensions SORP's guidelines, and, if not, to give details of any material departures. Although the

Pensions SORP's guidance is not mandatory, this provision, taken with the general status of a Pensions SORP issued in accordance with the ASB's code, has the effect of establishing a strong presumption that financial statements which meet the 2006 Regulations' requirement to show a true and fair view will normally follow the guidance contained in the Pensions SORP, taking into account any amendment judged to be necessary as a result of changes in financial reporting standards since its issue.

Other considerations

263. The trust deed establishing a scheme may establish additional requirements concerning the contents of its financial statements (but may not derogate from the statutory requirements). The scheme auditors therefore assess whether any such requirements are met. In addition, where the scheme auditors become aware of information which indicates that a transaction or transactions undertaken by the scheme may have breached any terms of its trust deed, they consider the implications for their reporting responsibilities following the guidance in the sections dealing with ISA (UK and Ireland) 250.

Examples of scheme auditors' reports

264. ISA (UK and Ireland) 700 sets out requirements for the content of auditors' reports on financial statements, including the circumstances in which additional explanatory material is necessary or the auditors' opinion is to be qualified. Examples of scheme auditors' reports showing different legislative requirements and illustrating each of the different forms of opinion are set out in Appendix 6.

Electronic publication of annual reports

265. An increasing number of pension schemes have made arrangements for members to obtain information about their schemes (including the scheme annual report) electronically: this may be via publicly accessible websites or on corporate intranet sites.

266. Auditors determine through discussion with trustees whether the annual report, and therefore their audit report, is to be "published" electronically. If electronic publication is proposed, auditors follow the guidance in Appendix 1 of ISA (UK and Ireland) 720 titled 'Electronic Publication of the Auditor's Report'. The main aim of the guidance is to ensure that the auditors' duty of care is not extended solely as a result of their report being published in electronic rather than hard copy form. In addition, as information published on websites is available in many countries with different legal requirements, it must be clear which legislation governs the preparation and dissemination of the financial statements.

ISA (UK and Ireland) 720 (Revised): Section A – Other information in Documents Containing Audited Financial Statements

Background note

The purpose of this ISA (UK and Ireland) is to establish standards and provide guidance on the auditor's consideration of other information, on which the auditor has no obligation to report, in documents containing audited financial statements. This ISA (UK and Ireland) applies when an annual report is involved; however, it may also apply to other documents.

The auditor should read the other information to identify material inconsistencies with the audited financial statements. (paragraph 2)

267. One of the fundamental principles set out in the Auditors' Code is that auditors do not allow their reports to be included in documents containing other information if they consider that the additional information is in conflict with the matters covered by their report or they have cause to believe it to be misleading.

268. Scheme auditors read the other information contained in the annual report in the light of the knowledge they have acquired during the audit. The scheme auditors are not expected to verify any of the other information. They read the other information with a view to identifying whether there are any apparent misstatements therein or matters which are inconsistent with the financial statements. It is important to ensure that the trustees are aware of the scheme auditors' responsibilities in respect of the other information, as set out in ISA (UK and Ireland) 720 and the extent of those responsibilities is specifically outlined in the engagement letter.

269. The 'other information' which may accompany the financial statements of a pension scheme and examples of the areas of potential concern are as follows:

- Trustees' report – membership reconciliation: are the changes in membership numbers consistent with the financial information – number of deaths, new contributors?

- Trustees' report – pension increases: is the rate of increase reflected in the benefit payments?

- Trustees' report: are details of the basis of calculation of transfer payments consistent with the actual basis of the amounts paid?

- Trustees' report: are references to the actuary's statement and funding certificate appropriate and consistent with the documents, which are appended to the annual report?

- Investment report: is the asset total and investment income/return reported by the investment manager consistent with the amounts shown in the financial statements?

270. The trustees may also distribute other documents together with the financial statements such as personal benefit statements, new rules booklets or newsletters. The scheme auditors have no statutory responsibility to consider these documents.

271. Practical considerations concerning the timing of work undertaken by the scheme auditors and actuaries are discussed in a subsequent section of this Practice Note, 'Liaison with the scheme actuary'.

> If, on reading the other information, the auditor identifies a material inconsistency, the auditor should determine whether the audited financial statements or the other information needs to be amended. (paragraph 11)
>
> If the auditor identifies a material inconsistency the auditor should seek to resolve the matter through discussion with those charged with governance. (paragraph 11-1)

272. Where the scheme auditors identify inconsistencies or apparent misstatements within the other information they consider whether an amendment is required to the financial statements or to the other information, and discuss the issues with those responsible for preparing the financial statements and annual report, and seek to resolve the situation. If the situation is not resolved, and involves information which the scheme auditors consider to be material, they make reference to the matter in their report on the financial statements and consider whether to report to the PB.

The Auditors' Statement of Opinions on Contributions

Requirement to provide the statement of opinions

273. The PA 1990 requires the trustees of a pension scheme to make available, not more than nine months after the end of the scheme year, financial statements which include an auditors' report on the scheme's financial statements. This report includes a statement by the scheme auditors as to whether, in their opinion, contributions payable to the relevant scheme during the scheme year have been received by the trustees within 30 days of the end of the scheme year and whether in the auditors' opinion such contributions have been paid in accordance with the rules of the relevant scheme and, if appropriate, with the recommendation of the actuary. If the opinions are negative or qualified, a statement of the reasons is required.

274. The statement of opinions has two elements,

- an opinion that contributions have been received within 30 days of the end of the scheme year, and

- an opinion that contributions have been paid in accordance with the scheme rules and, if appropriate, the recommendation of the actuary.

The work to support the opinions will draw on the scheme auditors' work performed in relation to contributions as part of the audit of the scheme's financial statements. Accordingly guidance to scheme auditors on providing the statement of opinions is set out in this Practice Note.

Additional Voluntary Contributions (AVCs)

275. AVCs are not required by law to be included in the fund account or net assets statement of the scheme at the end of the scheme year. They may instead be included in the notes to the financial statements. The statement of opinions on contributions will encompass the timing of all employee contributions, including AVCs to the extent deducted from payroll.

Materiality

276. The work undertaken by scheme auditors in respect of contributions takes into account both their obligation to report their opinion on the financial statements and, separately, their statement of opinions as to whether the contributions payable to the scheme during the scheme year have been received by the trustees within 30 days of the end of the scheme year, and have been paid in accordance with the rules of the scheme and, if appropriate, the recommendation of the actuary. This affects the determination of planning materiality, requiring the scheme auditors to consider more detailed aspects of the receipt of income from contributions than would be the case if reporting on the financial statements alone.

277. However, scheme auditors provide a statement of opinions in relation to contributions payable and therefore plan and carry out their work with a reasonable expectation of

detecting errors which are material to contributions due as a whole rather than, for example, at an individual member level. Therefore scheme auditors do need to consider materiality in relation to the statement of opinions in relation to contributions payable when planning and performing their work and also when assessing the results of their work.

278. The statement of opinions in relation to contributions payable requires assessment of whether specific conditions have been met. This narrower more factual focus entails close consideration of payment dates and amounts and hence a different level of materiality to that used for the audit of the scheme's financial statements is likely to be appropriate.

279. The legislation requiring the statement of opinions in relation to contributions payable does not refer to "materiality": as a result auditors issue qualified statements for very minor breaches. Since these minor breaches are not significant to contributions as a whole the auditors will not have planned and performed their work to detect them. However, having become aware of such breaches auditors refer to them in their statement of opinions in relation to contributions payable.

Work to be performed

280. In order to report on contributions, scheme auditors undertake procedures in order to obtain sufficient appropriate evidence to conclude on whether or not in their opinion contributions payable to the scheme have been paid in accordance with the recommendation of the actuary and the rules of the scheme, and received by the trustees within 30 days of the year end. In doing this the scheme auditors should have regard to both the amount of contributions received and the timing of those contributions.

281. Some issues that may require consideration include:

- changes in the rates of contributions payable and the timing of the implementation of the change in the employer payroll;

- changes in the definition of pensionable earnings;

- the use of an annual declaration or live payroll basis for calculating contributions;

- whether the trust deed and rules and the actuarial recommendation (where appropriate) are sufficiently clear in their drafting to allow the auditor to properly assess whether contributions have been paid in accordance with the requirements;

- the scheme's systems of recording and monitoring contributions;

- any reports to the PB by the trustees of late or inaccurate contributions; and

- whether there have been any member complaints about incorrect contributions, for example in response to annual benefit statements issued to members.

Reporting

282. The statement of opinions forms part of the auditors' report and the work performed by the scheme auditors to provide the opinions should form part of the audit work programmes.

Self investment

283. "Self investment" is defined in the PA 1990 as investment of all or part of the resources of a scheme in the business of the sponsoring employer or participating employer, any affiliate of those employers, or any director or shadow director of that employer or affiliate. This would include monies due to the scheme and held by the employer(s). Such monies include pension scheme contributions which have not yet been remitted to the trustees. The 2006 Regulations require that details of self investment by a scheme, at any time during the period covered by the report, be included in the notes to the financial statements, except where such monies are due for a period less than that provided for in section 58A of the Pensions Act 1990 ie:

   • employee contributions – within 21 days following the end of the month in which deduction of the contribution was made from the employee's salary;

   • employer contributions defined contribution schemes – within 21 days following the end of the month to which the contribution relates;

   • employer contributions defined benefit schemes – in accordance with the trust deed and rules or recommendation of the actuary or otherwise within 30 days of each year end.

284. Scheme auditors have no specific statutory reporting obligations in relation to self investment, save for the opinion that contributions have been received within 30 days of the scheme year end. Nevertheless, as full self investment information is required to be disclosed in the notes to the financial statements, so scheme auditors undertake procedures in order to obtain sufficient evidence to conclude as to whether appropriate disclosure has been made.

Trustee regulatory responsibilities

285. Under the PA 1990 trustees are required to ensure, in so far as is reasonable that contributions payable by the employer and the members of the scheme are received. The PA 1990 (section 58A of the Pensions Act 1990) requires that all employee contributions deducted in respect of defined benefit and defined contribution schemes and all employer contributions in respect of defined contribution schemes must be remitted to the trustees within 21 days from the end of the month in which the deduction was made or the contributions became due. The trustees are required to invest such contributions within 10 days of the latest date on which they should have been remitted or paid to the trustees by the employer. Employer contributions in respect of defined benefit schemes are required to be received in accordance with the timings noted by the actuary or stated in the trust deed and rules or otherwise within 30 days of the year end. Scheme auditors do not have an obligation to consider

adherence to these requirements as part of their work in relation to the financial statements except as noted above in relation to self investment and in relation to the auditors' statement of opinions on contributions. However, they may wish to consider breaches in the context of their audit work generally and as to whether they should bring them to the attention of the trustees and the PB in accordance with section 83 of the Pensions Act 1990.

Liaison with the scheme actuary

286. A scheme actuary is normally appointed only for defined benefit schemes.

287. The liability to pay pensions after the scheme year end, and the actuarial valuation of that liability, is not within the scope of the financial statements or of the audit, so scheme auditors have no responsibility for confirming the accuracy and appropriateness of the underlying data used by the actuary.

288. As noted in the discussion of ISA (UK and Ireland) 720, auditors read the other information contained in the annual report (which includes the actuarial funding certificate and statement, where appropriate) with a view to identifying whether there are any apparent misstatements therein or matters which are inconsistent with the financial statements. However, this does not require scheme auditors to carry out any checking of the basis of the actuary's funding certificate and statement.

289. Nonetheless, scheme auditors may agree (if requested) to undertake additional work to provide assurance to the trustees that information supplied to the scheme actuary is consistent with that used in the preparation of the financial statements. In these circumstances, the additional work will normally be the subject of a separate letter of engagement and will be reported on separately from the financial statements.

290. Auditors and actuaries look to the scheme trustees (rather than each other) as the primary source of information in relation to their professional roles. However, reference to arrangements for direct communication between scheme auditors and the scheme actuary is normally included in the engagement letters of both the scheme auditors and the actuary. Such access is relevant to a number of areas of the scheme auditors' responsibility:

(a) in planning the timing of audit procedures in the context of the trustees' timetable for the annual report, the scheme auditors may wish to liaise with the scheme actuary to understand the nature and timing of any planned actuarial statements or funding certificates;

(b) in relation to the contributions paid / payable during the year, the scheme auditors may require evidence to confirm that the contributions paid to the scheme were in accordance with the actuary's recommendation;

(c) in relation to benefit payments during the scheme year in respect of defined benefit schemes, the scheme auditors may seek to understand the nature and extent of the scheme actuary's involvement in the determination of benefits payable;

(d) in relation to any actuarial statement or funding certificate included in the annual report, the scheme auditors read the actuarial statement or certificate which accompanies their report on the scheme's financial statements and, if they become aware of any apparent misstatements therein, or identify any material inconsistencies with the audited financial statements, they seek to resolve the situation;

(e) when assessing whether a matter discovered by the scheme auditors is likely to be reportable to the PB, the scheme auditors may wish to consult with the scheme actuary in order to assist in forming their opinion as to whether a duty to report arises.

Concentration of investment

291. The PA 1990 requires details of any concentration of investment in excess of 5% of the resources of the scheme at the scheme year end to be disclosed in the notes to the financial statements. Investments greater than 5% in the following categories are not considered to be concentrations of investment: government securities; insurance policies; contracts of assurance; managed funds; unit trusts; and cash deposits.

292. However, paragraph 2.194 of the SORP states that only a concentration in UK Government Securities does not require to be disclosed. In the Irish context UK Government Securities is taken to include Irish and other Government Securities. Consequently, where advantage is being taken of the greater latitude permitted by the legislation, a note to the financial statements is required explaining why the trustees consider the limited disclosure to be more appropriate in the scheme's circumstances, as this is a breach of the SORP.

293. As a consequence scheme auditors undertake procedures in order to obtain sufficient evidence to conclude as to whether appropriate disclosure of any concentration of investment has been made in the financial statements.

Completion of the trustees' annual report

294. A practical consideration in completing the audit is the timing of issuing the scheme auditors' report and the scheme actuary's funding certificate and statement (where appropriate), all of which are required to be included in the trustees' annual report. ISA (UK and Ireland) 720 requires the scheme auditors to read other information included in the annual report and to seek to resolve any inconsistencies with the financial statements or possible misstatements which they identify, as set out above. ISA (UK and Ireland) 700 requires the financial statements and all other financial information in the annual report to have been approved by the trustees before the audit report is signed.

295. The trustees' annual report must be available within nine months of the end of the scheme year. It should include:

- the latest actuarial funding certificate (which, described briefly, gives the scheme actuary's opinion as to whether the scheme did or did not satisfy the funding standard at a defined date) is signed by the scheme actuary at least every three years. In the period between valuations, the scheme actuary may issue a revised certificate and it is the most recent version which must be included in the annual report but there is no requirement to issue a revised certificate annually;

- the actuarial statement (which, described briefly, confirms the scheme actuary's opinion as to whether if he were to prepare an actuarial funding certificate having an effective date of the last day of the period to which the annual report relates, he would certify whether or not the scheme would satisfy the funding standard) where required, must be made.

296. Where, in the most recent funding certificate, the actuary certifies that the scheme does not satisfy the funding requirement, and a funding proposal has been submitted to the PB, each annual report must include another form of actuarial statement (which, described briefly, confirms the scheme actuary's opinion that, at the last day of the period to which the annual report relates, the scheme will or will not satisfy the funding standard at the effective date of the next actuarial funding certificate).

297. These are not necessarily recent documents. Where a more recent funding certificate is in the course of preparation, the trustees may wish (providing that there is sufficient time within the statutory time limit of nine months) to delay the issue of the annual report until that certificate is available. However, there is no requirement to delay the annual report so that a more recent certificate can be included. Such documents are in any event required to be made available to the same categories of persons, including scheme members, as are entitled to see the annual report.

298. Close liaison and a good working relationship between the scheme auditors and the scheme actuary will enable both to carry out the work needed to arrive at their respective professional conclusions within the trustees' overall timetable for the preparation of the annual report.

299. Further guidance relevant to liaison with the scheme actuary is set out in the sections dealing with ISA (UK and Ireland) 210 'Terms of Engagement' and Section B of ISA (UK and Ireland) 250 'The Auditors' Right and Duty to Report to Regulators in the Financial Sector'. Professional guidance issued or adopted by the Society of Actuaries in Ireland also includes matters on which the actuary will wish to communicate with the auditors.

Appendix 1

List of principal relevant legislation

(Note that many of the statutes and regulations have subsequently been amended)

Statutes

Pensions Act, 1990
Social Welfare Act, 1991
Social Welfare Act, 1992
Social Welfare Act, 1993
Social Welfare (No. 2) Act, 1993
Pensions Amendment Act 1996
Social Welfare Act, 1997
Social Welfare Act, 1998
Social Welfare Act, 1999
Social Welfare Act, 2000
Pensions Amendment Act 2002
Social Welfare (Miscellaneous Provisions) Act, 2003
Social Welfare (Miscellaneous Provisions) Act, 2004
Social Welfare and Pensions Act, 2005
Social Welfare Law Reform and Pensions Act, 2006
Social Welfare and Pensions Act, 2007
Social Welfare and Pensions Act, 2008
Social Welfare and Pensions Act, (No. 10), 2009

Regulations

Pensions Act, 1990 (Sections 60 and 61) (Commencement) Order, 1990	S.I. No. 329 of 1990
Pensions Act, 1990 (Parts III, IV and V) (Commencement) Order, 1990	S.I. No. 330 of 1990
Pensions Act, 1990 (Parts I and II) (Commencement) Order, 1990	S.I. No. 331 of 1990
Pensions Act, 1990 (Part II) (Establishment Day) Order, 1990	S.I. No. 343 of 1990
Pensions Act, 1990 (Sections 59, 63 and 64) (Commencement) Order, 1991	S.I. No. 259 of 1991
Occupational Pension Schemes (Registration) Regulations, 1991	S.I. No. 325 of 1991
Occupational Benefit Schemes (Equal Treatment) Regulations, 1992	S.I. No. 365 of 1992
Pensions Act, 1990 (Part VII) (Commencement) Order, 1992	S.I. No. 366 of 1992
Occupational Pension Schemes (Funding Standard) Regulations, 1993	S.I. No. 419 of 1993
Occupational Pension Schemes (Member Participation in the Selection of Persons for Appointment as Trustees) (No. 3) Regulations, 1996	S.I. No. 376 of 1996
Occupational Pension Schemes (Oral Hearing) Regulations, 1997	S.I. No. 77 of 1997
Occupational Pension Schemes (Revaluation) Regulations, 1997	S.I. No. 76 of 1997
Pension Schemes (Family Law) Regulations, 1997	S.I. No. 107 of 1997
European Communities (Occupational Benefit Schemes) Regulations, 1997	S.I. No. 286 of 1997

Occupational Pension Schemes (Revaluation) Regulations, 1998	S.I. No. 35 of 1998
Occupational Pension Schemes (Disclosure of Information) (No. 2) Regulations, 1998	S.I. No. 349 of 1998
Occupational Pension Schemes (Funding Standard) (Amendment) (No. 2) Regulations, 1998	S.I. No. 568 of 1998
Occupational Pension Schemes (Revaluation) Regulations, 1999	S.I. No. 5 of 1999
Occupational Pension Schemes (Revaluation) Regulations, 2000	S.I. No. 13 of 2000
Occupational Pension Schemes (Preservation of Benefits) (Amendment) Regulations, 2000	S.I. No. 262 of 2000
Occupational Pension Schemes (Disclosure of Information) (Amendment) Regulations, 2000	S.I. No. 296 of 2000
Occupational Pension Schemes (Funding Standard) (Amendment) Regulations, 2000	S.I. No. 337 of 2000
Occupational Pension Schemes (External Schemes) (United Kingdom) Regulations, 2000	S.I. No. 469 of 2000
Occupational Pension Schemes (Schemes with External Members) (United Kingdom) Regulations, 2000	S.I. No. 470 of 2000
Occupational Pension Schemes (Revaluation) Regulations, 2001	S.I. No. 23 of 2001
Occupational Pension Schemes (Schemes with External Members) (United Kingdom) (Amendment) Regulations, 2001	S.I. No. 329 of 2001
Occupational Pension Schemes (Revaluation) Regulations, 2002	S.I. No. 18 of 2002
Pensions (Amendment) Act, 2002 (Part I and Sections 6, 9 to 12, 15 to 28, 30 to 36, 40, 44, 50 to 55 and 59) (Commencement) Order, 2002	S.I. No. 276 of 2002
Occupational Pension Schemes (Preservation of Benefits) Regulations, 2002	S.I. No. 279 of 2002
Occupational Pension Schemes (Preservation of Benefits) (Special Calculations) Regulations, 2002	S.I. No. 277 of 2002
Occupational Pension Schemes (Funding Standard) (Amendment) Regulations, 2002	S.I. No. 278 of 2002
Pensions (Amendment) Act, 2002 (Section 3 (In so far as it relates to the insertion of Sections 91 to 120 into the Pensions Act, 1990) and Sections 4, 7, 13, 14, 38, 56 and 57) (Commencement) Order, 2002	S.I. No. 502 of 2002
Personal Retirement Savings Accounts (Disclosure) Regulations, 2002	S.I. No. 501 of 2002
Personal Retirement Savings Accounts (Operational Requirements) Regulations, 2002	S.I. No. 503 of 2002
Personal Retirement Savings Accounts (Fees) Regulations, 2002	S.I. No. 506 of 2002
Pensions (Amendment) Act, 2002, (Certain Sections) (Commencement) Order, 2002	S.I. No. 609 of 2002
Occupational Pension Schemes (Fees) (Amendment) Regulations, 2002	S.I. No. 610 of 2002
Personal Retirement Savings Accounts (Functions of the Pensions Board) Regulations, 2002	S.I. No. 611 of 2002
Occupational Pension Schemes (Disclosure of Information) (Amendment) Regulations, 2003	S.I. No. 4 of 2003
Occupational Pension Schemes (Revaluation) Regulations, 2003	S.I. No. 77 of 2003
Pensions (Amendment) Act, 2002, (Sections 121 (3), (4), (5) and (6)) (Commencement) Order, 2003	S.I. No. 78 of 2003

Pensions (Amendment) Act, 2002 (Section 5, in so far as that section inserts sections 126 to 130, 146 and 147 of Part XI into the Pensions Act, 1990) (Commencement) Order, 2003	S.I. No. 119 of 2003
Pensions (Amendment) Act, 2002 (Sections 45 to 49) (Commencement) Order, 2003	S.I. No. 120 of 2003
Pensions (Amendment) Act, 2002 (Sections 29 and 37) (Commencement) Order, 2003	S.I. No. 128 of 2003
Social Welfare (Miscellaneous Provisions) Act, 2003 (Section 24) (Commencement) Order, 2000	S.I. No. 129 of 2003
Personal Retirement Savings Accounts (Operational Requirements) (Amendment) Regulations, 2003	S.I. No. 341 of 2003
Personal Retirement Savings Accounts (Disclosure) (Amendment) Regulations, 2003	S.I. No. 342 of 2003
Pensions (Amendment) Act, 2002, (Section 125) (Commencement) Order, 2003	S.I. No. 359 of 2003
Pensions (Amendment) Act, 2002 (Section 3 (In so far as it relates to the insertion of Sections 121 (Except in so far as that section is already in operation), 123, 124(1)) and 125 into the Pensions Act, 1990)) (Commencement) Order, 2003	S.I. No. 389 of 2003
Pensions Ombudsman Regulations, 2003	S.I. No. 397 of 2003
Pensions (Amendment) Act, 2002 (Section 5 (Except in so far as that section is already in operation) and Sections 8 and 58) (Commencement) Order, 2003	S.I. No. 398 of 2003
Social Welfare (Miscellaneous Provisions) Act, 2003 (Section 23) (Commencement) Order, 2003	S.I. No. 399 of 2003
Occupational Pension Schemes and Personal Retirement Savings Accounts (Transfer) Regulations, 2003	S.I. No. 429 of 2003
Occupational Pension Schemes and Personal Retirement Savings Accounts (Overseas Transfer Payments) Regulations, 2003	S.I. No. 716 of 2003
Pensions (Amendment) Act, 2002 (Section 3 (In so far as it relates to the insertion of Section 124(2) into the Pensions Act, 1990)) (Commencement) Order, 2003	S.I. No. 739 of 2003
Occupational Pension Schemes (Revaluation) Regulations, 2004	S.I. No. 49 of 2004
Social Welfare (Miscellaneous Provisions) Act, 2004 (Sections 22 & 23) (Commencement) Order, 2004	S.I. No. 141 of 2004
Occupational Pension Schemes (Annual Reports) Regulations, 2004	S.I. No. 223 of 2004
Occupational Pension Schemes (Revaluation) Regulations, 2005	S.I. No. 74 of 2005
Social Welfare and Pensions Act (Section 38 and 39) (Commencement) Order, 2005	S.I. No. 187 of 2005
Occupational Pension Schemes (Preservation of Benefits) (Amendment) Regulations	S.I. No. 188 of 2005
Occupational Pension Schemes (Fees) (Amendment) Regulations	S.I. No. 559 of 2005
Social Welfare and Pensions Act (Section 42) (Commencement) Order, 2005	S.I. No. 590 of 2005
Social Welfare and Pensions Act (Part 3) (Commencement) Order, 2005	S.I. No. 591 of 2005
Occupational Pension Schemes (Cross-Boarder) Regulations	S.I. No. 592 of 2005
Occupational Pension Schemes (Investments) Regulations	S.I. No. 593 of 2005
Occupational Pension Schemes (Trustees) Regulations	S.I. No. 594 of 2005

Occupational Pension Schemes (Funding Standard) (Amendment) Regulations	S.I. No. 595 of 2005
Occupational Pension Schemes (Revaluation) Regulations, 2006	S.I. No. 70 of 2006
Social Welfare Law Reform and Pensions Act 2006 (Section 39 (in so far as it inserts section 3B into the Pensions Act 1990)) (Commencement) Order, 2006	S.I. No. 169 of 2006
Social Welfare Law Reform and Pensions Act 2006 (Part 3) (Commencement) Order, 2006	S.I. No. 291 of 2006
Occupational Pension Schemes (Cross-Border) Regulations, 2006	S.I. No. 292 of 2006
Occupational Pension Schemes (Trustee) Regulations, 2006	S.I. No. 293 of 2006
Occupational Pension Schemes (Investment) Regulations, 2006	S.I. No. 294 of 2006
Occupational Pension Schemes (Funding Standard) (Amendment) Regulations, 2006	S.I. No. 295 of 2006
Occupational Pension Schemes (Disclosure of Information) Regulations 2006	S.I. No. 301 of 2006
Pensions Ombudsman Regulations, 2006	S.I. No. 302 of 2006
Social Welfare Law Reform and Pensions Act 2006 (Item 6 of Schedule 8) (Commencement) Order, 2006	S.I. No. 357 of 2006
Social Welfare Law Reform and Pensions Act 2006 (Section 40) (Commencement) Order, 2006	S.I. No. 437 of 2006
Personal Retirement Savings Accounts (Disclosure) (Amendment) Regulations, 2006	S.I. No. 567 of 2006
Occupational Pension Schemes (Disclosure of Information) (Amendment) Regulations, 2006	S.I. No. 582 of 2006
Occupational Pension Schemes (Revaluation) Regulations (2007)	S.I. No. 30 of 2007
Personal Retirement Savings Accounts (Disclosure) (Amendment) Regulations, 2007	S.I. No. 91 of 2007
Social Welfare Law Reform and Pensions Act 2006 (Section 42) (Commencement) Order, 2006	S.I. No. 136 of 2007
Occupational Pension Schemes (Review of Actuarial Work) Regulations, 2007	S.I. No. 137 of 2007
Social Welfare And Pensions Act 2007 (Section 37) (Commencement) Order, 2007	S.I. No. 181 of 2007
Trust RACs (Disclosure Of Information) Regulations 2007	S.I. No. 182 of 2007
Pensions Ombudsman Regulations 2007	S.I. No. 183 of 2007
Trust RACs (Cross-Border) Regulations 2007	S.I. No. 184 of 2007
Trust RACs (Investment) Regulations 2007	S.I. No. 185 of 2007
Trust RACs (Trustee) Regulations 2007	S.I. No. 186 of 2007
Trust RACs (Registration) Regulations 2007	S.I. No. 187 of 2007
Occupational Pension Schemes (Investment) (Amendment) Regulations, 2007	S.I. No. 188 of 2007
Social Welfare Law Reform and Pensions Act 2006 (Section 39) (Commencement) Order 2007	S.I. No. 631 of 2007
Social Welfare and Pensions Act 2007 (Section 37) (Commencement) (No. 2) Order 2007	S.I. No. 632 of 2007
Pensions Act (Notice of Alleged Offence) Regulations 2007	S.I. No. 633 of 2007
Trust RACs (Fees) Regulations 2007	S.I. No. 768 of 2007
Pensions Act (Disclosure of Information)(Amendment) Regulations, 2007	S.I. No. 842 of 2007

Pensions (Amendment) Act 2002 (Section 43) (Commencement) Order, 2007	S.I. No. 843 of 2007
Occupational Pension Schemes (External schemes and schemes with external members)(United Kingdom)(Revocation) Regulations, 2007	S.I. No. 844 of 2007
Occupational Pensions Schemes (Revaluation) Regulations, 2008	S.I. No. 20 of 2008
Social Welfare and Pensions Act, (sections 26, 29, 30 and 31) (Commencement) Order 2008.	S.I. No. 84 of 2008
Pensions Act, 1990 (Register or Administrators) Regulations, 2008	S.I. No. 275 of 2008
Pensions Act, 1990 (Registration and Renewal of Registration of Administrators) Regulations, 2008	S.I. No. 276 of 2008
Occupational Pension Schemes (Funding Standard)(Amendment) Regulations, 2008	S.I. No. 295 of 2008
Social Welfare and Pensions Act, 2008 (Section 27)(Commencement) (No.2) Order, 2008	S.I. No. 398 of 2008
Occupational Pension Schemes (Revaluation) Regulations, 2009	S.I. No. 22 of 2009
Occupational Pension Schemes (Funding Standard)(Amendment) Regulations, 2009	S.I. No. 62 of 2009
Occupational Pension Schemes (Preservation of Benefits) (Amendment) Regulations, 2009	S.I. No. 70 of 2009
Social Welfare and Pensions Act 2008 (sections 15 and 16)(Commencement) Order, 2009	S.I. No. 143 of 2009
Occupational Pension Schemes (Duties of Trustees in Connection with Bulk Transfer) Regulations 2009	S.I. No. 177 of 2009

Appendix 2

The legal and regulatory framework

1. This Appendix sets out a description of the major features of the legal and regulatory framework based on law as at 1 November 2008. It is intended to provide a general introduction for those unfamiliar with these major features and does not deal with any particular aspect in any depth. It is not intended to provide an interpretation of any aspect of the law or to substitute for direct reference to the legislation.

Types of pension scheme

2. Pension schemes may be divided into two main types: occupational schemes and personal schemes. Occupational schemes are those run by employers for the benefit of their employees and from an employee viewpoint, are linked with employment. On leaving the service of the employer, active membership normally ceases, though the employee may leave the benefits accrued to date in the scheme.

3. Personal pension plans are individual arrangements made by individuals who are self employed or in non-pensionable employment or not in an occupational scheme. They may accept contributions from the employer as well as the employee. In addition, in the absence of any other work-based pension provision, an employer may have to offer access to a personal retirement savings account (PRSA) to its employees by law. These types of arrangements are subject to specific requirements set out in the legislation which are different from occupational pension schemes and are not subject to the pension scheme audit regime.

Occupational pension schemes

4. Occupational schemes are very varied in their benefit structure. The main types are as follows:

    *   defined benefit (or earnings and service related) – a pension scheme where the benefit is calculated by reference to the member's pensionable earnings usually for a period ending at or before normal pension date or leaving service (hence the common description of such schemes as 'final salary' schemes), usually also based on pensionable service. Because of the uncertainties in determining the extent of future liabilities of such schemes, the trustees of such schemes are required to obtain regular actuarial assessments of the schemes' liabilities and estimated future costs;

    *   defined contribution (or money purchase) – a pension scheme where the individual member's benefit is determined by reference to contributions paid into the scheme in respect of that member, increased by an amount reflecting the investment return on those contributions. Because the scheme's commitment to pay future pensions is determined by the extent of funds available, no actuarial valuation is normally required;

- hybrid – a pension scheme which incorporates elements of both a defined benefit and defined contribution structure. Such a term may also be applied to a multiple benefit or mixed benefit scheme – a pension scheme in which there is both a defined benefit and defined contribution section; membership of the different sections need not necessarily be compulsory or complementary. For the purposes of the PA 1990 any such schemes are classified as defined benefit.

5. Schemes may provide the facility for members to pay additional voluntary contributions (AVCs). These may be on a defined benefit or defined contribution basis. Contributions providing defined benefits are generally paid into the scheme itself and can provide 'added years' at retirement. Defined contribution AVCs may be invested in the main fund or, more usually, invested with a third party such as an insurance company or building society. These investments remain under the control of, and are the responsibility of, the trustees of the scheme. If a scheme does not provide the facility for members to pay AVCs through the scheme it must provide the facility to do so through a PRSA.

Tax status

6. Pension schemes which have received the approval of the Revenue Commissioners, through the Retirement Benefits District, receive a number of valuable tax reliefs. It is therefore usual for pension schemes in Ireland to seek Revenue approval to become exempt approved schemes.

Insured schemes

7. Insured schemes are those where the long-term investment is an insurance policy. The trustees enter into a contract with a life assurance company under which premiums are paid to secure the benefits for the members and meet the costs of administering the scheme. Such schemes are generally used by small employers for ease of administration. The contract with the insurance company may be deposit administration or a with profits policy or the underlying investments may be pooled funds. An insured scheme may provide defined benefits or it may be a defined contribution scheme, in which case there may be a series of policies ear-marked for individual members, so that the policy provides all the benefits payable under the scheme for the particular member or their dependants.

8. A fully insured scheme is one under which insurance policies provide benefits corresponding at all times to those promised under the scheme. On retirement, the trustees of insured schemes arrange for an annuity to be purchased to settle the liability for the pension and in most cases, the responsibility for paying the pension is passed to the insurer. However, if the annuity policy is purchased in the name of the scheme the liability continues to rest with the scheme (although in practical terms it is generally assumed to be fully matched by the policy).

Managed funds

9. Some pension schemes use insurance company pooled funds as their investment vehicle. The arrangement consists essentially of an investment contract by means of

which an insurance company offers participation in one or more pooled funds. Such schemes are not insured schemes. However, insured schemes may be invested in internally managed funds of the insurance company.

Self administered schemes

10. Larger schemes generally directly manage the investment of their assets as they can usually achieve better returns and their size means that they are able to bear the long-term investment risks themselves. In such schemes, the trustees are free to invest in any form of investment permitted by the trust deed and legislation. Subject to being appropriately empowered by the trust documentation governing the scheme, the trustees will invest directly in investments (both in Ireland and overseas) such as equities, fixed interest and index-linked securities, property, managed funds and cash. The composition of the portfolio may be related to the age profile of scheme members and the liability of the scheme to pay pensions. The investment management is usually handled by third party investment managers and custodians. Other functions, such as scheme administration and the operation of the pensions payroll, may be handled in-house (by the scheme itself or by the employer) or by a third party administrator.

Small self-administered schemes

11. Generally a self-administered scheme is regarded by the Revenue Commissioners as small where the (up to 12) members are not at arms length i.e. they are family directors or directors who own more than 20% of the voting rights in the sponsoring employer (or parent of that employer). Such schemes are subject to special Revenue rules.

Pensions legislation

12. There is one major piece of legislation relating to pension schemes, the PA 1990. There have been a number of major amending Acts. There have also been numerous amendments to the main legislation made under the Social Welfare Acts. There are numerous sets of Regulations made under the PA 1990 (see Appendix 1).

Trust law

13. As most funded pension schemes are constituted under trusts for the purposes of obtaining exempt approval status from the Revenue Commissioners, they are subject to trust law. A trust is usually established by a legal document, the trust deed, under which the sponsoring employer establishing the scheme places the responsibility for the stewardship and custody of the assets on the trustees. The trustees are required to comply with the general requirements of the trust, general law and pensions legislation, some of whose provisions override those of the trust. The trustees are in a fiduciary position as regards the beneficiaries of the scheme. The trustees must therefore ensure that at all times they act in good faith and with proper care, act in the best interests of the beneficiaries, and always act in accordance with the terms of the trust. Certain general duties and powers of pension scheme trustees have also been codified in legislation (see paragraph 29 below).

14. The obligation not to delegate the performance of duties and powers is qualified in that trustees may be permitted to delegate matters either under statute or, if specifically authorised to do so, under the terms of their trust. As statutory provisions are limited, many trust deeds include wide powers of delegation. Permission to delegate does not release trustees from responsibility. Given they are fiduciaries, the trustees must take due care in selecting the delegate, in determining suitable guidelines for the performance of the matter delegated, and in monitoring the delegate's actual performance and compliance with the guidelines set. A distinction needs to be drawn between the delegation of the exercise or the performance of trustees' duties and powers with the employment of agents to carry out necessary activities on their behalf. The law has long recognised that trustees do not have to take all administrative steps themselves.

Financial reporting

15. Scheme trustees have a statutory duty under the PA 1990 and the 2006 Regulations to make available a scheme annual report within nine months of the end of the scheme year. The report will principally comprise:

    • a trustees' report, which provides a review of the management of the scheme, membership statistics and developments during the period;

    • an investment report, which reviews the investment policy and performance of the scheme;

    • except for schemes that are exempt, the financial statements, (referred to throughout the regulations as 'accounts') which should show a true and fair view of the financial transactions of the scheme during the period and of the disposition of its net assets at the period end, and contain the scheme auditors' report including the statement of opinions on contributions; and

    • where appropriate, an actuarial statement and actuarial funding certificate, which set out the actuary's opinions on the scheme's ability to satisfy the funding standard.

16. Whilst the individual components of the annual report are separate, it will be necessary for the user to read the whole report to gain a full and proper appreciation of the scheme's financial position.

Financial statements included in the annual report

17. As noted above, the annual report of a pension scheme should include, for certain types of schemes, the audited financial statements and the scheme auditors' report including the statement of opinions on contributions. The detailed requirements governing audited financial statements for inclusion in the annual report are contained in the 2006 Regulations.

Taxation

18. A pension scheme which has been approved by the Revenue Commissioners obtains a number of valuable tax reliefs, as do the employer and employee, and the advantages are such that most schemes conform to Revenue requirements to obtain the necessary approval.

19. The Retirement Benefits District (RBD) is responsible for granting and withdrawing approval. The Taxes Consolidation Act 1997 sets out certain basic conditions which must be satisfied before a scheme may be approved, but these are restricted, and virtually all schemes are approved under the Revenue's discretionary powers. General guidance on the exercise of these is set out in the Revenue's Pensions Manual. The RBD also has the power to withdraw approval at any time if it believes that the scheme is no longer meeting its requirements.

20. Exempt approved schemes are those approved by the RBD which are exempt from Irish taxation on investment income and capital gains arising out of their investments. Employer and employee contributions are also tax deductible. Once a scheme is approved, the RBD notifies the local inspector of taxes for the district in which the scheme is registered, and he deals with any tax payments or refunds

21. Taxation arises on pension arrangements, inter-alia, as follows:

    • where RBD approval has not been granted, has been withdrawn or has been limited;

    • where a surplus that has arisen in a scheme is returned to an employer;

    • generally, schemes are exempt and must pay VAT where it is charged;

    • stamp duty on investment transactions;

    • tax suffered at source on overseas investment income and gains may not be recoverable;

    • tax deductible from pension payments and refunds of contributions, including AVCs;

    • tax on commutation payments in excess of Revenue limits;

    • tax on activities which under the tax legislation constitute trading. Generally schemes would be prohibited from such activities.

22. Where a scheme's assets include shares in companies, those companies, even if wholly owned, do not necessarily enjoy the tax exemptions granted to the scheme.

Statutory rights and responsibilities of the various parties associated with pension schemes

23. The rights and responsibilities of the various parties associated with pension schemes are set out below. Most of the trustees' responsibilities originate in trust law and beneficiaries are able to take action for breach of trust and/or fiduciary duty in the civil courts. However, many of the duties and responsibilities of trustees (and also of other parties associated with occupational pension schemes) are now included in the PA 1990, and there are criminal penalties for failures to comply.

Trustees

Appointment and removal

24. Individual trustees are usually appointed and removed by deed, although the specific process will be set out in the scheme's trust documentation. Where a corporate entity is appointed trustee, directors' appointment and removal is dealt with under the terms of the memorandum and articles of the company. Trustees may be appointed as a result of a statutory requirement as well as the terms of the trust deed and rules of the scheme. Regulations made under the PA 1990 specify that members of most schemes have the right to nominate up to one half of the trustees, with a minimum of two member nominated trustees. The Occupational Pension Schemes (Member Participation in the Selection of Persons for Appointment as Trustees) (No. 3) Regulations, 1996 set out the detail of the requirements and the procedures for exemption. In the absence of a member invoking these Regulations, the selection and appointment of member trustees will be a matter for the employer and/or the trustees.

25. The High Court, on application by the PB, may make an order to remove or suspend a trustee. The PB may also appoint trustees to a scheme where there are no trustees or the trustees cannot be found.

Eligibility

26. The PA 1990 defines who is ineligible to act as a trustee.

27. Where the trustee board consists of one or more corporate trustees, the individual directors of the corporate trustee may be liable as if they were trustees of the scheme for the purposes of the PA 1990.

28. A person may not be qualified for appointment as auditor of a scheme if he is a member or a trustee of the scheme, a director or employee of any of the trustees of the scheme or the employer of any member employed or a director or employee of that employer or any affiliated employer.

Functions of Trustees under the PA 1990

29. In addition to the fiduciary duties imposed by general trust law and the provisions of the trust documentation, the PA 1990 imposes a number of statutory duties on trustees. The Act refers to trustees or administrator, so that where there are no trustees

because the scheme is not set up under trust e.g. public sector schemes, the administrator is responsible under the PA 1990 for compliance with the legislation. These statutory duties include, in general terms:

- ensuring contributions are paid to the scheme;

- ensuring benefits are paid in accordance with the rules of the scheme;

- providing for the proper investment of the resources of the scheme in accordance with the rules of the scheme (section 59);

- ensuring the preparation and making available of trustee annual reports (section 55) and , where appropriate, audited financial statements (section 56), actuarial valuations (section 56) and actuarial funding certificates (section 42);

- the keeping of proper membership and financial records (section 59);

- drawing up and implementing procedures for internal resolution of disputes (section132); and

- drawing up and implementing a statement of investment policy principles.

Sponsoring employers

30. Sponsoring employers have a duty under the PA 1990 to ensure that member contributions are remitted by the employer to the trustees within 21 days of the end of the month in which they are deducted from the employees' pay. Any employer contributions due in a defined contribution scheme must also be remitted by the employer to the trustees within 21 days of the end of the month in which they were due. Employer contributions in respect of defined benefit schemes are due as set out in the trust deed and rules or the recommendation of the actuary or otherwise within 30 days of the scheme's year end.

Registered Administrators

31. Trustees have a duty under the Social Welfare and Pensions Act 2008 to ensure that only Registered Administrators are involved in the activities restricted to Registered Administrators. Registered Administrators are Administrators who are registered with the PB. One of the responsibilities of a Registered Administrator of a Scheme is to prepare the financial statements and to present the financial statements to the Trustees within 8 months of the end of the accounting period.

Auditors

32. The 2006 Regulations require trustees of occupational pension schemes (other than small schemes) to cause the financial statements of the scheme to be audited by qualified auditors and the auditors' report to be prepared on the financial statements as soon as reasonably practicable after the end of the scheme year. A copy of the latest audited financial statements and the auditors' report on the financial statements

must be made available by the trustees not later than nine months after the end of the scheme year to which they relate.

33. The audit reporting requirements are set out in the 2006 Regulations. The scheme auditors' report on the financial statements must include:

- a statement as to whether, in their opinion, the audited financial statements contain the information specified in Schedule A of the 2006 Regulations;

- a statement as to whether, in their opinion, the financial statements show a true and fair view of the financial transactions of the relevant scheme during the scheme year and of the amount and disposition, at the end of the scheme year, of the assets and liabilities (other than liabilities to pay pensions and other benefits in the future);

- a statement as to whether, in their opinion, contributions payable to the relevant scheme during the scheme year have been received by the trustees within 30 days of the end of the scheme year and whether in their opinion such contributions have been paid in accordance with the rules of the relevant scheme and, if appropriate, with the recommendation of the actuary; and

- if any of the above three statements is qualified, a statement of the reasons.

The rights of the auditor in relation to information disclosure

34. It is required that trustees and any employer to whom the scheme relates should comply with any request from the actuary or scheme auditors for information that they may reasonably require for the purposes of their function under the PA 1990.

Actuaries

35. The PA 1990 sets out the framework for the legislation relating to the role of the actuary in relation to defined benefit schemes. The 2006 Regulations require ongoing actuarial valuations to be undertaken at least every three years. Trustees are also required under the PA 1990 to ensure an actuarial funding certificate is prepared at least every three years to certify whether the scheme does or does not meet the statutory minimum funding standard (i.e. whether or not the scheme could have met its liabilities if it had wound up at the effective date of the actuarial funding certificate. The PA 1990 specifies the liabilities of the scheme that must be calculated by the actuary in assessing whether, in his opinion, the funding standard is met on a specified date. The method by which these are calculated is set out in Guidance Notes issued by the Society of Actuaries in Ireland. A defined benefit scheme which does not meet the funding standard as at a valuation date must submit a Funding Proposal to the Pensions Board under which the employer and the trustees agree a structure of future funding over a period of three years which may be extended by the Pensions Board.

36. If the scheme year end falls after the date of the latest funding certificate the actuary is also required to make a statement confirming his opinion as to whether, if he were to

prepare a funding certificate having an effective date of the last day of the reporting period, he would certify whether or not the scheme would satisfy the funding standard.

37. The PA 1990 also requires the trustees of a defined contribution scheme (other than a one member arrangement) to value the liabilities of the scheme as at the last day of each scheme year and prepare a report on that valuation as soon as practicable thereafter.

The Pensions Board

38. The main powers conferred on the Pensions Board by the PA 1990 include:

- power to initiate prosecutions in respect of breaches of the requirements of the PA 1990 or, in lieu of the prosecution, to issue on-the-spot fines in relation to certain breaches of the Act with a notice to remedy that breach to the Board's satisfaction;

- power to apply to the High Court for injunctions to prevent persons from misappropriating or misusing scheme assets, prohibit investments or the disposal or selling of assets of the scheme;

- power to apply to the Court for orders to restore or dispose of assets;

- power to gather information and obtain warrants in relation to its investigative powers;

- power to apply to the High Court to have trustees removed and new trustees appointed or to have trustees suspended;

- power to appoint trustees where there are none or they cannot be found;

- power to order trustees to reduce the benefits in a scheme where an actuarial funding certificate or funding proposal have not been submitted to the Pensions Board;

- power to order an employer to pay arrears of contributions to a scheme; and

- the right to share information with other regulators.

Appendix 3

List of publications

The Pensions Board

The Pensions Board has issued a number of publications which scheme auditors may find useful in providing amplification of relevant areas of the regulations and in understanding the perspective of the regulator. Publications may be obtained on its website: www.pensionsboard.ie or by calling 01 – 6131900.

In particular it publishes a Trustee Handbook and Guidance Notes which set out good practice for and give guidance to trustees of schemes.

In addition the Pensions Board publishes numerous booklets and bulletins for trustees and members of schemes.

The Pensions Board also publishes a comprehensive legislation service. This contains a consolidated version of the pensions legislation and all of the regulations. This is subscription based service.

Accounting guidance

An industry SORP, Financial Reports of Pension Schemes, has been prepared by the Pensions Research Accountants Group (PRAG).

The SORP applies to all pension scheme financial statements which are intended to give a true and fair view and embraces all the information requirements of the 2006 Regulations. These Regulations require the inclusion of a statement whether the financial statements have been prepared in accordance with the SORP... 'and, if not, an indication of where there are any material departures from those guidelines'.

Pensions Terminology (Sixth edition)

A glossary of terminology for pension schemes, published by the Pensions Management Institute (PMI) and the Pensions Research Accountants Group (PRAG).
Available from:
Pensions Management Institute, PMI House, 4-10 Artillery Lane, London E1 7LS,
Telephone 0207 247 1452, Fax 0207 375 0603

Actuarial Guidance

The Society of Actuaries in Ireland issue guidance notes (GNs) to members; those that may be of interest to auditors of pension schemes include those in relation to actuarial funding certificates under the PA 1990, funding proposals under the PA1990, actuarial reports, transfer values and calculations required under the Family Law Act, 1995 or The Family Law (Divorce) Act, 1996. Copies of the guidance notes are available on the Society's website: www.actuaries.ie

Appendix 4

Illustrative examples of resignation letter and paragraphs for engagement letters

The illustrative examples of letters in this appendix have been drafted to apply to an occupational pension scheme that is subject to the requirement to make available audited financial statements under section 56 of the Pensions Act 1990. They are not necessarily comprehensive or appropriate to be used in relation to every pension scheme, and must be tailored to specific circumstances – for example, to any special reporting requirements imposed by regulation on particular types of scheme or by the scheme documentation. Note also that certain categories of occupational pension scheme are exempt from individual provisions of the various regulations made under the PA 1990 – the provisions of the regulations described in the following letters therefore do not apply to all occupational pension schemes.

Examples

1. Example resignation letter as scheme auditor

2. Example paragraphs for terms of engagement as scheme auditor to an occupational pension scheme that is required to make available audited financial statements under the PA 1990.

1. Example resignation letter as scheme auditor to an Occupational Pension Scheme

The Trustees
The (...) Pension Scheme

Date

Dear Sirs,

Resignation as Auditors of the (...) Pension Scheme

We acknowledge receipt of your letter dated ...... informing us of your intention to nominate .... as auditors to the scheme.

We hereby give you notice of our resignation as auditors to the scheme with effect from ....

Yours faithfully,

2. Example paragraphs for terms of engagement as scheme auditor to an Occupational Pension Scheme

Responsibilities of trustees and auditors

1.1 The respective statutory duties of trustees and scheme auditors in regard to financial statements and audit are contained in The Occupational Pension Schemes (Disclosure of Information) Regulations 2006 (the Regulations). In summary, under Regulation 4 of the Regulations, it is the duty of the trustees to make available audited financial statements within nine months of the end of the scheme year. Such financial statements should contain the information specified in Schedule A to the Regulations and show a true and fair view of the scheme's financial transactions during the year and of the amount and disposition at the end of the scheme year of its assets and liabilities, other than liabilities to pay benefits after the end of the scheme year.

1.2 It is the responsibility of the trustees to make appropriate arrangements to ensure that, in the preparation of the financial statements:

- the most appropriate accounting policies are selected and then applied consistently; and

- judgments and estimates are made that are reasonable and prudent.

1.3 The trustees are also responsible for safeguarding the assets of the scheme and for taking such steps as are reasonably open to them for the prevention and detection of fraud, error or non-compliance with law or regulations.

1.4 It is the responsibility of the Trustees to ensure that proper membership and financial records are kept in accordance with section 59 (1) (d) of the Pensions Act, 1990. These should include written records of trustees' meetings. You are also responsible for making available to us all the scheme's books, financial statements and records and other information as may reasonably be required for the performance of our duties, including minutes of all trustees' meetings. [Your accounting records are kept by (name) and we shall require direct access to those records.]

1.5 We shall also look to the trustees for assistance in relation to the provision of any information we may require from administrators, advisers, agents and, where appropriate, any person who may become involved in the winding up of the scheme.

1.6. You hereby undertake to notify us of matters which may be relevant to the financial affairs of the scheme which have been notified to you by the sponsoring employers or have otherwise come to your attention.

1.7 We confirm that we are Registered Auditors, eligible to conduct audits under the Regulations. We confirm that we will notify you immediately we become aware of the existence of any conflict of interest to which we are subject in relation to the scheme.

1.8 Our duty as scheme auditors is to report to you whether in our opinion:

- the financial statements presented to us for audit show a true and fair view of the financial transactions of the scheme during the scheme year and of the amount and disposition at the end of the scheme year of the scheme assets and of its liabilities, other than liabilities to pay benefits after the end of the scheme year, and whether the financial statements contain the information specified in Schedule A to the Regulations;

- contributions payable to the scheme during the scheme year have been paid in accordance with the rules of the scheme and, if appropriate, the recommendation of the actuary; and

- the contributions payable during the scheme year were received by the trustees within 30 days of the scheme year end.

1.9 We have a professional responsibility to report if the financial statements do not comply in any material respect with applicable accounting standards, unless in our opinion the non-compliance is justified in the circumstances. In determining whether or not the departure is justified we consider:

- whether the departure is required in order that the financial statements may show a true and fair view; and

- whether adequate disclosure has been made concerning the departure.

1.10 In addition, under the Regulations, the financial statements are required to include a statement as to whether they have been prepared in accordance with the Statement of Recommended Practice, 'Financial Reports of Pension Schemes', published by the Pensions Research Accountants Group, and if not to indicate where there are any material departures and the reasons for any such departures. Failure to comply in this respect will require us to qualify our opinion on whether the financial statements contain the information specified in the Regulations and may require us to qualify our "true and fair view" opinion.

1.11 Our professional responsibilities also include:

- including in our report a description of the trustees' responsibilities for the financial statements where the financial statements or accompanying information do not include such a description; and

- considering whether other information in documents containing audited financial statements is consistent with and does not undermine the credibility of the audited financial statements. In order to assist us with the examination of your financial statements, we shall request sight of all documents or statements which are due to be issued with the financial statements.

However, our responsibility in relation to any statements, certificates or reports by the scheme's actuary, or by other scheme advisers, issued with the audited financial statements is limited to that of understanding their implications for the scheme's financial statements.

1.12 Our audit report is made solely to the scheme's trustees, in accordance with Section 56 of the Pensions Act, 1990. Our audit work will be undertaken so that we might state to the scheme's trustees those matters we are required to state to them in an auditors' report and for no other purpose. To the fullest extent permitted by law, we do not accept or assume responsibility to anyone other than the trustees, for our audit work, for the audit report, or for the opinions we may form.

1.13 We have a statutory duty under section 83 of the Pensions Act, 1990 to report as soon as practicable to the Pensions Board if we have Reasonable Cause to Believe that a material misappropriation or a fraudulent conversion of the resources of the scheme has occurred, is occurring or is to be attempted. We may have to make this report without your knowledge and consent and we cannot undertake to you to fetter this discretion in any manner.

1.14 Section 83 does not require us to undertake work for the sole purpose of identifying breaches likely to be reportable to the Pensions Board. We shall fulfil our duty under this section in accordance with the requirements and guidance set out in ISA (UK and Ireland) 250: 'Section B – The Auditor's Right and Duty to Report to Regulators in the Financial Sector'. In considering the need to make a report, we may decide to consult other relevant persons. You hereby authorise us to communicate directly with other relevant persons for this purpose.

1.15 Under section 84 of the Pensions Act, 1990 where we make a report, whether in writing or otherwise, in good faith to the Pensions Board of any matter concerning the state and conduct of the scheme, whether or not the report is required to be made under section 83, no duty to which we may be subject shall be regarded as contravened and no liability or action shall lie against us in any Court for so doing.

1.16 Section 83 also places an obligation on the trustees and other advisers to report to the Pensions Board. If the trustees make a report to the Pensions Board or if the trustees are aware of such a report being made to the Pensions Board by one of their advisers, you agree to provide us with a copy of such a report.

Additional Legal Responsibilities

Criminal law

1.17 Where, in the course of conducting professional work, it comes to the attention of certain "relevant persons" (as defined), that information or documents indicate that an offence may have been committed under section 59 Criminal Justice (Theft and Fraud Offences) Act 2001, we have a reporting obligation to the An Garda Síochána. This applies regardless of the apparent materiality of the suspected offence, or whether the suspected offence has already been reported to the relevant authorities.

Money laundering reporting

1.18 The provision of audit, accounting and taxation services are businesses in the regulated sector under the Criminal Justice Act 1994 (Section 32) Regulations 2003 and, as auditors of the pension scheme we are required to report all knowledge or suspicion, or reasonable grounds to know or suspect, that a criminal offence giving rise to any direct or indirect benefit from criminal conduct has been committed, regardless of whether that offence has been committed by the scheme or by a third party. If as part of our normal work we have knowledge or suspicion, or have reasonable grounds to know or suspect, that such offences have been committed we are required to make a report to the An Garda Síochána and the Revenue Commissioners. In such circumstances it is not our practice to discuss such reports with you because of the potential offence of prejudicing an investigation within the provisions of the Anti-Money Laundering legislation.

Client identification

1.19 As with other professional services firms, we are under stringent requirements to identify our clients for the purposes of the anti-money laundering legislation. We are likely to request from you, and retain, some information and documentation for these purposes and/or to make searches of appropriate databases. If satisfactory evidence of your identity is not provided within a reasonable time, there may be circumstances in which we are not able to proceed with the audit appointment.

Scope of our work

2.1 Our audit will be conducted in accordance with International Standards on Auditing (UK and Ireland) issued by the Auditing Practices Board and will include such tests of transactions and of the verification of assets and liabilities as we consider necessary. Our work will include examination, on a test basis, of evidence relevant to the amounts of contributions payable to the scheme and the timing of those payments. We shall obtain an understanding of the accounting and control environment in order to assess their adequacy as a basis for the preparation of the financial statements and to develop an effective audit approach. We shall expect to obtain such appropriate evidence as we consider sufficient to enable us to draw reasonable conclusions there from.

2.2 The nature and extent of our procedures will vary according to our assessment of the scheme's accounting system and, where we wish to place reliance on it, the internal control system, and may cover any aspect of the scheme's operations that we consider appropriate, but we are not required to perform tests in connection with or report on:

- the scheme's long term pension liabilities; or

- the trustees' report, the investment report and any other reports accompanying the financial statements.

2.3 Our audit includes assessing the significant estimates and judgments made in the preparation of the financial statements and whether the accounting policies are appropriate to the scheme's circumstances, consistently applied and appropriately disclosed.

2.4 In forming our opinion, we shall also evaluate the overall adequacy of the presentation of information in the financial statements.

2.5 In order to carry out our duties as scheme auditors, we may need to consult with the scheme actuary, employer or other adviser appointed by you. You hereby authorise us to communicate directly with such persons for the purposes of performing our duties as scheme auditors.

2.6 The responsibility for safeguarding the assets of the scheme and for the prevention and detection of fraud, error and non-compliance with law or regulations rests with you. However, we shall endeavour to plan our audit so that we have a reasonable expectation of detecting material misstatements in the financial statements (including those resulting from fraud, error, non-compliance with law or regulations or breaches of trust), but our examination should not be relied upon to disclose all such material misstatements or frauds, errors or instances of non-compliance or breach of trust as may exist.

2.7 Once we have issued our report we have no further direct responsibility in relation to the financial statements for that financial year.

Representations by trustees and third parties

3.1 The information used by the trustees in preparing the financial statements will invariably include facts or judgements which are not themselves recorded in the accounting records. As part of our normal audit procedures, we shall request the trustees, those charged with governance, or senior officials/management involved in the administration of the scheme, to provide written confirmation each year of such facts or judgements and any other oral representations that we have received during the course of the audit on matters having a material effect on the financial statements.

3.2 In addition, we shall present to the trustees/those charged with governance, a schedule of any unadjusted misstatements that have come to our attention in the course of our audit work and if you decide not to adjust the financial statements for those misstatements we shall request you to explain in writing your reasons for not making the adjustments.

Reporting to those charged with governance

4.1 Our audit is not designed to identify all weaknesses in the Scheme's accounting and internal control systems. However, we shall report to the trustees in writing any/those material weaknesses in the scheme's systems or other business matters which come to our notice during the course of our normal audit work and which we consider should be brought to the attention of those charged with governance. Any oral or draft report on material weaknesses which we might provide will not constitute our definitive opinions and conclusions. Our review of internal financial control systems is only performed to the extent required for us to express an opinion on the Scheme's financial statements and the payment of contributions under the scheme. Therefore our comments on these systems will not necessarily address all possible improvements which might be suggested as a result of a more extensive special examination.

Electronic communications and reporting

5.1 We acknowledge that as Trustees of the Scheme you may wish to publish the Scheme's financial statements and the auditors' report on the Scheme's web site or distribute them to members by means such as e-mail. Should such a need arise, we will require that you advise us of any intended publication/distribution before it occurs and that additional engagement terms are agreed.

5.2 During the engagement we may, from time to time, communicate electronically with each other. However, the electronic transmission of information cannot be guaranteed to be secure or virus or error free and such information could be intercepted, corrupted, lost, destroyed, arrive late or incomplete, or otherwise be adversely affected or unsafe to use. We recognise that systems and procedures cannot be a guarantee that transmissions will be unaffected by such hazard.

We confirm that we each accept the risks of and authorise electronic communications between us. We each agree to use commercially reasonable procedures to check for the then most commonly known viruses before sending information electronically. We shall each be responsible for protecting our own systems and interests in relation to electronic communications.

Termination of appointment

6.1 Our appointment as scheme auditors may only be terminated, by you or by us, by notice in writing. The notice shall state the date with effect from which the appointment terminates.

Appendix 5

Illustrative example of representation letter

The following example of a management representation letter from the trustees of a scheme to its scheme auditors is in the form of a letter, but it is not intended to be a standard letter, nor to imply that management representations must necessarily be in the form of a letter from the trustees. Representations by management vary from one entity to another and from one year to the next.

Although seeking representations from the trustees on a variety of matters may serve to focus their attention on those matters, and thus cause them to specifically address those matters in more detail than would otherwise be the case, scheme auditors are cognisant of the limitations of management representations as audit evidence as set out in ISA (UK and Ireland) 580: 'Management Representations'.

(Scheme letterhead)

(Date)

(To the scheme auditors)

We confirm to the best of our knowledge and belief, and having made appropriate enquiries of others connected with the scheme, including participating employer(s) and service providers the following representations given to you in connection with your audit of the financial statements for the scheme year ended...............

We recognise that obtaining representations from us concerning the information in this letter is a significant procedure in enabling you to form an opinion on the financial statements. We also recognise that, as Trustees of the scheme, we have primary responsibility for the financial statements and therefore recognise our duty to make available audited financial statements within nine months of the end of the scheme year which contain the information specified in Schedule A to The Occupational Pension Schemes (Disclosure of Information) Regulations 2006 and show a true and fair view of the scheme's financial transactions during the year and of the amount and disposition at the end of the scheme year of its assets and liabilities, other than liabilities to pay benefits after the end of the scheme year.

1) You have been provided with all minutes of meetings of trustees held during the scheme year and subsequently.

2) Except as stated in the financial statements:

   −   there are no unrecorded liabilities, save for the liability to pay benefits in the future;

   −   none of the assets of the scheme has been assigned, pledged or mortgaged;

3) There have been no significant transactions with related parties [other than those disclosed to you in our memorandum dated ......] and we are not aware of any other such matters in relation to related parties required to be disclosed in the financial statements in accordance with Financial Reporting Standard 8 and with the recommendations of the Statement of Recommended Practice, 'Financial Reports of Pension Schemes' or any other requirements. We have confirmed this with all key managers and other individuals who are in a position to influence or are accountable for the stewardship of the scheme. We confirm that we are satisfied that the related party disclosures in the financial statements are complete and adequate.

4) All known, actual, or possible non-compliance with laws and regulations, together with the actual or contingent consequences which may arise therefrom have been disclosed to you.

5) We have not made any reports to the Pensions Board or other regulatory authority nor are we aware of any such reports having been made by any of our advisors. We also confirm that we are not aware of any matters which have arisen that would require a report to the Pensions Board or other regulatory authority.

6) We are not aware of any fraudulent acts or other irregularities which could have a material effect on the financial statements, or which we feel should be brought to your attention.

7) We have [not] commissioned advisory reports [on the following] which may affect the conduct of your work in relation to the Scheme's financial statements.

8) There have been no events since the scheme year end which necessitate revision of the figures included in the financial statements or inclusion of a note thereto. Should material events occur, which may necessitate revision of the figures included in the financial statements or inclusion of a note thereto, we will advise you accordingly.

9) We confirm that, except as disclosed in the financial statements:

- Contributions have been received and invested in accordance with the time scale specified in the legislation and in accordance with the trust deed and rules, and in accordance with the recommendation of the actuary, if appropriate;

- all contributions receivable in the year have been received within 30 days of the scheme year end;

- there was no other self investment by the scheme at any time during the year;

- there was no concentration of investments held by the scheme above 5% of the scheme's assets at ...

10) We confirm that the reasons why the misstatements that you have brought to our attention set out below have not been adjusted in the financial statements are as follows:

As discussed, approved and minuted by the board of trustees at its meeting on........... (date)

Chairman/Trustee............................... Secretary/Trustee...................................

Other signatories may include those with specific knowledge of the relevant matters, for example the chief financial officer.

Note

The paragraphs included in the example above relate to a specific set of circumstances. Set out below are some additional issues which, depending on the particular circumstances, the materiality of the amounts concerned to the financial statements and the extent of other audit evidence obtained, may be the subject of representations from management:

- Acknowledgement of responsibility for financial statements [where trustees do not include a statement of responsibilities in their annual report itself: for example we acknowledge as trustees our responsibilities for ensuring that financial statements are prepared which give a true and fair view and for making accurate representations to you]

- Confirmation of completeness of records [for example: you have been provided with all books and records relating to the administration of the scheme and have received all the information necessary for the audit of the financial statements. All transactions undertaken by the scheme have been properly reflected and recorded in the accounting records and the financial statements made available to you]

- Whether scheme documentation is fully up to date [for example: you have been informed of all changes to the scheme rules.]

- Confirmation of propriety of transactions [for example: no transactions have been made which are not in the interests of the scheme members or the scheme during the scheme year or subsequently.]

- Confirmation of particular disclosures [for example: there has been no 'self-investment' in a scheme employer or stock-lending.]

- Continuing tax status [for example: we are not aware of any reason why the tax status of the scheme may be jeopardised.]

- Material accounting estimates – confirming basis of estimation

- Lack of evidence – material representations where no other evidence available

- Trustees' opinions – confirmations of opinions concerning matters dealt with in the financial statements

- Accounting policies – confirming most appropriate, appropriately adopted and disclosed as required by Financial Reporting Standard 18

- Confirmation that all correspondence with Pensions Board and Pensions Ombudsman has been made available.

- Confirmation that the Trustees have access at all times to the Trustees' Handbook and Guidance Notes issued by the Pensions Board and that no costs or expenses were incurred by the scheme during the year in respect of trustee training.

Appendix 6

Illustrative examples of scheme auditors' reports

This appendix includes examples of auditors' reports for an occupational pension scheme.

1. Unqualified opinion on the financial statements of an occupational pension scheme.

2. Unqualified opinion on financial statements with a qualified opinion in relation to contributions.

Example 1: Unqualified opinion on the financial statements of a scheme.

Independent Auditors' report to the Trustees of the ABC Pension Scheme

We have audited the financial statements [that comprise the fund account, the net assets statement and the related notes/on pages a to z]. These financial statements have been prepared under the accounting policies set out [in the related notes/on page x].

Respective responsibilities of Trustees and Auditors

The Trustees' responsibilities for making available an annual report, including audited financial statements prepared in accordance with applicable Irish pension law and accounting standards generally accepted in Ireland, are set out in the statement of Trustees' responsibilities [on page y].

Our responsibility is to audit the financial statements in accordance with relevant legal and regulatory requirements and International Standards on Auditing (UK and Ireland).

We report to you our opinion as to whether the financial statements show a true and fair view of the financial transactions of the scheme during the scheme year and of the amount and disposition of its assets and liabilities, other than liabilities to pay benefits in the future, and whether the financial statements contain the information specified in Schedule A to the Occupational Pension Schemes (Disclosure of Information) Regulations, 2006. We also report to you whether in our opinion the contributions payable to the scheme during the scheme year have been received by the trustees within 30 days of the scheme year end and, in our opinion, have been paid in accordance with the scheme rules [and the recommendation of the actuary].

We read the other information contained in the annual report and consider the implications for our report if we become aware of any apparent misstatements or material inconsistencies with the financial statements. The other information comprises the Trustees' Report, the Investment Report, [the Actuarial statements][7] and the Compliance Statement [amend headings as applicable to match the document].

---

[7] In the case of a defined benefit scheme only.

FINANCIAL REPORTING COUNCIL

Basis of audit opinion

We conducted our audit in accordance with International Standards on Auditing (UK and Ireland) issued by the Auditing Practices Board. An audit includes examination, on a test basis, of evidence relevant to the amounts and disclosures in the financial statements. It also includes an assessment of the significant estimates and judgments made by or on behalf of the Trustees in the preparation of the financial statements, and of whether the accounting policies are appropriate to the Scheme's circumstances, consistently applied and adequately disclosed. Our work also included examination, on a test basis, of evidence relevant to the amounts of contributions payable to the scheme and the timing of those payments.

We planned and performed our audit so as to obtain all the information and explanations which we considered necessary in order to provide us with sufficient evidence to give reasonable assurance that the financial statements are free from material misstatement, whether caused by fraud or other irregularity or error, and that contributions have been paid in accordance with the scheme rules [and the recommendation of the actuary] and received within 30 days of the scheme year end. In forming our opinion we also evaluated the overall adequacy of the presentation of information in the financial statements.

Opinion

In our opinion the financial statements show a true and fair view of the financial transactions of the Scheme during the year ended [date], and of the amount and disposition at that date of its assets and liabilities, other than the liabilities to pay benefits in the future, and contain the information specified in Schedule A to the Occupational Pension Schemes (Disclosure of Information) Regulations, 2006.

In our opinion the contributions payable to the scheme during the year ended [date]

- have been received within 30 days of the end of the scheme year and

- have been paid in accordance with the scheme rules [and the recommendation of the actuary.]

Registered Auditors   Address

Date

Example 2: Unqualified opinion on the financial statements of a scheme with a qualified opinion in relation to contributions.

Independent Auditors' report to the Trustees of the ABC Pension Scheme

We have audited the financial statements [that comprise the fund account, the net assets statement and the related notes/on pages a to z]. These financial statements have been prepared under the accounting policies set out [in the related notes/on page x].

Respective responsibilities of Trustees and Auditors

The Trustees' responsibilities for making available an annual report, including audited financial statements prepared in accordance with applicable Irish pension law and accounting standards generally accepted in Ireland, are set out in the statement of Trustees' responsibilities [on page y].

Our responsibility is to audit the financial statements in accordance with relevant legal and regulatory requirements and International Standards on Auditing (UK and Ireland).

We report to you our opinion as to whether the financial statements show a true and fair view of the financial transactions of the scheme during the scheme year and of the amount and disposition of its assets and liabilities other than liabilities to pay benefits in the future and whether the financial statements contain the information specified in Schedule A to the Occupational Pension Schemes (Disclosure of Information) Regulations, 2006. We also report to you whether in our opinion the contributions payable to the scheme during the scheme year have been received by the trustees within 30 days of the scheme year end and, in our opinion, have been paid in accordance with the scheme rules [and the recommendation of the actuary].

We read the other information contained in the annual report and consider the implications for our report if we become aware of any apparent misstatements or material inconsistencies with the financial statements. The other information comprises the Trustees' Report, the Investment Report, [the Actuarial statements,][8] and the Compliance Statement [amend headings as applicable to match the document].

Basis of audit opinion

We conducted our audit in accordance with auditing standards issued by the Auditing Practices Board. An audit includes examination, on a test basis, of evidence relevant to the amounts and disclosures in the financial statements. It also includes an assessment of the significant estimates and judgments made by or on behalf of the Trustees in the preparation of the financial statements, and of whether the accounting policies are appropriate to the Scheme's circumstances, consistently applied and adequately disclosed. Our work also included examination, on a test basis, of evidence relevant to the amounts of contributions payable to the scheme and the timing of those payments.

---

[8] In the case of a defined benefit scheme only

We planned and performed our audit so as to obtain all the information and explanations which we considered necessary in order to provide us with sufficient evidence to give reasonable assurance that the financial statements are free from material misstatement, whether caused by fraud or other irregularity or error, and that contributions have been paid in accordance with the scheme rules [and the recommendation of the actuary] and received within 30 days of the scheme year end. In forming our opinion we also evaluated the overall adequacy of the presentation of information in the financial statements.

Opinion on financial statements

In our opinion the financial statements show a true and fair view of the financial transactions of the Scheme during the year ended [date], and of the amount and disposition at that date of its assets and liabilities, other than the liabilities to pay benefits in the future, and contain the information specified in Schedule A to the Occupational Pension Schemes (Disclosure of Information) Regulations, 2006.

Opinion on contributions: qualified in relation to late payment [where payment has subsequently been received]

In our opinion contributions amounting to €_____ in relation to the year ended [date] were not received by the trustees within 30 days of the year end but were received on [date]. Except for this matter, in our opinion, the contributions payable to the scheme during the year ended [date] have been received within 30 days of the end of the scheme year and in our opinion have been paid in accordance with the scheme rules [and the recommendation of the actuary]

Opinion on contributions: qualified in relation to late payment [where payment had not been received by the auditors' report date]

In our opinion, contributions amounting to €_____ in relation to the year ended [date] were not received by the trustees within 30 days of the year end and remain outstanding. Except for this matter, in our opinion, the contributions payable to the scheme during the year ended [date] have been received within 30 days of the end of the scheme year and in our opinion have been paid in accordance with the scheme rules [and the recommendation of the actuary]

Registered Auditors   Address

Date

Appendix 7

Illustrative example statement of trustees' responsibilities

The following illustrative wording may be used as the basis for preparing a statement for inclusion in a scheme's annual report.

The financial statements are the responsibility of the Trustees. Irish pension legislation requires the trustees to make the annual report of the scheme available for each scheme year, including audited financial statements and the report of the auditors. The financial statements are required to:

- show a true and fair view of the financial transactions of the scheme during the scheme year and of the amount and disposition at the end of that year of the assets and liabilities, other than liabilities to pay benefits in the future , and

- contain the information specified in the Schedule A to The Occupational Pension Schemes (Disclosure of Information) Regulations, 2006, including a statement as to whether the financial statements have been prepared in accordance with the Statement of Recommended Practice 'Financial Reports of Pension Schemes' (Revised May 2007) (the SORP).

Accordingly, the trustees must ensure that in the preparation of the scheme financial statements:

- suitable accounting policies are selected and then applied consistently;

- reasonable and prudent judgements and estimates are made; and

- the SORP is followed, or particulars of any material departures are disclosed and explained.

The trustees are responsible for ensuring that proper membership and financial records are kept and contributions are made to the scheme in accordance with the scheme rules and the requirements of legislation [and the recommendation of the actuary] and for safeguarding the assets of the pension scheme and hence for taking reasonable steps for the prevention and detection of fraud and other irregularities, including the maintenance of appropriate internal controls.

The maintenance and integrity of the [........ Pension Scheme] web site is the responsibility of the trustees'].

Appendix 8

Considerations for scheme auditors in relation to a scheme in the process of winding up

Introduction

In the Irish context the process of winding up pension schemes is determined by each scheme's Trust Deed & Rules and by the Pensions Acts 1990 – 2009 and relevant Regulations ('the Legislation').

In matters such as the compliance requirements in respect of annual report, incorporating where applicable financial statements, actuarial funding certificates and actuarial valuations, the Legislation makes very little distinction between active schemes and those in wind up.

An important distinction may however be made between schemes in wind up, where steps are being taken to terminate the schemes and to transfer their assets and liabilities elsewhere, and frozen or paid – up schemes that are merely closed to future benefit accrual. The main difference, from an accounting perspective, is that where a scheme is frozen before 1 January 1997 its trustees are no longer subject to the statutory requirement to have prepared annual reports (incorporating where applicable, audited financial statements). Scheme auditors should therefore take steps to determine whether schemes are actually in wind up or are simply frozen, as defined in the Legislation.

Timing of commencement of winding up

Wind up of a scheme may be triggered by a particular event described in a scheme's trust deed and rules (for example, a decision by the employer permanently to cease making contributions to the scheme or by a decision of the trustees). Where a scheme is being wound up as a result of a requirement in the scheme rules, wind up commences at the time set out in those rules or if there is no such provision in the rules, a time fixed by the trustees.

Requirement for audited financial statements to be prepared during wind up

Schemes that are in the process of winding up are not exempt, by that fact, from the requirements to produce an annual report, incorporating where applicable, statutory audited financial statements. However, certain indirect effects of a wind up may have an impact on the type of report prepared by some schemes. For example, the statutory requirement for trustees of schemes to cause an annual report to be prepared which incorporates audited financial statements applies to schemes other than small schemes. Hence this requirement continues for such schemes until their membership falls below these levels, which will happen to a scheme in wind up at some stage. Trust law and best practice indicate that trustees should continue to prepare financial statements which demonstrate their stewardship of the scheme up to the date on which the scheme is finally wound up. This is generally considered to be when all the assets of the scheme have been distributed to secure liabilities in accordance with the rules of the scheme and legal requirements, either a deed of determination or trustees' resolution has been executed, and the relevant regulatory authority has been notified.

Accounting policies

Once a scheme has commenced wind up, it is by definition no longer a going concern. Scheme auditors consider the issues in relation to going concern, set out in the ISA 570 section of the Practice Note. Specifically, the policy on the valuation of investments, particularly insurance policies, is reviewed and changed as necessary. Further guidance on this area is provided in the SORP.

Accounting periods for schemes in wind up

Schemes in wind up should continue to comply with the limits on accounting periods for statutory financial statements. The PA 1990 provides for a maximum period of 23 months in the final accounting period to wind up. In a wind up context financial statements may be prepared for any period up to the maximum without the prior authorisation of the Pensions Board.

Non statutory financial statements covering the wind-up process

Trustees will frequently require financial statements to be prepared up to the wind up date (a date at which all the assets and liabilities will have been disposed of). These financial statements would constitute the final financial statements required under the Pensions Acts in relation to the scheme. The trustees should remain in office until these financial statements have been signed. In situations where there are no longer trustees, scheme auditors may be requested by former trustees, employers or members, to carry out an audit of scheme financial statements for a period to the date at which the scheme was wound up. In such circumstances, scheme auditors put in place engagement terms for a non-statutory audit, as following the completion of wind up, there are no Pensions Act responsibilities. The non-statutory audit report should be addressed to whoever requests the audit, as set out in the engagement terms, and other wording in the financial statements and accompanying information should be consistent with those engagement terms.

Record keeping

The obligation of trustees to keep records continues throughout the wind up process.

Cessation of audit appointment

In order to avoid a situation where trustees inform scheme auditors that a scheme is wound up, when that is not the case, scheme auditors obtain evidence that a scheme is wound up, which may include obtaining a copy of the deed of determination or, trustee resolution. Once wind up is formally concluded, the scheme auditor's appointment automatically lapses without the need for formal resignation.

Appendix 9

Definitions

Terms in this Practice Note are used as defined in the Glossary of terms issued by the APB in conjunction with International Standards on Auditing (UK and Ireland), and Pensions Terminology – a Glossary for Pension Schemes (sixth edition) published by the Pensions Management Institute (PMI) and the Pensions Research Accountants Group (PRAG).

Terms and abbreviations in this Practice Note for frequently used terms are as follows:

FRS	*Financial Reporting Standard*
ISAs	*International Standards on Auditing*
PA 1990	*Pensions Act, 1990 to 2009 and associated regulations*
PB	*The Pensions Board*
Pension scheme	*An occupational pension scheme as defined by Part 1 Section 1 of the Pensions Act, 1990*
Pensions SORP	*The Statement of Recommended Practice 'Financial reports of pension schemes' (Revised May 2007)*
PRAG	*The Pensions Research Accountants Group*
Scheme	*An occupational pension scheme as defined by Part 1 Section 1 of the Pensions Act, 1990*
SSASs	*Small self-administered schemes*
The 2006 Regulations	*The Occupational Pension Schemes (Disclosure of Information) Regulations 2006*

Appendix 10

Some significant topics relevant to audits of pension schemes

Topic	Paragraph Numbers	Section
Statement of opinions on contributions	198 263 273 – 285	ISA (UK and Ireland) 320 ISA (UK and Ireland) 700 The Auditors' Statement of Opinions on Contributions
Reports to the Pensions Board	22 – 23 90 – 92 105 – 139 290	Introduction ISA (UK and Ireland) 250A ISA (UK and Ireland) 250B Liaison with the scheme actuary
Liaison with actuaries	28 – 30 254 286 – 299 35 – 36	Introduction ISA (UK and Ireland) 620 Liaison with the scheme actuary Appendix 2
Reliance on third parties	27 – 37 204 – 226 249 – 251 252 – 254	Introduction ISA (UK and Ireland) 402 ISA (UK and Ireland) 600 ISA (UK and Ireland) 620
Reporting to those charged with governance	62 93 – 94 141 – 142	ISA (UK and Ireland) 240 ISA (UK and Ireland) 250A ISA (UK and Ireland) 260
Trust deed	3, 4, 40 42 63 66, 73, 74 161, 167, 190 221, 223 228 233 252 256, 263 13	Introduction ISA (UK and Ireland) 210 ISA (UK and Ireland) 240 ISA (UK and Ireland) 250A ISA (UK and Ireland) 315 ISA (UK and Ireland) 402 ISA (UK and Ireland) 520 ISA (UK and Ireland) 550 ISA (UK and Ireland) 620 ISA (UK and Ireland) 700 Appendix 2
Taxation	5 18 – 22	Introduction Appendix 2

Topic	Paragraph Numbers	Section
Pensions SORP	14	Introduction
	72	ISA (UK and Ireland) 250A
	126	ISA (UK and Ireland) 250B
	160, 162	ISA (UK and Ireland) 315
	215	ISA (UK and Ireland) 402
	230, 232	ISA (UK and Ireland) 550
	235, 239	ISA (UK and Ireland) 570
	261, 262	ISA (UK and Ireland) 700
	–	Appendix 3
Appointment of scheme auditors	30	Introduction
	41 – 51	ISA (UK and Ireland) 210
	–	Appendix 4

PRACTICE NOTE 16 (REVISED)

BANK REPORTS FOR AUDIT PURPOSES IN THE UNITED KINGDOM

CONTENTS

Preface

This Practice Note summarises the process agreed between the UK auditing profession and the British Bankers Association (BBA) regarding the procedures auditors use when requesting confirmation of balances, transactions or arrangements from the bankers of an entity being audited.

In this Practice Note bank confirmations are described as 'bank reports'.

Introduction

Confirmations provided by banks and other financial institutions of balances and other banking arrangements usually provide the auditor with valuable audit evidence.

Over the years the auditing and banking professions have developed protocols and forms to assist this process. Practice Note 16: "Bank reports for audit purposes" formalises the process.

Following the publication of the clarified International Standards on Auditing (ISAs) (UK and Ireland) in October 2009, there was a need to update the APB's Practice Notes to reflect the new auditing standards. The changes required to PN 16 were relatively limited, the main one being to recognise that the requirement for the auditor to consider whether external confirmation procedures are to be performed is now included in ISA (UK and Ireland) 330, *The auditor's responses to assessed risks,* rather than ISA (UK and Ireland) 505, *External confirmations,* which now focuses on the design and performance of external confirmation procedures to obtain relevant and reliable audit evidence. No changes have been made to the process agreed between the UK auditing profession and the British Bankers Association (BBA) regarding the procedures auditors use when requesting confirmation of balances, transactions or arrangements from the bankers of an entity being audited.

Planning: Risk Assessment and Audit Evidence

1. The following International Standards on Auditing (UK and Ireland) are particularly relevant to the auditor's decisions as to whether to obtain a bank report and, where applicable, what information is to be covered by it:

    *   ISA (UK and Ireland) 300, *Planning an audit of financial statements*

    *   ISA (UK and Ireland) 315, *Identifying and assessing the risks of material misstatement through understanding the entity and its environment*

    *   ISA (UK and Ireland) 330, *The auditor's responses to assessed risks*

    *   ISA (UK and Ireland) 500, *Audit evidence*

    *   ISA (UK and Ireland) 505, *External confirmations*

2. ISA (UK and Ireland) 300 *Planning an audit of financial statements* states that the objective of the auditor [in complying with this standard] is to plan the audit so that it will be performed in an effective manner.

3. ISA (UK and Ireland) 315 *Identifying and assessing the risks of material misstatement through understanding the entity and its environment* requires the auditor to identify and assess the risks of material misstatement at the financial statement level, and at the assertion level for classes of transactions, account balances, and disclosures. Decisions on whether or not to request a bank report and, if so, the nature of evidence to be obtained are responses to the auditor's assessment of the risks of material misstatement.

4. ISA (UK and Ireland) 330, *The auditor's responses to assessed risks* requires the auditor to consider whether external confirmation procedures are to be performed as substantive audit procedures.

5. ISA (UK and Ireland) 500, *Audit evidence* considers the relative reliability of audit evidence obtained from different sources.

6. ISA (UK and Ireland) 505 *External confirmations* addresses the design and performance of external confirmation procedures to obtain relevant and reliable audit evidence.

7. During the planning phase of the audit the auditor therefore considers the risks in relation to relevant financial statement assertions including bank related information to be disclosed in the notes to the financial statements when deciding whether to obtain a bank report.

8. Many banks lay out the facilities the entity uses, or those made available to the entity, in an annual facilities letter. The auditor takes into account the banking facilities provided when assessing the risks in relation to relevant financial statement assertions and when deciding whether to obtain a bank report and, where applicable, what banking information is to be confirmed. Where there is no facilities letter, the auditor asks the entity's management what banking relationships are in place.

9. Given the importance of cash to an entity's business and its susceptibility to fraudulent misuse the auditor will usually conclude that, in the absence of a bank report regarding account balances, facilities and securities, it will not normally be practical to obtain sufficient appropriate audit evidence from other sources.

10. In rare circumstances where the banking transactions and relationships are very simple and sufficient appropriate audit evidence is likely to be available from other sources the auditor may consider that obtaining a bank report of account balances, facilities and securities is unnecessary.

Planning: the bank report request

11. Having decided to obtain a bank report, the auditor plans the submission of the request to the bank including:

    - determining the date by which the bank report is needed;

    - depending on the auditor's risk assessment, determining whether confirmation is needed on additional information such as trade finance transactions and balances;

    - deciding what type of report to use i.e. Standard (with or without additional information), Fast Track or Incomplete Information Requests;

    - making arrangements for assembling the necessary information to be included in the request including the main account sort code and number for each legal entity (that is, subsidiaries as well as the holding company, where a single letter is sent for all companies in a group). If the auditors have decided to confirm additional information (e.g. trade finance or derivative and commodity trading transactions and balances) a reference will be needed to a sample facility account number;

    - checking that the authorities provided to the banks to allow them to disclose information to the auditors are valid; and

    - ascertaining where to send the request. It is standard practice for banks to deal with requests for bank reports through a centralised delivery mechanism, using a dedicated query team. The addresses of units dealing with bank report requests for each bank are published on the BBA website at www.bba.org.uk. The designated unit will either respond on behalf of the bank or forward the request to a specialist department.

12. The normal purpose of bank reports is to provide confirmation of information already available to the auditors. In these circumstances, auditors send a Standard Request for information, including where appropriate a request for additional information. To assist banks retrieve the necessary information auditors provide the main account sort code and number for each legal entity named in the request and, where additional information is requested, a sample facility account number for trade finance or derivative and commodity trading information.

13. When the auditors are unable to provide the main account sort code and number for all the entities in a group or sufficient references to identify additional information required the auditors make a request using an Incomplete Information Request. Circumstances where such a request might be appropriate include:

    - because information is not available from the audited entity perhaps due to a break down in controls;

    - because the auditor suspects that full information has not been provided to them by the entity for example where there is prior experience of accounts or banking relationships not notified to the auditor or where the auditor suspects impropriety regarding the entity's use of financial instruments;

- where history shows poor record keeping, particularly of financial instruments that do not require an initial entry in the entity's records.

14. Auditors deciding to use an Incomplete Information Request need to be aware that banks cannot give information about legal entities that are not covered by an existing authority to disclose information. This means that details will be provided by the banks of all accounts and facilities relating to an entity listed on the request for a bank report, for which there is a current authority. The bank is under no obligation to tell the auditor that it holds an account or has other arrangements for an entity that is not listed in the request for information. Nor is the bank obliged to tell the auditor that it has withheld information about an entity not listed. Auditors therefore make enquiries of management and apply their understanding of the business to evaluate whether the list of entities to be included on all requests to banks, including the Incomplete Information Request, is complete.

15. Auditors also need to be aware that, where banks are asked to respond to an Incomplete Information Request, searches for possible relationships or facilities will take longer and the banks may charge their customers an additional fee. It is therefore sensible for auditors to use an Incomplete Information Requests only where their knowledge of the entity's business indicates that this is necessary.

16. Where the audit plan shows that a bank report is needed sooner than would be the case under normal procedures, the auditor requests a 'Fast Track' response. Fast Track responses are expected to be exceptional, for example where the entity has to meet a US reporting deadline within a month or less of the accounting year end. The process for Fast Track confirmation requests is considered in more detail in paragraph 30 below.

Authority to disclose

17. Banks require the explicit written authority of their customers to disclose the information requested. The BBA has requested that, where possible, this takes the form of an ongoing standing authority rather than as a separate authority each time information is requested. Auditors need to satisfy themselves that an authority is in place and up to date. A single authority can cover several legal entities provided that each entity is specified and the authorisation signatures are appropriate. Banks and building societies that are not members of the BBA may have different requirements for authority to disclose, which are ascertained by auditors before they submit their requests for information.[1]

---

[1] In addition, the BBA has indicated that it will disclose on its website details of credit institutions that do not currently retain authorities and therefore require an authority with each request.

18. A new authority will be needed in the case of a new audit entity. An updated authority will be needed if there are entity changes such as new group entities or auditor changes such as reorganisation as a limited liability partnership (LLP) or merger with another practice. An illustrative letter providing authority to a bank to disclose information to the entity's auditor is included as Appendix 2.

Guarantees and other third party securities

19. The provision of information about guarantees and other third party securities has, on occasion, resulted in significant delays in the completion of bank reports because banks have been unable to release the information sought without specific customer consent because of data protection regulations concerning the counter-parties. When banks do not have sufficient authority to provide full disclosure of the information requested, they advise the auditors of that fact and indicate, where that is the case, that such guarantees or third party securities exist. The auditors can then obtain details of the arrangement from the entity, for example by asking to see the relevant facility letter or loan agreement. In some cases, these procedures will suffice. In other cases, auditors will require further independent evidence, and if so they can ask banks for the specific information to be provided once consent from the guarantor or third party has been received.

Bank information

20. The key steps in the bank report process have been agreed with the BBA. The BBA has written to its members setting out guidance for them to follow in responding to requests for audit confirmations. This guidance note is reproduced in full in Appendix 3. A list of current BBA members may be viewed at the BBA's website, www.bba.org.uk. Where the entity's bank is not a BBA member, the auditor may still be able to get a positive response to a request for information. Where a bank report cannot be obtained, the auditors consider whether this represents a limitation of scope that should be referred to in the audit report.

Bank report request templates

21. The request for a bank report is issued on the auditors' own note paper using the appropriate template in Appendix 1.

22. The BBA's guidance to its members defining the information to be given in response to each type of request is set out in Appendix 3 of this Practice Note. The purpose of providing three different request forms is to reflect auditors' planning decisions as to the nature and timing of the information sought.

23. The Standard and Fast Track request templates specify:

- the names of all legal entities covered by the request, together with the main account sort code and number of each entity listed;

- reference to a sample facility account number for any additional information required. This will enable the bank to identify the units providing specialist services which need to be consulted. A full listing of all transactions or balances is not required;

- the date for which the auditor is requesting confirmation (i.e. the period end date) and the date at which the report request is made;

- a statement that neither the auditor's request nor the bank's response will create a contractual relationship between the bank and the auditor; and

- the auditor's contact details.

24. The template for Fast Track Requests includes a space for the auditor to explain the reason for the Fast Track requests and the date by which the reply is needed.

25. The Incomplete Information Request contains:

- the names of all legal entities covered by the request, together with the main account number and sort code of the parent company and for as many group entities as can be obtained by the auditor;

- the period end date for which the auditor is requesting confirmation;

- the date at which the report request is made;

- a statement that neither the auditor's request nor the bank's response will create a contractual relationship between the bank and the auditor; and

- the auditor's contact details.

The auditor accepts that banks will not be able to provide this information on an entity that is not covered by a valid authority to disclose.

26. The APB is of the view that the inclusion of a statement that neither the auditor's request nor the bank's response will create a contractual relationship between the bank and the auditor, does not impair the value of the information given as audit evidence. The information given by a bank ought not to be regarded as inaccurate or likely to be inaccurate simply because the giving of it is not actionable. Accordingly, the auditor can reasonably rely upon information given by the bank, provided it is not clearly wrong, suspicious or inconsistent in itself, ambiguous or in conflict with other evidence gathered in the course of the audit.

Timing of requests

27. Where practicable, the auditor sends the bank report request so as to reach the bank one month in advance of the period end date. It is advisable to allow more time at busy periods such as those covering December and March year ends.

28.   The BBA has indicated that banks providing acknowledgements of audit requests, if so required, will endeavour to do so within 5 working days of receipt. As part of the acknowledgement process, banks may indicate either a date by which they expect to send a reply to the auditor, or provide an indication of their standard service level agreement (SLA) for the process. The BBA has advised that no practical purpose is served by an auditor's chasing for a bank report until the expected date of receipt (as stated in the bank's acknowledgement or standard SLA) has passed. Banks that do not acknowledge receipt of audit requests are identified on the BBA's website and contact details given for pursuing enquiries.

29.   In straightforward circumstances the bank will endeavour to provide the information within a calendar month of the period end date. Where there is a request using an Incomplete Information Request or where a request has been made asking information about guarantees and other third party securities and specific consent is needed from a third party for such information to be released, a response may take longer.

30.   For listed companies and other entities subject to tight reporting deadlines the information may be needed sooner than the normal response time of a particular bank. The BBA has therefore agreed a process for fast track responses whereby auditors state why they need the information within less than a calendar month of the period end date. The Fast Track template in Appendix 1 includes a box to be completed by the auditor when seeking an accelerated response.

Minor omissions or discrepancies

31.   Minor omissions or discrepancies in the information provided by the bank may be dealt with informally by telephone or e-mail, although the auditor may request written confirmation of changes to the information provided.

Accrued interest and charges

32.   The provision of information about accrued interest and charges at the year end falls outside the scope of this Practice Note.

Appendix 1

Templates for auditor request forms

1. Standard Request (including additional information option)

2. Fast Track Request

3. Incomplete Information Request

4. Acknowledgement template

REQUEST FOR BANK REPORT FOR AUDIT PURPOSES – STANDARD

The request for a bank report is issued on the auditors' own note paper

Please note – Complete **section 6** only where additional information is required.

In accordance with the agreed practice for provision of information to auditors, please forward information on our mutual client(s) as detailed below on behalf of the bank, its branches and subsidiaries. This request and your response will not create any contractual or other duty with us.

1. BANK NAME & ADDRESS

2. AUDITOR CONTACT DETAILS

Name and
address
of auditor

Contact number

Contact name

Email address

Period end date
(DD/MM/YYYY)

Date of request
(DD/MM/YYYY)

3. Companies or other business entities

Company	Main account sort code	Main account number

4. Authority to disclose information

Authority already held [   ] **OR** Authority [   ]
and dated   Attached
(DD/MM/YYYY)

5. Acknowledgement

Please complete this section if an acknowledgement is required.

Acknowledgement [   ] by email   Reference number to [   ]
required   be quoted

OR   [   ] by post   (template attached)

6. Additional information required

Trade Finance [   ] One of the facility account numbers [   ]

Derivative & [   ] One of the facility account numbers [   ]
Commodity
Trading

REQUEST FOR BANK REPORT FOR AUDIT PURPOSES – FAST TRACK

The request for a bank report is issued on the auditors' own note paper

Please note – Complete **section 6** only where additional information is required.

In accordance with the agreed practice for provision of information to auditors, please forward information on our mutual client(s) as detailed below on behalf of the bank, its branches and subsidiaries. This request and your response will not create any contractual or other duty with us.

1. BANK NAME & ADDRESS

2. AUDITOR CONTACT DETAILS

Name and
address
of auditor

Contact number

Contact name

Email address

Period end date
(DD/MM/YYYY)

Date response required
(DD/MM/YYYY)

Date of request (DD/MM/YYYY)

Reason for Fast Track request

3. Companies or other business entities

Company	Main account sort code	Main account number

4. Authority to disclose information

Authority already held
and dated
(DD/MM/YYYY)   **OR**   Authority
                                     attached

5. Acknowledgement

Please complete this section if an acknowledgement is required.

Acknowledgement   by email   Reference number to
required   be quoted

OR   by post   (template attached)

6. Additional information required

Trade Finance   One of the facility account numbers

Derivative &   One of the facility account numbers
Commodity
Trading

REQUEST FOR BANK REPORT FOR AUDIT PURPOSES –
INCOMPLETE INFORMATION

The request for a bank report is issued on the auditors' own note paper

Please note – Complete **section 6** only where additional information is required.

In accordance with the agreed practice for provision of information to auditors, please forward information on our mutual client(s) as detailed below on behalf of the bank, its branches and subsidiaries. This request and your response will not create any contractual or other duty with us.

1. BANK NAME & ADDRESS

2. AUDITOR CONTACT DETAILS

Name and
address
of auditor

Contact number

Contact name

Email address

Period end date
(DD/MM/YYYY)

Date response required
(DD/MM/YYYY)

We confirm that there are exceptional circumstances that require us to ask for this request to be processed on the basis of incomplete account numbers, sort code and facility account numbers for all companies in the group and/or a facility account number for additional information. We understand that this may result in the search taking longer to complete than the standard request.

3. Companies or other business entities

Company	Main account sort code	Main account number

4. Authority to disclose information

Authority already held and dated [   ]   **OR**   Authority Attached [   ]

5. Acknowledgement

Please complete this section if an acknowledgement is required.

Acknowledgement required [   ] by email   Reference number to be quoted [   ]

OR [   ] by post   (template attached)

6. Additional information required

Trade Finance [   ] A facility account number if available [   ]

Derivative & Commodity Trading [   ] A facility account number if available [   ]

REQUEST FOR ACKNOWLEDGEMENT OF BANK REPORT FOR AUDIT PURPOSES

The request is issued on the auditors' own note paper

Please note – Part A is to be completed by the Auditor, Part B is to be completed by the Bank

PART A

This acknowledgement should be returned to:

Name and
address
of auditor

Please contact _____ if you have any queries on this letter

Contact number

Email Address

PART B

Thank you for your request for a bank report for audit purposes in respect of:

Customer Name	Main account sort code	Main account number

The request was received on (DD/MM/YYYY)

Your request is being processed and the report will be sent to you once we have gathered the information sought. In the event of your needing to contact us, please address any enquiries to:

Name and
address
of bank

Expected response date

Name of Individual or section responsible

Telephone number

Email address

Appendix 2

Authority to disclose information – Illustration

[*xxxxx Bank PLC*
25 xxx Street
Warrington
Cheshire WA1 1XQ]

[Parent Company Ltd,
Subsidiary 1 Ltd,
Subsidiary 2 Ltd]
Date

I/ We authorise [xxxx Bank PLC] including all branches and subsidiaries to provide to our auditor [*XXX Accountants*] any information that they may request from you regarding all and any of our accounts and dealings with you.

_____

signature(s)[1]

_____

signature(s)[1]

cc: The auditors

_____

[1]   Signatures according to current bank mandates with full authority to action this authorisation.

Appendix 3

British Bankers' Association guidance note for banks

1. PREFACE

Since the Auditing Practices Board (APB) revision of Practice Note 16 was issued for consultation in November 2005 there have been ongoing discussions between the BBA members and representatives of CCAB bodies.

The banks have found these discussions very useful and it has enabled them to understand the difficulties that the existing process presents to auditors. We have listened to the concerns and issues from the auditors' point of view. In turn, the auditors have listened to the banks. There is now an improved understanding of how auditors and banks can have a better working relationship, which will be to the mutual benefit of the client.

The new process is also expected to support the banks in providing an improved service.

1.1 Delivery of the bank confirmation request

Historically, banks have requested auditors to send the requests to a branch. However, many of the larger banks have now centralised such processes. That said, in the absence of a sort code and account number, the use of a branch address has at least given the banks some information to start the search process.

The acknowledgement, by the Auditing Practices Board, of the importance of providing primary sort codes and account numbers will facilitate the production of the bank response in a small number of service centres. This will enable auditors to send requests directly to a central address where this matches a bank's business model.

1.2 Acknowledgements

Banks providing acknowledgements, if requested, of audit requests will endeavour to do so within 5 working days of receipt. Where banks send acknowledgements via email, the audit firm's reference number for the client - and not the client's name – will be quoted for security reasons. Banks that do not acknowledge receipt of audit requests are identified on the BBA's website and contact details given for pursuing enquiries.

1.3 Enquiries

Many of the enquiries received by banks from auditors are classed as being pre-production, eg confirming receipt of the instruction. Many of these calls result from the acknowledgement process not working as well as it could. As banks receiving audit requests centrally are able to issue an acknowledgement earlier in the process, those operating in this way are likely to experience a reduced volume of pre-production enquiries.

For post-production enquiries, where possible, banks will provide a centralised enquiry point or details of how enquiries can be directed to the appropriate area.

1.4 Cooperation

The collaborative approach adopted by the working party of banks and auditors has been instrumental to the redesign of the request templates which will deliver improvements in the service provided. Having worked hard to discuss and understand the process and issues from both viewpoints, on-going cooperation between banks and auditors is seen as a key component to the smooth operation of the audit enquiry process. It is therefore proposed that the working group should be maintained and that liaison meetings should take place periodically, say once or twice per year, with the aim of providing a forum in which practical issues concerning the audit enquiry process can be raised.

1.5 Speed

The provision of primary account number information will address some of the issues experienced by the banks. It is essential that this information is provided, to enable the banks to commence their process more speedily. Account information is used for ensuring that the search is more robust but is also used to find information such as relationship details and allocate the request to the appropriate unit.

This will enable the banks to action the requests more quickly, not only reducing initial administration time but also the time spent locating the customers across the bank network. The banks are committed to reducing their current SLAs and this revised process will support that aspiration.

1.6 Scope

While the auditors have agreed on a best endeavours basis (see below), until periods ending on or after 26 December 2008, to provide primary sort code and account number information to subsidiary level, it is important that the banks commit to undertaking thorough searches of their records, in line with an authority to disclose, so that all evidence on a customer connection can be gathered. Auditors are not only looking for confirmation of what they already know but also evidence on what may have been omitted, deliberately or otherwise from information provided to them by their clients.

1.7 Timing

As it will take auditors at least one audit season to collect the main sort codes and account numbers for all group members, the BBA has agreed that banks will answer requests for bank reports on a best endeavours basis, until year ends on or after 26 December 2008. "Best endeavours" means that banks will search for information relating to all entities named on a request even if account numbers are not given.

1.8   Disclaimer from creating a contractual obligation

While information provided under PN16: Bank Reports for Audit Purposes does not constitute a contractual obligation between the bank and the auditor, it is a significant component of the evidence gathered in support of the audit and should be provided on a thorough and accurate basis. It is appropriate however for the bank to include a legal disclaimer in correspondence with auditors to the effect that the reply is given solely for the purpose of their audit without any responsibility on the part of the bank, its employees or agents and that it does not relieve the auditor from any other enquiry nor from the performance of any other duty.

2.   CHECKING FOR ACCOUNTS AND WHY THE ACCOUNT NUMBERS ARE IMPORTANT

2.1   Rather than undermine the search facility offered historically, the change in practice to auditors listing account information by legal entity provides a better platform on which to undertake the search for banking facilities in support of the third party audit verification.

2.2   In discussion with the auditors it has been explained that bank systems are designed around an account number record. While searches by name are possible, IT systems in banks typically are designed to search by account number and not by name. Name information is usually recorded in an abbreviated format, therefore for a 'name only' search to be successful there needs to be an exact match between the abbreviated name recorded and the entity name listed on the audit letter request. Auditors now appreciate that considerable processing time is lost in trying to locate accounts in this way and that it can often be a trial and error exercise.

2.3   It is important to stress that it is not intended that searches should be restricted to the main sort code and account number provided for each entity on the audit request. Instead, the information will be used to identify the relevant customer with greater accuracy and speed. In the case of most banks, information provided is used to identify a 'master account reference' for an entity. It is the master account reference which is then used to search for all connected accounts in that entity name. Therefore, the ability on the part of the auditor to provide primary account number information by legal entity will result in a more comprehensive search.

2.4   Banks will base their search on subsidiary companies listed on the request. However, if as part of these searches, an account is identified as belonging to a subsidiary that has not been listed on the audit letter request, banks should check whether the authority to disclose covers the entity in question. Providing it is listed on the authority as a subsidiary, and signatures are appropriate, then the banks may report the existence of such an account in the audit letter reply.

3. STANDARD AND ADDITIONAL INFORMATION

3.1 PN16 distinguishes between standard information that is likely to be needed in respect of most audit clients and supplementary information that is likely to be relevant in fewer instances.

3.2 **Standard information** which will be provided for all requests comprises:

- Balances as at the year-end (providing request received in advance)
- Details of accounts closed in the last 12 months
- Facilities
- Securities
- Other banking relationships

3.3 **Additional information** that may be requested comprises:

- Trade finance
- Derivatives and commodity trading

3.4 During discussions, the banks have highlighted to the auditors that some 70% of requests for supplementary information about trade finance, derivatives and commodity trading result in a nil return. The provision of a sample reference to a facility account number by the auditor will assist the bank to identify the units providing specialist services which need to be consulted. Banks can give information about these supplementary facilities reasonably easily provided that sample account or reference numbers for these facilities are given. The provision of reference details also ensures that supplementary information is only sought in circumstances where the facilities in question have been provided.

3.5 Given that it will not always be possible for auditors to obtain this information banks should still undertake this type of search where an incomplete information request is submitted by the auditor. It is, however, understood that this will lengthen the response time. It is a recommendation to auditors in the practice note that this type of request is only made after due consideration of the underlying customer's business as part of the audit planning process. Audit firms will endeavour to adopt an approach in which they provide banks with suitable reference details and not to request incomplete information searches in circumstances where their knowledge of the client makes it evident that such a search is unlikely to result in additional facilities being reported.

3.6 **Standard search**
Banks and auditors have agreed that this is likely to be the most used option.

- Auditors supply main sort codes and account numbers including subsidiary legal entities

- Banks able to identify connections using provided account numbers

- Where standard search includes request for additional information, the auditors will provide sufficient reference numbers to identify the additional facilities or transactions for which confirmation is required

- Searches for additional information directed to appropriate area using sample reference numbers.

The auditors are keen to ensure that the provision of account numbers will not detract from the thoroughness of the searches conducted. Instead, it provides the bank with the information needed to facilitate a detailed search for accounts. Same care, reduced time.

3.7 **Incomplete Information Requests**
This is likely to be used only rarely, usually when the auditor has been unable to obtain any of the required information other than the main sort code and account number. Where these details are held for some subsidiaries, then standard requests can be submitted by the auditor in respect of those entities.

- Auditors to supply a *minimum* of a main sort code and account number.

- Banks make searches using legal entity names supplied by auditor against bank records.

From a bank's perspective this process takes more time and is unlikely to be as accurate as banks' systems hold information by numeric reference, not alphabetical.

4. AUTHORITY TO DISCLOSE

4.1 It is the auditors' responsibility to ensure that their client has provided an authority addressed to the account holding bank and that this covers all relevant legal entities. Auditors will consider, as part of the audit planning process, whether there is a need for the authority to be updated.

4.2 Banks should conduct searches against the legal entities listed on the audit request and accounts which are found as a result of these searches checked against the authority to disclose held on bank records.

4.3 Due to client confidentiality obligations, the bank should only disclose to auditors accounts in the name of entities for which they have an express authority to do so.

4.4 Banks will check a new authority on receipt, or where the auditor indicates the existence of an authority from a previous year, against its records. If the authority cannot be verified it will be returned to the auditor together with any request for information for referral back to the client.

5. SERVICE LEVEL AGREEMENTS

5.1 Service Level Agreements (SLAs) are competitive between banks and are therefore not standard, with each bank having their own arrangements. However, banks are committed to reducing their SLAs in line with more information being provided by auditors.

6. ENQUIRIES

6.1 Banks receive a number of enquiries from auditors. The following guidance is intended to facilitate the enquiry process.

6.2 **Pre-production enquiries**
Banks should send an acknowledgement to the auditor within 5 working days of receipt by post or by email as requested. Where banks do not send acknowledgements on request, they are expected to publish a central enquiry point/make known who will deal with enquiries via the BBA's public website.

With this in mind, auditors diary for receipt of acknowledgement and if not received, chase the bank to confirm receipt (this will reduce the number of urgent requests after the year-end has passed).

Banks may indicate either an expected date when the auditor will receive the reply or provide an indication of their standard SLA for the process. Auditors have been requested to refrain from chasing for a response until the expected date of receipt has passed.

6.3 **Post-production enquiries**
Enquiry routes for individual banks will be identified on the BBA's public website. It is for each bank to ensure that the information provided remains up-to-date.

Banks should either provide a centralised enquiry point or make known that requests should be addressed to relationship managers.

Banks may provide a unique reference for each audit letter; where they do, auditors should use this reference when making post-production enquiries.

6.4 **Fast track requests**
Banks receive many requests from auditors for an urgent response. They appreciate that there are circumstances in which it may be necessary to provide a response for an audit letter in a shortened timescale eg group companies with shorter reporting timescales. This however can only be extended on a best endeavours basis as, with a finite resource, this effectively means that staff are diverted from working on requests which were received earlier. It has therefore been agreed that, where auditors require an urgent response, they state the reason on the information request form.

7. REQUIREMENTS

7.1 **Forms** – many BBA member banks use imaging technology for workflow management. Those banks may wish to make arrangements with auditors to use standard forms that have been tested for use in an image environment. These can be obtained from the BBA website or directly from the individual banks concerned. There are barriers at present on both the banking and the auditing side to requests being submitted securely using the internet.

7.2 **Submitting requests** – PN16 indicates that auditors deliver a request to the bank one month before the year end. The banks have underlined for the auditors the importance of this given the volumes of requests that they receive each month. This time is used to undertake preparatory work in advance of the year-end, such as sending out requests for completion by relevant departments.

7.3 **Account information** – auditors have been requested to provide, as a minimum, one main sort code and account number for each legal entity listed on the request. It is clearly explained within the practice note that the provision of sort codes and account numbers by legal entity will contribute significantly to the efficiency of the search.

7.4 **Authority to disclose** – while there is no need to provide an authority each time, the auditors have a responsibility for checking with the client that the authority is up-to-date. Banks should regard authorities as on-going unless rescinded by the client. (In Ireland the banks and auditors have agreed that a new authority to disclose should be provided by the auditors on each occasion.)

7.5 **Enquiries** – auditors have been encouraged to make use of the bank reference number provided in the bank response to the request. This should improve enquiry handling as banks will be able to locate the file much more quickly.

8. CLOSED ACCOUNTS

8.1 Where an account relationship existed at the audit date but has subsequently closed an appropriate fee will be required before the audit letter process can begin. In such cases, the bank should return the request to the auditor with a request for the appropriate fee to be provided. It should be made clear that work will not be carried out on the request until the fee is received. The standard SLA will apply from the date the fee is received or the audit date, whichever is the later.

ADDENDUM – INFORMATION PROVIDED IN BANK RESPONSES

The following tables set out the information that will be provided by banks in response to auditor requests. The banks are required to give the information in the order shown and if no information is available then this must be stated as 'None' in the response.

STANDARD INFORMATION REQUEST

1 **Account and Balance Details**

Give full titles of all Bank accounts including loans, (whether in sterling or another currency) together with their account numbers and balances. For accounts closed during the 12 months up to the audit report date give the account details and date of closure.

Note. Also give details where your Customer's name is joined with that of other parties and where the account is in a trade name.

State if any account or balances are subject to any restriction(s) whatsoever. Indicate the nature and extent of the restriction e.g. garnishee order.

2 **Facilities**

Give the following details of all loans, overdrafts, and associated guarantees and indemnities:

- term

- repayment frequency and/or review date

- details of period of availability of agreed finance i.e. finance remaining undrawn

- detail the facility limit.

3 **Securities**

With reference to the facilities detailed in (2) above give the following details:

- Any security formally charged (date, ownership and type of charge). State whether the security supports facilities granted by the Bank to the customer or to another party.

  Note. Give details if a security is limited in amount or to a specific borrowing or if to your knowledge there is a prior, equal or subordinate charge.

- Where there are any arrangements for set-off of balances or compensating balances e.g. back to back loans, give particulars (i.e. date, type of document and accounts covered) of any acknowledgement of set-off, whether given by specific letter of set-off or incorporated in some other document.

ADDITIONAL INFORMATION REQUEST

Request for Trade Finance information

1	**Trade Finance** Give the currencies and amounts of the following: (a) Letters of Credit (b) Acceptances (c) Bills discounted with recourse to the customer or any subsidiary or related party of the customer. (d) Bonds, Guarantees, Indemnities or other undertakings given to the Bank by the customer in favour of third parties (including separately any such items in favour of any subsidiary or related party of the customer). Give details of the parties in favour of whom guarantees or undertakings have been given, whether such guarantees or undertakings are written or oral and their nature. (e) Bonds, Guarantees, Indemnities or other undertakings given by you, on your customer's behalf, stating whether there is recourse to your customer and/or to its parent or any other company within the group. (f) Other contingent liabilities not already detailed. *Note. For each item state the nature and extent of any facility limits and details of period of availability of agreed facility.*
2	**Securities** With reference to the facilities detailed in the above section give the following: • Details of any security formally charged (date, ownership and type of charge). State whether the security supports facilities granted by the Bank to the customer or to another party. *Note. Give details if a security is limited in amount or to a specific borrowing or if to your knowledge there is prior, equal or subordinate charge.* • Where there are any arrangements for set-off of balances or compensating balances e.g. back to back loans, give particulars (i.e. date, type of document and accounts covered) of any acknowledgement of set-off, whether given by specific letter of set-off or incorporated in some other document.

Request for Derivatives and Commodity Trading information

On occasion Auditors may request Derivatives and Commodity Trading information. Responses must be given in the order as below and if no information is available then this must be stated as 'None' in the response:

1	**Derivatives and Commodity Trading** Give the currencies, amounts and maturity dates on a contract by contract basis of all outstanding derivative contracts including the following: (a)　foreign exchange contracts (b)　forward rate agreements (c)　financial futures (d)　interest rate swaps (e)　option contracts (f)　bullion contracts (g)　commodity contracts (h)　swap arrangements (near and far dates) (i)　credit derivatives including collateralised debt obligations (CDOs) (j)　others (indicate their nature). *Note. Indicate the nature and extent of any facility limits, detail period of availability of agreed facilities.*
2	**Securities** With reference to facilities detailed in the above section give the following: •　Details of any security formally charged (date, ownership and type of charge). State whether the security supports facilities granted by the Bank to the customer or to another party. Note. Give details if a security is limited in amount or to a specific borrowing or if to your knowledge there is prior, equal or subordinate charge. •　Where there are any arrangements for set-off balances of compensating balances e.g. back to back loans, give particulars (i.e. date, type of document and accounts covered) of any acknowledgement of set-off, whether given by specific letter of set-off or incorporated in some other document.

FINANCIAL REPORTING COUNCIL

PRACTICE NOTE 19(I)

THE AUDIT OF BANKS IN THE REPUBLIC OF IRELAND (REVISED)

CONTENTS

Preface

This Practice Note contains guidance on the application of auditing standards issued by the Auditing Practices Board (the '**APB**') to the audit of the financial statements of banks in the Republic of Ireland. Guidance is also given on:

* direct reports to the Irish Financial Services Regulatory Authority[1] (the '**Financial Regulator**'); and

* the conduct of auditors' periodic meetings with the Financial Regulator.

This Practice Note is supplementary to, and should be read in conjunction with, International Standards on Auditing ('**ISAs**') (UK and Ireland), which apply to all audits undertaken in the United Kingdom ('**UK**') and the Republic of Ireland in respect of accounting periods commencing on or after 15 December 2004. This Practice Note sets out the special considerations relating to the audit of banks which arise from individual ISAs (UK and Ireland) listed in the contents. It is not the intention of this Practice Note to provide step-by-step guidance to the audit of banks, so where no special considerations arise from a particular ISA (UK and Ireland), no material is included in this document.

This Practice Note has been prepared in consultation with the Financial Regulator and is based on the legislation and regulations in effect at 30 April 2008.

Changes currently under active consideration that will impact on the legal and regulatory environment affecting banks, auditors of banks and auditors of companies generally, include:

* the Companies Consolidation Bill whose purpose is to consolidate company law acts and regulations and to implement the recommendations of the Company Law Review Group[2];

* a project for the consolidation and modernisation of financial services legislation is ongoing and a Bill is expected to emerge from that project to streamline the existing legal framework for financial services regulation;

---

[1] The Central Bank of Ireland, which came into being in 1943, was re-structured and re-named as the Central Bank and Financial Services Authority of Ireland ('CBFSAI') on 1 May 2003. This body carries out all of the activities formerly carried out by the Central Bank of Ireland and additional regulatory and consumer protection functions for the financial services sector. The CBFSAI has two component entities:
* the Central Bank, which has responsibility for monetary policy functions, financial stability, economic analysis, currency and payment systems, investment of foreign and domestic assets and the provision of central services; and
* the Irish Financial Services Regulatory Authority (Financial Regulator), which is an autonomous entity within the CBFSAI and has responsibility for financial sector regulation and consumer protection.

[2] The Company Law Review Group is a statutory advisory expert body charged with advising the Minister for Enterprise, Trade & Employment on the review and development of company law in Ireland. The Review Group was accorded statutory advisory status by Part 7 of the Company Law Enforcement Act 2001.

- SEPA – Single European Payments Area. A project of the European banks, developed and managed by the banking industry, as represented by the European Payments Council. The intention is to harmonise bank systems throughout the European Union so as to make cross-border payments easier and eventually to facilitate banking from a single account in any one country;

- the Financial Regulator's 'Licensing and Supervision Requirements and Standards for Credit Institutions' ('the **Financial Regulator Standards**') are in the process of being updated. A 'consolidated' Administrative Notice to reflect the Capital Requirements Directive[3] ("**CRD**") is currently being drafted which will replace earlier Administrative Notices regarding solvency and capital adequacy.

Building societies

This Practice Note does not deal with specific matters requiring consideration in the course of auditing a building society's financial statements or with other aspects of auditors' obligations set out in the Building Societies Acts, 1989 to 2006.

Credit Unions

This Practice Note does not deal with specific matters requiring consideration in the course of auditing a credit union's financial statements. A separate Practice Note entitled "The Audit of Credit Unions in the Republic of Ireland" is being issued by the APB.

---

[3] The Capital Requirements Directive ('CRD') which is a term used to describe two EU Directives which transpose the Basel II Accord into a legal text for the purpose of its application to banks and investment firms across the European Economic Area (EEA). These directives are:
- Directive 2006/48/EC (recast) relating to the taking up and pursuit of the business of credit institutions; and
- Directive 2006/49/EC (recast) on the capital adequacy of investment firms and credit institutions.
Statutory Instruments (S.I.s) 660 and 661 of 2006 (which implement the CRD in Ireland) were signed into Irish law in December 2006 and have a commencement date of 1 January 2007
The CRD repeals Directive 2000/12/EC relating to the taking up and pursuit of business of credit institutions which had brought together:
- The First Banking Directive, 77/780/EEC;
- The Second Banking Directive, 89/646/EEC which was implemented in Ireland by S.I. 395 of 1992 – often referred to as the "Passporting Regulations";
- Own Funds Directive 89/299/EEC and Solvency Ratio Directive 89/647/EEC and amendments to those Directives by Directive 91/633/EEC, Directive 94/7/EC, Directive 95/15/EC, Directive 95/67/EC, Directive 89/299/EEC, Directive 96/10/EC, Directive 2004/69/EC, Directive 98/32/EC and Directive 98/33/EC;
- Consolidated Supervision Directive 92/30/EEC; and
- Large Exposures Directive 92/121/EC.
The CRD also repeals the Capital Adequacy Directive 93/6/EC and amending Directives 98/31/EC and 98/33/EC.
Details of specific articles of other Directives also repealed by the CRD can be found at Annex XIII Part A of Directive 2006/48/EC and Annex VIII Part A of Directive 2006/49/EC.

Introduction

1. Throughout this Practice Note, the term 'bank' refers to a credit institution (other than a building society) as defined by the CRD being an undertaking whose business is to receive deposits or other repayable funds from the public and to grant credits for its own account. Credit Unions and friendly societies are specifically excluded from the definition of a credit institution under the CRD and are not dealt with in this Practice Note.

2. As set out in the Preface above, the audit of building societies is specifically not covered by this Practice Note. However, banks and building societies share a number of common features and the regulatory approach of the Financial Regulator to building societies is broadly equivalent to that for banks. Consequently, the Practice Note's guidance on the statutory duty to report to the Financial Regulator is indicative of the duty to report under building societies' legislation and may be used by building society auditors to assist their judgments in this area, taking into account legislative differences in the detailed specification of matters to be reported to the Financial Regulator under the Building Societies Acts, 1989 to 2006; in particular section 88 of the Building Societies Act, 1989, dealing with the maintenance of satisfactory systems of internal controls, and sections 53 to 59 of the Building Societies Act, 1989, setting out specific audit requirements in relation to loans and transactions with directors.

3. Independent audit plays an important part in safeguarding the integrity of financial reports by directors of companies and other entities to the investing and business communities, both national and international. Additionally, auditors appointed to report on the financial statements of banks in the Republic of Ireland, and other members of the European Union, also contribute to the regulatory process.

4. In the case of overseas institutions which are not subject to the audit provisions of the Companies Act 1963 to 2006 and all Regulations to be construed as one with those Acts ('the Companies Acts'), the terms of engagement are a matter of contract between the auditors and their clients who may, for example, be local or head office management or the bank's home country auditors. Such engagements take many different forms: the auditors may be asked to report on the accounts of the Irish branch or only on particular aspects thereof, and the form of their opinion will also vary from case to case. The auditor undertaking such an assignment does not have to apply ISAs (UK and Ireland) but may find some of the guidance in this Practice Note of some assistance.

5. The Financial Regulator, established on 1 May 2003 pursuant to the Central Bank and Financial Services Authority of Ireland Act, 2003, ('**CBFSAI 2003**') is responsible for regulation of all financial services firms, including credit institutions, in Ireland. It also has an important role in the protection of the consumers of those firms. As the Financial Regulator its main tasks are to:

    *   help consumers to make informed decisions on their financial affairs in a safe and fair market; and

- foster sound, growing and solvent financial institutions which give consumers confidence that their deposits and investments are secure.

The Financial Regulator is a distinct component of the Central Bank and Financial Services Authority of Ireland (the 'CBFSAI'), with clearly defined regulatory responsibilities. These cover all Irish financial institutions including those previously regulated by the Central Bank, Department of Enterprise, Trade and Employment, Office of the Director of Consumer Affairs and Registrar of Friendly Societies. The Financial Regulator contributes to the work of the CBFSAI in discharging its responsibility in relation to overall financial stability.

6. The scope of the statutory audit of a bank's financial statements is no different from that of the generality of companies in the Republic of Ireland. However, the Oireachtas has, in addition, placed responsibility on auditors to provide reports to the Financial Regulator if they encounter circumstances that, in their opinion, meet certain criteria set out in statute[4], with the express purpose of making the regulator aware of matters that might jeopardise the stability of the banking and financial system or interests of depositors and others. ISA (UK and Ireland) 250, Section B, "The Auditor's Right and Duty to Report to Regulators in the Financial Sector" ('ISA (UK and Ireland) 250, Section B') deals generically with such reports to the Financial Regulator in its capacity as banking supervisor and further guidance is set out in Appendix 2.

7. Auditors of banks in the Republic of Ireland may also be asked to review and report on interim profits for capital adequacy purposes. This Practice Note therefore distinguishes between the two types of assignment relating to banks:

    - the audit of the financial statements in accordance with the Companies Act 1963 to 2006 and all regulations to be construed as one with those Acts (the 'Companies Acts'), including the auditor's duty to report directly to the Financial Regulator as a consequence of being the statutory auditor; and

    - the auditor's report on interim profits.

8. The Financial Regulator is entitled to hold periodic meetings with banks and their auditors. Such meetings are considered in paragraphs 163 to 170 of this Practice Note.

9. Section 25 of the Central Bank Act 1997[5] ('CBA 1997'), empowers the Financial Regulator to oblige a bank to provide a compliance statement to the Financial Regulator on request. If the Financial Regulator requests a compliance statement from a bank it may also, under Section 26 of the CBA 1997[6] request that the bank's auditor prepare a report about the relevant compliance statement. The Financial Regulator has not yet commenced the compliance statement regime. It is envisaged that this provision will be considered as part of the project for the consolidation and

---

[4] The Central Bank Act, 1989, the Supervision of Credit Institutions, Stock Exchange Member Firms and Investment Business Firms Regulations, 1996 and the Central Bank Act 1997 as amended by the Central Bank and Financial Services Authority of Ireland Act, 2004.

[5] As inserted by section 26 CBFSAI 2004.

[6] As inserted by section 26 CBFSAI 2004.

modernisation of financial services legislation mentioned in the Preface to this document.

The Relationship between the objectives of the Financial Regulator and the objectives of the auditor

10. In many respects the Financial Regulator, as the banking supervisor, and bank auditors have complementary concerns although the focus of their concerns may be different. In particular:

- the Financial Regulator is primarily concerned with maintaining the stability of the banking system and fostering the safety and soundness of individual banks in order to protect the interests of the depositors. The Financial Regulator monitors the present and future viability of banks and may use their financial statements in assessing their condition and performance. The auditor's primary responsibility is to report to shareholders his opinion as to whether the financial statements present a true and fair view, in the course of which they consider the appropriateness of the use of the going concern concept as a basis for the preparation of the financial statements;

- the Financial Regulator is concerned that banks maintain a sound system of internal control, including an adequately resourced, independent internal audit function, as a basis for safe and prudent management of a bank's business. The auditor is concerned with the assessment of internal control to determine the degree of reliance to be placed on the system in planning and performing the work necessary to express an opinion on a bank's financial statements; and

- the Financial Regulator must be satisfied that each bank maintains adequate records prepared in accordance with consistent accounting policies and practices that enable it to appraise the financial condition of the bank. The auditor is concerned with whether adequate and sufficiently reliable records are maintained in order to enable the entity to prepare financial statements that do not contain material misstatements.

Communications with bank auditors by the Financial Regulator

11. When making any disclosures of information, the Financial Regulator must ensure that it does so in a manner that accords with the CRD and section 33AK of the Central Bank Act 1942[7]. Under these provisions, information that is confidential and has been obtained by the Financial Regulator as supervisor of banks may be disclosed only in restricted circumstances. However, under the CRD the Financial Regulator is not precluded from disclosing information to the auditor of a bank supervised by the Financial Regulator in relation to that supervision, provided that the Financial Regulator can satisfy itself that the auditor has obligations with regard to professional

---

[7] As inserted by section 26 CBSFAI 2003. In accordance with this section the Financial Regulator may disclose confidential information to the auditor of a supervised entity in relation to that entity, in accordance with Supervisory Directives, provided such disclosure is not prohibited by the Rome Treaty, the ESCB Statute or the Supervisory Directives.

confidentiality or non-disclosure of information equivalent to the obligations imposed on the Financial Regulator itself.

Legislative and regulatory framework

12. The legal and regulatory framework within which banks operate in the Republic of Ireland is complex and involves:

    • Statutes;

    • Regulations implementing EU Directives in the banking sector;

    • Other Regulations;

    • Administrative Provisions and 'Licensing and Supervision Requirements and Standards for Credit Institutions' ('**Financial Regulator Standards**') issued by the Financial Regulator; and

    • Other guidance issued by the Financial Regulator.

    A summary of the legal and regulatory framework is set out in Appendix 1.

Financial statements

13. Financial statements of banks incorporated in the Republic of Ireland may be prepared under either of two reporting frameworks depending on the accounting policies adopted as follows:

    • International Financial Reporting Standards ('**IFRSs**') as adopted by the European Union ('**EU IFRSs**')[8];

    • Accounting standards issued by the Accounting Standards Board ('**ASB**') and promulgated by the Institute of Chartered Accountants in Ireland ('Generally Accepted Accounting Practice in Ireland, '**Irish GAAP**'). For entities using Irish GAAP a further complication arises as, depending on the accounting policies adopted and the nature of the investments held, an entity may fall within the scope of Financial Reporting Standard 25 "Financial Instruments: Disclosure and Presentation" (FRS 25), Financial Reporting Standard 26 "Financial Instruments: Measurement" (FRS 26) and Financial Reporting Standard 29 "Financial Instruments: Disclosures" (FRS 29).

14 Groups listed on an EU regulated market and incorporated In the Republic of Ireland (including relevant listed Irish banking groups) must prepare consolidated financial statements in accordance with EU IFRSs and those parts of the Companies Acts applicable to companies reporting under EU IFRSs. Irish companies or non listed groups, including Irish banks and banking groups, are permitted to voluntarily adopt

---

[8] Article 4 EC Regulation 1606/2002 – the IAS Regulation.

EU IFRSs for their financial statements. In preparing financial statements for banking institutions reference should be made to Statutory Instrument (S.I.) 116 of 2005, European Communities (International Financial Reporting Standards and Miscellaneous Amendments) Regulations 2005 and S.I. 765 of 2004, European Communities (Fair Value Accounting) Regulations, 2004.

15. The form and content of the financial statements prepared under Irish GAAP both including and excluding FRS 25, FRS 26 and FRS 29 is governed by the Companies Acts, Statements of Standard Accounting Practice ('**SSAPs**') and Financial Reporting Standards ('**FRSs**') issued by the ASB and Abstracts issued by the Urgent Issues Task Forces. Of particular relevance to banks in preparing financial statements is the European Communities (Credit Institutions: Accounts) Regulations, 1992 (the '**Bank Accounts Regulations, 1992**')[9] which includes the mandatory format for the financial statements of such entities. Entities should also refer to S.I. 765 of 2004, European Communities (Fair Value Accounting) Regulations, 2004. FRS 23 "The effects of changes in foreign exchange rates" and FRS 24 "Financial reporting in hyperinflationary economies" also apply if entities fall within the scope of FRS 26. Complex rules are in place to determine the applicability of FRS 26.

16. In addition, the British Bankers' Association and the Irish Bankers' Federation have jointly issued a Statement of Recommended Practice ('**SORP**') covering segmental reporting by banks to which the auditor reporting under Irish GAAP may refer.[10]

Prudential requirements

17. Banks are subject to certain prudential requirements of the Financial Regulator. These include requirements relating to capital adequacy, liquidity, large exposures (concentration risk), impairment and additional related aspects of systems and controls. Banks are also required to report to the Financial Regulator via regulatory which include:

- capital adequacy – ensuring sufficient capital resources in relation to risk requirements to absorb losses;

- liquidity – ensuring sufficient liquid assets or maturing assets to meet liabilities as they fall due;

- impairment;

- large exposures – avoiding undue credit risk concentrations; and

- sectoral limits.

---

[9] S.I. No. 294 of 1992.

[10] There were previously four additional banking SORPs issue covering the following: securities, advances, contingent liabilities and commitments, and derivatives. These SORPs were all withdrawn by the Accounting Standards Board on 31 December 2006.

The Audit of Financial Statements

ISAs (UK and Ireland) apply to the conduct of all audits. This includes audits of the financial statements of banks. The purpose of the following paragraphs is to identify the special considerations arising from the application of certain 'bold letter' requirements to the audit of banks, and to suggest ways in which these can be addressed (extracts from ISAs (UK and Ireland) are indicated by grey-shaded boxes below). This Practice Note does not contain commentary on all of the bold letter requirements included in the ISAs (UK and Ireland) and reading it should not be seen as an alternative to reading the relevant ISAs (UK and Ireland) in their entirety. In addition, where no special considerations arise from a particular ISA (UK and Ireland), no material is included.

ISA (UK and Ireland) 200: Objective and General Principles Governing an Audit of Financial Statements

Background note

The purpose of this ISA (UK and Ireland) is to establish standards and provide guidance on the objective and general principles governing an audit of financial statements.

The auditor should plan and perform an audit with an attitude of professional scepticism, recognising that circumstances may exist that cause the financial statements to be materially misstated. (paragraph 6)

18. Auditing standards include a requirement for auditors to comply with relevant ethical requirements relating to audit engagements. In the Republic of Ireland, the auditor should comply with the APB's Ethical Standards for Auditors (ESs) and relevant ethical guidance relating to the work of auditors issued by the auditor's professional body. A fundamental principle is that practitioners should not accept or perform work which they are not competent to undertake. The importance of technical competence is also underlined in the Auditors' Code[11], issued by the APB, which states that the necessary degree of professional skill demands an understanding of financial reporting and business. Practitioners should not undertake the audit of banks unless they are satisfied that they have, or can obtain, the necessary level of competence.

Independence

19. Independence issues can be complex for the auditor of a bank because of banking and other relationships that the auditor and/or its partners and staff may have with the bank. Threats and safeguards are outlined in the APB's Ethical Standard 2 – Financial, business, employment and personal relationships.

---

[11] This is appended to the APB's Scope and Authority of Pronouncements.

20. In addition auditors will be aware that the Financial Regulator (Financial Regulator Standards, paragraph 10.3) does not permit the auditor of a bank to act in any capacity other than that of auditor, consultant or share registrar. Auditors review the services provided by their audit firm to a bank to consider whether there are relationships which may affect this prohibition. Furthermore, paragraph 10.3(iii) of the Financial Regulator Standards states that a bank shall not grant an advance or a credit facility to its auditor.

21. Where the bank has operations in overseas countries, the auditor ensures that any firm of auditors whom work on overseas branches or subsidiaries also considers its banking relationships and maintains appropriate independence from both the local entity and the parent's wider international operations.

ISA (UK and Ireland) 210: Terms of Audit Engagements

Background note

The purpose of this ISA (UK and Ireland) is to establish standards and provide guidance on agreeing the terms of the engagement with the client.

The auditor and the client should agree on the terms of the engagement. (paragraph 2)

The terms of the engagement should be recorded in writing. (paragraph 2-1)

The auditor should ensure that the engagement letter documents and confirms the auditor's acceptance of the appointment, and includes a summary of the responsibilities of those charged with governance and of the auditor, the scope of the engagement and the form of any reports. (paragraph 5-1)

22. Matters which the auditor may decide to refer to in the engagement letter are as follows:

    * the responsibility of directors/senior management to comply with applicable financial services legislation and regulatory requirements;

    * the duty of the auditor to report directly to the Financial Regulator, in its role as banking supervisor, under section 47 of the CBA 1989, Regulation 7(c) of the Post-BCCI Regulations, and sections 27B to 27F of the CBA 1997[12] in particular circumstances (see the section on ISA (UK & Ireland) 250 Section B and Appendix 2 of this Practice Note);

    * the protection provided by section 47(6) of the CBA 1989, Regulation 9 of the Post-BCCI Regulations and section 27H of the CBA 1997 to auditors in respect of both fulfilling their duty to report and any disclosure of information required to respond to a query from the Financial Regulator on a matter relating to their audit;

    * the requirement under companies legislation (specifically sections 193(3), 196 and 197 of the Companies Act, 1990) and listing rules to co-operate with the auditor; and

    * that the auditor requests the bank to inform the auditor when it appoints a third party (including another department or office of the same audit firm) to review, investigate or report on any aspects of its business activities that may be relevant to the audit of the financial statements and to provide the auditor with copies of reports by such a third party promptly after their receipt.

---

[12] All references to sections 27B to 27F of the CBA 1997 refer to those sections inserted in the CBA 1997 by section 26 CBFSAI Act 2004.

23. In this connection the auditor is aware:

- that the Financial Regulator does not need to approve the appointment of an auditor;

- of the auditor's reporting obligations in certain circumstances arising under section 47 of the CBA 1989, section 27B to 27F of the CBA 1997[13] and Regulation 7 of the Post-BCCI Regulations; and

- that the auditor of a bank incorporated in the Republic of Ireland must give written notice, under section 47(1)(d-e) of the CBA 1989 and Regulation 7(c) of the Post-BCCI Regulations to the Financial Regulator if he:

  ○ resigns before expiration of his term of office;

  ○ does not seek re-appointment; or

  ○ decides to qualify the audit opinion.

---

[13] As inserted by section 26 CBFSAI 2004.

ISA (UK and Ireland) 220: Quality Control for Audits of Historical Financial Information

Background note

The purpose of this ISA (UK and Ireland) is to establish standards and provide guidance on specific responsibilities of firm personnel regarding quality control procedures for audits of historical financial information, including audits of financial statements.

Reference should also be made to ISQC 1 (UK and Ireland) – Quality Control for Firms that Perform Audits and Reviews of Historical Financial Information, and other Assurance and Related Services Engagements.

The engagement partner should be satisfied that the engagement team collectively has the appropriate capabilities, competence and time to perform the audit engagement in accordance with professional standards and regulatory and legal requirements, and to enable an auditor's report that is appropriate in the circumstances to be issued. (paragraph 19)

24. The nature of banking business is one of rapidly changing and evolving markets. Often banks develop new products and practices which require specialised auditing and accounting responses. It is therefore important that the auditor is familiar with current practice.

25. As well as ensuring that the engagement team has an appropriate level of knowledge of the industry and its corresponding products, the engagement partner also satisfies himself that the members of the engagement team have sufficient knowledge of the regulatory framework within which banks operate commensurate with their roles on the engagement.

ISA (UK and Ireland) 230: Audit Documentation

Background note

The purpose of this ISA (UK and Ireland) is to establish standards and provide guidance on audit documentation.

26. The auditor is aware that under section 27F of the CBA 1997[14] the Financial Regulator may:

> "by notice in writing, require an auditor of a regulated financial service provider, or an affiliate of the auditor, to provide the Bank with a copy of any record or information provided or obtained by the auditor or affiliate in connection with an audit of the financial service provider's accounts that is in the possession of the auditor or affiliate".

---

[14] As inserted by section 26 CBFSAI 2004.

ISA (UK and Ireland) 240: The Auditor's Responsibility to Consider Fraud in an Audit of Financial Statements

Background note

The purpose of this ISA (UK and Ireland) is to establish standards and provide guidance on the auditor's responsibility to consider fraud in an audit of financial statements and expand on how the standards and guidance in ISA (UK and Ireland) 315 and ISA (UK and Ireland) 330 are to be applied in relation to the risks of material misstatement due to fraud.

In planning and performing the audit to reduce audit risk to an acceptably low level, the auditor should consider the risks of material misstatements in the financial statements due to fraud. (paragraph 3)

The auditor should maintain an attitude of professional scepticism throughout the audit, recognising the possibility that a material misstatement due to fraud could exist, notwithstanding the auditor's past experience with the entity about the honesty and integrity of management and those charged with governance. (paragraph 24)

The auditor should make inquiries of management, internal audit, and others within the entity as appropriate, to determine whether they have knowledge of any actual, suspected or alleged fraud affecting the entity. (paragraph 38)

When obtaining an understanding of the entity and its environment, including its internal control, the auditor should consider whether the information obtained indicates that one or more fraud risk factors are present. (paragraph 48)

27. As with other entities fraudulent financial reporting (for example the manipulation of profits or the concealment of losses) or misappropriation of assets, can occur through a combination of management fraud, employee fraud or fraud perpetrated by third parties. However banks are particularly vulnerable to the misappropriation of assets by third parties, sometimes with the collusion of employees or vice versa. This arises in part due to the nature of their activities, a fraud risk factor, which ordinarily involves high values and volumes of disbursement of funds for a variety of purposes including:

    • drawdown on loans (including credit cards);

    • repayment of customer deposits;

    • settlement of financial transactions; and

    • funds transfer.

28. A further fraud risk factor is that banks also have custody of valuable and fungible assets including money. As a result fraud is an inherent cost of undertaking banking business. Frauds relating to most types of transactions can be facilitated by identity

theft and so 'know your customer' procedures are an important component of the procedures taken by banks to mitigate the risk of fraud.

29. Whilst remuneration policies can create excessive performance pressures in many industries, in certain types of banking (e.g. investment banking operations) performance related bonuses can be significant both in absolute terms and in relation to base remuneration. In addition significant bonus related remuneration can often extend beyond senior management, further down the organisation of banks, and can lead to more pervasive pressures that cause increased risks of fraud. Other examples of fraud risk factors include:

- valuation of complex financial instruments in an environment where there is inadequate segregation of duties and/or lack of supervision or independent review and/or understanding of the valuation techniques and associated inputs; and

- matters that are subject to significant judgment by management – e.g. allowances for impairment (particularly collective assessment of impairment) or customer compensation provisioning.

30. A bank is required by the Financial Regulator Standards to manage its business in accordance with sound administrative and accounting principles and to put in place and maintain internal control and reporting arrangements and procedures to ensure that the business is so managed. This includes the need to have comprehensive risk management systems commensurate with the scope, size and complexity of all the bank's activities including accurate and reliable management information systems and thorough control procedures. This will include appropriate systems to minimise the risk of losses to the bank from irregularities, fraud or error. Whilst the inherent risk of fraud may continue to exist, the establishment of accounting and internal control systems sufficient to meet these requirements frequently reduces the likelihood of fraud giving rise to material misstatements in the financial statements. Guidance on the auditor's consideration of accounting systems and internal controls is provided in the section of this Practice Note relating to ISA (UK and Ireland) 315, Understanding the Entity and Its Environment and Assessing the Risks of Material Misstatement. Examples of weaknesses in control that could give rise to fraud risk factors are also set out in paragraph 88.

When obtaining an understanding of the entity and its environment, including its internal control, the auditor should consider whether other information obtained indicates risks of material misstatement due to fraud. (paragraph 55)

31. The auditor considers reports or information obtained from the bank's compliance department, legal department, and money laundering reporting officer together with any reviews undertaken by third parties.

If the auditor has identified a fraud or has obtained information that indicates that a fraud may exist, the auditor should communicate these matters as soon as practicable to the appropriate level of management. (paragraph 93)

> The auditor should document communications about fraud made to management, those charged with governance, regulators and others. (paragraph 109)

32. The auditor is aware of its statutory duty to report directly to the Financial Regulator in certain circumstances (see the section of this Practice Note relating to ISA (UK and Ireland) 250 Section B and Appendix 2). The auditor is also aware of the auditor's duty to report suspected offences of money laundering or terrorist financing to the Garda Síochána and the Revenue Commissioners in accordance with section 57 of the Criminal Justice Act 1994. In addition section 59 of the Criminal Justice (Theft and Fraud Offences) Act 2001 requires an auditor to report to the Garda Síochána instances of suspected theft or fraud that come to their attention in the course of auditing the financial statements of bodies corporate and other entities. (See the Section of this Practice Note relating to ISA (UK and Ireland) 250 Section A).

ISA (UK and Ireland) 250: Section A – Consideration of Laws and Regulations in an Audit of Financial Statements

Background note

The purpose of this ISA (UK and Ireland) is to establish standards and provide guidance on the auditor's responsibility to consider laws and regulations in an audit of financial statements.

When designing and performing audit procedures and in evaluating and reporting the results thereof, the auditor should recognize that non compliance by the entity with laws and regulations may materially affect the financial statements. (paragraph 2)

In accordance with ISA (UK and Ireland) 200, "Objective and General Principles Governing an Audit of Financial Statements" the auditor should plan and perform the audit with an attitude of professional scepticism recognising that the audit may reveal conditions or events that would lead to questioning whether an entity is complying with laws and regulations. (paragraph 13)

In order to plan the audit, the auditor should obtain a general understanding of the legal and regulatory framework applicable to the entity and the industry and how the entity is complying with that framework. (paragraph 15)

33. Laws and regulations which are central to an entity's ability to conduct its business are those where either compliance is a prerequisite of obtaining a licence to operate or non-compliance may reasonably be expected to result in the entity ceasing operations, or call into question the entity's status as a going concern. In the context of banks, these two criteria indicate that laws and regulations are central to a bank's ability to conduct its business if non-compliance could cause the Financial Regulator to revoke or restrict authorisation. The auditor is alert to any indication that a bank is conducting business outside the scope of its authorisation by the Financial Regulator in accordance with the CRD or the bank is failing to meet requirements of the CBAs 1942 to 2004 or the Financial Regulator Standards. Such action may be a serious regulatory breach, which may result in fines, public censure, suspension or loss of authorisation. Banks may also be authorised to conduct investment business under the IIA, 1995 with the Financial Regulator also being the regulator of such entities. In this case, auditors also consider the laws and regulations central to the bank's ability to conduct investment business. The auditor is also aware of the bank's obligations pursuant to the Markets in Financial Instruments Directive 2004/39/EC ('**MiFID**') which was transposed into Irish legislation on 20 February 2007. MiFID replaces the existing Investment Services Directive ('**ISD**') and domestic regulations replace parts of the IIA, 1995. Appendix 1 of this Practice Note provides more detail on the legal and regulatory environment in which banks operate.

After obtaining the general understanding, the auditor should perform further audit procedures to help identify instances of non compliance with those laws and regulations where non compliance should be considered when preparing financial statements, specifically:

(a) Inquiring of management as to whether the entity is in compliance with such laws and regulations; and

(b) Inspecting correspondence with the relevant licensing or regulatory authorities.

(c) Enquiring of those charged with governance as to whether they are on notice of any such possible instances of non-compliance with law or regulations. (paragraph 18)

The auditor's procedures should be designed to help identify possible or actual instances of non-compliance with those laws and regulations which provide a legal framework within which the entity conducts its business and which are central to the entity's ability to conduct its business and hence to its financial statements. (paragraph 18-1)

34. Specific areas that audit procedures may address include the following:

- obtaining a general understanding of the legal and regulatory framework applicable to the bank and the banking industry, and of the procedures followed to ensure compliance with the framework;

- holding discussions with the bank's compliance officer and other personnel responsible for compliance;

- reviewing compliance reports prepared for the Board, audit committees and other committees;

- reviewing correspondence with the Financial Regulator and other regulators; and

- consideration of work on compliance matters carried out by internal audit.

Money laundering and the financing of terrorism

In the UK and Ireland, when carrying out procedures for the purpose of forming an opinion on the financial statements, the auditor should be alert for those instances of possible or actual non compliance with laws and regulations that might incur obligations for partners and staff in audit firms to report money laundering offences. (paragraph 22-1)

35. The law relating to the prevention of money laundering and terrorist financing is integral to the legal and regulatory framework within which banks conduct their business. By the nature of their business, banks are ready targets of those engaged in

money laundering activities and the financing of terrorism. Anti-money laundering legislation[15] in the Republic of Ireland makes it a criminal offence to provide assistance to those involved in money laundering or terrorist financing. In addition, section 57 of the Criminal Justice Act, 1994, as amended, (**'CJA 1994'**) requires banks and other bodies designated under that Act to report suspicions of money laundering or terrorist financing to the appropriate authorities, being the Garda Síochána and the Revenue Commissioners. It is also an offence under section 58(2) of the CJA 1994 to make a disclosure which is likely to prejudice any investigation arising from a report made under section 57 of that Act.

36. The anti-money laundering legislation in the Republic of Ireland also requires bodies designated for the purposes of that legislation, including banks, to meet certain requirements in the following areas:

   • the establishment and maintenance of policies, procedures and controls to deter and to recognise and report money laundering and terrorist financing activities;

   • taking reasonable measures to establish the identity of customers (often referred to as "know your customer" requirements);

   • retention of customer identification and transaction records for use as evidence in any future investigations into money laundering or terrorist financing; and

   • education and training of staff.

37. Detailed guidance on implementation of the requirements of anti-money laundering legislation, entitled "Money Laundering: Guidance Notes for Credit Institutions", has been issued with the approval of the Money Laundering Steering Committee[16]. New Guidance Notes will be published based on the legislation that will implement the 3rd Anti-Money Laundering Directive in Ireland.

38. Laws and regulations relating to money laundering and terrorist financing are therefore central to banks. When auditing the financial statements of a bank, the auditor needs to obtain a general understanding of how the bank ensures compliance with anti-money laundering legislation.

---

[15] Anti-money laundering legislation in the Republic of Ireland includes the following:
   • Criminal Justice Act 1994 – as amended;
   • S.I. No. 104 of 1995, Criminal Justice Act 1994 (Section 32(10)(a)) Regulations 1995;
   • Criminal Justice (Theft & Fraud Offences) Act 2001;
   • S.I. No. 216 of 2003, Criminal Justice Act 1994 (Section 32(10)(a)) Regulations 2003;
   • S.I. No. 242 of 2003, Criminal Justice Act 1994 (Section 32) Regulations 2003;
   • S.I. No. 416 of 2003, Criminal Justice Act 1994 (Section 32)(Amendment) Regulations 2003;
   • S.I. No. 3 of 2004, Criminal Justice Act 1994 (Section 32)(Prescribed Activities) Regulations 2004; and
   • Criminal Justice (Terrorist Offences) Act 2005.
[16] The Money Laundering Steering Committee is a committee chaired by the Department of Finance and comprises representatives of government departments, regulators and those bodies designated under the anti-money laundering legislation.

39. The auditor is aware of the auditor's own designation under the CJA 1994. If the auditor concludes that there is a possible breach of anti-money laundering legislation, or if he uncovers any suspicion that the bank has been involved, either knowingly or otherwise, in money laundering or terrorist financing offences, the auditor considers it, his statutory duty to report to the Garda Síochána and the Revenue Commissioners in accordance with the CJA 1994. In addition the auditor takes steps to assess the effect on the financial statements and the implications for other aspects of the audit. The auditor is aware that a suspicion of an offence of money laundering or terrorist financing may also give rise to a statutory duty to report directly to the Financial Regulator, separately to the Garda Síochána under section 59 of the Criminal Justice (Theft and Fraud Offences) Act, 2001, or to the Office of the Director of Corporate Enforcement in accordance with the Company Law Enforcement Act, 2001. In this regard the auditor needs to be mindful of the offence of prejudicing an investigation under section 58(2) of the CJA 1994.

Taxation

40. In the course of obtaining evidence sufficient to form an opinion on the view given by a bank's financial statements, auditors undertake procedures in relation to amounts relating to tax included in those statements in order to determine whether they are materially misstated. In addition to accounting for taxation arising on its own activities, a bank may have responsibilities under tax and stamp duty laws to operate various tax deductions and tax collection mechanisms. Whilst an audit of financial statements does not provide specific assurance on compliance by the entity with all provisions of tax law non-compliance can result in the risk of imposition of liabilities. Auditors of banks therefore:

   (a) make enquiries of the bank's directors, compliance officer and other personnel responsible for compliance with tax law and regulations as to how such duties are discharged and whether they are on notice of any possible instances of non-compliance;

   (b) review correspondence with the Revenue Commissioners; and

   (c) carry out procedures to obtain sufficient appropriate evidence that, in the context of the financial statements as a whole, tax charges, liabilities, assets and related disclosures are free from material mis-statement.

41. If auditors become aware of non-compliance with tax legislation, auditors consider the implications in the context of their 'whistle blowing' responsibilities under section 1079 of the Taxes Consolidation Act 1997.

**THE AUDITING
PRACTICES BOARD**

ISA (UK and Ireland) 250: Section B – The Auditors' Right and Duty to Report to Regulators in the Financial Sector

The auditor of a regulated entity should bring information of which the auditor has become aware in the ordinary course of performing work undertaken to fulfil the auditor's audit responsibilities to the attention of the appropriate regulator without delay when:

(a) The auditor concludes that it is relevant to the regulator's functions having regard to such matters as may be specified in statute or any related regulations; and

(b) In the auditor's opinion there is reasonable cause to believe it is or may be of material significance to the regulator. (paragraph 2)

Where an apparent breach of statutory or regulatory requirements comes to the auditor's attention, the auditor should:

(a) Obtain such evidence as is available to assess its implications for the auditor's reporting responsibilities;

(b) Determine whether, in the auditor's opinion, there is reasonable cause to believe that the breach is of material significance to the regulator; and

(c) Consider whether the apparent breach is criminal conduct that gives rise to criminal property and, as such, should be reported to the specified authorities. (paragraph 39)

Auditor's duty to report to the Financial Regulator

42. Section 47 of the CBA 1989 and Regulation 7 of the Post BCCI Regulations place a duty on auditors to report to the Financial Regulator without undue delay, where the auditor has reason to believe that:

- the continuous functioning of the bank may be affected; in particular, that there exist circumstances which are likely to affect materially its obligations to depositors or where there are issues relating to its ability to meet its financial obligations; or

- there are material defects in the financial systems and controls or accounting records of the bank; or

- there are material inaccuracies in, or omissions from, any financial returns made by the bank to the Financial Regulator; or

- there is a material breach of the laws, regulations or administrative provisions which lay down the conditions under which the bank has been authorised or of any laws, regulations or administrative provisions which govern its activities or of any condition or requirement imposed by the Financial Regulator; or

- there are circumstances such as preclude them from stating in their audit report that the annual financial statements give a true and fair view and have been properly prepared in accordance with the Companies Acts and all Regulations to be construed as one with those Acts; or

- where they have decided to resign or not seek re-election as auditor.

43. Under sections 27B to 27D of the CBA 1997[17], the auditor is required to provide to the Financial Regulator:

   - an annual confirmation as to whether there are matters to report in addition to and including any reports already submitted under 'prescribed enactments' (section 27B);

   - copies of any reports provided to the bank or those concerned with its management on matters that have come to the auditor's notice while auditing the financial statements of the bank or carrying out any work for the bank of any kind specified by the Financial Regulator (section 27C); and

   - copies of any reports issued to the Office of the Director of Corporate Enforcement (section 27D).

44. Further details of the auditor's duties noted in the two preceding paragraphs are set out in Appendix 2.

45. Information and opinions to be communicated are those meeting the specified criteria which relate to matters of which the auditor of the bank has become aware:

   - in his capacity as auditor of the bank (this limitation does not apply in the respect of reports required under section 27C as outlined above); and

   - if he is also the auditor of an entity who has close links[18] with the bank, in his capacity as auditor of that entity.

46. The duty to report opinions, as well as information, allows for circumstances where adequate information on a matter may not readily be forthcoming from the regulated entity, and where judgments need to be made. Where the auditor reports based on making a judgement rather on a matter of fact, a legal advice should be sought.

---

[17] All references made to sections 27B to 27D of the CBA are to those sections inserted by the CBFSAI 2004.

[18] Close links between two or more entities, as defined by Regulation 2 of the Post-BCCI Regulations, arise as a result of factors indicating either (a) participation: the ownership, direct or by way of control, or 20 per cent or more of the voting rights or capital of an undertaking; (b) control: the relationship between a parent undertaking and a subsidiary undertaking (including sub-subsidiaries). Additionally, close links exist if there is an arrangement whereby two or more persons are permanently linked to one and the same person by a control relationship.

Material significance

47.   The statutory reporting requirements referred to above do not require the auditor to perform any additional audit work nor is the auditor required specifically to seek out breaches of the requirements applicable to a particular regulated entity. However, in circumstances where the auditor identifies that a reportable matter may exist, the auditor carries out such extra work, as he considers necessary, to determine whether the facts and circumstances cause them 'reasonably to believe' that the matter does in fact exist. It should be noted that the auditor's work does not need to prove that the reportable matter exists.

48.   ISA (UK and Ireland) 250 Section B requires that, where an apparent breach of statutory or regulatory requirements comes to the auditor's attention, he should obtain such evidence as is available to assess the implications for the auditor's reporting responsibilities and determine whether, in his opinion, there is reasonable cause to believe that the breach has occurred and that it relates to a matter that is of material significance to the regulator.

49.   The reporting requirements under the CBA 1989 and the Post-BCCI Regulations refer to matters which are likely to be "material", with this word not being defined in law. In interpreting the matters giving rise to the duty to report, the definition of material significance from ISA (UK and Ireland) 250 Section B is applied.

'Material significance' is defined by ISA (UK and Ireland) 250 Section B as follows:

> "A matter or group of matters is normally of material significance to a regulator's functions when, due either to its nature or its potential financial impact, it is likely of itself to require investigation by the regulator."

50.   'Material significance' does not have the same meaning as materiality in the context of the audit of financial statements. Whilst a particular event may be trivial in terms of its possible effect on the financial statements of an entity, it may be of a nature or type that is likely to change the perception of the regulator.

51.   The determination of whether a matter is, or is likely to be, of material significance to the Financial Regulator inevitably requires the auditor to exercise his judgment. In forming such judgments, the auditor needs to consider not simply the facts of the matter but also their implications. In addition, it is possible that a matter, which is not materially significant in isolation, may become so when other possible breaches are considered.

52.   The auditor of a regulated entity bases his judgment of 'material significance' to the Financial Regulator solely on his understanding of the facts of which the auditor is aware without making any assumptions about the information available to the Financial Regulator in connection with any particular regulated entity.

53.   Minor breaches of the Financial Regulator's rules that, for example, are unlikely to jeopardise the entity's assets or amount to misconduct or mismanagement would not normally be of 'material significance'. ISA (UK and Ireland) 250 Section B however

requires the auditor of the bank when reporting on the bank's financial statements, to review information obtained in the course of the audit and to assess whether the cumulative effect is of 'material significance' such as to give rise to a duty to report to the regulator. In circumstances where the auditor is uncertain whether or not he is required to make a report, he may consider taking legal advice.

54. On completion of his investigations, the auditor ensures that the facts and circumstances, and the basis for his conclusion as to whether these are, or are likely to be, of 'material significance' to the Financial Regulator, are adequately documented such that the reasons for his decision to report or not, as the case may be, may be clearly demonstrated should the need to do so arise in future.

55. Whilst confidentiality is an implied term of the auditor's contract with a bank, section 47(6) of the CBA 1989, Regulation 9 of the Post-BCCI Regulations and section 27H of the CBA 1997[19] outline that an auditor does not contravene that duty of confidentiality in fulfilling his duty to report to the Financial Regulator. The protection afforded is given in respect of information obtained in his capacity as auditor.

Conduct of the audit

56. ISA (UK and Ireland) 250, Section B requires the auditor to ensure that all staff involved in the audit of a regulated entity 'have an understanding of

   (a)   the provisions of applicable legislation,

   (b)   the regulator's rules and any guidance issued by the regulator, and

   (c)   any specific requirements which apply to the particular regulated entity,

   appropriate to their role in the audit and sufficient (in the context of that role) to enable them to identify situations they encounter in the course of the audit which may give reasonable cause to believe that a matter should be reported to the regulator.'

57. Understanding, commensurate with the individual's role and responsibilities in the audit process, is required of :

   • the statutory provisions concerning the auditor's duty to report to the Financial Regulator;

   • the Standards and guidance in ISA (UK and Ireland) 250, Section B, and in this section of this Practice Note; and

   • relevant sections of the administrative provisions issued by the Financial Regulator, in particular, the Financial Regulator Standards.

---

[19]   As inserted by section 26 of the CBFSAI 2004.

THE AUDITING
PRACTICES BOARD

58. The auditor includes procedures within his planning process to ensure that members of the audit team have such understanding (in the context of their role) as to enable them to recognise potentially reportable matters, and that such matters are reported to the audit engagement partner without delay so that a decision may be made as to whether a duty to report arises.

59. An audit firm appointed as auditor of a bank needs to have in place appropriate procedures to ensure that the audit engagement partner is made aware of any other relationship which exists between any department of the audit firm and the regulated entity when that relationship could affect the audit firm's work as the auditor. (This matter is covered in more detail in Appendix 2 of ISA (UK and Ireland) 250, Section B). The auditor also requests the regulated entity to advise him when it appoints a third party (including another department or office of the same audit firm) to review, investigate or report on any aspects of its business activities that may be relevant to the audit of the financial statements and to provide the auditor with copies of reports by such a third party promptly after their receipt. This matter may usefully be referred to in the engagement letter.

Closely linked entities

60. Where the auditor of a bank is also the auditor of a closely linked entity[20] a duty to report arises directly in relation to information relevant to the bank of which the auditor becomes aware in the course of his work as the auditor of the closely linked entity.

61. The auditor establishes during audit planning whether the bank has one or more closely linked entities of which the audit firm is also the auditor. If there are such entities the auditor considers the significance of the closely linked entities and the nature of the issues that might arise which may be of material significance to the regulator of the bank. Such circumstances may involve:

- activities or uncertainties within the closely linked entity which might significantly impair the financial position of the bank;

- money laundering and if the closely linked entity is itself a bank or otherwise regulated; and/or

- matters that the auditor of the closely linked entity is intending to report to the Financial Regulator or another regulator.

62. Following the risk assessment above, the auditor of the bank identifies the closely linked entities for which the procedures in this paragraph are necessary. The engagement team of the bank communicates to the engagement team of the selected closely linked entities the audit firm's responsibilities to report to the Financial Regulator under the CBA 1989 and the Post-BCCI Regulations and notifies the engagement team of the circumstances that have been identified which, if found to exist, might be of material significance to the Financial Regulator as regulator of the

---

[20] See footnote 18.

bank. Prior to completion the auditor of the bank obtains details from the auditor of the closely linked entity of such circumstances or confirmation, usually in writing, that such circumstances do not exist. Where the closely linked entities are part of the inter-auditor group reporting process these steps can be built into that process.

63. Whilst confidentiality is an implied term of an auditor's contract with a bank, CBA 1989 and the Post-BCCI Regulations specify that an auditor of an entity closely linked to a bank who is also the auditor of that bank does not contravene that duty if he reports to the Financial Regulator information or his opinion, if he is acting in good faith and he reasonably believes that the information or opinion is relevant to any function of the Financial Regulator. The protection afforded is given in respect of information obtained in his capacity as auditor.

64. No duty to report is imposed on the auditor of an entity closely linked to a bank who is not also the auditor of the bank.

65. In circumstances where he is not also the auditor of the closely linked entity, the auditor of the bank decides whether there are any matters to be reported to the Financial Regulator relating to the affairs of the bank in the light of the information that they receive about a closely linked entity for the purpose of auditing the financial statements of the bank. If the auditor becomes aware of possible matters that may fall due to be reported, he may wish to obtain further information from the management or the auditor of the closely linked entity to ascertain whether the matter should be reported. To facilitate such possible discussions, at the planning stage of the audit, the auditor of the bank will have considered whether arrangements need to be put in place to allow them to communicate with the management and the auditor of the closely linked entity. If the auditor of the bank is unable to communicate with the management and the auditor of the closely linked entity to obtain further information concerning the matters he has identified he reports the matters, and that he has been unable to obtain further information, directly to the Financial Regulator.

Information received in a capacity other than as auditor

66. There may be circumstances where it is not clear whether information about a bank coming to the attention of the auditor is received in the capacity of the auditor or in some other capacity, for example as a general adviser to the entity. Appendix 2 to ISA (UK and Ireland) 250 Section B provides guidance as to how information obtained in non-audit work may be relevant to the auditor in the planning and conduct of the audit and the steps that need to be taken to ensure the communication of information that is relevant to the audit.

Discussing matters of material significance with the directors

67. The directors[21] are the persons principally responsible for the management of the bank. The auditor will therefore normally bring a matter of material significance to the

---

[21] This term would include the senior management of branches of foreign companies in the Republic of Ireland.

attention of the directors. ISA (UK and Ireland) 250 Section B emphasises that where the auditor concludes that a duty to report arises, he should bring the matter to the attention of the regulator without undue delay. The directors may also wish to report the matters identified to the Financial Regulator themselves and detail the actions taken or to be taken. While such a report from the directors may provide valuable information, it does not relieve the auditor of the statutory duty to report directly to the Financial Regulator. The auditor is aware that where the matter relates to a suspicion of an offence of money laundering or terrorist financing he is mindful of the offence of prejudicing an investigation under section 58(2) of the CJA 1994.

68. Section 47(4) of the CBA 1989 requires an auditor making a report to the Financial Regulator under section 47(1) or section 47(2) of that Act to provide a copy of the report to the bank concerned. However the auditor is aware that ISA (UK and Ireland) 250, Section B paragraph 54 states that:

> "When the matter giving rise to a statutory duty to make a report direct to a regulator casts doubt on the integrity of those charged with governance or their competence to conduct the business of the regulated entity, the auditor should, subject to compliance with legislation relating to 'tipping off', make the report to the regulator without delay and without informing those charged with governance in advance"

On a first reading section 47(4) of the CBA 1989 and ISA (UK and Ireland) 250 appear to conflict. However, section 47(4) of the CBA 1989 states that the "auditor of a holder of a licence shall send to the holder a copy of any report made by him to the Bank under subsection (1) or (2)."

It is clear that section 47(4) of the CBA 1989 will be complied with if the report is sent to the bank ("the holder of the licence") at the same time or immediately after a copy has been submitted to the Financial Regulator.

The auditor may consider seeking legal advice where the subject of a report required by the Financial Regulator relates to a suspicion of an offence of money laundering or terrorist financing and the auditor is therefore aware of the potential offence of 'prejudicing an investigation' under section 58(2) of the CJA 1994.

Timing of a report

69. The duty to report arises once the auditor has concluded that he reasonably believes that the matter is or is likely to be of material significance to the Financial Regulator's regulatory function. In reaching his conclusion the auditor may wish to take appropriate legal or other advice and consult with colleagues.

70. Section 47(1) of the CBA 1989 requires that the report should be made without undue delay once a conclusion has been reached. Unless the matter casts doubt on the integrity of the directors this should not preclude discussion of the matter with the directors and seeking such further advice as is necessary, so that a decision can be made on whether or not a duty to report exists. Such consultations and discussions are however undertaken on a timely basis to enable the auditor to conclude on the matter without undue delay.

Voluntary Reports to the Financial Regulator

71. Where there is a statutory duty to make a report under the CBA 1989, the CBA 1997 or the Post –BCCI Regulations, protection is afforded to the auditor by Section 47(6) of the CBA 1989, section 27(H) of the CBA 1997 and Regulation 9 of the Post-BCCI Regulations respectively.

72. There may be circumstances where the auditor concludes that a matter does not give rise to a statutory duty to report but nevertheless feels that in the public interest it should be brought to the attention of the Financial Regulator. Before making any such 'voluntary' report the auditor needs to consider whether any duty of confidentiality or other duty will be breached by making such a report. The common law may provide protection for disclosing certain matters to a proper authority in the public interest. This is discussed further at paragraphs 63 to 69 of Appendix 2 below.

73. Before making any such voluntary report the auditor may wish to take legal advice before deciding whether, and in what form, to make a report to the Financial Regulator, when not statutorily required to do so.

ISA (UK and Ireland) 300: Planning an Audit of Financial Statements

Background note

The purpose of this ISA (UK and Ireland) is to establish standards and provide guidance on the considerations and activities applicable to planning an audit of financial statements. This ISA (UK and Ireland) is framed in the context of recurring audits. In addition, matters the auditor considers in initial audit engagements are included in paragraphs 28 and 29.

The auditor should plan the audit so that the engagement will be performed in an effective manner. (paragraph 2)

The auditor should establish the overall audit strategy for the audit. (paragraph 8)

The auditor should develop an audit plan for the audit in order to reduce audit risk to an acceptably low level. (paragraph 13)

74. Matters the auditor of a bank considers as part of the planning process for the audit of the financial statements include:

    • the nature and scope of the bank's business;

    • the extent of head office control over networks of branches;

    • the bank's relationships with the Financial Regulator and any other regulators;

    • changes in applicable laws, regulations and accounting requirements;

    • the need to involve specialists in the audit;

    • the extent to which controls and procedures are outsourced to a third-party provider; and

    • issues relating to the auditor's statutory duty to report.

75. Guidance on the first four of these matters is set out in the section on ISA (UK and Ireland) 315 'Obtaining an Understanding of the Entity and its Environment and Assessing the Risks of Material Misstatement' below. Considerations in relation to the other matters in planning the audit are:

    • the nature and complexity of banking increases the likelihood that the auditor may consider it necessary to involve specialists in the audit process. For example, the auditor may wish to utilise the work of an expert in the valuation of derivative and other financial instruments not traded in an active market. The auditor considers the need to involve such specialists at an early stage in planning the audit work.

Where such specialists are to be used, they may be involved in the development of the audit plan and may take part in discussions with the management and staff, in order to assist in the development of knowledge and understanding relating to the business;

- the auditor considers the implications of the outsourcing of functions by the bank, and the sources of evidence available to the auditor for transactions undertaken by service organisations in planning the audit work. This may include the outsourcing of certain functions, such as the IT functions. Further guidance is contained in the section of the Practice Note dealing with ISA (UK and Ireland) 402 'Audit Considerations Relating to Entities Using Service Organisations'; and

- issues relating to the auditor's statutory duty to report include the adequacy of the audit team's understanding of the law and the identification of closely linked entities.

ISA (UK and Ireland) 315: Obtaining an Understanding of the Entity and its Environment and Assessing the Risks of Material Misstatement

Background note

The purpose of this ISA (UK and Ireland) is to establish standards and to provide guidance on obtaining an understanding of the entity and its environment, including its internal control, and on assessing the risks of material misstatement in a financial statement audit.

76. Banking can be complex and the auditor seeks to understand the business and the regulatory regime in which the bank operates. Generally, there is a close relationship between planning and obtaining an understanding of the business and the control environment, which is covered more fully below.

The auditor should obtain an understanding of relevant industry, regulatory, and other external factors including the applicable financial reporting framework. (paragraph 22)

The auditor should obtain an understanding of the nature of the entity. (paragraph 25)

77. When performing procedures to obtain an understanding of the bank's business, the auditor considers:

- the relative importance to the bank of each of its business activities. This includes an understanding of the type and extent of specialised activities, for example:

  - derivatives and other complex trading activities (where documentation, accounting and valuation aspects can be difficult);

  - trade finance, invoice discounting and factoring (where the documentation used can be complex and highly specialised); and

  - leasing (where there are particular accounting issues, especially relating to income recognition).

- the introduction of new categories of customers, or products or marketing and distribution channels;

- the relevant aspects of the bank's risk management procedures;

- the complexity of the bank's information systems;

- the legal and operational structure of the bank;

- a change in the market environment (for example, a marked increase in competition);

- the complexity of products;

- the consistency of products, methods and operations in different departments or locations; and

- the respective roles and responsibilities attributed to the finance, risk control, compliance and internal audit functions.

78. Many banks and banking groups are managed globally on product/business lines rather than focused around legal structure. Such 'matrix management' structures typically involve local reporting (often on a legal entity basis) on operational and compliance matters; and business/product based reporting (often globally) of activities undertaken. In addition, global trading activities may mean that transactions are entered into in one location but are recorded in another; it may even be the case that they are controlled and settled in a third location. Furthermore, parts of banks' operations may be undertaken through special purpose entities which may have structures and features that can mean they are excluded from financial statement consolidation. Given these factors, the auditor gains an understanding of how and where transactions are undertaken, recorded and controlled, in order to plan the audit.

79. Many banks operate a network of branches. In such instances, the auditor determines the degree of head office control over the business and accounting functions at branch level and the scope and effectiveness of the bank's inspection and/or internal audit visits. The extent and impact of visits from regulators is also relevant. Where branches maintain separate accounting records, the extent of audit visits and work on each branch is also dependent on the materiality of, and risks associated with, the operations of each branch and the extent to which controls over branches are exercised centrally. In the case of smaller branches, the degree to which exceptions to a bank's normal control procedures may be caused by minimal staffing levels (for example, the greater difficulty of ensuring adequate segregation of duties) and the consequent need for an increased level of control from outside the branch are relevant to assessing audit risk.

80. In obtaining an understanding of the regulatory factors the auditor considers:

- any formal communications between the Financial Regulator in its capacity as the regulator and the bank, including any new or interim risk assessments issued by the Financial Regulator, the results of any other supervisory visits conducted by Financial Regulator;

- the contents of any recent reports prepared by persons other than the auditor or by an inspector appointed to report on any aspect of the bank under financial services legislation;

- any formal communications between the bank and other regulators; and

- discussions with the bank's compliance officer together with others responsible for monitoring regulatory compliance.

The auditor should obtain an understanding of the entity's selection and application of accounting policies and consider whether they are appropriate for its business and consistent with the applicable financial reporting framework and accounting policies used in the relevant industry. (paragraph 28)

81. Accounting policies of particular relevance may include allowances for impairment, hedge accounting, classification of assets and liabilities (and thereby their measurement), embedded derivatives, revenue / expense recognition (including effective interest rates), offsetting and derecognition. The auditor undertakes procedures to consider whether the policies adopted are in compliance with applicable accounting standards and gains an understanding of the procedures, systems and controls applied to maintain compliance with them.

The auditor should obtain an understanding of the entity's objectives and strategies, and the related business risks that may result in material misstatement of the financial statements. (paragraph 30)

82. It is important for the auditor to understand the multi-dimensional nature and extent of the financial and business risks which are integral to the environment, and how the bank's systems record and address these risks. Although they may apply to varying degrees, the risks include (but are not limited to):

- credit risk: at its simplest, this is the risk that a borrower or other counterparty will be unable to meet its obligations. However, where credit risk is traded (in the form of secondary market loan trading or credit derivatives, for example), credit risk is often regarded as having two distinct elements:

    o spread risk: the risk arising from day to day changes in the price of a credit instrument because of changes in market perceptions about the credit standing of the debtor; and

    o default risk: the risk that a debtor will default on its obligations.
    Another form of credit risk is settlement risk which is the risk that a counterparty will be unable to settle its obligations under a transaction (in a securities settlement or payment system, for example) on the due date;

- liquidity risk: the risk that arises from the possibility that a bank has insufficient liquid funds to meet the demands of depositors or other counterparties;

- interest rate risk: the risk that arises where there is a mismatch between the interest reset dates or bases for assets and liabilities;

- currency risk: the risk that arises from the mismatching of assets, liabilities and commitments denominated in different currencies;

- market risk[22]: the risk that changes in the value of assets, liabilities and commitments will occur as a result of movements in relative prices (for example, as a result of changes in the market price of tradable assets). Market risk is a generic term which, in addition to interest rate and currency risk and, in some environments, spread risk, also includes equity risk and commodity price risk;

- operational risk is the risk of loss, arising from inadequate or failed internal processes, people and systems or from external events; and

- regulatory risk is the risk of public censure, fines (together with related compensation payments) and restriction or withdrawal of authorisation to conduct some or all of the bank's activities. In the Republic of Ireland this may arise from enforcement activity by the Financial Regulator.

Failure to manage the risks outlined above can also cause serious damage to a bank's reputation, potentially leading to loss of confidence in the bank, withdrawal of deposits or problems in maintaining liquidity (this is sometimes referred to as reputational risk or franchise risk).

The auditor should obtain an understanding of the measurement and review of the entity's financial performance. (paragraph 35)

83. The auditor obtains an understanding of the measures used by management to review the bank's performance. Further guidance in respect of key performance indicators is given in the section on ISA (UK and Ireland) 520.

The auditor should obtain an understanding of the internal control relevant to the audit. (paragraph 41)

The auditor should obtain an understanding of the control environment. (paragraph 67)

84. The quality of the overall control environment is dependent upon management's attitude towards the operation of controls. A positive attitude may be evidenced by an organisational framework which enables proper segregation of duties and delegation of control functions and which encourages failings to be reported and corrected. Thus, where a lapse in the operation of a control is treated as a matter of concern, the control environment will be stronger and will contribute to effective control systems; whereas a weak control onvironment will undermine detailed controls, however well designed.

---

[22] Some forms of market risk are 'non-linear' i.e. there is not a constant relationship between the profit and loss and the movement in the underlying price. For example, the relationship between an option's price and the price of its underlying instrument is 'non-linear'; the 'delta' measures the change in the price of an option for the unit change in the price of the underlying instrument whilst the 'gamma' indicates the extent of the 'non-linearity' (the change in 'delta' for a unit change in the price of the underlying instrument).

**THE AUDITING
PRACTICES BOARD**

85. Senior management is responsible for establishing and maintaining such systems and controls as are appropriate to the operations of the bank. The CRD together with the Financial Regulator Standards require that every person who has, or is to have, a qualifying holding (defined in Appendix 3), director, or senior manager of a bank is a fit and proper person in the context of the particular position which he holds or is to hold. In November 2006 the Financial Regulator published its "Fit and Proper Requirements" which applies a common framework for assessing the 'fitness and probity' of directors and senior managers across all the industry sectors, including the banking sector, subject to regulation by the Financial Regulator. Further information on this framework is available in Appendix 4.

86. The Financial Regulator requires banks to maintain systems and controls appropriate for its business. These include (but are not limited to):

•   clear and appropriate reporting lines which are communicated within the bank;

•   appropriate controls to ensure compliance with laws and regulations (this may mean a separate compliance function);

•   appropriate risk assessment process;

•   appropriate management information;

•   controls to ensure suitability of staff;

•   controls to manage tensions arising out of remuneration policies;

•   documented and tested business continuity plans;

•   documented business plans or strategies;

•   an internal audit function (where appropriate);

•   an audit committee (where appropriate); and

•   appropriate record keeping arrangements.

87. For large banks, the volume of transactions can be so great that it may be extremely difficult for the auditor to express an opinion without obtaining considerable assurance from adequate systems of control. Systems of internal control in a bank are important in ensuring orderly and prudent operations of the bank and in assisting the directors to prepare financial statements which give a true and fair view. The following features of the business of banks may be relevant to the auditor's assessment of such internal controls:

•   the substantial scale of transactions, both in terms of volume and relative value, makes it important that control systems are in place to ensure that transactions are recorded promptly, accurately and completely and are checked and approved, and that records are reconciled at appropriate intervals in order to identify and investigate differences promptly. Processing and accounting for complex transactions or high volumes of less complex transactions will almost inevitably involve the use of sophisticated technology. For example, transactions subject to 'straight through processing' involve little or no manual intervention after they have been initiated;

- a bank deals in money or near money instruments. In the case of most commercial organisations, most movements of funds are the result of a related movement of goods and some audit assurance may therefore be obtained by reference to this relationship. This is not available, however, in the case of banks and similar financial organisations. Management must therefore establish robust systems of control. As the centralised funds transfer departments which exist in larger banks will often process very high volumes and a high value of transactions each day, the need for strong and effective controls over this area is particularly important;

- the fact that banks deal in money and near money instruments makes proper segregation of duties between and amongst those entering into transactions, those recording the transactions, those settling them and where relevant, those responsible for their physical security particularly important;

- the geographical or organisational dispersal of some banks' operations means that, in order to maintain control over its activities, banks need to ensure not only that there are sufficient controls at each location, but also that there are effective communication and control procedures between the various locations and the centre. It is important that there should be clear, comprehensive reporting and responsibility lines, particularly where the business is managed using a 'matrix' structure;

- the activities of banks can typically result in the creation or use of derivatives and other complex transactions. The fact that the resultant cash flows may not take place for a considerable time creates the risk that wrongly recorded or unrecorded positions may exist and that these may not be detected for some time, thereby exposing the bank to risk of misstatement. The valuation of these instruments also poses risks of misstatement. Consequently, banks will normally have developed important operational controls to mitigate such risks;

- the provisions of the Irish tax legislation require banks to operate various tax deduction and collection arrangements, such as those relating to paying and collecting agents and tax deducted from interest paid to individuals. In addition, the VAT position of a bank can be particularly complex. These may give rise to significant liabilities if not properly dealt with. Accordingly, an effective control system is essential to ensure that the record-keeping requirements of the Irish tax legislation are satisfied, and that tax is accounted for promptly and accurately. Similar measures may be needed to address similar provisions arising in any other jurisdictions where the bank operates; and

- the Irish regulatory framework is both complex and evolving for banks. This may give rise to significant liabilities for compensation to clients if not properly dealt with. Accordingly, an effective control system is essential to ensure that the requirements of the Financial Regulator are satisfied. Measures may also be needed to address regulators in other jurisdictions.

> The auditor should obtain a sufficient understanding of control activities to assess the risks of material misstatement at the assertion level and to design further audit procedures responsive to assessed risks. (paragraph 90)

88. There is a wide variation between different banks in terms of size, activity and organisation, so that there can be no standard approach to internal controls and risk. The auditor assesses the adequacy of controls in relation to the circumstances of each entity. Examples of weaknesses that may be relevant to the auditor's assessment of the risk of material misstatement are as follows:

- complex products or processes inadequately understood by management; this includes undue concentration of expertise concerning matters requiring the exercise of significant judgment or capable of manipulation such as valuations of financial instruments or allowances for impairment;

- weaknesses in back office procedures contributing to completeness and accuracy of accounting records such as:

  - backlogs in key reconciliations, particularly those over correspondent bank accounts, settlement accounts and the custody of assets such as securities (either those held on own account or as collateral);

  - inadequate maintenance of suspense or clearing accounts; and

  - backlogs in confirmation processes relating to financial instrument transactions.

- weaknesses in new product approval procedures;

- lack of segregation of duties such as between critical dealing, operational, control, settlement and accounting functions; and

- weakness over payments systems, such as inadequate controls over access to payment systems and data.

89. Controls relating to outsourcing activities are considered in the ISA (UK and Ireland) 402 section.

> The auditor should obtain an understanding of how the entity has responded to risks arising from IT. (paragraph 93)

90. As a result of the type and complexity of transactions undertaken and records held by banks and the need for swift and accurate information processing and retrieval, many banking functions are highly automated, including: funds transfer systems, the

accounting function, the processing and recording of customer transactions, trading activity, regulatory reporting and the supply of management information.

91. The auditor assesses the extent, nature and impact of automation within the bank and plans and performs work accordingly. In particular the auditor considers:

- the required level of IT knowledge and skills may be extensive and may require the auditor to obtain advice and assistance from staff with specialist skills;

- the extent of the application of audit software and related audit techniques;

- general controls relating to the environment within which IT based systems are developed, maintained and operated; and

- external interfaces susceptible to breaches of security.

A single computer system rarely covers all of the bank's requirements. It is common for banks to employ a number of different systems and, in many cases, use PC-based applications (sometimes involving the use of complex spreadsheets) to generate important accounting and/or internal control information. The auditor identifies and understands the communication between computer systems in order to assess whether appropriate controls are established and maintained to cover all critical systems and the links between them and to identify the most effective audit approach.

The auditor should identify and assess the risks of material misstatement at the financial statement level, and at the assertion level for classes of transactions, account balances, and disclosures. (paragraph 100)

As part of the risk assessment, the auditor should determine which of the risks identified are, in the auditor's judgment, risks that require special audit consideration (such risks are defined as "significant risks"). (paragraph 108)

For significant risks, to the extent the auditor has not already done so, the auditor should evaluate the design of the entity's related controls, including relevant control activities, and determine whether they have been implemented. (paragraph 113)

92. Significant risks are likely to arise in those areas that are subject to significant subjective judgment by management or are complex and properly understood by comparatively few people within the bank.

93. Examples of significant risks that may arise include the following:

- allowances for impairment (particularly collective assessments of impairment) (see paragraphs 127 to 129) or customer compensation provisioning; and

- valuation of certain derivatives and other financial instruments (see paragraphs 132 and 133).

94. Weaknesses in the control environment and in controls such as those described in paragraph 88 could increase the risk of fraud.

95. The application of complex accounting standards such as IAS32, IAS39 and IFRS 7 (for banks using EU IFRS) and FRS 25, 26 and 29 (for banks using Irish GAAP) may also give rise to significant risk with respect to hedge accounting, classification of assets/liabilities, revenue/expense recognition (effective interest rates) and over the adequacy of financial statement disclosure.

ISA (UK and Ireland) 320: Audit Materiality

Background note

The purpose of this ISA (UK and Ireland) is to establish standards and provide guidance on the concept of materiality and its relationship with audit risk.

The auditor should consider materiality and its relationship with audit risk when conducting an audit. (paragraph 2)

Materiality should be considered by the auditor when:

(a) Determining the nature, timing and extent of audit procedures; and

(b) Evaluating the effect of misstatements. (paragraph 8)

96. The principles of assessing materiality in the audit are the same as those applying to the audit of any other entity. In particular the auditor's consideration of materiality is a matter of professional judgement, and is affected by the auditor's perception of the common information needs of users as a group[23].

97. Most banks are profit orientated and a profit based measure, such as a percentage of profit before tax is likely to be used. However, in applying materiality to the audit and assessment of transactions and balances which do not have a direct impact on profit, consideration is given to the extent any misstatement of these items would influence the economic decisions of users taken on the basis of the financial statements. For example, it is not uncommon for banks to encounter balance sheet misclassifications that do not affect profit, such as the offset of trading balances.

---

[23] The International Accounting Standards Board's 'Framework for the Preparation and Presentation of Financial Statements' indicates that, for a profit orientated entity, as investors are providers of risk capital to the enterprise, the provision of financial statements that meets their needs will also meet most of the needs of other users that financial statements can satisfy.

ISA (UK and Ireland) 330: The Auditor's Procedures in Response to Assessed Risks

Background note

The purpose of this ISA (UK and Ireland) is to establish standards and provide guidance on determining overall responses and designing and performing further audit procedures to respond to the assessed risks of material misstatement at the financial statement and assertion levels in a financial statement audit.

When, in accordance with paragraph 115 of ISA (UK and Ireland) 315, the auditor has determined that it is not possible or practicable to reduce the risks of material misstatement at the assertion level to an acceptably low level with audit evidence obtained only from substantive procedures, the auditor should perform tests of relevant controls to obtain audit evidence about their operating effectiveness. (paragraph 25)

98. In practice the nature and volume of transactions relating to the operations of banks often means that performing tests of relevant controls is the most efficient means of reducing audit risk to an acceptably low level.

99. Whilst some aspects of a bank's income statement and balance sheet lend themselves to the application of analytical procedures, income and expense resulting from trading activities is unlikely to be susceptible to these methods because of its inherent unpredictability.

When in accordance with paragraph 108 of ISA (UK and Ireland) 315, the auditor has determined that an assessed risk of material misstatement at the assertion level is a significant risk, the auditor should perform substantive procedures that are specifically responsive to that risk. (paragraph 51)

100. Examples of significant risks include the valuation of derivative and other financial instruments which are not traded in an active market and for which valuation techniques are required – see the section on ISAs (UK and Ireland) 545, and the section on ISA (UK and Ireland) 540 for estimates of allowances for impairment or customer compensation provisioning.

The auditor should perform audit procedures to evaluate whether the overall presentation of the financial statements, including the related disclosures, are in accordance with the applicable financial reporting framework. (paragraph 65)

101. Specific financial reporting standards can require extensive narrative disclosures in the financial statements of banks; for example, in relation to the nature and extent of risks arising from financial instruments. In designing and performing procedures to evaluate

these disclosures the auditor obtains audit evidence regarding the assertions about presentation and disclosure described in paragraph 17 of ISA (UK and Ireland) 500: Audit Evidence.

Disclosure of Market Risk Information under IFRS 7 and FRS 29

102. IFRS 7/FRS 29 Financial instruments: Disclosures may give rise to particular issues for the auditor, particularly in relation to market risk sensitivity analysis.

Understanding the risk measurement method adopted by the management

103. A bank applying IFRS 7/FRS 29, where appropriate, discloses a sensitivity analysis for each type of market risk to which the entity is exposed. Where a bank uses sensitivity analysis, such as value at risk ('**VAR**') that reflects interdependencies between risk variables and this is the method used to manage the financial risks of the business, disclosures based on these measures may be used instead of the standard method prescribed by IFRS 7/FRS 29 paragraph 40.

104. The auditor obtains an understanding of the method adopted by the management to develop the market price risk information to be disclosed. This may be done in conjunction with obtaining an understanding of the bank's accounting and internal control systems. For example, the auditor considers the independence of the bank's risk management function from the front office in the context of their understanding of the control environment.

Considering the skills needed by the audit team

105. The audit team is assembled on the basis of the skills needed. The auditor's approach to the market price risk disclosures is normally based on reviewing and testing the process used by the management to develop the information to be disclosed, rather than on re-performing the calculations (or making or obtaining an independent assessment). However, obtaining an understanding of that process and assumptions used may require technical knowledge of risk measurement methodologies; these can be complex, especially where a VAR model is adopted. Accordingly, when planning the audit, the auditor considers the skills needed in order to obtain and evaluate audit evidence in this part of the engagement.

106. The nature and extent of any technical knowledge of risk measurement methodologies that are required depends on the circumstances. The auditor takes into account such factors as the complexity of the models used and whether the models have received regulatory recognition. Where appropriate, the auditor may involve an expert in elements of this work (see the section of this Practice Note which relates to ISA (UK and Ireland) 620).

Considering the application of the risk measurement method

107. The auditor considers whether the risk measurement method adopted has been applied reasonably by, for example:

- reviewing, and where necessary testing, the internal controls relating to the operation of the bank's risk management system, in order to obtain evidence that the data used in developing the market price risk information are reliable. This may be done in conjunction with the auditor obtaining an understanding of control procedures including those over the data fed into the risk management system, pricing, and independent review of the algorithms. If the bank has applied for regulatory recognition of the method used, the auditor reviews correspondence with the regulator regarding such matters;

- reviewing, and where necessary testing, the internal controls relating to changes in the bank's risk management system (for example, controls over changes to algorithms and assumptions);

- if a VAR model is used, performing analytical review of the model's predictions during the year against actual outcomes (a process commonly referred to as 'backtesting'). The auditor normally reviews any comparisons made by the bank as part of its own backtesting procedures (for a bank to receive regulatory recognition of the model used it is required to undertake backtesting procedures); and

- agreeing the amount disclosed to the output of the risk management system.

108. If an approach based upon internal controls and backtesting proves to be unsatisfactory, the auditor may wish to consider testing the accuracy of the calculations used to develop the required information. However, this situation may indicate that it would be more appropriate for the bank to make disclosures on the simpler basis described in IFRS 7/FRS 29 paragraph 40.

Considering the adequacy of disclosures

109. Market price risk information is subject to a number of significant limitations which are inherent in the risk measurement methods used. For example:

- there are different VAR models and methods of presenting sensitivity analyses. It is to be expected that, in any particular case, the management of a bank will make an informed choice of the method that it considers to be most suitable. Normally, for the purpose of developing the market price risk information to be disclosed, the management will use the risk measurement method that is used in the bank's risk management system. It would, for example, be reasonable to expect the appropriateness of this method in the past to be supported by the bank's own backtesting procedures, where such procedures are performed. However, in the absence of recognised industry standards on VAR, there is no objective benchmark against which to assess the future appropriateness of management's choice;

- both VAR models and sensitivity analyses involve the management making a number of important assumptions in order to develop the disclosures. These are, by their nature, hypothetical and based on management's judgement (for example, when using a VAR model, assumptions are made concerning the appropriate holding period, confidence level and data set);

- both VAR models and, to a limited extent, sensitivity analyses are based on historical data and cannot take account of the fact that future market price movements, correlations between markets and levels of market liquidity in conditions of market stress may bear no relation to historical patterns; and

- each of the methods permitted for developing market price risk information may lead to a bank reporting significantly different information, depending on the choice made by the management. IFRS 7/FRS 29 paragraph 41 requires the market price risk information disclosed to be supplemented by other disclosures, including explanations of:

   ○ the method used in preparing such sensitivity analysis and of the main parameters and assumptions underlying the data provided in the disclosures; and

   ○ the objective of the method used and the limitations that may result in the information not fully reflecting the fair values of assets and liabilities involved.

110. The auditor considers the overall adequacy of the disclosures made by the bank in response to the requirements of IFRS 7/FRS 29 and whether the market risk information is presented fairly so that its limitations can be understood. In particular, the auditor considers whether it is sufficiently clear that:

- the market price risk information is a relative estimate of risk rather than a precise and accurate number;

- the market price risk information represents a hypothetical outcome and is not intended to be predictive (in the case of probability-based methods, such as VAR, profits and losses are almost certain to exceed the reported amount with a frequency depending on the confidence interval chosen); and

- future market conditions could vary significantly from those experienced in the past.

111. In many banks and related groups, market price risk is primarily managed at the level of individual business units rather than on a legal entity or group-wide basis. Therefore, the auditor considers the appropriateness of the basis on which the market risk information to be disclosed in the financial statements is to be compiled. It may well be inappropriate simply to aggregate the operating unit information to arrive at the information to be disclosed for the bank or group as a whole.

Considering the consistency of the risk measurement method adopted

112. The main purpose of the disclosure of market price risk information is to provide users of a bank's financial statements with a better understanding of the relationship between the bank's profitability and its exposure to risk. For example, an increase in

profitability may be achieved by taking on increased risk. IFRS 7/FRS 29 paragraph 40(c) requires disclosure of any changes in the methods and assumptions used and the reasons for the changes. Therefore, the auditor considers the consistency of the method, the main assumptions and parameters with those used in previous years.

113. If the method used for developing the market risk information is also used in the bank's risk management system, modifications will be made to the method as the need arises. If the bank performs its own backtesting procedures, this may lead to modification of, for example, the algorithm used, the assumptions and parameters specified or the parts of the trading book covered. Where modifications have been made, the auditor considers their effect on the market risk measures and whether appropriate disclosures about the changes have been made.

114. In some cases, re-statement may not be possible if the relevant data for the previous year cannot be constructed and in this case the auditor considers whether the disclosures provide sufficient information about the nature and extent of any change in the entity's risk profile. For example, as well as providing the current year figure on the 'new' basis, it may be relevant to show both the current year and the previous year figure on the 'old' basis. In all such cases, the auditor considers whether the disclosures contain sufficient narrative explanation of the change.

ISA (UK and Ireland) 402: Audit Considerations Relating to Entities Using Service Organisations

Background note

The purpose of this ISA (UK and Ireland) is to establish standards and provide guidance to an auditor where the entity uses a service organisation.

In obtaining an understanding of the entity and its environment, the auditor should determine the significance of service organization activities to the entity and the relevance to the audit. (paragraph 5)

Based on the auditor's understanding of the aspects of the entity's accounting system and control environment relating to relevant activities, the auditor should:

(a) Assess whether sufficient appropriate audit evidence concerning the relevant financial statement assertions is available from records held at the entity; and if not,

(b) Determine effective procedures to obtain evidence necessary for the audit, either by direct access to records kept by service organisations or through information obtained from the service organisations or their auditor. (paragraph 9-18)

If an auditor concludes that evidence from records held by a service organization is necessary in order to form an opinion on the client's financial statements and the auditor is unable to obtain such evidence, the auditor should include a description of the factors leading to the lack of evidence in the basis of opinion section of their report and qualify their opinion or issue a disclaimer of opinion on the financial statements. (paragraph 18-1)

115. In common with other industries the outsourcing of functions to third parties is becoming increasingly prevalent with banks. Some of the more common areas, such as customer call centres, may have no direct impact on the audit, while others such as IT functions may have a direct relevance. The auditor therefore gains an understanding of the extent of outsourced functions and their relevance to the financial statements. The bank is obliged to ensure that the auditor has appropriate access to records, information and explanations from material outsourced operations.

116. Whilst a bank may outsource functions to third parties the responsibility of these functions remains that of the bank. The bank should have appropriate controls in place over these arrangements including:

- risk assessment prior to contracting with the service provider, which includes a proper due diligence and periodic review of the appropriateness of the arrangement;

- appropriate contractual agreements or service level agreements;

- contingency plans should the provider fail in delivery of services;

- appropriate management information and reporting from the outsourced provider;

- appropriate controls over customer information; and

- right of access of the bank's internal audit to test the internal controls of the service provider.

117. If the auditor is unable to obtain sufficient audit evidence concerning outsourced operations the auditor considers whether it is necessary to report the matter directly to the Financial Regulator – see the section of this Practice Note relating to ISA (UK and Ireland) 250 Section B.

ISA (UK and Ireland) 505: External Confirmations

Background note

The purpose of this ISA (UK and Ireland) is to establish standards and provide guidance on the auditor's use of external confirmations as a means of obtaining audit evidence.

The auditor should determine whether the use of external confirmations is necessary to obtain sufficient appropriate evidence at the assertion level and how the audit evidence from other planned audit procedures will reduce the risk of material misstatement at the assertion level to an acceptably low level. (paragraph 2)

118. In general, external confirmation procedures may be useful as part of the audit of account balances and classes of transactions such as loans and deposits (including other receivables and payables such as settlement balances and nostro/vostro balances), securities held by third party custodians and derivative transactions. However, external confirmations may not always provide useful audit evidence in relation to:

   • retail loans and deposits; and

   • certain counterparties of wholesale market balances and transactions such as nostro/vostro balances, interbank loans and deposits and derivative transactions.

119. Retail loans and deposits typically comprise high volumes of comparatively low value amounts. Such third parties do not usually maintain independent records of their balances, largely depending on information already provided to them by the bank. Accordingly the auditor may consider the inherent reliability of such responses is comparatively low.

120. Wholesale counterparties incorporated in some jurisdictions outside the Republic of Ireland have countrywide policies of not responding to confirmation requests by auditors at all. Some counterparties will respond to requests to confirm specified balances and transactions but not to open requests for unspecified information.

121. If external confirmations are not used, the auditor seeks sufficient appropriate evidence from tests of control and other substantive procedures. For example, in relation to wholesale market balances and transactions most banks also have well developed transaction confirmation controls within their trading activities. The auditor may consider it more effective to test these controls rather than carry out their own confirmation procedures.

ISA (UK and Ireland) 520: Analytical Procedures

Background note

The purpose of this ISA (UK and Ireland) is to establish standards and provide guidance on the application of analytical procedures during an audit.

The auditor should apply analytical procedures as risk assessment procedures to obtain an understanding of the entity and its environment and in the overall review at the end of the audit. (paragraph 2)

122. Aspects of banking where there are high volumes of similar transactions or balances, such as interest receivable/payable or interest margins, may lend themselves to analytical procedures to highlight anomalies.

123. The auditor of a bank may wish to consider applying analytical procedures to the following, if the procedures are expected to yield useful audit evidence or where they are considered more efficient or effective than alternative procedures:

    - asset quality – e.g. ratio of non-performing loans to total loans and provisions for loan impairment to non-performing loans (overall and by portfolio type);

    - earnings/profitability – e.g. cost/income ratio, the ratio of interest income or expense to average interest bearing assets or liabilities and the ratio of net interest income to average interest bearing assets;

    - the exposure to and degree of mismatching arising from the market risks below and the comparison of the related risk positions to risk limits set by management. The auditor may find it helpful to consider risk information to be disclosed under IFRS 7/FRS 29:

        ○ liquidity;

        ○ interest rates;

        ○ foreign exchange; and

        ○ other market risks, such as equity and commodity prices;

    - the structure of the loan portfolio/credit exposure by industrial, geographic or other category, or by loan impairment provision;

    - regulatory compliance – e.g. complaints handling or reporting of suspicious transactions under the Money Laundering Regulations; and

    - operational risk measures – e.g. failed trade rates, volumes of unreconciled items.

124. Whilst some aspects of a bank's income statement and balance sheet lend themselves easily to analytical procedures, income and expense resulting from trading activities is unlikely to be susceptible to these methods because of its inherent unpredictability. Analytical procedures on income and expense items such as interest will be most effective if returns are calculated on the basis of average daily (or at least monthly) balance information.

125. When performing their review of the financial statements as a whole for consistency with their knowledge of the entity's business and the results of other audit procedures, the auditor considers transactions occurring either side of the year end, including:

- material short-term deposits which are re-lent on broadly similar terms; loan repayments which are received shortly before the year end then re-advanced shortly afterwards; material sale and repurchase transactions or other financing or linked transactions. Experience and judgement are required to identify and assess the implications, if any, of these transactions; they may, for example, be indicative of 'window dressing' of the balance sheet over the year end date;

- other transactions around the year end, apparently at rates which are significantly off market including those that appear or give rise to significant profits or losses;

- the value and nature of transactions between related parties/associated undertakings around the year end; and

- the reclassification of balances and transactions to achieve advantageous income recognition and balance sheet treatment/presentation.

126. Where non financial information or reports produced from systems or processes outside the financial statements accounting system are used in analytical procedures, the auditor considers the reliability of that information or those reports.

**THE AUDITING
PRACTICES BOARD**

ISA (UK and Ireland) 540: Audit of Accounting Estimates

Background note

The purpose of this ISA (UK and Ireland) is to establish standards and provide guidance on the audit of accounting estimates contained in financial statements.

The auditor should obtain sufficient appropriate audit evidence regarding accounting estimates. (paragraph 2)

The auditor should adopt one or a combination of the following approaches in the audit of an accounting estimate:

(a) Review and test the process used by management to develop the estimate;

(b) Use an independent estimate for comparison with that prepared by management; or

(c) Review of subsequent events which provide audit evidence of the reasonableness of the estimate made. (paragraph 10)

The auditor should make a final assessment of the reasonableness of the entity's accounting estimates based on the auditor's understanding of the entity and its environment and whether the estimates are consistent with other audit evidence obtained during the audit. (paragraph 24)

127. Accounting estimates are used for valuation purposes in a number of areas: the most common examples are allowances for loan losses, and the fair value measurement of financial instruments not traded on an active market. Estimates of allowances for impairment or customer compensation provisioning may represent significant risks.

128. In reviewing the adequacy of loan impairment provisions the auditor assesses whether the assumptions made by management in arriving at their estimate of likely cashflows to be received from the impaired loans have been made after due consideration and whether they are supported by relevant evidence, including evidence derived from backtesting. In the case of individual loan impairment calculations such evidence will be specific to the borrower but where impairment is estimated for a portfolio of similar loans the auditor considers observable data across the group of assets as a whole such as arrears statistics or economic conditions. IAS 39 (and its Irish GAAP equivalent FRS 26) gives guidance on the types of evidence to be considered. Banks will also refer to the Financial Regulator's "Credit Institutions Regulatory Document, Impairment Provisions for Credit Exposures" published in October 2005 for guidance in this area.

129. Loan impairment provisions are often calculated using extensive and sometimes complex spreadsheet models and the auditor assesses the control over the inputs to the models and the controls that ensure the consistency and integrity of the model.

130. Based on the audit evidence obtained, the auditor may conclude that the evidence points to an estimate that differs from management's estimate, and that the difference between the auditor's estimate or range and management's estimate constitutes a financial statement misstatement. In such cases, where the auditor has developed a range, a misstatement exists when management's estimate lies outside the auditor's range. The misstatement is measured as the difference between management's estimate and the nearest point of the auditor's range.

131. Management bias, whether unintentional or intentional, can be difficult to detect in a particular estimate. It may only be identified when there has been a change in the method for calculating estimates from the prior period based on a subjective assessment without evidence that there has been a change in circumstances, when considered in the aggregate of groups of estimates or all estimates, or when observed over a number of accounting periods. Although some form of management bias is inherent in subjective decisions, management may have no intention of misleading the users of financial statements. If, however, there is intention to mislead through, for example, the intentional use of unreasonable estimates, management bias is fraudulent in nature. ISA (UK and Ireland) 240, "The Auditor's Responsibility to Consider Fraud in an Audit of Financial Statements," provides standards and guidance on the auditor's responsibility to consider fraud in an audit of financial statements.

ISA (UK and Ireland) 545: Auditing Fair Value Measurements and Disclosures

Background note

The purpose of this ISA (UK and Ireland) is to establish standards and provide guidance on auditing fair value measurements and disclosures contained in financial statements.

The auditor should obtain sufficient appropriate audit evidence that fair value measurements and disclosures are in accordance with the entity's applicable financial reporting framework. (paragraph 3)

As part of the understanding of the entity and its environment, including its internal control, the auditor should obtain an understanding of the entity's process for determining fair value measurements and disclosures and of the relevant control activities sufficient to identify and assess the risks of material misstatement at the assertion level and to design and perform further audit procedures. (paragraph 10)

The auditor should evaluate whether the fair value measurements and disclosures in the financial statements are in accordance with the entity's applicable financial reporting framework. (paragraph 17)

132. The valuation of derivative and other financial instruments which are not traded in an active market and so for which valuation techniques are required is an activity that can give rise to significant audit risk. Such financial instruments are priced using valuation techniques such as discounted cashflow models, options pricing models or by reference to another instrument that is substantially the same as the financial instrument subject to valuation. The auditor reviews the controls, procedures and testing of the valuation techniques used by the bank. Controls and substantive testing could include focussing on:

- valuation technique approval and testing procedures used by the bank;

- the independence of review, sourcing and reasonableness of observable market data and other parameters used in the valuation techniques;

- calibration procedures used by the bank to test the validity of valuation techniques applied by comparing outputs to observable market transactions;

- completeness and appropriate inclusion of all relevant observable market data;

- the observability in practice of data classified by the bank as observable market data;

- the appropriateness and validity of classification of instruments designated as being traded in a non active and in an active market;

- the appropriateness and validity of the particular valuation technique applied to particular financial instruments;

- the appropriateness and validity of the parameters used by the bank to designate an instrument as substantially the same as the financial instrument being valued;

- mathematical integrity of the valuation model; and

- access controls over valuation models.

133. In the more subjective areas of valuation the auditor obtains an understanding of the assumptions used and undertakes a review of the estimates involved for reasonableness, consistency and conformity with generally accepted practices. In some cases, the auditor may use his own valuation techniques to assess the bank's valuations. See paragraphs 102 – 114 in this Practice Note concerning disclosure of market risk information. Given the complexities involved and the subjective nature of the judgments inherent the auditor may involve an expert in elements of this work (see ISA (UK and Ireland) 620 section of this Practice Note).

ISA (UK and Ireland) 550: Related Parties

Background note

The purpose of this ISA (UK and Ireland) is to establish standards and provide guidance on the auditor's responsibilities and audit procedures regarding related parties and transactions with such parties regardless of whether International Accounting Standard (IAS) 24, "Related Party Disclosures," or similar requirement, is part of the applicable financial reporting framework.

When planning the audit the auditor should assess the risk that material undisclosed related party transactions, or undisclosed outstanding balances between an entity and its related parties may exist. (paragraph 106-3)

134. Related party transactions are defined in FRS 8/IAS 24 'Related party disclosures'. Paragraph 16 of FRS 8 states that the 'disclosure provisions do not apply where to comply with them conflicts with the reporting entity's duties of confidentiality arising by operation of law'. IAS 24 contains no explicit corresponding exemption. However the potentially overriding impact of law concerning confidentiality in respect of disclosures under IAS 24 still needs to be considered. This is particularly relevant in a banking context: banks are usually under a strict duty of confidentiality (by operation of statute, contract or common law) regarding the affairs of their clients and, in respect of transactions entered into in certain overseas jurisdictions, this may even preclude a foreign entity from disclosing information to its parent, another group company or their auditor. A provider of finance (in the course of a business in that regard) and its customer are not 'related' simply because of that relationship.

135. Both when applying EU IFRS or Irish GAAP, under ISA (UK and Ireland) 550, the auditor is required to assess the risk that material undisclosed related party transactions may exist. It is in the nature of banking that transaction volumes are high but this factor will not, of itself, necessarily lead the auditor to conclude that the inherent risk of material undisclosed related party transactions is high.

136. Banks are required to report to the Financial Regulator changes in control in accordance with the 'acquiring transactions' provisions in the CBA 1989 (in some instances with prior Financial Regulator approval), changes in circumstances of existing controlling parties and changes in entities who are closely linked to the bank. As a result, it will therefore normally be the case that there are controls in place to ensure that this information is properly collated. However, the definition of 'controller and closely linked' for regulatory purposes is not congruent with the 'related party' definition in FRS 8/IAS 24 and the auditor therefore considers what controls have been in put in place by management to capture information on those parties which fall within the accounting definition only.

137. In reviewing related party information for completeness, the auditor may compare the proposed disclosures in the financial statements to information prepared for regulatory

reporting purposes (bearing in mind that the population may be different, as noted in the preceding paragraph).

138. Whilst related party transactions can arise in respect of banks generally they frequently arise in respect of deposits held by directors and/or persons connected with them and in respect of loans and other transactions with directors and/or persons connected with them. They may also arise in respect of the sale or arrangement of insurance products and in respect of the provision of professional and other services. The auditor is aware of Companies Acts provisions relating to transactions by companies with directors.

ISA (UK and Ireland) 560: Subsequent Events

Background note

The purpose of this ISA (UK and Ireland) is to establish standards and provide guidance on the auditor's responsibility regarding subsequent events.

The auditor should perform audit procedures designed to obtain sufficient appropriate audit evidence that all events up to the date of the auditor's report that may require adjustment of, or disclosure in, the financial statements have been identified. (paragraph 4)

139. Matters specific to banks which auditors may consider in their review of subsequent events include:

   • an evaluation of material loans and other receivables identified as being in default or potential default at the period end to provide additional evidence concerning period end loan impairment provisions;

   • an assessment of material loans and other receivables identified as (potential) defaults since the period end to consider whether any adjustment to the period end carrying value is required;

   • a review of movements in market prices and exchange rates, particularly in illiquid markets or where the bank has very large positions, to consider whether prices or rates used in period end valuations were realistic in relation to the size of positions held;

   • a review of correspondence with regulators and enquiries of management to determine whether any significant breaches of regulations or other significant regulatory concerns have come to light since the period end; and

   • a consideration of post year end liquidity reports for indications of funding difficulties.

ISA (UK and Ireland) 570: The Going Concern Basis in Financial Statements

Background note

The purpose of this ISA (UK and Ireland) is to establish standards and provide guidance on the auditor's responsibility on the audit of financial statements with respect to the going concern assumption used in the preparation of the financial statements, including management's assessment of the entity's ability to continue as a going concern.

When planning and performing audit procedures and in evaluating the results thereof, the auditor should consider the appropriateness of management's use of the going concern assumption in the preparation of the financial statements. (paragraph 2)

The auditor should consider any relevant disclosures in the financial statements. (paragraph 2-1)

140. In reviewing going concern issues, the auditor may consider the following areas in addition to those set out in ISA (UK and Ireland) 570:

   • capital adequacy ratios – review of management's analysis and rationale for ensuring that the bank is capable of maintaining adequate financial resources in excess of the minimum ;

   • operations/profitability indicators – e.g. review of the performance of loans in troubled industry sectors in which the bank has a high concentration of exposure;

   • liquidity indicators – e.g. review of the banks liquidity management process (e.g. maturity mismatch ladders) for signs of undue deterioration; and

   • reputational and other indicators – e.g. review of the financial press and other sources of market intelligence for evidence of deteriorating reputation; review of correspondence with regulators.

   Further details of possible factors that may indicate going concern issues in these areas are set out in Appendix 7 to this Practice Note.

141. The auditor also considers any undertakings which may have been provided to the Financial Regulator by the bank's parent or major shareholder. The Financial Regulator requires that parents or major shareholders provide an undertaking to the effect that the banking subsidiary incorporated and regulated in the State be in a position to meet its liabilities as they fall due for so long as the parent/shareholder continues to hold the majority of the equity of the subsidiary (the Financial Regulator Standards, paragraph 1.11).

142. If the auditor has any doubts as to the ability of a bank to continue as a going concern, the auditor considers whether he ought to make a report direct to the Financial Regulator.

143. Where the auditor intends to include an explanatory paragraph in an unqualified audit report, referring to a going concern issue, this would not, of itself, necessitate a report to the Financial Regulator under section 47 of the CBA, 1989 and Regulation 7(c) of the Post-BCCI Regulations (as it is not a qualification of the audit opinion). But in these circumstances the auditor considers whether the matter giving rise to the explanatory paragraph requires a report to the Financial Regulator under the statutory duty so to do.

ISA (UK and Ireland) 580: Management Representations

Background note

The purpose of this ISA (UK and Ireland) is to establish standards and provide guidance on the use of management representations as audit evidence, the procedures to be applied in evaluating and documenting management representations and the action to be taken if management refuses to provide appropriate representations.

Written confirmation of appropriate representations from management should be obtained before the audit report is issued. (paragraph 2-1)

The auditor should obtain written representations from management on matters material to the financial statements when other sufficient appropriate audit evidence cannot reasonably be expected to exist. (paragraph 4)

144. ISAs (UK and Ireland) 250, Section A and 550 require an auditor to obtain written confirmation in respect of completeness of disclosure to the auditor of:

- all known actual or possible non-compliance with laws and regulations (including breaches of the CBAs, the Financial Regulator Standards, anti-money laundering legislation, other regulatory requirements or any other circumstance that could jeopardise the authorisation of the bank) whose effects should be considered when preparing financial statements together with the actual or contingent consequences which may arise therefrom; and

- the completeness of information provided regarding the identification of related parties and the adequacy of related party disclosures in the financial statements.

145. In addition to the examples of other representations given in ISA (UK and Ireland) 580, the auditor also considers obtaining confirmation:

- as to the adequacy of provisions for loan impairment (including provisions relating to individual loans if material) and the appropriateness of other accounting estimates (such as derivatives valuations or adequate provisions for compensation concerning upheld complaints by customers);

- that all contingent transactions or commitments have been adequately disclosed and/or included in the balance sheet as appropriate; and

- that all correspondence with regulators has been made available to the auditor.

ISA (UK and Ireland) 600: Using the Work of Another Auditor

Background note

The purpose of this ISA (UK and Ireland) is to establish standards and provide guidance when an auditor, reporting on the financial statements of an entity, uses the work of another auditor on the financial information of one or more components included in the financial statements of the entity. This ISA (UK and Ireland) does not deal with those instances where two or more auditors are appointed as joint auditors nor does it deal with the auditor's relationship with a predecessor auditor. Further, when the principal auditor concludes that the financial statements of a component are immaterial, the standards in this ISA (UK and Ireland) do not apply. When, however, several components, immaterial in themselves, are together material, the procedures outlined in this ISA (UK and Ireland) would need to be considered.

When the principal auditor uses the work of another auditor, the principal auditor should determine how the work of the other auditor will affect the audit. (paragraph 2)

In the UK and Ireland, when planning to use the work of another auditor, the principal auditor's consideration of the professional competence of the other auditor should include consideration of the professional qualifications, experience and resources of the other auditor in the context of the specific assignment. (paragraph 7.1)

146. The principal auditor considers in particular the competence and capability of the other auditor having regard to the laws, regulation and industry practice relevant to the component to be reported on by the other auditor and whether the other auditor has access to relevant expertise, for example in the valuation of financial instruments, appropriate to the component's business.

147. Further procedures may be necessary for the auditor of an Irish bank where audit work in support of the audit opinion is undertaken by an audit firm that is not subject to the Irish audit regulatory regime. Where an overseas firm of the auditor (or an audit firm independent of the auditor) is undertaking audit procedures on a branch, or division or shared service centre of the bank, the auditor must have due regard to the requirements in the Audit Regulations[24] to ensure all relevant members of the engagement team are and continue to be fit and proper, are and continue to be competent, and are aware of and follow these Audit Regulations and any related procedures and requirements established by the audit firm. This includes the auditor's duty to report directly to the Financial Regulator in certain circumstances. More detailed consideration of the auditor's duty to report to the Financial Regulator is set out in the section of this Practice Note dealing with ISA (UK and Ireland) 250.

---

[24] Audit Regulations and Guidelines – December 2005 issued by the Institute of Chartered Accountants in England and Wales, the Institute of Chartered Accountants in Scotland and the Institute of Chartered Accountants in Ireland.

ISA (UK and Ireland) 610: Considering the Work of Internal Audit

Background note

The purpose of this ISA (UK and Ireland) is to establish standards and provide guidance to external auditors in considering the work of internal auditing. This ISA (UK and Ireland) does not deal with instances when personnel from internal audit assist the external auditor in carrying out external audit procedures. The audit procedures noted in this ISA (UK and Ireland) need only be applied to internal auditing activities which are relevant to the audit of the financial statements.

The external auditor should consider the activities of internal auditing and their effect, if any, on external audit procedures. (paragraph 2)

148. The CRD requires that every bank shall manage its business in accordance with sound administrative and accounting principles and shall put in place and maintain internal control and reporting arrangements and procedures to ensure that the business is so managed.

149. The Financial Regulator must be satisfied that:

- directors and senior management exercise adequate control over the bank;

- comprehensive risk management systems commensurate with the scope, size and complexity of all banking activities, including derivatives and associated risks, are in place, incorporating continuous measuring, monitoring, and controlling of risk, accurate and reliable management information systems, timely management reporting and thorough audit and control procedures; and

- where the size or nature of the operations of the bank warrant it, a properly staffed internal audit function exists which has direct access to the board of directors or an appropriate sub-committee of the board.

150. Internal audit services can be provided by an internal function, by the parent company or other group company, or by a third party.

151. Bank auditors understand the arrangements in place for internal audit and may develop, where appropriate, close liaisons with internal audit to ensure that the careful planning and execution of work avoids duplication and effects best use of resources.

ISA (UK and Ireland) 620: Using the Work of an Expert

Background note

The purpose of this ISA (UK and Ireland) is to establish standards and provide guidance on using the work of an expert as audit evidence.

When using the work performed by an expert, the auditor should obtain sufficient appropriate audit evidence that such work is adequate for the purposes of the audit. (paragraph 2)

152. Given the complexity, subjectivity and specialist nature of the valuation of derivatives and other financial instruments not traded in an active market, together with VAR (or similarly complex) market risk disclosures, the auditor may involve an expert in elements of the audit of these areas.

153. Where the auditor uses an expert as part of the audit, the auditor remains solely responsible for the audit of the bank's financial statements and will not refer to the work of the expert within the auditor's report.

ISA (UK and Ireland) 700: The Auditor's Report on Financial Statements

Background note

The purpose of this ISA (UK and Ireland) is to establish standards and provide guidance on the form and content of the auditor's report issued as a result of an audit performed by an independent auditor of the financial statements of an entity. Much of the guidance provided can be adapted to auditor reports on financial information other than financial statements.

In the UK and Ireland:

(a) The auditor should distinguish between the auditor's responsibilities and the responsibilities of those charged with governance by including in the auditor's report a reference to a description of the relevant responsibilities of those charged with governance when that description is set out elsewhere in the financial statements or accompanying information; or

(b) Where the financial statements or accompanying information do not include an adequate description of the relevant responsibilities of those charged with governance, the auditor's report should include a description of those responsibilities. (paragraph 9-1)

154. The auditor may report on the financial statements of a branch of a bank incorporated outside the Republic of Ireland. ISA (UK and Ireland) 700 (or aspects thereof) may remain applicable in these circumstances. However, in agreeing the form of the opinion for a branch audit, the auditor takes into account matters such as the nature and content of the financial statements to which the report relates, the extent to which transactions recorded in the branch may have been initiated in other locations (and, similarly, whether transactions initiated by the branch may have been recorded elsewhere), the specific terms of the engagement as agreed with the party which has commissioned the work (which may be local and/or head office management or the head office auditor, for example) and whether the report will be public or private.

Auditor's review reports on interim net profits

155. Banks are permitted to include interim profits in the capital base required to meet prudential supervision criteria only if such profits have been reported on by the bank's external auditors.

156. In undertaking the review the auditor normally performs the following procedures:

- satisfies himself that the figures forming the basis of the interim net profits have been properly extracted from the underlying accounting records;

- reviews the accounting policies used in calculating the interim net profits for the period under review so as to obtain comfort that they are consistent with those normally adopted by the bank in drawing up its annual financial statements and are in accordance with Irish GAAP applicable to banks or EU IFRS as appropriate;

- performs analytical procedures on the results to date which form the basis of calculating interim net profits, including comparisons of actual performance to date with budget and with the results of the prior period(s);

- performs analytical procedures on the results to date which form the basis of calculating interim net profits, including comparisons of actual performance to date with budget and with the results of prior period(s);

- discusses with management the overall performance and financial position of the deposit taker;

- obtains adequate comfort that the implications of current and prospective litigation, all known claims and commitments, changes in business activities, allowances for loan losses and other impairment provisions have been properly taken into account in arriving at interim net profits; and

- follows up significant matters of which the auditor is already aware in the course of auditing the bank's most recent financial statements.

The auditor may also consider obtaining appropriate representations from management.

157. As such reviews are undertaken specifically for regulatory purposes they do not fall within the scope of the APB's International Standard on Review Engagements (UK and Ireland) 2410 "Review of Interim Financial Information Performed by the Independent Auditor of the Entity" (ISRE 2410 (UK and Ireland)[25]. ISRE 2410 (UK and Ireland) provides guidance to auditors in reviewing and reporting on financial information in interim reports, produced by listed companies incorporated in the United Kingdom and the Republic of Ireland.

---

[25] ISRE 2410 (UK and Ireland) is effective for reviews of interim financial information for periods ending on or after 20 September 2007 and supersedes Bulletin 1999/4 'Review of Interim Financial Information'. Early adoption is permitted.

158. Where the scope of the work carried out by the auditor differs materially from that set out in paragraph 156, the Financial Regulator expects the auditor to provide details in the report.

159. In particular circumstances, the auditor may consider it appropriate to undertake further procedures before giving his report. For example:

- if the control environment surrounding the preparation of the interim profits as reported to the Financial Regulator is determined by the auditor to be weak;

- if the results of the initial procedures undertaken are not fully consistent with the interim profits as reported; or

- if there has been a significant change in the accounting systems.

160. It is often the case that the companies which are included in the consolidation or solo consolidation for Financial Regulator reporting purposes are not the same as those included for statutory accounts purposes. For example:

- 'non-financial' companies may be excluded from the consolidation for regulatory purposes; and/or

- 'financial' associates may be subject to full consolidation for regulatory purposes.

161. If the auditor is satisfied that the basis of consolidation of interim profits, although different from that used in the statutory accounts, reflects properly the Financial Regulator's requirements, this need not be referred to in the report. In other cases, the auditor considers including a paragraph in the report explaining the consolidation basis on which the interim profits have been prepared. A subsidiary's interim profits will be reported in the group quarterly regulatory returns of the parent if institutions have prior approval from the Financial Regulator to include them in Tier 1 capital.

162. Illustrative wording for such reports is set out in Appendix 6.

Meetings with the Financial Regulator

163. Under section 47(5) of the CBA 1989, the Financial Regulator has power to request information from the auditor of a bank on matters relating to the audit of its financial statements. The Financial Regulator uses its power under that section to meet with the auditors of banks to engage in dialogue in relation to the audit.

164. These meetings may take the form of both:

- *trilateral meetings:* periodic meetings called by the Financial Regulator, between the Financial Regulator, each bank and its auditor on a case by case basis. Such trilateral meetings are held in order to discuss audit related matters, particularly matters such as the bank's control environment, corporate governance procedures, internal audit procedures and risk profile; and

- *bilateral meetings:* the Financial Regulator may also initiate formal meetings with the auditor alone. Such meetings are used by the Financial Regulator for more detailed discussion of matters raised in the course of a trilateral meeting and to seek views of the auditor on matters of concern to the Financial Regulator or to the auditor, to the extent permitted under legislation. Section 33AK of the CBA 1942[26], provides a gateway for the Financial Regulator to disclose confidential information to an auditor of a bank. When participating in a bilateral meeting, the auditor does not, however, make supervisory judgments: such matters are for the decision of the Financial Regulator, having regard to all information at its disposal in relation to the bank concerned, not solely that provided by its auditor.

165. Following notification of a bilateral meeting, the auditor may wish to seek advance information from the Financial Regulator as to the matters it intends to discuss. Under current legislation, auditors of banks do not have a statutory right to disclose information to the Financial Regulator (other than information giving rise to a duty to report to Financial Regulator), but may be provided with protection from legal action arising from disclosure of information on a matter related to the audit, when responding to an enquiry by the Financial Regulator[27]. The common law may provide protection for disclosure of certain matters to an appropriate authority in the public interest. This is discussed further at paragraphs 63 to 69 of Appendix 2 below. However, it is unlikely that auditors in possession of information justifying disclosure in the public interest would be in the position of disclosing that information for the first time in the course of a bilateral meeting. Provision of information to the Financial Regulator is therefore made primarily under section 47(6) of the CBA 1989. In discussing issues in the course of a bilateral meeting, the auditor considers carefully the nature and extent of information to be provided to the Financial Regulator, taking into account:

---

[26] As inserted by section 26 CBSFAI 2003.
[27] Section 47(6) CBA, 1989.

- the auditor's duty of confidentiality to the bank concerned and the fact that the bank itself has primary responsibility for the provision of information required by the Financial Regulator;

- whether the matters concerned fall within the protection available to them in responding to questions from the Financial Regulator; and

- the desirability and benefits of a free exchange of views between the Financial Regulator and the auditor.

166. If uncertainty exists as to whether particular information may be disclosed to the Financial Regulator, the auditor may defer discussion of the relevant matter raised in order to consider whether the protection afforded by 47(6) of the CBA 1989, or other legal provisions apply, and may, if considered appropriate, take legal advice. In general terms, however, auditors who provide information to the Financial Regulator in response to questions from the Financial Regulator have effective protection from breach of confidentiality provided that they:

- report information in relation to the Financial Regulator's query in a balanced manner without selectivity or bias;

- indicate that information is provided under section 47(6) of the CBA 1989; and

- express any opinions in a neutral and responsible manner, making clear that they are opinions, not facts, and explaining the basis for them.

167. A contemporaneous record of the matters discussed at a tri- or bi-lateral meeting may be made and agreed subsequently with the representatives of the auditor and of the Financial Regulator who attended the meeting.

168. The auditor may not disclose information communicated to them by the Financial Regulator, including that received in bilateral discussions, except with the Financial Regulator's express agreement and, in some cases, that of other parties to which the information relates. The Financial Regulator will inform the auditor which parts of the bilateral discussion it permits them to communicate to the bank: if this information is not volunteered at the end of the bilateral meeting, the auditor asks the Financial Regulator to do so. Some information communicated to the auditor will relate only to the bank but many matters discussed may relate also to other parties, such as customers or employees. In addition, other information may have been received by the Financial Regulator from other regulators or in a capacity other than as banking supervisor, in which case there may be other restrictions on disclosure. Therefore, before communicating to the bank any information received during the bilateral meeting, the auditor considers carefully:

- whether the Financial Regulator's express permission has been received to communicate a particular item of information;

- whether the information relates to parties other than the bank, whose agreement is required prior to communication; and

- whether the information was received by the Financial Regulator in a capacity other than as banking supervisor or from another regulator, in which case permission may be required from the other party concerned.

169. The auditor can, however, disclose to the bank information which they have communicated to the Financial Regulator during the bilateral meeting (except where to do so would have the effect of disclosing information communicated by the Financial Regulator). If the auditor is in doubt as to whether particular information can be communicated consideration may be given to the procedures set out in the paragraph above and, in particular circumstances, to the need to take legal advice.

170. Matters communicated by the Financial Regulator during a bilateral meeting may be conveyed by representatives of an audit firm who attended the meeting to other partners and staff who need to know the information in connection with the firm's performance of its duties as auditor without the Financial Regulator's permission.

Appendix 1

Authorisation and Supervision of banks by the Financial Regulator: legislative and regulatory background

Authorisation of banks

1. In general terms, banking supervision is based on a system of licensing under which the supervisor is responsible for authorising entry into the banking system. Qualification for, and retention of, a banking licence is dependent on compliance with prudential and other requirements.

2. Under the CBA 1971 no entity may carry on the activity of taking deposits from the public without authorisation by the Financial Regulator. Before granting a banking licence, the Financial Regulator must be satisfied that the applicant meets the relevant criteria for authorisation and the applicant must undertake, once a licence is granted, that it will comply with the 'Financial Regulator Standards' on a continuous basis.

3. Many of the requirements applicable to Irish banks derive from European Directives. The most significant of these Directives is the Capital Requirements Directive ('**CRD**'). CRD is a term used to describe two EU Directives which transpose the Basel II Accord into a legal text for the purpose of its application to banks and investment firms across the European Economic Area ('**EEA**'). These Directives are Directive 2006/48/EC (recast) relating to the taking up and pursuit of the business of credit institutions and Directive 2006/49/EC (recast) on the capital adequacy of investment firms and credit institutions. Statutory Instruments ('**S.I.s**') 660 and 661 of 2006 were signed into Irish law to implement the CRD in Ireland in December 2006 and became effective from 1 January 2007.

4. The CRD repeals Directive 2000/12/EC relating to the taking up and pursuit of business of credit institutions which had brought together:

    *   The First Banking Directive, 77/780/EEC, on the co-ordination of laws, regulations and administrative provisions relating to the taking up and pursuit of the business of credit institutions;

    *   The Second Banking Directive, 89/646/EEC which was implemented in Ireland by S.I. 395 of 1992 – often referred to as the "Passporting Regulations";

    *   The Own Funds Directive 89/299/EEC and Solvency Ratio Directive 89/647/EEC and amendments to those Directives by Directive 91/633/EEC, Directive 94/7/EC, Directive 95/15/EC, Directive 95/67/EC, Directive 96/10/EC, Directive 2004/69/EC, Directive 98/32/EC and Directive 98/33/EC;

    *   The Consolidated Supervision Directive 92/30/EEC; and

    *   The Large Exposures Directive 92/121/EC

The CRD also repeals the Capital Adequacy Directive 93/6/EC and amending Directives 98/31/EC and 98/33/EC. Details of specific articles of other Directives also repealed by the CRD can be found at Annex XIII Part A of Directive 2006/48/EC and Annex VIII Part A of Directive 2006/49/EC.

5. The requirements for authorisation of credit institutions are contained in the CRD. The main provisions are as follows;

    a. Article 6 provides that Member States shall require Credit Institutions to obtain authorisation before commencing their activities and that they shall lay down requirements for such authorisations and notify them to the Commission.

    b. Article 7 provides that applications for authorisation must be accompanied by a programme of operations setting out, inter alia, the types of business envisaged and the structural organisation of the credit institutions.

    c. In accordance with Article 9 authorisation will not be granted when the credit institution does not possess separate own funds or in cases where initial capital is less than €5m.

    d. Article 23 provides that once a bank becomes authorised in a Member State (its 'Home State') it can establish a branch or do business/provide services by carrying on its activities within the industry, in any other Member State (**'Host State'**) without having to obtain an official authorisation from the banking regulator in the Host State.

    e. Articles 25-27 address the requirements to enable a credit institution to exercise its right of establishment in another Member State.

    f. Articles 28-37 address the information requirements and powers of the host Member State with regard to the provision of services by an institution from another member state.

6. Section 9(1) of CBA 1971[28] provides that the Financial Regulator may, at its discretion, grant or refuse a person's application for a banking licence. Section 10 of CBA 1971[29] provides that a licence is subject to such condition as the Financial Regulator may impose on the bank from time to time, being conditions which in the opinion of the Financial Regulator are calculated to promote the orderly and proper regulation of banking. The Financial Regulator's administrative provisions contained in its 'Financial Regulator Standards' set out the guidance for banks applying for authorisation by the Financial Regulator. "The Requirements for the Management of Liquidity Risk and Impairment Provisions for Credit Exposures" have been imposed as conditions on the licenses of credit institutions. Authorisation criteria are discussed in more detail in Appendix 2 in the context of an auditor's duty to report, in accordance with Regulation

---

[28] As amended by section 32 CBA 1989.
[29] As amended by section 532(2) and 33 CBA 1989.

7(a) of the Post-BCCI Regulations, breaches of laws, regulations or administrative provisions which set out the criteria under which the bank was authorised.

7.   Under the CRD banks authorised by a regulator in another Member State of the European Union (European banks) do not require authorisation under Irish law and regulations in order to accept deposits in the Republic of Ireland. A European Economic Area bank may conduct without further authorisation in the Republic of Ireland any activity which it is authorised to conduct in its home state, either as a branch or on a cross-border basis, provided that it has complied with the provisions of the CRD which include:

- that the bank has given to the relevant supervisory authority in its home state a notice of its intention to conduct business in the Republic of Ireland (the contents of which are prescribed);

- that the Financial Regulator has received from that authority a prescribed notice; and

- that either:

     (i)   the Financial Regulator has informed the bank that it may establish the branch or provide services on a cross border basis; or

     (ii)   a specified period has elapsed since the Financial Regulator received the notice from the home authority.

8.   The Financial Regulator's regulatory responsibilities extend to overseas branches of Irish authorised banks although, in discharging those responsibilities, it may seek to rely to some extent on the supervisory activities of other regulators.

9.   The CRD requires the Financial Regulator to supervise banking groups on a consolidated basis. This includes consideration of the potential impact of other group companies on the institution itself.

The Post BCCI Regulations

10.   The Post BCCI Regulations[30] implemented an EU Directive[31] issued after the failure of the Bank of Credit and Commerce International ('**BCCI**'). These Regulations require the Financial Regulator to consider, prior to the granting of authorisation to banks, its ability to exercise effectively its supervisory functions, taking into account:

- the existence of close links (see paragraph 11 below) between the bank and others; and

---

[30] Supervision of Credit Institutions, Stock Exchange Member Firms and Investment Business Firms Regulations, 1996, S.I. No. 267 of 1996, ('the Post BCCI Regulations').
[31] EU Directive 95/26/EEC of 19 July 1995, OJ L168 amended by EU Directives 2002/83/EC and 2000/12/EC.

- the laws, regulations or administrative provisions of a non-EU Member State governing one or more persons with which that bank has close links, or difficulties involved in their enforcement.

11. The Post BCCI Regulations also introduced a number of additional matters giving rise to a duty on auditors to report to the Financial Regulator. In particular, if the auditor of a bank is also appointed as auditor of entities which are 'closely linked' with the bank, the Regulations extended the duty to report to include matters coming to their attention in the course of their work as auditor of those entities.

Close links

12. Close links between two or more entities, as defined by Regulation 2 of the Post BCCI Regulations, arise as a result of factors indicating either —

- participation: the ownership, direct or by way of control, of 20 per cent or more of the voting rights or capital of an undertaking, or

- control: the relationship between a parent undertaking and a subsidiary undertaking (including sub-subsidiaries).

Additionally, close links exist if there is an arrangement whereby two or more persons are permanently linked to one and the same person by a control relationship.

The responsibility of directors and management of banks

13. The primary responsibility for the conduct of the business of a bank is vested in the board of directors and the management appointed by it. This responsibility includes:

- establishing adequate procedures and systems to ensure compliance with law applicable to banks, the 'Financial Regulator Standards' and other administrative provisions issued by the Financial Regulator, including Codes of Practice and other relevant law and regulations (including taxation law);

- the preparation of financial statements and compliance with other aspects of company law; and

- providing information to the Financial Regulator.

14. The CRD together with the Financial Regulator's 'Fit and Proper Requirements' published in November 2006 require that every person who has, or is to have, a qualifying holding (defined in Appendix 3), director, or senior manager of a bank is a fit and proper person in the context of the particular position which he holds or is to hold. For further details on the 'Fit and Proper Requirements' refer to Appendix 4.

Investment Business

15. The holding of a banking licence is generally sufficient authorisation in itself for a bank to conduct investment business (although the Financial Regulator may impose a

requirement, limit, or condition restricting the business that a bank may conduct.) Alternatively, a bank may conduct investment business through a separate subsidiary which must be authorised under the Investment Intermediaries Act 1995. Title 1 Article 1(2) of Directive 2004/39/EC – (MiFID) lists the provisions that apply to credit institutions authorised under Directive 2000/12/EC[32] when providing one or more investment services and/or performing investment activities.

The legal and regulatory framework

The legal and regulatory framework within which banks operate in the Republic of Ireland is complex and involves;

- Statutes;

- Regulations implementing EU Directives in the banking sector;

- Other Regulations;

- Administrative Provisions and Financial Regulator Standards; and

- Other guidance issued by the Financial Regulator.

Statutes

Central Bank Act, 1942;
Central Bank Act, 1971;
Central Bank Act, 1989;
Central Bank Act, 1997;
Central Bank Act, 1998;
Central Bank and Financial Services Authority of Ireland Act, 2003;
Central Bank and Financial Services Authority of Ireland Act, 2004;
Consumer Credit Act, 1995;
Dormant Accounts Act, 2001; and
Dormant Accounts (Amendment) Act, 2005

The main provisions of the CBAs deal with:

- the functions of the Financial Regulator and its Board of Directors;

- restrictions on the acceptance of deposits and on invitations to make deposits;

- the process of, and specific criteria for, authorisation of banks, including the requirement that the business should be conducted in a 'prudent manner';

- notification and other requirements relating to directors and persons who have a 'qualifying holding';

---

[32] Repealed by CRD.

- the powers of the Financial Regulator to require information, to instigate investigation procedures, to refuse, restrict or revoke authorisation and to give directions to, or impose conditions on, a bank during and after the revocation process;

- the auditor's duties to report to the Financial Regulator in certain circumstances;

- the operation of the Irish deposit protection scheme;

- restrictions on the use of banking names and descriptions;

- the requirements relating to overseas institutions with, or wishing to set up, representative offices in the Republic of Ireland; and

- restrictions on disclosure of information by the Financial Regulator

EU Directives and implementing Irish regulations as at 30 April 2008

Directive	Implemented in ROI
Annual Accounts Directive 86/635/EEC	European Communities (Credit Institutions Accounts) Regulations 1992, S.I. 294 of 1992
Branch Accounts Directive 89/117/EEC	Regulation 14 of S.I. 294 of 1992
Deposit Guarantee Scheme Directive 94/19/EC	European Communities (Deposit Guarantee Schemes) Regulations 1995, S.I. 168 of 1995 CBA 1997 and S.I. 468 of 1999
Directive Reinforcing Prudential Supervision Directive 95/26/EC (known as the Post-BCCI Directive)	Supervision of Credit Institutions, Stock Exchange Member Firms and Investment Business Firms Regulations, 1996, S.I. 267 of 1996
Distance Marketing Directive Directive 2002/65/EC concerning the distance marketing of consumer financial services	European Communities (Distance Marketing of Consumer Financial Services) Regulations 2004, S.I. 853 of 2004 European Communities (Distance Marketing of Consumer Financial Services) (Amendment) Regulations, 2005, S.I. No. 63 of 2005

Capital Requirements Directive Directive 2006/48/EC (recast) relating to the taking up and pursuit of the business of credit institutions and Directive 2006/49/EC (recast) on the capital adequacy of investment firms and credit institutions	European Communities (Capital Adequacy of Investment Firms) Regulations 2006, S.I. 660 of 2006 European Communities (Capital Adequacy of Credit Institutions) Regulations 2006, S.I. 661 of 2006
Markets in Financial Instruments Directive ("MiFID") Main Directive 2004/39/EC Supplementary Directive 2004/73/EC	S.I. 60 of 2007 European Communities (Markets in Financial Instruments) Regulations 2007; and Markets in Financial Instruments and Miscellaneous Provisions Act 2007
Money Laundering Directives 91/308/EEC	Implemented by the Criminal Justice Act 1994 and amended by the Criminal Justice (Miscellaneous Provisions) Act 1997
001/97/EEC	Implemented by the Criminal Justice (Theft and Fraud Offences) Act 2001 and S.I. 242 of 2003, Criminal Justice Act 1994 (Section 32) Regulations, 2003 as amended by S.I. 416 of 2003, Criminal Justice Act 1994 (Section 32)(Amendment) Regulations
2005/60/EC	Draft Scheme, Criminal Justice (Money Laundering) Bill, 2008 currently in issue for consultation. The Bill when passed will implement this Directive.

Other Regulations

Central Bank Act 1942 (Financial Services Ombudsman Council) Regulations 2005

Administrative provisions issued by the Financial Regulator

Licensing and Supervision Requirements and Standards for Credit Institutions	First issued in Winter Bulletin 1995 and later amended on 22 April 1998
Form for approval of directors	First issued in Winter Bulletin 1995 and later amended on 22 April 1998
Code of Practice on Transfer of Mortgages	First issued in Winter Bulletin 1995 and later amended on 22 April 1998
Asset Securitisation Notice	First issued in Winter Bulletin 1995 and later amended on 22 April 1998
Commercial Paper Notice BSD CP 1/98	First issued in Winter Bulletin 1995 and later amended on 22 April 1998
Assessment of Minimal Trading Book Activity	First issued in Winter Bulletin 1995 and later amended on 22 April 1998
Notice on Supervision of Bureaux de Change	First issued in Winter Bulletin 1995 and later amended on 22 April 1998
Code of Conduct for the Investment Business Services of Credit Exposures	Issued in June 2001 (Updated November 2001)
Regulatory Document on Impairment Provisions for Credit Institutions	Issued in October 2005
Requirements for Management of Liquidity Risk	Issued in June 2006
Minimum Competency Requirements	Issued in July 2006
Consumer Protection Code	Issued in August 2006
Fit and Proper Requirements	Issued in November 2006
Individual Questionnaire	Issued in November 2006

Other guidance issued by the Financial Regulator

In addition to the legislative and other publications listed above the Financial Regulator communicates directly with banks from time to time as and when issues arise which are of potential concern. These communications do not fall into the category of 'administrative provisions' and hence do not, of themselves, provide criteria for determining whether a duty to report to the Financial Regulator exists. However, their contents may be of assistance to auditors in forming an opinion as to whether that duty arises.

Note: This appendix sets out certain key provisions of law, regulation, and guidance. It is not an exhaustive list of legislation applicable to banks and is not a substitute for reference to the full text of relevant requirements. The Financial Regulator's website (www.financialregulator.ie) contains details of relevant legislation, regulations administrative provisions, and guidance.

Appendix 2

The Auditor's Duty to Report to the Financial Regulator in its Capacity as Banking Supervisor

1.   The Central Bank Act 1989 ('**CBA, 1989**') and the Supervision of Credit Institutions, Stock Exchange Member Firms and Investment Business Firms Regulations 1996 (the '**Post BCCI Regulations**') and the Central Bank Act, 1997 (**CBA 1997**)[33] place a duty on auditors of banks to report directly to the Financial Regulator in certain circumstances.

2.   The key factors for determining the scope of the statutory duty to report information are the capacity in which the accountant comes across the information and the nature of the information. It is only information that comes to the attention of the accountant as auditor that is of relevance for the duty to report. Relevant issues which apply to determining whether information is obtained in the capacity of auditor are whether the person who obtained the information also undertook the audit work and if so, whether it was obtained in the course of or as a result of undertaking the audit work.

3.   The purpose of this Appendix is to provide some detail in relation to the specific obligations of an auditor to report directly to the Financial Regulator.

MATTERS REQUIRING A REPORT BY AUDITORS TO THE FINANCIAL REGULATOR

4.   Section 47 of the CBA 1989 and Regulation 7 of the Post BCCI Regulations place a duty on auditors to report to the Financial Regulator where the auditor has reason to believe that:

(a)   the continuous functioning of the bank may be affected; in particular, that there exist circumstances which are likely to affect materially its obligations to depositors or where there are issues relating to its ability to meet its financial obligations; or

(b)   there are material defects in the financial systems and controls or accounting records of the bank; or

(c)   there are material inaccuracies in, or omissions from, any financial returns made by the bank to the Financial Regulator; or

(d)   there are circumstances such as preclude them from stating in their audit report that the annual financial statements give a true and fair view and have been properly prepared in accordance with the Companies Acts and all Regulations to be construed as one with those Acts; or

(e)   where they have decided to resign or not seek re-election as auditor; or

---

[33]   As amended by the CBFSAI 2004.

(f) there is a material breach of the laws, regulations or administrative provisions which lay down the conditions under which the bank has been authorised; or

(g) there is a material breach of any laws, regulations or administrative provisions which govern the bank's activities or of any condition or requirement imposed by the Financial Regulator.

5. Under sections 27B – 27D of the CBA 1997[34] the auditor is required to provide to the Financial Regulator:-

(a) An annual confirmation as to whether there are matters to report in addition to and including any reports already submitted under 'prescribed enactments' (section 27B);

(b) Copies of any reports provided to the bank or those concerned with its management on matters that have come to the auditor's notice while auditing the financial statements of the bank or carrying out any work for the bank of any kind specified by the Financial Regulator (section 27C); and

(c) Copies of any reports issued to the Office of the Director of Corporate Enforcement (section 27D).

a) Continuous functioning may be affected: Specifically, circumstances exist that are likely to affect obligations to depositors or issues relating to meeting financial obligations under the CBAs. *(Section 47(1) (a) of the CBA 1989 and Regulation 7(b) of the Post-BCCI Regulations)*

6. The auditor of a bank is required to report to the Financial Regulator where he has reasonable cause to believe that the continuous functioning of the institution may be affected. The duty specifically includes circumstances that are likely to affect the bank's ability to fulfil its obligations to depositors or to meet any of its financial obligations under the Central Bank Acts and Regulations. The procedures to be followed by the auditor in determining his concern (if any) about an entity's ability to continue as a going concern are set out in ISA (UK and Ireland) 570 and additional guidance on banks is provided in the commentary on ISA (UK and Ireland) 570 Section of this Practice Note.

b) Material defects in the financial systems and controls or accounting records *(Section 47(1)(b) of the CBA 1989)*

7. The CRD requires that every bank shall manage its business in accordance with sound administrative and accounting principles and shall put in place and maintain internal control and reporting management arrangements and procedures to ensure that the business is so managed.

---

[34] As inserted by section 26 CBFSAI 2004.

8. It is the management of a bank that is responsible for ensuring the appropriate financial systems and controls are put in place and accounting records are maintained. Weaknesses in systems, controls and records may be identified by management themselves, internal audit or by the auditor during the course of audit work. Where the auditor identifies weaknesses which have not previously been recognised by management, he considers whether there has been a failure in the bank's procedures for ensuring the effective operation of the systems and controls: this of itself may require a report to the Financial Regulator.

9. The Financial Regulator's 'Licensing and Supervision Requirements and Standards for Credit Institutions' (the '**Financial Regulator Standards**') state that the Financial Regulator seeks to satisfy itself that:

   • directors and senior management exercise adequate control over the bank;

   • comprehensive risk management systems commensurate with the scope, size and complexity of all the bank's activities, including derivatives and associated risks, are in place, incorporating continuous measuring, monitoring and controlling of risk, accurate and reliable management information systems, timely management reporting and thorough audit and control procedures; and

   • where the size or nature of the operations of the bank warrant it, a properly staffed internal audit function exists which has direct access to the board of directors or an appropriate sub-committee of the board.

10. The determination of those matters which require reporting is a matter of judgement for the auditor of each bank. There will be some weaknesses which will be reportable in the context of one bank but not for others. The decision to report a matter takes into account, for example:

   • the nature and volume of transactions occurring in the area where the weakness has arisen;

   • the seriousness of the risks to which the bank is exposed as a result of the weakness identified;

   • whether there are compensating systems and controls;

   • whether the weakness occurred for only a short period of time and has been rectified (although rectification does not of itself mean that the matter should not be reported); and

   • whether a weakness which has been identified, though not significant in itself, becomes so when considered in conjunction with other weaknesses.

11. If corrective action cannot be taken promptly, the weakness is more likely to be reportable because of its continuing nature. If the resulting exposure cannot be quantified and controlled in a relatively short time frame, the risk of loss to the bank is increased.

THE AUDITING
PRACTICES BOARD

12. If the situation can be rectified in a relatively short time frame and the auditor determines that on those grounds a report is not required at that time, he monitors the situation and confirms with the bank that appropriate action has been taken. If this proves not to be the case, then the auditor may need to re-consider the decision not to report. Failure of management to ensure that appropriate and effective action has been taken may also cause the auditor to consider whether there may have been a breach of the fit and proper criteria.

c) Material omissions from or inaccuracies in returns of a financial nature
(Section 47(1)(c) of the CBA 1989)

13. The examination by the auditor of returns made by a bank to the Financial Regulator is outside the scope of an audit of a bank's financial statements. However, where the auditor discovers a minor inaccuracy in financial information provided to the Financial Regulator, this would not normally give rise to a statutory duty to report unless it is indicative of a general and recurring lack of compliance with the Financial Regulator's requirements or otherwise casts doubt on the bank's compliance with the Financial Regulator's requirements. If the correction of an omission or inaccuracy in returns of a financial nature to the Financial Regulator would mean that the bank is then in breach of certain ratios or limits set by the Financial Regulator, this would be an indication that the matter is one of material significance to the Financial Regulator.

14. Where the auditor so requests, the Financial Regulator shall provide to him in writing details of such returns of a financial nature previously sent by the bank to the Financial Regulator for the purpose of enabling the auditor to comply with this duty[35].

d) Audit reports *(Section 47(1)(d) of the CBA 1989 and Regulation 7(c) of the Post-BCCI Regulations)*

15. The auditor of a bank is required to make a report to the Financial Regulator if he has reasonable cause to believe that the auditor will be precluded from stating in the auditor's report that the financial statements give a true and fair view and have been properly prepared in accordance with the Companies Acts 1963 to 2006 and all Regulations to be construed as one with those Acts. This requirement is dealt with in the commentary on ISA (UK and Ireland) 700, "The Auditor's Report on Financial Statements" in this Practice Note.

e) Decision to resign or not seek re-election as auditor *(Section 47(1)(e) of CBA 1989)*

16. Where a firm has made the decision to resign as auditor of a bank before the expiration of its term of office or intends not to seek reappointment it must report the matter to the Financial Regulator in writing without delay. All such instances require a report as they are presumed to be matters of material significance to the Financial Regulator. The Financial Regulator has requested that the auditor also sends to it a copy of the letter

---

[35] Section 47(3) CBA, 1989.

that is currently required to be sent to the Companies Registration Office in accordance with section 185(3) of the Companies Act, 1990.

f) Breaches of laws, regulations or administrative provisions which lay down the conditions under which the bank was authorised *(Regulation 7(a) of the Post-BCCI Regulations)*

17. The Financial Regulator Standards provide guidance relating to the Financial Regulator's authorisation criteria. This Practice Note and Appendices, although including explanatory material drawn from that publication, is not a substitute for it and should be read in conjunction therewith.

18. It is possible that a matter which is not materially significant to one of the criteria in isolation may become so when other criteria are considered. Therefore, auditors who become aware of a situation relating to one of the authorisation criteria consider its relevance to the others before determining whether it is of material significance and therefore reportable.

19. The following key authorisation criteria are considered below:

- matters for consideration of a new applicant;

- fit and proper persons;

- business to be conducted by at least two individuals;

- composition of the board of directors and management structures;

- business to be conducted in a prudent manner; and

- other criteria including:

    - acquisitions by banks;

    - general prudent conduct;

    - integrity and skill; and

    - minimum net assets.

Paragraphs 21 to 44 below consider each of the authorisation criteria in turn (some of these matters form part of the ongoing supervision of banks) and provide guidance on auditor's normal procedures which are likely to provide evidence of compliance or non-compliance. Examples of matters which might be considered materially significant are also given. It is important to consider these paragraphs in light of the guidance given in this Practice Note in relation to ISA (UK and Ireland) 250 Section A which sets out the level of work auditors are expected to carry out in the normal course of their audits.

THE AUDITING PRACTICES BOARD

20. A number of the Financial Regulator's initial authorisation requirements are unlikely to be considered or revisited by an auditor as part of his normal audit work. Therefore the duty to report is only likely to arise if a change in circumstances comes to the auditor's attention which, if in existence at the date of the initial application, would have caused the Financial Regulator to refuse that application.

Matters for consideration of a new applicant

21. Pursuant to Section 9 of the CBA Act 1971[36] an application for a licence shall be in such form and contain such particulars as the Financial Regulator may from time to time determine. Guidelines[37] on completing and submitting Banking Licence Applications have been issued by the Financial Regulator which outlines the steps that a potential applicant should take approaching the Financial Regulator to make an application for a banking licence. The key headings under which an applicant will be assessed are set out in this document, in addition to outlining how an application should be made and will be processed. The principal areas considered by the Financial Regulator in evaluating banking licence applications include:

- Overview of the parent/Group to which the applicant belongs;

- Consolidated Supervision of Parent/Group entities;

- Ownership Structure;

- Applicant's Objectives and Proposed Operations;

- Legal Structure;

- Organisation of the Applicant (including corporate governance arrangements, fitness and probity of key personnel etc.);

- Risk Oversight (e.g. audit, compliance, risk management, credit, liquidity, financial control, internal controls etc.);

- Capital, Funding and Solvency Projections;

- Financial Information and Projections; and

- Business Continuity.

The Financial Regulator's requirements, in relation to each of these headings, are detailed in the instructions paper entitled 'Checklist for completing and submitting Bank Licence Applications' (Checklist).

---

[36] As amended by section 32 CBA 1989.
[37] These Guidelines are available to download from the Financial Regulator's website – www.financialregulator.ie.

22. The Financial Regulator Standards detail issues that the Financial Regulator takes into account when considering a new applicant. The applicant must satisfy the Financial Regulator that:

- it has an acceptable legal form;

- the corporate structure of the group of which the applicant is part, or its relationship with other undertakings under common control, is clear and transparent and is not such as may result in the Financial Regulator being unable to exercise its supervisory responsibilities;

- it has clearly defined and adequately researched objectives and proposed operations which are consistent with the principles enshrined in banking legislation and in the Financial Regulator's licensing and supervision requirements and standards;

- it is independent of dominant persons;

- there will be cohesion, continuity and consistency in the manner in which the business of the bank is directed by its owners;

- the beneficial ownership of the bank is such as will ensure a capacity to provide such new capital for the bank as may be required in the future; and

- there is a willingness and capacity on the part of the bank to comply with the Financial Regulator's requirements.

23. The Financial Regulator's preference is that ownership be vested in one or more banks or other financial institutions of standing or, alternatively, that there be a wide spread of ownership. The Financial Regulator would not be receptive to a proposal from a general insurance entity to acquire a controlling shareholding in a bank.

24. In considering a proposal where ownership of a bank would vest in an industrial or commercial group, a range of additional considerations will apply, the more important of which may be summarised as follows:

- the Financial Regulator's assessment of the proposal will have regard to any additional risks arising from the ownership structure and, in particular, from relationships with non-bank elements of the group;

- the Financial Regulator will attach high importance to the degree of autonomy accorded to the applicant and to the degree of decision making to be located in the Republic of Ireland;

- only groups of the highest integrity and financial soundness (as evidenced by their trading record and international credit rating) will be considered;

- unless there are exceptional factors that warrant special attention, the Financial Regulator will require as a condition of granting a licence that there already exists, for some time, within the group, a separate financial entity, with its own management and financing structures and with skills and experience appropriate to banking;

- the minimum solvency ratio requirement for the bank (own funds as a percentage of risk assets) is likely to be set in excess of the minimum which applies to international banks;

- in general, funding for the bank should not include small retail deposits; if there is to be any dependence on group funding sources, due regard will need to be had to the continuity of those sources;

- in general, the bank would not be permitted to provide credit to or acquire assets from affiliated companies; and

- the principles of consolidated supervision will be applied by the Financial Regulator to the applicant group in the appropriate manner.

25. An application for authorisation from a branch or subsidiary of an international bank or international banking or financial group will be considered only where the supervisory authority in the country of origin of that bank or group exercises effectively its supervisory responsibilities on a consolidated basis.

26. The Financial Regulator will require from the parent or major shareholder of a bank subsidiary incorporated in the Republic of Ireland an undertaking that the subsidiary will be in a position to meet its liabilities as they fall due for as long as the parent/shareholder continues to hold the majority of the equity of the subsidiary. The stability of the shareholder will be considered by the auditor in addressing matters relating to the ability of the bank to continue as a going concern in accordance with ISA (UK and Ireland) 570.

Fit and Proper Persons

27. The CRD together with the Financial Regulator Standards and the Financial Regulator's 'Fit and Proper Requirements' published in November 2006 require that every person who has, or is to have, a qualifying holding (defined in Appendix 3), director, or senior manager of a bank is a fit and proper person in the context of the particular position which he holds or is to hold. The provisions are widely drawn and extend to shareholder controllers and indirect controllers of a bank as well as directors and senior executives. Further information on the 'Fit and Proper Requirements' is set out in Appendix 4.

28. Auditors cannot necessarily be expected to make judgements on matters of fitness and probity. In particular the auditor is not required to 'second guess' management decisions. However, there may be situations where there is clear evidence which calls into question the appropriateness of significant actions or decisions taken; such situations are normally reportable. For example, the auditor may question an individual's competence where he is of the opinion that, based on information which was, or should have been, available to that individual, there are no circumstances

under which the decision taken could have been appropriate. An instance could be where counsel's opinion has been sought on a particular matter and, without valid reasons so to do, the advice has been overridden.

29. In determining whether an individual is fit and proper for his or her position, the Financial Regulator has regard to the evidence arising over time. It may determine that a person is not fit and proper on the basis of several instances of behaviour each of which, if taken separately, might not have led to this conclusion. Thus, in determining whether a matter should be reported to the Financial Regulator, the auditor judges each instance on its own merits and in the light of previous evidence. Where the auditor of a bank has not been informed by the Financial Regulator of any matter, he cannot assume that there are no matters known to the Financial Regulator which could affect their judgment as to whether information is of material significance. In the absence of disclosure by the Financial Regulator, the auditor can only form their judgment in the light of evidence to which they have access.

Business to be directed by at least two individuals

30. Article 11(1) of the CRD states that authorisation shall only be granted to a bank where there are at least two persons who effectively direct its business activities. This requirement is expanded upon in the Financial Regulator Standards which state that the operations of the bank must be conducted from within the Republic of Ireland by at least two persons who are resident in the jurisdiction.

31. Where there is a single individual who is dominant in a bank, compliance with this criterion will be in doubt. There may, however, be other factors, such as any monitoring role, which may be fulfilled by a strong independent board of directors that includes non executive directors, audit committees or shareholders, which may act as a compensating mechanism.

32. A basic element of any audit is that the auditor obtains an understanding of the general control environment. Inter alia, this involves a consideration of the way in which the business is controlled and managed and the effects of changes in personnel or evolving structures or relationships. These procedures relating to the control environment are likely to provide evidence relating to this criterion.

33. If the auditor becomes aware of an area of the business where a particular individual is able to act alone, he addresses the question of whether the individual can act alone in respect of matters relating to strategy or significant operational decisions.

34. Where the auditor has reasonable cause to believe that this criterion is not being met this is likely to be of material significance to the Financial Regulator by virtue of its fundamental nature.

Composition of the board of directors and management structures

35. The Financial Regulator Standards' state that the Financial Regulator 'must be satisfied with the structure of the board and senior management of a bank and that internal control systems and reporting arrangements are such as to provide for the effective,

prudent and efficient administration of its assets and liabilities. In this respect, it is necessary for all banks to have in place such committees of directors and management and other management structures as are necessary to ensure that the business of the bank is being managed, conducted and controlled in a prudent manner and in accordance with sound administrative and accounting principles'.

36. The Financial Regulator has indicated that it is of the view that the appointment of non-executive directors to the board of directors and also the establishment of an internal audit function are matters of best practice which it takes into account in reviewing new applications.

37. Under normal circumstances, the auditor may assume that the Financial Regulator is aware of the composition of the board of directors of the bank. Therefore, the necessity to report under this criterion will arise only where the auditor becomes aware that a change in the membership of the board has not been notified to the Financial Regulator.

Business to be conducted in a prudent manner

38. The Financial Regulator requires that a bank conducts its business in a prudent manner. The Financial Regulator Standards include certain minimum standards which are stated to be prerequisite to this requirement. However, these are not exhaustive and are without prejudice to the general prudent conduct requirement. They cover the following areas:

- capital adequacy;

- liquidity;

- funding;

- lending and the adequacy of provisions;

- financial systems, internal controls and accounting records; and

- asset securitisations.

Acquisitions by banks

39. The legislative provisions relating to holdings by banks in other entities are set out in Part II, Chapter VI CBA 1989 and European Communities (Licensing and Supervision of Credit Institutions) Regulations 1992 (S.I. 395 of 1992). Notwithstanding these provisions, a bank should not acquire, directly or indirectly, more than ten per cent of the shares or other interests in another company without the prior approval of the Financial Regulator. The Financial Regulator would not be receptive to a proposal from a bank to acquire a qualifying holding in a general insurance company.

General prudent conduct

40. The matters discussed above are not exhaustive. Other issues which the Financial Regulator considers relevant in relation to general prudent conduct include the bank's:

    * management arrangements;

    * general strategy and objectives;

    * planning arrangements;

    * policies on accounting, lending and other exposures, and bad debt and tax provisions;

    * policies and practices on the taking and valuation of security, on the monitoring of arrears, on following up debtors in arrears, and interest rate matching;

    * recruitment, training and remuneration arrangements to ensure that the bank has an adequate number of experienced and skilled staff, appropriately incentivised and disciplined, to carry out its various activities in a prudent manner; and

    * approach to meeting the requirement of anti-money laundering legislation.

41. Other areas for consideration might be a bank's:

    * internal audit function; and

    * compliance arrangements.

Integrity and skill

42. The business of a bank should be carried on with integrity and the professional skills appropriate to the nature and scale of its business. This requirement, like that relating to prudent conduct, is concerned with the manner in which the business of the bank is carried on and is distinct from the fitness and propriety of the individuals controlling and managing that business. However, where the auditor of a bank has reason to believe that there is a material breach of the criterion relating to integrity and skill, it is expected that there will also be a breach of the fit and proper criterion. However, it may not be possible or practicable to establish to which individual within the bank this relates.

43. Criminal offences, breaches of statute, or the failure to comply with recognised ethical standards and codes of conduct by a bank will obviously call into question the bank's integrity. Of particular relevance are contraventions of any provision designed to protect against financial loss due to dishonesty, incompetence or malpractice. In considering whether a duty to report arises, auditors have regard to the seriousness of the breach, its resulting implications, and whether it was:

    * deliberate or unintentional;

THE AUDITING PRACTICES BOARD

- frequent or isolated; or

- systematic.

44. The skills requirement is concerned with whether a bank has available the range and depth of professional skills which are appropriate, given the size and nature of the business being conducted. In particular, evidence that there is insufficient experience within the board or at an appropriate level of senior management to understand fully the transactions being undertaken and the associated risks would be reportable.

Minimum net assets

45. The CRD contains a criterion relating to minimum net assets at the time of authorisation. This is not relevant for the purposes of considering initiating a report to the Financial Regulator. The continuing obligation on minimum net assets is dealt with under capital adequacy above.

g) Contravention of the provisions of laws and regulations (Regulation 7 of Post-BCCI Regulations)

46. The auditor of a bank also has a statutory duty to report to the Financial Regulator if he becomes aware of the possibility of breaches of laws, regulations or administrative provisions which specifically govern the activities of a bank or non-compliance with any condition or requirement imposed by the Financial Regulator on the bank which is likely to be of material significance to the Financial Regulator in the exercise of its function as banking supervisor.

47. The following list is not exhaustive but provides an indication of the type of matters which could become the subject of a report, and which are not covered by other, more specific requirements:

- failure to comply with a condition of authorisation issued under section 10 of CBA 1971;[38]

- failure to comply with a direction issued under section 38 of CBA 1989;

- failure to comply with the notification requirements relating to directors, qualifying holdings, acquisitions etc under the CBAs, the Transparency (Directive 2004/109/EC) Regulations 2007 (S.I. 277 of 2007), the Companies Act, 1990 and the Financial Regulator Standards;

- breach of the rules relating to advertising and invitations to make deposits set out in the Advertising Requirements applicable to Credit Institutions issued in accordance with section 117 of CBA 1989 and section 27 of CBA 1971[39] (as amended); and

---

[38] As amended by sections 32(2) and 33 CBA 1989.

[39] As amended by section 43 CBA 1989, Regulation 39(c) EC Licensing and Supervision of Credit Institutions 1992, section 70(e) CBA 1997 and Schedule 3 Part 4 CBFSAI 2004.

- where circumstances exist that could lead the Financial Regulator to revoke a bank's authorisation under section 11 of the CBA 1971[40] (as amended) and Regulation 4 of the Post-BCCI Regulations.

48. The duty to report does not specifically address situations where the CBAs and the regulations may give rise to a revocation of a licence.

49. Section 11(1)(b)(iv) of CBA 1971 as inserted by section 34 of the CBA 1989 allows the Financial Regulator to revoke authorisation if a bank or a person acting on its behalf has obtained the license through false statements or any other irregular means. There is no materiality test in connection with the criterion. In practice the Financial Regulator is not likely to exercise its powers just because of a minor inaccuracy. There would generally have to be a wider prudential concern, of which the inaccuracy may be a symptom. Therefore, the discovery by an auditor of a minor inaccuracy in information provided to the Financial Regulator would not normally give rise to a statutory duty to report unless it was indicative of a general lack of compliance with the Financial Regulator's requirements or otherwise cast doubt on the bank's compliance with the Financial Regulator's authorisation requirements.

Reporting under Section 27 of the CBA 1997

h) The annual statutory duty confirmation to the Financial Regulator *(section 27B of the CBA 1997)*

50. Section 27B of the CBA 1997[41] places a duty on auditors to make a written report to the Financial Regulator, within one month after the date of the auditor's report on the bank's financial statements or within such extended period as Financial Regulator allows, stating whether or not circumstances have arisen that require the auditor to report a matter to the Financial Regulator under a prescribed enactment and if such circumstances have arisen specify those circumstances (the "**Statutory Duty Confirmation**"). Prescribed enactments relating to banks are listed in Appendix 5A.

51. The Statutory Duty Confirmation is sent directly to the Financial Regulator and is a statement to the Financial Regulator that there is no matter, not already reported in writing to the Financial Regulator by the auditor, that has come to the attention of the auditor during the ordinary course of the audit that gives rise to a duty to report to the Financial Regulator. Where matters have already been reported to the Financial Regulator these are referred to in the Statutory Duty Confirmation. The Statutory Duty Confirmation does not in any way replace the auditor's obligations to report under other legislation and regulations as and when circumstances giving rise to the duty are identified in the course of audit work.

52. Although the Statutory Duty Confirmation is sent directly to the Financial Regulator, the auditor may send a copy of it to the bank. There may, however, be cases (for example

---

[40] As amended by Regulation 5 of EC Licensing Supervision of Bank Requirements 1979, section 34 CBA 1989 and section 71 CBA 1997.

[41] As inserted by section 26 CBFSAI 2004.

where a direct report has been made to the Financial Regulator without the bank's knowledge,) where this is inappropriate. The auditor should be aware of the potential conflict between section 47(4) of the CBA 1989 and ISA (UK and Ireland) 250 in this regard as outlined in paragraphs 67 and 68 of this Practice Note.

53. An example proforma Statutory Duty Confirmation is included in Appendix 5 of this Practice Note.

54. The Statutory Duty Confirmation should be submitted within one month of the date of the report of the auditor on the bank's financial statements. The latest date of submission of audited financial statements to the Head of Banking Supervision at the Financial Regulator is three months post year end. The period covered by the Statutory Duty Confirmation commences from the date of issue of the previous Statutory Duty Confirmation. It covers all matters that require the auditor to report to the Financial Regulator in respect of that period.

i) Other Reports to management *(section 27C of the CBA 1997)*

55. Section 27C of the CBA 1997[42] requires that if the auditor of a bank makes a report to the bank, or those concerned with its management, on any matter that has come to the auditor's notice during the course of the financial statement audit (or while carrying out any work of a kind specified by the Financial Regulator[43]), the auditor must provide the Financial Regulator with a copy of that report.

56. The copy must be provided at the same time as, or as soon as practicable after, the original is provided to the bank or those concerned in its management. Where no such report is to be sent to the bank section 27C (3) of the CBA 1997 requires the auditor to inform the Financial Regulator that such is the case i.e. a 'nil return'.

57. There is no definition contained in the legislation as to what constitutes 'a report' for the purpose of section 27C of the CBA 1997[44] or the meaning of the term 'those concerned in its management'. However the Financial Regulator has indicated that it would expect to receive under this section, copies of post audit reports prepared in accordance with International Standards on Auditing ('**ISA**') (UK & Ireland) 260, Communication with Those Charged with Governance, and that particular areas of interest include any concerns relating to solvency/capital adequacy or the bank's conduct of business with its clients.

58. In many cases, the post audit report required by ISA (UK & Ireland) 260 may constitute the only report made on matters arising from the audit. However, auditors will need to consider the nature of other communications and correspondence with the bank concerned and consider if they contain matters of a substantive nature, arising from the audit, such that they may be regarded as a report for the purposes of section 27C of the CBA 1997. In cases of uncertainty as to whether a particular communication to a

---

[42] As inserted by section 26 CBFSAI 2004.
[43] No work has yet been specified by the Financial Regulator for this purpose, hence the duty relates to reports on matters arising from the audit.
[44] As inserted by section 26 CBFSAI 2004.

financial institution constitutes a 'report' for the purposes of this section, auditors may wish to take legal advice.

59. The auditor may consider it prudent to include in any report to directors or management, as a matter of course, a statement that:

- the report has been prepared for the sole use of the bank;

- it must not be disclosed to another third party, other than the Financial Regulator;

- no responsibility is assumed by the auditor to any other person; and

- it does not purport to be a comprehensive record of all matters arising, all risks or all internal control weaknesses in the entity.

j) Reports to the Office of the Director of Corporate Enforcement (ODCE)
(Section 27D of the CBA 1997)

60. Section 27D of the CBA 1997[45] requires that auditors of regulated entities submit to the Financial Regulator copies of any reports sent to ODCE. Copies must be submitted at the same time or as soon as practicable after the report is made to ODCE.

Other reports to the Financial Regulator

61. In addition to the reports considered in this guidance, the Financial Regulator has the power to request specifically the auditors of a bank to provide reports listed in section 27E of the CBA 1997[46].

62. The auditor is also aware that under section 27F of the CBA 1997[47] the Financial Regulator may:

> *"by notice in writing, require an auditor of a regulated financial service provider, or an affiliate of the auditor, to provide the Bank with a copy of any record or information provided or obtained by the auditor or affiliate in connection with an audit of the financial service provider's accounts that is in the possession of the auditor or affiliate".*

PROTECTION FOR DISCLOSURE UNDER COMMON LAW

63. In cases of doubt, common law provides protection for disclosing certain matters to a proper authority in the public interest.

---

[45] As amended by section 26 CBFSAI 2004.
[46] As amended by section 26 CBFSAI 2004.
[47] As inserted by section 26 CBFSAI 2004.

64. Common law precedent in the UK[48] indicates that a degree of protection exists for disclosures of certain matters to an appropriate authority in the public interest. This UK case law which is only of persuasive authority in the Republic of Ireland, indicates that accounting firms are protected from the risk of liability from breach of confidence or defamation under general law even when carrying out work which is not clearly undertaken in the capacity of auditor provided that:

- in the case of breach of confidence:

  (a) disclosure is made in the public interest; and

  (b) such disclosure is made to an appropriate body or person; and

  (c) there is no malice motivating the disclosure; and

- in the case of defamation

  (a) the information disclosed was obtained in a proper capacity; and

  (b) there is no malice motivating the disclosure.

This principle of common law has received limited consideration in the courts in the Republic of Ireland.[49]

65. The same protection is given even if there is only a reasonable suspicion that non-compliance with law or regulations has occurred. Provided that it can be demonstrated that an accounting firm, in disclosing a matter in the public interest, has acted reasonably and in good faith, it would not be held by the court to be in breach of duty to the institution even if, an investigation or prosecution having occurred, it were found that there had been no breach of law or regulation.

66. When reporting to proper authorities in the public interest, it is important that, in order to retain the protection of qualified privilege, auditors report only to one who has a proper interest to receive the information. The Financial Regulator is the proper authority in the case of a bank.

67. 'Public interest' is a concept which is not capable of general definition. Each situation must be considered individually. In general circumstances, matters to be taken into account when considering whether disclosure is justified in the public interest may include:

---

[48] Initial Services and Putterill [1967] 3 All ER 145, Garthside –v- Outram [1856] 26 LJ Ch 113, British Steel Corp –v- Granada Television Ltd [1981] 1 All ER 417, Lion Laboratories Limited –v- Evans [1985] QB 526, AG –v- Guardian Newspapers Limited (No 2) [1988] 3 All ER 545, PriceWaterhouse (a firm) – v- BCCI Holdings (Luxembourg) S.A & Others [1992] BCLC 579.

[49] *National Irish Bank v RTE* [1998] 2 IR 465. See also *Glackin – v- TSB and McInerney* [1993] 3 IR 55 where consideration was given to the position of a statutory obligation to provide information where there was no explicit statutory protection against breach of duty.

- the extent to which the suspected non-compliance with law or regulations is likely to affect members of the public;

- whether the directors (or equivalent) have rectified the matter or are taking, or are likely to take, effective corrective action

- the extent to which non-disclosure is likely to enable the suspected non-compliance with law or regulations to recur with impunity;

- the gravity of the matter;

- whether there is a general management ethos within the entity of disregarding law or regulations; and

- the weight of evidence and the degree of the auditor's suspicion that there has been an instance of non-compliance with laws or regulations.

68. Determination of where the balance of public interest lies requires careful consideration. Auditors and reporting accountants need to weigh the public interest in maintaining confidential client relationships against the public interest in disclosure to a proper authority and to use their professional judgment to determine whether their misgivings justify them in carrying the matter further or are too insubstantial to deserve report.

69. In cases where it is uncertain whether the statutory duty requires an accounting firm to communicate a matter to the Financial Regulator in its capacity as supervisor of banks, it is possible that the firm may be able to rely on the defence of disclosure in the public interest if it communicates a matter to the Financial Regulator which could properly be regarded as having material significance in conformity with the guidance in ISA (UK and Ireland) 250 Section B and this Practice Note, although firms may wish to seek legal advice in such circumstances.

**THE AUDITING
PRACTICES BOARD**

Appendix 3

Persons who have qualifying holdings in a credit institution

1. The definition of a 'qualifying holding' in an applicant set out in the CRD is:

    'a direct or indirect holding in an undertaking which represents 10% or more of the capital or of the voting rights or which makes it possible to exercise a significant influence over the management of the undertaking.'

2. The Financial Regulator applies the same considerations of probity, competence, soundness of judgement and diligence to persons who have a qualifying holding that it applies when considering the fitness and propriety of directors and managers (see Appendix 4). However, the standards required of persons who have a qualifying holding will vary depending on:

    (a) the degree of influence which is, or could be, exercised by them; and

    (b) whether the bank is likely to be damaged by association with them.

3. A shareholder who has a qualifying holding and exercises a close control over the bank would be expected to possess the same range of skills and qualities as are expected of the executive directors. Similarly, the Financial Regulator expects a person who indirectly has a qualifying holding to satisfy standards which are at least as high as those expected of the person which he controls. When forming a judgement on whether a matter relating to a person who has a qualifying holding is likely to be of material significance, the auditor therefore applies the same considerations as those relating directly to those persons over whom control is, or could be, exercised.

Appendix 4

Fit and proper directors and senior executives

1. The Financial Regulator operates a 'fit and proper' test for all directors and senior managers of banks and other financial services firms. The framework applied by the Financial Regulator in this regard is set out in its "Fit and Proper Requirements" published in November 2006 and is supported by the "Individual Questionnaire" which must be completed by every applicant seeking appointment as a director or senior manager in a bank and returned to the Financial Regulator. Both the "Fit and Proper Requirements" and the "Individual Questionnaire" are available to download from www.financialregulator.ie, the Financial Regulator's website.

2. Consideration is given to criteria under three categories when assessing the fitness and probity of an individual;

    *   Competence and capability;

    *   Honesty, integrity, fairness and ethical behaviour; and

    *   Financial Soundness

Competence and capability

3. Some of the relevant factors that have a bearing on competence and capability include:

    *   the activities and size of the bank;

    *   the responsibilities of the position;

    *   whether the person has shown the capacity successfully to undertake the responsibilities of the position, taking into account the nature of those responsibilities, including the establishment of an effective control regime;

    *   whether the person has shown the capacity to fulfil his or her duties having regard to his or her other commitments where the position is not a full-time one;

    *   whether the person has a sound knowledge of the business and responsibilities he or she will be called upon to shoulder; and

    *   whether the appointee meets the standards set out in the "Minimum Competency Requirements" of June 2006.

Honesty, integrity, fairness and ethical behaviour

4. Honesty, integrity, fairness and ethical behaviour are the attributes used to describe "probity". Criminal offences, breaches of statute, censure or discipline by a

professional or regulatory body will obviously call into question the probity of an individual, as will business practices which appear to be deceitful, oppressive or otherwise improper. Of particular relevance are contraventions of any provision designed to protect members of the public against financial loss due to dishonesty, incompetence or malpractice. The auditor who becomes aware of any matters of this nature, other than in the case of trivial occurrences, will consider whether a report is required to the Financial Regulator in accordance with Regulation 7(a) of the Post-BCCI Regulations.

5. In contrast to the other elements of the fitness and propriety criterion, the probity requirement will tend to be much the same whatever position the individual holds. The Financial Regulator's "Individual Questionnaire" for approval of directors and senior executives sets out in some detail the types of matters it takes into account in determining if an individual is of good reputation and character.

Financial soundness

6. The Financial Regulator will enquire into issues relating to the financial soundness of an applicant for the position of director or senior manager of a bank. Such issues would include personal bankruptcy or similar and association with the bankruptcy or similar of a company. The existence of these issues in an applicant's past may raise questions in relation to his or her competence, honesty or integrity and therefore are important factors in the Financial Regulator's assessment of fitness and probity.

The "Individual Questionnaire"

7. The "Individual Questionnaire" which must be completed by every applicant for appointment as director or senior manager in a bank, consists of a number of sections. These are; Personal details; Qualifications and experience; Good reputation and character; Other business interests; Shareholdings in proposing firm; References; Appendix 1 – declarations to be signed by the applicant; Appendix 2 – declaration to be signed by the applicant firm (bank).

Appendix 5

Illustrative wording of a Statutory Duty Confirmation to the Financial Regulator

Name

Title: Head of Function (Banking Supervision Department)

The Financial Services Regulatory Authority

P.O. Box 9138

College Green

Dublin 2

Dear [Sir/Madam]:

Statutory Duty Confirmation: Statement by the auditor for [name of BANK] to the Financial Regulator

The letter and attached schedule constitute a report as required by section 27B of the Central Bank Act 1997[50] in relation to our statutory duty to report certain matters to the Financial Regulator, as specified in [*insert appropriate reference from list from footnote*[51]]. The schedule to this letter lists the reporting periods in which we acted as auditors of [*insert name of financial institution and related entities if appropriate*] and are therefore subject to the statutory duty from [*date of signing last statutory duty confirmation or date of appointment if later*] to [*date of signing current confirmation*].[52]

Respective responsibilities of directors and auditors

It is the responsibility of the directors of [*name of financial institution*]

- to take appropriate steps to provide reasonable assurance that the regulated entity complies with applicable legislation and the requirements of the Financial Regulator set out in Guidance Notes, Notices, Handbooks, Codes and other authoritative pronouncements (the Supervisory Requirements);

- to establish arrangements designed to detect non-compliance with the Guidance Notes, Notices, Handbooks, Codes and other authoritative pronouncements (the Supervisory Requirements and to report any breaches to you;

---

[50] As inserted by section 26 CBFSAI 2004.

[51] As discussed throughout this Practice Note, auditors of banks have a statutory duty to report specified matters to the Financial Regulator under the following provisions
- section 47 of the Central Bank Act 1989; or
- regulations 7, 8 and 9 of the Supervision of Credit Institutions, Stock Exchange Members Firms and Investment Business Firms Regulations 1996 (the Post-BCCI Regulations).

[52] Where the entity has no subsidiaries or close links with other entities the following sentence may be used:
"*we acted as auditor of X in the financial year ended [date] and we are therefore subject to the statutory duty from [date of signing last statutory duty confirmation or date of appointment if later] to [date of signing current confirmation].*"

- to report to the Financial Regulator any information which they know or have reasonable cause to believe is of material significance for the Financial Regulator's supervisory functions.

Our responsibilities are to report to you matters which come to our attention in the course of our work as auditors and are of regulatory concern to you, in accordance with *[insert appropriate reference from list in footnote 51]* and to report on an annual basis to you in relation to whether circumstances indicating such matters have been identified in the course of our work.

Basis of statement

In discharging our statutory duties to report to you we have had regard to matters identified in *[insert appropriate reference from footnote 52]* In doing so we are required to consider matters of which we have become aware in the capacities as auditors listed in the attached schedule to this letter.

Statement

[Except as already notified to you on [53] ......], no circumstances have come to our attention, in our capacities described in the schedule attached to this letter, that have given rise to a statutory duty on us to report to you under *[insert appropriate reference from footnote 51]* .

Our report is prepared solely for the confidential use of the Financial Regulator as required by section 27B of the Central Bank Act 1997[54]. It may not be relied upon by [name of regulated entity] or the Financial Regulator for any other purpose whatsoever. [Name of audit firm] neither owes nor accepts any duty to any other party and shall not be liable for any loss, damage, or expense of whatsoever nature which is caused by reliance on our report.

Yours faithfully

Dated [55]

---

[53] Insert list of reports issued and dates of such reports or delete as appropriate.
[54] As inserted by section 26 CBFSAI 2004.
[55] Where this confirmation letter is being provided for the first time the period covered is from the date of the previous audit report.

Schedule to Statutory Duty Confirmation: financial institutions to which the firm has acted as appointed auditor.

Capacity	Reporting period	Reference to basis of work
Auditor of [name of financial institution – XYZ Ltd]	Financial year ended	Audit report dated
Auditor of [name of financial institution – ABC Ltd]	Financial year ended	Audit report dated
Auditors of the following bodies closely linked by control to [name of financial institution (s) – XYZ Ltd and ABC Ltd Subsidiary 1 Ltd Subsidiary 2 Ltd	Financial year ended	Audit report dated
Auditor of the consolidated financial statements of [name of group - XYZ group]	Financial year ended	Audit report dated

THE AUDITING PRACTICES BOARD

Appendix 6

Pro-forma report on interim profits

The Financial Regulator has, in paragraph 2.1(iv) of the Central Bank Notice S 1/00, specified that an Irish incorporated bank may include interim profits in capital base for prudential supervision purposes only if such profits have been reported on by the bank's external auditors. The standard opinion is as follows:

Independent Review Report to the Directors of XXXXXX

We have been instructed by the [Name of Bank] to review the interim profit and loss account and balance sheet for the [Name of Bank] and its subsidiaries for the six months ended [Insert Date]. A copy of the interim profit and loss account and balance sheet are attached, initialled by us for identification purposes.

Directors' responsibilities

The interim profit and loss account and balance sheet are the responsibility of, and have been approved by, the directors. The Financial Regulator requires that the accounting policies and presentation applied to the interim figures should be consistent with those applied in preparing the latest statutory accounts for the year ended [Insert Date] except where any changes, and the reasons for them, are disclosed.

Review work performed

We conducted our review in accordance with guidance contained in Practice Note 19(I) - Banks in the Republic of Ireland issued by the Auditing Practices Board.

A review consists principally of making enquiries of group management and applying analytical procedures to the financial information and underlying financial data and based thereon, assessing whether the accounting policies and presentation have been consistently applied unless otherwise disclosed. A review excludes audit procedures such as tests of controls and verification of assets, liabilities and transactions. It is substantially less in scope than an audit performed in accordance with International Standards of Auditing (UK and Ireland) and therefore provides a lower level of assurance than an audit. Accordingly we do not express an audit opinion on the interim profit and loss account and balance sheet.

Review conclusion

On the basis of the results of our review, nothing came to our attention to indicate that:

(a) the interim profits as reported on the attached pages have not been calculated on the basis of the accounting policies adopted by the Bank in preparing its latest statutory accounts for the year ended [Insert Date];

(b) those accounting policies differ in any material respects from those required by Irish Generally Accepted Accounting Practices/International Financial Reporting Standards

THE AUDITING 1979
PRACTICES BOARD

adopted by the European Commission in accordance with EC Regulation No 1606/2002*; and

(c) the interim profits amounting to € xxxx, as so reported, are not reasonably stated.

Registered Auditor

DATE:

*delete as appropriate

Appendix 7

Possible factors that may indicate going concern issues

Capital adequacy ratios

- the bank operating at or near the limit of its minimum solvency ratio under the Financial Regulator's capital requirements, either on a group or solo basis;

- unjustified attempts to reduce the size of the buffer over and above the minimum solvency ratio that management has agreed to operate at;

Operations/profitability indicators

- marked decline in new lending/dealing volumes during the year or subsequently;

- marked decline in new business margins;

- severe overcapacity in markets leading to low pricing as well as low volumes;

- significant increase in loan defaults or seizure of collateral (e.g. house repossessions);

- excessive exposures to troubled industry sectors;

- unusually aggressive dealing positions and/or regular breaches of dealing or lending limits;

- redundancies, layoffs or failure to replace natural wastage of personnel;

Liquidity indicators

- unusually large maturity mismatch in the short term (say up to 3 months), either in total or across currencies;

- maturity mismatch ladders prepared on a basis which fail to recognise/use:

  - expected (as opposed to contractual) cash flows;

  - narrow gaps for near maturities;

  - anticipated defaults on loan repayments;

  - a cushion for market value of volatile investments; or

  - off balance sheet commitments;

- failure to put in place or renew sufficient committed standby facilities. (Bear in mind, however, that grounds for withdrawal of even 'committed' facilities can often be found when a bank suffers a major loss of confidence);

- dependence on a few large depositors (which may or may not be connected parties);

- withdrawal of (or reduction in) lines of credit by wholesale counterparties;

- regularly overdrawn nostro accounts;

- difficulty in meeting liquidity standards set on an individual basis by the Financial Regulator;

- uncompetitively low rates of interest offered to depositors (causing outflow of funds);

- very high rates of interest offered to depositors (to prevent outflow of funds, regardless of financial loss).

Reputational and other indicators

- adverse publicity which could lead to loss of confidence or reputation, including fines or public censure by the Financial Regulator;

- lowering of ratings by independent credit agencies;

- urgent attempts to remove assets from the balance sheet, apparently involving material loss of profits or at significant expense;

- deferral of investment plans or capitalisation of expenditure.

THE AUDITING PRACTICES BOARD

Appendix 8

Definitions

Terms and abbreviations used in practice note

Abbreviation Used	Description
APB	Auditing Practices Board
ASB	Accounting Standards Board
Administrative provisions	Notices or other forms of guidance issued by the Financial Regulator (or prior to May 2003 by the Central Bank) under its statutory powers, as set out in Appendix 1
Bank	A credit institution (other than a building society) as defined by the CRD being an undertaking whose business is to receive deposits or other repayable funds from the public and to grant credits for its own account.
Bank Accounts Regulations 1992	European Communities (Credit Institutions Accounts) Regulations 1992, S.I. 294 of 1992
CBA	Central Bank Act
CBAs	Central Bank Acts
CBFSAI	Central Bank and Financial Services Authority of Ireland
CJA	Criminal Justice Act 1994, as amended
Companies Acts	Companies Acts 1963 – 2006 and all regulations to be construed as one with those Acts
CRD	Capital Requirements Directive being the term applied to the EU Directives which transpose the Basel II Accord into a legal text for the purpose of its application to banks and investment firms across the European Economic Area (EEA). These directives are Directive 2006/48/EC (recast) relating to the taking up and pursuit of the business of credit institutions and Directive 2006/49/EC (recast) on the capital adequacy of investment firms and credit institutions.
EEA	European Economic Area
EU IFRSs	International Financial Reporting Standards as adopted by the European Union
FATF	Financial Action Task Force

Financial Regulator	The Irish Financial Services Regulatory Authority, an autonomous entity within the Central Bank and Financial Services Authority of Ireland having responsibility for financial sector regulation and consumer protection. Established 1 May 2003
Financial Regulator Standards	Licensing and Supervision Requirements and Standards for Credit Institutions issued by the Financial Regulator
FRS	Financial Reporting Standards issued by the ASB
IFRS	International Financial Reporting Standards issued by the International Accounting Standards Board
IIA 1995	Investment Intermediaries Act 1995
Irish GAAP	Generally accepted accounting practices in Ireland – accounting standards issued by the ASB and promulgated by the Institute of Chartered Accountants in Ireland
ISA(UK and Ireland)	International Standards on Auditing (UK and Ireland) issued by the APB
Material Significance	A matter or group of matters is normally of material significance to a regulator's function when, due either to its nature or its potential impact, it is likely of itself to require investigation by the regulator
MiFID	Markets in Financial Instruments Directive, 2004/39/EC
Post-BCCI Regulations	Supervision of Credit Institutions, Stock Exchange Member Firms and Investment Business Firms Regulations, 1996 S.I. 267 of 1996
SORPs	Statements of Recommended Practice issued jointly by the British Bankers Association and the Irish Banking Federation
VAR	Value at Risk

THE AUDITING PRACTICES BOARD

PRACTICE NOTE 20(I)

THE AUDIT OF INSURERS IN THE REPUBLIC OF IRELAND

CONTENTS

Preface

The purpose of Practice Notes issued by the Auditing Practices Board is to assist auditors in applying Auditing Standards of general application to particular circumstances and industries. They are persuasive rather than prescriptive. However they are indicative of good practice even though they may be developed without the full process of consultation and exposure used for Statements of Auditing Standards.

This Practice Note contains guidance on the application of Statements of Auditing Standards ('SASs') issued by the Auditing Practices Board ('APB') to the audit of financial statements of insurance companies in the Republic of Ireland, hereinafter referred to as Ireland for the purposes of this Practice Note. SASs contain the basic principles and essential procedures, referred to as Auditing Standards, with which auditors are required to comply in the conduct of any audit of financial statements. This Practice Note also contains guidance in relation to auditors' reports on regulatory returns.

The guidance in this Practice Note is supplementary to, and should be read in conjunction with, SASs. This Practice Note sets out the special considerations relating to the audit of insurers in Ireland that arise from individual SASs listed in the contents. It is not the intention of the Practice Note to provide step-by-step guidance to the audit of insurers, so where no special considerations arise from a particular SAS, no material is included. The Practice Note does not provide guidance for the audits of syndicates and other vehicles in the Lloyd's insurance market. Guidance for such audits is provided in the UK Practice Note 20 issued by the APB.

Auditing Standards include a requirement for auditors to comply with the ethical guidance issued by their relevant professional bodies in the conduct of any audit of financial statements. A fundamental principle embodied in such guidance is that practitioners do not accept or perform work which they are not competent to undertake. The importance of technical competence is also underlined in the Auditors' Code, issued by the APB, which states that the necessary degree of professional skill demands an understanding of financial reporting and business. Practitioners should not undertake the audit of insurers unless they are satisfied that they have, or can obtain, the necessary level of competence.

The Practice Note does not extend to audit appointments under legislation outside Ireland, nor does it give guidance to auditors of underwriting agents or brokers.

This Practice Note is based on legislation and related regulations and guidelines in effect at 31 May 2002. The legislation, regulatory arrangements and documents referred to in the Practice Note may change subsequent to publication.

This Practice Note has been prepared in consultation with the Department of Enterprise, Trade and Employment. References to the Department of Enterprise, Trade and Employment elsewhere in this Practice Note will be denoted by 'DETE'.

The guidance in this Practice Note is applicable to auditors of insurance companies in Ireland. The term 'insurance companies' is used in this document to refer to:

- Irish insurance companies authorised by the Department of Enterprise, Trade and Employment (insurers with their head offices in Ireland and Irish branches of insurers established outside the European Economic Area ('EEA')). Authorised insurers ('authorised insurers') are ones that hold an authorisation granted by the Minister under the Regulations of 1976[1], the Regulations of 1984[2], the Non-Life Regulations of 1994[3] or the Life Regulations of 1994[4] to carry on a specified class or description of business;

- pure reinsurance companies accepting reinsurance business in accordance with section 22 of the Insurance Act, 1989, as amended by section 5 of the Insurance Act, 2000; and

- Voluntary Health Insurance Board ('VHI').

The supervision of the insurance industry in Ireland, other than VHI, is the responsibility of the DETE, acting under the authority of the Minister of State for Science, Technology and Commerce. References in this Practice Note to the regulator include the Minister and the DETE.

Pure reinsurers are required to notify the Minister of their intention to carry on the business of reinsurance in Ireland but are not subject to the same regulatory reporting requirements as other insurers. VHI is subject to the provisions of the Health Insurance Acts and reports to the Minister of Health. It is not required to submit regulatory returns to the DETE. Throughout this Practice Note, references to an authorised insurer exclude pure reinsurers and VHI.

Recent and proposed legislation will affect the legal and regulatory environment affecting companies and their auditors. A number of these are currently at different stages of completion, namely:

- the Company Law Enforcement Act, 2001;

- the Criminal Justice (Theft and Fraud Offences) Act, 2001;

- a prospective bill to implement the recommendations of the Review Group on Auditing ('RGA') relating to companies generally and the regulation of the accountancy profession, including the establishment of an Irish Audit and Accountancy Supervisory Authority; and

- legislation to establish the single regulatory authority.[5]

---

[1] European Communities (Non-life Insurance) Regulations, 1976.
[2] European Communities (Life Assurance) Regulations, 1984.
[3] European Communities (Non-life Insurance) Framework Regulations, 1994.
[4] European Communities (Life Assurance) Framework Regulations, 1994.
[5] The Irish Financial Services Regulatory Authority, (IFSRA), is scheduled to assume the supervision responsibilities of the DETE.

The single regulatory authority may, in due course, introduce further changes in the regulatory environment in the course of carrying out its obligations. The guidance contained in this Practice Note will be reviewed and updated as appropriate in response to new legislation applicable to insurers as its provisions become known.

Introduction

1. This introduction summarises the key features of insurance business and of the environment within which auditors of insurers operate.

Types of insurance business

2. There is considerable variation in the types of business underwritten by insurers, the degree of risk involved, and in the way that business is conducted:

    Non-life insurance
    Non-life insurance may take many different forms, ranging from low risk (e.g. the property element of insurance) to high risk (e.g. the indemnity element of insurance or large commercial risks, such as those relating to oil exploration and extraction). Contracts for larger risks may involve participation by a number of insurers who each subscribe to a proportion of the risk;

    Life assurance
    Life assurance, whilst more homogeneous than non-life insurance business, is also underwritten in a number of ways, including pure life protection, savings products with life protection, pensions and annuities.

    Reinsurance involves an insurer underwriting risks accepted by other insurers or reinsurers. Contracts for reinsurance may relate either to particular individual risks (facultative reinsurance) or to specified portfolios of risks (treaty reinsurance).

3. The nature of records and control systems maintained by an insurer vary considerably in accordance with the types of business underwritten, the nature and degree of risk involved and the way in which the insurer conducts business as well as other factors such as the volume of business, the geographic areas in which the risks are situated, and the identity of counterparties concerned.

Non-life Business

4. Non-life business insurers provide protection against losses arising from various events (such as fire and theft or liabilities arising from injuries or damage to property). Premiums are, in the aggregate and taking one year with another, generally intended to cover anticipated claims costs (including claims handling expenses) resulting from insured events that occur during a fixed period of comparatively short duration. In some types of non-life business, the extent of claims can be established within a relatively short timescale, for example; most claims in relation to property damage. However, non-life business includes a number of areas in which claims may be slow to emerge and/or settle ('long tail business'), or are affected by legal decisions that have both extended the coverage of policies and lengthened the coverage period beyond those envisaged when the risk was underwritten (recent examples include latent diseases and environmental pollution).

Life Business

5. Insurers undertaking life business provide, inter alia, financial benefits at the time of death (or survival) or incapacity and savings products intended to provide benefits after a defined term. Premiums received include a combination of single and/or regular payments throughout the policy term, although the benefits and the services provided by the insurer are not expected to occur evenly over the term of the contract, which is generally an extended period. The term of the contract and the incidence of medical and health factors, and other uncertainties which may affect future claims result in the use of actuarial techniques in determining the provisions required in relation to policies in force.

6. Policyholder returns on life and other long term insurance policies may depend on investment returns. For some policies, investment risk is borne by the policyholder alone (e.g. unit linked policies); for others it is borne entirely by the insurer (e.g. fixed annuities); Ireland also has well developed 'with-profits' products where policyholders share in the investment risk but returns may be supported by guarantees.

Reinsurance

7. Reinsurance is a contract of insurance by which the original insurer transfers (or cedes) some or all of its risks to one or more other insurers. A reinsurer accepting the risk may in turn transfer some or all of its risks to other insurers. The primary purpose of reinsurance is to limit potential losses (particularly having regard to capital available to support underwriting and to avoid undue concentration of risks for one insurer in a single geographical area or market) so as to reduce exposure to the possibility of accumulation of a large number of claims from a single event, to large claims or to a series of events. Reinsurance may also be used for solvency management. The original insured party is normally unaware of the existence of reinsurance arrangements and the insurer's liability to the original insured is unaffected by reinsurance; consequently, where a reinsurer is unable to meet its obligations, the full cost of discharging the liability to the insured falls on the primary insurer which had taken out the reinsurance.

8. In the case of treaty reinsurance, information provided to the reinsurer relates only to the nature of business being reinsured -details of individual policies are not normally included. A reinsurer's decision as to whether to accept a reinsurance treaty is therefore likely to be based on an assessment of the perceived risks of the particular portfolio of business as a whole, rather than on the individual risks accepted by the insurer seeking reinsurance. Similarly, directors of the reinsurer do not normally have detailed information about specific policies when assessing the adequacy of provisions relating to treaty reinsurance. Implications for the way in which auditors obtain sufficient appropriate evidence in relation to treaty business are considered in the section dealing with SAS 400 'Audit evidence'.

Key Characteristics of Insurance Business

9. Insurance business differs in a number of fundamental ways from other types of business activity.

**THE AUDITING
PRACTICES BOARD**

10. The prime purpose of insurance is to spread risk. On the issue of a non-life insurance policy, the policyholder pays a premium as consideration for indemnity against the possible occurrence of a particular event during the period covered by the policy. A policy for life assurance provides financial protection against the uncertain timing of death or the occurrence of ill-health; in addition, many life policies also provide an important savings function, with proceeds from the policy being made available to the insured at its maturity.

11. Because it is not practicable for an insurer, when accepting a risk, to obtain a full understanding of its nature other than through information supplied by the policyholder, the doctrine of caveat emptor does not apply to insurance contracts in the same way as to other commercial contracts.

12. At the time at which the risk is underwritten, the insurer may not know whether or when a claim will result or, particularly for non-life insurance, how much will be paid. Consequently, insurers generally accumulate cash initially and settle claims over future periods, rather than incurring costs initially and subsequently receiving cash on sale of goods or delivery of services. This affects the nature of financial reporting by insurers in a number of ways, primarily:

   (a) in preparing the financial statements of a non-life insurer, applying the accounting principles of matching and prudence necessitates apportionment of premium income and acquisition costs over the period of cover, and estimation of both the final outcome of notified claims and of other claims payable in relation to events which have occurred whether or not notified to the insurer. For the financial statements of a life insurer, matching and prudence results in the deferral and amortisation of acquisition costs and consistency between the technical provisions and premiums and claims;

   (b) a significant element of insurers' accounting processes is driven not by the occurrence of events (such as delivery of goods or services) but by an assessment of the probable outcomes of liabilities, or potential liabilities, under existing contracts of insurance; and

   (c) the accumulation of premium income results in substantial investment portfolios, returns from which form an integral component of an insurer's financial result.

13. Insurers frequently delegate particular activities relating to their business to agents or other third parties, who may have power to act on their behalf. For example:

   • business may be conducted through intermediaries, rather than directly with policyholders;

   • underwriting or claims settlement may be carried out by third parties under delegated authority;

   • an insurer may outsource management of its investment portfolio, or custody of its investments; and

   • an insurer may outsource other functions.

14. Where an insurer conducts business through third parties, its auditors consider whether direct access to records and information maintained by them on the insurer's behalf is necessary in order to obtain sufficient appropriate audit evidence, as discussed in the sections of this Practice Note dealing with SAS 420 'Audit of accounting estimates' and SAS 480 'Service organisations'.

Inherent Uncertainty

15. Because claims for some types of business and their notification can arise over a long period, the degree of inherent uncertainty[6] and judgment involved in the preparation of an insurer's financial statements exceeds that of most organisations.

16. An insurer's obligations to meet uncertain future claims results in particular emphasis on its solvency. Hence, regulatory requirements provide safeguards not only in relation to minimum solvency margins but also by requiring compliance with statutory provisions concerning the admissibility and valuation of assets, and the valuation of liabilities.

17. Determining claims provisions may be subject to a high degree of inherent uncertainty and frequently involve statistical techniques. When reporting on a non-life business insurer's financial statements, auditors assess whether such uncertainties fall within the category of 'fundamental[7]' and so require to be disclosed in their report. In making this assessment, auditors take into account whether the financial statements provide a user with general information about the types of business written such that the overall level of inherent uncertainty likely to apply to those financial statements can be understood.

18. Further consideration of the impact of uncertainty on the work of the auditor is set out in the sections dealing with SAS 100 'Objectives and general principles governing the audit of financial statements' and SAS 220 'Materiality and the audit'.

Legislative and Regulatory Framework

19. In addition to the Companies Acts, 1963 to 2001, which apply to all companies, including insurance companies, the European Communities (Insurance Undertakings: Accounts) Regulations, 1996 apply to insurance and reinsurance undertakings and certain holding companies of such undertakings.

20. Insurers operate within a complex framework of law and regulation[8] that differs in a number of significant respects from that applicable to the generality of commercial enterprises. This framework involves statutory regulation of insurance activities

---

[6] "An uncertainty is inherent when its resolution is dependent upon certain future events outside the control of the reporting entity's directors at the date the financial statements are approved" (SAS 600, paragraph 12).

[7] "An uncertainty is fundamental when it is inherent **and** the magnitude of its potential impact is so great that, without clear disclosure of the nature and implications of the uncertainty, the view given by the financial statements would be seriously misleading" (SAS 600, paragraph 13).

[8] The Acts, Regulations and Guidelines which comprise the framework are listed in Appendix 5.

established by EU Directive, under which insurance regulators have powers to establish specific requirements as well as to institute investigations into insurers and to suspend or remove authorisation to conduct insurance business where appropriate.

21. Other than VHI, insurance business may not be carried on in Ireland without authorisation, or in the case of a pure reinsurer without notifying the regulator of the insurers' intention to carry on the business of reinsurance. Insurance may be undertaken by:

    (a) authorised insurers;

    (b) companies accepting pure reinsurance business; and

    (c) insurers authorised by other EEA member states, which may conduct insurance business in Ireland on a 'freedom of services' basis or through the establishment of branches.

22. The principal objective of insurance regulation is to provide appropriate protection to policyholders. The principal responsibilities of the regulator are:

    (a) to ensure that insurers are directed by 'persons of good repute with appropriate professional qualifications or experience';

    (b) to ensure that the insurers have administrative and accounting procedures and internal control mechanisms which are sound and adequate; and

    (c) to safeguard insurers' solvency.

23. Auditors of insurers need to be familiar with the relevant legal and regulatory requirements as well as guidelines issued by the DETE. The extent to which auditors consider compliance with regulatory requirements in the course of auditing an insurer's financial statements is discussed in the section dealing with SAS 120 'Consideration of law and regulations'. Guidance on auditors' responsibilities in relation to regulatory reporting is contained in the section 'Reporting on regulatory returns'.

24. Auditors have a statutory duty to report certain matters of which they become aware under section 35 of the Insurance Act, 1989 and guidance relating to this duty is included in the section dealing with SAS 620 'The Auditors Right and Duty to Report to Regulators'.

Solvency and adequacy of technical provisions

25. Much of the current regulatory framework consists of provisions intended to maintain the solvency of authorised insurers and so ensure their ability to meet future claims from policyholders. Accordingly, authorised insurers are required to comply with statutory solvency requirements and also to make annual or sometimes more frequent regulatory returns providing information concerning the value and type of assets held, claims arising under policies written and other financial information.

26. In the case of insurance companies undertaking life assurance business in Ireland, there is a statutory requirement to appoint an actuary (the 'Appointed Actuary') with responsibility, in particular, for conducting investigations into the financial condition of the insurance company's life business once in every period of twelve months and at any other time when there is to be a distribution of surplus from the life fund. In carrying out such investigations, the Appointed Actuary is required:

    (a) to value the liabilities attributable to life assurance business; and

    (b) to determine any excess over those liabilities of the assets representing the life assurance business fund.

    The Appointed Actuary is required to provide a certificate to accompany the regulatory return, setting out the results of this investigation[9].

27. In the case of insurers undertaking non-life business there is a requirement contained in a DETE Guideline for an actuary to 'certify' the adequacy of the provisions as stated in the annual returns to the regulator. This certification currently carries no responsibility for other aspects of solvency or technical solvency of the company and only applies to the provisions at that date.

    Exemption from certification may be sought by companies that have no third party business and who do not undertake motor, liability or financial guarantee business.

Financial reporting requirements

28. Directors of insurance companies are required to prepare financial statements complying with relevant legal and accounting requirements and giving a true and fair view of the company's results and its state of affairs.

29. In the case of insurance companies, relevant legal requirements are set out in the Companies Acts, 1963 to 2001 and the European Communities (Insurance Undertakings: Accounts) Regulations, 1996 and accounting requirements are set out in Financial Reporting Standards and Statements of Standard Accounting Practice adopted by the Accounting Standards Board('ASB') and statements from the Urgent Issues Task Force ('UITF')[10].

    The European Communities (Insurance Undertakings: Accounts) Regulations, 1996 require directors of insurance companies to state in their financial statements whether the financial statements have been prepared in accordance with applicable accounting standards. Some insurance companies choose to comply with the requirements of the

---

[9] The Appointed Actuary follows guidance set out in Guidance Notes GN1 ROI 'Actuaries and long term insurance business' and GN8 ROI 'Additional guidance for appointed actuaries and appropriate actuaries', issued by the Society of Actuaries in Ireland.

[10] The Urgent Issues Task Force Abstracts are applicable to financial statements of a reporting entity that are intended to give a true and fair view of its state of affairs at the balance sheet date and of it profit and loss account for the financial period ending at that date.

Statement of Recommended Practice 'Accounting for Insurance Business' adopted by the Association of British Insurers[11].

30. If an authorised insurer undertakes life assurance business, computation of the technical provision for life assurance business to be included in its financial statements must be made by an actuary 'on the basis of recognised actuarial methods with due regard to the actuarial principles laid down in Council Directive 92/96/EEC' (The Life Framework Directive). This requirement does not apply to any other technical provisions. The actuary carrying out the computation may, but is not required to, make a report in the financial statements relating to the provision.

Responsibilities of Directors

31. The primary responsibility for the conduct of the business of an insurer is vested in the board of directors and the management appointed by it. Directors of insurance companies are required to comply with provisions of company law in the same way as directors of companies generally. Consequently, they are responsible for the preparation of financial statements that give a true and fair view of the results and state of affairs of the insurance company and meet other requirements of the Companies Acts, 1963 to 2001 and the European Communities (Insurance Undertakings: Accounts) Regulations, 1996. In addition, they have significant responsibilities under the legislative and regulatory framework contained in the Insurance Acts and Regulations 1909-2001 and EU Directives, and as determined by the DETE. These include a requirement to:

   (a)   have administrative and accounting procedures and internal control mechanisms which are sound and adequate; and

   (b)   maintain specified margins of solvency.

   In compliance with section 11 of the Insurance Act, 1989, an authorised life assurance company is required to prepare regulatory returns in accordance with the requirements of the European Communities (Life Assurance) Framework Regulations, 1994. An authorised non-life insurance company is required to prepare regulatory returns in accordance with the requirements of the European Communities (Non-life Insurance) Framework Regulations, 1994. The form and content of the returns are determined in the case of life assurance, by the Life Framework Regulations, and in the case of non-life insurance by the European Communities (Non-life Insurance Accounts) Regulations, 1995.

Responsibilities of auditors

32. The primary objective of an audit of the financial statements of an insurance company by an external auditor is to enable an independent auditor to express an opinion in accordance with the requirements of the Companies Acts. The auditors opinion helps

---

[11]   The Statement of Recommended Practice on 'Accounting for Insurance Business' is issued by the Association of British Insurers in accordance with the ASB's Code of Practice for the development and issue of SORPs. This SORP does not apply in Ireland.

to establish the credibility of the financial statements. However it should not be interpreted as an assurance as to the future viability of the insurer or as an opinion as to the efficiency or effectiveness with which the management has conducted the affairs of the insurer, since these are not the objectives of the audit.

33. Auditors of insurers are required to possess the qualifications required of auditors under the Companies Act, 1990. Auditors normally qualify by virtue of membership of a recognised body of accountants and hence are required to comply with SASs issued by the APB and guidance relating to ethics issued by the relevant supervisory professional body.

In general terms, responsibilities of insurers' auditors are:

(a) to report on insurers' financial statements, as required by section 193 of the Companies Act, 1990 and the European Communities (Insurance Undertakings: Accounts) Regulations, 1996;

(b) for authorised insurers, to report on matters in relation to the insurer's regulatory returns, as required by the European Communities (Life Assurance) Framework Regulations, 1994 and the European Communities (Non-life Insurance Accounts) Regulations, 1995. Guidance on the auditors' work in relation to such returns is set out in the section of this Practice Note dealing with reporting on regulatory returns;

(c) for authorised insurers, to report direct to the regulator matters of material significance that come to their attention as required by section 35 of the Insurance Act, 1989. This requirement to report has been extended by the European Communities (Non-life Insurance) Framework (Amendment), Regulations, 1997 to matters likely to materially affect the insurers' ability to fulfil its obligations to policyholders or meet any of its material financial requirements under the Insurance Acts and Regulations while auditing an undertaking in a 'control relationship' with the insurer.[12] The 1997 Regulations implement the EC Directive 95/26/EC The Post BCCI Regulations. This duty does not require auditors of insurers to undertake additional work directed at identifying matters to report over and above the work necessary to fulfil their obligations to report on financial statements and regulatory returns. Guidance on the identification of matters to be reported to the regulators is set out in the section dealing with SAS 620 'The auditors' right and duty to report to regulators'; and

(d) to report to the Minister when, in accordance with section 35(3) of the Insurance Act, 1989, the Minister requires the auditor of authorised insurers to supply him

---

[12] An insurance company is in a 'control relationship' with:
- any person who is, or if he were an undertaking would be, its parent undertaking;
- any undertaking which is its subsidiary undertaking;
- any undertaking which is, or if any person falling within (a) were an undertaking would be, a fellow subsidiary undertaking; and
- any person in accordance with whose directions or instructions its directors are accustomed to act.

with such information as he may specify in relation to the audit of the business of an insurer. Guidance as to steps to be taken by the auditor following such a request from the Minister is set out in the section dealing with SAS 620 'The auditors' right and duty to report to regulators'.

34. Additionally auditors of insurance companies are required to comply with the provisions of legislation applicable to auditors generally including the Companies Acts, the Company Law Enforcement Act, 2001 and the Criminal Justice (Theft and Fraud) Act, 2001.

The Audit of Financial Statements

Auditing Standards, as set out in the SASs, apply to the conduct of the audit of the financial statements of any entity, irrespective of its size, legal form, or the nature of its activities. The commentary in this section identifies the special considerations arising from the application of individual SASs to the audit of insurers' financial statements, and indicates ways in which these can be addressed. The guidance it provides is relevant in the context of all insurers except when the text specifically limits a section or comment to a particular form or forms of insurers.

Where no special considerations arise from a particular SAS, no material is included.

For the specific requirements of Auditing Standards, auditors of insurers should refer to the SAS concerned.

This Practice Note is based on APB Statements of Auditing Standards in issue as at 31 July, 2002.

SAS 100: Objective and General Principles Governing the Audit of Financial Statements

Background note

In undertaking an audit of financial statements, SAS 100 requires that auditors carry out procedures designed to obtain sufficient appropriate evidence, in accordance with Auditing Standards, to determine with reasonable confidence that the financial statements are free of material misstatement. The SAS also requires that auditors should evaluate the overall presentation of the financial statements to ascertain whether they have been prepared in accordance with relevant legislation and accounting standards. The SAS requires that auditors should issue a report containing a clear expression of their opinion on the financial statements.

SAS 100 requires that auditors should comply with the ethical guidance issued by their relevant professional bodies in the conduct of any audit of financial statements.

1. Auditors are required to exercise their professional judgment within the framework provided by Auditing Standards in order to determine the extent of work necessary, in a particular instance, to provide reasonable assurance that the financial statements taken as a whole are free from material misstatement.

2. Financial statements of insurers are prepared following specific requirements set out in the European Communities (Insurance Undertakings: Accounts) Regulations, 1996[13].

3. An insurer's financial statements are required by statute to give a true and fair view of its profit or loss and of its state of affairs. Compliance with applicable financial reporting and accounting standards and UITF abstracts issued by the ASB is normally necessary to meet this requirement.

Inherent uncertainty

4. The preparation of insurers' financial statements involves a considerable degree of judgement as to the outcome of business written at the reporting date. In relation to any individual insurance transaction, there is typically uncertainty as to one or more of the following:

    (a) whether a claim will occur;

    (b) when it will occur;

    (c) what the cost will be; and

    (d) when it will be paid.

---

[13] This is in addition to the requirement for financial statements to be prepared in accordance with the relevant legislation (Companies Acts 1963 to 2001), Financial Reporting Standards, Statements of Standard Accounting Practice and UITF abstracts.

THE AUDITING PRACTICES BOARD 1999

5. Inherent uncertainty as to the final outcome of contracts of insurance is therefore a feature of the business. The degree of uncertainty varies according to a variety of factors including the type of business written and the insurer's arrangements for reinsurance.

6. Insurers writing non-life business, in particular those classes of business referred to as 'long tail', are generally subject to a far greater range of accounting estimates and potential outcomes than other insurers. Long tail business includes certain reinsurance business, employer's and general liability business, and may be affected by factors such as latent disease or pollution.

7. Auditors take account of uncertainties associated with a particular insurer when planning and conducting audit procedures and when considering the appropriateness of disclosure in the financial statements.

8. Auditors' opinions on the financial statements of an insurer are intended to provide reasonable assurance that those statements are free of material misstatement in the context of the inherent uncertainties relating to the business underwritten. Key elements in forming an opinion are:

    (a) the auditors' assessment of whether appropriate provisions for liabilities arising from business underwritten at the balance sheet date are included in the financial statements; and

    (b) the auditors' consideration of the adequacy of disclosures relating to risks and uncertainties.

SAS 110: Fraud and Error

Background note

The SAS requires that auditors should plan and perform their audit procedures, and evaluate the results thereof, recognising that fraud or error may materially affect the financial statements. The SAS requires that, when planning the audit, auditors should assess the risk that fraud or error may cause the financial statements to contain material misstatements. Based on their risk assessment, auditors should design audit procedures so as to have a reasonable expectation of detecting misstatements arising from fraud or error which are material to the financial statements.

Responsibilities

1. Responsibility for the prevention and detection of fraud and error lies with the directors of an insurance company even if they have delegated functions to third parties. In carrying out their responsibilities, the directors of authorised insurers have regard to statutory requirements for sound and prudent management (Regulation 9(2) of the Framework Regulations 1994)[14]. The European Communities (Life Assurance)

---

[14] The "Framework Regulations 1994" encompass the European Communities (Life Assurance) Framework Regulations 1994 – SI No.360 of 1994 and the European Communities (Non-life Insurance) Framework Regulations 1994 – SI No. 359 of 1994.

Framework Regulations 1994 and The European Communities (Non-life Insurance) Framework Regulations 1994 introduced into Irish insurance legislation the concept of 'persons of good repute with appropriate professional qualifications or experience' as a ground for refusing or withdrawing authorisation or for supervisory intervention.

2.   The Criminal Justice (Theft and Fraud Offences) Act, 2001 requires that auditors of all companies report to the Garda Siochana in certain specified circumstances; where during the course of an audit the auditor comes across an offence by the firm, partner, director, manager, secretary or other employee[15].

3.   The audit planning process includes an assessment of the risk of material misstatements, whether arising from fraud or error. Insurers may be subject to:

   (a) policyholder fraud;

   (b) fraud by directors and employees; and

   (c) fraud by agents, brokers or other related parties

4.   Under Regulation 10(3) (life) and 10(3) (non-life) of the Framework Regulations, 1994, authorised insurers should have administrative and accounting procedures and internal control mechanisms which in the opinion of the regulator are sound and adequate. The responsibility for the establishment and proper operation of administrative accounting controls and procedures and internal control mechanisms rests with the directors. Whilst the inherent risk of fraud may continue to exist, the establishment of accounting and internal controls systems sufficient to meet these requirements (particularly in the case of insurance companies that accept business involving a high volume of policies and claims of comparatively low individual financial value) frequently reduces the likelihood of such fraud giving rise to material misstatements in the financial statements. Guidance on the auditors' consideration of accounting systems and internal control is provided in SAS 300 'Accounting and internal control systems and audit risk assessments'.

5.   In the case of authorised insurers if auditors discover potential or actual fraud, they consider the regulatory implications, in particular their duty to report matters of material significance to the regulator. Any suspected or actual fraud involving directors or managers is likely to give rise to a statutory duty to report. A duty to report may also arise when:

   (a)   directors fail to take appropriate steps to minimise risks of external fraud; or

   (b)   employee fraud is discovered. Whilst employee fraud may not have the same significance as that relating to directors or senior management, it may be indicative of an unsatisfactory culture or weaknesses in the internal control environment.

---

[15] Section 59 of the Criminal Justice (Theft and Fraud Offences) Act, 2001.

THE AUDITING 2001
PRACTICES BOARD

Guidance on the circumstances giving rise to a duty to report to the regulator is an area contained in the section of this Practice Note dealing with SAS 620 'The auditors' right and duty to report to regulators'.

6. If auditors discover potential or actual fraud in the course of their work in respect of pure reinsurers or VHI, they consider whether the matter may be one that ought to be reported to a proper authority in the public interest. This consideration also applies to auditors of authorised insurers. Guidance on the circumstances in which matters are reported to a proper authority is contained within SAS 110[16].

Assessing the risk of fraud or error

7. Factors which may indicate that there is an increased risk of the existence of fraud or error include:

   (a) significant levels of high value surrenders of life policies;

   (b) unusual features in new business trends;

   (c) poor support for the calculation of provisions and a large number of adjustments;

   (d) an abnormally high use of suspense accounts, old reconciling items, and poor support for items included in suspense accounts;

   (e) unusual trends in commissions, including a long delay between the payment of commission and the initial premium payments and return premiums; and

   (f) directors or management displaying a lack of candour in dealing with policyholders, actuaries, regulators and auditors.

8. Guidance on the internal control procedures which can be put in place by insurance companies to minimise the risk of fraud or error occurring, is included in the section on SAS 300, 'Accounting and internal control systems and audit risk assessments'.

SAS 120 Consideration of Law and Regulations

Background note

The SAS requires that auditors plan and perform their audit procedures and evaluate and report on the results thereof, recognising that non-compliance by an entity with law or regulations may materially affect the financial statements.

The SAS requires that auditors should obtain sufficient appropriate audit evidence about compliance with those laws and regulations which relate directly to the

---

[16] SAS 110.10 – 110.12.

preparation of, or the inclusion or disclosure of specific items in, the financial statements.

The SAS requires that the auditors should perform specified procedures to help identify possible or actual instances of non-compliance with those laws and regulations, which provide a legal framework within which the entity conducts its business and which are central to the entity's ability to conduct its business and hence to its financial statements.

The SAS requires that, when carrying out their procedures for the purpose of forming an opinion on the financial statements, the auditors should in addition be alert for any instances of possible or actual non-compliance with law and regulations which may affect the financial statements.

The legal and regulatory framework

1. The legal and regulatory framework within which insurance companies conduct their business is summarised in the Introduction to the Practice Note. The present regulatory framework applicable to insurers is complex and involves a number of aspects of insurers' operations.

2. The principal purpose of prudential supervision is to ensure the protection of policyholders because of the promissory nature of transactions between insurers and the public. Much of the legislation for prudential supervision is based on EU Directives.

3. Prudential supervision of authorised insurers is carried out by the regulator under powers conferred by Insurance Acts and Regulations, 1909–2000 and EU Directives. Ongoing prudential supervision of authorised insurers is conducted in part by means of the annual regulatory returns submitted by all authorised insurers, within six months of their balance sheet date.

4. Part 111 of the Insurance Act, 1989 as amended by section 7 of the Insurance Act, 2000 provides for the making of detailed rules in relation to commission payments and disclosures to be made to life and non-life policyholders. Section 7 also makes provision for the furnishing of information to trustees of occupational pension schemes. The Life Assurance (Provision of Information) Regulations, 2001[17] prescribe the information to be provided to individual life policyholders resident in the state. Within one month of the end of each financial year, the insurer must submit to the regulator an actuary's certificate to the effect that certain of this information has been drawn up in accordance with the actuary's advice and relevant actuarial guidelines, and a declaration by the insurer that information required by the actuary for this purpose has been provided.

5. An Insurance Compensation Fund was established by statute in 1964. Section 31 of the Insurance Act, 1989 provides a mechanism whereby the liquidator of an insolvent

---

[17] SI no 15 of 2001.

non-life insurer may obtain funds to make payments to certain individuals who have claims against an insolvent insurer. Insurers may be required to contribute levies raised by these guarantee funds depending on the type of insurance business they undertake. There is also a compensation scheme set up under the Investor Compensation Act, 1998[18] which provides cover to customers of a wide variety of 'financial firms' including insurance brokers, agents and field agents of insurers but excludes insurers.

6. Life and non-life members of the Irish Insurance Federation abide by a series of Self Regulatory Codes of Practice. These codes together with the disclosure regulations provide a framework of guidelines and recommendations for policyholders' protection.

7. There are also consumer affairs bodies, such as the various Ombudsmen (who handle consumer complaints) and the Insurance Ombudsman which provide a direct means of redress for individual policyholders who have complaints against, or disputes with, insurers.

Classification of laws and regulations

8. SAS 120 states that laws and regulations relevant to the audit can be regarded as falling into two main categories:

(a) those relating directly to the preparation of the entity's financial statements, or the inclusion or disclosure of specific items in the financial statements; and

(b) those which provide a legal framework within which the entity conducts its business and which are central to the entity's ability to conduct its business and hence to the preparation of its financial statements.

Laws and regulations which do not fall into either category need not be taken into account in planning the audit work to be undertaken: however, auditors are required to remain alert to the possibility of breaches of other requirements and to consider the implications of any which come to their attention (SAS 120.4 and 120.5).

Laws relating directly to the preparation of the financial statements

9. SAS 120.2 requires auditors to obtain sufficient appropriate audit evidence about compliance with those laws and regulations which relate directly to the preparation of, or the inclusion or disclosure of specific items in, the financial statements.

10. The principal laws and regulations which relate directly to the preparation of financial statements of all insurance companies and insurance holding companies, and of which their auditors need to have an understanding, are, the Companies Acts 1963 to 2001, and the European Communities (Insurance Undertakings: Accounts) Regulations, 1996.

---

[18] A Scheme is run by the Investor Compensation Company Limited (c/o Central Bank of Ireland) and (in general) covers transactions carried out after 1 August 1998.

Laws and guidelines which are central to the insurer's conduct of its business

11. SAS 120.3 requires auditors to carry out specified steps to help identify possible or actual instances of non-compliance with those laws and regulations which fall into the category of those that are central to the entity's ability to conduct its business.

12. Non-compliance with laws and regulations that are central to an authorised insurer's activities is likely to give rise to a statutory duty, under section 35 of the Insurance Act, 1989, to report to the regulator. Such reports are made in accordance with the requirements of SAS 620 'The auditors' right and duty to report to regulators', following the guidance set out in the relevant section of this Practice Note.

13. Auditors need to consider whether to report non-compliance with laws and regulations that are central to a pure reinsurer's or VHI's activities to a proper authority in the public interest. This consideration also applies to auditors of authorised insurers.[19]

14. 'Central' is described in the SAS as relating to those laws and regulations where:

    (a) compliance is a pre-requisite of obtaining a licence or permission to operate; or

    (b) non-compliance may reasonably be expected to result in the insurer ceasing operations or call into question an insurance company's status as a going concern.

15. In the context of insurers, these two criteria indicate that laws and regulations are central to the conduct of business if breaches would have any of the following consequences:

    (a) removal of authorisation to carry out insurance business;

    (b) the imposition of fines or restrictions on business activities the significance of which is such that the ability of the insurer to continue as a going concern is threatened; or

    (c) intervention by the regulator.

16. The principal laws and regulations applicable to prudential supervision that are likely to give rise to such action by the regulator in relation to authorised insurance companies are the Insurance Act, 1989 as amended by the Insurance Act, 2000, the European Communities (Life Assurance) Framework Regulations 1994 and the European Communities (Non-life Insurance) Framework Regulations 1994.

17. These acts and regulations make provision for 'authorisation' including a minimum capital requirement, 'margins of solvency' and a 'matching requirement' in relation to insurance assets and liabilities In particular, this legislation contains:

---

[19] SAS 120.13–120.15.

(a)   the requirement for the insurer to be effectively run by persons of good repute with appropriate qualification or experience (Framework Regulations); and

(b)   provisions concerning prudential supervision.

For life assurance business, the provisions regarding prudential supervision consist of:

*   separation of life assurance assets and liabilities (section 14 – Insurance Act, 1989);

*   arrangements to avoid unfairness between separate insurance funds, etc. (section 14 – Insurance Act, 1989);

*   application of assets (section 15 – Insurance Act, 1989);

*   restrictions on dividends (section 15 – Insurance Act, 1989);

*   allocations to policyholders (section 15 – Insurance Act, 1989);

*   adequacy of premiums (Regulation 8 -1994 Regulations);

*   restriction on transactions with a related company (Part 2 Regulation 10(4) – 1994 Regulations);

*   margins of solvency (Regulation 12 (1(b)) – 1994 Regulations);

*   adequacy of assets (Regulation12 (4) – 1994 Regulations); and

*   a register of assets (Regulation12 (6) – 1994 Regulations);

In relation to non-life business, relevant provisions are:

*   adequacy of premiums (Regulation 8 (2) – 1994 Regulations);

*   margins of solvency (Regulation 13 (1(b)) – 1994 Regulations);

*   adequacy of assets (Regulation13 (5) – 1994 Regulations);

*   a register of assets (Regulation 13 (13) – 1994 Regulations); and

*   restriction on transactions with a related company (Regulation 15 – 1994 Regulations);

18.   The regulator, in July 2001, issued a series of guidelines to assist it supervise insurers.

The guidelines cover the following topics:

*   Actuarial Financial Condition Reports from Life Assurance Companies;

- Actuarial Certification of the Technical Reserves of Non-life Companies;

- Asset Management;

- Appointment of a Compliance Officer;

- Risk Management of Derivatives;

- Directors Compliance Certificates;

- On-Site Supervisory Visits.

19. Auditors need to understand the products offered by the insurer and the legal and regulatory requirements applying to those products. The nature of many life assurance products may include pension products and other vehicles for life assurance savings plans. Insurers authorised under the 1994 (or under the 1976 or 1984) EU Framework Regulations which provide such products may also be subject to further regulation in relation to the selling of life assurance business.

20. The regulator has certain intervention powers under sections 16 to 18 of the Insurance Act, 1989 in relation to authorised insurers. The 1989 Act defines these powers and lays down the grounds on which they may be exercised. Section 59 of this Act provides the Minister with powers to appoint an authorised officer. Section 10 of the Insurance Act, 2000 extends the Minister's powers to an authorised officer to inspect records and obtain information to enable the Minister exercise his functions under the Insurance Acts.

Money laundering

21. The law relating to money laundering is integral to the legal and regulatory framework within which life insurers conduct their business. By the nature of their business, life insurers are ready targets of those engaged in money laundering activities. Legislation in Ireland in this area makes it a criminal offence to provide assistance to those involved in money laundering. In addition, section 57 of the Criminal Justice Act, 1994 requires life insurers and other bodies designated under the Act to report suspicions of money laundering to the appropriate authorities, being the Garda Siochana. It is also an offence to prejudice further investigations by 'tipping off' those involved that a report has been made under s58(2) of that Act.

22. The legislation also requires financial sector businesses, including life insurers, to meet certain requirements in the following areas:

    (a) the establishment and maintenance of policies, procedures and controls to deter and to recognise and report money laundering activities;

    (b) evidence of customer identification (often referred to as 'know your customer' requirements);

(c) retention of customer identification and transaction records for use as evidence in future investigations; and

(d) education and training of staff.

Detailed guidance on implementation of the requirements has been issued by the Irish Insurance Federation (IIF) in its publication entitled 'Money Laundering'.

23. Laws and regulations relating to money laundering are therefore central to life insurers. When auditing the financial statements of life insurers, therefore, auditors need to obtain a general understanding of how the life insurer ensures compliance with the guidance in 'Money Laundering', as issued by the IIF. They also obtain from the directors written representations as to whether there have been any instances of non-compliance with the guidance.

24. If they conclude that there is a possible breach of the guidance in 'Money Laundering' or wider money laundering legislation; or if they uncover any suspicion that the life insurer has been involved, either knowingly or otherwise, in money laundering transactions, the auditors take steps to assess the effect on the financial statements and the implications for other aspects of their audit. In addition the auditors consider their statutory duty to report to the DETE (see SAS 620). When deciding on whether to report the matter, auditors need to be mindful of the offence of 'tipping off'.

Taxation

25. In the course of obtaining evidence sufficient to form an opinion on the view given by an insurer's financial statements, auditors undertake procedures in relation to amounts relating to tax included in those statements in order to determine whether they are materially misstated. In addition to accounting for taxation arising on its own activities, an insurer may have responsibilities under tax and stamp duty laws to operate various tax deduction and tax collection mechanisms. Whilst an audit of financial statements does not provide specific assurance on compliance by the entity with all provisions of tax law (SAS 120, paragraph 25), non-compliance can result in the risk of imposition of liabilities. Auditors of insurers therefore:

(a) make enquiries of the insurer's directors and other personnel responsible for compliance with tax law and regulations as to how such duties are discharged and whether they are on notice of any possible instance of non-compliance;

(b) review correspondence with the Revenue Commissioners; and

(c) carry out procedures to obtain sufficient appropriate evidence that, in the context of the financial statements as a whole, tax charges, liabilities, assets and related disclosures are free from material mis-statement.

26. If auditors become aware of non-compliance with tax legislation, auditors consider the implications in the context of their 'whistle blowing' responsibilities under Section 1079 of the Taxes Consolidation Act 1997.

27. In addition to procedures carried out in the course of their audit of the financial statements, auditors of insurers holding a licence to operate in the International Financial Services Centre may be required to provide additional reports to the Revenue Commissioners on compliance with specified tax legislation.

Non-compliance with company law

28. The Company Law Enforcement Act, 2001 established, with effect from 28 November 2001, a statutory duty on auditors of companies to report to the Director of Company Law Enforcement ('the Director') in the following terms:

> Where in the course of, and by virtue of, their carrying out an audit of the accounts of the company, information comes into the possession of the auditors of a company that leads them to form an opinion that there are reasonable grounds for believing that the company or officer or agent of it has committed an indictable offence under the Companies Acts, the auditor shall, forthwith after having formed it, notify that opinion to the Director and provide the Director with details of the grounds on which they formed that opinion[20].

SAS 120 specifically requires auditors who:

> '... become aware of a suspected or actual non-compliance with law and regulations which give rise to a statutory duty to report.... should make a report to the appropriate authority without undue delay,' (SAS 120.12)

Overseas activities

29. SAS 120.16 requires auditors to take steps to ensure that the audit work in relation to the detection and reporting of any non-compliance with local law and regulations is planned and carried out in accordance with the requirements of SAS 120.

Auditors of an authorised insurer that is a parent company therefore consider the impact of breaches of local laws and regulations on the trading status of the parent company, and of the overseas subsidiary/ branch only in so far as it affects the financial statements of the parent company. Regard is also had to the powers of intervention exercisable by the relevant regulatory authorities and the potential impact on the group financial statements. Guidance to auditors on assessing the materiality of the aggregate of uncorrected misstatements in evaluating whether the financial statements give a true and fair view is provided in the section of this Practice Note dealing with SAS 220 'Materiality and the audit'.

---

[20] Section 194(5) of the Companies Act, 1990, as inserted by section 74 of the Company Law Enforcement Act, 2001. See APB Bulletin 2002/01 for further information.

SAS 130: The Going Concern Basis in Financial Statements

Background note

The SAS requires that, when forming their opinion as to whether financial statements give a true and fair view, the auditors should consider the entity's ability to continue as a going concern, and any relevant disclosures in the financial statements.

The SAS requires that auditors should assess the adequacy of the means by which directors have satisfied themselves that it is appropriate for them to adopt the going concern basis and that the financial statements include such disclosures, if any, relating to going concern as are necessary for them to give a true and fair view. For this purpose, auditors should make enquiries of the directors, and examine appropriate available financial information. The auditors should also plan and perform procedures specifically designed to identify material matters which could indicate concern about the entity's ability to continue as a going concern, having regard to the future period to which the directors have paid particular attention in assessing going concern.

The SAS requires that the auditors should consider the need to obtain written confirmation of representations from the directors regarding the directors' assessment that the entity is a going concern, and any relevant disclosures in the financial statements.

The SAS requires that the auditors should consider whether the financial statements should include any disclosures relating to going concern in order to give a true and fair view.

1. The European Communities (Insurance Undertakings: Accounts) Regulations, 1996 presume the financial statements of insurance companies are prepared on the basis that the company is carrying on business as a going concern. If there are special reasons as to why the company's financial statements should not be prepared on a going concern basis, these reasons should be given in a note.

2. The directors are responsible for determining, on the basis of their own information and judgements, whether the going concern presumption is appropriate. SAS 130.2 requires that auditors assess the adequacy of the means by which directors have satisfied themselves that it is appropriate for them to adopt the going concern basis and that the financial statements include such disclosures, if any, relating to going concern as are necessary for them to give a true and fair view. With reference to insurance companies, specific audit procedures may include.

    *   reviewing the means whereby the board of directors and senior management of an insurance company satisfy themselves that the company will exceed its minimum solvency requirement for the foreseeable future;

    *   obtaining an understanding of the methods used by the company to manage its overall risk exposures, for example reinsurance programmes;

- considering whether the directors have evaluated the security of reinsurers;

- considering whether the period to which the directors have paid particular attention in assessing going concern is reasonable in the insurer's circumstances;

- evaluating budget and/or forecast information produced by the entity and the quality of the systems in place for producing this information and keeping it up to date;

- considering whether the key assumptions underlying the budgets and/or forecasts appear appropriate in the circumstances. Key assumptions will normally include claims projections (numbers, cost and timing), the profitability of business written (especially for life business) and the level of provisions required;

- for a life insurer, reviewing actuarial reports;

- considering an insurer's investment strategy, including the use of derivatives;

- reviewing correspondence with the regulator, and considering any actions taken by the regulator; and

- assessing the reasonable range of uncertainty in relation to the potential costs of settling claims (for instance uncertainty resulting from judicial decisions) and additional provisions.

3. Depending on the classes of business written and the products offered by the insurer, the effect of uncertainty and degree of estimation in financial reporting can vary significantly. SAS 210 requires that auditors should have or obtain a knowledge of the business of the entity to be audited which is sufficient to enable them to identify and understand the events, transactions and practices that may have a significant effect on the financial statements or the audit thereof. Such an understanding is particularly important in considering the appropriateness of the going concern assumption.

4. In certain circumstances the board of directors and the auditors may determine that the going concern assumption is appropriate but that fundamental uncertainty exists. Guidance to auditors on reporting fundamental uncertainty is contained in the section of this Practice Note dealing with SAS 600 'Auditors' reports on financial statements'.

SAS 140: Engagement Letters

Background note

The SAS requires that the auditors and the client should agree on the terms of the engagement, which should be recorded in writing. Auditors should agree the terms of their engagement with new clients in writing. Thereafter auditors should regularly review the terms of engagement and, if appropriate, agree any updating in writing.

The SAS also requires that auditors should confirm in the engagement letter their acceptance of the appointment and include a summary of the respective responsibilities of directors and auditors, the scope of the engagement and the form of any reports.

1. The basic principles used in drafting engagement letters apply in relation to the audit of insurers as to the audit of any entity. Practical considerations arising from the particular characteristics of authorised insurers are considered below.

2. SAS 140.4 requires auditors to ensure that the engagement letter documents and confirms their acceptance of the appointment. Matters specific to authorised insurers which may be dealt with in the engagement letter include:

    •   the directors' responsibilities to keep the regulator informed about the affairs of the business;

    •   the auditors' statutory duty under the Insurance Act, 1989 to report matters of material significance to the regulator as set out in section 35(i) of that Act; and,

    •   the auditors' statutory duty under section 35(ii) to supply the regulator with such information as the regulator may specify in relation to the audit of the business of the insurer, indicating that the regulator may require that in supplying such information the auditor shall act independently of the insurer.

3. The engagement letter makes it clear that the duty to report matters of material significance places an obligation on auditors to report such matters if found, and does not involve undertaking additional work to identify them.

SAS 150: Subsequent Events

Background note

The SAS requires that auditors perform procedures designed to obtain sufficient appropriate audit evidence that all material subsequent events up to the date of their report which require adjustment of, or disclosure in, the financial statements have been identified and are properly reflected therein.

1. With regard to authorised insurers, auditors consider events occurring:

    (a) between the period end and the date of the auditors' report on the insurer's financial statements; and

    (b) where appropriate, between the date of the auditors' report on the insurer's financial statements and the date of the auditors' report on the insurance company's regulatory returns.

2. Matters specific to insurers which auditors may consider in their review of subsequent events include:

    *   an evaluation of the impact of any material subsequent events on the required minimum margin of solvency for the company;

    *   an assessment of the influence of new information received relevant to claims provisions;

    *   an assessment of the impact of any regulatory developments since the balance sheet date; and

    *   a review of relevant correspondence with the regulator.

3. SAS 150 does not provide guidance on facts discovered after the laying of the financial statements before the members. If, in the course of their examination of the insurer's regulatory return, auditors become aware of subsequent events which, had they occurred or been known of at the date of their report on the financial statements, might have caused them to issue a different report, they and the directors consider the appropriate action to be taken. Where the auditors conclude that such a matter is likely to be of material significance to the regulator this may give rise to a duty to report to the regulator.

SAS 160: Other Information in Documents containing Audited Financial Statements (Revised)

Background note

The SAS requires that auditors should read the other information in documents containing audited financial statements. If, as a result, the auditors become aware of any apparent misstatements therein, or identify any material inconsistencies with the audited financial statements, they should seek to resolve them.

1. Insurance companies undertaking life assurance business may include an additional statement showing profits arising on that business calculated on an alternative basis to that used in drawing up the financial statements e.g. 'embedded value'[21] or 'achieved profits'[22] measurements are sometimes used or given in consolidated financial statements which include the financial statements of a life insurer. Without adequate

---

[21] "Embedded value" is a method of placing a value on life insurers. The embedded value equals the value of the in-force business plus the value of any net assets. The value of in-force business is calculated by discounting, using a risk discount rate, future cash flows based on best estimate assumptions.

[22] "Achieved profits" is a profit recognition basis for life insurers. It recognises as profit the cash released from the life assurance fund following the statutory actuarial valuation together with investment returns on future cash flows to shareholders and on assets in the fund not included in the cash release.

explanation, such statements may appear inconsistent with the audited financial statements. Auditors therefore consider whether an adequate explanation of the assumptions and different methodology has been provided in the annual report, and, if not, they consider including an additional comment in their report on the financial statements.

2. Insurers listed on the Irish or London Stock Exchange are required to include information on their compliance with corporate governance standards in the Annual report. The APB has issued guidance to auditors in the form of a Bulletin entitled 'The Combined Code: Requirements of auditors under the Listing Rules of the Irish Stock Exchange' (Q24) to provide guidance for auditors when reviewing the directors' report to shareholders concerning the directors' review of the effectiveness of internal control.

Planning, Controlling and Recording

SAS 200: Planning

Background note

The SAS requires that auditors should plan their work so as to perform the audit in an effective manner and should develop and document an overall audit plan, describing the expected scope and conduct of the audit. The SAS requires that auditors should develop and document the nature, timing, and extent of the planned audit procedures required to implement the overall audit plan. The SAS also requires that auditors should review the audit work planned and, if necessary, revise it during the course of the audit.

1. Insurance business can be complex. Consequently, in planning the audit of an insurer, it is necessary to obtain a detailed understanding of the particular types of insurance business undertaken. The planning process may include discussion with the insurer's management, in particular those with responsibility for:

    (a) determining, implementing and monitoring underwriting policy;

    (b) technical provisions;

    (c) managing investments; and

    (d) compliance and regulation.

2. General issues likely to require consideration in planning the audit of an insurer's financial statements are:

    (a) the need to involve specialists. The nature and complexity of insurance businesses increase the likelihood that auditors may consider it necessary, in order to obtain sufficient appropriate evidence on which to base their report, to involve specialists in the audit process. For example, auditors may wish to rely on the work of a statistician or an actuary to assist their consideration of an insurer's technical provisions. Similarly, the application of relevant tax legislation is likely to be complex, and hence auditors may wish to involve a tax specialist to assist the consideration of provisions for corporation and other taxes included in an insurer's financial statements.

Consequently, auditors of an insurer consider the need to involve such specialists at an early stage in planning their work. Where such specialists are to be used, they may be involved in the development of the audit plan and may take part in discussions with the insurer's management and staff, in order to assist in the development of knowledge and understanding relating to the insurer's business.

(b) the effect of delegated authorities granted by the insurer and the sources of evidence available to the auditors for transactions undertaken by those to whom such authority has been given. Auditors of insurers consider the implications of delegated authorities in planning their work. This may include the outsourcing of certain functions, such as investment management or the delegation of authority to underwrite and/or administer business, and to process and/or settle claims. Similar considerations apply in relation to captive insurance and reinsurance companies where a captive manager maintains financial records but is dependent on other parties (either within the captive's group or otherwise) for financial information and documentation. Further guidance on the extent of work, which may be appropriate, is contained in the section of the Practice Note dealing with SAS 480 'Service organisations'.

(c) the effect of industry wide factors, including claims experience and (in the case of nonlife business) significant catastrophes. Consideration of industry-wide factors assists the auditors' understanding of their impact upon the types of business undertaken by the insurance entity and its claims experience.

3. In developing the overall audit plan and the nature, extent and timing of necessary audit procedures, auditors of insurers consider the key areas of the insurance business as reflected in the financial statements. These are likely to include:

(a) underwriting strategy;

(b) reinsurance arrangements;

(c) insurance technical provisions; and

(d) investment strategy.

4. In auditing financial statements of most types of insurance business, technical provisions, both at the gross level and the reinsurers' share thereof, are usually of particular importance.

5. For insurance companies undertaking non-life business, technical provisions may form a material component of the insurer's net assets and significant changes in the level of technical provisions are likely to have a material effect upon the company's

reported results. The establishment of outstanding claims provisions (comprising provisions for notified outstanding claims and incurred but not reported claims), in particular when business underwritten is 'long tail', will involve the exercise of judgment by management due to uncertainty relating to the occurrence and quantum of claims. In addition, authorised insurers undertaking certain types of non-life business[23] are required to maintain statutory equalisation reserves, calculated on a prescribed basis, and to include these in technical provisions disclosed in their financial statements.

6.   Guidelines issued in July 2001 require that an annual opinion be provided by an actuary as to whether the total technical provisions of non-life insurers are greater than the sum of the expected future liabilities plus the expected profit margin in the unearned premium reserves as at the end of the financial year of the company. This opinion is to accompany the company's annual return to the regulator.

7.   The requirement for the annual actuarial opinion applies to all non-life insurers, including branches of third country insurance undertakings, but excluding VHI. The regulator will consider requests for exemption for the requirement from companies meeting the following criteria:

•   No third party business;

•   No motor, liability or financial guarantee business

8.   In the case of a company undertaking life assurance business, its actuary plays a central role in the determination of the life assurance business technical provision disclosed in its financial statements. Auditors may discuss elements of their audit plan with the actuary, in order to ensure that their audit procedures are co-ordinated with the actuary's work. Where the company appoints a separate actuary to fulfil the duties of an actuary in relation to the company's regulatory returns, the auditors also consider the need for liaison with this actuary. Further guidance on using the work of an actuary is contained in the section of this Practice Note dealing with SAS 520 'Using the work of an expert'.

9.   In view of their statutory responsibilities to report on regulatory returns, auditors of authorised insurers plan their work so as to carry out procedures necessary both to form an opinion on the financial statements and to report on matters included in the regulatory returns in an efficient and effective manner.

---

[23] The European Communities (Non-life Insurance) (Amendment) Regulations, 1991 require that companies undertaking Class 14 credit business should maintain statutory equalisation reserves.

SAS 210: Knowledge of the Business

Background note

The SAS requires that auditors should have or obtain a knowledge of the business of the entity to be audited which is sufficient to enable them to identify and understand the events, transactions and practices that may have a significant effect on the financial statements and the audit thereof.

The SAS also requires that the audit engagement partner should ensure that the audit team obtain such knowledge of the business of the entity being audited as may reasonably be expected to be sufficient to enable it to carry out the audit work effectively.

1. In order to identify and understand the events, transactions and practices which may have a significant effect upon the financial statements, auditors of insurers obtain a general understanding of the relevant parts of the insurance industry, in which the insurer operates, and a more detailed knowledge of the business of the insurer itself. The degree of knowledge required in order to understand the business varies according to the complexity of the business.

2. A feature of most types of insurance business is uncertainty, at the time of drawing up the financial statements, as to the ultimate amount and timing of claims payments. Uncertainty will be present in both non-life insurance business and life assurance business, although different factors are involved depending upon the type of business. Auditors obtain an understanding of the nature of uncertainties affecting the insurer's business in order to assess the impact of such uncertainties upon the financial statements. Uncertainties may be affected by industry-wide and economy-wide factors, or by factors specific to the insurer in question.

3. External factors relevant to the auditors' knowledge of an insurer's business may include:

   - the structure of the insurance market;

   - relevant economic developments;

   - relevant environmental factors; and

   - developments in relevant legislation and changes resulting from new judicial decisions.

4. Internal factors relevant to the auditors' understanding of an insurer's business may include:

   - the characteristics of its insurance products;

   - the methods by which business is transacted;

- whether the insurer participates with others in contracts for large commercial risks, and if so whether it transacts business as 'leader' in such contracts or as a 'follower';

- the underwriting policies adopted and changes therein;

- the reinsurance arrangements;

- the policies and procedures relating to the settlement of claims;

- its compliance record;

- the extent of outsourcing of certain functions, such as investment management, or the delegation of authority to underwrite and/or administer business and to process and/or settle claims, or quantify technical liabilities. Such factors are frequently applicable to captive insurers and captive reinsurance companies but can also apply to other insurers;

- 'fund accounting' in the determination of a captive insurer's and captive reinsurer's corporation tax liability;

- the policies and procedures relating to asset management; and

- the policies and procedures relating to risk management of derivatives.

5. Auditors' understanding of an insurer's business is developed from year to year in accordance with changes in the business and changes in external factors, which affect the business. Insurance policies written in previous years may continue to have an impact upon insurers' financial statements in subsequent years. For example, judicial decisions, the terms of the insurance cover provided and the reinsurance arrangements in force in a previous year are factors involved in the determination of technical provisions not only in the year in which the claims are incurred, but also in subsequent periods if the original estimates of the claims in question change.

6. The establishment of technical provisions frequently involves a degree of judgement by management of the insurer as well as statistical and actuarial techniques. Auditors use their understanding of the business, among other factors, in assessing the judgemental decisions made, together with the appropriateness of the statistical and actuarial methods used.

SAS 220: Materiality and the Audit

Background note

The SAS requires that auditors should consider materiality and its relationship with audit risk when conducting an audit. Materiality is not capable of general mathematical definition as it has both qualitative and quantitative aspects. Auditors are required to consider materiality when determining the nature, timing and extent of

> *audit procedures and should assess the materiality of the aggregate of uncorrected misstatements when evaluating whether the financial statements give a true and fair view.*

1. The principles of assessing materiality in the audit of an insurer are the same as those applying to the audit of any other entity. However, the focus of attention of users of the financial statements of an insurer may differ to that of other entities. In particular, the European Communities (Insurance Undertakings: Accounts) Regulations, 1996 require the use of a number of unique key headings within an insurer's financial statements which may be relevant to users of financial statements.

2. The financial statements of an insurance company, prepared under the European Communities (Insurance Undertakings: Accounts) Regulations 1996 include a profit and loss account in two parts, namely the technical account (for non-life insurance business and/or life assurance business), and the non-technical account; the former shows the results of the underwriting activities, whilst the latter shows the total results for the financial reporting period. There are a number of key headings within the profit and loss account relating to the underwriting activities, including gross premiums written, net earned premiums, net incurred claims and the balances on the technical accounts.

3. SAS 220 indicates that materiality is considered at both the overall financial statements level and in relation to individual account balances, classes of transactions and disclosures.

4. The profit and loss account of an insurance company shows amounts both gross and net of reinsurance and consideration of materiality is necessary at both levels.

5. Similarly, the balance sheet of an insurance company normally includes gross amounts of technical provisions within liabilities and reinsurers' shares of technical provisions within assets. As such, provisions and assets reflect estimated gross claims and recoveries at the balance sheet date, and will be subject to review and adjustment as individual claims are settled (over what may be a protracted period). They cannot be calculated to a high degree of precision, but instead are determined within a range of acceptable outcomes based on assessing available information at the date the financial statements are prepared.

6. Adjustments to an insurer's provisions will normally be more material to underwriting results than the provisions themselves. As a result, insurers' auditors regard the items in the balance sheet and those in the company's profit and loss account separately for the purpose of determining appropriate levels of materiality.

7. The auditors' use of materiality is also affected by the degree of uncertainty to which financial reporting by insurers is subject. In the case of many classes of insurance business, uncertainty relating to the ultimate cost of claims is an inherent feature of the business. As a result, whilst quantitative measures of materiality are of assistance in directing the focus of the auditors' work, qualitative factors relating to the extent and nature of disclosures in the financial statements will also be of importance. Where such

uncertainty is considered to be material, insurance entity auditors consider the disclosures made in the financial statements, and the effect upon the auditors' report. This is dealt with under SAS 600 'The auditors' report on financial statements'.

SAS 240: Quality Control for Audit Work (Revised)

Background note

SAS 240 requires that firms should establish and communicate quality control policy and processes; this involves the establishment of an appropriate structure within the firm and the appointment of a senior audit partner to take responsibility for these matters.

The SAS requires that, before accepting a new audit engagement, firms should ensure that they are competent to undertake the work and will be able to safeguard their objectivity and independence, that they assess the integrity of owners, managers and directors, and that they comply with ethical requirements in relation to changes in appointment. Firms should also ensure that they consider these matters, before the end of their term in office, in deciding whether they are willing to continue in office as auditor.

The SAS requires that firms should have sufficient audit partners and audit staff with the relevant competencies to meet their needs. An audit engagement partner should be appointed to each audit engagement undertaken by a firm to take responsibility for the engagement on behalf of the firm. Firms should establish procedures, and have sufficient resources, to facilitate consultation in relation to difficult or contentious matters; the results of the consultation that are relevant to audit conclusions should be documented.

The SAS requires that audit engagement partners should, in all cases, take responsibility on behalf of the audit firm for the quality of the audit engagements to which they are assigned. Audit engagement partners should consider whether adequate arrangements are in place to safeguard their objectivity and the firm's independence, and document their conclusions. They should ensure that audit work is directed, supervised and reviewed in a manner that provides reasonable assurance that the work has been performed competently.

The SAS requires that firms should ensure that an independent review is undertaken for all audit engagements where the audited entity is a listed company. In addition, firms should establish policies setting out the circumstances in which an independent review should be performed for other audit engagements, whether on the grounds of public interest or audit risk. The independent review should take place before the issue of the auditors' report and provide an objective, independent assessment of the quality of the audit performed; firms' policies should set out in detail the manner in which this objective is to be achieved. The SAS requires that firms should establish procedures for dealing with conflicting views between those associated with the audit regarding important matters.

> *The SAS requires that firms should appoint a senior audit partner or a suitably qualified external consultant to take responsibility for monitoring the quality of audits carried out by the firm.*

1. SAS 240 requires the audit of a listed company to have an independent review. Given the public interest nature of many non-listed insurance companies, it is likely that firms will establish policies to require that an independent review of the audit work is undertaken for all public interest insurance companies by a partner with sufficient experience and authority to fulfil that role.

2. The independent review partner may wish to consider:

   • how the engagement team has addressed its responsibilities to report matters of material significance to the regulator; and

   • communication between the non-audit departments of the firm and the audit engagement partner as commented on in the section dealing with SAS 620 'The auditors' right and duty to report to the regulator'.

3. SAS 240 also provides guidance on communication flows in relation to non-audit work. Paragraph 47 of the SAS indicates that a summary will be prepared of any factors that may reasonably be thought to bear on independence and objectivity, including a record of non-audit work. Furthermore, paragraph 48 sets out that a firm appointed as auditor needs to have in place appropriate procedures to ensure that the audit engagement partner is made aware of any other relationship which exists between the firm and its related entities and the client that may reasonably be thought to bear on the firms independence and the objectivity of the audit engagement partner and the audit staff.

Accounting Systems and Internal Controls

SAS 300: Accounting and Internal Control Systems and Audit Risk Assessments

Background note

> *The SAS requires that auditors should obtain an understanding of the accounting and internal control systems sufficient to plan the audit and develop an effective audit approach. The SAS requires that auditors should use their professional judgment to assess the components of audit risk and to design audit procedures which ensure it is reduced to an acceptably low level.*
>
> *The SAS requires that, in developing their audit approach and detailed audit procedures, auditors should assess inherent risk in relation to financial statement assertions about material account balances and classes of transactions, taking account of factors relevant both to the entity as a whole and to the specific assertions. The SAS requires that, in planning the audit, the auditors should obtain and document*

an understanding of the accounting system and control environment sufficient to determine their audit approach.

The SAS requires that auditors should consider the assessed levels of inherent and control risk in determining the nature, timing and extent of their substantive procedures required to reduce audit risk to an acceptable level. Regardless of the assessed levels of inherent and control risks, auditors should perform some substantive procedures for financial statement assertions of material account balances and transaction classes.

Control environment

1. As with all entities, the responsibility for the establishment and proper operation of systems of control in an insurer rests with its board of directors. The directors determine what is an appropriate level of control for a particular business. Accordingly, systems of control vary depending on the nature and scale of the insurance operations. The attitude, role and involvement of senior management and the board of directors are, however, likely to be fundamental when considering the effectiveness of the control environment.

2. An insurer's control environment consists of the overall attitude, awareness and actions of directors and management regarding internal controls and their importance in the entity. The control environment encompasses the management style, corporate culture and values shared by all employees. It provides the background against which the various other controls are operated.

3. As for the audit of other entities, auditors of insurers obtain an understanding of the control environment, in accordance with SAS 300, to enable them to assess the likely effectiveness of control procedures and develop an effective audit approach.

Inherent risk

4. In making an assessment of inherent risk, auditors of an insurer consider the specific features of the insurance business carried on in the year in question and in prior years. Whilst certain types of risk are common to many types of insurance business, the relative importance of such risks varies depending on the precise nature of the business.

5. Factors frequently encountered in insurance business that may increase the degree of inherent risk include:

    •   guarantees embedded in the life assurance contracts;

    •   complexity of products resulting in differing accounting bases for revenue recognition;

    •   uncertainty of judgements involved in establishing technical provisions and underwriting results;

- the security of investments held and matching investments to meet insurance liabilities;

- complex reinsurance contracts may give rise to errors in calculation of reinsurance premiums or recoveries recorded by the insurer;

- regulatory risks, including the complexity of legislation and the possibility of changes in regulations; and.

- the possibility of litigation arising out of inappropriate selling techniques.

6. Auditors of insurers, in making their assessment of inherent risk, pay particular attention to changes in the insurance business from one reporting period to another.

    Such changes may include:

- the levels or types of business underwritten;

- new lines of business; and

- the regulatory and legal environment.

Control risk

7. Responsibility for the establishment and proper operation of systems of control in an insurance company rests with its board of directors. Those systems of control will also need to have due regard to the requirements of the European Communities Framework Regulations 1994 (both life and non-life) that authorised insurers carry out their business in the manner that meets the criteria of sound and prudent management set out in Part 2 of the Framework Regulations 1994.

8. The assessment of control risk normally includes the identification of the principal ways in which the directors and senior management seek to ensure that the key business risks are identified, monitored and controlled.

9. In the context of an insurer, controls in the areas of underwriting (including premiums and claims), investment management, reinsurance and technical provisions are likely to be significant for audit purposes.

10. An effective control system over the administration of insurance business depends on the accurate collation, processing and storing of large volumes of data relating to:

- acceptance of risk;

- recording of policy details;

- collection of premiums;

- recording, investigation, evaluation and payment of claims;

- investment management and custody;

- identification of classes of business required to be disclosed in the insurer's regulatory returns; and

- transfer of data from the administration systems to the actuarial valuation system.

11. Insurers' auditors are concerned not only with the accurate derivation of amounts shown in the financial statements but also with the accuracy and consistency of statistics used in the establishment and evaluation of technical provisions.

12. Where third parties perform a significant role in an insurer's business, the insurer's auditors will normally assess the controls which management exercise over the use of such third parties and the implications for their overall assessment of control risk.

Accounting systems and control procedures

13. Many insurers are involved in retail markets, selling a high volume of business to individuals. As a result of the large number of transactions undertaken, and records held, by insurers and the need for swift and accurate information processing, retrieval, and presentation in different formats, many insurance functions are highly automated, including the accounting function, the processing and recording of insurance transactions, the recording of risks written and claims incurred, and the supply of management information.

14. In addition to providing a basis for preparation of the financial statements and meeting requirements for maintenance of adequate accounting records, a key feature of the information systems maintained by an insurer is the importance of reliable and properly coded historical statistical data to operate the business. Historical statistical data is important, for example, in providing unearned premium income and unexpired risk data, calculating provisions for outstanding claims and for providing analyses for regulatory returns.

15. The auditors assess the extent, nature and impact of automation within the insurer and plan and perform their work accordingly. In particular, the auditors consider:

   (a) the required level of technical computer knowledge and skills. This may be extensive and may require the auditors to obtain advice and assistance from staff with specialist skills;

   (b) the use of audit software and other types of computer assisted audit techniques; and,

   (c) the evaluation and testing of general controls relating to the environment within which computer based systems are developed, maintained, and operated.

16. Auditors normally require evidence of the effective operation of controls over premium and claims recording systems. They may also consider the controls exercised by the insurer in maintaining and testing the integrity of databases.

17.   SAS 300 requires auditors to obtain and document an understanding of the control environment. An important element of the control environment of an insurer consists of the arrangements whereby its board of directors monitors compliance with statutory requirements, and therefore auditors consider the overall adequacy of those arrangements in the course of their audit of the financial statements.

18.   Matters discovered in the course of the auditors' consideration of an insurer's control environment for the purposes of the audit of its financial statements that indicates material defects in the financial systems and controls or accounting records, which could materially affect the insurer's ability to fulfil its obligations to policyholders or meet any of its material financial requirements under the Insurance Acts, 1909-2000, is likely to be of material significance to the regulator and hence would normally give rise to a statutory duty to report the matter direct to the regulator. This duty (under section 35 of the Insurance Act, 1989) is considered under the heading of 'Reporting matters of material significance' in the section dealing with SAS 620 on 'The auditors' right and duty to report to the regulator'.

Evidence

SAS 400: Audit Evidence

Background note

SAS 400 requires that auditors should obtain sufficient appropriate audit evidence to be able to draw reasonable conclusions on which to base their audit opinion. The SAS also requires that, in seeking to obtain audit evidence from substantive procedures, auditors should consider the extent to which that evidence together with any evidence from tests of controls supports the relevant financial statement assertions.

1.   A key issue in the audit of insurers is the treatment of reinsurance, both with regard to those insurers ceding the business ('reinsurance outwards') and those underwriting it ('reinsurance inwards').

Reinsurance outwards

2.   An important aspect of the uncertainty to which a particular insurer is exposed is the nature and extent of its reinsurance programme[24]. Auditors consider the nature and coverage of any significant reinsurance programmes and, where material, the procedures adopted by the directors to determine the financial stability of reinsurers used. Auditors will normally consider the operation of any significant reinsurance programmes by reviewing whether the risks ceded and the resulting premium and

---

[24] Reinsurance business can be classified into the facultative and treaty methods. The facultative method of reinsurance involves the reinsurer assessing each individual risk offered and then accepting or rejecting it. Under the treaty method, an agreement is entered into between the insurer ceding the risk and the reinsurer whereby all risks written or claims incurred by the cedant that fall within the terms and limits of the treaty will be reinsured with the reinsurer automatically.

expense information are in accordance with the reinsurance contract. They may also consider the procedures in place for ensuring that material claims or balances, if any, disputed by reinsurers are resolved. Evidence may be obtained by reviewing correspondence with reinsurers or intermediaries and considering the quality and timeliness of reconciliations of reinsurer balances.

Reinsurance inwards

3. Reinsurers maintain records of all treaties and will receive regular statements from the cedant of premiums received, claims paid and other data relating to the treaty. The reinsurer will be reliant upon the cedant's statements to maintain accounting records of the underlying treaty transactions. The nature of treaty business affects the requirements for audit evidence particularly in relation to the assertions regarding the completeness of transactions and the measurement of transactions at the proper amount, and allocation of income and expenses to the proper period. Although a reinsurer may have contractual rights to inspect a cedant's books it is reasonable for directors to construct the financial records of the reinsurer from cedant statements. The contractual rights to inspect are designed to allow a reinsurer to investigate business ceded under treaty where, for example, the results are significantly different from those which were anticipated when the contract was written.

4. Auditors may obtain evidence that controls in relation to treaty reinsurance exist to ensure that:

    •   statements from the ceding insurer are received and processed on a regular basis;

    •   statements are reconciled to the reinsurer's accounting records where appropriate; and

    •   a procedure exists for the regular review of major treaty results.

5. The reinsurer is reliant upon the receipt of appropriate information from the cedant. In circumstances where auditors become aware of material deficiencies in this information, they consider whether sufficient appropriate audit evidence is available. In such circumstances, alternative sources of evidence might include any evidence of direct inspection by the reinsurer of the records maintained by the cedant.

Outsourcing functions

6. Many insurers outsource some of their activities, for instance captive managers maintain records of the captive's financial transactions and receive regular statements (Bordereaux) from a group risk manager, fronting company or broker contracted to the group, of premiums received, claims paid and other data relating to the business underwritten. The outsourcing of such functions within the group may affect the procedures for obtaining audit evidence.

SAS 420: Audit of Accounting Estimates

Background note

The SAS requires that auditors should obtain sufficient appropriate evidence regarding accounting estimates. Auditors should obtain sufficient appropriate audit evidence as to whether an accounting estimate is reasonable in the circumstances and, when required, is appropriately disclosed.

The SAS requires that auditors should adopt one or a combination of the following approaches in the audit of an accounting estimate:

(a) review and test the process used by management or by the directors for developing the estimate;

(b) use an independent estimate for comparison with that prepared by management or the directors; or

(c) review subsequent events.

The SAS requires that auditors should make a final assessment of the reasonableness of accounting estimates based on their knowledge of the business and whether the estimate is consistent with other audit evidence obtained during the audit.

1. For most insurers, the estimation of provisions for outstanding claims and other technical provisions (including unexpired risk provisions) is critical because it involves a high degree of judgement.

2. Although all types of insurance business are subject to some uncertainty there is usually more uncertainty associated with insurers writing 'long tail' business than other insurance. These types of business have a high degree of uncertainty in assessing the ultimate cost of claims, particularly as any assessment of overall claims provisions will include a substantial element for claims which have been incurred but not reported ('IBNR'). In the absence of details of the claims, the assessment of the liability relating to IBNR must be subjective.

3. The potential complexity of the calculation of provisions for outstandings and IBNR claims may well involve extensive use of statistical methods. Further guidance on the use of such expertise is given in this Practice Note in the section dealing with SAS 520, 'Using the work of an expert'.

4. In determining whether an insurer's approach to establishing claims provisions is reasonable, auditors need to obtain an understanding of the risks to which a particular insurer is exposed and the means by which those risks are controlled (including the use of reinsurance). The insurer should have detailed guidelines and procedures to support its underwriting strategy and audit evidence may be obtained from testing such controls.

5. Auditors obtain evidence to demonstrate that the insurer has procedures in place to ensure that information on claims is properly captured by its systems and appropriately recorded.

6. For all types of insurance business, the adequacy of assumptions made by management in the past will normally be tested by the auditors by reviewing the actual claims development. In the case of life assurance business, this would, for example, include testing mortality ratios against assumptions; whilst for non-life insurers, a key area of testing would be in the run-off of prior years claims provisions. This type of testing provides evidence of the effectiveness of the estimation processes developed by management.

7. Auditors may use industry data in order to assess whether the results of the insurers estimates (such as claims and operating ratios) are consistent with the experience of the industry. This type of evidence is likely to be useful for business such as motor insurance where, for many insurers, the data has a reasonable degree of homogeneity, rather than other business where the insurers are highly specialised and valid comparisons are accordingly difficult to make.

8. SAS 420.4 requires that auditors assess whether an estimate is consistent with other audit evidence obtained during the audit. The primary basis for the preparation of the key estimates contained within the financial statements is normally the statistical data maintained by the insurer including both the policy data and any statistical models. Where statistical models are used, auditors seek evidence that the source for statistical data has been reconciled with or analysed in comparison with the financial accounting data. In other situations, reliable statistics may not be available and directors will need to estimate claims provisions based on alternative methods, such as by using claim notification data or exposure analysis.

9. Where there is a high degree of uncertainty regarding an estimate, auditors may be concerned as to whether sufficient audit evidence can be obtained as to the appropriate level of provision. SAS 420.2 refers to whether an accounting estimate is reasonable in the circumstances and there will be variations across classes of business as to the precision with which an estimate can be made. Factors such as the information available to the insurer and the industry practice in relation to a particular type of estimate may be taken into account by the auditor in determining whether they have had access to all evidence which may reasonably be expected to be available in order to obtain sufficient evidence to assess the appropriateness of an estimate. Where there is not sufficient appropriate audit evidence, auditors will consider whether this results in a limitation in scope of their audit, which affects their audit opinion on the financial statements.

Non-life business

10. Financial statements of non-life insurance companies should indicate the basis of accounting used in their preparation, the reasons for its use and the policies adopted. Auditors consider the adequacy of such disclosures in the light of inherent uncertainties affecting the financial statements. Further guidance on this issue is

contained in the section dealing with SAS 600 'Auditors' reports on financial statements'.

11. An important source of evidence for auditors will be the appropriateness of the process by which an insurer undertaking non-life business uses the underwriting statistics, or other estimating methods, in arriving at claims provisions. An important element of the auditors' review relates to whether the insurer places undue reliance on one particular methodology and whether it is appropriate for the insurer's book of business. The auditors may assess the methodology by comparison with their knowledge of the business and, in particular, recent business developments.

12. SAS 420.3 refers to the use of an independent estimate for comparison with that prepared by the insurer. Where auditors have concerns regarding the methodology used by the insurer, auditors may prepare an independent estimate using an alternative or refined version of the methodology employed by the insurer. These independent estimates would then be used to evaluate the reasonableness of the estimates prepared by the insurer.

13. Auditors seek to obtain evidence of the accuracy of previous estimates made by management; in particular, analysing the run-off during the current year of prior period estimates such as outstanding claims and IBNR provisions by class of business or by large claim where appropriate.

14. SAS 420.3 also refers to a review of subsequent events when assessing an accounting estimate. For 'long tail' business, auditors may test the insurer's procedures to ensure that outstanding claims are reviewed on a regular basis and that claims provisions are updated when new information on a claim is received. For 'short tail' business, auditors may review claims developments since the end of the year, for example, for evidence of new loss development trends, claims backlogs at the year end or development of data on events (such as winter storms).

15. 'Long tail' non-life business, particularly when catastrophic events are covered, may present difficulties for insurers, as obtaining sufficient evidence to establish an appropriate estimate of the likely outcome can prove particularly difficult given the complexity of the risks underwritten. The audit approach is likely to focus on reviewing and testing the insurer's procedures for developing its estimate: preparation of an independent estimate and review of subsequent events may be of limited value. An insurer may construct claims models for particular disaster scenarios and obtain information from third parties such as brokers or other advisers. Where appropriate at the planning stage of the audit, auditors identify what process has been established by the insurer in order to provide an appropriate estimate of the potential claims exposure in the event of a particular type of catastrophe.

16. The motor insurance industry in the Republic of Ireland funds the payment of third party claims against uninsured and untraced drivers through the Motor Insurers' Bureau of Ireland ('MIBI'). The MIBI manages the settlement of uninsured claims by allocating the handling of the claims to the various insurers in the market. Motor insurers fund the cost of such claims in proportion to their share of the motor insurance market and the MIBI obtains these funds from the insurers by way of an annual levy

apportioned on a pro rata basis on gross premium income received by each insurer in respect of motor vehicle insurance risks underwritten in Ireland whether by way of freedom of services or through an establishment in the State.

Levies are called as required at the discretion of the MIBI. However, an individual insurer's ultimate liability to the MIBI in respect of claims outstanding is not limited to the amount of levies paid by the insurer in any one year. There is an ongoing contingent liability on all motor insurers to contribute to the cost of settling outstanding uninsured claims for as long as the insurer continues to write motor insurance.

Auditors of motor insurers need to be familiar with the arrangements for settling and funding uninsured claims and ensure that their client has appropriately accounted for the claims handled on behalf of the MIBI and for unsettled claims and the levy.

It is industry practice for motor insurers to include a provision in their financial statements for unsettled uninsured claims in proportion to their share of the motor market, based on the MIBI's most recent reported claims provisions.

The regulator has issued guidance to motor insurers to include in their financial statements provision for their total ultimate liabilities to the MIBI and to provide certain information in relation to these provisions and payments to the MIBI by footnote to form 8 (for motor business) of the annual insurance returns submitted to the regulator.

Life assurance

17. The most important consideration in the audit of the financial statements of an authorised insurer undertaking life assurance business is the valuation of life assurance liabilities. Directors of such companies are responsible for preparing financial statements which show a true and fair view: however, the valuation of the provision for life assurance liabilities is determined by the actuary, using assumptions relating, inter alia, to mortality and morbidity rates, interest rates, taxation rates and lapse and surrender rates.

18. The auditors seek to obtain evidence as to the appropriateness of the life assurance technical provisions for the purposes of giving a true and fair view opinion on the financial statements. Audit procedures may include a review of:

    (a) the appropriateness of the assumptions used;

    (b) the controls and procedures to ensure the completeness and integrity of the data; and

    (c) the calculation of the provisions.

19. The valuation process may include an analysis of the surplus for the financial period in which the insurer will analyse what factors have determined its emergence. This will enable the insurer to evaluate the divergence of actual experience from the assumed experience and accordingly to assess the validity of the assumptions. The analysis of

the surplus therefore provides auditors with audit evidence of the reasonableness of assumptions adopted by the insurer.

SAS 440: Management Representations

Background note

The SAS requires that auditors should obtain written confirmation of appropriate representations from management (including directors) before their report is issued. In particular, auditors should obtain evidence that the directors acknowledge their collective responsibility for the preparation of the financial statements and that they have approved them. The SAS also requires that auditors should obtain written confirmation of representations from management on matters material to the financial statements, when those representations are critical to gathering sufficient audit evidence.

1. SAS 440.1 requires auditors to obtain written confirmation of appropriate representations from management. These may take the form of a board minute or a representation letter and normally include a representation concerning the completeness of information made available to the auditors, including correspondence with the regulator. In addition, SAS 120 'Consideration of law and regulations' requires auditors to obtain written confirmation in respect of completeness of disclosure to the auditors of known events which involve possible non-compliance with laws and regulations (including the Criminal Justice Act, 1994 (Money Laundering)) together with the actual or contingent consequences which may arise therefrom (including compliance by subsidiaries and branches with overseas laws and regulations).

2. SAS 440.3 requires that auditors obtain written confirmation of representations from management on matters material to the financial statements when these representations are critical to obtaining sufficient appropriate audit evidence. For an insurer with material non-life business transactions, a board minute or representation letter may include a representation regarding management's procedures for assessing the adequacy of claims provisions and in particular the estimates for claims incurred but not reported. Additionally, there may be a number of assumptions supporting the directors' evaluation of the insurance company's going concern status which reflect commercial judgments such as the adequacy of the reinsurance programme. It may be appropriate for the auditors to obtain written representations on such judgements. Management representations may also be required in relation to matters contained in the directors' certificate included in the regulatory return of an authorised insurer undertaking life assurance business, or on matters which may affect the opinion by the Appointed Actuary on the life reserves included in such a return.

SAS 460: Related Parties

Background note

The SAS requires that auditors should plan and perform the audit with the objective of obtaining sufficient audit evidence regarding the adequacy of disclosure of related party transactions and control of the entity in the financial statements. The SAS requires that, when planning the audit, the auditors should assess the risk that material undisclosed related party transactions may exist.

The SAS requires that the auditors should review for completeness information provided by the directors identifying material transactions with those parties that have been related parties for any part of the financial period. In addition, the SAS requires that the auditors should be alert for evidence of related party transactions that are not included in the information provided by the directors.

The SAS requires that the auditors should obtain sufficient appropriate audit evidence that material identified related party transactions are properly recorded and disclosed in the financial statements. The SAS also requires that the auditors should obtain sufficient audit evidence that disclosures in the financial statements relating to control of the entity are properly stated.

The SAS requires that the auditors should obtain written representations from the directors concerning completeness of information provided regarding the related party and control disclosures in the financial statements.

1. Insurers are likely to have a particularly wide range of contractual arrangements because the nature of insurance is to spread risk. The directors will, in particular, need to consider how best to obtain information on related party interests in policies issued. In capturing this data it may be practical to establish criteria for evaluating materiality to the individuals concerned; the policies are, in many cases, unlikely to be material to the insurer. Auditors will need to consider the adequacy of these procedures in relation to the disclosures given in the financial statements. Many of the insurers in Ireland avail themselves of the exemptions provided in Financial Reporting Standard 8 (Related Party Disclosures) and do not disclose details in respect of related party transactions with group companies in their financial statements.

2. Regulation for insurance companies undertaking life assurance business with respect to related parties is also provided by Part 2 of the Framework Regulations 1994: 'transactions of a material nature with a related company or companies'. Reference should be made to these regulations. If there has been a contravention of these regulations, auditors also have regard to their duties under SAS 620 'The auditors' right and duty to report to regulators'[25].

---

[25] Regulation 10 (4) of SI No. 360 stipulates that prior notice of any transaction of a material nature with a related company must be given to the regulator.

SAS 480: Service Organisations

Background note

The SAS sets out a framework for determining the effect of outsourced activities on the audit, and the procedures, which may be followed to obtain audit evidence concerning those activities.

The SAS requires auditors to consider the arrangements put in place by the directors to monitor outsourced activities and to assess whether the evidence they need is available at the user entity. If not, the main alternatives for the auditors are to visit the service organisation in order to obtain the evidence they need, or to rely on work done by the service organisation's auditors.

1. Insurers, including captives, may outsource functions relating to administration, investment management, underwriting and claims. Captives may outsource many of these functions to a fellow group company. Information on the transactions undertaken on behalf of an insurer under such arrangements will typically be provided to the insurer in a summarised form. Although powers have been delegated, directors are still responsible for these transactions and will need to set up appropriate procedures to monitor them. Examples of outsourced services which may impact on the audit of the insurer include:

    *   accounting records;

    *   IT systems and infrastructure;

    *   risk management systems;

    *   internal audit functions; and

    *   investment management.

2. As part of assessing the affect of the outsourcing arrangements on the audit, auditors obtain an understanding of the way the insurer monitors those activities so as to ensure that it meets its fiduciary and other legal responsibilities. The absence of appropriate procedures may lead to a duty to report to the regulator.

3. Evidence obtained by auditors may include evaluation of these procedures, whether operated by the insurer's own staff or those of the agent. Alternatively, auditors may rely on work performed by internal audit or other compliance staff or instruct another firm of auditors to undertake work on their behalf, under guidance provided in relation to SAS 500 'Considering the work of internal audit' and SAS 510 'The relationship between principal auditor and other auditors' respectively.

Using the Work of Others

SAS 520: Using the Work of an Expert

Background note

SAS 520 establishes standards and provides guidance on using the work of an expert to obtain audit evidence.

1. The preparation of an insurer's financial statements frequently involves a need for the directors to obtain advice from experts, including:

    - property valuers and investment managers, in assessing the values of the insurer's investments at the balance sheet date;

    - loss adjustors and legal advisors, in determining the outcome of particular individual claims or portfolios of claims; and

    - statisticians and actuaries, in assessing the technical provisions required at the balance sheet date. In addition, authorised insurers undertaking life assurance business are required by statute to have an Appointed Actuary.

Using the work of an actuary

2. In conducting an audit of an insurer's financial statements, auditors may consider evidence provided by an actuary concerning the extent and adequacy of technical provisions included in those financial statements.

3. The involvement of an actuary in determining or advising on provisions to be included in an insurer's financial statements does not alter the responsibility of its directors to prepare financial statements which comply with relevant requirements and give a true and fair view of the insurer's profit or loss and its state of affairs. Similarly, the auditors remain solely responsible for conducting an audit of the insurer's financial statements, including meeting the requirements of Auditing Standards in the conduct of their work, and for expressing an independent opinion on them.

4. In applying the requirements of SAS 520 to technical provisions of an insurer computed, or reported on, by an actuary, auditors give particular attention to:

    (a) the formal lines of responsibility defined by the insurer between the board of directors and the actuary;

    (b) the independence of the actuary, their knowledge of the portfolio of business for which provision is being made and their experience of the market in which the insurer operates;

(c)   the role of the actuary whose work they aim to use and the scope of the work undertaken. The actuary's work may be performed in accordance with regulatory or legal requirements or specific engagement instructions; and

(d)   the approach which the actuary proposes to adopt in calculating provisions.

5.   In order to form an audit opinion on the financial statements, auditors need to understand, assess and, if appropriate, challenge the assumptions underlying the work of the actuary.

6.   In assessing the appropriateness of the actuary's work as audit evidence, auditors may consider it appropriate to:

(a)   make enquiries regarding any procedures undertaken by the actuary to establish whether the source data used is relevant, sufficient and reliable;

(b)   review or test data used by the actuary; and

(c)   assess the assumptions and computations used including the reasons for any changes in assumptions or computations compared with those used in prior periods.

7.   Auditors consider whether the assumptions and methods are reasonable, based on their knowledge of the business and the results of other audit procedures, and are compatible with those used for the preparation of the financial statements. If the auditors conclude that the assumptions or methods used by the actuary are not appropriate or consistent with other audit evidence, they discuss the circumstances with the actuary and, if appropriate, with the directors. Applying additional procedures, including possibly engaging another expert, may assist in resolving any apparent inconsistency.

8.   If the auditors are not satisfied that the work of an actuary provides sufficient appropriate audit evidence and there is no satisfactory alternative source of audit evidence, they consider the implications for their report.

9.   Auditors normally do not undertake work to provide the directors or actuary with assurance concerning the adequacy of source data used by the actuary. If the actuary wishes to place reliance on work performed by the auditor, the scope of this work is agreed in a separate formal engagement letter.

Life assurance business

10.   Regulation 26(4) of Chapter 3 of the European Communities (Insurance Undertakings: Accounts) Regulations 1996, which give effect to the EU Insurance Accounts Directive, provides that the computation of the life assurance provision in the financial statements 'shall be made on the basis of recognised actuarial methods annually by a Fellow Member of the Society of Actuaries in Ireland, with due regard to the actuarial principles laid down in Council Directive 92/96/EEC'. The reporting actuary for this purpose will usually be, but is not required to be, the company's Appointed Actuary. In

carrying out the annual valuation for the regulatory returns, the Appointed Actuary is required to comply with Guidance Notes 'Actuaries and Long Term Insurance Business (GN1 ROI)' and 'Additional Guidance for Appointed Actuaries (GN8 ROI)'. The statutory duty of the actuary in relation to the annual valuation does not extend to any technical provisions other than the life assurance provision.

11. For the purposes of expressing an opinion as required by the provisions of the European Communities (Insurance Undertakings: Accounts) Regulations, 1996 , auditors of an authorised insurer undertaking life assurance business take responsibility for expressing an opinion on the financial statements as a whole and, in doing so, form a view on the amount of the life assurance business provision and, accordingly, as to whether the calculation of the provision is appropriately made in the context of the financial statements. It will normally be appropriate for auditors to liaise with the any actuary concerned in order to plan their work.

12. Auditors obtain sufficient appropriate audit evidence that the actuary's scope of work is adequate for the purposes of their audit. The auditor will understand the approach which the actuary proposes to adopt in calculating the life assurance business provision. Whilst the statutory role of the actuary is restricted to the calculation of the life assurance business provision, actuaries are also frequently involved in calculating other balances such as the technical provisions for linked liabilities and the asset for deferred acquisition costs (including advising on the basis of amortisation). In order to obtain a detailed understanding of the effect of the underlying assumptions, auditors may review the results of projections prepared by the insurer which assess the effect of different possible assumptions or, where appropriate, re-perform projections using different assumptions.

13. Usually the life assurance business provision is derived from the mathematical reserves established by the Appointed Actuary for the purposes of regulatory returns. In such circumstances, auditors follow the guidance set out above to those reserves in considering the appropriateness of the amount of the life assurance business provision.

14. Auditors consider the Appointed Actuary's view of the future development of the fund and the risks to which it is exposed. Auditors normally discuss the authorised insurance company's financial condition with the Appointed Actuary as part of the audit of the financial statements. Auditors normally obtain a copy of the financial condition report (where prepared) and of any correspondence between the Appointed Actuary and the regulator.

Non-life insurance business

15. There is currently no statutory requirement for actuaries to be involved in the preparation of financial statements of non-life business insurance companies. Nonetheless, actuaries are frequently involved in assessing the claims outstanding provision and the unexpired risk provision. Furthermore the regulator will require an annual actuarial certification in respect of most non-life insurer's reserves to accompany the annual insurance return.

16. If an actuary has prepared a formal report on the technical provisions or on the financial soundness of a non-life insurance undertaking or has, before the auditor reports on the financial statements, prepared the certificate to accompany the annual insurance return, the auditor, where appropriate, reviews the report or reports to gain a better understanding of the scope of the work performed and of any limitations on any opinions expressed. If an actuary's report or certificate has not been prepared, it is necessary for auditors to ensure that the reliance on the work of the actuary reflects only such work undertaken by the actuary which is clearly defined. This is communicated by the auditor to the actuary concerned.

17. Due to the range of uncertainty inherent in the assumptions used to estimate the provisions for outstanding claims for non-life business insurance, particularly those established on a statistical basis and those associated with long tail claims, auditors consider the basis of the calculations and the sensitivity and validity of the underlying assumptions, including those related to discounting, if relevant, made by the actuary.

Reporting

SAS 600: Auditors' Reports on Financial Statements

Background note

The SAS requires that an auditors' report on financial statements should contain a clear expression of opinion, based on review and assessment of the conclusions drawn from the evidence obtained in the course of the audit.

The SAS requires that an auditors' report on the financial statements should include, as basic elements, the following:

(a) a title identifying the person or persons to whom the report is addressed;

(b) an introductory paragraph identifying the financial statements audited;

(c) separate sections, appropriately headed, dealing with:

  − *the respective responsibilities of directors, or equivalent persons, and auditors;*

  − *the basis of the auditors' opinion; and*

  − *the auditors' opinion on the financial statements.*

(d) the manuscript or printed signature of the auditors; and

(e) the date of the auditors' report.

In forming an opinion on the financial statements, the SAS requires that auditors should consider whether the view given by the financial statements could be affected by inherent uncertainties, which, in their opinion, are fundamental.

When an inherent uncertainty exists which:

(a) in the auditors' opinion is fundamental; and

(b) is adequately accounted for and disclosed in the financial statements,

the auditors should include an explanatory paragraph referring to the fundamental uncertainty in the section of their report setting out the basis of their opinion. When adding an explanatory paragraph, auditors should use words which clearly indicate that their opinion on the financial statements is not qualified in respect of its contents.

The SAS requires that auditors do not express an opinion on financial statements until those financial statements and all other financial information contained in a report of which the audited financial statements form a part have been approved by the directors, and the auditors have considered all necessary available evidence. The date of an auditors' report on a reporting entity's financial statements is the date on which the auditors signed their report expressing an opinion on those statements.

If the auditors disagree with the accounting or disclosures in the financial statements, or the scope of their work is limited so as to prevent them obtaining access to evidence reasonably expected to be available, the SAS requires them to issue a qualified opinion.

1. SAS 600 requires auditors' reports on financial statements to contain a clear expression of opinion based on review and assessment of the conclusions drawn from the evidence obtained in the course of the audit. Requirements of SAS 600 apply to reports on financial statements of insurance companies and statutory requirements affect the form of the auditors' report as discussed below.

2. Auditors of insurance companies, in common with other types of companies, are required to give an opinion as to whether the insurance company's financial statements give a true and fair view of its profit or loss and state of affairs. In forming their opinion, auditors take account of relevant accounting requirements. In determining whether a true and fair view is given, two particular issues may arise:

    (a) the treatment of inherent uncertainties; and

    (b) the inclusion of statutory equalisation reserves in financial statements of authorised insurers in a limited number of instances.

3. Financial statements of insurance companies are required by the Companies Acts, 1963 to 2001 and the European Communities (Insurance Undertakings: Accounts) Regulations, 1996 to give a true and fair view and comply with the requirements of this

legislation. Compliance with applicable financial reporting and accounting standards and UITF abstracts issued by the ASB is normally necessary to meet this requirement.

Inherent uncertainties

4.   The basis on which an insurance company's financial statements are prepared takes account of the extent of uncertainty inherent in the types of insurance business it underwrites. In the context of life assurance business, the outcome of inherent uncertainties existing at the reporting date can normally be estimated using statistical techniques. Financial statements of an authorised insurer undertaking life assurance business are therefore required to include a provision, determined by the company's Appointed Actuary, that takes into account risks and uncertainties at the reporting date, and to disclose the principal assumptions underlying the provision. In most circumstances, no further detailed disclosures of uncertainties are necessary in order to give a true and fair view.

5.   There are two acceptable bases for accounting for non-life business insurance transactions:

(a)   **the annual basis**, under which the underwriting result disclosed in the financial statements comprises the result for the current accounting period and any adjustments during the current accounting period to estimates used in prior accounting periods; or

(b)   **the fund basis**, under which a fund is created for each underwriting year to which written premiums for policies or contracts incepting that year are allocated, together with related claims and other expenditure. The recognition of profit on business written is deferred until sufficient information is available to provide reasonable certainty as to the profits (if any), which should be no later than the end of the third year following the inception of the underwriting year. Use of the fund basis is restricted to circumstances in which the annual basis is inappropriate because delays in the receipt of information concerning the results of underwriting business make it impracticable to prepare meaningful financial statements on the annual basis. This basis is therefore used in circumstances when the degree of inherent uncertainty is relatively high.

6.   When the fund basis is used, the reason for its adoption should be disclosed together with the categories of business accounted for in this way and the period before which any underwriting profit is recognised in respect of an underwriting year.

7.   Auditors reporting on financial statements of insurance companies undertaking non-life insurance business therefore consider:

(a)   whether appropriate disclosures have been made; and

(b)   when the fund basis is used, whether these disclosures are adequate and reflect relevant pronouncements of the Accounting Standards Board. Auditors consider, in particular, whether the explanation of reasons for using the fund basis provide a reader of the financial statements with sufficient information to appreciate the degree of risks involved. If the auditors disagree with disclosures relating to uncertainties and consider that the effect is material to the view given by the financial statements, they are required by SAS 600.8 to qualify their opinion.

8. Determining technical provisions is subject to a high degree of inherent uncertainty and frequently involves statistical techniques. When reporting on an insurer's financial statements, auditors assess whether such uncertainties fall within the category of fundamental, and so require to be disclosed in their report. In making this assessment, auditors take into account whether the financial statements provide a user with general information about the types of business written such that the overall level of inherent uncertainty likely to apply to those financial statements is apparent.

9. In addition to uncertainties arising from the types of insurance underwritten, there may be other uncertainties which the auditors conclude are fundamental to the view given by the financial statements or to which they wish to draw attention in their report (as envisaged by paragraph 29 of SAS 600). Such uncertainties may include:

- the outcome of legal disputes;

- the financial effect of regulatory action; and

- the outcome of disputes with reinsurers or counterparties to particular insurance contracts.

Statutory equalisation reserves

10. The European Communities (Non-life Insurance) (Amendment) Regulations 1991 (SI 5 of 1991), set out the type of non-life insurance business (Class 14 Credit Business) in respect of which equalisation reserves are required to be established and maintained by authorised insurers and the formulae to be used in calculating the amount of such reserves.

11. The European Communities (Insurance Undertakings: Accounts) Regulations, 1996 require equalisation reserves to be included in an authorised insurer's balance sheet as part of 'technical provisions' under the general heading 'liabilities' (Balance sheet format, item C5 and the related note 28). However, such equalisation reserves are not 'liabilities' as normally defined for the purposes of accounting standards.

12. Financial statements incorporating equalisation reserves should disclose:

(a) that the amounts provided are in addition to the provision required to meet the anticipated ultimate cost of settlement of outstanding claims at the balance sheet date, and that notwithstanding this, the European Communities (Insurance Undertakings: Accounts) Regulations, 1996 require the amounts to be included within technical provisions; and

(b) the impact of equalisation reserves on shareholders' funds and the effect of movements in the provisions on the results of the accounting period (and, if appropriate, an alternative earnings per share figure disregarding equalisation reserves).

13. Provided that adequate disclosure is made in financial statements which contain statutory equalisation reserves (and in the absence of other reasons to conclude that the financial statements do not give a true and fair view), it is appropriate to regard the financial statements incorporating such equalisation reserves as giving, in the particular circumstances, the required true and fair view. Consequently, unless special circumstances exist which are particular to the company or group concerned, auditors are justified in concluding that financial statements including such reserves give a true and fair view, and in expressing an unqualified opinion to that effect.

14. Notwithstanding that an unqualified opinion is expressed, it is appropriate for auditors to include reference to the particular legal requirements concerning equalisation reserves in their report, when the effect of those reserves is material to an insurance company's financial statements, in order to ensure that a reader is aware that their opinion is expressed in the context of those requirements.

15. Illustrative wording of such a paragraph to be included within the 'Basis of Audit Opinion' section of the audit report is as follows:

'Our evaluation of the presentation of information in the financial statements has had regard to the statutory requirement for insurance companies to maintain equalisation reserves in certain circumstances. The nature of the equalisation reserves, the amount set aside at (date), and the effect of the movement in those reserves during the year on the non-life business technical result and profit (loss) before tax, are disclosed in notes ...and ...respectively.'

SAS 610 (Revised): Communication of Audit Matters to Those Charged with Governance

Background note

SAS 610 requires that auditors communicate relevant matters relating to the audit of financial statements to those charged with governance. Such communications should be on a sufficiently prompt basis to enable appropriate action to be taken.

The SAS requires that auditors should plan with those charged with governance the form and timing of communications to them and determine whether there are particular persons to whom they should communicate certain matters.

1. If auditors of authorised insurers discover weaknesses in systems of control in the course of their work, they consider whether the circumstances raise doubt concerning compliance with regulatory requirements for accounting records and controls necessary to meet the requirement to have sound and adequate administrative and accounting procedures and internal control mechanisms.

2. Factors indicating a possible breach of the requirements to have sound and adequate procedures, records and controls which are likely to be of material significance to the regulator hence give rise to a duty (under section 35 of the Insurance Act, 1989) to report to the regulator. In addition (unless precluded by the requirement of SAS 620.6) the auditors take steps to bring the issues concerned to the attention of the board and audit committee of the insurance company.

3. Any communication to directors is confidential information. Thus auditors require the prior consent of the directors if they are to provide a copy of a communication to directors to a third party. This may be dealt with in the engagement letter. The DETE, as part of their on-site supervisory visits, may examine auditors' communications to directors or management. Against this background, auditors may consider it prudent to include in such reports to directors or management, as a matter of course, a statement that:

    (a) the report has been prepared for the sole use of the entity;

    (b) it must not be disclosed to another third party, or quoted or referred to, without the written consent of the auditors;

    (c) no responsibility is assumed by the auditors to any other person; and

    (d) it does not purport to be a comprehensive record of all matters arising, risks or internal control weaknesses in the entity.

SAS 620: The Auditors' Right and Duty to Report to Regulators

Background note

SAS 620 'The auditors' right and duty to report to regulators in the financial sector' establishes standards and provides guidance on the circumstances in which the auditors of an entity carrying on business in the financial sector report direct to a regulator.

The overall requirement of the SAS is as follows:

'Auditors of regulated entities bring information of which they have become aware in the ordinary course of performing work undertaken to fulfil their audit responsibilities to the attention of the appropriate regulator without delay when:

(a) they conclude that it is relevant to the regulator's functions having regard to such matters as may be specified in statute or any related regulations; and

(b) in their opinion there is reasonable cause to believe that it is or may be of material significance to the regulator. (SAS 620.1)'

There is no statutory 'right' for auditors to report to the regulator in Irish legislation.

1. The general requirement of SAS 620 is that auditors of regulated entities bring information of which they have become aware in the ordinary course of their work to the attention of the appropriate regulator when:

    • they conclude that it is relevant to the regulator's functions having regard to such matters as may be specified in statute or any related regulations; and

    • in their opinion there is reasonable cause to believe it may be of material significance to the regulator.

    However this general requirement must be considered in light of the specific provisions of section 35 of the Insurance Act,1989.

2. SAS 620 indicates that auditors of regulated entities may have special reporting responsibilities in addition to their responsibility to report on the financial statements and annual regulatory returns. These may take two forms:

    • a statutory **duty** to report certain information, relevant to the regulated activities of the insurer, that come to the auditors' attention in the course of their audit work; and

    • a statutory **right** to bring information to the attention of the regulator in particular circumstances which lie outside those giving rise to a statutory duty to initiate a direct report.

    A statutory **right** to report is not provided for under Irish insurance legislation. Therefore, auditors of Irish authorised insurers need only consider SAS 620 in the context of their **duty** to report.

The duty to report

3. The duty to report to the regulator does not require auditors to undertake additional work directed at identifying matters of material significance over and above that which are necessary to fulfil their obligations under the:

    • Companies Acts, 1963 to 2001;

    • European Communities (Insurance Undertakings: Accounts) Regulations, 1996;

    • European Communities (Non-life Insurance) Framework Regulations, 1994;

    • European Communities (Non-life Insurance Accounts) Regulations, 1995; and

    • European Communities (Life Assurance) Framework Regulations, 1994

    and any acts or instruments amending or supplementing these acts and regulations.

4. The regulator expects the primary source of information with regard to an authorised insurer to be the insurer itself. The normal reporting procedures will usually provide all the information necessary for the regulator to discharge its responsibilities.

5. Irish insurance legislation imposes a duty on auditors of authorised insurers to report in certain circumstances to the regulator.

    Section 35 of the Insurance Act, 1989 as amended by Regulation 5 of the European Communities (Non-life Insurance and Life Assurance) Framework (Amendment) Regulations, 1997, (the Post BCCI Regulations) sets out the circumstances in which auditors have a duty to report to the regulator.

    Section 35(1) places a duty on an auditor to report directly to the Minister in writing and without delay in circumstances where the auditor:

    (a) has reason to believe that there exist circumstances which are likely to affect materially the insurer's ability to fulfil its obligations to policyholders or meet any of its material financial requirements under the Insurance Acts; or

    (b) has reason to believe that there are material defects in the financial systems and controls or accounting records of the insurer which are likely to have that effect; or

    (c) proposes to qualify any certificate which he is to provide in relation to financial statements or returns of the insurer under the Companies Acts or Insurance Acts; or

    (d) decides to resign or not seek re-election as auditor;or

    (e) becomes aware of any facts or decisions which are likely to affect materially the insurer's ability to fulfil its obligations to policyholders or meet any of its material financial requirements under the Insurance Acts in the course of conducting an audit in an undertaking in a control relationship with the insurer.

6. Section 35(3) of the Insurance Act, 1989 provides that the Minister 'may require an auditor of an insurer to supply him with such information as he may specify in relation to the audit of the business of the insurer and the auditor shall comply with the requirement.'

7. Where auditors are reporting under Section 35(3) they specifically state that the information is supplied for the purposes of Section 35 (3) and that the information is commercially sensitive. Where they are reporting under section 35(3) in respect of an incomplete audit they emphasise that the report has been prepared on audit work to date and that the audit has not yet concluded.

8. When auditors receive a request from the regulator for information, consequent to section 35(3), they seek to ensure that they are in a position to inform the insurer of the request. A meeting between the auditors and the regulator will normally be necessary to clarify the specific information requested. The auditors consider whether the insurer

is invited to the meeting, unless the regulator specifically requires otherwise (as permitted by section 35(3)). If deemed appropriate, the auditors may furnish the insurer with a copy of all or part of the written response to the regulator, unless, as stated in section 35(3), the Minister requires that in supplying such information the auditor shall act independently of the insurer.

9. Where the regulator requests information about detailed audit procedures in specific areas, any written reply will emphasise that the auditors form their professional opinion on the basis of all the work carried out and all the information received during the audit, and not just on the basis of one or more tests in a specific area. The auditors' written response also states that the requested information is supplied on a confidential basis and on the understanding that it is not divulged to parties other than the regulator.

10. Auditors may not disclose information communicated to them by the regulator except with the regulator's express permission and, in some cases that of other parties to which the information relates, other than to partners and staff who need to be aware of the information in connection with the firm's performance as auditors.

11. Section 35(5) of the Insurance Act, 1989 affords protection to auditors in their communications with the Minister under section 35. This subsection states that:

> 'No duty to which an auditor of the insurer may be subject shall be regarded as contravened and no liability to the insurer, or to its shareholders, creditors, or other interested parties shall attach to the auditor, by reason of his compliance with any obligation imposed on him by or under this section'.

12. The Minister's powers under section 35(3) are restricted to information regarding 'the audit of the business of the insurer...'. Furthermore, the protection given to auditors by section 35(5), when making a report under section 35(3) is restricted to disclosure of information in their capacity as auditors of the insurer and in relation to the audit of the business of the insurer. Auditors consider carefully the nature and extent of information to be provided to the Minister, taking into account:

    (a) their duty of confidentiality to the insurer concerned; and

    (b) whether the matters concerned fall within the protection available in responding to the questions from the Minister.

13. There are circumstances in which section 35(5) will not provide protection, for example, where they could be held to have acted in bad faith or maliciously under section 35(1) or where they have supplied information following a request from the Minister which is outside the scope of section 35(3). Section 35(5) does not therefore provide auditors with complete immunity from legal action by any parties affected, or subsequently affected, by the auditors' action in reporting to the Minister.

    Auditors may therefore wish to consider taking legal or other professional advice from an appropriately qualified source before making the decision whether, or in what manner, to report. However, it should be borne in mind that speed of reporting may well be important to the regulator in order to allow it to protect the interests of existing and prospective policyholders.

Closely linked entities

14. Regulation 5 of the European Communities (Non-life Insurance and Life Assurance) Framework (Amendment) Regulations, 1997 amends section 35 by extending the duty to report to the Minister information of which auditors become aware in the context of their work as auditors of an entity which is in a 'control relationship' with the insurance company.

   An insurance company is in a 'control relationship' with:

   (a) any person who is, or if he were an undertaking would be, its parent undertaking;

   (b) any undertaking which is its subsidiary undertaking;

   (c) any undertaking which is, or if any person falling within (a) were an undertaking would be, a fellow subsidiary undertaking; and

   (d) any person in accordance with whose directions or instructions its directors are accustomed to act.

15. Auditors establish during audit planning whether the insurer has one or more closely linked entities of which the audit firm is also the auditor. If there are such entities the auditors consider the significance of the closely linked entities and the nature of the issues that might arise which may give rise to a duty on the auditors to report in accordance with Section 35 (1) of the Insurance Act, 1989 if the auditor becomes aware of any facts or decisions which are likely to affect materially the insurers ability to fulfil its obligations to policyholders or meet any of its material financial obligations under the Insurance Acts.

16. The audit engagement partner communicates to the audit engagement partner of the closely linked entity the audit firm's responsibilities to report to the regulator and notifies him of the circumstances that have been identified which, if they exist, might be of material significance to the regulator of the regulated entity. Prior to completion the auditors of the regulated entity obtain details from the auditors of the closely linked entity of such circumstances or confirmation, usually in writing, that such circumstances do not exist.

17. No duty to report is imposed on auditors of an entity closely linked to a regulated entity who are not also auditors of the regulated entity.

18. In circumstances where they are not also the auditors of the closely linked entity, the auditors of the insurer decide whether there are any matters to be reported to the regulator relating to the affairs of the insurer in the light of the information that they receive about a closely linked entity for the purpose of auditing the financial statements of the insurer, If the auditors become aware of possible matters that may fall due to be reported, they may wish to obtain further information from the management or auditors

of the closely linked entity to ascertain whether the matter should be reported. To facilitate such possible discussions, at the planning stage of the audit, the auditors of the insurer will have considered whether arrangements need to be in place to allow them to communicate with the management and the auditors of the closely linked entity. If the auditors of the insurer are unable to communicate with the management and auditors of the closely linked entity to obtain further information concerning the matters they have identified and if the matters identified give rise to a duty to report in relation to the insurer under Section 35 of the Insurance Act, 1989 they report the matters, and that they have been unable to obtain further information, direct to the regulator.

19.   Section 35(5) of the Insurance Act, 1989 provides protection in certain circumstance. There may be no legal protection where auditors are reporting on matters of which they became aware in the context of their work as auditors of an entity which is in a control relationship with an insurance company.

Matters of material significance to the regulator

20.   The inclusion in the paragraphs following of guidance on matters which the regulator might consider to be of material significance is not intended to imply that these matters will necessarily be covered in the normal audit. However auditors ensure that members of their staff undertaking work on an engagement as auditors of an authorised insurer (or, where relevant, as auditors of an entity with which the insurer is closely linked by control) when performing this work are able to recognise that they are required to report and that such matters are reported to the audit engagement partner of the insurer without delay.

Auditors are not expected to be aware of all circumstances which, had they known of them, would have led them to report to the regulator. Their obligation is limited to reporting those matters which come to their attention in the course of their work, and they are not expected to seek out matters that they are required to report to the regulator.

In circumstances where auditors identify that a reportable matter may exist they carry out such extra work as they consider necessary to determine whether facts and circumstances cause them to have reason to believe that the matter does in fact exist.

21.   A matter or group of matters is of material significance to a regulator's function when, due either to its nature or its potential financial impact, it is likely of itself to require investigation by the regulator[26]. The term 'material significance' when applied to matters arising from audits of insurers which may give rise to a duty to report to the regulator under section 35 of the Insurance Act, 1989 requires interpretation.

22.   'Material significance' does not have the same meaning as materiality in a normal auditing context. However, where quantitative aspects are being considered, the

---

[26]   SAS 620.14.

factors which need to be taken into account will be similar to those relevant to audit materiality in the context of financial statements.

23. The determination of whether a matter is likely to be of material significance inevitably requires auditors to exercise their judgement. Auditors base their judgement of 'material significance' solely on their understanding of the facts of which they are aware without making any assumptions about the information available to the regulator in connection with any insurer.

24. Whilst a particular event may be trivial when judged in purely financial terms, it may nevertheless be of a nature or of a type which is likely to change the perception of the regulator. For example, a small change may result in a particular solvency requirement being breached which, whilst not material in relation to other amounts in the financial statements, may be significant to the regulator.

25. SAS 620 notes that an apparent breach of statutory or regulatory requirements may not necessarily give rise to a duty to report and that there will normally be a need for some further investigation and discussion of the surrounding circumstances in order to determine whether a duty to report arises. In such investigations the auditors need not obtain the degree of evidence which would be a normal part of forming an opinion on financial statements; however, sufficient information to determine whether the matter is or may be of material significance to the regulator is necessary. Accordingly, although the duty to report may extend to information concerning the exposure of the auditors' client to another entity such as a reinsurer, a duty to report would not normally arise from matters such as unsubstantiated market rumours about a reinsurer with whom the insurer being audited places business. Such information is unlikely to form an acceptable standard of evidence and the auditors would be unlikely to have access to sufficient information about the reinsurer to form a proper judgement about the matter.

26. SAS 620 goes on to set out a number of detailed requirements within the general requirement set out above including:

- in gaining a knowledge of the business for the purposes of the audit, auditors of a regulated entity should obtain an understanding of its current activities, the scope of its authorisation and the effectiveness of its control environment;

- audit staff should have an understanding of applicable legislation, the role of the regulator and any guidance issued by the regulator and any specific requirements applicable to the particular entity appropriate to their role and sufficient (in the context of that role) to identify situations which may give reasonable cause to believe that a matter should be reported to the regulator;

- the steps to be taken where an apparent breach of requirements comes to the auditors' attention; and

- the timing and form of the auditors' report to the regulator.

Further guidance on the auditors' consideration of matters of material significance is set out in Appendix 1.

27. On completion of their investigations regarding matters which many need to be reported to the regulator, auditors ensure that the facts and circumstances, and the basis for their conclusion as to whether these are, or are likely to be, material matters which are required to be reported under Section 35, are adequately documented such that the reasons for their decision to report or not, as the case may be, may be clearly demonstrated should the need to do so arise in future.

Communications with auditors by the regulator

28. The regulator is mindful of the role of auditors and the supervisory benefits of close cooperation. The regulator has confirmed that, in appropriate cases, it will consider informing auditors of factors which may be relevant to their functions where there is no prohibition either in statute or in the common law relating to confidentiality.

29. Where such a matter has been brought to the attention of auditors, there may be implications for the conduct of their audit work and they may need to amend their approach accordingly. However, the fact that they may have been informed of a matter by the regulator does not, of itself, require auditors to change the scope of their work, nor does it necessarily require them to search actively for evidence in support of the situation communicated by the regulator.

30. The regulator has indicated that, for the avoidance of doubt, it still requires auditors to report matters of material significance which have occurred and of which the regulator is already aware, whether directly reported by the insurer or otherwise, and which may have been corrected. Normally such a report will refer to the earlier report from the insurer, where relevant, providing the auditors consider that it fully describes the matter concerned.

31. Accordingly in determining whether to make a report to the regulator, auditors will need to have regard to those matters, if any, which the regulator has brought to their attention. In considering what may be of material significance to the regulator, auditors will need to base their judgement on information which is available to them in their capacity as auditors without any regard to matters of which the regulator may independently be aware.

32. Auditors need to be aware that there are situations in which the regulator may conduct inquiries or investigations but about which neither they nor the particular insurer which they audit will necessarily be aware, since the regulator may decide not to take any action. Therefore, apparent inaction by the regulator should not be interpreted as meaning that a matter is not likely to be of material significance.

Discussing matters of material significance with the directors

33. The directors are the persons principally responsible for the management of the regulated entity. Auditors will therefore normally bring a matter of material significance to the attention of the directors and seek agreement on the facts and circumstances. Where the auditors conclude that a duty to report arises they should bring the matter to the attention of the regulator without delay. The directors may wish to report the matters identified to the regulator themselves and detail the actions taken or to be

taken. Whilst such a report from the directors may provide valuable information, it does not relieve the auditors of the statutory duty to report directly to the regulator.

Conduct of the audit

34. SAS 620.3 requires that all staff involved in an audit of a regulated entity should have an understanding of:

    (a) the provisions of applicable legislation;

    (b) the regulator's rules and any guidance issued by the regulator; and

    (c) any specific requirements which apply to the particular regulated entity,

    appropriate to their role in the audit in the context of that audit and sufficient to enable them to identify situations they encounter in the course of the audit which may give them reasonable grounds to believe that a matter should be reported to the regulator'.

35. As a minimum this understanding should extend to:

    (a) the provisions of section 35 of the Insurance Act, 1989, as amended by Regulation 5 of the European Communities (Non-life Insurance and Life Assurance) Framework (Amendment) Regulations, 1997; and

    (b) the contents of SAS 620 and this Practice Note.

36. Further understanding, commensurate with the individual's role and responsibilities in the audit process, may be required of the provisions of the following:

    •   The Insurance Acts, 1909 to 2000;

    •   European Communities (Non-life Insurance) Framework Regulations, 1994;

    •   European Communities (Non-life Insurance) Accounts Regulations, 1995;

    •   European Communities (Life Assurance) Framework Regulations, 1994;

    •   European Communities (Non-life Insurance and Life Assurance) Framework (Amendment) Regulations, 1997;

    •   European Communities (Insurance Undertakings: Accounts) Regulations, 1996;

    •   European Communities (Supplementary Supervision of Insurance Undertakings in an Insurance Group) Regulations, 1999;

    •   Life Assurance (Provision of Information) Regulations, 2001; and

    •   Guidelines issued by the regulator.

THE AUDITING PRACTICES BOARD

A complete listing of Irish Insurance Acts, Regulations and Guidelines as at 31 May 2002 issued by the regulator is set out at Appendix 5.

37. Auditors will also need to request from the insurer a copy of any relevant directions received from the regulator under Articles 3(2) of both the European Communities (Non-life Insurance) Framework Regulations, 1994 and the European Communities (Life Assurance) Framework Regulations, 1994.

38. Auditors include procedures within their planning process to ensure that members of the audit team have such understanding (in the context of their role) as to enable them to recognise potentially reportable matters, and that such matters are reported to the audit engagement partner without delay so that a decision may be made as to whether a duty to report arises.

Timing of a report

39. The duty to report arises once auditors have concluded that they reasonably believe that the matter is reportable under Section 35. In reaching their conclusion auditors may wish to take appropriate legal or other advice and consult with colleagues.

Information received in a capacity other than as auditor

40. There may be circumstances where it is not clear whether information about a regulated entity coming to the attention of the auditors is received in the capacity of auditor or in some other capacity, for example as a general adviser to the entity. Appendix 2 to SAS 620 provides guidance as to how information obtained in non-audit work may be relevant to the auditors in the planning and conduct of the audit and the steps that need to be taken to ensure the communication of information that is relevant to the audit.

Reporting on Regulatory Returns

1.   Auditors of authorised insurers are required to report on specified matters in relation to returns required from the insurer by the regulator. This section sets out guidance for auditors reporting on regulatory returns of authorised insurers.

2.   Auditors reporting on an insurer's regulatory returns normally also carry out an audit of its financial statements in accordance with Auditing Standards. Accordingly, the work that auditors perform on regulatory returns does not represent a second audit carried out in accordance with Auditing Standards, but represents a set of additional procedures which, in conjunction with the evidence drawn from the audit work carried out in relation to the financial statements, will enable them to report as required. When undertaking such additional procedures, auditors have regard to the general principles set out below.

3.   Auditors of authorised insurers have a duty to report direct to the regulator if they become aware, in the course of their work relating either to their report on an insurer's financial statements or to their report on its regulatory returns, of matters that they conclude are or may be of material significance to the regulator. Auditors fulfil this duty in accordance with the requirements of SAS 620 'The auditors' right and duty to report to regulators'.

General Principles

4.   The general principles applicable to reporting on regulatory returns are as follows:

   •   Auditors plan the work to be undertaken in relation to the regulatory returns so as to perform that work in an effective manner, taking into account their other reporting responsibilities.

   •   Auditors familiarise themselves with the regulations governing the preparation of the regulatory returns.

   •   Auditors comply with ethical guidance issued by their relevant professional bodies.

   •   Auditors agree the terms of the engagement with the insurer and record them in writing.

   •   Auditors consider materiality and its relationship with the risk of material misstatement in the regulatory returns in planning their work and in determining the effect of their findings on their report.

   •   Auditors undertake their work with an attitude of professional scepticism and carry out procedures designed to obtain sufficient appropriate evidence on which to base their opinion on the regulatory returns. In particular they:

      (a)   perform procedures designed to obtain sufficient appropriate evidence that all material subsequent events up to the date of their report on the regulatory returns which require adjustment of, or disclosure in, the returns have been identified and properly reflected therein;

(b)   apply analytical procedures in forming an overall conclusion as to whether the parts of the regulatory returns on which they report are consistent with their knowledge of the insurer's business; and

(c)   obtain written confirmation of appropriate representations from management before their report is issued.

- Auditors record in their working papers

  (a)   details of the engagement planning;

  (b)   the nature, timing and extent of the procedures performed in relation to their report on the regulatory returns, and the conclusions drawn; and.

  (c)   their reasoning and conclusions on all significant matters which require the exercise of judgment.

- Auditors issue a report containing a clear expression of their opinion on the regulatory returns.

- Auditors consider the matters which have come to their attention while performing the procedures on the returns and whether they should be included in a report to directors or management.

- If the auditors become aware of matters of material significance to the regulator which they have a duty to report under section 35 of the Insurance Act, 1989, they make a report direct to the regulator. In addition, when issuing such a report on the regulatory returns, auditors:

  (a)   consider whether there are consequential reporting issues affecting their opinion which arise from any report previously made direct to the regulator in the course of their appointment; and

  (b)   assess whether any matters encountered in the course of their work indicate a need for a further direct report.

- Auditors take steps to ensure that any delegated work is directed, supervised and reviewed in a manner which provides reasonable assurance that such work is performed competently.

- Auditors reporting on regulatory returns which include financial information on which other auditors have reported obtain sufficient appropriate evidence that the work of those other auditors is adequate for their purposes.

Authorised insurers

5. An insurer authorised to carry on business in Ireland is required, in the case of a life insurer, under Regulation 13(1) of the European Communities (Life Assurance) Framework Regulations 1994; and in the case of a non-life insurer, under Regulation 3 of the European Communities (Non-life Insurance Accounts) Regulations 1995, to submit a return (the regulatory return) to the regulator, within six months of the end of each financial year. The format of this return is prescribed by the 1995 Non-life Insurance Accounts Regulations (Nonlife Regulations) and the 1994 Life Assurance Regulations (Life Regulations)[27]. Insurers are required to complete different forms, depending on whether their head office is in Ireland, in another EEA country, outside the EEA, or in Switzerland. Pure reinsurers are not required to make a return, and the returns of those branches whose head offices are in the EEA are not subject to audit.

The form and content

6. Section 11 of the Insurance Act, 1989 states that the Minister may require 'any return or document submitted to him to be attested by a person of professional standing specified by the Minister'; the 1994/95 Regulations define the forms subject to audit and set out the contents of the auditors' report. The requirements of the Life and Non-life Regulations are different, and different reports are required in each case. The Non-life Regulations do not specify a form of report, whilst the Life Regulations do. Certain of the forms in the returns are available to the public through the Companies Office. Certain other forms are summarised in the annual report issued by the regulator.

7. The regulatory return comprises the following central elements:

    (a) Profit and loss account and balance sheet of the insurer;

    (b) Detailed analyses of the business of the insurer;

    (c) Detailed analyses of the funds of life insurers;

    (d) Solvency calculations and restatements of the assets of the insurer for the purposes of solvency calculations;

    (e) Actuarial reports;

    (f) Certificates by the directors and Appointed Actuary; and

    (g) Report by the auditors.

    A list of the contents of the regulatory returns for both life and non-life insurers is set out in Appendix 2.

---

[27] These are referred to as the 1994/95 Regulations.

8. The requirement to prepare regulatory returns is quite separate from the requirement for an Irish insurer to prepare financial statements under the Companies Acts, 1963 to 2001 and the European Communities (Insurance Undertakings: Accounts) Regulations, 1996; furthermore, it is common for the regulatory returns to be prepared some time after the financial statements have been approved. There is, however, a close correlation between the overall figures included in the two documents.

9. The principal differences between the regulatory returns and financial statements, copies of which are also provided to the regulator, are as follows:

   (a) the regulatory returns are primarily intended to demonstrate the solvency of an insurer;

   (b) the assets and liabilities used in the solvency calculations in the regulatory return may be stated at different values from those shown in the financial statements, arising from the application of prescribed rules in respect of:

   – the basic valuation principles to be applied to assets;

   – restrictions on the value of assets where the value arrived at by applying the basic valuation principles exceeds the permitted asset limits,

   – the determination of liabilities;

   – the treatment of certain types of hybrid capital; and

   – a provision for adverse changes where certain commitments are not strictly matched.

   (c) the income statement, particularly for non-life business, provides a large volume of detailed segmental information including a breakdown into specified accounting classes;

   (d) additional information is provided on a variety of topics including: -the abstract of the Appointed Actuary's valuation report for life insurers; -the annual actuarial opinion required in respect of certain non-life insurers; -reinsurance arrangements; -major non-life business reinsurers; and -the use of derivatives.

   (e) the regulatory returns are accompanied by a certificate signed by prescribed officers of the insurer ('the directors' certificate') which contains a number of statements. Specimen directors' certificates are set out in Appendix 4.

Auditors' responsibilities

10. The regulatory returns for life and non-life insurers are governed by different regulations, and the requirements of each is significantly different. Part 1 of Schedule 3 to the 1994 Life Regulations sets out the main elements of the report required of auditors on the life assurance regulatory returns. The 1995 Non Life

Regulations do not specify any particular format, but only state that 'A statement attesting the correctness of the information appearing on the Balance Sheet, Profit and Loss Account, Asset Analysis, Assets/Liabilities Summary (as appropriate) should be signed by the insurers' auditors'. The detailed reporting requirements of life and non-life returns are set out in the life and non-life sections below.

Standards to be applied by auditors

11. In the case of an authorised insurer, an audit of the financial statements will be conducted in accordance with Auditing Standards to enable the report required by section 193 of the Companies Act, 1990 to be given. Key areas in which auditors need to undertake procedures additional to those undertaken to report on the financial statements are:

   (a) the application of the prescribed valuation and admissibility rules to assets and liabilities for which existence, title, etc. has already been considered as a part of the audit of the insurer's financial statements;

   (b) presentation of the information in the prescribed forms; and

   (c) the specific additional disclosures that fall within the scope of the auditors' report.

12. If an audit of financial statements in accordance with Auditing Standards has not been undertaken (as may be the case in relation to the Irish branch of an insurance company, incorporated outside Ireland) the principal components of the regulatory returns will need to have been subjected to an audit in accordance with those standards in order to achieve an equivalent standard of evidence.

13. Work specific to the auditors' report on an authorised insurers regulatory returns may be undertaken concurrently with procedures designed to provide evidence for their report on its financial statements or at a later date. In either case, the auditors consider both aspects of their engagement when planning the audit of the financial statements.

14. The 1994/1995 Regulations draw a clear distinction between those parts of the regulatory returns which are required to be referred to in the auditors' report and those which are not.

15. In the case of life insurers there is no requirement for the auditors to report on the Appointed Actuary's report; the fact that the auditors' responsibilities do not extend to this part of the regulatory return is reinforced by Part 1 of Schedule 3 to the 1994 Life Assurance Regulations which enables the auditors in their report to express reliance on the actuary's certificate for the mathematical reserves and required minimum solvency margin figures. Where auditors avail themselves of the entitlement, they are required to state in their report on the regulatory return the extent to which they have relied on the certificate given by the Appointed Actuary. In such circumstances it is not necessary for the auditors to read the parts of the return falling outside their reports, and their reports on the regulatory return do not provide assurance on the Appointed Actuary's assessment of the mathematical reserves in the regulatory return.

16. The Non-life Regulations require auditors to report only on the 'Balance Sheet, Profit and Loss account, Asset Analysis, Assets/Liabilities Summary' and not the directors' certificate or other forms. The guidelines issued by the regulator in July 2001 in regard to actuaries' opinions on non-life provisions do not require the auditor to report on actuarial opinions. The auditors responsibilities do not extend to the forms which fall outside the scope of their reports. However they read these forms with a view to considering the implications for their report if they become aware of any apparent misstatement or material inconsistencies with the forms on which they do report or if there is any indication of a situation which may give rise to a requirement to report under Section 35 of the Insurance Act, 1989.

17. The 1995 Non-life Regulations state that 'A statement attesting the correctness of the information appearing on the Balance Sheet, Profit and Loss Account, Asset Analysis, Assets/ Liabilities Summary (as appropriate) should be signed by the insurers' auditors'. Auditors' examinations of regulatory returns are of a similar qualitative standard to the requirement of company law that financial statements give a true and fair view of a company's state of affairs and profit and loss, hence equivalent considerations of materiality apply. In evaluating whether the requirements of the 1994/1995 Regulations have been met, auditors therefore apply materiality in relation to the business as a whole, rather than in relation to the particular accounting class, business category or risk group within which a particular item is reported, except when considering figures which are required by the 1994/1995 Regulations to be derived from a prescribed source elsewhere in the return, or to be calculated on a specified basis, when (other than rounding differences) no concept of materiality applies. Following this approach, reliance on analytical review techniques is normally appropriate in relation to the segmental information provided within the regulatory returns.

Reporting

18. Auditors' reports on regulatory returns normally include the following matters:

   (a) a title identifying the persons to whom the report is addressed (which will normally be the Minister);

   (b) an introductory paragraph identifying the documents within the regulatory return which are covered by the report;

   (c) separate sections, appropriately headed, dealing with:

   — respective responsibilities of the company and the auditors, and

   — the bases of the auditors' opinions;

   — the auditors' opinions on the matters required by statute;

   — the signature of the auditors; and

   — the date of the auditors' report.

19. Appendix 3 sets out illustrative examples of reports on regulatory returns for life and nonlife insurers. These example wordings need to be tailored to reflect particular circumstances.

Subsequent events

20. There may be a substantial period between the date on which an insurer's statutory financial statements are approved and the date on which its regulatory returns are signed. Auditors do not sign their report on regulatory returns before they have signed their audit report on the financial statements. Statement of Standard Accounting Practice 17 'Accounting for post-balance sheet events' requires that material events arising after the balance sheet date should be adjusted for where they provide additional evidence of conditions that existed at the balance sheet date and materially affect the amounts to be included in the financial statements. The issue is not dealt with specifically in the 1994/1995 Regulations, however the requirement is not that the regulatory returns agree with the financial statements but that they fairly state the assets and liabilities. In practice, regulatory returns are more likely to require a post-balance sheet adjustment in respect of a material change in the determination of liabilities (where more information has become available) than in the case of the valuation of assets. Auditors undertake a review of post-balance sheet events up to the date of their report on the regulatory returns before signing that report.

Qualifications or references to fundamental uncertainties

21. When reporting on an insurer's regulatory returns, auditors include references to fundamental uncertainties or qualify their opinions as appropriate, following the principles in SAS 600 'Auditors' reports on financial statements'. It is possible for the auditors' opinion in their report on an insurer's financial statements to be qualified whilst that in their report on an insurer's regulatory returns is unqualified, and vice versa. This may occur where the grounds for qualification relate to the treatment of a particular item (for example, if an asset is included in the regulatory returns at a value which does not take account of the specific requirements of Annex III of the 1994 Non-life Regulations and Annex V of the 1994 Life Regulations). Any qualification or fundamental uncertainty paragraph in respect of technical provisions would (in the absence of exceptional circumstances such as a Court judgement clarifying liability after the signing of the financial statements) be expected to be reflected in both reports.

Resubmitted returns

22. If an insurer intends to resubmit the regulatory returns, or part thereof, where the original regulatory returns are considered to be inaccurate or incomplete, the auditors may be required to express an opinion on the amended or additional material. This can be done by either:

(a) withdrawing the original report and issuing a completely new report; or

(b) issuing a supplementary report on the amended material only, but including a reference to the original report.

The first option is preferable where the nature and volume of changes required gives rise to a resubmission of the complete return. The second option is preferable where the amendments are considered to be relatively minor or are few in number and only the amended forms, supplementary notes and/or statements are resubmitted.

Life insurance Returns

23. The main elements required in the auditor's report on life assurance regulatory returns are;

    (a) an opinion on whether the parts of the returns which are required to be audited (Forms 1 to 21) have been properly prepared in accordance with the provisions of the 1994 Life Regulations;

    (b) an opinion on whether the directors' certificate has been properly prepared in accordance with the regulations and whether it was reasonable for the directors to make the statements contained within it ; and

    (c) reference to the reliance which the auditors have placed, in giving their opinion, on the Appointed Actuary's certificate with respect to the mathematical reserves and required minimum solvency margin, and on the identity and value of implicit items included in the return.

The directors' compliance certificates

24. The directors' certificates are required to include a series of statements confirming compliance with requirements of statute and regulations where such statements can truthfully be made. Some of the statements in the certificate relate to documents and other information on which auditors do not report. Auditors of life insurers are required to state in their report whether, in their opinion and according to the information and explanations that they have received:

    (a) the certificate has been properly prepared in accordance with the 1994 Life Regulations; and

    (b) it was or was not reasonable for the persons giving the certificate to have made the statements therein.

25. The directors' certificate for a life insurer is only required to include positive statements concerning those requirements with which the insurer complies. Where the directors cannot confirm a particular matter, they omit it and add a footnote stating that fact. However, they are not required to comment further on the factors giving rise to non-compliance. The auditors' responsibilities are to consider the reasonableness of the statements made and they have no obligation to report on omissions. However, the factors giving rise to the omission of a particular statement in the directors' certificate may give rise to a statutory duty to report direct to the regulator under section 35 of the Insurance Act, 1989.

26. Each paragraph of the directors' compliance certificate needs to be considered separately to determine whether the 'reasonable' opinion can be given, and the rationale for the conclusions reached are recorded in the working papers.

27. Appropriate audit procedures may include:

- inspecting correspondence with the regulator and minutes of management meetings in relation to regulatory matters;

- considering the quality of the evidence available to the directors responsible for making such statements of compliance;

- enquiring of the directors as to whether they are aware of any instances of noncompliance; and

- assessing whether the directors' statements of compliance are consistent with the knowledge gained from the audit work on the rest of the regulatory returns and, where applicable, on the financial statements.

28. Some of the statements call for little or no audit work in addition to that necessary to determine whether the forms and notes subject to audit have been properly prepared.

29. Other aspects, such as compliance with the matching and localisation rules, are not directly documented on the forms specified for audit, and the auditors need to obtain evidence of the currency position and its monitoring throughout the year if the statement of compliance is to be regarded as reasonable.

30. The directors' certificate contains a general statement that, in relation to the audited documents within the return, an appropriate system of control has been established and maintained by the company over its transactions and records. Whilst the audit of the insurer's financial statements does not necessarily include tests of internal controls, the understanding of the accounting and internal control systems required by SAS 300 'Accounting and internal control systems and audit risk assessments,' for the purpose of developing an effective approach to the audit of the insurance company's financial statements may provide an adequate basis for the auditors' consideration of this statement. However, auditors will need to consider whether additional work needs to be carried out. Where work in relation to the operation of internal controls has been undertaken as part of the audit of the financial statements, auditors also take into account evidence from that work. Auditors will have already established, for the purposes of the audit of the financial statements, whether proper books and records have been kept.

31. Paragraph 5 of the directors' compliance certificate requires the directors to confirm that the company's life assurance business has been carried out in compliance with applicable legislation and with the written guidelines issued by the regulator[28]. This is a new and potentially onerous requirement both for directors in making the statement

---

[28] The written guidelines were issued by the regulator in July 2001.

and for auditors in considering its reasonableness. Auditors already plan and perform their audit procedures and evaluate and report on the results thereof in the context of the requirements of SAS 120 'Consideration of law and regulations'. However it is unlikely that their consideration of:

- laws relating directly to the preparation of the financial statements; and

- laws which are central to the insurer's conduct of it business

within the framework provided by SAS 120 will be sufficient to enable them to report on the directors' statement at paragraph 5 of the compliance certificate.

The directors will need to establish procedures which will enable them to provide the confirmation as required by paragraph 5 of the directors' compliance statement. Auditors review the directors procedures and may decide to undertake tests to establish that those procedures have been properly applied. The auditor will need to consider the implications for the auditors' opinion on the life assurance return if:

- there are no established procedures,

- in the opinion of the auditor the procedures are inadequate, or

- the company has not complied with the procedures.

Non-life Insurance Returns

32. The Non-life Regulations do not specify by number which forms in the non-life return are to be audited. Instead they state that the 'Balance Sheet, Profit and Loss account, Asset Analysis, Assets/Liabilities Summary (as appropriate)' should be the subject of the auditor's report which are forms 6, 10, 11 and 12.

33. The guidance issued by the regulator in July 2001 requiring non-life insurers to obtain actuaries' opinions in regard to the adequacy of their technical reserves makes no reference to a report upon them by auditors. Similarly there is no requirement for an auditor to make reference to the extent of their reliance on such opinions. Accordingly, audit reports make no reference to the actuaries' opinions.

The directors 'compliance certificate

34. Auditors of non-life insurers are not required to report on the directors' certificate, and so this certificate is not dealt with in this guidance but an example is included in Appendix 4 for information.

Appendix 1

Matters of material significance: Insurance companies

1. Matters likely to be of material significance to the regulator, and hence give rise to a duty to report in accordance with section 35(1) of the Insurance Act, 1989, fall under the following categories:

    (a) matters indicating the insurer's inability to meet its material policyholder obligations and/ or financial requirements under the Insurance Acts, 1909 to 2000 (paragraphs 2 to 23 below);

    (b) material defects in the financial systems and controls or accounting records of the insurer (paragraphs 24 to 30 below);

    (c) matters leading to the auditors' decision to issue a qualified opinion on the insurer's financial statements or annual return to the regulator (paragraphs 31 to 33 below); and

    (d) matters leading to the auditors' decision to resign or not seek re-election (paragraphs 34 and 35 below).

Inability to meet material policyholder obligations and/or financial requirements

2. A properly run authorised insurer should comply with all the provisions of insurance legislation at all times. Nevertheless, certain breaches are seen by the regulator as being of particular importance, and hence likely to be of material significance in the context of the duty to report under section 35(1) of the Insurance Act, 1989.

    Matters of this nature include:

    (a) breaches of solvency margin requirements;

    (b) submission of misleading or inaccurate information;

    (c) inadequate reinsurance;

    (d) the existence of matters that may lead to withdrawal of authorisation;

    (e) substantial departure from a proposal or forecast in an authorisation application;

    (f) adequacy of premiums for new life assurance business;

    (g) matters specific to linked contracts; and

    (h) other matters specifically dealing with policyholder protection.

    Each of these items is dealt with in more detail below.

THE AUDITING PRACTICES BOARD

3. In addition, the following may be of material significance in particular circumstances:

   (a) restriction of business to insurance;

   (b) restriction of business to classes for which the insurer is authorised;

   (c) adherence to admissibility, localisation and currency matching rules;

   (d) separation of assets and liabilities attributable to life assurance business;

   (e) application of assets of an insurer transacting life assurance business;

   (f) allocation to policyholders in life insurers and rules on transfers from and to the life fund;

   (g) legal restrictions on transactions with connected persons; and

   (h) compliance with guidelines issued by the regulator.

4. In considering all such matters, auditors are not required to change the scope of their work, nor the frequency and timing of their audit visits and do not have an obligation to seek out matters of material significance that may give rise to a duty to report to the regulator.

Solvency margin breach

5. A deterioration in the solvency position of an insurer may constitute a matter of material significance and so trigger a duty to report. Identification of this need not be dependent on the formal calculation of the required minimum solvency margin, as the regulator may consider it appropriate to intervene before the margin has been breached – in some cases well before the breach has occurred. The breach or potential breach may be evidenced by:

   (a) a significant decrease in the value of net assets (as determined in accordance with the provisions of the European Communities (Non-life Insurance) Framework Regulations, 1994 and the European Communities (Life Assurance) Framework Regulations, 1994);

   (b) a significant deterioration in claims experience; or

   (c) a significant increase in premium volumes.

   However, there will normally have been some event which has given rise to this deterioration.

6. The degree to which any deterioration in the solvency position should trigger the duty to report will depend on various factors, which will need to be given appropriate weight in each particular situation. The most relevant factors are likely to be the magnitude of the deterioration in absolute terms, the speed with which the deterioration has

occurred, the underlying trend of the change, the degree to which the change was unexpected and unique to a particular insurer, the degree of uncertainty surrounding the insurer's estimates of its liabilities or the values placed on its assets, and the closeness of the insurer to the required minimum margin of solvency. The relative importance of these factors is a matter for the professional judgement of the auditors.

7.   Auditors may become aware that an insurer is committed to using an accounting treatment or policy which has the effect of obscuring a deterioration in the underlying solvency of the company. This may be of material significance to the regulator and, if so, gives rise to a duty to report. However, the duty to report does not necessarily arise where a company seeks advice as to whether a particular accounting treatment is an appropriate one. The duty only arises where an insurer has committed itself to a treatment which may be misleading.

Misleading or inaccurate information

8.   Information is primarily submitted to the regulator annually in the regulatory return. The regulator has power to require the submission of returns on a more frequent basis or to require specific items of information. The primary responsibility for accuracy of regulatory returns rests with the directors of the insurer. The auditors' involvement arises only in connection with the expression of their opinion on that part of the annual regulatory returns which is required to be audited.

9.   Auditors are less likely to examine either that part of the annual regulatory return which is not required to be audited, or any other information requested by the regulator (e.g. quarterly returns required to be produced by newly authorised insurers) However, auditors may come across such information in the course of an audit in reviewing correspondence between the insurer and the regulator. They should be aware of the potential duty to report to the regulator if they become aware that any such information submitted appears to be inaccurate or misleading.

10. In considering whether there is a duty to report on the submission of inaccurate information, auditors will need to consider whether the inaccuracy, if known, might be of material significance to the regulator. In addition, new information may become available which indicates that information previously submitted to the regulator was inaccurate, or a fundamental error in reported information may be detected. Auditors need to exercise their judgement as to whether any such inaccuracy or error may be of material significance and hence whether a duty to report arises.

Inadequate reinsurance

11. The underwriting of insurance involves the identification and evaluation of risk and, in particular, the extent to which such risks should be retained by the insurer. The assessment of the degree to which the risks assumed by an insurer should be reinsured with other insurance companies is primarily one of underwriting judgement. This will depend on such factors as the underwriter's assessment of the likelihood of an insured event occurring, its magnitude, the possible extent of loss and the availability of reinsurance.

12. The function of financial statements is to report on directors' stewardship in a particular period – not to comment on management's judgements or, generally, to look forward to subsequent periods. Accordingly, the scope of an audit does not include an assessment of the appropriateness of reinsurance arrangements from an underwriting perspective. However, in carrying out their audit, auditors need to review the overall structure of the reinsurance programme to understand its operation and the interaction between the various arrangements.

13. Auditors do not generally consider the appropriateness of the nature or extent of reinsurance arrangements except insofar as they need to do so to assess the insurer's solvency position and the appropriateness of the going concern assumption. If there is material doubt as to the going concern assumption (for example in the case of a treaty where the timing of recovery was not matched to the timing of expected claims payments), then the directors will need to reflect this in the financial statements and it may need to be referred to in the auditors' report. In these circumstances, a statutory duty to report may arise before the formal approval of the financial statements.

Matters that may lead to withdrawal of authorisation

14. Under the provisions of the Insurance Act, 1989, the European Communities (Non-life Insurance) Framework Regulations, 1994 and the European Communities (Life Assurance) Framework Regulations, 1994, the regulator has the power to withdraw an insurer's authorisation to write new business in the following circumstances:

   (a) where the insurer fails to comply with an order issued by the regulator as a result of doubtful solvency or non-compliance with other significant provisions of the Insurance Acts, 1909 to 2000 (section 18 of the Insurance Act, 1989);

   (b) where the regulator is satisfied that no business has been carried on under the authorisation for the last two consecutive years, or if the insurer has reduced the scale of its business in a class or part of a class of business so as to amount in effect to a cessation of the carrying on of business in that class or part of a class (section 21 of the Insurance Act, 1989);

   (c) where a non-life insurer is convicted of an offence in relation to commission payments under section 37 or 38 of the Insurance Act, 1989 or section 39 of the Insurance Act, 1989; and

   (d) where an insurer has not used the authorisation for the last twelve months, has expressly renounced the authorisation, has ceased to carry on business covered by the authorisation for more than six months, no longer fulfils the conditions required by the Insurance Acts, 1909 to 2000 for the granting of an authorisation or fails seriously in its obligations under the Insurance Acts, 1909 to 2000 Regulation 17 of the European Communities (Non-life Insurance) Framework Regulations, 1994 and Regulation 37 of the European Communities (Life Assurance) Framework Regulations, 1994.

15. The regulator also has powers to revoke an insurer's authorisation under Regulation 23 of the European Communities (Non-life Insurance) Regulations, 1976 and

Regulation 25 of the European Communities (Life Assurance) Regulations, 1984. The circumstances set out in these regulations are similar to those outlined above.

16. The existence of any of the circumstances set out above is likely to be of material significance to the regulator and therefore gives rise to a duty to report.

17. In addition, if after authorisation to accept new business was withdrawn, the auditors became aware that an insurer had continued to accept new business, the duty to report would be triggered on the grounds of a contravention of the insurance legislation likely to be of material significance.

Substantial departure from a proposal/forecast in an authorisation application

18. Auditors would not generally expect to report to the regulator in the case of a departure from a proposal or forecast in an authorisation application, unless misleading or inaccurate information had been submitted in the initial proposal or a substantial departure became apparent subsequently, such that the regulator would need to consider taking action before receiving the annual or quarterly regulatory return in the normal course of events. A new insurer is usually required to submit returns on a quarterly basis for its first number of years in operation.

Premiums for new life assurance business

19. An Irish insurer writing life assurance business is required by Regulation 4 of Annex IV to the European Communities (Life Assurance) Framework Regulations, 1994 to ensure that premiums for new life business are sufficient, on the basis of reasonable actuarial assumptions, to enable the insurer to meet all its commitments. In doing so, account may be taken of all aspects of the insurer's financial situation, but only if this can be done without jeopardising the company's solvency position in the long-term. Whilst auditors' routine reporting responsibilities under the provisions of the European Communities (Life Assurance) Framework Regulations, 1994 do not include expression of an opinion on compliance with this requirement, circumstances which come to their attention indicating an actual or possible breach will normally be of material significance to the regulator.

Linked contracts

20. A life insurer entering into linked contracts must ensure that detailed requirements relating to provisions, set out in Regulation 2 of Annex V to the European Communities (Life Assurance) Framework Regulations, 1994 are followed. These require benefits provided by such contracts to be linked directly to assets and, where applicable, that the assets must be of appropriate security and marketability. A failure to follow these principles is likely to give rise to a duty to report.

Protection of policyholders

21. In addition to the matters discussed and referred to above, the Insurance Act, 1989, the European Communities (Non-life Insurance) Framework Regulations, 1994 and the European Communities (Life Assurance) Framework Regulations, 1994 lay down

various other requirements with which an insurer must comply in carrying on its business in the interests of protecting its policyholders. Examples include ensuring conformity with the general good in accordance with the laws of the European Union and policyholder disclosure rules and cancellation rights and the special requirements relating to third party motor liabilities.

22. Material breaches of these policyholder protection regulations are likely to be of interest to the regulator, and therefore be likely to give rise to a duty to report if auditors become aware of them during the normal course of their work.

23. In addition to the specific provisions of the Insurance Acts, 1909 to 2000, there may be particular circumstances where an insurer complies with specific requirements, but where it may be appropriate for certain issues to be reported to the regulator on the grounds that they may affect the insurer's ability to meet its material policyholder obligations. Examples of such circumstances include:

    (a) the solvency margin is achieved with assets that, although complying with admissibility rules, are not adequately matched with liabilities, thereby affecting the potential liquidity of the insurer;

    (b) there is a marked shift in investment strategy, particularly if there is a large concentration into a particular category of asset where the concentration may be such as to constitute an undue risk to policyholders; and

    (c) there are transactions before the year-end which are reversed early in the next period (as described in Statement of Standard Accounting Practice No. 17, 'Accounting for post balance sheet events') or there are other transactions with related parties for which there is no apparent commercial benefit to the insurer.

Material defects in the financial systems and controls

24. In accordance with Regulation 10 of the European Communities (Non-life Insurance) Framework Regulations, 1994 and Regulation 10 of the European Communities (Life Assurance) Framework Regulations, 1994, insurers are required to maintain administrative and accounting procedures and internal control mechanisms which are sound and adequate. In addition, the directors of both non-life and life insurers are required to certify that an appropriate system of control has been established and maintained by the insurer over its transactions and records as part of its annual regulatory returns.

25. Responsibility for ensuring that appropriate financial systems and controls are put in place and that proper accounting records are maintained therefore rests with the directors and management of the insurer.

26. Weaknesses in systems, controls and accounting records may be identified by management themselves, internal audit or auditors during the course of their work. Auditors are not required to change the scope of their work, nor the frequency and timing of their audit visits and do not have an obligation to seek out systems, controls and accounting weaknesses that may give rise to a duty to report to the regulator.

27. Where auditors identify such weaknesses, they consider:

    (a) whether there has been a failure in the insurer's procedures for ensuring the effective operation of the systems and controls – this of itself may trigger a duty to report to the regulator; and

    (b) whether the weakness is likely to affect the insurer's ability to meet its material policyholder obligations and/or financial requirements under the Insurance Acts, 1909 to 2000 – and hence give rise to a duty to report.

28. The determination of those weaknesses in systems, controls and/or accounting records which may give rise to a duty to report to the regulator is a matter of judgement for the auditors of each insurer. There may be some weaknesses which are reportable in the context of one insurer but not for others. The decision to report a matter may take into account, for example:

    (a) the effect on the insurer's ability to meet its material policyholder obligations and/or financial requirements under the Insurance Acts, 1909 to 2000;

    (b) the nature and volume of transactions occurring in the area where the weakness has arisen;

    (c) the seriousness of the risks to which the insurer is exposed as a result of the weakness identified;

    (d) whether there are compensating systems and controls;

    (e) whether the weakness occurred for only a short period of time and has been rectified (although rectification does not of itself mean that the matter should not be reported); and

    (f) whether a weakness which has been identified, though not significant in itself, becomes so when considered in conjunction with other weaknesses.

29. If corrective action cannot be taken promptly, the weakness is more likely to be reportable because of its continuing nature. If the resulting exposure cannot be quantified and controlled in a relatively short time frame, the risk to the insurer is increased.

30. If the insurer has taken steps to rectify the situation in a relatively short time frame and the auditors determine that on those grounds that a report is not required at that time, they monitor the situation and confirm with the insurer that appropriate action has been taken. If this proves not to be the case, then they may need to re-consider the decision not to report.

THE AUDITING PRACTICES BOARD

Decision to issue a qualified audit opinion

Financial statements or regulatory returns not properly prepared

31. If the auditors are proposing to qualify either the financial statements prepared in accordance with the Companies Acts, 1963 to 2001 and the European Communities (Insurance Companies: Accounts) Regulations, 1996 or the annual regulatory return prepared in accordance with the European Communities (Non-life Insurance Accounts) Regulations, 1995 or the European Communities (Life Assurance) Framework Regulations, 1994, on the grounds that either of these documents have not been properly prepared, the regulator should be advised immediately, and therefore not come to learn about the qualification only when the document in question is submitted.

Doubts regarding going concern

32. The continued functioning of an insurance company may be jeopardised by, amongst other things:

(a) breaches of its statutory obligations, leading to withdrawal of its authorisation;

(b) failure to maintain appropriate solvency margins; or

(c) reinsurance arrangements that prove inadequate in the light of its claims experience.

33. Each of these factors has been considered in preceding paragraphs. Other factors giving rise to doubts as to an insurer's status as a going concern may come to the auditors' attention in the course of their work, in particular when carrying out procedures to meet the requirements of SAS 130, 'The going concern basis in financial statements'. Where the auditors conclude that a reference to uncertainties as to whether the company is a going concern is necessary in their report on the company's financial statements, a duty to report to the regulator also arises.

Auditors' decision to resign or not seek re-election

34. Where the auditors of an insurer resign, or seek not to be re-elected, in accordance with section 185(1) of the Companies Act, 1990, they are required to serve notice in writing of their intention to do so to both the company and the Registrar of Companies. Such notice must contain either:

(a) a statement to the effect that there are no circumstances connected with the resignation that the auditors consider should be brought to the notice of the members or creditors of the company; or

(b) a statement of any such circumstances that may exist.

35. The resigning auditors should also notify the regulator of their intention to resign and, in the event of any statement as set out in (b) above being included in the notice under

section 185(1) of the Companies Act, 1990, need to consider whether or not these circumstances give rise to a duty to report to the regulator. Given that such circumstances are required to be notified to the members and creditors, they may be of material interest to the regulator and hence to give rise to a duty to report.

Appendix 2

Contents of regulatory returns

Non-life Insurance Business – Summary of Returns to be completed annually.

The contents of the regulatory returns of non-life insurance companies are specified by the European Communities (Non-life Insurance Accounts) Regulations, 1995.

	Returns required in respect of undertakings with their Head Office in Ireland	Returns required in respect of undertakings with their Head Office in either 1 or 2	
		1 Outside the EU	2 Switzerland
Form 1 Underwriting Account – One year business Gross and Net Figures	*	*	*
Form 2 Underwriting Account – One year business Net Figures	*	*	*
Form 3 Underwriting Account – Three year business Gross and Net Figures	*	*	*
Form 4 Underwriting Account – Three year business Net Figures	*	*	*
Form 5 Summary details of EU business	*		
Form 6 Asset analysis	*	*	*
Form 7 Currency Matching Analysis Net Figures	*	*	*
Form 8 Claims Settlement Analysis	*	*	*
Form 9 Statement of Method used to calculate UPR	*	*	*
Form 10 Balance Sheet	*	*	
Form 11 Profit and Loss Account	*	*	
Form 12 Asset/Liabilities Summary			*
Form 13 Employment Statistics	*	*	*
Form 14 Calculation of Solvency Margin	*	*	

Form 15	Details of Reinsurance Treaties	*	*	*
Form 16	Details of Facultative Reinsurance	*	*	*
Form 17	Certificate of Directors	*	*	*

* return specifically required.

Note: Forms highlighted in bold type are reported upon by auditors.

Appendix 2 contd.

Life Assurance Business – Summary of Returns to be completed annually

The contents of the regulatory returns of life assurance companies are specified by the European Communities (Life Assurance) Framework Regulations, 1994. Schedule 1 to the Regulations provides a summary of accounts (forms 1 to 24) to be completed annually, which are listed below. The Regulations require such of the forms 1 to 20 as are appropriate and form 23 to be audited by a duly qualified auditor who shall make a report in form 22 in accordance with the requirements of the Regulations.

Schedules 4 and 5 to the Regulations provide a summary of forms 25 to 44 which are completed by the Appointed Actuary, and which are not subject to audit.

Form No.

1	Revenue account
2	Analysis of premiums and expenses
2A	Analysis of premiums (by class of business)
3	Analysis of claims
4	Summary of changes in business – O.B.
5	Summary of changes in business – I.B.
6	Analysis of new business – O.B.
7	Analysis of new business – I.B.
8	Expected income from designated non-linked assets
9	Analysis of designated non-linked fixed-interest securities
10	Analysis of holdings in UCITS and in recognised unit trusts directly matching liabilities in respect of property linked benefits
11	Analysis of assets which are matching liabilities in respect of property linked benefits other than holdings in UCITS and in recognised unit trusts or internal linked funds
12	Balance sheet for internal linked funds
12A	Analysis of derivative instruments used in internal linked funds
13	Analysis of units in internal linked funds
14	Revenue account for internal linked funds
15	Asset analysis
15A	Analysis of derivative instruments
16	Life assurance business liabilities and margins
17	Liabilities which are not life assurance business liabilities

18	Statement of other income and expenditure
19	Statement of net assets
20	Statement of solvency
21	Employment statistics
22	Auditors' certificate
23	Directors' report[29]
24	Appointed actuary's certificate

Schedule 1 to the 1994 Regulations prescribes the requirements for returns to be made by the different categories of life assurance undertakings as follows:

1 Irish head office (1 to 24)

2 External branch undertaking Irish and global business (1 to 24)

3 Irish deposit undertaking Irish, Global and EC business (1 to 24, Form 20 on a Global and Community basis)

4 EC deposit undertaking Irish business (1 to 24)

---

[29] Directors Compliance Certificate. See Appendix 4.

Appendix 3

Illustrative examples of auditors' reports on regulatory returns

When reporting on an insurer's regulatory return, the example reports set out in this Appendix need to be adapted to meet the circumstances of that individual company.

Example 1 – Non-life Insurer

Auditors Report to the Minister for Enterprise Trade and Employment pursuant to the European Communities (Non-life Insurance Accounts) Regulations 1995

We have audited the information contained on Form 6 and the financial statements of [ ] for the period ended XXXXX, set out on Forms 10 and 11[30] which have been prepared pursuant to the European Communities (Non-life Insurance Accounts) Regulations, 1995.

Respective responsibilities of the directors and the auditors

The directors are responsible for the preparation of returns under the provisions of the European Communities (Non-life Insurance Accounts) Regulations, 1995. It is our responsibility to form an independent opinion, based on our audit, on Forms 6, 10 and 11 and to report our opinion to you.

Our responsibilities, as independent auditors, are established in Ireland by statute, the Auditing Practices Board and by our profession's ethical guidance.

Basis of Opinion

We conducted our audit in accordance with Auditing Standards issued by the Auditing Practices Board. An audit includes examination, on a test basis, of evidence relevant to the amounts and disclosures in Forms 6, 10 and 11. It also includes an assessment of the significant estimates and judgements made by the directors in Forms 6, 10 and 11.

We planned and performed our audit so as to obtain the information and explanations which we considered necessary in order to provide us with sufficient evidence to give reasonable assurance that Forms 6, 10 and 11 are free from material misstatement, whether caused by fraud or other irregularity or error. In forming our opinion we also evaluated whether the Forms 6, 10 and 11 have been prepared in the manner specified by the regulations and fairly state the information provided on the basis required.

Opinion

In our opinion (i) the information set out in Forms 6, 10 and 11 complies with the European Communities (Non-life Insurance Accounts) Regulations 1995, (ii) proper books of account

---

[30] Form 12. Assets/Liabilities Summary, which is required of insurance undertakings with their head office in Switzerland, is also subject to audit.

have been kept by the company and (iii) the financial information set out on Forms 10 and 11, are in agreement with the books of account. We have obtained all the information and explanations we consider necessary for the purposes of our audit.

Chartered Accountants and Registered Auditors

Date

Example 2 – Life Assurance Company

Auditors Report to the Minister for Enterprise, Trade and Employment pursuant to Article 31 of the European Communities (Life Assurance) Framework Regulations, 1994

We have audited the annual returns prepared pursuant to the European Communities (Life Assurance) Framework Regulations 1994, which are required to be audited by Article 31 of those Regulations. These comprise Forms 1 to 20* together with related notes in respect of the year ended [ ]

Respective responsibilities of the directors' and the auditors

The directors are responsible for the preparation of annual returns under the provisions of the European Communities (Life Assurance) Framework Regulations, 1994 as modified by the Ministerial direction issued pursuant to Article 3 of those regulations. It is our responsibility to form an independent opinion based on our audit, on the part of the returns which is subject to audit by reason of Article 31 of the 1994 Regulations, and to report our opinion to you.

Our responsibilities, as independent auditors, are established in Ireland by statute, the Auditing Practices Board and by our profession's ethical guidance.

Basis of Opinion

We conducted our audit in accordance with Auditing Standards issued by the Auditing Practices Board. An audit includes examination, on a test basis, of evidence relevant to the amounts and disclosures in the documents specified by Article 31. It also includes an assessment of the significant estimates and judgements made by the company in the preparation of these documents.

We planned and performed our audit so as to obtain all the information and explanations which we considered necessary in order to provide us with sufficient evidence to give reasonable assurance that the documents specified by Article 31 are free from material misstatement whether caused by fraud or other irregularity or error. In forming our opinion, we also evaluated whether the documents have been prepared in the manner specified by the European Communities (Life Assurance) Framework Regulations, 1994.

We read the information contained in the Directors' Certificate in Form 23 which is the responsibility of the directors. We review the procedures undertaken by the directors to enable them to certify Form 23 and undertake such tests as we consider appropriate to establish that these procedures have been properly applied. We consider the implications for our report on the regulatory returns if we become aware of any apparent misstatement or material inconsistencies within the directors certificate with the financial statements or forms 1 to 20 of the Regulatory Return.

In giving our opinion, we have relied on:

(i) The certificate of the actuary on Form 24 with respect to the mathematical reserves and required minimum solvency margin of the undertaking; and

(ii) The identity and value of any implicit items as they have been admitted in accordance with the 1994 Regulations.**

Opinion

In our opinion, Forms 1 to 20 together with related notes, have been properly prepared in accordance with the provisions of the European Communities (Life Assurance) Framework Regulations, 1994 *as modified by the Ministerial direction issued pursuant to Article 3 of those regulations**. We have obtained all the information and explanations we consider necessary for the purpose of our audit.

In our opinion and according to the information and explanations we have received:

(i) The directors' certificate on Form 23 annexed in accordance with Article 32(a) of the European Communities (Life Assurance) Framework Regulations, 1994 has been properly prepared in accordance with those regulations; and

(ii) It was reasonable for the persons giving the certificate to have made those statements required by Part 2 of the Schedule 3 to the European Communities (Life Assurance) Framework Regulations, 1994 therein.

Chartered Accountants and Registered Auditors.

Date

* The forms being reported on should be specifically referred to by number.

** This sentence is included only where the requirements apply.

Appendix 4

Contents of certificates required from directors

The form and content of the Directors Compliance Certificates set out in this Appendix accord with that prescribed in the Guidelines on Directors Compliance certificates issued by the regulator in July 2001.

Directors Compliance Certificate: Life (Head Office in Republic of Ireland)
Name of Company:

Global Business

Financial Year Ended:

We. the Directors of .... ('The Company') certify:

1.1 That for the purposes of preparing this return

    (i)   proper accounts and records have been maintained and adequate information has been obtained by the company; and

    (ii)   an appropriate system of control has been established and maintained by the company over its transactions and records.

1.2 That the value shown for each category of asset has been determined in conformity with Article 16 of the European Communities (Life Assurance) Framework Regulations, 1994 (the '1994 Regulations') and includes the value of only such assets or such parts thereof as are permitted to be taken into account.

1.3 That the amount shown for each category of liability (including contingent and prospective liabilities) has been determined in conformity with Article 16 of the 1994 Regulations.

1.4 That the assets held throughout the financial year enabled the company to comply with Annex VII of the 1994 Regulations.

2.1 Immediately following the end of the financial year the amount of the company's required minimum solvency margin was as shown in Form 20.

2.2 At the end of the financial year, the amount of the company's available assets and quantifiable contingent liabilities (other than those included in Forms 16 or 17) in accordance with paragraph 5 (1) of Schedule 2 and the identity and value of items admitted as implicit items in accordance with paragraph 2 (g) of Part A of Annex II to the 1994 Regulations, were as shown in Form 20.

3.1 That assets attributable to life assurance business, the income arising therefrom, the proceeds of any realisation of such assets and any other income or proceeds allocated to the life assurance business fund or funds have not been applied otherwise than for the purpose of the life assurance business.

3.2 That the register required by Article 12 (6) of the 1994 Regulations has been maintained throughout the year and, in respect of the assets listed in the register, the value of those assets on the closing date for which the accounts and balance sheets of the head office of the company are furnished to the competent supervisory authority, such values being those in such accounts and balance sheets.

3.3 That any amount payable from or receivable by the life assurance business fund or funds in respect of services rendered by or to any other business carried on by the company or by or to a connected company has been determined and, where appropriate, apportioned on terms which are believed to be no less than fair to that fund or those funds, and any exchange of assets representing such funds for other assets of the Company has been made at fair market value.

3.4 That all guarantees given by the company of the performance by a related company of a contract binding on the related company which would fall to be met by any life assurance business fund have been disclosed in the return, and that the fund or funds on which each such guarantee would fall have been identified therein.

3.5 (i)   The provisions of Article 6 (5) of the 1994 Regulations have been complied with;

and

(ii)   The returns in respect of life assurance business are not distorted by agreements between the companies concerned or by any arrangements which could affect the apportionment of expenses and income.

3.6 Proper accounts and records have been maintained in the State in respect of business supervised in the State.

4.   In relation to the company's reinsurance arrangements:

(i)   adequate information has been obtained as to the financial standing of each reinsurer concerned;

(ii)   adequate provision has been made where necessary (and detailed in the Annual Return) in respect of any doubtful recoveries and / or bad debts from the reinsurers concerned.

5.   The company's life assurance business has been carried out in compliance with applicable legislation and with the written guidelines issued by the insurance supervisory authority.

[alternative form of paragraph. 5 **for financial year 2001 only**:

5.   The company's life assurance business has been carried out in compliance with applicable legislation and with the written guidelines issued by the insurance

supervisory authority to the end of the year 2000. In relation to the written guidelines issued in July 2001, the company is taking steps to comply with the relevant guidelines.]

NOTE: Where, in the opinion of those signing the certificate, the circumstances are such that any of the above statements cannot truthfully be made, the relevant statements should be omitted, with an explanatory note as to why they have been omitted.

Directors Compliance Certificate: Non-life
Name of Company:

Global Business

Financial Year Ended:

We. the Directors of .... ('the Company') certify:

1.1   That for the purposes of preparing this Return

    (i)   proper accounts and records have been maintained and adequate information has been obtained by the company; and

    (ii)   an appropriate system of control has been established and maintained by the company over its transactions and records

1.2   That the value shown for each category of asset has been determined in conformity with Article 13 and Annex III of the European Communities (Non-life Insurance) Framework Regulations, 1994 (the1994 Regulations)and includes the value of only such assets or such parts thereof as are permitted to be taken into account.

1.3   That the amount shown for each category of liability has been determined in conformity with the European Communities (Insurance Undertakings: Accounts) Regulations, 1996

1.4   That the assets held throughout the financial year enabled the company to comply with Annex IV of the Regulations.

2.   Immediately following the end of the financial year the amount of the company's required minimum solvency margin was as shown in Form 14 of the European Communities (Non-life Insurance Accounts) Regulations, 1995.

3.1   That the register required by Article 13(13) of the 1994 Regulations has been maintained throughout the year and, in respect of the assets listed in the register, the value of those assets on the closing date for which the accounts and balance sheets of the head office of the company are furnished to the competent supervisory authority, such values being those in such accounts and balance sheets.

3.2   That any amount payable from or receivable by the non-life insurance reserves in respect of services rendered by or to any other business carried on by the company or by or to a connected company has been determined and, where appropriate, apportioned on items which are believed to be no less than fair to that reserve or reserves, and any exchange of assets representing such reserves for other assets of the company has been made at fair market value.

3.3   That all guarantees given by the company of the performance by a related company of a contract binding on the related company which would fall to be met by any non-life insurance reserve have been disclosed in the return, and that the reserves on which each such guarantee would fall have been identified therein.

3.4 The returns in respect of non-life insurance business are not distorted by agreements between the companies concerned or by any arrangements which could affect the apportionment of expenses and income.

3.5 Proper accounts and records have been maintained in the State in respect of business supervised in the State.

4. In relation to the company's reinsurance arrangements:

   (i) Adequate information has been obtained as to the financial standing of each reinsurer concerned;

   (ii) Adequate provision has been made where necessary (and detailed in the Annual Returns) in respect of any doubtful recoveries and / or bad debts from the reinsurers concerned

5. In relation to the preparation of the actuarial opinion on the technical reserves[31]:

   (i) No relevant information that would materially affect the company's reserves has been knowingly withheld from the certifying actuary;

   (ii) The data provided to the certifying actuary and underlying the reserves are accurate and complete and have been reconciled to the data used in preparing the statutory financial statements and supervisory returns for the period;

   (iii) The certifying actuary has been advised of all known changes in internal methods or procedures which would materially affect the determination of reserves; and

   (iv) Claims development data provided to the certifying actuary has been reconciled to the accounting information underlying the statutory financial statements.

6. The company's non-life assurance business has been carried out in compliance with applicable legislation and with the written guidelines issued by the insurance supervisory authority.

[alternative form of Par. 6 **for financial year 2001 only**:

6. The company's non-life assurance business has been carried out in compliance with applicable legislation and with the written guidelines issued by the insurance supervisory authority to the end of the year 2000. In relation to the written guidelines issued in July 2001, the company is taking steps to comply with the relevant guidelines.]

---

[31] This paragraph should be omitted where a company has been granted an exemption from the actuarial certification requirement.

THE AUDITING PRACTICES BOARD

NOTE: Where, in the opinion of those signing the certificate, the circumstances are such that any of the above statements cannot truthfully be made, the relevant statements should be omitted, with an explanatory note as to why they have been omitted.

Appendix 5

Acts, regulations and guidelines relevant to authorised insurers

GUIDE TO THE MAIN PROVISIONS OF SIGNIFICANT IRISH INSURANCE LEGISLATION

Legislation	Principal Provisions in Force
European Communities (Non-life Insurance) Framework Regulations, 1994 (S.I. No. 359 of 1994)	Transpose into Irish Law the Third (EU) Non-life Insurance Directive (92/49/EEC);
	Institute a single authorisation and supervision system throughout the EU whereby authorisation and supervision is done by the Member State in which the insurer's head office is located;
	Impose obligation on insurers in respect of reporting to the supervisory authority (the Minister for Enterprise, Trade & Employment);
	Prescribe rules for the valuation of underwriting liabilities and assets and requirements on the localisation of assets;
	Prescribe information and other requirements in the interests of the consumer;
	Prescribe fees to be paid by an insurer applying for an authorisation or an extension.
European Communities (Life Assurance) Framework Regulations, 1994 (S.I. No. 360 of 1994)	Transpose into Irish Law the Third (EU) Life Assurance Directive (92/96/EEC);
	Contain provisions similar to the Non-life Regulations described above;
	Implement relevant provisions of the Second (EU) Life Assurance Directive (90/619/EEC) concerning freedom of services to transact business on a cross-border basis throughout the EU;
	Prescribe the format for the statutory returns of life assurance undertakings.

European Communities (Insurance Undertakings Accounts) Regulations, 1996 (S.I. No. 23 of 1996)	Transpose into Irish Law the (EU) Insurance Accounts Directive (91/674/EEC) on the annual accounts and consolidated accounts of insurance undertakings.
European Communities (Non-life Insurance) Accounts Regulations, 1995 (S.I. No. 202 of 1995)	Prescribe the format for the statutory returns of non-life insurance undertakings.
Insurance Act, 1989 (Number 3 of 1989)	Principal framework in domestic legislation for the regulation of the insurance industry;
	Article 34 requires life assurance companies to have an appointed actuary whose duty is to carry out any function in relation to the business which is required to be undertaken by an actuary under the Act;
	Article 35 imposes a duty on an insurers' auditor to report independently to the Minister if circumstances exist which could e.g., affect the insurer's ability to fulfil its obligations to policyholders;
	Sections 59 and 60 authorise the Minister to appoint 'authorised officers' for the purpose of carrying out investigations.
European Communities (Non-life Insurance and Life Assurance) Framework (Amendment) Regulations, 1997	Implement the mandatory provisions of Directive 95/26/EC in respect of authorised insurance companies;
	Empower the regulator to seek information about companies related to insurance companies and requires auditors of those related companies to inform the regulator of any material circumstances in respect of such a company likely to lead to a breach of the Insurance Acts and Regulations in the insurance company;
	Require that the registered office of an insurer should be in the member state of its authorisation.

European Communities (Supplementary) Supervision of Insurance Undertakings in an Insurance Group) Regulations 1999 (S.I. No. 399 of 1999)	Transpose into Irish Law the (EU) Insurance Groups Directive (98/78/EC). Prescribe additional requirements to be met by insurance undertakings which are part of insurance groups.
Insurance Act, 1989 (Reinsurance) (Form of Notice) Regulations, 2000 (S.I. No. 473 of 2000)	Prescribes the format of the notification to be submitted by companies wishing to engage in the business of reinsurance in the State.
Life Assurance (Provision of Information) Regulations, 2001 (S.I. No. 15 of 2001)	Prescribe the information to be provided by life insurers to individual policyholders resident in the state.
Insurance Act 2000	The Insurance Act 2000 introduced a system of statutory authorisation and supervision of insurance and reinsurance intermediaries under the responsibility of the Central Bank from 1 April 2001. This Act also strengthened powers and authority in relation to reinsurance entities, including notification procedures.
	S.I. 473 prescribes the form of notice to be given to the regulator before writing reinsurance business and S.I.15 details the information to be furnished before the conclusion of a policy and during its term.

Insurance Acts 1909 – 2000

- Assurance Companies Act, 1909

- Local Authorities (Mutual Assurance) Act, 1926 (No. 34)

- Insurance Act, 1936 (No. 45)

- Insurance (Amendment) Act, 1938 (No. 31)

- The Industrial and Life Assurance Amalgamation Company (Acquisition of Shares) Act, 1947 (No. 6)

- Insurance Act, 1953 (No. 7) †

- Insurance Act, 1961 (No. 28) †

- Insurance Act, 1964 (No. 18)

- Insurance Act, 1969 (No. 5) †

- Insurance Act, 1971 (No. 10) †

- Insurance (Amendment) Act, 1978 (No. 30)

- Insurance Act, 1981 (No. 34)

- Insurance (Amendment) Act, 1983 (No. 5) †

- Insurance (No. 2) Act, 1983 (No. 29)

- Insurance (Miscellaneous Provisions) Act, 1988 (No. 22) †

- Insurance Act, 1989 (No. 3)

- Insurance Act, 1990 (No. 26)

- Insurance Act, 2000 (No. 42 of 2000)

† *These Acts relate to Export Credit Insurance only*

Insurance Regulations 1928–2001

- Assurance Companies Act, 1909 Adaptation Order, 1928 (No. 7).

- The Assurance Companies (Deposit of Securities) Rules, 1928 (No. 63).

- The Assurance Companies (Deposit in respect of Mechanically Propelled Vehicle Insurance Business) Rules, 1933 (No. 140).

- Insurance Act, 1936 (Parts I, II and IV) (Commencement) Order, 1937 (No. 17).

- Insurance (Amendment) Act, 1938 (Transfer Date) Order, 1939 (No. 250).

- Insurance (Amendment) Act, 1938 (Amendment of section 18) Order, 1939 (No. 367).

- Actuary (Qualification) Regulations, 1940 (No. 75).

- Industrial Assurance (Contents of Policies) Order, 1940 (No. 76).

- Insurance Acts, 1936 (Parts II, V and VII) Commencement Order, 1940 (No. 77)

- Insurance (Deposits) Rules, 1940 (No. 78).

- Insurance Regulations, 1940 (No. 80).

- Industrial Assurance (Fees for Determination of Disputes) Regulations, 1940 (No. 81)

- Decimal Currency (Friendly Society and Industrial Assurance Contracts) Regulations, 1971 (S.I. No. 64 of 1971).

- European Communities (Non-life Insurance) Regulations, 1976 (S.I. No. 115 of 1976).

- European Communities (Non-life Insurance) (Amendment) Regulations, 1976 (S.I. No. 276 of 1976).

- European Communities (Insurance Agents and Brokers) Regulations, 1978 (S.I. No.178 of 1978).

- European Communities (Insurance) (Non-life) Regulations, 1978 (S.I. No. 382 of 1978).

- European Communities (Co-Insurance) Regulations, 1983 (S.I. No. 65 of 1983).

- European Communities (Life Assurance) Regulations, 1984 (S.I. No. 57 of 1984).

- Motor Insurance Advisory Board, (Establishment) Order, 1984 (S.I. No. 299 of 1984)

- European Communities (Life Assurance) (Amendment) Regulations, 1985 (S.I. No. 296 of 1985).

- European Communities (Non-life Insurance) (Amendment) Regulations, 1985 (S.I. No. 297 of 1985).

- European Communities (Non-life Insurance) (Amendment) Regulations, 1986 (S.I. No. 309 of 1986).

- European Communities (Life Assurance Accounts, Statements and Valuations) Regulations, 1986 (S.I. No. 437 of 1986).

- European Communities (Life Assurance) (Amendment) Regulations, 1988 (S.I. No. 143 of 1988).

- European Communities (Non-life Insurance) (Amendment) Regulations, 1988 (S.I. No. 144 of 1988).

- Insurance Act, 1989 (Parts I, II, III and V) (Commencement) Order (S.I. No. 50 of 1989).

- Insurance Act, 1989 (Part IV) (Commencement) Order, 1990 (S.I. No. 136 of 1990).

- Insurance (Fees) Order, 1990 (S.I. No. 149 of 1990).

- European Communities (Life Assurance) (Amendment) Regulations, 1990 (S.I. No. 150 of 1990).

- Insurance (Bonding of Intermediaries) Regulations, 1990 (S.I. No. 191 of 1990).

- Insurance Act, 1990 (Commencement) Order, 1990 (S.I. No. 197 of 1990).

- European Communities (Non-life Insurance) (Amendment) Regulations, 1990 (S.I. No. 211 of 1990).

- European Communities (Life Assurance) (Amendment) (No. 2) Regulations, 1990, (S.I. No. 212 of 1990).

- European Communities (Non-life Insurance) (Amendment) Regulations, 1991 (S.I. No. 5 of 1991).

- European Communities (Non-life Insurance) (Amendment) (No. 2) Regulations, 1991 (S.I. No. 142 of 1991).

- European Communities (Non-life Insurance) (Legal Expenses) Regulations, 1991 (S.I. No. 197 of 1991).

- European Communities (Non-life Insurance) (Amendment) Regulations, 1992 (S.I. No. 244 of 1992).

- European Communities (Non-life Insurance) Framework Regulations, 1994 (S.I. No. 359 of 1994).

- European Communities (Life Assurance) Framework Regulations, 1994 (S.I. No. 360 of 1994).

- Insurance (Fees) Order, 1995 (S.I. No. 128 of 1995).

- European Communities (Non-life Insurance Accounts) Regulations, 1995 (S.I. No. 202 of 1995).

- European Communities (Insurance Undertakings Accounts) Regulations, 1996 (S.I. No. 23 of 1996).

- European Communities (Swiss Confederation Agreement) Regulations, 1996 (S.I. No. 25 of 1996).

- European Communities (Non-life Insurance and Life Assurance) Framework (Amendment) Regulations, 1997 (S.I. No. 457 of 1997).

- Insurance Act, 1989 (section 49(3)) Regulations, 1997 (S.I. No. 465 of 1997).

- European Communities (Supplementary Supervision of Insurance Undertakings in an Insurance Group) Regulations, 1999 (S.I. No. 399 of 1999)

- Insurance Act 1989, (Reinsurance)(Form of Notification) Regulations, 1999 (S.I. No 437 of 1999.)

- Insurance (Fees)(Amendment) Order, 2000 (S.I. No. 126 of 2000)

- Insurance Act, 2000 (Commencement) Order, 2000 (S.I. No. 472 of 2000)

- Insurance Act, 1989 (Reinsurance)(Form of Notice) Regulations, 2000 (S.I. No. 473 of 2000)

- Life Assurance (Provision of Information) Regulations, 2001 (S.I. No. 15 of 2001)

Insurance Guidelines

- 'IMF Actuarial Certificate Non-life Reserves' -Guidelines for Insurance Companies: Actuarial Certification of the Technical Reserves of Non-life Companies

- 'IMF Asset Management' – Guidelines for Insurance Companies on Asset Management

- 'IMF Compliance Officer' – Guidelines for Insurance Companies: Appointment of Compliance Officer

- 'IMF Derivatives' – Guidelines for Insurance Companies: Risk Management of Derivatives

- 'IMF Directors Compliance' – Guidelines for Insurance Companies: Directors Compliance Certificate

- 'IMF Financial Condition Reports for Life Companies' – Guidelines for Insurance Companies: Actuarial Financial Condition Reports from Life Assurance Companies

- 'IMF On Site Supervisory Visits' – Guidelines for Insurance Companies: On-site Supervisory Visits

- EU Insurance Groups Directive: Guidance Note

- European Communities (Life Assurance) Framework Regulations, 1994 : Guidance Note

- European Communities (Non-life insurance) Guidance Note.

PRACTICE NOTE 23 (REVISED JULY 2013)

SPECIAL CONSIDERATIONS IN AUDITING FINANCIAL INSTRUMENTS

> *This Practice Note is based on International Auditing Practice Note 1000 issued by the International Auditing and Assurance Standards Board. Supplementary FRC guidance is highlighted with grey shading.*

CONTENTS

Introduction

1. Financial instruments may be used by financial and non-financial entities of all sizes for a variety of purposes. Some entities have large holdings and transaction volumes while other entities may only engage in a few financial instrument transactions. Some entities may take positions in financial instruments to assume and benefit from risk while other entities may use financial instruments to reduce certain risks by hedging or managing exposures. This ~~International Auditing~~ Practice Note (IAPN) is relevant to all of these situations.

2. The following International Standards on Auditing (ISAs) (UK and Ireland) are particularly relevant to audits of financial instruments:

    (a) ISA (UK and Ireland) 540[1] deals with the auditor's responsibilities relating to auditing accounting estimates, including accounting estimates related to financial instruments measured at fair value;

    (b) ISA (UK and Ireland) 315[2] and ISA (UK and Ireland) 330[3] deal with identifying and assessing risks of material misstatement and responding to those risks; and

    (c) ISA (UK and Ireland) 500[4] explains what constitutes audit evidence and deals with the auditor's responsibility to design and perform audit procedures to obtain sufficient appropriate audit evidence to be able to draw reasonable conclusions on which to base the auditor's opinion.

3. The purpose of this PN is to provide:

    (a) Background information about financial instruments (Section I); and

    (b) Discussion of audit considerations relating to financial instruments (Section II).

    ~~IAPNs provide practical assistance to auditors. They are intended to be disseminated by those responsible for national standards, or used in developing corresponding national material. They also provide material that firms can use in developing their training programs and internal guidance.~~ PNs are persuasive rather than prescriptive and are indicative of good practice. They are intended to assist auditors in applying ISAs (UK and Ireland) to particular circumstances and industries. Auditors should be aware of and consider PNs applicable to the engagement. Auditors who do not consider and apply the guidance included in a relevant PN should be prepared to explain how the ISAs (UK and Ireland) have been complied with.

---

[1] ISA (UK and Ireland) 540, *Auditing Accounting Estimates, Including Fair Value Accounting Estimates, and Related Disclosures*.

[2] ISA (UK and Ireland) 315, *Identifying and Assessing the Risks of Material Misstatement through Understanding the Entity and Its Environment*.

[3] ISA (UK and Ireland) 330, *The Auditor's Responses to Assessed Risks*.

[4] ISA (UK and Ireland) 500, *Audit Evidence*.

FINANCIAL REPORTING COUNCIL

4.   This PN is relevant to entities of all sizes, as all entities may be subject to risks of material misstatement when using financial instruments.

5.   The guidance on valuation[5] in this PN is likely to be more relevant for financial instruments measured or disclosed at fair value, while the guidance on areas other than valuation applies equally to financial instruments either measured at fair value or amortized cost. This PN is also applicable to both financial assets and financial liabilities. This PN does not deal with instruments such as:

     (a) The simplest financial instruments such as cash, simple loans, trade accounts receivable and trade accounts payable;

     (b) Investments in unlisted equity instruments; or

     (c) Insurance contracts.

6.   Also, this PN does not deal with specific accounting issues relevant to financial instruments, such as ~~hedge accounting,~~ profit or loss on inception (often known as "Day 1" profit or loss), offsetting, risk transfers or impairment, including loan loss provisioning. Although these subject matters can relate to an entity's accounting for financial instruments, a discussion of the auditor's consideration regarding how to address specific accounting requirements is beyond the scope of this PN.

7.   An audit in accordance with ISAs (UK and Ireland) is conducted on the premise that management and, where appropriate, those charged with governance have acknowledged certain responsibilities. Such responsibilities subsume making fair value measurements. This PN does not impose responsibilities on management or those charged with governance nor override laws and regulation that govern their responsibilities.

8.   This PN has been written in the context of general purpose fair presentation financial reporting frameworks, but may also be useful, as appropriate in the circumstance, in other financial reporting frameworks such as special purpose financial reporting frameworks.

9.   This PN focuses on the assertions of valuation, and presentation and disclosure, but also covers, in less detail, completeness, accuracy, existence, and rights and obligations.

10.   Financial instruments are susceptible to estimation uncertainty, which is defined in ISA (UK and Ireland) 540 as "the susceptibility of an accounting estimate and related disclosures to an inherent lack of precision in its measurement."[6] Estimation uncertainty is affected by the complexity of financial instruments, among other factors. The nature and reliability of information available to support the measurement of financial instruments varies widely, which affects the estimation

---

[5]   In this PN, the terms "valuation" and "measurement" are used interchangeably.

[6]   ISA (UK and Ireland) 540, paragraph 7(c).

uncertainty associated with their measurement. This PN uses the term "measurement uncertainty" to refer to the estimation uncertainty associated with fair value measurements.

Section I—Background Information about Financial Instruments

11. Different definitions of financial instruments may exist among financial reporting frameworks. For example, International Financial Reporting Standards (IFRS) define a financial instrument as any contract that gives rise to a financial asset of one entity and a financial liability or equity instrument of another entity.[7] Financial instruments may be cash, the equity of another entity, the contractual right or obligation to receive or deliver cash or exchange financial assets or liabilities, certain contracts settled in an entity's own equity instruments, certain contracts on non-financial items, or certain contracts issued by insurers that do not meet the definition of an insurance contract. This definition encompasses a wide range of financial instruments from simple loans and deposits to complex derivatives, structured products, and some commodity contracts.

12. Financial instruments vary in complexity, though the complexity of the financial instrument can come from difference sources, such as:

   • A very high volume of individual cash flows, where a lack of homogeneity requires analysis of each one or a large number of grouped cash flows to evaluate, for example, credit risk (for example, collateralized debt obligations (CDOs)).

   • Complex formulae for determining the cash flows.

   • Uncertainty or variability of future cash flows, such as that arising from credit risk, option contracts or financial instruments with lengthy contractual terms.

   The higher the variability of cash flows to changes in market conditions, the more complex and uncertain the fair value measurement of the financial instrument is likely to be. In addition, sometimes financial instruments that, ordinarily, are relatively easy to value become complex to value because of particular circumstances, for example, instruments for which the market has become inactive or which have lengthy contractual terms. Derivatives and structured products become more complex when they are a combination of individual financial instruments. In addition, the accounting for financial instruments under certain financial reporting frameworks or certain market conditions may be complex.

13. Another source of complexity is the volume of financial instruments held or traded. While a "plain vanilla" interest rate swap may not be complex, an entity holding a large number of them may use a sophisticated information system to identify, value and transact these instruments.

---

[7] International Accounting Standard (IAS) 32, *Financial Instruments: Presentation*, paragraph 11.

Purpose and Risks of Using Financial Instruments

14.   Financial instruments are used for:

-   Hedging purposes (that is, to change an existing risk profile to which an entity is exposed). This includes:

    ○   The forward purchase or sale of currency to fix a future exchange rate;

    ○   Converting future interest rates to fixed rates or floating rates through the use of swaps; and

    ○   The purchase of option contracts to provide an entity with protection against a particular price movement, including contracts which may contain embedded derivatives;

-   Trading purposes (for example, to enable an entity to take a risk position to benefit from short term market movements); and

-   Investment purposes (for example, to enable an entity to benefit from long term investment returns).

15.   The use of financial instruments can reduce exposures to certain business risks, for example changes in exchange rates, interest rates and commodity prices, or a combination of those risks. On the other hand, the inherent complexities of some financial instruments also may result in increased risk.

16.   Business risk and the risk of material misstatement increase when management and those charged with governance:

-   Do not fully understand the risks of using financial instruments and have insufficient skills and experience to manage those risks;

-   Do not have the expertise to value them appropriately in accordance with the applicable financial reporting framework;

-   Do not have sufficient controls in place over financial instrument activities; or

-   Inappropriately hedge risks or speculate.

17.   Management's failure to fully understand the risks inherent in a financial instrument can have a direct effect on management's ability to manage these risks appropriately, and may ultimately threaten the viability of the entity.

18.   The principal types of risk applicable to financial instruments are listed below. This list is not meant to be exhaustive and different terminology may be used to describe these risks or classify the components of individual risks.

(a) Credit (or counterparty) risk is the risk that one party to a financial instrument will cause a financial loss to another party by failing to discharge an obligation and is often associated with default. Credit risk includes settlement risk, which is the risk that one side of a transaction will be settled without consideration being received from the customer or counterparty.

(b) Market risk is the risk that the fair value or future cash flows of a financial instrument will fluctuate because of changes in market prices. Examples of market risk include currency risk, interest rate risk, commodity and equity price risk.

(c) Liquidity risk includes the risk of not being able to buy or sell a financial instrument at an appropriate price in a timely manner due to a lack of marketability for that financial instrument.

(d) Operational risk relates to the specific processing required for financial instruments. Operational risk may increase as the complexity of a financial instrument increases, and poor management of operational risk may increase other types of risk. Operational risk includes:

(i) The risk that confirmation and reconciliation controls are inadequate resulting in incomplete or inaccurate recording of financial instruments;

(ii) The risks that there is inappropriate documentation of transactions and insufficient monitoring of these transactions;

(iii) The risk that transactions are incorrectly recorded, processed or risk managed and, therefore, do not reflect the economics of the overall trade;

(iv) The risk that undue reliance is placed by staff on the accuracy of valuation techniques, without adequate review, and transactions are therefore incorrectly valued or their risk is improperly measured;

(v) The risk that the use of financial instruments is not adequately incorporated into the entity's risk management policies and procedures;

(vi) The risk of loss resulting from inadequate or failed internal processes and systems, or from external events, including the risk of fraud from both internal and external sources;

(vii) The risk that there is inadequate or non-timely maintenance of valuation techniques used to measure financial instruments; and

(viii) Legal risk, which is a component of operational risk, and relates to losses resulting from a legal or regulatory action that invalidates or otherwise precludes performance by the end user or its counterparty under the terms of the contract or related netting arrangements. For example, legal risk could arise from insufficient or incorrect documentation for the contract, an inability to enforce a netting arrangement in bankruptcy, adverse changes in tax laws, or statutes that prohibit entities from investing in certain types of financial instruments.

(e) Model risk, which is the risk that imperfections and subjectivity of valuation models used to determine the value of certain types of financial instrument are not properly understood and accounted for or adjusted for. This includes the risk that undue reliance is placed by staff on information derived from valuation models, in managing financial instrument positions, with the result that they overlook the fundamentals of risk management and control of market, counterparty and operational risk for these types of transactions.

19.   Other considerations relevant to risks of using financial instruments include:

- The risk of fraud that may be increased if, for example, an employee in a position to perpetrate a financial fraud understands both the financial instruments and the processes for accounting for them, but management and those charged with governance have a lesser degree of understanding.

- The risk that master netting arrangements[8] may not be properly reflected in the financial statements.

- The risk that some financial instruments may change between being assets or liabilities during their term and that such change may occur rapidly.

The potential for rapid changes in prices, coupled with the structure of certain financial instruments, also can affect credit risk exposure. For example, highly leveraged financial instruments or financial instruments with longer maturity can result in credit risk exposure increasing quickly after a transaction has been undertaken.

Controls Relating to Financial Instruments

20.   The extent of an entity's use of financial instruments and the degree of complexity of the instruments are important determinants of the necessary level of sophistication of the entity's internal control. For example, smaller entities may use less structured products and simple processes and procedures to achieve their objectives.

21.   Often, it is the role of those charged with governance to set the tone regarding, and approve and oversee the extent of use of, financial instruments while it is management's role to manage and monitor the entity's exposures to those risks. Management and, where appropriate, those charged with governance are also responsible for designing and implementing a system of internal control to enable

---

[8]   An entity that undertakes a number of financial instrument transactions with a single counterparty may enter into a master netting arrangement with that counterparty. Such an agreement provides for a single net settlement of all financial instruments covered by the agreement in the event of default of any one contract.

the preparation of financial statements in accordance with the applicable financial reporting framework. An entity's internal control over financial instruments is more likely to be effective when management and those charged with governance have:

(a) Established an appropriate control environment, active participation by those charged with governance in controlling the use of financial instruments, a logical organizational structure with clear assignment of authority and responsibility, and appropriate human resource policies and procedures. In particular, clear rules are needed on the extent to which those responsible for financial instrument activities are permitted to act. Such rules have regard to any legal or regulatory restrictions on using financial instruments. For example, certain public sector entities may not have the power to conduct business using derivatives;

(b) Established a risk management process relative to the size of the entity and the complexity of its financial instruments (for example, in some entities a formal risk management function may exist);

(c) Established information systems that provide those charged with governance with an understanding of the nature of the financial instrument activities and the associated risks, including adequate documentation of transactions;

(d) Designed, implemented and documented a system of internal control to:

  ○ Provide reasonable assurance that the entity's use of financial instruments is within its risk management policies;

  ○ Properly present financial instruments in the financial statements;

  ○ Ensure that the entity is in compliance with applicable laws and regulations; and

  ○ Monitor risk.

  The Appendix provides examples of controls that may exist in an entity that deals in a high volume of financial instrument transactions; and

(e) Established appropriate accounting policies, including valuation policies, in accordance with the applicable financial reporting framework.

22. Key elements of risk management processes and internal control relating to an entity's financial instruments include:

• Setting an approach to define the amount of risk exposure that the entity is willing to accept when engaging in financial instrument transactions (this may be referred to as its "risk appetite"), including policies for investing in financial instruments, and the control framework in which the financial instrument activities are conducted;

- Establishing processes for the documentation and authorization of new types of financial instrument transactions which consider the accounting, regulatory, legal, financial and operational risks that are associated with such instruments;

- Processing financial instrument transactions, including confirmation and reconciliation of cash and asset holdings to external statements, and the payments process;

- Segregation of duties between those investing or trading in the financial instruments and those responsible for processing, valuing and confirming such instruments. For example, a model development function that is involved in assisting in pricing deals is less objective than one that is functionally and organizationally separate from the front office;

- Valuation processes and controls, including controls over data obtained from third-party pricing sources; and

- Monitoring of controls.

23. The nature of risks often differs between entities with a high volume and variety of financial instruments and those with only a few financial instrument transactions. This results in different approaches to internal control. For example:

- Typically, an institution with high volumes of financial instruments will have a dealing room type environment in which there are specialist traders and segregation of duties between those traders and the back office (which refers to the operations function that data-checks trades that have been conducted, ensuring that they are not erroneous, and transacting the required transfers). In such environments, the traders will typically initiate contracts verbally over the phone or via an electronic trading platform. Capturing relevant transactions and accurately recording financial instruments in such an environment is significantly more challenging than for an entity with only a few financial instruments, whose existence and completeness often can be confirmed with a bank confirmation to a few banks.

- On the other hand, entities with only a small number of financial instruments often do not have segregation of duties, and access to the market is limited. In such cases, although it may be easier to identify financial instrument transactions, there is a risk that management may rely on a limited number of personnel, which may increase the risk that unauthorized transactions may be initiated or transactions may not be recorded.

Completeness, Accuracy, and Existence

24. Paragraphs 25–33 describe controls and processes which may be in place in entities with a high volume of financial instrument transactions, including those with trading rooms. By contrast, an entity that does not have a high volume of financial instrument transactions may not have these controls and processes but may instead confirm their transactions with the counterparty or clearing house. Doing so may be

relatively straightforward in that the entity may only transact with one or two counterparties.

24-1.   Complete and accurate recording of financial instruments is an essential core objective on which many others are built. For example, without a process that completely and accurately records all financial instruments:

- Financial information may be incomplete and/or inaccurate;

- Risks may be improperly managed, because the entity's exposures will be inaccurately recorded;

- The entity may be unable to settle transactions accurately;

- Off-balance sheet instruments and their associated risks may not be appropriately treated.

Trade Confirmations and Clearing Houses

25.   Generally, for transactions undertaken by financial institutions, the terms of financial instruments are documented in confirmations exchanged between counterparties and legal agreements. Clearing houses serve to monitor the exchange of confirmations by matching trades and settling them. A central clearing house is associated with an exchange and entities that clear through clearing houses typically have processes to manage the information delivered to the clearing house.

26.   Not all transactions are settled through such an exchange. In many other markets there is an established practice of agreeing the terms of transactions before settlement begins. To be effective, this process needs to be run separately from those who trade the financial instruments to minimize the risk of fraud. In other markets, transactions are confirmed after settlement has begun and sometimes confirmation backlogs result in settlement beginning before all terms have been fully agreed. This presents additional risk because the transacting entities need to rely on alternative means of agreeing trades. These may include:

- Enforcing rigorous reconciliations between the records of those trading the financial instruments and those settling them (strong segregation of duties between the two are important), combined with strong supervisory controls over those trading the financial instruments to ensure the integrity of the transactions;

- Reviewing summary documentation from counterparties that highlights the key terms even if the full terms have not been agreed; and

- Thorough review of traders' profits and losses to ensure that they reconcile to what the back office has calculated.

Reconciliations with Banks and Custodians

27.   Some components of financial instruments, such as bonds and shares, may be held in separate depositories. In addition, most financial instruments result in payments of cash at some point and often these cash flows begin early in the contract's life. These cash payments and receipts will pass through an entity's bank account. Regular reconciliation of the entity's records to external banks' and custodians' records enables the entity to ensure transactions are properly recorded.

28.   It should be noted that not all financial instruments result in a cash flow in the early stages of the contract's life or are capable of being recorded with an exchange or custodian. Where this is the case, reconciliation processes will not identify an omitted or inaccurately recorded trade and confirmation controls are more important. Even where such a cash flow is accurately recorded in the early stages of an instrument's life, this does not ensure that all characteristics or terms of the instrument (for example, the maturity or an early termination option) have been recorded accurately.

29.   In addition, cash movements may be quite small in the context of the overall size of the trade or the entity's own balance sheet and may therefore be difficult to identify. The value of reconciliations is enhanced when finance, or other back office staff, review entries in all general ledger accounts to ensure that they are valid and supportable. This process will help identify if the other side to cash entries relating to financial instruments has not been properly recorded. Reviewing suspense and clearing accounts is important regardless of the account balance, as there may be offsetting reconciling items in the account.

30.   In entities with a high volume of financial instrument transactions, reconciliation and confirmation controls may be automated and, if so, adequate IT controls need to be in place to support them. In particular, controls are needed to ensure that data is completely and accurately picked up from external sources (such as banks and custodians) and from the entity's records and is not tampered with before or during reconciliation. Controls are also needed to ensure that the criteria on which entries are matched are sufficiently restrictive to prevent inaccurate clearance of reconciling items.

Other Controls over Completeness, Accuracy, and Existence

31.   The complexity inherent in some financial instruments means that it will not always be obvious how they should be recorded in the entity's systems. In such cases, management may set up control processes to monitor policies that prescribe how particular types of transactions are measured, recorded and accounted for. These policies are typically established and reviewed in advance by suitably qualified personnel who are capable of understanding the full effects of the financial instruments being booked.

32.   Some transactions may be cancelled or amended after initial execution. Application of appropriate controls relating to cancellation or amendment can mitigate the risks

of material misstatement due to fraud or error. In addition, an entity may have a process in place to reconfirm trades that are cancelled or amended.

33. In financial institutions with a high volume of trading, a senior employee typically reviews daily profits and losses on individual traders' books to evaluate whether they are reasonable based on the employee's knowledge of the market. Doing so may enable management to determine that particular trades were not completely or accurately recorded, or may identify fraud by a particular trader. It is important that there are transaction authorization procedures that support the more senior review.

Valuation of Financial Instruments

Financial Reporting Requirements

34. In many financial reporting frameworks, financial instruments, including embedded derivatives, are often measured at fair value for the purpose of balance sheet presentation, calculating profit or loss, and/or disclosure. In general, the objective of fair value measurement is to arrive at the price at which an orderly transaction would take place between market participants at the measurement date under current market conditions; that is, it is not the transaction price for a forced liquidation or distressed sale. In meeting this objective, all relevant available market information is taken into account.

35. Fair value measurements of financial assets and financial liabilities may arise both at the initial recording of transactions and later when there are changes in value. Changes in fair value measurements that occur over time may be treated in different ways under different financial reporting frameworks. For example, such changes may be recorded as profit or loss, or may be recorded in the other comprehensive income. Also, depending on the applicable financial reporting framework, the whole financial instrument or only a component of it (for example, an embedded derivative when it is separately accounted for) may be required to be measured at fair value.

36. Some financial reporting frameworks establish a fair value hierarchy to develop increased consistency and comparability in fair value measurements and related disclosures. The inputs may be classified into different levels such as:

- Level 1 inputs—Quoted prices (unadjusted) in active markets for identical financial assets or financial liabilities that the entity can access at the measurement date.

- Level 2 inputs—Inputs other than quoted prices included within level 1 that are observable for the financial asset or financial liability, either directly or indirectly. If the financial asset or financial liability has a specified (contractual) term, a level 2 input must be observable for substantially the full term of the financial asset or financial liability. Level 2 inputs include the following:

  ○ Quoted prices for similar financial assets or financial liabilities in active markets.

- ○ Quoted prices for identical or similar financial assets or financial liabilities in markets that are not active.

- ○ Inputs other than quoted prices that are observable for the financial asset or financial liability (for example, interest rates and yield curves observable at commonly quoted intervals, implied volatilities and credit spreads).

- ○ Inputs that are derived principally from, or corroborated by, observable market data by correlation or other means (market-corroborated inputs).

- Level 3 inputs—Unobservable inputs for the financial asset or financial liability. Unobservable inputs are used to measure fair value to the extent that relevant observable inputs are not available, thereby allowing for situations in which there is little, if any, market activity for the financial asset or financial liability at the measurement date.

In general, measurement uncertainty increases as a financial instrument moves from level 1 to level 2, or level 2 to level 3. Also, within level 2 there may be a wide range of measurement uncertainty depending on the observability of inputs, the complexity of the financial instrument, its valuation, and other factors.

37. Certain financial reporting frameworks may require or permit the entity to adjust for measurement uncertainties, in order to adjust for risks that a market participant would make in the pricing to take account of the uncertainties of the risks associated with the pricing or cash flows of the financial instrument. For example:

- Model adjustments. Some models may have a known deficiency or the result of calibration may highlight the deficiency for the fair value measurement in accordance with the financial reporting framework.

- Credit-risk adjustments. Some models do not take into account credit risk, including counterparty risk or own credit risk.

- Liquidity adjustments. Some models calculate a mid-market price, even though the financial reporting framework may require use of a liquidity adjusted amount such as a bid/offer spread. Another, more judgmental, liquidity adjustment recognizes that some financial instruments are illiquid which affects the valuation.

- Other risk adjustments. A value measured using a model that does not take into account all other factors that market participants would consider in pricing the financial instrument may not represent fair value on the measurement date, and therefore may need to be adjusted separately to comply with the applicable financial reporting framework.

Adjustments are not appropriate if they adjust the measurement and valuation of the financial instrument away from fair value as defined by the applicable financial reporting framework, for example for conservatism.

Observable and Unobservable Inputs

38.   As mentioned above, financial reporting frameworks often categorize inputs according to the degree of observability. As activity in a market for financial instruments declines and the observability of inputs declines, measurement uncertainty increases. The nature and reliability of information available to support valuation of financial instruments varies depending on the observability of inputs to its measurement, which is influenced by the nature of the market (for example, the level of market activity and whether it is through an exchange or over-the-counter (OTC)). Accordingly, there is a continuum of the nature and reliability of evidence used to support valuation, and it becomes more difficult for management to obtain information to support a valuation when markets become inactive and inputs become less observable.

39.   When observable inputs are not available, an entity uses unobservable inputs (level 3 inputs) that reflect the assumption that market participants would use when pricing the financial asset or the financial liability, including assumptions about risk. Unobservable inputs are developed using the best information available in the circumstances. In developing unobservable inputs, an entity may begin with its own data, which is adjusted if reasonably available information indicates that (a) other market participants would use different data or (b) there is something particular to the entity that is not available to other market participants (for example, an entity-specific synergy).

Effects of Inactive Markets

40.   Measurement uncertainty increases and valuation is more complicated when the markets in which financial instruments or their component parts are traded become inactive[8a]. There is no clear point at which an active market becomes inactive, though financial reporting frameworks may provide guidance on this issue. Characteristics of an inactive market include a significant decline in the volume and level of trading activity, available prices vary significantly over time or among market participants or the prices are not current. However, assessing whether a market is inactive requires judgment.

41.   When markets are inactive, prices quoted may be stale (that is, out of date), may not represent prices at which market participants may trade or may represent forced transactions (such as when a seller is required to sell an asset to meet regulatory or legal requirements, needs to dispose of an asset immediately to create liquidity or the existence of a single potential buyer as a result of the legal or time restrictions imposed). Accordingly, valuations are developed based on level 2 and level 3 inputs. Under such circumstances, entities may have:

[8a]   Guidance for auditors on issues that may arise in adverse market conditions is provided in Bulletins 2008/1 *Audit Issues When Financial Market Conditions are Difficult and Credit Facilities may be Limited* and 2008/10 *Going Concern Issues During the Current Economic Conditions*.

- Protocols for acquiring pricing indicators from as many different sources as possible;

- A valuation policy that includes a process for determining whether level 1 inputs are available;

- An understanding of how particular prices or inputs from external sources used as inputs to valuation techniques were calculated in order to assess their reliability. For example, in an active market, a broker quote on a financial instrument that has not traded is likely to reflect actual transactions on a similar financial instrument, but, as the market becomes less active, the broker quote may rely more on proprietary valuation techniques to determine prices;

- An understanding of how deteriorating business conditions affect the counterparty, as well as whether deteriorating business conditions in entities similar to the counterparty may indicate that the counterparty may not fulfill its obligations (that is, non-performance risk);

- Policies for adjusting for measurement uncertainties. Such adjustments can include model adjustments, lack of liquidity adjustments, credit risk adjustments, and other risk adjustments;

- The capability to calculate the range of realistic outcomes given the uncertainties involved, for example by performing a sensitivity analysis; and

- Policies for identifying when a fair value measurement input moves to a different level of the fair value hierarchy.

42. Particular difficulties may develop where there is severe curtailment or even cessation of trading in particular financial instruments. In these circumstances, financial instruments that have previously been valued using market prices may need to be valued using a model.

Management's Valuation Process

43. Techniques that management may use to value their financial instruments include observable prices, recent transactions, and models that use observable or unobservable inputs. Management may also make use of:

(a) A third-party pricing source, such as a pricing service or broker quote; or

(b) A valuation expert.

Third-party pricing sources and valuation experts may use one or more of these valuation techniques.

44. In many financial reporting frameworks, the best evidence of a financial instrument's fair value is found in contemporaneous transactions in an active market (that is, level 1 inputs). In such cases, the valuation of a financial instrument may be relatively

simple. Quoted prices for financial instruments that are listed on exchanges or traded in liquid over-the-counter markets may be available from sources such as financial publications, the exchanges themselves or third-party pricing sources. When using quoted prices, it is important that management understand the basis on which the quote is given to ensure that the price reflects market conditions at the measurement date. Quoted prices obtained from publications or exchanges may provide sufficient evidence of fair value when, for example:

(a) The prices are not out of date or "stale" (for example, if the quote is based on the last traded price and the trade occurred some time ago); and

(b) The quotes are prices at which dealers would actually trade the financial instrument with sufficient frequency and volume.

44-1. The pricing source should be independent and where possible there should be more than one provider of a quote. Prices should not come from quotations provided solely or primarily by the entity being audited.

44-2. It may also be necessary to adjust for factors not present in any market quotations. For example the credit spread of a particular counterparty may not be factored into a general market quote and may need to be adjusted for.

45. Where there is no current observable market price for the financial instrument (that is, a level 1 input), it will be necessary for the entity to gather other price indicators to use in a valuation technique to value the financial instrument. Price indicators may include:

• Recent transactions, including transactions after the date of the financial statements in the same instrument. Consideration is given to whether an adjustment needs to be made for changes in market conditions between the measurement date and the date the transaction was made, as these transactions are not necessarily indicative of the market conditions that existed at the date of the financial statements. In addition it is possible that the transaction represents a forced transaction and is therefore not indicative of a price in an orderly trade.

• Current or recent transactions in similar instruments, often known as "proxy pricing." Adjustments will need to be made to the price of the proxy to reflect the differences between them and the instrument being priced, for example, to take account of differences in liquidity or credit risk between the two instruments.

• Indices for similar instruments. As with transactions in similar instruments, adjustments will need to be made to reflect the difference between the instrument being priced and the instrument(s) from which the index used is derived.

46. It is expected that management will document its valuation policies and model used to value a particular financial instrument, including the rationale for the model(s)

used, the selection of assumptions in the valuation methodology, and the entity's consideration of whether adjustments for measurement uncertainty are necessary.

Models

47.   Models may be used to value financial instruments when the price cannot be directly observed in the market. Models can be as simple as a commonly used bond pricing formula or involve complex, specifically developed software tools to value financial instruments with level 3 inputs. Many models are based on discounted cash flow calculations.

48.   Models comprise a methodology, assumptions and data. The methodology describes rules or principles governing the relationship between the variables in the valuation. Assumptions include estimates of uncertain variables which are used in the model. Data may comprise actual or hypothetical information about the financial instrument, or other inputs to the financial instrument.

49.   Depending on the circumstances, matters that the entity may address when establishing or validating a model for a financial instrument include whether:

- The model is validated prior to usage, with periodic reviews to ensure it is still suitable for its intended use. The entity's validation process may include evaluation of:

  ○ The methodology's theoretical soundness and mathematical integrity, including the appropriateness of parameters and sensitivities.

  ○ The consistency and completeness of the model's inputs with market practices, and whether the appropriate inputs are available for use in the model.

- There are appropriate change control policies, procedures and security controls over the model.

- The model is appropriately changed or adjusted on a timely basis for changes in market conditions.

- The model is periodically calibrated, reviewed and tested for validity by a separate and objective function. Doing so is a means of ensuring that the model's output is a fair representation of the value that marketplace participants would ascribe to a financial instrument.

- The model maximizes the use of relevant observable inputs and minimizes the use of unobservable inputs.

- Adjustments are made to the output of the model to reflect the assumptions marketplace participants would use in similar circumstances.

**FINANCIAL
REPORTING COUNCIL**

- The model is adequately documented, including the model's intended applications and limitations and its key parameters, required data, results of any validation analysis performed and any adjustments made to the output of the model.

- Whether a model used to prepare actuarial information follows the principles in Technical Actuarial Standard M: Modelling[8b].

An Example of a Common Financial Instrument

50. The following describes how models may be applied to value a common financial instrument, known as an asset backed security.[9] Because asset backed securities are often valued based on level 2 or 3 inputs, they are frequently valued using models and involve:

- Understanding the type of security—considering (a) the underlying collateral; and (b) the terms of the security. The underlying collateral is used to estimate the timing and amounts of cash flows such as mortgage or credit card interest and principal payments.

- Understanding the terms of the security—this includes evaluating contractual cash flow rights, such as the order of repayment, and any default events. The order of repayment, often known as seniority, refers to terms which require that some classes of security holders (senior debt) are repaid before others (subordinated debt). The rights of each class of security holder to the cash flows, frequently referred to as the cash flow "waterfall," together with assumptions of the timing and amount of cash flows are used to derive a set of estimated cash flows for each class of security holder. The expected cash flows are then discounted to derive an estimated fair value.

51. The cash flows of an asset backed security may be affected by prepayments of the underlying collateral and by potential default risk and resulting estimated loss severities. Prepayment assumptions, if applicable, are generally based on evaluating market interest rates for similar collateral to the rates on the collateral underlying the security. For example, if market interest rates for mortgages have declined then the underlying mortgages in a security may experience higher prepayment rates than originally expected. Estimating potential default and loss severity involves close evaluation of the underlying collateral and borrowers to estimate default rates. For example, when the underlying collateral comprises residential mortgages, loss severities may be affected by estimates of residential housing prices over the term of the security.

[8b] Technical Actuarial Standards are issued by the Financial Reporting Council.

[9] An asset backed security is a financial instrument which is backed by a pool of underlying assets (known as the collateral, such as credit card receivables or vehicle loans) and derives value and income from those underlying assets.

Third-Party Pricing Sources

52. Entities may use third-party pricing sources in order to obtain fair value information. The preparation of an entity's financial statements, including the valuation of financial instruments and the preparation of financial statement disclosures relating to these instruments, may require expertise that management does not possess. Entities may not be able to develop appropriate valuation techniques, including models that may be used in a valuation, and may use a third-party pricing source to arrive at a valuation or to provide disclosures for the financial statements. This may particularly be the case in smaller entities or in entities that do not engage in a high volume of financial instruments transactions (for example, non-financial institutions with treasury departments). Even though management has used a third-party pricing source, management is ultimately responsible for the valuation.

53. Third-party pricing sources may also be used because the volume of securities to price over a short timeframe may not be possible by the entity. This is often the case for traded investment funds that must determine a net asset value each day. In other cases, management may have their own pricing process but use third-party pricing sources to corroborate their own valuations.

54. For one or more of these reasons most entities use third-party pricing sources when valuing securities either as a primary source or as a source of corroboration for their own valuations. Third-party pricing sources generally fall into the following categories:

- Pricing services, including consensus pricing services; and

- Brokers providing broker quotes.

Pricing services

55. Pricing services provide entities with prices and price-related data for a variety of financial instruments, often performing daily valuations of large numbers of financial instruments. These valuations may be made by collecting market data and prices from a wide variety of sources, including market makers, and, in certain instances, using internal valuations techniques to derive estimated fair values. Pricing services may combine a number of approaches to arrive at a price. Pricing services are often used as a source of prices based on level 2 inputs. Pricing services may have strong controls around how prices are developed and their customers often include a wide variety of parties, including buy and sell side investors, back and middle office functions, auditors and others.

56. Pricing services often have a formalized process for customers to challenge the prices received from the pricing services. These challenge processes usually require the customer to provide evidence to support an alternative price, with challenges categorized based on the quality of evidence provided. For example, a challenge based on a recent sale of that instrument that the pricing service was not aware of may be upheld, whereas a challenge based on a customer's own valuation technique may be more heavily scrutinized. In this way, a pricing service with a large

number of leading participants, both buy and sell side, may be able to constantly correct prices to more fully reflect the information available to market participants.

56-1. When considering whether a corrected price gives a suitable basis for valuation in the financial statements, consideration should be given to how long the challenge process has taken and whether the underlying data remains valid or there have been developments, such as market movements, to take account of.

Consensus pricing services

57. Some entities may use pricing data from consensus pricing services which differ from other pricing services. Consensus pricing services obtain pricing information about an instrument from several participating entities (subscribers). Each subscriber submits prices to the pricing service. The pricing service treats this information confidentially and returns to each subscriber the consensus price, which is usually an arithmetical average of the data after a data cleansing routine has been employed to eliminate outliers. For some markets, such as for exotic derivatives, consensus prices might constitute the best available data. However, many factors are considered when assessing the representational faithfulness of the consensus prices including, for example:

- Whether the prices submitted by the subscribers reflect actual transactions or just indicative prices based on their own valuation techniques.

- The number of sources from which prices have been obtained.

- The quality of the sources used by the consensus pricing service.

- Whether participants include leading market participants.

- Whether the market is one sided, where all the subscribers have positions in the same direction, causing the results to be skewed.

58. Typically consensus prices are only available to subscribers who have submitted their own prices to the service. Accordingly not all entities will have direct access to consensus prices. Because a subscriber generally cannot know how the prices submitted were estimated, other sources of evidence in addition to information from consensus pricing services may be needed for management to support their valuation. In particular, this may be the case if the sources are providing indicative prices based on their own valuation techniques and management is unable to obtain an understanding of how these sources calculated their prices.

Brokers providing broker quotes

59. As brokers provide quotes only as an incidental service for their clients, quotes they provide differ in many respects from prices obtained in pricing services. Brokers may be unwilling to provide information about the process used to develop their quote, but may have access to information on transactions about which a pricing service may not be aware. Broker quotes may be executable or indicative. Indicative quotes

are a broker's best estimate of fair value, whereas an executable quote shows that the broker is willing to transact at this price. Executable quotes are strong evidence of fair value. Indicative quotes are less so because of the lack of transparency into the methods used by the broker to establish the quote. In addition the rigor of controls over the brokers' quote often will differ depending on whether the broker also holds the same security in its own portfolio. Broker quotes are often used for securities with level 3 inputs and sometimes may be the only external information available.

59-1. Where brokers have not observed recent executed transactions the quality of their indicative quotations may be affected. If brokers do not hold positions the quality of their quotes will depend on their interactions with dealers in the specific market.

Further considerations relating to third-party pricing sources

60. Understanding how the pricing sources calculated a price enables management to determine whether such information is suitable for use in its valuation, including as an input to a valuation technique and in what level of inputs the security should be categorized for disclosure purposes. For example, third-party pricing sources may value financial instruments using proprietary models, and it is important that management understands the methodology, assumptions and data used.

61. If fair value measurements obtained from third-party pricing sources are not based on the current prices of an active market, it will be necessary for management to evaluate whether the fair value measurements were derived in a manner that is consistent with the applicable financial reporting framework. Management's understanding of the fair value measurement includes:

   • How the fair value measurement was determined—for example, whether the fair value measurement was determined by a valuation technique, in order to assess whether it is consistent with the fair value measurement objective;

   • Whether the quotes are indicative prices, indicative spread, or binding offers; and

   • How frequently the fair value measurement is estimated by the third-party pricing sources—in order to assess whether it reflects market conditions at the measurement date.

   Understanding the bases on which third-party pricing sources have determined their quotes in the context of the particular financial instruments held by the entity assists management in evaluating the relevance and reliability of this evidence to support its valuations.

62. It is possible that there will be disparities between price indicators from different sources. Understanding how the price indicators were derived, and investigating these disparities, assists management in corroborating the evidence used in developing its valuation of financial instruments in order to evaluate whether the valuation is reasonable. Simply taking the average of the quotes provided, without

doing further research, may not be appropriate, because one price in the range may be the most representative of fair value and this may not be the average. To evaluate whether its valuations of financial instruments are reasonable, management may:

- Look at the performance of price providers in the past. For example it may be that a price provider consistently over or under prices a particular asset class and that this would reduce the reliance being placed on that provider;

- Consider whether actual transactions represent forced transactions rather than transactions between willing buyers and willing sellers. This may invalidate the price as a comparison;

- Analyze the expected future cash flows of the instrument. This could be performed as an indicator of the most relevant pricing data;

- Depending on the nature of what is unobservable, extrapolate from observed prices to unobserved ones (for example, there may be observed prices for maturities up to ten years but not longer, but the ten year price curve may be capable of being extrapolated beyond ten years as an indicator). Care is needed to ensure that extrapolation is not carried so far beyond the observable curve that its link to observable prices becomes too tenuous to be reliable;

- Compare prices within a portfolio of financial instruments to each other to make sure that they are consistent among similar financial instruments;

- Use more than one model to corroborate the results from each one, having regard to the data and assumptions used in each; or

- Evaluate movements in the prices for related hedging instruments and collateral.

In coming to its judgment as to its valuation, an entity may also consider other factors that may be specific to the entity's circumstances.

Independent Price Verification Function

62-1. A feature of some entities' internal control is an independent price verification (IPV) function. This department is responsible for separately verifying the price of some financial instruments and may use alternative data sources, methodologies and assumptions. The IPV function, while not independent of the entity, often provides an objective management challenge to the pricing that has been developed in another part of the entity and is therefore often a key control over management's valuation process. To verify the price of financial instruments independently of management this function may:

- Perform revaluation of the entity's financial instruments using independent inputs and assumptions, comparing these values to those developed in another part of the entity.

- Compare the inputs used to develop financial instrument valuations by another part of the entity to independently obtained inputs (parameter based IPV).

- Make recommendations to management around adjustments to books and records to align valuations developed in another part of the entity with fair value.

- Assess the sufficiency and appropriateness of the information used, including evaluating third party pricing services such as consensus pricing services and broker quotes.

- Calculate fair value adjustments or other adjustments required to account for residual uncertainties in the valuation process.

Use of Valuation Experts

63.   Management may engage a valuation expert from an investment bank, broker, or other valuation firm to value some or all of its securities. Unlike pricing services and broker quotes, generally the methodology and data used are more readily available to management when they have engaged an expert to perform a valuation on their behalf. Even though management has engaged an expert, management is ultimately responsible for the valuation used.

Issues Related to Financial Liabilities

64.   Understanding the effect of credit risk is an important aspect of valuing both financial assets and financial liabilities. This valuation reflects the credit quality and financial strength of both the issuer and any credit support providers. In some financial reporting frameworks, the measurement of a financial liability assumes that it is transferred to a market participant at the measurement date. Where there is not an observable market price for a financial liability, its value is typically measured using the same method as a counterparty would use to measure the value of the corresponding asset, unless there are factors specific to the liability (such as third-party credit enhancement). In particular, the entity's own credit risk[10] can often be difficult to measure.

Presentation and Disclosure about Financial Instruments

65.   Most financial reporting frameworks require disclosures in the financial statements to enable users of the financial statements to make meaningful assessments of the effects of the entity's financial instrument activities, including the risks and uncertainties associated with financial instruments.

66.   Most frameworks require the disclosure of quantitative and qualitative information (including accounting policies) relating to financial instruments. The accounting requirements for fair value measurements in financial statement presentation and

---

[10] Own credit risk is the amount of change in fair value that is not attributable to changes in market conditions.

disclosures are extensive in most financial reporting frameworks and encompass more than just valuation of the financial instruments. For example, qualitative disclosures about financial instruments provide important contextual information about the characteristics of the financial instruments and their future cash flows that may help inform investors about the risks to which entities are exposed.

Categories of Disclosures

67.   Disclosure requirements include:

(a) Quantitative disclosures that are derived from the amounts included in the financial statements—for example, categories of financial assets and liabilities;

(b) Quantitative disclosures that require significant judgment—for example, sensitivity analysis for each type of market risk to which the entity is exposed; and

(c) Qualitative disclosures—for example, those that describe the entity's governance over financial instruments; objectives; controls, policies and processes for managing each type of risk arising from financial instruments; and the methods used to measure the risks.

68.   The more sensitive the valuation is to movements in a particular variable, the more likely it is that disclosure will be necessary to indicate the uncertainties surrounding the valuation. Certain financial reporting frameworks may also require disclosure of sensitivity analyses, including the effects of changes in assumptions used in the entity's valuation techniques. For example, the additional disclosures required for financial instruments with fair value measurements that are categorized within level 3 inputs of the fair value hierarchy are aimed at informing users of financial statements about the effects of those fair value measurements that use the most subjective inputs.

69.   Some financial reporting frameworks require disclosure of information that enables users of the financial statements to evaluate the nature and extent of the risks arising from financial instruments to which the entity is exposed at the reporting date. This disclosure may be contained in the notes to the financial statements, or in management's discussion and analysis within its annual report cross-referenced from the audited financial statements. The extent of disclosure depends on the extent of the entity's exposure to risks arising from financial instruments. This includes qualitative disclosures about:

•   The exposures to risk and how they arise, including the possible effects on an entity's future liquidity and collateral requirements;

•   The entity's objectives, policies and processes for managing the risk and the methods used to measure the risk; and

•   Any changes in exposures to risk or objectives, policies or processes for managing risk from the previous period.

Section II—Audit Considerations Relating to Financial Instruments

70. Certain factors may make auditing financial instruments particularly challenging. For example:

- It may be difficult for both management and the auditor to understand the nature of financial instruments and what they are used for, and the risks to which the entity is exposed.

- Market sentiment and liquidity can change quickly, placing pressure on management to manage their exposures effectively.

- Evidence supporting valuation may be difficult to obtain.

- Individual payments associated with certain financial instruments may be significant, which may increase the risk of misappropriation of assets.

- The amounts recorded in the financial statements relating to financial instruments may not be significant, but there may be significant risks and exposures associated with these financial instruments.

- A few employees may exert significant influence on the entity's financial instruments transactions, in particular where their compensation arrangements are tied to revenue from financial instruments, and there may be possible undue reliance on these individuals by others within the entity.

These factors may cause risks and relevant facts to be obscured, which may affect the auditor's assessment of the risks of material misstatement, and latent risks can emerge rapidly, especially in adverse market conditions[10a].

70-1. The auditor is required to obtain an understanding of the entity's objectives and strategies, the related business risks that may result in risks of material misstatement, and the entity's risk assessment process[10b]. For an entity transacting financial instruments, an understanding of the entity's related risk management processes and risk appetite may identify risks of material misstatement. It is not the job of the auditor to determine the amount of risk an entity should take on or how it should monitor and manage risk. However, obtaining an understanding of the risk management process is important for the auditor because poor risk management processes can affect the audit in a number of indirect ways by, for example:

- Exposing an entity to levels of risk that breach legal or regulatory restrictions. The auditor may have responsibilities in respect of such breaches as set out in

---

[10a] Guidance for auditors on issues that may arise in adverse market conditions is provided in Bulletins 2008/1 *Audit Issues When Financial Market Conditions are Difficult and Credit Facilities may be Limited* and 2008/10 *Going Concern Issues During the Current Economic Conditions*.
[10b] ISA (UK and Ireland) 315, paragraphs 11(d) and 15-17.

ISA (UK and Ireland) 250 Section B, *The auditor's Right and Duty to Report to Regulators in the Financial Sector*;

- Facilitating fraud or error;

- Making it more difficult to obtain an understanding of the impact of financial instruments on the entity as a whole;

- In extreme circumstances, increasing the risk of a going concern problem (for example, if financial instrument assets lose value or become illiquid or liability positions are developed to an extent that results in liquidity and/or solvency risks that threaten the ability of the entity to continue as a going concern).

Professional Scepticism[11]

71.   Professional scepticism is necessary to the critical assessment of audit evidence and assists the auditor in remaining alert for possible indications of management bias. This includes questioning contradictory audit evidence and the reliability of documents, responses to inquiries and other information obtained from management and those charged with governance. It also includes being alert to conditions that may indicate possible misstatement due to error or fraud and considering the sufficiency and appropriateness of audit evidence obtained in light of the circumstances.

71-1. Maintaining professional scepticism throughout the audit is necessary if the auditor is, for example, to reduce the risks of:

- Overlooking unusual circumstances.

- Over generalizing when drawing conclusions from audit observations.

- Using inappropriate assumptions in determining the nature, timing, and extent of the audit procedures and evaluating the results thereof.

- Not identifying management bias or over-optimism.

71-2. Evaluating audit evidence for assertions about some financial instruments requires considerable judgment because the assertions, especially those about valuation, may be based on highly subjective assumptions or be particularly sensitive to changes in the underlying assumptions. For example, valuation assertions may be based on assumptions about the occurrence of future events for which expectations are difficult to develop or about conditions expected to exist a long time. Accordingly, competent persons could reach different conclusions about valuation estimates or estimates of valuation ranges. Considerable judgment also may be required in evaluating audit evidence for assertions based on features of the financial instrument and applicable accounting principles, including underlying criteria, that are both extremely complex.

---

[11] ISA (UK and Ireland) 200, paragraph 15.

72.   Application of professional scepticism is required in all circumstances, and the need for professional scepticism increases with the complexity of financial instruments, for example with regard to:

- Evaluating whether sufficient appropriate audit evidence has been obtained, which can be particularly challenging when models are used or in determining if markets are inactive.

- Evaluating management's judgments, and the potential for management bias, in applying the entity's applicable financial reporting framework, in particular management's choice of valuation techniques, use of assumptions in valuation techniques, and addressing circumstances in which the auditor's judgments and management's judgments differ.

- Drawing conclusions based on the audit evidence obtained, for example assessing the reasonableness of valuations prepared by management's experts and evaluating whether disclosures in the financial statements achieve fair presentation.

Planning Considerations[12]

73.   The auditor's focus in planning the audit is particularly on:

- Understanding the accounting and disclosure requirements;

- Understanding the financial instruments to which the entity is exposed, and their purpose and risks;

- Determining whether specialized skills and knowledge are needed in the audit;

- Understanding and evaluating the system of internal control in light of the entity's financial instrument transactions and the information systems that fall within the scope of the audit;

- Understanding the nature, role and activities of the internal audit function;

- Understanding management's process for valuing financial instruments, including whether management has used an expert or a service organization; and

- Assessing and responding to the risk of material misstatement.

---

[12] ISA (UK and Ireland) 300, *Planning an Audit of Financial Statements*, deals with the auditor's responsibility to plan an audit of financial statements.

Materiality

73-1.   Determining materiality involves both quantitative and qualitative considerations. When planning the audit, materiality may be difficult to assess for an entity using particular financial instruments given some of their characteristics (e.g. where there is volatility of valuations). In particular, some financial instruments can be assets or liabilities depending on their valuation and this may change over the course of the audit. This factor may be relevant if, for example, materiality is initially determined prior to the period end reflecting estimates of period end valuations which subsequently change as at the actual period end.

Engagement Quality Control Review

73-2.   An engagement quality control review is required for all audits of financial statements of listed entities[12a]. Criteria that an audit firm considers when determining which audits other than those of listed entities are to be subject to an engagement quality control review include the identification of unusual circumstances or risks in the engagement[12b]. In this context, the auditor considers whether the attributes of the financial instruments used by the entity or market conditions make the appointment of an engagement quality control reviewer appropriate.

73-3.   The engagement quality control reviewer will need an understanding of the financial instruments used by the entity, including their purpose, nature and complexity.

Understanding the Accounting and Disclosure Requirements

74.   ISA (UK and Ireland) 540 requires the auditor to obtain an understanding of the requirements of the applicable financial reporting framework relevant to accounting estimates, including related disclosures and any regulatory requirements.[13] The requirements of the applicable financial reporting framework regarding financial instruments may themselves be complex and require extensive disclosures. Reading this PN is not a substitute for a full understanding of all the requirements of the applicable financial reporting framework. Certain financial reporting frameworks require consideration of areas such as:

- Hedge accounting;

- Accounting for "Day 1" profits or losses;

- Recognition and derecognition of financial instrument transactions;

- Own credit risk; and

[12a] ISA (UK and Ireland) 220, paragraph 19.
[12b] ISQC (UK and Ireland) 1, paragraph A41.
[13] ISA (UK and Ireland) 540, paragraph 8(a).

- Risk transfer and derecognition, in particular where the entity has been involved in the origination and structuring of complex financial instruments.

74-1. An entity's policies for accounting for financial instruments need to take into account the different purposes for which they can be transacted (such as trading, hedging or investment). Relevant accounting standards may be under review and entities need to monitor developments to ensure the correct accounting requirements, including possible transitional arrangements, are complied with. Having regard to disclosure requirements is important as they can play a key role in making the levels of holdings of financial instruments, their purpose and the underlying risk profile transparent.

Understanding the Financial Instruments

75. The characteristics of financial instruments may obscure certain elements of risk and exposure. Obtaining an understanding of the instruments in which the entity has invested or to which it is exposed, including the characteristics of the instruments, helps the auditor to identify whether:

- Important aspects of a transaction are missing or inaccurately recorded;

- A valuation appears appropriate;

- The risks inherent in them are fully understood and managed by the entity; and

- The financial instruments are appropriately classified into current and non-current assets and liabilities.

76. Examples of matters that the auditor may consider when obtaining an understanding of the entity's financial instruments include:

- To which types of financial instruments the entity is exposed.

- The use to which they are put.

- Management's and, where appropriate, those charged with governance's understanding of the financial instruments, their use and the accounting requirements.

- Their exact terms and characteristics so that their implications can be fully understood and, in particular where transactions are linked, the overall impact of the financial instrument transactions.

- Whether they are part of a structured arrangement designed to achieve a particular accounting or regulatory purpose. Specialist advice obtained by the entity may be an indicator of this.

- How they fit into the entity's overall risk management strategy.

- Whether there is a possibility of claims, that are material individually or in aggregate, against the entity for mis-selling financial instruments.

Inquiries of the internal audit function, the risk management function, if such functions exist, and discussions with those charged with governance may inform the auditor's understanding.

76-1. It may be appropriate for the auditor's understanding of relevant industry and regulatory factors in accordance with ISA (UK and Ireland) 315 to include inquiry of management as to whether there have been discussions with supervisors or other regulators during the year about its policies in respect of financial instruments, and whether management has reviewed its processes in the light of those discussions (for example if the regulator has expressed a view that the entity's valuations appear out of line with those of other entities or are not sufficiently prudent). The auditor reviews relevant correspondence, if any, with regulators.

76-2. For a regulated entity in the financial sector, it may be appropriate for the auditor to discuss matters related to the entity's use and disclosure of financial instruments directly with the regulator in bilateral and/or trilateral meetings (the latter involving representatives of the regulated entity). In July 2013 the FCA published its *Code of Practice for the relationship between the external auditor and the supervisor*. The Code of Practice sets out principles that establish, in the context of a particular regulated firm, the nature of the relationship between the supervisor and the auditor.

77. In some cases, a contract, including a contract for a non-financial instrument may contain a derivative. Some financial reporting frameworks permit or require such "embedded" derivatives to be separated from the host contract in some circumstances. Understanding management's process for identifying, and accounting for, embedded derivatives will assist the auditor in understanding the risks to which the entity is exposed.

77-1. While intended to mitigate risk, inappropriate hedge transactions can cause significant financial loss if the risks are not properly identified or managed. A simple example might be the hedging of baskets of bonds or shares with an index – if the basket does not match the index closely, price movements may not offset each other, therefore increasing risk not reducing it.

Using Those with Specialized Skills and Knowledge in the Audit[14]

78. A key consideration in audits involving financial instruments, particularly complex financial instruments, is the competence of the auditor. ISA (UK and Ireland) 220[15] requires the engagement partner to be satisfied that the engagement team, and any auditor's experts who are not part of the engagement team, collectively have the appropriate competence and capabilities to perform the audit engagement in accordance with professional standards and applicable legal and regulatory requirements and to enable an auditor's report that is appropriate in the circumstances to be issued. Further, relevant ethical requirements[16] require the auditor to determine whether acceptance of the engagement would create any threats to compliance with the fundamental principles, including the professional competence and due care. Paragraph 79 below provides examples of the types of matters that may be relevant to the auditor's considerations in the context of financial instruments.

79. Accordingly, auditing financial instruments may require the involvement of one or more experts or specialists, for example, in the areas of:

- Understanding the operating characteristics and risk profile of the industry in which the entity operates.

- Understanding the business rationale for the particular financial instruments used by the entity, the related risks and how they are managed.

- Understanding the financial instruments used by the entity and their characteristics, including their level of complexity. Using specialized skills and knowledge may be needed in checking whether all aspects of the financial instrument and related considerations have been captured in the financial statements, and evaluating whether adequate disclosure in accordance with the applicable financial reporting framework has been made where disclosure of risks is required.

---

[14] When such a person's expertise is in auditing and accounting, regardless of whether the person is from within or external to the firm, this person is considered to be part of the engagement team and is subject to the requirements of ISA (UK and Ireland) 220, *Quality Control for an Audit of Financial Statements*. When such a person's expertise is in a field other than accounting or auditing, such person is considered to be an auditor's expert, and the provisions of ISA (UK and Ireland) 620, *Using the Work of an Auditor's Expert*, apply. ISA (UK and Ireland) 620 explains that distinguishing between specialized areas of accounting or auditing, and expertise in another field, will be a matter of professional judgment, but notes the distinction may be made between expertise in methods of accounting for financial instruments (accounting and auditing expertise) and expertise in complex valuation techniques for financial instruments (expertise in a field other than accounting or auditing).

[15] ISA (UK and Ireland) 220, paragraph 14.

[16] IESBA *Code of Ethics for Professional Accountants* paragraphs 210.1 and 210.6.

Auditors in the UK and Ireland are subject to ethical requirements from two sources: the *APB Ethical Standards for Auditors*, issued by the Financial Reporting Council, concerning the integrity, objectivity and independence of the auditor, and the ethical pronouncements established by the auditor's relevant professional body. The ethical considerations relating to the fundamental principles of professional competence and due care are addressed in the pronouncements established by the professional bodies.

- Understanding the applicable financial reporting framework, especially when there are areas known to be subject to differing interpretations, or practice is inconsistent or developing.

- Understanding the legal, regulatory, and tax implications resulting from the financial instruments, including whether the contracts are enforceable by the entity (for example, reviewing the underlying contracts), may require specialized skills and knowledge.

- Understanding the differing regulatory requirements that may apply to group components and the implications for the audit. This may include where regulatory requirements for foreign branches are significantly different than for the entity the auditor is reporting on.

- Assessing the risks inherent in a financial instrument.

- Assisting the engagement team gather evidence to support management's valuations or to develop a point estimate or range, especially when fair value is determined by a complex model; when markets are inactive and data and assumptions are difficult to obtain; when unobservable inputs are used; or when management has used an expert.

- Evaluating information technology controls, especially in entities with a high volume of financial instruments. In such entities information technology may be highly complex, for example when significant information about those financial instruments is transmitted, processed, maintained or accessed electronically. In addition, it may include relevant services provided by a service organization.

The involvement of one or more experts or specialists may be needed especially when:

- The financial instruments are complex;

- Relatively simple financial instruments are combined to produce a more complex product; or

- The entity is engaged in active trading of complex financial instruments.

80. The nature and use of particular types of financial instruments, the complexities associated with accounting requirements, and market conditions may lead to a need for the engagement team to consult[17] with other accounting and audit professionals, from within or outside the firm, with relevant technical accounting or auditing expertise and experience, taking into account factors such as:

- The capabilities and competence of the engagement team, including the experience of the members of the engagement team.

---

[17] ISA (UK and Ireland) 220, paragraph 18(b), requires the engagement partner to be satisfied that members of the engagement team have undertaken appropriate consultation during the course of the engagement, both within the engagement team and between the engagement team and others at the appropriate level within or outside the firm.

- The attributes of the financial instruments used by the entity.

- The identification of unusual circumstances or risks in the engagement, as well as the need for professional judgment, particularly with respect to materiality and significant risks.

- Market conditions.

Understanding Internal Control

81. ISA (UK and Ireland) 315 establishes requirements for the auditor to understand the entity and its environment, including its internal control. Obtaining an understanding of the entity and its environment, including the entity's internal control, is a continuous, dynamic process of gathering, updating and analyzing information throughout the audit. The understanding obtained enables the auditor to identify and assess the risks of material misstatement at the financial statement and assertion levels, thereby providing a basis for designing and implementing responses to the assessed risks of material misstatement. The volume and variety of the financial instrument transactions of an entity typically determines the nature and extent of controls that may exist at an entity. An understanding of how financial instruments are monitored and controlled assists the auditor in determining the nature, timing and extent of audit procedures. The Appendix describes controls that may exist in an entity that deals in a high volume of financial instrument transactions.

81-1. An understanding of how the entity manages and controls its exposure to financial instruments includes how the entity ensures that:

- All instruments are completely and accurately recorded;

- Payments and receipts are monitored and made on time;

- Financial risks are analysed and monitored;

- Valuations are accurate, reviewed and used for monitoring purposes;

- Only competent and trained staff can enter into transactions;

- Risk limits are applied;

- Segregation of duties between those transacting, settling and accounting for financial instruments are maintained.

Understanding the Nature, Role and Activities of the Internal Audit Function[17a]

82.   In many large entities, the internal audit function may perform work that enables senior management and those charged with governance to review and evaluate the entity's controls relating to the use of financial instruments. The internal audit function may assist in identifying the risks of material misstatement due to fraud or error. However, the knowledge and skills required of an internal audit function to understand and perform procedures to provide assurance to management or those charged with governance on the entity's use of financial instruments are generally quite different from those needed for other parts of the business. The extent to which the internal audit function has the knowledge and skill to cover, and has in fact covered, the entity's financial instrument activities, as well as the competence and objectivity of the internal audit function, is a relevant consideration in the external auditor's determination of whether the internal audit function is likely to be relevant to the overall audit strategy and audit plan.

83.   Areas where the work of the internal audit function may be particularly relevant are:[18]

    •   Developing a general overview of the nature and extent of use of financial instruments;

    •   Understanding the control environment;

    •   Evaluating the appropriateness of policies and procedures and management's compliance with them;

    •   Evaluating the operating effectiveness of financial instrument control activities;

    •   Evaluating systems relevant to financial instrument activities; and

    •   Assessing whether new risks relating to financial instruments are identified, assessed and managed.

Understanding Management's Methodology for Valuing Financial Instruments

84.   Management's responsibility for the preparation of the financial statements includes applying the requirements of the applicable financial reporting framework to the valuation of financial instruments. ISA (UK and Ireland) 540 requires the auditor to obtain an understanding of how management makes accounting estimates and the data on which accounting estimates are based.[19] Management's approach to valuation also takes into account the selection of an appropriate valuation methodology and the level of the evidence expected to be available. To meet the

---

[17a] ISAs (UK and Ireland) 315 and 610 establish requirements regarding the auditor's understanding and use of the work of internal auditors. These include safeguards against inappropriate reliance on or over use of the work of internal auditors.

[18] Work performed by functions such as the risk management function, model review functions, and product control, may also be relevant.

[19] ISA (UK and Ireland) 540, paragraph 8(c).

objective of a fair value measurement, an entity develops a valuation methodology to measure the fair value of financial instruments that considers all relevant market information that is available. A thorough understanding of the financial instrument being valued allows an entity to identify and evaluate the relevant market information available about identical or similar instruments that should be incorporated into the valuation methodology.

Assessing and Responding to the Risks of Material Misstatement

Overall Considerations Relating to Financial Instruments

85.   ISA (UK and Ireland) 540[20] explains that the degree of estimation uncertainty affects the risk of material misstatement of accounting estimates. The use of more complex financial instruments, such as those that have a high level of uncertainty and variability of future cash flows, may lead to an increased risk of material misstatement, particularly regarding valuation. Other matters affecting the risk of material misstatement include:

- The volume of financial instruments to which the entity is exposed.

- The terms of the financial instrument, including whether the financial instrument itself includes other financial instruments.

- The nature of the financial instruments.

- The economics and business purpose of the entity's financial instrument activities.

- Whether the instruments are part of a structured arrangement designed to achieve a particular accounting or regulatory purpose.

- An entity's experience with the financial instrument.

- Whether the financial instrument is traded on national exchanges or across borders.

- Whether the financial instrument is traded on an exchange or 'over the counter'.

- The strength of the entity's control environment.

Fraud Risk Factors[21]

86.   Incentives for fraudulent financial reporting by employees may exist where compensation schemes are dependent on returns made from the use of financial instruments. Understanding how an entity's compensation policies interact with its risk appetite, and the incentives that this may create for its management and traders, may be important in assessing the risk of fraud.

---

[20] ISA (UK and Ireland) 540, paragraph 2.

[21] See ISA (UK and Ireland) 240, *The Auditor's Responsibilities Relating to Fraud in an Audit of Financial Statements*, for requirements and guidance dealing with fraud risk factors.

87.   Difficult financial market conditions may give rise to increased incentives for management or employees to engage in fraudulent financial reporting: to protect personal bonuses, to hide employee or management fraud or error, to avoid breaching regulatory, liquidity or borrowing limits or to avoid reporting losses. For example, at times of market instability, unexpected losses may arise from extreme fluctuations in market prices, from unanticipated weakness in asset prices, through trading misjudgments, or for other reasons. In addition, financing difficulties create pressures on management concerned about the solvency of the business.

88.   Misappropriation of assets and fraudulent financial reporting may often involve override of controls that otherwise may appear to be operating effectively. This may include override of controls over data, assumptions and detailed process controls that allow losses and theft to be hidden. For example, difficult market conditions may increase pressure to conceal or offset trades as they attempt to recover losses.

Assessing the Risk of Material Misstatement

89.   The auditor's assessment of the identified risks at the assertion level in accordance with ISA (UK and Ireland) 315 includes evaluating the design and implementation of internal control. It provides a basis for considering the appropriate audit approach for designing and performing further audit procedures in accordance with ISA (UK and Ireland) 330, including both substantive procedures and tests of controls. The approach taken is influenced by the auditor's understanding of internal control relevant to the audit, including the strength of the control environment and any risk management function, the size and complexity of the entity's operations and whether the auditor's assessment of the risks of material misstatement include an expectation that controls are operating effectively.

89-1.   An entity may have a control culture that is generally focused on maintaining a high level of internal control. Because of the complexity of some treasury activities, this culture may not pervade the group of personnel responsible for financial instrument activities. Alternatively, because of the risks associated with some financial instrument activities, management may enforce a more strict control environment than it does elsewhere within the entity. In entities without a treasury function, dealing in financial instruments may be rare and management's knowledge and experience limited. Accordingly, the auditor may need to consider in its risk assessment the control environment applicable to those responsible for functions dealing with financial instruments, particularly if the instruments are complex.

89-2.   In an entity with a complex organisational structure, lack of clarity of lines of responsibility may increase risks – for example, where there is not a clear delineation between front office and middle office control and back office functions in a complex trading environment.

90.   The auditor's assessment of the risk of material misstatement at the assertion level may change during the course of the audit as additional information is obtained. Remaining alert during the audit, for example, when inspecting records or documents may assist the auditor in identifying arrangements or other information that may indicate the existence of financial instruments that management has not

previously identified or disclosed to the auditor. Such records and documents may include, for example:

- Minutes of meetings of those charged with governance; and

- Specific invoices from, and correspondence with, the entity's professional advisors.

Factors to Consider in Determining Whether, and to What Extent, to Test the Operating Effectiveness of Controls

91. An expectation that controls are operating effectively may be more common when dealing with a financial institution with well-established controls, and therefore controls testing may be an effective means of obtaining audit evidence. When an entity has a trading function, substantive tests alone may not provide sufficient appropriate audit evidence due to the volume of contracts and the different systems used. Tests of controls, however, will not be sufficient on their own as the auditor is required by ISA (UK and Ireland) 330 to design and perform substantive procedures for each material class of transactions, account balance and disclosure.[22]

92. Entities with a high volume of trading and use of financial instruments may have more sophisticated controls, and an effective risk management function, and therefore the auditor may be more likely to test controls in obtaining evidence about:

- The occurrence, completeness, accuracy, and cutoff of the transactions; ~~and~~

- The existence, rights and obligations, and completeness of account balances; and

- The valuation of financial instruments where an independent price verification function exists.

93. In those entities with relatively few financial instrument transactions:

- Management and those charged with governance may have only a limited understanding of financial instruments and how they affect the business;

- The entity may only have a few different types of instruments with little or no interaction between them;

- There is unlikely to be a complex control environment (for example, the controls described in the Appendix may not be in place at the entity);

- Management may use pricing information from third-party pricing sources to value their instruments; and

- Controls over the use of pricing information from third-party pricing sources may be less sophisticated.

---

[22] ISA (UK and Ireland) 330, paragraph 18.

94. When an entity has relatively few transactions involving financial instruments, it may be relatively easy for the auditor to obtain an understanding of the entity's objectives for using the financial instruments and the characteristics of the instruments. In such circumstances, much of the audit evidence is likely to be substantive in nature, the auditor may perform the majority of the audit work at year-end, and third-party confirmations are likely to provide evidence in relation to the completeness, accuracy, and existence of the transactions.

95. In reaching a decision on the nature, timing and extent of testing of controls, the auditor may consider factors such as:

   • The nature, frequency and volume of financial instrument transactions;

   • The strength of controls, including whether controls are appropriately designed to respond to the risks associated with an entity's volume of financial instrument transactions and whether there is a governance framework over the entity's financial instrument activities;

   • The importance of particular controls to the overall control objectives and processes in place at the entity, including the sophistication of the information systems to support financial instrument transactions;

   • The monitoring of controls and identified deficiencies in control procedures;

   • The issues the controls are intended to address, for example, controls related to the exercise of judgments compared with controls over supporting data. Substantive tests are more likely to be effective than relying on controls related to the exercise of judgment;

   • The competency of those involved in the control activities, for example whether the entity has adequate capacity, including during periods of stress, and ability to establish and verify valuations for the financial instruments to which it is exposed;

   • The frequency of performance of these control activities;

   • The level of precision the controls are intended to achieve;

   • The evidence of performance of control activities; and

   • The timing of key financial instrument transactions, for example, whether they are close to the period end.

95-1. The population from which items are selected for detailed testing is not necessarily limited to the accounting records. Tested items may be drawn from other sources, for example counterparty confirmations and trader tickets, so that the possibility of omission of transactions in the recording procedure can be tested.

Substantive Procedures

96. Designing substantive procedures includes consideration of:

- The use of analytical procedures[23]—While analytical procedures undertaken by the auditor can be effective as risk assessment procedures to provide the auditor with information about an entity's business, they may be less effective as substantive procedures when performed alone. This is because the complex interplay of the drivers of the valuation often mask any unusual trends that might arise.

- Non-routine transactions—Many financial transactions are negotiated contracts between an entity and its counterparty (often known as "over the counter" or OTC). To the extent that financial instrument transactions are not routine and outside an entity's normal activities, a substantive audit approach may be the most effective means of achieving the planned audit objectives. In instances where financial instrument transactions are not undertaken routinely, the auditor's responses to assessed risk, including designing and performing audit procedures, have regard to the entity's possible lack of experience in this area.

- Availability of evidence—For example, when the entity uses a third-party pricing source, evidence concerning the relevant financial statement assertions may not be available from the entity.

- Procedures performed in other audit areas—Procedures performed in other financial statement areas may provide evidence about the completeness of financial instrument transactions. These procedures may include tests of subsequent cash receipts and payments, and the search for unrecorded liabilities.

- Selection of items for testing—In some cases, the financial instrument portfolio will comprise instruments with varying complexity and risk. In such cases, judgmental sampling may be useful.

97. For example, in the case of an asset-backed security, in responding to the risks of material misstatement for such a security, the auditor may consider performing some of the following audit procedures:

- Examining contractual documentation to understand the terms of the security, the underlying collateral and the rights of each class of security holder.

---

[23] ISA (UK and Ireland) 315, paragraph 6(b), requires the auditor to apply analytical procedures as risk assessment procedures to assist in assessing the risks of material misstatement in order to provide a basis for designing and implementing responses to the assessed risks. ISA (UK and Ireland) 520, *Analytical Procedures*, paragraph 6, requires the auditor to use analytical procedures in forming an overall conclusion on the financial statements. Analytical procedures may also be applied at other stages of the audit.

- Inquiring about management's process of estimating cash flows.

- Evaluating the reasonableness of assumptions, such as prepayment rates, default rates and loss severities.

- Obtaining an understanding of the method used to determine the cash flow waterfall.

- Comparing the results of the fair value measurement with the valuations of other securities with similar underlying collateral and terms.

- Reperforming calculations.

Dual-Purpose Tests

98. Although the purpose of a test of controls is different from the purpose of a test of details, it may be efficient to perform both at the same time by, for example:

- Performing a test of controls and a test of details on the same transaction (for example, testing whether a signed contract has been maintained and whether the details of the financial instrument have been appropriately captured in a summary sheet); or

- Testing controls when testing management's process of making valuation estimates.

Timing of the Auditor's Procedures[24]

99. After assessing the risks associated with financial instruments, the engagement team determines the timing of planned tests of controls and substantive audit procedures. The timing of planned audit procedures varies depending on a number of factors, including the frequency of the control operation, the significance of the activity being controlled, and the related risk of material misstatement.

100. While it is necessary to undertake most of the audit procedures in relation to valuation and presentation at the period end, audit procedures in relation to other assertions such as completeness and existence can usefully be tested at an interim period. For example tests of controls may be performed at an interim period for more routine controls, such as IT controls and authorizations for new products. Also, it may be effective to test the operating effectiveness of controls over new product approval by gathering evidence of the appropriate level of management sign-off on a new financial instrument for an interim period.

101. Auditors may perform some tests on models as of an interim date, for example, by comparing the output of the model to market transactions. Another possible interim

---

[24] Paragraphs 11–12 and 22–23 of ISA (UK and Ireland) 330 establish requirements when the auditor performs procedures at an interim period and explains how such audit evidence can be used.

procedure for instruments with observable inputs is to test the reasonableness of the pricing information provided by a third-party pricing source.

102. Areas of more significant judgment are often tested close to, or at, the period end as:

- Valuations can change significantly in a short period of time, making it difficult to compare and reconcile interim balances with comparable information at the balance sheet date;

- An entity may engage in an increased volume of financial instrument transactions between an interim period and year-end;

- Manual journal entries may only be made after the end of the accounting period; and

- Non-routine or significant transactions may take place late in the accounting period.

Procedures Relating to Completeness, Accuracy, Existence, Occurrence and Rights and Obligations

103. Many of the auditor's procedures can be used to address a number of assertions. For example, procedures to address the existence of an account balance at period end will also address the occurrence of a class of transactions, and may also assist in establishing proper cut-off. This is because financial instruments arise from legal contracts and, by verifying the accuracy of the recording of the transaction, the auditor can also verify its existence, and obtain evidence to support the occurrence and rights and obligations assertions at the same time, and confirm that transactions are recorded in the correct accounting period.

104. Procedures that may provide audit evidence to support the completeness, accuracy, and existence assertions include:

- External confirmation[25] of bank accounts, trades, and custodian statements. This can be done by direct confirmation with the counterparty (including the use of bank confirmations), where a reply is sent to the auditor directly. Alternatively this information may be obtained from the counterparty's systems through a data feed. Where this is done, controls to prevent tampering with the computer systems through which the information is transmitted may be considered by the auditor in evaluating the reliability of the evidence from the confirmation. If

---

[25] ISA (UK and Ireland) 505, *External Confirmations*, deals with the auditor's use of external confirmation procedures to obtain audit evidence in accordance with the requirements of ISA (UK and Ireland) 330 and ISA (UK and Ireland) 500, *Audit Evidence*. See also the IAASB Staff Audit Practice Alert, *Emerging Practice Issues Regarding the Use of External Confirmations in an Audit of Financial Statements*, issued in November 2009.

PN 16 (Revised), *Bank Reports for Audit Purposes in the United Kingdom*, summarises the process agreed between the UK auditing profession and the British Bankers Association regarding the procedures auditors use when requesting confirmation of balances, transactions or arrangements from bankers of an entity being audited.

confirmations are not received, the auditor may be able to obtain evidence by reviewing contracts and testing relevant controls. External confirmations, however, often do not provide adequate audit evidence with respect to the valuation assertion though they may assist in identifying any side agreements.

- Reviewing reconciliations of statements or data feeds from custodians with the entity's own records. This may necessitate evaluating IT controls around and within automated reconciliation processes and to evaluate whether reconciling items are properly understood and resolved.

- Reviewing operational data, such as reconciliation differences. To do this the auditor will have to obtain sufficient evidence to indicate that this data is reliable.

- Reviewing journal entries and the controls over the recording of such entries. This may assist in, for example:

  ○ Determining if entries have been made by employees other than those authorized to do so.

  ○ Identifying unusual or inappropriate end-of-period journal entries, which may be relevant to fraud risk.

- Reading individual contracts and reviewing supporting documentation of the entity's financial instrument transactions, including accounting records, thereby verifying existence and rights and obligations. For example, an auditor may read individual contracts associated with financial instruments and review supporting documentation, including the accounting entries made when the contract was initially recorded, and may also subsequently review accounting entries made for valuation purposes. Doing so allows the auditor to evaluate whether the complexities inherent in a transaction have been fully identified and reflected in the accounts. Legal arrangements and their associated risks need to be considered by those with suitable expertise to ensure that rights exist.

- Testing controls, for example by reperforming controls.

- Reviewing the entity's complaints management systems. Unrecorded transactions may result in the entity's failure to make a cash payment to a counterparty, and may be detected by reviewing complaints received.

- Reviewing master netting arrangements to identify unrecorded instruments.

105. These procedures are particularly important for some financial instruments, such as derivatives or guarantees. This is because they may not have a large initial investment, meaning it may be hard to identify their existence. For example, embedded derivatives are often contained in contracts for non-financial instruments which may not be included in confirmation procedures.

Valuation of Financial Instruments

Financial Reporting Requirements

106. Fair presentation financial reporting frameworks often use fair value hierarchies, for example those used in IFRS, ~~and~~ U.S. GAAP and in certain circumstances UK GAAP. This usually means that the volume and detail of the required disclosures increases as the level of measurement uncertainty increases. The distinction between the levels in the hierarchy may require judgment.

107. The auditor may find it useful to obtain an understanding of how the financial instruments relate to the fair value hierarchy. Ordinarily, the risk of material misstatement, and the level of audit procedures to be applied, increases as the level of measurement uncertainty increases. The use of level 3, and some level 2, inputs from the fair value hierarchy may be a useful guide to the level of measurement uncertainty. Level 2 inputs vary from those which are easily obtained to those which are closer to level 3 inputs. The auditor evaluates available evidence and understands both the fair value hierarchy and the risk of management bias in management's categorization of financial instruments in the fair value hierarchy.

108. In accordance with ISA (UK and Ireland) 540,[26] the auditor considers the entity's valuation policies and methodology for data and assumptions used in the valuation methodology. In many cases, the applicable financial reporting framework does not prescribe the valuation methodology. When this is the case, matters that may be relevant to the auditor's understanding of how management values financial instruments include, for example:

- Whether management has a formal valuation policy and, if so, whether the valuation technique used for a financial instrument is appropriately documented in accordance with that policy;

- Which models may give rise to the greatest risk of material misstatement;

- How management considered the complexity of the valuation of the financial instrument when selecting a particular valuation technique;

- Whether there is a greater risk of material misstatement because management has internally developed a model to be used to value financial instruments or is departing from a valuation technique commonly used to value the particular financial instrument;

- Whether a model used to prepare actuarial information follows the principles in Technical Actuarial Standard M: Modelling[26a];

- Whether management made use of a third-party pricing source;

---

[26] ISA (UK and Ireland) 540, paragraph 8(c).
[26a] Technical Actuarial Standards are issued by the Financial Reporting Council.

- Whether those involved in developing and applying the valuation technique have the appropriate skills and expertise to do so, including whether a management's expert has been used; and

- Whether there are indicators of management bias in selecting the valuation technique to be used.

108-1. UK banks and certain other regulated entities in the financial sector are required for regulatory purposes to prepare a Prudent Valuation Return, on a quarterly calendar year basis, to assist the regulator in assessing the capital resources of the entity and gaining a wider understanding of the nature and sources of measurement uncertainty in fair valued instruments. The information within these returns is not required to be included in the financial statements and is not required to be audited or reviewed by the auditor. A return may also not be prepared that coincides with the accounting reference date of the financial statements. However, the auditor of such an entity may find that consideration of the information in the returns assists the understanding of the uncertainties associated with the financial instruments used and disclosed by the entity.

Assessing the Risk of Material Misstatement Related to Valuation

109. When evaluating whether the valuation techniques used by an entity are appropriate in the circumstances, and whether controls over valuation techniques are in place, the factors considered by the auditor may include:

- Who developed the valuation techniques and whether design and implementation could have been unduly influenced by traders or others who may not be objective. Where the entity obtains input from traders without independent oversight the auditor considers whether that input is appropriate in the circumstances;

- Whether the valuation techniques are commonly used by other market participants and have been previously demonstrated to provide a reliable estimate of prices obtained from market transactions;

- Whether the valuation techniques operate as intended and there are no flaws in their design, particularly under extreme conditions, and whether they have been objectively validated. Indicators of flaws include inconsistent movements relative to benchmarks;

- Whether the valuation techniques take account of the risks inherent in the financial instrument being valued, including counterparty creditworthiness, and own credit risk in the case of valuation techniques used to measure financial liabilities;

- How the valuation techniques are calibrated to the market, including the sensitivity of the valuation techniques to changes in variables;

- Whether market variables and assumptions are used consistently and whether new conditions justify a change in the valuation techniques, market variables or assumptions used;

- Whether sensitivity analyses indicate that valuations would change significantly with only small or moderate changes in assumptions;

- The organizational structure, such as the existence of an internal department responsible for developing models to value certain instruments, particularly where level 3 inputs are involved. For example, a model development function that is involved in assisting in pricing deals is less objective than one which is functionally and organizationally segregated from the front office; and

- The competence and objectivity of those responsible for the development and application of the valuation techniques, including management's relative experience with particular models that may be newly developed.

The auditor (or auditor's expert) may also independently develop one or more valuation techniques to compare its output with that of the valuation techniques used by management.

Significant Risks

110. The auditor's risk assessment process may lead the auditor to identify one or more significant risks relating to the valuation of financial instruments, when any of the following circumstances exist:

- High measurement uncertainty related to the valuation of financial instruments (for example, those with unobservable inputs).[27]

- Lack of sufficient evidence to support management's valuation of its financial instruments.

- Lack of management understanding of its financial instruments or expertise necessary to value such instruments properly, including the ability to determine whether valuation adjustments are needed.

- Lack of management understanding of complex requirements in the applicable financial reporting framework relating to measurement and disclosure of financial instruments, and inability of management to make the judgments required to properly apply those requirements.

---

[27] Where the auditor determines that the high estimation uncertainty related to the valuation of complex financial instruments gives rise to a significant risk, ISA (UK and Ireland) 540 requires the auditor to perform substantive procedures and evaluate the adequacy of the disclosure of their estimation uncertainty. See ISA (UK and Ireland) 540, paragraphs 11, 15 and 20.

- The significance of valuation adjustments made to valuation technique outputs when the applicable financial reporting framework requires or permits such adjustments.

111. For accounting estimates that give rise to significant risks, in addition to other substantive procedures performed to meet the requirements of ISA (UK and Ireland) 330, ISA (UK and Ireland) 540[28] requires the auditor to evaluate the following:

   (a) How management has considered alternative assumptions or outcomes, and why it has rejected them, or how management has otherwise addressed measurement uncertainty in making the accounting estimate;

   (b) Whether the significant assumptions used by management are reasonable; and

   (c) Where relevant to the reasonableness of the significant assumptions used by management, or the appropriate application of the applicable financial reporting framework, management's intent to carry out specific courses of action and its ability to do so.

112. As markets become inactive, the change in circumstances may lead to a move from valuation by market price to valuation by model, or may result in a change from one particular model to another. Reacting to changes in market conditions may be difficult if management does not have policies in place prior to their occurrence. Management may also not possess the expertise necessary to develop a model on an urgent basis, or select the valuation technique that may be appropriate in the circumstances. Even where valuation techniques have been consistently used, there is a need for management to examine the continuing appropriateness of the valuation techniques and assumptions used for determining valuation of financial instruments. Further, valuation techniques may have been selected in times where reasonable market information was available, but may not provide reasonable valuations in times of unanticipated stress.

113. The susceptibility to management bias, whether intentional or unintentional, increases with the subjectivity of the valuation and the degree of measurement uncertainty. For example, management may tend to ignore observable marketplace assumptions or data and instead use their own internally-developed model if the model yields more favorable results. Even without fraudulent intent, there may be a natural temptation to bias judgments towards the most favorable end of what may be a wide spectrum, rather than the point in the spectrum that might be considered to be most consistent with the applicable financial reporting framework. Changing the valuation technique from period to period without a clear and appropriate reason for doing so may also be an indicator of management bias. Although some form of management bias is inherent in subjective decisions relating to the valuation of financial instruments, when there is intention to mislead, management bias is fraudulent in nature.

---

[28] ISA (UK and Ireland) 540, paragraph 15(a)-(b).

Developing an Audit Approach

113-1. Tests of valuation mainly fall under three headings:

- Verifying the external prices that are used to value financial instruments. External prices may be available directly from markets but it is likely for complex financial instruments that external price information will be used as inputs to valuation models. This is because many complex financial instruments are tailored for particular clients and are not therefore homogenous with each other;

- Confirming the validity of valuation models. Valuation models are used, where an instrument is not quoted in the market, but prices for its component parts can be derived from instruments that are quoted (where inputs to the model are observable) or from estimates of fair value (where inputs are unobservable);

- Evaluating the overall result and reserving for residual uncertainties. By their nature complex financial instruments are often not traded in active liquid markets and hence their valuation is often uncertain and requires considerable judgment. Once the detailed evidence has been gathered and valuations have been made on an instrument by instrument basis, it is important to review the overall result and consider whether there are residual uncertainties not taken into account by the valuation process that require further adjustment.

113-2. The entity being audited should have its own processes to undertake these tasks. The auditor reviews the output from these processes and considers what independent confirmation needs to be undertaken. If there are weaknesses in these processes, the auditor communicates them to those charged with governance. Where there are serious weaknesses, the auditor considers the impact on the audit and whether applicable law and regulations require a report to be made to a regulator.

114. In testing how management values the financial instrument and in responding to the assessed risks of material misstatement in accordance with ISA (UK and Ireland) 540,[29] the auditor undertakes one or more of the following procedures, taking account of the nature of the accounting estimates:

(a) Test how management made the accounting estimate and the data on which it is based (including valuation techniques used by the entity in its valuations).

(b) Test the operating effectiveness of the controls over how management made the accounting estimate, together with appropriate substantive procedures.

(c) Develop a point estimate or a range to evaluate management's point estimate.

(d) Determine whether events occurring up to the date of the auditor's report provide audit evidence regarding the accounting estimate.

---

[29] ISA (UK and Ireland) 540, paragraphs 12–14.

Many auditors find that a combination of testing how management valued the financial instrument, and the data on which it is based, and testing the operating effectiveness of controls, will be an effective and efficient audit approach. While subsequent events may provide some evidence about the valuation of financial instruments, other factors may need to be taken into account to address any changes in market conditions subsequent to the balance sheet date.[30] If the auditor is unable to test how management made the estimate, the auditor may choose to develop a point estimate or range.

115. As described in Section I, to estimate the fair value of financial instruments management may:

- Utilize information from third-party pricing sources;

- Gather data to develop their own estimate using various techniques including models; and

- Engage an expert to develop an estimate.

Management often may use a combination of these approaches. For example, management may have their own pricing process but use third-party pricing sources to corroborate their own values.

Audit Considerations When Management Uses a Third-Party Pricing Source

116. Management may make use of a third-party pricing source, such as a pricing service or broker, in valuing the entity's financial instruments. Understanding how management uses the information and how the pricing service operates assists the auditor in determining the nature and extent of audit procedures needed.

117. The following matters may be relevant where management uses a third-party pricing source:

- *The type of third-party pricing source* – Some third-party pricing sources make more information available about their process. For example, a pricing service often provides information about their methodology, assumptions and data in valuing financial instruments at the asset class level. By contrast, brokers often provide no, or only limited, information about the inputs and assumptions used in developing the quote.

- *The nature of inputs used and the complexity of the valuation technique* – The reliability of prices from third-party pricing sources varies depending on the observability of inputs (and accordingly, the level of inputs in the fair value hierarchy), and the complexity of the methodology for valuing a specific security

---

[30] Paragraphs A63-A66 of ISA (UK and Ireland) 540 provide examples of some of the factors that may be relevant.

or asset class. For example, the reliability of a price for an equity investment actively traded in a liquid market is higher than that of a corporate bond traded in a liquid market that has not traded on the measurement date, which, in turn, is more reliable than that of an asset-backed security that is valued using a discounted cash flow model.

- *The reputation and experience of the third-party pricing source* – For example, a third-party pricing source may be experienced in a certain type of financial instrument, and be recognized as such, but may not be similarly experienced in other types of financial instruments. The auditor's past experience with the third-party pricing source may also be relevant in this regard.

- *The objectivity of the third-party pricing source* – For example, if a price obtained by management comes from a counterparty such as the broker who sold the financial instrument to the entity, or an entity with a close relationship with the entity being audited, the price may not be reliable.

- *The entity's controls over the use of third-party pricing sources* – The degree to which management has controls in place to assess the reliability of information from third-party pricing sources affects the reliability of the fair value measurement. For example, management may have controls in place to:

  ○ Review and approve the use of the third-party pricing source, including consideration of the reputation, experience and objectivity of the third-party pricing source.

  ○ Determine the completeness, relevance and accuracy of the prices and pricing-related data.

- *The third-party pricing source's controls* – The controls and processes over valuations for the asset classes of interest to the auditor. For example, a third-party pricing source may have strong controls around how prices are developed, including the use of a formalized process for customers, both buy and sell side, to challenge the prices received from the pricing service, when supported by appropriate evidence, which may enable the third-party pricing source to constantly correct prices to more fully reflect the information available to market participants.

118. Possible approaches to gathering evidence regarding information from third-party pricing sources may include the following:

- For level 1 inputs, comparing the information from third-party pricing sources with observable market prices.

- Reviewing disclosures provided by third-party pricing sources about their controls and processes, valuation techniques, inputs and assumptions.

- Testing the controls management has in place to assess the reliability of information from third-party pricing sources.

- Performing procedures at the third-party pricing source to understand and test the controls and processes, valuation techniques, inputs and assumptions used for asset classes or specific financial instruments of interest.

- Evaluating whether the prices obtained from third-party pricing sources are reasonable in relation to prices from other third-party pricing sources, the entity's estimate or the auditor's own estimate.

- Evaluating the reasonableness of valuation techniques, assumptions and inputs.

- Developing a point estimate or a range for some financial instruments priced by the third-party pricing source and evaluating whether the results are within a reasonable range of each other.

- Obtaining a service auditor's report that covers the controls over validation of the prices.[31]

119. Obtaining prices from multiple third-party pricing sources may also provide useful information about measurement uncertainty. A wide range of prices may indicate higher measurement uncertainty and may suggest that the financial instrument is sensitive to small changes in data and assumptions. A narrow range may indicate lower measurement uncertainty and may suggest less sensitivity to changes in data and assumptions. Although obtaining prices from multiple sources may be useful, when considering financial instruments that have inputs categorized at levels 2 or 3 of the fair value hierarchy, in particular, obtaining prices from multiple sources is unlikely to provide sufficient appropriate audit evidence on its own. This is because:

(a) What appear to be multiple sources of pricing information may be utilizing the same underlying pricing source; and

(b) Understanding the inputs used by the third-party pricing source in determining the price may be necessary in order to categorize the financial instrument in the fair value hierarchy.

120. In some situations, the auditor may be unable to gain an understanding of the process used to generate the price, including any controls over the process of how reliably the price is determined, or may not have access to the model, including the assumptions and other inputs used. In such cases, the auditor may decide to undertake to develop a point estimate or a range to evaluate management's point estimate in responding to the assessed risk.

---

[31] Some pricing services may provide reports for users of its data to explain their controls over pricing data, that is, a report prepared in accordance with International Standard on Assurance Engagements (ISAE) 3402, *Assurance Reports on Controls at a Service Organization*. Management may request, and the auditor may consider obtaining, such a report to develop an understanding of how the pricing data is prepared and evaluate whether the controls at the pricing service can be relied upon.

Audit Considerations When the Entity has an Independent Price Verification Function

120-1. Where the entity has an independent price verification function in place (see paragraph 62-1), understanding the processes and controls performed by the function with respect to financial instrument valuations may assist the auditor in determining the nature and extent of procedures needed.

120-2. Audit procedures to test the entity's independent price verification function controls, may include:

* Testing the completeness of the price testing population.

* Testing the completeness, accuracy and existence of full revaluation or parameter based pricing differences.

* Testing the calculation of fair value adjustments in accordance with approved policies / methods.

* Testing controls for the reporting of pricing differences and adjustment to the entity's books and records.

Audit Considerations When Management Estimates Fair Values Using a Model

121. Paragraph 13(b) of ISA (UK and Ireland) 540 requires the auditor, if testing management's process of making the accounting estimate, to evaluate whether the method of measurement used is appropriate in the circumstances and the assumptions used by management are reasonable in light of the measurement objectives of the applicable financial reporting framework.

122. Whether management has used a third-party pricing source, or is undertaking its own valuation, models are often used to value financial instruments, particularly when using inputs at levels 2 and 3 of the fair value hierarchy. In determining the nature, timing and extent of audit procedures on models, the auditor may consider the methodology, assumptions and data used in the model. When considering more complex financial instruments such as those using level 3 inputs, testing all three may be a useful source of audit evidence. However, when the model is both simple and generally accepted, such as some bond price calculations, audit evidence obtained from focusing on the assumptions and data used in the model may be a more useful source of evidence.

123. Testing a model can be accomplished by two main approaches:

(a) The auditor can test management's model, by considering the appropriateness of the model used by management, the reasonableness of the assumptions and data used, and the mathematical accuracy; or

(b) The auditor can develop their own estimate, and then compare the auditor's valuation with that of the entity.

124. Where valuation of financial instruments is based on unobservable inputs (that is, level 3 inputs), matters that the auditor may consider include, for example, how management supports the following:

- The identification and characteristics of marketplace participants relevant to the financial instrument.

- How unobservable inputs are determined on initial recognition.

- Modifications it has made to its own assumptions to reflect its view of assumptions marketplace participants would use.

- Whether it has incorporated the best input information available in the circumstances.

- Where applicable, how its assumptions take account of comparable transactions.

- Sensitivity analysis of models when unobservable inputs are used and whether adjustments have been made to address measurement uncertainty.

125. In addition, the auditor's industry knowledge, knowledge of market trends, understanding of other entities' valuations (having regard to confidentiality) and other relevant price indicators informs the auditor's testing of the valuations and the consideration of whether the valuations appear reasonable overall. If the valuations appear to be consistently overly aggressive or conservative, this may be an indicator of possible management bias.

126. Where there is a lack of observable external evidence, it is particularly important that those charged with governance have been appropriately engaged to understand the subjectivity of management's valuations and the evidence that has been obtained to support these valuations. In such cases, it may be necessary for the auditor to evaluate whether there has been a thorough review and consideration of the issues, including any documentation, at all appropriate management levels within the entity, including with those charged with governance.

127. When markets become inactive or dislocated, or inputs are unobservable, management's valuations may be more judgmental and less verifiable and, as a result, may be less reliable. In such circumstances, the auditor may test the model by a combination of testing controls operated by the entity, evaluating the design and operation of the model, testing the assumptions and data used in the model, and comparing its output to a point estimate or range developed by the auditor or to other third-party valuation techniques.[32]

---

[32] ISA (UK and Ireland) 540, paragraph 13(d) describes requirements when the auditor develops a range to evaluate management's point estimate. Valuation techniques developed by third parties and used by the auditor may, in some circumstances be considered the work of an auditor's expert and subject to the requirements in ISA (UK and Ireland) 620.

128. It is likely that in testing the inputs used in an entity's valuation methodology,[33] for example, where such inputs are categorized in the fair value hierarchy, the auditor will also be obtaining evidence to support the disclosures required by the applicable financial reporting framework. For example, the auditor's substantive procedures to evaluate whether the inputs used in an entity's valuation technique (that is, level 1, level 2 and level 3 inputs) are appropriate, and tests of an entity's sensitivity analysis, will be relevant to the auditor's evaluation of whether the disclosures achieve fair presentation.

Evaluating Whether the Assumptions Used by Management Are Reasonable

129. An assumption used in a model may be deemed to be significant if a reasonable variation in the assumption would materially affect the measurement of the financial instrument.[34] Management may have considered alternative assumptions or outcomes by performing a sensitivity analysis. The extent of subjectivity associated with assumptions influences the degree of measurement uncertainty and may lead the auditor to conclude there is a significant risk, for example in the case of level 3 inputs.

130. Audit procedures to test the assumptions used by management, including those used as inputs to models, may include evaluating:

- Whether, and if so, how, management has incorporated market inputs into the development of assumptions, as it is generally preferable to seek to maximize the use of relevant observable inputs and minimize unobservable inputs;

- Whether the assumptions are consistent with observable market conditions, and the characteristics of the financial asset or financial liability;

- Whether the sources of market-participant assumptions are relevant and reliable, and how management has selected the assumptions to use when a number of different marketplace assumptions exist; and

- Whether sensitivity analyses indicate that valuations would change significantly with only small or moderate changes in assumptions.

See paragraphs A77 to A83 of ISA (UK and Ireland) 540 for further considerations relative to evaluating the assumptions used by management.

131. The auditor's consideration of judgments about the future is based on information available at the time at which the judgment is made. Subsequent events may result in outcomes that are inconsistent with judgments that were reasonable at the time they were made.

---

[33] See, for example, paragraph 15 of ISA (UK and Ireland) 540 for requirements relative to the auditor's evaluation of management's assumption regarding significant risks.

[34] See ISA (UK and Ireland) 540, paragraph A107.

132. In some cases, the discount rate in a present value calculation may be adjusted to account for the uncertainties in the valuation, rather than adjusting each assumption. In such cases, an auditor's procedures may focus on the discount rate, by looking at an observable trade on a similar security to compare the discount rates used or developing an independent model to calculate the discount rate and compare with that used by management.

Audit Considerations When a Management's Expert Is Used by the Entity

133. As discussed in Section I, management may engage a valuation expert to value some or all of their securities. Such experts may be brokers, investment bankers, pricing services that also provide expert valuation services, or other specialized valuation firms.

133-1. If the third party applies particular expertise, for example in the use of models, in making an estimate which the entity uses in preparing its financial statements, the third party is considered a management's expert. If, on the other hand, the third party merely provides price data regarding private transactions not otherwise available to the entity which the entity uses in its own estimation methods, such information, if used as audit evidence, is not considered to be evidence produced by a management's expert.

134. Paragraph 8 of ISA (UK and Ireland) 500 contains requirements for the auditor when evaluating evidence from an expert engaged by management. The extent of the auditor's procedures in relation to a management's expert and that expert's work depend on the significance of the expert's work for the auditor's purposes. Evaluating the appropriateness of management's expert's work assists the auditor in assessing whether the prices or valuations supplied by a management's expert provide sufficient appropriate audit evidence to support the valuations. Examples of procedures the auditor may perform include:

- Evaluating the competence, capabilities and objectivity of management's expert for example: their relationship with the entity; their reputation and standing in the market; their experience with the particular types of instruments; and their understanding of the relevant financial reporting framework applicable to the valuations;

- Obtaining an understanding of the work of the management's expert, for example by assessing the appropriateness of the valuation technique(s) used and the key market variables and assumptions used in the valuation technique(s);

- Evaluating the appropriateness of that expert's work as audit evidence. At this point, the focus is on the appropriateness of the expert's work at the level of the individual financial instrument. For a sample of the relevant instruments, it may be appropriate to develop an estimate independently (see paragraphs 136 to 137 on developing a point estimate or range), using different data and assumptions, then compare that estimate to that of the management's expert; and

- Other procedures may include:

  ○ Modeling different assumptions to derive assumptions in another model, then considering the reasonableness of those derived assumptions.

  ○ Comparing management's point estimates with the auditor's point estimates to determine if management's estimates are consistently higher or lower.

134-1. The auditor considers whether management has given proper consideration to the models used and, if not, the possible impacts on the risks related to these items and others and the implications for the audit. In such cases, the auditor's considerations may include whether:

- It is necessary and possible to obtain information directly, with management's authority, from the third party.

- A report on the third party's internal controls by their auditors is available covering control objectives applicable to the valuations.

135. Assumptions may be made or identified by a management's expert to assist management in valuing its financial instruments. Such assumptions, when used by management, become management's assumptions that the auditor needs to consider in the same manner as management's other assumptions.

Developing a Point Estimate or Range

136. An auditor may develop a valuation technique and adjust the inputs and assumptions used in the valuation technique to develop a range for use in evaluating the reasonableness of management's valuation. Paragraphs 106 to 135 of this PN may assist the auditor in developing a point estimate or range. In accordance with ISA (UK and Ireland) 540,[35] if the auditor uses assumptions, or methodologies that differ from management's, the auditor shall obtain an understanding of management's assumptions or methodologies sufficient to establish that the auditor's range takes into account relevant variables and to evaluate any significant differences from management's valuation. The auditor may find it useful to use the work of an auditor's expert to evaluate the reasonableness of management's valuation.

137. In some cases, the auditor may conclude that sufficient evidence cannot be obtained from the auditor's attempts to obtain an understanding of management's assumptions or methodology, for example when a third-party pricing source uses internally developed models and software and does not allow access to relevant information. In such cases, the auditor may not be able to obtain sufficient appropriate audit evidence about the valuation if the auditor is unable to perform other procedures to respond to the risks of material misstatement, such as developing a point estimate or a range to evaluate management's point estimate.[36]

---

[35] ISA (UK and Ireland) 540, paragraph 13(c).
[36] ISA (UK and Ireland) 540, paragraph 13(d).

ISA (UK and Ireland) 705[37] describes the implications of the auditor's inability to obtain sufficient appropriate audit evidence.

Evaluating the Overall Result and Adjusting for Valuation Uncertainties

137-1. Valuing complex financial instruments is not a precise science. Uncertainties over the reliability of market quotes, the validity of models and the accuracy of their calibration to actual market activity will exist, particularly for very complicated instruments that are not actively traded. If such instruments were sold, a buyer might reduce their price to reflect these uncertainties and the risks that (s)he was thereby assuming. Estimating the valuation adjustment required for such factors is very judgmental and will be specific to each entity. The auditor considers all the factors taken into account in the valuation process and uses experience and judgment to evaluate the amount of any adjustment required. The auditor may need to draw on expert help to assist in doing this.

137-2. One important factor in evaluating the overall result is to consider whether counterparty risk (the risk that a counterparty to a transaction will not perform their side of the bargain) has been properly taken into account in valuing the instrument. It is inherent in mark to market pricing that counterparty risk is taken into account in arriving at the market price and an entity's pricing process should therefore have already dealt with counterparty risk. However, the auditor considers whether there are any other aspects of counterparty risk that have not properly been addressed, such as the possible need for an impairment provision in respect of an accrual accounted component of a financial instrument (e.g. an interest accrual).

Hedge Accounting

137-3. Where hedge accounting techniques are used, the auditor gathers audit evidence to determine whether management's designation of a financial instrument as a hedge is appropriate and the accounting entries are consistent with the relevant accounting standards. The nature and extent of the evidence obtained by the auditor will vary depending on the nature of the hedged items and the hedging instruments. Generally, the auditor obtains evidence as to:

(a) Whether the financial instrument was designated as a hedge at the inception of the transaction;

(b) The nature of the hedging relationship;

(c) The entity's risk management objective and strategy for undertaking the hedge;

(d) The entity's assessment of the effectiveness of the hedge;

---

[37] ISA (UK and Ireland) 705, *Modifications to the Opinion in the Independent Auditor's Report.*

(e) Where the financial instrument is hedging a future transaction, the entity's assessment of the certainty of that future transaction; and

(f) Whether the hedging instrument, hedged item and hedging relationship are permitted under the relevant accounting standards.

If there is disagreement with management's use of hedge accounting the auditor considers whether to qualify the audit opinion on the financial statements.

137-4. The auditor gathers audit evidence to determine whether management complied with the applicable hedge accounting requirements of the financial reporting framework, including designation and documentation requirements. In addition, the auditor gathers audit evidence as to whether there is support for management's assessment that the hedging transaction has met the relevant effectiveness tests in accordance with the applicable accounting standards[37a]. The nature and extent of the documentation prepared by the entity will vary depending on the nature of the hedged items and the hedging instruments. If sufficient audit evidence to support management's use of hedge accounting is not available, or there is disagreement with management's use of hedge accounting, the auditor considers the implications for the auditor's report.

Presentation and Disclosure of Financial Instruments

138. Management's responsibilities include the preparation of the financial statements in accordance with the applicable financial reporting framework.[38] Financial reporting frameworks often require disclosures in the financial statements to enable users of the financial statements to make meaningful assessments of the effects of the entity's financial instrument activities, including the risks and uncertainties associated with these financial instruments[38a]. The importance of disclosures regarding the basis of measurement increases as the measurement uncertainty of

---

[37a] If the hedging relationship is no longer effective, the hedging instrument ceases to qualify for treatment as a hedge.

[38] See paragraphs 4 and A2 of ISA (UK and Ireland) 200.

[38a] For example, IAS 1, *Presentation of Financial Statements*, includes requirements to disclose:
- The judgments made in applying the entity's accounting policies that have the most significant effect on the amounts recognised in the financial statements;
- Information about the assumptions concerning the future; and
- Other major sources of estimation uncertainty at the end of the reporting period that have a significant risk of resulting in a material adjustment in the carrying amount of assets and liabilities within the next financial year.

Further, under UK and Irish company law, in relation to the use of financial instruments by the company, the directors' report is required to give an indication of:

(a) the financial risk management objectives and policies of the company, including the policy for hedging each major type of forecasted transaction for which hedge accounting is used, and

(b) the exposure of the company to price risk, credit risk, liquidity risk and cash flow risk,

unless such information is not material for the assessment of the assets, liabilities, financial position and profit or loss of the company. (In the UK: SI 2008/410 – The Large and Medium-sized Companies and Groups (Accounts and Reports) Regulations 2008, Schedule 7.6; in Ireland: Companies (Amendment) Act 1986, s13(1)(f).)

the financial instruments increases and is also affected by the level of the fair value hierarchy.

138-1. When evaluating compliance with presentation and disclosure requirements of the applicable financial reporting framework, the auditor determines whether management has had regard to related guidance and recommendations that may have been produced by relevant bodies (e.g. The European Securities and Markets Authority (ESMA), the Financial Stability Board and national regulators of entities providing financial services). The auditor considers whether related disclosures are needed and given for the financial statements as a whole to provide a true and fair view and enable users to obtain an understanding of the entity's position.

139. In representing that the financial statements are in accordance with the applicable financial reporting framework, management implicitly or explicitly makes assertions regarding the presentation and disclosure of the various elements of financial statements and related disclosures. Assertions about presentation and disclosure encompass:

(a) Occurrence and rights and obligations—disclosed events, transactions, and other matters have occurred and pertain to the entity.

(b) Completeness—all disclosures that should have been included in the financial statements have been included.

(c) Classification and understandability—financial information is appropriately presented and described, and disclosures are clearly expressed.

(d) Accuracy and valuation—financial and other information are disclosed fairly and at appropriate amounts.

The auditor's procedures around auditing disclosures are designed in consideration of these assertions.

Procedures Relating to the Presentation and Disclosure of Financial Instruments

140. In relation to the presentation and disclosures of financial instruments, areas of particular importance include:

- Financial reporting frameworks generally require additional disclosures regarding estimates, and related risks and uncertainties, to supplement and explain assets, liabilities, income, and expenses. The auditor's focus may need to be on the disclosures relating to risks and sensitivity analysis. Information obtained during the auditor's risk assessment procedures and testing of control activities may provide evidence in order for the auditor to conclude about whether the disclosures in the financial statements are in accordance with the requirements of the applicable financial reporting framework, for example about:

  ○ The entity's objectives and strategies for using financial instruments, including the entity's stated accounting policies;

- ○ The entity's control framework for managing its risks associated with financial instruments; and

- ○ The risks and uncertainties associated with the financial instruments.

- • Information may come from systems outside traditional financial reporting systems, such as risk systems. Examples of procedures that the auditor may choose to perform in responding to assessed risks relative to disclosures include testing:

- ○ The process used to derive the disclosed information; and

- ○ The operating effectiveness of the controls over the data used in the preparation of disclosures.

- • In relation to financial instruments having significant risk,[39] even where the disclosures are in accordance with the applicable financial reporting framework, the auditor may conclude that the disclosure of estimation uncertainty is inadequate in light of the circumstances and facts involved and, accordingly, the financial statements may not achieve fair presentation. ISA (UK and Ireland) 705 provides guidance on the implications for the auditor's opinion when the auditor believes that management's disclosures in the financial statements are inadequate or misleading.

- • Auditors may also consider whether the disclosures are complete and understandable, for example, all relevant information may be included in the financial statements (or accompanying reports) but it may be insufficiently drawn together to enable users of the financial statements to obtain an understanding of the position or there may not be enough qualitative disclosure to give context to the amounts recorded in the financial statements. For example, even when an entity has included sensitivity analysis disclosures, the disclosure may not fully describe the risks and uncertainties that may arise because of changes in valuation, possible effects on debt covenants, collateral requirements, and the entity's liquidity. ISA (UK and Ireland) 260[40] contains requirements and guidance about communicating with those charged with governance, including the auditor's views about significant qualitative aspects of the entity's accounting practices, including accounting policies, accounting estimates and financial statement disclosures.

140-1. The extent and nature of audit procedures has regard to whether the financial instrument disclosures are considered material to the users and the assessed risks of material misstatement. Disclosures are not deemed less significant simply by

---

[39] ISA (UK and Ireland) 540, paragraph 20, requires the auditor to perform further procedures on disclosures relating to accounting estimates that give rise to significant risks to evaluate the adequacy of the disclosure of their estimation uncertainty in the financial statements in the context of the applicable financial reporting framework.

[40] ISA (UK and Ireland) 260, *Communication with Those Charged with Governance.*

virtue of being disclosed in a note rather than on the face of the primary statements – for example, disclosures that measure the value of financial instruments on a different basis to the financial statement line item. If information subject to audit is considered to be material, the auditor plans and performs the audit to obtain reasonable assurance that it is not materially misstated on a consistent basis, whether the information is presented on the face of the primary statements or in the related notes.

141. Consideration of the appropriateness of presentation, for example on short-term and long-term classification, in substantive testing of financial instruments is relevant to the auditor's evaluation of the presentation and disclosure.

141-1. Practice Note 19 provides guidance on auditing disclosures of market risk information. It was written specifically for the audit of deposit takers, such as banks and building societies, but may also be helpful for auditors of other businesses that have significant financial instrument activity.

141-2. The auditor's conclusion as to whether the financial instruments are presented in conformity with relevant legislation, regulations and applicable financial reporting framework is based on the auditor's judgment as to whether:

- The accounting policies selected and applied are in conformity with the relevant financial reporting framework;

- Management's assumptions are reasonable and are used consistently and whether new conditions that may justify a change have been taken into account appropriately;

- Disclosure is adequate to ensure that the entity is in full compliance with the current disclosure requirements of relevant legislation, regulations and applicable financial reporting framework under which the financial statements are being reported;

- The information presented in the financial statements is classified and summarised in an appropriate and meaningful manner; and

- The financial statements show a true and fair view.

Other Relevant Audit Considerations

Written Representations

142. ISA (UK and Ireland) 540 requires the auditor to obtain written representations from management and, where appropriate, those charged with governance whether they believe significant assumptions used in making accounting estimates are

reasonable.[41] ISA (UK and Ireland) 580[42] requires that if, in addition to such required representations, the auditor determines that it is necessary to obtain one or more written representations to support other audit evidence relevant to the financial statements or one or more specific assertions in the financial statements, the auditor shall request such other written representations. Depending on the volume and degree of complexity of financial instrument activities, written representations to support other evidence obtained about financial instruments may also include:

- Management's objectives with respect to financial instruments, for example, whether they are used for hedging, asset/liability management or investment purposes;

- Representations about the appropriateness of presentation of the financial statements, for example the recording of financial instrument transactions as sales or financing transactions;

- Representations about the financial statement disclosures concerning financial instruments, for example that:

  ◦ The records reflect all financial instrument transactions; and

  ◦ All embedded derivative instruments have been identified;

- Whether all transactions have been conducted at arm's length and at market value;

- The terms of transactions;

- The appropriateness of the valuations of financial instruments;

- Whether there are any side agreements associated with any financial instruments;

- Whether the entity has entered into any written options;

- Management's intent and ability to carry out certain actions;[43] and

- Whether subsequent events require adjustment to the valuations and disclosures included in the financial statements.

---

[41] ISA (UK and Ireland) 540, paragraph 22. Paragraph 4 of ISA (UK and Ireland) 580, *Written Representations*, states that written representations from management do not provide sufficient appropriate audit evidence on their own about any of the matters with which they deal. If the auditor is otherwise unable to obtain sufficient appropriate audit evidence, this may constitute a limitation on the scope of the audit that may have implications for the auditor's report (see ISA (UK and Ireland) 705, *Modification to the Opinion in the Independent Auditor's Report*).

[42] ISA (UK and Ireland) 580 paragraph 13.

[43] Paragraph A80 of ISA (UK and Ireland) 540 provides examples of procedures that may be appropriate in the circumstances.

Communication with Those Charged with Governance and Others

143.   Because of the uncertainties associated with the valuation of financial instruments, the potential effects on the financial statements of any significant risks are likely to be of governance interest. The auditor may communicate the nature and consequences of significant assumptions used in fair value measurements, the degree of subjectivity involved in the development of the assumptions, and the relative materiality of the items being measured at fair value to the financial statements as a whole. In addition, the need for appropriate controls over commitments to enter into financial instrument contracts and over the subsequent measurement processes are matters that may give rise to the need for communication with those charged with governance.

144.   ISA (UK and Ireland) 260 deals with the auditor's responsibility to communicate with those charged with governance in an audit of financial statements. With respect to financial instruments, matters to be communicated to those charged with governance may include:

- A lack of management understanding of the nature or extent of the financial instrument activities or the risks associated with such activities;

- Significant deficiencies in the design or operation of the systems of internal control or risk management relating to the entity's financial instrument activities that the auditor has identified during the audit, including a lack of segregation of duties;[44]

- Significant difficulties encountered when obtaining sufficient appropriate audit evidence relating to valuations performed by management or a management's expert, for example, where management is unable to obtain an understanding of the valuation methodology, assumptions and data used by the management's experts, and such information is not made available to the auditor by management's expert;

- Significant differences in judgments between the auditor and management or a management's expert regarding valuations;

- The potential effects on the entity's financial statements of material risks and exposures required to be disclosed in the financial statements, including the measurement uncertainty associated with financial instruments;

---

[44] ISA (UK and Ireland) 265, *Communicating Deficiencies in Internal Control to Those Charged with Governance and Management*, establishes requirements and provides guidance on communicating deficiencies in internal control to management, and communicating significant deficiencies in internal control to those charged with governance. It explains that deficiencies in internal control may be identified during the auditor's risk assessment procedures in accordance with ISA (UK and Ireland) 315 or at any other stage of the audit.

- The auditor's views about the appropriateness of the selection of accounting policies and presentation of financial instrument transactions in the financial statements;

- The auditor's views about the qualitative aspects of the entity's accounting practices and financial reporting for financial instruments; or

- A lack of comprehensive and clearly stated policies for the purchase, sale and holding of financial instruments, including operational controls, procedures for designating financial instruments as hedges, and monitoring exposures.

The appropriate timing for communications will vary with the circumstances of the engagement; however, it may be appropriate to communicate significant difficulties encountered during the audit as soon as practicable if those charged with governance are able to assist the auditor to overcome the difficulty, or if it is likely to lead to a modified opinion.

Communications with Regulators and Others

145. In some cases, auditors may be required,[45] or may consider it appropriate, to communicate directly with regulators or prudential supervisors, in addition to those charged with governance, regarding matters relating to financial instruments. Such communication may be useful throughout the audit. For example, in some jurisdictions, banking regulators seek to cooperate with auditors to share information about the operation and application of controls over financial instrument activities, challenges in valuing financial instruments in inactive markets, and compliance with regulations. This coordination may be helpful to the auditor in identifying risks of material misstatement.

---

[45] For example, ISA (UK and Ireland) 250 Section A, *Consideration of Laws and Regulations in an Audit of Financial Statements*, requires auditors to determine whether there is a responsibility to report identified or suspected non-compliance with laws and regulations to parties outside the entity. In addition, requirements concerning the auditor's communication to banking supervisors and others may be established in many countries either by law, by supervisory requirement or by formal agreement or protocol.

Appendix

Examples of Controls Relating to Financial Instruments

1. The following provides background information and examples of controls that may exist in an entity that deals in a high volume of financial instrument transactions, whether for trading or investing purposes. The examples are not meant to be exhaustive and entities may establish different control environments and processes depending on their size, the industry in which they operate, and the extent of their financial instrument transactions. Further information on the use of trade confirmations and clearing houses is contained in paragraphs 25–26.

2. As in any control system, it is sometimes necessary to duplicate controls at different control levels (for example, preventative, detective and monitoring) to avoid the risk of material misstatement.

The Entity's Control Environment

Commitment to Competent Use of Financial Instruments

3. The degree of complexity of some financial instrument activities may mean that only a few individuals within the entity fully understand those activities or have the expertise necessary to value the instruments on an ongoing basis. Use of financial instruments without relevant expertise within the entity increases the risk of material misstatement.

Participation by Those Charged with Governance

4. Those charged with governance oversee and concur with management's establishment of the entity's overall risk appetite and provide oversight over the entity's financial instrument activities. An entity's policies for the purchase, sale and holding of financial instruments are aligned with its attitude toward risk and the expertise of those involved in financial instrument activities. In addition, an entity may establish governance structures and control processes aimed at:

   (a) Communicating investment decisions and assessments of all material measurement uncertainty to those charged with governance; and

   (b) Evaluating the entity's overall risk appetite when engaging in financial instrument transactions.

Organizational Structure

5. Financial instrument activities may be run on either a centralized or a decentralized basis. Such activities and related decision making depend heavily on the flow of accurate, reliable, and timely management information. The difficulty of collecting and aggregating such information increases with the number of locations and businesses in which an entity is involved. The risks of material misstatement associated with financial instrument activities may increase with greater

decentralization of control activities. This may especially be true where an entity is based in different locations, some perhaps in other countries.

Assignment of Authority and Responsibility

Investment and Valuation Policies

6. Providing direction, through clearly stated policies approved by those charged with governance for the purchase, sale, and holding of financial instruments enables management to establish an effective approach to taking and managing business risks. These policies are most clear when they state the entity's objectives with regard to its risk management activities, and the investment and hedging alternatives available to meet these objectives, and reflect the:

   (a) Level of management's expertise;

   (b) Sophistication of the entity's internal control and monitoring systems;

   (c) Entity's asset/liability structure;

   (d) Entity's capacity to maintain liquidity and absorb losses of capital;

   (e) Types of financial instruments that management believes will meet its objectives; and

   (f) Uses of financial instruments that management believes will meet its objectives, for example, whether derivatives may be used for speculative purposes or only for hedging purposes.

7. Management may design policies aligned with its valuation capabilities and may establish controls to ensure that these policies are adhered to by those employees responsible for the entity's valuation. These may include:

   (a) Processes for the design and validation of methodologies used to produce valuations, including how measurement uncertainty is addressed; and

   (b) Policies regarding maximizing the use of observable inputs and the types of information to be gathered to support valuations of financial instruments.

8. In smaller entities, dealing in financial instruments may be rare and management's knowledge and experience limited. Nevertheless, establishing policies over financial instruments helps an entity to determine its risk appetite and consider whether investing in particular financial instruments achieves a stated objective.

Human Resource Policies and Practices

9. Entities may establish policies requiring key employees, both front office and back office, to take mandatory time off from their duties. This type of control is used as a means of preventing and detecting fraud, in particular if those engaged in trading activities are creating false trades or inaccurately recording transactions.

Use of Service Organizations

10. Entities may also use service organizations (for example asset managers) to initiate the purchase or sale of financial instruments, to maintain records of transactions for the entity or to value financial instruments. Some entities may be dependent on these service organizations to provide the basis of reporting for the financial instruments held. However, if management does not have an understanding about the controls in place at a service organization, the auditor may not be able to obtain sufficient appropriate audit evidence to rely on controls at that service organization. See ISA (UK and Ireland) 402[46], which establishes requirements for the auditor to obtain sufficient appropriate audit evidence when an entity uses the services of one or more service organizations.

11. The use of service organizations may strengthen or weaken the control environment for financial instruments. For example, a service organization's personnel may have more experience with financial instruments than the entity's management or may have more robust internal control over financial reporting. The use of the service organization also may allow for greater segregation of duties. On the other hand, the service organization may have a poor control environment.

The Entity's Risk Assessment Process

12. An entity's risk assessment process exists to establish how management identifies business risks that derive from its use of financial instruments, including how management estimates the significance of the risks, assesses the likelihood of their occurrence and decides upon actions to manage them.

13. The entity's risk assessment process forms the basis for how management determines the risks to be managed. Risk assessment processes exist with the objective of ensuring that management:

    (a) Understands the risks inherent in a financial instrument before management enters into it, including the objective of entering into the transaction and its structure (for example, the economics and business purpose of the entity's financial instrument activities);

    (b) Performs adequate due diligence commensurate with the risks associated with particular financial instruments;

    (c) Monitors the entity's outstanding positions to understand how market conditions are affecting their exposures;

    (d) Has procedures in place to reduce or change risk exposure if necessary and for managing reputational risk; and

    (e) Subjects these processes to rigorous supervision and review.

---

[46] ISA (UK and Ireland) 402, *Audit Considerations Relating to an Entity Using a Service Organization.*

14.   The structure implemented to monitor and manage exposure to risks should:

(a) Be appropriate and consistent with the entity's attitude toward risk as determined by those charged with governance;

(b) Specify the approval levels for the authorization of different types of financial instruments and transactions that may be entered into and for what purposes. The permitted instruments and approval levels should reflect the expertise of those involved in financial instrument activities, demonstrating management's commitment to competence;

(c) Set appropriate limits for the maximum allowable exposure to each type of risk (including approved counterparties). Levels of allowable exposure may vary depending on the type of risk, or counterparty;

(d) Provide for the objective and timely monitoring of the financial risks and control activities;

(e) Provide for the objective and timely reporting of exposures, risks and the results of financial instrument activities in managing risk; and

(f) Evaluate management's track record for assessing the risks of particular financial instruments.

15.   The types and levels of risks an entity faces are directly related to the types of financial instruments with which it deals, including the complexity of these instruments and the volume of financial instruments transacted.

Risk Management Function

16.   Some entities, for example large financial institutions with a high volume of financial instrument transactions, may be required by law or regulation, or may choose, to establish a formal risk management function. This function is separated from those responsible for undertaking and managing financial instrument transactions. The function is responsible for reporting on and monitoring financial instrument activities, and may include a formal risk committee established by those charged with governance. Examples of key responsibilities in this area may include:

(a) Implementing the risk management policy set by those charged with governance (including analyses of the risks to which an entity may be exposed);

(b) Designing risk limit structures and ensuring these risk limits are implemented in practice;

(c) Developing stress scenarios and subjecting open position portfolios to sensitivity
analysis, including reviews of unusual movements in positions; and

(d) Reviewing and analyzing new financial instrument products. and

(e) Independent price verification.

17. Financial instruments may have the associated risk that a loss might exceed the amount, if any, of the value of the financial instrument recognized on the balance sheet. For example, a sudden fall in the market price of a commodity may force an entity to realize losses to close a forward position in that commodity due to collateral, or margin, requirements. In some cases, the potential losses may be enough to cast significant doubt on the entity's ability to continue as a going concern. The entity may perform sensitivity analyses or value-at-risk analyses to assess the future hypothetical effects on financial instruments subject to market risks. However, value-at-risk analysis does not fully reflect the extent of the risks that may affect the entity; sensitivity and scenario analyses also may be subject to limitations.

18. The volume and sophistication of financial instrument activity and relevant regulatory requirements will influence the entity's consideration whether to establish a formal risk management function and how the function may be structured. In entities that have not established a separate risk management function, for example entities with relatively few financial instruments or financial instruments that are less complex, reporting on and monitoring financial instrument activities may be a component of the accounting or finance function's responsibility or management's overall responsibility, and may include a formal risk committee established by those charged with governance.

18-1. To be effective, a risk management function needs to have sufficient resources and capabilities and status in the entity to control how risk is taken on and managed.

The Entity's Information Systems

19. The key objective of an entity's information system is that it is capable of capturing and recording all the transactions accurately, settling them, valuing them, and producing information to enable the financial instruments to be risk managed and for controls to be monitored. Difficulties can arise in entities that engage in a high volume of financial instruments, in particular if there is a multiplicity of systems that are poorly integrated and have manual interfaces without adequate controls.

19-1. The financial risks and exposures inherent in complex financial instruments cannot always be effectively captured in a balance sheet and profit and loss account. For example significant derivative contracts often have zero value at the outset since they are priced at prevailing market rates. The provision of additional information is often required by the financial reporting framework. Entities therefore need to have processes and controls to gather the information required by the applicable financial reporting framework so that it is complete and accurate.

20. Certain financial instruments may require a large number of accounting entries. As the sophistication or level of the financial instrument activities increases, it is necessary for the sophistication of the information system to also increase. Specific issues which can arise with respect to financial instruments include:

(a) Information systems, in particular for smaller entities, not having the capability or not being appropriately configured to process financial instrument transactions, especially when the entity does not have any prior experience in dealing with financial instruments. This may result in an increased number of manual transactions which may further increase the risk of error;

(b) The potential diversity of systems required to process more complex transactions, and the need for regular reconciliations between them, in particular when the systems are not interfaced or may be subject to manual intervention;

(c) The potential that more complex transactions, if they are only traded by a small number of individuals, may be valued or risk managed on spreadsheets rather than on main processing systems, and for the physical and logical password security around those spreadsheets to be more easily compromised;

(d) A lack of review of systems exception logs, external confirmations and broker quotes, where available, to validate the entries generated by the systems;

(e) Difficulties in controlling and evaluating the key inputs to systems for valuation of financial instruments, particularly where those systems are maintained by the group of traders known as the front office or a third-party service provider and/or the transactions in question are non-routine or thinly traded;

(f) Failure to evaluate the design and calibration of complex models used to process these transactions initially and on a periodic basis;

(g) The potential that management has not set up a library of models, with controls around access, change and maintenance of individual models, in order to maintain a strong audit trail of the accredited versions of models and in order to prevent unauthorized access or amendments to those models;

(h) The disproportionate investment that may be required in risk management and control systems, where an entity only undertakes a limited number of financial instrument transactions, and the potential for misunderstanding of the output by management if they are not used to these types of transactions;

(i) The potential requirement for third-party systems provision, for example from a service organization, to record, process, account for or risk manage appropriately financial instrument transactions, and the need to reconcile appropriately and challenge the output from those providers; and

(j) Additional security and control considerations relevant to the use of an electronic network when an entity uses electronic commerce for financial instrument transactions; and

(k) Difficulties in recruiting and retaining expert individuals to represent the accounting, processing and risk management of transactions correctly initially on systems and to validate periodically that they continue to be correctly recorded.

21. Information systems relevant to financial reporting serve as an important source of information for the quantitative disclosures in the financial statements. However, entities may also develop and maintain non-financial systems used for internal reporting and to generate information included in qualitative disclosures, for example regarding risks and uncertainties or sensitivity analyses.

The Entity's Control Activities

22. Control activities over financial instrument transactions are designed to prevent or detect problems that hinder an entity from achieving its objectives. These objectives may be either operational, financial reporting, or compliance in nature. Control activities over financial instruments are designed relative to the complexity and volume of transactions of financial instruments and will generally include an appropriate authorization process, adequate segregation of duties, and other policies and procedures designed to ensure that the entity's control objectives are met. Process flow charts may assist in identifying an entity's controls and lack of controls. This PN focuses on control activities related to completeness, accuracy and existence, valuation, and presentation and disclosure.

Authorization

23. Authorization can affect the financial statement assertions both directly and indirectly. For example, even if a transaction is executed outside an entity's policies, it nonetheless may be recorded and accounted for accurately. However, unauthorized transactions could significantly increase risk to the entity, thereby significantly increasing the risk of material misstatement since they would be undertaken outside the system of internal control. To mitigate this risk, an entity will often establish a clear policy as to what transactions can be traded by whom and adherence to this policy will then be monitored by an entity's back office. Monitoring trading activities of individuals, for example by reviewing unusually high volumes or significant gains or losses incurred, will assist management in ensuring compliance with the entity's policies, including the authorization of new types of transactions, and evaluating whether fraud has occurred.

24. The function of an entity's deal initiation records is to identify clearly the nature and purpose of individual transactions and the rights and obligations arising under each financial instrument contract, including the enforceability of the contracts. In addition to the basic financial information, such as a notional amount, complete and accurate records at a minimum typically include:

(a) The identity of the dealer;

(b) The identity of the person recording the transaction (if not the dealer), when the transaction was initiated (including the date and time of the transaction), and how it was recorded in the entity's information systems; and

(c) The nature and purpose of the transaction, including whether or not it is intended to hedge an underlying commercial exposure; and

(d) Information on compliance with accounting requirements related to hedging, such as:

- designation at inception as a hedge; and

- identification of the hedged item in a hedging relationship.

Segregation of Duties

25. Segregation of duties and the assignment of personnel is an important control activity, particularly when exposed to financial instruments. Financial instrument activities may be segregated into a number of functions, including:

    (a) Executing the transaction (dealing). In entities with a high volume of financial instrument transactions, this may be done by the front office;

    (b) Initiating cash payments and accepting cash receipts (settlements);

    (c) Sending out trade confirmations and reconciling the differences between the entity's records and replies from counterparties, if any;

    (d) Recording of all transactions correctly in the accounting records;

    (e) Monitoring risk limits. In entities with a high volume of financial instrument transactions, this may be performed by the risk management function; and

    (f) Monitoring positions and valuing financial instruments.

26. Many organizations choose to segregate the duties of those investing in financial instruments, those valuing financial instruments, those settling financial instruments and those accounting/recording financial instruments.

27. Where an entity is too small to achieve proper segregation of duties, the role of management and those charged with governance in monitoring financial instrument activities is of particular importance.

28. A feature of some entities' internal control is an independent price verification (IPV) function. This department is responsible for separately verifying the price of some financial instruments, and may use alternative data sources, methodologies and assumptions. The IPV provides an objective look at the pricing that has been developed in another part of the entity.

29. Ordinarily, the middle or back office is responsible for establishing policies on valuation and ensuring adherence to the policy. Entities with a greater use of financial instruments may perform daily valuations of their financial instrument portfolio and examine the contribution to profit or loss of individual financial instrument valuations as a test of the reasonableness of valuations.

Completeness, Accuracy, and Existence

30.   Regular reconciliation of the entity's records to external banks' and custodians' records enables the entity to ensure transactions are properly recorded. Appropriate segregation of duties between those transacting the trades and those reconciling them is important, as is a rigorous process for reviewing reconciliations and clearing reconciling items.

31.   Controls may also be established that require traders to identify whether a complex financial instrument may have unique features, for example embedded derivatives. In such circumstances, there may be a separate function that evaluates complex financial instrument transactions at their initiation (which may be known as a product control group), working in connection with an accounting policy group to ensure the transaction is accurately recorded. While smaller entities may not have product control groups, an entity may have a process in place relating to the review of complex financial instrument contracts at the point of origination in order to ensure they are accounted for appropriately in accordance with the applicable financial reporting framework.

Monitoring of Controls

32.   The entity's ongoing monitoring activities are designed to detect and correct any deficiencies in the effectiveness of controls over transactions for financial instruments and their valuation. It is important that there is adequate supervision and review of financial instrument activity within the entity. This includes:

(a) All controls being subject to review, for example, the monitoring of operational statistics such as the number of reconciling items or the difference between internal pricing and external pricing sources;

(b) The need for robust information technology (IT) controls and monitoring and validating their application; and

(c) The need to ensure that information resulting from different processes and systems is adequately reconciled. For example, there is little benefit in a valuation process if the output from it is not reconciled properly into the general ledger.

33.   In larger entities, sophisticated computer information systems generally keep track of financial instrument activities, and are designed to ensure that settlements occur when due. More complex computer systems may generate automatic postings to clearing accounts to monitor cash movements, and controls over processing are put in place with the objective of ensuring that financial instrument activities are correctly reflected in the entity's records. Computer systems may be designed to produce exception reports to alert management to situations where financial instruments have not been used within authorized limits or where transactions undertaken were not within the limits established for the chosen counterparties. However, even a sophisticated computer system may not ensure the completeness of the recording

of financial instrument transactions. Accordingly, management frequently puts additional procedures in place to increase the likelihood that all transactions will be recorded.

PRACTICE NOTE 25 (REVISED)

ATTENDANCE AT STOCKTAKING

CONTENTS

Introduction

1. International Standard on Auditing (ISA) (UK and Ireland) 501 'Audit Evidence – Specific Considerations for Selected Items' includes requirements and application material relating to inventory (stock and work in progress – 'stocks') and, in particular, obtaining audit evidence by attendance at physical inventory counting (stocktakes). Practice Note 25 contains further guidance, including how the requirements of other ISAs (UK and Ireland) may be applied in relation to attendance at stocktaking. The guidance is intended to assist auditors in applying the requirements of, and should be read in conjunction with, the ISAs (UK and Ireland) which apply to all audits undertaken in the United Kingdom and the Republic of Ireland.

2. The main assertions[1] relating to stocks are existence, rights to assets (ownership), completeness and valuation. Practice Note 25 is primarily concerned with audit evidence relating to the existence assertion.

3. ISA (UK and Ireland) 501, paragraph 4, requires that, if inventory is material to the financial statements the auditor shall obtain sufficient appropriate audit evidence regarding the existence and condition of inventory by, in addition to other procedures, attendance at physical inventory counting unless impracticable (see paragraphs 10 and 16 below).

4. While the principal reason for attendance at a stocktake is to obtain evidence to substantiate the existence of the stocks, attendance can also enhance the auditor's understanding of the business by providing an opportunity to observe the production process and/or business locations at first hand and providing evidence in relation to the:

    *   completeness and valuation of stocks;

    *   'cut-off' for recording stock inwards and outwards movements, and the resultant impact on revenues and costs; and

    *   design and operation of an entity's internal control relating to stocks.

5. It is the responsibility of those charged with governance of an entity to prepare financial statements that are free from material misstatement and, in so doing, to ensure that the amount at which stocks are recorded in the financial statements represents stocks physically in existence and includes all stocks of the entity. To achieve this, entities may maintain detailed records of stocks and check these by regular test counts. In some entities where the accounting records are less detailed, the amount of stocks may be determined by way of a full physical count of all stocks held at a date close to the entity's balance sheet date.

---

[1] 'Assertions' are the representations of those charged with governance that are embodied in the financial statements and are more fully described in ISA (UK and Ireland) 315 'Identifying and Assessing the Risks of Material Misstatement Through Understanding the Entity and its Environment,' paragraph A111.

6. In the case of a company incorporated under the Companies Act, management has specific responsibilities to keep adequate accounting records and to include any statements of stocktakings in those records[2].

Assessment of risks and internal controls

7. **ISA (UK and Ireland) 315: 'Identifying and Assessing the Risks of Material Misstatement Through Understanding the Entity and its Environment'** requires that the auditor shall identify and assess the risks of material misstatement at (a) the financial statement level, and (b) the assertion level for classes of transactions, account balances and disclosures to provide a basis for designing and performing further audit procedures. (paragraph 25)

8. Factors relating to the risk of material misstatement in the context of the existence of stocks include the:

    *   reliability of accounting and recording systems and related controls for stocks including, in relation to work in progress, the systems that track location, quantities and stages of completion;

    *   timing of stocktakes relative to the year-end date, and the reliability of records used in any 'roll-forward' of balances;

    *   location of stocks, including stocks on 'consignment,' stocks in transit and stocks held at third-party warehouses;

    *   physical controls over the stocks, and their susceptibility to theft or deterioration;

    *   objectivity, experience and reliability of the stocks counters and of those monitoring their work;

    *   degree of fluctuation in levels of stocks;

    *   nature of the stocks, for example whether specialist knowledge is needed to identify the quantity, quality, identity and/or stage of completion of items of stocks; and

    *   difficulty in carrying out the assessment of quantity and/or stage of completion of items of stocks, for example whether a significant degree of estimation is involved.

9. When planning the audit, the auditor also assesses the risks of material misstatement due to fraud[3]. Based on this risk assessment, the auditor designs audit procedures so

---

[2] In the United Kingdom – Section 386 of the Companies Act 2006; in the Republic of Ireland – Section 202.3(c)(ii) of the Companies Act 1990.
[3] ISA (UK and Ireland) 240 'The Auditor's Responsibilities Relating to Fraud in an Audit of Financial Statements.'

as to have a reasonable expectation of detecting material misstatements arising from fraud. Fraudulent activities which can occur in relation to stocks include:

- 'false sales' involving the movement of stocks not yet sold by the entity to a location not normally used for storing stocks;

- movement of stocks between entity sites with stocktakes at different dates;

- the appearance of stocks being misrepresented so that they seem to be of a higher value/greater quantity;

- the application of inappropriate estimation techniques;

- stocktake records prepared during stocktakes deliberately being incorrectly completed or altered after the event; and

- additional (false) stocktake records being added to those prepared during the count.

Audit evidence

10. **ISA (UK and Ireland) 501: 'Audit Evidence – Specific Considerations for Selected Items'** requires that, if inventory is material to the financial statements the auditor shall obtain sufficient appropriate audit evidence regarding the existence and condition of inventory by, in addition to other procedures, attendance at physical inventory counting unless impracticable. (paragraph 4)

11. Attendance at stocktaking can provide evidence to the auditor in respect of the existence, completeness and valuation assertions (including a consideration of possible obsolescence and deterioration).

12. The principal sources of evidence relating to the existence of stocks are:

- evidence from audit procedures which confirm the reliability of the accounting records upon which the amount in the financial statements is based;

- evidence from tests of the operation of control activities over stocks, including the reliability of counting procedures applied by the entity; and

- substantive evidence from the physical inspection tests undertaken by the auditor.

13. The nature and extent of the auditor's procedures during attendance at a stocktake will depend upon the auditor's assessment of the risks of material misstatement carried out in accordance with ISA (UK and Ireland) 315. In cases where the auditor's assessment of risks of material misstatement at the assertion level includes an expectation that relevant controls for confirming the existence of stocks are operating effectively (that is, the auditor intends to rely on the operating effectiveness of controls in determining the nature, timing and extent of substantive procedures), the auditor

may attend a stocktake to obtain evidence regarding the operating effectiveness of those controls as well as performing substantive procedures.

14. Where entities maintain detailed records of stocks and check these by regular test counts the auditor performs audit procedures designed to confirm whether management:

    • maintains adequate records of stocks that are kept up-to-date;

    • has satisfactory procedures for stocktaking and test-counting; and

    • investigates and corrects all material differences between the book records of stocks and the physical counts.

    The auditor attending a stocktake considers whether the checking of stocks as a whole is effective in confirming that accurate records of stocks are maintained. If the entity's records of stocks are not reliable the auditor may need to request management to perform alternative procedures which may include a full count at the year end.

15. In entities that do not maintain detailed records of stocks the quantification of stocks for financial statement purposes is likely to be based on a full physical count of all stocks at a date close to the entity's year end. In such circumstances the auditor recognises that the evidence of the existence of stocks provided by the stocktake is greater when the stocktake is carried out at the end of the financial year. Stocktaking carried out before or after the year end may also provide acceptable evidence for audit purposes provided the auditor is satisfied that the records of movements of stocks in the intervening period are reliable.

Procedures

16. When the auditor attends an inventory count in compliance with ISA (UK and Ireland) 501, the auditor is required to:

    (i) Evaluate management's instructions and procedures for recording and controlling the results of the entity's physical inventory counting;

    (ii) Observe the performance of management's count procedures;

    (iii) Inspect the inventory; and

    (iv) Perform test counts.

    The auditor is also required to perform audit procedures over the entity's final inventory records to determine whether they accurately reflect actual inventory count results. (paragraph 4)

17. The following paragraphs set out the principal procedures which may be carried out by auditors when attending a stocktake, but are not intended to provide a comprehensive list of the audit procedures which the auditor may find it necessary to perform during attendance at stocktaking.

Before the stocktake

18. The effectiveness of the auditor's attendance at stocktaking is increased by the use of audit staff who are familiar with the entity's business and where advance planning has been undertaken. Planning procedures include:

- performing analytical procedures, and discussing with management any significant changes in stocks over the year and any problems with stocks that have recently occurred, for example unexpected 'stock-out' reports and negative stock balances;

- discussing stocktaking arrangements and instructions with management;

- familiarisation with the nature and volume of the stocks, the identification of high value items, the method of accounting for stocks and the conditions giving rise to obsolescence;

- considering the locations of the stocks and assessing the implications of this for stock control and recording;

- considering the quantity and nature of work in progress, the quantity of stocks held by third parties, and whether expert valuers or stocktakers will be engaged (further guidance on these issues is set out in paragraphs 30-34 below);

- considering internal control relating to stocks, so as to identify potential areas of difficulty (for example cut-off and segregation of duties between entity staff carrying out the stocktake and those responsible for subsequent adjustments to stock records);

- considering any internal audit involvement, with a view to deciding the reliance which can be placed on it[4];

- considering the results of previous stocktakes made by the entity; and

- reviewing the audit working papers for the previous year.

19. The auditor examines the way the stocktake is organised and evaluates the adequacy of management's stocktaking instructions. Such instructions, preferably in writing, should cover all phases of the stocktaking procedures, be issued in good time and be discussed with the person responsible for the stocktake to check that the procedures

---

[4] ISA (UK and Ireland) 610 addresses 'Using the Work of Internal Auditors'.

are understood and that potential difficulties are anticipated. If the instructions are found to be inadequate, the auditor seeks improvements to them.

During the stocktake

20. During the stocktake, the auditor ascertains whether the entity's staff are carrying out management's instructions properly and undertakes test counts to obtain evidence that procedures and internal controls relating to the stocktake are working properly. If the manner of carrying out the stocktake or the results of the test-counts are not satisfactory, the auditor immediately draws the matter to the attention of management supervising the stocktake and may have to request a recount of part, or all of the stocks.

21. When carrying out test-counts, the auditor selects items both from count records and from the physical stocks and checks one to the other to obtain evidence as to the completeness and accuracy of the count records. In this context, the auditor gives particular consideration to those stocks which the auditor believes to have a high value either individually or as a category of stocks. The auditor also gives consideration to stocks that are susceptible to misappropriation. The auditor records in the audit working papers items for any subsequent testing considered necessary, such as copies of (or extracts from) stocktake records and details of the sequence of those records, and any differences noted between the records and the physical stocks counted.

22. The auditor determines whether the procedures for identifying damaged, obsolete and slow moving stocks operate properly. The auditor obtains (from observation and by discussion, for example with storekeepers and stock counters) information about the stocks' condition, age, usage and, in the case of work in progress, its stage of completion. In addition, the auditor ascertains that stocks held on behalf of third parties are separately identified and accounted for.

23. The auditor considers whether management has instituted adequate cut-off procedures, i.e. procedures intended to ensure that movements into, within and out of stocks are properly identified and reflected in the accounting records in the correct period. The auditor's procedures during the stocktake will depend on the manner in which the year end value of stocks is to be determined. For example, where stocks are determined by a full count and evaluation at the year end, the auditor tests the arrangements made to identify stocks that correspond to sales made before the cut-off point and the auditor identifies goods movement documents for reconciliation with financial records of purchases and sales. Where the full count and evaluation is at an interim date and year end stocks are determined by updating such an amount by the cost of subsequent purchases and sales, the auditor performs appropriate procedures during attendance at the stocktaking and in addition tests the financial cut-off (involving the matching of costs with revenues) at the year end[5].

---

[5] ISA (UK and Ireland) 501, paragraph 5, requires the auditor to obtain audit evidence about whether changes in inventory between the count date and the date of the financial statements are properly recorded.

24. The auditor's working papers include details of the auditor's observations and tests (for example, of physical quantity, cut-off date and controls over stocktake records), the manner in which points that are relevant and material to the stocks being counted or measured have been dealt with by the entity, instances where the entity's procedures have not been satisfactorily carried out and the auditor's conclusions.

25. Although the principal reason for attendance at a stocktake is usually to obtain evidence to substantiate the existence of the stocks, as noted in paragraph 4 above attendance can also enhance the auditor's understanding of the business by providing an opportunity to observe the production process and/or business locations at first hand and providing evidence regarding the completeness and valuation of stocks and the entity's internal control. Matters that the auditor may wish to observe whilst attending a stocktake include:

Understanding the business

- the production process;

- evidence of significant pollution and environmental damage;

- unused buildings and machinery.

Completeness and valuation of stocks

- physical controls;

- obsolete stock (for example goods beyond their sale date);

- scrap, and goods marked for re-work;

- returned goods.

Internal control

- exceptions identified by the production process (for example missing work tickets); and

- the operation of 'shop-floor' disciplines regarding the inputting of data such as movements of stocks into the computer systems.

26. Some entities use computer-assisted techniques to perform stocktakes; for example hand held scanners can be used to record items of stocks which update computerised records. In some situations there are no stocks-sheets, no physical count records, and no paper records available at the time of the count. In these circumstances, in addition to the other matters addressed in this Practice Note, the auditor considers the IT environment surrounding the stocktake and considers the need for specialist assistance when evaluating the techniques used and the controls over them. Relevant issues involve systems interfaces, and the controls over ensuring that the records of stocks are properly updated for the stocktake information.

The auditor considers the following aspects of the stocktake:

- how the test counts (and double counts where two people are checking) are recorded;

- how differences are investigated before the records of stocks are updated for the counts;

- how the records of stocks are updated, and how stocktake differences are recorded.

After the stocktake

27. After the stocktake, the matters recorded in the auditor's working papers at the time of the count or measurement, including apparent instances of obsolete or deteriorating stocks, are followed up. For example, details of the last serial numbers of goods inwards and outwards records and of movements during the stocktake may be used in order to check cut-off. In addition, copies of (or extracts from) the stocktake records obtained by the auditor during the stocktake and details of test counts, and of the sequence of stocktake records may be used to check that the results of the count have been properly reflected in the accounting records of the entity.

28. The auditor reviews whether continuous records of stocks have been adjusted to the amounts physically counted or measured and that differences have been investigated. Where appropriate, the auditor considers whether management has instituted procedures to ensure that all movements of stocks between the observed stocktake and the period end have been adjusted in the accounting records, and the auditor tests these procedures to the extent considered necessary to address the assessed risk of material misstatement. In addition, the auditor follows up queries and notifies management and those charged with governance of significant difficulties encountered during the stocktake.

29. In conclusion, the auditor considers whether attendance at the stocktake has provided sufficient appropriate audit evidence in relation to relevant assertions (principally existence) and, if not, the other procedures to be performed.

Work in progress

30. Management may place substantial reliance on internal controls designed to ensure the completeness and accuracy of records of work in progress. In such circumstances there may not be a stocktake which can be attended by the auditor. Nevertheless, inspection of the work in progress may assist the auditor in understanding the entity's relevant internal control. It will also assist the auditor in planning further audit procedures, and it may also help on such matters as the determination of the stage of completion of construction or engineering work in progress. For this purpose, the auditor identifies the accounting records that will be used by management to produce the work in progress figure in the year-end accounts and, where unfinished items are uniquely identifiable (for example by reference to work tickets or labels), the auditor physically examines items to obtain evidence that supports the recorded stage of

completion. In some cases, for example in connection with building projects, photographic evidence can also be useful evidence as to the state of work in progress, particularly if provided by independent third parties or the auditor.

The use of expert valuers and stocktakers

31. Prior to attending a stocktake, the auditor establishes whether expert help, such as that provided by a quantity surveyor, needs to be obtained by management to substantiate quantities, or to identify the nature and condition of the stocks, where they are very specialised. In cases where the entity engages a third party expert the auditor complies with the relevant requirements in ISA (UK and Ireland) 500, 'Audit Evidence', including evaluating the competence, capabilities and objectivity of the expert, obtaining an understanding of the work of the expert, and evaluating the appropriateness of the expert's work as audit evidence for the relevant assertion[6].

32. Management may from time to time appoint stocktakers from outside the entity, a practice common for stocks at, for example, farms, petrol stations and public houses. The use of independent stocktakers does not eliminate the need for the auditor to obtain audit evidence as to the existence of stocks. In addition, as well as considering the competence and objectivity of the independent stocktakers, the auditor considers how to obtain evidence as to the procedures followed by them to ensure that the stocktaking records have been properly prepared. In this connection the auditor also has regard, where relevant, to ISA (UK and Ireland) 402 'Audit Considerations Relating to an Entity Using a Service Organization'.

Stocks held by third parties or in public warehouses

33. If inventory under the custody and control of a third party is material to the financial statements, ISA (UK and Ireland) 501 requires the auditor to obtain sufficient appropriate audit evidence regarding the existence and condition of the inventory by performing one or both of:

    (a) requesting confirmation from the third party as to the quantities and condition of the inventory held on behalf of the entity;

    (b) performing inspection or other audit procedures appropriate in the circumstances. (paragraph 8)

34. ISA (UK and Ireland) 501 gives examples of other procedures that may be appropriate:

    • Attending, or arranging for another auditor to attend, the third party's physical counting of inventory, if practicable.

---

[6] ISA (UK and Ireland) 500, paragraph 8.

- Obtaining another auditor's report, or a service auditor's report, on the adequacy of the third party's internal control for ensuring that inventory is properly counted and adequately safeguarded.

- Inspecting documentation regarding inventory held by third parties, for example, warehouse receipts.

- Requesting confirmation from other parties when inventory has been pledged as collateral.

Other audit procedures may also include testing the entity's procedures for investigating the custodian and evaluating the custodian's performance. If the custodian is acting as a service organisation, ISA (UK and Ireland) 402 is relevant.

PRACTICE NOTE 26

GUIDANCE ON SMALLER ENTITY AUDIT DOCUMENTATION (REVISED)

CONTENTS

Introduction

1. This Practice Note provides guidance to auditors on the application of documentation requirements contained within the clarified International Standards on Auditing (ISAs) (UK and Ireland)[1] to the audit of financial statements of smaller entities in an efficient manner. It should be read in conjunction with the ISAs (UK and Ireland). It is not intended to be comprehensive guidance on the application of ISAs (UK and Ireland) to smaller audits[2].

2. The guidance in this Practice Note is directed to auditors of smaller, simpler entities. Typically these would be entities where:

    *   ownership is concentrated in a small number of individuals (sometimes a single individual) who are actively involved in managing the business; and

    *   the operations are uncomplicated with few sources of income and activities; and

    *   business processes and accounting systems are simple; and

    *   internal controls are relatively few and may be informal.

    Such entities are likely to include companies which are exempt from audit but which choose nonetheless to have a voluntary audit, small subsidiary companies, other smaller entities such as charities, as well as larger entities that are also relatively simple. However, a more detailed and rigorous approach may be necessary in smaller entities with complex operations or in respect of complex and subjective matters.

3. The guidance focuses on areas where feedback on the original implementation of the ISAs (UK and Ireland) in 2004 identified that further guidance on audit documentation could be helpful. For example, there can be uncertainty about the extent of documentation required to evidence the auditor's understanding of the entity, especially with regard to internal control[3].

4. There are many different ways in which audit documentation can be prepared to meet the requirements of ISA (UK and Ireland). The examples which are included in Appendix B to this document are illustrative of some of the possible ways in which

---

[1] The clarified ISAs (UK and Ireland) were issued by the APB in October 2009 and are effective for audits of financial statements for periods ending on or after 15 December 2010.

[2] The ISAs (UK and Ireland) also include guidance on considerations specific to smaller entities which may assist in the application of the standards.

[3] ISA (UK and Ireland) 315 requires the auditor to document key elements of understanding obtained regarding:
*   relevant industry, regulatory and other external factors including the applicable financial reporting framework;
*   the nature of the entity;
*   the entity's selection and application of accounting policies;
*   the entity's objectives and strategies;
*   the means by which the entity's financial performance is measured and reviewed; and
*   each of the internal control components (the control environment, the entity's risk assessment process, the information system, control activities, and monitoring controls).

compliance with the documentation requirements can be achieved. However, these illustrative examples are not mandatory.

Purposes of audit documentation

5. ISA (UK and Ireland) 230, "Audit Documentation," states that the objective of the auditor is to prepare documentation that provides:

    (a) A sufficient and appropriate record of the basis for the auditor's report; and

    (b) Evidence that the audit was planned and performed in accordance with ISAs (UK and Ireland) and applicable legal and regulatory requirements.

6. ISA (UK and Ireland) 230 explains that, in principle, compliance with the requirements of it will result in the audit documentation being sufficient and appropriate in the circumstances.

7. Some of the other ISAs (UK and Ireland) contain specific documentation requirements that are intended to clarify the application of ISA (UK and Ireland) 230 in the particular circumstances of those other standards. The absence of a documentation requirement in any particular ISA (UK and Ireland) is not intended to suggest that there is no documentation that will be prepared as a result of complying with that standard.

8. Importantly, ISA (UK and Ireland) 230 also explains that it is neither necessary nor practicable for the auditor to document every matter considered, or professional judgment made, in an audit. Further, it is unnecessary for the auditor to document separately (as in a checklist, for example) compliance with matters for which compliance is demonstrated by documents included within the audit file (e.g. the existence of an adequately documented audit plan demonstrates that the auditor has planned the audit).

9. The auditor is required to prepare audit documentation on a timely basis. ISA (UK and Ireland) 230 explains that preparing sufficient and appropriate audit documentation on a timely basis helps to enhance the quality of the audit and facilitates the effective review and evaluation of the audit evidence obtained and conclusions reached before the auditor's report is finalised. Documentation prepared after the audit work has been performed is likely to be less accurate than documentation prepared at the time such work is performed.

10. In addition to the objectives in paragraph 5, audit documentation serves a number of additional purposes, including:

    *   assisting the engagement team to plan and perform the audit;

    *   assisting members of the engagement team responsible for supervision to direct and supervise the audit work, and to discharge their review responsibilities in accordance with ISA (UK and Ireland) 220, "Quality Control for an Audit of Financial Statements";

- enabling the engagement team to be accountable for its work;

- retaining a record of matters of continuing significance to future audits;

- enabling the conduct of quality control reviews and inspections in accordance with International Standard on Quality Control (ISQC) (UK and Ireland) 1, "Quality Control for Firms that Perform Audits and Reviews of Financial Statements, and Other Assurance and Related Services Engagements"; and

- enabling the conduct of external inspections in accordance with applicable legal, regulatory or other requirements.

11. Complying with the documentation requirements of the ISAs (UK and Ireland) can also assist the auditor's consideration of the issues associated with significant matters arising during the audit. This often enhances the quality of the reasoning followed, the judgments made and the conclusions reached. In the UK and Ireland external monitoring of audits has consistently emphasised the need for high quality documentation of the rationale for the key audit judgments made in reaching the audit opinion. As noted in paragraph 13 below, documentation of significant professional judgements made in reaching important conclusions is now clearly identified as a requirement in ISA (UK and Ireland) 230.

Special considerations in the documentation of a smaller entity audit

12. The nature and extent of audit documentation that is appropriate for an audit of a smaller entity is influenced by special considerations which arise from:

- the qualitative indicators of a simpler entity as set out in paragraph 2:

  - concentration of ownership and management;

  - uncomplicated operations;

  - simple accounting systems; and

  - relatively small number and informal nature of controls; and

- the characteristics of a typical smaller entity audit team and the way in which they carry out the audit work, including:

  - the nature of the professional relationship between smaller entities and their auditors;

  - relatively small team size;

  - the use of proprietary audit systems.

13. Notwithstanding these special considerations, an audit of the financial statements for a smaller entity must still comply with the ISAs (UK and Ireland) and all audit documentation must be prepared in sufficient detail to enable an experienced auditor, having no previous connection with the audit, to understand:

   (a) The nature, timing, and extent of the audit procedures performed to comply with the ISAs (UK and Ireland) and applicable legal and regulatory requirements;

   (b) The results of the audit procedures performed, and the audit evidence obtained; and

   (c) Significant matters arising during the audit, the conclusions reached thereon and significant professional judgments made in reaching those conclusions.

Concentration of ownership and management

14. The ownership of a smaller entity is often concentrated in a small number of individuals, one or more of whom are actively involved in managing the business on a day-to-day basis. In these circumstances, the auditor's documentation of the entity's ownership and governance arrangements is likely to be relatively brief.

15. Particular consideration and documentation may be needed of matters, such as family and other close relationships, which may impact the auditor's risk assessments in relation to related parties.

Uncomplicated operations

16. Smaller entities often have a limited range of products or services and operate from a limited number of locations, with the consequence that their processes and structures are uncomplicated. In circumstances where an entity's business, processes and structures are uncomplicated, the documentation of the auditor's understanding of such an entity's operations and of the relevant industry, regulatory and other external factors required under ISA (UK and Ireland) 315 is likely to be simple in form and relatively brief.

17. This understanding may be documented using, for example, free-form narrative notes or by completing a structured form. The notes may be maintained separately or incorporated in the documentation of the overall audit strategy required by ISA (UK and Ireland) 300.

18. To comply with the ISAs (UK and Ireland), it is not necessary to document the entirety of the auditor's understanding of the entity and matters related to it. Key elements of the understanding documented by the auditor include those on which the auditor has based the assessment of the risks of material misstatement in the financial statements.

Simple accounting systems

19. Most smaller entities have a relatively uncomplicated accounting process. They are likely to employ few, if any, personnel solely engaged in record-keeping and there will be limited opportunities for segregation of duties.

20. Bookkeeping procedures and accounting records are often simple and there are usually no documented descriptions of accounting policies or procedures. Smaller entities are likely to use an off-the-shelf accounting package in producing their accounts. Understanding of the accounting package in question, including that gained from other audits, can help the auditor to identify and focus on areas of risk of misstatement that arise from the accounting system.

21. The audit documentation associated with the accounting system is likely to be relatively simple, focussing on how the main transaction cycles operate (including how a transaction originates and gets recorded) and highlighting the risks of material misstatement that arise from the nature of the systems in place[4].

Relatively small number and informal nature of controls

22. In the audit of a smaller entity, the auditor may decide that most of the audit evidence will be obtained from substantive tests of detail. Notwithstanding this, as part of the process of assessing the risks of material misstatement, the auditor is required by ISA (UK and Ireland) 315 to obtain and document an understanding of the components of the entity's internal control relevant to the audit (including, for example, the control environment, information systems relevant to financial reporting, and control activities).

23. Size and economic considerations in smaller entities often reduce the opportunity for formal control activities, although some basic control activities are likely to exist for the main transaction cycles such as revenues, purchases and employment costs. Management's direct control over key decisions and the ability to intervene personally at any time to ensure an appropriate response to changing circumstances are often important features of the management of any entrepreneurial venture. For example, management's sole authority for granting credit to customers and approving significant purchases can provide strong control over those important account balances and transactions, lessening or removing the need for more detailed control activities. Furthermore, management often has a personal interest in safeguarding the assets of the entity, measuring its performance and controlling its activities, and so they will apply their own controls and develop their own key indicators of performance.

24. However, the dominant position of management in a smaller entity may be abused and can result in the override of controls and inaccurate accounting records. Furthermore,

---

[4] Auditors of UK companies will be conscious of their responsibilities under Section 498 of the Companies Act 2006 to carry out such investigations as will enable them to form an opinion as to whether adequate accounting records have been kept by the company. Equivalent requirements for the Republic of Ireland relate to proper books of account and are contained in section 193 of the Companies Act 1990.

personal and business objectives can be inextricably linked in the mind of the owner-manager, which increases audit risk. For example, personal tax planning considerations might be important and could provide management with the motivation to bias the financial statements.

25. The extent and nature of management's involvement in internal control in a smaller entity is likely to be a key aspect in the documentation of the auditor's understanding of the entity and assessment of risk, including, for example:

- The evaluation of the control environment, including consideration of the attitude and motives of management based on prior year experience and the observation of management's actions during the audit.

- Specific control activities relevant to the audit. These are likely to be limited but may include management's direct involvement in, and/or supervision of, controls that mitigate risks of material misstatement.

- The key indicators used by management for evaluating financial performance.

Nature of the professional relationship between smaller entities and their auditors

26. Management of a smaller entity often need professional advice and assistance on a wide range of accounting and related financial and business issues which are not available "in-house", and it is common for the audit firm to provide non-audit services including accounting and taxation services. These services can enable the auditor to obtain useful information about the entity and about its objectives and strategies and the management style and ethos, as well as helping to keep the understanding of the entity up to date and so plan the audit efficiently.

27. In circumstances where the audit firm provides non-audit services, the auditor bears in mind the need to maintain objectivity when forming and expressing an opinion on the financial statements. When forming an opinion, but before issuing the report on the financial statements, the audit engagement partner reaches and documents an overall conclusion[5] that any threats to objectivity and independence have been properly addressed in accordance with APB Ethical Standards including, where appropriate, ES – Provisions Available for Small Entities[6].

28. The documentation considerations associated with providing non-audit services include the following:

- To achieve completeness of 'audit documentation', any information, gained as a result of the provision of other services, which is used as audit evidence needs to be incorporated or cross-referenced into the audit documentation.

---

[5] As required by paragraphs 48 and 64 of ES 1.

[6] ES – Provisions Available for Small Entities provides alternative provisions for auditors of Small Entities (size criteria for Small Entities are set out in paragraph 4) to apply in respect of certain threats arising from economic dependence and the provision of non-audit services and allows the option of exemptions from certain requirements in ES 1 to 5.

- The auditor's assessment of his or her objectivity and independence is documented, including a description of the threats identified and the safeguards applied to eliminate or reduce the threats to an acceptable level[7].

- The respective responsibilities of the directors (or equivalent) and the auditor are documented in an engagement letter. This is particularly important where the audit firm is involved in the preparation of the financial statements.

Relatively small audit team size

29. Audits of smaller entities may be conducted by small audit teams, possibly involving the audit engagement partner working with one audit assistant (or without any audit assistants).

30. ISA (UK and Ireland) 230 explains that the audit documentation for the audit of a smaller entity is generally less extensive than that for the audit of a larger entity. Further, in the case of an audit where the engagement partner performs all the audit work, the documentation will not include matters that might have to be documented solely to inform or instruct members of an engagement team, or to provide evidence of review by other members of the team (for example, there will be no matters to document relating to team discussions or supervision). Nevertheless, the engagement partner complies with the overriding requirement described in paragraph 13 above to prepare audit documentation that can be understood by an experienced auditor, as the audit documentation may be subject to review by external parties for regulatory or other purposes.

31. However, as the size of the engagement team increases, or where more inexperienced team members are introduced, more detailed documentation may assist the team in obtaining an appropriate understanding of the entity. There may also be more reviews performed in compliance with quality control policies and procedures, although the format of documentation for these reviews is not affected by the audit team size.

32. ISA (UK and Ireland) 230 suggests that when preparing audit documentation, the auditor of a smaller entity may find it helpful and efficient to record various aspects of the audit together in a single document, with cross-references to supporting working papers as appropriate. Examples of matters that may be documented together in the audit of a smaller entity include the understanding of the entity and its internal control, the overall audit strategy and audit plan, materiality determined in accordance with ISA (UK and Ireland) 320, "Materiality in Planning and Performing an Audit", assessed risks, significant matters noted during the audit, and conclusions reached.

Use of proprietary audit systems

33. Where the auditor of a smaller entity operates in a small practice, it is likely that use will be made of an audit methodology and/or audit software provided by an external supplier (proprietary systems). Proprietary systems are usually designed to deal with a

---

[7] As required by ES 1, paragraph 64, and ES 5, paragraph 37.

wide variety of client situations. To be used efficiently and effectively, the auditor needs to think carefully about how the system should be tailored to each individual client entity.

34. Documentation of the understanding of the entity including its controls is usually embedded into proprietary systems by use of optional check lists or 'white space' techniques. A risk exists that less experienced staff might think that it is compulsory to comply with all elements of these systems, without tailoring the approach to the needs of the particular entity, and thereby prepare excessive, and often irrelevant and costly, audit documentation. Proper training and supervision of junior staff and communication within the engagement team can help to overcome this risk.

35. Even where a proprietary system is used, a free-form planning memorandum can be a good way of documenting the auditor's understanding of the business and the basis for the risk assessments made. Such a memorandum can then easily be updated from one year to the next.

Audit documentation requirements in ISAs (UK and Ireland)

36. In addition to ISA (UK and Ireland) 230, several other ISAs (UK and Ireland) set out further specific audit requirements and guidance in relation to audit documentation.

37. Taking these requirements into account, the key matters to document are summarised in the table in Appendix A to the extent they apply in the context of the engagement. The requirements are summarised by audit phase:

- general;

- engagement acceptance and continuation;

- planning the audit;

- procedures performed in response to assessed risks;

- completion and review of the audit; and

- the auditor's report.

38. Where requirements are clearly not applicable, there is no need to include any references to them in the audit working papers. For example, where the entity uses no service organisations, there is no need to include any reference to ISA (UK and Ireland) 402.

Assembly of the final audit file

39. ISA (UK and Ireland) 230 and ISQC (UK and Ireland) 1 also set out specific requirements and guidance in relation to the assembly of the final audit file and the

confidentiality, safe custody, integrity, accessibility and retrievability and retention of engagement documentation.

40. With respect to individual engagements, ISA (UK and Ireland) 230 requires that:

- The auditor shall assemble the audit documentation in an audit file and complete the administrative process of assembling the final audit file on a timely basis after the date of the auditor's report (paragraphs 14 and A21-A22).

- After the assembly of the final audit file has been completed, the auditor shall not delete or discard audit documentation of any nature before the end of its retention period (paragraphs 15 and A23).

- In circumstances other than those envisaged in paragraph 13[8] of ISA (UK and Ireland) 230 where the auditor finds it necessary to modify existing audit documentation or add new audit documentation after the assembly of the final audit file has been completed, the auditor shall, regardless of the nature of the modifications or additions, document:

  (a) The specific reasons for making them; and

  (b) When and by whom they were made, and reviewed (paragraphs 16 and A24).

Changes to documentation after the date of the auditor's report

41. ISA (UK and Ireland) 230 recognises that in exceptional circumstances it may be necessary to change audit documentation after the date of the auditor's report. For example, when the auditor subsequently discovers facts that existed at the date of the auditor's report that, had the auditor been aware of them at the time, might have affected the auditor's report.

42. When such exceptional circumstances arise, requiring the auditor to perform new or additional audit procedures or leading the auditor to reach new conclusions, the auditor is required to document:

  (a) The circumstances encountered;

  (b) The new or additional audit procedures performed, audit evidence obtained, and conclusions reached, and their effect on the auditor's report; and

  (c) When and by whom the resulting changes to audit documentation were made, and reviewed (paragraphs 13 and A20).

---

[8] Paragraph 13 of ISA (UK and Ireland) 230 addresses exceptional circumstances where the auditor performs new or additional audit procedures.

Appendix A

Summary of documentation requirements and guidance in ISAs (UK and Ireland)

Subject Matter	ISA/ISQC (UK and Ireland) paragraphs setting out requirements	Key matters to document[9]	Example documentation included in this PN
General			
– Identification of who performed audit work	ISA (UK and Ireland) 230, "Audit Documentation" 9(b)	Who performed the audit work and the date it was completed	
– Departures, if any, from a relevant requirement in an ISA (UK and Ireland)	ISA (UK and Ireland) 230 12	How the alternative procedures performed achieve the aim of that requirement and the reasons for the departure[10]	
– Audit procedures performed	ISA (UK and Ireland) 230 8	Sufficient detail to enable an experienced auditor, having no previous connection with the audit, to understand[11]: (a) The nature, timing, and extent of the audit procedures performed to comply with the ISAs (UK and Ireland) and applicable legal and regulatory requirements;	Example 11

---

[9] This summarises the specific requirements in the ISAs (UK and Ireland), with footnote links to particular related guidance. It is necessary to refer to the relevant paragraphs in the standards for the full details of the specific documentation requirements and related guidance. UK and Ireland "pluses" in the standards are highlighted by shading.

[10] ISA (UK and Ireland) 230 indicates that this documentation requirement does not apply to requirements that are not relevant in the circumstances, e.g. those relating to internal audit where there is no such function, or where a requirement is conditional and the condition does not exist (paragraph A19).

[11] ISA (UK and Ireland) 230 indicates that the auditor need not include superseded drafts of working papers, notes that reflect incomplete or preliminary thinking, previous copies of documents corrected for typographical or other errors, and duplicates of documents (paragraph A4).

Subject Matter	ISA/ISQC (UK and Ireland) paragraphs setting out requirements	Key matters to document[9]	Example documentation included in this PN
		(b) The results of the audit procedures performed and the audit evidence obtained; and (c) Significant matters arising during the audit, the conclusions reached thereon, and significant professional judgments made in reaching those conclusions.	
– Consideration of ethical requirements and, in particular, independence	ISA (UK and Ireland) 220 "Quality Control for an Audit of Financial Statements" 24(a), 24(b)	Issues identified with respect to compliance with ethical requirements and how they were resolved. Conclusions on compliance with independence requirements that apply to the audit engagement, and any relevant discussions within the firm that support these conclusions.	
Engagement acceptance and continuation			
– Acceptance and continuance	ISA (UK and Ireland) 220 24(c) ISQC (UK and Ireland) 1, "Quality Control for Firms that Perform Audits and Reviews of Financial Statements, and Other Assurance and Related Services Engagements" 27(c)	Conclusions reached regarding the acceptance and continuance of client relationships and audit engagements. If issues are identified relating to a decision to accept or continue a client relationship or specific engagement, how those issues were resolved.	

Subject Matter	ISA/ISQC (UK and Ireland) paragraphs setting out requirements	Key matters to document[9]	Example documentation included in this PN
– Terms of the engagement	ISA (UK and Ireland) 210, "Agreeing the Terms of Audit Engagements" 10	The agreed terms of the engagement are required to be recorded in an engagement letter or other suitable form of contract and include[12]: (a) The objective and scope of the audit; (b) The responsibilities of the auditor; (c) The responsibilities of management[13]; (d) Identification of the applicable financial reporting framework for the preparation of the financial statements; and (e) Reference to the expected form and content of any reports to be issued by the auditor and a statement that there may be circumstances in which a report may differ from its expected form and content.	

---

[12] Paragraph 11 of ISA (UK and Ireland) 210, indicates that if law or regulation prescribes in sufficient detail the terms of the audit engagement referred to in paragraph 10, the auditor need not record them in a written agreement, except for the fact that such law or regulation applies and that management acknowledges and understands its responsibilities as set out in paragraph 6(b) (see footnote 13).The guidance in ISA (UK and Ireland) 210 sets out further matters that the auditor may make reference to.

[13] Paragraph 6(b) of ISA (UK and Ireland) 210 identifies those responsibilities of management where the auditor is required to obtain the agreement of management that it acknowledges and understands its responsibility.

Subject Matter	ISA/ISQC (UK and Ireland) paragraphs setting out requirements	Key matters to document[9]	Example documentation included in this PN
Planning the audit			
– Overall audit strategy	ISA (UK and Ireland) 300, "Planning an Audit of Financial Statements" 8, 12(a), 12(c)	The key decisions considered necessary to properly plan the audit and to communicate significant matters to the engagement team (e.g. regarding the overall scope, timing and conduct of the audit). Any significant changes made during the audit, the reasons therefore, and the overall strategy finally adopted; reflecting the appropriate response to the significant changes occurring during the audit. Paragraph 8[14] requires that in establishing the overall audit strategy, the auditor shall: (a) Identify the characteristics of the engagement that define its scope; (b) Ascertain the reporting objectives of the engagement to plan the timing of the audit and the nature of the communications required; (c) Consider the factors that, in the auditor's professional judgment, are significant in directing the engagement team's efforts;	Examples 1 and 2

---

[14] The guidance in ISA (UK and Ireland) 300 indicates that a suitable brief memorandum prepared at the completion of the previous audit, based on a review of the working papers and highlighting issues identified in the audit just completed, updated in the current period based on discussions with the owner-manager, can serve as the documented audit strategy for the current audit engagement if it covers the matters noted in paragraph 8 (paragraphs A11 and A19). The Appendix to the standard lists examples of considerations in establishing the overall audit strategy.

Subject Matter	ISA/ISQC (UK and Ireland) paragraphs setting out requirements	Key matters to document[9]	Example documentation included in this PN
		(d) Consider the results of preliminary engagement activities and, where applicable, whether knowledge gained on other engagements performed by the engagement partner for the entity is relevant; and (e) Ascertain the nature, timing and extent of resources necessary to perform the engagement.	
– Materiality	ISA (UK and Ireland) 320, "Materiality in Planning and Performing and Audit" 14	The following amounts and the factors considered in their determination: (a) Materiality for the financial statements as a whole; (b) If applicable, the materiality level or levels for particular classes of transactions, account balances or disclosures; (c) Performance materiality; and (d) Any revision of (a)-(c) as the audit progressed.	Examples 1 and 2
– Audit plan, including procedures to respond to assessed risks	ISA (UK and Ireland) 300 9, 12(b), 12(c)	A description of[15]: (a) The nature, timing and extent of planned risk assessment procedures, as determined under ISA (UK and Ireland) 315. (b) The nature, timing and extent of planned further audit	

---

[15] The guidance in ISA (UK and Ireland) 300 indicates that the auditor may use standard audit programs or audit completion checklists tailored as needed to reflect the particular engagement circumstances (paragraph A17).

Subject Matter	ISA/ISQC (UK and Ireland) paragraphs setting out requirements	Key matters to document[9]	Example documentation included in this PN
		procedures at the assertion level, as determined under ISA (UK and Ireland) 330. (c) Other planned audit procedures that are required to be carried out so that the engagement complies with the ISAs (UK and Ireland). Any significant changes made during the audit, the reasons therefore, and the audit plan finally adopted; reflecting the appropriate response to the significant changes during the audit.	
– Use of an auditor's expert	ISA (UK and Ireland) 620, "Using the Work of an Auditor's Expert" 11	The standard specifies matters to be agreed with the auditor's expert, in writing when appropriate[16]. Whilst not stipulated in the standard, it is reasonable to expect that copies of any such written agreements will be included in the audit documentation. The matters to be agreed are: (a) The nature, scope and objectives of that expert's work; (b) The respective roles and responsibilities of the auditor and that expert; (c) The nature, timing and extent of	

---

[16] The guidance in ISA (UK and Ireland) 620 indicates that matters relating to the nature, timing and extent of audit procedures may affect the level of detail and formality of the agreement with the auditor's external expert, including whether it is appropriate that the agreement be in writing (paragraph A24). The guidance also indicates that the agreement between the auditor and an auditor's external expert is often in the form of an engagement letter – the Appendix to the standard indicates matters that may be included in such an engagement letter, or in any other form of agreement with an external expert (paragraph A25).

Subject Matter	ISA/ISQC (UK and Ireland) paragraphs setting out requirements	Key matters to document[9]	Example documentation included in this PN
		communication between the auditor and that expert, including the form of any report to be provided by that expert; and (d) The need for the auditor's expert to observe confidentiality requirements.	
− Understanding of the entity and its environment	ISA (UK and Ireland) 315, "Identifying and Assessing the Risks of Material Misstatement Through Understanding the Entity and its Environment" 32(b)	Key elements of the understanding obtained regarding[17]: (a) Relevant industry, regulatory, and other external factors, including the applicable financial reporting framework. (b) Nature of the entity, including: (i) its operations; (ii) its ownership and governance structures; (iii) the types of investments that the entity is making and plans to make, including investments in special purpose entities; and (iv) the way the entity is structured and how it is financed. (c) Selection and application of	Examples 3 and 4 (re (a) to (e))

---

[17] The guidance in ISA (UK and Ireland) 315 indicates that the manner in which these matters are documented is for the auditor to determine using professional judgment. For example, in audits of small entities the documentation may be incorporated in the auditor's documentation of the overall strategy and audit plan. Similarly, for example, the results of the risk assessment may be documented separately, or may be documented as part of the auditor's documentation of further procedures (see below re paragraph 28 of ISA (UK and Ireland) 330) (paragraph A131).

Subject Matter	ISA/ISQC (UK and Ireland) paragraphs setting out requirements	Key matters to document[9]	Example documentation included in this PN
		accounting policies, including the reasons for changes thereto. (d) Objectives and strategies and those related business risks that may result in risks of material misstatement. (e) Measurement and review of the entity's financial performance.[18] (f) Internal control, including: (i) The control environment. (ii) The entity's risk assessment process. (iii) The information system, including the related business processes, relevant to financial reporting, and communication. (iv) Control activities relevant to the audit. (v) Monitoring of controls. The sources of information from which the understanding was obtained. The risk assessment procedures performed. These are required to include (para 6): • Inquiries of management and others within the entity who in the auditor's judgment	Examples 6 and 7 (re (f))

---

[18] Smaller entities often do not have processes to measure and review financial performance. However, enquiries of management may reveal that they rely on certain key indicators for evaluating financial performance and taking appropriate evidence.

Subject Matter	ISA/ISQC (UK and Ireland) paragraphs setting out requirements	Key matters to document[9]	Example documentation included in this PN
		may have information that is likely to assist in identifying risks of material misstatement due to fraud or error. • Analytical procedures. • Observation and inspection.	
– Use of a service organisation by the audited entity	ISA (UK and Ireland) 402, "Audit Considerations Relating to an Entity Using a Service Organisation" *This standard does not include any explicit documentation requirements. However, paragraph 9 stipulates matters the auditor obtains an understanding of, when an entity uses a service organisation, in meeting the requirements of paragraph 11 of ISA (UK and Ireland) 315. Paragraph 32(b) of ISA (UK and Ireland) 315 requires the auditor to document the key elements of the understanding of the entity identified in paragraph 11.*	(a) The nature of the services provided by the service organisation and the significance of those services to the user entity, including the effect thereof on the user entity's internal control; (b) The nature and materiality of the transactions processed or accounts or financial reporting processes affected by the service organisation; (c) The degree of interaction between the activities of the service organisation and those of the user entity; and (d) The nature of the relationship between the user entity and the service organisation, including the relevant contractual terms for the activities undertaken by the service organisation.	

Subject Matter	ISA/ISQC (UK and Ireland) paragraphs setting out requirements	Key matters to document[9]	Example documentation included in this PN
		(e) If the service organisation maintains all or part of a user entity's accounting records, whether those arrangements impact the work the auditor performs to fulfil reporting responsibilities in relation to accounting records that are established in law or regulation.	
– Assessment of the risks of material misstatement and, in particular, those risks related to fraud[19]	ISA (UK and Ireland) 315 32(a), 32(c), 32(d) ISA (UK and Ireland) 240, "The Auditor's Responsibilities Relating to Fraud in an Audit of Financial Statements" 44(a), 44(b), 47	The discussion among the engagement team regarding the susceptibility of the entity's financial statements to material misstatement due to error or fraud, the application of the applicable financial reporting framework to the entity's facts and circumstances, and the significant decisions reached[20]. The identified and assessed risks of material misstatements, due to error or fraud, at the financial statement level and at the assertion level. Significant risks identified, if any, and the related controls about which the auditor has obtained an understanding.	Example 5 (re planning meeting) Examples 8 and 9 (re risk assessment)

---

[19] ISA (UK and Ireland) 240 expands on the standards and guidance in ISAs (UK and Ireland) 315 and 330. Presenting ISA (UK Ireland) 240 separately, rather than embodying its content in ISAs (UK and Ireland) 315 and 330, emphasises the importance of the auditor's responsibility to consider fraud in an audit of financial statements. To comply with the requirements of ISA (UK and Ireland) 240, matters related to fraud need to be identifiable as such.

[20] The requirement for there to be a discussion among the engagement team does not apply where the audit is carried out entirely by the engagement partner.

Subject Matter	ISA/ISQC (UK and Ireland) paragraphs setting out requirements	Key matters to document[9]	Example documentation included in this PN
		The risks identified, and the related controls evaluated, where it is not possible or practicable to obtain sufficient appropriate audit evidence only from substantive procedures. If the auditor has concluded that there is not a significant risk due to fraud related to revenue recognition, the reasons for that conclusion.	
Procedures performed in response to assessed risks			
– Overall responses and specific procedures	ISA (UK and Ireland) 330, "The Auditor's Responses to Assessed Risks" 28(a), 28(b) ISA (UK and Ireland) 240 45(a)	The overall responses to address the assessed risks of material misstatements due to error or fraud at the financial statement level, and the nature, timing and extent of further audit procedures performed. The linkage of those procedures with the assessed risks of material misstatement due to error or fraud at the assertion level.	Examples 8 and 9 re overall responses
	ISA (UK and Ireland) 330 29	If the auditor plans to use audit evidence about the operating effectiveness of controls obtained in previous audits, the auditor shall document the conclusions reached about relying on such controls that were tested in a previous audit.	

Subject Matter	ISA/ISQC (UK and Ireland) paragraphs setting out requirements	Key matters to document[9]	Example documentation included in this PN
– Identifying characteristics of the specific matters or items being tested	ISA (UK and Ireland) 230 9(a)	In documenting the nature, timing and extent of audit procedures performed – the identifying characteristics of the specific items or matters tested[21].	
– Results	ISA (UK and Ireland) 330 28(c) ISA (UK and Ireland) 240 45(b)	Results, and conclusions where not otherwise clear, of audit procedures performed, including those designed to address the risk of management override of controls.	
– Agreement of financial statements to accounting records	ISA (UK and Ireland) 330 30	Demonstration that the financial statements agree or reconcile with the underlying accounting records.	
– Discussion of significant matters with management or others	ISA (UK and Ireland) 230 10	The significant matters discussed with management, those charged with governance, and others, including the nature of the significant matters discussed and when and with whom the discussions took place[22].	
– Information that is inconsistent with the auditor's final conclusion regarding a significant matter	ISA (UK and Ireland) 230 11	How the auditor addressed the inconsistency[23].	

[21] Identifying characteristics will vary with the nature of the audit procedure and the item or matter being tested. Paragraph A12 of ISA (UK and Ireland) 230 gives examples.

[22] The guidance in ISA (UK and Ireland) 230 indicates that the documentation may include records, such as agreed minutes, prepared by the entity. Others with whom the auditor may discuss significant matters may include other personnel within the entity, and external parties, such as persons providing professional advice to the entity (paragraph A14).

[23] The guidance in ISA (UK and Ireland) 230 indicates that the auditor does not need to retain documentation that is incorrect or superseded (paragraph A15).

Subject Matter	ISA/ISQC (UK and Ireland) paragraphs setting out requirements	Key matters to document[9]	Example documentation included in this PN
– Non compliance, if any, with laws and regulations	ISA (UK and Ireland) 250 Section A, "Consideration of Laws and Regulations in an Audit of Financial Statements" 29	Identified or suspected non-compliance with laws and regulations and the results of discussion with management and, where applicable, those charged with governance and other parties outside the entity[24].	
	Section B: "The Auditor's Right and Duty to Report to Regulators in the Financial Sector" 13, 16, A30	Some laws and regulations in the UK and Ireland impose a responsibility on the auditor to report actual or suspected non-compliances to an appropriate authority (e.g. in relation to money laundering offences). Other matters may be reported to an appropriate authority in the public interest[25]. Whilst not stipulated in the standard, it is reasonable to expect that copies of any such reports will be included in the audit documentation. Again, whilst not stipulated in the standard, it is reasonable to expect that copies of any reports made to a regulator will be included in the audit documentation. When	

---

[24] The guidance in ISA (UK and Ireland) 250, Section A, indicates that the documentation may include copies of records and documents, and minutes of discussions with management, those charged with governance or parties outside the entity (paragraph A21).

[25] The guidance in ISA (UK and Ireland) 250, Section A, indicates that where the auditor becomes aware of a suspected or actual instance of non-compliance with law or regulations, which does not give rise to a statutory duty to report to an appropriate authority the auditor considers whether the matter may be one that ought to be reported to a proper authority, in the public interest. If, having considered any views expressed on behalf of the entity and in the light of any legal advice obtained the auditor concludes that the matter ought to be reported to an appropriate authority in the public interest, the auditor notifies those charged with governance in writing of the view and, if the entity does not voluntarily do so itself or is unable to provide evidence that the matter has been reported, the auditor reports it (paragraphs A19-4 and A19-5).

Subject Matter	ISA/ISQC (UK and Ireland) paragraphs setting out requirements	Key matters to document[9]	Example documentation included in this PN
		the initial report is made orally, the auditor is required to make a contemporaneous written record of the report and to confirm the matter in writing to the regulator. Matters to be included when making or confirming a report direct to a regulator are set out in paragraph 16 of the requirements. The guidance in paragraph A30 indicates that where matters may be reportable to a regulator the auditor needs to ensure that the facts and the basis for the auditor's decision (whether to report or not) is adequately documented, such that the reasons for that decision may be clearly demonstrated should the need to do so arise in future.	
– Accounting estimates	ISA (UK and Ireland) 540, "Auditing Accounting Estimates Including Fair Value Accounting Estimates and Related Disclosures" 23	The basis for the auditor's conclusions about the reasonableness of accounting estimates (and their disclosure) that give rise to significant risks. Indicators of possible management bias, if any.	Example 10
– Related parties	ISA (UK and Ireland) 550, "Related Parties" 28	The names of identified related parties and the nature of the related party relationships.	

Subject Matter	ISA/ISQC (UK and Ireland) paragraphs setting out requirements	Key matters to document[9]	Example documentation included in this PN
– Groups	ISA (UK and Ireland) 600, "Special Considerations – Audits of Group Financial Statements (Including the Work of Component Auditors)" 50	(a) An analysis of components, indicating those that are significant, and the type of work performed on the financial information of the components. (b) The nature, timing and extent of the group engagement team's involvement in the work performed by the component auditors on significant components including, where applicable, the group engagement team's review of relevant parts of the component auditors' audit documentation and conclusions thereon. The guidance in paragraph A66-1 of ISA (UK and Ireland) 600 explains that in the UK the Companies Act 2006 requires that group auditors review for the purposes of the group audit the audit work conducted by other persons and record that review. (c) Written communications between the group engagement team and the component auditors about the group engagement team's requirements.	Example 13 (re (a) and (b))
– Internal audit	ISA (UK and Ireland) 610, "Using the Work of Internal Auditors" 13	If the external auditor uses specific work of internal auditors, the external auditor shall include in the audit documentation the	

Subject Matter	ISA/ISQC (UK and Ireland) paragraphs setting out requirements	Key matters to document[9]	Example documentation included in this PN
		conclusions reached regarding the evaluation of the adequacy of the work of the internal auditors, and the audit procedures performed by the external auditor on that work.	
– Concerns, if any, about going concern	ISA (UK and Ireland) 570, "Going Concern" A19-2 ISA (UK and Ireland) 230 8(c), A8	The guidance in these two standards makes clear that in complying with the requirements of ISA (UK and Ireland) 230, paragraph 8(c), to document significant matters arising during the audit, the auditor documents concerns (if any) about the entity's ability to continue as a going concern.	Example 11
– Directors' report	ISA (UK and Ireland) 720 Section B, "The Auditor's Statutory Reporting Responsibility in Relation to Directors' Reports" 12	Results of procedures performed to assess whether the information in the directors' report is consistent with the financial statements, including details of any material inconsistencies identified and how they were resolved. The conclusion reached as to whether the information in the directors' report is consistent with the financial statements.	
Completion and review of the audit			
– Consultation on difficult or contentious matters	ISA (UK and Ireland) 220 24(d)	Nature and scope of, and conclusions resulting from, consultations[26].	

---

[26] The guidance in ISA (UK and Ireland) 220 indicates that documentation that is sufficiently complete and detailed contributes to an understanding of the issue and the results of the consultation, including any decisions taken, the basis for those decisions and how they were implemented (paragraph A35).

Subject Matter	ISA/ISQC (UK and Ireland) paragraphs setting out requirements	Key matters to document[9]	Example documentation included in this PN
– Differences of opinion between members of the engagement team and/or others consulted	ISQC (UK and Ireland) 1 44(a)	The conclusions reached.	
– Evaluation of misstatements	ISA (UK and Ireland) 450, "Evaluation of Misstatements Identified During the Audit" 15	(a) The amount below which misstatements would be regarded as clearly trivial; (b) All misstatements accumulated during the audit and whether they have been corrected; and (c) The auditor's conclusion as to whether uncorrected misstatements are material, individually or in aggregate, and the basis for that conclusion.	Example 12
– Communications, if any, about fraud	ISA (UK and Ireland) 240 46	Communications about fraud with management, those charged with governance, regulators and others.	
– Significant deficiencies in internal control	ISA (UK and Ireland) 265 "Communicating Deficiencies in Internal Control to Those Charged with Governance and Management" 9, 10(a), 11	Significant deficiencies in internal control are required to be communicated in writing to those charged with governance. They should also be communicated in writing to an appropriate level of management unless it would be inappropriate to communicate directly to management in the circumstances[27]. Such written communications are required to include:	

---

[27] The guidance in ISA (UK and Ireland) 265 indicates that the level of detail at which to communicate significant deficiencies is a matter of the auditor's professional judgment in the circumstances. In the case of smaller entities, the auditor may communicate in a less structured manner with those charged with governance than in the case of larger entities (paragraphs A15 and A18).

Subject Matter	ISA/ISQC (UK and Ireland) paragraphs setting out requirements	Key matters to document[9]	Example documentation included in this PN
		(a) A description of the deficiencies and an explanation of their potential effects; and (b) Sufficient information to enable those charged with governance and management to understand the context of the communication. In particular, the auditor shall explain that: (i) The purpose of the audit was for the auditor to express an opinion on the financial statements; (ii) The audit included consideration of internal control relevant to the preparation of the financial statements in order to design audit procedures that are appropriate in the circumstances, but not for the purpose of expressing an opinion on the effectiveness of internal control; and (iii) The matters being reported are limited to those deficiencies that the auditor has identified during the audit and that the auditor has concluded are of sufficient importance to merit being	

Subject Matter	ISA/ISQC (UK and Ireland) paragraphs setting out requirements	Key matters to document[9]	Example documentation included in this PN
		reported to those charged with governance.	
– Communications with those charged with governance	ISA (UK and Ireland) 260 "Communication with Those Charged With Governance" 23	Matters required to be communicated by ISA (UK and Ireland) 260 that are communicated orally, including when and to whom they were communicated[28]. Copies of communications made in writing (e.g. regarding significant deficiencies in internal control – see above).	
– Identification of reviewer	ISA (UK and Ireland) 230 9(c)	Who reviewed the audit work and the date and extent of the review[29].	
– Engagement Quality Control Review[30]	ISQC (UK and Ireland) 1 42 ISA (UK and Ireland) 220 25	Confirmation that: (a) The procedures required by the firm's policies on engagement quality control review have been performed. (b) The engagement quality control review has been completed on or before the date of the auditor's report. (c) The reviewer is not aware of any unresolved matters that would cause the reviewer to believe that the significant	

---

[28] The guidance in ISA (UK and Ireland) 260 indicates that this documentation may take the form of a copy of minutes prepared by the entity where those minutes are an appropriate record of the communication (paragraph A45).

[29] The guidance in ISA (UK and Ireland) 230 indicates that the requirement to document who reviewed the audit work performed does not imply a need for each specific working paper to include evidence of review. The requirement, however, means documenting what audit work was reviewed, who reviewed such work, and when it was reviewed (paragraph A13).

[30] Engagement quality control reviews are not required for all audits. Further requirements on the nature and scope of these reviews are set out in paragraphs 35 to 41 of ISQC (UK and Ireland) 1, and paragraphs 19 to 21 of ISA (UK and Ireland) 220.

Subject Matter	ISA/ISQC (UK and Ireland) paragraphs setting out requirements	Key matters to document[9]	Example documentation included in this PN
		judgments the engagement team made and the conclusions they reached were not appropriate.	
– Management representations	ISA (UK and Ireland) 580, "Written Representations"	Written representations from management[31].	
The auditor's report			
	ISA (UK and Ireland) 700, "The Auditor's Report on Financial Statements"	Whilst not addressed by ISA (UK and Ireland) 700, it is reasonable to presume that the auditor will keep a copy of the auditor's report.	

---

[31] The guidance in ISA (UK and Ireland) 580 indicates that In view of their importance, it is appropriate for written representations that are critical to obtaining sufficient appropriate audit evidence to be provided by those charged with governance rather than the entity's management (paragraph A2-1).

Appendix B

Illustrative examples of audit documentation

This appendix includes a number of illustrative examples of audit documentation. The examples focus on:

(i) Elements of audit planning, including understanding of the entity, internal control and risk assessment. These represent the areas where most "new" requirements were added as a result of the introduction of ISAs (UK and Ireland) in 2004 and feedback indicated that further guidance on documentation would be particularly helpful.

(ii) Some of the documentation requirements introduced in the clarified ISAs (UK and Ireland) for audits of financial statements for periods ending on or after 15 December 2010. These examples cover materiality, evaluation of misstatements, and aspects of the planning memorandum for a group audit.

(iii) Audit procedures performed on an accounting estimate.

(iv) The auditor's conclusions on going concern.

There are a number of different ways in which the audit documentation requirements can be fulfilled. The examples illustrate this by demonstrating more than one technique in a number of areas for the audit of a fictitious company, Bulls Hotel and Restaurant Limited (with the exception of Example 13, which illustrates a group of companies). The examples do not represent a comprehensive set of audit working papers and do not necessarily identify all the risks associated with a business of the nature described. They are not intended to set a minimum standard of documentation and other approaches to documentation can be used in practice. For example, it would be possible to prepare one planning document covering all of the matters dealt with in examples 1 to 9. The level of documentation necessary on an audit will vary depending on the circumstances of the entity and the risks relating to a particular area.

Explanations are written out in full in these examples. Shorter bullet point lists, employing abbreviations, may be suitable in some circumstances provided that the meaning is unambiguous.

Area of documentation	Illustrative approach	Page
Audit strategy	Example 1 – Audit strategy memorandum Example 2 – Audit strategy referencing other documents on file	2213 2216
Understanding the entity	Example 3 – Free-form notes Example 4 - Based on a checklist	2218 2222
Audit team planning meeting	Example 5 – Excerpt from meeting using a pre-set agenda	2227
Controls documentation	Example 6 – Free-form notes Example 7 – Based on a checklist and systems diagrams	2230 2234
Risk assessment	Example 8 – Based on risks Example 9 – Based on assertions	2238 2240
Audit working papers	Example 10 – Property valuation Example 11 – Going concern	2242 2244
Completion	Example 12 – Evaluation of misstatements identified during the audit	2246

Example relating to a different case study entity:

Group audits	Example 13 – Excerpt from group planning memorandum	2248

Example documentation: for illustrative purposes only

Example 1 – Audit strategy memorandum[1]

Client: **Bulls Restaurant and Hotel Limited**
Year end: **31 January 20X1**

Characteristics of the engagement

- Small private company registered in England and Wales.

- Family company with two non-family shareholders and a number of related party transactions during the year.

- Accounts are prepared under the FRSSE.

- Accounting services, including payroll, provided by the part-time bookkeeper.

The permanent file documentation provides further information on understanding the business, the control environment and internal controls.

Timing of reporting

- Year end is 31st January.

- Audit fieldwork during May.

- Partner to meet with directors to discuss results and accounts signed in mid-June.

Significant factors

Materiality

Materiality for the financial statements as a whole
Materiality for the financial statements as a whole has been set at £13,500. This is based on 5% of an estimated profit before tax figure[2] of £270,000, which is a consistent basis to that used in previous audits. An unadjusted profit before tax figure is appropriate as there are no exceptional items affecting profit before tax and the levels of directors' remuneration are not abnormally high.

---

[1] Documentation requirement at ISA (UK and Ireland) 300 paragraph 12(a) and ISA (UK and Ireland) 320 paragraph 14.

[2] Profit before tax has been used in this example, but other bases (for example, turnover or balance sheet totals) and other percentages may be appropriate based on the auditor's judgment.

Example documentation: for illustrative purposes only

Lower levels of materiality for specific items
Users of the accounts are the shareholders and the bank. A lower level of materiality has been set in respect of the following classes of transactions, account balances and disclosures:

- Transactions between the company and individual family
  owners (relevant to the non-family shareholders)   £6,000

Performance materiality
In assessing the risks of material misstatement and determining the nature, timing and extent of further audit procedures performance materiality has been set at £10,000 (and £5,000 for transactions between the company and individual family owners). This is judged to be sufficient as, on the basis of past audit errors (which have been primarily of a cut-off nature), there is a low probability that the aggregate of uncorrected and undetected misstatements will exceed the overall materiality.

Internal control

- No past history of management override of controls. Audit staff will be briefed to remain alert to this risk.

- Managements' attitude towards internal control is very positive

- There are particular internal controls that we can plan to rely on.

- These are documented in the systems information (Ref: C43).

Results of previous audit
No matters were identified during the previous audit to suggest a significant change in audit approach is needed.

Developments in the business
The audit manager held a preliminary meeting with management on 18th January. The purpose of this meeting was to:

- discuss the nature, timing and extent of the audit work; and

- enquire whether there have been any developments in the business since the last audit that may impact the audit of the current period.

There have been no significant changes in the business activities since the last audit and no changes in the client's staff. The current poor economic climate has led to a downturn in trading (turnover reduced by 10% to £2.7m), but the directors believe the company is still performing relatively well given the circumstances and are confident that the ability to continue as a going concern is not threatened.

The Freehold property was re-valued last year. However, in light of general falls in property values since then the client believes that a significant reduction in value should be recognised in the accounts this year.

Example documentation: for illustrative purposes only

Risk assessment procedures performed
A preliminary analytical review of the December 20X0 management accounts was carried out (ref B34). The figures reflect a downturn in the current year's trading levels (consistent with fall in occupancy levels). No unusual relationships were identified in gross profit figures and business appears to be continuing as normal.

The significant risks are:

- Property valuation;

- Incomplete sales recording due to high volume of cash transactions.

Further details on these risks and other matters giving rise to significant risks and how they will be addressed are documented in the Understanding of the Entity (Ref: AB2).

Nature, timing and extent of resources allocated
Paul Cox has been the audit engagement partner for the past eight years. Sarah Cole has been the audit manager since the audit for the year ended 20W7. The main audit work this year will be carried out by a student in their final year of training.

The audit timetable is as follows:

Planning	• Amend audit strategy • Update permanent file information • Prepare audit programs	2 days	January 20X1
Stock-count	Junior member of staff to attend	1 day	1 February 20X1
Final audit	This will commence with the audit team planning meeting in the office before transferring to the client's premises Manager review Partner review	2 weeks	Commencing 10 May 20X1 19 May 20X1 21 May 20X1
Sign-off	Final meeting with client for approval of the accounts and signature Signing the audit report		Provisional date – 2 June 20X1 Mid-June 20X1

Prepared by Sarah Cole   Date 18ᵗʰ January 20X1

Approved by Paul Cox   Date 20ᵗʰ January 20X1

No revisions to these items were found to be necessary during the course of the audit.

Sarah Cole   Date 19ᵗʰ May 20X1

Paul Cox   Date 21ˢᵗ May 20X1

Example documentation: for illustrative purposes only

Example 2 – Audit strategy referencing other documents on file[3]

Client:	Bulls Restaurant and Hotel Limited
Year end:	31 January 20X1
Prepared by:	Sarah Cole
Approved by:	*Paul Cox* *20ᵗʰ January 20X1*
Information sources	*Meeting with management on 18 January 20x1*

Factors to consider	Notes		Ref
Characteristics of the engagement			
• Financial reporting framework • Industry specific reporting requirements • Need for expert	*Small family company. Accounts prepared using the FRSSE. Further detail is in understanding the business*		*AB1*
Reporting objectives, timing of the audit and nature of communications			
• Reporting timetable • Meetings with management and those charged with governance • Audit team communications	*Accounts to be signed by mid-June.* *Sign off meeting with directors provisionally arranged for 2 June 20X1* *Stock count 1 February 20x1.* *Audit team planning meeting 10 May 20x1.* *Manager review at client site 19 May 20x1.* *Partner review in the office 21 May 20x1.*		
Significant factors			
• Determination of materiality considering turnover, PBT and net assets	Materiality: Financial statements as a whole Specific items *Transactions with family members* Performance materiality: Financial statements as a whole Specific items: *Transactions with family members*	£13,500 £6,000 £ 10,000 £5,000	*AB10*

---

[3] Documentation requirement at ISA (UK and Ireland) 300, paragraph 12(a) and ISA (UK and Ireland) 320, paragraph 14.

Example documentation: for illustrative purposes only

Factors to consider	Notes	Ref
Result of preliminary engagement activities		
• Areas with high risk of material misstatement • Results of previous audits • Internal control • Significant business and other developments	December 20X0 management accounts reflect a downturn in trading (consistent with fall in occupancy levels). No unusual relationships were identified in gross profit figures and business is continuing as normal. The significant risks are: • Property valuation; • Incomplete sales recording due to high volume of cash transactions. See notes in understanding the business. No matters in previous audit suggesting a significant change in audit approach is needed. See controls documentation. No significant changes in business activities.	B34 AB2 C43
Nature and extent of resources		
• Engagement team • Budget	Engagement partner – Paul Cox Audit manager – Sarah Cole In-charge – Richard Cannon Total budgeted costs – £15,000	AD6

No revisions to these items were found to be necessary during the course of the audit.

Sarah Cole   Date 19th May 20X1

Paul Cox   Date 21st May 20X1

Example documentation: for illustrative purposes only

Example 3 – Free-form notes of Understanding the entity[4]

Client: **Bulls Restaurant and Hotel Limited**
Year end: **31 January 20X1**

Nature of the entity
Bulls Restaurant and Hotel Limited is a company that owns and operates a restaurant and hotel property in Manchester city centre. This property comprises a three storey building (wine bar on the ground floor, restaurant on the first floor and ballroom on the top floor) and an adjoining luxury hotel property of 10 en-suite rooms and 2 large family suites.

The company qualifies as a small company:

- Turnover is £3 million.

- Balance sheet total is £3.5 million.

- There are 25 permanent employees and a pool of approximately 15 casual staff who are used when special events are held.

The accounts have been audited for many years, despite an exemption being available prior to a property revaluation in 20X0. The directors chose to have a voluntary audit for a number of reasons. In particular, Lisa Swann (one of the shareholders) suggested it would be valuable from a control viewpoint and in order that future expansion might be eased. Once the property was reflected at its current market value in the accounts, the audit exemption was no longer available.

Revenue is generated from two sources – Food and Beverage (the wine bar, restaurant and function room) (70%) and Room revenue from the hotel (30%). A high proportion of transactions are cash based, which leads to a fraud risk that revenue is understated.

A local brewer supplies all alcohol and soft drinks – long established relationship. The hotel business is reliant on travel agent and internet related bookings.

Industry factors
Regeneration of Manchester city centre brought in a large number of competitors a few years ago. Occupancy rates of 80% and average room rate were maintained during this time but this resulted in a squeeze on margins as costs of supply increased.

---

[4] Documentation requirement at ISA (UK and Ireland) 315, paragraph 32(b).

Example documentation: for illustrative purposes only

Customers are now demanding a higher quality dining experience. Bulls is set up to provide this, and are not planning to apply for a change in their licence in order to be able to open later (currently 11 p.m. in the wine bar, 12 midnight in the restaurant and 1 a.m. in the function suite) in order to maintain their current clientele.

The business is subject to seasonal variation. This is most pronounced during December, when Christmas events increase turnover by over 100% and casual staff are employed for a large proportion of the time during this month.

Regulatory factors

- Environmental health inspections continue to be thorough and turn up areas for improvement.

- National minimum wage legislation is relevant.

- Tax treatment of gratuity payments was under dispute, but has now been agreed by HMRC.

- Health and Safety at work and fire safety legislation is relevant – there are a number of hazardous environments, especially in kitchen areas.

- A premises licence is held for the sale and supply of alcohol and provision of entertainment.

Ownership and governance
Single company owned by two family shareholders with a number of other shareholders. The directors and shareholders are as follows:

			Shareholding
Directors:	Fred Bull	Brother	40%
	Jo Giles	Sister	40%
Other shareholders:	Terry Bull	Father	10%
	Mark Quinn	Family friend	5%
	Lisa Swann	Family friend	5%

The directors are in a dominant position. However, past experience indicates that the non-director shareholders have an active involvement in the business and their professional capacities (a surveyor and accountant) help to prevent the directors from being able to abuse their position.

Related parties
A number of large functions have been held at the hotel for family and friends of the directors in the past. These have typically been invoiced at reduced rates compared to other customers, but have not been material and payments have been received promptly.

Example documentation: for illustrative purposes only

Terry Bull runs a local meat distribution company – Melville Foods. Much of the fresh meat used in the restaurant and for functions are supplied by this company, representing approximately 20% of the food costs of the company.

Fixed assets
The freehold property is continually refurbished in order to maintain its value.

Organisational structure and financing
Company originally set up with share finance and bank loans (now repaid). The company has an overdraft facility of £50,000. The maximum amount of this facility that is utilised during a year is typically £25,000. Annual meetings are held with a bank representative at which time the overdraft limit and covenants and any other loan facilities required for the forthcoming year are agreed.

Accounting policies
The company follows the FRSSE. The directors revalued the property last year and now need to keep this valuation up to date.

Objectives and strategies and related business risks
The operations have remained unchanged for a number of years, including the IT (EPOS and accounting) infrastructure. Management want to raise the standard of the restaurant and gain higher quality ratings in hotel and restaurant listings. Directors are researching the possibility of a second (rural) location: they propose to fund such expansion largely through bank finance.

Measurement and review of financial performance
Management review monthly management accounts prepared by a part-time bookkeeper, that include a comparison with budgets which are prepared by the directors. KPIs include occupancy, average room rate, covers served, turnover and rooms, food and beverage gross profit margins. Following a squeeze on margins a few years ago these have been steady for a number of years.

Originally prepared by *Sarah Cole* Date *June 20w8*

Sources of information referred to:

- discussion with Fred Bull and Jo Giles;
- share register;
- review of financial statements;
- management accounts;
- review of debtor and creditor listings; and
- company website (accessed on 16 June 20W8).

Updated for 20X1 audit by *Sarah Cole* Date *January 20X1*

Example documentation: for illustrative purposes only

Continuing relevance of the information above confirmed by discussion on 18th January with Fred Bull and Stacey Burrows, the bookkeeper.

Impact on the audit – risks of material misstatement relevant to audit for the year ended 31 January 20X1

At the Financial Statement Level

1. *No pervasive risks of material misstatement have been identified. The assessment of risk at the financial statement level is "low".*

At the Assertion Level

2. *Family company means related party transactions likely to occur, but may not be classified as such (R102).*

3. *Possible unrecorded liabilities resulting from fines and other liabilities arising from reviews by EHOs and HMRC – in the past few years there has been a potential liability relating to the tax treatment of gratuity payments (R101).*

4. *The directors believe that there has been a material change in the value of the property since it was re-valued last year for the first time. They will provide an estimated value for use in the accounts.* **This constitutes a significant risk (R103).**

5. *There is a high level of cash transactions leading to a potential loss through misappropriation.* **This constitutes a significant risk (R104).**

Example documentation: for illustrative purposes only

Example 4 – Understanding the entity based on a checklist[5]

Client:	Bulls Restaurant and Hotel Limited
Year end:	31 January 20X1
Objective:	To obtain an understanding of the entity and its environment sufficient to identify and assess the risks of material misstatement of the financial statements
Method:	Review notes from prior year audit, make enquiries of management, review recent industry press and management accounts.
Information sources:	Share register, management accounts, debtor and creditor listings, company website (accessed 16 June 20W8)

Factors to consider	Notes	Ref
Industry, regulatory and other external factors		
Industry conditions		
• Market and competition • Cyclical/seasonal activity • Product technology • Energy supply and cost	The company owns and operates a restaurant and hotel. Regeneration in Manchester brought in a large number of competitors and it is still a competitive market. Occupancy rates of 80% and average room rates have been maintained, but margins are tight. Customers are demanding a higher quality dining experience. Bulls is set up to provide this but it needs to be worked at in order to maintain this profile. The business is subject to seasonal variation. This is most pronounced during December when Christmas events increase turnover by over 100% and casual staff are employed for a large part of the month.	

---

[5] Documentation requirement at ISA (UK and Ireland) 315, paragraph 32(b).

Example documentation: for illustrative purposes only

Factors to consider	Notes	Ref
Regulatory environment		
• Accounting principles and industry specific practices • Legislation and regulation • Taxation • Government policies • Environmental requirements	Environmental health inspections continue to be thorough and highlight areas for improvement. National minimum wage, fire safety and health and safety legislation are relevant. Tax treatment of gratuity payments was under dispute but is now agreed by HMRC. Premises licence held.	R101
Other factors affecting the business		
• General level of economic activity • Interest rates • Inflation	The company has maintained performance during the current year and management accounts and forecasts indicate a small profit for the year is likely.	
Nature of the entity		
Business operations		
• Nature of revenue sources • Products, services and markets • Conduct of operations • Alliances, joint ventures and outsourcing activities • Involvement in e-commerce • Geographic dispersion • Industry segmentation • Key customers • Important suppliers • Employment • Research and development activities • Related parties	Revenue is generated from two sources — the wine bar, restaurant and function room (70%) and rooms in the hotel (30%). A high proportion of these are cash transactions. A local brewer supplies all alcohol and soft drinks and this is a long established relationship. The hotel business is reliant on travel agent and internet related bookings. This is a family company so related party transactions are likely to occur but may not be classified as such. One family shareholder runs Melville Foods which supplies meat to Bulls, representing approximately 20% of the food costs of the company.	R102

Example documentation: for illustrative purposes only

Factors to consider	Notes	Ref
Investments		
• Acquisitions/mergers/ disposals • Securities and loans • Capital investment activities • Investments in non-consolidated entities	The freehold property is continually refurbished to maintain value.	
Financing		
• Group structure • Debt structure • Leasing • Beneficial owners • Related parties • Use of derivative financial instruments	80% of the issued share capital is held by the directors (F Bull and J Giles) who are brother and sister. Three non-director shareholders each own 5-10% share capital and are effective in preventing management abusing their position. The company was originally set up with share finance and bank loans (now repaid) and now has an overdraft facility of £50K. The facility is fully utilised a couple of times a year but typically runs at £25K.	
Financial Reporting		
• Accounting principles and industry specific practices • Revenue recognition practices • Fair value accounting • Inventories • Foreign currency • Industry specific categories • Unusual or complex transactions • Financial statement presentation and disclosure	The company follows the FRSSE. The directors revalued the property for the first time last year and now this value must be kept up to date.	R103

Example documentation: for illustrative purposes only

Factors to consider	Notes	Ref
Objective and strategies and related business risks		
How does the client address industry, regulatory and other external factors: • Industry developments • New products and services • Expansion of the business • New accounting requirements • Regulatory requirements • Current and prospective financing requirements • Use of IT What effect will implementing this strategy have on the entity?	The operations have remained unchanged for a number of years, including the IT (EPOS and accounting) infrastructure. The management wish to raise the standard of the restaurant and gain higher quality ratings in hotel and restaurant listings. The board are researching the possibility of a second rural location.	
Measurement and review of the entity's financial performance		
• Key ratios and operating statistics • Key performance indicators • Employee performance measures and incentives • Trends • Use of forecasts, budgets and variance analysis • Analyst and credit rating reports • Competitor analysis • Period on period financial performance	Management review monthly accounts prepared by a part-time bookkeeper which include comparison with budgets. KPIs include occupancy, average room rate, turnover and gross profit margin. These have been steady for a number of years.	

Example documentation: for illustrative purposes only

Risks of material misstatement arising from Understanding the Entity

No pervasive risks of material misstatement have been identified. The assessment of risk at the financial statement level is "low".

R101 – Possible unrecorded liabilities resulting from fines and other liabilities arising from reviews by EHOs and HMRC – in the past few years there has been a potential liability relating to the tax treatment of gratuity payments.

R102 – Family company means related party transactions likely to occur, but may not be classified as such.

R103 – The high value of property and the need for an annual review for any material change in value represents a significant accounting estimate. This constitutes a significant risk.

R104 – There is a high level of cash transactions leading to a potential loss through misappropriation. This constitutes a significant risk.

Example documentation: for illustrative purposes only

Example 5 – Excerpt from Audit Team Planning Meeting using pre-set agenda[6]

Client:	Bulls Restaurant and Hotel Limited
Year end:	31 January 20X1
Date of meeting:	10th May 20X1

Persons in attendance

Name: Paul Cox   Position: PARTNER

Name: Sarah Cole   Position: MANAGER

Name: Richard Cannon   Position: SENIOR

Name: Position:

A. Susceptibility of the financial statements to material misstatements due to fraud

There are two types of fraud relevant to the auditor's considerations; fraudulent reporting and misappropriation of assets. For both types, the risk factors are further classified based on three conditions:

- Incentive or pressure for management or others to commit a fraud;

- Perceived or actual opportunity to commit a fraud, e.g. through management over-ride of controls; and

- Attitude, characters, culture, environment or set of ethical values that are consistent with a rationalisation by management or others to committing a fraud.

The auditor should maintain an attitude of professional scepticism throughout the audit, recognising the possibility that a material misstatement due to fraud could exist, notwithstanding the auditor's past experience with the entity and the auditor's belief about the honesty and integrity of management and those charged with governance.

1. Notes of team discussion on consideration of any known external and internal factors that may result in fraud:

(a) Due to the nature of the business there is a risk of cash and liquor stock theft (R104, R105).

---

[6] Documentation requirements at ISA (UK and Ireland) 315, paragraph 32(a), ISA (UK and Ireland) 240, paragraph 44(a).

Example documentation: for illustrative purposes only

(b) Generally, culture/environment is good with internal controls in place, but audit staff need to remain alert to management override of controls.

(c) Segregation of duties in place over sales with responsibilities split between restaurant manager, receptionist and bookkeeper.

(d) While management are in a dominant position, two directors' signatures are required on all cheques and non-director shareholders are actively involved in the business.

(e) Purchases from and sales to related parties (directors and Melville Foods) could be made not at arms length (R102).

(f) Fred Bull has complained about the amount of corporation tax and VAT the company is paying and has asked whether there are ways it could be reduced. He indicated, however, that he would not want the company to mislead HMRC deliberately and risk penalties (R106).

2. Team response to the assessed risks of material misstatement due to fraud including any additional work required

(a) Addressed in audit work on sales completeness.

(b) Confirm control consciousness of management by observation during the audit and be alert for management override of controls when testing journal entries and accounting estimates. Identify any transactions outside the normal course of business.

(c) Ensure that split of responsibilities is maintained by observation and walkthrough tests.

(d) Review Board meeting minutes to confirm attendance of non-director shareholders.

(e) Review invoicing for functions held for directors (unlikely to be material) and review invoices from Melville Foods.

(f) Remain alert for mis-accounting, particularly in relation to matters affecting tax, e.g. expenditure v capital.

B. Susceptibility of the financial statements to material misstatements due to error

The term 'error' refers to an unintentional misstatement in the financial statements, including the omission of an amount or a disclosure, such as:

• A mistake in gathering or processing data from which financial statements are prepared;

• An incorrect accounting estimate arising from oversight or misinterpretation of facts; or

• A mistake in the application of accounting principles relating to measurement, recognition, classification, presentation or disclosure.

Example documentation: for illustrative purposes only

1. Notes of team discussion on consideration of any known external and internal factors that may result in error

(a) Large number of small transactions so generally if errors arise should be small.

(b) Some manual processes, e.g. transfer of till rolls to spreadsheet, which could result in error. If material should be identified by sales review (R201).

(c) Lack of preparation of debtors listing could lead to errors arising due to bad debts not being identified (R202).

2. Team response to the assessed risks of material misstatement due to error together with additional testing required

(a) Generally susceptibility to error is low, subject to items b) and c) identified above.

(b) Unlikely to result in material misstatement: ensure that bank reconciliation control is operating effectively.

(c) Request directors to compile a year-end debtors listing and match invoices to cash received after year end.

C. Communication with other team members

The engagement partner shall determine which matters are to be communicated to engagement team members not involved in the discussion.

As all team members were present at the meeting, no further communication required.

OVERALL CONCLUSION
(subject to points carried forward in the final notes)

Specific risks of material misstatement and responses are noted above and have been recorded in risk assessment work papers. There is a limited risk of material misstatement at the financial statement level as there are few external users of the financial statements, the business is well-controlled and related parties are limited to family members.

Signed: P Cox

Date: 14th May 20X1

Example documentation: for illustrative purposes only

Example 6 – Free-form notes of controls documentation[7]

Client: Bulls Restaurant and Hotel Limited
Year end: 31 January 20X1

Control environment

Directors' meetings are held on a bi-monthly basis, where management accounts are reviewed and business operational matters are discussed. Non-director shareholders (including a professional accountant and surveyor) are personal friends or family of the two main directors and are invited to these meetings. A high level of reliance is placed on the part-time bookkeeper and the restaurant manager, who have been with the company for a number of years, and no significant problems with their work have been encountered in previous audits. The bookkeeper is a member of the Institute of Certified Bookkeepers.

Management's attitude to internal control is a very positive one. The two directors make a point of reviewing the records of the previous day's sales with key staff and holding regular staff meetings to emphasise the importance of maintaining both quality and control.

Risk assessment process

No formal process in place. Directors have an understanding of the key risks to the business:

Reputational risks:
- o Possible failure of health and safety systems, resulting in poor reputation and possible fines or requirements for capital investment (R101).
- o Loss of customers resulting from poor reviews or experience of "loutish behaviour" (R301).

Financial risks:
- o Losses due to stock shrinkage (R105).
- o High level of cash transactions leading to potential loss through misappropriation (R104).
- o Poor cash flow management (R302).
- o Credit facilities given to corporate clients who are not credit-worthy (R303).

---

[7] Documentation requirement at ISA (UK and Ireland) 315 paragraph 32(b).

Example documentation: for illustrative purposes only

Information system

Food and beverage transactions are recorded on EPOS terminals in situ. Room revenue is generated from a separate hotel computer system. All revenues are totalled daily and input manually to the ACT accounting system. All systems have been in place for a number of years. ACT has been experienced at a number of other small clients in the firm.

Monitoring controls

Formal monitoring controls consist of:
- The directors review the monthly stock-take information and follow up any shrinkage with bar staff.
- The monthly bank reconciliation is reviewed by one of the directors.

Originally prepared by Sarah Cole   Date June 20W8

Continuing relevance of the information above confirmed by discussion with Fred Bull and Stacey Burrows, the bookkeeper. These monitoring controls have been found by previous audits to have operated effectively in prior years. They will be tested again this year.

Internal control notes updated
for 20X1 audit by Sarah Cole   Date January 20X1

Impact on the audit – risks of material misstatement relevant to audit for the year ended 31 January 20X1

A high volume of cash transactions (combined with manual transfers of information from till rolls to a spreadsheet summary and then to the accounting system) increases the risks of inaccuracies in the sales cycles for all sources of revenue.

Example documentation: for illustrative purposes only

Information system and control activities – extract from notes relevant to sales cycle

This is an extract of information from the permanent audit file, which is relevant only to liquor sales in the wine bar, restaurant and function room.

Liquor sales

Sources of income

Wine bar (40%), restaurant (35%), function room (25%)

Methods of recording orders

Alcoholic and soft drinks are all served from the bar areas in the wine bar, restaurant and function room. In the wine bar and function room these are dealt either:

- On a cash basis, where details of the drinks served are input to the EPOS system terminal and payment is made by the customer at the time of serving.

- On credit, where a tab is opened on the EPOS terminal and either a credit card is retained behind the bar for use in settling the account when the guests are leaving or an invoice is made up on the following day from the details recorded.

In the restaurant, the orders are input to a waiter's terminal by waiting staff and paid for by the guest at the end of the meal. Drinks are served from the bar area in accordance with what has been input to the system.

Method of ensuring all sales are recorded

At the end of each day (or shift), all EPOS terminal till rolls are printed. A Z-reading is taken and the hash total at the bottom of the till roll is reconciled to the previous Z-reading. Beverage sales totals are input from the till rolls to a summary spreadsheet maintained by the restaurant manager, together with an analysis of credit card and cash takings and amounts to be invoiced.

Invoices are made up for credit sales in the function room by the restaurant manager or one of the directors using the information recorded by the EPOS terminal. These are handwritten and are taken from a pad with pre-printed serial numbers.

Accounting records and method of use

Information on sales totals is taken from the spreadsheet maintained by the restaurant manager and input directly to the ACT accounting system on a weekly basis by the bookkeeper.

Example documentation: for illustrative purposes only

At the end of each month an independent stocktake is carried out on all bar stocks (excluding hotel mini-bar stock). Closing stock values are input to the general ledger and gross profit margins monitored by the directors. Any variations in stock shrinkage from the norm are followed up with bar staff.

The bookkeeper reconciles the cash and credit card receipts with cash banked and receipts recorded on the bank statements. She also maintains a file of all unpaid invoices from the function room and where cash is received in the post, this is matched to these invoices. The file is reviewed on an ad hoc basis by one of the directors and clients are chased for payment where appropriate.

Impact on the audit – risks of material misstatement

R104   There is a fraud risk arising from the possible misappropriation of cash when cash sales are not input to an EPOS terminal. **This is a significant risk.** In relation to this, the independent monthly stocktake provides a mitigating control by highlighting stock shrinkages that are outside the norm (follow up of shrinkages has led to staff being dismissed in the past). **This control will be tested.**

R201   A high volume of cash transactions (combined with manual transfers of information from till rolls to a spreadsheet summary and then to the accounting system) increases the risks of inaccuracies in the sales cycle.

R202   No debtors listing is maintained and follow up of unpaid invoices is done on an ad hoc basis. This leads to a risk that bad debts are not provided for – past experience suggests a reluctance to accept that particular debts are "bad". Christmas and New Year functions are material and some debtors relating to this period are still outstanding two months after the year end.

R203   Deposit invoices raised in advance of a function may be treated as sales at the time of invoicing rather than the date of the function, creating a possible cut-off error.

Originally prepared by   Sarah Cole   Date   June 20W8

Continuing relevance of the information above confirmed by discussion with Fred Bull and Stacey Burrows, the bookkeeper.

Updated for 20X1 audit by   Sarah Cole   Date   January 20X1

Example documentation: for illustrative purposes only

Example 7 – Controls documentation based on a checklist and systems diagrams[8]

Client: Bulls Restaurant and Hotel Limited

Year end: 31 January 20X1

Objective: To obtain an understanding of internal control sufficient to identify and assess the risks of material misstatement of the financial statements

Method: Review notes from prior year audit, make enquiries of management and perform walk through tests on transaction cycles.

Factors to consider	Notes	Ref
Control environment		
• Communication and enforcement of integrity and ethical values • Commitment to competence • Participation by those charged with governance • Management's philosophy and operating style • Organisational structure • Assignment of authority and responsibility • Human resource policies and practices	Management's attitude to internal controls is a very positive one. Directors make a point of reviewing the records of the previous day's sales with key staff and holding regular staff meetings to emphasise the importance of maintaining both quality and control. Directors' meetings are held every two months where management accounts are reviewed and business operational matters are discussed. Non-director shareholders (including a professional accountant and surveyor) are invited to these meetings. A high level of reliance is placed on the part time bookkeeper and the restaurant manager (both have been with the co. for a number of years and no significant problems encountered in previous audits). The bookkeeper is a member of the Institute of Certified Bookkeepers.	

---

[8] Documentation requirement at ISA (UK and Ireland) 315, paragraph 32(b).

Example documentation: for illustrative purposes only

Factors to consider	Notes	Ref
Entity's risk assessment process		
• Changes in operating environment • New personnel or information systems • Rapid growth • New technology, business models, products or activities • Corporate restructurings • Expanded foreign ops • New accounting pronouncements	No formal process is in place. Directors have an understanding of the key risks to the business: • reputational risk (due to the failure of H&S systems & loss of customers from poor reviews), and • financial risks (due to stock shrinkage, misappropriation of cash, poor cash flow management and bad debts).	
Information system		
• Infrastructure and software • Document individual transaction cycles • Individual roles and responsibilities • Financial and accounting manuals	Food and beverage transactions recorded on EPOS terminals in situ. Room revenue is generated from a separate hotel computer system. Sales totals are taken from each system daily and input manually to the ACT accounting system. ACT accounting system is used by bookkeeper to prepare trial balance information.	R201
Control activities		
• Performance reviews • Information processing • Physical controls • Segregation of duties	See systems documentation on transaction cycles in Profit and Loss section: • Sales, Purchases, Payroll Segregation of duties in place over sales with responsibilities split between restaurant manager, receptionist and bookkeeper.	P20-23

Example documentation: for illustrative purposes only

Factors to consider	Notes	Ref
Monitoring of controls		
• Ongoing activities • Separate evaluations • Internal audit • Use of external information	Directors review monthly stock takes and follow up any shrinkage with bar staff. The monthly bank reconciliation is reviewed by one of the directors. These monitoring controls have been found by previous audits to have operated effectively in prior years. They will be tested again this year.	

Risks of material misstatement arising from Components of internal control

R201 – A high volume of transactions (combined with manual transfers of information from till rolls to a spreadsheet summary and then to the accounting system) increases the risks of inaccuracies in the sales cycle.

Arising from systems documentation of beverage sales at P20:

R104 – There is a fraud risk arising from the possible misappropriation of cash when cash sales are not input to an EPOS terminal. *This is a significant risk.* In relation to this the independent monthly stocktake provides a mitigating control by highlighting stock shrinkages that are outside the norm (follow up of shrinkages has led to staff being dismissed in the past). *This control will be tested.*

Example documentation: for illustrative purposes only

Ref: P20

Beverage sales cycle – systems documentation

Transaction initiation and processing	Responsibility	Frequency	Controls in place over assertions	Risk
Details of F&B input to EPOS. Master price list held in system and applied to each item automatically.	Bar and restaurant staff	As F&B are ordered	C – No detailed control in place. Directors review daily sales totals and follow up where lower than expected. O, A, L – Customer would complain if not served with F&B ordered or charged more than expected.	
Payment made by customer and input to EPOS.	Bar and restaurant staff	When F&B ordered or customer leaves	C – Directors review gross margins and monthly stock take and follow up any shrinkages with bar staff. O, A – total for cash taken is reconciled to total charges at the end of each shift and followed up by restaurant manager	R104- Misappropriation of cash at point of sale
Sales totals taken from till rolls and invoices and input to spreadsheet / Function room invoices prepared for credit sales from customer and notes on pricing kept in function diary	Restaurant manager	At end of each shift	C, F – Manager logs till roll from each terminal and checks Z-totals. Directors review daily sales totals and follow up where lower than expected. Function room invoices pre-numbered. O, A – Bank reconciliation performed monthly, reviewed by director.	R201 – Manual posting errors
Spreadsheet information used to update ACT	Bookkeeper	Weekly	C, O, A – Bank reconciliation performed monthly, reviewed by director.	

Key to assertions: O = Occurrence, C = Completeness, A = Accuracy, F = Cutoff, L = Classification

Example documentation: for illustrative purposes only

Example 8 – Risk assessment based on risks[9]

Beverage sales and debtors cycle
SALES and TRADE DEBTORS – SUMMARY of RISKS of MATERIAL MISSTATEMENT and AUDIT RESPONSE

Risk of material misstatement identified	Significant risk?	Mitigating internal controls	Likelihood of risk resulting in material misstatement	Assertions impacted	Audit procedures	Audit program reference
					These procedures are specific to this example only. They are not exhaustive and will not necessarily be useful in relation to similar risks in other circumstances.	
R104 – Misappropriation of cash at point of sale	✓ (this is a fraud risk)	Independent monthly stocktake to identify abnormal stock shrinkages	High	**Sales:** Completeness **Debtors:** Completeness	Review records of monthly stocktakes. Ascertain follow-up taken where margins out of line with expectation.	
R201 – Manual posting errors from till rolls and invoices to ACT via spreadsheet		Monthly bank reconciliation will identify cash received but no sale posted	Med	**Sales:** Completeness, Accuracy, Classification **Debtors:** Valuation	Review monthly bank reconciliations and ensure outstanding items clear during following month. For sample of dates, check sales totals from till rolls and invoices to spreadsheets and accounting system.	

---

[9] Documentation requirements at ISA (UK and Ireland) 315. paragraph 32(c) and (d), ISA (UK and Ireland) 240. paragraph 44(b) and 45(a), ISA (UK and Ireland) 330. paragraph 28(a) and (b).

Example documentation: for illustrative purposes only

Risk of material misstatement identified	Significant risk?	Mitigating internal controls	Likelihood of risk resulting in material misstatement	Assertions impacted	Audit procedures	Audit program reference
					These procedures are specific to this example only. They are not exhaustive and will not necessarily be useful in relation to similar risks in other circumstances.	
R202 – Bad debts not provided for or written off			Med	**Debtors:** Valuation	From client debtor listing match invoices to cash received after year end or include in discussion of bad debts.	
R203 – Sales not recorded or recorded in wrong period			Med	**Sales:** Completeness, Cutoff **Debtors:** Completeness	Check sample of function diary entries back to invoices to confirm sales recorded. Check sample of invoices back to function diary to confirm sales recorded in the correct period.	

Example documentation: for illustrative purposes only

Example 9 – Risk assessment based on assertions[10]

Beverage sales and debtors cycle

SALES and TRADE DEBTORS – RISK ASSESSMENT and AUDIT APPROACH SUMMARY

As a result of the issues considered during the planning, note here the risks of material misstatement associated with the audit of this section:

R104　(4) Due to the nature of the business there is a fraud risk of cash pilferage. Cash sales might not be input to EPOS at the point of sale and cash relating to these unrecorded sales stolen by bar and restaurant staff. This is a significant risk.

R201　(M) Manual transfer of amounts from invoices, till rolls and spreadsheets could create errors.

R202　(M) No debtors listing is maintained by the client with follow up of unpaid invoices not done systematically and bad debts not provided for.

R203　(M) Sales recorded in wrong period

Assertion	Risks of material misstatement	Control in operation	Tests of control (programme reference)	Substantive procedures (programme reference)
			These procedures are specific to this example only. They are not exhaustive and will not necessarily be useful in relation to similar risks in other circumstances.	
Sales				
Occurrence	None			
Completeness	R104 –ie. liquor sales	Monthly independent stocktake and review by directors will pick up significant amounts of pilferage.	Review records of monthly stocktakes. Ascertain follow up taken where margins out of line with expectation (TC 3).	Check sample of function diary entries back to invoices to confirm sales recorded.

---

[10] Documentation requirements at ISA (UK and Ireland) 315, paragraph 32(c) and (d), ISA (UK and Ireland) 240, paragraph 44(b) and 45(a), ISA (UK and Ireland) 330, paragraph 28(a) and (b).

Example documentation: for illustrative purposes only

Assertion	Risks of material misstatement	Control in operation	Tests of control	Substantive procedures
				These procedures are specific to this example only. They are not exhaustive and will not necessarily be useful in relation to similar risks in other circumstances.
	R201	Monthly bank reconciliation will identify cash received but no sale posted	Review monthly bank reconciliations and ensure outstanding items clear during following month (TC 6).	For sample of dates, check sales totals from till rolls and invoices to spreadsheets and accounting system (ST 4)
Accuracy	R201	See above – monthly bank reconciliation	See above – review monthly bank reconciliations	See above – test postings for a sample of dates
Cut off	R203	Pre-numbered function room invoices		Check sample of invoices back to function diary to confirm sales recorded in the correct period (ST 7)
Classification	R201	See above – monthly bank reconciliation	See above – review monthly bank reconciliations	See above – test postings for a sample of dates
Debtors				
Existence	None			
Rights and obligations	None			
Completeness	R204, R201, R203	See above – independent stocktake and gross profit review, monthly bank reconciliation and pre-numbered invoices	See above – review records of monthly stocktakes and review monthly bank reconciliations	See above – test postings for a sample of dates and check sample of invoices back to function diary
Valuation and allocation	R201	See above – monthly bank reconciliation	See above – review monthly bank reconciliations	See above – test postings for a sample of dates
	R202	None		From client debtor listing match invoices to cash received after year end or include in discussion of bad debts (DT 5)

Example documentation: for illustrative purposes only

Example 10 – Audit working paper: property valuation[11]

Client: **Bulls Restaurant and Hotel Limited**
Year end: **31 January 20X1**

Prepared by: Sarah Cole Date: 18 May 20X1

Reviewed by: Paul Cox   Date: 21 May 20X1

The freehold property was valued by XYZ surveyors last year at £2.5 million. Once revalued, the FRSSE requires a fixed asset to be carried at its market value at the balance sheet date. As property prices generally have reduced over the past year, the likely decline in the value of the property has been identified as a significant risk. Management confirm that they believe that there has been a material change in value this year, which should be recognised in the accounts.

Mark Quinn, a shareholder who is a qualified surveyor (confirmed with current list of RICS members) with a practice specialising in commercial property, has provided an estimate of the current value at £2 million. This was arrived at on the basis of his knowledge of a similar type of hotel property located outside the Manchester city centre being sold for £2.3 million in December 20X0. It was adjusted downwards due to that property being in better condition and slightly larger. The reduction in value of £500,000 has been properly accounted for and taken to the statement of recognised gains and losses in the accounts as it reverses a previous revaluation upwards.

While FRS15 requires an internal revaluation to be reviewed by an external qualified valuer, the FRSSE requires a revaluation to be undertaken by an <u>experienced</u> valuer and does not specify an external valuation. Bulls have therefore not engaged an external expert to advise on market value.

Work undertaken during the audit:

1. The basis for this estimate is set out in working paper E12. We have checked the sale price of the Manchester property, reviewed the sales particulars and discussed the assumptions underlying this estimate with Mark and they seem reasonable. Alternative assumptions were also discussed.

2. A range of possible values for the property was constructed from the following sources of information:

---

[11] Documentation requirement at ISA (UK and Ireland) 540, paragraph 23.

Example documentation: for illustrative purposes only

Source of information		Possible valuation
UK Quarterly Property Index	UK commercial property fell by 24% in 20X0	£1.9 million
XYZ Surveyors report on local property mkt.	12% fall in value for commercial property in Manchester over past year	£2.2 million
Christie & Co survey of hotel and pub property market	17.5% fall in values of hotels, restaurants and pubs in North of England to September 20X0	£2.06 million

3. Disclosures made in the accounts in connection with the fixed asset valuation and the movement on the revaluation reserve were reviewed. These make it clear that there is estimation uncertainty and that the current value is based on an internal estimate.

4. The valuation of the property will be included as a specific item in the written representation.

Conclusion:

1. The market value falls within a reasonable range.

2. Even though the valuation has been performed by a shareholder director, there is no evidence to suggest that the valuation is biased.

3. There is adequate disclosure of the estimation uncertainty in the financial statements.

Example documentation: for illustrative purposes only

Example 11 – Audit working paper: going concern[12]

Client: **Bulls Restaurant and Hotel Limited**
Year end: **31 January 20X1**

Prepared by: *Richard Cannon*   Date: *18 May 20X1*

Reviewed by: *Sarah Cole*   Date: *19 May 20X1*

Trading during the current economic conditions has been 10% down on previous years, although Bulls have been able to reduce costs. Management have prepared a cash flow forecast for the 12 months from the year end date (1 February 20X1 to 31 January 20X2) – file ref. L12. This exercise involved the shareholder, Lisa Swann (who is an accountant), in addition to Fred and Jo. It formed the basis of a discussion with the company's bankers at a meeting in February X1 where the overdraft facility was agreed for a further year to 28 February 20X2.

Work undertaken during the audit:

1. Discussed with management their plans for the company for the 18 months to 31 July 20X2 (more than 12 months after the expected date of approval of the accounts). They expect that there will be no further deterioration in trading levels, meaning that the maximum overdraft during the period will be £30,000, which is £20,000 short of the current overdraft facility. Budgets prepared by management in the past have proved to be reasonably accurate.

2. Reviewed figures included in the cash flow forecast for 12 months to 31 January 20X2. These have been prepared on the basis of:

   - Trading at January 20X1 levels continuing until late in 20X1, when a slow recovery is assumed.

   - Gross profit margins being maintained at recently experienced levels.

   - Previously planned expansion being delayed until late in 20X2 at the earliest.

3. Compared cash flow forecasts for the first three months of the year to actual results. No significant differences noted in turnover and gross profit margins.

4. Obtained a copy of the letter to the company agreeing the overdraft facilities to 28 February 20X2 (ref. F40). The directors have stated that they have no reason to believe that the overdraft facility (which is not dependent on the property valuation) will not be successfully renegotiated in February 20X2.

---

[12] Documentation requirement at ISA (UK and Ireland) 230 paragraph 8(c) – significant matters arising during the audit.

**FINANCIAL
REPORTING COUNCIL**

Example documentation: for illustrative purposes only

Conclusion: Although the current economic outlook is uncertain there are no indications that Bulls will not continue in operational existence for at least one year from the date of approval of the accounts. Disclosures made in the financial statements in connection with this matter are clear and understandable.

Example documentation: for illustrative purposes only

Example 12 – Evaluation of misstatements identified during the audit[13]

Client: **Bulls Restaurant and Hotel Limited**
Year end: **31 January 20X1**

All errors identified during audit testing are documented within the relevant audit papers. Misstatements below £100 are considered to be clearly trivial and have not been recorded below.

Schedule of audit adjustments

Adjusted
Errors which have been adjusted in the financial statements have a combined net effect of increasing profit by £995:

	Balance Sheet		Profit & loss		Cross
	Dr £	Cr £	Dr £	Cr £	reference
1 Profit and loss – administrative expenses			350		D24
Creditors – accruals		350			
Being under-accrual for electricity					
2 Creditors – taxation	2,345				L65
Profit and loss – taxation				2,345	
Being adjustment to tax computation					
3 Profit and loss – administrative expenses			1,000		D41
Creditors – accruals		1,000			
Being under-accrual for liquor licence fine					
Impact on profit – increase			**995**		

---

[13] Documentation requirement at ISA (UK and Ireland) 450, paragraph 15.

Example documentation: for illustrative purposes only

Unadjusted
The following error was also identified during our audit work.

	Balance Sheet		Profit & loss		Cross
	Dr	Cr	Dr	Cr	reference
	£	£	£	£	
1 Profit and loss – administrative expenses			5,000		F33
Debtors – trade debtors		5,000			
Being unprovided amount on disputed debt					
Impact on profit for the year – decrease			**5,000**		

When the bad debt was discussed with Fred Bull, there was a difference of view about the recoverability of this debtor balance and he decided not to adjust for it within the financial statements. We consider this to be over-optimistic. However, the impact is not material to the financial statements and the unadjusted misstatement from last year in respect of holiday pay (£3,580) has reversed through the profit and loss account this year, so mitigating the current year impact.

A written confirmation that the directors do not wish to make an adjustment to the financial statements in this respect and their reasons for not doing so are included in the letter of written representation (ref P13).

Overall conclusion
Uncorrected misstatements are not material, either individually or in aggregate.

Example documentation: for illustrative purposes only

Example 13 – Extract from Group planning memorandum[14]

This is an example for a different company to that illustrated elsewhere in this Practice Note. Although the group is small, they have chosen to produce group accounts and to have these audited although not all the subsidiaries need to be audited.

Group audit approach

Group materiality is set at £22,500. Performance materiality for the group accounts is £20,000 and materiality for the subsidiary audits is £15,000. We will audit the parent company's holdings of investments in the subsidiaries to a materiality of £15,000. The approach for each of the subsidiary companies is set out on the following page.

---

[14] Documentation requirement at ISA (UK and Ireland) 600, paragraph 50(a) and (b).

Example documentation: for illustrative purposes only

Component	Revenue – £m	Profit – £'000	Significant — Individual financial significance	Significant risks	Type of work	Auditors	Extent of involvement
Sub 1	2.0	100	✓		Full audit to materiality of £15,000	Network firm	• Phone call at planning stage to component management to understand developments in the business. • Phone network firm at planning stage to discuss and agree risk assessment. • Request memorandum from other audit firm regarding audit findings in respect of significant risks.
Sub 2	2.5	300	✓		Full audit to materiality of £15,000	Other auditors	• Meet component management at planning stage. • Meet other audit firm at planning stage to consider risks and review firm's risk documentation. • Review working papers at year end.
Sub 3	0.5	(10)			Review of financial statements	Group	–
Sub 4	0.4	20		✓	Audit of investments	Group	–
Sub 5	0.1	10			Analytical procedures at group level	Group	–
	5.5	450					

PRACTICE NOTE 27 (I)

THE AUDIT OF CREDIT UNIONS IN THE REPUBLIC OF IRELAND

CONTENTS

Preface

This Practice Note provides guidance to auditors on the application of International Standards on Auditing (UK and Ireland) (ISAs (UK and Ireland)) issued by the Auditing Practices Board ('the APB') to the audit of the financial statements of credit unions in the Republic of Ireland. It also contains guidance on special factors to be considered in the application of ISA (UK and Ireland) 250 – Section A – "Consideration of Laws and Regulations in an audit of financial statements" and "Section B the Auditor's right and duty to report to Regulators in the financial sector" to audits of credit unions in the Republic of Ireland.

The Practice Note is supplementary to, and is intended to be read in conjunction with, ISAs (UK and Ireland), and the explanatory and other material contained in the ISAs (UK and Ireland) which apply to all audits undertaken in the Republic of Ireland. This Practice Note supersedes previous guidance[1] issued by Consultative Committee of Accountancy Bodies Ireland ('CCAB-I')[2] accountancy bodies.

This Practice Note sets out the special considerations relating to the audit of credit unions which arise from individual ISAs (UK and Ireland) listed in the contents. It is not the intention of the Practice Note to provide step-by-step guidance on the audit of credit unions, so where no special considerations arise from a particular ISA (UK and Ireland), no material is included.

The Practice Note has been prepared in consultation with the Irish Financial Services Regulatory Authority ('the Financial Regulator')[3] and is based on the legislation in effect at 30 September 2008.

Introduction

1. This Practice Note addresses the responsibilities and obligations of the auditor concerning:

    • the audit of financial statements in accordance with the requirements of the CU Act, 1997 as amended; and

---

[1] Miscellaneous Technical Statement M22 'Credit Unions – Republic of Ireland' is now withdrawn.

[2] CCAB-I comprises the Association of Chartered Certified Accountants, the Chartered Institute of Management Accountants, the Institute of Certified Public Accountants in Ireland and the Institute of Chartered Accountants in Ireland.

[3] The Central Bank of Ireland, which came into being in 1943, was re-structured and re-named as the Central Bank and Financial Services Authority of Ireland ('CBFSAI') on 1 May 2003. This body carries out all of the activities formerly carried out by the Central Bank of Ireland and additional regulatory and consumer protection functions for the financial services sector. The CBFSAI has two component entities:

  • the Central Bank, which has responsibility for monetary policy functions, financial stability, economic analysis, currency and payment systems, investment of foreign and domestic assets and the provision of central services; and

  • The Irish Financial Services Regulatory Authority (Financial Regulator), which is an autonomous entity within the CBFSAI and has responsibility for financial sector regulation and consumer protection.

- the statutory duty to report directly to the Financial Regulator in certain circumstances.

2. A "credit union" in the context of this Practice Note is an industrial and provident society registered by virtue of the Credit Union Act, 1997 as amended ("the CU Act 1997"). A society which, prior to 1st October 1997, was registered as a credit union under the Industrial and Provident Societies Acts, 1893 to 1978, is deemed to be registered as a credit union under the Act.

3. Independent audit plays an important part in safeguarding the integrity of financial reports by directors of companies and other entities to the investing and business communities, both national and international. Additionally, auditors appointed to report on the financial statements of credit unions in the Republic of Ireland contribute to the regulatory process.

4. Registered auditors are required to comply with ISAs (UK and Ireland) when conducting audits. This principle applies in the context of credit unions in the same way as to entities in any sector, but the way in which ISAs (UK and Ireland) are applied needs to be adapted to suit the particular characteristics of the entity audited.

Features of credit unions

5. The CU Act 1997 outlines the overall aims and operation of credit unions. This includes day to day operation and control and the fundamental aims and aspirations of credit unions.

6. Credit unions have as their basic aims[4]

- the promotion of thrift among their members through the accumulation of savings;

- the creation of sources of credit for the mutual benefits of its members at fair and reasonable rate of interest;

- the use and control of members' savings for their mutual benefit;

- the training and education of its members in the wise use of money;

- the education of its members in their economic, social and cultural well-being as members of the community;

- the improvement of the well-being and spirit of the member's community; and

- the provision to its members of such additional services as are for their mutual benefit.

---

[4] Section (6)(2) of the CU Act 1997.

7. Members must be from the same locality, or be employed in the same industry or with the same employer or have some other "common bond" approved by the Financial Regulator[5]. To become a member of a credit union each individual must hold at least one fully paid up share in the credit union[6] and must qualify under the common bond set out in the credit union's rules.

8. The "Common Bond" between members of the credit union must be one of the following. Members must:

    - follow a particular occupation; or

    - reside in a particular locality; or

    - be employed in a particular locality; or

    - be employed by a particular employer or have retired from employment with a particular employer; or

    - be a member of a bona fide organisation or society which has been formed for purposes of other than that of registration as a credit union; or

    - have any other common bond approved by the Financial Regulator.

9. Credit unions therefore are mutual savings and loan organisations which are non-profit making and which operate solely for the benefit of their members. Any surpluses which are not distributed to members by way of dividend, or otherwise, are retained within the organisation for its future expansion. The members save by investing in the credit union's shares or making deposits. Like any other similar financial organisation, the savings and deposits which the credit union take in, provide a base and fund from which loans are granted to members.

10. Credit unions are obliged to send to the Financial Regulator a credit union annual return ('CUAR') and quarterly Prudential returns. The CUAR is not audited or signed by the credit union auditor. Annual financial statements are also required.

11. Credit unions are also required to have their annual financial statements audited[7].

The Management and Operation of Credit Unions

The responsibility of directors

12. The primary responsibility for the conduct of the business of a credit union is vested in the board of directors, who have responsibility for the general control, direction,

---

[5] Section (6)(3) of the CU Act 1997.
[6] Section (17)(3) of the CU Act 1997.
[7] Section 111(4) of the CU Act 1997.

management of the affairs, funds and records of the credit union, and the management appointed by it. This responsibility includes:

- establishing adequate procedures and systems to ensure compliance with the law applicable to credit unions and guidance issued by the Financial Regulator;

- the preparation of financial statements that give a true and fair view of the credit union's affairs for the year and compliance with other aspects of credit union law; and

- providing information to the Financial Regulator.

The role of the supervisory committee

13. Section 58 of the CU Act 1997 requires the establishment of a supervisory committee which must consist of three or five elected members who are all volunteers. This committee which is one of the most important from the internal governance perspective performs some similar functions to internal audit. Credit unions often also establish a credit committee to assess whether loans should be granted.

14. The responsibility of the supervisory committee who have the general duty of overseeing the performance by the directors of their functions includes the following:

- hold meetings with the board of directors at least four times a year to review the directors' performance of their functions;

- examine, at least twice a year, the books and documents of the credit union which shall include the inspection of securities, cash accounts and all records relating to loans;

- compare at least once a year the statement of accounts, of at least 10% of the members of the credit union on a random basis to the appropriate records of the credit union;

- ascertain that all actions and decisions of the officers relating to the affairs of the credit unions are in accordance with law and the registered rules for credit unions; and

- furnish a written report to the annual general meeting ('AGM') or to special general meetings of the results of its examination and enquiries.

15. The supervisory committee shall have access at all times to the books and documents of the credit union.[8]

---

[8] Section 60(2) of the CU Act 1997.

The role of the treasurer

16. The treasurer must be a director and may be voluntary or remunerated[9]. The primary responsibility of the treasurer is the monthly submission of an income and expenditure account and balance sheet to the board of directors[10]. The treasurer is also responsible, subject to the limitations and controls imposed by the board of directors, for the following[11]:

    • ensuring that proper systems of internal control are kept by the credit union;

    • maintaining custody of all funds, securities and documentation relating to the assets of the credit union;

    • providing, or causing to be provided, and maintaining full and complete records of all assets, liabilities, income and expenditure of the credit union;

    • submitting to the auditor such financial reports and returns as are required by the auditor;

    • ensuring all cash is deposited in accordance with the instructions of the board of directors;

    • reporting to the members of the credit union at the AGM; and

    • complying with any instruction of the board of directors.

Financial Statements

17. Section 111 of the CU Act 1997, requires the annual accounts of a credit union to give a true and fair view of its income and expenditure for the year, and of its state of affairs at the end of the year, and, in addition, to comply with section 110 of the CU Act 1997 in relation to the amounts included therein. The requirement for the accounts of Irish credit unions to give a true and fair view is usually regarded as also requiring compliance with the requirements of the relevant accounting standards of the Accounting Standards Board.

18. Section 110(1) of the CU Act 1997 requires that 'the amounts to be included in the accounts of a credit union in respect of items shown shall be determined in accordance with the following principles—

    (a) the credit union shall be presumed to be carrying on business as a going concern;

---

9   Section 68 of the CU Act 1997.
10 Section 64(1) of the CU Act 1997 "The treasurer of the credit unions shall act as the managing director of the credit union".
11 Section (6)(2) of the CU Act 1997.

(*b*) accounting policies shall be applied consistently from one financial year to the next;

(*c*) the amount of any item in the accounts shall be determined on a prudent basis and in particular—

(i) only surpluses realised at the balance sheet date shall be included in the income and expenditure account, and

(ii) all liabilities and losses which have arisen or are likely to arise in respect of the financial year to which the accounts relate, or the previous financial year, shall be taken into account, including those liabilities and losses which only become apparent between the balance sheet date and the date on which the accounts are signed in pursuance of *section 111*;

(*d*) all income and charges relating to the financial year to which the accounts relate shall be taken into account without regard to the date of receipt of payment; and

(*e*) in determining the aggregate amount of any item the amount of each individual asset or liability that falls to be taken into account shall be determined separately.'

19. Section 110(2) of the CU Act 1997 states 'If it appears to the directors of a credit union that there are special reasons for departing from any of the principles specified in *subsection (1)*, they may so depart, but particulars of the departure, the reasons for it and its effect on the balance sheet and income and expenditure account shall be stated in a note to the accounts, for the financial year concerned, of the credit union.'

20. The Financial Regulator is to issue a Guidance Note on "Matters Relating to Accounting for Investments and Distribution Policy" to directors of credit unions. A copy of the draft Guidance Note on Matters Relating to Accounting for Investments and Distribution Policy is available from the Financial Regulator's website. The Registrar is of the view that for the majority of credit unions, having regard to the nature of their operations and requirements of the CU Act 1997, the lower of cost and net realisable value will be the most appropriate method for the valuation of investments.

21. In relation to estimation techniques, FRS 18 requires the selection of estimation techniques that enable the accounts to give a true and fair view, and that are judged to be the most appropriate in the particular circumstances for the purpose of a true and fair view (FRS 18, paragraph 51). An example of an estimation technique given in FRS 18 is the method of estimating the proportion of debts that will not be recovered (FRS 18, paragraph 4).

22. FRS 18 also requires disclosure of:

• each material accounting policy;

• a description of its significant estimation techniques; and

- the effects of changes in accounting policies or material effects of changes in estimation techniques (FRS 18, paragraph 55).

Legislative and regulatory framework

23. The primary legislation is contained in the CU Act 1997 and in the Central Bank Act 1997 ('the CBA 1997') as amended by the Central Bank and Financial Services Authority of Ireland ('CBFSAI') Act, 2004. In addition many credit unions are subject to the Investment Intermediaries Act 1995 for some sections of their business. See appendix 2 for an indicative list of legislation applicable.

24. Credit unions are also subject to a number of guidance notes issued by the Financial Regulator. See appendix 2 for a list of those currently in issue.

25. The Financial Regulator, established on 1 May 2003 pursuant to the Central Bank and Financial Services Authority of Ireland ('CBFSAI') Act, 2003, is responsible for regulation of all financial services firms, including credit unions, in the Republic of Ireland. It also has an important role in the protection of the consumers of those firms. As the Financial Regulator its main tasks are to:

- help consumers to make informed decisions on their financial affairs in a safe and fair market; and

- foster sound, growing and solvent financial institutions which give consumers confidence that their deposits and investments are secure.

26. The Financial Regulator is a distinct component of the CBFSAI, with clearly defined regulatory responsibilities. These cover all Irish financial institutions including those previously regulated by the Central Bank, Department of Enterprise, Trade and Employment, Office of the Director of Consumer Affairs and Registrar of Friendly Societies. The Financial Regulator contributes to the work of the CBFSAI in discharging its responsibility in relation to overall financial stability. All credit unions must be registered with the Financial Regulator which is the statutory body established to administer the system of regulation and supervision of credit unions under the CU Act 1997.

27. Many credit unions are members of the Irish League of Credit Unions ('the League') which has its own rules with which League members are expected to comply. In addition the League publishes "Standard Rules for Credit Unions" for the guidance of and use by affiliated credit unions.

The role of external auditors

28. The primary objective of an audit of the financial statements of a credit union by external auditors is to enable them to express an independent opinion on the annual financial statements to the members of the credit union in accordance with the requirements of the CU Act 1997.

29. The auditors' opinion helps to establish the credibility of the financial statements. However, it should not be interpreted as an assurance as to the future viability of the credit union or an opinion as to the efficiency or effectiveness with which the management has conducted the affairs of the credit union, since these are not the objectives of the audit.

30. The scope of the statutory audit of a credit union's financial statements is no different from that of the generality of companies in the Republic of Ireland. However, the Oireachtas has, in addition, placed responsibility on auditors to provide reports to the Financial Regulator if they encounter circumstances that, in their opinion, meet certain criteria set out in statute[12]. The section of this Practice Note relating to ISA (UK and Ireland) 250, Section B, "The Auditor's Right and Duty to Report to Regulators in the Financial Sector" ('ISA (UK and Ireland) 250, Section B') provides guidance in relation to such reports to the Financial Regulator.

31. Section 25 of the CBA 1997 empowers the Financial Regulator to oblige a credit union to provide a compliance statement to the Financial Regulator on request. If the Financial Regulator requests a compliance statement from a credit union it may also, under Section 26 of the CBA 1997 request that the credit union's auditor prepare a report about the relevant compliance statement. The Financial Regulator has not yet commenced the compliance statement regime. It is envisaged that this provision will be considered as part of an anticipated project for the consolidation and modernisation of financial services legislation.

The relationship between the objectives of the Financial Regulator and the objectives of the auditors

32. In many respects the Financial Regulator, as the supervisor of credit unions, and credit union auditors have complementary concerns although the focus of their concerns may be different. These are outlined in the bullet points below:

- the purpose of the Financial Regulator is to regulate and supervise credit unions with a view to protection by each credit union of the funds of its members and the maintenance of the financial stability and well being of credit unions generally. The auditor is primarily concerned with reporting to the members on the credit union's financial statements;

- the Financial Regulator monitors the present and future viability of credit unions and may use their financial statements in assessing their condition and performance. The auditors' primary responsibility is to report to members their opinion as to whether the financial statements present a true and fair view, in the course of which they consider the appropriateness of the use of the going concern concept as a basis for the preparation of the financial statements;

---

[12] The CU Act 1997 and the CBA 1997 as amended by the Central Bank and Financial Services Authority of Ireland Act, 2004.

- the Financial Regulator is concerned that credit unions establish and maintain a sound system of control of the accounting and other records of its business such as to secure the credit unions' business. The auditors are concerned with the assessment of internal control to determine the degree of reliance to be placed on the system in planning and performing the work necessary to express an opinion on a credit union's financial statements; and

- the Financial Regulator must be satisfied that each credit union maintains adequate records to enable the preparation of financial statements that are in accordance with consistent accounting policies and practices. This enables the Financial Regulator assess the financial condition of the credit union. The auditors report whether proper books of account have been kept and whether the credit union annual financial statements are in agreement with these books of account. The auditors are concerned with whether adequate and sufficiently reliable records are maintained in order to enable the entity to prepare financial statements that do not contain material misstatements (section 108 of the CU Act 1997).

The Audit of Financial Statements

ISAs (UK and Ireland) apply to the conduct of all audits. This includes audits of financial statements of credit unions. The purpose of the following paragraphs is to identify the special considerations arising from the application of certain "bold letter" requirements (which are indicated by grey shaded boxes below) to the audit of credit unions and to suggest ways in which these can be addressed. This Practice Note does not contain commentary on all the bold letter requirements included in the ISAs (UK and Ireland) and reading it should not be seen as an alternative to reading the relevant ISAs (UK and Ireland) in their entirety. In addition, where no special considerations arise from a particular ISA (UK and Ireland) no material is included.

ISA (UK and Ireland) 200: Objective and General Principles Governing an Audit of Financial Statements

Background Note

The purpose of this International Standard on Auditing (UK and Ireland) (ISA (UK and Ireland)) is to establish standards and provide guidance on the objective and general principles governing an audit of financial statements.

The objective of an audit of financial statements is to enable the auditor to express an opinion whether the financial statements are prepared, in all material respects, in accordance with an applicable financial reporting framework (paragraph 2)

In the UK and Ireland the relevant ethical pronouncements with which the auditor should comply are the APB's Ethical Standards and the ethical pronouncements relating to the work of auditors issued by the auditor's relevant professional body. (paragraph 4-1).

The auditor should plan and perform an audit with an attitude of professional scepticism recognizing that circumstances may exist that cause the financial statements to be materially misstated (paragraph 6)

The term "scope of an audit" refers to the audit procedures deemed necessary in the circumstances to achieve the objective of the audit. The audit procedures required to conduct an audit in accordance with ISAs(UK and Ireland) should be determined by the auditor having regard to the requirements of ISAs (UK and Ireland), relevant professional bodies, legislation, regulations and, where appropriate, the terms of the audit engagement and reporting requirements. (paragraph 7)

33. Auditing standards include a requirement for auditors to comply with relevant ethical requirements relating to audit engagements. In the Republic of Ireland, the auditor should comply with the Auditing Practices Board's ('APB') Ethical Standards and relevant ethical guidance relating to the work of auditors issued by the auditor's

professional body. A fundamental principle is that practitioners should not accept or perform work which they are not competent to undertake. The importance of technical competence is also underlined in the Auditors' Code[13], issued by the APB, which states that the necessary degree of professional skill demands an understanding of financial reporting and business. Practitioners should not undertake the audit of Credit Unions unless they are satisfied that they have, or can obtain, the necessary level of competence.

34. In connection with possible independence issues auditors review any financial relationships that the firm or its partners and staff (and, separately, partners and staff assigned to that engagement) may have with that credit union to consider whether such relationships may affect independence.

35. The Financial Regulator has recommended that for credit unions there should be rotation of audit partner every 5 years. This was set out in the Financial Regulator's Guidance Note for the Auditors of Credit Unions which took the form of correspondence with Credit Union auditors in July 2004. The full text of that guidance note is set out in appendix 2 to this Practice Note.

---

[13] This is appended to the APB's Scope and Authority of Pronouncements.

ISA (UK and Ireland) 210: Terms of Audit Engagements

> **Background note**
>
> The purpose of this ISA (UK and Ireland) is to establish standards and provide guidance on:
>
> (a) agreeing the terms of the engagement with the client; and
>
> (b) the auditor's response to a request by a client to change the terms of an engagement to one that provides a lower level of assurance.
>
> The auditor and the client should agree on the terms of the engagement (paragraph 2).
>
> The terms of the engagement should be recorded in writing (paragraph 2-1)
>
> In the UK and Ireland, the auditor should ensure that the engagement letter documents and confirms the auditor's acceptance of the appointment, and includes a summary of the responsibilities of those charged with governance and of the auditor, the scope of the engagement and the form of any reports. (paragraph 5-1)

36. The same basic principles used in drafting engagement letters apply in relation to the audit of credit unions as to the audit of any entity. Practical considerations arising from the particular characteristics of credit unions are considered below.

37. The engagement letter for a credit union normally also refers to:

- the duty of the auditors to report directly to the Financial Regulator, in its role as supervisor, under section 122 of the CU Act 1997;

- the duty of the auditors to report directly to and to respond to the requests for information from the Financial Regulator under sections 27(B) to 27(F) of the CBA 1997[14]; and,

- the duty of auditors to inform the Financial Regulator of their resignation under section 118(2) of the CU Act 1997.

Guidance on reporting to the Financial Regulator is covered in more detail in the section on ISA (UK and Ireland) 250B below).

38. The engagement letter refers to the statutory obligations to report matters to the Financial Regulator as above and outlines that such obligations do not involve undertaking additional work to identify reportable matters.

---

[14] As inserted by section 26 of the CBFSAI 2004.

39. The engagement letter may also address the auditors' responsibility in respect of other information published with the financial statements in the annual report. See commentary on ISA (UK and Ireland) 720 (revised) below.

40. The engagement letter may note that a copy of the report to those charged with governance may be required to be sent by the auditor to the Financial Regulator.

41. The engagement letter may also refer to the reporting obligations imposed on auditors by section 59, Criminal Justice (Theft and Fraud Offences) Act, 2001 and by the anti-money laundering and terrorism financing provisions of the Criminal Justice Act 1994.

42. The directors and supervisory committee are volunteers and are unlikely to be experts in financial and accounting matters. It may be appropriate for the engagement letter to specify the role and responsibilities of the directors regarding accounts preparation, selection of accounting polices and the role of the auditor.

ISA (UK and Ireland) 220: Quality Control for Audits of Historical Financial Information (revised)

Background Note

The purpose of this ISA (UK and Ireland) is to establish standards and provide guidance on specific responsibilities of firm personnel regarding quality control procedures for audits of historical financial information, including audits of financial statements.

Reference should also be made to ISQC 1(UK and Ireland) – Quality Control for Firms that Perform Audits and Reviews of Historical Financial Information and other Assurance and Related Services Engagements.

The engagement partner should be satisfied that the engagement team collectively has the appropriate capabilities, competence and time to perform the audit engagement in accordance with professional standards and regulatory and legal requirements, and to enable an auditor's report that is appropriate in the circumstances to be issued. (paragraph 19)

43. The nature of financial service business is one of rapidly changing and evolving markets. Often credit unions and other financial service companies develop new products and practices which require specialised auditing and accounting responses. It is therefore important that the auditor is familiar with current practice.

44. As well as ensuring that the engagement team has an appropriate level of knowledge of the industry and its corresponding products, the engagement partner also satisfies himself that the members of the engagement team have sufficient knowledge of the regulatory framework within which credit unions operate commensurate with their roles on the engagement.

45. The Financial Regulator has recommended that for credit unions there should be rotation of audit partner every 5 years. This was set out in a letter to credit union auditors in July 2004 and is included in appendix 2 of this Practice Note.

46. Given the public interest nature of a credit union, firms may establish policies to require an independent review in relation to credit union audits to be undertaken by a partner with sufficient experience and authority to fulfil that role. In the case of sole practitioners and small firms a suitably qualified external consultant may perform the role of independent partner and carry out the independent review. In such circumstances, appropriate arrangements are made to safeguard client confidentiality.

ISA (UK and Ireland) 230: Audit Documentation

Background note

The purpose of this ISA (UK and Ireland) is to establish standards and provide guidance regarding documentation in the context of the audit of financial statements.

The auditor should prepare, on a timely basis, audit documentation that provides:

(a) A sufficient and appropriate record of the basis for the auditor's report; and

(b) Evidence that the audit was performed in accordance with ISAs (UK and Ireland) and applicable legal and regulatory requirements. (paragraph 2)

The auditor is aware that under section 27F of the CBA 1997[15] the Financial Regulator may:

> "by notice in writing, require an auditor of a regulated financial service provider, or an affiliate of the auditor, to provide the Bank with a copy of any record or information provided or obtained by the auditor or affiliate in connection with an audit of the financial service provider's accounts that is in the possession of the auditor or affiliate".

---

[15] As inserted by section 26 CBFSAI 2004.

ISA (UK and Ireland) 240 (Revised): The Auditor's Responsibility to Consider Fraud in an Audit of Financial Statements

Background note

The purpose of this ISA (UK and Ireland) is to establish standards and provide guidance on the auditor's responsibility to consider fraud in an audit of financial statements[16] and expand on how the standards and guidance in ISA (UK and Ireland) 315, "Understanding the Entity and its Environment and Assessing the Risks of Material Misstatement" and ISA (UK and Ireland) 330, "The Auditor's Procedures in Response to Assessed Risks" are to be applied in relation to the risks of material misstatement due to fraud.

The auditor should maintain an attitude of professional scepticism throughout the audit, recognising the possibility that a material misstatement due to fraud could exist, notwithstanding the auditor's past experience with the entity about the honesty and integrity of management and those charged with governance. (paragraph 24)

The auditor should make inquiries of management, internal audit and others within the entity as appropriate, to determine whether they have knowledge of any actual, suspected or alleged fraud affecting the entity. (paragraph 38)

When obtaining an understanding of the entity and its environment, including its internal control, the auditor should consider whether the information obtained indicates that one or more fraud risk factors are present. (paragraph 48)

When obtaining an understanding of the entity and its environment, including its internal control, the auditor should consider whether other information obtained indicates risks of material misstatement due to fraud.(paragraph 55)

The auditor should consider whether analytical procedures that are performed at or near the end of the audit when forming an overall conclusion as to whether the financial statement as a whole are consistent with the auditor's knowledge of the business indicate a previously unrecognised risk of material misstatement due to fraud (paragraph 85)

If the auditor has identified a fraud or has obtained information that indicates that a fraud may exist, the auditor should communicate these matters as soon as practicable to the appropriate level of management (paragraph 93)

The auditor should document communications about fraud made to management, those charged with governance, regulators and others. (paragraph 109)

---

[16] The auditor's responsibility to consider laws and regulations in an audit of financial statements is established in ISA (UK and Ireland) 250 "Consideration of Laws and Regulations".

47. As outlined in paragraphs 13 to 16 of ISA (UK and Ireland) 240, it is the responsibility of those charged with governance of the entity and management, to take such steps as are reasonably open to them to prevent and detect fraud. It is the auditors' responsibility to plan, perform and evaluate their audit work in order to have a reasonable expectation of detecting material misstatements in the financial statements arising from error or fraud.

48. Credit unions have custody of valuable and fungible assets including money. As a result fraud is an inherent risk of undertaking credit union business. Frauds relating to most types of transactions can be facilitated by identity theft and so 'know your customer' procedures are an important component of the procedures taken by credit unions to mitigate the risk of fraud.

49. Every credit union is required by law to establish and maintain a system of control of its business and records[17].This would include the appropriate control procedure to minimise the risk of losses to the credit union from irregularities or fraud.

50. Examples of conditions or events particularly relevant to credit unions which may increase the risk of fraud include:

- the non-participation in the running of the credit union on the part of some of the directors or officers leading to a small number of their colleagues dominating the credit union's management;

- excessive influence of one or a few officers or employees;

- inadequate segregation of duties between credit union staff;

- failure to document or follow the credit union's standard operating procedures;

- failure by the members of the supervisory committee to monitor the credit union's affairs on an ongoing basis during the year;

- loans granted in circumstances which do not appear to comply with the stated procedures of the credit union;

- failure to regularly reconcile funds received through payroll deductions particularly where the credit union's membership has an employment common bond;

- failure to prepare on a timely basis bank reconciliations and other control accounts in order to present monthly management accounts to the board of directors as required under section 64(1) of the CU Act 1997;

- funds disbursed, even if with board approval, in circumstances which do not appear to fall within the authorised activities of the credit union;

---

[17] Section 109 of the CU Act 1997.

- issuance of loans to, or failure to make appropriate bad debts provision in respect of, members already failing to meet the repayment schedule of existing loans;

- failure to properly control share withdrawals on dormant accounts;

- excessive influence on officers of a credit union by their extended family; or

- failure to exercise the same controls, both as regards physical safekeeping and reflecting transactions promptly in the credit union's records, to savings stamps as would be done to cash balances.

51. The auditor considers reports or information obtained from the credit union's money laundering reporting officer together with any reviews undertaken by third parties.

52. The auditor is aware of his statutory duty to report directly to the Financial Regulator in certain circumstances (see the Section of this Practice Note relating to ISA (UK and Ireland) 250 Section B). The auditor is also aware of the auditor's duty to report suspected offences of money laundering or terrorist financing to the Garda Síochána and the Revenue Commissioners in accordance with section 57 of the Criminal Justice Act 1994. In addition section 59 of the Criminal Justice (Theft and Fraud Offences) Act 2001 requires an auditor to report to the Garda Síochána instances of suspected theft or fraud that come to their attention in the course of auditing the financial statements of bodies corporate and other entities (see the Section of this Practice Note relating to ISA (UK and Ireland) 250 Section A).

ISA (UK and Ireland) 250: Section A – Consideration of Law and Regulations in an Audit of Financial Statements

Background note

The purpose of this ISA (UK and Ireland) is to establish standards and provide guidance on the auditor's responsibility to consider laws and regulations in the audit of financial statements.

When designing and performing audit procedures and in evaluating and reporting the results thereof, the auditor should recognise that non-compliance by the entity with laws and regulations may materially affect the financial statements. (paragraph 2)

In accordance with ISA (UK and Ireland) 200, "Objective and General Principles Governing an Audit of Financial Statements the auditor should plan and perform the audit with an attitude of professional scepticism recognising that the audit may reveal conditions or events that would lead to questioning whether an entity is complying with laws and regulations. (paragraph 13)

In order to plan the audit, the auditor should obtain a general understanding of the legal and regulatory framework applicable to the entity and the industry and how the entity is complying with that framework. (paragraph 15)

53. The directors of the Credit Union are responsible for ensuring that the necessary controls are in place to ensure compliance with applicable law and regulations, and to detect and correct any breaches that have occurred, even if they have delegated some of their executive functions to staff or professional advisors.

54. The regulatory framework within which a credit union operates, primarily the CU Act 1997 does not alter the nature of the auditors' responsibility to consider law and regulations in an audit of financial statements as described by ISA (UK and Ireland) 250, Section A. Appendix 2 of this Practice Note sets out the legislation relevant to Credit Unions. Guidance notes are also issued by the Financial Regulator from time to time on specific topics and a listing of these is also included in appendix 2.

55. The business activities that credit unions may undertake are set out in the CU Act 1997. The Financial Regulator may grant permission to certain credit unions to provide longer term loans. The auditor is alert to any indication that the business activities the credit unions is engaged in are outside the scope of the permissions granted to the credit union by the Financial Regulator and considers ISA (UK and Ireland) 250 Section A and where appropriate ISA (UK and Ireland) 250 Section B.

56. In order to obtain the general understanding of laws and regulations, the auditor would ordinarily:

- use their existing understanding of the credit union sector, regulatory and other factors;

- inquire of directors and management concerning the credit union's policies and procedures regarding compliance with laws and regulations; and

- discuss with management the policies or procedures adopted for identifying, evaluating and accounting for litigation claims and assessments; and (paragraph 17, ISA (UK and Ireland) 250).

After obtaining the general understanding, auditor should perform further audit procedures to help identify possible or actual instances of non-compliance with those laws and regulations where non-compliance should be considered when preparing financial statements, specifically:

(a) Inquiring of management as to whether the entity is in compliance with such laws and regulations;

(b) Inspecting correspondence with the relevant licensing or regulatory authorities;

(c) Enquiring of those charged with governance as to whether they are on notice of any such possible instances of non-compliance with laws or regulations.

(paragraph 18)

In the UK and Ireland, the auditor's procedures should be designed to help identify possible or actual instances of non-compliance with those laws and regulations which provide a legal framework within which the entity conducts its business and which are central to the entity's ability to conduct its business and hence to its financial statements. (paragraph 18-1)

57. Specific areas that auditors' procedures may address include the following:

- the adequacy of procedures to inform staff of the requirements of relevant legislation and the requirements of the Financial Regulator;

- the adequacy of procedures for authorisation of transactions;

- review of procedures for internal review of the entity's compliance with regulatory or other requirements;

- review of procedures to ensure that possible breaches of requirements are investigated by an appropriate person and are brought to the attention of senior management; and

- review of any compliance reports prepared for the directors or supervisory committee.

58. Under section 87 of the CU Act 1997 the Financial Regulator may exercise his power to direct a credit union to take specified measures. The auditor makes enquiry whether the Financial Regulator has issued any such directions to the Credit Union. Appendix 2 of this Practice Note sets out the text of section 87 of the CU Act 1997.

Money laundering and the financing of terrorism

In the UK and Ireland, when carrying out procedures for the purpose of forming an opinion on the financial statements, the auditor should be alert for those instances of possible or actual non compliance with laws and regulations that might incur obligations for partners and staff in audit firms to report money laundering offences. (paragraph 22-1)

59. The law relating to the prevention of money laundering and terrorist financing is integral to the legal and regulatory framework within which credit unions conduct their business. By the nature of their business, credit unions are ready targets of those engaged in money laundering activities and the financing of terrorism. Anti-money laundering legislation[18] in the Republic of Ireland makes it a criminal offence to provide assistance to those involved in money laundering or terrorist financing. In addition, section 57 of the Criminal Justice Act, 1994, as amended, ('CJA') requires credit unions and other bodies designated under that Act to report suspicions of money laundering or terrorist financing to the appropriate authorities, being the Garda Síochána and the Revenue Commissioners. It is also an offence under section 58(2) of the CJA to make a disclosure which is likely to prejudice any investigation arising from a report made under section 57 of that Act.

60. The anti-money laundering legislation in the Republic of Ireland also requires bodies designated for the purposes of that legislation, including credit unions, to meet certain requirements in the following areas:

- the establishment and maintenance of policies, procedures and controls to deter and to recognise and report money laundering and terrorist financing activities;

- taking reasonable measures to establish the identity of customers (often referred to as "know your customer" requirements);

- retention of customer identification and transaction records for use as evidence in any future investigations into money laundering or terrorist financing; and

---

[18] Anti-money laundering legislation in the Republic of Ireland includes the following:
- Criminal Justice Act 1994 – as amended
- S.I. No. 104 of 1995, Criminal Justice Act 1994 (Section 32(10)(a)) Regulations 1995
- Criminal Justice (Theft & Fraud Offences) Act 2001
- S.I. No. 216 of 2003, Criminal Justice Act 1994 (Section 32(10)(a)) Regulations 2003
- S.I. No. 242 of 2003, Criminal Justice Act 1994 (Section 32) Regulations 2003
- S.I. No. 416 of 2003, Criminal Justice Act 1994 (Section 32)(Amendment) Regulations 2003
- S.I. No. 3 of 2004, Criminal Justice Act 1994 (Section 32)(Prescribed Activities) Regulations 2004
- Criminal Justice (Terrorist Offences) Act 2005.

- education and training of staff.

61. Detailed guidance on implementation of the requirements of anti-money laundering legislation, entitled "Money Laundering: Guidance Notes for Credit Unions July 2004", has been issued by the Financial Regulator. New Guidance Notes will be published based on the legislation that will implement the 3rd Anti-Money Laundering Directive[19] in Ireland.

62. Laws and regulations relating to money laundering and terrorist financing are therefore central to credit unions. When auditing the financial statements of a credit union, the auditor needs to obtain a general understanding of how the credit union ensures compliance with anti-money laundering legislation.

63. The auditor is aware of the auditor's own designation under the CJA. If the auditor concludes that there is a possible breach of anti-money laundering legislation, or if they uncover any suspicion that the credit union has been involved, either knowingly or otherwise, in money laundering or terrorist financing offences, the auditor considers their statutory duty to report to the Garda Síochána and the Revenue Commissioners in accordance with the CJA. In addition the auditor takes steps to assess the effect on the financial statements and the implications for other aspects of the audit. The auditor is aware that a suspicion of an offence of money laundering or terrorist financing may also give rise to a statutory duty to report directly to the Financial Regulator or separately to the Garda Síochána under section 59 of the Criminal Justice (Theft and Fraud Offences) Act, 2001. In this regard the auditor needs to be mindful of the offence of prejudicing an investigation under section 58(2) of the CJA.

Tax Compliance

64. In the course of obtaining evidence sufficient to form an opinion on the view given by a credit union's financial statements, auditors undertake procedures in relation to amounts relating to tax included in those statements in order to determine whether they are materially misstated. A credit union may have responsibilities under tax and stamp duty laws to operate various tax deduction and tax collection mechanisms. Whilst an audit of financial statements does not provide specific assurance on compliance by the entity with all provisions of tax law non-compliance can result in the risk of imposition of liabilities. Auditors of credit unions therefore:

- make enquiries of the credit union's directors, Compliance Officer and other personnel responsible for compliance with tax law and regulations as to how such duties are discharged and whether they are on notice of any possible instances of non-compliance;

- review correspondence with the Revenue Commissioners; and

---

[19] EU Directive 2005/60/EC on the prevention of the use of the financial system for the purpose of money laundering and terrorist financing (the 3rd Anti-Money Laundering Directive) is due to be implemented in Ireland by December 2007.

- carry out procedures to obtain sufficient appropriate evidence that, in the context of the financial statements as a whole, liabilities, assets and related disclosures are free from material mis-statement.

65. If auditors become aware of non-compliance with tax legislation, auditors consider the implications in the context of their 'whistle blowing' responsibilities under Section 1079 of the Taxes Consolidation Act 1997.

ISA (UK and Ireland) 250: Section B – The Auditors' Right and Duty to Report to Regulators in the Financial Sector

Background Note

The auditor of a regulated entity should bring information of which the auditor has become aware in the ordinary course of performing work undertaken to fulfil the auditor's audit responsibilities to the attention of the appropriate regulator without delay when:

(a) The auditor concludes that it is relevant to the regulator's functions having regard to such matters as may be specified in statute or any related regulations; and

(b) In the auditor's opinion there is reasonable cause to believe it is or may be of material significance to the regulator. (paragraph 2)

Where an apparent breach of statutory or regulatory requirements comes to the auditor's attention, the auditor should:

(a) Obtain such evidence as is available to assess its implications for the auditor's reporting responsibilities;

(b) Determine whether, in the auditor's opinion, there is reasonable cause to believe that the breach is of material significance to the regulator; and

(c) Consider whether the apparent breach is criminal conduct that gives rise to criminal property and, as such, should be reported to the specified authorities. (paragraph 39)

Regulatory Framework

66. The legal framework within which credit unions operate is set out in appendix 2 and is primarily comprised of the CU Act 1997 and the CBA 1997. The CU Act 1997 assigned the Financial Regulator the role of monitoring and supervising the operations of the credit unions in accordance with the provisions of that Act. Both the CU Act 1997 and the CBA 1997 place a statutory duty on auditors of credit unions to report to the Financial Regulator in specified circumstances.

67. Section 118(2) of the CU Act 1997 places a duty on an auditor of a credit union to inform the Financial Regulator of his resignation.

68. Section 122(1) of the CU Act 1997 places a duty on auditors to report to the Financial Regulator in writing, where the auditor:[20] "at any time"

    (a) has reason to believe that there exist circumstances which are likely to affect materially the credit union's ability to fulfil its obligations to its members or meet any of its obligations under this Act;

    (b) has reason to believe that there are material defects in the accounting records, systems of control of the business and records of the credit union;

    (c) has reason to believe that there are material inaccuracies in or omissions from any returns made by the credit union to the Financial Regulator;

    (d) proposes to qualify any report which he is to provide under this Act; and

    (e) has reason to believe that there are material defects in the system for ensuring the safe custody of all documents of title, deeds and accounting records of the credit union.

69. The statutory duty to report does not require the auditors to extend the scope of their work in order to determine whether matters reportable under section 122 of the CU Act 1997 have arisen.

70. Section 122(2) of the CU Act 1997 allows the Financial Regulator to request reports from auditors setting out their opinion on a credit union's compliance with particular obligations under this Act as specified in the Financial Regulator's request.

71. Section 122(4) of the CU Act 1997, imposes a duty on auditors of a credit union to supply the Financial Regulator with such information as the Financial Regulator may specify in relation to the audit of the financial statements of the credit union. In supplying information for this purpose the Financial Regulator may require the auditor to act independently of the credit union[21].

72. Under section 27 of the CBA 1997, the auditor of a credit union is required to provide to the Financial Regulator:

    • an annual confirmation as to whether there are matters to report in addition to and including any reports already submitted under 'prescribed enactments' (section 27B); and

    • copies of any reports provided to the credit union or those concerned with its management on matters that have come to the auditor's notice while auditing the

---

[20] Section 122(1)(f) of the CU Act 1997 has not yet been commenced at the date of publication of this Practice Note. Section 122(1)(f) would require the auditor to report to the Financial Regulator where he "considers that the board of directors have failed to respond to any recommendations made by him".

[21] Section 122(5) of the CU Act 1997.

financial statements of the credit union or carrying out any work for the credit union of any kind specified by the Financial Regulator (section 27C).

73. In addition the Financial Regulator has the power to request specifically the auditors of a credit union to provide reports listed in section 27E of the CBA 1997.

Criteria for Reporting to the Financial Regulator

74. The inclusion in this section of guidance on matters which the Financial Regulator might consider to be material is not intended to imply that these matters will necessarily be identified in the normal audit. However, auditors ensure that members of their staff undertaking work on an engagement as auditors of a credit union are able to recognise situations that may indicate actual or possible breaches of the relevant law and regulation when performing their work and that such matters are reported to the audit engagement partner of the credit union without delay.

Reporting to the Financial Regulator in accordance with section 122(1) of the CU Act 1997

75. Auditors cannot be expected to be aware of all circumstances which may have led them, had they known of them, to make a report under section 122(1) of the CU Act 1997. That subsection does not require auditors to change the scope of their normal audit work, nor the frequency or timing of their audit visits, beyond that required to enable them to make a report on the financial statements of the credit union under the CU Act 1997. However, in circumstances where auditors identify that a reportable matter may exist, they carry out such extra work, as they consider necessary, to determine whether the facts and circumstances cause them "reason to believe" that the matter does in fact exist. It should be noted that the auditors' work does not need to prove that the reportable matter exists.

76. Appendix 2 to ISA (UK and Ireland) 250 Section B indicates that firms undertaking audits of a regulated entity need to have in place appropriate procedures to ensure that the partner responsible for the audit function is made aware of any other relationship which exists between any department of the firm and the regulated entity when that relationship could affect the firm's work as an auditor. The partner responsible for the audit needs to make appropriate enquiries in the process of planning and completing the audit. Such enquiries would be directed to those aspects of the non-audit work which might reasonably be expected to be relevant to the audit. Auditors should also consider whether any such relationships could result in a breach of Ethical Standards.

77. The statutory reporting requirements arising under section 122(1) of the CU Act 1997 refer to matters which are likely to be "material", although this word has not been defined in law. In interpreting the matters giving rise to the duty to report, the definition of material significance from paragraph 14 of ISA (UK & Ireland) 250 Section B may be useful to the auditor. It states that:

"The term 'material significance' requires interpretation in the context of the specific legislation applicable to the regulated entity. A matter or group of matters is normally of material significance to a regulator's functions when, due either to its nature or its potential financial impact, it is likely of itself to require investigation by the regulator".

78. "Material" for the purposes of reporting to the Financial Regulator does not necessarily have the same meaning as 'materiality' in the financial statement audit. Whilst a particular event may be trivial in terms of its possible effect on the financial statements of an entity, it may be of a nature or type that is likely to change the perception of the Financial Regulator. However, in the absence of any other information, where quantitative aspects are under consideration, the factors which are taken into account are similar to those considered in the context of a financial statement audit.

79. The determination of whether a matter is likely to be material inevitably requires the auditors to exercise their judgement. In forming such judgements, they consider not simply the facts of the matter but also their implications. In addition, it is possible that a matter, which is not material in isolation, may become so when other possible breaches are considered.

80. Auditors base their judgement of what is material solely on their understanding of the facts of which they are aware without making any assumptions about the information available to the Financial Regulator regarding an individual Credit Union.

81. On completion of their investigations, the auditor ensures that the facts and circumstances, and the basis for his conclusion as to whether these are, or are likely to be 'material' to the Financial Regulator, are adequately documented such that the reason for his decision to report or not, as the case may be, may be clearly demonstrated should the need to do so arise in the future.

82. Whilst confidentiality is an implied term of auditors contracts with a regulated entity, section 122 (6) of the CU Act 1997 states that an auditor does not contravene any duty by his compliance with any obligation of that Section.

Circumstances which are likely to affect the credit union's ability to fulfil its obligations to its members or meet any of its obligations under the CU Act 1997 (section 122(1)(a))

83. Auditors of a credit union are required to report to the Financial Regulator where they have reason to believe that circumstances exist which are likely to affect the credit union's ability to fulfil its obligations to members or to meet any of its financial obligations under the CU Act 1997. The procedures to be followed by auditors in determining their concern (if any) about an entity's ability to continue as a going concern are set out in ISA (UK and Ireland) 570 and additional guidance on matters particular to credit unions is provided in the commentary on ISA (UK and Ireland) 570 in this Practice Note.

Material defects in the accounting records, systems of control of the business and records of the credit union (section 122(1)(b))

84. It is the directors of a credit union who are responsible for ensuring that appropriate financial systems and controls are put in place and accounting records are maintained. Weaknesses in systems, controls and records may be identified by the directors themselves, management, the supervisory committee or by external auditors during the course of their work. Where the auditors identify weaknesses, or become aware of the identification of weaknesses by the aforementioned parties, they consider whether there has been a failure in the credit union's procedures for ensuring the effective operation of the systems and controls, this of itself may require a report to the Financial Regulator.

85. The determination of those matters which require reporting is a matter of judgement for the auditors of each credit union. There will be some weaknesses which will be reportable in the context of one credit union but not for another. The decision to report a matter takes into account, for example:

    - the nature and volume of transactions occurring in the area where the weakness has arisen;

    - the seriousness of the risks to which the credit union is exposed as a result of the weakness identified;

    - whether there are compensating systems and controls;

    - whether the weakness occurred for only a short period of time and has been rectified (although rectification does not of itself mean that the matter should not be reported); or

    - whether a weakness which has been identified, though not significant in itself, becomes so when considered in conjunction with other weaknesses.

Material inaccuracies in or omissions from any returns made by the credit union to the Financial Regulator (section 122(1)(c))

86. The examination by the auditors of returns made by a credit union to the Financial Regulator is outside the scope of an audit of a credit union's financial statements. However where the auditor becomes aware of a material inaccuracy in a return they have a reporting responsibility under this section of the act.

87. However, where the auditors discover a minor inaccuracy in information provided to the Financial Regulator, this would not normally give rise to a statutory duty to report unless:

    (i) it is indicative of a general and recurring lack of compliance with the Financial Regulator's requirements; or

(ii) otherwise casts doubt on the credit union's compliance with the Financial Regulator's requirements.

88. If the correction of an omission or inaccuracy in returns of a financial nature to the Financial Regulator would mean that the credit union is then in breach of certain ratios or limits set by the Financial Regulator, this would be an indication that the matter may be material to the Financial Regulator.

Qualified audit report (section 122(1)(d))

89. The auditors of a credit union are required to make a report to the Financial Regulator if they have reason to believe that they will be precluded from reporting that the accounts give a true and fair view and have been properly prepared in accordance with the CU Act 1997.

90. Where the auditors intend to include an explanatory paragraph in an unqualified audit report such as referring to a going concern issue, this would not of itself, necessitate a report to the Financial Regulator, as inclusion of that paragraph is not a qualification of the audit opinion. However, in those circumstances auditors consider whether the matter giving rise to the explanatory paragraph requires a report to the Financial Regulator under the duty so to do under Section 122(1)(a) of the CU Act 1997.

91. Auditors are mindful of the guidance to be issued by the Financial Regulator referred to in paragraph 28 above. If a Credit Union does not comply with the guidance, the auditors consider whether this has implications for the audit report. Where the auditor concludes that the issue will lead to a qualified audit report (as discussed in the section of this practice note on ISA (UK and Ireland) 700) there is an additional obligation to report immediately to the Financial Regulator under Section 122.

Material defects in the system for ensuring safe custody of all documents of title, deeds and accounting records of the Credit Union (section 122(1)(e))

92. If in the course of the audit, the auditor becomes aware of material defects in the system for ensuring safe custody of all documents of title deeds and accounting records of the credit union he has an obligation to report this to the Financial Regulator under section 122 (1) (e) of the CU Act 1997.

93. Section 108(9) of the CU Act 1997 specifies a credit union "shall take adequate precautions to ensure the safekeeping of the accounting records...". If records are kept other than at the registered offices of the credit union the treasurer must keep a written record of that location.

94. Failure by a credit union to establish and comply with appropriate record retention and retrieval procedures, inclusive of regular making of "back up" duplicates which are transferred to a secure "offsite" location, is likely to give rise to a statutory/duty to report.

Reports requested by the Financial Regulator in accordance with section 122(4) of the CU Act 1997

95. Section 122(4) of the CU Act 1997 empowers the Financial Regulator, where he considers that the exercise of his functions under the 1997 Act or the protection of the interests of the members of a credit union so requires, to ask the auditors to supply him "...with such information as he may specify in relation to the audit of the business of the credit union.". It should be noted that the Financial Regulator's powers under this subsection are restricted to information relating to "...the audit of the business of the credit union". Furthermore, the protection given to the auditor by section 122(6), when making a report under section 122(4), is restricted to disclosure of information in their capacity as auditors of the credit union and in relation to the audit of the business of the credit union. If auditors are reporting under Section 122(4) in respect of an incomplete audit they should emphasise that the report has been prepared based on audit work to date and that the audit has not yet concluded.

96. When a firm of auditors receives a request from the Financial Regulator for information in the context of section 122(4) they should seek to ensure that they are in a position to inform the credit union of this request. A meeting between the auditors and the Financial Regulator will normally be necessary to clarify the specific information requested.

97. Following the meeting the auditors will write to the Financial Regulator confirming the information requested and setting out their responses thereto. In drafting this response the auditors may feel it appropriate to obtain legal advice as to the protection provided to them by Section 122(6) of the CU Act 1997. If deemed appropriate, the auditors may furnish the credit union with a copy of all or part of the written response to the Financial Regulator, unless the Financial Regulator requires that the auditors, in supplying such information, are to act "...independently of the credit union.".

98. Where the Financial Regulator requests information about detailed audit procedures in specific areas any written reply will emphasise that auditors form their professional opinion on the basis of all the work carried out and all the information and explanations received during the audit, and not just on the basis of one or more results in a specific area. The auditors' written response should also state that the requested information is supplied on a confidential basis in the context of a "Section 122(4) CU Act 1997 request" and on the understanding it is not divulged to parties other than the Financial Regulator.

Matters giving rise to special reports under the CBA 1997

The annual statutory duty confirmation to the Financial Regulator (section 27B of the CBA 1997)

99. Under section 27B of the CBA 1997, the auditor of a credit union is required to make a report to the Financial Regulator within one month of the date of their audit report, or such extended period as the Financial Regulator permits. This report must state whether or not a reportable instance has arise in the context of section 122 of the CU Act 1997. This report is known as the "statutory duty confirmation".

100. The statutory duty confirmation is sent directly to the Financial Regulator and is a statement to the Financial Regulator that there is no matter, not already reported in writing to the Financial Regulator by the auditor, that has come to the attention of the auditor during the ordinary course of the audit that gives rise to a duty to report to the Financial Regulator. Where matters have already been reported to the Financial Regulator these are referred to in the statutory duty confirmation. The Statutory Duty Confirmation does not in any way replace the auditor's obligations to report under other legislation as and when circumstances giving rise to the duty are identified in the course of audit.

101. Although the statutory duty confirmation is sent directly to the Financial Regulator, the auditor may send a copy of it to the credit union. There may, however, be cases (for example where a direct report has been made to the Financial Regulator without the credit union's knowledge,) where this is inappropriate.

102. The period covered by the statutory duty confirmation commences from the date of issue of the previous statutory duty confirmation. It covers all matters that require the auditor to report to the Financial Regulator in respect of that period.

103. An illustrative wording for a statutory duty confirmation is included in Appendix 3 of this Practice Note.

Duty of auditor to provide the Financial Regulator with copies of certain reports (section 27C of the CBA 1997)

104. Section 27C of the CBA 1997 requires that if the auditor of a credit union makes a report to the credit union, or those concerned with its management, on any matter that has come to the auditor's notice during the course of the financial statement audit (or while carrying out any work of a kind specified by the Financial Regulator[22]), the auditor must provide the Financial Regulator with a copy of that report.

105. The copy must be provided at the same time as, or as soon as practicable after, the original is provided to the credit union or those concerned in its management. Where no such report is to be sent to the credit union, section 27C (3) of the CBA 1997 requires the auditor to inform the Financial Regulator that such is the case i.e. a 'nil return'.

106. There is no definition contained in the legislation as to what constitutes 'a report' for the purpose of section 27C of the CBA 1997 or the meaning of the term 'those concerned in its management'. However the Financial Regulator has indicated that it would expect to receive under this section, copies of post audit reports prepared in accordance with International Standards on Auditing ("ISA") (UK & Ireland) 260, Communication with Those Charged with Governance and that particular areas of interest include any concerns relating to solvency/capital adequacy or the credit union's conduct of business with its clients.

---

[22] No work has yet been specified by the Financial Regulator for this purpose, hence the duty relates to reports on matters arising from the audit.

107. In many cases, the post audit report required by ISA (UK & Ireland) 260 may constitute the only report made on matters arising from the audit. However, auditors will need to consider the nature of other communications and correspondence with the credit union concerned and consider if they contain matters of a substantive nature, arising from the audit, such that they may be regarded as a report for the purposes of Section 27C. In cases of uncertainty as to whether a particular communication to a credit union constitutes a 'report' for the purposes of this section, auditors may wish to take legal advice.

108. The auditor may consider it prudent to include in any report to directors or management, as a matter of course, a statement that:

- the report has been prepared for the sole use of the credit union;

- it must not be disclosed to another third party, other than the Financial Regulator;

- no responsibility is assumed by the auditor to any other person; and

- it does not purport to be a comprehensive record of all matters arising, risks or internal control weaknesses in the entity.

Requests by the Financial Regulator to provide certain reports (section 27E CBA 1997)

109. The Financial Regulator may request the auditor to provide him with a report on any or all of the following items:

(a) the credit unions accounting or other records;

(b) the systems (if any) in place by the credit union to ensure that it acts prudently in the interests of its members and the interests of those to whom the credit union provides financial services; and

(c) any other matter in respect of which the Financial Regulator requires information about the credit union's activities, to enable the Financial Regulator to perform a function imposed on it under an Act.

Requests by the Financial Regulator to provide certain documents (section 27F CBA 1997)

110. The Financial Regulator may request an auditor of a credit union to provide him with a copy of any record or information provided or obtained by the auditor in connection with an audit of the credit union's accounts in his possession.

111. The Financial Regulator may request that the auditor shall not disclose to the credit union the fact that they have received a request to provide certain reports or certain documents to the Financial Regulator or any information that may lead them to suspect that such a request has been received.

Communication with credit union auditors

112. The Financial Regulator will consider informing auditors of factors which may be relevant to their functions where there is no prohibition, either in statute or in the common law, relating to confidentiality. Disclosure of such information is to the auditors only; they are not generally free to pass that information to others, including the credit union.

113. Where such a matter has been brought to the attention of the auditors, there may be implications for the conduct of their audit work and they may need to amend their approach accordingly. However, the fact that they may have been informed of a matter by the Financial Regulator does not, of itself, require auditors to change the scope of their work, nor does it necessarily require them to search actively for evidence in support of the situation communicated by the Financial Regulator.

114. In determining whether particular circumstances are such as require them to make a report to the Financial Regulator auditors will need to have regard to those matters, if any, which the Financial Regulator has brought to their attention.

115. The Financial Regulator has indicated that, for the avoidance of doubt, he still requires auditors to report a "section 122 matter" which has come to their attention even though this has already been reported to the Financial Regulator by the credit union itself and has been corrected. Normally such a report by the auditors refers to the earlier report from the credit union, providing the auditors consider that it fully describes the matter concerned.

116. In considering what may be reportable to the Financial Regulator, auditors will need to base their judgement on information which is available to them in their capacity as auditors without any regard to matters of which the Financial Regulator independently may be aware.

Conduct of the Audit

The auditor should ensure that all staff involved in the audit of a regulated entity have an understanding of:

(a) The provisions of applicable legislation;

(b) The regulator's rules and any guidance issued by the regulator; and

(c) Any specific requirements which apply to the particular regulated entity,

appropriate to their role in the audit and sufficient (in the context of that role) to enable them to identify situations which may give reasonable cause to believe that a matter should be reported to the regulator. (paragraph 34)

117. As a basic minimum which would be expected of all staff involved, this understanding should extend to:

- the contents of ISA (UK and Ireland) 250 B and of this Practice Note; and

- the principal requirements of the CU Act, 1997.

118. Further understanding, commensurate with the individual's role and responsibilities in the audit process, is required of:

- relevant detailed provisions of the CU Act, 1997;

- relevant guidance issued by the Financial Regulator on the detailed provisions of the CU Act, 1997;

- Ministerial Regulations made under the CU Act, 1997;

- requirements or guidance issued by the Financial Regulator in relation to the activities and/or administration of credit unions; and

- the CBA 1997 as amended as it applies to credit unions.

119. Auditors should ensure that:

- all staff responsible for credit union assignments are aware of the provisions of section 122 of the CU Act 1997 and the content of this guidance and are able to identify situations in which they might operate; and

- satisfactory procedures exist to ensure that any information, which may be the subject of a regulatory report, obtained by the staff in the course of their work, is passed on to the person responsible without unnecessary delay.

Discussion with Management

120. Where the auditors are of the opinion that circumstances have arisen that appear to fall within the scope of section 122(1) of the CU Act 1997 they should consider discussing their concerns in the first instance with the credit union's directors or management to clarify, for the purposes of formulating their report, the extent and nature of the circumstances giving rise to concern, the probable financial impact of those matters, together with any action taken by the credit union to rectify the situation.

121. It may be inappropriate to have such discussions if initial consideration of the particular circumstances by the auditors lead them to conclude they no longer can have confidence in the integrity of management.

122. In conducting discussions with management the auditors should be conscious of the obligation to send the report to the Financial Regulator in writing without delay. When finalising their report, the auditors may need to consider obtaining legal advice on its contents and the protection provided to them by section 122(6) of the CU Act 1997.

**FINANCIAL
REPORTING COUNCIL**

123. The Financial Regulator may request that the auditor shall not disclose to the credit union the fact that they have received such a request or any information that may lead them to suspect that such a request has been received.

Statutory protection of reports by auditors

124. Section 122(6) of the CU Act 1997 Act affords protection to auditors in their communications with the Financial Regulator under section 122. The subsection states:

> "No duty to which the auditor of a credit union may be subject shall be regarded as contravened, and no liability to the credit union, its members, creditors or other interested parties shall attach to the auditor, by reason of his compliance with any obligation imposed on him by or under this Section.".

125. Auditors are protected in their communications with the Financial Regulator when making a formal report on those matters specified in section 122 of the CU Act 1997 relating to the credit union's affairs arising out of the audit of the business of the credit union.

126. Section 27H of the CBFSAI 2004 also provides for the immunity of the auditor from liability arising out of compliance with the requirements of Part IV of the CBA1997, including section 27 of that Act.

127. Auditors recognise that there are circumstances in which section 122(6) of the CU Act 1997 or section 27 of the CBA 1997 will not provide protection, for example, where they could be held to have acted in bad faith or maliciously in reporting under section 122(1) of the CU Act 1997, or where they have supplied information following a request from the Financial Regulator which is outside the scope of section 122(4) of the CU Act 1997. Section 122(6) of the CU Act 1997 does not, therefore, provide auditors with complete immunity from legal action by any parties affected, or subsequently affected, by the auditors action in reporting to the Financial Regulator. Auditors may, therefore, wish to consider taking legal or other professional advice from an appropriately qualified source before making the decision whether, or in what manner, to report. However, it should be borne in mind that speed of reporting may well be important in order to protect the interests of existing and prospective credit union members.

128. Although auditors cannot have the benefit of foresight when judging the potential effect on the interests of existing and prospective credit union members, they should satisfy themselves that the facts and circumstances, and the basis for the auditors' conclusion as to whether these are likely to be "material" to the Financial Regulator, adequately document their decision, whether or not to report and (if reporting) the nature of their report, will stand up to examination at a future date on the basis of the following considerations:

- what they knew at the time;

- what they could reasonably have been expected to know in the course of their audit;

- what they could reasonably have been expected to conclude; and

- what action they should have taken in the light of the above.

Voluntary Reports to the Financial Regulator

129. Where there is a statutory duty to make a report under the CU Act, 1997 or, the CBA 1997, protection is afforded to the auditor by section 122(6) of the CU Act, 1997 and section 27(H) of the CBA 1997[24].

130. There may be circumstances where the auditor concludes that a matter does not give rise to a statutory duty to report but nevertheless feels that in the public interest it should be brought to the attention of the Financial Regulator. Before making any such 'voluntary' report the auditor needs to consider whether any duty of confidentiality or other duty will be breached by making such a report. The common law may provide protection for disclosing certain matters to a proper authority in the public interest. This is discussed further in Appendix 5 below.

131. Before making any such voluntary report the auditor may wish to take legal advice before deciding whether, and in what form, to make a report to the Financial Regulator, when not statutorily required to do so.

ISA (UK and Ireland) 260: Communication of Audit Matters to those Charged with Governance

Background note

The purpose of this ISA (UK and Ireland) is to establish standards and provide guidance on communication of audit matters arising from the audit of financial statements between the auditor and those charged with governance of an entity.

The auditor should communicate audit matters of governance interest arising from the audit of financial statements to those charged with governance of an entity. (paragraph 2)

The auditor should determine the relevant persons who are charged with governance and with whom audit matters of governance interest are communicated. (paragraph 5)

The auditor should communicate audit matters of governance interest on a timely basis. This enables those charged with governance to take appropriate action. (paragraph 13)

The auditor should plan with those charged with governance the form and timing of communications to them. (paragraph 13-1)

132. The Supervisory Committee plays an important role in the governance of Credit Unions. Section 120 (2) requires the auditors of the Credit Union to meet with and report to the directors and the members of the Supervisory committee on the annual accounts and any matters relating to the accounts that the auditor feels should be drawn to their attention.

133. In common with the audit of financial statements of any type of organisation, auditors' consideration of the system of internal control is undertaken primarily for the purpose of forming an opinion on those statements. Therefore, in the first instance their assessment is focused on controls designed to prevent or detect material misstatements in the financial statements arising from fraud, or other irregularity or error.

134. Auditors obtain sufficient appropriate evidence that material weaknesses in control have not existed during the year. ISA (UK and Ireland) 260, Communication of Audit Matters to those charged with Governance, defines a material weakness as

" ...a condition which may result in a material misstatement in the financial statement".

135. ISA (UK and Ireland) 260 requires auditors to report any material weaknesses in the accounting and internal control system identified during the audit to directors on a timely basis.

136. Where significant matters raised in previous reports to directors or management have not been dealt with effectively, the auditors enquire why appropriate action has not been taken. If the point is still significant, consideration is given to repeating the point in the current report, otherwise there is a risk that they may give the impression that they are satisfied that the weakness has been corrected or is no longer significant.

137. As outlined under the section of this Practice Note providing guidance in relation to ISA (UK and Ireland) 250 Section B, an auditor is statutorily obliged to send copies of any reports provided to the credit union or those concerned with its management on matters that have come to the auditors' attention while auditing the financial statements of the credit union to the Financial Regulator. Such reports are likely to include copies of post audit reports prepared in accordance with ISA (UK & Ireland) 260.

ISA (UK and Ireland) 300: Planning an Audit of Financial Statements

Background note

The purpose of this ISA (UK and Ireland) is to establish standards and provide guidance on the considerations and activities applicable to planning an audit of financial statements. This ISA (UK and Ireland) is framed in the context of recurring audits. In addition, matters the auditor considers in initial engagements are included in paragraphs 28 and 29.

The auditor should plan the audit so that the engagement will be performed in an effective manner. (paragraph 2)

The auditor should establish the overall audit strategy for the audit. (paragraph 8)

The overall audit strategy and the audit plan should be updated and changed as necessary during the course of the audit. (paragraph 16)

The auditor should plan the nature, timing and extent of direction and supervision of engagement team members and review of their work. (paragraph 18)

138. Matters the auditors of a credit union may consider as part of the planning process for the audit of the financial statements include:

    - the nature and scope of the credit unions activities;

    - the complexity of the credit union's information systems;

    - the credit unions relationship with the Financial Regulator;

    - changes in applicable laws, regulations and accounting requirements;

    - the need to involve specialists in the audit;

    - the extent to which controls and procedures are outsourced to a third party provider;

    - issues relating to the auditors statutory duty to report; and

    - the appropriateness of the accounting policies adopted by the credit union.

139. Guidance on the first four of these matters is set out in the Section on ISA (UK and Ireland) 315 'Obtaining an Understanding of the Entity and its Environment and Assessing the Risk of Material Misstatement' below. Considerations in relation to other matters in planning the audit are:

    - the auditor considers the need to involve specialists in the audit, for example in the valuation of complex investments and loans;

- the auditor considers the implications of the outsourcing of functions by the credit union and the sources of evidence available to the auditors for transactions undertaken by service organisations in planning their work. This may include the outsourcing of certain functions such as the management of investment funds;

- issues relating to the auditors statutory duty to report include the adequacy of the audit teams understanding of the law; and

- the auditor considers the appropriateness and consistency of the application of the credit unions accounting policies particularly those applied to valuation of investments and loans.

140. When planning the work to be undertaken in respect of a credit union audit, it is important to identify those areas which are key to its operations as reflected in its financial statements. The key areas of credit unions' financial statements would include:

- shares held by members;

- deposits from members;

- loans to members and their recoverability;

- cash;

- funds invested; and

- fixed assets.

141. When considering the key areas it is also important to identify other possible sources of information available to the credit union auditors that may assist in the planning process. Significant sources of relevant information include:

- correspondence between the credit union and the Financial Regulator;

- reports of the supervisory committees;

- reports, where applicable, by the League;

- minutes of board, and other relevant committee, meetings;

- register of directors' interests;

- correspondence between the credit union and its solicitors;

- correspondence between the credit union and its investment advisors; and

- reports commissioned by the credit union or by the Financial Regulator from reporting accountants or other professional advisors.

ISA (UK and Ireland) 315: Obtaining an Understanding of the Entity and its Environment and Assessing the Risks of Material Misstatement

Background note

The purpose of this ISA (UK and Ireland) is to establish standards and to provide guidance on obtaining an understanding of the entity and its environment, including its internal control, and on assessing the risks of material misstatement in a financial statement audit.

142. Credit unions can be complex and the auditor seeks to understand the business and the regulatory regime in which they operate. Generally, there is a close relationship between planning and obtaining an understanding of the business and the control environment, which is covered more fully below.

The auditor should obtain an understanding of relevant industry, regulatory, and other external factors including the applicable financial reporting framework (paragraph 22)

The auditor should obtain an understanding of the nature of the entity (paragraph 25)

143. When performing procedures to obtain an understanding of the credit unions business, the auditor considers:

- The impact of recent legislation, government initiatives and guidance issued by the Financial Regulator;

- the relevant aspects of the credit union's risk management procedures;

- the complexity of the credit unions information systems;

- any changes in the market environment;

- the introduction of new categories of customers, or products or marketing and distribution channels;

- the complexity of products;

- the consistency of products, methods and operations in different departments or locations;

- the legal and operational structure of the credit union;

- the role and competence of volunteers;

- the number and location of branches;

- the respective roles and responsibilities attributed to the finance, risk control, compliance and internal audit functions; and

- the recruitment, competence, and experience of management.

144. In obtaining an understanding of the regulatory factors the auditor considers:

- any formal communications between the Financial Regulator and the credit union, the results of any supervisory visits conducted by the Financial Regulator or trade associations; and

- the contents of any publications from the Financial Regulator.

The auditor should obtain an understanding of the entity's selection and application of accounting policies and consider whether they are appropriate for its business and consistent with the applicable financial reporting framework and accounting policies used in the relevant industry. (paragraph 28)

145. Accounting policies of particular relevance may include allowances for impairment, classification of assets and liabilities (and thereby their measurement), revenue and expense recognition. The auditor undertakes procedures to consider whether the policies adopted are in compliance with applicable accounting standards, and the CU Act 1997, and gains an understanding of the procedures, systems and controls applied to maintain compliance with them.

The auditor should obtain an understanding of the entities objectives and strategies, and the related business risks that may result in material misstatement of the financial statements (paragraph 30)

146. It is important for the auditor to understand the nature and extent of the financial and business risks which are integral to the environment, and how the credit union's systems record and address these risks. Although they may apply to varying degrees, the risks include (but are not limited to):

- credit risk: at its simplest, this is the risk that a member will be unable to meet their obligations. Particular attention may be given to the overreliance by the credit union on mechanistic approaches to assessing doubtful loan provisions. Management and auditors exercise critical judgement in concluding on the adequacy of such provisions;

- liquidity risk: the risk that arises from the possibility that a credit union has insufficient liquid funds to its liabilities as they arise. Particular attention may be given to the nature of investments acquired by the credit union, in particular the maturity profile of investment products, and the appropriateness of acquisition control procedures and accounting policies in relation to such instruments;

- interest rate risk: the risk that arises where there is a mismatch between the interest rate contractual repricing dates or bases for assets and liabilities;

- currency risk: the risk that arises from the mismatching of assets and liabilities and commitments denominated in different currencies;

- operational risk is the risk of loss, arising from inadequate or failed internal processes, people and systems or from external events;

- investment risk: the risk of failure to comply with Regulatory Guidance regarding investments[23]; and

- regulatory risk is the risk of public censure, fines (together with related compensation payments) and restriction or withdrawal of authorisation to conduct some or all of the credit unions activities. This could arise from enforcement activity by the Financial Regulator.

147. Failure to manage the risks outlined above can also cause serious damage to a credit union's reputation, potentially leading to a loss of confidence in the credit union, withdrawal of shares and deposits or problems maintaining liquidity.

> The auditor should obtain an understanding of the measurement and review of the entity's financial performance. (paragraph 35)

148. The auditor obtains an understanding of the measures used by management to review the credit unions performance. Guidance on key performance indicators is included in the Section on ISA (UK and Ireland) 520 in this Practice Note.

> The auditor should obtain an understanding of internal control relevant to the audit. (paragraph 41)
>
> The auditor should obtain an understanding of the control environment. (paragraph 67)

149. Section 53 of the CU Act 1997 provides that the board of directors of the credit union have responsibility for the general control, direction and management of the affairs, funds and records of the credit union.

---

[23] The Financial Regulator published a guidance note for credit unions titled "Guidance Note on Investments by Credit Union" in October 2006. It lists the investment types that a credit union is authorised to make.

150. Section 109 of the CU Act 1997, requires a credit union to establish and maintain systems of control and safe custody. The systems of control must be such so as to secure that the credit union's business is so conducted and its records so kept that:

(a) the information necessary to enable the officers, the credit union and the auditor to discharge their functions is sufficiently accurate, and is available with sufficient regularity and with sufficient promptness for those purposes; and

(b) the information obtained by or furnished to the Financial Regulator is sufficiently accurate for the purposes for which it is obtained or furnished and is available as required by the Financial Regulator.

151. The supervisory committee is statutorily charged with the general duty of overseeing the performance by the directors of their functions.[24]

152. The quality of the overall control environment is dependent upon management's attitude towards the operation of controls. A positive attitude may be evidenced by an organisational framework which enables proper segregation of duties and delegation of control functions and which encourages failings to be reported and corrected. Thus, where a lapse in the operation of a control is treated as a matter of concern, the control environment will be stronger and will contribute to effective control systems; whereas a weak control environment will undermine detailed controls, however well designed.

153. No internal control system can by itself guarantee effective administration and completeness and accuracy of the credit union's records. However, the attitude, role and actions of the directors are fundamental in shaping the control environment of a credit union. Factors to consider include:

- the amount of time committed by individual directors;

- the skills, experience and qualifications of individual directors;

- the frequency and regularity of Board/Committee meetings;

- the degree of supervision of the credit union's transactions by individual directors; and

- in smaller credit unions the number of members of the management team and the consequent restriction on division of duties.

154. Systems and controls that may be appropriate for a credit union include the following:

- clear and appropriate reporting lines which are communicated within the credit union;

- appropriate controls to ensure compliance with laws and regulations;

---

[24] Section 58(1) of the CU Act 1997.

- appropriate risk assessment process;

- appropriate management information;

- controls to ensure the suitability of staff;

- documented business plans and strategies;

- an internal audit function (where appropriate); and

- appropriate record keeping arrangements.

> The auditor should obtain a sufficient understanding of control activities to assess the risks of material misstatement at the assertion level and to design further audit procedures responsive to assessed risks. (paragraph 90)

155. There is a wide variation between different credit unions in terms of size, activity and organisation, so that there can be no standard approach to internal controls and risk. In assessing whether there is a risk of material misstatement, the auditor may consider the factors outlined below in relation to the following:

(i) Control Environment

- inadequate segregation between front, middle and back offices;

- weaknesses in "know your customer" procedures;

- lack of an effective supervisory committee;

- inadequate definition of management responsibilities and supervision of staff and contractors;

- ineffective personnel practices;

- inadequate communication of information to management;

- voluntary nature of those charged with governance;

- non compliance with guidance[25] issued by the Financial Regulator;

- complex products or processes inadequately understood by management; this includes undue concentration of expertise concerning matters requiring the exercise of significant judgement or capable of manipulation such as valuations of financial instruments or allowances for impairments;

---

[25] The Financial Regulator has issued a number of guidance notes. See Appendix 2 for a list of these.

- weaknesses in back office procedures contributing to completeness and accuracy of accounting records; and

- Controls relating to outsourcing activities are considered in the ISA (UK and Ireland) 402 Section of this Practice Note.

(ii) Loans:

- inadequate procedures relating to loan approvals;

- lack of proper documentation;

- failure to systematically validate security or guarantees given in respect of loans;

- failure to regularly review loan policies and related procedures;

- failure to consistently take into account the borrower's ability to repay the loan in accordance with the agreed terms and conditions;

- single or lump sum repayment loans;

- rescheduling loans to a member as a means of addressing repayment difficulties encountered in respect of original loan; and

- failure to monitor loan book on a regular basis to ensure that the specific statutory requirements governing loans in excess of stated amounts, or for longer than stated periods, are not breached.

(iii) Deposits/shares of members

- inadequate monitoring procedures relating to dormant accounts;

- failure to monitor deposit levels on a regular basis and develop appropriate cash flow forecasts to ensure that the credit union's lending activities will not give rise to significant bank borrowing;

- an individual member holding more than one deposit account;

- payment of appropriate interest/dividend and where the credit union has allocated its depositors to differing categories, based on amounts deposited, confirmation that the appropriate rate has been paid to each category and the same rate to all members of a particular category; and

- where passbooks are not issued, failure to issue statements to members on a regular basis.

(iv) Distributions

- failure to distinguish correctly between realised and unrealised gains for the purpose of declaring a dividend; and

- desire to declare a dividend in line with members' expectations regardless of income and reserve levels.

The auditor should obtain an understanding of how the entity has responded to risks arising from IT. (paragraph 93)

156. The auditor assesses the extent, nature and impact of automation within the credit union and plans and performs work accordingly. In particular the auditor considers:

- the required level of IT knowledge and skills may be extensive and may require the auditor to obtain advice and assistance from staff with specialist skills;

- the extent of the application of audit software and related audit techniques;

- general controls relating to the environment within which IT based systems are developed, maintained and operated; and

- external interfaces susceptible to breaches of security.

The auditor should identify and assess the risks of material misstatement at the financial statement level, and at the assertion level for classes of transactions, account balances, and disclosures. (paragraph 100)

As part of the risk assessment as described in paragraph 100, the auditor should determine which of the risks identified are, in the auditors judgement, risks that require special audit consideration (such risks are defined as "significant risks"). (paragraph 108)

For significant risks, to the extent the auditor has not already done so, the auditor should evaluate the design of the entity's related controls, including relevant control activities, and determine whether they have been implemented. (paragraph 113)

157. Significant risks are likely to arise in those areas that are subject to significant judgement by management or are complex and are properly understood by comparatively few people in the credit union.

158. Examples of significant risks for credit unions requiring special audit consideration may include:

- allowances for impairment;

- valuation of investments; and

- assessment of going concern.

159. Weaknesses in the control environment and in controls such as those described above could increase the risk of fraud.

ISA (UK and Ireland) 330: The Auditors Procedures in Response to Assessed Risks

Background note

The purpose of ISA (UK and Ireland) is to establish standards and provide guidance on determining overall responses and designing and performing further audit procedures to respond to the assessed risks of material misstatement at the financial statement and assertion levels in a financial statement audit.

When, in accordance with paragraph 115 of ISA (UK and Ireland) 315, the auditor has determined that it is not possible or practicable to reduce the risks of material misstatement at the assertion level to an acceptably low level with audit evidence obtained only from substantive procedures, the auditor should perform tests of relevant controls to obtain audit evidence about their operating effectiveness. (paragraph 25)

160. As in the audit of other entities, the auditor obtains and documents an understanding of the accounting system and control environment to assess whether they are adequate as a basis for drawing up the financial statements and to determine their audit approach. If, having carried out this task, the auditor expects to be able to rely on the assessment of risk to reduce the extent of the substantive procedures, the auditor makes a preliminary assessment of risk for material financial statement assertions and plan and perform tests of control to support that assessment.

161. Control procedures designed to address specified controlled objectives are subject to inherent limitations and accordingly, errors or irregularities may occur and not be detected. Such control procedures cannot guarantee protection against fraud or collusion especially on the part of those holding positions of authority or trust.

When the auditor has determined that an assessed risk of material misstatement at the assertion level is a significant risk, the auditor should perform substantive procedures that are specifically responsive to that risk. (paragraph 51).

162. Examples of significant risks for credit unions requiring special audit consideration include the nature of and valuation of investments and other financial instruments for which valuation techniques are required – see the Section on ISA (UK and Ireland) 540 for estimates of allowances for impairment.

The auditor should perform audit procedures to evaluate whether the overall presentation of the financial statements, including the related disclosures, is in accordance with the applicable financial reporting framework. (paragraph 65).

163. Specific financial reporting standards can require extensive narrative disclosures in the financial statements of some credit unions; for example, in relation to the nature and extent of risks arising from financial instruments. In designing and performing procedures to evaluate these disclosures the auditor obtains audit evidence regarding the assertions about presentation and disclosure described in paragraph 17 of ISA (UK and Ireland) 500: Audit Evidence.

ISA (UK and Ireland) 402: Audit Considerations Relating to Entities using Service Organisations

Background note

The purpose of this ISA (UK and Ireland) is to establish standards and provide guidance to an auditor where the entity uses a service organisation.

In obtaining an understanding of the entity and its environment, the auditor should determine the significance of service organisation activities to the entity and the relevance to the audit. (paragraph 5)

164. The auditor gains an understanding of the extent of outsourced functions and their relevance to the financial statements. The Credit Union is obliged to ensure that the auditor has appropriate access to records, information and explanations from material outsourced operations.

165. In common with other industries the outsourcing of functions to third parties is becoming increasingly prevalent with credit unions albeit to a more limited degree for the smaller credit unions. Some of the more common areas may have a direct relevance to the audit such as IT services, investment management, payroll processing services and internal audit.

166. Whilst a credit union may outsource functions to third parties the responsibility for these functions remains that of the credit union. The credit union should have appropriate controls in place over these arrangements including:

- risk assessment prior to contracting with the service provider, which includes a proper due diligence and periodic review of the appropriateness of the arrangement;

- appropriate contractual agreements or service level agreements;

- contingency plans should the service provider fail in delivery of services;

- appropriate management information and reporting from the outsourced vendor;

- protection over member information; and

- right of access of the credit union's internal audit and external auditors to test the internal controls of the services provider.

167. If the auditor is unable to obtain sufficient appropriate audit evidence concerning outsourced operations the auditor considers whether it is necessary to report the matter direct to the Financial Regulator under section 122(1)(b) of the CU Act 1997 and section 122(1)(e) of the CU Act 1997 – see Section of this Practice Note relating to ISA (UK and Ireland) 250 Section B.

ISA (UK and Ireland) 501: Audit Evidence – Additional Considerations for Specific Items

Background Note

The purpose of this International Standard on Auditing (UK and Ireland) (ISA (UK and Ireland) is to establish standards and provide guidance additional to that contained in ISA (UK and Ireland) 500, "Audit Evidence" with respect to certain specific financial statement account balances and other disclosures.

When long-term investments are material to the financial statements, the auditor should obtain sufficient appropriate audit evidence regarding their valuation and disclosure. (paragraph 38)

168. When investments are classified as long term, audit procedures ordinarily include obtaining audit evidence as to whether the entity has the authority to hold the investments on a long term basis and obtaining written representations from directors[26].

169. The auditor ordinarily considers information, such as market quotations and related financial statements, which provide an indication of value and compares such values to the carrying amount of the investments up to the date of the auditor's report. If such values do not exceed the carrying amounts, the auditor would consider whether a write-down is required. If there is an uncertainty as to whether the carrying amount will be recovered, the auditor would consider whether appropriate adjustments and/or disclosures have been made.

170. In considering a write-down or adjustment, the auditor is cognisant of section 110 of the CU Act 1997 which requires that all liabilities and losses which have arisen or are likely to arise in respect of the financial year to which the accounts relate shall be taken into account. This section also requires that the amount of any item in the accounts shall be determined on a prudent basis. Discussion on the applicability of Fair Value Accounting to credit unions is outlined in at paragraph 20 of this Practice Note.

---

[26] See Guidance Note on Investments by Credit Unions – October 2006.

ISA (UK and Ireland) 505: External Confirmations

Background note

The purpose of this International Standard on Auditing (UK and Ireland) (ISA (UK and Ireland)) is to establish standards and provide guidance on the auditor's use of external confirmations as a means of obtaining evidence.

The auditor should determine whether the use of external confirmations is necessary to obtain sufficient appropriate evidence at the assertion level. In making this determination, the auditor should consider the assessed risk of material misstatement at the assertion level and how the audit evidence from other planned procedures will reduce the risk of material misstatement at the assertion level to an acceptably low level (paragraph 2)

171. The following types of balances and transactions are worthy of particular consideration:

   • members loans and shares/deposits; and

   • investments held with investment managers and custodians.

172. The supervisory committee is obliged to do a circularisation of a certain number of members' loans.[27] The auditor is aware of the timing of that circularisation and any potential evidence available from it.

173. Members' loans and shares/deposits typically comprise high volumes of comparatively low value amounts. Members may not maintain independent records of their balances but rather usually depend on information provided to them by the credit union. Accordingly the auditor may consider the inherent reliability of such responses is comparatively low.

174. As a result the auditor may conclude that undertaking confirmation procedures on their own may not make an effective contribution to reducing the risk of material misstatement of these account balances and transactions and instead will seek additional evidence from other audit procedures.

175. The credit union may obtain "certified" lists of investments held by custodians on a regular basis. Because these are sent directly to the credit union, they are not as conclusive as direct audit evidence. In the event that the audit determines that a confirmation letter should be obtained from the investment custodians, arrangements should be made for such custodians to mail directly to the auditor a copy of such lists and confirmation of other matters the auditor deems appropriate.

---

[27] Section 60(c) of the CU Act 1997.

ISA (UK and Ireland) 520: Analytical Procedures

Background note

The purpose of this ISA (UK and Ireland) is to establish standards and provide guidance on the application of analytical procedures during an audit.

The auditor should apply analytical procedures as risk assessment procedures to obtain an understanding of the entity and its environment and in the overall review at the end of the audit. (paragraph 2).

When analytical procedures identify significant fluctuations or relationships that are inconsistent with other relevant information or that deviate from predicted amounts, the auditor should investigate and obtain adequate explanations and appropriate corroborative audit evidence. (paragraph 17)

176. Credit unions are required to submit annual returns to the Financial Regulator which contain a comprehensive range of information and data which may assist auditors by providing an indication of trends and current ratios. In addition, detailed internal financial information produced for directors and management may provide a valuable source of evidence.

177. Examples of key ratios which auditors may wish to consider in carrying out analytical procedures on a credit union's results and balance sheet are as follows:

- bad debt provisions to total loans;

- total arrears to total net liabilities;

- non-performing loans to total loans;

- earnings cover of loan losses;

- liquid assets/total assets ratio;

- cost/income ratio;

- loans/shares ratio;

- investment income received/deposit interest paid ratio;

- share withdrawal trends;

- unattached shares/deposits ratio;

- staff costs/gross income ratio;

- average loan duration (months);

- value and number of re-scheduled loans;

- "weeks in arrears" value;

- capital (general reserves) to total assets;

- section 35(2)(a) of the CU Act 1997 lending ratio; and

- section 35(2)(b) of the CU Act 1997 lending ratio.

178. Key analytical procedures auditors may wish to perform include:

- reviewing total loan interest earned from members' borrowings and comparing with the average monthly outstanding balance for the year taken at the prevailing interest rate;

- comparing the total dividends paid on members' deposits with the credit union and testing against the dividend rate based on the average monthly deposit balance;

- comparing total payroll costs with previous years and obtaining explanations of variations;

- comparing the financial statements with budgets, forecasts, or management expectations;

- considering whether the financial statements adequately reflect any changes in the scope and nature of the credit union's activities of which the auditors are aware;

- enquiring into unexplained or unexpected features of the financial statements;

- where industry information is available, for example, PEARLS reports from the League, this may be used to benchmark income, resources and expenditure against other credit unions; and

- Key performance indicators could also include measures relating to regulatory compliance and operational risk measures.

179. When performing their review of the financial statements as a whole for consistency with their knowledge of the entity's activities and the results of other audit procedures, the auditor considers transactions occurring either side of the year end, including:

- loan repayments which are received shortly before the year end then re-advanced shortly afterwards; material sale and repurchase transactions or other financing or linked transactions. Experience and judgment are required to identify and assess the implications, if any, of these transactions; they may, for example, be indicative of 'window dressing' of the balance sheet over the year end date;

- other transactions around the year end, apparently at rates which are significantly off market including those that appear or give rise to significant profits or losses;

- the material rescheduling of loans; and

- the reclassification of balances and transactions to achieve advantageous income recognition and balance sheet treatment/presentation.

180. Where non financial information or reports produced from systems or processes outside the financial statements accounting system are used in analytical procedures, the auditor considers the reliability of that information or those reports.

ISA (UK and Ireland) 540: Audit of Accounting Estimates

Background note

The purpose of this ISA (UK and Ireland) is to establish standards and provide guidance on the audit of accounting estimates contained the financial statements.

The auditor should obtain sufficient appropriate audit evidence regarding accounting estimates (paragraph 2)

The auditor should adopt one or a combination of the following approaches in the audit of an accounting estimate:

(a) Review and test the process used by management to develop the estimate;

(b) Use an independent estimate for comparison with that prepared by management; or

(c) Review of subsequent events which provide audit evidence of the reasonableness of the estimate made.

(paragraph 10).

The auditor should make a final assessment of the reasonableness of the entity's accounting estimates based on the auditor's understanding of the entity and its environment and whether the estimates are consistent with other audit evidence obtained during the audit. (paragraph 24).

181. Accounting estimates are used for valuation purposes in a number of areas; the most common examples are for loan losses and valuation of investments not traded on an active market. Estimates of allowances for bad debts or loan impairments may represent significant risk.

182. A bad debt provision is calculated or an impairment review of the loan book is carried out depending on whether historic cost accounting or Fair Value Accounting is used. Further discussion on the applicability of Fair Value Accounting to credit unions is outlined in at paragraph 20 of this Practice Note.

183. Auditors' review of a credit union's methods for making provisions and writing off bad loans includes consideration of their reasonableness, consistency with prior years and conformity with generally accepted practices.

184. In reviewing the reasonableness of loan loss provisions, both specific and general, credit union auditors ascertain that management have properly exercised their judgement, followed a consistently applied policy in determining the level of provisions and not merely followed a standard formula/matrix calculation. Auditors need to be mindful of practices such as rescheduling, non-cash transfers or top-up lending that

can have the effect of understating provisions. In ascertaining the appropriateness of general provisions credit union auditors should take into consideration the level of risk inherent in the loan book and changes in the economic environment.

185. In reviewing the adequacy of loan impairment provisions the auditor assesses whether the assumptions made by management in arriving at their estimate of likely cash flows to be received from impaired loans and have been made after due consideration and whether they are supported by relevant evidence, including evidence derived from backtesting and the issue of enforceability of contracts in relation to collateral. In the case of individual loan impairment calculations such evidence will be specific to the borrower but where impairment is estimated for a portfolio of similar loans the auditor considers observable data across a group of assets as a whole such as arrears statistics or economic conditions.

186. Management bias whether intentional or unintentional, can be difficult to detect in a particular estimate. It may only be identified when there has been a change in the method for calculating estimates from the prior period based on a subjective assessment without evidence that there has been a change in circumstances, when considered in the aggregate of groups of estimates, or when observed over a number of accounting periods. Although some form of management bias is inherent in subjective decisions, management may have no intention of misleading the users of financial statements. If however, there is intention to mislead through, for example, the intentional use of unreasonable estimates, for instance because of excessive pressure to recommend a distribution, management bias may be fraudulent in nature. ISA (UK & Ireland) 240 "The Auditor's Responsibility to Consider Fraud in an Audit of Financial Statements", provides standards and guidance on the auditor's responsibility to consider fraud in an audit of financial statements.

ISA (UK and Ireland) 545: Auditing fair value measurements and disclosures

Background note

The purpose of this ISA (UK and Ireland) is to establish standards and provide guidance on auditing fair value measurements and disclosures contained in financial statements.

The auditor should obtain sufficient appropriate audit evidence that fair value measurements and disclosures are in accordance with the entity's applicable financial reporting framework. (paragraph 3)

As part of the understanding of the entity and its environment, including its internal control, the auditor should obtain an understanding of the entity's process for determining fair value measurements and disclosures and of the relevant control activities sufficient to identify and assess the risks of material misstatement at the assertion level and to design and perform further audit procedures. (paragraph 10)

The auditor should evaluate whether the fair value measurements and disclosures in the financial statements are in accordance with the entity's applicable financial reporting framework. (paragraph 17)

187. The valuation of derivative and other financial instruments which are not traded in an active market and so for which valuation techniques are required is an activity that can give rise to significant audit risk. Auditors of credit unions which may hold such instruments consider the guidance on audit procedures set out in the ISA (UK and Ireland) 545 section in PN 19: The audit of Banks in the Republic of Ireland (Revised).

ISA (UK and Ireland) 550: Related Parties

Background note

The purpose of this ISA (UK and Ireland) is to establish standards and provide guidance on the auditor's responsibilities and audit procedures regarding related parties and transactions with such parties regardless of whether International Accounting Standard (IAS) 24, "Related Party Disclosures," or similar requirement, is part of the applicable financial reporting framework.

When planning the audit the auditor should assess the risk that material undisclosed related party transactions or undisclosed outstanding balances between an entity and its related parties may exist. (paragraph 6-3)

188. The principles and procedures set out in ISA (UK and Ireland) 550 apply to the audit of credit unions as for other undertakings. However, the organisation of credit unions is such that the issue of a controlling shareholding of a credit union by any party will not arise. Related party transactions which are likely to arise include shares held by, deposits from and/or loans to directors or members of the supervisory committee of the credit union.

189. Related party transactions are defined in FRS 8 'Related party disclosures'. The financial statements need to disclose material transactions with directors and other related parties; these may be disclosed on an aggregated basis[28]. Paragraph 16 of FRS 8 states that the 'disclosure provisions do not apply where to comply with them conflicts with the reporting entity's duties of confidentiality arising by operation of law'. This is relevant in a credit union context: credit unions are usually under a strict duty of confidentiality (by operation of statute, contract or common law) regarding the affairs of their members.

190. Auditors will enquire as to the procedures, required under statute and under the rules of the individual credit union, governing the authorisation, recording and monitoring of any related party transactions. They will assess the operation of those procedures during the financial year and consider whether appropriate disclosure has been made in the financial statements.

191. Section 69 of the CU Act 1997 sets out rules regarding conflicts of interest. Accordingly the auditor's review of board minutes may reveal the existence of related parties and conflicts. Members should not be considered to be related parties simply by virtue of their being members of the credit union.

---

[28] Aggregate disclosures are allowed unless disclosure of an individual transaction, or connected transactions, is necessary for an understanding of the impact of the transactions.

ISA (UK and Ireland) 560: Subsequent Events

Background note

The purpose of this ISA (UK and Ireland) is to establish standards and provide guidance on the auditor's responsibility regarding subsequent events.

The auditor should perform audit procedures designed to obtain sufficient appropriate audit evidence that all events up to the date of the auditor's report that may require adjustment of, or disclosure in, the financial statements have been identified. (paragraph 4).

192. Matters specific to credit unions which auditors may consider in their review of subsequent events include:

- an evaluation of material loans and other receivables identified as being in default or potential default at the period end to provide additional evidence concerning period end loan impairment provisions;

- the accounting treatment of dividends declared after the year end[29];

- an assessment of material loans and other receivables identified as (potential) defaults since the period end to consider whether any adjustment to the period end carrying value is required; and

- the material impairment of investments, assets and securities held against loans;

- a review of correspondence with the Financial Regulator and enquiries of directors and management to determine whether any significant breaches of laws and regulations or other significant regulatory concerns have come to light since the period end.

---

[29] FRS 21 'Events after the Balance Sheet Date' (paragraph 12).

ISA (UK and Ireland) 570: Going Concern

Background note

The purpose of this ISA (UK and Ireland) is to establish standards and provide guidance on the auditor's responsibility on the audit of financial statements with respect to the going concern assumption used in the preparation of the financial statements, including considering management's[30] assessments of the entity's ability to continue as a going concern. (paragraph 1)

When planning and performing audit procedures and in evaluating the results thereof, the auditor should consider the appropriateness of management's[30] use of the going concern assumption in the preparation of the financial statements. (paragraph 2)

The auditor should consider any relevant disclosures in the financial statements. (paragraph 2-1).

In obtaining an understanding of the entity, the auditor should consider whether there are any events or conditions and related business risks which may cast significant doubt on the entity's ability to continue as a going concern. (paragraph 11)

The auditor should remain alert for audit evidence of events or conditions and related business risks which may cast significant doubt on the entity's ability to continue as a going concern in performing audit procedures throughout the audit. If such events or conditions are identified, the auditor should, in addition to performing the procedures set out in paragraph 26, consider whether they affect the auditor's assessment of the risks of material misstatement. (paragraph 12)

193. Section 110(1)(a) of the CU Act 1997 requires that 'the amounts to be included in the accounts of a credit union in respect of items shown shall be determined in accordance with the following principles—

    (a) the credit union shall be presumed to be carrying on business as a going concern; "

194. The directors are responsible for determining, on the basis of their own information and judgements, whether the going concern presumption is appropriate. ISA 570 (UK and Ireland) paragraph 17, requires that auditors evaluate managements assessment of the entity's ability to continue as a going concern and paragraph 17-1 requires the

---

[30] In the UK and Ireland, those charged with governance are responsible for the preparation of the financial statements and the assessment of the entity's ability to continue as a going concern.

auditor to assess the adequacy of the means by which directors have satisfied themselves that:

(a) it is appropriate for them to adopt the going concern basis and

(b) that the financial statements include such disclosures, if any, relating to going concern as are necessary for them to give a true and fair view.

195. When events or conditions have been identified which may cast significant doubt on a credit union's ability to continue as a going concern, the auditor should in accordance with ISA (UK and Ireland) 570, paragraph 26;

(a) review the directors' plans for future actions based on its going concern assessment;

(b) gather sufficient appropriate audit evidence to confirm or dispel whether or not a material uncertainty exists through carrying out audit procedures considered necessary, including considering the effect of any plans of directors and other mitigating factors; and

(c) seek written representations from directors regarding its plans for the future.

196. In reviewing going concern, the auditor may consider the following areas in addition to those set out in ISA (UK and Ireland) 570:

(a) capital adequacy ratios – review of management's analysis and rationale for ensuring that the credit union is capable of maintaining adequate financial resources in excess of the minimum;

(b) liquidity indicators – eg review of the credit union's liquidity management process for signs of undue deterioration; and

(c) reputational and other indicators – eg review of the financial press and other sources of market intelligence for evidence of deteriorating reputation; review of correspondence with regulators.

Further details of possible factors that may indicate going concern issues in these areas are set out in Appendix 4 to this Practice Note.

The auditor should consider the need to obtain written confirmation of representations from those charged with governance regarding:

(a) The assessment by those charged with governance that the company is a going concern;

(b) Any relevant disclosures in the financial statement.

(paragraph 26-1)

Based on the audit evidence obtained, the auditor should determine if, in the auditor's judgement, a material uncertainty exists related to events exists related to events or conditions that alone or in aggregate, may cast significant doubt on the entity's ability to continue as a going concern. (paragraph 30)

The auditor should document the extent of the auditor's concern (if any) about the entity's ability to continue as a going concern. (paragraph 30-1)

The auditor should consider whether the financial statements are required to include any disclosures relating to going concern in order to give a true and fair view. (paragraph 31-31)

Audit Conclusions and Reporting

197. Section 122 (1) of the CU Act 1997 specifically obliges the auditor of a credit union who:

"(a) Has reason to believe that there exists circumstances which are likely to affect materially the Credit Union's ability to fulfil its obligations to its members or meet any of its obligations under this Act"

to report directly to the Financial Regulator in writing and without delay. More detailed guidance on the procedures to be followed in such circumstances is set out in the ISA (UK and Ireland) 250 B Section of this Practice Note.

198. In their consideration of going concern auditors may become aware of matters concerning a credit union's funding or liquidity position that may give rise to a duty to report to the Financial Regulator. See the ISA (UK and Ireland) 250 B Section of this Practice Note.

199. Where the auditors intend to include an emphasis of matter paragraph in an unqualified audit report, referring to a going concern issue, this would not, of itself, necessitate a report to the Financial Regulator as inclusion of that paragraph is not qualification of the audit opinion. However, in those circumstances auditors consider whether the matter giving rise to the emphasis of matter paragraph requires a report to the Financial Regulator under the duty so to do under section 122(1)(a) of the CU 1997 Act.

ISA (UK and Ireland) 580: Management Representations

Background note

The purpose of this ISA (UK and Ireland) is to establish standards and provide guidance on the use of management representations as audit evidence, the procedures to be applied in evaluating and documenting management representations and the action to be taken if management refuses to provide appropriate representations.

Written confirmation of appropriate representations from management, as required by paragraph 4 below, should be obtained before the audit report is issued. (paragraph 2-1)

The auditor should obtain written representations from management on matters material to the financial statements when other sufficient appropriate audit evidence cannot reasonably be expected to exist. (paragraph 4)

200. ISA (UK and Ireland) 250 Section A and ISA (UK and Ireland) 550 require auditors to obtain written confirmation in respect of completeness of disclosure to the auditors of:

- all known actual or possible non-compliance with laws and regulations whose effects should be considered when preparing financial statements together with the actual or contingent consequences which may arise therefrom; and

- the completeness of information provided regarding the identification of related parties and the adequacy of related party disclosures in the financial statements.

201. In addition to the examples of other representations given in ISA (UK and Ireland) 580, the auditor also considers obtaining confirmation:

- as to the adequacy of provisions for loan impairment (including provisions relating to individual loans if material) and the appropriateness of other accounting estimates (such as investment valuations or adequate provisions for liabilities);

- that all contingent transactions or commitments have been adequately disclosed and/or included in the balance sheet as appropriate; and

- that all correspondence with regulatory bodies has been made available to the auditor.

ISA (UK and Ireland) 700: The Auditor's Report on Financial Statements

Background note

The purpose of this ISA (UK and Ireland) is to establish standards and provide guidance on the form and content of the auditor's report issued as a result of an audit performed by an independent auditor of the financial statements of an entity. Much of the guidance provided can be adapted to auditor reports on financial information other than financial statements.

The auditor should review and assess the conclusions drawn from the audit evidence obtained as the basis for the expression of an opinion on the financial statements. (paragraph 2)

The auditor's report should contain a clear written expression of opinion on the financial statements taken as a whole. (paragraph 4)

In the UK and Ireland, the auditor should not date the report earlier that the date on which all other information contained in a report of which the audited financial statements form a part have been approved by those charged with governance and the auditor has considered all necessary available evidence. (paragraph 24-1)

202. The form and content of auditors' report on the financial statements of credit unions follow the basic principles and procedures established by ISA (UK and Ireland) 700. An illustrative auditor's report for a credit union is included in appendix 1 of this Practice Note.

203. ISA (UK and Ireland) 700 requires that Independent Auditors Reports on Financial Statements identify the financial reporting framework used to prepare the financial statements. The expression Generally Accepted Accounting Practice in Ireland can be used to describe compliance with applicable Irish law and accounting standards issued by the Accounting Standards Board and published by the Institute of Chartered Accountants in Ireland.

204. If any significant matters of concern have arisen during the audit of a credit union, the auditors consider whether they have a duty to report the matter to the Financial Regulator in his capacity as the relevant supervisory authority.

205. If the auditors of a credit union decide to include a qualification in their audit report, written notice of that fact must be given to the Financial Regulator as required by section 122(1)(d) of the CU Act 1997. The decision to give written notice of a qualification will be taken only after extensive discussions with management, and when either a problem cannot be resolved or the circumstances indicate that the auditors intend to issue a qualified opinion.

206. Where the auditors intend to include an explanatory paragraph in an unqualified audit report, referring to a fundamental uncertainty, this does not necessitate a report to the Financial Regulator under section 122(1)(d) of the CU Act 1997 (because it is not a qualification of the audit opinion). However, auditors consider whether the matter giving rise to the uncertainty of itself gives rise to a duty to report under other parts of section 122(1) of the CU Act 1997.

Fair Value Accounting

207. The auditor is required to express an opinion on whether the financial statements have been properly prepared in accordance with the Credit Union Act 1997.Where the credit union has adopted fair values the auditor has regard to the draft guidance to directors of credit unions issued by the Financial Regulator (as discussed in the Introduction to this PN in paragraph 20).

208. If the auditor concludes that the law has not been complied with the auditor issues an adverse opinion together with the substantive reasons (normally provided by means of a cross reference to the notes to the accounts where the issue is described in detail) and, unless impracticable, a quantification of the possible effect(s) on the financial statements.

209. Where the auditor is uncertain as to whether or not the financial statements have been prepared in accordance with the law the auditor's report describes the limitation of scope (ie the uncertainty regarding the appropriate interpretation of the Credit Union Act) in the Basis of audit opinion section of the report and expresses an opinion that 'we were unable to determine whether the financial statements have been properly prepared in accordance with the Credit Union Act 1997'.

ISA (UK and Ireland) 720 (Revised): Other Information in Documents containing Audited Financial Statements

Background note

The purpose of this ISA (UK and Ireland) is to establish standards and provide guidance on the auditor's consideration of other information, on which the auditor has no obligation to report, in documents containing audited financial statements.

The auditor should read the other information to identify material inconsistencies with the audited financial statements. (paragraph 2)

If, as a result of reading the other information, the auditor becomes aware of any apparent misstatements therein, or identifies any material inconsistencies with the audited financial statements, the auditor should seek to resolve them. (paragraph 2-1)

210. Auditors are required to report on whether the information given in the report of the board of directors of a Credit Union is consistent with the financial statements in addition, one of the fundamental principles set out in the Auditors Code[13] is that auditors do not allow their reports to be included in documents containing other information if they consider that the additional information is in conflict with the matters covered by the report or they have cause to believe it to be misleading.

211. The auditors are not responsible for auditing the additional information. ISA(UK and Ireland) 720 does not require auditors to undertake additional procedures to corroborate other information in documents containing audited financial statements but rather to read the other information in the context of the knowledge they have obtained during the audit.

212. It is important to ensure that the directors are made aware of the auditors' responsibilities in respect of the other information, as set out in ISA(UK and Ireland) 720, and the extent of those responsibilities is specifically dealt with in the engagement letter.

213. The information which may accompany the financial statements of a credit union include:

- directors' report;

- supervisory committee report;

- treasurer's report;

- credit committee report;

- credit control report;

- membership committee report; and

- financial highlights for previous years.

214. The directors may also distribute other documents with the financial statements such as newsletters, new rules booklets, statement of member's balances of loans and/or shares/deposits in the credit union etc. The auditors have no responsibility to consider these documents.

Appendix 1

Illustrative Auditor's Report on financial statements for a Credit Union

Independent Auditor's Report to the Members of XYZ Credit Union

We have audited the financial statements of XYZ credit union for the year ended ....which comprise the Income and Expenditure Account, the Balance Sheet, the Statement of Total Recognised Gains and Losses and the related notes[31]. These financial statements have been prepared under the accounting policies set out in the Statement of Accounting Policies.

Respective responsibilities of directors and auditors

The directors' responsibilities for preparing the Annual Report and the financial statements in accordance with applicable law and the accounting standards issued by the Accounting Standards Board and promulgated by the Institute of Chartered Accountants in Ireland (Generally Accepted Accounting Practice in Ireland) are set out in the Statement of Directors' Responsibilities.

Our responsibility is to audit the financial statements in accordance with relevant legal and regulatory requirements and International Standards on Auditing (UK and Ireland).

We report to you our opinion as to whether the financial statements give a true and fair view and are properly prepared in accordance with Generally Accepted Accounting Practice in Ireland and the Credit Union Act 1997. We also report to you whether in our opinion proper accounting records have been kept by the credit union. In addition, we state whether we have obtained all the information and explanations necessary for the purposes of our audit and whether the credit union's financial statements are in agreement with the accounting records.

We read the other information contained in the annual report and consider whether it is consistent with the audited financial statements. The other information comprises only [the Directors' Report, the Treasurer's Report, the Supervisory Committee Reports, and the Credit Committee Report][32]. We consider the implications for our report if we become aware of any apparent misstatements or material inconsistencies with the financial statements. Our responsibilities do not extend to any other information.

---

[31] Auditor's reports of entities that do not publish their financial statements on a web site or publish them using 'PDF' format may continue to refer to the financial statements by reference to page numbers.

[32] The other information that is 'read' is the content of the printed Annual Report other than the financial statements. The description of the information that has been read is tailored to reflect the terms used in the Annual Report.

Basis of audit opinion

We conducted our audit in accordance with International Standards on Auditing (UK and Ireland) issued by the Auditing Practices Board. An audit includes examination, on a test basis, of evidence relevant to the amounts and disclosures in the financial statements. It also includes an assessment of the significant estimates and judgements made by the directors in the preparation of the financial statements and of whether the accounting policies are appropriate to the company's circumstances, consistently applied and adequately disclosed.

We planned and performed our audit so as to obtain all the information and explanations which we considered necessary in order to provide us with sufficient evidence to give reasonable assurance that the financial statements are free from material misstatement, whether caused by fraud or other irregularity or error. In forming our opinion we also evaluated the overall adequacy of the presentation of information in the financial statements.

Opinion

In our opinion the financial statements:

- give a true and fair view of the state of the affairs of the credit union as at .....and of its income and expenditure for the year then ended; and

- have been properly prepared in accordance with Generally Accepted Accounting Practice in Ireland and in accordance with the requirements of the Credit Union Act, 1997.

We have obtained all the information and explanations we consider necessary for the purpose of our audit. In our opinion, proper accounting records have been kept by the credit union. The financial statements are in agreement with the accounting records.

In our opinion the information given in the Directors' Report is consistent with the financial statements.

Accountants and Registered Auditors

Date:

Appendix 2

List of Legislation Relevant to Credit Unions

This appendix sets out the legislation and Financial Regulator guidance applicable to credit unions. It is not an exhaustive list and is not a substitute for reference to the full text of relevant requirements. This appendix also contains relevant extracts from key legislation together with the text of the Financial Regulator's Guidance Note for the Auditors or Credit Unions issued in July 2004.

Primary Legislation

- Credit Union Act 1997

- Central Bank Act 1942

- Central Bank and Financial Services Authority of Ireland Act 2003

- Central Bank and Financial Services Authority of Ireland Act 2004

- Consumer Information Act 1978

- Criminal Justice Act, 1994

- Criminal Justice [Miscellaneous Provisions] Act, 1997

- Criminal Justice [Theft and Fraud Offences] Act, 2001

- Criminal Justice (Terrorist Offences) Act 2005

- Data Protection Acts 1988 to 2003

- Finance Act 2001 [Sections 33 and 57 of the Finance Act 2001]

- Investment Intermediaries Acts 1995 to 2000

Statutory Instruments (The CU Act 1997)

- Credit Union Act, 1997 [Commencement] Order, 1997 No 403/1997

- Credit Union Act, 1997 [Commencement] Order, 2001 S.I. No 378/2001

- Credit Union Act, 1997 [Alteration of Financial Limit] Regulation, 1998 S.I. No 476/ 2001

- Credit Union Act, 1997 [Exemption from Additional Services Requirements] Regulation 2004 S. I. 223 of 2004

- Credit Union Act, 1997 [Alteration of Financial Limit] Order 2006 S.I. No 453 of 2006.

- Credit Union Act, 1997 [Alteration of Financial Limit] Regulation, 2006 S.I. 546/ 2006

- Credit Union Act, 1997 [Exemption from Additional Services Requirements] Regulation, 2007 S.I. No 107 of 2007.

- Credit Union Act, 1997 [Alteration of Financial Limits] Regulation, 2007 S.I. No 193 of 2007

Other Statutory Instruments

- Trustee (Authorised Investments) Order 1998 (Amendment) Order, 1998 S.I. No 28 of 1998.

- Trustee (Authorised Investments) Order 1998 (Amendment) Order, 2002 S.I. No 595 of 2002.

- Central Bank and Financial Services Authority of Ireland Act 2003 (Commencement) of Certain Provisions) Order 2003 S.I. 160 of 2003.

- Central Bank and Financial Services Authority of Ireland Act 2004 (Commencement) Order (No1) 2004 S.I. 454 of 2004.

- Central Bank and Financial Services Authority of Ireland Act 2004 (Commencement) Order 2004 S.I. 455 of 2004.

- Central Bank and Financial Services Authority of Ireland Act 2004 (Commencement) Order 2004 Order (No 2) 2004 S.I. 760 of 2004

Secondary Legislation

- Companies Acts, 1963 to date

- Companies [Auditing and Accounting] Act, 2001

Guidance Notes issued by the Financial Regulator[33]

- Guidance Notes for Credit Unions – The Criminal Justice Act, 1994 (as amended)- Money Laundering – July 2004[34]

- Guidance Note for the Auditors of Credit Unions- July 2004[35]*

---

[33] These Guidance Notes are available on Financial Regulator's website www.financialregulator.ie.

[34] Guidance Notes for Credit Unions – The Criminal Justice Act, 1994 (as amended) – Money Laundering – July 2004 – available from the Financial Regulator.

[35] *These Guidance Notes are available on the Financial Regulator website www.financialregulator.ie.

- Guidance on Obligations of Boards of Directors and Supervisory Committees – September 2004*

- Guidance Note on Investments by Credit Unions – January 2005*

- Guidance Note on the Control, Direction and Management of Credit Unions -May 2005*

- Guidance Note for Regulated Financial Service Providers in Reporting Compliance Concerns to the Financial Regulator – July 2005*

- Guidance Note on Investments by Credit Unions – October 2006*

- Draft Guidance Note for Credit Unions on Matters Relating to Accounting for Investments and Distribution Policy. – Draft issued July 2008*

Other Guidance

- Guidance on the Offence of Financing of Terrorism and the Financial Sanctions Regime for Bodies Designated under Section 32 of the Criminal Justice Act, 1994 – Issued with the approval of the Money Laundering Steering Committee – March 2005[36]

---

[36] These Guidance Notes are available on the Department of Finance website www.finance.gov.ie.

Relevant Extracts from the CU Act 1997 and the CBA 1997

The CU Act 1997 –

The following are relevant extracts section 87, section 118, section 120 and section 122 of the CU Act 1997.

Section 87 – Power of Registrar to give Regulatory Directions.

(1) If, with respect to a credit union, the Registrar is satisfied—

    (a) that the credit union has become, or is likely to become, unable to meet its obligations to its creditors or its members or suspends payments lawfully due from it, or

    (b) that it is expedient to do so in the public interest or in the interest of the orderly and proper regulation of the business of the credit union or in order to protect the savings of its members, or

    (c) that the credit union no longer possesses, or is not maintaining and is unlikely to be in a position to maintain, adequate capital resources and, in particular, no longer provides security for the funds entrusted to it, or

    (d) that the credit union is not a participant in a savings protection scheme approved by the Bank or, although a participant, has failed to make satisfactory arrangements with the management of such a scheme, or

    (e) that any member or group of members of the credit union have, or are likely to achieve, a position in relation to the credit union that would enable the member or group to exercise a significant influence over the management or operation of the credit union,

the Bank may give the credit union such regulatory directions as he thinks proper.

(2) The Bank may also give regulatory directions to a credit union if it appears to him—

    (a) that the credit union has failed to comply with any requirements imposed by or under this Act (including requirements imposed by the Bank by conditions, notices, directions or otherwise in the exercise of his powers under this Act); or

    (b) that the credit union has been convicted of an offence under *section 27 (2)* or *section 33 (6)* or an offence involving fraud, dishonesty or breach of trust; or

    (c) that, since the registration of the credit union, the factors taken into account in granting registration have so changed that, if the society were now applying for registration, it would be refused.

(3) For the purposes of this Act, "regulatory directions" are directions in writing given to a credit union by the Bank which do one or more of the following—

(a) prohibit the credit union, for such period not exceeding six months, to such extent, and subject to such conditions as may be specified, from carrying on all or any of the following activities, except with the written authority of the Bank—

    (i) the raising of funds (by whatever means);

    (ii) the making of payments;

    (iii) the acquisition or disposal of other assets or liabilities;

(b) require the credit union to refrain from making, or to realise within a specified period, investments of a specified class or description;

(c) specify, with respect to all loans which the credit union may make, the maximum amount of secured and unsecured loans which the credit union may make to its members, or the security or types of security which the credit union must require in respect of secured loans to its members;

(d) require the credit union to establish and maintain, with respect to all loans which the credit union may make, such ratio or ratios regarding loans to shares or loans to savings as may be specified;

and, in this subsection and *subsection (4)*, "specified" means specified by regulatory directions.

(4) Subject to any express provision in *subsection (3)*, regulatory directions—

(a) may be expressed to have effect, either generally or with respect to specified matters, for a specified period or until varied or revoked; and

(b) may make different provision for different classes of case (but not so as to make different provision for members, investments or loans within the same class).

(5) The giving of any regulatory directions shall not preclude a credit union—

(a) from receiving funds by way of voluntary non-repayable donation from its members or from such other person as may be approved by the Bank; or

(b) from setting off to any extent a member's share capital against his indebtedness to the credit union (such a set-off being regarded as a repayment of share capital).

FINANCIAL REPORTING COUNCIL

Section 118 – Resignation of Auditors

(1) An auditor of a credit union may, by a notice in writing which complies with *subsection (3)*, is served on the credit union and states his intention to do so, resign from the office of auditor to the credit union, and the resignation shall take effect on such date as may be specified in the notice, being not less than 28 days after the notice is served.

(2) A copy of a notice under *subsection (1)* shall be sent by the auditor to the Bank at the same time as it is served on the credit union.

(3) A notice under *subsection (1)* shall contain either—

(a) a statement to the effect that there are no circumstances connected with the resignation to which it relates that the auditor concerned considers should be brought to the notice of the members or creditors of the credit union; or

(b) a statement of any such circumstances.

(4) Subject to *subsection (5)*, where a notice under *subsection (1)* is served on a credit union and the notice contains a statement falling within *subsection (3) (b)*, the credit union shall, not later than 14 days after the date of that service, send a copy of the notice to every person who is entitled to notice of a general meeting of the credit union.

(5) Copies of a notice served on a credit union under *subsection (1)* need not be sent to the persons specified in *subsection (4)* if, on the application of the credit union concerned or any other person who claims to be aggrieved, the Bank is satisfied that the sending of the notice would be likely to diminish substantially public confidence in the credit union or that the rights conferred by this section are being abused to secure needless publicity for defamatory matter.

Section 120 – Auditor's report, right of access and to be heard

(1) The auditor of a credit union shall make a report to the members on the accounts examined by him, and on the annual accounts which are to be laid before the credit union at the annual general meeting during his tenure of office; and the auditor's report—

    (a)   shall be read at the annual general meeting of the credit union, and

    (b)   shall be open to inspection by any member of the credit union.

(2) Before signing his report, the auditor of a credit union shall meet with and report to the directors of the credit union and the members of the Supervisory Committee on the annual accounts and any matter relating thereto which he considers should be drawn to their attention.

(3) The auditor's report shall state whether—

    (a)   he has obtained all the information and explanations which, to the best of his knowledge and belief, were necessary for the purposes of his audit;

    (b)   he is of the opinion that proper accounting records have been kept by the credit union;

    (c)   the credit union's annual accounts are in agreement with the accounting records of the credit union;

    (d)   he is of the opinion that the credit union's annual accounts have been properly prepared so as to conform with any requirements made by or under this Act and give a true and fair view—

        (i)   in the case of the balance sheet, of the credit union's state of affairs as at the end of the financial year;

        (ii)   in the case of the income and expenditure account, of the income and expenditure of the credit union for the financial year; and

    (e)   the credit union's annual accounts contain any statement required under *section 111 (1)(c)* to be included by the body of accountants concerned.

(4) Without prejudice to *subsection (3)*, where the report of the auditor relates to any accounts other than the income and expenditure account for the financial year in respect of which he is appointed, that report shall state whether those accounts give a true and fair view of any matter to which they relate.

(5) It shall be the duty of the auditor in preparing his report under this section to carry out such investigations as will enable him to form an opinion as to whether—

    (a)   the credit union has kept proper accounting records, and

(b)   the credit union has maintained satisfactory systems of control of its business and records,

and where the auditor is of the opinion that the credit union has failed to keep proper accounting records or to maintain a satisfactory system of control of its business or records, he shall so state in his report.[37]

(6) Every auditor of a credit union shall have a right of access at all reasonable times to the books and documents of the credit union, and shall be entitled to require from the officers and voluntary assistants of the credit union such information and explanations that are within their knowledge or can be procured by them, as he thinks necessary for the performance of his duty as auditor.

(7) The auditor of a credit union shall be entitled—

(a)   to attend any general meeting of the credit union; and

(b)   to be heard at any general meeting on any part of the business which concerns him as auditor of the credit union;

and the credit union shall give its auditor the same notice of, and any other communications relating to, a general meeting that a member of the credit union is entitled to receive.

---

[37] At the date of publication of this Practice Note, this subsection has not yet commenced.

Section 122 Auditor's duty to report to the Registrar

(1) If at any time the auditor of a credit union—

    (a)   has reason to believe that there exist circumstances which are likely to affect materially the credit union's ability to fulfil its obligations to its members or meet any of its obligations under this Act,

    (b)   has reason to believe that there are material defects in the accounting records, systems of control of the business and records of the credit union,

    (c)   has reason to believe that there are material inaccuracies in or omissions from any returns made by the credit union to the Bank,

    (d)   proposes to qualify any report which he is to provide under this Act,

    (e)   has reason to believe that there are material defects in the system for ensuring the safe custody of all documents of title, deeds and accounting records of the credit union, or

    (f)   considers that the board of directors have failed to respond to any recommendations made by him,[38]

the auditor shall forthwith report the matter to the Bank in writing.

(2) The auditor of a credit union shall, if requested by the Bank, furnish to the Bank a report stating whether in his opinion and to the best of his knowledge the credit union has or has not complied with such requirements under this Act as the Bank may have requested the auditor to furnish a report on.

(3) The auditor of a credit union shall send to it, forthwith, a copy of any report made by him to the Bank under *subsection (1)* or *subsection (2)*.

(4) Whenever the Bank is of the opinion that the exercise of his functions under this Act or the protection of the interests of the members of a credit union so requires, he may require the auditor of the credit union to supply him with such information as he may specify in relation to the audit of the business of the credit union.

(5) The Bank may require that, in supplying information for the purpose of *subsection (4)*, the auditor shall act independently of the credit union.

(6) No duty to which the auditor of a credit union may be subject shall be regarded as contravened, and no liability to the credit union, its members, creditors or other interested parties shall attach to the auditor, by reason of his compliance with any obligation imposed on him by or under this section.

---

[38] At the date of publication of this Practice Note, this subsection has not yet commenced.

FINANCIAL REPORTING COUNCIL

Extracts from the CBA 1997

The following are relevant extracts from Section 27B to 27H of the CBA 1997 as inserted by section 26 of the CBFSAI Act 2004:

27B.— Auditor of regulated financial service provider to lodge annual report with Bank.

(1) This section applies to an auditor who is required by or in accordance with a prescribed enactment to report a matter to the Bank.

(2) Within 1 month after the date of the auditor's report on the financial service provider's accounts, or within such extended period as the Bank allows, the auditor of the service provider shall deliver a written report to the Bank—

    (a)   stating whether or not circumstances have arisen that require the auditor to report a matter to the Bank under a prescribed enactment and, if such circumstances have arisen, specify those circumstances, and

    (b)   where the service provider has, during that financial year, been required to provide the Bank with a compliance statement stating whether or not the requirement has been complied with.

(3) A report under this section must be in a form publicly notified by the Bank.

(4) The following are prescribed enactments for the purpose of this section:

    (a)   section 35 of the Insurance Act 1989;

    (b)   section 47 of the Central Bank Act 1989;

    (c)   section 89 of the Building Societies Act 1989;

    (d)   section 38 of the Trustee Savings Banks Act 1989;

    (e)   section 258 of the Companies Act 1990;

    (f)   section 15 of the Unit Trusts Act 1990;

    (g)   section 16 of the Investment Limited Partnership Act 1994;

    (h)   section 33 of the Investment Intermediaries Act 1995;

    (i)   section 34 of the Stock Exchange Act 1995;

    (j)   section 122 of the Credit Union Act 1997;

    (k)   regulations 7, 8 and 9 of the Supervision of Credit Institutions, Stock Exchange Members Firms and Investment Business Firms Regulations 1996;

    (*l*)   regulation 85 of the European Communities (Undertakings for Collective Investment in Transferable Securities) Regulations 2003;

    (*m*) any other provision of an Act or regulations declared under subsection (5) to be a prescribed enactment for the purpose of this section.

(5) The Bank may, by notice published in *Iris Oifigiuil*, declare a provision of an Act or regulations to be a prescribed enactment for the purpose of this section.

**FINANCIAL
REPORTING COUNCIL**

Section 27C – Duty of auditor to provide Bank with copies of certain reports

(1) If the auditor of a regulated financial service provider provides the financial service provider, or those concerned in its management, with a report on a matter that has come to the auditor's notice while auditing the accounts of the financial service provider or carrying out any other work for the financial service provider of a kind specified by the Bank, the auditor shall provide the Bank with a copy of the report. The copy must be provided at the same time as, or as soon as practicable after, the original is provided to the financial service provider or those concerned in its management.

(2) If—

(a) an auditor of a regulated financial service provider invites the financial service provider, or the persons concerned in its management, to comment on a draft of a report referred to in subsection (1), and

(b) the financial service provider or those persons comment on the draft in response to the invitation,

the obligation of the auditor under that subsection applies only to the final version of the report.

(3) If, in relation to the financial year of a regulated financial service provider, there has been no reason for the auditor of the service provider to provide such a report, the auditor shall nevertheless notify the Bank in writing that this is the case.

27E – Bank may request auditor of regulated financial service provider to provide Bank with report.

(1) The Bank may, by notice in writing, request an auditor of a regulated financial service provider, or an affiliate of the auditor, to provide the Bank with a report on all or any of the following:

    (a)   the service provider's accounting or other records;

    (b)   the systems (if any) that the service provider has in place to ensure that the service provider acts prudently in the interests of its members (if a company or firm) and the interests of those to whom the service provider provides financial services;

    (c)   any other matter in respect of which the Bank requires information about the service provider, or the service provider's activities, to enable the Bank to perform a function imposed on it by or under an Act.

(2) The auditor or affiliate shall comply with such a request within such period as is specified in the request, or within such extended period as the Bank may allow.

(3) If the Bank so directs, the auditor or affiliate shall not, without the consent of the Bank, disclose to the financial service provider concerned, or any person concerned in the management of, or employed by, that service provider—

    (a)   the fact that the auditor or affiliate has received a request under subsection (1), or

    (b)   any information that might lead that service provider, or any such person,

to suspect that the auditor or affiliate has received such a request.

Section 27F – Bank may require auditor of regulated financial service provider to provide certain documents

(1) The Bank may, by notice in writing, require an auditor of a regulated financial service provider, or an affiliate of the auditor, to provide the Bank with a copy of any record or information provided or obtained by the auditor or affiliate in connection with an audit of the financial service provider's accounts that is in the possession of the auditor or affiliate.

(2) The auditor or affiliate shall comply with such a request within such period as is specified in the request, or within such extended period as the Bank may allow.

(3) If the Bank so directs, the auditor or affiliate shall not, without the consent of the Bank, disclose to the financial service provider concerned, or any person concerned in the management of, or employed by, that service provider—

    (a)   the fact that the auditor or affiliate has received a request under subsection (1), or

    (b)   any information that might lead that service provider, or any such person, to suspect that the auditor or affiliate has received such a request.

FINANCIAL REPORTING COUNCIL

27G – Offences by auditors and affilates under this Chapter

(1) An auditor of a regulated financial service provider who, without reasonable excuse, fails to comply with section 27B (2), 27C(1), 27D, 27E(2) or 27F(2), or contravenes section 27E(3) or 27F(3), commits an offence and—

    (a)   if tried summarily, is liable on conviction to a fine not exceeding €2,000, or

    (b)   if tried on indictment, is liable on conviction to a fine not exceeding €75,000.

(2) An affiliate of an auditor of a regulated financial service provider who, without reasonable excuse, fails to comply with section 27E(2) or 27F(2), or contravenes section 27E(3) or 27F(3), commits an offence and—

    (a)   if tried summarily, is liable on conviction to a fine not exceeding €2,000, or

    (b)   if tried on indictment, is liable on conviction to a fine not exceeding €75,000.

(3) An auditor who, having been convicted of an offence of failing to comply with a provision of section 27B, 27C, 27D, 27E or 27F, continues to fail to comply with the provision commits a further offence on each day or part of a day during which the failure continues after that conviction and—

    (a)   if tried summarily, is liable on conviction to a fine not exceeding €200 for each such day or part of a day, or

    (b)   if tried on indictment, is liable on conviction to a fine not exceeding €7,500 for each such day or part of a day.

(4) An affiliate of an auditor who, having been convicted of an offence of failing to comply with a provision of section 27E or 27F, continues to fail to comply with the provision commits a further offence on each day or part of a day during which the failure continues after that conviction and—

    (a)   if tried summarily, is liable on conviction to a fine not exceeding €200 for each such day or part of a day, or

    (b)   if tried on indictment, is liable on conviction to a fine not exceeding €7,500 for each such day or part of a day

Section 27H: Auditors to have immunities from liability.

27H – An auditor or an affiliate of a regulated financial service provider does not—.

(a) contravene any duty of confidentiality owed to the service provider or to its creditors or clients or, if the service provider is an incorporated or unincorporated body, to its members, or

(b) incur any tortious liability, only because the auditor or affiliate complies with a duty imposed on the auditor or affiliate by this Part.

Guidance Note for Auditors of Credit Union issued by the Financial Regulator in July 2004

The following is a full extract of the guidance note for auditors of credit unions issued by the Financial Regulator in July 2004. The guidance note below is in the form of a correspondence letter from the Financial Regulator to credit union auditors and contains an appendix

27th July 2004

Re: Guidance Note for the Auditors of Credit Unions

Dear Sir / Madam,

At a time when the business of credit unions is growing in complexity and value we are concerned to ensure that auditing standards for the movement are operated to the highest possible level.

The purpose of this letter is to set out the requirements of the Irish Financial Services Regulatory Authority [IFSRA] regarding the auditing of credit unions. These requirements incorporate the recommendations contained in the report of the Review Group on Auditing [RGA] of July 2000, on the relationship between IFSRA and the external auditors of credit unions.

The Role of Credit Unions' External Auditors

Independent audit plays an important part in safeguarding the integrity of financial reports by directors of credit unions. The auditor's opinion helps to establish the credibility of the financial statements of credit unions. External auditors also contribute to the regulatory process. IFSRA relies on the external auditor's reports on the financial statements of credit unions.

Section 114 of the Credit Union Act, 1997 (the Act) states the qualifications necessary to be appointed as a credit union auditor. IFSRA requires auditors and the board of directors to ensure that no conflicts of interests arise which may affect the auditor's statutory independence and objectivity. IFSRA requires auditors to be in compliance with their professional ethical and other guidelines in all aspects of their relationship with a credit union. Auditors should be mindful of the resources and expertise necessary to audit credit unions when accepting assignments.

Section 120 of the Act sets out the obligation on the auditor to report to the members, the format and content of the auditor's report, the right of access by the auditor to the books and documents of the credit union and the right to be heard at the annual general meeting. The primary objective of an audit of the financial statements of a credit union is to enable an independent auditor to express an opinion in accordance with the Act. Section 120 [2] of the Act requires that the auditor, before signing his report, shall meet and report to the directors and the members of the Supervisory Committee on the annual accounts and on any matters relating thereto which he considers should be drawn to their attention. [Note Section 120 [5] of the Credit Union Act, 1997 has not been commenced.]

Duty of Auditors to report directly to IFSRA

Auditors have a statutory duty to report directly to IFSRA. Section 122 of the credit union Act, 1997 requires auditors to report, in writing, certain matters which they become aware of during the course of the audit, to IFSRA. These are detailed at appendix 1. Some credit unions may also be authorised under the Investment Intermediaries Act, 1995. Section 33 of the Investment Intermediaries Act, 1995 requires auditors to report, in writing, certain matters to IFSRA. These are detailed at appendix 2. [Note Section 122 [1] [f] of the Credit Union Act, 1997 has not been commenced.]

Recommendations of the Report of the Review Group on Auditing.

The Report of the Review Group on Auditing [RGA] contained certain recommendations regarding increased liaison between IFSRA and the external auditors of financial institutions. IFSRA fully supports these recommendations.

These recommendations include:

The requirement on the external auditors of a financial institution to provide "an annual positive statement" to IFSRA.

Increased liaison with the external auditors [bilateral/trilateral meetings].

The receipt of management letters by IFSRA from the external auditor.

IFSRA now requires that these recommendations, which are detailed in full at appendix 3, be implemented for credit unions commencing with the accounting period ending the 30th September 2004.

Rotation of the Auditor of Credit Unions

Finally it is recommended that in order to enhance the independence and objectivity of the audit process of credit unions there should be rotation of the audit partner responsible for the audit of the credit union every five years. I recognise the need for a transition period and accordingly I propose that full compliance with this recommendation should be implemented not later than the accounting period ending the 30th September 2007.

Should you have any queries in relation to this matter please contact Martin Johnson of this office. [Ph: 4104988, Fax 4104990, e-mail: martin.johnson@ifsra.ie]

Yours sincerely.

_____

Brendan F Logue

Registrar of Credit Unions

c.c. Chairman of the Boards of Credit Unions
c.c. Chairman of the Supervisory Committees of Credit Unions.

Appendix 3

Illustrative wording of a Statutory Duty Confirmation to the Financial Regulator

Title: Head of Function (relevant supervisory department)
The Financial Services Regulatory Authority
P.O. Box 9138
College Green
Dublin 2

Dear [Sir/Madam]:

Statutory Duty Confirmation: Statement by the auditors for [name REGULATED ENTITY] to the Financial Regulator

The letter and attached schedule constitute a report as required by section 27B of the Central Bank Act 1997[15] in relation to our statutory duty to report certain matters to the Financial Regulator, as specified in [insert appropriate reference from list in Appendix 1]. The schedule to this letter lists the reporting periods in which we acted as auditors of [insert name of credit union and related entities if appropriate] and are therefore subject to the statutory duty from [date of signing last statutory duty confirmation or date of appointment if later] to [date of signing current confirmation].[39]

Respective responsibilities of directors and auditors

It is the responsibility of the directors of [name of credit union]

- to take appropriate steps to provide reasonable assurance that the regulated entity complies with applicable legislation and the requirements of the Financial Regulator set out in Guidance Notes, Notices, Handbooks, Codes and other authoritative pronouncements (the Supervisory Requirements);

- to establish arrangements designed to detect non-compliance with the Guidance Notes, Notices, Handbooks, Codes and other authoritative pronouncements (the Supervisory Requirements and to report any breaches to you;

- to report to the Financial Regulator any information which they know or have reasonable cause to believe is of material for the Financial Regulator's supervisory functions.

Our responsibilities are to report to you matters which come to our attention in the course of our work as auditors and are of regulatory concern to you, in accordance with [insert

---

[39] Where the entity has no subsidiaries or close links with other entities the following sentence may be used:
"We acted as auditor of X in the financial year ended [date] and we are therefore subject to the statutory duty from [date of signing last statutory duty confirmation or date of appointment if later] to [date of signing current confirmation].

appropriate reference from list in Appendix 2A] and to report on an annual basis to you in relation to whether circumstances indicating such matters have been identified in the course of our work.

Basis of statement

In discharging our statutory duties to report to you we have had regard to matters identified in [*insert appropriate reference from list in Appendix 2A*][40] In doing so we are required to consider matters of which we have become aware in the capacities as auditors listed in the Annex to this letter.

Statement

[Except as already notified to you on [41] ......], no circumstances have come to our attention, in our capacities described in the schedule attached to this letter, that have given rise to a statutory duty on us to report to you under [*insert appropriate reference from list in Appendix 2A*] .

Our report is prepared solely for the confidential use of the Financial Regulator as required by section 27B of the Central Bank Act 1997[15]. It may not be relied upon by [name of regulated entity] or the Financial Regulator for any other purpose whatsoever. [Name of audit firm] neither owes nor accepts any duty to any other party and shall not be liable for any loss, damage, or expense of whatsoever nature which is caused by reliance on our report.

Yours faithfully

Dated [42]

---

[40] In addition the auditor should refer to Practice Note 19(I) Bank or Practice Note 20(I) Insurers where relevant.

[41] Insert list of reports issued and dates of such reports or delete as appropriate.

[42] Where this confirmation letter is being provided for the first time the period covered is from the date of the previous audit report.

Schedule to Statutory Duty Confirmation: financial institutions to which the firm has acted as appointed auditor.

Capacity	Reporting period	Reference to basis of work
Auditor of [name of financial institution – XYZ Ltd]	Financial year ended	Audit report dated
Auditor of [name of financial institution – ABC Ltd]	Financial year ended	Audit report dated
Auditors of the following bodies closely linked[43] by control to [name of financial institution (s) – XYZ Ltd and ABC Ltd Subsidiary 1 Ltd Subsidiary 2 Ltd	Financial year ended	Audit report dated

---

[43] The statutory duty of auditors of credit institutions, banks and Building Societies, Stock Exchange Member Firms and investment Business Firms extends to other entities with 'close links to the regulated entity. At the time of publication of this guidance, credit unions operate as stand alone entities and therefore are unlikely to have close links with another entity as defined. The term 'Close links' is defined in Regulation 2 of the Post BCCI Regulations. Close links between two or more entities, as defined by Regulation 2 of the Post-BCCI Regulations, arise as a result of factors indicating either — (a) participation: the ownership, direct or by way of control, of 20 per cent or more of the voting rights or capital of an undertaking, or (b) control: the relationship between a parent undertaking and a subsidiary undertaking (including sub-subsidiaries). Additionally, close links exist if there is an arrangement whereby two or more persons are permanently linked to one and the same person by a control relationship. For guidance, see Practice Note 19(I).

Appendix 4

Possible factors that may indicate going concern issues

Capital adequacy ratios

- the credit union operating at or near the limit of its individual capital guidance or limit otherwise set by management under the capital requirements;

- unjustified attempts to reduce the size of the buffer over and above the threshold solvency ratio that management has agreed to operate at;

Operations/profitability indicators

- marked decline in new lending/dealing volumes during the year or subsequently;

- marked decline in new business margins;

- severe overcapacity in markets leading to low pricing as well as low volumes;

- significant increase in loan defaults or seizure of collateral;

- excessive exposures to troubled industry sectors;

- unusually aggressive dealing positions and/or regular breaches of dealing or lending limits;

- redundancies, layoffs or failure to replace natural wastage of personnel;

- A high cost to income ratio

- Low return on assets

- Overtrading

Liquidity indicators

- low ratio of liquid assets to total relevant liabilities;

- mismatch between loans being issued and shares in the credit union;

- anticipated defaults on loan repayments;

- expected cash flows;

Reputational and other indicators

- adverse publicity which could lead to loss of confidence or reputation, including fines or public censure by a regulatory body;

- urgent attempts to remove assets from the balance sheet, apparently involving material loss of profits or at significant expense;

- deferral of investment plans or capitalisation of expenditure.

Appendix 5

Protection For Disclosure Under Common Law

1. In cases of doubt, common law provides protection for disclosing certain matters to a proper authority in the public interest.

2. Common law precedent in the UK[44] indicates that a degree of protection exists for disclosures of certain matters to an appropriate authority in the public interest. This UK case law which is only of persuasive authority in the Republic of Ireland, indicates that accounting firms are protected from the risk of liability from breach of confidence or defamation under general law even when carrying out work which is not clearly undertaken in the capacity of auditor provided that:

    •   in the case of breach of confidence:

        (a) disclosure is made in the public interest; and

        (b) such disclosure is made to an appropriate body or person; and

        (c) there is no malice motivating the disclosure; and

    •   in the case of defamation

        (a) the information disclosed was obtained in a proper capacity; and

        (b) there is no malice motivating the disclosure.

    This principle of common law has received limited consideration in the courts in the Republic of Ireland.[45]

3. The same protection is given even if there is only a reasonable suspicion that non-compliance with law or regulations has occurred. Provided that it can be demonstrated that an accounting firm, in disclosing a matter in the public interest, has acted reasonably and in good faith, it would not be held by the court to be in breach of duty to the institution even if, an investigation or prosecution having occurred, it were found that there had been no breach of law or regulation.

4. When reporting to proper authorities in the public interest, it is important that, in order to retain the protection of qualified privilege, auditors report only to one who has a

---

[44] Initial Services and Putterill [1967] 3 All ER 145, Garthside –v- Outram [1856] 26 LJ Ch 113, British Steel Corp –v- Granada Television Ltd [1981] 1 All ER 417, Lion Laboratories Limited –v- Evans [1985] QB 526, AG –v- Guardian Newspapers Limited (No 2) [1988] 3 All ER 545, PriceWaterhouse (a firm) – v- BCCI Holdings (Luxembourg) S.A & Others [1992] BCLC 579.

[45] National Irish Bank v RTE [1998] 2 IR 465. See also Glackin – v- TSB and McInerney [1993] 3 IR 55 where consideration was given to the position of a statutory obligation to provide information where there was no explicit statutory protection against breach of duty.

FINANCIAL REPORTING COUNCIL

proper interest to receive the information. The Financial Regulator is the proper authority in the case of a bank.

5. 'Public interest' is a concept which is not capable of general definition. Each situation must be considered individually. In general circumstances, matters to be taken into account when considering whether disclosure is justified in the public interest may include:

    •   the extent to which the suspected non-compliance with law or regulations is likely to affect members of the public;

    •   whether the directors (or equivalent) have rectified the matter or are taking, or are likely to take, effective corrective action;

    •   the extent to which non-disclosure is likely to enable the suspected non-compliance with law or regulations to recur with impunity;

    •   the gravity of the matter;

    •   whether there is a general management ethos within the entity of disregarding law or regulations;

    •   the weight of evidence and the degree of the auditor's suspicion that there has been an instance of non-compliance with laws or regulations.

6. Determination of where the balance of public interest lies requires careful consideration. Auditors and reporting accountants need to weigh the public interest in maintaining confidential client relationships against the public interest in disclosure to a proper authority and to use their professional judgment to determine whether their misgivings justify them in carrying the matter further or are too insubstantial to deserve report.

7. In cases where it is uncertain whether the statutory duty requires an accounting firm to communicate a matter to the Financial Regulator in its capacity as supervisor of banks, it is possible that the firm may be able to rely on the defence of disclosure in the public interest if it communicates a matter to the Financial Regulator which could properly be regarded as having material significance in conformity with the guidance in ISA (UK and Ireland) 250 Section B and this Practice Note, although firms may wish to seek legal advice in such circumstances.

Appendix 6

Definitions

Abbreviation Used	Description
ASB	Accounting Standards Board
APB	Auditing Practices Board
CBA 1997	Central Bank Act 1997
CBAs	Central Bank Acts
CBFSAI Act 2003	Central Bank and Financial Services Authority of Ireland Act 2003
CBFSAI Act 2004	Central Bank and Financial Services Authority of Ireland Act 2004
CJA	Criminal Justice Act 1994, as amended
Companies Acts	Companies Acts 1963 – 2006 and all regulations to be construed as one with those Acts
Credit Union	A "credit union" in the context of this Practice Note is a society registered as a credit union under the Credit Union Act, I997 as amended ("the CU Act 1997"). A society which, prior to 1st October 1997, was registered as a credit union under the Industrial and Provident Societies Acts, 1893 to 1978, is deemed to be registered as a Credit Union under the CU Act 1997. A credit union is a body corporate with perpetual succession which is known by its registered name.
CU Act 1997	The Credit Union Act 1997
CUAR	Credit Union Annual Return
CUDA	Credit Union Development Association
Financial Regulator	The Irish Financial Services Regulatory Authority, an autonomous entity within the Central Bank and Financial Services Authority of Ireland having responsibility for financial sector regulation and consumer protection. Established 1 May 2003
FRS	Financial Reporting Standards issued by the ASB
IFAC	International Federation of Accountants
IFRS	International Financial Reporting Standards issued by the International Accounting Standards Board
IIA 1995	Investment Intermediaries Act 1995

Irish GAAP	Generally accepted accounting practices in Ireland – accounting standards issued by the ASB and promulgated by the Institute of Chartered Accountants in Ireland
ISA(UK and Ireland)	International Standards on Auditing (UK and Ireland) issued by the APB
The League	The Irish League of Credit Unions

PROFESSIONAL SCEPTICISM

ESTABLISHING A COMMON UNDERSTANDING AND REAFFIRMING ITS CENTRAL ROLE IN DELIVERING AUDIT QUALITY

CONTENTS

Section 1 – Introduction

This paper sets out the APB's considered views on the nature of auditor scepticism and its role in the audit. Given the significance of scepticism to the quality of individual audits, and to the value of audit more generally, we believe that this document is an important point of reference on this topic and one which we hope all auditors will consider with great care.

It is written in an unusual format for an APB document, being much more discursive than is customary and drawing analogies from a diverse group of areas. This is because we believe that what is meant by scepticism needs to be more broadly understood and that drawing these analogies will assist in broadening that understanding. We are also keen to stimulate and provide input to an international debate on the issue of scepticism and believe that this broader and more discursive approach will provide a valuable input to that debate.

This document builds on the APB Discussion Paper published in August 2010 'Auditor Scepticism: Raising the Bar' and the subsequent Feedback Paper published in March 2011, which summarised the comments received and outlined the actions that the APB, and other parts of the FRC, intended to take in light of the responses received.

The Feedback Paper noted the following[1]:

- Responses suggested a wide range of views about what the initial mindset should be and raised concerns for the APB that there is a lack of consensus about the nature of professional scepticism and its role in the conduct of an audit.

- The APB did not accept that the auditor's role is limited to ensuring that management have appropriate evidence to support its assertions if this means accepting the evidence management present without subjecting it to robust challenge and comparison to alternative sources of evidence.

- The APB questioned whether a 'neutral mindset', or indeed just an 'inquiring mind', is appropriate for an auditor. The auditor's mindset is applied during audit planning to assess the risk of misstatement of the financial statements and such risk assessments determine the nature and extent of audit evidence to be obtained. It is also applied in assessing the validity of accounting estimates that are subject both to significant uncertainties and to considerable management judgment.

The first of the areas in which the APB proposed to undertake further work was ensuring that there is a consistent understanding of the nature of professional scepticism and its role in the conduct of an audit.

Section 2 considers the philosophical origins of scepticism in ancient Greece and how it later influenced scepticism in the scientific method that began to flourish in the 17th

---

[1] See 'Auditor scepticism: Raising the bar: Feedback Statement' – March 2011
http://www.frc.org.uk/apb/publications/pub2343.html.

Century. The relationship between scepticism and the disposition to believe or disbelieve is explored as well as the influences of evidence and behaviours on that disposition.

Section 3 seeks to provide insight into the mind-set required to develop the audit strategy and plan and to evaluate the audit evidence obtained, by demonstrating how another learning – science – has developed a sceptical approach that now commands respect.

Section 4 seeks to provide further insight into the mindset of the auditor by considering the nature of the agency relationships, and the resultant need for assurance, that gave rise to early auditing traditions in manorial households from the 14th Century.

Section 5 sets out the APB's conclusions from the foregoing analysis as to what a sceptical audit looks like. It suggests that professional scepticism is the cornerstone of audit quality – it defines the quality of each audit judgment and through these the overall effectiveness of the audit in meeting the needs of shareholders and other stakeholders.

Section 6 sets out the APB's views about the conditions that are necessary for auditors to demonstrate the appropriate degree of professional scepticism. It highlights the APB's expectations of individual auditors, engagement teams, audit firms and of the supporting role that can be played by audit committees, management and others.

Finally, Section 7 sets out how the APB proposes to take these matters forward.

Section 2 – Exploring the roots of scepticism and identifying lessons for its role in the conduct of an audit

Scepticism is derived from the Greek word "σκέψις" (skepsis), meaning[2]: *examination, inquiry into, hesitation or doubt, especially of the Sceptics or Pyrrhone philosophers.* Greek philosophical Scepticism was a school of thought from the 5th Century BC that doubted the certainty of knowledge. From this developed the philosophical viewpoint that it is not possible to gain certain knowledge (truth) about the natural world.

Scepticism in Greek philosophy

Beyond understanding the etymological basis for the modern term "scepticism", what more can we learn from early Greek philosophical scepticism?

- First, the essence of scepticism is doubt and that doubt stimulates informed challenge and inquiry. The sceptics' doubts arose from the many conflicting views that persisted about fundamental issues. Their doubt stimulated them to challenge conventional wisdom and to inquire after a better understanding of the nature of knowledge.

- Second, in the face of doubt they would suspend their judgment about the truth.

- Third, in its extreme forms scepticism is not pragmatic as it may lead to the conclusion that no judgments about the truth can be made[3].

The disposition to believe or disbelieve and its conditioning influences

Today, scepticism commonly means 'doubt as to the truth of some assertion or supposed fact'[4]. Doubt is unbelief, whose antonyms include belief and trust[5]. Neither doubt nor trust need be absolute. Each has expression in different degrees. Uncertainty lies between them and absolute trust (belief) and absolute distrust (disbelief) are at their extremes. Doubt, trust and uncertainty are passive concepts – states of mind. They describe an individual's disposition to believe or disbelieve an assertion.

The actual level of doubt or trust in the state of mind conditions the individual's response. When the levels of both trust and doubt are low, there is uncertainty which either may result

---

[2] Liddell & Scott Greek-English Lexicon.

[3] Bertrand Russell, in his 1958 book: "The Will to Doubt" illustrates such "heroic" scepticism by retelling the following: *"A story is told of Pyrrho, the founder of Pyrrhonism (which was the old name for scepticism). He maintained that we never know enough to be sure that one course of action is wiser than another. In his youth, when he was taking his constitutional one afternoon, he saw his teacher in philosophy (from whom he had imbibed his principles) with his head stuck in a ditch, unable to get out. After contemplating him for some time, he walked on, maintaining that there was no sufficient ground for thinking he would do any good by pulling the man out. Others, less sceptical, effected a rescue, and blamed Pyrrho for his heartlessness. But his teacher, true to his principles, praised him for his consistency.*

[4] The Shorter Oxford English Dictionary.

[5] See Roget's Thesaurus of synonyms and antonyms: categories 484 (Belief) and 485 (Unbelief; Doubt).

in a passive response – the indefinite suspension of judgment – or may stimulate an active inquiry to pursue the truth or falseness of the assertion. The results of that inquiry will further condition the state of mind and the process may be repeated. Only if and when a state of mind of trust or doubt is sufficiently high will the active response – acceptance or rejection of belief in the assertion – ensue.

The disposition to believe or disbelieve an assertion may be conditioned by many influences. These include not only the results of inquiry but also potentially the biases of the individual (whether conscious or sub-conscious) and the individual's perceptions and assessments of their self-interest. These other conditioning influences must be filtered out if objective truth is to be attained.

In the context of audit judgments, it may be helpful to understand the implications of the behavioural rules ('heuristics') underlying human decision-making and judgment processes. A number of heuristics have been proposed to help explain these processes, especially in the face of complex problems or incomplete information. It is also thought that they may, in some circumstances, introduce systematic errors or biases into these processes.

One illustration of these ideas may be found in a recent academic paper[6], which shows that people are less likely to adjust their beliefs in response to evidence that contradicts their optimistic beliefs than to evidence that contradicts their pessimistic beliefs.

What is needed to counteract this is a mechanism to encourage a structured consideration of the alternative point of view. One example of such a mechanism being applied in a financial services context is 'reverse stress testing'. In this form of stress testing, the directors consider what it would take to make the entity fail and then assess the evidence as to the likelihood of those circumstances arising.

Evidence based theories of knowledge and scientific scepticism

Later Sceptics were more pragmatic, arguing that there were ways of approaching (even if not quite attaining) the absolute truth. The Empirical school of thought proposed that the only or primary source of knowledge is experience gained through the senses. It therefore emphasised the role of empirical (observed) evidence in inducing knowledge rather than deducing knowledge from innate ideas and traditions.

Empiricism was highly influential in the development of science and the scientific method in the 17th Century. Scientific scepticism doubts the veracity of assertions that are not supported by empirical evidence that is reproducible and therefore seeks to exclude other influences from the scientific search for truth.

---

[6] See: *How unrealistic optimism is maintained in the face of reality*, by Sharot, Korn and Dolan, in Nature Neuroscience, Nov 2011. This and earlier research considering the impact of new evidence on existing beliefs is discussed in a recent Research Paper from Societe Generale: *In defence of the doom merchants: when hearing isn't listening*, Jan 2012 at: http://www.frc.org.uk/images/uploaded/documents/Societe%20Generale%20Research%20Paper%20January%202012.pdf. The Paper suggests that people have a natural tendency to take note of the evidence which backs their own theories and to ignore evidence which contradicts them. If anything, this tendency is exacerbated when they are exhorted to try harder.

Evidence, trust and agency in the audit process

An audit is an evidence-based process to assess and report on the truth and fairness of the financial statements prepared by the directors to whom capital resources are entrusted by the shareholders. The audit is entrusted to another agent of the shareholders – the auditor.

This description refers to two features of an audit which are relevant to scepticism – the evidence-based nature of the audit and the entrustment and agency relationships inherent in the audit. The role of scepticism in relation to each of these is explored further below. The evidence-based nature of the process suggests some parallels with, and is explored in the context of, the scientific method and scientific scepticism in Section 3. In Section 4, lessons about the expression of professional scepticism are also identified by considering the nature of the entrustment and agency relationships and the need for assurance that gave rise to the tradition of auditing servants in the manorial estates of the fourteenth century in the origins of the modern audit in the UK.

Section 3 – Scientific scepticism and the scientific method

The scientific method seeks to understand the causes and effects of natural processes by:

- **Empirical observation** of their behaviours in different conditions;

- Postulating how they work (**constructing theories** of cause and effect that are consistent with the observations) – an approach that relies on inductive logic.

- Predicting effects that would necessarily follow from the truth of a theory in specific conditions (**constructing hypotheses**) – an approach that relies on deductive logic.

- **Testing** those hypotheses by considering not only what evidence would support them but also what evidence would falsify them – accordingly, experiments are designed and performed to find such evidence.

- Each step of the process is **transparent and repeatable,** subject to the critical review of other scientists and capable of being challenged and retested by them.

- In the development of scientific knowledge in a new area, there may be several competing theories, each of which has survived hypothesis testing. The advancement of a theory to the status of accepted scientific knowledge requires a **'critical experiment'**, one capable of providing evidence that will prove the superiority of one theory over all the other competing theories.

This process can disprove a postulated theory but cannot absolutely prove it. If testing falsifies a hypothesis, then theories are reassessed in light of the new observations and if necessary new ones are postulated. A theory that survives rigorous testing remains plausible, for the time being. Scientific knowledge is therefore dynamic and constantly subject to challenge.

Prior to the development of the scientific method, knowledge of the natural world was largely based on accepted ancient wisdom (axiomatic truths) and advanced by developing consequential "knowledge" by logical deduction (the deductive method). A critical development in the evolution of the scientific method was the acceptance that there are no axiomatic truths that can be observed and that there is a continuing need to question and challenge all matters that may appear to be so.

Robert Boyle is widely recognised as the father of modern chemistry and an early proponent of the scientific method. His treatise on the new approach is aptly called 'The Sceptical Chymist'[7].

Scepticism in the scientific method can be described as a <u>systematic form of continual informed questioning</u> that requires the scientist:

---

[7] Robert Boyle, 1661: The Sceptical Chymist: or Chymico-Physical Doubts & Paradoxes Touching the Spagyrist's Principles Commonly call'd Hypostatical As they are wont to be Propos'd and Defended by the Generality of Alchemists.

- To critically appraise existing theories, actively looking for alternative plausible mechanisms of cause and effect that are consistent with their rigorous assessment of the empirical (observed) evidence;

- To undertake experiments that are repeatable and transparent, to look for evidence that contradicts rather than supports the validity of any given theory; and

- To suspend judgment about the validity of any given theory (ie to defer making an active decision to believe or disbelieve it) until it has both survived destructive testing and has been subjected to critical experiments the evidence from which makes it is possible to conclude that one theory is superior to all other current plausible theories.

There are many parallels between the scientific method and the audit and, whilst this analogy should, of course, not be taken too far, at a certain level there is much to learn from a consideration of the nature of scientific scepticism and the role it plays in the conduct of the scientific method. Scientific scepticism is the backbone of the scientific method, influencing every judgment in the process of learning and ultimately supporting the whole body of scientific knowledge.

However, the subject matters of scientific and audit inquiry are different in nature. The subject matter of Science is knowledge of the natural world, which experience shows to ordinarily behave in a systematic way. The subject matter of auditing is the outputs from the business performance and reporting systems of the entity, which though usually intended to operate systematically often do not as they are subject to the vagaries of external influences, as well as human error and fraud.

In science, the potential variables are identified and can be controlled and varied individually under laboratory conditions. In the audit, they cannot and the outputs of the business performance and reporting systems of the entity must be observed in real world (multivariate) conditions.

Notwithstanding these limitations to the analogy between the audit and the scientific method, elements of the scientific method suggest critical audit activities which will underpin appropriate scepticism in the audit:

- Empirical observation *suggests* developing a good understanding of the business of the audited entity and of the environment;

- Constructing falsifiable hypotheses *suggests* actively considering that material misstatements may exist and designing audit tests to identify them, rather than only considering how well the evidence obtained by management supports their conclusion that there are none; and

- Transparency and repeatability *suggest* the importance of documentation in underpinning transparency and repeatability of the audit work to internal reviewers and to external inspectors.

The comparison says less about how far the auditor should go in pursuing these activities:

- When should the active search for risks of material misstatement stop?

- How far should the auditor's understanding be pursued?

- How much testing and stress testing should the auditor undertake?

- When is the evidence sufficient?

The scientific analogy suggests there is no absolute level to which such matters should be pursued. Scientific scepticism is pursued up to the point where other similarly objective scientists would want to go before they accept or reject a hypothesis. In the scientific field, acceptance of a hypothesis only occurs when the level of trust in that hypothesis is approaching virtual certainty. This may not be the most appropriate point to which professional scepticism should be pursued in the audit. This is considered further in the next section in the context of the historical origins of the modern audit in the UK.

Section 4 – The origins of the modern audit

The origins of the modern audit can be seen in the tradition of auditing household servants in manorial estates that developed from the fourteenth century[8]. The auditor was the most trusted servant in the household and all other servants were required to account to the auditor for the resources entrusted to them.

In its simplest form, an account was required from each household servant of all money and other assets entrusted to them – they were "charged" with the assets when placed in their care and "discharged" when the auditor had heard and accepted their account.

When free incorporation joint stock companies were established in the Joint Stock Companies Act of 1844, there were default provisions for auditors to be appointed, that built on these traditions. Under the default provisions, at least one of the auditors should be appointed by the shareholders, their fees should be paid by the company but set by a government agency (the Commissioners of the Treasury) as they saw fit, and their report should be made publicly available. The auditor was neither required to be a shareholder nor a professional accountant but often was a shareholder and frequently employed professional accountants to assist them.

The Joint Stock Companies Act of 1856 enhanced the earlier default provisions to specifically allow the auditor to employ accountants to assist them at the company's expense and to prohibit the auditor from being a director or an officer of the company and from having any interest in any transaction of the company other than as a shareholder. The absolute requirement that companies should have an audit (initially just for joint stock banks but later extended to all companies) as opposed to optional default provisions, originated in the 1879 Companies Act following the collapse of the City Bank of Glasgow. In time, the practice of appointing shareholders as auditors fell away and public accountants were employed to undertake the role directly.

Looking back, it would seem that, in its origin, the audit was essentially a check, carried out on behalf of a principal by their trusted associate or agent, on the fidelity of other agents to whom the principal's resources were entrusted. The trust that existed between principal and auditor was a critical ingredient, if not the critical ingredient of the audit. The importance of professional skills only came later. The whole rationale for the audit was that the principal could not assume, and therefore sought assurance about, the fidelity of those to whom their assets were entrusted.

This may suggest how far the auditor should pursue professional scepticism in the audit. The strong bond of trust between the principal and the auditor and the principal's need for assurance about the fidelity of those to whom they had entrusted their assets would have determined the mindset of the auditor. That would have guided the appropriate degree of scepticism in the auditor when holding a hearing to question those entrusted with the principal's assets and to assess whether they had given a proper account of their handling of those assets. They would have asked the questions they would expect their principal to

---

[8] See *Be careful what you wish for: How accountants and Congress created the problem of auditor independence*, 2004, Sean M. O'Connor at: http://www.bc.edu/dam/files/schools/law/lawreviews/journals/bclawr/45_4/01_FMS.htm.

ask, they would have challenged where they would expect their principal to challenge and they would have pursued matters until they were satisfied that the evidence would satisfy their principal.

This is perhaps a fair lens through which to understand the necessary degree of scepticism in the modern audit. What would the shareholders (and other stakeholders) expect the auditor to ask, what matters would they expect them to challenge and what evidence would they need to satisfy those challenges?

Whilst fidelity may have been the issue in the 19th Century and much of the 20th Century (and remains an issue in the 21st Century), the development and increased complexity of business activity, and the increased size and reach of such businesses, combined with the arrival of the technological age mean that there are many other areas in relation to which shareholders (and other users) seek information and reassurance. For example, misalignment of their personal interests may simply lead to misalignment of risk taking appetite between the directors and shareholders.

This suggests that whilst the sceptical mindset is a constant, the degree of action taken by a sceptical auditor (by way of inquiry, challenge and testing) is responsive both to the expectations of shareholders (and other stakeholders) and to what emerges as the audit proceeds. This is the 'sliding scale' that was referred to in *Auditor Scepticism: Raising the Bar*.

Because of the need to consider their expectations, the perspective of shareholders and other stakeholders (as users) is embedded in the auditing standards in relation to materiality, and scepticism should embed that perspective in the making of all audit judgments. Against this background, the APB believes that when undertaking a modern audit the following factors accentuate the need for the auditor to be especially vigilant and aware of his or her responsibilities for the exercise of professional scepticism:

- There is potential for auditors not to be sceptical or thought not to be sceptical because they are engaged and paid by the company in a way that is relatively detached from shareholders. In addition, they have little, if any, direct contact with shareholders throughout the audit process; as a result, shareholders have no way of observing, and thereby gaining trust in, the audit process. This emphasises the need for strong governance generally and, in particular, the importance of the responsibility that audit committees have in both assessing and communicating to investors whether the auditors have executed a high quality, sceptical audit;

- Auditors necessarily have strong working relationships with management and audit committees, which may lead them to develop trust that may lead to either a lack of, or reduced, scepticism; and

- The audit firms' business models encourage a culture of building strong relationships with audited entities. This introduces the moral hazard of the auditor putting his or her interests ahead of those of shareholders and could lead the audit firm and the auditor to develop trust or self-interest motivations that may compromise either their objectivity or willingness to challenge management to the extent required.

It is perhaps not surprising that auditors often refer to the audited entity as the 'client', given the strength of these relationships and the all but formal appointment of the auditor by the directors and not by the shareholders. However, trust in management may compromise the auditor's exercise of scepticism because that trust may colour his/her judgement as to when and where a sceptical approach is required. It is important to lean against unjustified trust developing, just as it is important to address threats to the auditor's objectivity that may arise from the provision of non-audit services – it is interesting to note in this context that the auditor originally was not permitted to have any interest in any transaction with the company.

The factors described above are widely recognised to pose challenges to the reality and perception of auditors' professional integrity (including their objectivity and independence). The need to address these challenges gives rise to a variety of responses that seek to lean against them, including the responsibilities, liabilities and disclosures relating to the audit and the auditor established in the law and professional standards, including the Ethical Standards. This is also one of the principal reasons for the need for the application and demonstration of appropriate professional scepticism in the audit.

Despite the increasing role of audit committees as independent non-executive directors in monitoring and challenging the entity's financial information and controls (in effect as the representatives of the shareholders), there is also a risk that audit committees' views may be seen too readily by the auditor as a surrogate for those of the shareholders. Just addressing the concerns of the audit committee does not necessarily amount to meeting the expectations of shareholders (and other stakeholders).

For all of these reasons, the rigorous assessment of when, and the degree to which, professional scepticism is required is fundamental to an effective audit.

Section 5 – Conclusions about professional scepticism in the audit

In the growth and development of a living thing, the expression of its DNA in the formation of its cells defines its essence and its effectiveness in meeting the challenges of its environment. In the words of Richard Dawkins[9]:

DNA neither cares nor knows. DNA just is. And we dance to its music.

In the same way, the expression of professional scepticism by the audit team defines the essence of the particular audit. It defines the quality of each audit judgment and, through these, the overall effectiveness of the audit in addressing the challenges it faces in meeting the needs of shareholders (and other stakeholders) who rely on it. The reality and perception of the expression of professional scepticism define and underpin the confidence that others place in the audit and in turn the confidence they place in the audited financial statements.

The preceding analysis suggests that the appropriate application of professional scepticism in the audit requires a mindset which rigorously questions and challenges management's assertions with a degree of doubt that reflects the expectations of shareholders (and other stakeholders) for whose benefit it is performed. All judgments made in the course of the audit should be founded on the perspective of the shareholders (and other stakeholders). That mindset demands the sort of hard evidence – to back each audit judgment and, ultimately, the board's assertion that the financial statements give a true and fair view – that would be convincing and persuasive to shareholders (and other stakeholders), given the auditor's risk assessment.

The analysis suggests that in an appropriately sceptical audit:

- The auditor's risk assessment process should involve a <u>critical appraisal</u> of management's assertions, <u>actively looking for risks</u> of material misstatement.

  These may arise due to fraud or error and may reflect weaknesses in the design or the operation of management's system for controlling and reporting the entity's financial position and performance (such that relevant matters are not identified, or are not adequately controlled or reported, or that the design has not been implemented and operated effectively[10]).

- The auditor develops a high degree of knowledge of the audited entity's business and the environment in which it operates, sufficient to enable it to make its risk assessment through its own fresh and independent eyes rather than through the eyes of management.

- This enables the auditor to make informed challenge of consensus views and to consider the possible incidence of low probability high impact events. The

---

[9] Richard Dawkins: River Out of Eden: A Darwinian View of Life (1995), 133.

[10] This is not to suggest that the auditor must always test the operating effectiveness of the financial reporting system, rather than taking a substantive approach and testing the outputs from that system.

alternative would give rise to the risk of what is known in science as "hypothesis bias" which is an example of "group-think". The challenges in acquiring sufficient knowledge and experience should not be underestimated, especially in relation to complex business models. The traditional pyramid structure of the audit team may not always be appropriate and different models may need to be explored, such as including experienced business people on the team.

- The auditor designs audit procedures to <u>consider actively if there is any evidence that would contradict</u> management assertions not only to consider the extent to which management has identified evidence that is consistent with them. The opposite of a sceptical audit might be one in which the auditor merely rationalises and documents management's assertions.

- The auditor has strong skills in making evidence-based judgments and suspends judgment about whether the financial statements do or do not give a true and fair view until satisfied that:

  ○ There has been sufficient inquiry and challenge;

  ○ Sufficient testing of management's assertions has been undertaken;

  ○ The quality of the resulting evidence obtained has been critically appraised and judged by the auditor to be sufficiently persuasive; and

  ○ Where there are plausible alternative treatments of an item in the financial statements (such as different valuation bases), an assessment has been made as to whether one is superior and whether sufficient disclosure of the alternatives has been given, in order to give a true and fair view.

- The auditor approaches and documents audit judgments and audit review processes in a manner that facilitates challenge and demonstrates the rigour of that challenge.

The auditor's documentation of audit judgments is conclusive rather than conclusionary and therefore always sets out not only the auditor's conclusion but also their rationale for the conclusion, relating it to the nature of the challenges raised in the underlying work and reviews, the strength of the evidence obtained and the perspective of shareholders (and other stakeholders). The auditor needs strong skills in logical argument to do this effectively.

Section 6 – Fostering conditions necessary for auditors to demonstrate the appropriate degree of professional scepticism

The application of an appropriate degree of professional scepticism is a crucial skill for auditors. Unless auditors are prepared to challenge management's assertions they will not be able to confirm with confidence that a company's financial statements present a true and fair view.

The APB believes that in order to demonstrate the value of the audit, the auditor should perform a sceptical audit, evidence the exercise of appropriate scepticism in the audit documentation and convince audit committees and ultimately the shareholders (and other stakeholders) that it has done so.

The challenge for firms is to identify, develop and retain people with the necessary skills and to deploy them appropriately. It also involves nurturing the conditions that allow professional scepticism to flourish.

The prospects for a sceptical audit are likely to be enhanced if the environment in which the auditor operates also recognises and supports the important role that scepticism plays in the audit.

The APB considers that the conditions necessary for auditors to demonstrate the appropriate degree of professional scepticism are likely to include the following.

Individual auditors

- Develop a good understanding of the entity and its business.

- Have a questioning mind and are willing to challenge management assertions.

- Assess critically the information and explanations obtained in the course of their work and corroborate them.

- Seek to understand management motivations for possible misstatement of the financial statements.

- Investigate the nature and cause of deviations or misstatements identified and avoid jumping to conclusions without appropriate audit evidence.

- Are alert for evidence that is inconsistent with other evidence obtained or calls into question the reliability of documents and responses to inquiries.

- Have the confidence to challenge management and the persistence to follow things through to a conclusion – even if predisposed to agree with management's assertion, the auditor should actively consider the alternative views and challenge management to demonstrate that they are not more appropriate.

Engagement teams

- Have good business knowledge and experience.

- Actively consider in what circumstances management numbers may be misstated, whether due to fraud or error, and the possible sources of misstatement, notwithstanding existing knowledge and relationships.

- Develop a good understanding of the entity and its business in order to provide a basis for identifying unusual events or transactions and share information on a regular basis.

- Partners and managers are actively involved in assessing risk and planning the audit procedures to be performed – they think about the changes that are taking place in the entity and its environment and plan audit tests that are responsive to them.

- Partners and managers actively lead and participate in audit team planning meetings to discuss the susceptibility of the entity's financial statements to material misstatement including through fraud and the misuse of related parties.

- Partners and managers are accessible to other staff during the audit and encourage them to consult with them on a timely basis.

- Engagement teams document their key audit judgments and conclusions, especially those reported to the audit committee, in a way that clearly demonstrates that they have exercised an appropriate degree of challenge to management and professional scepticism. In particular, the reasons why the audit team concurs with management's assertions are clearly articulated in a way that, where appropriate, discusses the appropriateness of reasonably credible alternative views and the reasons why they have not been adopted.

- Partners and managers bring additional scepticism to the audit through taking the steps necessary to carry out, face to face where appropriate, a diligent challenge and review of the audit work performed, and the adequacy of the documentation prepared, by other members of the engagement team.

Audit firms

- The culture within the firm emphasises the importance of:

  ○ understanding and pursuing the perspective of the shareholders (and other stakeholders) of the audited entity in making audit judgments;

  ○ coaching less experienced staff to foster appropriate scepticism;

  ○ sharing experiences about difficult audit judgments within the firm;

  ○ consultation with others about difficult audit judgments; and

- ○ supporting audit partners when they need to take and communicate difficult audit judgements.

- Scepticism is embedded in the firm's training and competency frameworks used for evaluating and rewarding partner and staff performance.

- The firm requires rigorous engagement quality control reviews that challenge engagement teams' judgments and conclusions.

- Firm methodologies and review processes emphasise the importance of, and provide practical support for auditors in:

  - ○ developing a thorough understanding of the entity's business and its environment, sufficient to enable the auditor to carry out a robust risk assessment through their own fresh eyes;

  - ○ identifying issues early in the planning cycle to allow adequate time for them to be investigated and resolved;

  - ○ rigorously taking such steps as are appropriate to the scale and complexity of the financial reporting systems, to identify unusual transactions;

  - ○ changing risk assessments, materiality and the audit plan in response to audit findings;

  - ○ documenting audit judgments in a conclusive rather than a conclusionary manner and therefore setting out not only the conclusion but also the rationale for the conclusion, relating it to the nature of the challenges

  - ○ raised in the underlying work and reviews, the strength of the evidence obtained and the perspective of shareholders (and other stakeholders);

  - ○ raising matters with the Audit Committee (or those charged with governance) in relation to which the auditor believes the perspective of shareholders (and other stakeholders) about the treatment or disclosure of the matter in the financial statements or related narrative reports could well be different from that adopted by the entity; and

  - ○ ensuring that the disclosures relating to such matters are carefully assessed to ensure that those of relevance to shareholders (and other stakeholders) are sufficient and appropriate in the circumstances, having regard to the auditor's consideration of the true and fair view[11].

---

[11] See the FRC document: *True and Fair – July 2011* at:
http://www.frc.org.uk/images/uploaded/documents/Paper%20True%20and%20Fair1.pdf.

The role of Audit Committees and management

Whilst it is the responsibility of the auditor to ensure that an appropriate degree of professional scepticism is applied in an audit, the Audit Committee and management can have a significant influencing role.

The Audit Committee's role includes overseeing the integrity of financial reporting and the related processes (including internal financial controls, the independence and objectivity of the external auditor and the effectiveness of the audit process). In this role, the APB believes that Audit Committees should seek to foster appropriate professional scepticism in the external audit, for example, through:

- Promoting the development of a culture within the entity which elicits a constructive response from management and staff to auditor challenge;

- Challenging whether the auditor has developed an adequate understanding of the business and its environment and provided an appropriately informed fresh perspective in making its risk assessment;

- Ensuring that, where management and auditor have resolved either contentious issues or issues that involve significant judgment, these are brought to the audit committee's attention; and

- Seeking to understand in relation to issues brought to their attention (including issues where management and auditor agree the position) whether or not an appropriate degree of challenge was exercised by the auditor – for example, by demanding an explanation of the auditor's rationale for particular conclusions, what alternatives were considered and why the specific judgment was considered to be the most appropriate of the alternatives.

The APB believes that this is consistent with the FRC's *Effective Company Stewardship* proposals[12], under which it is proposed that Audit Committees should produce fuller reports for the Board, in particular setting out their advice on the integrity of the Annual Report and explaining how they discharged their responsibilities for this and other aspects of their remit (such as their oversight of the external audit process and appointment of external auditors). Taken together with the proposal for Boards to discuss these matters in the Annual Report, the effect should be to ensure that the Annual Report demonstrates that the audit addressed those matters of most interest to shareholders and other stakeholders with appropriate challenge and scepticism.

---

[12] See http://www.frc.org.uk/about/effcompsteward.cfm.

Section 7 – Taking these matters forward

The main purpose of this document is to explain the APB's views on professional scepticism and to encourage auditors to apply its principles in executing high quality sceptical audits and in documenting and demonstrating that they have done so. The APB has also considered the definition of professional scepticism and the extent and manner in which it has been dealt with in the ISAs (UK & I) and in ISQC 1 (UK &I), in light of the conclusions drawn in this Paper.

Although these standards contain many elements[13] that support the understanding of professional scepticism developed in this Paper, it is also possible for an auditor to follow the 'letter' of the standards without conducting a truly sceptical audit. The APB acknowledges that these standards may well need to be improved further to reflect better some of the conclusions reflected in this Paper and to be clearer about the performance, documentation and communication of professional scepticism.

Accordingly, whilst it has concluded that in taking these matters forward, the immediate emphasis should be on encouraging auditors and others to deliver a step change in behaviours that will achieve consistency in the manner in which professional scepticism is exercised in the conduct of their audits, it also intends to seek to influence the IAASB to enhance the auditing standards in due course.

The APB therefore proposes to:

- Stimulate debate and acceptance by stakeholders of the conclusions set out in this Paper about the nature and role of professional scepticism in the audit;

- Encourage the auditing profession and the audit firms to consider the implications of these conclusions for their business models and culture and for their approach to audits and to implement such changes as are necessary to respond to the challenges they identify – including the need to reflect the perspective of shareholders (and other stakeholders) in exercising their professional judgment;

- Promote these conclusions with Audit Committee members and management to encourage them to recognise and act on the important contribution that they can make to support the appropriate exercise of professional scepticism;

- Promote with those preparing the financial statements and Annual Report the benefits of open communication and consideration of the key judgments involved in doing so and in responding to the challenges raised in the audit; and

- Promote the conclusions set out in this Paper internationally, with a view to identifying ways in which the International Standards on Auditing might be developed to better reflect these conclusions, as part of the post Clarity ISA implementation review.

---

[13] See IAASB Staff Questions and Answers on "Professional Skepticism in an audit of Financial Statements" at:
http://www.ifac.org/sites/default/files/publications/files/IAASB%20Professional%20Skepticism%20Q andA-final.pdf.

Section 8: GLOSSARY OF TERMS[1]

(February 2015)

> This Glossary defines terms used in the ISAs (UK and Ireland), the ISQC (UK and Ireland) and APB Ethical Standards for Auditors issued by the FRC. It is based on the IAASB glossary of terms, with supplemental definitions used in the FRC standards shown in grey highlighted text.
>
> Separate glossaries are used in connection with the Standards for Investment Reporting (SIRs) and the Ethical Standard for Reporting Accountants (ESRA). These are included in SIR 1000 at Appendix 4 and in the ESRA at Appendix 1.

Access controls—Procedures designed to restrict access to on-line terminal devices, programs and data. Access controls consist of "user authentication" and "user authorization". "User authentication" typically attempts to identify a user through unique logon identifications, passwords, access cards or biometric data. "User authorization" consists of access rules to determine the computer resources each user may access. Specifically, such procedures are designed to prevent or detect:

(a)   Unauthorized access to on-line terminal devices, programs and data;

(b)   Entry of unauthorized transactions;

(c)   Unauthorized changes to data files;

(d)   The use of computer programs by unauthorized personnel; and

(e)   The use of computer programs that have not been authorized.

Accounting estimate—An approximation of a monetary amount in the absence of a precise means of measurement. This term is used for an amount measured at fair value where there is estimation uncertainty, as well as for other amounts that require estimation. Where ISA (UK and Ireland) 540[2] addresses only accounting estimates involving measurement at fair value, the term "fair value accounting estimates" is used.

Accounting records—The records of initial accounting entries and supporting records, such as checks and records of electronic fund transfers; invoices; contracts; the general and subsidiary ledgers, journal entries and other adjustments to the financial statements that are

---

[1]   In the case of public sector engagements, the terms in this glossary should be read as referring to their public sector equivalents.
Where accounting terms have not been defined in the pronouncements of the International Auditing and Assurance Standards Board, reference should be made to the Glossary of Terms published by the International Accounting Standards Board.

[2]   ISA (UK and Ireland) 540, "Auditing Accounting Estimates, Including Fair Value Accounting Estimates, and Related Disclosures".

not reflected in formal journal entries; and records such as work sheets and spreadsheets supporting cost allocations, computations, reconciliations and disclosures.

Accounting services—The provision of services that involve the maintenance of accounting records or the preparation of financial statements that are then subject to audit.

Affiliate—An entity that has any of the following relationships with the audited entity:

(a) An entity that has direct or indirect control over the audited entity if the audited entity is material, quantitatively or qualitatively, to such entity;

(b) An entity with a direct financial interest in the audited entity if that entity has significant influence over the audited entity and the interest in the audited entity is material, quantitatively or qualitatively, to such entity;

(c) An entity over which the audited entity has direct or indirect control;

(d) An entity in which the audited entity, or an affiliate of the audited entity under (c) above, has a direct financial interest that gives it significant influence over such entity and the interest is material, quantitatively or qualitatively, to the audited entity and its affiliate in (c); and

(e) An entity which is under common control with the audited entity client (a "sister entity") if the sister entity and the audited entity are both material, quantitatively or qualitatively, to the entity that controls both the audited entity and sister entity.

Factors that may be relevant in determining whether an entity or an interest in an entity is material to another entity include:

• the extent and nature of the relationships between the audited entity and the other entity and the impact these have on the relationships of either entity with the auditor of the audited entity, and

• the extent and nature of the relationship(s) between the auditor of the audited entity and the other entity and the impact that this has on their independence as auditor of the audited entity.

Agreed-upon procedures engagement—An engagement in which an auditor is engaged to carry out those procedures of an audit nature to which the auditor and the entity and any appropriate third parties have agreed and to report on factual findings. The recipients of the report form their own conclusions from the report by the auditor. The report is restricted to those parties that have agreed to the procedures to be performed since others, unaware of the reasons for the procedures may misinterpret the results.

Analytical procedures—Evaluations of financial information through analysis of plausible relationships among both financial and non-financial data. Analytical procedures also encompass such investigation as is necessary of identified fluctuations or relationships that are inconsistent with other relevant information or that differ from expected values by a significant amount.

Annual report—A document issued by an entity, ordinarily on an annual basis, which includes its financial statements together with the auditor's report thereon.

Anomaly—A misstatement or deviation that is demonstrably not representative of misstatements or deviations in a population.

Applicable financial reporting framework—The financial reporting framework adopted by management and, where appropriate, those charged with governance in the preparation of the financial statements that is acceptable in view of the nature of the entity and the objective of the financial statements, or that is required by law or regulation.

The term "fair presentation framework" is used to refer to a financial reporting framework that requires compliance with the requirements of the framework and:

(a) Acknowledges explicitly or implicitly that, to achieve fair presentation of the financial statements, it may be necessary for management to provide disclosures beyond those specifically required by the framework; or

(b) Acknowledges explicitly that it may be necessary for management to depart from a requirement of the framework to achieve fair presentation of the financial statements. Such departures are expected to be necessary only in extremely rare circumstances.

The term "compliance framework" is used to refer to a financial reporting framework that requires compliance with the requirements of the framework, but does not contain the acknowledgements in (a) or (b) above.

Application controls in information technology— Manual or automated procedures that typically operate at a business process level. Application controls can be preventative or detective in nature and are designed to ensure the integrity of the accounting records. Accordingly, application controls relate to procedures used to initiate, record, process and report transactions or other financial data.

Appropriateness (of audit evidence)—The measure of the quality of audit evidence; that is, its relevance and its reliability in providing support for the conclusions on which the auditor's opinion is based.

Arm's length transaction—A transaction conducted on such terms and conditions as between a willing buyer and a willing seller who are unrelated and are acting independently of each other and pursuing their own best interests.

Assertions—Representations by management, explicit or otherwise, that are embodied in the financial statements, as used by the auditor to consider the different types of potential misstatements that may occur.

Assess—Analyze identified risks of to conclude on their significance. "Assess", by convention, is used only in relation to risk. (also see *Evaluate*)

Association—(see *Auditor association with financial information*)

Assurance—(see *Reasonable assurance*)

Assurance engagement—An engagement in which a practitioner expresses a conclusion designed to enhance the degree of confidence of the intended users other than the responsible party about the outcome of the evaluation or measurement of a subject matter against criteria. The outcome of the evaluation or measurement of a subject matter is the information that results from applying the criteria (also see *Subject matter information*). Under the "International Framework for Assurance Engagements" there are two types of assurance engagement a practitioner is permitted to perform: a reasonable assurance engagement and a limited assurance engagement.

> *Reasonable assurance engagement*—The objective of a reasonable assurance engagement is a reduction in assurance engagement risk to an acceptably low level in the circumstances of the engagement[3] as the basis for a positive form of expression of the practitioner's conclusion.

> *Limited assurance engagement*—The objective of a limited assurance engagement is a reduction in assurance engagement risk to a level that is acceptable in the circumstances of the engagement, but where that risk is greater than for a reasonable assurance engagement, as the basis for a negative form of expression of the practitioner's conclusion.

Assurance engagement risk—The risk that the practitioner expresses an inappropriate conclusion when the subject matter information is materially misstated.

Audit documentation—The record of audit procedures performed, relevant audit evidence obtained, and conclusions the auditor reached (terms such as "working papers" or "workpapers" are also sometimes used).

Audit evidence—Information used by the auditor in arriving at the conclusions on which the auditor's opinion is based. Audit evidence includes both information contained in the accounting records underlying the financial statements and other information. (See *Sufficiency of audit evidence* and *Appropriateness of audit evidence*.)

Audit file—One or more folders or other storage media, in physical or electronic form, containing the records that comprise the audit documentation for a specific engagement.

Audit firm—(see *Firm*)

Audit opinion—(see *Modified opinion* and *Unmodified opinion*)

---

[3] Engagement circumstances include the terms of the engagement, including whether it is a reasonable assurance engagement or a limited assurance engagement, the characteristics of the subject matter, the criteria to be used, the needs of the intended users, relevant characteristics of the responsible party and its environment, and other matters, for example events, transactions, conditions and practices, that may have a significant effect on the engagement.

Audit risk—The risk that the auditor expresses an inappropriate audit opinion when the financial statements are materially misstated. Audit risk is a function of the risks of material misstatement and detection risk.

Audit sampling (sampling)—The application of audit procedures to less than 100% of items within a population of audit relevance such that all sampling units have a chance of selection in order to provide the auditor with a reasonable basis on which to draw conclusions about the entire population.

Audit team—For the purposes of APB Ethical Standards this is all audit professionals who, regardless of their legal relationship with the auditor or audit firm, are assigned to a particular audit engagement in order to perform the audit task (e.g. audit partner(s), audit manager(s) and audit staff).

Audited entity—The entity whose financial statements are subject to audit by the audit firm.

Auditor—"Auditor" is used to refer to the person or persons conducting the audit, usually the engagement partner or other members of the engagement team, or, as applicable, the firm. Where an ISA (UK and Ireland) expressly intends that a requirement or responsibility be fulfilled by the engagement partner, the term "engagement partner" rather than "auditor" is used. "Engagement partner" and "firm" are to be read as referring to their public sector equivalents where relevant.

Auditor association with financial information—An auditor is associated with financial information when the auditor attaches a report to that information or consents to the use of the auditor's name in a professional connection.

Auditor's expert—An individual or organization possessing expertise in a field other than accounting or auditing, whose work in that field is used by the auditor to assist the auditor in obtaining sufficient appropriate audit evidence. An auditor's expert may be either an auditor's internal expert (who is a partner[4] or staff, including temporary staff, of the auditor's firm or a network firm), or an auditor's external expert.

Auditor's point estimate or auditor's range—The amount, or range of amounts, respectively, derived from audit evidence for use in evaluating management's point estimate.

Auditor's range—(see *Auditor's point estimate*)

Business risk—A risk resulting from significant conditions, events, circumstances, actions or inactions that could adversely affect an entity's ability to achieve its objectives and execute its strategies, or from the setting of inappropriate objectives and strategies.

Chain of command—All persons who have a direct supervisory, management or other oversight responsibility over either any audit partner of the audit team or over the conduct of audit work in the audit firm. This includes all partners, principals and shareholders who may prepare, review or directly influence the performance appraisal of any audit partner of the

---

[4] "Partner" and "firm" should be read as referring to their public sector equivalents where relevant.

audit team as a result of that partner's involvement with the audit engagement. It does not include any non-executive individuals on a supervisory or equivalent board.

Close family—A non-dependent parent, child or sibling.

Comparative financial statements—Comparative information where amounts and other disclosures for the prior period are included for comparison with the financial statements of the current period but, if audited, are referred to in the auditor's opinion. The level of information included in those comparative financial statements is comparable with that of the financial statements of the current period.

Comparative information—The amounts and disclosures included in the financial statements in respect of one or more prior periods in accordance with the applicable financial reporting framework.

Compilation engagement—An engagement in which accounting expertise, as opposed to auditing expertise, is used to collect, classify and summarize financial information.

Complementary user entity controls—Controls that the service organization assumes, in the design of its service, will be implemented by user entities, and which, if necessary to achieve control objectives, are identified in the description of its system.

Compliance framework—(see *Applicable financial reporting framework* and *General purpose framework*)

Component—An entity or business activity for which group or component management prepares financial information that should be included in the group financial statements.

Component auditor—An auditor who, at the request of the group engagement team, performs work on financial information related to a component for the group audit.

Component management—Management responsible for the preparation of the financial information of a component.

Component materiality—The materiality for a component determined by the group engagement team.

Computer-assisted audit techniques—Applications of auditing procedures using the computer as an audit tool (also known as CAATs).

Connected parties—An audited entity's connected parties are:

a. its affiliates;

b. key members of management (including but not limited to directors and those charged with governance) of the audited entity and its significant affiliates, individually or collectively; and

c.   any person or entity with an ability to influence (other than in the capacity of professional advisors), whether directly or indirectly, key members of management or those charged with governance of the audited entity and its significant affiliates, individually or collectively, in relation to their responsibility for or approach to any matter or judgment that is material to the entity's financial statements.

Contingent fee basis—Any arrangement made under which a fee is calculated on a pre-determined basis relating to the outcome or result of a transaction, or other event, or the result of the work performed. A fee that is established by a court or other public authority is not a contingent fee.

Control activities—Those policies and procedures that help ensure that management directives are carried out. Control activities are a component of internal control.

Control environment—Includes the governance and management functions and the attitudes, awareness and actions of those charged with governance and management concerning the entity's internal control and its importance in the entity. The control environment is a component of internal control.

Control risk—(see *Risk of material misstatement*)

Corporate governance—(see *Governance*)

Corresponding figures—Comparative information where amounts and other disclosures for the prior period are included as an integral part of the current period financial statements, and are intended to be read only in relation to the amounts and other disclosures relating to the current period (referred to as "current period figures"). The level of detail presented in the corresponding amounts and disclosures is dictated primarily by its relevance to the current period figures.

Date of approval of the financial statements—The date on which all the statements that comprise the financial statements, including the related notes, have been prepared and those with the recognized authority have asserted that they have taken responsibility for those financial statements.

Date of report (in relation to ISQC (UK and Ireland) 1)—The date selected by the practitioner to date the report.

Date of the auditor's report—The date the auditor dates the report on the financial statements in accordance with ISA (UK and Ireland) 700[5].

Date of the financial statements—The date of the end of the latest period covered by the financial statements.

Date the financial statements are issued—The date that the auditor's report and audited financial statements are made available to third parties.

---

[5]   ISA (UK and Ireland) 700, "The Independent Auditor's Report on Financial Statements".

Deficiency in internal control—This exists when:

(a) A control is designed, implemented or operated in such a way that it is unable to prevent, or detect and correct, misstatements in the financial statements on a timely basis; or

(b) A control necessary to prevent, or detect and correct, misstatements in the financial statements on a timely basis is missing.

Detection risk—The risk that the procedures performed by the auditor to reduce audit risk to an acceptably low level will not detect a misstatement that exists and that could be material, either individually or when aggregated with other misstatements.

Direct assistance—The use of internal auditors to perform audit procedures under the direction, supervision and review of the external auditor.

The use of internal auditors to provide direct assistance is prohibited in an audit conducted in accordance with ISAs (UK and Ireland). See paragraph 5-1 of ISA (UK and Ireland) 610 (Revised June 2013), "Using the Work of Internal Auditors".

Emphasis of Matter paragraph—A paragraph included in the auditor's report that refers to a matter appropriately presented or disclosed in the financial statements that, in the auditor's judgment, is of such importance that it is fundamental to users' understanding of the financial statements.

Engagement documentation—The record of work performed, results obtained, and conclusions the practitioner reached (terms such as "working papers" or "workpapers" are sometimes used).

Engagement letter—Written terms of an engagement in the form of a letter.

Engagement partner[6]—The partner or other person in the firm who is responsible for the engagement and its performance, and for the report that is issued on behalf of the firm, and who, where required, has the appropriate authority from a professional, legal or regulatory body.

Engagement quality control review—A process designed to provide an objective evaluation, on or before the date of the report, of the significant judgments the engagement team made and the conclusions it reached in formulating the report. The engagement quality control review process is for audits of financial statements of listed entities and those other engagements, if any, for which the firm has determined an engagement quality control review is required.

Engagement quality control reviewer—A partner, other person in the firm, suitably qualified external person, or a team made up of such individuals, none of whom is part of the

---

[6] "Engagement partner", "partner", and "firm" should be read as referring to their public sector equivalents where relevant.

engagement team, with sufficient and appropriate experience and authority to objectively evaluate the significant judgments the engagement team made and the conclusions it reached in formulating the report.

Engagement team—All partners and staff performing the engagement, and any individuals engaged by the firm or a network firm who perform procedures on the engagement. This excludes external experts engaged by the firm or a network firm.[7]

For the purposes of APB Ethical Standards, engagement team comprises all persons who are directly involved in the acceptance and performance of a particular audit. This includes the audit team, professional personnel from other disciplines involved in the audit engagement and those who provide quality control (other than the engagement quality control reviewer) or direct oversight of the audit engagement, but it does not include any auditor's external experts contracted by the firm.

Entity in distress—An entity with actual or anticipated financial or operational difficulties that threaten the survival of that entity as a going concern.

Entity's risk assessment process—A component of internal control that is the entity's process for identifying business risks relevant to financial reporting objectives and deciding about actions to address those risks, and the results thereof.

Error—An unintentional misstatement in financial statements, including the omission of an amount or a disclosure.

Estimation uncertainty—The susceptibility of an accounting estimate and related disclosures to an inherent lack of precision in its measurement.

Ethics Partner—The partner or other person in the audit firm having responsibility for the adequacy of the firm's policies and procedures relating to integrity, objectivity and independence, their compliance with APB Ethical Standards and the effectiveness of their communication to partners and staff within the firm and providing related guidance to individual partners.

Evaluate—Identify and analyze the relevant issues, including performing further procedures as necessary, to come to a specific conclusion on a matter. "Evaluation", by convention, is used only in relation to a range of matters, including evidence, the results of procedures and the effectiveness of management's response to a risk. (also see *Assess*)

Exception—A response that indicates a difference between information requested to be confirmed, or contained in the entity's records, and information provided by the confirming party.

---

[7]   ISA (UK and Ireland) 620, "Using the Work of an Auditor's Expert", paragraph 6(a), defines the term "auditor's expert".

Experienced auditor—An individual (whether internal or external to the firm) who has practical audit experience, and a reasonable understanding of:

(a)   Audit processes;

(b)   ISAs (UK and Ireland) and applicable legal and regulatory requirements;

(c)   The business environment in which the entity operates; and

(d)   Auditing and financial reporting issues relevant to the entity's industry.

Expert—(see *Auditor's expert* and *Management's expert*)

Expertise—Skills, knowledge and experience in a particular field.

External confirmation—Audit evidence obtained as a direct written response to the auditor from a third party (the confirming party), in paper form, or by electronic or other medium.

Fair presentation framework—(see *Applicable financial reporting framework* and *General purpose framework*)

Financial interest—An equity or other security, debenture, loan or other debt instrument of an entity, including rights and obligations to acquire such an interest and derivatives directly related to such an interest.

Financial statements—A structured representation of historical financial information, including related notes, intended to communicate an entity's economic resources or obligations at a point in time or the changes therein for a period of time in accordance with a financial reporting framework. The related notes ordinarily comprise a summary of significant accounting policies and other explanatory information. The term "financial statements" ordinarily refers to a complete set of financial statements as determined by the requirements of the applicable financial reporting framework, but it can also refer to a single financial statement.

Firm—A sole practitioner, partnership or corporation or other entity of professional accountants.

For the purpose of APB Ethical Standards, audit firm includes network firms in the UK and Ireland which are controlled by the audit firm or its partners.

Forecast—Prospective financial information prepared on the basis of assumptions as to future events which management expects to take place and the actions management expects to take as of the date the information is prepared (best-estimate assumptions).

Fraud—An intentional act by one or more individuals among management, those charged with governance, employees, or third parties, involving the use of deception to obtain an unjust or illegal advantage.

Fraud risk factors—Events or conditions that indicate an incentive or pressure to commit fraud or provide an opportunity to commit fraud.

Fraudulent financial reporting—Involves intentional misstatements, including omissions of amounts or disclosures in financial statements, to deceive financial statement users.

General IT-controls—Policies and procedures that relate to many applications and support the effective functioning of application controls by helping to ensure the continued proper operation of information systems. General IT-controls commonly include controls over data center and network operations; system software acquisition, change and maintenance; access security; and application system acquisition, development, and maintenance.

General purpose financial statements—Financial statements prepared in accordance with a general purpose framework.

General purpose framework—A financial reporting framework designed to meet the common financial information needs of a wide range of users. The financial reporting framework may be a fair presentation framework or a compliance framework.

The term "fair presentation framework" is used to refer to a financial reporting framework that requires compliance with the requirements of the framework and:

(a) Acknowledges explicitly or implicitly that, to achieve fair presentation of the financial statements, it may be necessary for management to provide disclosures beyond those specifically required by the framework; or

(b) Acknowledges explicitly that it may be necessary for management to depart from a requirement of the framework to achieve fair presentation of the financial statements. Such departures are expected to be necessary only in extremely rare circumstances.

The term "compliance framework" is used to refer to a financial reporting framework that requires compliance with the requirements of the framework, but does not contain the acknowledgements in (a) or (b) above.[8]

Governance—Describes the role of person(s) or organization(s) with responsibility for overseeing the strategic direction of the entity and obligations related to the accountability of the entity.

Group—All the components whose financial information is included in the group financial statements. A group always has more than one component.

Group audit—The audit of group financial statements.

Group audit opinion—The audit opinion on the group financial statements.

---

[8] ISA (UK and Ireland) 200, "Overall Objectives of the Independent Auditor and the Conduct of an Audit in Accordance with International Standards on Auditing", paragraph 13(a).

Group engagement partner—The partner or other person in the firm who is responsible for the group audit engagement and its performance, and for the auditor's report on the group financial statements that is issued on behalf of the firm. Where joint auditors conduct the group audit, the joint engagement partners and their engagement teams collectively constitute the group engagement partner and the group engagement team.

Group engagement team—Partners, including the group engagement partner, and staff who establish the overall group audit strategy, communicate with component auditors, perform work on the consolidation process, and evaluate the conclusions drawn from the audit evidence as the basis for forming an opinion on the group financial statements.

Group financial statements—Financial statements that include the financial information of more than one component. The term "group financial statements" also refers to combined financial statements aggregating the financial information prepared by components that have no parent but are under common control.

Group management—Management responsible for the preparation of the group financial statements.

Group-wide controls—Controls designed, implemented and maintained by group management over group financial reporting.

Historical financial information—Information expressed in financial terms in relation to a particular entity, derived primarily from that entity's accounting system, about economic events occurring in past time periods or about economic conditions or circumstances at points in time in the past.

Immediate family—A spouse (or equivalent) or dependent.

Inconsistency—Other information that contradicts information contained in the audited financial statements. A material inconsistency may raise doubt about the audit conclusions drawn from audit evidence previously obtained and, possibly, about the basis for the auditor's opinion on the financial statements.

Independence

APB Ethical Standard 1 defines independence as freedom from situations and relationships which make it probable that a reasonable and informed third party would conclude that objectivity either is impaired or could be impaired. Independence is related to and underpins objectivity. However, whereas objectivity is a personal behavioural characteristic concerning the auditor's state of mind, independence relates to the circumstances surrounding the audit, including the financial, employment, business and personal relationships between the auditor and the audited entity.

Information system relevant to financial reporting—A component of internal control that includes the financial reporting system, and consists of the procedures and records established to initiate, record, process and report entity transactions (as well as events and conditions) and to maintain accountability for the related assets, liabilities and equity.

Informed management—Member of management (or senior employee) of the audited entity who has the authority and capability to make independent management judgments and decisions in relation to non-audit services on the basis of information provided by the audit firm.

Inherent risk—(see *Risk of material misstatement*)

Initial audit engagement—An engagement in which either:

(a)   The financial statements for the prior period were not audited; or

(b)   The financial statements for the prior period were audited by a predecessor auditor.

Inquiry—Inquiry consists of seeking information of knowledgeable persons, both financial and non-financial, within the entity or outside the entity.

Inspection (as an audit procedure)—Examining records or documents, whether internal or external, in paper form, electronic form, or other media, or a physical examination of an asset.

Inspection (in relation to quality control)—In relation to completed engagements, procedures designed to provide evidence of compliance by engagement teams with the firm's quality control policies and procedures.

Interim financial information or statements—Financial information (which may be less than a complete set of financial statements as defined above) issued at interim dates (usually half-yearly or quarterly) in respect of a financial period.

Internal audit function—A function of an entity that performs assurance and consulting activities designed to evaluate and improve the effectiveness of the entity's governance, risk management and internal control processes.

Internal auditors—Those individuals who perform the activities of the internal audit function. Internal auditors may belong to an internal audit department or equivalent function.

Internal control—The process designed, implemented and maintained by those charged with governance, management and other personnel to provide reasonable assurance about the achievement of an entity's objectives with regard to reliability of financial reporting, effectiveness and efficiency of operations, and compliance with applicable laws and regulations. The term "controls" refers to any aspects of one or more of the components of internal control.

International Financial Reporting Standards—The International Financial Reporting Standards issued by the International Accounting Standards Board.

Investigate—Inquire into matters arising from other procedures to resolve them.

IT environment—The policies and procedures that the entity implements and the IT infrastructure (hardware, operating systems, etc.) and application software that it uses to support business operations and achieve business strategies.

Key management position—Any position at the audited entity which involves the responsibility for fundamental management decisions at the audited entity (e.g. as a CEO or CFO), including an ability to influence the accounting policies and the preparation of the financial statements of the audited entity. A key management position also arises where there are contractual and factual arrangements which in substance allow an individual to participate in exercising such a management function in a different way (e.g. via a consulting contract).

Key partner involved in the audit—A partner, or other person in the engagement team (other than the audit engagement partner or engagement quality control reviewer) who either:

- is involved at the group level and is responsible for key decisions or judgments on significant matters or risk factors that relate to the audit of that audited entity, or

- is primarily responsible for the audit of a 'significant affiliate or division' (see separate definition) of the audited entity.

Limited assurance engagement—(see *Assurance engagement*)

Listed entity—An entity whose shares, stock or debt are quoted or listed on a recognized stock exchange, or are marketed under the regulations of a recognized stock exchange or other equivalent body.

For the purpose of APB Ethical Standards, listed company includes any company in which the public can trade shares on the open market, such as those listed on the London Stock Exchange (including those admitted to trade on the Alternative Investments Market), PLUS Markets and the Irish Stock Exchange (including those admitted to trade on the Irish Enterprise Exchange).

Management—The person(s) with executive responsibility for the conduct of the entity's operations. For some entities in some jurisdictions, management includes some or all of those charged with governance, for example, executive members of a governance board, or an owner-manager.

In the UK and Ireland, management will not normally include non-executive directors.

Management bias—A lack of neutrality by management in the preparation of information

Management's expert—An individual or organization possessing expertise in a field other than accounting or auditing, whose work in that field is used by the entity to assist the entity in preparing the financial statements.

Management's point estimate—The amount selected by management for recognition or disclosure in the financial statements as an accounting estimate.

Misappropriation of assets—Involves the theft of an entity's assets and is often perpetrated by employees in relatively small and immaterial amounts. However, it can also involve management who are usually more capable of disguising or concealing misappropriations in ways that are difficult to detect.

Misstatement—A difference between the amount, classification, presentation, or disclosure of a reported financial statement item and the amount, classification, presentation, or disclosure that is required for the item to be in accordance with the applicable financial reporting framework. Misstatements can arise from error or fraud. Where the auditor expresses an opinion on whether the financial statements are presented fairly, in all material respects, or give a true and fair view, misstatements also include those adjustments of amounts, classifications, presentation, or disclosures that, in the auditor's judgment, are necessary for the financial statements to be presented fairly, in all material respects, or to give a true and fair view.

Misstatement of fact—Other information that is unrelated to matters appearing in the audited financial statements that is incorrectly stated or presented. A material misstatement of fact may undermine the credibility of the document containing audited financial statements.

Modified opinion—A qualified opinion, an adverse opinion or a disclaimer of opinion.

Monitoring (in relation to quality control)—A process comprising an ongoing consideration and evaluation of the firm's system of quality control, including a periodic inspection of a selection of completed engagements, designed to provide the firm with reasonable assurance that its system of quality control is operating effectively.

Monitoring of controls—A process to assess the effectiveness of internal control performance over time. It includes assessing the design and operation of controls on a timely basis and taking necessary corrective actions modified for changes in conditions. Monitoring of controls is a component of internal control.

Negative confirmation request—A request that the confirming party respond directly to the auditor only if the confirming party disagrees with the information provided in the request.

Network—A larger structure:

(a)   That is aimed at cooperation, and

(b)   That is clearly aimed at profit or cost-sharing or shares common ownership, control or management, common quality control policies and procedures, common business strategy, the use of a common brand name, or a significant part of professional resources.

Network firm—A firm or entity that belongs to a network.

For the purpose of APB Ethical Standards, a network firm is any entity which is part of a larger structure that is aimed at co-operation and which is:

(i)   controlled by the audit firm; or

(ii)   under common control, ownership or management; or

(iii)   part of a larger structure that is clearly aimed at profit or cost sharing; or

(iv)   otherwise affiliated or associated with the audit firm through common quality control policies and procedures, common business strategy, the use of a common name or through the sharing of significant common professional resources.

Non-audit services – Any engagement in which an audit firm provides professional services to an audited entity, its affiliates or another entity in respect of the audited entity other than the audit of financial statements.

Non-compliance (in the context of ISA (UK and Ireland) 250[9]—Acts of omission or commission by the entity, either intentional or unintentional, which are contrary to the prevailing laws or regulations. Such acts include transactions entered into by, or in the name of, the entity, or on its behalf, by those charged with governance, management or employees. Non-compliance does not include personal misconduct (unrelated to the business activities of the entity) by those charged with governance, management or employees of the entity.

Non-response—A failure of the confirming party to respond, or fully respond, to a positive confirmation request, or a confirmation request returned undelivered.

Non-sampling risk—The risk that the auditor reaches an erroneous conclusion for any reason not related to sampling risk.

Observation—Consists of looking at a process or procedure being performed by others, for example, the auditor's observation of inventory counting by the entity's personnel, or of the performance of control activities.

Opening balances—Those account balances that exist at the beginning of the period. Opening balances are based upon the closing balances of the prior period and reflect the effects of transactions and events of prior periods and accounting policies applied in the prior period. Opening balances also include matters requiring disclosure that existed at the beginning of the period, such as contingencies and commitments.

Other information—Financial and non-financial information (other than the financial statements and the auditor's report thereon) which is included, either by law, regulation, or custom, in a document containing audited financial statements and the auditor's report thereon.

Other Matter paragraph—A paragraph included in the auditor's report that refers to a matter other than those presented or disclosed in the financial statements that, in the auditor's

---

[9]   ISA (UK and Ireland) 250 Section A, "Consideration of Laws and Regulations in an Audit of Financial Statements", and ISA (UK and Ireland) 250 Section B, "The Auditor's Right and Duty to Report to Regulators in the Financial Sector".

judgment, is relevant to users' understanding of the audit, the auditor's responsibilities or the auditor's report.

Outcome of an accounting estimate—The actual monetary amount which results from the resolution of the underlying transaction(s), event(s) or condition(s) addressed by the accounting estimate.

Overall audit strategy—Sets the scope, timing and direction of the audit, and guides the development of the more detailed audit plan.

Partner—Any individual with authority to bind the firm with respect to the performance of a professional services engagement.

Performance materiality—The amount or amounts set by the auditor at less than materiality for the financial statements as a whole to reduce to an appropriately low level the probability that the aggregate of uncorrected and undetected misstatements exceeds materiality for the financial statements as a whole. If applicable, performance materiality also refers to the amount or amounts set by the auditor at less than the materiality level or levels for particular classes of transactions, account balances or disclosures.

Person in a position to influence the conduct and outcome of the audit—This is:

(a)   Any person who is directly involved in the audit (the engagement team), including:

   (i)   the audit partners, audit managers and audit staff (the audit team);

   (ii) professional personnel from other disciplines involved in the audit (for example, lawyers, actuaries, taxation specialists, IT specialists, treasury management specialists);

   (iii) those who provide quality control or direct oversight of the audit;

(b)   Any person, who forms part of the chain of command for the audit within the audit firm;

(c)   Any person within the audit firm who, due to any other circumstances, may be in a position to exert such influence.

Personnel—Partners and staff.

Pervasive—A term used, in the context of misstatements, to describe the effects on the financial statements of misstatements or the possible effects on the financial statements of misstatements, if any, that are undetected due to an inability to obtain sufficient appropriate audit evidence. Pervasive effects on the financial statements are those that, in the auditor's judgment:

(a)   Are not confined to specific elements, accounts or items of the financial statements;

(b)   If so confined, represent or could represent a substantial proportion of the financial statements; or

(c)   In relation to disclosures, are fundamental to users' understanding of the financial statements.

Population—The entire set of data from which a sample is selected and about which the auditor wishes to draw conclusions.

Positive confirmation request—A request that the confirming party respond directly to the auditor indicating whether the confirming party agrees or disagrees with the information in the request, or providing the requested information.

Practitioner—A professional accountant in public practice.

Preconditions for an audit—The use by management of an acceptable financial reporting framework in the preparation of the financial statements and the agreement of management and, where appropriate, those charged with governance to the premise[10] on which an audit is conducted.

Predecessor auditor—The auditor from a different audit firm, who audited the financial statements of an entity in the prior period and who has been replaced by the current auditor.

Premise, relating to the responsibilities of management and, where appropriate, those charged with governance, on which an audit is conducted—That management and, where appropriate, those charged with governance have acknowledged and understand that they have the following responsibilities that are fundamental to the conduct of an audit in accordance with ISAs (UK and Ireland). That is, responsibility:

(a)   For the preparation of the financial statements in accordance with the applicable financial reporting framework, including where relevant their fair presentation;

(b)   For such internal control as management and, where appropriate, those charged with governance determine is necessary to enable the preparation of financial statements that are free from material misstatement, whether due to fraud or error; and

(c)   To provide the auditor with:

(i)   Access to all information of which management and, where appropriate, those charged with governance are aware that is relevant to the preparation of the financial statements such as records, documentation and other matters;

(ii)   Additional information that the auditor may request from management and, where appropriate, those charged with governance for the purpose of the audit; and

(iii)   Unrestricted access to persons within the entity from whom the auditor determines it necessary to obtain audit evidence.

---

[10]   ISA (UK and Ireland) 200, paragraph 13.

In the case of a fair presentation framework, (a) above may be restated as "for the preparation and *fair* presentation of the financial statements in accordance with the financial reporting framework", or "for the preparation of financial statements *that give a true and fair view* in accordance with the financial reporting framework".

The "premise, relating to the responsibilities of management and, where appropriate, those charged with governance, on which an audit is conducted" may also be referred to as the "premise".

Professional accountant

For the purpose of the ISAs (UK and Ireland) and APB Ethical Standards, *Professional accountants* are those persons who are members of a professional accountancy body, whether in public practice (including a sole practitioner, partnership or corporate body), industry, commerce, the public sector or education.

Professional accountant in public practice—A professional accountant, irrespective of functional classification (for example, audit, tax or consulting) in a firm that provides professional services. This term is also used to refer to a firm of professional accountants in public practice.

Professional judgment—The application of relevant training, knowledge and experience, within the context provided by auditing, accounting and ethical standards, in making informed decisions about the courses of action that are appropriate in the circumstances of the audit engagement.

Professional skepticism—An attitude that includes a questioning mind, being alert to conditions which may indicate possible misstatement due to error or fraud, and a critical assessment of evidence.

Professional standards—International Standards on Auditing (ISAs) (UK and Ireland) and relevant ethical requirements.

In the UK and Ireland, professional standards in the context of ISQC (UK and Ireland) 1 are the Ethical and Engagement Standards described in the Statement "The Financial Reporting Council – Scope and Authority of Audit and Assurance Pronouncements".

Projection—Prospective financial information prepared on the basis of:

(a) Hypothetical assumptions about future events and management actions which are not necessarily expected to take place, such as when some entities are in a startup phase or are considering a major change in the nature of operations; or

(b) A mixture of best-estimate and hypothetical assumptions.

Prospective financial information—Financial information based on assumptions about events that may occur in the future and possible actions by an entity. Prospective financial information can be in the form of a forecast, a projection or a combination of both. (see *Forecast* and *Projection*)

Public sector—National governments, regional (for example, state, provincial, territorial) governments, local (for example, city, town) governments and related governmental entities (for example, agencies, boards, commissions and enterprises).

Reasonable assurance (in the context of assurance engagements, including audit engagements, and quality control)—A high, but not absolute, level of assurance.

Reasonable assurance engagement—(see *Assurance engagement*)

Recalculation—Consists of checking the mathematical accuracy of documents or records.

Related party—A party that is either:

(a)   A related party as defined in the applicable financial reporting framework; or

(b)   Where the applicable financial reporting framework establishes minimal or no related party requirements:

   (i)   A person or other entity that has control or significant influence, directly or indirectly through one or more intermediaries, over the reporting entity;

   (ii)   Another entity over which the reporting entity has control or significant influence, directly or indirectly through one or more intermediaries; or

   (iii) Another entity that is under common control with the reporting entity through having:

      a.   Common controlling ownership;

      b.   Owners who are close family members; or

      c.   Common key management.

      However, entities that are under common control by a state (that is, a national, regional or local government) are not considered related unless they engage in significant transactions or share resources to a significant extent with one another.

In the UK and Ireland relevant definitions of "related party" are set out in the applicable financial reporting frameworks (for example, the definitions in International Accounting Standard 24, "Related Party Disclosures", Financial Reporting Standard 8, "Related Party Disclosures" or the Financial Reporting Standard for Smaller Entities).

Related services—Comprise agreed-upon procedures and compilations.

Relevant ethical requirements

In the UK and Ireland the relevant ethical pronouncements with which the auditor complies are the APB's Ethical Standards for Auditors and the ethical pronouncements relating to the work of auditors issued by the auditor's relevant professional body - see the Statement "The Financial Reporting Council – Scope and Authority of Audit and Assurance Pronouncements".

Reperformance—The auditor's independent execution of procedures or controls that were originally performed as part of the entity's internal controls.

Report on the description and design of controls at a service organization (referred to in ISA (UK and Ireland) 402[11] as a type 1 report)—A report that comprises:

(a)   A description, prepared by management of the service organization, of the service organization's system, control objectives and related controls that have been designed and implemented as at a specified date; and

(b)   A report by the service auditor with the objective of conveying reasonable assurance that includes the service auditor's opinion on the description of the service organization's system, control objectives and related controls and the suitability of the design of the controls to achieve the specified control objectives.

Report on the description, design, and operating effectiveness of controls at a service organization (referred to in ISA (UK and Ireland) 402 as a type 2 report)—A report that comprises:

(a)   A description, prepared by management of the service organization, of the service organization's system, control objectives and related controls, their design and implementation as at a specified date or throughout a specified period and, in some cases, their operating effectiveness throughout a specified period; and

(b)   A report by the service auditor with the objective of conveying reasonable assurance that includes:

(i)   The service auditor's opinion on the description of the service organization's system, control objectives and related controls, the suitability of the design of the controls to achieve the specified control objectives, and the operating effectiveness of the controls; and

(ii)   A description of the service auditor's tests of the controls and the results thereof.

Review (in relation to quality control)—Appraising the quality of the work performed and conclusions reached by others.

---

[11]   ISA (UK and Ireland) 402, "Audit Considerations Relating to an Entity Using a Service Organization".

Review engagement—The objective of a review engagement is to enable an auditor to state whether, on the basis of procedures which do not provide all the evidence that would be required in an audit, anything has come to the auditor's attention that causes the auditor to believe that the financial statements are not prepared, in all material respects, in accordance with an applicable financial reporting framework.

Review procedures—The procedures deemed necessary to meet the objective of a review engagement, primarily inquiries of entity personnel and analytical procedures applied to financial data.

Risk assessment procedures—The audit procedures performed to obtain an understanding of the entity and its environment, including the entity's internal control, to identify and assess the risks of material misstatement, whether due to fraud or error, at the financial statement and assertion levels.

Risk of material misstatement—The risk that the financial statements are materially misstated prior to audit. This consists of two components, described as follows at the assertion level:

(a)   Inherent risk—The susceptibility of an assertion about a class of transaction, account balance or disclosure to a misstatement that could be material, either individually or when aggregated with other misstatements, before consideration of any related controls.

(b)   Control risk—The risk that a misstatement that could occur in an assertion about a class of transaction, account balance or disclosure and that could be material, either individually or when aggregated with other misstatements, will not be prevented, or detected and corrected, on a timely basis by the entity's internal control.

Sampling—(see *Audit sampling*)

Sampling risk—The risk that the auditor's conclusion based on a sample may be different from the conclusion if the entire population were subjected to the same audit procedure. Sampling risk can lead to two types of erroneous conclusions:

(a)   In the case of a test of controls, that controls are more effective than they actually are, or in the case of a test of details, that a material misstatement does not exist when in fact it does. The auditor is primarily concerned with this type of erroneous conclusion because it affects audit effectiveness and is more likely to lead to an inappropriate audit opinion.

(b)   In the case of a test of controls, that controls are less effective than they actually are, or in the case of a test of details, that a material misstatement exists when in fact it does not. This type of erroneous conclusion affects audit efficiency as it would usually lead to additional work to establish that initial conclusions were incorrect.

Sampling unit—The individual items constituting a population.

Scope of a review—The review procedures deemed necessary in the circumstances to achieve the objective of the review.

Service auditor—An auditor who, at the request of the service organization, provides an assurance report on the controls of a service organization.

Service organization—A third-party organization (or segment of a third-party organization) that provides services to user entities that are part of those entities' information systems relevant to financial reporting.

Service organization's system—The policies and procedures designed, implemented and maintained by the service organization to provide user entities with the services covered by the service auditor's report.

Significance—The relative importance of a matter, taken in context. The significance of a matter is judged by the practitioner in the context in which it is being considered. This might include, for example, the reasonable prospect of its changing or influencing the decisions of intended users of the practitioner's report; or, as another example, where the context is a judgment about whether to report a matter to those charged with governance, whether the matter would be regarded as important by them in relation to their duties. Significance can be considered in the context of quantitative and qualitative factors, such as relative magnitude, the nature and effect on the subject matter and the expressed interests of intended users or recipients.

Significant affiliate—For the purposes of the APB Ethical Standards, an affiliate identified by the group audit team (i) that is of individual financial significance to the group, or (ii) that, due to its specific nature or circumstances, is likely to include significant risks of material misstatement of the group financial statements.

Significant component—A component identified by the group engagement team (i) that is of individual financial significance to the group, or (ii) that, due to its specific nature or circumstances, is likely to include significant risks of material misstatement of the group financial statements.

Significant deficiency in internal control—A deficiency or combination of deficiencies in internal control that, in the auditor's professional judgment, is of sufficient importance to merit the attention of those charged with governance.

Significant risk—An identified and assessed risk of material misstatement that, in the auditor's judgment, requires special audit consideration.

Smaller entity—An entity which typically possesses qualitative characteristics such as:

(a) Concentration of ownership and management in a small number of individuals (often a single individual – either a natural person or another enterprise that owns the entity provided the owner exhibits the relevant qualitative characteristics); and

(b) One or more of the following:

    (i) Straightforward or uncomplicated transactions;

    (ii) Simple record-keeping;

(iii) Few lines of business and few products within business lines;

(iv) Few internal controls;

(v) Few levels of management with responsibility for a broad range of controls; or

(vi) Few personnel, many having a wide range of duties.

These qualitative characteristics are not exhaustive, they are not exclusive to smaller entities, and smaller entities do not necessarily display all of these characteristics.

In the UK and Ireland, company law provides a lighter reporting regime for companies that are defined, by legislation, as small. A company qualifies as "small" if it meets particular thresholds in respect of turnover, balance sheet total/gross assets and number of employees and certain other criteria. The thresholds and other criteria are subject to change and reference to the relevant legislation should be made to determine what they are in respect of a particular accounting period.

For the purpose of APB Ethical Standards, a small entity is defined in "APB Ethical Standard – Provisions Available for Small Entities".

Special purpose financial statements—Financial statements prepared in accordance with a special purpose framework.

Special purpose framework—A financial reporting framework designed to meet the financial information needs of specific users. The financial reporting framework may be a fair presentation framework or a compliance framework.[12]

Staff—Professionals, other than partners, including any experts the firm employs.

Statistical sampling—An approach to sampling that has the following characteristics:

(a) Random selection of the sample items; and

(b) The use of probability theory to evaluate sample results, including measurement of sampling risk.

A sampling approach that does not have characteristics (a) and (b) is considered non-statistical sampling.

Stratification—The process of dividing a population into sub-populations, each of which is a group of sampling units which have similar characteristics (often monetary value).

Subsequent events—Events occurring between the date of the financial statements and the date of the auditor's report, and facts that become known to the auditor after the date of the auditor's report.

---

[12] ISA (UK and Ireland) 200, paragraph 13(a).

Subservice organization—A service organization used by another service organization to perform some of the services provided to user entities that are part of those user entities' information systems relevant to financial reporting.

Substantive procedure—An audit procedure designed to detect material misstatements at the assertion level. Substantive procedures comprise:

(a) Tests of details (of classes of transactions, account balances, and disclosures); and

(b) Substantive analytical procedures.

Sufficiency (of audit evidence)—The measure of the quantity of audit evidence. The quantity of the audit evidence needed is affected by the auditor's assessment of the risks of material misstatement and also by the quality of such audit evidence.

Suitably qualified external person—An individual outside the firm with the competence and capabilities to act as an engagement partner, for example a partner of another firm, or an employee (with appropriate experience) of either a professional accountancy body whose members may perform audits and reviews of historical financial information, or other assurance or related services engagements, or of an organization that provides relevant quality control services.

Supplementary information—Information that is presented together with the financial statements that is not required by the applicable financial reporting framework used to prepare the financial statements, normally presented in either supplementary schedules or as additional notes.

Test—The application of procedures to some or all items in a population.

Tests of controls—An audit procedure designed to evaluate the operating effectiveness of controls in preventing, or detecting and correcting, material misstatements at the assertion level.

Those charged with governance—The person(s) or organization(s) (for example, a corporate trustee) with responsibility for overseeing the strategic direction of the entity and obligations related to the accountability of the entity. This includes overseeing the financial reporting process. For some entities in some jurisdictions, those charged with governance may include management personnel, for example, executive members of a governance board of a private or public sector entity, or an owner-manager.[13]

In the UK and Ireland, those charged with governance include the directors (executive and non-executive) of a company and the members of an audit committee where one exists. For other types of entity it usually includes equivalent persons such as the partners, proprietors, committee of management or trustees.

---

[13] For discussion of the diversity of governance structures, see paragraphs A1-A8 of ISA (UK and Ireland) 260, "Communication with Those Charged with Governance".

Tolerable misstatement—A monetary amount set by the auditor in respect of which the auditor seeks to obtain an appropriate level of assurance that the monetary amount set by the auditor is not exceeded by the actual misstatement in the population.

Tolerable rate of deviation—A rate of deviation from prescribed internal control procedures set by the auditor in respect of which the auditor seeks to obtain an appropriate level of assurance that the rate of deviation set by the auditor is not exceeded by the actual rate of deviation in the population.

Uncertainty—A matter whose outcome depends on future actions or events not under the direct control of the entity but that may affect the financial statements.

Uncorrected misstatements—Misstatements that the auditor has accumulated during the audit and that have not been corrected.

Unmodified opinion—The opinion expressed by the auditor when the auditor concludes that the financial statements are prepared, in all material respects, in accordance with the applicable financial reporting framework.

User auditor—An auditor who audits and reports on the financial statements of a user entity.

User entity—An entity that uses a service organization and whose financial statements are being audited.

Walk-through test—Involves tracing a few transactions through the financial reporting system.

Written representation—A written statement by management provided to the auditor to confirm certain matters or to support other audit evidence. Written representations in this context do not include financial statements, the assertions therein, or supporting books and records.

Appendix: AUDIT AND ASSURANCE STANDARDS AND GUIDANCE AT 1 FEBRUARY 2015

		Publication date
Scope and Authority of Audit and Assurance Pronouncements		*February 2013*

Quality Control Standards

ISQC (UK and Ireland) 1 – Quality Control for Firms that Perform Audits and Reviews of Financial Statements, and other Assurance and Related Services Engagements		*October 2009*

Auditing Standards (ISAs (UK and Ireland))

200	Overall Objectives of the Independent Auditor and the Conduct of an Audit in Accordance with International Standards on Auditing (UK and Ireland)	*October 2009*
210	Agreeing the Terms of Audit Engagements	*October 2009*
220	Quality Control for an Audit of Financial Statements	*October 2009*
230	Audit Documentation	*October 2009*
240	The Auditor's Responsibilities Relating to Fraud in an Audit of Financial Statements	*October 2009*
250	Section A – Consideration of Laws and Regulations in an Audit of Financial Statements	*October 2009*
250	Section B – The Auditors' Right and Duty to Report to Regulators in the Financial Sector	
260	Communication With Those Charged With Governance	*September 2014*
265	Communicating Deficiencies in Internal Control to Those Charged With Governance	*October 2009*
300	Planning an Audit of Financial Statements	*October 2009*
315	Identifying and Assessing the Risks of Material Misstatement Through Understanding of the Entity and Its Environment *The June 2013 revision is effective for audits of financial statements for periods ending on or after 15 June 2014*	*June 2013*
320	Materiality in Planning and Performing an Audit	*October 2009*
330	The Auditor's Responses to Assessed Risks	*October 2009*
402	Audit Considerations Relating to an Entity Using a Service Organisation	*October 2009*
450	Evaluation of Misstatements Identified During the Audit	*October 2009*
500	Audit Evidence	*October 2009*

Ethical Standards

Provisions available for small entities (Revised)		*December 2010*
Ethical Standards for Reporting Accountants		*October 2006*

Statement of Standards for Reporting Accountants (UK and Ireland)

2410	Review of interim financial information performed by the independent auditor of the entity	*July 2007*

Standards for Investment Reporting

1000	Investment reporting standards applicable to all engagements in connection with an investment circular	*July 2005*
2000	Investment reporting standards applicable to public reporting engagements on historical financial information (Revised)	*March 2011*
3000	Investment reporting standards applicable to public reporting engagements on profit forecasts	*January 2006*
4000	Investment reporting standards applicable to public reporting engagements on pro forma financial information	*January 2006*
5000	Investment reporting standards applicable to public reporting engagements on financial information reconciliations under the Listing Rules	*February 2008*

Practice Notes

10	Audit of financial statements of public sector entities in the United Kingdom (Revised)	*October 2010*
10(I)	Audit of central government financial statements in the Republic of Ireland (Revised)	*August 2011*
11	The audit of charities in the United Kingdom (Revised)	*March 2012*
12	Money laundering – Guidance for auditors on UK legislation (Revised)	*September 2010*
14	The audit of housing associations in the United Kingdom	*January 2014*
15	The audit of occupational pension schemes in the United Kingdom (Revised)	*January 2011*
15(I)	The audit of occupational pension schemes in Ireland	*February 2010*
16	Bank reports for audit purposes (Revised)	*February 2011*
19	The audit of banks and building societies in the United Kingdom (Revised)	*March 2011*
19(I)	The audit of banks in the Republic of Ireland (Revised)	*June 2008*
20	The audit of insurers in the United Kingdom (Revised)	*January 2011*
20(I)	The audit of insurers in the Republic of Ireland	*August 2002*

21	The audit of investment businesses in the United Kingdom (Revised)	*December 2007*
22	The auditors' consideration of FRS 17 'Retirement Benefits' – Defined benefit schemes	*November 2001*
23	Special considerations in auditing financial instruments	*July 2013*
24	The audit of friendly societies in the United Kingdom (Revised)	*July 2011*
25	Attendance at stocktaking	*February 2011*
26	Guidance for smaller entity audit documentation (Revised)	*December 2009*
27	The audit of credit unions in the United Kingdom	*May 2011*
27(I)	The audit of credit unions in the Republic of Ireland	*December 2008*

Bulletins

2006/4	Regulatory and legislative background to the application of Standards for Investment Reporting in the Republic of Ireland	*April 2006*
2006/5	The Combined Code on Corporate Governance: Requirements of Auditors under the Listing Rules of the Financial Services Authority and the Irish Stock Exchange	*September 2006*
2007/2	The duty of auditors in the Republic of Ireland to report to the Director of Corporate Enforcement	*March 2007*
2008/1	Audit issues when financial market conditions are difficult and credit facilities may be restricted	*January 2008*
2008/2	The auditor's association with preliminary announcements made in accordance with the requirements of the UK and Irish Listing Rules	*February 2008*
2008/4	The special auditor's report on abbreviated accounts in the United Kingdom	*April 2008*
2008/5	Auditor's reports on revised accounts and reports in the United Kingdom	*April 2008*
2008/6	The 'senior statutory auditor' under the United Kingdom Companies Act 2006	*April 2008*
2008/9	Miscellaneous reports by auditors required by the United Kingdom Companies Act 2006	*October 2008*
2008/10	Going concern Issues during the current economic conditions	*December 2008*
2009/4	Developments in corporate governance affecting the responsibilities of auditors of UK Companies	*December 2009*
2010/1	XBRL Tagging of information in audited financial statements – guidance for auditors	*February 2010*

2010/2	Compendium of illustrative auditor's reports on United Kingdom private sector financial statements for periods ended on or after 15 December 2010 (Revised)	*March 2012*
2011/1	Developments in corporate governance affecting the responsibilities of auditors of companies incorporated in Ireland	*May 2011*
2011/2	Providing assurance on client assets to the Financial Services Authority	*October 2011*
1(I)[1]	Compendium of illustrative auditor's reports on Irish financial statements	*October 2012*
2	Guidance for reporting accountants of stakeholder pension schemes in the United Kingdom	*February 2013*
3	Providing assurance on client assets to the Financial Services Authority (Supplement addressing the use of Third Party Administrators)	*March 2013*
4	Recent developments in company law, the Listing Rules and auditing standards that affect United Kingdom auditor's reports	*April 2014*

Other

Briefing Paper	Professional Scepticism – Establishing a common understanding and reaffirming its central role in delivering audit quality	*March 2012*

---

[1] The number system for Bulletins was changed in 2012.